The Complete Directory to Prime Time Network TV Shows

1946–Present

The Complete Directory to Prime Time Network TV Shows
1946—Present
(Fourth Edition)

Tim Brooks and Earle Marsh

Ballantine Books • New York

Library of Congress Catalog Card Number: 87-91863

ISBN 0-345-35610-1

Cover design by James R. Harris
Photo credits: *I Love Lucy*—Viacom International; *Kate and Allie*—© 1988 CBS Inc.; Michael Landon—Charles William Bush; *Gilligan's Island*—© 1964 Gladasya-UATV; ALF—Lorimar Telepictures Corp. and Leisure Concepts, Inc.; Malcolm Jamal Warner—The Brokaw Company; Carol Burnett—Courtesy of Carol Burnett; *Dallas*—Lorimar Productions

Manufactured in the United States of America

First Edition: May 1979
Reprinted four times
Second (Revised) Edition: November 1981
Reprinted three times
Third (Revised) Edition: May 1985
Reprinted three times
Fourth (Revised) Edition: October 1988
10 9 8 7 6 5 4 3 2 1

CONTENTS

PREFACE TO THE FOURTH EDITION

Television is expanding rapidly, and so is this book. For the first time we have included the programs of the new Fox television network, as well as hundreds of new programs on ABC, CBS, and NBC, and more than 350 syndicated series that achieved national distribution. Also new with this edition are a ranking of the top 100 series of all time and the first listing of series reunion telecasts. As in previous editions we have continued to expand and improve the entries for earlier programs.

When we began compiling the information for the first *Complete Directory* thirteen years ago we sincerely believed that people would be interested in accurate information about TV shows of the past—even though many of the publishers we approached disagreed! However we never anticipated the explosion in interest that the 1980s would bring. The spread of cable TV has renewed and strengthened America's love affair with television, and many old favorites are finding new audiences on Nickelodeon, CBN, WTBS, and other cable channels. Revivals and reunions are rampant, and the rapid spread of home videotape recorders has helped spread classic TV as well. We hope that we have done your favorites justice.

Our goal is to give you the most accurate—and entertaining—directory to prime time network series possible. As always, your comments are appreciated, in care of the publisher.

—T.B. and E.M.

ACKNOWLEDGMENTS

Like the TV shows it lists, this new edition should have its own roll of credits, in acknowledgment of the help and encouragement we have received from many friends inside and outside the broadcasting industry. We are especially grateful to the patient and helpful staffs at the program information departments of the major networks, who have made their files and memories available to us: Chris Morgan, Eddie Cintron, Mike Schum and Jodi Barberi at ABC-TV; John Behrens at CBS-TV; Betty Jane Reed and Tom O'Brien at NBC-TV; and Marcy Baron at Fox. Also most helpful were NBC librarians Vera Mayer, Judy Friedman, and Doris Katz, who opened to us their unparalleled collection of trade literature from all periods of television history.

Others who contributed to the fourth edition in large ways and small include Asa Hoff and Cathy Korda of ABC-TV; Jim Sirmans, Mike Eisenberg and Dorothy Miller of CBS-TV; Curt Block, Matt Messina, Lissa Eichenberger, Ron Korda, Paul Wang, and Dana "Daytime" Herko of NBC-TV; Jack Fishman; actress/activist Fran Lee; humorist Carl Wolfson; George W. Woolery, author of the fine two-volume reference book *Children's Television;* Ron Simon of the Museum of Broadcasting in New York; Dan Einstein of the ATAS/UCLA Television Archives in Los Angeles; Catherine Heinz of the Broadcast Pioneers' Library in Washington; syndicated columnist Guy R. MacMillin ("The Videot"); and an eccentric but fascinating magazine about television history called *The TV Collector,* published by Stephen and Diane Albert (available from P.O. Box 188, Needham, MA 02192).

Our readers obviously love TV as much as we do, and continue to write in with (usually) good-natured comments and suggestions. We continue to appreciate and solicit the input of you, the viewer. All suggestions for additions and corrections are checked, although we can only use those that can be verified by original sources (memories, no matter how certain, are often mistaken!). We particularly want to thank the following correspondents, whose contributions will be found in the pages of this edition: Ms. Zita Carno, Adam Chan, Charlie Cino, Jon Alan Conrad, Daniel R. Eckman, Andrea Elenko (*Peyton Place*'s number one fan), Gary Gates, Charles Gersch, D.J. Hamburger, Dennis Hill, Jeff Jourdan, Gordon W. Leaworthy, David Lewis, Virgil Maringer, Miss J.M. Nazer, Mark Phillips, Norman Pomeroy, Howard H. Prouty, Deborah Puette, Jim Rayton, Marshall R. Saiger, Peter J. Stenhouse, Frederick Tucker, Howard J. White, Tom Wolf, and Jordan R. Young.

Finally, special thanks to some very patient and understanding folks at Ballantine Books, who have helped shape this sometimes unwieldy, ever-growing tome into a book you can use—Paul Anbinder and Carolyn Hart for the early editions, and Ann LaFarge and Virginia Faber for the later ones.

INTRODUCTION

"What's on TV tonight?"

Within these pages are 15,000 nights, a panorama of television programs and stars from the earliest pioneers of the mid-1940s to the very latest contemporary hits. What's on? A pretty, pixie-ish ingenue named Helen Parrish, introducing television's first "big time" series ever for a hardy little band of set owners in 1946 (see *Hour Glass*); a loud, brash comic who never quite made it in radio, becoming TV's first superstar, and causing millions of Americans to buy their first TV set (see *Milton Berle*); a laconic nonactor named Jack Webb droning "Just the facts, ma'am," and ushering in a whole era of grippingly real dramas (see *Dragnet*); a veteran actor who is to lose his career—and his life—when he is driven from his hit series by McCarthy-era blacklisting (see *The Goldbergs*); a towering, unknown actor in a role intended for John Wayne, opening an entire decade of "adult" westerns (see *Gunsmoke*); Richard M. Nixon saying "Sock it to me" on nationwide TV (see *Laugh-In*); a blue collar bigot railing about "spics and spades"—and changing the nature of TV comedy forever after (see *All in the Family*); the "Fonz" giving his thumbs-up signal and bringing a wave of nostalgia about the simpler days of the 1950s into our living rooms (see *Happy Days*).

They are all here, and a great many more. We have set out to give you the most complete and accurate history of nighttime television series ever assembled. But this is not simply a book of nostalgia, for current shows are here as well, and many of TV's great series of the past are still very much with us, in reruns. We suggest that you keep this book by your set, and when a favorite repeat or star turns up in your evening's viewing, take a moment to see what the background of that show was, its stars and story development during its run. You may even want to catch the movie or read the book on which it was based.

We hope that this book can help you enjoy today's TV a little more.

This volume has been carefully researched for the scholar who wants to know what happened and when. But it is also—like TV itself—for your enjoyment.

What Is in This Book

This is an encyclopedia listing (1) every regular series ever carried on the commercial broadcast networks during "prime time"—roughly, 7:30–11:00 P.M., E.S.T.; (2) all network series carried in the early evening (6:00–7:30 P.M.) and late night (after 11:00 P.M.) hours; and (3) the top syndicated programs of all time that were aired primarily in the evening hours. The book covers the entire history of TV networking in the U.S., from its inception on a regular basis in 1946 to 1988 (all programs premiering through April 15, 1988, are included). Our definition of a "series" is a program that ran for at least four consecutive weeks in the same time slot—or was intended to.

A few generic program types are found under general headings. Newscasts are summarized under *News;* sports events such as football, boxing, wrestling, etc., under the name of the sport; and feature film series under *Movies.* All other series are arranged by title in alphabetical order. There is a full index in the back to every cast member, plus appendixes listing the highest rated programs each season, network schedules for each season at a glance, major TV awards, and other information.

Network series are those that are fed out by ABC, CBS, NBC, or Fox (and, in the early days, DuMont). These are seen simultaneously across most of the country. Syndicated series are sold by their producers to individual stations, and are therefore seen at different times in different cities, and not at all in some areas. Thousands of syndicated programs have been produced over the years, many with very limited distribution. Only the principal ones are included here. Other programs that may have been seen in your city after 6:00 P.M.—but are not included here—are local programs and syndicated series which did not achieve widespread distribution.

This is the first book to trace programming back to the very founding of the networks, and, consequently, it includes some very early network series that were seen in only two or three cities on the East Coast. The networks spread quickly, however, first by sending out kinescopes (films) of their shows to nonconnected stations, and soon after with live connections to stations in the Midwest (in 1949) and on the West Coast (in 1951).

Under each series main heading you will find the following:

First/Last Telecast: The dates on which the series was first and last seen on a network. This includes repeats on a network, but not later reruns on local stations, which will be at a different time in each city, and may go on long after the program has ceased production. Generally the first and last telecast dates indicate the original production run of a network series.

Broadcast History: The days, times, and networks on which the series was carried (eastern time). Special episodes which ran for only one or two weeks in other than the normal time slot are not reflected. DUM indicates the DuMont TV network, and (OS) indicates that the program was off during the summer months. For syndicated series, we have indicated the years the program was in production, and when it was first released for telecast by local stations.

Cast: Regular cast members, those who were seen on a recurring basis, are listed along with the years in which they were seen during the original run. We have gone to considerable effort to separate regulars from guests making one-time only appearances, as the latter were not part of the continuing casts. Notable guests may be listed in the series description, however.

Principal sources of scheduling information were the files of the three major networks (ABC, CBS, NBC), cross-checked against detailed four-network logs maintained over the years by NBC and by the A. C. Nielsen Company. For the very earliest programs, listings in *TV Guide* and various newspapers were consulted, with listings in different cities being compared to establish network status. Cast and content data were drawn from network and syndicator files, press releases, listings in *TV Guide,* reviews in *Variety, Billboard,* and *Television* magazines, and elsewhere. To all of these organizations, we express our sincere gratitude.

—T.B. and E.M.

A Short History of Network Television
by Tim Brooks

Television goes back a good deal further than most people realize. There was no single inventor of television, although Dr. Vladimir Zworykin's invention of the iconoscope in 1923 provided a basic element, the "eye" of the TV camera. Demonstrations of various kinds of experimental TV were made in the late 1920s, including even primitive color television in 1929. General Electric began semiregular telecasts from its laboratories in Schenectady in May 1928, mostly for the benefit of a few nearby engineers who had receiving sets. NBC opened experimental TV station W2XBS in New York in 1930, followed by a similar CBS station in 1931. But for the next several years TV seemed to go nowhere. Pictures were fuzzy, screens tiny, and costs astronomical. In addition, there were several incompatible types of transmission, and engineers spent much time arguing over a single set of technical standards—something we take for granted today.

For the public at large the 1930s was the decade of radio, when virtually every home had a set, and superstars and hit shows became a familiar phenomenon. Comedies, dramas, quiz shows, and variety hours were all developed for a mass market, establishing formats that would later be transferred virtually intact to television. While radio and TV are only vaguely related technically, there is no doubt that the great radio networks of the 1930s were the direct entertainment predecessors of today's TV.

By the end of the 1930s interest in TV was picking up. In 1938 NBC transmitted several notable telecasts from its New York station, including scenes from the Broadway play *Susan and God* starring Gertrude Lawrence and Paul McGrath from the original cast. Also in that year the NBC station carried the first live, unscheduled coverage of a news event in progress. An NBC mobile unit happened to be working in a park in Queens, New York, when a fire broke out on Ward's Island, across the river. The TV crew swung their cameras around and telecast live pictures of the raging fire to surprised viewers.

Looking for a memorable event with which to inaugurate regular TV service, NBC decided upon the official opening of the World's Fair in New York on April 30, 1939. President Franklin D. Roosevelt was seen arriving and delivering the opening address, thus becoming the first incumbent president to appear on television. NBC announcer Bill Farren described the proceedings and also conducted interviews at the fairground. Thereafter, from 1939–1941, both NBC and CBS presented a surprisingly extensive schedule of programs over their New York stations for the several thousand sets then in use. There were few regular "series" however—every night was an event. If you had a set, you simply turned it on at night (there was seldom anything telecast during the day) and saw what was being sent out from the studios that night. Anything that moved was worth watching.

A sample night's entertainment, shortly after the World's Fair inaugural, was called simply *The Wednesday Night Program* and ran from 8:00–9:07 P.M. It opened with a fashion show described by commentators Renee Macredy and Nancy Turner, followed by songs by The Three Smoothies, a sketch called "The Smart Thing" (cast included Martha Sleeper, Ned Wever, and Burford Hampden), dancer Hal Sherman from the show *Helzapoppin',* and finally a magic act by Robert Reinhart, who also served as emcee of the program. If you've never heard of most of these names, neither had most viewers in 1939. Appearances by stars, especially the big names of radio, were few and far between, and television had to rely primarily on cabaret talent and young, lesser-known Broadway actors and actresses for many years to come.

Viewers didn't mind. There was a common bond of pioneering between viewers and broadcasters in those days, and in fact a good deal of communication both ways. NBC kept a card file listing every known set owner and sent out postcards each week listing the programs to be telecast, asking the viewer's opinion of each one. These were the first TV "ratings."

Most television programs were seen in New York only, which was, throughout the 1940s, America's TV "capital." It was the first city with more than one station operating, and it had by far the largest number of sets in people's homes. However, the possibility of networking, along the lines of the great radio chains, was pursued from the very beginning. As early as 1940 NBC began to relay some telecasts to the General Electric station in Schenectady, thus forming history's first network of sorts. (The feasibility of transmitting pictures between two widely separated cities had been demonstrated in 1927, when Secretary of Commerce Herbert Hoover, speaking in Washington, D.C., was seen in a New York laboratory, by special hookup.) The New York–Schenectady link was accomplished by the simple method of having General Electric pick up the signal off the air from New York, 130 miles away, and rebroadcast it. The picture quality thus obtained was not very good. In 1941 some NBC New York telecasts began to be fed to the Philco station in Philadelphia as well, giving NBC a three station "network." But all of this was intermittent, and there were still no regular series as we know them today.

Commercial television first saw the light of day in 1941, when both NBC and CBS were granted commercial licenses for their New York stations, both on July 1st (so neither could claim a "first"). NBC's call letters became WNBT on channel one (now WNBC-TV on channel four), and CBS got WCBW on channel two (now WCBS-TV).

Just as commercial television was beginning to take root, World War II put a stop to everything. Little was telecast during the war years, except for some training programs. The DuMont Laboratories, which had been experimenting with TV for years, received a commercial license in 1944 for WABD, New York (now WNYW-TV on channel five), serving as the cornerstone of that company's ill-fated network venture.

With the war over, work started anew. The year 1946 marked the true beginnings of regular network series. NBC's WNBT began feeding its programs on a more or less regular basis to Philadelphia and Schenectady, forming NBC's "East Coast Network." DuMont opened a second station, WTTG, in Washington, D.C., to which it fed programs—even though there were in mid-1946 only a bare dozen sets in the nation's capital. Network television's first major series effort, and the program which set many precedents for programs to come, was a regular Thursday night big budget variety hour called *Hour Glass,* which ran for ten months beginning in May 1946. It was a pioneer in many ways and helped spread the word that television could provide not only a novelty gadget for the gadget-minded, but regular high-quality family entertainment as well.

Several other network series began in 1946, including the long running *You Are an Artist,* Mrs. Carveth Wells' *Geographically Speaking, Television Screen Magazine* (an early version of *60 Minutes*), *Play the Game* (charades), *Cash and Carry* (quiz), *Face to Face* (drawings), *I Love to Eat* (cooking), and *Faraway Hill* (the first network soap opera). All of these programs can be found under their individual headings in this book.

Most early programming was quite experimental, just to see what would work in the new medium. Costs were kept to a minimum, and advertising agencies were given free time by the stations, to get them into the studio to try out TV. (Programs were often produced by the advertisers themselves.) Such visual formats as charades, cartooning, and fashion shows were favorites, along with sports events and adaptations of radio shows, telecast on a one-time tryout basis.

A landmark was the premiere of *Kraft Television Theater* in May 1947. This was not only the first regularly scheduled drama series to go out over a network, but was also blessed with sufficient money from a sponsor to insure uniformly high-quality productions.

Gradually stations were added to NBC's and DuMont's chains, two more stations in Washington, D.C., additional facilities in Philadelphia, then Baltimore, then Boston. Stations not connected with the East Coast opened in the Midwest and far west, often receiving network programs on kinescope.

But where were CBS and ABC?

Both were fully committed to the idea of networking, but each hung back for a different reason. ABC did not yet have a New York flagship station on the air from which to originate programming. ABC had in fact been buying time on other stations and producing programs on their schedules just to give its own technicians experience in studio production techniques, against the day when ABC would have its own station. An early example was *Play the Game* (1946),

which was produced by ABC using DuMont's facilities. In early 1948 ABC lined up a network of four stations, a curious amalgam of DuMont and independent stations, for a series called *On the Corner* with radio star Henry Morgan—which it now considers its first "network" program (although *Play the Game* was also seen over a network). Finally, in August 1948 ABC got its own New York station and production center on the air and began network service on a regular basis.

CBS delayed its entry into network television for quite a different reason. It had had an active New York station for years. But CBS was committed to the idea of color TV, and tried hard to get its own color system accepted by the Federal Communications Commission as the industry standard. This would have meant color TV from the start for everyone, and would also have made obsolete all of the equipment in use by CBS' rivals because the different systems were incompatible. The choice had to be color or black and white, but not both. Unfortunately, the CBS system was clumsy and unreliable compared with the fairly well-developed black-and-white TV of the day, and its adoption would probably have set TV back several years. (Eventually the CBS electromechanical system, with its spinning disc within every set, was discarded altogether. It is RCA's all-electronic, black-and-white compatible color system that we use today.) While the verdict was out, CBS delayed investment in a network.

Two events changed CBS' mind. First, a critical government decision went against the CBS color system. Then the NBC network's coverage of the 1947 World Series—the first World Series on TV—suddenly made it very apparent that an explosion in TV set ownership was about to take place. CBS, if it did not move quickly, was in danger of being left at the starting gate. A crash program of series development was instituted, and early in 1948 CBS began feeding programs out over its own small network.

The 1947 World Series brought in television's first mass audience. It was carried in New York, Philadelphia, Schenectady, and Washington, D.C., and was seen by an estimated 3.9 million people—3.5 million of them in bars! The TV set over the corner bar was a first introduction to the new medium for many people, and it helped sell thousands of sets for the home. After that, TV ownership was contagious. The first set on the block always brought in dozens of curious neighbors, who eventually went out and bought sets of their own.

By 1948 television networking was on its way. Several of the longest running programs included in this book premiered in that year, including Ted Mack's *Original Amateur Hour* in January, Milton Berle's *Texaco Star Theater* in June, Ed Sullivan's *Toast of the Town* in June, and *Arthur Godfrey's Talent Scouts* in December. NBC opened its midwest network of stations in September 1948, and in a special ceremonial telecast on January 11, 1949, east and midwest were linked. For a time Chicago was an important production center for network programs, but without the talent pool available in New York it could not compete for long. *Kukla, Fran & Ollie* and *Garroway at Large* were probably the most important series to come out of Chicago in its TV heyday.

In September 1951 the link was completed to the west coast, and America at last had nationwide television. Los Angeles was not to become the principal network production center until Hollywood-produced filmed dramatic shows became the TV norm during the second half of the 1950s, however.

In the early years of network operation NBC had the largest audiences, with *Milton Berle, Kraft Television Theater, Your Show of Shows, Dragnet,* and other top hits. But by the mid 1950s, through a combination of astute program development *(I Love Lucy, Ed Sullivan)* and carryovers from its top radio shows *(Arthur Godfrey, Jack Benny)* CBS took the lead, which it proudly retained for two decades thereafter. Nevertheless, NBC and CBS, the two giants of TV, were never far apart. ABC and DuMont were far behind, fighting for survival—for it was rapidly becoming apparent that there was room for only one other network in the U.S. There were several reasons for this. For one thing the talent pool available for successful TV shows was severely limited and very high priced. NBC and CBS had so many of the trump cards that there just wasn't very much left over for another network, much less for two others. Whenever a new talent emerged on DuMont or ABC, such as Ted Mack *(Original Amateur Hour)* or Jackie Gleason, he

would soon be stolen away by the "majors" with the promise of much more money.

Even more important, there were a limited number of stations to go around. Outside of New York and a few other large cities, very few places in the U.S. were serviced by more than two, or perhaps three, stations (some areas still aren't). NBC and CBS always got the best stations in each city, leaving ABC and DuMont to fight for the scraps, or perhaps be seen only part-time on a "shared" station.

In many ways DuMont seemed to be in a good position to become America's third network. The company was led by a brilliant and progressive engineer, Dr. Allen B. DuMont, who seemed to have made all the right decisions at the right times. He was involved in experimental television broadcasting from his laboratory in New Jersey in the early 1930s, long before ABC was even founded (in 1943, as a spin-off from NBC). DuMont had a base in manufacturing, and in fact marketed the first large screen (14 inch) home TV set in 1938. Knowing that large amounts of capital would be needed for television development, he obtained financing from giant Paramount Pictures in 1938 and began active TV programming in the early 1940s. DuMont was close on the heels of NBC in setting up a network in 1946-1947, and its production facilities were the most elaborate in the industry. What went wrong?

One important factor working against DuMont was the fact that the company did not operate a radio network, as did NBC, CBS, and ABC. An established radio network not only provided its competitors with a ready talent pool to draw on, but also gave them a foot in the door in signing up choice affiliates (which were usually associated with network radio stations) in many cities. Another devastating blow was a ruling by the government that DuMont, unlike the other three networks, could not own the legal maximum of five television stations.

Most of the affiliates over which the TV networks send their programs are locally owned. Each network could by law own outright only five VHF stations. These five were critically important because they provide the base of revenues to support the network (for years the networks themselves all lost money). They also guaranteed that all of the network's programs would be seen in at least those five markets. NBC, CBS, and ABC each obtained their quota of five stations early in the game. But because of a series of complicated legal rulings involving its relationship with Paramount Pictures (which also owned stations), DuMont could not, and thus was denied both the revenues and guaranteed program clearances that a full roster of five big market stations could provide. In addition, Paramount refused to give DuMont any further financial support after 1939.

ABC had financial problems too, but in 1953 it got the boost it needed by merging with United Paramount Theaters. With a heavy infusion of capital provided by the merger, ABC began developing programs in earnest, including the landmark deal in 1954 that brought *Walt Disney* to television and in 1955 the arrangement with Warner Brothers that produced many hit series (see under *Warner Brothers Presents*). With the ABC–Paramount Theaters merger, DuMont's fate was sealed, and the latter network finally went out of business in 1956.

Structurally, little has changed in TV networking since that time. In the mid 1950s compatible color TV was introduced, pushed hard by NBC (whose parent company, RCA, manufactured the sets). Video tape effected a behind-the-scenes revolution in the 1960s by freeing producers from the cumbersome aspects of film and the hectic uncertainty of live production. There was periodic talk of a fourth national network, such as the ill-fated Overmyer Network ("ON") in the 1960s, but nothing came of it until 20th Century–Fox launched its Fox Network in 1986 (with the ill-fated *Late Show Starring Joan Rivers*). Even network ownership remained unchanged until the 1980s. The giant conglomerate ITT and later billionaire Howard Hughes each tried to buy ABC, but no one succeeded until a cash rich station owner, Capital Cities Broadcasting, swallowed the network in January 1986. Five months later the giant General Electric Co. gobbled up RCA, and with it NBC. CBS was taken over by investor Lawrence Tisch three months after that.

It took ABC nearly thirty years to reach parity with CBS and NBC in audience size. It did not have a number-one rated series until *Marcus Welby, M.D.*, in the 1970s, and it did not rank number one as a network for a full season until 1976-1977, when long-time leader CBS was finally deposed. Later, in the mid-1980s, NBC moved into first place.

Trends in Programming: The Six Eras of Prime Time

Television programming has changed a great deal over the years, both in style and content. Each decade has had its program trends, reflecting not only the evolving tastes of the American public, but also important behind-the-scenes changes in the business that determines what we see. We have come a long way from the silly slapstick of Milton Berle to the social awareness of *All In The Family* and *The Facts of Life.*

Prime time program history can be divided into six principal eras.

The First Era: "Vaudeo" (1948–1957)

In the beginning there was Milton Berle. His time at the top was actually rather short—his series ranked number one for three seasons (1948–1951), in a period when relatively few people even had a TV set. Later major hits such as *I Love Lucy, Gunsmoke,* and *All In The Family* were number one for a longer time and were seen by far more people. But Uncle Miltie's influence was enormous. Not only was he TV's first superstar, but the excitement he created for the new medium helped television ownership spread like wildfire, from less than 2 percent of U.S. homes when he premiered in 1948 to over 70 percent by the time he left the air in 1956.

Berle's Tuesday night *Texaco Star Theater* was typical of the first wave of television programming—frantic, corny, but always highly visual. If ordinary people were going to spend $400 for a small-screen "radio with pictures," they wanted to see movement and action, and lots of it. Berle gave them fall-down slapstick with crazy costumes and sight gags galore. Ed Sullivan offered a three-ring circus of comedians, acrobats, opera singers, scenes from plays, and dancing bears. *The Ed Wynn Show, The All Star Revue* with Jimmy Durante, *Your Show of Shows* with Sid Caesar, *Fireball Fun-For-All* with Olsen and Johnson, and *The Colgate Comedy Hour* with practically everybody (Eddie Cantor, Martin and Lewis, Abbott and Costello, Bob Hope) all did the same. Such broadly played slapstick and variety looked so old fashioned that some called it "vaudeo"—a wedding of vaudeville and the new video medium.

Other types of series exploited the new medium's visual possibilities even further. *I'd Like To See* and *You Asked For It* brought viewers their own visual requests. *Photographic Horizons* showed models posing so that home viewers could take pictures of them right off the screen. Pantomime shows like Mike Stokey's *Pantomime Quiz* were popular.

Variety programs, however, drew the largest audiences. Talent shows proliferated, led by *Arthur Godfrey's Talent Scouts* (for up-and-coming professionals) and *The Original Amateur Hour* (for your local tap dancers and kazoo players). Future stars like Jack Klugman, Pernell Roberts, and Martin Balsam could be seen trying out on *Hollywood Screen Test*, but Godfrey's audition staff flunked a greasy-haired young singer named Elvis Presley before he could even get on the air!

Early situation comedies frequently used broadly played physical comedy. The number one hit in the mid 1950s was *I Love Lucy*, with the inspired mugging of Lucy and the continual exasperation of her bandleader husband, Desi. There were many others, including *The Life of Riley*, *The Stu Erwin Show*, Jackie Gleason's *Honeymooners*, and *Red Skelton*. Of the major stars of the day, only Jack Benny and Groucho Marx seemed to rely primarily on verbal humor. Another popular genre was the family comedy, full of warm, homey values and typified by *The Adventures of Ozzie & Harriet*, *The Danny Thomas Show (Make Room for Daddy)*, *Father Knows Best* and *Mama*. Such family shows have been among TV's longest running series.

Although vaudeville dominated early TV, some series tried a more intimate approach. Much of Arthur Godfrey's appeal was due to his folksy, down-to-earth humor, and his weekly variety show, *Arthur Godfrey & His Friends*, had an easygoing pace. Godfrey did not showcase stars; instead, his regular "family" of performers including Tony Marvin, the Chordettes, Julius LaRosa, and Frank Parker and Marion Marlowe were seen every week. Dave Garroway was also known for his wry, low-key style, while singer/host Perry Como was so relaxed that he became the butt of jokes: "Wake up, Perry!"

"Serious" television was represented mainly by dramatic anthology series, which offered a different play with a new cast each week. Some of these series had a unifying theme, like the newsworthiness of *Armstrong Circle Theatre* and *The Big Story*, but most simply presented good drama drawn from a variety of sources (original scripts, short stories, adaptations of the classics). Among the more popular of these stage-type series were *Kraft Television Theatre*, *General Electric Theater*, *Philco/Goodyear TV Playhouse*, *Ford Theatre*, *Fireside Theatre*, *Robert Montgomery Presents*, and *Studio One*. The last of these great series, *Playhouse 90*, left the air in 1961. Another kind of innovation was represented by the daring, though never highly popular, series of Ernie Kovacs, who experimented with the visual comedy effects possible in the new medium.

There were relatively few action or adventure shows in the early days, largely because of the studio-bound technical requirements of TV. *Dragnet* was the most popular police show, and one of the few series filmed in Hollywood—most of the big variety, comedy and playhouse series originated live from New York. But that was to change.

The "Adult Westerns" Era (1957–early 1960s)

Saturday, September 10, 1955, was an important night in television history. If you were watching CBS at 10 P.M. that evening you saw big John Wayne, standing by a corral, introducing a new series that he had been asked to star in. He couldn't take the role, but he had recommended a lanky young actor to take his place. It proved to be a lucky break for Jim Arness, who would star for the next 20 years in *Gunsmoke*. The series started off slowly in the ratings, but quickly gained momentum and was followed by a veritable stampede of others: *Cheyenne*; *Have Gun, Will Travel*; *Tales of Wells Fargo*; *Wagon Train*; *Rawhide*; *Wanted: Dead or Alive*; *The Virginian*. There were variations on the theme, including true-history Westerns (*Life & Legend of Wyatt Earp*), anthology-Westerns (*Zane Grey Theater*), "family" Westerns (*The Rifleman*) and even a Western that satirized the other Westerns (*Maverick*). By 1958–1959, seven out of the top ten series were

Westerns—a dominance seldom achieved by any program type.

What set these series apart from earlier kids' Westerns like *The Lone Ranger* and *Hopalong Cassidy* was that they were written for adults, in the style of such recent movie hits as *High Noon* and *Shane*. They often tackled adult subjects and relationships: just what *was* the relationship between Matt Dillon and Miss Kitty, anyway? Kids could still enjoy the action, while adults got something more than a Saturday-matinee plot and a moral.

TV violence took its first major upswing during the era of the adult Western, to the dismay of critics. The range of weapons used by TV's horseback crusaders was truly remarkable:

Series	Weapon
Wanted: Dead or Alive	Steve McQueen's sawed-off carbine
The Rifleman	Chuck Connors' fast-cocking Winchester with a large ring that supposedly allowed him to fire off the first round in three tenths of a second.
Wyatt Earp	Hugh O'Brian's oversized Buntline pistol.
Shotgun Slade	Scott Brady's unique two-in-one shotgun.
Adventures of Jim Bowie	Scott Forbes' Bowie knife
Cisco Kid	Pancho's bullwhip
Hotel de Paree	The shiny little discs in Earl Holliman's stetson, with which he could blind adversaries.

The adult Westerns signaled a major change in the source of prime-time TV programming. All of them were on film, and most of them were produced by the major Hollywood movie studios, which had previously avoided involvement with television as if it were the plague. From this time on most TV series would be products of Hollywood's dream factories rather than the live, theater-influenced New York stage. Like a product's switch from wood to plastic, this change made an important difference in the texture and "feel" of all future entertainment programs.

The last hurrah for live, eastern-originated programming was the big money quiz show fad which began in the summer of 1955 with the fabulous success of *The $64,000 Question*. The quiz shows were marvelous theater; a contestant agonized in an isolation booth while the host ticked off a complicated, multipart question which could be worth a fabulous amount of money. There was just one question per week, for ever greater amounts of money. The suspense from week to week was palpable, and contestant-heroes like Charles Van Doren on *Twenty-One* became national celebrities as they slowly climbed from obscurity to wealth before America's eyes—on live TV. Unfortunately some of the shows turned out to have been fixed (contestants were given the answers beforehand, and coached on how to triumph or fail on cue). They were all swept off the air in 1958–1959 in one of television's most embarrassing scandals.

While the adult Westerns were at their zenith another type of filmed program took root, a type that proved to be one of the most durable formats of all. The "swinging detectives" were sexy, as fast with a wisecrack as with a gun, and usually operated in an exotic locale. They began with *77 Sunset Strip* in 1958, which combined a couple of hip private eyes, some beautiful women, a colorful sidekick (Kookie), and the glamorous backdrop of L.A.'s Sunset Strip. In the wake of its success came *Hawaiian Eye, Peter Gunn, Checkmate, Burke's Law* and many others right up to *Magnum, P.I.* and *Remington Steele* in the 1980s.

By the early 1960s the flood of adult westerns was beginning to abate. There were simply too many of them on the air—as many as 31 in a single season—and new entries found it hard to attract attention. Does anyone today remember 1960–61's *Gunslinger* (Tony Young), *Stagecoach West* (Wayne Rogers), or *The Westerner* (Brian Keith with a mongrel dog)?

Number of Westerns In Prime Time, By Season
1955–1956:   9
1956–1957:   11

```
1957–1958:  20
1958–1959:  31
1959–1960:  30
1960–1961:  26
1961–1962:  16
1962–1963:  13
1963–1964:   8
1964–1965:   7
```

A second factor in the demise of the Westerns was concern over TV violence, which had centered on crime shows such as *The Untouchables* and *Bus Stop*, but which spilled over into Westerns as well. By 1961 Congress was holding hearings on the subject, and network executives were under heavy pressure to tone things down.

Even more important forces were at work behind the scenes—forces which would ultimately change all TV programming. The research companies that measured TV audiences were beginning to report those audiences in increasing detail—not only how many homes were tuned in, but detailed ages and incomes of the people who watched each show. It turned out that the adult Westerns were attracting older people, while young adults and kids were tuning to situation comedies. Since advertisers wanted to reach high-consuming young families, sitcoms were in.

The "Idiot Sitcom" Era (early to late 1960s)

The 1960s was the youth decade, and many of the comedies that poured onto the screen seemed to be aimed at the young. Most of them had a gimmick to attract attention. *Beverly Hillbillies*, the number-one program from 1962–1964, put hayseeds in high society, while *Gomer Pyle* had its bumpkin turning the Marine Corps upside down. In *Green Acres* the premise was reversed, with city folks out on the farm. *My Favorite Martian* offered reporter Bill Bixby the biggest story of his career, except that "Uncle Martin" wouldn't reveal his powers to anyone else; meanwhile pretty Samantha on *Bewitched* used her witchly powers more than husband Darrin would have liked. TV's sexiest genie, Barbara Eden, frustrated her "master" (Larry Hagman) and delighted viewers on *I Dream of Jeannie*. Bizarre, comical characters turned up on *The Addams Family*, *The Munsters*, *The Flying Nun*, and *Batman*, and slapstick silliness was alive and well on *Gilligan's Island, Mr.*

Ed, McHale's Navy, F Troop, Hogan's Heroes, and many other shows.

Kids themselves were the stars of some of the comedies as in *Dennis the Menace, Leave It To Beaver, The Donna Reed Show* and *The Many Loves of Dobie Gillis*. Kids like cartoons, so we had *The Flintstones* and *The Jetsons* in prime time; animals turned up on *Flipper* and *Daktari;* rock music on *Shindig* and *Hullabaloo;* science fiction on *Lost In Space* and *Star Trek*.

Of the many fads that swept America in the 1960s probably the biggest was the James Bond–super agent vogue, which started with the Bond movies in 1963–1964. The trend was soon reflected on the TV screen in such hits as *The Man From U.N.C.L.E., I Spy, Secret Agent*, and *Mission: Impossible*. One of the funniest comedies of the 1960s, *Get Smart*, satirized the whole genre.

A few westerns lingered on, notably *Bonanza* (the number-one series from 1964–1967) and *Gunsmoke*, which enjoyed a revival as a 7:30 P.M. kid's show. Drs. Kildare and Ben Casey kept women enthralled, as did the continuing anguish on prime time's first hit soap opera, *Peyton Place*. Men could find excitement on a wave of war shows, among them *Combat, Twelve O'Clock High*, and *Garrison's Gorillas*.

Was there anything serious on TV in the early 1960s? The answer is "not much"; even the network newscasts were only 15 minutes long until 1963. *The Dick Van Dyke Show* did offer comedy written on an adult level, and *The Defenders* sometimes presented serious, relevant drama. More typical was the fate of George C. Scott's first network TV series, *East Side/West Side*, a gritty 1963 drama about an inner-city social worker; it lasted a single season opposite *Sing Along with Mitch*. The following year, *That Was The Week That Was ("TW3")*, a pioneering attempt at social satire, was driven off the air by *Petticoat Junction*.

The Relevance Era (late 1960s–1975)

East Side/West Side and *TW3* were shows ahead of their time. America was changing, and the gap between TV's land of make believe and the real world was becoming a gulf. While Jed Clampett and Pvt. Gomer Pyle cavorted on our television screens, Kennedy and Khrushchev had brought the world to the brink of nuclear war over Cuba, and black Americans were burning and looting the slums of Los Angeles. Television, like many of society's other institutions, had to change.

The first major series of the period to acknowledge that there was a world beyond *Gilligan's Island* was *I Spy* in 1965, the series that reintroduced blacks to prime-time starring roles. Blacks had scarcely been seen on television since the early 1950s, and never in respectable, nondemeaning leading roles. *I Spy, Julia, Room 222,* and *The Mod Squad* changed all that, and dozens of black or minority series followed in the 1970s. The portrayal of women began to change as well, from the dependent housewives of *I Love Lucy* and *Donna Reed* to the liberated singles of *That Girl* and *Mary Tyler Moore.*

Direct political commentary within an entertainment format was a little longer in coming, but when it did it produced some enormous hits. *The Smothers Brothers Comedy Hour* premiered in February 1967 as a lightweight, youth-oriented variety show, but quickly swung toward biting, political satire which caused the CBS censors to have fits. On NBC, *Rowan & Martin's Laugh-In* premiered in 1968 with a similarly topical approach, and shot straight to the top of the ratings; it was the number one program on television from 1968–1970.

Ratings for the fall 1970 schedule seemed to suggest that "relevant TV" might have passed its peak. A slew of highly contemporary, youth-oriented shows were introduced that fall, among them *The Storefront Lawyers, The Young Lawyers, The Senator,* and *The Young Rebels* (the 1960s youth movement transplanted to the Revolutionary War). All of them failed. But a midseason replacement, scheduled with great trepidation by CBS, gave relevance new life. *All In The Family,* about a blue collar bigot and the folly of his ways, ranked number one among all series for five years, the longest time on top for any series in television history. In its wake came spin-offs *(Maude, The Jeffersons)* and a new wave of shows dealing with issues TV had scarcely ever touched before: interfaith marriage *(Bridget Loves Bernie),* anti-war sentiments *(M*A*S*H),* life at the bottom of the economic ladder *(Good Times, Chico & The Man).* Maude had an abortion, and Edith Bunker was attacked by a rapist—comedy had never been like this before!

Some shows stayed away from serious issues. Action-adventure was represented by the descendants of *77 Sunset Strip,* including *Mannix, Hawaii Five-O, Kojak, Columbo,* and *The Rockford Files. The Waltons* and *Little House On The Prairie* were gentle reminders of a simpler time, carrying a message about the value of love and the nuclear family.

A situation comedy that premiered on ABC in 1974 seemed to be even more of a throwback—but *Happy Days* would prove to be a harbinger of the next era of prime-time TV programming. Major changes were about to take place, in part due to government complaints about TV violence and the increasing frankness of the relevance shows, especially in time periods when children were watching. In 1975 the networks were forced to "sanitize" their early evening lineups with a curiously cynical concept called the 8:00–9:00 P.M. Family Viewing Time (cynical because children hardly view only between 8:00–9:00 P.M.). Henceforth, programs in that time slot would have to be suitable for "family viewing." No rapes and no abortions.

The ABC "Fantasy" Era (1975–1980)

As prime-time programming had swung like a pendulum from the escapism of the early 1960s to the relevance of the early 1970s, it now swung back again—at least part way. *Happy Days,* the perfect inoffensive 8:00 P.M. show, grew steadily in popularity, paralleling the vogue for one of its secondary characters, the Fonz. By 1976 it was the number-one program on television. At that time ABC's fortunes were in the hands of Fred Silverman, a master programmer who knew how to milk a rising series for all it was worth. Using *Happy Days* as his launching pad, he built a whole evening of similarly lightweight programs on Tuesdays with *Laverne & Shirley* at 8:30 followed by the progressively sexier *Three's Company, Soap,* and *Family.* The same thing worked on Wednesday, where *Eight Is Enough* captured the kids at 8 o'clock and *Charlie's Angels* gave adults something to leer at at nine.

Other hits were carefully nurtured in strategic places throughout the week, almost all of them thoroughly escapist comedy/action (for the kids) or sexually titillating. Thursday had *Welcome Back, Kotter* and *Barney Miller;* Friday, *Donny and Marie;* Saturday, *The Love Boat* and *Fantasy Island;* and Sunday, *The Six Million Dollar Man. Mork*

& Mindy was spun off from Happy Days, and The Bionic Woman from The Six Million Dollar Man. ABC, long the number-three network, vaulted to number one in the ratings for the first time in its history.

As ABC's fantasy and sex filled the air, the other two networks struggled to compete. They managed a few imitations of the ABC style (CBS' Dukes of Hazzard, NBC's CHiPs), but CBS survived mostly on carryovers from its glory days of the early 1970s (it had been in the vanguard of the relevance movement), while NBC floundered with an uneven hodgepodge typified by The Big Event. Few new "relevant" series were able to get a foothold; among them were Lou Grant and Quincy, M.E. "Serious" TV was relegated mostly to mini-series, such as the spectacularly successful Roots. In addition, 60 Minutes, an obscure CBS public affairs series that had been bumping around the schedule since 1968, enjoyed a remarkable surge in popularity, aided by fortuitous scheduling Sunday night at 7 P.M. It happened that a peculiarity in government regulations prevented the networks from competing with entertainment series in that time slot; only "public service" was allowed. Given this protection from normal competition, 60 Minutes caught on in a big way, eventually becoming the number-one program on television—the only news series ever to do so.

Soap Operas and the "Real People" Era (1980s)

By 1980 ABC's escapist hits were in decline, their novelty worn thin. Fred Silverman had defected to NBC, and new hits were hard to come by. In addition the competitive environment was changing radically. Cable TV networks were spreading across the country, and commercial broadcasters found an increasing portion of their audience siphoned off to watch commercial-free movies and specialty channels (all news, sports, rock music, etc.). With so many viewing alternatives, the commercial network schedules looked increasingly stale and derivative.

Gradually two new trends emerged. The soap opera, that serialized format so popular in daytime, became a hit in prime time as well, introducing a continuing-story element missing from most prime-time series. Dallas was the first major hit, followed by Dynasty,

Falcon Crest, and Knots Landing. Other series also began to work in continuing stories, such as the rocky romances on Hill Street Blues and Cheers.

The other trend was sparked by the much talked-about Real People in 1979 and was, in a sense, a swing back to reality. These programs set out to reflect the real world, especially its lighter, more entertaining aspects, without necessarily trying to change it (as the relevance shows had tended to do). That's Incredible and Ripley's Believe It Or Not followed closely in the spirit of Real People. 20/20 was a cross between 60 Minutes and a celebrity magazine, while TV's Bloopers and Practical Jokes was a close relation to that old snoop, Candid Camera. The number-one hit The Cosby Show presented a realistic view of child rearing; Hill Street Blues and St. Elsewhere brought reality to police and doctor shows. Numerous syndicated programs picked up on the reality trend, among them PM Magazine, Entertainment Tonight, and The People's Court.

There were still escapist fantasies like The A-Team, Knight Rider, The Fall Guy, and Magnum, P.I., some of them so slapstick they bordered on comedy. Wildly careening automobiles, a favorite since the days of Starsky & Hutch and The Dukes of Hazzard, were a favorite device. In Knight Rider, the vehicle (a talking Pontiac Trans-Am named KITT) could actually fly through the air. Landings were often hard, but no one ever got hurt.

Over the years America's love affair with television has matured from initial infatuation to an accepted, and pervasive, part of everyday life. It happened very fast. The percentage of U.S. homes with one or more TV sets leaped from 1 percent to 50 percent in five short years (1948–1953), and passed 90 percent in the early 1960s. Today 98 percent of U.S. homes have TV—it is everywhere. And the average home has its set on seven hours a day, every day, watching and taping. The explosion in cable channels has made the great shows of the past continuously available.

As for the programs we've watched, they're all in these pages. Leaf through the book, guided perhaps by the year-by-year network schedules and top program rankings in the back. A panorama of the series and the stars who captivated America for forty-plus years is on display.

The
Complete Directory
to Prime Time Network
TV Shows

1946–Present

A

ABC ALBUM
see *Plymouth Playhouse*

ABC BARN DANCE
Music
FIRST TELECAST: *February 21, 1949*
LAST TELECAST: *November 14, 1949*
BROADCAST HISTORY:
Feb 1949–Jun 1949, ABC Mon 8:30–9:00
Jul 1949–Oct 1949, ABC Mon 9:00–9:30
Oct 1949–Nov 1949, ABC Mon 9:30–10:00
EMCEE:
Hal O'Halloran
Jack Stillwell

The *National Barn Dance*, begun in 1924 on radio station WLS, Chicago, and long a radio favorite, was carried on ABC television in 1949 as the *ABC Barn Dance*. Among the *Barn Dance* favorites appearing on this half-hour Monday night version were the Sage Riders instrumental quartet, Lulu Belle and Scotty, Cousin Tifford, the De Zurick Sisters (a yodeling duet), caller John Dolce and comic Holly Swanson. The series was telecast from Chicago.

ABC COMEDY HOUR
Comedy Variety
FIRST TELECAST: *January 12, 1972*
LAST TELECAST: *August 9, 1972*
BROADCAST HISTORY:
Jan 1972–Apr 1972, ABC Wed 8:30-9:30
Jun 1972–Aug 1972, ABC Wed 9:30–10:30
REGULARS:
Rich Little
Frank Gorshin
George Kirby
Marilyn Michaels
Charlie Callas
Joe Baker
Fred Travalena

Most of the telecasts that were aired under the title *ABC Comedy Hour* featured a guest host plus a regular repertory company of impressionists called The Kopycats, listed above. (Fred Travalena replaced Charlie Callas in the company in mid-series.) The series also included a number of other comedy specials, among them two Friars' Roasts, an Alan King special, and an updated version of *Hellzapoppin'*. Reruns of the Kopycats episodes were aired during the summer of 1972 under the title *ABC Comedy Hour Presents the Kopycats*.

ABC COMEDY SPECIAL
Comedy Anthology
FIRST TELECAST: *June 6, 1986*

LAST TELECAST: *August 8, 1986*
BROADCAST HISTORY:
Jun 1986–Jul 1986, ABC Fri 9:30–10:00
Aug 1986   , ABC Fri 9:00–10:00

A collection of pilots for comedies that did not make ABC's Fall 1986 schedule. Among those starring in this particular crop of "busted pilots" were Caroline McWilliams, Annie Potts, Blair Brown, Ted Bessell, Robert Klein, Madeline Kahn, and Pat Harrington.

ABC DRAMATIC SHORTS—1952–1953
Dramatic Films

ABC had problems in the early 1950s. It had fewer stations than NBC or CBS, few advertisers, and therefore little revenue with which to pay for new programming. In order just to stay on the air, the "other network" was forced to schedule dozens of low-budget quiz shows, interview programs, and documentary films (most obtained free from government and industry). Needless to say, this did not attract much of an audience to the network. In 1952 ABC tried an experiment. It assembled a package of several dozen low-budget 30-minute dramatic films, most of them made by MCA Films in Hollywood. Many of them had been seen on TV before, on ABC *(Gruen Guild Theater)*, DuMont *(Gruen Playhouse)*, and some even on NBC *(Campbell Soundstage)*. These shopworn films were sprinkled liberally throughout the ABC schedule during the 1952–1953 season, on multiple "theater" series. Each film ran up to half a dozen times on different nights and on different series. Not every film would turn up on every series, but if you watched ABC long enough you would frequently get the impression that you had "seen that film before."

Most of the films were grade "B" productions, starring some Hollywood old-timers as well as lesser-known young actors and actresses (some of whom were to gain fame in later years). Among them were Buddy Ebsen, Raymond Burr, Cesar Romero, Ann Rutherford, Helen Parrish, Vincent Price, Anita Louise, Hans Conried, Cliff Arquette, Onslow Stevens, and many others. The scripts included mysteries (such as "The Cavorting Statue" with Cesar Romero), romantic tales ("A Little Pig Cried" with Frances Rafferty), and comedies.

Following is a list of the theater series among which the films rotated, mostly during 1952–1953. It is not guaranteed to be complete!

APPOINTMENT WITH LOVE
Dec 1952–Sep 1953, ABC Fri 9:00–9:30
CARNIVAL
Feb 1953–Sep 1953, ABC Thu 8:00–8:30
DARK ADVENTURE
Jan 1953–Jul 1953, ABC Mon 8:30–9:00
DOUBLE EXPOSURE
Jan 1953–Sep 1953, ABC Wed 9:00–9:30

FABLE FOR A SUMMER NIGHT
Jul 1953–Oct 1953, ABC Thu 10:30–11:00
FEAR AND FANCY
May 1953–Aug 1953, ABC Wed 8:00–8:30
FILM FESTIVAL
Jul 1953–Sep 1953, ABC Sun 6:30–7:00
GRUEN GUILD THEATER
Sep 1951–Dec 1951, ABC Thu 9:30–10:00
HALF HOUR THEATRE
Jun 1953–Sep 1953, ABC Fri 9:30–10:00
HOUR GLASS
Jan 1953–Sep 1953, ABC Wed 8:30–9:00
LITTLE THEATRE
Dec 1952–Jan 1953, ABC Wed 7:30–8:00
Aug 1953–Sep 1953, ABC Tue 9:00–10:30 (3 films)
PLAYHOUSE NUMBER 7
Oct 1952–Nov 1952, ABC Sun 9:00–9:30
Nov 1952–Jan 1953, ABC Wed/Sun 9:00–9:30
Jan 1953–Mar 1953, ABC Sun 7:30–8:00
RETURN ENGAGEMENT
Jul 1953–Sep 1953, ABC Mon 9:30–10:00
STRAW HAT THEATER
Jul 1953–Sep 1953, ABC Sun 7:30–8:00
SUMMER FAIR
Jun 1953–Sep 1953, ABC Thu 9:30–10:00
TURNING POINT, THE
Jan 1953–Mar 1953, ABC Thu 9:00–9:30
May 1953–Jun 1953, ABC Sat 7:30–8:00
TWENTIETH CENTURY TALES
Jan 1953–Jul 1953, ABC Wed 8:00–8:30
Jul 1953–Sep 1953, ABC Mon 8:30–9:00
WHITE CAMELLIA, THE
Jan 1953–Mar 1953, ABC Tue 8:30–9:30 (2 films)

ABC FEATURE FILM
see *Movies—Prior to 1961*

ABC LATE NIGHT
Various
FIRST TELECAST: *January 1, 1973*
LAST TELECAST: *October 21, 1982*
BROADCAST HISTORY:
Jan 1973–Nov 1979, ABC Mon–Fri 11:30–Conclusion
Nov 1979–Mar 1980, ABC Mon–Fri 11:50–Conclusion
Mar 1980–Jan 1981, ABC Mon–Thu 11:50–Conclusion + Fri 11:30–Conclusion
Jan 1981–Mar 1981, ABC Mon–Thu 12:00–Conclusion + Fri 11:30–Conclusion
Mar 1981–Oct 1982, ABC Mon–Fri 12:00–Conclusion

With the failure of Les Crane, Joey Bishop, or Dick Cavett to attract a substantial following for ABC in the late-night area, the network decided in 1973 to try a new tack. Johnny Carson could have the talk-show audience; ABC countered with a diversified potpourri that, it was hoped, would offer something of interest to everyone. ABC officially premiered *Wide World of Entertainment* on January 1, 1973, following a tryout run from November 21–December 8, 1972. There were nights, in fact whole weeks, with Cavett or Jack Paar hosting talk shows, but there were also comedy specials, mysteries, documentaries, rock-music shows, and just about anything else that could be done on a small budget. The first telecast was in two parts: "Let's Celebrate," a comedy-variety show starring Tony Roberts, followed by a short "Bedtime Story" in which a young married couple talked about their day as they prepared for bed. Other specials included "In Concert" (rock music), "Comedy News," Truman Capote interviewing convicts, and "The Roger Miller Show."

It soon became apparent that the improvisational comedy and offbeat specials were not attracting weary viewers, but the occasional mystery thrillers and TV-movie repeats were. Eventually these became the bulk of the presentations, followed in the later 1970s by reruns of prime-time series. With the change in program content, the umbrella title for this series was changed from *ABC Wide World of Entertainment* to *ABC Late Night* on January 12, 1976. During the fall, when ABC carried *Monday Night Football*, there was no *ABC Late Night* programming on that night.

Summarized below is a night-by-night history of *ABC Late Night*. In cases where there was a double feature on a given night, a semicolon is used to separate the first and second features. If more than one series alternated in the same time slot on different weeks they are separated by a slash.

CHRONOLOGY OF ABC LATE NIGHT
BY NIGHT OF THE WEEK

Monday
   Jan 1973–Sep 1973, Movie/*Jack Paar Tonight*/Movie/*Dick Cavett Show*
   Jan 1974–Aug 1974, ABC Late Night Special
   Jan 1975–Sep 1975, Wide World Mystery (Movie)
   Jan 1976–Sep 1976, ABC Monday Night Special
   Jan 1977–Apr 1977, The Streets of San Francisco; Dan August
   Apr 1977–Sep 1977, The Streets of San Francisco; Toma
   Jan 1978–May 1978, Police Story
   Jun 1978–Aug 1978, Soap; Police Story
   Dec 1978–Aug 1979, Police Story
   Jan 1980–Mar 1980, Barney Miller; Police Story
   Apr 1980–Jul 1980, Barney Miller; Police Woman
   Jul 1980–Aug 1980, Barney Miller
   Jan 1981–Aug 1981, Fantasy Island
   Jan 1982–Aug 1982, Movie

Tuesday
   Jan 1973–Oct 1973, ABC Late Night Special/*Jack Paar Tonight*/Movie/*Dick Cavett Show*

Nov 1973–Dec 1973, Movie/Dick Cavett Show
Dec 1973–Jan 1976, Wide World Mystery
  (Movie)
Jan 1976–May 1978, Tuesday Movie of the
  Week
Jun 1978–Aug 1978, Soap; Tuesday Movie of the
  Week
Aug 1978–Sep 1979, Tuesday Movie of the
  Week
Sep 1979–Dec 1979, Barney Miller; Tuesday
  Movie of the Week
Jan 1980–Apr 1980, Tuesday Movie of the Week
Apr 1980–Aug 1980, Soap; Tuesday Movie of the
  Week
Aug 1980–Sep 1981, Tuesday Movie of the
  Week
Sep 1981–Oct 1982, Fantasy Island

Wednesday
Jan 1973–Oct 1973, ABC Late Night Special/
  Jack Paar Tonight/ABC Late Night Special/
  Dick Cavett Show
Nov 1973–Dec 1973, ABC Late Night Special/
  Dick Cavett Show
Dec 1973–Sep 1975, Wide World Special
Sep 1975–Sep 1976, Wednesday Movie of the
  Week
Sep 1976–Aug 1977, The Rookies; Mystery of
  the Week (Movie)
Sep 1977–Dec 1977, Starsky and Hutch; Mys-
  tery of the Week (Movie)
Jan 1978–Aug 1978, Police Story; Mystery of the
  Week (Movie)
Sep 1978–Jan 1979, Police Woman; S.W.A.T.
Jan 1979–Jul 1979, Police Woman; Mannix
Jul 1979–Sep 1979, Police Woman; Baretta
Sep 1979–Sep 1980, Love Boat; Baretta
Sep 1980–Feb 1981, Love Boat; Police Woman
Mar 1981–Apr 1981, Love Boat; Joe Forrester
Apr 1981–Oct 1982, Love Boat

Thursday
Jan 1973–Nov 1973, ABC Late Night Special/
  Jack Paar Tonight/Movie/Dick Cavett Show
Nov 1973–May 1974, ABC Late Night Special/
  Dick Cavett Show
Jun 1974–Sep 1974, Good Night America/Dick
  Cavett Show
Sep 1974–Dec 1974, Wide World Special/Dick
  Cavett Show
Jan 1975–Sep 1975, Wide World Special
Oct 1975–Mar 1976, Mannix; Longstreet
Mar 1976–Sep 1976, Mannix; The Magician
Sep 1976–Dec 1976, The Streets of San Fran-
  cisco; Dan August
Jan 1977–Jun 1977, ABC Thursday Night Special
June 1977–Sep 1977, S.W.A.T.; ABC Thursday
  Night Special
Sep 1977–Dec 1977, Police Story; ABC Thurs-
  day Night Special
Jan 1978–Aug 1978, Starsky and Hutch; Toma

Sep 1978–Jan 1979, Starsky and Hutch;
  S.W.A.T.
Jan 1979–Jul 1979, Starsky and Hutch; Mannix
Jul 1979–Sep 1979, Starsky and Hutch; Baretta
Sep 1979–Apr 1980, Police Woman; Baretta
Apr 1980–Sep 1980, Charlie's Angels; Baretta
Sep 1980–Jan 1981, Charlie's Angels; Police
  Woman
Jan 1981–Sep 1981, Charlie's Angels
Oct 1981–Oct 1982, Vega$

Friday
Jan 1973–Nov 1973, In Concert/Jack Paar To-
  night/In Concert/Dick Cavett Show
Dec 1973–May 1975, In Concert/Movie
May 1975–Jan 1976, Wide World Special/
  Movie
Jan 1976–Sep 1976, The Rookies
Sep 1976–Apr 1977, S.W.A.T.
Apr 1977–Mar 1979, Baretta
Apr 1979–Jul 1979, Soap; Baretta
Jul 1979–Aug 1979, Soap
Sep 1979–Apr 1980, Charlie's Angels
Apr 1980–Oct 1982, Fridays

ABC MONDAY NIGHT COMEDY SPECIAL, THE
  Various
FIRST TELECAST: *May 16, 1977*
LAST TELECAST: *September 5, 1977*
BROADCAST HISTORY:
  May 1977–Sep 1977, ABC Mon 8:00–8:30

This was an umbrella title, covering an assortment of films for proposed series that did not
make the schedule and leftovers from series that
had been canceled. Included was a John Byner
situation comedy, an unusual rock music show (30
minutes of music—no dialogue), and leftover episodes from the canceled *Blansky's Beauties,
Nancy Walker Show,* and *Holmes and Yoyo.*

ABC NEWS REPORTS
  Documentary/Public Affairs
FIRST TELECAST: *July 7, 1963*
LAST TELECAST: *August 13, 1964*
BROADCAST HISTORY:
  Jul 1963–Dec 1963, ABC Sun 10:30–11:00
  Jan 1964–Aug 1964, ABC Thu 10:30–11:00
ANCHORMAN:
Bob Young (1963)

Some of the documentaries in this ABC News series were newly produced; others had been aired
previously under the title *ABC Closeup.* A major
production during August and September 1963
was a five-part series of special reports entitled
"Crucial Summer: The 1963 Civil Rights Crisis,"
produced by Bill Kobin and anchored by newsman Ron Cochran. From September through December 1963, correspondent Bob Young, who was
reportedly being groomed as a major on-camera
news "personality" by ABC, served as the regular

host. Later the anchor responsibilities rotated among various ABC correspondents.

ABC PENTHOUSE PLAYERS
see *ABC Television Players*

ABC PRESENTS
Documentary
FIRST TELECAST: *July 22, 1957*
LAST TELECAST: *October 3, 1957*
BROADCAST HISTORY:
Jul 1957–Sep 1957, ABC Mon 9:00–9:30
Sep 1957–Oct 1957, ABC Thu 8:00–8:30

A documentary film series seen during the summer of 1957. This program was also known as *Quest for Adventure*.

ABC ROCKS
Music Videos
FIRST TELECAST: *June 22, 1984*
LAST TELECAST: *August 2, 1985*
BROADCAST HISTORY:
Jun 1984–Aug 1985, ABC Fri 12:00 midnight–12:30 A.M.

One year after the premiere of NBC's *Friday Night Videos*, network television's first attempt to respond to the popularity of cable television's MTV (Music Television), ABC entered the fray with this half hour of music videos. Each weekly show consisted of a number of currently popular rock music videos, by such artists as Prince, The Cars, Cyndi Lauper, Bonnie Tyler, Eurythmics, Billy Idol, David Bowie, Huey Lewis and the News, and Flock of Seagulls.

ABC SATURDAY COMEDY SPECIAL, THE
Comedy Anthology
FIRST TELECAST: *June 24, 1978*
LAST TELECAST: *August 5, 1978*
BROADCAST HISTORY:
Jun 1978–Jul 1978, ABC Sat 8:30–9:00
Jul 1978–Aug 1978, ABC Sat 8:00–9:00

This was a collection of pilots for shows which did not make ABC's Fall 1978 schedule, along with miscellaneous reruns. Included were three Harvey Korman comedy episodes and a comedy-variety hour featuring characters from the Archie comic strip, with Dennis Bowen as Archie, Mark Winkworth as Reggie and Hilary Thompson as Veronica.

ABC SCOPE
Documentary/Public Affairs
FIRST TELECAST: *November 11, 1964*
LAST TELECAST: *March 2, 1968*
BROADCAST HISTORY:
Nov 1964–Sep 1965, ABC Wed 10:30–11:00
Sep 1965–Mar 1968, ABC Sat 10:30–11:00

Filmed reports, interviews, and roundtable discussions of current issues were all part of the format of this weekly public affairs series. ABC has also run many one-time documentary specials under this umbrella title over the years.

ABC SHOWCASE
Drama/Variety
FIRST TELECAST: *June 22, 1950*
LAST TELECAST: *July 26, 1950*
BROADCAST HISTORY:
Jun 1950–Jul 1950, ABC Thu 9:00–9:30
Jul 1950, ABC Wed 9:00–9:30

This was a blanket title for a series of dramatic and variety specials run during the summer of 1950 and starring, among others, Betty Furness, Peter Donald, and George O'Hanlon.

ABC STAGE 67
Various
FIRST TELECAST: *September 14, 1966*
LAST TELECAST: *May 11, 1967*
BROADCAST HISTORY:
Sep 1966–Jan 1967, ABC Wed 10:00–11:00
Jan 1967–May 1967, ABC Thu 10:00–11:00

This was an umbrella title for a potpourri of assorted specials. Among them were serious dramas with distinguished international casts, variety shows, an occasional documentary, and such unique formats as Jack Paar with examples of the Kennedy wit and David Frost on a tour of London with Peter Sellers, Albert Finney, and Laurence Olivier. The program had no regular host.

ABC TELEVISION PLAYERS
Dramatic Anthology
FIRST TELECAST: *January 16, 1949*
LAST TELECAST: *October 30, 1949*
BROADCAST HISTORY:
Jan 1949–Mar 1949, ABC Sun 9:00–9:30
Mar 1949–Oct 1949, ABC Sun 7:30–8:00
NARRATOR:
Don Gallagher

This was a series of low-budget live dramatic presentations from Chicago, fed to the East Coast network in the months immediately following the opening of the East-Midwest coaxial cable. Little-known Midwestern actors and actresses were used.

In April the title of the series was changed to *ABC Tele-Players*, and in August to *ABC Penthouse Players*.

ABC WIDE WORLD OF ENTERTAINMENT
see *ABC Late Night*

ABC'S NIGHTLIFE
Talk
FIRST TELECAST: *November 9, 1964*
LAST TELECAST: *November 12, 1965*
BROADCAST HISTORY:
Nov 1964–Nov 1965, ABC Mon-Fri 11:15–1:00

HOST:
Les Crane (Nov 1964–Feb 1965, Jun–Nov 1965)
REGULARS:
William B. Williams (1965)
Nipsey Russell (1965)
Jimmy Cannon (1965)
ORCHESTRA:
Cy Coleman (1965)
Donn Trenner (Mar–Jun 1965)
Elliot Lawrence (Jun–Nov 1965)

ABC's Nightlife was an early and abortive attempt by that network to compete in the late-night area long dominated by NBC's *Tonight Show.* The star was Les Crane, a handsome, young talk-show host from San Francisco who had attracted considerable attention there. Les's style was informal, highly spontaneous, and often controversial. The setting was a sort of studio-in-the-round, with the audience seated in circular tiers surrounding the stage, arena-style. Les, perched on his stool, often conversed with audience members by using a long-nosed "shotgun microphone," which he could focus on someone a long distance off. He strove for diversity and intelligence in his guests; the first show featured conservative commentator William Buckley and liberal Representative John V. Lindsay, actress Betsy Palmer, columnist Max Lerner, and comedian Groucho Marx, who acted as "instant critic" of the show.

Other critics were not very friendly, and Les left the show after only four months, to be replaced by a succession of guest hosts, including Shelley Berman, Dave Garroway, and Pat Boone, among others. Radio personality William B. Williams acted as aide-de-camp for all of them. At the end of June, however, Les was back, with Nipsey Russell as his sidekick. Soon after, the program moved from New York to Hollywood, but that couldn't save it. It ended its run just a year and three days after its premiere. Johnny Carson remained king of late-night television.

During its first four months the program was known as *The Les Crane Show.*

A.E.S. HUDSON STREET
Situation Comedy
FIRST TELECAST: *March 23, 1978*
LAST TELECAST: *April 20, 1978*
BROADCAST HISTORY:
Mar 1978–Apr 1978, ABC Thu 9:30–10:00
CAST:
Dr. Antonio "Tony" Menzies.. Gregory Sierra
Nurse Rosa Santiago .... Rosana Soto
J. Powell Karbo .... Stefan Gierasch
Ambulance Driver Foshko ...... Susan Peretz
Ambulance Aide Stanke .... Ralph Manza
Nurse Newton .... Ray Stewart
Dr. Mackler .... Bill Cort
Dr. Glick .... Allan Miller

This medical comedy starred Gregory Sierra as Dr. Menzies, the harried chief resident of an inner

city emergency ward; "A.E.S." stood for Adult Emergency Services. The location was Hudson Street, New York City, an area as run down as the hospital itself. Perpetually short of funds and surrounded by a staff of lunatics, Dr. Menzies nevertheless dealt with the various accident victims coming through the door as best he could, with good humor and only an occasional yearning to be somewhere else in the medical profession—anywhere else. Dr. Glick was the resident psychiatrist and J. Powell Karbo the bureaucratic hospital administrator.

A.K.A. PABLO
Situation Comedy
FIRST TELECAST: *March 6, 1984*
LAST TELECAST: *April 17, 1984*
BROADCAST HISTORY:
Mar 1984–Apr 1984, ABC Tue 8:30–9:00
CAST:
Paul (Pablo) Rivera .... Paul Rodriguez
Domingo Rivera .... Joe Santos
Rosa Maria Rivera............. Katy Jurado
Sylvia Rivera................. Alma Cuervo
Lucia Rivera Del Gato .... Martha Velez
Hector Del Gato .... Arnaldo Santana
Manuel Rivera.................. Bert Rosario
Carmen Rivera .... Maria Richwine
José Sanchez/Shapiro .... Hector Elizondo
Linda Rivera .... Edie Marie Rubio
Nicholas Rivera .... Antonio Torres
Anna Maria Del Gato ..... Claudia Gonzales
Susana Del Gato........... Martha Gonzales
Tomas Del Gato .... Mario Lopez
Mario Del Gato................. Beto Lovato
Elena Del Gato .... Michelle Smith
EXECUTIVE PRODUCER:
Norman Lear

Short-lived comedy about a struggling young Hispanic comedian and his large, noisy family, who rooted for his success while wanting him to treat his Mexican-American heritage with almost solemn dignity. Paul Rivera—still called Pablo by his family—used a lot of ethnic jokes in his act, which sometimes offended his traditionalist parents, Domingo and Rosa Maria. But every Mexican joke he used seemed to spring from his home situation, whether it was about sister Lucia and her swaggering husband Hector, stuffy brother Manuel and his coquettish wife Carmen, or unmarried (but anxious) sister Sylvia. José was Paul's fast-talking but inexperienced agent, while the rest of the regulars consisted of the Rivera/Del Gato children.

A-TEAM, THE
Adventure
FIRST TELECAST: *January 23, 1983*
LAST TELECAST: *June 14, 1987*
BROADCAST HISTORY:
Jan 1983, NBC Sun 10:00–11:00
Feb 1983–Aug 1986, NBC Tue 8:00–9:00

Aug 1986–Dec 1986, NBC Fri 8:00–9:00
Dec 1986, NBC Tue 8:00–9:00
May 1987–Jun 1987, NBC Sun 7:00–8:00

CAST:

Col. John "Hannibal" Smith . . George Peppard
Sgt. Bosco "B.A." Baracus . . . . Mr. T
Lt. Templeton Peck ("Faceman") (pilot only)
. . . . Tim Dunigan
Lt. Templeton Peck ("Faceman")
. . . . Dirk Benedict
Capt. H.M. "Howling Mad" Murdock
. . . . Dwight Schultz
Amy Allen (1983) . . . . Melinda Culea
Col. Lynch (1983–1984) . . . . . William Lucking
Col. Roderick Decker (1983–1986)
. . . . Lance LeGault
Tawnia Baker (1984) . . . . Maria Heasley
Gen. Hunt Stockwell (1986–1987)
. . . . Robert Vaughn
"Dishpan" Frankie Sanchez (1986–1987)
. . . . Eddie Velez
Carla (1986) . . . . Judy Ledford

MUSIC:

Mike Post and Pete Carpenter

It opened with machine-gun-like music, followed by the title stamped across the screen in stenciled, military-style letters, which were then punctured by bullet holes containing pictures of the stars. From opening title to closing credits, *The A-Team* was a veritable weekly demolition derby—and it was a smash hit.

The premise, like the plots, was standard-issue TV. A crack team of soldiers in Vietnam was caught while on a super-secret mission behind enemy lines. Seems that four days after the war had ended they had knocked over the Bank of Hanoi for one hundred million yen, but could not prove who had given them their orders, and so were imprisoned by their own government. They had escaped, but now were outcasts, pursued as criminals by a relentless Col. Lynch (and later by Col. Decker), who was determined to put them behind bars again. They not only managed to evade the colonel's clutches, however, but became freelance soldiers of fortune, righting wrongs across the country and in exotic foreign locales.

It was a colorful team. Col. Hannibal Smith, the cigar-chomping, remarkably fit leader, was a master of disguises. B.A. (officially "Bad Attitude," but you can use your imagination) was big, black, and menacing—and also an expert mechanic. Howling Mad Murdock was their pilot, whose sanity was seriously in question (they had to spring him from a mental hospital for their missions), but who could apparently fly anything from a crop duster to a 747. Faceman was the pretty boy, a smooth talker who could hustle practically anything they needed for their missions. Joining them in the first episode was Amy Allen, a pretty reporter who was understandably taken with this odd bunch and their far-flung adventures.

The destruction they wrought may have seemed appalling to some, but it was carried off with such panache, such a twinkle in the eye, that viewers knew it was not for real. Despite jeeps spinning through the air and buildings leveled in fiery explosions, hardly anyone—even the bad guys—ever got hurt. One furious chase scene ended with the pursuing villains' car in a spectacular high-speed crash. The camera lingered for a moment on the overturned wreck; one voice from inside grunted, "You okay, Al?" and another answered, "Yeah, I'm all right."

Nor were the team members ever at a loss for firepower, even when separated from their innocuous-looking but well-armed van. B.A. could build machine guns out of old washing machines, rocket launchers out of used water heaters, and an armored tank out of a broken-down school bus. Mr. T (as B.A.) was the cult hero of the show, with his macho chains (35 lbs. of gold) draped around his neck and his favorite scowling line. "You better watch out, sucker!" For all his threatening appearance, however, he did have one abiding fear—flying in a plane piloted by Howling Mad. So the team regularly drugged, hypnotized, or tricked him to get him to the scene of the action.

In the fall of 1986 the team's status changed dramatically. Tricked into capture by the mysterious Gen. Stockwell, they were tried and sentenced to die—but Stockwell arranged for them to "pay their debt" by becoming undercover government agents instead, under his heavy-handed control. Joining the team was a sneaky little special-effects expert known as "Dishpan" Frankie.

AARON'S WAY

Drama

FIRST TELECAST: *March 9, 1988*
LAST TELECAST: *May 25, 1988*
BROADCAST HISTORY:

Mar 1988–May 1988, NBC Wed 8:00–9:00

CAST:

Aaron Miller . . . . Merlin Olsen
Sarah Miller . . . . Belinda Montgomery
Roseanne Miller (age 15) . . Samantha Mathis
Martha Miller (12) . . . . Erin Chase
Frank Miller (11) . . . . Scott Curtis
Susannah Lo Verde . . . . Kathleen York
Connie Lo Verde . . . . Jessica Walter
Mickey Lo Verde (16) . . . . Christopher Gartin
Mr. Benvenuto . . . . Pierrino Mascarino

Merlin Olsen, best known for his roles in such "warm and wonderful" dramas as *Little House on the Prairie* and *Father Murphy,* starred in another one in 1988. Aaron Miller was a strict, bearded Amish patriarch who uprooted his tight-knit family from their cloistered environment in Pennsylvania and moved to California when his eldest son died there. Noah Miller had forsaken Amish ways, and when he perished in a surfing accident he left behind a pregnant girlfriend (Susannah) with a vineyard she couldn't maintain alone. So, unbidden, the Millers moved in to help.

Stories revolved around the Millers' culture shock as they adjusted to modern California ways, while trying to retain their deep-rooted moral values and peculiar style of dress; and conservative Aaron's clashes with free-spirited Susannah and her tart-tongued mother, Connie, who ran the local beauty salon. Underneath, of course, there was a lot of love. Susannah's teen-aged brother Mickey had his own plan for bridging the culture gap, with eyes for Miller daughter Roseanne.

ABBOTT AND COSTELLO SHOW, THE
Situation Comedy
BROADCAST HISTORY:
Syndicated and network daytime
30 minutes
Produced: *1951–1953* (52 episodes)
Released: *Fall 1952*
CAST:
Bud Abbott . . . . Himself
Lou Costello . . . . Himself
Hillary Brooke . . . . Herself
Sid Fields . . . . Himself
Mike the Cop . . . . Gordon Jones
Mr. Bacciagalupe . . . . Joe Kirk
Stinky . . . . Joe Besser
VARIOUS SUPPORTING ROLES:
Joan Shawlee
Bobby Barber
Milt Bronson
PRODUCER:
Alex Gottlieb
Pat Costello
DIRECTOR:
Jean Yarborough

Critics hated this show. Audiences found it screamingly funny, so much so that it became one of the most successful and most repeated syndicated programs in television history.

It certainly was low-brow slapstick in its purest form, full of terrible puns, improbable situations, and lots of knockabout, physical comedy. There was a story line of sorts, which had Bud (the tall, debonair one) and Lou (the short, silly one) as unemployed actors sharing an apartment in a rooming house run by Mr. Fields, who was always hounding them for back rent. Lou's girlfriend, Hillary, lived across the hall. Also living in the board-inghouse was Stinky, a malevolent brat who'd grab Lou's arm and threaten, "I'll harm you!" (Though a grown man, Stinky was always dressed in a Little Lord Fauntleroy outfit.) Other more or less regular characters were Mike the Cop and Mr. Bacciagalupe, who had different occupations depending on the episode. Appearing frequently in different roles were Joan Shawlee, Bobby

Barber (the short, bald one), and Milt Bronson.

Each program began with a premise, often some scheme of Lou's to make money or avoid paying bills, but soon disintegrated into a succession of unrelated skits and gags. Essentially, the series was a showcase for all the old material Bud and Lou had been using on stage and in films since the 1930s. They might be at a charity bazaar (where they could work in the "Lemon Bit"), or stranded in a haunted house (good excuse for the "Moving Candle" routine), or in an old folks' home full of loonies who were having a baseball game with an imaginary ball (up popped their classic "Who's on First?" routine). Some episodes were complete steals from old silent comedies, including a virtual re-enactment of Buster Keaton's 1920 short *One Week*, in which a jealous suitor sabotages the house Lou has built for his fiancée.

Lou Costello was the spark plug of all this frenzy. He was a natural comic, full of gags and practical jokes on screen and off. During filming, even when the action shifted elsewhere, the director kept one camera on Costello so as not to miss any impromptu bits of business. Lou owned the show, and after the first half dozen episodes installed his brother, Pat Costello, as producer.

After the first 26 episodes were filmed, changes were made. Brooke, Kirk, Besser, and Shawlee departed (as did the boys' pet, Bingo the Chimp, who had made the mistake of biting Costello), Director Jean Yarborough tried to get things more organized, with more consistent story lines and a new gag writer, Clyde Bruckman, for Abbott and Costello were running out of their old material. In all, only 52 episodes of the program were filmed, but these were highly popular—critics notwithstanding—and were rerun endlessly over the next decades (starting with six months on CBS's Saturday morning lineup from September 1954 to February 1955). One New York station is said to have aired each one of the 52 more than 200 times. It was one of the last great successes for the top comedy team of the 1940s, whose films, radio show, and *Colgate Comedy Hour* appearances entertained millions. The pair finally broke up in 1957. Costello, the human dynamo, was worn out by the time he reached his fifties; he died in 1959, at the age of 52. Abbott passed away in 1974.

A cartoon version of *The Abbott and Costello Show* was syndicated in 1966, with Abbott providing his own voice.

A detailed and appreciative account of Abbott and Costello's career, including full details on the TV series, can be found in *The Abbott and Costello Book* by Jim Mulholland, published in 1975.

ABE BURROWS' ALMANAC
Comedy Variety
FIRST TELECAST: *January 4, 1950*
LAST TELECAST: *March 29, 1950*
BROADCAST HISTORY:
Jan 1950–Mar 1950, CBS Wed 9:00–9:30

REGULARS:
Abe Burrows
Milton Delugg and His Orchestra

This live variety series starred comedian Abe Burrows, "the bald-headed baritone from Brooklyn," who chatted with orchestra leader Milton Delugg and welcomed different guest stars each week. Burrows had hosted two short-lived radio series in the late 1940s, but his greatest fame came as a writer-director for radio *(Duffy's Tavern)*, Broadway *(Guys and Dolls, How to Succeed in Business Without Really Trying)*, and Hollywood *(The Solid Gold Cadillac)*.

ACADEMY THEATRE
Dramatic Anthology
FIRST TELECAST: *July 25, 1949*
LAST TELECAST: *September 12, 1949*
BROADCAST HISTORY:
Jul 1949–Sep 1949, NBC Mon 8:00–8:30

This series of eight live half-hour dramas replaced *Chevrolet on Broadway* for the summer of 1949. It had a different cast each week, consisting of lesser-known actors and actresses in playlets by such authors as Thornton Wilder, Edna St. Vincent Millay, and Robert Finch. *Academy Theatre* was produced by Curtis Canfield, Professor of Dramatics at Amherst College.

ACAPULCO
Adventure
FIRST TELECAST: *February 27, 1961*
LAST TELECAST: *April 24, 1961*
BROADCAST HISTORY:
Feb 1961–Apr 1961, NBC Mon 9:00–9:30
CAST:
Patrick Malone . . . . Ralph Taeger
Gregg Miles . . . . James Coburn
Mr. Carver . . . . Telly Savalas
Chloe . . . . Allison Hayes
Bobby. . . . . Bobby Troup
Max . . . . Jason Robards, Sr.

Ralph Taeger and James Coburn starred as two Korean War buddies turned action-prone "beachcombers" in sunny Acapulco. Mr. Carver, a retired criminal lawyer, had supplied them with a beach cottage adjoining his sumptuous estate in return for their help in protecting him from enemies made during his career as a gang-busting lawyer. The two ex-GI's were constantly forced to give up their girl-chasing to protect Mr. Carver, but they still managed to spend much time at a small club run by musician Bobby Troup and at a more opulent club run by Chloe, a beautiful woman who knew everything about everybody in Acapulco.

ACCENT ON AN AMERICAN SUMMER
Travelogue
FIRST TELECAST: *June 7, 1962*

LAST TELECAST: *September 6, 1962*
BROADCAST HISTORY:
June 1962–Sep 1962, CBS Thu 7:30–8:00
HOST:
John Ciardi

Accent on an American Summer was a summer series that took viewers on tours of various places of historic or general interest. Hosted by John Ciardi, the series went to Monticello, Thomas Jefferson's home; the American Shakespeare Festival, to see excerpts from two plays; the wilds of Yellowstone National Park; the gambling environment of Reno, Nevada; and other varied locales.

ACCIDENTAL FAMILY
Situation Comedy
FIRST TELECAST: *September 15, 1967*
LAST TELECAST: *January 5, 1968*
BROADCAST HISTORY:
Sep 1967–Jan 1968, NBC Fri 9:30–10:00
CAST:
Jerry Webster . . . . Jerry Van Dyke
Sue Kramer . . . . Lois Nettleton
Sandy Webster . . . . Teddy Quinn
Tracy Kramer . . . . Susan Benjamin
Ben McGrath . . . . Ben Blue
Marty Warren . . . . Larry D. Mann

Jerry Van Dyke played nightclub comedian Jerry Webster, one of TV's many widowers, confronted with the problems of raising a young son, Sandy, played by Teddy Quinn. In this series Father decided literally to "farm out" his son by purchasing a farm in California's San Fernando Valley as a full-time home for the boy and part-time home for himself, between performing commitments. Farm manager Sue Kramer, a pretty divorcée whose daughter, Tracy, just happened to be Sandy's age, served as de facto governess for the boy and foil for Jerry. Ben McGrath, the farm handyman, and Marty Warren, Jerry's friend and lawyer, rounded out the cast of regulars.

ACCUSED
Courtroom Drama
FIRST TELECAST: *December 10, 1958*
LAST TELECAST: *September 30, 1959*
BROADCAST HISTORY:
Dec 1958–Sep 1959, ABC Wed 9:30–10:00
CAST:
Presiding Judge . . . . Edgar Allan Jones, Jr.
*Presiding Judge . . . . William Gwinn
Bailiff . . . . Tim Farrell
Clerk . . . . Jim Hodson
Reporter . . . . Violet Gilmore

*Occasional

Accused was a prime-time spin-off from *Day in Court*, a popular ABC daytime program that presented filmed reenactments of actual cases. Realism was the keynote of the series; the judge for

8

most of the trials was Edgar Allan Jones, Jr., a UCLA law professor, and the prosecution and defense attorneys were also real-life lawyers. Only the defendants and witnesses were actors, usually obscure ones but occasionally such well-known performers as Pamela Mason and Robert Culp (who appeared with his wife, actress Nancy Ash). The cases were almost invariably criminal proceedings.

Accused was produced by Selig J. Seligman, a former State Department attorney and ABC-TV Vice President, who kept a whole staff of lawyers and law students busy digging through court records and law books to provide authenticity for the show.

During its first few weeks on the air the nighttime series was known as *Day in Court*. The daytime version continued under that name from 1958 until 1965.

ACE CRAWFORD, PRIVATE EYE
Situation Comedy
FIRST TELECAST: *March 15, 1983*
LAST TELECAST: *April 12, 1983*
BROADCAST HISTORY:
  Mar 1983–Apr 1983, CBS Tue 8:00–8:30
CAST:
  Ace Crawford . . . . Tim Conway
  Toomey . . . . Joe Regalbuto
  Inch . . . . Billy Barty
  Luana . . . . Shera Danese
  Mello . . . . Bill Henderson
  Lt. Fanning . . . . Dick Christie

Imagine Bogie's Sam Spade played for laughs, and you've got *Ace Crawford*. A hard-nosed private detective, attired in the requisite trench coat, Ace was all business. But blind luck and fortuitous accidents were more responsible for his solving cases than his sleuthing skill. His incredible run of luck had given him an undeserved reputation and brought him a continuous stream of clients. It also made Ace irresistible to the ladies, although he was usually too busy fumbling through cases to pay any attention to them. Ace's bumbling part-time assistant Toomey, a full-time CPA, idolized Ace and hung out with his "boss" at the Shanty, a sleazy club located on the wharf. Inch (played by midget Billy Barty) was the owner and bartender at the Shanty, where Ace's not-quite-girlfriend Luana was the featured singer. Mello, Luana's blind accompanist, was played by jazz great Bill Henderson. Also featured was an incredulous Lt. Fanning, who couldn't understand how Ace seemed to solve difficult cases without any effort.

ACT IT OUT
  see *Say It with Acting*

ACTION AUTOGRAPHS
Documentary
FIRST TELECAST: *April 24, 1949*

LAST TELECAST: *January 8, 1950*
BROADCAST HISTORY:
  Apr 1949–Jun 1949, ABC Sun 10:00–10:15
  Sep 1949–Jan 1950, ABC Sun 6:30–6:45
HOST:
  Jack Brand *(Apr–Jun)*
  Ed Prentiss *(Sep–Jan)*

This short filmed program was sponsored by Bell & Howell Cameras, evidently to show how the medium of film could allow viewers to drop in on many interesting people and watch their activities. Interviews, demonstrations, and performances were included. Among the subjects were the national barbershop quartet champions, a water show, singer Burl Ives, and Dr. Beryl Orris psychoanalyzing the thoughts and actions of a character played by actor Richard Basehart in a scene from the play *She Walks at Night*.

ACTION TONIGHT
Dramatic Anthology
FIRST TELECAST: *July 15, 1957*
LAST TELECAST: *September 2, 1957*
BROADCAST HISTORY:
  Jul 1957–Sep 1957, NBC Mon 8:30–9:00

This series presented filmed reruns of dramas originally seen on *Schlitz Playhouse* and *Pepsi-Cola Playhouse*.

ACTORS STUDIO
Dramatic Anthology
FIRST TELECAST: *September 26, 1948*
LAST TELECAST: *June 23, 1950*
BROADCAST HISTORY:
  Sep 1948–Mar 1949, ABC Sun 8:30–9:00
  Mar 1949–Apr 1949, ABC Thu 8:30–9:00
  May 1949, ABC Thu 9:30–10:00
  Sep 1949–Oct 1949, ABC Wed 8:00–8:30
  Nov 1949–Jan 1950, CBS Tue 9:00–9:30
  Feb 1950–Jun 1950, CBS Fri 9:00–10:00
HOST:
  Marc Connelly
PRODUCER:
  Donald Davis

This was one of the first "prestige" dramatic showcases on the fledgling ABC network. It was produced live each week by the Actors Studio, Inc., a nonprofit organization for professional actors and actresses. Most productions were serious dramas, encompassing both adaptations of classic stories and occasional original scripts. Among the authors represented were William Saroyan, James Thurber, Ring Lardner, Edgar Allan Poe, Irwin Shaw, and Budd Schulberg. Performers included such first-rate talent as Julie Harris, Cloris Leachman, Martin Balsam, and Kim Hunter. The first telecast was "Portrait of a Madonna" and starred Jessica Tandy. Young Marlon Brando made his first television appearance here in January 1949.

Actors Studio made a strong impression during its first months on the air, and received a Peabody Award for its "uninhibited and brilliant pioneering in the field of televised drama" during the year of 1948.

During its final four months the program expanded to a full hour and was seen every other week, alternating with *Ford Theatre.* The series name was changed to *The Play's the Thing* in March 1950.

ACTUALITY SPECIALS
Documentary
FIRST TELECAST: *July 16, 1962*
LAST TELECAST: *September 13, 1968*
BROADCAST HISTORY:
   Jul 1962–Sep 1962, NBC Mon 10:00–11:00
   Oct 1965–Jun 1967, NBC Sun 6:30–7:30 (OS)
   Sep 1967–Sep 1968, NBC Fri 10:00–11:00

Actuality Specials was a collection of NBC News documentary specials. Some were reruns of programs shown earlier; others were new programs made specifically for this series. Narrators were usually NBC newsmen such as Robert MacNeil, Edwin Newman, Frank McGee, and Chet Huntley; however, celebrities such as Lorne Greene or Raymond Burr sometimes provided narration. *Actuality Specials* frequently alternated with other documentary series such as *NBC White Paper, NBC News Special, Campaign and the Candidates,* and *American Profile.*

AD LIBBERS
Improvisation
FIRST TELECAST: *August 3, 1951*
LAST TELECAST: *August 31, 1951*
BROADCAST HISTORY:
   Aug 1951, CBS Fri 8:00–8:30
HOST:
   Peter Donald
REGULARS:
   Charles Mendick
   Patricia Hosley
   Joe Silver
   Jack Lemmon
   Cynthia Stone
   Earl Hammond

This live series of improvisations was the 1951 summer replacement for *Mama.* Peter Donald, the host, would read a brief outline of a situation to the performers, who would then ad-lib dialogue to fit the situation. There were three or four sketches performed during each episode of this five-week show.

ADAM 12
Police Drama
FIRST TELECAST: *September 21, 1968*
LAST TELECAST: *August 26, 1975*

BROADCAST HISTORY:
   Sep 1968–Sep 1969, NBC Sat 7:30–8:00
   Sep 1969–Jan 1971, NBC Sat 8:30–9:00
   Jan 1971–Sep 1971, NBC Thu 9:30–10:00
   Sep 1971–Jan 1974, NBC Wed 8:00–8:30
   Jan 1974–Aug 1975, NBC Tue 8:00–8:30
CAST:
   Officer Pete Malloy . . . . Martin Milner
   Officer Jim Reed . . . . Kent McCord
   Sgt. MacDonald. . . . . William Boyett
   Officer Ed Wells . . . . Gary Crosby
   Dispatcher's voice . . . . Shaaron Claridge
   Officer Jerry Walters (1968–1969)
      . . . . William Stevens
   Sgt. Jerry Miller (1969) . . . . Jack Hogan
   Jean Reed (1969) . . . . Mikki Jamison
   Officer Norm Green (1970–1971)
      . . . . Claude Johnson
   Officer Grant (1974–1975) . . . . . William Elliott
   Officer Woods (1974–1975) . . . . Fred Stromsoe

Produced by Jack Webb, whose realistic portrayal of police work had scored a major hit in *Dragnet, Adam 12* dealt with the day-to-day working world of two uniformed policemen assigned to patrol-car duty. Officer Pete Malloy was a senior officer who at the start of the series was teamed with a probationary rookie cop, Jim Reed. As members of the Los Angeles Police Department, they encountered a wide range of cases in each episode, some serious, some trivial, some amusing, and some tragic. Running as it did for seven seasons, *Adam 12* saw changes in the status of the officers as the years passed. During the 1970–1971 season Jim Reed was promoted from rookie to officer, and in the following year Officer Malloy was upped to Policeman 3, one notch below the rank of sergeant.

ADAM'S RIB
Situation Comedy
FIRST TELECAST: *September 14, 1973*
LAST TELECAST: *December 28, 1973*
BROADCAST HISTORY:
   Sep 1973–Dec 1973, ABC Fri 9:30–10:00
CAST:
   Adam Bonner. . . . . Ken Howard
   Amanda Bonner . . . . Blythe Danner
   Gracie . . . . Dena Dietrich
   Asst. D.A. Roy Mendelsohn. . . . . . . Ron Rifkin
   Kip Kipple . . . . Edward Winter
   District Attorney Donahue. . . Norman Bartold
CREATOR/PRODUCER/DIRECTOR:
   Peter H. Hunt
THEME:
   "Two People," by Perry Botkin, Jr., and Gil Garfield

This romantic comedy was based on the Spencer Tracy–Katharine Hepburn movie classic of the same title. The show concerned a young Assistant D.A. and his wife, a junior partner in a law firm, whose jobs often put them on opposite sides in the courtroom as well as at home. *Adam's Rib* made overtures to the Women's Lib movement by building many stories around Amanda's crusades for women's rights (50 percent of the show's writers were women), but the program never found an audience.

Dena Dietrich ("Mother Nature" of commercials fame) played Amanda's secretary, and Edward Winter her law partner, while Norman Bartold and Ron Rifkin were on Adam's side.

ADDAMS FAMILY, THE
Situation Comedy
FIRST TELECAST: *September 18, 1964*
LAST TELECAST: *September 2, 1966*
BROADCAST HISTORY:
Sep 1964–Sep 1966, ABC Fri 8:30–9:00
CAST:
Morticia Frump Addams....... Carolyn Jones
Gomez Addams.................. John Astin
Uncle Fester Frump .... Jackie Coogan
Lurch .... Ted Cassidy
Grandmama Addams.......... Blossom Rock
Pugsley Addams .... Ken Weatherwax
Wednesday Thursday Addams... Lisa Loring
Cousin Itt .... Felix Silla
Thing .... Ted Cassidy

The strange, macabre, but somehow amusing cartoon characters created by Charles Addams for *The New Yorker* magazine made their live-action debut in the fall of 1964, one of two almost identical "ghoul comedies" to premiere that year (see also CBS' *Munsters*). Morticia was the beautiful but somber lady of the house. Her husband Gomez had strange eyes and rather destructive instincts, as did Uncle Fester. Lurch, the butler, was a seven-foot-tall warmed-over Frankenstein monster whose dialogue usually consisted solely of the two words, "You rang?" The children also had a rather ghoulish quality about them. Grandmama, although a witch, was the most normal-looking one of the bunch. They all lived in a musty, castlelike home full of strange objects—such as a disembodied hand, called "Thing," which kept popping out of a black box—and they scared almost everyone—except viewers—half to death.

An animated version of *The Addams Family* aired Saturday morning on NBC from September 1973 to August 1975.

ADDERLY
Comedy Drama
FIRST TELECAST: *September 24, 1986*
LAST TELECAST:
BROADCAST HISTORY:
Sep 1986–Jul 1987, CBS Wed 11:30–12:40A.M.
Aug 1987–Sep 1987, CBS Fri 10:00–11:00
*Sep 1987–   *, CBS Wed 11:30–12:40A.M.

CAST:
V.H. Adderly .... Winston Rekert
Melville Greenspan .... Jonathan Welsh
Mona Ellerby.................. Dixie Seatle
Major Jonathan B. Clack .... Ken Pogue

Adderly had been a top operative of the department of International Security and Intelligence (I.S.I.) until he lost the use of his left hand while being tortured by enemy agents. His superior, Major Clack, in order to keep him on the payroll, assigned him to work for the department of "Miscellaneous Affairs," which usually got involved with minor and harmless diplomatic assignments. V.H.'s new boss was a petty bureaucrat named Greenspan who had no desire to rock the boat and was exasperated by Adderly's predilection for making real cases out of seemingly mundane—and often nonsensical—assignments. Greenspan's secretary, Mona, who had a bit of a crush on Adderly, was more than willing to bypass normal channels and procedures to help V.H., despite the complaints from her boss.

Produced in Toronto.

ADMIRAL BROADWAY REVUE
Variety
FIRST TELECAST: *January 28, 1949*
LAST TELECAST: *June 3, 1949*
BROADCAST HISTORY:
Jan 1949–Jun 1949, NBC & DUM Fri 8:00–9:00
REGULARS:
Sid Caesar
Imogene Coca
Mary McCarty
Marge and Gower Champion
Tom Avera
Ronnie Cunningham
Judson Laire
Estelle Loring
Loren Welch

Sid Caesar won his first regular starring role in this program, which united him in a comedy team with Imogene Coca for the first time.

Neither of them was new to television in 1949, Caesar having guest-starred on Milton Berle's show during the previous fall and Coca having appeared on television as early as 1939.

Though short-lived, *Admiral Broadway Revue* was one of early television's most spectacular productions, completely dominating Friday night viewing the way that Milton Berle dominated Tuesday and Ed Sullivan, Sunday. The series was produced and directed by Max Liebman and was built along the lines of a Broadway music and comedy revue, with top-name guest stars and big production numbers. For example, the opening program included half a dozen comedy skits and closed with an elaborate burlesque on opera in the style of Billy Rose, called "No No Rigoletto." The program was telecast live from the newly completed International Theatre in New York and was one of the few major programs ever to be carried on two networks simultaneously (NBC and DuMont). It was seen in every city in the United States that had television facilities, either live from the networks or on kinescope in markets not yet having network connections.

Judson Laire, who was the featured baritone singer on *Admiral Broadway Revue,* turned up one month after this series left the air in a straight dramatic role on CBS's series *Mama.* He played Lars Hansen, the father figure in the show, for the next eight years.

ADMIRAL PRESENTS THE FIVE STAR REVUE—WELCOME ABOARD
see *Welcome Aboard*

ADMISSION FREE
see *Movies—Prior to 1961*

ADORN PLAYHOUSE
Dramatic Anthology
FIRST TELECAST: *May 13, 1958*
LAST TELECAST: *July 1, 1958*
BROADCAST HISTORY:
May 1958–Jul 1958, CBS Tue 8:30–9:00

This 1958 summer series consisted of reruns of episodes from other CBS anthologies, primarily *Schlitz Playhouse.*

ADVENTURE
Wildlife/Adventure
FIRST TELECAST: *June 28, 1953*
LAST TELECAST: *September 27, 1953*
BROADCAST HISTORY:
Jun 1953–Sep 1953, CBS Sun 6:00–7:00
NARRATOR:
Charles Collingwood

Produced in cooperation with the American Museum of Natural History, *Adventure* was composed of interviews with naturalists, anthropologists, and other authorities, coupled with filmed reports of expeditions to remote areas and primitive peoples. Charles Collingwood was the host of the series, which actually had its premiere as a late-Sunday-afternoon program on May 10, 1953. Following its run as an evening program, it returned to Sunday afternoons where it remained on the air until July 1956.

ADVENTURE PLAYHOUSE
see *Movies—Prior to 1961*

ADVENTURE SHOWCASE
Adventure Anthology
FIRST TELECAST: *August 11, 1959*
LAST TELECAST: *September 1, 1959*
BROADCAST HISTORY:
Aug 1959–Sep 1959, CBS Tue 9:00–9:30

This four-week summer series consisted of unsold pilots for proposed adventure series.

ADVENTURE THEATER
Adventure Anthology
FIRST TELECAST: *June 16, 1956*
LAST TELECAST: *August 31, 1957*
BROADCAST HISTORY:
Jun 1956–Sep 1956, NBC Sat 10:30–11:00
Jun 1957–Aug 1957, NBC Sat 10:30–11:00
HOST:
Paul Douglas

Aired as a summer replacement for *Your Hit Parade,* this program presented filmed, two-act plays that were produced in England. Host Paul Douglas introduced the plays, appearing as a storyteller who had been to England and returned with various objects such as a fur coat or a scarf, each of which led into the story with which it was associated. The 1957 series consisted of repeats of the 1956 episodes.

ADVENTURE THEATER
Dramatic Anthology
FIRST TELECAST: *August 4, 1960*
LAST TELECAST: *September 22, 1961*
BROADCAST HISTORY:
Aug 1960–Sep 1960, CBS Thu 10:00–10:30
Jul 1961–Sep 1961, CBS Fri 9:30–10:00

The dramas seen in this summer series were all reruns of episodes originally telecast on *Schlitz Playhouse.* There was no host.

ADVENTURES AT SCOTT ISLAND
see *Harbourmaster*

ADVENTURES IN JAZZ
Music
FIRST TELECAST: *January 28, 1949*
LAST TELECAST: *June 24, 1949*
BROADCAST HISTORY:
Jan 1949–Jun 1949, CBS Fri 8:00–8:30
HOST:
Fred Robbins
Bill Williams

Disc jockey Fred Robbins—noted for his unique chatter, concocted vocabulary, and floppy bow tie—was host of this live show, which brought jazz musicians and singers to television. After appearing on the show's premiere telecast, Robbins departed for other commitments and did not return to the series until May. Bill Williams hosted in Robbins' absence.

ADVENTURES IN PARADISE
Adventure
FIRST TELECAST: *October 5, 1959*
LAST TELECAST: *April 1, 1962*
BROADCAST HISTORY:
Oct 1959–Sep 1961, ABC Mon 9:30–10:30
Oct 1961–Apr 1962, ABC Sun 10:00–11:00

Capt. Adam Troy .... Gardner McKay
Oliver Lee (1959–1961)......... Weaver Levy
Renee (1960–1961)............ Linda Lawson
Bulldog Lovey (1960–1961) ...... Henry Slate
Clay Baker (1960–1962)........ James Holden
Trader Penrose (1960–1961) ... George Tobias
Sondi (1960–1961) .... Sondi Sodsai
Kelly (1960–1962) .... Lani Kai
Chris Parker (1961–1962) ..... Guy Stockwell
Inspector Bouchard (1961–1962)
.... Marcel Hillaire

This series featured handsome Gardner McKay as Adam Troy, the captain of a free-lance schooner plying the South Pacific in search of passengers, cargo, and adventure. Troy was a Korean War veteran who had found the Pacific to his liking. His schooner, the *Tiki,* ranged across the area from Hong Kong to Pitcairn Island with all sorts of adventurers, schemers, and island beauties aboard. Troy's original partner was a Chinese-American named Oliver Lee. In 1960 he hired a first mate named Clay Baker. The following season Baker went ashore to become manager of the Bali Miki hotel (replacing Trader Penrose), and Troy took on Chris Parker as his first mate. The females in the cast were young Tahitians and other lovely young women who seemed to abound in this series.

James A. Michener created *Adventures in Paradise* and sold the original idea to television, but then he apparently dropped out of the project. Critics complained that the series contained none of the scripting one would expect from such an eminent author. Even the sets looked like the 20th Century–Fox back lot—which it was—though after a couple of years, some location filming was actually done in the South Pacific.

ADVENTURES IN SHERWOOD FOREST
syndicated title for *Adventures of Robin Hood, The*

ADVENTURES OF CHAMPION, THE
Adventure
FIRST TELECAST: *September 30, 1955*
LAST TELECAST: *February 3, 1956*
BROADCAST HISTORY:
Sep 1955–Feb 1956, CBS Fri 7:30–8:00
CAST:
Ricky North .... Barry Curtis
Sandy North................... Jim Bannon
Will Calhoun .... Francis McDonald
Sheriff Powers .... Ewing Mitchell

This series was produced by Gene Autry and starred Champion the Wonder Horse, his mount. In *The Adventures of Champion,* the talented horse was owned by 12-year-old Ricky North, the only person Champion would allow to ride him. Ricky also owned a German Shepherd named Rebel, and both the horse and the dog were his

constant companions. Ricky, who lived on a ranch owned by his Uncle Sandy, had a penchant for getting involved in dangerous situations. But whether he was faced with natural disasters or with evil men who would steal, murder, or in some other way cause trouble, Champion and Rebel would come to his rescue by performing some feat not normally associated with horses or dogs.

ADVENTURES OF ELLERY QUEEN, THE
Detective Drama
FIRST TELECAST: *October 14, 1950*
LAST TELECAST: *September 5, 1976*
BROADCAST HISTORY:
Oct 1950–Dec 1951, DUM Thu 9:00–9:30 (OS)
Dec 1951–Mar 1952, ABC Sun 7:30–8:00
Apr 1952–Dec 1952, ABC Wed 9:00–9:30
Sep 1958–Aug 1959, NBC Fri 8:00–9:00
Sep 1975–Dec 1975, NBC Thu 9:00–10:00
Jan 1976–Sep 1976, NBC Sun 8:00–9:00
CAST:
Ellery Queen (1950–1951) ...... Richard Hart
Ellery Queen (1951–1952) .... Lee Bowman
Inspector Richard Queen (1950–1952)
.... Florenz Ames
Ellery Queen (1958–1959) ...... George Nader
Inspector Richard Queen (1958–1959)
.... Les Tremayne
Ellery Queen (1959) .... Lee Philips
Ellery Queen (1975–1976) .... Jim Hutton
Inspector Richard Queen (1975–1976)
.... David Wayne
Sgt. Velie (1975–1976) .... Tom Reese
Simon Brimmer (1975–1976).. John Hillerman
Frank Flannigan (1975–1976) ... Ken Swofford

Fictional mystery writer-supersleuth Ellery Queen had been the main character in a number of popular mystery novels, written by Frederic Dannay and Manfred Bennington Lee, before he became a regular feature on the CBS Radio Network in 1939. A decade later he made the first of four appearances on television. Ellery was a slightly absentminded mystery writer who would sort through a mass of evidence and a large collection of suspects to determine the guilty party in a crime, usually murder. His aid was regularly sought by his father, an inspector with the New York Police Department. Inspector Queen never ceased to marvel at the way his son could reach the proper conclusion by unearthing the most obscure clues—often left by the dying victim—and piecing them together.

Richard Hart was television's first Ellery Queen, portraying the role in *The Adventures of Ellery Queen,* a live series that premiered on Du-Mont in the fall of 1950. The following January, Hart died of a sudden and unexpected heart attack—he was in his 30s—and was replaced by Lee Bowman. Bowman stayed with the series when it moved to ABC in December of 1951 and played Ellery until its cancellation in December 1952. In 1954 a syndicated film version appeared, also titled *The Adventures of Ellery Queen*, and starring Hugh Marlowe, one of four actors who had played the role on film. Florenz Ames continued as Inspector Queen in these films. The title of the syndicated version was changed in 1956 to *Mystery Is My Business*.

Ellery returned to live network television on NBC in the fall of 1958 with George Nader in the title role. To distinguish it from its predecessors, this edition was titled *The Further Adventures of Ellery Queen* but, effective with the October 24, 1958 telecast, the title was shortened to *Ellery Queen*. When production of this edition shifted from Hollywood to New York, and went from live to videotape, both of the principal actors—George Nader and Les Tremayne—left the series. The role of Ellery was assumed by Lee Philips and that of Inspector Queen was dropped.

After a gap of 16 years, NBC once more brought the series back to television, with Jim Hutton in the title role. This version, also titled *Ellery Queen*, was done as a period piece set in New York City in the late 1940s. Sergeant Velie, the plainclothes assistant to Inspector Queen, was now a regular in the cast; he had appeared in the novels and the radio series, but had not been seen regularly in any of the previous TV versions. Also added to this latest TV cast were Simon Brimmer, a radio detective who vied with Ellery in trying to solve the murders, and newspaper columnist Frank Flannigan. At the climax of each episode, just before resolving the case, Ellery would turn to the television audience and ask, "Have you figured it out? Do you know who the murderer is?"

ADVENTURES OF FU MANCHU, THE

Crime Drama
BROADCAST HISTORY:
Syndicated only
30 minutes
Produced: *1955–1956* (39 episodes)
Released: *Early 1956*
CAST:
Dr. Fu Manchu .... Glen Gordon
Sir Dennis Nayland-Smith .. Lester Matthews
Dr. John Petrie .... Clark Howat
Betty Leonard .... Carla Balenda
Karamanch .... Laurette Luez
Kolb .... John George

The *Fu Manchu* series must be unique in that it starred the villain. An extraordinary villain he was, a brilliant and powerful scientist operating out of Macao and other points in the Orient, with one goal: the destruction, or at least discomfiture, of the Western democracies, to avenge old wrongs. Each week Dr. Fu sent his agents on missions of subversion, such as extorting secret information from a U.S. diplomat, waging germ warfare, undermining the U.S. currency, or subverting a peace conference. On the side, he engaged in smuggling and other criminal activities. Fu had apparently unlimited resources, including diaboli-

cal scientific devices of his own invention. Battling the evil genius was Sir Dennis Nayland-Smith of Scotland Yard, his sworn enemy for generations, who succeeded in foiling each scheme but never got Fu himself.

Fu Manchu has had a long and varied media history beginning with his invention in the stories and novels of Sax Rohmer around 1910. At that time he was the embodiment of the "Yellow Peril," threatening Western civilization, but the racial elements were later downplayed. He appeared in numerous silent movies and in sound films in the 1930s and 1940s, and was on radio from 1929 on. A pilot film for a TV series was made in 1952, starring Sir Cedric Hardwicke, but this did not make it to the screen. Finally in 1955 Sax Rohmer, then 72, sold the rights to his famous creation to Republic Pictures for $4 million, and another TV pilot was made. This one resulted in the syndicated series shown above. However, the series was not very successful, and only 39 episodes were made.

More recent appearances of Fu Manchu include a number of English movies made in the 1960s, starring Christopher Lee, and a 1980 feature starring Peter Sellers in his final appearance.

ADVENTURES OF HIRAM HOLIDAY, THE

Situation Comedy
FIRST TELECAST: *October 3, 1956*
LAST TELECAST: *February 27, 1957*
BROADCAST HISTORY:
Oct 1956–Feb 1957, NBC Wed 8:00–8:30
CAST:
Hiram Holiday .... Wally Cox
Joel Smith .... Ainslie Pryor

Hiram was a meek, mild-mannered proofreader for a New York newspaper who was discovered to possess physical and technical skills in a remarkable assortment of activities, such as fencing, scuba diving, airplane piloting, and art forgery. This so impressed his publisher that the newspaper sent him on a trip around the world, along with reporter Joel Smith as companion and recorder of his adventures.

ADVENTURES OF JIM BOWIE, THE

Western
FIRST TELECAST: *September 7, 1956*
LAST TELECAST: *August 29, 1958*
BROADCAST HISTORY:
Sep 1956–Aug 1958, ABC Fri 8:00–8:30
CAST:
Jim Bowie .... Scott Forbes
John James Audubon .... Robert Cornthwaite
Rezin Bowie .... Peter Hanson

This Western was unusual in at least two respects: it was based—somewhat loosely, to be sure—on a real historical character, and its hero wielded a knife instead of a gun. According to the scriptwriters, Jim Bowie invented his famous knife after an encounter with a grizzly bear in which his standard blade broke at a critical moment. His new Bowie knife became his favorite weapon, although ABC, sensitive to parental reaction, played down its explicit use as a weapon in this series.

The Adventures of Jim Bowie was set in the Louisiana Territory of the 1830s, which provided backdrops of French-American New Orleans, and backwoods settings. Bowie was a wealthy young planter and adventurer, and his path crossed those of many interesting people, including his good friend John James Audubon (the naturalist painter), pirate Jean Lafitte, Sam Houston, Andrew Jackson, and even Johnny Appleseed. In one episode Jim ran for Congress against Davy Crockett. A young Michael Landon appeared in a 1956 episode.

The show was adapted from the book, *Tempered Blade,* by Monte Barrett.

ADVENTURES OF KIT CARSON, THE
Western
BROADCAST HISTORY:
Syndicated only
30 minutes
Produced: *1951–1955* (104 episodes)
Released: *Fall 1951*
CAST:
Kit Carson .... Bill Williams
El Toro .... Don Diamond

One of the popular early kids' Westerns, with the famous frontier scout played by Hollywood leading man Bill Williams. His Mexican sidekick, El Toro, was played by Brooklyn-born Don Diamond. Kit and El Toro roamed the Old West, righting wrongs and eating dust from Wyoming to the Texas Panhandle, for 104 episodes. A couple of years later, when Williams was beginning work on a distinctly less rugged series, *Date With the Angels,* he remarked, "I never want to see or hear of Kit Carson again."

Hank Peterson played the occasional role of Sierra Jack.

ADVENTURES OF MCGRAW, THE
see *Meet McGraw*

ADVENTURES OF OKY DOKY
Children's
FIRST TELECAST: *November 4, 1948*
LAST TELECAST: *May 26, 1949*
BROADCAST HISTORY:
Nov 1948–Mar 1949, DUM Thu 7:00–7:30
Mar 1949–May 1949, DUM Tue/Thu 6:45–7:00
HOST/HOSTESS:
Wendy Barrie
Burt Hilber
REGULARS:
Pat Barnard
Mellodaires

VOICE OF OKY DOKY:
Dayton Allen

Oky Doky was a large (30-inch) mustachioed puppet created by Raye Copeland, which was first seen on a local New York kids' fashion show called *Tots, Tweens and Teens.* He later got his own show on the DuMont network, called first *Adventures of Oky Doky* and later *Oky Doky Ranch.* The setting was a dude ranch to which the kids flocked, to watch Oky's latest Western adventure and to take part in games and junior talent performances. There was a certain amount of roughhouse in Oky's sketches, with knock-down drag-out fights with the bad guys and lots of smashed furniture, but Oky triumphed in the end, thanks to his magic strength pills (they contained good wholesome MILK, kids!).

ADVENTURES OF OZZIE & HARRIET, THE
Situation Comedy
FIRST TELECAST: *October 3, 1952*
LAST TELECAST: *September 3, 1966*
BROADCAST HISTORY:
Oct 1952–June 1956, ABC Fri 8:00–8:30(OS)
Oct 1956–Sep 1958, ABC Wed 9:00–9:30
Sep 1958–Sep 1961, ABC Wed 8:30–9:00
Sep 1961–Sep 1963, ABC Thu 7:30–8:00
Sep 1963–Jan 1966, ABC Wed 7:30–8:00
Jan 1966–Sep 1966, ABC Sat 7:30–8:00
CAST:
Ozzie Nelson .... Himself
Harriet Nelson..................... Herself
David Nelson .... Himself
Eric "Ricky" Nelson .... Himself
"Thorny" Thornberry (1952–1958)
 .... Don DeFore
Darby (1955–1961)............... Parley Baer
Joe Randolph (1956–1966)........ Lyle Talbot
Clara Randolph (1956–1966). Mary Jane Croft
Doc Williams (1954–1965)........ Frank Cady
Wally (1957–1966)............... Skip Young
Butch Barton (1958–1960) ...... Gordon Jones
June (Mrs. David Nelson) (1961–1966)
 .... June Blair
Kris (Mrs. Rick Nelson) (1964–1966)
 .... Kristin Harmon
Fred (1958–1964) .... James Stacy
Mr. Kelley (1960–1962) .... Joe Flynn
Connie Edwards (1960–1966)
 .... Constance Harper
Jack (1961–1966) .... Jack Wagner*
Ginger (1962–1965) .... Charlene Salerno
Dean Hopkins (1964–1966) .... Ivan Bonar
Greg (1965–1966).............. Greg Dawson
Sean (1965–1966).............. Sean Morgan

*Played numerous other roles in late 1950s.
PRODUCER/DIRECTOR/HEAD WRITER:
Ozzie Nelson

One of TV's longest-running family comedies, this program was as much a picture of reality in its own way as the "relevance" comedies of the 1970s. *The Adventures of Ozzie & Harriet* was the real-life Nelson family on the air, with all the little adventures that an active and interesting middle-class American family might have, and two young boys growing up before their parents'—and the television audience's—eyes. Even the house they lived in was modeled on the Nelsons' real-life home in Hollywood. About the only liberties taken with reality, for dramatic purposes, was in Ozzie's role. On TV he had no defined source of income, and always seemed to be hanging around the house. In real life Ozzie Nelson was a hard worker indeed, having been the nation's youngest Eagle Scout at age 13, an honor student and star quarterback at Rutgers, and a nationally known bandleader in the 1930s. His wife, Harriet, had once been his band's vocalist.

Their two sons were the real stars of the program. When *The Adventures of Ozzie & Harriet* began on radio in 1944, the boys' roles were played by professional actors, but in 1949 Ozzie finally allowed his actual offspring to go on the air. From then until the TV version ended, America watched the two boys grow up. From 1952 to 1966 Ricky went from a crew-cut 11-year-old, to a real-life teenage singing idol, to a 25-year-old husband.

In the early episodes the stories revolved mostly around the four Nelsons, with only a few friends and neighbors featured—notably Thorny Thornberry, a holdover from radio days, who regularly offered Ozzie bits of ill-timed advice. Later, as the boys began to date, a succession of girlfriends and school buddies began to appear. In 1956 David went off to college, followed four years later by Ricky. In the meantime Ricky had begun a show business career of his own, which gave *The Adventures of Ozzie & Harriet* quite a boost among younger viewers. A fall 1956 episode had him organizing a rock 'n' roll band in high school. Then in an April 1957 telecast he picked up a guitar and sang a currently popular Fats Domino hit, "I'm Walkin' "—which, backed with "A Teenager's Romance," promptly became a real-life million-selling record for him. It was no flash-in-the-pan. Ricky went on to become one of the biggest stars of the rock era, and all of his songs were featured in *Ozzie & Harriet* episodes, or in an unconnected short segment tacked on to the end of the show.

In time both David and Ricky were married, and both real-life wives (June and Kris) appeared on the show. David emerged from "college" as a lawyer, and joined a law office, in which Ricky later worked as a part-time clerk. Their boss during most of this period was Mr. Kelley, and their secretary, Miss Edwards. Toward the end *The Adventures of Ozzie & Harriet* became almost a living exercise in nostalgia, with a number of episodes from the early 1950s being rerun during the last two seasons. The final original telecast in 1966 was wistful; it had Ozzie deciding to buy a

pool table and convert David and Ricky's now vacant bedroom into a game room—until he met with stiff opposition from Harriet.

For a short time in 1960 the series ran under the title *The Adventures of the Nelson Family.*

In 1973, the senior Nelsons returned with a syndicated series called *Ozzie's Girls.* With their sons married and away, Ozzie and Harriet took in two college-coed boarders—Susie Hamilton (played by Susan Sennett) and Brenda MacKenzie (Brenda Sykes). In the first few episodes Brenda's first name was Jennifer. Stories revolved around the problems of the parents of two sons adjusting to the presence of two "daughters."

ADVENTURES OF RIN TIN TIN, THE

Western

FIRST TELECAST: *October 15, 1954*
LAST TELECAST: *August 28, 1959*
BROADCAST HISTORY:
  Oct 1954–Aug 1959, ABC Fri 7:30–8:00
CAST:
  Rusty .... Lee Aaker
  Lt. Rip Masters .... James Brown
  Sgt. Biff O'Hara................. Joe Sawyer
  Cpl. Boone .... Rand Brooks
TRAINER:
  Lee Duncan

The Adventures of Rin Tin Tin was TV's "other" dog show. Despite some similarities to *Lassie*—it featured a heroic dog, with a small boy as his companion—there were considerable differences between the two shows. *Rin Tin Tin* was set in the Old West and was full of violent action, including gunfights, rampaging Indians, and the like. The boy, Rusty, had in fact been orphaned in an Indian raid, after which he and his dog Rin Tin Tin ("Yo ho, Rinty!") were adopted by the cavalry soldiers at Fort Apache, Arizona. The two were made honorary troopers and for the next five seasons proceeded to help the cavalry and the townspeople of nearby Mesa Grande establish law and order on the frontier.

Rin Tin Tin was a movie favorite of long standing, the first Rin Tin Tin feature having been made in 1922. Three different German Shepherds filled the role in the TV series, two of them descendants of the original Rinty (who died in 1932) and the other the offspring of another movie canine, Flame, Jr.

Reruns of *The Adventures of Rin Tin Tin* aired on ABC late afternoons from September 1959 to September 1961 and on CBS's Saturday morning lineup from September 1962 to September 1964.

When the old episodes of *Rin Tin Tin* were revived for a new life in reruns in 1976, former star James Brown came out of retirement to film new introductions for them. Remarkably, he looked only slightly older than he had two decades earlier when the series had been in production. Although the episodes were in black-and-white, the 1976 reruns had been tinted a light brown.

ADVENTURES OF ROBIN HOOD, THE

Adventure

FIRST TELECAST: *September 26, 1955*
LAST TELECAST: *September 22, 1958*
BROADCAST HISTORY:
Sep 1955–Sep 1958, CBS Mon 7:30–8:00
CAST:
Robin Hood .... Richard Greene
Maid Marian (1955–1957)
.... Bernadette O'Farrell
Maid Marian (1957–1958) .... Patricia Driscoll
Sir Richard..................... Ian Hunter
Friar Tuck............... Alexander Gauge
Little John (1955, 1956–1958) .. Archie Duncan
Little John (1955–1956)..... Rufus Cruikshank
Sheriff of Nottingham .... Alan Wheatley
Prince John............... Donald Pleasence

Filmed completely on location in England, *The Adventures of Robin Hood* brought the famous swashbuckler to American television. Robin and his Merry Men made their home in Sherwood Forest. Their efforts to rob from the rich to give to the poor were frowned upon by Prince John and the Sheriff of Nottingham. Robin's true love, Maid Marian, was a member of Prince John's court who provided Robin with useful information, which helped him frustrate the efforts of the sheriff to capture him.

CBS aired reruns of this series on Saturday mornings from October 1958 to September 1959.

ADVENTURES OF SIR FRANCIS DRAKE, THE

Adventure

FIRST TELECAST: *June 24, 1962*
LAST TELECAST: *September 9, 1962*
BROADCAST HISTORY:
Jun 1962–Sep 1962, NBC Sun 8:30–9:00
CAST:
Sir Francis Drake.......... Terence Morgan
Queen Elizabeth I............... Jean Kent
Richard Trevelyan....... Patrick McLoughlin
Walsingham................ Richard Warner
Morton, Earl of Lenox........ Ewan Roberts
Mendoza, the Spanish Ambassador
.... Roger Delgado
John Drake .... Michael Crawford
Diego .... Milton Reid
Grenville.................... Howard Lang
Bosun....................... Peter Diamond

Filmed in England, and used as a summer replacement for *Car 54, Where Are You?*, this series consisted of fictional stories about Sir Francis Drake, the 16th-century adventurer. His varied skills as a seaman, soldier, pirate, explorer, and spy made him an invaluable asset to the court of Queen Elizabeth I. Included in his exploits were the rescue of Sir Walter Raleigh's lost colony in Virginia; an attack on the Spanish fort at St. Augustine in what is now Florida; and the release of a captive Seminole Indian princess. The producers made every effort to replicate exactly Drake's ship, *The*

Golden Hind, and emphasis was placed on accuracy in historical detail.

ADVENTURES OF SIR LANCELOT, THE

Adventure

FIRST TELECAST: *September 24, 1956*
LAST TELECAST: *June 24, 1957*
BROADCAST HISTORY:
Sep 1956–Jun 1957, NBC Mon 8:00–8:30
CAST:
Sir Lancelot .... William Russell
Queen Guinevere .... Jane Hylton
King Arthur .... Ronald Leigh-Hunt
Merlin .... Cyril Smith
Leonides .... Peter Bennett
Brian .... Bobby Scroggins

This series, consisting of stories of the most famous knight of the Round Table, was filmed in England after extensive research had been done by Oxford University to guarantee the authenticity of the sixth- and seventh-century settings. Themes for the episodes came from assorted legends surrounding the chivalrous acts of Sir Lancelot and the other members of King Arthur's court.

ABC aired reruns of *The Adventures of Sir Lancelot* on Tuesday afternoons from October 1957 to September 1958.

ADVENTURES OF SUPERMAN, THE

Adventure

BROADCAST HISTORY:
Syndicated and network daytime
30 minutes
Produced: *July 1951–Nov 1957* (104 episodes)
Released: *Fall 1952*
CAST:
Superman/Clark Kent .... George Reeves
Lois Lane (1951) .... Phyllis Coates
Lois Lane (1953–1957) .... Noel Neill
Jimmy Olson .... Jack Larson
Perry White .... John Hamilton
Inspector William Henderson
.... Robert Shayne

"Faster than a speeding bullet!" exclaimed the announcer. "More powerful than a locomotive! Able to leap tall buildings at a single bound. . . . Superman . . . strange visitor from another planet who came to Earth with powers and abilities far beyond those of mortal men! Superman, who can change the course of mighty rivers, bend steel in his bare hands, and who, disguised as Clark Kent, mild-mannered reporter for a great metropolitan newspaper, fights a never-ending battle for truth, justice, and the American way!"

Superman was one of the most fabulously successful media creations of modern times—and, if you think about it, an interesting reflection on what we would like to be. Following a highly successful career in comic books, radio, and movies in the 1940s, he came to television in a syndicated (not network) version that was a major hit of the 1950s.

His now-familiar genealogy was spelled out in the first episode. Kal-El was born on the faraway planet Krypton, the son of scientist Jor-El and his wife Lara (played by Robert Rockwell and Aline Towne in "Superman on Earth," the establishing TV episode). When destruction of their planet became imminent, the parents of Kal-El sent the infant to Earth in a miniature rocket. The rocket landed in Smallville, U.S.A., where the infant was discovered and raised by a childless couple named Eben and Sarah Kent. They named him Clark. As he grew older, Clark began to discover that he was different from other children, endowed with superhuman powers. The Kents told him about his origin and Clark began to consider how he might use these powers for the good of mankind.

At age 25, after Eben Kent's death, Clark moved to Metropolis and landed a job as a reporter for *The Daily Planet,* a crusading newspaper. When danger loomed he quickly changed from mild-mannered Clark Kent to Superman, leapt out a convenient window, and flew to the rescue! His familiar red-and-blue costume had been given him by Mrs. Kent, who had made it from the blankets that had swaddled him in the rocket as an infant (with no explanation how she cut and sewed it, since the completed costume was bulletproof, tearproof, and virtually as indestructible as Superman himself).

Clark's boss at the newspaper was blustery editor Perry White, whose most common expletive was "Great Caesar's ghost!" Jimmy Olson was the ambitious, but timid, young cub reporter, and Lois Lane was the top reporter on the paper. She was chief competitor to Clark, and chief female admirer of Superman, but she never connected the two men. Lois was in fact rather hard-nosed and aggressive as portrayed by Phyllis Coates, but became more sensitive and vulnerable in the later characterization of Noel Neill. Inspector Henderson of the Metropolis Police Department was hard-working, but somehow never managed to solve a case without the help of Superman, the *Planet* staff, or both. Jimmy and Lois also seemed to depend on Superman's help—he was constantly called upon to rescue them from criminals—but no one suspected his true identity.

Superman did have an incredible collection of powers—super-strength, super-hearing, X-ray vision, telescopic and microscopic vision, superbreath—and the abilities to split himself into two functioning entities, to will himself through solid matter, to levitate people, and, most important, to fly. The only thing to which he was vulnerable was Kryptonite, fragments of green rock that were the remnants of his exploded home planet. The bad guys on *Superman,* including semiregulars Ben Welden, Herb Vigran, Tris Coffin, and Billy Nelson (they turned up in different roles on different episodes), used everything they could get

their hands on, including Kryptonite, to defeat and destroy Superman, but good always triumphed.

Although the first batch of 26 *Superman* films were made in 1951, the series did not reach local TV stations until late 1952. From 1953 to 1957 additional groups of films were made. Production, as with most non-network series, was low budget, and the actors wore virtually the same outfits all the time so that footage from different episodes could be shot at the same time without having to worry about matching costumes. The special effects were limited to having Superman crash through walls, lots of explosions, and scenes of Superman flying around—the latter accomplished by suspending him from invisible wires. The same flying sequences were used over and over, sometimes running as long as 30 or 40 seconds, to fill time. In one episode Superman changed direction while flying, which was accomplished by simply turning the film around—making the "S" on his uniform backward! There was a good deal of action and violence on *Superman* initially, but over the years it began to take itself less seriously and, by the last season, many of the episodes were played more for laughs than for action.

The media history of Superman is certainly varied. He was created by two teenagers, writer Jerry Siegel and artist Joe Shuster, in the 1930s, and was initially rejected by all the major newspaper syndicates. He finally appeared in a comic book in 1938, and became an instantaneous hit. This led to a regular newspaper strip that ran 28 years (1939-1967); a radio series from 1940 to 1951, with Bud Collyer initially providing the voice of Superman; 17 animated Paramount cartoons from 1941 to 1943; theatrical serials in 1948 and 1950; and a feature-length movie, *Superman and the Mole Men,* in 1951 (later re-edited and shown as a two-part episode of the TV series).

George Reeves, who had made his movie debut in *Gone With the Wind,* became so typecast by his TV Superman role that he could not get other work. Although there were conflicting stories surrounding his death on June 16, 1959—including one that the series was about to return to production—the coroner's verdict was that he had committed suicide by shooting himself in the head. Nothing, however, could end the fictional Superman's life. ABC reran the syndicated films from October 1957–September 1958 on Wednesday afternoons, and CBS revived the Man of Steel in animated form on its Saturday morning lineup in 1966 (with Bud Collyer again doing the voice). The CBS cartoons, under the titles *Superman,* or *The New Adventures of Superman,* or as part of *The Superman-Aquaman Hour* and *The Batman-Superman Hour,* ran until September 1970. Superman then moved to ABC on Saturday morning where he has been an integral part of the animated *Superfriends* since its inception in 1973. In 1978 Superman got his first big-budget production, *Superman—The Movie,* starring Christopher

Reeve, Margot Kidder, and Marlon Brando (with Noel Neill in an unbilled cameo role). It was a huge hit at the box office and precipitated a series of films about the superhero. There have also been a Superman play on Broadway, a novel, a Superman museum in Illinois, and endless nostalgia books about the Man of Steel. He will no doubt be seen on videodisks and on holographic TV in the year 2000. A thorough and comprehensive history of the Superman character can be found in *Superman—Serial to Cereal* by Gary Grossman, published by Popular Library in 1977.

ADVENTURES OF THE NELSON FAMILY, THE
see *Adventures of Ozzie & Harriet, The*

ADVENTURES OF TUGBOAT ANNIE, THE
Comedy Adventure
BROADCAST HISTORY:
Syndicated only
30 minutes
Produced: *1956* (39 episodes)
Released: *March 1958*
CAST:
Tugboat Annie.............. Minerva Urecal
Capt. Horatio Bullwinkle ...... Walter Sande

Salt spray, insults, and action marked this expensively produced comedy, which had a short but well-publicized run in syndication in the late 1950s. Rival tugboat captains in the Pacific Northwest, Annie, a widow, and Bullwinkle were both built like oxes. The two of them were constantly trading jibes, stealing jobs from one another, and sharing adventure. Pinto was the weakling cook on Annie's tug, the *Narcissus*.

The character of Tugboat Annie had been created many years earlier by Norman Reilly Raine in a long series of stories for *The Saturday Evening Post*. These were made into a famous movie in 1933, in which Marie Dressler traded salty insults with a drunken Wallace Beery. A Hollywood production company obtained TV rights to the stories in 1954, but had great trouble both in casting the leads and in the actual filming, on location in San Pedro Harbor and on the Pacific. The pilot episode was said by *Variety* in 1956 to have been the most expensive ever made, costing upward of $130,000. It took two more years to get the series on the air, and then it only lasted for 39 episodes.

ADVENTURES OF WILD BILL HICKOK, THE
Western
BROADCAST HISTORY:
Syndicated and network daytime
30 minutes
Produced: *1951–1958* (113 episodes)
Released: *April 1951*
CAST:
Marshal James Butler Hickok.. Guy Madison
Jingles .... Andy Devine

"James Butler Hickok, mister," the hero announced. Whereupon his fat sidekick, Jingles, would pipe up in his shrill, raspy voice, "That's *Wild Bill Hickok*, mister! The bravest, strongest, fightingest U.S. Marshal in the whole West!" It was just as well that Jingles kept filling people in, because Guy Madison, the star of this early oater, was so handsome he might otherwise have been mistaken for a Hollywood matinee idol (which, in fact, he was). Good looks aside, Wild Bill could beat up on the baddies with the best of them, while his 300-pound companion added comic relief and not a little serious help at times. Despite his girth and blundering manner, Jingles was good at disguises. Buckshot was Wild Bill's horse, while Jingles's suffering steed was named Joker.

There was a real Wild Bill Hickok in the 1800s, who was variously a Pony Express rider, Union scout during the Civil War, scout for Colonel Custer, and Marshal of Abilene, Kansas. He did *not* look like a matinee idol.

Begun as a syndicated program for local broadcast, *Wild Bill Hickok* was also seen on CBS from 1955–1958 and on ABC from 1957–1958, in the daytime or late afternoon. There was a concurrent radio version on Mutual from 1951–1956, also starring Madison and Devine.

AFTERMASH
Situation Comedy
FIRST TELECAST: *September 26, 1983*
LAST TELECAST: *December 18, 1984*
BROADCAST HISTORY:
Sep 1983–Mar 1984, CBS Mon 9:00–9:30
Apr 1984–Jun 1984, CBS Sun 8:00–8:30
Jul 1984–Oct 1984, CBS Tue 8:00–8:30
Dec 1984, CBS Tue 8:30–9:00
CAST:
Dr. Sherman Potter .... Harry Morgan
Max Klinger..................... Jamie Farr
Father Francis Mulcahy
.... William Christopher
Mildred Potter........... Barbara Townsend
Mildred Potter (1984).......... Ann Pitoniak
Soon-Lee Klinger............. Rosalind Chao
Mike D'Angelo............... John Chappell
Wally Wainwright (1984)
.... Peter Michael Goetz
Dr. Gene Pfeiffer............. Jay O. Sanders
Alma Cox .... Brandis Kemp
Nurse Coleman .... Lois Foraker
Bonnie Hornbeck .... Wendy Schaal
Bob Scannell .... Pat Cranshaw
Nurse Crown .... Shirley Lang
Dr. Boyer (1984) .... David Ackroyd
Sarah (1984)............... Carolsue Walker
Nurse Weber (1984)............. Susan Luck
Nurse Parker (1984).......... Joan Sweeny
Sunshine (1984)............ Sunshine Parker
Lenore Dudziak (1984)........ Wendy Girard

The Korean War was over and the men of the 4077th M.A.S.H. unit had returned to civilian life.

Most of them scattered to the four corners of the States but three—Sherman Potter, Max Klinger, and Father Mulcahy—were reunited on the staff of the General Pershing Veteran's Administration Hospital in River Bend, Missouri. Potter was chief of staff at the hospital, and it was through his recruiting efforts that Klinger joined the staff as his administrative assistant, and Mulcahy as the hospital chaplain. Others on staff included bureaucratic, ineffectual hospital administrator Mike D'Angelo; his pushy secretary Alma; another secretary, Bonnie; and a somewhat ingenuous young surgical resident named Gene. Most notable among the patients was absentminded old-timer Bob Scannell. Stories alternated between light comedy and serious depictions of the human wreckage created by war.

There was also a home scene. Klinger's Korean war bride, Soon-Lee, had come with him to America, and Potter's unassuming wife, Mildred, who was often talked about but never seen on *M*A*S*H* (except in a picture on Potter's desk), was on hand as well. By the spring of 1984 another cast member was on the way: Soon-Lee was about to give birth to her first child, a boy. The baby was born on the first episode of the show's second season but the series, despite a number of cast changes, including the arrival of a more serious administrator in the person of Wally Wainwright, died before the end of the year.

AIR POWER
Documentary
FIRST TELECAST: *November 11, 1956*
LAST TELECAST: *October 19, 1958*
BROADCAST HISTORY:
 Nov 1956–May 1957, CBS Sun 6:30–7:00
 May 1958–Oct 1958, CBS Sun 6:30–7:00
NARRATOR:
 Walter Cronkite

Air Power was a documentary series produced with the cooperation of the U.S. Air Force. Using filmed footage from all over the world, it traced the history of the airplane and gave an appraisal of its impact on the history and life-styles of the 20th century. From its infancy at the turn of the century to the jet planes that were flying when the series was produced in the 1950s, the airplane was portrayed as both a weapon and a servant. The 1958 summer series consisted of reruns of the 1956–57 films.

AIR TIME '57
Musical Variety
FIRST TELECAST: *December 27, 1956*
LAST TELECAST: *April 4, 1957*
BROADCAST HISTORY:
 Dec 1956–Apr 1957, ABC Thu 10:00–10:30
REGULARS:
 Vaughn Monroe
 Bobby Hackett
 Elliot Lawrence Orchestra

Singer Vaughn Monroe was the host and star of this live musical variety series, jazz trumpet player Bobby Hackett and his group were featured regulars, and there were one or more guest stars each week.

AIRWOLF
Adventure/Foreign Intrigue
FIRST TELECAST: *January 22, 1984*
LAST TELECAST: *July 23, 1986*
BROADCAST HISTORY:
 Jan 1984, CBS Sun 9:30–11:30
 Jan 1984–Apr 1984, CBS Sat 9:00–10:00
 Aug 1984–Jan 1985, CBS Sat 8:00–9:00
 Jan 1985–Jul 1985, CBS Sat 9:00–10:00
 Jul 1985–Mar 1986, CBS Sat 8:00–9:00
 May 1986–Jun 1986, CBS Sat 9:00–10:00
 Jun 1986–Jul 1986, CBS Wed 9:00–10:00(First-run on USA Cable Network in 1987)
CAST:
 Stringfellow Hawke (1984–1986)
  .... Jan-Michael Vincent
 Dominic Santini (1984–1986) . Ernest Borgnine
 Michael Archangel (1984–1986).... Alex Cord
 Marella (1984–1985) .... Deborah Pratt
 Caitlin O'Shannessy (1984–1986)
  .... Jean Bruce Scott
 St. John Hawke (1987)...... Barry Van Dyke
 Jason Lock (1987) .... Anthony Sherwood
 Jo Santini (1987) .... Michele Scarabelli
 Maj. Mike Rivers (1987)
  .... Geraint Wyn Davies

Nineteen eighty-four was the year of the helicopter. The success of the theatrical film *Blue Thunder* in the summer of 1983 resulted, the following spring, in series on all three networks featuring copters—CBS's *Airwolf*, ABC's *Blue Thunder*, and NBC's less serious *Riptide*.

Most advanced of all aircraft was Airwolf, a high-tech attack helicopter of the future. It could outrace conventional jets, travel halfway around the world, and blast away with enormous firepower. When its creator stole it and attempted to sell it to Libya, a supersecret U.S. Government agency known only as "The Firm" recruited reclusive pilot Stringfellow Hawke to get it back. He did, but then refused to turn it over until the government tracked down his brother, who was missing in action in Vietnam.

While the government was obligingly hunting up his brother, Hawke agreed to use Airwolf—which he had hidden in the Southwestern desert—on dangerous missions for The Firm. Hawke was not easy to deal with, however. A sullen and uncommunicative type, he could usually be found holed up in his mountain cabin, surrounded by his collection of impressionistic paintings, playing his cello. Women found this handsome loner fascinating, but he disdained them. His contact at The Firm was the suave, mysterious Archangel—identifiable by his white suit, eye patch, and cane. Helping Hawke on missions was his sensible, middle-aged war buddy, Dominic, and sometimes one of The Firm's agents, the beautiful Marella. Added to the cast at the start of the show's second season was spunky Caitlin O'Shannessy, a lady helicopter pilot who became part of the team.

When new episodes of *Airwolf* premiered on the USA Cable network in January of 1987, the cast was completely changed. In the storyline Dominic was killed and Stringfellow badly injured when one of their regular helicopters, sabotaged by foreign agents, exploded. Dom's niece, Jo; Archangel's replacement, Jason Locke; and a talented but hard-to-control young agent, Mike Rivers, took Airwolf on a mission to rescue Stringfellow's brother, St. John Hawke. After getting back to the states, St. John took over for his injured brother as head of the Airwolf team. They still hid the super copter from "The Company" (it used to be "The Firm"), but were willing to use it on assignments they felt were worthwhile.

In order to keep the budget down on the cable version of *Airwolf*, production was moved from Hollywood to various locations in Canada.

AL MORGAN
Music
FIRST TELECAST: *September 5, 1949*
LAST TELECAST: *August 30, 1951*
BROADCAST HISTORY:
Sep 1949–Feb 1951, DUM Mon 8:30–9:00
May 1951–Aug 1951, DUM Thu 8:00–8:30
HOST:
Al Morgan

This musical variety program from Chicago featured popular singer-pianist Al Morgan (whose big hit, in 1949, was a song called "Jealous Heart"). Most of the program consisted of Al's own easygoing playing and singing, although guests also appeared.

ALAN BURKE SHOW, THE
Talk
BROADCAST HISTORY:
Syndicated only
2 hours *(1966–1969)*, 1 hour *(1969–1970)*
Produced: *1966–1970*
Released: *Spring 1966*
HOST:
Alan Burke

Alan Burke, former news editor, ad man, and real estate broker, was the caustic host of this New York-based discussion program. It was representative of the "crackpot" school of talk shows, generally eschewing celebrity or serious political guests for more bizarre or sensational subjects—witchcraft, UFOs, censorship, political extremists, belly dancers, and the like. Originally two hours in length, it was later cut to an hour without noticeable improvement. Seen mostly in large cities.

ALAN DALE SHOW, THE
Music
FIRST TELECAST: *August 10, 1948*
LAST TELECAST: *January 16, 1951*
BROADCAST HISTORY:
Aug 1948–Sep 1948, DUM Tue 7:00–7:15
Jun 1950–Nov 1950, CBS Fri 11:00–11:30
Dec 1950–Jan 1951, CBS Mon/Wed/Fri 6:30–6:45 and Tue/Thu 6:30–7:00
HOST:
Alan Dale
REGULARS:
Janie Ford (1948)
Milt Green Trio (1950–1951)

Young Alan Dale (whose real name was Aldo Sigismundi) was considered one of the more promising crooners of the late 1940s and early 1950s. He was only 21 when he began his first local television show over DuMont's New York station in May 1948. The setting was a record shop supposedly run by Alan and his singing partner Janie Ford, which gave him plenty of opportunities to demonstrate his smooth baritone (actually he lip-synched to his own recordings). This series, which continued until March 1949, was fed out over the DuMont network for a time during the fall of 1948. Later Alan Dale was seen on CBS, in late-night and early-evening shows. Guest singers and comedians also appeared on his shows.

ALAN YOUNG SHOW, THE
Comedy Variety
FIRST TELECAST: *April 6, 1950*
LAST TELECAST: *June 21, 1953*
BROADCAST HISTORY:
Apr 1950–Mar 1952, CBS Thu 9:00–9:30 (OS)
Feb 1953–June 1953, CBS Sun 9:30–10:00
REGULARS:
Alan Young . . . . Himself
Kay Prindall (1953) . . . . Dawn Addams
WRITERS:
Leo Solomon, David R. Schwartz, Alan Young

Young Canadian comedian Alan Young seemed to have a very bright future when he first moved to the new medium of television in 1950 (he had previously been on radio for a number of years). Critics applauded his gentle, intelligent humor, his versatility, and the excellent writing for his shows. "The Charlie Chaplin of television," *TV Guide* called him. "Without benefit of purloined gags, squirting seltzer, bad grammar, insults, references to his family, wornout guest stars, or women's hats, [he has] quietly become the rave of a growing legion of loving fans."

Young generally played a well-meaning young man who constantly wound up in a predicament. His half-hour shows consisted of a brief monologue, a song or two by a vocalist, and two complete skits—ranging from the first-time airline passenger who turns a peaceful flight into chaos, to a small boy in a world of very large furniture.

Despite his talents, Young's shows never really caught on. After two and a half seasons of the skits format, he returned in the spring of 1953 in a situation comedy, cast as a bank teller, with a girlfriend played by Dawn Addams. This version of the *Alan Young Show* was aired on alternate weeks with the *Ken Murray Show* under the umbrella title, *Time to Smile*. After two unsuccessful months Young returned to his familiar two-skit format, but this failed to save the series from final cancellation in June 1953.

ALASKANS, THE
Adventure
FIRST TELECAST: *October 4, 1959*
LAST TELECAST: *September 25, 1960*
BROADCAST HISTORY:
Oct 1959–Sep 1960, ABC Sun 9:30–10:30
CAST:
Silky Harris .... Roger Moore
Reno McKee...................... Jeff York
Nifty Cronin................... Ray Danton
Rocky Shaw............... Dorothy Provine

The Alaskan gold rush of the 1890s brought adventurers Silky Harris and Reno McKee to less-than-beautiful Skagway, Alaska, in search of their fortunes. With them went a singer friend, Rocky Shaw. Hunting for gold did not really appeal to the trio—it was too much like work—so they cast about for other means of obtaining money. Rocky went to work for saloon owner Nifty Cronin, who was only slightly more devious than Rocky's two friends but noticeably less honest. Silky and Reno would fleece their victims gently and rarely did anything completely harmful. Nifty would resort to robbery, murder, and any other means to attain his ends.

ALCOA HOUR, THE
Dramatic Anthology
FIRST TELECAST: *October 16, 1955*
LAST TELECAST: *September 22, 1957*
BROADCAST HISTORY:
Oct 1955–Sep 1957, NBC Sun 9:00–10:00

One of the major drama series of TV's "Golden Age," *The Alcoa Hour* was telecast live from New York on alternate Sundays. The premiere presented Ann Todd in her American TV debut in "The Black Wings," co-starring Wendell Corey. Among the others who performed on *Alcoa* during its two-year run were Laurence Harvey (in his United States TV debut), Martin Balsam, Walter Matthau, Joanne Woodward, Sal Mineo, Helen Hayes, Eddie Albert, and Maureen Stapleton.

Although the majority of plays presented on *Alcoa Hour* were dramas, there were some musicals as well. These included "Amahl and the Night Visitors"; an adaptation of Dickens's *Christmas Carol* entitled "The Stingiest Man in Town," starring Vic Damone, Johnny Desmond, and Basil Rathbone (singing!); and an original TV musical entitled "He's for Me," with Roddy McDowall, Jane Kean, and Larry Blyden.

ALCOA PREMIERE
Dramatic Anthology
FIRST TELECAST: *October 10, 1961*
LAST TELECAST: *September 12, 1963*
BROADCAST HISTORY:
Oct 1961–Sep 1962, ABC Tue 10:00–11:00
Oct 1962–Sep 1963, ABC Thu 10:00–11:00
HOST:
Fred Astaire

This filmed dramatic series featured Fred Astaire as host and occasional star. The premiere telecast was "People Need People," a powerful drama about the rehabilitation of psychologically disturbed war veterans, starring Lee Marvin and Arthur Kennedy and directed by Alex Segal. Subsequent telecasts maintained this high standard, with appearances by Charlton Heston, Brian Keith, Shelley Winters, Cliff Robertson, Janis Paige, Telly Savalas, and many others. Among the notable productions were "End of a World," a big-budget documentary drama about the assassination of Archduke Ferdinand, the event that triggered World War I; "Hornblower," based on the C. S. Forester books and pilot for a series that never materialized; "The Jail," by science-fiction writer Ray Bradbury; and "Flashing Spikes," a baseball drama starring James Stewart and real-life pitcher Don Drysdale, directed by movie giant John Ford.

Astaire generally appeared in dramatic roles too, but perhaps his most notable performance was in a comedy called "Mr. Lucifer," co-starring Elizabeth Montgomery—in which he played the Devil, in six different disguises.

ALCOA PRESENTS
Occult Anthology
FIRST TELECAST: *January 20, 1959*
LAST TELECAST: *October 3, 1961*
BROADCAST HISTORY:
Jan 1959–Oct 1961, ABC Tue 10:00–10:30
HOST:
John Newland

Actual case histories of supernatural phenomena and the occult were dramatized for this filmed series. Confrontations with ghosts and various forms of ESP were frequent themes, and the stories were always told with a suitably eerie and mysterious air. The subtitle of the show (later used as the title when the series went into syndication) was more descriptive of its contents: *One Step Beyond*.

Almost two decades later a much grayer John Newland turned up as the host of a new syndicated series of tales of the occult and supernatural, *The Next Step Beyond*. Unlike the original series, which was in black-and-white, the syndicated version was shot in color. This may have actually hurt its chances, because it lacked the moody texture of the original. At any rate, it was in production only during 1978 and never attracted much of an audience.

ALCOA THEATRE
Dramatic Anthology
FIRST TELECAST: *October 7, 1957*
LAST TELECAST: *September 19, 1960*
BROADCAST HISTORY:
   Oct 1957–Sep 1960, NBC Mon 9:30–10:00
ROTATING STARS:
   David Niven (1957–1958)
   Robert Ryan (1957–1958)
   Jane Powell (1957–1958)
   Jack Lemmon (1957–1958)
   Charles Boyer (1957–1958)

When Alcoa transferred its dramatic efforts from Sunday (see *Alcoa Hour*) to Monday nights in 1957, several major changes were made. A rotating company of five stars was introduced, and the format was reduced from a full hour live to half an hour on film. Though the quality remained high, the program had a less spectacular air. Many of the presentations were dramas, with titles such as "On Edge," "Circumstantial," "In the Dark," and "Ten Miles to Doomsday." However, there were occasional light comedies as well.

In 1958 the rotating stars were dropped and the program became a true anthology once again, featuring such varied talents as Cornel Wilde, Janet Blair, John Cassavetes, Jack Carson, Cliff Robertson, Agnes Moorehead, Walter Slezak, and Gary Merrill, among others. Throughout its run *Alcoa Theatre* was seen on alternate weeks. During its first four months it alternated with *Goodyear Theatre* under the umbrella title *A Turn of Fate*.

ALDRICH FAMILY, THE
Situation Comedy
FIRST TELECAST: *October 2, 1949*
LAST TELECAST: *May 29, 1953*
BROADCAST HISTORY:
   Oct 1949–Jun 1951, NBC Sun 7:30–8:00
   Sep 1951–May 1953, NBC Fri 9:30–10:00
CAST:
Henry Aldrich (1949–1950) ..... Robert Casey
Henry Aldrich (1950–1951) ..... Richard Tyler
Henry Aldrich (1951–1952) ..... Henry Girard
Henry Aldrich (1952) .... Kenneth Nelson
Henry Aldrich (1952–1953) .... Bobby Ellis
Mr. Sam Aldrich .... House Jameson*
Mrs. Alice Aldrich (1949–1950) .. Lois Wilson
Mrs. Alice Aldrich (1950–1951)
   .... Nancy Carroll
Mrs. Alice Aldrich (1951) .... Lois Wilson
Mrs. Alice Aldrich (1951–1953)
   .... Barbara Robbins
Mary Aldrich (1949–1950) ...... Charita Bauer
Mary Aldrich (1950–1952) ...... Mary Malone
Mary Aldrich (1952–1953) .... June Dayton
Homer Brown (1949–1951) ...... Jackie Kelk*

Homer Brown (1951–1952) ...... Robert Barry
Homer Brown (1952–1953) ..... Jackie Grimes
Mrs. Brown .... Leona Powers*
Mr. Brown .... Howard Smith
Kathleen .... Marcia Henderson
Aunt Harriet .... Ethel Wilson
Anna Mitchell .... Ann Sorg
George Bigelow .... Lionel Wilson
Mr. Bradley (1949) .... Richard Midgley
Mr. Bradley (1950–1953) .... Joseph Foley
Eleanor (1952–1953) .... Loretta Leversee

*Same role in radio series.

This television version of the long-running radio situation comedy concerned the adventures of teenager Henry Aldrich, his "typical American family," his high school buddies (including best friend Homer Brown), and his puppy loves. The locale was the Aldrich household on Elm Street, Centerville. There was considerable turnover in casting of the principal roles, with only House Jameson remaining throughout the television run as Henry's long-suffering father. Viewers must have wondered at Mr. Aldrich's marital life, what with five different sons, three daughters, and three wives all within the space of four years!

Still another actress was supposed to play the role of Henry's mother, but was dropped at the last minute in one of the television industry's most celebrated cases of political blacklisting. Jean Muir, a movie and radio actress for nearly 20 years, was hired during the summer of 1950 to portray Mrs. Aldrich in the coming season. Immediately, protests began to come in from right-wing groups, accusing Miss Muir of left-wing sympathies—it seems her name was listed in *Red Channels*, a vicious pamphlet that cited the alleged left-wing activities of dozens of performers. The sponsor, General Foods, and its advertising agency, Young and Rubicam, canceled the opening episode of the season as a result, and Miss Muir was summarily fired—with no opportunity to defend herself. Later, before a Congressional committee, she stated that she was not and had never been a Communist. But the truth didn't really matter. As in the cases of Philip Loeb of *The Goldbergs* and Ireene Wicker, *The Singing Lady*, the accusations alone had been enough virtually to destroy her career.

The Aldrich Family was created by Clifford Goldsmith, based on his play *What A Life*. The opening lines each week became something of a national catch phrase, with Mrs. Aldrich's call, "Henry! Henry Aldrich!," and Henry's pained reply, "Coming, Mother!"

ALF
Situation Comedy
FIRST TELECAST: *September 22, 1986*
LAST TELECAST:
BROADCAST HISTORY:
   Sep 1986–   , NBC Mon 8:00–8:30

CAST:
ALF (Gordon Shumway) (voice only)
.... Paul Fusco
Willie Tanner .... Max Wright
Kate Tanner............... Anne Schedeen
Lynn Tanner................. Andrea Elson
Brian Tanner................ Benji Gregory
Dorothy Halligan (1987) .... Anne Meara
Raquel Ochmonek .... Liz Sheridan
Trevor Ochmonek............. John LaMotta

Well, what would you do if an alien's spaceship crashed into your garage? Call the police? If you lived in a TV sitcom, you would probably do just what the Tanners did—hide him in the kitchen and enjoy years of laughs. Actually, there was little more to the plot of ALF than that. The furry little creature, nicknamed ALF (for "Alien Life Form"), landed on the Tanner's garage when his spacecraft went out of control. Unfortunately the ship couldn't be fixed, and anyway, his home planet of Melmac had just blown up, so ALF took up residence in the pleasant suburban Tanner home, disrupting their formerly boring life and commenting sarcastically (in a gravelly voice provided by the show's co-creator Paul Fusco) on the foibles of earthlings. The dense neighbors, the Ochmoneks, like all sitcom neighbors, never figured out what was going on.

ALF was a novelty hit in the 1986–87 season, leading to ALF dolls and other kid's paraphernalia. NBC even issued an official biography of its Monday night star. He was said to be 229 years old ("I've got dandruff older than your country") and had attended Melmac high school for 122 years, where he majored in software and was co-captain of the Bouillabaiseball team. Adult occupations included Assistant Boxleitner, part-time male model, and operator of his own phlegm dealership. Hobbies included gerrymandering and snacking on cats, a Melmackian delicacy (the Tanner's cat, Lucky, was often seen scurrying from the room). Height: "Fluctuates with weight." Weight: "Till the Sun Shines Nellie."

The creators of this fanciful comedy were Fusco and actor/producer Tom Patchett; a frequent director was TV comic Peter Bonerz. A three-foot tall midget by the name of Michu Meszaros was inside the ALF costume (when scenes called for it to walk around) during the first season.

An animated version of Alf premiered on NBC's Saturday morning lineup in September 1987.

ALFRED HITCHCOCK PRESENTS
Suspense Anthology
FIRST TELECAST: October 2, 1955
LAST TELECAST: July 20, 1986
BROADCAST HISTORY:
Oct 1955–Sep 1960, CBS Sun 9:30–10:00
Sep 1960–Sep 1962, NBC Tue 8:30–9:00
Sep 1962–Dec 1962, CBS Thu 10:00–11:00
Jan 1963–Sep 1963, CBS Fri 9:30–10:30
Sep 1963–Sep 1964, CBS Fri 10:00–11:00

Oct 1964–Sep 1965, NBC Mon 10:00–11:00
Sep 1985–Jul 1986, NBC Sun 8:30–9:00
(First-run on U.S.A. Cable Network in 1987)
HOST:
Alfred Hitchcock
MUSICAL THEME:
Based on Gounod's "Funeral March of a Marionette"

The benign countenance of pudgy film director Alfred Hitchcock welcomed viewers to stories of terror, horror, suspense, and twisted endings for an entire decade. His clipped British accent and catlike theme music became television standbys as the series appeared on two different networks and was later seen for years in syndication. The stories would often appear to end with evil triumphant, in strict violation of the television code of ethics. This situation was always resolved following the last commercial, when Hitchcock would return to explain, in his deadpan sardonic way, what silly mistake or chance occurrence had finally done the villain in. When the show was expanded to an hour in the fall of 1962, the title was changed to The Alfred Hitchcock Hour.

Twenty years after the original series left the air, and five years after Hitchcock's death, the famous director achieved a unique distinction: he became the first person in history to return from the dead to host a new series. Films of his original black-and-white introductions were computer processed into color and used to introduce new episodes. Some of the color films made for the 1985 revival series were new stories, while others were remakes of original scripts. Hitchcock's black humor took on an eerie quality coming, as it were, from the grave. It was the sort of macabre touch the master would have enjoyed.

Following a one-year network run, additional episodes were filmed for the U.S.A. Cable Network beginning in 1987.

ALIAS SMITH AND JONES
Western
FIRST TELECAST: January 21, 1971
LAST TELECAST: January 13, 1973
BROADCAST HISTORY:
Jan 1971–Sep 1971, ABC Thu 7:30–8:30
Sep 1971–Aug 1972, ABC Thu 8:00–9:00
Sep 1972–Jan 1973, ABC Sat 8:00–9:00
CAST:
Hannibal Heyes (Joshua Smith) (1971–1972)
.... Peter Deuel
Hannibal Heyes (Joshua Smith) (1972–1973)
.... Roger Davis
Jed "Kid" Curry (Thaddeus Jones)
.... Ben Murphy
Clementine Hale................. Sally Field
NARRATOR:
Roger Davis (1971–1972)
Ralph Story (1972–1973)
CREATOR/PRODUCER:
Glen A. Larson

The main characters in this Western adventure were two gallant and amiable ex-outlaws trying to go straight. The governor had promised them a pardon for their past crimes if they could stay out of trouble for one year, but what with a price still on their heads, a lot of grudges against them, and a bit of larceny still in their hearts, that was no easy proposition. Chased across two TV seasons by posses, bounty hunters, and old outlaw friends who wanted them to join in on some escapade, they never did get their pardon. The occasional role of Clementine Hale, another lovable rogue, was added in October 1971 to give the program some continuing female interest.

On December 31, 1971, star Peter Deuel, age 31, was found shot to death in his Hollywood Hills apartment, an apparent suicide. With only a few episodes already in the can, the role of Joshua Smith quickly had to be recast. Roger Davis, who had been doing the program's opening and closing narrations, was chosen, and a partially completed episode was finished with Davis redoing scenes already filmed by Deuel.

ALICE

Situation Comedy
FIRST TELECAST: *August 31, 1976*
LAST TELECAST: *July 2, 1985*
BROADCAST HISTORY:
  Aug 1976, CBS Mon 9:30–10:00
  Sep 1976–Oct 1976, CBS Wed 9:30–10:00
  Nov 1976–Sep 1977, CBS Sat 9:30–10:00
  Oct 1977–Oct 1978, CBS Sun 9:30–10:00
  Oct 1978–Feb 1979, CBS Sun 8:30–9:00
  Mar 1979–Sep 1982, CBS Sun 9:00–9:30
  Oct 1982–Nov 1982, CBS Wed 9:00–9:30
  Mar 1983–Apr 1983, CBS Mon 9:00–9:30
  Apr 1983–May 1983, CBS Sun 9:30–10:00
  Jun 1983–Jan 1984, CBS Sun 8:00–8:30
  Jan 1984–Dec 1984, CBS Sun 9:30–10:00
  Jan 1985–Mar 1985, CBS Tue 8:30–9:00
  Jun 1985–Jul 1985, CBS Tue 8:30–9:00
CAST:
  Alice Hyatt.................... Linda Lavin
  Tommy Hyatt................ Philip McKeon
  Mel Sharples .... Vic Tayback
  Florence Jean Castleberry ("Flo") (1976–1980)
    .... Polly Holliday
  Vera Louise Gorman .... Beth Howland
  Belle Dupree (1980–1981) .... Diane Ladd
  Jolene Hunnicutt (1981–1985)... Celia Weston
  Carrie Sharples (1982–1984).... Martha Raye
  Eliot Novak (1983–1985) .... Charles Levin
  Nicholas Stone (1984–1985) .. Michael Durrell
  Henry (1977–1985)............ Marvin Kaplan
  Andy (1976–1978) .... Pat Cranshaw
  Jason (1978–1979) .... Patrick J. Cronin
  Cecil (1978–1979).............. Bob McClurg
  Earl Hicks (1978–1985) .... Dave Madden
  Chuck (1978–1985)........ Duane R. Campbell
  Marie (1978–1980)........... Victoria Carroll
  Mike (1979–1980)............ Michael Ballard
  Brian (1979–1980) .... Alan Haufrect

  Charlie (1979–1981)............. Ted Gehring
  Ralph (1979–1981)....... Michael Alldredge
  Raleigh (1979–1981) .... Raleigh Bond
  Mitch Aames (1981–1982).... Phillip R. Allen
  Jerry (1981–1982)................ Jerry Potter
  Artie (1982–1985)................ Tony Longo
  Danny (1984–1985) .... Jonathan Prince
  Doug (1984–1985)............ Doug Robinson
THEME:
  "There's a New Girl in Town," by Alan and Marilyn Bergman and David Shire, sung over the opening credits by Linda Lavin.

When this comedy premiered in 1976, it was the story of a recently widowed aspiring singer with a very precocious 12-year-old son. Alice Hyatt had moved from her home in New Jersey to look for work in Phoenix. While attempting to find a singing job, she kept her household together by working as a waitress at Mel's Diner. The two other waitresses at Mel's provided quite a contrast. Flo, the old hand, was lusty, outspoken, and crude (her favorite expression was "Kiss my grits"), but had difficulty hiding a soft heart. Vera, on the other hand, was young, impressionable, and rather quiet. Mel Sharples, the owner of the diner, was also its cook and the creator of Mel's Famous Chili, which was so popular in the area that it (along with fun-loving Flo) attracted a loyal and regular clientele. In fact, all of the listed cast members from Henry on down (with the exception of Mel's sometime girlfriend Marie) were regulars at the diner.

The series was based on the movie *Alice Doesn't Live Here Anymore,* the title role of which was played by Ellen Burstyn, who received an Academy Award for her performance. The only member of the movie cast to make the transition to the TV series in 1976 was Vic Tayback, recreating his role as the crusty owner of Mel's Diner. He was joined in the spring of 1980 by Diane Ladd, who had played Flo in the movie but turned up as Belle in the TV series. Belle was hired by Mel as a waitress when Flo moved to Houston to run her own restaurant (see the spinoff series *Flo*). She was from Mississippi, wrote country-and-western songs, and lived in the Phoenix Palms Apartments, where Alice and Tommy also resided. Belle admirably filled the void left by Flo—the accent may have been different, but her earthy outlook on life and aggressive personality endeared her to Mel's regulars. She left after one year and was replaced by Jolene. Carrie, Mel's pushy, loudmouthed mother, moved to Phoenix after her divorce, took up residence with her son, and practically took over the diner. Next to her, Mel was a real softie. In the fall of 1983, after a whirlwind courtship, shy Vera married policeman Elliot Novak and the following fall found Alice with a new boyfriend, Nicholas Stone.

In the last original episode of the series (March 19, 1985) Mel sold the diner and, despite his reputation for cheapness over the years, gave each of his waitresses a $5,000 farewell bonus. All worked out for the best, however, since Jolene was planning to quit to open a beauty shop, Vera had become pregnant and was looking forward to becoming a fulltime mother, and Alice, after all the years at the diner, was moving to Nashville as lead singer with a band.

CBS aired reruns of *Alice* on weekday mornings from June 1980 to September 1982.

ALICE PEARCE
Musical Variety
FIRST TELECAST: *January 28, 1949*
LAST TELECAST: *March 4, 1949*
BROADCAST HISTORY:
Jan 1949–Mar 1949, ABC Fri 9:45–10:00
REGULARS:
Alice Pearce
Mark Lawrence, piano

This short—and short-lived—program presented fifteen minutes of music and comedy, hosted by comedienne Alice Pearce.

ALKALI IKE
Comedy
FIRST TELECAST: *April 17, 1950*
LAST TELECAST: *May 11, 1950*
BROADCAST HISTORY:
Apr 1950–May 1950, CBS Mon/Thu/Fri 7:45–8:00
REGULARS:
Al Robinson
Beverly Fite
The Slim Jackson Quartet

Ventriloquist Al Robinson was a discovery of Arthur Godfrey's. For a short time in the spring of 1950 he had his own live show featuring his Western dummy, Alkali Ike. Ike was trying to learn to live a varied and interesting life with the help of Al and an attractive female tutor. The action took place at Ike's ranch "somewhere in the West" and included vocal numbers by Beverly Fite and The Slim Jackson Quartet.

ALL AROUND THE TOWN
Interview
FIRST TELECAST: *November 10, 1951*
LAST TELECAST: *June 7, 1952*
BROADCAST HISTORY:
Nov 1951–Jan 1952, CBS Sat 6:00–6:45
May 1952–Jun 1952, CBS Sat 9:00–9:30
REGULARS:
Mike Wallace
Buff Cobb

Mike Wallace and his wife Buff Cobb hosted this live interview show on CBS during the 1951–1952 season. They traveled around New York City to places such as Coney Island, the New York City Ballet, and numerous restaurants from which they telecast their informal interviews with patrons and promoters.

The series began as a thrice-weekly late-afternoon entry in June 1951, then moved into the evening hours in November.

ALL IN ONE
Comedy Variety
FIRST TELECAST: *December 27, 1952*
LAST TELECAST: *April 2, 1953*
BROADCAST HISTORY:
Dec 1952–Jan 1953, CBS Sat 9:00–9:30
Apr 1953, CBS Thu 8:00–8:30
HOST:
George de Witt

In addition to functioning as host, George de Witt participated in sketches with the guest comics who were the stars of this short-lived variety show. Everything was done on a bare stage, and the audience was required to use its imagination to visualize sets and props. *All in One* had a four-week run and then returned in April for a single encore. It originated live from New York.

ALL IN THE FAMILY
Situation Comedy
FIRST TELECAST: *January 12, 1971*
LAST TELECAST: *September 21, 1983*
BROADCAST HISTORY:
Jan 1971–Jul 1971, CBS Tue 9:30–10:00
Sep 1971–Sep 1975, CBS Sat 8:00–8:30
Sep 1975–Sep 1976, CBS Mon 9:00–9:30
Sep 1976–Oct 1976, CBS Wed 9:00–9:30
Nov 1976–Sep 1977, CBS Sat 9:00–9:30
Oct 1977–Oct 1978, CBS Sun 9:00–9:30
Oct 1978–Mar 1983, CBS Sun 8:00–8:30
Mar 1983–May 1983, CBS Mon 8:00–8:30
May 1983, CBS Sun 8:00–8:30
Jun 1983, CBS Mon 9:30–10:00
Jun 1983–Sep 1983, CBS Wed 8:00–8:30
CAST:
Archie Bunker .... Carroll O'Connor
Edith Bunker (Dingbat) (1971–1980)
.... Jean Stapleton
Gloria Bunker Stivic (1971–1978)
.... Sally Struthers
Mike Stivic (Meathead) (1971–1978)
.... Rob Reiner
Lionel Jefferson (1971–1975) ..... Mike Evans
Louise Jefferson (1971–1975) ... Isabel Sanford
Henry Jefferson (1971–1973) ..... Mel Stewart
George Jefferson (1973–1975)
.... Sherman Hemsley
Irene Lorenzo (1973–1975) ...... Betty Garrett
Frank Lorenzo (1973–1974)
.... Vincent Gardenia
Bert Munson (1972–1977) .... Billy Halop
Tommy Kelsey (1972–1973) ... Brendon Dillon
Tommy Kelsey (1973–1977) .... Bob Hastings
Justin Quigley (1973–1976) .... Burt Mustin
Barney Hefner (1973–1983) ..... Allan Melvin
Jo Nelson (1973–1975) .... Ruth McDevitt

Stretch Cunningham (1974) . James Cromwell
Teresa Betancourt (1976–1977) .... Liz Torres
Stephanie Mills (1978–1983)
.... Danielle Brisebois
Harry Snowden (1977–1983).. Jason Wingreen
Hank Pivnik (1977–1981)..... Danny Dayton
Murray Klein (1979–1981).... Martin Balsam
Mr. Van Ranseleer (1978–1983).... Bill Quinn
Veronica Rooney (1979–1982) ... Anne Meara
Jose (1979–1983).......... Abraham Alvarez
Linda (1980–1981) .... Heidi Hagman
Raoul (1980–1983) .... Joe Rosario
Ellen Canby (1980–1982)..... Barbara Meek
Polly Swanson (1980–1981)
.... Janet MacLachlan
Ed Swanson (1980–1981)........ Mel Bryant
Billie Bunker (1981–1983) ...... Denise Miller
Gary Rabinowitz (1981–1983) .. Barry Gordon
Bruce (1982–1983) .... Bob Okazaki
Marsha (1982–1983) .... Jessica Nelson

THEME:
"Those Were the Days," by Strouse and
Adams, sung at the opening of each show by
Archie and Edith until 1979, replaced by an
instrumental version after that.

PRODUCER:
Norman Lear

All in the Family changed the course of television
comedy. It brought a sense of harsh reality to a TV
world which previously had been populated
largely by homogenized, inoffensive characters
and stories that seemed to have been laundered
before they ever got on the air. Its chief character,
Archie Bunker, was anything but bland. A typical
working-class Joe, he was uneducated, preju-
diced, and blatantly outspoken. He was constantly lambasting virtually every minority group
in existence. His views on blacks (or, as he often
called them, "jungle bunnies" or "spades"),
Puerto Ricans ("spics"), Chinese ("chinks"), and
any other racial or religious group not his own,
were clear and consistent. Archie believed in
every negative racial and ethnic stereotype he
had ever heard.

Unfortunately, he could never get away from
the people he despised. Archie was a dock foreman for the Prendergast Tool and Die Company,
and he had to work with a racially mixed group
of people. Next door to his small house at 704
Houser Street, in the Corona section of Queens,
New York, lived a black family, the Jeffersons. His
daughter Gloria had married a Pole. On top of it
all, Archie, the bigoted arch-conservative, even
had to share his house with his egghead liberal
son-in-law, Mike Stivic. (Mike was studying for
his degree in sociology, and so was unemployed.)
Completing the Bunker household was Archie's
slow-witted but honest and unprejudiced wife,
Edith.

The Jefferson family next door consisted of
Louise, one of Edith's closest friends, her husband
George, who ran a small dry-cleaning store, and
their son Lionel, a close friend of Mike's. Lionel
loved to come to the Bunker house to tease Archie
about his prejudices, while George Jefferson's
brother Henry, who was as opinionated from the
black point of view as Archie was from the white,
also provided conflict.

Over the years changes took place. Edith's
cousin Maude Findlay, played by Bea Arthur, appeared in several episodes, provoking Archie
with her loud, liberal opinions. She got her own
show, *Maude,* in 1972. The Jeffersons moved
away to Manhattan and into their own show, *The
Jeffersons,* early in 1975, whereupon Mike, who
had finally graduated from college, moved into
their old house. This allowed Mike to continue to
torment Archie, but as a next-door neighbor. Then
Gloria became pregnant; the baby, Joey, was born
in December 1975. The Lorenzos, an Italian couple, moved in as neighbors for a while. Frank
Lorenzo loved to clean and cook (woman's work,
according to Archie) while his wife Irene was an
accomplished fixer of anything mechanical. Irene
also possessed a sarcastic wit, with which she put
down Archie regularly. When Archie was temporarily laid off from his job in October 1976, the
Bunkers were forced to take in a Puerto Rican
boarder, Teresa Betancourt, which provided still
another source of irritation.

The 1977–1978 season brought a major change
to *All in the Family.* In the opening three-part
story, Archie gave up his job to pursue the American dream of owning his own business. Along
with Harry the bartender, he purchased Kelsey's
Bar from an ailing Tommy Kelsey and reopened
it as Archie's Place. This season included episodes with some very adult themes, including one
in which an intruder attempted to rape Edith.
Then at the end of the season Rob Reiner and
Sally Struthers announced that they were leaving
All in the Family for ventures of their own. The
final episode of the season saw Mike, Gloria, and
little Joey (played by twins Jason and Justin Draeger) moving to California, where Mike was to take
a teaching position. The episode was a tearful and
sentimental farewell, leaving Archie and Edith
with an "empty nest." Temporarily, as it turned
out, for in the fall of 1978, Archie and Edith were
joined by little Stephanie Mills, a niece who had
been abandoned by her father.

During the 1979–1980 season the program grew
even further away from its original format, as the
action shifted to Archie's bar. Edith was seen only
infrequently—Jean Stapleton, feeling that she had
exhausted the potential of her character, wished
to be phased out of the series. New regulars were
introduced at the bar, as Archie expanded it to
include a short-order restaurant and took on a
Jewish partner named Murray Klein. Murray's liberal intellectual background was in sharp contrast to, and sometimes in sharp conflict with, Archie's views. The ethnic mix at Archie's Place
included Veronica, the sardonic Irish cook, Jose,
the Puerto Rican busboy, and a wide variety of

27

customers. Coincident with these changes, in the fall of 1979, the name of the series was changed to *Archie Bunker's Place*.

Then came a development which in the early days of the series would have seemed unthinkable. Edith died suddenly, of a stroke. This was not treated directly; rather, in the premiere episode of the 1980–1981 season Archie and Stephanie—whom the Bunkers had adopted—were seen grieving over Edith's unexpected death. Life did go on, however, and Archie hired a black housekeeper, Ellen Canby, to help look after his niece. Mrs. Canby was the sister-in-law of one of his neighbors, Polly Swanson. With Edith gone, Archie gingerly moved into the dating scene, for the first time in more than 25 years.

In the spring of 1981, Archie took over sole operation of the bar when partner Murray moved to San Francisco with his new wife (Martin Balsam had tired of his limited role in the series and wanted to bow out). That fall, without the business expertise of his now-absentee partner, Archie got needed financial help from young lawyer/business manager Gary Rabinowitz. Gary's involvement was more than strictly business, however, since he was dating Archie's 18-year-old niece, Billie. She had arrived at the start of the season on a visit, only to become a permanent member of the Bunker household and a waitress at Archie's Place.

Throughout all of these changes *All in the Family* remained one of the top hits on television. It did not begin that way, however. It took 1971 audiences several months to adjust to the blunt, outrageous humor of the show. There was considerable publicity about Archie's railings against "spics and spades," and it seemed possible that the show might be canceled. But by the summer of 1971 *All in the Family* had become a controversial hit, and the number-one program on television—a position it retained for five years. Part of its appeal was based on the fact that it could be interpreted in several different ways. Liberals and intellectuals could cite it as an example of the absurdity of prejudice, while another large segment of the viewing audience could agree with Archie's attitudes and enjoy him as their kind of guy. Like *The Honeymooners'* Ralph Kramden in the 1950s, the loud-mouthed yet vulnerable Archie Bunker was a man for all audiences.

All in the Family was based on the British series, *Till Death Do Us Part*.

CBS telecast reruns of *All in the Family* weekdays from December 1975 to September 1979.

ALL IS FORGIVEN
Situation Comedy
FIRST TELECAST: *March 20, 1986*
LAST TELECAST: *June 12, 1986*
BROADCAST HISTORY:
  Mar 1986, NBC Thu 9:30–10:00
  Mar 1986–Apr 1986, NBC Sat 9:30–10:00
  May 1986–Jun 1986, NBC Thu 9:30–10:00

CAST:
  Paula Russell .... Bess Armstrong
  Matt Russell .... Terence Knox
  Nicolette Bingham .... Carol Kane
  Sonia Russell .... Shawnee Smith
  Lorraine Elder .... Valerie Landsburg
  Cecile Porter-Lindsey ... Judith-Marie Bergan
  Oliver Royce .... David Alan Grier
  Wendell Branch .... Bill Wiley
  Sherry Levy .... Debi Richter

"She has a love nest at home and a cuckoo's nest at work," read the ad for this short-lived comedy. Paula Russell went through two of life's great traumas on the same day, March 29th—getting married and starting a new job. The new hubby was Matt, a young donut executive who came complete with a loud and somewhat jealous teenage daughter named Sonia. The job was that of producer of the soap opera *All Is Forgiven* (yes, the same title as this series), providing a crew of loony co-workers. Nicolette, a spaced-out, syrupy transplanted Southern belle, was the head writer; Wendell, the insecure director; Cecile, the pushy star who did everything possible to make sure that no one usurped her status; Oliver, the talented but unsure new member of the writing staff; Sherry, one of the production assistants; and Lorraine, the receptionist/secretary who seemed to be eternally preoccupied with her social life.

For some reason NBC repeated the premiere episode of this forgettable series as a "special presentation" on August 23, 1986, two months after the regular run had ended.

ALL STAR REVUE
Comedy Variety
FIRST TELECAST: *October 4, 1950*
LAST TELECAST: *April 18, 1953*
BROADCAST HISTORY:
  Oct 1950–Jul 1951, NBC Wed 8:00–9:00
  Sep 1951–Apr 1953, NBC Sat 8:00–9:00
STARS:
  Ed Wynn (1950–1952)
  Danny Thomas (1950–1952)
  Jack Carson (1950–1952)
  Jimmy Durante (1950–1953)
  Martha Raye (1951–1953)
  George Jessel (1952–1953)
  Tallulah Bankhead (1952–1953)

This variety series originally featured a rotating roster of four famous comedians—Ed Wynn, Danny Thomas, Jack Carson, and Jimmy Durante—who alternated as hosts. First known as *Four Star Revue*, the series was retitled *All Star Revue* in the fall of 1951 when a number of additional entertainers began to headline episodes. Among them were Martha Raye (who starred in four episodes), Olsen & Johnson, Spike Jones, Victor Borge, Bob Hope, the Ritz Brothers, and Paul Winchell.

During the summer of 1952 there was no regular

star and the program adopted a vaudeville flavor, with both new and established performers appearing. This summer version was titled *All Star Summer Revue*. When the fall season began there was a new lineup of regular hosts, with only Jimmy Durante remaining from prior seasons. The other performers starring in single episodes of the series in 1952–1953 were Dennis Day, the Ritz Brothers, Walter O'Keefe, Perry Como, Sonja Henie, and Ben Blue.

ALL'S FAIR
Situation Comedy
FIRST TELECAST: *September 20, 1976*
LAST TELECAST: *August 15, 1977*
BROADCAST HISTORY:
  Sep 1976–Aug 1977, CBS Mon 9:30–10:00
CAST:
  Richard C. Barrington . . . . Richard Crenna
  Charlotte (Charley) Drake . Bernadette Peters
  Lucy Daniels . . . . Lee Chamberlain
  Allen Brooks . . . . J. A. Preston
  Ginger Livingston . . . . Judy Kahan
  Sen. Wayne Joplin . . . . Jack Dodson
  Lanny Wolf (1977) . . . . Michael Keaton

As if the difference in their ages wasn't enough of a problem, 49-year-old political columnist Richard Barrington and his vivacious 23-year-old girlfriend Charley, a free-lance photographer, were also at the opposite ends of the political spectrum: he was an archconservative and she was a "liberated" liberal. Love somehow managed to keep them together, despite the stormy outbursts that occurred when the subject of government and governmental policies happened to come up, which was quite often, since this series was set in Washington, D.C. Al Brooks was Richard's black assistant; his girlfriend Lucy was a reporter for CBS News in Washington. Charley's roommate Ginger was involved with a married Congressman; Wayne Joplin was a liberal senator and a friend of Richard's who usually sided with Charley in any disagreement between the couple. When Richard became a special assistant to President Carter, Ginger became his secretary and "superhip" Carter aide Lanny Wolf became a permanent member of the cast.

ALMOST ANYTHING GOES
Competition
FIRST TELECAST: *July 31, 1975*
LAST TELECAST: *April 10, 1976*
BROADCAST HISTORY:
  July 1975–Aug 1975, ABC Thu 8:00–9:00
  Jan 1976–Apr 1976, ABC Sat 8:00–9:00
PLAY BY PLAY:
  Charlie Jones
COLOR COMMENTATOR:
  Lynn Shackleford
FIELD INTERVIEWER:
  Dick Whittington (1975)
  Regis Philbin (1976)

Originally conceived as a one-month summer fill-in show, this uninhibited free-for-all was sufficiently popular to win a regular season tryout in early 1976 and also give birth to a Saturday morning kid's edition (called *Junior Almost Anything Goes*.) The format was an expansion of the old *Beat the Clock*, pitting teams from different towns and states against each other in all sorts of bizarre stunts. The setting was outdoors and the coverage was handled as in a sports event, complete with play-by-play, color, and field interviews. Winning teams got to participate in regional championships.

The first telecast, for example, had contestants carry a loaf of bread while sliding across a greased pole suspended over a pool; balance an egg on the head while riding down an obstacle course in a golf cart; and dive into a pool and climb onto a raft to dress up in formal garb. Greased runways, swimming pools filled with peanuts, and chocolate pies in the face were also stock-in-trade for this series.

ALOHA PARADISE
Situation Comedy
FIRST TELECAST: *February 25, 1981*
LAST TELECAST: *April 29, 1981*
BROADCAST HISTORY:
  Feb 1981–Apr 1981, ABC Wed 9:00–10:00
CAST:
  Sydney Chase . . . . Debbie Reynolds
  Curtis Shea . . . . Bill Daily
  Fran Linhart . . . . Pat Klous
  Evelyn Pahinui . . . . Mokihana
  Richard Bean . . . . Stephen Shortridge

Aloha Paradise was a rather obvious clone of *The Love Boat*, and was produced by the same people. The captain in this case was Sydney Chase, the female manager of the glamorous Paradise Village resort in sundrenched Hawaii. As on *The Love Boat*, there was a perky social director (Fran) and an understanding bartender (Evelyn), who dispensed tropical drinks and wise counsel. Also on board—or on hand—were Curtis, the somewhat uncertain assistant manager and Richard, the handsome lifeguard.

The plot also bore more than a passing resemblance to *Love Boat's*: three or four different stories were told within each episode, each about people in love, out of love, or looking for love, and finding that their dreams could come true—at any age—in a romantic vacation setting. The guest stars who appeared in these little stories were mostly retreads from other TV series, also a *Love Boat* practice. Even the lush theme song sounded like *Love Boat's*.

One almost expected *Aloha Paradise* to toot its whistle and set sail.

ALVIN SHOW, THE
Cartoon
FIRST TELECAST: *October 4, 1961*

LAST TELECAST: *September 5, 1962*
BROADCAST HISTORY:
  Oct 1961–Sep 1962, CBS Wed 7:30–8:00
VOICES:
  Ross Bagdasarian
  Shepard Menken

Ross Bagdasarian, whose professional name was David Seville, had a huge success with a novelty record "The Chipmunk Song." In the seven weeks following its original release in 1958, it sold over four million copies. Subsequent success with chipmunk albums and singles eventually resulted in this animated series. Bagdasarian was the voice of three chipmunks; Alvin, an aggressive, ambitious, impulsive, and often foolish little fellow and his more conservative brothers Simon and Theodore. Bagdasarian was also the voice of the animated David Seville in whose home Alvin and his brothers lived. In addition to stories about their relationship and one or two musical numbers, each episode included an adventure of Clyde Crashcup, a nutty inventor who took credit for inventing anything and everything. His voice was done by Shepard Menken.

Reruns of *The Alvin Show* aired on Saturday mornings on CBS from June 1962 to September 1965 and were revived on NBC's Saturday morning lineup from March to November 1979.

An all-new animated series, *Alvin & the Chipmunks* premiered on NBC's Saturday morning lineup in September of 1983, with Ross Bagdasarian, Jr. filling the role his late father had filled in the original series. The new version is still on the air.

AMANDA'S
Situation Comedy
FIRST TELECAST: *February 10, 1983*
LAST TELECAST: *May 26, 1983*
BROADCAST HISTORY:
  Feb 1983–Mar 1983, ABC Thu 8:30–9:00
  May 1983, ABC Thu 9:30–10:00
CAST:
  Amanda Cartwright .... Beatrice Arthur
  Marty Cartwright .... Fred McCarren
  Arlene Cartwright........... Simone Griffeth
  Earl Nash .... Rick Hurst
  Aldo .... Tony Rosato
  Clifford Mundy .... Keene Curtis
  Zack Cartwright .... Kevin McCarthy

Bea Arthur returned briefly to series television in this obvious (though unacknowledged) copy of the popular British series *Fawlty Towers.* Amanda was the formidable owner of "Amanda's By The Sea," a homey little hotel overlooking the Pacific. Her fractious staff included Marty, her hotel-management-graduate son; Arlene, his spoiled and citified wife; Earl, the excitable chef; and Aldo, the confused bellhop of indeterminate foreign extraction. Stories concerned burnt steaks, fussy guests, travel-guide writers who had

to be impressed, and the threatening banker, Mr. Mundy, who was always about to foreclose. In the last few episodes brother-in-law Zack showed up to meddle and to woo Amanda.

AMATEUR HOUR, THE
  see *Original Amateur Hour, The*

AMAZING DUNNINGER, THE
Mind Reading/Audience Participation
FIRST TELECAST: *June 25, 1955*
LAST TELECAST: *October 10, 1956*
BROADCAST HISTORY:
  Jun 1955–Sep 1955, NBC Sat 8:30–9:00
  May 1956–Oct 1956, ABC Wed 8:30–9:00
REGULAR:
  Joseph Dunninger

Titled *The Dunninger Show* on NBC and *The Amazing Dunninger* on ABC, this summer series featured the unique skills of the famed mentalist. His ability to read minds was tested each week by celebrity guests and by members of the studio audience.

AMAZING MR. MALONE, THE
Crime Drama
FIRST TELECAST: *September 24, 1951*
LAST TELECAST: *March 10, 1952*
BROADCAST HISTORY:
  Sep 1951–Mar 1952, ABC Mon 8:00–8:30
CAST:
  John J. Malone................... Lee Tracy

Lee Tracy, who perhaps was better known as *Martin Kane—Private Eye,* enacted the role of the "brilliant criminal lawyer" John J. Malone in this live mystery series. Malone, who had been a cynical, humorless character on radio, became a lighthearted sleuth with a ready quip and an affinity for pretty girls in this TV version.

It was based on the Malone novels by Craig Rice, and on the radio series which began in 1947; the TV version alternated with *Mr. District Attorney.*

AMAZING POLGAR, THE
Hypnosis
FIRST TELECAST: *September 16, 1949*
LAST TELECAST: *October 21, 1949*
BROADCAST HISTORY:
  Sep 1949–Oct 1949, CBS Fri 7:45–7:55
STAR:
  Dr. Franz Polgar

This extremely short, live series—it was only ten minutes long and was on the air for five weeks—examined the effects of hypnosis, the power of suggestion, the immunity to pain, the ability to recall incidents that the conscious mind does not remember, and other mental feats. It starred professional hypnotist Dr. Franz Polgar, who possessed doctorates in psychology and economics.

AMAZING SPIDER-MAN, THE

Adventure

FIRST TELECAST: *April 5, 1978*
LAST TELECAST: *May 3, 1978*
BROADCAST HISTORY:

Apr 1978–May 1978, CBS Wed 8:00–9:00

CAST:

Peter Parker/Spider-Man
.... Nicholas Hammond
Capt. Barbera .... Michael Pataki
J. Jonah Jameson........... Robert F. Simon
Rita Conway .... Chip Fields

Spider-Man, the Marvel comic creation of Stan Lee, was brought to life for this limited run CBS series. Peter Parker was a young college science major and a part-time news photographer for the *Daily Bugle*. When he was accidently bitten by a radioactive spider, he suddenly found himself endowed with superhuman abilities. He could sense the presence of danger and possessed strength far superior to that of ordinary men; he could scale sheer walls without ropes and had a magic web concealed in a wrist band that helped him to "fly" and to subdue attackers. But the transformation to Spider-Man was a mixed blessing for young Peter. He was, by nature, a rather simple, nonviolent man who found himself forced to lead a double life, possessing powers he didn't quite understand and didn't really want. Peter's boss at the *Daily Bugle* was publisher J. Jonah Jameson. Jameson's secretary, Rita, was Peter's good friend and protector.

Spider-Man returned to the air in the fall of 1978, but as a number of specials rather than as a regular series. For these seven new episodes, the last of which aired on July 6, 1979, Ellen Bry was added to the cast as free-lance photographer Julie Mason.

An animated *Spider-Man* series ran on ABC's Saturday morning lineup from September 1967 to August 1969, and on its Sunday morning lineup from March to September 1970. Spider-Man then resurfaced in animation as part of NBC's Saturday morning lineup for five seasons beginning in September 1981.

AMAZING STORIES

Fantasy Anthology

FIRST TELECAST: *September 29, 1985*
LAST TELECAST: *May 15, 1987*
BROADCAST HISTORY:

Sep 1985–Jun 1986, NBC Sun 8:00–8:30
Jun 1986–Feb 1987, NBC Mon 8:30–9:00
Mar 1987–May 1987, NBC Fri 8:30–9:00

EXECUTIVE PRODUCER:

Steven Spielberg

As a child, Steven Spielberg was a fan of such TV anthology series as *The Outer Limits, One Step Beyond,* and *The Twilight Zone.* He began his career at age 21 (1969) as a director of the pilot for Rod Serling's *Night Gallery,* and first gained attention for his unusual TV movie *Duel* (between

a man and a mysterious truck), in 1971. Then he moved on to the big screen to create such monster hits as *Jaws, Close Encounters of the Third Kind, Raiders of the Lost Ark,* and *E.T.*

In 1985 NBC lured him back to produce a series that was supposed to mark the revival of the kind of short story TV anthologies he had loved as a child. It didn't, but during its two-year run *Amazing Stories* did provide innovative, sometimes scary, sometimes whimsical "little films" from some of Hollywood's leading talents—people who otherwise had little to do with television. Episode directors included Spielberg himself ("Ghost Train," "The Mission"), Martin Scorsese, Clint Eastwood, Paul Bartel, and Burt Reynolds. Among the guest stars were Drew Barrymore, Kevin Costner, Sid Caesar, Mark Hamill, Sam Waterston, Milton Berle, David Carradine, Stan Freberg, and Charlie Sheen.

AMAZING WORLD OF KRESKIN, THE

Mind Reading/Audience Participation

BROADCAST HISTORY:

Syndicated only
30 minutes
Produced: *1971–1975* (90 episodes)
Released: *1971*

STAR:

Kreskin

HOST:

Bill Luxton

This was one of those sideshows that TV sometimes puts forth. Like Dunninger and Kuda Bux in the 1950s, Kreskin specialized in mind reading and ESP—he knew where you had been that morning, what was in the sealed envelope, where the lady in the third row went for her vacation. Celebrity guests ranging from William Shatner to Meadowlark Lemon dropped in. *Kreskin* was taped in Canada, for broadcast on the CTV network, and was syndicated in the U.S. A later batch of episodes, made in 1975, were called *The New Kreskin Show.*

AMEN

Situation Comedy

FIRST TELECAST: *September 27, 1986*
LAST TELECAST:
BROADCAST HISTORY:

Sep 1986–Apr 1987, NBC Sat 9:30–10:00
Jun 1987–   , NBC Sat 9:30–10:00

CAST:

Deacon Ernest Frye .... Sherman Hemsley
Rev. Reuben Gregory......... Clifton Davis
Thelma Frye.......... Anna Maria Horsford
Casietta Hetebrink..... Barbara Montgomery
Amelia Hetebrink.................. Roz Ryan
Rolly Forbes................. Jester Hairston
*Lorenzo Hollingsworth....... Franklyn Seales
*Leola Forbes............... Rosetta LeNoire

*Occasional

Amen was a breakthrough of sorts—the first hit comedy in TV history to be based on religion. Sherman Hemsley, who played pushy, egotistical George Jefferson on *The Jeffersons* for ten years, played a similar character here as an insufferable deacon (and lawyer) whose father had founded the First Community Church of Philadelphia, and who intended to keep it under his thumb. Unfortunately the new minister, Rev. Gregory, had other ideas and every week he quietly deflated the strutting deacon. Both, of course, really had the church's best interests at heart. Thelma was the deacon's 30-year-old, unmarried, romantically frustrated daughter, who eventually began dating the handsome new pastor; Casietta and Amelia, chattering sisters who were members of the Church board; and Rolly, the board's wise old voice of reason. A running story in the second season involved the arrival at the church of a charismatic 12-year-old preacher, Rev. Johnny Tolbert (played by real-life child minister Rev. William Hudson III).

Actor Clifton Davis, best known as the star of the 1974 series *That's My Mama,* was also a real-life minister. While appearing in the top-rated *Amen* he served as assistant pastor at the Loma Linda, Calif., Seventh-Day Adventist Church.

AMERICA
Documentary
FIRST TELECAST: *November 14, 1972*
LAST TELECAST: *April 10, 1973*
BROADCAST HISTORY:
  Nov 1972–Apr 1973, NBC Tue 10:00–11:00
HOST:
  Alistair Cooke

Through pictures and the commentary of Englishman Alistair Cooke, these documentaries traced the history of the United States from the last of the Mohicans to the hippies of the 1970s; they were filmed on location over a period of two years. Cooke, who had spent the last 35 years living in the United States as a foreign correspondent and reporter, narrated the series, which he regarded as a "personal history of America."

America was one of the few series ever to be shown first on commercial television and later rerun on public television (the Public Broadcasting Service network).

AMERICA IN VIEW
Travelogue
FIRST TELECAST: *May 31, 1951*
LAST TELECAST: *October 28, 1953*
BROADCAST HISTORY:
  May 1951–Jul 1951, ABC Thu 10:30–11:00
  Aug 1951–Oct 1951, ABC Fri 10:30–11:00
  Jan 1952–Mar 1952, ABC Sat 10:45–11:00
  Jun 1952–Jun 1953, ABC Sun 9:00–9:30 (most weeks)
  Oct 1953, ABC Wed 8:00–8:30

Film travelogues of the United States.

AMERICA SONG
Music
FIRST TELECAST: *April 21, 1948*
LAST TELECAST: *April 25, 1949*
BROADCAST HISTORY:
  Apr 1948–Jul 1948, NBC Wed 8:00–8:15
  Jul 1948–Sep 1948, NBC Tue 7:30–7:50
  Oct 1948–Feb 1949, NBC Mon 7:30–7:50
  Mar 1949–Apr 1949, NBC various 15-minute spots
REGULARS:
  Paul Arnold
  Nellie Fisher, dancer
  Ray Harrison, dancer

A program of traditional American folk songs and dances, hosted by singer-guitarist Paul Arnold. A number of singers and dancers rotated in and out of the cast during the program's run, including 12-year-old Jimsey Somers and 8-year-old Dickie Orlan in early 1949. The program was renamed *American Songs* during its last four months.

AMERICA SPEAKS
Opinion Poll
FIRST TELECAST: *September 5, 1948*
LAST TELECAST: *October 31, 1948*
BROADCAST HISTORY:
  Sep 1948–Oct 1948, CBS Sun 10:00–10:15
HOST:
  Dr. George Gallup

George Gallup is probably the most famous poll taker in America. In the fall of 1948, a presidential election year, he was the star of a nine-week live series in which he presented the results of a series of public opinion polls he had taken to the television audience. In addition to displaying the results, the series showed reenactments of the actual polling techniques.

AMERICA 2-NIGHT
  see *Fernwood 2-Night*

AMERICAN BANDSTAND
Music
FIRST TELECAST: *October 7, 1957*
LAST TELECAST: *December 30, 1957*
BROADCAST HISTORY:
  Oct 1957–Dec 1957, ABC Mon 7:30–8:00
HOST:
  Dick Clark

Dick Clark's *American Bandstand* is best known as the networks' longest-running (30 years) afternoon show for teens, but it did have a short run in prime time as well, as indicated above. The show had begun as a local dance program in Philadelphia in 1952, moving to the full ABC network as a Monday–Friday late afternoon entry in August 1957. Its immediate success prompted ABC to give it a brief run on Monday nights that fall.

The nighttime version was identical to its daytime counterpart. Clark hosted one or two guest performers whose records were currently on the pop charts. They lip-synched their hits, chatted about their careers, and signed autographs. Most of these young singers and groups were at the beginnings of their careers, and Clark wisely kept the tapes of their appearances and got full permission to use them in the future. These clips are often seen in rock music retrospectives today, and in some cases are the only film available of some rock legends (and "one-shot" wonders) early in their careers.

During the remainder of the show Clark played current hits, while the studio audience danced to the music. There was also the infamous "rate-a-record" feature ("Umm, it's got a good beat . . . I'll give it a 95").

The daytime network version of *American Bandstand* continued on ABC's weekday lineup until August 1963, and then became a once-a-week Saturday afternoon show from 1963–1987. In the fall of 1987 it was finally canceled by ABC, but Clark continued production of original episodes for syndication, which were seen on many stations in the same time period—Saturday afternoons. In the 1950s and early '60s the show (both daytime and nighttime versions) originated live from Philadelphia; production moved to Hollywood in February 1964. For a loving, illustrated history of the program see *The History of American Bandstand* by Michael Shore with Dick Clark (Ballantine, 1985).

Dick Clark has also produced and hosted a number of other prime-time rock music shows, including the Saturday night *Dick Clark Show* (q.v.), which ran from 1958 until 1960.

AMERICAN DREAM
Drama
FIRST TELECAST: *April 26, 1981*
LAST TELECAST: *June 10, 1981*
BROADCAST HISTORY:
    Apr 1981, ABC Sun 9:30–11:00
    Apr 1981, ABC Mon 9:00–10:00
    May 1981–June 1981, ABC Wed 9:00–10:00
CAST:
    Danny Novak . . . . Stephen Macht
    Donna Novak . . . . Karen Carlson
    Casey Novak . . . . Tim Waldrip
    Todd Novak . . . . Michael Hershewe
    Jennifer Novak . . . . Andrea Smith
    Abe Berlowitz . . . . Hans Conried
    Sam Whittier . . . . John McIntire

Family drama about the Novaks, who made the unusual decision to move from the sunny suburbs back into the grimy inner city, partly of necessity, partly to put a little "reality" into their lives. Danny Novak's decision came about when he began looking for a new house—to accommodate an expected baby, and Donna's aging father Sam—and found that the only place the family could afford was a creaky old structure in downtown Chicago. It was a far cry from the neat lawns of Park Ridge, and most of the family was apprehensive, particularly 17-year-old Casey, a pasty-faced youth who seemed to have a great deal of trouble adjusting. Todd, the 12-year-old, was a natural-born "operator" and could adjust anywhere. Jennifer, the 5-year-old, thought it was all great fun. Abe Berlowitz was the neighborhood old-timer who had sold them the house, and who became their new best friend.

Filmed on location in Chicago and Park Ridge, Illinois.

AMERICAN FORUM OF THE AIR
Discussion
FIRST TELECAST: *February 4, 1950*
LAST TELECAST: *September 21, 1952*
BROADCAST HISTORY:
    Feb 1950–Sep 1950, NBC Sat 7:00–7:30
    Sep 1950–Oct 1950, NBC Sat 6:00–6:30
    Jul 1951–Sep 1951, NBC Sun 10:00–10:30
    May 1952–Sep 1952, NBC Sun 10:30–11:00
MODERATOR:
    Theodore Granik

This long-running discussion program was founded and moderated by Theodore Granik. It originated in Washington, D.C., usually before a live audience, with Granik interviewing two distinguished guests, one on each side of a major national or international issue. *Forum* began on radio in 1928 and appeared on television from 1949 to 1957, generally on Sunday afternoons. However, during the periods indicated above it was a prime-time series. Granik, who was also founder and moderator of *Youth Wants to Know*, relinquished the role of moderator in 1953 due to ill health, but continued to produce the program with newsman Stephen McCormick as moderator.

AMERICAN GIRLS, THE
Adventure/Drama
FIRST TELECAST: *September 23, 1978*
LAST TELECAST: *November 10, 1978*
BROADCAST HISTORY:
    Sep 1978–Nov 1978, CBS Sat 9:00–10:00
CAST:
    Rebecca Tomkins . . . . Priscilla Barnes
    Amy Waddell . . . . Debra Clinger
    Francis X. Casey . . . . David Spielberg
    Jason Cook . . . . William Prince

Rebecca and Amy were two very attractive young reporters working for *The American Report*, a fictitious TV news magazine similar to the real-life *60 Minutes*. Rebecca was the older and more experienced of the two, a witty and sophisticated big-city girl. Amy was fresh out of college, a small-town girl who was eager to succeed. The two of them traveled around the country on assignments in an elaborately equipped van that provided them with a remote production studio to work on their stories. Casey was the show's producer in New York, who gave the girls their assignments and helped them out of dangerous or embarrassing situations. The on-air personality who anchored *The American Report* was Jason Cook.

AMERICAN INVENTORY
Documentary/Drama
FIRST TELECAST: *July 1, 1951*
LAST TELECAST: *August 23, 1952*
BROADCAST HISTORY:
   Jul 1951–Aug 1951, NBC Sun 8:00–8:30
   Jun 1952–Aug 1952, NBC Sat 7:30–8:00
HOST:
   Ray Morgan (1951)

Produced by NBC in cooperation with the Alfred P. Sloan Foundation, *American Inventory* was an experimental series that tried out new techniques in adult education. Episodes included panel discussions on various issues, documentary films, ballet, drama, and other features to make it, according to its producers, "the living newspaper." It premiered as a Sunday evening show in July of 1951 and moved to an earlier time period on Sunday afternoons in September. The host of the original series was Ray Morgan, who left in May 1952 when the program ended. When returned to nighttime television on June 28, 1952, it was as a series of documentary-style dramatizations under the broad subtitle "American Gallery." The dramatizations dealt with the people who contributed, in their modest ways, to the betterment of American society—doctors, lawyers, teachers, and so on. In September 1952 it again moved into an earlier time slot on Sunday afternoons, where it remained on the air until December 1955.

AMERICAN MINSTRELS OF 1949
Variety
FIRST TELECAST: *January 13, 1949*
LAST TELECAST: *March 17, 1949*
BROADCAST HISTORY:
   Jan 1949–Mar 1949, ABC Thu 8:00–9:00
EMCEE:
   Jack Carter
REGULARS:
   Pick and Pat (Pick Malone and Pat Padgett)
   Mary Small
   Jimmy Burrell
   Estelle Sloane

This was more vaudeville than a true minstrel show, but it featured some real oldtime acts, such as Smith and Dale in their "Doctor Kronkheit" routine. Regulars included blackface comics Pick and Pat, singers Mary Small and Jimmy Burrell, and dancer Estelle Sloane. Also seen were such big-time TV acts as Nelson's Cats.

AMERICAN ODYSSEY
Documentary
FIRST TELECAST: *March 24, 1958*
LAST TELECAST: *June 9, 1958*
BROADCAST HISTORY:
   Mar 1958–June 1958, ABC Mon 7:30–8:00

American Odyssey focused on the various roles played by American institutions and individuals and presented a half-hour filmed documentary on a given topic each week. Subjects ranged from the grueling experiences of a plebe at West Point to dramatized cases from the files of the American Medical Association to a tour of the famous sights in Washington, D.C.

AMERICAN PARADE, THE
Magazine
FIRST TELECAST: *March 27, 1984*
LAST TELECAST: *September 5, 1984*
BROADCAST HISTORY:
   Mar 1984–May 1984, CBS Tue 8:00–9:00
   Jun. 1984–Sep 1984, CBS Wed 8:00–9:00
ANCHORMEN/HOSTS:
   Charles Kuralt
   Bill Moyers
CORRESPONDENTS:
   Morton Dean
   Andrew Lack
   Bill Kurtis
   Diane Sawyer
   Maria Shriver
   Art Buchwald

This unabashedly patriotic magazine series featured stories about the triumphs and tragedies of individuals both well known and obscure. It was dedicated to an exploration of the "vitality of the American spirit." Most weeks the show was a potpourri of pieces ranging from the likes of Muhammed Ali or ex-president Richard Nixon to a report on a Vietnamese refugee's accomplishments as a female cadet at West Point. Humorist Art Buchwald was also seen with his irreverent, satirical views of the American scene, and host Kuralt did whimsical features on the quirky and eccentric folks he had encountered over the years doing his "on the road" featurettes for CBS News. After dismal early ratings Bill Moyers was added as co-host, covering more serious subjects. The show was retitled *Crossroads* and moved to Wednesdays in June, but none of this seemed to help and the revamped show ground to a halt by the end of the summer.

AMERICAN PROFILE
Documentary
FIRST TELECAST: *September 29, 1967*
LAST TELECAST: *July 5, 1968*
BROADCAST HISTORY:
   Sep 1967–Jul 1968, NBC Fri 10:00–11:00

Various aspects of American life and the natural beauty of the country were covered in this series of seven documentaries, which were aired on a rotating basis with *The Bell Telephone Hour, Actuality Specials*, and *NBC News Reports*. The subjects included an examination of endangered species of American wildlife, discussions of politics, and a tour through the National Gallery of

Art in Washington, D.C. NBC newsmen narrated most of the telecasts; however, Eddy Arnold was host for "Music from the Land" and Robert Culp led the tour through the National Gallery of Art.

AMERICAN SCENE, THE
Documentary
FIRST TELECAST: *July 6, 1952*
LAST TELECAST: *September 28, 1952*
BROADCAST HISTORY:
Jul 1952–Sep 1952, ABC Sun 6:30–7:00

American Scene presented documentary films on assorted subjects. The title was also used by ABC for various one-time telecasts of films in 1952–1953.

AMERICAN WEEK, THE
News/Commentary
FIRST TELECAST: *April 4, 1954*
LAST TELECAST: *October 10, 1954*
BROADCAST HISTORY:
Apr 1954–Oct 1954, CBS Sun 6:00–6:30
CORRESPONDENT:
Eric Sevareid

A summary of the major happenings in the world during the previous week was presented each Sunday evening by CBS News' chief Washington correspondent, Eric Sevareid. In addition to summarizing the news, Mr. Sevareid included observations and analysis of his own. The show featured original filmed interviews with people prominent in the week's news. Although it left the nighttime slot in the middle of October 1954, this series remained on the air in an earlier time period on Sunday afternoons until the following June.

AMERICAN YOUTH FORUM
see *Youth Wants to Know*

AMERICANA
Quiz
FIRST TELECAST: *December 8, 1947*
LAST TELECAST: *July 4, 1949*
BROADCAST HISTORY:
Dec 1947, NBC Mon 8:10–8:40
Jan 1948–Apr 1948, NBC Wed 8:00–8:30
Apr 1948–Nov 1948, NBC Mon 8:30–9:00
Dec 1948–Jul 1949, NBC Mon 9:30–10:00
MODERATOR:
John Mason Brown (Dec 1947–Jan 1948)
Ben Grauer (1948–1949)

This quiz program dealt with American history and folklore, using questions submitted by viewers. The person submitting "the most interesting question of the week" received a set of the *Encyclopedia Americana*. At first the questions were put to a panel of adult experts, but in February 1948 this was changed to teams of high school students.

AMERICANS, THE
Civil War Drama
FIRST TELECAST: *January 23, 1961*
LAST TELECAST: *September 11, 1961*
BROADCAST HISTORY:
Jan 1961–Sep 1961, NBC Mon 7:30–8:30
CAST:
Ben Canfield............... Darryl Hickman
Jeff Canfield .... Dick Davalos

Two young brothers who grew up in Harpers Ferry, then in the state of Virginia, were faced with a major decision when Virginia seceded from the Union in 1861. Jeff, the younger brother, somewhat impetuous and rebellious, decided to fight for the Confederacy. Ben, the elder brother, was torn between loyalty to his home state and loyalty to the Union. After their father died in a fire during the first episode, Ben swam across the river to Maryland and enlisted in the Union Army. During the remainder of the series each brother was showcased on alternate weeks, Ben fighting for the Union and Jeff with the Confederates in the Virginia Militia.

AMERICA'S GREATEST BANDS
Music
FIRST TELECAST: *June 25, 1955*
LAST TELECAST: *September 24, 1955*
BROADCAST HISTORY:
Jun 1955–Sep 1955, CBS Sat 8:00–9:00
HOST:
Paul Whiteman

Serving as the 1955 summer replacement for *The Jackie Gleason Show*, *America's Greatest Bands* presented four different big-name bands each week. Appearing on a giant rotating stage, each of the bands took turns performing. The permanent host of the series was bandleader Paul Whiteman, whose own band was featured on the first telecast. Among the other bands that appeared were those of Duke Ellington, Sammy Kaye, Xavier Cugat, Perez Prado, Bob Crosby, Les Brown, and Count Basie.

AMERICA'S HEALTH
Documentary
FIRST TELECAST: *August 20, 1951*
LAST TELECAST: *March 6, 1952*
BROADCAST HISTORY:
Aug 1951–Sep 1951, ABC Mon 10:00–10:30
Sep 1951–Oct 1951, ABC Sat 9:30–10:00
Feb 1952–Mar 1952, ABC Thu 10:00–10:15

This series consisted of documentary films on health subjects, provided by such organizations as the Veterans Administration and the American Cancer Society. A sample title was "Doctor Speaks His Mind."

AMERICA'S MOST WANTED
Public Service

FIRST TELECAST: *April 10, 1988*
LAST TELECAST:
BROADCAST HISTORY
   Apr 1988–   , FOX Sun 8:00–8:30
HOST:
   John Walsh

This series billed itself as a "weekly nationwide criminal manhunt." In cooperation with law enforcement agencies ranging from the F.B.I. to local municipalities, *America's Most Wanted* provided the general public with detailed information about violent criminals on the loose. Each week two or three cases were covered with recreations of the crimes, interviews with victims and law officers, and, if available, pictures of the actual criminals themselves. Viewers were given a toll-free number to call (1-800-CRIME-88) if they had information that might help in apprehending the criminals.

   The show certainly got off to a good start. Four days after the first episode aired (in February 1988 on the Fox-owned stations), calls from viewers led to the capture of one of the criminals depicted—David James Roberts, a murderer and rapist on the F.B.I.'s ten most wanted list. Over the next few months several other criminals wanted by the F.B.I. were captured with the help of viewers. In early April, *America's Most Wanted* became a prime-time series on the Fox network.

AMERICA'S TOWN MEETING
Debate
FIRST TELECAST: *October 5, 1948*
LAST TELECAST: *July 6, 1952*
BROADCAST HISTORY:
   Oct 1948–Jun 1949, ABC Tue 8:30–9:30
   Jan 1952–Jul 1952, ABC Sun 6:30–7:00
MODERATOR:
   George V. Denny, Jr. (1948–1952)
   John Daly (Apr–Jul 1952)

This venerable radio series, which began in 1935 and ran for 21 years thereafter, had two runs on network television, in 1948–1949 and in 1952. The format was the same as that of the radio show, consisting of debates by politicians, writers, and other prominent persons on such topics as "Are We Too Hysterical About Communism?", "Has the Korean War Been a Failure?", and "Should We Have Uniform Federal Divorce Laws?" The program originated from New York's Town Hall Auditorium before a vociferous and involved audience. George V. Denny, Jr., who created the series, served as moderator for all telecasts except for a brief period in 1952 when ABC newsman John Daly took over.

AMOS BURKE—SECRET AGENT
   see *Burke's Law*

AMOS 'N' ANDY
Situation Comedy

FIRST TELECAST: *June 28, 1951*
LAST TELECAST: *June 11, 1953*
BROADCAST HISTORY:
   Jun 1951–Jun 1953, CBS Thu 8:30–9:00
CAST:
   Amos Jones................ Alvin Childress
   Andrew Hogg Brown ("Andy")
   .... Spencer Williams, Jr.
   George "The Kingfish" Stevens .. Tim Moore
   Lawyer Algonquin J. Calhoun .... Johnny Lee
   Sapphire Stevens .... Ernestine Wade
   Lightnin'
   ..... Horace Stewart (a.k.a. Nick O'Demus)
   Sapphire's Mama (Ramona Smith)
   .... Amanda Randolph
   Madame Queen............ Lillian Randolph
THEME:
   "The Perfect Song" by Clarence Lucas

Amos 'n' Andy, one of the most popular and long-running radio programs of all time, was brought to television in the summer of 1951. The series was produced by Freeman Gosden and Charles Correll, the two actors who had created and starred in the radio version. Since they were white, and the entire cast of the show on television had to be black, a much ballyhooed search was held, over a period of four years, to find the right actors to play the pasts. Only Ernestine Wade and Amanda Randolph were brought over from the radio cast.

   Set in Harlem, *Amos 'n' Andy* centered around the activities of George Stevens, a conniving character who was always looking for a way to make a fast buck. As head of the Mystic Knights of the Sea Lodge, where he held the position of "Kingfish," he got most of the lodge brothers involved in his schemes. That put him at odds not only with them, but with his wife, Sapphire, and her mother. Mama, in particular, didn't trust him at all. Andy Brown was the most gullible of the lodge members, a husky, well-meaning, but rather simple soul. The Kingfish was constantly trying to swindle him in one way or another, but the "big dummy" (as Kingfish called him) kept coming back for more. More often than not, Kingfish would get them both into trouble, but win Andy's cooperation with an appeal to fraternal spirit—"Holy mackerel, Andy! We's all got to stick together in dis heah thing...remember, we is brothers in that great fraternity, the Mystic Knights of the Sea."

   Amos was actually a rather minor character, the philosophical cabdriver who narrated most of the episodes. Madame Queen was Andy's girlfriend and Lightnin' was the slow-moving janitor at the lodge.

   Civil rights groups such as the NAACP had long protested the series as fostering racial stereotypes, to little avail. *Amos 'n' Andy* drew sizable audiences during its two-year CBS run, and was widely rerun on local stations for the next decade. The turning point came in 1963 when CBS Films, which was still calling *Amos 'n' Andy* one of its most widely circulated shows, announced that the program had been sold to two African countries, Kenya and Western Nigeria. Soon afterward, an official of the Kenya government announced that the program would be banned in his country. This focused attention anew on the old controversy and in the summer of 1964, when a Chicago station announced that it was resuming reruns, there were widespread and bitter protests. CBS found its market for the films suddenly disappearing, and in 1966 the program was withdrawn from sale, as quietly as possible.

As to whether the program was in fact racist, there was no agreement on that. The creators certainly didn't think so, and actor Alvin Childress (Amos) was quoted as saying, "I didn't feel it harmed the Negro at all. . . . Actually the series had many episodes that showed the Negro with professions and businesses like attorneys, store owners, and so on, which they never had in TV or movies before. . . ." Others pointed out that the situations were no different than those found in many comedy programs with white characters. Nevertheless the humor certainly derived from the fact that these were shiftless, conniving, not-too-bright *blacks.* The very stereotypes that had so long been unfairly applied to an entire race were used throughout. As a result, it is unlikely that *Amos 'n' Andy* will ever be seen again on television.

For an interesting, but disguised, sequel by Correll and Gosden, see *Calvin and the Colonel.*

AMY PRENTISS
Police Drama
FIRST TELECAST: *December 1, 1974*
LAST TELECAST: *July 6, 1975*
BROADCAST HISTORY:
    Dec 1974–Jul 1975, NBC Sun 8:30–10:30
CAST:
    Amy Prentiss . . . . Jessica Walter
    Det. Tony Russell . . . . Steve Sandor
    Det. Rod Pena . . . . Arthur Metrano
    Det. Contreras . . . . Johnny Seven
    Jill Prentiss . . . . Helen Hunt
    Joan Carter . . . . Gwenn Mitchell

When the chief of detectives of the San Francisco Police Department died unexpectedly, the person at the top of the service list was Amy Prentiss, an attractive 35-year-old widow with a young daughter. There had never been a woman chief of detectives before, and many of the male officers who suddenly found themselves reporting to Amy resented it. A measure of grudging respect gradually emerged, however, when her skill as an investigator became apparent in a series of cases that otherwise constituted standard crime-show fare. Unfortunately, viewers took less readily to the idea of woman as boss, and the program was canceled after a short run.

Amy Prentiss was one of the four rotating elements that made up the 1974–1975 edition of *NBC*

Sunday Mystery Movie. The others were *Columbo, McCloud,* and *McMillan and Wife.*

AND EVERYTHING NICE
Fashions
FIRST TELECAST: *March 15, 1949*
LAST TELECAST: *January 2, 1950*
BROADCAST HISTORY:
    Mar 1949–June 1949, DUM Tue 7:00–7:30
    Jul 1949–Aug 1949, DUM Mon 8:30–9:00
    Sep 1949–Jan 1950, DUM Mon 9:00–9:30
HOSTESS:
    Maxine Barrat

This was an early program that presented fashions, style tips, and guests.

AND HERE'S THE SHOW
Comedy Variety
FIRST TELECAST: *July 9, 1955*
LAST TELECAST: *September 24, 1955*
BROADCAST HISTORY:
    Jul 1955–Sep 1955, NBC Sat 10:00–10:30
REGULARS:
    Ransom Sherman
    Jonathan Winters
    The Double Daters
    John Scott Trotter, musical director
    Bob LeMond, announcer

This live variety program served as a summer replacement for the *George Gobel Show.* Ransom Sherman and Jonathan Winters were the co-stars, with Sherman also acting as host. Both of the stars functioned as monologists and appeared together in skits. The Double Daters introduced the guest stars and the comedy skits and performed a featured musical number each week. The program's title was derived from one of George Gobel's familiar lines.

ANDROS TARGETS, THE
Newspaper Drama
FIRST TELECAST: *January 31, 1977*
LAST TELECAST: *July 9, 1977*
BROADCAST HISTORY:
    Jan 1977–May 1977, CBS Mon 10:00–11:00
    Jul 1977, CBS Sat 10:00–11:00
CAST:
    Mike Andros . . . . James Sutorius
    Sandi Farrell . . . . Pamela Reed
    Chet Reynolds . . . . Roy Poole
    Norman Kale . . . . Alan Mixon
    Wayne Hillman . . . . Ted Beniades
    Ted Bergman . . . . Jordan Charney

Mike Andros was an investigative reporter for *The New York Forum.* Much in the style of the real-life reporters who had become celebrities in the aftermath of the Watergate scandal, Andros focused his efforts on the corruption in the biggest city in the nation. Unethical use of amphetamines by doctors, underworld activities in areas of pornography, prostitution, and narcotics, and unusual criminal cases that had been hushed up by the police all came under his scrutiny. Sandi Farrell was Mike's young assistant and Chet and Norman were the managing and city editors, respectively, of *The New York Forum*. Wayne Hillman was a fellow reporter and friend, and Ted Bergman was the paper's metropolitan editor.

ANDY AND DELLA RUSSELL
Music
FIRST TELECAST: *December 18, 1950*
LAST TELECAST: *June 15, 1951*
BROADCAST HISTORY:
   Dec 1950–Jun 1951, ABC Mon–Fri 7:00–7:05
REGULARS:
   Andy Russell
   Della Russell
   Mort Lippman, piano

Andy Russell, a radio and recording star of the 1940s, and his wife Della hosted this brief but pleasant musical interlude, which originated live from New York every weeknight. A month after its premiere the series' name was changed to *Cook's Champagne Party*, in honor of the sponsor.

ANDY GRIFFITH SHOW, THE
Situation Comedy
FIRST TELECAST: *October 3, 1960*
LAST TELECAST: *September 16, 1968*
BROADCAST HISTORY:
   Oct 1960–Jul 1963, CBS Mon 9:30–10:00 (OS)
   Sep 1963–Sep 1964, CBS Mon 9:30–10:00
   Sep 1964–June 1965, CBS Mon 8:30–9:00
   Sep 1965–Sep 1968, CBS Mon 9:00–9:30
CAST:
   Andy Taylor .... Andy Griffith
   Opie Taylor .... Ronny Howard
   Barney Fife (1960–1965) .... Don Knotts
   Ellie Walker (1960–1961) .... Elinor Donahue
   Aunt Bee Taylor .... Frances Bavier
   Clara Edwards .... Hope Summers
   Gomer Pyle (1963–1964) .... Jim Nabors
   Helen Crump (1964–1968) ..... Aneta Corsaut
   Goober Pyle (1965–1968) ..... George Lindsey
   Floyd Lawson .... Howard McNear
   Otis Campbell (1960–1967) ...... Hal Smith
   Howard Sprague (1966–1968) .... Jack Dodson
   Emmett Clark (1967–1968) ..... Paul Hartman
   Thelma Lou (1960–1965) .... Betty Lynn
   Warren Ferguson (1965–1966) ..... Jack Burns
   Clara Edwards .... Hope Summers
   Mayor Stoner (1962–1963) .... Parley Baer
   Jud Crowley (1961–1966) .... Burt Mustin

The small town of Mayberry, North Carolina, was the setting of this highly successful homespun situation comedy. Sheriff Andy Taylor was a widower with a young son, Opie. They lived with Andy's Aunt Bee, a combination housekeeper and foster mother for Opie. Andy's deputy was his cousin Barney Fife, the most inept, hypertense deputy sheriff ever seen on television. The tone of the show was very gentle, giving Andy the opportunity to state and practice his understanding, philosophical outlook on life. Since there was practically no crime in Mayberry, the stories revolved mostly around the personal relationships of its citizens.

Two of the show's regulars graduated to series of their own. The first was Jim Nabors. He had become a member of the cast in the spring of 1963 in the role of Gomer Pyle, the naive, lovable gas station attendant at Wally's filling station. After a year and a half he left to join the marines and become *Gomer Pyle, U.S.M.C.* Co-star Don Knotts left the show in 1965 for his own variety series, *The Don Knotts Show*. Among the other regulars, Andy's original girlfriend, druggist Ellie Walker, was seen only during the first season, and for the following three years Andy had no regular romantic interest. Schoolteacher Helen Crump filled the void in 1964, and, when Andy Griffith decided to quit the show in 1968, she also provided his means of escape. On the first episode of *Mayberry R.F.D.*, the successor to *The Andy Griffith Show*, Andy and Helen married and moved away, leaving the supporting cast to carry on with a new star, Ken Berry, in the role of Sam Jones—another widower with a young son.

Daytime reruns of this series, as well as some syndicated versions, were titled *Andy of Mayberry*. CBS aired weekday daytime reruns from October 1964 to September 1970, with the title reverting to *The Andy Griffith Show* when the prime-time version left the air. A nostalgic reunion of the series' original cast—the made-for-TV film "Return to Mayberry"—aired in April 1986 and was the highest-rated movie of the entire 1985–1986 season.

ANDY OF MAYBERRY
   see *Andy Griffith Show, The*

ANDY WILLIAMS AND JUNE VALLI SHOW, THE
Music
FIRST TELECAST: *July 2, 1957*
LAST TELECAST: *September 5, 1957*
BROADCAST HISTORY:
   Jul 1957–Sep 1957, NBC Tue/Thu 7:30–7:45
REGULARS:
   Andy Williams
   June Valli
   Alvy West, orchestra conductor
THEME:
   "On a Summer Evening"

On this live summer series, Andy Williams and June Valli sang both individually and together.

ANDY WILLIAMS PRESENTS RAY STEVENS
Comedy Variety
FIRST TELECAST: *June 20, 1970*

LAST TELECAST: *August 8, 1970*
BROADCAST HISTORY:
Jun 1970–Aug 1970, NBC Sat 7:30–8:30
REGULARS:
Ray Stevens
Lulu
Dick Curtis
Steve Martin
Carol Robinson
Solari and Carr
Billy Van
"Mama" Cass Elliot

Singer-composer-comedian-impressionist Ray Stevens starred in this summer replacement for *The Andy Williams Show*. Ray, who was a frequent guest on Andy's show, was featured in production numbers and comedy skits in the summer program, which was taped in Toronto. The skits tended to be very broad and often verged on the physical violence associated with Mack Sennett slapstick.

ANDY WILLIAMS SHOW, THE
Musical Variety
FIRST TELECAST: *July 3, 1958*
LAST TELECAST: *July 17, 1971*
BROADCAST HISTORY:
Jul 1958–Sep 1958, ABC Thu 9:00–9:30
Jul 1959–Sep 1959, CBS Tue 10:00–11:00
Sep 1962–Jun 1963, NBC Thu 10:00–11:00
Sep 1963–May 1964, NBC Tue 10:00–11:00
Oct 1964–May 1966, NBC Mon 9:00–10:00
Sep 1966–May 1967, NBC Sun 10:00–11:00
Sep 1969–Jul 1971, NBC Sat 7:30–8:30 (OS)
STAR:
Andy Williams
REGULARS:
Dick Van Dyke (1958)
The Bob Hamilton Trio (1958)
The Mort Lindsey Orchestra (1958)
The Dick Williams Singers (1959)
The Peter Gennaro Dancers (1959)
The Jack Kane Orchestra (1959)
Randy Sparks and the New Christy Minstrels (1962–1963)
Jimmy Gaines (1962–1963)
Marian Mercer (1962–1963)
R. G. Brown (1962–1963)
The Osmond Brothers (1962–1971)
The Colin Romoff Orchestra (1962–1963)
The Dave Grusin Orchestra (1963–1966)
The Allyn Ferguson Orchestra (1966–1967)
The Mike Post Orchestra (1969–1971)
The Good Time Singers (1963–1966)
Jonathan Winters (1965–1967, 1970–1971)
Irwin Corey (1969–1970)
Janos Prohaska (1969–1971)
Ray Stevens (1969–1971)
The Lennon Sisters (1970–1971)
Charlie Callas (1970–1971)
The Nick Castle Dancers (1963–1966)
The James Starbuck Dancers (1966–1967)

The Jaime Rogers Dancers (1969–1970)
The Andre Tayri Dancers (1970–1971)
THEME (after 1962):
"Moon River," by Henry Mancini and Johnny Mercer

Smooth-voiced popular singer Andy Williams starred in a number of variety shows in the late 1950s and 1960s. The first two were summer shows, in 1958 and 1959, followed by his own regular season series on NBC beginning in 1962. Big-name guest stars appeared, usually of the adult variety (rarely a rock act), and a large number of regulars were seen. Originally the New Christy Minstrels were the chief backup act, but they were soon superseded by a quartet of talented youngsters discovered by Williams performing at Disneyland (they had also appeared once on a *Disneyland* TV special). The Osmond Brothers, billed as "youthful barbershop harmony group from Ogden, Utah," were first seen on December 20, 1962, singing "I'm a Ding Dong Daddy from Dumas" and "Side by Side." They stayed with Williams for the rest of his run. The original four were periodically augmented by brothers and sisters, with six-year-old Donny Osmond making his debut on December 10, 1963.

In 1967 Andy cut back to a schedule of only three specials per year, but in 1969 he returned with a regular weekly series once again. This time the look was decidedly contemporary, including rock acts, psychedelic lighting, and a futuristic set that had the audience seated on movable platforms which followed Andy around through the show. Among the regular features were "The Informal Spot" and "The Williams Weirdos"—Little General, Walking Suitcase, Big Bird, and The Bear.

Williams's 1958 summer show, which had filled in for vacationing Pat Boone, was titled *The Chevy Showroom Starring Andy Williams*. All of his subsequent series were simply titled *The Andy Williams Show*, including a syndicated half-hour musical variety series he hosted during the 1976–1977 season. The only featured regular on the syndicated show was comic/ventriloquist Wayland Flowers.

ANGEL
Situation Comedy
FIRST TELECAST: *October 6, 1960*
LAST TELECAST: *September 20, 1961*
BROADCAST HISTORY:
Oct 1960–Dec 1960, CBS Thu 9:00–9:30
Dec 1960–Apr 1961, CBS Thu 8:00–8:30
Apr 1961–Sep 1961, CBS Wed 9:00–9:30
CAST:
Angel .... Annie Farge
John Smith .... Marshall Thompson
Susie....................... Doris Singleton
George .... Don Keefer

Angel was a petite French girl who had just moved to America and become the bride of a young architect, John Smith. Her efforts to adjust to the American way of life provided the humor in this series. Her problems with English, misunderstanding of situations, and attempts to be a responsible housewife all contributed to the amusement of her husband and their next-door neighbors, Susie and George, who were also their closest friends.

ANGIE

Situation Comedy
FIRST TELECAST: *February 8, 1979*
LAST TELECAST: *October 2, 1980*
BROADCAST HISTORY:
Feb 1979–Aug 1979, ABC Thu 8:30–9:00
Sep 1979–Jan 1980, ABC Tue 8:30–9:00
Jan 1980–Feb 1980, ABC Mon 8:30–9:00
Apr 1980, ABC Sat 8:00–8:30
Jul 1980–Oct 1980, ABC Thu 8:30–9:00
CAST:
Angie Falco Benson . . . . Donna Pescow
Brad Benson . . . . Robert Hays
Theresa Falco . . . . Doris Roberts
Marie Falco . . . . Debralee Scott
Joyce Benson . . . . Sharon Spelman
Randall Benson . . . . John Randolph
Diedre "DiDi" Malloy . . . . Diane Robin
Hillary (1979) . . . . Tammy Lauren
Phipps . . . . Emory Bass
Mary Mary . . . . Valri Bromfield
Mary Grace . . . . Susan Duvall
Mary Katherine . . . . Nancy Lane
Gianni . . . . Tim Thomerson
THEME:
"Different Worlds," by Gimbel and Fox, sung by Maureen McGovern

Cinderella-story comedy about a pert young waitress who finds her handsome—and rich—young prince. When Brad Benson first walked into the Liberty Coffee Shop, Angie thought he was poor and began slipping him pastries. It turned out he was not only a pediatrician from the medical building across the street, but scion of one of Philadelphia's richest families. They fell in love and were married, much to the dismay of Brad's overbearing big sister, Joyce, and stuffy father, Randall, and to the bemusement of Angie's down-to-earth mama, Theresa. Mr. Falco had walked out 19 years earlier—"He went to get the paper"—but Theresa still kept a place at the table for him. She had raised Angie and younger sister Marie by running a newsstand. The Bensons had a different set of problems. Snobbish Joyce was three times divorced and undergoing therapy with a psychiatrist who hated her. DiDi was Angie's big-hearted, big-mouthed best friend at the coffee shop, and Phipps was the butler.

The newlyweds moved into Brad's mansion, but the palatial surroundings were too much so they later bought a smaller house, where Brad set up his practice on the first floor. At first Angie bought the coffee shop, to keep herself busy, but later she traded it for a beauty parlor, where Gianni was the pleasure-seeking hairstylist.

ABC aired reruns of *Angie* on weekday mornings from June–September 1985.

ANIMAL CRACK-UPS

Wildlife/Nature
FIRST TELECAST: *August 8, 1987*
LAST TELECAST: *September 12, 1987*
BROADCAST HISTORY:
Aug 1987–Sep 1987, ABC Sat 8:00–8:30
HOST:
Alan Thicke

What does an orangutan eat for lunch? Why do giraffes neck? Does an elephant have eyelashes? For those who have always wanted to know the answers to such questions, ABC presented this nature documentary cum quiz show about comical oddities of the animal world. A panel of guest celebrities made educated guesses, then viewers saw the answers in film clips supplied by the Tokyo Broadcasting System. The series moved to a more appropriate time slot (for kids) on Saturday morning effective September 12, 1987.

ANIMAL KINGDOM

see *Animal World*

ANIMAL SECRETS

Wildlife Documentary
FIRST TELECAST: *July 2, 1967*
LAST TELECAST: *August 27, 1967*
BROADCAST HISTORY:
Jul 1967–Aug 1967, NBC Sun 7:00–7:30
HOST:
Dr. Loren Eiseley

The mysteries of animal behavior were explored in this nature series hosted by Dr. Loren Eiseley, Professor of Anthropology at the University of Pennsylvania. Each episode dealt with a specific mystery—why do birds migrate, what makes bees buzz, how do fish talk. NBC got a lot of mileage out of this pleasant little series. It first ran on Saturday afternoons from October 1966 to April 1967, was rerun Sunday at 7 P.M. during the summer of 1967, then was rerun again on Sunday afternoons from January until May 1968.

ANIMAL WORLD

Wildlife Documentary
FIRST TELECAST: *June 16, 1968*
LAST TELECAST: *September 12, 1971*
BROADCAST HISTORY:
Jun 1968–Sep 1968, NBC Sun 6:30–7:00
May 1969–Sep 1969, CBS Thu 7:30–8:00
Apr 1970–Sep 1970, ABC Thu 7:30–8:00
Jul 1971–Sep 1971, CBS Sun 7:30–8:00
HOST:
Bill Burrud

Bill Burrud, who had previously made several true-life adventure films for theatrical release, produced and hosted this nature series, which showed wild animals in their natural habitats from locations all over the world. The title of the series was originally *Animal Kingdom,* but was changed to *Animal World* with the telecast that was aired on August 11, 1968. After a season on NBC, it moved to CBS as a late Sunday afternoon series in the fall of 1968. It returned to prime time on three occasions; on CBS in the summers of 1969 and 1971, and on ABC in the summer of 1970, followed by a final network run on Sunday afternoons on NBC from January to September of 1972. *Animal World* then went into syndication, with a mixture of reruns and new episodes. The last of the new episodes were produced in 1976.

ANN SOTHERN SHOW, THE

Situation Comedy
FIRST TELECAST: *October 6, 1958*
LAST TELECAST: *September 25, 1961*
BROADCAST HISTORY:
    Oct 1958–Jul 1960, CBS Mon 9:30–10:00 (OS)
    Oct 1960–Dec 1960, CBS Thu 9:30–10:00
    Dec 1960–Mar 1961, CBS Thu 7:30–8:00
    Jul 1961–Sep 1961, CBS Mon 9:30–10:00
CAST:
    Katy O'Connor .... Ann Sothern
    Jason Macauley (1958–1959) .... Ernest Truex
    Olive Smith .... Ann Tyrrell
    Johnny Wallace (1958–1960) .. Jack Mullaney
    Paul Martine (1958–1959) ...... Jacques Scott
    Flora Macauley (1958–1959)...... Reta Shaw
    James Devery (1959–1961)........ Don Porter
    Dr. Delbert Gray (1960–1961)...... Louis Nye
    Woody (1960–1961)............... Ken Berry
    Oscar Pudney (1960–1961) .... Jesse White

Katy O'Connor was the assistant manager of the plush Bartley House Hotel in New York. Her first boss, Jason Macauley, was transferred to Calcutta in the March 9, 1959, episode, but Katy's hopes of succeeding him as manager were torpedoed when James Devery arrived to fill the job. Katy's secretary, roommate, and best friend was Olive Smith, who developed a romantic interest during the 1960–1961 season in the person of dentist Delbert Gray. Don Porter and Ann Tyrrell had been Ann Sothern's co-stars in her previous series, *Private Secretary,* and they joined her here in amusing tales of the problems encountered in running a big-city hotel.

ANNA AND THE KING

Situation Comedy
FIRST TELECAST: *September 17, 1972*
LAST TELECAST: *December 31, 1972*
BROADCAST HISTORY:
    Sep 1972–Dec 1972, CBS Sun 7:30–8:00
CAST:
    King of Siam .... Yul Brynner
    Anna Owens .... Samantha Eggar
    Kralahome .... Keye Luke
    Louis Owens .... Eric Shea
    Crown Prince Chulalongkorn .... Brian Tochi
    Lady Thiang........................ Lisa Lu

It was in 1951, while preparing for his starring role in Rodgers and Hammerstein's new musical *The King And I,* that Yul Brynner first shaved his head, to add realism to his portrayal. The role and the bald pate both became Brynner trademarks; he brought them to the film version of the musical in 1956 and to this short-lived television comedy version in 1972. Based on Margaret Landon's novel *Anna and the King of Siam,* the story was set in the 1860s and involved a young schoolteacher, a widow with a 12-year-old son, who had been hired by the King of Siam to educate his royal offspring. (The King's many wives, of whom Lady Thiang was most important, had borne him a whole schoolful of children.) There was much conflict between the autocratic king and the stubborn, strong-willed teacher, but there was also a developing respect and affection.

ANNIE OAKLEY

Western
BROADCAST HISTORY:
    Syndicated and network daytime
    30 minutes
    Produced: *Apr 1953–Dec 1956* (81 episodes)
    Released: *January 1954*
CAST:
    Annie Oakley..................... Gail Davis
    Deputy Sheriff Lofty Craig..... Brad Johnson
    Tagg Oakley............... Jimmy Hawkins

Pigtails and pistols were the formula in one of the 1950s' more unusual Westerns. Five-foot-two, 95 pounds, and cute as a button, Annie was also a crack shot and the scourge of badmen around her hometown of Diablo, where she lived with her kid brother, Tagg (the rest of the immediate family was unaccounted for). Towering Deputy Lofty Craig was her friend and silent suitor, and Annie's uncle, Luke MacTavish, was the seldom-seen town sheriff. Co-starring were the horses— Annie's Target, Lofty's Forest, and Tagg's Pixie.

Gail Davis was discovered by Gene Autry, who featured her in nearly 20 of his movies, 30 of his own program's episodes, and then spun her off into this series of her own, which was produced by his company. She really was a good rider and trick shot, performing in Autry's traveling rodeo as well. She once said, "So far as I'm concerned, I'm going to be Annie Oakley for the rest of my born days," and apparently she was right. Today she manages other celebrities.

The real Annie Oakley lived from 1859 to 1926, and was an exhibition sharpshooter for Buffalo Bill and other traveling shows. She traveled around the world, and once shot a cigarette from the mouth of Kaiser Wilhelm II.

Annie Oakley reruns were seen on ABC on Saturday and Sunday daytime from 1959 to 1960, and 1964 to 1965.

ANOTHER DAY
Situation Comedy
FIRST TELECAST: *April 8, 1978*
LAST TELECAST: *April 29, 1978*
BROADCAST HISTORY:
  Apr 1978, CBS Sat 9:00–9:30
CAST:
  Don Gardner .... David Groh
  Ginny Gardner .... Joan Hackett
  Olive Gardner .... Hope Summers
  Kelly Gardner .... Lisa Lindgren
  Mark Gardner .... Al Eisenmann

Don Gardner was a somewhat old-fashioned young businessman trying to live up to his expectations of the American dream despite limited finances. Even with the extra income provided by his wife Ginny, who had recently returned to work, there never seemed to be enough money. With an inhibited 12-year-old son, Mark, and a totally uninhibited teenage daughter, Kelly, things were never normal in the Gardner family. Adding to the confusion was Don's complaining mother, Olive, who completed the household.

ANSWER YES OR NO
Quiz
FIRST TELECAST: *April 30, 1950*
LAST TELECAST: *July 23, 1950*
BROADCAST HISTORY:
  Apr 1950–Jul 1950, NBC Sun 10:30–11:00
EMCEE:
  Moss Hart

This quiz show featured a celebrity panel. Arlene Francis was the only panelist to remain for the entire three-month run of the program. The typical question asked of the panel was "What would you do in this situation?", to which they responded with comic answers.

ANSWERS FOR AMERICANS
Discussion
FIRST TELECAST: *November 11, 1953*
LAST TELECAST: *February 24, 1954*
BROADCAST HISTORY:
  Nov 1953–Feb 1954, ABC Wed 8:30–9:00
MODERATOR:
  Hardy Burt
PERMANENT PANEL:
  Brig. General Frank Howley, Vice Chancellor, New York University
  Devin Garrity, publisher
  John K. Norton, Columbia University
  Dr. Charles Hodges, New York University

This public affairs program was presented in cooperation with *Facts Forum*. The prestigious panel discussed with equally prestigious guests such lofty issues as "Where Does the Eisenhower

Administration Stand Today?", "Should Red China Be Admitted to the UN?", and "What Can Be Done About Korea?" After a brief prime-time run the program continued on Sunday afternoon until June 1954.

ANYBODY CAN PLAY
Quiz/Audience Participation
FIRST TELECAST: *July 6, 1958*
LAST TELECAST: *December 8, 1958*
BROADCAST HISTORY:
  Jul 1958–Sep 1958, ABC Sun 8:30–9:00
  Oct 1958–Dec 1958, ABC Mon 9:30–10:00
EMCEE:
  George Fenneman
ASSISTANT:
  Judy Bamber (Nov–Dec)

In this quiz show, four studio contestants competed for cash and prizes by answering questions on a point system. The questions ranged over many subjects; for instance, contestants were asked to name a celebrity, identify a song or movie from short clips, or identify an object solely by touch. Contestants remained on the show for four weeks (later reduced to two), and viewers at home had the opportunity to participate in a $10,000 jackpot competition by sending in estimates of the contestants' age, weight, ability, and related data. Judy Bamber joined George Fenneman as co-host during the program's final month.

ANYONE CAN WIN
Quiz/Audience Participation
FIRST TELECAST: *July 14, 1953*
LAST TELECAST: *September 1, 1953*
BROADCAST HISTORY:
  Jul 1953–Sep 1953, CBS Tue 9:00–9:30
MODERATOR:
  Al Capp

Each week a different panel of four celebrities competed in a general quiz, with cartoonist Al Capp serving as moderator. Before the show started, all members of the studio audience were asked to pick which celebrity they thought would answer the most questions correctly. At the end of each show, those who had correctly guessed the winner shared $2,000 in cash.

ANYWHERE, U.S.A.
Documentary Drama
FIRST TELECAST: *November 9, 1952*
LAST TELECAST: *December 14, 1952*
BROADCAST HISTORY:
  Nov 1952–Dec 1952, ABC Sun 10:30–11:00
CAST:
  Doctor .... Eddie Dowling

Dramatized documentary films on health subjects, produced by the Health Information Foundation, covered such topics as physical therapy, the need for checkups, and new drugs. Robert Preston also appeared as a doctor on some telecasts of this series.

APPLE PIE
Situation Comedy
FIRST TELECAST: *September 23, 1978*
LAST TELECAST: *September 30, 1978*
BROADCAST HISTORY:
Sep 1978, ABC Sat 8:30–9:00
CAST:

Ginger-Nell Hollyhock	Rue McClanahan
"Fast Eddie" Murtaugh	Dabney Coleman
Grandpa Hollyhock	Jack Gilford
Anna Marie Hollyhock	Caitlin O'Heaney
Junior Hollyhock	Derrel Maury

"You can't pick your own relatives" goes the old saying, but that's exactly what a lonely hairdresser named Ginger-Nell Hollyhock did in this 1978 comedy. Placing classified ads in the local papers, she recruited a con man husband ("Fast Eddie"), a tap-dancing daughter (Anna Marie), a son who wanted to fly like a bird (Junior), and a tottering old grandfather (Grandpa), all of whom came to live together—for the laughs. The setting was Kansas City, Missouri, in 1933, which added period color.

The program was based on the play "Nourish the Beast," by Steve Tesich.

APPLE'S WAY
General Drama
FIRST TELECAST: *February 10, 1974*
LAST TELECAST: *January 12, 1975*
BROADCAST HISTORY:
Feb 1974–Jan 1975, CBS Sun 7:30–8:30
CAST:

George Apple	Ronny Cox
Barbara Apple	Lee McCain
Paul Apple	Vincent Van Patten
Cathy Apple	Patti Cohoon
Patricia Apple (1974)	Franny Michel
Patricia Apple (1974–1975)	Kristy McNichol
Steven Apple	Eric Olson
Grandfather Aldon	Malcolm Atterbury

This drama concerned the successful architect George Apple, who decided to leave the rat race of big-city life and return with his wife Barbara and their four children to his home town of Appleton, Iowa. This small rural community, which had been founded by George's ancestors, was a far cry from Los Angeles. It provided even more adjustment problems for George's city-bred children than for his wife and himself, but in time the entire family came to appreciate their new surroundings. George was an idealist, with compassion for his fellow man and strong religious convictions, and he found himself getting involved in numerous causes, sometimes being looked upon by the townspeople as a bit of a kook.

APPOINTMENT WITH ADVENTURE
Dramatic Anthology
FIRST TELECAST: *April 3, 1955*
LAST TELECAST: *April 1, 1956*
BROADCAST HISTORY:
Apr 1955–Apr 1956, CBS Sun 10:00–10:30

This live half-hour series, using studio sets, took viewers to various parts of the world, as well as different locations in the United States. Its contemporary and period stories were set in such locales as World War II Europe and Civil War America. Among the better-known performers who appeared in these plays were Polly Bergen, Betsy Palmer, Gena Rowlands, Phyllis Kirk, Dane Clark, Tony Randall, Gene Barry, and Paul Newman.

APPOINTMENT WITH LOVE
see *ABC Dramatic Shorts—1952–1953*

AQUANAUTS, THE
Adventure
FIRST TELECAST: *September 14, 1960*
LAST TELECAST: *September 27, 1961*
BROADCAST HISTORY:
Sep 1960–Sep 1961, CBS Wed 7:30–8:30
CAST:

Drake Andrews	Keith Larsen
Larry Lahr	Jeremy Slate
Mike Madison	Ron Ely
The Captain (1961)	Charles Thompson

Taking the same format as the highly successful syndicated series *Sea Hunt*, *The Aquanauts* told stories of the adventures of two professional salvage divers based in Southern California. The human and marine perils they faced on assignments created the suspense and action. Drake Andrews and Larry Lahr were the two young divers at the start of the season. Andrews was last seen in the episode that was aired on January 18. The following week Larry Lahr recruited Mike Madison as a replacement. On February 15, the title of the series was changed to *Malibu Run*. Although the principals still participated in salvage operations, they had moved into the Malibu Beach area and set up an aquatic sports shop. A new member of the cast was the Captain, an old salt who lived nearby and who became their good friend.

ARCHER
Detective Drama
FIRST TELECAST: *January 30, 1975*
LAST TELECAST: *March 13, 1975*
BROADCAST HISTORY:
Jan 1975–Mar 1975, NBC Thu 9:00–10:00
CAST:

Lew Archer	Brian Keith
Lt. Barney Brighton	John P. Ryan

Lew Archer was the antithesis of the slick, sexy, superefficient detective so often seen on television. He was a real person, a man of simple tastes, who used his analytic ability rather than brute strength or gimmicks to solve crimes. Although he was a former cop, and generally worked with the police, Archer was not above bending the law if it would help him nail the culprit. Perhaps the lack of gimmicks is why the program failed to catch on.

The series was based on the central character in Ross MacDonald's highly successful mystery novels.

ARCHIE BUNKER'S PLACE
see *All in the Family*

ARE YOU POSITIVE
Sports Quiz/Audience Participation
FIRST TELECAST: *July 6, 1952*
LAST TELECAST: *August 24, 1952*
BROADCAST HISTORY:
Jul 1952–Aug 1952, NBC Sun 6:00–6:30
EMCEE:
Bill Stern (7/6–7/20)
Frank Coniff (7/27–8/24)
REGULAR PANELISTS:
Jimmy Cannon (New York *Post* columnist)
Frank Fisch (radio and TV sports commentator)

This weekly live sports quiz program, which premiered as *Bill Stern's Sports Quiz*, featured Stern and a panel of three people familiar with all aspects of sports. The panelists were asked to identify a sports personality from photographs taken when he/she was a child, or occasionally from a negative of a photograph. Suggestions for personalities to be used were sent in by the viewing audience. Frank Coniff replaced Bill Stern as emcee on July 27.

ARMCHAIR DETECTIVE
Detective Drama
FIRST TELECAST: *July 6, 1949*
LAST TELECAST: *September 28, 1949*
BROADCAST HISTORY:
Jul 1949–Sep 1949, CBS Wed 9:00–9:30
CAST:
Mr. Crime Interrogator
.... John Milton Kennedy
Mr. Crime Authority .... H. Allen Smith

Each week two one-act whodunit plays were presented in this series of films. The plays contained clues that pointed to the solution, which was explained in detail at the end of each story by H. Allen Smith, a member of the California State Legislature.

ARMED FORCES HOUR, THE
Musical Variety
FIRST TELECAST: *February 4, 1951*
LAST TELECAST: *May 6, 1951*
BROADCAST HISTORY:
Feb 1951–May 1951, DUM Sun 8:00–9:00

This was a frankly promotional half-hour for the U.S. Armed Forces, produced by the Department of Defense and using a musical variety format to lure viewers to watch short films about the services. Entertainment was by servicemen-performers such as The Singing Sergeants and the U.S. Navy Dance Band appearing on a USO Club set, joined by professional entertainers such as Frances Langford and Marion Morgan. Acts were interspersed with films about the army, the navy, and the air force.

ARMSTRONG BY REQUEST
Dramatic Anthology
FIRST TELECAST: *July 8, 1959*
LAST TELECAST: *September 16, 1959*
BROADCAST HISTORY:
Jul 1959–Sep 1959, CBS Wed 10:00–11:00

The summer 1959 replacement for *Armstrong Circle Theatre* was a series of repeats of six documentary dramas that had been presented on that program during the 1958–1959 season. The program alternated with *The U.S. Steel Hour*.

ARMSTRONG CIRCLE THEATRE
Dramatic Anthology
FIRST TELECAST: *June 6, 1950*
LAST TELECAST: *August 28, 1963*
BROADCAST HISTORY:
Jun 1950–Jun 1955, NBC Tue 9:30–10:00
Sep 1955–Jun 1957, NBC Tue 9:30–10:30
Oct 1957–Aug 1963, CBS Wed 10:00–11:00 (OS)
HOST/NARRATOR:
Nelson Case (1950–1951)
Joe Ripley (1952–1953)
Bob Sherry (1953–1954)
Sandy Becker (1954–1955)
John Cameron Swayze (1955–1957)
Douglas Edwards (1957–1961)
Ron Cochran (1961–1962)
Henry Hamilton (1962–1963)

Armstrong Circle Theatre was one of the major dramatic anthology series of television's "Golden Age." At the outset it featured original dramas set in the contemporary world, many by noted writers. Serious treatments of such sensitive subjects as mental illness and racial intolerance alternated with occasional spoofs and comedies. Violence and morbidity were specifically avoided as Armstrong intended its program to be suitable for family viewing. Among the early telecasts was "The Parrot" (March 24, 1953), the first operetta commissioned for commercial television.

In 1955, when *Armstrong Circle Theatre* expanded to an hour, the format was changed to emphasize dramas based on real-life events, both headline-making ("S.O.S. from the *Andrea Doria*") and personal ("I Was Accused," the story of an immigrant threatened with deportation). One of the most notable telecasts of this period was "Nightmare in Red," a documentary on the history of Communism in Russia (December 27, 1955).

When it moved to CBS in 1957, as the program alternating with *The U.S. Steel Hour, Armstrong Circle Theatre* retained the documentary-drama format. The most popular topics during this period were related to the cold war: "The Vanished," about an Iron Curtain victim; "Thunder Over Berlin"; "Security Risk," about army counterintelligence; "The Spy Next Door"; "Crime Without a Country," about Interpol; "Window on the West," about Radio Free Europe; "Tunnel to Freedom," about refugees escaping to West Berlin; and "The Assassin," about a Soviet espionage agent. The other most prevalent format was the exposé: "The Meanest Crime in the World," about fraudulent medical practices; "Sound of Violence: The Juke Box Rackets"; "Full Disclosure," about security swindles; "The Antique Swindle"; "Smash-Up," about auto insurance company fraud; and "The Thief of Charity," among others.

ARNIE
Situation Comedy
FIRST TELECAST: *September 19, 1970*
LAST TELECAST: *September 9, 1972*
BROADCAST HISTORY:
Sep 1970–Sep 1971, CBS Sat 9:00–9:30
Sep 1971–Dec 1971, CBS Mon 10:30–11:00
Dec 1971–Sep 1972, CBS Sat 9:30–10:00
CAST:
Arnie Nuvo .... Herschel Bernardi
Lillian Nuvo .... Sue Ane Langdon
Hamilton Majors, Jr. .... Roger Bowen
Felicia Farfiss .... Elaine Shore
Neil Ogilvie .... Herb Voland
Richard Nuvo.................... Del Russel
Andrea Nuvo .... Stephanie Steele
Julius .... Tom Pedi
Fred Springer................... Olan Soule
Randy Robinson (1971–1972)
.... Charles Nelson Reilly

Arnie Nuvo, a perfectly content loading dock foreman for the Continental Flange Company, unexpectedly found himself promoted to head of the Product Improvement Division. The sudden shift from blue-collar worker to white-collar executive made many drastic changes in Arnie's life. Suddenly he had all sorts of new challenges, new responsibilities, new sources of aggravation, and a substantial increase in pay. His social status was changed, and, with the exception of his good friend Julius, he was removed from contact with his former co-workers. The adjustments he and his wife Lillian had to make, and the problems they had making them, provided the material for the comedy in this series.

AROUND THE TOWN
see *Girl about Town* for 1949 program by this name

AROUND THE TOWN
Documentary
FIRST TELECAST: *January 7, 1950*
LAST TELECAST: *February 18, 1950*
BROADCAST HISTORY:
Jan 1950–Feb 1950, NBC Sat 9:30–10:00
HOST:
Bob Stanton

In this program, a mobile unit visited interesting places around New York City.

ARREST AND TRIAL
Crime Drama
FIRST TELECAST: *September 15, 1963*
LAST TELECAST: *September 6, 1964*
BROADCAST HISTORY:
Sep 1963–Sep 1964, ABC Sun 8:30–10:00
CAST:
Det. Sgt. Nick Anderson .... Ben Gazzara
Attorney John Egan .... Chuck Connors
Deputy D.A. Jerry Miller .... John Larch
Assistant Deputy D.A. Barry Pine .. John Kerr
Det. Sgt. Dan Kirby .... Roger Perry
Det. Lt. Bone .... Noah Keen
Mitchell Harris .... Don Galloway
Jake Shakespeare .... Joe Higgins
Janet Okada .... Jo Anne Miya

Arrest and Trial was actually two separate but interwoven 45-minute programs, the first showing the commission of a crime, the police investigation, and the arrest; and the second depicting the trial. Ben Gazzara starred as Los Angeles police detective Nick Anderson in the first part, while Chuck Connors portrayed defense attorney John Egan (who tried to get Anderson's arrestees off the hook) in the second.

ARROW SHOW, THE
Comedy Variety
FIRST TELECAST: *November 24, 1948*
LAST TELECAST: *May 19, 1949*
BROADCAST HISTORY:
Nov 1948–Dec 1948, NBC Wed 8:30–9:00
Dec 1948, NBC Wed 7:30–7:55
Nov 1948–May 1949, NBC Thu 8:00–8:30
HOST:
Phil Silvers (Nov 1948–Mar 1949)
Hank Ladd (Apr–May 1949)
REGULAR:
Jack Gilford

This was a comedy variety show with guest stars and a rotating stable of "regulars," of whom only Jack Gilford remained for the full season. Also known as *The Phil Silvers Arrow Show* and *Arrow Comedy Theatre.*

ART BAKER SHOW, THE
see *You Asked For It*

45

ART FORD ON BROADWAY

Interview

FIRST TELECAST: *April 5, 1950*
LAST TELECAST: *June 30, 1950*
BROADCAST HISTORY:
  Apr 1950–Jun 1950, ABC Wed/Thu/Fri 7:15–7:30
HOST:
  Art Ford

On this short-lived Broadway chatter program, host Art Ford interviewed such guests as the manager of the Astor Hotel, a Broadway detective, and the author of a new book. During its final month on the air the program's title was altered to *Art Ford on the Broadways of the World.*

ART FORD SHOW, THE

Quiz/Audience Participation

FIRST TELECAST: *July 28, 1951*
LAST TELECAST: *September 15, 1951*
BROADCAST HISTORY:
  Jul 1951–Sep 1951, NBC Sat 7:30–8:00
EMCEE:
  Art Ford

Each week three disc jockeys from stations around the country served as panelists trying to guess composers, vocalists, and orchestras of various records played on the air. The disc jockey with the most correct answers at the end of the program received a special "Disc Jockey Oscar." Mr. Ford, himself a disc jockey on radio station WNEW in New York, also introduced each week a recording artist with a "million seller" who performed on the show.

An unusual feature of this program was that it also sought to publicize the good works done by many disc jockeys, such as their support of charities and their involvement in other public service activities.

ART LINKLETTER SHOW, THE

Quiz/Audience Participation

FIRST TELECAST: *February 18, 1963*
LAST TELECAST: *September 16, 1963*
BROADCAST HISTORY:
  Feb 1963–Sep 1963, NBC Mon 9:30–10:00
HOST:
  Art Linkletter
REGULARS:
  Carl Reiner (Apr–Sep)
  Jayne Meadows (Apr–Sep)

This short-lived variation on *Candid Camera* presented amusing incidents in everyday life, some filmed with a hidden camera and some acted out by a group of players. Celebrity guests and the studio audience then tried to guess the outcome; by April the guessing was being done by a celebrity panel alone. In a typical episode, the panel had to guess whether a woman would buy an atrocious hat, if told it was by a famous French designer; whether a man with both his arms in slings could persuade a stranger to feed him ice cream; and if a customer in a pet shop would be willing to conduct his business with a chimpanzee, in the absence of the proprietor.

ART LINKLETTER'S HOLLYWOOD TALENT SCOUTS

See *Hollywood Talent Scouts*

ARTHUR GODFREY AND HIS FRIENDS

Musical Variety

FIRST TELECAST: *January 12, 1949*
LAST TELECAST: *April 28, 1959*
BROADCAST HISTORY:
  Jan 1949–Jun 1957, CBS Wed 8:00–9:00 (OS)
  Sep 1958–Apr 1959, CBS Tue 9:00–9:30
HOST:
  Arthur Godfrey
REGULARS:
  Tony Marvin
  The Chordettes (Virginia Osborn, Dorothy Schwartz, Carol Hagedorn, Janet Ertel) (1949–1953)
  Janette Davis (1949–1957)
  Bill Lawrence (1949–1950)
  The Mariners (Jim Lewis, Tom Lockard, Nat Dickerson, Martin Karl) (1949–1955)
  Haleloke (1950–1955)
  Frank Parker (1950–1956)
  Marion Marlowe (1950–1955)
  Julius LaRosa (1952–1953)
  Lu Ann Simms (1952–1955)
  The McGuire Sisters (Christine, Dorothy, Phyllis) (1952–1957)
  Carmel Quinn (1954–1957)
  Pat Boone (1955–1957)
  The Toppers (1955–1957)
  Miyoshi Umeki (1955)
  Frank Westbrook Dancers (1958–1959)
ORCHESTRA:
  Archie Bleyer (1949–1954)
  Jerry Bresler (1954–1955)
  Will Roland and Bert Farber (1955–1957)
  Bernie Green (1958–1959)

The arrival of Arthur Godfrey on television was the most widely publicized event of the 1948–1949 season. Godfrey had been one of the biggest stars on radio in the late 1940s, and his folksy, person-to-person style looked like a natural for TV. It was.

Both *Arthur Godfrey and His Friends* and its companion show, *Arthur Godfrey's Talent Scouts*, shot to the top of the TV ratings and stayed there for several years. Part of the appeal was in Godfrey's repertory company of singers, all of them good clean kids who had been lifted out of obscurity by Godfrey (he never hired an established performer as a regular). But mostly it was "the old redhead" himself that the viewers adored. Ben Gross of the New York *Daily News* summed up his appeal: "It is his friendliness, his good cheer, his small-boy mischievousness and his kindly philosophy ... or maybe it's his magnetism, his personal attractiveness." As on radio, Godfrey frequently kidded his sponsors and refused to advertise any product for which he could not personally vouch. Frequently he would throw away the script and improvise his way through a testimonial. When Godfrey talked about how much he liked that cup of Lipton Tea, he sounded like he meant it.

The show itself was a variety hour built around Godfrey and his "friends." Frank Parker and Marion Marlowe were the mature, romantic duet, Julius LaRosa was the bright young boy singer, Haleloke the shy, exotic Hawaiian, and the Chordettes the well-scrubbed young barbershop harmonizers from Sheboygan, Wisconsin. Tony Marvin was the deep-voiced announcer who added a certain urbanity to the show. In and out of the proceedings flitted Godfrey, sometimes plunking his ukulele, sometimes singing (the term is used generously), sometimes just adding encouragement or folksy chatter.

For several years there seemed to be no stopping him. Arthur Godfrey was practically deified by the press. When he underwent surgery in May 1953 for an old hip injury (the painful result of an auto smashup 20 years before), the whole country, it seemed, sent get-well cards.

Then, in one of the most dramatic turnarounds in any star's history, Godfrey became the subject of tremendous controversy, vilified by the same columnists who had heaped praise on him only a few years before. Probably no personality got more press coverage in the mid-1950s, often with sensational headlines. Godfrey brought it on himself. Most publicized was his firing of the "little Godfreys," one by one, for what often seemed petty reasons. By far the most dramatic incident was the on-the-air-dismissal in October 1953 of Julius LaRosa, who, Godfrey said, had gotten to be too big a star. His remark to the press that LaRosa had lost his "humility" was to haunt Godfrey for the rest of his days. (LaRosa, who had only humble praise for his former boss, immediately went on to some well-publicized appearances on the *Ed Sullivan Show,* several hit records, and a series of his own, but his career faded after a few years.) Others who got the ax included orchestra leader Archie Bleyer, who was running a record company on the side and who made the mistake of recording Godfrey's archrival, Don McNeill (Bleyer's dating of Chordette Janet Ertel, whom he later married, was also given as a reason); producer Larry Puck (who was dating Marion Marlowe); and the Chordettes (they never could figure out why). Then, in April 1955, in one fell swoop he fired Marion Marlowe, Haleloke, and the Mariners, plus three writers.

All this might not have been so bad if Godfrey had not been so thin-skinned about press criticism. A regular feud erupted, with the vituperous star variously labeling his detractors as "Dope!" (Ed Sullivan), "Liar!" (or words to that effect, for Dorothy Kilgallen), "Fatuous ass!" (John Crosby), "These jerk newspapermen!" and "Muckrakers!" for all and sundry. When his private pilot's license was suspended because he allegedly buzzed an airport tower in his private DC-3, the papers had a field day with that, too.

Godfrey's bad press adversely affected his goodwill, and his ratings began to drop. The fired "friends" were all replaced, almost on a one-for-one basis. Pretty Marion Marlowe with her long, flowing black hair was replaced by pretty Carmel Quinn with long, flowing red hair; earnest young Julius LaRosa by earnest young Pat Boone; the harmonizing Chordettes by the harmonizing McGuire Sisters. Godfrey even signed up a Japanese girl, Miyoshi Umeki, to take the place of the Hawaiian Haleloke. It was not quite the same, though, and while Godfrey kept both his shows until he voluntarily decided to give them up, their popularity in the later days never matched that of the spectacular early 1950s.

After a final season in a half-hour format in 1958–1959, with only Tony Marvin as a regular, Godfrey left nighttime TV. He turned up briefly on *Candid Camera* in 1960–1961, then continued on radio for many years, until a tearful farewell broadcast on CBS in 1972. Having survived a bout with cancer, he devoted himself to conservationist causes until his death in 1983.

ARTHUR GODFREY AND HIS UKULELE
Instruction
FIRST TELECAST: *April 4, 1950*
LAST TELECAST: *June 30, 1950*
BROADCAST HISTORY:
  Apr 1950, CBS Tue/Thu 7:45–8:00
  Apr 1950–Jun 1950, CBS Tue/Fri 7:45–8:00
STAR:
  Arthur Godfrey

For a three-month period in 1950, in addition to his other CBS radio and television programs, Arthur Godfrey appeared twice a week to give lessons on how to play the ukulele to his television audience. For the first three weeks these live lessons ran on Tuesday and Thursday nights at 7:45, after which the Thursday lesson moved to Friday.

ARTHUR GODFREY SHOW, THE
  see *Arthur Godfrey and His Friends*

ARTHUR GODFREY'S TALENT SCOUTS
Talent
FIRST TELECAST: *December 6, 1948*
LAST TELECAST: *July 21, 1958*
BROADCAST HISTORY:
  Dec 1948–Jul 1958, CBS Mon 8:30–9:00 (OS)
HOST:
  Arthur Godfrey

Tony Marvin
ORCHESTRA:
Archie Bleyer (1948–1954)
Jerry Bresler (1954–1955)
Will Roland and Bert Farber (1955–1958)

Arthur Godfrey was the only personality in TV history to have two top-rated programs running simultaneously in prime time for an extended period (eight and a half seasons). On Mondays viewers could see him on the *Talent Scouts,* on Wednesdays on *Arthur Godfrey and His Friends. Talent Scouts* was slightly higher-rated, reaching No. 1 for the 1951–1952 season. But it was hard to tell the two programs apart. In 1952–1953 *Talent Scouts* and *Friends* ranked No. 2 and 3 among all programs on TV, just behind *I Love Lucy.*

Talent Scouts had "scouts" bring on their discoveries to perform before a live national audience. Most of these "discoveries" were aspiring professionals with some prior experience, and the quality of the acts was therefore quite high. Godfrey's folksy banter and interviews added the icing to the cake. Winners for each show were chosen by an audience applause meter. Several of the winners were invited to join Godfrey as regulars on his other show, and of these some went on to become major stars in their own right. Among the Godfrey regulars who were discovered on *Talent Scouts* were the Chordettes, Carmel Quinn, Pat Boone, and the McGuire Sisters.

Others who appeared here before they became famous included Rosemary Clooney, Tony Bennett, and 13-year-old Connie Francis (playing her accordion), all in 1950; Steve Lawrence and Al Martino in 1951; Marian McPartland and Leslie Uggams in 1952; the Diamonds and Roy Clark in 1956; and Patsy Cline in 1957. The Godfrey screening staff missed a few big ones, though. Elvis Presley (in early 1955) and Buddy Holly (in 1956) both flunked auditions for the show.

ARTHUR MURRAY PARTY, THE
Musical Variety
FIRST TELECAST: *July 20, 1950*
LAST TELECAST: *September 6, 1960*
BROADCAST HISTORY:
Jul 1950–Sep 1950, ABC Thu 9:00–9:30
Oct 1950–Jan 1951, DUM Sun 9:00–10:00
Jan 1951–Mar 1951, DUM Sun 9:00–9:30
Apr 1951–Jun 1951, ABC Mon 9:00–9:30
Sep 1951–Dec 1951, ABC Wed 9:00–9:30
Jan 1952–May 1952, ABC Sun 9:00–9:30
Jul 1952–Aug 1952, CBS Fri 8:00–8:30
Oct 1952–Apr 1953, DUM Sun 10:00–10:30
Jun 1953–Oct 1953, CBS Sun 9:30–10:00
Oct 1953–Apr 1954, NBC Mon 7:30–7:45
Jun 1954–Sep 1954, NBC Tue 8:30–9:00
Jun 1955–Sep 1955, NBC Tue 8:30–9:00
Apr 1956–Sep 1956, CBS Thu 10:00–10:30
Apr 1957–Jun 1957, NBC Tue 8:00–8:30
Jul 1957–Sep 1957, NBC Mon 9:30–10:00

Sep 1958–Sep 1959, NBC Mon 10:00–10:30
Sep 1959–Jan 1960, NBC Tue 9:00–9:30
Jan 1960–Sep 1960, NBC Tue 9:30–10:00
REGULARS:
Kathryn Murray
Arthur Murray
The Arthur Murray Dancers
The Stanley Melba Orchestra (1950)
The Emil Coleman Orchestra (1951–1952)
The Ray Carter Orchestra (1953–1960)

This was, without a doubt, the longest-running commercial in the history of television. For a full decade, Arthur and Kathryn Murray built an entire program around dancing as an incentive for viewers to take courses with the Arthur Murray Dance Studio. In the early years, through spring of 1953, the show was actually sponsored by the dance studios. A regular feature was a mystery dance segment, in which viewers could win two free lessons at their nearest Arthur Murray Studio by mailing in a postcard correctly identifying the week's mystery dance.

Throughout its long run, the format of *The Arthur Murray Party* remained virtually unchanged. The setting was a large party at which Kathryn was the cheerful, vivacious hostess. There were always one or two guest stars on hand, from the world of show business or sports, and a substantial group of Arthur Murray dance instructors from the various studios in the New York area. Kathryn chatted with the guests; they in turn sang, danced, and occasionally participated in comedy sketches. Arthur acted as the instructor who taught the home audience, and often the guest stars as well, a particular dance step. The instructors who appeared in the party group would often be singled out to demonstrate their proficiency at unusual or complex dances. As the show drew to a close, Arthur and Kathryn would glide majestically into a Strauss waltz with the rest of the party group joining in. There were subtle additions and subtractions to the format over the years but the basic structure remained intact. Kathryn's closing line each week was, "Till then, to put a little fun in your life, try dancing."

The Arthur Murray Party was the perennial summer replacement series. It was easy to produce and always attracted a respectable audience. It was one of only four series to appear, at one time or another, on four television networks. For its premiere on ABC in 1950 it was called *Arthur Murray Party Time.* That fall, the first DuMont version was titled *The Arthur Murray Show,* but by the autumn of 1951 it had become *The Arthur Murray Party,* the name it retained throughout the rest of its ten years on the air.

ASIA PERSPECTIVE
Documentary/Public Affairs
FIRST TELECAST: *September 4, 1966*
LAST TELECAST: *September 25, 1966*

BROADCAST HISTORY:
Sep 1966, CBS Sun 6:00–6:30

The four documentaries that were shown under the collective title *Asia Perspective* covered the then-current ideological purges in Communist China, the elections taking place in South Vietnam, and a two-part history of the political, economic, and social changes that had taken place on the Chinese mainland since the fall of Manchuria in 1931. Various CBS correspondents contributed to the reports.

ASK DR. RUTH
Discussion/Advice
BROADCAST HISTORY:
Syndicated and cable only
30 Minutes
Produced: *1987–*
Released: *January 1987*
HOSTESS:
Dr. Ruth Westheimer
CO-HOST:
Larry Angelo

Diminutive psychologist Dr. Ruth Westheimer's subject was sex—"good sex"—and coming from this sweet, grandmotherly lady with a thick German accent, the sometimes graphic discussions of physical and emotional performance problems, techniques, and other ways to make your sex life enjoyable caused quite a sensation. Starting with a late night local radio show in New York in the early 1980s, she had by the middle of the decade become a national phenomenon, with cable and syndicated series, a best-selling book, and scores of personal appearances. The kindest compliment was being lampooned by dozens of comics, notably Johnny Carson on *The Tonight Show*.

In this syndicated series, Dr. Ruth talked with celebrity guests and experts on various aspects of sexuality, and took questions from her studio audience. Naturally, because of the explicit subject matter, most of the stations carrying *Ask Dr. Ruth* aired it very late at night.

ASK ME ANOTHER
Quiz/Audience Participation
FIRST TELECAST: *July 3, 1952*
LAST TELECAST: *September 25, 1952*
BROADCAST HISTORY:
Jul 1952–Sep 1952, NBC Thu 10:30–11:00
EMCEE:
Joe Boland
REGULAR PANELISTS:
Johnny Lujack (football player)
Warren Brown (sports editor, *Chicago Tribune*)
Kay Westfall (TV actress)
Tom Duggan (sports commentator)

The four panelists on this quiz show tried to guess the identities of famous sports personalities, who appeared as guests. Each guest would stand behind a shadow curtain while the panelists asked questions to try to figure out his or her identity. A special feature of the show was the appearance of one "performing guest" each week, who would perform his or her specialty behind the shadow curtain while the panelists tried to guess who it was.

ASPEN
see *Innocent and the Damned, The*

ASPHALT JUNGLE, THE
Police Drama
FIRST TELECAST: *April 2, 1961*
LAST TELECAST: *September 24, 1961*
BROADCAST HISTORY:
Apr 1961–Sep 1961, ABC Sun 9:30–10:30
CAST:
Matthew Gower .... Jack Warden
Capt. Gus Honochek .... Arch Johnson
Sgt. Danny Keller .... Bill Smith

Fighting crime in a big city is often a job that requires specialists. Deputy Police Commissioner Matthew Gower was one of them. Helping him break up the large organized crime rings that infiltrated his town was a special squad of select men headed by Gus Honochek and Danny Keller. Often they had undercover assignments, and Commissioner Gower, not one to leave the dirty work to his men, would pitch in and go undercover with them. The most memorable aspect of this police series was the background music, composed by the great jazz musician Duke Ellington.

ASSIGNMENT DANGER
see *Martin Kane, Private Eye*

ASSIGNMENT FOREIGN LEGION
Adventure Anthology
FIRST TELECAST: *October 1, 1957*
LAST TELECAST: *December 24, 1957*
BROADCAST HISTORY:
Oct 1957–Dec 1957, CBS Tue 10:30–11:00
HOSTESS:
Merle Oberon

Actress Merle Oberon was the narrator of and occasional performer in this British dramatic series about the French Foreign Legion. Each episode opened with Miss Oberon, as a foreign correspondent stationed in North Africa, introducing a story about the officers and men of the Legion. Occasionally, as the foreign correspondent, she appeared in the story as well. The series was filmed on location in Morocco, Algiers, and Spain and was first seen on British television.

ASSIGNMENT MANHUNT
see *Manhunt*

ASSIGNMENT VIENNA
Spy Drama

FIRST TELECAST: *September 28, 1972*
LAST TELECAST: *June 9, 1973*
BROADCAST HISTORY:
> *Sep 1972–Dec 1972,* ABC Thu 9:00–10:00
> *Jan 1973–Jun 1973,* ABC Sat 10:00–11:00

CAST:
> Jake Webster .... Robert Conrad
> Maj. Caldwell .... Charles Cioffi
> Inspector Hoffman .... Anton Diffring

This international spy drama was one of three rotating elements of the series *The Men.* It starred Robert Conrad as Jake Webster, a rugged, independent American expatriate with a shady past who operated Jake's Bar & Grill in Vienna. Jake's bistro was only a cover for his undercover work for the United States government, however, as he tracked down assorted spies and international criminals in convoluted plots. He maintained an uneasy liaison with Major Caldwell of U.S. Intelligence, who in return for Jake's services kept the American out of jail. The series was filmed on location in Vienna.

ASSOCIATES, THE
Situation Comedy
FIRST TELECAST: *September 23, 1979*
LAST TELECAST: *April 17, 1980*
BROADCAST HISTORY:
> *Sep 1979–Oct 1979,* ABC Sun 8:30–9:00
> *Mar 1980–Apr 1980,* ABC Thu 9:30–10:00

CAST:
> Emerson Marshall ...... Wilfred Hyde-White
> Eliot Streeter .... Joe Regalbuto
> Leslie Dunn .... Alley Mills
> Tucker Kerwin .... Martin Short
> Sara James .... Shelley Smith
> Johnny Danko .... Tim Thomerson

THEME:
"Wall Street Blues" by Albert Brooks, sung by B. B. King

ABC had high hopes for this lawyer-comedy show, which, though well received by critics, never attracted a large audience. It revolved around three young law school graduates who had just joined the prestigious Wall Street firm of Bass and Marshall as associates, beginning their five- to seven-year trial period. Daughter of a poor New York family, Leslie was recently graduated from Columbia, and felt for the oppressed. Bass and Marshall did not usually represent the oppressed. Tucker, Leslie's beau, was a Midwesterner slightly out of step with his Ivy League colleagues, a little naive but very charming. Sara was a Boston blueblood, bright as well as sexy. They were all at the mercy of a heirarchy including such oddballs as formidable but slightly dotty Senior Partner Emerson Marshall, 81 (played to perfection by British character actor Wilfred Hyde-White), and dedicated Junior Partner Eliot Streeter, who had only one goal—to take over the firm. Waving his hand he exclaimed, in the first

episode, "I love this firm. . . . I never told it so, but it *knows.*"

Counterpointing all this class was Johnny Danko, the 21-year-old mailboy, whose one goal was to make time with beautiful chicks.

AT EASE
Situation Comedy
FIRST TELECAST: *March 4, 1983*
LAST TELECAST: *July 15, 1983*
BROADCAST HISTORY:
> *Mar 1983–Jul 1983,* ABC Fri 8:30–9:00

CAST:
> Sgt. Val Valentine .... Jimmie Walker
> PFC Tony Baker .... David Naughton
> Col. Clapp .... Roger Bowen
> Maj. Hawkins .... Richard Jaeckel
> Cpl. Lola Grey .... Jourdan Fremin
> Cpl. Wessel .... George Wyner
> Maxwell .... Joshua Mostel
> Cardinal .... John Vargas
> Maurice .... Jeff Bannister

This short-lived military comedy was billed as the 1980s version of the classic Sgt. Bilko series *(The Phil Silvers Show).* Without a strong lead to match Phil Silvers, it attracted few viewers. As in the original, the setting was a sleepy peacetime army post in the heartland—this time a computer base called Camp Tar Creek, in Texas. The scheming Sgt. Bilko was replaced by scheming Sgt. Valentine and his buddy PFC Baker, and the dense Col. Hall by the equally credulous Col. Clapp. The greatest threat to Val and his pals in Company J was the Colonel's by-the-book security chief, Maj. Hawkins, whose informant was the weasely Cpl. Wessel. Hawkins was always trying to close down Val's scams and shape things up, but to no avail. A little sex appeal was added by Baker's luscious girlfriend Lola, and a contemporary slant by the computers from Apple Computer Co. But some things never change: the platoon also had a klutzy, always-hungry private named Maxwell (remember Doberman?).

AT HOME SHOW
see *Earl Wrightson Show*

AT ISSUE
Interview
FIRST TELECAST: *July 12, 1953*
LAST TELECAST: *February 24, 1954*
BROADCAST HISTORY:
> *Jul 1953–Aug 1953,* ABC Sun 9:00–9:15
> *Oct 1953–Feb 1954,* ABC Wed 8:00–8:15

HOST:
Martin Agronsky

News commentator Agronsky interviewed public figures on important issues of the day in this 15-minute public-affairs program. After its primetime run the program continued on Sunday afternoons until June 1954.

AT LIBERTY CLUB
Music
FIRST TELECAST: *June 25, 1948*
LAST TELECAST: *September 16, 1948*
BROADCAST HISTORY:
Jun 1948–Jul 1948, NBC Fri 8:00–8:30
Jul 1948–Sep 1948, NBC Thu 8:00–8:15
HOSTESS:
Jacqueline (Turner)

This short musical interlude was set in a mythical nightclub for "at liberty" youngsters, presided over by Parisian singer Jacqueline, with guests. The program was formerly local on WPTZ, Philadelphia.

AT THE MOVIES
Commentary
BROADCAST HISTORY:
Syndicated only
30 minutes
Produced: *1982–*
Released: *September 1982*
HOSTS:
Roger Ebert (1982–1986)
Gene Siskel (1982–1986)
Rex Reed (1986–   )
Bill Harris (1986–   )

Film critics Roger Ebert of the *Chicago Sun-Times* and Gene Siskel of the *Chicago Tribune* first gained national notoriety in 1977 as the contentious hosts of the popular PBS series *Sneak Previews*. In 1982 they left public television to launch this syndicated program for commercial stations, using virtually the same format and theater setting. Each week, from "the balcony," they watched clips from several new movies, argued about them, and then individually gave a "thumbs up/thumbs down" evaluation of each one.
When Ebert and Siskel ran into contractual difficulties with Tribune Entertainment, the producer of the show, in the fall of 1986, they departed for a new movie review series, *Siskel & Ebert & the Movies. At the Movies* acquired two new hosts, movie critic Rex Reed and critic/gossip columnist Bill Harris. Added to the format, in addition to the movie reviews, were show business news and short pieces on movie production.

AUCTION-AIRE
Auction
FIRST TELECAST: *September 30, 1949*
LAST TELECAST: *June 23, 1950*
BROADCAST HISTORY:
Sep 1949–Jun 1950, ABC Fri 9:00–9:30
EMCEE:
Jack Gregson
REGULAR:
"Rebel" (Charlotte) Randall
COMMERCIAL ANNOUNCER:
Durward Kirby

In this fast-paced auction program from Chicago, the audience had a chance to bid on valuable merchandise—using, instead of cash, the labels from products of The Libby Company, the program's sponsor. Among the bargains was a $250 home freezer that went for 88 labels, a $355 refrigerator for 225 labels, and a $450 sterling silver set for 225 labels. Out-of-town viewers could call their bids in to their local station, which relayed them to the stage of the Ritz Theater in New York, where the program originated live. There was also a "Mystery Chant," in which contestants who could identify the total of the numbers rattled off in an auctioneer's chant won an automobile. Auction-Aire Gregson's assistant, buxom model "Rebel" Randall, was mainly decorative.

AUTHOR MEETS THE CRITICS
Book Discussion
FIRST TELECAST: *April 4, 1948*
LAST TELECAST: *October 10, 1954*
BROADCAST HISTORY:
Apr 1948–Mar 1949, NBC Sun 8:00–8:30
Mar 1949–Jul 1949, NBC Sun 8:30–9:00
Oct 1949–Nov 1949, ABC Mon 7:30–8:00
Nov 1949–Dec 1949, ABC Wed 9:00–9:30
Dec 1949–Mar 1950, ABC Thu 9:30–10:00
Mar 1950–Sep 1950, ABC Wed 8:30–9:00
Sep 1951–Dec 1951, NBC Mon 10:00–10:30
Mar 1952–Oct 1952, DUM Thu 10:30–11:00
Oct 1952–May 1953, DUM Thu 10:00–10:30
May 1953–Oct 1953, DUM Wed 9:30–10:00
Mar 1954–Jul 1954, DUM Sun 7:00–7:30
Jul 1954–Oct 1954, DUM Sun 10:00–10:30
MODERATOR:
John K. M. McCaffery (1948–1951)
Faye Emerson (1952)
Virgilia Peterson (1952–1954)

An author defending his current work against a panel of critics was the premise of this durable program, which began on local television in New York on July 10, 1947, and later saw service on an assortment of nights and networks. The critics, one pro and one con each week, were generally literary figures, although some were TV celebrities as well, such as Bennett Cerf and Dr. Mason Gross. Authors ranged from Ezra Stone and Cornelia Otis Skinner to Henry Morgan (whose latest movie was dissected) and cartoonist Al Capp. Their debates sometimes generated real verbal fireworks.
In addition to current books, such as *U.S.A. Confidential* and *The Execution of Private Slovik*, occasional movies and magazine articles were considered. John K. M. McCaffery, who had been one of the hosts of *Author Meets the Critics* on radio, where it originated in 1946, was the first host of the TV series; he was later succeeded by actress Faye Emerson and then by Virgilia Peterson.

AUTOMAN
Police/Science Fiction

FIRST TELECAST: *December 15, 1983*
LAST TELECAST: *April 2, 1984*
BROADCAST HISTORY:
  Dec 1983–Jan 1984, ABC Thu 8:00–9:00
  Mar 1984–Apr 1984, ABC Mon 8:00–9:00
CAST:
  Walter Nebicher .... Desi Arnaz, Jr.
  Automan .... Chuck Wagner
  Lt. Jack Curtis .... Robert Lansing
  Capt. Boyd .... Gerald S. O'Loughlin
  Roxanne .... Heather McNair

Computers are becoming part of everyday life, from the checkout counter and the automatic bank teller to home-video games, and *Automan* tried to make them part of television fantasy as well. Walter Nebbish—er, Nebicher—was a mousy police computer expert who liked to develop computer games in his spare time. One day he really blew his circuits: a computer creation called "Automan" jumped right off the screen and started Walter on a career as an international crime fighter. Since Walter had programmed in everything that Automan knew, this handsome superhero in his sparkling uniform was really Walter's alter ego, but able to do all the things that Walter couldn't. He could walk through walls, make objects appear and disappear, and make beautiful women swoon (Automan's broad smile showed more teeth than an Osmond brother). Automan also had lots of friends; practically any computer he ran into would help him out, which was handy for commandeering elevators and causing security systems to keep their bells quiet. If Walter and his creation got into serious trouble while on a case, Walter could even merge into Automan for a time and evade flying bullets!

As if Automan were not enough, there was also Cursor—the little glowing dot that normally moves around a computer screen to show you where you are. This Cursor followed Automan and Walter, and on their command would outline a superfast getaway car or even a tank (which would then materialize, ready for use).

There were, of course, problems. Automan used so much energy that lights tended to dim around him. He faded away entirely at daybreak, when the city's electrical consumption began to rise, often leaving Walter in some dangerous predicament. Then there was Walter's grumpy, old-fashioned boss, Capt. Boyd, who thought that all computers were worthless, to say nothing of the people who ran them. Neither he nor Walter's protector on the force, Lt. Curtis, knew about Automan, but Curtis knew that somehow Walter was able to crack cases and he shamelessly used Walter's leads to further his own career.

AVENGERS, THE
Spy Drama

FIRST TELECAST: *March 28, 1966*
LAST TELECAST: *September 15, 1969*
BROADCAST HISTORY:
  Mar 1966–Jul 1966, ABC Mon 10:00–11:00
  Jul 1966–Sep 1966, ABC Thu 10:00–11:00
  Jan 1967–Sep 1967, ABC Fri 10:00–11:00
  Jan 1968–Sep 1968, ABC Wed 7:30–8:30
  Sep 1968–Sep 1969, ABC Mon 7:30–8:30
CAST:
  Jonathan Steed .... Patrick Macnee
  Emma Peel (1966–1968) .... Diana Rigg
  Tara King (1968–1969) .... Linda Thorson
  "Mother" (1968–1969) .... Patrick Newell
  Purdey (1976) .... Joanna Lumley
  Mike Gambit (1976) .... Gareth Hunt

The Avengers first appeared on British television more than five years before it was imported to the United States in 1966. Pure escapist entertainment, it centered on Jonathan Steed, a suave, imperturbable, and very proper British secret agent, who was joined after a few episodes by a female partner, Mrs. Peel. Their missions, whether planned or accidental, involved all sorts of diabolical geniuses who planned to take over the world through various fantastic schemes. Improbable technical devices, wittily absurd villains, and the clever and efficient Steed combined to make this fantasized espionage series unique. Like the American-made *Man From U.N.C.L.E.,* it attempted to out-James-Bond James Bond.

Macnee's original female partner in the British version of the series was Honor Blackman, who played Pussy Galore in the James Bond film *Goldfinger.* By the time *The Avengers* reached American audiences she had been replaced by the lithe, jumpsuited Diana Rigg. Steed and Mrs. Peel were separated in the March 20, 1968, episode, when the lady agent was reunited with her long-lost husband. Linda Thorson, a younger and more voluptuous woman, then became the female partner.

The series was resurrected in Britain in 1976 with a new title, *The New Avengers,* and a new supporting cast for Mr. Steed—young agents Purdey and Gambit. It was this version that joined the CBS late-night lineup in the fall of 1978, the only original programming (at least to American audiences) amid CBS' late-night movie reruns and episodes of former prime-time network series.

The popularity of this late-night *Avengers* prompted CBS to subsequently rerun both it and the earlier version that had aired on ABC in the 1960s. The end date above refers to the original ABC prime-time run of *The Avengers.* For information on the later reruns see *The CBS Late Movie.*

AWARD THEATER
syndicated title for *Alcoa Theatre* and *Goodyear Theater*

AWAY WE GO
Musical Variety
FIRST TELECAST: *June 3, 1967*
LAST TELECAST: *September 2, 1967*
BROADCAST HISTORY:
Jun 1967–Sep 1967, CBS Sat 7:30–8:30
REGULARS:
George Carlin
Buddy Greco
Buddy Rich
The Miriam Nelson Dancers
The Allyn Ferguson Orchestra

Comedian George Carlin, singer Buddy Greco, and drummer Buddy Rich and his orchestra were the stars of this variety show, which was the 1967 summer replacement for *The Jackie Gleason Show*. The series title was based on one of Gleason's pet expressions, "And away we go!"

B

B.A.D. CATS
Police Drama
FIRST TELECAST: *January 4, 1980*
LAST TELECAST: *February 8, 1980*
BROADCAST HISTORY:
Jan 1980–Feb 1980, ABC Fri 8:00–9:00
CAST:
Officer Nick Donovan .... Asher Brauner
Officer Ocee James............. Steve Hanks
Officer Samantha Jensen ... Michelle Pfeiffer
Capt. Eugene Nathan........... Vic Morrow
Rodney Washington.......... Jimmie Walker
Ma .... LaWanda Page

Another of TV's hot-rod cops series. Nick and Ocee were ex-racing drivers who had been recruited by the Los Angeles Police Department for its B.A.D. C.A.T. squad (Burglary Auto Detail, Commercial Auto Thefts)—apparently on the theory that if you can't catch the crooks peaceably, run 'em down in the streets. Bystanders dove for cover as Nick and Ocee went chasing miscreants down the streets of L.A. in their souped-up Nova, tires squealing. Like all good TV cops, they were willing to "bend the rules" (which they hardly knew anyway) to get their prey. Helping were shapely lady cop Samantha, crusty Captain Nathan, restaurant owner Ma, and gangling Rodney, a comic car-thief-turned-auto-repossessor.

The series was canceled after only five telecasts, leading producer Everett Chambers to admit ruefully, "It was an ill-conceived and ineptly executed series. The network is responsible for some of it and I'm responsible for some of it. We bought $40,000 worth of cars to smash up, and we never got a chance to smash them up. I think that's kind of immoral, $40,000 worth of cars to smash up when people are starving in India." He concluded, "I'm not putting this on my credits."

B.J. AND THE BEAR
Comedy Adventure
FIRST TELECAST: *February 10, 1979*
LAST TELECAST: *August 1, 1981*
BROADCAST HISTORY:
Feb 1979–Mar 1980, NBC Sat 9:00–10:00 (OS)
Mar 1980–Aug 1980, NBC Sat 8:00–9:00
Jan 1981–Apr 1981, NBC Tue 9:00–10:00
Apr 1981–Aug 1981, NBC Sat 9:00–10:00
CAST:
B.J. (Billie Joe) McCay .... Greg Evigan
Sheriff Elroy P. Lobo (1979).... Claude Akins
Deputy Perkins (1979) .... Mills Watson
Sheriff Masters (1979) .... Richard Deacon
Sheriff Cain (1979–1980) .... Ed Lauter
Sgt. Beauregard Wiley (1979) ... Slim Pickens
Wilhelmina "The Fox" Johnson (1979–1980)
.... Conchata Ferrell
Deputy Higgins (1979–1980) .... Otto Felix
Tommy (1979–1980) .... Janet Louise Johnson
Bullets (1979–1980) .... Joshua Shelley
Rutherford T. Grant (1981). Murray Hamilton
Lt. Jim Steiger (1981) .... Eric Server
Stacks (1981) .... Judy Landers
Callie (1981).............. Linda McCullough
Samantha (1981) .... Barbra Horan
Teri Garrison (1981).......... Candi Brough
Geri Garrison (1981) .... Randi Brough
Cindy Grant (1981).......... Sherilyn Wolter
Angie Cartwright (1981) ..... Sheila DeWindt
THEME:
"B.J. and the Bear," written by Glen A. Larson and sung by Greg Evigan

In the mid-1970s NBC had aired an adventure series about two truckers traveling around the country, titled *Movin' On*. A few years later, and about the same time CBS premiered its hit "good ole boy" rural adventure series *The Dukes of Hazzard*, this countrified version of *Movin' On* turned up on NBC. *B.J. and the Bear* was played more for laughs than adventure, and did seem to put stronger emphasis on pretty girls and wild car and truck chases, but it had a distinct family resemblance to its predecessor on NBC.

B.J. McCay was a good-looking young tucker who traveled around the country in his big red-and-white rig, with a single companion, his pet chimp Bear. Although he logged a lot of miles, B.J. was based in rural Georgia, where he was confronted by a succession of corrupt local sheriffs—Elroy P. Lobo (who was later given his own series, *Lobo*), followed in the fall of 1979 by Sgt. Wiley of Winslow County and his two fellow lawmen, Sheriffs Cain and Masters. The only honest cop B.J. seemed to encounter was the Fox, who spent much of her time trying to trap the crooked local cops. Tommy was a lady trucker friend of B.J.'s and Bullets ran the local hangout, the Country Comfort Truck Stop.

When *B.J. and the Bear* returned for its second season in January 1981 (delayed several months by an actors' strike), B.J. had settled down to run a trucking business in Los Angeles called Bear Enterprises. For B.J., however, corruption seemed to follow wherever he went. His new adversary was Rutherford T. Grant, a corrupt politician who headed the state Special Crimes Action Team. Grant was a silent partner in TransCal, the largest trucking firm in the state, and stopped at nothing to stamp out potential competition. Because of Grant's intervention, B.J. found it impossible to get regular male truck drivers to work for him and had to settle for a crew of seven young, beautiful lady truckers (in the cast credits from Stacks to Angie), including a pair of identical twins, and Grant's daughter, Cindy.

BAA BAA BLACK SHEEP
War Drama
FIRST TELECAST: *September 21, 1976*

54

LAST TELECAST: *September 1, 1978*
BROADCAST HISTORY:
Sep 1976–Aug 1977, NBC Tue 8:00–9:00
Dec 1977–Mar 1978, NBC Wed 9:00–10:00
Mar 1978–Apr 1978, NBC Thu 9:00–10:00
Jul 1978, NBC Wed 9:00–10:00
Aug 1978–Sep 1978, NBC Fri 8:00–9:00
CAST:
Maj. Gregory "Pappy" Boyington
.... Robert Conrad
Col. Lard, USMC............... Dana Elcar
Capt. James W. Gutterman (1976–1977)
.... James Whitmore, Jr.
Lt. Jerry Bragg................. Dirk Blocker
Lt. T. J. Wiley .... Robert Ginty
Lt. Bob Anderson .... John Larroquette
Lt. Lawrence Casey .... W. K. Stratton
Gen. Moore................. Simon Oakland
Hutch (1976–1977)............. Joey Aresco
Lt. Don French................. Jeff MacKay
Lt. Bob Boyle................. Larry Manetti
Sgt. Andy Micklin (1977–1978) .... Red West
Cpl. Stan Richards (1977–1978)
.... Steve Richmond
Capt. Tommy Harachi (1977–1978)
.... Byron Chung
Capt. Dottie Dixon (1977–1978)
.... Katherine Cannon
Lt. Jeb Pruitt (1978)............. Jeb Adams
Nurse Samantha Green (1978)
.... Denise DuBarry
Nurse Ellie (1977–1978)..... Kathy McCullen
Nurse Susan (1977–1978)...... Brianne Leary
Nurse Nancy Gilmore (1977–1978)
.... Nancy Conrad
TECHNICAL ADVISOR:
Gregory Boyington

Based loosely on the book *Baa Baa Black Sheep*, by the World War II Marine Corps flying ace Gregory Boyington, this series was the story of a squadron of misfit flyers in the South Pacific. Squadron 214 was composed of men who had been on the verge of court martial before Boyington provided them with reprieves. They had been charged with everything from fighting with officers, to stealing booze, to being general nuisances and nonconformists. Pappy (he was so named because at age 35 "he was an old man" by the standards of his men) maintained almost no discipline, ignored military regulations, and did not care what his men did when they weren't on missions. As long as they could fly and do the job when necessary, nothing else mattered. Given this personal code, Pappy was completely at home with his men, whether they were chasing women, getting into brawls, conning the military hierarchy or civilian populations, or—in a more serious vein—intercepting the Japanese.

Baa Baa Black Sheep was dropped from the NBC lineup at the end of the 1976–1977 season, only to be revived in December 1977 when most of the new 1977–1978 series failed and the net-

work ran short of programming. It was retitled *Black Sheep Squadron*, and Capt. Dottie Dixon was added to the cast. She was in charge of the nursing force on Vella La Cava, the island where Pappy and his men were based, and her young charges were seemingly always available for fun and games with the men of the 214th Squadron. Four of the girls became regular cast members in early 1978. They were christened "Pappy's Lambs," perhaps as a parody of ABC's popular *Charlie's Angels*, who were scheduled opposite *Black Sheep Squadron*. One of the lambs, Nurse Nancy, was played by the daughter of Robert Conrad.

BABY, I'M BACK
Situation Comedy
FIRST TELECAST: *January 30, 1978*
LAST TELECAST: *August 12, 1978*
BROADCAST HISTORY:
Jan 1978–Aug 1978, CBS Mon 8:30–9:00
CAST:
Raymond Ellis.............. Demond Wilson
Olivia Ellis................. Denise Nicholas
Luzelle Carter .... Helen Martin
Angie Ellis .... Kim Fields
Jordan Ellis................... Tony Holmes
Col. Wallace Dickey .... Ed Hall

Seven years after he had deserted his wife because he couldn't take the pressures of being married, Raymond Ellis discovered that she had just had him declared legally dead. His interest in reconciliation suddenly revived, Raymond moved into the apartment building where his ex-wife, Olivia, lived with her two young children, Angie and Jordan, and her mother Luzelle. Not only did Ray try to rekindle a romance with his estranged wife, but he also had to contend with a mother-in-law who had never thought very much of him in the first place, and with Olivia's fiancé, Col. Dickey. Col. Dickey was a Pentagon official for whom Olivia worked and to whom she was planning to get married—until Ray showed up. A backdrop to this romantic conflict was Ray's attempts to have himself legally declared alive.

BABY MAKES FIVE
Situation Comedy
FIRST TELECAST: *April 1, 1983*
LAST TELECAST: *April 29, 1983*
BROADCAST HISTORY:
Apr 1983, ABC Fri 8:00–8:30
CAST:
Eddie Riddle .... Peter Scolari
Jennie Riddle .... Louise Williams
Blanche Riddle .... Janis Paige
Edna Kearney .... Priscilla Morrill
Michael Riddle .... André Gower
Laura Riddle .... Emily Moultrie
Annie Riddle .... Brandy Gold

Babies and other small children were the focus of this super-cute family comedy. Accountant Eddie Riddle was the young husband who found his family growing faster than expected; his wife Jennie was about to give birth to twins to add to the three small children already creating havoc in their household. Eddie's madcap mother Blanche and Jennie's stodgy, old-fashioned mom Edna were also on hand.

BACHELOR FATHER
Situation Comedy
FIRST TELECAST: *September 15, 1957*
LAST TELECAST: *September 25, 1962*
BROADCAST HISTORY:
  Sep 1957–Jun 1959, CBS Sun 7:30–8:00 (OS)
  Jun 1959–Sep 1961, NBC Thu 9:00–9:30
  Oct 1961–Sep 1962, ABC Tue 8:00–8:30
CAST:
  Bentley Gregg .... John Forsythe
  Kelly Gregg .... Noreen Corcoran
  Peter Tong .... Sammee Tong
  Ginger Farrell/Loomis/Mitchell
      .... Bernadette Withers
  Howard Meechim (1958–1961)... Jimmy Boyd
  Elaine Meechim (1959) .... Joan Vohs
  Cal Mitchell (1960–1962)......... Del Moore
  Adelaide Mitchell (1960–1962)... Evelyn Scott
  Cousin Charlie Fong (1961–1962)
      .... Victor Sen Yung
  Warren Dawson (1962) .... Aron Kincaid
  Vickie (1957–1958) .... Alice Backus
  Kitty Deveraux (1958–1959) .. Shirley Mitchell
  Kitty Marsh (1959–1961) ... Sue Ane Langdon
  Suzanne Collins (1961) .... Jeanne Bal
  Connie (1961–1962)......... Sally Mansfield

Bentley Gregg was a wealthy, successful Hollywood attorney, whose clients included many glamorous and available women. He lived with his niece Kelly, his houseboy Peter, and a large shaggy dog named Jasper in posh Beverly Hills. Uncle Bentley had become Kelly's legal guardian after her parents had been killed in an automobile accident when she was 13 years old. Between his large and active law practice, his social life with beautiful women, and the responsibilities of raising a teenage girl, Bentley's time was more than adequately filled. Peter, the helpful but often inscrutable Oriental houseboy, was a jack-of-all-trades who ran the Gregg home and was indispensible to his boss.

Kelly was a typical teenager—exuberant and enthusiastic—who at times tried to find a wife for her uncle. During her high school years she had a regular boyfriend, lanky Howard Meechim. Her best friend was Ginger, whose parents and last name were changed twice during the five-year run of the show; only the last set of parents, Cal and Adelaide Mitchell, appeared often enough to be listed as regulars. At the end of the 1960–1961 season, in the last episode aired on NBC, Kelly graduated from high school. Two weeks later,

when new episodes began on ABC, she had started college. The following spring brought her true love, in the person of Warren Dawson, a young lawyer who became Bentley's junior partner and Kelly's fiancé. *Bachelor Father* concluded its network run at the end of that season, however, so that Kelly and Warren never did get married.

As for Bentley, he may have been an irresistible ladies' man, but he certainly had trouble holding on to a secretary. Five different actresses filled that role in succession: Alice Backus, Shirley Mitchell, Sue Ane Langdon, Jeanne Bal, and Sally Mansfield.

In what would later become a bit of irony, actress Linda Evans appeared in one episode of *Bachelor Father* as a girlfriend of Bentley's niece Kelly. Two decades later, on the series *Dynasty*, she and John Forsythe, who had played Bentley, were man and wife.

BACK THAT FACT
Audience Participation
FIRST TELECAST: *October 22, 1953*
LAST TELECAST: *November 26, 1953*
BROADCAST HISTORY:
  Oct 1953–Nov 1953, ABC Thu 9:00–9:30
EMCEE:
  Joey Adams
ASSISTANTS:
  Al Kelly
  Hope Lange
  Carl Caruso

As host of this short-lived audience-participation show, Joey Adams interviewed members of the studio audience about such matters as their backgrounds, hobbies, and accomplishments. From time to time an offstage voice (Carl Caruso) would challenge a statement they made, calling on them to "back that fact." If they could (in the estimation of a panel chosen from the audience), they won a prize. The program was presented live from New York.

BACKGROUND
News/Documentary
FIRST TELECAST: *August 16, 1954*
LAST TELECAST: *September 6, 1954*
BROADCAST HISTORY:
  Aug 1954–Sep 1954, NBC Mon 8:30–9:00
COMMENTATOR:
  Joseph C. Harsch

On this program, Joseph C. Harsch each week presented an analysis of a different issue of current world importance. Special film reports produced by NBC News were used; the thrust of the program was to take the audience beyond the headlines to the people who were actually living the news. After a brief run in prime time the series moved to Sunday afternoons, where it continued until June 1955.

BACKSTAGE WITH BARRY WOOD

Variety
FIRST TELECAST: *March 1, 1949*
LAST TELECAST: *May 24, 1949*
BROADCAST HISTORY:
  Mar 1949–May 1949, CBS Tue 10:00–10:15
HOST:
  Barry Wood

Singer Barry Wood was the producer and host of this series, which gave young entertainers an opportunity to perform on live television to a full network audience. The slogan of the show was that it "featured tomorrow's stars today."

BACKSTAIRS AT THE WHITE HOUSE

Documentary/Drama
FIRST TELECAST: *January 29, 1979*
LAST TELECAST: *February 19, 1979*
BROADCAST HISTORY:
  Jan 1979–Feb 1979, NBC Mon 9:00–11:00
CAST:
  Maggie Rogers.................. Olivia Cole
  Lillian Rogers (as a child).... Tania Johnson
  Lillian Rogers Parks (as an adult)
  .... Leslie Uggams
  Levi Mercer .... Louis Gossett, Jr.
  Ike Hoover .... Leslie Nielsen
  Mrs. Jaffray .... Cloris Leachman
  Mays .... Robert Hooks
  Coates .... Hari Rhodes
  Dixon .... David Downing
  Jackson .... Bill Overton
  Annie .... Helena Carroll
  Pres. William Howard Taft.... Victor Buono
  Helen "Nellie" Taft .... Julie Harris
  Pres. Woodrow Wilson....... Robert Vaughn
  Ellen Wilson .... Kim Hunter
  Edith Galt Wilson .... Claire Bloom
  Pres. Warren Harding...... George Kennedy
  Florence Harding .... Celeste Holm
  Pres. Calvin Coolidge .... Ed Flanders
  Grace Coolidge .... Lee Grant
  Pres. Herbert Hoover........... Larry Gates
  Lou Hoover..................... Jan Sterling
  Pres. Franklin D. Roosevelt... John Anderson
  Eleanor Roosevelt............ Eileen Heckart
  Pres. Harry S Truman........ Harry Morgan
  Bess Truman .... Estelle Parsons
  Pres. Dwight D. Eisenhower
  .... Andrew Duggan
  Mamie Eisenhower........... Barbara Barrie

This miniseries presented an unusual glimpse into the private lives of eight American Presidents—from Taft to Eisenhower—as seen through the eyes of the permanent White House staff. The central characters were Chief Maid Maggie Rogers and her daughter, Lillian, who succeeded her. A continuing subplot concerned Maggie's efforts to hold her own little family together, despite many problems: a missing husband, survival on the edge of poverty (White House servants,

though they worked amid the trappings of wealth and power, were paid very little), a son permanently scarred by wartime service, and daughter Lillian's affliction with polio. Lillian, though occasionally hotheaded, overcame her affliction and went on to a long and successful career serving the Presidents and their sometimes more demanding wives.

Others on the White House staff included Mrs. Jaffray, the head housekeeper; Ike Hoover, the chief usher; and Levi Mercer, the serving man. Coates and Dixon were butlers, Mays and Jackson, doormen, and Annie, another maid.

Based on *My Thirty Years Backstairs at the White House*, by Lillian Rogers Parks with Frances Spatz Leighton, a book which created a furor when first released because of its frank and intimate portrayal of presidential families. At the beginning of each episode of the mini-series it was announced that in some instances real names and settings had been changed to advance the story.

BAD NEWS BEARS, THE

Situation Comedy
FIRST TELECAST: *March 24, 1979*
LAST TELECAST: *July 26, 1980*
BROADCAST HISTORY:
  Mar 1979–Sep 1979, CBS Sat 8:00–8:30
  Sep 1979–Oct 1979, CBS Sat 8:30–9:00
  Jun 1980, CBS Sat 8:00–8:30
  Jul 1980, CBS Sat 8:30–9:00
CAST:
  Morris Buttermaker .... Jack Warden
  Dr. Emily Rappant .... Catherine Hicks
  Roy Turner.................. Phillip R. Allen
  Leslie Ogilvie............... Sparky Marcus
  Tanner Boyle .... Meeno Peluce
  Rudi Stein...................... Billy Jacoby
  Regi Tower................. Corey Feldman
  Timmy Lupus............. Shane Butterworth
  Ahmad Abdul Rahim....... Christoff St. John
  Mike Engelberg............. J. Brennan Smith
  Miguel Agilar................. Charles Nunez
  Jose Agilar .... Danny Nunez
  Amanda Whirlitzer .... Tricia Cast
  Frosty......................... Bill Lazarus
  Kelly Leek .... Gregg Forrest
  Josh Matthews.................... Rad Daly

Former minor-league baseball player Morris Buttermaker was trying to make a living as a swimming-pool cleaner, but his temper got him another, part-time job. When one of his clients refused to pay him, Morris drove the client's car into the pool. Dragged into court, he was given the alternative of "volunteering" to coach the baseball team at Hoover Junior High or going to jail. He chose baseball, but soon found that jail might have been more rewarding—the Hoover Bears was as sorry a pack of youthful misfits and bumblers as could be found anywhere. It was a miracle that he managed to get them to accomplish anything. Dr. Emily Rappant was Hoover's principal, Roy

Turner, the coach of the hated rival Lions, and Amanda Whirlitzer, the Bears' star pitcher. Morris had dated Amanda's mother at one time, and Amanda was always looking for ways to get them back together. The only member of the Bears who was not on the team when the series premiered was Josh Matthews, who transferred to Hoover in the fall of 1979.

Based on the 1976 motion picture, *The Bad News Bears,* starring Walter Matthau and Tatum O'Neal. Two sequels to the theatrical movie, *The Bad News Bears in Breaking Training* and *The Bad News Bears Go to Japan,* were released prior to the start of the television series.

BADGE 714
syndicated title for *Dragnet* (before 1967)

BAILEYS OF BALBOA, THE
Situation Comedy
FIRST TELECAST: *September 24, 1964*
LAST TELECAST: *April 1, 1965*
BROADCAST HISTORY:
   Sep 1964–Apr 1965, CBS Thu 9:30–10:00
CAST:
   Sam Bailey....................... Paul Ford
   Buck Singleton............ Sterling Holloway
   Jim Bailey.................... Les Brown, Jr.
   Stanley....................... Clint Howard
   Commodore Cecil Wyntoon..... John Dehner
   Barbara Wyntoon............... Judy Carne

Paul Ford portrayed crusty old Sam Bailey, a widower who ran a small charter fishing boat called *The Island Princess.* The boat was based on a little island Sam owned in the middle of Balboa, a fictitious exclusive yachting community. Sam's unpretentious nature and dislike for fancy society trappings antagonized the surrounding community, particularly the aristocratic Commodore Wyntoon. Sam's son Jim was infatuated with the commodore's daughter Barbara, however, and their romance forced a degree of civility on the two fathers. Buck was the forgetful first mate and entire crew of *The Island Princess,* and Stanley was an obnoxious little boy who was one of Sam's neighbors.

BAKER'S DOZEN
Situation Comedy
FIRST TELECAST: *March 17, 1982*
LAST TELECAST: *April 21, 1982*
BROADCAST HISTORY:
   Mar 1982–Apr 1982, CBS Wed 9:30–10:00
CAST:
   Mike Locasale.................... Ron Silver
   Terry Munson............ Cindy Weintraub
   O.K. Otis Kelly............... Alan Weeks
   Harve Schoendorf.......... Sam McMurray
   Desk Sgt. Martin............. Thomas Quinn
   Jeff Diggins................. John Del Regno
   Capt. Florence Baker.......... Doris Belack

Much in the style of *Barney Miller, Baker's Dozen* sought to show the human and often funny side of police work. It followed the off-beat activities of an undercover anti-crime unit of the N.Y.P.D. under the direction of no-nonsense Capt. Florence Baker. Mike and Terry, two of the undercover cops, struggled to maintain their rather rocky romantic relationship, though their assignments often got in the way. Kelly and Harve were also members of Baker's team and Jeff Diggins, one of the many street people they dealt with, was a neighborhood con man who sometimes helped them out with information. Sgt. Martin, the precinct philosopher, was forever spouting homilies and making long-winded observations about life to anyone who would sit still and listen.

The program was filmed on location in New York City.

BALANCE YOUR BUDGET
Quiz/Audience Participation
FIRST TELECAST: *October 18, 1952*
LAST TELECAST: *May 2, 1953*
BROADCAST HISTORY:
   Oct 1952–May 1953, CBS Sat 10:00–10:30
EMCEE:
   Bert Parks

Contestants on *Balance Your Budget* were asked to describe what had caused "their personal or family budgets to slip into the red"; they were then given an opportunity to win some money by answering a series of questions asked by emcee Bert Parks. Winners were also given the opportunity to pick from among a large number of keys, one of which would open the show's "Treasure Chest," containing an additional jackpot of $1,500 or more. Because the contestants had the chance to explain why they needed the money, CBS billed this as a "human interest" quiz show.

BALL FOUR
Situation Comedy
FIRST TELECAST: *September 22, 1976*
LAST TELECAST: *October 27, 1976*
BROADCAST HISTORY:
   Sep 1976–Oct 1976, CBS Wed 8:30–9:00
CAST:
   Jim Barton...................... Jim Bouton
   "Cap" Capogrosso .... Jack Somack
   Bill Westlake........... David-James Carroll
   "Rhino" Rhinelander.......... Ben Davidson
   Coach Pinky Pinkney ...... Bill McCutcheon
   Lenny "Birdman" Siegel...... Lenny Schultz
   Rayford Plunkett............. Marco St. John
   Orlando Lopez................. Jaime Tirelli
   C. B. Travis .... Sam Wright

Ball Four was truly "locker-room" comedy, since most of its action took place in the locker room of a major league baseball team, the Washington Americans. In the first episode pitcher Jim Barton informed his teammates and coaches that he was going to write a series of articles on baseball life "off the field." Manager Capogrosso and most of the others were not very keen on the idea, and neither was the viewing audience. The show folded after less than two months on the air. *Ball Four* was based on a book of the same title by former major league pitcher Jim Bouton. Not only did he star in a semi-autobiographical role in the series, he was also one of the writers.

BANACEK
Detective Drama
FIRST TELECAST: *September 13, 1972*
LAST TELECAST: *September 3, 1974*
BROADCAST HISTORY:
 Sep 1972–Dec 1973, NBC Wed 8:30–10:00
 Jan 1974–Sep 1974, NBC Tue 8:30–10:00
CAST:
 Thomas Banacek .... George Peppard
 Jay Drury .... Ralph Manza
 Felix Mulholland .... Murray Matheson
 Carlie Kirkland (1973–1974)
 .... Christine Belford

The gimmick in this private-eye series was ethnic: Banacek was a cool, smooth, shrewd Polish-American. His game was collecting rewards from insurance companies by solving crimes involving stolen property, and he was successful enough to live in the exclusive Beacon Hill section of Boston. Banacek's buddies were his chauffeur Jay and his good friend Felix, who ran a bookstore. During the show's second season Carlie, an insurance agent, was added for romantic interest. Polish proverbs were liberally sprinkled throughout the series, and the positive image of its hero made the show very popular with such groups as the Polish-American Congress, which gave the program an award for portraying Polish-Americans in a positive manner. *Banacek* originally aired as one of the rotating segments of NBC's *Wednesday Mystery Movie.*

BAND OF AMERICA
 see *Cities Service*

BAND OF THE WEEK
 see *Music at the Meadowbrook*

BANK ON THE STARS
Quiz/Audience Participation
FIRST TELECAST: *June 20, 1953*
LAST TELECAST: *August 21, 1954*
BROADCAST HISTORY:
 Jun 1953, CBS Sat 9:00–9:30
 Jun 1953–Aug 1953, CBS Sat 9:30–10:00
 May 1954–Aug 1954, NBC Sat 8:00–8:30
EMCEE:
 Jack Paar (1953)
 Bill Cullen (May–July 1954)
 Jimmy Nelson (Jul–Aug 1954)

Contestants on this game show were drawn from the studio audience and divided into teams. Each two-person team would be shown a film clip from a famous motion picture and asked questions about the scene, for cash prizes. A bonus round involved answering more difficult questions about a different movie scene, which the contestants could only hear and not see.

BANYON
Detective Drama
FIRST TELECAST: *September 15, 1972*
LAST TELECAST: *January 12, 1973*
BROADCAST HISTORY:
 Sep 1972–Jan 1973, NBC Fri 10:00–11:00
CAST:
 Miles C. Banyon .... Robert Forster
 Peggy Revere .... Joan Blondell
 Lt. Pete McNeil .... Richard Jaeckel
 Abby Graham .... Julie Gregg

This period private-eye series was set in Los Angeles during the late 1930s. Banyon, a tough but honest detective, would take on any case, from murder to missing persons, for $20 a day. Peggy Revere, whose secretarial school was located in the same building as Banyon's office, provided him each week with a new free secretary, ranging from sexpot to country farm girl. Banyon's eyes were fixed on his girlfriend Abby Graham, a nightclub singer—though he successfully evaded her constant efforts to get him to marry and settle down.

BARBARA MCNAIR SHOW, THE
Musical Variety
BROADCAST HISTORY:
 Syndicated only
 60 minutes
 Produced: *1969–1971* (52 episodes)
 Released: *Fall 1969*
HOSTESS
 Barbara McNair

This was one of those pleasant musical variety shows that made the rounds in the late 1960s and early 1970s. Barbara McNair, a good-looking black songstress, hosted such diverse musical guests as John Gary and the Turtles, along with such comics as Bob Hope, Soupy Sales, and Rich Little.

BARBARA MANDRELL & THE MANDRELL SISTERS
Musical Variety
FIRST TELECAST: *November 18, 1980*
LAST TELECAST: *June 26, 1982*
BROADCAST HISTORY:
 Nov 1980, NBC Tue 10:00–11:00
 Nov 1980–Jan 1982, NBC Sat 8:00–9:00
 Jan 1982–Feb 1982, NBC Sat 9:00–10:00

Mar 1982, NBC Tue 10:00–11:00
Apr 1982–Jun 1982, NBC Sat 9:00–10:00
REGULARS:
Barbara Mandrell
Louise Mandrell
Irlene Mandrell
The Krofft Puppets

Country-and-western music star Barbara Mandrell hosted this variety series with the help of her talented younger sisters, Louise and Irlene. All three sang and played musical instruments: Barbara the banjo, steel guitar, piano, and saxophone; Louise, the banjo and fiddle; and Irlene, the drums. They engaged in a certain amount of tongue-in-cheek sibling rivalry, and throughout each telecast there was byplay between the sisters, including comedy sketches describing their relationship over the years. Barbara was usually portrayed as the serious, pushy sister, and Irlene the sexy, vain one.

The main emphasis of the show was on music, however, with such well-known country stars as Dolly Parton, Marty Robbins, Tennessee Ernie Ford, Kenny Rogers, and Charley Pride making appearances. A group of life-size Krofft puppets called Truck Shackley & the Texas Critters—five musicians and a dog—served as the resident band. The series was produced by Sid and Marty Krofft.

Midway through the second season, series star Barbara Mandrell announced that the show would cease production in early 1982. The weekly grind was more work than she had anticipated and, in conjunction with her busy concert schedule, left her on the verge of exhaustion. Health problems, not ratings problems, canceled this series.

BARBARA STANWYCK SHOW, THE
Dramatic Anthology
FIRST TELECAST: *September 19, 1960*
LAST TELECAST: *September 11, 1961*
BROADCAST HISTORY:
Sep 1960–Sep 1961, NBC Mon 10:00–10:30
HOSTESS/STAR:
Barbara Stanwyck

Hollywood leading lady Barbara Stanwyck hosted this anthology of original 30-minute filmed teleplays and starred in all but four of them. The four were pilots for possible series and starred Lloyd Nolan ("The Seventh Miracle"), Milton Berle ("Dear Charlie"), Peggy Cass ("Call Me Annie"), and Andy Devine ("Big Jake"). None of them made it on to the next fall's schedule.

The dramas in which Miss Stanwyck appeared tended to be on the serious side. Three of them were pilots for a proposed new series of her own, in which she would star as an American adventuress running an import-export business in exotic Hong Kong. The original pilot was aired on November 14, 1960, as "The Miraculous Journey of

'Tadpole Chan' " and established the character of Josephine Little. Viewers were requested to write to the network if they liked the idea, and the response was strong enough to result in two other episodes, in January and March. However, the Josephine Little series never went into full production.

BARBARY COAST, THE
Western
FIRST TELECAST: *September 8, 1975*
LAST TELECAST: *January 9, 1976*
BROADCAST HISTORY:
Sep 1975–Oct 1975, ABC Mon 8:00–9:00
Oct 1975–Jan 1976, ABC Fri 8:00–9:00
CAST:
Cash Conover .... Doug McClure
Jeff Cable .... William Shatner
Moose Moran................. Richard Kiel
Thumbs, the piano player ...... Dave Turner

This Western was set in the 1870s in a square-mile section of San Francisco called the Barbary Coast, a wide-open, rip-roaring district whose inhabitants ranged from flashy ladies to sourdoughs. Cable was a special agent working for the Governor of California, gathering information on criminals in the district. He traveled incognito and was a master of disguise. Conover was the flamboyant owner of the Golden Gate Casino (which he had won in a poker game) and was Cable's unlikely ally.

BARE ESSENCE
Drama
FIRST TELECAST: *February 15, 1983*
LAST TELECAST: *April 29, 1983*
BROADCAST HISTORY:
Feb 1983–Mar 1983, NBC Tue 9:00–10:00
Mar 1983–Apr 1983, NBC Fri 10:00–11:00
CAST:
Tyger Hayes.................. Genie Francis
Lady Bobbi Rowan.......... Jennifer O'Neill
Ava Marshall................ Jessica Walter
Hadden Marshall .... John Dehner
Niko Theophilus .... Ian McShane
Sean Benedict .... Michael Woods
Marcus Marshall .... Jonathan Frakes
Muffin Marshall .... Wendy Fulton
Laura Parker .... Penny Fuller
Margaret Marshall........... Susan French
Barbara Fisher .... Jaime Lyn Bauer
Cathy...................... Laura Bruneau
Natasha................. Anulka Dziubinska
Larry DeVito .... Morgan Stevens

The perfume business was the setting for this tale of corruption, sex, and power. Tyger Hayes—young and beautiful, ambitious and energetic—was entering the business world after the death of her wealthy playboy husband, Chase Marshall. Chase's father, Hadden, was the patriarch of the Marshall family and the head of Kellico, the family's privately held conglomerate. With the help of her staunchest supporter, Hadden's sister Margaret, Tyger attempted to make a name for herself developing "Ma Femme" perfume. But she soon found herself in conflict with her conniving in-laws. Ava, the widow of Hadden's other son, Hugh, was determined to see her ineffectual son Marcus take over Kellico. Marcus' wife Muffin agreed. Ava's efforts to secure the Marshall empire for her son led her to woo and eventually marry Hadden himself (her father-in-law). Meanwhile Tyger's mother, international beauty Lady Bobbi, was having an affair with Niko Theophilus, a Greek millionaire with a long-standing vendetta against the Marshalls. He hoped to use this liaison as a means of destroying them.

This series was the continuation of a highly popular TV movie of the same name seen on CBS in October 1982. It was based on a popular novel, and starred one of the hottest young stars of the daytime soap-opera world, *General Hospital*'s Genie Francis. Despite a heavy infusion of jet-set glamour (settings included Manhattan, the Marshalls' country estate, Niko's yacht, and locations in Paris and along the Mediterranean) the audience for this weekly series was small, and *Bare Essence* soon left the air.

BAREFOOT IN THE PARK
Situation Comedy
FIRST TELECAST: *September 24, 1970*
LAST TELECAST: *January 14, 1971*
BROADCAST HISTORY:
Sep 1970–Jan 1971, ABC Thu 9:00–9:30
CAST:
Paul Bratter . . . . Scoey Mitchlll
Corie Bratter . . . . Tracy Reed
Mabel Bates . . . . Thelma Carpenter
Honey Robinson . . . . Nipsey Russell
Mr. Kendricks . . . . Harry Holcombe
Mr. Velasquez . . . . Vito Scotti

This all-black version of Neil Simon's hit play and movie concerned two young newlyweds trying to establish their life on a shoestring budget in New York. Their home was a one-room walk-up apartment on the top floor of an old brownstone. At least they had each other—plus Corie's busybody mother Mabel, Mabel's persistent suitor Honey, Paul's boss Mr. Kendricks, and the bumbling building superintendent Mr. Velasquez.

BARETTA
Police Drama
FIRST TELECAST: *January 17, 1975*
LAST TELECAST: *June 1, 1978*
BROADCAST HISTORY:
Jan 1975–Mar 1975, ABC Fri 10:00–11:00
Apr 1975–Jul 1975, ABC Wed 10:00–11:00
Sep 1975–Aug 1977, ABC Wed 9:00–10:00
Aug 1977–Jan 1978, ABC Wed 10:00–11:00
Feb 1978–Jun 1978, ABC Thu 10:00–11:00

CAST:
Det. Tony Baretta . . . . Robert Blake
Inspector Shiller (1975) . . . . Dana Elcar
Lt. Hal Brubaker . . . . Edward Grover
Billy Truman . . . . Tom Ewell
Rooster . . . . Michael D. Roberts
Fats . . . . Chino Williams
THEME:
"Keep Your Eye on the Sparrow," sung by Sammy Davis, Jr.

Baretta was half-a-spin-off from another detective show. Robert Blake had originally been scheduled to take over the lead role in *Toma* after Tony Musante left that series. But *Toma* had not been a big hit, and rather than risk being tied to an unsuccessful series the title was changed and alterations were made in the locale and other details. In essence, *Toma* became *Baretta*, moved to California.

Tony Baretta was, like Toma, an unconventional cop. He was streetwise, single, with a decidedly funky life-style: he holed up in a run-down old hotel when he wasn't on the job, which was seldom. He was usually seen in T-shirt and jeans, with his trademark cap pulled down over his forehead. The orphaned son of poor Italian immigrants, Tony knew the city inside out. He was a master of disguise, and because of his rough appearance was able to infiltrate such groups as motorcycle gangs and even "the Mob." Needless to say, he refused to have a partner and always worked alone. Inspector Shiller was his original boss, later succeeded by Lt. Brubaker. Billy Truman was a retired cop who was a combined manager and house detective at the hotel where Baretta lived.

There was plenty of hard action in this series, despite Blake's public protestations that he opposed wanton violence on TV. The show had a "with-it" light sense of humor; comic relief was provided by Tony's fancy-dude informant-friend Rooster and by Fred, Tony's pet cockatoo. Blake's real-life wife Sondra Blake was an occasional guest star.

BARNABY JONES
Detective Drama
FIRST TELECAST: *January 28, 1973*
LAST TELECAST: *September 4,* 1980
BROADCAST HISTORY:
Jan 1973–Jun 1974, CBS Sun 9:30–10:30
Jul 1974–Sep 1974, CBS Sat 10:00–11:00
Sep 1974–Aug 1975, CBS Tue 10:00–11:00
Sep 1975–Nov 1975, CBS Fri 10:00–11:00
Dec 1975–Nov 1979, CBS Thu 10:00–11:00
Dec 1979–Sep 1980, CBS Thu 9:00–10:00
CAST:
Barnaby Jones . . . . Buddy Ebsen
Betty Jones . . . . Lee Meriwether
Jedediah Romano (J.R.) Jones (1976–1980)
. . . . Mark Shera

Lt. Joe Taylor (1973).......... Vince Howard
Lt. John Biddle (1974–1980) ...... John Carter
EXECUTIVE PRODUCER:
Quinn Martin

After a long and successful career as a private investigator, Barnaby Jones had retired, leaving the business to his son Hal. When Hal was murdered while on a case, Barnaby came out of retirement to help track down his son's killer. Hal's widow, Betty, worked with her father-in-law to solve the case and remained with him, as his assistant, when he deciced to keep his Los Angeles-based firm in operation. His keen analytic skills were often masked by a homespun exterior, drawing guilty parties into a false sense of security that led to their downfall. Until *Cannon*—another Los Angeles detective series—went off the air in the fall of 1975, there was occasional interplay between it and *Barnaby Jones*.

In the fall of 1976 Barnaby's young cousin J.R. joined the firm, initially to track down the murderer of *his* father, but eventually as a permanent partner. One of the things that most fascinated him was Barnaby's home crime laboratory, something rarely seen in other detective series. It was in the lab that various clues were analyzed and possible bits of evidence evaluated. J.R., in addition to his work with Barnaby, was also studying to pass the bar exam and become a lawyer.

BARNEY BLAKE, POLICE REPORTER

Crime Drama
FIRST TELECAST: *April 22, 1948*
LAST TELECAST: *July 8, 1948*
BROADCAST HISTORY:
Apr 1948–Jul 1948, NBC Thu 9:30–10:00
CAST:
Barney Blake............... Gene O'Donnell
Jennifer Allen................. Judy Parrish

Reporter Barney Blake, assisted by his secretary Jennifer, solved assorted homicides in this live series, which NBC claims was television's first regularly scheduled mystery series. It set at least one precedent when it was canceled by the sponsor, American Tobacco Company, after only thirteen weeks.

BARNEY MILLER

Situation Comedy
FIRST TELECAST: *January 23, 1975*
LAST TELECAST: *September 9, 1982*
BROADCAST HISTORY:
Jan 1975–Jan 1976, ABC Thu 8:00–8:30 (OS)
Jan 1976–Dec 1976, ABC Thu 8:30–9:00 (OS)
Dec 1976–Mar 1982, ABC Thu 9:00–9:30
Mar 1982–Apr 1982, ABC Fri 8:30–9:00
Apr 1982–Sep 1982, ABC Thu 9:00–9:30
CAST:
Capt. Barney Miller............. Hal Linden
Det. Phil Fish (1975–1977)....... Abe Vigoda

Det. Sgt. Chano Amenguale (1975–1976)
.... Gregory Sierra
Det. Stanley Wojohowicz ("Wojo")
.... Maxwell Gail
Det. Nick Yemana (1975–1978) ..... Jack Soo
Det. Ron Harris................. Ron Glass
Elizabeth Miller (pilot only) .... Abby Dalton
Elizabeth Miller (1975–1976) .. Barbara Barrie
Rachael Miller (1975) ...... Anne Wyndham
David Miller (1975) .... Michael Tessier
Bernice Fish (1975–1977).... Florence Stanley
Det. Janice Wentworth (1975–1976)
.... Linda Lavin
Inspector Frank Luger........ James Gregory
Officer Carl Levitt (1976–1982) .... Ron Carey
Det. Baptista (1976–1977) .... June Gable
Det. Arthur Dietrich (1976–1982)
.... Steve Landesberg
Lt. Scanlon (1978–1982)..... George Murdock

Barney Miller grew out of a rejected comedy pilot called "The Life and Times of Captain Barney Miller," which aired as part of an ABC summer anthology called *Just for Laughs* in 1974. In that pilot the action revolved equally around Barney's problems at the police precinct house and his home life, with his wife Elizabeth and kids prominently featured. But when *Barney Miller* made it to the regular ABC schedule the following January, the family played a much smaller role (eventually they were written out) and the locale became the Greenwich Village station house where Barney and his motley crew spent their day.

Three actors besides Hal Linden came over from the pilot to the series: Barney's two kids, David and Rachael, who soon disappeared, and a broken-down old cop named Fish. Fish was the hit of the show. Not only did he look incredible, he sounded and acted like every breath might be his last. Fish was always on the verge of retirement, and his worst day was when the station house toilet broke down. He was constantly complaining about everything, especially his seldom-seen wife Bernice.

There were ironies in Abe Vigoda's portrayal of Fish. Vigoda, 54, was in real life an active athlete (he jogged and played handball), and the role for which he was previously best known was quite different indeed—that of the ruthless Mafia leader Tessio, in *The Godfather*. Vigoda became so popular that he eventually got his own series, *Fish*, though he also continued on *Barney Miller* for a time. He left the series ("retiring" from the police force) in September 1977.

Others around the 12th Precinct station house were Det. Amenguale, the Puerto Rican; Wojo, the naive, trusting one; Yemana, the philosophical one who made coffee for them all; Dietrich, the know-it-all; and Harris, the wisecracking, ambitious black. Seen occasionally were Inspector Luger, the sometimes incoherent superior; Levitt, the 5'3" uniformed officer who wanted to be a detective, but was "too short"; Lt. Scanlon of Internal Affairs; and female officers Wentworth and Baptista. A continuous parade of crazies, crooks, conmen, hookers, juvenile muggers, and other street denizens passed through.

Among the notable events of later seasons were Harris' emergence as a published author, with a lurid novel about police work called *Blood on the Badge;* and, in January 1979, the death of actor Jack Soo. Soo was last seen as Yemana in October 1978, but was so loved that a special episode was devoted to him the following May, with clips from past shows and reminiscences by the cast. At the end they all raised their coffee cups in a poignant farewell toast.

As the series declined in audience share during 1981–1982, the producers decided to end its run with an ironic twist. The discovery of an antique gun in the precinct house revealed that the building had been the headquarters of Teddy Roosevelt when he was president of the New York Police Board in the 1890s. In fact, Barney's office may have been President Roosevelt's office. As a result, the building was declared a historic landmark and the precinct forced to vacate. In the last episode, Barney received the long-awaited phone call from headquarters. The news was bittersweet: Barney was promoted to deputy inspector and Levitt had finally made sergeant; but the men of the precinct would be scattered to different locations throughout the city. The 12th was no more.

BARON, THE
Spy Drama
FIRST TELECAST: *January 20, 1966*
LAST TELECAST: *July 14, 1966*
BROADCAST HISTORY:
Jan 1966–Jul 1966, ABC Thu 10:00–11:00
CAST:
John Mannering, "The Baron".. Steve Forrest
Cordelia Winfield............... Sue Lloyd
John Alexander Templeton-Green
.... Colin Gordon
David Marlowe................ Paul Ferris

John Mannering, otherwise known as "The Baron," was the handsome, cultured, American-born owner of fine antique shops in London, Paris, and Washington, D.C. When not appraising expensive objets d'art for his exclusive clientele, he was pursuing dangerous missions around the world on behalf of British Intelligence. He was called in whenever priceless art objects were involved, as often seemed to happen in cases of espionage, blackmail, and murder. His contact at British Intelligence was John Templeton-Green, to whom the beautiful secret agent Cordelia Winfield also reported. David Marlowe served occasionally as Mannering's assistant. The name "The Baron" derived from the Mannering family's sprawling ranch in Texas, where John grew up.

The series was filmed in England and was based on the novels of John Creasey.

BASEBALL
Sports
FIRST TELECAST: *May 26, 1951*
LAST TELECAST:
BROADCAST HISTORY:
May 1951–Sep 1951, ABC Sat 9:00–11:00
May 1952–Jun 1952, ABC Sat 8:30–10:30
Jun 1972–Sep 1975, NBC Mon 8:15–Conclusion (summers only)
Apr 1976–Aug 1982, ABC Mon 8:30–Conclusion (summers only)
Jun 1983– , ABC Mon 8:00–Conclusion (summers only)
SPORTSCASTERS:
Pat Flanagan (1951)
Don Dunphy (1952)
Bob Finnegan (1952)
Curt Gowdy (1972–1975)
Tony Kubek (1972–1975)
Jim Simpson (1972–1975)
Sandy Koufax (1972)
Maury Wills (1973–1975)
Joe Garagiola (1975)
Bob Prince (1976)
Warner Wolf (1976–1977)
Bob Uecker (1976–1982)
Al Michaels (1976–   )
Norm Cash (1976)
Bob Gibson (1976–1977)
Bill White (1977–1979)
Howard Cosell (1977–1985)
Keith Jackson (1978–1982, 1986)
Don Drysdale (1978–1985)
Jim Lampley (1978–1979)
Lou Brock (1980)
Earl Weaver (1983–1984)
Steve Stone (1983)
Jim Palmer (1984–   )
Tim McCarver (1984–   )
Gary Bender (1987–   )

Baseball has always had a home on television, at both the local and the network level. The first baseball game ever telecast was a college, rather than a professional, game. On May 17, 1939, NBC telecast a game between Princeton and Columbia to the few sets in operation in the New York City area. In 1947 the World Series had its first network telecast, over a four-station NBC network; it has been a popular fall attraction ever since. Although locally originated baseball networks were set up in the late 1940s and early 1950s, they were primarily weekend afternoon games and were beamed to the limited area in which the originating team had most of its fans. Later, on both local stations and networks, Saturday and Sunday afternoons were reserved for "the national pastime."

The first nighttime network baseball series, aired on ABC in 1951 and 1952, featured women

63

rather than men. There was a women's professional league at that time, and the ABC series, known popularly as *Girls' Baseball,* was officially titled *National Women's Professional Baseball League Games.* In 1951 it was telecast from Chicago and followed the home games of the Queens of America. The following year it originated from New York, with Don Dunphy doing the play-by-play and Bob Finnegan providing color commentary on the home games of the Arthur Murray Girls.

It was not until two decades later that NBC decided to bring men's major league baseball to prime-time television as the regular summer replacement for *NBC Monday Night at the Movies.* Curt Gowdy and Tony Kubek provided coverage of the major game telecast each week, with other sportscasters covering secondary games. After four years on NBC, *Monday Night Baseball* moved to ABC in the spring of 1976. ABC expanded the number of people in the broadcast booth from two to three, as they had done with *Monday Night Football,* and during the summer of 1976 the primary game team was composed of Bob Prince, Warner Wolf, and Bob Uecker. Others seen frequently on the "first team" in subsequent years included Al Michaels, Howard Cosell, Keith Jackson, Don Drysdale, and former Baltimore Orioles manager Earl Weaver.

BASEBALL CORNER
Sports Discussion
FIRST TELECAST: *June 1, 1958*
LAST TELECAST: *August 27, 1958*
BROADCAST HISTORY:
  Jun 1958–Jul 1958, ABC Sun 9:00–9:30
  Jul 1958–Aug 1958, ABC Wed 9:30–10:00
HOST:
  Buddy Blattner

Buddy Blattner broadcast sports news, narrated films, and conducted interviews with a panel of four guests. The program emanated from Chicago.

BASEBALL WORLD OF JOE GARAGIOLA, THE
Sports Commentary
FIRST TELECAST: *June 12, 1972*
LAST TELECAST: *September 1, 1975*
BROADCAST HISTORY:
  Jun 1972–Sep 1975, NBC Mon 8:00–8:15 (Summers Only)
HOST:
  Joe Garagiola

Former major league baseball player Joe Garagiola was the host of this show that preceded the Monday night *NBC Major League Baseball* game. The show featured interviews with players and the humorous anecdotes and observations of Mr. Garagiola.

BASKETBALL
Sports
FIRST TELECAST: *November 13, 1948*
LAST TELECAST: *March 15, 1952*
BROADCAST HISTORY:
  Nov 1948–Mar 1949, NBC Sat 9:00–Conclusion
  Feb 1949–Mar 1949, CBS Thu 9:00–Conclusion
  Dec 1951–Mar 1952, ABC Sat 9:00–Conclusion

Basketball has rarely been seen on a regular basis on nighttime network television, and not at all in the last 25 years. Back in the early days of network television it was tried by three different networks, all four networks if its frequent appearance on DuMont's *Saturday Night at the Garden* is considered.

The earliest appearance of network basketball was on NBC during the 1948–1949 season, with Bob Stanton announcing the games of the semipro New York Gothams. That same spring CBS gave Mel Allen the mike to cover various college games during the college tournament season. College games did somewhat better than the semipros in terms of audience appeal, and ABC gave them another try during the 1951–1952 college season, with Curt Gowdy and Vince Garrity doing the play-by-play.

BAT MASTERSON
Western
FIRST TELECAST: *October 8, 1959*
LAST TELECAST: *September 21, 1961*
BROADCAST HISTORY:
  Oct 1958–Sep 1959, NBC Wed 9:30–10:00
  Oct 1959–Sep 1960, NBC Thu 8:00–8:30
  Sep 1960–Sep 1961, NBC Thu 8:30–9:00
CAST:
  Bat Masterson . . . . Gene Barry

Bat Masterson was a lawman, Indian fighter, scout, and professional gambler. He was also, by Western standards, quite a dandy. With a derby hat, a gold-topped cane, and clothes that were more at home in New York than in Tombstone, Arizona, he did not look like he belonged in the Old West. Preferring to use his wits and his cane to disarm opponents, rather than his gun, Masterson provided quite a contrast to the general run of violent Western heroes. He was a debonair charmer of women and roamed the Southwest romancing the ladies and helping to protect the innocent, especially in situations where they had been wrongly accused of crimes. The real William Bartley "Bat" Masterson may not have been quite as glamorous a personality as Gene Barry's portrayal indicated, but he was quite a character in his own right. The derby, cane, and a specially designed gun were presented to him by the grateful citizens of Dodge City during his tenure as sheriff; he was a close friend of Wyatt Earp, another legendary Western hero; and his exploits created the legend upon which this series was based.

BATMAN

Fantasy Adventure

FIRST TELECAST: *January 12, 1966*
LAST TELECAST: *March 14, 1968*
BROADCAST HISTORY:

> *Jan 1966–Aug 1967,* ABC Wed/Thu 7:30–8:00
> *Sep 1967–Mar 1968,* ABC Thu 7:30–8:00

CAST:

> *Bruce Wayne (Batman)* . . . . Adam West
> *Dick Grayson (Robin)* . . . . Burt Ward
> *Alfred Pennyworth* . . . . Alan Napier
> *Aunt Harriet Cooper* . . . . Madge Blake
> *Police Commissioner Gordon* . Neil Hamilton
> *Chief O'Hara* . . . . Stafford Repp
> *Barbara Gordon (Batgirl) (1967–1968)*
> . . . . Yvonne Craig

MUSICAL THEME:

"Batman," by Neal Hefti

Cartoonist Bob Kane's *Batman* first appeared in comic-book form in *Detective Comics* in 1939 and was featured on radio's *Superman* series and in two movie serials in the 1940s. In January of 1966 it took television by storm. But in slightly over two years it blew itself out. *Batman* was the ultimate "camp" show of the 1960s and was definitely not to be taken seriously, even by those who acted in it. The fight scenes were punctuated by animated "Pows," "Bops," "Bangs," and "Thuds" that flashed on the screen when a blow was struck, obliterating the actors. The situations were incredibly contrived and the acting was intentionally overdone by everyone except Adam West, who was so wooden that he was hilarious.

The general structure of the series was true to Bob Kane's original comics. Bruce Wayne had been orphaned in his teens when his parents were killed by a criminal. Inheriting their fortune, Bruce built a complex crime lab under the Wayne mansion and, as the mysterious Batman, waged war on the evil-doers who plagued Gotham City. His young ward, the orphaned Dick Grayson, joined him; they were known individually as the Caped Crusader and The Boy Wonder, and together as The Dynamic Duo. The only person who knew their real identity was the Wayne family butler, Alfred, who had raised Bruce after his parents' murder. In addition to the underground Batlab (where every device was carefully labeled with its function), they used a marvelously equipped car, the Batmobile, to chase and apprehend criminals. Whenever their services were needed, Police Commissioner Gordon could summon them with the searchlight-like Batsignal or call them on the special Batphone.

Batman was an overnight sensation when it premiered in 1966, airing two-part stories that ran on Wednesday and Thursday. The climax of the first part always left the pair in a dire predicament from which they managed to extricate themselves on the following night. The public's fancy was caught by the silliness, the absurdity, and Robin's horrible puns (attempting to scale a building with

Batman in the first episode, he was heard to say, "Holy fire escape, Batman!"). Both the Wednesday and Thursday episodes ranked among the ten most popular programs of the 1965–1966 season. Appearing as a guest villain on the show became something of a status symbol. Among the more celebrated foes were The Penguin (Burgess Meredith), The Joker (Cesar Romero), The Riddler (Frank Gorshin and, later, John Astin), Egghead (Vincent Price), King Tut (Victor Buono), and the Catwoman (played variously by Julie Newmar, Lee Ann Meriwether, and Eartha Kitt).

By the fall of 1967, however, the novelty had passed and the ratings began to fall. A new role was added, the part of Commissioner Gordon's daughter Barbara, a young librarian who fought crime on her own as Batgirl and who regularly teamed up with Batman and Robin (she had also been in Kane's comics). But it didn't help. Cut back to once a week in the fall of 1967, the surprise hit of 1966 was gone by the following spring.

The Dynamic Duo didn't completely disappear from network television, however. Six months after the ABC prime-time series faded from the air, the animated *Batman-Superman Hour* premiered on CBS's Saturday morning schedule. This first animated version lasted two seasons. Batman and Robin surfaced again on ABC's *Super Friends* in the fall of 1973. From February 1977 to September 1978 CBS aired *The New Adventures of Batman* with Adam West and Burt Ward providing the voices, and *Super Friends* on ABC, despite numerous title changes, remained on the air.

BATTLE OF THE AGES

Talent

FIRST TELECAST: *January 1, 1952*
LAST TELECAST: *November 29, 1952*
BROADCAST HISTORY:

> *Jan 1952–Jun 1952,* DUM Tue 9:00–9:30
> *Sep 1952–Nov 1952,* CBS Sat 10:30–11:00

EMCEE:

> John Reed King (Jan–Jun)
> Morey Amsterdam (Sep–Nov)

Each week *Battle of the Ages* presented two teams of professional performers competing for audience applause. The teams' distinguishing characteristic was the age of the participants. All members of one team had to be over 35 (veterans), and all members of the other team under 35 (youngsters). When the older team won the sponsor made a donation to the Actors Fund of America, and when the younger team won a similar donation was made to the Scholarship Fund of the Professional Children's School.

BATTLE REPORT

Documentary/Public Affairs

FIRST TELECAST: *August 13, 1950*
LAST TELECAST: *August 31, 1951*

BROADCAST HISTORY:
Aug 1950–Sep 1950, NBC Sun 8:00–8:30
Jun 1951–Aug 1951, NBC Fri 9:30–10:00
HOST:
Robert McCormick

This weekly documentary program on the United States' involvement in the Korean War used filmed interviews and reports from both the home front and battle front. Although produced by NBC News, it was virtually an official government presentation, with regular weekly commentary by Dr. John Steelman, assistant to President Truman, and reports from many high-ranking officials. The series was telecast on Sunday afternoon during most of its 1950–1952 run, but moved to prime time during the periods shown above.

BATTLESTAR GALACTICA
Science Fiction
FIRST TELECAST: *September 17, 1978*
LAST TELECAST: *August 17, 1980*
BROADCAST HISTORY:
Sep 1978–Apr 1979, ABC Sun 8:00–9:00
Jun 1979–Aug 1979, ABC Sat 8:00–9:00
Jan 1980–Aug 1980, ABC Sun 7:00–8:00
CAST:
Commander Adama . . . . Lorne Greene
Capt. Apollo (1978–1979) . . . . . . Richard Hatch
Lt. Starbuck (1978–1979) . . . . Dirk Benedict
Lt. Boomer (1978–1979) . . . . Herb Jefferson, Jr.
Athena (1978–1979) . . . . Maren Jensen
Flight Sgt. Jolly (1978–1979) . . . . . Tony Swartz
Boxey (1978–1979) . . . . Noah Hathaway
Col. Tigh (1978–1979) . . . . Terry Carter
Cassiopea (1978–1979) . . . . Laurette Spang
Count Baltar (1978–1979) . . . . John Colicos
Sheba (1979) . . . . Anne Lockhart
Capt. Troy (1980) . . . . Kent McCord
Lt. Dillon (1980) . . . . Barry Van Dyke
Jamie Hamilton (1980) . . . . Robyn Douglass
Dr. Zee (1980) . . . . Robbie Risk
Dr. Zee (1980) . . . . Patrick Stuart
Col. Sydell (1980) . . . . Allan Miller
Xavier (1980) . . . . Richard Lynch
SPECIAL EFFECTS:
John Dykstra
MUSIC:
The Los Angeles Philharmonic Orchestra

Battlestar Galactica was the most highly publicized new series of the fall 1978 schedule. Reported to have cost one million dollars per hour to produce—the highest budget ever for a regular series—it used spectacular special effects to depict a mighty life and death struggle between the forces of good and evil in outer space, thousands of years in the future. Lasers flashed, majestic spaceships lumbered through deep space, and dashing, caped heroes fought half-human, half-robot villains for no less than the survival of mankind.

If this sounds like a copy of the movie *Star Wars*, it was. *Battlestar Galactica* was such a literal imitation of *Star Wars* that the producers of the movie sued ABC for "stealing" their film. Part of the similarity lay in the special effects, such as laser battles and closeups of the spacecraft, which were created by John Dykstra, the same man who worked on *Star Wars*.

The setting was the seventh millennium, A.D. Galactica was the only surviving battlestar after a surprise attack by the evil Cylons, aided by the treacherous Count Baltar, had shattered the interplanetary peace and wiped out most of humankind. Now the Cylons were pursuing Galactica and her attendant fleet of 220 smaller spacecraft as they sped through space toward a last refuge, a distant, unknown planet called Earth.

Commanding the mile-wide Galactica was the stoic, silver-haired Adama. His son Apollo led Galactica's fighter squadron (another son was killed off by the Cylons in the premiere). Starbuck was his ace pilot, as well as a smooth-talking con artist and ladies' man. Muffit was the mechanical canine daggit. Many other characters came and went from the large cast, including the singing Android Sisters, who entertained with two sets of mouths apiece, in a surrealistic outer-space bar peopled by oddly shaped creatures from other civilizations (remember *that* scene in *Star Wars?*).

Despite the hype, the audience for *Galactica* declined sharply, until eventually only the kids were left watching. It left the air after a single season, then returned in early 1980 retitled *Galactica 1980*.

This new series of films was set 30 years later, and only Lorne Greene remained from the original regular cast. Galactica had finally reached Earth, only to find that the Cylons were planning to destroy that, too. Capt. Troy (Boxey as an adult) and Lt. Dillon were sent to the planet's surface, incognito, to enlist the aid of California's high-powered Pacific Institute of Technology in preparing Earth for the forthcoming battle. Novice TV newswoman Jamie Hamilton of United Broadcasting latched on to them, and, sensing a big story, insisted that she accompany them when they were called back to the mother ship. Also in the revamped cast were Dr. Zee, a 14-year-old boy genius, and Xavier, a renegade member of Galactica's 12-man ruling council.

BAXTERS, THE
Situation Comedy/Audience Participation
BROADCAST HISTORY:
Syndicated only
30 minutes
Produced: *1979–1981*
Released: *September 1979*
CAST (1979–1980):
Fred Baxter . . . . Larry Keith
Nancy Baxter . . . . Anita Gillette
Naomi Baxter (19) . . . . Derin Altay
Jonah Baxter (14) . . . . Chris Petersen
Rachael Baxter (10) . . . . Terri Lynn Wood

CAST (1980–1981)

Jim Baxter	Sean McCann
Susan Baxter	Terry Tweed
Allison Baxter (19)	Marianne McIsaac
Gregg Baxter (14)	Sammy Snyders
Lucy Baxter (10)	Megan Follows

Surely one of the most unusual programs telecast nationally in the U.S. in recent years, this comedy gave viewers the chance to do "instant analysis" of a program they'd just seen, and to do it on the air. The format consisted of an 11-minute vignette about the Baxters, a middle-class family living in a suburb of St. Louis, as they faced a controversial issue. In one episode they had to decide whether to commit Mother Baxter to a nursing home; in another, whether the fact that Jonah's teacher was a homosexual would harm their son; in another, Fred faced a dilemma over whether to turn a small, money-losing apartment house he owned into condominiums, thus forcing out some of the tenants.

This short episode was played as a situation comedy, but it always ended with several options open. A studio audience assembled at the local station where the program was being carried, then discussed what *they* thought should be done. In some cities, viewers could call in and voice their reactions.

In the vignettes, Fred Baxter was an insurance salesman and Mary a housewife. Naomi (adopted) was their college-aged daughter, and Jonah and Rachael the youngsters. The discussion moderator in the second segment was, of course, different in each city.

Despite its good intentions, *The Baxters* came across as rather heavy-handed, and never reached a very large audience. The program had begun as a local production at WCVB-TV, Boston, in early 1977, where it had been created by an ex-divinity student named Hubert Jessup as part of his Sunday morning public-affairs show. Jessup persuaded station management to try it in the early evening, and to everyone's surprise it attracted a loyal, if not large, cult following. Producer Norman Lear happened to find out about it, offered to produce the program in Hollywood, and put it into nationwide syndication for the 1979–1980 season—a move that, because of Lear's many past hits, attracted wide attention. High costs and a generally disappointing reception caused Lear to withdraw after a year, and for the 1980–1981 season the program reverted to its Boston originators, who syndicated it themselves. The 1980-1981 episodes were produced in Toronto with an all-new cast, and even new first names for the Baxters. Mr. Baxter became a schoolteacher and Mrs. Baxter returned to work, but otherwise the format was essentially the same.

BAY CITY BLUES, THE

Drama

FIRST TELECAST: *October 25, 1983*

LAST TELECAST: *November 15, 1983*

BROADCAST HISTORY:

Oct 1983–Nov 1983, NBC Tue 10:00–11:00

CAST:

Joe Rohner	Michael Nouri
Sunny Hayward	Kelly Harmon
Ray Holtz	Pat Corley
Ozzie Peoples	Bernie Casey
Frenchy Nuckles	Perry Lang
Terry St. Marie	Patrick Cassidy
Angelo Carbone	Dennis Franz
Lynwood Scott	Larry Flash Jenkins
Judy Nuckles	Michele Greene
Rocky Padillo	Ken Olin
Lee Jacoby	Tony Spiridakis
Deejay Cunningham	Mykel T. Williamson
Vic Kresky	Jeff McCracken
Mitch Klein	Peter Jurasik
Cathy St. Marie	Sharon Stone
Lynn Holtz	Sheree North
Bird	Marco Rodriguez
Mickey Wagner	Barry Tubb

The private and public lives of the members of a minor-league baseball team provided the focus for this highly touted but short-lived series. The working-class town of Bay City, California, was the setting, and the Bluebirds were the local pro baseball team. Practically everyone on the team wanted to get out of Bay City and into the majors, including manager Joe Rohner, who meanwhile did his best to nurture the promising young players and deal with the frustrations of the older has-beens and never-weres who were also on the team. Ray Holtz was the Bluebirds' slippery owner, who also ran a local used car lot; Ozzie Peoples and Angelo Carbone were two coaches; Mitch Klein was the team's motor-mouth announcer; and Bird, the colorful mascot, who paraded around the stands decked out as "The Bluebird of Happiness."

There was a lot of sex in this series, including Joe's clandestine affair with Sunny, the wife of a local banker. There were personal problems galore, among them the hotshot young pitcher's secret agony—he regularly wet his bed. *Bay City Blues* was produced by the people responsible for *Hill Street Blues*, and attempted the same gritty realism, but succeeded mostly in being depressing and so had a short run.

BE OUR GUEST

Musical Variety

FIRST TELECAST: *January 27, 1960*

LAST TELECAST: *June 1, 1960*

BROADCAST HISTORY:

Jan 1960–Jun 1960, CBS Wed 7:30–8:30

HOST:

George De Witt (Jan–Mar)

Keefe Brasselle (Mar–Jun)

REGULARS:

Mary Ann Mobley

Ray McKinley and the Glenn Miller Orchestra

A number of performers, some well known and some not, some professional and some amateur, some very young and others very old, were invited each week to *Be Our Guest* and participate in this informal musical variety program. George De Witt was the original host, replaced by Keefe Brasselle on March 16; Mary Ann Mobley (a former Miss America) was the featured singer.

BEACON HILL
Drama
FIRST TELECAST: *August 25, 1975*
LAST TELECAST: *November 4, 1975*
BROADCAST HISTORY:
Aug 1975, CBS Mon 9:00–11:00
Sep 1975–Nov 1975, CBS Tue 10:00–11:00
CAST:
Trevor Bullock.................. Roy Cooper
Robert Lassiter .... David Dukes
Benjamin Lassiter............ Stephen Elliott
Richard Palmer.......... Edward Herrmann
Mary Lassiter .... Nancy Marchand
Maude Palmer.............. Maeve McGuire
Emily Bullock .... Deann Mears
Giorgio Bellonci .... Michael Nouri
Betsy Bullock.................... Linda Purl
Mr. Hacker.................... George Rose
Terence O'Hara .... David Rounds
Brian Mallory .... Paul Rudd
Harry Emmet.................. Barry Snider
Mrs. Hacker............... Beatrice Straight
Eleanor .... Sydney Swire
Marilyn Gardiner.......... Holland Taylor
Fawn Lassiter .... Kathryn Walker
William Piper .... Richard Ward
Rosamond Lassiter............. Kitty Winn

Hoping to capitalize on the success that public television had had with the British import *Upstairs, Downstairs,* CBS launched this lavish, period soap opera in prime time in the fall of 1975. *Beacon Hill* was set in Boston in the early 1920s. The various continuing storylines revolved around the lives of the wealthy Lassiter family and the members of their household staff, led by Mr. Hacker, the Lassiters' head butler. The cast was huge, the sets and production values the best, and a special two-hour advance premiere on August 2 received top ratings. But after that the audience shrank steadily with each succeeding episode. CBS, which had hoped to parlay a successful British program into a new trend in American television (as it had done with *All in the Family*), was forced to cancel the program after only 13 episodes.

BEANY & CECIL
see *Matty's Funday Funnies*

BEARCATS
Adventure
FIRST TELECAST: *September 16, 1971*
LAST TELECAST: *December 30, 1971*

BROADCAST HISTORY:
Sep 1971–Dec 1971, CBS Thu 8:00–9:00
CAST:
Hank Brackett.................. Rod Taylor
Johnny Reach................. Dennis Cole

Set in the American Southwest around 1914, *Bearcats* was the story of two adventurers who traveled around looking for lucrative, difficult, and dangerous assignments. Their mode of transportation was a fancy Stutz Bearcat. Rather than charge a fee for taking on an assignment, they requested a blank check from each of their clients. After completing the job they filled in the amount according to what they felt their services were worth. In one episode they were hired to find out who was setting fire to oil wells in a small border town; in another, their task was to stop mercenaries from sabotaging medical supplies that were being shipped overseas to the Allies during World War I.

BEAT THE CLOCK
Quiz/Audience Participation
FIRST TELECAST: *March 23, 1950*
LAST TELECAST: *February 16, 1958*
BROADCAST HISTORY:
Mar 1950, CBS Thu 9:45–10:30
Apr 1950–Sep 1950, CBS Sat 8:00–9:00
Sep 1950–Mar 1951, CBS Fri 10:30–11:00
Mar 1951–Sep 1956, CBS Sat 7:30–8:00
Sep 1956–Feb 1957, CBS Sat 7:00–7:30
Feb 1957–Sep 1957, CBS Fri 7:30–8:00
Oct 1957–Feb 1958, CBS Sun 6:00–6:30
EMCEE:
Bud Collyer
ASSISTANT:
Roxanne (1950–1955)
Beverly Bentley (1955–1958)
PRODUCERS:
Mark Goodson and Bill Todman

This durable game show started on CBS radio in 1949 with Bud Collyer as emcee and moved to television in March 1950. The format was certainly simple. Contestants were chosen from the studio audience and attempted to perform various stunts within a given time limit (in most cases 60 seconds or less), depending on the difficulty of the stunt. Prizes were awarded for succeeding within the time limit, and occasionally there was a bonus if the contestant completed it faster than that. A large clock ticked off the seconds so that the audience and contestants could see how much time was left.

What made *Beat the Clock* a hit were the stunts themselves, which were full of whipped cream, custard pies, and exploding balloons, always frantic yet always ingenious. Most of them were dreamed up by production staffers Frank Wayne and Bob Howard, who maintained "a stunt factory" where each feat was tried out before the show to make sure that it wasn't either too hard or too easy. Unemployed actors were used for the testing (including a young unknown named James Dean, who was described as so well-coordinated he could do *anything* the producers dreamed up). The stunts were so popular that the sponsor even issued a book of them.

A typical stunt had a contestant put on an over-size set of long underwear, then try to stuff 12 inflated balloons into it without breaking any, all in 45 seconds. Another presented the contestant with a fishing pole and line, with a frankfurter tied at the end. He would then have to lower the frank-furter onto a series of mousetraps and try to spring a total of six of them in 40 seconds. His teammate would release the frankfurter from each trap after it sprang. Yet a third stunt, one that was pretty messy, involved three marshmallows and a bowl of Jell-O. The marshmallows were buried deep in the bowl and the contestant had to dig out two of them with a spoon held in his mouth, and deposit them carefully on the table next to the bowl. If a marshmallow fell off the spoon it was reburied in the gelatin (time limit: 35 seconds). Some stunts were even messier. One interesting statistic quoted in 1955 was that, up to that point, approximately 1,100 gallons of whipped cream had been squirted into the faces of hapless contestants on the program, an average of three and a half gallons per week.

Before the advent of the big-money quiz shows in 1955, the prizes on *Beat the Clock* had always been secondary to the game. Even the "bonus stunt," which was harder than most, had rarely been worth more than $100. By 1956, however, with competition from NBC's *The Big Surprise,* the ante for successfully completing the "bonus stunt" had gone up considerably, starting at $5,000 and rising by $1,000 for every attempt until some-body finally managed to complete it successfully. In September 1956 one winning couple took home $64,000, by far the biggest prize ever given on the show.

Bud Collyer's original assistant and the show's official photographer, who snapped photos of con-testants amid the debris after their stunts, was a shapely blonde named Roxanne (real name: Dolores Rosedale). She became a celebrity in her own right, often appearing in magazine articles about beauty or fashion and making personal ap-pearance tours with her boss. At one time there were rumors that her celebrity status did not en-dear her to Collyer, who was, after all, supposed to be the star of the show. In August 1955 she left the show on maternity leave and was replaced by Beverly Bentley.

Bud Collyer also hosted the network daytime version of *Beat the Clock,* which ran on CBS from September 1957 to September 1958 and on ABC from October 1958 to January 1961. A syndicated version was in production from 1969 to 1975, with Jack Narz emceeing for the first three years and Gene Wood, who had been the announcer for Narz, taking over as emcee for the last three. *Beat*

the Clock returned briefly to CBS' weekday day-time lineup in the fall of 1979. Monty Hall hosted this last version, which ran from September to February.

BEAUTIFUL PHYLLIS DILLER SHOW, THE
Comedy Variety
FIRST TELECAST: *September 15, 1968*
LAST TELECAST: *December 22, 1968*
BROADCAST HISTORY:
Sep 1968–Dec 1968, NBC Sun 10:00–11:00
REGULARS:
Phyllis Diller
Norm Crosby
Rip Taylor
Dave Willock
Bob Jellison
Merryl Joy
The Curtain Calls
The Jack Regas Dancers
The Jack Elliott Orchestra

This comedy variety hour had as its star the come-dienne Phyllis Diller, known for her fright-wig hair and rasping cackle; the supporting performers were comics Norm Crosby and Rip Taylor, guest stars, and the Curtain Calls, a song-and-dance group. Each week's show featured a big produc-tion-number "salute" to a famous person, ranging from Ponce de León to Luther Burbank to P.T. Barnum—all classified, at least as far as Phyllis was concerned, as forgotten Americans.

BEAUTY AND THE BEAST
Fantasy/Drama
FIRST TELECAST: *September 25, 1987*
LAST TELECAST:
BROADCAST HISTORY:
Sep 1987, CBS Fri 10:00–11:00
Oct 1987– , CBS Fri 8:00–9:00
CAST:
Asst. D.A. Catherine Chandler
 .... Linda Hamilton
Vincent .... Ron Perlman
Father .... Roy Dotrice
Deputy D.A. Joe Maxwell....... Jay Acavone
Edie .... Ren Woods
Kipper (pilot only) .... Jason Allen
Kipper .... Cory Danziger
Mouse (1988–) .... David Greenlee

New York City was the setting for this unusual romantic fantasy. Catherine was a young attorney who had been attacked by criminals and left to die in Central Park. It was there that she was found by Vincent, a powerful but sensitive man-beast with the facial features of a lion, who lived in a strange, serene world of caverns and tunnels deep beneath Manhattan Island. He took her to this underground tunnel world to nurse her back to health. Although she returned to the surface world after her recovery, Catherine and Vincent had fallen in love—despite his beastly appearance, the vast differences in their worlds, and their lack of physical contact—and they developed a strong psychic bond. He could sense when she was in danger and always reached her before she could be hurt, sometimes riding on the tops of subway cars (so he wouldn't be seen in public). Her new job, working in the D.A.'s office under Joe Maxwell, seemed to put her in jeopardy regularly.

Edie was Catherine's researcher, Father the brilliant recluse who had raised Vincent from infancy and was the nominal leader of the "Tunnel World" people, and Kipper and Mouse two of its other residents who often ran errands for Father.

BEHIND CLOSED DOORS
Spy Drama
FIRST TELECAST: *October 2, 1958*
LAST TELECAST: *April 9, 1959*
BROADCAST HISTORY:
    Oct 1958–Apr 1959, NBC Thu 9:00–9:30
CAST:
    Commander Matson........... Bruce Gordon

Incidents of American counterespionage were dramatized in this series based on the files of Rear Admiral Ellis M. Zacharias, USN (Ret.), who had spent 25 years in naval intelligence. The stories were connected with the cold war, which required updating and relocating the real-life incidents supplied by Adm. Zacharias, who served as technical consultant for the series. Commander Matson was the program host and was occasionally featured in the stories themselves.

BEHIND THE NEWS WITH HOWARD K. SMITH
News Analysis
FIRST TELECAST: *April 12, 1959*
LAST TELECAST: *September 20, 1959*
BROADCAST HISTORY:
    Apr 1959–Jun 1959, CBS Sun 6:00–6:30
    Sep 1959, CBS Sun 6:00–6:30
HOST:
    Howard K. Smith

The purpose of this series was to take the most significant news story of the previous week and do an in-depth analysis of its background, significance, and consequences. CBS News Washington correspondent Howard K. Smith served as analyst, host, moderator, or discussion leader, depending on the way in which the story was prsented. Film coverage, interviews, and roundtable discussions were all used at one time or another. The program was originally seen on Sunday afternoons, beginning in January 1959.

BEHIND THE SCREEN
Drama
FIRST TELECAST: *October 9, 1981*
LAST TELECAST: *January 8, 1982*
BROADCAST HISTORY:
    Oct 1981–Jan 1982, CBS Fri 11:30–12:05 A.M.

CAST:
    Evan Hammer .... Mel Ferrer
    Zina Willow .... Joanne Linville
    Gerry Holmby .... Joshua Bryant
    Dory Ranfield Holmby .... Loyita Chapel
    Bobby Danzig .... Bruce Fairbairn
    Lynette Porter .... Debbi Morgan
    Sally Dundee .... Catherine Parks
    Brian Holmby .... Michael Sabatino
    Janie-Claire Willow .... Janine Turner
    Jeanne .... Momo Yashima
    Karl Madison.................. Mark Pinter
    Tony, the Director .... Terry Alexander
    Joyce.......................... Erica Yohn
    Jordan Willow............... Scott Mulhern
    Merritt Madison .... Warren Stevens
    Angela Aries .... Claudette Nevins

The behind-the-scenes activities and manipulations of people involved with a successful daytime soap opera provided the focus of this short-lived late-night soap opera. Gerry Holmby was the creator/producer of the daytime drama *Generations*. His wife Dory was a screenwriter, and Brian, his son by a former wife, was one of *Generations'* actors. Brian's girlfriend, on and off the soap opera, was Janie-Claire Willow. Writer Jordan Willow was Janie-Claire's brother, and Zina their invalid mother. Brian's former girlfriend Sally Dundee was an actress sharing an apartment with another young actress, Lynette Porter. Unscrupulous Evan Hammer served as personal manager to both Janie-Claire and Lynette. Evil Merritt Madison was the overbearing head of a major movie studio and the father of Dory's former lover, Karl. And on, and on, and on . . .

BELIEVE IT OR NOT
    see *Ripley's Believe It Or Not*

BELL AND HOWELL CLOSEUP
Documentary
FIRST TELECAST: *November 14, 1961*
LAST TELECAST: *June 4, 1963*
BROADCAST HISTORY:
    Nov 1961–Dec 1961, ABC Tue 10:30–11:00
    Oct 1962–Dec 1962, ABC Tue 10:30–11:00
    Apr 1963–Jun 1963, ABC Tue 10:30–11:00

This series of documentaries, produced by ABC News, covered subjects ranging from international politics to a day in the life of a concert pianist. It began on an occasional basis in September 1960 and was seen in sporadic regular runs from 1961–1963.

BELL SUMMER THEATRE
    see *Bell Telephone Hour, The*

BELL TELEPHONE HOUR, THE
Music
FIRST TELECAST: *October 9, 1959*
LAST TELECAST: *April 26, 1968*

BROADCAST HISTORY:

Oct 1959–Apr 1960, NBC Fri 8:30–9:30
Sep 1960–Apr 1961, NBC Fri 9:00–10:00
Sep 1961–Apr 1962, NBC Fri 9:30–10:30
Oct 1963–May 1965, NBC Tue 10:00–11:00
Sep 1965–Apr 1967, NBC Sun 6:30–7:30 (OS)
Sep 1967–Apr 1968, NBC Fri 10:00–11:00

FEATURING:

The Bell Telephone Orchestra conducted by
Donald Voorhees

EXECUTIVE PRODUCER:

Barry Wood (1959–1967)
Henry Jaffe (1967–1968)

THEME:

"The Bell Waltz," by Donald Voorhees

For nearly a decade *The Bell Telephone Hour*
provided a prestigious television showcase for
fine music, always presented with elegance and
style. The music ranged across the spectrum from
popular to jazz to classical, performed by the top
names among established Broadway, Hollywood,
and recording stars (no rock 'n' roll here). A different host presided over each telecast. The featured performers appearing over the years included Benny Goodman, Mahalia Jackson, Carol
Lawrence, Paul Whiteman (conducting "Rhapsody in Blue"), Marge and Gower Champion, the
Kingston Trio, Ray Bolger, Richard Tucker, and
Bing Crosby.

Among the classical highlights were the American TV debuts of ballet dancer Rudolf Nureyev in
January 1961 (he was a last-minute substitute for
the injured Erik Bruhn), Joan Sutherland in March
1961, and pianists Albert Casadesus in February
1964 and Clifford Curzon in April 1965.

Just as the performers tended to be standard
adult favorites, so did the music. *The Bell Telephone Hour*, though certainly classy, was not
overly adventuresome. During the first few seasons, popular and show music predominated,
though there was usually a classical spot in each
telecast. Programs were built around tributes to
popular composers such as Gershwin, Berlin, and
Porter, or around holiday themes or topics such as
small-town shindigs. In 1966 a new format was
introduced—that of filmed musical documentaries, generally of great performers—and the emphasis was shifted to more classical music.
Among the subjects were Van Cliburn, Pablo Cas-
als, Zubin Mehta, Arturo Toscanini, Duke Ellington, and even George Plimpton (in his brief career
as a percussionist with the New York Symphony
Orchestra).

The Bell Telephone Hour had been a radio
standby for 19 years when it moved to television
in 1959, first as a series of specials in the spring
and then as a regular alternate weekly series in
the fall. Bell had previously sponsored a series of
science specials and for a time these alternated
with the music hour. Later, news and other programs ran on the alternate weeks; *Bell* continued
as a biweekly or monthly series throughout its

television history. During the summer of 1964 the
program featured some newer talent and was subtitled *The Bell Summer Theatre*.

Conductor Donald Voorhees, who was associated with the program throughout its radio
and TV history, was also the composer of its lilt-
ing theme, "The Bell Waltz."

BEN CASEY

Medical Drama

FIRST TELECAST: *October 2, 1961*
LAST TELECAST: *March 21, 1966*
BROADCAST HISTORY:

Oct 1961–Sep 1963, ABC Mon 10:00–11:00
Sep 1963–Sep 1964, ABC Wed 9:00–10:00
Sep 1964–Mar 1966, ABC Mon 10:00–11:00

CAST:

Dr. Ben Casey .... Vince Edwards
Dr. David Zorba (1961–1965) .... Sam Jaffe
Dr. Maggie Graham .... Bettye Ackerman
Dr. Ted Hoffman .... Harry Landers
Nick Kanavaras .... Nick Dennis
Nurse Wills .... Jeanne Bates
Jane Hancock (1965) .... Stella Stevens
Dr. Mike Rogers (1965) .... Ben Piazza
Dr. Daniel Niles Freeland (1965–1966)
.... Franchot Tone
Dr. Terry McDaniel (1965–1966)
.... Jim McMullan
Sally Welden (1965–1966) ..... Marlyn Mason

One of the great medical dramas in television history, *Ben Casey* premiered in October 1961 and
quickly became the most popular program on the
ABC network. Much of its success was due to its
lead, the handsome, virile Vince Edwards, who
was discovered by Bing Crosby (the show was
produced by Crosby's production company).
Casey's original mentor, in the Kildare-Gillespie
tradition, was Dr. David Zorba, who guided the
gifted young resident surgeon in his battles with
disease and the medical establishment. *Ben
Casey* frequently tackled controversial subjects
and exuded a feeling of realism and tension,
which was emphasized by extreme closeup shots
in moments of crisis. A *Time* review noted that it
"accurately captures the feeling of sleepless intensity in a metropolitan hospital."

Some important changes took place at County
General Hospital at the beginning of the 1965–
1966 season. Dr. Zorba departed and was replaced as Chief of Surgery by Dr. Daniel Freeland.
A greater thread of continuity from week to week
was introduced, including some "cliff-hangers,"
and Casey was even allowed a brief love affair
with Jane Hancock, a beautiful young woman
who had just awakened from a 13-year coma. This
was established in a five-part story early in the
season, which involved a romantic triangle between Casey, Hancock, and the young intern
Mike Rogers. (There had always been a hint of
love between Casey and Dr. Maggie Graham, but
it was not openly stated.) There was also a stormy

71

romance between the new doctor Terry McDaniel and a disturbed patient, Sally Welden. The role of the orderly Nick Kanavaras was downplayed, although quiet, likable Dr. Ted Hoffman and Nurse Wills remained.

Ben Casey was produced by James Moser, who also created *Medic.* Reruns were aired on ABC's weekday daytime lineup from September 1965 to March 1967.

BEN GRAUER SHOW, THE
Talk
FIRST TELECAST: *January 3, 1950*
LAST TELECAST: *June 27, 1950*
BROADCAST HISTORY:
   Jan 1950–Jun 1950, NBC Tue 11:00–11:15
HOST:
   John Gnagy (Jan)
   Warren Hull (Jan–Feb)
   Ben Grauer (Feb–Jun)

This show was nothing more than an extended commercial for its sponsor, the book publishers Doubleday and Company. It started as a local program in New York, with John Gnagy as the host and the title *You Are an Artist,* the same title as Gnagy's previous art-instruction program on NBC. In this case, since Doubleday had published Gnagy's new book, the emphasis was on convincing the viewing audience to run out and buy it to help them learn to draw. The show started in October of 1949 and went network at the start of the new year.

At the end of January, Warren Hull took over, with the title changed to *The Warren Hull Show.* Hull had no book to plug but, instead, chatted each week about a new book (offered by Doubleday) and then interviewed the author. Hull left the show after a month and was replaced by Ben Grauer. Again the title was changed, to identify the host, but the format remained the same. Grauer would interview authors about their new books, and there were plugs for both the books themselves and the various Doubleday book clubs—such as the Doubleday Dollar Book Club and the Mystery Guild—through which they could be obtained at discount.

BEN VEREEN . . . COMIN' AT YA
Musical Variety
FIRST TELECAST: *August 7, 1975*
LAST TELECAST: *August 28, 1975*
BROADCAST HISTORY:
   Aug 1975, NBC Thu 8:00–9:00
HOST:
   Ben Vereen
REGULARS:
   Lola Falana
   Liz Torres
   Avery Schreiber
   Arte Johnson
   Lee Lund
   The Jack Elliott and Allyn Ferguson Orchestra

This was a summer musical variety hour hosted by the versatile black actor/singer Ben Vereen.

BENNY HILL SHOW, THE
Comedy
BROADCAST HISTORY:
   Syndicated only
   30 minutes
   Produced (U.K.): *1969–*
   Released (U.S.): *January 1979*
REGULARS:
   Benny Hill
   Henry McGee
   Bob Todd
   Jackie Wright
   Nicholas Parsons

A pudgy comedian named Benny Hill, who had been convulsing British TV audiences for a decade, suddenly became a cult hit on American screens in 1979. The shows were all edited versions of his British programs, but the humor was universal. Sly, lecherous, and good at slapstick, knock-about comedy, Benny appeared in several skits per show, in roles ranging from a passenger on a Cunard liner in the 1930s to an astronaut about to blast off with a bevy of beautiful "helpers." In fact, leggy girls in skimpy outfits abounded in the sketches, as in Benny as a shepherd with three naughty shepherdesses, or Benny as a nervous bridegroom. Stock characters included Capt. Fred Scuttle, Prof. Marvel, and the Firemen's Choir. In the supporting cast, along with the girls, were Jackie Wright (the little bald guy) and Henry McGee (the straight man/announcer).

With all the mugging and sight gags, Benny, at times, resembled a slightly blue version of Red Skelton, on occasion even using Skelton's sincere closing, "Good night, God bless." Benny Hill specials continue to be produced in Britain, so there's more to come.

BENNY RUBIN SHOW, THE
Comedy/Variety
FIRST TELECAST: *April 29, 1949*
LAST TELECAST: *June 24, 1949*
BROADCAST HISTORY:
   Apr 1949–Jun 1949, NBC Fri 9:00–9:30
HOST:
   Benny Rubin
REGULARS:
   Vinnie Monte
   Mady Sullivan
   Charlie Ford, the organist
   The Creators
   The Rex Maupin Orchestra

In this comedy variety program, a succession of singers, dancers, and comedians visited Benny Rubin's Theatrical Agency to show him their latest routines. Vinnie Monte played the young office boy at the agency and Mady Sullivan served as Benny's secretary.

BENSON

Situation Comedy

FIRST TELECAST: *September 13, 1979*
LAST TELECAST: *August 30, 1986*
BROADCAST HISTORY:

Sep 1979–Jul 1980, ABC Thu 8:30–9:00
Aug 1980–Mar 1983, ABC Fri 8:00–8:30
Mar 1983–Apr 1983, ABC Thu 8:00–8:30
May 1983–Mar 1985, ABC Fri 8:00–8:30
Mar 1985–Sep 1985, ABC Fri 9:00–9:30
Oct 1985–Jan 1986, ABC Fri 9:30–10:00
Jan 1986–Aug 1986, ABC Sat 8:30–9:00

CAST:

Benson DuBois .... Robert Guillaume
Governor James Gatling .... James Noble
Katie Gatling .... Missy Gold
Gretchen Kraus .... Inga Swenson
Marcy Hill (1979–1981)
.... Caroline McWilliams
John Taylor (1979–1980) .... Lewis J. Stadlen
Clayton Endicott III (1980–1986)
.... René Auberjonois
Pete Downey (1980–1985) ...... Ethan Phillips
Frankie (1980–1981) .... Jerry Steinfeld
Denise Stevens Downey (1981–1985)
.... Didi Conn
Mrs. Cassidy (1984–1986) .... Billie Bird
Sen. Diane Hartford (1985–1986)
.... Donna LaBrie

In this spin-off from *Soap*, Benson the black butler—the only sane member of the Tate household—was sent by Jessica Tate to help her widowed cousin, Gov. James Gatling. Benson found himself moved from one loony bin to another.

Gov. Gatling was a sweet, well-meaning man, but terribly naive; Katie, his precocious daughter; Gretchen, the formidable German housekeeper; and Marcy, his secretary (married in a February 1981 episode). Benson, though theoretically only in charge of the governor's household, kept order around the executive mansion, did constant battle with Gretchen, helped raise little Katie, and generally assisted the meek governor in deciding what to do, both politically and personally. Of less help to the chief executive were his political aide Taylor (replaced by Clayton), bumbling press assistant Pete, and messenger boy Frankie.

In 1981 Benson was appointed state budget director, giving him added responsibilities as well as his own secretary, Denise (who later married Pete). The promotion came just in time for Benson to help the governor in his campaign for a second term, which fortunately for the series he won, as an Independent—after his party dumped him. Benson's former employer, Jessica Tate, showed up in ghostly form in 1983 to remind him how far he had progressed. Benson's remarkable rise continued. In 1984 he was elected Lieutenant Governor, and in 1986—in the series' final original episodes—he ran against his mentor Gov. Gatling for the governorship itself, with his new fiancée

Diane serving as his campaign manager. The bitter campaign strained the two men's friendship, but in the end they reconciled, reminisced, and settled in to watch the election results together. In true TV cliffhanger tradition, the outcome was not revealed, so viewers never did find out who won. However one thing was clear—Benson the insolent butler had come a long way.

ABC aired reruns of *Benson* on weekday mornings from September 1983–June 1984.

BERRENGER'S

Drama

FIRST TELECAST: *January 5, 1985*
LAST TELECAST: *March 9, 1985*
BROADCAST HISTORY:

Jan 1985–Mar 1985, NBC Sat 10:00–11:00

CAST:

Billy Berrenger .... Robin Strand
Paul Berrenger .... Ben Murphy
Simon Berrenger .... Sam Wanamaker
Shane Bradley .... Yvette Mimieux
Babs Berrenger .... Anita Morris
Stacey Russell .... Jonelle Allen
Laurel Hayes .... Laura Ashton
Melody Hughes .... Claudia Christian
John Higgins................... Jeff Conaway
Todd Hughes .... Art Hindle
Cammie Springer .... Leslie Hope
Nick Morrison .... Steve Kahan
Gloria Berrenger......... Andrea Marcovicci
Danny Krucek .... Jack Scalia
Julio Morales .... Eddie Velez
Connie Morales............. Connie Ramirez
Mami Morales............... Alma Beltran
Ana Morales .... Jeannie Linero
Max Kaufman .... Alan Feinstein
Mr. Allen............... Michael David Lally
Frank Chapman........... Richard Sanders
Allison Harris .... Donna Dixon

This short-lived nighttime soap opera attempted to find sex and scandal at a fancy New York department store, but instead went out of business in two months. Sam Wanamaker portrayed ruthless Simon Berrenger, the head of the high-class store that bore his name (why didn't they call it Wanamaker's?). His two sons were both working in the business—Paul, the president of Berrenger's, who was trapped in a loveless marriage to his wife Gloria and was carrying on an affair with Shane Bradley, the chain's merchandise v.p.; and Billy, in charge of P.R., who was fighting a losing battle with booze and gambling. Simon's daughter, Babs, was a divorcée who had spent her entire life trying to win her father's love and respect. Babs' daughter, Melody, was married to ambitious Todd Hughes, who ran Berrenger's only branch store. They, and the others on the payroll of Berrenger's, were all involved in the licit and illicit affairs, power stuggles, and assorted other intrigues that were the staple of all serial dramas. Telecast so briefly, however, *Berrenger's* never

73

had the opportunity to become as convoluted as its more successful brethren.

BERT D'ANGELO/SUPERSTAR
Police Drama
FIRST TELECAST: *February 21, 1976*
LAST TELECAST: *July 10, 1976*
BROADCAST HISTORY:
Feb 1976–Jul 1976, ABC Sat 10:00–11:00
CAST:
Sgt. Bert D'Angelo .... Paul Sorvino
Inspector Larry Johnson .... Robert Pine
Capt. Jack Breen .... Dennis Patrick
EXECUTIVE PRODUCER:
Quinn Martin

The superstar in this case was a TV cop, this one a 10-year veteran of the New York City force who had transferred to new turf—San Francisco. Tough, direct, and often in trouble with his superiors, D'Angelo handled cases that cut across departmental lines, including homicides, narcotics, and robberies. He found lots of action but not much audience, and was canceled after half a season.

BEST IN MYSTERY, THE
Dramatic Anthology
FIRST TELECAST: *July 16, 1954*
LAST TELECAST: *August 31, 1956*
BROADCAST HISTORY:
Jul 1954–Sep 1954, NBC Fri 9:00–9:30
Jul 1955–Sep 1955, NBC Fri 9:00–9:30
Jul 1956–Aug 1956, NBC Fri 9:00–9:30

This program was aired for three years as a summer replacement for *The Big Story.* During 1954 and 1955 it was a true anthology composed of reruns from other dramatic series. The suspense dramas during this period included "Lullaby," starring Agnes Moorehead and Tom Drake; "Death Makes a Pass," starring Jay Novello and Lloyd Corrigan; "Accounts Closed," starring George Nader and Carolyn Jones; and "Passage Home," starring John Doucette, James McCallion, and Brian Keith. The 1956 version, however, consisted solely of episodes of *Four Star Playhouse,* seen previously on CBS, starring Dick Powell as the gambling-house owner Willie Dante. See also under series: *Dante.*

BEST OF BROADWAY, THE
Anthology
FIRST TELECAST: *September 15, 1954*
LAST TELECAST: *May 4, 1955*
BROADCAST HISTORY:
Sep 1954–May 1955, CBS Wed 10:00–11:00

Hard as it may be to believe, this series of classic Broadway plays and musical comedies shared its time period with one of the more popular boxing shows on network television. Every fourth Wednesday, for the entire 1954–1955 season,

Pabst Blue Ribbon Bouts was preempted by *The Best of Broadway*—one of the more unlikely marriages in television history. Produced live in New York, the plays included *The Royal Family* with Helen Hayes, Fredric March, Claudette Colbert, and Charles Coburn; *The Man Who Came to Dinner* with Monty Woolley, Merle Oberon, Joan Bennett, and Bert Lahr; *The Philadelphia Story* with Dorothy McGuire, John Payne, Richard Carlson, and Mary Astor; and *Arsenic and Old Lace* with Helen Hayes, Boris Karloff, Peter Lorre, Billie Burke, Orson Bean, and Edward Everett Horton.

CBS was very proud of its ability to present these plays in color, utilizing a giant new color studio recently completed in New York. They even ballyhooed the fact that "for the first time the Westinghouse product demonstrations will be done in color by Betty Furness."

BEST OF GROUCHO, THE
see *You Bet Your Life*

BEST OF THE WEST
Situation Comedy
FIRST TELECAST: *September 10, 1981*
LAST TELECAST: *August 23, 1982*
BROADCAST HISTORY:
Sep 1981, ABC Thu 8:00–8:30
Sep 1981–Jan 1982, ABC Thu 8:30–9:00
Feb 1982, ABC Fri 9:00–9:30
Jun 1982–Aug 1982, ABC Mon 8:00–8:30
CAST:
Marshal Sam Best .... Joel Higgins
Elvira Best .... Carlene Watkins
Daniel Best .... Meeno Peluce
Parker Tillman .... Leonard Frey
Doc Jerome Kullens .... Tom Ewell
Laney Gibbs .... Valri Bromfield
Frog .... Tracey Walter
Mayor Fletcher .... Macon McCalman

The brave marshal, the evil saloonkeeper who "owns" the town, the drunken old sawbones—*Best of the West* was a rollicking spoof of the clichés of TV Westerns. "Best" was Sam Best, a Civil War veteran from Philadelphia who journeyed west in 1865. With him were his ten-year-old son Daniel and his new wife Elvira, a Southern belle whom he had met while burning her father's plantation to the ground. Fluttery Elvira and smart-mouthed Daniel were not exactly at home on the rough-and-tumble frontier. Elvira did her best to tidy up their new cabin, though. Dabbing daintily at the floor with a broom, she sighed, "I just can't seem to get the dirt off this floor"—to which Sam deadpanned, "It's a dirt floor." And from city kid Daniel came: "I want you to understand, Dad, I'm never going outside."

But Sam's problems weren't confined to home. First there was the Calico Kid, an incompetent gunfighter who terrorized the town until Sam accidentally drove him off, thereby earning himself the job of town marshal. A more continuing source of aggravation was Parker Tillman, the villainous proprietor of the Square Deal Saloon (and of most of the rest of Copper Creek). Though his fastidious, prissy demeanor seemed totally out of place in the West, Tillman had his manicured fingers in every racket imaginable. When his construction company put up the new jail, the building promptly collapsed; when the townspeople had to fight a flood, he rented them shovels.

Also in the cast was Tillman's dim-witted henchman Frog, bawdy mountain woman Laney Gibbs, and—of course—drunk old Doc Kullens.

BEST TIMES, THE
Drama
FIRST TELECAST: *April 19, 1985*
LAST TELECAST: *June 7, 1985*
BROADCAST HISTORY:
Apr 1985–Jun 1985, NBC Fri 8:00–9:00
CAST:

Joanne Braithwaite	Janet Eilber
Mia Braithwaite	Beth Ehlers
Dan Bragen	Jim Metzler
Tony Younger	Jay Baker
Annette Dimetriano	Liane Curtis
Chris Henson	Darren Dalton
Dionne MacAllister	LaSaundra Hall
Giselle Kraft	Tammy Lauren
Neil "Trout" Troutman	David Packer
Dale Troutman	K.C. Martel
Joy Villafranco	Melora Hardin

Southern California's John F. Kennedy High School was the setting for this drama about teachers, students, and the trials of growing up. Divorcée Joanne Braithwaite and her daughter Mia had both just entered the school—Joanne as a nervous new English teacher, and Mia as a student trying hard to fit in. Joanne, at least, found support and a fledgling love interest in science teacher Dan Bragen. Among the students who were seen regularly were Tony, a fast-talking jock who was not very interested in classwork; Annette, Mia's tough-talking friend who didn't want to be in school at all; Chris, a former dropout who had returned to complete his education; Dionne and Giselle (Mia's best friend), both of whom worked part-time at the Potato Palace fast food restaurant; "Trout," the ambitious young night manager at the Potato Palace who was going steady with Joy; and Trout's trouble-prone younger brother, Dale.

BETTER DAYS
Situation Comedy
FIRST TELECAST: *October 1, 1986*
LAST TELECAST: *October 29, 1986*
BROADCAST HISTORY:
Oct 1986, CBS Wed 8:30–9:00
Oct 1986, CBS Wed 8:00–8:30
CAST:

Brian McGuire	Raphael Sbarge
Harry Clooney	Dick O'Neill

Luther Cain	Chip McAllister
Anthony "The Snake" Johnson . . .	Guy Killum
Harriet Winners	Randee Heller
Terence Dean	Randall Batinkoff
Beat-Box	Richard McGregor

Brian was a blond California teenager whose world was turned upside down when his parents suffered severe financial reversals. To help ease the burden, he moved in with his grandfather, Harry, and tried to adjust to life in Brooklyn, New York—a far cry from the sunny surfer's life he had led in Beverly Hills. Helping him to adjust, although they never completely accepted him, were Luther and the Snake, two of his street-smart teammates on the Braxton High School basketball team. Miss Winners was their cynical, no-nonsense English teacher.

The first casualty of the 1986–1987 season, this culture-shock comedy lasted only five weeks.

BETTER HOME SHOW, THE
Instruction
FIRST TELECAST: *May 5, 1951*
LAST TELECAST: *April 26, 1952*
BROADCAST HISTORY:
May 1951–Apr 1952, ABC Sat 6:30–7:00
REGULARS:
Norman Brokenshire
Dick Wilson
Doreen Wilson

An interesting "how-to" program with kindly old radio announcer Norman Brokenshire, assisted by his neighbors the Wilsons, who often dropped in. "Broke's" topics ranged from how to build cabinets out of orange crates to how to use luminous paint on garden tools and how to get bats out of your belfry. The program was previously aired locally.

BETTER LIVING TV THEATRE
Documentary/Discussion
FIRST TELECAST: *April 21, 1954*
LAST TELECAST: *August 29, 1954*
BROADCAST HISTORY:
Apr 1954–Jun 1954, DUM Wed 10:30–11:00
Jun 1954–Aug 1954, DUM Sun 10:30–11:00
HOST:
Fischer Black

This program promoted private industry through interviews, discussions, and film clips illustrating the contribution made by industry toward better living in the United States. Fischer Black, editor of *Electrical World*, served as moderator. The show had originally aired Sundays at noon on ABC for two months in the summer of 1953, and then turned up almost a year later in prime time on DuMont.

BETTY HUTTON SHOW, THE
Situation Comedy

FIRST TELECAST: *October 1, 1959*
LAST TELECAST: *June 30, 1960*
BROADCAST HISTORY:
Oct 1959–Jun 1960, CBS Thu 8:00–8:30
CAST:
Goldie Appleby .... Betty Hutton
Pat Strickland .... Gigi Perreau
Nicky Strickland.............. Richard Miles
Roy Strickland.................. Dennis Joel
Lorna .... Joan Shawlee
Rosemary .... Jean Carson
Howard Seaton .... Tom Conway
Hollister .... Gavin Muir

The leading character in this comedy was Goldie, an outspoken showgirl turned manicurist. When Mr. Strickland, one of her regular customers, died suddenly, Goldie found herself the inheritor of his considerable estate, as well as legal guardian of his three teenage children. The adjustments made by all concerned—Goldie to the luxury and social status of her new wealth, the children to their unsophisticated and unconventional guardian, and family lawyer Howard Seaton to his new employer—created many comic story situations. Goldie's ex-roommates, Lorna and Rosemary, also spent time at the Strickland mansion and remained her closest friends.

BETTY WHITE SHOW, THE
Comedy Variety
FIRST TELECAST: *February 5, 1958*
LAST TELECAST: *April 30, 1958*
BROADCAST HISTORY:
Feb 1958–Apr 1958, ABC Wed 9:30–10:00
REGULARS:
Betty White
Johnny Jacobs
Del Moore
Reta Shaw
Frank Nelson
Frank DeVol Orchestra

After the cancellation of her situation comedy *Date with the Angels*, comedienne Betty White filled the same time slot by starring for a few months in this comedy variety show. Each show generally consisted of three skits, in which Miss White portrayed a variety of roles, assisted by her regulars and guest stars, such as Charles Coburn and Billy DeWolfe. Jimmy Boyd, who had played the role of Wheeler in *Angels,* was a regular guest, and orchestra leader Frank DeVol also took part in the skits.

BETTY WHITE SHOW, THE
Situation Comedy
FIRST TELECAST: *September 12, 1977*
LAST TELECAST: *January 9, 1978*
BROADCAST HISTORY:
Sep 1977–Nov 1977, CBS Mon 9:00–9:30
Dec 1977–Jan 1978, CBS Mon 9:30–10:00

CAST:
Joyce Whitman .... Betty White
John Elliot.................. John Hillerman
Mitzi Maloney................ Georgia Engel
Tracy Garrett................... Caren Kaye
Doug Porterfield .... Alex Henteloff
Fletcher Huff .... Barney Phillips
Hugo Muncy...:............. Charles Cyphers

Betty White and Georgia Engel, two alumnae from *The Mary Tyler Moore Show,* starred in this comedy spoof of television and the people who work in it. Joyce Whitman was a fortyish movie actress whose career had been on the decline until she was offered the starring role in a new television series *Undercover Woman* (a loose parody on the real TV series, *Police Woman*). Joyce jumped at the chance, only to discover that the director was her suave, sarcastic ex-husband, John Elliot. None of the mutual antagonism that had ended their marriage had ebbed, and the two of them spent much of their time on the set putting each other down. Others working on *Undercover Woman* were Joyce's TV "partner," Tracy Garrett, a sexy young actress who was mindlessly clawing her way to the top, using anybody and anything to get there; Fletcher Huff, a fidgety actor who played the police chief for whom Undercover Woman worked; and Hugo Muncy, her stuntman double. Also wandering around the set was Doug Porterfield, the network liaison man assigned to the series by CBS (yes, they did refer to the network producing the mythical series as CBS). Doug was forever trying to assert himself as a network "executive," but his weak, bumbling personality kept getting in his way, making it difficult for anyone to take him seriously.

Away from the studio, Joyce's best friend was flaky Mitzi Maloney, a lovable dumb blonde (virtually the same role Georgia Engel had played on *The Mary Tyler Moore Show*). Mitzi had worked at the unemployment office when Joyce was collecting unemployment checks, prior to getting the part in *Undercover Woman,* and she subsequently became Joyce's roommate.

BEULAH
Situation Comedy
FIRST TELECAST: *October 3, 1950*
LAST TELECAST: *September 22, 1953*
BROADCAST HISTORY:
Oct 1950–Sep 1953, ABC Tue 7:30–8:00
CAST:
Beulah (1950–1952) .... Ethel Waters
Beulah (1952–1953) .... Louise Beavers
Harry Henderson (1950–1952)
.... William Post, Jr.
Harry Henderson (1952–1953) ... David Bruce
Alice Henderson (1950–1952).... Ginger Jones
Alice Henderson (1952–1953)..... Jane Frazee
Donnie Henderson (1950–1952)
.... Clifford Sales
Donnie Henderson (1952–1953) .. Stuffy Singer

Oriole.................. Butterfly McQueen
Bill Jackson (1950–1951) .. Percy (Bud) Harris
Bill Jackson (1951–1953) ...... Dooley Wilson

"Somebody bawl fo' Beulah?" she exclaimed, as TV's favorite black maid came once again to the rescue of her ever-bumbling employers. *Beulah,* one of the most popular comedy characters of the 1940s and 1950s, originated as a supporting role on radio's *Fibber McGee and Molly* program in 1944. Its creator was a white male actor, Marlin Hurt, who eventually began a separate *Beulah* series on radio. When ABC brought the popular show to television in 1950 the role was filled by veteran singer-actress Ethel Waters, with Percy Harris as her shiftless boyfriend Bill and Butterfly McQueen as her girlfriend Oriole. Her employers, the Hendersons, were a virtual caricature of a white middle-class family, giving Beulah plenty to do as one crisis after another overtook the household (such as Mr. Henderson's burning the steaks at a picnic, falling into the water while fishing, or trying to stop his young son Donnie from running away from home).

In April 1952, there was a major cast change. Hattie McDaniel, another Hollywood veteran *(Gone with the Wind),* was scheduled to take over the role of Beulah, but she suddenly became ill and the part went to Louise Beavers, who had a long list of movie credits of her own. At the same time the entire Henderson family changed faces. *Beulah* was still receiving high ratings in September 1953 when it went off the air because Miss Beavers decided to leave the role.

BEVERLY HILLBILLIES, THE
Situation Comedy
FIRST TELECAST: *September 26, 1962*
LAST TELECAST: *September 7, 1971*
BROADCAST HISTORY:
Sep 1962–Sep 1964, CBS Wed 9:00–9:30
Sep 1964–Sep 1968, CBS Wed 8:30–9:00
Sep 1968–Sep 1969, CBS Wed 9:00–9:30
Sep 1969–Sep 1970, CBS Wed 8:30–9:00
Sep 1970–Sep 1971, CBS Tue 7:30–8:00
CAST:
Jed Clampett .... Buddy Ebsen
Daisy Moses (Granny) .... Irene Ryan
Elly May Clampett.......... Donna Douglas
Jethro Bodine.................. Max Baer, Jr.
Milburn Drysdale .... Raymond Bailey
Jane Hathaway .... Nancy Kulp
Cousin Pearl Bodine (1962–1963)
  .... Bea Benaderet
Mrs. Margaret Drysdale (1962–1969)
  .... Harriet MacGibbon
Jethrene Bodine (1962–1963).... Max Baer, Jr.
John Brewster (1962–1966) ..... Frank Wilcox
Edythe Brewster (1965–1966)... Lisa Seagram
Jasper DePew (1962–1963) ...... Phil Gordon
Ravenswood, the butler (1962–1965)
  .... Arthur Gould Porter
Marie, the maid (1962–1963) .... Sirry Steffen

Sonny Drysdale (1962)............ Louis Nye
Janet Trego (1963–1965)......... Sharon Tate
Lawrence Chapman (1964–1967)
  .... Milton Frome
Studio Guard (1964–1966)....... Ray Kellogg
John Cushing (1964–1967) .... Roy Roberts
Dash Riprock (nee Homer Noodleman) (1965–1969)........................ Larry Pennell
Homer Cratchit (1968–1971).... Percy Helton
Elverna Bradshaw (1969–1971) . Elvia Allman
Shorty Kellems (1969–1971)
  .... George "Shug" Fisher
Miss Switzer (1969–1970) .... Judy Jordan
Helen Thompson (1969–1971).. Danielle Mardi
Miss Leeds (1969)........... Judy McConnell
Susan Graham (1969–1971).... Mady Maguire
Gloria Buckles (1969–1971).... Bettina Brenna
Shifty Shafer (1969–1971) .... Phil Silvers
Flo Shafer (1969–1971)..... Kathleen Freeman
Joy Devine (1970–1971) .... Diana Bartlett
Mark Templeton (1970–1971)... Roger Torrey

One of CBS' longest-running situation comedies, this was the slapstick treatment of the Clampetts, an Ozark hillbilly family who struck it rich (an oil well sprouted in their front yard) and moved to a Beverly Hills mansion. They deposited the $25 million given them by John Brewster, of the OK Oil Company, for drilling rights to their land, in Milburn Drysdale's Commerce Bank. As Drysdale's biggest depositors, they received special treatment. The banker, concerned about their naivete and ignorance of "big city ways," moved them into the mansion next door to his own home, in hopes of keeping an eye on them and helping them become more civilized.

The Clampetts were quite a group. Jed was the patriarch of the clan, a widower with much more common sense than anyone else in his slightly scatterbrained family. Jed's mother-in-law, Granny, spent most of her time concocting potions and trying to find a husband for Elly May. Elly May was a gorgeous young thing who loved "critters" (from cats and dogs to skunks and goats) and was incredibly naive. Many viewers put up with the inane stories just to see her in a pair of jeans that looked like they were painted on. Cousin Jethro Bodine was a hulking giant of a man, as stupid as he was strong, always chasing any attractive lady he saw. The Clampetts' encounters with corrupt politics, unfamiliar fashions, indoor plumbing, and the other trappings of modern life provided grist for years of comedy.
  Mrs. Drysdale, the banker's wife, could not stand living next door to the Clampetts. A socially prominent, status-conscious lady, she could never civilize them and, at one point, suffered the indignity of having her prize poodle Claude bear a litter fathered by Jed's lazy bloodhound, Duke. Despite her constant efforts, she could never get the Clampetts to move away. That her husband fawned over them, and indulged them as his best customers, only made matters worse. To help him with

77

the monumental task of dealing with the Clampetts, Mr. Drysdale had the able help of his highly efficient assistant, Jane Hathaway.

In its first season, *The Beverly Hillbillies* spent much time in the hill country, as well as in Los Angeles. Jethro's mother, Cousin Pearl Bodine, was a prominent member of the cast, and there was a running story line covering the romance of Jethro's sister, Jethrine, with Jasper DePew. In later years, when *Petticoat Junction* was on the air, the Clampetts would travel to Hooterville around Christmastime to spend the holidays with their friends "back home." They were even there in the fall of 1970, after *Petticoat Junction* had been canceled as a regular series.

In June of 1966 Jethro finally got his grade-school diploma and began a succession of schemes to become successful in business and, more important, as a playboy. None of his schemes worked but, since the oil kept flowing (by the last season the Clampett fortune had swelled to $95,000,000), it really didn't matter. In the fall of 1964 Mr. Drysdale purchased controlling interest in Mammoth Studios for the Clampetts, who spent the next several seasons giving studio boss Lawrence Chapman fits. Elly May even found a long-term, but unsuccessful, suitor in movie star Dash Riprock, who tried to help Jethro in his quest to become a playboy. There was also an extended running battle between Mr. Drysdale and John Cushing, who ran the Merchant's Bank in Beverly Hills, since the latter was always trying to get the Clampetts to move their funds to his bank. In the last season *The Beverly Hillbillies* was in production Elly May had a serious beau in Mark Templeton, a navy frogman, something Granny never quite understood. Interestingly, during the previous season, the same actor had played a backwoods hillbilly named Matthew Templeton during a story line in which Granny returned home to Bug Tussle with Elly May to find her a husband.

The Beverly Hillbillies was an instantaneous hit, and during its first two seasons ranked as the number-one program on television, attracting as many as 60 million viewers per week. It entertained audiences for nine years in prime time but was finally canceled because its ratings declined gradually and its audience was too heavily concentrated in rural areas to suit Madison Avenue advertisers.

The theme song, "The Ballad of Jed Clampett," was especially composed for the program by bluegrass musicians Lester Flatt and Earl Scruggs, and was on the national hit parade in early 1963. Not only did they sing the theme song, but Flatt and Scruggs made annual appearances on the show, playing themselves as friends of the Clampetts. These annual appearances, which ran until 1968, included actress Joi Lansing in the role of Gladys Flatt, Lester's wife, an ambitious but untalented singer and actress.

CBS aired reruns of *The Beverly Hillbillies*

weekday mornings from September 1966 to September 1972.

BEVERLY HILLS BUNTZ
Situation Comedy
FIRST TELECAST: *November 5, 1987*
LAST TELECAST: *April 22, 1988*
BROADCAST HISTORY:
Nov 1987–Jan 1988, NBC various previews
Mar 1988–Apr 1988, NBC Fri 9:30–10:00
CAST:
Norman Buntz .... Dennis Franz
Sidney Thurston .... Peter Jurasik
Rebecca Giswold .. Dana Wheeler-Nicholson
Lt. James Pugh................... Guy Boyd

Television lost its most beloved police series but gained two seedy private eyes in this spin-off from the much honored *Hill Street Blues*. In the final *Hill Street* episode Buntz punched out pompous Chief Daniels and resigned. He then moved with his friend Sid "the Snitch" to sunnier climes, opening his own low-rent private detective business in Los Angeles. Fish out of water in trendy L.A. ("Knights in shining polyester," the ads called them), the two shifty sleazeballs took on the dregs of detective work, but somehow managed to get things done when higher priced talent could not. Sid, true to his code, cooked up a succession of scams to augment their meagre income.

Neither drama nor outright comedy, *Beverly Hills Buntz* confused critics and viewers alike. NBC was so uncertain of its chances that it ran four "try out" episodes in various time periods from November to January, before beginning a regular run in March.

BEWITCHED
Situation Comedy
FIRST TELECAST: *September 17, 1964*
LAST TELECAST: *July 1, 1972*
BROADCAST HISTORY:
Sep 1964–Jan 1967, ABC Thu 9:00–9:30
Jan 1967–Sep 1971, ABC Thu 8:30–9:00
Sep 1971–Jan 1972, ABC Wed 8:00–8:30
Jan 1972–Jul 1972, ABC Sat 8:00–8:30
CAST:
Samantha Stephens/Serena
.... Elizabeth Montgomery
Darrin Stephens (1964–1969) ...... Dick York
Darrin Stephens (1969–1972) .... Dick Sargent
Endora .... Agnes Moorehead
*Maurice .... Maurice Evans
Larry Tate .... David White
Louise Tate (1964–1966) .... Irene Vernon
Louise Tate (1966–1972) .... Kasey Rogers
Tabitha Stephens (1966–1972)
.... Erin and Diane Murphy
Adam Stephens (1971–1972)
.... David and Greg Lawrence
Abner Kravitz .... George Tobias
Gladys Kravitz (1964–1966)
.... Alice Pearce (d. 3/66)

Gladys Kravitz (1966–1972) .... Sandra Gould
Aunt Clara (1964–1968) .... Marion Lorne
*Uncle Arthur (1965–1972) .... Paul Lynde
*Esmerelda (1969–1972) .... Alice Ghostley
Dr. Bombay (1967–1972) .... Bernard Fox

*Occasional role
PRODUCER/DIRECTOR:
William Asher

Bewitched was a comedy about an exceptionally pretty young witch named Samantha and her earnest attempts to abandon her witchcraft to please her mortal husband, Darrin. The couple was married on the first telecast, but that was the last "normal" event in their union. Samantha was continually tempted to use her witchly powers, invoked by a twitch of her nose, to get her way around the house. There was also a bevy of her relatives, none of whom wanted her to go straight: her mother Endora, her father Maurice, practical-joking Uncle Arthur, and forgetful Aunt Clara, witches and warlocks all. Esmerelda the housekeeper, who came along in 1969, was also a witch, but her powers were declining; a timid soul, she would fade away when spoken to harshly. Samantha's mischievous look-alike, cousin Serena, was also played by Miss Montgomery.

Also in the cast were Larry Tate, Darrin's long-suffering boss at the New York advertising agency of McMann and Tate, Larry's wife Louise, and the Stephens' easygoing but somewhat nosy neighbors, the Kravitzes.

Samantha's first child, Tabitha, was "born" on the telecast of January 13, 1966. The newborn infant was played briefly by identical twins Heidi and Laura Gentry and then by Tamar and Julie Young; beginning in the fall of 1966, two-year-old Erin and Diane Murphy assumed the role (later it was played by Erin alone). A son, Adam, came along on the night of October 16, 1969, although he was not seen regularly until the 1971–1972 season.

Visitors to the Stephens household included Julius Caesar (summoned up by mistake when Samantha asked Esmerelda to make a Caesar salad), George Washington, and Henry VIII.

Bewitched was an imaginative and well-written show that earned several Emmys. Extremely popular, it was in fact the biggest hit series produced by the ABC network up to that time (it ranked number two among all programs on the air during its first season). Reruns have entertained viewers for many years, on the ABC weekday schedule from January 1968 to July 1973, on ABC's Saturday morning lineup from September 1971 to September 1973, and on local stations.

Elizabeth Montgomery, the star of the series, was in real life married to its producer/director, William Asher.

BEYOND WESTWORLD
Science Fiction
FIRST TELECAST: *March 5, 1980*
LAST TELECAST: *March 19, 1980*
BROADCAST HISTORY:
Mar 1980, CBS Wed 8:00–9:00
CAST:
John Moore.................. Jim McMullan
Simon Quaid .... James Wainwright
Joseph Oppenheimer .... William Jordan
Pamela Williams .... Connie Sellecca
Foley .... Severn Darden
Roberta .... Ann McCurry

The Delos Corporation was the world's largest and most powerful multinational company. Among its many enterprises was the futuristic amusement park, Westworld, where visitors were waited on by sophisticated robots that looked and acted exactly like real people. With their help, Westworld's visitors could live out their wildest fantasies.

Enter the mad scientist, Simon Quaid, who with Joseph Oppenheimer had invented these lifelike robots for Delos. Quaid, an unstable genius, decided to reprogram his children "to take over the world (what else!) and turn it into a utopian" society under his guidance. Charged with foiling this fiendish plot were John Moore, head of Delos Security, and his lovely assistant, Pamela Williams. Actually, Quaid's efforts were thwarted more by this series' viewers than by anything else. There were so few of them that it was canceled after only three episodes.

Beyond Westworld was an offshoot of the 1973 movie *Westworld*, in which the robots ran amok (with no explanation why) and destroyed the amusement park, killing many of the guests in the process. Yul Brynner, as one of the robots, was the star of the movie *Westworld* and was its only cast member to appear in its sequel, *Futureworld*.

BID 'N' BUY
Quiz/Audience Participation
FIRST TELECAST: *July 1, 1958*
LAST TELECAST: *September 23, 1958*
BROADCAST HISTORY:
Jul 1958–Sep 1958, CBS Tue 10:00–10:30
EMCEE:
Bert Parks

At the start of each telecast of this auction game show, each of four contestants was given $10,000 in real money, which they then used to bid for clues that would help them identify a silhouette of some common object. The winner received an expensive prize, such as a sportscar, a fancy wardrobe, or a cabin cruiser, plus the right to return the following week.

BIFF BAKER U.S.A.
Adventure
FIRST TELECAST: *November 13, 1952*
LAST TELECAST: *March 26, 1953*
BROADCAST HISTORY:
Nov 1952–Mar 1953, CBS Thu 9:00–9:30

79

CAST:
Biff Baker .... Alan Hale, Jr.
Louise Baker .... Randy Stuart

Traveling all over the world in search of goods for his profitable importing business, Biff Baker often found himself involved in some form of international intrigue. Never looking for trouble, he nevertheless encountered it with remarkable frequency, and was always ready to deal with it. Biff and his wife Louise, with whom he traveled, most often found themselves caught up in some form of espionage, which was bad for the importing business but good for the plot.

BIG BEAT, THE
Music
FIRST TELECAST: *July 12, 1957*
LAST TELECAST: *August 2, 1957*
BROADCAST HISTORY:
  Jul 1957–Aug 1957, ABC Fri 10:00–10:30
HOST:
  Alan Freed

Alan Freed was the New York City disc jockey who is credited with coining the term "rock 'n' roll" and who did much to popularize "the big beat" in the mid-1950s. A flamboyant showman and promoter, Freed packaged this series of four rock spectaculars for ABC in the summer of 1957. The list of guests reads like a Who's Who of rock in the 1950s; the first show alone starred Connie Francis, The Everly Brothers ("Bye Bye Love"), Ferlin Husky ("Gone"), Don Rondo ("White Silver Sands"), the Billy Williams Quartet ("I'm Gonna Sit Right Down and Write Myself a Letter"), Nancy Wiskey ("Freight Train"), and Johnny and Joe ("Over the Mountain"). Later guests included Andy Williams, Chuck Berry, Frankie Lymon and the Teenagers, Bobby Darin, the Fontane Sisters, Fats Domino, Clyde McPhatter, Dale Hawkins, Gogi Grant, Mickey and Sylvia, Jerry Lee Lewis, and more—all in four half-hour telecasts! The Big Beat was probably a better representation of the current hit parade, all with original artists doing their own hits, than was ever heard on *Your Hit Parade*. In addition to serving as host, Freed led his own orchestra on the show, which included star saxophonists "Big Al" Sears and Sam "the Man" Taylor.

BIG EDDIE
Situation Comedy
FIRST TELECAST: *August 23, 1975*
LAST TELECAST: *November 7, 1975*
BROADCAST HISTORY:
  Aug 1975–Sep 1975, CBS Sat 8:30–9:00
  Sep 1975–Nov 1975, CBS Fri 8:00–8:30
CAST:
Eddie Smith .... Sheldon Leonard
Honey Smith .... Sheree North
Ginger Smith .... Quinn Cummings
Monte "Bang Bang" Valentine ... Billy Sands
Jessie Smith .... Alan Oppenheimer
Raymond McKay .... Ralph Wilcox

Eddie Smith was a reformed gambler who was trying to make it as the owner-promoter of New York's Big E Sports Arena. Despite the gruff exterior, accentuated by the thickest New York accent ever heard on television, Eddie was a softie at heart and really wanted to broaden his intellectual horizons and improve his manners. His family consisted of his wife Honey, an ex-stripper; his granddaughter Ginger; and his brother Jessie, the accountant for Eddie's business. Bang Bang was Eddie's cook, and Raymond a stereotyped, jive-talking young black man working for Eddie. *Big Eddie* was given a preseason preview run on Saturday nights before moving into a Friday time period, but it faded quickly when pitted against *Sanford and Son,* its regular competition, in September.

BIG EVENT, THE
Various
FIRST TELECAST: *September 26, 1976*
LAST TELECAST: *September 27, 1981*
BROADCAST HISTORY:
  Sep 1976–Sep 1981, NBC Sun Various times
  Jan 1978–Sep 1979, NBC Tue Various times

The Big Event was NBC's regular weekly showcase for special programming. Many of the specials lumped under this generic title were two hours in length, and some were even longer. "The First Fifty Years," a retrospective of NBC's half-century in broadcasting, occupied the entire evening of November 21, 1976, from 7:00 to 11:30 P.M. Major theatrical motion pictures were aired as *Big Events; Earthquake, 2001: A Space Odyssey,* and *Gone with The Wind* made their network television debuts here. In addition several major original television films were produced for the show (*Sybil, The Moneychangers, Holocaust,* and *Jesus of Nazareth*—the latter having previously aired in Europe) as well as more standard specials ("An Evening with Diana Ross," "The Father Knows Best Reunion," "The Story of Princess Grace").
The *Big Event* concept soon spread to other nights of the week as NBC, which was suffering from a shortage of hit series at the time, sought to boost its ratings with short-run but spectacular programming. A number of two- and three-part series such as "Harvest Home" and "The Godfather Saga" (an amalgam of the two *Godfather* theatrical films plus unused footage left over from the making of the films), ran partly or entirely under the *Big Event* title, usually extending from Saturday through Monday or Tuesday nights. A second regular *Big Event* night was added on Tuesday from 1978 to 1979.

BIG GAME, THE
Quiz/Audience Participation

FIRST TELECAST: *June 13, 1958*
LAST TELECAST: *September 12, 1958*
BROADCAST HISTORY:
 Jun 1958–Sep 1958, NBC Fri 7:30–8:00
EMCEE:
 Tom Kennedy

An unusual variation on quiz shows, this program tried to create the atmosphere of a big-game hunt. Each contestant was first given three plastic animals to place wherever he chose in his "jungle" (game board). He then answered multi-part questions, giving him opportunities to "shoot" at his opponent's animals. Although unable to see his opponent's board, a contestant could "shoot" at specific locations on the board (marked by a grid), hoping that the animals had been placed there. The first hunter to bag all of his opponent's animals won $2,000 and the right to face a new challenger.

BIG HAWAII
 Adventure
FIRST TELECAST: *September 21, 1977*
LAST TELECAST: *November 16, 1977*
BROADCAST HISTORY:
 Sep 1977–Nov 1977, NBC Wed 10:00–11:00
CAST:
 Mitch Fears .... Cliff Potts
 Barrett Fears .... John Dehner
 Karen "Keke" Fears........... Lucia Stralser
 Oscar Kalahani................. Bill Lucking
 Lulu Kalahani .... Elizabeth Smith
 Garfield Kalahani................ Moe Keale
 Kimo Kalahani .... Remi Abellira

The sprawling Paradise Ranch on the island of Hawaii was the private domain of autocratic Barrett Fears. He had built it into an empire that had made him one of the richest and most powerful men in all the Hawaiian islands. Recently returned to help him run the ranch was his only son, 29-year-old Mitch, a free spirit whose antiestablishment, radical attitudes were a source of constant conflict with his traditional father. Mitch's best friend, and the mediator between the two strong-willed Fears men, was Oscar Kalahani, the foreman of Paradise Ranch. Keke was Mitch's spoiled, tomboyish 18-year-old cousin who also lived on the ranch; Big Lulu, Oscar's mother and the family housekeeper, whose son Garfield did odd jobs around the ranch; and Kimo, Lulu's son and a good friend of Keke. Stories revolved around the problems of running the ranch, the conflicts between its owners, and the adjustments forced on the traditional Hawaiian life-style by the inroads of change.

BIG IDEA, THE
 Inventions
FIRST TELECAST: *December 15, 1952*
LAST TELECAST: *October 15, 1953*

BROADCAST HISTORY:
 Dec 1952–May 1953, DUM Mon 9:00–9:30
 May 1953–Oct 1953, DUM Thu 10:00–10:30
HOST:
 Donn Bennett
REGULAR PANELIST:
 Ray Wood

This unusual program displayed new inventions, with commentary by a panel and interviews with guest inventors. The presentations were entirely straight, and most of the inventions shown were useful, if prosaic, aids to everyday life, though there were some screwball exceptions. A sample of what the viewer might see on *The Big Idea*: a woman's inflatable bathing suit, an inflatable coat hanger, a dart board that lit up, a golf bag that stood up by itself, a complete miniature orchestra, a lunch box with self-contained hot plate, a refrigerated lunch box, a self-snuffing ashtray, a collapsible smoking pipe, spring-loaded shoe heels, rotating shoe heels, a clothesline with permanently attached clothespins, a device for preventing storm windows from falling off, a device to allow cars to park sideways, the "Dickey-Dout" (a device to hold blouses and shirts in place), and individual plastic nose filters for allergy sufferers.
 The Big Idea was first scheduled against CBS's *I Love Lucy*, where it was probably seen by nobody except friends and families of the inventors. It later moved to Thursday night but expired after a year's run.

BIG ISSUE, THE
 Public Affairs
FIRST TELECAST: *April 7, 1953*
LAST TELECAST: *January 18, 1954*
BROADCAST HISTORY:
 Apr 1953–Jun 1953, DUM Tue 8:30–9:00
 Sep 1953–Jan 1954, DUM Mon 8:30–9:00
MODERATOR:
 Martha Rountree
REGULAR PANELIST:
 Lawrence E. Spivak

This discussion program covered important issues of the day and was moderated for most of its run by Martha Rountree, who is better known for her *Meet the Press*. Two guests, on opposing sides of the "big issue," appeared on each telecast. DuMont considered this to be "throwaway" programming, scheduling it first against *Milton Berle* on Tuesday and then opposite *Arthur Godfrey's Talent Scouts* on Monday.

BIG MOMENT, THE
 Sports Drama
FIRST TELECAST: *July 5, 1957*
LAST TELECAST: *September 13, 1957*
BROADCAST HISTORY:
 Jul 1957–Sep 1957, NBC Fri 9:30–10:00
HOST:
 Bud Palmer

81

Films of sports highlights from the early 1920s to the present were featured on this summer replacement for *The Big Story.* Among the stories covered were famous finishes, arguments and riots, upsets, comebacks, sports characters, and women athletes.

BIG PARTY, THE
Variety
FIRST TELECAST: *October 8, 1959*
LAST TELECAST: *December 31, 1959*
BROADCAST HISTORY:
  Oct 1959–Dec 1959, CBS Thu 9:30–11:00

The full title of this biweekly series was *The Big Party by Revlon,* paying homage to its sponsor. Each telecast presented a different host or hostess and a large roster of guest stars in a lavish 90-minute variety show. The program filling the alternate weeks was the prestigious *Playhouse 90.* Originally there were to have been a total of 20 of these live variety shows, but the series was canceled with the New Year's Eve telecast. Despite the appearance of such well-known performers as Rock Hudson, Tallulah Bankhead, Sammy Davis, Jr., Mort Sahl, and Esther Williams, all of whom were on the first telecast, *The Big Party* never found a big audience.

BIG PAYOFF, THE
Quiz/Audience Participation
FIRST TELECAST: *June 29, 1952*
LAST TELECAST: *September 27, 1953*
BROADCAST HISTORY:
  Jun 1952–Sep 1952, NBC Sun 8:00–9:00
  Jun 1953–Sep 1953, NBC Sun 8:00–9:00
EMCEE:
  Randy Merriman
HOSTESS:
  Bess Myerson

Contestants for this summer series were selected from letters in which men told why the women in their lives deserved the wonderful prizes offered by the program. The Big Payoff itself included jewelry, clothes, a mink coat for the woman, a new car for the man, and a trip to anywhere in the world via Pan American World Airways. To win, the man had to answer a series of progressively more difficult questions. Added features were the Big Little Payoff for children and the Turn About Payoff, in which women had a chance to win prizes for their men. Randy Merriman was also the emcee of the daytime version of this show, which premiered December 31, 1951. Bess Myerson appeared on both the daytime and the nighttime versions, chatting with contestants and displaying prizes.

The daytime version ran on NBC until March 1953 and was then carried by CBS until it went off the air in October 1959. Hosts who succeeded Mr. Merriman on the daytime version were Burt

Parks, Mort Lawrence, and Robert Paige. When Miss Myerson left the daytime version of *The Big Payoff* her role as assistant/model was taken by Betty Ann Grove and later by Denise Lor.

BIG PICTURE, THE
Documentary
FIRST TELECAST: *October 5, 1953*
LAST TELECAST: *September 30, 1959*
BROADCAST HISTORY:
  Oct 1953–Dec 1954, ABC Mon 9:30–10:00
  Jan 1954–Aug 1954, ABC Wed 9:00–9:30
  Aug 1954–Feb 1955, ABC Sun 8:30–9:00
  Mar 1955–Jun 1955, ABC Sat 7:30–8:00
  Aug 1955, ABC Tue 8:30–9:00
  Sep 1955–Jan 1956, ABC Mon 10:00–10:30
  Mar 1956–Apr 1956, ABC Sun 10:00–10:30
  Jun 1956–Oct 1956, ABC Tue 10:00–10:30
  Jul 1957, ABC Thu 8:00–8:30
  Aug 1957–Oct 1957, ABC Fri 10:00–10:30
  Sep 1958–Oct 1958, ABC Fri 9:00–9:30
  Jun 1959–Aug 1959, ABC Sat 10:00–10:30
  Aug 1959–Sep 1959, ABC Wed 7:30–8:00
NARRATOR:
  Capt. Carl Zimmerman

Many films produced by government and industry to promote their own interests were shown on television during the 1950s, especially by the impoverished ABC and DuMont networks. Probably no such series had as long a run or was as well received by viewers as the U.S. Army's *Big Picture.* This program aired straight documentary films produced by the Army Pictorial Center and depicting various facets of the U.S. Army in action, including great battles, biographies of generals, new weaponry, and the roles played by various divisions and branches. Professional actors were rarely used; instead most of the footage came from the army's own vast historical and training film libraries.

The Big Picture was the brainchild of Lt. Carl Bruton, a commercial broadcaster called to active duty at the Pentagon during the Korean War. Seeing the vast amount of film available, and realizing the impact made by such privately made documentaries as *Crusade in Europe,* he sensed an excellent public relations opportunity for the army. (The films were also used for training purposes and were shown to foreign audiences.) The series began on WTOP in Washington, D.C., in 1951 and was soon being offered free to stations all over the country, to be shown in any manner they pleased. ABC picked it up in 1953 and ran it off and on for six years, seemingly whenever there was a hole to plug in the network schedule.

BIG QUESTION, THE
News/Discussion
FIRST TELECAST: *September 9, 1951*
LAST TELECAST: *October 21, 1951*
BROADCAST HISTORY:
  Sep 1951–Oct 1951, CBS Sun 6:00–6:30

Charles Collingwood

This live discussion program, which originated from Washington, D.C., attempted to cover a major issue of domestic or world importance each week. CBS White House correspondent Charles Collingwood served as moderator. When the subject warranted, the program might be filmed in advance on location, as in the case of a discussion with the delegates to the San Francisco conference on the Japanese Peace Treaty. At the end of October 1951 the program moved to an afternoon time slot, where it remained until early 1952.

BIG RECORD, THE
Music
FIRST TELECAST: *September 18, 1957*
LAST TELECAST: *June 11, 1958*
BROADCAST HISTORY:
Sep 1957–Mar 1958, CBS Wed 8:00–8:30
Mar 1958–Jun 1958, CBS Wed 8:30–9:00
HOSTESS:
Patti Page

Singer Patti Page, who had sold millions of her own records, was the hostess of this live musical showcase. The program's guest stars were well-established recording artists singing their biggest-selling or trademark songs; those currently on the popular record charts; and up-and-coming young singers who were, in the words of the producers, "due to hit the jukebox jackpot within the near future." The range of selections included show music and standards in addition to rock 'n' roll, then a fairly new trend in music. Emphasis was placed on standards, however, to attract a wider audience than the teenage-oriented top-40 songs.

BIG SHAMUS, LITTLE SHAMUS
Detective Drama
FIRST TELECAST: *September 29, 1979*
LAST TELECAST: *October 6, 1979*
BROADCAST HISTORY:
Sep 1979–Oct 1979, CBS Sat 9:00–10:00
CAST:
Arnie Sutter . . . . Brian Dennehy
Max Sutter . . . . Doug McKeon
George Korman . . . . George Wyner
Stephanie Marsh . . . . Kathryn Leigh Scott
Jerry Wilson . . . . Ty Henderson
Jingles Lodestar . . . . Cynthia Sikes

Atlantic City's Ansonia Hotel would have gone bankrupt were it not for the legalization of gambling in that seaside resort community. With new management and a brand-new casino to help bring in money, the Ansonia had a new lease on life. One of the survivors from the Ansonia's past was its veteran house detective, Arnie Sutter. With his 13-year-old son, Max, he attempted to cope with the tremendous increase in crime accompanying the legalization of gambling. Along

with the bettors came an influx of prostitutes, thieves, and con men, all trying to "hit it big" in their own way. George Korman was Arnie's boss, the security chief at the Ansonia; Stephanie Marsh was the new assistant manager; Jerry Wilson was the desk clerk; and Jingles Lodestar an undercover security agent posing as a cocktail waitress. *Big Shamus, Little Shamus* was so poorly done, and so poorly received, that it was canceled after only two episodes had aired.

BIG SHOW, THE
Variety
FIRST TELECAST: *March 4, 1980*
LAST TELECAST: *June 3, 1980*
BROADCAST HISTORY:
Mar 1980–Jun 1980, NBC Tue 9:00–10:30
REGULARS:
Joe Baker
Graham Chapman
Paul Grimm
Charlie Hill
Mimi Kennedy
Edie McClurg
Pamela Myers
Owen Sullivan
Adolfo Quinones and his dance group, Shabba-Doo
The Big Show Water Ballet
The Big Show Ice Skaters
The Tony Charmoli Dancers
The Nick Perito Orchestra

NBC tried gamely to bring back the big, splashy variety show with this 1980 series. It offered lavish sets, big budgets, major stars, and a full 90 minutes (sometimes two hours) of entertainment every week. There was a regular company of resident comedians for sketches, a huge pool for water ballets, a giant rink for ice-skating numbers, and a pair of big-name co-hosts each week. Steve Allen hosted on three occasions, and other hosts included Dean Martin, Tony Randall, Victor Borge, Gene Kelly, Flip Wilson, and Don Rickles. Singers Mel Tillis and Debby Boone made multiple guest appearances, as did comics Sid Caesar and Gallagher, and ice skaters Peggy Fleming and Dorothy Hamill. The reviewers thought it was wonderful, but the viewing audience stayed with ABC's Tuesday night comedies, leading to *The Big Show*'s early demise.

BIG STORY, THE
Dramatic Anthology
FIRST TELECAST: *September 16, 1949*
LAST TELECAST: *June 28, 1957*
BROADCAST HISTORY:
Sep 1949–Mar 1951, NBC Fri 9:30–10:00
Mar 1951–Jul 1956, NBC 9:00–9:30 (OS)
Sep 1956–Jun 1957, NBC Fri 9:30–10:00
NARRATOR:
Bob Sloane (1949–1954)

Norman Rose (1954–1955)
Ben Grauer (1955–1957)

This long-running documentary-drama series was based on the actual case histories of reporters who solved crimes, uncovered corruption, or otherwise performed significant public service through their diligent reporting. Some episodes were local human-interest stories, and some were national scandals, such as the story of labor columnist Victor Riesel, who was blinded by racketeers for his exposé. Each week, the sponsor, American Tobacco Company, gave a $500 cash award (initially called the Pall Mall Award) to the reporter whose story was used. Starting in 1955 Ben Grauer appeared in a newsroom at the beginning and end of each episode, in the role of the program's editor. He introduced the evening's "big story," and then, after the drama, would present the real-life reporter with his "Big Story Award." The series was presented on alternate weeks during part of its run.

Following its cancellation by NBC in 1957, *The Big Story* continued in production for another season as a syndicated series. Burgess Meredith narrated the syndicated version.

BIG SURPRISE, THE

Quiz/Audience Participation
FIRST TELECAST: *October 8, 1955*
LAST TELECAST: *April 2, 1957*
BROADCAST HISTORY:
  Oct 1955–Jun 1956, NBC Sat 7:30–8:00
  Sep 1956–Apr 1957, NBC Tue 8:00–8:30
EMCEE:
  Jack Barry (1955–1956)
  Mike Wallace (1956–1957)

In the wake of the sudden and dramatic success of CBS' *The $64,000 Question*, which had premiered during the summer of 1955, NBC brought out its own big-money quiz show that fall. During its first six months on the air *The Big Surprise* underwent numerous modifications in format. There was a period during which the contestant could be "rescued" if he or she missed a question, by having someone else correctly answer a substitute question; the "rescuer" then got 10 percent of the regular contestant's total winnings. There was a period when the contestant could be asked easy or hard questions. Missing an easy question cost the contestant all his or her winnings, while missing a hard one cost only half the winnings. There were other variations as well. In April 1956 the program finally settled down with a less complicated format. The subject area was chosen by the contestant. There were ten questions ranging in value from $100 to $100,000, and the contestant could also answer two insurance questions. Correct answers to the insurance questions guaranteed the contestants all the money they had won up to that point, regardless of future misses.

Unlike *The $64,000 Question,* there were no isolation booths on *The Big Surprise*. Contestants stood on a pedestal while pondering the answers to questions. Jack Barry left the show on March 3, 1956, and was replaced the following week by Mike Wallace.

BIG TOP

Circus
FIRST TELECAST: *July 1, 1950*
LAST TELECAST: *January 6, 1951*
BROADCAST HISTORY:
  Jul 1950–Sep 1950, CBS Sat 7:00–8:00
  Sep 1950–Jan 1951, CBS Sat 6:30–7:30
REGULARS:
  Jack Sterling
  Dan Lurie
  Ed McMahon
  Chris Keegan

Each week a full hour of live circus acts was presented on this series, which originated from the Camden, New Jersey, Convention Hall. Jack Sterling was the ringmaster, Ed McMahon (later of *The Tonight Show*) and Chris Keegan were the resident clowns, and Dan Lurie was the strongman. In addition to the regulars, at least six different acts, ranging from trapeze to trained animals, were presented on each show. After its six-month run at night, *Big Top* moved to Saturday afternoons (noon–1:00 P.M.), where it remained a fixture on the CBS lineup for the next seven years.

BIG TOWN

Newspaper Drama
FIRST TELECAST: *October 5, 1950*
LAST TELECAST: *October 2, 1956*
BROADCAST HISTORY:
  Oct 1950–Sep 1954, CBS Thu 9:30–10:00
  Feb 1953–Jul 1953, DUM Fri 8:00–8:30
  Oct 1954–Sep 1955, NBC Wed 10:30–11:00
  Sep 1955–Oct 1956, NBC Tue 10:30–11:00
CAST:
  Steve Wilson (1950–1954) . . . . . Patrick McVey
  Steve Wilson (1954–1956) . . . . . . Mark Stevens
  Lorelei Kilbourne (1950–1951)
   . . . . Mary K. Wells
  Lorelei Kilbourne (1951–1952) . . . Julie Stevens
  Lorelei Kilbourne (1952–1953) . . . . . Jane Nigh
  Lorelei Kilbourne (1953–1954) . . Beverly Tyler
  Lorelei Kilbourne (1954–1955) . . . Trudy Wroe
  Charlie Anderson (1954–1956) . . . Barry Kelley
  Lt. Tom Greggory (1954–1955) . . John Doucette
  "Rush" (1954–1955) . . . . Lyn Stalmaster
  Diane Walker (1955–1956) . . . . . . Doe Avedon

This long-running melodrama centered on *The Illustrated Press,* the largest and most influential newspaper in Big Town, whose driving force was crusading editor Steve Wilson. Steve's concerns were thwarting the spread of organized crime, exposing political corruption, establishing various types of reforms, and any other cause that seemed worthy. His star reporter was Lorelei Kilbourne, who had a certain romantic interest in her boss. *Big Town* had run from 1937 to 1948 on radio (where Steve Wilson had once been played by Edward G. Robinson), and when it moved to television as a live weekly series in 1950 it was an immediate hit. In April 1952 series production moved from New York to Hollywood, and *Big Town* was thereafter a filmed rather than live show. Patrick McVey portrayed editor Wilson throughout the CBS run, but Lorelei Kilbourne's face kept changing. After the end of its first season on NBC, her part was dropped completely from the show and Steve's love interest became Diane Walker, a commercial artist. City editor Charlie Anderson was also added as a regular cast member by NBC, as was ambitious young cub reporter "Rush."

Repeats of *Big Town* were seen on DuMont under the title *City Assignment* while the program was still running on CBS. The DuMont episodes starred Patrick McVey, as did other episodes later syndicated under the title *Heart of the City*. The episodes in which Mark Stevens had starred were later syndicated as *Headline* (1954–1955 episodes) and *Byline Steve Wilson* (1955–1956 episodes).

BIG VALLEY, THE
Western
FIRST TELECAST: *September 15, 1965*
LAST TELECAST: *May 19, 1969*
BROADCAST HISTORY:
   Sep 1965–Jul 1966, ABC Wed 9:00–10:00
   Jul 1966–May 1969, ABC Mon 10:00–11:00
CAST:
   Victoria Barkley .... Barbara Stanwyck
   Jarrod Barkley .... Richard Long
   Nick Barkley .... Peter Breck
   Heath Barkley .... Lee Majors
   Audra Barkley .... Linda Evans
   Silas .... Napoleon Whiting

This action-filled Western adventure was set on the sprawling Barkley ranch in California's San Joaquin Valley in the 1870s. The matriach of the clan was Victoria Barkley, who ran the family empire with a strong hand and the help of her four adult offspring; lawyer Jarrod, bold, brawling young Nick, ruggedly handsome Heath, and beautiful daughter Audra. (Another son, 19-year-old Eugene, played by Charles Briles, was seen occasionally in early episodes.) Like other settlers, the Barkleys were continually fighting the lawless elements of the Old West, and *Big Valley* stories were peopled with schemers, murderers, bank robbers, Mexican revolutionaries, and con men; one of the latter was delightfully portrayed by Milton Berle, in a guest appearance.

The *Big Valley* was Lee Majors's first TV se-

ries, and was in fact the first acting role he read for after completing a mere six months of drama instruction. He played the illegitimate son of Victoria's late husband, Tom.

BIGELOW SHOW, THE
Variety
FIRST TELECAST: *October 14, 1948*
LAST TELECAST: *December 28, 1949*
BROADCAST HISTORY:
   Oct 1948–Jul 1949, NBC Thu 9:30–10:00
   Oct 1949–Dec 1949, CBS Wed 9:00–9:30
REGULARS:
   Paul Winchell and Jerry Mahoney
   Dunninger

This two-part program featured the ventriloquist Paul Winchell and his dummy Jerry Mahoney in one segment, and mental telepathist Dunninger in another. Winchell and Mahoney did a regular weekly comedy routine, sometimes with the aid of a guest star. Dunninger's act consisted of reading the minds of members of the studio audience or special guests, and sometimes other tricks, always with a noted personality present to judge the honesty of the performance; he had a standing offer of $10,000 to anyone who could prove that he used an accomplice. In one telecast a United States Congressman was shown on the steps of the Capitol in Washington, while from New York Dunninger read his mind—via split screen.

BIGELOW THEATRE, THE
Dramatic Anthology
FIRST TELECAST: *December 10, 1950*
LAST TELECAST: *December 27, 1951*
BROADCAST HISTORY:
   Dec 1950–Jun 1951, CBS Sun 6:00–6:30
   Sep 1951–Dec 1951, DUM Thu 10:00–10:30

This series of filmed dramas appeared first on CBS before moving to DuMont. Some of the telecasts in the DuMont run had originally been seen on CBS—among them, "The Big Hello" with Cesar Romero, "Charming Billy" with Spring Byington, and "A Man's First Debt" with Lloyd Bridges; others were originals appearing for the first time. Ward Bond, Gig Young, Lynn Bari, Chico Marx, and Gale Storm appeared in episodes.

BILL COSBY SHOW, THE
Situation Comedy
FIRST TELECAST: *September 14, 1969*
LAST TELECAST: *August 31, 1971*
BROADCAST HISTORY:
   Sep 1969–May 1971, NBC Sun 8:30–9:00
   Jun 1971–Aug 1971, NBC Tue 7:30–8:00
CAST:
   Chet Kincaid .... Bill Cosby
   Rose Kincaid (1969–1970) ... Lillian Randolph
   Rose Kincaid (1970–1971) ..... Beah Richards
   Brian Kincaid .... Lee Weaver

Verna Kincaid	Olga James
Mr. Langford	Sid McCoy
Mrs. Marsha Peterson	Joyce Bulifant
Max Waltz	Joseph Perry

Comic Bill Cosby, who scored his first TV success in the adventure series *I Spy*, played a high school physical education teacher and coach, Chet Kincaid, in this warmhearted comedy. The setting was a school in a lower-middle-class neighborhood of Los Angeles. Chet's relationships with family, students, and fellow teachers were emphasized, giving free reign to Cosby's gentle sense of humor and philosophy. His family life with his mother, Rose, his brother, Brian, and his sister-in-law, Verna, were as much a part of the program as his professional life with the principal, Mr. Langford; the guidance counselor, Mrs. Peterson; and lots of kids.

BILL DANA SHOW, THE
Situation Comedy
FIRST TELECAST: *September 22, 1963*
LAST TELECAST: *January 17, 1965*
BROADCAST HISTORY:
  Sep 1963–Sep 1964, NBC Sun 7:00–7:30
  Sep 1964–Jan 1965, NBC Sun 8:30–9:00
CAST:
Jose Jimenez	Bill Dana
Mr. Phillips	Jonathan Harris
Eddie (1963–1964)	Gary Crosby
Byron Glick	Don Adams
Susie	Maggie Peterson

Writer-comedian Bill Dana, whose character Jose Jimenez had a very successful career on records and in nightclubs following its creation on *The Steve Allen Show*, brought him to life for this series. Jose was a Mexican immigrant who worked as a bellhop at the Park Central Hotel. Not only did he work there, it was practically his entire world: he lived in special bachelor quarters provided for hotel employees, ate in the hotel kitchen, and had social contact only with employees and guests of the hotel. In his goodhearted naivete he saw only the good in the people around him. His biggest problems were his fellow bellhop Eddie, who was constantly trying to get him to wise up; the less-than-understanding hotel manager Mr. Phillips; and the not-too-brilliant hotel detective Byron Glick. Walter Mitty-like dream sequences were occasionally used to extricate Jose from the hotel environment.

BILL GWINN SHOW, THE
Audience Participation
FIRST TELECAST: *February 5, 1951*
LAST TELECAST: *April 21, 1952*
BROADCAST HISTORY:
  Feb. 1951–Mar 1951, ABC Mon 10:30–11:00
  Mar 1951–Jun 1951, ABC Mon 8:30–9:30
  Jun 1951–Sep 1951, ABC Wed 9:00–9:30

  Oct 1951–Mar 1952, ABC Mon 10:00–10:30
  Mar 1952–Apr 1952, ABC Mon 9:30–10:00
EMCEE:
  Bill Gwinn

In this audience-participation show, three couples competed for prizes by enacting scenes showing how favorite songs had influenced their lives. The program underwent several title changes, beginning as *It Could Be You*, changing to *This Could Be You* two weeks later, *The Bill Gwinn Show* in April 1951, and *This Is My Song* shortly before its demise in April 1952.

BILL STERN'S SPORTS QUIZ
  see *Are You Positive?*

BILLY
Situation Comedy
FIRST TELECAST: *February 26, 1979*
LAST TELECAST: *April 28, 1979*
BROADCAST HISTORY:
  Feb 1979–Mar 1979, CBS Mon 8:00–8:30
  Mar 1979–Apr 1979, CBS Sat 8:30–9:00
CAST:
Billy Fisher	Steve Guttenberg
George Fisher	James Gallery
Alice Fisher	Peggy Pope
Gran	Paula Trueman
Norval Shadrack	Michael Alaimo
Arthur Milliken	Bruce Talkington

There were many ways of looking at 19-year-old Billy Fisher. His mother, Alice, thought he had a vivid imagination; his father, George, was sure he was a compulsive liar; and his grandmother put it more succinctly than either of his parents—as far as she was concerned, Billy was just "nuts." Billy's real world revolved around his menial job as an assistant mortician's clerk at the funeral home of Shadrack and Shadrack. In his fantasy life, however, he was everything from a famous surgeon, to a rock-music superstar appearing on *The Merv Griffin Show*, to the world's most irresistible bachelor. In Billy's daydreams, at least two of which were shown in each episode of this short-lived series, appeared such personalities as Don Adams, Suzanne Somers, and football star Larry Czonka—all playing themselves.

BILLY BOONE AND COUSIN KIB
Children's
FIRST TELECAST: *July 9, 1950*
LAST TELECAST: *August 27, 1950*
BROADCAST HISTORY:
  Jul 1950–Aug 1950, CBS Sun 6:30–7:00
REGULARS:
  Carroll "Kib" Colby
  Patti Milligan

As the 1950 summer replacement for *Mr. I Magination*, another children's show, this series featured cartoonist "Kib" Colby and Patti Milligan as

Suzy, his ten-year-old helper and friend. Each episode consisted of Billy Boone comic strips sketched by Mr. Colby, drawing games with members of the studio audience, and children's folk songs sung by the audience.

BILLY CRYSTAL COMEDY HOUR, THE
Comedy Variety
FIRST TELECAST: *January 30, 1982*
LAST TELECAST: *February 27, 1982*
BROADCAST HISTORY:
Jan 1982–Feb 1982, NBC Sat 10:00–11:00
REGULARS:
Billy Crystal
Phyllis Katz
Monica Ganas
Tino Insana
Jane Anderson
Brother Theodore Gottlieb
The Dee Dee Wood Dancers
The Van Dyke Parks Orchestra

Veteran nightclub comic (and former star of *Soap*) Billy Crystal starred in this short-lived variety hour. Each episode included comedy monologues, celebrity impersonations, and comedy skits, as well as an occasional musical number. In addition to the resident comedians, Billy played host to a wide range of guest performers—actors Robert Urich and Morgan Fairchild, funny men Rob Reiner and Gallagher, and musical performers Smokey Robinson and the Manhattan Transfer.

BILLY DANIELS SHOW, THE
Music
FIRST TELECAST: *October 5, 1952*
LAST TELECAST: *December 28, 1952*
BROADCAST HISTORY:
Oct 1952–Dec 1952, ABC Sun 6:30–6:45
FEATURING:
Billy Daniels
Benny Payne Trio
HOST:
Jimmy Blaine

This brief program consisted of songs performed by "That Old Black Magic" singer, Billy Daniels, with rhythm accompaniment.

BILLY GRAHAM CRUSADE, THE
Religion
FIRST TELECAST: *June 1, 1957*
LAST TELECAST: *April 11, 1959*
BROADCAST HISTORY:
Jun 1957–Aug 1957, ABC Sat 8:00–9:00
May 1958–Jun 1958, ABC Sat 10:00–11:00
Sep 1958–Oct 1958, ABC Sat 8:00–9:00
Feb 1959–Apr 1959, ABC Sat 10:00–11:00
HOST:
Rev. Billy Graham

On four occasions in the late 1950s, the world-famous evangelist Dr. Billy Graham had a regular series of televised religious services from his various crusades.

BILLY ROSE SHOW, THE
Dramatic Anthology
FIRST TELECAST: *October 3, 1950*
LAST TELECAST: *March 27, 1951*
BROADCAST HISTORY:
Oct 1950–Mar 1951, ABC Tue 9:00–9:30
DIRECTOR:
Jed Harris

Billy Rose, the legendary Broadway producer and songwriter, had a brief fling with television in this early dramatic series, most of whose stories were adaptations from his syndicated newspaper column, "Pitching Horseshoes." Sample titles were "The Night They Made a Bum out of Helen Hayes" and "The Night Billy Rose Shoulda Stood in Bed." Billy had a reputation for doing things in a big way. The talent he used here was respectable—Burgess Meredith, Alfred Drake, Leo G. Carroll—but the project never quite measured up to the Rose reputation. What did Billy, the producer of so many theatrical spectaculars, finally think of the new medium? "It shapes up like a shortcut to an ulcer," he told *TV Guide*, "... but a darn interesting one."

BILLY WALKER'S COUNTRY CARNIVAL
see *Grand Ole Opry*

BING CROSBY SHOW, THE
Situation Comedy
FIRST TELECAST: *September 14, 1964*
LAST TELECAST: *June 14, 1965*
BROADCAST HISTORY:
Sep 1964–Jun 1965, ABC Mon 9:30–10:00
CAST:
Bing Collins .... Bing Crosby
Ellie Collins .... Beverly Garland
Janice Collins.................. Carol Faylen
Joyce Collins .... Diane Sherry
Willie Walters.............. Frank McHugh

Bing Collins was a former singer who had left the hectic world of show business to settle down with his family and work as an electrical engineer. But life around the Collins household was hardly peaceful. Bing's wife Ellie had visions of making it in show business herself. Their two daughters provided quite a contrast: Janice was a normal, boy-crazy 15-year-old, but 10-year-old Joyce was so intellectual she seemed to belong in college. Willie Walters was the family's live-in handyman. Bing managed to sneak a song into almost every episode of this series, in between mediating disputes and dispensing sage advice to all.

BIOGRAPHY
Documentary
BROADCAST HISTORY:
Syndicated only

30 minutes
Produced: 1961–1964, 1979 (91 episodes)
Released: *February 1962*
NARRATOR:
Mike Wallace (1961–1964)
David Janssen (1979)
PRODUCERS:
David Wolper
Jack Haley, Jr.

Biography was pretty much what the title implied, filmed biographies of great men of the twentieth century, assembled from film clips, still photos, and recordings. It covered politicians such as Fiorello La Guardia, Huey Long, Sen. Joseph McCarthy, and all the modern presidents; world leaders (Churchill, Hitler, etc.); sports figures (Babe Ruth, Knute Rockne); as well as generals, explorers, authors, scientists, actors, and humanitarians. A modest and rather obvious project, it nevertheless became a very popular syndicated feature in the 1960s, and many of its episodes are still used as the "standard" filmed biographies of the subjects involved.

Narrator and script consultant in the original series was Mike Wallace, who was then at a low point in his career. Originally an actor and game-show host, Wallace had made his name in news as a fire-breathing interviewer in the late 1950s, but was made to tone down his approach by nervous network executives, and eventually forced out of network news work altogether. The considerable success of *Biography* helped reestablish his name. Soon he landed a position with CBS News, and a few years later he emerged once again as a biting, relentless inquisitor on CBS's *60 Minutes.*

A 1979 revival of *Biography,* covering a new set of celebrities ranging from Idi Amin to Walt Disney, was narrated by David Janssen.

BIONIC WOMAN, THE
Adventure
FIRST TELECAST: *January 14, 1976*
LAST TELECAST: *September 2, 1978*
BROADCAST HISTORY:
Jan 1976–May 1977, ABC Wed 8:00–9:00
Sep 1977–Mar 1978, NBC Sat 8:00–9:00
May 1978–Sep 1978, NBC Sat 8:00–9:00
CAST:
Jaime Sommers, the Bionic Woman
.... Lindsay Wagner
Oscar Goldman .... Richard Anderson
Dr. Rudy Wells .... Martin E. Brooks
Jim Elgin (1976) .... Ford Rainey
Helen Elgin (1976) .... Martha Scott

The Bionic Woman was one of a wave of comic-book-style superheroes brought to TV in the wake of the enormous success of *The Six Million Dollar Man. The Bionic Woman* was in fact a spin-off from, and closely linked to, that program. Jaime Sommers was originally introduced on *The Six*

Million Dollar Man as Steve Austin's one-time fiancée. The couple had drifted apart when Steve became an astronaut, while Jaime went to college and then became a successful tennis pro. Then Jaime was nearly killed in a sky-diving accident, and the doctors who had reconstructed Steve bionically after his accident decided to try again with Jaime. Steve and Jaime renewed their romance, but too late it seemed, for when the four-part story ended in early 1975 Jaime was in a coma and apparently near death.

Unbeknownst to Steve, Jaime recovered and began a new life as a schoolteacher on an army base near her home town of Ojai, California. Her bionic operation had given her superhuman abilities—two legs for great speed, a right arm of great strength, and an ear for acute, long-distance hearing. Grateful for having been saved, she, like Steve, undertook dangerous underground missions for the government's Office of Scientific Information (OSI), fighting international spies, smugglers, kidnappers, and an occasional extraterrestrial being. Among her disguises were those of a nun, a roller-derby queen, and a lady wrestler.

When Steve Austin learned of all this he rushed to her, but Jaime's problems had left her with a partial memory loss, and she had forgotten her love for Steve. So for the time being there was no bionic marriage. They sometimes were seen jointly on missions, however, and Jaime for a time lived in an apartment over the coach house at the farm of Steve's mother and stepfather, the Elgins, in Ojai.

Other regulars in the cast were Oscar Goldman, Jaime's supervisor at OSI, and Dr. Rudy Wells, who had devised the bionic operations, both of whom also appeared on *The Six Million Dollar Man.* Peggy Callahan (played by Jennifer Darling) was seen occasionally as Oscar's secretary on both series.

When *The Bionic Woman* moved to NBC another regular character was added to the cast in the person of Max, the bionic dog, a German Shepherd that became Jaime's loyal pet. Toward the end of that NBC season, with the popularity of science fiction movies on theater screens, more and more episodes of *The Bionic Woman* found Jaime encountering visitors from other planets.

The series was based on the novel *Cyborg,* by Martin Caidin.

BIRTHDAY PARTY
Children's
FIRST TELECAST: *May 15, 1947*
LAST TELECAST: *June 23, 1949*
BROADCAST HISTORY:
May 1947–Jan 1948, DUM Thu 7:30–8:00
Jan 1948–Aug 1948, DUM Thu 7:00–7:30
Sep 1948–Mar 1949, DUM Wed 7:00–7:30
Mar 1949–May 1949, DUM Sun 6:00–6:30
May 1949–Jun 1949, DUM Thu 7:00–7:30

Bill Slater (1947)
Aunt Grace (1948)
Ted Brown as "King Cole" (1949)

This early children's show was built around a birthday party for a visiting child, complete with ice cream and cake, with performances by talented youngsters. Although it began on DuMont's New York station in May 1947, the exact date when it was first fed over the network is not known; it was a network entry by early in 1948. It was also known as *King Cole's Birthday Party*.

BISHOP SHEEN PROGRAM, THE
syndicated title for *Life Is Worth Living*

BLACK ROBE, THE
Courtroom Reenactments
FIRST TELECAST: *May 18, 1949*
LAST TELECAST: *March 30, 1950*
BROADCAST HISTORY:
May 1949–Aug 1949, NBC Wed 8:30–9:00
Aug 1949–Oct 1949, NBC Mon Various times
Nov 1949–Dec 1949, NBC Sat 10:00–10:30
Jan 1950–Mar 1950, NBC Thu 8:00–8:30
REGULARS:
Judge .... Frank Thomas
Police Officer .... John Green

Dramatic reenactments of cases tried in New York City's Police Night Court. Although the judge and court officers were portrayed by actors, the persons appearing in court were often actual defendants and witnesses re-creating their own cases; their names and appearance were "altered for reasons in the public interest." Various public figures appeared as guests of the court, and on at least one occasion a remorseful criminal was induced to surrender to authorities as the result of an appeal made on the show. The appearance of three orphans on another telecast drew 500 offers of adoption in the New York City area. *The Black Robe* received a number of commendations for its public service and humanitarian work, but could not find a sponsor and so was canceled after ten months on the air.

BLACK SADDLE
Western
FIRST TELECAST: *January 10, 1959*
LAST TELECAST: *September 30, 1960*
BROADCAST HISTORY:
Jan 1959–Sep 1959, NBC Sat 9:00–9:30
Oct 1959–Sep 1960, ABC Fri 10:30–11:00
CAST:
Clay Culhane .... Peter Breck
Marshal Gib Scott .... Russell Johnson
Nora Travers .... Anna Lisa

Clay Culhane came from a family of gunfighters, but after losing his brothers in a shootout he decided that the practice of law might be a less violent way to settle personal disputes. Carrying his law books in his saddle bags, he traveled throughout the New Mexico Territory during the post–Civil War years, helping those in need of legal assistance. U.S. Marshal Gib Scott, who could not quite believe that Clay had really given up the gun for good, was never far behind.

BLACK SHEEP SQUADRON
see *Baa Baa Black Sheep*

BLACKE'S MAGIC
Detective Drama
FIRST TELECAST: *January 5, 1986*
LAST TELECAST: *June 11, 1986*
BROADCAST HISTORY:
Jan 1986, NBC Sun 9:00–11:00
Jan 1986–Jun 1986, NBC Wed 9:00–10:00
CAST:
Alexander Blacke .... Hal Linden
Leonard Blacke .... Harry Morgan

Old pros Hal Linden and Harry Morgan were teamed in this rather thin series about a magician-detective and his dad. Alexander Blacke was the debonair detective, who had recently retired as a society magician (after he almost killed himself in a particularly difficult stunt) and who now used his bag of tricks to nab murderers and other scoundrels. His understanding of illusion and deception often proved useful in figuring out how seemingly impossible crimes had been committed. Assisting Alexander was his father Leonard, a not quite reformed flim-flam man and master of disguise, whose skills came in handy in setting up ways to expose the bad guys. Unfortunately dad still found it difficult to stay on the right side of the law, requiring his son to periodically bail him out.

Most of the magic tricks performed on this series were real, performed by star Hal Linden, who had no previous experience as an illusionist.

BLANSKY'S BEAUTIES
Situation Comedy
FIRST TELECAST: *February 12, 1977*
LAST TELECAST: *May 21, 1977*
BROADCAST HISTORY:
Feb 1977–May 1977, ABC Sat 8:00–8:30
CAST:
Nancy Blansky .... Nancy Walker
Bambi Benton .... Caren Kaye
Ethel "Sunshine" Akalino.. Lynda Goodfriend
Emilio .... Johnny Desmond
Joey DeLuca .... Eddie Mekka
Anthony DeLuca .... Scott Baio
Horace "Stubbs" Wilmington
.... George Pentecost
Hillary S. Prentiss .... Taaffe O'Connell
Arkansas .... Rhonda Bates
Lovely Carson .... Bond Gideon
Jackie Outlaw .... Gerri Reddick
Gladys "Cochise" Littlefeather
.... Shirley Kirkes

Sylvia Silver .... Antoinette Yuskis
Misty Karamazov .... Jill Owens
Bridget Muldoon .... Elaine Bolton
Arnold .... Pat Morita

Nancy Blansky was den mother to a bevy of beautiful Las Vegas showgirls in this short-lived comedy. In addition to keeping order in the chaotic apartment complex where they all lived, Nancy staged the girls' big numbers at the Oasis Hotel, where her boss—the second-in-command at the hotel—was Horace Wilmington. Emilio, the maître d', was Nancy's boyfriend. To help Nancy defray the costs of her apartment, Sunshine and Bambi shared it with her, along with her nephews Joey DeLuca (a choreographer) and leering, 12-year-old ("going on 28") Anthony. Anthony was forever trying to make time with Bambi, who much to his chagrin treated him like a kid brother, as did almost all of Nancy's girls. Also sharing Nancy's apartment was a huge Great Dane named Black Jack.

Pat Morita, after the failure of his series *Mr. T. and Tina*, was added to the cast as Arnold, the same name (and virtually the same character) he had had in a similar supporting role on *Happy Days*. There he had run a drive-in restaurant, while here he ran the coffee shop at the Oasis. His presence on *Blansky's Beauties* gave both him and star Nancy Walker the dubious distinction of being in two program failures in the same season; she had starred in *The Nancy Walker Show* five months before the premiere of *Blansky's Beauties*.

BLIND DATE
Audience Participation
FIRST TELECAST: *May 5, 1949*
LAST TELECAST: *September 15, 1953*
BROADCAST HISTORY:
 May 1949–Jul 1949, ABC Thu 7:30–8:00
 Jul 1949–Sep 1949, ABC Thu 9:30–10:00
 Sep 1949–Feb 1950, ABC Fri 8:30–9:00
 Mar 1950–Jun 1950, ABC Thu 9:00–9:30
 Aug 1950–Sep 1951, ABC Thu 9:30–10:00
 Jun 1952–Jul 1952, NBC Sat 9:00–9:30
 May 1953–Sep 1953, DUM Tue 8:00–8:30
EMCEE:
 Arlene Francis (1949–1952)
 Melvyn Douglas (May–Jun 1953)
 Jan Murray (Jun–Sep 1953)
REGULAR:
 Ray Bloch Orchestra (1953)

College boys attempted to win a date with an unseen—but beautiful—model in this audience-participation program, which was adapted from the radio series of the same name. The boys and their quarry were separated by a wall, but they could talk to each other via a special telephone hookup. The boys with the best "line" won the date and a night on the town. During the Korean War the program did its patriotic bit by substitut-

ing eager young servicemen for the college crowd, as its radio predecessor had done during World War II.

After a two-year run on ABC, *Blind Date* returned in 1952 as an NBC summer replacement and in 1953 as a DuMont summer show. The DuMont version began under the title *Your Big Moment*, with a slightly different format; the host helped arrange blind dates for people writing in requesting a certain type of individual—a sort of TV dating service. After a few weeks the title was changed back to *Blind Date* and the duties of host passed from Melvyn Douglas to Jan Murray.

BLONDIE
Situation Comedy
FIRST TELECAST: *January 4, 1957*
LAST TELECAST: *January 9, 1969*
BROADCAST HISTORY:
 Jan 1957–Sep 1957, NBC Fri 8:00–8:30
 Sep 1968–Jan 1969, CBS Thu 7:30–8:00
CAST (1957):
 Dagwood Bumstead .... Arthur Lake
 Blondie .... Pamela Britton
 J. C. Dithers .... Florenz Ames
 Alexander .... Stuffy Singer
 Cookie .... Ann Barnes
 Cora Dithers .... Elvia Allman
 Herb Woodley .... Hal Peary
 Mr. Beasley .... Lucien Littlefield
CAST (1968):
 Dagwood Bumstead .... Will Hutchins
 Blondie .... Patricia Harty
 J. C. Dithers .... Jim Backus
 Alexander .... Peter Robbins
 Cookie .... Pamelyn Ferdin
 Cora Dithers .... Henny Backus
 Tootsie Woodley .... Bobbi Jordan
 Mr. Beasley .... Bryan O'Bourne

There were two attempts to bring to television the adventures of the Bumstead household, long a favorite of comic-strip readers and movie fans. In 1957 NBC brought Dagwood, Blondie, their children Alexander and Cookie, and Daisy and the other dogs to TV. Arthur Lake, the Dagwood of this version, had played the role in the movie series of the 1940s. The stories were all familiar to regular readers of the strip, with Dagwood getting into misunderstandings both at home and at work with Mr. Dithers, his boss. CBS gave *Blondie* a second chance a decade later, with a completely different cast, but that version also failed to catch on.

BLUE ANGEL, THE
Variety
FIRST TELECAST: *July 6, 1954*
LAST TELECAST: *October 12, 1954*
BROADCAST HISTORY:
 Jul 1954–Aug 1954, CBS Tue 10:30–11:00
 Sep 1954–Oct 1954, CBS Tue 8:30–9:00

Orson Bean
Norman Paris Trio

This variety series was the 1954 summer replacement for *See It Now*. In a nightclub setting patterned after the famous Blue Angel in the 1930 movie of the same title, host Orson Bean introduced and chatted with the various guest stars and occasionally added his own humor to the show. After *See It Now* returned to the air, *The Blue Angel* was given another four-week run at an earlier time.

BLUE ANGELS, THE

Adventure
BROADCAST HISTORY:
Syndicated only
30 minutes
Produced: *1960* (39 episodes)
Released: *Fall 1960*
CAST:
Cdr. Arthur Richards.......... Dennis Cross
Cdr. Donovan................. Morgan Jones
Capt. Wilbur Scott............ Warner Jones
Lt. Russ MacDonald ...... Michael Galloway
Lt. Hank Bertelli............... Don Gordon

This was an adventure series tracing the "exploits" of the U.S. Navy's four-man precision flying team, the Blue Angels. Cdr. Richards was the original skipper (replaced after the first 12 episodes by Cdr. Donovan), and Scott, MacDonald, and Bertelli his fellow pilots. There were no other continuing characters, but one of the more frequent supporting actors, appearing in various roles, was Burt Reynolds (in three episodes). For the precision flying scenes, films were used of the real Blue Angels tooling around in their Grumman F-111's.

Since the real Blue Angels spent most of their time simply flying, at one air show after another, considerable ingenuity was needed to lend this series variety. The producers managed to concoct all sorts of unlikely plots, such as having the pilots, on the spur of the moment, chase smugglers, romance pretty bystanders, fly life-saving supplies to a dying woman, scare a juvenile delinquent into going straight by giving him a wild airplane ride, and even stop a holdup—much of this off duty. The U.S. Navy, which cooperated in the production of the series, protested some of this, but producer Sam Gallu barked back, "How the hell does the Pentagon know what happens to a Blue when he's off duty?"

BLUE KNIGHT, THE

Police Drama
FIRST TELECAST: *December 17, 1975*
LAST TELECAST: *October 27, 1976*
BROADCAST HISTORY:
Dec 1975–Oct 1976, CBS Wed 10:00–11:00

CAST:
Bumper Morgan............ George Kennedy
Sgt. Newman .... Phillip Pine
Sgt. Cabe (1976)............. Charles Siebert
Lt. Hauser (1976).............. Lin McCarthy

Joseph Wambaugh, the author of the novel *The Blue Knight*, had once been a member of the Los Angeles Police Department, and his portrayal of police officers at work bore a note of strong realism missing from many TV police series. Wambaugh's first brush with TV was as consultant for NBC's police anthology *Police Story*, where he continued to write about the day-to-day world of big-city cops. Bumper Morgan, *The Blue Knight*'s leading character, first came to television in an NBC mini-series of the same name in the spring of 1973, with William Holden in the lead role. In both the mini-series and the series itself, Bumper Morgan was a cop who walked his beat, had no squad car for transportation, and knew virtually everyone in his territory. He was not beyond overlooking the existence of "good" prostitutes and other harmless types living on the fringes of the law, for his main concern was maintaining order in his inner-city neighborhood. He was stubborn, loyal, and determined, often resorting to physical force when it served his needs. An old-fashioned cop, he had a certain amount of trouble adjusting to the red tape and concern for suspects' rights that had grown up over the years.

BLUE LIGHT

Spy Drama
FIRST TELECAST: *January 12, 1966*
LAST TELECAST: *August 31, 1966*
BROADCAST HISTORY:
Jan 1966–Aug 1966, ABC Wed 8:30–9:00
CAST:
David March .... Robert Goulet
Suzanne Duchard .... Christine Carere

Filmed in Germany and set in Europe during World War II, *Blue Light* was the story of American espionage agent David March. March posed as a foreign correspondent who had officially renounced his American citizenship, but he actually belonged to a highly secret organization called "Code: Blue Light," whose purpose was to infiltrate the German high command and pass information on to the Allies. In addition to eluding German counterintelligence, who managed to uncover and execute 17 members of the Blue Light unit, March also had to watch out for Allied intelligence agencies, who never seemed to realize that he was on their side. Suzanne Duchard was his Girl Friday.

BLUE MEN, THE

see *Brenner*

BLUE RIBBON BOUTS

see *Boxing*

BLUE THUNDER
Police Drama
FIRST TELECAST: *January 6, 1984*
LAST TELECAST: *September 7, 1984*
BROADCAST HISTORY:
> *Jan 1984–Mar 1984*, ABC Fri 9:00–10:00
> *Apr 1984*, ABC Mon 8:00–9:00
> *May 1984–Jun 1984*, ABC Fri 9:00–10:00
> *Aug 1984–Sep 1984*, ABC Fri 9:00–10:00
CAST:
> *Frank Chaney* .... James Farentino
> *Clinton Wonderlove ("Jafo")* ... Dana Carvey
> *Lyman "Bubba" Kelsey* .... Bubba Smith
> *Richard "Ski" Butowski* .... Dick Butkus
> *Capt. Braddock* .... Sandy McPeak
> *J. J. Douglas* .... Ann Cooper

One of the hit movies of the summer of 1983 was *Blue Thunder*, an action adventure "starring" a seemingly impregnable police helicopter. Perfect for television, someone said, so six months later ABC and CBS both produced television copies, the CBS version called *Airwolf* and this one direct from the movie. Honcho of the Blue Thunder team was Frank Chaney, an argumentative, determined pilot who was constantly in trouble with his boss, Capt. Braddock. Flying with him in the high-tech chopper was a youthful electronics whiz named Clinton, who was simultaneously awed and frustrated by do-it-my-way Chaney ("Please stop calling me Jafo!" "Sorry, Jafo.") Two other members of the team drove a truck—for some reason this super-helicopter had to be followed around on the ground by a mobile support vehicle. The two, Bubba and Ski, both ex-football players and built like mountains, helped out in the pinches and added comic relief during the dull spots.

The real star of the show, as of the movie, was the ominous black chopper. It could eavesdrop at 10,000 feet, "map" the interior of other aircraft, switch to a "whisper mode" and tiptoe through the sky undetected, deflect machine-gun fire, or blaze away with its own awesome firepower. It could not, however, outrace conventional jet aircraft—as Airwolf could.

BLUES BY BARGY
Music
FIRST TELECAST: *April 23, 1949*
LAST TELECAST: *April 22, 1950*
BROADCAST HISTORY:
> *Apr 1949–Aug 1949*, CBS Sat 7:45–8:00
> *Aug 1949–Feb 1950*, CBS Sat 7:45–7:55
> *Mar 1950–Apr 1950*, CBS Sat 7:15–7:30
HOSTESS:
> Jean Bargy

Jean Bargy, daughter of veteran pianist-conductor Roy Bargy, sang ballads and played the piano in this short musical interlude that ran for a full year on CBS. She was also seen locally in New York on other nights of the week in an end-of-the-evening "filler" program on WCBS-TV.

BOB & CAROL & TED & ALICE
Situation Comedy
FIRST TELECAST: *September 26, 1973*
LAST TELECAST: *November 7, 1973*
BROADCAST HISTORY:
> *Sep 1973–Nov 1973*, ABC Wed 8:00–8:30
CAST:
> *Bob Sanders* .... Robert Urich
> *Carol Sanders* .... Anne Archer
> *Ted Henderson* .... David Spielberg
> *Alice Henderson* .... Anita Gillette
> *Sean Sanders, son* .... Brad Savage
> *Elizabeth Henderson, daughter* .. Jodie Foster

This comedy concerned two Los Angeles couples who were close friends, but rather distant in values and attitudes. Filmmaker Bob Sanders and his wife Carol were in their twenties, "young, aware, and with-it." Lawyer Ted Henderson and his wife Alice, in their thirties, were much more conventional. Overly cute stories about nude swimming, premarital sex, and unmarried friends living together helped hasten this generation-gap comedy to an early end. The program was based on the movie of the same name.

BOB AND RAY
Comedy Variety
FIRST TELECAST: *November 26, 1951*
LAST TELECAST: *September 28, 1953*
BROADCAST HISTORY:
> *Nov 1951–Feb 1952*, NBC Mon–Fri 7:15–7:30
> *Feb 1952–May 1952*, NBC Tue/Thu 7:15–7:30
> *Jul 1952–Aug 1952*, NBC Sat 7:30–8:00
> *Apr 1953–Sep 1953*, NBC Mon 7:30–7:45
REGULARS:
> Bob Elliott
> Ray Goulding
> Audrey Meadows
> Cloris Leachman (1952)

Satirists Bob Elliott and Ray Goulding were already well known to radio audiences when they first appeared on television in the early 1950s. Although their gentle, intelligent humor had always relied more on puns and vocal delivery than on sight gags, they nevertheless adapted well enough to the new medium to survive nearly two years on NBC, first on a Monday-through-Friday show, then on Tuesdays and Thursdays, and later once a week. Among their stock characters were Mary Margaret McGoon, cooking "expert," commentator, and all-purpose giver of advice; Tex, the drawling cowboy; and an assortment of travesties on current radio and TV personalities. Singer and actress Audrey Meadows played the part of Linda Lovely in Bob and Ray's continuing satire of soap operas. During the summer of 1952, when the show served as summer replacement for the soap opera *One Man's Family* (their version was *One Feller's Family*), Miss Meadows's place was taken by Cloris Leachman. Her primary role was in their spoof *Mary Backstage, Noble Wife* (a takeoff on the indomitable heroine of the radio serial *Mary Noble, Backstage Wife*). Audrey Meadows returned to the cast in the spring of 1953.

BOB CRANE SHOW, THE
Situation Comedy
FIRST TELECAST: *March 6, 1975*
LAST TELECAST: *June 19, 1975*
BROADCAST HISTORY:
  Mar 1975–Jun 1975, NBC Thu 8:30–9:00
CAST:
  Bob Wilcox .... Bob Crane
  Ellie Wilcox.................... Trisha Hart
  Marvin Susman............... Todd Susman
  Dean Lyle Ingersoll .... Jack Fletcher
  Mr. Ernest Busso .... Ronny Graham
  Pam Wilcox .... Erica Petal
  Jerry Mallory............... James Sutorius

In this short-lived series, Bob Crane played a fortyish insurance executive who abruptly decided to quit his job and enter medical school. The family pitched in, but the problems inherent in being twice the age of the other students and dependent on his working wife Ellie created constant comic situations, as did such resident characters as the overzealous Dean Ingersoll and nutty landlord Mr. Busso.

BOB CROSBY SHOW, THE
Musical Variety
FIRST TELECAST: *June 14, 1958*
LAST TELECAST: *September 6, 1958*
BROADCAST HISTORY:
  Jun 1958–Sep 1958, NBC Sat 8:00–9:00
REGULARS:
  Bob Crosby
  The Bobcats
  Gretchen Wyler
  The Peter Gennaro Dancers
  The Clay Warnick Singers
  The Carl Hoff Orchestra

Singer-bandleader Bob Crosby hosted and starred in this 1958 summer replacement for *The Perry Como Show*. With Bob were his band, The Bobcats, and musical-comedy star Gretchen Wyler.

BOB CUMMINGS SHOW, THE
Situation Comedy
FIRST TELECAST: *January 2, 1955*
LAST TELECAST: *September 15, 1959*
BROADCAST HISTORY:
  Jan 1955–Sep 1955, NBC Sun 10:30–11:00
  Jul 1955–Sep 1957, CBS Thu 8:00–8:30
  Sep 1957–Sep 1959, NBC Tue 9:30–10:00
CAST:
  Bob Collins.................. Bob Cummings
  Margaret MacDonald .... Rosemary DeCamp
  Charmaine "Shultzy" Schultz .. Ann B. Davis
  Chuck MacDonald .... Dwayne Hickman

  Pamela Livingston .... Nancy Kulp
  Paul Fonda .... Lyle Talbot
  Collette DuBois .... Lisa Gaye
  Francine Williams (1955–1956)
    .... Diane Jergens
  Harvey Helm (1955–1958)..... King Donovan
  Ruth Helm (1956–1958) ...... Mary Lawrence
  Mary Beth Hall (1956–1957).. Gloria Marshall
  Shirley Swanson (1956–1959)..... Joi Lansing
  Olive Sturgess (1956–1957).... Carol Henning
  Ingrid Goude, Miss Sweden 1956 (1957–1958)
    .... Herself
  Tammy Johnson (1959)
    .... Tammy Lea Marihugh

Clean-cut Bob Cummings played swinging bachelor Bob Collins in this comedy about a professional photographer who spent all his working time with beautiful models. In his spare time Bob squired the lovely ladies around town, but he never seemed able to settle on any one woman, causing endless problems at home and "in the harem." Bob lived with his widowed sister Margaret and her son Chuck; Margaret never quite understood her brother's social life, and Chuck was always trying to get in on Uncle Bob's action, despite the fact that he had attractive, wholesome girlfriends of his own (Francine and later Olive). Bob's devoted assistant was Shultzy, who had a crush on her boss but couldn't compete with glamorous models like Collette, Mary Beth, Shirley, and Ingrid.

Bob had his own private plane and occasionally flew to his home town of Joplin, Missouri, to visit his grandfather, Josh Collins (also played by Bob Cummings). Despite his age, the elder Collins had not lost his eye for the ladies, which he proved when it was his turn to visit his grandson—and all the sexy young models at the photography studio. When this series moved to daytime after concluding its evening run, the title was changed to *Love That Bob*, the same title later used in syndication. The network daytime run was on ABC from October 1959 to December 1961.

BOB CUMMINGS SHOW, THE
Comedy Adventure
FIRST TELECAST: *October 5, 1961*
LAST TELECAST: *March 1, 1962*
BROADCAST HISTORY:
  Oct 1961–Jan 1962, CBS Thu 8:30–9:00
  Feb 1962–Mar 1962, CBS Thu 7:30–8:00
CAST:
  Bob Carson.................. Bob Cummings
  Lionel........................ Murvyn Vye
  Hank Gogerty .... Roberta Shore

Bob Cummings, long an airplane enthusiast, managed to mix his avocation with his vocation in this adventure series. Bob Carson was a suave, high-living adventurer who made his living as a combination charter pilot and amateur detective. His assignments, both with and without passengers, took him all over the world. When his travels were short domestic hops close to his California base, Bob flew an aerocar, an unusual vehicle that could be used as an automobile or, when its removable wing was attached, converted into a small single-engine aircraft. When carrying passengers or traveling longer distances, Bob used a more luxurious twin-engine plane. His operating motto was that he would do anything that wasn't "illegal, immoral, or underpaid" and, with his expensive life-style, keeping in the black financially demanded regular employment. Lionel was his bodyguard/assistant and Hank the teenage daughter of the owner of the airstrip where Bob kept his planes. A tomboy, who rode a motor scooter to the airstrip every day, she spent much of her time flirting with Bob and trying to get him to take her on assignments. Effective with the episode that aired on December 28, 1961, the title of this series was changed to *The New Bob Cummings Show*.

BOB HOPE PRESENTS THE CHRYSLER THEATRE

Dramatic Anthology
FIRST TELECAST: *September 27, 1963*
LAST TELECAST: *September 6, 1967*
BROADCAST HISTORY:
 Sep 1963–Sep 1965, NBC Fri 8:30–9:30
 Sep 1965–Sep 1967, NBC Wed 9:00–10:00
HOST:
 Bob Hope

A mixed bag of drama, variety, and "event" specials, all involving Bob Hope in one role or another. In addition to serving as host on the dramatic telecasts, he starred in several of them. Among the more memorable telecasts of the series were "One Day in the Life of Ivan Denisovich," starring Jason Robards, Jr., Albert Paulsen, and Harold J. Stone (from the novel by Alexander Solzhenitsyn, later made into a movie); "The Seven Little Foys," with Mickey Rooney, Eddie Foy, Jr., and the Osmond Brothers; and "Think Pretty," a musical with Fred Astaire and Barrie Chase. Performers who starred in at least two of the episodes in this series were Peter Falk, Hugh O'Brian, Shelley Winters, Cliff Robertson, John Cassavetes, Jack Lord, William Shatner, Angie Dickinson, Suzanne Pleshette, Robert Stack, Dina Merrill, Darren McGavin, Broderick Crawford, and Stuart Whitman.

The variety shows were pure Hope, full of his topical one-liners, beautiful girls, sports heroes, and elaborate skits. The title of the variety hours was altered slightly to *Chrysler Presents a Bob Hope Special.* The highlight of the year, however, must be classed as one of TV's annual "events." This was the Bob Hope Christmas Show, filmed before an audience of G.I.s in Vietnam and carried as a 90-minute special telecast in January.

BOB NEWHART SHOW, THE

Comedy Variety
FIRST TELECAST: *October 10, 1961*
LAST TELECAST: *June 13, 1962*
BROADCAST HISTORY:
 Oct 1961–Jun 1962, NBC Wed 10:00–11:00
REGULARS:
 Bob Newhart
 Mickey Manners (1961)
 Joe Flynn
 Jackie Joseph
 Andy Albin
 Dan Sorkin
 Kay Westfall (1961)
 Jack Grinnage (1961)
 Ken Berry (1962)
 Paul Weston and His Orchestra

On the heels of the success of his "Button Down Mind" comedy albums, the young comic Bob Newhart was given this variety hour in the fall of 1961. Borrowing the format of his nightclub and album routines, each telecast opened with a monologue in which Newhart talked on the telephone with an unseen, and unheard, adversary. The conversation usually concluded with Newhart's regular tag line, "Same to you, fella." The show featured guest musical talent and a large group of comic actors and actresses who appeared in various sketches about contemporary life. None of them were truly regulars appearing on each telecast, but those listed above showed up at least half a dozen times during the season.

BOB NEWHART SHOW, THE

Situation Comedy
FIRST TELECAST: *September 16, 1972*
LAST TELECAST: *August 26, 1978*
BROADCAST HISTORY:
 Sep 1972–Oct 1976, CBS Sat 9:30–10:00
 Nov 1976–Sep 1977, CBS Sat 8:30–9:00
 Sep 1977–Apr 1978, CBS Sat 8:00–8:30
 Jun 1978–Aug 1978, CBS Sat 8:00–8:30
CAST:
 Robert (Bob) Hartley . . . . Bob Newhart
 Emily Hartley . . . . Suzanne Pleshette
 Howard Borden . . . . Bill Daily
 Jerry Robinson . . . . Peter Bonerz
 Carol Kester Bondurant . . . . . Marcia Wallace
 Margaret Hoover (1972–1973) . Patricia Smith
 Dr. Bernie Tupperman (1972–1976)
  . . . . Larry Gelman
 Ellen Hartley (1974–1976) . . . . Pat Finley
 Larry Bondurant (1975–1977)
  . . . . Will Mackenzie
 Elliot Carlin . . . . Jack Riley
 Mrs. Bakerman . . . . Florida Friebus
 Miss Larson (1972–1973) . . . . . Penny Marshall
 Michelle Nardo (1973–1976) . . . . Renee Lippin
 Mr. Peterson (1973–1978) . . . . John Fiedler
 Mr. Gianelli (1972–1973) . . . . Noam Pitlik
 Mr. Vickers (1974–1975) . . . . Lucien Scott
 Mr. Herd (1976–1977) . . . . Oliver Clark

Bob Hartley was a successful Chicago psychologist who lived in a high-rise apartment with his wife Emily, an elementary school teacher. Bob shared the services of his receptionist Carol with a bachelor dentist, Jerry Robinson. Carol was a brash, nutty individual who could dish it out pretty well to both her bosses. In the fall of 1975, she married Larry Bondurant, a travel agent, after a whirlwind courtship. Originally two of the Hartleys' neighbors were seen on a regular basis: Howard Borden, a divorced commercial airline pilot who had an annoying habit of barging into their apartment without knocking; and Margaret Hoover, a friend of Emily's. For a period Bob's sister Ellen lived with him and Emily, and at one point almost married Howard, but that passed.

Bob was a very low-key fellow, which was handy at the office but did not always prove effective in dealings with his wife and friends. He had a number of regular patients, including all of the above cast of characters from Elliot Carlin to the bottom of the list. Bob's patients had problems ranging from ordinary, everyday neuroses to homosexuality to extreme paranoia. They were all trying to find themselves. The character who appeared most regularly—and the one with the biggest problems—was Elliot, without doubt one of the most neurotic individuals ever seen on television. He was completely lacking in self-confidence, had a persecution complex, and was forever putting himself down.

In addition to treating his patients individually, Bob was a firm believer in group therapy, and his patients interacted in various groups in hilarious fashion.

BOBBIE GENTRY SHOW, THE
Musical Variety
FIRST TELECAST: *June 5, 1974*
LAST TELECAST: *June 26, 1974*
BROADCAST HISTORY:
Jun 1974, CBS Wed 8:00–9:00
REGULARS:
Bobbie Gentry
Michael Greer
Earl Pomerantz
Valri Bromfield

The star and host of this short summer variety series was country and western singer Bobbie Gentry, whose biggest hit was "Ode to Billy Joe," a ballad she had written herself.

The series was also known as *Bobbie Gentry's Happiness*.

BOBBY DARIN AMUSEMENT COMPANY, THE
see *Dean Martin Presents The Bobby Darin Amusement Company*

BOBBY DARIN SHOW, THE
Musical Variety
FIRST TELECAST: *January 19, 1973*
LAST TELECAST: *April 27, 1973*

BROADCAST HISTORY:
Jan 1973–Apr 1973, NBC Fri 10:00–11:00
REGULARS:
Bobby Darin
Dick Bakalyan
Geoff Edwards
Tommy Amato

Pop singer Bobby Darin appeared as both a singer and a sketch comedian in this short-lived series. In the sketches he became Groucho, Dusty John the hippie poet, Angie the tenement dweller, or the Godmother. He also performed several musical numbers each week, backed by a full orchestra. A consistent theme of the show was a salute to a different city each week, in song and in blackout comedy sketches.

BOBBY GOLDSBORO SHOW, THE
Music
BROADCAST HISTORY:
Syndicated only
30 minutes
Produced: 1972–1975 (78 episodes)
Released: *Early 1973*
HOST:
Bobby Goldsboro

Mop-topped young singer Bobby Goldsboro, who looked like a rock 'n' roller but did strictly middle-of-the-road material, hosted this pleasant little half-hour of songs. His guests were generally non-rock artists such as Johnny Mathis, Bobby Vinton, the Lennon Sisters, and B. J. Thomas. He also had a hand puppet named Jonathan Rebel to contribute to the patter.

BOBBY SHERMAN SHOW, THE
see *Getting Together*

BOBBY VINTON SHOW, THE
Musical Variety
BROADCAST HISTORY:
Syndicated only
30 minutes
Produced: *1975–1978* (52 episodes)
Released: *Fall 1975*
HOST:
Bobby Vinton
REGULARS:
Freeman King (1975–1976)
Jack Duffy (1975–1976)
Billy Van (1975–1976)
Jimmy Dale Orchestra
The Peaches (1976–1978)

Popular singer Bobby Vinton, who had a long string of ballad hits in the 1960s ("Roses Are Red, My Dear," "Blue on Blue," "Mr. Lonely"), was host of this slick musical-comedy series produced in Toronto. He has described his style as "sentimental and sincere," and so was most of the music presented here. There were also sketches, comedy blackouts, and short animated sequences, and most of the guests were comedians—Arte Johnson, Foster Brooks, John Byner, and Henny Youngman making multiple appearances.

During the first season there was a cast of regulars, and a lot of "Polish Power" jokes (Bobby is of Polish extraction). Both these elements were dropped in the second season, to give the boyish star broader appeal. A shapely backup group called the Peaches was also added.

BOING BOING SHOW, THE
Cartoon
FIRST TELECAST: *May 30, 1958*
LAST TELECAST: *October 3, 1958*
BROADCAST HISTORY:
  May 1958–Oct 1958, CBS Fri 7:30–8:00
NARRATOR:
  Bill Goodwin

The Gerald McBoing-Boing cartoon series—a combination of animation and live action—made its debut on CBS in December of 1956, on Sunday afternoons. Unable to talk, little Gerald would make himself understood by using pantomime and various noises rather than speech. When this didn't work, actor-announcer Bill Goodwin was always on hand to serve as a live interpreter. The series was aired in prime time during the summer of 1958.

BOLD JOURNEY
Travel Documentary
FIRST TELECAST: *July 16, 1956*
LAST TELECAST: *August 31, 1959*
BROADCAST HISTORY:
  Jul 1956–Feb 1957, ABC Mon 7:30–8:00
  Feb 1957–Jun 1957, ABC Thu 9:30–10:00
  Jun 1957–Aug 1959, ABC Mon 8:30–9:00
HOST:
  John Stephenson (1955–1957)
  Jack Douglas (1957–1959)

Home movies were shown on this series, but not normal everyday home movies. These films were taken by explorers and adventurers on trips to remote or highly unusual places around the world. The host of the show would introduce each week's guest, interview him about his experiences during the expedition, and then help narrate the film that had been taken during the trip. Los Angeles personality, Jack Douglas, took over as host on October 28, 1957.

BOLD ONES, THE
Drama
FIRST TELECAST: *September 14, 1969*
LAST TELECAST: *June 22, 1973*
BROADCAST HISTORY:
  Sep 1969–Sep 1972, NBC Sun 10:00–11:00
  Sep 1972–Jan 1973, NBC Tue 9:00–10:00
  May 1973–Jun 1973, NBC Fri 10:00–11:00

The Bold Ones was the umbrella title for a number of rotating series that were aired within the same time slot. During the 1969–1970 season there were three elements in the program: *The New Doctors, The Lawyers,* and *The Protectors.* In its second season, *The Senator* replaced *The Protectors.* For 1971–1972 only two elements were aired—*The New Doctors* and *The Lawyers*—and in its last season the program was composed solely of new episodes of *The New Doctors.* For information on specific elements in this series, see their respective titles.

BOLD VENTURE
Adventure
BROADCAST HISTORY:
  Syndicated only
  30 minutes
  Produced: *1958–1959* (39 episodes)
  Released: *January 1959*
CAST:
  Slate Shannon . . . . Dane Clark
  Sailor Duval . . . . Joan Marshall
  King Moses . . . . Bernie Gozier

Swaying palms, beautiful women, and high adventure filled this action series set in the Caribbean. Slate Shannon was an expatriate American, owner of a hotel called Shannon's Place and a 60-foot sloop named *The Bold Venture.* His constant companion was Sailor Duval, a good-looking young woman who had been left as his ward by her deceased father, Slate's best friend (although why, in her 20s, she needed to be anybody's ward was never explained). From their base in Trinidad, Slate and his charge stumbled into one adventure after another, involving smugglers, killers, and the other shady characters who populate series such as this.

An unusual feature of the series was its calypso music, which not only served as background but sometimes tied the story together through bits of narrative by calypso singer King Moses.

Bold Venture originated as a syndicated radio series in 1951–1952, in which Humphrey Bogart and Lauren Bacall wisecracked their way around the West Indies. They were a hard act to follow, and only 39 episodes of this television sequel were filmed.

BON VOYAGE
see *Treasure Quest*

BONANZA
Western
FIRST TELECAST: *September 12, 1959*
LAST TELECAST: *January 16, 1973*
BROADCAST HISTORY:
  Sep 1959–Sep 1961, NBC Sat 7:30–8:30
  Sep 1961–Sep 1972, NBC Sun 9:00–10:00
  May 1972–Aug 1972, NBC Tue 7:30–8:30
  Sep 1972–Jan 1973, NBC Tue 8:00–9:00

Ben Cartwright .... Lorne Greene
Little Joe Cartwright .... Michael Landon
Eric "Hoss" Cartwright (1959–1972)
.... Dan Blocker
Adam Cartwright (1959–1965)
.... Pernell Roberts
Hop Sing .... Victor Sen Yung
Sheriff Roy Coffee (1961–1971) ..... Ray Teal
Candy (1967–1970, 1972–1973) .. David Canary
Dusty Rhoades (1970–1972) ...... Lou Frizzel
Jamie Hunter (1970–1973) .... Mitch Vogel
Griff King (1972–1973) .... Tim Matheson

THEME SONG:
"Bonanza," by Jay Livingston and Ray Evans

Set in the vicinity of Virginia City, Nevada, during the years of the Civil War, soon after the discovery of the fabulous Comstock Silver Lode, Bonanza was the story of a prosperous family of ranchers. Widower Ben Cartwright was the patriarch of the all-male clan and owner of the thousand-square-mile Ponderosa Ranch. Each of his three sons had been borne by a different wife, none of whom was still alive. Adam, the oldest of the half brothers, was the most serious and introspective, the likely successor to his father as the controlling force behind the sprawling Cartwright holdings. Hoss, the middle son, was a mountain of a man who was as gentle as he was huge, at times naive, and not particularly bright. Little Joe was the youngest, most impulsive, and most romantic of the Cartwright offspring. The adventures of these men, individually and collectively, their dealings with the mining interests and the ranching interests, and the people whose paths crossed theirs made up the stories on Bonanza.

The program was not a traditional shoot-em-up Western; it relied more on the relationships between the principals and the stories of the characters played by weekly guest stars than it did on violence. Many of the episodes explored serious dramatic themes.

Bonanza premiered on Saturday night in the fall of 1959, and was the first Western to be televised in color. It was at first only moderately successful, but two years later, when it moved to Sunday night as the replacement for The Dinah Shore Chevy Show, it soared in popularity. For most of the 1960s Bonanza ranked as one of the highest-rated programs on television, placing number one for three seasons between 1964–1967. Its driving theme song, written by two Hollywood songsmiths who had written many top movie hits of the 1940s and 1950s, was on the hit parade. Bonanza finished second only to Gunsmoke as the longest-running, most successful Western in the history of television.

There were cast changes over the years. Pernell Roberts left the series at the end of the 1964–1965 season and his role was written out of the show. At the start of the 1967–1968 season a wanderer named Candy was hired as a ranch hand for the Cartwrights and practically became one of the family. Three years later, when Candy left the series (he later returned), two other new cast members arrived to join the Ponderosa household. Dusty Rhoades was a friend of Ben's, and Jamie Hunter, his charge, was an orphaned teenaged son of a rainmaker who had been killed. Prior to the start of production for the 1972–1973 season Dan Blocker died unexpectedly. His loss, coupled with a move to a new day and time, after 11 years on Sunday night, may have contributed to the poor rating performance that resulted in Bonanza's cancellation in the middle of its 14th season.

During the summer of 1972, while Bonanza was still being aired on Sundays, reruns from the 1967–1970 period were shown on Tuesdays at 7:30 P.M. under the title Ponderosa. Bonanza itself moved to Tuesdays that September.

BONINO

Situation Comedy
FIRST TELECAST: September 12, 1953
LAST TELECAST: December 26, 1953
BROADCAST HISTORY:
Sep 1953–Dec 1953, NBC Sat 8:00–8:30
CAST:

Bonino .... Ezio Pinza
Edward .... Conrad Janis
Doris .... Lenka Peterson
Jerry .... Chet Allen
Jerry (beg. 11/18 1953)........ Donald Harris
Carlo .... Oliver Andes
Francesco .... Gaye Huston
Andrew .... Van Dyke Parks
Martha, the maid .... Mary Wickes
Rusty, the former valet .... Mike Kellin
Walter Rogers .... David Opatoshu
John Clinton .... Fred (Anthony) Eisley

This live situation comedy starred the operatic basso Ezio Pinza as Bonino, a world-famous concert singer. Bonino's wife had died, leaving him with eight children to support. He abandoned his professional touring—much to the chagrin of his concert manager, Walter Rogers, and his valet—but found that his children had grown very independent during his absence. Mr. Pinza sang once during each episode.

BONKERS

Comedy
BROADCAST HISTORY:
Syndicated only
30 minutes
Produced: 1978–1979 (24 episodes)
Released: September 1978
CAST:
The Hudson Brothers (Bill, Brett, Mark)
Bob Monkhouse
The Bonkettes

"But *who* are the Hudson Brothers?" asked the *TV Guide* reporter, echoing a question that has bedeviled this talented comedy trio throughout their career. Despite a network summer series in 1974, the Saturday morning *Hudson Brothers Razzle Dazzle Show* in 1974–1975, this syndicated entry in 1978, a number of moderately popular records, and innumerable guest spots, they still are not—well, household names.

On *Bonkers* they did their usual thing, which is frantic, knockabout comedy somewhat reminiscent of the Marx Brothers, combined with contemporary music, real and parodied. Guest stars, a dazzling chorus line called the Bonkettes, and production by the company responsible for *The Muppets* didn't help.

BONNY MAID VERSATILE VARIETIES
see *Versatile Varieties*

BOOK OF LISTS, THE
Variety
FIRST TELECAST: *May 4, 1982*
LAST TELECAST: *May 25, 1982*
BROADCAST HISTORY:
May 1982, CBS Tue 8:00–9:00
HOST:
Bill Bixby

Each week host Bill Bixby, along with a co-host and a couple of other assistants, brought to life some of the odd, unusual, and intriguing facts gleaned from *The Book of Lists* and *The Book of Lists II*, two best-sellers compiled by David Wallechinsky, Irving Wallace, and Amy Wallace. Other items were tailored to the guest personalities who appeared on the show. Guest helper Ruth Buzzi described the "Ten Physical Attributes Women Most Admire in Men," Shecky Greene told "His Five Favorite Stories," Foster Brooks explained his "Favorite Hangover Cures," co-host Lorna Patterson sang a medley of "Songs Made Famous by Blondes," and co-host Steve Allen discussed the "Seven Things Married Couples Fight About Most."

This summer series lasted four weeks and may well turn up itself someday on a list of "Ten Most Obscure TV Series."

BOONE
Drama
FIRST TELECAST: *September 26, 1983*
LAST TELECAST: *August 11, 1984*
BROADCAST HISTORY:
Sep 1983–Dec 1983, NBC Mon 8:00–9:00
Jul 1984–Aug 1984, NBC Sat 10:00–11:00
CAST:
Boone Sawyer .... Tom Byrd
Rome Hawley .... Greg Webb
Merit Sawyer................. Barry Corbin
Faye Sawyer .... Elizabeth Huddle
Susannah Sawyer.............. Kitty Moffat
Squirt Sawyer .... Amanda Peterson
Uncle Link .... William Edward Phipps
Aunt Dolly .... Ronnie Claire Edwards
Mr. Johnson .... Davis Roberts
Banjo .... Julie Anne Haddock
Norman .... Chris Hebert
Amanda...................... Robyn Lively

Boone Sawyer was a young man with a guitar and a dream. It was 1953, in rural Trinity, Tennessee, not far from Nashville, and Boone was about to graduate from high school. He was an earnest and decent young man, and his family had down-to-earth plans for him. But Boone had other ideas. Upbeat country music, the kind that would soon evolve into rockabilly, was his first love, and he hoped it would be his ticket to stardom. Unfortunately the management of the Grand Ole Opry thought otherwise—they threw him out on his ear. Boone's father, Merit, who ran a local garage, and his loving mother, Faye, were not very supportive either, preferring that Boone stay close to home and either take over dad's gas station or become a minister—the career intended for his older brother Dwight, who had been killed in World War II. Parents never understand.

Boone found encouragement elsewhere, however, especially from his best buddy, leather-jacketed, motorcycle-riding Rome Hawley, who backed him on stage and shared wild times with him. Older sister Susannah and younger sister Squirt were sympathetic to his ambitions, too, as were Aunt Dolly and Uncle Link, who ran Link's Lounge, a local saloon where Boone and Rome hung out and sometimes performed. Mr. Johnson was an old, blind black man, a former blues guitarist who gave Boone helpful advice. Follow your dream, he said, so Boone kept a-pickin' and a-grinnin'—right up to the time this *Waltons*-esque series bit the dust after only three and a half months.

BORDEN SHOW, THE
Various
FIRST TELECAST: *July 6, 1947*
LAST TELECAST: *September 28, 1947*
BROADCAST HISTORY:
Jul 1947–Sep 1947, NBC Sun 9:00–9:30
DIRECTOR:
Fred Coe

The Borden Show was the overall title for a 1947 series, sponsored by Borden, that presented a different format each week. Such "sampler" programs were typical in the early days of TV broadcasting when networks and sponsors alike were experimenting with the new medium. Among the formats tried out on *The Borden Show* were variety shows, dramas, films, and marionette shows. The first telecast, subtitled "Borden Club," is illustrative. Set in an intimate supper club, it opened outside the club with a shot of a group of autograph-seekers besieging an unseen celebrity—who turned out to be Elsie the Borden Cow, in marionette form. The camera then moved inside where emcee Wally Boag entertained with his rubber balloons, followed by singer Lisa Kirk, impressionist Patricia Bright, and the Dominicans dance team.

The Elsie marionette also appeared on other *Borden Show* telecasts, providing a thread of continuity for the series.

BORN FREE
Adventure
FIRST TELECAST: *September 9, 1974*
LAST TELECAST: *December 12, 1974*
BROADCAST HISTORY:
   Sep 1974–Dec 1974, NBC Mon 8:00–9:00
CAST:
   George Adamson............... Gary Collins
   Joy Adamson .... Diana Muldaur
   Makedde .... Hal Frederick
   Nuru .... Peter Lukoye
   Awaru .... Nelson Kajuna
   Joe Kanini.................. Joseph De Craft

Filmed entirely on location in East Africa, where the action took place, *Born Free* chronicled the adventures of George and Joy Adamson with the lioness Elsa. The Adamsons were game wardens whose job was to watch over the wildlife in the area and protect the animals from poachers and natural disasters. The show was based on the popular book and movie of the same name.

BORN TO THE WIND
Adventure
FIRST TELECAST: *August 19, 1982*
LAST TELECAST: *September 5, 1982*
BROADCAST HISTORY:
   Aug 1982, NBC Thu 8:00–9:00
   Aug 1982, NBC Sat 8:00–9:00
   Aug 1982–Sep 1982, NBC Sun 7:00–8:00
CAST:
   Painted Bear .... Will Sampson
   Low Wolf .... A Martinez
   One Feather.................... Dehl Berti
   Star Fire .... Rose Portillo
   Prairie Woman .... Linda Redfearn
   White Bull .... Emilio Delgado
   Two Hawks .... Guillermo San Juan

This summer series had an unusual setting: a small Indian tribe somewhere in North America, around 1800, prior to the arrival of white settlers. The Indians' attempts to cope with an often hostile environment, relationships with each other, and the strong moral and ethical code by which they lived were all explored. Painted Bear was the leader (but not designated chief) of the group, and made most of the major decisions. Prairie Woman was his squaw, Star Fire his daughter, and Two Hawks his teenage son. One Feather was the village medicine man, and Low Wolf and White Bull were two other prominently featured braves.

BOSOM BUDDIES
Situation Comedy
FIRST TELECAST: *November 27, 1980*
LAST TELECAST: *September 15, 1984*
BROADCAST HISTORY:
   Nov 1980–Sep 1981, ABC Thu 8:30–9:00
   Oct 1981, ABC Thu 9:00–9:30
   Nov 1981–Jan 1982, ABC Fri 8:30–9:00
   Feb 1982–Mar 1982, ABC Thu 8:30–9:00
   May 1982–Jun 1982, ABC Thu 8:30–9:00
   Jul 1984–Sep 1984, NBC Sat 9:00–9:30
CAST:
   Henry Desmond/Hildegarde .... Peter Scolari
   Kip Wilson/Buffy .... Tom Hanks
   Amy Cassidy .... Wendie Jo Sperber
   Sonny Lumet .... Donna Dixon
   Isabelle .... Telma Hopkins
   Lilly Sinclair (1980–1981) ..... Lucille Benson
   Ruth Dunbar .... Holland Taylor
THEME:
   "My Life," written by Billy Joel

The old guys-in-drag gag was revived in this 1980 sex farce. Henry and Kip were two young studs working at a New York City advertising agency, Henry as a junior copywriter (and aspiring novelist) and Kip as a junior illustrator (and aspiring painter). They were also roommates, but one day they found a wrecking ball in the bedroom—seems the building was being demolished. Office receptionist Amy, who was smitten with Henry, came up with the bright idea that they move into her building, which just happened to be an all-girl residence—the Susan B. Anthony Hotel. Henry and Kip liked the low rent and the idea of being surrounded by beautiful women in various stages of undress, so in they went, gussied up as Hildegarde and Buffy. Amy was the only one who knew their true identities, even though Henry and Kip kept showing up at the hotel as themselves (passed off as Hildegarde's and Buffy's brothers). Sonny and Isabelle were two sexpots at the hotel, and Lilly Sinclair its fearsome manager. Ruth Dunbar was the idea-appropriating boss at the office.

Eventually the boys revealed their ruse to the girls at the hotel, but nobody else seemed to catch on. They also went into the commercial production business with Amy, taking over the failing firm owned by Henry's Uncle Mort. Sonny pursued her career as a nurse, while being pursued by Kip, and Isabelle took over as manager of the hotel, while waiting for her big break as an actress.

NBC aired reruns of *Bosom Buddies* during the summer of 1984.

BOSS LADY
Situation Comedy
FIRST TELECAST: *July 1, 1952*
LAST TELECAST: *September 23, 1952*
BROADCAST HISTORY:
   Jul 1952–Sep 1952, NBC Tue 9:00–9:30

99

CAST:

Gwen F. Allen	Lynn Bari
Gwen's Father	Nicholas Joy
Jeff Standish	Glenn Langan
Chester Allen	Charlie Smith
Aggie	Lee Patrick
Roger	Richard Gainer

In this summer replacement of *Fireside Theatre*, Lynn Bari played Gwen F. Allen, the beautiful chief executive of a highly successful construction firm, Hillandale Homes. Her two major problems, around which most of the stories were based, were finding a general manager who would not fall in love with her and maintaining her well-intentioned but inept father in his position as chairman of the board.

BOSTON BLACKIE
Detective Drama
BROADCAST HISTORY:
Syndicated only
30 minutes
Produced: *1951–1953* (58 episodes)
Released: *September 1951*
CAST:

Boston Blackie	Kent Taylor
Mary Wesley	Lois Collier
Inspector Faraday	Frank Orth

Boston Blackie, hero of more than a dozen 1940s B-movies, a B radio series, and B-grade magazine stories dating back decades, appeared in a memorable B-grade television series in the early 1950s. The term "B" is used in all the best senses: a certain vitality and sense of humor substituted more than adequately for the normal criteria of expensive production and famous stars.

Blackie, "enemy of those who make him an enemy, friend of those who have no friend," was a dapper reformed crook living in Los Angeles. Aided by his helper and girlfriend Mary, he regularly solved crimes several steps ahead of the local police, who were represented by the somewhat dimwitted Inspector Faraday. There were a lot of wisecracks and light asides along with the murders, and the whole series looked a little like a stock-company version of *Mr. and Mrs. North*, or Nick and Nora Charles in *The Thin Man* (Blackie and Mary had a dog too, named Whitey). Some episodes, in fact, were played more for comedy than crime.

The original Boston Blackie was a rather disreputable character, created by Jack Boyle in the pages of *Cosmopolitan* and *Redbook* magazines in the early 1900s (though the character was possibly inspired by black-eyed Blackie Daw, an elegant con man who was a major character in the "Get-Rich-Quick Wallingford" stories of George Randolph Chester, beginning in 1908). Boyle's Blackie was a burglar and bank robber by trade, and though well educated and extremely clever, he spent a lot of time in prison while Mary patiently waited. After one particularly brutal incarceration, he decided to go straight and started solving crimes instead of committing them. He was a popular character, appearing in several silent movies of the 1910s and 1920s, and in the feature-film series of the 1940s starring Chester Morris. There was also a 1940s radio series with Morris and, later, Richard Kollmar.

BOTH SIDES
Debate
FIRST TELECAST: *March 15, 1953*
LAST TELECAST: *June 21, 1953*
BROADCAST HISTORY:
Mar 1953–Jun 1953, ABC Sun 10:30–11:00
MODERATOR:
Quincy Howe

This public-affairs debate was sponsored by the American Federation of Labor. Prominent politicians, organized into opposing teams of two members each (the debater and his "counsel"), engaged in lively verbal jousting on a major issue of the day. On the first telecast Sen. Hubert Humphrey (D—Minn.) and Sen. Homer Ferguson (R—Mich.) practically tore each other apart.

BOURBON STREET BEAT
Detective Drama
FIRST TELECAST: *October 5, 1959*
LAST TELECAST: *September 26, 1960*
BROADCAST HISTORY:
Oct 1959–Sep 1960, ABC Mon 8:30–9:30
CAST:

Cal Calhoun	Andrew Duggan
Rex Randolph	Richard Long
Melody Lee Mercer	Arlene Howell
Kenny Madison	Van Williams

Bourbon Street Beat was the least successful of the imitation *77 Sunset Strip* detective shows churned out by Warner Brothers for ABC in the late 1950s and early 1960s. It had the requisite team of detectives (Cal and Rex), the aspiring young junior-grade detective (Kenny), the attractive female (Melody), and was set in an interesting locale (New Orleans), but somehow it just never caught on. The only casualty from its passing, however, was senior partner Cal Calhoun. Rex Randolph moved to Los Angeles and joined the detectives at *77 Sunset Strip* and Kenny Madison moved to Miami Beach to set up his own agency. He remained in the same time slot in the fall of 1960 as one of the stars of *Surfside Six*.

BOWLING HEADLINERS
Sports
FIRST TELECAST: *January 2, 1949*
LAST TELECAST: *October 30, 1949*
BROADCAST HISTORY:
Jan 1949–Apr 1949, ABC Sun 10:00–10:30
May 1949–Jun 1949, ABC Sun 10:15–11:00

Jul 1949–Oct 1949, ABC Sun 10:30–11:00 (OS)
Oct 1949, ABC Sun 11:00–12:00
ANNOUNCERS:
Al Cirillo
Jimmy Powers
Joe Hasel

This show, broadcast live from the Rego Park Lanes in Queens, New York, has the distinction of being television's first regularly scheduled bowling show. Each week two nationally known professional bowlers competed in matches of a round-robin elimination tournament. There was prize money, but it was minimal by today's standards, since bowling in the late 1940s was still a sport with limited appeal that was trying to change its lower-middle-class image. It was during this period, as a matter of fact, that the first major effort to change bowling terminology was launched to give it universal appeal; "lanes" was substituted for "alleys," "channel ball" for "gutter ball," and so on.

Al Cirillo, who produced the show, was the announcer throughout its run, assisted by sportswriter Jimmy Powers until the middle of March, and by Joe Hasel thereafter. For a two-month period, from mid-July until mid-September, when the heat in an unair-conditioned bowling establishment became unbearable, the show took a summer break.

BOWLING STARS
see *National Bowling Champions*

BOXING
Sports
FIRST TELECAST: *November 8, 1946*
LAST TELECAST: *September 11, 1964*
BROADCAST HISTORY:
Monday—
    Nov 1946–May 1949, NBC 9:00–Conclusion
    Mar 1949–May 1949, DUM 10:00–Conclusion
    May 1952–Aug 1956, DUM 9:00–Conclusion
    May 1954–May 1955, ABC 9:30–11:00
Tuesday—
    July 1948–Jan 1949, DUM 9:00–11:00
    Jan 1949–Sep 1950, ABC 10:00–Conclusion
    Apr 1949–May 1949, DUM 9:30–Conclusion
    Feb 1953–Aug 1953, ABC 9:00–10:00
Wednesday—
    Jul 1948–Jan 1949, DUM 9:00–11:00
    Jun 1949–Aug 1949, DUM 9:30–Conclusion
    Oct 1948–May 1949, CBS 9:00–Conclusion
    Oct 1949–May 1950, CBS 9:30–Conclusion
    Sep 1950–May 1955, CBS 10:00–Conclusion
    Jun 1955–Sep 1960, ABC 10:00–Conclusion
Thursday—
    Aug 1949–Sep 1950, DUM 9:30–Conclusion
    Jan 1952–Jun 1952, ABC 9:30–10:00
    Mar 1953–Jun 1953, ABC 9:00–10:00
Friday—
    Nov 1946–Jan 1949, NBC 9:30–Conclusion
    Jan 1949–May 1949, NBC 10:00–Conclusion

Sep 1949–Jun 1960, NBC 10:00–Conclusion (OS)
Sep 1949–Jul 1950, DUM 10:00–Conclusion
Oct 1963–Sep 1964, ABC 10:00–Conclusion
Saturday—
    Jan 1953–Jan 1955, ABC 9:00–Conclusion
    Oct 1960–Sep 1963, ABC 10:00–Conclusion

Boxing was an institution in early television for several reasons. It was easy to produce, the camera-coverage area was limited to the relatively small space occupied by the ring, and it had tremendous appeal to the first purchasers of television sets in the late 1940s—bars. Even a TV with a ten-inch screen could become a magnet to sportsminded drinkers. All the great names of the era—Sugar Ray Robinson, Rocky Marciano, Willie Pep, Rocky Graziano, and Archie Moore—appeared on the screen, as well as multitudes of lesser-known boxers who would probably not have had careers if it were not for the voracious appetite of television. Unlike today, when the main interest is in the heavyweight class, boxers in all weight divisions had strong fan appeal when television was new.

There were periods in the late 1940s and early 1950s when it was common to have as many as five or six network boxing shows on during the same week, not to mention the local shows that were also available. Those who complain about the saturation of football on television today need only look at the boxing picture in the early 1950s to see what *real* saturation was. A summary of the boxing shows carried by each network follows.

NBC was the first network to carry televised boxing. *Cavalcade of Sports* began on local TV in the mid-1940s and added network coverage in 1946, with Bob Stanton at the TV mike from St. Nicholas Arena in Manhattan on Mondays and from Madison Square Garden on Fridays. The Friday telecasts, which became the *Gillette Cavalcade of Sports* in 1948, ran for 14 years, by far the longest continuous run of any televised boxing show. When Stanton, who worked with Ray Forrest for part of the 1948–1949 season, left the series in 1949, he was replaced by Jimmy Powers. Powers remained the principal NBC announcer until the show went off the air in 1960. In its later years, the *Gillette Cavalcade of Sports* traveled all over the country to cover top bouts, and other announcers occasionally substituted for Powers.

CBS' boxing coverage was aired exclusively on Wednesday nights. Russ Hodges was the first CBS announcer for bouts originating from White Plains, New York, and St. Nicholas Arena. The series was given the title *International Boxing Club Bouts* in the fall of 1949, not long before Hodges left to be replaced by Ted Husing in March of 1950. Husing remained for roughly 16 months; Hodges returned in the summer of 1951, when the title was changed to *Blue Ribbon Bouts;* and Jack Drees arrived in 1954. Drees and Hodges shared announcing duties during that last CBS year and both stayed with the show when ABC took it over in June of 1955. As was true on NBC, coverage was extended beyond the New York area in the early 1950s, to locations where the most promotable fights were being staged.

DuMont's programming was heavy with both boxing and wrestling in the late 1940s and early 1950s. With its limited finances, inexpensive programming that had a ready audience was something that DuMont could not resist. Dennis James was DuMont's sports announcer for boxing and wrestling. The DuMont boxing shows, however, could not afford traveling to locations where there were no DuMont stations, so that most of them originated from the New York area. Dennis James covered bouts from Jamaica Arena, Queens, on Mondays, from Park Arena on Tuesdays, from White Plains, New York, on Wednesdays, and from Sunnyside Gardens and Dexter Arena on Thursdays. The longest-running DuMont boxing show, however, did not have James at the helm. Ted Husing was the announcer when *Boxing from Eastern Parkway* (Brooklyn) went on the air in May of 1952. He left in March of 1953 and was replaced by young Chris Schenkel. When ABC picked up the show in May of 1954, DuMont and Schenkel moved shop to St. Nicholas Arena where they stayed until DuMont went out of the network business in 1956. *Boxing from St. Nicholas Arena* was the last DuMont network series, its last network telecast coming on August 6, 1956, though it remained on as a local program in New York for another two months.

ABC's first major entry into the boxing wars came with *Tomorrow's Boxing Champions,* a show featuring young, unranked boxers that was aired on Tuesday nights in 1949. It originated from Chicago, with Bob Elson at the mike. January of 1952 brought *Meet the Champ,* a collection of bouts involving members of the armed forces, on Thursday nights, with Wally Butterfield announcing. In 1953 ABC's boxing coverage really expanded. In January *The Saturday Night Fights* premiered with Bill Stern doing the blow-by-blow; Jack Gregson took over from Stern in the fall. In February a series of *Boxing from Ridgewood Grove* bouts began on Tuesdays, with Jason Owen as the announcer in the first month and Bob Finnegan taking over until its cancellation in August. March brought *Motor City Boxing* from Detroit for three months of Thursdays, with Don Wattrick at the mike. In 1954 *Boxing from Eastern Parkway* moved to ABC from DuMont, with the announcing chores taken over by Tommy Logran, occasionally helped by Bob Finnegan and Fred Sayles. ABC also picked up the CBS *Blue Ribbon Bouts* when it was canceled and renamed it *The Wednesday Night Fights.* Russ Hodges and Jack Drees both stayed with the show, but Hodges left in October and Drees was the only regular announcer for the five years it stayed on ABC. When it moved to Saturday, and eventually Friday, the

title was again changed, this time to *The Fight of the Week.* Don Dunphy, released from NBC radio with the cancellation of the *Cavalcade of Sports* show on Fridays, took over the television commentary in the fall of 1960 and remained with it until it faded in September of 1964, the last regular nighttime network boxing series on the air.

BOYS WILL BE BOYS
see *Second Chance*

BRACKEN'S WORLD
Drama
FIRST TELECAST: *September 19, 1969*
LAST TELECAST: *December 25, 1970*
BROADCAST HISTORY:
   Sep 1969–Dec 1970, NBC Fri 10:00–11:00
CAST:
   Sylvia Caldwell (1969–1970) .. Eleanor Parker
   Kevin Grant .... Peter Haskell
   Davey Evans (1969–1970) .... Dennis Cole
   Laura Deane................ Elizabeth Allen
   John Bracken (voice only; 1969–1970)
     .... Warren Stevens
   John Bracken (1970).......... Leslie Nielsen
   Diane Waring .... Laraine Stephens
   Rachel Holt .... Karen Jensen
   Paulette Douglas............ Linda Harrison
   Marjorie Grant (1969–1970) .... Madlyn Rhue
   Tom Hudson (1970) .... Stephen Oliver
   Grace Douglas (1970)......... Jeanne Cooper
   Mark Grant (1970) .... Gary Dubin

The personal and professional lives of fictitious people in the movie business were the focus of this melodrama. Filmed at 20th Century–Fox, and featuring many real-life movie stars in cameo roles, *Bracken's World* was set at fictional Century Studios. Studio head John Bracken, though never seen, dominated the lives of the principals in the series through his executive secretary, Sylvia Caldwell. Among his many scheming underlings were writer-producer Kevin Grant; Laura Deane, who ran the studio's new-talent school; stunt man Davey Evans; and a number of aspiring young actors and starlets.

Bracken's World was only moderately successful during its first season, and so major surgery was performed at the start of the second. Bracken, now played by Leslie Nielsen, became visible as he struggled to guide the studio through troubled economic times. Gone were his executive secretary, stunt man Evans, and Kevin Grant's alcoholic wife Marjorie—who was killed off in the season's premiere episode. The series itself outlived her by only three months.

BRADY BRIDES, THE
Situation Comedy
FIRST TELECAST: *February 6, 1981*
LAST TELECAST: *April 17, 1981*
BROADCAST HISTORY:
   Feb 1981–Apr 1981, NBC Fri 8:30–9:00

CAST:

Marcia Brady Logan ... Maureen McCormick
Jan Brady Covington .... Eve Plumb
Wally Logan .... Jerry Houser
Philip Covington III .... Ron Kuhlman
Alice Nelson .... Ann B. Davis
Harry .... Keland Love
Carol Brady .... Florence Henderson

In this spin-off from the successful ABC comedy of the early 1970s, *The Brady Bunch*, the two older Brady girls, Marcia and Jan, got married. They then began house-hunting with the help of their mother, Carol, who became a real estate agent after the kids had grown up. But Los Angeles was an expensive place to live, and the only solution seemed to be to set up housekeeping together in a big old house that they had all fallen in love with. This created some problems, as their life-styles were rather different—Marcia and her toy-salesman husband Wally were much less traditional than Jan and her college-instructor husband Philip. There were also the little strains of new marriages. Helping work things out, as in the old days, was Alice, their former housekeeper, who lived nearby. Harry was a kid from the slums who had been befriended by Wally.

BRADY BUNCH, THE
Situation Comedy
FIRST TELECAST: *September 26, 1969*
LAST TELECAST: *August 30, 1974*
BROADCAST HISTORY:
Sep 1969–Sep 1970, ABC Fri 8:00–8:30
Sep 1970–Sep 1971, ABC Fri 7:30–8:00
Sep 1971–Aug 1974, ABC Fri 8:00–8:30
CAST:

Mike Brady .... Robert Reed
Carol Brady .... Florence Henderson
Alice Nelson .... Ann B. Davis
Marcia Brady .... Maureen McCormick
Jan Brady .... Eve Plumb
Cindy Brady .... Susan Olsen
Greg Brady .... Barry Williams
Peter Brady .... Christopher Knight
Bobby Brady .... Mike Lookinland

The Brady Bunch was one of the last of the old-style fun-around-the-house situation comedies, full of well-scrubbed children, trivial adventures, and relentlessly middle-class parents. The premise here was a kind of conglomerate family, formed by a widow with three daughters who married a widower with three sons; a nutty housekeeper, Alice, thrown in to act as referee; plus, of course, the family cat and a shaggy dog, Tiger.

All of these smiling faces lived in a four-bedroom, two-bathroom house in the Los Angeles suburbs, from which Dad pursued his nice, clean profession as a designer and architect. Typical stories revolved around the children going steady, family camping trips, competition for the family

telephone (at one point Dad installed a pay phone), and of course war in the bathroom.

The children ranged in age from 7 to 14 at the series' start, and the oldest son, Greg, played by Barry Williams, soon became something of a teen-age idol; he was receiving 6,500 fan letters per week during 1971. Barry and several of the others tried to parlay their TV success into recording careers in the early 1970s, but without notable success.

Reruns of *The Brady Bunch* were aired as part of ABC's weekday daytime lineup from July 1973 to August 1975, and an animated spinoff titled *The Brady Kids* ran Saturday mornings on ABC from September 1972 to August 1974.

BRADY BUNCH HOUR, THE
Comedy Variety
FIRST TELECAST: *January 23, 1977*
LAST TELECAST: *May 25, 1977*
BROADCAST HISTORY:
Jan 1977–Feb 1977, ABC Sun 7:00–8:00
Mar 1977–Apr 1977, ABC Mon 8:00–9:00
May 1977, ABC Wed 8:00–9:00
CAST:

Carol Brady .... Florence Henderson
Mike Brady .... Robert Reed
Alice .... Ann B. Davis
Marcia Brady .... Maureen McCormick
Jan Brady .... Geri Reischl
Cindy Brady .... Susan Olsen
Greg Brady .... Barry Williams
Peter Brady .... Christopher Knight
Bobby Brady .... Mike Lookinland

This was an attempt to revive the *Brady Bunch* comedy of the early 1970s, in hour-long format. The original cast returned intact except for Eve Plumb, who was replaced by Geri Reischl as Jan. The format now contained more variety than situation comedy, as father Mike had given up his career as an architect so that the family could star in their own TV variety show. The setting also changed, to a new beachfront home in California, and a group called the Water Follies Swimmers made regular appearances.

Originally scheduled to be seen only every fifth week in the *Nancy Drew/Hardy Boys Mysteries* time slot on Sunday, *The Brady Bunch Hour* later turned up in various ABC time periods on different nights.

BRAINS & BRAWN
Quiz/Audience Participation
FIRST TELECAST: *September 13, 1958*
LAST TELECAST: *December 27, 1958*
BROADCAST HISTORY:
Sep 1958–Dec 1958, NBC Sat 10:30–11:00
EMCEE:
Jack Lescoulie ("brawn")
Fred Davis ("brains")

103

Each team on this unusual show consisted of an athlete (the "brawn") and someone with high intellectual skills (the "brains"). The teams were determined by lot before the show went on the air. Two such teams were then pitted against each other, the "brawn" competing in athletic events and the "brains" answering questions. Two emcees handled the two parts of the competition.

BRANDED
Western
FIRST TELECAST: *January 24, 1965*
LAST TELECAST: *September 4, 1966*
BROADCAST HISTORY:
  Jan 1965–Sep 1966, NBC Sun 8:30–9:00 (OS)
CAST:
  Jason McCord .... Chuck Connors

Set in America in the 1880s, this series told the story of Jason McCord, who had had a successful military career following his graduation from West Point. He had risen to the rank of captain before he was dismissed from the service after being unjustly accused of cowardice. McCord traveled around the country in his attempt to gain proof that he was not a coward. In his travels he encountered people who believed in him and others who accepted his cowardice as fact. His previous experience as an engineer and mapmaker also led him into assorted adventures.

BRAVE EAGLE
Western
FIRST TELECAST: *September 28, 1955*
LAST TELECAST: *June 6, 1956*
BROADCAST HISTORY:
  Sep 1955–Jun 1956, CBS Wed 7:30–8:00
CAST:
  Brave Eagle .... Keith Larsen
  Keena.................... Keena Nomkeena
  Morning Star .... Kim Winona
  Smokey Joe.................. Bert Wheeler

In a turnabout from the normal pattern of TV Westerns, *Brave Eagle* presented the white man's expansion into the American Southwest during the middle of the 19th century from the Indian point of view. Brave Eagle was the young chief of a peaceful tribe of Cheyenne, Keena was his foster son, Morning Star was the attractive young Indian girl in whom he showed some romantic interest, and Smokey Joe was an old half-breed who was the tribal sage. Stories told in the series detailed their struggles with nature, other Indian tribes, and the ever-encroaching white man.

BREAK THE BANK
Quiz
FIRST TELECAST: *October 22, 1948*
LAST TELECAST: *January 15, 1957*
BROADCAST HISTORY:
  Oct 1948–Sep 1949, ABC Fri 9:00–9:30
  Oct 1949–Jan 1952, NBC Wed 10:00–10:30

  Jan 1952–Feb 1953, CBS Sun 9:30–10:00
  Jun 1953–Sep 1953, NBC Tue 8:30–9:00
  Jan 1954–Oct 1955, ABC Sun 10:00–10:30
  Oct 1955–Jun 1956, ABC Wed 9:30–10:00
  Oct 1956–Jan 1957, NBC Tue 10:30–11:00
HOST:
  Bert Parks
CO-HOST:
  Bud Collyer (1948–1953)
PAYING TELLER:
  Janice Wolfe (1949–1953)
  Janice Gilbert (1953–1957)
MUSIC:
  Peter Van Steeden Orchestra
  The Song Spinners

This popular quiz show began on radio in 1945 and started television simulcasts in 1948. Bert Parks, who had begun as one of *Break the Bank's* several radio hosts in 1945, when he was fresh out of the army, was closely associated with the program throughout its television run.

Break the Bank was always considered a big-money show, with cash prizes sometimes running over $10,000 even in the early days. The questions were tough, too. Contestants, who were drawn from the studio audience, chose a category and were asked a series of questions in that category for increasing amounts of money. If successful, they eventually had a chance to "break the bank," which was usually worth thousands of dollars (depending on how long it was since it had last been "broken").

A number of gimmicks were added to the show from time to time, including guest celebrities during the early years, and a "Wish Bowl Couple." These were viewers chosen by postcard drawing who won an expense-paid trip to New York to compete on the show.

In October 1956 *Break the Bank* jumped on the super-money bandwagon and was renamed *Break the $250,000 Bank.* Instead of studio contestants, "experts" were brought in to answer complex questions worth thousands of dollars. They did this while standing in a specially designed "Hall of Knowledge" and could sometimes be assisted by members of their families seated to the side of the stage. Among the unusual contestants during this period were two Hungarian refugees just arrived in the United States (their category was "Fight for Freedom") and the veteran actress-singer Ethel Waters, who said she needed the money to pay off back taxes (she won $10,000). No one ever reached $250,000 during the program's brief run.

Efforts to launch other versions of this old warhorse have been notably unsuccessful. Bert Parks hosted an NBC daytime version that ran from March to September 1953, while Tom Kennedy gamely tried a revival on ABC from April to July 1976. There was also a syndicated version hosted by Jack Barry in 1976 and another hosted by Gene Rayburn for the 1985–1986 season.

BREAKING AWAY

Situation Comedy
FIRST TELECAST: *November 29, 1980*
LAST TELECAST: *July 6, 1981*
BROADCAST HISTORY:
Nov 1980–Jan 1981, ABC Sat 8:00–9:00
Jun 1981–Jul 1981, ABC Mon 8:00–9:00
CAST:
Dave Stohler .... Shaun Cassidy
Ray Stohler .... Vincent Gardenia
Evelyn Stohler.............. Barbara Barrie
Moocher .... Jackie Earle Haley
Cyril.......................... Thom Bray
Mike......................... Tom Wiggin
Roy........................... John Ashton

Breaking Away was another example of the fact
that hit movies do not necessarily make hit TV
series. The setting was the college town of Bloom-
ington, Indiana, where four high school buddies
spent their time playing pranks on the lordly University of Indiana fraternity men (who disdain-
fully called them "cutters," after the town's blue-
collar stone cutters), dealing with their parents,
and just growing up. Dave was the central character, an intelligent, dreamy boy whose great passion was bicycle racing, and whose prized possession was a $1,200 La Strada bike he'd won. His
buddies were easygoing Moocher, sardonic Cyril,
and aggressive football star Mike. Dave's father
was Ray, a stone-cutter-turned-used-car-sales-
man who wished Dave would settle down to a
meat-and-potatoes existence like his own. Evelyn
was the mediating mother, and Roy was buddy
Mike's brother, a campus cop.

Re-creating their roles from the film *Breaking
Away* were Barrie (who had been nominated for
an Academy Award), Haley, and Ashton.

BREAKING POINT

Medical Drama
FIRST TELECAST: *September 16, 1963*
LAST TELECAST: *September 7, 1964*
BROADCAST HISTORY:
Sep 1963–Sep 1964, ABC Mon 10:00–11:00
CAST:
Dr. McKinley Thompson....... Paul Richards
Dr. Edward Raymer.......... Eduard Franz

McKinley Thompson, called Dr. Mac by almost
everyone on the staff, was the chief resident psychiatrist at fictitious York Hospital in Los Angeles. His superior, the director of the hospital's
psychiatric clinic, was Dr. Edward Raymer. Running what amounted to an out-patient service for
the emotionally distraught, they tried to help the
various people who came to the clinic. Their roles
in the series were rather peripheral, as the action
dealt more with the situations that had caused
people to seek their help than with life at the hospital.

BRENNER

Police Drama
FIRST TELECAST: *June 6, 1959*
LAST TELECAST: *September 13, 1964*
BROADCAST HISTORY:
June 1959–Oct 1959, CBS Sat 9:00–9:30
Jun 1961–Sep 1961, CBS Mon 10:30–11:00
Jun 1962–Sep 1962, CBS Thu 9:00–9:30
May 1964–Sep 1964, CBS Sun 9:30–10:00
CAST:
Det. Lt. Roy Brenner .... Edward Binns
Officer Ernie Brenner....... James Broderick

Filmed entirely on location in New York, *Brenner*
was the story of two generations of police officers
learning from each other. Roy Brenner was a career cop who had risen to the rank of detective
lieutenant. His son Ernie was a rookie patrolman.
The approach of the veteran father, who had been
hardened by the experiences of more than 20
years on the force, was often radically different
from that of the young, inexperienced, and idealistic son. Nevertheless, their love and respect for
each other enabled both of them to grow as individuals and learn from each other. The series
was produced in 1959 and selected reruns were
aired by CBS in the summers of 1961, 1962, and
1964. In order to freshen the series during its 1964
run, ten new episodes were produced and aired in
addition to the original 1959 shows.

BRET MAVERICK

Western
FIRST TELECAST: *December 1, 1981*
LAST TELECAST: *August 24, 1982*
BROADCAST HISTORY:
Dec 1981–Mar 1982, NBC Tue 9:00–10:00
Mar 1982–Jul 1982, NBC Tue 8:00–9:00
Jul 1982–Aug 1982, NBC Tue 9:00–10:00
CAST:
Bret Maverick .... James Garner
Tom Guthrie..................... Ed Bruce
Philo Sandine.............. Stuart Margolin
Mary Lou Springer............ Darleen Carr
Cy Whittaker............. Richard Hamilton
Rodney Catlow .... David Knell
Sheriff Mitchell Dowd.......... John Shearin
Elijah Crow .... Ramon Bieri
Jack, the bartender............. Jack Garner
Shifty Delgado............... Luis Delgado
Deputy Sturgess .... Tommy Bush
Mrs. Springer............... Priscilla Morrill
Kate Hanrahan .... Marj Dusay
Jasmine DuBois (1982)....... Simone Griffeth

More than 20 years after leaving *Maverick*, the
TV series that had made him a star, James Garner
returned to the role that had launched his career.
Set in the town of Sweetwater, in the Arizona
Territory, during the late 1880s, this series pro-
vided a more mature, less adventuresome Bret
Maverick than the one who had wandered from
town to town in search of poker games and excite-

ment. The sense of humor and friendliness were still there, but Bret had become a solid citizen and fulltime resident of a community trying to shed its untamed rural Western image. He owned a ranch outside Sweetwater and was part owner of the Red Ox Saloon in town. Cranky, irritable Cy Whittaker was the caretaker at the Lazy Ace, Bret's ranch, and former sheriff Tom Guthrie was his partner in the saloon. Guthrie, an old-fashioned lawman, had recently lost the sheriff's election to young, ambitious Mitchell Dowd, who struggled to bring "civilization" to Sweetwater with the marginal help of his stupid deputy, Sturgess. Feisty Mary Lou Springer ran the local newspaper, the *Territorian*, with the help of her mother and young printer's apprentice, Rodney Catlow. Also seen regularly were the local banker, Elijah Crow, who was not above stretching the law to his advantage; Shifty Delgrado, the house dealer at the Red Ox who cheated at cards whenever he thought he could get away with it; and Philo Sandine, a self-styled Indian scout who was more smalltime con man than anything else (a role similar to the one Stuart Margolin had played on Garner's previous series, *The Rockford Files*). The actor playing the bartender at the Red Ox was James Garner's brother, Jack.

BRIAN KEITH SHOW, THE
Situation Comedy
FIRST TELECAST: *September 15, 1972*
LAST TELECAST: *August 30, 1974*
BROADCAST HISTORY:
Sep 1972–Aug 1973, NBC Fri 8:30–9:00
Sep 1973–May 1974, NBC Fri 9:30–10:00
May 1974–Aug 1974, NBC Fri 8:30–9:00
CAST:
Dr. Sean Jamison .... Brian Keith
Dr. Anne Jamison .... Shelley Fabares
Nurse Puni .... Victoria Young
Ronnie (1972–1973) .... Michael Gray
Alfred Landis (1972–1973)...... Steven Hague
Stewart .... Sean Tyler Hall
Dr. Austin Chaffee (1973–1974) . Roger Bowen
Mrs. Gruber (1973–1974) .... Nancy Kulp

Titled *The Little People* during its first season, this was a "heartwarming" comedy about two pediatricians, a father and a daughter, who ran a free clinic as well as private practices on the Hawaiian island of Oahu. The concern that the Jamisons had for their "little people" formed the crux of most of the stories. The type of humor was similar to that on *Family Affair*, Mr. Keith's previous hit series. In its second season the situation changed somewhat, as did the title, which became *The Brian Keith Show*. The very proper Dr. Chaffee now shared office space with Sean and found that adjusting to Sean's informality could be rather difficult. Wealthy widow Mrs. Gruber, owner of the free clinic, as well as of much of Hawaii, was added to the cast to help provide

problem situations for the easygoing doctor and his attractive and equally competent daughter.

BRIDGES TO CROSS
Drama
FIRST TELECAST: *April 24, 1986*
LAST TELECAST: *June 12, 1986*
BROADCAST HISTORY:
Apr 1986–Jun 1986, CBS Thu 9:00–10:00
CAST:
Tracy Bridges .... Suzanne Pleshette
Peter Cross .... Nicolas Surovy
Morris Kane .... Jose Ferrer
Maria Talbot .... Eva Gabor
Norman Parks .... Roddy McDowall

Fictional *World/Week* magazine, a major news weekly headquartered in Washington, D.C., was the focal point of this romantic drama. Veteran reporter Tracy Bridges' accumulated contacts gave her entree to the movers and shakers in the capital's political and economic circles. One of Tracy's fellow reporters was her former husband, Peter Cross, with whom she continually sparred, romantically and professionally. Keeping *World/Week* on schedule was hard-nosed editor Morris Kane; keeping Tracy on schedule was her efficient male executive secretary, Norman. One of Tracy's closest friends, and an invaluable contact, was Washington socialite Maria Talbot.

This was CBS' second attempt to place Miss Pleshette in a series as a reporter, after they had failed with the comedic approach of *Suzanne Pleshette Is Maggie Briggs* in the spring of 1984.

BRIDGET LOVES BERNIE
Situation Comedy
FIRST TELECAST: *September 16, 1972*
LAST TELECAST: *September 8, 1973*
BROADCAST HISTORY:
Sep 1972–Sep 1973, CBS Sat 8:30–9:00
CAST:
Bernie Steinberg .... David Birney
Bridget Fitzgerald Steinberg
.... Meredith Baxter
Sam Steinberg .... Harold J. Stone
Sophie Steinberg............ Bibi Osterwald
Amy Fitzgerald .... Audra Lindley
Walt Fitzgerald .... David Doyle
Uncle Moe Plotnick .... Ned Glass
Father Mike Fitzgerald ..... Robert Sampson
Otis Foster .... William Elliott
Charles the butler................ Ivor Barry

This show was part of a wave of ethnic comedies in the early 1970s that followed on the success of *All in the Family* and *Sanford and Son*. Bernie was Jewish, a struggling young writer who supplemented his income by driving a cab. Bridget, his young bride, was an elementary school teacher whose parents were wealthy Irish Catholics. The couple shared a small apartment above a New

York City delicatessen owned by Bernie's parents. The widely divergent ethnic, cultural, and social backgrounds of the Steinberg and Fitzgerald families, and their attempts to reconcile for the sake of the young couple, provided most of the plot situations. Any resemblance to the vintage Broadway play *Abie's Irish Rose* was hardly coincidental.

Despite reasonably good ratings, *Bridget Loves Bernie* was canceled at the end of its first season. One contributing factor may have been the furor created by the unhappiness of religious groups, primarily Jewish, over the show's condoning and publicizing mixed marriages. An interesting sidelight is that the two stars of the series, David Birney and Meredith Baxter, later married each other in real life.

BRING 'EM BACK ALIVE
Adventure
FIRST TELECAST: *September 24, 1982*
LAST TELECAST: *June 21, 1983*
BROADCAST HISTORY:
 Sep 1982, CBS Fri 9:00–10:00
 Sep 1982–Dec 1982, CBS Tue 8:00–9:00
 Jan 1983–Feb 1983, CBS Sat 8:00–9:00
 May 1983–Jun 1983, CBS Tue 8:00–9:00
CAST:
 Frank Buck . . . . Bruce Boxleitner
 Gloria Marlowe . . . . Cindy Morgan
 H.H., the Sultan of Johore . . . . Ron O'Neal
 Myles Delany . . . . Sean McClory
 G. B. VonTurgo . . . . John Zee
 Ali . . . . Clyde Kusatsu
 Bhundi . . . . Harvey Jason
 Chaing, the bartender . . . George Lee Cheong

Inspired by the box-office success of the film *Raiders of the Lost Ark,* CBS brought this period adventure series to TV viewers the following year. Frank Buck was a legendary guide and Great White Hunter, living in Malaya during the years just prior to World War II. Operating out of the Raffles Hotel bar in Singapore, an establishment run by his good friend Myles Delaney, Frank donned pith helmet and ventured forth every week to deal with the baddies of Southeast Asia. His foes ran the gamut from smugglers, warlords, and bounty hunters to spies, strutting Nazis, and menacing Japs. Lantern-jawed Frank dispatched them all with élan, although G. B. VonTurgo, top man in the Singapore underworld, did manage to create recurring problems for Frank and his friends. On the side of the good guys were Gloria Marlowe, the pretty new American vice consul in Singapore; the regal Sultan of Johore; and Frank's loyal assistant, Ali. Bhundi was an associate of VonTurgo who, though essentially a criminal, would switch sides if he thought it would benefit him.

There was a real Frank Buck, a famous animal trapper in the 1940s, and the book which provided the title for this series was about his exploits. Any resemblance, however, between the real Buck and the character portrayed in this series, was purely coincidental.

BRINGING UP BUDDY
Situation Comedy
FIRST TELECAST: *October 10, 1960*
LAST TELECAST: *September 25, 1961*
BROADCAST HISTORY:
 Oct 1960–Sep 1961, CBS Mon 8:30–9:00
CAST:
 Aunt Violet Flower . . . . Enid Markey
 Aunt Iris Flower . . . . Doro Merande
 Buddy Flower . . . . Frank Aletter

Making his home with two lovable but wacky maiden aunts kept investment counselor Buddy Flower pretty busy. As if he didn't have enough to cope with at the office, when he came home he was likely to discover that they had found the perfect girl for him to marry, had made some other major decision about the way he was to live, or had gotten themselves into some kind of trouble from which he would have to extricate them.

BRISTOL-MYERS TELE-VARIETIES
Various
FIRST TELECAST: *January 5, 1947*
LAST TELECAST: *April 13, 1947*
BROADCAST HISTORY:
 Jan 1947–Mar 1947, NBC Sun 8:15–8:30
 Mar 1947–Apr 1947, NBC Sun 8:00–8:15

This was a series of short program tryouts by sponsor Bristol-Myers in the new medium of television. The variety show was the most common format, using an assortment of little-known talent, but perhaps the most successful experiment was a TV adaptation in March of Tex and Jinx McCrary's radio talk show, *Hi Jinx.* The McCrarys were naturals for TV, and with their combination of friendly chatter, interviews, and features, they later became two of the leading personalities in the new medium.

Tele-Varieties was first seen as a local show in New York in December 1946.

BROADSIDE
Situation Comedy
FIRST TELECAST: *September 20, 1964*
LAST TELECAST: *September 5, 1965*
BROADCAST HISTORY:
 Sep 1964–Sep 1965, ABC Sun 8:30–9:00
CAST:
 Lt. (j.g.) Anne Morgan . . . . Kathy Nolan
 Cdr. Rogers Adrian . . . . Edward Andrews
 Lt. Maxwell Trotter . . . . Dick Sargent
 Machinist's Mate Molly McGuire
  . . . . Lois Roberts
 Machinist's Mate Selma Kowalski
  . . . . Sheila James

Machinist's Mate Roberta Love .. Joan Staley
Machinist's Mate Marion Botnik
.... Jimmy Boyd
Ship's Cook 1st Class Stanley Stubbs (1965)
.... Arnold Stang
Ensign Beasley .... George Furth
Nicky D'Angelo (1964)........ Don Edmonds

This military comedy featured a group of U.S. Navy WAVES who were assigned to a South Pacific island during World War II and found themselves surrounded by thousands of sailors and an unappreciative CO. As an experiment, Lt. Morgan and her girls had been sent to Ranakai Island as replacements for male motor pool personnel, but Cdr. Adrian, the base CO, did not appreciate the resulting disruption. Ranakai was one of the quietest posts in the Pacific, and until they arrived Adrian had had a soft tour, complete with a Persian rug in his office, Rolls-Royce staff car, and gourmet meals (prepared by his eccentric but world-famous chef, Stanley Stubbs).

Most episodes consisted of Adrian's attempts to get the WAVES to transfer Stateside, by such clever ploys as cutting off their lipstick supply. Some concerned the "plight" of M/M Marion Botnik, who had been assigned to the WAVES by mistake when a personnel clerk mistook his name for that of a female.

Broadside was produced by the creator of *McHale's Navy*, Edward J. Montagne.

BROADWAY JAMBOREE
Musical Variety
FIRST TELECAST: *May 10, 1948*
LAST TELECAST: *June 28, 1948*
BROADCAST HISTORY:
May 1948–Jun 1948, NBC Mon 8:00–8:30

This early live variety show was originally conceived as network television's first all-black series. The first telecast was described by NBC as an "all colored revue ... featuring the Deep River Boys, colored quartet dressed in regular business suits and singing the songs popular with a minstrel show, and Derby Wilson, colored tap rhythm dancer." The second week offered the Deep River Boys, Maxine Sullivan, Tom Fletcher, Theodore Hines, and the dance team of Carl & Haryette. Thereafter the format suffered some turmoil, and featured both black and white performers. The third telecast was a straight variety show, and the next two starred Jack Albertson as a Broadway columnist trying to fend off his job-hunting girlfriend while talking about various acts (who then performed). The final week tied together the acts by leafing through the pages of *Variety*, then cutting to performers who were named in ads or stories. Among those appearing during the later telecasts were comedian Gus Van, dancers Ellsworth and Fairchild, the Melodeers (a black quintet) and a square-dance team from New Rochelle.

The series was originally called *Broadway*

Minstrels (for the first two, all-black episodes), and thereafter *Broadway Jamboree*.

BROADWAY MINSTRELS
see *Broadway Jamboree*

BROADWAY OPEN HOUSE
Talk/Variety
FIRST TELECAST: *May 29, 1950*
LAST TELECAST: *August 24, 1951*
BROADCAST HISTORY:
May 1950–May 1951, NBC Mon–Fri 11:00–12:00
May 1951–Aug 1951, NBC Tue/Thu/Fri 11:00–12:00
REGULARS:
Jerry Lester
Morey Amsterdam (1950)
Dave Street
Jane Harvey (1950)
Andy Roberts
The Mellolarks
Bob Warren (1951)
Richard Hayes (1951)
Helen Wood (1951)
Elaine Dunn (1951)
Jack Leonard (1951)
Eileen Barton (1951)
Buddy Greco (1951)
The Milton Delugg Quartet
Dagmar
Ray Malone
Wayne Howell
The Honeydreamers
Dell and Abbott (1951)
Estelle Sloane (1951)
Earl Barton (1951)
The Kirby Stone Quintet (1951)
Maureen Cannon (1951)
Marion Colby (1951)
Frank Gallop (1951)
Barbara Nichols (1951)

Broadway Open House was the granddaddy of all of television's informal talk shows, and preceded *The Tonight Show* as NBC's post-11 P.M. nightly attraction. Actually, however, it was two shows in one. Jerry Lester was on three days a week (Tuesday, Thursday, and Friday), while Morey Amsterdam was the initial emcee on Mondays and Wednesdays. They each had their own group of regulars, the most famous being the statuesque "dumb" blonde Dagmar, on Lester's nights. Stars were invited to drop in and chat, or perform if they felt like it, and the regulars performed in comedy skits, songs, and dances. There was also byplay with orchestra leader/accordionist Milton Delugg. Delugg was a songwriter as well and at least one of his numbers, "Orange Colored Sky," was plugged so much on this show that it became a major record hit—probably the first song ever to become a hit through television exposure.

Morey Amsterdam left in November of 1950,

and the cast on his two nights underwent a number of changes. Finally, in May 1951, Jerry Lester also left the show; he was replaced by Jack Leonard as star, and the entire show was cut back to three nights a week. Original cast member Dagmar was retained, new singers, dancers, and musicians were added, and the Kirby Stone Quintet moved over from the canceled Monday and Wednesday show.

The circumstances surrounding Jerry Lester's departure from *Broadway Open House* involved an ongoing feud with Dagmar, the show's biggest star next to Jerry. A young actress named Jennie Lewis (although her real name was Virginia Ruth Egnor), Dagmar had been signed by Jerry to do a walk-on early in the run of the show, reading inane poetry with a deadpan delivery. It was for that part that Jerry renamed her Dagmar. She was an instant hit and became a regular feature, her salary rising quickly to the point where only Jerry made more. A veteran performer, Jerry resented the publicity and popularity of what he felt was his "creation" and tried to minimize her role. In the spring of 1951, to divert attention from Dagmar, he even added another statuesque blonde to the cast, Barbara Nichols (whom he renamed Agathon). The friction became intolerable, for Dagmar had become Jerry's Frankenstein monster, too popular for him to deal with, and Jerry abandoned the series to pursue other interests. Neither the show nor Dagmar's newfound career survived without him.

BROADWAY SPOTLIGHT

Variety
FIRST TELECAST: *March 10, 1949*
LAST TELECAST: *September 4, 1949*
BROADCAST HISTORY:
 Mar 1949–Apr 1949, NBC Wed 8:00–8:30
 May 1949–Jul 1949, NBC Sun 7:00–7:30
 Jul 1949–Sep 1949, NBC Sun 7:30–8:00
HOST:
 Danton Walker (Mar–Jun)
 Richard Kollmar (Jun–Sep)
REGULARS:
 Ving Merlin Orchestra
 Joey Faye, comedian (Jun–Sep)
 June Taylor Dancers (Jul–Sep)

This live variety program was originally hosted by Broadway columnist Danton Walker, later by radio personality Richard Kollmar. Singers, comedians, and stage actors and actresses appeared as guests, with the emphasis on past and present stars of the Broadway stage. One early feature involved a major star performing one of his or her great successes of the past, together with a newcomer whom that star had discovered. The title of the series varied from *Show Business, Inc.* (March–April) to *Danton Walker's Broadway Scrapbook* (April–June) to *Broadway Spotlight* (June–September).

BROADWAY TO HOLLYWOOD—HEADLINE CLUES

News/Interview/Quiz
FIRST TELECAST: *July 20, 1949*
LAST TELECAST: *July 15, 1954*
BROADCAST HISTORY:
 Jul 1949–Sep 1949, DUM Wed 8:30–9:00
 Oct 1949–May 1950, DUM Fri 8:30–9:00
 May 1950–Jan 1951, DUM Wed 10:00–10:30
 Jan 1951–Jul 1954, DUM Thu 8:30–9:00
HOST:
 George F. Putnam (1949–1951)
 Bill Slater (1951–1953)
 Conrad Nagel (1953–1954)

This magazine show featuring news, gossip, and quiz elements ran for five years on the DuMont TV network. Early in the program's history the quiz element was stressed; host-commentator George Putnam would call viewers at home and offer prizes for the correct answers to news-related questions or identification of photos shown on the air. There were also guest celebrities and new talent discoveries; Eddie Fisher is said to have made his first TV appearance on this show.

By the time Bill Slater took over as host in March 1951, the quiz segment had been dropped, and emphasis was placed on late-breaking news stories and timely features on world and national issues and show business. The day assassins attempted to kill President Truman, for instance, *Headline Clues* flew an eyewitness to its New York studios to give a firsthand account of the incident. Human-interest stories were also featured, as in the meeting—on the show—of two doctors who had developed the wonder drug cortisone and a little girl who had been cured of a crippling infirmity by their discovery. New movies and nightclub acts were reviewed, and guest celebrities performed

First known simply as *Headline Clues*, the program changed its name to *Broadway to Hollywood—Headline Clues* in October 1949.

BROKEN ARROW

Western
FIRST TELECAST: *September 25, 1956*
LAST TELECAST: *September 18, 1960*
BROADCAST HISTORY:
 Sep 1956–Sep 1958, ABC Tue 9:00–9:30
 Apr 1960–Sep 1960, ABC Sun 7:00–7:30
CAST:
 Tom Jeffords.................... John Lupton
 Cochise .... Michael Ansara
 Duffield .... Tom Fadden
 Nukaya .... Steven Ritch

The cowboys and Indians got together to battle injustice in this Western, which starred John Lupton as Indian agent Tom Jeffords and Michael Ansara as Apache Chief Cochise. Jeffords was originally an army officer given the assignment of getting the U.S. Mail safely through Apache territory in Arizona. Adopting the novel approach of making friends with the Indians instead of shooting at them, Jeffords soon became blood brother to Cochise. Together they fought both renegades from the Chiricahua Reservation and dishonest "white eyes" who preyed upon the Indians. The show was based on the novel *Blood Brother,* by Elliott Arnold, which had been made into a movie in 1950.

Repeats of *Broken Arrow* were seen on the network on Sunday afternoons in 1959–1960 and in an early-evening time slot during the summer of 1960.

BRONCO
Western
FIRST TELECAST: *September 23, 1958*
LAST TELECAST: *August 20, 1962*
BROADCAST HISTORY:
   Sep 1958–Sep 1960, ABC Tue 7:30–8:30
   Oct 1960–Aug 1962, ABC Mon 7:30–8:30
CAST:
   Bronco Layne.................... Ty Hardin

Bronco, as portrayed by newcomer Ty Hardin, was born of the fight between Clint Walker and Warner Brothers Studios over the series *Cheyenne* (see *Cheyenne* for details). When Walker quit his successful series in 1958, Hardin was brought in to replace him. Although the series continued under the title *Cheyenne,* Hardin starred in it as Bronco Layne, an ex-Confederate Army captain who had wandered west after the war in search of adventure. There were no other regulars, but the handsome young Bronco did encounter plenty of interesting characters in his exploits, including Billy the Kid, Jesse James (played by James Coburn), Cole Younger, Belle Starr, and Wild Bill Hickok.

In 1959 Clint Walker returned to *Cheyenne,* and *Bronco* became a separate series. In both the 1958–1959 and 1959–1960 seasons Hardin's series alternated with another Western, *Sugarfoot.* Then in 1960 *Bronco* was brought back under the *Cheyenne* umbrella title, as part of a rotating anthology consisting of Walker's *Cheyenne,* Will Hutchins' *Sugarfoot,* and Hardin's *Bronco;* the three stars were seen separately, in different episodes. *Sugarfoot* was dropped from the rotation in 1961, leaving only *Bronco* and *Cheyenne* to alternate in 1961–1962.

BRONK
Detective Drama
FIRST TELECAST: *September 21, 1975*
LAST TELECAST: *July 18, 1976*
BROADCAST HISTORY:
   Sep 1975–Jul 1976, CBS Sun 10:00–11:00
CAST:
   Lt. Alex Bronkov............... Jack Palance
   Mayor Pete Santori .... Joseph Mascolo
   Harry Mark .... Henry Beckman

   Sgt. John Webber .... Tony King
   Ellen Bronkov .... Dina Ousley

Tough guy Jack Palance, who frequently played heavies in movies, turned contemplative cop for this single-season series. Pipe-smoking Lt. Alex Bronkov had been enlisted by his old friend Pete Santori, mayor of Ocean City, in Southern California, to help clean up that corruption-ridden town. Bronk worked on special assignments from the mayor, with the assistance of fellow officer Sgt. John Webber. Also featured in the cast were retired policeman Harry Mark, a close friend of Bronk's who was now in the auto-junkyard business, and Bronk's crippled daughter Ellen, who had been confined to a wheelchair by an accident that had crippled her and killed Bronk's wife.

BRONX ZOO, THE
Drama
FIRST TELECAST: *March 19, 1987*
LAST TELECAST:
BROADCAST HISTORY:
   Mar 1987, NBC Thu 10:10–11:10
   Mar 1987–May 1987, NBC Wed 10:00–11:00
   Aug 1987–Sep 1987, NBC Wed 9:00–10:00
   Dec 1987–Jan 1988, NBC Wed 10:00–11:00
   Mar 1988–Apr 1988, NBC Wed 10:00–11:00
   Jun 1988–   , NBC Wed 10:00–11:00
CAST:
   Principal Joe Danzig .... Edward Asner
   Jack Felspar .... Nicholas Pryor
   Sara Newhouse .... Kathryn Harrold
   Harry Barnes .... David Wilson
   Mary Caitlin Callahan ...... Kathleen Beller
   Matthew Littman .... Jerry Levine
   Gus Butterfield .... Mykel T. Williamson
   Carol Danzig .... Janet Carroll
   Roz .... Gail Boggs
   Roberta .... Tyra Ferrell
   Virginia Biederman .... Betty Karlen
   Snyder .... Adam Carl
   Chris Barnes (1988-   ) ...... Chelsea Field

"Are you *bad?*" sneered the smart-mouthed black girl to the new principal. "Can be," he shot back, smiling. Ed Asner, stung by the quick cancellation of his lightweight 1985 sitcom *Off the Rack,* essayed a meatier role in this tough-as-nails drama. It was set in an inner city high school whose violent atmosphere made viewers wince. The producer called it "a show of small victories," and that's the most viewers got amid the muggings, vandalism, and worse (Asner's character was even shot in one episode). Despite the problems, Principal Joe Danzig was determined to keep order and perhaps impart a little hope to the mostly poor and underprivileged students who (sometimes) attended Benjamin Harrison High. Jack was the often insufferable but basically decent Vice Principal, who had wanted Danzig's job; Sara the beautiful, upper-class English teacher, dubious about her assignment to such a hell-hole; Harry the street-wise history teacher who helped, and romanced, her; Callahan the free-spirited art and drama teacher; Littman a drop-out lawyer and neophyte math teacher; and Gus the black basketball coach and science teacher. Carol was Joe's wife of 29 years, who wished he would get out of such a dangerous assignment, but understood his idealism. She passed away shortly after giving birth to a late-in-life baby, leaving him with an additional burden.

BROTHERS, THE
Situation Comedy
FIRST TELECAST: *October 2, 1956*
LAST TELECAST: *September 7, 1958*
BROADCAST HISTORY:
Oct 1956–Mar 1957, CBS Tue 8:30–9:00
Jun 1958–Sep 1958, CBS Sun 7:30–8:00
CAST:
Harvey Box .... Gale Gordon
Gilmore Box .... Bob Sweeney
Dr. Margaret Kleeb .... Ann Morriss
Capt. Sam Box (1956) .... Frank Orth
Capt. Sam Box (1956–1957) . Howard McNear
Marilee Dorf .... Nancy Hadley
Carl Dorf...................... Oliver Blake
Barrington Steel .... Robin Hughes

Harvey and Gilly Box were two brothers who owned a photography studio in San Francisco. Harvey, the older brother, was somewhat blustery and overbearing, but at heart was a good man whose bark was worse than his bite. Gilly was a shy, naive, and inoffensive soul who seemed happy to let his older brother run things. Both of them had girlfriends whose personalities seemed well matched to those of their men, Harvey's the strong-willed Dr. Margaret Kleeb, and Gilly's the quiet Marilee Dorf. Most of the episodes of *The Brothers* revolved around their social and personal lives, their friends, and family. During the summer of 1958, reruns of this series alternated with *Bachelor Father*.

BROTHERS AND SISTERS
Situation Comedy
FIRST TELECAST: *January 21, 1979*
LAST TELECAST: *April 6, 1979*
BROADCAST HISTORY:
Jan 1979, NBC Sun 8:10–8:40
Jan 1979–Feb 1979, NBC Fri 8:30–9:00
Feb 1979–Apr 1979, NBC Fri 9:00–9:30
CAST:
Milos "Checko" Sabolcik ..... Chris Lemmon
Ronald Holmes III .... Randy Brooks
Stanley Zipper.................. Jon Cutler
Harlan Ramsey............. Larry Anderson
Mary Lee.................... Amy Johnston
Suzi Cooper .... Mary Crosby
Seymour .... Roy Teicher

Larry Krandall............. William Windom
Isabel St. Anthony .... Susan Cotten

Following the success of the movie *Animal House* in 1978, all three networks came up with their televersions of college life. ABC had *Delta House*, CBS had *Co-Ed Fever*, and NBC had *Brothers and Sisters*. None of them succeeded.

The setting for this comedy was the campus of Larry Krandall College, run by its founder and namesake. Living at Pi Nu Fraternity were three buddies, Checko, Ronald, and Zipper. They inhabited the frat house's boiler room, nicknamed "Le Dump," and made quite a group. Checko was sincere and dedicated to getting an education, Ron was the fraternity's token black, and Zipper its resident slob. The Pi Nu president, Harlan Ramsey, was as obnoxious and overbearing as he was rich. Harlan's girlfriend, the social-climbing and equally obnoxious Mary Lee, was a member of Gamma Iota sorority, as was Zipper's dream girl, Suzi Cooper. Stories centered around activities at the two houses, with emphasis on pranks and social activities.

BUCCANEERS, THE
Adventure
FIRST TELECAST: *September 22, 1956*
LAST TELECAST: *September 14, 1957*
BROADCAST HISTORY:
Sep 1956–Sep 1957, CBS Sat 7:30–8:00
CAST:
Captain Dan Tempest .... Robert Shaw
Lt. Beamish .... Peter Hammond
Crewman Armando .... Edwin Richfield
Crewman Gaff.............. Brian Rawlinson
Crewman Taffy .... Paul Hansard
Crewman Van Bruch........... Alex Mango
Crewman Dickon .... Wilfrid Downing

Set in the West Indies during the early 1700s, *The Buccaneers* featured adventure on the high seas as well as swashbuckling on land. After clearing the island of New Providence (Nassau) of pirates, the original governor was sent back to England by the Admiralty and replaced by young Lt. Beamish. Fresh out of the Royal Navy's Midshipman's School, the inexperienced Beamish found that, with Blackbeard threatening to take over the island, the situation there was more than he could handle. To cope with it, he made an ally of Dan Tempest, a reformed pirate who had been pardoned by the previous governor. Tempest helped rout the pirates and enjoyed himself so much in the process that he decided to return permanently to the sea on his ship *The Sultana*. His travels to places as far away as New York, and battles with pirates and Spaniards, provided the central plots of episodes of this series. *The Buccaneers* was filmed entirely in England.

ABC aired reruns on Monday afternoons from September 1957 to September 1958.

BUCK JAMES

Medical Drama

FIRST TELECAST: *September 27, 1987*
LAST TELECAST: *May 5, 1988*
BROADCAST HISTORY:

Sep 1987–Jan 1988, ABC Sun 10:00–11:00
Mar 1988–May 1988, ABC Thu 10:00–11:00

CAST:

Dr. Buck James . . . . Dennis Weaver
Clint James . . . . Jon Maynard Pennell
Dinah James . . . . Elena Stiteler
Jenny James . . . . Shannon Wilcox
Vittorio . . . . Dehl Berti
Dr. Rebecca Meyer . . . . Alberta Watson
Henry Carliner . . . . John Cullum

Dennis Weaver starred in this routine medical drama, which resembled *McCloud* in a surgical gown. Buck James was a dedicated trauma surgeon at Holloman University hospital in Texas. His laconic, down home manner and common sense approach to the constant crises in the emergency room made him an excellent doctor—despite a certain amount of verbal sparring with newcomer Rebecca (who was female, East-Coast, and Jewish) and hospital administrator Henry, a well-meaning bureaucrat. When Buck put on his stetson and drove home to the ranch things did not go smoothly, however. His ex-wife Jenny still loved him, but their marriage had ended in divorce due to his total dedication to his work. Daughter Dinah, 22, had come home unmarried and pregnant; son Clint, 19, worked at the ranch and felt alienated from his busy father. Vittorio was the ranch foreman, who dispensed sage advice and had become a kind of second father to Clint. "It's not that I like my job more than my family," opined Buck. "I'm just better at my job."

BUCK ROGERS

Science Fiction

FIRST TELECAST: *April 15, 1950*
LAST TELECAST: *January 30, 1951*
BROADCAST HISTORY:

Apr 1950–Sep 1950, ABC Sat 7:00–7:30
Sep 1950–Jan 1951, ABC Tue 8:30–9:00

CAST:

Buck Rogers (1950) . . . . Kem Dibbs
Buck Rogers (1950–1951) . . . . . Robert Pastene
Wilma Deering . . . . Lou Prentis
Dr. Huer . . . . Harry Sothern
Black Barney . . . . Harry Kingston

This was the first TV version of the famous hero of comic books, radio, and movie serials, also known as *Buck Rogers in the 25th Century*. As in the other versions Buck alone was responsible for the safety of the universe; aided by various pseudo-scientific gadgets, he always managed to outwit such interstellar villains as Killer Kane. Lou Prentis played Buck's beautiful companion Wilma; Harry Sothern his ally, the brilliant Dr. Huer; and Harry Kingston his Martian crony, Bar-

ney. His home base was Niagara, capital of the world. Handsome Kem Dibbs first played the role of Buck on television with suitable derring-do, but was nevertheless replaced after a few months by Robert Pastene.

Production was on the cheap side, though perhaps not as cheap as for DuMont's long-running hit *Captain Video*, which *Buck Rogers* preceded on Saturdays for a time. *Buck Rogers* was also seen in later years as a local series, consisting of edited versions of the movie serials starring Buster Crabbe in the title role.

BUCK ROGERS IN THE 25TH CENTURY

Science Fiction

FIRST TELECAST: *September 20, 1979*
LAST TELECAST: *April 16, 1981*
BROADCAST HISTORY:

Sep 1979–Jul 1980, NBC Thu 8:00–9:00
Aug 1980–Sep 1980, NBC Sat 8:00–9:00
Jan 1981–Apr 1981, NBC Thu 8:00–9:00

CAST:

Capt. William "Buck" Rogers . . . . . Gil Gerard
Col. Wilma Deering . . . . Erin Gray
Dr. Huer (1979–1980) . . . . Tim O'Connor
Twiki . . . . Felix Silla
Twiki's voice . . . . Mel Blanc
Twiki's voice (1981 temporary replacement)
. . . . Bob Elyea
Dr. Theopolis (voice only) (1979–1980)
. . . . Eric Server
Princess Ardala (1979–1980) . Pamela Hensley
Kane (1979) . . . . Henry Silva
Kane (1979–1980) . . . . Michael Ansara
Hawk (1981) . . . . Thom Christopher
Dr. Goodfellow (1981) . . . Wilfred Hyde-White
Admiral Asimov (1981) . . . . Jay Garner
Crichton (voice only) (1981) . . . . Jeff David
Lt. Devlin (1981) . . . . Paul Carr

This updated *Buck Rogers* was far more elaborate than the version aired on ABC almost 30 years earlier. It benefited from much-improved technology, the interest generated by theatrical films like *Star Wars* and *Close Encounters of the Third Kind*, and a budget that enabled the utilization of fancy special effects. Also, unlike earlier versions of *Buck*, in the comics and on film, radio, and television, this series didn't take itself seriously. It was good escapist entertainment with a tongue-in-cheek quality that prevented it from getting pretentious.

Capt. Buck Rogers was an astronaut whose deep-space probe, launched in 1987, was lost for 500 years. Fortunately for Buck, he was frozen in suspended animation, awakening when his craft was discovered by Draconians in the year 2491. The Draconians, led by beautiful but evil Princess Ardala and her henchman, Kane, hoped to take over Earth and thought that Buck was a spy. So, too, did the Earth Defense Directorate, based in the city of New Chicago. Buck, using a combination of wit, charm, brains, and brute strength, eventually prevented the Draconians from achieving their ends (though they did keep reappearing with new plans to defeat Earth) and became a valued ally in defending Earth. He became a good friend of Dr. Huer, the most renowned scientist on Earth, and of Wilma Deering, the beautiful commander in charge of Earth's defenses. Dr. Huer provided Buck with a small robot aide, Twiki, and the services of a talking computer, Dr. Theopolis (usually seen in the form of a large disk around Twiki's neck). Together, they fought the Draconians and others who threatened peace and security. Buck's acclimation to the world of the 25th century was not always easy and his use of 20th-century slang tended to rub off on both Twiki and his human associates.

When *Buck Rogers in the 25th Century* returned for its second season in 1981 (delayed several months by an actors' strike), it had been completely overhauled. No longer based on Earth, Buck and Wilma were now crew members aboard the *Searcher*, an interstellar spaceship seeking survivors of the "great holocaust" that had sent many Earthmen into space not long after Buck's original probe had been lost. In many respects this new format had elements of both *Star Trek* and *Battlestar Galactica*. Other members of the *Searcher*'s crew included its commander, Admiral Asimov (descended from science-fiction writer Isaac Asimov); Lt. Devlin, Asimov's assistant; Dr. Goodfellow, an elderly, eccentric scientist with an insatiable curiosity; and Hawk, part man and part bird, searching for other members of his race. In addition to Twiki, the *Searcher* carried Crichton, a highly intelligent but very obnoxious robot that could not believe it had been built by humans, and especially by its creator, Dr. Goodfellow. Missing from the second season, in addition to the departed cast members, was the narration provided by William Conrad during *Buck Rogers'* initial year.

The pilot for this series, titled *Buck Rogers in the 25th Century*, was released theatrically in March 1979, six months before the series premiered on NBC.

BUCKSKIN
Western
FIRST TELECAST: *July 3, 1958*
LAST TELECAST: *August 29, 1965*
BROADCAST HISTORY:
Jul 1958–Sep 1958, NBC Thu 9:30–10:00
Oct 1958–Jan 1959, NBC Fri 7:30–8:00
Jan 1959–Sep 1959, NBC Mon 7:30–8:00
Jul 1965–Aug 1965, NBC Sun 8:30–9:00
CAST:
Jody O'Connell .... Tommy Nolan
Mrs. Annie O'Connell .... Sallie Brophy
Marshal Tom Sellers .... Michael Road
Ben Newcomb (1959) .... Michael Lipton

Jody O'Connell was a ten-year-old boy living in his mother's boardinghouse in the frontier town of

Buckskin, Montana, in 1880. Annie's boardinghouse was the center of social and business activity for the area, and the series showed life through the eyes of young Jody as he became involved both with guests passing through town and with residents of Buckskin. The series ran for about a year in 1958–1959 and was rerun during the summer of 1965.

BUDWEISER SUMMER THEATRE
see *Movies—Prior to 1961*

BUFFALO BILL
Situation Comedy
FIRST TELECAST: *May 31, 1983*
LAST TELECAST: *April 5, 1984*
BROADCAST HISTORY:
May 1983–Aug 1983, NBC Wed 9:30–10:00
Dec 1983–Apr 1984, NBC Thu 9:30–10:00
CAST:
Bill Bittinger............... Dabney Coleman
Jo Jo White.................. Joanna Cassidy
Woody........................ John Fiedler
Karl Shub .... Max Wright
Wendy Killian................ Geena Davis
Newdell..................... Charles Robinson
Tony........................ Meshach Taylor
Stan Fluger............... Claude Earl Jones

Surely one of the most unusual comedies of recent years, *Buffalo Bill* flouted a basic rule of series TV—that the leading character must, if nothing else, be likable. Bill Bittinger was arrogant, insensitive, and a thorough cad. As the garrulous host of an inexplicably popular local TV talk show in Buffalo, New York, he regularly played the role of "star," shamelessly used everyone around him, and blamed others for anything that went wrong. He did all this, it must be said, with style; Bill, as played by the talented Dabney Coleman, was a fascinating character, even if he did make you squirm at times. And—honoring one of TV's other basic rules, that good *must* win out in the end—he usually failed to get his way. Practically everybody was on to him, and Bill spent many a lonely night after his latest scheme or attempted amorous conquest had fallen through.

Among the people Bill worked with at WBFL-TV were Jo Jo, the beautiful director of his show, with whom he had an on-again, off-again romantic involvement. She harbored no illusions about his nature, however. Once he had proposed to her, with the gallant comment, "You're better than 90 percent of the bimbos out there." Woody was his mousy stage manager, who seemed incredibly naive (he worshiped Bill) but underneath it all, understood. Just to rub it in, the little guy happened to be extremely successful on the side, owning an auto dealership and Bill's apartment building. Karl was the nervous station manager at Channel 12, constantly beset by lawsuits brought on by Bill's outrageous on-air comments; Wendy, the ingenuous research assistant; and Newdell, the black makeup man, who took no grief from anyone, Bill included. Seen occasionally was Bill's daughter Melanie, portrayed by Pippa Pearthree. Some rather sensitive subjects were dealt with in this comedy setting, including Jo Jo's abortion (after Bill had pompously decided for her that she should have the child), and Bill's racist dream, after he had had a run-in with Newdell. The dream was filled with Zulu warriors, pushy black hookers, and other outrageous stereotypes, all in pursuit of Bill, accompanied by the music of Ray Charles' "Hit the Road, Jack."

BUGS BUNNY/ROADRUNNER SHOW, THE
Cartoon
FIRST TELECAST: *April 27, 1976*
LAST TELECAST: *June 1, 1976*
BROADCAST HISTORY:
  Apr 1976–Jun 1976, CBS Tue 8:00–8:30

For a five-week period in the spring of 1976, CBS aired a collection of cartoon shorts from the Warner Brothers cartoon library as a prime-time series. Although titled *The Bugs Bunny/Roadrunner Show,* the series included appearances by such famous cartoon characters as Elmer Fudd, Sylvester and Tweety, Yosemite Sam, Daffy Duck, and Pepe le Pew. Voice characterizations were done by veteran Mel Blanc. This series ran concurrently with other Warner Bros. cartoons that were aired on Saturday mornings by CBS under the same title.

BUGS BUNNY SHOW, THE
Cartoon
FIRST TELECAST: *October 11, 1960*
LAST TELECAST: *September 25, 1962*
BROADCAST HISTORY:
  Oct 1960–Sep 1962, ABC Tue 7:30–8:00
HOST:
  Dick Coughlan
VOICES:
  Mel Blanc

Bugs Bunny and the entire Warner Brothers inventory of theatrical cartoon characters first appeared on network television in this prime-time series, which premiered in the fall of 1960, the same season that saw the premiere of ABC's most successful venture in prime-time animation, *The Flintstones.* Along with Bugs were Porky Pig, Tweety and Sylvester, Yosemite Sam, the Roadrunner, Henry Hawk, Hippity Hopper, Daffy Duck, and others. All voices were done by veteran Mel Blanc. By the time this series departed from prime time in September 1962 a Saturday morning version had already started (in April 1962). That Saturday morning version, still on the air, has become the longest continuously running Saturday morning children's program in the history of network television.

BUICK ACTION THEATER
Dramatic Anthology
FIRST TELECAST: *August 22, 1958*
LAST TELECAST: *October 3, 1958*
BROADCAST HISTORY:
  Aug 1958–Oct 1958, ABC Fri 9:30–10:00

The plays telecast in this short summer series consisted of filmed reruns of episodes from other anthology series.

BUICK BERLE SHOW, THE
  see *Milton Berle Show, The*

BUICK CIRCUS HOUR, THE
Musical Drama
FIRST TELECAST: *October, 7, 1952*
LAST TELECAST: *June 16, 1953*
BROADCAST HISTORY:
  Oct 1952–Jun 1953, NBC Tue 8:00–9:00
CAST:
  The Clown .... Joe E. Brown
  Bill Sothern .... John Raitt
  Kim O'Neill .... Dolores Gray
  The Ringmaster............... Frank Gallop

Set within the framework of a circus, this was the story of an aging clown who tries to help a young singer, Kim O'Neill, who has just joined the troupe. Kim had joined the circus to be near its owner, Bill Sothern, a boisterous, fun-loving giant of a man with whom she had fallen in love. Musical production numbers as well as real circus acts were featured in this series, all interwoven with the stories of the personal and professional conflicts of circus life. Originating live from New York, the series was aired every fourth week in the time slot normally occupied by Milton Berle's *Texaco Star Theatre.*

BULLWINKLE SHOW, THE
Cartoon
FIRST TELECAST: *September 24, 1961*
LAST TELECAST: *September 16, 1962*
BROADCAST HISTORY:
  Sep 1961–Sep 1962, NBC Sun 7:00–7:30
VOICES:
  Bullwinkle J. Moose, Dudley Doright,
    Mr. Peabody.................... Bill Scott
  Rocky Squirrel, Natasha Fatale .. June Foray
  Boris Badenov .... Paul Frees
  Aesop...................... Charles Ruggles
  Snidley Whiplash............. Hans Conried
  Sherman .... Walter Tetley
  Narrator of "Fractured Fairy Tales".
    .... Edward Everett Horton
  Narrator of "Bullwinkle" segments
    .... William Conrad

This cartoon show included clever satire designed to appeal to adults as well as children. The principal characters in the series were Bullwinkle and his friend Rocket J. (Rocky) Squirrel. Boris and Natasha were the cynical but rather ineffectual spies with whom they were most often involved. Other featured segments, not seen in every episode, included "Fractured Fairy Tales"; "Peabody's Improbable History," in which a wealthy dog, Mr. Peabody, traveled back through time with his adopted boy, Sherman; "Adventures of Dudley Doright," a noble mountie confronted with the evil Snidley Whiplash; and "Aesop and Son," in which fables were recounted in unusual ways.

The characters of Rocky and Bullwinkle had originally appeared in a series called *Rocky and His Friends,* in ABC's weekday afternoon lineup during the 1959–1960 season. That series, which had different supporting segments than *The Bullwinkle Show,* ran on ABC until September 1961. *The Bullwinkle Show* then appeared on NBC, Sunday at 7 P.M. from 1961–1962 (above); moved to NBC's Sunday afternoon and then Saturday morning schedule in 1962–1964; and finally went back to ABC, where it remained on Sunday mornings until September 1973. *The Bullwinkle Show* returned home to NBC's Saturday morning lineup almost a decade later, for the 1981–1982 season.

BURKE'S LAW
Police/Detective Drama
FIRST TELECAST: *September 20, 1963*
LAST TELECAST: *January 12, 1966*
BROADCAST HISTORY:
   Sep 1963–Sep 1964, ABC Fri 8:30–9:30
   Sep 1964–Sep 1965, ABC Wed 9:30–10:30
   Sep 1965–Jan 1966, ABC Wed 10:00–11:00
CAST:
   Capt. Amos Burke.............. Gene Barry
   Det. Tim Tilson (1963–1965).... Gary Conway
   Det. Sgt. Les Hart (1963–1965). Regis Toomey
   Henry (1963–1965).............. Leon Lontoc
   Sgt. Ames (1964–1965) .... Eileen O'Neill
   "The Man" (1965–1966) ..... Carl Benton Reid

Gene Barry played a Los Angeles chief of detectives who also was a millionaire, a role not unlike his cowboy-dandy in the earlier *Bat Masterson* series. The character of Amos Burke was first seen two seasons earlier in a *Dick Powell Theatre* presentation ("Who Killed Julia Greer"), where it was played by Dick Powell. As portrayed by Barry, Amos Burke was high-living, elegant, and witty, yet cagey and tough when required. He lived in a palatial mansion and habitually arrived at the scene of a crime in a Rolls-Royce driven by his chauffeur, Henry. Burke also had a magnetic attraction for beautiful women, and interrupted his romances only for interesting homicide cases, usually involving the elite.

His sidekicks were Det. Tim Tilson, a smart, young college type; Det. Les Hart, a seasoned veteran of the force; and in 1964–1965 a pretty policewoman, Sgt. Ames. *Amos Burke* was highly pro-

moted during its first season and featured dozens of Hollywood stars as guests, ranging from Annette Funicello to Sir Cedric Hardwicke; 63 stars appeared in the first eight episodes, according to one press release.

An important change in format and title was made in September 1965. Glamour and sophistication remained the series' trademarks, but Amos Burke severed his connection with the police and became a debonair, globe-trotting secret agent for a United States intelligence agency. His only contact at the agency, and the only other regular during the last season, was known simply as "The Man." The title of the series was simultaneously changed to *Amos Burke—Secret Agent.*

BURNS AND ALLEN SHOW, THE
   see *George Burns and Gracie Allen Show, The*

BURNS AND SCHREIBER COMEDY HOUR, THE
Comedy Variety
FIRST TELECAST: *June 30, 1973*
LAST TELECAST: *September 1, 1973*
BROADCAST HISTORY:
   Jun 1973–Sep 1973, ABC Sat 9:00–10:00
REGULARS:
   Jack Burns
   Avery Schreiber
   Teri Garr
   Frank Welker
   Fred Willard
   Frank Link
   Lisa Todd
   Jack Elliott and Allyn Ferguson Orchestra
   Tony Mordente Dancers

Comedians Jack Burns (the thin one) and Avery Schreiber (the rotund, mustachioed one) starred in this summer series, which featured their own brand of off-beat humor in sketches and blackouts. Various guest stars, including many popular singers, also appeared.

BUS STOP
Drama
FIRST TELECAST: *October 1, 1961*
LAST TELECAST: *March 25, 1962*
BROADCAST HISTORY:
   Oct 1961–Mar 1962, ABC Sun 9:00–10:00
CAST:
   Grace Sherwood .... Marilyn Maxwell
   Will Mayberry .... Rhodes Reason
   Elma Gahringer............... Joan Freeman
   Glenn Wagner........... Richard Anderson

The bus stop of this series was a diner in Sunrise, Colorado, a small town in Rocky Mountain country. The continuing characters included Grace Sherwood, the working owner of the diner; Elma Gahringer, its only waitress; Sheriff Will Mayberry; and District Attorney Glenn Wagner. The stories revolved around the people passing through Sunrise, and many an unusual character stepped off that interstate bus. The program earned national notoriety—and probably an early cancellation—due to an episode titled "A Lion Walks Among Us," which was based on a Tom Wicker novel and starred rock singer Fabian Forte as a youthful psychopath bent on murder and mayhem. This segment was widely denounced for its explicit violence and sadism and was cited in Congressional hearings on violence in television. The president of ABC-TV, when challenged by an angry senator as to whether he allowed his own children to watch such a series, stammered and admitted no—he did not.

Bus Stop was based on the successful play of the same name and had the original playwright, William Inge, as a script consultant.

BUSTIN' LOOSE
Situation Comedy
BROADCAST HISTORY:
Syndicated Only
30 Minutes
Produced: 1987–
Released: September 1987
CAST:
Sonny Barnes................ Jimmie Walker
Mimi Shaw................. Vonetta McGee
Rudey Butler .... Larry Williams
Trish Reagan .... Tyren Perry
Nikky Robison.................. Aaron Lohr
Sue Anne Tyler .... Marie Lynn Wise

Sonny Barnes was a small-time con man in Philadelphia with a penchant for telling tall tales about his nonexistent exploits and relationships with famous people. When one of his scams landed him in court the judge sentenced him to five years' community service—helping social worker Mimi Shaw take care of the four orphans who lived with her. Sonny moved into the basement of her home and took over, however reluctantly, most of the work around the house. He also endeared himself to the orphans, who were fascinated by his bragging. Rudey, the oldest, was a well-meaning klutz who was blind without his glasses; Trish was a popular teen who was the most "adult" of the group; Nikki was street-smart and had the potential to become a junior-grade Sonny; and little Sue Anne was just too cuddly and adorable for words.

Based loosely on the 1981 movie of the same name starring Richard Pryor.

BUSTING LOOSE
Situation Comedy
FIRST TELECAST: *January 17, 1977*
LAST TELECAST: *November 16, 1977*
BROADCAST HISTORY:
Jan 1977–May 1977, CBS Mon 8:30–9:00
Jul 1977–Nov 1977, CBS Wed 8:30–9:00

CAST:
Lenny Markowitz .... Adam Arkin
Melody Feebeck .... Barbara Rhoades
Sam Markowitz.............. Jack Kruschen
Pearl Markowitz................. Pat Carroll
Lester Bellman .... Danny Goldman
Allan Simmonds .... Steve Nathan
Vinnie Mordabito........... Greg Antonacci
Woody Warshaw .... Paul Sylvan
Ralph Cabell .... Paul B. Price
Raymond St. Williams .... Ralph Wilcox
Jackie Gleason.............. Louise Williams

After graduating from engineering school, young Lenny Markowitz decided it was time to find his own place, away from his overprotective parents Sam and Pearl. He secretly moved into a run-down apartment building and set up housekeeping. Since he could not even afford to cover up the ducks on the wallpaper left by the previous tenant, it was not exactly a swinger's pad. It did have compensations, however, most notably his next-door neighbor Melody, a beautiful young woman who worked for an escort service. To make money on a temporary basis, until he could find more suitable employment, Lenny went to work as a salesman at Mr. Cabell's shoe store, where he worked with a "hip" black named Raymond. Lenny's buddies, Lester, Allan, Vinnie, and Woody, were frequent visitors to his place and partners in mischief, as when they left the New York setting of the series to hunt girls at a fashionable Catskills resort. In the fall of 1977, Lenny found a regular girlfriend in a curvaceous young beauty named "Jackie Gleason" (no relation, or resemblance, to the famous TV comedian).

BUZZY WUZZY
Comedy Variety
FIRST TELECAST: *November 17, 1948*
LAST TELECAST: *December 8, 1948*
BROADCAST HISTORY:
Nov 1948–Dec 1948, ABC Wed 7:30–7:45
HOST:
Jerry Bergen
Imogene Coca

Hollywood comedian Jerry Bergen had just finished work on *The Pirate*, a Judy Garland film, when he was recruited to try television in this short comedy variety show. It lasted only four weeks. Imogene Coca was seen with him.

BY POPULAR DEMAND
Variety
FIRST TELECAST: *July 2, 1950*
LAST TELECAST: *September 22, 1950*
BROADCAST HISTORY:
Jul 1950–Aug 1950, CBS Sun 7:30–8:00
Aug 1950–Sep 1950, CBS Fri 10:00–10:30
Sep 1950, CBS Fri 10:30–11:00
REGULARS:
Robert Alda

Arlene Francis (Sep)
The Harry Sosnik Orchestra

Robert Alda was the master of ceremonies for this series, which featured four professional entertainment acts competing with each other in an elimination competition to determine which act would return the following week. Winners were determined by the applause-meter vote of the studio audience. Robert Alda left the show at the beginning of September and was replaced by Arlene Francis for the last three telecasts.

BYLINE

Drama
FIRST TELECAST: *November 4, 1951*
LAST TELECAST: *December 9, 1951*
BROADCAST HISTORY:
   Nov 1951–Dec 1951, ABC Sun 7:30–8:00

CAST:
   Betty Furness

Betty Furness starred in this brief series of live mysteries, which filled in ABC's Sunday 7:30 P.M. time slot until *Ellery Queen* moved over from DuMont in December 1951. Miss Furness was introduced in the first episode as a reporter on the trail of international criminals.

The official title of the program must surely be one of the longest in TV history: *Your Kaiser Dealer Presents Kaiser-Frazer "Adventures in Mystery" Starring Betty Furness in "Byline."*

For two weeks prior to its evening run, the program had run Saturday at noon under the rather simpler title *News Gal.*

BY-LINE—STEVE WILSON

syndicated title for Big Town

C

CBS CARTOON THEATRE

Cartoons
FIRST TELECAST: *June 13, 1956*
LAST TELECAST: *September 5, 1956*
BROADCAST HISTORY:
Jun 1956–Sep 1956, CBS Wed 7:30–8:00
HOST:
Dick Van Dyke

This summer cartoon series featured the characters from Hollywood's "Terrytoons," Heckle and Jeckle, Gandy Goose, Sour Puss, Dinky Duck, and Little Roquefort. Through the use of special film techniques, host Dick Van Dyke was seen chatting with the animated characters between cartoons.

CBS LATE MOVIE, THE

Various
FIRST TELECAST: *February 14, 1972*
LAST TELECAST:
BROADCAST HISTORY:
Feb 1972–   , CBS Mon–Fri 11:30–Conclusion

In the early 1970s CBS had attempted to compete in the late-night audience sweepstakes with *The Merv Griffin Show*. When *Griffin* failed to make a significant dent in the ratings of NBC's highly successful *Tonight Show*, CBS decided to take a different approach to late-night programming, airing the same thing local stations had been showing for years—movies. *The CBS Late Movie* at first consisted of theatrical and made-for-television films, mostly reruns of material that had previously been seen in prime time. In the fall of 1976 reruns of *Kojak* started airing two nights a week and by the end of the 1970s, despite the umbrella title *The CBS Late Movie*, the bulk of CBS' late-night lineup actually consisted of reruns of former prime-time series (*Kojak, Hawaii Five-O, Barnaby Jones, The Jeffersons*, etc.). There were also first American runs of such British series as *The New Avengers* and *Return of the Saint*, and limited runs of original programming (*NBA Basketball Playoffs* and *No Holds Barred*). In the fall of 1985, finally acknowledging the obvious, the series' title was changed to *CBS Late Night*.

Summarized below is a night-by-night history of *The CBS Late Movie*. In cases where there was a double feature on a given night, a semicolon is used to separate the first and second features. If more than one series alternated in the same time slot on different weeks they are separated by a slash.

Monday
Feb 1972–Jan 1977, Movie
Jan 1977–Sep 1977, *Kojak;* Movie
Sep 1977–Sep 1978, Movie
Sep 1978–Sep 1979, *The Rockford Files;* Movie
Sep 1979–Dec 1979, *Harry-O; McMillan & Wife*
Jan 1980–Sep 1980, *Harry-O;* Movie
Sep 1980–Oct 1980, *Quincy, M.E.; The Saint*
Oct 1980–Mar 1981, *Quincy, M.E.; The New Avengers*
Mar 1981–Nov 1981, *Quincy, M.E.; Harry-O*
Dec 1981–Feb 1982, *Quincy, M.E.; Banacek*
Feb 1982–Sep 1982, *Quincy, M.E.; Columbo*
Sep 1982–Jun 1983, *Trapper John, M.D.; Columbo*
Jun 1983–Jul 1983, *Hart to Hart; Columbo*
Jul 1983–Sep 1983, *Hart to Hart;* Movie
Sep 1983–Jun 1984, *Hart to Hart; Columbo*
Jul 1984–Aug 1984, *Magnum, P.I.;* Movie
Sep 1984–May 1985, *Simon & Simon; McMillan & Wife*
May 1985–Aug 1985, *Simon & Simon; Columbo*
Aug 1985–Sep 1985, *Simon & Simon;* Movie
Sep 1985–May 1986, *Remington Steele;* Movie
Jun 1986–Sep 1986, *Magnum, P.I.;* Movie
Sep 1986–Aug 1987, *Simon & Simon;* Movie
Sep 1987–   , Hunter; Movie

Tuesday
Feb 1972–Sep 1976, Movie
Sep 1976–Jan 1977, *Kojak;* Movie
Jan 1977–Sep 1977, Movie
Sep 1977–Nov 1977, *Kojak;* Movie
Nov 1977–Aug 1978, Movie; *Kojak*
Aug 1978–Sep 1978, Movie
Sep 1978–May 1980, *Barnaby Jones;* Movie
May 1980–Jun 1980, *Barnaby Jones; Mary Hartman, Mary Hartman*
Jul 1980–Sep 1980, *Cannon; Barnaby Jones*
Sep 1980–Mar 1981, *Lou Grant;* Movie
Mar 1981–May 1981, *Columbo; NBA Basketball Playoffs*
May 1981–Jul 1981, *Columbo*
Jul 1981–Sep 1981, *Cannon; The Saint*
Sep 1981–Jan 1982, *Alice; McCloud*
Jan 1982–Jul 1982, *Alice; WKRP In Cincinnati; McCloud*
Aug 1982–Sep 1982, *Alice; McCloud*
Sep 1982–Aug 1983, *Quincy, M.E.; McMillan & Wife*
Aug 1983–Sep 1983, Movie
Sep 1983–Jun 1984, *Magnum, P.I.; McCloud*
Jul 1984–Aug 1984, *McGarrett; Columbo*
Sep 1984, *Campaign '84; McGarrett; Columbo*
Oct 1984, *Campaign '84; The Fall Guy; Columbo*
Nov 1984–May 1985, *The Fall Guy; Columbo*
May 1985   , The Fall Guy; McCloud
Jun 1985–Sep 1985, *Magnum, P.I.; McCloud*
Sep 1985–Oct 1985, *Simon & Simon;* Movie

Oct 1985–Nov 1985, Simon & Simon; Cool Million
Nov 1985–Dec 1985, Simon & Simon; McCoy
Jan 1986   , Simon & Simon; Madigan
Feb 1986–Sep 1986, Simon & Simon; Movie
Sep 1986–Dec 1986, Hot Shots; Movie
Dec 1986–Sep 1987, T.J. Hooker; Movie
Sep 1987–   , Diamonds; Movie

Wednesday
Feb 1972–Sep 1977, Movie
Sep 1977–Nov 1977, Hawaii Five-O; Movie
Dec 1977–Aug 1978, Hawaii Five-O; Kojak
Aug 1978–Sep 1978, Hawaii Five-O; Movie
Sep 1978–Nov 1978, Hawaii Five-O; Kojak
Nov 1978–Dec 1978, Movie; Kojak
Jan 1979–Apr 1979, The Rockford Files; Kojak
May 1979, The Rockford Files; Hawaii Five-O
Jun 1979–Sep 1979, Switch; Kojak
Sep 1979–Oct 1979, Switch; Hawaii Five-O
Oct 1979–Dec 1979, Black Sheep Squadron; Hawaii Five-O
Dec 1979–Jan 1980, Black Sheep Squadron; Movie
Jan 1980–Mar 1980, Mary Hartman, Mary Hartman; Movie
Mar 1980–Jun 1980, Black Sheep Squadron; Movie
Jul 1980, The Saint; Black Sheep Squadron
Jul 1980–Sep 1980, The Saint; Movie
Sep 1980–Nov 1980, Campaign Countdown; Movie
Nov 1980–Mar 1981, Movie
Apr 1981, NBA Basketball Playoffs
May 1981–Sep 1981, Movie
Sep 1981–Jan 1982, WKRP In Cincinnati; Movie
Jan 1982–Sep 1982, Movie
Sep 1982–Dec 1982, Archie Bunker's Place; Movie
Dec 1982–Jun 1983, Hart to Hart; Movie
Jun 1983–Sep 1983, Police Story
Sep 1983–Jun 1984, Police Story; Movie
Jun 1984–Aug 1984, The New Avengers; McCloud
Sep 1984–May 1985, Magnum, P.I.; Movie
Jun 1985–Jul 1985, Night Heat; Movie
Jul 1985–Sep 1985, Movie; The New Avengers
Sep 1985–Sep 1986, T.J. Hooker; Movie
Sep 1986–Jul 1987, Adderly; Movie
Jul 1987–Sep 1987, Hot Shots; Movie
Sep 1987–   , Adderly; Movie

Thursday
Feb 1972–Sep 1976, Movie
Sep 1976–Sep 1977, Kojak; Movie
Sep 1977–Mar 1978, Movie
Mar 1978–Sep 1979, M*A*S*H; Movie
Sep 1979–Jan 1980, Columbo; McCloud/Banacek/Madigan
Jan 1980–Mar 1980, Columbo; Black Sheep Squadron

Mar 1980–Apr 1980, Columbo; Mary Hartman, Mary Hartman
May 1980–Sep 1980, The Jeffersons; Movie
Sep 1980–May 1981, The Jeffersons; McMillan & Wife
Jun 1981–Aug 1981, The Jeffersons; Hec Ramsey
Aug 1981–Sep 1981, The Jeffersons; Madigan
Sep 1981–Feb 1982, Quincy, M.E.; The Saint
Feb 1982–Sep 1982, Quincy, M.E.; McMillan & Wife
Sep 1982–Jul 1983, Quincy, M.E.; McCloud
Jul 1983–Sep 1983, Movie
Sep 1983–Jun 1984, Trapper John, M.D.; Movie
Jul 1984–Aug 1984, Hart to Hart; Movie
Sep 1984–Jan 1985, Newhart; Movie
Jan 1985–Mar 1985, Night Heat; Movie
Mar 1985–Apr 1985, Newhart; Movie
May 1985   , Night Heat; Movie
Jun 1985–Jul 1985, The Fall Guy; Movie
Jul 1985–Aug 1985, The New Avengers; Movie
Aug 1985–Sep 1985, Columbo; The New Avengers
Sep 1985–Jul 1987, Night Heat; Movie
Aug 1987–Sep 1987, Movie
Sep 1987–   , Night Heat; Movie

Friday
Feb 1972–Sep 1977, Movie
Sep 1977–Dec 1977, M*A*S*H; Kojak
Dec 1977–Mar 1978, M*A*S*H; Movie
Mar 1978–May 1978, NBA Basketball Playoffs
May 1978–Sep 1978, Movie
Sep 1978–Mar 1979, The New Avengers; Movie
Mar 1979–May 1979, NBA Basketball Playoffs
May 1979–Jul 1979, Kolchak: The Night Stalker; Movie
Jul 1979–Aug 1979, Hawaii Five-O; Movie
Sep 1979–Dec 1979, Kolchak: The Night Stalker; Movie
Dec 1979–Mar 1980, The Avengers; Return of the Saint
Mar 1980–Apr 1980, NBA Basketball Playoffs
May 1980–Aug 1980, The Avengers; Return of the Saint
Aug 1980–Sep 1980, The Avengers; Movie
Sep 1980–Oct 1980, No Holds Barred; The New Avengers
Oct 1980–Mar 1981, Movie
Mar 1981–May 1981, NBA Basketball Playoffs
Jun 1981–Sep 1981, The Night Stalker; Movie
Sep 1981–Oct 1981, Movie
Oct 1981–Jan 1982, Behind the Screen; Movie
Jan 1982–Mar 1982, Movie
Mar 1982–May 1982, NCAA/NBA Basketball Playoffs
May 1982–Apr 1983, Movie
Apr 1983–May 1983, NBA Basketball Playoffs
May 1983–Jan 1986, Movie
Feb 1986   , Magnum, p.i.
Feb 1986–Mar 1986, Magnum, p.i.; Movie
Mar 1986–May 1986, Magnum, p.i.; McGarrett
Jun 1986–Sep 1986, Movie

Sep 1986–Dec 1986, T.J. Hooker; Movie
Jan 1987–Jun 1987, Keep On Cruisin'; McGarrett
Jun 1987–Aug 1987, In Person from the Palace;
  Movie
Aug 1987–Sep 1987, Movie
Sep 1987–Mar 1988, Top of the Pops; Kolchak:
  The Night Stalker
Apr 1988– , Movie

CBS NEWCOMERS
Variety
FIRST TELECAST: *July 12, 1971*
LAST TELECAST: *September 6, 1971*
BROADCAST HISTORY:
  Jul 1971–Sep 1971, CBS Mon 10:00–11:00
REGULARS:
  Dave Garroway
  David Arlen
  Cynthia Clawson
  Raul Perez
  Rex Allen, Jr.
  Gay Perkins
  Peggy Sears
  The Californians
  Joey Garza
  Rodney Winfield
  The Good Humor Company
  Nelson Riddle and His Orchestra

This summer variety show marked the return to a
regular network series of Dave Garroway after a
nine-year absence. He introduced performances
by a wide range of young entertainers, all new to
network television, who had been discovered in
nightclubs and theaters during the previous year.
None of them, alas, went on to become a major
star.

CBS NEWS ADVENTURE
Documentary
FIRST TELECAST: *March 20, 1970*
LAST TELECAST: *April 17, 1970*
BROADCAST HISTORY:
  Mar 1970–Apr 1970, CBS Fri 7:30–8:30
NARRATOR:
  Charles Kuralt

This adventure documentary series examined in
depth one or two subjects each week. Among the
topics were an auto race from London, England, to
Sydney, Australia; people who dive to remarkable
depths without diving equipment; and a round-
the-world sailing trip by five men and a woman,
using a 47-foot boat.

CBS NEWS RETROSPECTIVE
Documentary/Public Affairs
FIRST TELECAST: *July 8, 1973*
LAST TELECAST: *September 1, 1974*
BROADCAST HISTORY:
  Jul 1973–Sep 1973, CBS Sun 6:00–7:00
  Jul 1974–Sep 1974, CBS Sun 6:00–7:00

HOST:
  John Hart

The documentaries that were aired in this summer
series had originally been telecast during the
1950s and 1960s and were considered classics of
TV journalism. Many of them came from Edward
R. Murrow's *See It Now;* others were from the
CBS News Reports and *CBS News Special* series
that succeeded it. John Hart was the host, setting
the background for the period in which the specials had originally been aired and putting them in
historical perspective.

CBS REPORTS/NEWS HOUR/NEWS SPECIAL
Documentary
FIRST TELECAST: *January 5, 1961*
LAST TELECAST: *September 7, 1971*
BROADCAST HISTORY:
  Jan 1961–Sep 1962, CBS Thu 10:00–11:00
  Sep 1962–Dec 1964, CBS Wed 7:30–8:30
  Dec 1964–Aug 1965, CBS Mon 10:00–11:00
  Sep 1965–Jun 1970, CBS Tue 10:00–11:00
  Apr 1966–May 1966, CBS Fri 10:00–11:00
  Sep 1970–Sep 1971, CBS Tue 10:00–11:00

On October 27, 1959, fifteen months after the demise of Edward R. Murrow's *See It Now,* the CBS
News Department premiered a new, incisive, in-
depth documentary program entitled *CBS Reports.* It was patterned after Murrow's precedent-
setting program and employed many of the same
production staff, including Murrow's former partner Fred Friendly. It was aired during 1959–60 on
an irregular basis as a series of specials. Murrow
himself appeared on the first telecast, "Biography
of a Missile," though he was later only an infrequent participant in the new series.
  In January of 1961 CBS began airing *CBS Reports* as a regular alternate-week series on Thursday nights, opposite ABC's enormously successful
The Untouchables. The rationale seemed to be
that since CBS could not compete for the escapist-
entertainment audience, it would at least telecast
something worthwhile opposite the violence on
ABC. For almost a full decade *CBS Reports* remained a regular series on various nights, at times
alternating with *CBS News Hour, CBS News Special,* and other shows and at times as a weekly
series. It remained CBS' most prestigious news
analysis program and generally ran for a full hour,
while the other CBS news programs varied between 30 and 60 minutes depending on subject.
CBS Reports has continued to appear since 1971
on an irregular basis, in the form of specials.
  During its ten-year run as a regular series, a
number of the documentaries aired on *CBS Reports* won Emmy awards. Among them were
"KKK—The Invisible Empire" (1966), "Eric Hoffer,
the Passionate State of Mind" (1968), "CBS Reports: What About Ronald Reagan" (1968), "Gauguin in Tahiti: The Search for Paradise" (1968),

"CBS Reports: Hunger in America" (1969), "Justice Black and the Bill of Rights" (1969), "The Great American Novel" (1969), "The Japanese" (1970), and "The Selling of the Pentagon" (1971).

CBS SUMMER PLAYHOUSE
Dramatic Anthology
FIRST TELECAST: *June 12, 1987*
LAST TELECAST:
BROADCAST HISTORY:
Jun 1987–Sep 1987, CBS Fri 8:00–9:00
Jun 1988–   , CBS Tue 8:00–9:00
HOSTS:
Tim Reid (1987)
Daphne Maxwell Reid (1987)

This summer anthology series was comprised entirely of pilot episodes for series—both comedy and drama—that CBS had not picked for its fall lineup. In an unusual twist, viewers were given the opportunity to say whether or not they liked each of the pilots by voting via special "900" phone numbers after each evening's pilot (or pilots) had aired.

The series' hosts, married couple Tim and Daphne Maxwell Reid, took advantage of their role here to promote *Frank's Place,* the CBS series on which they would co-star in September. Among the more familiar faces featured in the pilots (none of which were "saved" by viewer call-ins) were Kevin Tighe, Valerie Perrine, Brenda Vaccaro, Barbara Bain, Buddy Ebsen, Linda Purl, and Darren McGavin.

When *CBS Summer Playhouse* returned in 1988 it was without hosts or viewer voting.

C.P.O. SHARKEY
Situation Comedy
FIRST TELECAST: *December 1, 1976*
LAST TELECAST: *July 28, 1978*
BROADCAST HISTORY:
Dec 1976–Jan 1977, NBC Wed 8:00–8:30
Feb 1977–Apr 1977, NBC Wed 9:00–9:30
Jul 1977–Aug 1977, NBC Wed 9:00–9:30
Oct 1977–Jan 1978, NBC Fri 8:30–9:00
Feb 1978–Apr 1978, NBC Fri 8:30–9:00
Jun 1978–Jul 1978, NBC Fri 8:00–8:30
CAST:
C.P.O. Otto Sharkey............ Don Rickles
Seaman Pruitt .... Peter Isacksen
Daniels .... Jeff Hollis
Kowalski...................... Tom Ruben
Skolnick .... David Landsberg
Capt. Quinlan (1976–1977) ... Elizabeth Allen
Chief Robinson .... Harrison Page
Mignone (1976–1977) .... Barry Pearl
Apodaca (1977–1978) .... Philip Simms
Rodriguez .... Richard Beauchamp
Lt. Whipple................. Jonathan Daly
Chief Gypsy Koch .... Beverly Sanders
Capt. "Buck" Buckner (1977–1978)
.... Richard X. Slattery

Insult comic Don Rickles found the perfect vehicle for his humor in this situation comedy, in which he was cast as Chief Petty Officer Sharkey of the U.S. Navy. Sharkey, a 24-year veteran of navy service, was stationed at the Navy Training Center in San Diego, California. He was in charge of a company of new recruits, and it was his job to make sailors out of a collection of diverse ethnic types, most of whom had never been away from home before. The various ethnic backgrounds and stereotypes were all targets for Sharkey's verbal barbs, but beneath that harsh, nasty exterior beat the heart of an old softie, especially when he sensed the suffering of a recruit who either could not take his bluster or was suffering the problems of adjusting to life away from home. Sharkey's immediate superior was the long-winded and overbearing Lt. Whipple; the base commander was Capt. Quinlan, who was, of all things, an attractive woman.

When *C.P.O. Sharkey* returned in October 1977, to replace the short-lived *The Sanford Arms,* Sharkey had a new, and male, commanding officer in Capt. "Buck" Buckner.

CACTUS JIM
Children's
FIRST TELECAST: *October 31, 1949*
LAST TELECAST: *October 26, 1951*
BROADCAST HISTORY:
Oct 1949–Oct 1951, NBC Mon–Fri 6:00–6:30
HOST:
Cactus Jim (1949–1951) .... Clarence Hartzell
Cactus Jim (1951) .... Bill Bailey

This children's program was built around Western feature movies, which were shown in segments on succeeding days. Cactus Jim, a "range-riding old-timer," introduced each episode and spun a few yarns. The program emanated from WNBQ, Chicago. It later turned up on NBC's Saturday morning lineup for a brief run from January to March 1952.

CADE'S COUNTY
Police Drama
FIRST TELECAST: *September 19, 1971*
LAST TELECAST: *September 4, 1972*
BROADCAST HISTORY:
Sep 1971–Aug 1972, CBS Sun 9:30–10:30
Aug 1972–Sep 1972, CBS Mon 10:00–11:00
CAST:
Sam Cade .... Glenn Ford
J. J. Jackson .... Edgar Buchanan
Arlo Pritchard .... Taylor Lacher
Rudy Davillo .... Victor Campos
Pete............................. Peter Ford
Joannie Little Bird (1971) .... Sandra Ego
Betty Ann Sundown........ Betty Ann Carr

Sprawling Madrid County, California, was the setting for this contemporary Western/police drama. Sheriff Sam Cade, based in the town of Madrid, was responsible for law enforcement throughout the county. He was assisted by veteran deputy J. J. Jackson and three younger deputies, Arlo, Rudy, and Pete. Sandra Ego initially had the role of police dispatcher but was replaced early on by Betty Ann Carr. Both of them were American Indians. The role of Pete, one of Cade's young deputies, was played by the son of Glenn Ford, the show's star.

CAESAR PRESENTS
Comedy Variety
FIRST TELECAST: *July 4, 1955*
LAST TELECAST: *September 12, 1955*
BROADCAST HISTORY:
  Jul 1955–Sep 1955, NBC Mon 8:00–9:00
HOST:
  Bobby Sherwood
CAST:
  Charles Williams .... Phil Foster
  Barbara Williams .... Barbara Nichols
  Sandy Williams .... Sandra Deel
  Vocalist .... Bill Hayes
  Various Parts .... Sid Gould
  Various Parts .... Cliff Norton
  Various Parts .... Judy Tyler

This combination variety and situation-comedy show was a summer replacement for *Caesar's Hour.* In addition to production numbers and comedy skits, a weekly feature of the program was the situation-comedy sketch "The Pharmacist," starring Phil Foster as an overworked and underpaid pharmacist with problems at home and at work. Sid Caesar, who produced this show, appeared live to introduce each episode.

CAESAR'S HOUR
Comedy Variety
FIRST TELECAST: *September 27, 1954*
LAST TELECAST: *May 25, 1957*
BROADCAST HISTORY:
  Sep 1954–Jun 1956, NBC Mon 8:00–9:00
  Sep 1956–May 1957, NBC Sat 9:00–10:00
CAST:
  Bob Victor .... Sid Caesar
  George Hansen .... Carl Reiner
  Fred Brewster .... Howard Morris
  Ann Victor (1954–1956) ...... Nanette Fabray
  Betty Hansen (1954–1955) .... Virginia Curtis
  Betty Hansen (1955–1956) .... Sandra Deel
  Betty Hansen (1956–1957) ...... Shirl Conway
  Alice Brewster (1954–1956) ...... Ellen Parker
  Alice Brewster (1956–1957) .... Pat Carroll
  Jane Victor (1956–1957) .... Janet Blair
REGULARS:
  William Lewis (1955–1957)
  Earl Wild (1955–1957)
  Dave Caesar (1955–1957)
  Paul Reed (1955–1957)
  Milt Kamen (1956–1957)
  Bea Arthur (1956–1957)
  Hugh Downs (1956–1957), announcer

The highly imaginative and creative comedy of Sid Caesar was the moving force in this successor to his famous *Your Show of Shows,* With him in this venture, also from *Your Show of Shows,* were comedians Carl Reiner and Howard Morris. The format of the series varied from a full hour of situation comedy, to musical revues, to a variety show or any combination of the three. Although the three male leads remained the same throughout the duration of the series, there was considerable turnover among the women.

The most successful sketch used in the series was "The Commuters," in which Caesar, Reiner, and Morris typified the suburbanite who takes the same train to work in the big city every morning and the same train home every evening. The lives of these people became to *Caesar's Hour* what "The Honeymooners" was to *The Jackie Gleason Show.* A featured part of the program, on occasion this sketch was expanded to fill the entire hour. The cast credits above are for the parts played by the participants in this sketch. Other featured comedy skits were "The Three Haircuts," in which Caesar, Reiner, and Morris satirized rock 'n' roll musicians, and Caesar's characterization of "The Professor."

CAGNEY & LACEY
Police Drama
FIRST TELECAST: *March 25, 1982*
LAST TELECAST:
BROADCAST HISTORY:
  Mar 1982–Apr 1982, CBS Thu 9:00–10:00
  Oct 1982–Sep 1983, CBS Mon 10:00–11:00
  Mar 1984–Dec 1987, CBS Mon 10:00–11:00
  Jan 1988–Apr 1988, CBS Tue 10:00–11:00
  Apr 1988–Jun 1988, CBS Mon 10:00–11:00
  Jun 1988–   , CBS Thu 10:00–11:00
CAST:
  Det. Mary Beth Lacey .... Tyne Daly
  Det. Chris Cagney (1982) .... Meg Foster
  Det. Chris Cagney (1982–   ) . Sharon Gless
  Lt. Bert Samuels .... Al Waxman
  Det. Mark Petrie .... Carl Lumbly
  Det. Victor Isbecki .... Martin Kove
  Det. Paul La Guardia (1982–1985)
    .... Sidney Clute
  Deputy Inspector Marquette (1982–1983)
    .... Jason Bernard
  Desk Sergeant Ronald Coleman
    .... Harvey Atkin
  Harvey Lacey .... John Karlen
  Harvey Lacey, Jr. .... Tony La Torre
  Michael Lacey .... Troy Slaten
  Sgt. Dory McKenna (1984–1985)
    .... Barry Primus
  Insp. Knelman (1984–   ) .. Michael Fairman
  Det. Jonah Newman (1985–1986) .... Dan Shor
  David Keeler (1985–   ) ..... Stephen Macht
  Alice Lacey (1985–1987)
    .... Dana & Paige Bardolph
  Alice Lacey (1987–   ) ...... Michelle Sepe

Det. Manny Esposito (1986–)
.... Robert Hegyes
Det. Al Corassa (1986–).... Paul Mantee
Josie (1986–)................. Jo Corday
Kazak (1986–1987) .... Stewart Coss
Beverley Faverty (1986–1987)
.... Beverley Faverty
Tom Basil (1986–)........... Barry Laws
Verna Dee Jordan (1987–)
.... Merry Clayton

"We had a shot," said producer Barney Rosenzweig, "at television history." *Cagney & Lacey* was certainly unusual for commercial TV, asserting that two women could be best buddies in the Starsky-and-Hutch, Paul Newman–Robert Redford tradition and do a "man's job" just as well as any man could. With male leads it would have been a rather ordinary TV police series. Mary Beth Lacey was the married one, trying to be a wife and mother, as well as a New York City police officer. Chris Cagney was single, ambitious, and full of the joys of living. Though beautiful, she was often disappointed in love. Despite their different life-styles, Mary Beth and Chris were partners and fast friends, determined to break the stereotypes often ascribed to women in jobs not traditionally associated with them. They fought criminals, the chauvinism of their male fellow officers, the ignorance of their friends regarding their unusual careers, and sometimes each other—with shouting sessions in the ladies' room. Working primarily as undercover cops, they infiltrated criminal organizations and sometimes served as decoys to capture street criminals.

Not all of the cases worked out, either. Like *Hill Street Blues* and other "reality" shows, *Cagney & Lacey* reflected the real world of the big-city cop.

The offscreen troubles of this series were almost as dramatic as the onscreen problems of its stars. Conceived by Rosenzweig with the help of feminists Barbara Corday and Barbara Avedon in 1974, it was turned down as a series by all three networks, finally airing as a made-for-TV movie on CBS in October 1981 with Loretta Swit as Cagney. The movie drew a tremendous audience, and a limited-run series was commissioned for the following spring. Loretta Swit was unavailable, so Meg Foster was cast as Cagney. This time the ratings were poor, and CBS thought it knew why. "They were too harshly women's lib," said an unnamed CBS executive in *TV Guide*, "too tough, too hard, and not feminine." "The American public doesn't respond to the bra burners, the fighters, the women who insist on calling manhole covers peoplehole covers," he continued. "We perceived them as dykes."

That last remark set off a storm of protest, but the role of Cagney was once again recast, this time with beautiful Sharon Gless, who was to provide a softer, more feminine counterpart for Lacey. Gay groups protested *that* ("She's from the Copacabana school of acting," complained the

Gay Media Task Force, "very kittenish and feminine . . ."), but the decision stuck.

Despite the changes, audiences were disappointingly small in 1982–1983, and the series was canceled at the end of the season amid a flurry of publicity about the cop show that had tried to be "different." Loyal viewers thereupon inundated CBS with letters, and summer reruns began to pick up new viewers who were curious about the fuss. In September the show won an Emmy. Much to everyone's surprise, CBS relented and the series surfaced once again in the spring of 1984—accompanied by the *TV Guide* headline "Welcome Back, *Cagney & Lacey*," and advertising that proclaimed "You Want Them! You've Got Them!"

The series flourished after being brought back and the personal lives of Cagney and Lacey became more prominent in the story lines. Mary Beth had another child, a daughter named Alice. Chris' social life, first her relationship with drug-addicted fellow cop Dory McKenna and later with attorney David Keeler, were featured. At one point she was even the victim of date rape. Her personal problems, including the fear of never marrying and having a family and a bout with alcoholism, were also depicted. Chris' father Charlie (Dick O'Neill) also turned up from time to time, until he passed away in the spring of 1987. That year she was promoted to sergeant.

CAIN'S HUNDRED
Police Drama
FIRST TELECAST: *September 19, 1961*
LAST TELECAST: *September 11, 1962*
BROADCAST HISTORY:
Sep 1961–Sep 1962, NBC Tue 10:00–11:00
CAST:
Nicholas "Nick" Cain . (Peter) Mark Richman

Nick Cain had spent years as a gangland lawyer. He knew who the important people in organized crime were; and now that he had become an agent of the federal government, he was determined to ferret out and bring to prosecution the 100 men controlling the many-tentacled monster of organized crime in America. Roving about the country with a special squad of assistants, Nick Cain assembled the necessary evidence to help the government bring big-time gangsters to justice. Based on actual case histories, *Cain's Hundred* dramatized, often in quasi-documentary fashion, the personalities, lives, and methods of the members of the underworld fraternity in the United States.

CALIFORNIA FEVER
Adventure
FIRST TELECAST: *September 25, 1979*
LAST TELECAST: *December 11, 1979*
BROADCAST HISTORY:
Sep 1979–Dec 1979, CBS Tue 8:00–9:00
CAST:
Vince Butler............... Jimmy McNichol
Ross Whitman.............. Marc McClure

Laurie Newman..............	Michele Tobin
Rick	Lorenzo Lamas
Bobby.......................	Cosie Costa
Sue	Lisa Cori

This is what middle-aged network executives think is meant by the term "youth appeal." Vince, Ross, and Laurie were three high school students living the carefree life in suburban Los Angeles. With a background of disco music, surfing, souped-up cars, and cruising the Sunset Strip, this series followed the adventures of Vince and Ross. Vince was into music, and ran an underground radio station from the back room of Rick's, the local hangout that served snacks and rented roller skates. Ross was the mechanic supreme, and drove a personally customized monstrosity that he had named "The Grossmobile." Together they sought fun and excitement in the sun-drenched, fad-oriented environment of Southern California. Like the fads, however, *California Fever* didn't have much staying power.

CALIFORNIANS, THE
Western
FIRST TELECAST: *September 24, 1957*
LAST TELECAST: *August 27, 1959*
BROADCAST HISTORY:
Sep 1957–Mar 1959, NBC Tue 10:00–10:30
Apr 1959–Jun 1959, NBC Tue 9:00–9:30
Jul 1959–Aug 1959, NBC Thu 7:30–8:00
CAST:
Dion Patrick (1957–1958).....	Adam Kennedy
Jack McGivern (1957–1958) ...	Sean McClory
Martha McGivern (1957–1958).....	Nan Leslie
Sam Brennan (1957–1958)....	Herbert Rudley
Matthew Wayne............	Richard Coogan
Schaab (1957–1958)..........	Howard Caine
Wilma Fansler (1958–1959) .	Carole Mathews
Jeremy Pitt (1958–1959)......	Arthur Fleming

Set in San Francisco during the 1850s, at the height of the Gold Rush, *The Californians* was the story of the honest men trying to clean up a wild city overrun by criminals and con men. Dion Patrick had been drawn to San Francisco by the prospect of Gold Rush riches, but went to work instead as a crusading reporter for newspaperman Sam Brennan—and also joined storekeeper Jack McGivern's vigilantes, the only functioning law-enforcement organization in town. In the middle of the first season Matthew Wayne arrived and was elected sheriff of San Francisco; he became the leading character as vigilantes Patrick and McGivern were eased out of the show. In the second season Wayne, by then city marshal, continued his fight against crime with a newly reorganized 50-man police force. He remained the focal point with the addition of love interest Wilma Fansler, a young widow who ran a gambling house, and attorney Jeremy Pitt, friend and foil to the marshal.

CALL MR. D
Syndicated title for *Richard Diamond, Private Detective*

CALL OF THE WEST
see *Death Valley Days*

CALL TO GLORY
Drama
FIRST TELECAST: *August 13, 1984*
LAST TELECAST: *February 12, 1985*
BROADCAST HISTORY:
Aug 1984–Dec 1984, ABC Mon 8:00–9:00
Jan 1985–Feb 1985, ABC Tue 10:00–11:00
CAST:
Col. Raynor Sarnac	Craig T. Nelson
Vanessa Sarnac	Cindy Pickett
RH Sarnac	Gabriel Damon
Jackie Sarnac................	Elisabeth Shue
Wesley Sarnac	David Hollander
Carl Sarnac	Keenan Wynn
Patrick Thomas............	Thomas O'Brien
Airman Tom Bonelli	David Lain Baker
General Hampton..............	J.D. Cannon
Lillie.......................	Priscilla Pointer

The Cold War of the early 1960s provided the backdrop for this drama about a military family headed by patriotic Air Force Colonel Raynor Sarnac. Sarnac commanded a group of jet pilots, and he seemed to become involved in many of the earthshaking events of the time, from the Cuban Missile Crisis to the incipient U.S. involvement in Vietnam. He also faced turmoil at home, from his worried wife, Vanessa, and his three growing children: Jackie, 15, who was dating a somewhat confused young man named Patrick; Wesley, the fun-loving 14-year-old; and RH, the 8-year-old. They all felt the pressures of military life, with its danger and constant relocation. Carl was the colonel's walrus-mustached dad, who offered sage advice about duty to family and country.

Bits of 1960s songs, vintage newsfilm, and references to such issues of the day as air raid drills and the Civil Rights movement helped give the series a period flavor.

CALUCCI'S DEPARTMENT
Situation Comedy
FIRST TELECAST: *September 14, 1973*
LAST TELECAST: *December 28, 1973*
BROADCAST HISTORY:
Sep 1973–Dec 1973, CBS Fri 8:00–8:30
CAST:
Joe Calucci	James Coco
Shirley Balukis	Candy Azzara
Ramon Gonzales.................	Jose Perez
Cosgrove	Jack Fletcher
Elaine Fusco.....................	Peggy Pope
Woods	Bill Lazarus
Frohler.....................	Bernard Wexler
Mitzi Gordon	Rosetta LeNoire

Roly-poly comic James Coco portrayed the supervisor of a branch of the New York State Unemployment Office in this ethnic sitcom. Calucci had to cope with the problems of unemployed claimants, the frictions among various members of his staff (who were carefully picked to represent every race, religion, and creed imaginable), and the frustrations of governmental red tape. As if that wasn't enough, he was in love with his secretary, Shirley—or at least infatuated with her—but the series was canceled before their relationship really developed. Apparently most Americans did not find an unemployment office very amusing.

CALVIN AND THE COLONEL
Cartoon
FIRST TELECAST: *October 3, 1961*
LAST TELECAST: *September 22, 1962*
BROADCAST HISTORY:
Oct 1961–Nov 1961, ABC Tue 8:30–9:00
Jan 1962–Sep 1962, ABC Sat 7:30–8:00
VOICES:
The Colonel .... Freeman Gosden
Calvin .... Charles Correll
Maggie Belle .... Virginia Gregg
Sister Sue .... Beatrice Kay
Oliver Wendell Clutch .... Paul Frees

This animated feature concerned the exploits of a bunch of animals from the Deep South who had taken up residence in a large Northern city. The Colonel was a very foxy fox, and Calvin was his best friend, a lovable but not particularly bright bear. Other regulars on the series were the Colonel's wife Maggie Belle, her sister Sue, and Oliver Wendell Clutch, a lawyer who was a weasel. If the plot line sounds vaguely like that of *Amos 'n' Andy*, don't be surprised. Gosden and Correll, the creators and principal voices of this series, played *Amos 'n' Andy* on radio for years. The use of animals here avoided creating what could have been a touchy racial situation in the early 1960s.

CAMEL CARAVAN
see *Vaughn Monroe Show, The*

CAMEO THEATRE
Dramatic Anthology
FIRST TELECAST: *May 16, 1950*
LAST TELECAST: *August 21, 1955*
BROADCAST HISTORY:
May 1950–Sep 1950, NBC Wed 8:30–9:00
Jun 1951–Aug 1951, NBC Mon 8:00–8:30
Jan 1952–Apr 1952, NBC Sun 10:00–10:30
Jul 1955–Aug 1955, NBC Sun 10:00–10:30
CREATOR AND PRODUCER:
Albert McCleery

An interesting early experiment in the unique dramatic possibilities of television, this occasional series of live plays was produced in the round, using a minimum of props. It made considerable use of closeups and other camera techniques to focus attention on the characterizations of individual actors. High-quality scripts were used, both originals and adaptations for television. The first telecast was "It Takes a Thief," by Arthur Miller; later presentations included a three-part adaptation of Ibsen's *Peer Gynt* and a version of the Broadway musical *Dark of the Moon*.

After an absence of three years the series returned for a final run during the summer of 1955, as a replacement for *The Loretta Young Show*.

CAMP RUNAMUCK
Situation Comedy
FIRST TELECAST: *September 17, 1965*
LAST TELECAST: *September 2, 1966*
BROADCAST HISTORY:
Sep 1965–Sep 1966, NBC Fri 7:30–8:00
CAST:
Senior Counselor Spiffy ...... Dave Ketchum
Commander Wivenhoe .... Arch Johnson
Mahala May Gruenecker........ Alice Nunn
Pruett....................... David Madden
Doc Joslyn .... Leonard Stone
Caprice Yeudleman .... Nina Wayne
Eulalia Divine .... Hermione Baddeley
Malden .... Mike Wagner
The Sheriff .... George Dunn

Nuttiness abounded in this comedy of two summer camps for children, Camp Runamuck for boys and, on the other side of the lake bordering it, Camp Divine for girls. The four characters in charge of the boys' camp, Spiffy, Wivenhoe, Pruett, and Doc Joslyn, created constant chaos in their own camp and maintained a strong, and often hilarious, rivalry with the counselors of Camp Divine.

Bandleader Frank DeVol was originally scheduled to play Doc, and did so in the first episode, but health problems forced him to quit the series. Leonard Stone replaced him.

CAMPAIGN AND THE CANDIDATES, THE
News
FIRST TELECAST: *September 17, 1960*
LAST TELECAST: *November 5, 1960*
BROADCAST HISTORY:
Sep 1960–Nov 1960, NBC Sat 9:30–10:30
ANCHORMAN:
Frank McGee

This series of weekly summaries followed the campaigns of presidential candidates John F. Kennedy and Richard M. Nixon as they stated their cases to the American public in the fall of 1960. Coverage was narrated by numerous NBC reporters assigned to the campaigns, with Frank McGee acting as host and coordinator.

CAMPAIGN COUNTDOWN
News

FIRST TELECAST: *September 10, 1980*
LAST TELECAST: *November 5, 1980*
BROADCAST HISTORY:
  Sep 1980–Nov 1980, CBS Wed 11:30–12:00
ANCHORMAN:
  Walter Cronkite

As the 1980 Presidential campaign reached its final stages, CBS aired this weekly wrap-up of political news. Four regular features were: summaries of the campaign activities of the candidates; "Inside Politics," dealing with the impact of finances, media consultants, and polls; latest results of the CBS News—*New York Times* poll; and interviews conducted by George Crile, discussing the major issues. Various CBS news correspondents contributed reports.

CAMPAIGN ROUNDUP
News Analysis
FIRST TELECAST: *May 12, 1958*
LAST TELECAST: *June 9, 1958*
BROADCAST HISTORY:
  May 1958–Jun 1958, ABC Mon 8:00–8:30
MODERATOR:
  Quincy Howe

Continuing analysis of the various congressional and gubernatorial campaigns taking place throughout the country was provided by the ABC news staff during the 1958 primary season. Different correspondents contributed information regarding the races in different parts of the country.

CAMPAIGN '72
News
FIRST TELECAST: *June 25, 1972*
LAST TELECAST: *September 17, 1972*
BROADCAST HISTORY:
  Jun 1972–Sep 1972, CBS Sun 6:00–7:00

During the summer of 1972, a presidential election year, CBS aired a regular series of reports on the activities of both parties as they prepared for their conventions, planned their campaign strategies, and sought to determine the way in which their respective nominees would handle themselves in the post-convention campaign.

CAMPAIGN '76
News
FIRST TELECAST: *September 3, 1976*
LAST TELECAST: *October 31, 1976*
BROADCAST HISTORY:
  Sep 1976–Oct 1976, CBS Fri 7:30–8:00

As the 1976 presidential campaign drew to a close, CBS News provided a weekly report on the activities of Gerald Ford and Jimmy Carter in their "race for the White House." In addition to the latest poll results, CBS correspondents were shown on location with the candidates and in various parts of the country discussing issues with

citizens and evaluating how regional climate of opinion was affected by the rhetoric. Various CBS News correspondents served as anchormen on individual telecasts.

CAMPAIGN '84
News
FIRST TELECAST: *September 11, 1984*
LAST TELECAST: *October 30, 1984*
BROADCAST HISTORY:
  Sep 1984–Oct 1984, CBS Tue 11:30–12:00
ANCHORMAN:
  Dan Rather

This weekly program updated viewers on the presidential campaigns of Republican President Ronald Reagan and Democratic challenger Walter Mondale. Dan Rather coordinated the proceedings, which included coverage of the preceding week's major political stories and features on various aspects of the campaigns—economic, ideological, social, and political.

CAMPBELL PLAYHOUSE
see *Campbell Soundstage*

CAMPBELL SOUNDSTAGE
Dramatic Anthology
FIRST TELECAST: *June 6, 1952*
LAST TELECAST: *September 3, 1954*
BROADCAST HISTORY:
  Jun 1952–Aug 1952, NBC Fri 9:30–10:00
  Jul 1953–Sep 1954, NBC Fri 9:30–10:00

This dramatic series premiered in 1952 as the summer replacement for the vacationing *Aldrich Family*. Initially it was a collection of filmed dramas under the title *Campbell Playhouse*. Among the dramas were "The Cavorting Statue," starring Cesar Romero and Ann Rutherford, "Return to Vienna," with Ruth Warrick and Cameron Mitchell, and "This Little Pig Cried," with Frances Rafferty and Robert Rockwell.

The show returned in 1953 under the title *Campbell Soundstage*, this time as the permanent replacement for the canceled *Aldrich Family*. With the new name came a change in format. The plays were produced live in New York, starred bigname talent, and all had surprise endings reminiscent of O. Henry's short stories. Among the performers who starred in these live plays were Jack Lemmon, Walter Matthau, James Dean, E. G. Marshall, Betsy Palmer, Roddy McDowall, Brian Keith, and Lillian Gish.

On June 4, 1954, the title became *Campbell Summer Soundstage* and the presentations reverted to film. Many of these were reruns of episodes previously aired on *Ford Theatre*.

CAMPUS CORNER
Music
FIRST TELECAST: *March 18, 1949*
LAST TELECAST: *April 11, 1949*

BROADCAST HISTORY:
  Mar 1949–Apr 1949, CBS Mon/Fri 7:45–8:00
REGULAR SINGERS:
  Beverly Fite
  Frank Stevens
  Buzz Davis
  Dean Campbell
  Bob Burkhardt

Singer Beverly Fite was the hostess and star of this short-lived musical series, which was aired twice a week in the spring of 1949. She sang, with a quartet as backup, and chatted with a guest or two. The series was also called *The Quadrangle.*

CAMPUS HOOPLA
  Sports/Variety
FIRST TELECAST: *December 27, 1946*
LAST TELECAST: *December 19, 1947*
BROADCAST HISTORY:
  Dec 1946–Dec 1947, NBC Fri 8:00–8:30 (OS)
HOST:
  Bob Stanton
COMMERCIALS:
  Eva Marie Saint

Campus Hoopla was a combination sports and variety show aimed at teenage viewers. The setting was a campus soda shop, complete with "cheerleaders" and "students" who talked about sports, participated in quiz segments, and sang and danced to the music of a jukebox. The latest sports scores were given by NBC sportscaster Bob Stanton, who also narrated films of recent games.

CAN DO
  Quiz/Audience Participation
FIRST TELECAST: *November 26, 1956*
LAST TELECAST: *December 31, 1956*
BROADCAST HISTORY:
  Nov 1956–Dec 1956, NBC Mon 9:00–9:30
EMCEE:
  Robert Alda

This short-lived game show offered contestants the opportunity to win up to $50,000 for correctly guessing whether famous show-business personalities could successfully perform certain stunts. The first round was worth $1,500, with the prize doubling on each successive round. A contestant could quit at any time, with the threat of losing most of his winnings to be weighed against doubling his money. An incorrect guess meant that the contestant only took home 10 percent of the amount he was trying for, or roughly 20 percent of what he had already won. Among the celebrities featured were Sal Mineo operating a construction crane and Rory Calhoun performing an archery feat.

CAN YOU TOP THIS?
  Comedy
FIRST TELECAST: *October 3, 1950*

LAST TELECAST: *March 26, 1951*
BROADCAST HISTORY:
  Oct 1950–Dec 1950, ABC Tue 9:30–10:00
  Dec 1950–Mar 1951, ABC Mon 8:00–8:30
EMCEE:
  Ward Wilson
PANEL:
  Joe Laurie, Jr.
  Harry Hershfield
  Peter Donald
  "Senator" Ed Ford

In the simple format of this show, four old-time gagsters sat around a table and told funny stories, including some sent in by viewers. A laugh meter measured the audience reaction to each and determined the winner of each round. The program was based on the radio show of the same name.

Here's a typical story: A very fussy school inspector arrived to inspect a little country schoolhouse. Hearing a commotion in one of the classrooms, he walked in and found the boys and girls raising a ruckus. One of them, a little taller than the rest, was making most of the noise. So the inspector promptly took this lad into another room, bent him over his knee, and spanked him. "Now, you stand in that corner and behave yourself or else I'll spank you again," the inspector warned sternly. So the fellow stood in the corner. A while later, there was a timid knock on the door. A little girl stuck her head in and said, "Please, sir, can we have our teacher back now?"

During the 1969–1970 season, almost two decades after the network version left the air, *Can You Top This?* returned in a syndicated version. Wink Martindale (replaced during the season by Dennis James) was the emcee, Richard Dawson assisted, and Morey Amsterdam was the only permanent panelist.

CANDID CAMERA
  Humor
FIRST TELECAST: *August 10, 1948*
LAST TELECAST: *September 3, 1967*
BROADCAST HISTORY:
  Aug 1948–Sep 1948, ABC Sun 8:00–8:30
  Oct 1948, ABC Wed 8:30–8:45
  Nov 1948–Dec 1948, ABC Fri 8:00–8:30
  May 1949–Jul 1949, NBC Sun 7:30–8:00
  Jul 1949–Aug 1949, NBC Thu 9:00–9:30
  Sep 1949–Sep 1950, CBS Mon 9:00–9:30
  Jun 1953, NBC Tue 9:30–10:00
  Jul 1953, NBC Wed 10:00–10:30
  Oct 1960–Sep 1967, CBS Sun 10:00–10:30
PRODUCER AND HOST:
  Allen Funt
CO-HOST:
  Arthur Godfrey (1960–1961)
  Durward Kirby (1961–1966)
  Bess Myerson (1966–1967)

A patron at a bowling alley would roll a ball, and back down the chute it would come—minus finger holes. *Candid Camera* viewers watched as the poor fellow tried to figure out *what the*—!

A tiny foreign car would pull into a service station and the driver would casually ask for a "fill up." The hidden camera focused on the attendant's growing astonishment as the midget auto practically drained the station dry. (There was a tank concealed in the trunk).

"Smile, you're on *Candid Camera!*"

The premise of Allen Funt's long-running *Candid Camera* was simply to snoop on unsuspecting citizens with hidden cameras and see how they would react to bizarre situations. Cars were a favorite device. In one sequence, innocent-looking Dorothy Collins (frequently seen on the show during the 1960s) would come driving down a hill and pull up in front of a passerby, asking for help—the car "won't seem to start." Up went the hood to reveal . . . no engine. Other ploys included vending machines that talked back, actors who got into unbelievable predicaments and then asked passersby for help, diners served impossibly small portions, and so on—*ad infinitum.* The reactions of the surprised victims were often hilarious.

Allen Funt, who appeared in many of the gags, may have been one of the nerviest actors in TV history. Yet he got few rejections, much fewer punches in the nose, for his presumptions upon innocent citizens. His greatest coup was a special filmed in Moscow—without the permission, or even knowledge, of the Russian authorities. Funt managed to smuggle himself, cameramen, hidden cameras, and 90,000 feet of film into and out of the Soviet Union undetected (the border guards, taking him for a tourist, never opened his bags). On the streets of the Russian capital he staged many of his favorite stunts, including the newspaper routine (start reading someone's paper over their shoulder, gradually get your hands on it to position it better, and then work it away from them entirely) and the two-suitcase caper. (A pretty girl with two suitcases asks a passing male to help her carry one; hers is empty, his is filled with 200 pounds of concrete. To Funt's astonishment, a burly Russian blithely picked up the trick suitcase and trotted off with it, never blinking an eye.)

Some of the best sequences were not setups, but simply cameos from life; for instance, the husky traffic cop at a busy intersection who seemed to perform a classical ballet as he motioned cars hither and yon.

Allen Funt first brought his established *Candid Microphone* radio program to television in 1948, and it continued off and on for 30 years thereafter. The first TV version was in fact called *Candid Microphone,* but the title was changed to *Candid Camera* when it moved to NBC in 1949. In addition to its prime-time runs, listed above, *Candid Camera* was aired as a local program in New York in the mid-1950s; as part of the commercials within *Pontiac Presents Playwrights '56* in 1955–1956; as a segment within the *Garry Moore Show* in 1959–1960; and in reruns on CBS

daytime TV, from September 1966 to September 1968.

Six years later, Allen Funt brought *Candid Camera* back in a syndicated version that included both new and old material. The syndicated version, which ran from 1974 to 1978, utilized the services of Phyllis George, Jo Ann Pflug, and John Bartholomew Tucker as co-hosts with Funt, and comedienne Fannie Flagg as a semi-regular participant in the setups.

CANNON
Detective Drama
FIRST TELECAST: *September 14, 1971*
LAST TELECAST: *September 19, 1976*
BROADCAST HISTORY:
  Sep 1971–Sep 1972, CBS Tue 9:30–10:30
  Sep 1972–Sep 1973, CBS Wed 10:00–11:00
  Sep 1973–Jul 1976, CBS Wed 9:00–10:00
  Jul 1976–Sep 1976, CBS Sun 10:00–11:00
CAST:
  Frank Cannon . . . . William Conrad

Balding, middle-aged, and portly, detective Frank Cannon represented quite a change from the traditional suave, handsome private detectives TV had brought to its viewers. He occasionally let his conscience dictate his choice of cases, but more often his wallet took precedence. To most clients he charged a high fee, in order to provide himself with the money to indulge in personal luxuries such as an expensive convertible and fine cuisine. Cannon rarely fired a shot, was in no condition to beat up his adversaries, and was generally seen driving around Los Angeles in his big, shiny Continental. The car took more physical abuse than Cannon did, often getting dented, scraped, and mangled during chase sequences.

William Conrad, the only regular in the series, had previously been more familiar to the ears than to the eyes of Americans. During the 1950s he had been the voice of Matt Dillon in the radio version of *Gunsmoke,* but was manifestly unsuited to portray the tough Western marshal when the series moved to television—so young James Arness got the role, in what became the longest-running dramatic series in TV history.

CAPITOL CAPERS
Music
FIRST TELECAST: *August 1, 1949*
LAST TELECAST: *September 7, 1949*
BROADCAST HISTORY:
  Aug 1949–Sep 1949, NBC Mon/Wed 7:30–7:45
REGULARS:
  Cliff Quartet, instrumental
  Gene Archer, baritone

This live musical program emanated from NBC's Washington, D.C., studios.

CAPITOL CLOAK ROOM
Public Affairs/Discussion

FIRST TELECAST: *October 14, 1949*
LAST TELECAST: *September 8, 1950*
BROADCAST HISTORY:
    Oct 1949–Sep 1950, CBS Fri 10:30–11:00
PANELISTS:
    Griffing Bancroft
    Eric Sevareid
    Bill Shadel

CBS simulcast this live political discussion program from Washington, D.C., on both its television and radio networks. Each week a key political figure was interviewed by a panel of three CBS correspondents. The panel was chaired by Griffing Bancroft. Following its prime-time run, *Capitol Cloak Room* moved to Sunday afternoons, where it remained until the following January.

CAPTAIN AND TENNILLE, THE
Musical Variety
FIRST TELECAST: *September 20, 1976*
LAST TELECAST: *March 14, 1977*
BROADCAST HISTORY:
    Sep 1976–Mar 1977, ABC Mon 8:00–9:00
REGULARS:
    Daryl Dragon
    Toni Tennille

This youth-oriented variety hour was built around the "soft rock" husband-and-wife team of Daryl Dragon and Toni Tennille, who had several big record hits in 1975–1976 and who, ABC hoped, might become another Sonny and Cher on TV. They didn't.

Toni was a pretty but somewhat antiseptic version of Cher, while Daryl ("The Captain," after his ever-present captain's hat) was decidedly quieter than Sonny. In fact, he scarcely said a word, and much of the comedy was built around his extremely taciturn nature. He also had a chance to show off his musical wizardry—he was a master of all sorts of keyboard instruments. Daryl came from a background of music, if not comedy, being the son of the well-known concert conductor Carmen Dragon.

Among the featured segments on the show were "The Charcoal House," with Daryl and Toni as two struggling young performers, and "Masterjoke Theater." The only other regulars on the show were the Dragons' two English bulldogs, Elizabeth and Broderick.

CAPTAIN BILLY'S MISSISSIPPI MUSIC HALL
Variety
FIRST TELECAST: *October 1, 1948*
LAST TELECAST: *November 26, 1948*
BROADCAST HISTORY:
    Oct 1948–Nov 1948, CBS Fri 8:30–9:00
REGULARS:
    Ralph Dumke
    Betty Brewer
    Johnny Downs
    Juanita Hall

George Jason
Bibi Osterwald
The Vic Smalley Orchestra

Loosely based on incidents related in the book *Old Man River and His Chillun*, written by Captain Billy Bryant, this live variety series was set on a Mississippi paddlewheel showboat. It was hosted by Ralph Dumke, in the role of Captain Billy, and included musical numbers, comedy, and dramatic interludes performed by guest stars. The series had premiered on August 16 as a local show under the title *Captain Billy's Showboat*, changed its name on September 17, and two weeks later became a network program.

CAPTAIN NICE
Situation Comedy
FIRST TELECAST: *January 9, 1967*
LAST TELECAST: *August 28, 1967*
BROADCAST HISTORY:
    Jan 1967–Aug 1967, NBC Mon 8:30–9:00
CAST:
    Carter Nash (Captain Nice). William Daniels
    Mrs. Nash.................... Alice Ghostley
    Sgt. Candy Kane............... Ann Prentiss
    Mayor Finney .... Liam Dunn
    Chief Segal................ William Zuckert
    Mr. Nash.................... Byron Foulger

Captain Nice was created and written by Buck Henry, co-creator of *Get Smart*, and it was to superheroes what *Get Smart* was to secret agents—a parody. Carter Nash was a police department chemist who had accidentally discovered a liquid that, when drunk, would transform him into Captain Nice. Unfortunately Captain Nice was no stronger a personality than Carter was normally—shy, quiet, unassuming, and mother-dominated. In fact if it had not been for his mother, who demanded that her son wage war on the evil forces that constantly threatened society, he would not have gotten actively involved in fighting crime at all. The sight of Captain Nice trying to maintain his composure while flying over Bigtown (he had an acute fear of heights) in his baggy, moth-eaten, red-white-and-blue leotards (made for him by his mother) did not exactly terrify evil-doers.

CAPTAIN VIDEO AND HIS VIDEO RANGERS
Children's
FIRST TELECAST: *June 27, 1949*
LAST TELECAST: *April 1, 1955*
BROADCAST HISTORY:
    Jun 1949–Aug 1949, DUM Mon/Tu/Thu/Fri 7:00–7:30
    Aug 1949–Sep 1953, DUM Mon–Fri 7:00–7:30
    Sep 1953–Apr 1955, DUM Mon–Fri 7:00–7:15
    also
    Feb 1950–Sep 1950, DUM Sat 7:30–8:00
    Sep 1950–Nov 1950, DUM Sat 7:00–7:30

Captain Video (1949–1950) . . . Richard Coogan
Captain Video (1951–1955) . . . . Al Hodge
The Ranger . . . . Don Hastings
Dr. Pauli (1949) . . . . Bran Mossen
Dr. Pauli (later) . . . . Hal Conklin

CREATOR/PRODUCER:
James Caddigan

WRITER:
Maurice C. Brock

THEME:
Overture to *The Flying Dutchman,* by Richard Wagner

"Guardian of the Safety of the World"—on a prop budget of $25 per week! *Captain Video* was one of the low-budget wonders of television history, and one of the most popular children's programs of the early 1950s. It was the first of a trio of "space operas" popular at the time—*Space Patrol* and *Tom Corbett—Space Cadet* were mere imitations—and the one most frequently seen (Monday–Friday during most of its run).

Captain Video, as played by handsome, jut-jawed Richard Coogan, and later by handsome, jut-jawed Al Hodge (formerly the voice of radio's *Green Hornet*), was a scientific genius who took it upon himself, as a private citizen, to insure the safety of the universe. Operating from his secret, mountaintop headquarters, sometime in the 21st or 22nd century, he controlled a vast network of "Video Rangers" as well as an impressive arsenal of futuristic weaponry of his own invention. His sidekick The Ranger—idol of half the kids in America—was played by young Don Hastings, who was 15 when the series began.

Captain Video's adversaries were legion, among them Nargola, Mook the Moon Man, Kul of Eos, Heng Foo Seeng, Dr. Clysmok, and Dahoumie. But the most persistent was Dr. Pauli, head of the Astroidal Society and an evil genius whose scientific weaponry was almost equal to Video's own.

Captain Video and The Ranger were constantly coming up with new devices with which to fight off these assorted villains. The Opticon Scillometer (which looked suspiciously like a length of pipe with some spare parts bolted on) allowed one to see through things; the Atomic Rifle could blow up almost anything; the Discatron was a sort of portable TV set; the Radio Scillograph was a long-range two-way radio that fit in the palm of the hand; and the Cosmic Ray Vibrator a handy device that literally shook adversaries into submission—seldom was anyone killed outright on *Captain Video.* Not to be outdone, Dr. Pauli countered with his Trisonic Compensator, which could curve bullets around a house; his Barrier of Silence, so he couldn't be heard; and the Cloak of Invisibility—how many kids would have liked to get their hands on *that!*

Perhaps the most terrifying piece of machinery seen on *Captain Video,* however, was Tobor ("robot" spelled backward). Designed as the ultimate, unstoppable, indestructible robot to work for the good of mankind, he had been appropriated by a beautiful villainess named Atar. She programmed him, naturally, to "get Captain Video." But the captain also managed to get on Tobor's secret frequency and in a magnificent climactic scene, the hulking brute was reduced to a pile of scrap metal by conflicting orders from Atar and Video.

Since DuMont was perpetually impoverished, the sets and props on *Captain Video* were constructed on the smallest possible budget. Most of the controls in the captain's spaceship, the *Galaxy,* were painted on, and one suspected that a single swift kick at his master control board would destroy the entire headquarters. The unkindest limitations were on the network of Video Rangers, whom the captain would look in on, using his Remote Carrier Beam, once during each telecast. Most of them looked exactly like cowboys in the Old West—DuMont was running pieces of ancient Westerns to pad out the half hour! (This practice ceased after a time.)

There was tremendous viewer interest in *Captain Video,* heightened by offers of premiums such as plastic replicas of the captain's weapons, his decoder ring, and his space helmet. A theatrical serial was made based on his exploits. The program won several awards from impressed adults, too, for the captain's regular short talks to "Rangers at home" on the value of tolerance, fair play, and personal integrity.

Captain Video was, in all, a splendid example of innovative programming that was perfect for the TV medium. Had DuMont been able to devise more such breakthroughs, the network might have survived longer than it did. As it was, *Captain Video and His Video Rangers* lasted until the network itself crumbled away, in 1955. During the last stages of its run it was also known as *The Secret Files of Captain Video.*

The reader interested in a detailed, and loving, description of *Captain Video* and other "space operas" is referred to *The Great Television Heroes,* by Donald F. Glut and Jim Harmon.

CAPTAINS AND THE KINGS
Drama

FIRST TELECAST: *September 30, 1976*
LAST TELECAST: *April 25, 1977*
BROADCAST HISTORY:
Sep 1976–Nov 1976, NBC Thu 9:00–10:00
Mar 1977–Apr 1977, NBC Thu 9:00–11:00
Apr 1977, NBC Mon 9:00–11:00
CAST:
Joseph Armagh . . . . Richard Jordan
Katherine Hennessey . . . . Joanna Pettet
Big Ed Healey . . . . Charles Durning
Martinique . . . . Barbara Parkins
Tom Hennessey . . . . Vic Morrow
Harry Zieff . . . . Harvey Jason
Miss Emmy . . . . Beverly D'Angelo

Charles Desmond	Robert Vaughn
Elizabeth Healey Hennessey	Blair Brown
Bernadette Hennessey Armagh	
	Patty Duke Astin
Moira/Mary Armagh	Katherine Crawford
Marjorie Chisholm Armagh	Jane Seymour
Rory Armagh	Perry King
Claudia Desmond	Cynthia Sikes
Kevin Armagh	Douglas Heyes, Jr.

Adapted from Taylor Caldwell's novel, *Captains and the Kings* was the saga of Joseph Armagh, a poor Irish immigrant who rose to great prominence in America in the latter part of the nineteenth century. Episodes chronicled the period from his arrival in New York as a young man in 1857 till the death of his last son around 1912. His rise to wealth and power through investments in the oil industry, his affairs both public and private, and his consuming desire to have one of his sons become the first Irish Catholic president of the United States were all woven into the story. That latter plan, on the verge of success, was abruptly destroyed when Rory was assassinated during the campaign.

Captains and the Kings was one of the four novels dramatized under the collective title *NBC's Best Sellers*. Although most of the chapters ran only one hour, as indicated in the broadcast history above, the first and last chapters ran from 9–11 P.M. It was also the only one of the four novels to be rerun, in the spring of 1977, with all rerun installments running two hours in length. The concluding chapter of the *Captains and the Kings* reruns aired on Monday night, April 25, 1977.

CAPTURED
syndicated title for *Gangbusters*

CAR 54, WHERE ARE YOU?
Situation Comedy
FIRST TELECAST: *September 17, 1961*
LAST TELECAST: *September 8, 1963*
BROADCAST HISTORY:
Sep 1961–Sep 1963, NBC Sun 8:30–9:00
CAST:

Officer Gunther Toody	Joe E. Ross
Officer Francis Muldoon	Fred Gwynne
Lucille Toody	Bea Pons
Captain Martin Block	Paul Reed
Officer O'Hara	Albert Henderson
Officer Anderson (1961–1962)	Nipsey Russell
Officer Antonnucci (1961–1962)	
	Jerome Guardino
Officer Riley (1961–1962)	Duke Farley
Officer Murdock (1961–1962)	Shelley Burton
Officer Steinmetz	Joe Warren
Officer Leo Schnauser	Al Lewis
Officer Kissel	Bruce Kirby
Officer Ed Nicholson	Hank Garrett
Officer Nelson	Jim Gormley
Sylvia Schnauser	Charlotte Rae

Officer Wallace (1962–1963)
.... Frederick O'Neal
CREATOR AND PRODUCER:
Nat Hiken

Officers Toody and Muldoon were among the most unlikely patrol-car partners ever seen on a police force. Toody was short, stocky, friendly, and just a bit nosy, a marked contrast to the tall, quiet Muldoon. Although they were assigned to New York's 53rd precinct—a run-down area in the Bronx not generally considered a hotbed of hilarity—they always seemed to encounter more comedy than crime. Much of the action took place in the precinct house itself, particularly in the locker room as the officers got into uniform, and the comedy was invariably of the broad slapstick variety reminiscent of Mack Sennett.

One unusual aspect of this series was the partners' patrol car, which looked identical to those used by real-life New York City police—but only because the show was filmed in black and white. The car was actually painted red and white to distinguish it from real police cars during the shooting (all of which was done on location). On the home screen the red and white car looked identical to the dark green and white of genuine New York City police cars.

Nat Hiken of the *Phil Silvers Show* was the creator, producer, and one of the writers of *Car 54, Where Are You?*

CARA WILLIAMS SHOW, THE
Situation Comedy
FIRST TELECAST: *September 23, 1964*
LAST TELECAST: *September 10, 1965*
BROADCAST HISTORY:
Sep 1964–Apr 1965, CBS Wed 9:30–10:00
May 1965–Sep 1965, CBS Fri 8:30–9:00
CAST:

Cara Bridges/Wilton	Cara Williams
Frank Bridges	Frank Aletter
Damon Burkhardt	Paul Reed
Mrs. Burkhardt	Reta Shaw
Fletcher Kincaid	Jack Sheldon
Mary Hammilmeyer	Jeanne Arnold
Agnes	Audrey Christie

A secret marriage in the face of a company rule against employing married couples provided the basis for much of the comedy in this series. Cara and Frank Bridges, the secret spouses, had to pretend to be singles as they went to work each day at Fenwick Diversified Industries. Frank was the company efficiency expert, and Cara, who used her maiden name of Wilton in the office, was a secretary with an incredibly complex filing system. She was indispensable to her boss, Mr. Burkhardt, because she was the only one who could find anything in her files. The Bridges' problems at home and at work, as they tried to protect their secret, made for amusing and complicated situations.

131

CARIBE

Police Drama

FIRST TELECAST: *February 17, 1975*
LAST TELECAST: *August 11, 1975*
BROADCAST HISTORY:
Feb 1975–Aug 1975, ABC Mon 10:00–11:00
CAST:
Lt. Ben Logan.................. Stacy Keach
Sgt. Mark Walters .... Carl Franklin
Deputy Commissioner Ed Rawlings,
   Miami P.D. .... Robert Mandan

This action-adventure was set in Miami and throughout the Caribbean. Ben Logan and his black partner, Sgt. Mark Walters, constituted a two-man law-enforcement unit working for Caribbean Force, an international agency fighting crime wherever Americans were involved.

CARMEL MYERS SHOW, THE

Interviews

FIRST TELECAST: *June 26, 1951*
LAST TELECAST: *February 21, 1952*
BROADCAST HISTORY:
Jun 1951–Oct 1951, ABC Tue 7:15–7:30
Oct 1951–Feb 1952, ABC Thu 10:45–11:00
HOSTESS:
Carmel Myers

Carmel Myers, formerly a queen of the silent movies, hosted this weekly 15-minute program of interviews, chats, and reminiscences on ABC in 1951–1952. Among her guests were Abe Burrows, Jule Styne, and Richard Rodgers.

CARNIVAL

see *ABC Dramatic Shorts—1952–1953*

CAROL BURNETT SHOW, THE

Comedy Variety

FIRST TELECAST: *September 11, 1967*
LAST TELECAST: *September 8, 1979*
BROADCAST HISTORY:
Sep 1967–May 1971, CBS Mon 10:00–11:00 (OS)
Sep 1971–Nov 1972, CBS Wed 8:00–9:00 (OS)
Dec 1972–Dec 1977, CBS Sat 10:00–11:00 (OS)
Dec 1977–Mar 1978, CBS Sun 10:00–11:00
Jun 1978–Aug 1978, CBS Wed 8:00–9:00
Aug 1979–Sep 1979, ABC Sat 8:00–9:00
REGULARS:
Carol Burnett
Harvey Korman (1967–1977)
Lyle Waggoner (1967–1974)
Vicki Lawrence
Tim Conway (1975–1979)
The Ernest Flatt Dancers
The Harry Zimmerman Orchestra (1967–1971)
The Peter Matz Orchestra (1971–1978)
Dick Van Dyke (1977)
Kenneth Mars (1979)
Craig Richard Nelson (1979)
THEME:
"It's Time to Say Goodbye"

In an era in which variety shows were rapidly disappearing from television, *The Carol Burnett Show* survived for more than a decade. The life span for other variety series in the 1970s rarely exceeded two seasons, and their total number had dwindled substantially from the heyday of variety shows in the 1950s. Only Carol managed to remain popular and successful. The small nucleus of her regular cast remained constant for several years, with none of her original supporting troupes leaving until 1974. Their chemistry helped hold the show together. The binding force, however, was Carol, one of television's most versatile variety performers, who could sing, dance, act, clown, and mime with equal facility.

Over the years certain basic aspects of the show remained the same. There was one point in each telecast, usually at the beginning, when Carol and the evening's guest star would answer questions from the studio audience. There were comedy sketches that spoofed TV series, popular movies, or other forms of mass entertainment. Among Carol's extensive repertoire of comic characterizations were a few recurring sketches that persisted for years. In "Mr. Tudball and Mrs. Wiggins" she played an inept, blonde office worker with a frustrated, ever-suffering boss played by Tim Conway. In "Ed & Eunice" (which several years later ran as a series titled *Mama's Family* on NBC) she and Harvey Korman were an uptight married couple constantly at odds with Eunice's mother, played by Vicki Lawrence. In "Old Folks at Home" Carol and Roger, played by Miss Burnett and Harvey Korman, were an unhappily married couple who fought almost all the time and had problems with Carol's kid sister Chrissy, played by Vicki Lawrence (who, disconcertingly, looked enough like Carol to really have been her sister). "As the Stomach Turns" was a continuing soap-opera satire.

Jim Nabors, one of Carol's close friends, was her good-luck charm and always appeared as the guest star on the opening telecast of each season. Tim Conway, who had been a frequent guest in *The Carol Burnett Show*'s early years, joined the regular cast in the fall of 1975. Harvey Korman decided to leave the series in the spring of 1977, a loss that was felt deeply by Carol, who had worked so well with him for so long. The resulting need for a strong lead actor-comic was met by Dick Van Dyke, who was signed to be Carol's co-star that fall.

The chemistry that had existed between Carol and Harvey Korman was not present with her new co-star and Dick Van Dyke left the show only three months after he had arrived. For the first time in years, Carol's ratings faltered, forcing the move to Sunday nights in December of 1977. Semiregular guest stars Ken Berry and Steve Lawrence tried to help fill the void caused by the lack of a strong male lead, but by the following spring after eleven years on the air, Carol decided to give up the weekly grind. In a special two-hour finale, on

March 29, 1978, highlights from past shows were intermixed with new material.

This was not quite the end, however. Reruns were aired during the summer of 1978, and during the summer of 1979 four new episodes were produced for ABC featuring two new regulars, and aired under the title *Carol Burnett & Company*. Also in 1979, the comedy sketches (only) from the original CBS programs were edited into a series of half-hour shows and syndicated to local stations to be rerun under the title *Carol Burnett and Friends*.

CAROLYN GILBERT SHOW, THE
Music
FIRST TELECAST: *January 15, 1950*
LAST TELECAST: *July 30, 1950*
BROADCAST HISTORY:
    Jan 1950–Jul 1950, ABC Sun 7:30–7:45
REGULARS:
    Carolyn Gilbert
    Don Tennant

This musical variety program was hosted by singer-pianist Carolyn Gilbert. The young puppeteer and vocalist Don Tennant provided skits to introduce Miss Gilbert's numbers.

CARTER COUNTRY
Situation Comedy
FIRST TELECAST: *September 15, 1977*
LAST TELECAST: *August 23, 1979*
BROADCAST HISTORY:
    Sep 1977–Mar 1978, ABC Thu 9:30–10:00
    May 1978–Aug 1978, ABC Tue 9:30–10:00
    Sep 1978, ABC Sat 8:00–8:30
    Oct 1978–Jan 1979, ABC Sat 8:30–9:00
    Mar 1979–Aug 1979, ABC Thu 9:30–10:00
CAST:
    Chief Roy Mobey .... Victor French
    Sgt. Curtis Baker............. Kene Holliday
    Mayor Teddy Burnside........ Richard Paul
    Deputy Jasper DeWitt, Jr...... Harvey Vernon
    Deputy Harley Puckett .... Guich Koock
    Cloris Phebus................ Barbara Cason
    Lucille Banks............... Vernee Watson
    Tracy Quinn (1978–1979) .... Melanie Griffith
    Julia Mobey (1978–1979) ... Amzie Strickland

This racial comedy was set in the small Georgia town of Clinton Corners, "just down the road from Plains" (home of President Jimmy Carter). Chief Roy Mobey was the lovable redneck police chief and Sgt. Curtis Baker his ultra-sharp black deputy, who had been trained in big-city police methods in New York. Despite the obvious points of conflict—black *vs.* white, big city *vs.* backwoods—the two had a basic respect for each other. Also on the force was Cloris Phebus, a man-hungry policewoman; young Harley, and "good ole boy" Jasper. Teddy Burnside was the chubby, weak-willed mayor, a mama's boy who was elected because nobody else wanted the job. He

also ran the local bank, Burnside Savings & Loan, though he usually preferred to pass the buck; his favorite departing words were: "Handle it!" Curtis was always trying to make time with the mayor's secretary, Lucille, and finally, in May 1979, they were married.

Added to the cast in the second season were Tracy Quinn, a cub reporter, and Roy's mother, Julia Mobey.

CARTOON TELETALES
Children's
FIRST TELECAST: *November 14, 1948*
LAST TELECAST: *September 24, 1950*
BROADCAST HISTORY:
    Nov 1948–Sep 1949, ABC Sun 6:00–6:30
    May 1950–Aug 1950, ABC Sun 6:30–7:00
    Aug 1950–Sep 1950, ABC Sun 6:00–6:30
HOSTS:
    Chuck Luchsinger
    Jack Luchsinger

This children's program was hosted by cartoonist Chuck Luchsinger and his brother Jack. Jack, a professional actor, narrated stories from the big *Cartoon TeleTales* storybook while his brother drew amusing illustrations to match. For a time the program was highly popular with both children and their parents, and a continuing art contest drew as many as 5,600 entries a month during 1949. Among the characters introduced were Usta the Rooster, Bumsniff the Bloodhound, Madcap the Mountain Goat, and Mimi the Mole. *Cartoon TeleTales* began in Philadelphia in May 1948, moved to New York as a late-afternoon entry in June, and became a 6:00 P.M. network entry in November.

CASABLANCA
International Intrigue
FIRST TELECAST: *September 27, 1955*
LAST TELECAST: *September 3, 1983*
BROADCAST HISTORY:
    Sep 1955–Apr 1956, ABC Tue 7:30–8:30
    Apr 1983, NBC Sun 10:00–11:00
    Aug 1983–Sep 1983, NBC Sat 10:00–11:00
CAST (1955–1956):
    Rick Jason................ Charles McGraw
    Capt. Renaud................. Marcel Dalio
    Ferrari .... Dan Seymour
    Sasha .... Michael Fox
    Sam .... Clarence Muse
    Ludwig .... Ludwig Stossel
CAST (1983):
    Rick Blaine.................... David Soul
    Capt. Louis Renault .... Hector Elizondo
    Ferrari .... Reuven Bar-Yotam
    Sacha .... Ray Liotta
    Sam .... Scatman Crothers
    Carl .... Arthur Malet
    Major Heinrik Strasser....... Patrick Horgan
    Lt. Heinz .... Kai Wulff

Casablanca, based on the classic 1942 film of the same name, presented stories of romance and adventure in a North African setting. Rick was an American expatriate and owner of the Club Americain in Casablanca, a bistro that attracted both intrigue and beautiful women. Despite his gruff and indifferent exterior, Rick had a penchant for getting involved in other people's problems. He also worked, quietly, to undermine the activities of the Nazis who were occupying Casablanca during World War II. Capt. Renaud/Renault was the unsympathetic police captain, Ferrari a black marketeer, Sasha/Sacha the bartender at Rick's place, and Sam the inimitable piano player.

Casablanca first surfaced as a series in 1955 as one of three rotating elements airing under the umbrella title *Warner Brothers Presents.* In this version Rick's last name was Jason; when NBC revived the program as a weekly series in 1983, the name had changed to Blaine, the one used by Humphrey Bogart in the film. The names of some of the other regulars were also spelled differently in the two series. Seen regularly in the 1983 version were Nazi commander Strasser and his aide, Heinz.

CASE HISTORIES OF SCOTLAND YARD
syndicated title for *Scotland Yard*

CASH AND CARRY
Quiz/Audience Participation
FIRST TELECAST: *June 20, 1946*
LAST TELECAST: *July 1, 1947*
BROADCAST HISTORY:
  Jun 1946–Jan 1947, DUM Thu 9:00–9:30
  Apr 1947–Jul 1947, DUM Tue 7:30–8:00
EMCEE:
  Dennis James

Sponsored by Libby's, this early quiz show was set in a grocery store, its shelves lined with cans of the sponsor's products to which were attached questions worth $5, $10, or $15. There were also studio stunts, such as a man assigned to pantomime a woman taking off her clothes for a bath, or a blindfolded wife trying to feed her husband ice cream. At home viewers could also participate, via phone, in a segment that involved guessing what was under a large barrel.

As with some other early programs, it is not known whether this was fed over a network from the start, though it was being networked by early 1947 at the latest.

CASSIE & COMPANY
Detective Drama
FIRST TELECAST: *January 29, 1982*
LAST TELECAST: *August 20, 1982*
BROADCAST HISTORY:
  Jan 1982–Feb 1982, NBC Fri 10:00–11:00
  Jun 1982–Jul 1982, NBC Tue 10:00–11:00
  Jul 1982–Aug 1982, NBC Fri 10:00–11:00

CAST:
  Cassie Holland .... Angie Dickinson
  Lyman "Shack" Shackelford .... John Ireland
  Meryl Foxx.................... Dori Brenner
  Benny Silva .... A Martinez
  Mike Holland.................... Alex Cord

This series could have been subtitled *"Police Woman* Goes Private," since the role played by star Angie Dickinson was essentially the Pepper Anderson character she had played in the earlier series. Though no youngster, former police officer Cassie Holland was a private detective who took advantage of her looks and sex appeal as well as her analytical skills to solve cases. She had taken over the business of retired private eye Shack Shackelford, and often sought his help with tough cases. Young ex-con Meryl worked as Cassie's secretary, and part-time gym manager Benny was her leg-man, doing most of the physical work. Cassie's friendship with her ex-husband, City District Attorney Mike Holland, came in handy when she needed to get her hands on inside information.

CAVALCADE OF AMERICA
Dramatic Anthology
FIRST TELECAST: *October 1, 1952*
LAST TELECAST: *June 4, 1957*
BROADCAST HISTORY:
  Oct 1952–Jun 1953, NBC Wed 8:30–9:00
  Sep 1953–Jun 1955, ABC Tue 7:30–8:00 (OS)
  Sep 1955–Jun 1957, ABC Tue 9:30–10:00 (OS)

Cavalcade of America was one of the most prestigious dramatic shows of network radio, sponsored for 18 years (1935–1953) by DuPont as a means of enhancing the company's image and bringing great events in American history to an audience of millions. In 1952 DuPont brought the *Cavalcade* to TV, and viewers were treated to the same meticulously accurate stories of American heroes both famous and obscure, in historical periods ranging from colonial days to the Revolution to the early 1900s. The first telecast was a humorous piece about Benjamin Franklin's lighter side.

In 1955 the format was modified to include contemporary stories, such as a biography of Dr. Ralphe Bunche and an account of a 1948 Olympic swimming star's battle with polio. In this season and the one following, an increasing number of episodes dealt with ordinary people unconnected with great events, but triumphing over some adversity or showing some act of courage.

Actors and actresses appearing on *Cavalcade* were generally lesser-known talent, as the focus was always on the story.

For the first season the program was seen every two weeks, alternating with *Scott Music Hall.* In 1955 it changed its name to *DuPont Cavalcade Theater* and in 1956 to *DuPont Theater.*

CAVALCADE OF BANDS
Musical Variety

FIRST TELECAST: *January 17, 1950*
LAST TELECAST: *September 25, 1951*
BROADCAST HISTORY:
    Jan 1950–Sep 1951, DUM Tue 9:00–10:00
EMCEE:
    Fred Robbins (Jan 1950)
    Warren Hull (Jan–Apr 1950)
    Ted Steele (May 1950–Feb 1951)
    Buddy Rogers (Feb–Sep 1951)

This was one of the DuMont network's major efforts in the musical variety field, and was designed to lure some of the NBC audience away following the top-rated Milton Berle hour (which ran Tuesday 8–9 P.M.). The "star" of this series was a different big-name band each week, ranging from the "sweet" music of Guy Lombardo and Lawrence Welk to the big-band swing of Lionel Hampton and Duke Ellington. Virtually every major dance band in the country appeared on this program at one time or another.

In addition to the "Band of the Week," top-line singers and comedians filled out the bill, including such names as Jackie Gleason, Kitty Kallen, and Peggy Lee, as well as a number of lesser lights. Four different hosts presided over the *Cavalcade of Bands* during its year-and-a-half run: New York disc jockey Fred Robbins at the beginning, replaced almost immediately by Warren Hull, who was followed by Ted Steele and finally by former matinee idol Buddy Rogers.

CAVALCADE OF SPORTS
    see *Boxing* and *Gillette Summer Sports Reel*

CAVALCADE OF STARS
    Comedy Variety
FIRST TELECAST: *June 4, 1949*
LAST TELECAST: *September 26, 1952*
BROADCAST HISTORY:
    Jun 1949–Sep 1950, DUM Sat 9:00–10:00
    Sep 1950–Sep 1952, DUM Fri 10:00–11:00
EMCEE:
    Jack Carter (1949–1950)
    Jerry Lester (1950)
    Jackie Gleason (1950–1952)
    Larry Storch (summer 1951, 1952)
REGULARS:
    Art Carney (1950–1952)
    Pert Kelton (1950–1952)
    June Taylor Dancers (1950–1952)
    Sammy Spear/Charlie Spear Orchestra

Big-budget variety shows seemed to be taking over television in 1949. DuMont's answer to such hits as NBC's *Texaco Star Theatre* and CBS' *Ed Sullivan Show* was the *Cavalcade of Stars*, which gave early exposure to a number of talented performers who later became major TV celebrities.

The first host was Jack Carter, who maintained a lightning pace throughout the 60 minutes, mugging, tossing off gags, and working with the guests in skits. Just as he began to build a following, NBC stole him away in February 1950, to front the first hour of its *Saturday Night Revue*, on the same night as *Cavalcade*. His replacement was round-faced comic Jerry Lester, who was no less manic but who remained on the show for only four months, until July 1950. (He later became TV's first late-night star, on NBC's original *Broadway Open House*.) Lester's replacement, and one of the major talents on DuMont during the next two years, was Jackie Gleason.

Gleason, who had starred in the first, unsuccessful version of *The Life of Riley* in 1949–1950, immediately began to build a large and loyal following, a process that was helped when *Cavalcade* moved to a more propitious time period on Friday night, away from the competition of Saturday's Sid Caesar–Imogene Coca hour. One of the chief delights of *Cavalcade* was the variety of comic characterizations Gleason introduced on the show, many of which he was to continue throughout his TV career. The first to become enormously popular, in 1950, was "The Bachelor," in which he portrayed a helpless, spouseless male bedeviled by the necessities of housekeeping for one. Typical routines, all in pantomime, were "The Bachelor Gets His Own Breakfast," "Doing the Laundry," and "Dressing for a Date," all to the soft music of "Somebody Loves Me."

Later additions included the dissolute, top-hatted playboy Reggie Van Gleason III; The Poor Soul; the garrulous Joe the Bartender, talking about his patrons Crazy Guggenheim, Moriarty the undertaker, Duddy Duddleston, and Bookshelf Robinson; the continually oppressed Fenwick Babbitt; and Charlie Bratten, "The Loudmouth." The best, however, was probably "The Honeymooners," introduced in the fall of 1951. Bus driver Ralph Kramden was the perfect incarnation of the always boastful, always scheming, always thwarted "poor slob" who would never get away from his dingy apartment and nagging wife.

Part of Gleason's success lay with his excellent supporting cast—which included Pert Kelton as the original Alice Kramden and Art Carney as his foil in many of the sketches—and his stable of topnotch writers (Joe Bigelow and Harry Crane helped him develop "The Honeymooners"). But most of the appeal lay with Gleason himself, and when CBS lured him away in 1952—with a reported offer of $8,000 per week instead of the $1,600 he was getting from DuMont—there was nowhere for *Cavalcade* to go but down. After lingering through the summer with comedian Larry Storch as host, it ended in September 1952.

CAVALIER THEATRE
    Dramatic Anthology
FIRST TELECAST: *December 5, 1951*
LAST TELECAST: *December 26, 1951*
BROADCAST HISTORY:
    Dec 1951, NBC Wed 10:30–11:00

A short-lived anthology series that filled NBC's Wednesday 10:30 P.M. time slot between the last telecast of *The Freddy Martin Show* and the premiere of *Pantomime Quiz* on January 2, 1952.

CAVANAUGHS, THE
Situation Comedy
FIRST TELECAST: *December 1, 1986*
LAST TELECAST: *March 9, 1987*
BROADCAST HISTORY:
  Dec 1986–Mar 1987, CBS Mon 9:30–10:00
CAST:
  Francis "Pop" Cavanaugh ... Barnard Hughes
  Kit Cavanaugh .... Christine Ebersole
  Chuck Cavanaugh .... Peter Michael Goetz
  Mary Tanner Cavanaugh .... Mary Tanner
  Father Chuck Cavanaugh, Jr. ...... John Short
  Kevin Cavanaugh .... Danny Cooksey
  John Cavanaugh .... Parker Jacobs

Crotchety old Barnard Hughes played crotchety old "Pop" Cavanaugh—as Irish as a shillelagh, and about as blunt—in this ethnic family comedy. His daughter Kit had left Boston 20 years earlier in search of fame, but now she was back, an aging and much-divorced showgirl, to help raise her widowed brother Chuck's family. Sparks flew between strong-willed Pop and his wayward daughter, but underneath there was a lot of love. Often caught in the comic crossfire were Chuck, a busy executive with the family-run Cavanaugh Construction Company, and his four kids: Chuck, Jr., a young priest with the demeanor of a talk show host; Mary Margaret, a shy teenager who idolized the freewheeling Kit; and the obnoxious young twins, Kevin and John. A frequent guest star was Art Carney as Pop's brother James "the weasel" Cavanaugh, the owner of Cavanaugh Construction and Chuck's boss.

CELANESE THEATRE
Dramatic Anthology
FIRST TELECAST: *October 3, 1951*
LAST TELECAST: *June 25, 1952*
BROADCAST HISTORY:
  Oct 1951–Dec 1951, ABC Wed 10:00–11:00
  Dec 1951–Jun 1952, ABC Wed 10:00–10:30

A live dramatic series telecast from New York, *Celanese Theatre* presented high-quality plays by leading playwrights. The first *Celanese* telecast was Eugene O'Neill's *Ah, Wilderness!,* followed by such classics as O'Neill's *Anna Christie,* Maxwell Anderson's *Winterset,* and Elmer Rice's *Street Scene.* Stars appearing included Alfred Drake, David Niven, Mickey Rooney, and Lillian Gish. *Celanese Theatre* appeared on alternate weeks throughout its run.

CELEBRITY CHALLENGE OF THE SEXES
Sports
FIRST TELECAST: *January 31, 1978*
LAST TELECAST: *February 28, 1978*

BROADCAST HISTORY:
  Jan 1978–Feb 1978, CBS Tue 8:00–8:30
HOST:
  Tom Brookshier
COACHES:
  McLean Stevenson (men)
  Barbara Rhoades (women)

This series was an offshoot of the CBS Sunday afternoon sports series *Challenge of the Sexes.* As the title implies, *Celebrity Challenge of the Sexes* pitted show business personalities against each other in various sporting events. To make the contests more competitive, the men were given handicaps to compensate for their superior size or strength. Sports announcer Tom Brookshier acted as host and commentator, while McLean Stevenson and Barbara Rhoades coached the competitors, although the "coaches" played their roles primarily for laughs. Among the stars participating were Karen Black and Don Adams in ping pong, Barbi Benton and baseball star Reggie Jackson in a bicycle race, and Elke Sommer and Pat Harrington on an obstacle course.

CELEBRITY GAME, THE
Quiz/Audience Participation
FIRST TELECAST: *April 5, 1964*
LAST TELECAST: *September 9, 1965*
BROADCAST HISTORY:
  Apr 1964–Sep 1964, CBS Sun 9:00–9:30
  Apr 1965–Sep 1965, CBS Thu 9:30–10:00
EMCEE:
  Carl Reiner

At times this series seemed more like a comedy variety program than a quiz show. There were three contestants each week and a rotating panel of nine celebrities. Reiner would pose a question such as "Can a man love two women at the same time?," "Should nude scenes be banned from Hollywood movies?," or "Can most women keep a secret?" The individual panelists decided yes or no, and each contestant tried to guess which way a given panelist had voted, and why. The "why" gave the panelists the opportunity to make funny responses. Contestants won money for correct guessing but the money was incidental to the humor.
Reruns were aired by CBS on Sunday afternoons from October 1967 to June 1968.

CELEBRITY TALENT SCOUTS
Variety
FIRST TELECAST: *August 1, 1960*
LAST TELECAST: *September 26, 1960*
BROADCAST HISTORY:
  Aug 1960–Sep 1960, CBS Mon 9:00–9:30
HOST:
  Sam Levenson

This series was the 1960 summer replacement for *The Danny Thomas Show.* Each week Sam Levenson introduced three or four celebrities who had new young "discoveries" they felt deserved national television exposure. The "discoveries" then performed their specialties, generally comedy, singing, or dancing.

CELEBRITY TIME
Quiz/Audience Participation
FIRST TELECAST: *January 23, 1949*
LAST TELECAST: *September 21, 1952*
BROADCAST HISTORY:
Jan 1949–Mar 1949, CBS Sun 8:30–9:00
Mar 1949–Jun 1949, ABC Sun 8:30–9:00
Jul 1949–Mar 1950, ABC Sun 10:00–10:30
Apr 1950–Jun 1950, CBS Sun 10:00–10:30
Oct 1950–Sep 1952, CBS Sun 10:00–10:30
EMCEE:
Conrad Nagel
PANELISTS:
John Daly (1948–1950)
Ilka Chase (1948–1950)
Kyle MacDonnell (1950–1951)
Herman Hickman (1950–1952)
Martha Wright (1950–1951)
Mary McCarty (1951–1952)
Jane Wilson (1951–1952)

This program began as a combination guessing game and battle of the sexes, teaming regular panelists with guest celebrities of their own sex to compete against a similar team of the opposite sex. Guests ranged from Sir Thomas Beecham to Slapsie Maxie Rosenbloom. At first the questions were reasonably intelligent, involving, for example, guessing names in the news, identifying famous places from film clips, or providing information about live demonstrations or skits performed on the show. Later, skits and performances by the guests began to predominate until the proceedings more resembled a variety show than a quiz. Finally, in June 1952, the panel was dropped altogether; during its final months *Celebrity Time* became a straight musical variety program, with Conrad Nagel as host.

The series underwent quite a few title changes during its career, beginning in November 1948 as a local New York program called *The Eyes Have It* (Douglas Edwards, host), quickly changing to *Stop, Look and Listen* (Paul Gallico, host), then *Riddle Me This* in December 1948 (with Nagel), *Goodrich Celebrity Time* in March 1949, and finally *Celebrity Time* in April 1950.

CENTENNIAL
Historical Drama
FIRST TELECAST: *October 1, 1978*
LAST TELECAST: *October 25, 1980*
BROADCAST HISTORY:
Oct 1978–Feb 1979, NBC Sun (or Sat) Various times
Sep 1980–Oct 1980, NBC Sat (& other days) Various times

CAST:
Pasquinel .... Robert Conrad
Alexander McKeag..... Richard Chamberlain
Bockweiss.................... Raymond Burr
Lisa Bockweiss .... Sally Kellerman
Clay Basket .... Barbara Carrera
Lame Beaver .... Michael Ansara
Levi Zandt .... Gregory Harrison
Elly Zahm.............. Stephanie Zimbalist
Lucinda .... Cristina Raines
Jake Pasquinel............ Stephen McHattie
Mike Pasquinel .... Kario Salem
Maxwell Mercy.............. Chad Everett
Hans Brumbaugh .... Alex Karras
John McIntosh .... Mark Harmon
R. J. Poteet .... Dennis Weaver
Oliver Seccombe............ Timothy Dalton
Col. Frank Skimmerhorn..... Richard Crenna
John Skimmerhorn .... Cliff DeYoung
Nate Person .... Glynn Turman
Bufe Coker .... Les Lannom
Axel Dumire.................... Brian Keith
Clemma................. Adrienne LaRussa
Nacho..................... Rafael Campos
Mervin Wendell .... Anthony Zerbe
Philip Wendell .... Doug McKeon
Charlotte Buckland Seccombe Lloyd
.... Lynn Redgrave
Jim Lloyd................. William Atherton
Maude Wendell.............. Lois Nettleton
Tranquilino.................... A Martinez
Paul Garrett .... David Janssen
Morgan Wendell............. Robert Vaughn
Lew Vernor .... Andy Griffith
Sidney Enderman .... Sharon Gless

This epic television series (twenty-four hours in all), which reportedly cost more than $20,000,000 to produce, faithfully transferred James A. Michener's massive novel *Centennial* to the screen. Michener himself appeared at the beginning of the first episode to ask the viewing audience if it was aware of the way in which the land on which man depends was being used and exploited. Citing the historical events described in *Centennial*, Michener reminded viewers that their actions (and inactions) have an impact on the quality of life for future generations.

Centennial chronicled the settlement and development of and the controversies surrounding a piece of land in the Rocky Mountain area, from 1795 to the present day. It began with the arrival of the first white men to stake claims on the land, French trapper Pasquinel and Scottish trader Alexander McKeag. Over the years the area, which would eventually become the town of Centennial, Colorado, attracted all types of men. Some were settlers who cared for the land and tried to co-exist with the original Pawnee and Cheyenne Indian inhabitants. Among these were Mennonite Levi Zandt, founder of the town, German immigrant Hans Brumbaugh, the first to raise crops in the area, and Englishman Oliver Seccombe, who saw the potential of the land as a grazing area for vast herds of cattle. As more people arrived, the land began to lose its unspoiled natural beauty. Many later arrivals wanted to manipulate events for their own ends, some out of greed and others out of a mistaken sense of righteousness. The unscrupulous Wendell family was willing to do anything to gain the power and wealth offered by Centennial, while the misguided Col. Frank Skimmerhorn was convinced that only white men belonged, and that the remaining Indians must be driven off or killed. Many of these basic struggles continued for generations and some were still apparent in the Colorado of today, where rancher Paul Garrett, whose family line could be traced all the way back to Pasquinel, fought to prevent the senseless exploitation of the land by wealthy businessman Morgan Wendell.

Originally aired during the 1978–1979 season, *Centennial* was repeated in the fall of 1980, when an actors' strike delayed the availability of new programs.

CENTER STAGE
Dramatic Anthology
FIRST TELECAST: *June 1, 1954*
LAST TELECAST: *September 21, 1954*
BROADCAST HISTORY:
   Jun 1954–Sep 1954, ABC Tue 9:30–10:30

Center Stage consisted of filmed dramas presented on alternate weeks during the summer of 1954, as a replacement for *Motorola TV Theatre*. An assortment of notable actors and actresses were seen, including Walter Matthau, Lee Marvin, Vivian Blaine, and Charles Coburn.

CHAMBER MUSIC HOUR
   see *Chicago Symphony Chamber Orchestra*

CHAMPAGNE AND ORCHIDS
Music
FIRST TELECAST: *September 6, 1948*
LAST TELECAST: *January 10, 1949*
BROADCAST HISTORY:
   Sep 1948–Nov 1948, DUM Mon 8:00–8:15
   Nov 1948–Jan 1949, DUM Mon 7:45–8:00
HOSTESS:
   Adrienne (Meyerberg)
ANNOUNCER:
   Robert Turner
ALSO:
   David Lippman at the theremin

This musical interlude featured Adrienne, a svelte brunette who sang sultry torch songs in French, Spanish, and English. The setting was a fancy nightclub, and the atmosphere of elegance was enhanced by Adrienne's glamorous gowns, lent by some of New York's leading stores. Even the announcer, with whom she sometimes danced, wore a tux.

Seen originally as a local New York show beginning in December 1947, *Champagne and Orchids* was sent out over the DuMont network beginning in September 1948.

CHAMPIONS, THE
Adventure
FIRST TELECAST: *June 10, 1968*
LAST TELECAST: *September 9, 1968*
BROADCAST HISTORY:
   Jun 1968–Sep 1968, NBC Mon 8:00–9:00
CAST:
   Craig Stirling .... Stuart Damon
   Sharon Macready .... Alexandra Bastedo
   Richard Barrett .... William Gaunt
   Tremayne .... Anthony Nicholls

Craig, Sharon, and Richard were three international crime fighters with special "powers," which had been given to them by members of an unknown race from a lost civilization deep in the wastelands of Tibet. The powers included extraordinary mental abilities, the ability to see in the dark, superhuman strength, and assorted other physical talents. All these special skills were put to good use by the trio in their missions for Nemesis, a Geneva-based international agency similar to Interpol. Tremayne, head of Nemesis, was their boss and principal contact.

CHANCE OF A LIFETIME
Quiz/Audience Participation
FIRST TELECAST: *September 6, 1950*
LAST TELECAST: *November 28, 1951*
BROADCAST HISTORY:
   Sep 1950–Nov 1951, ABC Wed 7:30–8:00
EMCEE:
   John Reed King
REGULARS:
   Dick Collier
   Russell Arms
   Liza Palmer
   Joseph Biviano Orchestra

This quiz show, which was also heard on radio, used singers and comedians to provide clues for contestants. A female contestant might be placed in a mock-Egyptian setting and wooed by rotund comic Dick Collier, to hint that the correct answer was "Cleopatra." Or, a couple of professional wrestlers might come on stage and the contestant would be asked to name the holds they were using. Singers Russell Arms and Liza Palmer gave musical clues.

Thirty-five years after this series went off the air another quiz show using essentially the same title, *The $1,000,000 Chance of a Lifetime*, turned up in the first-run syndication market, emceed by Jim Lange.

CHANCE OF A LIFETIME
Talent
FIRST TELECAST: *May 8, 1952*

LAST TELECAST: *June 23, 1956*
BROADCAST HISTORY:
  May 1952–Aug 1953, ABC Thu 8:30–9:00
  Sep 1953–Jun 1955, DUM Fri 10:00–10:30
  Jul 1955–Feb 1956, ABC Sun 9:00–9:30
  Mar 1956–Jun 1956, ABC Sat 10:00–10:30
EMCEE:
  Dennis James
REGULAR:
  Bernie Leighton Orchestra

This talent show gave network exposure to aspiring young performers who had some prior professional experience. Winners, chosen by the studio audience, got $1,000 and a week's engagement at New York's Latin Quarter, while runners-up often landed bookings at lesser night spots. Those competing ranged from banjo players to opera singers, but surprisingly, despite their professional orientation, few seem to have gone on to become big names in show business. According to a review of the show after its first year, the top "find" up to that time was a comedienne named Helen Halpin, who subsequently had a minor career on Broadway and TV. A more notable later find was teenage singer Diahann Carroll, who won three weeks in a row.

CHANNING
Drama
FIRST TELECAST: *September 18, 1963*
LAST TELECAST: *April 8, 1964*
BROADCAST HISTORY:
  Sep 1963–Apr 1964, ABC Wed 10:00–11:00
CAST:
  Dean Fred Baker.............. Henry Jones
  Prof. Joseph Howe .... Jason Evers

Mythical Channing University was the setting for this series of dramas revolving around life on a college campus. Fred Baker was the school's dean, and Joseph Howe was a professor of English. Their personal and professional lives provided the basis for many stories, as they related to students, faculty, and the nonacademic world. At times the action focused more strongly on the students or other faculty members.

CHARADE QUIZ
Charades
FIRST TELECAST: *December 4, 1947*
LAST TELECAST: *June 23, 1949*
BROADCAST HISTORY:
  Dec 1947–May 1948, DUM Thu 8:30–9:00
  May 1948–Jul 1948, DUM Thu 8:00–8:30
  Aug 1948–Jan 1949, DUM Thu 8:30–9:00
  Jan 1949–Apr 1949, DUM Wed 8:00–8:30
  May 1949–Jun 1949, DUM Thu 8:30–9:00
EMCEE:
  Bill Slater
PANEL:
  Minnabess Lewis
  Herb Polesie

Bob Shepard
Jackson Beck
REPERTORY COMPANY:
  Allan Frank
  Richard Seff
  Ellen Fenwick

Charades were a favorite type of program on early television, since they were so obviously visual. This show used subjects suggested by viewers and acted out by a varying repertory company of young actors (those remaining on the show for several months are listed above). If the actors stumped the panel, the viewer who sent in the suggestion got $15.

CHARLES IN CHARGE
Situation Comedy
FIRST TELECAST: *October 3, 1984*
LAST TELECAST: *July 24, 1985*
BROADCAST HISTORY:
  Oct 1984–Apr 1985, CBS Wed 8:00–8:30
  Apr 1985, CBS Sat 8:00–8:30
  Jun 1985–Jul 1985, CBS Wed 8:00–8:30
  (In first-run syndication from January 1987–)
CAST:
  Charles .... Scott Baio
  Jill Pembroke (1984–1985)......... Julie Cobb
  Stan Pembroke (1984–1985) .. James Widdoes
  Lila Pembroke (1984–1985)..... April Lerman
  Douglas Pembroke (1984–1985)
    .... Jonathan Ward
  Jason Pembroke (1984–1985)
    .... Michael Pearlman
  Buddy Lembeck............... Willie Aames
  Gwendolyn Pierce (1984–1985)
    .... Jennifer Runyon
  Walter Powell (1987–)... James Callahan
  Ellen Powell (1987–)...... Sandra Kerns
  Jamie Powell (1987–) ...... Nicole Eggert
  Sarah Powell (1987–)........ Josie Davis
  Adam Powell (1987–)
    .... Alexander Polinsky
  Lillian (1987–) .... Ellen Travolta

One of two 1984 series featuring hunky guys working as domestics (the other was ABC's *Who's the Boss*), *Charles in Charge* was the saga of a 19-year-old college student who went to work as a male governess for a busy working couple. In exchange for room, board, and a little spending money, Charles tried valiantly to keep a rein on Stan and Jill's three rambunctious children: cute, boy-crazy Lila (14); sarcastic Douglas (12); and happy-go-lucky Jason (10). Charles worked hard at the job and at his studies, but still managed to find time to hang out with his best friend Buddy and to pursue the girl of his dreams, beautiful, sexy coed Gwendolyn Pierce.

  When *Charles in Charge* returned to the air as a first-run syndicated series in early 1987, only Charles and Buddy were left from the original

139

cast. The Pembrokes had moved to Seattle and sold their house to the Powells, who became Charles' new employers. The man of the house was not Mr. Powell, a Navy commander stationed in the South Seas, but his cranky father Walter, himself a retired career Navy man. Also in the house were Walter's daughter-in-law Ellen, and his three grandchildren, Jamie (14), Sarah (13), and Adam (12). Jamie was much more outgoing, worldly, and boy-crazy than her younger sister and seemed to be forever preoccupied with getting Sarah out of her shell, while Sarah was moving at a much slower, but for her more comfortable, pace. Rambunctious Adam could have been a clone of Jason Pembroke.

That fall Charles' loving mother, Lillian, came from Scranton for a short visit. She bought his favorite hangout, Sid's Pizza Parlor, and took up permanent residence in New Brunswick. Not only did he have to deal with her good-natured meddling, but picking up girls at Sid's, when she was there, was not what it used to be.

CHARLEY WEAVER SHOW, THE
see *Hobby Lobby*

CHARLIE CHAN
see *New Adventures of Charlie Chan, The*

CHARLIE & CO.
Situation Comedy
FIRST TELECAST: *September 18, 1985*
LAST TELECAST: *July 23, 1986*
BROADCAST HISTORY:
Sep 1985–Dec 1985, CBS Wed 9:00–9:30
Jan 1986, CBS Tue 8:30–9:00
Apr 1986–Jun 1986, CBS Fri 8:00–8:30
Jun 1986–Jul 1986, CBS Wed 8:30–9:00
CAST:
Charlie Richmond............... Flip Wilson
Diana Richmond............. Gladys Knight
Lauren Richmond (15)........ Fran Robinson
Charlie Richmond, Jr. (16) ... Kristoff St. John
Robert Richmond (9)........... Jaleel White
Walter Simpson .... Ray Girardin
Milton Bieberman........... Richard Karron
Ronald Sandler.................... Kip King
Jim Coyle .... Terry McGovern
Miguel Santana................ Eddie Velez
Aunt Rachel (1986).............. Della Reese

Chicago's south side was the setting for this domestic comedy which many critics accused of being a poor-man's version of NBC's highly successful *The Cosby Show*. Charlie Richmond was an administrative assistant with the Chicago Department of Highways. He and his wife Diana, an elementary school teacher, had three outspoken children—Junior, Lauren, and Robert. Since none of them were afflicted with shyness, life at home, particularly at meals, tended to resemble a verbal free-for-all. Walter Simpson was Charlie's boss, and Bieberman, Sandler, Coyle, and Miguel were

his co-workers. Early in 1986 Diana's sarcastic Aunt Rachel, not one of Charlie's favorite people, turned up, adding to the already contentious atmosphere in Charlie's home.

CHARLIE FARRELL SHOW, THE
Situation Comedy
FIRST TELECAST: *July 2, 1956*
LAST TELECAST: *September 19, 1960*
BROADCAST HISTORY:
Jul 1956–Sep 1956, CBS Mon 9:00–9:30
Jul 1957–Sep 1957, NBC Mon 8:00–8:30
Aug 1960–Sep 1960, CBS Mon 7:30–8:00
CAST:
Charlie Farrell.................... Himself
Dad Farrell.............. Charles Winninger
Sherman Hull............... Richard Deacon
Mrs. Papernow .... Kathryn Card
Pierre......................... Leon Askin
Rodney .... Jeff Silver
Doris Mayfield................ Noreen Nash

The Charlie Farrell Show was originally telecast as the 1956 summer replacement for *I Love Lucy*. It was the semi-autobiographical story of its star, as the stories were all based on actual incidents that had occurred at the Racquet Club, the exclusive Palm Springs, California, resort owned and managed by Mr. Farrell. Charlie had problems with everybody—the resort's manager, Sherman Hull; the chef, Pierre; his nephew, Rodney; his housekeeper, Mrs. Papernow; and even his lovable father. Reruns of the series were aired by NBC in 1957 and by CBS in 1960.

CHARLIE WILD, PRIVATE DETECTIVE
Detective Drama
FIRST TELECAST: *December 22, 1950*
LAST TELECAST: *June 19, 1952*
BROADCAST HISTORY:
Dec 1950–Mar 1951, CBS Fri 9:00–9:30
Apr 1951–Jun 1951, CBS Wed 9:00–9:30
Sep 1951–Mar 1952, ABC Tue 8:00–8:30
Mar 1952–Jun 1952, DUM Thu 10:00–10:30
CAST:
Charlie Wild (1950–1951) .. Kevin O'Morrison
Charlie Wild (1951–1952) ..... John McQuade
Effie Perrine............... Cloris Leachman

Charlie Wild was a tough New York City private eye who got into a fight in almost every episode of this live detective series, one of many on the air in the late 1940s and early 1950s. The series had started on CBS radio in the late 1940s, and was brought to television with Kevin O'Morrison, in the lead. He was replaced in May 1951 by John McQuade, who remained in the part through the show's rapid movement from CBS to ABC to DuMont. The show's only other regular cast member was Charlie's secretary, Effie Perrine.

CHARLIE'S ANGELS
Detective Drama

FIRST TELECAST: *September 22, 1976*
LAST TELECAST: *August 19, 1981*
BROADCAST HISTORY:
Sep 1976–Aug 1977, ABC Wed 10:00–11:00
Aug 1977–Oct 1980, ABC Wed 9:00–10:00
Nov 1980–Jan 1981, ABC Sun 8:00–9:00
Jan 1981–Feb 1981, ABC Sat 8:00–9:00
Jun 1981–Aug 1981, ABC Wed 8:00–9:00
CAST:
Sabrina Duncan (1976–1979) ... Kate Jackson
Jill Munroe (1976–1977)
.... Farrah Fawcett-Majors
Kelly Garrett .... Jaclyn Smith
Kris Munroe (1977–1981)........ Cheryl Ladd
Tiffany Welles (1979–1980)..... Shelley Hack
Julie Rogers (1980–1981) ...... Tanya Roberts
John Bosley .... David Doyle
Charlie Townsend (voice only)
.... John Forsythe

Sex, pure and simple, seemed to be the principal ingredient in the considerable success of this detective show. Denunciations of "massage parlor television" and "voyeurism" only brought more viewers to the screen, to see what the controversy was about. Often they were rather disappointed, as a lot more seemed to be promised than delivered, but *Charlie's Angels* nevertheless ended its first season as one of the top hits on television.

The plot involved three sexy police-trained detectives working for an unseen boss named Charlie, who relayed assignments by telephone. Charlie's assistant, Bosley, was on hand to help the girls and fret about costs, but he hardly seemed likely to make a pass at any of them. Most of the cases involved health spas, Las Vegas night spots, or other places where the girls could appear in bikinis or other scanty attire.

Sabrina was the cool, multilingual leader, Jill the athletic type, and Kelly the former showgirl who had "been around." Usually they worked as an undercover team. When they investigated a killing in the army, Jill and Kelly became recruits and Sabrina a base nurse; when it was the death of a roller-derby queen, Sabrina posed as an insurance investigator, Kelly as a magazine writer, and Jill as a derby competitor.

Farrah Fawcett-Majors was the last of the Angels to be cast (the show needed a blonde) and was little known compared to the lead, Kate Jackson, when the series began. Farrah quickly became the object of a tremendous fad, based partially on her gorgeous, flowing blond hair, and partially on some cheesecake publicity photos, including one now-famous swimsuit pose which showed the fine points of her anatomy in marvelous detail. Farrah Fawcett-Majors dolls were marketed, as were T-shirts with her picture and dozens of other gimmicks. Heady with all the sudden adulation, she walked out on the series, with the intention of launching a career in feature films. This started a series of lawsuits, which ended when she finally agreed to make a limited number

of guest appearances on the show during the next three seasons. Thereafter, the introduction of a new "Angel" became an almost annual occurrence. First, Jill was replaced by her spunky younger sister, Kris (1977); two years later, Sabrina left and was replaced by Tiffany Welles, daughter of a Connecticut police chief (1979); a year after that, Tiffany was out, replaced by street-smart Julie Rogers (1980).

CHARMINGS, THE
Situation Comedy
FIRST TELECAST: *March 20, 1987*
LAST TELECAST: *February 11, 1988*
BROADCAST HISTORY:
Mar 1987–Apr 1987, ABC Fri 8:00–8:30
Aug 1987–Jan 1988, ABC Thu 8:30–9:00
Jan 1988–Feb 1988, ABC Thu 8:00–8:30
CAST:
Snow White Charming (Spring 1987)
.... Caitlin O'Heaney
Snow White Charming .... Carol Huston
Prince Eric Charming ...... Christopher Rich
Queen Lillian White .... Judy Parfitt
Thomas Charming .... Brandon Call
Cory Charming .... Garette Ratliffe
Luther....................... Cork Hubbert
The Mirror .... Paul Winfield
Sally Miller .... Dori Brenner
Don Miller .... Paul Eiding

Snow White and Prince Charming fell asleep in the Enchanted Forest and woke up in 20th century California in this slightly off-center continuation of the Brothers Grimm fairy tale. According to the legend, the beautiful couple threw Snow's wicked stepmother, Queen Lillian, into a bottomless pit and lived happily ever after. Unfortunately the pit was not really bottomless, just very, very deep, and when the furious Queen managed to climb out she cast a spell so powerful that even she couldn't control it. Everybody—Snow White, the Prince, their two young sons, the dwarf, the Magic Mirror, and even the Queen herself—fell asleep for centuries.

They all woke up in 1987 in Van Oaks, California, and found themselves coping with the modern, not-so-quaint world of American suburbia. The handsome Prince, still in his tights and referring to his "castle" (a suburban home), became a writer of children's stories; Snow a dress designer; and their young sons Thomas and Cory schoolchildren. The dwarf Luther helped around the house. Spoiling the fun was Queen Lillian, a vain, vengeful, and still powerful in-law who lived upstairs. Jealous of the happy lovebirds, she would periodically cast spells to disrupt their plans and alarm the neighbors, who didn't understand the new couple on the block at all. A botched attempt to send everyone back to the Forest just brought Cinderella into the 20th Century, to flirt with Eric; a few magic beans carelessly thrown out her window produced Jack and the

Beanstalk in their yard. Even Lillian's sole companion, the Magic Mirror (which had a sarcastic personality of its own), failed to calm her down.

Sally and Don were the befuddled neighbors who, in true sitcom fashion, never caught on.

CHASE
Police Drama
FIRST TELECAST: *September 11, 1973*
LAST TELECAST: *August 28, 1974*
BROADCAST HISTORY:
> *Sep 1973–Jan 1974,* NBC Tue 8:00–9:00
> *Jan 1974–Aug 1974,* NBC Wed 8:00–9:00
CAST:
> Capt. Chase Reddick .... Mitchell Ryan
> Officer Norm Hamilton .... Reid Smith
> Officer Steve Baker ..... Michael Richardson
> Officer Fred Sing .... Brian Fong
> Sgt. Sam MacCray .... Wayne Maunder
> Inspector Frank Dawson .... Albert Reed
> Officer Ed Rice .... Gary Crosby
> Officer Tom Wilson .... Craig Gardner

One of the variations on the police-show format so popular in the early 1970s was the "special cop," the policeman or unit with special skills solving otherwise unsolvable crimes with unconventional means. Capt. Chase Reddick's plain-clothes unit, though nominally part of the Los Angeles Police Department, was accountable only to the Chief of Detectives and had a virtual free hand in solving cases none of the other police divisions could crack. Reddick had only four men, each with a useful skill: Sam MacCray, a specialist in the training and handling of police dogs; Norm Hamilton, a former Vietnam War helicopter pilot; Steve Baker, a hot-rod car driver; and Fred Sing, an expert motorcycle rider. Occasional "straight" cops also appeared in the series, including officer Ed Rice, played by Gary Crosby—who on other duty tours turned up in Jack Webb's *Adam 12,* the model of the "straight cop" genre.

CHECK IT OUT
Situation Comedy
BROADCAST HISTORY:
> USA Cable Network and Syndicated
> 30 minutes
> Produced: *1985–*
> Released: *Spring 1986*
CAST:
> Howard Bannister .... Don Adams
> Edna Moseley .... Dinah Christie
> Jack Christian .... Jeff Pustil
> Marlene Weimaraner ...... Kathleen Laskey
> Jennifer Woods (1985–1986) .. Tonya Williams
> Leslie Rappaport .... Aaron Schwartz
> Marvin (1985) .... Jason Warren
> Murray Amherst (1985–1987)
> .... Simon Reynolds
> Alf Scully (1985–1986) .... Henry Beckman
> *Mrs. Alfreda Cobb (1985–1986)
> .... Barbara Hamilton

> Viker (1986–   ) .... Gordon Clapp
> T.C. Collingwood (1987) .... Elizabeth Hanna

*Occasional

Don Adams returned to series television as a bumbling supermarket manager in this low-budget sitcom. The setting was Cobb's, part of a chain of stores in the town of Brampton. Jack was the ambitious, obnoxious young assistant manager; Marlene, Jennifer, and overtly homosexual Leslie worked the checkout registers; Marvin, and later Murray, were both bagboys and stock clerks; Alf was the ancient security guard who had been working in the same store for more than 40 years; and Edna was Howard's secretary. They had been having an affair, which the entire town knew about, for more than six years. Although she would have loved to become Mrs. Bannister, Edna was resigned to tolerating Howard's inability to make a binding commitment. Mrs. Cobb, the overbearing owner of the small grocery chain, turned up periodically to disrupt the already less-than-efficient operation of the store.

Viker was added to the cast in the second season as Cobb's inept handyman and T.C. Collingwood arrived in the fall of 1987 as the ambitious young v.p. of corporate development for Cendrax Corporation, the conglomerate to whom Mrs. Cobb had sold the chain. T.C. was all business, and determined to make her name by turning around the slipshod operation. Fat chance.

Check It Out was based on the British series *Tripper's Day.* It had originally been produced in Toronto as a joint venture of the CTV Television Network in Canada and the USA Cable Network in the United States. It aired first-run on both, with the reruns sold into syndication in the United States.

CHECKING IN
Situation Comedy
FIRST TELECAST: *April 9, 1981*
LAST TELECAST: *April 30, 1981*
BROADCAST HISTORY:
> *Apr 1981,* CBS Thu 8:00–8:30
CAST:
> Florence Johnston .... Marla Gibbs
> Lyle Block .... Larry Linville
> Elena Beltran .... Liz Torres
> Earl Bellamy .... Patrick Collins
> Hank Sabatino .... Robert Costanzo
> Betty .... Ruth Brown
> Dennis, the bellboy .... Jordan Gibbs

In this comedy spin-off from *The Jeffersons,* Florence, the Jeffersons' outspoken maid, left domestic work to become executive housekeeper at the St. Frederick, one of Manhattan's better hotels. Her new responsibilities included managing most of the hotel's staff. Elena was her efficient assistant; Earl, the barely competent house detective; Hank, the beefy chief engineer in charge of heat,

142

air conditioning, and plumbing; and Betty, one of the floor supervisors. Florence's biggest problem, however, and the target of the most of her jibes, was her stuffy boss, hotel manager Lyle Block. Block was in fact reminiscent of another character played by actor Larry Linville in the series *M*A*S*H,* the insufferable Major Frank Burns.

CHECKMATE
Detective Drama
FIRST TELECAST: *September 17, 1960*
LAST TELECAST: *September 19, 1962*
BROADCAST HISTORY:
  Sep 1960–Sep 1961, CBS Sat 8:30–9:30
  Oct 1961–Sep 1962, CBS Wed 8:30–9:30
CAST:
  Don Corey................. Anthony George
  Jed Sills..................... Doug McClure
  Carl Hyatt................. Sebastian Cabot
  Chris Devlin (1962).............. Jack Betts

Checkmate, Inc., was the name of a very fancy, very expensive investigative agency operated in San Francisco by Don Corey and Jed Sills. The goal of the company was to prevent crimes and to forestall death. In most of their cases, Don and Jed tried to protect the lives of people who had been threatened or who suspected they were possible targets of criminals. Helping them with the analytical side of the operation was Carl Hyatt, a bearded and very British former Oxford professor of criminology, who acted as special consultant to the firm. Added to the firm in 1962, on an irregular basis, was investigator Chris Devlin.

CHEER TELEVISION THEATRE
Dramatic Anthology
FIRST TELECAST: *May 30, 1954*
LAST TELECAST: *June 27, 1954*
BROADCAST HISTORY:
  May 1954–Jun 1954, NBC Sun 7:00–7:30

This five-week series of filmed dramas filled the period between the cancellation of *The Paul Winchell Show* and the start of *Kollege of Musical Knowledge.*

CHEERS
Situation Comedy
FIRST TELECAST: *September 30, 1982*
LAST TELECAST:
BROADCAST HISTORY:
  Sep 1982–Dec 1982, NBC Thu 9:00–9:30
  Jan 1983–Dec 1983, NBC Thu 9:30–10:00
  Dec 1983–   , NBC Thu 9:00–9:30
CAST:
  Sam Malone................... Ted Danson
  Diane Chambers (1982–1987).... Shelley Long
  Carla Tortelli................. Rhea Perlman
  Ernie "Coach" Pantusso (1982–1985)
  .... Nicholas Colasanto
  Norm Peterson.............. George Wendt
  Cliff Clavin.............. John Ratzenberger

  Dr. Frasier Crane (1984–   )
  .... Kelsey Grammer
  Woody Boyd (1985–   ) .. Woody Harrelson
  Rebecca Howe (1987–   ) ..... Kirstie Alley
  *Dr. Lilith Sternin (1986–   ).. Bebe Neuwirth
  *Evan Drake (1987–   )........ Tom Skerritt

*Occasional
THEME:
  "Where Everybody Knows Your Name," by Judy Hart Angelo and Gary Portnoy, sung by Gary Portnoy

The witty gang at a Boston bar called Cheers provided the focus of this comedy. Sam was the owner and bartender, a tall, rugged, and rather self-assured man with a knack for good conversation, an eye for the ladies, and an interesting past. Once a pitcher for the Boston Red Sox, he'd had a bout with alcoholism but was now sworn off the stuff for good. Helping him out behind the great oak bar was "Coach," a kindly, absentminded gent who had been in pro ball as a coach and manager, and who regaled the customers with his experiences. Carla was a wise-cracking waitress, while Norm (an accountant) and Cliff (the mailman) were regular patrons.

Into this bastion of locker-room chatter came Diane, a bright, attractive graduate student whose interests leaned toward the arts. Stopping by one snowy evening with her fiancé, literature professor Sumner Sloan, on his way to the Caribbean to be married, Diane expected never to see the place again. But her fiancé jilted her, and Diane found herself in need of immediate employment. Sam hired her for the only job she was qualified to do, that of waitress. She despised him at first, and the barbs flew thick and fast, but in time a romantic attraction grew. By the beginning of the second season Sam and Diane—despite their sarcastic jibes—were the latest "item" at Cheers.

Their off-again, on-again romance lasted only about a year until, in the fall of 1984, Diane found a new boyfriend in obnoxious, insecure psychologist Frasier Crane. They went to Europe to get married but, unable to get Sam out of her mind, Diane jilted Frasier and eventually returned to working at Cheers. Meanwhile in early 1985 "Coach" passed away (actor Nicholas Colasanto had died), and a new bartender joined the ensemble. Young Woody, a naive farmboy from Indiana, had been taking a mail-order course in bartending from Coach and had come to Cheers to meet him. The dejected Frasier also joined the gang.

The 1985–1986 season ended with a cliffhanger worthy of a prime-time soap opera. Sam's whirlwind romance with attractive city councilwoman Janet Eldridge (Kate Mulgrew) was coming to a head and Sam was ready to propose—but to whom? In the last scene of the season he was on the phone asking someone to marry him. It turned out to be Diane, but she said no and the two returned to another season of sparring, ending when Diane announced in 1987 she was leaving for "just six months" to write her long-awaited novel. As she walked out the door—and out of his life—a knowing Sam whispered after her, "have a good life."

Sam then sold the bar and embarked on an around-the-world trip in a sailboat, but the boat sank and he was soon back looking for a job at the establishment he once ran. The new manager was Rebecca, a buxom, determined lady who took him in, but only on *her* terms. A new, and very different, romantic relationship was in the offing for macho Sam.

CHER
Musical Variety
FIRST TELECAST: *February 16, 1975*
LAST TELECAST: *January 4, 1976*
BROADCAST HISTORY:
  Feb 1975–Jun 1975, CBS Sun 7:30–8:30
  Sep 1975–Jan 1976, CBS Sun 8:00–9:00
REGULARS:
  Cher Bono
  Gailard Sartain
  The Tony Charmoli Dancers (1975)
  The Anita Mann Dancers (1975–1976)
  The Jimmy Dale Orchestra (1975)
  The Jack Eskew Orchestra (1975–1976)

Following their divorce in 1974, pop singers Sonny and Cher Bono, who had formerly starred together on *The Sonny and Cher Comedy Hour*, each hosted a series of their own. His was a short-lived variety series on ABC in the fall of 1974 (see *The Sonny Comedy Revue*), and hers was *Cher*, a musical variety hour with guest stars that premiered the following February. Steve Martin, Teri Garr, and Sonny and Cher's daughter Chastity were frequent guest stars during Cher's solo period.

The magic Sonny and Cher had had together did not survive the transition to singles. Cher's solo venture limped along on CBS for almost a year, with a new dance group and orchestra in the fall of 1975, by which time she and Sonny decided to try it again as a team, at least professionally. One month after *Cher* left the air, *The Sonny and Cher Show* reappeared in the time period that had been vacated.

CHESTERFIELD PRESENTS
Dramatic Anthology
FIRST TELECAST: *January 10, 1952*
LAST TELECAST: *March 6, 1952*
BROADCAST HISTORY:
  Jan 1952–Mar 1952, NBC Thu 9:00–9:30

This dramatic anthology series, also known as *Dramatic Mystery*, alternated with *Dragnet* on Thursday nights during the latter's first two months on network television.

CHESTERFIELD SOUND OFF TIME
Comedy Variety
FIRST TELECAST: *October 14, 1951*
LAST TELECAST: *January 6, 1952*
BROADCAST HISTORY:
  Oct 1951–Jan 1952, NBC Sun 7:00–7:30
STARS:
  Bob Hope
  Jerry Lester
  Fred Allen

This half-hour comedy variety series was emceed on a rotating basis by three major stars. The programs involved skits, monologues, and production numbers keyed to each star's brand of comedy. The original version of *Dragnet* was previewed as a special edition of *Chesterfield Sound Off Time* on December 16, 1951. Jack Webb starred in the preview, while his superior was played by Raymond Burr, later of *Perry Mason* and *Ironside*.

CHESTERFIELD SUPPER CLUB
  see *Perry Como*

CHET HUNTLEY REPORTING
News/Documentary
FIRST TELECAST: *December 22, 1957*
LAST TELECAST: *June 18, 1963*
BROADCAST HISTORY:
  Dec 1957–Sep 1959, NBC Sun 6:30–7:00
  Jan 1962–Sep 1962, NBC Fri 10:30–11:00
  Oct 1962–Jun 1963, NBC Tue 10:30–11:00
HOST/REPORTER:
  Chet Huntley

This documentary series premiered on Sunday afternoons in April 1956 under the title *Outlook*. It began as a weekend news program that included news headlines and covered four or five stories at greater length, with filmed reports. Narration and commentary was by Huntley. When the program moved to Sunday evenings in December 1957, the format was changed to provide indepth exploration of a single subject. From 1959 to 1961 the program was aired on Sunday afternoons at 5:30 P.M. On January 12, 1962, it moved to Friday nights and continued in the evening hours for another year and a half, retaining the same newsdocumentary format with Huntley interviewing news personalities and exploring topical issues in depth.

The program title changed several times during its seven-year run. Originally *Outlook*, it later became *Chet Huntley . . . Reporting* (November 1958) and *Time: Present . . . Chet Huntley Reporting* (October 1959) before going back to *Chet Huntley Reporting* (September 1960).

CHEVROLET ON BROADWAY
Musical Variety
FIRST TELECAST: *July 17, 1956*
LAST TELECAST: *September 13, 1956*
BROADCAST HISTORY:
  Jul 1956, NBC Tue/Thu 7:30–7:45
  Aug 1956–Sep 1956, NBC Thu 7:30–7:45

Snooky Lanson
Mellolarks, vocal quartet
The Hal Hastings Orchestra

This summer replacement for *The Dinah Shore Show* featured Snooky Lanson, star of the popular *Your Hit Parade*. For its first three weeks it ran as a twice-weekly series on Tuesdays and Thursdays, then switched to once a week for the duration of the summer.

CHEVROLET SHOWROOM
see *Your Chevrolet Showroom*

CHEVROLET TELE-THEATRE
Dramatic Anthology
FIRST TELECAST: *September 27, 1948*
LAST TELECAST: *June 26, 1950*
BROADCAST HISTORY:
Sep 1948–Jan 1949, NBC Mon 8:00–8:30
Feb 1949–Apr 1949, NBC Mon 8:30–9:00
May 1949–Jun 1950, NBC Mon 8:00–8:30

Chevrolet Tele-Theatre was a big-budget, live dramatic series that presented an original play or adaptation each week during the 1948–1949 and 1949–1950 seasons. Top-flight writers and actors were used, the latter including such names as Paul Muni, Eddie Albert, Nanette Fabray, Basil Rathbone, Mercedes McCambridge, Rex Harrison, and E.G. Marshall. Gertrude Berg made her TV debut on the October 18, 1948, telecast in the comedy "Whistle, Daughter, Whistle." This was based on her highly popular radio series *The Goldbergs* and became the prototype for the TV series of the same name which premiered a few months later. *Chevrolet Tele-Theatre* was known as *Chevrolet on Broadway* during parts of the 1948–1949 season.

CHEVY MYSTERY SHOW, THE
Dramatic Anthology
FIRST TELECAST: *May 29, 1960*
LAST TELECAST: *September 17, 1961*
BROADCAST HISTORY:
May 1960–Sep 1960, NBC Sun 9:00–10:00
Jul 1961–Sep 1961, NBC Sun 9:00–10:00
HOSTS:
Walter Slezak
Vincent Price (1960)

Aired as a summer replacement for *The Dinah Shore Chevy Show*, these dramas were hosted by Walter Slezak through September 4, 1960, and by Vincent Price for the last three telecasts that year. The host introduced the program, introduced each act, and then closed the program. Reruns of the plays hosted by Walter Slezak were aired the following summer under the title *Sunday Mystery Hour*. Among the plays, which emphasized suspense and mystery without resorting to violence, were: "The Summer Hero," written by Charlotte Armstrong and starring Zachary Scott and Patty

McCormack; "Dead Man's Walk," starring Robert Culp and Abby Dalton; "Trial by Fury," starring Agnes Moorehead and Warren Stevens; and an adaptation of the A. A. Milne story "The Perfect Alibi," starring Janet Blair.

CHEVY SHOW, THE
Variety
FIRST TELECAST: *October 4, 1955*
LAST TELECAST: *September 4, 1956*
BROADCAST HISTORY:
Oct 1955–Sep 1956, NBC Tue 8:00–9:00

There was no regular star on this variety series, which aired every third Tuesday during the 1955–1956 season on a rotating basis with *The Milton Berle Show* and *The Martha Raye Show*. Bob Hope and Dinah Shore—who later had her own *Chevy Show* series—appeared frequently during the winter season, and Betty Hutton and Ethel Merman each starred in one show apiece. During the summer of 1956 *The Chevy Show* continued to appear every third week, alternating with assorted specials. Gisele Mackenzie, Fred Waring, and Janet Blair appeared as hosts for the summer edition.

CHEVY SHOW, THE
Musical Variety
FIRST TELECAST: *June 22, 1958*
LAST TELECAST: *September 27, 1959*
BROADCAST HISTORY:
Jun 1958–Sep 1958, NBC Sun 9:00–10:00
Jun 1959–Sep 1959, NBC Sun 9:00–10:00
REGULARS:
Janet Blair
John Raitt
Edie Adams (1958)
Dorothy Kirsten
Stan Freberg (1958)
Rowan and Martin (1958)
The Harry Zimmerman Orchestra

This *Chevy Show* was the summer replacement for *The Dinah Shore Chevy Show* in 1958 and 1959. The format was a mixed bag of popular and classical music, skits, and monologues. During the summer of 1958 the show had three musical-comedy stars—Janet Blair, John Raitt, and Edie Adams—who appeared each week and took turns as host. The opera singer Dorothy Kirsten was a featured regular; Stan Freberg and Rowan and Martin provided humor. During the summer of 1959 Blair and Raitt returned as co-hosts, with Miss Kirsten the only other returning regular.

CHEVY SHOWROOM STARRING ANDY WILLIAMS, THE
see *Andy Williams Show, The*

CHEYENNE
Western
FIRST TELECAST: *September 20, 1955*
LAST TELECAST: *September 13, 1963*

BROADCAST HISTORY:
Sep 1955–Sep 1959, ABC Tue 7:30–8:30
Sep 1959–Dec 1962, ABC Mon 7:30–8:30
Apr 1963–Sep 1963, ABC Fri 7:30–8:30
CAST:
Cheyenne Bodie .... Clint Walker
Smitty (1955–1956) .... L. Q. Jones

The behind-the-scenes story of this series was fully as interesting as what appeared on the screen. Probably no series in TV history has undergone so much production turmoil and absorbed and spun off as many other series as did *Cheyenne.*

The on-screen story was simple enough. Cheyenne Bodie was a tall, strapping Western adventurer in the days following the Civil War—he was 6'7", or 6'5", or 6'8", depending on the press release—and a mean hombre. He drifted from job to job, encountering plenty of villains, beautiful girls, and gunfights. In one episode he could be seen as the foreman on a ranch, in another as trail scout for a wagon train, in another as a recently deputized lawman. The show was lavishly produced, movie-style, by Warner Brothers, but the attraction was obviously Clint Walker himself. He had a sidekick, Smitty, for the first season, but after that he worked alone.

Cheyenne was first seen as one of three rotating elements of *Warner Brothers Presents,* the studio's first venture into TV, and quickly emerged as the most popular of the three. Hour-long Westerns were difficult to produce on a once-a-week basis, however, so the program continued to alternate with other series, first *Conflict* (1956–1957) and then *Sugarfoot* (1957–1959). In fact, Clint Walker's *Cheyenne* was seldom seen on an every-week basis at any time during its original run.

In 1958 the brooding fighter of the screen walked out on Warner Brothers, after they refused to release him from some of the more stringent requirements of his contract, which had been signed before *Cheyenne* became a hit. Among other things Walker did not want to have to kick back 50 percent of all personal-appearance fees to the studio, wanted higher payment for reruns, and wanted permission to make records for labels other than Warners' own. Stripped of its star, the studio nevertheless refused to give an inch and continued the series under the name *Cheyenne,* with an unknown actor named Ty Hardin in the leading role which was now that of Bronco Layne. Walker, meanwhile, was legally prevented from working anywhere.

In early 1959 Walker and the studio finally came to terms, and Walker returned to the series. Ty Hardin continued in a series of his own called *Bronco.* Clint Walker was obviously not happy with the settlement, for although the pot had been sweetened somewhat he felt he had simply worn out the Cheyenne character and was becoming typecast. But the program was in the top 20, and

Warner Brothers was not about to let him go. "I am like a caged animal," he complained to reporters.

For part of the 1959–1960 season *Cheyenne* alternated with *Shirley Temple's Storybook.* Then for 1960–1961 *Cheyenne* became *The Cheyenne Show,* a rotating anthology in which Walker was seen on a majority of weeks, interspersed with episodes of Ty Hardin as *Bronco* and Will Hutchins as *Sugarfoot.* In 1961–1962 *Sugarfoot* was dropped and only *Cheyenne* and *Bronco* were seen. Finally, in the fall of 1962, for the last three months, the series consisted of episodes of Walker's *Cheyenne* alone. Reruns of *Cheyenne* episodes were also seen during the summer of 1963.

Cheyenne was based, rather loosely, on a 1947 movie of the same name that starred Dennis Morgan.

See *Bronco* and *Sugarfoot* for details of those series, including the period when they ran under the *Cheyenne* title.

CHICAGO JAZZ
Music
FIRST TELECAST: *November 26, 1949*
LAST TELECAST: *December 31, 1949*
BROADCAST HISTORY:
Nov 1949–Dec 1949, NBC Sat 8:30–8:45
REGULARS:
Art Van Damme Quintette
The Tailgate Seven

A live musical interlude from Chicago, this short-lived program was also known as *Sessions.* The Art Van Damme Quintette was featured on the first telecast, and The Tailgate Seven on the rest.

CHICAGO STORY
Drama
FIRST TELECAST: *March 6, 1982*
LAST TELECAST: *August 27, 1982*
BROADCAST HISTORY:
Mar 1982–Apr 1982, NBC Sat 8:30–10:00
Apr 1982–Aug 1982, NBC Fri 8:30–10:00
CAST:
Dr. Judith Bergstrom .... Maud Adams
Lou Pellegrino .... Vincent Baggetta
Megan Powers .... Molly Cheek
Officer Joe Gilland .... Dennis Franz
Annie Gilland .... Connie Foster
Det. Frank Wajorski ..... Daniel Hugh-Kelly
Det. O. Z. Tate .... Richard Lawson
Kenneth A. Dutton .... Craig T. Nelson
Dr. Max Carson .... Kristoffer Tabori
Lt. Roselli .... John Mahoney
Carol .... Jill Shellabarger

Set in Chicago, this series followed the professional and personal lives of three groups of people—doctors, lawyers, and police officers—whose paths often crossed. Judith Bergstrom and Max Carson were surgeons in the trauma unit at Cook

County Hospital. Lou Pellegrini was a stubborn public defender whose penniless clients were often prosecuted by young assistant D.A. Kenneth Dutton. Outside the courtroom Lou and Ken were good friends, but in it they were sworn enemies, a situation that tended to make things uncomfortable for their mutual friend and fellow attorney, Megan Powers. The Chicago police included hardworking, married beat cop Joe Gilland and two plainclothes detectives, old pro O.Z. Tate and young partner Frank Wajorski. When the people being pursued by the police got hurt they often ended up in the Cook County Hospital trauma unit and, when they got out of the hospital, they went to trial. Because of the 90-minute format of the show, each of the principals in *Chicago Story* was regularly featured, along with plenty of Chicago scenery.

CHICAGO SYMPHONY
Music
FIRST TELECAST: *January 6, 1954*
LAST TELECAST: *April 6, 1955*
BROADCAST HISTORY:
Jan 1954–Mar 1954, DUM Wed 8:30–9:00
Sep 1954–Apr 1955, DUM Wed 9:00–10:00
CONDUCTORS:
Fritz Reiner
George Schick
COMMENTATOR:
George Kuyper

George Kuyper, orchestra manager of the Chicago Symphony, introduced the various pieces performed in this weekly classical-music series. During the intermissions, he also provided commentary and information about the composers and their works from "The Music Room." The principal conductor of the Chicago Symphony at this time was Fritz Reiner, who for most of this series shared the podium with associate conductor George Schick. During the first four weeks of the 1954–1955 season, before the start of the Chicago Symphony season, this time period was occupied by *Concert Tonight*, performances by the New York Concert Choir and Orchestra under the baton of Margaret Hillis.

CHICAGO SYMPHONY CHAMBER ORCHESTRA
Music
FIRST TELECAST: *September 25, 1951*
LAST TELECAST: *March 18, 1952*
BROADCAST HISTORY:
Sep 1951–Mar 1952, ABC Tue 10:30–11:00
ANNOUNCER:
Ken Nordine

With 25 to 30 members of the Chicago Symphony under the baton of Rafael Kubelik, this program featured soloists from the orchestra and guest vocalists. Some of the presentations were not carried over the full ABC network. ABC also carried occasional telecasts of the Chicago Symphony during the fall of 1948 under the titles *Chamber Music Hour* and *Chamber Music*. The 1951–1952 series was also known simply as *The Symphony*.

CHICAGO TEDDY BEARS, THE
Situation Comedy
FIRST TELECAST: *September 17, 1971*
LAST TELECAST: *December 17, 1971*
BROADCAST HISTORY:
Sep 1971–Dec 1971, CBS Fri 8:00–8:30
CAST:
Linc McCray .... Dean Jones
Nick Marr .... Art Metrano
Marvin .... Marvin Kaplan
Duke .... Mickey Shaughnessy
Lefty .... Jamie Farr
Julius .... Mike Mazurki
Dutch .... Huntz Hall
Uncle Latzi .... John Banner

Linc McCray and his Uncle Latzi were partners in a Chicago speakeasy during the late 1920s in this period comedy. The speakeasy did good business and was coveted by a small-time gangster, Big Nick Marr, whose efforts to muscle in on the operation provided much of the action. It was all a family affair, since Linc and Nick were cousins and both were nephews of Uncle Latzi, who couldn't believe that his nephew Nicholas could be anything but a nice young man. Everyone else was terrified of Big Nick, however, including Marvin, Linc's bookkeeper, and the club's four inept bodyguards, Duke, Lefty, Julius, and Dutch.

CHICAGOLAND MYSTERY PLAYERS
Police Drama
FIRST TELECAST: *September 18, 1949*
LAST TELECAST: *July 30, 1950*
BROADCAST HISTORY:
Sep 1949–Jul 1950, DUM Sun 8:00–8:30
CAST:
Jeffrey Hall .... Gordon Urquhart
Sgt. Holland .... Bob Smith

Chicagoland Mystery Players was a good example of Chicago-based dramatic programming in the early days of television. The format was that of a straight crime drama, with criminologist Jeffrey Hall and his partner, Sgt. Holland, tracking down criminals in stories such as "The Fangs of Death," "Tryst with a Dummy," and "Kiss of Death." The program had been seen locally on Chicago television for two years before its network run. During its local days viewers were not shown the solution of the night's crime, but were told to pick up a copy of the next day's *Chicago Tribune* for the outcome—a nice commercial tie-in.

CHICO AND THE MAN
Situation Comedy
FIRST TELECAST: *September 13, 1974*

147

LAST TELECAST: *July 21, 1978*
BROADCAST HISTORY:
 Sep 1974–Jan 1976, NBC Fri 8:30–9:00
 Jan 1976–Mar 1976, NBC Wed 9:00–9:30
 Apr 1976–Aug 1976, NBC Wed 9:30–10:00
 Aug 1976–Feb 1978, NBC Fri 8:30–9:00
 Jun 1978–Jul 1978, NBC Fri 8:30–9:00
CAST:
 Ed Brown (The Man)......... Jack Albertson
 Chico Rodriguez (1974–1977).. Freddie Prinze
 Louie .... Scatman Crothers
 Mabel (1974–1975) .... Bonnie Boland
 Mando (1974–1977).............. Isaac Ruiz
 Rev. Bemis (1975–1976)...... Ronny Graham
 Della Rogers (1976–1978) .... Della Reese
 Raul Garcia (1977–1978) ...... Gabriel Melgar
 Aunt Charo (1977–1978).............. Charo
THEME:
"Chico and the Man," written and performed by
Jose Feliciano

Set in the barrio of East Los Angeles, *Chico and the Man* was the story of two men from radically different cultural backgrounds who grew to respect each other. Chico, the enterprising young Chicano, was determined to go into partnership with cranky, sarcastic, cynical Ed Brown. Ed operated a small, run-down garage and spent most of his time complaining and alienating people. A lonely widower, he at first fought Chico's determined efforts to help him make the business work, but underneath it all he was both flattered and touched to have someone show genuine interest in him. Chico cleaned the place up, moved into a beat-up old truck in the garage, and brought in business. As often as Ed complained about Chico, and as often as he made token efforts to get rid of him, he felt an attachment that he would never publicly admit.

Regularly seen were Louie the garbageman, Mabel the mailwoman, and Chico's friend Mando. Della Rogers was added to the cast in the fall of 1976 as the civic-minded owner of the diner across the street from Ed's Garage, who also happened to be the new owner of the property on which the garage was located. She was more than capable of dishing out as much as she took from Ed.

When Freddy Prinze took his own life early in 1977, prior to the completion of the season's episodes, there was serious consideration given to the cancellation of the series. That was not done, however, as a new "Chico" was added to the cast for the following fall.

He was not an adult, though, or even someone whose name was really Chico. In the opening episode of the 1977–1978 season it was established that Chico had left Ed's garage to go into business with his successful father, a character introduced the previous year and played by Cesar Romero. Later, Ed and Louie returned from a fishing trip to Tijuana to discover a 12-year-old stowaway in their car trunk. The boy, Raul, ingratiated himself

with Ed and became his personal resident alien. At the end of that first episode, when the two of them were preparing to go to bed, Ed inadvertently said "Good night, Chico" to his new friend and, when corrected, simply said, "You're all Chicos to me." Thus a new "Chico" for "The Man." Ed eventually adopted Raul and found himself contending with Raul's protective, and very sexy, Aunt Charo, an entertainer who had recently arrived from Spain to work in Los Angeles. She spent so much time at Ed's garage with her nephew that she, too, became part of the family.

NBC aired reruns of *Chico and the Man* from May to December 1977 in its weekday daytime lineup.

CHILDREN'S SKETCH BOOK
Children's
FIRST TELECAST: *January 7, 1950*
LAST TELECAST: *February 4, 1950*
BROADCAST HISTORY:
 Jan 1950–Feb 1950, NBC Sat 7:00–7:30
STORYTELLER:
 Edith Skinner
ILLUSTRATOR:
 Lisl Weil

In this live children's program, Edith Skinner told stories in rhyme, accompanied by songs and drawings made by Lisl Weil. The show had formerly been on the network during the afternoon.

CHILD'S WORLD
Children's Discussion
FIRST TELECAST: *November 1, 1948*
LAST TELECAST: *April 27, 1949*
BROADCAST HISTORY:
 Nov 1948–Jan 1949, ABC Tue 7:30–7:45
 Jan 1949–Apr 1949, ABC Wed 7:15–7:30
HOSTESS:
 Helen Parkhurst

Child's World was an experiment in drawing out children's real feelings through spontaneous discussions. Youngsters ranging in age from 8 to 13 met in Miss Parkhurst's apartment and discussed such topics as jealousy, God, prejudice, and school.

CHINA SMITH
Adventure
BROADCAST HISTORY:
 Syndicated only
 30 minutes
 Produced *Jun 1952–1955* (52 episodes)
 Released: *Fall 1952*
CAST:
 China Smith................... Dan Duryea
 Inspector Hobson .... Douglas Dumbrille
 Shira ("Empress").............. Myrna Dell

Tough-guy movie actor Dan Duryea, who made a name for himself slugging Joan Bennett in *The*

Woman in the Window (1944), carried on in two-fisted style in this 1950s syndicated adventure. China Smith was an opportunistic con artist and sometimes private eye, operating out of a bar in Singapore, who roamed the Orient in search of adventure and a fast buck. He had an eye for beautiful women, and they all seemed to fall for his wisecracks and Irish brogue, despite—or perhaps because of—his tendency to play rough. Douglas Dumbrille was the very British police inspector, and Myrna Dell the scheming and powerful "Empress."

Two groups of *China Smith* films were made, the first 26 in 1952 (shot in Mexico), and the second 26 in 1954–1955, the latter being syndicated as *The New Adventures of China Smith.* Also known as *The Affairs of China Smith.*

CHiPS
Police Drama
FIRST TELECAST: *September 15, 1977*
LAST TELECAST: *July 17, 1983*
BROADCAST HISTORY:
Sep 1977–Mar 1978, NBC Thu 8:00–9:00
Apr 1978, NBC Sat 8:00–9:00
May 1978–Aug 1978, NBC Thu 8:00–9:00
Sep 1978–Mar 1980, NBC Sat 8:00–9:00
Mar 1980–Mar 1983, NBC Sun 8:00–9:00
Apr 1983–May 1983, NBC Sun 7:00–8:00
May 1983–Jul 1983, NBC Sun 8:00–9:00
CAST:
Officer Jon Baker (1977–1982) .. Larry Wilcox
Officer Frank "Ponch" Poncherello
.... Erik Estrada
Sgt. Joe Getraer................ Robert Pine
Officer Gene Fritz (1977–1981)
.... Lew Saunders
Officer Baricza (1977–1982) ..... Brodie Greer
Officer Sindy Cahill (1978–1979)
.... Brianne Leary
Harlan (1978–1983)............. Lou Wagner
Officer Grossman .... Paul Linke
Officer Bonnie Clark (1979–1982)
.... Randi Oakes
Officer Turner (1980–1982) ..... Michael Dorn
Officer Bobby Nelson (1982–1983)
.... Tom Reilly
Officer Kathy Linahan (1982–1983)
.... Tina Gayle
Cadet Bruce Nelson (1982–1983)
.... Bruce Penhall
Officer Webster (1982–1983)
.... Clarence Gilyard, Jr.

CHiPs, an acronym for California Highway Patrol, was the motorcycle equivalent to a previous episodic police series, *Adam 12.* Jon Baker and "Ponch" Poncherello were two state motorcycle patrolmen, both young bachelors, whose adventures helping citizens, fighting crime, and leading active social lives were all woven into the series. The two men worked as a team, and spent most of their working time around the vast Los Angeles

freeway system. Each episode was a composite of four or five separate incidents, both on the job and off, with violence downplayed in favor of human interest and the humorous elements of their work. Jon was rather straight and serious, while "Ponch" was the romantic free spirit, whose happy-go-lucky attitude did not always sit well with their superior, Sgt. Getraer. Added in 1978 were Harlan, a police mechanic who worked on their "choppers," and Sindy, a female "Chippie" who worked out of a patrol car. She was replaced, the following fall, by another female "Chippie," Bonnie Clark.

Former Olympic decathlon champion Bruce Jenner appeared as Officer Steve McLeish in several episodes in the fall of 1981 as a temporary replacement for Erik Estrada, who was embroiled in a salary dispute with *CHiPs'* producers. When Estrada returned, Jenner left the show. The fall of 1982 brought a number of cast changes. Larry Wilcox, who had had a stormy relationship with Estrada for several years, quit the series. Ponch got a new partner, Bobby Nelson, and Nelson's kid brother Bruce (played by professional motorcycle racer Bruce Penhall) joined the force as a trainee. The new resident "Chippie" was Kathy Linahan.

NBC aired reruns of *CHiPS* on weekday afternoons from April 1980–September 1980.

CHISHOLMS, THE
Western
FIRST TELECAST: *March 29, 1979*
LAST TELECAST: *March 15, 1980*
BROADCAST HISTORY:
Mar 1979–Apr 1979, CBS Thu 8:00–9:00
Jan 1980–Mar 1980, CBS Sat 8:00–9:00
CAST:
Hadley Chisholm .... Robert Preston
Minerva Chisholm .... Rosemary Harris
Will Chisholm................. Ben Murphy
Gideon Chisholm (1979) .... Brian Kerwin
Gideon Chisholm (1980) .... Brett Cullen
Bo Chisholm............. James Van Patten
Bonnie Sue Chisholm (1979) ... Stacey Nelkin
Bonnie Sue Chisholm (1980) ..... Delta Burke
Annabel Chisholm (1979) .... Susan Swift
Mercy Hopwell (1980) .... Susan Swift
Cooper Hawkins (1980) .... Mitchell Ryan
Kewedinok .... Victoria Racimo
Lester Hackett (1979)........ Charles Frank
Lester Hackett (1980)............ Reid Smith
Betsy O'Neal (1980) .... Devon Ericson
Frank O'Neal (1980)............ Guich Koock
Jeremy O'Neal (1980).......... Les Lannom
McVeety (1980) .... Frank Noel
Tehohane (1980) .... Nick Ramus

Originally aired as a four-part mini-series in the spring of 1979, *The Chisholms* attracted a sufficiently large audience to encourage CBS to bring it back the following January. It was soap-opera-cum-Western. The Chisholm clan, led by patriarch Hadley and his wife Minerva, were a poor but industrious Virginia family of the 1840s who lost their land in a legal dispute. With little money but a lot of gumption they began a journey to California, in search of a new life. The original mini-series chronicled the arduous trip from Virginia to Fort Laramie, Wyoming, in the course of which the youngest daughter Annabel died during an Indian attack; son Will married an Indian woman, Kewedinok; and daughter Bonnie Sue had an illegitimate child by con man and gambler Lester Hackett, who had joined them in Louisville. When *The Chisholms* returned in 1980, the family was part of a wagon train, led by Cooper Hawkins, traveling from Fort Laramie to California. En route Hadley, having fallen ill, passed away. Not long thereafter, so did the entire series.

CHOPPER ONE
Police Drama
FIRST TELECAST: *January 17, 1974*
LAST TELECAST: *July 11, 1974*
BROADCAST HISTORY:
  Jan 1974–Jul 1974, ABC Thu 8:00–8:30
CAST:
  Officer Don Burdick.......... Jim McMullan
  Officer Gil Foley.............. Dirk Benedict
  Capt. McKeegan .... Ted Hartley
  Mitch .... Lou Frizzel

In this action drama, two young "chopper cops" were assigned to police helicopter duty in a large California city. Among their adversaries were rooftop snipers, muggers in the parks, and other desperados foolish enough to work in the open— including one sniper whose goal in life was to shoot down police helicopters. Lou Frizzel played Mitch, the copter mechanic.

CHRONICLE
Documentary
FIRST TELECAST: *October 2, 1963*
LAST TELECAST: *April 22, 1964*
BROADCAST HISTORY:
  Oct 1963–Apr 1964, CBS Wed 7:30–8:30
HOST:
  Charles Collingwood

Chronicle was aired during the 1963–1964 season on an alternating basis with *CBS Reports*. Whereas *CBS Reports* was known for its hard-news documentaries, *Chronicle* sought to look at the cultural side of contemporary society and the roots from which that culture developed. Episodes in the series covered such diverse subjects as the British music hall, the writings of Edgar Allan Poe, political and social revolution in the 20th century, and the Constitution of the United States.

CHRONOLOG
see *First Tuesday*

CHRONOSCOPE
Discussion

FIRST TELECAST: *June 11, 1951*
LAST TELECAST: *April 29, 1955*
BROADCAST HISTORY:
  Jun 1951–Sep 1951, CBS Mon 11:00–11:15
  Sep 1951–Jun 1953, CBS Mon/Wed/Fri 11:00–11:15
  Aug 1953–Apr 1955, CBS Mon/Wed/Fri 11:00–11:15
MODERATOR:
  Frank Knight (1951)
  William Bradford Huie (1951–1953)
  Edward P. Morgan (1953)
  Larry Le Sueur (1953–1955)

Current issues in world affairs were discussed on this late evening series. Each telecast featured a guest who was either personally involved in, or an expert on, a situation of major significance on the world scene—politics, finance, natural disasters, or the Korean War, for example. Two other panelists from a rotating group of journalists chatted with the guest panelist about the implications of the event or trend under discussion.

CHRYSLER THEATRE
see *Bob Hope Presents The Chrysler Theatre*

CHUCK BARRIS RAH RAH SHOW, THE
Comedy Variety
FIRST TELECAST: *February 28, 1978*
LAST TELECAST: *April 11, 1978*
BROADCAST HISTORY:
  Feb 1978–Apr 1978, NBC Tue 8:00–9:00
REGULARS:
  Chuck Barris
  Jaye P. Morgan
  Milton Delugg Orchestra

The Chuck Barris Rah Rah Show was one of the less conventional variety shows of recent years, as well as one of the shortest lived. Barris was a longtime producer of game shows who had first been seen on camera on *The Gong Show*, a parody on talent shows which was seen on the NBC daytime lineup. He was supposed to be simply the program's producer, but had taken over as host at the last minute before the premiere when the original host proved unsuitable. He was perfect in the role.

The *Gong Show* idea—a succession of no-talent amateurs doing dreadful acts (and often getting "gonged" off the stage)—caught on, and soon produced both a syndicated version and this nighttime adaptation. Unlike *Gong* the *Rah Rah Show* included professional acts, doing their bits in quick succession on a simple stage. Barris' choice of guests was a bit odd, combining old-timers such as Slim Gaillard ("Flat Foot Floogie") and Cab Calloway with 1950s rock artists such as The Coasters and Chuck Berry, along with contemporary talent such as Jose Feliciano and Anson Williams. Comics Fred Travalena and Henny Youngman made repeat appearances, and singer Jaye P. Morgan was a regular. In addition there were always several amateurs displaying their questionable talents, such as the lady who chirped and barked while singing "The Sound of Music" and Dr. Flame-O, who played "Smoke Gets in Your Eyes" on a row of burning candles.

CIMARRON CITY
Western
FIRST TELECAST: *October 11, 1958*
LAST TELECAST: *September 16, 1960*
BROADCAST HISTORY:
Oct 1958–Sep 1959, NBC Sat 9:30–10:30
Jun 1960–Sep 1960, NBC Fri 7:30–8:30
CAST:
Matthew Rockford . . . . . . George Montgomery
Beth Purcell . . . . Audrey Totter
Lane Temple . . . . John Smith
Art Sampson . . . . Stuart Randall
Martin Kingsley . . . . Addison Richards
Burt Purdy . . . . Fred Sherman
Alice Purdy . . . . Claire Carleton
Tiny Budinger . . . . Dan Blocker
Jesse Williams . . . . George Dunn
Dody Hamer . . . . Pete Dunn
Silas Perry . . . . Tom Fadden
Jed Fame . . . . Wally Brown

George Montgomery was both star and narrator of this saga of a boom town on the western frontier during the 1890s. Oil and gold had created a booming economy in the Oklahoma Territory, and Cimarron City had mushroomed into a sprawling, roughhewn metropolis, with hopes of becoming the capital of the future state of Oklahoma. Matthew Rockford, son of the town's founder, was mayor and a leading cattle rancher, Beth Purcell, the owner of a boardinghouse; and Lane Temple, the town sheriff. These three, singly or together, were the focus of most episodes. Dan Blocker, who later starred as Hoss on *Bonanza,* was featured as a local citizen who often helped the sheriff in the cause of law and order. Montgomery narrated the episodes from the perspective of an older man recalling the adventures and happenings of his younger days. Those that were telecast during the summer of 1960 were reruns of earlier shows.

CIMARRON STRIP
Western
FIRST TELECAST: *September 7, 1967*
LAST TELECAST: *September 7, 1971*
BROADCAST HISTORY:
Sep 1967–Sep 1968, CBS Thu 7:30–9:00
Jul 1971–Sep 1971, CBS Tue 8:30–10:00
CAST:
U.S. Marshal Jim Crown . . . . . Stuart Whitman
Mac Gregor . . . . Percy Herbert
Francis Wilde . . . . Randy Boone
Dulcey Coopersmith . . . . Jill Townsend

The Cimarron Strip was the border region between the Kansas Territory and Indian territory during the late 19th century. Patrolling this vast area was the job of U.S. Marshal Jim Crown, who was based in Cimarron City. Marshal Crown had no full-time deputies but he often availed himself of the assistance of Mac Gregor, an itinerant Scot, and Francis Wilde, a young photographer. Also seen as a regular in this series was Dulcey, a young woman from the East who had moved to the frontier to take over an inn that had been run by her late father. *Cimarron Strip* was an attempt by CBS to copy the success of NBC's *The Virginian* (the first 90-minute Western series), and like *The Virginian* it centered largely on characters acted by guest stars. Reruns of the original series aired during the summer of 1971.

CINEMA VARIETIES
see *Movies—Prior to 1961*

CINEMA-SCOPE
see *Movies—Prior to 1961*

CIRCLE OF FEAR
see *Ghost Story*

CIRCLE THEATER
see *Armstrong Circle Theater*

CIRCUIT RIDER
Religion
FIRST TELECAST: *March 5, 1951*
LAST TELECAST: *May 7, 1951*
BROADCAST HISTORY:
Mar 1951–May 1951, ABC Mon 11:00–11:30
NARRATOR:
Rex Marshall
MODERATOR:
Rev. George Pigueron

This series began with dramatizations of the efforts of clergymen to bring religion to the early American frontier, and later broadened to dramatizations emphasizing the significance of Christianity in everyday life. There was also a weekly guest who discussed current religious problems and activities. Sponsored by America for Christ, Inc.

CIRCUS
Variety
BROADCAST HISTORY:
Syndicated only
30 minutes
Produced: *1971–1973* (52 episodes)
Released: *Fall 1971*
HOST:
Bert Parks

Leading European circus acts were taped on location for this series, which was much in the style of the earlier *International Showtime* (by the same producers).

CIRCUS BOY
Adventure
FIRST TELECAST: *September 23, 1956*
LAST TELECAST: *September 11, 1958*
BROADCAST HISTORY:
    Sep 1956–Sep 1957, NBC Sun 7:30–8:00
    Sep 1957–Sep 1958, ABC Thu 7:30–8:00
CAST:
    Corky .... Mickey Braddock
    Joey, the Clown .... Noah Beery, Jr.
    Big Tim Champion ,.......... Robert Lowery
    Hank Miller .... Leo Gordon
    Little Tom, the Midget............ Billy Barty
    Swifty........................ Olin Howlin
    Barker .... Eddie Marr
    Big Boy .... Guinn Williams

Circus life at the turn of the century as seen through the eyes of a young boy. Corky, a 12-year-old orphan, had been adopted by the members of a traveling circus owned by Big Tim Champion. His life with the colorful performers and behind-the-scenes workers, as the circus traveled from town to town, formed the basis for the series. Corky's personal pet was Bimbo, a baby elephant, for whom he was water boy.

Although the series left prime time after two seasons on two networks, reruns continued on Saturday mornings until September 1960.

Nearly a decade after *Circus Boy* left the air, its star, Mickey Braddock, surfaced again on another series. Now an adult, and using his real last name, Dolenz, he was one of the four stars of *The Monkees.*

CIRCUS TIME
Variety
FIRST TELECAST: *October 4, 1956*
LAST TELECAST: *June 27, 1957*
BROADCAST HISTORY:
    Oct 1956–Jun 1957, ABC Thu 8:00–9:00
REGULARS:
    Paul Winchell
    Betty Ann Grove (1957)
    Ralph Herman Orchestra

This variety show with the flavor of a traditional circus presented both circus performers and traditional entertainment acts. Paul Winchell was the "ringmaster-host," assisted by his dummies Jerry Mahoney and Knucklehead Smith. Guests included popular music acts such as Mickey and Sylvia and the Dell Vikings.

CISCO KID, THE
Western
BROADCAST HISTORY:
    Syndicated only
    30 minutes

Produced: *1950–1956* (156 episodes)
Released: *Late 1950*
CAST:
    The Cisco Kid .... Duncan Renaldo
    Pancho........................ Leo Carrillo

One of the most popular kids' Westerns of early television never ran on a network. Sold individually to local stations, *The Cisco Kid* was not only the first big syndicated film hit, but was in fact one of the first popular filmed programs on TV (most shows at that time were done live). Eventually 156 half-hour episodes were made by Ziv Television, surprisingly all of them in color, although most stations showed them in black-and-white during the 1950s.

The Cisco Kid was a Mexican adventurer who ranged the old Southwest with his trusty sidekick, Pancho. Dressed immaculately in a highly embroidered black outfit, and endowed with an excess of Latin charm, he usually swept some *señorita* off her feet after running the criminals to earth. All she got was a kiss and a dashing sweep of the sombrero, however, before the two knights on horseback rode off with a laugh. Cisco's horse was Diablo, and Pancho's was Loco.

Fat old Pancho was always ready with a crack and some fractured English that kids loved to imitate ("Ceesco? Let's went! The shereef, he ees getting closer!"). But he was brave in a fight, and an expert with the bullwhip. They saw a lot of action together, but relatively little gunplay. Usually Cisco's fast draw was to shoot the gun out of the bad guy's hand. The ready, fun-loving camaraderie between Cisco and Pancho was what made the series work.

The Cisco Kid had a long and glorious history before coming to TV. Invented by O. Henry in the short story "The Caballero's Way," he was originally a scruffy bandito who victimized the rich and helped the poor. He turned up in early silent movies, and then in many sound features beginning with *In Old Arizona* in 1929 (for which Warner Baxter, as Cisco, won one of the first Academy Awards). Dozens of films followed with Cesar Romero, Gilbert Roland, and Duncan Renaldo in the lead role, and there was a popular radio series off and on during the 1940s. Beginning simultaneously with the TV series, there was also a comic strip, which lasted until 1968.

Renaldo was in his 50s and Leo Carrillo in his 70s when the TV films were made, but they nevertheless did much (though not all) of the hard riding and stunts themselves. They were both excellent horsemen. Years after production finally ended, Renaldo continued to tour with the aging Diablo, and he will always be, in his own and the public's eye, the Cisco Kid. Carrillo died in 1961 at the age of 81.

CITIES SERVICE BAND OF AMERICA
Music
FIRST TELECAST: *October 17, 1949*

LAST TELECAST: *January 9, 1950*
BROADCAST HISTORY:
  Oct 1949–Jan 1950, NBC Mon 9:30–10:00
CONDUCTOR:
  Paul Lavalle
ANNOUNCER:
  Ford Bond

This simulcast of the popular NBC radio program featured Paul Lavalle and the 48-piece Band of America. Various soloists from the band were spotlighted, as well as the Green and White Vocal Quartette and a 12-voice glee club. Baton-twirling majorettes and an occasional film clip were added as a concession to television, but the program faced withering competition from *The Goldbergs,* running opposite it on CBS, and was soon canceled.

CITY ASSIGNMENT
  see *Big Town*

CITY DETECTIVE
  Police Drama
BROADCAST HISTORY:
  Syndicated only
  30 minutes
  Produced: *1953–1955* (65 episodes)
  Released: *Fall 1953*
CAST:
  Det. Lt. Bart Grant............ Rod Cameron

This bare-knuckles detective show was one of several such vehicles for lanky Rod Cameron *(State Trooper, Coronado 9),* of whom *TV Guide* once remarked, "Most of his acting ability is in his fists." Despite the "city" in the title, Lt. Grant ranged far and wide fighting crime, from Mexico to the Mojave Desert to New York City. Most episodes involved murder, extortion, or similar crimes.

CITY HOSPITAL
  Medical Drama
FIRST TELECAST: *March 25, 1952*
LAST TELECAST: *October 1, 1953*
BROADCAST HISTORY:
  Mar 1952–Jun 1953, CBS Tue 9:00–9:30
  Jun 1953–Oct 1953, CBS Thu 10:30–11:00
CAST:
  Dr. Barton Crane .... Melville Ruick
  Dr. Kate Morrow................. Ann Burr

The daily crises of a large metropolitan hospital, and the personal and professional lives of its staff members, were dramatized in this live series. Dr. Barton Crane was the medical director of City Hospital, and it was from his position, either as an active participant or advisor to those involved, that the stories were developed. The presence of a female doctor, Kate Morrow, was rather uncommon for medical shows of this period.

City Hospital was aired on a biweekly basis throughout its run, alternating with *Crime Syndicated* on Tuesdays and with *Place the Face* on Thursdays. It had originally been seen as a Saturday afternoon series on ABC, where it ran from November 1951 to April 1952, barely overlapping the start of its prime-time run on CBS.

CITY OF ANGELS
  Detective Drama
FIRST TELECAST: *February 3, 1976*
LAST TELECAST: *August 10, 1976*
BROADCAST HISTORY:
  Feb 1976–Aug 1976, NBC Tue 10:00–11:00
CAST:
  Jake Axminster .... Wayne Rogers
  Marsha .... Elaine Joyce
  Lt. Murray Quint.............. Clifton James
  Michael Brimm .... Philip Sterling

Set in Los Angeles (the "City of Angels") in the 1930s, this period detective series was patterned after the hit motion picture *Chinatown.* It concerned the exploits of Jake Axminster, an often broke but always free-wheeling private investigator who was not above stretching the law and his ethics to get the information he wanted. Possibly as a reflection of his own standards, Jake trusted nobody completely, not even his attorney, Michael Brimm. Jake's office was run by a beautiful but daffy secretary, Marsha, who also ran a switchboard that took messages for call girls. A midseason replacement, *City of Angels* was notable more for its vintage automobiles and period fashions than for dramatic involvement, and it was soon canceled.

CLAUDIA, THE STORY OF A MARRIAGE
  Drama
FIRST TELECAST: *January 6, 1952*
LAST TELECAST: *June 30, 1952*
BROADCAST HISTORY:
  Jan 1952–Mar 1952, NBC Sun 6:30–7:00
  Mar 1952–Jun 1952, CBS Mon 9:30–10:00
CAST:
  Claudia Naughton.......... Joan McCracken
  David Naughton .... Hugh Reilly
  Mrs. Brown............. Margaret Wycherly
  Bertha .... Lilia Skala
  Julia Naughton.................. Faith Brook
  Harley Naughton .... Alex Clark
  Fritz .... Paul Andor
  Roger .... Mercer McCloud

Claudia was a study in contrasts, at once both very childish and remarkably mature for her age. She married aspiring architect David Naughton at the age of 18, and the problems and joys of their young marriage were explored realistically in this series. Claudia's dealings with her new family, including David's sister Julia and brother Harley, and her attempts to break away from her possessive mother, Mrs. Brown, all served as subject matter. The series was broadcast live from New York.

Claudia had had a highly successful career before coming to TV, having been the heroine in three novels by Rose Franken (published between 1939–1941), a Broadway play, a radio series, and two movies starring Dorothy McGuire and Robert Young. On television, however, her story was brief.

CLIFF EDWARDS SHOW, THE
Music
FIRST TELECAST: *May 23, 1949*
LAST TELECAST: *September 19, 1949*
BROADCAST HISTORY:
  May 1949–Sep 1949, CBS Mon/Wed/Fri 7:45–8:00
  Sep 1949, CBS Mon 7:45–8:00
REGULARS:
  Cliff Edwards
  The Tony Mottola Trio

Show-business veteran Cliff "Ukulele Ike" Edwards was the host of this informal live musical series, which filled out the remainder of the half-hour in which CBS aired its nightly network news program. Cliff would recount homespun stories, play his ukulele, and model some of his huge collection of unusual hats. He also sang songs and occasionally chatted with a guest. Some of the songs were no doubt taken from Cliff's long career on records, radio, and in movies, during which he had introduced such hits as "Fascinating Rhythm" (in a 1924 Broadway show), "Singin' in the Rain" (in a 1929 movie musical), and "When You Wish Upon A Star" (in the 1939 Disney feature *Pinocchio*, for which Edwards provided the voice of Jiminy Cricket).

CLIFF HANGERS
Serials
FIRST TELECAST: *February 27, 1979*
LAST TELECAST: *May 1, 1979*
BROADCAST HISTORY:
  Feb 1979–May 1979, NBC Tue 8:00–9:00

From the 1910s to the 1950s, cliff hangers were a stable form of movie entertainment for America's young. Saturday afternoons meant a trip to the neighborhood theater where the latest chapter of the current *Zorro, Superman,* or *Commando Cody* serial was on display. All of the movie serials—whether Westerns, melodramas, science fiction, or gothic horror stories—had one element in common. At the end of each episode (full serials ran 10 to 15 episodes) the hero or heroine was left in a perilous, potentially fatal situation. Miraculously, however, the first minutes of the succeeding episode would show how he or she had escaped. The kids at the Saturday matinees knew their heroes would survive, the only question was how. Not knowing gave them something to talk about all week until they faithfully returned to the movie house the following week to find out.

More than two decades after the last movie serial was produced, NBC tried the format on television. *Cliff Hangers* was the umbrella title for three separate serials all sharing the same hour on Tuesday nights. Each week viewers saw the latest 20-minute chapter of *Stop Susan Williams, The Secret Empire,* and *The Curse of Dracula.* To add to the "in progress" feeling, each of the three was picked up at a different stage on February 27, 1980: *Stop Susan Williams* at Chapter II, *The Secret Empire* at Chapter III, and *The Curse of Dracula* at Chapter VI. The idea was to begin new serials while others were still in progress, but only *The Curse of Dracula* managed to reach its conclusion in the brief time *Cliff Hangers* was on the air. For more detail, see the individual serial titles.

CLIMAX
Dramatic Anthology
FIRST TELECAST: *October 7, 1954*
LAST TELECAST: *June 26, 1958*
BROADCAST HISTORY:
  Oct 1954–Jun 1958, CBS Thu 8:30–9:30
HOSTS:
  William Lundigan
  Mary Costa (1956–1958)

Climax was one of the longer-running dramatic series aired on network television during the 1950s. Hosted by William Lundigan, who was joined by permanent co-host Mary Costa in the summer of 1956, each week it presented a one-hour drama originating from CBS' facilities in Hollywood. When it first went on the air, *Climax* was done live every week, but as time wore on, filmed (and later taped) productions were added to the mix. Even in its last season, however, there were several live programs presented. Among the plays aired were adaptations of *Casino Royale,* with Barry Nelson playing an American James Bond; *A Farewell to Arms,* with Guy Madison and Diana Lynn; and *Dr. Jekyll and Mr. Hyde,* with Michael Rennie playing the dual role.

CLOAK OF MYSTERY
Dramatic Anthology
FIRST TELECAST: *May 11, 1965*
LAST TELECAST: *August 8, 1965*
BROADCAST HISTORY:
  May 1965, NBC Tue 9:30–10:00
  May 1965–Aug 1965, NBC Tue 9:00–10:00

This summer anthology series consisted of reruns of episodes of *Alcoa Premiere, Alfred Hitchcock Presents, Pepsi-Cola Playhouse,* and *G. E. Theatre.* In addition, two episodes were pilots for series that never made it to the schedule.

CLOCK, THE
Suspense Anthology
FIRST TELECAST: *May 16, 1949*
LAST TELECAST: *January 9, 1952*

BROADCAST HISTORY:

May 1949–Aug 1949, NBC Mon 8:30–9:00
Aug 1949–Mar 1950, NBC Wed 8:30–9:00
Apr 1950–Feb 1951, NBC Fri 9:30–10:00
Jul 1951–Aug 1951, NBC Fri 8:30–9:00
Oct 1951–Jan 1952, ABC Wed 9:30–10:00

NARRATOR:

Larry Semon

THEME:

"Sands of Time"

"Sunrise and sunset, promise and fulfillment, birth and death—the whole drama of life is written in the Sands of Time." So began this mystery-suspense series, composed for the most part of live original dramas written for TV and starring a wide range of guest actors and actresses. A clock was prominently featured, and time played a vital role in each story. Typically, murder or insanity was the theme. The program was based on a preceding ABC radio series (1946–1948).

CLORETS SUMMER THEATRE

Dramatic Anthology
FIRST TELECAST: *July 12, 1955*
LAST TELECAST: *August 23, 1955*
BROADCAST HISTORY:
Jul 1955–Aug 1955, NBC Tue 9:00–9:30

Clorets Summer Theatre alternated with *Kleenex Summer Theatre* as a replacement series for *Fireside Theatre.* The dramas shown were all filmed reruns of episodes from *Four Star Playhouse.*

CLUB EMBASSY

Variety
FIRST TELECAST: *October 7, 1952*
LAST TELECAST: *June 23, 1953*
BROADCAST HISTORY:
Oct 1952–Jun 1953, NBC Tue 10:30–10:45
REGULARS:
Bob Elliott (Oct–Dec)
Ray Goulding (Oct–Dec)
Audrey Meadows (Oct–Dec)
Florian Zabach
Julia Meade (Oct–Dec)
Mindy Carson (Dec–May)
The Embassy Quartet (Dec–Jun)
Danny Hoctor (Dec–June)
Connie Russell (May–June)

This comedy variety show originally starred Bob and Ray doing their own brand of off-beat, satirical humor, in the setting of a nightclub (the first telecast was under the title *Embassy Club*). Audrey Meadows sang and acted in various skits, violinist Florian Zabach (famous for his showpiece number "The Hot Canary") was the featured instrumental soloist, and Julia Meade was the emcee and cigarette girl. On December 30, 1952, the cast and format underwent major changes. Bob and Ray, Audrey Meadows, and Julia Meade were replaced by singer Mindy Car-

son, and the emphasis was shifted from comedy to music. Backing up Miss Carson were the Embassy Quartet and dancer Danny Hoctor. On May 19, 1953, Miss Carson was in turn replaced by singer Connie Russell, but the "club" closed down a month later.

CLUB OASIS

Variety
FIRST TELECAST: *September 28, 1957*
LAST TELECAST: *September 6, 1958*
BROADCAST HISTORY:
Sep 1957–Aug 1958, NBC Sat 9:00–9:30
Sep 1958, NBC Sat 10:30–11:00
REGULARS:
Spike Jones and His City Slickers (1958)
Helen Grayco (1958)
Joyce Jameson (1958)
Billy Barty (1958)

Club Oasis was a simulated nightclub that headlined a different popular entertainer each week. Depending on the performer, the material might be comedy or singing or full-scale production numbers. Among those featured were Jimmy Durante, Martha Raye, Eddie Fisher, Jo Stafford, Dean Martin, Kay Starr, and Frank Sinatra, along with supporting acts each week to fill out the bill. During the summer of 1958 Spike Jones became the permanent star of the show and the title was changed to *Club Oasis Starring Spike Jones*. Featured along with Spike's lunatic band were his wife, singer Helen Grayco; comedienne Joyce Jameson; and midget comic Billy Barty. *Club Oasis* was a biweekly series throughout its run, first alternating with *The Polly Bergen Show* and during the summer of 1958 with *Opening Night*.

CLUB SEVEN

Musical Variety
FIRST TELECAST: *August 12, 1948*
LAST TELECAST: *August 24, 1951*
BROADCAST HISTORY:
Aug 1948–Sep 1948, ABC Thu 8:00–8:30
Oct 1948, ABC Thu 8:30–9:00
Nov 1948–Jan 1949, ABC Wed 8:00–8:30
Jan 1949–Mar 1949, ABC Thu 10:30–11:00
Sep 1950–Aug 1951, ABC Mon–Fri 7:00–7:30
REGULARS:
Johnny Thompson (1948–1949)
Bobby Byrne Orchestra (1948–1949)
Tony Bavaar (1950–1951)
Eadie and Rack, piano team (1950–1951)

This informal, low-budget musical variety program in the early days of the ABC network featured new talent, ranging from singers and dancers to acrobats and "Hank the Mule." After a hiatus in 1949–1950 the program returned as a nightly feature, hosted by vocalist Tony Bavaar. This later version varied in length from 10 to 30 minutes, since it was often truncated by five- or ten-minute newscasts or other series on either end.

CODE NAME: FOXFIRE
Foreign Intrigue/Secret Agent
FIRST TELECAST: *January 27, 1985*
LAST TELECAST: *March 22, 1985*
BROADCAST HISTORY:
Jan 1985, NBC Sun 8:00–10:00
Feb 1985–Mar 1985, NBC Fri 8:00–9:00
CAST:
Elizabeth "Foxfire" Towne... Joanna Cassidy
Larry Hutchins .... John McCook
Maggie Bryan .... Sheryl Lee Ralph
Danny O'Toole .... Robin Johnson
Phillips .... Henry Jones

The fate of the nation (or at least of NBC's Friday night schedule) rested in the hands of three sexy government agents in this hard-action cross between the James Bond movies and *Charlie's Angels.* The leader was former CIA operative Liz "Foxfire" Towne, who had just served four years in prison for a crime she hadn't committed. She had been sprung by Larry Hutchins, the brother of the President, to organize a special counterespionage team reporting directly to him. Liz's partners were Maggie "the cat," a reformed thief from Detroit and Danny "the driver," a resourceful, street-wise, former hansom cab driver from New York. They were hard-nosed and tough, or elegant and sophisticated, as the assignment demanded. Also on Liz's mind, understandably, was tracking down the former lover who had abandoned her in Bogota and thereby been responsible for her imprisonment. Phillips was Hutchins' stuffy valet who helped out at unexpected times.

CODE R
Adventure
FIRST TELECAST: *January 21, 1977*
LAST TELECAST: *June 10, 1977*
BROADCAST HISTORY:
Jan 1977–Jun 1977, CBS Fri 8:00–9:00
CAST:
Rick Wilson .... James Houghton
George Baker .... Martin Kove
Walt Robinson .... Tom Simcox
Suzy .... Susanne Reed
Ted Milbank .... Ben Davidson
Bobby Robinson .... Robbie Rundle
Harry .... W. T. Zacha

Scenic Channel Island, off the southern California coast, was the setting for this adventure series, which resembled NBC's *Emergency* but was laid in a self-contained locale. Rick Wilson was the fire chief, George Baker the chief of beaches, and Walt Robinson the police chief on Channel Island. They all managed to get involved in at least one of the several stories that unfolded in any given episode. Suzy was the dispatcher for the Island's Emergency Services Department and doubled as

secretary to all three men, since their offices were in the same building. Ted was a deputy of police, Bobby was Walt's ten-year-old son, and Harry was the owner and bartender at the Lighthouse Bar, a favorite off-duty hangout of the three chiefs. Typical situations included rescuing two young boys floating out to sea on a homemade raft, tracking down a bootleg whiskey operation, coping with an arsonist, and helping a man trapped in the water in his dune buggy.

CODE RED
Adventure
FIRST TELECAST: *September 20, 1981*
LAST TELECAST: *September 12, 1982*
BROADCAST HISTORY:
Sep 1981, ABC Sun 8:00–9:30
Nov 1981–Mar 1982, ABC Sun 7:00–8:00
Jul 1982–Sep 1982, ABC Sun 7:00–8:00
CAST:
Battalion Chief Joe Rorchek ... Lorne Greene
Ann Rorchek .... Julie Adams
Ted Rorchek............... Andrew Stevens
Chris Rorchek .... Sam J. Jones
Haley Green............... Martina Deignan
Danny Blake .... Adam Rich
Capt. Mike Benton .... Joe Maross
Rags Harris .... James Crittenden
"Stuff" Wade .... Dennis Haysbert
Al Martelli .... Jack Lindine
PRODUCER:
Irwin Allen

Lorne Greene headed a family of firefighters in this instructional series. Joe Rorchek was a 30-year veteran of the Los Angeles City Fire Department who specialized in arson investigations. His sons were also firemen—Ted on the ground and Chris from the air, as a helicopter pilot. Haley was a young woman trying to prove herself as the city's first female "smoke eater," and Danny was a homeless 13-year-old adopted by the Rorcheks. Naturally he joined the fire department's Explorer Program so he could learn all about firefighting, too.

Along with lessons in fire safety, viewers saw examples of the work of paramedics, rescue operations, and even "scuba diving for underwater fire prevention"—a danger most people would find unlikely!

CO-ED FEVER
Situation Comedy
FIRST TELECAST: *February 4, 1979*
LAST TELECAST: *February 4, 1979*
BROADCAST HISTORY:
Feb 1979, CBS Sun 10:00–11:00
CAST:
Tuck .... David Keith
Mousie .... Alexa Kenin
Doug .... Christopher S. Nelson
Elizabeth................... Cathryn O'Neil
Gobo .... Michael Pasternak

Hope	Tacey Phillips
Mrs. Selby	Jane Rose
Sandi	Heather Thomas
Mr. Peabody	Hamilton Camp
Melba	Jillian Kesner

One of the biggest theatrical movie hits of 1978 was a slapstick look at college life titled *Animal House*. Whether by pure coincidence or not, each of the three networks rushed to television early in 1979 a comedy series that centered around college hijinx. ABC had *Delta House* and NBC, *Brothers and Sisters*, but to CBS went the distinction of a series so dreadful that it never even made it to its regular time slot (on Monday). *Co-Ed Fever* was seen just once, as a "special preview" on Sunday, February 4, 1979.

The setting for *Co-Ed Fever* was a co-educational dormitory at rustic Baxter College. The dormitory, Brewster House, was peopled by a wide assortment of kooky college students, one ultra-sexy blonde named Sandi, and a spaced-out housemother, Mrs. Selby.

COKE TIME WITH EDDIE FISHER
Music
FIRST TELECAST: *April 29, 1953*
LAST TELECAST: *February 22, 1957*
BROADCAST HISTORY:
Apr 1953–Feb 1957, NBC Wed/Fri 7:30–7:45 (OS)
REGULARS:
Eddie Fisher
Don Ameche (1953)
Freddy Robbins
Axel Stordahl and His Orchestra
The Echoes (1956–1957)

Handsome young Eddie Fisher was fresh out of the army and at the height of his career when this popular 15-minute show began in 1953. The idol of bobbysoxers all over the country, he sang many of his million-selling recordings here, including "I'm Walking Behind You" (which reached number one on the hit parade shortly after the series began), "Oh! My Papa," and "Anytime." Each live telecast—occasionally the show was filmed in advance or on location—opened with Eddie singing his theme song, "May I Sing to You." Guest stars appeared frequently and a permanent backup group, the Echoes, was added in the fall of 1956. Actor Don Ameche was the original host of the show, through October 23, 1953. Freddy Robbins, who had been announcing the commercials, subsequently took on the added duty of host.

COLBYS, THE
Drama
FIRST TELECAST: *November 20, 1985*
LAST TELECAST: *March 26, 1987*
BROADCAST HISTORY:
Nov 1985, ABC Wed 10:00–11:00
Nov 1985–Mar 1987, ABC Thu 9:00–10:00

CAST:
Jason Colby	Charlton Heston
Sable Scott Colby	Stephanie Beacham
Francesca Scott Colby Hamilton Langdon	
	Katherine Ross
Jeff Colby	John James
Fallon Carrington Colby	Emma Samms
Monica Colby	Tracy Scoggins
Miles Colby	Maxwell Caulfield
Bliss Colby	Claire Yarlett
Zachary Powers	Ricardo Montalban
Constance Colby (1985–1986)	
	Barbara Stanwyck
Lord Roger Langdon	David Hedison
Garrett Boydston (1985–1986)	Ken Howard
Hutch Corrigan (1985–1986)	
	Joseph Campanella
Sean McAllister (1985–1986)	
	Charles Van Eman
Neil Kittredge (1985–1986)	Philip Brown
Henderson Palmer (1985–1986)	Ivan Bonar
Arthur Cates (1985–1986)	Peter White
Wayne Masterson (1986)	Gary Morris
L.B. ("Little Blake") Colby (1986)	
	Ashley Mutrux; also Brandon Bluhm
Spiros Koralis (1986)	Ray Wise
Asst. D.A. John Moretti (1986)	
	Vince Baggetta
Channing Carter Colby (1986–1987)	
	Kim Morgan Greene
Sen. Cash Cassidy (1986–1987)	
	James Houghton
Adrienne Cassidy (1986–1987)	Shanna Reed
Kolya (Nikolai) Rostov (1986–1987)	
	Adrian Paul
Anna Rostov (1986–1987)	Anna Levine
Sacha Malenkov (1986)	Judson Scott
Lucas Carter (1986–1987)	Kevin McCarthy
Dr. Waverly (1986–1987)	Georgann Johnson
Phillip Colby (a.k.a. Hoyt Parker) (1987)	
	Michael Parks

A strong emphasis on glamour and the trappings of the super-rich marked this close copy of (and spin-off from) ABC's hit soap opera *Dynasty*. Perhaps it was too close a copy; *The Colbys* never caught on as its parent program had, and was canceled after only two seasons.

At the center of the turmoil was Jason Colby, head of giant Colby Enterprises, a multinational conglomerate with interests in oil, shipping, real estate, and the aerospace industry. The family's opulent estate Belvedere, overlooking Los Angeles, was a veritable hotbed of intrigue, much of it between Jason's glamorous, scheming wife Sable and her much-married sister Francesca ("Frankie"), her rival for Jason's affections. Maintaining a degree of civility between the squabbling sisters was Jason's sensible older sister Constance, who owned half of Colby Enterprises.

Stories during the first season included the arrival (from *Dynasty*) of Jason's nephew Jeff, to take his place in the family empire and to search for his missing bride Fallon, who had developed amnesia; Sable's scheme to have Constance declared incompetent so she couldn't leave her half of the family fortune to Jeff; Connie's relationship with rancher Hutch and Francesca's short marriage to British diplomat Roger Langdon; Zach Powers' incessant plotting against the Colbys'; and the revelation that Jeff was in fact Jason's son, the product of a tryst with Francesca many years before. Along the way each of Jason and Sable's three children had their own entanglements: lawyer Monica with blind country singer Wayne and married man Neil (with whom she worked at Titania Records); playboy Miles with Fallon, whom he maneuvered into marriage; and sexy young Bliss with Clean Earth activist Sean. As the season ended, Jason and Sable were embroiled in a messy divorce proceeding, sons Miles and Jeff were accused of murdering minor characters, and Jason was in jail for wife beating and attempted murder.

During the second season Sable plotted to hold on to Jason, but was ultimately unsuccessful as he prepared to marry Francesca. At the last minute Frankie's long-lost husband (and Jason's brother) Phillip showed up, however, spoiling that idea. Monica had an affair with Senator Cash Cassidy, whose wife Adrienne and young son Scott were not pleased; Miles bedded and then married a magazine reporter named Channing, who found that before she could get the lurid story of the Colbys into print she had become part of it; and Bliss fell in love with a Russian ballet dancer named Kolya, who cheerfully defected on her behalf. There was death and birth: word of Constance Colby's death in Nepal was received, while Fallon gave birth to a baby girl prematurely after a fall, as current husband Jeff and her ex, Miles, wondered which of them was the father. As if that was not enough, poor Fallon soon after found herself in one of the most bizarre end-of-season cliffhangers ever devised for a prime-time soap: driving down a remote country road, she was abducted and carried away in an alien spaceship! (In retrospect, that was probably not a bad thing; the aliens transported her back to *Dynasty* the following season, while most of the other characters in *The Colbys* disappeared as the show was canceled.)

So that viewers would have no doubt about its origins, the series was officially called *Dynasty II—The Colbys* during its first two months.

COLGATE COMEDY HOUR, THE
Variety
FIRST TELECAST: *September 10, 1950*
LAST TELECAST: *December 25, 1955*
BROADCAST HISTORY:
Sep 1950–Dec 1955, NBC Sun 8:00–9:00
PRINCIPAL HOSTS:
Eddie Cantor (1950–1954)
Dean Martin and Jerry Lewis (1950–1955)
Fred Allen (1950)

Donald O'Connor (1951–1954)
Abbott and Costello (1951–1954)
Bob Hope (1952–1953)
Jimmy Durante (1953–1954)
Gordon MacRae (1954–1955)
Robert Paige (1955)

This big-budget series of comedy spectaculars, featuring most of the top names in show business, was NBC's first successful counterprogramming against *The Ed Sullivan Show*, which ran opposite it on Sunday nights. It boasted numerous television firsts, and was the first starring vehicle for such names as Eddie Cantor, Fred Allen, Abbott and Costello, Spike Jones, Tony Martin, and Ray Bolger. It was also the first commercial series to originate in Hollywood (September 30, 1951), and it included the first network color telecast, on November 22, 1953 (as an experimental test of RCA's new compatible color system, under special permission from the FCC).

When *The Colgate Comedy Hour* began in the fall of 1950 the intention was to have three rotating elements, each a complete series of its own, starring Eddie Cantor, Martin and Lewis, and Fred Allen, respectively. Allen was dropped in December 1950, and the series thereafter began to include other big-name hosts on an occasional basis, in addition to the principals, who appeared approximately once a month. Among those hosting one or two shows during 1950–1951, for example, were Abbott and Costello, Jerry Lester, Spike Jones, Tony Martin, and Phil Silvers. In September 1951 the program began telecasts from the El Capitan Theatre in Hollywood, though there continued to be occasional telecasts from the International Theatre in New York.

In September 1952 Eddie Cantor suffered a heart attack immediately following one of his telecasts and was off the air for several months. He returned in January 1953 and completed one more season with the show. Beginning with the 1952–1953 season Colgate also began to vary the revue format, with occasional "book" musicals, such as *Anything Goes*, starring Ethel Merman and Frank Sinatra (February 28, 1954); *Revenge With Music*, with Anna Maria Alberghetti (October 24, 1954); and *Roberta*, with Gordon MacRae (April 10, 1955). In early 1954 the program began to "hit the road," with special broadcasts from all over the United States, including Pebble Beach, California; the Cocoanut Grove and Hollywood Bowl in Hollywood; Miami; Las Vegas; Jones Beach, New York; and the liner *S.S. United States* docked at a pier in New York. Some shows featured special events, such as the Ice Capades or various awards presentations and salutes. Always the emphasis was on big names and "event" television.

In the summer of 1955 Colgate began a tie-in with Paramount Pictures, in which scenes from a new film were shown, and stars from the movie appeared. Charlton Heston even hosted several telecasts. The name of the series was changed at this time to *Colgate Variety Hour*. However, a superbudget series such as this proved harder and harder to sustain, and in December 1955 one of TV's most notable early comedy variety programs finally reached the end of its run—with a December 25th hour devoted to Christmas music by Fred Waring and his Pennsylvanians, from Hollywood.

COLGATE THEATRE
Dramatic Anthology
FIRST TELECAST: *January 3, 1949*
LAST TELECAST: *October 7, 1958*
BROADCAST HISTORY:
Jan 1949–Oct 1949, NBC Mon 9:00–9:30
Oct 1949–Jun 1950, NBC Sun 8:30–9:00
Aug 1958–Oct 1958, NBC Tue 9:00–9:30

The first program to use this name was a live dramatic series presenting adaptations of short stories and plays, as well as scripts especially written for television. Comedies, dramas, and mysteries alternated, and a wide variety of talent appeared (usually not top names, however). A "Broadway Theater" theme opened the show, with the camera following theatergoers into their seats, scanning the program for the title of the night's production, and then focusing on the stage as the curtain began to rise. Among the first season's productions were the first TV adaptations of two popular radio series, *Mr. and Mrs. North* (July 4, 1949) and *Vic and Sade* (July 11–July 25, 1949).

The second *Colgate Theatre* was a summer film series in 1958, consisting primarily of pilots for projected series that did not make it to the network's fall schedule. However, one episode, "Fountain of Youth," written, directed, and narrated by Orson Welles, won a Peabody Award.

COLGATE VARIETY HOUR, THE
see *Colgate Comedy Hour, The*

COLGATE WESTERN THEATRE
Western Anthology
FIRST TELECAST: *July 3, 1959*
LAST TELECAST: *September 4, 1959*
BROADCAST HISTORY:
Jul 1959–Sep 1959, NBC Fri 9:30–10:00

This summer series consisted of reruns of films of Western dramas originally seen, for the most part, on *G.E. Theatre* and *Schlitz Playhouse*.

COLISEUM
Variety
FIRST TELECAST: *January 26, 1967*
LAST TELECAST: *June 1, 1967*
BROADCAST HISTORY:
Jan 1967–Jun 1967, CBS Thu 7:30–8:30

Each week a different star hosted this variety series, which traveled around the world to film such spectacles as the New Vienna Ice Extravaganza and the Moscow State Circus. In addition there

were many New York–based programs featuring popular entertainers in a straight variety format.

COLLEGE BOWL, THE
Musical Comedy
FIRST TELECAST: *October 2, 1950*
LAST TELECAST: *March 26, 1951*
BROADCAST HISTORY:
Oct 1950–Mar 1951, ABC Mon 9:00–9:30
REGULARS:
Chico Marx
Jimmy Brock
Stanley Prager
Barbara Ruick
Kenny Buffert
Evelyn Ward
Andy Williams
Paula Huston
Tommy Morton
Joan Holloway
Lee Lindsey
PRODUCER:
Martin Gosch

A weekly miniature musical comedy featuring Chico Marx, of the Marx Brothers, as the proprietor of a campus soda fountain. The supporting cast was a lively group of young actors and actresses from Broadway shows and nightclubs, most notably 18-year-old Andy Williams. The show was telecast live from New York.

COLLEGE OF MUSICAL KNOWLEDGE, THE
see *Kay Kyser's Kollege of Musical Knowledge*

COLLEGE PRESS CONFERENCE
see *Junior Press Conference*

COLONEL HUMPHREY FLACK
Situation Comedy
FIRST TELECAST: *October 7, 1953*
LAST TELECAST: *July 2, 1954*
BROADCAST HISTORY:
Oct 1953–Dec 1953, DUM Wed 9:00–9:30
Jan 1954–May 1954, DUM Sat 10:00–10:30
May 1954–Jul 1954, DUM Fri 10:30–11:00
CAST:
Col. Humphrey Flack........ Alan Mowbray
Uthas P. Garvey .... Frank Jenks

By 1953, Britisher Alan Mowbray was one of Hollywood's most experienced character actors, having appeared in nearly 300 B-films since 1923. (Contrary to popular belief, in only five of them did he play the butler.) DuMont could not have picked a more suitable performer to play Col. Humphrey Flack, a dapper, witty, somewhat paunchy modern-day Robin Hood. Flack was a con man's con man, outswindling assorted swindlers in order to aid the poor—and retaining a percentage for himself, of course, to "cover expenses." His sidekick was Uthas P. (for Patsy)

Garvey, who was no slouch himself, but not up to the colonel's suave standards.

The program was based on a series of *Saturday Evening Post* stories by Everett Rhodes Castle and was telecast live. In 1958 a filmed syndicated version, simply titled *Colonel Flack,* starring Mowbray and Jenks, was released. This series was also known as *The Fabulous Fraud.*

COLT .45
Western
FIRST TELECAST: *October 18, 1957*
LAST TELECAST: *September 27, 1960*
BROADCAST HISTORY:
  Oct 1957–Dec 1957, ABC Fri 10:00–10:30
  Jan 1958–Apr 1958, ABC Fri 8:30–9:00
  Oct 1958–Sep 1959, ABC Sun 9:00–9:30
  Oct 1959–Mar 1960, ABC Sun 7:00–7:30
  Apr 1960–Sep 1960, ABC Tue 9:30–10:00
CAST:
  Christopher Colt . . . . Wayde Preston
  Sam Colt, Jr. (1959–1960) . . . . Donald May

Christopher Colt was a handsome young government undercover agent posing as a gun salesman in this Western adventure. Most of his missions involved tracking down notorious outlaws, and in the process he had plenty of opportunities to use his famous Colt .45 pistol.

Not long after the series began, Warner Brothers Studios began to have trouble with its star. Eventually Wayde Preston joined the growing list of "Warner Brothers walkouts" (for some others see *Cheyenne, Maverick,* and *77 Sunset Strip*), and a considerable number of repeats had to be interspersed with original episodes to keep the series on the air through the 1958–1959 season. In 1959 Christopher Colt was gradually replaced as the leading character by his cousin Sam Colt, Jr. Also a government agent, Sam was the focal point of some episodes and appeared jointly with Christopher Colt at least once. Although actor Preston did rejoin the fold, Donald May eventually took over as the lead full time.

COLUMBIA UNIVERSITY SEMINAR
Instruction
FIRST TELECAST: *October 4, 1952*
LAST TELECAST: *January 3, 1953*
BROADCAST HISTORY:
  Oct 1952–Jan 1953, ABC Sat 6:30–7:00
INSTRUCTOR:
  Donald N. Bigelow

This was a course on American Civilization, presided over by Donald N. Bigelow, Assistant Professor of History at Columbia University. Prof. Bigelow and his eleven students were seen seated at a round table. Academic credit was also given to viewers actively participating in the course. After its prime-time run the series continued on Sunday afternoons until May 1953.

COLUMBO
Police Drama
FIRST TELECAST: *September 15, 1971*
LAST TELECAST: *September 4, 1977*
BROADCAST HISTORY:
  Sep 1971–Sep 1972, NBC Wed 8:30–10:00
  Sep 1972–Jul 1974, NBC Sun 8:30–10:00
  Aug 1974–Aug 1975, NBC Sun 8:30–10:30
  Sep 1975–Sep 1976, NBC Sun 9:00–11:00
  Oct 1976–Sep 1977, NBC Sun 8:00–9:30
CAST:
  Lt. Columbo . . . . Peter Falk

At the beginning of each *Columbo* episode the audience witnessed a clever murder and saw the ingenious measures the murderer took to prevent detection by the police. Then into the case came Lt. Columbo (he never did have a first name). He drove a beat-up old car, wore a dirty, rumpled trench coat that looked at least ten years old, and acted for all the world like an incompetent bumbler. He was excessively polite to everyone, went out of his way not to offend any of the suspects, and seemed like a hopeless choice to solve any crime, especially a well-conceived murder. But all that was superficial, designed to lull the murderer into a false sense of security. Despite his appearance, Columbo was one of the shrewdest, most resourceful detectives on the Los Angeles police force. Slowly and methodically he pieced together the most minute clues leading to the identity of the killer, who, when his guilt was revealed, was always incredulous that such an unlikely cop had managed to find him out.

Columbo was one of the three original rotating elements of the *NBC Sunday Mystery Movie,* the other two being *McMillan and Wife* and *McCloud.* It was by far the most popular of the elements and would have become a separate series in its own right if actor Peter Falk had permitted it to. But a 60- or 90-minute movie every week was too much for one actor to carry, not to mention the dangers of being typecast in such a distinctive role. Toward the end of the program's run Falk was said to be making more than a quarter of a million dollars per episode, but even at that he refused to do more than a few per year. He continued to film an occasional new episode after the last date shown above.

An interesting sidelight is that Peter Falk was the producers' second choice to portray Columbo. The first actor approached for the role was Bing Crosby. Crosby, 67 years old and a millionaire many times over, declined, reportedly because it would interfere with his golf game. And so Falk got the part, and stardom.

COMBAT
War Drama
FIRST TELECAST: *October 2, 1962*
LAST TELECAST: *August 29, 1967*
BROADCAST HISTORY:
  Oct 1962–Aug 1967, ABC Tue 7:30–8:30

CAST:

Lt. Gil Hanley .... Rick Jason
Sgt. Chip Saunders .... Vic Morrow
Caje (Caddy Cadron) .... Pierre Jalbert
Pvt. William G. Kirby (1963–1967)
.... Jack Hogan
Littlejohn (1963–1967) .... Dick Peabody
Doc Walton (1962–1963) ...... Steven Rogers
Doc (1963–1965) .... Conlan Carter
Pvt. Braddock (1962–1963) .... Shecky Greene
Pvt. Billy Nelson (1963–1964) .... Tom Lowell

Combat depicted the exploits of a U.S. Army platoon fighting its way across Europe during World
War II, following D-Day. Realism was the keynote
of this mud-splattered series, whose cast was sent
to army camp for a week of actual "boot camp"
training before production began. Original World
War II battle footage was included in some episodes. The stories ranged from straight combat
adventure to human interest and sometimes humorous themes. Among the regulars were Pvt.
Braddock, the platoon comic and resident hustler,
played by nightclub comedian Shecky Greene;
Caje, the sly, dark-haired Cajun; and Doc Walton,
the young, sensitive medical aidman. Out in front
were the tough, hard-boiled leaders, Lt. Gil Hanley and Sgt. Chip Saunders.

COMBAT SERGEANT
War Drama
FIRST TELECAST: *June 29, 1956*
LAST TELECAST: *September 27, 1956*
BROADCAST HISTORY:
Jun 1956–Aug 1956, ABC Fri 8:00–8:30
Sep 1956, ABC Thu 9:00–9:30
CAST:
Sgt. Nelson .... Michael Thomas
Gen. Harrison .... Cliff Clark
Abdulla .... Dominick Delgarde

This wartime adventure was set in North Africa
during World War II. Sgt. Nelson, receiving his
orders direct from Gen. Harrison, found himself
involved in various dangerous assignments, including coordination between the Allied forces,
espionage against the Germans, and sometimes
even romance. Actual World War II film footage
was used in this series.

COME CLOSER
Quiz/Audience Participation
FIRST TELECAST: *September 20, 1954*
LAST TELECAST: *December 13, 1954*
BROADCAST HISTORY:
Sep 1954–Dec 1954, ABC Mon 8:00–8:30
EMCEE:
Jimmy Nelson
DUMMIES:
Danny O'Day
Humphrey Higby
Farfel the Dog

This audience-participation show starred the ventriloquist Jimmy Nelson and his dummies, with
questions calling for comic answers by studio
contestants. The contestant "coming closest" to
the correct answer won cash and prizes. A jackpot prize, based on a clue given in song by "Danny
O'Day," was also featured.

COMEBACK STORY, THE
Drama/Interview
FIRST TELECAST: *October 2, 1953*
LAST TELECAST: *February 5, 1954*
BROADCAST HISTORY:
Oct 1953–Feb 1954, ABC Fri 9:30–10:00
EMCEE:
George Jessel (Oct 1953–Jan 1954)
Arlene Francis (Jan–Feb 1954)

This heartwarming series presented, through interviews and dramatizations, the stories of persons stricken with physical disabilities or bad fortune who had fought to rebuild their lives. Some
of the guests were ordinary people, but most were
notable personalities such as Norman Brokenshire, the pioneer radio announcer who won his
battle with alcoholism; athlete Mildred "Babe"
Didrikson Zaharias; and blind jazz pianist George
Shearing. The program was telecast live from
New York.

COMEDY BREAK
Comedy Variety
BROADCAST HISTORY:
Syndicated only
30 minutes
Produced: *1985–1986*
Released: *Fall 1985*
HOSTS:
Mack Dryden
Jamie Alcroft

Comedians Dryden and Alcroft hosted this collection of comedy skits, stand-up routines, and funny
clips from old TV shows. Their guests were primarily veteran comics like Morey Amsterdam,
Rose Marie, Ruth Buzzi, Bill Dana, and Arte Johnson along with current TV series regulars like
John Larroquette, Tim Reid, John Hillerman,
Christopher Hewett, Markie Post, Katherine Helmond, and Marla Gibbs.

COMEDY CIRCUS
Films
FIRST TELECAST: *July 13, 1951*
LAST TELECAST: *September 28, 1951*
BROADCAST HISTORY:
Jul 1951, ABC Fri 7:30–8:00
Aug 1951–Sep 1951, ABC Fri 8:00–8:30

Comedy Circus consisted of vintage comedy films
starring such actors as Buster Keaton and Harry
Langdon.

COMEDY FACTORY, THE

Comedy Anthology
FIRST TELECAST: *June 21, 1985*
LAST TELECAST: *August 9, 1985*
BROADCAST HISTORY:
  Jun 1985–Aug 1985, ABC Fri 8:30–9:00
REGULARS:
  Mary Ann McDonald
  Geoffrey Bowes
  Derek McGrath
  Mary Long

This unusual summer series featured a repertory company of players, plus a guest star, in a different half-hour situation comedy sketch each week. The guest stars included Bill Daily, Avery Schreiber, Judy Landers, Pat Harrington, and Richard Kline.

COMEDY HOUR SPECIAL

Comedy Variety
FIRST TELECAST: *July 29, 1963*
LAST TELECAST: *September 16, 1963*
BROADCAST HISTORY:
  Jul 1963–Sep 1963, CBS Mon 9:00–10:00

Reruns of eight specials formed the contents of this summer series. Originally aired during the 1959–1960 season, they starred Jack Benny and Phil Silvers, appearing both separately and together.

COMEDY PARADE

see *Movies—Prior to 1961*

COMEDY PLAYHOUSE

Comedy Anthology
FIRST TELECAST: *August 1, 1971*
LAST TELECAST: *September 5, 1971*
BROADCAST HISTORY:
  Aug 1971–Sep 1971, CBS Sun 8:00–8:30

The situation comedies that made up this 1971 summer anthology were all pilots for proposed series that had not made it to the fall schedule. Around the networks this kind of summer runoff of busted pilots—which every network has in quantity—is irreverently known as "garbage can theater."

COMEDY SHOP, THE

Comedy
BROADCAST HISTORY:
  Syndicated only
  30 minutes
  Produced: *1978* (25 episodes)
  Released: *Fall 1978*
HOST:
  Norm Crosby

Stand-up comics, most of them little known, had a chance to do their stuff before a studio audience in this 1978 series. Some established comedians

also appeared, among them Larry Storch, Shirley Hemphill, Ted Knight, and Red Buttons. The format called for a three-minute monologue from each performer.

COMEDY SPOT, THE

Comedy Anthology
FIRST TELECAST: *June 28, 1960*
LAST TELECAST: *September 18, 1962*
BROADCAST HISTORY:
  Jun 1960–Sep 1960, CBS Tue 9:30–10:00
  Jul 1961–Sep 1961, CBS Tue 9:00–9:30
  Jul 1962–Sep 1962, CBS Tue 9:00–9:30
HOST:
  Art Gilmore (1960)

This series filled in for *The Red Skelton Show* for three consecutive summers. The 1960 and 1962 versions were called *The Comedy Spot,* while the 1961 edition was titled *Comedy Spotlight.* Although some of the episodes were reruns of previously aired episodes from other anthologies, most were pilots for proposed comedy series that had not made it to the fall schedule. There was one notable exception: the July 19, 1960, comedy titled "Head of the Family," starring Carl Reiner as a television comedy writer, Robert Petrie. This was the pilot for what would become, the following season, *The Dick Van Dyke Show.* Reiner, the creator of the show, was the only member of the pilot's cast to have a role in *The Dick Van Dyke Show* when it went on the air, though it was not the role he had had in the pilot. Instead of the series' star, he played Rob's tyrannical boss, Alan Brady (Alan Sturdy in the pilot), star of the variety show for which Rob was head writer.

COMEDY THEATER

Comedy Anthology
FIRST TELECAST: *July 17, 1981*
LAST TELECAST: *August 28, 1981*
BROADCAST HISTORY:
  Jul 1981–Aug 1981, NBC Fri 8:30–9:00

Each episode of this summer series was a pilot for a series that NBC had decided not to carry on its regular fall lineup. Among the series pilots shown were "Pals" starring Tony Lo Bianco and Jeffrey Tambor, "The Grady Nutt Show" starring Rev. Grady Nutt and Elinor Donahue, and "Dear Teacher" starring Melinda Culea, Rebecca York, and Ted Danson.

COMEDY THEATRE

Comedy Anthology
FIRST TELECAST: *July 26, 1976*
LAST TELECAST: *June 28, 1979*
BROADCAST HISTORY:
  Jul 1976–Sep 1976, NBC Mon 8:00–9:00
  May 1979–Jun 1979, NBC Thu 8:30–9:00

This was a collection of pilot episodes from series that were not purchased for regular weekly presentation. Among the more recognizable names who appeared in these proposed shows were Don Knotts and Peter Isacksen in "Piper's Pets," Cleavon Little and Adam Wade in "Uptown Saturday Night," and Carol Wayne and William Daniels in "Heaven on Earth."

COMEDY TIME
Comedy Anthology
FIRST TELECAST: *July 6, 1977*
LAST TELECAST: *September 1, 1977*
BROADCAST HISTORY:
Jul 1977, NBC Wed 9:30–10:00
Jul 1977–Sep 1977, NBC Thu 8:00–9:00

NBC used this blanket title for a collection of situation-comedy pilots that were aired during the summer of 1977 on two different nights. All of them were half-hour shows, with two different pilots running back-to-back on Thursdays. None of them made the fall schedule as regular series.

COMEDY TONIGHT
Comedy Variety
FIRST TELECAST: *July 5, 1970*
LAST TELECAST: *August 23, 1970*
BROADCAST HISTORY:
Jul 1970–Aug 1970, CBS Sun 9:00–10:00
REGULARS:
Robert Klein
Peter Boyle
Macintyre Dixon
Judy Graubart
Madeline Kahn
Lynn Lipton
Marty Barris
Barbara Cason
Boni Enten
Laura Greene

Comedian Robert Klein was the host and star of this summer comedy series that spoofed such things as soap operas, politics, and almost anything else that its cast felt topical and worth satirizing. The tone was highly improvisational. Two members of the cast, Peter Boyle and Madeline Kahn, went on to successful careers in motion pictures.

COMEDY TONIGHT
Comedy Variety
BROADCAST HISTORY:
Syndicated only
30 minutes
Produced: *1985–1986*
Released: *Fall 1985*
HOST:
Bill Boggs

New York talk-show personality Bill Boggs hosted this series which featured stand-up comedians doing their routines. Although some veteran comedians (Rich Little, Henny Youngman, and

George Burns among them) appeared, most of the performers were relatively new faces like Pudgy, Rita Rudner, Marsha Warfield, Dennis Wolfberg, Harvey Fierstein, Yakov Smirnoff, Paul Provenza, Danitra Vance, Eric Bogosian, Bob Saget, John Mulrooney, Sinbad, and Bob Duback.

COMEDY ZONE
Comedy
FIRST TELECAST: *August 17, 1984*
LAST TELECAST: *September 7, 1984*
BROADCAST HISTORY:
Aug 1984–Sep 1984, CBS Fri 8:00–9:00
REGULARS:
Bob Gunton
Ann Lange
Mark Linn-Baker
Joe Mantegna
Audrie J. Neenan
Bill Randolph

Comedy Zone was a collection of short sketches, ranging in length from two to twelve minutes apiece, performed by a repertory company of comic actors and guest stars. There was no host. The show tried to achieve a fresh look by originating from New York and featuring the work of Broadway and Off-Broadway comedy writers rather than using the Hollywood-based writers employed by most TV series. Some of their ideas were certainly unusual: a musical production number, "They've Got No Cocaine In Cancun," performed by a full mariachi band and dancers; "The Blind Dating Game"; and a musical takeoff on the Heimlich Maneuver. In between the skits there were short blackouts; often two stick figures on a roadsign (representing pedestrians) who came to life and did strange things to each other. Apparently the audience didn't notice much difference between this and traditional TV comedy, and the show soon disappeared.

COMING OF AGE
Situation Comedy
FIRST TELECAST: *March 15, 1988*
LAST TELECAST: *March 29, 1988*
BROADCAST HISTORY:
Mar 1988, CBS Tue 9:00–9:30
CAST:
Dick Hale .... Paul Dooley
Ginny Hale .... Phyllis Newman
Ed Pepper .... Alan Young
Trudie Pepper .... Glynis Johns
Brian Binker .... Kevin Pollak
Pauline Spencer .... Ruta Lee
Marvel Whitsett .... Pearl Shear
Wilma Salzgaber .... Lenore Woodward

Dick Hale was an airline pilot forced into an unwanted retirement at age 60 by company policy. He and his wife Ginny moved to The Dunes, an Arizona retirement community, to begin a new life. She had a positive outlook but Dick, whose grumpy personality did not help, found it difficult to make the adjustment. He didn't like retirement, he didn't like the climate, he didn't like condescending young Brian Binker, who managed The Dunes, and he wasn't particularly fond of many of his fellow residents. Their next-door neighbors—and the walls between the apartments were so thin you could hear right through them—were perpetually perky Ed and Trudie Pepper. Among the other residents were Marvel, whose life revolved around her little dog, Krystle; and Pauline, The Dunes' resident sexpot.

COMMAND POST
Instruction
FIRST TELECAST: *February 14, 1950*
LAST TELECAST: *April 4, 1950*
BROADCAST HISTORY:
    Feb 1950–Apr 1950, CBS Tue 8:00–9:00

Produced by and for the U.S. Army, this series was designed as an eight-week course to train the army reserves via television. Subjects covered in the series included planning attacks, self-defense, and combat theory and technique.

COMMENT
Public Affairs
FIRST TELECAST: *June 17, 1954*
LAST TELECAST: *September 10, 1972*
BROADCAST HISTORY:
    Jun 1954–Aug 1954, NBC Mon 8:30–9:00
    Jan 1958–Aug 1958, NBC Fri 10:45–11:00
    Jan 1971–Sep 1971, NBC Sun 6:00–6:30
    Jan 1972–Sep 1972, NBC Sun 6:00–6:30
HOST:
    Edwin Newman (1971–1972)

In the first two series aired by NBC under the title *Comment*, NBC News correspondents made personal observations about current news issues. That was in 1954 and 1958. More than a decade later, when *Comment* returned to the NBC lineup, the personal opinions voiced were those of spokesmen for various causes or noted public figures discussing significant issues. NBC newsman Edwin Newman was the host for the 1970s version of *Comment* but rarely voiced any opinions of his own on the series.

COMPASS
Travelogue
FIRST TELECAST: *October 23, 1954*
LAST TELECAST: *October 6, 1957*
BROADCAST HISTORY:
    Oct 1954–Feb 1955, ABC Sat 7:30–8:00
    Mar 1955–Sep 1955, ABC Sat 10:00–10:30
    Jul 1956–Sep 1956, ABC Thu 10:00–10:30
    Jun 1957–Jul 1957, ABC Thu 9:30–10:00
    Jul 1957–Oct 1957, ABC Sun 9:00–9:30

These documentary travel films were fed out over the ABC network for the benefit of stations that did not wish to schedule local series in these time periods. *Compass* was never carried on ABC's flagship station in New York.

CONCENTRATION
Quiz/Audience Participation
FIRST TELECAST: *October 30, 1958*
LAST TELECAST: *September 11, 1961*
BROADCAST HISTORY:
    Oct 1958–Nov 1958, NBC Thu 8:30–9:00
    Apr 1961–Sep 1961, NBC Mon 9:30–10:00
EMCEE:
    Jack Barry (1958)
    Hugh Downs (1961)

Concentration, a fixture on the NBC daytime lineup from August 1958 until March 1973, had two runs as a nighttime network series. It first appeared in the fall of 1958 as a temporary replacement for *Twenty-One*, after the latter was suddenly pulled off the air because of the quiz-show scandals that were developing at the time. The host of this version of *Concentration*, which ran for only four weeks, was Jack Barry, who had been host of the suspended *Twenty-One*. *Concentration* made its second appearance on the nighttime schedule as a summer show in 1961, with Hugh Downs, who had hosted the daytime version since its inception.

The format of the show was based on an old children's game of the same name. Two contestants were faced with a game board containing 30 squares. Behind each square was a prize. There were two squares on the board for each prize, and to win the prize the contestant had to match the two correct squares. In order to keep the prizes, however, the contestant also had to be first to guess a rebus, which was gradually revealed as the chosen squares were rotated.

After Hugh Downs left the daytime edition of *Concentration* early in 1969, he was replaced by Bob Clayton, who had been the announcer and substitute host on the show for more than five years. Clayton emceed *Concentration* for the remainder of its network run (except for six months in 1969 when Ed McMahon held the reins). Others who filled in as substitute emcees over the years were Art James, Jim Lucas, and Bill Mazur. James and Lucas were *Concentration* announcers when the regular emcee was around.

The series returned to NBC's weekday daytime lineup under the title *Classic Concentration* in May of 1987, with Alex Trebek as emcee.

CONCERT TONIGHT
see *Chicago Symphony*

CONCRETE COWBOYS
Adventure
FIRST TELECAST: *February 7, 1981*
LAST TELECAST: *March 21, 1981*

BROADCAST HISTORY:
Feb 1981, CBS Sat 10:00–11:00
Feb 1981–Mar 1981, CBS Sat 9:00–10:00
CAST:
Jimmy Lee (J.D.) Reed .... Jerry Reed
Will Ewbanks .... Geoffrey Scott
THEME:
"Breakin' Loose," written and performed by Jerry Reed

This was a countrified version of the early 1960s hit *Route 66*. J.D. and Will were two carefree cowpokes traveling around the country in search of adventure. J.D. was the fast-talking instigator, who usually made the decisions, while Will was his sidekick, more inhibited and more romantic than his buddy. They were slick operators in a card game, but when their gambling luck failed them they could still pick up a few bucks by taking on various odd jobs. Never staying long in one place, they roamed the concrete trails of modern-day America, sometimes finding trouble, always looking for adventure. Their home on wheels was a beat-up old camper.

Country music star Jerry Reed starred in the series and also served as its narrator. There was usually at least one opportunity in each episode for him to grab his guitar and do a little pickin'.

CONDO
Situation Comedy
FIRST TELECAST: *February 10, 1983*
LAST TELECAST: *June 16, 1983*
BROADCAST HISTORY:
Feb 1983–Mar 1983, ABC Thu 8:00–8:30
Mar 1983–Apr 1983, ABC Thu 8:30–9:00
May 1983–Jun 1983, ABC Thu 8:00–8:30
CAST:
James Kirkridge .... McLean Stevenson
Kiki Kirkridge .... Brooke Alderson
Scott Kirkridge .... Mark Schubb
Billy Kirkridge .... Marc Price
Jesse Rodriguez .... Luis Avalos
Maria Rodriguez .... Yvonne Wilder
Linda Rodriguez .... Julie Carmen
Jose Montoya .... James Victor

The declining fortunes of an opinionated WASP brought him next door to an upwardly mobile Latino family in this 1983 comedy. Insurance salesman James Kirkridge found it necessary to move his All-American family from their rambling house to a smaller condominium, where his next-door neighbor turned out to be Jesse Rodriguez, whose success in the landscaping business had recently allowed him to move up from the barrio. As if the clash of cultures weren't enough for traditionalist Kirkridge, his son Scott and Jesse's daughter Linda soon announced that they were getting married and expecting a baby. Race and religion jokes flew thick and fast between James and Jesse, but not fast enough to save this series.

CONFESSION
Interview/Discussion
FIRST TELECAST: *June 19, 1958*
LAST TELECAST: *January 13, 1959*
BROADCAST HISTORY:
Jun 1958–Sep 1958, ABC Thu 10:00–10:30
Sep 1958–Jan 1959, ABC Tue 10:00–10:30
HOST:
Jack Wyatt

This series sought to probe the underlying causes of criminal acts. Filmed in Dallas, Texas, and moderated by Jack Wyatt, each show opened with an interview between Mr. Wyatt and a convicted criminal. Following the interview, Mr. Wyatt led a discussion group that attempted to analyze the reasons for the crime. The discussion group consisted of a lawyer, a clergyman, a penologist or sociologist, and a psychiatrist or psychologist.

CONFIDENTIAL REPORT
syndicated title for *Dragnet*

CONFLICT
Dramatic Anthology
FIRST TELECAST: *September 18, 1956*
LAST TELECAST: *September 3, 1957*
BROADCAST HISTORY:
Sep 1956–Sep 1957, ABC Tue 7:30–8:30

These hour-long dramas, produced in Hollywood by Warner Brothers, featured varying casts and were seen on alternate weeks with *Cheyenne*. The general theme was people in conflict, in settings ranging across time from Elizabethan England to the present. One of the better productions was "The Magic Brew," starring Jim Backus as a medicine-show pitchman attempting to peddle his wares in a small town. At least two episodes served as prototypes for future series; in one, Will Hutchins appeared as an inept cowboy (his role a year later in *Sugarfoot*), and in the other Efrem Zimbalist, Jr., portrayed private detective Stuart Bailey (as he did in 1958's *77 Sunset Strip*). Among the others seen on *Conflict* were Tab Hunter, Virginia Mayo, and Jack Lord.

CONGRESSIONAL REPORT
Discussion
FIRST TELECAST: *June 15, 1969*
LAST TELECAST: *August 31, 1969*
BROADCAST HISTORY:
Jun 1969–Aug 1969, NBC Sun 6:00–6:30
MODERATOR:
Bill Monroe

Each week four members of Congress participated in a round-table discussion of an issue of current interest to the congressmen and their constituencies. Two members of the panel supported the issue and the other two opposed it. NBC newsman Bill Monroe was the moderator of this series, which had premiered as a Sunday afternoon show on April 13, 1969.

CONTENDER, THE
Drama
FIRST TELECAST: *April 3, 1980*
LAST TELECAST: *May 1, 1980*
BROADCAST HISTORY:
    Apr 1980–May 1980, CBS Thu 10:00–11:00
CAST:
    Johnny Captor .... Marc Singer
    Jill Sindon .... Katherine Cannon
    George Beifus .... Moses Gunn
    Brian Captor .... Alan Stock
    Alma Captor................. Louise Latham
    Missy Dinwittie.............. Tina Andrews
    Harry........................ Don Gordon
    Andy....:................ William Watson
    Lucinda (Lou) Waverly .... Susan Walden

Johnny Captor was from a middle-class Oregon family. While he was in college, his father, a lumberjack, was paralyzed in a freak mill accident and committed suicide rather than face a life of total dependency on others. Johnny, trying to decide what to do with his life, and with the added burden of supporting his mother and his kid brother, Brian, decided to leave college and concentrate on a boxing career. This did not sit well with his girlfriend, Jill Sindon, a teacher at the college, who failed to understand why an intelligent person would want to earn a living in such a dangerous way. Former fighter George Beifus was Johnny's trainer and manager and Missy Dinwittie, the teenaged sister of "Killer" Dinwittie, another fighter. Missy seemed more interested in Johnny's career than in her brother's. Lou Waverly was a sportswriter working on an article about Johnny.

CONTINENTAL, THE
Romantic Monologue
FIRST TELECAST: *January 22, 1952*
LAST TELECAST: *January 6, 1953*
BROADCAST HISTORY:
    Jan 1952–Apr 1952, CBS Tue/Thu 11:15–11:30
    Oct 1952–Jan 1953, ABC Tue/Fri 11:00–11:15
HOST:
    Renzo Cesana

For bored housewives looking to add a little excitement to their lives, CBS offered this live program, which followed the 11:00 P.M. local news twice a week. Suave, debonair, sultry-voiced Renzo Cesana, Italian by birth but American by choice, was the only performer. Each night, in a glamorous setting, he would provide a romantic monologue directed to the women in the audience. He was promoted as an Italian count and member of one of the leading families of Rome, and had been doing a similar program on a local station in Los Angeles for several months before CBS

brought him to New York to perform on the network.

After a short tenure on that network he showed up on ABC in the fall for another brief run, this time meeting with couples out on their first date.

CONTINENTAL SHOWCASE
Variety
FIRST TELECAST: *June 11, 1966*
LAST TELECAST: *September 10, 1966*
BROADCAST HISTORY:
    Jun 1966–Sep 1966, CBS Sat 7:30–8:30
REGULARS:
    Jim Backus
    The Kessler Twins
    Heidi Bruhl
    Bibi Johns
    Esther & Abi Ofarim
    The Peanuts
    The Continental Showcase Dancers
    The Hazy Osterwald Sextet
    The Harry Segers Orchestra

Continental Showcase was the 1966 summer replacement for *The Jackie Gleason Show*. Host Jim Backus traveled throughout Europe with the production company filming many popular local acts, including singers, dancers, acrobats, and other European (and occasionally Oriental) performers. Although they were not officially regulars, the artists shown above appeared on more than half of the shows.

CONVERSATIONS WITH ERIC SEVAREID
Discussion
FIRST TELECAST: *July 13, 1975*
LAST TELECAST: *August 31, 1975*
BROADCAST HISTORY:
    Jul 1975–Aug 1975, CBS Sun 6:00–7:00
HOST:
    Eric Sevareid

CBS News correspondent Eric Sevareid had an informal chat each Sunday with a person who had a background in, and understanding of, world affairs. Their talks usually dealt with developing economic and political situations. Among the guests were former West German President Willy Brandt and novelist Leo Rosten.

CONVOY
War Drama
FIRST TELECAST: *September 17, 1965*
LAST TELECAST: *December 10, 1965*
BROADCAST HISTORY:
    Sep 1965–Dec 1965, NBC Fri 8:30–9:00
CAST:
    Comdr. Dan Talbot.............. John Gavin
    Merchant Capt. Ben Foster ...... John Larch
    Chief Officer Steve Kirkland ... Linden Chiles
    Lt. Dick O'Connell .... James Callahan

The problems of transporting troops and supplies across the high seas during World War II provided the thrust for this series. Commander Dan Talbot of the U.S. Navy Destroyer Escort *DD 181* was responsible for insuring the safety of a convoy of merchant ships, while civilian Captain Ben Foster ran the merchant freighter *Flagship*, the nerve center for the entire convoy. These two men, one military and one civilian, contended with the problems caused by war—air and U-boat attacks—as well as fogs, high seas, and other perils of the ocean. Foster's chief aide was Chief Officer Steve Kirkland; his counterpart on the destroyer escort was Lt. Dick O'Connell.

COOK'S CHAMPAGNE PARTY
see *Andy and Della Russell*

COOL MILLION
Detective Drama
FIRST TELECAST: *October 25, 1972*
LAST TELECAST: *July 11, 1973*
BROADCAST HISTORY:
  Oct 1972–Jul 1973, NBC Wed 8:30–10:00
CAST:
  Jefferson Keyes .... James Farentino
  Elena .... Adele Mara
  Tony Baylor.................... Ed Bernard

Jefferson Keyes was a former CIA agent who had become an extremely successful private investigator. He was so successful, in fact, that he demanded a $1-million fee for his services. With that kind of money he could afford to have his own executive jet, which he piloted himself to whatever destination, business or pleasure, he had in mind. His popularity as a raconteur as well as a sleuth created strong demands on his time whenever he was not occupied professionally. *Cool Million* was one of the three elements in the 1972–1973 version of *NBC Wednesday Mystery Movie*, along with *Banacek* and *Madigan*.

COP AND THE KID, THE
Situation Comedy
FIRST TELECAST: *December 4, 1975*
LAST TELECAST: *March 4, 1976*
BROADCAST HISTORY:
  Dec 1975, NBC Thu 8:30–9:00
  Jan 1976–Mar 1976, NBC Thu 8:00–8:30
CAST:
  Officer Frank Murphy ...... Charles Durning
  Lucas Adams .... Tierre Turner
  Mrs. Brigid Murphy .... Patsy Kelly
  Mary Goodhew .... Sharon Spelman
  Shortstuff..................... Curtiz Willis
  Mouse .... Eric Laneuville
  Sgt. Zimmerman .... William Pierson

This was another of the ethnic comedies so popular in the 1970s. Through a strange circumstance, portly, middle-aged Irish cop Frank Murphy found himself assigned custody of Lucas, a young, black, street-wise orphan. Murphy had suffered an asthma attack while chasing Lucas following a shoplifting incident. Knowing that the asthma could be cause for Murphy's dismissal from the force, Lucas blackmailed Murphy into asking for leniency for him at his trial. Murphy did this so well that the court made him Lucas's guardian. The efforts of Murphy and his mother to reform young Lucas provided the comedy.

CORLISS ARCHER
see *Meet Corliss Archer*

CORNER BAR, THE
Situation Comedy
FIRST TELECAST: *June 21, 1972*
LAST TELECAST: *September 7, 1973*
BROADCAST HISTORY:
  Jun 1972–Aug 1972, ABC Wed 8:30–9:00
  Aug 1973–Sep 1973, ABC Fri 9:30–10:00
CAST:
  Harry Grant (1972)............. Gabriel Dell
  Fred Costello .... J. J. Barry
  Phil Bracken .... Bill Fiore
  Joe (1972)....................... Joe Keyes
  Peter Panama (1972) ...... Vincent Schiavelli
  Meyer Shapiro............... Shimen Ruskin
  Mary Ann (1972).......... Langhorn Scruggs
  Mae (1973) .... Anne Meara
  Frank Flynn (1973) .... Eugene Roche
  Donald Hooten (1973) .... Ron Carey
EXECUTIVE PRODUCER:
  Alan King
PRODUCER:
  Howard Morris

This comedy about contemporary life focused on the patrons who frequented Grant's Toomb, a neighborhood tavern in New York City. During the summer of 1972 Gabriel Dell (one of the original Bowery Boys) portrayed bartender-owner Harry Grant, but in 1973 the place was taken over by Mae and Frank (Anne Meara and Eugene Roche). The regular patrons in one or both seasons were Fred, a griping, hard-hat cabdriver; Phil, a scheming Wall Street lawyer; Peter Panama, a gay set designer; and Donald, a flamboyant actor. The hired help included Joe, the "liberated" black cook; Meyer, the long-suffering waiter; and Mary Ann, the sexy and slightly daft waitress.

CORONET BLUE
Mystery
FIRST TELECAST: *May 29, 1967*
LAST TELECAST: *September 4, 1967*
BROADCAST HISTORY:
  May 1967–Sep 1967, CBS Mon 10:00–11:00
CAST:
  Michael Alden.............. Frank Converse
  Anthony...................... Brian Bedford
  Max Spier........................ Joe Silver

Michael Alden was not his real name. It was the name he used because he had suffered almost total amnesia after having been dumped off a freighter in New York harbor by someone trying to kill him. The only clue he could remember was that he had been mumbling the words "Coronet Blue" when the police fished him out of the water. In his attempt to ascertain his identity, Alden was befriended by a monk named Anthony and a coffee-shop owner named Max Spier. Danger and intrigue were the key notes of this summer series as the unknown villians who had dumped Alden into the river pursued him to finish the job. *Coronet Blue* never made it to a full season's run and no conclusion was ever filmed, so Alden—and the viewers—never did find out the meaning of those mysterious words.

CORRUPTORS, THE

see *Target! The Corruptors*

COS

Comedy Variety
FIRST TELECAST: *September 19, 1976*
LAST TELECAST: *November 7, 1976*
BROADCAST HISTORY:
   Sep 1976–Nov 1976, ABC Sun 7:00–8:00
REGULARS:
   Bill Cosby
   Jeffrey Altman
   Tim Thomerson
   Marion Ramsey
   Buzzy Linhart
   Willie Bobo
   Mauricio Jarrin

Cos was one of the few attempts in recent years to design a prime-time television series specifically for two- to twelve-year-olds. It was essentially a variety program, with guest celebrities, sports stars, puppets, and comedy and music that would appeal to the younger set. Bill Cosby opened each show with a monologue, which he never got to finish, because he was invariably interrupted in some fashion. Then he went through a "magic door" to various adventures. A "Cos" Repertory Company of youngsters was on hand to assist in the skits.

COSBY SHOW, THE

Situation Comedy
FIRST TELECAST: *September 20, 1984*
LAST TELECAST:
BROADCAST HISTORY:
   Sep 1984–   , NBC Thu 8:00–8:30
CAST:
   Dr. Heathcliff (Cliff) Huxtable .... Bill Cosby
   Clair Huxtable.............. Phylicia Rashad
   Denise Huxtable (16) (1984–1987).. Lisa Bonet
   Theodore Huxtable (14)
   .... Malcolm-Jamal Warner
   Vanessa Huxtable (8) ..... Tempestt Bledsoe
   Rudy Huxtable (5) .... Keshia Knight Pulliam

   Sondra Huxtable Tibideaux (20)
   .... Sabrina Le Beauf
   *Peter Chiara (1985–   )........ Peter Costa
   *Anna Huxtable.............. Clarice Taylor
   *Russell Huxtable.............. Earl Hyman
   *Elvin Tibideaux (1986–   )
   .... Geoffrey Owens
   *Kenny ("Bud") (1986–   )... Deon Richmond
   *Cockroach (1986–   )... Carl Anthony Payne
   *Denny (1987–   )............ Troy Winbush

*Occasional

This gentle yet hip family comedy was the number one program on television during the mid 1980s, and a striking reminder that TV series don't have to be built on gimmicks to succeed. Most of the action took place at the Huxtable residence, a New York City brownstone where Cliff (an obstetrician) also maintained his office. He and his wife Clair (a legal aid attorney) tried to bring up the kids with a combination of love and parental firmness, while leading their own active professional lives. Sondra, the oldest daughter, was a senior at Princeton University during the first season, graduating early in the second; Denise and Theo ("No problem!") were the know-it-all teenagers; Vanessa the rambunctious 8-year-old; and Rudy the adorable, if mischievous, little girl. "I just hope they get out of the house before we die," murmured an exhausted Cliff as he sank into bed at the end of the premiere episode.

Although the main focus was on the immediate family, a number of other characters were seen occasionally. Cliff's parents Anna and Russell and Claire's folks Carrie and Al Hanks turned up once in a while, as did Rudy's little friends Peter (one of the few whites in the cast), Bud, and Kenny, and Theo's buddy Cockroach. Sondra was eventually married to Elvin, whom she had met at Princeton.

The Cosby Show had an interesting history. Originally proposed as a comedy about a blue-collar worker, it was turned down by ABC and NBC. Bill Cosby's wife reportedly urged the comedian to change the lead characters to upscale professionals, whereupon the show was again rejected by ABC but was picked up by NBC, which agreed to Cosby's condition that, unlike most network series, it would be taped in New York (he disliked working in Hollywood). Cosby also insisted on total creative control, which he used to shape the series into a showcase for the educational and child-rearing theories he had developed while pursuing his doctorate in education in the 1970s (the actor proudly included the redundant line "Dr. William H. Cosby, Jr., Ed.D." in the credits for each episode). Not everyone agreed with his approach; *The Cosby Show* was criticized for its unrealistic portrayal of blacks as wealthy, well-educated professionals, and for its lack of attention to black-white relations. Others defended it as providing role models for what blacks could achieve, and lessons for all races in how to raise a family in a calm and loving manner.

COSMOPOLITAN THEATRE
Dramatic Anthology
FIRST TELECAST: *October 2, 1951*
LAST TELECAST: *December 25, 1951*
BROADCAST HISTORY:
  Oct 1951–Dec 1951, DUM Tue 9:00–10:00

This major dramatic effort by DuMont presented live TV adaptations of stories from the pages of *Cosmopolitan* magazine, many of them mysteries or romantic dramas. Among the stars that appeared were Lee Tracy, Marsha Hunt, and Lon Chaney, Jr.

COUNTERATTACK: CRIME IN AMERICA
Information/Public Affairs
FIRST TELECAST: *May 2, 1982*
LAST TELECAST: *May 23, 1982*
BROADCAST HISTORY:
  May 1982, ABC Sun 7:00–8:00
HOST:
  George Kennedy

This unusual program featured a national telephone hotline intended to help solve real-life crimes. It was produced in cooperation with WeTip, a California organization that had been operating such a similar statewide hot line for ten years. Operators were seen standing by as host George Kennedy described recent crimes around the country that had baffled police, among them the "Catch Me Killer" in St. Paul, Minnesota, and the "Rotten Tooth .45-caliber Thief" in Nassau County, New York. Reenactments were also shown, and tips given on how to prevent crime.

COUNTRY CARNIVAL/COUNTRY MUSIC CARAVAN/COUNTRY MUSIC MEMORIES/COUNTRY SHOW, THE
see *Grand Ole Opry*

COUNTRY MUSIC JUBILEE
see *Ozark Jubilee*

COUNTRY STYLE
Musical Variety
FIRST TELECAST: *July 29, 1950*
LAST TELECAST: *November 25, 1950*
BROADCAST HISTORY:
  Jul 1950–Nov 1950, DUM Sat 8:00–9:00
REGULARS:
  Peggy Ann Ellis
  Gordon Dilworth
  Pat Adair
  Emily Barnes
  Bob Austin
  The Folk Dancers
  Alvy West and the Volunteer Firemen, band

This rustic musical variety hour was designed to simulate a Saturday night's entertainment in a small town. The town bandstand, manned by the Volunteer Fireman's band, was the setting around which musical numbers, square dancing, and comedy vignettes took place.

COUPLE OF JOES, A
Variety
FIRST TELECAST: *October 27, 1949*
LAST TELECAST: *July 12, 1950*
BROADCAST HISTORY:
  Oct 1949–Dec 1949, ABC Thu 11:15–12 Mid
  Dec 1949–Feb 1950, ABC Wed 8:00–9:00
  Mar 1950–Jul 1950, ABC Wed 9:00–9:30
REGULARS:
  "Big" Joe Rosenfield
  Joe Bushkin
  Joan Barton (Sep–Feb)
  Warren Hull (Dec–Mar)
  Beryl Richards (Mar–Jul)
  Pat Harrington (Mar–May)
  Allyn Edwards (Mar–Jul)
  Morgan the Dog
  Mike Reilly Orchestra
  Bobby Sherwood Orchestra (1950)

This combination music, variety, and giveaway program starred "Big" Joe Rosenfield and jazz pianist Joe Bushkin, with an assortment of regulars that included singer Joan Barton and, later, comic Pat Harrington. One of the biggest stars of the show seemed to be Morgan the Dog, who attracted much publicity and survived numerous cast changes. *A Couple of Joes* premiered as a local New York show in August 1949, moved to the network in a late-night time slot in October, and in December became a prime-time entry.

COURT-MARTIAL
Drama
FIRST TELECAST: *April 8, 1966*
LAST TELECAST: *September 2, 1966*
BROADCAST HISTORY:
  Apr 1966–Sep 1966, ABC Fri 10:00–11:00
CAST:
  Capt. David Young . . . . Bradford Dillman
  Maj. Frank Whittaker . . . . Peter Graves
  M/Sgt. John MacCaskey . . Kenneth J. Warren
  Sgt. Wendy . . . . Diane Clare

At the center of this World War II drama were the officer-lawyers of the U.S. Army Judge Advocate General's Office, headquartered in England, who investigated and prosecuted crimes committed during wartime. The court-martial itself, the climactic part of each show, was preceded by lengthy investigations ranging across war-torn Europe. The series was filmed in England.

COURT OF CURRENT ISSUES
Debate
FIRST TELECAST: *February 9, 1948*

BROADCAST HISTORY:
  Feb 1948–Jul 1948, DUM Tue 8:00–8:30
  Jul 1948–Nov 1948, DUM Mon 9:30–10:00
  Nov 1948–Jan 1949, DUM Mon 8:00–9:00
  Jan 1949–Feb 1949, DUM Mon 10:00–11:00
  Mar 1949–Apr 1949, DUM Mon 9:00–10:00
  May 1949–Jun 1949, DUM Wed 9:00–10:00
  Jun 1949–Jun 1951, DUM Tue 8:00–9:00
CREATOR/PRODUCER:
  Irvin Paul Sulds

Court of Current Issues was one of a number of early programs that presented debates on public affairs, this one within the framework of a courtroom trial. A real judge or attorney sat on the bench, prominent persons on each side of the issue represented opposing counsel and witnesses, and a jury of 12 drawn from the audience handed down a verdict. During its last two years *Court* was scheduled on Tuesday night, opposite NBC's Milton Berle, and a reviewer complained that a fine public-affairs show was being wasted—not a single person called in an audience survey was watching it.

The program was known during its early months as *Court of Public Opinion*.

COURT OF LAST RESORT, THE
Crime Drama
FIRST TELECAST: *October 4, 1957*
LAST TELECAST: *February 17, 1960*
BROADCAST HISTORY:
  Oct 1957–Apr 1958, NBC Fri 8:00–8:30
  Aug 1959–Sep 1959, ABC Wed 8:00–8:30
  Oct 1959–Feb 1960, ABC Wed 7:30–8:00
CAST:
  Sam Larsen .... Lyle Bettger
  Erle Stanley Gardner............ Paul Birch
  Dr. LeMoyne Snyder ...... Charles Meredith
  Raymond Schindler .... Robert H. Harris
  Harry Steeger .... Carleton Young
  Marshall Houts .... John Launer
  Alex Gregory .... John Maxwell
  Park Street, Jr.............. Robert Anderson

The Court of Last Resort, in real life, was a committee of crime experts who investigate cases in which there was a possibility that the convicted prisoner was innocent. This series dramatized some of the actual cases taken on by this renowned group, founded in the early 1950s by the famous mystery writer Erle Stanley Gardner. Each episode depicted the crime for which a given person was imprisoned, and then followed the efforts of the members of the Court of Last Resort to verify his guilt or find evidence of his innocence. The names of the people involved were changed, since the cases were all based on real situations.

In the series Sam Larsen was a special investigator working with the seven members of the Court in their search for truth. At the close of each story, the actual seven-member board was seen briefly and one of them would discuss a specific point of law that was crucial in the drama just finished. On occasion this function was taken over by judges, law-enforcement officers, or district attorneys.

The ABC telecasts consisted of reruns from the original NBC series.

COURT OF PUBLIC OPINION
  see *Court of Current Issues*

COURTSHIP OF EDDIE'S FATHER, THE
Situation Comedy
FIRST TELECAST: *September 17, 1969*
LAST TELECAST: *June 14, 1972*
BROADCAST HISTORY:
  Sep 1969–Sep 1970, ABC Wed 8:00–8:30
  Sep 1970–Sep 1971, ABC Wed 7:30–8:00
  Sep 1971–Jan 1972, ABC Wed 8:30–9:00
  Jan 1972–Jun 1972, ABC Wed 8:00–8:30
CAST:
  Tom Corbett...................... Bill Bixby
  Eddie Corbett................. Brandon Cruz
  Mrs. Livingston .... Miyoshi Umeki
  Norman Tinker .... James Komack
  Tina Rickles............... Kristina Holland
THEME:
  "Best Friend," by Harry Nilsson

Magazine publisher Tom Corbett was one of television's many widowers saddled with the responsibility of running a motherless household. In this case his son, freckle-faced young Eddie (played by Brandon Cruz, who was seven years old when the series began), did most of the plotting. Eddie had a special penchant for getting his father romantically involved with prospective brides, which led to many warm and comic moments. Mrs. Livingston was Tom's dependable, philosophical, but sometimes confused housekeeper; Tina his secretary; and Norman Tinker a mod photographer at the magazine. Although not a regular on the show, young Jodie Foster appeared from time to time as Eddie's friend, Joey Kelly. The series was based on a novel by Mark Toby, and had a theme song ("Best Friend") written by pop singer Harry Nilsson.

COVER UP
Detective/Foreign Intrigue
FIRST TELECAST: *September 22, 1984*
LAST TELECAST: *July 6, 1985*
BROADCAST HISTORY:
  Sep 1984–Apr 1985, CBS Sat 10:00–11:00
  May 1985–Jul 1985, CBS Sat 8:00–9:00
CAST:
  Mac Harper (1984).......... Jon-Erik Hexum
  Danielle Reynolds .... Jennifer O'Neill
  Henry Towler .... Richard Anderson
  Jack Striker .... Antony Hamilton
  Rick .... Mykel T. Williamson
  Gretchen .... Ingrid Anderson

Billie	Irena Ferris
Ashley	Dana Sparks
Cindy (1984)	Heather McNair

They traveled around the world on fashion assignments—Dani, the gorgeous professional photographer, and Mac, her handsome male model. At least that was their public job; actually they were secret agents working on a free-lance basis for a mysterious U.S. government agency. They were well-suited to their clandestine roles—Mac was a former Green Beret who had served in Vietnam and was a specialist in karate, chemical interrogation, and foreign languages. Dani was no novice either, having been married to an agent whose death she and Mac avenged in the series' premiere episode. Under the loose supervision of Towler they traveled from country to country, staging fashion shows and photo sessions with their scantily clad models, while rescuing Americans from dangerous situations. Rick was Dani's photographic assistant and helped both her and Mac on espionage assignments, while Gretchen, Billie, Ashley, and Linda were her most frequently used models.

Antony Hamilton replaced Jon-Erik Hexum as Dani's partner after Hexum's tragic death following an accident in which he had shot himself in the head on the set of *Cover Up*.

COWBOY IN AFRICA
Adventure
FIRST TELECAST: *September 11, 1967*
LAST TELECAST: *September 16, 1968*
BROADCAST HISTORY:
  Sep 1967–Sep 1968, ABC Mon 7:30–8:30
CAST:

Jim Sinclair	Chuck Connors
John Henry	Tom Nardini
Wing Comdr. Howard Hayes	
	Ronald Howard
Samson	Gerald Edwards

After TV had run through adult Westerns, dude Westerns, "empire" Westerns, contemporary Westerns, and comedy Westerns, ABC decided to try an African Western. *Cowboy in Africa* starred Chuck Connors as the world champion rodeo cowboy Jim Sinclair, who had been hired by an English landowner, Commander Hayes, to bring modern ranching methods to his game ranch in Kenya. Sinclair was assisted by his Navajo blood brother John Henry and was "adopted" by an orphaned, ten-year-old Kikuyu native boy named Samson.

The series was based on Ivan Tors' theatrical film *Africa—Texas Style* and was shot in Africa (for the backgrounds) and the Africa, U.S.A., park in southern California.

COWBOY THEATRE
Western Anthology
FIRST TELECAST: *June 9, 1957*

LAST TELECAST: *September 15, 1957*
BROADCAST HISTORY:
  Jun 1957, NBC Sun 6:30–7:00
  Jun 1957–Sep 1957, NBC Sun 6:30–7:30
HOST:
  Monty Hall

Re-edited Western feature films produced by Columbia Pictures in the 1930s and 1940s provided the material for this anthology, which was hosted and narrated by Monty Hall. The series began on Saturday afternoons in September 1956.

COWBOYS, THE
Western
FIRST TELECAST: *February 6, 1974*
LAST TELECAST: *August 14, 1974*
BROADCAST HISTORY:
  Feb 1974–Aug 1974, ABC Wed 8:00–8:30
CAST:

Jebediah Nightlinger	Moses Gunn
Mrs. Annie Andersen	Diana Douglas
U.S. Marshal Bill Winter	Jim Davis
Cimarron	A Martinez
Slim	Robert Carradine
Jimmy	Sean Kelly
Homer	Kerry MacLane
Steve	Clint Howard
Hardy	Mitch Brown
Weedy	Clay O'Brien

The Cowboys was a kind of teenage Western in which seven young boys, aged 9 to 17 years, faced the trials of growing into manhood while helping a widow run a ranch in the New Mexico Territory of the 1870s. The ranch foreman, Jebediah Nightlinger, and the widow, Mrs. Andersen, were around for adult supervision as the boys fought off teenage Comanches and adult rustlers. The series was based on the novel by William Dale Jennings and the movie starring John Wayne. Four of the boys in the series—Martinez, Carradine, Kelly, and O'Brien—also appeared in the film.

COWBOYS & INJUNS
Children's
FIRST TELECAST: *October 15, 1950*
LAST TELECAST: *December 31, 1950*
BROADCAST HISTORY:
  Oct 1950–Dec 1950, ABC Sun 6:00–6:30
HOST:
  Rex Bell

This was an unusually informative children's show, consisting of demonstrations of real cowboy and Indian folklore. It was filmed in an outdoor corral and an Indian village as well as in indoor settings. Originally it was a local program in Los Angeles.

COWTOWN RODEO
Rodeo
FIRST TELECAST: *August 1, 1957*

171

LAST TELECAST: *September 8, 1958*
BROADCAST HISTORY:
    Aug 1957–Sep 1957, ABC Thu 8:00–9:00
    Jun 1958–Sep 1958, ABC Mon 7:30–8:30
COMMENTATORS:
    Marty Glickman
    Howard "Stony" Harris

Top rodeo performers competed for cash prizes on this summertime show. Bronco busting, saddle and bareback riding, and calf roping were among the featured events. The program was produced at Cowtown Ranch in New Jersey, whose owner, Stony Harris, was one of the commentators.

CRASH CORRIGAN'S RANCH
Children's
FIRST TELECAST: *July 15, 1950*
LAST TELECAST: *September 29, 1950*
BROADCAST HISTORY:
    Jul 1950–Aug 1950, ABC Sat 7:00–7:30
    Aug 1950–Sep 1950, ABC Sun 6:30–7:00
    Sep 1950, ABC Fri 7:30–8:00
HOST:
    Ray (Crash) Corrigan

This variety show for children, starring Ray (Crash) Corrigan, featured musical and other acts in a Western setting.

CRAWFORD MYSTERY THEATRE
Drama/Quiz
FIRST TELECAST: *September 6, 1951*
LAST TELECAST: *September 27, 1951*
BROADCAST HISTORY:
    Sep 1951, DUM Thu 9:30–10:00
HOST/MODERATOR:
    John Howard
    Warren Hull

Detective-fiction writers and other guests guessed solutions to filmed mysteries in this early series, which was sponsored by Crawford Clothes. John Howard was host for the first two telecasts, after which he was replaced by Warren Hull (Howard later appeared as an actor in some of the dramas). The program was also known as *Public Prosecutor*. It was under the latter title that it remained on the air locally in New York until the end of February 1952.

CRAZY LIKE A FOX
Detective
FIRST TELECAST: *December 30, 1984*
LAST TELECAST: *September 4, 1986*
BROADCAST HISTORY:
    Dec 1984–Jan 1986, CBS Sun 9:00–10:00
    Jan 1986–Mar 1986, CBS Wed 9:00–10:00
    Apr 1986–Jun 1986, CBS Sat 8:00–9:00
    Jun 1986–Jul 1986, CBS Thu 8:00–9:00
    Aug 1986–Sep 1986, CBS Thu 9:00–10:00
CAST:
    Harry Fox .... Jack Warden
    Harrison K. Fox .... John Rubinstein
    Cindy Fox .... Penny Peyser
    Josh Fox .... Robby Kiger
    Allison Ling (1984–1985) .... Lydia Lei
    Allison Ling (1985–1986)
        .... Patricia Ayame Thomson
    Lt. Walker (1985–1986) .... Robert Hanley
    Ernie (1985–1986) .... Theodore Wilson

Harrison K. Fox was a conservative young attorney trying to develop a successful law practice in San Francisco to support his wife, Cindy, and his young son, Josh. Unfortunately his life was endlessly complicated by his unconventional father Harry, a loveable con artist and private eye who was constantly getting involved in murder cases. Harry was a real character. When he got involved in a dicey case, he would inevitably drag Harrison in with him—sometimes to get free legal advice (he had, after all, paid for Harrison's education), sometimes to get Harrison to take on one of his trouble-prone friends as a client, most often to help with the legwork. That usually meant chasing people, breaking into offices, and getting shot at—just the sort of diversion a conservative attorney enjoys! Harrison's secretary Allison grew used to seeing Harry barge into the office, interupting important meetings.

Despite all this, and regardless of his better judgment, Harrison could never turn Harry down. He was, after all, a loveable old coot.

CRIME PHOTOGRAPHER
Newspaper Drama
FIRST TELECAST: *April 19, 1951*
LAST TELECAST: *June 5, 1952*
BROADCAST HISTORY:
    Apr 1951–Jun 1952, CBS Thu 10:30–11:00
CAST:
    Casey (Apr–Jun 1951) .... Richard Carlyle
    Casey (Jun 1951–1952) ...... Darren McGavin
    Ethelbert (Apr–Jun 1951) .... John Gibson
    Ethelbert (Jun 1951–1952) .... Cliff Hall
    Ann Williams .... Jan Miner
    Captain Logan .... Donald McClelland
    Jack Lipman .... Archie Smith

The adventures of Casey, crack photographer for *The Morning Express*, were told in this series, which moved to television after a highly successful run on radio in the 1940s. Casey hung out at the Blue Note Cafe, where the music was provided by the Tony Mottola Trio, and was friendly with Ethelbert the bartender, to whom he recounted his various exploits. Richard Carlyle and John Gibson portrayed the roles when the series premiered in April 1951, but by June they were replaced by Darren McGavin and Cliff Hall. Ann Williams, a reporter on *The Morning Express*, was Casey's girlfriend. During the summer of 1951, he acquired a partner in cub reporter Jack Lipman, who wrote copy to go with Casey's pictures. This live series was set in, and broadcast from, New York City. It was based on the *Casey* novels by George Harmon Coxe.

CRIME STORY

Serial Drama

FIRST TELECAST: *September 18, 1986*
LAST TELECAST: *May 10, 1988*
BROADCAST HISTORY:

Sep 1986, NBC Thu 9:00–11:00
Sep 1986, NBC Fri 10:00–11:00
Sep 1986–Nov 1986, NBC Tue 9:00–10:00
Dec 1986–Mar 1987, NBC Fri 10:00–11:00
Jun 1987–Sep 1987, NBC Fri 10:00–11:00
Sep 1987–May 1988, NBC Tue 10:00–11:00

CAST:

Lt. Mike Torello .... Dennis Farina
Ray Luca................. Anthony Denison
Pauli Taglia .... John Santucci
Atty. David Abrams........... Stephen Lang
Det. Danny Krychek .... Bill Smitrovich
Det. Joey Indelli .... William Campbell
Det. Walter Clemmons .... Paul Butler
Det. Nate Grossman............. Steve Ryan
Frank Holman .... Ted Levine
Manny Weisbord .... Joseph Wiseman
Cori Luca .... Johann Carlo
Max Goldman .... Andrew Clay
Julie Torello (1986–1987).... Darlanne Fluegel
Inga Thorson (1986–1987)
.... Patricia Charbonneau
Ted Kehoe (1986–1987) .... Mark Hutter
Chief Kramer (1986–1987)........ Ron Dean
Phil Bartoli (1986–1987)........... Jon Polito
Steven Kordo (1987–1988)..... Jay O. Sanders

THEME:
"Runaway," sung by Del Shannon

Crime Story was an unusual serialized police drama. It began in Chicago in the early 1960s, where Lt. Mike Torello was head of the city's MCU (Major Crime Unit), and rising young gangster Ray Luca his chief target. Liberal prosecutor David Abrams, the son of a mobster himself, had forsaken the underworld and joined Torello in pursuing Luca. Julie was Torello's estranged wife (they were divorced after a few episodes, whereupon Torello had an affair with Inga); Danny, Joey, Walter, and Nate his team of hard-bitten detectives. Despite their efforts—and his own blundering sidekick Pauli—Luca prospered, building a violent criminal empire with nationwide tentacles. Old-line crime lords Manny Weisbord and Phil Bartoli provided support. When Luca moved his base of operations to Las Vegas, Torello followed, as part of a federal task force headed by Abrams. Although Torello dogged Luca's every step, he never could shut him down completely; the resilient gangster even survived an A-bomb blast at the end of the first season when he fled across Yucca Flats in the middle of a test.

Period flavor was a major component of this series, as was authenticity. Star Dennis Farina had been a real-life cop in Chicago for 18 years before shifting his beat to TV.

CRIME SYNDICATED

Police Anthology

FIRST TELECAST: *September 18, 1951*
LAST TELECAST: *June 23, 1953*
BROADCAST HISTORY:

Sep 1951–Jun 1953, CBS Tue 9:00–9:30

NARRATOR:
Rudolph Halley
Herbert R. O'Conor

Dramatizations of actual cases from the files of the Senate Crime Investigating Committee, the FBI, and local law-enforcement agencies were presented each week on this live series. Rudolph Halley, former chief counsel for the Senate Crime Investigating Committee, was the original host. When he became president of the New York City Council in late 1951 he decided to alternate narrator responsibilities with Sen. Herbert R. O'Conor of Maryland, former chairman of the Senate Crime Investigating Committee. In March 1952 *Crime Syndicated* was cut back from a weekly series to a biweekly series, alternating with *City Hospital*.

CRIME WITH FATHER

Police Drama

FIRST TELECAST: *August 31, 1951*
LAST TELECAST: *January 18, 1952*
BROADCAST HISTORY:

Aug 1951–Jan 1952, ABC Fri 9:00–9:30

CAST:

Capt. Jim Riland................ Rusty Lane
Chris Riland.................. Peggy Lobbin

This father-and-daughter detective show revolved around the cases of Capt. Jim Riland of the homicide squad. Jim's daughter Chris was of greater help in solving cases than any of his plainclothesmen.

CRISIS

syndicated title for *Kraft Mystery Theater*

CRISIS, THE

Drama

FIRST TELECAST: *October 5, 1949*
LAST TELECAST: *December 28, 1949*
BROADCAST HISTORY:

Oct 1949–Dec 1949, NBC Wed 8:00–8:30

INTERVIEWER:
Adrian Spies

"DIRECTOR":
Arthur Peterson (Oct)
Bob Cunningham (Nov–Dec)

This unusual series used a real-life crisis as the subject of a studio dramatization. First a guest would describe for interviewer Spies the events leading up to a critical moment in his or her life. At the major turning point in the story the guest's narrative was stopped, and professional actors—who were unaware of what actually happened next—would carry on, playing the scene as they imagined it might have been resolved. The actors worked unrehearsed and without scripts, improvising dialogue. An on-camera "director" provided some instructions and called for props. After each scene was played, the guest would return to explain what had actually happened. The show was produced live in Chicago and was directed by Norman Felton.

CRITIC AT LARGE
Discussion
FIRST TELECAST: *August 18, 1948*
LAST TELECAST: *April 20, 1949*
BROADCAST HISTORY:
  Aug 1948–Nov 1948, ABC Wed 7:30–8:00
  Nov 1948–Jan 1949, ABC Thu 8:30–9:00
  Jan 1949–Apr 1949, ABC Wed 8:30–9:00
MODERATOR:
  John Mason Brown

Author and critic John Mason Brown, who once commented that "some television programs are so much chewing gum for the eyes," offered this intellectual alternative in 1948–1949. It consisted of an informal living-room discussion on the arts with two or three guests, of the caliber of author James Michener, producer Billy Rose, publisher Bennett Cerf, and critic Bosley Crowther. The subjects ranged from modern art to new novels, films, the theater, and fashions.

CROSS CURRENT
see *Foreign Intrigue*

CROSS QUESTION
see *They Stand Accused*

CROSSROADS
Dramatic Anthology
FIRST TELECAST: *October 7, 1955*
LAST TELECAST: *September 27, 1957*
BROADCAST HISTORY:
  Oct 1955–Sep 1957, ABC Fri 8:30–9:00

Crossroads would have been indistinguishable from many other competently done dramatic anthologies of the early and mid-1950s were it not for its unusual subject matter. The series dealt exclusively with dramatizations of the experiences of clergymen. The problems they faced in both their personal and professional lives were depicted by many fine actors, Vincent Price and Luther Adler among them. Clergymen of all faiths were treated at one time or another, and the dramas successfully made the point that these were real people, as well as representatives of their respective faiths.

CROSSROADS
see *American Parade, The*

CROSS-WITS, THE
Quiz/Audience Participation
BROADCAST HISTORY:
  Syndicated only

30 minutes
Produced: *1975–1980, 1986–1987*
Released: *Fall 1975*
HOST:
  Jack Clark (1975–1980)
  David Sparks (1986–1987)
EXECUTIVE PRODUCER:
  Ralph Edwards

This popular syndicated quiz show was a word game, based on a crossword puzzle. Two teams, each composed of two celebrities and one civilian, competed to fill in words in a crossword puzzle, from clues provided by the host. Points were awarded, and the winner advanced to the "Crossfire" finale, where he or she was assisted by a celebrity of his choice. The object here was to fill in 10 words in 60 seconds. The grand prize on the premiere was a trip to Paris.

Among the celebrities making frequent appearances were Alice Ghostley, Jo Anne Worley, Jamie Farr, Stu Gilliam, and Vicki Lawrence.

Six years after the original series had left the air, *The New Cross-Wits* surfaced, with David Sparks replacing the original host, Jack Clark.

CRUSADE IN EUROPE
Documentary
FIRST TELECAST: *May 5, 1949*
LAST TELECAST: *October 27, 1949*
BROADCAST HISTORY:
  May 1949–Oct 1949, ABC Thu 9:00–9:30
NARRATOR:
  Westbrook Van Voorhis
  Maurice Joyce
PRODUCER:
  Richard de Rochemont
ADAPTED BY:
  Fred Feldkamp

This film documentary series on the European theater of action during World War II was assembled from combat footage shot during the war. *Crusade in Europe* was one of the first major documentary series produced especially for television (by the March of Time film unit), and was based on General Dwight D. Eisenhower's best-selling book of the same name. Its success led to a syndicated sequel titled *Crusade in the Pacific*. Westbrook Van Voorhis provided narration, while Maurice Joyce read quotes from Eisenhower's book.

CRUSADER
International Intrigue
FIRST TELECAST: *October 7, 1955*
LAST TELECAST: *December 28, 1956*
BROADCAST HISTORY:
  Oct 1955–Dec 1956, CBS Fri 9:00–9:30
CAST:
  Matt Anders . . . . Brian Keith

Free-lance writer Matt Anders devoted much of his time to one cause: helping the oppressed peoples living under dictatorial or Communist regimes escape to free countries. The reason for his devotion to this cause was simple. After overthrowing the Polish government, the Communists had kept his mother in Poland and sent her to a concentration camp, where she died. Holding the Communists responsible for her death, Matt used every means at his disposal to help save others from her fate.

CRYSTAL ROOM
Variety
FIRST TELECAST: *August 15, 1948*
LAST TELECAST: *September 12, 1948*
BROADCAST HISTORY:
Aug 1948–Sep 1948, ABC Sun 8:30–9:00
HOSTESS:
Maggi McNellis

This short-lived variety program was set in an imaginary nightclub and featured Maggi McNellis, one of early TV's ubiquitous personalities, and guests.

CURSE OF DRACULA, THE
Serial
FIRST TELECAST: *February 27, 1979*
LAST TELECAST: *May 1, 1979*
BROADCAST HISTORY:
Feb 1979–Mar 1979, NBC Tue 8:40–9:00
Mar 1979–May 1979, NBC Tue 8:00–8:20
CAST:
Count Dracula . . . . Michael Nouri
Kurt von Helsing . . . . Stephen Johnson
Mary Gibbons . . . . Carol Baxter
Antoinette . . . . Antoinette Stella
Darryl . . . . Mark Montgomery
Christine . . . . Bever-Leigh Banfield
Amanda Gibbons . . . . Louise Sorel

In this contemporary serial, Count Dracula was "undead and well, and living in California." The 500-year-old vampire was located in San Francisco and teaching a course in European history at South Bay College (Evening Division). One of the principal advantages of his teaching post was that it brought him in contact with attractive young students—Antoinette, Christine, and Darryl—who could be turned into vampires and join the legions of the undead. Seeking to destroy Dracula was Kurt von Helsing, grandson of Prof. von Helsing, a former nemesis of the count. Helping Kurt was Mary Gibbons, whose mother had been turned into a vampire by Dracula years before. Mary herself almost fell victim to the fatal charm of the count, but was saved by the intervention of her vampire mother, Amanda. In the climactic chapter, Mary drove a wooden stake through the heart of her mother, freeing her from the curse of the undead, and Kurt shot Dracula with a wooden arrow from a crossbow, destroying him.
The Curse of Dracula was one of three serials aired under the umbrella title *Cliff Hangers*, and was the only one to reach its conclusion by the time the series was canceled.

CURTAIN CALL
syndicated title for *Lux Video Theater*

CURTAIN CALL
Dramatic Anthology
FIRST TELECAST: *June 20, 1952*
LAST TELECAST: *September 26, 1952*
BROADCAST HISTORY:
Jun 1952–Sep 1952, NBC Fri 8:00–8:30

Curtain Call, the 1952 summer replacement for *The RCA Victor Show*, was composed of live plays telecast from Hollywood.

CURTAIN UP
see *Movies—Prior to 1961*

CURTAIN TIME
syndicated title for *Telephone Time*

CUSTER
Western
FIRST TELECAST: *September 6, 1967*
LAST TELECAST: *December 27, 1967*
BROADCAST HISTORY:
Sep 1967–Dec 1967, ABC Wed 7:30–8:30
CAST:
Lt. Col. George A. Custer . . . Wayne Maunder
California Joe Milner . . . . Slim Pickens
Sgt. James Bustard . . . . Peter Palmer
Crazy Horse . . . . Michael Dante
Brig. Gen. Alfred Terry . . . . . Robert F. Simon
Capt. Miles Keogh . . . . Grant Woods

This action Western was based on the career of George A. Custer between 1868 and 1875, the year before his death in the Battle of the Little Big Horn. In 1868, after losing his Civil War rank of brevet major general, Custer was posted to Fort Hays, Kansas, to take command of the 7th Cavalry Regiment. The 7th was a ragtag outfit of low reputation, made up of ex-Confederates, thieves, and renegades. With the help of California Joe Milner, a leathery old army scout and friend; Capt. Keogh, a shrewd and witty Irishman; and towering Sgt. Bustard, Custer managed to whip this sorry regiment into an effective force capable of protecting the settlers on the surrounding plains. Gen. Terry, commanding officer of Fort Hays, disliked Custer's unconventional methods and appearance (including his shoulder-length blond hair), but supported him in his battles with Crazy Horse's Sioux.

CUTTER TO HOUSTON
Medical Drama
FIRST TELECAST: *October 1, 1983*
LAST TELECAST: *December 31, 1983*
BROADCAST HISTORY:
Oct 1983, CBS Sat 8:00–9:00
Dec 1983, CBS Sat 8:00–9:00

Dr. Andy Fenton	Jim Metzler
Dr. Beth Gilbert	Shelley Hack
Dr. Hal Wexler	Alec Baldwin
Nurse Connie Buford	K Callan
Mayor Warren Jarvis	Noble Willingham
Nurse Patty Alvarez	Susan Styles

TV's hotshot young doctors usually work their miracles in sprawling urban medical centers, but in this series three of them were dumped in the boondocks—with varying reactions. Rural Cutter, Texas, pop. 5231, was only 60 miles from Houston, but it seemed like a million miles to ambitious young surgeon Beth Gilbert, who had to serve her apprenticeship in the town's newly opened clinic before returning to the prestigious Texas Medical Center. Andy Fenton didn't mind it, though; he was a local boy and was eager to repay the townsfolk who had encouraged his career. Internist Hal Wexler hadn't made up his mind about Cutter. Since he had been convicted of writing illegal prescriptions and was serving his probation in Cutter, he was glad to be working at all.

Though the town was small it was mighty proud of its new facility, and provided plenty of business, including victims of bar brawls, oilwell explosions, and crimes, as well as normal cases of pregnancy and disease. Whenever things got worse than could be handled with Cutter's limited equipment, Houston's Texas Medical Center could be reached by helicopter, radio, or computer linkup (hence the call, "Cutter to Houston . . .").

D

D.A., THE
Courtroom Drama
FIRST TELECAST: *September 17, 1971*
LAST TELECAST: *January 7, 1972*
BROADCAST HISTORY:
Sep 1971–Jan 1972, NBC Fri 8:00–8:30
CAST:
Deputy D.A. Paul Ryan .... Robert Conrad
Chief Deputy D.A. "Staff" Stafford
.... Harry Morgan
D.A. Investigator Bob Ramirez .. Ned Romero
Public Defender Katherine Benson
.... Julie Cobb

Collecting the evidence necessary to bring criminals to trial and following the course of the trial provided the thrust for this short-lived series. The program had two segments: first Deputy D.A. Ryan and his team would investigate the crime, then Ryan would function as prosecuting attorney. His courtroom adversary in most cases was Public Defender Katherine Benson, representing the accused. The courtroom portion of the series was done in quasi-documentary style with Ryan doing voice-over narration to explain legal terminology and procedures to the audience. The series was replaced after a few months by the highly successful *Sanford and Son.*

D.A.'S MAN, THE
Police Drama
FIRST TELECAST: *January 3, 1959*
LAST TELECAST: *August 29, 1959*
BROADCAST HISTORY:
Jan 1959–Aug 1959, NBC Sat 10:30–11:00
CAST:
Shannon .... John Compton
Al Bonacorsi .... Ralph Manza
Frank LaValle .... Herb Ellis

Working as an undercover investigator for the New York City District Attorney's Office, ex-private eye Shannon spent most of his time infiltrating the New York underworld. Hijacking rings, prostitution, narcotics, and any other source of "mob" income were appropriate targets for his sleuthing. Shannon's contact at the D.A.'s office was First Assistant D.A. Al Bonacorsi.

D.C. FOLLIES
Situation Comedy
BROADCAST HISTORY:
Syndicated only
30 minutes
Produced: *1987–*
Released: *September 1987*
REGULARS:
Fred Willard
The Krofft Puppets
VOICES:
Louise DuArt
John Roarke
Maurice LaMarche
Joe Alaskey

D.C. Follies was a bar located in Washington not far from the White House. Its owner and bartender was Fred Willard, who was, in fact, the only live regular on this series—the patrons were virtually all puppets designed by Sid and Marty Krofft. They included dummies (no pun intended) of President and Mrs. Reagan; former presidents Carter, Ford, and Nixon; other political personalities; assorted news types like Andy Rooney, Dan Rather, and Ted Koppel; and celebrities such as Woody Allen, Jack Nicholson, and Oprah Winfrey. The humor tended to be on the satirical side, often taking pot shots at politicians and the political process. In addition to the puppets, each episode brought a celebrity guest into the bar, with Martin Mull, Robin Leach, Bob Uecker, and Betty White appearing early on.

DADS
Situation Comedy
FIRST TELECAST: *December 5, 1986*
LAST TELECAST: *June 27, 1987*
BROADCAST HISTORY:
Dec 1986–Jan 1987, ABC Fri 9:00–9:30
Jan 1987–Feb 1987, ABC Fri 9:30–10:00
Jun 1987, ABC Sat 9:30–10:00
CAST:
Rick Armstrong .... Barry Bostwick
Louie Mangiotti .... Carl Weintraub
Kelly Armstrong (age 13) .... Skye Bassett
Allan Mangiotti (16) .... Eddie Castrodad
Kenny Mangiotti (12) .... Jason Naylor

Two single fathers shared a house in Philadelphia, and the joys of child-rearing, in this short-lived comedy. Yuppie Rick, a reporter, worried a lot about his teenage daughter Kelly, while his blue-collar pal Louie, a stonemason, just played it loose with his young sons Kenny and Allan.

DAGMAR'S CANTEEN
Variety
FIRST TELECAST: *March 22, 1952*
LAST TELECAST: *June 14, 1952*
BROADCAST HISTORY:
Mar 1952–Jun 1952, NBC Sat 12:15–12:45 A.M.
REGULARS:
Dagmar (Jennie Lewis)
Ray Malone
Tim Herbert
Jeanne Lewis
Milton Delugg and His Orchestra

Dagmar, the statuesque, well-endowed blonde made famous on Jerry Lester's *Broadway Open House,* starred in this late-night live variety show as the hostess of a real canteen for servicemen. She interviewed, sang songs, and danced, but the most amusing part of the show was her weekly reading of one of her original plays (similar to her hilarious "poetry readings" on *Broadway Open House*). Roles in the plays were also read by servicemen chosen from the audience, as well as by the other cast members. One of the regulars was Dagmar's sister Jeanne, who was the assistant hostess.

DAKOTAS, THE
Western
FIRST TELECAST: *January 7, 1963*
LAST TELECAST: *September 9, 1963*
BROADCAST HISTORY:
  Jan 1963–Sep 1963, ABC Mon 7:30–8:30
CAST:
  Marshal Frank Ragan . . . . Larry Ward
  Deputy J. D. Smith . . . . Jack Elam
  Deputy Del Stark . . . . Chad Everett
  Deputy Vance Porter . . . . Mike Greene

This Western adventure depicted the efforts of a U.S. marshal and his three deputies to maintain law and order across the Black Hills and Badlands of the Dakota Territory. The deputies were a study in contrasts: young, volatile Del Stark; big, gruff Vance Porter; and J. D. Smith, an ex-gunfighter.

DAKTARI
Adventure
FIRST TELECAST: *January 11, 1966*
LAST TELECAST: *January 15, 1969*
BROADCAST HISTORY:
  Jan 1966–Sep 1968, CBS Tue 7:30–8:30
  Sep 1968–Jan 1969, CBS Wed 7:30–8:30
CAST:
  Dr. Marsh Tracy . . . . Marshall Thompson
  Paula Tracy . . . . Cheryl Miller
  Jack Dane (1966–1968) . . . . Yale Summers
  Hedley . . . . Hedley Mattingly
  Mike . . . . Hari Rhodes
  Bart Jason (1968–1969) . . . . Ross Hagen
  Jenny Jones (1968–1969) . . . . Erin Moran

Filmed at Africa, U.S.A., a wild-animal park near Los Angeles, *Daktari* told the story of an American doctor and his daughter living in Africa. "Daktari" is a native word for doctor. Marsh Tracy was a veterinarian who ran an animal study center with the assistance of his daughter Paula, an American named Jack Dane, and a native named Mike. The Tracys had two distinctive pets, a lion named Clarence and a chimpanzee named Judy. (Clarence had previously starred in an Ivan Tors movie called *Clarence the Cross-eyed Lion*.) Also featured was Hedley, the British game warden, who often called on Marsh for help in dealing with animals, natives, and poachers. Added to the cast in 1968 were Bart Jason, a for-

mer ranger and hunter who had become a guide for camera safaris, and Jenny Jones, a seven-year-old orphan who became part of the Tracy household.

DALLAS
Drama
FIRST TELECAST: *April 2, 1978*
LAST TELECAST:
BROADCAST HISTORY:
  Apr 1978, CBS Sun 10:00–11:00
  Sep 1978–Oct 1978, CBS Sat 10:00–11:00
  Oct 1978–Jan 1979, CBS Sun 10:00–11:00
  Jan 1979–Nov 1981, CBS Fri 10:00–11:00
  Dec 1981–May 1985, CBS Fri 9:00–10:00
  Sep 1985–May 1986, CBS Fri 9:00–10:00 (OS)
  Sep 1986–May 1988, CBS Fri 9:00–10:00
CAST:
  John Ross (J.R.) Ewing, Jr. . . . . Larry Hagman
  Eleanor Southworth (Miss Ellie)
    Ewing (1978–1984, 1985–   )
    . . . . Barbara Bel Geddes
  Eleanor Southworth (Miss Ellie)
    Ewing (1984–1985) . . . . Donna Reed
  John Ross (Jock) Ewing (1978–1981)
    . . . . Jim Davis
  Bobby Ewing (1978–1985, 1986–   )
    . . . . Patrick Duffy
  Pamela Barnes Ewing (1978–1987)
    . . . . Victoria Principal
  Lucy Ewing Cooper (1978–1985)
    . . . . Charlene Tilton
  Sue Ellen Ewing . . . . Linda Gray
  Ray Krebbs . . . . Steve Kanaly
  Cliff Barnes . . . . Ken Kercheval
  Julie Grey (April 1978) . . . . Tina Louise
  Willard "Digger" Barnes (1978)
    . . . . David Wayne
  Willard "Digger" Barnes (1979–1980)
    . . . . Keenan Wynn
  Gary Ewing (1978–1979) . . . . David Ackroyd
  Gary Ewing (1979–1981) . . . . Ted Shackelford
  Valene Ewing (1978–1981) . . . . . Joan Van Ark
  Liz Craig (1978–1982) . . . . . . Barbara Babcock
  Willie Joe Garr (1978–1979) . . . . . John Ashton
  Jeb Amos (1978–1979) . . . . Sandy Ward
  Kristin Shepard (1979–1981) . . . . Mary Crosby
  Mrs. Shepard (1979) . . . . Martha Scott
  Dusty Farlow (1979–1982, 1985) . . Jared Martin
  Alan Beam (1979–1980) . . . . . Randolph Powell
  Dr. Ellby (1979–1981) . . . . Jeff Cooper
  Donna Culver Krebbs (1979–1987)
    . . . . Susan Howard
  Dave Culver (1979–1982, 1986–1987)
    . . . . Tom Fuccello
  Harve Smithfield . . . . George O. Petrie
  Vaughn Leland (1979–1984) . . . Dennis Patrick
  Connie (1979–1981) . . . . Jeanna Michaels
  Louella (1979–1981) . . . . Meg Gallagher
  Jordan Lee (1979–   ) . . . . Don Starr
  Mitch Cooper (1979–1982) . . . Leigh McCloskey
  John Ross Ewing III (1980–1983) . Tyler Banks
  John Ross Ewing III (1983–   ) . . . Omri Katz

Punk Anderson (1980–   )
.... Morgan Woodward
Mavis Anderson (1982–   ).... Alice Hirson
Brady York (1980–1981)........ Ted Gehring
Alex Ward (1980–1981)........ Joel Fabiani
Les Crowley (1980–1981)....... Michael Bell
Marilee Stone (1980–1987) ....Fern Fitzgerald
Afton Cooper (1981–1984)....Audrey Landers
Arliss Cooper (1981)........... Anne Francis
Clint Ogden (1981) .... Monte Markham
Leslie Stewart (1981)........ Susan Flannery
Rebecca Wentworth (1981–1983)

.... Priscilla Pointer
Craig Stewart (1981) .... Craig Stevens
Jeremy Wendell (1981, 1984–   )
.... William Smithers
Clayton Farlow (1981–   ).... Howard Keel
Jeff Farraday (1981–1982) .... Art Hindle
Katherine Wentworth (1981–1984)

.... Morgan Brittany
Charles Eccles (1982)........... Ron Tomme
Bonnie Robertson (1982)...... Lindsay Bloom
Blair Sullivan (1982) .... Ray Wise
Holly Harwood (1982–1984)...... Lois Chiles
Mickey Trotter (1982–1983)

.... Timothy Patrick Murphy
Walt Driscoll (1982–1983)........ Ben Piazza
Jarrett McLeish (1982–1983)

.... J. Patrick McNamara
Thornton McLeish (1982–1983)

.... Kenneth Kimmins
Eugene Bullock (1982–1983) ..... E. J. Andre
Mark Graison (1983–1984, 1985–1986)

.... John Beck
Aunt Lil Trotter (1983–1984)....... Kate Reid
Roy Ralston (1983).............. John Reilly
Serena (1983–1985) ..... Stephanie Blackmore
Peter Richards (1983–1984)

.... Christopher Atkins
Paul Morgan (1983–1984, 1988–   )
.... Glenn Corbett
Jenna Wade (1983–   )..... Priscilla Presley
Charlie Wade (1983–   )... Shalane McCall
Edgar Randolph (1983–1984)

.... Martin E. Brooks
Armando Sidoni (1983–1984) .. Alberto Morin
Sly (1983–   ) .... Deborah Rennard
Betty (1984–1985)............. Kathleen York
Eddie Cronin (1984–1985) ...... Fredric Lehne
Pete Adams (1984–1985) .... Burke Byrnes
Dave Stratton (1984) ...... Christopher Stone
Jessica Montford (1984)........ Alexis Smith
Mandy Winger (1984–1987) . Deborah Shelton
Jamie Ewing Barnes (1984–1986)

.... Jenilee Harrison
Christopher Ewing (1984–   )
.... Joshua Harris
Scotty Demarest (1985–1986) .. Stephen Elliott
Jack Ewing (1985–1987)........ Dack Rambo
Angelica Nero (1985–1986) .. Barbara Carrera
Dr. Jerry Kenderson (1985–1986)

.... Barry Jenner
Nicholas (1985–1986) .... George Chakiris

Grace (1985–1986)....... Marete Van Kamp
Matt Cantrell (1986)............ Marc Singer
Luis Rueda (1986)............ Alejandro Rey
Tony (1986)............. Solomon Smaniotto
April Stevens (1986–   )... Sheree J. Wilson
Ben Stivers/Wes Parmalee (1986)

.... Steve Forrest
B. D. Calhoun (1986–1987) .. Hunter von Leer
Ozwald Valentine (1986–1987)

.... Derek McGrath
Bruce Harvey (1986–1987)

.... Jonathan Goldsmith
Senator Dowling (1986–1987).. Jim McMullan
Mrs. Scottfield (1987)........ Karen Carlson
Nicholas Pearce (1987–   ) ..... Jack Scalia
Casey Denault (1987–   ).. Andrew Stevens
"Dandy" Dandridge (1987)...... Bert Remsen
Kimberly Cryder (1987–   )
.... Leigh Taylor-Young
Lisa Alden (1987–   ) .... Amy Stock
Laurel Ellis (1988–   )... Annabel Schofield
Sen. Henry Harrison O'Dell (1988–   )
.... Howard Duff
Brett Lomax (1988–   )
.... Mark Lindsay Chapman
Kay Lloyd (1988–   )........ Karen Kopins

Soap operas have always been a staple of day-time television, but ABC's mid-1960s *Peyton Place* was the last prime-time soap opera to be a major viewer attraction—until *Dallas.* It was not a big hit when it premiered in 1978, but *Dallas*'s audience continued to build and, by the 1980–1981 season, it was the runaway most popular series on network television, having spawned one spin-off *(Knots Landing)* and a host of imitators, including *Dynasty, Flamingo Road,* and *Secrets of Midland Heights.*

Dallas had all of the elements that make for a successful soap opera—characters that were larger than life, conflicts based on the struggle for money and power, and lots and lots of sex. It was appropriate that the series was set in Texas, with its reputation for the excesses of the wealthy. Patriarch of the Ewing clan was Jock Ewing, who 40 years before had struck it rich as an oil wildcatter and then maneuvered his partner Digger Barnes out of both his share of their company and his true love, Eleanor Southworth. Jock and Miss Ellie had three sons, J.R., Jr., Bobby, and Gary. J.R., the eldest, was the man viewers loved to hate. He was power-hungry, unscrupulous, and conniving in his business dealings, and continually unfaithful to his wife, Sue Ellen—even after she bore him a son, J.R. Ewing III, in the 1979–1980 season. When J.R. wanted something or someone, he stopped at nothing to attain his goal. Bobby, the youngest brother, had the morals and integrity his older brother lacked, and was a constant thorn in J.R.'s side. Bobby was married to Digger Barnes' sexy young daughter Pamela, and seemed to J.R. to represent a continual threat to his control of Ewing Oil. Jock, J.R., Bobby, and their families all lived

179

under one roof, a sprawling ranch owned by the Ewings called Southfork, which was located outside the city in rural Braddock, Texas.

The middle Ewing brother, Gary, was rarely seen on *Dallas*. Unable to compete with his strong-willed brothers, and suffering from emotional instability, Gary only appeared occasionally to see his daughter Lucy (he eventually got his own series, *Knots Landing*). Lucy also lived at Southfork and spent most of her time seducing every man in sight, a not too difficult task in light of her blond sexiness. Management of the Southfork ranch fell to Ray Krebbs, one of Lucy's first conquests. Cliff Barnes, the son of Jock's ex-partner Digger Barnes, had become a Ewing in-law when his sister Pam married Bobby. But Cliff was an assistant district attorney and was determined to avenge his father's ruination by the Ewings, so he spent most of his time working with the government attempting to expose the family's corruption of public officials and other illegal business practices.

Most of the major conflicts on *Dallas* centered around J.R., aptly described in *Time* magazine as "that human oil slick." He had, among other things, sold worthless Asian oil leases to the family banker Vaughn Leland and a number of other investors, mortgaged Southfork without telling his parents, attempted to get Sue Ellen institutionalized for alcoholism, thwarted the efforts of unscrupulous Alan Beam to marry Lucy and get his hands on part of the Ewing fortune, and left a trail of disillusioned mistresses whom he had discarded like so much garbage. It was one of these mistresses, his wife's sister Kristin (played briefly in early 1979 by Colleen Camp), who became the focal point of the major TV story of 1980. In the last original episode of the 1979–1980 season, J.R. was shot by an unknown assailant and rushed to the hospital in critical condition. All summer the question raged—"Who shot J.R.?" *Dallas* was by this time a huge international hit, and all over the world viewers were trying to figure out which of the 15 or so characters who had just cause had actually pulled the trigger. Betting parlors took in millions of dollars in wagers. Security was extraordinarily tight at the studio where *Dallas* was filmed, and even the actors themselves did not know for sure (several alternative endings had been filmed). Finally, on November 21, 1980, the world found out: Kristin had pulled the trigger. Pregnant with J.R.'s child, and about to be framed by him for prostitution because she refused his order to get out of Dallas, she shot him for revenge. The episode in which her guilt was revealed was seen by more people than any program in the history of television up to that time. Nearly 80 percent of all viewers watching television that night were tuned to *Dallas*.

In true *Dallas* style, however, J.R. lived and Kristin was never prosecuted, although she did finally leave town. J.R. recovered and waged a new war to unseat his brother Bobby, who had taken over Ewing Oil during his convalescence. There were also two Ewing marriages that season. Lucy married young pre-med student Mitch Cooper, and Ray Krebbs (who was revealed to be Jock's illegitimate son, and therefore a Ewing) married attractive, politically powerful widow Donna Culver. J.R. was as malevolent as ever, engineering a foreign coup to regain some of his holdings as well as hiring a sexy (of course) public-relations woman to promote a new image for himself as an "All-American Businessman." If she could pull that off, she would deserve an Academy Award!

As time passed, marriages alternated with divorces. J.R. and Sue Ellen divorced and later remarried, although neither remained faithful to the other. Lucy and Mitch also divorced, and she subsequently had an ill-fated romance with Mickey Trotter. Mickey was grievously injured in a car accident caused by a drunken Sue Ellen; while he was lying brain-dead at the hospital, Ray Krebbs pulled the plug on his life-support system. The jury called it manslaughter. Meanwhile, Pam had an emotional breakdown, separated from, and eventually divorced Bobby (while retaining custody of their adopted son Christopher, Kristin and J.R.'s child).

Pam's brother Cliff proved to be just as greedy as everyone else—if somewhat less talented at it—when he went to work for his mother. His manipulations became more complicated as the stakes got higher and, when he became president of Barnes/Wentworth Oil, he even had hopes of besting J.R. in the world of dirty deals. His conniving and beautiful half sister Katherine Wentworth first tried to ally herself with J.R. to break Cliff, and then fell in love with Bobby—who by that time was back together with an old girlfriend, Jenna Wade (played once in 1978 by Morgan Fairchild and a few times in early 1980 by Francine Tacker).

Even Miss Ellie found a new romance, after Jock passed away in 1981 (actor Jim Davis had died), marrying the wealthy Clayton Farlow. Through it all her sons J.R. and Bobby fought over control of Ewing Oil. Eventually, to neither's satisfaction, they ended up running the family business together, constantly trying to outmaneuver each other to gain total control.

The 1984–1985 season saw the arrival of still another troublemaker, cousin Jamie, who teamed with Cliff Barnes to fight J.R. for a piece of Ewing Oil; eventually she and Cliff were married. Donna struck oil in an independent venture, introducing strains in her marriage to Ray; and J.R., in between battles with everyone, found time to pursue hard-to-get Mandy Winger. Brother Bobby had a bad season all around. First he was shot by an assassin who was gunning for J.R., then he broke up with Jenna (who married and then was convicted of murdering Marchetta), and finally he was "killed" in a hit-and-run accident.

Bobby's demise left a major hole in *Dallas*. During 1985–1986 his two loves tried to find happiness in new relationships, Pam with the long–missing Mark Graison and Jenna with Jamie's brother Jack Ewing. The season's major new manipulator was Marinos Shipping executive Angelica, who allied with Cliff while flirting with Jack. J.R.'s boozy wife Sue Ellen was committed to a sanitarium (her mother Patricia bailed her out), had a fling with Dusty, and wound up in a nasty custody fight with J.R. over little John Ross. But still the memory of Bobby lingered. It was renewed when a childhood friend named Matt turned up looking for an extension of the financing Bobby had given him for an emerald mine in South America. Pam obliged and a series of adventures in the jungle ensued.

What Pam—and viewers—longed for, of course, was not ghosts from Bobby's past but Bobby himself. With ratings sagging, star Larry Hagman made a personal appeal to Patrick Duffy to rejoin the cast. No matter that his character had been killed and buried in an elaborate funeral. In one of the most celebrated cop-outs in soap opera history the 1986–1987 season opened with a very live Bobby lathering up in Pam's shower. How did he get there? It seems she had *dreamt* the entire 1985–1986 season, and Bobby had not died at all! With that minor detail out of the way it was back to normal, with Bobby torn as ever between Pam (whom he remarried) and Jenna. Pam, however, was grievously injured in a fiery auto accident and then disappeared, while Jenna was preoccupied with her trouble-prone teenaged daughter Charlie. Over in J.R.'s story, a bitter Sue Ellen found a new way to embarrass him by manufacturing a line of "Valentine's Girl" erotic lingerie—which became an instant hit with Mandy as the model. Inspired, perhaps, by Bobby's miraculous resurrection, a ranchhand named Parmalee surfaced claiming to be the long-dead Jock Ewing, causing great distress in the family. The Krebbs' marriage disintegrated further when Donna went to Washington as a lobbyist, and flirted with some between-the-sheets lobbying with Senator Dowling. Back home Jack's ex-wife April was the latest newcomer scheming to snag a piece of Ewing Oil.

The Ewings suffered a major setback in 1987 when proof of J.R.'s illegal dealings finally caused him to lose partial control of Ewing Oil. Ever resourceful but on the defensive, wily J.R. worked with Casey Denault to regain some of his lost power. He also tried his celebrated bedroom ploy with Kimberly Cryder, the beautiful wife of his new nemesis Winston Cryder. Jenna and Ray were married; Bobby was pursued by Lisa (who sought custody of his son, Christopher) and by April; and Miss Ellie threw Clayton out of the house. Sue Ellen had the right product for them all—she pursued the lingerie business with intimate help from banker Nicholas Pearce.

DALTON'S CODE OF VENGEANCE
Adventure
FIRST TELECAST: *July 27, 1986*

LAST TELECAST: *August 24, 1986*
BROADCAST HISTORY:
  July 1986–Aug 1986, NBC Sun 8:00–9:00
CAST:
  David Dalton . . . . Charles Taylor

A short-run series about a rootless young Vietnam veteran who prowled around the country stumbling upon wrongs to right. The character was originally seen in two TV movies, telecast in June 1985 and May 1986; the first of these was chopped in two and rerun as two episodes of the series' four-episode run in the summer of 1986, which was the last network viewers saw of Dalton.

DAMON RUNYON THEATRE
Dramatic Anthology
FIRST TELECAST: *April 16, 1955*
LAST TELECAST: *June 30, 1956*
BROADCAST HISTORY:
  Apr 1955–Jun 1956, CBS Sat 10:30–11:00
HOST:
  Donald Woods

Most of the episodes in this filmed anthology were based on the short stories of Damon Runyon. Best known through the musical *Guys and Dolls,* which was adapted from his writings, Runyon was unique in his use of hip New York language and characters. Vivian Blaine, who created the role of Adelaide in *Guys and Dolls,* appeared in a variation on that role in the premiere episode of the program.

DAN AUGUST
Police Drama
FIRST TELECAST: *September 23, 1970*
LAST TELECAST: *June 25, 1975*
BROADCAST HISTORY:
  Sep 1970–Jan 1971, ABC Wed 10:00–11:00
  Jan 1971–Aug 1971, ABC Thu 9:30–10:30
  May 1973–Oct 1973, CBS Wed 9:00–10:00
  Apr 1975–Jun 1975, CBS Wed 10:00–11:00
CAST:
  Det. Lt. Dan August . . . . Burt Reynolds
  Sgt. Charles Wilentz . . . . Norman Fell
  Sgt. Joe Rivera . . . . Ned Romero
  Chief George Untermeyer . . Richard Anderson
  Katy Grant . . . . Ena Hartmann

Burt Reynolds portrayed Dan August, a police detective, in this straight police-action show. Since August had grown up with many of the people he had to deal with officially in Santa Luisa, California, he became more personally involved in his cases than would most big-city detectives. Despite—or perhaps because of—this, he always got his man, in true TV-detective fashion.

Dan August was aired on ABC during the 1970–1971 season to mediocre ratings and was not renewed. However, shortly thereafter Reynolds became a major celebrity through feature-film and other exposure, and CBS telecast reruns during two subsequent summers to larger audiences than had seen the original series.

DAN RAVEN
Police Drama
FIRST TELECAST: *September 23, 1960*
LAST TELECAST: *January 6, 1961*
BROADCAST HISTORY:
Sep 1960–Jan 1961, NBC Fri 7:30–8:30
CAST:
Lt. Dan Raven .... Skip Homeier
Det. Sgt. Burke .... Dan Barton
Perry Levitt .... Quinn Redeker

The Sunset Strip in Hollywood provided the setting for this police-action series. Lt. Dan Raven and his partner Sgt. Burke were assigned by the Los Angeles sheriff's office (West Hollywood Division) to the maze of jazz spots, nightclubs, coffee houses, and other entertainment emporiums that lined the famous Strip. While covering his beat, Raven often became involved with show business personalities—such as Bobby Darin, Paul Anka, Buddy Hackett, and Gogi Grant—who worked on the Strip. The plots often revolved around these guest stars, some of whom played themselves and some of whom portrayed fictional characters. Magazine photographer Perry Levitt, who also had the Hollywood beat, was often seen where the action was.

DAN TEMPEST
see *Buccaneers, The*

DANCE FEVER
Dance
BROADCAST HISTORY:
Syndicated only
30 minutes
Produced: *1978–1987*
Released: *January 1979*
HOST:
Deney Terrio (1979–1985)
Adrian Zmed (1985–1987)
REGULARS:
Freeman King (1979–1980)
Motion—Dianne Day (1979–1980, 1981–1985)
    Flo Solder (1980–1981)
    Toni Yuskis (1979–1980)
    Janet Marie Jones (1980–1985)
    Debra Johnson (1985–1987)
    Jeanie Thompson (1985–1987)
    Debby Harris (1985–1987)
    Cindy Millican (1985–1987)

This pulsating series offered the best amateur disco dancers from around the country a chance for national exposure. Each week four couples competed and were rated by a guest panel of show-business celebrities. The top-rated team could go on to win as much as $50,000 if they made it to the annual Grand Prix finals. The music was hot and continuous, with flashing lights and spectacular routines straight out of *Saturday Night Fever*. A rock music act and the show's own dancers (Terrio and two women called "Motion") also performed each week. Freeman King was the show's "video disc jockey" during the first two seasons. When Terrio left *Dance Fever* in 1985 he was replaced by actor Adrian Zmed, who had previously been a celebrity panelist on the show.

DANCIN' TO THE HITS
Music
BROADCAST HISTORY:
Syndicated only
30 minutes
Produced: *1986*
Released: *September 1986*
HOST:
Lorenzo Lamas
DANCERS:
Sweet Dreams
        (Jeff, Cheryl, Eartha, Aurorah, Priscilla, Barry, Andrea, Bill)

Music series which emphasized the athletic and erotic dancing of its regular troupe of young, attractive dancers. Hosted by sexy Lorenzo Lamas, star of CBS' *Falcon Crest*, *Dancin' to the Hits* looked like *American Bandstand* with professional dancers and choreography. In addition to dancing to current top-40 recordings, each episode included a live song by such new performers as the S.O.S. band, the Stabilizers, Melissa Morgan, the Rainmakers, Dramarama, Jean Carn, and Howard Hewitt.

DANCING ON AIR
Instruction
FIRST TELECAST: *February 2, 1947*
LAST TELECAST: *March 2, 1947*
BROADCAST HISTORY:
Feb 1947–Mar 1947, NBC Sun 8:00–8:15
EMCEE:
Ed Sims

Dancing on Air was a five-week dance-instruction program, with instructors from the Fred Astaire Studios.

DANGER
Dramatic Anthology
FIRST TELECAST: *September 19, 1950*
LAST TELECAST: *May 31, 1955*
BROADCAST HISTORY:
Sep 1950–Aug 1954, CBS Tue 10:00–10:30
Aug 1954–Dec 1954, CBS Tue 9:30–10:00
Jan 1955–May 1955, CBS Tue 10:00–10:30
HOST/NARRATOR:
Richard Stark

The title of this series was fully descriptive of its content. Psychological dramas and various types of murder mysteries were the weekly fare in these live plays telecast from New York. "Death and

Murder," in fact, might have been an even more appropriate title, since those words kept popping up in titles of individual episodes. There were "Murder Takes the 'A' Train," "Operation Murder," "Murder's Face," "Motive for Murder," and "Inherit Murder" on the one hand, and "Death Gamble," "Death Among the Relics," "Death Beat," "Prelude to Death," "Death for the Lonely," "Flowers of Death," and "Death Signs an Autograph" on the other. The players were not particularly well known and, at the time, neither were the directors. Three of the directors subsequently did become highly successful. Yul Brynner, who worked frequently as a director in the early days of television, was the director of *Danger* when it went on the air in the fall of 1950. He was replaced early on by Sidney Lumet, who later gave way to John Frankenheimer.

Among the young performers featured on *Danger* were several who would go on to successful careers in the movies. They included John Cassavetes, James Dean, Charlton Heston, Paul Newman, Walter Matthau, Jack Lemmon, Rod Steiger, and Anthony Quinn. On the distaff side, Grace Kelly, Lee Grant, Carroll Baker, Nina Foch, Kim Stanley, and Cloris Leachman appeared.

DANGER MAN
International Intrigue
FIRST TELECAST: *April 5, 1961*
LAST TELECAST: *September 13, 1961*
BROADCAST HISTORY:
  Apr 1961–Sep 1961, CBS Wed 8:30–9:00
CAST:
  John Drake .... Patrick McGoohan

Filmed on diverse locations around the world, ranging from major European capitals to remote African jungles, *Danger Man* told of the exploits of John Drake, an internationally famous security investigator whose services were available only to governments or highly placed government officials. Working in affiliation with NATO, the suave, calculating, and highly efficient Mr. Drake was equally at home in the best restaurants or eating raw meat with a native tribe in some remote outpost as he pursued his quarry to the four corners of the earth. This British-produced series was the first of three similar series starring Patrick McGoohan to reach American audiences in the 1960s. The other two were *Secret Agent* and *The Prisoner*.

DANGEROUS ASSIGNMENT
Foreign Intrigue
BROADCAST HISTORY:
  Syndicated only
  30 minutes
  Produced: *1951–1952* (39 episodes)
  Released: *Early 1952*
CAST:
  Steve Mitchell .... Brian Donlevy

Action and intrigue in exotic places marked the exploits of Steve Mitchell, undercover agent for the U.S. government. In each episode he was dispatched by "The Commissioner" to a place like Mexico City, Casablanca, or Burma, or behind the Iron Curtain, to tidy up some international problem. The scenery was nice, but only a backdrop for violence. In the first episode, for example, he was sent to pick up a turncoat's son in Stockholm. He got slugged with an automatic, leapt from a speeding car just before it hurtled over a cliff and burst into flames, and finally zapped the villain with the bare wires of a light fixture. Nice trip.

Donlevy also starred in an NBC radio version of *Dangerous Assignment* from 1950 to 1953.

DANIEL BOONE
Western
FIRST TELECAST: *September 24, 1964*
LAST TELECAST: *August 27, 1970*
BROADCAST HISTORY:
  Sep 1964–Aug 1970, NBC Thu 7:30–8:30
CAST:
  Daniel Boone .... Fess Parker
  Yadkin (1964–1965) .... Albert Salmi
  Mingo (1964–1968) .... Ed Ames
  Rebecca Boone .... Patricia Blair
  Jemima Boone (1964–1966)
     .... Veronica Cartwright
  Israel Boone .... Darby Hinton
  Cincinnatus .... Dal McKennon
  Jericho Jones (1965–1966) ...... Robert Logan
  Gideon (1968–1969) .... Don Pedro Colley
  Gabe Cooper (1969–1970) .... Roosevelt Grier
  Josh Clements (1968–1970) ...... Jimmy Dean

Fess Parker, who gained fame portraying Davy Crockett for Walt Disney in the mid-1950s, became even more successful as another frontiersman, Daniel Boone, in the 1960s. Like Crockett, Daniel Boone was one of America's great folk heroes. He lived in the North Carolina-Tennessee-Kentucky area just before and during the Revolutionary War, and his exploits were legendary. The stories in this series revolved around Boone's encounters with Indians, both friendly and hostile, his survey work and pioneering expeditions, and his relationships with family and friends.

The family included his wife Rebecca, his daughter Jemima, and his son Israel. The friends were originally his traveling companion Yadkin, his Indian friend Mingo, and Cincinnatus, tavernkeeper of Boonesborough, Daniel's home base. Only Cincinnatus remained through the entire six-year run of the show. Later added to the cast were young pioneer Jericho Jones; Gideon, a black Indian; Josh Clements, a fur trapper; and Gabe Cooper, a runaway slave living with the Indians.

DANNY KAYE SHOW, THE
Musical Variety
FIRST TELECAST: *September 25, 1963*
LAST TELECAST: *June 7, 1967*

Sep 1963–Jun 1967, CBS Wed 10:00–11:00 (OS)

REGULARS:
Danny Kaye
Harvey Korman (1964–1967)
Joyce Van Patten (1964–1967)
Laurie Ichino (1964–1965)
Victoria Meyerink (1964–1967)
The Johnny Mann Singers (1963–1964)
The Earl Brown Singers (1964–1967)
The Tony Charmoli Dancers
Paul Weston and His Orchestra

The multitalented Danny Kaye starred for four seasons in his own musical comedy-variety series on CBS. He did monologues, pantomime, and comedy sketches; he sang, danced, and even played an instrument or two. The most remarkable aspect of the series was its use of inventive comedy sketches with Danny's guest stars. Although neither Harvey Korman nor Joyce Van Patten appeared on every episode during the three years in which they frequented the series, they were given featured-performer status by CBS in all press releases about the show, as were child performers Laurie Ichino and Victoria Meyerink.

DANNY THOMAS HOUR, THE

Various

FIRST TELECAST: *September 11, 1967*
LAST TELECAST: *June 10, 1968*
BROADCAST HISTORY:
Sep 1967–Jun 1968, NBC Mon 9:00–10:00
HOST/STAR:
Danny Thomas

This weekly series was a potpourri of different entertainment forms. Included were musical-variety specials, dramatic plays, and light comedies. Danny Thomas starred in all the musical-variety episodes and comedies and was host of the serious dramas. A number of comedies were long versions of his own previous hit series, *Make Room for Daddy (The Danny Thomas Show)*.

DANNY THOMAS SHOW, THE

Situation Comedy

FIRST TELECAST: *September 29, 1953*
LAST TELECAST: *September 2, 1971*
BROADCAST HISTORY:
Sep 1953–Jun 1956, ABC Tue 9:00–9:30
Oct 1956–Feb 1957, ABC Mon 8:00–8:30
Feb 1957–Jul 1957, ABC Thu 9:00–9:30
Oct 1957–Sep 1964, CBS Mon 9:00–9:30 (OS)
Apr 1965–Sep 1965, CBS Mon 9:30–10:00
Sep 1970–Jan 1971, ABC Wed 8:00–8:30
Jan 1971–Sep 1971, ABC Thu 9:00–9:30
CAST:
Danny Williams .... Danny Thomas
Mrs. Margaret Williams (1953–1956)
.... Jean Hagen
Mrs. Kathy Williams ("Clancey") (1957–1971)
.... Marjorie Lord

Rusty Williams .... Rusty Hamer
Terry Williams (1953–1958) ... Sherry Jackson
Terry Williams (1959–1960) ... Penney Parker
Linda Williams (1957–1971)

.... Angela Cartwright
Louise (1953–1964) .... Amanda Randolph
Horace (1953–1954)........ Horace McMahon
Benny (1953–1957)................ Ben Lessy
Jesse Leeds (1955–1957).......... Jesse White
Uncle Tonoose (1958–1971)..... Hans Conried
Phil Brokaw (1959–1961).... Sheldon Leonard
Pat Hannigan (1959–1960).. Pat Harrington, Jr.
Gina (1959) .... Annette Funicello
"Uncle Charley" Halper (1959–1971)
.... Sid Melton
Bunny Halper (1961–1964) .... Pat Carroll
Rosey Robbins (1970–1971) .. Roosevelt Grier
Michael (1970–1971)........ Michael Hughes
Henry (1970–1971)
.... Stanley Myron Handleman
THEME:
"Danny Boy" ("Londonderry Air")

Danny Thomas' first major exposure on television had been as one of the hosts of NBC's *All Star Revue*. His nightclub routine was a flop on TV, as a result of which he blasted the new medium as being suitable "only for idiots" and vowed never to return. But return he did, in 1953, with one of the longest-running family comedies of the 1950s and 1960s. *Make Room for Daddy*, as it was called for its first three seasons, was a reflection of Danny's own life as an entertainer and the problems created by his frequent absences from his children. The title came from a phrase used in the real-life Thomas household: whenever Danny returned home from a tour, his children had to shift bedrooms, to "make room for Daddy." In the series, Danny played nightclub entertainer Danny Williams, a sometimes loud but ultimately softhearted lord of the household, who was constantly being upstaged by his bratty but lovable kids. The kids were, at the outset, 6-year-old Rusty and 11-year-old Terry. Jean Hagen played Danny's loving wife, Margaret.

A number of major changes took place as the show matured. In 1956 Jean Hagen quit. Instead of replacing her, Danny had her written out of the show as having died, which led to a season (1956–1957) of his courting eligible women—with frequent assistance from the kids. He eventually proposed to an Irish lass, Kathy. The wedding did not take place on the show, but when the program returned in the fall of 1957 Danny and Kathy were just returning from their honeymoon, and little Linda, Kathy's daughter by a previous marriage, had also joined the Williams household.

Sherry Jackson left the cast in 1958. At first the character she played, Terry, was supposed to be away at school, but in 1959 a new actress assumed the role. Terry then had a season-long courtship with a young nightclub performer named Pat Hannigan, whom she eventually married. Terry then left the household for good.

A number of other youngsters also passed through the series, including Gina, a foreign exchange student living in the Williams home. Piccola Pupa, a young Italian singer discovered by Danny, was also seen in a few episodes. Other regulars included a succession of Danny's agents, the first played by Horace McMahon, later ones by Jesse White—who simultaneously was appearing as the agent on *Private Secretary*—and Sheldon Leonard. (Leonard was the real-life producer of *The Danny Thomas Show* and had appeared in 1953 episodes as Danny's masseur.) Benny was Danny's original accompanist, Louise the family housekeeper, and Charley Halper the owner of the Copa Club, where Danny Williams frequently performed.

No doubt the most memorable regular was Hans Conried in the role of Uncle Tonoose, eccentric patriarch of the Williams family. Conried had previously been seen in several guest roles on the show, including those of ne'er-do-well Cousin Carl, Uncle Oscar, and visiting Derik Campbell, before he turned up as Tonoose in a fall 1958 telecast. The role was perfect, and he continued to appear in it, periodically, for the rest of the series' run. Others who made guest appearances were songwriter Harry Ruby as himself, Bill Dana as José Jiminez, the elevator operator, and many top names from the entertainment world, playing themselves.

The Danny Thomas Show ended its original run in 1964, although repeat telecasts were seen on CBS during 1965. Then in 1970 Danny Williams returned in a new series called *Danny Thomas in Make Room for Granddaddy*, complete with Kathy, Rusty (now 23 and married), and Linda (now 17) from the original cast. A newcomer was a roguishly cute little terror named Michael, age 6. Michael made Danny the "Granddaddy," since he was cast as Terry's son, left with the Williamses while Terry and her soldier husband were abroad. Charley Halper and Uncle Tonoose were back, joined by a new accompanist (played by ex-football star Roosevelt Grier) and Henry, the neurotic elevator operator in Danny's apartment building. Despite guest appearances by such stars as Bob Hope, Frank Sinatra, Milton Berle, and Lucille Ball, the format was rather old-hat for the 1970s, and *Make Room for Granddaddy* expired after a single season.

NBC aired reruns of *The Danny Thomas Show*, under the title *Make Room for Daddy*, as part of its weekday daytime lineup from October 1960–March 1965 and as part of its Saturday morning lineup from September 1961–October 1964.

DANTE
Mystery Adventure
FIRST TELECAST: *October 3, 1960*
LAST TELECAST: *April 10, 1961*
BROADCAST HISTORY:
Oct 1960–Apr 1961, NBC Mon 9:30–10:00

CAST:
Willie Dante .... Howard Duff
Stewart Styles .... Alan Mowbray
Biff .... Tom D'Andrea
Inspector Loper .... James Nolan

Adventurer Willie Dante had a history of running clip joints and gambling casinos around the country, a reputation he planned to change when he opened his own legitimate nightclub in San Francisco. With him were his two sidekicks from the gambling days, Biff the bartender and Stewart the maître d'. Unfortunately, neither the police nor the underworld believed that Dante had really gone straight, and his confrontations with both provided much of the action of the show. Played in a tongue-in-cheek manner, *Dante* had more humor than violence. The contrast between the three leads—suave, urbane, ladies' man Willie Dante; Biff, who kept bringing up incidents from their sordid past; and Stewart, whose proper British image did not fit with his encyclopedic knowledge of underworld characters and activities—was the source of much of the humor.

The role of Willie Dante had been played by Dick Powell in a number of episodes of *Four Star Playhouse* during the 1950s.

DARK ADVENTURE
see *ABC Dramatic Shorts—1952-1953*

DARK OF NIGHT
Dramatic Anthology
FIRST TELECAST: *October 10, 1952*
LAST TELECAST: *May 1, 1953*
BROADCAST HISTORY:
Oct 1952–May 1953, DUM Fri 8:30–9:00

The stars of this unusual drama series were its locations. *Dark of Night* was telecast live each week from locations all over the New York City area, such as stores, factories, railroad yards, docks, and hospitals. Apparently most of the budget was used in getting the cameras and crew to the locations, since the performers and writers were for the most part unknown. Among the starring locations were Brentano's Book Store on Fifth Avenue, a hangar at Idlewild (now Kennedy) Airport, an old English-style castle in Paterson, New Jersey, the Parke-Bernet art galleries in Manhattan, a Coca-Cola bottling plant, a coffee company (for a comedy about the trials of a coffee taster), the F. & M. Shaeffer Brewing Company, and the American Red Cross Blood Bank. Appropriately, the final telecast was from the DuMont television set factory in East Paterson, New Jersey.

During a two-month period, from mid-November 1952 to mid-January 1953, *Dark of Night* was seen on alternate weeks.

DARKROOM
Occult Anthology
FIRST TELECAST: *November 27, 1981*

185

LAST TELECAST: *July 8, 1982*
BROADCAST HISTORY:
   Nov 1981–Jan 1982, ABC Fri 9:00–10:00
   Jul 1982, ABC Thu 8:00–9:00
HOST:
   James Coburn

An imaginative teenager suspects that her sister's handsome boyfriend is a vampire; a Vietnam veteran gives his son an army of toy soldiers, only to have them come to life and attack him; a ruthless young hoodlum finds himself stalked by an eerie black cat; a French rogue tries to escape the guillotine by an ingenious plot to execute the executioner. Stories of suspense and terror characterized this short-run anthology series, which featured different guest stars each week. Among those appearing were Steve Allen, Esther Rolle, Lawrence-Hilton Jacobs, David Carradine, and June Lockhart.

DATE WITH JUDY, A
   Situation Comedy
FIRST TELECAST: *July 10, 1952*
LAST TELECAST: *September 30, 1953*
BROADCAST HISTORY:
   Jul 1952–Oct 1952, ABC Thu 8:00–8:30
   Jan 1953–Sep 1953, ABC Wed 7:30–8:00
CAST:
   Judy Foster .... Mary Linn Beller
   Melvyn Foster .... John Gibson
   Dora Foster .... Flora Campbell
   Randolph Foster .... Peter Avramo
   Oogie Pringle .... Jimmy Sommers
WRITER:
   Aleen Leslie

The trials of a hyperactive bobbysoxer and her harassed parents were the subject of this live situation comedy, which was the TV version of a popular radio series begun in 1941. In addition to Judy and her sedate, middle-class parents, the characters included her pesky younger brother Randolph and her boyfriend Oogie. First seen as a Saturday daytime series on June 2, 1951 (with Pat Crowley as Judy), *A Date with Judy* changed casts and moved to prime time in July 1952.

DATE WITH THE ANGELS
   Situation Comedy
FIRST TELECAST: *May 10, 1957*
LAST TELECAST: *January 29, 1958*
BROADCAST HISTORY:
   May 1957–Jun 1957, ABC Fri 10:00–10:30
   Jul 1957–Dec 1957, ABC Fri 9:30–10:00
   Jan 1958, ABC Wed 9:30–10:00
CAST:
   Vicki Angel .... Betty White
   Gus Angel .... Bill Williams
   Wilma Clemson .... Natalie Masters
   George Clemson .... Roy Engle
   Mrs. Cassie Murphy .... Maudie Prickett
   Mr. Murphy (Murph) .... Richard Reeves

   Mrs. Drake .... Lillian Bronson
   Dr. Gordon .... Gage Clark
   Mr. Finley .... Burt Mustin
   Roger Finley .... Richard Deacon
   Wheeler .... Jimmy Boyd

Betty White starred in this domestic comedy about a new bride and her husband, an insurance salesman. An unusually wide assortment of neighbors and friends passed through the series, usually serving as foils for one of Vicki's or Gus' schemes. Most frequently seen were their friend Murph, the Clemsons, and an erratic neighbor, Mr. Finley. Jimmy Boyd appeared periodically as their teenage nephew Wheeler.

DATELINE EUROPE
   see *Foreign Intrigue*

DATING GAME, THE
   Quiz/Audience Participation
FIRST TELECAST: *October 6, 1966*
LAST TELECAST: *January 17, 1970*
BROADCAST HISTORY:
   Oct 1966–Jan 1967, ABC Thu 8:30–9:00
   Jan 1967–Jan 1970, ABC Sat 7:30–8:00
HOST:
   Jim Lange
PRODUCER:
   Chuck Barris

The premise of *The Dating Game* was to take one young person plus three "candidates" of the opposite sex and arrange a date. There were two rounds in each show, one in which a girl asked questions of three guys, and one in which a guy asked questions of three girls. The questioner could not see the three candidates, which eliminated appearance as a consideration. At the end of each round the questioner picked the date he or she thought would be most interesting, and the newly matched pair were then sent off on a night on the town or an expense-paid trip to some exotic fun spot. (Follow-up reports in later months told how many of these first dates blossomed into romance and marriage.) The questions, which were prepared by the show's staff, were generally of the titillating variety.

Originally a daytime program on ABC, *The Dating Game* came to prime time as a stop-gap replacement for *The Tammy Grimes Show,* the first casualty of the 1966–1967 season. It was popular enough to remain on the nighttime lineup for more than three years, after which it continued in daytime only. The daytime edition of *The Dating Game* ran on ABC from December 1965 to July 1973. It then turned up in a number of syndicated versions. Jim Lange hosted the first two, during the 1973–1974 season and from 1977–1980. In the fall of 1986 Elaine Joyce served as hostess of *The New Dating Game.* A year later it had a new name, *The All New Dating Game;* a new host, Jeff MacGregor; and a modified format. In addition to

186

the quiz segments, some of the daters returned together to tell all about their date, in a manner similar to the highly successful syndicated daytime series *Love Connection.*

For the companion program by the same producers, which ran in the adjacent time slot on Saturday night, see *The Newlywed Game.*

DAVE GARROWAY SHOW, THE
see *Garroway at Large*

DAVE KING SHOW, THE
see *Kraft Music Hall Presents the Dave King Show*

DAVID BRINKLEY'S JOURNAL
Documentary
FIRST TELECAST: *October 11, 1961*
LAST TELECAST: *August 26, 1963*
BROADCAST HISTORY:
  Oct 1961–Sep 1962, NBC Wed 10:30–11:00
  Oct 1962–Aug 1963, NBC Mon 10:00–10:30
COMMENTATOR:
  David Brinkley

David Brinkley, who had been the coanchor of NBC's nightly *Huntley-Brinkley Report* since 1956, hosted his own prime-time documentary series in the early 1960s. From one to three stories were examined each week, each of them treated from Brinkley's own unique perspective. His caustic wit and incisive observations gave the program a very personal flavor, quite different from the run of TV documentaries. The subject matter ranged from light pieces on professional wrestler Antonino Rocca, the birth of a Broadway musical, and after-dinner speeches by political figures, to probing evaluations of domestic and foreign political issues.

The critical response to *David Brinkley's Journal* was positive, and the program won Emmy Awards in both 1962 and 1963 as the best public-affairs series on television. However, viewership was low and the series survived as a weekly entry for only two seasons. It was later seen on an occasional basis, until 1965.

DAVID CASSIDY—MAN UNDERCOVER
Police Drama
FIRST TELECAST: *November 2, 1978*
LAST TELECAST: *August 2, 1979*
BROADCAST HISTORY:
  Nov 1978–Jan 1979, NBC Thu 10:00–11:00
  Jul 1979–Aug 1979, NBC Thu 10:00–11:00
CAST:
  Officer Dan Shay .... David Cassidy
  Joanne Shay .... Wendy Rastatter
  Cindy Shay .... Elizabeth Reddin
  Sgt. Walt Abrams .... Simon Oakland
  Officer T. J. Epps .... Ray Vitte
  Officer Paul Sanchez ..... Michael A. Salcido

Dan Shay was a policeman in his late 20s working as part of an undercover team headed by Sgt.

Abrams. As an undercover cop, Dan generally played the youth angle, infiltrating a gang of young bank robbers, posing as a college student to crack an illegal adoption racket, pretending to be a drug addict to nail a doctor selling narcotics prescriptions. Dan's wife Joanne worried constantly, but kept a stiff upper lip for the sake of their little girl, Cindy. The setting for this series, as with most televised police shows over the years, was Los Angeles.

DAVID FROST REVUE, THE
Comedy
BROADCAST HISTORY:
  Syndicated only
  30 minutes
  Produced: *1971–1973* (52 episodes)
  Released: *Fall 1971*
REGULARS:
  David Frost
  Marcia Rodd
  Jack Gilford
  Jim Catusi
  George S. Irving
  Lynn Lipton
  Cleavon Little
  Whitney Blake

In this program of satire, David Frost returned to the format that had made him famous. Each week's skits concentrated on a different subject, such as sports, medicine, women's lib, the telephone company, or TV talk shows. There were barbs and blackouts, but little of the topical bite with which Frost had made his name. Celebrity guests included Alan Alda, Lucille Ball, Jack Klugman, and Arte Johnson.

DAVID FROST SHOW, THE
Talk
BROADCAST HISTORY:
  Syndicated only
  90 minutes
  Produced: *1969–1972*
  Released: *Summer 1969*
REGULARS:
  David Frost
  Billy Taylor Orchestra

David Frost, the *enfant terrible* of British and American political satire in the 1960s (see *That Was The Week That Was*), here tried to become a celebrity talk-show host in the Merv Griffin-Johnny Carson mold. The program originated in New York and ran 60 to 90 minutes, depending on the local station. Guests ranged across the map, and included the likes of Paul Newman, Gore Vidal, Billy Graham, Averill Harriman, and Dr. Timothy Leary, musicians Pete Seeger, James Brown, Tex Ritter, and the Rolling Stones, actors Burt Reynolds, Shirley MacLaine, and Elizabeth Taylor, comics Rich Little and Henny Youngman, *et al.* A minor tempest raged among critics as to whether Frost had "sold out," but all remarked on his singular interviewing style: hunched forward, staring at the guest with rapt attention, like a "bemused and slightly undernourished bird of prey transfixed by a being it finds too fascinating to attack" (in the words of Peter Heller). He seemed constantly enthralled by everyone, regularly exclaiming, "Marvelous! Smashing! Terrific! It's been a *joy* having you here!"

The program ran for three years, while Frost jetted back and forth across the Atlantic (he was simultaneously hosting a weekly variety show in England). Produced by the Westinghouse station group, *The David Frost Show* got its start when Merv Griffin left afternoon and evening syndication for a late-night network run on CBS; Frost filled the gap on many stations. When Griffin returned to local syndication in 1972, Frost folded.

DAVID NIVEN SHOW, THE
Dramatic Anthology
FIRST TELECAST: *April 7, 1959*
LAST TELECAST: *September 15, 1959*
BROADCAST HISTORY:
   Apr 1959–Sep 1959, NBC Tue 10:00–10:30
HOST:
   David Niven

David Niven appeared before each episode of this summer anthology series to introduce the drama being presented, and personally starred in one of the episodes.

DAVID STEINBERG SHOW, THE
Comedy Variety
FIRST TELECAST: *July 19, 1972*
LAST TELECAST: *August 16, 1972*
BROADCAST HISTORY:
   Jul 1972–Aug 1972, CBS Wed 8:00–9:00
REGULAR:
   David Steinberg

Controversial comedian David Steinberg was referred to in *TV Guide* as "off beat, racy, outrageous and establishment-baiting—all of which makes him a particular favorite of the young and disenchanted." In 1972 he starred in his own summer comedy series, introducing two or three guest stars each week and performing with them.

DAVID SUSSKIND SHOW, THE
Talk
BROADCAST HISTORY:
   Syndicated only
   2 hours
   Produced: *1958–1987*
   Released: *1961*
HOST:
   David Susskind

David Susskind talked on television for a very long time. An aggressive former talent agent and Broadway and TV producer (responsible for

many of the top TV plays of the 1950s), he began the chatter in October 1958 with a local show in New York. It was called *Open End,* because it started at 11 P.M. and ran until the subject—or participants—were exhausted (which led unkind critics to dub it "Open Mouth"). The guests were literate, provocative, and often controversial. In perhaps his most celebrated confrontation, Susskind took on Nikita Khrushchev during the latter's visit to the U.S. in 1960; the leader of the Communist world made mincemeat of him.

Over the years, topics ranged across all sorts of social problems (race relations, the draft, organized crime, etc.) as well as less weighty subjects such as clairvoyants, sex-change operations, and testing your I.Q. In the early 1960s the program was mercifully cut to two hours (though the name remained *Open End* for several years more), and went into national syndication. In later years it was seen largely on PBS stations, although it was on commercial channels in some cities.

Mr. Susskind passed away in 1987.

DAY BY DAY
Situation Comedy
FIRST TELECAST: *February 29, 1988*
LAST TELECAST:
BROADCAST HISTORY:
   Feb 1988–Mar 1988, NBC Mon/Thu 8:30–9:00
   Mar 1988–May 1988, NBC Sun 8:30–9:00
CAST:
   Brian Harper .... Douglas Sheehan
   Kate Harper .... Linda Kelsey
   Ross Harper .... C.B. Barnes
   Eileen Swift .... Julia Louis-Dreyfus
   Kristin Carlson ...... Courtney Thorne-Smith
   Molly .... Thora
   Blake .... Garrett Taylor
   Dana............................. J.P. Dizon
   Justin O'Donnell .... Chris Finefrock
   Sammy Schrom .... Robert Chavez
   Buddy Schrom .... Mark Gordon
   Stiv Miltman .... Gino de Mauro
THEME:
   "Day By Day" by Sammy Cahn, Axel Stordahl, and Paul Weston (1945 popular song), sung by Clydine Jackson

One of the wave of "yuppie comedies" that swept TV in the late '80s, *Day By Day* was about a couple of suburban overachievers who dropped out and opened a daycare center in their home. Why? Well, with the arrival of their second child, stockbroker Brian and his wife Kate, a lawyer, decided that they were missing their children's best years and wanted to be at home. Gangly teenager Ross, who enjoyed his independence and girl chasing, was not sure that was such a good idea—especially the "quality time" his underfoot dad now wanted to spend with him. But there were compensations, notably the sexy 19-year-old assistant Kristin whom his parents had hired to help run the center.

Eileen, Brian's single and sarcastic former business associate, could not understand the Harpers' decision at all (observing the children in organized activities: "Oh, you've got them to march around in a circle. Are you going to enter them in a show?"). Numerous cute kids were seen, including super-smart little Molly, whom the Harpers hoped would not turn out as they almost had.

DAY DREAMING WITH LARAINE DAY
Interviews/Variety
FIRST TELECAST: *May 17, 1951*
LAST TELECAST: *July 19, 1951*
BROADCAST HISTORY:
  May 1951–Jul 1951, ABC Thu 7:15–7:30
HOSTESS:
  Laraine Day

Celebrity interviews, songs, and Broadway and Hollywood gossip with actress Laraine Day were the features of this program. Among other things, Miss Day asked her guests to describe alternative careers they might prefer to have chosen. A similar series with Miss Day ran concurrently on Saturday afternoons.

DAY IN COURT
see *Accused*

DAYS AND NIGHTS OF MOLLY DODD, THE
Comedy/Drama
FIRST TELECAST: *May 21, 1987*
LAST TELECAST:
BROADCAST HISTORY:
  May 1987–Aug 1987, NBC Thu 9:30–10:00
  Mar 1988–Apr 1988, NBC Thu 9:30–10:00
  May 1988–Jun 1988, NBC Wed 9:00–9:30
  Jun 1988–   , NBC Wed 9:30–10:00
CAST:
  Molly Dodd .... Blair Brown
  Florence Bickford .... Allyn Ann McLerie
  Fred Dodd .... William Converse-Roberts
  Mamie Grolnick .... Sandy Faison
  Davey McQuinn .... James Greene
  Nina Shapiro .... Maureen Anderman
  Dennis Widmer............... Victor Garber
  Moss Goodman (1988–   )
   .... David Strathairn

Critics loved this mellow, reality-based "dramedy" (combination drama and comedy) about the life and times of an attractive divorced woman in her mid-30s, living in New York City. Molly spent a good deal of time musing about herself—her love life, her goals, her ever-changing career, her apartment, her . . . you get the idea. Molly changed jobs rather often. First she was a singer with Fred Dodd's band, then she sold real estate (Dennis was her boss), and then worked at a Greenwich Village book store (where Moss was the boss). All of her bosses were also sometime love interests. Fred was her irresponsible ex-husband, a jazz saxophone player, who kept hanging around; Florence her worrywart mother; Mamie her unhappily married sister; Davey the philosophical elevator operator; and Nina her best friend.

Producer Jay Tarses appeared occasionally as the garbageman, Nick Donatello.

DEADLINE FOR ACTION
see *Wire Service*

DEALER'S CHOICE
Quiz/Audience Participation
BROADCAST HISTORY:
  Syndicated only
  30 minutes
  Produced: *1973–1975*
  Released: *Early 1974*
HOST:
  Bob Hastings
  Jack Clark

Syndicated game show taped at the Tropicana Hotel in Las Vegas, and built around various gambling-casino games—blackjack, roulette, slot machines, etc. Garish surroundings and the betting fever prevalent in Las Vegas helped add excitement. The original host, Bob Hastings, was later replaced by Jack Clark.

DEAN MARTIN COMEDY WORLD, THE
Comedy Variety
FIRST TELECAST: *June 6, 1974*
LAST TELECAST: *August 15, 1974*
BROADCAST HISTORY:
  Jun 1974–Aug 1974, NBC Thu 10:00–11:00
HOSTS:
  Jackie Cooper
  Nipsey Russell
  Barbara Feldon

Jackie Cooper served as "anchorman in the control room from the center of the comedy world," coordinating and introducing many of the comedy acts that appeared on this summer replacement for *The Dean Martin Comedy Hour*. The show included taped performances by new comedy talent from all over the world, excerpts from both old and new comedy films, and performances by well-established comedy stars. Nipsey Russell and Barbara Feldon were on location to do introductions from such diverse spots as London, Hollywood, and San Francisco.

DEAN MARTIN PRESENTS
Musical Variety
FIRST TELECAST: *June 20, 1968*
LAST TELECAST: *September 6, 1973*
BROADCAST HISTORY:
  Jun 1968–Sep 1968, NBC Thu 10:00–11:00
  Jul 1969–Sep 1969, NBC Thu 10:00–11:00
  Jul 1970–Sep 1970, NBC Thu 10:00–11:00
  Jul 1972–Sep 1972, NBC Thu 10:00–11:00
  Jul 1973–Sep 1973, NBC Thu 10:00–11:00

Joey Heatherton (1968)
Frank Sinatra, Jr. (1968)
Paul Lynde (1968–1969)
The Golddiggers (1968–1970)
Barbara Heller (1968)
Stu Gilliam (1968)
Stanley Myron Handleman (1968, 1969)
Skiles and Henderson (1968)
Times Square Two (1968)
Gail Martin (1969)
Allison McKay (1969)
Darleen Carr (1969)
Fiore and Eldridge (1969)
Lou Rawls (1969)
Tommy Tune (1969–1970)
Albert Brooks (1969)
Danny Lockin (1969)
Joyce Ames (1969)
Charles Nelson Reilly (1970)
Marty Feldman (1970)
Julian Chagrin (1970)
Bobby Darin (1972)
Rip Taylor (1972)
Steve Landesberg (1972)
Sara Hankboner (1972)
Cathy Cahill (1972)
Dick Bakalyan (1972)
Schnecklegruber (1972)
Loretta Lynn (1973)
Lynn Anderson (1973)
Jerry Reed (1973)
Ray Stevens (1973)
Les Brown and His Band (1968–1969)
The Jack Parnell Orchestra (1970)
The Eddie Karam Orchestra (1972)

Dean Martin Presents . . . was the umbrella title for a series of summer replacements for *The Dean Martin Show*. They were all musical variety shows featuring mostly young talent; their actual titles were as follows:

1968—*Dean Martin Presents the Golddiggers*
1969—*Dean Martin Presents the Golddiggers*
1970—*Dean Martin Presents the Golddiggers in London*
1972—*Dean Martin Presents the Bobby Darin Amusement Co.*
1973—*Dean Martin Presents Music Country*

The regular casts of these summer shows remained relatively stable through 1972. The country and western version aired during the summer of 1973 had, in addition to the four regulars who appeared in almost every episode, a large number of country music performers who appeared irregularly. The Golddiggers also had a syndicated variety show in 1971.

DEAN MARTIN SHOW, THE
Comedy Variety
FIRST TELECAST: *September 16, 1965*
LAST TELECAST: *May 24, 1974*

190

BROADCAST HISTORY:
Sep 1965–Jul 1973, NBC Thu 10:00–11:00 (OS)
Sep 1973–May 1974, NBC Fri 10:00–11:00
REGULARS:
Dean Martin
The Golddiggers (1967–1971)
The Ding-a-Ling Sisters (1970–1973)
Kay Medford (1970–1973)
Lou Jacobi (1971–1973)
Marian Mercer (1971–1972)
Tom Bosley (1971–1972)
Dom DeLuise (1972–1973)
Nipsey Russell (1972–1973)
Rodney Dangerfield (1972–1973)
Ken Lane
Les Brown and His Band

Singer-comedian Dean Martin was host and star of this long-lived variety hour, which was for most of its run a fixture on the NBC Thursday night lineup. At first Dean had no regular supporting cast other than his accompanist, pianist Ken Lane. Guest stars were featured each week in comedy skits and songs, both alone and with Dean. Some of the young talent appearing during the regular season also starred in Dean's summer replacement series, *The Dean Martin Summer Show* and later *Dean Martin Presents*. A bevy of pretty young dancers called the Golddiggers were added as regulars in 1967, and four of these later became the Ding-a-Ling Sisters (1970–1973).

Beginning in 1970 a supporting cast of comics and singers was gradually assembled around Dean, some of whom appeared regularly (see credits) and others occasionally, such as Foster Brooks with his "drunk" routine. The hallmark of the show remained Dean's own easy informality, as he welcomed guests into his cozy living room through the ever-present door, or sang or clowned beside (or on, or under) Ken Lane's grand piano. In fact, a stipulation in Dean's contract helped foster this air of informality by allowing Dean not to show up until the day of the taping each week, when the show would be done with only minimal rehearsal.

In 1973 the title and format were changed, as well as the time slot. The new title was *The Dean Martin Comedy Hour*, and Dean and Ken Lane were once again the only regulars. Two new features were added. The first was a country music spot, with top-name country performers, to hold some of the audience that had been attracted to Dean's summer replacement in 1973, *Dean Martin Presents Music Country*. The second was the "Man of the Week Celebrity Roast," in which several celebrities seated at a banquet dais tossed comic insults at the guest of honor. This feature proved so popular that after Dean's regular series ended in 1974, the "roasts" continued on NBC as a series of occasional specials.

DEAN MARTIN SUMMER SHOW, THE
Variety

FIRST TELECAST: *June 16, 1966*
LAST TELECAST: *August 19, 1971*
BROADCAST HISTORY:
  Jun 1966–Sep 1966, NBC Thu 10:00–11:00
  Jun 1967–Sep 1967, NBC Thu 10:00–11:00
  Jul 1971–Aug 1971, NBC Thu 10:00–11:00
REGULARS:
  Dan Rowan (1966)
  Dick Martin (1966)
  Dom DeLuise (1966)
  Lainie Kazan (1966)
  Frankie Randall (1966)
  Judi Rolin (1966)
  Wisa D'Orso (1966)
  Vic Damone (1967)
  Carol Lawrence (1967)
  Gail Martin (1967)
  Don Cherry (1967)
  Les Brown and His Band

Nearly two years before their hit *Laugh-In,* comedians Dan Rowan and Dick Martin starred as the 1966 summer replacements for Dean Martin. Because of the stars, the emphasis was more on comedy than on music. The 1967 replacement, however, which was aired under the title *The Dean Martin Summer Show Starring Your Host Vic Damone,* relied more on music. Selected episodes of the Vic Damone series were rerun as Dean's summer replacement during the summer of 1971.

DEAR DETECTIVE
Police Drama
FIRST TELECAST: *March 28, 1979*
LAST TELECAST: *April 18, 1979*
BROADCAST HISTORY:
  Mar 1979–Apr 1979, CBS Wed 9:00–10:00
CAST:
  Det. Sgt. Kate Hudson .... Brenda Vaccaro
  Prof. Richard Weyland ... Arlen Dean Snyder
  Det. Brock .... Michael McRae
  Det. Clay .... John Dennis Johnston
  Det. Chuck Morris .... Jack Ging
  Det. Schwartz .... Ron Silver
  Mrs. Hudson .... Lesley Woods
  Lisa .... Jet Yardum
  Capt. Gorcey .... M. Emmet Walsh

Kate Hudson juggled three roles—policewoman, lover, and mother—in this short-lived series. Det. Sgt. Hudson was a dedicated professional, who also happened to be in love with Prof. Richard Weyland, a teacher of English literature at U.C.-L.A. The fact that she was always "on call" complicated their relationship, as did his distinct lack of enthusiasm for the police and their methods. Kate was also saddled with the responsibility of raising young Lisa, her daughter from a dissolved marriage.

DEAR PHOEBE
Situation Comedy

FIRST TELECAST: *September 10, 1954*
LAST TELECAST: *September 11, 1956*
BROADCAST HISTORY:
  Sep 1954–Sep 1955, NBC Fri 9:30–10:00
  Jun 1956–Sep 1956, NBC Tue 8:00–8:30
CAST:
  Bill Hastings .... Peter Lawford
  Mickey Riley .... Marcia Henderson
  Mr. Fosdick .... Charles Lane
  Humphrey Humpsteader .... Joe Corey

In this comedy, a college instructor gave up teaching to become the writer of the advice-to-the-lovelorn column in The *Los Angeles Daily Blade.* Bill Hastings, who wrote under the name Phoebe Goodheart, had a lovelorn admirer of his own in the person of the paper's female sports writer, Mickey Riley. Mickey tried to hide her affection by being extremely competitive with Bill for choice assignments from Mr. Fosdick, the flinty old managing editor. Bill made no secret of his love for Mickey, however, and many of the episodes developed around their rocky romance. Humphrey Humpsteader was the typical copyboy trying to make it in the newspaper game. The 1956 edition of *Dear Phoebe* was composed entirely of reruns.

DEATH VALLEY DAYS
Western Anthology
BROADCAST HISTORY:
  Syndicated only
  30 minutes
  Produced: *1952–1975* (558 episodes)
  Released: *Fall 1952*
HOST:
  Stanley Andrews ("The Old Ranger")
    (1952–1965)
  Ronald Reagan (1965–1966)
  Robert Taylor (1966–1968)
  Dale Robertson (1968–1972)
  Merle Haggard (1975)

This modestly produced but very popular anthology was one of the longest-running series in the history of television—and of radio. It began on radio in 1930, as a means of promoting the products of sponsor 20 Mule Team Borax. The stories were all based in fact, and revolved around the legends and lore of Death Valley, California, where borax was mined. Mostly they tended to be human-interest stories, sometimes little more than vignettes, from the days when miners and homesteaders first fanned across the western United States in search of a better life. There was both gentle comedy and drama, for example the story of the Bennett-Arcane party trapped in the sweltering, arid valley in 1849; that of a prospector who bought a white hearse believing that it was a pleasure vehicle; and that of Tiger Lil, the queen of Virginia City in gold-rush days. Hundreds of actors appeared in the series, most of them not big names; the emphasis was clearly on the story.

The only regular, in fact, was the host and narrator, originally Stanley Andrews as "The Old Ranger." When Andrews left the series in the mid-1960s he was succeeded by a number of hosts, including Ronald Reagan, who dropped out after he was elected governor of California in 1966. Other familiar aspects of the show were the opening bugle call, the scenes of the 20-mule team hauling the borax wagons out of the desert, and Rosemary DeCamp doing the homey commercials for the product. Nearly 600 episodes were filmed, most of them on location in Death Valley.

Death Valley Days was created in 1930 by Ruth Woodman, a New York advertising-agency script-writer who had never seen the place. After the series went on the air she became fascinated with the area, and made many trips there to gather lore and ideas for stories. She even found a real "old ranger," a grizzled old desert rat named Wash Cahill, who seemed to know everybody and everything in the valley, and who served as her guide on many of the trips. For Mrs. Woodman, *Death Valley Days* became a career, and she wrote scripts throughout its long radio run (1930–1945) and when it began on TV as well. In 1960 she claimed that there had never been a script without a solid basis in fact. When asked about the show's extraordinary durability, she remarked, "Sometimes it seems it will go on forever."

Death Valley Days has been seen in reruns under a variety of titles and with various hosts, including *Call of the West* (John Payne), *Frontier Adventure* (Dale Robertson), *The Pioneers* (Will Rogers, Jr.), *Trails West* (Ray Milland), and *Western Star Theatre* (Rory Calhoun).

DEBBIE REYNOLDS SHOW, THE
Situation Comedy
FIRST TELECAST: *September 16, 1969*
LAST TELECAST: *September 1, 1970*
BROADCAST HISTORY:
    Sep 1969–Sep 1970, NBC Tue 8:00–8:30
CAST:
    Debbie Thompson.......... Debbie Reynolds
    Jim Thompson .... Don Chastain
    Charlotte Landers............ Patricia Smith
    Bob Landers..................... Tom Bosley
    Bruce Landers .... Bobby Riha

Debbie Reynolds made her series television debut in this comedy about the unpredictable wife of a successful sports columnist for the *Los Angeles Sun*. Debbie's efforts to create more excitement for herself than her life in the suburbs offered got her into all sorts of strange situations, much to the consternation of her husband Jim. Debbie's schemes, which were in some ways reminiscent of Lucille Ball's screwball exploits in the old *I Love Lucy* series, were often helped along by her sister Charlotte. The long-suffering members of

Charlotte's family were her husband Bob and their son Bruce.

DECEMBER BRIDE
Situation Comedy
FIRST TELECAST: *October 4, 1954*
LAST TELECAST: *April 20, 1961*
BROADCAST HISTORY:
    Oct 1954–Jun 1958, CBS Mon 9:30–10:00 (OS)
    Oct 1958–Sep 1959, CBS Thu 8:00–8:30
    Jul 1960–Sep 1960, CBS Fri 9:30–10:00
    Apr 1961, CBS Thu 7:30–8:00
CAST:
    Lily Ruskin................. Spring Byington
    Ruth Henshaw............. Frances Rafferty
    Matt Henshaw................... Dean Miller
    Hilda Crocker .... Verna Felton
    Pete Porter .... Harry Morgan

Lily Ruskin was that truly rare individual, a mother-in-law who could live with and be loved by her son-in-law. An attractive widow who was very popular with the older set—hence her potential as a "December bride"—Lily's social life revolved around her family as well. Her daughter Ruth and son-in-law Matt were always looking for suitable marriage prospects for Lily, as was her friend and peer, Hilda Crocker. Pete Porter, the next-door neighbor who couldn't stand *his* mother-in-law, was often seen around the Henshaw household, and he became so popular that he eventually got his own series, *Pete and Gladys*, after *December Bride* went off the air. Pete complained constantly about his wife, Gladys, but she was never seen on *December Bride*—only heard. Reruns of this series were aired in prime time during 1960 and 1961 and had been part of the CBS weekday morning lineup from October 1959 to March 1961.

DECISION
Dramatic Anthology
FIRST TELECAST: *July 6, 1958*
LAST TELECAST: *September 28, 1958*
BROADCAST HISTORY:
    Jul 1958–Sep 1958, NBC Sun 10:00–10:30

This series of filmed dramas was the 1958 summer replacement for *The Loretta Young Show*. Half the shows were reruns of episodes from other dramatic-anthology series; the remainder were pilots for proposed series. One of the latter was a short version of *The Virginian* starring James Drury, who played the same role when the show became a series in the fall of 1962.

DECISION '80
News
FIRST TELECAST: *September 14, 1980*
LAST TELECAST: *November 2, 1980*
BROADCAST HISTORY:
    Sep 1980–Nov 1980, NBC Sun 11:30–12:00

Robert Abernethy

NBC News presented this series of campaign reports leading up to the 1980 Presidential election. There were also discussions of other important races, and each week a special report centered on voter attitudes in a different key state.

DEFENDERS, THE
Courtroom Drama
FIRST TELECAST: *September 16, 1961*
LAST TELECAST: *September 9, 1965*
BROADCAST HISTORY:
  Sep 1961–Sep 1963, CBS Sat 8:30–9:30
  Sep 1963–Nov 1963, CBS Sat 9:00–10:00
  Nov 1963–Sep 1964, CBS Sat 8:30–9:30
  Sep 1964–Sep 1965, CBS Thu 10:00–11:00
CAST:
  Lawrence Preston . . . . E. G. Marshall
  Kenneth Preston . . . . Robert Reed
  Helen Donaldson (1961–1962) . . Polly Rowles
  Joan Miller (1961–1962) . . . . Joan Hackett

The law firm of Preston & Preston was composed of a father and son, two lawyers involved in a weekly courtroom drama. Lawrence, the father, was a knowledgeable, seasoned attorney with more than 20 years of experience at the bar. Kenneth, the son, was a recent law school graduate. The learning process he went through as his father's partner was an integral part of this series. During the first season the firm's secretary, Helen Donaldson, and Kenneth's girlfriend, Joan Miller, had regular featured roles.

At a time when most TV entertainment series avoided any hint of controversy or topicality, *The Defenders* occasionally addressed such real-life issues as abortion, mercy killing, and the U.S. government's restriction of its citizens' right to travel to unfriendly countries. A January 1964 episode entitled "Blacklist" was TV's first hard look at its own practice of political blacklisting, and won actor Jack Klugman and writer Ernest Kinoy Emmy awards.

The Defenders was based on an original story by Reginald Rose, which was first telecast as a two-part episode of *Studio One* in February–March, 1957. That presentation was titled "The Defender," and starred Ralph Bellamy and William Shatner as the father and son attorneys, with Steve McQueen as a young defendant accused of murder.

DELL O'DELL SHOW
Variety
FIRST TELECAST: *September 14, 1951*
LAST TELECAST: *December 14, 1951*
BROADCAST HISTORY:
  Sep 1951–Dec 1951, ABC Fri 10:00–10:30
EMCEE:
  Dell O'Dell

Lady magician Dell O'Dell performed on this short-lived variety program, which included audience participation in the stunts as well as special guests. Wonder if she sawed any men in half?

DELORA BUENO
Music
FIRST TELECAST: *March 10, 1949*
LAST TELECAST: *May 5, 1949*
BROADCAST HISTORY:
  Mar 1949–May 1949, DUM Thu 7:00–7:15
HOSTESS:
  Delora Bueno

Songs and piano stylings were performed by Delora Bueno, a Latin beauty born in Dubuque, Iowa. (She was raised, however, in Brazil.)

DELPHI BUREAU, THE
Spy Drama
FIRST TELECAST: *October 5, 1972*
LAST TELECAST: *September 1, 1973*
BROADCAST HISTORY:
  Oct 1972–Jan 1973, ABC Thu 9:00–10:00
  Mar 1973–Sep 1973, ABC Sat 10:00–11:00
CAST:
  Glenn Garth Gregory . . . . Laurence Luckinbill
  Sybil Van Loween . . . . Anne Jeffreys

The Delphi Bureau was an obscure government agency ostensibly intended to do research for the President of the United States; in fact it carried out super-secret missions to protect and defend the security of the nation against various foes. Its office was a moving limousine, and its chief operative, Glenn Gregory, a most reluctant hero. Gregory's only contact at the Delphi Bureau was Sybil Van Loween, a delightful but slightly mysterious Washington hostess. Secret ciphers, hidden islands, and bizarre international operators showed up regularly in the plots.

Celeste Holm was originally announced to play the role of Sybil, but she never appeared in the series, being replaced by Anne Jeffreys. *The Delphi Bureau* was one of three rotating elements of *The Men.*

DELTA HOUSE
Situation Comedy
FIRST TELECAST: *January 18, 1979*
LAST TELECAST: *April 28, 1979*
BROADCAST HISTORY:
  Jan 1979, ABC Thu 8:30–9:00
  Jan 1979–Mar 1979, ABC Sat 8:00–8:30
  Mar 1979–Apr 1979, ABC Sat 8:30–9:00
CAST:
  Dean Vernon Wormer . . . . John Vernon*
  Kent "Flounder" Dorfman . . . . Stephen Furst*
  Daniel Simpson Day ("D-Day")
  . . . . Bruce McGill*
  Robert Hoover . . . . James Widdoes*
  Jim "Blotto" Blutarsky . . . . Josh Mostel

Eric Stratton ("Otter")	Peter Fox
Doug Neidermayer	Gary Cookson
Larry Kroger ("Pinto")	Richard Seer
Mandy Pepperidge	Susanna Dalton
Muffy	Wendy Goldman
Greg Marmalard	Brian Patrick Clarke
Einswine	Lee Wilkof
Prof. Dave Jennings	Peter Kastner
The Bombshell	Michelle Pfeiffer

*Played same role in the movie

Following the enormous success of the movie *Animal House*, all three networks rushed imitations onto the small screen. ABC had a leg up on the competition, however, as it had acquired the production team responsible for the movie as well as rights to the story—everything except the title itself. So *Delta House* was *Animal House* brought to TV.

The setting was the same, Faber College in the early 1960s, where the riotous members of Delta House fraternity pulled pranks on Dean Wormer (who was constantly trying to get them kicked off campus) and his allies, the stuffy, rich brothers of Omega House. The series opened with the arrival of Blotto, younger brother of the legendary Bluto Blutarsky (John Belushi's unforgettable character in the film). Belushi wasn't available for the TV series, so the role was played by Josh Mostel, Zero Mostel's son. The other Deltas included portly Flounder, greasy, mustachioed D-Day, and Hoover. Doug Neidermayer and Greg Marmalard represented Omega House, and there were assorted girlfriends and faculty (although nobody studied much).

It all was a pretty pale imitation without Belushi, and it lasted only about three months. That was longer than NBC's *Brothers and Sisters* (two and a half months) or CBS' *Co-Ed Fever* (one telecast)!

DELVECCHIO
Police Drama
FIRST TELECAST: *September 9, 1976*
LAST TELECAST: *July 17, 1977*
BROADCAST HISTORY:
   Sep 1976, CBS Thu 9:00–10:00
   Sep 1976–Jul 1977, CBS Sun 10:00–11:00
CAST:
Sgt. Dominick Delvecchio	Judd Hirsch
Sgt. Paul Shonski	Charles Haid
Lt. Macavan	Michael Conrad
Tomaso Delvecchio	Mario Gallo
Sgt. Rivera	Jay Varela
Asst. D.A. Dorfman	George Wyner

Delvecchio was the story of a tough, independent big-city police detective fighting crime in Los Angeles. Delvecchio and his partner Shonski were assigned cases that ranged from narcotics investigations to murders to auto thefts. His boss, and the man who assigned most of his cases, was Lt.

Macavan. Also seen regularly was Delvecchio's father, Tomaso, an Old World type who ran a small barbershop and was constantly perplexed about why his stubborn, determined son had become a cop. The series was shot on location in Los Angeles.

DEMPSEY & MAKEPEACE
Police Drama
BROADCAST HISTORY:
   Syndicated only
   60 minutes
   Produced: *1985* (19 episodes)
   Released: *September 1985*
CAST:
Lt. James Dempsey	Michael Brandon
Det. Sgt. Harriet Makepeace (Harry)	Glynis Barber
Chief Superintendant Gordon Spikings	Ray Smith
Det. Sgt. Charles Jarvis (Chas)	Tony Osoba

Produced in England, *Dempsey & Makepeace* chronicled the exploits of two members of SI-10, a special undercover group working out of London's Scotland Yard. Jim Dempsey was a New York City cop who had discovered corruption in the New York City police force and had been sent to England for his own protection. He was brash, impetuous, occasionally obnoxious, and much quicker to use his gun than the British. His reluctant partner was Lady Harriet Makepeace, a member of royalty who, for reasons never clearly explained on the show, had decided to make a career out of police work. Her connections with those in high places often proved handy when they were looking for information or assistance on various cases. Although a grudging mutual respect developed between them, and there was a certain sexual tension, a social relationship never materialized. Spikings was the blustery head of SI-10 and Chas was one of the other members of the team.

DENNIS DAY SHOW, THE
   see *RCA Victor Show, The*

DENNIS O'KEEFE SHOW, THE
Situation Comedy
FIRST TELECAST: *September 22, 1959*
LAST TELECAST: *June 7, 1960*
BROADCAST HISTORY:
   Sep 1959–Jun 1960, CBS Tue 8:00–8:30
CAST:
Hal Towne	Dennis O'Keefe
Sarge	Hope Emerson
Randy Towne	Rickey Kelman
Karen Hadley	Eloise Hardt
Eliot	Eddie Ryder

This comedy starred Dennis O'Keefe as the syndicated columnist Hal Towne, one of TV's many widowers, with a precocious, friendly ten-year-old son named Randy. Helping Hal keep his home together while he was out getting material for his column was a housekeeper aptly named Sarge. Karen Hadley, an aggressive, career-oriented publicity agent, was Hal's regular girlfriend, but his work on his column, called "All Around Towne," was constantly introducing Hal to some very attractive competition. The story was set in Los Angeles.

DENNIS THE MENACE
Situation Comedy
FIRST TELECAST: *October 4, 1959*
LAST TELECAST: *September 22, 1963*
BROADCAST HISTORY:
   Oct 1959–Sep 1963, CBS Sun 7:30–8:00
CAST:
   Dennis Mitchell. . . . . Jay North
   Henry Mitchell . . . . Herbert Anderson
   Alice Mitchell . . . . Gloria Henry
   George Wilson (1959–1962) . . . Joseph Kearns
   Martha Wilson (1959–1962) . . . . . Sylvia Field
   Joey McDonald (1959–1960) . . . . Gil Smith
   Mrs. Lucy Elkins. . . . . Irene Tedrow
   Tommy Anderson . . . . Billy Booth
   Margaret Wade. . . . . Jeannie Russell
   Mr. Quigley . . . . Willard Waterman
   Miss Esther Cathcart (1959–1961)
      . . . . Mary Wickes
   Grandma Mitchell (1961)
      . . . . Kathleen Mulqueen
   Sgt. Theodore Mooney (1961–1963)
      . . . . George Cisar
   Seymour (1962–1963) . . . . Robert John Pittman
   John Wilson (1962–1963) . . . . Gale Gordon
   Eloise Wilson (1962–1963) . . . . . . Sara Seegar

Cartoonist Hank Ketcham's mischievous imp was brought to television in 1959 in the person of Jay North. *Dennis the Menace* had been a comic-strip fixture for years, with its little boy who was always trying to help out but who usually managed to make everything worse. Dennis' long-suffering parents put up with him as best they could, which was more than could be said for Mr. Wilson, their next-door neighbor in suburban Hillsdale. If Mr. Wilson planted some fancy tulips, Dennis was sure to uproot them and plant some "prettier" potatoes in their place. If Dennis happened upon some of Mr. Wilson's rare coins, he was sure to donate them to the March of Dimes. Adding to the general confusion was Dennis' dog, Freemont.

Joseph Kearns, the first Mr. Wilson, died before filming was completed for the 1961–1962 season. He was replaced in May 1962 by Gale Gordon, who was initially introduced as Mr. Wilson's brother John, a house guest of Mrs. Wilson. The next fall, John returned complete with a wife of his own, Eloise, as if he had always been the sole Mr. Wilson.

Reruns of *Dennis the Menace* aired Saturday mornings on NBC from October 1963 to September 1965. A quarter-century after the live-action

Dennis the Menace left the air CBS brought an animated version to its Saturday morning lineup in January 1988.

DEPUTY, THE
Western
FIRST TELECAST: *September 12, 1959*
LAST TELECAST: *September 16, 1961*
BROADCAST HISTORY:
   Sep 1959–Sep 1961, NBC Sat 9:00–9:30
CAST:
   Marshal Simon Fry . . . . Henry Fonda
   Clay McCord . . . . Allen Case
   Marshal Herk Lamson (1959–1960)
      . . . . Wallace Ford
   Fran McCord (1959–1960) . . . . Betty Lou Keim
   Sgt. Hapgood Tasker (1960–1961)
      . . . . Read Morgan

Set in the Arizona Territory in the early 1880s, *The Deputy* was built around the conflict in ideals between Chief Marshal Simon Fry, a dedicated lawman, and young storekeeper Clay McCord. Although an expert shot, Clay was opposed to the use of weapons because they contributed to the high level of violence on the frontier. Despite his pacifist feelings, however, Clay was frequently persuaded to serve as "the deputy" in Silver City to help the aging town marshal, Herk Lamson, defend the local populace when Marshal Fry was out of town. The basis for many of the stories was the ongoing conflict between the oldtimers in Silver City and the younger townspeople, who wanted to see it settle down, grow, and prosper. Added to the cast at the start of the second season was "Sarge" Tasker, an army sergeant assigned to set up a supply office in Silver City. At the same time, Herk Lamson and Clay's younger sister Fran were dropped from the cast. Henry Fonda appeared as narrator in all episodes but was featured in the cast only when Marshal Fry was in town.

DES O'CONNER SHOW, THE
   see *Kraft Music Hall Presents The Des O'Conner Show*

DESIGNING WOMEN
Situation Comedy
FIRST TELECAST: *September 29, 1986*
LAST TELECAST:
BROADCAST HISTORY:
   Sep 1986–Nov 1986, CBS Mon 9:30–10:00
   Dec 1986–Jan 1987, CBS Thu 9:30–10:00
   Feb 1987, CBS Sun 9:00–9:30
   Mar 1987–Feb 1988, CBS Mon 9:30–10:00
   Feb 1988–Jun 1988, CBS Mon 8:30–9:00
   Jun 1988–   , CBS Mon 9:30–10:00
CAST:
   Suzanne Sugarbaker . . . . Delta Burke
   Julia Sugarbaker . . . . Dixie Carter
   Charlene Winston. . . . . Jean Smart
   Mary Jo Shively . . . . Annie Potts

Anthony Bouvier........... Meshach Taylor
*Claudia Shively............. Priscilla Weems
*Quinton Shively................ Brian Lando
*Reese Watson .... Hal Holbrook
*J.D. Shackleford............ Richard Gilliland

*Occasional

Designing Women was the story of the four out-spoken women who ran Sugarbakers, a recently opened interior decorating business in Atlanta, which they operated out of an attractive suburban home that served as both office and showplace for their work. The founder, guiding force, and most sharp-tongued of the four was widowed Julia Sugarbaker. She was bright, classy, and had great taste and good connections. Her younger sister Suzanne was sexy, flashy, and prone to use her physical charms to mask a limited knowledge of decorating. A former beauty contest winner, she flirted with any and all attractive, successful, and/or wealthy men—and was collecting alimony from three ex-husbands. Their two partners were Mary Jo, a recent divorcee with a teenaged daughter, Claudia, and a young son, Quinton; and Charlene, the firm's business manager who had never been married but was not averse to the prospect if the right man came along. There was plenty of good-natured bitchiness and, by the standards of network TV, a lot of sexual innuendo. Helping them with the heavy work was their handyman, Anthony, a cheerful, black ex-con. Reese (played by Ms. Carter's real-life husband, Hal Holbrook) was Julia's boyfriend and J.D. (played by Ms. Smart's husband Richard Gilliland—they had met on the *Designing Women* set) was dating Mary Jo.

The critics loved *Designing Women,* and so did its loyal audience. They howled when CBS moved the show all over the schedule following initial ratings success on Monday nights, and then canceled it in the spring of 1987. Viewer protests (encouraged by the network's own publicity) prompted the programmers to reconsider, and *Designing Women* was saved from the Nielsen axe.

DESILU PLAYHOUSE
see *Westinghouse Desilu Playhouse*

DESTINY
Dramatic Anthology
FIRST TELECAST: *July 5, 1957*
LAST TELECAST: *September 26, 1958*
BROADCAST HISTORY:
   Jul 1957–Sep 1957, CBS Fri 8:30–9:00
   Jul 1958–Sep 1958, CBS Fri 8:30–9:00
HOST:
   Francis L. Sullivan

Reruns of episodes from other anthologies were aired by CBS in this time slot for two summers, as replacement for *Dick Powell's Zane Grey Theater.*

DESTRY
Western
FIRST TELECAST: *February 14, 1964*
LAST TELECAST: *September 11, 1964*
BROADCAST HISTORY:
   Feb 1964–Sep 1964, ABC Fri 7:30–8:30
CAST:
   Harrison Destry .... John Gavin

At the center of this comedy-Western was Harrison Destry, a tall, easygoing chap who wasn't exactly a coward—just a mite careful. He'd just as soon dive under the table as shoot it out. Young Destry, the son of famed lawman Tom Destry, had once been a sheriff, until he was packed off to prison on a trumped-up embezzlement charge. In this series he wandered about the West trying to stay out of further trouble as he looked for the scalawags who had framed him.

The Destry character has had a lengthy career; he was portrayed in films by Tom Mix, James Stewart (in a 1939 movie classic co-starring Marlene Dietrich), and Audie Murphy and later in a hit Broadway musical starring Andy Griffith. The character was originally based on the Max Brand novel, *Destry Rides Again.*

DETECTIVE IN THE HOUSE
Detective
FIRST TELECAST: *March 15, 1985*
LAST TELECAST: *April 19, 1985*
BROADCAST HISTORY:
   Mar 1985–Apr 1985, CBS Fri 8:00–9:00
CAST:
   Press Wyman................... Judd Hirsch
   Diane Wyman .... Cassie Yates
   Todd Wyman................. Meeno Peluce
   Deborah Wyman.............. Mandy Ingber
   Dunc Wyman................. R.J. Williams
   Nick Turner .... Jack Elam

This was not your everyday mid-life crisis. Press Wyman was a successful engineer who wanted to be a private detective. Since he knew very little about sleuthing, Press sought the assistance of retired private eye Nick Turner. In his time, Nick had been a legend—in retirement he was a bit loony, living on his unkempt estate furnished completely with lawn furniture. While Press bumbled his way through cases and did most of the household chores when he wasn't busy, his loving wife Diane went back to work to provide them with a regular income. Todd, Deborah, and Link were their three children, who didn't really understand why their father was doing this.

DETECTIVE SCHOOL
Situation Comedy
FIRST TELECAST: *July 31, 1979*
LAST TELECAST: *November 24, 1979*
BROADCAST HISTORY:
   Jul 1979–Aug 1979, ABC Tue 8:30–9:00
   Sep 1979–Nov 1979, ABC Sat 8:30–9:00

CAST:

Nick Hannigan	James Gregory
Eddie Dawkins	Randolph Mantooth
Charlene Jenkins............	LaWanda Page
Teresa Cleary (Jul–Aug)	Jo Ann Harris
Maggie Ferguson (Sep–Nov) ..	Melinda Naud
Leo Frick.........................	Pat Proft
Robert Redford	Douglas V. Fowley
Silvio Galindez	Taylor Negron

James Gregory (Inspector Luger of *Barney Miller*) headed the cast in this short-lived comedy. Nick Hannigan's flea-bitten detective school and agency was supposed to be a night school for sleuths, nothing more. Unfortunately his motley collection of students was constantly getting involved in real cases, to comic effect, and Nick more than once had to bail them out. Sometimes they had to bail *him* out. Dawkins was an enthusiastic young man who worked in a shoe store; Jenkins, a black housewife with a smart mouth, often aimed at aging fellow student Robert Redford (who was obviously no kin to the movie star!). Frick sold vacuum cleaners door-to-door; Galindez was an oily Argentinian hooked on the disco scene. Petite Teresa Cleary, the sixth student, was replaced by gorgeous Maggie Ferguson in September.

The show did well in the summer, against soft competition, but died when it was added to the regular schedule in the fall.

DETECTIVE'S DIARY
see *Mark Saber*

DETECTIVES, STARRING ROBERT TAYLOR, THE
Police Drama
FIRST TELECAST: *October 16, 1959*
LAST TELECAST: *September 21, 1962*
BROADCAST HISTORY:
Oct 1959–Sep 1961, ABC Fri 10:00–10:30
Sep 1961–Sep 1962, NBC Fri 8:30–9:30
CAST:

Capt. Matt Holbrook	Robert Taylor
Lt. John Russo	Tige Andrews
Lt. James Conway (1959–1960).......	Lee Farr
Lt. Otto Lindstrom (1959–1961)	
....	Russell Thorson
Sgt. Chris Ballard (1960–1962)	
....	Mark Goddard
Lisa Bonay (1960–1961)........	Ursula Thiess
Sgt. Steve Nelson (1961–1962) ...	Adam West

Screen star Robert Taylor played a humorless, hard-nosed, doggedly effective captain on a big-city police force in this unassuming series. He led a team of three plainclothes detectives, which allowed individual episodes of the program to vary the lead (seldom were all four men assigned to the same case). The original trio consisted of Lt. Jim Conway of Homicide, a young ladies' man; Lt. Johnny Russo of Burglary, cigar-smoking and tough-talking; and Lt. Otto Lindstrom of the Bunco squad, an old-timer. Each week one or more of them would tackle a murder, con game, drug operation, or other crime.

Capt. Holbrook was a widower with little time for anything but his job. His only romantic involvement during the three-year run of the series was a brief, antiseptic affair with a police reporter named Lisa Bonay—played by Taylor's real-life wife, German actress Ursula Thiess.

During its season on NBC the program was retitled *Robert Taylor's Detectives*.

DETECTIVE'S WIFE
Detective Comedy
FIRST TELECAST: *July 7, 1950*
LAST TELECAST: *September 29, 1950*
BROADCAST HISTORY:
Jul 1950–Sep 1950, CBS Fri 8:30–9:00
CAST:

Connie Conway..................	Lynn Bari
Adam Conway................	Donald Curtis

Detective's Wife was the live summer replacement in 1950 for the popular detective series *Man Against Crime*. Adam Conway was a private detective who wanted to run a peaceful little agency but had received so much publicity after solving a murder that homicides were the only kind of cases he could get. The emphasis in this series was mostly on Adam's wife Connie, who got more involved in his cases than either of them would have preferred.

DEVLIN CONNECTION, THE
Detective Drama
FIRST TELECAST: *October 2, 1982*
LAST TELECAST: *December 25, 1982*
BROADCAST HISTORY:
Oct 1982–Dec 1982, NBC Sat 10:00–11:00
CAST:

Brian Devlin...................	Rock Hudson
Nick Corsello...................	Jack Scalia
Lauren Dane	Leigh Taylor-Young
Lt. Earl Borden	Louis Giambalvo
Mrs. Watanabe.....................	Takayo
Otis Barnes	Herb Jefferson, Jr.

The contrast was striking. Brian Devlin was suave, debonair, and independently wealthy, leading a life of quiet elegance. After retiring from a most successful career as a private investigator, he had taken on the distinctly civilized position of Director of the Los Angeles Cultural Arts Center. Into this classy world burst coarse and impetuous Nick Corsello, 28, an aspiring private eye of the "tough" school—and Brian's long-lost son! Nick had been raised in New York by his mother, and now wanted to make it on his own as a gumshoe—though he still worked part time as a racquetball pro at a health club.

Understandably taken aback, Dad still wanted to get to know this rough gem of a son a little better. Keeping an eye on Nick's cases, he helped out wherever possible, preferably without Nick's knowledge or damage to the Mercedes. Usually they wound up solving the cases together, each using his own special skills.

Lauren was Brian's beautiful assistant at the arts center, and Mrs. Watanabe his efficient housekeeper and cook. Lt. Borden was the friendly, if less than competent, contact on the L.A.P.D. and Otis was Nick's nightclub owner friend.

The series was originally scheduled to premiere in 1981, but was delayed when Rock Hudson underwent open-heart surgery.

DIAGNOSIS: UNKNOWN
Detective Drama
FIRST TELECAST: *July 5, 1960*
LAST TELECAST: *September 20, 1960*
BROADCAST HISTORY:
Jul 1960–Sep 1960, CBS Tue 10:00–11:00
CAST:
Dr. Daniel Coffee .... Patrick O'Neal
Doris Hudson.............. Phyllis Newman
Dr. Motilal Mookerji .... Cal Bellini
Link .... Martin Huston
Det. Capt. Max Ritter .... Chester Morris

Daniel Coffee, the head pathologist at a large metropolitan hospital, worked closely with the police department to solve bizarre murders. Working with him were his two close friends and assistants, Motilal Mookerji and Doris Hudson. Also seen regularly was Link, the young boy who cleaned up the lab and worked as a handyman for Dr. Coffee. Dr. Coffee's contact on the New York City police department was Captain Ritter.

DIAHANN CARROLL SHOW, THE
Musical Variety
FIRST TELECAST: *August 14, 1976*
LAST TELECAST: *September 3, 1976*
BROADCAST HISTORY:
Aug 1976–Sep 1976, CBS Sat 10:00–11:00
STAR:
Diahann Carroll
The Carl Jablonski Dancers
The Earl Brown Orchestra

Singer Diahann Carroll was the star of this four-week mini-series, which included comedy and repartee with guest performers as well as musical numbers.

DIAMONDS
Detective
FIRST TELECAST: *September 22, 1987*
LAST TELECAST:
BROADCAST HISTORY:
Sep 1987–   , CBS Tue 11:30–12:40 A.M.
CAST:
Mike Devitt .... Nicholas Campbell
Christina Towne .... Peggy Smithhart

Lt. Lou Gianetti .... Tony Rosato
Darryl .... Alan Feiman

A TV series about TV private eyes who decided to tackle the real thing. Mike and Christina had been married and played married private detectives on their once-popular TV detective series *Diamonds.* Now that they were divorced and their series had been canceled, they decided to try and make a go of it as real-life detectives, opening an agency appropriately called "Two of Diamonds." Helping them was Darryl, the special-effects expert from their former studio, whose plans and tricks got them into and out of numerous tight situations. Also providing assistance was Mike's cousin, police Lt. Gianetti.

Produced in Toronto.

DIANA
Situation Comedy
FIRST TELECAST: *September 10, 1973*
LAST TELECAST: *January 7, 1974*
BROADCAST HISTORY:
Sep 1973–Jan 1974, NBC Mon 8:30–9:00
CAST:
Diana Smythe .... Diana Rigg
Norman Brodnik .... David Sheiner
Howard Tolbrook .... Richard B. Shull
Norma Brodnik .... Barbara Barrie
Marshall Tyler .... Robert Moore
Holly Green .... Carol Androsky
Jeff Harmon .... Richard Mulligan
Smitty, the bellboy............. Liam Dunn

Diana Rigg had been introduced to American audiences as Emma Peel in the British spy-adventure series *The Avengers.* In *Diana* she played an English divorcée in her mid-30s who had moved to New York to begin a new life and a new career. Soon after taking over her absent brother's Manhattan apartment, however, Diana discovered that a number of his men friends had duplicate keys to the place, a situation that resulted in both embarrassing and comic confrontations. Commercial model Holly Green was Diana's friendly neighbor, helping her cope with the unexpected visitors. Diana's co-workers at Butley's Department Store on Fifth Avenue, where she was employed as a fashion coordinator, included Norman Brodnik, the president of the store; Norma, his wife; Howard Tolbrook, a cantankerous copywriter who shared an office with Diana; and Marshall Tyler, a window dresser. Jeff Harmon was a mystery-writer friend of hers.

DIANE DOXEE SHOW, THE
Music
FIRST TELECAST: *August 6, 1950*
LAST TELECAST: *September 24, 1950*
BROADCAST HISTORY:
Aug 1950–Sep 1950, ABC Sun 7:30–8:00

Diane Doxee
Jimmy Blade

This program featured songs by Miss Doxee, accompanied by Jimmy Blade on piano.

DICK AND THE DUCHESS
Comedy Adventure
FIRST TELECAST: *September 28, 1957*
LAST TELECAST: *May 16, 1958*
BROADCAST HISTORY:
  Sep 1957–Mar 1958, CBS Sat 8:30–9:00
  Mar 1958–May 1958, CBS Fri 7:30–8:00
CAST:
  Dick Starrett .... Patrick O'Neal
  Jane Starrett.................. Hazel Court
  Peter Jamison............... Richard Wattis
  Inspector Stark .... Michael Shepley
  Mathilda .... Beatrice Varley
  Rodney .... Ronnie Stevens

Dick Starrett was an American living in London and married to Jane, an English duchess. He often found himself in perplexing situations with members of Jane's upper-crust family, who were less than enchanted with her marriage to a commoner—and an American at that. Dick was employed as an insurance investigator/adjustor by a large multinational company, and to complicate matters, Jane frequently managed to get herself involved in his claims investigations, trying to help but only causing problems. Peter Jamison was Dick's friend and associate at the office, and Inspector Stark was a Scotland Yard investigator with whom he often worked.

DICK CAVETT SHOW, THE
Talk/Variety
FIRST TELECAST: *May 26, 1969*
LAST TELECAST: *December 29, 1972*
BROADCAST HISTORY:
  May 1969–Sep 1969, ABC Mon/Tue/Fri 10:00–11:00
  Dec 1969–Dec 1972, ABC Mon-Fri 11:30 P.M.–1:00 A.M.
HOST:
  Dick Cavett
REGULARS:
  Bobby Rosengarden
  Fred Foy

Dick Cavett was one of the few TV personalities ever to star in major programs in daytime, prime time, and late nighttime, all in quick succession, and to fail to attract a large audience with any of them. His shows were well received by the critics and were generally acknowledged to be witty, intelligent, and interesting as compared to what was scheduled around them. Perhaps it was his intelligence that did Cavett in, for he never hesitated to bring in thought-provoking people as well as show-biz types as guests. Viewers, evidently, didn't much care to have their thoughts provoked.

All three of Cavett's ABC shows were essentially talk programs with some singing or performing guests. The daytime version was a 90-minute affair, five days a week, and lasted from March 1968 until January 1969. The prime-time summer show was on three nights a week from May until September 1969, and the late-night edition (11:30 P.M.–1:00 A.M.) lasted from December 1969 until December 1972. Guests in prime time included the usual run of movie and sports stars (including a full hour with Groucho Marx) mixed in with such heady fare as political pundit I. F. Stone, maverick Federal Communications Commission member Nicholas Johnson, and Cavett's own former philosophy professor, Paul Weiss.

In December 1969 Cavett moved to late-night television, with Bobby Rosengarden as orchestra leader and Fred Foy as announcer. The guests continued to be diverse. At one point Cavett presented a series of one-guest shows with Anthony Quinn, Fred Astaire, Charlton Heston, Jack Lemmon, and Woody Allen, followed by a program on which a group of children gave their views of contemporary life. On another famous occasion, in December 1971, former Governor Lester Maddox of Georgia walked off the show when challenged on his segregationist views.

While the show continued to receive excellent reviews, ABC continued to run a poor third behind NBC and CBS in late-night viewership. Finally in April 1972 the network announced that unless audience levels improved by July 28th, the program would be canceled. This set off a controversy almost unparalelled in TV history. ABC was deluged with more than 15,000 letters in a few weeks, running nine to one in favor of Cavett. Several ABC affiliates ran "Save the Dick Cavett Show" advertisements, and notable public figures urged that the series be continued. Columnists around the country had a field day, castigating ABC and the Nielsen audience measurement system, and lauding Cavett as—in the words of one—"infinitely more valuable than another old movie." Perhaps Cavett could not attract as many viewers as Johnny Carson, editorialized *Time* magazine, but "should the more than 3,200,000 viewers who want his brand of intelligent alternative programming be summarily disenfranchised?"

Viewership did not increase significantly, and after a temporary reprieve, *The Dick Cavett Show* was cut back to occasional status in January 1973, when it became part of the new *ABC Wide World of Entertainment*. It left ABC entirely in 1975.

DICK CAVETT SHOW, THE
Variety
FIRST TELECAST: *August 16, 1975*
LAST TELECAST: *September 6, 1975*
BROADCAST HISTORY:
  Aug 1975–Sep 1975, CBS Sat 10:00–11:00

HOST:
Dick Cavett
REGULARS:
Leigh French
Marshall Efron

Host Dick Cavett did a little bit of everything in this four-week summer series. He interviewed guest stars, sang a little, and acted in comedy sketches with comedienne Leigh French and comedian Marshall Efron. Mr. Efron, in addition to performing, was one of the writers of the show.

DICK CAVETT SHOW, THE
Talk/Discussion
FIRST TELECAST: *September 23, 1986*
LAST TELECAST: *December 30, 1986*
BROADCAST HISTORY:
Sep 1986–Dec 1986, ABC Tue/Wed 12:00 MID–1:00 A.M.
HOST:
Dick Cavett

Dick Cavett returned to network TV in 1986, briefly, with another of his wide-ranging, thought-provoking, and little-viewed discussion shows. Part of an ABC plan to provide meatier fare for late-night viewers (*Nightline* at 11:30 P.M., followed by Cavett on Tuesday and Wednesday, and Jimmy Breslin on Thursday and Friday), *The Dick Cavett Show* featured authors, screenwriters, politicians, and thinkers along with some interesting actors (Lily Tomlin, Carol Burnett, Veronica Hamel). The last telecast consisted of a group of children explaining their views on a number of issues.

DICK CLARK PRESENTS THE ROCK AND ROLL YEARS
Music
FIRST TELECAST: *November 28, 1973*
LAST TELECAST: *January 9, 1974*
BROADCAST HISTORY:
Nov 1973–Jan 1974, ABC Wed 8:00–8:30
HOST/EXECUTIVE PRODUCER:
Dick Clark
REGULARS:
Jeff Kutash Dancers

This series presented a nostalgic portrait of the rock 'n' roll era through performances by its top artists, laced with chatter about the styles, dances, and news events of the period. Each program consisted of three acts taped before a live audience at Santa Monica Civic Auditorium in California, five acts from the past shown in film clips, and one spot titled "The Immortal," in which a superstar of the past performed. Many of the top recording stars of the 1950s and 1960s appeared, such as Chuck Berry, Pat Boone, Danny and the Juniors, the Shirelles, Duane Eddy, and Little Richard; there were also some more recent acts, such as Chicago and Three Dog Night. The

"Immortals" (most of them deceased) included Jimi Hendrix, James Dean, Clyde McPhatter, and Jim Croce. Unfortunately, Clark never managed to sign Elvis.

DICK CLARK SHOW, THE
Music
FIRST TELECAST: *February 16, 1958*
LAST TELECAST: *September 10, 1960*
BROADCAST HISTORY:
Feb 1958–Sep 1960, ABC Sat 7:30–8:00
HOST:
Dick Clark

Dick Clark, host of the highly successful afternoon series *American Bandstand*, was featured in this nighttime derivative of his daytime show. Each week a number of recording artists, whose records were currently on the "Top 40" charts, performed their hits on *The Dick Clark Show*. Although some of them actually sang on the show, most of them lip-synched to their own recordings. Some of the numbers were performed simply; others were done as production numbers. The highlight of the show was the unveiling of the "American Bandstand Top Ten" records for the following week at the conclusion of the program. The series was also known as *The Dick Clark Saturday Night Beechnut Show.*

DICK CLARK'S LIVE WEDNESDAY
Variety
FIRST TELECAST: *September 20, 1978*
LAST TELECAST: *December 27, 1978*
BROADCAST HISTORY:
Sep 1978–Dec 1978, NBC Wed 8:00–9:00
HOST/PRODUCER:
Dick Clark

Dick Clark, who was a major force in bringing rock 'n' roll to TV in the 1950s, became the chief exponent of nostalgia for the music of that decade, 20 years later. Looking just as young as he had on *American Bandstand* in 1957, Clark hosted a series of highly popular specials which led to his own live prime-time musical variety series in 1978. The program featured a mix of current popular music and that of the 1950s and 1960s, performed by the original artists. Sometimes singers would be introduced with clips of themselves performing years before, as when Ricky Nelson was seen as a child on *The Adventures of Ozzie & Harriet*, before he came on to perform. There was chatter about the fads of the past, and a feature called "Where Are They Now?", but all was not nostalgia. Current stars performed as well. Dozens of famous faces flashed across the screen each week, many in cameo appearances, ranging from such current teenage favorites as Jimmy and Kristy McNichol to old pros like Bob Hope and Danny Kaye, and old rock 'n' rollers like Chuck Berry and Bo Diddley. To emphasize the show's live origination (from Hollywood), a death-defying stunt was performed on each telecast by a professional stuntman.

Six months after it left the air, *Dick Clark's Live Wednesday* returned for a single telecast on July 11, 1979.

DICK CLARK'S NIGHTTIME
Musical Variety
BROADCAST HISTORY:
  Syndicated only
  60 minutes
  Produced: *1985–1986* (26 episodes)
  Released: *September 1985*
HOST:
  Dick Clark

Dick Clark, host of ABC's long-running *American Bandstand,* produced and hosted this late-night syndicated music series. The format was a mix of performances and interviews with rock artists, videos, and *Bandstand*-style in-studio dancing to recorded music. Most of the stations carrying the show aired it on Saturday nights after their late-evening local news.

DICK CLARK'S WORLD OF TALENT
Variety
FIRST TELECAST: *September 27, 1959*
LAST TELECAST: *December 20, 1959*
BROADCAST HISTORY:
  Sep 1959–Dec 1959, ABC Sun 10:30–11:00
REGULARS:
  Dick Clark
  Jack E. Leonard

Each week Dick Clark was the host to three young performers, who presented their acts to the viewing audience and a panel composed of Jack E. Leonard and two celebrity guests. The panel would then comment on the performances and offer suggestions to the entertainers. Most of the performers had already begun their professional careers; they ranged from 15-year-old concert pianist Lorin Hollander to folk singers Bud and Travis. Comedians, dancers, and soloists were also seen (despite Clark's identification with the current hit parade, there were few rock acts). Some of the performers had been in show business quite a while, in fact, stretching the "young artist" theme a bit; among these were singers Don Cornell, Della Reese, Alan Dale, and the Four Aces.

DICK POWELL SHOW, THE
Dramatic Anthology
FIRST TELECAST: *September 26, 1961*
LAST TELECAST: *September 17, 1963*
BROADCAST HISTORY:
  Sep 1961–Sep 1962, NBC Tue 9:00–10:00
  Sep 1962–Sep 1963, NBC Tue 9:30–10:30
HOST/STAR:
  Dick Powell

Dick Powell, the boyish star of some of the 1930s' most glittering movie musicals, was a seasoned veteran when he appeared in this, his last TV series. Many of the episodes aired were pilots, and two of them actually became regular series in their own right. Powell himself starred in the first telecast, "Who Killed Julie Greer," playing the role of wealthy policeman Amos Burke; the following fall Gene Barry took on the same role in the series *Burke's Law.* "Savage Sunday" starred Nick Adams as a crusading New York newspaper reporter, a role he kept when *Saints and Sinners* premiered the next fall. Among the pilots that didn't succeed was "Safari," based on the movie *The African Queen* and starring Glynis Johns and James Coburn. A noteworthy episode was "The Price of Tomatoes," for which a young Peter Falk won an Emmy.

In addition to serving as host, Powell periodically appeared in individual episodes. During the first season he co-starred with his wife June Allyson in a play called "A Time to Die." It is not known whether Powell knew at the time that he had cancer, but by the beginning of the second season he was in declining health. His last acting role was in "The Court-Martial of Captain Wycliff," which was aired on December 12, 1962, and his last appearance as host (on film) was on New Year's Day 1963. He died the following day. In deference to his family the filmed introductions that he had already prepared for future telecasts were deleted, and a succession of guest stars appeared as hosts for the remainder of the season. The title of the program was also changed to *The Dick Powell Theatre.*

DICK POWELL'S ZANE GREY THEATER
Western Anthology
FIRST TELECAST: *October 5, 1956*
LAST TELECAST: *September 20, 1962*
BROADCAST HISTORY:
  Oct 1956–Jul 1958, CBS Fri 8:30–9:00 (OS)
  Oct 1958–Sep 1960, CBS Thu 9:00–9:30
  Oct 1960–Jul 1961, CBS Thu 8:30–9:00
  Apr 1962–Sep 1962, CBS Thu 9:30–10:00
HOST/STAR:
  Dick Powell

During its early seasons, *Dick Powell's Zane Grey Theater* was comprised completely of adaptations of the short stories and novels of famous Western author Zane Grey. Eventually, when the Grey material began to run out, Western stories from other authors were included. Host Dick Powell was frequently the star of individual episodes, more often in the early years than later in its run. The episodes telecast in the summer of 1962 were all reruns.

DICK TRACY
Police Drama
FIRST TELECAST: *September 11, 1950*
LAST TELECAST: *February 12, 1951*

Sep 1950–Oct 1950, ABC Wed 8:30–9:00
Oct 1950–Dec 1950, ABC Mon 8:30–9:00
Jan 1951–Feb 1951, ABC Tue 8:00–8:30
CAST:
Dick Tracy .... Ralph Byrd
Sam Catchem.................... Joe Devlin

Chester Gould's famous comic-strip hero appeared briefly on network television in 1950–1951 in this very violent series. With him were the famous supporting characters, including his sidekick Sam Catchem, Chief Murphy, and an array of incredible villains ranging from The Mole (a counterfeiter who tunneled underground) to the laughing Joker. Ralph Byrd, who had been slugging it out in Dick Tracy theatrical movies and serials since the 1930s, also appeared in this TV version.

Byrd continued to make new *Tracy* films for TV syndication after the series left the network, until his death in 1952. Joe Devlin co-starred. *Dick Tracy* had also been heard on radio from 1935–1948, the latter part of its run on ABC. Edited versions of theatrical movies, as well as a cartoon version, have been seen on TV in more recent years.

DICK VAN DYKE SHOW, THE
Situation Comedy
FIRST TELECAST: *October 3, 1961*
LAST TELECAST: *September 7, 1966*
BROADCAST HISTORY:
Oct 1961–Dec 1961, CBS Tue 8:00–8:30
Jan 1962–Sep 1964, CBS Wed 9:30–10:00
Sep 1964–Sep 1965, CBS Wed 9:00–9:30
Sep 1965–Sep 1966, CBS Wed 9:30–10:00
CAST:
Rob Petrie................... Dick Van Dyke
Laura Petrie .... Mary Tyler Moore
Sally Rogers.................... Rose Marie
Maurice "Buddy" Sorrell . Morey Amsterdam
Ritchie Petrie............... Larry Mathews
Melvin Cooley.............. Richard Deacon
Jerry Helper .... Jerry Paris
Millie Helper .... Ann Morgan Guilbert
Alan Brady..................... Carl Reiner
CREATOR:
Carl Reiner
PRODUCER/DIRECTOR/WRITER (VARIOUS EPISODES):
Carl Reiner
Sheldon Leonard
Jerry Paris

This highly successful series is often considered one of television's classic comedies, primarily because of its first-class scripting and excellent casting. Most of the principals were show-business veterans and several went on to star in series of their own. The setting, appropriately enough, was behind the scenes on a mythical TV comedy show. Rob Petrie was the head comedy writer for *The Alan Brady Show*, a popular New York-based comedy-variety series whose neurotic star

was seldom seen here. Working with Rob were two other writers, Sally and Buddy, both of whom were close friends of Rob and his wife Laura. Their nemesis at the office, and the butt of much humor, was balding Melvin Cooley, the pompous producer of *The Alan Brady Show* and the brother-in-law of its star. Episodes generally revolved around the problems of the writers and the home life of the Petries in New Rochelle. Early episodes often included flashbacks to Rob and Laura's courtship, while Rob was still in the army, the early days of their marriage, and the development of Rob's career. Frequently seen were their next-door neighbors, Jerry and Millie Helper. Writer-director Carl Reiner played the occasional role of Alan Brady, who was heard but never seen until the show had been on for several seasons.

The Dick Van Dyke Show took several seasons to develop into a major hit and was still very popular in 1966, when it finally left the air because Van Dyke and other cast members wanted to try new material. Van Dyke was never able to repeat the spectacular success of this series, but his co-star Mary Tyler Moore went on to greater fame on her own *Mary Tyler Moore Show* in the 1970s. See the index for other series starring Morey Amsterdam and Sheldon Leonard.

Reruns of *The Dick Van Dyke Show* were a staple on the CBS weekday daytime lineup from August 1965 to September 1969.

DIFF'RENT STROKES
Situation Comedy
FIRST TELECAST: *November 3, 1978*
LAST TELECAST: *August 30, 1986*
BROADCAST HISTORY:
Nov 1978–Oct 1979, NBC Fri 8:00–8:30
Oct 1979–Oct 1981, NBC Wed 9:00–9:30
Oct 1981–Aug 1982, NBC Thu 9:00–9:30
Aug 1982–Aug 1985, NBC Sat 8:00–8:30
Sep 1985–Mar 1986, ABC Fri 9:00–9:30
Jun 1986–Aug 1986, ABC Sat 8:00–8:30
CAST:
Philip Drummond .... Conrad Bain
Arnold Jackson .... Gary Coleman
Willis Jackson................ Todd Bridges
Kimberly Drummond (1978–1984). Dana Plato
Mrs. Edna Garrett (1978–1979)
.... Charlotte Rae
Adelaide Brubaker (1980–1982)... Nedra Volz
Pearl Gallagher (1982–1986).. Mary Jo Catlett
Aunt Sophia (1981–1982)..... Dody Goodman
Dudley Ramsey (1981–1986)..... Shavar Ross
Mr. Ted Ramsey (1981–1985)........ Le Tari
Miss Chung (1982–1983) ..... Rosalind Chao
Charlene DuPrey (1981–1982) .. Janet Jackson
Robbie Jason (1982–1983) ...... Steven Mond
Lisa Hayes (1982–1986)........ Nikki Swasey
Sam McKinney (1984–1986) .. Danny Cooksey
Maggie McKinney (1984–1985) .. Dixie Carter
Maggie McKinney (1985–1986)
.... Mary Ann Mobley
Charlie (1985–1986)........... Jason Hervey

Pint-sized Gary Coleman was one of the comedy discoveries of the late 1970s. Pudgy cheeks, twinkling eyes, and flawless timing made him seem like an old pro packed into the body of a small child—and he helped turn this improbable comedy into one of the hits of the 1978–1979 season.

Eight-year-old Arnold and his 12-year-old brother Willis were two black kids from Harlem who found themselves quite suddenly in the lap of luxury. Their dying mother, a housekeeper for wealthy Philip Drummond, had extracted from her employer the promise that he would look after her boys. Unlike some of TV's other accidental parents (see, for example, *Family Affair*), Drummond didn't mind at all, and welcomed the two into his Park Avenue apartment as his own. No matter that there were endless double takes when the rich, white Drummond, president of the huge conglomerate Trans Allied, Inc. (though he never seemed to work much), introduced the two spunky black kids as his "sons." They didn't care. There was always plenty of love around—though Willis seemed a bit reserved—and everybody learned little lessons in Living Right in each episode. There were also episodes on such serious subjects as child abuse and the dangers of hitchhiking. First lady Nancy Reagan appeared in a 1983 episode dealing with drug abuse. Rounding out the household was widower Drummond's 13-year-old daughter, Kimberly, and the new housekeeper, the scatterbrained Mrs. Garrett.

As years passed, new characters were introduced. Mrs. Garrett left to become a housemother at the prestigious Eastland School for Girls, which Kimberly was attending, in a spin-off series called *The Facts of Life*. She was replaced as housekeeper first by the somewhat grumpy Adelaide, and then by cheerful Pearl. Dudley arrived on the scene in 1981 as Arnold's best buddy, while Charlene was Willis' girlfriend for a time. Perhaps the most notable addition to all their lives came in 1984. After years of fruitless matchmaking by his sister Sophia and by the kids, Drummond finally fell in love—with a feisty TV-exercise-show hostess named Maggie. They were married in February 1984, adding her young son Sam to the Drummond household. In the fall of 1984 Kimberly graduated from high school and went away to study in Paris.

When *Diff'rent Strokes* premiered NBC had few comedies on its schedule, and it used its new hit to help out some of the others. First *Facts of Life* began with a crossover episode. Then Drummond just happened to buy the Portland, Oregon, radio station where Larry Adler (principal character on *Hello, Larry*) was a talk-show host, leading to some visits there; Larry and Philip, it seemed, were old army buddies.

Coleman was 10 when this series began. He was born with a congenital kidney problem and received a kidney transplant at the age of five, which resulted in his being smaller than normal for his age (a condition that would continue throughout his life). An uncommonly bright and articulate youngster, he seemed quite happy to be alive, and became a frequent and popular guest on talk shows and other series.

NBC aired reruns of *Diff'rent Strokes* on weekdays from April 1982 to December 1983 and from July to September 1984.

DIFFERENT WORLD, A
Situation Comedy
FIRST TELECAST: *September 24, 1987*
LAST TELECAST:
BROADCAST HISTORY:
Sep 1987–   , NBC Thu 8:30–9:00
CAST:

Denise Huxtable	Lisa Bonet
Jaleesa Vinson	Dawnn Lewis
Maggie Lauten	Marisa Tomei
Whitley Gilbert	Jasmine Guy
Dwayne Wayne	Kadeem Hardison
Stevie Rallen	Loretta Devine
J. T. Rallen, her son	Amir Williams
Lettie Bostic (1988–)	Mary Alice
Ron Johnson	Darryl Bell
Millie	Marie-Alise Recasner
Walter Oakes	Sinbad
Gloria	Bee-be Smith
Allison	Kim Wayans
Gregory (1988–)	Kevin Vavasseur

Fresh from her movie debut in the controversial film *Angel Heart,* 19-year-old Lisa Bonet starred in this spin-off from the top-rated *Cosby Show.* The "different world" for Denise Huxtable was college, where for the first time in her life she was out from under the protective wing of her family and trying to make it on her own. As the series began she was a sophomore at Hillman College, a mostly black institution which both her father and grandfather had attended. Dad (Bill Cosby) and the family were only a phone call away, but Denise was determined to show that she was "all grown up" and wasn't going to come running home for money and support at every crisis. That wasn't easy, since the crises came every week, sitcom-style. Denise's roommates were Jaleesa, a 26-year-old freshman who had already been married and divorced, and who had a no-nonsense attitude toward life; and Maggie, a flighty, naive, eternally optimistic chatterbox (and one of the few whites at Hillman).

There were a number of cast changes early in the show's run, with various professors passing through and dorm director Stevie being replaced by Lettie—a colorful woman who had left Hillman to "walk on the wild side" but now had returned to finish her education. Whitley, an uppity Southern belle, and super-cool Dwayne were among the most prominently featured students.

DINAH AND HER NEW BEST FRIENDS
Musical Variety
FIRST TELECAST: *June 5, 1976*

BROADCAST HISTORY:
Jun 1976–Jul 1976, CBS Sat 10:00–11:00
STAR:
Dinah Shore
REGULARS:
Diana Canova
Bruce Kimmel
Gary Mule Deer
Mike Neun
Leland Palmer
Michael Preminger
Avelio Falana
Dee Dee Rescher

This 1976 summer variety series, a replacement for the vacationing Carol Burnett, starred the most successful female variety series performer of the 1950s and 1960s, the versatile Dinah Shore. Working with Miss Shore was a company of regular players who had had little, if any, previous television exposure. They participated in comedy sketches, did their own solos, and blended their talents with those of the guest stars for the week.

DINAH SHORE CHEVY SHOW, THE
Musical Variety
FIRST TELECAST: *October 5, 1956*
LAST TELECAST: *May 12, 1963*
BROADCAST HISTORY:
Oct 1956–Jun 1957, NBC Fri 10:00–11:00
Oct 1957–Jun 1961, NBC Sun 9:00–10:00 (OS)
Oct 1961–Jun 1962, NBC Fri 9:30–10:30
Dec 1962–May 1963, NBC Sun 10:00–11:00
REGULARS:
Dinah Shore
The Skylarks (1956–1957)
The Even Dozen (1961–1962)
The Tony Charmoli Dancers (1957–1962)
The Nick Castle Dancers (1962–1963)
The Harry Zimmerman Orchestra (1957–1961, 1962–1963)
Frank DeVol and His Orchestra (1961–1962)

Dinah Shore, one of the few women to achieve major success as a variety-series host on TV, starred in her own full-hour musical variety show on NBC for seven seasons, following a successful run with the much simpler and shorter *Dinah Shore Show*, which was only 15 minutes long. A full hour enabled Dinah to play host to top-name guest stars, include skits and large production numbers, and expand on her own varied talents. Besides her warm and friendly style, her trademarks on this series were the theme song "See the U.S.A. in your Chevrolet" and the resounding kiss she gave the audience at the end of each show.

When *The Dinah Shore Chevy Show* premiered in 1956 it was as a series of monthly specials. The following fall it moved to Sunday night and became a weekly series. It vacated the Sunday time slot to *Bonanza* in 1961, moved to Friday with the new title *The Dinah Shore Show,* and continued on a rotating basis with assorted specials for two more seasons.

DINAH SHORE SHOW, THE
Music
FIRST TELECAST: *November 27, 1951*
LAST TELECAST: *July 18, 1957*
BROADCAST HISTORY:
Nov 1951–Jul 1957, NBC Tue/Thu 7:30–7:45 (OS)
REGULARS:
Dinah Shore
The Notables, vocal quintet (1951–1955)
The Skylarks, vocal quintet (1955–1957)
Ticker Freeman, pianist
The Vic Schoen Orchestra (1951–1954)
The Harry Zimmerman Orchestra (1954–1957)

Twice weekly for six years, Dinah Shore starred in this live 15-minute musical show that occupied the remainder of the half hour that included the NBC network news. Dinah sang, often gave her accompanist Ticker Freeman a chance to do featured solos, and occasionally had guest stars with whom she chatted and performed.

DINNER DATE WITH VINCENT LOPEZ
see *Vincent Lopez*

DIONE LUCAS SHOW, THE
see *To The Queen's Taste*

DIRTY SALLY
Western
FIRST TELECAST: *January 11, 1974*
LAST TELECAST: *July 19, 1974*
BROADCAST HISTORY:
Jan 1974–Jul 1974, CBS Fri 8:00–8:30
CAST:
Sally Fergus . . . . Jeanette Nolan
Cyrus Pike . . . . Dack Rambo

Dirty Sally was a far cry from the traditional violent Western. Sally Fergus was a hard-drinking, crusty old lady who was traveling west to the California gold fields in a wagon pulled by her faithful mule, Worthless. Her traveling companion was Cyrus Pike, a young ex-gunfighter. His desire to reach their destination met with constant frustration from Sally, who got herself involved in the lives of almost everyone they met along the way.

DISC MAGIC
see *Musical Merry-Go-Round*

DISNEYLAND
see *Walt Disney*

DO IT YOURSELF
Comedy/Information
FIRST TELECAST: *June 26, 1955*
LAST TELECAST: *September 18, 1955*
BROADCAST HISTORY:
Jun 1955–Sep 1955, NBC Sun 7:30–8:00

Dave Willock
Cliff Arquette (as Charley Weaver)

Do It Yourself was a short-lived attempt to mix situation comedy with useful household information. Hobbyist-builder Dave Willock was seen each week in his workshop with two or three projects on his schedule, ranging from the repair of broken appliances to building various objects from scratch. He was "helped" by his friend Charley Weaver, who spent most of the time clowning around, and by other friends who happened to drop by. Despite the horseplay, Willock managed to convey all the information needed to build or repair the projects at hand.

DO YOU TRUST YOUR WIFE?

Quiz/Audience Participation
FIRST TELECAST: *January 3, 1956*
LAST TELECAST: *March 26, 1957*
BROADCAST HISTORY:
Jan 1956–Mar 1957, CBS Tue 10:30–11:00
EMCEE:
Edgar Bergen
ANNOUNCER:
Ed Reimers

Ventriloquist Edgar Bergen was the host of this comedy quiz show, which derived its title from the fact that when Mr. Bergen asked each married team of contestants to answer questions on a given topic, the husband had to decide whether he—or his wife—would try to answer. The jackpot available at the end of each telecast was $100 per week for a full year. Featured on the series along with Mr. Bergen were his assorted dummies: Charlie McCarthy, Mortimer Snerd, and Effie Klinker. The program later moved to daytime where it was seen under the title *Who Do You Trust?* During most of its run as a daytime show, Johnny Carson was the emcee and Ed McMahon the onstage announcer. The daytime version ran from September 1957 to December 1963. When Carson left it to take over *The Tonight Show* in the fall of 1962, he was replaced by Woody Woodbury.

DOBIE GILLIS

syndicated title for *Many Loves of Dobie Gillis, The*

DOC

Situation Comedy
FIRST TELECAST: *August 16, 1975*
LAST TELECAST: *October 30, 1976*
BROADCAST HISTORY:
Aug 1975–Oct 1976, CBS Sat 8:30–9:00
CAST:
"Doc" Joe Bogert............Barnard Hughes
Annie Bogert...............Elizabeth Wilson
Miss Tully..................Mary Wickes
"Happy" Miller...............Irwin Corey

Laurie Bogert Fenner............Judy Kahan
Fred Fenner..................John Harkins
Ben Goldman..................Herbie Faye
Janet Scott (1976)............Audra Lindley
Stanley Moss (1976).....David Ogden Stiers
Woody Henderson (1976)..........Ray Vitte
Teresa Ortega (1976)........Lisa Mordente

During its first season, *Doc* was the story of an old-fashioned doctor practicing medicine in New York City. Joe Bogert was a kindly, soft-spoken doctor who was more concerned with his patients' health than with his fees (similar to *The Practice*, which premiered the following January). He was happily married to a woman who was much tougher with his patients than he was; his daughter and son-in-law (a fellow he disliked intensely) rented the apartment above his. Doc often sought refuge in the company of his friends Ben and Happy.

Marginal ratings during the first season prompted a major overhaul in the fall of 1976. Doc now worked at the Westside Clinic, run by Stanley Moss, and had a new nurse in Janet Scott. Gone were his wife and family and friends from the previous season. The new characters in the series consisted of the people who worked at the clinic with him, including Woody and Teresa. The change didn't help the show, which lasted only two months in the new format before being canceled.

DOC CORKLE

Situation Comedy
FIRST TELECAST: *October 5, 1952*
LAST TELECAST: *October 19, 1952*
BROADCAST HISTORY:
Oct 1952, NBC Sun 7:30–8:00
CAST:
Doc Corkle..................Eddie Mayehoff
Melinda.......................Billie Burke
Winfield Dill..................Arnold Stang
Nellie Corkle................Hope Emerson
Laurie Corkle..............Connie Marshall

Doc Corkle was a neighborhood dentist who was continually beset with money problems and a collection of nutty relatives. The wackiest was his stepsister Melinda, whose well-meaning blunders got Doc and his sister Nellie in all sorts of trouble. His teenage daughter Laurie was engaged to marry Winfield Dill, a youthful millionaire who had inherited six businesses.

This filmed series ran only three weeks. The sponsor, Reynolds Metals, was so disappointed with it that it was quickly canceled and replaced with *Mr. Peepers*. The part of Melinda was played by the famous and, by this time, aging film and theater star, Billie Burke.

DOC ELLIOT

Medical Drama
FIRST TELECAST: *January 23, 1974*

LAST TELECAST: *August 14, 1974*
BROADCAST HISTORY:
  Jan 1974–Aug 1974, ABC Wed 10:00–11:00
CAST:
  Dr. Benjamin Elliot. . . . . James Franciscus
  Mags Brimble . . . . Neva Patterson
  Barney Weeks . . . . Noah Beery
  Eldred McCoy . . . . Bo Hopkins
PRODUCER:
  Sandor Stern, M.D.
MAIN THEME:
  by Marvin Hamlisch

This contemporary drama concerned a drop-out
doctor who gave up his career in New York City
to become a blue-jeaned G.P. in Gideon,
Colorado. Doc's new patients, most of them as
independent as he, were spread over a 600-
square-mile area of rugged terrain, and his house
calls (better named cabin calls) were made by
plane or in a four-wheel-drive camper outfitted
with medical equipment. Mags Brimble was the
widow of the area's former G.P. and Doc's helper
and confidante; Barney Weeks the owner of the
general store; and Eldred McCoy a bush pilot.
There was lots of attractive mountain scenery in
this series.

DOCTOR, THE
Medical Anthology
FIRST TELECAST: *August 24, 1952*
LAST TELECAST: *June 28, 1953*
BROADCAST HISTORY:
  Aug 1952–Jun 1953, NBC Sun 10:00–10:30
CAST:
  The Doctor . . . . Warner Anderson

The Doctor was a series of dramas centering
more on situations of high emotional stress than
on physical ailments. An assortment of actors and
actresses appeared, among them Jay Jostyn, Anne
Jackson, Ernest Truex, Mildred Natwick, and Lee
Marvin. Except for the infrequent occasions on
which he also starred in the story, Warner Anderson appeared only at the beginning and end of
each episode, to set the scene and discuss the
outcome.

DR. FIX-UM
Information
FIRST TELECAST: *May 3, 1949*
LAST TELECAST: *August 6, 1950*
BROADCAST HISTORY:
  May 1949–Jun 1949, ABC Tue 9:30–10:00
  Nov 1949–Jan 1950, ABC Sun 6:45–7:00
  Jan 1950–Aug 1950, ABC Sun 7:45–8:00
HOST:
  Arthur Youngquist
  Ed Prentiss

Dr. Fix-Um was a program of helpful household
hints in which Arthur Youngquist showed how to
repair broken gadgets and gave solutions to vari-

ous other household problems. The program was
telecast from Chicago, where it continued to be
seen as a local program after the network run.

DR. HUDSON'S SECRET JOURNAL
Medical Drama
BROADCAST HISTORY:
  Syndicated only
  30 minutes
  Produced: *1955–1957* (78 episodes)
  Released: *Fall 1955*
CAST:
  Dr. Wayne Hudson . . . . John Howard
  Kathy Hudson . . . . Cheryl Callaway
  Mrs. Grady . . . . Olive Blakeney
  Nurse Ann Talbot . . . . Frances Mercer
  Dr. Bennett . . . . Jack Kelly

This syndicated medical series was based on a
character in one of the best-selling novels of the
20th century. Dr. Wayne Hudson was killed off at
the start of Lloyd C. Douglas's *Magnificent Obsession* (1929), but his private journal, written in a
secret code, helped guide young Bobby Merrick
spiritually and professionally as he struggled to
become a doctor and save the eyesight of Hudson's widow. A subsequent book by Douglas, *Dr.
Hudson's Secret Journal* (1939), reprinted the journal in full, and served as the basis for this program.
The TV series largely dispensed with the religious overtones of Douglas' books (as had the two
weepy movie versions of *Magnificent Obsession*,
made in 1935 and 1954). Nevertheless it was clear
that Hudson, a noted neurosurgeon at Center Hospital, had a strange and rather mysterious gift in
his ability to help others psychologically as well
as physically. He needed such talents, as he encountered a succession of shattered lives as well
as shattered bodies in his weekly rounds. A widower, he lived with his young daughter, Kathy,
and their housekeeper, Mrs. Grady.
An unusual aspect of the series was the nationwide competition held in the pages of *TV Guide*
in 1955 to find a young actor to play the role of
Hudson's protégé, Tim Watson, in several episodes. Those entering had to submit a photograph
and a recording ("professional or amusement-
park type") in which they read some emotional
dialogue. The winner, one Joe Walker, does not
appear to have found fame in show business,
however.

DOCTOR I.Q.
Quiz/Audience Participation
FIRST TELECAST: *November 4, 1953*
LAST TELECAST: *March 23, 1959*
BROADCAST HISTORY:
  Nov 1953, ABC Wed 9:30–10:00
  Dec 1953–Jan 1954, ABC Thu 9:00–9:30
  Jan 1954–Mar 1954, ABC Mon 8:30–9:00
  Apr 1954–Oct 1954, ABC Sun 9:30–10:00
  Dec 1958–Mar 1959, ABC Sun 9:30–10:00

Jay Owen (1953–1954)
James McClain (1954)
Tom Kennedy (1958–1959)

Doctor I.Q., one of radio's more popular quiz shows, came to television for two brief runs in the 1950s. "The Doctor" stood behind a podium on the stage and fired questions at people seated in the studio audience. Roving assistants with hand microphones located the contestants and shot back to the Doctor such familiar phrases as "I have a lady in the balcony, Doctor." The questions were reasonably intelligent, and winners were always paid off in silver dollars ("Give that lady ten silver dollars!").

DOCTOR IN THE HOUSE
Situation Comedy
BROADCAST HISTORY:
Syndicated only
30 minutes
Produced: *1970–1973* (78 episodes)
Released (U.S.): *Fall 1971*
CAST:
Dr. Michael Upton (1970–1972) .. Barry Evans
Dr. Duncan Waring .... Robin Nedwell
Dr. Dick Stuart-Clark .... Geoffrey Davies
Prof. Geoffrey Loftus .... Ernest Clark
The Dean .... Ralph Michael
Paul Collier .... George Layton
Huw Evans................... Martin Shaw
Dave Briddock................. Simon Cuff
Danny Hooley .... Jonathan Lynn
Dr. Bingham............. Richard O'Sullivan
Nurses
  Donna Reading, Sammie Winmill, Siobhan Quinlan, Madeline Smith, others

This English comedy about a group of madcap medical students was set at crumbling St. Swithin's Teaching Hospital in London—which, as the Dean informed us in the opening episode, "is not one of the oldest but was founded in 1560, after a severe outbreak of venereal disease that followed closely on the discovery of America."

The three principals were newly arrived and youthful Dr. Michael Upton, his newfound friend Duncan Waring, and perpetual malingerer Dick Stuart-Clark. Their nemesis was the crochety and ever put-upon Prof. Loftus. The boys were constantly in trouble, whether hatching schemes or pranks, throwing up in anatomy class, or chasing the shapely nurses who populated St. Swithin's. A large cast of semi-regulars also appeared.

Doctor in the House was originally a series of books popular in England in the early 1950s. The author, a newly graduated and bored Dr. Richard Gordon, wrote the first while he was a ship's doctor on a cargo vessel en route to Australia. The books led to a hugely successful (in England) series of movies starring Dirk Bogarde, and, around 1970, to a London Weekend Television network

series which became a national craze. The TV scripts were supervised by Dr. Gordon himself, and the show was taped before a live audience. Although it was quickly exported to, and popular in, many other countries, cracking the U.S. market was difficult. American station managers resisted (1) anything English and (2) anything making fun of doctors. It finally made it to the U.S. and became a popular program here for several seasons.

DR. KILDARE
Medical Drama
FIRST TELECAST: *September 28, 1961*
LAST TELECAST: *August 30, 1966*
BROADCAST HISTORY:
  Sep 1961–Sep 1965, NBC Thu 8:30–9:30
  Sep 1965–Aug 1966, NBC Mon/Tue 8:30–9:00
CAST:
Dr. James Kildare...... Richard Chamberlain
Dr. Leonard Gillespie ..... Raymond Massey
Dr. Simon Agurski (1961–1962) .. Eddie Ryder
Dr. Thomas Gerson (1961–1962) ... Jud Taylor
Receptionist Susan Deigh (1961–1962)
  .... Joan Patrick
Nurse Zoe Lawton (1965–1966) .... Lee Kurty
PRODUCER:
Norman Felton

Dr. Kildare came to television after having been an extremely successful series of movies in the 1940s. There was something immensely appealing about the story of a young intern in a large metropolitan hospital trying to learn his profession, deal with the problems of the patients, and win the respect of the senior doctor in his specialty, internal medicine. Kildare was the young intern, Dr. Gillespie the father figure, and Blair General the hospital in which they practiced medicine. The series did not flinch from realistic portrayals of hospital life and the life-and-death aspect of the work. Interestingly, both *Dr. Kildare* and *Ben Casey,* possibly the two most successful medical shows ever aired on television, arrived in the same season.

During the course of its run, *Dr. Kildare* went through an evolutionary process. By the third season Kildare was promoted to resident. His intern buddies from the first season, Drs. Agurski and Gerson, were not seen in subsequent seasons as the program came to center more closely on the patients and their families. In the 1965–1966 season the show was aired twice a week as a half-hour program rather than once a week for an hour, as previously. Although each episode was self-contained, the series began to take on more of a serial nature, with consecutive episodes developing an overall story. Some of these extended stories ran for only two episodes, others for as many as six.

The Kildare stories were also seen in a 1972 syndicated series called *Young Dr. Kildare,* starring Mark Jenkins as Kildare and Gary Merrill as Gillespie.

DR. SIMON LOCKE
Medical Drama

BROADCAST HISTORY:
Syndicated only
30 minutes
Produced: *1971–1974*
Released: *Fall 1971*

CAST:

Dr. Simon Locke	Sam Groom
Dr. Sellers *(1971–1972)*	Jack Albertson
Nurse Wynn *(1971–1972)*	Nuala Fitzgerald
Chief/Det. Lt. Dan Palmer *(1971–1973)*	
	Len Birman
Lt. Jack Gordon *(1973–1974)*	Larry D. Mann

This Canadian-produced medical drama was very cheaply made, and critics found it awful, but nevertheless it survived for three seasons in syndication in the U.S. In the first season Dr. Simon Locke was an earnest young physician newly arrived in the small town of Dixon Mills, where his mentor was the crusty Dr. Sellers. Despite the rural locale, Locke encountered all sorts of excitement, such as murders, battered children, and a typhoid epidemic. In its second season the show moved to the city, where Locke was assigned to the police emergency unit, finding even more crime-oriented (though generally nonviolent) stories. Chief Palmer of Dixon Mills came along as his tough-talking police boss. ("Remember," he growled at Locke, "you're only second line. Don't become a hero.") The title was changed to *Police Surgeon*. In the final season, Lt. Gordon became Locke's police superior. A guest-star policy was also instituted in the second and third seasons, with such well-known actors as William Shatner, Leslie Nielsen, Keenan Wynn, and Susan Strasberg appearing.

The behind-the-scenes story of *Dr. Simon Locke* is an interesting, if extreme, case study in how syndicated programs get on the air. It isn't simply a matter of a producer having a bright idea, followed by the audience voting yea or nay. This one began when the Federal Communications Commission announced that starting in the fall of 1971, the networks had to cut back their evening programming, and local stations would have to fill the vacated time—generally 7:30–8:00 P.M.—with original shows (not reruns). The idea was to encourage localized programming, but that didn't happen. Syndicators, who sell their programs station to station, rushed out all sorts of first-run candidates. The problem was that they had to be very cheap, because without network financing and guaranteed exposure, the risk capital simply wasn't available for big-budget production. As a result, what the public got was mostly inexpensive game shows and nature documentaries. However, the Colgate-Palmolive Co., sponsor of *Dr. Kildare* and the daytime serial *The Doctors*, was persuaded by its advertising agency to finance a dramatic show about a young doctor who moves to a rural town.

The first necessity was to get production out of Hollywood, where expenses were astronomical. The second was to find a way to sell the program to other countries, to help defray costs. Unfortunately many countries had recently instituted severe quotas on the amount of programming that could be imported from the U.S. So production was moved to Toronto, thus qualifying the series as "Canadian"—okay for Canada and the British Empire—and cheap enough for the U.S. Little-known Sam Groom, a refugee from *Another World,* provided an inexpensive lead. Jack Albertson was lured away from Hollywood as the only "name" in the cast.

Still, budgets were so skinflinty that when Albertson arrived to do location filming he found he literally had to change his pants in the bushes. The director refused to screen the results of each day's filming for him (again, to save money), and he never saw a show until the first three were edited and complete. When he did, he was furious at the mess—incredibly sloppy production, microphones in camera range, bad lighting, choppy editing, dreadful scripts. He promptly quit to save his reputation. "You have a contract," insisted the producer. "After what I just saw," exploded Albertson, "there's not a jury in the world that would convict me!"

Albertson was mollified, at least temporarily, but when critics saw the results on the air they were even madder. "Sub-sub par . . . unbelievable . . . It is literally impossible to assume that any viewer would return for a second look. . . . No way, no way!" cried *Variety.* "A syndie quickie," groaned *TV Guide.* "The only way [the producers] could break even with this show would be if they gave something away with it."

So how did it survive? Economics. It was not only cheap, the producers actually *gave* it to stations—with the understanding that two of the commercials in each episode remain with them (called "barter" in the trade). These went to Colgate, who had put up the cash. Although audiences weren't sizable, they did contain a fair number of young women (Colgate's clientele), and the sponsor liked Sam Groom and thought perhaps the show could be juiced up with the move to the city. Things limped along this way until 1974, when Colgate finally found better things to do with its money, and Dr. Locke closed up shop. Without the benefit of the legislative and economic accident that put it on the air, *Dr. Simon Locke* was scarcely seen at all in reruns.

DOCTORS AND THE NURSES, THE
see *Nurses, The*

DOCTORS' HOSPITAL
Medical Drama

FIRST TELECAST: *September 10, 1975*
LAST TELECAST: *January 14, 1976*
BROADCAST HISTORY:
Sep 1975–Jan 1976, NBC Wed 9:00–10:00

CAST:
 Dr. Jake Goodwin........... George Peppard
 Dr. Norah Purcell............ Zohra Lampert
 Dr. Felipe Ortega .... Victor Campos
 Janos Varga .... Albert Paulsen
 Dr. Chaffey................... Russ Martin
 Dr. Paul Herman........... John Larroquette
 Dr. Danvers .... John Pleshette
 Dr. Anson Brooks.......... James Almanzar
 Nurse Connie Kimbrough... Elizabeth Brooks
 Nurse Hester Stanton .... Adrian Ricard
 Nurse Forester............. Barbara Darrow
 Nurse Wilson................ Elaine Church
 Nurse Franklin .... Susan Franklin
 Barney...................... Larry Watson
 Scotty...................... Maxine Stuart

Set at fictitious Lowell Memorial Hospital in Los Angeles, this medical series sought a unique approach to hospital life: it examined all aspects of that life—the good and the bad—through the eyes of the doctors rather than those of the patients. Dr. Jake Goodwin was the chief of neurosurgical services at the hospital, and Norah Purcell was a second-year resident and his most gifted student. Dr. Ortega was the chief resident at Lowell Memorial and Janos Varga its director. To minimize the roles of the patients, a large number of them were treated in each episode, thereby shifting the emphasis to the work and personalities of the doctors and the other members of the hospital staff.

DOCTORS' PRIVATE LIVES
Medical Drama
FIRST TELECAST: *April 5, 1979*
LAST TELECAST: *April 26, 1979*
BROADCAST HISTORY:
 Apr 1979, ABC Thu 10:00–11:00
CAST:
 Dr. Michael Wise................ Ed Nelson
 Dr. Jeffrey Latimer.............. John Gavin
 Dr. Rick Calder............ Randolph Powell
 Kenny Wise................... Phil Levien
 Sheila Castle .... Gwen Humble
 Nurse Diane Cooper .... Eddie Benton

This series focused on the personal and professional crises of two famous heart surgeons, Chief Surgeon Dr. Michael Wise and cardiovascular unit chief Dr. Jeffrey Latimer. Worrying along with them were young Dr. Rick Calder, medical students Kenny Wise and Shelia Castle, and Nurse Cooper.

DOG AND CAT
Police Drama
FIRST TELECAST: *March 5, 1977*
LAST TELECAST: *May 14, 1977*
BROADCAST HISTORY:
 Mar 1977–May 1977, ABC Sat 10:00–11:00

CAST:
 Det. Sgt. Jack Ramsey.......... Lou Antonio
 Officer J. Z. Kane .... Kim Basinger
 Lt. Arthur Kipling............... Matt Clark

This was a police show with a light sense of humor. It had to be, to team an experienced veteran plainclothes cop (Ramsey) with a bright, sexy, and, of course, competent female rookie (Kane) and expect nothing but police work to occur. Lt. Kipling was the boss. The program was filmed in Southern California.

DOLLAR A SECOND
Quiz/Audience Participation
FIRST TELECAST: *September 20, 1953*
LAST TELECAST: *September 28, 1957*
BROADCAST HISTORY:
 Sep 1953–Apr 1954, DUM Sun 10:00–10:30
 Apr 1954–Jun 1954, DUM Mon 8:00–8:30
 Jul 1954–Aug 1954, NBC Sun 10:00–10:30
 Oct 1954–Jun 1955, ABC Fri 9:00–9:30
 Jul 1955–Aug 1955, NBC Tue 9:30–10:00
 Sep 1955–Sep 1956, ABC Fri 9:00–9:30
 Jun 1957–Sep 1957, NBC Sat 9:30–10:00
 Sep 1957, NBC Sat 10:00–10:30
EMCEE:
 Jan Murray

In this comedy quiz show the contestant could win money in two ways: he or she won a dollar for every correct answer and another dollar for every second he stayed on the show. There was a catch, however, and that was called "the outside event." While the contestant was answering questions, and paying funny but embarrassing penalties for wrong answers (as in *Truth or Consequences*), something was going on outside the studio that might cause him or her to forfeit all winnings. The contestant could choose to quit at any time and keep all winnings up to that point, or continue in the hope that the outside event would not take place until after the show was over. The contestant did not know the nature of the outside event, but viewers did. It might be the arrival of a train at a specified point, or the landing of a given plane at LaGuardia Airport, or the birth of a baby at a designated hospital. A remote camera looked in periodically on the event about to take place, to heighten the suspense for the viewing audience.

$1.98 BEAUTY SHOW, THE
Comedy
BROADCAST HISTORY:
 Syndicated only
 30 minutes
 Produced: *1978–1980*
 Released: *September 1978*
HOST:
 Rip Taylor
EXECUTIVE PRODUCER:
 Chuck Barris

Critics howled with disgust, but audiences seemed to enjoy this intentionally tacky travesty on the traditional American beauty pageant. "Chuck Barris [the producer] seems determined to become the leading purveyor of bad taste on the tube," groaned *Variety*. The format called for six contestants, some sexy, some gross, to vie for a crown. First they were introduced, to good-natured ribbing by chubby, mustachioed host Rip Taylor and the rambunctious panel; then came the "talent" competition, in which 200-pound lady plumbers did the "Dance of the Sugar Plum Fairies," and off-key singers bellowed their way through hapless ballads (shades of *The Gong Show!*); and finally there was the swimsuit competition, in which the girls purred, nervously tiptoed, or defiantly waddled through their paces "deprived of all their worldly goods." Hoots and cheers from the audience! Some of the contestants were pretty sexy, but the fat ladies always seemed to do best in this last segment.

The winner got $1.98 plunked into her hand, and a tacky crown. In his gaudy vest, host Taylor presided over the tumult with unctuous charm. Frequent celebrity panelists included Jaye P. Morgan, Jamie Farr, Louis Nye, Marty Allen, and the Unknown Comic (Murray Langston).

DOLLY
Music
BROADCAST HISTORY:
    Syndicated only
    30 minutes
    Produced: *1976* (52 episodes)
    Released: *February 1976*
HOSTESS:
    Dolly Parton

Country superstar Dolly Parton, with her generous bust, mountainous wig, and sequinned pseudo-cowgirl outfit, hosted this half-hour of music taped in Nashville. Guests included country-pop talent such as Tennessee Ernie Ford, Bobby Goldsboro, Lynn Anderson, Rod McKuen, and even Captain Kangaroo. Though Miss Parton was a major star in the country field, she had not yet emerged into the popular mainstream at this time; as her fame spread over the next few years, the program was widely repeated.

DOLLY
Musical Variety
FIRST TELECAST: *September 27, 1987*
LAST TELECAST: *May 7, 1988*
BROADCAST HISTORY:
    Sep 1987–Jan 1988, ABC Sun 9:00–10:00
    Jan 1988–May 1988, ABC Sat 8:00–9:00
REGULARS:
    Dolly Parton
    A Cappella (singing group)

ABC made a valiant attempt to revive the concept of a big, splashy prime-time variety show in this 1987 series headlined by country superstar Dolly Parton. The petite (5'2") Miss Parton, in her towering blonde wigs and skin-tight fashions, never looked better ("It takes a lot of money to make me look this cheap," she cracked). The accent was on music "with a lot of heart," mostly of the country or country-pop variety, often in cozy settings such as Dolly's rustic living room with its roaring fireplace, rather than on a stage. There were also comedy sketches in recurring settings including Dixie's Place Cafe (with Dolly as a waitress), the Vanity Fair Beauty Salon, "D.P.'s" country music club, or on "Dolly's Date."

Guests included Burt Reynolds, country groups Alabama and The Oak Ridge Boys, Whoopi Goldberg, Willie Nelson, the Smothers Brothers, and Kermit the Frog. A Cappella was Dolly's backup group, consisting of Richard Dennison, Gene Miller, Dave Rowland, and Howard Smith.

DOM DELUISE SHOW, THE
Comedy Variety
FIRST TELECAST: *May 1, 1968*
LAST TELECAST: *September 18, 1968*
BROADCAST HISTORY:
    May 1968–Sep 1968, CBS Wed 10:00–11:00
REGULARS:
    Dom DeLuise
    Marian Mercer
    Bill McCutcheon
    Carol Arthur
    Paul Dooley
    Mike and Joe Gentry
    Dick Lynn
    The June Taylor Dancers
    Sammy Spear and His Orchestra

Pudgy comedian Dom DeLuise hosted and starred in this summer variety series. The emphasis was on comedy, with DeLuise's pantomime routines frequently featured. Guest stars appeared on each telecast, along with a cast of regulars. One of the regulars, Carol Arthur, was Dom's wife.

DOM DELUISE SHOW, THE
Situation Comedy
BROADCAST HISTORY:
    Syndicated only
    30 minutes
    Produced: *1987–*
    Released: *September 1987*
CAST:
    Dom .... Dom DeLuise
    George Henry Wallace ...... George Wallace
    Maureen .... Maureen Murphy
    Penny .... Angela Aames
    Michael Chambers .... Michael Chambers
    Blanche Maxwell .... Lois Foraker
    Rosa .... Lauren Woodland
    Charlie .... Charlie Callas
    Billy (1987) .... Billy Scudder

This series described itself as "almost, but not quite, a situation comedy" and did so with good reason. Although the regulars, most of whom had considerable experience as stand-up comics, all stayed in character, individual scenes frequently tended to look like variety-show comedy sketches or comedy monologues. On top of everything else, star Dom DeLuise (and on occasion others in the cast) sometimes talked directly to the viewing audience, much as George Burns had done three decades earlier on *The George Burns and Gracie Allen Show*.

Most of the action took place in Dom's Barber Shop, where Dom and his black partner George held court for their customers and friends. Among them were Maureen, their spaced-out manicurist; Penny, the sexy young aerobics instructor who worked nearby; Michael, the loose-limbed pizza delivery boy who could dance up a storm; Charlie, the paranoid, trenchcoated private detective; and Billy, the Chaplinesque (including tramp costume and walk) little man who advertised Dom's Barber Shop with a small sign on his back. Dom, a widower who took pride in being a gourmet cook, lived behind the barber shop with his cute 10-year-old daughter Rosa. His girlfriend Blanche owned a neighborhood pet shop and had given him Max, his pet chimpanzee, as a Christmas present. Located near the big movie studios in Hollywood, the barber shop was visited by celebrities like Burt Reynolds, Sherman Hemsley, Zsa Zsa Gabor, Dean Martin, and Tom Jones.

DOMESTIC LIFE
Situation Comedy
FIRST TELECAST: *January 4, 1984*
LAST TELECAST: *September 11, 1984*
BROADCAST HISTORY:
Jan 1984–Feb 1984, CBS Wed 8:00–8:30
Mar 1984–Apr 1984, CBS Sun 8:00–8:30
Jul 1984–Sep 1984, CBS Tue 8:30–9:00
CAST:
Martin Crane .... Martin Mull
Harold Crane .... Christian Brackett-Zika
Didi Crane .... Megan Follows
Cliff Hamilton .... Robert Ridgely
Candy Crane .... Judith-Marie Bergan
Jane Funakubo .... Mie Hunt
Rip Steele .... Hoyt Axton
Jeff, the floor manager .... J. Alan Thomas
EXECUTIVE PRODUCER:
Steve Martin

Comedian Steve Martin produced this comedy about a slightly offbeat family, which was turned down by one network (NBC) and then had a short and unsuccessful run on another (CBS). Martin Crane had just arrived in Seattle to take a job as a commentator for station KMRT-TV. His regular spot on the station's evening news was called "Domestic Life," and dealt with the humorous side of home and family life. He certainly had a lot to talk about! His wife Candy was a sucker for

other people's problems, and vaguely dissatisfied with their own limited finances. Daughter Didi was a typical, semicontrollable 15-year-old. Harold, their chubby ten-year-old son, talked like a businessman, had an office in his room, and had already netted thousands from wise investments. In some ways he was more mature than his parents, though he still wanted a hug and a kiss when he gave them a loan.

Martin's life was usually in an uproar both at home and at the station, where Cliff and Jane were fellow reporters and Rip Steele—an ex-cowboy star of "B" movies—was the colorful, guitar-strumming station owner.

DON ADAMS' SCREEN TEST
Comedy/Audience Participation
BROADCAST HISTORY:
Syndicated only
30 minutes
Produced: *1974–1975* (26 episodes)
Released: *Fall 1975*
HOST/"DIRECTOR":
Don Adams

Comedian Don Adams hosted this original but high-decibel audience-participation show, in which pre-selected studio contestants were paired with guest stars to reenact famous movie scenes. First the original scene was shown, via a film clip. Then the contestant and celebrity did it, usually for laughs (in the beach scene from *From Here to Eternity*, for example, everybody got drenched with buckets of water). Don Adams served as "director" and sometimes participant in the scenes. A professional TV or movie director picked the winner, who got a bit part in an upcoming real production—although that part was incidental to the laughs. Among the stars appearing were Milton Berle, Mel Brooks, Bob Newhart, and Greg Morris; the movies parodied included *On the Waterfront*, *Pillow Talk*, *Bride of Frankenstein*, and *The African Queen*.

DON AMECHE'S MUSICAL PLAYHOUSE
see *Holiday Hotel*

DON KIRSHNER'S ROCK CONCERT
Music
BROADCAST HISTORY:
Syndicated only
90 minutes
Produced: *1973–1981*
Released: *September 1973*
HOST:
Don Kirshner

This was one of the two principal showcases for rock music in the mid- and late-1970s. Although it was syndicated for local airing anywhere on a station's schedule, it usually ran late at night, like NBC's *Midnight Special*. The emphasis was on progressive rock bands, such as the Allman Brothers, Fleetwood Mac, Black Sabbath, Led Zeppelin, and the Ramones, but a wide variety of contemporary talent appeared—Paul McCartney and Wings, Dr. Hook, Blondie, Chuck Berry, etc. Mick Jagger and the Rolling Stones headlined the much-heralded premiere in 1973. In the later 1970s soft-pop acts started to creep in (Captain and Tennille, Johnny Nash, Shaun Cassidy, even Debby Boone), but the program never abandoned the non-top-40 side of rock. Some hip comics also were seen, among them Martin Mull, the Village Idiots, and Natural Gas.

Don Kirshner had begun his career with Bobby Darin in the 1950s, and was a major figure in the music business by this time (he was responsible for the Monkees, among others). ABC hired him in late 1972 as impresario for its short-lived *In Concert,* but he left to start his own show a few months later. Some of the executives at ABC, he remarked, didn't seem to know the difference between the Allman Brothers and the Osmond Brothers.

There was no regular host at first. Beginning with the second season, Kirshner himself began to do brief introductions (on camera but offstage).

DON KNOTTS SHOW, THE
Comedy Variety
FIRST TELECAST: *September 15, 1970*
LAST TELECAST: *July 6, 1971*
BROADCAST HISTORY:
  Sep 1970–Jan 1971, NBC Tue 7:30–8:30
  Jan 1971–Jul 1971, NBC Tue 8:00–9:00
REGULARS:
  Don Knotts
  Elaine Joyce
  Bob Williams and his dog Louie
  Frank Welker
  Ken Mars
  Mickey Deems
  John Dehner
  Eddie Carroll
  Gary Burghoff
  The Nick Perito Orchestra

Don Knotts hosted and starred in this comedy variety show. There were two regular features each week: Don and his guest stars in skits about his frustrations caused by the grind of doing a weekly TV show, and "The Front Porch," in which Don and his guest star would sit in rocking chairs and exchange "philosophies."

DON McNEILL TV CLUB
Variety
FIRST TELECAST: *September 13, 1950*
LAST TELECAST: *December 19, 1951*
BROADCAST HISTORY:
  Sep 1950–Jun 1951, ABC Wed 9:00–10:00
  Sep 1951–Dec 1951, ABC Wed 9:00–9:30
  (alternate weeks)
REGULARS:
  Don McNeill

  Johnny Desmond
  Fran Allison
  Sam Cowling
  Patsy Lee
  Eddie Ballantine Orchestra

Don McNeill seemed like a natural for TV. His easygoing, homey style was much like that of Arthur Godfrey, who in 1950 was scoring an enormous hit with his *Arthur Godfrey and His Friends* and *Talent Scouts* programs. McNeill, like Godfrey, had been a radio fixture for years; his *Breakfast Club,* which began in 1933, had almost single-handedly turned early-morning network radio into a profitable medium. Thus, in the fall of 1950 ABC brought McNeill and his *Breakfast Club* gang to nighttime network television, live from his hometown of Chicago.

Music and variety acts were featured, all delivered with the down-home charm and sincerity that had endeared McNeill to millions of radio fans. Among the regulars were Fran Allison doing her rural Aunt Fanny characterization, singer Johnny Desmond, portly comic Sam Cowling, singer-comedienne Patsy Lee, plus show-business guests. The guests never overshadowed the regular cast. Perhaps that was part of the problem; perhaps there was only room for one Godfrey. In any event, McNeill never caught on in television, and after a season and a half in prime time and an attempt at a daytime version of the *Breakfast Club* in 1954, he abandoned the medium to concentrate solely on his radio show (which had continued in the meantime). He continued with it until 1968, a run of over 34 years. His signature was the same on radio and television: "Be good to yourself."

DON RICKLES SHOW, THE
Comedy Variety
FIRST TELECAST: *September 27, 1968*
LAST TELECAST: *January 31, 1969*
BROADCAST HISTORY:
  Sep 1968–Jan 1969, ABC Fri 9:00–9:30
REGULARS:
  Don Rickles
  Pat McCormick
  Vic Mizzy Orchestra

This was a kind of one-man roast, in which Don Rickles directed his famous "insult humor" at guests and audience. Everyone was a "dummy" to Don. Pat McCormick was his gargantuan foil-announcer-factotum, as well as one of the writers of the show. Apparently the viewing audience did not take kindly to this kind of assault, and the show was soon canceled. Those involved bore no grudge, however; at the end of the final telecast the writers and the entire crew and staff carried Rickles off the stage on their shoulders. What they did with him afterward was not revealed.

DON RICKLES SHOW, THE

Situation Comedy

FIRST TELECAST: *January 14, 1972*
LAST TELECAST: *May 26, 1972*

BROADCAST HISTORY:

Jan 1972–May 1972, CBS Fri 10:30–11:00

CAST:

Don Robinson .... Don Rickles
Barbara Robinson.............. Louise Sorel
Janie Robinson .... Erin Moran
Tyler Benedict................ Robert Hogan
Audrey...................... Judy Cassmore
Jean Benedict............. Joyce Van Patten
Conrad Musk .... Barry Gordon

The life and endless problems of a New York advertising-agency executive were the premise for this comedy starring Don Rickles. Don Robinson's loving wife Barbara and his cute young daughter Janie stood by more or less helplessly while Don, the master of insult humor, did constant battle with the frustrations of corporate society. Battlegrounds included his office at Kingston, Cohen and Vanderpool, Inc., and his pleasant Long Island home. Apparently viewers quickly wearied of the fray, as the series was canceled after only four months.

DONALD O'CONNOR TEXACO SHOW, THE

Situation Comedy

FIRST TELECAST: *October 9, 1954*
LAST TELECAST: *September 10, 1955*

BROADCAST HISTORY:

Oct 1954–Sep 1955, NBC Sat 9:30–10:00

CAST:

Donald O'Connor .... Himself
Sid Miller........................ Himself
Doreen...................... Joyce Smight

During the 1954–1955 season the *Texaco Star Theatre* consisted of two alternating series, *The Donald O'Connor Show* and *The Jimmy Durante Show.* O'Connor's half of the venture, which was subtitled "Here Comes Donald," was a loosely structured situation comedy whose primary function was to let Donald perform as a singer and dancer with his songwriting partner Sid Miller. The basic story line presented Donald and Sid as two young songwriters trying to find buyers for their songs and winding up in situations where they had the opportunity to sing, dance, and be comedians. Joyce Smight had the continuing role of their secretary, Doreen.

DONNA REED SHOW, THE

Situation Comedy

FIRST TELECAST: *September 24, 1958*
LAST TELECAST: *September 3, 1966*

BROADCAST HISTORY:

Sep 1958–Sep 1959, ABC Wed 9:00–9:30
Oct 1959–Jan 1966, ABC Thu 8:00–8:30
Jan 1966–Sep 1966, ABC Sat 8:00–8:30

CAST:

Donna Stone.................... Donna Reed
Dr. Alex Stone..................... Carl Betz
Mary Stone (1958–1963) ..... Shelley Fabares
Jeff Stone...................... Paul Petersen
Trisha Stone (1963–1966) ..... Patty Petersen
Dr. Dave Kelsey (1963–1965) ...... Bob Crane
Midge Kelsey (1963–1966)....... Ann McCrea
Karen Holmby (1964–1965)..... Janet Langard
Smitty (1965–1966) .... Darryl Richard

PRODUCER/EXEC. PRODUCER:

Tony Owen

THEME SONG:

"Happy Days," by William Loose and John Seely

At the center of this family comedy were Donna Stone, her husband Alex, a pediatrician, and their rambunctious teenage kids. The adventures of the Stone family were similar to those of other TV families—measles, girlfriends, school problems, little white lies, and so on—compounded by the fact that Dr. Alex was always running off at odd hours to attend to his patients. The show was set in the small town of Hilldale, and it had a wholesome quality that endeared it to audiences. It won many awards from youth, women's, educational, and medical groups; the president of the American Medical Association even appeared in a cameo role in one telecast.

Over the years changes in the series took place. Mary, the older child, went off to college in 1962, followed by Jeff two years later. About the time that Mary left the series for good, in 1963, the character of Trisha, an eight-year-old orphan who "adopted" the Stones, was added. Played by Patty Petersen, Paul's real-life sister, she was first seen in a January 1963 telecast and stayed for the rest of the series. Dave Kelsey was Alex's colleague and the Stones' next-door neighbor, and Midge was Dave's wife. Various friends and romances of Mary and Jeff appeared from time to time, the most regular of whom were Paul's girlfriend Karen and his college buddy Smitty.

Both of Donna Reed's original TV offspring had short but spectacular recording careers in 1962–1963 with songs introduced on the series. On a January 1962 telecast Paul Petersen sang the novelty ditty "She Can't Find Her Keys," as part of a dream sequence in which Jeff dreamed he was a teenage recording star out on a date. His recording of the song became a major hit during early 1962. Later he had several other best sellers, including the top-ten hit "My Dad," about Dr. Alex. Shelley Fabares did even better with a teenage love song called "Johnny Angel," which went to number one on the charts in early 1962 and earned her a gold record, denoting sales of more than a million copies.

Reruns of *The Donna Reed Show* were telecast weekdays on ABC from December 1964 to March 1968.

DONNY AND MARIE

Musical Variety

FIRST TELECAST: *January 16, 1976*
LAST TELECAST: *May 6, 1979*
BROADCAST HISTORY:

Jan 1976–May 1977, ABC Fri 8:00–9:00
Jun 1977–Aug 1977, ABC Wed 8:00–9:00
Aug 1977–Jan 1979, ABC Fri 8:00–9:00 (OS)
Jan 1979–Mar 1979, ABC Sun 7:00–8:00
May 1979, ABC Sun 7:00–8:00

REGULARS:

Donny Osmond
Marie Osmond
Alan Osmond
Wayne Osmond
Merrill Osmond
Jay Osmond
Johnny Dark (1978–1979)
Jimmy Osmond
The Ice Vanities (1976–1977)
The Ice Angels (1977–1978)
The Disco Dozen (1978–1979)
Jim Connell
Larry Larsen

Sid and Marty Krofft of animated cartoon fame originally produced this teenage variety hour. Eighteen-year-old Donny and his 16-year-old sister Marie were co-hosts of the show, which also featured other members of the popular musical family, ranging in age from Jimmy (12) to Alan (26). Despite his youth, Donny was a show-business veteran by the time the program premiered, having made his TV debut at the age of four singing "You Are My Sunshine" on *The Andy Williams Show.* In order to keep up the clan's youthful appearance, Merrill introduced another Osmond—his six-month old son Travis—to the cast on an early telecast.

The format was the usual mixture of comedy and songs, with a liberal sprinkling of the Osmonds' teenybopper hits. The comedy often made fun of Donny's toothy, super-wholesome appearance, as when his brothers ganged up and dumped him into a gigantic nine-foot whipped cream pie in one 1976 broadcast. "I think I finally made a big splash on television," Donny said. Although not credited as a regular, Paul Lynde appeared as a guest star on many of the *Donny and Marie* episodes.

The second season brought changes, as a new production team took over in an attempt to give the show a more "adult" look. Much was made of Marie's stunning new wardrobe, designed by Bob Mackie (Cher's former designer), and her eighteenth birthday party was telecast in October. However, *Donny and Marie* remained, at heart, a homey affair. Tired of the tinsel and glitter of Hollywood, the entire Osmond clan packed up and moved back to their hometown of Orem, Utah, in late 1977; all subsequent telecasts originated from the elaborate studio facility built there by the Osmonds at a cost of $2.5 million, to house their various TV and film activities. The first episode taped in Orem was the 1977 Christmas show, which starred Paul Lynde, the Mormon Tabernacle Choir, and 28 members of the Osmond family.

Midway through the final season, Donny turned 21 (and to prove it he had his wife Debbie on the show!). In January 1979 the series moved to Sunday night and was retitled *The Osmond Family Show.*

DON'T CALL ME CHARLIE

Situation Comedy

FIRST TELECAST: *September 21, 1962*
LAST TELECAST: *January 25, 1963*
BROADCAST HISTORY:

Sep 1962–Jan 1963, NBC Fri 9:30–10:00

CAST:

Judson McKay .... Josh Peine
Pat Perry .... Linda Lawson
Col. U. Charles Barker .... John Hubbard
First Sgt. Wozniak .... Cully Richards
Gen. Steele .... Alan Napier
Cpl. Lefkowitz .... Arte Johnson
Selma Yossarian .... Louise Glenn
Madame Fatima .... Penny Santon

This "military" comedy centered on Judson McKay, a young veterinarian from Iowa, who was drafted by mistake and assigned to a U.S. Army veterinary station in Paris. The principal conflict was between good-natured country boy McKay and his pompous commander, Col. U. Charles Barker, the "Charlie" of the title. Arte Johnson played the supporting role of Cpl. Lefkowitz. Pat Perry was the general's secretary, Selma Yossarian another secretary, and Mme. Fatima the concierge.

DOODLES WEAVER

Comedy Variety

FIRST TELECAST: *June 9, 1951*
LAST TELECAST: *September 1, 1951*
BROADCAST HISTORY:

Jun 1951–Jul 1951, NBC Sat 10:00–10:15
Aug 1951–Sep 1951, NBC Sat 10:00–10:30

REGULARS:

Doodles Weaver
Marion Colby
Milton Delugg and His Orchestra
Red Marshall
Dick Dana
Peanuts Mann

In the premiere telecast, Doodles Weaver was informed that he had to put together a low-budget summer show without sets, scenery, or dancing girls. He was left with an empty television studio and discarded sets and props from other shows. Although this was supposed to be a joke, it set the tone for a rather formless improvisational comedy series. Veteran burlesque comics Marshall, Dana, and Mann contributed laughs and singer Marion Colby provided musical support.

DOOR WITH NO NAME
see *Doorway To Danger*

DOORWAY TO DANGER
International Intrigue
FIRST TELECAST: *July 6, 1951*
LAST TELECAST: *October 1, 1953*
BROADCAST HISTORY:
Jul 1951–Aug 1951, NBC Fri 9:00–9:30
Jul 1952–Aug 1952, NBC Fri 9:00–9:30
Jul 1953–Oct 1953, ABC Thu 8:30–9:00
CAST:
John Randolph (1951)............. Mel Ruick
John Randolph (1952)........ Roland Winters
John Randolph (1953)..... Raymond Bramley
Doug Carter (1951).......... Grant Richards
Doug Carter (1953)............. Stacy Harris
NARRATOR:
Westbrook Van Voorhis (1951)

Doorway to Danger was a summer replacement series during the early 1950s. It told, in quasi-documentary style, stories of international intrigue involving operatives of federal agencies. The title referred to the door to the office of John Randolph, chief of a top-secret government agency, who supervised the agents assigned to track down enemies of the United States. These enemies might be either domestic criminals or agents of a foreign power; smugglers and spies seemed to be the usual opponents in this series.

Doug Carter was Randolph's number one agent during the first and third seasons, and episodes followed Carter around the world on his dangerous assignments. During the second season there was no regular agent, and each week Chief Randolph sent a different trench-coated operative scurrying off to defend the nation.

During its first season this series was known as *Door With No Name*.

DOORWAY TO FAME
Talent
FIRST TELECAST: *May 2, 1947*
LAST TELECAST: *July 11, 1949*
BROADCAST HISTORY:
May 1947–Sep 1947, DUM Fri 7:30–8:00 (approximately)
Oct 1947–Mar 1948, DUM Mon 7:00–7:30
Mar 1949–Jul 1949, DUM Mon 8:30–9:00
REGULARS:
Johnny Olsen
Ned Harvey Orchestra

This was one of the many talent shows that populated early television. Through the doorway came all manner of hopefuls, plus one guest star each week who offered words of encouragement. Some 20,000 New York-area residents were said to have auditioned for the show during its first year, but none are known to have gone on to stardom.

DORIS DAY SHOW, THE
Situation Comedy
FIRST TELECAST: *September 24, 1968*
LAST TELECAST: *September 10, 1973*
BROADCAST HISTORY:
Sep 1968–Sep 1969, CBS Tue 9:30–10:00
Sep 1969–Sep 1973, CBS Mon 9:30–10:00
CAST:
Doris Martin .... Doris Day
Buck Webb (1968–1970)........ Denver Pyle
Aggie Thompson (1968)........... Fran Ryan
Leroy B. Simpson (1968–1969)
.... James Hampton
Billy Martin (1968–1971)........ Philip Brown
Toby Martin (1968–1971)........ Todd Starke
Juanita (1968–1969)........... Naomi Stevens
Myrna Gibbons (1969–1971)...... Rose Marie
Michael Nicholson (1969–1971)
.... McLean Stevenson
Ron Harvey (1969–1971) .... Paul Smith
Angie Palucci (1970–1971) ..... Kaye Ballard
Louie Palucci (1970–1971)...... Bernie Kopell
Cy Bennett (1971–1973) .... John Dehner
Jackie Parker (1971–1973)...... Jackie Joseph

When *The Doris Day Show* premiered in the fall of 1968, Miss Day was cast as a widow with two young sons who had decided to move back to the family ranch after spending most of her life in big cities. The adjustments to rural living provided much of the comedy. The ranch was run by her father Buck, their hired hand Leroy, and the housekeeper Aggie (replaced in December by a new housekeeper, Juanita).

At the start of the second season Doris became a commuter. She got a job as a secretary at *Today's World* magazine in San Francisco and commuted daily from the farm. Mr. Nicholson, the editor of the magazine, was her boss, and Myrna Gibbons was a secretary with whom she became friendly. At the start of the third season Doris, her two boys, and their huge dog Lord Nelson left the farm and moved into a San Francisco apartment owned by the Paluccis, who ran an Italian restaurant on the ground floor. Doris' activities expanded from merely being Mr. Nicholson's secretary to include some writing for the magazine, on assignment from the assistant editor, Ron Harvey.

Still another major change was made at the start of the fourth season, in the fall of 1971, as the show edged still closer to the urban-career-girl format popularized by Mary Tyler Moore. Doris continued to work for *Today's World*, but she suddenly became a carefree, single staff writer; the children, the dog, and the entire cast from previous seasons disappeared. Her new boss was editor Cy Bennett, and the only other regular was his secretary Jackie.

At the end of the fifth season the entire show disappeared.

DOROTHY
Situation Comedy

FIRST TELECAST: *August 8, 1979*
LAST TELECAST: *August 29, 1979*
BROADCAST HISTORY:
Aug 1979, CBS Wed 8:00–8:30
CAST:
Dorothy Banks . . . . Dorothy Loudon
Frankie . . . . Linda Manz
Meredith . . . . Susan Brecht
Cissy . . . . Elissa Leeds
Margo. . . . . Michele Greene
Burton Foley . . . . Russell Nype
Jack Landis. . . . . Kenneth Gilman
Lorna Cathcart . . . . Priscilla Morrill

Fresh from winning a Tony Award for her role in the musical *Annie,* Dorothy Loudon turned up on this summer comedy series as a divorced former showgirl who took a position as music and drama teacher at the exclusive Hannah Hunt School for Girls, a rather stuffy Eastern school. Her background and undisciplined approach to teaching were not always appreciated by the administration, especially by headmaster Burton Foley. But the girls were delighted, and Dorothy was tickled by the chance to do some of her routines for such an appreciative (if underage) audience. Jack and Lorna were two other teachers at the school.

DO'S AND DON'TS
Instruction
FIRST TELECAST: *July 3, 1952*
LAST TELECAST: *August 28, 1952*
BROADCAST HISTORY:
Jul 1952–Aug 1952, ABC Thu 9:30–10:00

This was a brief series of films on safety.

DOTTO
Quiz/Audience Participation
FIRST TELECAST: *July 1, 1958*
LAST TELECAST: *August 12, 1958*
BROADCAST HISTORY:
Jul 1958–Aug 1958, NBC Tue 9:00–9:30
EMCEE:
Jack Narz

In *Dotto* two contestants competed to guess the identity of a famous personality whose caricature was drawn on a screen by connecting fifty dots on each contestant's "Dotto" board. The contestants answered questions that allowed them progressively to connect the dots, and the first to identify the picture of the person won. There was also a home game in which viewers sent in postcards, hoping to be called on the phone to identify a special dotted caricature shown on the air. *Dotto's* biggest claim to fame was that a disgruntled former contestant on the daytime version of the show (which had begun earlier and ran concurrently with this nighttime version) started the famous quiz show scandals by publicly declaring that the game was rigged. His name was Edward Hilgemeier, Jr., and, ironically, he had never actu-

ally appeared on the show at all. While waiting in the studio for his opportunity to go on as a contestant, he found a notebook belonging to a woman contestant that contained answers to questions she had been asked on the show. He informed the contestant who had been defeated by the woman and both he and the defeated contestant confronted the producers. They were both paid off but, when Mr. Hilgemeier found out the defeated contestant had been given $4000 while he had only been given $1500, he got angry and precipitated the quiz show scandals by protesting to the New York State Attorney General's office.

DOTTY MACK SHOW, THE
Music
FIRST TELECAST: *February 16, 1953*
LAST TELECAST: *September 3, 1956*
BROADCAST HISTORY:
Feb 1953–Jun 1953, DUM Mon 10:45–11:00
Jul 1953–Aug 1953, DUM Tue 9:00–9:30
Aug 1953–Oct 1953, ABC Thu 9:00–9:30
Oct 1953–Mar 1954, ABC Sat 6:30–7:00
Apr 1954–Oct 1954, ABC Sat 7:30–8:00
Oct 1954–Jun 1955, ABC Sat 8:00–9:00
Jun 1955–Sep 1955, ABC Tue 9:30–10:00
Sep 1955–Mar 1956, ABC Mon 9:00–9:30
Apr 1956–Jul 1956, ABC Thu 10:00–10:30
Jul 1956–Sep 1956, ABC Mon 8:00–8:30
REGULARS:
Dotty Mack
Bob Braun
Colin Male

Dotty Mack had one of the simpler acts on early television: she pantomimed to other performers' hit records. She began her miming on *The Paul Dixon Show* out of Cincinnati, then landed a 15-minute spot by herself on DuMont called, appropriately, *Girl Alone.* Four months later, in July 1953, the program was expanded to 30 minutes, two assistants (Bob Braun and Colin Male) were added, and the title was changed to *The Dotty Mack Show.* Shortly thereafter ABC picked it up. At times the program was a full hour in length, although 30 minutes was normal.

Most of the songs pantomimed were currently popular favorites or novelty songs by such stars as Eddie Fisher, Perry Como, or Patti Page; sometimes puppets or other visual aids accompanied the pantomimes. Things began to get complicated when rock 'n' roll started taking over the hit parade in 1955. Although Dotty gamely included such records as "Rock Around the Clock" in her repertoire, the sight of pleasant young people pantomiming to Bill Haley or Elvis Presley records became slightly ludicrous, and the show quietly passed from the scene in 1956.

DOUBLE DARE
Detective
FIRST TELECAST: *April 10, 1985*
LAST TELECAST: *May 22, 1985*

Apr 1985–May 1985, CBS Wed 8:00–9:00
CAST:
Billy Diamond . . . . Billy Dee Williams
Ken Sisko . . . . Ken Wahl
Sylvester . . . . Joe Maher
Lt. Samantha Warner (pilot only)
. . . . Jennifer Warren
Lt. Samantha Warner . . . . Janet Carroll

Billy Diamond was the most successful thief in San Francisco. He lived lavishly on the fruits of his illicit activities—until he got caught in the act by Lt. Samantha Warner of the S.F.P.D. To avoid going to jail he agreed to become an undercover operative for the San Francisco police. It was either that or give up his life-style for a drab, dirty prison cell. The one concession that he was able to get from Warner was to have his former partner, Ken Sisko, released from San Quentin to work with him again. Sylvester was Billy's butler.

DOUBLE DARE
see *Family Double Dare*

DOUBLE EXPOSURE
see *ABC Dramatic Shorts—1952–1953*

DOUBLE LIFE OF HENRY PHYFE, THE
Situation Comedy
FIRST TELECAST: *January 13, 1966*
LAST TELECAST: *September 1, 1966*
BROADCAST HISTORY:
Jan 1966–Sep 1966, ABC Thu 8:30–9:00
CAST:
Henry Wadsworth Phyfe . . . . Red Buttons
Gerald B. Hannahan . . . . Fred Clark
Judy Kimball . . . . Zeme North
Mrs. Florence Kimball . . . . . . Marge Redmond
Mr. Hamble . . . . Parley Baer

This short-lived comedy focused on the adventures of Henry Phyfe, a mild-mannered accountant who was recruited by the CIS, a United States counterintelligence agency, to impersonate U-31, a recently deceased foreign agent to whom Henry bore a striking resemblance. The trouble was that U-31 in most other respects had been the opposite of Henry: bon vivant, Don Juan, master linguist, and crack shot. Henry's girlfriend Judy, his future mother-in-law Florence, and his boss at the accounting firm had no idea of his double life. Only Gerald B. Hannahan, the balding, bombastic regional director of CIS, linked him with the world of spies and adventure. Judy and her mother were phased out of the series in March.

DOUBLE OR NOTHING
Quiz/Audience Participation
FIRST TELECAST: *June 5, 1953*
LAST TELECAST: *July 3, 1953*
BROADCAST HISTORY:
Jun 1953–Jul 1953, NBC Fri 9:30–10:00
EMCEE:
Bert Parks
Bob Williams (asst.)

The summer of 1953 brought this familiar radio quiz show—and its emcee, Bert Parks—to television for a five-week stay. Each contestant was asked a series of four questions, respectively worth $10, $20, $40, and double or nothing, for a possible total of $140 in the first round. All contestants, whether or not they were successful in the first round, then participated in the "Red and White Sweepstakes" at the end (the colors referred to those on the label of the sponsor's product, Campbell soups). In the sweepstakes, a question was asked and each contestant wrote his or her answer on a card shaped like a horse. The "race" was won by whomever could provide the correct answer first.

The daytime version of *Double or Nothing* had started on CBS in October 1952 and ran until July 1954.

DOUBLE TROUBLE
Situation Comedy
FIRST TELECAST: *April 4, 1984*
LAST TELECAST: *August 21, 1985*
BROADCAST HISTORY:
Apr 1984–May 1984, NBC Wed 9:30–10:00
Jul 1984–Sep 1984, NBC Wed 8:00–8:30
Dec 1984–May 1985, NBC Sat 8:30–9:00
Jun 1985–Aug 1985, NBC Wed 9:30–10:00
CAST:
Kate Foster . . . . Jean Sagal
Allison Foster . . . . Liz Sagal
Art Foster (1984) . . . . Donnelly Rhodes
Beth McConnell (1984) . . Patricia Richardson
Michael Gillette (1984) . . . . Jon Caliri
Aunt Margo . . . . Barbara Barrie
Billy Batalato . . . . Jonathan Schmock
Charles Kincaid . . . . James Vallely
Mr. Arrechia . . . . Michael D. Roberts
Aileen Lewis . . . . Anne-Marie Johnson

The adventures of a pair of teenage twins were explored in this light comedy. Kate and Allison were 16, identical in appearance, but opposites in personality. Allison was the sober, responsible one, and Kate the spunky troublemaker who often got them both into hot water. Pretending to be Allison was one of Kate's favorite ploys. Art was their widower father, who ran a gym and dance studio in their hometown of Des Moines, Iowa, Beth was one of his adult instructors, and Michael was Kate's boyfriend.

When *Double Trouble* returned for a second season, in December 1984, Kate and Allison had moved to New York to pursue separate careers. Kate wanted to become an actress, while her more practical sister was enrolled in the Fashion Institute of Technology studying design. They lived in a spacious townhouse with their kooky Aunt Margo, a successful writer of children's stories. Also living in the townhouse were Billy and Charles, two aspiring actors and kindred spirits of Kate's. Mr. Arrechia was an obnoxious, overbearing instructor at the Fashion Institute and Aileen was Allison's fellow student and best friend.

DOUGLAS FAIRBANKS, JR., PRESENTS
Anthology
BROADCAST HISTORY:
Syndicated only
30 minutes
Produced: *1952–1957* (117 episodes)
Released: *January 1953*
HOST:
Douglas Fairbanks, Jr.

Douglas Fairbanks, Jr., a Hollywood star since the 1920s, hosted one of television's classiest and most successful anthology series during the 1950s. He also served as executive producer and starred in approximately a fourth of the episodes. The scripts were first-rate and unusually wide-ranging, from psychological studies to light farce, with an occasional murder yarn. Actors were generally lesser known. The series was filmed in England, with an eye to authenticity—if they needed a castle, they went out and got one!

DOWN AND OUT IN BEVERLY HILLS
Situation Comedy
FIRST TELECAST: *April 26, 1987*
LAST TELECAST: *September 12, 1987*
BROADCAST HISTORY:
Apr 1987, FOX Sun 9:00–9:30
Jul 1987–Aug 1987, FOX Sat 8:00–8:30
Aug 1987–Sep 1987, FOX Sat 9:00–9:30
CAST:
Dave Whiteman .... Hector Elizondo
Barbara Whiteman............. Anita Morris
Jerry Baskin .... Tim Thomerson
Max Whiteman (17).......... Evan Richards
Jenny Whiteman (20).......... Eileen Seeley
Carmen, the maid............... April Ortiz

Dave Whiteman had made his fortune selling clothes hangers and had moved his family into a sumptuous Beverly Hills mansion. Although he still had middle-class roots and understood the value of a dollar, such could not be said for his flighty wife Barbara or his social-climbing daughter Jenny. Max, his son, was not coping well with either his new peer group at Beverly Hills High or his own adolescence. Into this unsettled household came Jerry Baskin, a flower child of the '60s who had become a derelict in the '80s. When his attempt to commit suicide in the Whiteman pool failed—he was pulled out by Dave—Jerry stayed on to live the good life with them and dispense philosophical and sometimes cryptic answers to the unending questions posed by the Whitemans.

Based on the 1985 feature film starring Richard Dreyfuss, Bette Midler, and Nick Nolte, which in turn was based on characters from the play

"Bondu Sauve des Eaux" by Rene Fauchois. Reprising his role in the movie as the nasty pooch Matisse was a black-and-white Scottish Border collie known professionally as Mike the Dog.

DOWN YOU GO
Quiz/Panel
FIRST TELECAST: *May 30, 1951*
LAST TELECAST: *September 8, 1956*
BROADCAST HISTORY:
May 1951–Jul 1951, DUM Wed 9:00–9:30
Jul 1951–Sep 1951, DUM Thu 9:00–9:30
Sep 1951–Jun 1952, DUM Fri 9:00–9:30
Jul 1952–Sep 1952, DUM Fri 8:00–8:30
Oct 1952–Apr 1954, DUM Fri 10:30–11:00
May 1954–Jun 1954, DUM Wed 9:30–10:00
Sep 1954–Jan 1955, DUM Wed 10:00–10:30
Jan 1955–May 1955, DUM Fri 10:30–11:00
Jun 1955–Sep 1955, CBS Sat 9:30–10:00
Sep 1955–Jun 1956, ABC Thu 9:30–10:00
Jun 1956–Sep 1956, NBC Sat 7:30–8:00
EMCEE:
Dr. Bergen Evans (1951–1956)
Bill Cullen (1956)
REGULAR PANELISTS:
Francis Coughlin
Prof. Robert Breen (1951–1954)
Toni Gilman (1951–1954)
Carmelita Pope (1951–1954)
Fran Allison (1954)
Phil Rizzuto (1954–1955)
Boris Karloff (1954–1955)
Jean Kerr (1955)
Patricia Cutts (1955–1956)
Basil Davenport (1955)
Phyllis Cerf (1955)
Sherl Stern (1955)
John Kieran, Jr. (1955)
Arthur Treacher (1956)
Hildy Parks (1956)
Jimmy Nelson (1956)
Jayne Mansfield (1956)

Widely regarded as one of the wittiest, most intelligent panel shows on television, *Down You Go* was a deceptively simple word game whose charm derived from its participants. The rules were simple: the panel was asked to guess a word or phrase that had been submitted by a viewer. A few cryptic clues were offered, and then the panelists filled in the words, letter by letter, on a "magic board." An incorrect guess by a panelist and "down you go," out of play until the next round. Viewers received $5 for submitting a phrase that was used, and $25 for one that stumped the panel (later these amounts were increased, but money was never the principal appeal of the show).

Dr. Bergen Evans, a witty and charming professor of English at Northwestern University, was the longtime host of *Down You Go*, which at first was telecast from Chicago over the DuMont network. The program became quite popular, and in

1954 a *Down You Go* game was being sold in stores, complete with tiles, board, and clock. In December 1954 the program moved to New York, with only Evans and Francis Coughlin, a Chicago radio editor, remaining from the original cast. During 1955 and 1956 a succession of regular and guest panelists appeared, but none of these later panels seemed to catch the flavor of the original. Nevertheless the program survived the end of the DuMont network, making a grand tour of the networks from CBS to ABC to NBC before it was canceled in September 1956.

The last version of *Down You Go* little resembled the original. Bergen Evans was replaced for the last two months of the show by Bill Cullen, and the panel was filled by such "literati" as Jimmy Nelson and his dummies, and Jayne Mansfield.

DOWNTOWN
Police Drama
FIRST TELECAST: *September 27, 1986*
LAST TELECAST: *September 5, 1987*
BROADCAST HISTORY:
> Sep 1986–Dec 1986, CBS Sat 8:00–9:00
> Aug 1987–Sep 1987, CBS Sat 8:00–9:00
CAST:
> Det. John Forney............. Michael Nouri
> Terry Corsaro .... Blair Underwood
> Harriet Conover .... Millicent Martin
> Jesse Smith............... Mariska Hargitay
> Dennis Shothoffer.......... Robert Englund
> Delia Bonner .... Virginia Capers
> Capt. David Kiner........... David Paymer

In addition to fighting crime in Los Angeles, police Det. John Forney was saddled with the responsibility of serving as probation officer for four parolees living together in a sort of half-way house as part of an experimental program administered by social worker Delia Bonner. Forney's charges were Terry, a likeable young black and former pickpocket; Harriet, a classy older woman whose financial reverses had prompted her to get involved in land fraud; Jesse, a young woman whose tough, street-smart exterior hid a yearning to be accepted; and Dennis, a neurotic with a penchant for impersonating others. Being a part-time probation officer did not appeal to Forney, but he made the best of it, trying to keep the four of them out of trouble and find them jobs. Their repeated attempts to help him solve cases did not make it any easier. Capt. Kiner was Forney's boss.

DRAGNET
Police Drama
FIRST TELECAST: *January 3, 1952*
LAST TELECAST: *September 10, 1970*
BROADCAST HISTORY:
> Jan 1952–Dec 1955, NBC Thu 9:00–9:30
> Jan 1956–Sep 1958, NBC Thu 8:30–9:00
> Sep 1958–Jun 1959, NBC Tue 7:30–8:00

> Jul 1959–Sep 1959, NBC Sun 8:30–9:00
> Jan 1967–Sep 1970, NBC Thu 9:30–10:00
CAST:
> Sgt. Joe Friday.................. Jack Webb
> Sgt. Ben Romero (1951)... Barton Yarborough
> Sgt. Ed Jacobs (1952) .... Barney Phillips
> Officer Frank Smith (1952)....... Herb Ellis
> Officer Frank Smith (1953–1959)
> .... Ben Alexander
> Officer Bill Gannon (1967–1970)
> .... Harry Morgan
THEME:
> "Dragnet" (also known as "Dragnet March" and "Danger Ahead"), by Walter Schumann
DIRECTOR:
> Jack Webb

Dragnet was probably the most successful police series in the history of television. By providing the prototype of the realistic action series, it marked a major turning point for a medium that had, for its first few years, been dominated by comedy and vaudeville. *Dragnet's* hallmark was its appearance of realism, from the documentary-style narration by Joe Friday, to the cases drawn from the files of a real police department (Los Angeles, which provided the locale), to its careful attention to the details of police work ("It was 3:55 ... We were working the day watch out of homicide"). Viewers were reminded of the unglamorous dead ends and the constant interruptions of their private lives that plague real policemen, and this made the final shootout and capture of the criminal all the more exciting. At the end of each episode, after the criminal was apprehended, an announcer would describe what happened at the subsequent trial and the severity of the sentence.

The concept, as created by laconic actor-director Jack Webb, caught on immediately, perhaps because it stood out so sharply against the police-private eye caricatures then on the air. *Dragnet* became an enormous hit. Its catch phrases and devices became national bywords and were widely satirized. There was Webb's terse "My name's Friday—I'm a cop," and "Just the facts, ma'am"; the jargon—the criminal's "M.O.," "Book him on a 358"—and, of course, that arresting theme music, with possibly the most famous four-note introduction since Beethoven's Fifth Symphony ("Dum-de-dum-dum"). Music was an important part of *Dragnet's* success, even aside from the theme. It was laced throughout every episode, dark and tension-filled, then erupting in a loud, sudden "stinger" after an especially significant revelation or denouement. In fact, *Dragnet* inspired two hit records in 1953: a recording of the theme music by Ray Anthony and His Orchestra, and the hilarious "St. George and the Dragonet" by Stan Freberg—probably the only parody of a current TV series ever to sell a million copies and reach number one on the hit parade. (The record's opening intoned, "The legend you are about to

219

hear is true; only the needle should be changed to protect the record . . .")

Dragnet began on radio in 1949 and, after a special TV preview on *Chesterfield Sound Off Time* in December 1951, opened its official TV run on January 3, 1952. Friday's partner in the preview was played by Barton Yarborough, of the radio series. He died suddenly of a heart attack a few days after the telecast, and four actors subsequently portrayed Friday's sidekick: Barney Phillips in the spring of 1952, Herb Ellis in the fall, Ben Alexander for the remainder of the seven-and-a-half-year original run, and Harry Morgan for the revival in 1967–1970.

During most of its first 12 months on the air *Dragnet* ran every other Thursday, alternating with *Gangbusters,* another transplanted radio police show. From January of 1953 until 1959 it was a weekly series. In 1967, after a hiatus of more than seven years, it returned to the air under the slightly modified title *Dragnet '67,* to distinguish it from the reruns of the original series still being played on many stations. (Reruns were also known as *Badge 714,* after Friday's badge number.) Jack Webb returned to the role of Friday but with a new partner, Officer Bill Gannon. The format was essentially the same as the original *Dragnet* but there was somewhat stronger emphasis on the noncrime aspects of police work, such as community involvement and helping individuals in trouble. Today, more than a quarter century after its first telecast, reruns of *Dragnet* can still be seen on some local stations.

DRAMA AT EIGHT
Dramatic Anthology
FIRST TELECAST: *July 9, 1953*
LAST TELECAST: *July 30, 1953*
BROADCAST HISTORY:
Jul 1953, DUM Thu 8:00–8:30

This was a series of filmed dramas featuring lesser-known actors and actresses. The July 30 telecast, a comedy entitled "Uncle Charlie," presented an early TV version of Cliff Arquette's Charley Weaver characterization. That was the last network airing of the program, though it continued locally in New York through October 1, 1953.

DRAMATIC MYSTERY
see *Chesterfield Presents*

DRAW ME A LAUGH!
Cartoon Quiz/Panel
FIRST TELECAST: *January 15, 1949*
LAST TELECAST: *February 5, 1949*
BROADCAST HISTORY:
Jan 1949–Feb 1949, ABC Sat 8:30–9:00
EMCEE:
Walter Hurley
Patricia Bright

REGULARS:
Mel Casson
Jay Irving
Oscar Brand

The object of this show was for the participants, who were cartoonists, to draw cartoons based on ideas sent in by viewers. The show's regular cartoonist, Mel Casson, was given a description of the cartoon to be drawn but not the caption; simultaneously, the caption but not the description was given to another cartoonist, who made up his own illustration. The two cartoons were then compared and an audience panel voted on which was funnier. Other segments of the show included making cartoons out of scribbles, drawing blind, and "singing captions" by folk singer Oscar Brand.

The program lasted exactly four weeks.

DRAW TO WIN
Cartoon Quiz/Panel
FIRST TELECAST: *April 22, 1952*
LAST TELECAST: *June 10, 1952*
BROADCAST HISTORY:
Apr 1952–Jun 1952, CBS Tue 8:30–9:00
EMCEE:
Henry Morgan
PANELISTS:
Bill Holman
Abner Dean

Home viewers here were asked to send in slogans, names of objects, or anything else that could be described through a series of cartoon clues. The panel, composed of three cartoonists and a celebrity guest, would then try to guess the solution to the cartoon clues. Depending on how long it took them to identify correctly the meaning of the clues, the sender would receive a prize of up to $25.

DREAM GIRL, U.S.A.
Beauty Contest
BROADCAST HISTORY:
30 minutes
Syndicated only
Produced: *1986*
Released: *Fall 1986*
HOST:
Ken Howard
ANNOUNCER:
Danny Dark
CHOREOGRAPHER:
Kevin Carlisle
DANCERS:
Alexander Cole
Scott Grossman
Michael Thompson
Jerald Vincent

This prerecorded beauty pageant (the entire series was taped during a few weeks in 1986) featured a series of elimination rounds with four participants in each episode competing in swimsuit, evening gown, and other events.

DREAM HOUSE
Quiz
FIRST TELECAST: *March 27, 1968*
LAST TELECAST: *September 19, 1968*
BROADCAST HISTORY:
  Mar 1968–Aug 1968, ABC Wed 8:30–9:00
  Sep 1968, ABC Thu 9:30–10:00
EMCEE:
  Mike Darrow

Young married couples were offered a roomful of furniture for correct answers on this quiz show. Winners of four consecutive rounds (rooms) received a house worth up to $40,000 as well. The "dream house" might take several forms, a traditional house, mobile home, ski lodge, houseboat, or even a private island. *Dream House* was also seen in a daytime edition that premiered a few weeks after the prime-time version and remained on the air until January 1970.

Thirteen years later, in April 1983, a new version of *Dream House* surfaced on NBC's weekday daytime lineup. The revived version, hosted by Bob Eubanks, ran until June 1984. The cost of housing had gone up considerably over the years. The grand prize "dream house" in the new version of the show was worth $100,000.

DREAMS
Situation Comedy
FIRST TELECAST: *October 3, 1984*
LAST TELECAST: *October 31, 1984*
BROADCAST HISTORY:
  Oct 1984, CBS Wed 8:30–9:00
CAST:
  Gino Minnelli .... John Stamos
  Martha Spino.................... Jami Gertz
  Phil Taylor .... Cain Devore
  Morris Weiner.............. Albert Macklin
  Lisa Copley .... Valerie Stevenson
  Louise Franconi............. Sandy Freeman
  Frank Franconi .... Ron Karabatsos
  Torpedo..................... Bill Henderson

Gino Minnelli, 22, was a welder by day and a rock musician by night. He and the other young members of his group "Dreams" hoped that their music would be the ticket out of their blue-collar Philadelphia neighborhood. Gino was lead singer, lead guitarist, and resident ladykiller. Martha sang backup, Phil wrote most of their songs and also played guitar, and Weiner was the flaky keyboard player. The newest member of "Dreams" was Lisa, whose father was a wealthy U.S. senator, and who had been recruited mostly for her money. The pleasant surprise for all was that Lisa could really belt out a song. While they worked for their big break, "Dreams" performed regularly at a small neighborhood club owned by Gino's

Uncle Frank. Music video segments were incorporated into each episode of *Dreams* in an attempt to merge a traditional situation comedy format with the hot new fad for music videos.

DRESS REHEARSAL
Various
FIRST TELECAST: *March 21, 1948*
LAST TELECAST: *August 31, 1948*
BROADCAST HISTORY:
  Mar 1948–Apr 1948, NBC Thu 8:00–8:30
  Jul 1948–Aug 1948, NBC Mon 8:00–8:30
  Aug 1948, NBC Tue 9:00–9:30
"DIRECTOR" (on camera):
  Richard Goode

This was an umbrella title for a series of one-time and experimental programs that took the form of dress rehearsals. It included musical revues, quiz shows, and an occasional drama. Perhaps the best show was the last, entitled "Swap Night," which featured the first TV appearance of veteran radio commentator Norman Brokenshire, dressed as a rural Yankee trader and presiding over a swap session between cast members and viewers at home.

DREW PEARSON
Commentary
FIRST TELECAST: *May 4, 1952*
LAST TELECAST: *March 18, 1953*
BROADCAST HISTORY:
  May 1952–Nov 1952, ABC Sun 11:00–11:15
  Dec 1952–Mar 1953, DUM Wed 7:30–7:45
COMMENTATOR:
  Drew Pearson

The famous columnist Drew Pearson, who covered the 1952 political conventions and the subsequent presidential election for ABC, presented commentary and his "Predictions of Things to Come" in these network telecasts in 1952–1953.

DROODLES
Cartoon Quiz/Audience Participation
FIRST TELECAST: *June 21, 1954*
LAST TELECAST: *September 17, 1954*
BROADCAST HISTORY:
  Jun 1954–Sep 1954, NBC Mon 8:00–8:30
  Sep 1954, NBC Fri 8:00–8:30
EMCEE:
  Roger Price
PANELISTS:
  Marc Connelly
  Carl Reiner
  Denise Lor

"Droodles" were simple line drawings that depicted an object or scene, often from a rather strange perspective. Roger Price, who had written a book called *Droodles*, was the emcee. The three regular panelists were joined by a fourth guest panelist, who started the show by drawing his or her own droodle for the other panelists to try to figure out. After this the guest joined the other panelists in guessing what was depicted in selected droodles submitted by home viewers (who won prizes if they stumped the panel) and some drawn by Price. In addition, there was a "Hundred Dollar Droodle" drawn by Price at the end of each show. Viewers were invited to send in postcards with possible titles for it, and the best title won the $100.

DUCK FACTORY, THE
Situation Comedy
FIRST TELECAST: *April 12, 1984*
LAST TELECAST: *July 11, 1984*
BROADCAST HISTORY:
Apr 1984–May 1984, NBC Thu 9:30–10:00
Jun 1984–Jul 1984, NBC Wed 9:30–10:00
CAST:
Skip Tarkenton .... Jim Carrey
Mrs. Sheree Winkler .... Teresa Ganzel
Brooks Carmichael............. Jack Gilford
Aggie Aylesworth .... Julie Payne
Andrea Lewin .... Nancy Lane
Marty Fenneman................. Jay Tarses
Roland Culp .... Clarence Gilyard, Jr.
Wally Wooster .... Don Messick

The Duck Factory was set in a small, rundown Hollywood animation studio peopled by the loony crew who produced a TV cartoon show called *Dippy Duck*. The newest employee was Skip Tarkenton, an eager young cartoonist fresh from the Midwest and bursting with excitement at his first professional job. His wide-eyed innocence contrasted sharply with the cynicism of his co-workers: Brooks, the fatherly artist full of doubts about his own brilliance; Andrea, the sarcastic, man-hungry film editor; Marty, the two-bit gag writer; Roland, the only black storyboard artist in the business; and Wally, the voice-over narrator who had a repertoire of so many cartoon voices that he had long since forgotten his own voice. Buddy Winkler, the tyrannical owner of the studio, had just died and the place was virtually leaderless when Skip arrived, so the whole crew turned to the reluctant newcomer to save *Dippy Duck*—which was constantly on the verge of cancellation by the network. This brought the enmity of Aggie, the pushy, penny-pinching business manager who thought she should be in charge, but also the appreciation of Mrs. Winkler, the sexy young bimbo whom Buddy had met and married only three weeks before his demise—and who was, therefore, now the studio's owner.

DUET
Comedy/Drama
FIRST TELECAST: *April 19, 1987*
LAST TELECAST:
BROADCAST HISTORY:
Apr 1987–May 1987, FOX Sun 9:30–10:00
May 1987–Sep 1987, FOX Sun 8:30–9:00

Sep 1987–Oct 1987, FOX Sat 9:30–10:00
Oct 1987–   , FOX Sun 9:30–10:00
CAST:
Ben Coleman .... Matthew Laurance
Laura Kelly .... Mary Page Keller
Richard Phillips .... Chris Lemmon
Linda Phillips .... Alison LaPlaca
Jane Kelly....................... Jodi Thelen
Geneva .... Arleen Sorkin
Cooper Hayden .... Larry Poindexter

This episodic comedy revolved around the intertwined romantic lives of two couples. Ben and Laura were establishing a new relationship while Richard and Linda were trying to maintain one. When *Duet* premiered Ben was an unpublished writer of mystery novels (his first published novel, "Death in the Fast Lane," did become a best seller) and Laura was running a catering business with the "help" of her flighty younger sister Jane. As their relationship evolved from casual dating to serious dating to living together, Ben and Laura went through periods of uncertainty and misgiving—at one point they even stopped dating—but their love kept bringing them back together. Interspersed through the story of their courtship were Ben's daydream sequences, in black and white, in which he imagined himself as one of his own Sam Spade-like detective creations winning his moll.

Ben's best friend Richard and his wife Linda were stereotypical Yuppies, preoccupied with financial success and status. Linda was an executive at World Wide Studios, and had a difficult time dealing with Richard's abrupt decision to quit his lucrative job selling patio furniture for his father and become a professional pianist. She was also not nearly as enthusiastic about their impending parenthood as was Richard (in fact, the prospect terrified her), but after their daughter Amanda was born she became a doting mother. Geneva was the Phillips' sexy, sharp-tongued maid who took great pleasure in putting down her employers, especially Linda; Cooper was Linda's boss at World Wide, who for some reason was infatuated with Jane; and Reuben was Ben's large dog and, prior to the arrival of Laura in his master's life, Ben's closest confidante.

DUKE, THE
Situation Comedy
FIRST TELECAST: *July 2, 1954*
LAST TELECAST: *September 3, 1954*
BROADCAST HISTORY:
Jul 1954–Sep 1954, NBC Fri 8:00–8:30
CAST:
"The Duke" London .... Paul Gilbert
Johnny .... Allen Jenkins
Rudy Cromwell .... Claude Stroud
Sam Marco................ Sheldon Leonard
Gloria........................ Phyllis Coates

The "Duke" in this comedy was a streetwise professional boxer who had, in his spare time, become an accomplished painter. Through that hobby he met Harvard graduate Rudy Cromwell, who offered to help him expand his intellectual and cultural horizons. Rudy was admirably suited to the purpose and enjoyed introducing Duke to "high-brow" forms of entertainment and diversion. The fighting side of the Duke's life kept intruding, however, in the persons of his trainer, Johnny, and fight promoter Sam Marco, both of whom wanted him to give up his pursuit of the finer things in life and return to what he knew best, boxing. Society blonde Gloria, the Duke's girlfriend, also played a prominent part.

DUKE, THE

Detective Drama

FIRST TELECAST: *April 5, 1979*
LAST TELECAST: *May 18, 1979*
BROADCAST HISTORY:
  Apr 1979, NBC Thu 9:30–11:30
  Apr 1979–May 1979, NBC Fri 10:00–11:00
CAST:
  Oscar "Duke" Ramsey .... Robert Conrad
  Joe Cadillac .... Larry Manetti
  Sgt. Mick O'Brien .... Red West
  Dedra Smith .... Patricia Conwell

After losing a bout to a man almost half his age, 38-year-old prizefighter Duke Ramsey decided to give up the ring and spend more time with outside interests, such as running Duke and Benny's Corner, a bar and grill in his native Chicago. Benny Lyle, his manager and friend, was the person who shared billing on the eatery, but by the time it opened he had been murdered. Duke tracked down his killer, and thereby found himself a new calling—private detective. Friends from his fight days, on both sides of the law, gave him access to numerous sources of information. One of these was Joe Cadillac, a flashy young bookie. Dedra was a jet-setting socialite with romantic designs on tough-guy Duke.

DUKES OF HAZZARD, THE

Comedy Adventure

FIRST TELECAST: *January 26, 1979*
LAST TELECAST: *August 16, 1985*
BROADCAST HISTORY:
  Jan 1979–Nov 1981, CBS Fri 9:00–10:00
  Dec 1981–Feb 1985, CBS Fri 8:00–9:00
  Jun 1985–Aug 1985, CBS Fri 8:00–9:00
CAST:
  Luke Duke .... Tom Wopat
  Bo Duke..................... John Schneider
  Daisy Duke................. Catherine Bach
  Uncle Jesse Duke .... Denver Pyle
  Sheriff Roscoe P. Coltrane .... James Best
  Jefferson Davis "Boss" Hogg ... Sorrell Booke
  Deputy Enos Strate (1979–1980, 1982–1985)
    .... Sonny Shroyer
  Cooter .... Ben Jones

Deputy Cletus (1980–1983) .... Rick Hurst
Lulu Hogg .... Peggy Rea
Miz Emma Tisdale (1981–1983)... Nedra Volz
Sheriff Little (1981–1984)... Don Pedro Colley
Laverne (1981–1985).............. Lila Kent
Emery Potter (1981–1985) .... Charlie Dell
Coy Duke (1982–1983) .... Byron Cherry
Vance Duke (1982–1983).. Christopher Mayer
The Balladeer (voice only).. Waylon Jennings
THEME:
"The Dukes of Hazzard," written and sung by Waylon Jennings

Rural comedies such as *The Beverly Hillbillies* had been a staple of the CBS lineup in the 1960s. *The Dukes of Hazzard* signaled a revival of the "good ol' boy" comedy, nearly a decade later. Luke and Bo Duke were cousins and buddies in Hazzard County, located "east of the Mississippi and south of the Ohio" (no mention of the state, but there is a real Hazard, Kentucky—a city not a county). Their nemesis was Boss Hogg, a fat, blustery, and thoroughly corrupt local politician always seen in a white flannel suit. The Dukes easily managed to avoid capture by dimwitted Sheriff Coltrane, Boss Hogg's brother-in-law, while acting as Robin Hoods of the county. The boys hot-rodded all over Hazzard County in their souped-up Dodge Charger, "General Lee," occasionally pausing for some sage advice from their wise old Uncle Jesse. Moonshine, wild car chases and crashes, and lots of scantily clad young women, including the Duke's gorgeous cousin Daisy, populated the series. Country star Waylon Jennings served as offscreen narrator, to the accompaniment of fast-paced banjo music.

The considerable success of *Dukes* spawned several imitations, including *Lobo, Harper Valley P.T.A.,* and a spinoff from *Dukes* itself starring Sheriff Coltrane's grinning deputy Enos (see *Enos*). When Enos departed the series he was replaced by a new deputy, Cletus.

In the spring of 1982, series stars Tom Wopat and John Schneider walked out on *The Dukes of Hazzard* in a contract dispute over their salaries and share of the merchandising rights royalties from *Dukes* toys, games, T-shirts, and other paraphernalia that were selling like hotcakes to children around the country. The production company, Warner Brothers, held a nationwide hunt to find two new Dukes to fill their places in the series and, after screening 2,230 applicants, settled on Byron Cherry and Christopher Mayer. In the premiere episode that fall, it was explained that Luke and Bo had left Hazzard to try their luck on the NASCAR racing circuit, and that their cousins Coy and Vance had returned home, after a six-year absence, to help Uncle Jesse run the farm. Deputy Enos Strate was back, but it just wasn't the same. For those who were convinced that the real star of the series was the "General Lee," it must have come as a surprise to learn that the car's drivers made any difference. The program's ratings and Wopat's and Schneider's careers all suffered as a result of the feud, so a settlement was finally reached and Luke and Bo returned to Hazzard County the following February. That fall Coy and Vance were gone.

The series also took its toll in real automobiles, as a result of all those chases and crashes. Although onscreen the General Lee never seemed to have a scratch, almost 300 look-alikes were wrecked during filming. A regular stable of identically painted Dodge Chargers was kept on hand during production of each episode, so as not to hold things up.

The theme song from this series, sung by Waylon Jennings, was on the charts during 1980. An animated version of the show, titled *The Dukes*, aired on CBS' Saturday morning lineup from February to November 1983 with the series' regulars providing the voices.

DUMONT ROYAL THEATER
Dramatic Anthology
FIRST TELECAST: *April 12, 1951*
LAST TELECAST: *June 26, 1952*
BROADCAST HISTORY:
Apr 1951–Jul 1951, DUM Thu 9:30–10:00
Apr 1952–Jun 1952, DUM Thu 9:00–9:30

This was a series of low-budget 30-minute dramatic films featuring an assortment of lesser-known talent, such as Edgar Barrier, Mary Sinclair, and Hugh O'Brian (later of *Wyatt Earp* fame). The 1952 version alternated with *Gruen Playhouse*. The series was also known as *Royal Playhouse*.

DUMPLINGS, THE
Situation Comedy
FIRST TELECAST: *January 28, 1976*
LAST TELECAST: *March 24, 1976*
BROADCAST HISTORY:
Jan 1976–Mar 1976, NBC Wed 9:30–10:00
CAST:
Joe Dumpling .... James Coco
Angela Dumpling .... Geraldine Brooks
Charles Sweetzer .... George S. Irving
Frederic Steele .... George Furth
Stephanie .... Marcia Rodd
Cully........................ Mort Marshall
Bridget McKenna .... Jane Connell
The prude .... Wil Albert

There was a message in *The Dumplings*—fat people can be as kind, good, industrious, and lovable as anyone else. Joe and Angela were a chubby married couple running a lunch counter in a large office building in Manhattan. Among their regular customers were a city councilman, Mr. Steele; an executive of a large corporation with offices in the building, Mr. Sweetzer; his secretary, Bridget; and Angela's sister Stephanie. Joe and Angela were madly in love with life and each other, exuded good cheer and enthusiasm, and never had a bad word for each other.

DUNDEE AND THE CULHANE
Western
FIRST TELECAST: *September 6, 1967*
LAST TELECAST: *December 13, 1967*
BROADCAST HISTORY:
Sep 1967–Dec 1967, CBS Wed 10:00–11:00
CAST:
Dundee .... John Mills
Culhane.................... Sean Garrison

Although their law offices were in Sausalito, across the bay from San Francisco, British attorney Dundee and his apprentice lawyer, The Culhane, traveled throughout the West to help their clients. Dealing with the sort of haphazard justice prevalent in much of the West during the latter part of the 19th century proved more of a problem than the actual courtroom defense. Judges were bribed, prisoners broke out of jails, and many citizens took the law into their own hands.

DUNNINGER SHOW, THE
see *Amazing Dunninger, The*

DUPONT CAVALCADE THEATER
see *Cavalcade of America*

DUPONT SHOW OF THE WEEK, THE
Various
FIRST TELECAST: *September 17, 1961*
LAST TELECAST: *September 6, 1964*
BROADCAST HISTORY:
Sep 1961–Sep 1964, NBC Sun 10:00–11:00

The DuPont Show of the Week presented a potpourri of various types of entertainment and informational programs. For three seasons it was NBC's late Sunday evening "class" showcase, with sponsor E. I. DuPont using the best available talent, both in front of and behind the cameras, to present everything from dramatic plays and documentaries to light comedies and musical revues. One of the aims of the series was to show the latitude and potential of the television medium as a means of communication. This format represented a change in the sponsor's philosophy. For the four years before the start of this weekly NBC series, DuPont had sponsored *DuPont Show of the Month*, an irregularly scheduled collection of culturally impressive 90-minute dramas on CBS. During the CBS period, adaptations of such classics as *Don Quixote, Hamlet, A Tale of Two Cities*, and *The Browning Version* had been aired. At the time, that was CBS' answer to NBC's *Hallmark Hall of Fame*.

The first telecast on NBC was the documentary "Hemingway," narrated by Chet Huntley, with Andrew Duggan providing Ernest Hemingway's voice. Later, retired actor Ken Murray presented his edited home movies of the stars at home in "Hollywood—My Home Town"; clown Emmett Kelly narrated a documentary on the universal appeal of the circus; and Peter Lind Hayes was narrator of a musical special, "Regards to George

M. Cohan." Dramatic programs were not omitted; in fact, they became the primary staple of the series during its last two years. Starring were such people as Richard Conte, Claude Rains, Walter Matthau, Zachary Scott, Teresa Wright, Eddie Albert, Martha Scott, Lloyd Nolan, James Daly, Peter Falk, Arthur Kennedy, and Oscar Homolka. Documentaries also continued; one of the most interesting was "Comedian Backstage," a *cinéma-vérité* look at the real life of comedian Shelley Berman.

DUPONT SHOW WITH JUNE ALLYSON, THE
Dramatic Anthology
FIRST TELECAST: *September 21, 1959*
LAST TELECAST: *June 12, 1961*
BROADCAST HISTORY:
Sep 1959–Sep 1960, CBS Mon 10:30–11:00
Sep 1960–Dec 1960, CBS Thu 10:30–11:00
Jan 1961–Jun 1961, CBS Mon 10:30–11:00
HOSTESS/STAR:
June Allyson

Actress June Allyson was the regular hostess and occasional star of this filmed dramatic-anthology series. The plays, which ranged from light comedy to melodrama, told stories of contemporary American life. The budget for this show was lavish, and it attracted many Hollywood stars, including Ginger Rogers, Bette Davis, David Niven, Joseph Cotten, and Jane Powell. Among the telecasts were "A Summer's Ending," in which Miss Allyson and her husband Dick Powell made their first joint television appearance; "Slip of the Tongue," in which Italian actor Rossano Brazzi made his American television debut; and "Silent Panic," with Harpo Marx in a rare dramatic appearance as a deaf mute.

DUPONT THEATER
see *Cavalcade of America*

DUSTY'S TRAIL
Situation Comedy
BROADCAST HISTORY:
Syndicated only
30 minutes
Produced: *1973* (26 episodes)
Released: *Fall 1973*
CAST:
Dusty .... Bob Denver
Mr. Callahan .... Forrest Tucker
Mr. Brookhaven .... Ivor Francis
Mrs. Brookhaven.............. Lynn Wood
Lulu McQueen .... Jeannine Riley
Betsy .... Lori Saunders
Andy........................... Bill Cort

Bob Denver starred in this slapstick comedy, which was rather reminiscent of his earlier hit *Gilligan's Island*—only set in the West. In fact it was an almost exact copy, character for character. Bumbling their way across the prairie in a wagon train were Dusty (Gilligan), wagonmaster

Callahan (the Skipper), the rich socialites the Brookhavens (the Thurston Howells), two sexy girls, sassy Lulu (Ginger) and sweet young Betsy (Mary Ann), and the nice young man (the Professor). The simpleminded, knockabout humor was also the same. Despite saturation coverage when it premiered, *Dusty's Trail* was a derivative flop.

DYNASTY
Drama
FIRST TELECAST: *January 12, 1981*
LAST TELECAST:
BROADCAST HISTORY:
Jan 1981–Apr 1981, ABC Mon 9:00–10:00
Jul 1981–Sep 1983, ABC Wed 10:00–11:00
Sep 1983–May 1984, ABC Wed 9:00–10:00
Aug 1984–May 1986, ABC Wed 9:00–10:00
Sep 1986–May 1987, ABC Wed 9:00–10:00
Sep 1987–Mar 1988, ABC Wed 10:00–11:00
CAST:
Blake Carrington.............. John Forsythe
Krystle Jennings Carrington..... Linda Evans
Alexis Carrington Colby........ Joan Collins
Fallon Carrington Colby (1981–1984)
.... Pamela Sue Martin
Fallon Carrington Colby (1985, 1987–   )
.... Emma Samms
Steven Carrington (1981–1982)...... Al Corley
Steven Carrington (1982–   ).. Jack Coleman
Adam Carrington/Michael Torrance
(1982–   ) .... Gordon Thomson
Cecil Colby (1981–1982) ...... Lloyd Bochner
Jeff Colby (1981–1985, 1987–   ). John James
Claudia Blaisdel (1981–1986)
.... Pamela Bellwood
Matthew Blaisdel (1981)........ Bo Hopkins
Lindsay Blaisdel (1981)...... Katy Kurtzman
Walter Lankershim (1981) ... Dale Robertson
Joseph Anders (1981–1983)...... Lee Bergere
Kirby (1982–1984) .... Kathleen Beller
Andrew Laird (1981–1984)
.... Peter Mark Richman
Sammy Jo Dean........... Heather Locklear
Michael Culhane (1981, 1986–1987)
.... Wayne Northrop
Dr. Nick Toscanni (1981–1982)
.... James Farentino
Mark Jennings (1982–1984).... Geoffrey Scott
Cong. Neal McVane (1982–1984, 1987)
.... Paul Burke
Chris Deegan (1983)......... Grant Goodeve
Tracy Kendall (1983–1984).... Deborah Adair
Farnsworth "Dex" Dexter (1983–   )
.... Michael Nader
Peter de Vilbis (1983–1984) ... Helmut Berger
Amanda Carrington (1984–1986)
.... Catherine Oxenberg
Amanda Carrington (1986–1987)
.... Karen Cellini
Dominique Deveraux (1984–1987)
.... Diahann Carroll
Gerard (1984–   )......... William Beckley
Gordon Wales (1984–   ).... James Sutorius
Luke Fuller (1984–1985).... William Campbell

225

THEME:
by Bill Conti

One of the most successful prime-time soap operas inspired by *Dallas* was this lavish entry. The setting was Denver, but true to the form, practically everyone was either filthy rich and disgusting or not-so-rich and disgusting.

As in *Dallas,* the money flowed from Big Oil (in fact, the series was originally going to be called *Oil*). Blake Carrington ran his vast holdings from an opulent, 48-room mansion. As the story began, however, his empire was tottering on the brink of collapse because Mideast revolutionaries had expropriated his tankers. Blake's unhappy wife was Krystle, a beautiful former secretary he had wooed and won, but whom he now treated like any other possession. Fallon was his spoiled, arrogant daughter and Steve his homosexual son (both by a previous marriage). Matthew Blaisdel, a crack geologist with the Carrington firm, was Krystle's former lover, but now had his hands full with a psychologically disturbed wife (Claudia) and a sexually blossoming daughter (Lindsay).

As the spring 1981 season ended Blake found himself on trial for the murder of Steven's male lover, Ted. Into the courtroom swept an unexpected witness for the prosecution, a mysterious, veiled woman. Not until the fall did viewers learn her identity; it was none other than Blake's former wife, the glamorous and vengeful Alexis. From that time on, much of the action on *Dynasty* centered on the rivalry between Krystle and Alexis, as Alexis schemed to displace the younger

woman and secure her place in the Carrington dynasty.

Alexis soon insinuated herself into everyone's affairs. When her efforts failed to win Blake she wed his archrival, oil tycoon Cecil Colby—who promptly died of a heart attack. Then she schemed to destroy Blake professionally as well as personally, through a merger of Denver-Carrington with Colby's Colbyco. Alexis did tempt Blake briefly, but ultimately he realized the strength of his love for Krystle and Alexis was once again foiled. The war between the two beautiful women continued unabated; Alexis causing Krystle to lose her baby, Krystle attacking Alexis in a spectacular fight in a lily pond, the two of them trapped together in a burning cabin and battling it out in the mud.

On the fringes of this battle royal other stories unfolded. There was Steven's somewhat confused love life, from his homosexual affair with Ted to his marriages with Sammy Jo (who bore him a child, Danny) and Claudia. In 1982 he disappeared into exile in Indonesia, where he was injured in an explosion, necessitating "plastic surgery." His new face solved nothing, however. Always the black sheep of the family, on his return Steven found himself fighting Blake, who thought him unfit for the custody of Danny.

Meanwhile, fickle Fallon knew exactly what *she* wanted, bedding down successively with Michael the chauffeur, Nick the doctor, Jeff the junior executive, and Peter the playboy. Jeff, whom she married briefly and bore a child, L.B. ("Little Blake"), was the one who really loved her. But it seemed that he might have to settle for Kirby (the butler's daughter!) instead.

A third Carrington offspring arrived in October 1982, calling himself Michael Torrance. He turned out to be Adam Carrington, Blake's long-lost son, who had returned to claim his birthright and whatever ladies were available. Others passing through the early stories included blustery wildcatter Walter Lankershim, an old foe of Blake's who arrived at Blake and Krystle's wedding with gun in hand; Joseph, the majordomo (Kirby's father); lawyer Andrew Laird; Krystle's ex, handsome Mark Jennings; and ruthless Congressman Neal McVane.

After a slow start *Dynasty* rose quickly to the top of the ratings, only slightly behind its prototype *Dallas.* What it may have lacked in depth of characterization and story as compared to the older serial, it made up in style and glamour, as exemplified by that gorgeous mansion (actually the Filoli estate, south of San Francisco). And if "class" is measured by the company one keeps, *Dynasty* won hands down. It was probably the first soap opera in history in which an ex-President and Secretary of State of the United States played onscreen roles: former President and Mrs. Gerald Ford and Henry Kissinger all appeared in a December 1983 episode set at Denver's glittering, real-life Carousel Ball.

As *Dynasty* matured, however, its "campy" approach to soap opera began to wear a little thin. The 1984–1985 season saw Blake fighting to regain his empire from Alexis, who had finally ruined him by undermining his South China Sea oil deal; Alexis herself was convicted of murdering Mark (actually Neal McVane did it, in a wig that made him look like Alexis). New on the scene was black singer Dominique, who arrived with her record-mogul husband Brady Lloyd (played by Billy Dee Williams) to reveal, to Blake's discomfort, that she too was a Carrington—his father's illegitimate daughter! Blake's old man Tom Carrington, seen in a riotous deathbed scene, had apparently been a world-class philanderer. Blake and Krystle's marriage had its problems; after giving birth to their first child, Krystina, Krystle dallied with handsome horsebreeder Daniel Reece (played by Rock Hudson in his last role), while Blake was seen with jet-set photographer Lady Ashley. Son Steven, as sexually confused as ever, alternated between wife Claudia and boyfriend Luke, and Jeff spent most of the season searching for true love Fallon, who had disappeared. The climactic event of the season—and for many the most preposterous story yet—involved the arrival of Alexis' lost daughter Amanda, who made a few passes at Alexis' new husband Dex and was then fixed up with Prince Michael of Moldavia. The Carringtons trooped off to the picturesque European principality for a royal wedding, but in the season finale revolutionaries burst into the palace and machine gunned them all!

After a certain amount of intrigue in the cardboard kingdom, everybody got out and Prince Michael and King Galen became part of the Denver scene. Other major stories of 1985–1986 included a drawn-out scheme by evil producer Joel and greedy Sammy Jo to abduct Krystle and substitute a lookalike actress named Rita inside the Carrington mansion (Blake didn't seem to notice the difference, even in bed); several episodes featuring the cast of the spin-off serial *The Colbys* (q.v.); and the appearance of Blake's estranged younger brother Ben and Alexis' sister Caress. Caress wrote a scandalous book about Alexis called *Sister Dearest;* there was plenty to write about, but Alexis squashed the project by buying the publisher. Also introduced were the Fallmonts, Sena-

tor Buck, indiscreet wife Emily, sons Clay (who eventually married Sammy Jo) and Bart (who made a pass at Steven). Alexis once again "destroyed" Blake, this time throwing him "and that blonde tramp" (Krystle) out of the mansion entirely. The season ended with a distraught Blake attempting to physically strangle his ex, while across town his resort hotel La Mirage was engulfed in a fire accidently touched off by Claudia, who perished in the flames.

The following season saw the marriages of Sammy Jo to Clay and Dana to Adam (who turned out not to be Blake's long-lost son, but was adopted by him anyhow); a story in which three-year-old Krystina needed a heart transplant, then was abducted by the donor's mother, Sarah; the return of Ben's sexy daughter Leslie; and a surreal interlude in which Blake, suffering from "soap opera amnesia" after an accident, thought he was married to Alexis. She loved it. The writers apparently suffered amnesia too, bringing back three characters long since disposed of: Michael Culhane, the sleazy chauffeur from the first season, now with $50 million in his pocket; Neal McVane, who was sprung from prison long enough to blackmail Adam over his non-Carrington parentage; and supposedly deceased Matthew Blaisdel, who burst in on the Adam/Dana wedding reception with a gang of tuxedo-clad gunmen determined to carry off Krystle. At least Blake got his company back from Alexis.

Another spectre appeared in the fall of 1987 in the person of Sean, son of the butler Joseph (who had committed suicide) and brother of Kirby (fled to Europe), seeking revenge against Alexis. Fallon and Jeff were back, having escaped the sinking *Colbys* series; Blake ran for governor against Alexis, enduring her mud-slinging attacks on him in her paper the *Denver Mirror* (in the end both lost the election to a third candidate); Adam and Dana, unable to conceive, hired Karen to be a surrogate mother and got into a nasty court fight when Karen decided to keep the child; and Alexis and Krystle fell into yet another hair-pulling fight in the mud. *Plus ça change, plus c'est la même chose.*

DYNASTY II—THE COLBYS
  see *The Colbys*

E

E/R
Situation Comedy
FIRST TELECAST: *September 16, 1984*
LAST TELECAST: *July 24, 1985*
BROADCAST HISTORY:
   Sep 1984, CBS Sun 8:00–9:00
   Sep 1984–Oct 1984, CBS Tue 8:30–9:00
   Nov 1984–Apr 1985, CBS Wed 8:30–9:00
   Apr 1985, CBS Sat 8:30–9:00
   Jun 1985–Jul 1985, CBS Wed 8:30–9:00
CAST:
   Dr. Howard Sheinfeld .... Elliott Gould
   Dr. Eve Sheridan (pilot only)
   .... Marcia Strassman
   Dr. Eve Sheridan .... Mary McDonnell
   Nurse Joan Thor .... Conchata Ferrell
   Nurse Julie Williams .... Lynne Moody
   Maria Amardo .... Shuko Akune
   Nurse Cory Smith .... Corinne Bohrer
   Off. Fred Burdock .... Bruce A. Young
   Dr. Thomas Esquivel .... Luis Avalos
   Harold Stickley .... Jason Alexander
   Ace .... George Clooney
   Richard, the orderly ..... William G. Schilling
   Bert, the paramedic .... Jeff Doucette

Chicago's Clark Street Hospital was the setting
for this comedy about the staff and patients populating the hospital's emergency room. Howard
Sheinfeld was the sarcastic, talkative doctor who
oversaw most of the emergency-room treatment.
An ear-nose-and-throat specialist, he moon-
lighted at Clark Street Hospital doing 48-hour
shifts to help him keep up with alimony payments
to two ex-wives. Eve, his no-nonsense boss at the
hospital, wished he would take things a little more
seriously and not work such long shifts. Harold
Stickley was the hospital administrator and Ace
the inexperienced young physician recently assigned to emergency-room duty. Joan Thor was
the head nurse, Julie her industrious assistant,
and Cory the perpetually confused floater nurse.
Maria was the lazy, smart-mouthed receptionist,
and Fred was her boyfriend. Into their emergency
room came a constant stream of the sick and the
injured, some with minor problems and others in
critical condition, in this awkward mixture of gag
comedy and serious illness.

E.S.P.
Audience Participation/Anthology.
FIRST TELECAST: *July 11, 1958*
LAST TELECAST: *August 22, 1958*
BROADCAST HISTORY:
   Jul 1958–Aug 1958, ABC Fri 9:00–9:30
EMCEE/HOST:
   Vincent Price

E.S.P. premiered as a contest show to determine
the amount of extrasensory perception possessed
by contestants, all of whom were first screened by
a staff of psychologists. After only three telecasts
the quiz format was replaced by dramas entitled
Tales of E.S.P., which depicted people with the
abilities that the quiz show had been trying to
find. Vincent Price was host of both programs.

EARL WRIGHTSON SHOW, THE
Music
FIRST TELECAST: *November 27, 1948*
LAST TELECAST: *February 21, 1952*
BROADCAST HISTORY:
   Nov 1948–Jan 1949, ABC Sat 7:45–8:00
   Jan 1949–Apr 1949, ABC Mon 7:15–7:30
   Sep 1949–Jun 1950, CBS Wed 7:45–8:00
   Sep 1950–Jun 1951, CBS Mon 11:00–11:15
   Aug 1951–Feb 1952, ABC Thu 10:30–10:45
REGULARS:
   Earl Wrightson
   Buddy Weed, piano and trio (1948–1949)
   Norman Paris Trio and Orchestra (1949–1951)

Concert baritone Earl Wrightson was a familiar
figure in the early days of television, appearing on
his own 15-minute program of songs on both ABC
and CBS. Wrightson's forte was Broadway show
tunes and music from operettas such as *The Student Prince* and *H.M.S. Pinafore*, and he performed these in program segments called "Spotlight on Showtime" and "Masland Showtime."
Guest stars were also featured.
   The title of this program changed several times,
from the original *Earl Wrightson Show* to *Earl
Wrightson at Home* (September 1949), *At Home*
(October 1949), *At Home Show* (September 1950),
and finally, in honor of the sponsor, *Masland At
Home Party* (August 1951).
   In later years Wrightson made frequent guest
appearances on other programs.

EARN YOUR VACATION
Quiz/Audience Participation
FIRST TELECAST: *May 23, 1954*
LAST TELECAST: *September 5, 1954*
BROADCAST HISTORY:
   May 1954–Sep 1954, CBS Sun 7:00–7:30
EMCEE:
   Johnny Carson
   Young comedian Johnny Carson hosted this
summer quiz show, which asked members of the
studio audience where they would most like to go
on a vacation and why. The people with the most
interesting answers won the chance to become
contestants and answer a series of four progres-
sively more difficult questions, which could win
them their dream vacation.

EAST SIDE/WEST SIDE
Drama

FIRST TELECAST: *September 23, 1963*
LAST TELECAST: *September 14, 1964*
BROADCAST HISTORY:
  Sep 1963–Sep 1964, CBS Mon 10:00–11:00
CAST:
  Neil Brock .... George C. Scott
  Frieda Hechlinger .... Elizabeth Wilson
  Jane Foster .... Cicely Tyson

This dramatic series starred George C. Scott as Neil Brock, a young social worker in the New York slums. The stories involved child abuse, the welfare syndrome, problems of aging, drug addiction, and crime, situations all too familiar to Neil Brock in his daily routine. Frieda Hechlinger was the head of the welfare agency branch for which he worked, and Jane Foster was the office secretary. Critics appreciated the gritty realism of this series in the midst of TV's land of make-believe, but its downbeat subjects proved deadly with viewers and it was dropped after a single season.

EASY ACES
  Humor
FIRST TELECAST: *December 14, 1949*
LAST TELECAST: *June 14, 1950*
BROADCAST HISTORY:
  Dec 1949–Jun 1950, DUM Wed 7:45–8:00
REGULARS:
  Goodman Ace
  Jane Ace
  Betty Garde

This was a video version of the longtime radio favorite, featuring Goodman and Jane Ace in comedy chatter. As on radio, "Ace" was his witty, intelligent self, and his wife, Jane, was a charming bundle of malapropisms. *Easy Aces* went on the DuMont network in December 1949, but lasted for only six months. Goodman Ace went on to make a much greater impression on the new medium as a top comedy writer for such stars as Perry Como. *Easy Aces* was filmed, and was syndicated to other local stations even while it was on the DuMont network.

EASY DOES IT . . . STARRING FRANKIE AVALON
  Musical Variety
FIRST TELECAST: *August 25, 1976*
LAST TELECAST: *September 15, 1976*
BROADCAST HISTORY:
  Aug 1976–Sep 1976, CBS Wed 8:30–9:00
REGULARS:
  Frankie Avalon
  Annette Funicello
  The War Babies (Marsha Meyers, Susan Nesbitt, Tim Reid, Renny Temple)
  Vic Glazer

Frankie Avalon, a pop singer and star of numerous "beach-party" movies in the early 1960s, was the star of this four-week mini-series. With him each week was Annette Funicello, his co-star in several of those movies. In addition to the musical numbers, the show featured blackouts and silly comedy sketches with an improvisational group, The War Babies. Also on camera, in many of the sketches, was the show's musical director, Vic Glazer.

EASY STREET
  Situation Comedy
FIRST TELECAST: *September 15, 1986*
LAST TELECAST: *May 27, 1987*
BROADCAST HISTORY:
  Sep 1986, NBC Sat 9:30–10:00
  Sep 1986–Nov 1986, NBC Sun 8:00–8:30
  Nov 1986–Mar 1987, NBC Sun 8:30–9:00
  Mar 1987–Apr 1987, NBC Tue 9:30–10:00
  Apr 1987–May 1987, NBC Wed 9:30–10:00
CAST:
  L.K. McGuire .... Loni Anderson
  Uncle Alvin "Bully" Stevenson .... Jack Elam
  Ricardo Williams .... Lee Weaver
  Eleanor Standard .... Dana Ivey
  Quentin Standard .... James Cromwell
  Bobby, the butler .... Arthur Malet
THEME:
  "Easy Street" (1941 popular song)

This routine clash-of-cultures comedy starred Loni Anderson as a former Las Vegas showgirl who had married a rich playboy ("we were really in love"), and promptly inherited half of his Beverly Hills mansion when he unexpectedly died. The other half was owned and occupied by L.K.'s snooty sister-in-law Eleanor and her milquetoast husband, Quentin, who wished L.K. was out of the house—and their lives. Also sharing the manse was L.K.'s only living relative, elderly Uncle Bully, and his pal Ricardo, who had been pried out of their rundown retirement home to come keep her company in the lonely lap of luxury. Bully and Ricardo's earthy ways vs. Eleanor's pretensions formed the basis of most of the comedy.

ED SULLIVAN SHOW, THE
  Variety
FIRST TELECAST: *June 20, 1948*
LAST TELECAST: *June 6, 1971*
BROADCAST HISTORY:
  Jun 1948, CBS Sun 9:00–10:00
  Jul 1948–Aug 1948, CBS Sun 9:30–10:30
  Aug 1948–Mar 1949, CBS Sun 9:00–10:00
  Mar 1949–Jun 1971, CBS Sun 8:00–9:00
REGULARS:
  Ed Sullivan
  Ray Bloch and His Orchestra
  The June Taylor Dancers

If any program in the history of American television could be called an institution, it would probably be *The Ed Sullivan Show*. Every Sunday night for more than two decades this homely newspaper columnist with peculiar diction and awkward gestures brought an incredible variety of entertainment into American homes. No pandering to the lowest common denominator here—there was grand opera and the latest rock stars, classical ballet and leggy Broadway showgirls, slapstick comedy and recitations from great dramatic writings, often juxtaposed on a single telecast. Viewers loved it.

It began simply enough. Originally titled *Toast of the Town* (it was going to be called *You're the Top,* but that title was dropped before the first telecast), the program was one of many variety shows on early television—most of which had noticeably short lives. The first telecast, in the summer of 1948, was produced on a meager budget of $1,375. Only $375 was allocated for talent, and the two young stars of that show, Dean Martin and Jerry Lewis, split the lion's share of that—$200. But Ed had class. Also on that first telecast was concert pianist Eugene List, Richard Rodgers and Oscar Hammerstein II, and the six original June Taylor Dancers (then called the Toastettes). The critics of the early Sullivan shows were not kind. They complained about his deadpan delivery, his lack of any noticeable talent as a performer, and the strange collections of acts he put together for a single program. That very variety, and a newspaperman's nose for "events," made Sullivan's show a resounding success. The format only seemed to be that of an old-fashioned vaudeville revue (Ed himself stoutly denied that it was "vaudeo"). Where in vaudeville would you have the Bolshoi Ballet one week, scenes from a hit Broadway show with the original cast on another, and dancing bears on a third?

Numerous performers made their American television debuts on the show, including Charles Laughton, Bob Hope, Lena Horne, Martin and Lewis, Dinah Shore, Eddie Fisher, the Beatles, and Walt Disney. Disney's appearance was ironic. He was featured in a full-hour special edition of *Toast of the Town* on February 8, 1953. The following year he began his own show, on ABC, and it was that program that finally surpassed *Ed Sullivan* as the longest-running prime-time network show. It will be noted that Elvis Presley is missing from the above list of firsts. Although he is best remembered for his appearances on *The Ed Sullivan Show* in the fall of 1956, Elvis actually made his TV debut in January 1956, on Tommy and Jimmy Dorsey's *Stage Show.* No matter. To play Sullivan was to make headlines, and Presley's appearance just at the moment he was revolutionizing popular music did just that. So did the Beatles seven years later.

In addition to the firsts, virtually every "name" act in American music, comedy, theater, and film appeared over the years. There were also a few who never did make it out from under Ed's wing: Topo Gigio, the mechanical Italian mouse, and Señor Wences and his talking box ("S-all right?"

"S-all right!") Those celebrities not appearing on the stage were in the audience. To be picked out by Ed from the stage and introduced on nationwide television was a high honor indeed.

Sullivan's mannerisms became legendary, the butt of a thousand comics. He himself participated in a parody record called "It's a Reeally Big SHEW Tonight!" in the mid-1950s, and his program was brilliantly satirized in the Broadway musical *Bye Bye Birdie* in the early 1960s—in which an all-American family reaches spiritual ecstasy when they learn, "We're going to be on . . . Ed Sullivan!"

The show itself changed little over the years, though its scope certainly widened. The title was changed officially to *The Ed Sullivan Show* on September 18, 1955. Some telecasts and segments originated from foreign countries, including Japan, the Soviet Union, Italy, France, England, Spain, Portugal, Ireland, Mexico, Israel, Cuba, and Hong Kong. Some shows were mini-spectaculars, such as the 90-minute tribute to songwriter Irving Berlin, which ended in true Sullivan fashion with a huge American flag in fireworks and the entire cast singing "God Bless America."

Sullivan's run finally ended in 1971, the victim not so much of falling ratings as of a desire by CBS to "modernize" its programming (Ed's appeal had increasingly been to older viewers). There followed some Ed Sullivan specials and a 25th-anniversary special in 1973, but shortly thereafter Sullivan was dead. He will not soon be forgotten.

ED WYNN SHOW, THE
Comedy Variety
FIRST TELECAST: *October 6, 1949*
LAST TELECAST: *July 4, 1950*
BROADCAST HISTORY:
Oct 1949–Dec 1949, CBS Thu 9:00–9:30
Jan 1950–Mar 1950, CBS Sat 9:00–9:30
Apr 1950–Jul 1950, CBS Tue 9:00–9:30
REGULARS:
Ed Wynn
Lud Gluskin

One year after being named by his fellow comedians as "the greatest visual comedian of our day," and more than 40 years after he began his career in vaudeville, Ed Wynn became a regular television performer with his own variety show. Although the show had guest stars, its main focus was Ed himself, in his giggling "Perfect Fool" characterization and in other roles he had created over the years on stage and radio. Ed's guests included many of the great names in film comedy. Ben Blue, Buster Keaton, Lucille Ball and Desi Arnaz (before *I Love Lucy*), Leon Errol, the Three Stooges (Moe Howard, Shemp Howard, and Larry Fine), Joe E. Brown, Ben Wrigley, and Marie Wilson all made guest appearances on the show.

The Ed Wynn Show was the first regular show to originate from Hollywood, carried live on the West Coast and kinescoped for rebroadcast from

New York to the CBS Eastern and Midwest networks. This was the reverse of the normal procedure of that day, in which live shows were aired from New York and had kinescoped repeats fed from Hollywood.

ED WYNN SHOW, THE
Situation Comedy
FIRST TELECAST: *September 25, 1958*
LAST TELECAST: *January 1, 1959*
BROADCAST HISTORY:
Sep 1958–Jan 1959, NBC Thu 8:00–8:30
CAST:
John Beamer...................... Ed Wynn
Laurie.................... Jacklyn O'Donnell
Midge...................... Sherry Alberoni
Ernest Henshaw .... Herb Vigran

Ed Wynn came out of semi-retirement to make one final try at a regular series on television, and this short-lived situation comedy was the result. As John Beamer, he was an elderly widower whose children had also died, leaving him with the responsibility of raising his two granddaughters—Laurie, age 18, and Midge, age 9. With unbounded enthusiasm and optimism he helped not only his own family, but his friends, his neighbors, and anyone else he met. At one point he even got himself elected to the city council.

EDDIE CANTOR COMEDY THEATRE
Comedy Variety
BROADCAST HISTORY:
Syndicated only
30 minutes
Produced: *1954–1955* (38 episodes)
Released: *January 1955*
HOST:
Eddie Cantor

Eddie Cantor's trademark during 50 years in show business was always manic activity—prancing around the stage, waving his hands, rolling his banjo eyes. He was still at it in the early 1950s on *The Colgate Comedy Hour,* but after a heart attack in 1952 he was forced to slow down. This was his last series, a relatively leisurely, filmed half-hour incorporating many of his old routines, but leaving much of the work to numerous guest stars. Many of the episodes consisted of little playlets, with Cantor only hosting. The guest stars were many and varied—Billie Burke, Eddie Fisher, Peter Lorre, Stan Freberg, Helen O'Connell, Charles Coburn, Buster Keaton, and the Three Stooges among them.

On the variety stanzas viewers got all of Cantor's old chestnuts: "If You Knew Susie," "Ma!," "Mandy" (he never seemed to sing anything written after 1930); Cantor with a chorus line of leggy beauties; Cantor behind the wheel of a cab as Maxie the Taxi. It all seemed pretty old hat, and a little weary. But these syndicated films got tremendous circulation, and a great deal of press

coverage. As Steve Allen remarked, "Let no one underestimate the importance of being venerable. . . ."

EDDIE CAPRA MYSTERIES, THE
Lawyer/Detective Drama
FIRST TELECAST: *September 8, 1978*
LAST TELECAST: *September 7, 1979*
BROADCAST HISTORY:
Sep 1978–Jan 1979, NBC Fri 10:00–11:00
Jun 1979–Sep 1979, NBC Fri 10:00–11:00
CAST:
Eddie Capra................ Vincent Baggetta
Lacey Brown .... Wendy Phillips
J.J. Devlin .... Ken Swofford
Harvey Winchell .... Michael Horton
Jennie Brown .... Seven Ann McDonald

Capra was introduced as a detective show in the "classic style." No fancy frills, just a straightforward homicide at the opening of each show, followed by an hour in which the viewer could watch the young lawyer-sleuth uncover clues one by one. Eddie Capra, the unconventional star, worked for the conventional, and very prestigious, law firm of Devlin, Linkman and O'Brien. Lacey was his secretary, close to her boss both on the job and off; Harvey was his enthusiastic young legman; J.J. Devlin, the irascible senior partner in the firm; and Jennie was Lacey's precocious daughter.

EDDIE CONDON'S FLOOR SHOW
Music
FIRST TELECAST: *January 1, 1949*
LAST TELECAST: *Jun 24, 1950*
BROADCAST HISTORY:
Jan 1949–Jul 1949, NBC Sat 8:30–9:00
Jul 1949–Sep 1949, NBC Sat 9:30–10:00
May 1950–Jun 1950, CBS Sat 7:30–8:00
HOST:
Eddie Condon
Carl Reiner (1950)

Guitarist Eddie Condon hosted this informal weekly jam session, one of the first network series devoted to jazz music. It had run previously on WPIX-TV, New York, and before that on WNBT-TV, New York, during the war, making it one of television's oldest features. Guests included many of the top names in jazz, such as Gene Krupa, Woody Herman, Sidney Bechet, Ella Fitzgerald, Louis Armstrong, and dozens of others, as well as such up-and-coming vocalists as Patti Page and Rosemary Clooney. A special feature during the summer of 1949 was a series of programs dramatizing—musically—great moments in jazz history. During the program's brief run on CBS, Condon was joined by Carl Reiner, who chatted with the guests about their careers.

EDDIE FISHER SHOW, THE
Musical Variety

FIRST TELECAST: *September 24, 1957*
LAST TELECAST: *March 17, 1959*
BROADCAST HISTORY:
   Sep 1957–Mar 1959, NBC Tue 8:00–9:00 (OS)
REGULARS:
   Eddie Fisher
   George Gobel
   Buddy Bregman and His Orchestra
   The Bill Thompson Singers (1957–1958)
   The Johnny Mann Singers (1959)

After toiling in a limited-format 15-minute program for several years (see *Coke Time*), popular singer Eddie Fisher got his own full-hour variety show in the fall of 1957. It lasted for two seasons, alternating on Tuesdays with *The George Gobel Show*. Although there were no regulars on the show other than Fisher, George Gobel participated in comedy skits in most of the telecasts. To reciprocate, Eddie made frequent guest appearances on George's show.

EDDY ARNOLD SHOW, THE
   Musical Variety
FIRST TELECAST: *July 14, 1952*
LAST TELECAST: *September 28, 1956*
BROADCAST HISTORY:
   Jul 1952–Aug 1952, CBS Mon/Wed/Fri 7:45–8:00
   Jul 1953–Oct 1953, NBC Tue/Thu 7:30–7:45
   Apr 1956–Jun 1956, ABC Thu 8:00–8:30
   Jun 1956–Sep 1956, ABC Wed 9:30–10:00
REGULARS:
   Eddy Arnold
   The Russ Case Orchestra (1952)
   The Dickens Sisters (1953)
   Chet Atkins (1956)
   The Paul Mitchell Quintet (1956)

Country and western singer Eddy Arnold spent two summers filling in for vacationing singers with regularly scheduled song shows: Perry Como on CBS in 1952 and Dinah Shore on NBC in 1953. In both cases, these 15-minute programs, which filled the remainder of the half-hours in which the networks presented their news programs, provided little opportunity for anything but two or three songs. In the spring of 1956, with a full half-hour on ABC, Mr. Arnold could talk with special guest stars and do more involved production numbers as well as perform solos. Chet Atkins provided instrumental solos and the Paul Mitchell Quintet instrumental backup for this later series, which featured both popular and classical numbers, as well as the soft ballads for which Arnold was famous.

EDIE ADAMS SHOW, THE
   Musical Variety
FIRST TELECAST: *September 26, 1963*
LAST TELECAST: *March 19, 1964*
BROADCAST HISTORY:
   Sep 1963–Mar 1964, ABC Thu 10:00–10:30

REGULARS:
   Edie Adams
   Don Chastain
   Peter Hanley
   The Paul Godkin Dancers
   The Randy Rayburn Singers
   The Peter Matz Orchestra

Singer Edie Adams starred in this half-hour musical variety series that alternated with *The Sid Caesar Show* on Thursday nights during the 1963–1964 season. Edie and her guest stars sang, danced, and did comedy sketches. To start the season both Edie and Sid Caesar appeared together in a full-hour variety special that aired from 10:00–11:00 P.M. on September 19. This show was also known by the title *Here's Edie*.

EDITOR'S CHOICE
   News Analysis
FIRST TELECAST: *June 25, 1961*
LAST TELECAST: *September 24, 1961*
BROADCAST HISTORY:
   Jun 1961–Sep 1961, ABC Sun 10:30–11:00
HOST:
   Fendall Yerxa

Each week, in either a filmed report, a filmed report with interviews, or interviews alone, members of the ABC News staff sought to treat a current news story or issue in greater depth than was possible within the framework of the regular nightly newscast. *Editor's Choice* returned to the air on Sunday afternoons in January 1962, where it remained until February 1963.

EDWIN NEWMAN REPORTING
   News/Documentary
FIRST TELECAST: *June 5, 1960*
LAST TELECAST: *September 4, 1960*
BROADCAST HISTORY:
   Jun 1960–Sep 1960, NBC Sun 6:30–7:00
HOST/REPORTER:
   Edwin Newman

This series was the 1960 summer replacement for *Time Present: Chet Huntley Reporting*. Edwin Newman, then chief of the NBC News Paris bureau, filled in for Chet Huntley, focusing each week on one or two issues of current interest.

EIGHT IS ENOUGH
   Comedy/Drama
FIRST TELECAST: *March 15, 1977*
LAST TELECAST: *August 29, 1981*
BROADCAST HISTORY:
   Mar 1977–May 1977, ABC Tue 9:00–10:00
   Aug 1977–Mar 1981, ABC Wed 8:00–9:00
   Mar 1981–Aug 1981, ABC Sat 8:00–9:00
CAST:
   Tom Bradford . . . . Dick Van Patten
   Joan Bradford (1977) . . . . Diana Hyland

Sandra Sue Abbott ("Abby") Bradford
.... Betty Buckley
Nicholas Bradford (age 8) .... Adam Rich
Tommy Bradford (age 14)...... Willie Aames
Elizabeth Bradford (age 15)
.... Connie Needham (Newton)
Nancy Bradford (age 18).........Dianne Kay
Susan Bradford Stockwell (age 19)
.... Susan Richardson
Joannie Bradford (age 20).... Laurie Walters
Mary Bradford (age 21)........ Lani O'Grady
David Bradford (age 23) ..... Grant Goodeve
Dr. Greg Maxwell (1977–1979)
.... Michael Thoma
Daisy Maxwell (1977–1979) . Virginia Vincent
Donna (1978–1981) .... Jennifer Darling
Merle "The Pearl" Stockwell (1979–1981)
.... Brian Patrick Clarke
Janet Bradford (1979–1981)...... Joan Prather
Ernie Fields (1979–1981) ... Michael Goodrow
Jeremy Andretti (1980–1981)... Ralph Macchio

This comedy-drama focused on a family with eight very independent children, aged 8 to 23. When the series began, Tom, the father, was a newspaper columnist for the Sacramento, California, *Register,* and Joan was his wife of 25 years. The death of actress Diana Hyland during production of the spring 1977 episodes of *Eight Is Enough* forced major changes, however. Hyland had completed only four shows and was written out of the remainder as being "away." When the series returned with new episodes that fall, Tom Bradford had become a widower, his wife having died, at least in the storyline, about "a year ago." With the help of his best friend Doc Maxwell, Tom set about keeping order among his large brood while re-entering, in middle age, the singles world. He soon found romance in the person of Abby, a pretty school-teacher who came to the Bradford home to tutor one of the youngsters. Their romance blossomed, and on a special two-hour telecast on November 9, 1977, Tom and Abby were married.

As the series continued, Abby pursued and got her Ph.D. in education and began counseling work at Memorial High (as well as at home!). The Bradford kids all became involved with various friends and romances as they grew, and in a special episode in September 1979 David and Susan each got married, in a double wedding—David to attorney Janet, and Susan to pro baseball pitcher Merle "The Pearl" Stockwell (who later signed with the New York Mets). David then went to work for a construction firm, while Susan set about producing the first Bradford grandchild—Sandra Sue, born in October 1980. Meanwhile Joannie got a job at a television station, and became engaged to Jeffrey Trout (played by Nicholas Pryor).

The series was based on the book *Eight Is Enough* by Thomas Braden.

87TH PRECINCT
Police Drama

FIRST TELECAST: *September 25, 1961*
LAST TELECAST: *September 10, 1962*
BROADCAST HISTORY:
Sep 1961–Sep 1962, NBC Mon 9:00–10:00
CAST:
Det. Steve Carella .... Robert Lansing
Det. Bert Kling................. Ron Harper
Det. Roger Havilland....... Gregory Walcott
Det. Meyer Meyer .... Norman Fell
Teddy Carella .... Gena Rowlands

Manhattan's 87th precinct was the base for the police detectives of this rather grim, violent series that was based on the mystery stories of Ed McBain (pseudonym of Evan Hunter), which were popular in the 1950s and 1960s. In addition to the various aspects of police work normally seen in action series of this type, the personal lives of the officers provided much of the side drama. Detective Steve Carella was married to a beautiful woman who unfortunately was a deaf mute; Bert Kling was the young detective learning the ropes; Roger Havilland the hardened old pro; and Meyer Meyer the older officer who, having "seen it all," often injected a dry humor into otherwise serious business. Most of the stories started in the precinct office where all of the detectives gathered to write up reports and wait for assignments.

EISCHIED
Police Drama
FIRST TELECAST: *September 21, 1979*
LAST TELECAST: *September 2, 1983*
BROADCAST HISTORY:
Sep 1979–Dec 1979, NBC Fri 10:00–11:00
Dec 1979–Jan 1980, NBC Sun 10:00–11:00
June 1983–Sep 1983, NBC Fri 10:00–11:00
CAST:
Chief Earl Eischied .... Joe Don Baker
Capt. Finnerty .... Alan Oppenheimer
Dep. Commissioner Kimbrough... Alan Fudge
Chief Inspector Ed Parks .... Eddie Egan
Carol Wright .... Suzanne Lederer
Rick Alessi................. Vincent Bufano
Det. Malfitano .... Joe Cirillo

Working for the New York City Police Department could harden anyone, and nobody was more hardened than Chief of Detectives Earl Eischied, in this violent, gritty series. A tough, dedicated career cop, Eischied (pronounced "Eye-shyed") knew the rule book and how to get around it when necessary to break a case. Eischied's methods worried politically ambitious, "by-the-book" Deputy Commissioner Kimbrough, but fortunately Earl's friend, Chief Inspector Ed Parks, could serve as a buffer between them. Carol Wright and Rick Alessi were two members of the special squad reporting directly to Eischied, as was trusted friend Capt. Finnerty. They were all dedicated to Eischied, though their only reward was an occasional, gruff "You done good," delivered in his inimitable Southern drawl. A bachelor, Eischied's constant companion both at home and at work was his pet cat, P.C.

Three years after the conclusion of its unsuccessful original run, NBC aired reruns of *Eischied* as a summer replacement series in 1983.

EISENHOWER & LUTZ
Situation Comedy
FIRST TELECAST: *March 14, 1988*
LAST TELECAST: *June 20, 1988*
BROADCAST HISTORY:
   Mar 1988–Jun 1988, CBS Mon 9:30–10:00
CAST:
   Barnett M. "Bud" Lutz, Jr. ...... Scott Bakula
   Megan O'Malley .... DeLane Matthews
   Kay "K.K." Dunne ...... Patricia Richardson
   Millie Zamora .... Rose Portillo
   Dwayne Spitler .... Leo Geter
   Barnett M. "Big Bud" Lutz
      .... Henderson Forsythe

Bud Lutz had barely made it through law school and, after failing to establish a practice in Las Vegas, had returned home to Palm Springs, California, to open a law office there. The office, located in a former hot tub showroom (with a leftover sample in his reception area) in a mini-mall on the outskirts of town, did not attract a high-class clientele—mostly whiplash victims and illegal aliens. Bud's girlfriend Megan, who had returned with him from Vegas, was a cocktail waitress at the nearby Kon Tiki Lounge. Her relationship with Bud was threatened by his high school sweetheart Kay, a partner in the high-powered local law firm of Griffin, McKendrick & Dunne, who still had the hots for him. Others in the cast were Millie, the secretary who Bud never seemed to pay; Dwayne, the eager young law student who did odd jobs for free in order to watch a real lawyer at work (some example!!) and Bud's free-spirited father Big Bud, an eccentric sign painter. It was Big Bud's idea to call his son's firm Eisenhower & Lutz because the Eisenhower name was well respected in the desert. Unfortunately, too many prospective clients asked for the nonexistent Mr. Eisenhower and not enough for Mr. Lutz.

ELDER MICHAUX
Religion
FIRST TELECAST: *October 31, 1948*
LAST TELECAST: *January 9, 1949*
BROADCAST HISTORY:
   Oct 1948–Jan 1949, DUM Sun 6:00–6:30
PREACHER:
   Elder Lightfoot Solomon Michaux

The black preacher Lightfoot Solomon Michaux (pronounced "Me-show") and his foot-stomping, hand-clapping revival meetings had been heard on radio since the very early days of that medium. The broadcasts emanated from his hometown of Washington, D.C., where he was pastor of the

Church of God, and featured his Happy-Am-I Choir and an enthusiastic congregation that shouted ecstatic encouragement as the Elder preached. He became a regular feature on local Washington TV soon after the first station opened there, and his broadcasts were periodically fed over the DuMont network beginning in 1947. The network telecasts included a semi-regular run in 1948–1949, as shown above.

ELEVENTH HOUR, THE
Medical Drama
FIRST TELECAST: *October 3, 1962*
LAST TELECAST: *September 9, 1964*
BROADCAST HISTORY:
   Oct 1962–Sep 1964, NBC Wed 10:00–11:00
CAST:
   Dr. Theodore Bassett (1962–1963)
      .... Wendell Corey
   Dr. Paul Graham .... Jack Ging
   Dr. L. Richard Starke (1963–1964)
      .... Ralph Bellamy

The role of psychiatry in helping people cope with the world, as well as its use in law-enforcement areas, provided the grist for this dramatic series. Drs. Bassett and Graham were two psychiatrists sharing an office, and the patients who came to them "in the eleventh hour"—on the verge of some form of breakdown—provided the stories. Various forms of analysis and psychotherapy were used, and the two doctors often disagreed on the proper course to take with a specific patient. Dr. Bassett was also an advisor to the State Department of Correction and the police department and was often called upon to evaluate the mental competency of accused criminals.

During the first season the majority of stories dealt with Dr. Bassett's criminal cases. When Wendell Corey left the series, Ralph Bellamy took over his responsibilities, as Dr. Starke, and the emphasis was shifted to involve both of the doctors directly in more of the cases.

ELGIN TV HOUR, THE
Dramatic Anthology
FIRST TELECAST: *October 5, 1954*
LAST TELECAST: *June 14, 1955*
BROADCAST HISTORY:
   Oct 1954–Jun 1955, ABC Tue 9:30–10:30

This one-hour Tuesday night series of dramatic presentations on ABC replaced the previous season's *Motorola TV Theatre*. The dramas were telecast live from New York and featured such top actors as Ralph Bellamy, Gertrude Berg, Franchot Tone, Boris Karloff, Polly Bergen, John Cassavetes, and John Forsythe, to name a few. The series alternated with *The U.S. Steel Hour*.

ELLEN BURSTYN SHOW, THE
Situation Comedy
FIRST TELECAST: *September 20, 1986*

LAST TELECAST: *September 12, 1987*
BROADCAST HISTORY:
Sep 1986–Nov 1986, ABC Sat 8:30–9:00
Aug 1987–Sep 1987, ABC Sat 8:30–9:00
CAST:
Ellen Brewer .... Ellen Burstyn
Sydney Brewer .... Elaine Stritch
Molly Brewer Ross.......... Megan Mullally
Nick Ross .... Jesse Tendler
Tom Hines .... Barry Sobel

Ellen Burstyn starred as a best-selling author whose life seemed to consist mostly of one-liners, in this multigenerational comedy. Sharing her Baltimore brownstone were her acerbic mother, Sydney; her divorced, 25-year-old daughter Molly; and her cute 5-year-old grandson Nick. Tom was an impoverished student who was taking the seminar Ellen taught at a nearby college. Quips flew thick and fast around the kitchen table, but not fast enough to save this series.

ELLERY QUEEN
see *Adventures of Ellery Queen, The*

EMERALD POINT N.A.S.
Military Drama
FIRST TELECAST: *September 26, 1983*
LAST TELECAST: *March 12, 1984*
BROADCAST HISTORY:
Sep 1983–Mar 1984, CBS Mon 10:00–11:00
CAST:
Rear Adm. Thomas Mallory . Dennis Weaver
Maggie Farrell............... Maud Adams
Deanna Kincaid .... Jill St. John
Lt. Glenn Matthews........ Andrew Stevens
Lt. Cmdr. Jack Warren .... Charles Frank
Lt. Simon Adams ... Richard Dean Anderson
Hilary Adams .... Sela Ward
Ensign Leslie Mallory .... Doran Clark
Kay Mallory Matthews... Stephanie Dunnam
Celia Mallory Warren............ Susan Dey
Harlan Adams (1983)........ Patrick O'Neal
Harlan Adams (1983–1984).... Robert Vaughn
Lt. Alexi Gorichenko .... Michael Carven
Adm. Yuri Bukharin.......... Robert Loggia
Scott Farrell................ Darryl Cooksey
David Marquette........... Michael Brandon

The interlocking worlds of the military and big business provided the backdrop for this prime-time soap opera. Commanding officer at the Emerald Point Naval Air Station was Admiral Thomas Mallory, a widowed career military man with three beautiful young daughters—Celia, married to brilliant military lawyer Jack Warren; Kay, who in midseason wed Glenn Matthews, a former pilot who had been discharged from the navy after being convicted of manslaughter; and youngest daughter Leslie, recently graduated from Annapolis. The local business magnate, appropriately unscrupulous, was Harlan Adams, president of Adams Industries. Harlan's son, navy pilot

Simon Adams, was as honorable and good as his father and sister Hilary were bad. There was the usual mix of maneuvering for power, sleeping around, and horrible revelations about flawed characters and hidden pasts, along with the intrigue added by the military setting. Admiral Mallory's bitchy but beautiful sister-in-law, Deanna Kincaid, who wanted power and wealth, had her heart set on marrying Harlan. In the meantime she got involved with KGB spy Yuri Bukharin and, when caught by naval intelligence, became a double agent. The love life of Admiral Mallory was shared with Maggie Farrell, the liaison between the town's military affairs council and the naval base. She and Mallory, who were good friends at the start of the season, were about to be married at its end. The wedding never took place, however, since she was kidnapped by a mentally disturbed David Marquette in the cliffhanger season-ending episode. Since the series was not renewed, viewers never did find out what happened.

EMERGENCY
Drama
FIRST TELECAST: *January 22, 1972*
LAST TELECAST: *September 3, 1977*
BROADCAST HISTORY:
Jan 1972–Jul 1972, NBC Sat 8:00–9:00
Sep 1972–Sep 1977, NBC Sat 8:00–9:00
CAST:
Dr. Kelly Brackett .... Robert Fuller
Nurse Dixie McCall............ Julie London
Dr. Joe Early .... Bobby Troup
Paramedic Roy DeSoto......... Kevin Tighe
Paramedic John Gage ... Randolph Mantooth
Dr. Morton .... Ron Pinkhard
Captain Stanley (1973–1977) .. Michael Norell
Fireman Chet Kelly (1973–1977)
.... Tim Donnelly
Fireman Lopez (1973–1977)..... Marco Lopez
Fireman Stoker (1973–1977)..... Mike Stoker
Officer Vince (1976–1977)..... Vince Howard
EXECUTIVE PRODUCER:
Jack Webb

Done in the semi-documentary style for which Jack Webb had become famous with *Dragnet*, *Emergency* followed the efforts of Squad 51 of the Los Angeles County Fire Department's Paramedical Rescue Service. Paramedics DeSoto and Gage were usually at the center of the action, while the emergency staff of Rampart Hospital provided backup assistance. Each telecast depicted several interwoven incidents, some humorous, some touching, others tragic. A typical night's work might have the paramedics called on to help an overweight woman who was having trouble breathing because her girdle was too tight, or aiding a maintenance worker who had broken his back in a 100-foot fall from a smokestack he was painting. Another night they might be saving children trapped in an abandoned building when a wrecking crew began demolishing the place, or

235

rescuing a woman parachutist who had gotten caught in a tree. One of the specialties of the paramedics, in fact, seemed to be saving "danglers"—people trapped in precarious positions because of faulty rigging, collapsing scaffolding, or the like.

Former bandleader Bobby Troup, who played neurosurgeon Joe Early, was in real life married to Julie London, who played Rampart's head nurse. (She had previously been married to producer Jack Webb.) Squad 51's mascot was a dog named Boots.

Although *Emergency* ended its run as a series in 1977, special two-hour movie versions, newly filmed, were periodically aired during the following season.

An animated Saturday morning spinoff of this series, titled *Emergency + 4*, aired on NBC from September 1973 to September 1976.

EMPIRE
Western
FIRST TELECAST: *September 25, 1962*
LAST TELECAST: *September 6, 1964*
BROADCAST HISTORY:
  Sep 1962–Sep 1963, NBC Tue 8:30–9:30
  Mar 1964–Sep 1964, ABC Sun 7:30–8:30
CAST:
  Jim Redigo .... Richard Egan
  Constance Garret .... Terry Moore
  Lucia Garret .... Anne Seymour
  Tal Garret .... Ryan O'Neal
  Chuck Davis (1963) .... Warren Vanders
  Paul Moreno (1963) .... Charles Bronson

This drama was set on the sprawling Garret ranch in contemporary New Mexico. The ranch was indeed an empire, a multi-million-dollar operation covering half a million acres and including oil, mining, lumber, and crop-raising industries, plus cattle-, sheep-, and horse-breeding. All of these gave Jim Redigo, the foreman, plenty of opportunity for dramatic adventure.

Production of *Empire* ceased at the end of the 1962–1963 season, but ABC aired reruns of the original episodes during mid-1964. The main character, Jim Redigo, was saved by NBC for a shorter version of this series, simply titled *Redigo*, that was aired in the fall of 1963 but lasted only 13 weeks. (See *Redigo* for details.)

EMPIRE
Situation Comedy
FIRST TELECAST: *January 4, 1984*
LAST TELECAST: *February 1, 1984*
BROADCAST HISTORY:
  Jan 1984–Feb 1984, CBS Wed 8:30–9:00
CAST:
  Ben Christian .... Dennis Dugan
  Calvin Cromwell .... Patrick Macnee
  Peg .... Maureen Arthur
  Jackie Willow .... Christine Belford
  Meredith .... Caren Kaye

  Jack Willow .... Richard Masur
  Edward Roland .... Michael McGuire
  Arthur Broderick .... Dick O'Neill
  Roger Martinson .... Howard Platt
  T. Howard Daniels .... Edward Winter
  Renee .... Patricia Elliott
  Bill .... Paul Wilson
  Amelia Lapidus .... Francine Tacker

Empire was a wild satire on the shenanigans and paranoia of corporate America. Board of directors meetings at giant Empire Industries resembled open house at a lunatic asylum. Calvin Cromwell was the autocratic chairman of the board who delighted in making his underlings squirm; Meredith was the manipulative director of public relations; Jack Willow, the incompetent sales v.p. whose ambitious wife, Jackie, had to give him detailed instructions on what to say at board meetings (which sometimes backfired when an unexpected question was asked). In addition, Arthur Broderick was the over-the-hill head of marketing, who plastered his hair with artificial coloring in a hopeless attempt to look young; Tom Martinson, the thoroughly unprincipled chief counsel; and Howard Daniels, the neurotic security chief who kept an oxygen mask by his side during board meetings. Edward Roland was another board member rather obviously trying to unseat Cromwell and take over the entire business.

Into this nest of bumbling schemers came naive young Ben Christian, whom Cromwell had just appointed to be vice-president of research and development. Friendly toward the company's workers, honest, and with the boss' confidence as well, Ben posed a major threat to the others. Played in serial fashion, and strictly for laughs, *Empire* featured back-stabbing, double-dealing, and even an off-handed murder committed by Martinson as board members jockeyed for power.

ENCORE PLAYHOUSE
  see *Movies—Prior to 1961*

ENCORE THEATRE
Dramatic Anthology
FIRST TELECAST: *July 7, 1956*
LAST TELECAST: *September 14, 1957*
BROADCAST HISTORY:
  Jul 1956–Sep 1956, NBC Sat 10:00–10:30
  Jul 1957–Sep 1957, NBC Sat 10:00–10:30

Encore Theatre was the 1956 summer replacement for *The George Gobel Show* and ran in the summer of 1957 after Gobel left the Saturday schedule. The 1956 version consisted of reruns of episodes of *Pepsi-Cola Playhouse* and *Studio 57*. The 1957 version was made up of reruns of episodes of *Ford Theatre*.

ENCOUNTER
Dramatic Anthology
FIRST TELECAST: *October 5, 1958*

BROADCAST HISTORY:
 Oct 1958–Nov 1958, ABC Sun 9:30–10:30

Encounter was a live dramatic series, telecast from Toronto and produced by the Canadian Broadcasting Corporation. For a five-week period in the fall of 1958 these dramas were aired simultaneously by the CBC in Canada and by ABC in the United States, one of the few instances of a live "international network" involving the U.S.

The stories varied between romance, mystery, and adventure, but all involved Canadians as characters and featured such Canadian and British actors as Patrick Macnee and Barry Morse.

END OF THE RAINBOW, THE
Audience Participation
FIRST TELECAST: *January 11, 1958*
LAST TELECAST: *February 15, 1958*
BROADCAST HISTORY:
 Jan 1958–Feb 1958, NBC Sat 10:00–10:30
EMCEE:
 Art Baker (Jan)
 Bob Barker (Feb)
PRODUCER:
 Ralph Edwards

The End of the Rainbow was a poor man's traveling version of *This Is Your Life* and was produced by the same man, Ralph Edwards. Each week during its brief run, an unsuspecting person or couple would be surprised in their hometown and honored for being good citizens who had made an outstanding contribution to the community. The chosen people were given "The Surprise of Their Lives," a gift, award, or opportunity that they could only have expected to find "at the end of the rainbow." As on *This Is Your Life,* the subjects were surprised by friends and relatives who were invited to participate in telling their story. The original emcee, Art Baker, left the show after three telecasts and was replaced by Bob Barker for the final three.

ENGELBERT HUMPERDINCK SHOW, THE
Musical Variety
FIRST TELECAST: *January 21, 1970*
LAST TELECAST: *September 19, 1970*
BROADCAST HISTORY:
 Jan 1970–Jun 1970, ABC Wed 10:00–11:00
 Jul 1970–Sep 1970, ABC Sat 9:30–10:30
REGULARS:
 Engelbert Humperdinck
 Irving Davies Dancers
 The Jack Parnell Orchestra

ABC's success with *This Is Tom Jones,* an English musical variety hour, prompted the network to try this London-based revue starring another singer of similar background and musical style, Engelbert Humperdinck. The star (whose real name was Arnold George Dorsey) was a handsome, likable chap popular in both England and the United States. He had done well enough in an ABC special in December 1969, but his regular series failed to make the grade. It ceased production after six months, although reruns were aired on Saturday nights through the summer.

ENOS
Police Comedy
FIRST TELECAST: *November 5, 1980*
LAST TELECAST: *September 19, 1981*
BROADCAST HISTORY:
 Nov 1980–May 1981, CBS Wed 8:00–9:00
 May 1981–Sep 1981, CBS Sat 8:00–9:00
CAST:
 Officer Enos Strate........... Sonny Shroyer
 Officer Turk Adams....... Samuel E. Wright
 Lt. Jacob Broggi................ John Dehner
 Capt. Dempsey .... John Milford
 Det. Bigalow (1980) .... C. Pete Munro
 Sgt. Theodore Kick........... Leo V. Gordon

Enos Strate was the reincarnation of Gomer Pyle—a gullible, trusting Southerner who had his own hilarious way of coping with urban life. Enos had been a Hazzard County deputy sheriff on CBS' highly successful series, *The Dukes of Hazzard.* When he accidentally captured two mostwanted criminals, the Los Angeles Police Department was so impressed it offered him a job with the newly organized Special Branch of its Metro Squad. Los Angeles was not quite the same after country bumpkin Enos arrived. His street-smart black partner Turk Adams couldn't believe how naive he was, and their superior, Lt. Broggi, had as much trouble with him as the Marines had with Gomer Pyle. Enos always had an ear-to-ear grin on his face, a Southern homily for every situation, and a love for fast cars and wild chases (and crashes). Dumb, maybe, but by the final scene he always seemed to run down the crooks. His friends from Hazzard made occasional visits to L.A. and Enos narrated each episode as he wrote letters to Daisy telling her what was happening to him in the big city.

ENSIGN O'TOOLE
Situation Comedy
FIRST TELECAST: *September 23, 1962*
LAST TELECAST: *September 10, 1964*
BROADCAST HISTORY:
 Sep 1962–Sep 1963, NBC Sun 7:00–7:30
 Mar 1964–Sep 1964, ABC Thu 9:00–9:30
CAST:
 Ensign O'Toole .... Dean Jones
 Chief Petty Officer Homer Nelson
 .... Jay C. Flippen
 Lt. (jg) Rex St. John .... Jack Mullaney
 Seaman Gabby Di Julio .... Harvey Lembeck
 Lt. Cdr. Virgil Stoner........ Jack Albertson
 Seaman Howard Spicer .... Beau Bridges
 Seaman Claude White .... Bob Sorrells

This military comedy followed along the same lines as *McHale's Navy* (which also premiered in 1962), but it was set in peacetime. O'Toole was a junior officer aboard the destroyer *Appleby,* clever and an expert on almost everybody's subject, but seldom to be found when there was work to be done. His foils were the usual assortment of lunatic crew members and the overbearing and ambitious supply officer, Lt. Rex St. John. The ship's executive officer was Lt. Cdr. Virgil Stoner. He relayed orders from the captain, who was never seen but only heard, barking orders over the "squawk box."

Based on two books by Bill Lederer, *All the Ships at Sea* and *Ensign O'Toole and Me.* Lederer served as consultant for the series.

The ABC run consisted of reruns of episodes previously aired by NBC.

ENTERPRISE
Documentary
FIRST TELECAST: *October 19, 1952*
LAST TELECAST: *June 8, 1958*
BROADCAST HISTORY:
Oct 1952–Dec 1952, ABC Sun 7:30–8:00
Dec 1952–Mar 1953, ABC Sun 10:30–10:45
Jan 1954–Sep 1954, ABC Sat 8:00–8:30
Oct 1954–Jan 1955, ABC Wed 9:30–10:00
Jul 1957, ABC Thu 8:30–9:00
Aug 1957–Oct 1957, ABC Fri 9:00–9:30
Mar 1958–Apr 1958, ABC Sun 7:00–7:30
Apr 1958–Jun 1958, ABC Sun 9:30–10:00

These documentary films on American industry were run by ABC to fill various holes in the schedule. The original 1952–1953 series was billed in an interesting fashion: "These films, presented in cooperation with such industries as Bethlehem Steel and General Electric, will point out that America is out to prove democracy in industry and to fight communism in industry."

ENTERTAINERS, THE
Variety
FIRST TELECAST: *September 25, 1964*
LAST TELECAST: *March 27, 1965*
BROADCAST HISTORY:
Sep 1964–Dec 1964, CBS Fri 8:30–9:30
Jan 1965–Mar 1965, CBS Sat 9:00–10:00
REGULARS:
Carol Burnett
Caterina Valente
Bob Newhart (1964)
Tessie O'Shea (1964)
Art Buchwald (1964)
Don Crichton (1964)
Ruth Buzzi
John Davidson
Dom DeLuise
The Ernie Flatt Dancers (1964)
The Peter Gennaro Dancers (1965)
The Lee Hale Singers
The Harry Zimmerman Orchestra

The format of this variety series was designed to allow each of its three stars—Carol Burnett, Caterina Valente, and Bob Newhart—at least one week off each month. Sometimes all three of them were on a given episode, sometimes only two, and occasionally only one. There was no formal host; instead, each performer introduced the act to follow at the conclusion of his own act. In an effort to simulate a live show, the taping was done on the same evening that the program was actually aired. The regular repertory company of singers, dancers, and comedians was augmented by one or two guest stars each week.

By the end of 1964 one of the three costars, Bob Newhart, had left the series, along with several members of its regular cast, and Carol Burnett and Caterina Valente were seen together as co-stars on every episode in 1965. One interesting sidelight is that on November 13, 1964, *The Entertainers* presented a full-hour documentary on the Beatles' 1964 American tour.

ENTERTAINMENT TONIGHT
News/Gossip
BROADCAST HISTORY:
Syndicated only
30 minutes weeknights/60 minutes weekends
Produced: *1981–*
Released: *September 14, 1981*
HOSTS:
Ron Hendren (1981–1984)
Marjorie Wallace (1981)
Tom Hallick (1981)
Dixie Whatley (1981–1984)
Mary Hart (1982–   )
Steve Edwards (1982–1983)
Alan Arthur (1983–1984)
Robb Weller (1984–   )
Leeza Gibbons (1984–   )
John Tesh (1986–   )

The latest news items and gossip from the world of show business were presented in straight newscast fashion on *Entertainment Tonight.* To stay up-to-the-minute, *ET* was fed daily by satellite to stations around the country, most of whom carried it live. Many of the stories hardly deserved that urgency—who was leaving what series, who was seen going out with whom, hype for the latest movies and shows—but an audience anxious for the latest celebrity scuttlebutt, no matter how trivial, made the program a hit from coast to coast.

There has been a certain amount of turmoil in host assignments on *ET.* When the series premiered, actor Tom Hallick, former Miss World Marjorie Wallace, and critic Ron Hendren were the weeknight anchors. Only Hendren survived; Hallick was dropped as host after a month, Wallace was replaced by Dixie Whatley a month after that, and then Whatley was replaced by Mary Hart in September 1982. A one-hour weekend recap called *Entertainment This Week* was hosted for the first season by the same team that did the weeknight version. In 1982 Dixie Whatley and Steve Edwards took over, and in 1983 Alan Arthur replaced Edwards. Fall of 1984 brought young Robb Weller to both the weekday and weekend editions as male co-host, with Leeza Gibbons replacing the female member of the weekend anchor team. Although no longer serving as weekend hosts, both Dixie Whatley and Alan Arthur remained with the show as contributing correspondents, along with movie critic Leonard Maltin, who had been with *Entertainment Tonight* since its premiere.

In the summer of 1985 Rona Barrett, the queen of gossip, joined the series as a regular contributor, replacing Bill Harris, whose gossip pieces had been a regular feature for the previous year. Miss Rona left when her one-year contract was not renewed, with Jeanne Wolf filling the void left by her departure. In the fall of 1986 former CBS reporter John Tesh replaced Weller as Mary Hart's co-host on *Entertainment Tonight*, with Weller holding onto the male host's position on *Entertainment This Week*.

EQUALIZER, THE
Detective
FIRST TELECAST: *September 18, 1985*
LAST TELECAST:
BROADCAST HISTORY:
  Sep 1985–Mar 1986, CBS Wed 10:00–11:00
  Mar 1986–Aug 1986, CBS Tue 10:00–11:00
  Sep 1986–Feb 1987, CBS Wed 10:00–11:00
  May 1987–Jun 1988, CBS Wed 10:00–11:00
  Jun 1988–   , CBS Wed 9:00–10:00
CAST:
  Robert McCall.......... Edward Woodward
  Control...................... Robert Lansing
  Lt. Burnett (1985) .... Steven Williams
  Lt. Isadore Smalls (1986–1987) ... Ron O'Neal
  *Scott McCall (1986–   ) ..... William Zabka
  Mickey Kostmayer (1986–   )
    .... Keith Szarabajka
  Sgt. Alice Shepherd (1987–   )
    .... Chad Redding
  Pete O'Phelan (1987–   )
    .... Maureen Anderman

*Occasional

He had served as a secret agent for the government, but Robert McCall had grown disillusioned by all the double-dealing that he had seen over the years. Now retired, McCall, who had been known throughout his espionage career as "The Equalizer," attempted to be just that for people who found themselves facing seemingly hopeless situations. Operating his one-man security force from a plush Manhattan apartment, he found his clients through ads he placed in the local newspapers urging people in dire straits to contact The Equalizer. He was both detective and bodyguard, and was only occasionally helped by his former

Agency boss, known only as Control. McCall sought to do good on a personal level—as a form of penance for his previous life—often for little or no pay.

Also seen were Mickey, who did much of McCall's legwork; Scott, his impulsive young son; and assorted members of the N.Y.P.D. Turning up late in 1987, as the owner of a little bistro which McCall began to frequent, was a former friend from his Agency days, Pete O'Phelan.

ERN WESTMORE SHOW, THE
  see *Hollywood Backstage*

ERNIE IN KOVACSLAND
Comedy Variety
FIRST TELECAST: *July 2, 1951*
LAST TELECAST: *August 24, 1951*
BROADCAST HISTORY:
  Jul 1951–Aug 1951, NBC Mon–Fri 7:00–7:30
REGULARS:
  Ernie Kovacs
  Tony DeSimone Trio
  Edith Adams

Emanating from Philadelphia during the summer of 1951, *Ernie in Kovacsland* was an unstructured live comedy show that highlighted its star's incredible repertoire of nutty characterizations. The humor was slapstick and almost entirely visual, and was a forerunner of the later Kovacs shows. Appearing as vocalist on *Ernie in Kovacsland* was one Edith Adams, who would later marry the star and shorten her first name to Edie.

ERNIE KOVACS SHOW, THE
Comedy Variety
FIRST TELECAST: *December 30, 1952*
LAST TELECAST: *September 10, 1956*
BROADCAST HISTORY:
  Dec 1952–Apr 1953, CBS Tue 8:00–9:00
  Jul 1956–Sep 1956, NBC Mon 8:00–9:00
REGULARS:
  Ernie Kovacs
  Edith Adams
  Ernie Hatrak (1952–1953)
  Trigger Lund (1952–1953)
  Andy McKay (1952–1953)
  Bill Wendell (1956)
  Peter Hanley (1956)
  Henry Lascoe (1956)
  Al Kelly (1956)
  Barbara Loden (1956)

Ernie Kovacs, one of the most original TV comedians of the 1950s, turned up on the CBS network for a few months in 1952–1953 in this live hour of comedy sketches (at first titled *Kovacs Unlimited*, the same as his local show). With him were many of the regulars from his local show, including singer Edith (not yet Edie) Adams, pianist Ernie Hatrak, and straight men Trigger Lund and Andy McKay. After an absence of three years Ernie re-

239

turned in 1956, cigar in hand, as the summer replacement for *Caesar's Hour* on NBC. By then he and Edie were married. The supporting cast was different but the humor was the same, largely visual and always offbeat. Among the regular features were *You Asked to See It*, Percy Dovetonsils, the Nairobi Trio, Mr. Question Man, and Clowdy Faire, Your Weather Girl.

ESCAPE
Dramatic Anthology
FIRST TELECAST: *January 5, 1950*
LAST TELECAST: *March 30, 1950*
BROADCAST HISTORY:
   Jan 1950–Mar 1950, CBS Thu 9:00–9:30

This live dramatic series was the television counterpart to a successful CBS radio series of the same name. The plays depicted people attempting to deal with danger, the supernatural, or some fantasized situation, allowing the viewer to escape from reality.

ESCAPE
Adventure Anthology
FIRST TELECAST: *February 11, 1973*
LAST TELECAST: *September 9, 1973*
BROADCAST HISTORY:
   Feb 1973–Apr 1973, NBC Sun 10:00–10:30
   Aug 1973–Sep 1973, NBC Sun 10:00–10:30
NARRATOR:
   Jack Webb

Narrow escapes from danger, both natural and man-made, formed the subject matter of this brief semi-documentary adventure series narrated by Jack Webb. Only four original episodes were aired during February–April 1973, dealing with a submarine trapped on the ocean's floor, a demolition expert racing to avert disaster, two children lost in the woods, and an orphan who saves an American official during the Korean war. The four were repeated during the summer of 1973.

ESPIONAGE
Spy Drama
FIRST TELECAST: *October 2, 1963*
LAST TELECAST: *September 2, 1964*
BROADCAST HISTORY:
   Oct 1963–Sep 1964, NBC Wed 9:00–10:00

Filmed on location throughout Europe, *Espionage* was an anthology of spy stories, all based on actual case histories. The periods ranged from World War I to the then-current cold war, and covered all forms of international intrigue, civil war, and underground resistance movements. Although most of the performers in these dramas were Europeans unfamiliar to American audiences, some fairly well-known names were also featured, such as Dennis Hopper, Patricia Neal, Arthur Kennedy, Jim Backus, Anthony Quayle, and, in a small supporting role in one episode, author Ian Fleming (of James Bond fame).

ETHEL AND ALBERT
Situation Comedy
FIRST TELECAST: *April 25, 1953*
LAST TELECAST: *July 6, 1956*
BROADCAST HISTORY:
   Apr 1953–Dec 1954, NBC Sat 7:30–8:00 (OS)
   Jun 1955–Sep 1955, CBS Mon 9:30–10:00
   Oct 1955–Jul 1956, ABC Fri 10:00–10:30
CAST:
   Ethel Arbuckle................... Peg Lynch
   Albert Arbuckle .... Alan Bunce

Ethel and Albert was one of many popular radio shows of the 1940s that had a second life on television in the 1950s. The format was extremely simple and down-to-earth, following the middle-aged Ethel and Albert Arbuckle through the minor triumphs and crises of everyday life. A gentle realism was the keynote of this series, with blown fuses, burnt-out lightbulbs, and ruined dinners being about the worst things that happened in Sandy Harbor, where the couple lived. On radio the Arbuckles had generally been the only characters heard, but a few friends and neighbors wandered through the TV version from time to time.

Peggy Lynch, who had created the characters *Ethel and Albert* in the 1930s, played the role of Ethel on TV, and Alan Bunce, also a holdover from radio, was Albert. They first appeared on TV as a featured sketch on *The Kate Smith Hour*, before launching their own series.

EVE ARDEN SHOW, THE
Situation Comedy
FIRST TELECAST: *September 17, 1957*
LAST TELECAST: *March 25, 1958*
BROADCAST HISTORY:
   Sep 1957–Mar 1958, CBS Tue 8:30–9:00
CAST:
   Liza Hammond .... Eve Arden
   George Howell................. Allyn Joslyn
   Nora....................... Frances Bavier
   Jenny .... Gail Stone
   Mary .... Karen Greene

Following Eve Arden's long association with *Our Miss Brooks*, which had ended the previous season, this comedy series cast the actress as novelist Liza Hammond. Liza was a widow who supplemented her writing income by giving lectures, and George Howell was the head of the lecture bureau that booked her tours. While Liza was out lecturing the population, her 12-year-old twin daughters, Jenny and Mary, were at home being looked after by her mother, Nora. The series was based on the autobiography of the writer Emily Kimbrough.

EVERYBODY'S BUSINESS
Documentary
FIRST TELECAST: *July 2, 1951*
LAST TELECAST: *September 28, 1952*

BROADCAST HISTORY:
Jul 1951–Aug 1951, ABC Sun 10:30–11:00
Jul 1952–Sep 1952, ABC Sun 7:30–8:00
HOST:
Oscar Ewing (1951)

This documentary film series on education, health, and social services was presented in cooperation with the Federal Security Agency during the summers of 1951 and 1952. The host was Oscar Ewing, Federal Security Administrator.

EVERYTHING'S RELATIVE
Situation Comedy
FIRST TELECAST: *October 3, 1987*
LAST TELECAST: *November 7, 1987*
BROADCAST HISTORY:
Oct 1987–Nov 1987, CBS Sat 8:30–9:00
CAST:
Julian Beeby .... Jason Alexander
Scott Beeby .... John Bolger
Emily Cabot .... Gina Hecht
Mickey Murphy .... Tony Deacon Nittoli
Rae Matthews .... Anne Jackson

A short-lived comedy about two brothers sharing a loft apartment in the Soho section of lower Manhattan. Julian was older and more sensible, a divorced 33-year-old with a small business that tested consumer products for advertising agencies and companies. Scott was a carefree hunk, a 25-year-old construction worker who was irresistable to women. Stories revolved around their divergent values, life-styles, and social lives. Julian's partner Emily wanted their relationship to be more than just business, and was vocal about letting him know it; Mickey was the young guy who ran errands for both of the brothers and marvelled at Scott's womanizing; and Rae was their mother. Stencilled on door of their loft apartment was the Latin phrase "Tutto E Possibile" (Everything is Possible).

EXCLUSIVELY YOURS
see *Igor Cassini Show, The*

EXECUTIVE SUITE
Drama
FIRST TELECAST: *September 20, 1976*
LAST TELECAST: *February 11, 1977*
BROADCAST HISTORY:
Sep 1976–Jan 1977, CBS Mon 10:00–11:00
Jan 1977–Feb 1977, CBS Fri 10:00–11:00
CAST:
Don Walling .... Mitchell Ryan
Howell Rutledge .... Stephen Elliott
Helen Walling .... Sharon Acker
Brian Walling .... Leigh McCloskey
Mark Desmond .... Richard Cox
Astrid Rutledge .... Gwyda DonHowe
Tom Dalessio .... Paul Lambert
Pearce Newberry .... Byron Morrow
Yvonne Holland .... Trisha Noble
Stacey Walling .... Wendy Phillips

Glory Dalessio .... Joan Prather
Hilary Madison .... Madlyn Rhue
Malcolm Gibson .... Percy Rodriguez
Anderson Galt .... William Smithers
Marge Newberry .... Maxine Stuart
Summer Johnson .... Brenda Sykes
Harry Ragin .... Carl Weintraub

Corporate intrigue, family problems, and all sorts of emotional involvements were part of the mix in this nighttime soap opera about the lives of people working for, and affected by, the huge Cardway Corporation. Don Walling was the president, Howell Rutledge the vice-president and chief rival to Walling, and their families, business associates, and personal entanglements all had their parts in this short-lived series.

EXPEDITION
Wildlife/Archeology
FIRST TELECAST: *September 20, 1960*
LAST TELECAST: *April 23, 1962*
BROADCAST HISTORY:
Sep 1960–Jun 1961, ABC Tue 7:00–7:30
Sep 1961–Apr 1962, ABC Mon 7:00–7:30
HOST:
Col. John D. Craig

Filmed accounts of safaris to Africa, meetings with remote and primitive tribes, archeological expeditions to ruined cities of antiquity, and studies of animals in their natural habitats were all part of this series. Col. Craig was widely seen in later years in a similar, syndicated series called *Of Lands and Seas*.

EXPLORERS, THE
Documentary
BROADCAST HISTORY:
Syndicated only
30 minutes
Produced: *1972–1973* (22 episodes)
Released: *Fall 1972*
HOST:
Leslie Nielsen

True-life adventure films of explorers, scientists, and others in various remote corners of the world.

EXPOSÉ
syndicated title for *Target: The Corruptors*

EYE ON HOLLYWOOD
Magazine
FIRST TELECAST: *August 4, 1983*
LAST TELECAST: *July 18, 1986*
BROADCAST HISTORY:
Aug 1983–Sep 1983, ABC Thu 8:00–8:30
Feb 1984–Jun 1984, ABC Mon–Fri 12:00–12:30 A.M.
Jun 1984–Aug 1985, ABC Mon–Thu 12:00–12:30 A.M.
Aug 1985–Dec 1985, ABC Tue–Fri 12:00–12:30 A.M.

HOSTS:
Tawny Schneider (1983–1984)
Chuck Henry
Paul Moyer (1984)
Jann Carl (1985–1986)
CORRESPONDENT:
Johnny Mountain

For those who cannot get enough of showbiz glamour, this fast-paced magazine series brought video reports on such burning questions as what the truly rich in Los Angeles spend their money on (gold-plated handguns and mink bedspreads, it seems) and "California Girls, the Myth and the Reality." One of the regular features was "Pressed for Time," a 60-second montage of clips showing a famous L.A. location like Sunset Boulevard or Disneyland. The series was based on the local Los Angeles television program "Eye on L.A.," seen on KABC-TV.

EYE TO EYE
Detective
FIRST TELECAST: *March 21, 1985*
LAST TELECAST: *May 2, 1985*
BROADCAST HISTORY:
Mar 1985–May 1985, ABC Thu 9:00–10:00
CAST:
Oscar Poole .... Charles Durning
Tracy Doyle .... Stephanie Faracy

Action series about a mismatched pair of private eyes. Oscar was an overweight, over-the-hill L.A. gumshoe who was semiretired until his ex-partner was murdered, and the man's sexy young daughter insisted that Oscar help her solve the case. They then solved several more, with Tracy providing tight dresses and enthusiasm, and Oscar puffing along behind.

EYE WITNESS
Documentary
FIRST TELECAST: *November 6, 1947*
LAST TELECAST: *April 13, 1948*
BROADCAST HISTORY:
Nov 1947–Dec 1947, NBC Thu various times
Jan 1948–Apr 1948, NBC Thu 8:00–8:30
HOST:
Ben Grauer

One of the earliest regularly scheduled network programs was this behind-the-scenes introduction to the television medium itself. The program was telecast live with film inserts, and frequently went on location. Subjects included how a TV set works, how a TV studio operates, mobile units on location, and the problems of networking. One telecast, in February 1948, traced the history of television from Joseph May's experiments in 1873 to the present day.

EYE WITNESS
Dramatic Anthology
FIRST TELECAST: *March 30, 1953*
LAST TELECAST: *June 29, 1953*
BROADCAST HISTORY:
Mar 1953–Jun 1953, NBC Mon 9:00–9:30
PRODUCER:
Robert Montgomery

A live dramatic-anthology series produced by Robert Montgomery, with emphasis on the supernatural and strange twists of fate. Scripts were both originals written for TV and adaptations of stories. The guest host or hostess for each program, who was introduced at the start of the show by Mr. Montgomery, starred the following week on Montgomery's principal series, *Robert Montgomery Presents* (Monday 9:30–10:30 P.M.).

EYES HAVE IT, THE
see *Celebrity Time*

EYES HAVE IT, THE
Quiz/Panel
FIRST TELECAST: *November 20, 1948*
LAST TELECAST: *January 27, 1949*
BROADCAST HISTORY:
Nov 1948–Jan 1949, NBC Sat 8:00–8:30
MODERATOR:
Ralph McNair

This quiz program required panelists to identify a famous place or face from a portion of a picture—a picture in pieces, an unusual angle shot, extreme close-up, or a close shot of the eyes, gradually widening to reveal other parts of a face. The program emanated from NBC's station in Washington, D.C., where it had begun as a local show in September 1948. After its prime-time run it continued on the network on Sunday afternoons until June 1949.

EYEWITNESS TO HISTORY
News Analysis
FIRST TELECAST: *September 23, 1960*
LAST TELECAST: *August 2, 1963*
BROADCAST HISTORY:
Sep 1960, CBS Fri 9:00–9:30
Sep 1960–Jun 1961, CBS Fri 10:30–11:00
Sep 1961–Aug 1963, CBS Fri 10:30–11:00
ANCHORMAN:
Charles Kuralt (1960–1961)
Walter Cronkite (1961–1962)
Charles Collingwood (1962–1963)

An in-depth analysis of a major current news story was presented each Friday night on *Eyewitness to History*. The program was originally aired as a series of specials beginning in September 1959, then moved into a regular weekly time slot a year later. The title of the series was shortened to *Eyewitness* in September 1961.

F

F.B.I., THE
Police Drama
FIRST TELECAST: *September 19, 1965*
LAST TELECAST: *September 8, 1974*
BROADCAST HISTORY:
Sep 1965–Sep 1973, ABC Sun 8:00–9:00
Sep 1973–Sep 1974, ABC Sun 7:30–8:30
CAST:
Inspector Lewis Erskine . Efrem Zimbalist, Jr.
Arthur Ward .... Philip Abbott
Barbara Erskine (1965–1966) .... Lynn Loring
Special Agent Jim Rhodes (1965–1967)
.... Stephen Brooks
Special Agent Tom Colby (1967–1973)
.... William Reynolds
Agent Chris Daniels (1973–1974)
.... Shelly Novack
EXECUTIVE PRODUCER:
Quinn Martin
MUSICAL THEME:
"F.B.I. Theme," by Bronislaw Kaper

The Federal Bureau of Investigation has been the subject of several highly popular radio and TV shows (remember *The F.B.I. in Peace and War*?), but none portrayed the cool, professional operation of the agency so thoroughly as this long-running series starring Efrem Zimbalist, Jr., as Inspector Lewis Erskine. Zimbalist personified the calm, business-suited government agent who always tracked his quarry down, scientifically and methodically, and with virtually no emotion whatever.

The cases were supposedly based on real FBI files. They ranged across the United States and involved counterfeiters, extortionists, organized crime, Communist spies, and radical bombings (during the era of Vietnam dissent). Arthur Ward was the assistant to the FBI director and the man to whom Inspector Erskine reported, while several agents served as Erskine's sidekick over the years. Barbara Erskine, his daughter, appeared only during the first season, later being written out apparently because there was no room for anything so fallible as family ties in *The F.B.I.*

The program always portrayed the agency in a favorable light. It won the commendation of real-life FBI Director J. Edgar Hoover, who gave the show full government cooperation and even allowed filming of some background scenes at the FBI headquarters in Washington. Bringing the program even closer to real life, many telecasts closed with a short segment asking the audience for information on the FBI's most-wanted men (including, in April 1968, the fugitive James Earl Ray).

Associated with the program as sponsor throughout its run was the Ford Motor Company, which accounted for the fact that those agents were always seen driving Ford cars.

F.D.R.
Documentary
FIRST TELECAST: *January 8, 1965*
LAST TELECAST: *September 10, 1965*
BROADCAST HISTORY:
Jan 1965–Jun 1965, ABC Fri 9:30–10:00
Jun 1965–Sep 1965, ABC Fri 8:00–8:30
NARRATORS:
Arthur Kennedy
Charlton Heston
EXECUTIVE PRODUCER:
Robert D. Graff
PRODUCER:
Ben Feiner, Jr.

Created by the same team that had produced the acclaimed *Winston Churchill: The Valiant Years* several years before, *F.D.R.* was a presentation and analysis of the life of Franklin Delano Roosevelt. Eleanor Roosevelt, FDR's widow, acted as consultant during the development of the program and intended to appear on the telecasts, but she died before the series reached the air. Before her death she was filmed relating her reminiscences of FDR's early days, and these sequences were included in some of the early telecasts of the series. Arthur Kennedy narrated, and Charlton Heston read from the late president's writings.

F TROOP
Situation Comedy
FIRST TELECAST: *September 14, 1965*
LAST TELECAST: *August 31, 1967*
BROADCAST HISTORY:
Sep 1965–Aug 1966, ABC Tue 9:00–9:30
Sep 1966–Aug 1967, ABC Thu 8:00–8:30
CAST:
Capt. Wilton Parmenter .... Ken Berry
Sgt. Morgan O'Rourke .... Forrest Tucker
Cpl. Randolph Agarn .... Larry Storch
Wrangler Jane .... Melody Patterson
Chief Wild Eagle .... Frank deKova
Crazy Cat .... Don Diamond
Bugler Hannibal Dobbs...... James Hampton
Trooper Duffy .... Bob Steele
Trooper Vanderbilt .... Joe Brooks
CREATOR/PRODUCER:
Richard M. Bluel

The "stars" of this military farce were the gallant incompetents of F Troop at Fort Courage, somewhere west of the Missouri, in post–Civil War days. The CO was the wide-eyed, bumbling Capt. Parmenter, who had been promoted from private during the closing days of the war when he accidentally led a charge in the wrong direction—toward the enemy. Unbeknownst to the captain, Sgt. O'Rourke had already negotiated a secret—and highly profitable—treaty with the Hekawi Indians, from whom he also had an exclusive franchise to sell their souvenirs to tourists. There was no peace treaty with the Shugs, however, and they sometimes caused trouble. Cpl. Agarn was O'-Rourke's chief aide and assistant schemer, and Wrangler Jane the hard-riding, fast-shooting cowgirl who was out to marry Parmenter.

A lot of colorful Indians and others passed through this series in one-time special appearances, including Roaring Chicken (Edward Everett Horton); 147-year-old Flaming Arrow (Phil Harris); Bald Eagle (Don Rickles); Wise Owl (Milton Berle), an Indian detective; Sgt. Ramsden (Paul Lynde), a singing mountie; and Wrongo Starr (Henry Gibson), a jinxed cavalry trooper.

F.Y.I.
Public Affairs
FIRST TELECAST: *June 5, 1960*
LAST TELECAST: *September 25, 1960*
BROADCAST HISTORY:
Jun 1960–Sep 1960, CBS Sun 6:00–6:30
HOST:
Douglas Edwards

F.Y.I. (For Your Information) premiered as a Sunday morning informational program on CBS in January 1960. It moved to Sunday evenings for the summer of 1960, providing filmed reports and interviews covering such subjects as the political problems of shifting city populations, the pressures leading to mental breakdowns, and European attitudes toward the American way of electing political leaders.

FABLE FOR A SUMMER NIGHT
see *ABC Dramatic Shorts—1952–1953*

FABULOUS FRAUD, THE
see *Colonel Humphrey Flack*

FACE IS FAMILIAR, THE
Quiz/Audience Participation
FIRST TELECAST: *May 7, 1966*
LAST TELECAST: *September 3, 1966*
BROADCAST HISTORY:
May 1966–Sep 1966, CBS Sat 9:30–10:00
EMCEE:
Jack Whitaker

This summer game show featured two teams of contestants, each consisting of a celebrity guest and a non-celebrity contestant. The teams competed to guess the identity of a familiar face from scrambled sections of a photograph of that face. As each team correctly answered questions from the emcee, increasing sections of the face were revealed. The first team to guess the correct identity won $200 and the chance to win an additional $500 by correctly identifying which sets of eyes, noses, and mouths belonged to specific predesignated celebrities.

FACE OF DANGER, THE
Dramatic Anthology
FIRST TELECAST: *April 18, 1959*
LAST TELECAST: *May 30, 1959*
BROADCAST HISTORY:
Apr 1959–May 1959, CBS Sat 9:00–9:30

The filmed dramas telecast in this short-lived series were all reruns of episodes previously aired in the series *Playhouse of Stars*.

FACE THE MUSIC
Music
FIRST TELECAST: *May 3, 1948*
LAST TELECAST: *May 19, 1949*
BROADCAST HISTORY:
May 1948, CBS Mon/Wed 7:15–7:30
May 1948, CBS Mon/Wed/Fri 7:15–7:30
May 1948–Jun 1948, CBS Mon/Wed/Thu/Fri 7:15–7:30
Jun 1948–Aug 1948, CBS Mon–Fri 7:15–7:30
Aug 1948–Feb 1949, CBS Mon–Fri 7:45–8:00
Feb 1949–Mar 1949, CBS Mon/Tue/Thu/Fri 7:45–8:00
Mar 1949–Apr 1949, CBS Tue/Thu 7:45–8:00
Apr 1949–May 1949, CBS Tue/Thu 7:15–7:30
REGULARS:
Johnny Desmond (1948)
Shaye Cogan (1948)
Carole Coleman
Tony Mottola Trio

This live musical show premiered as a twice-a-week feature starring vocalists Johnny Desmond and Shaye Cogan with music by the Tony Mottola Trio. Within six weeks of its premiere it had expanded to a five-day-a-week schedule. On December 13, 1948, the title was changed to *Make Mine Music* and Carole Coleman took over as featured singer.

FACE THE NATION
Interview
FIRST TELECAST: *October 2, 1960*
LAST TELECAST: *April 6, 1961*
BROADCAST HISTORY:
Oct 1960–Nov 1960, CBS Sun 6:00–6:30
Nov 1960–Dec 1960, CBS Mon 10:30–11:00
Jan 1961–Apr 1961, CBS Thu 10:00–10:30
MODERATOR:
Stuart Novins (1960)
Howard K. Smith (1960–1961)

CBS' well-respected public-affairs program, in which leading politicians and other public figures were subjected to questioning by a panel of newsmen, premiered on Sunday, November 7, 1954. Though it has spent most of its long career as a Sunday daytime program, it was seen for short periods in the early 1960s as a nighttime show. When *Face the Nation* premiered in late 1954, CBS newsman Ted Koop was the moderator. He was replaced the following August by Stuart Novins, who was still moderating the show when it moved to prime time in 1960. Howard K. Smith took over in November 1960. His successors have been Paul Niven (1963–1965), Martin Agronsky (1965–1969), George Herman (1969–1983), and Leslie Stahl (since 1983).

FACE TO FACE
Cartoon Quiz
FIRST TELECAST: *June 9, 1946*
LAST TELECAST: *January 26, 1947*
BROADCAST HISTORY:
Jun 1946–Jan 1947, NBC Sun 8:00–8:20
REGULARS:
Eddie Dunn
Bill Dunn
"Sugar"

The idea of this early game show was for an artist to draw a picture of an unseen person from verbal clues, then compare the results with the actual person, when he came into the studio. At first the subject was in a separate room, unseen by viewers and heard only over a telephone line; later he sat on the opposite side of a curtain from the artist, and viewers could compare the sketch as it progressed. There was also a quiz element, with prizes for identifying a celebrity from various clues. Bill Dunn did the sketching and Eddie Dunn the interviewing, with a woman named Sugar present on later telecasts as a kind of emcee.

As with some other early programs, it is not known whether this was carried over the NBC network from the start; however, it was a network feature by early November 1946 at the latest.

FACTS OF LIFE, THE
Situation Comedy
FIRST TELECAST: *August 24, 1979*
LAST TELECAST:
BROADCAST HISTORY:
Aug 1979–Sep 1979, NBC Fri 8:30–9:00
Mar 1980–May 1980, NBC Fri 8:30–9:00
Jun 1980–Jul 1980, NBC Wed 9:30–10:00
Aug 1980–Oct 1980, NBC Fri 8:30–9:00
Nov 1980–Oct 1981, NBC Wed 9:30–10:00
Oct 1981–Aug 1985, NBC Wed 9:00–9:30
Sep 1985–Jun 1986, NBC Sat 8:30–9:00
Jun 1986–May 1987, NBC Sat 8:00–8:30
Jun 1987–Jul 1987, NBC Wed 9:00–9:30
*Jul 1987–   *, NBC Sat 8:00–8:30
CAST:
Edna Garrett (1979–1986) . . . . . . Charlotte Rae
Blair Warner . . . . Lisa Whelchel
Dorothy "Tootie" Ramsey . . . . Kim Fields
Natalie Green . . . . Mindy Cohn
Jo Polniaczek (1980–   ) . . . . Nancy McKeon
Steven Bradley (1979–1980) . . . . . John Lawlor
Miss Emily Mahoney (1979) . . . Jenny O'Hara
Nancy Olson (1979–1982) . . . . Felice Schacter
Sue Ann Weaver (1979–1982) . Julie Piekarski
Cindy Webster (1980–1982)
. . . . Julie Anne Haddock

Molly Parker (1979–1980) . . . . Molly Ringwald
Howard (1980–1981) . . . . Hugh Gillin
Mr. Charles Parker (1981–1983) . . Roger Perry
*Geri Warner (1981–1984) . . . . Geri Jewell
Kelly Affinado (1983–1984) . . . . . Pamela Segall
Cliff (1983–1984) . . . . Woody Brown
George Burnett (1985–1986) . . George Clooney
Andy Moffet (1985–   ) . . . . MacKenzie Astin
Beverly Ann Stickle (1986–   )
. . . . Cloris Leachman
Pippa McKenna (1987–   ) . . . . Sherrie Krenn
Jeff Williams (1987–   ) . . . . Todd Hollowell
Snake Robinson (1987–   )
. . . . Robert Romanus
Casey Clark (1987–   ) . . . . . . Paul Provenza
Rick Bonner (1988–   ) . . . . Scott Bryce

*Occasional
THEME:
"The Facts of Life," by Alan Thicke, Gloria Loring, and Al Burton, sung by Gloria Loring

This spin-off from the popular NBC comedy *Diff'rent Strokes* originally focused on Mrs. Garrett, who had been the Drummonds' housekeeper prior to taking a job as housemother at the prestigious Eastland school for young women. Mrs. Garrett was kind and understanding, serving as both confidante and surrogate parent to the girls in her charge, who at the start of the series ranged in age from 11 to 15. Blair, 15, was wealthy, attractive, and spoiled; Nancy, 14, was well-rounded; Sue Ann, 14, was cute and boy-crazy; Tootie, 11, was the resident gossip; and Natalie, the other principal student, was plump and impressionable. The headmaster at Eastland was Mr. Bradley, and Miss Mahoney was a teacher seen only during the tryout run of *The Facts of Life* in the summer of 1979.

As the seasons passed, the series evolved. By 1980 Mrs. Garrett had taken on the additional responsibilities of dietician at Eastland, and there were two new cast members: Jo, a 16-year-old street kid from the Bronx who maintained a tough exterior to hide her insecurities; and Howard, the cook at Eastland. Mr. Bradley was succeeded as headmaster by the seldom-seen Mr. Harris (Kenneth Mars), and then by Mr. Parker. It was Parker's callousness toward Mrs. Garrett that led to a major change in 1983. Frustrated at having been underpaid and taken for granted for so long, Edna vented her frustration to her beloved son Raymond, an accountant who stunned her by offering to buy a run-down store in the nearby town of Peekskill, New York, and letting her reopen it as a gourmet food shop. Thus was born Edna's Edibles. Blair and Jo (who were now attending nearby Langley College) and Tootie and Natalie (still at Eastland) moved in, and their good times continued.

In 1985 a fire destroyed the store and Mrs. Garrett and the girls rebuilt it into a completely new business—an updated version of a 1950s malt

245

shop, selling everything from ice cream to records and T-shirts, and called "Over Our Heads." It was the perfect hangout for students at Langley, and the girls were all partners. Young Andy was the errand boy, and George the good-looking young carpenter who helped with the rebuilding. The following year Mrs. Garrett remarried and tearfully moved away; she was replaced by her chatterbox sister, Beverly Ann, who became the new "housemother" and stepmother to Andy.

By 1987–1988 the "girls" had become young women. It was announced that this would be *The Facts of Life*'s last season, and each of the regulars was seen embarking on adult life, each in her own way. Natalie, the aspiring author, got her first taste of a writer's life in New York City, and was also the first to lose her virginity when she spent the night with her boyfriend Snake. Shortly thereafter Jo, who was headed for a business career, was married to freewheeling musician Rick. Tootie, who was engaged to Jeff, planned to become an actress, and enrolled at the prestigious Royal Academy of Dramatic Arts in London. But the most surprising was wealthy Blair, by now enrolled at Langley Law School. Watching in despair as her alma mater Eastland went steadily downhill, she decided to do something about it. Putting all her assets on the line, she bought the school and assumed the position of headmistress, planning major changes—including a coed student body—to put Eastland back on the map.

The stories on *The Facts of Life* were funny, but also often touching. The girls faced problems with their parents, including lack of communication, divorce, and death; they also experienced growing pains in a realistic way (it seemed as if teenager Tootie's braces would never come off). Blair's 23-year-old cousin Geri, who was determined to become a comedienne despite the handicap of cerebral palsy, was occasionally seen (played by Geri Jewell, a real-life CP victim). Also seen infrequently were Blair's divorced parents, David and Monica Warner (played by Nicolas Coster and Marj Dusay), and Jo's folks Charlie and Rose Polniaczek (Alex Rocco, Claire Malis).

NBC aired reruns of *The Facts of Life* on weekdays from December 1982 until June 1985.

FACTS WE FACE, THE

Documentary
FIRST TELECAST: *August 27, 1950*
LAST TELECAST: *August 19, 1951*
BROADCAST HISTORY:
  Aug 1950–Sep 1950, CBS Sun 9:30–10:00
  Sep 1950, CBS Sun 10:15–11:00
  Jul 1951–Aug 1951, CBS Sun 6:00–6:30
MODERATOR:
  Bill Shadel (1950)
  Walter Cronkite (1951)

The Facts We Face was originally a five-week series designed to inform the American public of the impact that the then-current Korean War mo-

bilization would have on their lives. Through filmed reports and interviews the program covered the selective service, production and allocation of resources and manpower, rationing, economic prospects, and civil defense. Following its prime-time run the series moved to Sunday afternoons. It returned to nighttime television during the following summer, with Walter Cronkite as moderator and a new title, *Open Hearing*.

FAIR EXCHANGE

Situation Comedy
FIRST TELECAST: *September 21, 1962*
LAST TELECAST: *September 19, 1963*
BROADCAST HISTORY:
  Sep 1962–Dec 1962, CBS Fri 9:30–10:30
  Mar 1963–Sep 1963, CBS Thu 7:30–8:00
CAST:
  Eddie Walker................. Eddie Foy, Jr.
  Dorothy Walker .... Audrey Christie
  Patty Walker.................. Lynn Loring
  Larry Walker..................... Flip Mark
  Tommy Finch............... Victor Maddern
  Sybil Finch................. Diana Chesney
  Heather Finch .... Judy Carne
  Neville Finch .... Dennis Waterman
  Willie Shorthouse........ Maurice Dallimore

This hands-across-the-sea comedy concerned two middle-class families, the Eddie Walkers of New York City, U.S.A., and the Thomas Finches of London, England, who agreed to swap teenage daughters for a year. Eddie and Tommy had been wartime buddies, and now each had a lovely wife (Dorothy and Sybil), a son, and a daughter. The scene alternated between New York and London as the two daughters, Patty and Heather, explored their new friends and surroundings.

Begun as an unusual experiment in full-hour comedy, *Fair Exchange* ran for only three months and was canceled. The unexpected volume of mail from the show's audience prompted CBS to give it another try. It was trimmed to half an hour and, after a three-month hiatus, returned in March 1963. The shorter format didn't work either, and the program left the air for good at the end of the season.

FALCON CREST

Drama
FIRST TELECAST: *December 4, 1981*
LAST TELECAST:
BROADCAST HISTORY:
  Dec 1981–May 1985, CBS Fri 10:00–11:00
  *Sep 1985–   *, CBS Fri 10:00–11:00 (OS)
CAST:
  Angela Channing .... Jane Wyman
  Chase Gioberti (1981–1987) . Robert Foxworth
  Maggie Gioberti Channing.... Susan Sullivan
  Lance Cumson.............. Lorenzo Lamas
  Tony Cumson (1981–1982, 1986–)
  .... John Saxon
  Cole Gioberti (1981–1986).. William R. Moses

Victoria Gioberti Hogan (1981–1983)
.... Jamie Rose
Victoria Gioberti Hogan Stavros (1986–   )
.... Dana Sparks
Julia Cumson (1981–1986) .... Abby Dalton
Gus Nunouz (1981–1982) .... Nick Ramus
Phillip Erikson (1981–1984) .... Mel Ferrer
Emma Channing .... Margaret Ladd
Douglas Channing (1981–1982)
.... Stephen Elliott
Sheriff Turk Tobias (1981–1982)
.... Robert Sampson
Mario (1981–1982).......... Mario Marcelino
Chau-Li .... Chau-Li Chi
Melissa Agretti Cumson (1982–   )
.... Ana Alicia
Richard Channing (1982–   ) .. David Selby
Carlo Agretti (1982) .... Carlos Romero
Diana Hunter (1982–1983)... Shannon Tweed
John Costello (1982–1985) .... Roger Perry
Nick Hogan (1982–1983) .... Roy Thinnes
Jacqueline Perrault (1982–1983).. Lana Turner
Darryl Clayton (1982–1983)
.... Bradford Dillman
Lori Stevens (1982–1983)..... Maggie Cooper
Dr. Howell (1982–1983) .... Richard Eastham
Sheriff Robbins (1982–1985) ...... Joe Lambie
Linda Caproni (1982–1984)
.... Mary Kate McGeehan
Vince Caproni (1982–1984) ...... Harry Basch
Dr. Michael Ranson (1983–1984)
.... Cliff Robertson
Dr. Hooks (1983–1984) .. Raymond St. Jacques
Dr. Lantry (1983–1984)........... Ron Rifkin
Pamela Lynch (1983–1985) .... Sarah Douglas
Terry Hartford Ranson (1983–1986)
.... Laura Johnson
Corene Powers (1983–1984) . Victoria Racimo
Dr. Foster (1983–1984) ..... Thomas Callaway
Valerie (1983–1984).......... Tina Andrews
Joseph Gioberti (1983–1987).. Jason Goldberg
Norton Crane (1983–1984).... Jordan Charney
Spheeris (1983–1985) .... Ken Letner
Padgett (1984) .... Don Matheson
Francesca Gioberti (1984).. Gina Lollobrigida
Lorraine Prescott (1984–1985) ... Kate Vernon
Greg Reardon (1984–1986)
.... Simon MacCorkindale
Joel McCarthy (1984–1985). Parker Stevenson
Gustav Riebmann (1984–1985)
.... J. Paul Freeman
Alan Caldwell (1984)...... George McDaniel
Max Hartman (1984–1985) .... John Carter
Father Bob (1985–   ) .... Bob Curtis
Connie Giannini (1985) .... Carla Borelli
Cassandra Wilder (1985) ...... Anne Archer
Robin Agretti (1985–1986)... Barbara Howard
Jordan Roberts (1985–1986)
.... Morgan Fairchild
Father Christopher (1985–1986)..... Ken Olin
Apollonia (1985–1986)
.... Patricia "Apollonia" Kotero
Peter Stavros (1985–1987) ..... Cesar Romero

Anna Rossini (1985).......... Celeste Holm
Sheriff Gilmore (1985–1986)
.... John Bennett Perry
Al Hurley (1985) .... Mike Genovese
B. Riley Wicker (1985–1986) .... Henry Jones
Dwayne Cooley (1985–1986)... Daniel Greene
Julian J. Roberts (1985–1986) .. John McMartin
Sofia Stavros (1986)............ Julie Carmen
Eric Stavros (1986–   )...... John Callahan
Erin Jones (1986)............... Jill Jacobson
Jeff Wainwright (1986)........ Edward Albert
Kit Marlowe (1986–1987)......... Kim Novak
Dan Fixx (1986–   )......... Brett Cullen
Meredith Braxton (1986–1987).... Jane Badler
Vince Karlotti (1986–1987)... Marjoe Gortner
Guy Stafford (1986–1987) .... Jeff Kober
Dina Wells (1986–1987)........ Robin Greer
Mrs. Whitaker (1986–1987)... Laurel Schaefer
Sheriff Jack North (1987) .... John Aprea
Garth (1987–   )............ Carl Heid
Jay Spence (1987–   )... John David Carson
Gabrielle Short (1987–   )... Cindy Morgan
Kolinski (1987)............. Jonathan Banks
Roland Saunders (1987) .... Robert Stack
Fred Wilkinson (1987)........ Dick O'Neill
Allison (1987–   )........... Maggie Cooper
Carly Fixx (1988–   ) .... Mariska Hargitay
Rosemont (1988–   ) ... Roscoe Lee Browne

Airing in the time slot following CBS' immensely popular *Dallas, Falcon Crest* sought to hold on to the soap-opera addicts with yet another saga of the rich and greedy fighting for power and sex. The setting was the fictitious Tuscany Valley, located in the beautiful Napa Valley region outside San Francisco, and the industry around which the action centered was wine-making. *Falcon Crest* had all the requisite characters: autocratic, evil power broker Angela Channing, industrious good guy Chase Gioberti, lazy young playboy Lance Cumson, and ambitious newspaper owner Richard Channing, among many others.

The matriarch and principal empire-builder on *Falcon Crest* was powerful Angela Channing, played by veteran actress Jane Wyman. Respected and feared by almost everyone whose life she touched, Angela ran the Falcon Crest winery with an iron hand and lived regally in a palatial house near her sprawling vineyards. Angela tried to manipulate everyone to suit her purposes. As the series began, her nephew Chase had just inherited 50 acres of vineyards from his late father, Angela's brother Jason. Angela was convinced the land should be hers, to add to her already vast holdings, but Chase brought his wife Maggie and two children, Cole and Victoria, west from New York to live in the valley and manage his land. Angela and Chase were constantly in conflict. She first tried to ruin Chase by blocking a badly needed bank loan; then she attempted to undermine his relationship with his son, Cole, by implying that Cole might someday inherit all of Falcon Crest. When she couldn't get her hands on

Chase's land, she pushed her grandson, Lance Cumson, into marrying Melissa Agretti, to help her consolidate the large Agretti and Falcon Crest wineries under her control. When she eventually lost control of Falcon Crest to Chase, in a complicated legal maneuver, she devoted her life to getting it back.

Compared to Angela, Chase Gioberti was a knight in shining armor. His concerns were with his family and all the people of the valley, and he fought hard to keep the power-hungry from taking over. When he became a county supervisor, Chase did everything in his power to stop Angela from monopolizing the water supply for the entire Tuscany Valley, which could have bankrupted most of the other vintners there. His mother, Jacqueline Perrault, showed up occasionally, to give him advice on how to deal with Angela, and in the cliff-hanger finale of the 1982–1983 season, the two of them ended up getting shot (fatally for Jacqueline) by Angela's mentally disturbed daughter, Julia Cumson (Lance's mother). Julia had earlier killed another figure who was in her mother's way, Melissa Agretti's father Carlo. Chase eventually recovered and Julia went first to prison and later into a mental institution.

Lance Cumson was the archetypal good-looking, ne'er-do-well playboy. He wanted power and money from Falcon Crest, but was too lazy to work for it. Although he chafed at the control Angela had over him, Lance was tied to her. He had married Melissa, who had plenty of ambition and greed in her own right, but he never stopped fooling around with other women. When he found out that Melissa's newborn son, Joseph, had been fathered not by him but by Cole, he disappeared with his old girlfriend, Lori Stevens. Before long a lack of money brought Lance back to his wife and the luxury he craved.

The only character on *Falcon Crest* who approached Angela in nastiness was Richard Channing. He arrived in San Francisco to run the *Globe,* a newspaper which had been owned by his late father, Angela's ex-husband Douglas Channing. Richard inherited 50 percent, while Angela's two daughters, Julia Cumson and Emma Channing, got the other half. Richard was ambitious and unprincipled. Not only did he want all of the paper, but Carlo Agretti's land and Falcon Crest as well. He worked with Jacqueline (whom he subsequently discovered was his mother) to fight Angela, and connived with Julia to get control of Falcon Crest. When all else failed, he fought for, and got, a permit to build a race track in the Tuscany Valley that could destroy the area's entire wine industry.

Others with recurring major roles were Angela's lawyer, Phillip Erikson; Chase's wife, Maggie, who worked as a reporter at the San Francisco *Globe;* Jacqueline's nephew, Dr. Michael Ranson, a neurosurgeon who arrived to help Chase recover from his gunshot wound; and Terry Hartford, Maggie's hooker sister who arrived to get in on the action and found it by moving in with Dr. Ranson.

Murders, bombings, and other violent criminal activity became a trademark of *Falcon Crest* in later seasons. A major story in 1984–1985 involved The Cartel, a shadowy international syndicate headed by an exceptionally vicious man named Gustav Riebmann, who was after wartime Nazi booty that had been buried on the Falcon Crest lands. After assorted plane crashes, bombings, buggings and—when that didn't work—seductions, the Cartel (which had been co-founded by Richard's late mother Jacqueline) was finally smashed. Other main stories that season involved Angela's takeover of Richard's newspaper, *The Globe,* with Lance being installed as Editor; Richard's plot to frame Lance for the attempted murder of Angela; Richard's acquisition of a one-third interest in Falcon Crest from Angela's half-sister, Francesca; Cole and Melissa's stormy marriage; and Cassandra's vendetta against Angela for past wrongs to her family.

Cassandra was quite successful, leaving both Angela and her partner/enemy Richard in dire financial straits. Angela fought back by calling on an old flame, shipping magnate Peter Stavros, to bail her out. He did—after being abducted by his own daughter Sophia (who wanted the money herself)—and then persuaded Angela to marry him. It was either that, or he would become her landlord! Peter's son Eric later became an important character. Meanwhile Richard managed to claw his way back to solvency by skimming profits from the Tuscany Downs race track, until Terry found out and blackmailed him into marriage. Other main stories of 1985–1986 included Richard's schizophrenic lady attorney Jordan, a hooker ("Monica") by night; Maggie's lapse into amnesia, during which she secretly wrote, then forgot she had written, a tell-all novel about the inhabitants of Tuscany Valley; her subsequent pursuit by crazed book publicist Jeff; and Cole and Melissa's plan to hire a surrogate mother, which backfired when the sexy surrogate (Robin) seduced Cole and then kept the baby. Emma's distraction for the season was rough-hewn trucker Dwayne, while Lance's was rock singer Apollonia ("Babylonia" to his disgusted grandmother Angela). The season ended with a major earthquake shaking the valley.

Richard's private investigator Miss Jones was practically a one-person crime wave in 1986–1987, framing her boss for attempted murder, trying to kill Chase, and blowing up Jeff. Richard finally shipped her off to a prison in Borneo, only to have her sister Meredith show up seeking revenge. Melissa, meanwhile, dabbled in a singing career, then made off with Chase and Maggie's newborn baby Kevin (Chase was killed during the rescue at the end of the season). Emma had an even more bizarre year, dallying with a con man/spiritualist named Karlotti. A new arrival was Kit, a mysterious woman of many disguises, at first thought to be Peter's long-lost daughter Skylar. Instead she was on the run from Eastern criminals who arrived in the person of evil billionaire Roland Saunders. He met an untimely end; Kit poisoned his cigar just before Peter bonked him on the head with a heavy wrench. Another newcomer was Dan Fixx, who schemed to displace Lance as Angela's heir apparent. The Richard-Angela infighting continued, but the squabbling wine moguls had more in common than they realized. As Peter departed for Greece (having "amicably" divorced Angela), he revealed that archenemy Richard was actually her son—the one she had been told was stillborn!

Falcon Crest edged even closer to becoming the *Crime Story* of nighttime serials in 1987–1988 as Richard became deeply involved with a murderous underworld group known as "The Thirteen." Maggie, his new wife, was increasingly disturbed by his shady connections, not to mention the bombs going off on their estate. Angela, who had a few shady connections of her own, continued to fight Richard for control of the valley, but expended most of her energy luring runaway grandson Lance back into the fold—Dan having defected and allied with Melissa. (In a curious subplot, Angela tried to drive Melissa crazy by having a special effects expert make Melissa think there were ghosts in her house.) Emma had a fling running a call girl business, then tried to sell her experience as a movie, while Vickie was dragged off by a Yugoslavian white slavery ring. Reality, it seems, was never the hallmark of *Falcon Crest*.

FALL GUY, THE
Adventure
FIRST TELECAST: *November 4, 1981*
LAST TELECAST: *May 2, 1986*
BROADCAST HISTORY:
Nov 1981–Mar 1983, ABC Wed 9:00–10:00
Apr 1983–Jul 1985, ABC Wed 8:00–9:00
Sep 1985–Oct 1985, ABC Thu 8:00–9:00
Nov 1985–Jan 1986, ABC Sat 8:00–9:00
Jan 1986–May 1986, ABC Fri 10:00–11:00
CAST:
Colt Seavers .... Lee Majors
Howie Munson .... Douglas Barr
Jody Banks .... Heather Thomas
Samantha "Big Jack" Jack (1981–1982)
.... Jo Ann Pflug
Terri Shannon/Michaels (1982–1985)
.... Markie Post
Pearl Sperling (1985–1986) .... Nedra Volz
THEME:
"The Unknown Stuntman," by David Somerville, Gail Jensen, and Glen Larson, sung by Lee Majors

Spectacular stunt work was the hallmark of this action series, which was rugged Lee Majors' fifth successful prime-time offering. Majors was cast, appropriately enough, as Hollywood stuntman

Colt Seavers, who picked up a little extra money by using his special skills to track down and capture bail jumpers. Helping out were Colt's inexperienced but eager younger cousin, Howie, and stunning stuntwoman Jody. They got their assignments from a sexy bail bondswoman named Big Jack, later replaced by Terri Shannon (whose last name was changed to Michaels in 1983) and then by a feisty old lady named Pearl.

Each episode began with one of Colt's daredevil (and usually high-speed) movie stunts, then shifted to his pursuit of the bail jumper—during which Colt often used the same stunts he had used in the movie. None of these assignments turned out to be as simple as Big Jack or Terri claimed they would be, but with so many beautiful women, famous stars, and exotic locales to see along the way, Colt did not complain—much.

FAME
Drama
FIRST TELECAST: *January 7, 1982*
LAST TELECAST: *August 4, 1983*
BROADCAST HISTORY:
Jan 1982–Aug 1983, NBC Thu 8:00–9:00
(In first-run syndication from fall 1983–fall 1987)
CAST:
Lydia Grant .... Debbie Allen
Coco Hernandez (1982–1983) ... Erica Gimpel
Danny Amatullo .... Carlo Imperato
Bruno Martelli (1982–1984) .... Lee Curreri
Doris Schwartz (1982–1985)
.... Valerie Landsburg
Leroy Johnson .... Gene Anthony Ray
Montgomery MacNeil (1982) .... P. R. Paul
Elizabeth Sherwood (1982–1986)
.... Carol Mayo Jenkins
Mr. Benjamin Shorofsky .... Albert Hague
Julie Miller (1982–1983) .... Lori Singer
Mr. Crandall (1982) .... Michael Thoma
Mrs. Charlotte Miller (1982–1983)
.... Judy Farrell
Angelo Martelli (1982–1983).. Carmine Caridi
David Reardon (1982–1983) .. Morgan Stevens
Dwight (1982–1985).......... David Greenlee
Mrs. Gertrude Berg (Alice Bowman)
.... Ann Nelson
Holly Laird (1983–1986)........ Cynthia Gibb
Christopher Donlon (1983–1987) . Billy Hufsey
Quentin Morloch (1983–1985) .. Ken Swofford
Cleo Hewitt (1984–1985) .... Janet Jackson
Jesse Valesquez (1984–1987) .... Jesse Borrego
Nicole Chapman (1984–1987)..... Nia Peeples
Mr. Lou Mackie (1985–1987) ..... Dick Miller
Laura Mackie (1986–1987) ... Carolyn J. Silas
Dusty Tyler (1985–1987) .... Loretta Chandler
Mr. Bob Dyrenforth (1985–1987)
.... Graham Jarvis
Reggie Higgins (1986–1987) . Carrie Hamilton
Kate Riley (1986) .... Page Hannah
Ian Ware (1986–1987) ...... Michael Cerveris
Jillian Beckett (1986–1987) .... Elisa Heinsohn
Mr. Paul Seeger (1986–1987) ... Eric Pierpoint

Maxie (1986–1987) .... Olivia Barash
Miltie Horowitz (1986–1987)
.... Robert Romanus
THEME:
"Fame," written by Michael Gore and Dean
Pitchford, and sung by Erica Gimpel

New York City's renowned High School for the
Performing Arts was the setting for this series
about the hopes and aspirations of a group of
students planning to become singers, dancers, actors, musicians, and comedians. Geared specifically to provide a curriculum that would prepare
its graduates for careers in show business, the
School for the Performing Arts attracted a student
body with tremendous talent, energy, and ambition. It was there that they learned to deal with
competition and rejection, as well as the problems
of growing up.

Among the featured students were Bruno, a talented but somewhat arrogant keyboard artist and
composer; Coco, a singer-dancer driven to succeed and in a rush to get into the professional
world; Danny, a bright comedian who would
break into a monologue at the drop of a hat; Doris,
an actress-writer-comedienne whose easy-going
manner belied an ego as strong and determined as
anyone's; Leroy, a talented dancer from the ghettos of New York, who graduated and became an
assistant dance instructor at the school himself;
Montgomery, trying to follow in the path of his
successful actress mother; and Julie, the outsider
from Grand Rapids, Michigan, who was an accomplished cellist adjusting both to the school
and the high-energy environment of New York.

If anything, the faculty was even more dedicated than the students, with hard-driving, beautiful dance teacher Lydia Grant the most prominent. Other teachers included Mr. Shorofsky, the
bearded music teacher; Mr. Crandall, the drama
instructor; and English teacher Elizabeth Sherwood.

Fame was an immediate hit with the critics.
They lauded its talented cast of young performers,
the well-choreographed production numbers, and
its realistic portrayal of the problems of growing
up in contemporary society. Unfortunately it attracted a small audience, and after a year and a
half on NBC it was finally canceled in the spring
of 1983. Undaunted, the producers continued production of new episodes and sold them on a syndicated basis to local stations, which generally
aired them on Saturday or Sunday in the early
evening.

There were changes in the cast. David Reardon
replaced Mr. Crandall (Michael Thoma had died)
as drama teacher (later replaced by Paul Seeger);
Mrs. Berg, the scatterbrained school secretary,
became a regular; and Quentin Morloch, an officious principal (later replaced by Bob Dyrenforth)
who gradually came to understand that this was
not an ordinary high school, was added. New students included Dwight, an awkward, fat tuba

player; Holly, a vivacious drama major; Jesse, an
hispanic dancer who became Leroy's protege;
Nicole, a beautiful black singer and dancer who
was tragically killed in an auto accident; Christopher, a talented but cocky dancer; and Ian, an
English guitarist who loved rock music. In later
years Lou's bowling alley/restaurant became a
regular hangout for the students.

Fame was based on the movie of the same
name, with a number of its cast members—Debbie Allen, Albert Hague, Gene Anthony Ray, and
Lee Curreri—reprising their roles in the series.

FAMILY
Drama
FIRST TELECAST: *March 9, 1976*
LAST TELECAST: *June 25, 1980*
BROADCAST HISTORY:
Mar 1976–Feb 1978, ABC Tue 10:00–11:00 (OS)
May 1978, ABC Tue 10:00–11:00
Sep 1978–Mar 1979, ABC Thu 10:00–11:00
Mar 1979–Apr 1979, ABC Fri 8:00–9:00
May 1979, ABC Thu 10:00–11:00
Dec 1979–Feb 1980, ABC Mon 10:00–11:00
Mar 1980, ABC Mon 9:00–10:00
Jun 1980, ABC Wed 8:00–9:00
CAST:
Kate Lawrence .... Sada Thompson
Doug Lawrence .... James Broderick
Nancy Lawrence Maitland (1976)
.... Elayne Heilveil
Nancy Lawrence Maitland (1976–1980)
.... Meredith Baxter-Birney
Willie Lawrence .... Gary Frank
Letitia "Buddy" Lawrence .. Kristy McNichol
Jeff Maitland .... John Rubinstein
Mrs. Hanley (1976–1978)
.... Mary Grace Canfield
Salina Magee (1976–1977)..... Season Hubley
Annie Cooper (1978–1980)... Quinn Cummings
Timmy Maitland (1978–1980)
.... Michael David Schackelford

Family was a prime-time soap opera that followed the travails of the middle-class Lawrence
family in Pasadena, California. Doug was the father, a highly independent lawyer, and Kate his
quiet, steadfast wife. The series opened with
daughter Nancy discovering that her husband Jeff
was untrue (she walked in on him making love to
another woman!) and it was all downhill from
there. Nancy had a baby (Timmy), divorced Jeff,
then began having affairs of her own. Later she
went to work for a law firm, which seemed more
interested in her body than in her brains. Brother
Willie, age 17, vulnerable and idealistic, was confronted with his first love, an unwed mother (Salina), then married a girl with a terminal illness
(Lizzy). Little sister Buddy, age 13, feeling unwanted, ran away from home. Before Kate could
worry about *that,* she discovered that she had
breast cancer, after which Doug was temporarily
blinded in an automobile accident. An 11-year-old

waif named Annie joined the household, only to reject everyone's affections. Then there was the dying grandmother, Doug's alcoholic sister, and so on, and on, and on . . .

FAMILY AFFAIR
Situation Comedy
FIRST TELECAST: *September 12, 1966*
LAST TELECAST: *September 9, 1971*
BROADCAST HISTORY:
   Sep 1966–Sep 1969, CBS Mon 9:30–10:00
   Sep 1969–Sep 1971, CBS Thu 7:30–8:00
CAST:
   Bill Davis .... Brian Keith
   Mr. (Giles) French .... Sebastian Cabot
   Buffy .... Anissa Jones
   Jody .... Johnnie Whitaker
   Cissy .... Kathy Garver
   Emily Turner (1970–1971) ..... Nancy Walker

Bill Davis' carefree existence as a swinging bachelor was just about perfect. A highly paid consulting engineer, he maintained an elegant apartment off Fifth Avenue in Manhattan and had his domestic needs cared for by a very English gentleman's gentleman, Mr. French. Into this life of independence came three young orphans, the 6-year-old twins Buffy and Jody and 15-year-old Cissy. Their parents, Bill's brother and sister-in-law, had died in an accident, and other relatives felt that Bill could best provide for them. Despite initial misgivings, Bill and French became very attached to the children and learned to adjust their life-style to make room for the new members of the household. Mr. French, a stickler for neatness and order, had the toughest adjustment to make—he was with the children all the time while Bill was often out of town on assignments—but he and the children managed to compromise and learn to live with each other.

For a period during the show's first season, co-star Sebastian Cabot was taken ill and was replaced in nine episodes by John Williams. In the story line, Giles French was called away to special service of the Queen of England and his brother Niles arrived at the Davis residence to serve the family during his absence. Although not a full-time member of the cast, Nancy Walker appeared in the continuing role of Mr. Davis' part-time housekeeper, Emily, during the last season.

CBS aired reruns of *Family Affair* on weekdays from September 1970 to January 1973.

FAMILY DOUBLE DARE
Quiz
FIRST TELECAST: *April 3, 1988*
LAST TELECAST:
BROADCAST HISTORY:
   Apr 1988, FOX Sun 8:00–8:30
   Apr 1988–   , FOX Sat 8:00–8:30
EMCEE:
   Marc Summers

Start with *Family Feud,* pour on a bucket of *Beat the Clock,* and add a gooey topping of *Truth or Consequences* and you have a pretty good idea what *Family Double Dare* was like—one of the messiest "stunt shows" on television. Two families (parents and two children) competed. In the opening rounds the families tried to best each other in a stunt, for example by being the first to fill a cup sitting on one of the parent's heads with seltzer, from six feet away. The winning family won a cash prize and then was asked a question worth a specified amount. They could either answer or dare the other family to do so for twice as much money; the second family could take the challenge or "double dare" the first family to answer (and the amount would double again). An incorrect answer gave the money and first chance on the next question to the other family.

The family "double-dared" had another option, which was frequently taken. Instead of the question they could choose "the physical challenge," another stunt that had to be completed in a limited time. At the end the family winning the most money ran an obstacle course for grand prizes. The object of most of the stunts and challenges seemed to be to make as big a mess as possible, with the various family members wading through water balloons, puddings and syrups, eggs, pies, and green and red slime. It was no accident that the emcee, while attired in a tuxedo, also wore tennis shoes!

Family Double Dare began as *Double Dare* on the Nickelodeon cable channel in 1986. On the cable version all the contestants were children, and the show was a big hit with Nickelodeon's young audience. Early in 1988 a limited number of Fox television stations began airing a new version of *Double Dare* and a couple of months later *Family Double Dare,* including adults, premiered on the Fox network. If there was one thing young viewers liked more than seeing other kids covered with slop, it was seeing parents making a mess of themselves.

FAMILY FEUD
Quiz/Audience Participation
BROADCAST HISTORY:
   Syndicated and network daytime
   30 minutes
   Produced: 1977–
   Released: *Fall 1977*
HOST:
   Richard Dawson

Family Feud was one of the most popular game shows to come along in the 1970s. A hit on ABC's daytime lineup from its debut in July 1976; it quickly spun off this syndicated nighttime version a year later.

Two families of five members each (parents, children, cousins, aunts and uncles, etc.) were introduced at the start of each show, seated opposite each other as if posing for family portraits.

Host Richard Dawson spent at least the first five minutes of the show talking to them, asking about their backgrounds and interests, and cracking little jokes. Then the game began. The families were presented with a question; for example: "Name a purchase on which most families spend a great deal of money." The object was to guess how most people would have answered, based on a prior survey. Points were awarded according to what percentage of the survey, if any, gave the same answer (for example, if the family said "buying a house" and 60 percent of the survey said the same thing, the family got 60 points). The family with the most points on the initial answer was given the option of trying to guess all the answers the survey had generated, accumulating points until they had either gotten them all, or gotten three wrong answers. In that case, the other team could win the accumulated points by coming up with one of the remaining correct answers. Preliminary rounds were played until one of the families had won at least 300 points. That family played the final round in which, if successful, they walked away with the $10,000 grand prize and $1 for every point accumulated in the preliminary rounds.

The format was identical to that used in daytime, except for the grand prize ($5,000 in the daytime version). The host of both was Richard Dawson, an English comedian who got his start in the U.S. as Newkirk in *Hogan's Heroes*. It was Dawson's glib familiarity and ready wit that helped make *Family Feud* a hit. The ABC network periodically telecast prime-time specials based on the show, with celebrity casts from various series substituting for the families.

The network version left ABC's daytime lineup in June 1985.

FAMILY HOLVAK, THE
General Drama
FIRST TELECAST: *September 7, 1975*
LAST TELECAST: *June 28, 1977*
BROADCAST HISTORY:
  Sep 1975, NBC Sun 7:30–8:30
  Sep 1975–Oct 1975, NBC Sun 8:00–9:00
  Oct 1975, NBC Mon 8:00–9:00
  Dec 1975, NBC Sun 8:00–9:00
  May 1977–Jun 1977, CBS Tue 8:00–9:00
CAST:
  Rev. Tom Holvak .... Glenn Ford
  Elizabeth Holvak .... Julie Harris
  Ramey Holvak .... Lance Kerwin
  Julie Mae Holvak .... Elizabeth Cheshire
  Chester Purdle .... Ted Gehring
  Ida .... Cynthia Howard
  Deputy Jim Shanks .... William McKinney

Life in the South during the Depression was hard on everyone, and a preacher was no exception. Rev. Tom Holvak was the poverty-stricken clergyman trying to scrape together enough money to support his wife Elizabeth and his two children,

13-year-old Ramey and 8-year-old Julie Mae. To add to his meager income, he sold produce grown on a small plot of land owned by the church. This unsuccessful series was, in many ways, patterned after the highly successful CBS series *The Waltons,* in that it stressed how love and understanding helped a Depression family survive, even though they lacked many of the comforts that most people now take for granted.

Reruns of *The Family Holvak* were aired briefly on CBS during the summer of 1977.

FAMILY MAN
Situation Comedy
FIRST TELECAST: *March 18, 1988*
LAST TELECAST: *April 29, 1988*
BROADCAST HISTORY:
  Mar 1988–Apr 1988, ABC Fri 9:30–10:00
CAST:
  Shelly Tobin .... Richard Libertini
  Andrea Tobin .... Mimi Kennedy
  Rosie Tobin (age 10) .... Alison Sweeney
  Josh Tobin (7) .... Whitby Hertford
  Sara Tobin (3) ...... Keeley Mari Gallagher

A routine family comedy with lots of close-ups of cute kids. Shelly was a tall, balding TV comedy writer who worked at home, where he was evidently surrounded by comedy one-liners. Wife Andrea provided loyal support, along with two children from her previous marriage (Rosie, Josh) and one of their own (Sara).

FAMILY TIES
Situation Comedy
FIRST TELECAST: *September 22, 1982*
LAST TELECAST:
BROADCAST HISTORY:
  Sep 1982–Mar 1983, NBC Wed 9:30–10:00
  Mar 1983–Aug 1983, NBC Mon 8:30–9:00
  Aug 1983–Dec 1983, NBC Wed 9:30–10:00
  Jan 1984–Aug 1987, NBC Thu 8:30–9:00
  Aug 1987–Sep 1987, NBC Sun 8:00–9:00
  Sep 1987–   , NBC Sun 8:00–8:30
CAST:
  Elyse Keaton .... Meredith Baxter-Birney
  Steve Keaton .... Michael Gross
  Alex P. Keaton .... Michael J. Fox
  Mallory Keaton............ Justine Bateman
  Jennifer Keaton .... Tina Yothers
  Andrew Keaton (1986–   ).... Brian Bonsall
  Irwin "Skippy" Handelman ...... Marc Price
  Ellen Reed (1985–1986) .... Tracy Pollan
  Nick Moore (1985–   ) .... Scott Valentine
  Lauren Miller (1987–   )..... Courteney Cox
THEME:
  "Without Us," by Jeff Barry and Tom Scott, sung by Johnny Mathis and Deniece Williams

The mellow 1960s clashed with the conservative 1980s in this generation-gap comedy, set in suburban Columbus, Ohio. The generations had their roles reversed, however. Elyse and Steve Keaton were one-time flower children who still espoused the liberal values of the idealistic '60s, though they were now parents and professionals (she an architect, he the manager of public TV station WKS-TV). Their children's ideals were something else. Seventeen-year-old Alex was Mr. Conservative, habitually dressed in suit and tie and with a picture of William F. Buckley, Jr., over his bed. Mallory, 15, was into designer jeans, boys, and junk food, while cute little Jennifer, 9, just wanted to be a kid. They were a loving family, though the kids never could understand those Bob Dylan records their parents kept playing.

During the 1984–1985 season Elyse gave birth to baby Andrew, and by the following fall superstudent Alex had entered college espousing, what else, the virtues of the Reagan administration's supply-side economics. There he became seriously involved with another student, perky Ellen Reed, while back home sister Mallory was dating a poorly educated aspiring sculptor named Nick Moore. Mallory, an academic underachiever, narrowly graduated from high school in 1986, and set her sights on a career in fashion design, more or less. In 1987 another love interest entered Alex's life in the person of psychology student Lauren Miller. Alex's chief sidekick, though, was little brother Andrew (already four years old!), who idolized him. Skippy was Alex's rather dense friend.

NBC aired reruns of *Family Ties* on weekday mornings from December 1985 to January 1987.

FAMILY TREE, THE
Drama
FIRST TELECAST: *January 22, 1983*
LAST TELECAST: *August 10, 1983*
BROADCAST HISTORY:
  Jan 1983–Feb 1983, NBC Sat 10:00–11:00
  Jul 1983–Aug 1983, NBC Wed 10:00–11:00
CAST:
  Kevin Nichols .... Frank Converse
  Annie Benjamin Nichols .... Anne Archer
  Jake Nichols.................. James Spader
  Toby Benjamin .... Jonathan Hall Kovacs
  Tess Benjamin .... Melora Hardin
  Sam Benjamin .... Martin Hewitt
  Dr. David Benjamin .... Alan Feinstein
  Elizabeth Nichols .... Joanna Cassidy
  Molly Nichols Tanner ...... Ann Dusenberry

Remarriage for divorced people with children takes understanding and patience from all the family members involved. That was the theme of *The Family Tree*. Kevin Nichols, owner of a successful lumber company, and Annie Benjamin, who worked part-time selling real estate, were the couple starting a second life together. Kevin's grown daughter Molly was married, and his teenaged son Jake lived with Kevin's ex-wife, Elizabeth. Annie's three children were all still part of her household, with Toby, her deaf young son, particularly upset about the divorce from her first

husband, David. Annie's children were still very close to their father and had problems adjusting to the arrival of their stepfather. Coping with the altered relationships caused by divorce and remarriage provided the focus for this series.

FAMOUS ADVENTURES OF MR. MAGOO, THE
Cartoon
FIRST TELECAST: *September 19, 1964*
LAST TELECAST: *August 7, 1965*
BROADCAST HISTORY:
  Sep 1964–Dec 1964, NBC Sat 8:00–8:30
  Jan 1965–Aug 1965, NBC Sat 8:30–9:00
VOICES:
  Mr. Quincy Magoo .... Jim Backus
  Various .... Marvin Miller,
                Howard Morris, Paul Frees

Mr. Magoo, that clumsy, crusty, nearsighted old man, has had a long history of success in theatrical cartoons and on TV. At Christmastime in 1962 and 1963, NBC aired a feature-length cartoon version of Dickens's *The Christmas Carol*, featuring "Mr. Magoo as Ebeneezer Scrooge and retitled Mr. Magoo's Christmas Carol." This prompted the development of a series in which Magoo played assorted characters of historic significance, both fictional and real. Long John Silver, Friar Tuck, William Tell, Dr. Watson (of the Sherlock Holmes stories), and Rip Van Winkle were among the characters played by Magoo in this humorous animated series.

FAMOUS FIGHTS
Sports
FIRST TELECAST: *September 15, 1952*
LAST TELECAST: *December 17, 1957*
BROADCAST HISTORY:
  Sep 1952–Dec 1952, DUM Mon 9:45–10:00
  Jul 1957–Dec 1957, ABC Wed 10:45–11:00
COMMENTATOR:
  Jimmy Powers (1952)

Filmed highlights of outstanding boxing matches in the history of Madison Square Garden were shown preceding or following the live fights in 1952 and 1957.

FAMOUS FILM FESTIVAL
  see *Movies—Prior to 1961*

FAMOUS JURY TRIALS
Courtroom Drama
FIRST TELECAST: *October 12, 1949*
LAST TELECAST: *March 12, 1952*
BROADCAST HISTORY:
  Oct 1949–May 1950, DUM Wed 9:30–10:00
  May 1950–May 1951, DUM Wed 9:00–9:30
  Nov 1951–Mar 1952, DUM Wed 9:00–9:30

This series presented reenactments of real-life criminal trials and the crimes that led to them. Typically the story would open in the courtroom.

While opposing witnesses related their versions of the events, the scene would shift to another set and a reenactment of the crime according to each witness's version. At the end the jury was given the case, and the viewer found out what really happened. Staged with little-known actors on a minuscule budget, this DuMont production nevertheless managed to survive off and on for two and a half years.

FANFARE
Dramatic Anthology
FIRST TELECAST: *July 7, 1959*
LAST TELECAST: *September 8, 1959*
BROADCAST HISTORY:
   Jul 1959–Sep 1959, NBC Tue 9:00–9:30
HOST:
   Richard Derr

This summer series consisted of repeats of *Loretta Young Show* plays in which Miss Young had not appeared. Actor Richard Derr was the host, introducing each play and giving a summary of the following week's offering at the conclusion of the telecast.

FANFARE
Musical Variety
FIRST TELECAST: *June 19, 1965*
LAST TELECAST: *September 11, 1965*
BROADCAST HISTORY:
   Jun 1965–Sep 1965, CBS Sat 7:30–8:30
REGULARS:
   Al Hirt
   The Don McKayle Dancers
   The Mort Lindsey Orchestra

Al Hirt, the hefty, bearded New Orleans trumpet player, was the host and star of this summer musical variety series. In addition to his own flashy renditions of popular and classical trumpet pieces, Hirt presented various guest stars, all of whom participated in some type of musical number, whether or not they were themselves musicians.

FANTASTIC JOURNEY
Science Fiction
FIRST TELECAST: *February 3, 1977*
LAST TELECAST: *April 13, 1977*
BROADCAST HISTORY:
   Feb 1977–Apr 1977, NBC Thu 8:00–9:00
CAST:
   Varian .... Jared Martin
   Dr. Fred Walters.............. Carl Franklin
   Scott Jordan .... Ike Eisenmann
   Liana .... Katie Saylor
   Dr. Jonathan Willaway.... Roddy McDowall

This science-fantasy series began with a group of university scientists exploring the area of the Bermuda Triangle. Their boat ran aground on an uncharted land mass, which turned out to be the source of a strange "time and space warp" in which past, present, and future were all intermingled. One of the scientists, Dr. Fred Walters, was drawn into the warp, where he met four people from various eras, each of whom was trying to find the way back to his or her own time. The four were Varian, a telepathic individual from the 23rd century; Liana, a survivor from the lost continent of Atlantis; Scott, a young boy from the present day who had occult abilities; and Dr. Jonathan Willaway, a scientist from the 1960s who was living with androids. The adventures of these wanderers in time and space, the bizarre creatures they encountered, and the conflicts between them were all interwoven in the series.

FANTASY ISLAND
Romantic Drama
FIRST TELECAST: *January 28, 1978*
LAST TELECAST: *August 18, 1984*
BROADCAST HISTORY:
   Jan 1978–Aug 1979, ABC Sat 10:00–11:00
   Aug 1979–Oct 1979, ABC Fri 8:00–9:00
   Oct 1979–Aug 1984, ABC Sat 10:00–11:00
CAST:
   Mr. Roarke .... Ricardo Montalban
   Tattoo (1978–1983) .... Herve Villechaize
   Julie (1981–1982) .... Wendy Schaal
   Lawrence (1983–1984) ... Christopher Hewett

When ABC realized it had a major hit with *Love Boat*, it immediately began developing a second program using a similar theme. That program was *Fantasy Island*, and, scheduled right after *Love Boat* on Saturday night, it soon became an equally big hit.

Both programs were episodic, consisting of several different stories each week played out against a common background. The backdrop of *Fantasy Island* was romantic indeed; a remote island resort, where each visitor could have one lifelong dream come true. A homely young man wanted to become, during his stay, a sex symbol to beautiful girls (bikini-clad beauties abounded on *Fantasy Island*); a frustrated salesman whose career was going nowhere wanted to score the business coup of his life; a henpecked family man wanted a weekend of respect from his clan. Many of the stories involved glamour and excitement for ordinary people whose lives normally had none, and ABC obviously felt that viewers would relate this to their own lives. There was sometimes an element of danger, or a twist of fate, but everything always worked out for the best.

Overseeing the two or three little dramas each week was the island's owner, the suave and slightly mysterious Mr. Roarke, and his midget helper Tattoo (replaced in 1983 by Lawrence). In later seasons, Roarke became increasingly mysterious, in fact, dispensing magic spells and potions, calling up events from the past and future, and even doing battle with the devil. The plots got ever more fanciful. Visitors on the island were played by a wide range of guest stars, among them Henry

Gibson, Georgia Engel, Christopher George, Marcia Strassman, Dennis James, and Roddy McDowall (as Mephistopheles). Mr. Roarke's god-daughter Julie was seen as a regular for a single season.

Fantasy Island was originally filmed at a real tropical paradise, a public park called the Ar-boretum, 25 miles from Los Angeles.

FARADAY AND COMPANY
Detective Drama
FIRST TELECAST: *September 26, 1973*
LAST TELECAST: *August 13, 1974*
BROADCAST HISTORY:
   Sep 1973–Jan 1974, NBC Wed 8:30–10:00
   Apr 1974–Aug 1974, NBC Tue 8:30–10:00
CAST:
   Frank Faraday.................. Dan Dailey
   Steve Faraday .... James Naughton
   Holly Barrett .... Sharon Gless
   Lou Carson .... Geraldine Brooks

Frank Faraday was a private detective who had served 25 years in a South American jail for a crime that he had not committed. When he was finally released he was forced to adjust to a world very much changed, including a son, Steve, he had never known (born to his secretary, Lou Carson, after his imprisonment). After tracking down and bringing to justice the man who had actually committed the crime for which he had been imprisoned, Frank joined forces with his son—who had himself become a detective—in operating a Los Angeles detective agency that specialized in security investigations. The contrast in styles between the two men created constant tensions and strains in the relationship, for father Frank often resorted to old-style physical force against a new generation of technologically and legally astute criminals. *Faraday and Company* was one of the four rotating elements in the 1973–1974 version of the *NBC Wednesday Mystery Movie*. The others were *Banacek, The Snoop Sisters,* and *Tenafly.*

FARADAY HILL
Romantic Drama
FIRST TELECAST: *October 2, 1946*
LAST TELECAST: *December 18, 1946*
BROADCAST HISTORY:
   Oct 1946–Dec 1946, DUM Wed 9:00–9:30
CAST:
   Karen St. John .... Flora Campbell
ALSO:
   Mel Brandt
   Ann Stell
   Lorene Scott
   Frederic Meyer
   Melville Galliart
   Jacqueline Waite
   Jack Halloran
   Ben Low
   Bill Gale
   Vivian King

Eve McVeagh
Julie Christy
Hal Studer
Barry Doig
Munroe Gabler
WRITER/DIRECTOR:
   David P. Lewis

Faraway Hill was the first example on network television of a durable and tear-stained program type—the soap opera. The network wasn't very big (New York and Washington) and the program didn't last very long (12 weeks), but it had all the elements that today's serial viewers have come to know and love—two women after the same man, family jealousies, incredible complications, and the inevitable "tune in next time" to find out what happened.

Some of the specifics, such as character names, have been lost in the mists of history. The basic plot concerned a wealthy New York woman who, following the death of her husband, traveled to the country to visit relatives and get away from it all. The relatives, who lived on a farm, turned out to be a little more rural than she had expected, which resulted in conflict between her sophistication and their lack of it. Staying with them was an adopted farm boy, with whom the widow soon became romantically involved. Unfortunately, he was already promised to the farmer's daughter, which led to the inevitable romantic triangle. Widow St. John tried all her wiles to win him away, but—well, tune in next week.

Flora Campbell, a Broadway actress with numerous credits, played the leading role of Karen St. John, and Mel Brandt was the object of her affections.

Faraway Hill was an experiment to see how this kind of series would look on TV, and some of the devices used were interesting. On the initial episode the various characters were introduced with their names and relationships shown on the screen, so that viewers could keep everyone straight. Each subsequent episode began with a recap of what had gone before (illustrated by slides from the shows) and a reminder of who was who, narrated in emotional tones by Karen. Within the show an off-screen voice would relate Karen's thoughts, to serve as a bridge between scenes, and occasional film sequences were worked into the otherwise live show to depict such details as passing trains. The whole production was done on an absolutely minimal budget of $300 per week.

Though *Faraway Hill* was the first soap opera to be carried on a network, it was not the first one on television. During the summer of 1946 WRGB, the pioneering General Electric station in Schenectady, aired a 13-part serial called *War Bride,* about a GI returned from the war with a new love, much to the consternation of his mother and his former fiancée. There may have been a few others, also telecast on a local basis. In any event it was not until the networks moved into daytime telecasting in a big way in the 1950s that the TV soap opera really caught on, and the serialized grief has been endless ever since.

FARMER'S DAUGHTER, THE
Situation Comedy
FIRST TELECAST: *September 20, 1963*
LAST TELECAST: *September 2, 1966*
BROADCAST HISTORY:
  Sep 1963–Nov 1963, ABC Fri 9:30–10:00
  Dec 1963–Sep 1964, ABC Wed 8:30–9:00
  Sep 1964–Jun 1965, ABC Fri 8:00–8:30
  Jun 1965–Oct 1965, ABC Mon 9:30–10:00
  Nov 1965–Sep 1966, ABC Fri 9:30–10:00
CAST:
  Katrin "Katy" Holstrum .... Inger Stevens
  Congressman Glen Morley.. William Windom
  Agatha Morley, Glen's Mother
  .... Cathleen Nesbitt
  Steve Morley .... Mickey Sholdar
  Danny Morley .... Rory O'Brien
  Cooper, the Butler (1963–1964)
  .... Philip Coolidge

This comedy concerned Katy, a naive, sexy farm girl of Swedish descent, who came to Washington, D.C., to look for help from her congressman. Instead she wound up working for him, as governess of his two motherless boys, Danny (age 8) and Steve (age 14). Through simple charm and native intelligence Katy managed to loosen up the sometimes stuffy politicians around her and to further Glen's bumbling political career. On the telecast of November 5, 1965, Katy married Glen, but this failed to reverse the declining ratings, and the show concluded its run at the end of that season.

The program was based on the 1947 movie of the same name starring Loretta Young, for which Miss Young won an Oscar.

FASHION STORY, THE
Fashion/Comedy
FIRST TELECAST: *November 4, 1948*
LAST TELECAST: *March 1, 1949*
BROADCAST HISTORY:
  Nov 1948–Jan 1949, ABC Thu 8:00–8:30
  Jan 1949–Mar 1949, ABC Tue 7:30–8:00
REGULARS:
  Marilyn Day
  Carl Reiner
  Don Saxon
  Pamela O'Neill
  Dennis Bohan
  Doris Lane
  Patsy Davis
  Elaine Joyce
  Aina Shields
  Hayes Gorden
MUSIC:
  Walter Fleicher Trio
  Roger Stearns, piano

This was a fashion show combined with a slight comedy story line to provide continuity. Marilyn Day was seen in the role of Lucky Marshall, a young model who hoped to break into show business as a singer (thus providing an excuse for periodic songs). Her young boss, who was forever causing problems, was played by Dennis Bohan. A bevy of fashion models paraded through each show, providing its main reason for being. Pamela O'Neill was the fashion commentator. Carl Reiner, as a comic photographer, was also a regular, but his talents were largely wasted, causing one reviewer to remark that he and Miss Day deserved "a good spot of their own on a variety show, without the drawback of tying together a fashion show." They both got one, working together two months later on *The Fifty-fourth Street Revue.* For Miss Day that was the end of the network line, but Carl Reiner went on to *Your Show of Shows* and a long succession of writing/performing/producing jobs in television.

FASHIONS ON PARADE
Fashion/Variety
FIRST TELECAST: *August 20, 1948*
LAST TELECAST: *January 7, 1949*
BROADCAST HISTORY:
  Aug 1948–Jan 1949, DUM Fri 8:00–8:30
NARRATOR:
  Adelaide Hawley

This combination fashion show and musical revue featured guest celebrities and the famous Conover (Modeling Agency) Cover Girls as models. A thin story line each week tied together the performances and the showing of the latest fashions. Among the guests were Vincent Lopez and Jerry Wayne.

The show was also seen locally in New York during various periods in 1948 and 1949.

FAST TIMES
Situation Comedy
FIRST TELECAST: *March 5, 1986*
LAST TELECAST: *April 23, 1986*
BROADCAST HISTORY:
  Mar 1986–Apr 1986, CBS Wed 8:00–8:30
CAST:
  Jeff Spicoli .... Dean Cameron
  Mr. Arnold Hand .... Ray Walston
  Mike Damone .... Patrick Dempsey
  Mark Ratner.................. Wally Ward
  Stacey Hamilton ..... Courtney Thorne-Smith
  Brad Hamilton................ James Nardini
  Linda Barrett .... Claudia Wells
  Mr. Hector Vargas .... Vincent Schiavelli
  Ms. Leslie Melon .... Kit McDonough
  Barbara DeVilbiss .... Moon Zappa
  Dennis Taylor .... Paul Wilson
  The Surfer.................... Bill Calvert
  Curtis Spicoli................. Jason Hervey
THEME:
  "Fast Times" written by Danny Elfman and performed by Oingo Boingo

This contemporary high-school comedy was centered around the lives of the students and faculty at Ridgemont High in Los Angeles' San Fernando Valley. The students included spaced-out Spicoli, who would rather go surfing than waste his time in school; Brad Hamilton, a popular guy who worked at the burger stand in the neighborhood shopping mall; Stacey, Brad's cute but somewhat insecure younger sister; Linda Barrett, a beautiful, popular cheerleader and Stacey's best friend; Damone, the school's resident con man and source for anything from a phony ID to tickets for a sold-out rock concert; and Ratner, a shy guy who worked as a ticket taker at the movie theater in the mall. The faculty members showing up regularly were Mr. Hand, a disciplinarian history teacher frustrated by the casual attitude of so many of his students; Mr. Vargas, the eccentric science teacher; and Ms. Melon, the Life Studies teacher with a penchant for getting personally involved in the personal lives of her students.

Based on the theatrical feature "Fast Times at Ridgemont High," with Ray Walston and Vincent Schiavelli recreating the roles they played in the film. Cameron Crowe, who had written the article on which a book, and later the film, had been based, served as creative consultant for the series.

FATHER KNOWS BEST
Situation Comedy
FIRST TELECAST: *October 3, 1954*
LAST TELECAST: *April 5, 1963*
BROADCAST HISTORY:

> *Oct 1954–Mar 1955,* CBS Sun 10:00–10:30
> *Aug 1955–Sep 1958,* NBC Wed 8:30–9:00
> *Sep 1958–Sep 1960,* CBS Mon 8:30–9:00
> *Oct 1960–Sep 1961,* CBS Tue 8:00–8:30
> *Oct 1961–Feb 1962,* CBS Wed 8:00–8:30
> *Feb 1962–Sep 1962,* CBS Mon 8:30–9:00
> *Sep 1962–Dec 1962,* ABC Sun 7:00–7:30
> *Dec 1962–Apr 1963,* ABC Fri 8:00–8:30

CAST:

> *Jim Anderson* .... Robert Young
> *Margaret Anderson* .... Jane Wyatt
> *Betty Anderson (Princess)* ... Elinor Donahue
> *James Anderson, Jr. (Bud)* ..... Billy Gray
> *Kathy Anderson (Kitten)* ...... Lauren Chapin
> *Miss Thomas* .... Sarah Selby
> *Ed Davis (1955–1959)* .... Robert Foulk
> *Myrtle Davis (1955–1959)* .... Vivi Jannis
> *Dotty Snow (1954–1957)* .... Yvonne Lime
> *Kippy Watkins (1954–1959)* .... Paul Wallace
> *Claude Messner (1954–1959)* .... Jimmy Bates
> *Doyle Hobbs (1957–1958)* .... Roger Smith
> *Ralph Little (1957–1958)* .... Robert Chapman
> *April Adams (1957–1958)* .... Sue George
> *Joyce Kendall (1958–1959)*
> .... Jymme (Roberta) Shore

Father Knows Best was the classic wholesome family situation comedy. It was set in the typical Midwestern community of Springfield, where Jim Anderson was an agent for the General Insurance

Company. Every evening he would come home from work, take off his sports jacket, put on his comfortable sweater, and deal with the everyday problems of a growing family. In contrast with most other family comedies of the period, in which one or the other of the parents was a blundering idiot, both Jim and his wife Margaret were portrayed as thoughtful, responsible adults. When a family crisis arose, Jim would calm the waters with a warm smile and some sensible advice.

When *Father Knows Best* went on television in 1954, the three children were aged 17 (Betty), 14 (Bud), and 9 (Kathy). As the seasons passed two of them graduated from high school, first Betty (1956) and then Bud (1959). Neither left home, however, both electing to go to Springfield's own State College.

The Andersons were truly an idealized family, the sort that viewers could relate to and wish to emulate. The children went through the normal problems of growing up, including those concerning school, friends, and members of the opposite sex. They didn't always agree with their parents and occasionally succeeded in asserting their independence (as when Jim and Margaret almost succeeded in pushing Betty into going to their alma mater, until they realized that she had to make her own decisions and let her choose State instead). But the bickering was minimal, and everything seemed to work out by the end of the half-hour.

Father Knows Best began as an NBC radio series in 1949, with Robert Young in the starring role. He was the only member of the radio cast that made the transition to TV in 1954. The TV series was not particularly successful at first, and CBS canceled it in March 1955. A flood of viewer protest, demanding that the program be reinstated and moved to an earlier time slot so that the whole family could watch it, prompted NBC to pick it up for the following season with an 8:30 P.M. starting time. *Father Knows Best* prospered for the next five years.

The series became such a symbol of the "typical" American family that the U.S. Treasury Department commissioned the producers to film a special episode to help promote the 1959 U.S. Savings Bond Drive. The story, "24 Hours in Tyrant Land," told how the Anderson children attempted to live for a day under a make-believe dictatorship. Never aired on television, this special episode was distributed to churches, schools, and civic organizations to show the importance of maintaining a strong American democracy.

During the 1959–1960 season, its last with original episodes, *Father Knows Best* had its most successful year, ranking sixth among all television programs. By the end of that season, however, star Robert Young had tired of the role, which he had been playing for 11 years, and decided it was time to move on to other things. This was one of the rare occasions in the history of television when production on a series ceased when it was at the peak of its popularity. CBS scheduled rerun episodes in prime time for another two years, also a rarity, and ABC reran them for another season after that. From November 1962 until February 1967, reruns were also seen on ABC daytime.

FATHER MURPHY
Drama
FIRST TELECAST: *November 3, 1981*
LAST TELECAST: *June 17, 1984*
BROADCAST HISTORY:
Nov 1981–Mar 1982, NBC Tue 8:00–9:00
Mar 1982–Jul 1982, NBC Sun 7:00–8:00
Jul 1982–Dec 1982, NBC Tue 8:00–9:00
Apr 1984–Jun 1984, NBC Sun 7:00–8:00
CAST:
John Michael Murphy .... Merlin Olsen
Moses Gage .... Moses Gunn
Mae Woodward Murphy .. Katherine Cannon
Will Adams .... Timothy Gibbs
Lizette Winkler .... Lisa Trusel
Ephram Winkler .... Scott Mellini
Eli (1982) .... Chez Lister
Howard Rodman .... Charles Tyner
Miss Tuttle .... Ivy Bethune
Father Joe Parker .... Richard Bergman
Dr. Thompson .... Warren Munson
Sheriff .... Charles Cooper
CREATOR/PRODUCER:
Michael Landon

Michael Landon created and produced this wholesome series about love and caring on the American frontier featuring Merlin Olsen, his beefy co-star from *Little House on the Prairie*. Set in the Dakota Territory town of Jackson during the 1870s, the story began when drifter John Murphy sought to rally the local prospectors against the depredations of the town boss. The boss and his henchmen retaliated by blowing up the miners' camp, thereby creating a new career for Murphy—establishing and running an orphanage for two dozen now-parentless children. To make the orphanage appear legitimate, the bearded frontiersman had to pose as a priest, hence he became "Father" Murphy.

With Murphy at the Gold Hill School were a young teacher named Mae and a friendly dog named Mine. Danger was constantly at their doorstep. While Murphy and Mae attempted to teach and care for the orphans, they were constantly threatened by two pompous and officious representatives of the Dakota Territory Authority, Mr. Rodman and Miss Tuttle, who sought to have the children sent to the territorial workhouse at Claymore. In the spring of 1982, when Murphy's deception was exposed, he and Mae got married, adopted all the orphans, and continued to struggle to hold the "family" together. Black miner Moses Gage was Murphy's good friend, and Will, Lizette, and Ephram were the most prominently seen of the 25 children under Murphy's care. Eli, an orphaned young black boy, became part of the household at the start of *Father Murphy's* second season. Episodes of *Father Murphy* were rerun in 1984.

FATHER OF THE BRIDE
Situation Comedy
FIRST TELECAST: *September 29, 1961*
LAST TELECAST: *September 14, 1962*
BROADCAST HISTORY:
Sep 1961–Sep 1962, CBS Fri 9:30–10:00
CAST:
Stanley Banks .... Leon Ames
Ellie Banks .... Ruth Warrick
Kay Banks Dunston .... Myrna Fahey
Tommy Banks .... Rickie Sorensen
Buckley Dunston .... Burt Metcalfe
Herbert Dunston .... Ransom Sherman
Doris Dunston .... Lurene Tuttle
Delilah .... Ruby Dandridge

The adjustments parents must make when their children grow up and seek a life of their own were the subject of this comedy. Attorney Stanley Banks was not quite ready to accept his daughter Kay's decision when she announced that she was engaged to Buckley Dunston. Despite the enthusiasm of his wife, Ellie, his son, Tommy, his maid, Delilah, and almost everyone else, Stanley was not happy about it at all. Episodes on the series involved Stanley's tribulations at getting used to his prospective son-in-law and the son-in-law's parents, the planning and carrying out of the wedding, and learning to live without Kay around.

FATHERS AND SONS
Situation Comedy
FIRST TELECAST: *April 6, 1986*
LAST TELECAST: *May 4, 1986*
BROADCAST HISTORY:
Apr 1986–May 1986, NBC Sun 7:30–8:00
CAST:
Buddy Landau .... Merlin Olsen
Lanny Landau .... Jason Late
Ellen Landau .... Kelly Sanders
Sean Flynn .... Andre Gower
Matty Bolen .... Ian Fried
Dr. Richard Bolen .... Nicholas Guest
Brandon Russo .... Hakeem

The focus of this limited-run series was on the relationships of a group of adolescent boys with each other and with Buddy Landau, one of the boys' fathers. Buddy, a former athlete, loved sports and served as the coach of various little league teams. The boys included Buddy's chubby son Lanny, whose involvement in sports seemed to be more a function of his father's enthusiasm than his own; Sean, the budding ladies' man of the group; Matt, the resident intellectual whose father was unable to spend as much time with his son as he would have liked; and Brandon, a diminutive ball of fire who almost made up in energy and determination what he lacked in size.

FAVORITE STORY
Dramatic Anthology
BROADCAST HISTORY:
Syndicated only
30 minutes
Produced: 1952–1954 (78 episodes)
Released: January 1953
HOST/OCCASIONAL STAR:
Adolphe Menjou

Debonair Adolphe Menjou hosted and sometimes starred in this popular syndicated anthology series. Stories were adapted from the classics and ranged from farce to tragedy, sometimes treading a delicate line between the two. The scripts and casting were generally first-rate. Raymond Burr played a land-hungry Russian peasant in the first episode, a little morality play adapted from Tolstoy and called "How Much Land Does a Man Need?"

Adapted from the *Favorite Story* radio series of 1946–1949, hosted by Ronald Colman. Menjou presided over another, somewhat different TV anthology series in the late 1950s—see *Target*.

FAY
Situation Comedy
FIRST TELECAST: *September 4, 1975*
LAST TELECAST: *June 2, 1976*
BROADCAST HISTORY:
Sep 1975–Oct 1975, NBC Thu 8:30–9:00
May 1976–Jun 1976, NBC Wed 9:30–10:00
CAST:
Fay Stewart .... Lee Grant
Lillian .... Audra Lindley
Jack Stewart...................... Joe Silver
Linda Stewart Baines ..... Margaret Willock
Dr. Elliott Baines .... Stewart Moss
Danny Messina .... Bill Gerber
Letty Gilmore................ Lillian Lehman
Al Cassidy .... Norman Alden

The exploits of an attractive, fortyish divorcée who decides to become a swinging single were the subject of this short-lived and somewhat risqué comedy. After divorcing Jack, her philandering husband of 25 years, Fay first got herself a job as secretary to two off-the-wall attorneys, Danny Messina and Al Cassidy. She then moved into an apartment of her own and started dating. Onlookers to Fay's new life-style were Jack, who kept trying to get her back again, daughter Linda and son-in-law Elliott, who were appalled, and Fay's unhappily married friend Lillian, who lived vicariously through Fay's affairs.

FAYE EMERSON SHOW, THE
Interview
FIRST TELECAST: *March 13, 1950*
LAST TELECAST: *December 23, 1950*
BROADCAST HISTORY:
Mar 1950–Apr 1950, CBS Mon 11:00–11:15

May 1950–Jul 1950, CBS Sun various 15-minute spots
Apr 1950–May 1950, NBC Sat 10:30–10:45
Jun 1950–Aug 1950, NBC Wed 8:00–8:15
Sep 1950–Dec 1950, CBS Tue/Thu/Sat 7:45–8:00
HOSTESS:
Faye Emerson

Faye Emerson seemed to be everywhere on early television. In addition to numerous guest appearances on fashion, quiz, and dramatic shows, she hosted her own 15-minute "chat" on a variety of nights in 1950, sometimes appearing on two networks simultaneously. The format of *The Faye Emerson Show* was informal and gossipy, with Miss Emerson discussing fashions, the theater, and current celebrities and welcoming a guest from some area of show business. Perhaps her most widely publicized contribution to the new medium, however, were the gowns she wore—her trademark plunging neckline was the subject of considerable controversy during television's formative years.

From June to August 1950 Miss Emerson's NBC series was known as *Fifteen with Faye*. She also hosted several similarly formatted local programs in New York, prior to and following her network run.

FAYE EMERSON'S WONDERFUL TOWN
Variety
FIRST TELECAST: *June 16, 1951*
LAST TELECAST: *April 12, 1952*
BROADCAST HISTORY:
Jun 1951–Apr 1952, CBS Sat 9:00–9:30
HOSTESS:
Faye Emerson

Each week Faye Emerson spotlighted a different city in America, using musical, dramatic, and narrative elements to convey the flavor of the city, both past and present. Guest stars for each telecast either were born in the city or had some strong association with it. In time, the scope of the show expanded to include interesting foreign cities, such as Paris and Mexico City.

FEAR AND FANCY
see *ABC Dramatic Shorts—1952–1953*

FEARLESS FOSDICK
Children's
FIRST TELECAST: *July 13, 1952*
LAST TELECAST: *September 28, 1952*
BROADCAST HISTORY:
Jul 1952–Sep 1952, NBC Sun 6:30–7:00
PUPPETS:
The Mary Chase Marionettes

Straight from Al Capp's comic strip "Li'l Abner" came this filmed summer series using puppets and animation. Fosdick—a parody of Dick Tracy—was Li'l Abner's favorite detective and, according

259

to him, the world's greatest. The lantern-jawed Fosdick was abused by his boss on the police force and made barely enough money to live on, but he valiantly fought on against crime and evil. *Fearless Fosdick* premiered on June 15, 1952, on Sunday afternoon and later moved into an evening slot.

FEATHER AND FATHER GANG, THE
Crime Drama
FIRST TELECAST: *March 7, 1977*
LAST TELECAST: *August 6, 1977*
BROADCAST HISTORY:
  Mar 1977–Apr 1977, ABC Mon 10:00–11:00
  May 1977–Aug 1977, ABC Sat 10:00–11:00
CAST:
  Toni "Feather" Danton . . . . . . Stefanie Powers
  Harry Danton. . . . . Harold Gould
  Enzo . . . . Frank Delfino
  Margo. . . . . Joan Shawlee
  Michael . . . . Monte Landis
  Lou . . . . Lewis Charles

"Feather" was a beautiful young attorney, her father a suave, shrewd ex-con man. Together with their little band of grafters and bunco artists they comprised a crack investigative team, determined to "cheat the cheaters," the swindlers and murderers who were the targets of their investigations. Lots of disguises and elaborate ruses were used.

Harold Gould, the "father" in this show, was a rarity in show business—a Ph.D. and a former full professor of drama at UCLA who decided to practice what he taught.

FEATURE PLAYHOUSE
see *Movies—Prior to 1961*

FEATURE THEATRE
see *Movies—Prior to 1961*

FEDERAL MEN
syndicated title for *Treasury Men in Action*

FELONY SQUAD
Police Drama
FIRST TELECAST: *September 12, 1966*
LAST TELECAST: *January 31, 1969*
BROADCAST HISTORY:
  Sep 1966–Sep 1968, ABC Mon 9:00–9:30
  Sep 1968–Jan 1969, ABC Fri 8:30–9:00
CAST:
  Det. Sgt. Sam Stone . . . . Howard Duff
  Det. Jim Briggs. . . . . Dennis Cole
  Desk Sgt. Dan Briggs . . . . Ben Alexander
  Capt. Nye . . . . Frank Maxwell
  Capt. Franks (1967–1968) . . . . . Barney Phillips
  Det. Cliff Sims (1968–1969) . . . . . Robert DoQui
THEME:
  "Felony Squad Theme," by Pete Rugulo

This police action drama was set in a large city in the West. The principals were 20-year veteran Sam Stone, his young partner Jim Briggs, and Briggs' father, Desk Sgt. Dan Briggs, a kind of paunchy housemother to the younger cops in the station house. Capt. Nye was their commanding officer during the first and last seasons, temporarily replaced by Capt. Franks in 1967–1968. The series was filmed on location in the Los Angeles area.

FERNWOOD 2-NIGHT
Satire
BROADCAST HISTORY:
  Syndicated only
  30 minutes
  Produced: *1977–1978* (125 episodes)
  Released: *July 1977*
CAST:
  Barth Gimble . . . . Martin Mull
  Jerry Hubbard . . . . Fred Willard
  Happy Kyne . . . . Frank DeVol
FREQUENT GUESTS:
  Garth Gimble, Sr. . . . . Robert B. Williams
  Verne Taylor . . . . Verne Rowe
  Virgil Sims . . . . Jim Varney
  Aunt Edity . . . . Irma Seigel
  Linda Barry . . . . Barrie Youngfellow
  Tony Roletti . . . . Bill Kirchenbauer
CREATED BY:
  Norman Lear

Introduced as the summer replacement for *Mary Hartman, Mary Hartman*, this was one of the most talked-about programs of 1977. In it, denizens of Fernwood, Ohio (Mary's home town), mounted a talk show on local station WZAZ-TV, Channel 6, down on Acacia Street. It did look like an ordinary talk show, with desk and couch, slick, smiling host and his eager sidekick, and guests like a piano player, an insufferable child dancer, and a couple who had lost their son to a religious cult. But the pianist was rolled out in an iron lung, and proceeded to play a Mozart sonata upside down and backward while the Shirley Temple look-alike tap-danced alongside; the son, whom the parents complained had been programmed to keep "falling on his knees and mumbling in a foreign tongue," and who always dressed in black and kept "leading cockamamie parades down church aisles," turned out to be a Catholic priest.

Fernwood 2-Night was a wild, and some said patently offensive, parody on TV talk shows. The host, Barth Gimble, was natty and egotistical, his sidekick, Jerry Hubbard, a fatuous idiot ("Any comparison to Johnny Carson and Ed McMahon is, of course, purely intentional," smirked *Time* magazine). Martin Mull had previously appeared on *Mary Hartman, Mary Hartman* as Garth Gimble, a wife beater who eventually impaled himself on an aluminum Christmas tree in the closet. Barth was presented here as his twin brother, and there were occasional visits by their father, Garth, Sr. The guests were parodies of every mind-numbing act that ever paraded across the Carson/Douglas/Griffin shows, from Vietnamese refugee Mian Co

260

Tiam, who had written a patriotic book titled *Yankee Doodle Gook,* to a housewife who was campaigning to have her late Aunt Dora made a saint because she made "remarkable raisin bread," to a Jewish man named Morton Rose who had been caught speeding through all-WASP Fernwood. He was brought on because Barth was sure many of the local viewers had never seen "a person of the Jewish persuasion." "What tribe are you from?" asked Hubbard. "I'm originally from Toledo," responded the guest eagerly. Then they opened the phone lines for a "Talk-to-a-Jew" call-in segment, in which one woman wanted to know, "When is Barbra Streisand's next movie coming out?"

The writers spared no one. "We will offend the sensitivities of a number of Americans, for which we apologize out front," admitted producer Alan Thicke. "But we're not being discriminating in our satire," he added cheerfully, "we're offending everybody, regardless of race, creed, color, or income level." A few jokes, though very few, were off limits. A line about recent suicide Freddie Prinze was deleted; as was a skit about two brothers fighting over whether to pull the plug on their comatose mother. ("Now," interjected Gimble, "is it Mom or the money you want?")

Other guests included Linda Barry, owner of the Fernwood Nudist Colony, mechanic Virgil Sims, Barth's Aunt Edity, a couple discussing the La Fromage method of childbirth, the founder of the Church of the Divine Lemonade, and the Salvation Army Singers performing "Da Do Ron Ron." Happy Kyne led the ragged, four-piece studio band, the Mirth Makers, when not touting his franchised dental service.

Although this bizarre program was only marginally successful in its summer 1977 run, Norman Lear brought it back in April 1978 as *America 2-Night.* Barth and Jerry had moved to Alta Coma, California, "the unfinished furniture capital of the world," and hoped to boost the show with appearances by major Hollywood stars. (Many did appear, playing parodies of themselves, including Charlton Heston, Robin Williams, George Gobel, Elke Sommer, and Gary Burghoff.) The new series got off to a grand start with a week-long buildup for "Electrocution Night '78," in which a convict was to be executed on stage while his wife lined up book, movie, and T-shirt deals. Viewers had a chance to participate by entering an "I would like to throw the switch because . . ." contest.

FESTIVAL OF STARS
Dramatic Anthology
FIRST TELECAST: *June 30, 1956*
LAST TELECAST: *September 17, 1957*
BROADCAST HISTORY:
  Jun 1956–Sep 1956, NBC Sat 9:30–10:00
  Jul 1957–Sep 1957, NBC Tue 8:00–8:30
HOST:
  Jim Ameche (1957)

The 1956 edition of this summer series of dramas was made up of reruns of episodes of *Ford*

Theatre. When it returned the following summer, *Festival of Stars* consisted of reruns of episodes from *The Loretta Young Show* in which Miss Young had not appeared. Jim Ameche served as host of the latter series.

FIBBER MCGEE AND MOLLY
Situation Comedy
FIRST TELECAST: *September 15, 1959*
LAST TELECAST: *January 19, 1960*
BROADCAST HISTORY:
  Sep 1959–Jan 1960, NBC Tue 8:30–9:00
CAST:
  Fibber McGee .... Bob Sweeney
  Molly McGee .... Cathy Lewis
  Doc Gamble .... Addison Richards
  Mayor La Trivia .... Harold Peary
  Teeny .... Barbara Beaird
  Hazel Norris .... Elisabeth Fraser
  Roy Norris .... Paul Smith
  Fred Nitney .... Jack Kirkwood

Fibber McGee and Molly was one of the most popular radio shows of all time, running from 1935 until 1957. In the fall of 1959 it came to television, but with much less success. The McGees were the residents of 79 Wistful Vista and, as on radio, had to cope with friends and neighbors who made life rather hilarious. Fibber's tendency to overstate— some people called it fibbing—constantly got him into trouble. Fortunately, Molly's common sense and talents as a peacemaker prevented most situations from getting out of hand. Symptomatic of the problems involved in bringing *Fibber McGee and Molly* to television was McGee's famous overcrowded hall closet, which always unleashed its contents in a crash whenever it was opened. Somehow this was not as funny seen on television as it had been when only heard on radio.

Most of the actors in the TV version had not been associated with the show on radio, but one did have an interesting connection with the earlier version. Harold Peary had created the role of Throckmorton P. Gildersleeve on *Fibber McGee and Molly* in 1939, later moving it to a series of his own as *The Great Gildersleeve.* When *Fibber McGee* came to TV, he returned as Mayor La Trivia.

FIFTEEN WITH FAYE
  see *Faye Emerson Show, The*

FIFTY-FOURTH STREET REVUE, THE
Variety
FIRST TELECAST: *May 5, 1949*
LAST TELECAST: *March 25, 1950*
BROADCAST HISTORY:
  May 1949–Sep 1949, CBS Thu 8:00–9:00
  Sep 1949–Jan 1950, CBS Fri 9:00–10:00
  Jan 1950–Mar 1950, CBS Sat 8:00–9:00
HOST:
  Jack Sterling (1949)
  Al Bernie (1949)

Billy Vine (1949–1950)
Joey Faye (1950)
REGULARS:
Russell Arms
Marilyn Day
Carl Reiner (1949)
Pat Bright (1949)
Cliff "Ukulele Ike" Edwards (1949)
Wynn Murray (1949)
Mort Marshall
Joe Silver
Joan Diener
Fosse and Niles
Virginia Gorski
Harry Sosnik Orchestra

This live musical and comedy revue derived its name from the street address of the New York studio in which it was produced. Its regular cast changed constantly, depending on what other jobs its members could find that were more substantial than employment in early television. Jack Sterling was the original host, soon replaced by Al Bernie. Bernie lasted until December 1949, to be replaced by Billy Vine, who lasted only two months, and finally by Joey Faye. Carl Reiner, Pat Bright, Cliff Edwards, and Marilyn Day were also early departures, with Miss Day returning for a second stint during Joey Faye's tenure as host.

The male half of the young dance team of Fosse and Niles was Bob Fosse, who would become a very successful choreographer and director of Broadway musicals and films in the 1960s and 1970s.

FIGHT BEAT
Sports Commentary
FIRST TELECAST: *April 4, 1958*
LAST TELECAST: *December 26, 1958*
BROADCAST HISTORY:
Apr 1958–Dec 1958, NBC Fri 10:45–11:00
HOST:
Bud Palmer

Bud Palmer interviewed the winning fighters and other boxing celebrities in this short sports commentary program designed to fill the time remaining between the conclusion of the featured bout on *Cavalcade of Sports* and the 11 o'clock news. The title of the program was originally *Post Fight Beat*, but this was shortened to *Fight Beat* on May 23.

FIGHT OF THE WEEK, THE
see *Boxing*

FIGHT TALK
Sports Commentary
FIRST TELECAST: *January 24, 1953*
LAST TELECAST: *January 15, 1955*
BROADCAST HISTORY:
Jan 1953–Jan 1955, ABC Sat 9:45–10:00

COMMENTATORS:
Don Dunphy
Red Smith (1953–1954)
Bob Cook (1954–1955)

This show followed ABC's *Saturday Night Fights* and provided its two commentators with an opportunity to analyze the bout that had just been seen and make predictions and observations about other major fights that were coming up in the near future. Don Dunphy was with the show throughout its run, while Red Smith left and was replaced by Bob Cook.

FILM FAIR
see *Movies—Prior to 1961*

FILM FESTIVAL
see *ABC Dramatic Shorts—1952–1953*

FILM SHORTS
see *Movies—Prior to 1961*

FILM THEATRE OF THE AIR
see *Movies—Prior to 1961*

FILTHY RICH
Situation Comedy
FIRST TELECAST: *August 9, 1982*
LAST TELECAST: *June 15, 1983*
BROADCAST HISTORY:
Aug 1982, CBS Mon 9:30–10:00
Oct 1982–Nov 1982, CBS Mon 9:30–10:00
Jan 1983–Feb 1983, CBS Mon 8:30–9:00
Jun 1983, CBS Wed 8:30–9:00
CAST:
Big Guy Beck (1982) . . . . Slim Pickens
Big Guy Beck . . . . Forrest Tucker
Kathleen Beck . . . . Delta Burke
Carlotta Beck . . . . Dixie Carter
Stanley Beck . . . . Charles Frank
Wild Bill Weschester . . . . Jerry Hardin
Marshall Beck . . . . Michael Lombard
Bootsie Weschester . . . . Ann Wedgeworth
Winona "Mother B" Beck . . . . Nedra Volz
George Wilhoit (pilot only) . . . . . David Healy
George Wilhoit . . . . Vernon Weddle

Filthy Rich was an unabashed sendup of the *Dallas/Dynasty/Falcon Crest* school of prime-time soap opera about the machinations of the unscrupulous rich. The founder of the family fortune, Tennessee land baron Big Guy Beck, was dead, but he still controlled the lives of his heirs. Before dying, and being cryogenically frozen, he had produced a living will on videotape, and each week another section of it was played for the family. The terms of the will were hardest on socially prominent elder son Marshall and his equally status-conscious wife Carlotta. They were forced to welcome Big Guy's illegitimate son, Wild Bill Weschester, and Bill's flaky wife, Bootsie, into the family mansion, Toad Hall. For the simple Weschesters this was paradise, but for the Becks it was humiliating. Big Guy's greedy, social-climbing, sexy young widow, Kathleen, was looking for a new meal ticket, while his first wife, elderly Mother B, belied her age by repeatedly escaping from the nursing home where she was living. Only Big Guy's younger son, Stanley, who was independently wealthy, seemed to be normal. He was considerate and charming, and spent much of his time foiling the devious plans of Marshall and Carlotta to rid themselves of both the Weschesters and the constraints of the will. George Wilhoit was the attorney who administered Big Guy's taped will.

When this limited-run series returned to the air in October 1982 Forrest Tucker was seen as Big Guy in the tapes, since actor Slim Pickens had died after the first few episodes had been produced.

FINDER OF LOST LOVES

Detective Drama
FIRST TELECAST: *September 22, 1984*
LAST TELECAST: *August 24, 1985*
BROADCAST HISTORY:
  Sep 1984–Aug 1985, ABC Sat 10:00–11:00
CAST:
  Cary Maxwell .... Tony Franciosa
  Daisy Lloyd .... Deborah Adair
  Rita Hargrove .... Anne Jeffreys
  Brian Fletcher .... Richard Kantor
  Lyman Whittaker (1985) . Larry Flash Jenkins

Mix a little bit of *Love Boat* with a touch of *Fantasy Island*, wrap the entire package as a detective series, and you have *Finder of Lost Loves*. Cary Maxwell was a wealthy widower who, after the untimely death of his beloved wife Kate, had decided to devote the remainder of his working life reuniting star-crossed lovers and tracking down old flames. With the help of his beautiful assistant, Daisy (Kate's sister), his young trainee, Brian, and his efficient office manager, Rita, Cary sought to bring romance back into the lives of others. In this high-tech contemporary world it was not surprising that his most valued asset was Oscar, the computer he used to tie pieces of information together and locate the missing people his clients sought. Each episode contained two or three separate stories, and most resolved themselves into appropriately satisfying happy endings, the trademark of producer Aaron Spelling, who was also responsible for the aforementioned *Love Boat* and *Fantasy Island*.

FIREBALL FUN-FOR-ALL

Comedy Variety
FIRST TELECAST: *June 28, 1949*
LAST TELECAST: *October 27, 1949*
BROADCAST HISTORY:
  Jun 1949–Aug 1949, NBC Tue 8:00–9:00
  Sep 1949–Oct 1949, NBC Thu 9:00–10:00

REGULARS:
  Ole Olsen and Chick Johnson
  Bill Hayes
  Marty May
  June Johnson
  J. C. Olsen
  The Buick Belles
  Al Goodman Orchestra (Jun–Jul)
  Charles Sanford Orchestra (Jul–Oct)

This comedy free-for-all, hosted by old-time vaudevillians Olsen and Johnson, was based on their Broadway hit *Hellzapoppin'*. Gimmick props, midgets running frantically across the stage, leggy showgirls, seltzer water, and custard pies were all the stock-in-trade of this noisy and unpredictable revue, which generally resembled organized mayhem. At the beginning many of the gags took place in the studio audience, but when the show returned after a brief summer hiatus the action tended to be more confined to the stage.

The program was directed and staged by Ezra Stone, one of the stars of the *Henry Aldrich* series. June Johnson and J. C. Olsen were the daughter and son, respectively, of the show's hosts.

FIREHOUSE

Adventure
FIRST TELECAST: *January 17, 1974*
LAST TELECAST: *August 1, 1974*
BROADCAST HISTORY:
  Jan 1974–Aug 1974, ABC Thu 8:30–9:00
CAST:
  Capt. Spike Ryerson .... James Drury
  Hank Myers .... Richard Jaeckel
  Sonny Caputo .... Michael Delano
  Billy Dalzell .... Brad David
  Cal Dakin .... Bill Overton
  Scotty Smith..................... Scott Smith

In 1972 a crudely written but true-to-life book titled *Report from Engine Co. 82*, whose author was a real-life fireman, shot to the top of the bestseller list. About a year and a half later, a crudely produced but hopefully true-to-life television series called *Firehouse* premiered on the ABC network. Was it coincidence? Where do you suppose TV producers find their inspirations?

James Drury portrayed the father figure to the young smoke-eaters of Engine Co. 23 in this action drama. They encountered various disasters and performed various rescues each week; one of the more interesting of these was a man in traction whose house was about to slide off a hill. The firemen couldn't get into his room to maneuver him out without setting off the tilting house. How did they get him out? Sorry, series canceled.

FIRESIDE ARENA THEATRE

Dramatic Anthology
FIRST TELECAST: *July 3, 1951*
LAST TELECAST: *August 21, 1951*

BROADCAST HISTORY:
Jul 1951–Aug 1951, NBC Tue 9:00–9:30
PRODUCER/DIRECTOR:
Albert McCleery

This summer replacement for *Fireside Theater* was quite a different program, presenting eight weeks of live drama in a theater-in-the-round setting. A minimum of scenery and props was used, as the camera focused closely on the actors and the story.

FIRESIDE THEATRE
Dramatic Anthology
FIRST TELECAST: *April 5, 1949*
LAST TELECAST: *September 8, 1963*
BROADCAST HISTORY:
Apr 1949–Jun 1957, NBC Tue 9:00–9:30 (OS)
Sep 1957–May 1958, NBC Thu 10:30–11:00
Jun 1963–Sep 1963, ABC Sun 8:00–8:30
HOST:
Frank Wisbar (1952–1953)
Gene Raymond (1953–1955)
Jane Wyman (1955–1958)

Fireside Theatre was one of the earliest filmed dramatic shows produced especially for television. However, for its first three months this series was a showcase of new program ideas, some live and some on film, which were being tried out for possible inclusion on the network schedule. These included dramas, comedies, and musical revenues. The very first episode was a situation comedy, "Friend of the Family," starring Virginia Gilmore, Yul Brynner, and Peter Barry. One of the musical revues was Leonard Sillman's "New Faces." Win Elliot was the original announcer for the show, but he left after eight telecasts, after which there was no regular announcer or host for the next few years.

In the fall of 1949 *Fireside Theatre* switched to filmed stories, mostly dramas, featuring a wide range of actors and actresses (generally not big names). According to *TV Guide* these were "quickie" films, each one ground out in two or three days at the Hal Roach studios in Hollywood. Most of them were produced by Frank Wisbar. During the 1949–1950 season the majority of these little dramas were 15 minutes long (there were two per week), but beginning in the fall of 1950 and for the rest of the series each telecast was a self-contained 30-minute presentation.

In the fall of 1952 producer Frank Wisbar began appearing at the start of each week's telecast, in an effort to give the series greater continuity. From 1953–1955 actor Gene Raymond was the host, in addition to appearing in many of the dramas. For the 1954–1955 season an effort was also made to develop a regular repertory company of actors and actresses, including William Bendix, George Brent, and Dorothy Malone.

The hostess who is most identified with the show in viewers' minds—Jane Wyman—made her first appearance in 1955. The movie actress also starred in many of the episodes during her association with the show. The program was renamed in her honor (eventually it became simply *The Jane Wyman Show*) and special theme music was written for her. Well-known actors and actresses were engaged for the weeks when Miss Wyman did not star, among them Keenan Wynn, Peter Lawford, Dan Duryea, Ozzie Nelson, John Ireland, Gene Lockhart, Imogene Coca, Gene Barry, Joseph Cotten, and Vincent Price, plus many lesser-known Hollywood standbys. The program continued until the spring of 1958, when it was finally retired—to begin a very long run in syndication.

Reruns were shown on NBC as a summer replacement in 1954 and on the ABC network during the summer of 1963 (as *Jane Wyman Presents*).

Fireside Theatre, with and without Miss Wyman, was one of the most durable dramatic anthologies of the 1950s. Though generally not rising to the star-studded heights of *Studio One* or *Robert Montgomery Presents*, it did produce hundreds of fine dramas and also proved the practicality and value of a filmed series for the TV medium.

FIRST CAMERA
see *Monitor*

FIRST DATE
see *Continental, The*

FIRST NIGHTER
see *Movies—Prior to 1961*

FIRST PERSON
see *Gulf Playhouse: 1st Person*

FIRST TUESDAY
News Magazine
FIRST TELECAST: *January 7, 1969*
LAST TELECAST: *August 8, 1973*
BROADCAST HISTORY:
Jan 1969–Sep 1971, NBC Tue 9:00–11:00
Oct 1971–Jul 1972, NBC Fri 9:00–11:00
Sep 1972–Aug 1973, NBC Tue 10:00–11:00
ANCHORMAN:
Sander Vanocur (1969–1970)
Garrick Utley (1971–1972)

First Tuesday premiered four months after CBS' *60 Minutes*, but its roots went back to the early 1960s when *David Brinkley's Journal* provided viewers with a magazine/documentary format. Unlike all of the other magazine series, *First Tuesday* ran for a full two hours. With that much time to fill, the number of stories covered in each telecast often ran from six to eight. Among the subjects treated in depth were chemical-biological warfare, student revolts, occultism, the rise in beef prices, and the miracle of heart transplants. *First Tuesday* also had its lighter side, covering such topics as baton twirling, bathrooms in America, the romantic mystique surrounding stewardesses, and honeymoon trips to Guam.

Sander Vanocur was the original anchorman/reporter on *First Tuesday* which, as the title indicates, aired in place of the NBC Tuesday movie once a month. When Vanocur left, he was replaced by Garrick Utley, who stayed with the series when it moved to the fourth Friday of every month and was retitled *Chronolog.* After a season on Fridays, it returned to its original day and title, but was trimmed to an hour in length. For its last season on the air, *First Tuesday* had no regular anchorman, although reporters Tom Pettit and Patrick Trese made frequent appearances. NBC did not give up on the news-magazine concept, trying in later years with *Weekend, Prime Time Sunday,* and, returning to the source, with *NBC Magazine With David Brinkley.*

FISH

Situation Comedy
FIRST TELECAST: *February 5, 1977*
LAST TELECAST: *June 8, 1978*
BROADCAST HISTORY:
Feb 1977–May 1977, ABC Sat 8:30–9:00
Jun 1977–Aug 1977, ABC Thu 9:30–10:00
Aug 1977–Nov 1977, ABC Sat 8:00–8:30
Jan 1978–Apr 1978, ABC Thu 8:30–9:00
May 1978–Jun 1978, ABC Thu 9:30–10:00
CAST:
Det. Phil Fish . . . . Abe Vigoda
Bernice Fish . . . . Florence Stanley
Mike . . . . Lenny Bari
Loomis . . . . Todd Bridges
Victor Kreutzer . . . . John Cassisi
Jilly Papalardo . . . . Denise Miller
Diane Pulaski . . . . Sarah Natoli
Charlie Harrison . . . . Barry Gordon

Detective Fish, the dilapidated cop in the hit series *Barney Miller,* got his own show in 1977. It was unusual in that he not only remained in character, but for several months continued to appear in *Barney Miller* as well. *Fish* simply presented the domestic side of his life.

Fish and his wife Bernice had decided to move out of their New York apartment and into a run-down house, in order to become foster parents to five P.I.N.S.—the social workers' term for "Persons in Need of Supervision." The term was an understatement, for the five racially mixed street kids were constantly causing problems. Loomis was the cut-up of the lot, the preteen hipster who befriended the dead cat in Fish's basement. Mike was the oldest, charming but streetwise. Victor was the blustery tough guy, Jilly the angelic con artist, and Diane the young TV addict. Psychologist Charlie Harrison (played by one-time child star Barry Gordon) tended to be too impractical to help very much, leaving huffing, puffing Fish and chattering Bernice to quell each uproar and reestablish normalcy.

FISHING AND HUNTING CLUB

Sports
FIRST TELECAST: *September 30, 1949*
LAST TELECAST: *March 31, 1950*
BROADCAST HISTORY:
Sep 1949–Mar 1950, DUM Fri 9:00–9:30
HOST:
Bill Slater

This sports interview and demonstration program featured Bill Slater and experts from various fields. The title was changed on January 20, 1950, to *Sports for All.*

FITZ AND BONES

Comedy/Drama
FIRST TELECAST: *October 24, 1981*
LAST TELECAST: *November 14, 1981*
BROADCAST HISTORY:
Oct 1981–Nov 1981, NBC Sat 10:00–11:00
CAST:
Ryan Fitzpatrick . . . . Dick Smothers
Bones Howard . . . . Tom Smothers
Terri Seymour . . . . Diana Muldaur
Robert Whitmore . . . . Mike Kellin
Lt. Rosie Cochran . . . . Lynette Mettey
Lawrence Brody . . . . Roger C. Carmel

Ryan Fitzpatrick and Bones Howard were an oddly matched pair. Ryan was an aggressive investigative reporter for Newsline 3, on a San Francisco television station, and Bones was his somewhat inept cameraman. Together they pursued a wide range of leads throughout the city, from human-interest vignettes about little kids to deadly serious stories of terrorism, racism, and crime. Ryan's style was unorthodox and he would stop at nothing to get a scoop on his rival, Lawrence Brody, who worked for a competing station. He also had to contend with his director at the station, Robert Whitmore, and the no-nonsense news editor, Terri, who often thought he was off on another wild goose chase. One connection that often helped was Fitz's good relationship with his ex-wife, Rosie, whose position on the police force enabled her to feed him leads.

FITZPATRICKS, THE

Drama
FIRST TELECAST: *September 5, 1977*
LAST TELECAST: *January 10, 1978*
BROADCAST HISTORY:
Sep 1977, CBS Mon 9:00–10:00
Sep 1977–Jan 1978, CBS Tue 8:00–9:00
CAST:
Mike Fitzpatrick . . . . Bert Kramer
Maggie Fitzpatrick . . . . Mariclare Costello
Sean Fitzpatrick . . . . Clark Brandon
Jack Fitzpatrick . . . . . James Vincent McNichol
Maureen (Mo) Fitzpatrick . . . . Michele Tobin
Max Fitzpatrick . . . . Sean Marshall
R.J. . . . . Derek Wells
Kerry Gerardi . . . . Helen Hunt

Flint, Michigan, was the setting for this warm family drama about a middle-class Catholic family trying to make ends meet. The father, Mike Fitzpatrick, was a steelworker who put in lots of overtime, and mother Maggie worked part-time at a diner to help supplement the family income. The rest of the family consisted of four children—Sean (16), Jack (15), Mo (14), and Max (10)—and a mangy dog named Detroit. Seen regularly were Max's best friend R.J. and Kerry, the cute girl next door whose flirting with both of the older Fitzpatrick boys intensified their sibling rivalry. The stories were often little lessons in morality and growing up, making this series something like a modern-day *Waltons*. Previewed by CBS on a Monday night early in September, *The Fitzpatricks* moved into its regular Tuesday time slot two weeks later.

FIVE FINGERS
Spy Drama
FIRST TELECAST: *October 3, 1959*
LAST TELECAST: *January 9, 1960*
BROADCAST HISTORY:
  Oct 1959–Jan 1960, NBC Sat 9:30–10:30
CAST:
  Victor Sebastian . . . . David Hedison
  Simone Genet . . . . Luciana Paluzzi
  Robertson . . . . Paul Burke

Victor Sebastian was an American counterspy posing as a Communist agent in Europe. His code name was "Five Fingers," and his mission, to feed information on Communist activities to the United States government. Sebastian's public cover was that of a theatrical booking agent who placed musical talent in clubs and cafés all over the Continent. In this capacity he traveled with a beautiful young fashion model, Simone Genet, who aspired to become a singer. Romance blossomed between them, which complicated their relationship since she was not aware of his espionage activities. The only person who did know was Robertson, Sebastian's American contact. Victor and Simone's relationship provided both humorous and romantic counterpoint to the main theme of international intrigue.

The series was based, rather loosely, on a successful 1952 film of the same name directed by Joseph L. Mankiewiez and starring James Mason and Danielle Darrieux.

FIVE STAR JUBILEE
Musical Variety
FIRST TELECAST: *March 17, 1961*
LAST TELECAST: *September 22, 1961*
BROADCAST HISTORY:
  Mar 1961–Apr 1961, NBC Fri 8:00–8:30
  May 1961–Sep 1961, NBC Fri 8:30–9:00
STARS:
  Snooky Lanson
  Tex Ritter
  Jimmy Wakely

Carl Smith
Rex Allen
REGULARS:
The Promenaders
The Wagon Wheelers
The Jubilaires
The Tall Timber Trio
Slim Wilson and His Jubilee Band

The five stars of this country music variety show appeared separately, on a rotating basis. The program featured square dancing as well as guest stars and originated from Springfield, Missouri. Although a network offering, *Five Star Jubilee* was never telecast in New York because of its primarily rural appeal.

FLAMINGO ROAD
Drama
FIRST TELECAST: *January 6, 1981*
LAST TELECAST: *July 13, 1982*
BROADCAST HISTORY:
  Jan 1981–Mar 1981, NBC Tue 10:00–11:00
  Jun 1981–Aug 1981, NBC Mon 9:00–10:00
  Nov 1981–Mar 1982, NBC Tue 10:00–11:00
  Mar 1982–Jun 1982, NBC Tue 9:00–10:00
  Jun 1982–Jul 1982, NBC Tue 10:00–11:00
CAST:
  Sheriff Titus Semple . . . . Howard Duff
  Sam Curtis . . . . John Beck
  Claude Weldon . . . . Kevin McCarthy
  Eudora Weldon . . . . Barbara Rush
  Skipper Weldon . . . . Woody Brown
  Constance Weldon Carlyle
  . . . . Morgan Fairchild
  Fielding Carlyle . . . . Mark Harmon
  Jasper, the butler . . . . Glenn Robards
  Elmo Tyson . . . . Peter Donat
  Lane Ballou . . . . Cristina Raines
  Lute-Mae Sanders. . . . . Stella Stevens
  Michael Tyrone. . . . . David Selby
  Sande Swanson. . . . . Cynthia Sikes
  Julio Sanchez . . . . Fernando Allende
  Alicia Sanchez . . . . Gina Gallego
  Christie Kovacs. . . . . Denise Galik
  Alice Kovacs . . . . Marcia Rodd
  Beth MacDonald. . . . . Sandra Kearns
  Deputy Tyler . . . . John Shearin

Produced by the same company responsible for CBS' *Dallas*, *Flamingo Road* was a similar mix of corruption, sex, financial manipulation, and political jockeying, albeit on a smaller scale. Here the setting was the sleepy town of Truro, Florida. Most of the action involved Sheriff Titus Semple, a crafty power broker who had a vast knowledge of potentially embarrassing or incriminating facts about most of the town's residents. Truro's wealthiest family was the Weldons, residing on exclusive Flamingo Road. Claude Weldon had made his money from the family paper mill, which his son Skipper now ran. Claude's spoiled, adopted daughter Constance was married to Fielding Carlyle, the ambitious protégé of Sheriff Semple, who had orchestrated Fielding's successful campaign for state senator. Semple had insisted that Fielding marry into the influential Weldon family, despite the young man's love for Lane Ballou, a pretty singer at Lute-Mae Sanders' casino-cum-bordello. Lane still harbored romantic feelings for Fielding, though she was also involved with Sam Curtis, a successful construction-company developer. Elmo Tyson was the publisher of the *Clarion,* Truro's newspaper.

The fall of 1981 brought ruthless tycoon Michael Tyrone to Truro, intent on avenging the execution, many years before, of his father for a murder he had not committed. Michael stopped at nothing to achieve his goal. When money, power, and deceit were not enough, he used black magic and murder (including that of his sister, reporter Sande Swanson) to get revenge on the citizens of Truro. Fielding had an affair with Sande and Michael ended up in bed with both Lute-Mae and Constance (who, it had been revealed, was Lute-Mae's illegitimate daughter). The only healthy relationship was that of Constance's brother, Skipper, and Alicia Sanchez, younger sister of one of Constance's former lovers, Julio. Skipper and Alicia, truly in love, eloped and tried to make a life for themselves despite the turmoil around them.

Flamingo Road was based on the best-selling novel by Robert Wilder and the 1949 movie starring Joan Crawford.

FLASH GORDON
Science Fiction
BROADCAST HISTORY:
Syndicated only
30 minutes
Produced: *1953–1954* (39 episodes)
Released: *Fall 1953*
CAST:
Flash Gordon . . . . Steve Holland
Dale Arden . . . . Irene Champlin
Dr. Zharkov . . . . Joe Nash

Flash Gordon was one of the great comic-book heroes of the 1930s and 1940s, fighting daring intergalactic battles with merciless foes for the safety of mankind. In this syndicated TV version, produced in Germany, he was portrayed by an obscure actor named Steve Holland. His companions, as always, were the lovely Dale and the bearded Dr. Zharkov. Together they battled the androids and death rays of such exotic enemies as the Evil Queen of Cygnil, the archcriminal Bizdar, the Great God Em of Odin, and the Mad Witch of Neptune.

The blond hero was created for a comic strip in 1934 by Alex Raymond. Science-fiction heroes were very popular at the time (*Buck Rogers* had begun five years earlier), and Flash captured the imagination of the nation's youth. He was introduced as a Yale graduate and polo player who set off with Dale and Dr. Zharkov to the planet Mongo, where the fearsome Emperor Ming was plotting to destroy the Earth. In wild and woolly battles they managed to defeat Ming and his legions, then set about dealing with other villains of the galaxy. *Flash Gordon* quickly became a radio serial in 1935 (starring Gale Gordon), and was immortalized in a series of three movie serials starring Buster Crabbe, made between 1936 and 1940. These movies have been widely shown on television since the early 1950s, and are probably more familiar to viewers than the Steve Holland TV films.

In 1979 *Flash Gordon* was seen as a Saturday morning cartoon series on NBC. In 1980 an expensive, frequently witty theatrical film of *Flash Gordon* was released, but it failed to attract a public large enough to make it a financial success.

FLATBUSH
Situation Comedy
FIRST TELECAST: *February 26, 1979*
LAST TELECAST: *March 12, 1979*
BROADCAST HISTORY:
Feb 1979–Mar 1979, CBS Mon 8:30–9:00
CAST:
Presto Prestopopolos . . . . Joseph Cali
Socks Palermo . . . . Adrian Zmed
Turtle Romero . . . . Vincent Bufano
Joey Dee . . . . Randy Stumpf
Figgy Figueroa . . . . Sandy Helberg
Esposito . . . . Antony Ponzini
Mrs. Fortunato . . . . Helen Verbit
Detective Bosko . . . . Jack Murdock
Clean Otto . . . . John Quade

The exploits of five recent high school graduates living in a middle-class Italian neighborhood in the Flatbush district of Brooklyn, New York. Presto was a cab-driver, Socks worked in a local clothing store and was the fashion plate of the group, Figgy worked at a supermarket delivering groceries on his bike, Joey was an apprentice plumber studying at night to become a lawyer, and Turtle worked in his family's restaurant. Together, as the Flatbush Fungos, their local club/gang, they wandered the neighborhood in search of innocent fun and excitement. The ethnic stereotypes that appeared in this series so offended the real-life Brooklyn borough president that he publicly demanded the series be taken off the air, before it gave Brooklyn a bad name. CBS beat him to it and canceled it after three episodes, before it gave *them* a bad name.

FLIGHT #7
Travelogue
FIRST TELECAST: *June 14, 1954*
LAST TELECAST: *August 31, 1957*
BROADCAST HISTORY:
Jun 1954–Aug 1954, ABC Mon 7:30–7:45
Aug 1954–Feb 1955, ABC Sun 8:00–8:30
Jun 1955–Sep 1955, ABC Sat 7:00–7:30
Jun 1957–Aug 1957, ABC Sat 7:30–8:00

This summer series presented travel films, generally of areas outside the continental United States.

FLIGHT TO RHYTHM
Music
FIRST TELECAST: *May 15, 1949*
LAST TELECAST: *September 22, 1949*
BROADCAST HISTORY:
May 1949–Jul 1949, DUM Sun 6:30–7:00
Aug 1949–Sep 1949, DUM Thu 8:00–8:30
REGULARS:
Delora Bueno
Miguelito Valdez Orchestra
Larry Carr

This 1949 summer series featured latin music, with vocalist Delora Bueno. It was set in "Club Rio," a Brazilian nightclub.

FLINTSTONES, THE
Cartoon
FIRST TELECAST: *September 30, 1960*
LAST TELECAST: *September 2, 1966*
BROADCAST HISTORY:
Sep 1960–Sep 1963, ABC Fri 8:30–9:00
Sep 1963–Dec 1964, ABC Thu 7:30–8:00
Dec 1964–Sep 1966, ABC Fri 7:30–8:00
VOICES:
Fred Flintstone .... Alan Reed
Wilma Flintstone .... Jean Vander Pyl
Barney Rubble.................... Mel Blanc
Betty Rubble (1960–1964) ..... Bea Benaderet
Betty Rubble (1964–1966) ..... Gerry Johnson
Dino the Dinosaur .... Mel Blanc
Pebbles (1962–1966) .... Jean Vander Pyl
Bamm Bamm (1963–1966) .... Don Messick
CO-PRODUCERS:
Bill Hanna, Joe Barbera

The Flintstones was a parody on modern suburban life, set in the Stone Age. The characters in the cartoon series all behaved and spoke in a contemporary manner, though they lived in the prehistoric city of Bedrock. Fred worked as operator of a dinosaur-powered crane at the Rock Head & Quarry Cavé Construction Co. (slogan: "Own Your Own Cave and Be Secure"). Around their split-level cave the Flintstones enjoyed such conveniences as Wilma's Stoneway piano, a hi-fi on which Fred could play his "rock" music (it consisted of a turntable and a bird with a long beak to serve as the needle), a vacuum cleaner (a baby elephant with a long trunk), and an automatic garbage-disposal unit (a famished buzzard stashed under the sink). Their car, which sported tail fins, also came equipped with steamroller wheels—to smooth out the rocky road.

At first the Flintstones had only Dino, their pet dinosaur, around the cave to play with. Then one day in 1962 they were blessed with a baby daughter, whom they named Pebbles. Not to be outdone, their neighbors the Rubbles adopted an orphan boy named Bamm Bamm. (The two kids later had a Saturday morning cartoon series of their own, *Pebbles and Bamm Bamm.*)

The Flintstones was always as much adult satire as children's fun. In many respects it resembled Jackie Gleason's popular *Honeymooners*, especially in the relationships of the principals. A wide range of caricatures passed through the stories: Lollobrickida, a pretty cook; Ann-Margrock, whose voice was supplied by Ann-Margret; attorney Perry Masonry (he never lost a case); Ed Sullystone, a TV host; Eddy Brianstone, a teenage impresario; and Weirdly and Creepella Gruesome, the strange couple who with their son Goblin moved into a cave nearby (this was a parody on *The Addams Family* and *The Munsters*, then popular). The Gruesomes thought that they were normal, and everyone *else* in Bedrock was odd.

In addition to being the longest-running animated series in prime-time history, *The Flintstones* and its spin-offs have had a highly successful run on Saturday mornings—on NBC from January 1967–September 1970, on CBS from September 1972–January 1974, back on NBC from February 1979–September 1984, and most recently on ABC with *The Flintstone Kids* since September 1986.

FLIP WILSON SHOW, THE
Comedy Variety
FIRST TELECAST: *September 17, 1970*
LAST TELECAST: *June 27, 1974*
BROADCAST HISTORY:
Sep 1970–Jun 1971, NBC Thu 7:30–8:30
Sep 1971–Jun 1974, NBC Thu 8:00–9:00 (OS)
REGULARS:
Flip Wilson
The Jack Regas Dancers
The George Wyle Orchestra

Comic Flip Wilson was the first black performer to achieve major popularity as host of his own variety hour. *The Flip Wilson Show* was an enormous hit, placing number two among all programs on television during its first two seasons. Although music and guests were an important part of the format, Flip's comedy was the real focal point of the series. In various skits he played a collection of stock characters, which included: Geraldine Jones, sassy, swinging, liberated woman with a very jealous boyfriend named "Killer"; Reverend LeRoy of the Church of What's Happening Now, a gospel preacher who seemed to be slightly less than honest and just a touch lecherous; Danny Danger, private detective; and Herbie, the Good Time Ice Cream Man. Flip's best-known expression was a wide-eyed "The Devil made me do it!"

FLIPPER
Adventure
FIRST TELECAST: *September 19, 1964*
LAST TELECAST: *September 1, 1968*

Sep 1964–Sep 1967, NBC Sat 7:30–8:00
Jan 1968–Jun 1968, NBC Sun 6:30–7:00
Jun 1968–Sep 1968, NBC Sun 7:00–7:30
CAST:
Porter Ricks . . . . Brian Kelly
Sandy Ricks . . . . Luke Halpin
Bud Ricks . . . . Tommy Norden
Hap Gorman (1964–1965) . . . . . . Andy Devine
Ulla Norstrand (1965–1966) . . Ulla Stromstedt

Porter "Po" Ricks was the chief ranger of Coral Key Park, Florida, responsible for protecting both the game fish and the skin divers in the park. A widower, he lived with his two children, 15-year-old Sandy and 10-year-old Bud, in a cottage near the shore. The real star of the series was the boys' pet dolphin, Flipper, who was both friend and helper in their weekly adventures. The stories generally revolved around Flipper and his two young companions, with Bud involved more often than Sandy. Also regularly seen during the first season was Hap Gorman, an old marine carpenter with endless numbers of stories about sea life and adventures. During the second season Ulla Norstrand, an attractive oceanographer, was a regular character.

The role of Flipper was played by a dolphin named Suzy.

FLO
Situation Comedy
FIRST TELECAST: *March 24, 1980*
LAST TELECAST: *July 21, 1981*
BROADCAST HISTORY:
Mar 1980–Apr 1980, CBS Mon 9:30–10:00
Jul 1980–Jan 1981, CBS Mon 8:00–8:30
Feb 1981, CBS Sat 9:00–9:30
Mar 1981–May 1981, CBS Sat 8:30–9:00
Jun 1981–Jul 1981, CBS Tue 8:30–9:00
CAST:
Florence Jean (Flo) Castleberry
. . . . Polly Holliday
Earl Tucker . . . . Geoffrey Lewis
Farley Waters . . . . Jim B. Baker
Mama Velma Castleberry . . . . Sudie Bond
Fran Castleberry . . . . Lucy Lee Flippin
Miriam Willoughby . . . . Joyce Bulifant
Randy Stumphill . . . . Leo Burmester
Les Kincaid . . . . Stephen Keep
Wendell Tubbs (1980) . . . . Terry Wills
Chester . . . . Mickey Jones

After four seasons as the feisty, hot-blooded waitress at Mel's Diner on *Alice*, Flo "Kiss My Grits" Castleberry got her own place to run. While passing through her hometown of Cowtown, Texas, on her way to a hostess job in Houston, Flo impulsively bought a run-down old roadhouse she remembered from her rambunctious youth, and determined to make it a viable business. Not used to being the boss, Flo had her troubles running the place, renamed Flo's Yellow Rose. Earl, the bar-

tender, hated the idea of working for a woman, and Farley was the obnoxious skinflint who held the mortgage. Les was the resident piano player and Randy the mechanic who worked at the garage located next door. Being back home meant spending time with Mama, in whose raucous image Flo was molded, and with an introverted, clutzy sister, Fran; and long-lost best friend Miriam. Wendell was Fran's fiancé, the owner of a feed supply business, and Chester was a regular customer at the Yellow Rose.

FLOOR SHOW, THE
see *Eddie Condon's Floor Show*

FLYING HIGH
Adventure
FIRST TELECAST: *September 29, 1978*
LAST TELECAST: *January 23, 1979*
BROADCAST HISTORY:
Sep 1978–Dec 1978, CBS Fri 10:00–11:00
Jan 1979, CBS Tue 10:00–11:00
CAST:
Marcy Bowers . . . . Pat Klous
Lisa Benton . . . . Connie Sellecca
Pam Bellagio . . . . Kathryn Witt
Capt. Doug March . . . . Howard Platt
Raymond Strickman . . . . Ken Olfson

Marcy, Lisa, and Pam were three sexy young girls who had just graduated from flight attendant school. As stewardesses for Sunwest Airlines, they had romantic, interesting, and occasionally dangerous adventures. All three worked on the same jumbo jet, and reported to Captain Doug March. Sometimes episodes centered on the girls' working hours and sometimes on their active social lives. Doug, despite his constant efforts, was never quite the ladies' man he thought he was. His romantic interludes always seemed to fall apart, or get him into trouble with somebody. Raymond was the passenger relations agent who worked ground crew in Los Angeles, where Sunwest was based.

The three actresses who played the leads in this series were all former New York City–based models, with little previous acting experience. In an effort to make their roles more believable, they met with groups of real flight attendants prior to starting production on the series, to hear about actual incidents that had taken place on real flights and the manner in which the stewardesses had handled them. It didn't help—*Flying High* barely got off the ground before it was canceled.

FLYING NUN, THE
Situation Comedy
FIRST TELECAST: *September 7, 1967*
LAST TELECAST: *September 18, 1970*
BROADCAST HISTORY:
Sep 1967–Jan 1969, ABC Thu 8:00–8:30
Feb 1969–Sep 1969, ABC Thu 7:30–8:00

Sep 1969–Jan 1970, ABC Wed 7:30–8:00
Jan 1970–Sep 1970, ABC Fri 7:30–8:00

CAST:

Sister Bertrille................... Sally Field
Sister Jacqueline........... Marge Redmond
Mother Superior....... Madeleine Sherwood
Carlos Ramirez............. Alejandro Rey
Sister Sixto................ Shelley Morrison
Sister Ana................... Linda Dangcil
Police Capt. Gaspar Formento (1968–1969)
.... Vito Scotti
Marcello, the orphan boy (1969–1970)
.... Manuel Padilla, Jr.

The subject of this comedy was Sister Bertrille, a bright, effusive young novice—the former Elsie Ethington—who brightened the lives of all at the ancient Convent San Tanco, situated on a hilltop near San Juan, Puerto Rico. Not the least of Sister Bertrille's attributes was that she could fly. How? Well, "when lift plus thrust is greater than load plus drag," any object can fly, including Sister Bertrille, who weighed only 90 pounds. Whenever a stiff wind caught the starched cornette worn by her order, off she went.

These aerodynamics were not always pleasant. Occasionally Sister Bertrille would get dunked in the ocean or be thrust in the midst of unlikely goings-on, and once she was almost shot down as an enemy aircraft (a pelican once fell in love with her, too). Least impressed was her staid, conservative Mother Superior. But Sister Bertrille got along well with the wise and humorous Sister Jacqueline, and with Sister Sixto, the Puerto Rican nun who fought a running battle with the English language. Sister Bertrille was also admired—from a distance—by Carlos Ramirez, the rich, handsome playboy owner of a discotheque in town who was a patron of the convent.

Believe it or not, The Flying Nun was commended by some religious orders—for "humanizing" nuns and their work. It was based on the book The Fifteenth Pelican, by Tere Rios.

FLYING TIGERS, THE
see Major Dell Conway of the Flying Tigers

FOCUS
Documentary
FIRST TELECAST: March 18, 1952
LAST TELECAST: October 10, 1957

This was a blanket title for documentary films carried by ABC in various 15-minute and half-hour time slots, usually for short periods of time, between 1952 and 1957.

FOCUS ON AMERICA
Documentary
FIRST TELECAST: June 27, 1961
LAST TELECAST: September 10, 1963
BROADCAST HISTORY:
Jun 1961–Sep 1961, ABC Tue 7:00–7:30

Jul 1962–Sep 1962, ABC Wed 8:00–8:30
Jul 1963–Sep 1963, ABC Tue 10:30–11:00

HOST:
Bill Shadel (1962)
Don Goddard (1963)

Documentaries that had originally been produced and aired by local ABC affiliates were telecast over the entire ABC network during three summers in the early 1960s. They were selected by members of the ABC News Department as examples of the best of locally originated informational programming, and ranged from "Clipper Ships and Paddle Wheelers" (KGO-TV, San Francisco) to "Cows, Cowboys and Cow Country" (KOCO-TV, Oklahoma City) to "To The Moon and Beyond" (WTVN-TV, Columbus).

FOLEY SQUARE
Situation Comedy
FIRST TELECAST: December 11, 1985
LAST TELECAST: July 23, 1986
BROADCAST HISTORY:
Dec 1985–Feb 1986, CBS Wed 8:30–9:00
Mar 1986–Apr 1986, CBS Tue 9:30–10:00
Jun 1986–Jul 1986, CBS Wed 8:00–8:30

CAST:
Asst. D.A. Alex Harrigan..... Margaret Colin
D.A. Jesse Steinberg......... Hector Elizondo
Denise Willums..... Vernee Watson-Johnson
Peter Newman............ Michael Lembeck
Asst. D.A. Molly Dobbs....... Cathy Silvers
Asst. D.A. Carter DeVries.... Sanford Jensen
Angel Gomez................... Israel Juarbe
Mole........................... Jon Lovitz
Spiro Papadopolis....... Richard C. Serafian

Foley Square was the location of the Manhattan District Attorney's office, the setting for this short-lived legal comedy. Jesse was an old-timer, a career public servant who had seen it all and was now in charge of a bureau with three assistant D.A.s. They were: Alex, who was perky, dedicated and single; Carter, ambitious and overbearing; and Molly, the neophyte just out of law school. Helping out was Denise, Alex's secretary; Angel, a young office messenger who was an ex-con; and—in the first several episodes—Mole, an investigator for the D.A.'s office. Mr. Papadopolis ran the neighborhood coffee shop where they all hung out.

On the personal side, Peter was a school teacher who lived in Alex's Upper West Side apartment building, and was her good friend. Although many of the episodes dealt with criminal cases at the office, nearly as much time was spent on Alex's uneven social life.

FOLLOW THAT MAN
syndicated title for Man Against Crime

FOLLOW THE LEADER
Quiz/Audience Participation

FIRST TELECAST: *July 7, 1953*
LAST TELECAST: *August 4, 1953*
BROADCAST HISTORY:
Jul 1953–Aug 1953, CBS Tue 9:00–9:30
HOSTESS:
Vera Vague

This live show, which was telecast from Hollywood, gave members of the studio audience the opportunity to see how well they could imitate a scene pantomimed by actress Vera Vague (whose real name was Barbara Jo Allen).

FOLLOW THE SUN
Adventure
FIRST TELECAST: *September 17, 1961*
LAST TELECAST: *September 9, 1962*
BROADCAST HISTORY:
Sep 1961–Sep 1962, ABC Sun 7:30–8:30
CAST:
Ben Gregory...................... Barry Coe
Paul Templin .... Brett Halsey
Eric Jason .... Gary Lockwood
Katherine Ann Richards........ Gigi Perreau
Lt. Frank Roper.................. Jay Lanin

This adventure series focused on the exploits of two footloose, handsome, free-lance magazine writers living in Hawaii. Ben and Paul's bachelor pad was a plush penthouse in Honolulu, and they both led active social lives when not facing danger in pursuit of a story (their articles were not intended for the faint of heart). Helping them was Eric Jason, who did much of the legwork for their articles; Kathy Richards, who was a part-time secretary and full-time student at the University of Honolulu; and Lt. Roper of the Honolulu Police, who bailed them out whenever they got in over their heads.

FOOT IN THE DOOR
Situation Comedy
FIRST TELECAST: *March 28, 1983*
LAST TELECAST: *May 2, 1983*
BROADCAST HISTORY:
Mar 1983–May 1983, CBS Mon 8:30–9:00
CAST:
Jonah Foot .... Harold Gould
Jim Foot................... Kenneth Gilman
Harriet Foot .... Diana Canova
Mrs. Griffin................. Marian Mercer

Following the death of his abstemious wife after 40 years of marriage, widower Jonah Foot moved from Pitts Valley, N.H., to the New York City co-op apartment of his son Jim and daughter-in-law Harriet and proceeded to become a liberated, skirt-chasing swinger. This created no end of problems for conservative Jim, an advertising agency copywriter, and sweet Harriet, a buyer for a Manhattan department store. It also failed to endear him to Mrs. Griffin, the cynical president

of the board of directors of the building in which the Foots lived.

Adapted from the British comedy *Tom, Dick & Harriet.*

FOOTBALL
Sports
FIRST TELECAST: *October 3, 1950*
LAST TELECAST:
BROADCAST HISTORY:
Oct 1950–Jan 1951, ABC Tue 8:00–8:30
Sep 1953–Dec 1953, ABC Sun 7:45–9:00
Oct 1953–Nov 1953, DUM Sat 8:00–Conclusion
Oct 1954–Nov 1954, DUM Sat 8:00–Conclusion
Oct 1957–Nov 1957, ABC Sun 10:00–10:30
Nov 1957–Dec 1957, ABC Sun 9:30–10:00
Aug 1959–Oct 1959, ABC Sat 11:00–Conclusion
Sep 1970–   , ABC Mon 9:00–Conclusion
(Sep–Dec each year)
ANNOUNCERS:
Bill Fisher (1950–1951)
Harry Wismer (1953)
Ford Bond (1953)
Chuck Thompson (1954, 1959)
Chick Hearn (1957)
Howard Cosell (1959, 1970–1983)
Keith Jackson (1970)
Don Meredith (1970–1973, 1977–1984)
Frank Gifford (1971–   )
Fred Williamson (1974)
Alex Karras (1974–1976)
Fran Tarkenton (1979–1982)
O. J. Simpson (1983–1985)
Joe Namath (1985)
Al Michaels (1986–   )
Dan Dierdorf (1987–   )

The 1950–1951 season brought a weekly highlight film of a major college football game to ABC. Titled *The Game of the Week,* it was narrated by Bill Fisher. Three years later, ABC was back with a nighttime football series featuring the most popular college team in football history. *Notre Dame Football,* with Harry Wismer and Ford Bond doing the play-by-play, was still a highlight film, but a more extensive one than the half-hour series aired in 1950. It was edited to 75 minutes in length, leaving out only dull and uneventful plays. Wismer did double duty that fall, also announcing the weekly *Pro Football* game carried live by DuMont on Saturday nights. This was the same Harry Wismer who, a decade later, was the original owner of the New York Titans of the fledgling American Football League (later to become the New York Jets). DuMont was back with *Pro Football* in 1954, but Chuck Thompson had replaced Wismer at the mike. The year 1957 saw the revival of ABC's first football series, as *The All-American Football Game of the Week,* which highlighted a major college game of the weekend, this time narrated by Chick Hearn.

Professional football made its first appearance on ABC in the fall of 1959, but it wasn't until a decade later that it really became successful as a prime-time series. The 1959 series, which ran at 11:00 P.M. on Saturday nights, consisted of a full-length videotape replay of a game that had been played earlier that day. Commentators were Chuck Thompson and Howard Cosell. When, in the spring of 1970, ABC secured the rights from the National Football League to carry a regularly scheduled *Monday Night Football* game that fall, it was around Cosell's caustic personality that the announcing team was organized. Whereas the traditional way of covering football was with two people, a play-by-play announcer and a color man to add insights and observations, ABC decided to put three people in the booth. Keith Jackson did the play-by-play during the first season, with Frank Gifford assuming that role in 1971. The other two commentators, Cosell and Don Meredith, were there to inform, observe, and entertain. It was this last aspect of their work that offended sports traditionalists. At times, especially during boring games, the men in the booth seemed to lose touch completely with what was happening on the field. They were accused of turning a sport into an entertainment show, but as long as the ratings were high enough (which they always were), they received full support from ABC's management.

Later years saw periodic changes in the broadcast booth, as new faces (usually former athletes) were brought in to do color. Easygoing Frank Gifford was for many years the play-by-play announcer, switching to color in 1986. Howard "The Mouth" Cosell got most of the press, however, and it marked the end of an era when he retired in 1983. ABC briefly tried a two-man team in 1986 (Gifford and Al Michaels), reverting to the former three-person arrangement the following year.

FOOTBALL NEWS
see *New York Giants Quarterback Huddle*

FOOTBALL SIDELINES
Sports
FIRST TELECAST: *October 6, 1952*
LAST TELECAST: *December 29, 1952*
BROADCAST HISTORY:
Oct 1952–Dec 1952, DUM Mon 9:30–9:45
HOST:
Harry Wismer

Football Sidelines filled half of a 30-minute sports block that preceded the Monday night fights on DuMont in 1952. (The second half consisted of film clips of *Famous Fights*.) Here Wismer commented on filmed highlights from the previous weekend's football action.

FOOTBALL THIS WEEK
Sports
FIRST TELECAST: *October 11, 1951*
LAST TELECAST: *December 6, 1951*
BROADCAST HISTORY:
Oct 1951–Dec 1951, DUM Thu 10:45–11:00

This program featured filmed highlights of the major college football games of the preceding weekend.

FOOTLIGHTS THEATER
Dramatic Anthology
FIRST TELECAST: *July 4, 1952*
LAST TELECAST: *September 11, 1953*
BROADCAST HISTORY:
Jul 1952–Sep 1952, CBS Fri 9:30–10:00
Jul 1953–Sep 1953, CBS Fri 9:30–10:00

For two summers this anthology series aired on CBS, presenting adaptations of plays and novels as well as original stories. The 1952 version was broadcast live from New York, while 1953 saw filmed dramas presented under the same title. Lesser-known and predominantly younger actors and actresses were featured in the plays, with various episodes starring Victor Jory, Gig Young, Lloyd Bridges, Gale Storm, Barbara Hale, and Lynn Bari.

FOR LOVE AND HONOR
Drama
FIRST TELECAST: *September 23, 1983*
LAST TELECAST: *December 27, 1983*
BROADCAST HISTORY:
Sep 1983–Nov 1983, NBC Fri 10:00–11:00
Dec 1983, NBC Tue 10:00–11:00
CAST:
First Sgt. Eugene Allard .... Cliff Potts
Platoon Sgt. James "China" Bell
.... Yaphet Kotto
Capt. Carolyn Engel........... Shelley Smith
Capt. Stephen Wiecek......... Gary Grubbs
Cpl. Grace Pavlik............ Rachel Ticotin
Pvt. Chris Dolan............. Pete Kowanko
Pvt. Duke Johnson .... Keenan Ivory Wayans
Pvt. Dominick Petrizzo .... John Mengatti
Pvt. Utah Wilson .... Tony Becker
Sharon........................... Amy Steel
Mary Lee..................... Kelly Preston
Phyllis Wiecek .... Shanna Reed

For Love and Honor was a cross between the highly successful film *An Officer and a Gentleman* and the nighttime soap operas so popular in the early 1980s. The setting was the U.S. Army's Fort Geller, Texas, headquarters for the 88th Airborne Division, where paratroopers were trained for possible combat duty. In command of the unit around which most of the stories centered was bigoted Captain Stephen Wiecek, whose adulterous wife Phyllis was an alcoholic. Sgt. Allard was a compassionate drill instructor who was having a secret affair with Carolyn Engel, the base medical officer. The other drill instructor, China Bell, was an embittered former boxer and Vietnam veteran. Among their new recruits were con man Chris Dolan, who dated Sharon, a pretty local civilian; Duke Johnson, a young black who wanted China to help him become a professional boxer; Utah, a willing and gullible country boy; Utah's roommate, buddy, and protector, Dominick Petrizzo; and the unit's only female recruit, pretty but tough Puerto Rican Grace Pavlik. The base commander's adopted daughter Mary Lee was an oversexed teenager who flirted with most of the guys.

FOR THE PEOPLE
Police Drama
FIRST TELECAST: *January 31, 1965*
LAST TELECAST: *May 9, 1965*
BROADCAST HISTORY:
    Jan 1965–May 1965, CBS Sun 9:00–10:00
CAST:
    David Koster .... William Shatner
    Anthony Celese .... Howard Da Silva
    Frank Malloy .... Lonny Chapman
    Phyllis Koster .... Jessica Walter

William Shatner played David Koster, a strong-willed New York City assistant district attorney. David's passion for justice often brought him more trouble than he could handle, both from his superiors and from members of the criminal underground, who had little love for his obsessive dedication. Trying to keep David under tight rein, despite his admiration for the young prosecutor's zeal, was bureau chief Anthony Celese, his immediate boss. Helping David to ferret out criminals was detective Frank Malloy. David's wife, Phyllis, was a viola player in a classical string quartet, and had a life and priorities of her own that sometimes conflicted with his.

FOR YOUR PLEASURE
Music
FIRST TELECAST: *April 15, 1948*
LAST TELECAST: *September 10, 1949*
BROADCAST HISTORY:
    Apr 1948–Jun 1948, NBC Thu 8:00–8:15
    Jul 1948–Sep 1948, NBC Wed 8:00–8:15
    Jul 1949–Sep 1949, NBC Sat 8:30–9:00
REGULARS:
    Kyle MacDonnell
    Norman Paris Trio
DANCERS:
    Jack and Jill (Apr–Jun 1948)
    Blaire and Deane (Jun–Sep 1948)
ORCHESTRA:
    Earl Shelton (1949)

This live studio musical program featured Kyle MacDonnell, the pretty singing star of Broadway's *Make Mine Manhattan* and one of the most frequently seen "personalities" on early TV screens. The program was set in a nightclub with Kyle strolling among the tables, chatting with guests and singing a song or two. TV-set owners in 1948 had to put up with a lot of inconveniences to watch the winsome Miss MacDonnell, however. A *New York Times* reviewer complained that

"the lighting has been particularly erratic, at times almost blotting out Miss MacDonnell and the other artists in a haze of whiteness, and at other moments reflecting both skill and thought. More rehearsal . . . should correct such defects."

See *Girl About Town* for the continuation of this program in similar format.

FORD FESTIVAL
Musical Variety
FIRST TELECAST: *April 5, 1951*
LAST TELECAST: *June 26, 1952*
BROADCAST HISTORY:
    Apr 1951–Dec 1951, NBC Thu 9:00–10:00
    Jan 1952–Jun 1952, NBC Thu 9:30–10:30
REGULARS:
    James Melton
    Dorothy Warrenskjold
    Vera Vague
    The Wiere Brothers
    Billy Barty

Ford Festival was originally a loosely structured "book" show in which a simple plot served to tie together performances by the singing star of the show, James Melton, and his semi-regulars, singer Dorothy Warrenskjold, comedienne Vera Vague (Barbara Jo Allen), and comedy singers The Wiere Brothers. On June 7, 1951, the format was changed to that of a straight revue, and all pretense of plot was dropped. Billy Barty was added to the cast of regulars the following week and The Wiere Brothers were dropped.

FORD SHOW, THE
Musical Variety
FIRST TELECAST: *October 4, 1956*
LAST TELECAST: *June 29, 1961*
BROADCAST HISTORY:
    Oct 1956–Jun 1961, NBC Thu 9:30–10:00 (OS)
REGULARS:
    Tennessee Ernie Ford
    The Voices of Walter Schumann (1956–1957)
    The Top Twenty (1957–1961)
    The Harry Geller Orchestra

Tennessee Ernie Ford was host, singer, comedian, and star of this variety show, whose title referred not to him, but to its sponsor, the Ford Motor Company. Ernie's informal, friendly quality set the tone for the program, which included his reminiscences about growing up in Bristol, Tennessee, and his homespun catch phrases ("Bless your pea-pickin' hearts!"). The musical portion of the program consisted mostly of country and western and gospel music, for which Ernie was famous, and the show generally ended with a hymn. The choral group "The Voices of Walter Schumann" backed Ernie during his first season; "The Top Twenty," a more contemporary mixed singing group, performed those duties for the remainder of the show's run.

273

FORD STAR JUBILEE
Various
FIRST TELECAST: *September 24, 1955*
LAST TELECAST: *November 3, 1956*
BROADCAST HISTORY:
Sep 1955–Nov 1956, CBS Sat 9:30–11:00 (OS)

This series of "spectaculars," which aired roughly once per month, was CBS' "class" series for the 1955–1956 season. The material and the stars were all first-rate. Judy Garland (in her first network TV starring vehicle) hosted the premiere telecast "The Judy Garland Show," and other musical telecasts in the series included Mary Martin and Noel Coward in "Together with Music"; Eddie Fisher, Debbie Reynolds, Nat "King" Cole, Bobby Van, Ella Fitzgerald, and Red Skelton in "I Hear America Singing"; and Louis Armstrong, Dorothy Dandridge, and Shirley Jones in a tribute to Cole Porter titled "You're the Top." There was also drama—Lloyd Nolan, Barry Sullivan, and Frank Lovejoy in *The Caine Mutiny Court-Martial;* Jack Lemmon, Raymond Massey, Lillian Gish, and Charles Laughton in *The Day Lincoln Was Shot;* and Orson Welles, Betty Grable, and Keenan Wynn in *Twentieth Century.* The last telecast of *Ford Star Jubilee,* however, was really something special. It was the first airing of what has since become a television tradition—Judy Garland's classic 1939 film *The Wizard of Oz,* with Judy's 10-year-old daughter Liza Minnelli and Bert Lahr (the cowardly lion from the film) on hand to introduce it.

FORD STAR REVUE
Comedy Variety
FIRST TELECAST: *July 6, 1950*
LAST TELECAST: *March 29, 1951*
BROADCAST HISTORY:
Jul 1950–Sep 1950, NBC Thu 9:00–10:00
Jan 1951–Mar 1951, NBC Thu 9:00–10:00
REGULARS:
Jack Haley
Havel Brothers (Jul–Sep 1950)
Dr. Roy K. Marshall
Mindy Carson (Jan–Mar 1951)
Carl Hoff Orchestra (Jan–Mar 1951)
Ted Adolphus Dancers (Jan–Mar 1951)

This musical comedy–variety series began as a summer replacement for *Kay Kyser's Kollege of Musical Knowledge,* then was given its own regular season slot (briefly) in early 1951. Many famous guest stars and semi-regular performers came and went during the life of the show. Haley, who is perhaps best known for his role as the Tin Woodman in the 1939 movie classic *The Wizard of Oz,* failed to catch on as a TV host and the program was soon canceled.

Among the writers for the 1951 edition was Norman Lear.

FORD STARTIME
see *Startime*

FORD THEATRE
Dramatic Anthology
FIRST TELECAST: *October 7, 1949*
LAST TELECAST: *July 10, 1957*
BROADCAST HISTORY:
Oct 1949–Jun 1951, CBS Fri 9:00–10:00 (OS)
Oct 1952–Sep 1956, NBC Thu 9:30–10:00
Oct 1956–Jul 1957, ABC Wed 9:30–10:00

Ford Theatre began as a monthly series of live hour-long dramatic plays on CBS on October 17, 1948. It became a regular series a year later, airing on alternate Friday nights with other dramatic shows. The live CBS edition used New York–based actors and actresses, primarily those working on Broadway. Among the plays aired during this period were an adaptation of *Little Women,* with Peggy Ann Garner, Kim Hunter, and June Lockhart; *Twentieth Century,* with Fredric March and Lilli Palmer; and *One Sunday Afternoon,* with Hume Cronyn and Burgess Meredith.

After a season's absence, *Ford Theatre* returned to the air on NBC in October 1952, as a filmed series of half-hour plays. This version of the show remained on NBC for four years and then moved to ABC for a final season. With the shift to film, the production moved to Hollywood and the episodes starred motion-picture performers. The scope ranged from light comedy to heavy drama and consisted of adaptations of plays and novels as well as original stories. Such familiar names as Charles Coburn, Barry Sullivan, Peter Lawford, Thomas Mitchell, Ann Sheridan, Claudette Colbert, Ida Lupino, and Teresa Wright starred in these shows. Ronald Reagan and his wife Nancy Davis made their first professional appearance together in this series, on February 5, 1953, in a teleplay titled "First Born."

FOREIGN INTRIGUE
Intrigue
BROADCAST HISTORY:
Syndicated only
30 minutes
Produced: *1951–1955* (156 episodes)
Released: *Fall 1951*
CAST:
Robert Cannon (1951–1953) ..... Jerome Thor
Helen Davis (1951–1953)........ Synda Scott
Michael Powers (1953–1954) ..... James Daly
Patricia Bennett (1953–1954) ... Anne Preville
Christopher Storm (1954–1955) .. Gerald Mohr

This syndicated mystery, filmed in Europe, owed its popularity more to its authentic locations and European flavor than to its stars (of whom it had five in four years). When it began, Jerome Thor played a trench-coated European correspondent for an American wire service whose assignments took him across the Continent, and involved him with political provocateurs, old war criminals, and neo-Nazis. There was a heavily political flavor to many of the episodes. His friendly rival was reporter Helen Davis, and their base of operations, Stockholm.

Thor was replaced after two seasons by James Daly, whose pipe-smoking correspondent for Associated News was a rougher yet less serious hero. Anne Preville, who played a correspondent for Consolidated Press, became his female foil, and production moved to Paris. Both Thor and Daly took "vacations" from time to time, Thor being spelled in some episodes by another correspondent (played by Bernard Farrel) and Daly by Miss Preville.

In 1954 the lead and location changed again. This time Gerald Mohr starred as the American owner of a hotel in Vienna, and a fast man both with a gun and with his fists. In the opening episodes he was involved in smashing a counterfeiting ring dealing in American currency.

Foreign Intrigue was created, produced, directed, and sometimes written by an ambitious young New Yorker named Sheldon Reynolds. It was repeated in later years under a variety of names: *Dateline Europe* for the Thor episodes, *Overseas Adventure* for the Daly episodes, and *Cross Current* for the Mohr episodes. Also known as *Foreign Assignment*.

FOREIGN LEGION
see *Assignment: Foreign Legion*

FOREVER FERNWOOD
see *Mary Hartman, Mary Hartman*

FORTUNE DANE
Police Drama
FIRST TELECAST: *February 15, 1986*
LAST TELECAST: *March 27, 1986*
BROADCAST HISTORY:
   Feb 1986–Mar 1986, ABC Sat 9:00–10:00
CAST:
   Fortune Dane .... Carl Weathers
   Mayor Amanda Harding........ Penny Fuller
   Kathy "Speed" Davenport
   .... Daphne Ashbrook
   Perfect Tommy .... Joe Dallesandro

This rather violent series centered on an imposing black police detective who turned in his badge when the gangland killing he was investigating revealed a connection between his banker-father, whom he idolized, and the mob. Following the hit man to a west coast metropolis called Bay City, Dane solved the case and then became a troubleshooter for that city's lady mayor, who was almost as tough as he was.

48 HOURS
Documentary
FIRST TELECAST: *January 19, 1988*
LAST TELECAST:
BROADCAST HISTORY:
   Jan 1988–Feb 1988, CBS Tue 8:00–9:00
   *Mar 1988–   *, CBS Thu 8:00–9:00

ANCHORMAN:
   Dan Rather
CORRESPONDENT:
   Bernard Goldberg

Not since the *CBS News Hour* left the air in 1971 had any network aired a regularly scheduled prime-time news series that focused on a single topic each week. The premise of *48 Hours* was to give viewers a cinéma vérité look at a news story, following correspondents and crews as each story was developed and filmed over a two-day period. Although the series often dealt with issues of topical interest, it did not necessarily focus on the hottest current news story. The first three episodes, for instance, covered Miami's struggle to overcome its image as a center for drug trafficking, the congestion at Denver's busy Stapleton Airport over New Year's weekend, and the work of the doctors, nurses, and staff at Dallas' Parkland Memorial Hospital. Dan Rather was the series' in-studio anchorman and Bernard Goldberg was its sole full-time correspondent. Various CBS reporters contributed each week.

FOUL PLAY
Detective
FIRST TELECAST: *January 26, 1981*
LAST TELECAST: *August 23, 1981*
BROADCAST HISTORY:
   Jan 1981–Feb 1981, ABC Mon 10:00–11:00
   Aug 1981, ABC Sun 8:00–8:30
CAST:
   Gloria Munday .... Deborah Raffin
   Det. Tucker Pendleton....... Barry Bostwick
   Capt. Vito Lombardi ...... Richard Romanus
   Stella .... Mary Jo Catlett
   Ben .... Greg Rice
   Beau .... John Rice

Based on the movie of the same name starring Chevy Chase and Goldie Hawn, *Foul Play* concerned a TV talk-show hostess (Gloria) and a concert-violinist-turned-cop (Tucker) who teamed up to solve crimes in San Francisco. Capt. Lombardi was Tucker's boss, and Ben and Beau a couple of helpful midgets. The series had none of the raucous comedy of the movie, and was soon canceled.

FOUL-UPS, BLEEPS & BLUNDERS
Comedy
FIRST TELECAST: *January 10, 1984*
LAST TELECAST: *August 11, 1985*
BROADCAST HISTORY:
   Jan 1984–Oct 1984, ABC Tue 8:00–8:30
   Nov 1984–Mar 1985, ABC various (occasional)
   Apr 1985–Jul 1985, ABC Tue 8:30–9:00
   Aug 1985, ABC Sun 10:30–11:00
HOSTS:
   Don Rickles
   Steve Lawrence
FOREIGN CORRESPONDENT:
   Noel Edmunds

ABC seemed to be one step behind in the TV-outtakes craze. NBC started it all with its highly successful "Bloopers" specials, and ABC followed with its "Life's Most Embarrassing Moments" specials. Then NBC discovered that a special made up of commercials could be funny, and ABC copied that with its own "great commercials" specials. Finally NBC turned its good thing into a weekly Monday night series called *TV's Bloopers & Practical Jokes*, and ABC followed suit a day later with the practically identical *Foul-Ups, Bleeps & Blunders.*

The format was simply to string together outtakes from movies, TV shows, local newscasts, commercials, and elsewhere that showed supposed professionals—many of them major stars—fluffing their lines, falling over props, breaking up, etc. Interspersed were some *Candid Camera*-style segments in which ordinary citizens were given equal time to make fools of themselves.

NBC had the last laugh in all this, however. Running against NBC's super hit *The A-Team*, *Foul-Ups* barely survived, while the Monday night NBC version attracted large audiences.

FOUR IN ONE
Drama
FIRST TELECAST: *September 16, 1970*
LAST TELECAST: *September 8, 1971*
BROADCAST HISTORY:
  Sep 1970–Sep 1971, NBC Wed 10:00–11:00

Four in One was the umbrella title for a group of four mini-series, each of which was aired for a period of six consecutive weeks and then was rerun on a rotating basis. See *McCloud, San Francisco International Airport, Night Gallery,* and *The Psychiatrist.*

FOUR SEASONS, THE
Situation Comedy
FIRST TELECAST: *January 29, 1984*
LAST TELECAST: *July 29, 1984*
BROADCAST HISTORY:
  Jan 1984–Feb 1984, CBS Sun 8:00–8:30
  Mar 1984–Jul 1984, CBS Sun 8:30–9:00
CAST:
  Danny Zimmer . . . . Jack Weston
  Ted Bolen . . . . Tony Roberts
  Claudia Zimmer . . . . Marcia Rodd
  Lorraine Elliot . . . . Barbara Babcock
  Boris Elliot . . . . Alan Arbus
  Pat Devon . . . . Joanna Kerns
  Lisa Callan . . . . Beatrice Alda
  Beth Burroughs . . . . Elizabeth Alda
  Sharon Hogan . . . . Lori Carrell
EXECUTIVE PRODUCERS:
  Alan Alda and Martin Bregman

Danny Zimmer was a born-and-bred New Yorker, a dentist, and a hypochondriac. He worried about almost everything, including the decision to move to California and establish a new practice in Los Angeles.

Danny dreaded change of any kind, and the adjustment was traumatic although it was eased by the new friends he made in Los Angeles. Ted Bolen was his aggressive real-estate-salesman pal, who lived the "California" life-style and had a live-in relationship with stunt woman Pat Devon. Danny's other close friend was Boris Elliot, a successful attorney who had given up the practice of law for the less pressured life of a bicycle-shop owner after suffering a heart attack. Boris' wife, Lorraine, was a professor of orthopedics at the UCLA School of Medicine and a good sport, despite a rather stuffy exterior. Also seen regularly were Beth Burroughs, the daughter of Danny's best friend from New York, and Beth's friend Lisa, who moved to California to find fame and fortune. Sharon was the girl with whom Beth and Lisa shared an apartment. They all shared little middle-class adventures, often involving Danny's beloved Mercedes automobile, and counterpointed by the music of Vivaldi—*The Four Seasons*, of course.

The Four Seasons was based on the Alan Alda movie of the same name, with Jack Weston and Alda's daughters Beatrice and Elizabeth re-creating the roles they had played in the movie.

FOUR SQUARE COURT
Discussion
FIRST TELECAST: *March 16, 1952*
LAST TELECAST: *June 29, 1952*
BROADCAST HISTORY:
  Mar 1952–May 1952, ABC Sun 7:30–8:00
  May 1952–Jun 1952, ABC Sun 9:00–9:30
MODERATOR:
  Norman Brokenshire

Many TV entertainment series have dealt with criminals of various types. This was probably the only network series ever to star the real thing: masked ex-convicts out on parole, who appeared each week to discuss their crimes and rehabilitation. No doubt the parolees watched their language on this live, coast-to-coast show, as state parole board officials appeared on the panel with them. The program emanated from New York.

FOUR STAR PLAYHOUSE
Dramatic Anthology
FIRST TELECAST: *September 25, 1952*
LAST TELECAST: *September 27, 1956*
BROADCAST HISTORY:
  Sep 1952–Sep 1954, CBS Thu 8:30–9:00
  Oct 1954–Sep 1956, CBS Thu 9:30–10:00
REGULARS:
  David Niven
  Charles Boyer
  Dick Powell
  Ida Lupino

When *Four Star Playhouse* was announced, the four stars who were supposed to appear on a rotating basis were Charles Boyer, Dick Powell, Rosalind Russell, and Joel McCrea. Russell and McCrea never made it and were replaced by David Niven and Ida Lupino. Although *Four Star Playhouse* was essentially an anthology, one continuing character did make numerous appearances. That was nightclub owner Willie Dante, portrayed by Dick Powell. A later series based on Powell's characterization, *Dante,* appeared on NBC in 1960 with Howard Duff in the title role.

The format of the individual episodes varied greatly, with the content ranging from comedy to drama. The four stars were not the only headliners, especially during the first two seasons. Others who were featured over the years were Ronald Colman, Merle Oberon, Joan Fontaine, Teresa Wright, and Frank Lovejoy.

Four Star Playhouse was originally an alternate-week series, expanding to a weekly basis in September 1953.

FOUR STAR REVUE
see *All Star Revue*

FRANK LEAHY SHOW, THE
Sports Commentary
FIRST TELECAST: *September 27, 1953*
LAST TELECAST: *December 6, 1953*
BROADCAST HISTORY:
Sep 1953–Dec 1953, ABC Sun 7:45–8:00
HOST:
Frank Leahy

The Frank Leahy Show was the pregame show leading up to *Notre Dame Football* in 1953. Notre Dame coach Frank Leahy would interview the coach of the team that Notre Dame had played the previous day. Following their discussion, the highlights of the game itself were shown on *Notre Dame Football.*

FRANK SINATRA SHOW, THE
Musical Variety
FIRST TELECAST: *October 7, 1950*
LAST TELECAST: *April 1, 1952*
BROADCAST HISTORY:
Oct 1950–Jun 1951, CBS Sat 9:00–10:00
Oct 1951–Apr 1952, CBS Tue 8:00–9:00
REGULARS:
Frank Sinatra
Ben Blue (1950–1951)
Joey Walsh (1950–1951)
Axel Stordahl and His Orchestra
Sid Fields (1950–1951)
Roberta Lee (1950–1951)
Pat Gaye (1950–1951)

A good deal of publicity attended Frank Sinatra's initial plunge into television in 1950. He certainly had superstar credentials from music, radio, and films (though his greatest films were still to come); would he make it in the new medium of TV? The answer was no, although there was never a clear reason why Sinatra didn't, when such other singers as Perry Como and Dinah Shore did. *The Frank Sinatra Show* was telecast live from New York and featured top-line guest stars and plenty of Frankie's singing, assisted and backed by an assortment of female vocalists and backup groups. There was also, at least for the first three months, a regular supporting cast of comedians to help provide variety.

One factor that certainly didn't help was the competition. Sinatra was first scheduled opposite Sid Caesar's *Your Show of Shows,* then a red-hot sensation. For the second season he was moved to Tuesday, against *The Texaco Star Theater* with Milton Berle—the number one show in television! Frank moved the show to Hollywood in November 1951, but it was hopeless.

There were no regulars other than host Sinatra during the second season.

FRANK SINATRA SHOW, THE
Variety/Drama
FIRST TELECAST: *October 18, 1957*
LAST TELECAST: *June 27, 1958*
BROADCAST HISTORY:
Oct 1957–Jun 1958, ABC Fri 9:00–9:30
REGULARS:
Frank Sinatra
Nelson Riddle and His Orchestra

After his first, unsuccessful plunge into television in 1950–1952, singer-actor Frank Sinatra generally steered clear of the medium for several years. But despite the lack of success of his early variety show, he was considered a "hot property" and was actively sought for special appearances and another series of his own. His career in recording and movies had taken a considerable upturn in the mid-1950s, including his Academy Award for *From Here to Eternity.* Finally in 1957 he consented to do a regular weekly series for ABC, provided that he was given *carte blanche* to do it exactly as he wanted to. ABC paid $3 million for the honor of having him on its network.

What Sinatra had in mind was an unusual drama-plus-variety format, originally planned to include one-third variety shows, one-third dramas starring himself, and one-third dramas starring others, which he would host. Unfortunately he apparently approached the project with the attitude that all he had to do was appear, and TV success would be automatic. He rehearsed little, devoting most of his time to movie and other activities. The result was a disaster of the first magnitude, as *The Frank Sinatra Show* ran second or third in audience in its time period. Around December Sinatra buckled down to try to save the show. The number of musicals was increased, the show switched to filming before a live audience, and Sinatra himself began guesting on other

277

shows to promote his program. Unfortunately it was too late.

Nelson Riddle, who had helped spark Sinatra's comeback on records with his imaginative arranging, was musical director on the variety episodes, whose guest stars included such names as Bob Hope, Peggy Lee, and the professional debut of Sinatra's daughter Nancy—aged 17—on November 1, 1957.

FRANK'S PLACE
Situation Comedy
FIRST TELECAST: *September 14, 1987*
LAST TELECAST:
BROADCAST HISTORY:
Sep 1987–Nov 1987, CBS Mon 8:00–8:30
Dec 1987–Feb 1988, CBS Mon 8:30–9:00
Feb 1988–Mar 1988, CBS Mon 9:30–10:00
Mar 1988, CBS Tue 8:00–8:30
*Jul 1988–   *, CBS Sat 8:30–9:00
CAST:
Frank Parrish..................... Tim Reid
Sy "Bubba" Weisburger...... Robert Harper
Hannah Griffin .... Daphne Maxwell Reid
Anna-May............. Francesca P. Roberts
Miss Marie............. Frances E. Williams
Mrs. Bertha Griffin-Lamour .. Virginia Capers
Big Arthur..................... Tony Burton
Tiger Shepin.............. Charles Lampkin
Reverend Deal............ Lincoln Kilpatrick
Cool Charles .... William Thomas, Jr.
Shorty La Roux .... Don Yesso

One of the mellowest, most offbeat "comedies" of recent years, an easygoing mélange of eccentric characters set in a small Creole restaurant in New Orleans. Frank Parrish was not really cut out to run such a place. In fact, he had never been to New Orleans until he found out he had inherited Chez Louisiane from a father he had not seen since he was two years old. Raised in New England, and most recently a professor of Renaissance history in Boston, Frank had quite an adjustment to make—to New Orleans, to the restaurant business, and to a staff that at times resented him as an outsider and at other times tried to help him adjust to his new surroundings. The restaurant's staff included Big Arthur, the head chef; Shorty, the assistant chef; Tiger, the bartender; Anna-May, the head waitress; Miss Marie, the frail elderly "waitress emeritus"; and Cool Charles, the versatile handyman. The regulars at Chez Louisiane were Bubba Weisberger, a friendly lawyer; Reverend Deal, who appeared to be more con man than minister; Mrs. Griffin-Lamour, domineering owner of the neighborhood funeral parlor; and her beautiful daughter Hanna (played by star Tim Reid's real-life wife Daphne), a mortician and embalmer whose profession almost, but not quite, prevented Frank from becoming romantically involved with her.

Critics loved the rule-bending show, which offered no canned laughter, a slow, Dixieland-flavored musical background, and dramatic moments along with the comedy. Viewers were not so sure what to make of it.

FRANKIE LAINE TIME
Musical Variety
FIRST TELECAST: *July 20, 1955*
LAST TELECAST: *September 19, 1956*
BROADCAST HISTORY:
Jul 1955–Sep 1955, CBS Wed 8:00–9:00
Aug 1956–Sep 1956, CBS Wed 8:00–9:00
REGULARS:
Frankie Laine
The Lynn Duddy Singers (1955)
The James Starbuck Dancers (1955)
The Jimmy Carroll Orchestra (1955)
The Mellolarks (1956)
The Edith Barstow Dancers (1956)
The Russ Case Orchestra (1956)

Popular singer Frankie Laine spent two summers on television as the replacement for *Arthur Godfrey and His Friends*. He sang, introduced, and performed with assorted guest stars, and acted in comedy sketches.

FRED ASTAIRE PREMIERE THEATER
syndicated title for *Alcoa Premiere*

FRED WARING SHOW, THE
Musical Variety
FIRST TELECAST: *April 17, 1949*
LAST TELECAST: *May 30, 1954*
BROADCAST HISTORY:
Apr 1949–Jan 1952, CBS Sun 9:00–10:00 (OS)
Jan 1952–May 1954, CBS Sun 9:00–9:30 (OS)
REGULARS:
Fred Waring and His Pennsylvanians
THEME:
"Sleep," by Earl Lebieg

Fred Waring, and his orchestra and large chorus, had been an American institution for several decades when he first entered TV on a regular basis in 1949. Slotted right after the high-rated Ed Sullivan *Toast of the Town*, he quickly became a Sunday night standby. The entire Waring organization made up the regular TV cast of more than 60 members. In addition to standard instrumental and vocal numbers, the show included dancing (during the 1949–1950 season there was a dance contest titled "Video Ballroom" as a regular feature); sketch material that was musically related; and interpretations of fairy tales. Although all the members of the Pennsylvanians had solos at one time or another during the show's five-year run, those most frequently spotlighted were Jane Wilson, Joanne Wheatley, Joe Marine, Daisy Bernier, Keith and Sylvia Textor, Hugh "Uncle Lumpy" Brannum, Virginia Morley and Livingston Gearhart, and Poley McClintock (with whom Fred had founded his first band in 1915).

The Fred Waring Show was performed before

a live studio audience during its first and last seasons, and without a live audience for the three seasons in between. In its last season it was cut back to alternate-week status, with *G.E. Theatre* airing on the alternate Sundays.

FREDDY MARTIN SHOW, THE
Musical Variety
FIRST TELECAST: *July 12, 1951*
LAST TELECAST: *November 28, 1951*
BROADCAST HISTORY:
Jul 1951–Aug 1951, NBC Thu 10:00–10:30
Sep 1951–Nov 1951, NBC Wed 10:30–11:00
REGULARS:
Freddy Martin and His Orchestra
Merv Griffin
Murray Arnold
The Martin Men

Saxophone player and orchestra leader Freddy Martin was the star of this musical variety show, which featured, in addition to a guest female vocalist each week, the Freddy Martin Orchestra, a young male vocalist named Merv Griffin (later to have great success as a talk-show host), pianist Murray Arnold, and the Martin Men, a vocal quintet. Sponsored by Hazel Bishop cosmetics, this series was also known as *The Hazel Bishop Show*.

FREE COUNTRY
Situation Comedy
FIRST TELECAST: *June 24, 1978*
LAST TELECAST: *July 22, 1978*
BROADCAST HISTORY:
Jun 1978–Jul 1978, ABC Sat 8:00–8:30
CAST:
Joseph Bresner.................. Rob Reiner
Anna Bresner................... Judy Kahan
Sidney Gewertzman........ Fred McCarren
Ida Gewertzman.............. Renee Lippin
Leo Gold...................... Larry Gelman
Louis Peschi................. Joe Pantoliano

Rob Reiner assumed the dual role of a young Lithuanian immigrant, and the same man at age 89, in this summer series. Reiner opened each episode as the elderly Joseph Bresner, reminiscing about the days when he was a young man newly arrived in the U.S.A. The scene then shifted to New York City's Lower East Side in the early 1900s, where Joseph and his bride Anna struggled to understand the customs of their adopted homeland. Ida and Sidney Gewertzman were their neighbors, Louis was a friend, and Leo Gold a border. Rob Reiner was co-writer and co-producer of this series, as well as its star.

FREEBIE AND THE BEAN
Police
FIRST TELECAST: *December 6, 1980*
LAST TELECAST: *January 17, 1981*

BROADCAST HISTORY:
Dec 1980–Jan 1981, CBS Sat 9:00–10:00
CAST:
Det. Sgt. Tim Walker (Freebie).. Tom Mason
Det. Sgt. Dan Delgado (Bean)
.......................Hector Elizondo
D.A. Walter W. Cruikshank
.... William Daniels
Rodney Blake ("Axle")........ Mel Stewart

Freebie and the Bean were two plainclothes police officers working on special assignments for San Francisco District Attorney Walter Cruikshank. As a team, the two seemed totally mismatched. Freebie was a swinging single, always looking for angles and not above bending the law a little to help their investigations. Bean was introverted and serious, a family man with a wife and two children who believed in doing things more or less "by the book." They were often in conflict, with Freebie usually convincing the Bean that his way would work. It just seemed that every time Bean let himself get talked into one of Freebie's off-the-wall plans, *he* wound up on the short end. Their unorthodox methods, and history of destroying police property (mostly cars in wild chases), did not endear them to the D.A., but they got results, and that's what counted. Axle was the mechanic at the police garage who had the unenviable task of trying to salvage the cars they used in the chases.

Unfortunately this series was such a mishmash of comedy and drama, slapstick and reality, that it soon sank without a trace. The fact that it was scheduled opposite ABC's *The Love Boat*—which had no trouble defining what *it* wanted to be—probably didn't help. *Freebie and the Bean* was based on the 1974 movie of the same name, starring James Caan and Alan Arkin.

FRIDAY COMEDY SPECIAL, THE
Comedy Anthology
FIRST TELECAST: *March 14, 1975*
LAST TELECAST: *May 23, 1975*
BROADCAST HISTORY:
Mar 1975–May 1975, CBS Fri 8:00–8:30

The situation comedies telecast in this series were a collection of unsold pilots for projected regular series.

FRIDAY NIGHT VIDEOS
Music
FIRST TELECAST: *July 29, 1983*
LAST TELECAST:
BROADCAST HISTORY:
Jul 1983–Jun 1987, NBC Fri 12:30–2:00 A.M.
Jun 1987–   , NBC Fri 1:30–2:30 A.M.
ANNOUNCER (OFF CAMERA):
Nick Michaels (1983–1985)
Scott Muni (1985)

279

This late-night series was commercial television's answer to the considerable popularity of cable TV's MTV (Music Television) network. Like MTV, *Friday Night Videos* consisted primarily of the latest rock music videos, most of them by currently hot artists such as Culture Club, the Police, John Cougar Mellencamp, Styx, Quarterflash, and Paul McCartney. Mixed in were "Hall of Fame Videos" by stars of the 1960s and 1970s (the Beatles, Hollies, Doors, etc.); "Private Reel," a profile of a major star; and "Video Vote," in which viewers got to vote for one of two selected videos, using nationwide 900-numbers. On the series' premiere, Duran Duran's "Hungry Like the Wolf" trounced David Bowie's "Let's Dance" by 59,000 to 37,000 calls. On later telecasts the combined vote ran as high as 200,000 calls. A highlight of each show was a "World Premiere Video," the first network showing of a major artist's clip. The program got banner ratings in December 1983 when it premiered Michael Jackson's million-dollar "Thriller" video under this heading.

Initially there was no on-camera host or announcer for *Friday Night Videos*, with the songs being introduced by off-camera announcers. However a policy of on-camera celebrity guests was begun in the fall of 1985; among those hosting were stars of currently popular TV series (Phylicia Rashad, Lisa Bonet, Harry Anderson, Susan Saint James, Tony Danza, Michael Warren, etc.), movie actors, and some singers (Whitney Houston, Stevie Wonder).

FRIDAY THE 13TH
Horror/Drama
BROADCAST HISTORY:
Syndicated only
30 minutes
Produced: *1987–*
Released: *October 1987*
CAST:
Micki Foster........................ Robey
Ryan Dallion .... John D. Le May
Jack Marshak................ Chris Wiggins

Lewis Vendredi was an antiques dealer who had made a deal with the devil to sell cursed antiques in return for material wealth. When Lewis died, his niece Micki inherited the antique store which she renamed "Curious Goods." With the help of her cousin Ryan and their partner, retired magician Jack Marshak, Micki attempted to recover the cursed antiques and seal them away in the basement under the store so that they could cause no more damage. The antiques they recovered always seemed to cause deaths—for example, a scalpel that could work miracles on the living, but only after it had been used to kill someone; and a cupid's statue that compelled women to fall in love with the owner but made him kill them after making love.

Although this TV series used the title of a very popular series of horror movies—and was even advertised as "Friday the 13th—The Series"—it actually had nothing to do with the movies.

FRIDAYS
Comedy Variety
FIRST TELECAST: *April 11, 1980*
LAST TELECAST: *October 22, 1982*
BROADCAST HISTORY:
Apr 1980–Mar 1981, ABC Fri 11:30–12:40 A.M.
Apr 1981–Sep 1981, ABC Fri 12:00–1:10 A.M.
Sep 1981–Oct 1982, ABC Fri 12:00–1:40 A.M.
REGULARS:
Mark Blankfield
Maryedith Burrell
Melanie Chartoff
Larry David
Darrow Igus
Brandis Kemp
Bruce Mahler
Michael Richards
John Roarke

ABC's answer to NBC's *Saturday Night Live*—in fact, an out-and-out carbon copy of *Saturday Night Live*—was this live late-night program called *Fridays*. As on the prototype, there was a rambunctious cast of bright young comedians, heavy emphasis on satirical and sometimes raunchy humor, rock musicians as guests, and even a "Weekend Update"–style parody newscast. A guest host presided each week.

Some of the early sketches were so gross, in fact, that a number of network affiliates dropped the show. Among the offensive bits were a skit called "Diner of the Living Dead," in which the actors ate human flesh, and another entitled "Women Who Spit." Later things got a bit more sophisticated, with one of the highlights being an elaborate, 17-minute musical comedy satirizing the cult film *The Rocky Horror Show* (called "The Ronny Horror Show," and starring a mock President Reagan). John Roarke's Reagan was a regular feature, as was Mark Blankfield's speed-freak pharmacist, Larry David's rabbi, Bruce Mahler's Spanish announcer, and the "Rasta Chef" of Darrow Igus (the only black in the cast). A certain cynical commercialism remained, however, as when an apparently real on-camera fist fight between guest star Andy Kaufman and one of the show's producers turned out to have been staged to generate publicity.

The young repertory company was hard-working and inventive, and some of the writing (supervised by Jack Burns of *The Muppet Show*) was first-rate, but the program's reputation as a rip-off and its failure to provide an attention-getting new star (like Chevy Chase in *Saturday Night Live*'s first season) hindered its chances of becoming the breakthrough hit the earlier program had been.

FRIENDS
Comedy/Drama
FIRST TELECAST: *March 25, 1979*

LAST TELECAST: *April 22, 1979*
BROADCAST HISTORY:
  Mar 1979–Apr 1979, ABC Sun 7:00–8:00
CAST:
  Pete Richards .... Charles Aiken
  Nancy Wilks .... Jill Whelan
  Randy Summerfield .... Jarrod Johnson
  Mr. Frank Richards .... Andy Romano
  Mrs. Pamela Richards........ Karen Morrow
  Cynthia Richards .... Alicia Fleer
  Mr. Charley Wilks .... Dennis Redfield
  Mr. Warren Summerfield .... Roger Robinson
  Mrs. Jane Summerfield .... Janet MacLachlan

Supercute comedy-drama about life as seen through the eyes of three 11-year-olds from differing backgrounds: Pete; Nancy, from a broken home; and Randy, a black youth and son of a lawyer. All about dating, learning to succeed, the meaning of friendship, etc.

FRIENDS OF MAN
Documentary
BROADCAST HISTORY:
  Syndicated only
  30 minutes
  Produced: *1973–1974* (45 episodes)
  Released: *Fall 1975*
NARRATOR:
  Glenn Ford

This documentary series about animals as the "friends of man" was aimed primarily at younger viewers.

FRIGIDAIRE SUMMER THEATER
Dramatic Anthology
FIRST TELECAST: *June 20, 1958*
LAST TELECAST: *August 1, 1958*
BROADCAST HISTORY:
  Jun 1958–Aug 1958, ABC Fri 9:30–10:00

This program was a collection of filmed reruns of episodes from other anthology series.

FROM A BIRD'S EYE VIEW
Situation Comedy
FIRST TELECAST: *March 29, 1971*
LAST TELECAST: *August 16, 1971*
BROADCAST HISTORY:
  Mar 1971–Aug 1971, NBC Mon 7:30–8:00
CAST:
  Millie Grover.............. Millicent Martin
  Maggie Ralston.................. Pat Finley
  Mr. Clive Beauchamp .... Peter Jones
  Uncle Bert Quigley........ Robert Cawdron
  Miss Fosdyke................... Noel Hood

The misadventures of two young stewardesses for an international airline based in London, England. Britisher Millie was so good-natured and well-meaning that she could never resist helping people. Every time she tried to help, however, some-

thing went wrong, and the more she tried to straighten things out, the more complicated they became. Maggie, her level-headed American friend, spent most of her time trying to get Millie out of her predicaments. Also featured was the girls' boss, Mr. Beauchamp, a harassed middle-management executive for the airline.

FROM HERE TO ETERNITY
War Drama
FIRST TELECAST: *February 14, 1979*
LAST TELECAST: *August 16, 1980*
BROADCAST HISTORY:
  Feb 1979, NBC Wed 9:00–11:00
  Mar 1980–Apr 1980, NBC Wed 10:00–11:00
  Aug 1980, NBC Various times
CAST:
  Master Sgt. Milt Warden ... William Devane
  Karen Holmes (1979) .... Natalie Wood
  Karen Holmes (1980) .... Barbara Hershey
  Pvt. Robert E. Lee Prewitt (1979)
  .... Steve Railsback
  Capt./Maj. Dana Holmes .... Roy Thinnes
  Pvt. Angelo Maggio (1979) .... Joe Pantoliano
  Lorene Rogers .... Kim Basinger
  Sgt. Cheney .... Will Sampson
  Mrs. Kipfer (1979)............. Salome Jens
  Lt./Capt. Ross .... David Spielberg
  Fatso Judson (1979) .... Peter Boyle
  Jefferson Davis Prewitt (1980)... Don Johnson
  Pfc. Ignacio Carmona (1980)
  .... Rocky Echevarria
  Emily Austin (1980) .... Lacey Neuhaus
  Lt. Kenneth Barrett (1980) .... John Calvin
  Mrs. Austin (1980) .... Priscilla Pointer
  Mr. Austin (1980) .... Richard Roat
  Dr. Anne Brewster (1980)....... Claire Malis
  Aimee (1980) .... Joann Gordon
  Kurt Von Nordlund (1980) .. Richard Erdman

James Jones' classic novel first came to television as a six-hour mini-series in the spring of 1979. *From Here to Eternity* was a story of World War II military life on Hawaii in 1941, prior to and just after the Japanese attack on Pearl Harbor. Sgt. Milt Warden was faced with two problems. He was having a torrid love affair with his commanding officer's wife, Karen Holmes; and he was trying to instill confidence in Pvt. Robert Prewitt, a sensitive young man in his unit, whose lack of aggression caused him to be ridiculed by the other men. The mini-series generally followed the lengthy Jones novel more accurately than did the 1953 theatrical movie version starring Burt Lancaster and Deborah Kerr.

  The ratings success of the mini-series prompted NBC to introduce a regular weekly series that took up where the novel left off. It took place in Honolulu during 1942, with the city under martial law following the Japanese attack. Sgt. Warden was still having his affair with Karen, but now had to deal with Robert Prewitt's brother Jefferson. (The AWOL Robert had been killed while tryin' to return to base on Warden's advice.) Jefferson Prewitt became romantically involved with Lorene Rogers, the prostitute who had been Robert's girlfriend, and eventually married her. Meanwhile Warden and Maj. Holmes had a showdown over Holmes's treatment of his wife, after which Warden suffered a minor heart attack. Karen Holmes thereupon left Honolulu to spend the duration of the war on the U.S. mainland.

This weekly soap opera drew few viewers, and was abruptly pulled from the schedule after less than a month. The resolution of the story, as described here, did not take place until August 1980, when the remaining original episodes were aired as specials.

FRONT PAGE, THE
Newspaper Drama
FIRST TELECAST: *September 29, 1949*
LAST TELECAST: *January 26, 1950*
BROADCAST HISTORY:
  Sep 1949–Jan 1950, CBS Thu 8:00–8:30
CAST:
  Walter Burns . . . . John Daly
  Hildy Johnson . . . . Mark Roberts

Adapted from the famous Hecht-MacArthur play about a small-town newspaper editor and his star reporter, Hildy Johnson. The love-hate relationship between the two of them was the focal point of the story, as Hildy was always threatening to quit the *Center City Examiner* to find "a normal job." Despite what they said about each other, however, Walter and Hildy were loyal friends. The John Daly in this live series was the same person who worked for CBS and later ABC as a news correspondent. It was felt that his actual journalistic experience would give this dramatic role a sense of authenticity.

FRONT PAGE DETECTIVE
Newspaper Drama
FIRST TELECAST: *July 6, 1951*
LAST TELECAST: *November 13, 1953*
BROADCAST HISTORY:
  Jul 1951–Feb 1952, DUM Fri 9:30–10:00
  Oct 1953–Nov 1953, DUM Fri 8:00–8:30
CAST:
  David Chase. . . . . Edmund Lowe
  David's Girlfriend. . . . . Paula Drew

Movie actor Edmund Lowe, known both for his matinee-idol roles and his portrayal of the grimy Sgt. Quirt in *What Price Glory?*, starred in this early filmed series as David Chase, a newspaper columnist who "couldn't be bought." David's stories usually involved murders, which he was unusually good at solving. Paula Drew played his girlfriend, a fashion designer.

Front Page Detective was primarily a syndicated series seen on local stations at various times, but it was carried on the DuMont network for two periods, as shown.

FRONT ROW CENTER
Musical Variety
FIRST TELECAST: *March 25, 1949*
LAST TELECAST: *April 9, 1950*
BROADCAST HISTORY:
  Mar 1949–Jun 1949, DUM Fri 9:00–9:30
  Jun 1949–Sep 1949, DUM Fri 8:00–9:00
  Oct 1949–Apr 1950, DUM Sun 7:00–8:00
REGULARS:
  Phil Leeds
  Monica Moore
  Cass Franklin
  Hal Loman
  Bibi Osterwald
  Joan Fields
  Danny Shore
  The Sammy Spear Orchestra

This was one of DuMont's early attempts to produce a big weekly variety show, and it starred numerous guests from Broadway and the nightclub circuit. Frank Fontaine hosted the first telecast, with special guest star Marilyn Maxwell in her TV debut. Various hosts appeared thereafter, along with a large and constantly changing supporting cast of regulars. Some of those with longer runs are listed above.

FRONT ROW CENTER
Dramatic Anthology
FIRST TELECAST: *June 1, 1955*
LAST TELECAST: *September 21, 1955*
BROADCAST HISTORY:
  Jun 1955–Sep 1955, CBS Wed 10:00–11:00

Live full-hour adaptations of Broadway plays were presented under the title *Front Row Center* on CBS during the summer of 1955, starting with the acclaimed *Dinner at Eight*. The series aired weekly throughout June and then became an alternate-week program when *The U.S. Steel Hour* moved in to share its time slot in July. It returned to the air the following January on Sunday afternoons where it stayed until April.

FRONTIER
Western Anthology
FIRST TELECAST: *September 25, 1955*
LAST TELECAST: *September 9, 1956*
BROADCAST HISTORY:
  Sep 1955–Sep 1956, NBC Sun 7:30–8:00
NARRATOR:
  Walter Coy

Walter Coy's opening and closing lines, the same for each episode, were descriptive of this anthology series about the West: "This is the West. This is the land of beginning again. This is the story of men and women facing the frontier. This is the way it happened." And finally, "It happened that way . . . moving west."

There was no glamour in *Frontier*. It depicted real people with real problems moving into, and coping with, a new territory. Indians were not the only villains; roving criminals, rustlers, and the sometimes harsh environment also beset the settlers. In addition to serving as narrator, Walter Coy acted in some of the episodes.

FRONTIER ADVENTURE
see *Death Valley Days*

FRONTIER CIRCUS
Circus Drama
FIRST TELECAST: *October 5, 1961*
LAST TELECAST: *September 20, 1962*
BROADCAST HISTORY:
Oct 1961–Jan 1962, CBS Thu 7:30–8:30
Feb 1962–Sep 1962, CBS Thu 8:00–9:00
Sep 1962, CBS Thu 7:30–8:30
CAST:
Col. Casey Thompson .... Chill Wills
Ben Travis .... John Derek
Tony Gentry................ Richard Jaeckel

Set in the Southwest during the late 1800s, *Frontier Circus* was a cross between a circus drama and a traditional Western. The T&T Circus, operated by Col. Casey Thompson, traveled from town to town in a wagon train. Two handsome hunks of masculinity typical of the TV West were at the center of much of the action: Ben Travis, the straw boss, who supervised the workmen, and Tony Gentry, the advance man, who scouted likely stopping places for the circus. The stories involved the relationships between the performers and workmen of the circus, and their encounters with assorted frontier types. Where did the name T&T come from? From Thompson and Travis, who were actually partners, despite their divergent functions.

FRONTIER JUSTICE
Western Anthology
FIRST TELECAST: *July 7, 1958*
LAST TELECAST: *September 28, 1961*
BROADCAST HISTORY:
Jul 1958–Sep 1958, CBS Mon 9:30–10:00
Jul 1959–Sep 1959, CBS Mon 9:00–9:30
Aug 1961–Sep 1961, CBS Thu 8:30–9:00
HOST:
Lew Ayres (1958)
Melvyn Douglas (1959)
Ralph Bellamy (1961)

For three summers, CBS aired reruns of episodes originally telecast on Dick Powell's *Zane Grey Theater*—in 1958 as the summer replacement for *December Bride,* in 1959 for *The Danny Thomas Show,* and in 1961 for the series from which they were taken, *Dick Powell's Zane Grey Theater.* Each season's host was a different actor.

FRONTIER THEATER
see *Movies—Prior to 1961*

FROSTY FROLICS
Musical Variety
FIRST TELECAST: *September 19, 1951*
LAST TELECAST: *October 10, 1951*
BROADCAST HISTORY:
Sep 1951–Oct 1951, ABC Wed 8:00–9:00

This four-week series of musical variety shows on ice included the Ice Follies, Ice Capades, and Icelandia Skaters.
From Hollywood.

FUGITIVE, THE
Drama
FIRST TELECAST: *September 17, 1963*
LAST TELECAST: *August 29, 1967*
BROADCAST HISTORY:
Sep 1963–Aug 1967, ABC Tue 10:00–11:00
CAST:
Dr. Richard Kimble .... David Janssen
Lt. Philip Gerard.............. Barry Morse
Donna Taft .... Jacqueline Scott
Fred Johnson, the One-Armed Man
.... Bill Raisch
EXECUTIVE PRODUCER:
Quinn Martin

Dr. Richard Kimble had been accused, tried, convicted, and sentenced to die for a crime he did not commit—the murder of his wife. Kimble was being taken by Lt. Gerard to prison to be executed when the train in which they were riding was derailed and the lieutenant was knocked unconscious. Kimble escaped. For the next four highly successful seasons, while Gerard searched for Kimble, Kimble searched for the one-armed man he had seen actually murder his wife. Back and forth across the country, taking odd jobs and new identities, and constantly on the verge of being caught by the relentless Gerard, Kimble kept looking for the real killer. Only on rare occasions could the doctor return furtively to his former life (through contacts with his married sister Donna), and rarely did he glimpse his quarry, the one-armed man.

In a move unique among series of this type, *The Fugitive* actually resolved the situation that had sustained suspense throughout its run. In a special two-part story, aired on the last two Tuesdays that the show was seen on the network, Kimble found the one-armed man, Gerard found Kimble, and the doctor was exonerated of the crime—despite the death of the one-armed man. In a climactic chase scene, Kimble and the one-armed man cornered each other atop a tower. Lt. Gerard, in hot pursuit on the ground, realized he had been wrong about Kimble and shot the one-armed man to save the doctor's life. The one-armed man plunged to his death before he could be captured.

This final episode of *The Fugitive,* which aired on August 29, 1967, was seen by more people than any single episode of a regular series in the history of television until that time, and its 72 percent share of all television viewers that night set a regular series record which was not exceeded until the *Dallas* episode in which J.R.'s attacker was revealed, 13 years later.

The deep, resonant voice of the narrator on *The Fugitive,* who kept viewers apprised of Richard Kimball's situation, belonged to rotund actor William Conrad.

Reruns of *The Fugitive* aired weekday afternoons on ABC from April 1967 to March 1968.

FU MANCHU
see *Adventures of Fu Manchu, The*

FULL HOUSE
Situation Comedy
FIRST TELECAST: *September 22, 1987*
LAST TELECAST:
BROADCAST HISTORY:
Sep 1987, ABC Tue 8:30–9:00
Sep 1987–Feb 1988, ABC Fri 8:00–8:30
Mar 1988–   , ABC Fri 8:30–9:00
CAST:
Danny Tanner .... Bob Saget
Uncle Jesse Cochran .... John Stamos
Joey Gladstone .... David Coulier
D.J. (Donna Jo) Tanner (age 10)
    .... Candace Cameron
Stephanie Tanner (5) .... Jodie Sweetin
Michelle Tanner (6 mos.)
    .... Mary Kate & Ashley Fuller
                        Olsen (alternating)

Three young men and three kids formed the latest of TV's unlikely "families" in this light comedy, set in San Francisco. The children belonged to TV sportscaster Danny, who was left with his hands full when his wife died suddenly. Moving in to help (?) were Danny's brother-in-law Jesse, a long-haired rock 'n' roller who wanted to PARTY!; and friend Joey, an aspiring stand-up comic given to loud jackets and nonsensical reactions to diapers.

FUN FOR THE MONEY
Quiz/Audience Participation
FIRST TELECAST: *June 17, 1949*
LAST TELECAST: *December 9, 1949*
BROADCAST HISTORY:
Jun 1949–Dec 1949, ABC Fri 9:30–10:00
EMCEE:
Johnny Olsen

This audience-participation quiz show was modeled along the lines of baseball, with stunts and games.

FUNNY FACE
Situation Comedy
FIRST TELECAST: *September 18, 1971*

LAST TELECAST: *December 11, 1971*
BROADCAST HISTORY:
Sep 1971–Dec 1971, CBS Sat 8:30–9:00
CAST:
Sandy Stockton .... Sandy Duncan
Alice McRaven .... Valorie Armstrong
Kate Harwell .... Kathleen Freeman
Pat Harwell .... Henry Beckman

Sandy Duncan was considered one of the most promising new stars in television when this comedy series was launched in the fall of 1971. She was cast as Sandy Stockton, a pert young UCLA student majoring in education who made ends meet by working part-time as an actress in TV commercials. The big-city life of Los Angeles was a constant challenge for Sandy, who hailed from the small town of Taylorville, Illinois. Helping her cope were her next-door neighbor and best friend, Alice McRaven, and Mr. and Mrs. Harwell, the nosy landlords. *Funny Face* did not make the grade, but the character of Sandy Stockton was to return the following season in a similar venture called *The Sandy Duncan Show.*

FUNNY SIDE, THE
Comedy Variety
FIRST TELECAST: *September 14, 1971*
LAST TELECAST: *December 7, 1971*
BROADCAST HISTORY:
Sep 1971–Nov 1971, NBC Tue 9:30–10:30
Nov 1971–Dec 1971, NBC Tue 8:30–9:30
HOST:
Gene Kelly
REGULARS:
John Amos and Teresa Graves
Warren Berlinger and Pat Finley
Dick Clair and Jenna McMahon
Michael Lembeck and Cindy Williams
Burt Mustin and Queenie Smith

Comedy sketches, musical vignettes, and production numbers were the basic elements of this variety show, which each week looked at the funny side of a specific aspect of married life. Topics covered ranged from health to financial problems to sexual attitudes, and were seen from the perspectives of five married couples. John and Teresa were the minority couple, Warren and Pat represented blue-collar people, Dick and Jenna were wealthy, Michael and Cindy were counterculture teenagers, and Burt and Queenie were senior citizens. Gene Kelly was the regular host and participated in many of the sketches and production numbers.

FURTHER ADVENTURES OF ELLERY QUEEN, THE
see *Adventures of Ellery Queen, The*

G

G.E. COLLEGE BOWL, THE
Quiz/Audience Participation
FIRST TELECAST: *January 7, 1968*
LAST TELECAST: *June 14, 1970*
BROADCAST HISTORY:
Jan 1968–Jun 1968, NBC Sun 6:00–6:30
Jan 1969–Jun 1969, NBC Sun 6:00–6:30
Jan 1970–Jun 1970, NBC Sun 6:30–7:00
HOST/MODERATOR:
Robert Earle

G.E. College Bowl, one of the most intelligent of TV's many quiz shows, was seen through most of its long run as a Sunday afternoon program. However, on three occasions between 1968 and 1970 it was scheduled in the evening hours.

The format was simple, although the questions were not. Two teams of four scholars each, representing different colleges, were pitted against each other and the buzzer. Questions ranged across mathematics, science, engineering, literature, and philosophy and often sent viewers at home scurrying for their encyclopedias. The team amassing the most points won scholarship money for its college and the right to return the following week. A team winning for five consecutive weeks won a special trophy and was retired as an undefeated champion. Awards to a championship team could amount to as much as $19,500.

G.E. College Bowl premiered on Sunday afternoon, January 4, 1959, on CBS with Allen Ludden as host. He was succeeded by Robert Earle, who followed the program when it moved to NBC in 1963. In addition to this network series' 11-year run (1959–1970) the same format was used locally in many cities with area high schools competing. The local high school version was usually titled *It's Academic.*

G.E. GUEST HOUSE
Quiz/Panel
FIRST TELECAST: *July 1, 1951*
LAST TELECAST: *August 26, 1951*
BROADCAST HISTORY:
Jul 1951–Aug 1951, CBS Sun 9:00–10:00
EMCEE:
Oscar Levant
Durward Kirby

A different panel of four celebrities from four areas of show business—a critic, a writer, a performer, and a producer—appeared each week to answer assorted questions on this live summer game show. The object of the game was to determine which of the four areas produced people most knowledgeable about show business. Emcee Oscar Levant, a pianist, played a number of musical selections and conducted a musical quiz during each show. When he left the series, after its first three telecasts, Durward Kirby assumed the role of emcee.

GABRIELLE
Music
FIRST TELECAST: *July 13, 1948*
LAST TELECAST: *August 12, 1948*
BROADCAST HISTORY:
Jul 1948–Aug 1948, ABC Tue/Thu 7:00–7:15
HOSTESS:
Gabrielle

This was a musical interlude with songs in the French style by Gabrielle.

GALACTICA 1980
see *Battlestar Galactica*

GALE STORM SHOW, THE
Situation Comedy
FIRST TELECAST: *September 29, 1956*
LAST TELECAST: *March 24, 1960*
BROADCAST HISTORY:
Sep 1956–Apr 1959, CBS Sat 9:00–9:30
Oct 1959–Mar 1960, ABC Thu 7:30–8:00
CAST:
Susanna Pomeroy .... Gale Storm
Esmerelda Nugent .... ZaSu Pitts
Capt. Huxley .... Roy Roberts
Cedric (1956–1959) .... Jimmy Fairfax

Susanna Pomeroy was the social director of the luxury liner S.S. *Ocean Queen.* She spent much of her time in cahoots with her close friend Esmerelda "Nugey" Nugent, operator of the ship's beauty salon, and their alliance confounded the liner's rather stuffy Capt. Huxley. Adding to the captain's frustrations was the ship's steward, an impish little fellow named Cedric (who went overboard when the series moved to ABC). This filmed comedy was subtitled *Oh Susanna,* and that was the title it later adopted when it went into syndication.

Network reruns of this series appeared weekdays on ABC from April 1959 to September 1961.

GALEN DRAKE SHOW, THE
Children's Variety
FIRST TELECAST: *January 12, 1957*
LAST TELECAST: *May 11, 1957*
BROADCAST HISTORY:
Jan 1957–May 1957, ABC Sat 7:00–7:30
REGULARS:
Galen Drake
Stuart Foster
Rita Ellis

This unusual variety show was aimed directly at children. Galen Drake was a popular radio personality who was known for the pleasant way in which he told stories. Here he sang a little, interviewed guests, and introduced songs by the show's regular singers, Stuart Foster and Rita Ellis. Guests on this live series were people presumably of interest to youngsters, such as puppeteer Bil Baird, the president of an art school, and a young girl who had run away from home because she was in love with Elvis Presley.

GALLANT MEN, THE
War Drama
FIRST TELECAST: *October 5, 1962*
LAST TELECAST: *September 14, 1963*
BROADCAST HISTORY:
  Oct 1962–Dec 1962, ABC Fri 7:30–8:30
  Dec 1962–Sep 1963, ABC Sat 7:30–8:30
CAST:
  Conley Wright............ Robert McQueeney
  Capt. Jim Benedict........ William Reynolds
  Lt. Frank Kimbro .... Robert Ridgely
  1st Sgt. John McKenna ... Richard X. Slattery
  PFC Pete D'Angelo........... Eddie Fontaine
  Private Ernie Lucavich ..... Roland LaStarza
  Private Sam Hanson .... Robert Gothie
  Private Roger Gibson .... Roger Davis

One of the TV trends of the early 1960s that never really got off the ground was the wartime action drama. ABC premiered two such shows in 1962, *Combat* and *The Gallant Men*.

The Gallant Men was set in Italy during World War II and followed the progress of a front-line infantry company, part of the 36th Infantry ("Texas") Division, as it fought its way up the peninsula. The company was led by a determined young captain named Jim Benedict, and the action was seen through the eyes of a war correspondent, Conley Wright. Other principals included free-swinging 1st Sergeant McKenna; handsome, guitar-playing ladies' man D'Angelo (the company's "operator"); the inseparable Lucavich and Hanson; and the callow young driver, Gibson.

The Gallant Men offered action, heroics, and a kind of gritty realism, plus plenty of sexy Italian girls along the way, but it failed to establish a beachhead against either *Rawhide* on Friday night or *Jackie Gleason* on Saturday, and soon disappeared.

GALLERY OF MME. LUI-TSONG, THE
Crime Drama
FIRST TELECAST: *September 3, 1951*
LAST TELECAST: *November 21, 1951*
BROADCAST HISTORY:
  Sep 1951–Oct 1951, DUM Mon 8:30–9:00
  Oct 1951–Nov 1951, DUM Wed 9:00–9:30
CAST:
  Mme. Lui-Tsong .... Anna May Wong

Chinese-American actress Anna May Wong (whose real name was Wong Lui-Tsong) portrayed the owner of a far-flung chain of art galleries who doubled as an exotic—and beautiful—sleuth in this short-lived series. Stolen treasure, international intrigue, and shady operators all provided material for the stories. Effective October 10, 1951, the program's title was shortened to *Mme. Lui-Tsong*.

GAMBLE ON LOVE
Quiz/Audience Participation
FIRST TELECAST: *July 16, 1954*
LAST TELECAST: *August 6, 1954*
BROADCAST HISTORY:
  Jul 1954–Aug 1954, DUM Fri 10:30–11:00
HOSTESS:
  Denise Darcel

In this short-lived summer quiz, three couples who were "married, about to be married, or just in love" were first interviewed on their "gamble on love." They then had a chance at the wheel of fortune, with one partner spinning the wheel and the other answering the questions. Top prize was a mink coat, or the like. Curvaceous actress Denise Darcel hosted. Ernie Kovacs replaced her in the same time period with a new format and title (see *Time Will Tell*).

GAME OF THE WEEK, THE
see *Football*

GAMES PEOPLE PLAY
Sports
FIRST TELECAST: *August 21, 1980*
LAST TELECAST: *September 24, 1981*
BROADCAST HISTORY:
  Aug 1980–Dec 1980, NBC Thu 8:00–9:00
  Jun 1981–Aug 1981, NBC Sat 10:00–11:00
  Sep 1981, NBC Thu 8:00–9:00
REGULARS:
  Bryant Gumbel
  Cyndy Garvey
  Mike Adamle
  Johnny Bench
  Donna DeVarona
  Gary Owens
  Arte Johnson

These were not everyday sporting events. They were "games" played for novelty and amusement, often with an eye for the bizarre or ridiculous. Some of the "competitions" shown for such titles or in such events as "America's Toughest Bouncer," "World Bellyflopping Championship," "The Billiards Battle of the Generations," "Backwards Motor Racing," "Taxi Cab Demolition Derby," "Three-Ton Tug of War," and the "Disk Jockey Invitational Talk-Off." Bryant Gumbel and Cyndy Garvey were co-hosts; Mike Adamle, Johnny Bench, Donna DeVarona, and Arte Johnson were regular field reporters at the locations around the country where the events had taken place; and Gary Owens was the announcer. In addition to the regulars, there were weekly guest stars serving as commentators, among them athletes such as Dorothy Hamill, Bruce Jenner, and Reggie Jackson, sports announcers such as Marv

Albert and Joe Garagiola, and entertainment celebrities such as Darren McGavin, Tanya Tucker, Erik Estrada, and James Coburn.

GANGBUSTERS
Police Anthology
FIRST TELECAST: *March 20, 1952*
LAST TELECAST: *December 25, 1952*
BROADCAST HISTORY:
  Mar 1952–Dec 1952, NBC Thu 9:00–9:30
CREATOR/WRITER/NARRATOR:
  Phillips H. Lord

Gangbusters was one of the all-time classics of radio, running for some 21 years (1936–1957) on various networks. However, its history on television was short, for unusual reasons.

The format was the same as in the radio version. Action-packed stories on the apprehension of major criminals, taken from "actual police and FBI files," were presented in semi-documentary style. There was no continuing cast, but Phillips H. Lord, creator and writer of the show, appeared each week as narrator. At the end of each telecast a photo of one of the nation's most-wanted criminals was shown, and anyone having knowledge of his whereabouts was asked to phone the local police, the FBI, or *Gangbusters*. (Over the years the "most-wanted" feature of the radio *Gangbusters* resulted in the apprehension of several hundred criminals.)

Gangbusters premiered on TV in March 1952, alternating on Thursday nights with *Dragnet*. Both shows were phenomenally successful, completely overwhelming their competition. (In fact the other three networks virtually gave up trying to compete, and scheduled political-discussion programs opposite them.) During the fall of 1952 *Gangbusters* averaged a 42 rating, garnering virtually all of the audience available in its time slot and ranking number eight among all programs on TV. Nevertheless, it left the air in December—making it probably the highest-rated program ever to be canceled in the history of television.

The reason for the cancellation appears to be that *Gangbusters* was never intended to be a full-time TV series, but merely a stopgap provided by the sponsor to fill in the weeks when *Dragnet* wasn't on. Jack Webb even appeared at the end of each telecast to plug the next week's *Dragnet* episode. Webb could not at first provide a new *Dragnet* film every week, but when he could, *Dragnet* (which was even more popular than *Gangbusters*) went weekly and *Gangbusters* had to make way.

GANGSTER CHRONICLES, THE
Drama
FIRST TELECAST: *February 21, 1981*
LAST TELECAST: *May 8, 1981*
BROADCAST HISTORY:
  Feb 1981–Mar 1981, NBC Sat 9:00–10:00
  Apr 1981–May 1981, NBC Fri 10:00–11:00

CAST:
  Charles "Lucky" Luciano ..... Michael Nouri
  Benjamin "Bugsy" Siegel .... Joe Penny
  Michael Lasker .... Brian Benben
  Stella Siegel .... Kathleen Lloyd
  Ruth Lasker .... Madeline Stowe
  Joy Osler .... Chad Redding
  Chris Brennan .... Markie Post
  Goodman .... Alan Arbus
  Al Capone .... Louis Giambalvo
  Frank Costello .... James Andronica
  Vito Genovese .... Robert Davi
  Salvatore Maranzano .... Joseph Mascolo
  Vincent "Mad Dog" Coll ...... David Wilson
  Thomas E. Dewey .... Kenneth Tigar
  Giuseppe "Joe the Boss" Masseria
  .... Richard Castellano
  Thomas "Three Finger Brown" Lucchese
  .... Jon Polito
  Dutch Schultz .... Jonathan Banks
NARRATOR:
  E. G. Marshall

Dramatizations of the constant "warfare" between criminals and law-enforcement agencies are almost invariably shown from the perspective of the "good guys." However, the success of the two *Godfather* movies, both theatrically and on TV, inspired NBC to dramatize the Mafia from the inside, showing the relationships of gangland figures with each other and their families. *The Gangster Chronicles*, though based on historical fact, was a dramatization of the lives of three crime figures who had grown up together in New York and worked together as bootleggers and racketeers during the Prohibition era. Lucky Luciano was the suave, cultured organizer; Bugsy Siegel, the violent, amoral enforcer; and Michael Lasker (a composite of several real people), the soft-spoken family man who was the brains of the operation. As with the *Godfather* movies, their personal lives were also explored. Unlike *The Untouchables* of 20 years before, which had drawn two-dimensional caricatures of Prohibition's gangsters, *The Gangster Chronicles* combined slam-bang action with a portrait of the hoods as real—though not necessarily very pleasant—people, and as products of their environment.

GARLUND TOUCH, THE
  see *Mr. Garlund*

GARRISON'S GORILLAS
War Drama
FIRST TELECAST: *September 5, 1967*
LAST TELECAST: *September 17, 1968*
BROADCAST HISTORY:
  Sep 1967–Sep 1968, ABC Tue 7:30–8:30
CAST:
  Lt. Craig Garrison .... Ron Harper
  Actor .... Cesare Danova
  Casino .... Rudy Solari

Goniff	Christopher Cary
Chief	Brendon Boone

This action series focused on a motley group of commandos recruited from stateside prisons to use their special skills against the Germans in World War II. They had been promised a presidential pardon at the end of the war if they worked out; if not, they could expect a firing squad. The four were Actor, a handsome, resonant-voiced con man; Casino, a tough, wiry safecracker; Goniff, a slender, likable cat burglar; and Chief, a rugged, somber American Indian proficient with a switchblade. Led by West Pointer Craig Garrison, and headquartered in a secluded spot in England, this slippery group ranged all over Europe in exploits that often took them behind enemy lines.

GARROWAY AT LARGE

Variety
FIRST TELECAST: *April 16, 1949*
LAST TELECAST: *June 25, 1954*
BROADCAST HISTORY:
> *Apr 1949–Jul 1949*, NBC Sat 10:00–10:30
> *Jul 1949–Jun 1951*, NBC Sun 10:00–10:30 (OS)
> *Oct 1953–Jun 1954*, NBC Fri 8:00–8:30

REGULARS:
> Dave Garroway
> Jack Haskell
> Cliff Norton
> Bette Chapel (1949–1951)
> Carolyn Gilbert (1949)
> Connie Russell (1949–1951)
> Jill Corey (1953–1954)
> Shirley Harmer (1953–1954)
> Songsmiths Quartet (1949)
> The Daydreamers (1950)
> The Cheerleaders (1953–1954)

DANCERS:
> Russell and Aura (1950–1951)
> Ken Spaulding and Diane Sinclair (1953–1954)

ORCHESTRA:
> Joseph Gallichio (1949–1951)
> Skitch Henderson (1953–1954)

THEME:
> "Sentimental Journey," by Bud Green, Les Brown, and Ben Homer

A former disc jockey and onetime NBC page, Dave Garroway first brought his relaxed brand of humor to network audiences in 1949, with this easygoing musical revue. The program, which was telecast live from Chicago, had Garroway chatting with guests and casually strolling from set to set, past cameras, props, and technicians. No attempt was made at elaborate production. Entertainment was provided by guest stars and a regular supporting cast of singers and musicians. Sometimes the guest or setting was unusual, as in the 1950 New Year's Eve show when Dave's guests were the cleaning women of NBC's Chicago studios, "who work on New Year's Eve while others play"; and a May 1950 telecast that moved up onto the roof of the studio building for a view of the Chicago skyline at night.

Perhaps most evocative of Dave's sincere, straightforward style was his regular closing, when he would turn to the camera, raise his hand, and bid farewell with a simple, "Peace."

In January 1952 Garroway began his long run as host of NBC's pioneering *Today Show*. He returned to prime time for the 1953–1954 season, with a revue similar to his 1949–1951 series but this time emanating from New York and titled simply *The Dave Garroway Show*. Singer Jack Haskell and comedian Cliff Norton returned from the earlier show, but otherwise the supporting cast was new. Unfortunately this second series was faced with overwhelming competition from *Mama* and *Ozzie & Harriet*, which were running opposite on CBS and ABC, and it lasted only a single season.

GARRY MOORE SHOW, THE

Variety
FIRST TELECAST: *June 26, 1950*
LAST TELECAST: *December 27, 1951*
BROADCAST HISTORY:
> *Jun 1950–Jul 1950*, CBS Mon–Fri 7:00–7:30
> *Jul 1950–Sep 1950*, CBS Mon/Tue/Thu/Fri 7:00–7:30
> *Aug 1950–Sep 1950*, CBS Wed 8:00–9:00
> *Oct 1951–Dec 1951*, CBS Thu 8:00–8:30

REGULARS:
> Garry Moore
> Ken Carson
> Denise Lor
> Durward Kirby

The pace of the early, live *Garry Moore Show* was slow and relaxed, and very informal. Included were songs, poems, comedy sketches, chats with regulars and guests, and anything else that came to mind while the show was on the air. Ken Carson and Denise Lor were the featured vocalists while Durward Kirby doubled as announcer and comedian. The program was simulcast on television and radio, five days a week, during the summer of 1950. In August 1950 the Wednesday 7:00–7:30 P.M. telecast was moved (and expanded) to 8:00–9:00 P.M., to fill in for the vacationing Arthur Godfrey, who normally occupied that time slot.

The fall 1951 version of *The Garry Moore Show*, in the same format and with the same regulars, was aired once a week under the title *The Garry Moore Evening Show*, to distinguish it from Garry's highly successful daytime show on CBS.

GARRY MOORE SHOW, THE

Variety
FIRST TELECAST: *September 30, 1958*
LAST TELECAST: *January 8, 1967*
BROADCAST HISTORY:
> *Sep 1958–Jun 1964*, CBS Tue 10:00–11:00 (OS)
> *Sep 1966–Jan 1967*, CBS Sun 9:00–10:00

REGULARS:
Garry Moore
Durward Kirby
Marion Lorne (1958–1962)
Carol Burnett (1959–1962)
Dorothy Loudon (1962–1964)
Allen Funt (1959–1960)
John Byner (1966–1967)
Jackie Vernon (1966–1967)
Chuck McCann (1966–1967)
Pete Barbutti (1966–1967)
Buster Davis Singers (1958–1959)
George Becker Singers (1959–1964)
Paul Godkin Dancers (1958–1959)
Ernest Flatt Dancers (1959–1963)
Carol Henry Dancers (1963–1964)
Bob Hamilton Dancers (1966–1967)
Howard Smith Orchestra (1958–1959)
Irwin Kostal Orchestra (1959–1964)
Bernie Green Orchestra (1966–1967)

This Garry Moore variety series ran very successfully for six seasons in the late 1950s and early
1960s. Among other things, it made a star out of
Carol Burnett, brought back Allen Funt's Candid
Camera (as a regular feature), and showcased
many fine musical and comedic talents. And then
there was, of course, the friendly humor of the
bow-tied, crewcut Moore himself. From 1958 to
1963 the highlight of the show was "That Wonderful Year," consisting of film clips, comedy
sketches, and production numbers based on the
events and styles of a given year. This often filled
from one-third to one-half of the show.

The Garry Moore Show left the air in 1964, not
because of low ratings but because Garry wanted
to get away from the weekly grind and have some
time to relax. After two years of well-earned rest
(he had begun on network radio in 1939 and had
been on television continuously since 1950) Garry
returned in the fall of 1966 as host of a program
featuring Durward Kirby and a rotating cast of
comedians and guests. This was short-lived, however (partially due to the withering competition of
Bonanza), and thereafter Garry was known primarily as a daytime TV personality.

GAS COMPANY PLAYHOUSE
Dramatic Anthology
FIRST TELECAST: July 5, 1960
LAST TELECAST: September 13, 1960
BROADCAST HISTORY:
Jul 1960–Sep 1960, NBC Tue 8:30–9:00
HOSTESS:
Julia Meade

This summer series was composed of reruns of
Goodyear TV Playhouse, The David Niven Show,
Colgate Theatre, and Alcoa Theatre. It was
hosted by Julia Meade and alternated on Tuesday
evenings with NBC Playhouse.

GAVILAN
Adventure

FIRST TELECAST: October 26, 1982
LAST TELECAST: March 18, 1983
BROADCAST HISTORY:
Oct 1982–Dec 1982, NBC Tue 9:00–10:00
Mar 1983, NBC Fri 10:00–11:00
CAST:
Robert Gavilan .... Robert Urich
Milo Bentley .... Patrick Macnee
Marion Jaworski .... Kate Reid

His years as a CIA agent had made Robert Gavilan a little bit cynical, but not enough to stop him
from fighting for what was right and just. In his
current capacity, as inventor and consultant to
California's DeWitt Institute of Oceanography,
Gavilan helped rescue people in trouble, worked
on underwater projects, and occasionally got involved with exactly the type of espionage activities that had caused him to leave the Agency. He
shared his Malibu beach house with Milo Bentley,
a suave, conniving travel agent who regularly
helped Gavilan on his adventures. Mrs. Jaworski,
Gavilan's boss at the Institute, was impressed by
his talents but bothered by his tendency to get
into dangerous situations. He did, it must be said,
have to deal with more than his share of evil des-
pots and foreign agents, as well as a never-ending
stream of beautiful women, in this formula adventure.

GAY NINETIES REVUE, THE
Musical Variety
FIRST TELECAST: August 11, 1948
LAST TELECAST: January 14, 1949
BROADCAST HISTORY:
Aug 1948–Oct 1948, ABC Wed 8:00–8:30
Nov 1948–Jan 1949, ABC Fri 8:30–9:00
REGULARS:
Joe Howard
Lulu Bates
The Floradora Girls
Ray Bloch Orchestra

Joe Howard was about as authentic an old-timer
as TV could get for a show like this—and probably the oldest performer ever to headline a TV
variety series. He had been in vaudeville since the
1890s, and, as a songwriter, his biggest hit had
been "Hello Ma Baby," in 1899. At 81 years of age
he was still a spry performer (he lived to be 93)
and he emceed this old-fashioned variety show
with period style. Lulu Bates added boisterous
Gay Nineties vocals, and the Floradora Girls
(named after the hit 1900 Broadway show) provided female harmonizing. The setting was an old
gaslight nightclub. The program was adapted
from the radio series of the same name that Howard had emceed in the early 1940s—when he was
only in his 70s.

Joe Howard's trademark song, which he sang
and used as a theme on all these programs, turned
out to be one of the most durable cases of fraud
in music-business history. For 40 years he had
sung "I Wonder Who's Kissing Her Now," and

regaled audiences with stories about how he had been inspired to write it by a chance remark he heard in 1909. Twentieth Century–Fox even called his 1947 screen biography *I Wonder Who's Kissing Her Now*, and played up the story of the song's composition in the film. That brought forth someone named Harold Orlob, who proved that he, when a young man, had written the song for Howard, who then appropriated credit for it and sang it for the next half-century. Howard died while singing "Let Me Call You Sweetheart" on the stage of a Chicago theater in 1961.

GEMINI MAN
Action/Adventure
FIRST TELECAST: *September 23, 1976*
LAST TELECAST: *October 28, 1976*
BROADCAST HISTORY:
  Sep 1976–Oct 1976, NBC Thu 8:00–9:00
CAST:
  Sam Casey .... Ben Murphy
  Leonard Driscoll .... William Sylvester
  Abby Lawrence .... Katherine Crawford

Sam Casey was an agent for INTERSECT, a government think-tank and operations center specializing in missions requiring the utmost secrecy. While on a diving assignment, Sam was affected by the radiation from an underwater explosion. The radiation rendered him invisible, and it was only through the combined efforts of computer expert Abby Lawrence and Leonard Driscoll, Sam's boss at INTERSECT, that a way was devised to control his invisibility. Sam was fitted with a computerized watchlike contraption that kept him visible. He could, however, switch it off and become invisible again, for short periods. If he did this for more than 15 minutes in any 24-hour period, he would die. Needless to say, the ability to become invisible, despite the time limits, made Sam a very effective agent indeed.

Unfortunately, stiff competition from ABC and CBS rendered the ratings for this program almost invisible, and it did a fast fade-out after only one month on the air.

GENE AUTRY SHOW, THE
Western
FIRST TELECAST: *July 23, 1950*
LAST TELECAST: *August 7, 1956*
BROADCAST HISTORY:
  Jul 1950–Jul 1953, CBS Sun 7:00–7:30
  Jul 1953–Sep 1954, CBS Tue 8:00–8:30
  Sep 1954–Aug 1956, CBS Sat 7:00–7:30
REGULARS:
  Gene Autry
  Pat Buttram
THEME:
  "Back in the Saddle Again," by Ray Whitley and Gene Autry

Gene Autry, the singing cowboy, made the transition from feature-length movies to half-hour TV films in the early 1950s and became very wealthy doing it. For six seasons he and his sidekick, Pat Buttram, rode from town to town in the Southwest helping maintain law and order. Each episode provided opportunities for Gene to sing, his sidekick Pat to get into some silly predicament, and his horse Champion to show off the training that made him a very talented hunk of horseflesh.

GENERAL ELECTRIC SUMMER ORIGINALS
Dramatic Anthology
FIRST TELECAST: *July 3, 1956*
LAST TELECAST: *September 18, 1956*
BROADCAST HISTORY:
  Jul 1956–Sep 1956, ABC Tue 9:00–9:30

This summer series consisted of 30-minute dramatic films never before seen on television, featuring such Hollywood standbys as Vivian Blaine, Joe E. Brown, Zachary Scott, and Ronald Reagan.

GENERAL ELECTRIC THEATER
Dramatic Anthology
FIRST TELECAST: *February 1, 1953*
LAST TELECAST: *September 16, 1962*
BROADCAST HISTORY:
  Feb 1953–Sep 1962, CBS Sun 9:00–9:30
HOST/STAR:
  Ronald Reagan (1954–1962)

This long-running filmed anthology series premiered in February 1953 as an alternate-week program with *The Fred Waring Show*. There was no host when it first went on the air, Ronald Reagan taking over that role at the start of the 1954–1955 season. He occasionally added the role of episode star to his regular function as host and commercial spokesman. At first, not all of the dramas were filmed, but, as Mr. Reagan said many years later, the problems inherent in live drama on television gave the live episodes a less finished look than the filmed ones. Eventually all of the shows were filmed in advance.

The range of material covered was vast, with one week's story a contemporary adventure, like "Ride the River" with Broderick Crawford and Neville Brand, and the next week's a period Biblical drama, like "The Stone" starring Tony Curtis. Everything from light bedroom comedy to heavy melodrama showed up on *General Electric Theater* and when Westerns became very popular in the late 1950s they were well represented too— "Saddle Tramp in the Old West" starring James Stewart and "Too Good with a Gun" starring Robert Cummings and young Michael Landon (pre-*Bonanza*) among them.

Although most of the stories used on *General Electric Theater* were either original teleplays or adaptations from lesser-known authors, there were occasional exceptions. Phyllis Thaxter and Patric Knowles starred in "Nora," based on Henrik Ibsen's *A Doll's House;* Burgess Meredith starred in a condensed version of the motion picture *Edison, the Man;* Teresa Wright and Richard Boone had the leads in "Love Is Eternal," based on Irving Stone's novel of the same name; and Ronald Reagan and his wife Nancy Davis starred in "Money and the Minister," written by Charlotte Armstrong.

In its eight-plus years, however, *General Electric Theater*'s emphasis was primarily on simple dramas and diversionary entertainment. It was there to entertain, not to preach or educate, and most of the stories were not memorable. However, the list of famous performers appearing was formidable. In addition to those mentioned above, such people as Sir Cedric Hardwicke, Ward Bond, June Havoc, Alan Ladd, Barry Fitzgerald, Jane Wyman, Cornel Wilde, Myrna Loy, Jack Benny, Bette Davis, Anne Baxter, and Barbara Stanwyck starred at one time or another.

General Electric Theater was syndicated under the title *Star Showcase,* with new introductions by Edward Arnold.

GENERAL ELECTRIC TRUE
Dramatic Anthology
FIRST TELECAST: *September 30, 1962*
LAST TELECAST: *September 22, 1963*
BROADCAST HISTORY:
Sep 1962–Sep 1963, CBS Sun 9:30–10:00
HOST/NARRATOR:
Jack Webb

The distinction between this series and its predecessor, *General Electric Theater,* was that all of the stories presented in this series were based on actual incidents and were dramatized with as much fidelity to the original as possible. The stories tended to be in the adventure-suspense vein, and many had military themes. All were taken from the files of *True* magazine.

Jack Webb, who was the host and narrator for the entire series, was the closest thing to a major star to appear in *General Electric True.* In "Code-Name Christopher," a two-part story which he also directed, Webb played an American agent planning the sabotage of a Nazi factory during World War II. Among the few other familiar names that appeared in these dramas were Jerry Van Dyke, Arte Johnson, Robert Vaughn, and Victor Buono.

GENERATION GAP, THE
Quiz
FIRST TELECAST: *February 7, 1969*
LAST TELECAST: *May 23, 1969*
BROADCAST HISTORY:
Feb 1969–May 1969, ABC Fri 8:30–9:00
EMCEE:
Dennis Wholey (Feb–Apr)
Jack Barry (Apr–May)

Quiz in which two teams, one composed of three teenagers and the other of three adults, were each asked questions about the other generation's life-styles and fads. The teenagers were quizzed about such things as the Edsel, Shirley Temple, Senator Claghorn, Carmen Miranda, and the like; the adults (all over 30) would have to answer questions about the boogaloo, current draft law, "hanging five," and so on. Film clips, photos, and recordings illustrated the questions. Celebrity parents and their offspring often appeared on opposing teams.

GENTLE BEN
Adventure
FIRST TELECAST: *September 10, 1967*
LAST TELECAST: *August 31, 1969*
BROADCAST HISTORY:
Sep 1967–Aug 1969, CBS Sun 7:30–8:00
CAST:
Tom Wedloe .... Dennis Weaver
Mark Wedloe................. Clint Howard
Ellen Wedloe.................. Beth Brickell
Henry Boomhauer............ Rance Howard
Willie (1968–1969)........ Angelo Rutherford

Ben was a 650-pound American black bear who, fortunately, was as friendly and lovable as he was large. He lived in the Everglades of Florida with his "family," the Wedloes. Ben's constant companion was eight-year-old Mark Wedloe, whose father, Tom, was a wildlife officer. Henry Boomhauer, portrayed by young star Clint Howard's real father Rance, was a backwoodsman who was both friend and advisor to the Wedloes.

GEOGRAPHICALLY SPEAKING
Travelogue
FIRST TELECAST: *October 27, 1946*
LAST TELECAST: *December 1, 1946*
BROADCAST HISTORY:
Oct 1946–Dec 1946, NBC Sun 8:15–8:30
HOSTESS:
Mrs. Carveth Wells

This early series began locally on NBC's New York station on June 9, 1946, and was fed to the small NBC East Coast network in October, sponsored by Bristol-Myers. It consisted of travel films taken and narrated by Mrs. Carveth Wells, and it ended when she ran out of film.

GEORGE BURNS AND GRACIE ALLEN SHOW, THE
Situation Comedy
FIRST TELECAST: *October 12, 1950*
LAST TELECAST: *September 22, 1958*
BROADCAST HISTORY:
Oct 1950–Mar 1953, CBS Thu 8:00–8:30
Mar 1953–Sep 1958, CBS Mon 8:00–8:30
CAST:
George Burns...................... Himself
Gracie Allen....................... Herself
Blanche Morton.............. Bea Benaderet
Harry Morton (1950–1951) .... Hal March
Harry Morton (1951) .... John Brown

Harry Morton (1951–1953) .... Fred Clark
Harry Morton (1953–1958) ..... Larry Keating
Bill Goodwin (1950–1951) .... Himself
Harry Von Zell (1951–1958) .... Himself
Mr. Beasley, the Mailman ...... Rolfe Sedan
Ronnie Burns (1955–1958) .... Himself
Bonnie Sue McAfee (1957–1958)
.... Judi Meredith
THEME:
"Love Nest," by Louis A. Hirsch and Otto Harbach

George Burns and Gracie Allen had one of the most enduring acts in the history of show business. They were headliners in vaudeville in the 1920s, on radio in the 1930s and 1940s, and for almost a full decade on television in the 1950s. The factor which finally terminated the act was not loss of audience appeal, but Gracie's decision to retire in 1958.

The format of the TV Burns and Allen show was simple enough. It was set in the Burns home, and cast George in the dual role of on-screen narrator of the proceedings and straight man for Gracie's scatterbrained but delightful involvements with various people and situations. Gracie's cohort in many of her predicaments was neighbor Blanche Morton, whose long-suffering accountant husband Harry was as infuriated by the girls' escapades as George was tolerant. George was unflappable. He would simply turn to the camera, cigar in hand, and philosophize to the audience.

When it first came to television in 1950 The George Burns and Gracie Allen Show was produced live in New York and aired every other Thursday night. Members of the radio cast who followed the show to television were Bill Goodwin, the commercial announcer who doubled as George and Gracie's friend; Bea Benaderet, as neighbor Blanche Morton; Hal March as Blanche's husband Harry; and Rolfe Sedan as the mailman to whom Gracie gossiped. There was considerable turnover in the role of Harry Morton during the series' early years. March left the show in January 1951, to be replaced by John Brown. Brown lasted six months and was replaced in June by Fred Clark, who was in turn replaced in the fall of 1953 by Larry Keating. Harry Von Zell joined the cast at the start of the 1951–1952 season as replacement for Bill Goodwin, doing the commercials and playing a friend of the family. In the fall of 1952 the series became a weekly filmed feature originating from the West Coast.

GEORGE BURNS COMEDY WEEK
Comedy Anthology
FIRST TELECAST: *September 18, 1985*
LAST TELECAST: *December 25, 1985*
BROADCAST HISTORY:
Sep 1985–Dec 1985, CBS Wed 9:30–10:00
HOST:
George Burns

Veteran funnyman George Burns, who was 89 years old when this series was on the air, served as both host and narrator of this comedy anthology series. Among the more familiar names appearing were Joe Piscopo, Robert Klein, Martin Mull, Don Rickles, Don Knotts, Fannie Flagg, Candy Clark, Howard Hesseman, Laraine Newman, James Whitmore, Roddy McDowall, and Samantha Eggar. One of the episodes, which had starred Harvey Korman and Valerie Perrine, surfaced as the series *Leo & Liz in Beverly Hills* four months after *George Burns Comedy Week* left the air.

GEORGE BURNS SHOW, THE
Situation Comedy
FIRST TELECAST: *October 21, 1958*
LAST TELECAST: *April 14, 1959*
BROADCAST HISTORY:
Oct 1958–Apr 1959, NBC Tue 9:00–9:30
CAST:
George Burns .... Himself
Blanche Morton .... Bea Benaderet
Harry Morton .... Larry Keating
Harry Von Zell .... Himself
Ronnie Burns .... Himself
Judi Meredith .... Herself
Miss Jenkins .... Lisa Davis

Following his wife Gracie's retirement from show business, George Burns attempted a series of his own, including most of the regulars from the highly successful *Burns and Allen Show*. George played a theatrical producer beset with the usual problems of casting, booking, eccentric stars, and a complement of helpful friends who tended to create more problems than they solved. Blanche was George's secretary; Harry, her husband; and Harry Von Zell, a bumbling friend. George's real-life son Ronnie also appeared in the series, while Judi Meredith portrayed an aspiring actress who was Ronnie's steady girlfriend. Although Gracie Allen did not appear on this program, she was referred to. Blanche was a close friend of Gracie's, and as such was always trying to keep George from becoming involved with the attractive young starlets he constantly met—including a certain sexy secretary named Miss Jenkins.

Beginning in December and running through mid-February 1959, the format was altered to include a live variety show within almost every episode, featuring the regular cast and guest stars.

GEORGE GOBEL SHOW, THE
Comedy Variety
FIRST TELECAST: *October 2, 1954*
LAST TELECAST: *June 5, 1960*
BROADCAST HISTORY:
Oct 1954–Jun 1957, NBC Sat 10:00–10:30 (OS)
Sep 1957–Mar 1959, NBC Tue 8:00–9:00 (OS)
Oct 1959–June 1960, CBS Sun 10:00–10:30
HOST:
George Gobel

Alice (1954–1958). . . . . Jeff Donnell
Alice (1958–1959). . . . . Phyllis Avery
Peggy King (1954–1956)
Johnny Mann Singers (1957–1958)
Shirley Harmer (1957–1958)
John Scott Trotter Orchestra (1954–1958, 1959–1960)
Frank DeVol Orchestra (1958–1959)
Eddie Fisher (1957–1958)
The Kids Next Door (1958–1959)
Joe Flynn (1958–1959)
Anita Bryant (1959–1960)
The Modernaires (1959–1960)
Harry Von Zell (1959–1960)
THEME:
"Gobelues," by John Scott Trotter

Low-key comedian George Gobel, known affectionately as "Lonesome George," starred in his own live variety series for six years. It opened with George's monologue, included a sketch with or performance by the week's guest star, and always a sketch about George's family problems with his wife, Alice. Alice was his real-life wife's name, but on television she was portrayed first by Jeff Donnell and later by Phyllis Avery. (The Alice sketches were finally dropped when the series moved to CBS.)

For a time Gobel was one of TV's top hits, and his familiar sayings ("Well, I'll be a dirty bird!," "You don't hardly get those no more") became bywords. But then *Gunsmoke* came along, running opposite on CBS, and Gobel's star began to fade. During the two seasons that the show aired on Tuesday nights for a full hour, it alternated with *The Eddie Fisher Show*, and both stars were regular guests on each other's programs. When Gobel moved to CBS for a final season, he alternated with *The Jack Benny Show*.

GEORGE JESSEL SHOW, THE
Variety
FIRST TELECAST: *September 13, 1953*
LAST TELECAST: *April 11, 1954*
BROADCAST HISTORY:
Sep 1953–Apr 1954, ABC Sun 6:30–7:00
HOST:
George Jessel
WRITERS:
George Jessel
Sam Carlton

George Jessel's most famous act, which he used throughout his long career, was that of the after-dinner speaker, and it was in that role that he appeared here. Each week Jessel, the self-proclaimed "Toastmaster General of the United States," was seen in a mock testimonial dinner, paying comic homage to the assembled guests of honor. In most cases these were personalities from the field of entertainment, such as Sophie

Tucker, Mitzi Gaynor, and Margaret O'Brien. Live from New York.

GEORGE MICHAEL SPORTS MACHINE, THE
Sports Highlights
FIRST TELECAST: *September 2, 1984*
LAST TELECAST:
BROADCAST HISTORY:
Sep 1984–   , NBC Sun 11:30–12:00
HOST:
George Michael

A fast-paced, irreverent weekly wrap-up of major happenings in the world of sports, hosted by the sports reporter for NBC's Washington TV station, WRC-TV. Michael made extensive use of video-taped highlights from the week's games, along with player profiles, sports bloopers, and intentionally funny coverage of such non-mainstream "sports" as wrestling and rodeo.

GEORGE SANDERS MYSTERY THEATER, THE
Dramatic Anthology
FIRST TELECAST: *June 22, 1957*
LAST TELECAST: *September 14, 1957*
BROADCAST HISTORY:
June 1957–Sep 1957, NBC Sat 9:00–9:30
HOST:
George Sanders

George Sanders served as host for all of these filmed dramas and appeared occasionally as an actor in them.

GEORGE SCHLATTER'S COMEDY CLUB
Comedy Variety
BROADCAST HISTORY:
Syndicated only
30 minutes
Produced: *1987–*
Released: *September 1987*
HOST:
George Schlatter

When he produced *Rowan & Martin's Laugh-In* two decades earlier, George Schlatter had altered the face of television comedy by making it hip and topical, and drastically increasing the pace. His 1987 series had no regular cast—each week a different group of young comics was featured—but the look was very reminiscent of his former hit. The individual monologues and sketches tended to be very short, with each change to a new performer or skit seeming to almost chop off the end of the previous one. The action took place on a large stage with different people doing different things, while the camera zoomed from one to another. There were background dancers and activities which never seemed to get any attention and the overall mood was one of frenzied confusion. Mr. Schlatter himself, who had not appeared on *Laugh-In*, opened and closed each episode from an on-camera "director's chair."

GEORGETOWN UNIVERSITY FORUM
Discussion
FIRST TELECAST: *July 3, 1951*
LAST TELECAST: *October 11, 1953*
BROADCAST HISTORY:
  Jul 1951–Oct 1951, DUM Tue 8:00–8:30
  Oct 1951–Nov 1951, DUM Thu 8:00–8:30
  Dec 1951–Mar 1952, DUM Sun 6:30–7:00
  Mar 1952–Oct 1953, DUM Sun 7:00–7:30
MODERATOR:
  Frank Blair

Round-table discussions of topics of current interest, by members of the Georgetown University faculty and expert guests. At first the topics were political-social ("Is Our National Transportation Policy Outmoded?"), but later more popular subjects ("Flying Saucers") and descriptive programs on advances in medicine and daily living were featured as often as the debates. From Washington, D.C.

GEORGIA GIBBS AND HER MILLION RECORD SHOW
Music
FIRST TELECAST: *July 1, 1957*
LAST TELECAST: *September 2, 1957*
BROADCAST HISTORY:
  Jul 1957–Sep 1957, NBC Mon 7:30–7:45
REGULARS:
  Georgia Gibbs
  The Eddie Safranski Orchestra

"Her Nibs" Miss Georgia Gibbs (the nickname was given to her by Garry Moore) hosted this 15-minute summer show during 1957. In addition to introducing promising young singers, Georgia sang a number of popular songs, at least two of which were million sellers on record. Included, no doubt, were her own three gold records, "Kiss of Fire," "Tweedle Dee," and "Dance with Me, Henry." Occasionally, before doing her rendition of someone else's big hit, she would play an excerpt from the original recording which had sold a million.

GERTRUDE BERG SHOW, THE
Situation Comedy
FIRST TELECAST: *October 4, 1961*
LAST TELECAST: *April 5, 1962*
BROADCAST HISTORY:
  Oct 1961–Jan 1962, CBS Wed 9:30–10:00
  Jan 1962–Apr 1962, CBS Thu 9:30–10:00
CAST:
  Sarah Green.................. Gertrude Berg
  Professor Crayton..... Sir Cedric Hardwicke
  Maxfield .... Mary Wickes
  Joe Caldwell.................... Skip Ward
  Susan Green (1961)............. Marion Ross
  Jerry Green (1961)................ Leo Penn

  George Howell.................. Paul Smith
  Irma Howell................. Aneta Corsaut
  Carol .... Karyn Kupcinet

Gertrude Berg had become famous on radio and television in a series called *The Goldbergs*. Sarah Green, the character she played in this situation comedy, was in many ways an older version of her inimitable Molly Goldberg. Sarah was a matronly widow whose thirst for knowledge led her to enroll in college, despite her advancing years. Her English teacher, Professor Crayton, was an exchange teacher from Cambridge University. Maxfield ran the boardinghouse where Mrs. Green lived, and Joe Caldwell was an 18-year-old freshman in her class. The program was originally titled *Mrs. G. Goes to College*, but this was changed to *The Gertrude Berg Show*, in January 1962.

GET CHRISTIE LOVE
Police Drama
FIRST TELECAST: *September 11, 1974*
LAST TELECAST: *July 18, 1975*
BROADCAST HISTORY:
  Sep 1974–Mar 1975, ABC Wed 10:00–11:00
  Apr 1975–Jul 1975, ABC Fri 10:00–11:00
CAST:
  Det. Christie Love............ Teresa Graves
  Lt. Matt Reardon (1974) .... Charles Cioffi
  Capt. Arthur P. Ryan (1975)....... Jack Kelly
  Det. Joe Caruso.............. Andy Romano
  Det. Steve Belmont........... Dennis Rucker
  Det. Valencia................. Scott Peters
  Sgt. Pete Gallagher (1975) .... Michael Pataki
TECHNICAL ADVISOR/SOMETIME WRITER:
  Det. Olga Ford, NYPD

Action series with black, sexy Teresa Graves as supercop Christie Love of the Special Investigations Division, Los Angeles Police Department. Most of Christie's assignments were undercover jobs, giving her plenty of latitude for her slick, "with-it," rule-breaking style. Her hard-nosed boss was Lt. Matt Reardon, later replaced by Capt. Ryan, and her sidekick was Sgt. Pete Gallagher.

GET SMART
Situation Comedy
FIRST TELECAST: *September 18, 1965*
LAST TELECAST: *September 11, 1970*
BROADCAST HISTORY:
  Sep 1965–Sep 1968, NBC Sat 8:30–9:00
  Sep 1968–Sep 1969, NBC Sat 8:00–8:30
  Sep 1969–Feb 1970, CBS Fri 7:30–8:00
  Apr 1970–Sep 1970, CBS Fri 7:30–8:00
CAST:
  Maxwell Smart, Agent 86........Don Adams
  Agent 99 .... Barbara Feldon
  Thaddeus, the Chief........... Edward Platt
  Agent 13 (1966–1967) .... Dave Ketchum
  Carlson (1966–1967) .... Stacy Keach

Conrad Siegfried (1966–1969)... Bernie Kopell
Starker (1966–1969)............ King Moody
Hymie, the C.O.N.T.R.O.L. robot (1966–1969)
.... Dick Gautier
Agent 44 .... Victor French
Larrabee (1967–1970) .... Robert Karvelas
99's Mother (1968–1969)........... Jane Dulo
DEVELOPERS/WRITERS:
Mel Brooks
Buck Henry

James Bond would have turned over in his grave. Here was secret agent Maxwell Smart, willing but inept, enthusiastic but confused, somehow stumbling through to defeat the evil agents of K.A.O.S. who, led by their mastermind Siegfried and his assistant Starker, planned to take over the world. Max worked for "The Chief," head of the Washington-based U.S. intelligence agency C.O.N.-T.R.O.L., and had a beautiful and brilliant young partner known as Agent 99. Love blossomed and this mismatched pair married during the 1968–1969 season. During the next season, after the show had moved from NBC to CBS, 99 gave birth to twins, a boy and a girl.

Get Smart was a sophomoric, but highly successful, spoof of the secret-agent genre that had been spawned by James Bond movies in the 1960s, and was probably best typified by Max's pet expression "Would you believe?"—used whenever an agent of K.A.O.S. or someone on his own side didn't seem to accept one of his fabrications and he was trying to come up with a more acceptable alternative. That catch-phrase became very popular with young people in the late 1960s.

GETTING TOGETHER
Situation Comedy
FIRST TELECAST: *September 18, 1971*
LAST TELECAST: *January 8, 1972*
BROADCAST HISTORY:
Sep 1971–Jan 1972, ABC Sat 8:00–8:30
CAST:
Bobby Conway .... Bobby Sherman
Lionel Poindexter .... Wes Stern
Jennifer Conway .... Susan Neher
Officer Rudy Colcheck .... Jack Burns
Rita Simon .... Pat Carroll
THEME:
"Getting Together," by Helen Miller and Roger Atkins

Recording star Bobby Sherman played a young songwriter struggling to make it in the popular music business in this youth-oriented comedy. Bobby had the melodies, and his tone-deaf, offbeat friend Lionel wrote the lyrics. Bobby's mod-rock world was not without responsibilities, however, as he was legal guardian of his freckle-faced, 12-year-old sister Jennifer. The three of them, Bobby, Lionel, and Jennifer, lived in an antique shop (it was cheap—but occasionally the furniture got sold out from under them) while

Bobby worked as a recording engineer, and the boys tried to peddle their songs. Rita was their motherly landlady, and Rudy her policeman-boyfriend.

Getting Together would seem to have been a perfect vehicle for Sherman to use in launching new hits, but in fact his real-life recording career went into something of a slump when the series went on the air. He did have one moderately popular disc derived from the program, however—titled "Jennifer"—and an album named after the show.

Getting Together was previewed on a March 1971 telecast of *The Partridge Family,* in which the Partridges introduced Bobby and Lionel to each other.

GHOST AND MRS. MUIR, THE
Situation Comedy
FIRST TELECAST: *September 21, 1968*
LAST TELECAST: *September 18, 1970*
BROADCAST HISTORY:
Sep 1968–Sep 1969, NBC Sat 8:30–9:00
Sep 1969–Jan 1970, ABC Tue 7:30–8:00
Jan 1970–Sep 1970, ABC Fri 8:30–9:00
CAST:
Mrs. Carolyn Muir .... Hope Lange
Capt. Daniel Gregg......... Edward Mulhare
Martha Grant................... Reta Shaw
Candice Muir............... Kellie Flanagan
Jonathan Muir .... Harlen Carraher
Claymore Gregg ...... Charles Nelson Reilly

Somewhere along a desolate stretch of New England coastline, overlooking Schooner Bay, sat a charming little house known as Gull Cottage. It was charming except for one slight problem—it was haunted by the ghost of a previous owner, Capt. Daniel Gregg, a 19th-century sea captain. Every time his nephew Claymore, the current owner, tried to rent the cottage to someone, the captain scared them off. Into Gull Cottage moved attractive widow Carolyn Muir with her two young children (aged 8 and 9), their pet dog Scruffy, and Martha, a housekeeper. The captain resented the invasion—Carolyn was sleeping in *his* bedroom—and he tried to scare them off. Eventually, however, they established a truce, and even developed a fondness for each other. *The Ghost and Mrs. Muir* was picked up by ABC for a second season after being canceled by NBC.

Based on the 1947 movie starring Gene Tierney and Rex Harrison.

GHOST STORY
Supernatural Anthology
FIRST TELECAST: *September 15, 1972*
LAST TELECAST: *June 22, 1973*
BROADCAST HISTORY:
Sep 1972–Jun 1973, NBC Fri 9:00–10:00
HOST:
Sebastian Cabot (as *Winston Essex;* 1972)

When *Ghost Story* premiered in September 1972 it dealt exclusively with tales of ghosts, vampires, witches, and various other aspects of the supernatural. It was hosted by Sebastian Cabot in the role of Winston Essex. Essex would open the show by taking the audience to Essex House and introducing the story as something that could happen to anyone. As the story unfolded, however, it turned into a bizarre nightmare of one kind or another. On January 5, 1973, the title was changed to *Circle of Fear.* Under the new title stories of suspense could be included that did not have supernatural overtones. In addition, the narrator was no longer part of the program.

GIANT STEP
Quiz/Audience Participation
FIRST TELECAST: *November 7, 1956*
LAST TELECAST: *May 29, 1957*
BROADCAST HISTORY:
  Nov 1956–May 1957, CBS Wed 7:30–8:00
EMCEE:
  Bert Parks

Giant Step was somewhat different from the other big-money quiz shows of its time in that all of its contestants were students, mostly of high-school age, who competed for a free college education. The students picked their topic and then tried to answer enough questions successfully to win a four-year scholarship, and an all-expense-paid vacation to Europe after graduation. There were eight steps involved in reaching the final victory. As with *The $64,000 Question,* suspense was built by having the contestants—after their initial appearance—answer only one big question per week.

GIBBSVILLE
Drama
FIRST TELECAST: *November 11, 1976*
LAST TELECAST: *December 30, 1976*
BROADCAST HISTORY:
  Nov 1976–Dec 1976, NBC Thu 10:00–11:00
CAST:
  Jim Malloy .... John Savage
  Ray Whitehead.................. Gig Young
  Dr. Malloy .... Biff McGuire
  Mrs. Malloy .... Peggy McCay
  Pell.......................... Bert Remsen

This short-lived dramatic series centered around the activities of Jim Malloy in the small Pennsylvania town of Gibbsville, where he was cub reporter for the *Gibbsville Courier,* during the 1940s. Jim worked with senior reporter Ray Whitehead (both of them accountable to editor Pell) and made his home with his folks. Whitehead had started his career at the *Courier* and then moved on to more prestigious papers in larger cities. Unfortunately, he had lost a long bout with the bottle and was back in Gibbsville trying to salvage what was left of a once-promis-

ing career. Jim Malloy's father was the town physician. The stories and characters in this series were developed from the writings of John O'Hara.

GIDGET
Situation Comedy
FIRST TELECAST: *September 15, 1965*
LAST TELECAST: *September 1, 1966*
BROADCAST HISTORY:
  Sep 1965–Jan 1966, ABC Wed 8:30–9:00
  Jan 1966–Sep 1966, ABC Thu 8:00–8:30
CAST:
  Francine "Gidget" Lawrence...... Sally Field
  Professor Russ Lawrence .... Don Porter
  Anne Cooper .... Betty Conner
  John Cooper .... Peter Deuel
  Larue ....Lynette Winter
  Peter Stone ("Siddo") ....Mike Nader
THEME:
  Sung by Johnny Tillotson

There was lots of California sun and surf in this frothy comedy about the adventures of a bright, winsome teenager. Gidget was age 15½, the daughter of Prof. Russ Lawrence, a widower. Despite the best efforts of her overly protective older sister, Anne, and Anne's husband John (a psychology student who practiced on the family), Gidget and her best friend Larue managed to find endless fun in the sun. Gidget's boyfriend Jeff (Stephen Mines) was "off to college" and seldom seen.

Sally Field was plucked from obscurity for the starring role in this series. Only 18 when the show began, she had enrolled in a Columbia Pictures actors' workshop as a summertime lark after completing high school and before beginning college. It proved to be a direct path to TV and, later, movie stardom.

Based on the *Gidget* series of movies, the first of which (1959) starred Sandra Dee in the title role. See *The New Gidget* for a 1980s sequel.

GILLETTE CAVALCADE OF SPORTS
  see *Boxing*

GILLETTE SUMMER SPORTS REEL
Sports/Sports Commentary
FIRST TELECAST: *June 2, 1950*
LAST TELECAST: *August 19, 1955*
BROADCAST HISTORY:
  Jun 1950–Aug 1955, NBC Fri 10:00–10:30 (summers only)
COMMENTATORS:
  Don Dunphy (1950)
  Jimmy Powers (1951)
  Clem McCarthy (1953)
  Ken Banghart (1953)
  Ray Barrett (1953, 1955)
  Jim Leaming (1954)
  Bob Wilson (1953–1955)
  Gene Kelly (1954)
  Byrum Saam (1954)

Fred Caposella (1954–1955)
Lindsay Nelson (1955)
Radcliff Hall (1955)

For five years this series was the summer replacement for the Gillette *Cavalcade of Sports* Friday night boxing matches. There were very few live bouts scheduled during these summers, so the *Summer Sports Reel* used other sports programming to fill the time slot. The basic element of the show, and the one that was kept throughout its run, was the showing of newsreel highlights of major sports events from around the world.

In 1950, under the title *Cavalcade of Sports,* the show was hosted by Don Dunphy, who was the radio announcer for the boxing matches during the regular season. He made observations about the films shown as well as introducing the various events. This same format was used in 1951, under the title *Sports Newsreel,* when Jimmy Powers, the television announcer for winter boxing on Gillette *Cavalcade of Sports,* replaced Dunphy. In 1952 the stories stood on their own, with only the newsreel announcers providing explanations of the action and no commentary. The 1952 title was *Gillette Summer Sports Reel,* as it was the following summer when a regular group of commentators was used to discuss the various events shown on film. This same format with a group of commentators, not all of whom were seen every week, was used in 1954 and 1955 under the title *Sportsreel.*

GILLIGAN'S ISLAND
Situation Comedy
FIRST TELECAST: *September 26, 1964*
LAST TELECAST: *September 4, 1967*
BROADCAST HISTORY:
Sep 1964–Sep 1965, CBS Sat 8:30–9:00
Sep 1965–Sep 1966, CBS Thu 8:00–8:30
Sep 1966–Sep 1967, CBS Mon 7:30–8:00
CAST:
Gilligan .... Bob Denver
Jonas Grumby (The Skipper) ... Alan Hale, Jr.
Thurston Howell III .... Jim Backus
Mrs. Lovey Howell .... Natalie Schafer
Ginger Grant .... Tina Louise
Roy Hinkley (The Professor)
.... Russell Johnson
Mary Ann Summers .... Dawn Wells
THEME:
"The Ballad of Gilligan's Island," by George Wyle and Sherwood Schwartz

The small charter boat *Minnow* had been on a sight-seeing party when it was caught in a storm and wrecked on the shore of an uncharted South Pacific island. Marooned together on the island were: the good-natured skipper; a somewhat blustery millionaire and his vacuous wife; a sexy movie star named Ginger; a high-school science teacher known as The Professor; a sweet, naive country girl named Mary Ann; and Gilligan. Gilligan was the boat's sole crew member, aside from

the skipper. He was well-meaning but inept in his attempts to find a means of returning to civilization. As a result, and perhaps even more because this simple-minded farce became a top hit, the little band was stranded on that island for three full seasons. One question that never got answered, however, concerned the luggage. In the first episode, and in the theme song, it was pointed out that the cruise was only supposed to be for three hours. How, then, did the passengers have enough clothing to last three years?

Gilligan's biggest fans were kids, and when the series finally went into repeats on local stations they made it one of the biggest rerun hits of the 1960s and 1970s. An animated cartoon version called *The New Adventures of Gilligan* was produced for ABC, and ran on that network's weekend daytime schedule from 1974 to 1977.

Then in 1978 NBC had the bright idea of bringing the original cast back together for a reunion special, in which they were finally rescued. All agreed to appear except Tina Louise (who wanted too much money, and so was replaced by Judith Baldwin). "Rescue From Gilligan's Island" aired in October 1978 as a two-part special, and was a phenomenal hit. They did finally get off the island, and returned to a triumphant homecoming. But then they made the mistake of going on a reunion cruise on the *Minnow II,* only to wind up stranded back on the same island—the result of another freak storm! "Castaways on Gilligan's Island," a follow-up special aired in 1979, had them converting the island into a tourist resort. And in still another sequel in 1981, The Harlem Globetrotters dropped in. There was talk of reviving the series, but audiences for the 1979 and 1981 sequels were not very large, and the plans never materialized.

GIMME A BREAK
Situation Comedy
FIRST TELECAST: *October 29, 1981*
LAST TELECAST: *May 12, 1987*
BROADCAST HISTORY:
Oct 1981–Aug 1982, NBC Thu 9:30–10:00
Sep 1982, NBC Thu 9:00–9:30
Oct 1982–Dec 1982, NBC Sat 9:00–9:30
Jan 1983–Aug 1983, NBC Thu 9:00–9:30
Aug 1983–Sep 1984, NBC Thu 8:00–8:30
Sep 1984–Nov 1984, NBC Sat 8:30–9:00
Dec 1984–Aug 1985, NBC Sat 9:00–9:30
Sep 1985–Jun 1986, NBC Sat 8:00–8:30
Jun 1986–Mar 1987, NBC Wed 9:30–10:00
Mar 1987–May 1987, NBC Tue 9:00–9:30
CAST:
Nellie Ruth "Nell" Harper .... Nell Carter
Chief Carl Kanisky (1981–1985)
.... Dolph Sweet
Katie Kanisky (1981–1986) .. Kari Michaelson
Julie Kanisky Maxwell (1981–1986)
.... Lauri Hendler
Samantha "Sam" Kanisky .... Lara Jill Miller
Officer Ralph Simpson (1981–1986)
.... Howard Morton

Grandpa Stanley Kanisky (1982–1987)
.... John Hoyt
Grandma Mildred Kanisky (1982–1983)
.... Jane Dulo
Uncle Ed Kanisky (1982–1983) .. Pete Schrum
Joey Donovan (1983–1987) .... Joey Lawrence
Addy Wilson (1984–1987) .... Telma Hopkins
Jonathan Maxwell (1984–1986)
.... Jonathan Silverman
Matthew Donovan (1986–1987)
.... Matthew Lawrence
Marty/Esteban (1986–1987) .... Paul Sand
Maybelle Harper (1986–1987)
.... Rosetta LeNoire
Maggie O'Brien (1986–1987). Rosie O'Donnell

A rotund black housekeeper maintained order in the home of a portly white police chief in this old-fashioned comedy set in the fictional town of Glen Lawn, California. Policeman Carl's beloved wife Margaret had died only months before, leaving him with three winsome daughters, ranging in age from cute grade-schooler to troublesome teen. Wisecracks and fat jokes abounded, but there was a lot of love as Nell tried to be friend and surrogate mother to the clan. Officer Simpson was a dopey police officer who was frequently seen, and Joey was a six-year-old orphan and junior-grade hustler who joined the household in the third season.

As the 1985–1986 season opened the chief had passed away, and Nell became both mother and father to the Kaniski brood. The man of the house was now Jonathan, who had married Julie at the end of the previous season and moved in. By 1986, with the Kanisky girls grown and/or college-bound, Nell and her best friend Addy decided to leave Glen Lawn for New York City, with Grandpa and little Joey in tow. There they discovered Joey's irresponsible father Tim, who turned over Joey's younger brother Matthew (played by Joey Lawrence's real-life brother) and departed, adding a second child to the shifting household. Marty was Nell's nutty New York landlord, who also owned the restaurant El Gaspacho downstairs, where he put on a phony Spanish accent and called himself "Esteban."

GIRL ABOUT TOWN
Music
FIRST TELECAST: *September 8, 1948*
LAST TELECAST: *June 11, 1949*
BROADCAST HISTORY:
Sep 1948–Jan 1949, NBC Wed 8:00–8:30
Feb 1949–Jun 1949, NBC Sun 10:00–10:30
REGULARS:
Kyle MacDonnell
Johnny Downs (1948)
Earl Wrightson (1948–1949)
Norman Paris Trio

Live musical program built around singer Kyle MacDonnell. The songs and chatter were interspersed with films of Kyle as a glamorous New Yorker, visiting chic night spots and attending Broadway shows, sailing on Long Island Sound, etc. Johnny Downs was her first co-host, replaced by baritone Earl Wrightson about a month after the program began. During its final three months the program was known as *Around the Town.*

GIRL ALONE
see *Dotty Mack Show, The*

GIRL FROM U.N.C.L.E., THE
Spy Spoof
FIRST TELECAST: *September 13, 1966*
LAST TELECAST: *August 29, 1967*
BROADCAST HISTORY:
Sep 1966–Aug 1967, NBC Tue 7:30–8:30
CAST:
April Dancer .... Stefanie Powers
Mark Slate .... Noel Harrison
Alexander Waverly .... Leo G. Carroll
Randy Kovacs .... Randy Kirby

Following the success of *The Man from U.N.C.L.E.* (U.N.C.L.E. stood for the United Network Command for Law and Enforcement), NBC decided in the fall of 1966 to create *The Girl from U.N.C.L.E.*, a companion James Bond–type spy spoof. Organization head Alexander Waverly teamed American April Dancer, a young, attractive, and very resourceful agent, with Mark Slate, recently transferred from U.N.C.L.E.'s London office to its New York headquarters. In the fight against THRUSH and other enemies of the world community, this new team would add its skills and enthusiasm. If *The Man from U.N.C.L.E.* seemed rather far-fetched to fans of spy and espionage stories, *The Girl from U.N.C.L.E.* was even sillier and more implausible, and it soon disappeared.

GIRL OF THE WEEK
see *Sportswoman of the Week*

GIRL WITH SOMETHING EXTRA, THE
Situation Comedy
FIRST TELECAST: *September 14, 1973*
LAST TELECAST: *May 24, 1974*
BROADCAST HISTORY:
Sep 1973–Dec 1973, NBC Fri 8:30–9:00
Jan 1974–May 1974, NBC Fri 9:00–9:30
CAST:
John Burton .... John Davidson
Sally Burton .... Sally Field
Anne........................ Zohra Lampert
Jerry Burton .... Jack Sheldon
Owen Metcalf .... Henry Jones
Stuart Kline .... William Windom
Angela .... Stephanie Edwards
Amber .... Teri Garr

Marriages often have rocky starts, but *The Girl with Something Extra* posed an unusual dilemma for her new spouse. On their wedding night Sally informed her husband John that she possessed E.S.P. and could read his mind. After deciding that their love was more important than the problems her mind-reading might cause, John and Sally settled down to a decidedly abnormal marriage. Her ability to read minds, his as well as everyone else's, created embarrassing and amusing situations which formed the basis for most of the stories in this series. Featured were John's brother Jerry and Sally's friend Anne, both single, and platonic friends of each other. John was employed as an attorney with the firm of Metcalf, Kline, and Associates.

GIRLS, THE
Situation Comedy
FIRST TELECAST: *January 1, 1950*
LAST TELECAST: *March 25, 1950*
BROADCAST HISTORY:
Jan 1950–Mar 1950, CBS Sun 7:00–7:30
CAST:
Cornelia Otis Skinner (Jan–Feb)
.... Bethel Leslie
Cornelia Otis Skinner (Feb–Mar)
.... Gloria Stroock
Emily Kimbrough .... Mary Malone
Todhunter Smith II .... Kenneth Forbes

Based on the autobiographical novel *Our Hearts Were Young and Gay* by Cornelia Otis Skinner and Emily Kimbrough, this early live comedy series followed the adventures of the two young Bryn Mawr graduates as they returned to New York in search of their careers, following a postgraduate fling in Europe. They moved to Greenwich Village at the height of the "Roaring 20s" and started looking for work, Miss Skinner as an actress and Miss Kimbrough as a writer. Bethel Leslie left the series in February to accept a role in a new play (that was considered far better work than television!), and was replaced by Gloria Stroock, the sister of actress Geraldine Brooks. The original title of this series was *Young and Gay*, changed to *The Girls* after the first two episodes had aired.

GIRLS' BASEBALL
see *Baseball*

GISELE MACKENZIE SHOW, THE
Musical Variety
FIRST TELECAST: *September 28, 1957*
LAST TELECAST: *March 29, 1958*
BROADCAST HISTORY:
Sep 1957–Mar 1958, NBC Sat 9:30–10:00
REGULARS:
Gisele MacKenzie
Jack Narz (1957–1958)
Tom Kennedy (1958)
The Curfew Boys
The Joe Pryor Group
The Axel Stordahl Orchestra

Canadian-born songstress Gisele MacKenzie made her starring debut in her own variety series in the fall of 1957, after being dropped from *Your Hit Parade* (along with the rest of the cast) in a "modernization" move. In addition to her singing and violin-playing, talents which she had regularly displayed in the past, she danced and acted with the guest stars who appeared each week. There was a small group of regular singers (The Joe Pryor Group) and dancers (The Curfew Boys) plus a regular announcer who was seen on camera. Initially the announcer was Jack Narz, who left the series on January 11, 1958, to be succeeded by his own brother, Tom Kennedy.

GLADYS KNIGHT & THE PIPS SHOW, THE
Musical Variety
FIRST TELECAST: *July 10, 1975*
LAST TELECAST: *July 31, 1975*
BROADCAST HISTORY:
Jul 1975, NBC Thu 8:00–9:00
REGULARS:
Gladys Knight & the Pips
(Merald Knight, William Guest, Edward Pattern)
The George Wyle Orchestra

Gladys Knight and the Pips had been one of the top rock recording groups for nearly 15 years when they were chosen to headline this four-week summer variety series in 1975. Miss Knight, a onetime child prizewinner on *Ted Mack's Original Amateur Hour*, was joined by the Pips (all relatives of hers) as hosts and singing stars of the show. Each week they sang a number of their record hits and joined guest stars in musical and comedy routines.

GLAMOUR-GO-ROUND
Interview
FIRST TELECAST: *February 16, 1950*
LAST TELECAST: *August 10, 1950*
BROADCAST HISTORY:
Feb 1950–Aug 1950, CBS Thu 9:30–9:45
HOSTS:
Ilka Chase
Durward Kirby
Bill Nalle

Ilka Chase, described in a CBS press release as a "recognized authority on style and beauty," hosted this informal talk show along with Durward Kirby. The setting was Miss Chase's drawing room where she and Durward, along with pianist Bill Nalle, welcomed distinguished visitors from New York's fashion world, show business, and various fields of cultural endeavor.

GLEN CAMPBELL GOODTIME HOUR, THE
Musical Variety
FIRST TELECAST: *January 29, 1969*
LAST TELECAST: *June 13, 1972*

BROADCAST HISTORY:
  Jan 1969–Dec 1969, CBS Wed 7:30–8:30 (OS)
  Dec 1969–Jun 1971, CBS Sun 9:00–10:00 (OS)
  Sep 1971–Jun 1972, CBS Tue 7:30–8:30
REGULARS:
  Glen Campbell
  Ron Poindexter Dancers (1969–1971)
  Denny Vaughn Singers (1969–1970)
  Marty Paich Orchestra
  Larry McNeeley (1970–1972)
  Jerry Reed (1970–1972)
  Mike Curb Congregation (1971–1972)
  Dom DeLuise (1971–1972)
THEME:
  "Gentle on My Mind," by John Hartford

Country-popular singer Glen Campbell looked like a potential successor to Perry Como when this weekly variety hour was launched in 1969. He had a long string of enormously successful records in the late 1960s (including his theme, "Gentle on My Mind"), was popular with both teenagers and adults, and had an easy, ingratiating style which had won him a wide TV following during his frequent appearances on *The Smothers Brothers Show.* His own show was reminiscent of Como's, too, in a contemporary way—relaxed, informal, and down-home friendly. In addition to hosting, he sang many of his hits (two of which, "Wichita Lineman" and "Galveston," were on the charts about the time this series began) and did instrumental solos (he was a first-rate guitarist). Guests on the show tended to be country singers and sketch comedians. Although not usually credited as a regular, comedian Dom DeLuise appeared in more than half the show's telecasts during the final season. Composer-singer John Hartford, who had written Glen's theme song and was a close personal friend, was likewise not a regular but made frequent guest appearances throughout the show's run.

GLEN CAMPBELL MUSIC SHOW, THE
  Music
BROADCAST HISTORY:
  Syndicated only
  30 minutes
  Produced: *1982–1983* (24 episodes)
  Released: *Fall 1982*
HOST:
  Glen Campbell

Pop singer Glen Campbell presided over this amiable half-hour of songs with a minimum of chatter and a maximum of informality. He was joined by middle-of-the-road musical guests such as Willie Nelson, Chuck Mangione, and Leo Sayer.

GLENN MILLER TIME
  Music
FIRST TELECAST: *July 10, 1961*
LAST TELECAST: *September 11, 1961*
BROADCAST HISTORY:
  Jul 1961–Sep 1961, CBS Mon 10:00–10:30

REGULARS:
  Johnny Desmond
  Ray McKinley
  Patty Clark
  The Castle Singers
THEME:
  "Moonlight Serenade," by Glenn Miller and Mitchell Parish

Johnny Desmond and Ray McKinley were co-hosts of this summer music series that featured the style and sounds of the Glenn Miller Orchestra. Each telecast included a medley of "something old, something new, something borrowed, something blue," a regular feature of the band during the days when it had a regularly scheduled radio series during World War II. In addition to starring in this live series, Ray McKinley was then touring with "The Original Glenn Miller Orchestra" (Miller himself had died in 1944).

GLITTER
  Drama
FIRST TELECAST: *September 13, 1984*
LAST TELECAST: *December 27, 1985*
BROADCAST HISTORY:
  Sep 1984, ABC Thu 9:00–10:00
  Dec 1984, ABC Tue 9:00–10:00
  Dec 1985, ABC Tue–Fri 12:00–1:00 A.M.
CAST:
  Sam Dillon .... David Birney
  Kate Simpson .... Morgan Brittany
  Pete Bozak .... Christopher Mayer
  Jennifer Douglas .... Dianne Kay
  Chester "Chip" Craddock
    .... Timothy Patrick Murphy
  Angela Timini .... Tracy Nelson
  Shelley Sealy .... Barbara Sharma
  Clive Richlin .... Arte Johnson
  Earl Tobin .... Dorian Harewood
  Terry Randolph.............. Melinda Culea
  Charles Hardwick .... Arthur Hill

Any resemblance between *People* magazine and the fictional *Glitter* magazine was purely intentional. As ABC's press department described it, *"Glitter,* the hottest magazine on the newsstands, sends its teams of reporters to probe the nation's most glamorous places and people." The series was flashy and unabashedly romantic, with happy endings in most of its subplots and a revolving door full of guest stars who seemed to be on their way to or from appearances on *The Love Boat.* Sam Dillon and Kate Simpson were the magazine's star reporters, covering the juiciest stories. Other reporters on the staff were Pete Bozak, Jennifer Douglas, Earl Tobin, and Terry Randolph. Shelley Sealy was the romance and health editor, Clive Richlin the chief photographer, and Charles Hardwick the magazine's publisher. Even the little people on the *Glitter* staff showed up on the air. Chip the mail clerk and pretty receptionist Angela Timini were madly in love with each other and their romance was a continuing thread amid the glamour of the stories featuring the weekly guest stars.

One of the first casualties of the 1984–1985 season, *Glitter* resurfaced briefly as part of ABC's late-night lineup a year later, airing seven original episodes not previously seen in prime time.

GLORIA
Situation Comedy
FIRST TELECAST: *September 26, 1982*
LAST TELECAST: *September 21, 1983*
BROADCAST HISTORY:
Sep 1982–Apr 1983, CBS Sun 8:30–9:00
Jun 1983–Sep 1983, CBS Wed 8:30–9:00
CAST:
Gloria Bunker Stivic .... Sally Struthers
Dr. Willard Adams........ Burgess Meredith
Clark V. Uhley, Jr. .... Lou Richards
Dr. Maggie Lawrence .... Jo de Winter
Joey Stivic................. Christian Jacobs

Her marriage to Mike Stivic had crumbled when he left her to live on a commune with a flower child; she was back from California. Archie Bunker's little girl Gloria (see *All in the Family*) wanted to start a new life in fresh surroundings. Not wanting to be completely out of touch with her father, and hoping to become a vet, Gloria found a job as an assistant trainee to a couple of veterinarians in the rural upstate New York town of Foxridge. Crusty old Dr. Willard Adams was not only her boss but her landlord as well. Maggie Lawrence was Dr. Adams' partner at the clinic, a true liberated woman, and Clark Uhley was their other assistant. For Clark, becoming a vet seemed a ludicrous aim—he seemed to be feared or hated by almost every creature that came into the clinic.

The adjustments were not easy for Gloria, or for her eight-year-old son Joey. But her new friends—and all those cuddly animals—helped brighten things up for Archie's daughter, who never lost her little-girl innocence.

GLYNIS
Situation Comedy
FIRST TELECAST: *September 25, 1963*
LAST TELECAST: *September 6, 1965*
BROADCAST HISTORY:
Sep 1963–Dec 1963, CBS Wed 8:30–9:00
Jul 1965–Sep 1965, CBS Mon 9:00–9:30
CAST:
Glynis Granville .... Glynis Johns
Keith Granville .... Keith Andes
Chick Rogers .... George Mathews

Keith Granville was a very successful attorney who had two problems, a scatterbrained wife and a penchant for getting involved in criminal cases as an amateur detective. With his wife joining him, they made a rather wacky pair of semi-pro sleuths who always managed to stumble onto the solution of whatever crime they were investigating. His wife's background as a mystery-story writer may have been of some help, but it was

their incredible luck more than anything else that saved the day. Reruns of this series were aired by CBS during the summer of 1965.

GO LUCKY
Quiz/Audience Participation
FIRST TELECAST: *July 15, 1951*
LAST TELECAST: *September 2, 1951*
BROADCAST HISTORY:
Jul 1951–Sep 1951, CBS Sun 7:30–8:00
EMCEE:
Jan Murray

This comedy game show, the summer replacement in 1951 for *This Is Show Business*, gave contestants the challenge of identifying an activity—fishing, bowling, burping a baby, etc.—by asking questions of the host. The studio and home audience had seen what the activity was, and the host would only answer yes or no to the questions. Each contestant worked with a team of two celebrities, the three of them trying to narrow the subject down until they could identify the activity. Small prizes were awarded for guessing correctly within a short time limit.

GOING MY WAY
Situation Comedy
FIRST TELECAST: *October 3, 1962*
LAST TELECAST: *September 11, 1963*
BROADCAST HISTORY:
Oct 1962–Sep 1963, ABC Wed 8:30–9:30
CAST:
Father Chuck O'Malley.......... Gene Kelly
Father Fitzgibbon .... Leo G. Carroll
Tom Colwell..................... Dick York
Mrs. Featherstone.......... Nydia Westman

Clerical comedy-drama based on the 1944 movie, with Gene Kelly assuming the role created in the film by Bing Crosby. Father O'Malley, a lighthearted, progressive young priest, was assigned to a parish in a lower-class New York City neighborhood to aid the crusty old pastor, Father Fitzgibbon. There he encountered boyhood friend Tom Colwell (who ran the local community center), humor, and a great deal of warmth. Mrs. Featherstone was the housekeeper at the rectory.

GOING PLACES WITH BETTY BETZ
Discussion
FIRST TELECAST: *February 20, 1951*
LAST TELECAST: *May 15, 1951*
BROADCAST HISTORY:
Feb 1951–May 1951, ABC Tue 7:15–7:30
MODERATOR:
Betty Betz

Teenage panel show in which panelists and guests discussed career opportunities and other topics of interest to young people. Betty Betz was a nationally syndicated columnist for the Hearst newspapers, and an "authority" on teenagers.

GOLD SEAL PLAYHOUSE

Dramatic Anthology

FIRST TELECAST: *September 17, 1953*
LAST TELECAST: *October 8, 1953*
BROADCAST HISTORY:

Sep 1953–Oct 1953, ABC Thu 10:00–10:30

This was a short series of filmed dramas.

GOLDBERGS, THE

Situation Comedy

FIRST TELECAST: *January 10, 1949*
LAST TELECAST: *October 19, 1954*
BROADCAST HISTORY:

Jan 1949–Feb 1949, CBS Mon 8:00–8:30
Mar 1949–Apr 1949, CBS Mon 9:00–9:30
Apr 1949–Jun 1951, CBS Mon 9:30–10:00
Feb 1952–Jul 1952, NBC Mon/Wed/Fri 7:15–7:30
Jul 1953–Sep 1953, NBC Fri 8:00–8:30
Apr 1954–Oct 1954, DUM Tue 8:00–8:30

CAST:

Molly Goldberg . . . . Gertrude Berg
Jake Goldberg (1949–1951) . . . . Philip Loeb
Jake Goldberg (1952) . . . . Harold J. Stone
Jake Goldberg (1953–1954) . . Robert H. Harris
Sammy Goldberg (1949–1952)
. . . . Larry Robinson
Sammy Goldberg (1954) . . . . Tom Taylor
Rosalie Goldberg . . . . Arlene McQuade
Uncle David . . . . Eli Mintz
Mrs. Bloom (1953) . . . . Olga Fabian

Gertrude Berg had conceived the role of Molly Goldberg and made her a popular radio character for almost 20 years. In January 1949 the entire Goldberg clan moved to television. Living in Apartment 3B at 1030 East Tremont Avenue in the Bronx, they were a middle-class Jewish family with middle-class problems. Molly's husband Jake was in the clothing business, and their two children, Sammy and Rosalie, were active teenagers. Molly was a housewife, prone to gossip with her neighbors across the inside courtyard of the apartment building. Her call to her favorite cohort in gossip—"Yoo-hoo, Mrs. Bloom"—came whenever she had something juicy to spread, which was quite regularly. Also living with the family was the educated and philosophical Uncle David, patriarch of the family. Molly was a good soul and was constantly involved in trying to help everybody in the neighborhood solve their problems.

The Goldbergs was a live series during the years it ran on CBS, NBC, and DuMont. In the fall of 1955 a filmed version was produced for syndication to local stations, using the same cast as had appeared on DuMont in 1954. In this last version, Molly and the family moved from the Bronx to the suburban community of Haverville. It lasted for one season.

The program ended its CBS run in 1951 under a cloud of controversy. Principal Philip Loeb had been blacklisted for alleged left-wing sympathies, causing sponsor General Foods to drop the series.

Mrs. Berg fought to keep him, but to no avail—nervous sponsor and network executives said that either Loeb went or *The Goldbergs* would never be seen again. Thus when the series reappeared in 1952, it was without Loeb.

The charges against Loeb were never proven—indeed, he declared under oath that he was not a Communist Party member—but his career went into a sharp decline. He had become "controversial," and advertisers steered clear of him. He appealed to his union for help, with no result. His career in a shambles, Loeb became increasingly depressed and embittered. In 1955, alone in a hotel room, he took a fatal overdose of sleeping pills. Four years after he had been driven from TV, Philip Loeb was dead, a suicide.

GOLDDIGGERS, THE

see *Dean Martin Presents The Golddiggers*

GOLDEN GAME, THE

Religion

FIRST TELECAST: *April 9, 1950*
LAST TELECAST: *May 7, 1950*
BROADCAST HISTORY:

Apr 1950–May 1950, ABC Sun 6:30–7:00

Biblical charades. Two teams of laymen representing different nationalities and creeds acted out charades based on Biblical stories or proverbs. At the end they explained why they picked their subjects, and what these subjects meant to their lives.

GOLDEN GIRLS, THE

Situation Comedy

FIRST TELECAST: *September 14, 1985*
LAST TELECAST:
BROADCAST HISTORY:

Sep 1985– , NBC Sat 9:00–9:30

CAST:

Dorothy Zbornak . . . . Bea Arthur
Rose Nylund . . . . Betty White
Blanche Devereaux . . . . Rue McClanahan
Sophia Petrillo . . . . Estelle Getty

For those who thought NBC's drug-drenched crime show *Miami Vice* was giving Miami a bad name, the network launched this equally popular comedy—nicknamed "Miami Nice." It centered on four mature, single women living together in the sunny city of retirees, and enjoying their "golden years" to the hilt. Dorothy was the outspoken divorcée, a substitute teacher whose strong personality often seemed to overpower her housemates. Rose was a flaky, naive, soft-spoken widow given to hilarious misinterpretations of almost everything that was said in her presence. She worked, believe it or not, as a grief counselor. Blanche, who owned the house, was also a widow, but of a different stripe. She was lusty, man-hungry, and dripping with charm, a Southern belle who never aged—in her own mind, at least.

All in their 50s and 60s, the three were joined by Dorothy's elderly mother Sophia, who moved in when her retirement home burned to the ground. Sophia had the saltiest mouth in the house. She had had a stroke, it was said, that destroyed the "tact" cells in her brain.

Herb Edelman was seen occasionally as Dorothy's no-good ex-husband Stan, who had dumped her for a young bimbo.

GOLDEN TOUCH OF FRANKIE CARLE, THE
Music
FIRST TELECAST: *August 7, 1956*
LAST TELECAST: *October 29, 1956*
BROADCAST HISTORY:
  Aug 1956, NBC Tue 7:30–7:45
  Sep 1956, NBC Mon/Tue 7:30–7:45
  Oct 1956, NBC Mon 7:30–7:45
REGULAR:
  Frankie Carle

Pianist Frankie Carle starred in this live music show, originating from Hollywood, that filled the remainder of the half-hour in which NBC aired its network news program during the summer of 1956. Guest vocalists appeared on a regular basis and the selections of songs, both instrumental and vocal, ranged from standards to currently popular numbers.

GOLDIE
  see *Betty Hutton Show, The*

GOMER PYLE, U.S.M.C.
Situation Comedy
FIRST TELECAST: *September 25, 1964*
LAST TELECAST: *September 9, 1970*
BROADCAST HISTORY:
  Sep 1964–Jun 1965, CBS Fri 9:30–10:00
  Sep 1965–Sep 1966, CBS Fri 9:00–9:30
  Sep 1966–Aug 1967, CBS Wed 9:30–10:00
  Sep 1967–Sep 1969, CBS Fri 8:30–9:00
  Jul 1970–Sep 1970, CBS Wed 8:00–8:30
CAST:
  Pvt. Gomer Pyle .... Jim Nabors
  Sgt. Vince Carter .... Frank Sutton
  Pvt. Gilbert "Duke" Slater ..... Ronnie Schell
  Corp. Chuck Boyle (1965–1968) .... Roy Stuart
  Frankie Lombardi (1966) .... Ted Bessell
  Bunny Olsen. .... Barbara Stuart
  Pvt. Lester Hummel ..... William Christopher
  Col. Edward Gray. .... Forrest Compton
  Sgt. Hacker (1965–1969) .... Allan Melvin
  Cpl. Nick Guccinello (1964–1965)
  .... Tommy Leonetti
  Larry (1964–1965) .... Larry Hovis

After little more than a season playing Gomer Pyle on *The Andy Griffith Show,* Jim Nabors got his own series built around the same character. Gomer was a likable, naive, bumbling rural character who gave up his job as a gas station attendant in Mayberry to join the peacetime Marine Corps, which stationed him at Camp Henderson, California. His nemesis in the Marines Corps was his immediate superior, Sgt. Carter, who tried hard to be a cynical, tough leatherneck, but was constantly confounded by Gomer's wide-eyed innocence and trust in practically everyone. At first Carter believed that Gomer was trying to make a fool out of him, but he later realized that it was just Gomer's nature to be the way he was. Sgt. Carter eventually became Gomer's friend and protector, a role belying his gruff exterior. That is not to say, however, that Gomer did not continue to drive him crazy on a relatively regular basis.

The episodes aired during the summer of 1970 in prime time and later in daytime were all reruns. The CBS daytime run began in August 1969 and ended in March 1972.

GONG SHOW, THE
Comedy/Audience Participation
BROADCAST HISTORY:
  Syndicated and network daytime
  30 minutes
  Produced: *1976–1980*
  Released: *Fall 1976*
HOST:
  Gary Owens (1976–1977)
  Chuck Barris (1977–1980)
PANELISTS:
  Jaye P. Morgan
  Jamie Farr
  Rex Reed
  Phyllis Diller
  Arte Johnson
  Rip Taylor
  Steve Garvey
  Ken Norton
  Dr. Joyce Brothers
REGULAR:
  Milton Delugg Orchestra

Possibly the most bizarre program to air on American television in recent years, *The Gong Show* was a wild and sometimes raunchy parody on amateur programs. It consisted, simply enough, of a succession of amateurs demonstrating their dubious talents. Anyone could audition, but sometimes it seemed that only certifiable crazies need apply. Typical of the acts was a girl who whistled through her nose, a dentist who played "Stars and Stripes Forever" with his drill, a man who played lighted bulbs that blinked on and off, a dancer with four arms, a comedian who performed inside a barrel, a musician who blew a trumpet through his navel, another who meowed to the tune "Alley Cat," an endless parade of fat ladies who did unlikely things (tap-dancing, playing the tuba, belching to music, singing "On the Good Ship Lollipop"), and someone who broke eggs on his head while making faces through a distorting glass. And of course there was the lady in the tutu who stood on her head on a cup and spun slowly around, while playing "Old Folks at Home" on the mandolin.

Looking on during all this insanity, and sometimes joining in, was a rowdy panel of three celebrities who were supposed to rate each act on a scale of one to ten, or, if it was bad enough, gong it off the stage. (Some acts were gonged so fast there was eventually a minimum time limit imposed.) The act with the highest score got a prize of $712.05 ($516.32 on the daytime version), and a golden gong. About one-third of the acts were gonged, and on some shows they all were, leaving no winners at all.

There were also interludes with regulars, such as Gene-Gene the Dancing Machine (a big, black stagehand who came on dancing frantically, and was usually pelted with assorted objects thrown by the panel), and the Unknown Comic, who wore a paper bag over his head, the better to avoid responsibility for his corny jokes (he was later unmasked—or debagged—on *Real People* as one Murray Langston). It was, as one of the writers put it, "a cuckoo's nest without walls."

Jaye P. Morgan and Jamie Farr were virtually regular panelists, joined frequently by Arte Johnson, Rex Reed, Rip Taylor, Steve Garvey, Phyllis Diller, and others at home with this kind of mayhem. The show was created by Chris Bearde and Chuck Barris, and premiered on the NBC daytime lineup in June 1976, remaining there until July 1978. A syndicated nighttime version was added in the fall of 1976. Curly-headed Chuck "Chuckie Baby" Barris, one of the most successful game-show producers in Hollywood (*Dating Game, Newlywed Game*), was the host of the daytime version throughout its run, and replaced Gary Owens on the syndicated version after its first year.

GOOD COMPANY
Interview
FIRST TELECAST: *September 7, 1967*
LAST TELECAST: *December 21, 1967*
BROADCAST HISTORY:
  Sep 1967–Dec 1967, ABC Thu 10:00–10:30
HOST:
  F. Lee Bailey
EXECUTIVE PRODUCER:
  David Susskind

In a style reminiscent of Edward R. Murrow's *Person to Person*, famed criminal lawyer F. (for Francis) Lee Bailey visited the home of a different celebrity each week and chatted about his host's life and career. The principal difference was that Bailey was filmed at the home of the interviewee, rather than talking long-distance from the studio, as Murrow had done on his live program. Among those Bailey interviewed were actor Tony Curtis, publisher Hugh Hefner (at his million-dollar Chicago mansion), Senator Everett Dirksen, and Jack Paar (who was such a good talker that he required two telecasts).

GOOD GUYS, THE
Situation Comedy
FIRST TELECAST: *September 25, 1968*
LAST TELECAST: *January 23, 1970*
BROADCAST HISTORY:
  Sep 1968–Sep 1969, CBS Wed 8:30–9:00
  Sep 1969–Jan 1970, CBS Fri 8:00–8:30
CAST:
  Rufus Butterworth .... Bob Denver
  Bert Gramus .... Herb Edelman
  Claudia Gramus .... Joyce Van Patten
  Andy Gardner (1968) .... Ron Masak
  Hal Dawson (1968–1969) .... George Furth
  Big Tom (1969) .... Alan Hale, Jr.
  Gertie (1969) .... Toni Gilman

Fresh from his success in *Gilligan's Island*, Bob Denver moved into the role of Rufus Butterworth in this 1968 comedy series. Rufus and Bert Gramus had been friends since they were children. Bert was married and ran a diner, "Bert's Place," while Rufus was single and worked as a cabdriver. Rufus also helped his friend out around the diner, and was constantly coming up with money-making schemes, none of which ever seemed to pan out—but all of which got the two of them into endless predicaments. Rufus gave up his cabdriving at the start of the second season to become a full-time partner in the diner, which closed its doors forever with the cancellation of the series in January 1970.

GOOD HEAVENS
Situation Comedy
FIRST TELECAST: *March 8, 1976*
LAST TELECAST: *June 26, 1976*
BROADCAST HISTORY:
  Mar 1976–Apr 1976, ABC Mon 8:30–9:00
  May 1976–Jun 1976, ABC Sat 8:00–8:30
CAST:
  Mr. Angel .... Carl Reiner
EXECUTIVE PRODUCER:
  Carl Reiner

Gentle comedy starring Carl Reiner as a warm and witty business-suited angel who descended to earth to bestow one wish on a different mortal each week—any wish except money. Thanks to Mr. Angel, and to themselves, a sporting-goods salesman got his long-dreamt-of tryout in the big leagues; a young woman who couldn't decide between two suitors got a new beau who combined the best qualities of each; and an unsuccessful author got an adventure to which everyone wanted the literary rights.

GOOD LIFE, THE
Situation Comedy
FIRST TELECAST: *September 18, 1971*
LAST TELECAST: *January 8, 1972*
BROADCAST HISTORY:
  Sep 1971–Jan 1972, NBC Sat 8:30–9:00

CAST:
Albert Miller .... Larry Hagman
Jane Miller .... Donna Mills
Charles Dutton .... David Wayne
Grace Dutton .... Hermione Baddeley
Nick Dutton .... Danny Goldman

Albert and Jane Miller were a middle-class American couple who decided that the dull routine of their lives needed a change. Instead of dropping out, however, they contrived to "drop up"—obtaining work as butler and cook, respectively, for an extremely wealthy family. Amid the opulence of a millionaire's mansion, they hoped to share at least some of the benefits of "the good life." Their new employer, industrialist Charles Dutton, was unaware of their middle-class background. He recognized their inexperience but found them pleasant enough company. His stuck-up sister Grace was upset with their lack of proper training, however, and constantly looked for ways to get them fired. Dutton's teenage son Nick was the only member of the household who discovered the truth about the Millers, but he thought that their charade was great fun and helped them through the many catastrophes caused by their unfamiliarity with social etiquette among the wealthy.

GOOD MORNING, WORLD
Situation Comedy
FIRST TELECAST: *September 5, 1967*
LAST TELECAST: *September 17, 1968*
BROADCAST HISTORY:
Sep 1967–Sep 1968, CBS Tue 9:30–10:00
CAST:
Dave Lewis .... Joby Baker
Larry Clarke .... Ronnie Schell
Roland B. Hutton, Jr. .... Billy DeWolf
Linda Lewis .... Julie Parrish
Sandy Kramer .... Goldie Hawn

Comedy about "Lewis and Clarke," two early-morning radio disc jockeys who worked together as a team at a small Los Angeles station owned by the overbearing Roland B. Hutton, Jr. Their adventures both on and off the air were the subjects of stories in this series. Dave was happily married, while Larry, a single, fancied himself quite a swinger. Goldie Hawn, in her pre-*Laugh-In* days, played the Lewises' gossiping neighbor Sandy.

GOOD TIME HARRY
Situation Comedy
FIRST TELECAST: *July 19, 1980*
LAST TELECAST: *September 13, 1980*
BROADCAST HISTORY:
Jul 1980, NBC Sat 10:00–11:00
Aug 1980–Sep 1980, NBC Sat 10:30–11:00
CAST:
Harry Jenkins .... Ted Bessell
Jimmy Hughes .... Eugene Roche

Carol Younger .... Marcia Strassman
Billie Howard .... Jesse Welles
Stan .... Barry Gordon
Sally .... Ruth Manning
Martin Springer .... Steven Peterman
Lenny the bartender .... Richard Karron

Harry Jenkins was a sportswriter for the San Francisco *Sentinel,* whose dates with beautiful women tended to get in the way of his assignments for the paper. His extracurricular activities did not endear him to his editor, Jimmy Hughes, who had once fired him because of it. Harry's skill at his craft got him his job back, but his continuing playboy escapades made for an adversary relationship between him and his boss. Sally was Hughes' secretary; Carol, a sympathetic fellow reporter; Martin, the enthusiastic young copy boy; and Billie, a cocktail waitress. Living next door to Harry, and jealous of his success with beautiful women, was Stan, a rather bland insurance salesman who was always trying to get Harry to fix him up with dates. One of Harry's favorite haunts was Danny's Bar, a watering hole very popular with San Francisco writers.

GOOD TIMES
Situation Comedy
FIRST TELECAST: *February 1, 1974*
LAST TELECAST: *August 1, 1979*
BROADCAST HISTORY:
Feb 1974–Sept 1974, CBS Fri 8:30–9:00
Sep 1974–Mar 1976, CBS Tue 8:00–8:30
Mar 1976–Aug 1976, CBS Tue 8:30–9:00
Sep 1976–Jan 1978, CBS Wed 8:00–8:30
Jan 1978–May 1978, CBS Mon 8:00–8:30
Jun 1978–Sep 1978, CBS Mon 8:30–9:00
Sep 1978–Dec 1978, CBS Sat 8:30–9:00
May 1979–Aug 1979, CBS Wed 8:30–9:00
CAST:
Florida Evans (1974–1977, 1978–1979)
.... Esther Rolle
James Evans (1974–1976) .... John Amos
James Evans, Jr. (J.J.) .... Jimmie Walker
Willona Woods .... Ja'net DuBois
Michael Evans .... Ralph Carter
Thelma Evans Anderson .. BernNadette Stanis
Carl Dixon (1977) .... Moses Gunn
Nathan Bookman (1977–1979) . Johnny Brown
Penny Gordon Woods (1977–1979)
.... Janet Jackson
Keith Anderson (1978–1979) ...... Ben Powers
Sweet Daddy (1978–1979) .. Theodore Wilson
PRODUCER:
Norman Lear

Good Times was a spin-off from *Maude,* which in turn was a spin-off from *All in the Family.* Florida Evans was originally Maude Findlay's maid until, in the spring of 1974, she got a show of her own. Florida and James Evans were lower-middle-class blacks living with their three children in a high-rise ghetto on the South Side of Chicago. J.J.

was the oldest (17 when the series started), Thelma was a year younger than him, and Michael was 10. Trying to make ends meet on the erratic income provided by James, who was always in and out of jobs, made life difficult, but there was plenty of love in the family. J.J. was an accomplished amateur painter who, though going to trade school, was always looking for some get-rich-quick scheme that would help get him and his family out of the ghetto. He formed a rock group, managed a young comic, and tried various other money-making ideas after he got out of school. He did manage to earn money with his painting and was also quite popular with the girls, something his mother viewed with mixed emotions. His catch-phrase "Dy-No-Mite" became very popular in the mid-1970s. Florida's neighbor and best friend was Willona Woods.

At the start of the 1976–1977 season there was a major change in the cast. James had found a job working as a partner in a garage in Mississippi when he was killed in an auto accident. The entire family, which had been planning to move to their new home and start a new life, was now fatherless. J.J. became the man of the house and was even more determined to find a way out of the ghetto for his family, whether by means that were entirely legal or not. Some of his schemes became decidedly shady. Meanwhile Florida found a new man in her life in the spring of 1977, in the person of Carl Dixon, the owner of a small appliance repair shop. They were married during the summer of 1977 (though the wedding was not seen), and in the fall were referred to on the show as being "on their honeymoon."

Series star Esther Rolle had become disenchanted with the role model for young blacks provided by J.J.'s "jive-talking," woman-chasing, less-than-honest character and, on the pretense of illness, left the series prior to the start of the 1977–1978 season. In the story line, Florida became ill and was living with Carl Dixon in a Southern location that was better for her health. Friend and neighbor Willona became a surrogate mother to the Evans household. Little Penny Gordon, a victim of child abuse, became Willona's adopted daughter. J.J. was working full time at a small ad agency, a job he had gotten during the 1976–1977 season, and Bookman, the building superintendent, became a more prominent member of the cast.

The following fall Esther Rolle returned to the cast (sans Carl), with the promise that J.J. would be a more respectable character, and daughter Thelma married football star Keith Anderson. J.J., who was paying for the wedding, had lost his job at the advertising agency when a business slowdown forced them to lay him off. He had to borrow money from loan shark Sweet Daddy to pay for the wedding and, to make matters worse, accidentally tripped Keith during the ceremony, resulting in a leg injury that jeopardized Keith's million-dollar pro-football contract. Money was hard to come by,

and the newlyweds were living in the Evans apartment while Keith recuperated. Though depressed by his physical problems, Keith drove a taxi to help out, while Florida got a job as a school-bus driver and J.J. taught art at home.

With falling ratings, *Good Times* was pulled from the CBS schedule in December. It returned in the spring and, in the last original episode (there were no reruns aired in the last season), everything worked out for the series principals. Keith got his big contract as a running back and moved into his own place with Thelma, who was expecting their first child; J.J. sold the comic strip he had developed to a syndicate for a healthy advance; and neighbor Willona got promoted to head buyer at the clothing boutique where she worked.

GOODNIGHT, BEANTOWN
Situation Comedy
FIRST TELECAST: *April 3, 1983*
LAST TELECAST: *September 2, 1984*
BROADCAST HISTORY:
   Apr 1983–May 1983, CBS Sun 8:00–8:30
   Aug 1983–Jan 1984, CBS Sun 9:30–10:00
   Jul 1984, CBS Sun 8:00–8:30
   Aug 1984–Sep 1984, CBS Sun 8:30–9:00
CAST:

Matt Cassidy	Bill Bixby
Jennifer Barnes	Mariette Hartley
Susan Barnes	Tracey Gold
Dick Novak (1983)	George Coe
Sam Holliday (1983)	Charles Levin
Albert Addelson	G. W. Bailey
Valerie Wood	Stephanie Faracy
Frank Fletcher	Jim Staahl
Augie Kleindab	Todd Susman

Although infrequently used as the setting for a TV series, Boston was the setting of three shows that ran concurrently in the early 1980s: *St. Elsewhere, Cheers,* and *Goodnight, Beantown.* Much like *The Mary Tyler Moore Show, Goodnight, Beantown* dealt with the staff of a local television newsroom. Matt Cassidy and Jenny Barnes were co-anchors on the WYN evening news show, somewhat antagonistic but friendly competitors on the job, and sometimes lovers in private life. Amazingly, their professional rivalry seemed to have little negative impact on their romance. Others on the WYN staff were news director Dick Novak (replaced in the fall by anxiety-ridden Albert Addelson), news producer Sam Holliday, sexy feature reporter Valerie Wood, obnoxious sports reporter Frank Fletcher, and cameraman Augie Kleindab. The only regular away from the newsroom was the divorced Jenny's young daughter, Susan.

GOODRICH CELEBRITY TIME
   see *Celebrity Time*

GOODTIME GIRLS
Situation Comedy
FIRST TELECAST: *January 22, 1980*

LAST TELECAST: *August 29, 1980*
BROADCAST HISTORY:
Jan 1980–Feb 1980, ABC Tue 8:30–9:00
Apr 1980, ABC Sat 8:30–9:00
Aug 1980, ABC Fri 8:30–9:00
CAST:
Edith Bedelmeyer .... Annie Potts
Betty Crandall .... Lorna Patterson
Loretta Smoot .... Georgia Engel
Camille Rittenhouse .... Francine Tacker
Irma Coolidge .... Marcia Lewis
George Coolidge .... Merwin Goldsmith
Benny Loman .... Peter Scolari
Frankie Millardo .... Adrian Zmed
Skeeter .... Sparky Marcus

Comedy set in Washington, D.C., during World War II (1942), where three young women (Edith, Betty, Loretta) descended on the same scarce one-room apartment. Snobbish Camille, doing a magazine story on the apartment shortage, was much amused until she found out that she'd lost hers and had to move in with them, making it four in the cramped attic room.

Edith, employed at the Office of Price Administration, was the group's unofficial leader; Betty, from Sioux City, Iowa, worked in a Baltimore defense plant; and shy Loretta, a war bride, worked for Gen. Culpepper, a Pentagon bureaucrat. The Coolidge House boarding facility where they lived was tightly run by George and Irma Coolidge. Frankie was the hustling cabbie who brought the girls there—because he lived downstairs.

Ration stamps, big bands, and the jitterbug provided the social backdrop.

GOODYEAR SUMMERTIME REVUE
see *Paul Whiteman's Goodyear Revue*

GOODYEAR TV PLAYHOUSE
Dramatic Anthology
FIRST TELECAST: *October 14, 1951*
LAST TELECAST: *September 12, 1960*
BROADCAST HISTORY:
Oct 1951–Sep 1957, NBC Sun 9:00–10:00
Sep 1957–Sep 1960, NBC Mon 9:30–10:00
PRODUCER:
Fred Coe (1951–1955)

For six years, from the fall of 1951 through the fall of 1957, *Goodyear TV Playhouse* presented full-hour live dramas, originating from New York, on Sunday evenings. Some were original plays for television and some were adapted from other media. The series ran on alternate weeks with *Philco Television Playhouse*. In the fall of 1955, the title was shortened to *Goodyear Playhouse* and a new sponsor took the alternate Sundays with *The Alcoa Hour*.

Young playwright Paddy Chayefsky wrote several original dramas for this series, two of which were later made into feature films. "The Catered Affair" appeared in 1955 as a TV drama with Thelma Ritter, Pat Henning, and J. Pat O'Malley. The following year it was made into a movie with Bette Davis, Debbie Reynolds, and Ernest Borgnine. Chayefsky's other effort that became a successful theatrical feature was probably the single most acclaimed live drama in the history of television. It aired on May 24, 1953, with Rod Steiger in the title role of "Marty." There were no Emmy awards in 1953 for performances in a single telecast, only for series, so "Marty," ironically, won no TV awards. However, the 1955 movie version won Oscars for best picture and best performance by an actor (Ernest Borgnine). In addition to Rod Steiger, performers who starred in at least two *Goodyear TV Playhouse* productions during these live years included Roddy McDowall, Walter Matthau, Cyril Ritchard, Kim Stanley, Eva Marie Saint, Martin Balsam, Eli Wallach, Ralph Bellamy, Philip Abbott, and Tony Randall. Julie Harris, Paul Newman, Grace Kelly, Veronica Lake, and the Gish sisters (Lillian and Dorothy in separate but consecutive telecasts in 1953) also appeared.

In the fall of 1957, the series moved to Monday nights, was reduced to half an hour, and was on film rather than live. It was still alternating with Alcoa and, although the title of the Goodyear episodes was *Goodyear Theater*, the overall title for the series was *A Turn of Fate*, a designation that was dropped in February 1958. Initially there was to be a rotating roster of regular stars (David Niven, Robert Ryan, Jane Powell, Jack Lemmon, and Charles Boyer) but that concept petered out by the end of the first season. Stars featured during the last two seasons were Paul Douglas, Eddie Albert, Gig Young, Jackie Cooper, Ray Milland, James Mason, Edward G. Robinson, Peter Lawford, Errol Flynn, and Thomas Mitchell. In the spring of each of the last two seasons several of the episodes were pilots for proposed series. One of these was "Christobel" starring Arthur O'Connell as John Monroe, author James Thurber's harried hero. More than a decade later, the Thurber-based John Monroe character reappeared in the weekly series *My World and Welcome to It* starring William Windom.

GORDON MACRAE SHOW, THE
Music
FIRST TELECAST: *March 5, 1956*
LAST TELECAST: *August 27, 1956*
BROADCAST HISTORY:
Mar 1956–Aug 1956, NBC Mon 7:30–7:45
REGULARS:
Gordon MacRae
The Cheerleaders
The Van Alexander Orchestra

The set used for this live musical program was a replica of Gordon MacRae's living room, with a large picture window looking out on a scene appropriate for the songs being performed on a given evening. Backing up MacRae, and occasionally with a featured number of their own, was a vocal group called the Cheerleaders. This show originated from Hollywood and was used to fill the remainder of the half-hour in which NBC aired its network news.

GOVERNOR & J.J., THE
Situation Comedy
FIRST TELECAST: *September 23, 1969*
LAST TELECAST: *August 11, 1972*
BROADCAST HISTORY:
  Sep 1969–Sep 1970, CBS Tue 9:30–10:00
  Sep 1970–Dec 1970, CBS Wed 8:30–9:00
  Jun 1972–Aug 1972, CBS Fri 10:30–11:00
CAST:
  Gov. William Drinkwater .... Dan Dailey
  Jennifer Jo ("J.J.") Drinkwater . Julie Sommars
  Maggie McLeod .... Neva Patterson
  George Callison .... James Callahan
  Sara Andrews .... Nora Marlowe

One of the needs of any man in high political office is someone to organize social functions and serve as first lady. For Governor William Drinkwater, the chief executive of a small Midwestern state, and a widower, that someone was his attractive young daughter Jennifer Jo. Despite the problems caused by their generation gap (J.J. was in her early 20s), J.J. served her father as a charming and efficient first lady. Bright and opinionated, she was always ready to debate issues with him, too. J.J. also had a regular job as assistant curator at a zoo, which presented a nice counterpoint to politics. It may also explain her fondness for the stray basset hound she brought into the family in January 1970 and named, appropriately, Guv. Around the executive mansion she sought and received assistance from the governor's secretary Maggie, his press secretary George, and the housekeeper, Sara. During the summer of the 1972 presidential election year, CBS aired reruns of this series.

GRADY
Situation Comedy
FIRST TELECAST: *December 4, 1975*
LAST TELECAST: *March 4, 1976*
BROADCAST HISTORY:
  Dec 1975, NBC Thu 8:00–8:30
  Jan 1976–Mar 1976, NBC Thu 8:30–9:00
CAST:
  Grady Wilson .... Whitman Mayo
  Ellie Wilson Marshall .... Carol Cole
  Hal Marshall .... Joe Morton
  Laurie Marshall .... Roseanne Katan
  Haywood Marshall .... Haywood Nelson
  Mr. Pratt .... Jack Fletcher
  Rose Kosinski .... Alix Elias

In this short-lived spin-off from *Sanford and Son*, Grady Wilson, one of Fred Sanford's friends, moved out of Watts and into a racially mixed middle-class neighborhood in Los Angeles to be with his daughter and her family. His daughter Ellie was married and had two children, Laurie and Haywood. Mr. Pratt was their landlord and Rose was one of their neighbors.

GRAND OLE OPRY
Country Music
FIRST TELECAST: *October 15, 1955*
LAST TELECAST: *September 15, 1956*
BROADCAST HISTORY:
  Oct 1955–Sep 1956, ABC Sat 8:00–9:00
REGULARS:
  Carl Smith
  Ernest and Justin Tubb
  Hank Snow
  Minnie Pearl
  Chet Atkins
  Goldie Hill
  Marty Robbins
  Rod Brasfield
  Cousin Jody
  Roy Acuff
  June Carter
  Jimmy Dickens
  Louvin Brothers

In the world of country music an appearance on the *Grand Ole Opry* has long been considered a symbol of ultimate success. Oddly enough, the *Opry* has never become a regular feature on national TV although other, "lesser" country music shows have had long runs (see for example *Ozark Jubilee*). During 1955–1956 ABC carried an hour of the *Opry* (it goes on all night) on a monthly basis, live from its longtime home in Nashville, Tennessee. The *Opry* troupe numbers in the dozens, and is constantly changing, and only those members most frequently seen during the ABC run are listed above.

The program's history has been primarily in syndication, enabling it to maximize its availability in areas where country music is popular. Over the last 30 years there have been numerous syndicated country music shows using the Grand Ole Opry as a backdrop, some original and others just repackaged episodes from other shows. Among the most successful series were *Billy Walker's Country Carnival*, *Classic Country Featuring Stars of the Grand Ole Opry*, *Country Carnival*, *Country Music Caravan*, *Country Music Memories*, *The Country Show*, and *Hayride*.

The *Opry* began on radio in Nashville in 1925, was first heard on network radio in 1939, and is still going strong today. It will probably continue forever, with or without network TV.

GRANDPA GOES TO WASHINGTON
Situation Comedy
FIRST TELECAST: *September 7, 1978*
LAST TELECAST: *January 16, 1979*
BROADCAST HISTORY:
  Sep 1978–Jan 1979, NBC Tue 8:00–9:00

CAST:
```
Senator Joe Kelley ........... Jack Albertson
Major General Kevin Kelley ... Larry Linville
Rosie Kelley .............. Sue Ane Langdon
Kathleen Kelley ............. Michele Tobin
Kevin Kelley, Jr. ............ Sparky Marcus
Madge ..................... Madge Sinclair
Tony De Luca ................ Tom Mason
```

Jack Albertson portrayed a maverick freshman
senator in this hour-long comedy series. Joe Kelley was a former political science professor who
had been forcibly retired at age 66, and who
promptly got himself elected to the U.S. Senate
when the regular candidates were both exposed
as crooks. Kelley's style was certainly unusual for
Washington. He drove around in a Volkswagen,
played drums for relaxation, and his campaign
pledge was honesty in government (and he meant
it!). His chief political asset was a network of
"friends in low places," former students of his
who regularly fed him inside political information.
Kelley lived with his son, a bland, empty-headed
Air Force general ("My son the fathead,") and his
son's family, consisting of wife Rosie, daughter
Kathleen, and son Kevin, Jr. Madge was the senator's trusty secretary, and Tony his aide.

GRAY GHOST, THE
Adventure
BROADCAST HISTORY:
Syndicated only
30 minutes
Produced: *1957* (39 episodes)
Released: *October 1957*
CAST:
```
Maj. John Singleton Mosby .... Tod Andrews
Lt. St. Clair.................. Phil Chambers
```

Civil War action series focusing on the true exploits of John Singleton Mosby, one of the South's
most colorful heroes. A young lawyer who originally supported the Union, Mosby changed his
mind when the South seceded, joined the 43rd
Battalion of the 1st Virginia Cavalry, and began a
series of lightning-swift raids on Union positions.
So elusive was he that he became known as the
"Gray Ghost."
    Although this was basically an adventure se-
ries, with lots of galloping horses, gunplay, and
derring-do, advertisers were extremely nervous
about portraying a Confederate hero at a time of
civil-rights strife, when Federal troops were in Little Rock. The series was originally intended for
the CBS-TV network, but three times potential
sponsors backed out. Finally CBS decided to syndicate it to local stations, and to everyone's surprise it both failed to stir up regional animosities
and was a big hit in all parts of the country, especially with younger viewers. Tod Andrews, a New
Yorker, was received as a hero when he toured
the South.
    The series was based on the book *Gray Ghosts*

and Rebel Raiders by Virgil Carrington Jones,
and Jones himself served as technical advisor.

GREAT ADVENTURE, THE
Dramatic Anthology
FIRST TELECAST: *September 27, 1963*
LAST TELECAST: *April 23, 1965*
BROADCAST HISTORY:
Sep 1963–Sep 1964, CBS Fri 7:30–8:30
Mar 1965–Apr 1965, CBS Fri 8:30–9:30
NARRATOR:
Van Heflin

A great moment in American history was dramatized each week in this series. Careful attention
was paid to the historical accuracy of each play,
and all of them were produced with the cooperation and assistance of the National Education
Association. Many well-known performers
participated in the dramas—Joseph Cotten and
Ricardo Montalban in "The Massacre at
Wounded Knee," Lloyd Bridges in "Wild Bill
Hickok—The Legend and the Man," Victor Jory
and Robert Culp in "The Testing of Sam Houston," Jackie Cooper in "The Hunley" (the first submarine to sink an enemy warship), and Robert
Cummings and Ron Howard in "The Plague"
(about the discovery of anti-smallpox vaccine).

GREAT GHOST TALES
Occult Anthology
FIRST TELECAST: *July 6, 1961*
LAST TELECAST: *September 21, 1961*
BROADCAST HISTORY:
Jul 1961–Sep 1961, NBC Thu 9:30–10:00

This series of ghost stories was the 1961 summer
replacement for *The Ford Show Starring Tennessee Ernie Ford.* Each of the plays was produced
live in New York, something of a rarity for a dramatic show in the early 1960s. Among the actors
who appeared were Robert Duvall, Arthur Hill,
Lois Nettleton, Lee Grant, and a young Richard
Thomas.

GREATEST AMERICAN HERO, THE
Adventure
FIRST TELECAST: *March 18, 1981*
LAST TELECAST: *February 3, 1983*
BROADCAST HISTORY:
Mar 1981–May 1981, ABC Wed 8:00–9:00
Aug 1981–Aug 1982, ABC Wed 8:00–9:00
Sep 1982–Nov 1982, ABC Fri 9:00–10:00
Jan 1983–Feb 1983, ABC Thu 8:00–9:00
CAST:
```
Ralph Hinkley (Hanley) ........ William Katt
Bill Maxwell ................... Robert Culp
Pam Davidson .............. Connie Sellecca
Tony Villicana ................ Michael Pare
Rhonda Blake .................. Faye Grant
Cyler Johnson ............... Jesse D. Goins
Rodriguez ................... Don Cervantes
Kevin Hinkley (1981) ...... Brandon Williams
```

THEME:
    "The Greatest American Hero (Believe It Or Not)," by Mike Post and Stephen Geyer, sung by Joey Scarbury

This superhero parody was beset by trouble practically from the time it premiered in March 1981. First, the owners of the Superman copyright threatened to sue, charging that the program had stolen their character. Then a man with the same last name as the hero made a real-life assassination attempt on the President of the United States, causing scripts to be hurriedly rewritten. Then the ratings started to fall.

Superman advocates may have cried "Thief!," but others suggested that the program was more of a steal from *Mr. Terrific* and *Captain Nice*, two bumbling superhero shows of the mid-1960s. Ralph Hinkley was a curly-haired young high-school teacher in Los Angeles, who was set upon by extraterrestrial beings while on a field trip into the desert. The aliens presented him with an incredible red flying suit, which, when donned, gave him (and only him) the ability to fly. A neurotic FBI agent, Maxwell, convinced Ralph to use the suit to help him fight crime. Unfortunately Ralph promptly lost the instruction book for the suit, and had to spend succeeding episodes flailing about in the air trying to master aerodynamics while crashing into walls and plummeting into bushes. He also discovered other powers of the suit—often at inopportune times—such as the power to become invisible, and the power to see at great distances and through solid walls.

The only adult besides Ralph and Maxwell who knew of the suit's powers was Ralph's girlfriend, attorney Pam Davidson (kids knew, but who would believe them?). Anybody else who came upon Ralph while he was trying to jump off a roof in his red jammies just naturally assumed he was crazy.

Kevin was Ralph's young son by a former marriage; Tony, Rhonda, Cyler, and Rodriguez were street-tough students in Ralph's remedial education class. The students shared many of Ralph's adventures during the 1981–1982 season, but were phased out the following season, as Ralph and Pam were finally married. As for Ralph's last name, it was abruptly changed to "Mr. H" (sometimes "Mr. Hanley") for a time after John Hinckley (with a "c") made an attempt on the life of President Reagan on March 30, 1981. Eventually it reverted back to Hinkley.

The theme song of this series was a major record hit during the summer of 1981.

GREATEST FIGHTS OF THE CENTURY
Sports
FIRST TELECAST: *October 15, 1948*
LAST TELECAST: *July 23, 1954*
BROADCAST HISTORY:
    Oct 1948–Jan 1949, NBC Fri 10:45–11:00
    Apr 1949–Jun 1950, NBC Fri 10:45–11:00 (OS)
    Sep 1950–Jul 1954, NBC Fri 10:45–11:00

NARRATOR:
    Jim Stevenson

This program was used to fill the time between the conclusion of the boxing match on *Gillette Cavalcade of Sports* and the start of the 11:00 P.M. local news. Jim Stevenson narrated newsreel films of some of the major boxing matches of the 20th century.

GREATEST MAN ON EARTH, THE
Quiz/Audience Participation
FIRST TELECAST: *December 3, 1952*
LAST TELECAST: *February 19, 1953*
BROADCAST HISTORY:
    Dec 1952–Feb 1953, ABC Thu 8:00–8:30
EMCEE:
    Ted Brown (Dec–Jan)
    Vera Vague (Jan–Feb)
ASSISTANT:
    Miss Pat Conway

Five men chosen from the studio audience competed for the title of *The Greatest Man on Earth* by performing stunts and answering questions, in this live, New York–based quiz show. Finalists and their wives were eligible for a new car, a trip to Europe, or other prizes. Ted Brown was the original emcee, replaced on January 22 by comedienne Vera Vague.

GREATEST MOMENTS IN SPORTS, THE
Sports Commentary
FIRST TELECAST: *July 30, 1954*
LAST TELECAST: *February 4, 1955*
BROADCAST HISTORY:
    Jul 1954–Sep 1954, NBC Fri 10:30–10:45
    Sep 1954–Feb 1955, NBC Fri 10:45–11:00
HOST:
    Walter Kiernan

Greatest Moments in Sports was a 15-minute program comprised of interviews with famous sports personalities and film clips of memorable events in the world of sports. Walter Kiernan was the host to the various guests and served as narrator for the filmed portions of the program. It premiered on a regular basis at 10:30 P.M. and when the Gillette *Cavalcade of Sports* boxing bouts resumed in September was used to fill the time between the conclusion of the bout and 11:00 P.M.

GREATEST SHOW ON EARTH, THE
Circus Drama
FIRST TELECAST: *September 17, 1963*
LAST TELECAST: *September 8, 1964*
BROADCAST HISTORY:
    Sep 1963–Sep 1964, ABC Tue 9:00–10:00
CAST:
    Johnny Slate...................Jack Palance
    Otto King ....Stu Erwin
THEME:
    "March of the Clowns," by Richard Rodgers

The Ringling Brothers Barnum & Bailey Circus—"The Greatest Show on Earth"—provided the background for this behind-the-scenes drama of circus performers. Hard-driving Johnny Slate was the working boss of the circus, whose job included, among other things, maintaining peace among a large group of individualistic performers. Otto King was the circus money man. Each week's story centered around the problems of a specific group—clowns, strongmen, aerialists, animal trainers, etc. Actual Ringling Brothers Barnum & Bailey performers were seen regularly in this series.

GREATEST SPORT THRILLS
Sports
FIRST TELECAST: *January 23, 1954*
LAST TELECAST: *September 27, 1956*
BROADCAST HISTORY:
Jan 1954–Sep 1954, ABC Sat 8:30–9:00
Jun 1955–Sep 1955, ABC Mon 7:30–8:00
Jul 1955–Sep 1955, ABC Thu 9:30–10:00
Jul 1955–Sep 1955, ABC Fri 8:00–8:30
Jul 1955–Aug 1955, ABC Fri 9:00–9:30
Jul 1955, ABC Sun 7:30–8:00
Nov 1955–Jan 1956, ABC Thu 10:00–10:30
Jun 1956–Sep 1956, ABC Thu 9:30–10:00
HOSTS:
Marty Glickman
Stan Lomax

Filmed highlights of sports events that had taken place at Madison Square Garden in New York City over the years were narrated and discussed by Marty Glickman and Stan Lomax on *Greatest Sport Thrills.* Used primarily as a filler program, during the summer of 1955 it was being offered as often as five times per week on the ABC network—often with the same episode repeated on different days. Many ABC stations, including the one in New York, often chose to carry other syndicated or local programming in its place.

GREEN ACRES
Situation Comedy
FIRST TELECAST: *September 15, 1965*
LAST TELECAST: *September 7, 1971*
BROADCAST HISTORY:
Sep 1965–Sep 1968, CBS Wed 9:00–9:30
Sep 1968–Sep 1969, CBS Wed 9:30–10:00
Sep 1969–Sep 1970, CBS Sat 9:00–9:30
Sep 1970–Sep 1971, CBS Tue 8:00–8:30
CAST:
Oliver Wendell Douglas . . . . Eddie Albert
Lisa Douglas . . . . Eva Gabor
Mr. Haney . . . . Pat Buttram
Eb Dawson . . . . Tom Lester
Hank Kimball . . . . Alvy Moore
Fred Ziffel . . . . Hank Patterson
Doris Ziffel (1965–1969) . . . . . . Barbara Pepper
Doris Ziffel (1969–1970) . . . . Fran Ryan
Sam Drucker . . . . Frank Cady
Newt Kiley (1965–1970) . . . . Kay E. Kuter
Alf Monroe (1966–1969) . . . . Sid Melton

Ralph Monroe (1966–1971)
. . . . Mary Grace Canfield
Darlene Wheeler (1970–1971)
. . . . Judy McConnell

One of the most successful of CBS' rural situation comedies of the 1960s, *Green Acres* was closely intertwined with *Petticoat Junction,* another show produced by the same people. Oliver Wendell Douglas was a highly successful Manhattan lawyer who, despite his good life in New York City, longed to get closer to nature. Ignoring the objections of his socialite wife Lisa, Oliver bought a 160-acre farm, sight unseen, from Mr. Haney. The farm was located outside the town of Hooterville (the setting for *Petticoat Junction*). It was in horrible shape. It had not been worked in years, the house was run-down, unfurnished, and in desperate need of major repairs.

Lisa wanted to turn right around and go back to their Park Avenue penthouse, but Oliver persisted in his determination to give it a chance. They found a shy, gawky handyman named Eb Dawson to help them get the place back into shape, and utilized the services of the Monroes, a sister-and-brother carpenter team, to rebuild the house and barn. Lisa never quite adjusted to the rural life. She kept applying the standards of sophisticated socialites to the ingenuous populace of Hooterville. Even her wardrobe, long flowing gowns and lots of jewelry, seemed out of place on Oliver's Green Acres. She did, however, grow quite fond of the animals they owned, giving names to all the chickens, cows, etc., on the farm. During the second season a pig, though not theirs, became a featured member of the cast. One of the Douglas' neighbors, pig farmer Fred Ziffel, had a pet pig named Arnold who watched television, could do various tricks on cue, and was so intelligent that Fred treated him like a son.

Until *Petticoat Junction* left the air in the fall of 1970, there was always a certain amount of interplay between it and *Green Acres,* with characters from one series making guest appearances on the other. *Green Acres* itself, though still successful, was canceled in 1971 as part of CBS' general purging of rural comedies from its schedule.

GREEN HORNET, THE
Crime Drama
FIRST TELECAST: *September 9, 1966*
LAST TELECAST: *July 14, 1967*
BROADCAST HISTORY:
Sep 1966–Jul 1967, ABC Fri 7:30–8:00
CAST:
Britt Reid/The Green Hornet . . Van Williams
Kato . . . . Bruce Lee
Lenore "Casey" Case . . . . Wende Wagner
Mike Axford . . . . Lloyd Gough
District Attorney F. P. Scanlon
. . . . Walter Brooke
CREATED BY:
George W. Trendle (on radio, in 1936)

THEME:

An updated arrangement of Rimsky-Korsakov's "Flight of the Bumble Bee," played by Al Hirt.

"Faster, Kato!" Then, with a roar of Black Beauty's mighty engine, and the squeal of tires, *The Green Hornet* strikes again!

The TV version of this radio favorite of the 1930s and 1940s was launched close on the flying heels of *Batman,* in 1966, and was produced by the same production team. The plot outline was familiar: Britt Reid, crusading editor and publisher of *The Daily Sentinel,* fought crime in the secret guise of The Green Hornet. Only his faithful manservant Kato and the D.A. knew that Reid and the Hornet were one and the same. Even Reid's admiring secretary Casey and his hardnosed crime reporter Mike never made the connection.

Some changes were made in adapting *The Green Hornet* to television, and to the 1960s. In addition to *The Daily Sentinel,* Britt owned a TV station. The evil he fought often involved organized crime (not the bizarre villains of *Batman*), and of course the crime-fighting gadgetry was brought up to date.

The chief piece of hardware was the Hornet's souped-up car, the Black Beauty (actually a 1966 Chrysler Imperial, rebuilt, at a cost of $50,000, by Hollywood customizer Dean Jeffries). Among its features were a built-in TV camera which could "see" four miles ahead, a kind of exhaust apparatus which spread ice over the road to foil pursuers, and brushes behind the rear wheels which lowered to sweep away tire tracks. For face-to-face combat, the Hornet had a special nonlethal gas gun which immobilized adversaries, and a sting gun which penetrated steel.

It is not generally known that *The Green Hornet* was directly related to George Trendle's other major hit, *The Lone Ranger,* whose plot line it closely paralleled. In fact, Britt Reid was originally introduced to radio audiences as the son of Dan Reid, the Lone Ranger's nephew.

GRIFF

Detective Drama
FIRST TELECAST: *September 29, 1973*
LAST TELECAST: *January 5, 1974*
BROADCAST HISTORY:
 Sep 1973–Jan 1974, ABC Sat 10:00–11:00
CAST:
 Wade Griffin .... Lorne Greene
 S. Michael (Mike) Murdoch..... Ben Murphy
 Gracie Newcombe .... Patricia Stich
 Capt. Barney Marcus.......... Vic Tayback

Lorne Greene tried to discard his *Bonanza* image and shift to a more contemporary role in this short-lived detective series. He played Wade Griffin, a veteran police captain who had resigned from the force after 30 years—over a matter of principle—and gone into business on his own, as

Wade Griffin Investigations. His home base was the swinging, youth-oriented Westwood section of Los Angeles, and his assistant was a young man named Mike Murdoch. Aided by their secretary Gracie, and Wade's many contacts in officialdom and in the streets, they tackled the usual array of murders, kidnappings, extortion schemes, etc.

GRINDL

Situation Comedy
FIRST TELECAST: *September 15, 1963*
LAST TELECAST: *September 13, 1964*
BROADCAST HISTORY:
 Sep 1963–Sep 1964, NBC Sun 8:30–9:00
CAST:
 Grindl...................... Imogene Coca
 Anson Foster .... James Millhollin

In this single-season comedy series Imogene Coca played Grindl, a highly efficient, well-organized domestic worker who was constantly put upon by a world that seemed determined to make life difficult for her. Grindl worked for Foster's Temporary Employment Service, and each week she found herself in a different job. She was, at one time or another, a maid, a laundress, a ticket-taker at a theater, a baby sitter, a cook, or anything else that Anson Foster could find for her to do.

GRIZZLY ADAMS

see *Life and Times of Grizzly Adams, The*

GROUCHO SHOW, THE

see *You Bet Your Life*

GROWING PAINS

Situation Comedy
FIRST TELECAST: *September 24, 1985*
LAST TELECAST:
BROADCAST HISTORY:
 Sep 1985–Mar 1986, ABC Tue 8:30–9:00
 May 1986–Mar 1988, ABC Tue 8:30–9:00
 Mar 1988–   , ABC Wed 8:00–8:30
CAST:
 Dr. Jason Seaver .... Alan Thicke
 Maggie Seaver............... Joanna Kerns
 Mike Seaver (15).............. Kirk Cameron
 Carol Seaver (14) .... Tracey Gold
 Ben Seaver (9)............... Jeremy Miller
 Richard Stabone ("Boner")
  .... Josh A. (Andrew) Koenig
 Eddie .... K.C. Martel
 Debbie (1987–   )............... Lisa Capps
 Shelley (1987–   ).......... Rachael Jacobs
 Coach Lubbock (1987–   )
  .... Bill Kirchenbauer
THEME:
 "As Long As We Got Each Other," sung by B.J. Thomas & Jennifer Warnes.

If *Father Knows Best* had been revived in the 1980s, it would have been called *Growing Pains.*

As amiable and wise as Jim Anderson had been, Jason Seaver was more so—and a little hipper to boot. This father was a psychiatrist (who better to deal with teenage traumas?) who had moved his office into his suburban New York home when his wife Maggie went back to work, in order to keep an eye on the kids. The young Seavers were Mike, a gangly teenager who was more interested in having a good time than in responsibility ("a hormone with feet," his mother called him); shy Carol, his brainy sister; and their cute little brother Ben, no slouch himself at getting into scrapes. Dad was always available with sage advice while Mom, who had become a reporter for the Long Island Herald (later a TV reporter, as "Maggie Malone"), rushed off to work. Mike and Carol attended school at Thomas E. Dewey High.

Fourteen-year-old Kirk Cameron, formerly unnoticed as a regular on Two Marriages, became something of a teenage heartthrob on this hit series, receiving 10,000 letters a month. "I'm still nervous and shy when I meet girls," he told a reporter. "The only thing that's changed is that I've gotten the chance to meet more girls because they introduce themselves to me."

GROWING PAYNES, THE
Situation Comedy
FIRST TELECAST: *October 20, 1948*
LAST TELECAST: *August 3, 1949*
BROADCAST HISTORY:
   Oct 1948–Aug 1949, DUM Wed 8:30–9:00
CAST:
   Mr. Payne (1948–1949) . . . . John Harvey*
   Mr. Payne (1949) . . . . Ed Holmes
   Mrs. Payne (1948–1949) . . . . Judy Parrish
   Mrs. Payne (1949) . . . . Elaine Stritch
ALSO:
   David Anderson
   Warren Parker
   Lester Lonergan, Jr.
   Ann Sullivan
ORIGINAL MUSIC:
   Bill Wirges

*Also given as John Henry

This was an early live domestic comedy about the trials of an insurance salesman (John Harvey), his screwball wife (Judy Parrish), and young kids. Often it was Birdie, the maid, who saved the day. The setting was the family's apartment. Plugs for the sponsor, Wanamaker's Department Store, were worked into the early stories, as was the custom at the time.

GRUEN GUILD THEATER
   see *ABC Dramatic Shorts—1952–1953*

GRUEN PLAYHOUSE
Dramatic Anthology
FIRST TELECAST: *January 17, 1952*
LAST TELECAST: *July 3, 1952*

BROADCAST HISTORY:
   Jan 1952–Jul 1952, DUM Thu 9:00–9:30

Filmed dramas featuring such talent as Patrick O'Neal, Elisabeth Fraser, and Bobby Jordan. At least some of these films also appeared on ABC at about the same time on the various series listed under *ABC Dramatic Shorts.* Seen on alternate weeks.

GUESS AGAIN
Quiz/Audience Participation
FIRST TELECAST: *June 14, 1951*
LAST TELECAST: *June 21, 1951*
BROADCAST HISTORY:
   June 1951, CBS, Thu 8:30–9:00
MODERATOR:
   Mike Wallace
ACTORS:
   Joey Faye
   Mandy Kaye
   Bobby Martin

This short-lived game show—it only aired for two weeks—had a panel of three celebrities, each of whom was paired with a studio-audience contestant. Together the teams attempted to answer questions about a series of vignettes done by three actors, with each correct answer giving them the chance to tackle the next question and "guess again." The first correct answer was worth $10 and each succeeding answer was worth $5 more than the last, up to four questions worth a total of $70. Contestants kept their winnings and celebrity panelists donated theirs to their favorite charities.

GUESS WHAT
Quiz/Panel
FIRST TELECAST: *July 8, 1952*
LAST TELECAST: *August 26, 1952*
BROADCAST HISTORY:
   Jul 1952–Aug 1952, DUM Tue 9:00–9:30
EMCEE:
   Dick Kollmar
PANELISTS:
   Quentin Reynolds
   Virginia Peine
   Mark Hanna
   Audrey Christie

Summer quiz show in which a panel of celebrities was given a series of cryptic quotations and asked to guess: "What is it?" Numerous personalities appeared on the panel during the short run of this show, of whom the above four were most frequently seen.

GUESS WHAT HAPPENED
   see *What Happened*

GUESTWARD HO!
Situation Comedy

FIRST TELECAST: *September 29, 1960*
LAST TELECAST: *September 21, 1961*
BROADCAST HISTORY:
  Sep 1960–Sep 1961, ABC Thu 7:30–8:00
CAST:
  Babs Hooten................... Joanne Dru
  Hawkeye.................... J. Carrol Naish
  Bill Hooten.................... Mark Miller
  Brook Hooten................... Flip Mark
  Lonesome .... Earle Hodgins
  Pink Cloud .... Jolene Brand
  Rocky................. Tony Montenaro, Jr.

Fed up with the hustle and bustle of New York City, the Hootens decided to look for someplace else to live and work. Their dream house proved to be *Guestward Ho,* a dude ranch in New Mexico. They bought it, sight unseen, and moved west, only to find a rather run-down establishment in need of much work. The only source of supplies in the area was a store run by an Indian named Hawkeye. Hawkeye read the *Wall Street Journal,* sold Indian trinkets that had been made in Japan, and was bound and determined to find a way to return the country to its rightful owners, *his* people. He was not really militant, just industrious and conniving, and his relationship with the Hootens, including their young son Brook, provided the basis for many amusing situations.

GUIDE RIGHT
  Variety
FIRST TELECAST: *February 25, 1952*
LAST TELECAST: *October 30, 1953*
BROADCAST HISTORY:
  Feb 1952–Dec 1952, DUM Mon 9:00–9:30
  Dec 1952–Jul 1953, DUM Thu 8:00–8:30
  Jul 1953–Oct 1953, DUM Fri 8:30–9:00
EMCEE:
  Don Russell
CONDUCTOR:
  Elliot Lawrence

Korean War–era variety show designed to aid enlistments, and featuring both military and civilian talent. Some telecasts originated from military bases. Many of the Army and Air Force bands seen on *Guide Right* were unaccustomed to studio performances, and conductor Elliot Lawrence recalls that he was brought in after the first few telecasts specifically to rehearse the military musicians and direct them on the air. Among the civilian talent "doing their bit" for enlistments were Teresa Brewer, Denise Lor, Morey Amsterdam, Steve Lawrence and Eydie Gorme, Tony Bennett, and Chandu the Magician. Perhaps the hottest popular singer of the day came from the ranks, however—PFC Eddie Fisher, then serving his own enlistment, appeared in October 1952. Military talent such as The Airmen of Note and The Singing Sergeants were also seen.

GUINNESS GAME, THE
  Quiz/Audience Participation

BROADCAST HISTORY:
  Syndicated only
  30 minutes
  Produced: *1979* (24 episodes)
  Released: *September 1979*
HOST:
  Don Galloway

This was another of those noisy early-evening game shows, but with a twist. Each telecast featured four live, onstage attempts to break a world's record in some specialty, and thus qualify the record-breaker for inclusion in *The Guinness Book of World Records.*

At the start of the program three contestants won money by answering a series of questions based on *Guinness.* They then used the money to bet, pro or con, on whether the attempts to break a world's record would succeed. The records challenged were often pretty bizarre. One man had to eat 17 bananas in less than two minutes; another, to jump rope 50 times on a wire suspended 33 feet above the stage; another, to make 256 five-foot-long noodles in under 63 seconds; and four burly men attempted to change all four tires on a sedan in less than two minutes. The race against the clock was followed as in a sports competition, and if it was successful the audience would erupt in great tumult as the screen flashed on and off, "New World's Record—Tire Changing—1:48.8!"

The producers insisted that *Guinness* was not intended to be a freak show, and the record challengers certainly seemed serious. On hand to authenticate new records was David Boehm, American editor of the book. Also on hand were giant nets, paramedics, and two husky "catchers" who tried to stop anyone falling or prevent other kinds of live, onstage disaster.

GULF PLAYHOUSE: 1ST PERSON
  Dramatic Anthology
FIRST TELECAST: *October 3, 1952*
LAST TELECAST: *September 11, 1953*
BROADCAST HISTORY:
  Oct 1952–Dec 1952, NBC Fri 8:30–9:00
  Jul 1953–Sep 1953, NBC Fri 8:30–9:00

When *Gulf Playhouse* was originally aired in the fall of 1952 it was a conventional live dramatic anthology. It was replaced by *The Life of Riley* and was back again in the summer of 1953 as *Riley's* summer replacement. The format had changed, however. Although it was still a live anthology series, under the new title *Gulf Playhouse: 1st Person* the camera itself became one of the actors, through whose "eyes" all of the action was seen. It had a voice, and could have been a person or an object or an animal. The other actors addressed the camera as if it were a live member of the cast and gave the viewer a sense of participation in these plays.

GULF ROAD SHOW STARRING BOB SMITH, THE

Variety/Talent

FIRST TELECAST: *September 2, 1948*
LAST TELECAST: *June 30, 1949*
BROADCAST HISTORY:
  Sep 1948–Jun 1949, NBC Thu 9:00–9:30
REGULARS:
  Bob Smith
  Eve Young (1949)
  Heathertones (1949)
ORCHESTRA:
  Enoch Light (1948)
  Johnny Guarnieri (1948–1949)
  Bobby Wren (1949)

Bob Smith, originator (in 1947) of TV's long-running *Howdy Doody Show*, hosted this prime-time talent/variety series during the 1948–1949 season. The program was notable for its frequent changes of format. There were three such changes during the first month alone, and five in all. In order, viewers were treated to a straight musical variety revue (first two weeks), a musical quiz show (one week), a series subtitled *What's New* featuring new talent, inventions, movies, books, etc. (three months), a straight talent show (four and a half months), and finally back to the original musical revue, with guest stars and the audience-participation segment (last two months).

Howdy Doody made a couple of appearances on the show, singing "All I Want for Christmas Is My Two Front Teeth" on the Christmas show, and the new talent included such notable attractions as young songstress Patti Page and "Miss Television Tube of 1949" (comedienne Patricia Bright).

GUN SHY

Situation Comedy

FIRST TELECAST: *March 15, 1983*
LAST TELECAST: *April 19, 1983*
BROADCAST HISTORY:
  Mar 1983–Apr 1983, CBS Tue 8:30–9:00
  Apr 1983, CBS Tue 8:00–8:30
CAST:
  Russell Donovan .... Barry Van Dyke
  Theodore Ogilvie .... Tim Thomerson
  Amos Tucker .... Geoffrey Lewis
  Clovis .... Keith Mitchell
  Clovis .... Adam Rich
  Celia .... Bridgette Anderson
  Homer McCoy .... Henry Jones
  Nettie McCoy .... Janis Paige
  Colonel Mound .... Pat McCormick

Set in the small California town of Quake City in 1869, this comedy Western revolved around the lives of a good-natured gambler, the two young children he won in a card game, and the townsfolk in Quake City. Russell Donovan was the gambler, caring for his two young wards, Celia and Clovis (the latter played by Keith Mitchell in the first four episodes of this limited series and by Adam Rich in the last two). Theodore and Amos were two bumbling would-be desperados, vainly attempting to build reputations as outlaws, and Homer McCoy was Quake City's barber, sheriff, and justice of the peace. Homer's ex-wife Nettie ran the only hotel in town, and Col. Mound was the owner of the local stagecoach line. Russell's attempts to bring up two precocious children, and the hapless antics of Theodore and Amos, provided the focus of this series.

Based on the Walt Disney films *The Apple Dumpling Gang* and *The Apple Dumpling Gang Rides Again*, in which Bill Bixby played Donovan and Don Knotts and Tim Conway played Theodore and Amos.

GUNG HO

Situation Comedy

FIRST TELECAST: *December 5, 1986*
LAST TELECAST: *June 27, 1987*
BROADCAST HISTORY:
  Dec 1986–Jan 1987, ABC Fri 9:30–10:00
  Jan 1987–Feb 1987, ABC Fri 9:00–9:30
  Jun 1987, ABC Sat 9:00–9:30
CAST:
  Hunt Stevenson .... Scott Bakula
  Kaz Kazuhiro .... Gedde Watanabe
  Buster .... Stephen Lee
  Mr. Saito .... Sab Shimono
  Googie .... Clint Howard
  Ito .... Rodney Kageyama
  Randi .... Heidi Banks
  Umeki Kazuhiro .... Patti Yasutake
  Yukiko Saito .... Emily K. Kuroda
  Kenji .... Scott Atari

East and West comically clashed in a Hadleyville, Pennsylvania, auto plant in this short-lived comedy. Assan Motors of Japan had reopened the closed plant, and the workers were thankful for that, but problems were inevitable. Kaz was the newly installed plant manager, trying to balance his country's traditions, the unfamiliar customs of the U.S.A., and the demands of his management back in Japan; Saito was his conservative Japanese assistant, who didn't want to adapt at all. Kaz's wife Umeki, though properly subservient to her husband, sometimes flirted with the freedom accorded American women, while Saito's Yukiko was much more conservative. Hunt was the freewheeling go-between with the plant's American workers, who gave the new managers an introduction to America they would never forget.

Based on the 1986 movie of the same name, in which Gedde Watanabe also played the role of Kaz.

GUNS OF WILL SONNETT, THE

Western

FIRST TELECAST: *September 8, 1967*
LAST TELECAST: *September 15, 1969*
BROADCAST HISTORY:
  Sep 1967–May 1969, ABC Fri 9:30–10:00
  Jun 1969–Sep 1969, ABC Mon 8:30–9:00

Will Sonnett................ Walter Brennan
Jeff Sonnett.................... Dack Rambo

A grizzled old ex-cavalry scout and his grandson searched the West for the boy's father in this unusual Western, set in the 1870s. James Sonnett had disappeared 19 years before, leaving the infant Jeff in Will's care. As the years passed the boy had grown into manhood determined to find his father, who had meanwhile become a notorious, but elusive, gunfighter. The old man (played by character actor Walter Brennan, then 73) and his grandson followed James' trail, finding many who knew of him, some with bitterness and hatred, others with gratitude and awe. James Sonnett (played by Jason Evers) was seen fleetingly in a few episodes, but Will and Jeff never did catch up with him—although in the last original episode they met the man who claimed to have killed him. *Sic transit* gunfighters.

GUNSLINGER
Western
FIRST TELECAST: *February 9, 1961*
LAST TELECAST: *September 14, 1961*
BROADCAST HISTORY:
Feb 1961–Sep 1961, CBS Thu 9:00–10:00
CAST:
Cord.......................... Tony Young
Capt. Zachary Wingate....... Preston Foster
Pico McGuire.................. Charles Gray
Billy Urchin.................... Dee Pollock
Amby Hollister .... Midge Ware
Sgt. Major Murdock............. John Picard

Set in the Southwest in the decade following the conclusion of the Civil War, *Gunslinger* was the story of Cord, a fast gun who worked on undercover assignments for Capt. Zachary Wingate, the commandant of Fort Scott, New Mexico. Pico and Billy were Cord's two close friends, who often went with him on assignments, and Amby Hollister ran the general store at the fort.

GUNSMOKE
Western
FIRST TELECAST: *September 10, 1955*
LAST TELECAST: *September 1, 1975*
BROADCAST HISTORY:
Sep 1955–Sep 1961, CBS Sat 10:00–10:30
Sep 1961–Sep 1967, CBS Sat 10:00–11:00
Oct 1961–Jun 1964, CBS Tue 7:30–8:00
Sep 1967–Sep 1971, CBS Mon 7:30–8:30
Sep 1971–Sep 1975, CBS Mon 8:00–9:00
CAST:
Marshal Matt Dillon .... James Arness
Dr. Galen (Doc) Adams....... Milburn Stone
Kitty Russell (1955–1974) ..... Amanda Blake
Chester Goode (1955–1964)... Dennis Weaver
Festus Haggen (1964–1975)........ Ken Curtis
Quint Asper (1962–1965) ...... Burt Reynolds

Sam, the bartender (1962–1974)
.... Glenn Strange
Clayton Thaddeus (Thad) Greenwood
  (1965–1967) .... Roger Ewing
Newly O'Brien (1967–1975)...... Buck Taylor
Mr. Jones (1955–1960) .... Dabbs Greer
Louie Pheeters................ James Nusser
Barney........................ Charles Seel
Howie .... Howard Culver
Ed O'Connor .... Tom Brown
Percy Crump .... John Harper
Hank (1957–1975) .... Hank Patterson
Ma Smalley (1962–1975) .... Sarah Selby
Nathan Burke (1964–1975) .... Ted Jordan
Mr. Bodkin (1965–1975)......... Roy Roberts
Mr. Lathrop (1966–1975) ... Woody Chamblis
Halligan (1967–1975) .... Charles Wagenheim
Miss Hannah (1974–1975)......... Fran Ryan
MUSICAL THEME:
"Gunsmoke" (also known as "Old Trails"), by Glenn Spencer and Rex Koury

The few Westerns seen on television during the early 1950s starred old-style movie heroes such as the Lone Ranger and Hopalong Cassidy, and had little to do with the real West. Westerns were considered another form of obvious fantasy, strictly for the kids. Two shows, *Gunsmoke* and *The Life and Legend of Wyatt Earp*, changed all that. These two programs, which premiered during the same week in 1955, introduced the "adult Western" to TV, and began an enormous wave of Westerns on TV over the next ten years.

Gunsmoke had its genesis on CBS radio in the spring of 1952, with William Conrad in the role of the resolute, determined Marshal Matt Dillon. Conrad, who later became TV's *Cannon* in the 1970s, remained the radio voice of Matt Dillon for a total of nine years, but when CBS decided to add a video version of the series the first choice for the role was John Wayne. Wayne would probably have done very well in the role, but he did not want to commit himself to the rigors of a weekly television series and suggested James Arness, a young, relatively unknown actor friend of his. Wayne even offered to introduce the program's first episode, an offer which was quickly accepted by the CBS brass. James Arness, six feet seven inches in height, was even bigger physically than John Wayne, and he proved to be perfect casting for the role of the heroic marshal.

Gunsmoke was set in Dodge City, Kansas, around 1880. Crusty old Doc Adams, the only cast member besides Arness to stay with the show for its entire run, was the town's kindly, sympathetic physician. Doc spent most of his spare time, as did many of Dodge City's residents, at the Longbranch Saloon, which was owned and operated by Kitty Russell. Kitty was extremely softhearted, beneath what could be a very businesslike exterior, and would have willingly become romantically involved with Matt. In the radio version the implication was that she was a prostitute, but on TV Matt and Kitty exchanged no more than smiles. Matt's loyal, well-meaning deputy was Chester Goode, who walked with a pronounced limp, talked with a twang ("Mister Dillon!"), and brewed a mean pot of coffee—which was often seen behind the closing credits.

Gunsmoke was not an immediate hit. It premiered on Saturday night against the established *George Gobel Show* and did not make TV's top 15 during its first season. In its second year it jumped to No. 8, however, and for the next four years—1957 to 1961—it was the top-rated program in all of TV. *Gunsmoke* precipitated a deluge of Westerns in the late 1950s (at one time there were more than 30 prime-time network Westerns on in the same season), but it outlived them all. It went into a considerable decline in the mid-1960s, after being expanded to an hour, and was about to leave the air when CBS gave it one more chance, moving it to Monday night in 1967. The result was a stunning comeback that put the show in the top ten once again, where it stayed well into the 1970s. It is ironic that when it finally did leave the air in 1975, it was the last Western left on network television at that time. In all, *Gunsmoke* ran for 20 years, longer than any other series with continuing characters in the history of the medium.

Over the years there were changes in the supporting cast. Chester (Dennis Weaver) left in 1964 to be replaced by Festus Haggen, the scruffy hillbilly deputy who remained for the rest of the run. Half-breed Indian Quint Asper was featured for a while as the town blacksmith, as were gunsmith Newly O'Brien and Matt's friend Thad Greenwood.

In addition to the principal cast members, there was an extensive supporting cast of Dodge City residents who appeared from time to time. Miss Hannah ran the Long Branch Saloon after Kitty's departure. Jones and Lathrop were storekeepers; Halligan and O'Connor, local ranchers; Louie, the town drunk; Barney, the telegraph agent; Howie, the hotel clerk; Percy, the Dodge City undertaker; Hank, the stableman; Nathan, the freight agent; Mr. Bodkin, the banker; and Ma Smalley, the boardinghouse owner.

As the years passed, less and less was seen of Matt. Stories often revolved around other members of the cast while he was out of town, and, to some extent, *Gunsmoke* frequently resembled an anthology as stories often came to center on guest stars, using Dodge City simply as a background. "Hard" social issues of the 1960s, such as the rights of minorities, social protest, and crimes such as rape, began to be tackled in stories adapted to the Dodge City setting.

Matt Dillon set the tone of the show throughout its long life, however, standing for justice, sincerity, and truth. The opening of the show (during its early seasons) said it all. There was Matt in a fast-draw showdown in the main street of Dodge City. The other man fired a fraction of a second faster, but missed completely, while Matt's aim was true. Matt could be beaten up, shot, and ambushed, but that indomitable will would never be defeated.

For the first three seasons following the expansion of *Gunsmoke* from half an hour to a full hour on Saturday nights, CBS aired reruns of the original half-hour version on Tuesdays under the title *Marshal Dillon*.

GUY LOMBARDO'S DIAMOND JUBILEE

Musical Variety
FIRST TELECAST: *March 20, 1956*
LAST TELECAST: *June 19, 1956*
BROADCAST HISTORY:
    Mar 1956–Jun 1956, CBS Tue 9:00–9:30
REGULAR:
    Guy Lombardo and His Royal Canadians

Viewers of this series were asked to send in letters describing how a specific song had played an important role in their lives. Each week four of the people who had written in were selected to appear on the live show as Guy's guests and watch as their stories were dramatized. In addition to the viewer guests there was one celebrity guest who appeared on the show in connection with "the song of his life." The viewers who appeared on the show won, in addition to the free trip to New York, diamond jewelry and other gifts.

For the two years prior to this network exposure, Guy Lombardo had starred in a syndicated half-hour show titled *Guy Lombardo and His Royal Canadians*, playing "the sweetest music this side of heaven."

GUY MITCHELL SHOW, THE

Musical Variety
FIRST TELECAST: *October 7, 1957*
LAST TELECAST: *January 13, 1958*
BROADCAST HISTORY:
    Oct 1957–Jan 1958, ABC Mon 8:00–8:30
REGULARS:
    Guy Mitchell
    Dolores Hawkins
    The Guy Mitchell Singers
    The Ted Cappy Dancers
    The Van Alexander Orchestra

Singer Guy Mitchell hosted and starred in this short-lived musical variety series. Dolores Hawkins, not originally a cast regular, became one during the middle of the show's four-month run. Guest stars were featured and the focus of the show was on singing, which worked much better than the contrived comedy sketches that were also part of the format.

317

H

HAGEN
Detective Drama
FIRST TELECAST: *March 1, 1980*
LAST TELECAST: *April 24, 1980*
BROADCAST HISTORY:
Mar 1980–Apr 1980, CBS Sat 10:00–11:00
Apr 1980, CBS Thu 9:00–10:00
CAST:
Paul Hagen.................. Chad Everett
Carl Palmer .... Arthur Hill
Jody .... Aldine King
Mrs. Chavez................ Carmen Zapata

Paul Hagen and Carl Palmer made an interesting, if somewhat mismatched, team. Paul was a lover of the great outdoors, a hunter, and an accomplished tracker. Carl was a well-known San Francisco attorney, cosmopolitan, and attuned to all the subtle nuances of the legal system. Merging their respective skills, they teamed to solve difficult criminal cases, Paul doing most of the legwork and Carl handling the legal complications. Jody was Carl's secretary and Mrs. Chavez his housekeeper.

HAGGIS BAGGIS
Quiz/Audience Participation
FIRST TELECAST: *June 30, 1958*
LAST TELECAST: *September 29, 1958*
BROADCAST HISTORY:
Jun 1958–Sep 1958, NBC Mon 7:30–8:00
EMCEE:
Jack Linkletter

Contestants on *Haggis Baggis* faced a large game board consisting of 25 squares. The object was to guess the identity of the celebrity whose picture was revealed, bit by bit, as the squares were uncovered. The contestants picked questions corresponding to different squares, and upon answering correctly got to see what was behind that square. The winner (first to name the celebrity) had his choice of either of two groups of prizes, one labeled haggis (luxury items) and the other, baggis (utilitarian items). If the runner-up could guess which group the winner had taken, he got the other.
Haggis Baggis was also seen on NBC daytime, where it continued until June 1959.

HAIL THE CHAMP
Children's
FIRST TELECAST: *September 22, 1951*
LAST TELECAST: *June 14, 1952*
BROADCAST HISTORY:
Sep 1951–Dec 1951, ABC Sat 6:30–7:00
Dec 1951–Jun 1952, ABC Sat 6:00–6:30

EMCEE:
Herb Allen

Children's program in which six youngsters competed for prizes in games and stunts. Also seen on Saturday daytime from 1952–1953. From Chicago.

HAIL TO THE CHIEF
Situation Comedy
FIRST TELECAST: *April 9, 1985*
LAST TELECAST: *July 30, 1985*
BROADCAST HISTORY:
Apr 1985–May 1985, ABC Tue 9:30–10:00
Jun 1985–Jul 1985, ABC Tue 9:30–10:00
CAST:
President Julia Mansfield........ Patty Duke
Gen. Oliver Mansfield.......... Ted Bessell
Premier Dmitri Zolotov/Ivan Zolotov
.... Dick Shawn
Sec. of State LaRue Hawkes.. Glynn Turman
Helmut Luger.............. Herschel Bernardi
Gen. Hannibal Stryker .... John Vernon
Sen. Sam Cotton.......... Murray Hamilton
Doug Mansfield........... Ricky Paul Goldin
Lucy Mansfield .... Quinn Cummings
Willy Mansfield .... Taliesin Jaffe
Lenore .... Maxine Stuart
Rev. Billy Joe Bickerstaff ...... Richard Paul
Darlene the spy............. Alexa Hamilton
Randy .... Joel Brooks
Raoul the butler .... Chick Vennera

The President of the United States was surrounded by a cabinet of crazies in this comedy about life in the White House under the first woman chief executive. Created by the creator of *Soap* (Susan Harris), it used the same type of semiserialized storylines as the earlier hit, and even some similar plots. Madame President was confronted by such ongoing crises as her husband Oliver's inability to make love; a lunatic major threatening to start World War III; an equally lunatic Russian Premier Zolotov on the hotline; the blackmailing of her husband by KGB head Ivan (the Premier's twin brother) after Oliver was caught in a compromising position with sexy spy Darlene; son Doug's impregnating of General Stryker's daughter; and an attempt to impeach her by ranting Rev. Billy Joe, who maintained that Satan had put this woman in the White House.
Hawkes was the sensible black Secretary of State, who was often outshouted by National Security Advisor Luger and Gen. Stryker. The President's three children were tennis pro Doug, Lucy (who had the hots for Raoul the butler) and little Willy; Lenore was Julia's bedazzled mom, and Randy her chief Secret Service agent. The whole ensemble was voted out of TV office after only seven episodes.

HAL IN HOLLYWOOD
see *Sawyer Views Hollywood*

½ HOUR COMEDY HOUR, THE
Comedy Variety
FIRST TELECAST: *July 5, 1983*
LAST TELECAST: *August 9, 1983*
BROADCAST HISTORY:
  Jul 1983–Aug 1983, ABC Tue 8:00–8:30
HOSTS:
  Thom Sharp
  Arsenio Hall
REGULARS:
  John Moschitta
  Peter Isacksen
  John Paragon
  Vic Dunlop
  Jan Hooks
  Victoria Jackson
  Barry Diamond
  Diane Stilwell

Sight gags, one-liners, and skits were packed into this frantic summer comedy show, which was on and off the schedule faster than one of John Moschitta's motormouthed monologues. (Moschitta was known at the time for his incredibly fast-talking commercials.) Routines on the premiere included "Bonan the Barbarian," "Jennifer Holiday-In," and "In Search of the Ridiculous." Besides the repertory company of comics, there was an assortment of guest stars including Henny Youngman—who must have felt right at home, since he had practically invented the TV one-liner years before.

HALF HOUR THEATRE
  see *ABC Dramatic Shorts—1952–1953*

HALF NELSON
Detective Comedy/Drama
FIRST TELECAST: *March 24, 1985*
LAST TELECAST: *May 10, 1985*
BROADCAST HISTORY:
  Mar 1985, NBC Sun 9:00–11:00
  Mar 1985–May 1985, NBC Fri 9:00–10:00
CAST:
  Rocky Nelson..................... Joe Pesci
  Chester Long .... Fred Williamson
  Annie O'Hara .... Victoria Jackson
  Kurt .... Dick Butkus
  Beau......................... Bubba Smith
  Det. Hamill................... Gary Grubbs
  Dean Martin...................... Himself

"Why doesn't someone stand up to all the corruption in Beverly Hills?" read the ad. Next page: "He *is* standing up!" Rocky Nelson was a short detective, a former New York City undercover cop who moved to Beverly Hills where he got a job with an expensive private security service for the rich and famous, while trying to break into acting. His police experience certainly came in handy, though it did not endear him to either his boss, Chester Long, or Det. Hamill of the Beverly Hills Police. Rocky was supposed to guard bejeweled poodles

and manicured lawns, not solve crimes. However, he found that his short stature allowed him to sneak into secret places and obtain clues, simply because nobody took such a "little guy" seriously. Kurt and Beau were two of his fellow guards at the Patrol—all muscle and no brains—and Annie was the slightly daffy secretary at the office. Rocky liked the job mostly for the contact it gave him with celebrities, including client and confidante Dean Martin. Maybe one of them would give the little guy his big break?

HALLMARK SUMMER THEATRE
Dramatic Anthology
FIRST TELECAST: *July 6, 1952*
LAST TELECAST: *August 31, 1952*
BROADCAST HISTORY:
  Jul 1952–Aug 1952, NBC Sun 10:00–10:30
PRODUCER/DIRECTOR:
  Albert McCleery

The individual was the focus of this live summer drama series, which was sponsored by Hallmark Cards. The plays were produced using the theater-in-the-round technique, with a minimum of props to suggest time periods ranging from the American Revolution to the present day. Stories usually involved a crisis or act of courage in one person's life. The actors appearing were generally lesser-known performers from the Broadway stage.

HALLS OF IVY, THE
Situation Comedy
FIRST TELECAST: *October 19, 1954*
LAST TELECAST: *September 29, 1955*
BROADCAST HISTORY:
  Oct 1954–Jul 1955, CBS Tue 8:30–9:00
  Jul 1955–Sep 1955, CBS Thu 10:30–11:00
CAST:
  Dr. William Todhunter Hall . Ronald Colman
  Vicky Hall .... Benita Hume
  Alice........................ Mary Wickes
  Clarence Wellman .... Herb Butterfield
  Dr. Merriweather (1954) .... Ray Collins
  Dr. Merriweather (1954–1955) .... James Todd
THEME:
  "Halls of Ivy," by Henry Russell and Vick Knight

Dr. William Todhunter Hall was president of scenic Ivy College, somewhere in the Midwest, in this filmed comedy about a literate, witty college administrator. The school's students, its faculty, and its board of governors all figured in the stories, as did Dr. Hall's wife Vicky ("a former actress"), their housekeeper, Alice, and Chairman of the Board of Governors Clarence Wellman. *The Halls of Ivy* was adapted from the radio series of the same name (1950–1952), with Ronald Colman and his wife Benita Hume re-creating their radio roles. However, its very literacy and lack of physi-

cal action militated against it in the video me-
lium, and it soon disappeared.

One of the more memorable elements of the
series was its theme ("We love the Halls of Ivy/
That surround us here today . . ."), rendered in
suitably collegiate fashion by a male chorus. The
song achieved some popularity on records during
the early 1950s.

HAMPTONS, THE
Drama
FIRST TELECAST: *July 27, 1983*
LAST TELECAST: *August 24, 1983*
BROADCAST HISTORY:
Jul 1983–Aug 1983, ABC Wed 9:00–10:00
CAST:

Peter Chadway	Michael Goodwin
Lee Chadway	Leigh Taylor-Young
Brian Chadway	Craig Sheffer
Jay Mortimer	John Reilly
Adrienne Duncan Mortimer	Bibi Besch
Tracy Mortimer	Holly Roberts
Cheryl Ashcroft	Kate Dezina
David Landau	Phil Casnoff
Nick Atwater	Daniel Pilon
Karen Harper	Kathleen Buse
Penny Drake	Jada Rowland
Ada	Fran Carlon

Daytime soap-opera maven Gloria Monty produced this prime-time serial, which had a short
run during the summer of 1983. As in other prime-
time soaps, the principal characters were rich and
miserable, but at least the setting was different:
New York City and the fashionable nearby resort,
the Hamptons. Two old-line families, the Chad-
ways and the Duncan Mortimers, were linked
both by romance and co-ownership of the chic
Duncan-Chadway department store chain. Corporate intrigue and sexual scandal swirled through
the short summer run, and by the fifth and final
episode "good guy" Peter Chadway stood accused of murdering Penny Drake during his battle
to retain control of Duncan-Chadway; conniving
Jay Mortimer, who was trying to take the company away from him, was exposed as having an
incestuous relationship with his step-daughter
Tracy (Jay: "You know I'd do anything for you."
Tracy: "Then stay out of my bedroom, Daddy!");
Jay's drunken wife Adrienne was enraged; and
suave mogul Nick Atwater was making a strong
play for Peter's loyal wife, Lee.

HANDLE WITH CARE
see *Mail Story, The*

HANDS OF MYSTERY
Suspense Anthology
FIRST TELECAST: *September 30, 1949*
LAST TELECAST: *December 11, 1951*
BROADCAST HISTORY:
Sep 1949–Jul 1950, DUM Fri 8:00–8:30
Jul 1950–Sep 1951, DUM Fri 9:00–9:30
Sep 1951–Dec 1951, DUM Tue 10:00–10:30

The TV plays in this live series generally revolved
around a theme of murder or suspense, with episode titles such as "Don't Go Out Alone" and
"Vulture of the Waterfront." Included were some
stories of the supernatural and stories based on
true incidents, such as "The Man Who Killed Hitler." A novel aspect of the series, no doubt suggested to producer Larry Menkin by DuMont's
minimal budget, was the almost complete absence of props and sets, with inventive camera
angles and lighting used instead to suggest the
locale. Lesser-known actors and actresses were
featured.

The title of this series was changed twice, from
the original *Hands of Murder* to *Hands of Destiny*
in April 1950 and finally to *Hands of Mystery* in
August 1950.

HANGING IN
Situation Comedy
FIRST TELECAST: *August 8, 1979*
LAST TELECAST: *August 29, 1979*
BROADCAST HISTORY:
Aug 1979, CBS Wed 8:30–9:00
CAST:

Louis Harper	Bill Macy
Maggie Gallagher	Barbara Rhoades
Sam Dickey	Dennis Burkley
Pinky Nolan	Nedra Volz
Rita Zefferelli	Darian Mathias

EXECUTIVE PRODUCER:
Norman Lear

Even educators have to cope with politics, or so
this summer comedy series seemed to say. Lou
Harper was a former pro football star who had
subsequently devoted himself to helping the poor
and underprivileged through various community
projects. When he was offered the presidency of
Braddock University, he brought his humanitarian attitudes with him, not realizing the problems this could create with the University board,
prominent fund raisers, and the university staff.
Helping Harper, and often providing a practical
solution to the problems he created, were Maggie Gallagher, Dean of Faculty; Sam Dickey, Director of Development and the university's
highly manipulative public-relations man; and
Pinky Nolan, Harper's diminutive but outspoken
housekeeper.

The story of how this series got on the air is
even more interesting than the program itself. The
original concept was not about college politics,
but about government politics in Washington,
D.C. Early in 1978, when it became apparent that
the long-running comedy *Maude* was getting
stale, that series' producers decided to liven
things up by moving their star to Washington.
Maude was appointed to fill out the term of a
congressman who had recently died, moved to
Washington with her husband Walter (Bill Macy),
and began to confront her inherited staff with her
liberal outlook. After only two episodes in this
new setting, however, Beatrice Arthur decided

that she did not want to continue as Maude, and the series abruptly left the air.

The production company still believed the idea was workable and they filmed another series pilot, titled *Onward and Upward,* using essentially the same script and supporting cast. The only difference was that the Maude character had become a black former pro football star, played by John Amos. Creative differences between Mr. Amos and the producers led to his departure and a new series lead was sought. During this period the title was changed to *Mr. Dooley* and then again to *Mr. Dugan.* Cleavon Little was hired to star and a third pilot was filmed, still with the same supporting cast. *Mr. Dugan* was scheduled to premiere on CBS in March of 1979—it even had on-air promotion—but was pulled at the last minute, when the producers received a generally negative reaction from a number of real-life black politicians who had been given a preview of the first episode. The politicians felt that the show's comic portrayal of a black politician was demeaning to all blacks.

Undaunted, the producers reworked the project again, finally coming up with *Hanging In.* The premise was the same, but now the setting had been changed to a college. Ironically, *Maude*'s Bill Macy resurfaced as the star of the version that finally did air. The supporting cast, except for Darian Mathias, had been in all four versions of the pilot and must have known their lines pretty well by the time they got to *Hanging In.*

After all this travail, *Hanging In* lasted just four weeks.

HANK

Situation Comedy
FIRST TELECAST: *September 17, 1965*
LAST TELECAST: *September 2, 1966*
BROADCAST HISTORY:
   Sep 1965–Sep 1966, NBC Fri 8:00–8:30
CAST:
   Hank Dearborn .... Dick Kallman
   Doris Royal .... Linda Foster
   Dr. Lewis Royal .... Howard St. John
   Prof. McKillup .... Lloyd Corrigan
   Tina Dearborn .... Katie Sweet
   Franny .... Kelly Jean Peters
   Ossie Weiss .... Dabbs Greer
   Mrs. Ethel Weiss .... Sheila Bromley
   Miss Mittleman .... Dorothy Neumann
   Asst. Coach Gazzari .... Lou Wills, Jr.

Dick Kallman, a promising young Broadway and Hollywood comic of the 1950s and 1960s who never quite made it to major stardom, was showcased in this single-season campus comedy. He played Hank Dearborn, a resourceful young man determined to get a college education despite his lack of funds or family support (his parents had been killed in a car accident when he was 15, leaving him to support his baby sister, Tina). Hank simply "dropped in" to classes at Western State University, filling the seats of students he knew would be absent, and wearing a variety of ingenious disguises.

To support himself and Tina, he engaged in a number of money-making schemes, including running a campus laundry service, a watch and shoe repair shop, a dating agency, etc. He was always one step ahead of Dr. Royal, the registrar, who was bent on tracking down the campus phantom. Just about everyone else was in on the secret, however, including Doris, Hank's girlfriend and Dr. Royal's daughter; Prof. McKillup; and Franny, Tina's baby-sitter. The track coach, Ossie Weiss, after seeing Hank sprint to classes, wanted him to join the track team.

HANK MCCUNE SHOW, THE

Situation Comedy
FIRST TELECAST: *September 9, 1950*
LAST TELECAST: *December 2, 1950*
BROADCAST HISTORY:
   Sep 1950–Dec 1950, NBC Sat 7:00–7:30
CAST:
   Hank McCune
   Larry Keating
   Arthur Q. Bryan
   Sara Berner
   Frank Nelson
   Tammy Kiper

This early filmed situation comedy starred "likable blunderer" Hank McCune, who was constantly getting himself into comic predicaments of his own making. For example, on the first telecast Hank attended a convention held by his sponsor, Peter Paul candy bars, in Atlantic City, where he proceeded to foul up the hotel reservations, infuriate lifeguards, and disrupt the neighboring convention of a mystic fraternal order. Larry Keating played Hank's sidekick. The program was filmed in Hollywood and first ran as a local series in the fall of 1949.

The comedy on *The Hank McCune Show* was slapstick, and the show quickly disappeared from the air. However one aspect of it has remained with us, with a vengeance. Toward the end of its review of the first telecast, *Variety* noted, almost incidentally, that the program

   ... has an innovation in a sound track that contains audience laughter. Although the show is lensed on film without a studio audience, there are chuckles and yocks dubbed in. Whether this induces a jovial mood in home viewers is still to be determined, but the practice may have unlimited possibilities if it's spread to include canned peals of hilarity, thunderous ovations and gasps of sympathy.

HANNA-BARBERA HAPPY HOUR, THE

Comedy Variety
FIRST TELECAST: *April 13, 1978*
LAST TELECAST: *May 4, 1978*
BROADCAST HISTORY:
   Apr 1978–May 1978, NBC Thu 8:00–9:00

Honey and Sis (puppets)
The Rudy Baga Band
PUPPETRY BY:
Iwao Takamoto
EXECUTIVE PRODUCER:
Joseph Barbera

William Hanna and Joseph Barbera, famous for such cartoon creations as the Flintstones and Yogi Bear, tried their hands at a prime-time variety hour with this short-lived series. The program was certainly unusual. Instead of a live host, it had as emcees two life-sized puppets, Honey (the flashy blonde) and Sis (the insecure redhead), who participated in skits and songs with such live guests as Tony Randall, Dan Haggerty, Twiggy, and Leif Garrett. Regular features were "The Disco of Life," where puppets and stars swapped gags, and "The Truth Tub," where guests could confess their comic problems.

The appearance of the show was that of a normal, slickly produced, live comedy-variety hour, and Honey and Sis appeared remarkably lifelike. (They were animated by a team of six men who stood behind them but who could not be seen on screen, due to an electronic masking technique called chroma-key.) However, TV viewers apparently preferred human hosts, for this series attracted a small audience and was canceled after four weeks.

HAPPILY EVER AFTER
see *With This Ring*

HAPPY
Situation Comedy
FIRST TELECAST: *June 8, 1960*
LAST TELECAST: *September 8, 1961*
BROADCAST HISTORY:
Jun 1960–Sep 1960, NBC Wed 9:00–9:30
Jan 1961–Sep 1961, NBC Fri 7:30–8:00
CAST:
Happy .... David/Steven Born
Sally Day .... Yvonne Lime
Chris Day .... Ronnie Burns
Charlie Dooley .... Lloyd Corrigan
Clara Mason .... Doris Packer

Sally and Chris Day were a young married couple who were managers and part-owners (with Clara Mason) of the Desert Palm Motel, a very posh resort. Their efforts to keep the hotel running smoothly were often complicated by the well-meaning but not always useful assistance of Uncle Charlie. The most novel aspect of this show revolved around the Days' infant son, Happy, who was played by the Born twins. All of the goings-on at the hotel, business and personal, were observed by Happy, who regularly voiced his reactions through facial expressions and an off-screen voice—a variation on the observer-speaking-to-

the-camera device used by George Burns in the *Burns and Allen Show,* and elsewhere.

HAPPY DAYS
Variety
FIRST TELECAST: *June 25, 1970*
LAST TELECAST: *August 27, 1970*
BROADCAST HISTORY:
Jun 1970–Aug 1970, CBS Thu 8:00–9:00
REGULARS:
Louis Nye
Bob Elliott
Ray Goulding
Chuck McCann
Julie McWhirter
Alan Copeland
The Happy Days Singers
The Wisa D'Orso Dancers
The Happy Days Band with Jack Elliott and
Allyn Ferguson
Laara Lacey
Clive Clerk
Bill O'Berlin
Jim McGeorge
Jerry Dexter

Songs, dance numbers, and comedy blackouts and sketches were all part of this summer variety series hosted by comedian Louis Nye. All of the material, comedic and musical, was based on the 1930s and 1940s, the period referred to in the title as the "happy days." Sounds of the big bands—including appearances by Duke Ellington—Bob and Ray satirizing old radio shows, as well as real excerpts from actual shows of the era and parties hosted by such comicstrip characters as Mandrake the Magician and Little Orphan Annie were all woven into the show. There were even filmed interviews with major motion picture stars George Raft, Edward G. Robinson, and Charles Laughton talking about their memories of the period. Louis Nye had a regular spot as a song tester, trying to pick big potential hits; and Chuck McCann performed as The Great Voodini, the world's worst, and clumsiest, escape artist.

HAPPY DAYS
Situation Comedy
FIRST TELECAST: *January 15, 1974*
LAST TELECAST: *July 12, 1984*
BROADCAST HISTORY:
Jan 1974–Sep 1983, ABC Tue 8:00–8:30
Sep 1983–Jan 1984, ABC Tue 8:30–9:00
Apr 1984–May 1984, ABC Tue 8:30–9:00
Jun 1984–Jul 1984, ABC Thu 8:00–8:30
CAST:
Richie Cunningham (1974–1980)
.... Ron Howard
Arthur "Fonzie" Fonzarelli.... Henry Winkler
Howard Cunningham............ Tom Bosley
Marion Cunningham .... Marion Ross
Warren "Potsie" Weber (1974–1983)
.... Anson Williams

Ralph Malph (1974–1980)	Donny Most
Joanie Cunningham	Erin Moran
Chuck Cunningham (1974) ..	Gavan O'Herlihy
Chuck Cunningham (1974–1975)	
....	Randolph Roberts
Bag (1974–1975)	Neil J. Schwartz
Marsha (1974–1976)	Beatrice Colen
Gloria (1974–1975)	Linda Purl
Wendy (1974–1975)	Misty Rowe
Trudy (1974–1975)	Tita Bell
Arnold (Matsuo Takahashi)	
(1975–1976, 1982–1983)	Pat Morita
Alfred Delvecchio (1976–1982) ...	Al Molinaro
Charles "Chachi" Arcola (1977–1984)	
....	Scott Baio
Lori Beth Allen Cunningham (1977–1982)	
....	Lynda Goodfriend
Jenny Piccalo (1980–1983)	Cathy Silvers
Roger Phillips (1980–1984)	Ted McGinley
Flip Phillips (1982)	Billy Warlock
K. C. Cunningham (1982–1983)	
....	Crystal Bernard
Ashley Pfister (1982–1983)	Linda Purl
Heather Pfister (1982–1983)	
....	Heather O'Rourke
Officer Kirk (occasional)	Ed Peck

MUSIC:

"Rock Around the Clock" (original recording by Bill Haley & His Comets); "Happy Days" (Gimbel-Fox); and recordings by Fats Domino, Connie Francis, Johnnie Ray, Kay Starr, and other stars of the 1950s and 1960s

Nostalgia for the 1950s became big business in the mid-1970s, and leading the wave was this updated version of teenage life in the mid-1950s. It started modestly and built in popularity until in the 1976–1977 season *Happy Days* was the number one program in all of television. Along the way it made a major star out of one of its supporting actors.

Happy Days changed dramatically from the series that premiered in 1974. Originally it was the story of two high-school kids, Richie Cunningham and his pal Potsie Weber, at Jefferson High in Milwaukee, Wisconsin. Howard Cunningham, Richie's father, ran a hardware store while Chuck was Richie's college-bound older brother and Joanie his 13-year-old kid sister. Richie and most of his friends hung out at Arnold's Drive-In, a malt shop near the school.

Richie was supposed to be the innocent teenager and Potsie his more worldly pal. So as not to make the show too much like *Ozzie & Harriet*, however, the producers added some slightly more extreme counterpoint in the person of the greasy-haired motorcycle kid, Fonzie. That was the move that made the show a hit. Instead of the fairly hackneyed Richie-Potsie relationship, the show came to center on the relationship between the "cool" dropout Fonz, and the "straight" kids represented by Richie. Henry Winkler made the character of Fonzie three-dimensional, vulnerable

as well as hip. One of the classic episodes, which ran traditionally every Christmas, was the one that first showed the Fonz's own pad, a dingy, cluttered room with his motorcycle in the middle of the floor—and only a tiny, pathetic tree to indicate that it was Christmas. Too proud to admit to being alone for the holiday, the Fonz—whose father had deserted him at the age of three—nevertheless allowed himself to be brought into the Cunninghams' home to share in their celebration.

As Fonzie's popularity spread (his thumbs-up gesture and "aaayyh!" became trademarks), the show became a bigger and bigger hit. Winkler moved from his original fifth billing to third, then second behind Ron Howard and finally first when Howard left in 1980. But ABC claimed that there would be no spin-off series, because without the Richie-Fonzie contrast there would be no *Happy Days*. Not only did Fonzie's billing change as the series grew, but so did his residence. During the 1975–1976 season he moved into a small apartment over the Cunningham garage. He was thus always available to give Richie advice about life and girls (the Fonz made every girl in Milwaukee swoon).

Changes in the cast were fairly minor in the early years. Dozens of high school kids came and went, and Richie's older brother disappeared from the family early on, never to be referred to again. Arnold, the Japanese who owned Arnold's, first showed his face in 1975 but was replaced by a new owner, Alfred, in 1976. (Pat Morita had gotten his own series that fall, *Mr. T. and Tina.* He returned for occasional episodes beginning in 1982.) Two lower-middle-class girls who turned up briefly in late 1975—on a double date with Richie and Fonzie—quickly went on to a series of their own, *Laverne & Shirley.* Chachi arrived in 1977, as Fonzie's young cousin, the same season that Richie began going steady with Lori Beth, with the performers who played both roles turning up together on an NBC series, *Who's Watching the Kids,* the following fall as well.

One of the most popular characters passing through was Pinky Tuscadero (played by Roz Kelly), the sexy motorcycle queen who wrapped the Fonz around her little finger—as "cool" as he was, she was "cooler." An old girlfriend of his, she roared into town in September 1976 with her Pinkettes (Tina and Lola, played by Doris Hess and Kelly Sanders) to join the Fonz in a demolition derby. A season later her sister Leather Tuscadero (played by rock star Suzi Quatro) turned up on a couple of episodes with her rock group, the Suedes. More nostalgic guests on the show ranged from Buffalo Bob Smith *(Howdy Doody)* to John Hart *(The Lone Ranger),* Frankie Avalon, and Jack Smith, onetime emcee of *You Asked For It.* Jack played the host of the mythical *You Wanted to See It* show in an episode where Fonzie set a new world's record by leaping his motorcycle over 14 garbage cans behind Arnold's Drive-In, on live TV.

As the 1976–1977 season ended, Richie and the gang graduated from high school and it seemed that Fonzie, the dropout, might be left behind. But at the last minute it turned out that the Fonz, while working days at various garages, had been going to night school and would get his diploma too. Richie, Potsie, and Ralph enrolled at the University of Wisconsin at Milwaukee, with Fonzie still around (though not enrolled) to advise them on love and life. Richie enrolled as a journalism student and Potsie as a psychology major, while Ralph followed in his father's footsteps to become an eye doctor—though he really wanted to be a comedian.

In 1980 major changes began to take place in both the cast and story line of *Happy Days*. Richie and Ralph graduated from college, joined the army, and were shipped off to Greenland (Ron Howard and Donny Most had left the show). From there the unseen Richie corresponded with and eventually married Lori Beth—by telephone, with Fonz as his stand-in. Lori Beth visited him from time to time and in 1981 gave birth to a son, Richie, Jr. Back in Milwaukee the Fonz had become so straight that he was now a co-owner of Arnold's, a shop teacher at Jefferson High, and operator of Bronco's Garage. "Mr. Cool" had a close brush with serious romance in 1982–83 when he fell for divorcée Ashley Pfister and her cute daughter Heather, but it didn't last. In 1983 he joined Marion's nephew Roger Phillips, an English teacher and basketball coach at Jefferson High, in a new career. Roger had just been appointed principal of the rowdy George S. Patton Vocational High School, and Fonz joined him there as Dean of Boys!

Potsie, the perennial college student, went to work for Mr. C. at Cunningham Hardware. But by this time it was the 1960s and the focus of the program turned increasingly to the next generation, particularly the rocky teenage love of Joanie and Chachi. They had their own spin-off show, *Joanie Loves Chachi*, for a time in 1982, but they never left *Happy Days* entirely. After a try at a singing career, Joanie enrolled in college and signed on as a trainee teacher at Roger's vocational school. Others of the '60s generation were Joanie's independent, boy-crazy friend Jenny Piccalo, who was finally seen after years of only being referred to; Roger's rambunctious younger brother Flip; and Howard's teenaged niece K.C., who lived with the Cunninghams for a year.

The final season was a time of reunions and farewells. Richie and Lori Beth returned in the fall for a visit, with Richie, Jr., in tow, and another baby on the way. Then Richie headed for Hollywood to pursue his dream of becoming a screenwriter. In the series' final episode Richie and other former regulars returned one last time as Fonzie bought a home and adopted a young orphan named Danny, and Joanie and Chachi were finally married—by Al's lookalike brother, Father Delvecchio. With "both" their children now married

(even *they* had forgotten Chuck), Howard and Marion thanked the audience for being part of their family, and made a tearful farewell.

In its later years *Happy Days* became something of an institution. In 1980 it was announced that the Fonz's leather jacket was being enshrined in the Smithsonian Institution. Three years later the *Happy Days* cast visited the real-life city of Milwaukee, and some 150,000 residents lined the streets to welcome them "home." Mr. C. got the key to the city, and the Fonz said "Aaayyh!"

The origin of this immensely successful series was a skit that appeared on *Love, American Style* in February 1972, titled "Love and the Happy Days," and starring Ron Howard and Anson Williams. The original theme song for the series was Bill Haley's famous 1955 hit record "Rock Around the Clock," which promptly became a best-seller all over again in 1974 as a result of its exposure on the show. It was later superseded as the theme by an original composition, "Happy Days," which was itself on the hit parade in 1976.

ABC aired reruns of *Happy Days* on its daytime lineup from September 1975 to March 1979, and an animated Saturday morning version from November 1980 to September 1983.

HARBOR COMMAND
Police Drama
BROADCAST HISTORY:
Syndicated only
30 minutes
Produced: *1957–1958* (39 episodes)
Released: *September 1957*
CAST:
Capt. Ralph Baxter. . . . . Wendell Corey

Harbor Command was a straight police-action show, set in the harbor of a large city. Capt. Baxter was the plainclothes chief of the Harbor Command, fighting dope smugglers, murderers, and other assorted villains with the help of his uniformed officers.

HARBOURMASTER
Adventure
FIRST TELECAST: *September 26, 1957*
LAST TELECAST: *June 29, 1958*
BROADCAST HISTORY:
Sep 1957–Dec 1957, CBS Thu 8:00–8:30
Jan 1958–Jun 1958, ABC Sun 8:30–9:00
CAST:
Capt. David Scott . . . . Barry Sullivan
Jeff Kittridge. . . . . Paul Burke
Anna Morrison . . . . Nina Wilcox
Cap'n Dan. . . . . Michael Keens
Danny . . . . Evan Elliott

Off the New England coast lay Scott Island, an idyllic little place far removed from the hustle and bustle of the mainland. David Scott's family had settled the island generations ago and had lived there ever since. A bachelor, David was the "Harbourmaster" for the island, arranging dock space for boats, anchorages, and serving as a one-man rescue squad and police force.

His hobby, which he pursued between storms, fires, and other problems, was running a boat-yard. Here, with the help of young Jeff Kittridge, David repaired and rented small boats. Nearby was the Dolphin Restaurant, run by winsome Anna, a young woman whose interest in David was obvious to all but him. When the series moved to ABC in the middle of its one-season run, the title was changed to *Adventures at Scott Island*.

HARD COPY
Newspaper Drama
FIRST TELECAST: *February 1, 1987*
LAST TELECAST: *July 3, 1987*
BROADCAST HISTORY:
    Feb 1987, CBS Sun 10:00–11:00
    May 1987–Jul 1987, CBS Fri 10:00–11:00
CAST:
    Andy Omart . . . . Michael Murphy
    David Del Valle . . . . Dean Devlin
    Blake Calisher . . . . Wendy Crewson
    William Boot . . . . Charles Cooper
    Lt. Guyla Cook . . . . Fionnula Flanagan
    Scoop Webster . . . . George O. Petrie
    John Freed . . . . Jeffrey Kramer
    Lt. Brian Packer . . . . E. Erich Anderson
    Larry Coverson . . . . Jim McDonnell

The Morning Post was a Los Angeles newspaper with a reputation for hard-hitting journalism and a highly competitive staff of crime reporters. The lead reporter was veteran Andy Omart, who had seen just about everything in his years with the paper. A recent addition to the staff, fresh out of journalism school, was young David Del Valle, an eager beaver who found it difficult to compete with ambitious Blake Calisher, William Boot, Scoop Webster, and the other, more experienced reporters on the paper. Local TV anchorman Larry Coverson was forever trying to break major stories before the print reporters, but almost never succeeded.

HARDCASTLE & McCORMICK
Detective/Adventure
FIRST TELECAST: *September 18, 1983*
LAST TELECAST: *July 23, 1986*
BROADCAST HISTORY:
    Sep 1983–Dec 1984, ABC Sun 8:00–9:00
    Dec 1984–May 1985, ABC Mon 8:00–9:00
    Aug 1985–May 1986, ABC Mon 8:00–9:00
    Jun 1986–Jul 1986, ABC Wed 9:00–10:00
CAST:
    Judge Milton G. Hardcastle . . . . . . Brian Keith
    Mark "Skid" McCormick . Daniel Hugh-Kelly
    Sarah Wicks (1983) . . . . Mary Jackson
    Lt. Michael Delaney (1984–1985)
    . . . . John Hancock
    Lt. Frank Harper (1985–1986) . . . . . . Joe Santos

Vigilante justice reached new extremes in this action series, in which an athletic retired judge decided to track down "the ones that got away"—presumed criminals who had beaten the rap in his courtroom over the previous 30 years thanks to smart lawyers, lack of evidence, and other "legal loopholes." Although Judge Hardcastle was still remarkably fit at 65, he needed some help in this crusade, so he recruited a handsome, young two-time loser named Mark, who just happened to be a hotshot racing driver. The deal was that Hardcastle would get the lad off the hook for his latest conviction (auto theft), if Mark would help the judge track down his quarry. "I figure it takes one to catch one," growled Hardcastle.

Mark agreed, partially just to be around such a colorful character. Hardcastle, who used to wear loud shirts and tennis shorts under his robes while on the bench, was now given to wearing T-shirts with slogans like NO PLEA BARGAINING IN HEAVEN and FIND 'EM AND HANG 'EM. He raced around in a macho red sportscar (macho because you had to crawl in through the windows) with license plates reading DE JUDGE. Amid a steady stream of wisecracks and car crashes, he still knew how to lean on his many contacts in the judiciary and on the streets to help him crack cases. Home base for the series was the judge's palatial estate (he had evidently invested well). Presided over by housekeeper Sarah, it was the scene of his weekly poker game.

Of course there were a few "buts," presumably to keep the ACLU off his back. Mark hadn't really committed that crime, and Hardcastle only went after offenders for their current offenses. Once he even took on a trio of fellow judges who had decided simply to kill ex-cons as they were released from prison. But the criminal element presumably got the message: watch out for judges wearing T-shirts reading BLAST 'EM, TONTO!

HARDY BOYS MYSTERIES, THE
Adventure
FIRST TELECAST: *January 30, 1977*
LAST TELECAST: *August 26, 1979*
BROADCAST HISTORY:
    Jan 1977–Jan 1979, ABC Sun 7:00–8:00
    Jun 1979–Aug 1979, ABC Sun 7:00–8:00
CAST:
    Joe Hardy . . . . Shaun Cassidy
    Frank Hardy . . . . Parker Stevenson
    Fenton Hardy . . . . Edmund Gilbert
    Callie Shaw (1977) . . . . Lisa Eilbacher
    Aunt Gertrude (1977–1978) . . . . Edith Atwater
    Nancy Drew (1977–1978) . . Pamela Sue Martin
    Nancy Drew (1978) . . . . . Janet Louise Johnson
    Carson Drew (1977–1978)
    . . . . William Schallert
    George Fayne (1977–1978) . . . . Susan Buckner
    Bess (1977–1978) . . . . Ruth Cox
    Harry Gibbon (1978–1979) . . . Phillip R. Allen
    Harry Hammond (1978–1979) . . . . . . Jack Kelly

The adventures of 16-year-old Joe and 18-year-old Frank Hardy, the teenage detective sons of world-famous investigator Fenton Hardy, were the basis of this series. Their exploits were usually on the nonviolent side, involving ghosts, missing persons, smugglers, and other "mysteries" rather than violent action. Often they had a contemporary youth orientation, to appeal to the teenagers who made up much of the audience to this show, as when the boys traveled to Europe to Transylvania to attend a rock concert at Dracula's Castle, where they encountered strange goings-on. Helping out were Callie, who worked part-time in Fenton Hardy's detective agency, and Aunt Gertrude. Added in 1978 were federal agent Harry Gibbon and CIA operative Harry Hammond.

At first the series alternated on Sunday nights with *The Nancy Drew Mysteries*, which starred Pamela Sue Martin in the title role. In the fall of 1977 the Hardy Boys and Nancy Drew appeared jointly in some episodes, and then in February 1978, the two programs were combined into one, with all three leads appearing together regularly. Unhappy with the elimination of her separate series, Pamela Sue Martin left the program and was briefly replaced by 18-year-old Janet Louise Johnson. The character of Nancy Drew was dropped altogether in the fall of 1978, and the title was shortened to *The Hardy Boys*.

In addition to his adventures, Shaun Cassidy found time to launch a singing career while on this program, much as his older brother David Cassidy had done while on another TV series, *The Partridge Family*, seven years earlier. Shaun sang "Da Do Ron Ron" on an April 1977 telecast, and saw it become a number one record hit.

The Hardy Boys mystery books, on which this series was based, were supposedly written by "Franklin W. Dixon," but in fact there was no such person. They were actually the product of a remarkable "writing factory" founded in the early 1900s by Edward Stratemeyer, which was also responsible for the Nancy Drew, Tom Swift, Rover Boys, and Bobbsey Twins series, and hundreds of other juvenile adventure best-sellers. Stratemeyer and his daughter Harriet Adams wrote or oversaw the writing of all of them, using more than 60 pseudonyms. "Franklin W. Dixon" was used for the Hardy novels, and "Carolyn Keene" for Nancy Drew. Several Nancy Drew movies were made in the late 1930s, and early television producers were also interested in using the stories. However, Harriet Adams insisted on script approval, and not until 1977 did Universal Studios agree to this condition, resulting in the ABC series.

HARNESS RACING
Sports
FIRST TELECAST: *May 27, 1949*
LAST TELECAST: *August 19, 1958*
BROADCAST HISTORY:
May 1949–Sep 1949, NBC Fri 10:00–Conclusion

Jul 1949–Sep 1949, NBC Tue 9:30–Conclusion
Jun 1950–Aug 1950, NBC Thu 10:00–Conclusion
Jun 1950–Sep 1950, NBC Sat 10:00–Conclusion
Sep 1951–Nov 1951, ABC Sat Various times (9:00, 9:30, 10:00 starts)
Jun 1958–Aug 1958, ABC Fri 10:00–10:30
Aug 1958, ABC Tue 10:00–10:30

Back in the relatively early days of network television, NBC aired live coverage of races from New York's Roosevelt Raceway, usually two or three races each night. Veteran horse-race announcer Clem McCarthy called the races, described them prior to the start of each race, and talked about various horse owners and trainers. To keep viewers from being bored, there was a quiz game conducted between races with contestants from a studio audience. The quiz was conducted by Ray Barrett and Bill Stern, and was only used by NBC in the 1950 edition of *Trotting Races,* not the original in 1949.

ABC covered the trotters in 1951 and 1958 under the title *Harness Racing.* Races aired in 1951 originated from Maywood Park in Chicago until late October, and then shifted to Yonkers Raceway near New York City. The 1958 series, on ABC, originated only from the New York area, with individual telecasts aired from either Roosevelt Raceway or Yonkers Raceway.

HAROLD ROBBINS' "THE SURVIVORS"
see *Survivors, The*

HARPER VALLEY P.T.A.
Situation Comedy
FIRST TELECAST: *January 16, 1981*
LAST TELECAST: *August 14, 1982*
BROADCAST HISTORY:
Jan 1981–Aug 1981, NBC Fri 8:00–8:30
Oct 1981–Nov 1981, NBC Thu 8:00–8:30
Dec 1981–Jan 1982, NBC Sat 8:00–8:30
Jan 1982–Feb 1982, NBC Sat 8:30–9:00
Apr 1982–Jun 1982, NBC Sat 8:00–8:30
Jul 1982–Aug 1982, NBC Sat 8:30–9:00
CAST:
Stella Johnson .... Barbara Eden
Dee Johnson .... Jenn Thompson
Flora Simpson Reilly .... Anne Francine
Cassie Bowman .... Fannie Flagg
Mayor Otis Harper, Jr. .... George Gobel
Wanda Reilly Taylor .... Bridget Hanley
Scarlett Taylor .... Suzi Dean
Bobby Taylor .... Rod McCary
Tom Meechum .... Christopher Stone
Norman Clayton (1981) .... Gary Allen
Vivian Washburn (1981) .... Mari Gorman
Willamae Jones (1981) .... Edie McClurg
Cliff Willoughby (1981) .... Robert Gray
George Kelly (1981) .... Vic Dunlop
Coach Burt Powell (1981) ..... Kevin Scannell
Winslow Homer (Uncle Buster) Smith (1981–1982) .... Mills Watson

"Harper Valley P.T.A.," written by Tom T. Hall

This was one of only two series in network television history to be based on a phonograph record (the other: *The Alvin Show*). Jeannie C. Riley's huge 1968 record hit "Harper Valley P.T.A." told of the struggles of a liberated woman fighting hypocrisy in a small Southern town. The song served as the basis for a 1978 theatrical movie starring Barbara Eden as the outspoken Stella Johnson. The film was only a modest success in theaters, but it attracted a large audience when aired on television. This prompted NBC to develop it into a weekly situation comedy with Miss Eden re-creating her movie role.

Stella was a very attractive widow with a 13-year-old daughter (Dee) living in sleepy little Harper Valley—a very staid and proper community on the surface, but actually full of miscreants, adulterers, and cheerful alcoholics. Stella was a real individual who did what she pleased, regardless of what anybody thought. Independent but principled, her approach to life endlessly distressed the self-righteous members of the P.T.A. board, to which she had been elected. Her short skirts, flirting, and "radical" ideas convinced the other board members that she made a disgusting role model for their children, not to mention a temptation for their husbands (who thought Stella was jus' fine). The stuffy matrons waged a constant struggle to have her removed from the board, while Stella fought back with a succession of hilarious put-downs that got them every time. Stella's principal adversary was wealthy Flora Simpson Reilly, the leader of Harper Valley "society." The entire Reilly family, in fact, shared Flora's pompous attitudes, including daughter Wanda; son-in-law Bobby, the town's leading attorney; and granddaughter Scarlett, a classmate of Dee's. Stella's one ally was beauty-parlor operator Cassie, who helped her with her schemes. In order to make a living, Stella sold Angelglow cosmetics door to door.

When the series returned in the fall of 1981 there were several changes. Since the P.T.A. meetings and involvement had been dropped, the title of the show was shortened to *Harper Valley*. Stella's relationship with Dee became more prominent, and a new character, Stella's Uncle Buster, a bumbling, eccentric inventor, came to town and moved in with his niece. Buster's "inventions" never seemed to work the way they were supposed to; the results were usually catastrophic and hilarious.

HARRIGAN AND SON
Situation Comedy
FIRST TELECAST: *October 14, 1960*
LAST TELECAST: *September 29, 1961*
BROADCAST HISTORY:
Oct 1960–Sep 1961, ABC Fri 8:00–8:30

CAST:

James Harrigan, Sr.	Pat O'Brien
James Harrigan, Jr.	Roger Perry
Gypsy	Georgine Darcy
Miss Claridge	Helen Kleeb

James Harrigan, Sr., had been practicing law, as a criminal attorney, since before his son was born. Now his boy had just graduated from Harvard Law School and joined the firm as a junior partner. Junior's problem was that he tried to do everything by the book and was constantly at odds with his father who was not above playing angles that would help his case. The two lawyers had secretaries that matched their styles completely. Senior had fiery, flip, effervescent Gypsy and Junior had sedate, efficient Miss Claridge.

HARRIS AGAINST THE WORLD
Situation Comedy
FIRST TELECAST: *October 5, 1964*
LAST TELECAST: *January 4, 1965*
BROADCAST HISTORY:
Oct 1964–Jan 1965, NBC Mon 8:00–8:30
CAST:

Alan Harris	Jack Klugman
Kate Harris	Patricia Barry
Deedee Harris	Claire Wilcox
Billy Harris	David Macklin
Helen Miller	Fay DeWitt
Norm Miller	Sheldon Allman

Jack Klugman played Alan Harris, a plant superintendent at a huge movie studio who lived at 90 Bristol Court with his wife, Kate, and his two children, Deedee and Billy. Coping with life was a full-time job for Alan. His bosses, debts, taxes, and people in general always seemed to be one up on him. His wife was a champion spender who always managed to find him part-time jobs to work at in the spare time he didn't really have. But much as he complained about almost everything and everybody, Alan was really an old softie at heart.

Harris Against the World was the middle component of a series of three comedies that ran from 7:30–9:00 P.M. on Monday evenings under the blanket title *90 Bristol Court*, which referred to the fashionable apartment block where all three shows were set. *Karen* ran from 7:30–8:00 and *Tom, Dick and Mary* from 8:30–9:00.

HARRIS AND COMPANY
Family Drama
FIRST TELECAST: *March 15, 1979*
LAST TELECAST: *April 5, 1979*
BROADCAST HISTORY:
Mar 1979–Apr 1979, NBC Thu 8:00–9:00
CAST:

Mike Harris	Bernie Casey
David Harris	David Hubbard
Liz Harris	Renee Brown
Juanita Priscilla (J.P.) Harris	Lia Jackson

```
Tommy Harris............. Eddie Singleton
Richard Allen Harris.......... Dain Turner
Harry Foreman................ James Luisi
Louise Foreman............... Lois Walden
Charlie Adams ............... Stu Gilliam
Angie Adams............. C. Tillery Banks
```

Following the death of his wife, black assembly-line worker Mike Harris and his five children decided to move from Detroit to Los Angeles and build a new life. As with every decision in the Harris household, all family members were consulted and it was put to a vote (hence the "company" in the series title). In L.A. Mike went into partnership with Harry Foreman running a garage. Stories revolved around problems with work and the comic difficulties of a single parent raising a family. The Harris children ranged in age from college-student Liz to 6-year-old Richard. Charlie and Angie Adams were cousins who helped Mike with the kids.

Harris and Company was an unusual attempt to build a dramatic series around a loving, caring black family. It attracted a small audience and had a short run.

HARRY
Situation Comedy
FIRST TELECAST: *March 4, 1987*
LAST TELECAST: *March 25, 1987*
BROADCAST HISTORY:
Mar 1987, ABC Wed 8:30–9:00
CAST:
```
Harry Porschak.................. Alan Arkin
Richard Breskin ............. Richard Lewis
Bobby Kratz................... Matt Craven
Dr. Sandy Clifton ............. Barbara Dana
Nurse Ina Duckett .......... Holland Taylor
Wyatt Lockhart............... Kurt Knudson
Lawrence Pendelton............. Thom Bray
```

Alan Arkin starred as a wheeler-dealer supply clerk in a large hospital in this short-lived comedy. Kidney-stone pools and outpatient poker were the order of the day in Harry's basement domain at County General Hospital; overbearing Nurse Duckett and her meek, bow-tied toady Lawrence were his chief nemeses, and Wyatt Lockhart the bemused hospital administrator.

HARRY'S GIRLS
Situation Comedy
FIRST TELECAST: *September 13, 1963*
LAST TELECAST: *January 3, 1964*
BROADCAST HISTORY:
Sep 1963–Jan 1964, NBC Fri 9:30–10:00
CAST:
```
Harry Burns.................. Larry Blyden
Rusty ........................... Susan Silo
Lois....................... Dawn Nickerson
Terry ..................... Diahn Williams
```

Harry Burns was a vaudeville entertainer with an act that featured three beautiful girl dancers,

Rusty, Lois, and Terry. Although his act was much too old-fashioned to be successful in the United States, it was reasonably popular in Europe. Harry, in addition to being the star of the act, had to do the booking, handle finances, and try to keep tabs on the girls. The last was not always easy. Rusty was incredibly gullible and constantly falling in love, Lois was distressingly naive and often acted like a country girl on her first trip to the big city, and Terry was too sophisticated for her own good. Filmed on location throughout Europe, this series followed the travels of *Harry's Girls* as the act played in various continental cities. Occasional excerpts from the act were shown, but only as they fit into the story.

HARRY-O
Detective Drama
FIRST TELECAST: *September 12, 1974*
LAST TELECAST: *August 12, 1976*
BROADCAST HISTORY:
Sep 1974–Aug 1976, ABC Thu 10:00–11:00
CAST:
```
Harry Orwell................ David Janssen
Det. Lt. Manuel (Manny) Quinlan (1974–1975)
.......................... Henry Darrow
Lt. K. C. Trench (1975–1976)
.......................... Anthony Zerbe
Sgt. Don Roberts (1975–1976)..... Paul Tulley
Lester Hodges (1975–1976) ...... Les Lannom
Dr. Fong (1976) .................. Keye Luke
```

Harry Orwell was one of TV's more bohemian private eyes, living in a beachfront cottage near San Diego and often using the city bus for transportation (his car didn't work). An ex-Marine and ex-cop pensioned from the force after being injured in the line of duty, he augmented his income by taking cases that especially interested him. These usually involved luscious girls—none of whom seemed to matter much to Harry, however.

Harry's sometime nemesis, sometime ally, was Lt. Manny Quinlan of the San Diego Police Department. Manny was killed off in a February 1975 telecast, after which Harry moved his base of operations to Santa Monica. There, he inherited a new official nemesis, Lt. Trench, plus occasional unsolicited help with his cases from amateur criminologists Lester Hodges and Dr. Fong.

Infrequently seen, but highly visible on those occasions when she did appear, was Harry's girl-next-door, Farrah Fawcett.

HART TO HART
Adventure
FIRST TELECAST: *August 25, 1979*
LAST TELECAST: *July 31, 1984*
BROADCAST HISTORY:
Aug 1979–Oct 1979, ABC Sat 10:00–11:00
Oct 1979–Jul 1984, ABC Tue 10:00–11:00
CAST:
```
Jonathan Hart .............. Robert Wagner
Jennifer Hart ............... Stefanie Powers
Max ....................... Lionel Stander
```

Jonathan and Jennifer Hart were rich, stylish, and supersleuths. He was a self-made millionaire, head of the huge Hart Industries conglomerate (which never seemed to require his attention); she was an internationally known free-lance journalist. From their mansion in Beverly Hills, they rekindled their continuing love affair by setting out each week on a new adventure. They roamed the glamour spots of the world in their private jet, hobnobbed with the rich, famous, and not-so-famous, and along the way solved crimes that baffled more pedestrian souls. Gravel-voiced Max was their chauffeur and confidant; Freeway, their dog.

The series was created by best-selling novelist Sidney Sheldon.

HARTMANS, THE
Situation Comedy
FIRST TELECAST: *February 27, 1949*
LAST TELECAST: *May 22, 1949*
BROADCAST HISTORY:
Feb 1949–May 1949, NBC Sun 7:30–8:00
CAST:
Grace Hartman .... Herself
Paul Hartman .... Himself
The handyman.............. Harold J. Stone
Their brother-in-law .... Loring Smith
Their nephew................. Bob Shawley
The man next door.............. Gage Clark
Grace's sister.............. Valerie Cossart

Grace and Paul Hartman, the famous dance satirists, played straight comedy in this early live series about the trials of a young married couple living in a suburb called Forest Heights.

HATHAWAYS, THE
Situation Comedy
FIRST TELECAST: *October 6, 1961*
LAST TELECAST: *August 31, 1962*
BROADCAST HISTORY:
Oct 1961–Aug 1962, ABC Fri 8:00–8:30
CAST:
Elinore Hathaway .... Peggy Cass
Walter Hathaway.............. Jack Weston
Jerry Roper................ Harvey Lembeck
Thelma Brockwood .... Barbara Perry
Amanda Allison .... Mary Grace Canfield
Mrs. Harrison .... Belle Montrose

The Hathaways were a family of five, all of them wearing normal clothes and eating together at the same table, but only two of them were people. Walter Hathaway was a real-estate agent and Elinore was his wife. Charlie, Enoch, and Cindy were chimps—the Marquis Chimps—and very bright chimps at that. Elinore, besides treating them like her children, was booking agent for their show-business act, which included riding bicycles and making faces. (They also had a formal talent agent named Jerry Roper.) Walter had mixed emotions about the whole arrangement, wondering if the chimps meant more to his wife than he did,

and their suburban neighbors also had some difficulty adjusting to "the kids next door." One of the neighbors was played by Belle Montrose, the mother of comedian Steve Allen.

HAVE GUN WILL TRAVEL
Western
FIRST TELECAST: *September 14, 1957*
LAST TELECAST: *September 21, 1963*
BROADCAST HISTORY:
Sep 1957–Sep 1963, CBS Sat 9:30–10:00
CAST:
Paladin .... Richard Boone
Hey Boy (1957–1960; 1961–1963) ... Kam Tong
Hey Girl (1960–1961) .... Lisa Lu
THEME:
"The Ballad of Paladin," by Johnny Western, Richard Boone, and Sam Rolfe, sung on the soundtrack by Johnny Western

Have Gun Will Travel was one of the most popular programs of the late 1950s, and the chief prototype of a rash of dapper heroes invented by TV to populate the Old West. Paladin was certainly not your normal, everyday illiterate gunslinger. He was college-educated, having attended West Point in pursuit of a military career. Instead, after serving in the Civil War, he headed west to become a high-priced "gun for hire," a kind of Old West troubleshooter. He was based at the fancy Hotel Carlton in San Francisco and his calling card bore the figure of a paladin (the white chess knight) and the inscription, "Have Gun, Will Travel . . . Wire Paladin, San Francisco."

Paladin was a man of culture, enjoying the finest clothes, epicurean meals, and literate company—except when he was on assignment. Then, dressed all in black, he became a very intimidating figure indeed. Despite his somewhat violent profession, he had a sense of ethics that dictated what he would and would not do; it occasionally led him to seek out the very people who had hired him if they in fact were the guilty parties. Hey Boy, the Oriental working at the Hotel Carlton, was seen at the beginning of most episodes bringing a message to Paladin from a prospective client. (During the 1960–1961 season, while Kam Tong was involved in a more substantial role in another series, *The Garlund Touch,* he was replaced by Lisa Lu. He returned to *Have Gun Will Travel* after his new venture was canceled.)

Have Gun Will Travel was an overnight hit, ranking among the top five programs during its first season on the air. From 1958–1961 it was the number three program on television, behind two other Westerns—*Gunsmoke* and *Wagon Train.* Its theme song, "The Ballad of Paladin," was a hit single in the early 1960s.

HAVING BABIES
Medical Drama
FIRST TELECAST: *March 7, 1978*
LAST TELECAST: *June 26, 1979*

BROADCAST HISTORY:
Mar 1978–Apr 1978, ABC Tue 10:00–11:00
June 1979, ABC Tue 10:00–11:00

CAST:
Dr. Julie Farr .... Susan Sullivan
Dr. Blake Simmons............ Mitchell Ryan
Dr. Ron Danvers .... Dennis Howard
Kelly........................ Beverly Todd

This medical drama was one of several new programs which got short-run try-outs during the
spring of 1978 to test their potential as regular fall
series. Dr. Julie Farr was a dedicated physician at
Lake General Hospital whose practice brought
her into contact with couples from all walks of
life, many of whom had one thing in common: the
joy and pain of childbirth. Several stories were
usually seen in each episode, at least one of which
always dealt with childbirth: for example, the illegal alien who wanted her baby to be born in the
United States, even though she was suffering from
malaria; the "storybook marriage" that threatened to crumble with the prospect of pregnancy;
the wealthy father who had never learned to
enjoy his success.

Dr. Simmons was the experienced older doctor,
and Dr. Danvers the eager intern.

Having Babies was first seen as a series of
movie specials from 1976–1978. Effective with the
March 28, 1978, episode its title was changed to
Julie Farr, M.D. The series was canceled with the
April 18, 1978, telecast, but three additional origi-
nal episodes were aired in June 1979.

HAWAII FIVE-O
Police Drama
FIRST TELECAST: *September 26, 1968*
LAST TELECAST: *April 26, 1980*
BROADCAST HISTORY:
Sep 1968–Dec 1968, CBS Thu 8:00–9:00
Dec 1968–Sep 1971, CBS Wed 10:00–11:00
Sep 1971–Sep 1974, CBS Tue 8:30–9:30
Sep 1974–Sep 1975, CBS Tue 9:00–10:00
Sep 1975–Nov 1975, CBS Fri 9:00–10:00
Dec 1975–Nov 1979, CBS Thu 9:00–10:00
Dec 1979–Jan 1980, CBS Tue 9:00–10:00
Mar 1980–Apr 1980, CBS Sat 9:00–10:00
CAST:
Det. Steve McGarrett.............. Jack Lord
Det. Danny Williams (1968–1979)
.... James MacArthur
Det. Chin Ho Kelly (1968–1978) ... Kam Fong
Det. Kono Kalakaua (1968–1972) .... Zulu
Governor Philip Grey ...... Richard Denning
Det. Ben Kokua (1972–1974).... Al Harrington
Che Fong (1970–1977)........... Harry Endo
Doc Bergman (1970–1976)........... Al Eben
May (1968–1969) .... Maggi Parker
Jenny Sherman (1969–1976) ...... Peggy Ryan
Luana (1978–1980)............... Laura Sode
Duke Lukela (1972–1980)
.... Herman Wedemeyer

Att. Gen. Walter Stewart (1968–1969)
.... Morgan White
Att. Gen. John Manicote (1972–1977)
.... Glenn Cannon
James "Kimo" Carew (1979–1980)
.... William Smith
Truck Kealoha (1979–1980)........ Moe Keale
Lori Wilson (1979–1980) ...... Sharon Farrell

Though based in the Iolani Palace in downtown
Honolulu, the men of Hawaii's Five-O group were
not members of the Honolulu Police Department.
They worked instead as part of the Hawaiian
State Police and were accountable directly to the
governor. Stolid, unemotional Steve McGarrett
was the head of Five-O, and worked with his own
men and the local police in solving various individual crimes and fighting the organized forces of
the Hawaiian underworld. Most hated of all the
evil men in the islands was the criminal genius
Wo Fat (played by Khigh Dhiegh). He would pop
up periodically to make life difficult for McGarrett, who was bound and determined to put him in
jail. Though Steve did manage to interfere with
Wo Fat's illegal operations, he couldn't piece together sufficient evidence to bring him to court.

Hawaii Five-O was filmed entirely on location
and it may well have been the beautiful scenery
as well as the action and adventure that made it
so popular. Whatever the causes, *Hawaii Five-O*
was immensely successful. It was the longest continuously running police show in the history of
television. Surprisingly, there was very little turnover among the leads. Steve did have several
secretaries—May being replaced by Jenny, with
Luana turning up later, and one of his assistants,
Kono, left after four seasons, but for most of the
cast the working conditions in Hawaii were too
pleasant to give up. After ten seasons, however,
Kam Fong tired of the role of Chin Ho Kelly and
was written out of the show by having his character killed in the final episode of the 1977–1978
season.

At the end of the following season, James
MacArthur decided he had enough of playing
McGarrett's top assistant, Danny "Danno" Williams, and he too left *Hawaii Five-O.* That fall
three new members were added to the Five-O
team, including former policewoman Lori Wilson.
The ratings were falling, and the infusion of new
people didn't help. It became obvious to all that
this would be *Hawaii Five-O*'s last season. Near
the end of the run, on April 5, 1980, McGarrett's
most bitter enemy was finally brought to justice.
Disguised as a scientist, McGarrett sprung a trap
that sent Wo Fat, seen for the first time in five
years, to jail.

The Iolani Palace, which in this series was the
seat of the Hawaiian government, had at one
time housed the Hawaiian Legislature. That time
was long gone, however, as it had been a museum for many years prior to the start of *Hawaii
Five-O.*

Reruns from the last season's episodes aired under the title *McGarrett* on *CBS Late Night*.

HAWAIIAN EYE
Detective Drama
FIRST TELECAST: *October 7, 1959*
LAST TELECAST: *September 10, 1963*
BROADCAST HISTORY:
Oct 1959–Sep 1962, ABC Wed 9:00–10:00
Oct 1962–Sep 1963, ABC Tue 8:30–9:30
CAST:

Tom Lopaka .... Bob Conrad
Tracy Stele (1959–1962) ...... Anthony Eisley
Cricket Blake .... Connie Stevens
Kazuo Kim .... Poncie Ponce
Greg MacKenzie (1960–1963)
   .... Grant Williams
Quon (1960–1963) .... Mel Prestidge
Moke (1960–1963) .... Doug Mossman
Philip Barton (1962–1963) ..... Troy Donahue

Hawaiian Eye has been called "*77 Sunset Strip* played in Hawaii." There certainly were similarities. Both shows were produced by the same studio (Warner Brothers), both featured two handsome, free-swinging young detectives as alternate leads, both had simple melodramatic plots set against glamorous backgrounds, and both made use of nutty sidekicks for comic relief.

Base of operations for Tom Lopaka and Tracy Stele was a swank, poolside office at the Hawaiian Village Hotel. Their sidekicks were a pert, somewhat addled young singer-photographer named Cricket, and a colorful cabbie named Kim. Kim, the operator of a one-man taxi service, was especially helpful as he had seemingly dozens of relatives scattered around the islands ready to help out if one of his employers needed some local assistance. Kim's trademarks were his *pupule* ("crazy") straw hat, dumb jokes, and ukulele.

A new detective named Greg MacKenzie arrived in December 1960, while Philip Barton joined the cast of characters in 1962 as the hotel's social director. Quon was the contact on the Honolulu police force. Fellow gumshoe Stu Bailey of *77 Sunset Strip* made an occasional visit from the mainland, possibly to get a closer look at some of the beautiful girls who peopled every *Hawaiian Eye* plot. But then he had beautiful girls in his series, too.

HAWAIIAN HEAT
Police Drama
FIRST TELECAST: *September 14, 1984*
LAST TELECAST: *December 21, 1984*
BROADCAST HISTORY:
Sep 1984–Dec 1984, ABC Fri 9:00–10:00
CAST:

Andy Senkowski .... Jeff McCracken
Mac Riley .... Robert Ginty
Irene Gorley .... Tracy Scoggins
Maj. Taro Oshira .... Mako
Harker .... Branscombe Richmond

Talk about a change of scenery! Andy and Mac were two street cops from Chicago who, fed up with the weather and the frustrations of their jobs, moved to sun-drenched Hawaii—no more snow, no more city grime, no more sleazy street criminals to chase. And what did they get with the move? Sand, surf, beaches full of well-filled bikinis, and jobs working as undercover detectives for the friendly Honolulu police.

The two cops were a study in contrasts. Mac was brash, impulsive, and pugnacious, while Andy was introspective and cautious. They were assigned to cases ranging from murder, to smuggling, to underworld drug trafficking. Their boss, police Maj. Oshiro, had his misgivings about the two young *haoles* (mainlanders), but they did seem to get the job done. The living arrangements weren't too bad either, as they shared a beach house with a number of bikini-clad beauties, including sexy helicopter pilot Irene Gorley.

HAWK
Police Drama
FIRST TELECAST: *September 8, 1966*
LAST TELECAST: *August 11, 1976*
BROADCAST HISTORY:
Sep 1966–Dec 1966, ABC Thu 10:00–11:00
Apr 1976–Aug 1976, NBC Wed 10:00–11:00
CAST:

Lt. John Hawk .... Burt Reynolds
Det. Dan Carter .... Wayne Grice
Asst. D.A. Murray Slaken ..... Bruce Glover
Asst. D.A. Ed Gorton .... Leon Janney

Hawk was a police story with a twist. John Hawk was a full-blooded Iroquois Indian working the night beat for the New York District Attorney's Office with his partner Det. Carter. Filmed on location in and around New York City at night, the cases in which he was involved sent him to the rich and the poor, from the exclusive penthouses along Park Avenue to the run-down tenements of the West Side. The star of this series, Burt Reynolds, was himself part Indian. *Hawk* was originally aired by ABC in the fall of 1966. Almost a decade later, hoping to capitalize on Burt Reynolds' later development into a celebrity, NBC aired reruns of the ABC series during the summer of 1976 (as CBS had done with *Dan August*, another ABC series in which Reynolds had starred).

HAWKINS
Law Drama
FIRST TELECAST: *October 2, 1973*
LAST TELECAST: *September 3, 1974*
BROADCAST HISTORY:
Oct 1973–Sep 1974, CBS Tue 9:30–11:00
CAST:

Billy Jim Hawkins .... James Stewart
R. J. Hawkins .... Strother Martin

Billy Jim Hawkins had given up his position as a deputy district attorney to enter private legal practice in rural West Virginia. His small-town location did not keep fancy clients away, however, as his fame as a specialist in murder cases attracted clients from far and wide. His pleasant, slow-talking, homespun qualities belied the shrewd, determined attorney that he really was, and he often traveled great distances with his cousin and investigative assistant R.J. in search of evidence that would clear his clients of guilt and lead to the apprehension of the real culprits.

Hawkins was one of the three rotating elements that filled the 9:30–11 P.M. time slot on Tuesday nights for CBS during the 1973–1974 season. The other two were *Shaft* and *The New CBS Tuesday Night Movies.*

HAWKINS FALLS, POPULATION 6,200
Comedy/Drama
FIRST TELECAST: *June 17, 1950*
LAST TELECAST: *October 12, 1950*
BROADCAST HISTORY:
    June 1950–Aug 1950, NBC Sat 8:00–9:00
    Aug 1950–Oct 1950, NBC Thu 8:30–9:00
CAST:
    Clate Weathers .... Frank Dane
    The Judge .... Phil Lord
    Laif Flaigle .... Win Stracke
    Mrs. Catherwood .... Hope Summers

This series, which later became a straight-forward daytime soap opera, began as a prime-time summer replacement show containing an odd mixture of situation comedy, light drama, and musical entertainment. The setting was the "typical" small town of Hawkins Falls, U.S.A. (patterned after real-life Woodstock, Illinois). The format called for the local newspaper editor, Clate Weathers, to describe the latest events in town, which were then dramatized. Each weekly episode was complete in itself; for example, the uproar when the town loafer (Laif) was put forward as a candidate for mayor, and the events surrounding a typical country auction. Mrs. Catherwood was the president of the garden club.

Hawkins Falls returned to the air in April 1951, as a Monday–Friday daytime serial, retaining many of the same cast members. The daytime version lasted until July 1955.

HAYLOFT HOEDOWN
Country Music
FIRST TELECAST: *July 10, 1948*
LAST TELECAST: *September 18, 1948*
BROADCAST HISTORY:
    Jul 1948–Sep 1948, ABC Sat 9:30–10:00
REGULARS:
    Elmer Newman
    Jack Day
    Murray Sisters
    Jesse Rogers
    Stuff Jumpers
    Wesley Tuttle

Ranch Square Dancers
The Sleepy Hollow Gang (instrumental)

One of the earliest examples of country music on network television, and one of ABC's first series, was this bush-league production from Town Hall in Philadelphia, telecast on Saturday nights during the summer of 1948. The talent was little known even in the country field, but everyone pitched in with enthusiasm with square dancing, yodeling, comedy routines, and the like. Emcee Elmer Newman doubled as "Pancake Pete."

The program had been a radio favorite for several years, beginning on Philadelphia's WFIL in December 1944, and moving to the ABC radio network in 1945.

HAYRIDE
see *Grand Ole Opry*

HAZEL
Situation Comedy
FIRST TELECAST: *September 28, 1961*
LAST TELECAST: *September 5, 1966*
BROADCAST HISTORY:
    Sep 1961–Jul 1964, NBC Thu 9:30–10:00 (OS)
    Sep 1964–Sep 1965, NBC Thu 9:30–10:00
    Sep 1965–Sep 1966, CBS Mon 9:30–10:00
CAST:
    Hazel Burke .... Shirley Booth
    George Baxter (1961–1965) ...... Don DeFore
    Dorothy Baxter (1961–1965) ... Whitney Blake
    Rosie .... Maudie Prickett
    Harvey Griffin .... Howard Smith
    Harold Baxter .... Bobby Buntrock
    Harriet Johnson (1961–1965)... Norma Varden
    Herbert Johnson (1961–1965) .. Donald Foster
    Deidre Thompson (1961–1965)... Cathy Lewis
    Harry Thompson (1961–1965).. Robert P. Lieb
    Mona Williams (1965–1966).... Mala Powers
    Millie Ballard (1965–1966) .... Ann Jillian
    Steve Baxter (1965–1966) .... Ray Fulmer
    Barbara Baxter (1965–1966)..... Lynn Borden
    Susie Baxter (1965–1966)...... Julia Benjamin

George Baxter was a highly successful corporation lawyer who was always in control of everything at the office, but of almost nothing at home. When he returned from the office at day's end, to his wife, Dorothy, and his young son, Harold, he entered the world of Hazel. Hazel was the maid/housekeeper who ran the Baxter household more efficiently than George ran his office. She was always right, knew exactly what needed doing, and preempted his authority with alarming, though justified, regularity. The Johnsons were the Baxters' nutty neighbors.

When this series moved to CBS in 1965, Hazel changed families. George and Dorothy had been "transferred" to the Middle East on an assignment leaving Hazel and son Harold to live with George's brother's family—which consisted of brother Steve, his wife Barbara, and daughter

Susie. Steve Baxter was a real-estate agent who had never understood why George had let Hazel take over his home. He soon found out.

Hazel was based on the *Saturday Evening Post* cartoons of Ted Key.

HAZEL BISHOP SHOW, THE
see *Freddy Martin Show, The*

HAZEL SCOTT
Music
FIRST TELECAST: *July 3, 1950*
LAST TELECAST: *September 29, 1950*
BROADCAST HISTORY:
Jul 1950–Sep 1950, DUM Mon/Wed/Fri 7:45–8:00
HOSTESS:
Hazel Scott

This summer music show was hosted by Trinidad-born singer and pianist Hazel Scott, who performed café favorites and show tunes. Miss Scott, a striking beauty who had appeared in nightclubs, on radio, and in a few movies and Broadway shows, was in private life the wife of New York Congressman Adam Clayton Powell, Jr. She also appeared on local television in New York for a time.

HE & SHE
Situation Comedy
FIRST TELECAST: *September 6, 1967*
LAST TELECAST: *September 11, 1970*
BROADCAST HISTORY:
Sep 1967–Sep 1968, CBS Wed 9:30–10:00
Jun 1970–Sep 1970, CBS Fri 8:00–8:30
CAST:
Paula Hollister .... Paula Prentiss
Dick Hollister .... Richard Benjamin
Oscar North .... Jack Cassidy
Harry Zarakardos............ Kenneth Mars
Andrew Hummel............ Hamilton Camp
Norman Nugent............... Harold Gould

Dick Hollister was a successful cartoonist whose creation, "Jetman," had been turned into a TV show starring Oscar North in the title role. Oscar was a bit on the arrogant, smug, egocentric side, and was constantly disagreeing with Dick about the proper interpretation of "Jetman." Paula, Dick's scatterbrained, social-worker wife, had problems of her own which always seemed to end up being shared by the two of them. Andrew Hummel was the fumbling superintendent of the New York apartment building in which Dick and Paula lived, and Harry was their fireman friend.

Paula Prentiss and Richard Benjamin were husband and wife in real life. Reruns of this series, which bore more than a passing resemblance to the classic *Dick Van Dyke Show,* were aired by CBS in the summer of 1970.

HEAD OF THE CLASS
Situation Comedy

FIRST TELECAST: *September 17, 1986*
LAST TELECAST:
BROADCAST HISTORY:
Sep 1986–Feb 1987, ABC Wed 8:30–9:00
Apr 1987–   , ABC Wed 8:30–9:00
CAST:
Charlie Moore .... Howard Hesseman
Dr. Harold Samuels ..... William G. Schilling
Bernadette Meara......... Jeannetta Arnette
Arvid Engen................ Dan Frischman
Maria Borges................... Leslie Bega
Simone Foster .... Khrystyne Haje
Jawaharlal Choudhury .... Jory Husain
Eric Mardian .... Brian Robbins
Janice Lazarotto .... Tannis Vallely
Alan Pinkard .... Tony O'Dell
Darlene Merriman .... Robin Givens
Dennis Blunden.......... Daniel J. Schneider
Sarah Nevins.............. Kimberly Russell
*Lori Applebaum............. Marcia Christie

*Occasional

This popular comedy was the flipside of *Welcome Back, Kotter.* Instead of underachieving "sweathogs," its focus was the overachieving honors students at Manhattan's Monroe High School. They were so brainy, in fact, that most of their former teachers had just read books while they taught themselves. Enter substitute teacher Charlie Moore, who realized that while these kids were long on facts, they were painfully short on maturity, and could use a few lessons from "the Book of Life" before they faced the real world.

Dr. Samuels was the principal, wary of Charlie's disruption of academic routine but generally supportive; and Bernadette, the energetic assistant principal. The class included Arvid, the classic nerd with glasses, pocket slide rule, and polyester pants; Maria, so driven that when she got a "B" she grounded herself; Simone, the poet; Jawaharlal, the word-mangling exchange student; Eric, the "cool dude" who hated being so smart that he was put with the geeks; Janice, a 12-year-old genius who hasn't had time to grow up; Alan the proto-yuppie; Darlene, the uptown rich girl; and Dennis, the chunky chemistry whiz who was overly fond of pizza.

HEADLINE
syndicated title for *Big Town*

HEADLINE CLUES
see *Broadway to Hollywood—Headline Clues*

HEADLINERS WITH DAVID FROST
Talk/Interview
FIRST TELECAST: *May 31, 1978*
LAST TELECAST: *July 5, 1978*
BROADCAST HISTORY:
May 1978–Jul 1978, NBC Wed 9:00–10:00
REGULARS:
David Frost

Liz Smith
Kelly Garrett

Celebrity interviewer David Frost hosted this 1978 summer series, which originated live from the NBC studios in New York. Those interviewed were generally show-business stars, with a few political figures thrown in, making the format an odd combination of superficial and serious subjects. Guests on the first show, for example, were the rock group the Bee Gees, actor John Travolta, and former C.I.A. chief Richard Helms. An additional feature was Headliners Forum, where Frost would pose a question such as "What is the secret of a happy marriage," and a succession of show business, literary, and political figures would be seen (on tape) giving short, humorous answers. Liz Smith contributed a weekly gossip segment and Kelly Garrett sang of recent events in a "That Was the Week That Was" segment.

HEADMASTER, THE
Drama
FIRST TELECAST: *September 18, 1970*
LAST TELECAST: *September 10, 1971*
BROADCAST HISTORY:
Sep 1970–Jan 1971, CBS Fri 8:30–9:00
Jun 1971–Sep 1971, CBS Fri 8:30–9:00
CAST:
Andy Thompson .... Andy Griffith
Jerry Brownell.............. Jerry Van Dyke
Mr. Purdy .... Parker Fennelly
Margaret Thompson........ Claudette Nevins
Judy .... Lani O'Grady
THEME:
"Only a Man," by Gordon and Williams

Andy Thompson was the headmaster of the Concord School, a private high school with high academic standards. His wife was one of the school's English teachers and his best friend, Jerry Brownell, was the physical-education teacher and coach. Andy's professional life at the school, dealing with the problems of teachers and students, provided the central focus of this folksy series.

Andy Griffith's past television success had been in a very different, country-boy role, and the viewing public did not accept him in this more dignified dramatic setting. In January 1971 he tried to revert to his earlier type of portrayal on a series called *The New Andy Griffith Show*, but that too proved unsuccessful and reruns of *The Headmaster* returned to the time slot in June.

HEART OF THE CITY
Police Drama
FIRST TELECAST: *September 20, 1986*
LAST TELECAST: *July 2, 1987*
BROADCAST HISTORY:
Sep 1986–Jan 1987, ABC Sat 9:00–10:00
Jun 1987–Jul 1987, ABC Thu 9:00–10:00

CAST:
Det. Wes Kennedy .... Robert Desiderio
Robin Kennedy (age 15) . Christina Applegate
Kevin Kennedy (16) .... Jonathan Ward
Lt. Ed Van Duzer .... Dick Anthony Williams
Det. Rick Arno................. Kario Salem
Sgt. Luke Halui ...... Branscombe Richmond
Det. Stanley .... Robert Alan Browne

Det. Wes Kennedy was a cop with problems. His wife had been murdered by a crazed killer, leaving Wes with recurrent flashbacks of the grisly event as well as with two teenagers to raise— Robin, a sullen, rebellious girl who blamed him for her mother's death, and Kevin, a better-adjusted youth who was mostly interested in girls. Wes had transferred from the L.A.P.D.'s S.W.A.T. team to the night shift in order to have more time for his son and daughter, but his coworkers—especially Lt. Van Duzer—sometimes had little patience for his family problems, like bailing the kids out of jail.

HEART OF THE CITY
syndicated title for *Big Town*

HEARTBEAT
Medical Drama
FIRST TELECAST: *March 23, 1988*
LAST TELECAST:
BROADCAST HISTORY:
Mar 1988–Apr 1988, ABC Wed 10:00–11:00
Apr 1988, ABC Thu 10:00–11:00
CAST:
Dr. Joanne Springsteen .... Kate Mulgrew
Dr. Eve Autrey .... Laura Johnson
Dr. Leo Rosetti .... Ben Masters
Dr. Stan Gorshalk................ Ray Baker
Priscilla Gorshalk........ Katherine Cannon
Dr. Cory Banks .... Lynn Whitfield
Nurse Marilyn McGrath..... Gail Strickland
Dr. Paul Jared .... Darrell Larson
Receptionist Robin Flowers
.... Claudette Sutherland
Caroline Petrie .... Shanna Reed

Feminism met the TV doctor show met soap opera in this 1988 series. Women's Medical Arts was a new clinic founded by Doctors Joanne and Eve, who believed that women should chart their own direction in the traditionally male-dominated world of medicine. They emphasized women treating women (though there were men on their staff), and an unintimidating relationship between patient and doctor. At WMA, patients were encouraged to call physicians by their first names ("Don't I call her 'doctor'?" "Not around here ... it's too much of a barrier between patient and doctor").

Dr. Springsteen ... er, Joanne ... was a gynecologist and the driving force behind WMA; Eve, a surgeon; Leo, a handsome pediatrician and Joanne's love interest; Stan, a worried psychiatrist; Cory, a young black doctor and mother of two; and Paul, the group's fertility specialist. Their battles were fought in the clinic, at male-dominated Bay General Hospital, with which they were affiliated, and sometimes in the bedroom.

HEAVEN FOR BETSY
Situation Comedy
FIRST TELECAST: *September 30, 1952*
LAST TELECAST: *December 23, 1952*
BROADCAST HISTORY:
Sep 1952–Dec 1952, CBS Tue/Thu 7:45–8:00
CAST:
Pete Bell . . . . Jack Lemmon
Betsy Bell . . . . Cynthia Stone

This early live domestic comedy starred real-life newlyweds Jack Lemmon and Cynthia Stone as Pete and Betsy Bell, newlyweds who were adjusting to married life. Pete was assistant buyer in the toy department of a suburban New York department store. His biggest problem was a tendency to jump into a situation before realizing its ramifications. His wife, Betsy, a secretary turned full-time homemaker, was not really occupied maintaining their two-room apartment, but had plenty to do getting Pete out of various scrapes. Lemmon and Stone worked together in several TV series in the early 1950s, before he began his highly successful movie career in 1954.

HEC RAMSEY
Western
FIRST TELECAST: *October 8, 1972*
LAST TELECAST: *August 25, 1974*
BROADCAST HISTORY:
Oct 1972–Aug 1974, NBC Sun 8:30–10:00
CAST:
Hec Ramsey . . . . Richard Boone
Sheriff Oliver B. Stamp . . . . Richard Lenz
Doc Amos Coogan . . . . Harry Morgan
Arne Tornquist . . . . Dennis Rucker

Hec Ramsey was a grizzled old gunfighter, living around the turn of the century, who had become interested in the "newfangled" science of criminology and spent years learning all he could about it. He still carried a gun, but had come to rely on a trunk full of paraphernalia that included finger-printing equipment, magnifying glasses, scales, and other odds and ends to track down culprits. As the series began Hec arrived in New Prospect, Oklahoma, to take a job as deputy sheriff. He soon discovered that the sheriff, Oliver B. Stamp, was very young and inexperienced. Stamp, fearing that Hec's legendary "fast gun" would attract trouble, was uncertain about his new partner, but young sheriff and old deputy eventually learned to make good use of Hec's novel methods.

Hec Ramsey spent two seasons as one of the four rotating elements of the *NBC Sunday Mystery Movie*. The other three elements were *Columbo, McCloud,* and *McMillan and Wife.*

HEE HAW
Variety
FIRST TELECAST: *June 15, 1969*
LAST TELECAST: *July 13, 1971*
BROADCAST HISTORY:
Jun 1969–Sep 1969, CBS Sun 9:00–10:00
Dec 1969–Jun 1970, CBS Wed 7:30–8:30
Sep 1970–Jul 1971, CBS Tue 8:30–9:30
(Syndicated since 1971)
HOSTS:
Roy Clark
Alvis Edgar "Buck" Owens (1969–1986)
ORIGINAL REGULARS (1969):
Cathy Baker
Jennifer Bishop (1969–1971)
Archie Campbell (1969–1987)
Jim Hager (1969–1986)
Jon Hager (1969–1986)
Don Harron (1969–1986)
Gunilla Hutton
Louis M. "Grandpa" Jones (1969–1987)
Claude "Jackie" Phelps (1969–1986)
Don Rich (1969–1975)
Jimmy Riddle (1969–1983)
Jeannine Riley (1969–1971)
Alvin "Junior" Samples (1969–1984)
Diana Scott (1969–1970)
Lulu Roman
Stringbean (a.k.a. David Akeman) (1969–1974)
Gordie Tapp
Mary Taylor (1969–1970)
Sheb Wooley (1969)
The Buckaroos (1969–1986)
The Hee Haw Band
The Nashville Edition
LATER REGULARS (IN ORDER THEY JOINED):
Minnie Pearl (1970–   )
Lisa Todd (1970–1986)
Barbi Benton (1971–1976)
Sherry Miles (1971–1972)
Ray Sanders (1971–1972)
Harry Cole (1972–1976)
George Lindsey (1972–   )
Ann Randall (1972–1973)
Marianne Gordon Rogers (1972–   )
Misty Rowe (1972–   )
Gailard Sartain (1972–   )
Roni Stoneman (1973–   )
Kenny Price (1974–   )
John Henry Faulk (1975–1982)
Buck Trent (1975–1982)
Charlie McCoy (1976–   )
Linda Thompson (1977–   )
Mackenzie Colt (1978–1982)
Rev. Grady Nutt (1979–1983)
Roy Acuff (1980–1985)
Victoria Hallman (1980–   )
Rodney Lay (1980–1987)
The Wild West & Fanci (1980–   )
Diana Goodman (1981–1985)
Slim Pickens (1981–1983)
Chase Randolph (1981–1982)
Nancy Taylor (1981–1982)

Jonathan Winters (1983–1984)
Kelly Billingsley (1984–1987)
Irlene Mandrell (1984–   )
Jeff Smith (1984–   )
Jackie Waddell (1984–1987)
Patricia McKinnon (1985–1986)
Dub Taylor (1985–   )
Mike Snyder (1987–   )

Hee Haw was country music's answer to *Rowan & Martin's Laugh-In*. Blackouts, nutty running gags, cameos by assorted guest stars, and some of the worst "corny" one-liners imaginable, appropriately delivered from a cornfield, all contributed to the mix. An animated donkey was used on a regular basis to react to the humor, and to provide the "hee haw" of the title.

Although the humor was purposely cornball, the music on *Hee Haw* was first-rate country material. Co-hosts Buck Owens and Roy Clark were both major country stars, Clark being one of the best banjoist-guitarists in the business. Other big names from the country field, both current and long-established, were also featured regularly. *Hee Haw* was in the top 20 nationally when it was dropped from the network in 1971, a victim of CBS' decision to "de-ruralize" its programming (national advertisers want only young, urban audiences). Like Lawrence Welk, which was dropped by ABC for similar reasons, it promptly went into syndication with all-new shows and has been a major hit ever since on a non-network basis. When co-host Buck Owens left the show after the 1985–1986 season he was not replaced. Instead, a policy of having Roy Clark joined by weekly guest co-hosts was instituted.

HEE HAW HONEYS
Comedy Variety
BROADCAST HISTORY:
Syndicated only
30 minutes
Produced: *1978–1979* (26 episodes)
Released: *September 1978*
CAST:
Kathie Honey........... Kathie Lee Johnson
Misty Honey .... Misty Rowe
Willie Billie Honey .... Gailard Sartain
Lulu Honey.................... Lulu Roman
Kenny Honey.................. Kenny Price

In this spin-off from *Hee Haw,* five members of that show's cast appeared as operators of the Hee Haw Honeys Club, a Nashville nightspot. Lulu and Kenny Honey were the parents of good ole boy Willie, sexy Misty, and cute Kathie. The setting was little more than an excuse for a cornball variety show, along the lines of *Hee Haw* itself, with rustic jokes and country music performed by such guests as Loretta Lynn, the Oak Ridge Boys, Conway Twitty, and the Statler Brothers.

HELEN O'CONNELL SHOW, THE
Music
FIRST TELECAST: *May 29, 1957*
LAST TELECAST: *September 6, 1957*
BROADCAST HISTORY:
May 1957–Sep 1957, NBC Wed/Fri 7:30–7:45
REGULAR:
Helen O'Connell

Big-band singer Helen O'Connell was on the air twice a week with this live musical show that occupied the remainder of the half-hour in which NBC telecast its network news program. The show originated from New York and gave Miss O'Connell the opportunity to sing several songs, occasionally with a guest star but more often without.

HELEN REDDY SHOW, THE
Musical Variety
FIRST TELECAST: *June 28, 1973*
LAST TELECAST: *August 16, 1973*
BROADCAST HISTORY:
Jun 1973–Aug 1973, NBC Thu 8:00–9:00
REGULARS:
Helen Reddy
The Jaime Rogers Dancers
Nelson Riddle and His Orchestra
THEME:
"I Am Woman," by Helen Reddy (lyrics) and Ray Burton (music)

Australian singer Helen Reddy, who became something of a symbol of the Women's Liberation movement through her best-selling recording "I Am Woman" ("I am strong, I am invincible . . ."), was the star of this 1973 summer series. The format of the show included comedy skits and musical numbers with guest stars. Each show closed with a question-and-answer session, with the questions coming from members of the studio audience.

HELL TOWN
Drama
FIRST TELECAST: *September 4, 1985*
LAST TELECAST: *December 25, 1985*
BROADCAST HISTORY:
Sep 1985–Dec 1985, NBC Wed 9:00–10:00
CAST:
Father Noah "Hardstep" Rivers
 .... Robert Blake
One Ball .... Whitman Mayo
Lawyer Sam..................... Jeff Corey
Mother Maggie .... Natalie Core
Sister Indigo................ Vonetta McGee
Sister Angel Cake............ Isabel Grandin
Stump.......................... Tony Longo
Sister Daisy .... Rhonda Dodson
Crazy Horse.................. Zitto Kazann
Poco Loco .... Eddie Quillan

"If I ever catch you down here sellin' garbage," the burly priest shouted at the startled drug dealer, "I'll tear your arms out." Ahem. "Are you really a priest?" he was later asked. "Why, soitanly. On Sunday, I even wear a dress. Come inta'da church and see."

Father Hardstep was *Baretta* as a priest. Sleeves rolled up, shooting pool, mangling the English language, he was surely the most unusual clergyman seen on TV, but one dedicated to bringing a little hope into the impoverished East Los Angeles parish of St. Dominic's. Hardstep was an ex-con, and a perfect choice for such a tough neighborhood. He had grown up there and knew all of the petty crooks, gangs, and others who preyed on the honest parishioners. Helping out with legal matters (Hardstep was often short of funds, or trying to bend the rules a bit) was Sam, a retired lawyer. One Ball, Stump, and Crazy Horse aided him when more physical assistance was needed. But it was "Father Brassknuckles" himself who laid down the law: "In Hell Town, nobody kills nobody for no reason. Nobody dies in Hell Town, unless it's from old age."

HELLO, LARRY

Situation Comedy
FIRST TELECAST: *January 26, 1979*
LAST TELECAST: *April 30, 1980*
BROADCAST HISTORY:
Jan 1979–Feb 1979, NBC Fri 9:30–10:00
Feb 1979–Aug 1979, NBC Fri 8:30–9:00
Oct 1979, NBC Fri 8:30–9:00
Oct 1979–Apr 1980, NBC Wed 9:30–10:00
CAST:

Larry Alder	McLean Stevenson
Diane Alder (1979)	Donna Wilkes
Diane Alder (1979–1980)	Krista Errickson
Ruthie Alder	Kim Richards
Morgan Winslow	Joanna Gleason
Earl	George Memmoli
Meadowlark Lemon	Himself
Tommy Roscini	John Femia
Henry Alder (1980)	Fred Stuthman
Leona Wilson	Ruth Brown

Following the breakup of his marriage, radio talk-show host Larry Alder moved from Los Angeles to Portland, Oregon, to get a fresh start. He landed a job at radio station KLOW, where Morgan Winslow became the producer of his phone-in talk show. Earl was Larry's obese engineer. Larry had been given custody of his two daughters, 13-year-old Ruthie and 16-year-old Diane. Glib and in total control on the air, he was much less sure of himself at home as the single parent of two maturing girls. Leona, a schoolteacher and neighbor, tried to bring a little of the woman's touch to this chaotic household. Larry's ex-wife Marion (Shelley Fabares) also turned up occasionally. Added to the regular cast in the fall of 1979 were former Harlem Globetrotters basketball star Meadowlark Lemon, playing himself as owner of a sporting goods store, and Tommy, a 14-year-old neighbor. In February 1980 Larry's retired father, Henry, also moved in.

Hello, Larry's time slot on the NBC schedule was right after the much more popular *Diff'rent Strokes*. Since both shows were produced by Tandem Productions, and *Larry* needed a boost, it was established that Larry Alder and *Diff'rent Strokes'* Philip Drummond were old army buddies, and that Drummond's company had purchased the radio station where Larry worked. The producers hoped that by having the casts of the two shows appear together in crossover episodes the much larger *Diff'rent Strokes* audience would be attracted to *Hello, Larry.* It never happened.

HENNESEY

Comedy/Drama
FIRST TELECAST: *September 28, 1959*
LAST TELECAST: *September 17, 1962*
BROADCAST HISTORY:
Sep 1959–Sep 1962, CBS Mon 10:00–10:30 (OS)
CAST:

Charles J. "Chick" Hennesey	Jackie Cooper
Martha Hale	Abby Dalton
Capt. Walter Shafer	Roscoe Karns
Max Bronski	Henry Kulky
Harvey Spencer Blair III	James Komack
Seaman Shatz	Arte Johnson
Dr. Dan Wagner (1960–1962)	Herb Ellis
Dr. Owen King (1960)	Robert Gist
Pulaski (1960–1962)	Norman Alden
Mrs. Shafer	Meg Wyllie

Stationed at a naval base in San Diego, Lt. Chick Hennesey was a young medical officer who treated the base personnel and their families. He worked for crusty Capt. Shafer (who during the course of the series would be promoted to admiral), and had attractive Martha Hale for an understanding and romantically interested nurse. Their romance blossomed and they became engaged, with the wedding taking place in the episode that aired on May 7, 1962. The biggest "character" in the entire medical department was Harvey Spencer Blair III, a young naval dentist whose society background and financial independence grated on all concerned. Blair was always looking for angles and gimmicks, much in the style of Ernie Bilko in *The Phil Silvers Show* but, unlike Bilko, fancied himself a real ladies' man.

HENNY AND ROCKY SHOW, THE

Comedy Variety
FIRST TELECAST: *June 1, 1955*
LAST TELECAST: *August 10, 1955*
BROADCAST HISTORY:
Jun 1955–Aug 1955, ABC Wed 10:45–11:00
REGULARS:
Rocky Graziano
Henny Youngman

Marion Colby
Bobby Hackett
Buddy Weed

Designed to fill the time slot between the end of *The Wednesday Night Fights* and the start of the eleven o'clock local news, *The Henny and Rocky Show* provided the singing of Marion Colby and the playing of a jazz combo featuring Bobby Hackett on trumpet and Buddy Weed on piano. Comedy was supplied by Henny Youngman and ex-middleweight boxing champion Rocky Graziano. Featured in the show was a recap of the night's fight and "Ribber's Digest" in which Henny satirized the current news. Henny left the show following the June 29 telecast and it was retitled *Rocky's Corner*.

HENRY MORGAN'S GREAT TALENT HUNT
Comedy Variety
FIRST TELECAST: *January 26, 1951*
LAST TELECAST: *June 1, 1951*
BROADCAST HISTORY:
  Jan 1951–Mar 1951, NBC Fri 9:00–9:30
  Mar 1951–Jun 1951, NBC Fri 9:30–10:00
REGULARS:
  Henry Morgan
  Dorothy Claire
  Kaye Ballard
  Dorothy Jarnac
  Arnold Stang (as "Gerard")
  Art Carney
  Pert Kelton

This program started as a satire on the *Original Amateur Hour*-type program with Henry Morgan introducing people with offbeat "talents"—a man who played the violin by picking the strings with his teeth, a girl who tap-danced while playing an instrument, a woman who had taught her dog to talk, etc. Arnold Stang was Henry's helper, supposedly tracking down all of the "talented" guests on the show. Morgan opened the show with a monologue and, after the acts had performed, the winner was chosen by the applause level of the studio audience. On April 20, 1951, the title of this live program was shortened to *The Henry Morgan Show* and the format changed. It became a comedy variety show with the emphasis on satiric comedy skits. Singer Dorothy Claire and dancer Dorothy Jarnac provided musical numbers between the skits.

HERALD PLAYHOUSE
  syndicated title for *Schlitz Playhouse of Stars*

HERB SHRINER SHOW, THE
Comedy Variety
FIRST TELECAST: *November 7, 1949*
LAST TELECAST: *December 4, 1956*
BROADCAST HISTORY:
  Nov 1949–Feb 1950, CBS Mon/Tue/Thu/Fri/Sat 7:55–8:00

  Oct 1951–Apr 1952, ABC Thu 9:00–9:30
  Oct 1956–Dec 1956, CBS Tue 9:00–9:30
REGULAR:
  Herb Shriner

Herb Shriner was a humorist who had become famous on radio in the late 1940s with his folksy monologues on rural life back home in Indiana, interspersed with harmonica solos. His homespun philosophy, and his disarming, ingenuous personality often led to comparisons with the late Will Rogers. During the 1948–1949 season Shriner had a Monday–Friday daytime show on CBS and in the fall of 1949 he moved into nighttime television with a five-a-week series of short monologues called *The Herb Shriner Show*. ABC brought him back in 1951 as the host of an evening half-hour entitled *Herb Shriner Time*. The longer format gave him a chance to play his harmonica and work in skits with guest stars, as well as deliver his tall tales. It was essentially this same format that was tried again in the fall of 1956 on CBS in *The Herb Shriner Show*.

HERBIE, THE LOVE BUG
Situation Comedy
FIRST TELECAST: *March 17, 1982*
LAST TELECAST: *April 14, 1982*
BROADCAST HISTORY:
  Mar 1982–Apr 1982, CBS Wed 8:00–9:00
CAST:
  Jim Douglas .... Dean Jones
  Susan MacLane.............. Patricia Harty
  Bo Phillips .... Richard Paul
  Julie MacLane .... Claudia Wells
  Robbie MacLane.......... Douglas Emerson
  Matthew MacLane.............. Nicky Katt
  Jason .... Bryan Utman
  Randy Bigelow .... Larry Linville
  Mrs. Bigelow .... Natalie Core

Herbie, a Volkswagen Beetle with a mind of its own, was the star of this lighthearted comedy series. Herbie had "adopted" its owner, Jim Douglas, and spent much of its time looking out for his welfare, including finding him an attractive young wife. Julie MacLane, a divorcée with three young children, was the chosen bride, discovered by Herbie and Jim when they thwarted a bank robbery in which she was being held hostage. Despite the efforts of her former boyfriend, Randy Bigelow, to disrupt her new romance, Jim prevailed and the two were married in the April 7 episode. Jim ran a driving school with help from easygoing Bo Phillips, but his limited income from this venture forced him also to teach driver education at a local high school.

Based on the *Love Bug* movies produced by Walt Disney Productions from 1969 to 1980, with Dean Jones reprising the role he had played in two of them—*The Love Bug* (1969) and *Herbie Goes to Monte Carlo* (1977).

HERE AND NOW

Documentary

FIRST TELECAST: *September 29, 1961*
LAST TELECAST: *December 29, 1961*
BROADCAST HISTORY:

Sep 1961–Dec 1961, NBC Fri 10:30–11:00
HOST:

Frank McGee

Frank McGee narrated the three or four stories that were covered in each telecast of this magazine-format news program. The subjects were people involved in major news stories in varied areas ranging from politics to medicine to the arts. Emphasis was placed on how the people involved were affected by the news events, not simply upon the events themselves.

HERE COME THE BRIDES

Comedy Adventure

FIRST TELECAST: *September 25, 1968*
LAST TELECAST: *September 18, 1970*
BROADCAST HISTORY:

Sep 1968–Sep 1969, ABC Wed 7:30–8:30
Sep 1969–Sep 1970, ABC Fri 9:00–10:00
CAST:

Jason Bolt .... Robert Brown
Jeremy Bolt................. Bobby Sherman
Joshua Bolt...................... David Soul
Lottie Hatfield .... Joan Blondell
Candy Pruitt................. Bridget Hanley
Aaron Stempel................ Mark Lenard
Big Swede..................... Bo Svensen
Biddie Cloom................ Susan Tolsky
Capt. Charley Clancey ...... Henry Beckman
Miss Essie Gillis................ Mitzi Hoag
Ben Jenkins .... Hoke Howell
Christopher Pruitt (1969–1970)..... Eric Chase
Molly Pruitt (1969–1970) .... Patti Cohoon

THEME:

"Seattle," by Jack Keller, Hugo Montenegro, and Ernie Sheldon

Comedy-adventure set in boomtown Seattle (pop. 152) in the 1870s. Logging camp operator Jason Bolt and his young brothers Jeremy and Joshua were in danger of losing their timberland, at Bridal Veil Mountain, because their men were in near revolt—over the lack of women in Seattle. Jason contrived an ingenious scheme. Using funds borrowed from rival saw-mill operator Aaron Stempel, he sailed back to New Bedford, Massachusetts, and persuaded 100 prospective brides to return with him to the frontier. The girls, led by "straw boss" Candy Pruitt, returned with Jason aboard Capt. Clancey's decrepit ship, and Seattle was never the same again.

There was a catch, however. If any of the 100 girls left before a year was up, Jason would forfeit his land to Stempel. It was quite a year, but Jason won his wager.

Bobby Sherman and David Soul were both looked on as promising young singers when

Brides was cast. Boosted by exposure on the series, Sherman went on to become a highly popular recording star beginning in 1969, and subsequently appeared in other TV series (see Index). Blond-haired David Soul, who had his first regular TV exposure as the hooded "mystery singer" on *The Merv Griffin Show* from 1966–1967, later became Hutch on the enormously popular *Starsky and Hutch*. He also married (in real life) one of the "brides" he met on this series' set, actress Karen Carlson.

HERE WE GO AGAIN

Situation Comedy

FIRST TELECAST: *January 20, 1973*
LAST TELECAST: *June 16, 1973*
BROADCAST HISTORY:

Jan 1973–Jun 1973, ABC Sat 8:00–8:30
CAST:

Richard Evans............... Larry Hagman
Susan Evans.................... Diane Baker
Jerry Standish .... Dick Gautier
Judy Evans .... Nita Talbot
Jeff......................... Chris Beaumont
Cindy .... Leslie Graves
Jan........................... Kim Richards

Divorce-as-comedy; the trials of a newly married couple whose former mates lived nearby, and kept intruding on their connubial bliss. Susan's first husband was Jerry Standish, a free-swinging restauranteur, owner of Jerry's Polynesian Paradise. Richard's ex-wife was Judy, a rather domineering magazine editor. Adding to the general confusion were the children, Susan's two little girls, Cindy and Jan (who lived with the Evanses), and Richard's teenage son, Jeff (who lived with his mother, Judy).

HERE'S BOOMER

Adventure

FIRST TELECAST: *March 14, 1980*
LAST TELECAST: *August 14, 1982*
BROADCAST HISTORY:

Mar 1980–Aug 1980, NBC Fri 8:00–8:30
Sep 1981–Nov 1981, NBC Sun 7:30–8:00
Jul 1982–Aug 1982, NBC Sat 8:00–8:30
BOOMER'S TRAINERS:

Bryan Renfro and Ray Berwick

Boomer was television's answer to Benji. He was a mixed-breed little stray who had no owner, and who spent much of his time scrounging for food as he wandered from place to place. Boomer never stayed long in any one spot, but before he left he usually managed to solve somebody's problem. He saved two young campers from harm, helped a young aspiring jockey win his first race, broke up a ring of dognappers, and helped a little girl prove to adults that she was not mentally retarded, but simply suffering from a hearing impairment. Like Lassie and Rin Tin Tin before him, Boomer was an uncommonly intelligent dog.

Boomer was supposed to return in the fall of 1980 with a new wrinkle—viewers could hear what he was thinking via an off-screen voice. (Not so new, actually, as viewers in the 1950s could hear Jackie Cooper's basset hound on *The People's Choice* musing in much the same way.) Unfortunately Boomer couldn't talk network executives into renewing his series on a regular basis, and he was heard on only one episode, aired as a special on December 7, 1980. When more new episodes of *Here's Boomer* did surface on NBC during the 1981–1982 season, Boomer's thoughts were all his own again. You could watch him, but had no idea what he was thinking.

HERE'S EDIE
see *Edie Adams Show, The*

HERE'S LUCY
see *Lucy Show, The*

HERITAGE
Music and Art
FIRST TELECAST: *August 1, 1951*
LAST TELECAST: *September 5, 1951*
BROADCAST HISTORY:
    Aug 1951–Sep 1951, NBC Wed 8:00–9:00
HOST:
    Frank Blair

The National Gallery of Art in Washington, D.C., was the setting for this cultural series telecast live during the summer of 1951. The program consisted primarily of classical selections played by the 30-piece National Gallery Orchestra, with commentary by one of its members, pianist Rose d'Amore. During the first intermission, chief curator of the museum John Walker or a member of his staff discussed the paintings currently on exhibit, while the camera gave viewers a chance to see them. During the second intermission Miss d'Amore interviewed one of the composers whose work was being performed that night.

HERMAN HICKMAN SHOW, THE
Sports Commentary
FIRST TELECAST: *October 3, 1952*
LAST TELECAST: *March 27, 1953*
BROADCAST HISTORY:
    Oct 1952–Mar 1953, NBC Fri 7:00–7:15
REGULARS:
    Herman Hickman
    Rex Marshall

Herman Hickman was the star of this program which featured football predictions, reminiscences of his days as head football coach at Yale University, other stories in the sports vein, and an occasional poetic recitation. Actor Rex Marshall was a regular on the show and helped in its presentation. Sports and entertainment personalities served as guests, chatting with Herman on sports and other topics.

HERO, THE
Situation Comedy
FIRST TELECAST: *September 8, 1966*
LAST TELECAST: *January 5, 1967*
BROADCAST HISTORY:
    Sep 1966–Jan 1967, NBC Thu 9:30–10:00
CAST:
    Sam Garret................ Richard Mulligan
    Ruth Garret .... Mariette Hartley
    Paul Garret................... Bobby Horan
    Fred Gilman.................. Victor French
    Burton Gilman.................... Joey Baio
    Dewey .... Marc London

The real world and the make-believe world of television are two completely different things. That was the message of this unusual TV self-satire. Sam Garret was a hugely popular TV star with his own (fictional) Western series, *Jed Clayton—U.S. Marshal.* The real Sam differed somewhat from the coolly imperturbable hero of the TV screen, however. To his wife Ruth and his son Paul, as well as to their neighbors, the Gilmans, Sam was a nice guy who, among other things, was afraid of horses, allergic to sagebrush, and all thumbs when it came to any activity requiring coordination.

HE'S THE MAYOR
Situation Comedy
FIRST TELECAST: *January 10, 1986*
LAST TELECAST: *March 21, 1986*
BROADCAST HISTORY:
    Jan 1986–Mar 1986, ABC Fri 9:30–10:00
CAST:
    Mayor Carl Burke .... Kevin Hooks
    Alvin Burke .... Al Fann
    Wardell Halsey.......... Wesley Thompson
    Kelly Enright .... Margot Rose
    Councilman Nash .... David Graff
    Ivan Bronski.................. Stanley Brock
    Chief Walter Padget .... Pat Corley
    Paula Hendricks .... Mari Gorman

Fun and games at City Hall was the premise of this 1986 comedy. Mayor Carl Burke, a black, had been elected at age 25 and found running things a little more difficult than criticizing from the outside. His "kitchen cabinet" consisted of his father Alvin, who was the City Hall janitor, and best friend Wardell, hizzoner's chauffeur.

HEY JEANNIE
Situation Comedy
FIRST TELECAST: *September 8, 1956*
LAST TELECAST: *September 30, 1960*
BROADCAST HISTORY:
    Sep 1956–May 1957, CBS Sat 9:30–10:00
    Jun 1960–Sep 1960, ABC Thu 9:00–9:30
CAST:
    Jeannie MacLennan .... Jeannie Carson
    Al Murray................... Allen Jenkins
    Liz Murray .... Jane Dulo

Jeannie MacLennan was a sweet, naive young Scottish lass who had arrived in the United States with no job and no place to live. After clearing immigration (which evidently didn't mind her lack of employment) she went on a tour of New York with cabdriver Al Murray. For reasons he never fully understood, he offered to become her sponsor. Jeannie moved in with Al and his sister Liz, and then set about learning about her adopted country, its strange customs, and stranger people.

Three years after this filmed series ended its run on CBS it was brought back, in reruns, as an ABC summer series, under the title *The Jeannie Carson Show.*

HEY LANDLORD
Situation Comedy
FIRST TELECAST: *September 11, 1966*
LAST TELECAST: *May 14, 1967*
BROADCAST HISTORY:
    Sep 1966–May 1967, NBC Sun 8:30–9:00
CAST:
    Woody Banner .... Will Hutchins
    Chuck Hookstratten .... Sandy Baron
    Timothy Morgan .... Pamela Rodgers
    Kyoko Mitsui .... Miko Mayama
    Jack Ellenhorn .... Michael Constantine

Woody, the landlord in this comedy series, was not the usual bumbling old codger but a young, trusting Ohio lad fresh out of college, who had come to New York to find out more about life. His building, inherited from an uncle, was a brownstone in Manhattan's East 30s which was peopled with the usual assortment of lunatics generally found on TV comedies. Woody shared his own apartment with Chuck Hookstratten, an aspiring young comic who was born and raised in the city, and who was constantly amazed at Woody's blind faith in people. Woody planned to manage the building while living off the proceeds. Far from supporting him, however, he found that he had to go to work to support the brownstone—its condition and age caused constant and costly problems. Meanwhile his tenants, including photographer Jack, glamorous Timothy, and her roommate Kyoko, yelled, "Hey landlord!"

HEY MULLIGAN
    see *Mickey Rooney Show, The*

HIGH ADVENTURE WITH LOWELL THOMAS
Adventure/Travelogue
FIRST TELECAST: *June 16, 1964*
LAST TELECAST: *September 15, 1964*
BROADCAST HISTORY:
    Jun 1964–Sep 1964, CBS Tue 8:00–9:00
HOST:
    Lowell Thomas

This summer series was a collection of reruns of selected specials, telecast under the same title, that had originally aired in the late 1950s. Lowell Thomas—newsman, adventurer, and explorer—had led these filmed expeditions to remote and exotic locations around the world. Among them were a visit to the capital of Tibet, a tour through the casbah of Morocco, and an expedition to the Australian Outback.

HIGH CHAPARRAL, THE
Western
FIRST TELECAST: *September 10, 1967*
LAST TELECAST: *September 10, 1971*
BROADCAST HISTORY:
    Sep 1967–Sep 1968, NBC Sun 10:00–11:00
    Sep 1968–Dec 1970, NBC Fri 7:30–8:30
    Feb 1971–Sep 1971, NBC Fri 7:30–8:30
CAST:
    Big John Cannon .... Leif Erickson
    Buck Cannon .... Cameron Mitchell
    Billy Blue Cannon (1967–1970) ... Mark Slade
    Manolito Montoya .... Henry Darrow
    Victoria Cannon .... Linda Cristal
    Don Sebastian Montoya (1967–1970)
    .... Frank Silvera
    Sam Butler .... Don Collier
    Reno (1967–1970)............. Ted Markland
    Pedro (1967–1970) .... Roberto Contreras
    Joe............................ Robert Hoy
    Wind (1970–1971) .... Rudy Ramos

High Chaparral was the name given to the ranch owned and operated by the Cannon family in the Arizona Territory during the 1870s. Stubborn, determined Big John Cannon was the patriarch of the family, and his driving ambition to establish a flourishing cattle empire in the rugged, Indian-infested Arizona Territory was the thrust of the entire show. His younger brother Buck was a good-natured carouser who could outdrink, outshoot, outfight, and when properly motivated outwork any man alive—with the possible exception of his brother. John's son, Billy Blue, was a young man in his 20s whose mother was killed by an Apache arrow in the first episode of the series. After his first wife's death, Big John married Victoria, daughter of Don Sebastian Montoya and heiress to his extensive cattle holdings. Her brother Manolito accompanied her to the Cannon ranch and became a permanent member of the household. Sam was the foreman, while Reno, Pedro, and Joe were ranch hands.

The marriage of John and Victoria also united the Cannons and the Montoyas in their efforts to tame the land. Family differences, the conflicts between the Mexicans and the Americans, and the ever-present threats from rustlers and renegade Indians all provided material for the stories in this series.

A number of cast changes occurred in the program's last season. The character of Billy Blue Cannon was dropped. Frank Silvera, who played Victoria's father, had died and his character was written out of the show by having Don Sebastian also pass away. Added to the cast was Wind, a half-breed youth who became a member of the Cannon household after helping Big John avoid a major disaster during a roundup.

HIGH FINANCE
Quiz/Audience Participation
FIRST TELECAST: *July 7, 1956*
LAST TELECAST: *December 15, 1956*
BROADCAST HISTORY:
Jul 1956–Dec 1956, CBS Sat 10:30–11:00
EMCEE:
Dennis James

Contestants on *High Finance* were asked questions based on news items that had appeared in their local papers during the preceding week. Each contestant was given a cash stake to start with and then invested part of it on the assumption that he could answer the questions correctly. Correct answers yielded high returns and the money could be invested again and again until the contestant had achieved his desired objective. There were pitfalls involved and contestants could lose everything by not "investing" wisely. There were prizes available as well as cash, and the ultimate amount that any one contestant could win was set at $110,000. Nobody ever came within $50,000 of the upper limit but there were many winners in the $10,000–$25,000 range.

HIGH MOUNTAIN RANGERS
Adventure
FIRST TELECAST: *January 2, 1988*
LAST TELECAST: *July 9, 1988*
BROADCAST HISTORY:
Jan 1988–July 1988, CBS Sat 8:00–9:00
CAST:
Jesse Hawkes................ Robert Conrad
Matt Hawkes.............. Christian Conrad
Cody Hawkes .... Shane Conrad
Frank Avila (White Eagle)..... Tony Acierto
Robin Kelly .... P.A. Christian
Cutler........................ Russell Todd
Hart .... Eric Eugene Williams
Izzy Flowers................. Timothy Erwin
Jackie Hawkes.............. Robyn Peterson
Sheriff McBride.................. Med Flory

Three decades ago, Jesse Hawkes had formed a mountain rescue/service team called the High Mountain Rangers. Based in the foothills of the Sierra Nevada mountains near Lake Tahoe, the rangers used the latest in high-tech equipment, along with their knowledge of mountaineering and survival techniques, to protect the human residents and visitors, as well as the animal life that lived in the mountains.

Jesse was now semiretired, living with his teen-aged son Cody in a cabin high in the mountains. His older son Matt was running the operation, along with fellow rangers Robin, Cutler, Hart, full-blooded Shoshone Frank Avila, and Izzy the young apprentice. Matt kept in close contact with

his dad by short-wave radio—there were no phone lines that far up the mountains—and sought Jesse's advice and help when needed, which seemed to be every week. Jesse and his wife Jackie, a blackjack dealer at one of the casinos in South Lake Tahoe, had been separated for years, primarily because she was not interested in living the relatively isolated life-style that appealed to her husband.

High Mountain Rangers was a real family affair for star Robert Conrad. His two sons on the series were his real-life sons, his daughter Joan was the series' executive producer, and her husband, Timothy Erwin, had a featured role. Filmed on location in the Sierra Nevada mountains near Lake Tahoe.

HIGH PERFORMANCE
Adventure
FIRST TELECAST: *March 2, 1983*
LAST TELECAST: *March 23, 1983*
BROADCAST HISTORY:
Mar 1983, ABC Wed 8:00–9:00
CAST:
Brennan Flannery............. Mitchell Ryan
Kate Flannery .... Lisa Hartman
Shane Adams................. Rick Edwards
Blue Stratton .... Jack Scalia
Fletch...................... Jason Bernard

A trio of athletic young instructors at a school for chauffeur/bodyguards hired out for free-lance security and rescue missions in this action series. Using the Flannery School as their base, martial arts expert Kate, stunt driver Shane, and ex-military intelligence man Blue raced, parachuted, and helicoptered into adventures around the world. Their assignments came from Kate's father Brennan Flannery, and their high-tech gadgets from mechanical wizard Fletch.

HIGH ROAD, THE
see *John Gunther's High Road*

HIGHCLIFFE MANOR
Situation Comedy
FIRST TELECAST: *April 12, 1979*
LAST TELECAST: *May 3, 1979*
BROADCAST HISTORY:
Apr 1979–May 1979, NBC Tue 8:30–9:00
CAST:
Helen Blacke .... Shelley Fabares
Rev. Ian Glenville......... Stephen McHattie
Frances Kiskadden..... Eugenie Ross-Leming
Dr. Felix Morger............. Gerald Gordon
Wendy Sparkes............. Audrey Landers
Rebecca...................... Jenny O'Hara
Bram Shelley............ Christian Marlowe
Dr. Lester .... David Byrd
Dr. Sanchez .... Luis Avalos
Smythe...................... Ernie Hudson
Cheng...................... Harold Sakata

This short-lived comedy was a sendup of the old, Gothic horror tales. The setting was Highcliffe Manor, a huge stone mansion located on an island off the coast of Massachusetts. Helen Blacke had inherited the place, and controlling interest in the Blacke Foundation, when her husband died in an explosion in his laboratory. Despite the fact that everyone there seemed to be plotting her demise, Helen cheerily went about running Highcliffe, oblivious to all that was going on around her. Populating the manor was a collection of eccentrics, including Rev. Glenville, a girl-chasing clergyman from South Africa; Frances, a mad scientist working her evil magic on freshly stolen corpses; Felix, the former assistant to Helen's husband; Bram, an attractive Frankenstein monster created by Frances, with limbs lifted from an erector set and a virtually nonexistent memory; Cheng, Frances' gigantic servant; and Dr. Lester and Dr. Sanchez, two evil men trying to take over the Foundation. Wendy was the girl-next-door secretary who was romantically attracted to Rev. Glenville, and Rebecca was the eerie maid.

HIGH-LOW

Quiz/Audience Participation
FIRST TELECAST: *July 4, 1957*
LAST TELECAST: *September 19, 1957*
BROADCAST HISTORY:
  Jul 1957–Sep 1957, NBC Thu 9:30–10:00
EMCEE:
  Jack Barry
SEMI-REGULARS:
  Burl Ives
  John Van Doren
  Patricia Medina
  Walter Slezak
  Hank Bloomgarden

This live quiz show was the 1957 summer replacement for *The Ford Show*. Contestants pitted their knowledge against that of the members of the panel, which consisted of three celebrities each week. The contestant was in an isolation booth and both he and the panelists were asked the same multi-part question. First the panelists each indicated how many parts of the question they could answer. Then the contestant could either attempt to answer as many parts as the "high" panelist, and triple his money, or answer as many parts as the "low" panelist, and double his money. If he failed to answer as many parts as the chosen panel member, however, he lost all but 10 percent of his previous winnings.

HIGHWAY PATROL

Police Drama
BROADCAST HISTORY:
  Syndicated only
  30 minutes
  Produced: *1955–1959* (156 episodes)
  Released: *September 1955*

CAST:
  Chief Dan Matthews .... Broderick Crawford
NARRATOR:
  Art Gilmore

Beefy, gravel-voiced Broderick Crawford was the no-nonsense chief of the Highway Patrol in this action series, which was one of the most popular syndicated programs in television history (156 episodes were made, run, and rerun endlessly for years). The stories were stright crime dramas, with the chief and his uniformed officers nailing hijackers, smugglers, and robbers. In a typical episode a young newlywed couple were witnesses to a café holdup in which the proprietor was murdered. The Highway Patrol was at first stymied by their chief suspect's airtight alibi, but Matthews managed to get him in the end in a suspenseful chase, when the crook went after the couple who were the only witnesses to the crime. In another episode, a bank messenger absconded with $50,000 and took it home to his wife, only to have her slug him and make off with the loot herself. Chief Matthews put out an all-points bulletin and eventually nabbed them both.

Most of *Highway Patrol*'s action took place outdoors, on the sprawling highway system of an unidentified western state (those official-looking emblems on the police cars read simply "Highway Patrol"). There were lots of hardware—patrol cars, motorcycles, and occasional helicopters—and Chief Matthews was always leaning on the side of a car, microphone in hand, bellowing orders ("Ten-four, ten-four!"). There were no other regular characters in the long-running series, although actor William Boyett, later a regular on *Adam-12*, was seen frequently in various supporting roles.

HIGHWAY TO HEAVEN

Drama
FIRST TELECAST: *September 19, 1984*
LAST TELECAST:
BROADCAST HISTORY:
  Sep 1984–Mar 1988, NBC Wed 8:00–9:00
  Mar 1988–May 1988, NBC Wed 9:00–10:00
  *Jun 1988–   *, NBC Wed 8:00–9:00
CAST:
  Jonathan Smith .... Michael Landon
  Mark Gordon .... Victor French
EXECUTIVE PRODUCER/WRITER:
  Michael Landon

Jonathan was a probationary angel with a very unusual mission on earth—to bring a little love and understanding into the lives of people who were in trouble. Although he had angelic powers he seldom used them, preferring to rely on persuasion and example as he slipped into and out of the lives of children and old folks, rich people and poor. It might be a mother whose child was dying of cancer, a young black boxer being pressured to sabotage a fight, or a Vietnamese child facing prejudice in her new American hometown. Each of them learned a little about coping with life through love.

Jonathan traveled around the country as an itinerant laborer. His only companion was a burly ex-cop named Mark, who had been a bitter, defeated man until Jonathan helped turn him around. Now he wanted to help his newfound friend in his heavenly mission. Tender, emotional stories about the value of kindness in life dominated this series created by Michael Landon, but there was also room for a twinkle in the eye. A notable example of the latter was an October 1987 Halloween episode lampooning Landon's first, famous movie role in *I Was a Teenage Werewolf* (1957)—called, what else, "I Was a Middle-Aged Werewolf."

HIGHWAYMAN, THE
Adventure
FIRST TELECAST: *March 4, 1988*
LAST TELECAST: *May 6, 1988*
BROADCAST HISTORY:
Mar 1988–Apr 1988, NBC Fri 8:00–9:00
Apr 1988–May 1988, NBC Fri 9:00–10:00
CAST:
The Highwayman .... Sam Jones
Jetto .... Jacko
D.C. Montana..................... Tim Russ
Tania Winthrop................. Jane Badler

Fantasy-action series starring a big, high-tech truck. The giant 18-wheeler, which looked a bit like a misshapen hot dog, was heavily armed, virtually impregnable, and equipped with such niceties as a cab that converted into a helicopter, allowing nifty escapes from danger. (In the 1987 TV movie on which this series was based the truck could also become invisible, but that was dispensed with.) Piloting this monster rig along the highways of America was a muscular, leather-clad crime fighter called only The Highwayman, one of a team of special federal marshals ("Highwaymen") empowered to right wrongs "where ordinary laws do not reach"—and to haul sensitive government cargo. Jetto was his growling, break-down-the-doors Australian partner, and Ms. Winthrop the beautiful but tough "controller" who gave him his rolling orders. D.C. was the hip, black electronics wizard who kept all the toys working.

Produced by Glen A. Larson, who also brought us—couldn't you guess?—*Knight Rider.*

HILL STREET BLUES
Police Drama
FIRST TELECAST: *January 15, 1981*
LAST TELECAST: *May 19, 1987*
BROADCAST HISTORY:
Jan 1981, NBC Thu/Sat 10:00–11:00
Jan 1981–Apr 1981, NBC Sat 10:00–11:00
Apr 1981–Aug 1981, NBC Tue 9:00–10:00

Oct 1981–Nov 1986, NBC Thu 10:00–11:00
Dec 1986–Feb 1987, NBC Tue 9:00–10:00
Mar 1987–May 1987, NBC Tue 10:00–11:00
CAST:
Capt. Frank Furillo........ Daniel J. Travanti
Sgt. Phil Esterhaus (1981–1984)
.... Michael Conrad
Officer Bobby Hill .... Michael Warren
Officer Andy Renko .... Charles Haid
Joyce Davenport .... Veronica Hamel
Det. Mick Belker............... Bruce Weitz
Lt. Ray Calletano .... Rene Enriquez
Det. Johnny (J.D.) LaRue......... Kiel Martin
Det. Neal Washington...... Taurean Blacque
Lt. Howard Hunter............ James Sikking
Sgt./Lt. Henry Goldblume .... Joe Spano
Officer/Sgt. Lucille Bates ...... Betty Thomas
Grace Gardner (1981–1985) . Barbara Babcock
Fay Furillo (1981–1986) ...... Barbara Bosson
*Capt. Jerry Fuchs (1981–1984)
.... Vincent Lucchesi
Det./Lt. Alf Chesley (1981–1982). Gerry Black
Officer Leo Schnitz (1981–1985)
.... Robert Hirschfield
Officer Joe Coffey (1981–1986) ... Ed Marinaro
Chief Fletcher P. Daniels .... Jon Cypher
Officer Robin Tataglia (1983–1987)
.... Lisa Sutton
Asst. D.A. Irwin Bernstein (1982–1987)
.... George Wyner
*Jesus Martinez............... Trinidad Silva
*Judge Alan Wachtel .... Jeffrey Tambor
Det. Harry Garibaldi (1984–1985)... Ken Olin
Det. Patricia Mayo (1984–1985).. Mimi Kuzyk
Mayor Ozzie Cleveland (1982–1985)
.... J.A. Preston
Sgt. Stanislaus Jablonski (1984–1987)
.... Robert Prosky
Lt. Norman Buntz (1985–1987).. Dennis Franz
Celeste Patterson (1985–1986) . Judith Hansen
Sidney (Sid the Snitch) Thurston (1985–1987)
.... Peter Jurasik
Officer Patrick Flaherty (1986–1987)
.... Robert Clohessy
Officer Tina Russo (1986–1987)
.... Megan Gallagher
Officer Raymond (1987)....... David Selburg

*Occasional
THEME:
"Hill Street Blues," by Mike Post

This critically acclaimed series focused on the officers of Hill Street Station, located in the blighted ghetto area of a large, unnamed Eastern city. In command was Capt. Frank Furillo, a quiet yet forceful man with the patience of Job. Every day and long into the night, he dealt with the sleazy characters living in his precinct, which was rife with drugs, prostitution, burglary, murder, and the decay of a rotting neighborhood. As if that weren't enough, Frank had to cope with police bureaucracy and a chaotic personal life—an ex-wife (Fay) who constantly badgered him for more alimony, and a contentious public defender (Joyce) who was also his secret lover. The crazy assortment of cops under his command included the vaguely maniacal Belker, a scruffy little undercover officer who sometimes bit offenders and barked at startled dogs—but who called home regularly to his mom. To surly criminals he was a terror ("Would you like to sit down, hairball, or would you prefer internal bleeding?"). Henry Goldblume was the dedicated and idealistic community affairs officer, who sometimes took the brutality he saw around him too much to heart; Howard Hunter was the trigger-happy leader of the precinct's SWAT team, ready to blast away at any excuse; Ray Calletano was the second-in-command at the precinct; and J.D. LaRue a cash-poor vice cop who was frequently in trouble. Hill and Renko were two young partners—one black, one white—who were shot in the first episode and had difficulty adjusting to life on the streets after that. There was also an assortment of cocky street-gang leaders, notably the pushy Jesus Martinez, with whom Furillo had to deal almost as an equal. Only tall, fatherly Phil Esterhaus, the head sergeant, provided a haven of calm in the storm. He ended each roll call with the same words, "And, hey—let's be careful out there."

Viewers followed dramatic turns in the lives of their favorite characters as stories unfolded from episode to episode in semiserial fashion. Chesley and Goldblume were promoted to lieutenant, with Chesley moving on after the first full season. Frank and Joyce finally went public with their relationship, and were married in the 1983–1984 season—in a quickie, lunch-hour ceremony. The manipulative Chief Daniels, to whom Furillo reported, ran for mayor that same season, but lost in a bitter contest, to everyone's relief. In another story in early 1984, a despondent Hunter attempted suicide, only to survive when it turned out that his co-workers had removed the bullets from his service revolver. In one of the most famous episodes, in 1982, the normally quiet Ray Calletano, who was proud and sensitive about his Colombian heritage and unhappy about the status of Hispanics in American society, was honored as the department's "Hispanic Officer of the Year." At his testimonial banquet, after being misidentified as Puerto Rican and served Mexican food, he threw away his acceptance speech and told his stunned audience: "Why is it . . . that I look around this room—full of ranking officers—and the only other hispanics I see are waiters and busboys?"

Probably the most dramatic development was the sudden death of kindly Sgt. Esterhaus in the middle of the 1983–1984 season (following the death of actor Michael Conrad). He had been having a passionate affair with Grace Gardner, the middle-aged widow of a fellow officer, and according to the story he suffered a heart attack while making love to her. "The Blues" were deeply touched by his passing.

Hill Street Blues was a most unusual mixture of drama and comedy, fast-paced and deliberately choppy, as was life at the station house (each episode began with 7 A.M. roll call and ended late at night, with several stories interwoven). Although conceptually similar to ABC's *Barney Miller,* its rough texture and hard reality gave it a greater sense of honesty. The humor in it was the nervous humor of frustration and life in the streets. If *Barney Miller* was a police comedy with occasional dramatic overtones, *Hill Street Blues* was a police drama with occasional comedic moments.

Although the city in which the series took place was never mentioned, the real-life station house seen in exterior shots was the Maxwell Street Precinct in Chicago. The theme song from the series was on the record charts in late 1981.

HIPPODROME
Circus Variety
FIRST TELECAST: *July 5, 1966*
LAST TELECAST: *September 6, 1966*
BROADCAST HISTORY:
Jul 1966–Sep 1966, CBS Tue 8:30–9:30

Filmed in England, this summer replacement for *The Red Skelton Hour* featured a different celebrity host each week who introduced an assortment of acts that included many circus stalwarts (animal acts, aerialists, clowns, etc.) as well as the more traditional variety-show staples (singers, dancers, and comedians). Hosts included Allan Sherman, Woody Allen, and Merv Griffin.

HIRAM HOLIDAY
see *Adventures of Hiram Holiday, The*

HIZZONNER
Situation Comedy
FIRST TELECAST: *May 10, 1979*
LAST TELECAST: *June 14, 1979*
BROADCAST HISTORY:
May 1979–June 1979, NBC Thu 8:00–8:30
CAST:
Mayor Cooper .... David Huddleston
James Cooper................... Will Seltzer
Annie Cooper............... Kathy Cronkite
Timmons .... Don Galloway
Ginny........................ Diana Muldaur
Melanie .... Gina Hecht
Nails........................ Mickey Deems

Mayor Cooper was a widower with two grown children: Annie, a feminist civil-rights attorney, and James, a hippie affiliated with a communal organization called the Wilderness Cult. As the well-loved chief executive of a small Midwestern city, Cooper was basically honest, but not above doing things that were politically to his advantage. Timmons was his chief of staff; Ginny, his personal secretary; Melanie, one of the other secretaries at city hall; and Nails, the childhood friend who served as both bodyguard and chauffeur. When things started to get out of hand, Mayor Cooper would break into song, and there was one musical number in each episode of this short-lived series. Actress Kathy Cronkite, who played Annie, is the daughter of CBS News' Walter Cronkite.

HOBBY LOBBY
Comedy
FIRST TELECAST: *September 30, 1959*
LAST TELECAST: *March 23, 1960*
BROADCAST HISTORY:
   Sep 1959–Mar 1960, ABC Wed 8:00–8:30
STAR:
   Cliff Arquette (*as Charley Weaver*)

Hobby Lobby gave Charley Weaver the opportunity to chat each week with two people, one a celebrity and one not, about their interesting or amusing hobbies. Zsa Zsa Gabor discussed her love of fencing on one telecast and Gypsy Rose Lee sang the praises of sport fishing on another. Charley also made joking references to the hobbies of residents of his fictional hometown of Mount Idy, Ohio. The jokes were more interesting than the hobbies and the hobbies were eventually dropped. Effective with the November 25, 1959, telecast the title was changed to *The Charley Weaver Show.* Each week Charley had one or two guest celebrities come to visit with him in Mount Idy and chat about the activities of such local residents as Elsie Krack, Birdie Rudd, Wallace Swine, Clara Kimball Moots, and Grandpa Snider.

HOGAN FAMILY, THE
see *Valerie*

HOGAN'S HEROES
Situation Comedy
FIRST TELECAST: *September 17, 1965*
LAST TELECAST: *July 4, 1971*
BROADCAST HISTORY:
   Sep 1965–Sep 1967, CBS Fri 8:30–9:00
   Sep 1967–Sep 1969, CBS Sat 9:00–9:30
   Sep 1969–Sep 1970, CBS Fri 8:30–9:00
   Sep 1970–Jul 1971, CBS Sun 7:30–8:00
CAST:
   Col. Robert Hogan .... Bob Crane
   Col. Wilhelm Klink ...... Werner Klemperer
   Sgt. Hans Schultz .... John Banner
   Louis LeBeau .... Robert Clary
   Peter Newkirk .... Richard Dawson
   Sgt. James Kinchloe (1965–1970).. Ivan Dixon
   Sgt. Richard Baker (1970–1971)
   .... Kenneth Washington
   Sgt. Carter .... Larry Hovis
   Helga (1965–1966)............. Cynthia Lynn
   Hilda (1966–1970) .... Sigrid Valdis

Hogan's Heroes set out to prove that, at least in the world of televised situation comedies, life in

a Nazi POW camp during World War II could be fun. Commandant of the camp was the incompetent, monocled Col. Klink, and guarding Stalag 13, where the American-led resistance forces were housed, was the equally inept Sgt. Schultz. Under the direction of Col. Robert Hogan, the prisoners were actually in complete control of the camp. They had rigged the barbed-wire fence so that it could be opened and closed like a garage door. They fed classified information to the Allied forces on the outside, helped fugitives escape from Germany, printed counterfeit money, and did anything else imaginable to confound the Germans. Their living conditions were more reminiscent of a fancy hotel than a POW camp. They had a French chef, a steam room, a barber shop, and more comforts than they would have had at home. Since they were more important to the Allied cause in the camp than out of it, they had no desire to escape, especially considering the fun and comforts they had there.

HOLD IT PLEASE
Quiz/Audience Participation
FIRST TELECAST: *May 8, 1949*
LAST TELECAST: *May 22, 1949*
BROADCAST HISTORY:
   May 1949, CBS Sat 7:00–7:30
EMCEE:
   Gil Fates
REGULARS:
   Bill McGraw
   Mort Marshall
   Cloris Leachman

Contestants on this short-lived quiz program—it only lasted three weeks—were asked to answer questions that were acted out by the show's regulars. The questions might relate to events in history or be fictional in nature. The regulars often danced and sang, as well as acted, to illustrate the questions. The contestant who successfully answered the basic quiz questions won an opportunity to go for the $1,000 jackpot, as well as the prizes already won. If a contestant won the jackpot, he remained on the program as assistant emcee until there was a new jackpot winner.

HOLD THAT CAMERA
Game/Variety
FIRST TELECAST: *August 27, 1950*
LAST TELECAST: *December 15, 1950*
BROADCAST HISTORY:
   Aug 1950–Sep 1950, DUM Sun 7:30–8:00
   Sep 1950–Dec 1950, DUM Fri 8:30–9:00
EMCEE:
   Jimmy Blaine
   Kyle MacDonnell
ORCHESTRA:
   Ving Merlin

Hold That Camera began as a game show in which viewers at home played an important role.

A home viewer, contacted by telephone, would give directions over the phone to an on-camera contestant who performed stunts for prizes. The contestant completing the stunts in the least amount of time won for both himself and his telephone "partner." Interspersed with the games were songs by host Jimmy Blaine.

After only about a month, both Blaine and the game-show format were scrapped and *Hold That Camera* became a straight variety show, hosted by songstress Kyle MacDonnell. The setting was a nightclub called "The Camera Room," in which Miss MacDonnell and visiting guest stars performed.

HOLD THAT NOTE
Quiz/Audience Participation
FIRST TELECAST: *January 22, 1957*
LAST TELECAST: *April 2, 1957*
BROADCAST HISTORY:
Jan 1957–Apr 1957, NBC Tue 10:30–11:00
EMCEE:
Bert Parks
ANNOUNCER/HOST:
Johnny Olsen

Hold That Note appeared rather suddenly on January 22, 1957, as an unannounced and unexplained replacement for *Break the $250,000 Bank*, which had aired in the same time slot on the previous Tuesday. Bert Parks was the emcee of both programs, and informed viewers of the first telecast of *Hold That Note* that the contestants who were still on from last week's edition of *Break the $250,000 Bank* had been paid their winnings and given the opportunity to become contestants on the new show, which two of them did. There was really no mystery surrounding the sudden departure of *Break the $250,000 Bank*. It had been doing poorly in the ratings and seemed not to be working too well, so the producers decided to try another giveaway show in its place.

The object of *Hold That Note*, much like that of the somewhat similar but longer-lasting *Name That Tune*, was for the contestants to recognize a particular tune as soon as possible. The fewer notes played, the more the tune was worth. The first person to correctly identify three tunes was the winner of the round and the accumulated money in that round. There was a jackpot as an inducement for a winning contestant to keep playing, but also the possibility that he could lose some of his accumulated winnings. Bert Parks sang a song during each show and questions about the song he sang were worth extra money to the contestants.

HOLIDAY HANDBOOK
Travelogue
FIRST TELECAST: *April 4, 1958*
LAST TELECAST: *June 20, 1958*
BROADCAST HISTORY:
Apr 1958–Jun 1958, ABC Fri 10:00–10:30

Travel films, mostly of Western Europe, and keyed to what a visitor might find in local entertainment and culture.

HOLIDAY HOTEL
Musical Variety
FIRST TELECAST: *March 23, 1950*
LAST TELECAST: *October 4, 1951*
BROADCAST HISTORY:
Mar 1950–Jun 1950, ABC Thu 9:30–10:00
Sep 1950–Oct 1951, ABC Thu 9:00–9:30
REGULARS:
Edward Everett Horton (1950)
Don Ameche (1950–1951)
Leonore Lonergan (1950)
Betty Brewer
Bill Harrington (1950)
Walter Dare Wahl (1950)
Don Saddler (1950)
Dorothy Greener (1951)
Florence Halop (1951)
Joshua Shelley (1951)
June Graham Dancers
Charles Tate Dancers (1951)
Bernie Green Orchestra
Don Craig's Chorus

Holiday Hotel premiered in the spring of 1950 as a musical variety show set in a Park Avenue hotel. Edward Everett Horton was the beleaguered manager of the hotel, running things for the absent Mr. Holiday, and trying to keep the bizarre tenants and guests under control. Leonore Lonergan provided comic counterpoint as the hotel's switchboard operator. After a comic sketch by the regulars the scene would shift to the ballroom for entertainment by the week's guest stars, and musical production numbers staged by Gordon Jenkins. Even the sponsor (Packard Motors) got into the act, with a Packard showroom conveniently located on the ground floor of the hotel.

Despite a big budget, the program received poor reviews, and for the fall Edward Everett Horton was replaced by Don Ameche as manager of the hotel. In July 1951 the hotel motif was dropped and the title changed to *Don Ameche's Musical Playhouse*. The setting became a playhouse run by "manager" Ameche, but otherwise format and cast were the same as for *Holiday Hotel*.

HOLIDAY LODGE
Situation Comedy
FIRST TELECAST: *June 25, 1961*
LAST TELECAST: *October 8, 1961*
BROADCAST HISTORY:
Jun 1961–Oct 1961, CBS Sun 9:30–10:00
CAST:
Johnny Miller . . . . Johnny Wayne
Frank Boone . . . . Frank Shuster
Dorothy Jackson . . . . Maureen Arthur
Woodrow . . . . Charles Smith
J. W. Harrington . . . . Justice Watson

The Canadian comedy team of Johnny Wayne and Frank Shuster starred as Johnny Miller and Frank Boone in this situation comedy about the adventures of two men working as social directors at a posh summer resort. All of the regulars in this series were employees of the hotel, with Dorothy Jackson the girlfriend of Johnny Miller as well. The stories revolved around the wealthy, not-so-wealthy, and suspicious guests of the resort and the ways in which their activities involved them with the social directors.

HOLLYWOOD ADVENTURE TIME
see *Movies—Prior to 1961*

HOLLYWOOD AND THE STARS
Documentary
FIRST TELECAST: *September 30, 1963*
LAST TELECAST: *September 28, 1964*
BROADCAST HISTORY:
Sep 1963–Sep 1964, NBC Mon 9:30–10:00
HOST:
Joseph Cotten

Hollywood and the Stars looked at all aspects of the motion-picture industry, in documentary form. Each telecast surveyed a particular theme or subject, such as biographies of famous stars, specific types of films and film cycles, the people behind the scenes, and depictions of movies actually being made. Among the stars whose lives and careers were profiled were Rita Hayworth, Paul Newman, Natalie Wood, Bette Davis, and Humphrey Bogart. Other individual telecasts treated Westerns, musicals, gangster movies, war movies, teenage idols, great comedians, movie lovers, and glamour girls. One entire program was spent on location with Elizabeth Taylor and Richard Burton as Burton filmed *The Night of the Iguana*.

HOLLYWOOD BACKSTAGE
Beauty Tips
FIRST TELECAST: *August 7, 1955*
LAST TELECAST: *September 11, 1955*
BROADCAST HISTORY:
Aug 1955–Sep 1955, ABC Sun 7:30–8:00
HOST:
Ern Westmore

Ern Westmore, dean of Hollywood makeup artists, gave demonstrations and advice to women in this series, which was also seen in daytime at various times during the mid-1950s. A regular feature of the show called for a woman from the studio audience to be glamorized with the full Westmore Treatment. Ern would also demonstrate how a screen star was made up for a famous role.

The program was known in daytime as *The Ern Westmore Show*.

HOLLYWOOD BEAT
Police Drama

FIRST TELECAST: *September 21, 1985*
LAST TELECAST: *November 23, 1985*
BROADCAST HISTORY:
Sep 1985–Nov 1985, ABC Sat 8:00–9:00
CAST:
Det. Nick McCarren............. Jack Scalia
Det. Jack Rado................. Jay Acavone
George Grinsky.............. John Matuszak
Capt. Wes Biddle .... Edward Winter

Nick and Jack were undercover cops working the seedy side of Hollywood with fast cars and to the sound of loud rock music, in this knock-off of *Miami Vice*. Using sometimes bizarre disguises, they operated out of a business operated by George Grinsky, a hulking brute who was openly gay, but so big that no one dared say anything about it. Bag ladies, pimps, and winos were their street contacts, and Capt. Biddle the usual tough superior.

HOLLYWOOD FILM THEATRE
see *Movies—Prior to 1961*

HOLLYWOOD HOUSE
Variety
FIRST TELECAST: *December 4, 1949*
LAST TELECAST: *March 5, 1950*
BROADCAST HISTORY:
Dec 1949–Jan 1950, ABC Sun 7:30–8:00
Jan 1950–Mar 1950, ABC Sun 6:30–7:00
REGULARS:
Dick Wesson
Jim Backus
Gale Robbins

Comedy variety show set in a medium-sized Hollywood hotel, where anyone could wander in and anything could happen. Evidently not enough did, as the show was dropped after three months.

HOLLYWOOD MOVIE TIME
see *Movies—Prior to 1961*

HOLLYWOOD MYSTERY TIME
see *Movies—Prior to 1961*

HOLLYWOOD OFF BEAT
see *Steve Randall*

HOLLYWOOD OPENING NIGHT
Dramatic Anthology
FIRST TELECAST: *July 20, 1951*
LAST TELECAST: *March 23, 1953*
BROADCAST HISTORY:
Jul 1951–Mar 1952, CBS Fri 10:30–11:00
Oct 1952–Mar 1953, NBC Mon 9:00–9:30
HOST:
Jimmy Fidler (1952–1953)

The dramas aired in this CBS series during the 1951–1952 season were half-hour films made especially for television. For the second season, however, the sponsor moved the show to NBC and the dramas became live productions. This was in fact the first live dramatic show to originate from the West Coast and the first program to make use of NBC's recently completed Burbank studios. Hollywood columnist Jimmy Fidler opened each show in a "theater" lobby and invited the television audience to join him inside to see the play. At the end of each week's performance he gave a brief preview of the next week's offering.

The fare was quite varied, ranging from serious dramas such as "Delaying Action" starring John Hodiak, John Agar, and Tab Hunter, and "The Pattern" starring Gloria Swanson, to light comedies like "Uncle Fred Flits By" with David Niven and "Legal Affairs" with Franchot Tone. With the Hollywood talent pool to draw from, the casts in this series were generally quite impressive.

HOLLYWOOD PALACE, THE
Variety
FIRST TELECAST: *January 4, 1964*
LAST TELECAST: *February 7, 1970*
BROADCAST HISTORY:
   Jan 1964–May 1967, ABC Sat 9:30–10:30
   Sep 1967–Jan 1968, ABC Mon 10:00–11:00
   Jan 1968–Feb 1970, ABC Sat 9:30–10:30 (OS)
ORCHESTRA:
   Les Brown (1964)
   Mitchell Ayres (1964–1969)
EXECUTIVE PRODUCER:
   Nick Vanoff

The Hollywood Palace was a lavish, big-budget, big-name variety show of the 1960s which attempted to become to Saturday night what *The Ed Sullivan Show* was to Sunday. It premiered amid much hoopla in January 1964, live from the recently rebuilt ABC Palace Theater (formerly the El Capitan) in Hollywood. The first telecast headlined Bing Crosby as host, with Mickey Rooney, Bobby Van, Nancy Wilson, Bob Newhart, and Gary Crosby, as well as singers, dancers, magicians, balancing acts, and even clowns.

A different host topped the bill each week, but some returned more often than others. Bing Crosby was most frequently seen (30-plus appearances), while Fred Astaire, Milton Berle, Jimmy Durante, Sid Caesar and Imogene Coca, Sammy Davis, Jr., and Don Adams also made multiple appearances as host. Other acts on the *Palace* bill ranged from old-timers Groucho Marx and Ed Wynn to Frank Sinatra with the Basie band, to Judy Garland, to the Rolling Stones. The strictly vaudeville acts (acrobats, etc.) were seen less often during later years, as the show became more of a straight musical-comedy variety hour. A highlight of every season was the Christmas holiday show, usually presided over by Bing Crosby (sometimes with his family), and also the glamorous billboard girls (at one time including the then-unknown Raquel Welch).

Though *The Hollywood Palace* featured top-line talent, and attracted a substantial audience, it never developed the loyal following of the other great variety hours, probably because of the lack of a central figure as continuing host.

The show was known during its first few weeks as *The Saturday Night Hollywood Palace.* Attempts were made in both 1973 and 1977 to revive this series with syndicated versions. Each time the revivals lasted but a single season.

HOLLYWOOD PREMIERE
Variety
FIRST TELECAST: *September 22, 1949*
LAST TELECAST: *November 17, 1949*
BROADCAST HISTORY:
   Sep 1949–Nov 1949, NBC Thu 8:00–8:30

A short-lived series of half-hour programs showcasing established talent in comedic and dramatic material. There was no continuing cast. Among those appearing were Pinky Lee, Howard Da Silva, and Sterling Holloway. The programs were produced in Hollywood and shown via kinescope on the Eastern and Midwestern NBC networks.

HOLLYWOOD PREMIERE THEATRE
see *Hollywood Theatre Time*

HOLLYWOOD SCREEN TEST
Talent
FIRST TELECAST: *April 15, 1948*
LAST TELECAST: *May 18, 1953*
BROADCAST HISTORY:
   Apr 1948–May 1948, ABC Thu 8:00–8:30
   May 1948–Jun 1948, ABC Sun 6:30–7:00
   Aug 1948–Sep 1948, ABC Sun 7:30–8:00
   Oct 1948–May 1949, ABC Sun 8:00–8:30
   May 1949–Sep 1950, ABC Sat 7:30–8:00
   Sep 1950–May 1953, ABC Mon 7:30–8:00 (OS)
HOST:
   Bert Lytell (1948)
   Neil Hamilton (1948–1953)
ASSISTANT:
   Robert Quarry (1949)

"You, the public, make the stars" was the oft-repeated slogan of this long-running talent show of TV's early years. Unlike many TV talent shows, the production values here were commendably high. The young talent appearing on *Hollywood Screen Test* all had previous professional experience, and were looking for the "big break" that would bring them stardom. They were paired with established stars in dramatic sketches and comedy skits written especially for the program, as well as scenes adapted from famous plays and novels. The behind-the-scenes ambience of the show was heightened by the setting, a Hollywood sound stage, with silent film actor Bert Lytell as the original "producer" and Neil Hamilton as his assistant. (Lytell left after a few months and Hamilton took over the show.)

Several newcomers got the break they were

looking for, landing Hollywood contracts as a result of their appearance on the show. Among the program's Hollywood-bound alumni were Grace Kelly, Jack Klugman, Gene Barry, Pernell Roberts, Betsy Palmer, Martin Balsam, Susan Cabot, and Robert Quarry (who also served as assistant on the show). Better known (at the time) were the guest stars with whom they played their scenes, including Mercedes McCambridge, Jeff Morrow, Edward Everett Horton, and others.

HOLLYWOOD SQUARES

Quiz/Audience Participation
FIRST TELECAST: *January 12, 1968*
LAST TELECAST: *September 13, 1968*
BROADCAST HISTORY:
Jan 1968–Sep 1968, NBC Fri 9:30–10:00
EMCEE:
Peter Marshall
REGULARS:
Cliff Arquette (*Charley Weaver*)
Wally Cox

This nighttime version of the highly popular NBC daytime game show (which premiered in October 1966) was seen on the network in 1968. The host, as in the daytime version, was Peter Marshall.

The Hollywood Squares set resembled a huge tic-tac-toe board, with a different celebrity in each of the nine squares. Two contestants took turns choosing celebrities. The chosen celebrity would be asked a question—sometimes serious, sometimes strange, often ridiculous—by emcee Marshall, and would give an answer. The contestant would then have to state whether the answer given was right or wrong. If the contestant guessed correctly, he won that square. If not, his opponent won it, unless that square would give the opponent three squares in a row and a victory. The first contestant to win three squares in a row won the round. Often, however, nobody noticed who won, as the quiz element in *Hollywood Squares* was distinctly secondary to the quips and jokes of the celebrities. Paul Lynde, who was to become the star "center square" regular of the daytime version of *Hollywood Squares*, was not yet a regular when the nighttime version was on. He appeared only six times during its run and became a regular on the daytime show roughly one month after the nighttime show left the air.

In addition to the daytime version, a syndicated once-a-week nighttime edition was begun in the fall of 1971. The daytime *Hollywood Squares* finally left the air in June 1980—after a 14-year run—but the syndicated nighttime edition continued, expanded to five nights a week until the fall of 1982. A year later *Hollywood Squares* returned to the NBC weekday daytime lineup as part of *The Match Game—Hollywood Squares Hour*. The host of this version was Jon Bauman, formerly of the singing group Sha Na Na. He was the first person other than Peter Marshall—who had hosted all previous versions of the series—to

emcee *Hollywood Squares. The Match Game—Hollywood Squares Hour* left the air in July of 1984.

A new syndicated version of *Hollywood Squares* premiered in the fall of 1986 with John Davidson as emcee. Regulars in this version included JM J. Bullock, who also filled in for Davidson as substitute emcee; Joan Rivers, who became the permanent "center square" in 1987; and the show's announcer, Shadoe Stevens.

HOLLYWOOD SUMMER THEATRE

Dramatic Anthology
FIRST TELECAST: *August 3, 1956*
LAST TELECAST: *September 28, 1956*
BROADCAST HISTORY:
Aug 1956–Sep 1956, CBS Fri 8:00–8:30
HOST:
Gene Raymond

This filmed summer anthology series was made up of original dramas, never before seen on television, and was hosted by Gene Raymond. Appearing were such performers as Merle Oberon, Laraine Day, Joanne Dru, Rod Cameron, Ricardo Montalban, and Preston Foster.

HOLLYWOOD TALENT SCOUTS

Variety
FIRST TELECAST: *June 22, 1965*
LAST TELECAST: *September 5, 1966*
BROADCAST HISTORY:
Jun 1965–Sep 1965, CBS Tue 8:30–9:30
Dec 1965–Sep 1966, CBS Mon 10:00–11:00
HOST:
Art Linkletter

The performers in this variety series were young unknowns who had been seen by celebrities and brought by those celebrities to *Hollywood Talent Scouts* to get their first national television exposure. Each week there were four or five guest celebrities who chatted briefly with host Art Linkletter and then introduced their discoveries.

During its initial summer run there were a few discoveries who actually became successful in future years, but not always doing what they did on this show. Tom Smothers brought a young comic named Pat Paulsen (later to work on the Smothers Brothers' variety show), actor Bob Crane presented a young singer named Marilyn McCoo (later the lead singer with The Fifth Dimension), and Carl Reiner brought one of the writers from his *Dick Van Dyke Show*, Garry Marshall. Marshall, who went on the show to try his luck as a comedian, later became the producer of *Happy Days* and *Laverne & Shirley*. Most of the young talents never made it, though, and some were not so young. Cliff Arquette, as Charley Weaver, introduced the Frivolous Five, a Dixieland jazz group composed entirely of women over sixty.

When this series returned in December, the title had been altered to *Art Linkletter's Hollywood*

Talent Scouts and on-location interviews with celebrities were included in the format. Singer Donna Theodore was the most notable talent presented in this run. Virtually the same program, with different hosts, aired under the title *Celebrity Talent Scouts*.

HOLLYWOOD THEATRE TIME
Various
FIRST TELECAST: *October 8, 1950*
LAST TELECAST: *October 20, 1951*
BROADCAST HISTORY:
Oct 1950–Dec 1950, ABC Sun 8:00–8:30
Dec 1950–Oct 1951, ABC Sat 7:00–7:30

This series was a showcase for an assortment of variety shows, dramatic presentations, scenes from famous plays, and situation comedies, all produced in Hollywood. Frequently seen during the first few months was "The Gil Lamb Show," a half-hour musical variety show hosted by the screen comedian. Other presentations included "Mr. and Mrs. Detective" starring Gale Storm and Don DeFore, and "The Spectre" starring Marjorie Reynolds.

During its first two months the series was known as *Hollywood Premiere Theatre*.

HOLMES AND YOYO
Situation Comedy
FIRST TELECAST: *September 25, 1976*
LAST TELECAST: *December 11, 1976*
BROADCAST HISTORY:
Sep 1976–Dec 1976, ABC Sat 8:00–8:30
CAST:
Det. Alexander Holmes..... Richard B. Shull
Gregory "Yoyo" Yoyonovich.... John Schuck
Capt. Harry Sedford............ Bruce Kirby
Officer Maxine Moon ...... Andrea Howard

This was billed as the revival of the classic two-man comedy team. Said producer Leonard Stern, "For over thirty years we had the marvelous antics of Laurel & Hardy, Abbott & Costello, Hope & Crosby, Martin & Lewis, Gleason & Carney, and then suddenly came an unexplainable gap. But now, hopefully, Schuck & Shull will fill the comedy void."

Schuck & Shull did not become another Laurel & Hardy; their series *Holmes and Yoyo* lasted a brief three months. Holmes was an accident-prone cop who never got hurt himself, but kept sending partners to the hospital. So the department decided to try its latest development, a lifelike robot "computerperson" named Yoyo (after its inventor, Dr. Yoyonovich). Holmes was not supposed to know that his new partner was a robot. He did, secretly, but few others were aware of it, certainly not Officer Maxine Moon who kept making amorous advances to Yoyo. Yoyo did have his strong points, including a photographic memory, an independent power source, a silent trash compressor which permitted him to digest

anything, and the ability to produce color prints. But there were drawbacks, too. Nobody could lift him because he weighed 427 pounds. And although he was uninjurable, an assailant's bullet once shorted out his rhythm system, causing him to tapdance out of control during a chase.

HOMETOWN
Comedy/Drama
FIRST TELECAST: *August 22, 1985*
LAST TELECAST: *October 15, 1985*
BROADCAST HISTORY:
Aug 1985–Sep 1985, CBS Thu 10:00–11:00
Sep 1985–Oct 1985, CBS Tue 8:00–9:00
CAST:
Mary Newell Abbott .... Jane Kaczmarek
Ben Abbott...................... Franc Luz
Christopher Springer .... Andrew Rubin
Barbara Donnelly......... Margaret Whitton
Peter Kincaid............ John Bedford-Lloyd
Jane Parnell .... Christine Estabrook
Joey Nathan .... Daniel Stern
Jennifer Abbott .... Erin Leigh Peck
Tess Abbott .... Donna Vivino
Dylan Nathan .... Mikey Viso

Hometown was an obvious, and unsuccessful, attempt to bring the feel of the highly successful 1983 movie "The Big Chill" to television. It was the story of seven close friends, who had been practically inseparable during their college days in the 1960s, trying to cope with the realities of their maturing lives in the 1980s. Mary and Ben got married in the series' premiere episode, after having lived together since their college days and raising two daughters. He was a successful businessman, while she wanted to renew her long-abandoned dancing career. Christopher was a wealthy rock star with an unhappy personal life; Barbara, an insecure divorcée trying to start a new life; Peter and Jane, both college professors and, in her case, a Presidential advisor as well; and Joey, a single parent and restaurant cook who was more content with his modest means than any of his materially more successful friends.

HONDO
Western
FIRST TELECAST: *September 8, 1967*
LAST TELECAST: *December 29, 1967*
BROADCAST HISTORY:
Sep 1967–Dec 1967, ABC Fri 8:30–9:30
CAST:
Hondo Lane .... Ralph Taeger
Angie Dow .... Kathie Browne
Johnny Dow .... Buddy Foster
Buffalo Baker............... Noah Beery, Jr.
Capt. Richards................ Gary Clarke
Chief Vittoro .... Michael Pate
Col. Crook.................... William Bryant

Ralph Taeger played the title role of a cavalry scout in the Arizona Territory, *ca.* 1870, in this

Western adventure. Hondo was an embittered loner. He had once been a Confederate Cavalry captain, and had lived with the Apaches for a time under the aegis of Chief Vittoro, only to see his Indian bride—Vittoro's daughter—slain by the army in a massacre. Now he traveled with a dog named Sam, troubleshooting for the army and trying to avert further bloodshed in the campaign against renegade Indians, land grabbers, gunmen, and bandits around Fort Lowell. Capt. Richards was the young martinet commander of the fort; Buffalo Baker, a colorful scout; Angie Dow, Hondo's romantic interest, and Johnny, her nine-year-old son.

Based on Louis L'Amour's story, and the 1953 John Wayne movie derived from it.

HONESTLY CELESTE
Situation Comedy
FIRST TELECAST: October 10, 1954
LAST TELECAST: December 5, 1954
BROADCAST HISTORY:
Oct 1954–Dec 1954, CBS Sun 9:30–10:00
CAST:
Celeste Anders .... Celeste Holm
Bob Wallace .... Scott McKay
Marty Gordon .... Mike Kellin
Mr. Wallace................. Geoffrey Lumb
Mr. Wallace's Secretary....... Mary Finney

Vivacious Celeste Anders had given up her position teaching journalism in the Midwest to come to New York and take a job as a reporter for The New York Express, to get some "real" experience. What she found was a new boyfriend (Bob Wallace, the publisher's son), a friendly cabbie named Marty who took her to many of her reporting assignments, and all sorts of predicaments. Despite the attraction of film star Celeste Holm and much favorable pretelecast publicity, this filmed comedy series lasted less than three months.

HONEY WEST
Detective Drama
FIRST TELECAST: September 17, 1965
LAST TELECAST: September 2, 1966
BROADCAST HISTORY:
Sep 1965–Sep 1966, ABC Fri 9:00–9:30
CAST:
Honey West.................. Anne Francis
Sam Bolt...................... John Ericson
Aunt Meg .... Irene Hervey

Honey West was a true rarity in 1965, a female private detective. She had inherited the family detective business and partner Sam Bolt from her late father, and she made quite a fetching female James Bond. Honey was skilled at judo, proficient at karate, owned a weapons arsenal full of the most amazing devices, and used a specially modified lipstick that contained a radio transmitter. Her traveling office was a specially equipped spy van labeled "H.W. Bolt & Co., TV Service." She

had everything necessary to track down the bad guys—even a trench coat. The love of her life was her pet ocelot, Bruce, much to the consternation of partner Sam, who would willingly have married her.

Honey West was introduced to TV audiences in an April 1965 episode of Burke's Law, in which the sexy sleuth outwitted even that dapper investigator.

HONEYMOONERS, THE
Situation Comedy
FIRST TELECAST: October 1, 1955
LAST TELECAST: May 9, 1971
BROADCAST HISTORY:
Oct 1955–Feb 1956, CBS Sat 8:30–9:00
Feb 1956–Sep 1956, CBS Sat 8:00–8:30
Jan 1971–May 1971, CBS Sun 10:00–11:00
CAST:
Ralph Kramden.............. Jackie Gleason
Ed Norton...................... Art Carney
Alice Kramden (1955–1956)
.... Audrey Meadows
Trixie Norton (1955–1956).... Joyce Randolph
Alice Kramden (1971) .... Sheila MacRae
Trixie Norton (1971)............. Jane Kean

Although The Honeymooners is one of the best-remembered comedy highlights of TV's golden age, it was seen for most of its history as a segment within other programs. Oddly enough, on the few occasions when it was presented as an independent series, it was not successful. Yet practically anyone who has ever sat in front of a TV set has seen a bit of the saga of Ralph and Alice Kramden, the not-so-newlyweds living in a run-down apartment in Brooklyn. The surroundings were grimy and spartan, quite unlike the happy middle-class homes of most TV situation comedies. Ralph, a portly New York City bus driver, was one of life's colorful losers—blustery, ambitious, avaricious, and constantly searching for the one great money-making scheme that would make him rich. Always willing to help was his best friend Ed Norton, who lived upstairs. Norton was no better off than "Ralphie-boy"—he worked in the city's sewers—but he was a veritable fountain of cheer and encouragement. Unfortunately Norton negated through incompetence and naivete the benefits of his blind enthusiasm, and he was a constant source of grief and aggravation to Ralph. Their schemes never worked out, usually causing friction between Ralph and his more practical wife, Alice. Ralph's reaction, whenever Alice proved him wrong or disapproved of one of his great ideas, was to threaten to belt her, with such lines as "To the moon, Alice," or "One of these days, Alice, one of these days . . . Pow! Right in the kisser!" But Alice understood Ralph, and in the end, at the final curtain, he would beam and admit, "Alice . . . you're the greatest."

The Honeymooners was first seen in 1951 as a sketch within DuMont's Cavalcade of Stars, with

Pert Kelton originating the role of Alice and Art Carney as Ed Norton. When the show moved to CBS as *The Jackie Gleason Show* Audrey Meadows assumed the role of Alice. *The Honeymooners* finally became a series in its own right in 1955. Jackie Gleason wanted a respite from the rigors of a full-hour live weekly variety show and was also interested in becoming a packager of other programs. It was decided to film a full season (39 episodes) of half-hour *Honeymooners* shows and fill the other half of what had been Gleason's regular hour in the CBS schedule with *Stage Show*, a program owned by Jackie. All of *The Honeymooners* episodes were filmed before a live audience, two episodes per week, using an advanced filming system called the Electronicam. This was one of the first examples of live audience, single-set filmed situation comedy, so prevalent today (though it was not the first—see *I Love Lucy*). In 1956, with the failure of *Stage Show*, the less-than-anticipated response to *The Honeymooners*, and the strong competition from *The Perry Como Show* on NBC, Gleason returned to a regular variety format.

In 1966 *The Honeymooners*, which had only been seen on a very occasional basis since Art Carney's departure as a regular on *The Jackie Gleason Show* in 1957, was revived in the form of full-hour episodes of Gleason's then-current variety series. Carney was back, with Sheila MacRae and Jane Kean playing the wives. These episodes, in which the Kramdens and the Nortons traveled together in addition to getting into trouble at home in New York, were done on a grander scale than the 1955–1956 series, complete with songs and production numbers. They accounted for roughly half the total output of *The Jackie Gleason Show* during its last four years on the air. A collection of reruns of these hour episodes was aired as another *Honeymooners* series in 1971. In addition, reruns of the original 39 half-hour episodes from the 1955–1956 season continue to be shown, and will probably run forever, on local stations.

Those 39 episodes got a lot of company in the 1980s when "The Lost Episodes" of *The Honeymooners* surfaced on Showtime's pay-cable network. The episodes weren't really lost at all. They were actually Honeymooners sketches that had aired on *The Jackie Gleason Show* in the 1950s. Gleason had kinescopes of the sketches and released the material to Viacom, Showtime's parent company, in 1984. Although as sketches they varied in length from a few minutes to almost a full half hour, they were edited together to produce 68 new Honeymooners half hours. After airing on Showtime in 1984 and 1985, these "new" episodes subsequently went into syndication along with the original 39.

HONG KONG
Adventure
FIRST TELECAST: *September 28, 1960*
LAST TELECAST: *September 20, 1961*

BROADCAST HISTORY:
  Sep 1960–Sep 1961, ABC Wed 7:30–8:30
CAST:
  Glenn Evans .... Rod Taylor
  Neil Campbell .... Lloyd Bochner
  Tully .... Jack Kruschen
  Fong (1960) .... Harold Fong
  Ling (1960–1961) .... Gerald Jann
  Ching Mei .... Mai Tai Sing

The British Crown Colony of Hong Kong was the locale for the adventures of Glenn Evans, an American journalist living and working amid the intrigue of that exotic city. His search for stories led him into encounters with smugglers, murderers, dope peddlers, and slinky women disappearing behind beaded curtains. A source of stories, as well as a friend, was Neil Campbell, chief of the Hong Kong police. Tully ran the swank nightclub where Glenn spent much of his free time. Glenn's original houseboy was Fong, who was replaced by Ling within a month after the series premiered. By the end of the year Ching Mei had joined the cast as the hostess at the Golden Dragon, Tully's nightclub.

HOOPERMAN
Police
FIRST TELECAST: *September 23, 1987*
LAST TELECAST:
BROADCAST HISTORY:
  Sep 1987– , ABC Wed 9:00–9:30
CAST:
  Det. Harry Hooperman .... John Ritter
  Susan Smith .... Debrah Farentino
  Capt. Celeste (C.Z.) Stern .... Barbara Bosson
  Off. Boris "Bobo" Pritzger ... Clarence Felder
  Off. Maureen "Mo" DeMott ... Sydney Walsh
  Off. Rick Silardi .... Joseph Gian
  Insp. Clarence McNeil .... Felton Perry
  Betty Bushkin .... Alix Elias

The mid-1980s vogue for "dramedies" (half-hour comedy/dramas) was perhaps best exemplified by this odd cross between *Hill Street Blues* and *Barney Miller*, which combined humorous moments with hard action. Hooperman was a little like Lt. Goldblume of *Hill Street*, a thoughtful cop who hated to use his gun. His superior on the San Francisco P.D. was Capt. Stern, whose demanding manner masked basic insecurities, especially about her failed marriage. Mo was a female officer dedicated to "saving" her handsome-but-gay partner Rick, Bobo was the office redneck, and Betty the cheerful dispatcher.

Hooperman's private life was just as colorful. His landlady had been murdered, leaving him her broken-down apartment building and her yapping little dog Bijoux—so he also had rebellious tenants to placate. Susan was the building handyman and aspiring writer with whom he had a somewhat rocky romantic relationship, but who, by early 1988, was about to bear his child.

HOOTENANNY
Music
FIRST TELECAST: *April 6, 1963*
LAST TELECAST: *September 12, 1964*
BROADCAST HISTORY:
Apr 1963–Sep 1963, ABC Sat 8:30–9:00
Sep 1963–Sep 1964, ABC Sat 7:30–8:30
HOST:
Jack Linkletter
THEME:
"Hootenanny Saturday Night," by Alfred Uhry
and Richard Lewine

A traveling musical jamboree, taped before a live
audience at a different college campus each week,
and featuring the popularized "folk music" of the
early 1960s. Artists were generally commercial
pop-folk groups such as the Limeliters, the Chad
Mitchell Trio, and the Smothers Brothers, but also
included some traditional performers such as Josh
White and the Carter Family.

Interestingly, several major stars refused to appear on this program because it continued the
1950s practice of "blacklisting" certain performers with alleged left-wing views (such as Pete Seeger and the Weavers). This, it was said, was due
to sponsor pressure. Among those who refused to
appear were the Kingston Trio, Joan Baez, and
Peter, Paul and Mary.

HOPALONG CASSIDY
Western
FIRST TELECAST: *June 24, 1949*
LAST TELECAST: *December 23, 1951*
BROADCAST HISTORY:
Jun 1949–Oct 1949, NBC Fri 8:00–9:00
(some telecasts local)
Apr 1950–Dec 1951, NBC Sun 6:00–7:00
CAST:
Hopalong Cassidy............. William Boyd
Red Connors .... Edgar Buchanan

Theatrical films of the adventures of Hopalong
Cassidy had been shown on New York television
at least as early as 1945, and became a regular
local series in November 1948. The first films seen
on TV were edited versions of his old "B" features, with Boyd adding narration and occasionally even a new scene or two (it is remarkable that
a man of 50 could match scenes that he had filmed
15 years before, and look no different!). His sidekick in these old theatrical films was usually either Gabby Hayes or Andy Clyde. Then Boyd
made a new series of TV films, with Edgar Buchanan as his sidekick, which ran on NBC for a
time and then went into syndication for many
years thereafter.

The plots were the same as in the old "B" films,
with Hoppy, silver-haired and dressed all in
black, chasing villains to their doom on his faithful horse Topper. He was a true Knight of the
West—and a far cry from the profane, unwashed,

gimpy-legged cowpoke originally created in the
stories of Clarence E. Mulford.

William Boyd had been wise enough to buy the
TV rights to his theatrical films during the 1940s,
and it was television—not Hollywood features—
that made him a millionaire. He died in 1972.

HORACE HEIDT SHOW, THE
Talent
FIRST TELECAST: *October 2, 1950*
LAST TELECAST: *September 24, 1951*
BROADCAST HISTORY:
Oct 1950–Sep 1951, CBS Mon 9:00–9:30
HOST:
Horace Heidt

This series, begun by the veteran bandleader on
radio in 1947 as *Horace Heidt's Youth Opportunity Program,* added a television version in 1950.
As with *The Original Amateur Hour,* the emphasis of the show was on finding young talent and
exposing it to a national audience. At the end of
each live show, the acts were voted upon by the
studio audience, and the winner, as measured by
applause meter, came back the following week to
defend his championship.

HORIZONS
Discussion
FIRST TELECAST: *December 2, 1951*
LAST TELECAST: *March 6, 1955*
BROADCAST HISTORY:
Dec 1951, ABC Sun 6:00–6:30
May 1952–Jun 1952, ABC Sun 7:30–8:00
Dec 1954–Mar 1955, ABC Sun 9:15–9:30
HOST:
Dr. Louis H. Bauer (1954–1955)
PRODUCERS:
Erik Barnouw and Jack Pacey (1951–1952)
DIRECTOR:
Leslie Gorall (1951–1952)

Live lecture series in which prominent professors
from Columbia University and occasional outside
experts spoke on likely future developments in
their specialties. Included during the 1951–1952
season were Prof. Mark Van Doren on "The Future of Poetry," anthropologist Margaret Mead on
"The Future of the Family," and Dr. Philip E. Mosley on "The Future of Soviet Diplomacy." For part
of its run the 1951–1952 series aired on Sunday
afternoons.

The title *Horizons* was revived in 1954 for a
similarly erudite series of short talks on advances
in medicine, presided over by Dr. Louis H. Bauer,
past president of the American Medical Association and Secretary General of the World Medical
Association.

HOT L BALTIMORE
Situation Comedy
FIRST TELECAST: *January 24, 1975*

LAST TELECAST: *June 6, 1975*
BROADCAST HISTORY:
Jan 1975–Jun 1975, ABC Fri 9:00–9:30
CAST:
Bill Lewis	James Cromwell
Clifford Ainsley	Richard Masur
April Green	Conchata Ferrell
Charles Bingham	Al Freeman, Jr.
Suzy Marta Rocket	Jeannie Linero
Millie	Gloria Le Roy
Jackie	Robin Wilson
Mr. Morse	Stan Gottlieb
George	Lee Bergere
Gordon	Henry Calvert
Mrs. Bellotti	Charlotte Rae

Hot L Baltimore was one of the most controversial comedies of the 1970s. Based on the award-winning off-Broadway play of the same name, and produced for TV by trendsetter Norman Lear (of *All in the Family* fame), it brought sexual innuendo and racy dialogue to the home screen. The setting was the lobby of the once grand but now dilapidated Hotel Baltimore (the "e" in the sign had burned out and had never been replaced). Among its denizens were desk clerk Bill and his love, April; the harried manager, Clifford; the philosophical Charles; Suzy Marta Rocket, the Colombian prostitute; Millie, the unemployed waitress; Jackie, the tomboy; Mr. Morse, the septugenarian always on the brink of expiring; George and Gordon, the homosexual couple; and eccentric Mrs. Bellotti. Often heard but never seen on-screen was Mrs. Bellotti's 26-year-old prankster son Moose, who delighted in such escapades as buttering the hallways, staging *The Poseidon Adventure* in the bathtub, and collecting unlikely pets. Once when the lobby habitués protested a rent increase, Moose glued himself to the ceiling of his room in sympathy.

HOT PURSUIT
Drama
FIRST TELECAST: *September 22, 1984*
LAST TELECAST: *December 28, 1984*
BROADCAST HISTORY:
Sep 1984–Nov 1984, NBC Sat 10:00–11:00
Dec 1984, NBC Fri 10:00–11:00
CAST:
Kate Wyler/Cathy Ladd	Kerrie Keane
Jim Wyler	Eric Pierpoint
Estelle Modrian	Dina Merrill
Alec Shaw	Mike Preston

Love on the run was the theme of this 1984 adventure series. Kate and Jim were the young couple, very much in love, who seemed to have it all—he was a veterinarian, she was a top auto engineer developing a new, high-performance car. Then, in a sudden nightmare, Kate was accused and convicted of the murder of her avaricious employer, auto magnate Victor Modrian.

Jim then learned that Kate had been framed by Modrian's devious widow, Estelle, using an exact lookalike named Cathy Ladd. As Kate was being taken to prison, Jim staged a daring ambush to free her from custody, and the two of them set out on a cross-country pursuit to find the double—the one person who could prove Kate's innocence. As they followed their quarry from one city to another, they often became involved in the lives of people they met. But they could not stay long, because hot on their heels were not only the police but a vicious, one-eyed assassin named Shaw, who had been hired by the widow Modrian.

Although this series was admittedly reminiscent of *The Fugitive*, its emphasis on the close relationship between the leads gave it a somewhat different flavor from the earlier program.

HOT SEAT, THE
Interview
FIRST TELECAST: *April 18, 1952*
LAST TELECAST: *December 29, 1952*
BROADCAST HISTORY:
Apr 1952–Jul 1952, ABC Fri 8:00–8:30
Oct 1952–Nov 1952, ABC Sun 7:30–8:00
Nov 1952–Dec 1952, ABC Mon 8:30–9:00
HOST:
Stuart Scheftel

Lively interview show in which public figures were grilled by ABC newsman Stuart Scheftel and a guest. Subjects ranged from radio-TV personality Tex McCrary to Senator Joseph McCarthy.

HOT SHOTS
Magazine Drama
FIRST TELECAST: *September 23, 1986*
LAST TELECAST: *September 9, 1987*
BROADCAST HISTORY:
Sep 1986–Dec 1986, CBS Tue 11:30–12:40 A.M.
Jul 1987–Sep 1987, CBS Wed 11:30–12:40 A.M.
CAST:
Amanda Reed	Dorothy Parke
Jason West	Booth Savage
Nicholas Broderick	Paul Burke
Al Pendleton	Clark Johnson
Cleo	Heather Smith
Receptionist	Mung Ling

Amanda and Jason were two young, ambitious reporters for *CrimeWorld* magazine. In their quest for titillating stories they were often teamed together. Despite their competitive bickering and complaints about having to work together, they did respect each other's abilities and, though they would never admit it, were sexually attracted to each other. Nicholas Broderick was the editor and publisher of *CrimeWorld* magazine, Al his talented researcher, and Cleo his secretary.

Produced in Toronto.

HOTEL

Drama

FIRST TELECAST: *September 21, 1983*
LAST TELECAST:
BROADCAST HISTORY:

Sep 1983–May 1984, ABC Wed 10:00–11:00
Jun 1984–Jul 1984, ABC Tue 9:00–10:00
Aug 1984–Mar 1987, ABC Wed 10:00–11:00
May 1987–Sep 1987, ABC Wed 10:00–11:00
Sep 1987–Jan 1988, ABC Sat 10:00–11:00
Mar 1988–May 1988, ABC Thu 9:00–10:00
Jun 1988–   , ABC Sat 10:00–11:00

CAST:

Peter McDermott . . . . James Brolin
Christine Francis . . . . Connie Sellecca
Mark Danning (1983–1986) . . . . . . Shea Farrell
Billy Griffin . . . . Nathan Cook
Dave Kendall (1983–1987) . . . . Michael Spound
Megan Kendall (1983–1987) . . . . . Heidi Bohay
Julie Gillette . . . . Shari Belafonte-Harper
Victoria Cabot (1983–1986) . . . . . . Anne Baxter
Kei (1984–   ) . . . . Michael Yama
Harry the bartender (1984–   )
. . . . Harry George Phillips
Charles Cabot (1986) . . . . . Efrem Zimbalist Jr.
Elizabeth Bradshaw Cabot (1986)
. . . . Michelle Phillips
Cheryl Dolan (1987–   ) . Valerie Landsburg
Ryan Thomas (1987–   ) . . . . Susan Walters
Eric Lloyd (1987–   ) . . . . Ty Miller

THEME:

by Henry Mancini

San Francisco's St. Gregory was an elegant hostelry indeed. Its marble columns rose up over a cavernous lobby and elegant restaurants; above lay plush suites serviced by an attentive staff. This was the setting for romance, drama, and occasional comedy in the weekly series *Hotel*. Produced by the same people responsible for *Love Boat*, *Hotel* bore a certain resemblance to that seagoing series. There were different guests each week, usually in gentle stories of the heart, almost all with happy endings. Sometimes the drama was a little heavier, as when a prostitute was brought into the hotel and then gang-raped by some students; or lighter, as when the kindly old gentleman died in the dining room but was left propped up until after lunch so as not to disturb the other patrons.

The staff included Victoria Cabot, a wealthy aristocrat who oversaw the operation on behalf of her sister-in-law, Laura Trent; Peter McDermott, the suave, bearded general manager; Christine, his beautiful assistant and later lover; Mark, the handsome and likable public-relations director; and Billy Griffin, a black ex-con who had gone straight and now served as the hotel's security director. Julie was in charge of the information center, while cheerful newlyweds Dave and Megan were a bellhop and desk clerk, respectively, who left the series when, after a long struggle, he graduated from law school.

Among the familiar faces appearing as guests were Morgan Fairchild, Shirley Jones, Pernell Roberts, Arte Johnson, Liberace, Donald O'Connor, McLean Stevenson, Stewart Granger, Connie Stevens, Peter Marshall, and Lynn Redgrave. Prior to the series' debut there was much publicity about the signing of Bette Davis for the recurring role of Laura Trent; however, due to illness she was seen only on the premiere and then departed on an "extended trip," leaving Victoria in charge.

When *grande dame* Victoria died in the middle of the 1985–1986 season it was revealed that she had left her half interest in the St. Gregory to her loyal assistant Peter. He promptly made *his* loyal assistant—and growing love interest—Christine the new general manager, while eager Megan became the new assistant manager. All this happiness was temporarily interrupted by a battle for control of the hotel waged by members of the Cabot family who owned the other half—Charles (played by Efrem Zimbalist, Jr.), Jessica (Dina Merrill), and Jake (Ralph Bellamy)—but in the end Peter managed to buy them out.

The series was based, more or less, on Arthur Hailey's best-selling novel of sex and scandal, and was also known as *Arthur Hailey's "Hotel."* The real hotel that served as its model was the regal Fairmont Hotel on Nob Hill in San Francisco, whose imposing façade was seen in exterior shots and whose giant lobby was re-created on a Hollywood sound stage.

HOTEL BROADWAY

Variety

FIRST TELECAST: *January 20, 1949*
LAST TELECAST: *March 17, 1949*
BROADCAST HISTORY:
Jan 1949–Mar 1949, DUM Thu 8:30–9:00
REGULARS:
The Striders

Low-budget musical variety program featuring different singers and comedians each week, generally of less-than-top-name caliber. Among those who appeared were Johnny Desmond, Jean Darling, and Harry Ranch's Orchestra. There was no host, but a quartet called The Striders was used to introduce each act.

HOTEL DE PAREE

Western

FIRST TELECAST: *October 2, 1959*
LAST TELECAST: *September 23, 1960*
BROADCAST HISTORY:
Oct 1959–Sep 1960, CBS Fri 8:30–9:00
CAST:

Sundance . . . . Earl Holliman
Monique . . . . Judi Meredith
Annette Deveraux . . . . Jeanette Nolan
Aaron Donager . . . . Strother Martin

Western centered in the Hotel de Paree, the fanciest (and only) lodging in Georgetown, Colorado, and its chief hero-in-residence, Sundance. Sundance had come to Georgetown via a rather circuitous route. After accidentally killing a man there, he had spent 17 years in prison. He nevertheless returned to the town upon his release, *ca.* 1870, to find the Hotel de Paree being operated by two rather attractive relatives of the dead man, Annette Deveraux and her niece, Monique. Their hotel was a little bit of European dignity in the midst of the Old West. They needed a strong arm (and fast gun) to keep things quiet, and Sundance was their man. Among his trademarks was a string of polished silver discs in the hatband of his black stetson, with which to blind his adversaries.

HOUR GLASS
see *ABC Dramatic Shorts—1952–1953*

HOUR GLASS
see *Movies—Prior to 1961*

HOUR GLASS
Variety
FIRST TELECAST: *May 9, 1946*
LAST TELECAST: *March 6, 1947*
BROADCAST HISTORY:
May 1946–Mar 1947, NBC Thu 8:00–9:00
EMCEE:
Helen Parrish (1946)
Eddie Mayehoff
PRODUCER:
Howard Reilly
DIRECTOR:
Ed Sobel

Hour Glass was one of the most important pioneers in the early history of television. Yet its very existence, much less its place in the development of the medium, has scarcely been acknowledged anywhere until now. It was the first hour-long entertainment series of any kind produced for network television, the first show to develop its own star, the first big variety series, and the most ambitious production by far ever attempted up to its time. Milton Berle, Ed Sullivan, *Your Show of Shows,* Carol Burnett, and dozens of others are all its lineal descendants, as is, in a sense, the whole concept of "big-time" television.

To understand the breakthrough that *Hour Glass* represented we might first remember the other shows on the air in 1946. Commercial television was still in its infancy, with only a few thousand sets in use, mostly in New York and a few other large cities. New York was the only city with more than one station, and was the nation's TV "capital." The week in which *Hour Glass* premiered looked like this, in New York. Monday: one station on the air for one hour, with a 30-minute fashion show and a 30-minute excerpt from a grade-B Western film (*The Fighting Deputy* with Fred Scott). Tuesday: one station on for 90 minutes, 30 minutes of informal skits, 30 minutes of travel films, and 30 minutes of a disc-jockey

show called *King's Record Shop.* Wednesday: two stations on, one with film shorts and the other with 90 minutes of mixed films and studio chatter. Thursday: the other two channels offered a cartoonist, a newscast, and an adaptation of the radio show *Famous Jury Trials.* Friday: three stations on, with some very obscure grade-B films, a short studio game show, and boxing from St. Nicholas Arena. This, pretty much, had been typical of TV programming up to that time.

Hour Glass was sponsored by a major company, Standard Brands (Chase & Sanborn Coffee, Tender Leaf Tea), which poured more money into it than TV had ever seen before—reportedly $200,000 over the show's ten-month run. For the first time there was money for elaborate sets, specially made films, and reasonably respectable talent. Of course everything they tried was an experiment, since no one had attempted such a show before. The premiere telecast, on May 9, 1946, opened with a song by recording star Evelyn Knight, followed by a seriocomic sketch starring actor Paul Douglas, set in a cabin. Next came a live commercial for Chase and Sanborn coffee—two and a half minutes long! Comedian Joe Besser then appeared with several supporting players in a hilarious take-off on the military entitled "The Rookie," followed in quick succession by a ballroom-dancing sequence, a brief talk about TV and a booklet available on the subject from NBC, another song by Evelyn Knight, a monologue by fast-talking comic Doodles Weaver (a well-known personality in the 1940s), and finally a film of South American dancing. The end commercial, which included film of coffee-growing country, ran for four and a half minutes.

Subsequent shows tightened up the commercials quite a bit, and also brought on such acts as Bert Lahr, the singing Merry Macs, Dennis Day, Jerry Colonna, Joey Faye, and Peggy Lee. In November the show added TV's first regular chorus line, a group of leggy beauties. Compared to the nightclub rejects generally seen on TV in the late 1940s this was big talent indeed. Perhaps the biggest coup was the TV debut, on November 14, 1946, of ventriloquist Edgar Bergen (and Charlie McCarthy). This was one of the earliest instances of a top radio star bringing his act to television, a practice which was to become quite prevalent in the years to come, until TV developed its own galaxy of stars.

The hostess on the first *Hour Glass* telecast was Evelyn Eaton, and guest hosts appeared thereafter until a pretty young actress named Helen Parrish was signed as permanent "femcee." She was bright, pixieish, and as fresh as the medium itself, and she made quite a hit with TV viewers of 1946 (just about all of whom watched *Hour Glass* on Thursday night). The sponsor gave her a substantial publicity build-up, and it was said that she became as well known, at least in the cities which had TV, as the top radio stars of the day. She left the show in November to have a

357

baby, after which her co-host Eddie Mayehoff took over.

Standard Brands was well aware that the limited viewership of television at this time did not justify such a large investment on a purely financial basis. But they, and NBC, wanted to see what could be done with the new medium, and the lessons they learned have influenced what we see today. They learned, for example, not to let single commercials run for four to five minutes; that money is better spent on obtaining "star" talent than on fancy, highly visual sets; that viewers liked the idea of a regular host (or hostess) providing continuity from week to week; and that TV in general was a medium which demanded staging and pacing far different from movies, the stage, or radio.

The network history of *Hour Glass* is sketchy, due to incomplete records for this very early period. NBC's network consisted of three stations at the time, in New York, Philadelphia, and Schenectady, and while it is not known whether *Hour Glass* was being fed to all three at the start (it originated in New York) it definitely was on the network by early November at the latest.

More than a year was to pass after the demise of *Hour Glass* before another sponsor could be induced to put similar amounts of money into television for a big-time variety hour. That one, drawing on the lessons learned here, brought TV out of its infancy and produced its first superstar: Milton Berle. And what became of Helen Parrish? She returned to Hollywood, where she had been a child star in the 1930s, and made a few more films. She died in 1959 at the age of 35.

HOUR OF DECISION
Religion
FIRST TELECAST: *September 30, 1951*
LAST TELECAST: *February 28, 1954*
BROADCAST HISTORY:
  Sep 1951–Mar 1952, ABC Sun 10:00–10:30
  Jul 1952–Sep 1953, ABC Sun 10:00–10:15
  Sep 1953–Feb 1954, ABC Sun 10:30–10:45
HOST:
  Rev. Billy Graham

Almost from its inception as a mass medium, evangelist Billy Graham has made frequent use of television to publicize his religious crusades. During 1951–1954 the Billy Graham Evangelical Association sponsored regular weekly Sunday night talks by Dr. Graham on the ABC network.

HOUR OF STARS
  syndicated title for *20th Century-Fox Hour, The*

HOUSE CALLS
Situation Comedy
FIRST TELECAST: *December 17, 1979*
LAST TELECAST: *September 13, 1982*
BROADCAST HISTORY:
  Dec 1979–Mar 1980, CBS Mon 9:30–10:00
  May 1980–Sep 1982, CBS Mon 9:30–10:00

CAST:
Dr. Charley Michaels .... Wayne Rogers
Ann Anderson (1979–1981) .... Lynn Redgrave
Jane Jeffries (1982) .... Sharon Gless
Dr. Norman Solomon .... Ray Buktenica
Dr. Amos Weatherby .... David Wayne
Conrad Peckler (1980–1982) ... Marc L. Taylor
Mrs. Phipps .... Deedy Peters
Head Nurse Bradley .... Aneta Corsaut
Nurse Sally Bowman (1979–1980)
  .... Diane Lander
Nurse Nancy (1980–1982) .... Beth Jacobs
Nurse Shirley Bryan (1980–1982)
  .... Suzanne Hunt

Dating someone with whom you work can create problems, as Charley Michaels and Ann Anderson learned. He was a surgeon at Kensington General Hospital in San Francisco, a good doctor but less than enthusiastic about conforming to hospital rules and regulations. She was the hospital's new administrative assistant, an English lady with a commitment to keeping the hospital running efficiently. They were romantically involved but often at odds when Charley's concern for his patients conflicted with Ann's concern for the business side of Kensington. Others in the cast were Norman Solomon, a neurotic young obstetrician; Amos Weatherby, the brilliant but absentminded (some would say senile) chief of surgery; Ann's stuffy boss, Conrad Peckler; and Mrs. Phipps, a flighty hospital volunteer who provided patients with books, candy, and other inexpensive odds and ends.

A contract dispute between series co-star Lynn Redgrave and *House Calls'* producers prompted her departure in 1981. In the series' story line Ann Anderson suddenly disappeared from Kensington General but sent the staff a letter indicating that she had returned to England and her former husband. Ann's replacement, Jane Jeffries, turned out to be one of Charley's former love interests. Conveniently, his relationship with Jane was not noticeably different than the one he had had with Ann.

Based on the motion picture starring Walter Matthau and Glenda Jackson.

HOUSTON KNIGHTS
Police Drama
FIRST TELECAST: *March 12, 1987*
LAST TELECAST: *June 6, 1988*
BROADCAST HISTORY:
  Mar 1987–Apr 1987, CBS Wed 10:00–11:00
  Jul 1987–Sep 1987, CBS Tue 9:00–10:00
  Sep 1987–Dec 1987, CBS Tue 8:00–9:00
  Jan 1988–Feb 1988, CBS Sat 9:00–10:00
  Apr 1988–Jun 1988, CBS Tue 8:00–9:00
CAST:
Sgt. Joey La Fiamma .... Michael Pare
Sgt. Levon Lundy .... Michael Beck
Clarence ("Chicken") .... John Hancock
Lt. Joanne Beaumont .... Robyn Douglass
Sgt. Joe-Bill McCandless.... James Crittenden

Annie .... Madlyn Rhue	Laura Macahan .... Kathryn Holcomb
Carol ("Legs") .... Nancy Everhard	Josh Macahan .... William Kirby Cullen
Sgt. Nat Holliday .... Brian Mitchell	Jessie Macahan .... Vicki Schreck
Sgt. Estaban Gutierrez ..... Efrain Figueroa	
Jamie Kincaid .... D. Franki Horner	
Eric Kincaid .... Dana Young	

A youth-oriented police-action series, in the *Starsky & Hutch* mold. Following the murder of his partner in an organized crime hit, high-strung, aggressive Chicago cop Joey La Fiamma transferred to the Houston Police Department to get away from the hoods who were still after him. La Fiamma's partner on the Houston force, and the person assigned to help the short-tempered Chicagoan adjust to Houston, was his opposite in temperament, laid-back Levon Lundy. Although neither of these young men was particularly fond of the other's methods, they were intensely loyal to each other. Others who worked out of their precinct were their boss, Lt. Beaumont; male officers McCandless, Holliday, and Gutierrez; and two female officers, sexy Carol and Annie, who had been confined to a wheelchair since being shot while on duty several years earlier. Chicken, who ran the rib joint where La Fiamma and Lundy hung out on their off hours, was their most reliable tipster. Lundy was dating Jamie Kincaid, a widow with a 12-year-old son, who had misgivings about dating another cop since her first husband had been killed while on duty.

HOW DID THEY GET THAT WAY
Discussion
FIRST TELECAST: *July 24, 1951*
LAST TELECAST: *March 10, 1952*
BROADCAST HISTORY:
  Jul 1951–Sep 1951, ABC Tue 8:00–8:30
  Sep 1951–Jan 1952, ABC Tue 8:30–9:00
  Feb 1952–Mar 1952, ABC Mon 9:30–10:00
MODERATOR:
  Isabelle Leighton

Public-service program dealing with emotional problems, utilizing medical films and discussions by psychiatrists and guests. Among the topics covered were "Gossip," "Hostility," "Feelings of Rejection," and "Why Tommy Won't Eat." During its first few months the program was known as *What's on Your Mind*.

HOW THE WEST WAS WON
Western
FIRST TELECAST: *February 12, 1978*
LAST TELECAST: *April 23, 1979*
BROADCAST HISTORY:
  Feb 1978–May 1978, ABC Sun 8:00–9:00
  Jul 1978–Aug 1978, ABC Sun 8:00–9:00
  Jan 1979–Apr 1979, ABC Mon 9:00–11:00
CAST:
  Zeb Macahan .... James Arness
  Aunt Molly Culhane ..... Fionnula Flanagan
  Luke Macahan .... Bruce Boxleitner

James Arness, Marshal Dillon of the long-running *Gunsmoke* series, returned to TV screens in 1978 in this mixture of Western adventure and soap opera. Zeb Macahan was a rugged mountain man who had spent ten years in the Dakota Territory before returning to Virginia, where his brother's family was preparing to make the long trek west. No sooner had they set out than the Civil War broke out. Zeb's brother Timothy returned east and his wife Kate was subsequently killed in an accident, leaving the four Macahan children in Zeb's care. Luke, the eldest, had killed three men in self-defense, and was a fugitive from the law; Laura was pretty and ready for womanhood; Jessie was the tomboyish 12-year-old; and teenager Josh was exuberant and anxious to become the man of the family. Aunt Molly, Kate's widowed sister, came from Boston to help them on the long journey, through dangers and hardships caused by Indians, renegades, nature, and the other perils of an untamed West. After an initial run in 1978, the series returned in early 1979 with 11 new two-hour episodes depicting the Macahans as they homesteaded a ranch in the Tetons, and began to raise Appaloosa horses.

Adding to the epic scope of the series was the spectacular setting; the program was filmed on location in Utah, Colorado, Arizona, and Southern California. The executive producer was John Mantley, who had also been the producer of *Gunsmoke*. The series was based on the 1963 motion picture of the same name, which was directed by John Ford and featured an all-star cast, including John Wayne.

HOW TO
Informational
FIRST TELECAST: *July 10, 1951*
LAST TELECAST: *September 11, 1951*
BROADCAST HISTORY:
  Jul 1951–Sep 1951, CBS Tue 9:00–9:30
MODERATOR:
  Roger Price
PANEL:
  Leonard Stern
  Stanley Adams
  Anita Martell

The solutions that moderator Roger Price and his panel of experts had for the various questions that were asked of them were not the most sensible in the world. To the person who asked "How to" open a beer can with a thumbtack the response was "place the tack on top of the can and hit it with a large ax." The obvious way to keep a faucet from leaking was to turn it on. Such pearls of wisdom were dispensed weekly on both radio and television (though not simulcast) during the summer of 1951.

HOW TO MARRY A MILLIONAIRE

Situation Comedy

BROADCAST HISTORY:

Syndicated only

30 minutes

Produced: *1957–1959* (52 episodes)

Released: *October 1958*

CAST:

"Mike" McCall	Merry Anders
Loco Jones	Barbara Eden
Greta (1957–1958)	Lori Nelson
Gwen Kirby (1958–1959)	Lisa Gaye

Cheerful comedy about three sexy New York career girls living in a swank penthouse apartment they can barely afford, and out to snare rich husbands by any scheme they can concoct. The series was based on the hit 1953 movie of the same name, with Barbara Eden as Loco, the dimwitted blonde who was so nearsighted she kept walking into walls (the Marilyn Monroe role); Lori Nelson as Greta, the breezy manhunter (Betty Grable); and Merry Anders as Mike, the ringleader of the group (Lauren Bacall). The names of the girls were somewhat different in the film (Pola, Loco, and Schatz), but the glamorous gold-digging theme was the same.

Lori Nelson, upset that her role wasn't bigger, quit after the first season to do "heavier" stuff, and was written out as having married and moved away; she was replaced by Lisa Gaye. Miss Nelson was never heard from again (she was married for a time to musician Johnny Mann, but has never done another TV series or movie). Lisa and Merry—who had a bit part in the 1953 movie—didn't fare much better after this series, making a few B-pictures in the 1960s and then disappearing (Anders' last film was *Women of the Prehistoric Planet* in 1966). However, Barbara Eden went on to TV stardom in the long-running *I Dream of Jeannie,* and later returned to TV on *Harper Valley P.T.A.*

HOWARD K. SMITH—NEWS AND COMMENT

News Commentary

FIRST TELECAST: *February 14, 1962*

LAST TELECAST: *June 16, 1963*

BROADCAST HISTORY:

Feb 1962–Sep 1962, ABC Wed 7:30–8:00

Sep 1962–Jun 1963, ABC Sun 10:30–11:00

NEWSMAN:

Howard K. Smith

In his first regular television assignment for ABC, after severing a 20-year relationship with CBS News, Howard K. Smith presented this weekly news and commentary program. It featured a summary of the week's major news events, commentary and analysis by Mr. Smith, and interviews with prominent people in the news.

HUCK FINN

see *New Adventures of Huck Finn, The*

HUDSON BROTHERS SHOW, THE

Variety

FIRST TELECAST: *July 31, 1974*

LAST TELECAST: *August 28, 1974*

BROADCAST HISTORY:

Jul 1974–Aug 1974, CBS Wed 8:00–9:00

REGULARS:

The Hudson Brothers (Bill, Brett, and Mark)

Ronny Graham

Gary Owens

Stephanie Edwards

Ron Hull

The Jaime Rogers Dancers

The Jack Eskew Orchestra

Katee McClure

The Hudson Brothers were, according to series producer Alan Blye, "a cross between the Marx Brothers and the Beatles." They sang reasonably well and did sketch and monologue comedy in this short-lived summer variety series. They were all in their 20s and much of their material was aimed at the under-35 audience.

HULLABALOO

Music

FIRST TELECAST: *January 12, 1965*

LAST TELECAST: *August 29, 1966*

BROADCAST HISTORY:

Jan 1965–May 1965, NBC Tue 8:30–9:30

Jun 1965–Aug 1965, NBC Tue 10:00–11:00

Sep 1965–Aug 1966, NBC Mon 7:30–8:00

REGULARS:

The Hullabaloo Dancers (6 girls, 4 boys)

MUSIC DIRECTOR:

Peter Matz

PRODUCER:

Gary Smith

Hullabaloo was one of TV's few attempts to give rock 'n' roll a big-budget, top-quality showcase all its own in prime time. (Another, seen at about the same time, was *Shindig.*) Each week top popular recording artists performed their current hits, backed by elaborate production and the frenetic, miniskirted Hullabaloo Dancers. The whole affair was very youth-oriented, with a great deal of noise and motion, and the general atmosphere was that of a discotheque in full swing—in fact, one segment was called "Hullabaloo A-Go-Go." (Just for the record, "the girl in the cage" doing a perpetual frug was Lada Edmund, Jr.) A different host presided each week, including Paul Anka, Jack Jones, Frankie Avalon and Annette Funicello, and Jerry Lewis (with his rock-star son, Gary). Performing were such acts as the Supremes, the Ronettes, Sonny and Cher, and many others. A special feature during the first three months was a weekly segment taped in London, hosted by rock impresario Brian Epstein and presenting top English acts such as Gerry and the Pacemakers, Marianne Faithful, Herman's Hermits, and the Moody Blues. Brian never brought on the biggest English superstars of all, however—his own protégés, the Beatles. (They finally did appear after Brian had left the show, in a January 1966 telecast.)

HUMBLE REPORT, THE
Documentary
FIRST TELECAST: *March 1, 1964*
LAST TELECAST: *September 15, 1964*
BROADCAST HISTORY:
Mar 1964–May 1964, NBC Sun 10:00–11:00
Jun 1964–Sep 1964, NBC Tue 10:00–11:00

This series of full-hour documentaries on various subjects, ranging from political issues to a profile of baseball player Willie Mays, aired on alternate weeks during the spring and summer of 1964. It was sponsored by the Humble Oil Company.

HUNTER
Foreign Intrigue
FIRST TELECAST: *February 18, 1977*
LAST TELECAST: *May 27, 1977*
BROADCAST HISTORY:
Feb 1977–May 1977, CBS Fri 10:00–11:00
CAST:
James Hunter............. James Franciscus
Marty Shaw.................. Linda Evans
Gen. Baker................. Ralph Bellamy

Working for top Federal intelligence chief General Baker, James Hunter and his partner Marty Shaw were called upon to fight a multitude of international foes in their jobs as undercover counterespionage agents. Sometimes they fought with Communists, sometimes with underworld organizations, and occasionally with other U.S. intelligence agencies. Their assignments took them all over the world.

HUNTER
Police Drama
FIRST TELECAST: *September 18, 1984*
LAST TELECAST:
BROADCAST HISTORY:
Sep 1984, NBC Tue 9:00–10:00
Sep 1984–Jan 1985, NBC Fri 9:00–10:00
Mar 1985–Feb 1986, NBC Sat 10:00–11:00
Mar 1986–Aug 1986, NBC Tue 9:00–10:00
Aug 1986–Dec 1987, NBC Sat 10:00–11:00
Dec 1987–Mar 1988, NBC Tue 9:00–10:00
Mar 1988– , NBC Sat 10:00–11:00
CAST:
Det. Sgt. Rick Hunter............ Fred Dryer
Det. Sgt. Dee Dee McCall.. Stepfanie Kramer
Sgt. Bernie Terwilliger (1984–1986)
.... James Whitmore, Jr.
Capt. Lester Cain (pilot)
.... Michael Cavanaugh
Capt. Lester Cain (1984) ... Arthur Rosenberg
Captain Dolan (1984–1985)....... John Amos
Capt. Wyler (1985–1986)...... Bruce Davison

Capt. Charlie Devane (1986–   )
.... Charles Hallahan
Lt. Ambrose Finn (1985–   ) ... John Shearin
*Carlos (1985–1987)...... Richard Beauchamp
Arnold "Sporty" James (1986–   )
.... Garrett Morris
*Barney (1987–   ).............. Perry Cook
Reuben Garcia (1987–   ) ..... Rudy Ramos

*Occasional

One of the biggest box-office draws of the 1970s and 1980s was Clint Eastwood in his characterization of the violent, give-'em-no-quarter cop, Dirty Harry. Perhaps it was inevitable that television would produce its own version of this popular character, only slightly softened for the home screen. "Make my day," growled Harry as he aimed his pistol at a felon about to flee; "works for me" was Hunter's catchphrase. Both had magnum revolvers big enough to send speeding cars into spectacular crashes. Hunter's was called Simon ("Says who?" scowled the crook; "Simon says," replied Hunter, brandishing the weapon). Both were saddled with incompetent superiors who didn't understand their forceful ways and were constantly after their badges.

There were some differences. Hunter had a partner, a beautiful but rather tough lady cop named Dee Dee—otherwise known as "the brass cupcake." He also had an unusual family, most of them mobsters, who sometimes gave him grief. Another source of aggravation was Bernie, the inept senior detective to whom he was occasionally assigned. At least our hero had the satisfaction of knowing that his fatuous superiors in the L.A.P.D. came and went; three different actors portrayed Hunter's captain in the first six episodes.

Providing information to help crack cases were Carlos, an assistant at the morgue, and street hustler Sporty James.

HUNTER, THE
International Intrigue
FIRST TELECAST: *July 3, 1952*
LAST TELECAST: *December 26, 1954*
BROADCAST HISTORY:
Jul 1952, CBS Thu 9:00–9:30
Jul 1952–Sep 1952, CBS Wed 9:30–10:00
Jul 1954–Dec 1954, NBC Sun 10:30–11:00
CAST:
Bart Adams (1952–1954) .... Barry Nelson
Bart Adams (1954) .... Keith Larsen

Bart Adams was a wealthy, attractive young American businessman whose interests caused him to become involved in suspenseful adventures in exotic places all over the world. In order to move about unnoticed, he was a master of disguise, changing his appearance for each show. Most of the episodes in the series had Bart rescue someone who was in the clutches of Communist agents or thwart some evil plan that Communist agents had concocted to cause trouble for the Free World. The way he identified himself to friends in the European underground was by whistling "Frère Jacques," and ending it with a wolf whistle.

This filmed series was originally a CBS summer show, but films continued to be produced for syndication after the end of its network run. The episodes aired on NBC during the summer of 1954 were drawn from these syndicated films. Some new episodes were aired on NBC in the fall of 1954, with Keith Larsen replacing Barry Nelson in the role of Bart Adams.

HUSBANDS, WIVES & LOVERS
Situation Comedy
FIRST TELECAST: *March 10, 1978*
LAST TELECAST: *June 30, 1978*
BROADCAST HISTORY:
  Mar 1978–Jun 1978, CBS Fri 10:00–11:00
CAST:
  Helene Willis.................. Jesse Welles
  Ron Willis .... Ron Rifkin
  Murray Zuckerman .... Stephen Pearlman
  Paula Zuckerman .... Cynthia Harris
  Harry Bellini .... Eddie Barth
  Joy Bellini .... Lynne Marie Stewart
  Lennie Bellini .... Mark Lonow
  Rita DeLatorre............... Randee Heller
  Dixon Carter Fielding .... Charles Siebert
  Courtney Fielding.......... Claudette Nevins

One format that has rarely worked in television, despite numerous attempts, has been the hour-long situation comedy. This one followed the lives of five couples, all friends, who lived in the San Fernando Valley suburbs outside of Los Angeles. Murray Zuckerman was a traveling salesman for a pharmaceutical firm and spent much of his time out of town; Harry Bellini was a rough-hewn, self-taught garbage truck tycoon with a young, naive second wife; Lennie was Harry's younger brother who was living with Rita DeLatorre, with whom he ran a stylish jean boutique; Ron Willis was a dentist who had an amicable relationship with his wife Helene, from whom he was separated; and Dixon Carter Fielding was Ron's best friend, a corporate attorney who was also representing Helene in the separation proceedings. Carter's wife, Courtney, was a spendthrift who managed to go through even more money than his substantial income provided.

The series was created by comedienne Joan Rivers.

I

I COVER TIMES SQUARE
Newspaper Drama
FIRST TELECAST: *October 5, 1950*
LAST TELECAST: *January 11, 1951*
BROADCAST HISTORY:
   Oct 1950–Jan 1951, ABC Thu 10:00–10:30
CAST:
   Johnny Warren . . . . Harold Huber
PRODUCER:
   Harold Huber

Harold Huber, a veteran actor who had portrayed dozens of squint-eyed, scheming villains on radio and in films (including the Charlie Chan pictures), was cast as a crusading Broadway columnist in this early series. His favorite hangout was the out-of-town newspaper stand in Times Square, and his beat, the seamy side of show business. In the first episode, for example, he was out to break up a gambling syndicate that controlled the boxing business in New York. The real-life prototype for Huber's role was said to be Walter Winchell.

After its prime-time run *I Cover Times Square* moved to Saturday afternoon, where it continued until late 1951.

I DREAM OF JEANNIE
Situation Comedy
FIRST TELECAST: *September 18, 1965*
LAST TELECAST: *September 1, 1970*
BROADCAST HISTORY:
   Sep 1965–Sep 1966, NBC Sat 8:00–8:30
   Sep 1966–Aug 1967, NBC Mon 8:00–8:30
   Sep 1967–Aug 1968, NBC Tue 7:30–8:00
   Sep 1968–Aug 1969, NBC Mon 7:30–8:00
   Sep 1969–Sep 1970, NBC Tue 7:30–8:00
CAST:
   Jeannie . . . . Barbara Eden
   Capt. Tony Nelson . . . . Larry Hagman
   Capt. Roger Healey . . . . Bill Daily
   Dr. Alfred Bellows . . . . Hayden Rorke
   Gen. Wingard Stone (1965–1966) . Philip Ober
   Melissa Stone (1965–1966) . . . . . Karen Sharpe
   Gen. Martin Peterson (1965–1969)
   . . . . Barton MacLane
   Amanda Bellows (1966–1970)
   . . . . Emmaline Henry
   Gen. Winfield Schaeffer (1969–1970)
   . . . . Vinton Hayworth

Astronaut Tony Nelson was on a space mission that aborted, forcing him to parachute onto a desert island. While waiting for a rescue team he came across an old bottle that had apparently washed ashore. When he opened the bottle, out popped a 2,000-year-old (but remarkably well-preserved) genie, who promptly accepted him as her master, since he had set her free.

Returning to Cocoa Beach, Florida, with the rescue team, Tony found that nobody would believe that he had found a luscious, sexy genie. The base psychiatrist, Dr. Bellows, was convinced that Tony had suffered delusions caused by exposure. Complicating the matter, the genie, appropriately named Jeannie, refused to perform magic or ever appear for anyone but Tony. Her efforts to serve him often resulted in rather confusing situations, caused in part by her lack of familiarity with 20th-century American customs.

I Dream of Jeannie ran for five seasons. In its first year Tony was engaged to General Stone's daughter Melissa. Since Jeannie was in love with Tony she went out of her way to make his relationship with Melissa extremely difficult. By the second season, Melissa was gone, as was her father, and Tony had a new commanding officer in General Peterson. His social life was at this point involved with his girl-crazy buddy, and fellow astronaut, Roger Healey, the only person other than Tony who realized that Jeannie existed and had magical powers. Roger was always getting Tony into situations that aggravated the very jealous Jeannie. After four seasons of trying, Jeannie finally succeeded in convincing Tony that he loved her enough to marry her and they were wed in the episode telecast on December 2, 1969.

Roger and Tony, originally captains, were both promoted to major during the run of the show.

An animated version of this series, simply titled *Jeannie*, aired Saturday mornings on CBS from September 1973 to August 1975.

I HAD THREE WIVES
Detective Comedy/Drama
FIRST TELECAST: *August 14, 1985*
LAST TELECAST: *September 13, 1985*
BROADCAST HISTORY:
   Aug 1985–Sep 1985, CBS Wed 8:00–9:00
   Sep 1985, CBS Fri 8:00–9:00
CAST:
   Jackson Beaudine . . . . Victor Garber
   Mary Parker . . . . Maggie Cooper
   Liz . . . . Shanna Reed
   Samantha . . . . Teri Copley
   Andrew Beaudine . . . . David Faustino
   Lt. Gomez . . . . Luis Avalos

This short-lived summer detective series, set in Los Angeles, followed the cases of Jackson Beaudine, a private investigator who made the most of his extended family. A three-time loser in the marital wars, Jackson was on very good terms with his ex-wives. Mary, his first wife and the only one who had remarried, was an attorney and had custody of their 10-year-old son, Andrew. Her legal advice always proved helpful. Sam—wife number two—was an actress, master of disguise, and martial arts expert, and loved to help Jackson out whenever he needed her assistance; and third wife Liz, a newspaper reporter with keen analytical skills and a host of useful contacts, also came in handy. The three of them, all too chummy to believe, seemed more than willing to work individually or together to assist Jackson in his investigations on this rather lighthearted show.

I LED THREE LIVES
Intrigue
BROADCAST HISTORY:
Syndicated only
30 minutes
Produced: *May 1953–mid-1956* (117 episodes)
Released: *September 1953*
CAST:
Herbert Philbrick	Richard Carlson
Eva Philbrick	Virginia Stefan
Special Agent Jerry Dressler	John Zaremba
Special Agent Henderson	Ed Hinton
*Constance Philbrick	Patricia Morrow
*Special Agent Steve Daniels	John Beradino
*Special Agent Mike Andrews	
	William Hudson
*Special Agent Joe Carey	Charles Maxwell

*Occasional

This product of the McCarthy era contained what was perhaps the most explicit political propaganda ever found in a popular dramatic series on American television. Today it stands as a genuine period piece, reflecting the stereotypes that were all too prevalent during the Red Scare of the 1940s and early 1950s. In this show, Communist spies really were behind every bush, and anyone with liberal views was indeed suspect.

The program had a documentary flavor, opening with an announcer booming, "This is the fantastically true story of Herbert A. Philbrick, who for nine frightening years did lead three lives—average citizen, member of the Communist Party, and counterspy for the FBI. For obvious reasons the names, dates, and places have been changed, but the story is based on fact."

Philbrick was a pipe-smoking Boston advertising executive who infiltrated the local CP organization in order to provide information to the U.S. government. He was constantly called upon to take part in nefarious plots against the U.S., and always ran the risk of discovery and perhaps elimination as a traitor. The Communist schemes included sabotage of vital industries, stealing government secrets, dope-smuggling (to poison the nation's youth), and spreading the party line through infiltration of organizations such as labor unions, university faculties, and even churches. Sometimes Philbrick was ordered to carry out the plans himself, perhaps using his position in the advertising agency; sometimes he was just a courier. Schemes were constantly being smashed and party members arrested wherever he went, but the party hierarchy—a rather thick lot—never seemed to catch on. Still, there was constant danger, to himself, his wife Eva, and their children. Dark alleyways and secret cell meetings in base-

ments were part of every episode. So was suspicion. Any indication of left-wing views would cause a raised eyebrow, and the whispered comment "Maybe he is . . . a Communist."

In one episode a mother reported her daughter's boyfriend, Paul, because she thought he had caused her daughter to start talking about how she hated bombing and wars and such. "Where did my daughter get the outrageous ideas she's been expressing?" the mother worried. Philbrick tracked down the real Commie—an art dealer the daughter knew—and at the end noted with relief that the girl was "not only safe and sound, but cured of her Communist infection, a real dividend for her mother and Paul."

To heighten the dramatic impact, Philbrick was also the narrator, referring to himself in the third person. Even though there was little violence seen, he always emphasized the danger ("This could be a trap, Philbrick."). Politics aside, it was fascinating melodrama, tensely scripted and realistically staged, with many outdoor scenes on busy streets and on lonely highways. Occasionally Philbrick would even be sent to Europe or South America.

The only regulars besides Philbrick and his wife were the FBI agents with whom he rendezvoused, played most frequently by John Zaremba (a regular after the first few episodes) and Ed Hinton. The Reds got arrested so regularly that none of them lasted long.

Observers today might wonder how viewers in the 1950s could take so seriously the idea that "your best friend may be a traitor" (as opposed to the dangers of international Communism). The series got much of its impact from the fact that it was based on a true story, as told by the real Herbert A. Philbrick in his best-selling book *I Led Three Lives*. Philbrick himself served as technical consultant. The program even had the approval of J. Edgar Hoover and the FBI, which reviewed all scripts. In later episodes, as the writers began to run out of material, the stories strayed further and further from actual events. One episode even had the Commies plotting to undermine the U.S. guided-missile program by converting vacuum cleaners into bomb launchers.

This type of topical politico-drama was by no means new. Several popular radio series during World War II depicted scheming Nazis infiltrating the U.S., and there had already been a movie (1951) and a radio series (1952) titled *I Was A Communist for the F.B.I.*, based on a story similar to Philbrick's. Then too, many viewers, especially younger ones (including this writer), saw it as simply a good detective yarn with lots of suspense and no real political overtones at all. The very fact that it was on television, surrounded by all kinds of adventure fantasies, encouraged this attitude.

As for those involved in the series, they saw the program primarily as a profit-maker. "We're not trying to deliver a message," stated the production company, Ziv. "That's not our field. Our chief purpose is to find good story properties, turn them into good films, and sell them." Richard Carlson, when queried, invariably rattled off the financial advantages (he got a piece of the profits) and the benefits of a filmed series in allowing him time for other pursuits. "I'm just an actor," he insisted. "Philbrick is the guy who made the contribution, not me." Still, he admitted, he did see it as a "public service." Virginia Stefan expressed amazement at the seriousness with which some viewers took the show. "It's hard to believe, but people actually write us and ask us to investigate Communists in their neighborhood." The letters were turned over to the FBI.

Most politically motivated was author Philbrick, whose new career as a lecturer and writer on the Communist menace was boosted no end by this hit series. Philbrick continues to lecture to this day, and currently puts out a newsletter from Washington, D.C.

Whatever the motives of those involved, *I Led Three Lives* was one of the major syndicated hits of television history. Breweries were its most frequent sponsors, but oil and steel companies, banks and utilities felt that it was an excellent public-service program for their patriotic "image" advertising and continued to sponsor reruns well into the 1960s. Today, however, *I Led Three Lives* is simply an especially interesting reflection of a very different time.

I LOVE LUCY

Situation Comedy

FIRST TELECAST: *October 15, 1951*
LAST TELECAST: *September 24, 1961*
BROADCAST HISTORY:

Oct 1951–Jun 1957, CBS Mon 9:00–9:30 (OS)
Apr 1955–Oct 1955, CBS Sun 6:00–6:30
Oct 1955–Apr 1956, CBS Sat 6:30–7:00
Sep 1957–May 1958, CBS Wed 7:30–8:00
Jul 1958–Sep 1958, CBS Mon 9:00–9:30
Oct 1958–May 1959, CBS Thu 7:30–8:00
Jul 1959–Sep 1959, CBS Fri 8:30–9:00
Sep 1961, CBS Sun 6:30–7:00

CAST:

Lucy Ricardo .... Lucille Ball
Ricky Ricardo .... Desi Arnaz
Ethel Mertz.................. Vivian Vance
Fred Mertz .... William Frawley
Little Ricky Ricardo (1956–1957)
.... Richard Keith
Betty Ramsey (1957) .... Mary Jane Croft
Ralph Ramsey (1957).......... Frank Nelson

THEME:

"I Love Lucy," by Harold Adamson and Eliot Daniel

Lucille Ball had spent three seasons on CBS radio as the female lead in the situation comedy *My Favorite Husband* when she decided to give the new medium, television, a try. In her radio role as Liz Cooper, she perfected many of the mannerisms that she would use in *I Love Lucy*, including the scatterbrained quality and the loud crying fits

when things weren't going her way. CBS was enthusiastic about the concept of the show, but the network nabobs had two major objections—they were positive nobody would believe Desi was her husband (despite the fact that they were married in real life), and they wanted the show done live from New York, like most of the other early television comedies. Lucy was determined to use Desi and had no desire to commute from Hollywood to New York for the show. In the summer of 1950 the two of them went on tour performing before live audiences to prove that Desi was believable as her husband, and early in 1951 they produced a film pilot for the series with $5,000 of their own money. The pilot convinced the CBS brass that they had something special and *I Love Lucy* was given a berth on the fall schedule.

The premise of *I Love Lucy* was not that much different from that of other family situation comedies on television and radio—a wacky wife making life difficult for a loving but perpetually irritated husband—but the people involved made it something very special. Lucy Ricardo was an American of Scottish ancestry (maiden name MacGillicuddy) married to a Cuban bandleader. Husband Ricky was employed at the Tropicana Club and since she was constantly trying to prove to him that she could be in show business too, he spent much of his time trying to keep Lucy off the nightclub's stage. Ricky just wanted her to be a simple housewife. Whenever he became particularly exasperated with one of her schemes, Ricky's already broken English would degenerate into a stream of Spanish epithets. The Tropicana Club was in Manhattan, and so was the Ricardo apartment, in a middle-class building in the East 60s where their neighbors, best friends, and landlords were Fred and Ethel Mertz. Lucy's partner in mischief was Ethel, and both Ricky and Fred had to endure the foolishness perpetrated by their wives.

I Love Lucy was an immediate smash hit and, during its six years in originals, never ranked lower than third in popularity among all television programs. The plots, by writers Madelyn Pugh and Bob Carroll, Jr., were superb, the gags were inventive, and Lucy's clowning the *pièce de résistance* that took *I Love Lucy* beyond the realm of other contemporary comedies. As wacky as she was, audiences could empathize with and adore her. Watching *I Love Lucy* in the early 1950s became as much a part of life as watching Milton Berle's *Texaco Star Theater* had been in the late 1940s. It was a national event when, on January 19, 1953, Lucy Ricardo gave birth to Little Ricky on the air, the same night that Lucille Ball gave birth to her second child, Desiderio Alberto Arnaz IV.

Over the years, within the context of the show, Ricky became more successful. He got a movie offer that prompted a cross-country trip by car, with the Mertzes, during the 1954–1955 season. During the 1955–1956 season they took a trip to Europe, also with the Mertzes, and at the start of the 1956–1957 season Ricky opened his own club, the Ricky Ricardo Babaloo Club. He had also gotten a TV show and, with his good fortune, bought a country home in Connecticut early in 1957. (See *Lucy in Connecticut* for complete description.) It was also during the 1956–1957 season that Little Ricky was added to the regular cast. He had been played on a very occasional basis in the previous seasons by a pair of infant twins, Joseph David Mayer and Michael Lee Mayer.

Everyone has certain favorite episodes of *I Love Lucy,* and there were so many memorable ones that trying to cite the "best" is particularly difficult. Even CBS executives had problems doing it. During the summer of 1958 there was a collection of reruns titled *The Top Ten Lucy Shows*— there were 13 different episodes in that "top 10." There was the show in which Lucy maneuvered her way onto Ricky's TV show to do a health-tonic commercial, and got drunk sampling the high-alcohol-content product. There was the time she tried to bake her own bread, and was pinned to the far wall of her kitchen when the loaf—into which she had thrown two entire packages of yeast—was released from the oven. While looking for souvenirs to take back to New York from their trip to Hollywood, Lucy and Ethel tried to pry loose the block of cement with John Wayne's footprints from in front of Grauman's Chinese Theatre. There was the time Lucy tried to get into Ricky's nightclub show by impersonating a clown. When they were going to be interviewed on the TV show *Face to Face* they almost got into a fight with the Mertzes because Ricky's new agent wanted them to move into a classier apartment. The messiest episode, however, had to be one that was part of their trip to Europe. Lucy had been offered a minor role in a film by an Italian producer and, in an effort to absorb atmosphere, ended up in a vat of unpressed grapes fighting with a professional grape stomper.

The success of *I Love Lucy* is unparalleled in the history of television. The decision to film it, rather than do it live, made it possible to have a high-quality print of each episode available for endless rebroadcasts, as opposed to the poor-quality kinescopes of live shows. The reruns, sold to independent stations after *I Love Lucy* left the network, and translated into virtually every language for foreign distribution, made millions. This set the pattern for all of television. The appeal of reusable filmed programs, all started by *I Love Lucy,* eventually resulted in the shift of television production from New York, where it had all started, to Hollywood, where the film facilities were. *I Love Lucy* was practically unique in that it was filmed before a live audience, something that did not become widespread in the situation comedy world until the 1970s, and the technique of simultaneously using three cameras during the filming to allow for editing of the finished product was also a *Lucy* first.

By the end of the 1956–1957 season, despite the fact it was still the number one program in all of television, *I Love Lucy* ceased production as a weekly series. For the two years prior to the suspension of production, both Lucy and Desi had been seeking to cut down on their workload. They finally succeeded. After the fall of 1957 there was no *I Love Lucy,* but there were a number of *Lucille Ball-Desi Arnaz Shows,* full-hour specials about the continuing travels and tribulations of the Ricardos and the Mertzes. Reruns of *I Love Lucy* had aired during the summer of 1955 as *The Sunday Lucy Show* and during the 1955–1956 season on Saturdays as *The Lucy Show.* With the original show out of production, prime-time reruns of *I Love Lucy* were aired for another two years on CBS, showed up briefly in 1961, and ran in daytime on CBS until 1967. The syndicated reruns have been running continuously ever since, and there is no end in sight.

I LOVE TO EAT
Cooking
FIRST TELECAST: *August 30, 1946*
LAST TELECAST: *May 18, 1947*
BROADCAST HISTORY:
  Aug 1946–Oct 1946, NBC Fri 8:15–8:30 (approximately)
  Nov 1946–Mar 1947, NBC Fri 8:30–8:45
  Apr 1947–May 1947, NBC Thu 8:30–9:00
HOST:
  James Beard

This Borden-sponsored program opened with a sketch of Elsie, the famed Borden cow. Then James Beard took over to demonstrate the preparation of some of his unique dishes for the television audience. Beard's cooking demonstrations were seen earlier as a segment of NBC-TV's *Radio City Matinee.*

I MARRIED DORA
Situation Comedy
FIRST TELECAST: *September 22, 1987*
LAST TELECAST:
BROADCAST HISTORY:
  Sep 1987, ABC Tue 9:30–10:00
  Sep 1987–Jan 1988, ABC Fri 8:30–9:00
  May 1988–   , ABC Fri 9:30–10:00
CAST:
  Peter Farrell............. Daniel Hugh-Kelly
  Dora Calderon.............. Elizabeth Pena
  Kate Farrell (age 13).......... Juliette Lewis
  Will Farrell (11) .... Jason Horst
  Hughes Whitney Lennox .... Henry Jones
  Dolf Menninger.............. Sanford Jensen
  Marisol Calderon .... Evelyn Guerrero

This short-lived sitcom wins the Trivia Award both for the most outrageous premise of 1987, and for the most bizarre final episode. The idea, you see, was that busy Los Angeles architect and single dad Peter was faced with the loss of his efficient young housekeeper, a Central American refugee named Dora. The feds had discovered that she was an illegal alien and were about to deport her. So Peter, ever the practical type, married her—so that she could continue to be his maid. "No love," he kept reassuring her, "this is just a formality." Dora, a feisty young woman who assumed she would be shot if she were sent back to her native country, went along.

When it was pointed out to ABC that marrying an alien for the purpose of avoiding deportation was a direct violation of U.S. law, the network nonchalantly inserted a full-screen announcement in the premiere episode; it stated that what the series was depicting constituted a federal offense, and then helpfully added "You should not try this in your own home"! Peter (who apparently did not see the notice) then proceeded to marry Dora, while the laugh track roared. So much for love and legality.

Looking on were Peter's young kids Kate and Will, who really liked Dora and thought it was all a neat idea, legal or not. Mr. Lennox was Peter's doddering boss at the office, and Marisol was Dora's occasionally seen sister.

I Married Dora had a short run, and one of TV history's most surprising final episodes. In the last original telecast Peter received a lucrative offer for a two-year job in Bahrein, packed his bags, and prepared to leave Dora and the family. Dora pleaded with him not to go and couldn't believe he'd actually get on the plane, but he did. Then, to everyone's surprise, he got off again.

Peter: "It's been canceled."
Dora: "The flight?"
Peter: "No, our series!"

The camera then pulled back revealing the stage and crew as everyone waved goodbye to the few remaining viewers. Now that's how a failed sitcom *should* end!

I MARRIED JOAN

Situation Comedy
FIRST TELECAST: *October 15, 1952*
LAST TELECAST: *April 6, 1955*
BROADCAST HISTORY:
    Oct 1952–Apr 1955, NBC Wed 8:00–8:30
CAST:
    Joan Stevens.................... Joan Davis
    Judge Bradley Stevens........... Jim Backus
    Minerva Parker (1952–1953)... Hope Emerson
    Beverly (1953–1955) .... Beverly Wills
    Mabel (1953–1954) .... Geraldine Carr
    Janet Tobin (1954–1955)...... Sheila Bromley
    Kerwin Tobin (1954–1955)........ Dan Tobin

Bradley Stevens served as a judge in domestic court. Each episode opened with Judge Stevens on the bench. In the course of trying to resolve the problems of those who came before him, he would explain to them how he had dealt with a similar type of problem with his own beloved but slightly wacky wife, Joan. As he started to tell the story, the courtroom scene would fade into his home

and the situation would be enacted. During the first season, Joan's next-door neighbor and partner-in-mischief was Minerva Parker. The following two seasons Joan Davis's real daughter was the only other regular in the cast, playing the part of Joan Stevens's much younger college-student sister, Beverly. Mabel and Janet, two of Joan's friends, also turned up frequently during the next two years.

I REMEMBER MAMA

see *Mama*

I SPY

Adventure/Espionage
FIRST TELECAST: *September 15, 1965*
LAST TELECAST: *September 2, 1968*
BROADCAST HISTORY:
    Sep 1965–Sep 1967, NBC Wed 10:00–11:00
    Sep 1967–Sep 1968, NBC Mon 10:00–11:00
CAST:
    Kelly Robinson .... Robert Culp
    Alexander Scott .... Bill Cosby

I Spy was a departure from the traditional type of show about espionage. Both of its leads were realistically conceived characters and could see the humor in situations, enabling them to have fun with their work. It had its share of cloak-and-dagger action, but never took itself too seriously. Comedian Bill Cosby, who provided much of the subtle humor in the show, proved he was an accomplished serious actor and had the added distinction of being the first black performer to have a starring role in a regular dramatic series on American television.

Kelly Robinson and Alexander Scott were a team of American agents. The cover used by Kelly was that of a top-seeded tennis player traveling around the world for tournaments. A former law student at Princeton, he had played on two Davis Cup teams. Alexander Scott's cover was as trainer and traveling companion to Robinson. A graduate of Temple and a Rhodes scholar, his knowledge of languages was often useful in dealing with people all over the world. Both of them were dedicated to government service and America, but their dedication did not stop them from often questioning the motives and purposes behind some of the maneuvers in which they were involved. Their casual approach to life, and job, was a very refreshing contrast to the nature of their work.

ICE PALACE

Musical Variety
FIRST TELECAST: *May 23, 1971*
LAST TELECAST: *July 25, 1971*
BROADCAST HISTORY:
    May 1971–Jul 1971, CBS Sun 10:00–11:00

Each week the cast was different but the format remained the same; a guest celebrity host, one or two featured musical or comedy acts, and a selection of performers from The Ice Capades. Everything was tied to and revolved around the skating acts, which made this variety series somewhat different from most.

ICHABOD AND ME
Situation Comedy
FIRST TELECAST: *September 26, 1961*
LAST TELECAST: *September 18, 1962*
BROADCAST HISTORY:
  Sep 1961–Sep 1962, CBS Tue 9:30–10:00
CAST:
  Robert Major . . . . Robert Sterling
  Ichabod Adams . . . . George Chandler
  Abigail Adams . . . . Christine White
  Benjie Major . . . . Jimmy Mathers
  Aunt Lavinia . . . . Reta Shaw
  Jonathan Baylor . . . . Jimmy Hawkins
  Martin Perkins . . . . Guy Raymond
  Olaf . . . . Burt Mustin
  Colby . . . . Forrest Lewis

Tiring of the rat race of newspaper work in New York City, reporter Bob Major bought the only paper in a small rural town called Phippsboro, and moved there with his six-year-old son, Benjie. The man from whom Bob had purchased the paper, and who still owned most of the town, was Ichabod Adams. Ichabod still kept his finger in the operation of the paper, while his attractive young daughter Abigail kept her eye on the highly eligible Mr. Major. Bob, a widower, spent most of his time winding down to the snail's pace of Phippsboro and of the small *Phippsboro Bulletin.*

I'D LIKE TO SEE
Demonstration
FIRST TELECAST: *November 5, 1948*
LAST TELECAST: *March 29, 1949*
BROADCAST HISTORY:
  Nov 1948–Dec 1948, NBC Fri 9:00–9:30
  Dec 1948–Mar 1949, NBC Tue 9:00–9:30
HOST:
  Ray Morgan
REGULAR:
  Kuda Bux (Jan–Mar)

Viewer-participation program, which was the prototype for the long-running DuMont/ABC series *You Asked for It* (1950–1959). Viewers were asked to write in suggestions for unusual places or things they would like to see, and these were then presented via a combination of films and live studio demonstrations. The first show, for example, included scenes of the United Nations building, an Edgar Bergen–Charlie McCarthy routine, and film clips of presidents of the U.S. from McKinley to Truman. In January Indian performer Kuda Bux, "the man with the X-ray vision," was added as a regular and viewers were asked what feats they would like to see him perform blindfolded.

IDENTIFY
Quiz
FIRST TELECAST: *February 14, 1949*
LAST TELECAST: *May 9, 1949*
BROADCAST HISTORY:
  Feb 1949–May 1949, ABC Mon 9:00–9:15
HOST:
  Bob Elson

This short-lived sports picture quiz originated in Chicago. Each week three contestants attempted to identify scenes from the sports world, through films, drawings, and photographs.

IF YOU HAD A MILLION
syndicated title for *The Millionaire*

IGOR CASSINI SHOW, THE
Interview
FIRST TELECAST: *October 25, 1953*
LAST TELECAST: *March 3, 1954*
BROADCAST HISTORY:
  Oct 1953–Jan 1954, DUM Sun 6:00–6:30
  Jan 1954–Mar 1954, DUM Sun 6:15–6:30
HOST:
  Igor Cassini

Igor Cassini, who as Cholly Knickerbocker wrote a society gossip column for the Hearst papers, hosted this interview program which was filmed in the homes of the guests. Typical of Cassini's guests was his first, Mrs. Gwen Cafritz, Washington's leading hostess. Society and literary types made up the bulk of the interviews. Cassini also reviewed current films and plays. The program was also known as *Exclusively Yours.*

ILONA MASSEY SHOW, THE
Music
FIRST TELECAST: *November 1, 1954*
LAST TELECAST: *January 3, 1955*
BROADCAST HISTORY:
  Nov 1954–Jan 1955, DUM Mon 8:00–8:30
REGULARS:
  Ilona Massey
  Irving Fields Trio

Hungarian-born movie actress Ilona Massey sang sultry ballads in a nightclub atmosphere in this short-lived musical show. The Irving Fields Trio provided instrumental backing to her intimate song styling.

I'M A BIG GIRL NOW
Situation Comedy
FIRST TELECAST: *October 31, 1980*
LAST TELECAST: *July 24, 1981*
BROADCAST HISTORY:
  Oct 1980–July 1981, ABC Fri 8:30–9:00
CAST:
  Diana Cassidy . . . . Diana Canova
  Dr. Benjamin Douglass . . . . . . Danny Thomas
  Rebecca "Becky" Cassidy . . . . Rori King

Walter Douglass	Michael Durrell
Neal Stryker	Martin Short
Karen Hawks	Deborah Baltzell
Edie McKendrick	Sheree North

THEME:

"I'm a Big Girl Now," by George Aliceson Tipton and Leslie Bricusse, sung by Diana Canova

Danny Thomas returned to television in this gentle father-daughter comedy. He was Dr. Benjamin Douglass, a cantankerous dentist made all the more so by the fact that his wife had just run off to Spain with his partner, Ira. At the same time his pretty daughter, Diana, divorced her husband. Both a bit shell-shocked, father and daughter decided to live under the same roof for a while, for mutual support. The problem was for *her* to convince *him* she wasn't his little girl anymore, and to stop trying to run her life. Since they were both dating from time to time, she had some ammunition. With them was Diana's cute little scene-stealing seven-year-old daughter, Becky. Walter was Benjamin's neurotic son; and Edie, the hypertense boss at the research institute where Diana worked, in downtown Washington, D.C.

I'M DICKENS—HE'S FENSTER

Situation Comedy

FIRST TELECAST: *September 28, 1962*
LAST TELECAST: *September 13, 1963*
BROADCAST HISTORY:
 Sep 1962–Sep 1963, ABC Fri 9:00–9:30
CAST:

Arch Fenster	Marty Ingels
Harry Dickens	John Astin
Kate Dickens	Emmaline Henry
Mel Warshaw	Dave Ketchum
Mulligan	Henry Beckman
Myron Bannister	Frank DeVol

Comedy bordering on the slapstick with Dickens and Fenster, two carpenter-construction workers who were constantly getting into dangerous situations on and off the job. Single Arch Fenster was the more scatterbrained of the two, married Harry Dickens the responsible one. Warshaw and Mulligan were friends on the job. Bandleader Frank DeVol portrayed the balding building contractor in this series.

I'M THE LAW

Police Drama

BROADCAST HISTORY:
 Syndicated only
 30 minutes
 Produced: *1952–1953* (26 episodes)
 Released: *Early 1953*
CAST:

Lt. George Kirby	George Raft

Movie tough guy George Raft, who portrayed criminals in most of his screen roles, was a tough

New York City police lieutenant in this syndicated series. There were a lot of fistfights and shootouts as he tracked down murderers and thieves all over the city, from the waterfront to Central Park. Raft also served as narrator.

Also known (incorrectly) as *I Am the Law*.

IMMORTAL, THE

Adventure

FIRST TELECAST: *September 24, 1970*
LAST TELECAST: *September 8, 1971*
BROADCAST HISTORY:
 Sep 1970–Jan 1971, ABC Thu 10:00–11:00
 May 1971–Sep 1971, ABC Wed 9:30–10:30
CAST:

Ben Richards	Christopher George
Fletcher	Don Knight
Arthur Maitland	David Brian
Sylvia	Carol Lynley

Handsome racing driver Ben Richards seemed to have everything in this adventure series, youth, health—and immortality. That last attribute was due to some peculiar antibodies in his blood which made him immune to disease or aging. Immortality was something that a lot of people wanted for their own purposes, however, so Richards was constantly pursued, principally by ruthless billionaire Arthur Maitland and his henchman Fletcher. Like *The Fugitive*, this was essentially a "chase" show, as Richards kept one step ahead of his relentless pursuers while living the life of a footloose young racing driver. Maitland and Ben's fiancée, Sylvia, were seen only occasionally in this series.

The Immortal was based on a TV movie aired in 1969, which had a somewhat different cast.

IMOGENE COCA SHOW, THE

Comedy Variety

FIRST TELECAST: *October 2, 1954*
LAST TELECAST: *June 25, 1955*
BROADCAST HISTORY:
 Oct 1954–Jun 1955, NBC Sat 9:00–9:30
REGULARS:

Betty Crane	Imogene Coca
Helen Milliken (1955)	Bibi Osterwald
Jerry Crane (1955)	Hal March
Harry Milliken (1955)	David Burns

MUSIC:
 The Carl Hoff Orchestra

The Imogene Coca Show never quite figured out what it wanted to be. Initially it went on the air as a situation comedy with Miss Coca essentially playing herself as an actress whose comic adventures in "real life," away from the TV cameras, formed the basis for stories. After only two weeks in this format, the show was altered to become a comedy variety show with sketches, production numbers, and guest stars. On February 19, 1955, the format was overhauled again. It was now a situation comedy about a newlywed couple, the

Cranes, and the adventures they had with their neighbors, the Millikens. All the changes and tinkering with format never gave the show a solid audience and it was canceled at the end of its first season.

IN CONCERT
see *ABC Late Night*

IN PERSON FROM THE PALACE
Variety
FIRST TELECAST: *June 12, 1987*
LAST TELECAST: *August 21, 1987*
BROADCAST HISTORY:
  Jun 1987–Aug 1987, CBS Fri 11:30–12:40 A.M.
HOST:
  Bobby Colomby
EXECUTIVE PRODUCER:
  Dick Clark

Each week a number of singers and rock bands performed in a taped concert setting from the Palace theater in Hollywood. Bobby Colomby, a former rock star himself with the group Blood, Sweat & Tears, served as host and interviewed the performers. Among those appearing were Jody Watley, Anita Baker, the Heaters, Level 42, the Charlie Daniels Band, the Beastie Boys, the Nylons, Eddie Money, and Smokey Robinson.

IN RECORD TIME
see *Art Ford Show, The*

IN SEARCH OF . . .
Documentary
BROADCAST HISTORY:
  Syndicated only
  30 minutes
  Produced: *1976–1982* (144 episodes)
  Released: *Fall 1976*
HOST/NARRATOR:
  Leonard Nimoy

This documentary series dealt with bizarre phenomena on the fringes of science, such as ghosts and witchcraft, UFOs and ESP, the Lost City of Atlantis, and the Loch Ness Monster. It was presented in perfectly straightforward fashion with film clips, interviews, and occasional dramatizations. Host Leonard Nimoy appeared on camera at the end to explain that there were many possible explanations for what you had just seen, and we couldn't be sure which one was right, could we? Maybe Bigfoot, Amelia Earhart, and Count Dracula are out there, after all.

IN THE BEGINNING
Situation Comedy
FIRST TELECAST: *September 20, 1978*
LAST TELECAST: *October 18, 1978*
BROADCAST HISTORY:
  Sep 1978–Oct 1978, CBS Wed 8:30–9:00

CAST:
Father Daniel M. Cleary.. McLean Stevenson
Sister Agnes................. Priscilla Lopez
Sister Lillian .... Priscilla Morrill
Willie....................... Olivia Barash
Jerome Rockefeller.......... Bobby Ellerbee
Msgr. Francis X. Barlow........ Jack Dodson

This comedy was a kind of updated *Going My Way*, focusing on the conflict between the pompous, traditionalist, and continually exasperated Father Cleary and the street-wise nun assigned to him, Sister Agnes. They worked in a storefront mission-community center in an inner-city section of Baltimore. It was Sister Aggie's home neighborhood, and she loved the assignment, but Father Cleary found both her and the neighborhood hookers, hustlers, and winos more than he could stand. He kept trying to get reassigned, hoping to get as far away as possible from the Sister he called "Attila the Nun."

IN THE FIRST PERSON
Interview
FIRST TELECAST: *January 29, 1949*
LAST TELECAST: *October 10, 1950*
BROADCAST HISTORY:
  Jan 1949–Dec 1949, CBS Sat 7:30–7:45
  Feb 1950–Mar 1950, CBS Sat 7:15–7:30
  Mar 1950–Jun 1950, CBS Thu 10:30–10:45
  Jun 1950–Jul 1950, CBS Sun 9:45–10:00
  Jul 1950–Aug 1950, CBS Sun 9:15–9:30
  Sep 1950–Oct 1950, CBS Tue 10:45–11:00
HOST:
  Quincy Howe
  Ned Calmer (1950)

Each week *In the First Person*'s host introduced and chatted informally with a celebrity or someone in the news. Entertainers, politicians, corporation heads, and others appeared on this live 15-minute program. Quincy Howe was the host from its inception through August 1950. He was replaced by Ned Calmer during the program's six-week run that fall.

IN THE HEAT OF THE NIGHT
Police Drama
FIRST TELECAST: *March 6, 1988*
LAST TELECAST: *May 3, 1988*
BROADCAST HISTORY:
  Mar 1988, NBC Sun 9:00–11:00
  Mar 1988–May 1988, NBC Tue 9:00–10:00
CAST:
Chief Bill Gillespie........ Carroll O'Connor
Chief of Det. Virgil Tibbs.... Howard Rollins
Althea Tibbs .... Anne-Marie Johnson
Dep. Bubba Skinner............. Alan Autry
Dep. Parker Williams .... David Hart
Dep. Junior Abernathy.... Christian Le Blanc
Dep. Horace Goode .... Peter Gabb
Dep. Jamison .... Hugh O'Connor

Mayor Findley . . . . Dennis Lipscomb
Barbara Giles . . . . Jill Carroll

A white Southern police chief and his new, black Chief of Detectives—forced on him by a mayor seeking the black vote—found they had more in common than they imagined in this moody crime series. Chief Bill Gillespie was a gruff old-timer who knew the streets and people of Sparta, Mississippi, like the back of his weathered hand. Virgil Tibbs, though he had been born in Sparta, had learned the latest techniques in scientific criminology as a big-city cop in Philadelphia. Now Virgil was back, and he found that Sparta was still living in another era in terms of police work and race relations. But his sleepy hometown was evidently a hotbed of crime (a murder or major drug bust every week, it seemed), so Virgil and the Chief—a fair man—learned to work together and ignore the rednecks in the town and on the force. Althea was Virgil's worried wife, and Barbara the chief's beloved goddaughter.

Based on the Academy Award–winning 1967 movie starring Sidney Poitier and Rod Steiger, and filmed in and around Hammond, La. The role of Jamison was played by Carroll O'Connor's son, Hugh.

IN THE KELVINATOR KITCHEN
Instruction
FIRST TELECAST: *May 21, 1947*
LAST TELECAST: *June 30, 1948*
BROADCAST HISTORY:
    May 1947–Jun 1948, NBC Wed 8:30–8:45
HOSTESS:
    Alma Kitchell

Cooking program seen during the very early days of network television.

IN THE MORGAN MANNER
Musical Variety
FIRST TELECAST: *March 1, 1950*
LAST TELECAST: *July 30, 1950*
BROADCAST HISTORY:
    Mar 1950–Apr 1950, ABC Sun 10:00–10:30
    Jul 1950, ABC Sun 8:00–8:30
HOST:
    Russ Morgan and His Orchestra
THEME:
    "Does Your Heart Beat for Me," by Mitchell Parish and Russ Morgan

This low-budget musical variety show originated in Chicago and featured Russ Morgan, who led one of the more popular dance bands of the late 1940s. Morgan was extremely big on the popular record charts at the time (at one point during 1949 he had six of the top 10 tunes, including the million-seller "Cruising Down the River"). That plus his easygoing personality made him a natural for

television. This show was also seen on Sunday afternoons for a time.

Morgan's slogan was "Music in the Morgan Manner," hence the program's title.

INA RAY HUTTON SHOW, THE
Musical Variety
FIRST TELECAST: *July 4, 1956*
LAST TELECAST: *September 5, 1956*
BROADCAST HISTORY:
    Jul 1956–Sep 1956, NBC Wed 10:30–11:00
REGULARS:
    Ina Ray Hutton and Her All-Girl Band
    Diane Brewster
    Mickey Anderson

This may have been the first "Women's Lib" program on television. Ina Ray Hutton and Her All-Girl Band were the stars and principal performers. Miss Hutton, in addition to leading the band, sang and danced with guest stars in production numbers. Not only were the regulars on this show all women, but so were all of the guest stars, including Judy Canova, the King Sisters, Gogi Grant, Rose Marie, and Yma Sumac. Even the announcer was a woman, actress Diane Brewster. It was no wonder that the program was subtitled "No Men Allowed."

The most prominent member of Miss Hutton's 13-piece band was Mickey Anderson who, in addition to playing saxophone, clarinet, and flute, also did comic vocals. The remaining dozen members of the group were Dee Dee Ball, piano and organ; Helen Smith, bass; Margaret Rinker, drums; Jane Davies, guitar; Harriet Blackburn, saxophone and conga drums; Judy Von Euer, saxophone and clarinet; Evie Howeth, saxophone and clarinet; Helen Wooley, saxophone and clarinet; Lois Cronin, trombone and vibraphone; and trumpet players Peggy Fairbanks, Helen Hammond, and Zoe Ann Willy.

INCREDIBLE HULK, THE
Adventure/Drama
FIRST TELECAST: *March 10, 1978*
LAST TELECAST: *June 2, 1982*
BROADCAST HISTORY:
    Mar 1978–Jan 1979, CBS Fri 9:00–10:00
    Jan 1979, CBS Wed 8:00–9:00
    Feb 1979–Nov 1981, CBS Fri 8:00–9:00
    May 1982–Jun 1982, CBS Wed 8:00–9:00
CAST:
    David Bruce Banner . . . . Bill Bixby
    The Incredible Hulk . . . . Lou Ferrigno
    Jack McGee . . . . Jack Colvin

David Banner was a research scientist who had been experimenting with various means of determining the effects of stress on physical strength. In a freak accident in his laboratory, David was exposed to a massive dosage of radiation that had a dramatic effect on his physiology. Normally a quiet, peaceful man, David now found that every time he became angered he turned into *The Incredible Hulk*, a huge, greenish, manlike monster of immense strength and primitive passions. David knew what was happening when the transformation started to take place but, when he calmed down and returned to normal, had no recollection of what he had done when he was the creature. Traveling around the country in search of a cure, and taking odd jobs to keep himself fed and clothed, David sought to avoid the pursuit of investigative reporter Jack McGee, who suspected his secret but who had no real proof.

The Incredible Hulk was based on the comic-book character created by Stan Lee in 1962. From September 1982 to September 1985, NBC aired an animated version of *The Incredible Hulk* as part of its Saturday morning lineup.

INDUSTRIES FOR AMERICA
Documentary
FIRST TELECAST: *May 31, 1951*
LAST TELECAST: *September 19, 1957*
BROADCAST HISTORY:
  May 1951–Jul 1951, ABC Thu 10:00–10:30
  Jul 1951–Sep 1951, ABC Sun 10:00–10:30
  Oct 1951–Dec 1951, ABC Fri 10:30–11:00
  Feb 1952, ABC Thu 10:15–10:30
  Jun 1957–Sep 1957, ABC Thu 9:30–10:00

Documentary films which ABC ran during the early and mid-1950s, mostly, it seems, to fill time. The central theme was American industry on parade, with such provocative titles as "The Magic of Lumber," "Drama of Portland Cement," and "The Cranberry Story."

INFORMATION PLEASE
Quiz/Audience Participation
FIRST TELECAST: *June 29, 1952*
LAST TELECAST: *September 21, 1952*
BROADCAST HISTORY:
  Jun 1952–Sep 1952, CBS Sun 9:00–9:30
EMCEE:
  Clifton Fadiman
PANELISTS:
  Franklin P. Adams
  John Kieran

Information Please had had a long and successful run on radio, but its only appearance on television was as the 1952 summer replacement for *The Fred Waring Show*. Viewers submitted questions to be answered by the members of the panel, two permanent and one guest. The viewer received a $10 certificate good for the purchase of books or magazines if his question was used, and a $50 certificate if it stumped the panel. Emcee/moderator Clifton Fadiman had long been associated with the radio version of this literate series, as had panelists Adams and Kieran.

INNOCENT AND THE DAMNED, THE
Drama
FIRST TELECAST: *May 31, 1979*
LAST TELECAST: *June 28, 1979*
BROADCAST HISTORY:
  May 1979–Jun 1979, NBC Thu 10:00–11:00
CAST:
  Tom Keating................... Sam Elliott
  Lee Bishop .... Perry King
  Carl Osborne .... Gene Barry
  Gloria Osborne .... Michelle Phillips
  Max Kendrick .... Roger Davis
  Abe Singer .... George DiCenzo
  Alex Budde.............. Anthony Franciosa
  Kit Pepe..................... Jessica Harper
  Jon Osborne .... Douglas Matthew Heyes
  Budd Townsend................. Bo Hopkins
  Owen Keating .... John McIntire
  Len Ralston .... Angus Duncan
  Joseph Drummond .... John Houseman
  Judge Kendrick .... William Prince
  Angela Morelli .... Debi Richter
  Joan Carolinian .... Martine Beswick
  Sheriff Dinehart.......... Lee Jones-deBroux

The central focus of this mini-series was the 1964 trial of Lee Bishop for the rape-murder of 15-year-old Angela Morelli, a crime he didn't commit. Bishop was nevertheless convicted and young lawyer Tom Keating spent eight years working behind the scenes to get him freed from Colorado's death row. Woven into the legal maneuvering was the secondary story of manipulation by entrenched real-estate interests, including tycoon Carl Osborne (with whose daughter, Gloria, Bishop had been having an affair), to transform the sleepy town of Aspen into a major ski resort.

Adapted from the novels *Aspen* by Bert Hirschfield and *The Adversary* by Bart Spicer, this mini-series originally aired November 5–7, 1977, under the title *Aspen*.

INSIDE AMERICA
Magazine
FIRST TELECAST: *April 4, 1982*
LAST TELECAST: *April 25, 1982*
BROADCAST HISTORY:
  Apr 1982, ABC Sun 7:00–8:00
HOST:
  Dick Clark

Dick Clark produced and hosted this magazine show filled with "fluff" pieces on show business. Among the subjects were "Who's Sexier: Tom Selleck or Burt Reynolds?," Rex Reed on the Ten Worst Movies of 1981, "Inside Graceland," and "Where Are Joey Dee & the Starliters Now?"

INSIDE DETECTIVE
see *Rocky King—Inside Detective*

INSIDE PHOTOPLAY
see *Wendy Barrie Show, The*

INSIDE U.S.A. WITH CHEVROLET
Musical Variety
FIRST TELECAST: *September 29, 1949*
LAST TELECAST: *March 16, 1950*
BROADCAST HISTORY:
Sep 1949–Mar 1950, CBS Thu 8:30–9:00
REGULARS:
Peter Lind Hayes
Mary Healy
Mary Wickes
Sheila Bond
Jay Blackton Orchestra
PRODUCER:
Arthur Schwartz

Songwriter and producer Arthur Schwartz brought his hit musical *Inside U.S.A.* to network television in the fall of 1949, as an alternate-week series. The program was done in revue style, with Peter Lind Hayes hosting in the role of a contemporary American minstrel, and each telecast included songs, comedy sketches, dance, and lavish production numbers. As the minstrel, Hayes would travel across the country and provide background to the individual program elements as he observed the splendor of America's natural beauty and the diversity of its people. Featured in the regular cast was his wife, singer-actress Mary Healy. There was also a big-name "star of the week" for every show, with such varied talents as Lucille Ball, Boris Karloff, Ethel Merman, David Niven, and Oscar Levant starring in individual telecasts.

INSIDERS, THE
Newspaper Drama
FIRST TELECAST: *September 25, 1985*
LAST TELECAST: *June 23, 1986*
BROADCAST HISTORY:
Sep 1985–Jan 1986, ABC Wed 8:00–9:00
Jun 1986, ABC Mon 8:00–9:00
CAST:
Nick Fox .... Nicholas Campbell
James Mackey .... Stoney Jackson
Alice West .... Gail Strickland

The fast-paced adventures of a pair of hip investigative reporters for a national magazine; each week they wormed their way inside a target, usually the mob or some other criminal organization, using disguises and help from street contacts from their checkered pasts. Nick, who looked a lot like rock star Sting, was a rebellious product of the '60s; his partner Mackey, a cool, young black dude who resembled rock star Prince, was a "reformed" ex-con (although he made much use of the tricks of his former trade, like hot-wiring cars). All of this was accompanied by an ample dose of violence, car chases, and loud rock music.

INSPECTOR MARK SABER—HOMICIDE SQUAD
see *Mark Saber*

INTERLUDE
see *Summer Theater*

INTERNATIONAL PLAYHOUSE
see *Movies—Prior to 1961*

INTERNATIONAL SHOWTIME
Variety
FIRST TELECAST: *September 15, 1961*
LAST TELECAST: *September 10, 1965*
BROADCAST HISTORY:
Sep 1961–Sep 1965, NBC Fri 7:30–8:30
HOST:
Don Ameche

Circuses, ice shows, magic shows, and other similar types of spectaculars, from all over Europe, were shown each week on *International Showtime*. Some episodes focused on a specific talent—clowns, daredevils, etc.—and compiled the best examples from different performers into a single show. Don Ameche was the host of the series throughout its four-season run. He would introduce each act and then sit back as part of the audience to enjoy it. He traveled around Europe with the production crew and was actually present when each act was taped.

INTERNS, THE
Medical Drama
FIRST TELECAST: *September 18, 1970*
LAST TELECAST: *September 10, 1971*
BROADCAST HISTORY:
Sep 1970–Sep 1971, CBS Fri 7:30–8:30
CAST:
Dr. Peter Goldstone ..... Broderick Crawford
Dr. Greg Pettit .... Stephen Brooks
Dr. Pooch Hardin .... Christopher Stone
Dr. Cal Barrin .... Hal Frederick
Dr. Lydia Thorpe .... Sandra Smith
Dr. Sam Marsh .... Mike Farrell
Dr. Hugh Jacoby .... Skip Homeier
Bobbe Marsh .... Elaine Giftos

Broderick Crawford starred in this medical series as the father figure to a nicely mixed group of five young interns (one black, one woman, one young married man, two swingers). New North Hospital was the setting, and the personal and professional lives of the young doctors provided the stories.

INVADERS, THE
Science Fiction
FIRST TELECAST: *January 10, 1967*
LAST TELECAST: *September 17, 1968*
BROADCAST HISTORY:
Jan 1967–Jan 1968, ABC Tue 8:30–9:30
Jan 1968–Sep 1968, ABC Tue 10:00–11:00

CAST:
David Vincent .... Roy Thinnes
Edgar Scoville .... Kent Smith
EXECUTIVE PRODUCER:
Quinn Martin

One of the most durable science-fiction ideas is the one that questions the very reality of what we see around us. Could there be aliens in our midst? Architect David Vincent certainly thought so. He had witnessed the landing of a flying saucer, and stumbled onto an incredible secret: that scattered throughout the world's population, disguised as humans, was an advance guard of alien creatures from a dying planet, who were preparing to conquer the earth!

Convincing his fellow citizens of this was of course no easy task, so Vincent went on a one-man crusade to obtain solid evidence and warn mankind of the dangers it faced—while trying not to fall into the clutches of the aliens. Identifying the enemy was tricky, but it could be done. Sometimes the invaders would have slightly mutated hands, such as a little finger jutting out awkwardly; sometimes, though rarely, they would begin to glow when they were in need of regeneration to retain their human form. And of course, they had no pulse or heartbeat—because they had no hearts.

For the first few months of the series Vincent fought a lonely, largely undercover battle. Eventually, feeling that he was a bit too lonely to be plausible, the producers gave him some allies, a group of seven others who also learned the secret and wanted to help. His chief confederate, who joined the show in December 1967, was Edgar Scoville, the head of an electronics firm.

Could it really happen? Well, you never know, but actor Roy Thinnes, in a bit of promotional hype released by the ABC press department, claimed that he had actually seen a UFO during the filming of the series. Then again, maybe *he* is one of *them.* . . .

INVESTIGATOR, THE
Detective Drama
FIRST TELECAST: *June 3, 1958*
LAST TELECAST: *September 2, 1958*
BROADCAST HISTORY:
Jun 1958–Sep 1958, NBC Tue 8:00–9:00
CAST:
Jeff Prior .... Lonny Chapman
Lloyd Prior .... Howard St. John

Jeff Prior was a swinging private investigator in his early 30s whose ability to track down clues and resolve mysteries had made him very successful. He had learned his skills from his father, Lloyd, a retired newspaperman who had a reputation of his own for solving mysteries when he was a young reporter in the 1920s. Jeff dug up most of the facts in each case and, with his father's help, tied them all together to nail the culprits. This live

detective series aired as a summer replacement in 1958.

INVESTIGATORS, THE
Detective Drama
FIRST TELECAST: *October 5, 1961*
LAST TELECAST: *December 28, 1961*
BROADCAST HISTORY:
Oct 1961–Dec 1961, CBS Thu 9:00–10:00
CAST:
Russ Andrews .... James Franciscus
Steve Banks .... James Philbrook
Maggie Peters .... Mary Murphy
Bill Davis .... Al Austin

With offices on the fashionable East Side of New York, the firm of "Investigators, Inc." was a highly successful and highly specialized operation. The cases dealt with by its staff were all tied in to very large insurance claims. As a team of insurance investigators, Russ, Steve, and Bill became involved with the underworld, the police, and others as they tracked down clues to determine whether or not claims were legitimate. Helping back at the office, and occasionally as an undercover operative, was Maggie Peters, their girl Friday.

INVISIBLE MAN, THE
International Intrigue
FIRST TELECAST: *November 4, 1958*
LAST TELECAST: *September 22, 1960*
BROADCAST HISTORY:
Nov 1958–May 1959, CBS Tue 8:00–8:30
May 1959–Jul 1959, CBS Thu 7:30–8:00
Jul 1960–Sep 1960, CBS Thu 7:30–8:00
CAST:
Dr. Peter Brady .... Anonymous
Diane Brady .... Lisa Daniely
Sally Brady .... Deborah Watling

Dr. Peter Brady was an English scientist working with the principles that govern the refraction of light when he discovered a means of making himself invisible. The only problem was that after becoming invisible, he could not make himself visible again. Having decided to make the best of his handicap, Peter became an adventurer/agent, working with British Intelligence to thwart the efforts of evil organizations and their agents throughout Europe (he had no trouble getting through customs). Seen regularly were his sister Diane and his niece Sally.

The actor playing Peter was never seen at all, being concealed in bandages or only heard off-screen. His identity was kept a close secret by the producers and to this day no one has revealed his name (not that very many are asking anymore).

The episodes aired during the summer of 1960 were not repeats but an additional group of original episodes. The series was produced in England.

INVISIBLE MAN, THE

Adventure

FIRST TELECAST: *September 8, 1975*
LAST TELECAST: *January 19, 1976*
BROADCAST HISTORY:

Sep 1975–Jan 1976, NBC Mon 8:00–9:00

CAST:

Dr. Daniel Westin .... David McCallum
Walter Carlson .... Craig Stevens
Dr. Kate Westin .... Melinda Fee

In an attempt to update the classic H.G. Wells story, this series brought us Dr. Daniel Westin, a scientist who had discovered a means of making any object invisible—including himself. When he found out that the government planned to use his technique for military purposes, he memorized his secret formula, destroyed his equipment, and turned himself invisible to escape. Unfortunately his method for becoming visible again failed to work, and he was temporarily stuck in invisibility. Seeking the aid of a scientist friend, he had a wig, highly realistic face mask, and plastic hands made to conceal his invisibility, enabling him to resume a somewhat normal public life.

Daniel and his wife Kate then went to work for the KLAE Corporation, where he continued his experiments in order to find his way back. He also undertook an assortment of dangerous security missions for his boss, Walter Carlson. Whenever the situation got tight Daniel could take off his mask and clothes and "disappear." This did not always prove to be as helpful as it might seem, however, as when he was trapped in the house of a blind man, extraordinarily sensitive to sound, who was out to kill him.

IRON HORSE, THE

Western

FIRST TELECAST: *September 12, 1966*
LAST TELECAST: *January 6, 1968*
BROADCAST HISTORY:

Sep 1966–Sep 1967, ABC Mon 7:30–8:30
Sep 1967–Jan 1968, ABC Sat 9:30–10:30

CAST:

Ben Calhoun................ Dale Robertson
Dave Tarrant.................. Gary Collins
Barnabas Rogers.............. Bob Random
Nils Torvald (1966–1967)....... Roger Torrey
Julie Parsons (1967–1968) .... Ellen McRae

Ben Calhoun was a hard-driving ladies' man who had the good fortune to win a railroad in a poker game. Unfortunately, the Buffalo Pass, Scalplock, and Defiance Line was only half built and on the brink of bankruptcy, so it was up to Ben to finish the job. Helping him push the line to completion through the wild, untamed West of the 1880s were Dave, his young construction engineer; Nils, the giant crewman; and Barnabas, a young orphan who idolized Ben and served as his clerk. Julie Parsons arrived in the second season as the freight station operator and proprietor of the Scalplock General Store.

There was plenty of action in this epic of a railroad moving west, with crooked financiers, rampaging Indians, and assorted desperadoes peopling the stories.

IRONSIDE

Police Drama

FIRST TELECAST: *September 14, 1967*
LAST TELECAST: *January 16, 1975*
BROADCAST HISTORY:

Sep 1967–Sep 1971, NBC Thu 8:30–9:30
Sep 1971–Nov 1971, NBC Tue 7:30–8:30
Nov 1971–Jan 1975, NBC Thu 9:00–10:00

CAST:

Robert Ironside .... Raymond Burr
Det. Sgt. Ed Brown........... Don Galloway
Eve Whitfield (1967–1971)

.... Barbara Anderson
Mark Sanger .... Don Mitchell
Fran Belding (1971–1975) ..... Elizabeth Baur
Commissioner Dennis Randall ... Gene Lyons
Lt. Carl Reese (1969–1975) ..... Johnny Seven
Diana Sanger (1974–1975)....... Joan Pringle

Robert Ironside had been chief of detectives for the San Francisco Police Department for many years, and a member of the force for 25, when a would-be assassin's bullet grazed his spine and left him paralyzed from the waist down. Forced to leave the force as a regular member, he convinced Police Commissioner Randall to appoint him to a position as special consultant. Helping him wage his unrelenting war against crime were two former assistants, Sgt. Ed Brown and Policewoman Eve Whitfield, and an ex-delinquent (Mark Sanger) who became his aide and bodyguard. Confined to a wheelchair, Ironside made use of a specially equipped police van for transportation and some unused office space at police headquarters as a base of operations. When Barbara Anderson left the series at the end of the 1970–1971 season over a contract dispute, she was replaced by Elizabeth Baur as Policewoman Fran Belding. Mark, who had found time to go to law school while working for Chief Ironside, graduated at the start of the 1974–1975 season and got married.

ISLANDERS, THE

Adventure

FIRST TELECAST: *October 2, 1960*
LAST TELECAST: *March 26, 1961*
BROADCAST HISTORY:

Oct 1960–Mar 1961, ABC Sun 9:30–10:30

CAST:

Sandy Wade .... William Reynolds
Zack Malloy............... James Philbrook
Wilhelmina Vandeveer...... Diane Brewster
Naja .... Daria Massey
Shipwreck Callahan............ Roy Wright

Sandy and Zack were pilots flying for their own one-plane airline, based in the Spice Islands of the East Indies. Part of the spice was Wilhelmina "Steamboat Willie" Vandeveer, their beautiful, blonde, self-appointed business manager. Something of an operator herself, Willie was not above playing all the angles when it came to landing business for the boys. Unfortunately for Sandy and Zack, the results were designed more to benefit Willie than themselves. Whether flying passengers or cargo, the results were usually other than originally planned. Smugglers, escaped convicts, stolen goods, and mysterious, beautiful women were always keeping things busy.

IT COULD BE YOU
see *Bill Gwinn Show, The*

IT COULD BE YOU
Quiz/Audience Participation
FIRST TELECAST: *July 2, 1958*
LAST TELECAST: *September 27, 1961*
BROADCAST HISTORY:
Jul 1958–Sep 1958, NBC Wed 10:00–10:30
Nov 1958–Mar 1959, NBC Thu 8:30–9:00
Sep 1959–Jan 1960, NBC Sat 10:30–11:00
Jun 1961–Sep 1961, NBC Wed 10:00–10:30
EMCEE:
Bill Leyden
ASSISTANT:
Wendell Niles

Unsuspecting members of the studio audience were reunited with friends or relatives, called upon to perform stunts, or given the opportunity to meet guest celebrities on this program. As on *This Is Your Life,* research was done on the "victims" before the show, and anecdotes about their lives and pictures from their childhood were brought out. Being in the audience was always exciting, because you never knew when "It Could Be You." Bill Leyden was also the host of the daytime version of this show, which premiered in June 1956 and ran until December 1961.

IT HAPPENED IN SPORTS
Sports Commentary
FIRST TELECAST: *July 3, 1953*
LAST TELECAST: *January 19, 1954*
BROADCAST HISTORY:
Jul 1953–Aug 1953, NBC Fri 10:45–11:00
Sep 1953–Jan 1954, NBC Tue 10:45–11:00
HOST:
Bud Palmer

It Happened in Sports was used to fill the time between the conclusion of the boxing bout that started at 10 P.M. and the local news at 11 P.M. Bud Palmer was the host and presided over both live and filmed interviews with famous sports personalities as well as films of historic events in the world of sport.

IT PAYS TO BE IGNORANT
Quiz/Audience Participation
FIRST TELECAST: *June 6, 1949*
LAST TELECAST: *September 27, 1951*
BROADCAST HISTORY:
Jun 1949–Sep 1949, CBS Mon 8:30–9:00
Jul 1951–Sep 1951, NBC Thu 8:00–8:30
EMCEE:
Tom Howard
PANELISTS:
Lulu McConnell
Harry McNaughton
George Shelton

It was appropriate that *It Pays to Be Ignorant* was the summer replacement for *You Bet Your Life* in 1951, for neither was really a quiz show—both were primarily vehicles for comedy. *It Pays to Be Ignorant* had started as a radio series in 1942 and aired on TV once before, in the summer of 1949. The four cheerful lunatics who comprised host and panel were the same on radio and TV. "Professor" Tom Howard, a spry, 65-year-old ex-vaudevillian, posed extremely simple questions to the panel and got replies that ranged from the ridiculous to the absurd. The frustrated emcee would watch as the "experts" stumbled through an improbable answer, interrupted each other, and found that they had changed the subject completely. Members of the studio audience were invited to pull questions out of a dunce cap for the experts. If the experts failed to answer the question correctly, and the studio contestant could squeeze the right answer into the mayhem, the contestant won a nominal award.

More than two decades after it left the air, *It Pays to Be Ignorant* returned in a syndicated version that lasted the 1973–1974 season. Joe Flynn was the emcee; Jo Anne Worley, Billy Baxter, and Charles Nelson Reilly were regular panelists. The format was somewhat modified from the original.

IT TAKES A THIEF
International Intrigue
FIRST TELECAST: *January 9, 1968*
LAST TELECAST: *September 14, 1970*
BROADCAST HISTORY:
Jan 1968–Aug 1969, ABC Tue 8:30–9:30
Aug 1969–Jan 1970, ABC Thu 10:00–11:00
Jan 1970–Sep 1970, ABC Mon 7:30–8:30
CAST:
Alexander Mundy. . . . . Robert Wagner
Noah Bain (1968–1969) . . . . . . Malachi Throne
Wallie Powers (1969–1970). . . . Edward Binns
Alister Mundy (1969–1970) . . . . . . Fred Astaire

Alexander Mundy was a cat burglar and professional thief who had style, class, and great talent. He had made only one mistake—getting caught. While serving a sentence in San Jobel Prison, he was contacted by representatives of U.S. Government spy agency, the SIA. They offered to get him out if he would put his talents to work stealing for the government. Accepting the offer, he worked closely with an SIA department head, Noah Bain, who was his boss, aide, associate, friend, and watchdog. Filmed throughout Europe, *It Takes a Thief* saw Al Mundy on various assignments as a master thief for the SIA, romancing beautiful women, and generally being his relaxed, handsome self.

At the start of the 1969–1970 season there were a few changes. Whereas previously Mundy had been under house confinement when not on an assignment, he was now a free agent. His SIA contact had become Wallie Powers, and his father, played by Fred Astaire, became a semi-regular. Al's father was the retired thief from whom he had learned all his skills, and who occasionally teamed with his son on special jobs.

IT TAKES TWO
Situation Comedy
FIRST TELECAST: *October 14, 1982*
LAST TELECAST: *September 1, 1983*
BROADCAST HISTORY:
   Oct 1982–Sep 1983, ABC Thu 9:30–10:00
CAST:
   Dr. Sam Quinn .... Richard Crenna
   Molly Quinn............... Patty Duke Astin
   Lisa Quinn .... Helen Hunt
   Andy Quinn .... Anthony Edwards
   Mama......................... Billie Bird
   Walter Chaiken.......... Richard McKenzie
   Decker .... Randy Dreyfuss
   Judge Caroline Phillips .... Della Reese

A pair of overachievers found that dual careers can get in the way of family life in this contemporary comedy. Dr. Sam Quinn was chief of surgery at a Chicago hospital, working long hours but able to come home to a devoted wife—until she got her law degree. Now that Molly had embarked on her own busy career as an assistant D.A., Sam found his dinners cold, his shirts unironed, and his love life decidedly wanting. In bed, his wife just fell asleep. To complain would be chauvinistic, so Sam coped as best he could, which is more than could be said for the couple's teenaged kids, shy Lisa and aspiring rock musician Andy.

New careers brought new opinions, too. While Sam remained a dedicated liberal, Molly's exposure to street criminals had turned her into something of a hard-liner. One psychopathic offender caused her to erupt, "Says it's because he comes from a broken home. Of course he comes from a broken home—he killed his father!" Surprisingly, the one island of calm in this disrupted household was Molly's dippy mama, whose nutty responses sometimes helped make everyone else forget their complaints.

IT WAS A VERY GOOD YEAR
Documentary
FIRST TELECAST: *May 10, 1971*
LAST TELECAST: *August 30, 1971*
BROADCAST HISTORY:
   May 1971–Aug 1971, ABC Mon 8:30–9:00
HOST:
   Mel Torme

An exercise in nostalgia. *It Was a Very Good Year* compiled old film clips, memorabilia, and interviews with famous personalities to provide a capsule summary of the news, fashions, and songs of a given year in the 20th century. Mel Torme was the host and, in addition to providing narration for some of the material and singing a song or two, he chatted with people who had been prominent in the year being covered. The years treated ranged from 1919 to 1964, but were mostly of the pre-rock 'n' roll era, so the show appealed primarily to older adults.

IT'S A BUSINESS?
Situation Comedy
FIRST TELECAST: *March 19, 1952*
LAST TELECAST: *May 21, 1952*
BROADCAST HISTORY:
   Mar 1952–May 1952, DUM Wed 9:00–9:30
CAST:
   Bob Haymes
   Leo DeLyon
   Dorothy Loudon

This situation comedy with music was set at the turn of the century and concerned the activities of a couple of Broadway song publishers. They had plenty of opportunities to demonstrate their wares (grand old favorites like "After the Ball"), as well as to welcome visiting vaudevillians to their offices. Bob Haymes, the brother of big-band singer Dick Haymes, and Leo DeLyon played the song-publisher partners and Dorothy Loudon played their secretary.

IT'S A GREAT LIFE
Situation Comedy
FIRST TELECAST: *September 7, 1954*
LAST TELECAST: *June 3, 1956*
BROADCAST HISTORY:
   Sep 1954–Sep 1955, NBC Tue 10:30–11:00
   Sep 1955–Jun 1956, NBC Sun 7:00–7:30
CAST:
   Denny David .... Michael O'Shea
   Steve Connors .... William Bishop
   Uncle Earl.................... James Dunn
   Mrs. Amy Morgan .... Frances Bavier
   Kathy Morgan .... Barbara Bates

Denny David and Steve Connors were two recently discharged GIs who decided to room together while trying to find civilian jobs. They headed for Southern California because Steve had been stationed there during World War II, and loved the weather. Once in California, they found lodgings in the home of widow Amy Morgan, whose household also included her daughter Kathy and her brother Earl. Stories revolved around Denny and Steve's problems in adjusting to civilian life, their problems with various jobs, and the trouble they got into by repeatedly letting the conniving Uncle Earl lure them into his money-making schemes.

IT'S A LIVING
Situation Comedy
FIRST TELECAST: *October 30, 1980*
LAST TELECAST: *September 10, 1982*
BROADCAST HISTORY:
  Oct 1980–Jan 1981, ABC Thu 9:30–10:00
  Jul 1981–Aug 1981, ABC Tue 9:30–10:00
  Sep 1981–Oct 1981, ABC Fri 8:30–9:00
  Oct 1981–Jan 1982, ABC Sat 8:30–9:00
  Feb 1982, ABC Fri 9:30–10:00
  Jun 1982–Sep 1982, ABC Fri 8:30–9:00
  (In first-run syndication since September 1985)
CAST:
  Nancy Beebe .... Marian Mercer
  Lois Adams (1980–1981) ...... Susan Sullivan
  Dot Higgins .... Gail Edwards
  Vicki Allen (1980–1981) .... Wendy Schaal
  Cassie Cranston (1980–1986) ..... Ann Jillian
  Jan Hoffmeyer Gray ...... Barrie Youngfellow
  Sonny Mann (née Manishevitz)
  .... Paul Kreppel
  Mario (1980–1981) .... Bert Remsen
  Maggie McBurney (1981–1982) . Louise Lasser
  Dennis Hubner (1981–1982) .... Earl Boen
  Amy Tompkins (1985–   ) .. Crystal Bernard
  Howard Miller (1985–   ) .... Richard Stahl
  Ginger St. James (1986–   )
  .... Sheryl Lee Ralph

This sexy comedy was about five pretty waitresses working at a posh Los Angeles restaurant (so posh that in one scene an enraged customer received a bill for $540, for six people). Nancy was the disciplinarian supervisor, trying to get a day's work out of Lois, Dot, Vicki, Cassie (the brassy one), Jan, and Sonny, the self-absorbed lounge pianist. Along with battling customers and chattering about their home life, the girls all giggled a lot, paraded around in skimpy outfits, and made jokes about who had "done it" the previous night.

ABC evidently had faith in this show. Despite a shaky first season, it was renewed, given a new name *(Making a Living)* and two new cast members, and tried out in several time periods. It didn't help.

Three years after leaving ABC, with its original title and most of the original cast, *It's a Living* returned to the air with new episodes produced for the syndicated market. Added to the cast were Amy, a naive, new young waitress; a new chef named Howard who was the constant, and disinterested, object of Nancy's amorous advances; and the infrequently seen Richie Gray (played by Richard Kline), an electrician who eventually married Jan. In the fall of 1986 an outspoken, sexy black waitress named Ginger joined the other waitresses at Above the Top. Late in 1987, in a

moment of weakness, sarcastic Howard finally started dating Nancy and, to the surprise of everyone on the staff including himself, the two of them got married in Las Vegas.

IT'S A MAN'S WORLD
Situation Comedy
FIRST TELECAST: *September 17, 1962*
LAST TELECAST: *January 28, 1963*
BROADCAST HISTORY:
  Sep 1962–Jan 1963, NBC Mon 7:30–8:30
CAST:
  Wes Macauley .... Glenn Corbett
  Howie Macauley............... Mike Burns
  Tom-Tom DeWitt .... Ted Bessell
  Vern Hodges .... Randy Boone
  Houghton Stott................ Harry Harvey
  Irene Hoff...................... Jan Norris
  Mrs. Iona Dobson............ Kate Murtaugh
  Virgil Dobson.................. Scott White
  Alma Jean Dobson .... Jeanine Cashell
  Nora........................ Ann Schuyler

Comedy set in a small Midwestern college town where two college students (Wes and Tom-Tom), one kid brother (Howie), and one footloose guitarist (Vern) lived together in a houseboat. The stories, which ranged from light comedy to drama, involved their problems with school, girls, jobs, and each other.

IT'S A SMALL WORLD
Travelogue
FIRST TELECAST: *June 27, 1953*
LAST TELECAST: *July 27, 1953*
BROADCAST HISTORY:
  Jun 1953–Jul 1953, DUM Sat 7:30–8:00
  Jul 1953, DUM Mon 8:00–8:30
HOST:
  Dick Noel

Travel films narrated by Dick Noel. The program became a local New York presentation for the remainder of the summer.

IT'S ABOUT TIME
Quiz/Panel
FIRST TELECAST: *March 4, 1954*
LAST TELECAST: *May 2, 1954*
BROADCAST HISTORY:
  Mar 1954, ABC Thu 8:00–8:30
  Apr 1954–May 1954, ABC Sun 7:30–8:00
EMCEE:
  Dr. Bergen Evans
PANELISTS:
  Robert Pollack
  Ruthie Duskin
  Sherl Stern
  Vim Gottschalk
  Fran Allison

Panelists on this quiz show were asked to identify well-known events of the past. Clues were given in the form of scrambled headlines, dramatic vignettes, old phonograph records, etc. There was also a mystery guest.

IT'S ABOUT TIME
Situation Comedy
FIRST TELECAST: *September 11, 1966*
LAST TELECAST: *August 27, 1967*
BROADCAST HISTORY:
Sep 1966–Aug 1967, CBS Sun 7:30–8:00
CAST:
Hector .... Jack Mullaney
Mac .... Frank Aletter
Shad .... Imogene Coca
Gronk......................... Joe E. Ross
Boss .... Cliff Norton
Mrs. Boss .... Kathleen Freeman
Clon .... Mike Mazurki
Mlor .... Mary Grace
Breer .... Pat Cardi
Mr. Tyler..................... Alan DeWitt
Gen. Morley (1967)............ Frank Wilcox

After their space capsule made a wrong turn somewhere, and cracked the time barrier, astronauts Hector and Mac discovered that they were headed back to a world quite different from the one they had left. They landed in a swamp smack in the middle of Earth's Stone Age, not far from a tribe of cave dwellers. Among their new prehistoric neighbors were a friendly couple, Shad and Gronk; their two children, Mlor and Breer; the tribal bully, Clon; and the suspicious chief, Boss. In the episode of January 22, the astronauts finally managed to repair their spaceship and return to the 20th century, bringing Shad, Gronk, and their children back with them. The cave people had even more trouble adjusting to modern-day Los Angeles than the astronauts did to the prehistoric world.

IT'S ALEC TEMPLETON TIME
Music
FIRST TELECAST: *June 10, 1955*
LAST TELECAST: *August 26, 1955*
BROADCAST HISTORY:
Jun 1955, DUM Fri 10:30–11:00
Jul 1955–Aug 1955, DUM Fri 10:00–10:30
HOST:
Alec Templeton

This summer musical series was hosted by Alec Templeton, the blind pianist-satirist, who introduced guest singers, dancers, and musicians, and chatted with them following their numbers.

IT'S ALWAYS JAN
Situation Comedy
FIRST TELECAST: *September 10, 1955*
LAST TELECAST: *June 30, 1956*
BROADCAST HISTORY:
Sep 1955–Jun 1956, CBS Sat 9:30–10:00

CAST:
Janis Stewart .... Janis Paige
Pat Murphy .... Patricia Bright
Val Marlowe .... Merry Anders
Josie Stewart .... Jeri Lou James
Stanley Schreiber............. Arte Johnson
Harry Cooper.................. Sid Melton

Musical-comedy star Janis Paige starred in this comedy series about the problems of a single parent. Nightclub singer Janis Stewart had lost her husband during the war and had a 10-year-old daughter (Josie) to raise. Not possessed of very much money, Jan and Josie lived in a small apartment with two of Jan's friends. Pat was secretary to a theatrical producer and Val was an aspiring actress and model. Stanley Schreiber was the son of the man who owned the neighborhood delicatessen. The format of this series allowed Miss Paige the opportunity to sing a song in most episodes.

IT'S GARY SHANDLING'S SHOW
Situation Comedy
FIRST TELECAST: *March 6, 1988*
LAST TELECAST:
BROADCAST HISTORY:
Mar 1988–   , FOX Sun 9:00–9:30
CAST:
Gary Shandling............. Gary Shandling
Mrs. Shandling .... Barbara Cason
Nancy Bancroft................. Molly Cheek
Pete Schumaker .... Michael Tucci
Jackie Schumaker......... Bernadette Birkett
Grant Schumaker .... Grant Nemes
Leonard Smith................. Paul Willson

In the 1970s and 1980s television saw an increasing number of shows that mocked TV's own conventions—*Saturday Night Live, Fernwood 2-Night, Late Night With David Letterman, Max Headroom,* and *Moonlighting,* among others. One of the most innovative was this slice-of-life comedy that was so unconventional it was reportedly rejected by all three major commercial networks, before premiering on the Showtime cable network in the fall of 1986.

The focus, more or less, was the fictionalized personal life of offbeat comic Gary Shandling. Gary played himself, a friendly, rather neurotic young single coping not too successfully with the outside world. His main problems were his general insecurity, his limited success with women, and a tendency to have things fall apart around him. Most of the action took place in a set that was a replica of Gary's real-life living room. His platonic friend Nancy, his mother, his best married friend Pete, and Pete's intellectual young son Grant came by to help Gary deal with his problems. Leonard was the nosy next-door neighbor.

What made *It's Gary Shandling's Show* so different was its point of view. Gary knew he was on television. As George Burns had done three decades before, he opened each show talking directly to the audience and, as the story progressed, regularly paused to make observations to the camera. Not only did Gary know, but so did all the others in the cast, and stories were written to take advantage of this awareness. If Gary was leaving home he might invite the studio audience to use his living room while he was away—and they did—until he came back and they returned to their seats. At times he would leave the set and go into the audience to get personal reactions to what was going on or "take a call from a viewer" (a la *Donahue*). Sometimes the other actors, in character, chided Gary for paying too much attention to the camera and not enough to the plot. Gary and his writers were all too familiar with the standard elements of traditional sitcoms—including the "fourth wall" (between fictional character and real life)—and went out of their way to make fun of them, while still presenting a reasonably coherent, and funny, story. This extended even to the show's self-mocking theme song; Gary's fictional neighbor might drop by to complain that it was being played too loud—again!

It's Gary Shandling's Show received rave reviews from critics bored with standard TV fare, and did reasonably well on the limited-distribution Showtime cable service. In early 1988, in an effort to bolster its Sunday night lineup, the new Fox network secured the rights to air reruns of the Showtime episodes not less than one month after they had aired on Showtime, and all America could see what the fuss was about.

IT'S MAGIC
Magic
FIRST TELECAST: *July 31, 1955*
LAST TELECAST: *September 4, 1955*
BROADCAST HISTORY:
  Jul 1955–Sep 1955, CBS Sun 7:00–7:30
HOST:
  Paul Tripp

Each week on this summer series, three famous magicians appeared to perform some of their tricks before a studio audience. The host of the show, Paul Tripp, had been the producer and star of the popular children's program *Mr. I Magination*.

IT'S NEWS TO ME
Quiz/Audience Participation
FIRST TELECAST: *July 2, 1951*
LAST TELECAST: *August 27, 1954*
BROADCAST HISTORY:
  Jul 1951–Mar 1952, CBS Mon 9:30–10:00
  Apr 1952–Jun 1952, CBS Fri 9:30–10:00
  Jul 1952–Aug 1952, CBS Sun 6:30–7:00
  Sep 1952, CBS Fri 10:30–11:00
  Sep 1952–Nov 1952, CBS Sat 6:30–7:00
  Dec 1952–Sep 1953, CBS Sat 10:30–11:00
  Jul 1954–Aug 1954, CBS Fri 10:30–11:00

MODERATOR:
  John Daly (1951–1953)
  Walter Cronkite (1954)
PANELISTS:
  John Henry Faulk
  Anna Lee
  Quincy Howe (1951–1952)
  Quentin Reynolds
  Nina Foch (1954)

The object of this quiz show was for the celebrity panelists to describe what news story was represented by a visual or verbal clue. The stories were always current news items and members of the studio audience could win small amounts of money by determining whether or not the celebrity panelists were correct. John Daly was the original host/moderator and was succeeded by Walter Cronkite when the series was revived as a summer replacement for *Person to Person*.

IT'S NOT EASY
Situation Comedy
FIRST TELECAST: *September 29, 1983*
LAST TELECAST: *October 27, 1983*
BROADCAST HISTORY:
  Sep 1983–Oct 1983, ABC Thu 9:30–10:00
CAST:
  Jack Long . . . . Ken Howard
  Ruth Long . . . . Jayne Meadows
  Carol Long . . . . Rachael Jacobs
  Johnny Long . . . . Evan Cohen
  Sharon Long Townsend . . . . . Carlene Watkins
  Neal Townsend . . . . Bert Convy
  Matthew Townsend . . . . Billy Jacoby

Divorce with a laugh track was the premise of this short-lived comedy, which seemed to suggest that even the kids don't mind it when parents split. Jack and Sharon were the divorced couple who decided to live across the street from one another so they could share custody of their cute children, 8-year-old Johnny and 11-year-old Carol. Sharon had since remarried, and her stepson, Matthew, age 14, was also mixed into the stew. They all ran into and out of each other's kitchens—and lives—as did Sharon's new hubby, Neal (who wondered if his new family was really his) and Jack's meddling mother, Ruth. One of the favorite pursuits was trying to fix up the athletic Jack with someone new, so that everything would be symmetrical again.

IT'S POLKA TIME
see *Polka Time*

IT'S SHOWTIME AT THE APOLLO
Musical Variety
BROADCAST HISTORY:
  Syndicated only
  60 minutes
  Produced: *1987–*
  Released: *September 1987*

REGULARS:
Sandman Sims
Rick Aviles
The Apollo Dancers

Taped before a live audience at Harlem's famous Apollo Theatre, this variety series was a showcase primarily for black performers. Each telecast featured a celebrity guest host. Regulars included dancer Sandman Sims, comic Rick Aviles, and the long-stemmed Apollo Dancers. Among those appearing as guests and guest hosts were Melba Moore, The Beastie Boys, Natalie Cole, Expose, Al Jarreau, Bill Cosby, James Brown, Stephen Bishop, Mary Wilson, Stephanie Mills, and Freddie Jackson. There was a regular amateur night segment (just as at the real Apollo) as well as tributes to great former Apollo stars like Billie Holiday, Sam Cooke, The Nicholas Brothers, Pearl Bailey, and Moms Mabley.

A similar series, hosted by Willie Bryant and titled simply *Showtime At the Apollo*, had been syndicated briefly in 1954. This earlier series provided a rare showcase for black jazz and rhythm and blues talent in the pre–rock 'n' roll days, and footage from it—sometimes the only existing film of legendary performers—is often seen in documentaries.

IT'S YOUR MOVE
Situation Comedy
FIRST TELECAST: *September 26, 1984*
LAST TELECAST: *August 10, 1985*
BROADCAST HISTORY:
Sep 1984–Jan 1985, NBC Wed 9:30–10:00
Jan 1985–Mar 1985, NBC Sat 9:30–10:00
Jun 1985–Aug 1985, NBC Sat 8:30–9:00
CAST:

Matthew Burton	Jason Bateman
Norman Lamb	David Garrison
Eileen Burton	Caren Kaye
Julie Burton	Tricia Cast
Eli	Adam Sadowsky
Lou Donatelli	Ernie Sabella
Principal Dwight Ellis	Garrett Morris

Comedy about a smooth-talking, 14-year-old con artist who met his match when an equally slick writer moved in next door. Matt always had a scam going—selling term papers, arranging dates, bugging his sister Julie's slumber party so he could sell the girls' secrets at school. He had his single mother Eileen in the palm of his hand. Then in moved Norman, a would-be writer, always broke, who began to date Matt's mother. Norman neatly countered every one of Matt's plans to break up the incipient romance. A steady stream of pranks, schemes, and counterschemes followed, as Matt and Norman tried to outmaneuver each other. Eli was Matt's chubby, dim-witted companion.

IVAN THE TERRIBLE
Situation Comedy
FIRST TELECAST: *August 21, 1976*
LAST TELECAST: *September 18, 1976*
BROADCAST HISTORY:
Aug 1976–Sep 1976, CBS Sat 8:30–9:00
CAST:

Ivan	Lou Jacobi
Olga	Maria Karnilova
Vladimir	Phil Leeds
Tatiana	Despo
Federov	Christopher Hewett
Sascha	Matthew Barry
Nikolai	Alan Cauldwell
Sonya	Caroline Kava
Raoul	Manuel Martinez
Svetlana	Nana Tucker

Ivan was the headwaiter at the Hotel Metropole in contemporary Moscow in this five-week summer mini-series. His biggest problem was the congestion in his 3½ room apartment, inhabited by nine people and a ferocious, but unseen, dog named Rasputin. Living with Ivan were his wife, Olga; their children, Sonya, Nikolai, and Sascha; Olga's first husband, Vladimir, and her mother, Tatiana. Also in the household were Nikolai's wife Svetlana and a Cuban named Raoul. All of them except young Sascha and Raoul had various jobs in Moscow.

I'VE GOT A SECRET
Quiz/Audience Participation
FIRST TELECAST: *June 19, 1952*
LAST TELECAST: *July 5, 1976*
BROADCAST HISTORY:
Jun 1952–Jun 1953, CBS Thu 10:30–11:00
Jul 1953–Sep 1961, CBS Wed 9:30–10:00
Sep 1961–Sep 1962, CBS Mon 10:30–11:00
Sep 1962–Sep 1966, CBS Mon 8:00–8:30
Sep 1966–Apr 1967, CBS Mon 10:30–11:00
Jun 1976–Jul 1976, CBS Tue 8:00–8:30
MODERATOR:
Garry Moore (1952–1964)
Steve Allen (1964–1967)
Bill Cullen (1976)
PANELISTS:
Louise Allbritton (1952)
Laura Hobson (1952)
Walter Kiernan (1952)
Orson Bean (1952)
Melville Cooper (1952)
Bill Cullen (1952–1967)
Kitty Carlisle (1952–1953)
Henry Morgan (1952–1976)
Laraine Day (1952)
Eddie Bracken (1952)
Faye Emerson (1952–1958)
Jayne Meadows (1952–1959)
Betsy Palmer (1957–1967)
Bess Myerson (1958–1967)
Pat Collins (1976)
Richard Dawson (1976)
Elaine Joyce (1976)

THEME:
"Plink, Plank, Plunk," by Leroy Anderson
PRODUCERS:
Mark Goodson and Bill Todman
ASSOCIATE PRODUCER:
Allan Sherman (1952–1958)

The format of *I've Got a Secret* was both simple and durable. Four panelists took turns questioning the person with the secret to determine what the secret was. A nominal financial award was given to a contestant whose secret (flashed on the TV screen for the viewing audience) could not be guessed by the panel. Each show gave three regular contestants an opportunity to stump the panel, and also had one celebrity guest with his own secret to hide.

The program had a rocky start—the premiere telecast used a courtroom set, with Garry Moore as the judge, the guest in a defendant's dock, and the panelists questioning like lawyers as they stood before the bench. This complicated setup was scrapped by the second telecast, when *Secret* adopted a standard panel-show set. The series went on to a 15-year network run, and was probably the most successful quiz show in the history of the medium. It placed in the top ten for four consecutive years during the late 1950s, and remained quite popular during the following decade as well, a record that no other quiz program has approached. Almost a decade after the final telecast of its original run, it was brought back for a short summer run in 1976, with Bill Cullen, one of the earliest regular panelists, in the role of moderator. It was also seen in a syndicated version during the 1972–1973 season, hosted by Steve Allen.

As with any panel show, the secret of *Secret*'s success lay with the chemistry of its regulars. After considerable turnover in 1952, the show settled down to a well-balanced and familiar crew. Through the 1950s it was grinning Bill Cullen and acerbic Henry Morgan, balanced on the female side by Faye Emerson and Jayne Meadows. In the 1960s the two men remained, but the women were replaced by Betsy Palmer and Bess Myerson. The repartee was witty and spontaneous, although the unplanned quality was occasionally shattered, as on the occasion when Monty Woolley appeared as guest celebrity. His secret was that he slept with his beard inside the covers. When asked why, he replied, "As a matter of fact I don't. That's merely the secret they decided upon for me." Garry Moore, for once, was speechless.

J

J.J. STARBUCK

Adventure
FIRST TELECAST: *September 26, 1987*
LAST TELECAST:
BROADCAST HISTORY:
  Sep 1987, NBC Sat 9:30–11:00
  Sep 1987–Dec 1987, NBC Tue 9:00–10:00
  Dec 1987–Feb 1988, NBC Sat 10:00–11:00
  Jun 1988–   , NBC Tue 9:00–10:00
CAST:
  J.J. (Jerome Jeremiah) Starbuck
  .... Dale Robertson
  E.L. "Tenspeed" Turner (1988–   )
  .... Ben Vereen
  Charlie Bullets................. Jimmy Dean
  *Jill Starbuck .... Shawn Weatherly

*Occasional

"I reckon a diamond is just a hunk of coal that stuck to the job. . . . If you want something done, find the busiest person to do it. . . . You look happier than a termite in a sawmill. . . ." Mumbling a constant stream of such homey aphorisms, eccentric Texas billionaire J.J. Starbuck set out to solve crimes using his natural charm, down-home manner, and, when necessary, his vast wealth and connections. J.J. was one of TV's outrageous characters. Apparently Marklee Industries, the San Antonio–based corporation that was the source of his wealth, ran itself, freeing J.J. to drive around the country alone in his 1961 Lincoln convertible, complete with steer horns on the hood and a horn that blared "The Eyes of Texas." Old J.J. never charged a fee, and usually helped those who had been framed or abandoned by the system. Local law enforcement officials were not sure what to make of this superrich meddler, but J.J. just charmed their badges off. After all, if they told him to move on, he'd just chew a bit and observe, "Well sir, the Lord never closes one door without openin' another."

Early in 1988 J.J. picked up a sidekick in the person of "Tenspeed" Turner, a con man whose tricks and disguises came in handy at times (Ben Vereen had played the same character in the failed 1980 series *Tenspeed and Brown Shoe*, marking one of TV's more unusual character revivals). Jill was J.J.'s infrequently seen niece.

JACK AND MIKE

Comedy/Drama
FIRST TELECAST: *September 16, 1986*
LAST TELECAST: *May 28, 1987*
BROADCAST HISTORY:
  Sep 1986–Mar 1987, ABC Tue 10:00–11:00
  Apr 1987–May 1987, ABC Thu 9:00–10:00
CAST:
  Jackie Shea................... Shelley Hack
  Mike Brennan .... Tom Mason
  Carol .... Holly Fulger
  Nora Adler.............. Jacqueline Brookes
  Anthony Kubecek.............. Kevin Dunn
  Rick Scotti .... Vincent Baggetta
  Belinda .... Noelle Bou-Sliman

Jack and Mike was one of several attempts by ABC to produce another young, trendy, romantic drama to follow its established Tuesday night hit *Moonlighting*. Jackie was a glamorous, dynamic newspaper columnist for the *Chicago Mirror*, who was always after a hot lead for an exposé, or sometimes just a warm human-interest story; Mike was a successful restauranteur, who operated two of the city's trendiest watering holes and was about to open a third. Though they were married and very much in love, their high-energy careers (her tips, his hors d'oeuvres) kept getting in the way.

Nora was the city editor and Anthony a reporter at the *Mirror,* and Carol the head waitress at Mike's new "Brennan's Grill." Rick was an occasionally seen attorney friend. The series was filmed on location in Chicago.

JACK BENNY SHOW, THE

Comedy
FIRST TELECAST: *October 28, 1950*
LAST TELECAST: *August 30, 1977*
BROADCAST HISTORY:
  Oct 1950–Jun 1959, CBS Sun 7:30–8:00 (OS)
  Oct 1959–Jun 1960, CBS Sun 10:00–10:30
  Oct 1960–Jun 1962, CBS Sun 9:30–10:00 (OS)
  Sep 1962–Jun 1963, CBS Tue 9:30–10:00
  Sep 1963–Sep 1964, CBS Tue 9:30–10:00
  Sep 1964–Sep 1965, NBC Fri 9:30–10:00
  Aug 1977, CBS Tue 8:00–8:30
REGULARS:
  Jack Benny
  Eddie "Rochester" Anderson
  Don Wilson
  Dennis Day
  Mary Livingstone
  Frank Nelson
  Artie Auerbach
  Mel Blanc
THEME:
  "Love in Bloom," by Leo Robin and Ralph Rainger

Jack Benny had been a regular network-radio personality since 1932. When he made his first tentative forays into television in 1950, it was with a series of specials that aired on an infrequent basis in what would eventually become his regular Sunday nighttime slot. Ten of them aired during the 1950–1951 and 1951–1952 seasons. From October 5, 1952, through the following January his show was televised once every four weeks, and when he returned again, on September 13, 1953, it was on an alternate-week basis that lasted through June of 1960. For his last five seasons, *The Jack Benny Show* aired every week.

The format of the show, and the personality of its star, so well honed in two decades on radio, made the transition to television almost intact. Jack's stinginess, vanity about his supposed age of 39, basement vault where he kept all his money, ancient Maxwell automobile, and feigned ineptness at playing the violin were all part of the act—and were, if anything, bolstered by their visibility on the TV show. Added to Jack's famous pregnant pause and exasperated "Well!" were a rather mincing walk, an affected hand to the cheek, and a pained look of disbelief when confronted by life's little tragedies.

The two regulars who were with Jack throughout his television run were Eddie "Rochester" Anderson as his valet and Don Wilson as his announcer and friend. Appearing on a more irregular basis were Dennis Day, Artie Auerbach, Frank Nelson, Mary Livingstone (Mrs. Benny), and Mel Blanc, all veterans from the radio show. Blanc, the master of a thousand voices (including Bugs Bunny), was both heard as the engine of Jack's Maxwell and seen as Prof. Le Blanc, his long-suffering violin teacher.

Jack's underplayed comedy was as popular on television as it had been on radio. After fifteen years as a more or less regular television performer, he cut back his schedule to an occasional special and continued to appear until the year of his death, 1974. CBS brought back four episodes from *The Jack Benny Show,* originally filmed in the early 1960s, for a limited run in August 1977.

CBS had also aired reruns of this series on weekday afternoons from October 1964 to September 1965 as *The Jack Benny Daytime Show* and on Sunday afternoons from October 1964 to March 1965 as *Sunday with Jack Benny.*

JACK CARTER SHOW, THE
Variety
FIRST TELECAST: *February 25, 1950*
LAST TELECAST: *June 2, 1951*
BROADCAST HISTORY:
 Feb 1950–Jun 1951, NBC Sat 8:00–9:00 (OS)
REGULARS:
 Jack Carter
 Don Richards
 Bill Callahan
 Lou Breese Orchestra (1950)
 Harry Sosnik Orchestra (1950–1951)

NBC's innovative Vice President of Programs Pat Weaver introduced several novel concepts to television in the early 1950s, perhaps the best-remembered of which are the *Today* and *Tonight* shows. Another was the *Saturday Night Revue,* a package of two big-name variety shows on a single evening, one originating live from Chicago and the other live from New York. Comedian Jack

Carter hosted the Chicago element from 8:00–9:00 P.M., while Sid Caesar and Imogene Coca starred from 9:00–10:30 P.M. in the New York segment, titled *Your Show of Shows.*

Jack Carter was a fast-rising young talent in 1950, having appeared on several programs, including his own series of specials on ABC in 1949. His element of the *Saturday Night Revue* was a music-comedy-variety hour, opening with a stand-up routine by Jack followed by guest stars and skits by a constantly changing supporting cast. Among the longer-lasting regulars were baritone Don Richards and dancer Bill Callahan. Memorable routines included a satire of current TV stars (Garroway, Godfrey, Berle, *et al.*) and elaborate musical productions such as "Gravediggers of 1950: A Musical Extravagangster" starring Carter, Cesar Romero, and the whole cast.

Both segments of the *Saturday Night Revue* were quite popular at the outset, blitzing the competition, but gradually the Caesar-Coca portion began to dominate. Carter's segment moved to New York at the start of the 1950–1951 season, but by the following summer it was dropped in favor of *The All Star Revue.*

JACK DREES SPORTS SHOW, THE
Sports News
FIRST TELECAST: *July 2, 1956*
LAST TELECAST: *August 24, 1956*
BROADCAST HISTORY:
 Jul 1956–Aug 1956, ABC Mon–Fri 7:00–7:15
REPORTER:
 Jack Drees

Jack Drees, who was also the announcer for ABC's *Wednesday Night Fights,* brought audiences up to date on the latest sports news with this nightly report. He also interviewed sports celebrities when they were available.

JACK LEONARD
Music
FIRST TELECAST: *March 10, 1949*
LAST TELECAST: *May 5, 1949*
BROADCAST HISTORY:
 Mar 1949–May 1949, DUM Thu 7:15–7:30
REGULARS:
 Jack Leonard
 Virginia Oswald, vocals
 Bob Curtis, piano

Songs by the former big-band singer.

JACK PAAR PROGRAM, THE
Variety
FIRST TELECAST: *September 21, 1962*
LAST TELECAST: *September 10, 1965*
BROADCAST HISTORY:
 Sep 1962–Sep 1965, NBC Fri 10:00–11:00
REGULARS:
 Jack Paar
 Jose Melis Orchestra

This was, in many respects, a prime-time version of Jack's earlier late-night talk show (*The Tonight Show*), which he had hosted from 1957–1962. It was somewhat more diversified, however, including topical films and recorded interviews, comedy sketches, musical segments, and home movies of Jack's travels with his wife, Miriam, and his teen-age daughter, Randy. Each telecast opened with a Paar monologue and then, depending on the guest stars, went to either sketches, songs, or chats. The films of the Paar family's various trips to Africa, Europe, and Russia were often shown, with daughter Randy present to help with the narration.

Among the more notable moments were Richard Nixon playing a composition of his own on the piano on March 8, 1963 (his first public appearance since losing the gubernatorial race in California in 1962); Barry Goldwater discussing his chances of defeating Lyndon Johnson in the 1964 presidential race, one month after having announced his candidacy; and a filmed interview in Africa with Dr. Albert Schweitzer. In a precursor of what would become one of the most popular television series of the 1970s, Paar presented a condensed 20-minute episode from the British comedy series *Steptoe and Son* on his April 24, 1964, telecast. That series was the basis for the American situation comedy *Sanford and Son*. Although not classified as a regular, Jonathan Winters was a frequent guest during *The Jack Paar Program*'s first two seasons.

JACK PAAR SHOW, THE
see *Tonight Show, The*

JACK PAAR SHOW, THE
Variety
FIRST TELECAST: *July 17, 1954*
LAST TELECAST: *September 4, 1954*
BROADCAST HISTORY:
Jul 1954–Sep 1954, CBS Sat 9:30–10:00
REGULARS:
Jack Paar
Betty Clooney
Johnny Desmond
Pupi Campo's Orchestra
Jose Melis

In addition to hosting a regular daytime series, which had started in November 1953, comedian Jack Paar served as host for this live summer replacement for *My Favorite Husband*. Jose Melis, who was to spend many years with Jack when he became host of *The Tonight Show* later in the 1950s, had started with him on the daytime show and appeared on this series. The format included monologues by Jack, appearances by guest stars, and songs by his regular singers.

JACKIE GLEASON SHOW, THE
Comedy Variety
FIRST TELECAST: *September 20, 1952*

LAST TELECAST: *September 12, 1970*
BROADCAST HISTORY:
Sep 1952–Jun 1955, CBS Sat 8:00–9:00 (OS)
Sep 1956–Jun 1957, CBS Sat 8:00–9:00
Oct 1958–Jan 1959, CBS Fri 8:30–9:00
Sep 1962–May 1968, CBS Sat 7:30–8:30 (OS)
Sep 1968–Sep 1970, CBS Sat 7:30–8:30
REGULARS:
Jackie Gleason
Art Carney (1952–1957; 1966–1970)
Joyce Randolph (1952–1957)
Audrey Meadows (1952–1957)
Buddy Hackett (1958–1959)
Frank Fontaine (1962–1966)
Sue Ane Langdon (1962–1963)
Barbara Heller (1963–1965)
Horace McMahon (1963–1964)
Alice Ghostley (1962–1964)
Helen Curtis (1964–1966)
Sid Fields (1964–1966)
Phil Bruns (1964–1966)
George Jessel (1965–1966)
Sheila MacRae (1966–1970)
Jane Kean (1966–1970)
The June Taylor Dancers
The Glea-Girls (1956–1970)
Ray Bloch & His Orchestra (1952–1959)
Sammy Spear & His Orchestra (1962–1970)
ANNOUNCERS:
Jack Lescoulie (1952–1959)
Johnny Olsen (1962–1970)
THEME:
"Melancholy Serenade," by Jackie Gleason (written in 1953)

The lure of money brought *The Jackie Gleason Show* to CBS in the fall of 1952. The rotund comic had been starring in *The Cavalcade of Stars* on DuMont since the summer of 1950 and had developed into one of the few genuine successes on that money-poor network. When CBS offered him a staggering increase in weekly pay—reportedly $8,000 compared to the $1,600 that DuMont could afford—coupled with the funding to make his show a much more elaborate production, he could scarcely refuse.

Jackie's original CBS variety hour, done live from New York, bore a strong similarity to his previous show on DuMont, albeit with a much larger budget. His second banana, Art Carney, made the move with him, as did the June Taylor Dancers and Ray ("the Flower of the Musical World") Bloch's Orchestra. Audrey Meadows and Joyce Randolph were added to the cast of regulars, primarily in "The Honeymooners" sketches (see separate entry for details of *The Honeymooners*), and most of the characters that Gleason had developed on DuMont were honed to perfection on CBS. Among them, in addition to "The Honeymooners" Ralph Kramden, were The Poor Soul, Joe the Bartender, The Loudmouth, Reggie Van Gleason III, Rudy the Repairman, and Fenwick Babbitt. The Great One, as Jackie was called, opened each telecast with a monologue and then led into the first sketch with "And awa-a-aay we go," as he left the stage. His other catchphrase, used in reaction to almost anything at all, was "How sweet it is!"

The original *Jackie Gleason Show* ran three seasons and was replaced, for the 1955–1956 season, with a half-hour situation comedy version of *The Honeymooners*. When the variety show returned the following fall, it was with the same basic cast and format, plus some decorative additions in "Glea-Girls," 16 young models who did little else than look beautiful and introduce various sketches. There was no Gleason variety series during the 1957–1958 season, but Jackie was back in the fall of 1958 with a modified half-hour format. Gone were all the regular cast members from previous seasons and Buddy Hackett was added as Jackie's second banana. The chemistry wasn't there and, after only three months on the air, this short version of *The Jackie Gleason Show* expired.

In the fall of 1962, following an abortive failure with a quiz show *(You're in the Picture)* and the talk show *(The Jackie Gleason Show)* that replaced it in 1961, Jackie was back with a lavish full-scale variety show—*The Jackie Gleason Show: The American Scene Magazine.* His new second banana was Frank Fontaine (as Crazy Guggenheim in Joe the Bartender sketches), who could sing quite well when not in character and released a number of moderately successful record albums during his tenure with Gleason. Not only were most of Jackie's standard characters in evidence, but a new "Agnes and Arthur" sketch about two lovelorn tenement residents (with Alice Ghostley as Agnes) was added as a semi-regular feature. The beautiful "Glea-Girls," including Barbara Heller as "Christine Clam," were still in evidence introducing the segments of each show, but there was a considerable turnover in the supporting cast. There was more topical satire in this show than in Jackie's previous efforts, and more appearances by name guest stars. In keeping with the title, there were entire episodes that were done as musical comedies with book, lyrics, songs, dances, and sketches reflecting "the American scene." At Jackie's insistence, the entire production moved from New York to Miami Beach before the start of the 1964–1965 season, and remained a Florida-based show throughout the remainder of its run. A feature added the following year was a nationwide talent hunt, in which George Jessel traveled around the country auditioning young performers who would get their first national exposure on Jackie's variety show.

The 1966–1967 season brought a basic change in format, a modified title, and a different supporting cast. The title was shortened to *The Jackie Gleason Show,* Art Carney was back with Gleason on a regular basis after a nine-year absence, and Sheila MacRae and Jane Kean were the only other cast regulars. "The Honeymooners" was brought

back as the principal source of program material. There were still variety shows with sketches and guest stars, special shows devoted to single subjects like circuses or tributes to show-business greats, and book musicals, but throughout this last four-year run over half of the telecasts were full-hour "Honeymooners" episodes. Sometimes they were done without music and other times they were done as musical comedies with songs and production numbers. They took place in Brooklyn, around New York, and in different locations around the world. They were done with and without guest stars, but the constants were always there, the Kramdens (Jackie as Ralph and Sheila as Alice) and the Nortons (Art as Ed and Jane as Trixie), middle-class schlepps bumbling their way through life.

JACKIE GLEASON SHOW, THE

Talk

FIRST TELECAST: *January 27, 1961*
LAST TELECAST: *March 24, 1961*
BROADCAST HISTORY:
   Jan 1961–Mar 1961, CBS Fri 9:30–10:00
HOST:
   Jackie Gleason

Jackie Gleason had been absent from network television for slightly over two years when he premiered a quiz show titled *You're in the Picture* on January 20, 1961. The program was a total failure and, on the following Friday, *The Jackie Gleason Show* was on in its place. The first telecast was simply a chat between Gleason and his television audience. It was an apology for *You're in the Picture,* made before a nationwide audience. For the next two months Gleason conducted an informal talk show in the time slot. Each telecast was devoted to a single guest who reminisced with Jackie about past experiences, both professional and personal. Among the guests were Mickey Rooney, Art Carney, Bobby Darin, and Jayne Mansfield.

JACKPOT BOWLING STARRING MILTON BERLE

Sports

FIRST TELECAST: *January 9, 1959*
LAST TELECAST: *March 13, 1961*
BROADCAST HISTORY:
   Jan 1959–Jun 1960, NBC Fri 10:45–11:00
   Sep 1960–Mar 1961, NBC Mon 10:30–11:00
HOSTS:
   Leo Durocher (1959)
   Mel Allen
   Bud Palmer (1959)
   Milton Berle (1960–1961)

Under its original title, *Phillies Jackpot Bowling,* this program was used to fill the time between the conclusion of the bout on *Cavalcade of Sports* and the start of the 11 P.M. local news. Top professional bowlers competed for a $1,000 weekly prize with a special bonus awarded to the bowler able to throw six strikes in a row. Leo Durocher was the host for the first two telecasts, and Mel Allen took over until April 10, 1959, when he was replaced by Bud Palmer. Palmer stayed through October 2, 1959, and Mel Allen returned the following week and continued as host throughout the remainder of its Friday night run, which ended on June 24, 1960.

On September 19, 1960, the program returned under the new title *Jackpot Bowling Starring Milton Berle,* essentially the same show moved to Monday nights. Funnyman Berle was the host and there were two matches each week instead of the single match played when the show had been on Friday nights. An added feature of the new version was the appearance of a show-business celebrity each week who bowled for his favorite charity between the two regular matches.

JACKSONS, THE
Musical Variety
FIRST TELECAST: *June 16, 1976*
LAST TELECAST: *March 9, 1977*
BROADCAST HISTORY:
Jun 1976–Jul 1976, CBS Wed 8:00–8:30
Jan 1977–Mar 1977, CBS Wed 8:30–9:00
REGULARS:
Michael Jackson
Jackie Jackson
Tito Jackson
Marlon Jackson
Randy Jackson
LaToya Jackson
Rebie (Maureen) Jackson
Janet Jackson
Jim Samuels (1976)
Marty Cohen (1976)
Emmett Ashford (1977)
Tom Biener (1977)
Johnny Dark (1977)
Biff Manard (1977)

Five male members of the Jackson Family (aged 16–24) formed a rock combo called The Jackson Five, which had had numerous hit records in the early 1970s. In 1976 the boys were joined by three of their sisters in a four-week summer variety show. The emphasis was on comedy and popular music, with guest stars each week participating in both aspects of the show. The program returned for an additional run in the spring of 1977 with a different group of supporting regulars appearing in comic sketches.

JACQUES FRAY MUSIC ROOM, THE
Music/Talent
FIRST TELECAST: *February 19, 1949*
LAST TELECAST: *October 16, 1949*
BROADCAST HISTORY:
Feb 1949–Apr 1949, ABC Sat 8:00–8:30
May 1949–Aug 1949, ABC Sun 8:00–8:30
Sep 1949–Oct 1949, ABC Sun 9:30–10:00

REGULARS:
Jacques Fray
Charles Stark (Feb–Jul)
Conrad Thibault (Aug–Oct)
John Gart, organ

This unusual program was essentially a longhair vaudeville/talent show. Pianist Fray, who specialized in concert numbers and show tunes, would play a bit, but most of the program consisted of performances by aspiring "high-brow" talent, rated by two judges in the studio and one at home (by telephone). It was all very classy. In August Conrad Thibault was brought in as emcee, replacing Charles Stark. Among those guesting were Marguerite Piazza, Bess Myerson, and Russell & Aura.

Also known as *The Music Room.*

JAKE AND THE FATMAN
Legal Drama
FIRST TELECAST: *September 26, 1987*
LAST TELECAST:
BROADCAST HISTORY:
Sep 1987, CBS Sat 10:00–11:00
Sep 1987–Feb 1988, CBS Tue 9:00–10:00
Mar 1988–May 1988, CBS Wed 9:00–10:00
Jun 1988–   , CBS Wed 8:00–9:00
CAST:
Jason Lochinvar "Fatman" McCabe
.... William Conrad
Jake Styles .... Joe Penny
Derek Mitchell .... Alan Campbell
Gertrude .... Lu Leonard

J.L. "Fatman" McCabe was the tough district attorney in what CBS described as "a large Southern California city" (could they have meant Los Angeles?). A former cop who was noted for his earthy language, lack of tact, dogged persistence, and willingness to skirt strict legal procedures when it suited his purpose, the Fatman had a remarkable record of convictions and a long list of enemies. Jake Styles was his special investigator, a flashy, high-living young stud who often went undercover to get evidence for the cases they were working on. Also on McCabe's staff were Derek Mitchell, a novice, overly enthusiastic young assistant D.A.; and Gertrude, the Fatman's sassy secretary. McCabe's ancient pet bulldog, Max—who somewhat resembled his owner—was J.L.'s constant companion.

JAMBOREE
see *Windy City Jamboree.*

JAMES AT 15
Drama
FIRST TELECAST: *October 27, 1977*
LAST TELECAST: *July 27, 1978*
BROADCAST HISTORY:
Oct 1977–Mar 1978, NBC Thu 9:00–10:00
Jun 1978–Jul 1978, NBC Thu 9:00–10:00

CAST:

James Hunter................. Lance Kerwin
Mr. Paul Hunter.............. Linden Chiles
Mrs. Joan Hunter............. Lynn Carlin
Sandy Hunter................. Kim Richards
Kathy Hunter............. Deirdre Berthrong
Sly Hazeltine.............. David Hubbard
Marlene Mahoney............ Susan Myers
Mr. Shamley.................... Jack Knight

James at 15 was one of TV's more honest attempts to portray the pains and joys of growing up in the 1970s. Fifteen-year-old James Hunter was a bright, sensitive boy who found his world completely disrupted when his father, a college professor, moved the family from Oregon to Boston, Mass., in order to accept a new teaching position. At first James tried to run away; then he began to learn how to cope with life in a new, city environment. Among his new friends at Bunker Hill High were a hip black named Sly, who always had a little sage advice, or "slychology," when James needed it; and Marlene, a plain but very intelligent girl who always took the intellectual point of view. Sandy was James' teenage sister, and Kathy their older sister.

James was an avid photographer and also a daydreamer. One of the novel elements of the series was his periodic lapses into daydreaming of himself as he would like to be—heroic, suave, etc.—portrayed in special dreamlike sequences. Although there was comedy in *James at 15*, none of the main characters were caricatures, and likewise the subject matter was sometimes rather serious: a young friend who was dying of cancer, teenage alcoholism, venereal disease, the discovery that Kathy was having a pre-marital affair. Perhaps the most controversial episode was one in which James lost his own virginity in an affair with a Swedish exchange student, Christina Kollberg (portrayed by Kirsten Baker). Although the subject matter in the series was tastefully handled, and NBC had high hopes for the show, it did not attract a large audience and was canceled after a single season.

Effective February 9, 1978, the episode dealing with James' affair, the series' title was changed to *James at 16*.

JAMES GARNER AS NICHOLS
see *Nichols*

JAMES MICHENER'S ADVENTURES IN PARADISE
see *Adventures in Paradise*

JAMIE
Situation Comedy
FIRST TELECAST: September 28, 1953
LAST TELECAST: October 4, 1954
BROADCAST HISTORY:
Sep 1953–Oct 1954, ABC Mon 7:30–8:00 (OS)

CAST:

Jamison Francis McHummer (Jamie)
.... Brandon De Wilde
Grandpa .... Ernest Truex
Aunt Laurie .... Polly Rowles
Cousin Liz.................... Kathy Nolan
Annie Moakum .... Alice Pearce
*Aunt Ella............... Kathleen Comegys

*Occasional

Brandon De Wilde was one of the child-star discoveries of the 1950s. A sensitive lad, and a natural actor, he was signed by ABC for his own series three years after his professional debut (at age 8) in the hit Broadway play *A Member of the Wedding. Jamie,* which had previewed to rave reviews as an episode of *ABC Album* during the previous season, looked like a surefire winner as a series. De Wilde was cast as a likable orphan who had been shunted from one uncaring relative to another, until he landed in Aunt Laurie's household. There he met a kindred spirit in Grandpa (played to perfection by 63-year-old character actor Ernest Truex), who was similarly ignored by his kin. Grandpa, twinkle-eyed and with a zest for life, became Jamie's bosom buddy, sharing escapades, and the joys of growing up and of growing old. Others in the cast included Liz, Jamie's teenage cousin, and Annie, Aunt Laurie's helper in the catering business.

Jamie was a live weekly series and there was some publicity at the time about the problems of a youngster, however gifted, being so deeply involved in an adult profession during his formative years. De Wilde's parents had a special contract which allowed him to drop out of the series on short notice if he wanted to, or if his parents felt it was impairing his emotional growth. *Jamie* did indeed end abruptly two weeks into its second season, but it was not due to concern over Master De Wilde, but rather to a fight between network and sponsor over mundane business matters. An attempt was made to locate the popular program in another time slot or on another network, but this did not transpire.

The ending was unhappy in the long run for the tow-headed young star, as well. Never able to sustain the success of his youth into adulthood, Brandon De Wilde died in 1972, at the age of 30, in a traffic accident.

JAN MURRAY TIME
Variety
FIRST TELECAST: February 11, 1955
LAST TELECAST: May 6, 1955
BROADCAST HISTORY:
Feb 1955–May 1955, NBC Fri 10:45–11:00
REGULARS:
Jan Murray
Tina Louise
The Novelites
Fletcher Peck

This short and short-lived variety series was used to fill the time between the conclusion of the bout on *Cavalcade of Sports* and the start of the local 11 P.M. news, in the spring of 1955. It starred comedian Jan Murray and featured singer Tina Louise, the singing and instrumental group The Novelites, and pianist Fletcher Peck. There was no set format for this live show, since the length varied depending on how long the fight took. There were occasional guest stars and, time permitting, comedy sketches, in addition to Jan Murray's shorter comedy bits and musical numbers by his supporting cast.

JANE FROMAN'S U.S.A. CANTEEN
Musical Variety
FIRST TELECAST: *October 18, 1952*
LAST TELECAST: *June 23, 1955*
BROADCAST HISTORY:
Oct 1952–Dec 1952, CBS Sat 9:00–9:30
Dec 1952–Jan 1954, CBS Tue/Thu 7:45–8:00 (OS)
Jan 1954–Jun 1955, CBS Thu 7:45–8:00 (OS)
REGULARS:
Jane Froman
The Peter Birch Dancers
The Alfredo Antonini Orchestra (1952–1953)
The Hank Sylvern Orchestra (1953–1954)

Singer Jane Froman, who had worked long and hard entertaining the troops during the Second World War, featured men in uniform on her CBS network television series. In cooperation with the Department of Defense, the program sought out talented servicemen who competed for the opportunity to perform on this live program. The setting was a re-creation of a U.S.O. Canteen, and it was there that Miss Froman sang, chatted with her guests, and introduced young performing servicemen to the nation.

At the start of the 1953–1954 season the title of the program was shortened to *The Jane Froman Show*, the servicemen were dropped, and the emphasis shifted to a straight musical variety show.

Although Miss Froman was perhaps best known for her signature tune, "With a Song in My Heart" (which was also the title of her 1952 movie biography), this series was more notable for the introduction of another song—one of the first songs to be made a hit by the new medium of television. It was "I Believe," a semi-religious number written especially for this series and sung incessantly on it by Miss Froman, which went on to become one of the top hits of 1953.

JANE PICKENS SHOW, THE
Music
FIRST TELECAST: *January 31, 1954*
LAST TELECAST: *September 12, 1954*
BROADCAST HISTORY:
Jan 1954–Apr 1954, ABC Sun 9:15–9:30
Apr 1954–Jul 1954, ABC Sun 6:30–6:45
Jul 1954–Sep 1954, ABC Sun 9:15–9:30
REGULARS:
Jane Pickens
The Vikings

Songstress Jane Pickens starred in this informal 15-minute musical show, backed by a male singing group called The Vikings.

JANE WYMAN SHOW, THE
see *Fireside Theater*

JANET DEAN, REGISTERED NURSE
Medical Drama
BROADCAST HISTORY:
Syndicated only
30 minutes
Produced: *1953–1955* (39 episodes)
Released: *February 1954*
CAST:
Janet Dean .... Ella Raines

Medical drama about an earnest young nurse who believed in treating patients' hopes and fears as well as their broken bones. Recently discharged from the Air Force, Nurse Dean traveled around the country on private assignments, involving herself in all sorts of human dramas. At the end of each episode she also appeared in a little spot promoting the nursing profession.

The series was filmed in New York.

JAYE P. MORGAN SHOW, THE
Music
FIRST TELECAST: *June 13, 1956*
LAST TELECAST: *August 24, 1956*
BROADCAST HISTORY:
Jun 1956–Aug 1956, NBC Wed/Fri 7:30–7:45
REGULARS:
Jaye P. Morgan
The Morgan Brothers
The Joel Herron Orchestra

Jaye P. Morgan starred in this 1956 summer replacement for *Coke Time*. The informal quarter-hour was filled with popular songs sung by Miss Morgan and a vocal quartet made up of her four brothers.

JEAN ARTHUR SHOW, THE
Situation Comedy
FIRST TELECAST: *September 12, 1966*
LAST TELECAST: *December 5, 1966*
BROADCAST HISTORY:
Sep 1966–Dec 1966, CBS Mon 10:00–10:30
CAST:
Patricia Marshall .... Jean Arthur
Paul Marshall .... Ron Harper
Morton..................... Leonard Stone
Richie Wells .... Richard Conte

Attractive Patricia Marshall was the best defense attorney in town and, as a widow, one of the most eligible women as well. Her 25-year-old son Paul had recently graduated from law school and returned home to practice law with her. Patricia's comic involvements with her clients and family provided the stories in this series. An almost silent member of the cast was her chauffeur, Morton, who would probably have had more to say if his boss had ever stopped talking long enough for him to get a word in.

JEAN CARROLL SHOW, THE
see *Take It from Me*

JEANNIE CARSON SHOW, THE
see *Hey Jeannie*

JEFFERSON DRUM
Western
FIRST TELECAST: *April 25, 1958*
LAST TELECAST: *April 23, 1959*
BROADCAST HISTORY:
Apr 1958–Sep 1958, NBC Fri 8:00–8:30
Sep 1958–Oct 1958, NBC Fri 7:30–8:00
Oct 1958–Apr 1959, NBC Thu 7:30–8:00
CAST:
Jefferson Drum................ Jeff Richards
Lucius Coin .... Cyril Delevanti
Joey Drum.................... Eugene Martin
Big Ed .... Robert Stevenson

The lawless frontier town of Jubilee, a mining community somewhere in the West during the 1850s, was the setting for *Jefferson Drum*. Jefferson was the editor of the local newspaper who, although he believed that the pen was mightier than the sword, was quite a gunfighter when he had to be. A widower with a young son, Jefferson had a sense of great responsibility to his community and the law-abiding people who lived there. His efforts to maintain a decent town were aided by his printer, Lucius Coin, and by Big Ed, the bartender in the town saloon.

JEFFERSONS, THE
Situation Comedy
FIRST TELECAST: *January 18, 1975*
LAST TELECAST: *July 23, 1985*
BROADCAST HISTORY:
Jan 1975–Aug 1975, CBS Sat 8:30–9:00
Sep 1975–Oct 1976, CBS Sat 8:00–8:30
Nov 1976–Jan 1977, CBS Wed 8:00–8:30
Jan 1977–Aug 1977, CBS Mon 8:00–8:30
Sep 1977–Mar 1978, CBS Sat 9:00–9:30
Apr 1978–May 1978, CBS Sat 8:00–8:30
Jun 1978–Sep 1978, CBS Mon 8:00–8:30
Sep 1978–Jan 1979, CBS Wed 8:00–8:30
Jan 1979–Mar 1979, CBS Wed 9:30–10:00
Mar 1979–Jun 1979, CBS Wed 8:00–8:30
Jun 1979–Sep 1982, CBS Sun 9:30–10:00
Sep 1982–Dec 1984, CBS Sun 9:00–9:30
Jan 1985–Mar 1985, CBS Tue 8:00–8:30
Apr 1985, CBS Tue 8:30–9:00
Jun 1985, CBS Tue 8:30–9:00
Jun 1985–Jul 1985, CBS Tue 8:00–8:30

CAST:
George Jefferson .... Sherman Hemsley
Louise Jefferson.............. Isabel Sanford
Lionel Jefferson (1975, 1979–1981)
.... Mike Evans
Lionel Jefferson (1975–1978).... Damon Evans
Helen Willis................... Roxie Roker
Tom Willis.................. Franklin Cover
Jenny Willis Jefferson ...... Berlinda Tolbert
Harry Bentley (1975–1981, 1983–1985)
.... Paul Benedict
Mother Olivia Jefferson (1975–1978)
.... Zara Cully
Ralph the Doorman .... Ned Wertimer
Florence Johnston.............. Marla Gibbs
Marcus Garvey (1977–1979)
.... Ernest Harden, Jr.
Allan Willis (1978–1979)........ Jay Hammer
Jessica Jefferson (1984–1985) ... Ebonie Smith
Charlie (1984–1985)............ Danny Wells
THEME:
"Moving on Up," by Jeff Barry and Ja'net DuBois
PRODUCER:
Norman Lear

George Jefferson was the black Archie Bunker. In fact, he had been Archie's next-door neighbor in Queens for several years, a situation that created quite a turmoil between the two opinionated, blustery, bigoted individuals. George had started a small dry-cleaning business and his success resulted in expansion to a small chain. It was at that point that this spin-off from *All in the Family* started, with George, his level-headed wife Louise, and their college-student son Lionel moving into a luxury high-rise apartment on Manhattan's East Side.

One of the Jeffersons' neighbors was an erudite Englishman, Harry Bentley; another was Tom Willis, a white man with a black wife (Helen). Their daughter Jenny became Lionel's girlfriend, fiancée, and finally wife when they were married in the 1976 Christmas show. George's quickly acquired wealth enabled his natural snobbishness to assert itself, and he was often pretty intolerable. He resented Lionel's involvement with the child of a mixed marriage and was continually at odds with Tom and Helen. Adding to the general level of discord in the Jefferson apartment was their wise-cracking maid, Florence.

Mike Evans, who had played the role of Lionel on *All in the Family* and stayed with it when *The Jeffersons* first went on the air, left the show in the fall of 1975. He was replaced by Damon Evans, another young black actor, to whom he was not related. Early in the 1977–1978 season a young, street-wise black named Marcus Garvey was added to the cast as an employee of the branch of George Jefferson's chain of cleaning stores that was located in the lobby of the building in which the Jeffersons lived. The following fall brought Allan Willis, Jenny's white brother, back from a commune to become a regular member of the cast and source of irritation to both his own father and George Jefferson. Damon Evans had left the cast and, although Lionel was occasionally referred to in various episodes, he was no longer seen until Mike Evans, the original Lionel, returned to the series in the fall of 1979. Lionel and Jenny had a baby girl, Jessica, the following spring. After graduation from college, Lionel found a job as an electrical engineer for Teletex Electronics. His career was moving along but his marriage was faltering, and in the fall of 1981 Lionel and Jenny separated. Although Lionel no longer appeared on *The Jeffersons*, Jenny, who had become a fashion designer, continued to show up periodically. Neighbor Bentley returned in late 1983, after a two-year stay in Russia, still his very proper self, and George's business, as well as *The Jeffersons'* ratings, continued to prosper. In 1984 George went into partnership, along with Tom Willis, in Charlie's Bar, a little place that became their leisure-time hangout, and the following January Lionel and Jenny filed for divorce. That summer, after a run of more than a decade, *The Jeffersons* finally faded from the CBS prime-time schedule.

CBS aired reruns of *The Jeffersons* as part of its weekday daytime lineup from February 1980 to September 1981.

JEFF'S COLLIE
syndicated title for *Lassie*.

JENNIFER SLEPT HERE
Situation Comedy
FIRST TELECAST: *October 21, 1983*
LAST TELECAST: *September 5, 1984*
BROADCAST HISTORY:
Oct 1983–Dec 1983, NBC Fri 8:30–9:00
Apr 1984–May 1984, NBC Sat 8:30–9:00
Jul 1984–Sep 1984, NBC Wed 8:30–9:00
CAST:
Jennifer Farrell .... Ann Jillian
Joey Elliot.................. John P. Navin, Jr.
Susan Elliot .... Georgia Engel
George Elliot .... Brandon Maggart
Marilyn Elliot .... Mya Akerling
Marc....................... Glenn Scarpelli

Shades of *Topper*. When George Elliot, his wife Susan, and their two children moved from New York to Beverly Hills they had no idea that the sumptuous home they had bought was haunted. The resident ghost was not a sheet-shrouded apparition, however, but the beautiful and sexy former owner, deceased movie star Jennifer Farrell. Jennifer decided to take 14-year-old Joey Elliot under her wing and help him adjust to life in California. She also thought he could use some help with girls, especially if he wanted to keep up with his much more worldly next-door neighbor and new friend, Marc. Under normal circumstances, Joey was the only one who could see Jennifer, which meant that his habit of talking to the furni-

ture confused and worried his family and friends. There was the requisite walking through walls and objects floating in midair, but the focus of the show was on Jennifer's relationship with Joey and the spectacular wardrobe worn by Ann Jillian.

JEOPARDY!
Quiz/Audience Participation
BROADCAST HISTORY:
Syndicated and Network Daytime
30 minutes
Produced: *1974–1975, 1984–*
Released: *September 1974*
EMCEE:
Art Fleming (1974–1975)
Alex Trebek (1984–   )

Jeopardy! is a game-show classic based on the simple premise of guessing the question to go with a given answer. In the first round three contestants faced a game board containing six categories; each category had five different hidden answers, worth different dollar amounts. A contestant picked a category and dollar amount, the "answer" was revealed, and all three contestants had the opportunity to be the first to guess the question that went with it. A correct guess got the designated dollar amount added to the winner's score, while an incorrect one subtracted that amount. A contestant's winnings were always in jeopardy! The second round was "double Jeopardy," with six new categories and the dollar amounts doubled. Then came "final Jeopardy," in which contestants who had anything left at this point could wager all or part of their accumulated winnings on the question that went with a single answer in a category chosen by the emcee.

Unlike most game shows, *Jeopardy!* prided itself on the difficulty of its questions and the intelligence of its contestants. It was a favorite among college students and a fixture on NBC's weekday daytime lineup from March 1964–January 1975. Art Fleming emceed the NBC series and the prime-time syndicated version during the 1974–1975 season. He was still with the show when it returned briefly to NBC daytime as *The All New Jeopardy!* from October 1978–March 1979.

Five years later, in the fall of 1984, *Jeopardy!* returned to the syndication market with Alex Trebek as both executive producer and emcee. The new version followed the same format as the original, although the dollar amounts were now ten times what they had been two decades earlier. *Jeopardy!* has been a major hit ever since—second in popularity only to the mega-hit *Wheel of Fortune* among syndicated game shows in the mid-1980s. Ironically, both series were created by the same person, talk-show host Merv Griffin.

JERICHO
War Drama
FIRST TELECAST: *September 15, 1966*
LAST TELECAST: *January 19, 1967*

BROADCAST HISTORY:
Sep 1966–Jan 1967, CBS Thu 7:30–8:30
CAST:
Franklin Sheppard	Don Francks
Jean-Gaston André	Marino Mase
Nicholas Gage	John Leyton

Three undercover agents representing three countries worked together as Allied troubleshooters during the Second World War in this series. Their code name: *Jericho.* Franklin Sheppard was a captain in the American Army Intelligence, Jean-Gaston André an officer in the Free French Air Force, and Nicholas Gage a lieutenant in the British Navy. Specially trained, and having worked together since early in the war, they tackled assignments that ranged from sabotage to espionage to intelligence-gathering.

JERRY COLONNA SHOW, THE
Comedy Variety
FIRST TELECAST: *May 28, 1951*
LAST TELECAST: *November 17, 1951*
BROADCAST HISTORY:
May 1951–Jun 1951, ABC Mon 8:00–8:30
Jun 1951–Aug 1951, ABC Fri 8:00–8:30
Aug 1951–Sep 1951, ABC Thu 10:00–10:30
Oct 1951–Nov 1951, ABC Sat 7:30–8:00
EMCEE:
Jerry Colonna
REGULARS:
Barbara Ruick
Gordon Polk
"Cookie" Fairchild's Band

A program of music, comedy, and variety hosted by the famous comedian with the booming voice and the walrus mustache. From Hollywood.

JERRY LEWIS SHOW, THE
Talk/Variety
FIRST TELECAST: *September 21, 1963*
LAST TELECAST: *December 21, 1963*
BROADCAST HISTORY:
Sep 1963–Dec 1963, ABC Sat 9:30–11:30
REGULARS:
Jerry Lewis
Del Moore
Lou Brown Orchestra

This two-hour weekly marathon was possibly the most spectacular attempt at big-name variety programming in TV history—and also the most colossal flop. It was preceded by a great deal of fanfare, including the revelation that ABC had committed $8,000,000 in production costs for the first year alone. Headlining was Jerry Lewis, long a TV series holdout, and guesting were all sorts of big names. The first telecast, live from Hollywood's El Capitan Theatre, co-starred Mort Sahl, Kay Stevens, Jack Jones, and Harry James. Later telecasts featured Sammy Davis, Jr., the Count Basie Orchestra, heavyweight challenger Cassius Clay (discussing his upcoming title fight with the champ, Sonny Liston), and the all-star cast of the movie *It's A Mad, Mad, Mad, Mad World.*

Whether it was simply too big, whether the controversial Lewis grated on too many viewers, or whether the scheduling was bad (NBC and CBS viewers had to leave in the middle of *The Defenders* or the *Saturday Night Movie* to catch the beginning), the initial airings garnered terrible reviews and disastrously low ratings. A considerable uproar ensued, in which the president of ABC flew to the West Coast for intensive conferences with Lewis and his writers (who included the young Dick Cavett) on how to save the show. Subsequent telecasts improved, but the ratings did not and the colossus folded after 13 weeks.

Two weeks later, *The Hollywood Palace,* a similar show—but sans Lewis—took over the theater and the first half of the time slot, and ran for six years.

JERRY LEWIS SHOW, THE
Comedy Variety
FIRST TELECAST: *September 12, 1967*
LAST TELECAST: *May 27, 1969*
BROADCAST HISTORY:
Sep 1967–May 1968, NBC Tue 8:00–9:00
Sep 1968–May 1969, NBC Tue 7:30–8:30
REGULARS:
Jerry Lewis
Lou Brown & His Orchestra
The George Wyle Singers
The Nick Castle Dancers (1967–1968)

Jerry Lewis starred in this comedy variety series that featured guest stars with primary appeal to young adults, teens, and children. The Osmond Brothers made a number of appearances on the show during its two seasons on the air and many other groups and individual performers popular with young people were occasional guests. Jerry's collection of comic characters, originally seen in his movies, all made their presence felt in short vignettes and longer comedy sketches. Among them were The Nutty Professor, The Poor Soul, The Shoeshine Boy, and, new for the TV series, Ralph Rotten. During the first season individual numbers and routines were recorded separately and pieced together to produce the hour-long show. In an attempt to generate a more spontaneous feeling, all shows for the second season were taped continuously in front of a live studio audience.

JERRY REED WHEN YOU'RE HOT YOU'RE HOT HOUR, THE
Comedy Variety
FIRST TELECAST: *June 20, 1972*
LAST TELECAST: *July 25, 1972*
BROADCAST HISTORY:
Jun 1972–Jul 1972, CBS Tue 7:30–8:30

REGULARS:
Jerry Reed
Spencer Quinn
Cal Wilson
Norman J. Andrews
Merie Earle
John Twomey
The George Wyle Orchestra

This five-week summer variety series starred the versatile Jerry Reed—comedian, singer, and songwriter. His musical success had been primarily in country music and the entire show had a country flavor. Comedy skits, songs, and production numbers were all part of the format. The most unusual regular on the show was John Twomey, a Chicago attorney who made music with his bare hands.

JESSE JAMES
see *Legend of Jesse James, The*

JESSICA NOVAK
Drama
FIRST TELECAST: *November 5, 1981*
LAST TELECAST: *December 3, 1981*
BROADCAST HISTORY:
Nov 1981–Dec 1981, CBS Thu 10:00–11:00
CAST:
Jessica Novak .... Helen Shaver
Max Kenyon................. David Spielberg
Phil Bonelli.................. Andrew Rubin
Ricky Duran................. Eric Kilpatrick
Audrey Stiles.................. Nina Wilcox
Vince Halloran .... Kenneth Gilman
Katie Robbins .... Lara Parker

KLA-TV news reporter Jessica Novak handled feature stories that ranged from gentle human-interest pieces to exposés on such topics as gambling addiction, the pressures that cause high school students to contemplate suicide, and the frustrations that prompt husbands separated from their families to kidnap their children. Her boss, news director Max Kenyon, usually sent her out on harmless little "fluff" pieces, but Jessica was determined to show that she was as good as the best of them and always managed to wind up with a Big Scoop instead. Respected by her associates for her persistence and dedication, Jessica worked with a crew consisting of cameraman Phil Bonelli, sound man Ricky Duran, and tape editor Audrey Stiles.

Between assignments she tried to maintain a semblance of a social life, in hopes of finding the right man. Katie was a friend of Jessica's, as was public defender Vince Halloran.

JESSIE
Police Drama
FIRST TELECAST: *September 18, 1984*
LAST TELECAST: *November 13, 1984*
BROADCAST HISTORY:
Sep 1984–Nov 1984, ABC Tue 10:00–11:00
CAST:
Dr. Jessie Hayden.......... Lindsay Wagner
Lt. Alex Ascoli .... Tony Lo Bianco
Molly Hayden .... Celeste Holm
Officer Hubbell .... Tom Nolan
Ellie .... Renee Jones
Phil.................... James David Hinton
Sgt. Mac McClellan .... William Lucking
Officer Floyd Comstock....... Peter Isacksen

Jessie Hayden was staff psychiatrist for an unnamed Southern California police department. As such, she attempted to help the police deal with mentally unstable criminals, ranging from petty thieves to psychopathic killers, and assisted in counseling victims of crime. Jessie's faith in her understanding methods often put her at odds with Lt. Ascoli, particularly when it placed her in physical danger, as it often seemed to in this action series. Her mother Molly, with whom she lived, was also outspoken and opinionated, particularly when it came to the dangers of Jessie's chosen profession.

Star Lindsay Wagner had wanted *Jessie* to be rather cerebral, exploring psychiatric and medical themes, but ABC's programming executives felt that the pilot was too talky and boring, forcing the producers to cram in more chases, fights, and gunplay, and make the show generally more like other police action series.

The series was based in part on the book *Psychologist With a Gun*, by Detective Harvey Schlossberg, Ph.D., and Lucy Freeman.

JETSONS, THE
Cartoon
FIRST TELECAST: *September 23, 1962*
LAST TELECAST: *September 8, 1963*
BROADCAST HISTORY:
Sep 1962–Sep 1963, ABC Sun 7:30–8:00
VOICES:
George Jetson............. George O'Hanlon
Jane Jetson .... Penny Singleton
Judy Jetson .... Janet Waldo
Elroy Jetson .... Daws Butler
Astro .... Don Messick
ALSO:
Mel Blanc, Howard Morris, Herschel Bernardi, Howard McNear, and Frank Nelson
PRODUCERS:
William Hanna and Joseph Barbera

This cartoon series about a middle-class family of the future was the 21st-century equivalent of *The Flintstones*, and was produced by the same people. George Jetson worked for Spacely Sprockets, Inc., commuting to the job in an atomic-powered bubble. He lived with his wife, Jane, and their children in Skypad Apartments, which were raised and lowered on huge hydraulic lifts to stay clear of bad weather. A robot maid packed son, Elroy, off to school in a pneumatic tube each morning, while teenybopper daughter, Judy, spent her free time learning the latest dance, the Solar Swivel. Astro was the family dog. Appearing occasionally was George's boss, Cosmo G. Spacely, voiced by the versatile Mel Blanc.

After leaving prime time, *The Jetsons* proved to be remarkably durable as a Saturday morning children's show, despite the fact that only 24 episodes had been produced. Reruns aired on ABC (1963–1964), CBS (1964–1965 and 1969–1970), and NBC (1965–1967, 1971–1976, and 1979–1983). In 1985, to make the series more viable in the syndication marketplace, 41 new episodes of *The Jetsons* were produced, bringing the total to 65.

JIGSAW
Police Drama
FIRST TELECAST: *September 21, 1972*
LAST TELECAST: *August 11, 1973*
BROADCAST HISTORY:
  Sep 1972–Dec 1972, ABC Thu 9:00–10:00
  Feb 1973–Aug 1973, ABC Sat 10:00–11:00
CAST:
  Lt. Frank Dain . . . . James Wainwright

Frank Dain was a special investigator for the California State Police Department's Bureau of Missing Persons. A rebel who broke the rules when necessary, he was tough, dry, and sardonic. Naturally he got the most difficult and intriguing cases, and solved them all. *Jigsaw* was one of three rotating elements of *The Men*.

JIGSAW JOHN
Police Drama
FIRST TELECAST: *February 2, 1976*
LAST TELECAST: *September 6, 1976*
BROADCAST HISTORY:
  Feb 1976–Sep 1976, NBC Mon 10:00–11:00
CAST:
  John St. John ("Jigsaw John") . . Jack Warden
  Sam Donner . . . . Alan Feinstein
  Maggie Hearn . . . . Pippa Scott
  Frank Chen . . . . James Hong

Jigsaw John dealt with the cases tackled by Los Angeles Police Department Special Investigator John St. John. He had received the nickname Jigsaw John because of the way in which he slowly, methodically, and precisely fitted together each of the seemingly unrelated pieces that collectively led to the determination of guilt in his homicide investigations. The highly individualistic way in which he and his partner, Sam Donner, worked did not always sit well with the police department bureaucracy, but the results could not be faulted. John's commitment to his job always took priority over the other things in his life, most noticeably his long-running romance with nursery-school teacher Maggie Hearn.

JIM BOWIE
see *Adventures of Jim Bowie, The*

JIM NABORS HOUR, THE
Comedy Variety
FIRST TELECAST: *September 25, 1969*
LAST TELECAST: *May 20, 1971*
BROADCAST HISTORY:
  Sep 1969–May 1971, CBS Thu 8:00–9:00 (OS)
REGULARS:
  Jim Nabors
  Frank Sutton
  Ronnie Schell
  Karen Morrow
  The Nabors Kids
  The Tony Mordente Dancers
  Paul Weston & His Orchestra

Jim Nabors, the twangy, rural comedian of *The Andy Griffith Show* and *Gomer Pyle—U.S.M.C.*, surprised everyone when in the mid-1960s he opened his mouth and began to sing. His voice was a rich baritone, and he proceeded to make quite a splash in the record field with several best-selling LPs. After *Gomer Pyle* had run its course, his versatility earned him this Thursday night variety hour. With him were two of his former co-stars from *Gomer Pyle,* Frank Sutton and Ronnie Schell. There were also guest stars, comedy sketches, and musical numbers on the show. One continuing comedy sketch was "The Brother-in-Law," in which Karen Morrow played Jim's sister and Frank Sutton her husband. Frank's role was that of a self-centered, insecure neurotic trying to cope with what he perceived as a hostile world.

JIM ROCKFORD, PRIVATE INVESTIGATOR
syndicated title for *Rockford Files, The*

JIM STAFFORD SHOW, THE
Comedy Variety
FIRST TELECAST: *July 30, 1975*
LAST TELECAST: *September 3, 1975*
BROADCAST HISTORY:
  Jul 1975–Sep 1975, ABC Wed 10:00–11:00
REGULARS:
  Jim Stafford
  Valerie Curtin
  Richard Stahl
  Phil MacKenzie ("Adam")
  Deborah Allen
  Cyndi Wood
  Jeanne Sheffield
  Tom Biener
  Jean Anne Chapman
  Eddie Karam Orchestra

Jim Stafford, an amiable, ingratiating young singer-composer with hits about such unlikely subjects as "My Girl Bill" and "Spiders and Snakes," hosted this summer variety hour. "Some people think I'm weird," he remarked. "I'm not really weird—unless you're picky." Rodney the robot, an insulting bag of transistors, also appeared on the show.

JIMMIE RODGERS SHOW, THE
Musical Variety
FIRST TELECAST: *March 31, 1959*
LAST TELECAST: *September 1, 1969*
BROADCAST HISTORY:
Mar 1959–Sep 1959, NBC Tue 8:30–9:00
Jun 1969–Sep 1969, CBS Mon 10:00–11:00
REGULARS:
Jimmie Rodgers
Connie Francis (1959)
Kirby Stone Four (1959)
The Clay Warnick Singers (1959)
Buddy Morrow Orchestra (1959)
Frank Comstock Orchestra (1969)
Burgundy Street Singers (1969)
Lyle Waggoner (1969)
Vicki Lawrence (1969)
Nancy Austin (1969)
Bill Fanning (1969)
Don Crichton (1969)

In 1959 folk-popular singer Jimmie Rodgers was riding the crest of a wave of success with a string of hit records, most notably "Honeycomb" and "Kisses Sweeter Than Wine." NBC signed him for a variety show in the hopes of making him a TV star as well, as ABC had done with Pat Boone. However, the show never caught on. By the summer, regulars Connie Francis and the Kirby Stone Four had abandoned ship, and the show was soon canceled.

A decade later, after recovering from a mysterious auto accident that almost cost him his life and which occasioned a long gap in his career, Rodgers returned to television as the summer replacement for Carol Burnett, with a new variety series called *Carol Burnett Presents the Jimmie Rodgers Show.* Two of the regulars from Carol's series, Lyle Waggoner and Vicki Lawrence, also served as regulars on the summer show.

JIMMY BLAINE'S JUNIOR EDITION
Music
FIRST TELECAST: *January 1, 1951*
LAST TELECAST: *August 31, 1951*
BROADCAST HISTORY:
Jan 1951–Feb 1951, ABC Mon/Wed/Fri 6:15–6:30
Jan 1951–Feb 1951, ABC Tue/Thu 6:15–6:45
Feb 1951–Jun 1951, ABC Mon–Fri 6:45–7:00
Jul 1951–Aug 1951, ABC Mon/Wed/Fri 6:45–7:00
REGULARS:
Jimmy Blaine
Mary Crosby
Buddy Weed Trio

Jimmy Blaine, featured vocalist on *Stop the Music,* hosted this short music and talk program featuring songs for teenagers.

JIMMY BRESLIN'S PEOPLE
Talk/Interview
FIRST TELECAST: *September 25, 1986*
LAST TELECAST: *January 2, 1987*
BROADCAST HISTORY:
Sep 1986–Jan 1987, ABC Thu/Fri 12:00 MID–1:00 A.M.
HOST:
Jimmy Breslin

This talkfest was part of an abortive ABC attempt to bring relevance to the late-night schedule, with *Nightline* at 11:30 P.M. followed by Dick Cavett on Tuesday and Wednesday and Jimmy Breslin on Thursday and Friday. Breslin, a gruff, gravelly voiced syndicated columnist who had long been part of the New York scene, did his part with hard-hitting shows on AIDS, the criminal justice system, the excesses of fandom, etc. Unfortunately many local stations delayed or preempted the show in favor of rock videos and old movies. In Breslin's home town of New York it was not seen until as late as 2:00 A.M., or only one night a week. Disgusted, Jimmy announced he was "canceling the network" and ended the series after only three months.

JIMMY DEAN SHOW, THE
Musical Variety
FIRST TELECAST: *June 22, 1957*
LAST TELECAST: *April 1, 1966*
BROADCAST HISTORY:
Jun 1957–Sep 1957, CBS Sat 10:30–11:00
Sep 1963–Mar 1964, ABC Thu 9:00–10:00
Mar 1964–Aug 1964, ABC Thu 9:30–10:30
Sep 1964–Sep 1965, ABC Thu 10:00–11:00
Sep 1965–Apr 1966, ABC Fri 10:00–11:00
REGULARS:
Jimmy Dean
Texas Wildcats (1957)
The Country Lads (1957)
Jo Davis (1957)
Jan Crockett (1957)
Mary Klick (1957)
Chuck Cassey Singers (1963–1966)
Doerr-Hutchinson Dancers (1964–1965)
Tony Mordente Dancers (1965–1966)
Peter Matz Orchestra (1963–1965)
Don Sebesky Orchestra (1965–1966)

Country singer Jimmy Dean was frequently seen on daytime and nighttime television in the late 1950s and 1960s. A lanky, drawling Texan, he is best known for a Nashville-pop sound typified by his own most famous hit, "Big Bad John" (1961). The first *Jimmy Dean Show* was a half-hour daytime variety series, based in Washington, D.C., which ran on CBS from April to December 1957, and from September 1958 to June 1959. In addition, Jimmy hosted a prime-time summer show in 1957, also from Washington. This was a low-budget affair which generally featured guest country acts such as Johnny Cash and Jim Reeves, plus some rather out-of-date popular talent (the Andrews Sisters, Gene Austin).

Then from 1963–1966 Dean fronted his own big-league variety hour on ABC. Guests on this series also included country-and-western standbys such as Eddy Arnold, Homer and Jethro, and Molly Bee, but were more frequently popular talent. His first ABC telecast headlined comic Dick Shawn and cartoon character Fred Flintstone. A continuing character on the ABC series was Jim Henson's muppet hound, Rowlf, with whom Dean joked and bantered ("My ol' buddy"). Other semi-regulars included Ron Martin, the accident-prone singer who never seemed to finish a song, Lud and Lester (Roger Price and Mort Marshall) doing a Lum and Abner–type spot, and the Jubilee Four gospel quartet. The Chuck Cassey Singers, with their stetsons and guitars, provided vocal support.

In an effort to "jazz up" the show during its final season, special telecasts originated from the stage of the Grand Ole Opry (September), Miami Beach (November), and Carnegie Hall (December), while an October 1965 telecast played host to the first annual Country Music Awards presentations.

A syndicated half-hour *Jimmy Dean Show* was produced from 1973 to 1975.

JIMMY DURANTE PRESENTS THE LENNON SISTERS
Musical Variety
FIRST TELECAST: *September 26, 1969*
LAST TELECAST: *July 4, 1970*
BROADCAST HISTORY:
   Sep 1969–Jan 1970, ABC Fri 10:00–11:00
   Feb 1970–Jul 1970, ABC Sat 9:30–10:30
REGULARS:
   Jimmy Durante
   Dianne Lennon
   Peggy Lennon
   Kathy Lennon
   Janet Lennon
   Jack Regas Dancers
   George Wyle Orchestra

The year after they ended their long association with Lawrence Welk the four Lennon Sisters co-starred with veteran comedian Jimmy Durante in this weekly musical variety hour. The show normally opened with Durante at the piano, leading into a segment of friendly chatter and songs with the Lennons. Some big-name guests appeared, including Jack Benny, Glen Campbell, Bob Hope, and Phyllis Diller, but it didn't help much. The combination of old trouper and sweet young talent never quite worked and the show was canceled at the end of its first season.

JIMMY DURANTE SHOW, THE
Comedy Variety
FIRST TELECAST: *October 2, 1954*
LAST TELECAST: *September 21, 1957*
BROADCAST HISTORY:
   Oct 1954–Jun 1956, NBC Sat 9:30–10:00

Jun 1957–Sep 1957, CBS Sat 8:00–8:30
Sep 1957, CBS Sat 8:30–9:00
REGULARS:
   Jimmy Durante
   Eddie Jackson
   Jules Buffano
   Jack Roth
   The Durante Girls
   The Roy Bargy Orchestra

The basic setting of *The Jimmy Durante Show* was a small nightclub, owned and operated by Jimmy and appropriately called the Club Durant. In the role of club operator, Jimmy interviewed and auditioned talent, coped with the headaches involved in dealing with his employees, and occasionally performed himself. His raspy voice and large "schnozzola" (nose, to the uninitiated) were his trademarks. With him were his long-time friend and partner from vaudeville days, Eddie Jackson, and two actor-musicians, Jules Buffano (piano) and Jack Roth (drums), along with a chorus line composed of The Durante Girls. At the end of each show, Jimmy would be seen walking off the stage, through a series of spotlights, after saying his perennial closing line: "And good night Mrs. Calabash, wherever you are."

During its first season *The Jimmy Durante Show* aired on alternate weeks with Donald O'-Connor, under the umbrella title *Texaco Star Theatre*. Jimmy's shows were all live and Donald's were on film. The Durante show was seen weekly during 1955–1956. The CBS summer series in 1957 was made up of kinescopes from the live series on NBC.

JIMMY HUGHES, ROOKIE COP
Police Drama
FIRST TELECAST: *May 8, 1953*
LAST TELECAST: *July 3, 1953*
BROADCAST HISTORY:
   May 1953–Jul 1953, DUM Fri 8:30–9:00
CAST:
   Officer Jimmy Hughes . . . . . . William Redfield
   Officer Jimmy Hughes . . . . Conrad Janis
   Inspector Ferguson . . . . Rusty Lane
   Betty Hughes . . . . Wendy Drew

In the opening telecast of this crudely produced series Jimmy Hughes (William Redfield) was introduced as a young soldier just returned from Korea after his father, a policeman, was killed in a gun battle. Jimmy joined the police force to avenge his father's death, and won his father's badge. In the process of tracking down the killers he learned that teamwork is more important than individual action. In later episodes Jimmy tackled cases ranging from narcotics to teenage gangs to kidnaping. Rusty Lane played Inspector Ferguson, his hard-boiled mentor, and Wendy Drew played his sister.

Redfield was replaced by Conrad Janis in later episodes.

JIMMY STEWART SHOW, THE

Situation Comedy

FIRST TELECAST: *September 19, 1971*
LAST TELECAST: *August 27, 1972*
BROADCAST HISTORY:
  Sep 1971–Aug 1972, NBC Sun 8:30–9:00
CAST:
  Prof. James K. Howard . . . . Jimmy Stewart
  Martha Howard . . . . Julie Adams
  Peter Howard. . . . . Jonathan Daly
  Wendy Howard. . . . . Ellen Geer
  Dr. Luther Quince. . . . . John McGiver
  Jake Howard . . . . Kirby Furlong
  Teddy Howard . . . . Dennis Larson

Anthropology professor James Howard was a good-natured soul, but his home life became suddenly complicated when he offered to let his 29-year-old son Peter temporarily move his family in, after Peter's home had been destroyed by fire. Howard senior and junior coped as best they could with the conflicts arising in the somewhat overcrowded household, with three generations of the same family living under one roof. The fact that James and his wife, Martha, had a second son, Teddy, who was the same age (8) as their grandson Jake, only added to the complications. Teddy did, indeed, feel funny referring to Jake as his uncle.

The setting for *The Jimmy Stewart Show* was beautiful Easy Valley, California, home of Josiah Kessel College, founded by Prof. Howard's grandfather and the institution where both James and his good friend Dr. Quince taught.

JO STAFFORD SHOW, THE

Music

FIRST TELECAST: *February 2, 1954*
LAST TELECAST: *June 28, 1955*
BROADCAST HISTORY:
  Feb 1954–Jun 1955, CBS Tue 7:45–8:00 (OS)
REGULARS:
  Jo Stafford
  The Starlighters
  Paul Weston & His Orchestra

Singer Jo Stafford starred in this live 15-minute show that filled the remainder of the half hour in which CBS aired its network news program. Miss Stafford sang, chatted with occasional guest stars, and performed with them. The orchestra was under the direction of her husband, Paul Weston.

JOAN EDWARDS SHOW, THE

Music

FIRST TELECAST: *July 4, 1950*
LAST TELECAST: *October 26, 1950*
BROADCAST HISTORY:
  Jul 1950–Oct 1950, DUM Tue/Thu 7:45–8:00
HOSTESS:
  Joan Edwards

Singer-pianist Joan Edwards, a familiar voice on radio and records during the 1940s (she had a long

stint on *Your Hit Parade*), entertained on this 1950 musical interlude. She was actually something of a TV veteran, having starred on a local version of *Girl About Town* on New York television in 1941 during TV's early experimental period.

JOANIE LOVES CHACHI

Situation Comedy

FIRST TELECAST: *March 23, 1982*
LAST TELECAST: *September 13, 1983*
BROADCAST HISTORY:
  Mar 1982–Apr 1982, ABC Tue 8:30–9:00
  Sep 1982–Dec 1982, ABC Thu 8:00–8:30
  May 1983–Sep 1983, ABC Tue 8:30–9:00
CAST:
  Chachi Arcola . . . . Scott Baio
  Joanie Cunningham . . . . Erin Moran
  Al Delvecchio . . . . Al Molinaro
  Louisa Delvecchio . . . . Ellen Travolta
  Uncle Rico . . . . Art Metrano
  Bingo . . . . Robert Peirce
  Mario . . . . Derrel Maury
  Annette . . . . Winifred Freedman
THEME:
  "You Look at Me," by Pamela Phillips and James P. Dunne, sung by Erin Moran and Scott Baio

Teenage heartthrob Scott Baio starred in this short-lived spin-off from *Happy Days*, which saw Fonzie's young cousin move to Chicago with his mother, Louisa, and stepfather, Al, and try to start a singing career. With him were best girl Joanie, who shared the vocals, and his backup band: a spaced-out drummer named Bingo, a chubby cousin named Annette, and another cousin, Mario. Mario and Annette's father, Uncle Rico, was their agent. Joanie and Chachi sang several numbers in each episode, usually at Al and Louisa's newly opened restaurant. Though there were new songs introduced in each episode, and Chachi had girls in the audience swooning, neither the songs nor the show caught on. Most of the cast soon returned to Milwaukee and *Happy Days*.

JOE & MABEL

Situation Comedy

FIRST TELECAST: *June 26, 1956*
LAST TELECAST: *September 25, 1956*
BROADCAST HISTORY:
  Jun 1956–Sep 1956, CBS Tue 9:00–9:30
CAST:
  Joe Sparton. . . . . Larry Blyden
  Mabel Spooner . . . . Nita Talbot
  Mrs. Spooner . . . . Luella Gear
  Sherman Spooner . . . . Michael Mann
  Mike the Cabbie. . . . . Norman Fell
  Dolly Armstrong . . . . Shirl Conway

The course of true love never quite ran smooth for Joe and Mabel. Joe was a big-city cabdriver and Mabel was his girlfriend. Although he eventually planned to marry her, Joe's idea of when did not seem soon enough for Mabel. She was always trying to trap him into proposing and setting a date for the wedding. Mabel lived at home with her mother and her little brother, who helped her scheme to trap Joe. Joe's best friend was Mike, another cabdriver, who thought Joe was better off preventing the inevitable as long as possible.

JOE AND SONS
Situation Comedy
FIRST TELECAST: *September 9, 1975*
LAST TELECAST: *January 13, 1976*
BROADCAST HISTORY:
Sep 1975–Jan 1976, CBS Tue 8:30–9:00
CAST:
Joe Vitale	Richard Castellano
Gus Duzik	Jerry Stiller
Aunt Josephine	Florence Stanley
Estelle	Bobbi Jordan
Mark Vitale	Barry Miller
Nick Vitale	Jimmy Baio

Italian-American widower Joe Vitale lived in Hoboken, New Jersey, with two teenage sons. His best friend, Gus Duzik, worked with him at the Hoboken Sheet and Tube Company. As a typical middle-class factory worker, Joe did the best he could to raise his boys, hold his job, and conduct some semblance of a social life, though the latter was rather limited. Helping him with the boys, and cooking an occasional meal for the entire family, was Estelle, the cocktail waitress who lived in the apartment across the hall.

JOE & VALERIE
Situation Comedy
FIRST TELECAST: *April 24, 1978*
LAST TELECAST: *January 19, 1979*
BROADCAST HISTORY:
Apr 1978–May 1978, NBC Mon 8:30–9:00
May 1978, NBC Wed 8:30–9:00
Jan 1979, NBC Fri 8:30–9:00
REGULARS:
Joe Pizo	Paul Regina
Valerie Sweetzer	Char Fontane
Frank Berganski (1978)	Bill Beyers
Frank Berganski (1979)	Lloyd Alann
Paulie Barone	David Elliott
Thelma Medina	Donna Ponterotto
Stella Sweetzer (1978)	Pat Benson
Stella Sweetzer (1979)	Arlene Golonka
Vincent Pizo	Robert Costanzo

Young love and its pitfalls was the theme of this comedy series, which attempted to cash in on the disco craze of the late 1970s. Joe and Valerie had fallen in love at a New York City disco, but theirs was still a probing, tentative, teenage affair, which was constantly being upset by their nutty friends. Joe shared an apartment with the macho Frankie, who worked at a health spa, and simple-minded Paulie, who drove a hearse for a living. Valerie lived at home with her divorced mother,

Stella. Thelma was Valerie's man-hungry best friend. By day Joe worked at his father Vincent Pizo's plumbing store, and Valerie was a clerk at a cosmetics counter, but by night, when they met on the disco's glittering dance floor, they were Cinderella and her Prince Charming.

This series aired briefly in the spring of 1978 and then returned with new episodes for a few weeks the following January. During the January 1979 run Joe and Valerie got married.

JOE BASH
Situation Comedy
FIRST TELECAST: *March 28, 1986*
LAST TELECAST: *May 10, 1986*
BROADCAST HISTORY:
Mar 1986–May 1986, ABC Fri 9:30–10:00
May 1986, ABC Sat 8:30–9:00
CAST:
Off. Joe Bash	Peter Boyle
Off. Willie Smith	Andrew Rubin

This peculiar series didn't seem to know what it wanted to be—drama or comedy. Joe was a balding, older New York City street cop near the end of his career, who just wanted to go out peacefully and with a nice, safe pension. Cynical about the system, he wasn't above a little larceny; in one episode he tried to keep the bag of cash he found in a dead woman's ratty apartment. Willie was his enthusiastic young partner, who was supposed to learn from him, but spent most of his time keeping Joe more or less honest. Lorna (DeLane Matthews) was Joe's hooker-girlfriend. A gritty, "mean streets" look and unappealing characters kept this series from attracting much of an audience.

JOE FORRESTER
Police Drama
FIRST TELECAST: *September 9, 1975*
LAST TELECAST: *August 30, 1976*
BROADCAST HISTORY:
Sep 1975–Jan 1976, NBC Tue 10:00–11:00
Feb 1976–Aug 1976, NBC Mon 9:00–10:00
CAST:
Joe Forrester	Lloyd Bridges
Georgia Cameron	Patricia Crowley
Sgt. Bernie Vincent	Eddie Egan
Jolene Jackson	Dwan Smith
Det. Will Carson	Taylor Lacher

Unlike most of the police series on television, *Joe Forrester* looked at the life of a regular cop on the beat, a patrolman who had been working the same district for many years. Joe felt that the friendships and information sources he had cultivated were worth much more than the comfort of a patrol car or the status of detective. He occasionally overlooked minor infractions of the law, but was known, respected, and trusted by everyone on his beat. When something serious took place, he could count on them for help in providing information. He had a girlfriend, Georgia Cameron, a good buddy in watch commander Bernie Vincent (who was played by former New York policeman Eddie Egan), and had become friendly with members of the black community in his district, including young student Jolene Jackson. The locale of the series was never any more specific than "a large city in California."

JOE'S WORLD
Situation Comedy
FIRST TELECAST: *December 28, 1979*
LAST TELECAST: *July 26, 1980*
BROADCAST HISTORY:
Dec 1979, NBC Fri 10:00–11:00
Jan 1980, NBC Wed 9:30–10:00
May 1980–Jul 1980, NBC Sat 9:30–10:00
CAST:
Joe Wabash .... Ramon Bieri
Katie Wabash .... K Callan
Steve Wabash .... Christopher Knight
Maggie Wabash .... Melissa Sherman
Jimmy Wabash .... Michael Sharrett
Rick Wabash................... Ari Zeltner
Linda Wabash............... Missy Françis
Brad Hopkins................. Russ Banham
Judy Wilson .... Misty Rowe
Andy....................... Frank Coppola

This family comedy centered around an old-fashioned family man, a strict disciplinarian who was trying to cope with a changing world both at home and on the job. Joe Wabash was a Detroit house painter. He and his wife, Katie, had five children. The oldest was Steve, an apprentice painter on Joe's crew whom Joe hoped would someday carry on the family tradition. Steve wasn't so sure. Maggie, an attractive 16-year-old, gave her folks some anxious moments with the guys she was dating, while the three younger children had all the normal sibling rivalries of a large family. At work, Joe's paint crew included Brad, self-proclaimed stud; Judy, a sexy, blond mother who nursed her baby during lunch breaks; and Joe's long time friend, Andy.

JOEY & DAD
Musical Variety
FIRST TELECAST: *July 6, 1975*
LAST TELECAST: *July 27, 1975*
BROADCAST HISTORY:
Jul 1975, CBS Sun 7:30–8:30
REGULARS:
Joey Heatherton
Ray Heatherton
Pat Paulsen
Henny Youngman
Pat Proft
Bob Einstein
The Lex de Azevedo Orchestra

Sexy singer-dancer Joey Heatherton teamed with her father Ray in this short-lived summer variety series. Ray, who had been *The Merry Mailman* on television in the 1950s, was by this time more

commonly known to TV viewers as the commercial spokesman for Tropicana Orange Juice. Father and daughter sang, danced, and did comedy sketches with the other regulars on the show and with their guest stars.

JOEY BISHOP SHOW, THE
Situation Comedy
FIRST TELECAST: *September 20, 1961*
LAST TELECAST: *September 7, 1965*
BROADCAST HISTORY:
Sep 1961–Jun 1962, NBC Wed 8:30–9:00
Sep 1962–Sep 1964, NBC Sat 8:30–9:00
Sep 1964–Dec 1964, CBS Sun 9:30–10:00
Dec 1964–Sep 1965, CBS Tue 8:00–8:30
CAST:
Joey Barnes .... Joey Bishop
J. P. Willoughby (1961) .... John Griggs
Mrs. Barnes (1961–1962) .... Madge Blake
Barbara Simpson (1961–1962) . Nancy Hadley
Frank (1961–1962) .... Joe Flynn
Betty (1961–1962)........... Virginia Vincent
Larry Barnes (1961–1962) .. Warren Berlinger
Stella Barnes (1961–1962).... Marlo Thomas
Ellie Barnes (1962–1965)........ Abby Dalton
Mr. Jillson (1962–1965)............ Joe Besser
Charles Raymond (1962).......... Bill Bixby
Freddie (1962) .... Guy Marks
Hilda (1962–1965) .... Mary Treen
Larry Corbett (1963–1965).... Corbett Monica
Dr. Sam Nolan (1964–1965) ..... Joey Forman

When it premiered in the fall of 1961, *The Joey Bishop Show* focused on Joey Barnes, a young assistant to Los Angeles press agent J. P. Willoughby. Barnes, as played by dead-pan comic Joey Bishop, was a softhearted, nice guy who had tried to build up his importance in the eyes of his family. Unfortunately, the members of that family often tried to take advantage of Joey's nonexistent influence with the big names of show business, and Joey spent much of his time getting into trouble while trying to help out his family. The program seemed to have too many regular characters, and by the middle of the first season, four of them were gone: Joey's older sister Betty; her husband Frank, an unsuccessful salesman; Mr. Willoughby's secretary, Barbara, and Willoughby himself. Joey's mother, stage-struck sister Stella, and kid brother Larry remained to the end of the first season.

At the start of the second season both the format and the supporting cast were changed completely. Joey Barnes was now the host of a *Tonight Show*-type talk program that originated in New York. Stories revolved around his personal and professional life as a TV celebrity, and many guest stars appeared, playing themselves. Joey was now married to a Texas girl named Ellie, had a manager named Freddie (later Larry Corbett became his manager), and lived in a fancy Manhattan apartment. In 1963 Ellie gave birth to a baby boy, who later was seen on the show, played by Abby Dalton's real-life infant son, Matthew

Smith. Dr. Sam Nolan, a pediatrician neighbor, was added to the cast in 1964.

The Joey Bishop Show is one sitcom of the 1960s that is not likely to be seen again. Part of the run was filmed in black & white and part in color, so it was never widely rerun. Then in the mid-1980s, reportedly at the request of Mr. Bishop himself, all prints of the series were destroyed.

JOEY BISHOP SHOW, THE
Talk
FIRST TELECAST: *April 17, 1967*
LAST TELECAST: *December 26, 1969*
BROADCAST HISTORY:
  Apr 1967–Dec 1969, ABC Mon–Fri 11:30–1:00 A.M.
REGULARS:
  Joey Bishop
  Regis Philbin
  Johnny Mann, Musical Director

The Joey Bishop Show was one of several attempts by ABC to establish a strong late-night talk show. Joey had been quite successful as a substitute host for Johnny Carson on NBC, and it was hoped that perhaps he could lure some of Carson's audience away permanently.

The beginning was not auspicious. The program was originally done live and, on premiere night, guest Governor Ronald Reagan showed up 14 minutes late. Petite actress Debbie Reynolds, demonstrating how to help someone on fire, tackled announcer Regis Philbin and threw him to the floor (to smother the "flames"). On the second night Joey gave a big introduction to guest Buddy Greco, only to be left gesturing toward an empty curtain—seems Buddy was still in the dressing room. Worse than the first-week gaffes, however, was a series of events on NBC. Just as Joey premiered, Johnny Carson staged a dramatic walkout, garnering reams of publicity. A few weeks later he returned triumphantly, and of course all eyes were on NBC to see what would happen (nothing further did).

With his thunder thus stolen at the outset, Joey limped along for more than two years, never posing much of a threat to the mighty *Tonight Show*. In 1969 ABC finally gave up the ghost. For the last month guest hosts were used.

JOEY FAYE'S FROLICS
Comedy Variety
FIRST TELECAST: *April 5, 1950*
LAST TELECAST: *April 12, 1950*
BROADCAST HISTORY:
  Apr 1950, CBS Wed 9:30–10:00
REGULARS:
  Joey Faye
  Audrey Christie
  Mandy Kaye
  Danny Dayton
  Joe Silver

Comic Joey Faye starred in this comedy variety show that obviously did not work too well. It only lasted two weeks.

JOHN BYNER COMEDY HOUR, THE
Comedy Variety
FIRST TELECAST: *August 1, 1972*
LAST TELECAST: *August 29, 1972*
BROADCAST HISTORY:
  Aug 1972, CBS Tue 7:30–8:30
REGULARS:
  John Byner
  Patti Deutsch
  R.G. Brown
  Linda Sublette
  Gary Miller
  Dennis Flannigan
  The Ray Charles Orchestra

Comedian John Byner was the host and star of this short-lived summer variety series. In order to utilize his ability as an impressionist, the majority of comedy sketches were of the spoof variety. A continuing feature was "The Bland Family," satirizing situation comedies, while individual telecasts included takeoffs on *The Godfather,* soap operas, Fred Astaire–Ginger Rogers musicals (with Michele Lee as Ginger), Frank Sinatra, and George C. Scott's characterization of *Patton* shifted to the presidency of a toy company.

JOHN CONTE'S LITTLE SHOW
see *Van Camp's Little Show*

JOHN DAVIDSON SHOW, THE
Musical Variety
FIRST TELECAST: *May 30, 1969*
LAST TELECAST: *June 14, 1976*
BROADCAST HISTORY:
  May 1969–Sep 1969, ABC Fri 8:00–9:00
  May 1976–Jun 1976, NBC Mon 8:00–9:00
REGULARS:
  John Davidson
  Rich Little (1969)
  Mireille Mathieu (1969)
  Aimi MacDonald (1969)
  Jack Parnell Orchestra (1969)
  Pete Barbutti (1976)
  Lenny Stark Orchestra (1976)

Handsome singer John Davidson has starred in two summer variety series. The 1969 version originated in London and placed the accent on youth, with popular music stars and up-and-coming comedians as guests. In 1976, doing a four-week mini-series on NBC that originated from Los Angeles, Davidson added an element of audience participation to the traditional variety aspects of his show. He would wander into the audience and choose people at random to appear in small parts in comedy sketches and to help introduce his guest stars.

JOHN FORSYTHE SHOW, THE

Situation Comedy
FIRST TELECAST: *September 13, 1965*
LAST TELECAST: *August 29, 1966*
BROADCAST HISTORY:
Sep 1965–Aug 1966, NBC Mon 8:00–8:30
CAST:
Major John Foster .... John Forsythe
Miss Margaret Culver .... Elsa Lanchester
Miss Wilson .... Ann B. Davis
Ed Robbins .... Guy Marks
Joanna .... Peggy Lipton
Kathy .... Darleen Carr
Pamela .... Pamelyn Ferdin
Susan .... Tracy Stratford
Norma Jean .... Brooke Forsythe
Marcia .... Page Forsythe

Air Force Major John Foster had been a bachelor all his life and his dealings with women had been exclusively social. When he retired from the air force he became the headmaster of the Foster School, an exclusive San Francisco school for girls that he had recently inherited from his Aunt Victoria. Helping him run the school was a former air force sergeant and friend, Ed Robbins. The clash of these two men with an alien environment produced unexpected results. Misunderstandings between them and Miss Culver, the school principal, were frequent and often hilarious. John Forsythe's two daughters, Brooke (aged 11) and Page (aged 14) were among the young actresses portraying students at the school.

In the spring of 1966 there was a change in format. The Foster School was no longer the center of attention as John and Ed became world-traveling undercover agents for the U.S. government using the school only as a base from which to start, or end, their adventures. Their missions were not heavy cloak-and-dagger stuff, but were definitely more serious, and romantic, than anything that had happened at the school. No matter, the series never made it to a second season.

JOHN GARY SHOW, THE

Musical Variety
FIRST TELECAST: *June 22, 1966*
LAST TELECAST: *September 7, 1966*
BROADCAST HISTORY:
Jun 1966–Sep 1966, CBS Wed 10:00–11:00
REGULARS:
John Gary
Mitchell Ayres Orchestra
The Jimmy Joyce Singers
The Jack Regas Dancers

Singer John Gary was the star and host of this summer variety show that filled in for the vacationing Danny Kaye (who was Gary's special guest on both the first and last telecasts of this series). There was a pretty fair balance between music and comedy, with each week's guest stars encompassing both fields. The singers were gen-

erally middle-of-the-road (not rock 'n' roll), like Vikki Carr, Vic Damone, and Joanie Sommers, while several of the comedians were regulars in TV series of their own (Tim Conway, Bob Crane, and Morey Amsterdam).

JOHN GUNTHER'S HIGH ROAD

Travelogue
FIRST TELECAST: *September 7, 1959*
LAST TELECAST: *September 17, 1960*
BROADCAST HISTORY:
Sep 1959, ABC Mon 8:30–9:00
Sep 1959–Sep 1960, ABC Sat 8:00–8:30
HOST:
John Gunther

Noted author and world traveler John Gunther served as host and narrator for this series. The filmed trips to interesting places around the world were of two categories: those made specifically for the series and those that had been made by some other group but were purchased for use in the series. Gunther had been to many of the places shown, but very little of the film had been made on his own trips.

JOHNNY CARSON SHOW, THE

see *Tonight Show, The*

JOHNNY CARSON SHOW, THE

Comedy Variety
FIRST TELECAST: *June 30, 1955*
LAST TELECAST: *March 29, 1956*
BROADCAST HISTORY:
Jun 1955–Mar 1956, CBS Thu 10:00–10:30
REGULARS:
Johnny Carson
Virginia Gibson
Barbara Ruick
Jill Corey
Jack Prince
The Lud Gluskin Orchestra

In the mid-1950s the CBS Press Department was hailing Johnny Carson as "a bright young comic." He had begun his TV career in Omaha in 1948, then turned up in Los Angeles in 1951 with a well-received local show called *Carson's Cellar*. His big break came when he began writing monologues for Red Skelton. This led to a stint as host of the 1954 summer quiz show *Earn Your Vacation*, and a CBS daytime series titled *The Johnny Carson Show* early in 1955. By the spring of 1955 it was decided by the network that he was ready for prime time. The format of the nighttime *Johnny Carson Show* relied heavily on comedy sketches and singing, with more of the former than the latter. Johnny created many of the sketches himself and, in addition to his weekly guests, used comediennes Virginia Gibson and Barbara Ruick in them. Two sketches that kept popping up on a semi-regular basis were parodies of other successful TV shows (*You Are There, Person to Per-*

401

son, and *What's My Line* among them) and his "catch up with the news" feature in which he acted as a roving reporter doing interviews. Whom did he interview? One week it was the inhabitants of a flying saucer, another week a man about to be shot out of a cannon, and yet a third such divergent subjects as a butcher trapped for two weeks in an icebox, a dentist trying to relieve a whale's toothache, and a dog being rescued from a 500-foot-deep well. Johnny's then wife Jody was seen as the female singer for a few weeks at the beginning of the series, but Jill Corey took over that role. Jack Prince provided male vocals.

JOHNNY CASH PRESENTS THE EVERLY BROTHERS SHOW
Musical Variety
FIRST TELECAST: *July 8, 1970*
LAST TELECAST: *September 16, 1970*
BROADCAST HISTORY:
 Jul 1970–Sep 1970, ABC Wed 9:00–10:00
REGULARS:
 Don Everly
 Phil Everly
 Joe Higgins
 Ruth McDevitt

Rock 'n' roll singers Don and Phil Everly spent the summer of 1970 as the replacement for *The Johnny Cash Show.* Although their songs were generally known as top-40 hits, the sources of much of their material were country and gospel music and many of their guest stars were performers from that idiom. The emphasis of the series was on currently popular recordings, with Joe Higgins and Ruth McDevitt providing regular comic relief.

JOHNNY CASH SHOW, THE
Musical Variety
FIRST TELECAST: *June 7, 1969*
LAST TELECAST: *September 19, 1976*
BROADCAST HISTORY:
 Jun 1969–Sep 1969, ABC Sat 9:30–10:30
 Jan 1970–May 1971, ABC Wed 9:00–10:00 (OS)
 Aug 1976–Sep 1976, CBS Sun 8:00–9:00
HOST:
 Johnny Cash
REGULARS (1969–1971):
 Mother Maybelle & The Carter Family (June, Helen, Anita)
 Statler Brothers
 Carl Perkins
 The Tennessee Three (Marshall Grant, bass; W. S. Holland, drums; Bob Wooton, guitar)
 Bill Walker Orchestra
REGULARS (1976):
 June Carter Cash
 Steve Martin
 Jim Varney
 Howard Mann
 Bill Walker Orchestra

THEME:
 "Folsom Prison Blues" (opening theme)
 "I Walk the Line" (Closing theme)

To date, one of the major attempts to bridge the gap between country music and the mass audience was made by Johnny Cash in 1969–1971. Unlike such earlier efforts as *Ozark Jubilee* (strictly for the sticks) and *The Jimmy Dean Show* (more pop than country), *The Johnny Cash Show* was true to its roots, yet packaged in a manner acceptable to most urban viewers. Part of its success lay with Cash himself, one of the few true superstars of both country and popular music, and a dramatic figure in his Lincolnesque "man in black" outfit. His craggy-featured authenticity, honed in real-life hardship, made him believable in such segments as "Ride This Train." Backing him were the members of his regular road show, the Carter Family (one of the legendary groups in country music history; Cash was married to one of the daughters, June), the Statler Brothers, Carl "Blue Suede Shoes" Perkins, and the Tennessee Three. Guest stars included first-rate talent from almost every musical genre, ranging from Louis Armstrong to Arlo Guthrie, Jose Feliciano, Glen Campbell, Rod McKuen, Pete Seeger, Linda Ronstadt, Merle Haggard, James Taylor, and Minnie Pearl.

One of the highlights of the 1969–1971 series was a two-part telecast in January 1971 tracing the "Country Music Story." Practically everybody who was anybody in country music appeared in this music documentary, which included film clips of such stars of the past as the original Jimmie Rodgers, Hank Williams, and Jim Reeves, and live performances by others ranging across the generations from Roy Acuff to Tammy Wynette.

In 1976 Johnny returned with a four-week summer series which, like the 1969–1971 program, originated from Nashville. This time guest stars were almost exclusively from the country field.

JOHNNY JUPITER
Children's
FIRST TELECAST: *March 21, 1953*
LAST TELECAST: *June 13, 1953*
BROADCAST HISTORY:
 Mar 1953–Jun 1953, DUM Sat 7:30–8:00
REGULARS:
 Ernest P. Duckweather .... Vaughn Taylor
 His Boss .... Gilbert Mack
PUPPETEER:
 Carl Harms

This imaginative puppet show was produced by the company responsible for *Howdy Doody,* but it had a much shorter run. Its premise was a satirical view of our civilization as seen through eyes of another planet's residents.

The initial setting was a TV studio, where E. P. Duckweather, an inquisitive janitor who liked to fiddle with the equipment, accidentally brought in Jupiter on one of the control-room consoles. He then talked with Johnny Jupiter and his friend B-12 (the puppets) and discovered that both Jupiterians were quite mystified about Earthling civilization—based on what they had seen on Earth's TV shows. Later the tables were turned and Duckweather became something of a personality on Jupiterian TV.

JOHNNY MANN'S STAND UP AND CHEER
Music
BROADCAST HISTORY:
Syndicated only
30 minutes
Produced: *1971–1973* (48 episodes)
Released: *Fall 1971*
REGULARS:
Johnny Mann
The Johnny Mann Singers

The well-scrubbed and youthful Johnny Mann Singers had a minor career on records in the 1960s doing pleasant, inoffensive versions of pleasant, upbeat songs like "Up Up and Away." They brought their act to TV in 1971 in this musical half-hour that featured a lot of patriotic flag-waving and middle-of-the-road guests such as Patti Page, Jack Jones, Bobby Goldsboro, and Andy Griffith. Sometimes a guest star would also do a recitation—like Milton Berle reading "Desiderata." As host, Johnny Mann leapt about the stage "like a man possessed" *(Variety)*, while the boys and girls in their collegiate sweaters sang "Yankee Doodle Dandy."

Mama don't want no rock 'n' roll around here!

JOHNNY RINGO
Western
FIRST TELECAST: *October 1, 1959*
LAST TELECAST: *September 29, 1960*
BROADCAST HISTORY:
Oct 1959–Sep 1960, CBS Thu 8:30–9:00
CAST:
Johnny Ringo .... Don Durant
Laura Thomas .... Karen Sharpe
Cully........................ Mark Goddard
Case Thomas .... Terence de Marney

Johnny Ringo was a gunfighter-turned-lawman. Folks around Velardi, Arizona, apparently didn't mind their sheriff's past, and in fact one of them— pretty young Laura—thought he was a right handsome hunk of man. Case Thomas, Laura's father, was an old drunk who also happened to own the general store. Helping Johnny protect the people of Velardi, and filling in for him when he was busy fending off Laura, was the young deputy, Cully.

There really was a gunfighter-turned-lawman named Johnny Ringo in the 1880s, though it is doubtful that his exploits resembled those portrayed in this series.

JOHNNY STACCATO
Detective Drama

FIRST TELECAST: *September 10, 1959*
LAST TELECAST: *September 25, 1960*
BROADCAST HISTORY:
Sep 1959–Mar 1960, NBC Thu 8:30–9:00
Mar 1960–Sep 1960, ABC Sun 10:30–11:00
CAST:
Johnny Staccato .... John Cassavetes
Waldo .... Eduardo Ciannelli

When this series premiered in September 1959 its title was simply *Staccato*. Set in New York City, it centered on jazz pianist Johnny Staccato, who supplemented his meager income as a musician by working as a private detective. An important background for many episodes was "Waldo's," a small jazz club in Greenwich Village where Johnny Staccato spent much of his spare time and met most of his clients. Working at the club, and often featured in musical numbers, was the jazz combo of Pete Candoli which included Barney Kessel, Shelly Manne, Red Mitchell, Red Norvo, and Johnny Williams. After *Johnny Staccato* was canceled by NBC, ABC picked it up and aired reruns of the NBC episodes through September 1960.

JOHNS HOPKINS SCIENCE REVIEW, THE
Information
FIRST TELECAST: *December 31, 1948*
LAST TELECAST: *September 2, 1954*
BROADCAST HISTORY:
Dec 1948–May 1949, CBS Fri 9:00–9:30
Oct 1950–Oct 1951, DUM Tue 8:30–9:00
Oct 1951–Apr 1953, DUM Mon 8:30–9:00
Apr 1953–Apr 1954, DUM Wed 8:00–8:30
Apr 1954–Sep 1954, DUM Thu 9:00–9:30
HOST:
Lynn Poole (1948–1949)
Robert Cochrane (1949)

This half hour of learned scientific discussion and demonstrations was what is known in the trade as a "time-filler." During its long run on CBS and DuMont it was scheduled against such hit shows as *Break the Bank, Milton Berle, Arthur Godfrey,* and *Dragnet,* programs from which its network had little chance of luring away viewers.

Anyone who did happen to tune over from *Godfrey et al.* was treated to a genuinely worthwhile program, however. Conducted by members of the Johns Hopkins University faculty and other experts, and using films as well as discussions, it ranged across such topics as snails, TV, polio, X-rays, baby-feeding, cancer, human fear, transistors, sunburn, and "Electrons at Work in a Vacuum."

When it left prime time, *Johns Hopkins Science Review* moved to Sunday afternoons, where it remained on DuMont until March 1955. Twenty months later it was back on Sunday afternoons with a new title *(Johns Hopkins File 7)* on a new network (ABC). It left the air for good in September 1960.

JOHNSON'S WAX THEATRE
Dramatic Anthology
FIRST TELECAST: *June 18, 1958*
LAST TELECAST: *September 17, 1958*
BROADCAST HISTORY:
Jun 1958–Sep 1958, CBS Wed 8:30–9:00

The filmed half-hour plays aired in this series were all repeats of episodes previously seen on *Schlitz Playhouse.*

JOKER'S WILD, THE
Quiz/Audience Participation
BROADCAST HISTORY:
Syndicated and network daytime
30 minutes
Produced: *1976–1986*
Released: Fall 1976
HOST:
Jack Barry (1976–1984)
Bill Cullen (1984–1986)

A giant mock-up of a Las Vegas slot machine dominated this quiz show's set. By pulling the lever the two competing contestants spun the wheel and determined a category, then got questions in that category worth $50 or more. A "joker" on the machine could double or triple the loot, or allow the contestant to choose a category not showing on the slot machine. The first contestant to reach $500 won the game and got to play a bonus round worth more money.

The Joker's Wild ran on the CBS daytime schedule from September 1972 until June 1975, also with Jack Barry as host. In 1979 a children's version called *Joker! Joker! Joker!* appeared in syndication. It ran until 1981. When Jack Barry (who, with his longtime partner Dan Enright, also produced *The Joker's Wild*) died suddenly in the spring of 1984, veteran game-show emcee Bill Cullen was chosen to take over *The Joker's Wild* when it resumed production that fall.

JONATHAN WINTERS SHOW, THE
Comedy Variety
FIRST TELECAST: *October 2, 1956*
LAST TELECAST: *June 25, 1957*
BROADCAST HISTORY:
Oct 1956–Jun 1957, NBC Tue 7:30–7:45
REGULARS:
Jonathan Winters
Don Pardo (1956–1957)
Wayne Howell (1957)
The Eddie Safranski Orchestra

Comedian Jonathan Winters starred in this 15-minute series that occupied the remainder of the half hour in which NBC aired its network news program. Assisting him in sketches and comedy blackouts was the announcer, Don Pardo, until March 1957, when Wayne Howell succeeded him. Jonathan also had guest stars, primarily singers and musicians, who both performed on their own

and participated with him in assorted comedy bits. Most telecasts opened with a Winters monologue, contained a song by the evening's guest star, and closed with a sketch. Among the subjects that got the Winters treatment were Hollywood movie premieres, Robin Hood, and General Custer. Typical was an interview (in the *You Are There* tradition) between Edward R. Murrow and Napoleon, with Winters playing both parts.

JONATHAN WINTERS SHOW, THE
Comedy Variety
FIRST TELECAST: *December 27, 1967*
LAST TELECAST: *May 22, 1969*
BROADCAST HISTORY:
Dec 1967–Dec 1968, CBS Wed 10:00–11:00 (OS)
Dec 1968–May 1969, CBS Thu 8:00–9:00
REGULARS:
Jonathan Winters
Abby Dalton
Dick Curtis
Pamela Rodgers (1968)
Alice Ghostley (1968–1969)
Paul Lynde (1968–1969)
Georgene Barnes (1968–1969)
Jerry Rannow (1968–1969)
Cliff Arquette (1968–1969)
The Establishment (1968–1969)
Bob Banas Dancers (1967–1968)
Tony Charmoli Dancers (1968)
Wisa D'Orso Dancers (1968–1969)
Paul Weston Dancers (1967–1969)
Earl Brown Orchestra (1968–1969)

Inventive sketch comedian Jonathan Winters was the star of his own one-hour variety show for two seasons. Regular characters portrayed by Jonathan included Maude Frickert, Willard (in the "Couple Up the Street" sketches with Abby Dalton as his wife Margaret), and various strange people he played in "Face the Folks" sketches. Another regular feature was a satire on a well-known movie. The addition of a new regular sketch in the second season, "Jack Armstrong—The All-American Boy," featuring Jonathan as Jack, brought three new regulars to the cast: Cliff Arquette as Uncle Charley Weaver, Jerry Rannow as Billy, and Georgene Barnes as Betty, in addition to the other regulars who participated in non-recurring sketches.

JONNY QUEST
Cartoon
FIRST TELECAST: *September 18, 1964*
LAST TELECAST: *September 9, 1965*
BROADCAST HISTORY:
Sep 1964–Dec 1964, ABC Fri 7:30–8:00
Dec 1964–Sep 1965, ABC Thu 7:30–8:00
VOICES:
Jonny Quest .... Tim Matheson
Dr. Benton Quest (1964) .... John Stephenson
Dr. Benton Quest (1964–1965) ...Don Messick

Race Bannon .... Mike Road
Hadji .... Danny Bravo
PRODUCERS:
William Hanna and Joseph Barbera

This rather realistic cartoon-adventure series, which later ran successfully as a Saturday morning children's show, spent one full season as a prime-time entry. The hero was 11-year-old Jonny Quest, who traveled the world with his scientist father, Dr. Benton Quest, on various missions. With them were Roger "Race" Bannon, their personal bodyguard; Hadji, a young Indian friend of Jonny's; and Bandit, the Quests' miniature bulldog. The Saturday morning run was on CBS from 1967 to 1970, ABC from 1970 to 1972, and NBC from 1979 to 1980.

JOSEPH COTTEN SHOW, THE
Dramatic Anthology
FIRST TELECAST: September 14, 1956
LAST TELECAST: September 21, 1959
BROADCAST HISTORY:
Sep 1956–Sep 1957, NBC Fri 9:00–9:30
Jun 1958–Aug 1958, NBC Sat 10:30–11:00
Jul 1959–Sep 1959, CBS Mon 9:30–10:00
HOST/STAR:
Joseph Cotten

The filmed half-hour plays in this anthology were all based on records of actual legal cases from various parts of the world, and various periods of history. The host and occasional star was Joseph Cotten. Others starring in individual episodes included Joan Fontaine, Keenan Wynn, Dane Clark, Kim Hunter, Hoagy Carmichael, June Lockhart, and MacDonald Carey.

When this series first aired in the fall of 1956 its title was On Trial. Joseph Cotten became so identified with the series that its title was changed, effective February 1, 1957, to The Joseph Cotten Show—On Trial. NBC reran episodes from the series in the summer of 1958 as The Joseph Cotten Show, and CBS used that title again during the summer of 1959 for an anthology that included reruns from this series, General Electric Theater, and Schlitz Playhouse.

JOSEPH SCHILDKRAUT PRESENTS
Dramatic Anthology
FIRST TELECAST: October 28, 1953
LAST TELECAST: January 21, 1954
BROADCAST HISTORY:
Oct 1953–Dec 1953, DUM Wed 8:30–9:00
Jan 1954, DUM Thu 8:00–8:30
HOST/STAR:
Joseph Schildkraut

Joseph Schildkraut, an actor who had appeared in many prestigious Broadway and Hollywood productions over the years, hosted and sometimes starred in this dramatic anthology series during the fall of 1953. Schildkraut's stage and screen roles had ranged from comedy to romance to classical drama, and he displayed a fairly wide range of talents here as well. But DuMont, evidently carried away with the very fact of his presence on its fledgling network (his name was always preceded by the glowing term "noted" or "distinguished"), failed to provide him with decent scripts, and the program folded after only three months.

Also known as Personal Appearance Theatre.

JOURNEY TO THE UNKNOWN
Suspense Anthology
FIRST TELECAST: September 26, 1968
LAST TELECAST: January 30, 1969
BROADCAST HISTORY:
Sep 1968–Jan 1969, ABC Thu 9:30–10:30
EXECUTIVE PRODUCER:
Joan Harrison

This series of melodramas focused on the psychological horrors experienced by warped and twisted minds, and the terrors that can confront people in situations that are all too real. The executive producer was a former aide to Alfred Hitchcock, and the producer of the Hitchcock television series, and she obviously tried to invoke the master's touch in this series—with only middling success. Among the stories: a mannequin comes to life for its loving admirer, but leads him into a nightmare; a mysterious man is seen in the crowd just before several disasters; and tales of witches, hallucinations, and deserted islands.

Journey to the Unknown was produced in England.

JUBILEE U.S.A.
see Ozark Jubilee

JUDD, FOR THE DEFENSE
Law Drama
FIRST TELECAST: September 8, 1967
LAST TELECAST: September 19, 1969
BROADCAST HISTORY:
Sep 1967–May 1969, ABC Fri 10:00–11:00
May 1969–Sep 1969, ABC Fri 9:00–10:00
CAST:
Clinton Judd .... Carl Betz
Ben Caldwell .... Stephen Young

Clinton Judd was a high-priced, high-powered criminal attorney modeled along the lines of such real-life legal superstars as F. Lee Bailey and Percy Foreman. Based in Houston, Texas, he traveled all over the U.S. with his young assistant Ben, defending wealthy tycoons and flower children. The series had a highly contemporary ring, as Judd was often involved in cases which mirrored recent headlines, such as draft evasion, Mexican-American labor activism, and civil rights murders.

JUDGE FOR YOURSELF
Quiz/Audience Participation

FIRST TELECAST: *August 18, 1953*
LAST TELECAST: *May 11, 1954*
BROADCAST HISTORY:
   Aug 1953–May 1954, NBC Tue 10:00–10:30
EMCEE:
   Fred Allen
ANNOUNCER:
   Dennis James
REGULARS:
   Bob Carroll (1954)
   The Skylarks (1954)
   Milton Delugg & His Orchestra
   Kitty Kallen (1954)
   Judy Johnson (1954)

Three professional acts—singers, dancers, musicians, comedians, etc.—performed on this show each week. The three acts were rated in 1-2-3 order by two panels of judges, one composed of three show-business personalities and the other made up of three members of the studio audience. If one of the amateur judges rated the acts in the same order as the professional (show-business) judges, he or she won $1,000. The only acts that performed on this show that also had some professional success were two instrumental jazz groups—vibraphonist Terry Gibbs and the Marian McPartland Trio.

On January 5, 1954, the format of the show was changed. Gone were the professional judges, and the amateur judges were now rating new songs to determine which would become big hits. The winning judge was determined by his or her agreement with applause voting by the studio audience. Songs were performed by a regular cast consisting of Bob Carroll, the Skylarks, and Kitty Kallen. Miss Kallen was only with the show for two weeks, leaving the female vocalist spot to guest singers until Judy Johnson joined the cast at the end of February.

JUDY GARLAND SHOW, THE
   Musical Variety
FIRST TELECAST: *September 29, 1963*
LAST TELECAST: *March 29, 1964*
BROADCAST HISTORY:
   Sep 1963–Mar 1964, CBS Sun 9:00–10:00
REGULARS:
   Judy Garland
   Jerry Van Dyke (1963)
   Ken Murray (1964)
   The Mort Lindsey Orchestra
   The Ernie Flatt Dancers (1963)
   The Nick Castle Dancers (1963)
   The Peter Gennaro Dancers (1963–1964)
MUSICAL ADVISOR:
   Mel Tormé

Throughout its short history, *The Judy Garland Show* was a series desperately looking for a format. When it first went into production under the guidance of young George Schlatter (who would later do *Rowan and Martin's Laugh-In*) it was to be modeled after Judy's highly successful special

that had aired in the spring of 1963—glossy, full of big production numbers, with a brassy driving quality. Schlatter was relieved of the production responsibilities after five shows had been taped, and was replaced by Norman Jewison. His efforts were geared to make Judy's show more folksy, in the style of *The Garry Moore Show*, in the hope that that approach would attract some of the audience of its primary competition, NBC's top-rated *Bonanza*. By the time it left the air in March of 1964, *The Judy Garland Show* had gone through two more producers, still without making even a dent in *Bonanza*'s audience.

At the outset Judy was aided by comic Jerry Van Dyke, but he was gone by the end of 1963. For a while there was a regular "Tea for Two" segment in which Judy chatted with guest stars about show business and various personal experiences. Among the guests were her young daughter Liza Minnelli; her co-star from Andy Hardy days, Mickey Rooney; and Ray Bolger, who had played the scarecrow in *The Wizard of Oz*. Early in 1964 Ken Murray was a regular contributor, with his home movies of Hollywood stars. Nothing seemed to work. Judy was at her best just singing, and several of the shows during the last two months were just that—no guest stars, no regulars, but a full hour of Judy. That may have been the best format, but it was too little too late.

A fascinating behind-the-scenes account of this show, from its creation to its demise, is contained in the 1970 book *The Other Side of the Rainbow* by Judy's friend, fellow artist, and "musical advisor" Mel Tormé.

JUDY SPLINTERS
   Children's
FIRST TELECAST: *June 13, 1949*
LAST TELECAST: *August 5, 1949*
BROADCAST HISTORY:
   Jun 1949–Aug 1949, NBC Mon–Fri 7:00–7:15
HOST:
   Shirley Dinsdale

Pretty 21-year-old ventriloquist Shirley Dinsdale and her saucy, pigtailed dummy Judy Splinters hosted this live program, which served as the 1949 summer replacement for *Kukla, Fran & Ollie*. The program was first seen in 1947 as a local entry in Los Angeles, moved to Chicago for its summer network run, and then to New York for nine months as a late afternoon show in 1949–1950.

JUKE BOX JURY
   see *Peter Potter Show, The*

JULIA
   Situation Comedy
FIRST TELECAST: *September 17, 1968*
LAST TELECAST: *May 25, 1971*
BROADCAST HISTORY:
   Sep 1968–Jan 1971, NBC Tue 8:30–9:00
   Jan 1971–May 1971, NBC Tue 7:30–8:00

CAST:
Julia Baker .... Diahann Carroll
Dr. Morton Chegley .... Lloyd Nolan
Marie Waggedorn .... Betty Beaird
Corey Baker .... Marc Copage
Earl J. Waggedorn .... Michael Link
Melba Chegley .... Mary Wickes
Sol Cooper .... Ned Glass
Carol Deering (1968–1969) ...... Allison Mills
Hannah Yarby (1968–1970)..... Lurene Tuttle
Eddie Edson .... Eddie Quillan
Paul Cameron (1968–1970) ..... Paul Winfield
Len Waggedorn .... Hank Brandt
Steve Bruce (1970–1971) .... Fred Williamson
Roberta (1970–1971) .... Janear Hines
Richard (1970–1971) .... Richard Steele
Kim Bruce (1970–1971)...... Stephanie James

This comedy was more notable for its casting than
its content. Singer Diahann Carroll became the
first black female to star in her own comedy series
in a "prestige" role (i.e., not as a domestic such as
Beulah, or a second banana). Julia was an independent woman, a young, widowed nurse whose
husband had been killed in Vietnam. After his
death she moved to Los Angeles and found a job
in the medical office of Astrospace Industries.
There she met fellow nurse Hannah Yarby, and
feisty Dr. Chegley, whose bark was much worse
than his bite. Life at the office coupled with her
home and social lives provided the material for
the stories.
   The show was thoroughly integrated, and after
this attracted some initial attention as a novelty,
it met with immediate acceptance—to the relief of
nervous network executives. Julia lived in a modern, integrated apartment building with her little
boy, Corey, whose best friend was white Earl J.
Waggedorn, one of their neighbors. Paul Cameron
was Julia's romantic interest for the first two seasons, and was replaced by Steve Bruce during the
series' final year.

JULIE ANDREWS HOUR, THE
Musical Variety
FIRST TELECAST: September 13, 1972
LAST TELECAST: April 28, 1973
BROADCAST HISTORY:
   Sep 1972–Jan 1973, ABC Wed 10:00–11:00
   Jan 1973–Apr 1973, ABC Sat 9:00–10:00
REGULARS:
   Julie Andrews
   Rich Little
   Alice Ghostley
   Tony Charmoli Dancers
   The Dick Williams Singers
   Nelson Riddle Orchestra

British musical-comedy star Julie Andrews hosted
this hour of sweetness-and-light which lasted for
a single season on ABC. There were songs, skits,
and blackouts, with Julie re-creating some of her
famous roles such as Eliza Doolittle (from My Fair
Lady) and Mary Poppins. Comedians Rich Little

and Alice Ghostley constituted a semi-regular
comedy repertory company. Little's career received quite a boost on this series. Jack Benny so
liked Rich's impersonation of him on the show
that he sent the young comic an 18-carat-gold
money clip and the message, "With Bob Hope
doing my walk and you doing my voice, I can be
a star and do nothing."

JULIE FARR, M.D.
   see Having Babies

JULIUS LAROSA SHOW, THE
Music
FIRST TELECAST: June 27, 1955
LAST TELECAST: September 23, 1955
BROADCAST HISTORY:
   Jun 1955–Sep 1955, CBS Mon/Wed/Fri 7:45–8:00
REGULARS:
   Julius LaRosa
   The Debutones
   The Russ Case Orchestra

Singer Julius LaRosa was the star of this thrice-
weekly live summer music show that filled the
remainder of the half hour in which CBS aired its
network news program. He sang, as did the female quartet, the Debutones, and introduced his
guest stars.

JULIUS LAROSA SHOW, THE
Musical Variety
FIRST TELECAST: July 14, 1956
LAST TELECAST: September 7, 1957
BROADCAST HISTORY:
   Jul 1956–Aug 1956, NBC Sat 8:00–9:00
   Jun 1957–Sep 1957, NBC Sat 8:00–9:00
REGULARS:
   Julius LaRosa
   Frank Lewis Dancers (1956)
   The Spellbinders (1956)
   Carl Hoff & His Orchestra (1956)
   Louis Da Pron Dancers (1957)
   Artie Malvin Singers (1957)
   Mitchell Ayres & His Orchestra (1957)

Julius LaRosa spent two summers filling in for the
vacationing Perry Como. During the summer of
1956, LaRosa, Patti Page, and Tony Bennett each
spent about one month headlining a musical variety hour with the same supporting cast: the Spellbinders, the Frank Lewis Dancers, and Carl Hoff
& His Orchestra. During the summer of 1957,
LaRosa was the sole star and had Como's regular
dancers and orchestra as part of his supporting
cast.

JUNE ALLYSON SHOW, THE
   see DuPont Show with June Allyson, The

JUNIOR PRESS CONFERENCE
Interview
FIRST TELECAST: October 5, 1953
LAST TELECAST: December 13, 1954

BROADCAST HISTORY:
Oct 1953–Dec 1954, ABC Mon 9:00–9:30
MODERATOR:
Ruth Geri Hagy

Public-service program in which politicians and other personalities in the news were interviewed by a panel of four college correspondents from various campus newspapers. *Junior Press Conference* was first seen in October 1952, as a Sunday daytime entry, and continued on Sundays after its prime-time run until November 1960. In October 1954 the title was changed to *College Press Conference.* From Philadelphia.

JUST IN TIME
Situation Comedy
FIRST TELECAST: *April 6, 1988*
LAST TELECAST: *May 18, 1988*
BROADCAST HISTORY:
Apr 1988–May 1988, ABC Wed 9:30–10:00
CAST:
Harry Stadlin................ Tim Matheson
Joanna G. Farrell .... Patricia Kalember
Jack Manning................ Kevin Scannell
Steven Birnbaum........... Alan Blumenfeld
Isabel Miller .... Nada Despotovich
Carly Hightower ..... Ronnie Claire Edwards
Nick Thompson.............. Patrick Breen

Romantic comedy about an aggressive, modish young editor who is hired to shake up sagging *West Coast Review* magazine by making it, well, a bit livelier. That put him directly at odds with his top political columnist, smart but oh-so-serious Joanna. The romantic sparring began almost immediately. Harry says he'll print anything of hers that's a little more sensational? She gives him an exposé of his own amorous exploits back in Chicago. And so on.

Also on the staff were fact-bending sportswriter Jack, experienced right-hand man Steve, and enthusiastic young assistant Isabel. Carly was the drawling Southern secretary, and Nick the scruffy photographer.

JUST OUR LUCK
Situation Comedy
FIRST TELECAST: *September 20, 1983*
LAST TELECAST: *December 27, 1983*
BROADCAST HISTORY:
Sep 1983–Dec 1983, ABC Tue 8:00–8:30
CAST:
Shabu........................ T. K. Carter
Keith Barrow .... Richard Gilliland
Meagan Huxley............... Ellen Maxted
Nelson Marriott................ Rod McCary
Chuck...................... Richard Schaal
Professor Bob............... Hamilton Camp
Jim Dexter.................. Leonard Simon

The genie-in-the-bottle story has seldom been done with as many twists as in this 1983 comedy.

First of all, the genie—Shabu—was a hip black man disgusted at having fallen into the hands of a wishy-washy young TV reporter. Shabu's previous assignments had been much more glamorous, serving the likes of Cleopatra, Napoleon, and King Arthur. His new master, Keith, was not so keen on the arrangement, either, especially since the fun-loving Shabu was given to practical jokes and throwing spells around at all the wrong times. Keith was more interested in trying to save his job at KPOX-TV, where he had just been replaced as weatherman by Professor Bob. The officious program director, Meagan Huxley, thought Keith lacked charisma ("You just stick on the screen. Like old gum."), so Shabu gave him enough for ten people. When Keith needed to throw a party to impress the station manager, Mr. Mariott, Shabu conjured up a night none of them would forget.

There were lots of surprises on this show, including cameos by such people as Roy Orbison, Dr. Joyce Brothers, and Wink Martindale (doing a burlesque quiz show in which he couldn't seem to give away anything). Unfortunately, Shabu's magic didn't work against *The A-Team,* running opposite on NBC. Just his luck.

JUSTICE
Law Drama
FIRST TELECAST: *April 8, 1954*
LAST TELECAST: *March 25, 1956*
BROADCAST HISTORY:
Apr 1954–Jun 1955, NBC Thu 8:30–9:00
Oct 1955–Mar 1956, NBC Sun 10:30–11:00
CAST:
Jason Tyler (1954–1955)......... Gary Merrill
Richard Adams (1955–1956)... William Prince
PRODUCER:
David Susskind

Taken from the files of the National Legal Aid Society, the dramas presented in this live series were the stories of poor people in need of legal help, either criminal or civil in nature, with the emphasis on the former. There were no regulars in the cast when the series began but Legal Aid attorney Jason Tyler became the permanent lawyer on the series in the fall of 1954. He was replaced for the 1955–1956 season by a new attorney, Richard Adams.

A 1955 episode about song sharks in the music business, starring *Your Hit Parade* star Gisele MacKenzie, had an unexpected by-product. The song used in the drama, "Hard to Get," became quite a big seller on the real-life hit parade.

JUVENILE JURY
Quiz/Audience Participation
FIRST TELECAST: *April 3, 1947*
LAST TELECAST: *September 14, 1954*
BROADCAST HISTORY:
Apr 1947–Jul 1947, NBC Thu 8:00–8:30
Jun 1951–Sep 1951, NBC Tue 8:30–9:00
Jun 1952–Oct 1952, NBC Wed 8:00–8:30

Jul 1953–Sep 1953, NBC Mon 9:00–9:30
Jun 1954–Sep 1954, CBS Tue 8:30–9:00
EMCEE:
Jack Barry

Juvenile Jury was created by radio announcer Jack Barry, who served as its emcee on both radio and television. The format was simple and highly effective. A panel of five children, ranging in age from 3 to 12, was presented with "problems" sent in by viewers and asked to comment, or think up solutions. The kids were utterly uninhibited, and their answers were sometimes serious, sometimes funny, and always totally unpredictable. A typical exchange went like this. A mother wrote in, "My little girl wakes up very early every morning so she won't be late for school. But school is only two blocks away and she awakens the whole family, then arrives at school so early she has to sit on the steps and wait for the doors to open." To which the "jury" replied:

Richard (10): "Well, there's one good thing about her getting up so early—the rest of the family won't have to get in line for the bathroom!"

Mai-Lan (7): "Instead of keeping everyone else awake, why doesn't she go out and walk around the block a few thousand times?"

Elberta (6½): "Her teacher must be Gregory Peck or something . . ."

David (6): "Maybe she gets ready fast and early now—but wait till she gets older. Wait till she starts putting lipstick on and wearing a girdle."

Barry picked his kids carefully, and the results were always entertaining. (A similar format was used for years by Art Linkletter on a segment of his *House Party* show.) Once a sweet young child told him that when she grew up she wanted to be a doctor. "Why?" asked Barry. "Because," she answered, full of sincerity, "I like to stick needles in people."

Perhaps the best exchange, though, came after Barry had just finished delivering a commercial for the sponsor's health tonic, in which he was obliged to take a couple swigs of the stuff. As he walked over to the panel to begin his next interview, the young subject eyed him suspiciously, sniffed the air, and piped up accusingly, "Have you been drinking?"

Juvenile Jury began on radio in 1946 and had a brief run on NBC's early East Coast TV network in mid-1947. It was seen again on network television, this time nationwide, for four summers from 1951–1954. It continued as a Sunday afternoon show until March 27, 1955. Fifteen years later Jack Barry revived *Juvenile Jury* as a syndicated series during the 1970–1971 season.

K

KAISER ALUMINUM HOUR, THE
Dramatic Anthology
FIRST TELECAST: *July 3, 1956*
LAST TELECAST: *June 18, 1957*
BROADCAST HISTORY:
Jul 1956–Jun 1957, NBC Tue 9:30–10:30

Live hour-long dramas were presented every other week on *The Kaiser Aluminum Hour*. It alternated on Tuesday evenings with *The Armstrong Circle Theatre* prior to the latter program's move to CBS. The format was varied to include both serious and light subjects, with both well-known and lesser-known actors. The first production, "Army Game," was headlined by Paul Newman. Others who were featured in this series included Eli Wallach, Robert Culp, Natalie Wood, Forrest Tucker, Jack Warden, MacDonald Carey, Claude Rains, Henry Hull, Hume Cronyn, Franchot Tone, Geraldine Brooks, Kim Hunter, and Ralph Bellamy.

KALLIKAKS, THE
Situation Comedy
FIRST TELECAST: *August 3, 1977*
LAST TELECAST: *August 31, 1977*
BROADCAST HISTORY:
Aug 1977, NBC Wed 9:30–10:00
CAST:
Jasper T. Kallikak .... David Huddleston
Venus Kallikak .... Edie McClurg
Bobbi Lou Kallikak .... Bonnie Ebsen
Junior Kallikak .... Patrick J. Peterson
Oscar Heinz.................. Peter Palmer
THEME:
"Beat the System," by Stanley Ralph Ross, sung by Roy Clark

In the hopes of finding his fortune out West, Jasper T. Kallikak had moved his family from their native Appalachia, where he had worked as a coal miner, to the small town of Nowhere, California. He had inherited a small, two-pump gas station there and figured that, as his own boss, he would improve his lot. Conniving and avaricious, Jasper lived by the theme song of this mini-series, always looking for a way to beat the system. With his overly affectionate wife Venus, his social-climbing teenage daughter, and his mechanical genius preteen son, not to mention his German hired hand Oscar who could barely speak English, Jasper had quite a household. One member of the cast should have felt right at home with this hill-billies-move-west format. Bonnie Ebsen's father Buddy had spent most of the 1960s as Jed Clampett on *The Beverly Hillbillies*.

KAREN
Situation Comedy
FIRST TELECAST: *October 5, 1964*
LAST TELECAST: *August 30, 1965*
BROADCAST HISTORY:
Oct 1964–Aug 1965, NBC Mon 7:30–8:00
CAST:
Karen Scott .... Debbie Watson
Steve Scott .... Richard Denning
Barbara Scott................ Mary LaRoche
Mimi Scott .... Gina Gillespie
Janis .... Bernadette Withers
Candy .... Trudi Ames
Peter........................ Teddy Quinn
Spider Gibson .... Murray MacLeod
David Rowe III .... Richard Dreyfuss

Karen was one of the three half-hour situation comedies that comprised the 90-minute *90 Bristol Court* series in the fall of 1964. The concept of *90 Bristol Court* was to link together three separate families living in the same Southern California apartment complex, each with their own story and own half-hour show each week. *Karen* was the only one of the three that made it through the entire 1964–1965 season, however, the other two *(Harris Against the World* and *Tom, Dick and Mary)* being dropped in January.

Karen Scott was an energetic 16-year-old whose activities constantly confounded her tolerant parents, Steve and Barbara. Karen's tomboyish younger sister Mimi created a different set of problems for the elder Scotts, and the situations she became involved in functioned as counterpoint to those of her older sister. Handyman Cliff Murdock, the only character appearing in all three parts of *90 Bristol Court*, did not appear in *Karen* after the other two comedies were dropped.

KAREN
Situation Comedy
FIRST TELECAST: *January 30, 1975*
LAST TELECAST: *June 19, 1975*
BROADCAST HISTORY:
Jan 1975–Jun 1975, ABC Thu 8:30–9:00
CAST:
Karen Angelo.............. Karen Valentine
Dale Busch (first telecast) ...... Denver Pyle
Dale Busch .... Charles Lane
Dena Madison .... Dena Dietrich
Cissy Peterson................. Aldine King
Adam Cooperman.............. Will Seltzer
Jerry Siegel.................... Oliver Clark
Cheryl Siegel .... Alix Elias

This contemporary situation comedy centered around Karen Angelo, a single, bright, involved young woman who worked for a citizens' action organization called Open America, headquartered in Washington, D.C. Helping Karen uncover crooked politicians and lobby for citizens' legislation were crusty Dale Busch, founder of Open America; Dena, the group's cynical office manager; Adam, a young student working for the organization; and Cissy, Karen's roommate. Jerry and Cheryl were Karen's neighbors in Georgetown.

KAREN'S SONG
Situation Comedy
FIRST TELECAST: *July 18, 1987*
LAST TELECAST: *September 12, 1987*
BROADCAST HISTORY:
 Jul 1987–Sep 1987, FOX Sat 9:30–10:00
CAST:
 Karen Matthews .... Patty Duke
 Claire Steiner .... Lainie Kazan
 Steven Foreman .... Lewis Smith
 Laura Matthews (18) .... Terri Hatcher
 Michael Brand................ Charles Levin
 Zach Matthews .... Granville Van Dusen

Ten years after her divorce, Karen Matthews' life was pretty good. She had just been promoted to editor for a Los Angeles book publisher and her daughter, Laura, had started college at UCLA. Then she fell in love with Steve, the owner of a small catering service called A Catered Affair. He was bright, friendly, interesting, loving, and 28 years old—12 years younger than Karen. Daughter Laura thought dating a younger man disgusting and best friend Claire thought it was great. Karen's neighbor and former lover, real-estate salesman Michael, was supportive but thought she and Steve should get married. As for Karen herself, she was alternately content and confused, unsure of whether a relationship with a younger man made sense or had a future. The relationship might have, but the series failed after only two months.

KATE & ALLIE
Situation Comedy
FIRST TELECAST: *March 19, 1984*
LAST TELECAST:
BROADCAST HISTORY:
 Mar 1984–May 1984, CBS Mon 9:30–10:00
 Aug 1984–Sep 1986, CBS Mon 9:30–10:00
 Sep 1986–Sep 1987, CBS Mon 8:00–8:30
 Sep 1987–Nov 1987, CBS Mon 8:30–9:00
 Dec 1987–Jun 1988, CBS Mon 8:00–8:30
 *July 1988–   *, CBS Sat 8:00–8:30
CAST:
 Kate McArdle .... Susan Saint James
 Allie Lowell .... Jane Curtin
 Emma McArdle .... Ari Meyers
 Chip Lowell .... Frederick Koehler
 Jennie Lowell .... Allison Smith
 *Charles Lowell (1984–1986)...... Paul Hecht
 Ted Bartelo (1984–1985, 1987–   )
 .... Gregory Salata
 Bob Barsky (1987–   ).......... Sam Freed

*Occasional

Kate and Allie were two divorcées who had been friends since high school. In an effort to save money and provide mutual emotional support,

they decided to share an apartment in New York's Greenwich Village. Of course, there were problems. Between them they had three young children who caused a certain amount of turmoil, and Kate and Allie themselves had decidedly different life-styles. Kate was glamorous, contemporary, and a bit frivolous, while Allie was old-fashioned, proper, and industrious to a fault. Stories revolved around the problems of adjusting to communal life, raising children in the city, and Allie's rocky love life. She had never dated much, and now more than ever needed the help of her more worldly friend.

Allie's ex-husband Charles was seen occasionally, picking up the kids; later, he remarried. Kate did find romance in 1985, in the unlikely person of plumber Ted Bartelo. They actually got engaged that spring, but broke up after a short time.

Allie's hard-earned bachelor's degree proved of little help in getting her a good job, and Kate became bored with being a travel agent, so in the spring of 1987 they started their own catering business. That fall both of their daughters enrolled at Columbia University. Emma subsequently moved into a dormitory, giving her more freedom than her friend Jennie. Allie was forced to face the reality that her daughter was becoming a woman, and reluctantly gave Jennie some of the same freedom at home that Emma had at the dorm. Kate's old boyfriend Ted was back, and Allie was dating sportscaster Bob Barsky.

KATE LOVES A MYSTERY
Detective Drama
FIRST TELECAST: *February 26, 1979*
LAST TELECAST: *December 6, 1979*
BROADCAST HISTORY:
 Feb 1979, NBC Mon 9:00–11:00
 Mar 1979, NBC Thu 10:00–11:00
 Aug 1979–Dec 1979, NBC Thu 10:00–11:00
CAST:
 Kate Columbo/Callahan...... Kate Mulgrew
 Jenny Columbo/Callahan......... Lili Haydn
 Josh Alden .... Henry Jones
 Sgt. Mike Varrick.............. Don Stroud

One of the biggest hits of the early 1970s was *Columbo*, the disheveled detective who always got his man. He often mentioned his wife ("the missus"), but she was never seen. *Columbo* finally ran its course, but the producers, unwilling to let a good (and profitable) idea die, decided to concoct a Mrs. Columbo who was also a sleuth, on a show of her own. Kate Columbo was the mother of a seven-year-old daughter and, to avoid the monotony of housework, a reporter for *The Valley Advocate,* a suburban weekly newspaper edited by crusty old Josh Alden. It may seem a little farfetched, but working for the paper somehow got Kate involved in numerous murder mysteries, all of which she solved in much the same manner of her celebrated spouse.

After a mixed reception in early 1979, the series

underwent three title changes, from the original *Kate Columbo*, to *Kate the Detective*, to *Kate Loves a Mystery*. The producers apparently felt that tying Kate to *Columbo* had been a mistake, so they gave her a new last name, Callahan, and all references to a husband were dropped. She still worked at the paper, and Sgt. Varrick was added to the cast as her contact on the police force. It didn't help, and the program was canceled by early December.

KATE MCSHANE
Law Drama
FIRST TELECAST: *September 10, 1975*
LAST TELECAST: *November 12, 1975*
BROADCAST HISTORY:
  Sep 1975–Nov 1975, CBS Wed 10:00–11:00
CAST:
  Kate McShane .... Anne Meara
  Pat McShane .... Sean McClory
  Ed McShane .... Charles Haid

Kate McShane was the first network dramatic series to feature a woman lawyer in the lead role. As played by Anne Meara, Kate was single, independent, aggressive, and softhearted. She had a tendency to become emotionally involved with her clients, which was not always a good idea. When she encountered problems (which was every week) she could turn to her father, Pat, a former cop who served as her investigator, or to her brother Ed, a Jesuit priest and law professor who helped her with the stickier legal and moral questions.

Miss Meara was half of the husband-and-wife comedy team of Stiller and Meara, which appeared on many variety shows during the 1970s. This was her first dramatic series.

KATE SMITH EVENING HOUR, THE
Musical Variety
FIRST TELECAST: *September 19, 1951*
LAST TELECAST: *June 11, 1952*
BROADCAST HISTORY:
  Sep 1951–Jun 1952, NBC Wed 8:00–9:00
REGULARS:
  Kate Smith
  Ted Collins
  The Jack Allison Singers
  The Johnny Butler Dancers
  The Jack Miller Orchestra

Kate Smith, one of radio's favorite and most familiar personalities, made only two brief excursions into a nighttime television series (she also had a daytime show from 1950 to 1954). *The Kate Smith Evening Hour* was a live weekly variety show which featured Broadway and Hollywood stars in excerpts from famous plays, as well as musical numbers, comedy sketches, and the other traditional components of a variety show. Ted Collins, who was Miss Smith's manager and producer of this show, served as the host of the program. The

semi-regular feature "Ethel and Albert," starring Peg Lynch and Alan Bunce, later became a series in its own right and ran for several seasons.

Two of Kate's guests on this series were making their television debuts: singer Josephine Baker and the Tommy Dorsey Orchestra. In contrast to her daytime theme, "When the Moon Comes Over the Mountain," Miss Smith opened her prime-time show with her stirring and familiar rendition of "God Bless America."

KATE SMITH SHOW, THE
Musical Variety
FIRST TELECAST: *January 25, 1960*
LAST TELECAST: *July 18, 1960*
BROADCAST HISTORY:
  Jan 1960–Jul 1960, CBS Mon 7:30–8:00
REGULARS:
  Kate Smith
  Neal Hefti and His Orchestra
  The Harry Simeone Chorus

Kate Smith returned to nighttime television, after an absence of almost a decade, with this musical variety show. She sang, introduced her guest stars, and participated with them in production numbers. Most of the guests were popular singers, dancers, or musicians.

KAY KYSER'S KOLLEGE OF MUSICAL KNOWLEDGE
Quiz/Audience Participation
FIRST TELECAST: *December 1, 1949*
LAST TELECAST: *September 12, 1954*
BROADCAST HISTORY:
  Dec 1949–Dec 1950, NBC Thu 9:00–10:00 (OS)
  Jul 1954–Sep 1954, NBC Sun 7:00–7:30
EMCEE:
  Kay Kyser (1949–1950)
  Tennessee Ernie Ford (1954)
REGULARS (1949–1950):
  Ish Kabbible
  Liza Palmer
  Sue Bennett
  Michael Douglas
  Honeydreamers
  Dr. Roy K. Marshall (announcer)
  Ben Grauer (announcer)
  Diane Sinclair
  Ken Spaulding
  Carl Hoff (orchestra director)
REGULARS (1954):
  The Cheerleaders Quintet
  Frank DeVol Orchestra
  Jack Narz (announcer and "Dean")
THEME (1949–1950):
  "Thinking of You," by Walter Donaldson and Paul Ash

Kay Kyser was one of several bandleaders who had developed an audience-involvement "gimmick" while touring dance halls across the country in the 1930s, and then brought his routine suc-

412

cessfully to radio in the 1940s (another was Sammy Kaye with his *So You Want to Lead a Band* routine). When television came along, hungry for programming, the bandleaders were ready with their pretested and already successful entertainment packages.

The *Kollege of Musical Knowledge* was a musical quiz show. "Professor" Kay, garbed in cap and gown, recruited contestants from the studio audience and posed musical questions, which were performed or acted out by members of the band and special guests. Three bearded judges, dressed in tails and somewhat resembling the Smith Brothers, sat behind a long desk and comically "judged" the answers (all three speaking in perfect unison). The band was dressed in sweaters and beanies. Contestants were sometimes required to give a totally incorrect answer, upon which Kay would shout, "That's right, you're wrong," or "That's wrong, you're right," as might be the case. The whole atmosphere was somewhat antic, with Kay constantly mugging for the audience and comedy and musical routines interpolated.

Assisting with the musical questions were "dumb" comedian Ish Kabbible (real name: Merwyn Bogue) and several of the band's regular vocalists, including young Michael (Mike) Douglas—later of TV talk show fame.

After a year's run the program was involved in a dispute between sponsor and network, which resulted in its cancellation. It probably could have been revived in another time slot or on another network, but Kyser, tired of years of the showbiz grind, threw in the towel and retired not only from TV but from the entertainment world entirely. He pursued religious activities for the rest of his life.

The *Kollege of Musical Knowledge* idea was revived in 1954 as a summer show, with Tennessee Ernie Ford as host. Kay Kyser was listed as "consultant" for the 1954 revival, and even appeared as special guest on one telecast, but without the regular presence of Kay and his maniac crew the program had lost its spark, and was not renewed.

KAY O'BRIEN

Medical Drama
FIRST TELECAST: *September 25, 1986*
LAST TELECAST: *November 13, 1986*
BROADCAST HISTORY:
 Sep 1986–Nov 1986, CBS Thu 10:00–11:00
CAST:
 Dr. Kay O'Brien ("Kayo") . Patricia Kalember
 Dr. Robert Moffitt .... Lane Smith
 Dr. Josef Wallach .... Jan Rubes
 Dr. Michael Kwan .... Keone Young
 Dr. Mark Doyle .... Brian Benben
 Dr. Cliff Margolis .... Tony Soper
 Nurse Rosa Villanueva .... Priscilla Lopez
 Sam .... Franc Luz
 Nat .... Michael Rogers
 Anesthesiologist .... Myra Fried
 O.R. Nurse .... Arlene Duncan

Fictional Manhattan General Hospital was the setting for this medical drama. Kayo was a 28-year-old surgical resident at the hospital; her stress-filled professional life, and, to a lesser extent, her personal life, provided the focus of most episodes. Others on the staff included Dr. Moffitt, the attending surgeon and Kayo's teacher; Dr. Doyle, an obnoxious fellow surgical resident who felt women shouldn't be surgeons; Dr. Margolis, the intern working under Kayo; Dr. Kwan, the senior resident physician on staff; and Dr. Wallach, the imposing head of surgery. Chief Emergency Room nurse Rosa was Kayo's best friend and confidante; Sam, the former boyfriend who left her because he didn't like taking second place in her life after medicine; and Nat was a helpful black orderly.

KAZ

Law/Detective Drama
FIRST TELECAST: *September 10, 1978*
LAST TELECAST: *August 19, 1979*
BROADCAST HISTORY:
 Sep 1978–Oct 1978, CBS Sun 10:00–11:00
 Oct 1978–Jan 1979, CBS Sun 9:00–10:00
 Jan 1979–Apr 1979, CBS Wed 10:00–11:00
 Jul 1979–Aug 1979, CBS Sun 10:00–11:00
CAST:
 Martin "Kaz" Kazinsky .... Ron Leibman
 Samuel Bennett .... Patrick O'Neal
 Katie McKenna .... Linda Carlson
 Mary Parnell .... Gloria Le Roy
 Peter Colcourt .... Mark Withers
 Illsa Fogel .... Edith Atwater
 D.A. Frank Revko .... George Wyner
 Malloy .... Dick O'Neill

Kaz had an unusual background for an attorney—he had earned his law degree while serving time in prison. Upon his release he had managed to secure a position as a junior partner with the prestigious Los Angeles law firm of Bennett, Rheinhart and Alquist. The pay wasn't very good (as he frequently reminded senior partner Samuel Bennett), but someone with his background and inexperience had little choice. Kaz did have one advantage, however. Having been on the other side of the law himself, he had an understanding of the criminal mind not usually found in attorneys. His girlfriend was court reporter Katie McKenna, and his pad a small apartment over the Starting Gate, a jazz music nightclub owned by his friend Mary Parnell. Kaz often hung out at the Starting Gate, and sat in with the band as a drummer. Working with him at the law firm was another young attorney, Peter Colcourt.

KEANE BROTHERS SHOW, THE

Musical Variety
FIRST TELECAST: *August 12, 1977*
LAST TELECAST: *September 2, 1977*
BROADCAST HISTORY:
 Aug 1977–Sep 1977, CBS Fri 8:30–9:00

REGULARS:
  Tom Keane
  John Keane
  Jimmy Caesar
  The Anita Mann Dancers
  The Alan Copeland Orchestra

If ABC could make series stars out of teenagers Donny and Marie Osmond, CBS figured they could try a summer mini-series with two performers who were even younger. Probably the youngest co-stars ever on a network variety series, piano-playing Tom was 13, and his drummer brother John was only 12. They sang and played popular tunes and performed with assorted guest stars. Impressionist Jimmy Caesar provided comic relief.

KEEFE BRASSELLE SHOW, THE
Musical Variety
FIRST TELECAST: *June 25, 1963*
LAST TELECAST: *September 17, 1963*
BROADCAST HISTORY:
  Jun 1963–Sep 1963, CBS Tue 10:00–11:00
REGULARS:
  Keefe Brasselle
  Noelle Adam
  Ann B. Davis
  Sammy Kaye
  Rocky Graziano
  The Bill Foster Dancers
  Charles Sanford Orchestra

Keefe Brasselle was pushed hard as a "coming star" on television in the 1960s, but he never did seem to make the big time. In addition to producing programs and appearing in dramatic presentations, he starred in this variety series which was the summer replacement for *The Garry Moore Show*. Probably the highlight of the series was the premiere, on which a young guest named Barbra Streisand belted out "Soon It's Gonna Rain" from *The Fantastiks*.

Brasselle, who also worked in an executive capacity for CBS, later turned novelist and wrote a sex-and-scandal bestseller focusing on an unnamed TV network. The book was entitled *The CanniBalS*.

KEEP IT IN THE FAMILY
Quiz
FIRST TELECAST: *October 12, 1957*
LAST TELECAST: *February 8, 1958*
BROADCAST HISTORY:
  Oct 1957–Feb 1958, ABC Sat 7:30–8:00
EMCEE:
  Keefe Brasselle (1957)
  Bill Nimmo
ANNOUNCER:
  Johnny Olsen

This quiz show pitted two families against each other. Each team, which might comprise several generations within one family, was presented with a multi-part question. Each member of the family, starting with the youngest, then had to answer one part. Winning families continued on the program until defeated. Keefe Brasselle was the host on the first telecast of this show, but was replaced for the remainder of the run by Bill Nimmo.

KEEP ON CRUISIN'
Variety
FIRST TELECAST: *January 9, 1987*
LAST TELECAST: *June 5, 1987*
BROADCAST HISTORY:
  Jan 1987–Jun 1987, CBS Fri 11:30 P.M.–12:30 A.M.
HOSTS:
  Stephen Bishop
  Jimmy Aleck
  Sinbad
EXECUTIVE PRODUCER:
  Dick Clark

Musical and comedy performers were featured on this variety series aired from a different location in the Los Angeles area each week. Singer-songwriter Stephen Bishop co-hosted with young comic Sinbad. When the show returned in April after a brief hiatus, Bishop had been replaced by comic Jimmy Aleck. The locations included the Santa Monica pier, Hollywood Boulevard, Johnny Rocket's Hollywood Diner, Mann's Chinese Theater, and Knotts' Berry Farm. Appearing were musical guests like the New Edition, Little Anthony, Billy Vera and the Beaters, Eddie Money, Oingo Boingo, and Ronnie Spector, and hip young comedians Rick Overton, Frank Welker, Lois Bromfield, and Rick Ducommun.

KEEP ON TRUCKIN'
Comedy Variety
FIRST TELECAST: *July 12, 1975*
LAST TELECAST: *August 2, 1975*
BROADCAST HISTORY:
  Jul 1975–Aug 1975, ABC Sat 8:00–9:00
CAST:
  Franklyn Ajaye
  Rhonda Bates
  Kathrine Baumann
  Jeannine Burnier
  Didi Conn
  Charles Fleischer
  Wayland Flowers
  Larry Ragland
  Marion Ramsey
  Rhilo Fahir
  Jack Riley
  Fred Travalena
  Gailard Sartain
  Richard Lee Sung

This four-week summer variety series featured a repertory company of 14 bright young comics, who did rapid-fire gags and satirical sketches, and

414

indulged in general buffoonery. Each telecast was to be introduced by respected writer-actor Rod Serling, but Serling died two weeks before the premiere and his pretaped segments were omitted from the actual telecasts.

KEEP POSTED
Public Affairs
FIRST TELECAST: *October 9, 1951*
LAST TELECAST: *March 31, 1953*
BROADCAST HISTORY:
Oct 1951–Mar 1953, DUM Tue 8:30–9:00
MODERATOR:
Martha Rountree
REGULAR PANELIST:
Lawrence Spivak

Martha Rountree moderated this public-affairs program in which a panel of citizens, chaired by Lawrence Spivak, questioned a leading public figure. Among the guests was Rep. Richard M. Nixon (R-Calif), whose topic was "Fighting Communism." The program originated from Washington, D.C.

KEEP TALKING
Quiz/Audience Participation
FIRST TELECAST: *July 15, 1958*
LAST TELECAST: *May 3, 1960*
BROADCAST HISTORY:
Jul 1958–Sep 1958, CBS Tue 8:30–9:00
Sep 1958–Oct 1958, CBS Tue 8:00–8:30
Nov 1958–Feb 1959, CBS Sun 10:00–10:30
Feb 1959–Sep 1959, CBS Wed 8:00–8:30
Sep 1959–May 1960, ABC Tue 10:30–11:00
EMCEE:
Monty Hall (1958)
Carl Reiner (1958–1959)
Merv Griffin (1959–1960)
REGULARS:
Joey Bishop
Ilka Chase (1958–1959)
Audrey Meadows (1958–1959)
Elaine May (1958–1959)
Paul Winchell
Danny Dayton
Morey Amsterdam
Peggy Cass
Pat Carroll
Orson Bean (1959–1960)

The players on *Keep Talking* were divided into two teams of three each. The emcee gave each player a different secret phrase, which the player was then required to incorporate into a story. After the phrase had been used the emcee would stop the story and ask the other team what the phrase was. Guessing the phrase won the team a point and the team with the most points at the end of the show was the winner. The object, therefore, was to ad-lib so skillfully that the phrases were masked from the other team. Monty Hall was the original emcee but was replaced by Carl Reiner

when the show moved to Sunday nights in November 1958. When the series moved to ABC in September 1959, Merv Griffin took over as emcee.

KELLY MONTEITH SHOW, THE
Comedy Variety
FIRST TELECAST: *June 16, 1976*
LAST TELECAST: *July 7, 1976*
BROADCAST HISTORY:
Jun 1976–Jul 1976, CBS Wed 8:30–9:00
REGULARS:
Kelly Monteith
Nellie Bellflower
Henry Corden

Kelly Monteith's forte was the comic monologue, with which he opened each episode of this four-week summer mini-series. Nellie Bellflower and Henry Corden, and a weekly guest star, also assisted Kelly in assorted sketches.

KEN BERRY "WOW" SHOW, THE
Musical Variety
FIRST TELECAST: *July 15, 1972*
LAST TELECAST: *August 12, 1972*
BROADCAST HISTORY:
Jul 1972–Aug 1972, ABC Sat 10:00–11:00
REGULARS:
Ken Berry
Teri Garr
Billy Van
Carl Gottlieb
Don Lane
Steve Martin
Barbara Joyce
Laara Lacey
Cheryl Stoppelmoor (Cheryl Ladd)
Gene Merlino
Tom Kenny
Ted Zeigler
The New Seekers
Jaime Rogers Dancers
Jimmy Dale Orchestra

Ken Berry's previous exposure to a national television audience was almost exclusively as an actor in situation comedies, most notably *The Andy Griffith Show*, *Mayberry R.F.D.*, and *F Troop*. This contemporary summer series gave him an opportunity to show off his skills as a dancer and singer as well. Satires and lampoons of movies and TV shows were frequent features.

KEN MURRAY SHOW, THE
Variety
FIRST TELECAST: *January 7, 1950*
LAST TELECAST: *June 21, 1953*
BROADCAST HISTORY:
Jan 1950–Jun 1952, CBS Sat 8:00–9:00 (OS)
Feb 1953–Jun 1953, CBS Sun 9:30–10:00
REGULARS:
Ken Murray
Darla Hood (1950–1951)

Joe Wong (1950–1951)
Tony Labriola (1950–1951)
Jack Mulhall (1950–1951)
Betty Lou Walters (1950–1951)
The Enchanters (1950–1951)
Joe Besser (1950–1951)
Art Lund (1951–1952)
Laurie Anders
Pat Conway (1951–1952)
Jane Bergmeier (1951–1952)
Lillian Farmer (1951–1952)
Anita Gordon (1951–1953)
Johnny Johnston (1953)

Old trouper Ken Murray, who had begun his career in vaudeville in the teens and who appeared on the first commercial program on television, in 1930, hosted his own comedy-variety series on CBS from 1950–1953. Murray was also a producer of some note, and his show featured top-name guest stars and elaborate sets—including his trademark Hollywood and Vine backdrop. He had a large cast of regular singers and dancers, including cowgirl Laurie "Ah love the wide open spaces" Anders and a bevy of long-stemmed "Glamourlovelies." Ken bridged the various acts with informal chatter and humor. The series began as an alternate-week entry, switched to weekly in the fall of 1950, and then back to alternate weeks in 1953. During the 1953 run it alternated with *The Alan Young Show* under the umbrella title *Time to Smile*.

KENTUCKY JONES
Comedy/Drama
FIRST TELECAST: *September 19, 1964*
LAST TELECAST: *September 11, 1965*
BROADCAST HISTORY:
  Sep 1964–Dec 1964, NBC Sat 8:30–9:00
  Jan 1965–Sep 1965, NBC Sat 8:00–8:30
CAST:
  "Kentucky" Jones . . . . Dennis Weaver
  Ike Wong . . . . Ricky Der
  Seldom Jackson . . . . Harry Morgan
  Annie Ng . . . . Cherylene Lee
  Mr. Ng . . . . Arthur Wong
  Thomas Wong . . . . Keye Luke
  Edith Thorncroft . . . . Nancy Rennick

Kenneth Yarborough Jones was a veterinarian and owner of a 40-acre ranch in Southern California. He had acquired the nickname Kentucky because of the way he signed his name: "K. Y. Jones." His wife had applied to adopt a nine-year-old Chinese orphan who arrived shortly after her sudden death. Kentucky's situation as a widower made him have second thoughts about taking the orphan, Dwight Eisenhower "Ike" Wong, into his household. Although reluctant to accept the responsibility, Kentucky came to love Ike. Seldom Jackson was the handyman around the ranch, Edith Thorncroft, the social worker looking after Ike's welfare. The other regulars were members of the local Chinese community.

KEY CLUB PLAYHOUSE
Dramatic Anthology
FIRST TELECAST: *May 31, 1957*
LAST TELECAST: *August 23, 1957*
BROADCAST HISTORY:
  May 1957–Aug 1957, ABC Fri 9:00–9:30

The filmed dramas presented in this series were selected reruns of episodes from *Ford Theatre*.

KEY TO THE AGES
Discussion
FIRST TELECAST: *February 27, 1955*
LAST TELECAST: *May 22, 1955*
BROADCAST HISTORY:
  Feb 1955–May 1955, ABC Sun 8:00–8:30
HOST:
  Dr. Theodore Low

Ancient Greek poets, great novels, and other literary or cultural subjects were examined on this ABC program, which ran opposite Ed Sullivan for a few months in 1955. It originated from Baltimore and was produced in cooperation with the Enoch Pratt Free Library and the Walters Art Gallery.

KEY TO THE MISSING
Interview
FIRST TELECAST: *August 8, 1948*
LAST TELECAST: *September 16, 1949*
BROADCAST HISTORY:
  Aug 1948–Oct 1948, DUM Sun 6:30–7:00
  Oct 1948–Mar 1949, DUM Fri 7:00–7:30
  Mar 1949–Apr 1949, DUM Thu 8:30–9:00
  May 1949–Jun 1949, DUM Fri 9:30–10:00
  Jun 1949–Sep 1949, DUM Fri 9:00–9:30
HOST:
  Archdale J. Jones

This was a kind of missing persons bureau of the air. Archdale Jones interviewed relatives and friends and showed pictures, handwriting specimens, etc., of missing persons, and then appealed to viewers to call in any information they might have on the vanished person's whereabouts. Although some of the cases went back generations, quite a few long-lost kin were reunited this way. The wartime radio program upon which the show was based (called *Where Are They Now?*) claimed a success rate of 68 percent.

KHAN
Detective Drama
FIRST TELECAST: *February 7, 1975*
LAST TELECAST: *February 28, 1975*
BROADCAST HISTORY:
  Feb 1975, CBS Fri 8:00–9:00
CAST:
  Khan . . . . Khigh Dhiegh
  Anna Khan . . . . Irene Yah-Ling Sun
  Kim Khan . . . . Evan Kim
  Lt. Gubbins . . . . Vic Tayback

Based in San Francisco's Chinatown, private detective Khan, with the help of his two children, unraveled mysterious crimes in a style that could best be described as contemporary Charlie Chan. Daughter Anna was finishing a Ph.D. in criminology and son Kim was also a college grad. Using their mix of modern and traditional techniques, the three Khans made a highly efficient team. Unfortunately, they did not attract an audience and the show was canceled after only four weeks on the air.

KID GLOVES
Sports
FIRST TELECAST: *February 24, 1951*
LAST TELECAST: *August 4, 1951*
BROADCAST HISTORY:
    Feb 1951–Mar 1951, CBS Sat 7:30–8:00
    Mar 1951–Aug 1951, CBS Sat 6:30–7:00
REGULARS:
    Frank Goodman
    Bill Sears
    John De Grosa

Originating live from Philadelphia, where it had been a successful local show for several months prior to its moving to the full CBS network, *Kid Gloves* gave young children an opportunity to display their skills as boxers. Contestants ranged in age from 3 to 12 and fought three-round matches. The length of each round was between 30 seconds and one minute, depending on the age of the contestants. Frank Goodman was the referee, the judge, and the matchmaker. Bill Sears was the ringside announcer, and John De Grosa of the Pennsylvania State Athletic Commission interviewed celebrities from the sports world between rounds.

KIERAN'S KALEIDOSCOPE
Documentary
BROADCAST HISTORY:
    Syndicated only
    15 minutes
    Produced: *1949–1952* (104 episodes)
    Released: *Early 1949*
HOST:
    John Kieran

John Kieran, longtime sports columnist for the *New York Times*, gained national fame with his incredibly wide range of knowledge on radio's *Information Please* in the 1930s and 1940s. In this series of early TV films (the first widely seen syndicated series) he augmented his erudite and witty comments with still photographs and films of various subjects, from the solar system to wood carving to the life of the beetle. One topic was discussed per program.

KIERNAN'S CORNER
Interview
FIRST TELECAST: *August 16, 1948*
LAST TELECAST: *March 30, 1949*
BROADCAST HISTORY:
    Aug 1948–Sep 1948, ABC Mon 8:00–8:30
    Sep 1948–Jan 1949, ABC Mon 7:30–8:00
    Jan 1949–Mar 1949, ABC Mon 8:00–8:30
HOST:
    Walter Kiernan

Newspaperman and radio commentator Walter Kiernan, a familiar face on early television, conducted this talk show. He interviewed tourists in New York and visited interesting places around the city with the ABC cameras.

KING COLE'S BIRTHDAY PARTY
see *Birthday Party*

KING FAMILY SHOW, THE
Musical Variety
FIRST TELECAST: *January 23, 1965*
LAST TELECAST: *September 10, 1969*
BROADCAST HISTORY:
    Jan 1965–Sep 1965, ABC Sat 7:30–8:30
    Sep 1965–Jan 1966, ABC Sat 8:00–8:30
    Mar 1969–Sep 1969, ABC Wed 8:30–9:00
CAST:
    The King Sisters (Yvonne, Luise, Marilyn, Alyce, Maxine, Donna), *et al.*
ORCHESTRA:
    Alvino Rey Orchestra directed by Mitchell Ayres (1965–1966)
    Ralph Carmichael (1969)
EXECUTIVE PRODUCER:
    Nick Vanoff (1965–1966)
    Yvonne King Burch and Luise King Rey (1969)

Thirty-seven—count 'em—37 King family members all singing on one stage at one time! Or was it 36? Or 41? Whatever it was, there was a lot of kin in this wholesome family musical series, which was a spin-off from a special appearance the Kings had made on *The Hollywood Palace* in August 1964. That appearance had drawn a reported 53,000 letters and a King Family series was assured.

At the center of things were the six King Sisters, a singing group popular since the early 1940s, when they had been part of Alvino Rey's orchestra. (Alvino was in fact married to one of them, Luise.) Sisters, brothers, husbands, nephews, cousins, and masses of kids were featured on this series (each of the King Sisters had from two to five offspring). Ages ranged from seven months to 79 years. The oldster was William King Driggs, the father, an old-time vaudevillian who had begun the family's musical tradition in 1921. Music ranged from semi-classical to semi-rock, interspersed with lots of gentle family humor. Alvino Rey had a regular spot with his talking guitar. A "Family Circle" segment, exploring in verse and song the meaning of familial happiness, was a regular feature. Each telecast ended with the family *en masse* singing "Love at Home."

All this built up an intensely loyal following. One viewing family, knowing what would move a sponsor's cold heart, wrote in that "the King Family program was beautiful, talented, and completely entertaining. We are buying Clairol and Wisk tomorrow." Apparently not enough Clairol and Wisk was sold, however, for the show was canceled after only a year.

A brief revival in 1969 spotlighted a more contemporary sub-group, the King Cousins, along with the sisters, Alvino, and the rest of the family.

KING OF DIAMONDS
Crime Drama
BROADCAST HISTORY:
Syndicated only
30 minutes
Produced: *1961–1962* (39 episodes)
Released: *September 1961*
CAST:
John King .... Broderick Crawford
Al Casey .... Ray Hamilton

Broderick Crawford attempted to repeat his recent success on *Highway Patrol* with this bare-knuckles private-eye series, without much luck. He played John King, "Chief of Security for the diamond industry," traveling around the world solving crimes and taking on other dangerous assignments relating to the diamond trade. Casey was his young sidekick. Thieves, smugglers, and fences abounded, and King met them with a great deal of violence, even beating up some of the shadier women (while making passes at the others). His recurring enemy was something called, incredibly enough, the Illegal Diamond Buyers' Syndicate.

KING'S CROSSING
Drama
FIRST TELECAST: *January 16, 1982*
LAST TELECAST: *February 27, 1982*
BROADCAST HISTORY:
Jan 1982–Feb 1982, ABC Sat 8:00–9:00
CAST:
Paul Hollister............. Bradford Dillman
Nan Hollister................... Mary Frann
Lauren Hollister .... Linda Hamilton
Carey Hollister .... Marilyn Jones
Billy McCall................... Daniel Zippi
Jillian .... Doran Clark
Louisa Beauchamp .... Beatrice Straight
Willa Bristol .... Dorothy Meyer

Unlike most prime-time soap operas, *King's Crossing* focused on the travails of the young, principally teenagers Lauren and Carey Hollister. They were the daughters of Paul and Nan Hollister, a couple who had moved their family to the small town of King's Crossing, California, in an effort to make a fresh start. Paul was an alcoholic teacher and writer trying to set his life straight, and Nan his supportive wife. Problems came from 19-year-old Lauren, who was ambitious and impetuous, and 17-year-old Carey, wide-eyed and

having her first affair, with fun-loving stableboy Billy McCall.

Entwined with their lives were wealthy Aunt Louisa, who resented her niece's return to King's Crossing to claim the family house; Louisa's housekeeper Willa; and the Hollister girls' beautiful but disturbed young cousin Jillian, crippled in body and mind but slowly making her way back to a normal life, despite the callousness of the local teens toward her.

KING'S CROSSROADS
see *Movies—Prior to 1961*

KINGS ROW
Drama
FIRST TELECAST: *September 13, 1955*
LAST TELECAST: *January 17, 1956*
BROADCAST HISTORY:
Sep 1955–Jan 1956, ABC Tue 7:30–8:30
CAST:
Dr. Parris Mitchell............... Jack Kelly
Randy Monaghan .... Nan Leslie
Drake McHugh .... Robert Horton
Dr. Tower .... Victor Jory
Grandma .... Lillian Bronson
Dr. Gordon .... Robert Burton

Romantic drama (soap opera, if you prefer) about young Dr. Parris Mitchell, who returned to his hometown at the turn of the century to set up a psychiatric practice. There he encountered considerable resistance to his new methods, due to the superstitious citizenry and the tradition-bound medical practices of the day. Based on the Henry Bellamann novel and 1941 movie classic.

Kings Row was seen approximately every third week, being one of three rotating elements of *Warner Brothers Presents.*

KINGSTON: CONFIDENTIAL
Newspaper Drama
FIRST TELECAST: *March 23, 1977*
LAST TELECAST: *August 10, 1977*
BROADCAST HISTORY:
Mar 1977–Aug 1977, NBC Wed 10:00–11:00
CAST:
R. B. Kingston .... Raymond Burr
Tony Marino .... Art Hindle
Beth Kelly................. Pamela Hensley
Jessica Frazier................ Nancy Olson

San Francisco was the home base of the Frazier Group, a communications conglomerate that owned and operated 26 newspapers and 9 radio and TV stations around the country. Jessica Frazier was the chief operating officer and R. B. Kingston was one of her top executives, with a long history as one of the finest investigative reporters in the country. Despite his high status, Kingston was more than willing to leave the office and do his own digging to help unearth a particularly difficult or juicy story. His two young assistants, Tony and Beth, often went undercover to help track down useful information.

KIRBY STONE QUINTET, THE
see *Strictly for Laughs*

KIT CARSON
see *Adventures of Kit Carson, The*

KLEENEX SUMMER THEATRE
Dramatic Anthology
FIRST TELECAST: *July 5, 1955*
LAST TELECAST: *August 16, 1955*
BROADCAST HISTORY:
Jul 1955–Aug 1955, NBC Tue 9:00–9:30

Kleenex Summer Theatre alternated with *Clorets Summer Theatre* as a 1955 summer replacement series for *Fireside Theater*. The dramas shown were all reruns of episodes from *Four Star Playhouse*.

KLONDIKE
Adventure
FIRST TELECAST: *October 10, 1960*
LAST TELECAST: *February 6, 1961*
BROADCAST HISTORY:
Oct 1960–Feb 1961, NBC Mon 9:00–9:30
CAST:
Mike Halliday .... Ralph Taeger
Jeff Durain .... James Coburn
Kathy O'Hara .... Mari Blanchard
Goldie .... Joi Lansing

Skagway, Alaska, at the turn of the century, was the setting of this action-adventure series. In Alaska in search of gold and excitement during the famous gold rush of 1897–1899, rugged Mike Halliday spent much of his time trying to outwit Jeff Durain, a gambler and scoundrel whose efforts to make money often put him on the wrong side of the law. Durain owned and ran a hotel in Skagway that provided miners with a place to lose their earnings in games of chance that were not always on the up-and-up. The town's honest hotel was run by Kathy O'Hara, who often worked with Mike to foil Durain's illegal schemes. Mike was not quite ready to settle down with a good woman and raise a family and was involved with a number of ladies, including Durain's girlfriend and accomplice in crime, the beautiful but greedy Goldie.

KNIGHT RIDER
Adventure
FIRST TELECAST: *September 26, 1982*
LAST TELECAST: *August 8, 1986*
BROADCAST HISTORY:
Sep 1982, NBC Sun 8:00–10:00
Oct 1982–Aug 1983, NBC Fri 9:00–10:00
Aug 1983–Mar 1985, NBC Sun 8:00–9:00
Mar 1985–Apr 1985, NBC Fri 8:00–9:00
Apr 1985–Aug 1985, NBC Sun 8:00–9:00
Aug 1985–Dec 1985, NBC Fri 8:00–9:00
Jan 1986–Apr 1986, NBC Fri 9:00–10:00
May 1986–Aug 1986, NBC Fri 8:00–9:00
CAST:
Michael Knight .... David Hasselhoff
Devon Miles .... Edward Mulhare
Bonnie Barstow (1982–1983, 1984–1986)
.... Patricia McPherson
April Curtis (1983–1984) .... Rebecca Holden
Voice of KITT .... William Daniels
Reginald Cornelius III "RC3" (1985–1986)
.... Peter Parros

Brandon Tartikoff, youthful head of programming at NBC, once gave *California* magazine this version of the creation of *Knight Rider:* It seems he and one of his assistants were discussing the problems of casting handsome leading men in series, because many of them can't act. Why not have a series, they mused, called "The Man of Six Words," which would begin with the guy getting out of a woman's bed and saying "Thank you." Then he would chase down some villains and say "Freeze!" Finally the grateful almost-victims would thank him, and he would murmur, "You're welcome." End of show. In between, the car could do the talking.

The series that made it to the air as *Knight Rider* was scarcely less preposterous than that, but it was played with such a twinkle in the eye that viewers—especially kids—made it one of the hits of the 1982 season. The opening episode told the story of how a dying millionaire named Wilton Knight rescued a young undercover cop who had been shot in the face. After plastic surgery, officer Michael Young had a new face, a new identity (Michael Knight), and a new mission in life: to fight for law and justice in Knight's incredible super-car, the Knight Industries Two Thousand—or KITT, for short. It was love at first sight between Michael and KITT. The car, a sleek, black, customized Pontiac Trans-Am, was impervious to attack, could cruise at 300 mph, could leap up to 50 feet through the air, and was loaded with such armaments as flamethrowers, smoke bombs, and infrared sensing devices. Best of all, it could talk, and in fact had a personality all its own; peevish, a bit haughty, but totally protective of Michael. He could summon the car when in trouble, and it would come crashing through walls to get him.

Its deceased inventor had left behind a huge fortune to finance the crime-fighting, and a trusted associate, the suave Devon, to look after things. Based at a palatial estate, called somewhat grandly the Foundation for Law and Government, Michael (and often Devon) went forth each week, trailed by a large maintenance van that served as a sort of mobile command post. Rounding out the crew was a beautiful mechanic, variously Bonnie or April, and "RC3," a street-wise black mechanic who joined the team in the fall of 1985. (Behind the scenes, the same Hollywood customizers who

419

built Batman's Batmobile and the Green Hornet's Black Beauty worked on KITT.)

Though the gimmick in the series was the car, much of the show's appeal was due to actor David Hasselhoff, a tall, handsome former soap-opera heartthrob (on *The Young and The Restless*) who joked and kidded with his computerized companion. While he had more to say than "The Man of Six Words," his tight jeans, wavy hair, and laid-back style (his favorite phrase was "You got it") made women melt.

KNOTS LANDING
Drama
FIRST TELECAST: *December 20, 1979*
LAST TELECAST:
BROADCAST HISTORY:

Dec 1979–Mar 1980, CBS Thu 10:00–11:00
Jun 1980–Mar 1981, CBS Thu 10:00–11:00
Jun 1981–Oct 1981, CBS Thu 10:00–11:00
Nov 1981–Mar 1982, CBS Thu 9:00–10:00
Mar 1982–Mar 1983, CBS Thu 10:00–11:00
Jun 1983–Jun 1986, CBS Thu 10:00–11:00
Sep 1986–Nov 1986, CBS Thu 9:00–10:00
Nov 1986–   , CBS Thu 10:00–11:00 (OS)
CAST:

Gary Ewing .... Ted Shackelford
Valene Ewing................. Joan Van Ark
Sid Fairgate (1979–1981) .... Don Murray
Karen Fairgate MacKenzie ..... Michele Lee
Richard Avery (1979–1983).... John Pleshette
Laura Avery Sumner (1979–1987)
.... Constance McCashin
Kenny Ward (1979–1983) ... James Houghton
Ginger Ward (1979–1983) ...... Kim Lankford
Diana Fairgate (1979–1984) .. Claudia Lonow
Michael Fairgate................ Pat Petersen
Eric Fairgate (1979–1987) .... Steve Shaw
Jason Avery (1979–1980) .... Justin Dana
Jason Avery (1980–1982) .... Danny Gellis
Jason Avery (1983–1985) ...... Danny Ponce
Jason Avery (1986–1987) .. Matthew Newmark
Abby Cunningham Ewing (1980–   )
.... Donna Mills
Brian Cunningham (1980–1985)
.... Bobby Jacoby
Brian Cunningham (1986–   )
.... Brian Greene
Olivia Cunningham (1980–   )
.... Tonya Crowe
Judy Trent (1980–1981)............ Jane Elliot
Earl Trent (1980–1981)............ Paul Rudd
Sylvie (1980–1981)........... Louise Vallance
Linda Striker (1980–1981)....... Denise Galik
Roy Lance (1980–1982) .... Steven Hirsch
Lilimae Clements (1981–1987) .... Julie Harris
Scooter Warren (1981–1982)..... Allan Miller
Joe Cooper (1982–1983) .... Stephen Macht
Amy (1981–1983) .... Jill Cohen
M. (Mack) Patrick MacKenzie (1982–   )
.... Kevin Dobson
Wayne Harkness (1982) ...... Harry Northup
Ciji Dunne (1982–1983) .... Lisa Hartman

Jeff Munson (1982–1983) .... Jon Cypher
Chip Roberts (1982–1983) .. Michael Sabatino
Janet Baines (1983)............ Joanna Pettet
Mitchell Casey (1983) .... Edward Bell
Ben Gibson (1983–1987)..... Douglas Sheehan
Nick Morrison (1983–1984)...... Steve Kahan
Jim Westmont (1983) .... Joseph Hacker
Gregory Sumner (1983–   )
.... William Devane
Cathy Geary Rush (1983–1986)
.... Lisa Hartman
Mary-Frances Sumner (1983–1984)
.... Danielle Brisebois
Jane Sumner (1983–1984)...... Millie Perkins
Ray Geary (1984) .... Bruce Fairbairn
Mark St. Claire (1984)...... Joseph Chapman
Joshua Rush (1984–1985)....... Alec Baldwin
Carol (1984) .... Gigi Vorgan
P.K. Kelly (1984–1985) ..... Wendel Meldrum
Tom Jezik (1984–1985)............ Peter Fox
Rev. Kathrun (1984–1985) ..... Sandy Kenyon
Mary Kathrun (1984) ...... Whitney Kershaw
Paul Galveston (1984–1985) .... Howard Duff
Ruth Galveston (1985)......... Ava Gardner
John Coblentz (1985) .... Madison Mason
Harry Fisher (1985) .... Joe Regalbuto
Sheila Fisher (1985) .... Robin Ginsburg
Frank Elliot (1985) ..... Jonathan Goldsmith
Peter Hollister (1985–1987)....... Hunt Block
Jill Bennett (1985–   )......... Teri Austin
Linda Martin (1985–1986) ....Leslie Hope
Sylvia Lean (1986) .... Ruth Roman
Det. Behar (1986) .... Allen Williams
Paige Matheson (1986–   )
.... Nicollette Sheridan
Jean Hackney (1986–1987) .... Wendy Fulton
Tina (1986–   )................ Tina Lifford
Peggy (1986–   )....... Victoria Ann-Lewis
Marsha (1986–   ) .... Marcia Solomon
Anne W. Matheson (1987) .. Michelle Phillips
Al Baker (1987)............ Red Buttons
Bobby Gibson (1987–   )
.... Christian/Joseph Cousins
Betsy Gibson (1987–   )
.... Kathryn/Tiffany Lubran
Carlos (1987–   ) .... Carlos Cantu
Jody Campbell (1987–   )... Kristy Swanson
Barbara (1987–   )........... Ronne Troup
Ana (1987–   ).......... Movita Castenada
Johnny Rourke (1988–   )..... Peter Reckell
Patricia Williams (1988–   ).. Lynne Moody
Frank Williams (1988–   )...... Larry Riley
Julie Williams (1988–   )
.... Kent Masters-King
Harold Dyer (1988–   )..... Paul Carafotes
Manny Vasquez (1988–   ) ..... John Aprea

Hoping to ride the crest of its success with *Dallas*, CBS spun off this series featuring the black sheep of the Ewing family, Gary. Gary was a weak-willed reformed alcoholic who had deserted his wife, Val, and then remarried her and moved to Southern California to escape the formidable pressures of life with the Ewings in Dallas. All the principals in this series lived on the same cul-de-sac in the quiet little community of Knots Landing. In addition to being neighbors, their lives intertwined in other ways. Gary worked for Sid Fairgate, owner of Knots Landing Motors, the local classic car dealership. Sid and his wife Karen had three teenaged children. The other two couples on the cul-de-sac were young recording executive Kenny Ward and his attractive wife, Ginger, and Richard and Laura Avery. Richard was an obnoxious, aggressive, unprincipled attorney who was always lusting after other women and resented Laura's success selling real estate. One of her customers, who arrived in the fall of 1980, was Sid Fairgate's recently divorced sister, Abby Cunningham. She moved onto the cul-de-sac with her two kids and immediately began undermining the relationships of her married neighbors, spreading gossip about affairs, both real and imagined, and setting her own sights on Richard Avery. Gary, a member of Alcoholics Anonymous, sponsored a new member, Earl Trent, and ended up having an affair with Judy, Earl's passionate wife.

In the fall of 1981 Sid Fairgate was paralyzed and later died as the result of an auto accident, leaving his wife Karen to run Knots Landing Motors with Abby Cunningham and Gary Ewing. Abby started to set her sights on Gary, while his wife Val wrote a novel, *Capricorn Crude,* that was a thinly disguised chronicle of the manipulations of his family in the oil business. Eventually Gary divorced Val, married Abby, and inherited part of Jock Ewing's fortune. Val became quite a celebrity with her book and began dating reporter Ben Gibson.

Another plot involved Chip Roberts, who worked for Val's press agent and who was simultaneously having affairs with Diana Fairgate and Ciji Dunne, a pretty singer. When Ciji got pregnant, Chip killed her, but because of circumstantial evidence Gary Ewing was indicted for the crime. Diana and Chip skipped town together; later she returned alone and moved in with Abby. Chip was subsequently caught and convicted of Ciji's murder, escaped from prison, and died in a freak accident at Gary Ewing's ranch where he was hiding out with Diana.

Meanwhile, Richard Avery's marriage and career were falling apart. His wife Laura wanted to leave him but held off due to her pregnancy and his nervous breakdown. Richard's attempt to open a restaurant, "Daniel's," financed by Gary and Abby, was unsuccessful and his philandering with Abby finally caused Laura to divorce him. Abby, on the other hand, continued to build her power base. She had part of Knots Landing Motors, was married into Gary Ewing Enterprises (although living on Gary's ranch was something she could barely tolerate), was heavily into the Lotus Point real estate development, and was having another affair—this one with powerful, underworld-connected State Senator Gregory Sumner. Sumner was an old friend of Attorney Mack MacKenzie (Karen Fairgate's new husband); not anticipating honesty from a *Knots Landing* regular, he offered Mack a job as crime commissioner. When he realized that his friend could be a serious roadblock to his own schemes, Sumner sought to discredit Mack.

The 1984–1985 season brought problems for three of *Knots Landing*'s leading women. Karen was shot with a bullet meant for Gary, and was paralyzed for a period; Abby was taken hostage by St. Claire, who was eventually killed by Sumner; and Val gave birth to twins (by her ex, Gary). The babies were stolen from the hospital and sold in a black market scheme that took an entire season to unravel. Sen. Sumner continued his political machinations, pressuring Mack to drop his investigation of unscrupulous tycoon Paul Galveston (Sumner's father) and trying to force Gary out of the Empire Valley development project. The Senator also made a play for Laura, and they were married.

Handsome Joshua Rush (son of Lilimae, half-brother of Val) entered the scene as a preacher turned successful local TV personality, wooing Cathy and proposing to her on the air. However, when she got more fan mail than he did he had a mental breakdown and then committed suicide (or was it murder?). That's show biz. Other main stories in 1985–1986 involved young Olivia's bout with drugs; Val's rocky marriage to Ben; Cathy's flirtation with Ben; and more dirty doings at the Empire Valley project. Abby's latest conquest was Peter, an up-and-coming politico who claimed to be Sen. Sumner's brother.

Politics was a major focus in 1986–1987, as Gary ran against Peter for the Senate and lost both the campaign and his wife Abby to his opponent. Karen was kidnapped by Phil, who wanted to get even with her crimebusting husband Mack; and sexy young Paige, Mack and Anne's illegitimate daughter, caused problems for all. The young generation, in fact, was being seen more often on *Knots Landing.* Paige had affairs with Michael (Karen's son) and Peter, and there was a continuing story about Olivia's drug problem. Peter also tried to seduce Olivia, before he met a violent end at the close of the season.

The investigation of Peter's murder dominated the fall of 1987, with Abby confessing to cover for her daughter Olivia. (Actually, Paige did it.) Abby had by this time divorced Gary, receiving $2 million in the settlement, and had rekindled a romance with a long-ago lover named Charles Scott. Gary, now at liberty, took up with Jill, though viewers knew that Val would always be his true love. On the youth scene, Michael formed a rock band and a relationship with Jody, while both Paige and Olivia found themselves involved with seedy criminal types. Older cast members were gradually phased out. Ben disappeared in South America in early 1987, and Laura died of a brain tumor. She was mourned in unusual "improvised" episodes. Symbolically, her home on the cul-de-sac was then occupied by newcomers Patricia and Frank Williams and their young daughter Julie—all hiding out in the federal Witness Protection Program!

By 1988 none of the original four couples who lived on the cul-de-sac when *Knots Landing* premiered were still there, and together; only three of the eight spouses even remained with the show (Gary, Val, and Karen, all in new relationships). This willingness of *Knots Landing* to evolve, combined with first-rate writing and an emphasis on characters as real, relatable people, contributed to a growing perception in the late 1980s that this serial had become the best of the nighttime soaps.

There was a certain interplay between *Knots Landing* and *Dallas,* with Gary's brothers turning up occasionally in Knots Landing, while he and Valene made infrequent visits to Southfork, the Ewing ranch near Dallas, to see their daughter Lucy.

KOBB'S KORNER
Musical Variety
FIRST TELECAST: *September 29, 1948*
LAST TELECAST: *June 15, 1949*
BROADCAST HISTORY:
Sep 1948–Jan 1949, CBS Wed 8:00–8:30
Jan 1949–Feb 1949, CBS Thu 8:00–8:30
Feb 1949, CBS Wed 9:00–9:30
Mar 1949–Jun 1949, CBS Wed 9:30–10:00
REGULARS:
Stan Fritts and His Korn Kobblers
Hope Emerson
Jo Hurt
Betty Garde (1949)

This live series originated from New York but, if you could believe it, was supposed to come from Shufflebottom's General Store, U.S.A. The Korn Kobblers were a group of accomplished musicians who, in addition to playing straight music, used mouth harps, whistles, sirens, cowbells, jugs, washboards, and anything else that would make a noise. Actress Hope Emerson played Maw Shufflebottom, the owner of the general store, and Jo Hurt played her daughter Josiebelle. It was a little bit like a cross between *Hee Haw* and *Spike Jones* although it preceded them both, at least on television.

KODAK REQUEST PERFORMANCE
Dramatic Anthology
FIRST TELECAST: *April 13, 1955*
LAST TELECAST: *September 28, 1955*
BROADCAST HISTORY:
Apr 1955–Sep 1955, NBC Wed 8:00–8:30
HOST:
Jack Clark

The dramas presented on *Kodak Request Performance* were all reruns of episodes of dramatic series that had aired originally during the 1954–1955 television season, primarily on *Ford Theatre* and *Fireside Theater.* Jack Clark provided live introductions to the filmed dramas.

KODIAK
Police Drama
FIRST TELECAST: *September 13, 1974*
LAST TELECAST: *October 11, 1974*
BROADCAST HISTORY:
Sep 1974–Oct 1974, ABC Fri 8:00–8:30
CAST:
Cal "Kodiak" McKay . . . . Clint Walker
Abraham Lincoln Imhook. . . Abner Biberman
Mandy . . . . Maggie Blye

Clint Walker was a cop with an unusual beat in this short-lived series. Kodiak was a member of the Alaska State Patrol, responsible for 50,000 square miles of rugged country and all the criminals, avalanche victims, and squabbling miners contained therein. He worked alone most of the time, traveling by four-wheel-drive truck, snowmobile, on skis, or snowshoes, as appropriate. Abraham Lincoln Imhook was his Eskimo friend and confidant. Filmed on location in Alaska.

KOJAK
Police Drama
FIRST TELECAST: *October 24, 1973*
LAST TELECAST: *April 15, 1978*
BROADCAST HISTORY:
Oct 1973–Sep 1974, CBS Wed 10:00–11:00
Sep 1974–Sep 1975, CBS Sun 8:30–9:30
Sep 1975–Jan 1977, CBS Sun 9:00–10:00
Jan 1977–Sep 1977, CBS Mon 10:00–11:00
Sep 1977–Dec 1977, CBS Sun 10:00–11:00
Dec 1977–Apr 1978, CBS Sat 10:00–11:00
CAST:
Lt. Theo Kojak. . . . . Telly Savalas
Frank McNeil. . . . . Dan Frazer
Lt. Bobby Crocker . . . . Kevin Dobson
Det. Stavros . . . . George Savalas
Det. Rizzo (1974–1977). . . . . Vince Conti
Det. Saperstein (1974–1977) . . . . Mark Russell

When they started out together in the New York Police Department, Theo Kojak and Frank McNeil had worked closely together and, for a number of years, been partners. Over the years Frank had worked his way up the hierarchy to the point where he was now chief of detectives for the 13th Precinct in the Manhattan South district. Kojak, who had a cynical sense of humor and was determined to do things his way regardless of what his bosses thought, was now working for him. Kojak was outspoken and streetwise, and was not above stretching the literal interpretation of the law if it would help him crack a case. Working closely with him was plainclothes detective Bobby Crocker, as close to a regular partner as he had.

The supporting role of Detective Stavros was

played by Telly Savalas's brother George who, during the first two seasons the show was on the air, was billed as Demosthenes in the credits rather than by his real name. Starting with the 1976–1977 season, considerable location filming was done in New York with Kojak seen all over the city licking his trademark lollipops. *Kojak* received much favorable publicity from police departments around the country for its realistic portrayal of police work.

KOLCHAK: THE NIGHT STALKER
Occult
FIRST TELECAST: *September 13, 1974*
LAST TELECAST: *August 30, 1975*
BROADCAST HISTORY:
 Sep 1974–Dec 1974, ABC Fri 10:00–11:00
 Jan 1975–Aug 1975, ABC Fri 8:00–9:00
CAST:
 Carl Kolchak .... Darren McGavin
 Tony Vincenzo .... Simon Oakland
 Ron Updyke .... Jack Grinnage
 Emily Cowles................ Ruth McDevitt
 Gordy Spangler................ John Fiedler
 Monique Marmelstein .... Carol Ann Susi

Stories of the bizarre and supernatural, seen through the eyes of Carl Kolchak, crime reporter for Chicago's Independent News Service. The series was an odd mixture of reality and fantasy, with wisecracking reporter Kolchak and his common-sense investigations juxtaposed with inexplicable happenings. Instead of the usual hoods, Kolchak kept running into vampires, werewolves, zombies, and other esoteric phenomena. If he was sent to cover a crooked politician, he would find that the man had sold his soul to the Devil—literally. If he was covering a museum opening, a 500-year-old Aztec mummy would come to life. Kolchak's main trouble was convincing his skeptical editor, Tony Vincenzo, to print his incredible revelations.
 Kolchak was based on the highly successful TV-movie of the same name. It premiered, appropriately enough, on Friday the 13th, but lasted for only a single season.

KOLLEGE OF MUSICAL KNOWLEDGE, THE
 see *Kay Kyser's Kollege of Musical Knowledge*

KOPYCATS, THE
 see *ABC Comedy Hour*

KOVACS UNLIMITED
 see *Ernie Kovacs Show, The*

KRAFT MUSIC HALL, THE
Musical Variety
FIRST TELECAST: *September 13, 1967*
LAST TELECAST: *May 12, 1971*
BROADCAST HISTORY:
 Sep 1967–May 1969, NBC Wed 9:00–10:00
 Sep 1969–May 1971, NBC Wed 9:00–10:00

ANNOUNCER:
 Ed Herlihy
ORCHESTRA:
 Peter Matz
CHOREOGRAPHY:
 Peter Gennaro

From 1933 to 1949 *The Kraft Music Hall* was one of the most popular variety shows on radio. Bing Crosby was probably its most famous host, at the helm from 1936–1946. When Kraft moved into television in 1947, it switched to weekly dramatic productions as *Kraft Television Theatre*. The music-hall format first appeared on television in the 1958–1959 season as *Milton Berle Starring in the Kraft Music Hall* and *Kraft Music Hall Presents: The Dave King Show*. *Perry Como's Kraft Music Hall* filled the Wednesday 9:00–10:00 P.M. hour for the next four seasons and there was a *Kraft Summer Music Hall* in 1966.
 All of the above variations of *The Kraft Music Hall* had regular hosts, but beginning in the fall of 1967 each program became self-contained and featured a different host. During its first season there were a number of "theme" programs. Rock Hudson narrated "The Hollywood Musical," Lorne Greene hosted the musical potpourri "How the West Was Swung," George Burns did "Tin Pan Alley Today," and Dinah Shore did "The Nashville Sound." Although the title emphasized music, there were telecasts that were all comedy—"Woody Allen Looks at 1967" and Groucho Marx hosting "A Taste of Funny." In the spring and summer of 1968 there were periods when the same host appeared for a number of weeks—Eddy Arnold with the series subtitled "County Fair" from April 24–June 5; John Davidson for the next three weeks; and Ed McMahon from July 3–September 4. While Eddy Arnold was hosting there was one regular along with him, comic John Byner.
 Several performers who starred during the series' first season appeared during each of the succeeding seasons. In addition to Eddy Arnold, Don Rickles, and Alan King—the three stars who would appear most often throughout *The Kraft Music Hall*'s run—Steve Lawrence and Eydie Gorme were annual visitors. Others with multiple telecasts were Mitzi Gaynor, Bobby Darin, Roy Rogers, and Dale Evans, Wayne Newton, and Johnny Cash. The Country Music Association Awards were telecast each year on *The Kraft Music Hall* and it was on this series that the Friars Club Roasts (later to become a semi-regular series of specials as "The Dean Martin Celebrity Roasts") first had national exposure. Johnny Carson, Milton Berle, Jack Benny, Don Rickles, and Jerry Lewis were all "roasted" over the years. During the last season there were two appearances by the Kopycats, talented impressionists who were later featured on *The ABC Comedy Hour*.
 Summer replacements for the 1967–1971 ver-

sions of the *Kraft Music Hall* were Sandler and Young, and Don Ho in 1969, and English star Des O'Connor in 1970 and 1971.

KRAFT MUSIC HALL PRESENTS SANDLER & YOUNG
Variety
FIRST TELECAST: *May 14, 1969*
LAST TELECAST: *August 13, 1969*
BROADCAST HISTORY:
May 1969–Aug 1969, NBC Wed 9:00–10:00
REGULARS:
Tony Sandler
Ralph Young
Jack Parnell and His Orchestra
Judy Carne
Norman Wisdom

The 1969 summer replacement for *The Kraft Music Hall* was this taped variety show from London, hosted by singers Tony Sandler and Ralph Young. A regular feature of the series was "Hands Across the Sea," a combination of messages to America from London and a salute to a foreign country. Des O'Connor was originally slated to host this series. He got his chance in a London-originated summer series of his own during the following two summers (see *Kraft Music Hall Presents the Des O'Connor Show*).

KRAFT MUSIC HALL PRESENTS: THE DAVE KING SHOW
Variety
FIRST TELECAST: *May 20, 1959*
LAST TELECAST: *September 23, 1959*
BROADCAST HISTORY:
May 1959–Sep 1959, NBC Wed 9:00–9:30
REGULARS:
Dave King
Sid Greene
Dick Hills
Alan MacAteer
Jim Boles
Barney Martin
Bobby Gale
The Jerry Packer Singers
The Bill Foster Dancers
Vic Schoen Orchestra

English comedian/singer Dave King made his American television debut in this summer variety series. The format varied from music to skits, comic monologues, and pantomime, depending on the talents of his weekly guest stars. The variety was reflected in the show's theme song—"Anything Goes." One unusual aspect of this series was that its two writers, Sid Greene and Dick Hills, were also regular members of the on-air cast.

KRAFT MUSIC HALL PRESENTS THE DES O'CONNOR SHOW
Variety

FIRST TELECAST: *May 20, 1970*
LAST TELECAST: *September 1, 1971*
BROADCAST HISTORY:
May 1970–Sep 1970, NBC Wed 9:00–10:00
Jun 1971–Sep 1971, NBC Wed 9:00–10:00
REGULARS:
Des O'Connor
Jack D. Douglas
The MacGregor Brothers (1970)
Jim Coulton and Rex (1970)
Patrick Newell (1970)
The Mike Sammes Singers
Jack Parnell and His Orchestra
Joe Baker (1971)
Connie Stevens (1971)
The New Faces (1971)

British TV personality Des O'Connor was the host and star of this London-originated summer replacement for *The Kraft Music Hall*. With Des was his long-time partner, Jack D. Douglas, whose regular role on the series was that of Alf Ippittimus, a stage-struck buffoon. When the series returned for its second summer run in 1971, the title was shortened to *The Des O'Connor Show* and included two new recurring weekly features—"Dandy Sandy" and "I Say I Say." The former was a satire on a children's television show and the latter a situation in which members of the cast would interrupt Des' attempt to recite something with snappy one-line jokes.

KRAFT MYSTERY THEATER
Dramatic Anthology
FIRST TELECAST: *June 14, 1961*
LAST TELECAST: *September 25, 1963*
BROADCAST HISTORY:
Jun 1961–Sep 1961, NBC Wed 9:00–10:00
Jun 1962–Sep 1962, NBC Wed 9:00–10:00
Jun 1963–Sep 1963, NBC Wed 9:00–10:00
HOST:
Frank Gallop (1961)

Filmed dramatic-anthology series, which served as summer replacement for *Perry Como's Kraft Music Hall.* The 1961 version consisted of mystery-suspense dramas, most of them filmed in England, originally for English television and theatrical distribution. Frank Gallop was host for the series. In 1962 American films shot at the Desilu Studios in Hollywood were used, some of them originals and some having already been seen on CBS' *Westinghouse Desilu Playhouse* from 1958–1960. Many top Hollywood actors were seen. In 1963 the films were provided by Hollywood's Revue Studios, some of them having been aired previously on *Alcoa Playhouse* from 1961–1963.

KRAFT MYSTERY THEATRE
see *Kraft Television Theatre* for 1958 series

KRAFT SUMMER MUSIC HALL, THE
Variety

FIRST TELECAST: *June 6, 1966*
LAST TELECAST: *August 29, 1966*
BROADCAST HISTORY:
Jun 1966–Aug 1966, NBC Mon 9:00–10:00
REGULARS:
John Davidson
George Carlin
Jackie and Gayle
The Five King Cousins
The Lively Set
Jimmie Haskell Orchestra

Handsome young singer John Davidson was the host and star of this summer variety series which placed its emphasis on youth. Most of the guest stars, as well as the series regulars, were performers in their 20s. Comedian George Carlin, in addition to performing on the show himself, wrote all of the comedy material. The Five King Cousins were members of the huge King family, which had had its own series on ABC.

KRAFT SUSPENSE THEATER
Dramatic Anthology
FIRST TELECAST: *October 10, 1963*
LAST TELECAST: *September 9, 1965*
BROADCAST HISTORY:
Oct 1963–Sep 1965, NBC Thu 10:00–11:00

Kraft, which had used both dramatic and musical offerings to promote its products on TV over the years, mixed the two formats in the 1963 and 1964 seasons. The emphasis was on drama, preempted by a Perry Como *Kraft Music Hall* special approximately once a month, all in the Thursday 10:00–11:00 P.M. time period (this in itself was a major change, as Kraft had "owned" the Wednesday 9:00–10:00 P.M. hour on NBC for the previous 15 years).

The dramas, which were filmed in Hollywood, employed top-name talent, with Lee Marvin, Gig Young, and Lloyd Bridges headlining during the first month that the series was on the air. Most of the plots concerned murder, psychological terror, or other stories of danger and mystery. Among these was "Rapture at Two Forty," presented in April 1965, the pilot for the later series *Run For Your Life.*

KRAFT TELEVISION THEATRE
Dramatic Anthology
FIRST TELECAST: *May 7, 1947*
LAST TELECAST: *October 1, 1958*
BROADCAST HISTORY:
May 7, 1947–Dec 1947, NBC Wed 7:30–8:30
Jan 1948–Oct 1958, NBC Wed 9:00–10:00 (OS)
Oct 1953–Jan 1955, ABC Thu 9:30–10:30
ANNOUNCER:
Ed Herlihy (1947–1955)
Charles Stark (1955)
REGULAR PRODUCERS/DIRECTORS:
Stanley Quinn
Maury Holland

Harry Hermann
Richard Dunlap
Fielder Cook
William Graham
Norman Morgan
David Susskind
Robert Herridge
Alex March
George Roy Hill
Buzz Kulik

Kraft Foods Co. was one of the major supporters of live television drama during the 1950s, before switching to musical offerings in 1958. The *Kraft Television Theatre* was one of television's most prestigious showcases, winning top ratings and many awards, and becoming a Wednesday night institution. By the end of its run, more than 650 plays, drama and comedy, both originals and adaptations for TV, had been presented. At one time *two* Kraft Theatre series were airing simultaneously on NBC and ABC. All of these plays were live (although kinescopes and a very few videotapes were made for delayed transmission purposes), so most of these dramatic presentations are lost to us today.

Kraft skimped on nothing. The casts were large, the sets often elaborate, and the playwrights and producers first-rate. One "event" production in 1956 about the sinking of the *Titanic* almost seemed to have an actor for each of the 1,502 souls who went down with that ill-fated ship! (Actually there were 107 in the cast.) A brief sampling of the actors and actresses who starred over the years would include E. G. Marshall (frequently), Jack Lemmon, Cyril Ritchard (his first U.S. TV appearance, in 1951), Rod Steiger, James Dean, Lee Remick, Art Carney, Joanne Woodward, Grace Kelly, Anthony Perkins—and many, many more. A number of performers who would later become film and TV stars gained early exposure on *Kraft,* including Cloris Leachman (1949), Martin Milner (1949), and Paul Newman (1952).

Scripts ranged from the classics (Shakespeare, Ibsen) to Tennessee Williams, Agatha Christie, and Rod Serling. Many new or unknown writers were given exposure too, and during the 1955–1956 season Kraft offered a $50,000 prize for the best original play presented during the year. Judges were Helen Hayes, Walter Kerr, and Maxwell Anderson. The prize went to William Noble for "Snap Finger Creek," telecast on February 22, 1956.

During the mid-1950s quite a few youth-oriented episodes were presented, mostly dramas revolving around popular music. Among the popular singers playing dramatic (and singing) roles were Gisele MacKenzie (1955), Ferlin Husky (1957), and Julius LaRosa (1957). Even more rock-oriented were actor-singer Tommy Sands, who starred in an Elvis Presley–type role in "The Singing Idol" in January 1957 (the featured song on this telecast, "Teenage Crush," went on to become a million-selling record); and Sal Mineo, who introduced his biggest hit, "Start Movin'," on the Kraft dramatic presentation "Drummer Man" in May 1957.

Another notable landmark in the series' history was the use of color, which began intermittently in April 1954 and became permanent in July 1956.

In April 1958 *Kraft Television Theatre* was taken over by a new production company and its title was shortened to *Kraft Theatre*. In June 1958 the title was changed again to *Kraft Mystery Theatre* (not to be confused with the filmed series of the same name in the early 1960s).

At the end of Kraft's long run in live TV drama, *TV Guide* summoned up a few statistics. In 11½ years *Kraft* had presented 650 plays culled from 18,845 scripts, starred or featured 3,955 actors and actresses in 6,750 roles, used up 26,000 hours of rehearsal time and employed 5,236 sets. Costs had risen from $3,000 for the first production on May 7, 1947 (a play called "Double Door" starring John Baragrey) to $165,000 by 1958. Ed Rice, the script editor for *Kraft* throughout the program's run, observed that the entire studio facilities used in 1947 were half the size of the space used just to produce the commercials in 1958.

But *Kraft's* contribution to television is not measured in statistics alone. Quite simply, the series presented superlative live drama throughout television's "Golden Age."

KREISLER BANDSTAND
Music
FIRST TELECAST: *March 21, 1951*
LAST TELECAST: *June 13, 1951*
BROADCAST HISTORY:
   Mar 1951–Jun 1951, ABC Wed 8:30–9:00
EMCEE:
   Fred Robbins

Big-name dance bands were featured each week on this program, hosted by New York disc jockey Fred Robbins. Among those appearing were Ralph Flanagan, Sammy Kaye, Duke Ellington, Benny Goodman, Art Mooney, and Cab Calloway, as well as such singers as Patti Page, Ella Fitzgerald, and Margaret Whiting.

KRYPTON FACTOR, THE
Quiz/Audience Participation
FIRST TELECAST: *August 7, 1981*
LAST TELECAST: *September 4, 1981*
BROADCAST HISTORY:
   Aug 1981–Sep 1981, ABC Fri 8:30–9:00
HOST:
   Dick Clark

Four contestants really worked for their prizes on this summer quiz show. First the four faced a memory test: after seeing clips from a current movie, they had to recall specific dialogue and identify one of the actors in a lineup with impostors. Then their reflexes were challenged by a difficult video or computer game; their physical stamina by a race through an obstacle course in speedboats, dune buggies, or motortrikes; their mental agility through brain-teaser problems and general-knowledge questions. If they survived all that, they had a shot at the $50,000 grand prize in the championship finals held on the last telecast.

A contestant's score was called his or her "Krypton Factor."

KUDA BUX, HINDU MYSTIC
Magic
FIRST TELECAST: *March 25, 1950*
LAST TELECAST: *June 17, 1950*
BROADCAST HISTORY:
   Mar 1950–Jun 1950, CBS Sat 6:30–6:45
REGULARS:
   Kuda Bux (real name: Khudah Bukhsh)
   Rex Marshall
   Janet Tyler

Kuda Bux, "the man with the X-ray eyes," was one of the favorite novelty acts on early television. After appearing as a regular on several series (including the appropriately named *I'd Like to See*), he had his own 15-minute network show in the spring of 1950. Feats of magic, mind reading, and other illusions were performed weekly by the man from Kashmir, India (who had been plying his trade in Europe for years before coming to the U.S.). The highlight always came when Kuda Bux's eyes were wrapped in bandages, tin foil, lead, and just about anything one might conceive of. On one show, sponsored by a bakery, he had his eyes covered with baker's dough. He would then proceed to "see" through it all to thread needles, hit bull's-eyes, and perform other feats.

Every viewer had a theory about how he did it. One lad said it was obvious that Kuda saw through his nose. A lady said Kuda marked off places on the floor just before he was blindfolded, and then just felt his way around. A little boy wrote in to say he believed Kuda swiveled his head completely around, and then saw out the back. Kuda Bux just laughed, and looked mystifying.

Rex Marshall served as announcer and interpreter on this series, and Janet Tyler was Kuda's helper and assistant.

KUKLA, FRAN & OLLIE
Children's
FIRST TELECAST: *November 29, 1948*
LAST TELECAST: *August 31, 1957*
BROADCAST HISTORY:
   Nov 1948–Nov 1951, NBC Mon–Fri 7:00–7:30 (OS)
   Nov 1951–Jun 1952, NBC Mon–Fri 7:00–7:15
   Sep 1954–Aug 1957, ABC Mon–Fri 7:00–7:15 (OS)
HOSTESS:
   Fran Allison
PUPPETEER:
   Burr Tillstrom

MUSICAL DIRECTOR:
  Jack Fascinato
PUPPETS:
  Kukla
  Ollie (Oliver J. Dragon)
  Fletcher Rabbit
  Mme. Ophelia Oglepuss
  Buelah Witch
  Cecil Bill
  Col. Crackie
  Mercedes
  Dolores Dragon (1950–1957)
  Olivia Dragon (1952–1957)

This whimsical puppet show was one of television's longest-running and most loved children's programs. It was always done live, and the dialogue was unscripted, with Fran and her little friends reacting to each other in an entirely spontaneous manner.

Burr Tillstrom created Kukla, the first of his "Kuklapolitan Players," in 1936. The name Kukla was supposedly bestowed by the famous Russian ballerina Tamara Toumanova when she first saw the puppet perform (it means "doll" in Russian). The Kuklapolitan troupe was seen on experimental television as early as 1939, and the *Kukla, Fran & Ollie* series (originally known as *Junior Jamboree*) began locally on Chicago's WBKB-TV on October 13, 1947. It was fed to NBC's newly established Midwest network beginning in November 1948, and as soon as coaxial cables were opened to the East Coast (1949) and West Coast (1951) it was seen live in those regions as well.

The members of the Kuklapolitan Players were as follows: Kukla, a solemn, bulb-nosed little fellow with a perpetually worried expression, who knew nothing of his own past; Fran, a Chicago actress and singer, and the only live character seen (the puppets performed on a miniature stage, with Fran standing in front of it); Oliver J. Dragon, a carefree, extroverted, one-toothed dragon who was born in Vermont, where his parents ran Dragon Retreat (there had been no fire-breathing dragons in Ollie's family since his great-great-great-great-grandfather swam the Hellespont, gulped some water, and doused the flame); Fletcher Rabbit, the mailman, whose ears drooped so badly they had to be starched for formal occasions; Ophelia Oglepuss, a haughty ex-opera star; Buelah Witch, who had studied electronics and who patrolled the coaxial cable, while not buzzing around on her jet-propelled broomstick; Cecil Bill, the stage manager who spoke a language all his own; Col. Crackie, the long-winded Southern-Gentleman emcee of the company, and Mme. Oglepuss' escort; Mercedes, the troupe's little girl; Dolores Dragon, infant daughter of Ollie's long-lost Uncle Dorchester (Ollie considered her a horrible little monster); and Olivia Dragon, Ollie's elderly mother, who had hair 75 yards long, *two* fine teeth, and a sharp New England accent.

In addition to episodes focusing on day-to-day experiences and songs, the Players sometimes presented full-dress productions, ranging from mild satires ("Martin Dragon, Private Tooth") to established operettas. *The Mikado*, with Kukla as Nanki Poo, Fran as Yum Yum, and Ollie as the Lord High Executioner, was an annual event for several years. There were also original musical plays, such as *St. George and the Dragon*, presented in June 1953, complete with musical accompaniment by Arthur Fiedler and the Boston Pops and Boston Mayor John B. Hines as special guest. This show was repeated in August 1953 as one of the first experimental telecasts in compatible color.

In addition to its prime-time telecasts, listed above, *Kukla, Fran & Ollie* appeared Sunday afternoons on NBC from August 1952 to June 1954; in a five-minute week-day spot on NBC from September 1961 to June 1962; on PBS (Public Television) from 1969 to 1971; and in a syndicated version during the 1975–1976 season.

KUNG FU
Western
FIRST TELECAST: *October 14, 1972*
LAST TELECAST: *June 28, 1975*
BROADCAST HISTORY:

  Oct 1972–Nov 1972, ABC Sat 8:00–9:00
  Jan 1973–Aug 1974, ABC Thu 9:00–10:00
  Sep 1974–Oct 1974, ABC Sat 9:00–10:00
  Nov 1974–Jan 1975, ABC Fri 8:00–9:00
  Jan 1975–Jun 1975, ABC Sat 8:00–9:00

CAST:

  Kwai Chang Caine . . . . David Carradine
  Master Po . . . . Keye Luke
  Master Kan . . . . Philip Ahn
  Caine (as a youth) . . . . Radames Pera
  Margit McLean . . . . Season Hubley

*Occasional

Kung Fu could probably best be classified as a philosophical Western. It attracted quite a bit of notoriety and a cult following in the early 1970s, due to its unusual protagonist. Caine was a shaven-headed Buddhist monk, and a hunted man. He had been born in China in the mid-1800s of Chinese and American parents, and was raised as an orphan by the monks of Shaolin Temple. They tutored him in a mystic philosophy of internal harmony and the "oneness of all things," and a code of nonviolence. They also taught him the martial arts of kung fu—just in case.

Then one day young Caine was involved in an incident in which he was forced to kill a member of the Chinese royal family. Fleeing China, he landed in the American West where he began a search for a long-lost brother—while he himself was pursued by Chinese imperial agents and American bounty hunters.

Besides his background, there were many other unusual things about this particular Western hero.

He spoke very little, uttering occasional cryptic statements about the nature of being and universal harmony ("Remember," his teachers had said, "the wise man walks always with his head bowed, humble, like the dust."); his use, when cornered, of the ancient Chinese martial arts instead of a gun; his pariah status—a Chinaman, as well as a hunted man. *Kung Fu* used many gimmicks to lend it a surreal aspect, such as slow-motion photography, and included frequent flashbacks to Caine's days as a youth in China (in which his teachers, Master Po and Master Kan, appeared, as well as Caine as a young boy). Caine was usually a loner, although in the final season an American cousin, Margit, began to make occasional appearances.

The star, David Carradine, was responsible for much of the publicity surrounding this show. A member of a respected theatrical family (his father, John Carradine, had appeared in many famous movies of the 1930s and 1940s), David dropped out of Hollywood's glittering world and lived a decidedly unconventional life in a ramshackle old house in the hills, reflecting the same philosophy of mysticism and "oneness with nature" that Caine represented.

Kung Fu, incidentally, translates roughly as "accomplishment technique," and is China's ancient science of personal combat, from which karate and judo are derived. It enjoyed quite a vogue in the U.S. during the late 1960s and early 1970s as a result of the movies of Chinese-American actor Bruce Lee.

L

L. A. LAW
Law Drama
FIRST TELECAST: *October 3, 1986*
LAST TELECAST:
BROADCAST HISTORY:
  Oct 1986–Nov 1986, NBC Fri 10:00–11:00
  Dec 1986–   , NBC Thu 10:00–11:00
CAST:
  Leland McKenzie . . . . Richard Dysart
  Douglas Brackman, Jr. . . . . Alan Rachins
  Michael Kuzak . . . . Harry Hamlin
  Dep. D.A. Grace Van Owen . . . . Susan Dey
  Ann Kelsey . . . . Jill Eikenberry
  Arnie Becker . . . . Corbin Bernsen
  Stuart Markowitz . . . . Michael Tucker
  Victor Sifuentes . . . . Jimmy Smits
  Abby Perkins . . . . Michele Greene
  Roxanne Melman . . . . Susan Ruttan
  Elizabeth Brand . . . . Ellen Drake
  *Sheila Brackman . . . . Joanna Frank
  *Hilda Brunschweiger . . . . Patricia Huston
  *Iris Hubbard (1986–1987) . . . . . . Cynthia Harris
  Benny Stulwicz (1987–   ) . . . . . Larry Drake
  Jonathan Rollins (1987–   )
    . . . . Brian Underwood

*Occasional

This critically acclaimed ensemble drama was
one of the hits of the 1986 season. Created by
Steven Bochco (creator of *Hill Street Blues*) and
Terry Louise Fisher (producer of *Cagney and
Lacey*, and a former Deputy D.A. herself), it
looked like *Hill Street* in a fancy law office, with
many characters and stories intertwined in each
episode. The high-powered Los Angeles law firm
of McKenzie, Brackman, Chaney and Kuzak took
on cases of all types, criminal and civil, usually
for high fees (though they also did some "pro
bono" work for the poor). Leland McKenzie was
the esteemed, fatherly senior partner; Brackman,
the vain, insufferable, balding partner struggling
to fill his late father's formidable shoes; Kuzak,
the savvy but compassionate younger partner;
Van Owen, the idealistic Deputy D.A. who was
Kuzak's lover and sometime courtroom opponent;
Ann, another idealistic attorney; Stuart, the firm's
nebbishy little tax attorney, who had a heart of
gold and also had the hots for Ann; Arnie, the
sleazy, womanizing divorce lawyer (whose object
was often to create discord in order to produce a
more profitable case); Victor, the uptight young
hispanic brought into the firm to meet racial
quotas, and he knew it; Abby, the unsure-of-her-
self young intern; and Roxanne, the motherly receptionist. Added in early 1987 was Benny, a retarded office worker—one of the few continuing

portrayals in TV series history of a retarded person.
Plenty of office politics and sexual adventures
were mixed in with the cases (Markowitz and
Kelsey angling to become partners, Kuzak lusting
after Van Owen, Markowitz after Kelsey, Becker
after everybody). Perhaps the series' most publicized early episode was the one in which a biga-
mist-client taught Stuart a secret sexual maneuver
guaranteed to melt down any woman—the
"Venus Butterfly." Viewers never learned what it
was, but Ann was his.

LADIES BE SEATED
Quiz/Audience Participation
FIRST TELECAST: *April 22, 1949*
LAST TELECAST: *June 10, 1949*
BROADCAST HISTORY:
  Apr 1949–Jun 1949, ABC Fri 8:30–9:00
EMCEE:
  Tom Moore
ASSISTANT:
  Phil Patton

This TV version of the long-running radio show
featured a quiz and penalty stunts for members of
the studio audience. The stunts were similar to
those generally found on such shows, such as a
blindfolded couple after an apple on a string, a
man racing to put on women's clothes, etc. From
Chicago.

LADIES' MAN
Situation Comedy
FIRST TELECAST: *October 27, 1980*
LAST TELECAST: *February 21, 1981*
BROADCAST HISTORY:
  Oct 1980–Jan 1981, CBS Mon 8:30–9:00
  Feb 1981, CBS Sat 9:30–10:00
CAST:
  Alan Thackeray . . . . Lawrence Pressman
  Amy Thackeray . . . . Natasha Ryan
  Elaine Holstein . . . . Louise Sorel
  Betty Brill . . . . Karen Morrow
  Gretchen . . . . Simone Griffeth
  Susan . . . . Allison Argo
  Andrea Gibbons . . . . Betty Kennedy
  Reggie . . . . Herb Edelman

It seemed as if everyone in Alan Thackeray's life
was a woman. He was a single parent, raising a
precocious eight-year-old daughter (Amy), and
often had to seek the advice of Betty, a friendly
housewife who lived in his apartment building.
His job was that of a feature writer for *Women's
Life* magazine, where his boss was sophisticated,
dominant Elaine Holstein, and his co-workers, all
extremely attractive, were serious Gretchen, militant feminist Susan, and romantic Andrea. His
first assignment there was to write an article
called "Sexual Harassment and the Working
Woman," a subject for which firsthand research

was a little difficult. The only other male around was *Women's Life*'s harried bookkeeper, Reggie.

LADY BLUE
Police Drama
FIRST TELECAST: *September 15, 1985*
LAST TELECAST: *January 25, 1986*
BROADCAST HISTORY:
Sep 1985, ABC Sun 9:00–11:00
Sep 1985–Oct 1985, ABC Thu 9:00–10:00
Nov 1985–Jan 1986, ABC Sat 9:00–10:00
CAST:
Det. Katy Mahoney .... Jamie Rose
Chief Det. Terry McNichols ... Danny Aiello
Sgt. Gina Ginelli .... Ron Dean
Cassady.................... Bruce A. Young
Capt. Flynn.................... Ralph Foody

This tough lady detective reminded a lot of critics of someone else ("Skirty Harry"? "Dirty Harriet"?). Working the seedier side of Chicago, she tracked down drug pushers, money launderers, rapists, and other slime, blasting away with her .357 magnum more often than Internal Affairs would have liked (but, of course, those she blew away were always guilty). Though she could be reasonably sexy, the violence in her life tended to get in the way of any truly sensitive relationships. Terry was her worried-but-supportive boss, and Gina a fellow officer.

Filmed on location in Chicago.

LAMB'S GAMBOL, THE
Musical Variety
FIRST TELECAST: *February 27, 1949*
LAST TELECAST: *May 22, 1949*
BROADCAST HISTORY:
Feb 1949–Mar 1949, NBC Sun 8:30–9:00
Mar 1949–May 1949, NBC Sun 8:00–8:30

Musical variety program using the resources of New York's famed theatrical association, the Lamb's Club. Broadway stars, old vaudevillians, and newcomers appeared each week to do their turns, or to reverse roles (such as a tragedian doing a song-and-dance routine). A different host presided each week, and there were no regulars.

LANCER
Western
FIRST TELECAST: *September 24, 1968*
LAST TELECAST: *September 9, 1971*
BROADCAST HISTORY:
Sep 1968–Jun 1970, CBS Tue 7:30–8:30
May 1971–Sep 1971, CBS Thu 8:00–9:00
CAST:
Johnny Madrid Lancer .... James Stacy
Scott Lancer............... Wayne Maunder
Murdoch Lancer .... Andrew Duggan
Teresa O'Brien .... Elizabeth Baur
Jelly Hoskins (1969–1970) ...... Paul Brinegar

Set in California during the 1870s, *Lancer* was the story of the struggles of a landowner against locals who were trying to take over his property by force. Old Murdoch Lancer was no longer able to defend his cattle and sheep ranch in the San Joaquin Valley by himself, and even trying to run it with only the help of his attractive young ward, Teresa, had become difficult. At his behest his two sons (from different marriages) came to the ranch to help their father. The half brothers had never met each other and had widely divergent backgrounds. Johnny was a drifter/gunfighter who had spent most of his life wandering around the border towns of the Southwest. Scott was a sophisticated college graduate who had been living in Boston. Despite their differences, they learned to respect each other and help their father manage his vast real estate holdings. Jelly Hoskins, a crochety old ranch hand, became a regular member of the cast for the second season. The episodes telecast during the summer of 1971 were all reruns.

LAND OF THE GIANTS
Science Fiction
FIRST TELECAST: *September 22, 1968*
LAST TELECAST: *September 6, 1970*
BROADCAST HISTORY:
Sep 1968–Sep 1970, ABC Sun 7:00–8:00
CAST:
Capt. Steve Burton .... Gary Conway
Mark Wilson .... Don Matheson
Barry Lockridge .... Stefen Arngrim
Dan Erikson .... Don Marshall
Valerie Scott .... Deanna Lund
Betty Hamilton .... Heather Young
Cdr. Alexander Fitzhugh....... Kurt Kasznar
Inspector Kobrick.............. Kevin Hagen
CREATOR/PRODUCER:
Irwin Allen

This science-fiction fantasy concerned seven very small people in a very large world. Seven Earthlings had been on a suborbital flight from the U.S. to London in the mid-1980s when their craft was drawn into a "space warp." They landed in a strange world, much like Earth but with inhabitants 12 times their size. As the space castaways attempted to repair their rocketship in order to try and get home, they were continually menaced by giant children, huge pets and insects, and inhabitants who would exhibit them as freaks or experiment on them.

Capt. Steve Burton, his co-pilot Dan Erikson, and stewardess Betty Hamilton made up the crew of the lost craft, while on the passenger roster were engineer-tycoon Mark Wilson, jet-set (rocket-set?) heiress Valerie Scott, 12-year-old Barry and his dog Chipper, and mystery passenger Cdr. Fitzhugh. Tracking the Earth people down in the giant world was the responsibility of Inspector Kobrick of S.I.B., a security agency.

LANIGAN'S RABBI

Police Drama

FIRST TELECAST: *January 30, 1977*
LAST TELECAST: *July 3, 1977*
BROADCAST HISTORY:
  Jan 1977–Jul 1977, NBC Sun Various times
CAST:
  Chief Paul Lanigan.............. Art Carney
  Rabbi David Small........... Bruce Solomon
  Kate Lanigan .... Janis Paige
  Miriam Small................ Janet Margolin
  Bobbie Whittaker........... Barbara Carney
  Lt. Osgood .... Robert Doyle

Paul Lanigan was the police chief of the small town of Cameron, California. A local rabbi and close personal friend of his was David Small. David was an amateur criminologist who had become quite good at analyzing clues and deducing the perpetrator of a crime. He had become so good, in fact, that his friend Paul had become somewhat dependent on his assistance in cracking tough cases. Not only did they work together, they spent many evenings socializing with their wives, who tended to get rather aggravated when the conversation inevitably turned to the latest case. The role of the persistent local reporter, Bobbie Whittaker, was played by Art Carney's daughter Barbara.

Lanigan's Rabbi was based on a series of novels by Harry Kemelman, the first of which was *Friday the Rabbi Slept Late.* In 1977 it aired in rotation with *Columbo, McCloud,* and *McMillan* under the umbrella title *The NBC Sunday Mystery Movie.*

LANNY ROSS SHOW, THE

  see *Swift Show, The*

LARAMIE

Western

FIRST TELECAST: *September 15, 1959*
LAST TELECAST: *September 17, 1963*
BROADCAST HISTORY:
  Sep 1959–Sep 1963, NBC Tue 7:30–8:30
CAST:
  Slim Sherman .... John Smith
  Jess Harper................... Robert Fuller
  Jonesy (1959–1960) .... Hoagy Carmichael
  Andy Sherman (1959–1961)
  .... Bobby Crawford, Jr.
  Mike Williams (1961–1963) .. Dennis Holmes
  Daisy Cooper (1961–1963).... Spring Byington
  Mort Corey (1960–1963)....... Stuart Randall

Two brothers determined to maintain the family ranch after the death of their father were the central characters in this Western, which was set in the Wyoming Territory of the 1870s. After their father had been shot by a land-grabber, the responsibility of running the ranch had fallen to Slim and his 14-year-old brother Andy. Although possessed of great potential, the ranch had been barely able to provide a living for the Shermans before their father's death. Only Jonesy, a friend of their father who had helped raise them, was around to help run the ranch. In the first episode, however, a drifter named Jess Harper wandered in and was persuaded to settle down and throw in his lot with them. In addition to raising cattle, the Shermans used their ranch as a relay station for stagecoach traffic into and out of nearby Laramie, which accounted for many a desperado passing through.

There were cast changes. Jonesy, played by veteran singer-composer Hoagy Carmichael, left the show at the start of the second season while Sheriff Mort Corey of Laramie became a regular. Young Andy, who had previously left the ranch and appeared only occasionally, was gone entirely by 1961, at the same time that two new members were added to the household. Mike Williams, an orphan whose parents had been killed by Indians, joined the family, and Daisy Cooper took over the job of housekeeper and surrogate mother in the previously all-male household.

LAREDO

Western

FIRST TELECAST: *September 16, 1965*
LAST TELECAST: *September 1, 1967*
BROADCAST HISTORY:
  Sep 1965–Sep 1966, NBC Thu 8:30–9:30
  Sep 1966–Sep 1967, NBC Fri 10:00–11:00
CAST:
  Reese Bennett .... Neville Brand
  Chad Cooper .... Peter Brown
  Joe Riley .... William Smith
  Capt. Edward Parmalee .... Philip Carey
  Erik Hunter (1966–1967) ..... Robert Wolders

Stories of the Texas Rangers in the post–Civil War era were told with humor as well as action in this series. The stories centered around three members of Company B and their senior officer, Capt. Parmalee. Former Union Army officer Reese Bennett was already in his 40s when he joined the Rangers, and his age was quite a source of amusement to the two much younger rangers who were his partners. Riley had been a gunfighter whose activities were not always completely legal, and he had joined the Rangers because he liked action but wanted sanctuary from lawmen in other territories who were after him. Cooper, a Boston native and wartime member of the Border Patrol, joined the Rangers after the war to continue his hunt for the American gunrunners who had sold arms to the Mexicans who had wiped out most of his comrades. All three retained a sense of humor about life, however, and Capt. Parmalee, a stern man who assigned them their missions, sometimes found their jokes and horseplay rather frustrating. Erik Hunter was added to the cast in the second season as a new Ranger.

LARRY STORCH SHOW, THE

Comedy Variety
FIRST TELECAST: *July 11, 1953*
LAST TELECAST: *September 12, 1953*
BROADCAST HISTORY:
 Jul 1953–Sep 1953, CBS Sat 8:00–9:00
REGULARS:
 Larry Storch
 Ray Bloch and His Orchestra

Young nightclub comic Larry Storch was the star of this live 1953 summer replacement for *The Jackie Gleason Show.* Guest stars were featured along with Larry's odd assortment of sketch characters, built up from his club act. Among the characters were Victor, a 10-year-old troublemaking monster; Smilie Higgins, a TV cowboy; and Railroad Jack, a philosophical hobo.

LASH OF THE WEST

Western
FIRST TELECAST: *January 4, 1953*
LAST TELECAST: *April 26, 1953*
BROADCAST HISTORY:
 Jan 1953–Apr 1953, ABC Sun 6:30–6:45
CAST:
 Marshal Lash La Rue .... Lash La Rue
 Deputy Fuzzy Q. Jones .. Al "Fuzzy" St. John
 Flapjack........................ Cliff Taylor
 Stratton .... John Martin

Cowboy star Lash La Rue recycled his B-grade Western movies of the late 1940s via this early, 15-minute TV series. Lash appeared at the opening of each show in his modern-day U.S. marshal's office and related a story about his grandfather—who looked just like him, was also a marshal, and was also named Lash La Rue. The scene then shifted to clips from Lash's old Westerns, in which his black-garbed "granddad" tracked down villains with the help of his bullwhip and his faithful, bewhiskered sidekick, Fuzzy Q. Jones.

The cheaply made 15-minute films were originally put together for syndication in 1952, but turned up on the ABC network on Sundays in early 1953, and on ABC's Saturday morning schedule from March to May 1953.

LASSIE

Adventure
FIRST TELECAST: *September 12, 1954*
LAST TELECAST: *September 12, 1971*
BROADCAST HISTORY:
 Sep 1954–Jun 1955, CBS Sun 7:00–7:30
 Sep 1955–Sep 1971, CBS Sun 7:00–7:30
 In first-run syndication from fall 1971–fall 1974
CAST:
 Jeff Miller (1954–1957) .... Tommy Rettig
 Ellen Miller (1954–1957) .... Jan Clayton
 "Gramps" Miller (1954–1957)
 .... George Cleveland
 Sylvester "Porky" Brockway (1954–1957)
 .... Donald Keeler

 Matt Brockway (1954–1957)..... Paul Maxey
 Timmy (1957–1964).............. Jon Provost
 Doc Weaver (1954–1964)....... Arthur Space
 Ruth Martin (1957–1958).... Cloris Leachman
 Paul Martin (1957–1958) .... Jon Shepodd
 Uncle Petrie Martin (1958–1959)
 .... George Chandler
 Ruth Martin (1958–1964)....... June Lockhart
 Paul Martin (1958–1964) .... Hugh Reilly
 Boomer Bates (1958–1959) ...... Todd Ferrell
 Cully Wilson (1958–1964)....... Andy Clyde
 Corey Stuart (1964–1969)....... Robert Bray
 Scott Turner (1968–1970)........... Jed Allan
 Bob Erickson (1968–1970)..... Jack De Mave
 Garth Holden (1972–1973)....... Ron Hayes
 Ron Holden (1972–1974) .... Skip Burton
 Mike Holden (1972–1974) ...... Joshua Albee
 Dale Mitchell (1972–1974)...... Larry Wilcox
 Keith Holden (1973–1974)...... Larry Pennell
 Lucy Baker (1973–1974)...... Pamelyn Ferdin
 Sue Lambert (1973–1974)..... Sherry Boucher
LASSIE'S TRAINER:
 Rudd Weatherwax

The one constant in this favorite long-running children's adventure series was Lassie, a brave, loyal, and remarkably intelligent collie. Lassie was always alert, ready to help her masters and protect them from evil and adversity. In fact, her heroics were often incredible—leading lost persons to safety, warning of all sorts of impending disasters, tending the sick and manipulating various human devices with ease. Fortunately Lassie was able to shift her allegiances periodically, for she was required to go through several sets of owners during her long career.

As originally conceived, *Lassie* was the story of a young boy and his companion collie. The boy was Jeff Miller, who lived on a small modern farm outside the town of Calverton with his widowed mother and his grandfather. In the spring of 1957 a runaway orphan boy named Timmy was brought in by Lassie and joined the Miller household. That fall Gramps died suddenly (actor George Cleveland in fact died soon after the start of the season). Ellen Miller found that she and Jeff could not work the farm alone, so she sold it to the Martins and moved to the city. Lassie and the orphan Timmy remained behind in the care of the Martins, who were childless, and Timmy became Lassie's new companion in weekly adventures.

By 1964 the Martins decided to leave the farm, responding to an advertisement for free land in Australia. Timmy went with them but Lassie could not go—due to animal quarantine regulations. The collie was left for a time in the care of an elderly friend of the family, Cully Wilson, but he subsequently suffered a heart attack. Lassie trotted off to get help from forest ranger Corey Stuart, and soon found herself with a new master. By this time Lassie was beginning to get the feeling that human masters are a temporary thing. In her adventures with ranger Corey, the scope of

432

her exploits widened considerably, as she traveled with him to various parts of the country and situations far more exotic than those encountered around the farm. The premise of a small boy and his dog was gone completely.

In the fall of 1968 Corey was seriously hurt fighting a forest fire, and the Forest Service chief assigned two other rangers, Scott Turner and Bob Erickson, to watch over Lassie. By this time, however, her exploits were often independent of human help, and her contact with the two new rangers was not as frequent as it had been with Corey. By the start of the final season Lassie had become a wanderer without any human companionship at all. The ultimate step in her progression to independence came in a special seven-part story that began the 1970–1971 season. Lassie met a male collie, fell in love, and bore him a litter of puppies. In reality that would have been quite a trick, for all of the many collies that had portrayed Lassie over the years were male.

Although no longer on CBS, *Lassie* remained in production as a syndicated series for three more seasons—during the first as a wanderer similar to her final network season, and in the last two with a new family on the Holden ranch in Solvang, California. Garth Holden ran the ranch with the help of his sons, Ron and Mike, and his assistant Dale Mitchell. When Garth left to start up another ranch, at the start of the 1973–1974 season, his brother Keith arrived to watch over the ranch and his nephews. Lucy Baker was the little deaf girl who lived nearby and Sue Lambert was the local veterinarian. CBS brought Lassie back in an animated version, *Lassie's Rescue Rangers*, which ran on Saturday mornings from September 1973 to August 1975.

Lassie originated in *Lassie Come Home*, a best-selling 1940 novel by Eric Knight which told the story of a poor family forced to sell its beloved collie, who then managed to make her way back to them against all odds. The book was made into a very successful 1943 movie starring a young Roddy McDowall and Elizabeth Taylor, among others, and this was followed by more *Lassie* movies and a radio series from 1947 to 1950.

LASSIE AND TIMMY
syndicated title for *Lassie*

LAST CONVERTIBLE, THE
   Drama
FIRST TELECAST: *June 28, 1981*
LAST TELECAST: *July 20, 1981*
BROADCAST HISTORY:
   Jun 1981, NBC Sun 9:00–11:00
   Jun 1981–Jul 1981, NBC Mon 10:00–11:00
CAST:
   Russ Currier...................... Perry King
   George Virdon............. Bruce Boxleitner
   Chris Farris .... Deborah Raffin
   Ron "Dal" Dalrymple .... Edward Albert
   Terry Garrigan .... John Shea

Nancy Van Breymer .... Caroline Smith
Ann Rowan..................... Kim Darby
Kay Haddon .... Sharon Gless
Liz Baynor .... Tracy Brooks Swope
Paul McCreed .... Fred McCarren
Sheilah Garrigan.............. Stacey Nelkin
Rob Dalrymple .... Shawn Stevens
Jean R. G. R. desBarres ...... Michael Nouri

The Last Convertible was an adaptation of Anton Myrer's romantic novel following the loves and lives of five Harvard University roommates from their arrival on campus in 1940 through their 25th reunion in 1969. Calling themselves "The Five Fusiliers," the young men shared good times, a luxurious Packard convertible dubbed "The Empress," and the love of a beautiful Radcliffe student named Chris. Jean, the original owner of the car, died while fighting with the Free French during World War II, but roommates Russ, George, Terry, and Dal (who married Chris during the war) all survived. During the years that followed their lives continued to intertwine, with Chris at the center of much of the jealousy and passion, and the car as the symbol of their lost youth.

The Last Convertible originally aired as a three-part mini-series in September 1979, and was rerun in weekly installments in 1981.

LAST OF THE WILD
   see *Lorne Greene's Last of the Wild*

LAST PRECINCT, THE
   Situation Comedy
FIRST TELECAST: *April 11, 1986*
LAST TELECAST: *May 30, 1986*
BROADCAST HISTORY:
   Apr 1986–May 1986, NBC Fri 9:00–10:00
CAST:
   Captain Rick Wright .... Adam West
   Sgt. Price Pascall .... Jonathan Perpich
   Off. William Raider ("Raid")
      .... Rick Ducommun
   Det. Sgt. Tremaine "Night Train" Lane
      .... Ernie Hudson
   Off. Mel Brubaker............. Randi Brooks
   Alphabet (Shivaramanbhai Poonchwalla)
      .... Vijay Amritraj
   King .... Pete Willcox
   Butch .... Keenan Wynn
   Sundance...................... Hank Rolike
   Off. Rina Starland .... Lucy Lee Flippin
   Lt. Ronald Hobbs .... Wings Hauser
   Sgt. Martha Haggerty .... Yana Nirvana
   Justin Dial.................. Geoffrey Elliott
   Chief Bludhorn .... James Cromwell

Adam 12 was never like this. The title *The Last Precinct* referred to both the location of Los Angeles' 56th precinct (on the jurisdictional border between the L.A.P.D. and the county sheriff's office) and the fact that it was the dumping ground for all the eccentrics and misfits of the L.A.P.D. In charge of the precinct, more or less, was straight-arrow Capt. Rick Wright, who often seemed oblivious to the goings-on around him. His officers included handsome Price Pascall, the closest the 56th had to an effective, relatively normal policeman; Raid, a bumbling, overweight motorcycle cop; Rina, the records clerk with the hots for Raid; Night Train, a black plainclothes officer who dressed like a pimp; Mel Brubaker, a sexy, miniskirted officer who had been a man before his/her sex-change operation; King, an Elvis Presley impersonator; Alphabet, a stereotypically polite Indian exchange officer; and over-the-hill veterans Butch and Sundance. The 56th was always in competition with the nearby county sheriff's office, run by Lt. Hobbs and his Nazi-like assistant Sgt. Haggerty.

LAST RESORT, THE
Situation Comedy
FIRST TELECAST: *September 19, 1979*
LAST TELECAST: *March 17, 1980*
BROADCAST HISTORY:
   Sep 1979–Oct 1979, CBS Wed 8:00–8:30
   Dec 1979–Mar 1980, CBS Mon 8:30–9:00
CAST:
   Michael Lerner .... Larry Breeding
   Gail Collins .... Stephanie Faracy
   Duane Kaminsky .... Zane Lasky
   Zach Comstock .... Walter Olkewicz
   Jeffrey Barron .... Ray Underwood
   Mrs. Trilling................ Dorothy Konrad
   Kevin .... John Fujioka
   Murray.................... Robert Costanzo

Summer resorts in the Catskill Mountains of upstate New York have always depended on college students as a source of cheap, unskilled labor, and the Last Resort was no exception. Four of the college students working there for the summer were bright, romantic premed Michael Lerner; bookish Duane Kaminsky; bumbling, overweight Zach Comstock; and snobbish Jeffrey Barron. Also on the staff were Gail Collins, a young woman who had run away from her wealthy husband and become the pastry chef despite a minimal knowledge of baking; Kevin, the Japanese chef who pretended not to understand English when it suited him; and Murray the maitre d', who ran the kitchen staff like an army unit, criticizing everybody and screaming continuously. Fortunately for the rest of the staff, Murray was not very bright and could easily be tricked by almost anyone.

A ratings failure when it premiered, *The Last Resort* was pulled from the CBS schedule after only three episodes. It returned two months later on a different night, but never found an audience and was permanently canceled in the spring.

LAST WORD, THE
Informational/Panel
FIRST TELECAST: *June 2, 1957*
LAST TELECAST: *May 25, 1958*
BROADCAST HISTORY:
   Jun 1957–Sep 1957, CBS Sun 6:00–6:30
   Mar 1958–May 1958, CBS Sun 6:00–6:30
HOST:
   Dr. Bergen Evans

The wonderful world of grammar and language was explored each week in this series which requested viewers to send in questions to be discussed by Dr. Evans and a rotating panel of linguistic experts. As the CBS press release announcing its premiere said, "the series would cover . . . such things as euphemisms, regional dialects, occupational lingo, metaphors and similes, pronunciation, British versus American words and usage, cliché, figures of speech, slang, secret languages (like pig Latin), journalese . . ." The series premiered in January as a Sunday afternoon entry but moved into evening hours for the summer of 1957 and the spring of 1958. *The Last Word*'s final Sunday afternoon telecast took place in October 1959.

LAST WORD, THE
News
FIRST TELECAST: *October 26, 1982*
LAST TELECAST: *April 22, 1983*
BROADCAST HISTORY:
   Oct 1982–Apr 1983, ABC Mon–Fri 12:00–1:00 A.M.
REGULARS:
   Greg Jackson
   Phil Donahue

This late-night informational series was telecast live from New York, and hosted by newsman Greg Jackson, who interviewed notables from politics, sports, and other fields, and invited viewers' opinions via toll-free national telephone lines. Phil Donahue contributed a taped interview segment from Chicago.

LATE NIGHT WITH DAVID LETTERMAN
Talk
FIRST TELECAST: *February 2, 1982*
LAST TELECAST:
BROADCAST HISTORY:
   Feb 1982–May 1987, NBC Mon–Thu 12:30–1:30 A.M.
   Jun 1987–   , NBC Mon–Fri 12:30–1:30 A.M.
HOST:
   David Letterman
BANDLEADER:
   Paul Shaffer
WITH:
   Calvert DeForest as Larry "Bud" Melman

Late Night with David Letterman was to TV talk shows as Salvador Dali was to traditional painting. It was a real talk show, the elements were all there, but something was a bit off. The pleasant-looking young host would come out each evening, in sports jacket and tie, tell a joke, banter meaninglessly with his spaced-out bandleader, and sit down at his desk to welcome the night's first guest. Then, with mock-serious demeanor, Letterman might interview a mechanic about "celebrities and their auto repairs," or solicit movie reviews from unlikely "experts"—a dentist, for example, about the movie *Reds*. He might present "Small Town News," an ironic perusal of unintentionally funny items from local newspapers; "Stupid Pet Tricks," a demonstration of nonsensical tricks which ordinary people had tried (often unsuccessfully) to teach their pets; "Brush with Greatness" (who was that?); or "Nightcap Theater," one minute's worth of campy clips from old, bad movies, which viewers were presumably missing by watching this show. There were elevator races in the studio building, and walking tours of the streets of New York City (where the show was produced). Many of the bits poked fun at TV's fascination with new technology, in the best tradition of Ernie Kovacs; for example, the "Monkey-cam" (a live camera strapped to the back of a chimpanzee set loose in the studio), and "the 360 degree show" (in which the home picture made one complete rotation in the hour, so that half way through David and his guests appeared upside down—NBC received a lot of calls about that one).

Letterman also had straight celebrity guests, who were often quite at sea when faced with the host's non-interview style; the guest did all the work. The introductions could be unnerving, too. Sir Alec Guinness was introduced just after the host tossed a carton of eggs into a giant electric fan.

The show had an unstructured, rambling quality. One evening Letterman let the studio audience vote on what it wanted to do that night; another time, he brought a woman up from the audience and let her take over the show—for real—while he disappeared for a lengthy time "to find my false tooth."

Regulars on the show were bandleader Paul Shaffer and a rotund little man with thick-framed glasses named Larry "Bud" Melman, who performed various chores—at the city's main bus terminal handing out hot towels to incoming passengers, or outside the Soviet Consulate distributing pamphlets urging defection and offering American appliances and pornography.

Others seen periodically included Jay Leno, Richard Lewis, Pee-wee Herman, Rita Rudner, Elayne Boosler, Brother Theodore, Carol Leifer, George Muller, and Sandra Bernhard. Appearing in skits from time to time were several of the show's writers, especially Chris Elliott ("Guy under the seats," "the fugitive," etc.). Other writers seen included Gerard Mulligan, Larry Jacobson, and Steve O'Donnell.

Late Night with David Letterman in some ways resembled *Fernwood 2-Night,* but instead of being make-believe, it was the real thing. The show *The New York Times* called "an absurdist parody of mass culture" went over the heads of many viewers—who simply didn't find it funny—but a loyal core of fans made it a cult favorite on the late-night schedule.

LATE SHOW, THE
Talk
FIRST TELECAST: *October 9, 1986*
LAST TELECAST:
BROADCAST HISTORY:
  Oct 1986–Dec 1987, FOX Mon–Fri 11:00–12:00 MID
  Jan 1988– , FOX Mon–Fri 11:00–12:00 MID
HOST:
  Joan Rivers (1986–1987)
  Arsenio Hall (1987)
  Ross Shafer (1988)
REGULARS:
  Clint Holmes (1986–1987)
  Mark Hudson and the Party Boys (1986–1987)
  Daniel Rosen (1988)
  Mark Campbell (1988–)
  Jack Mack & the Heart Attack (1988–)

This was the inaugural series in Fox Broadcasting's effort to start a fourth national television network and, initially at least, it was a ratings disaster.

The original star was caustic comedienne Joan Rivers, whose career had skyrocketed when she became the "permanent" guest host on *The Tonight Show Starring Johnny Carson* in 1983. The announcement in the spring of 1986 that Joan was leaving *Tonight* to become Johnny's competition that fall was a major media event, providing Fox with much desired publicity—including a heavily promoted feud between Joan and her mentor Carson.

Unfortunately for both Fox and Joan, after the initial curiosity about her show (which looked like a carbon copy of *Tonight* despite claims that it would be different), the audience departed. *The Late Show Starring Joan Rivers* never proved to be serious competition for Carson and Joan left after the May 15, 1987 telecast. The title was shortened to *The Late Show* and an assortment of rotating guest hosts—most frequently Suzanne Somers and young, black comics Robert Townsend and Arsenio Hall—took over. By the end of the summer Hall had effectively become the regular host, staying until *The Late Show* was replaced by *The Wilton North Report* at the end of the year. Announcer Clint Holmes and orchestra leader Mark Hudson were with the series for its entire 14-month run.

When *The Wilton North Report* was yanked from the Fox schedule after only four weeks on the air, selected reruns of *The Late Show* (primarily with Rivers and Hall) returned until it could be revived with new regulars. Two months later, with virtually no publicity, the revamped *Late Show* premiered on March 10, 1988, with a new announcer (Daniel Rosen), a new band (Jack Mack & the Heart Attack), and a redesigned set.

Although there was no permanent host, comedians Jeff Joseph and John Mulrooney were given most of the on-air tryouts early on, until Ross Shafer became the regular host later that spring.

LATE SUMMER EARLY FALL BERT CONVY SHOW, THE
Musical Variety
FIRST TELECAST: *August 25, 1976*
LAST TELECAST: *September 15, 1976*
BROADCAST HISTORY:
Aug 1976–Sep 1976, CBS Wed 8:00–8:30
REGULARS:
Bert Convy
Henry Polic II
Sallie Janes
Marty Barris
Donna Ponterotto
Lenny Schultz
Perry Botkin Orchestra

Bert Convy, who was the host of the CBS daytime game show *Tattletales*, was the singing and comedy star of this four-week summer mini-series. The only guest star to appear on the show was Don Knotts, on the premiere telecast. Bert and his comedy troupe, featuring Lenny Schultz as Lenny the Bionic Chicken, performed all of the musical and comedy numbers.

LAUGH-IN
see *Rowan and Martin's Laugh-In*

LAUGH-IN
Comedy Variety
FIRST TELECAST: *June 6, 1979*
LAST TELECAST: *July 4, 1979*
BROADCAST HISTORY:
Jun 1979–Jul 1979, NBC Wed 8:00–9:00
REGULARS:
Nancy Bleiweiss
Ed Bluestone
Kim Braden
Claire Faulkonbridge
Wayland Flowers and Madam
June Gable
Jim Giovanni
Ben Powers
Bill Rafferty
Michael Sklar
Lenny Schultz
Antoinette (Toad) Atell
Robin Williams
Sergio Aragones

Producer George Schlatter had struck gold with the original *Rowan & Martin's Laugh-In* in the late 1960s (see separate listing). Its irreverent humor, fast pacing, and resident cast of nuts made it a huge success—the highest-rated program on television at the time.

Hoping that lightning would strike twice in the same format, Schlatter assembled a new cast of relatively obscure comics and revived *Laugh-In* as a series of specials aired by NBC during the 1977–1978 season. What had been fresh in the original seemed stale in the revival, and *Laugh-In* was not a significant audience attraction in its second incarnation. One of the comics, however, was a fellow named Robin Williams. He went on to star in the comedy smash of the 1978–1979 season, *Mork & Mindy*, which may well have prompted NBC to rerun the specials as a series during the summer of 1979. It was hardly accidental that the promotion for these repeat telecasts seemed to suggest that Robin Williams was the star of the show, even though his contribution had in fact been rather minor.

LAUGH LINE
Quiz/Audience Participation
FIRST TELECAST: *April 16, 1959*
LAST TELECAST: *June 11, 1959*
BROADCAST HISTORY:
Apr 1959–Jun 1959, NBC Thu 9:00–9:30
EMCEE:
Dick Van Dyke
REGULAR:
Dorothy Loudon

A changing group of comedians enacted a silent comedy routine submitted by a viewer in this short-lived show. The celebrity panel would then suggest punch lines for the routine. Prizes for the person submitting the routine were determined by which punch line was funnier, the one submitted with the sketch or the one supplied by the pros. The panelists were generally comedians or comedy writers, with Dorothy Loudon the only regular. The young comedy team of Mike Nichols and Elaine May, though not regulars, made several appearances.

LAUGHS FOR SALE
Comedy
FIRST TELECAST: *October 20, 1963*
LAST TELECAST: *December 22, 1963*
BROADCAST HISTORY:
Oct 1963–Dec 1963, ABC Sun 10:00–10:30
EMCEE:
Hal March

Each week a panel composed of prominent comics and comediennes participated in this series which sought to give young comedy writers exposure and help. The material that the writers submitted—sketches, monologues, routines, etc.—was performed by the members of the panel who then discussed the strong and weak points they perceived in it. Panel members changed each week, but Shecky Greene, Mickey Rooney, and Phil Foster appeared frequently.

LAVERNE & SHIRLEY
Situation Comedy
FIRST TELECAST: *January 27, 1976*

LAST TELECAST: *May 10, 1983*
BROADCAST HISTORY:
Jan 1976–Jul 1979, ABC Tue 8:30–9:00
Aug 1979–Dec 1979, ABC Thu 8:00–8:30
Dec 1979–Feb 1980, ABC Mon 8:00–8:30
Feb 1980–May 1983, ABC Tue 8:30–9:00
CAST:
Laverne De Fazio . . . . Penny Marshall
Shirley Feeney (1976–1982) . . Cindy Williams
Carmine Ragusa . . . . Eddie Mekka
Frank De Fazio . . . . Phil Foster
Andrew "Squiggy" Squiggman
. . . . David L. Lander
Lenny Kosnowski* . . . . Michael McKean
Mrs. Edna Babish De Fazio (1976–1981)
. . . . Betty Garrett
Rosie Greenbaum (1976–1977)
. . . . Carole Ita White
Sonny St. Jacques (1980–1981) . . . Ed Marinaro
Rhonda Lee (1980–1983) . . Leslie Easterbrook

**called "Kolowski" in earlier episodes
THEME:
"Making Our Dreams Come True," by Norman
Gimbel and Charles Fox; sung by Cyndi Grecco

This slapstick 1950s-era comedy was about two
spunky girls from lower-class backgrounds, without much education, with no money, but with the
determination to get ahead. They worked on an
assembly line in the bottle-cap division of the
Shotz Brewery in Milwaukee. Laverne was the
quick-tempered, defensive one, always afraid of
getting hurt (which she usually did)—a glib real-
ist. Shirley was naive and trusting, a sucker for a
sad story. Others in the cast included Lenny and
Squiggy, the girls' screwball neighbors and truck
drivers at the plant; amorous Carmine, "The Big
Ragu"; Laverne's father, Frank, owner of the Pizza
Bowl, a local hangout; Mrs. Babish, the sardonic
landlady who was first seen in the fall of 1976
(replacing the original landlady, Mrs. Haven-
wurst, played by Helen Page Camp, seen in only
a couple of episodes); and Rosie, an uppity friend.
Laverne & Shirley was a spin-off of sorts from
Happy Days, in which the girls appeared only
briefly. It was set in the same city and period, and
the girls' friend Fonzie sometimes stopped by to
say hello. With friends like that *Laverne & Shirley*
shot to the top of the ratings. Critics called it TV
junk food; ABC program chief Fred Silverman responded by comparing it to the classic satire of
the 17th-century French playwright Molière. No
matter what anyone said, the public loved it. During the 1977–1978 season it was the number one
program on television.
With the 1978–1979 season, the program moved
into the 1960s. Frank De Fazio and Mrs. Babish,
both single, began dating, and in the fall of 1979
they were married. Then, in the fall of 1980, the
whole crew picked up and moved to Burbank,
California, all seeking to better their lot in a new
environment. The girls began trying to get into the

movies. Frank and Edna opened a restaurant,
Cowboy Bill's. Carmine just wanted to be near his
best girl, Shirley. New neighbors included
Rhonda, a caustic dancer and model, and Sonny,
a stuntman, and their apartment building manager.
Life behind the scenes on *Laverne & Shirley*
had always been tumultuous, due to an intense
rivalry between its two stars. Demands were
made, writers fired, feuds erupted. Finally in 1982
Cindy Williams, who was pregnant, left the series. Her character, Shirley, married an army
medic named Walter Meany who was assigned
overseas. Laverne tried to go it alone, but, faced
with withering competition from *The A-Team* on
NBC, *Laverne & Shirley* quietly expired the following spring.
The theme song of this series was on the hit
parade in 1976 in a recording by Cyndi Grecco,
who was also heard on the show. Reruns of *Laverne & Shirley* were on ABC's daytime lineup
from April 1979 to June 1980, and a Saturday
morning cartoon version was seen from October
1981 to September 1983.

LAW AND HARRY MCGRAW, THE
Detective
FIRST TELECAST: *September 27, 1987*
LAST TELECAST: *February 10, 1988*
BROADCAST HISTORY:
Sep 1987, CBS Sun 9:00–11:00
Sep 1987–Dec 1987, CBS Tue 10:00–11:00
Jan 1988–Feb 1988, CBS Wed 8:00–9:00
CAST:
Harry McGraw . . . . Jerry Orbach
Ellie Maginnis . . . . Barbara Babcock
Steve Lacey . . . . Shea Farrell
E. J. Brunson . . . . Juli Donald
Deputy D.A. Tyler Chase . . . . . . Peter Haskell
Howard . . . . Earl Boen
Cookie, the bartender . . . . Marty Davis

Harry McGraw was not the classiest private detective in Boston. He was disorganized, disheveled, irritable, and surly. On the other hand, he
was a bright guy with good analytical skills and
a dogged determination to stick with a case until
he found what he was looking for. The best thing
Harry had going for himself, however, was his
friendship with attorney Ellie Maginnis, whose
office was across the hall from his. There was a
certain nepotism here—Harry's niece E.J. worked
as his assistant/secretary and Ellie's nephew
Steve was the junior partner in her legal office.
Gilhooley's was the saloon where Harry spent
much of his free time.
Harry McGraw had appeared a few times on
Murder, She Wrote before getting a series of his
own.

LAW AND MR. JONES, THE
Law Drama
FIRST TELECAST: *October 7, 1960*

LAST TELECAST: *October 4, 1962*
BROADCAST HISTORY:
Oct 1960–Sep 1961, ABC Fri 10:30–11:00
Apr 1962–Oct 1962, ABC Thu 9:30–10:00
CAST:
Abraham Lincoln Jones..... James Whitmore
Marsha Spear .... Janet De Gore
C. E. Carruthers .... Conlan Carter

That a man with a name like Abraham Lincoln Jones was honest was a foregone conclusion. This particular Abe was an attorney with great compassion for people, and a willingness to fight both literally and figuratively for his clients. His penchant for quoting Oliver Wendell Holmes did nothing to lessen his appeal. His cases rarely involved violence, however. Fraud, embezzlement, and jurisdictional disputes were the issues he most frequently addressed. Abe's law clerk was young C. E. Carruthers, and his winsome secretary was Marsha Spear.

ABC canceled this series after its initial season, but viewer response, in the form of thousands of angry letters, was so strong that it was brought back the following April. Alas, the size of its audience did not increase and it was canceled again in October.

LAW OF THE PLAINSMAN
Western
FIRST TELECAST: *October 1, 1959*
LAST TELECAST: *September 24, 1962*
BROADCAST HISTORY:
Oct 1959–Sep 1960, NBC Thu 7:30–8:00
Jul 1962–Sep 1962, ABC Mon 8:30–9:00
CAST:
Deputy U.S. Marshal Sam Buckhart
.... Michael Ansara
Marshal Andy Morrison..... Dayton Lummis
Tess Logan.................. Gina Gillespie
Martha Commager.......... Nora Marlowe

The struggle to reconcile Indian and white man in the wild New Mexico Territory of the 1880s was the subject of this series. The plainsman was Deputy U.S. Marshal Sam Buckhart, a lawman with a unique past. Born an Apache Indian, and known among the Indians as Buck Heart, he had befriended and nursed back to health a cavalry captain who had been wounded in an Indian ambush. When the captain died two years later, he left the youth money for an education at private schools and Harvard University.

Having acquired tremendous respect for the white man's laws and the U.S. Constitution, Sam returned to the troubled territory where he had spent his youth, determined to become a marshal. He served under Marshal Andy Morrison in Santa Fe, while living in a rooming house run by Martha Commager. The only other female in his life was eight-year-old Tess Logan, an orphan he had rescued from a stagecoach mishap. Martha served as a kind of surrogate mother for both Sam and his young ward.

Reruns of this NBC series were aired on ABC during the summer of 1962. It's pilot had aired on *The Rifleman* early in 1959.

LAWLESS YEARS, THE
Police Drama
FIRST TELECAST: *April 16, 1959*
LAST TELECAST: *September 22, 1961*
BROADCAST HISTORY:
Apr 1959–Jun 1959, NBC Thu 8:00–8:30
Jul 1959–Sep 1959, NBC Thu 8:30–9:00
Oct 1959–Mar 1960, NBC Thu 10:30–11:00
May 1961–Sep 1961, NBC Fri 9:00–9:30
CAST:
Barney Ruditsky............. James Gregory
Max .... Robert Karnes

The setting of this police drama was wide-open New York City in the Roaring Twenties, city of speakeasies, gangsters, bathtub gin, and flappers. The exploits of Police Detective Barney Ruditsky in his fight against organized crime were portrayed. *The Lawless Years* had a certain claim to authenticity, both in its meticulous attention to period detail and in the fact that it was based (loosely) on actual cases of a real-life New York cop named Barney Ruditsky. The careers of real gangsters of the period were depicted, although with fictitious names.

Six months after *The Lawless Years* premiered, *The Untouchables*, treating the same subject but with Chicago rather than New York as the background, began on ABC. *The Lawless Years* folded soon after, but the success of *The Untouchables* inspired a revival with new episodes in the summer of 1961.

The real Barney Ruditsky, who had retired from police work in 1941 and was running a West Coast detective agency, was the technical advisor for *The Lawless Years*.

LAWMAN, THE
Western
FIRST TELECAST: *October 5, 1958*
LAST TELECAST: *October 2, 1962*
BROADCAST HISTORY:
Oct 1958–Apr 1962, ABC Sun 8:30–9:00
Apr 1962–Oct 1962, ABC Sun 10:30–11:00
CAST:
Marshal Dan Troop .... John Russell
Deputy Johnny McKay .... Peter Brown
Dru Lemp (1958–1959) .... Bek Nelson
Lily Merrill (1959–1962)......... Peggy Castle
Jake (1961–1962) .... Dan Sheridan

The "lawman" in this straightforward Western was Marshal Dan Troop of Laramie, a granitejawed, taciturn type. With his string tie and fatherly mustache, John Russell looked the part. There were no tricks or gimmicks in *Lawman*, just simple stories of desperadoes brought to justice by the long, stern arm of the law. Playing off Troop's fatherly image was his young deputy, Johnny McKay. Lily Merrill arrived in town during the second season to open the Birdcage Saloon and help the righteous marshal unbend a bit.

LAWRENCE WELK SHOW, THE
Music

FIRST TELECAST: *July 2, 1955*
LAST TELECAST: *September 4, 1971*
BROADCAST HISTORY:
Jul 1955–Sep 1963, ABC Sat 9:00–10:00
Sep 1963–Jan 1971, ABC Sat 8:30–9:30
Jan 1971–Sep 1971, ABC Sat 7:30–8:30
(New episodes syndicated from 1971–1982)
HOST:
Lawrence Welk
MUSICAL DIRECTOR:
George Cates
CHAMPAGNE LADY:
Alice Lon (1955–1959)
Norma Zimmer (1960–1982)
ORIGINAL REGULARS (1955):
Aladdin, violin (1955–1967)
Jerry Burke, piano-organ (1955–1965)
Dick Dale, saxophone, vocals (1955–1982)
Myron Floren, accordion (1955–1982)
Larry Hooper, piano, bass vocals (1955–1982)
Dick Kesner, violin (1955–1959)
Bob Lido, violin (1955–1982)
Tiny Little, Jr., piano (1955–1959)
Buddy Merrill, guitar (1955–1974)
Jim Roberts, vocals (1955–1982)
Rocky Rockwell, trumpet, gravel-voiced vocals (1955–1962)
Sparklers Quartet (1955–1957)
LATER REGULARS (in order they joined):
Lennon Sisters (Dianne, Peggy, Kathy, Janet) (1955–1968)
Larry Dean, vocals (1956–1960)
Frank Scott, piano, arranger (1956–1969)
Maurice Pearson, vocals (1957–1960)
Joe Feeney, Irish tenor (1957–1982)
Jack Imel, tap dancer (1957–1982)
Alvan Ashby, hymn singer (1957–1959)
Pete Fountain, Dixieland clarinet (1957–1959)
Jo Ann Castle, ragtime piano (1959–1969)
Jimmy Getzoff, violin (1960–1962)
Bobby Burgess and Barbara Boylan, dancers (1961–1967)
  (Boylan replaced by Cissy King (1967–1978) then by Elaine Niverson (1979–1982))
Joe Livoti, violin (1962–1982)
Bob Ralston, piano-organ (1963–1982)
Art Duncan, dancer (1964–1982)
Steve Smith, vocals (1965–1969)
Natalie Nevins, vocals (1965–1969)
The Blenders, vocal quartet (1965–1967)
Lynn Anderson, vocals (1967–1968)
Andra Willis, vocals (1967–1969)
Tanya Falan Welk, vocals (1968–1977)

Sandi Jensen, vocals (1968–1980)
Salli Flynn, vocals (1968–1972)
Hotsy Totsy Boys (1969–1980)
Clay Hart, vocals (1969–1975)
Ralna English Hovis (1969–1982)
Guy Hovis (1970–1982)
Peanuts Hucko (1970–1972)
Anacani (1972–1982)
Tom Netherton (1973–1981)
Ava Barber (1974–1982)
Kathy Sullivan (1976–1982)
Sheila & Sherry Aldridge (1977–1982)
David & Roger Otwell (1977–1982)
Jim Turner (1979–1982)
THEME:
"Bubbles in the Wine" (1955–1970), by Lawrence Welk, Frank Loesser, and Bob Calame; "Champagne Fanfare" (1971–1982), by George Cates

Lawrence Welk's Champagne Music was first heard on network television as a summer replacement program in 1955. The critics were not impressed. Reviewing the program at the end of the summer, *TV Guide* remarked smugly: "The program lacks the necessary sparkle and verve to give it a chance against any really strong competition. But it has been a satisfactory summertime entry. . . ." That proved to be the misjudgment of the year. Welk went on to a phenomenal 16-year network run on Saturday nights, and became one of the major musical success stories in all of TV history. From 1956 to 1959 he had *two* weekly hours on ABC, and he maintained good ratings throughout his run. In fact, when his program was finally canceled by ABC in 1971 it was primarily because his audience was "too old"—not too small. Welk then assembled a syndicated network of his own and continued to produce new programs that attracted bigger audiences than many network shows.

The Welk formula was good, old-fashioned, melodic music, unadorned and straightforwardly presented. Old folks loved it. This was the one place on TV—probably in all of modern media—where "I Love You Truly" could be heard sung completely straight. Moreover, everyone on the show was completely good, clean, and wholesome (or else they were fired). Welk himself had about as much stage presence as Ed Sullivan, but that did not stop either of them. The maestro read stiffly through the brief introductions, and his thick accent was the butt of endless jokes. But when he played his accordion (which was rarely) or danced with one of the ladies in the audience, viewers loved it.

Much of the appeal of the program lay with its close-knit family of performers. Practically every player in the band was given a chance to solo from time to time, though some (listed above) were seen more often than others. Welk, who was highly sensitive to viewers' letters, kept a "fever chart" on which each comment on a performer, pro or con, was carefully tallied. Performers with a lot of favorable comments were featured more, and those in disfavor with the letter-writing public tended to disappear from view. The viewer, too, was part of the "family."

Probably the most famous of Welk's alumni were "da lovely Lennon Sisters," who were first brought to his attention in 1955 by his son, Lawrence, Jr., who was dating Dianne Lennon at the time. Lawrence, Sr., signed them immediately. They first appeared on his Christmas Eve 1955 broadcast, and stayed for more than 12 years. Dianne left to get married in 1960, and the quartet was only a trio until her return in 1964.

Other favorites included accordionist Myron Floren, who was also the assistant conductor; deep-voiced singer-pianist Larry Hooper (who was off the show from 1967–1971 due to heart trouble; he died in 1983); dancers Bobby Burgess and Barbara Boylan; and Aladdin (real name: Aladdin Abdullah Achmed Anthony Pallante), the mustachioed violinist who also did dramatic readings. High point of the season was the annual Christmas show, when all the band members brought their children and Larry Hooper dressed up as Santa Claus for fun and gifts.

Most of Welk's musical family stayed with him for years, but there were a few highly publicized walkouts. Welk has always been a very strait-laced individual, and his moral as well as musical regimentation grated on some performers. Perhaps the most traumatic incident for Welk was his firing of Champagne Lady Alice Lon in July 1959, because she showed "too much knee" on camera. "Cheesecake does not fit our show," charged an angry Welk. "All I did was sit on a desk and cross my legs," replied Miss Lon. "That is the way a lady sits down." Welk got thousands of angry letters for his action, which evidently caused him second thoughts. He tried to get Alice back, but to no avail. After a year and a half of guest Champagne Ladies, soprano Norma Zimmer was hired on a permanent basis.

Hardly less painful was the departure of the Lennon Sisters in 1968, to build a career of their own. Dixieland clarinetist Pete Fountain, one of the most jazz-oriented musicians ever to star with Welk, quit when the maestro refused to let him jive up a carol on a Christmas show. He later built a successful career on his own, as have Jo Ann Castle and country singer Lynn Anderson.

During his later years Lawrence Welk made a conscious effort to add younger, reasonably contemporary performers to his troupe. The success of his record "Calcutta" in 1960 evidently convinced him that good music and something remotely resembling a contemporary beat were not necessarily incompatible. Dancers Burgess and Boylan joined after winning a "Calcutta" dance contest in 1961, and added later were Sandi and Salli, Tanya Falan (who married Welk's son),

and tap dancer Art Duncan, the only black face in the crowd.

After leaving the network *The Lawrence Welk Show* continued in production for 11 more years, remaining one of the top-rated programs on American television—a tribute to the unwavering maestro of the "uh-one, uh-two" and his continued popularity with millions of viewers. The last original episode was produced in February 1982. In later years early programs were repackaged with new introductions by Welk, and aired under the title *Memories With Lawrence Welk*.

The Lawrence Welk Show was seen on local television in Los Angeles for two years before going on the network in 1955. It was known for a time in 1958 as *The Dodge Dancing Party*.

LAWRENCE WELK'S TOP TUNES AND NEW TALENT
Talent
FIRST TELECAST: *October 8, 1956*
LAST TELECAST: *May 27, 1959*
BROADCAST HISTORY:
  Oct 1956–Jun 1958, ABC Mon 9:30–10:30
  Sep 1958–May 1959, ABC Wed 7:30–8:30
REGULARS:
  Lawrence Welk
  The Lawrence Welk Orchestra
  Lawrence Welk's Little Band (1958–1959)

In addition to his familiar Saturday night show, Lawrence Welk had a second hour on ABC between 1956 and 1959, featuring "top tunes and new talent." Some of the performers discovered in the talent-show portion of the series later became Welk regulars, among them Joe Feeney, Jack Imel, and Maurice Pearson. Also featured were Welk's regular orchestra and soloists.

In 1958 the title of the show was changed to *The Plymouth Show*, and the Lawrence Welk "Little Band" was added as a regular feature. This second band was composed of talented youngsters ranging in age from 12 to 20, and included such solo talent as drummer Cubby O'Brien (12), a former *Mickey Mouse Club* mouseketeer.

LAWYERS, THE
Law Drama
FIRST TELECAST: *September 21, 1969*
LAST TELECAST: *August 20, 1972*
BROADCAST HISTORY:
  Sep 1969–Aug 1972, NBC Sun 10:00–11:00
CAST:
  Walter Nichols .... Burl Ives
  Brian Darrell .... Joseph Campanella
  Neil Darrell .... James Farentino

Three attorneys with different skills, interests, and approaches joined forces to form the law firm of Nichols, Darrell and Darrell. Walter Nichols had been practicing law since before either of his two young partners was born. His vast experience gave him a perspective and patience that neither of the Darrell brothers had. Shrewd and effective, Walter functioned as a stabilizing influence, consultant, and sometimes father figure to his partners. Brian, the older of the Darrell brothers, was a superb researcher and detail man who did everything by the book. Neil, the younger brother, was more sympathetic to unpopular causes and more unorthodox than either of his partners. He was not above stretching a law to achieve a desired end. The blending of these three diverse personalities caused occasional conflict among the attorneys but resulted in a very effective team. *The Lawyers* was one of the rotating elements that comprised *The Bold Ones*.

LAYTONS, THE
Situation Comedy
FIRST TELECAST: *August 11, 1948*
LAST TELECAST: *October 13, 1948*
BROADCAST HISTORY:
Aug 1948–Oct 1948, DUM Wed 8:30–9:00
CAST:
Amanda Randolph
Vera Tatum

Black actress Amanda Randolph, better known as Sapphire's Mama on both the radio and TV versions of *Amos 'n' Andy*, starred in this short-lived domestic comedy on DuMont. It had been previously seen as a local program in New York, in May–June 1948.

LAZARUS SYNDROME, THE
Medical Drama
FIRST TELECAST: *September 4, 1979*
LAST TELECAST: *October 9, 1979*
BROADCAST HISTORY:
Sep 1979–Oct 1979, ABC Tue 10:00–11:00
CAST:
Dr. MacArthur St. Clair .... Louis Gossett, Jr.
Joe Hamill.................... Ronald Hunter
Gloria St. Clair .... Sheila Frazier
Virginia Hamill............... Peggy Walker
Stacy .... Peggy McKay

This rather grim medical drama was one of the earliest casualties of the 1979–1980 season. Dr. MacArthur St. Clair, a tall, bald, black man with a somewhat ominous demeanor, was Chief of Cardiology at Webster Memorial Hospital. His life seemed to be a series of conflicts, both with the idealistic hospital administrator, Joe Hamill, who had signed on to help him fight the bureaucracy, and with his wife, Gloria, who wanted him to have a little more home life.

The term "Lazarus Syndrome" refers to a belief that doctors are omnipotent beings who can work miracles.

LEAVE IT TO BEAVER
Situation Comedy

FIRST TELECAST: *October 4, 1957*
LAST TELECAST: *September 12, 1963*
BROADCAST HISTORY:
Oct 1957–Mar 1958, CBS Fri 7:30–8:00
Mar 1958–Sep 1958, CBS Wed 8:00–8:30
Oct 1958–Jun 1959, ABC Thu 7:30–8:00
Jul 1959–Sep 1959, ABC Thu 9:00–9:30
Oct 1959–Sep 1962, ABC Sat 8:30–9:00
Sep 1962–Sep 1963, ABC Thu 8:30–9:00
CAST:
June Cleaver............. Barbara Billingsley
Ward Cleaver .... Hugh Beaumont
Beaver (Theodore) Cleaver .... Jerry Mathers
Wally Cleaver.................... Tony Dow
Eddie Haskell .... Ken Osmond
Miss Canfield (1957–1958) ... Diane Brewster
Miss Landers (1958–1962)....... Sue Randall
Larry Mondello (1958–1960)
.... Rusty Stevens
Whitey Whitney............. Stanley Fafara
Clarence "Lumpy" Rutherford (1958–1963)
.... Frank Bank
Mr. Fred Rutherford......... Richard Deacon
Gilbert Bates (1959–1963) .... Stephen Talbot
Richard (1960–1963) .... Richard Correll

This family comedy focused on life through the eyes of a young boy. Beaver Cleaver was 7 when the series began, and his brother Wally, 12. Beaver was a typically rambunctious youth, more interested in pet frogs than in girls, but Wally, just entering his teens, was beginning to discover other things in life. The counterpoint between the two, plus some good writing and acting, lent the series its charm. The boys' parents, June and Ward Cleaver, were one of those nice, middle-class couples so often seen in this kind of program. Larry, Whitey, and Gilbert (among others) were Beaver's pals, Eddie and Lumpy were Wally's buddies. Eddie was one of the more memorable characters, unctuous and oily to adults ("Good evening, Mr. and Mrs. Cleaver"), but a bully to little kids—a thoroughgoing rat. Miss Canfield and Miss Landers were Beaver's schoolteachers. The locale was the suburban town of Mayfield.

As the years passed and Beaver got older, the stories naturally moved away from the little-boy premise until, in the final season, Beaver was about to enter his teens and Wally was ready for college.

In 1987, in the midst of a *Leave It to Beaver* revival, the original 1957 pilot episode for the series surfaced, containing a somewhat different cast than most people remembered. Billingsley and Mathers were there, but Ward Cleaver was played by Casey Adams, Wally by Paul Sullivan, and "Frankie"—the Eddie Haskell–type character—by Harry Shearer, who years later would become a regular on *Saturday Night Live*. For the further adventures of the Cleaver clan in the '80s, see *The New Leave It to Beaver*.

LEAVE IT TO LARRY

Situation Comedy

FIRST TELECAST: *October 14, 1952*
LAST TELECAST: *December 23, 1952*
BROADCAST HISTORY:

Oct 1952–Dec 1952, CBS Tue 8:00–8:30

CAST:

Larry Tucker .... Eddie Albert
Mr. Koppel .... Ed Begley
Amy Tucker .... Betty Kean
Stevie Tucker................ Glenn Walken
Harriet Tucker.............. Lydia Schaeffer

The problems of a young man working for his father-in-law formed the basis of this comedy. Larry Tucker, a pleasant enough fellow with a wife (Amy) and two children, faced Amy's father every morning in the shoe store where he worked. He faced Mr. Koppel every night, too, since Amy's father also owned and lived in the two-family house where Larry and his family lived. Too much family, all of the time, made Larry's life a bit hectic. Someone in the family always had it in for someone else, and he was always in the middle.

Leave It to Larry had premiered with a different cast supporting Albert and Begley—Katherine Bard (as Amy), Olive Templeton, Bradley Houston, Gene Lee, and Patsy Bruder. These were replaced almost immediately by the cast listed above.

LEAVE IT TO THE GIRLS

Discussion

FIRST TELECAST: *April 27, 1949*
LAST TELECAST: *March 27, 1954*
BROADCAST HISTORY:

Apr 1949–May 1949, NBC Wed 8:00–8:30
May 1949–Aug 1949, NBC Sun 8:00–8:30
Aug 1949–Oct 1949, NBC Sun 8:30–9:00
Oct 1949–Sep 1951, NBC Sun 7:00–7:30
Oct 1951–Dec 1951, NBC Sun 10:30–11:00
Oct 1953–Mar 1954, ABC Sat 7:30–8:00

MODERATOR:

Maggi McNellis

PANELISTS:

Eloise ("The Mouth") McElhone
Vanessa Brown
Florence Pritchett
Lisa Ferraday
Ann Rutherford
Harriet Van Horne
Janet Blair
John Henry Faulk (1954)

CREATOR/PRODUCER:

Martha Rountree

This bit of piffle was created by Martha Rountree, the same woman responsible for *Meet the Press* and other deadly serious public-affairs shows. Indeed, when it was first heard on radio in 1945, *Leave It to the Girls* was conceived as a serious discussion of male-female problems by career women. However, it soon degenerated into a one-sided battle of the sexes, and by the time it got to TV the subject matter was mostly what was wrong with men, how to marry them, and clever jokes about their foibles. A lone male was generally present to "defend the honor of his sex," and he was given a toy horn with which to signal his intention to speak (which was often the only way to break in on the chatterbox panel).

The female panelists changed frequently. All were "of the Stork Club ilk," as *TV Guide* put it—glamorous, well-dressed, showbiz types. Eloise McElhone was the most constant panel member over the years, with Vanessa Brown and Florence Pritchett also closely associated with the show. Male guests were generally panel-show types, such as Henry Morgan, Morey Amsterdam, and George Jessel. A "permanent" male defender, John Henry Faulk, was added during the last months.

Leave It to the Girls was first seen on local television in New York in 1947, and moved to the network in 1949. Oddly enough, it was sponsored through part of its run by a tobacco company. Almost a decade later, during the 1962–1963 season, Miss McNellis returned to moderate a syndicated weekday daytime version of *Leave It to the Girls*. Regular panelists were Sue Oakland and Rita Hayes.

LEG WORK

Detective

FIRST TELECAST: *October 3, 1987*
LAST TELECAST: *November 7, 1987*
BROADCAST HISTORY:

Oct 1987–Nov 1987, CBS Sat 9:00–10:00

CAST:

Claire McCarron............. Margaret Colin
Willie Pipal .... Frances McDormand
Lt. Fred McCarron ..... Patrick James Clarke

This series was an odd cross between *Designing Women* and *Miami Vice*, about a young, single woman in the big city who spent her time chattering with her girlfriends about love and life, in between high-speed chases and shootouts. Claire was a former assistant district attorney who had decided to become a private detective. She was much better at tracking down people and uncovering information for her clients than she was at managing her own finances. Claire's expensive Manhattan apartment, fancy (and too often in the shop) Porsche, and tendency to overspend on her credit cards, kept her busy juggling creditors. Willie was her best friend and confidant and Fred her loving brother, conveniently placed in the public information office of the N.Y.P.D. Although the title of this series was supposed to refer to the tedious part of detective work, it could just as well have referred, as many reviewers pointed out, to the attractive mini-skirted legs of star Margaret Colin.

LEGEND OF CUSTER
see *Custer*

LEGEND OF JESSE JAMES, THE
Western
FIRST TELECAST: *September 13, 1965*
LAST TELECAST: *September 5, 1966*
BROADCAST HISTORY:
Sep 1965–Sep 1966, ABC Mon 8:30–9:00
CAST:
Jesse James............... Christopher Jones
Frank James.................... Allen Case
Cole Younger.................. John Milford
Bob Younger.................. Tim McIntire
Marshal Sam Corbett .... Robert Wilke
Mrs. James .... Ann Doran

Television is apparently capable of making a hero out of anyone. This Western sympathetically portrayed the murderous James brothers, notorious in the Old West as robbers and desperadoes, as latter-day Robin Hoods driven to violence against their will. Christopher Jones played young, handsome, romantic Jesse, while Allen Case played his steadier older brother Frank. Occasionally featured in stories were Cole and Bob Younger, another pleasant pair drawn from Western history, and Marshal Sam Corbett. The Jameses' adventures, and attempts to show that they weren't all that bad, lasted for a single season on ABC.

LEGMEN
Detective Drama
FIRST TELECAST: *January 20, 1984*
LAST TELECAST: *March 16, 1984*
BROADCAST HISTORY:
Jan 1984–Feb 1984, NBC Fri 8:00–9:00
Feb 1984–Mar 1984, NBC Fri 9:00–10:00
CAST:
Jack Gage .... Bruce Greenwood
David Taylor .... J. T. Terlesky
Oscar Armismendi .... Don Calfa
Tom Bannon.................. Claude Akins

Take two Southern California college students looking for a little extra income and a good time, add a seedy private eye who needed someone to do his legwork cheap, and you have the plot for *Legmen*. Jack and David usually started out on simple car-repossession or process-serving errands, but ended up involved in dangerous cases with flying bullets and beautiful women. Oscar was their original employer, replaced after a few episodes by the more demanding Tom Bannon.

LEO & LIZ IN BEVERLY HILLS
Situation Comedy
FIRST TELECAST: *April 25, 1986*
LAST TELECAST: *June 6, 1986*
BROADCAST HISTORY:
Apr 1986–Jun 1986, CBS Fri 8:30–9:00

CAST:
Leo Green.................. Harvey Korman
Liz Green .... Valerie Perrine
Diane Fedderson.......... Deborah Harmon
Jerry Fedderson........... Kenneth Kimmins
Mitzi Green .... Sue Ball
Lucille Trumbley............... Julie Payne
Leonard.................. Michael J. Pollard

Leo & Liz in Beverly Hills had a certain family resemblance to *The Beverly Hillbillies*. Both series dealt with the comedic problems of folks from back East adjusting to the life-style in affluent Beverly Hills. Unlike the Clampetts of *Hillbillies* fame, however, who were oblivious to what they were doing wrong, the Greens wanted desperately to fit in. Having worked hard to make something of their lives in their native New Jersey, nouveau riche Leo and Liz moved to Beverly Hills to enjoy the fruits of their labors. Along with the normal problems of moving into a new place with a different social structure, they had to deal with the pretentious family into which their daughter Mitzi had married and two batty servants, Lucille the maid and Leonard the handyman. The Feddersons were their next-door neighbors.

Created, written, co-produced, and directed by veteran comedian Steve Martin, *Leo & Liz in Beverly Hills* was first seen as an episode of *George Burns Comedy Week* in the fall of 1985.

LES CRANE SHOW, THE
see *ABC's Nightlife*

LESLIE UGGAMS SHOW, THE
Musical Variety
FIRST TELECAST: *September 28, 1969*
LAST TELECAST: *December 14, 1969*
BROADCAST HISTORY:
Sep 1969–Dec 1969, CBS Sun 9:00–10:00
REGULARS:
Leslie Uggams
Dennis Allen
Lillian Hayman
Lincoln Kilpatrick
Allison Mills
Johnny Brown
The Howard Roberts Singers
The Donald McKayle Dancers
Nelson Riddle and His Orchestra

Singer Leslie Uggams was the star of this musical-variety series. In addition to her singing and dancing, and turns by weekly guest stars, a regular feature of the program was a continuing comedy sketch called "Sugar Hill." It dealt with the lives of a middle-class black family in a large city. The family consisted of Henrietta (Leslie Uggams), her husband B.J. (Lincoln Kilpatrick), her mother (Lillian Hayman), her brother Lamar (Johnny Brown), and her sister Oletha (Allison Mills). The only white regular on the show was sketch comedian Dennis Allen.

443

LESSON IN SAFETY

Instruction

FIRST TELECAST: *September 8, 1951*
LAST TELECAST: *October 20, 1951*
BROADCAST HISTORY:
   Sep 1951–Oct 1951, ABC Sat 9:00–9:30

Accident-prevention films, covering such subjects as fire safety, driving, bicycling, and freight handling.

LET THERE BE STARS

Musical Variety

FIRST TELECAST: *October 16, 1949*
LAST TELECAST: *November 27, 1949*
BROADCAST HISTORY:
   Oct 1949–Nov 1949, ABC Sun 9:00–10:00

The premiere telecast of this hour-long musical revue was a producer's dream: big budget, cast of bright, talented young newcomers, top-notch production, and a rave review in the next morning's issue of *Variety* ("Here's a show to make the detractors of Hollywood's video entries eat their words."). The talent was rounded up by a Rodgers and Hammerstein talent scout in the process of casting R&H shows, and included Patti Brill, Jane Harvey, Tom Noonan, and Peter Marshall. One of the novel (for the time) production devices used on the program was "Teleparencies," a projected background effect that moved, dissolved, and faded in and out with the action.

Subsequent shows apparently did not live up to the premiere, and the series folded after a few weeks. It was seen in the East via kinescope, having premiered on West Coast television on September 21, 1949.

LET'S DANCE

Music

FIRST TELECAST: *September 11, 1954*
LAST TELECAST: *October 16, 1954*
BROADCAST HISTORY:
   Sep 1954–Oct 1954, ABC Sat 8:00–9:00
REGULARS

(New York):
   Ralph Flanagan Orchestra
   Julius LaRosa
   Martha Wright
(Chicago):
   Art Mooney Orchestra
   June Valli
   Fran Allison

Short-lived dance-music series originating from both New York and Chicago. Featured bands were Ralph Flanagan from New York's Hotel New Yorker and Art Mooney from Chicago's Aragon Ballroom, with vocalists and guest celebrities. Celebrities, seated at a "VIP table" near the bandstand, were interviewed by Martha Wright in New York and Fran Allison (of *Kukla, Fran & Ollie* fame) in Chicago. Added features were a "Sing a Song for TV" segment in New York and a "Dance for TV" interlude in Chicago, in which a member of the audience was caught in the spotlight and invited to perform on live nationwide television. For the final telecast, Art Mooney was replaced on the Chicago end by Billy May's Orchestra.

LET'S MAKE A DEAL

Quiz/Audience Participation

FIRST TELECAST: *May 21, 1967*
LAST TELECAST: *August 30, 1971*
BROADCAST HISTORY:
   May 1967–Sep 1967, NBC Sun 8:30–9:00
   Feb 1969–May 1969, ABC Fri 9:00–9:30
   May 1969–Jan 1970, ABC Fri 7:30–8:00
   Jan 1970–Jan 1971, ABC Sat 7:30–8:00
   Jan 1971–Aug 1971, ABC Mon 7:30–8:00
EMCEE:
   Monty Hall
ANNOUNCER:
   Jay Stewart

Let's Make a Deal premiered on the NBC daytime lineup in December 1963, and first moved to nighttime in 1967. The basic format had emcee Monty Hall open the show by choosing contestants from among members of the studio audience—who came dressed in outrageous costumes to attract his attention. The contestants chosen could trade something that they had brought with them for a first prize. They then had the opportunity to trade this first modest prize for objects hidden in boxes or behind curtains on the stage.

The hidden prizes could be trips, money, expensive jewelry, or other valuable merchandise—or they could be "zonks," worthless nonsense prizes. Many of the contestants were offered multiple options to test their greed in "trading" what they had already won for something possibly more expensive—or possibly a "zonk." At the end of the show the "Big Deal of the Day" gave two of the biggest winners the chance to trade their loot for whatever was behind one of three curtains. Although there was rarely a "zonk" at this point, a big winner could end up trading his current prizes for something worth much less.

In addition to its 13-year daytime run (1963–1968 on NBC, 1968–1976 on ABC), *Let's Make a Deal* appeared in prime time as a summer-replacement series in 1967 and as a regular series from 1969–1971. There was also a syndicated evening series from 1971–1976, a Vancouver-based revival in 1980, and another revival that premiered in the fall of 1984 and ran for two seasons. The following January it moved to the U.S.A. Cable network where it has been airing regularly ever since. Monty Hall, who was one of the creators and producers of *Let's Make a Deal*, presided over all versions as emcee.

LET'S PLAY THE GAME

see *Play the Game*

444

LET'S RHUMBA

Dance Instruction
FIRST TELECAST: *November 15, 1946*
LAST TELECAST: *January 17, 1947*
BROADCAST HISTORY:
  Nov 1946–Jan 1947, NBC Fri 8:15–8:30 (approx.)
HOST:
  D'Avalos

Dance-instruction program by D'Avalos, whose accent and oily good looks added a distinct Latin flavor to this early series. The featured dance was the "Ranchero."

LET'S SEE

Quiz
FIRST TELECAST: *July 14, 1955*
LAST TELECAST: *August 25, 1955*
BROADCAST HISTORY:
  Jul 1955–Aug 1955, ABC Thu 10:00–10:30
EMCEE:
  John Reed King

A short-lived, oddly formatted quiz show filmed at Convention Hall in Atlantic City, New Jersey. Panelists attempted to discover through indirect questions what attractions contestants had seen in Atlantic City. Sponsored by the Atlantic City Chamber of Commerce.

LETTER TO LORETTA, A

see *Loretta Young Show, The*

LEWIS & CLARK

Situation Comedy
FIRST TELECAST: *October 29, 1981*
LAST TELECAST: *July 30, 1982*
BROADCAST HISTORY:
  Oct 1981–Nov 1981, NBC Thu 8:30–9:00
  Dec 1981–Jan 1982, NBC Sat 8:30–9:00
  Jul 1982, NBC Fri 8:00–8:30
CAST:
  Stewart Lewis .... Gabe Kaplan
  Roscoe Clark .... Guich Koock
  Alicia Lewis.................... Ilene Graff
  John, the bartender....... Michael McManus
  Wendy, the waitress ...... Wendy Holcombe
  Silas Jones .... Clifton James
  Kelly Lewis .... Amy Linker
  Keith Lewis .... David Hollander
  Lester...................... Aaron Fletcher

Stu Lewis had a dream. Even though he was a city kid, he was fed up with the hustle and bustle of New York, so he packed up his wife Alicia and their two children and moved to sleepy Luckenback, in the Texas Panhandle. The wife and kids hated the idea, but no matter, Stu could at last realize his dream: owning a country-and-western club. He named it the Nassau County Café, after his former home in the New York suburbs. The place had been through so many owners that it sported a sign reading ALWAYS UNDER NEW MAN-

AGEMENT, and the big night of the week was when they had armadillo races. That was just fine with Stu, who had finally found a place where even his weak one-liners could draw a laugh.

Adjusting to the slower pace and the wide-open spaces took some doing for all the Lewises, but they did grow to appreciate the place. Along with the café came a manager, Roscoe Clark—the hick with the dopey grin on his face who was really a mite smarter than he looked. Then there was John, the bartender; Wendy, the goofy waitress; Silas Jones, the local beer distributor; and Lester, the town drunk. They all went out of their way to make the transplanted Easterners feel at home, whatever they thought of those jokes.

LEWISOHN STADIUM CONCERT

Music
FIRST TELECAST: *June 26, 1950*
LAST TELECAST: *August 7, 1950*
BROADCAST HISTORY:
  Jun 1950–Aug 1950, NBC Mon 9:30–10:30

Live concerts from New York's Lewisohn Stadium, featuring the New York Philharmonic Orchestra with various conductors and soloists.

LIAR'S CLUB

Quiz/Audience Participation
BROADCAST HISTORY:
  Syndicated only
  30 minutes
  Produced: *1969; 1976–1978*
  Released: *1969; September 1976*
HOST:
  Rod Serling *(1969)*
  Bill Armstrong *(1976–1977)*
  Allen Ludden *(1977–1978)*
PANELISTS *(1976–1978)*:
  Larry Hovis
  Betty White
  Dick Gautier
  Fannie Flagg
  Norm Crosby
  Joey Bishop
  Dody Goodman

Contestants on this game show were shown an unusual-looking object, then each of a panel of four celebrities gave an outlandish but plausible explanation as to its use. The contestant then had to wager all or part of an initial $100 on which panelist was telling the truth.

Rod Serling hosted an early and rather obscure version of the show. It returned in 1976 with Bill Armstrong and then Allen Ludden as host. Larry Hovis was the regular panelist on the later show, joined frequently by Betty White, Dick Gautier, and others.

LIBERACE SHOW, THE

Musical Variety
FIRST TELECAST: *July 1, 1952*

LAST TELECAST: *September 16, 1969*
BROADCAST HISTORY:
Jul 1952–Aug 1952, NBC Tue/Thu 7:30–7:45
Jul 1969–Sep 1969, CBS Tue 8:30–9:30
REGULARS:
Liberace
George Liberace and Orchestra (1952)
Richard Wattis (1969)
Georgina Moon (1969)
Jack Parnell Orchestra (1969)

Flamboyant pianist "Lee" Liberace (real name: Wladziu Valentino Liberace) appeared frequently on television during the 1950s and 1960s. His trademarks were always the same, and always the butt of innumerable jokes: the outlandish and very expensive wardrobe, the curly hair and pearly-tooth smile, and a florid piano style. Atop his Steinway was always perched an ornate candelabra (imitation Louis XIV). Women, especially older ones, loved it. The critics were not kind, but Liberace did not mind. "I cried," he remarked in one of show business' more memorable quotes, "all the way to the bank."

Liberace's first television exposure was on a local program in Los Angeles in 1951, followed by a 15-minute network summer series in 1952. The following year he began a syndicated series (filmed 1953–1955) that received extremely wide circulation and made him a great deal of money. These films were rerun for years and are said to have aired on more stations than any network or syndicated program up to that time. Later programs included an ABC daytime series in 1958–1959, and a network summer show in 1969, the latter a full hour in length. With him in the early years was violinist brother George, who led the orchestra. The 1969 variety show, which originated in London, featured guest stars and two regulars, Richard Wattis and Georgina Moon, who portrayed Liberace's butler and maid in a regular sketch sequence each week.

In later years Liberace concentrated on personal appearances, especially in Las Vegas, where he entertained a loyal, if aging, following.

LIBRARY OF COMEDY FILMS
see *Movies—Prior to 1961*

LIE DETECTOR
Discussion
BROADCAST HISTORY:
Syndicated only
30 minutes
Produced: *1983* (5 per week; 170 episodes total)
Released: *January 1983*
HOST:
F. Lee Bailey

Famed criminal lawyer and showman F. Lee Bailey hosted this rather peculiar series, in which guests were allowed to substantiate their claims by taking an on-camera polygraph test. Guests

were generally people who had been in the news, or on its fringes, due to claims of UFO sightings, reincarnation, involvement in scandals, etc.

LIEUTENANT, THE
Drama
FIRST TELECAST: *September 14, 1963*
LAST TELECAST: *September 5, 1964*
BROADCAST HISTORY:
Sep 1963–Sep 1964, NBC Sat 7:30–8:30
CAST:
Lt. William (Bill) Rice....... Gary Lockwood
Capt. Ray Rambridge .... Robert Vaughn
Lt. Samwell (Sanpan) Panosian (1963)
.... Steve Franken
Lt. Harris .... Don Penny
Lily........................ Carmen Phillips
Various roles .... Chris Noel
Sgt. Kagey..................... John Milford
Maj. Barker .... Henry Beckman
Col. Hiland............... Richard Anderson

The Lieutenant sought to convey what life was like for a newly commissioned officer in the peacetime Marine Corps. Bill Rice had graduated from Annapolis and gone through Marine Officers' Training School at Quantico, Virginia. After leaving Quantico, he was stationed as a second lieutenant at Camp Pendleton, California. Bill's friendly, easygoing manner made him popular with the recruits at Camp Pendleton and with the many girls he dated in an active off-duty social life. Bill's immediate superior was Capt. Ray Rambridge, who was harshly critical not because he disliked Bill, but because he wanted to make a good officer out of him. Also seen regularly was Lily, the owner of the nightclub frequented by Bill when he was off duty. Steve Franken was originally cast as one of Bill's fellow lieutenants, but left the show after five episodes were filmed and was replaced by Don Penny. Actress Chris Noel kept popping up as a recurring regular, but in a different role each time. In one episode she would be a nurse, in another a lady Marine, and in a third one of Bill's girlfriends. Sometimes her role was substantial and sometimes she was only peripherally involved in the story.

LIFE AND LEGEND OF WYATT EARP, THE
Western
FIRST TELECAST: *September 6, 1955*
LAST TELECAST: *September 26, 1961*
BROADCAST HISTORY:
Sep 1955–Sep 1961, ABC Tue 8:30–9:00
CAST:
Wyatt Earp................... Hugh O'Brian
Bat Masterson (1955–1957)
.... Mason Alan Dinehart III
Ben Thompson (1955–1956)...... Denver Pyle
Bill Thompson (1955–1956)....... Hal Baylor
Abbie Crandall (1955–1956).... Gloria Talbot
Marsh Murdock (1955–1956) ... Don Haggerty
Doc Fabrique (1955–1956).... Douglas Fowley

*Ned Buntline.................. Lloyd Corrigan
Jim "Dog" Kelly (1956–1958) ... Paul Brinegar
Jim "Dog" Kelly (1958–1959) .. Ralph Sanford
Mayor Hoover (1956–1957)... Selmer Jackson
Deputy Hal Norton (1957–1958)
.... William Tannen
Doc Holliday (1957–1961).... Douglas Fowley
Doc Holliday (temporary; 1959)
.... Myron Healy
Kate Holliday (1957–1958) .... Carol Stone
Shotgun Gibbs (1958–1961)
.... Morgan Woodward
Morgan Earp (1959–1961) .... Dirk London
Virgil Earp (1959–1961) .... John Anderson
Nellie Cashman (1959–1960) ... Randy Stuart
Old Man Clanton (1959–1961)
.... Trevor Bardette
Emma Clanton (1959–1960)... Carol Thurston
Sheriff Johnny Behan (1959)..... Lash La Rue
Sheriff Johnny Behan (1959–1961)
.... Steve Brodie
Curley Bill Brocius (1959–1961)
.... William Phipps
Johnny Ringo (1960–1961)...... Britt Lomond
Mayor Clum (1960–1961)........ Stacy Harris
Doc Goodfellow (1959–1961)
.... Damian O'Flynn

*Occasional

In the make-believe world of TV Westerns, *Wyatt Earp* was unique. Not only was it based on fact (more or less—there was a real Marshal Wyatt Earp, and he did have a very colorful life), but it developed its characters over a period of six years in a continuing story involving politics and family relationships as well as standard Western action. It was in many respects a serial drama. Part of the reason for this orientation was no doubt author-playwright Frederick Hazlitt Brennan, who wrote the scripts from the start.

The series began in 1955 with an episode titled "Mr. Earp Becomes a Marshal," in which Wyatt's friend, Marshal Whitney of Ellsworth, Kansas, was killed by a gunman. Wyatt accepted his badge and avenged his death. Wyatt's friend, famed showman and writer Ned Buntline, then provided him with his trademark, two "Buntline Special" pistols—.45s with extra-long barrels—with which to keep the peace. (The first time Wyatt saw them he locked Buntline in the pokey for carrying "over-sized pistols.") Their recoil was pretty ferocious, but their extra range allowed the marshal to drop an opponent from the other side of town. They proved handy, for during the rest of the first season Wyatt faced an array of foes in and around Ellsworth, including the murderous John Wesley Hardin and—most frequently—the outlaw Thompson brothers.

But Ellsworth was too small for Wyatt's talents, and for the second season he moved on to Dodge City to become marshal there (with no reference made to the fact that Matt Dillon already had that

job, at least on Saturday nights). Young Bat Masterson joined him as deputy for a while, before becoming a county sheriff in his own right. Wyatt then tried out Bat's brother Ed Masterson as a sidekick, but finally settled on Hal Norton as his deputy. Another character introduced in the 1956–1957 season was Wyatt's pal Jim "Dog" Kelly, who eventually got himself elected mayor of Dodge City, replacing Mayor Hoover. The 1957–1958 season brought an even more colorful real-life character to Dodge, the notorious Doc Holliday, a physician turned gambler and schemer (played by the same actor who had previously been Ellsworth's Doc Fabrique). Wyatt's brothers Virgil and Morgan Earp began to turn up in occasional episodes, usually requiring a steadying hand from their older brother.

In the 1959–1960 season Wyatt moved again, this time to Tombstone, Arizona, and the greatest battle of his career. Tombstone was a rough-and-ready town run by Old Man Clanton, leader of the "Ten Percent Gang." Clanton ruled the territory with an iron hand, exacting tribute from citizens and masterminding gunrunning schemes across the Mexican border. Johnny Behan was his hand-picked sheriff in Tombstone, and he had a private army of gunslingers to enforce his will. For two years, Earp, as marshal, battled the Clanton gang through political and legal means. Shotgun Gibbs, a peace-loving frontiersman, followed Wyatt from Dodge City to Tombstone to become his deputy. Some of Dodge's less respectable citizens showed up too, including Doc Holliday and gunslinger Curley Bill Brocius. Nellie Cashman provided some love interest for a season (Wyatt was always handy with the womenfolk) as the operator of the Birdcage Saloon.

The final showdown, again based on fact, came at the end of the last season, in 1961. In a five-part story that concluded *Wyatt Earp*'s original run, Wyatt discovered that the Clanton gang was using the O.K. corral as a center and fortress for their illegal activities. Wyatt tried to prevent bloodshed, but events moved rapidly toward a climactic shootout in which Wyatt, his brothers Morgan and Virgil, and Doc Holliday broke the power of the Clanton gang in the famous gunfight at the O.K. corral.

LIFE AND TIMES OF GRIZZLY ADAMS, THE
Adventure
FIRST TELECAST: *February 9, 1977*
LAST TELECAST: *July 26, 1978*
BROADCAST HISTORY:
   Feb 1977–Jul 1978, NBC Wed 8:00–9:00
CAST:
   James "Grizzly" Adams .... Dan Haggerty
   Mad Jack...................... Denver Pyle
   Nakuma....................... Don Shanks
   Robbie Cartman .... John Bishop

Set in the western United States during the late 1800s, *The Life and Times of Grizzly Adams* was the story of a man accused of a crime he had not committed, who sought refuge in the wilderness and discovered that life there suited him better than life in the city. With the help of a friend named Mad Jack and an Indian blood brother, Nakuma, Grizzly built a sturdy cabin and determined to live in harmony with nature. A grizzly bear cub that he had rescued from a ledge became his roommate. The bear was christened Ben, and though he grew to be an imposing animal weighing several hundred pounds, he remained as friendly as a child. With Ben as his constant companion, the bearded Grizzly Adams found wilderness adventure in dealing with nature, the elements, and strangers passing through. A frequent visitor was young Robbie Cartman, the son of a farmer living in the area, who loved to listen to Grizzly's tales.

Dan Haggerty, who starred in this series, played the same role in the movie *The Life and Times of Grizzly Adams,* and a similar role in another film, *The Adventures of Frontier Freemont.* Haggerty was originally an animal trainer rather than an actor, and was chosen for the film roles partly because of his remarkable rapport with bears. Denver Pyle appeared as his co-star in both films.

There was a real Grizzly Adams, upon whom this series was loosely based. He was born in Massachusetts in 1812, and spent many years in the Sierra Nevada after having gone bankrupt through a series of unfortunate business deals. The real Grizzly was a bit less altruistic than his TV counterpart. Having deserted his wife and children, he spent much of his time hunting and killing animals and capturing others for zoos (a few of the larger beasts almost killed *him* on one occasion or another). The real Ben died in a zoo that Adams himself opened in San Francisco in the 1850s. But Adams also loved animals and cared for many of them throughout his wilderness days. He died while on tour with P. T. Barnum in 1860.

LIFE BEGINS AT EIGHTY
Discussion
FIRST TELECAST: *January 13, 1950*
LAST TELECAST: *February 25, 1956*
BROADCAST HISTORY:
> *Jan 1950–Mar 1950,* NBC Fri 9:30–10:00
> *Apr 1950–Jul 1950,* NBC Sat 7:30–8:00
> *Jul 1950–Aug 1950,* NBC Fri 9:00–9:30
> *Oct 1950–Dec 1950,* ABC Tue 10:00–10:30
> *Dec 1950–Sep 1951,* ABC Tue 9:30–10:00
> *Oct 1951–Mar 1952,* ABC Mon 8:30–9:00
> *Mar 1952–Jun 1952,* DUM Fri 8:30–9:00
> *Jul 1952–Jun 1954,* DUM Fri 9:00–9:30
> *Sep 1954–Jul 1955,* DUM Sun 9:30–10:00
> *Aug 1955–Oct 1955,* ABC Sun 9:30–10:00
> *Oct 1955–Dec 1955,* ABC Sun 10:00–10:30
> *Jan 1956–Feb 1956,* ABC Sat 10:00–10:30
EMCEE:
Jack Barry

REGULAR PANELISTS:
Mrs. Georgiana Carhart
Fred Stein

Jack Barry created a radio version of *Life Begins at 80* in 1948, as a copy of his successful *Juvenile Jury*—substituting octogenarians for the youngsters. A panel of oldsters was posed questions submitted by viewers, and given the opportunity to expound on life from the vantage point of their years. They often provided hilarious quips and insights, and needed little prompting from Barry. An additional highlight of the show, which became more prominent toward the later years of the TV run, was the "Footlight Favorite." This was a show-business personality who performed for the audience. Some of these guests were themselves old-timers, like vaudevillians Joe Howard and Smith & Dale, singer Morton Downey and cornetist Vincent Buono (who performed with other original members of the Sousa Band); others, such as Lanny Ross and Faye Emerson, were younger.

Much of the appeal of *Life Begins at 80* lay in the chemistry of its panelists, the most delightful of whom were Mrs. Georgiana Carhart, an engaging flirt who told stories with an Irish brogue ("Why worry," she quipped, "you'll never get out of life alive anyway."), and Fred Stein, an active realtor who viewed life with similar enthusiasm. The two of them were with the show throughout its history, though both were nearing 90 by the end of the run. (The ages given for individual panelists vary somewhat, according to the source!) Oddly enough, continuity of panel members was less a problem on this show than on those with younger panels. The panelists might eventually die off, but none seemed to give up voluntarily. Among those appearing for extended periods were Joseph Rosenthal (85), John Draney (89), pianist Paolo Gallico (82), vaudevillian Lorna Standish (80), and Thomas Clark (81).

Emcee Barry (32) sometimes closed the show with a quote from Julia Ward Howe, who said of old age that "all the sugar is at the bottom of the cup."

LIFE IS WORTH LIVING
Religious Talk
FIRST TELECAST: *February 12, 1952*
LAST TELECAST: *April 8, 1957*
BROADCAST HISTORY:
> *Feb 1952–Apr 1955,* DUM Tue 8:00–8:30 (OS)
> *Oct 1955–Apr 1956,* ABC Thu 8:00–8:30
> *Oct 1956–Apr 1957,* ABC Mon 9:00–9:30
HOST:
Bishop Fulton J. Sheen

There was a time when anything was possible in prime-time television, even a weekly half hour featuring a charming, well-spoken Catholic bishop offering anecdotes and little lessons in morality ("sermons" would be too stuffy a word) for a large and devoted following. *Life Is Worth Living* was probably the most widely viewed religious series in TV history, and sponsors often paid a premium to have their commercials next to it (since they couldn't get *in* it). Its "star" and only "regular" was the Most Reverend Fulton J. Sheen, Auxiliary Bishop of New York, a modest, middle-level cleric who had long been heard on radio. On TV he was seen in a simulated study, punctuating his points with drawings scrawled on a blackboard. (One of his "angels," his TV crew, would slip in when he moved away, to clean off the board; the identity of this unseen hand was a great source of speculation among viewers). The bishop's famous sign-off: "God love you."

Many of Bishop Sheen's talks revolved around the evils of world communism, and perhaps the series' most dramatic incident came in early 1953 when he delivered a hair-raising reading of the burial scene from *Julius Caesar,* with the names of Caesar, Cassius, Marc Antony, and Brutus replaced by "Stalin, Beria, Malenkov, and Vishinsky. Stalin," Sheen intoned, with hypnotic forcefulness, "must one day meet his judgment." A few days later the Russian dictator suffered a sudden stroke, and a week later he was dead. There was never any comment from Sheen's office on this remarkable coincidence, which was widely reported in the press.

Four years after leaving ABC, Bishop Sheen returned with a half-hour syndicated series, *The Bishop Sheen Program,* which ran from 1961 to 1968. Despite the name change, it was virtually indistinguishable in format from *Life Is Worth Living.*

LIFE OF LEONARDO DA VINCI, THE
Historical Drama
FIRST TELECAST: *August 13, 1972*
LAST TELECAST: *September 10, 1972*
BROADCAST HISTORY:
Aug 1972–Sep 1972, CBS Sun 9:30–10:30
CAST:
Leonardo Da Vinci .... Philippe Leroy

This five-part dramatization of the life, achievements, and explorations of one of the greatest geniuses the world has ever known was originally produced in Italy. It was the Grand Prize winner at the 1972 Monte Carlo International Television Festival and was brought to American television by CBS in the summer of 1972.

LIFE OF RILEY, THE
Situation Comedy
FIRST TELECAST: *October 4, 1949*
LAST TELECAST: *August 22, 1958*
BROADCAST HISTORY:
Oct 1949–Mar 1950, NBC Tue 9:30–10:00
Jan 1953–Sep 1956, NBC Fri 8:30–9:00 (OS)
Oct 1956–Dec 1956, NBC Fri 8:00–8:30
Jan 1957–Aug 1958, NBC Fri 8:30–9:00

CAST (1949–1950):
Chester A. Riley .... Jackie Gleason
Peg Riley .... Rosemary DeCamp
Junior .... Lanny Rees
Babs .... Gloria Winters
Jim Gillis .... Sid Tomack
Digby "Digger" O'Dell .... John Brown
CAST (1953–1958):
Chester A. Riley .... William Bendix
Peg Riley .... Marjorie Reynolds
Junior .... Wesley Morgan
Babs Riley Marshall .... Lugene Sanders
Jim Gillis (1953–1955, 1956–1958)
.... Tom D'Andrea
Honeybee Gillis (1953–1955, 1956–1958)
.... Gloria Blondell
Egbert Gillis (1953–1955)... Gregory Marshall
Cunningham .... Douglas Dumbrille
Dangle .... Robert Sweeney
Riley's boss .... Emory Parnell
Waldo Binney .... Sterling Holloway
Otto Schmidlap .... Henry Kulky
Calvin Dudley (1955–1956)
.... George O'Hanlon
Belle Dudley (1955–1956)
.... Florence Sundstrom
Don Marshall (1957–1958) ..... Martin Milner

Television's original lovable bumbler was Chester A. Riley, a hardhat with a soft heart and a genius for unwittingly turning order into chaos. The role had been created on radio in 1943 by William Bendix. However, when the time came for the move to television, Bendix was tied up with movie commitments, and the opportunity went to young Jackie Gleason—his first TV series.

Riley worked in an aircraft plant in California, but viewers usually saw him at home, cheerfully disrupting life with his malapropisms and ill-timed intervention into minor problems. His stock answer to every turn of fate became a catch-phrase: "What a revoltin' development this is!" Riley's long-suffering wife, Peg, and their children, Babs and Junior, somehow saw that it always came out all right in the end. Others seen were Gillis, Riley's sarcastic friend, and "Digger" O'-Dell, the smiling undertaker ("Guess I'd better be shoveling off ..."), played by John Brown, the only member of the radio cast to make the transition to TV.

Jackie Gleason's bug-eyed portrayal of Riley did not catch on, and the program was canceled after only one season. Three years later it returned with an entirely new cast, headed by William Bendix, and ran for five years. The cast was relatively stable through the second run, although a few neighbors came and went and Babs eventually left to get married and Junior to go to college. Both kids returned occasionally to visit.

The show was filmed in Hollywood.

LIFE WITH ELIZABETH
Situation Comedy

BROADCAST HISTORY:
Syndicated only
30 minutes
Produced: *1953–1955* (65 episodes)
Released: *October 1953*
CAST:
Elizabeth...................... Betty White
Alvin .... Del Moore
Mrs. Chlorine *"Chloe"* Skinridge
.... Lois Bridge
Richard .... Dick Garton
Mr. Fuddy.................. Ray Erlenborn
ANNOUNCER:
Jack Narz

This domestic comedy was the first starring vehicle for Betty White. Each program consisted of three separate episodes in the life of a married couple, with the emphasis placed on gentle comedy and more talk than action. Alvin was the husband, a junior executive; Chloe, their neighbor; Richard, Alvin's not-too-bright friend; and Mr. Fuddy, Alvin's boss. Stormy was the couple's 185-pound St. Bernard, and Bandie, their Pekinese.

Betty White was fresh from local TV in Los Angeles, where she had originated *Life With Elizabeth* on KLAC-TV a year earlier. Hailed for her girl-next-door good looks (*TV Guide* called her a candidate for "America's Sweetheart"), she soon had her own daytime show on NBC, then graduated to several nighttime series (see Index).

LIFE WITH FATHER
Situation Comedy
FIRST TELECAST: *November 22, 1953*
LAST TELECAST: *July 5, 1955*
BROADCAST HISTORY:
Nov 1953–May 1954, CBS Sun 7:00–7:30
Aug 1954–Dec 1954, CBS Tue 10:00–10:30
Jan 1955–Jul 1955, CBS Tue 8:00–8:30
CAST:
Clarence Day, Sr.............. Leon Ames
Vinnie Day................... Lurene Tuttle
Clarence Day, Jr. (1953–1954) .... Ralph Reed
Clarence Day, Jr. (1954–1955) . Steven Terrell
Whitney Day (1953–1954)...... Ronald Keith
Whitney Day (1954–1955)...... B. G. Norman
Whitney Day (1955)....... Freddy Ridgeway
Harlan Day .... Harvey Grant
John Day (1953–1954)........ Freddie Leiston
John Day (1954–1955)....... Malcolm Cassell
Margaret.................. Dorothy Bernard
Nora........................ Marion Ross

Clarence Day, Jr.'s nostalgic autobiographical articles in *The New Yorker* were very successful in the 1920s. They later led to a best-selling novel, hit play, Hollywood movie, and in 1953 to this live television series. Set in New York City in the 1880s, *Life with Father* was the story of Clarence Day, Sr., a stern but loving Victorian father, his wife Vinnie, and their four red-headed sons. Despite the fact that he ruled with an iron hand, and

was a staunch traditionalist, Father Day dealt fairly with his family and earned their lifelong respect.

The turnover in actors playing the Day children in this series was rather high, although the adult members of the cast lasted longer. This was the first live color series for network TV originating in Hollywood.

LIFE WITH LINKLETTER
Variety/Audience Participation
FIRST TELECAST: *October 6, 1950*
LAST TELECAST: *April 25, 1952*
BROADCAST HISTORY:
Oct 1950–Apr 1952, ABC Fri 7:30–8:00 (OS)
EMCEE:
Art Linkletter
REGULAR:
Muzzy Marcellino Orchestra

This was a nighttime version of Linkletter's long-running *House Party* show, a daytime standby on radio and television from 1945 until 1970. All of the familiar Linkletter elements were present, including the mad stunts performed by members of the studio audience for prizes, and the interviews with children. Guest stars also appeared, but the center of attraction was always Art himself, one of broadcasting's all-time favorite personalities. The program originated in Hollywood, and for a time in 1951–1952 alternated with *Say It with Acting*.

LIFE WITH LUCY
Situation Comedy
FIRST TELECAST: *September 20, 1986*
LAST TELECAST: *November 15, 1986*
BROADCAST HISTORY:
Sep 1986–Nov 1986, ABC Sat 8:00–8:30
CAST:
Lucy Barker .... Lucille Ball
Curtis McGibbon .... Gale Gordon
Margo Barker McGibbon ... Ann Dusenberry
Ted McGibbon............. Larry Anderson
Becky McGibbon .... Jenny Lewis
Kevin McGibbon.......... Philip J. Amelio II
Leonard Stoner .... Donovan Scott
THEME:
sung by Eydie Gorme

Probably the most widely anticipated new series—and most embarrassing flop—of the 1986 season was this ill-conceived comedy that marked the return of Lucille Ball to series television after 12 years. In order to get her, ABC had to promise a huge salary, complete creative control, no pilot or testing before preview audiences, and a guaranteed time slot on the fall schedule. What it got was an unimaginative rehash of the Lucy shows of many years before, only this time with a 75-year-old star.

Lucy was cast as a free-spirited grandmother whose husband Sam had died, leaving her half interest in M&B Hardware in South Pasadena, Calif. Lucy decided to move in and help run the place, but her idea of "help"—like arranging all the merchandise in alphabetical order on the shelves—was not appreciated by her late husband's partner, blustery old Curtis McGibbon (played by Ms. Ball's longtime foil Gale Gordon, then 80). To further complicate matters Lucy's daughter Margo was married to Curtis' son Ted, a law student, and all of them, plus Lucy's young grandchildren Becky and Kevin, lived in the building together. With one bathroom. Leonard was an employee at the store.

There was plenty of slapstick, sight gags, and Lucy celebrity chasing, as in days of old; Ms. Ball was in fine shape, but unfortunately the scripts were not. The series disappeared abruptly after less than two months, never to be seen again.

LIFE WITH LUIGI
Situation Comedy
FIRST TELECAST: *September 22, 1952*
LAST TELECAST: *December 22, 1952*
BROADCAST HISTORY:
Sep 1952–Dec 1952, CBS Mon 9:30–10:00
CAST:
Luigi Basco . . . . J. Carrol Naish
Pasquale . . . . Alan Reed
Rosa . . . . Jody Gilbert
Miss Spalding . . . . Mary Shipp
Schultz . . . . Sig Ruman
Olson . . . . Ken Peters
Horwitz . . . . Joe Forte

Irish-American actor J. Carroll Naish became typecast as an Italian after playing the role of Luigi Basco for several years, first on CBS radio starting in 1948, and for a short period on a live TV series in 1952. Luigi was a newly arrived Italian immigrant who was learning to love his new homeland. He did not always understand what everything meant, and often took things too literally, but his sweet, gentle nature won everyone over. The setting alternated between Luigi's antique shop and his friend Pasquale's restaurant. Pasquale, a fellow immigrant who had been in this country for several years, had paid Luigi's boat fare to America in hopes that he might be able to marry off his fat daughter Rosa to his impressionable countryman.

Despite its popularity on radio, *Life with Luigi* had only a short career on TV. Its extreme ethnic stereotyping was found offensive by some, and sponsor troubles provided the *coup de grâce*.

LIFE WITH SNARKY PARKER
Children's
FIRST TELECAST: *January 9, 1950*
LAST TELECAST: *August 30, 1950*
BROADCAST HISTORY:
Jan 1950–Mar 1950, CBS Mon/Tue/Thu/Fri 7:45–8:00
Apr 1950–Aug 1950, CBS Mon–Fri 6:15–6:30

PUPPETEERS:
Bil Baird
Cora Baird
PRODUCER/DIRECTOR:
Yul Brynner

The marionettes of puppeteers Bil and Cora Baird performed in this "saga" of life in the Old West. Snarky Parker was the deputy sheriff of the town of Hot Rock. He was in love with the local schoolteacher, rode a horse named Heathcliffe, and fought with Ronald Rodent, the local villain. Also seen regularly in this live series were Slugger, the piano player in the Bent Elbow Saloon, and Paw, the father of the schoolteacher. Yul Brynner, later more successful as a performer, was the producer and director of this show. After leaving evening hours in August, it remained on the air for another month as a late-afternoon weekday entry.

LIFE WITH THE ERWINS
see *Stu Erwin Show, The*

LIFELINE
Medical Documentary
FIRST TELECAST: *September 9, 1978*
LAST TELECAST: *December 30, 1978*
BROADCAST HISTORY:
Sep 1978, NBC Thu 10:00–11:00
Oct 1978–Nov 1978, NBC Sun 10:00–11:00
Dec 1978, NBC Sun 9:00–10:00
PRODUCER:
Alfred Kelman
DIRECTOR OF PHOTOGRAPHY:
Robert Elfstrom
NARRATOR:
Jackson Beck

This unusual program used no actors. It was essentially a medical documentary, focusing on a different real-life doctor in a different city each week, as he met one medical emergency after another. To produce the programs a camera crew followed each doctor for several months, filming him with his family and at work, including actual operating room and emergency room scenes where lives often hung in the balance. Viewers got to know the doctor and his patients, heightening the sense of real-life drama. The hard realities of medical life apparently depressed viewers to the point where they simply would not watch *Lifeline*. Acclaimed for its quality, that same dedication to gruesome detail led to *Lifeline*'s cancellation by year's end. The series was produced by the company that had produced the highly acclaimed "Body Human" specials during the 1977–1978 season.

LIFE'S MOST EMBARRASSING MOMENTS
Comedy
FIRST TELECAST: *August 2, 1985*
LAST TELECAST: *September 10, 1985*

Aug 1985–Sep 1985, ABC Fri 10:00–11:00
Sep 1985, ABC Tue 10:00–11:00
HOST:
Steve Allen

ABC's *Life's Most Embarrassing Moments* specials, which originally aired on an irregular basis
beginning in 1983, were rerun as a weekly series
during the summer of 1985. Hosted by veteran
comic Steve Allen, each episode consisted primarily of celebrity outtakes, much in the manner
of NBC's *TV's Bloopers & Practical Jokes* and
ABC's less successful *Foul-Ups, Bleeps & Blunders.*

LIFESTYLES OF THE RICH AND FAMOUS
Magazine
FIRST TELECAST: *July 21, 1986*
LAST TELECAST: *September 19, 1986*
BROADCAST HISTORY:
Jul 1986–Aug 1986, ABC Mon–Fri 12:00 MID–
12:30 A.M.
Sep 1986, ABC Tue–Fri 12:00 MID–12:30 A.M.
HOST/NARRATOR:
Robin Leach

Some people have built an entire life's career out
of One Big Idea—for example, Allen Funt's *Candid Camera,* or Ross Bagdasarian's squeaky-
voiced *Alvin & the Chipmunks.* Celebrity reporter
Robin Leach's Big Idea may not prove as durable
as that, but it certainly received a lot of exposure
in the mid-1980s. It consisted simply of documentary-style tours of the most opulent homes in the
world, especially those of show-biz celebrities,
accompanied by gushing narrative and endless
paeans to the glories of wealth. Everything seen
on this show was "elegant," "glamorous," "luxurious," "exclusive," or all of the above. As *TV
Guide* remarked, "If you're into envy at all, it's a
fudge sundae."
Leach, a British expatriate who was formerly a
celebrity-chaser for *Entertainment Tonight, People* magazine, and the Cable News Network, narrated this hymn to avarice with such outrageous
enthusiasm that he resembled a human press release. *Lifestyles of the Rich and Famous* began as
a syndicated series in 1984, and aired concurrently
on the ABC network in daytime from April to September 1986 and in late night from July to September 1986. A modified version continued in ABC
daytime from September 1986 to May 1987 under
the title *Fame, Fortune and Romance.* Still another
variation was syndicated in early 1987 with the
title *Runaway With the Rich and Famous.*

LIGHTS, CAMERA, ACTION
Talent
FIRST TELECAST: *July 4, 1950*
LAST TELECAST: *August 20, 1950*
BROADCAST HISTORY:
Jul 1950–Aug 1950, NBC Sun 10:00–10:30

EMCEE:
Walter Woolf King

Summer talent show originating in Hollywood
and shown via kinescope over the NBC East and
Midwest networks. Professional young talent and
a panel of "name" judges were featured. Walter
Woolf King, a matinee idol of the 1930s, emceed.

LIGHTS OUT
Suspense Anthology
FIRST TELECAST: *July 19, 1949*
LAST TELECAST: *September 29, 1952*
BROADCAST HISTORY:
Jul 1949–Aug 1949, NBC Tue 9:00–9:30
Nov 1949–Sep 1952, NBC Mon 9:00–9:30
NARRATOR:
Jack LaRue (1949–1950)
Frank Gallop (1950–1952)
SPECIAL MUSICAL EFFECTS:
Paul Lipman, theremin (1949)
Arlo Hults, organ (1949–1952)
Doris Johnson, harp (1950–1952)

Live dramatic show featuring stories of mystery,
suspense, and the supernatural. At the beginning
of each episode viewers would see only a close
shot of a pair of eyes, then a bloody hand reaching
to turn out the lights, followed by an eerie laugh
and the words, "Lights out, everybody . . ."
The plays themselves were a combination of
adaptations and dramas written especially for
TV. Spooky houses, loved ones returned from the
dead, and lonely country roads were frequent elements of *Lights Out.* At first lesser-known actors
and actresses were featured, but beginning in
1950 a "guest star" policy brought in such names
as Boris Karloff, Burgess Meredith, Billie Burke,
Leslie Nielsen, Basil Rathbone, Eddie Albert, Raymond Massey, and Yvonne DeCarlo.
Lights Out began on radio in 1934 and had been
seen on television in 1946 as a series of four specials produced by Fred Coe.

LIME STREET
Adventure/Detective
FIRST TELECAST: *September 21, 1985*
LAST TELECAST: *October 26, 1985*
BROADCAST HISTORY:
Sep 1985–Oct 1985, ABC Sat 9:00–10:00
CAST:
James Greyson Culver .... Robert Wagner
Edward Wingate .... John Standing
Henry Wade Culver .... Lew Ayres
Elizabeth Culver .... Samantha Smith
Margaret Ann Culver .... Maia Brewton
Celia Wesphal .... Julie Fulton
Evelyn Camp .... Anne Haney

A year after *Hart to Hart* left the air, Robert Wagner returned playing another glamorous, globe-
trotting investigator in this short-lived series. Like
Jonathan Hart, James Greyson Culver was very

rich, and very fond of adventure. Operating out of his sprawling ranch in Virginia, where he bred horses, Culver was half of a team investigating international cases of insurance fraud for a large, London-based insurance company. His partner was Edward Wingate, a British aristocrat who lived in a castle outside London and who had been James' roommate at Oxford. Elizabeth and Margaret Ann were widower James' two adorable children; Henry, his dapper father; Celia, his private secretary; and Evelyn, the family housekeeper and surrogate mom.

Limited audiences and an off-screen tragedy contributed to the early demise of this series. Samantha Smith, a Maine schoolgirl who had become famous when she wrote to Soviet leader Yuri Andropov urging peace and then was invited to visit the U.S.S.R., was signed to play Elizabeth; however, the 13-year-old was killed in a plane crash after only a few episodes were filmed.

LINEUP, THE
Police Drama
FIRST TELECAST: *October 1, 1954*
LAST TELECAST: *January 20, 1960*
BROADCAST HISTORY:
   Oct 1954–Jun 1958, CBS Fri 10:00–10:30 (OS)
   Sep 1958–Sep 1959, CBS Fri 10:00–10:30
   Sep 1959–Jan 1960, CBS Wed 7:30–8:30
CAST:
   Det. Lt. Ben Guthrie .... Warner Anderson
   Inspector Matt Grebb (1954–1959) . Tom Tully
   Inspector Fred Asher (1954–1959)
     .... Marshall Reed
   Inspector Dan Delaney (1959–1960)
     .... William Leslie
   Inspector Charlie Summers (1959–1960)
     .... Tod Barton
   Officer Pete Larkin (1959–1960) ... Skip Ward
   Policewoman Sandy McAllister (1959–1960)
     .... Rachel Ames

Produced in cooperation with the San Francisco Police Department, *The Lineup* sought to give realistic semi-documentary portrayals of the work of law officers in the beautiful Bay City. Ben Guthrie and Matt Grebb were the officers who tracked down criminals throughout most of the series' run. The stories were all based on actual cases from the files of the S.F.P.D., and generally included a police lineup where the victims of the crime attempted to pick out the perpetrators.

When the series expanded to an hour in the fall of 1959, there were a number of changes in the cast. Matt Grebb and Fred Asher were gone, replaced by two new inspectors. In addition, Officer Pete Larkin and Policewoman Sandy McAllister became regulars.

LITTLE HOUSE ON THE PRAIRIE
Adventure/Drama
FIRST TELECAST: *September 11, 1974*
LAST TELECAST: *March 21, 1983*

BROADCAST HISTORY:
   Sep 1974–Sep 1976, NBC Wed 8:00–9:00
   Sep 1976–Mar 1983, NBC Mon 8:00–9:00
CAST:
   Charles Ingalls (1974–1982) .. Michael Landon
   Caroline Ingalls (1974–1982) .. Karen Grassle
   Laura Ingalls Wilder .... Melissa Gilbert
   Mary Ingalls Kendall (1974–1981)
     .... Melissa Sue Anderson
   Carrie Ingalls (alternating; 1974–1982)
     .... Lindsay Greenbush
   Carrie Ingalls (alternating; 1974–1982)
     .... Sidney Greenbush
   Lars Hanson (1974–1978) ...... Karl Swenson
   Nels Oleson .... Richard Bull
   Harriet Oleson. .... Katherine MacGregor
   Nellie Oleson Dalton (1974–1981)
     .... Alison Arngrim
   Willie Oleson (1975–1983) .. Jonathan Gilbert
   Dr. Baker .... Kevin Hagen
   Rev. Robert Alden .... Dabbs Greer
   Eva Beadle Simms (1974–1978)
     .... Charlotte Stewart
   Mr. Isaiah Edwards (1974–1977, 1982–1983)
     .... Victor French
   Ebenezer Sprague (1975–1976)... Ted Gehring
   Grace Edwards (1976–1977)... Bonnie Bartlett
   Jonathan Garvey (1977–1981)... Merlin Olsen
   Andy Garvey (1977–1981)
     .... Patrick Laborteaux
   Alice Garvey (1977–1980) ..... Hersha Parady
   Albert Ingalls (1978–1982)
     .... Matthew Laborteaux
   Adam Kendall (1978–1981) .. Linwood Boomer
   Grace Ingalls (alternating; 1978–1982)
     .... Wendy Turnbeaugh
   Grace Ingalls (alternating; 1978–1982)
     .... Brenda Turnbeaugh
   Larrabee (1978–1979) ...... Don "Red" Baker
   Hester Sue Terhune (1978–1983)
     .... Ketty Lester
   Almanzo Wilder (1979–1983) ..... Dean Butler
   Eliza Jane Wilder (1979–1982)
     .... Lucy Lee Flippin
   Percival Dalton (1980–1981) ..... Steve Tracy
   James Cooper (1981–1982) ..... Jason Bateman
   Cassandra Cooper (1981–1982)
     .... Missy Francis
   Nancy Oleson (1981–1983) .... Allison Balson
   Jenny Wilder (1982–1983) .. Shannen Doherty
   John Carter (1982–1983)............ Stan Ivar
   Sarah Carter (1982–1983) ...Pamela Roylance
   Jeb Carter (1982–1983)..... Lindsay Kennedy
   Jason Carter (1982–1983)..... David Friedman
   Etta Plum (1982–1983) .... Leslie Landon

The time was the late 1870s, and the locale was the American West, but *Little House on the Prairie* was not a Western in the usual sense. There were no cowboys, Indians, or cowtown saloons in this version of frontier life—it was more like *The Waltons* in a different setting, the story of a loving family in trying times.

Charles Ingalls was a homesteader struggling to make a living for his family on a small farm near the town of Walnut Grove, Plum Creek, Minnesota. The Ingalls had moved from the great plains of Kansas to Walnut Grove in search of a future in a young and growing community. With Charles were his wife, Caroline, and their three daughters, teenagers Mary and Laura, and little Carrie (played alternately by a pair of identical twins). Stories related the experiences of family life and growing children, the constant struggle against natural disasters and ruined crops, and the dealings with other members of the little community in which they lived. Among the Ingalls' new friends were Mr. Hanson, the mill owner; Nels Oleson, the proprietor of the general store; and Mr. Edwards, a nearby farmer who became a good friend, despite his rather harsh exterior.

A lot happened on *Little House* after that simple beginning, as the program came to resemble a serial. First, Mr. Edwards left in 1977 (Victor French got his own series, *Carter Country*), and was replaced by Jonathan Garvey (played by former Los Angeles Rams star Merlin Olsen). Garvey had a wife named Alice and a young son, Andy. In 1978 Caroline gave birth to a fourth daughter, Grace, but oldest daughter Mary lost her sight and was sent to a school for the blind. Mary promptly fell in love with her instructor, Adam Kendall, and they moved off to the Dakotas.

No sooner were they gone than the town of Walnut Grove fell on hard times, and Charles and his family (along with some other regulars) had to pack up and move to the bustling frontier city of Winoka, where their household was enlarged again by the addition of Albert, a young orphan they adopted. City life didn't sit well with the family, however, so they all moved back to Walnut Grove, which had miraculously recovered from his problems. Mary and Adam moved back too, and had a baby boy, who unfortunately perished (along with Alice Garvey) when the school for the blind where Mary was teaching burned down.

Feeling left out amid all this travail, daughter Laura decided to become a teacher, and was courted by and eventually married Almanzo Wilder, in the fall of 1980. Even nasty Nellie Oleson got married, although problems arose when it was discovered that her husband, Percival, was really Jewish (Isaac Cohen) and a decision had to be made about how to raise their children. Since Nellie had twins, everything was resolved by deciding they raise the son as a Jew and the daughter as a Christian!

Jonathan Garvey, now a widower, moved to nearby Sleepy Eye to manage a warehouse, and convinced Charles to set up a freight business between there and Walnut Grove. Meanwhile, over in the Adam and Mary subplot, Adam regained his sight in a freak accident, and was accepted to law school.

In the fall of 1981, Adam's father offered him a job with his law firm in New York, and Adam and Mary left Walnut Grove forever. Nellie and Percival were also in New York, where he had taken over his late father's business. Jonathan and Andy Garvey were no longer seen, while Hester Sue Terhune, who had worked at the Sleepy Eye school for the blind, moved to Walnut Creek to work, along with Caroline Ingalls, at Mrs. Oleson's restaurant.

There were more adoptions in the 1981–1982 season, with Charles and Caroline adding recently orphaned James and Cassandra Cooper to their household, and lonely Mrs. Oleson taking in an orphan named Nancy—who bore a striking resemblance to her departed Nellie, in both looks and nastiness. Mr. Edwards, whose problems with drinking had cost him his marriage, returned to Walnut Creek the following spring, and Laura gave birth to a daughter, Rose.

Michael Landon's decision to leave *Little House* prompted a number of changes in the fall of 1982. The title was changed to *Little House: A New Beginning,* and Laura and Almanzo became the principal stars. Economic problems forced Charles to sell the "little house" and move to Burr Oak, Iowa, where he had found a job. Moving into the former Ingalls home were John and Sarah Carter, who ran the town newspaper, and their sons Jeb and Jason. Laura gave up her teaching job to raise both Rose and Jenny, who was orphaned when Almanzo's brother Royal died. Laura's replacement at the school, Etta Plum, was portrayed by Michael Landon's daughter Leslie.

The series' audience had been declining for several years, and the revised version lasted only a single season.

The stories told on *Little House* were originally based on the "Little House" books by Laura Ingalls Wilder, which contained her recollections of growing up on the American frontier. On the TV series, the actress playing Laura functioned as the narrator. Michael Landon, who starred in this series, was also its executive producer.

LITTLE PEOPLE, THE
see *Brian Keith Show, The*

LITTLE REVUE, THE
Music
FIRST TELECAST: *September 4, 1949*
LAST TELECAST: *April 21, 1950*
BROADCAST HISTORY:
Sep 1949–Mar 1950, ABC Sun 8:30–9:00
Mar 1950–Apr 1950, ABC Fri 9:30–10:00
REGULARS:
Nancy Evans
Dick Larkin
Bill Sherry
Gloria Van
Billy Johnson
Nancy Doran and Dick France, dancers
Bill Weber Marionettes
Rex Maupin's Orchestra

A program of smooth, relaxed music and assorted variety-show elements from Chicago.

LITTLE SHOW, THE
see *Van Camp's Little Show*

LITTLE THEATRE
see *ABC Dramatic Shorts—1952-1953*

LITTLE WOMEN
Drama
FIRST TELECAST: *February 8, 1979*
LAST TELECAST: *March 8, 1979*
BROADCAST HISTORY:
　Feb 1979–Mar 1979, NBC Thu 8:00–9:00
CAST:
　Marmee March . . . . Dorothy McGuire
　Rev. John March . . . . William Schallert
　Jo March . . . . Jessica Harper
　Meg March Brooke . . . . Susan Walden
　Amy March Laurence . . . . . . Ann Dusenberry
　John Brooke . . . . Cliff Potts
　Theodore Laurie Laurence . . Richard Gilliland
　Prof. Friedrich Bhaer . . . . David Ackroyd
　Aunt Kathryn March . . . . Mildred Natwick
　Melissa Jane Driscoll ("Lissa") . . . Eve Plumb
　Hannah . . . . Virginia Gregg
　James Laurence . . . . Robert Young
　Amanda . . . . Maggie Malooly

In October 1978 NBC had aired a two-part movie adaptation of the Louisa May Alcott novel *Little Women.* The following spring this short-lived series, with most of the original movie cast, continued the saga of the March family where Miss Alcott's novel left off. Two of the three March daughters were married, Meg to John Brooke and Amy to the grandson of Rev. March's wealthy neighbor, Mr. Laurence. Headstrong aspiring writer Jo was engaged to the German-born Friedrich Bhaer, and a new member was added to the March household, in the person of young cousin Lissa, who was an eerie look-alike for the deceased daughter, Beth. The others living in the 19th-century New England home were old maid Aunt March and the housekeeper, Hannah.

LIVE LIKE A MILLIONAIRE
Talent/Variety
FIRST TELECAST: *January 5, 1951*
LAST TELECAST: *February 7, 1953*
BROADCAST HISTORY:
　Jan 1951–Apr 1951, CBS Fri 9:30–10:00
　Apr 1951–Jun 1951, CBS Fri 9:00–9:30
　Jul 1951–Mar 1952, CBS Fri 10:00–10:30
　Oct 1952–Feb 1953, ABC Sat 7:30–8:00
EMCEE:
　Jack McCoy (1951)
　John Nelson
ASSISTANT:
　Michael O'Halloran (1951)
　Connie Clawson (1951–1952)

The format of *Live Like a Millionaire* was a variation on Arthur Godfrey's *Talent Scouts.* Each week three or four sets of talented parents performed on the show, after being introduced by their children. The winning parent or parents won the chance to "live like a millionaire" for an entire week. They were waited on, sent on trips, provided with expensive cars, or whatever else they might desire.

Jack McCoy was the original emcee and, when he left at the end of March 1951, he was replaced by the show's announcer, John Nelson. At the outset, Michael O'Halloran played Merton the Butler, waiting on the winners, but he was soon replaced by hostess Connie Clawson. When ABC picked up *Live Like a Millionaire* in the fall of 1952, only emcee Nelson was with the show. The basic format was retained but the prize became purely monetary. The winning parents received one week's interest on $1,000,000, plus an all-expenses-paid vacation.

LIVELY ONES, THE
Musical Variety
FIRST TELECAST: *July 26, 1962*
LAST TELECAST: *September 12, 1963*
BROADCAST HISTORY:
　Jul 1962–Sep 1962, NBC Thu 9:30–10:00
　Jul 1963–Sep 1963, NBC Thu 9:30–10:00
REGULARS:
　Vic Damone
　Joan Staley ("Tiger," 1962)
　Shirley Yelm ("Charley," 1962)
　Quinn O'Hara ("Smitty," 1963)
　Gloria Neil ("Melvin," 1963)
　Jerry Fielding Orchestra

Vic Damone was host of this big, brash, swinging musical variety show which aired during the summers of 1962 and 1963. Each show presented established stars and new talent, appearing in different, often offbeat locations around the country. The only regulars on the series, other than Vic Damone, were his two "dates," Tiger and Charley in 1962 and Smitty and Melvin in 1963.

LLOYD BRIDGES SHOW, THE
Dramatic Anthology
FIRST TELECAST: *September 11, 1962*
LAST TELECAST: *August 27, 1963*
BROADCAST HISTORY:
　Sep 1962–Aug 1963, CBS Tue 8:00–8:30
CAST:
　Adam Shepherd and various others
　 . . . . Lloyd Bridges

Lloyd Bridges narrated and starred in this dramatic-anthology series. Each episode began with free-lance journalist Adam Shepherd digging into a story, sometimes current and sometimes historical. Shepherd then imagined himself as the primary protagonist (also played by Bridges), and the drama unfolded.

LOBO

Police Comedy

FIRST TELECAST: *September 18, 1979*
LAST TELECAST: *August 25, 1981*
BROADCAST HISTORY:

Sep 1979–Mar 1980, NBC Tue 8:00–9:00
Dec 1980–Aug 1981, NBC Tue 8:00–9:00

CAST:

Sheriff Elroy P. Lobo . . . . Claude Akins
Deputy Perkins . . . . Mills Watson
Deputy Birdwell "Birdie" Hawkins
. . . . Brian Kerwin
Sarah Cumberland (1979–1980)
. . . . Leann Hunley
Rose Lobo Perkins (1979–1980)
. . . . Cydney Crampton
Margaret Ellen (1979–1980)
. . . . Janet Lynn Curtis
Chief J. C. Carson (1980–1981)
. . . . Nicolas Coster
Sgt. Hildy Jones (1980–1981) . . . . . Nell Carter
Peaches (1980–1981) . . . . Amy Botwinick
Brandy (1980–1981) . . . . Tara Buckman

Lobo was a slapstick parody on police shows. Sheriff Elroy P. Lobo of Orly County, Georgia, was not really a crook. He might be a bit larcenous in intent, but somehow he always wound up doing the right thing, in spite of himself. Time and time again, he set off on a money-making scheme and wound up catching crooks and recovering loot—which he never got to keep. Of dubious help was his bumbling, idiot brother-in-law, Deputy Perkins. A bit brighter was the handsome, college-educated mayor's son, Deputy Birdie Hawkins, though he too was on the naive side. He somehow managed to believe in the integrity of his boss, despite mounting evidence to the contrary. Birdie dated pretty Sarah Cumberland, who ran the Orly Hotel. Sexy Margaret Ellen was a waitress who showed up regularly at the sheriff's office stuffed into one skimpy costume or another, bringing meals for prisoners and staff. As with *B.J. and the Bear,* from which it was spun off, *Lobo* had wild car chases and sexy women populating almost every episode.

When *Lobo* returned late in 1980 to start its second season there were a number of changes. The title, which had been *The Misadventures of Sheriff Lobo* during the first season, was shortened to *Lobo.* Elroy and his two deputies had moved to Atlanta, where they were appointed to a special police task force. In true *Lobo* fashion, they were there because the governor had been impressed by the low crime rate in Orly County under Lobo's regime, a misunderstanding caused by Lobo's neglecting to send crime statistics to the state capitol. In Atlanta their presence was resented by Chief of Detectives Carson, who couldn't understand how the hicks from Orly were going to help his overworked force. Nevertheless Lobo and his boys bumbled their way to success fighting urban crime. Most of the Atlanta

cops, including Carson's aide, sarcastic Sgt. Hildy Jones, didn't get along too well with the country bumpkins. About the only exceptions were Peaches and Brandy, two sexy undercover cops who worked with Lobo and his men on special assignments.

LOCK UP

Law Drama
BROADCAST HISTORY:

Syndicated only
30 minutes
Produced: *1959–1961* (78 episodes)
Released: *August 1959*

CAST:

Herbert L. Maris . . . . Macdonald Carey
Casey . . . . Olive Carey
Jim Weston . . . . John Doucette

This rather straightforward lawyer series starred Macdonald Carey as Herbert L. Maris, a real-life corporation lawyer whose passion was defending those he believed had been unjustly convicted of crimes. Typically the program opened with the accused, or a friend of the accused, approaching Maris with a last-ditch appeal for help, whereupon the attorney set about obtaining evidence of his innocence.

Casey was Maris' middle-aged secretary, who was always trying to match him up with a "nice young girl" (actress Olive Carey was no relation to the show's star, but was the wife of Western star Harry Carey). The real Maris, 79 years old and semiretired when the series was made, opined that it was "well enough done that it won't—shall we say—do me any harm."

LOGAN'S RUN

Science Fiction
FIRST TELECAST: *September 16, 1977*
LAST TELECAST: *January 16, 1978*
BROADCAST HISTORY:

Sep 1977, CBS Fri 9:00–10:00
Oct 1977–Jan 1978, CBS Mon 8:00–9:00

CAST:

Logan . . . . Gregory Harrison
Jessica . . . . Heather Menzies
Rem . . . . Donald Moffat
Francis . . . . Randy Powell

The Earth of 2319 was radically different from that of the 20th century. There had been a nuclear holocaust that had devastated much of the planet. The remnants of civilization were living in isolated cities, each with its own life-style, separated from each other by vast stretches of wasteland and ruins. One of the surviving communities was the City of Domes, where all residents lived entirely for their own pleasure. It would have been idyllic were it not mandated that nobody could live past his 30th birthday. Logan was one of the city's citizens, a Sandman (elite policeman) who had fled as his 30th birthday approached. Together with a young girl named Jessica, who had helped him escape from the city, and an android (humanlike robot) named Rem, Logan searched for a purported utopia called Sanctuary. Pursuing them was a dedicated Sandman (Francis) who wanted to take them back to the City of Domes to die in the ritual ceremony known as Carousel. The chase of the fugitives by their pursuer, and their encounters with the diverse and strange remnants of human civilization, both in modern cities and in the wilds between them, provided the subject matter for this series.

It was based on a novel by William F. Nolan and George Clayton Johnson and a feature-length movie, both also titled *Logan's Run.*

LONE RANGER, THE
Western
FIRST TELECAST: *September 15, 1949*
LAST TELECAST: *September 12, 1957*
BROADCAST HISTORY:
Sep 1949–Sep 1957, ABC Thu 7:30–8:00
Jun 1950–Sep 1950, ABC Fri 10:00–10:30
CAST:
The Lone Ranger (1949–1952, 1954–1957)
.... Clayton Moore
The Lone Ranger (1952–1954) ..... John Hart
Tonto .... Jay Silverheels
THEME:
"William Tell Overture," by G. Rossini (composed in 1829)

The Lone Ranger was typical of the first wave of Westerns to hit TV, in the early 1950s. Characters and plots were simple—good guys *vs.* bad guys— and there was none of the character development that marked the later "adult" Westerns.

The Lone Ranger had begun as a local radio show in 1933, and had quickly spread to a nation-wide hookup (it was, in fact, the cornerstone of the then new Mutual Radio Network). In 1949 it was brought to TV in a series of half-hour films, made in Hollywood especially for the new medium. The opening episode, on September 15, 1949, told the familiar story of how the Lone Ranger got his name and his mission in life. He had been one of a posse of six Texas Rangers tracking a gang of desperadoes. The Rangers were lured into an ambush in a canyon, and five of them were slaughtered. The sixth, young John Reid, was left for dead. But Reid managed to crawl to safety near a water hole, where he was found and nursed back to health by a friendly Indian named Tonto. Reid had once helped Tonto and the Indian now vowed to stay with him as the "lone" Ranger sought to avenge the deaths of his comrades. "You kemo sabe," said Tonto; "it mean 'trusty scout.' " Avenge they did, cornering the outlaw Butch Cavendish in a dramatic battle.

Reid buried his past at the graves of the five dead Rangers, donned a mask, and set out with Tonto to avenge wrongs throughout the Old West. He had no visible means of support (he never accepted payment for his good deeds), but subsisted on the income from a silver mine that he and his brother—who was one of the deceased Rangers—had discovered. Periodically he returned to the mine, which was run for him by an honest old man, to collect the proceeds and stock up on silver bullets. Then, with a hearty "Hi-yo Silver, away!" he would sally forth once again, like some idealized Don Quixote, with faithful Tonto at his side and their faithful mounts Silver and Scout.

Although the Lone Ranger never killed anyone (sometimes his adversaries killed themselves and each other), there was plenty of action, and the show was a great favorite with the younger audience. Parents liked it too, because of the lack of overt killing and the hero's faultless grammar— which in itself was unique for the Old West. *The Lone Ranger* was in fact the biggest hit ABC had in its early years, and when the A. C. Nielsen Company first began compiling national ratings for network programs in 1950 it was the only ABC program to rank in the top 15. Everything else was on NBC or CBS. Reruns of *The Lone Ranger* aired during the day on Saturdays from June 1953 to September 1960 on CBS and then on NBC for another year, as well as on ABC late afternoons for four years ending in September 1961 (the first three on Sunday and the last year on Wednesday). An animated version of *The Lone Ranger* aired Saturday mornings on CBS for three years ending in September 1969, and was revived in 1980 as part of *The Tarzan/Lone Ranger Hour.*

The Lone Ranger was created by George W. Trendle and Fran Striker, who were also responsible for *The Green Hornet,* and there was an unusual link between the two programs. John Reid's nephew Dan was supposed to be the father of Britt Reid, who became the avenger of crime in another era as *The Green Hornet.*

Clayton Moore was the best-known TV Lone Ranger (he also filled the role in two feature films made in the late 1950s), but the character was also played by veteran actor John Hart for a couple of seasons. Tonto was always played to poker-faced perfection by Jay Silverheels, a mixed-blood Mohawk Indian who in later years became quite successful as a horse breeder and racer. Asked once if he would consider racing Scout, he smiled and replied, "Heck, I can beat Scout."

LONER, THE
Western
FIRST TELECAST: *September 18, 1965*
LAST TELECAST: *April 30, 1966*
BROADCAST HISTORY:
Sep 1965–Apr 1966, CBS Sat 9:30–10:00
CAST:
William Colton .... Lloyd Bridges

At the conclusion of the Civil War, ex-Union cavalry officer William Colton decided to head west in search of adventure and a new life. As he wandered the frontier, looking for something that would give his life meaning, his encounters with people both honest and dishonest, hardworking and fast-buck, gave him an expanded understanding of himself and of human beings in general.

LONG, HOT SUMMER, THE
Drama
FIRST TELECAST: *September 16, 1965*
LAST TELECAST: *July 13, 1966*
BROADCAST HISTORY:
  Sep 1965–Jan 1966, ABC Thu 10:00–11:00
  Jan 1966–Jul 1966, ABC Wed 10:00–11:00
CAST:
  "Boss" Will Varner (1965) .. Edmond O'Brien
  "Boss" Will Varner (1966) .... Dan O'Herlihy
  Ben Quick...................... Roy Thinnes
  Clara Varner .... Nancy Malone
  Jody Varner .... Paul Geary
  Minnie Littlejohn .... Ruth Roman
  Eula Harker .... Lana Wood

Adult drama set in small, Deep South community of Frenchman's Bend, dominated by aging, tyrannical Will Varner, who owned the town, and young Ben Quick, who had returned after 13 years to reclaim his father's farm and challenge Varner's absolute authority. Ben's father had been "destroyed" by Varner, but Ben was determined to settle the fight from which his father ran. Also featured were Varner's troubled, sensitive daughter Clara, his weak, immature son Jody, his mistress Minnie, and Eula, the sexy young daughter of the local postmaster.

The Long, Hot Summer was based on material by William Faulkner, primarily the novel *The Hamlet* and the short story "Barn Burning," which were adapted for a hit movie in 1958.

LONGSTREET
Detective Drama
FIRST TELECAST: *September 9, 1971*
LAST TELECAST: *August 10, 1972*
BROADCAST HISTORY:
  Sep 1971–Aug 1972, ABC Thu 9:00–10:00
CAST:
  Mike Longstreet .... James Franciscus
  Nikki Bell .... Marlyn Mason
  Duke Paige .... Peter Mark Richman
  Mrs. Kingston .... Ann Doran

Mike Longstreet was a New Orleans insurance-company investigator. While on a case he had the double misfortune of having his wife killed and his eyesight destroyed by people determined that he not solve the case. Despite his injury, Mike refused to quit the business. With his German shepherd guide dog Pax to help him get around, and an electronic cane to judge distances, Longstreet remained a remarkably successful investigator. If anything, blindness sharpened his other senses and analytical skills. Mike's girl Friday, Nikki, was his biggest booster; his insurance-com-

pany friend Duke Paige worked with him on many cases.

Kung Fu expert Bruce Lee appeared in this series as Longstreet's self-defense instructor.

LOOK MA, I'M ACTING
  see *Say It With Acting*

LOOK PHOTOCRIME
  see *Photocrime*

LORETTA YOUNG SHOW, THE
Dramatic Anthology
FIRST TELECAST: *September 20, 1953*
LAST TELECAST: *September 10, 1961*
BROADCAST HISTORY:
  Sep 1953–Jun 1958, NBC Sun 10:00–10:30 (OS)
  Oct 1958–Sep 1961, NBC Sun 10:00–10:30
HOSTESS/STAR:
  Loretta Young

The Loretta Young Show's trademark, one that was often lampooned by comedians, was the dramatic entrance Miss Young made at the beginning of each episode. She would come sweeping through a doorway with her full-skirted dress swirling around her and move into the center of the room to introduce the evening's play. Equally distinctive was the program's close, when she would return and read a few lines of poetry or a passage from the Bible that amplified or restated the message of the play just telecast. Miss Young starred in over half the plays aired during this filmed series' eight-season run, playing everything from nuns to housewives. The periods and locations varied, the story may have been serious, amusing, or touching, but all of the tales told on *The Loretta Young Show* were uplifting. They portrayed the nobler side of the human spirit and were designed to teach as well as entertain. Episodes in which Miss Young had not starred were rerun under various titles as summer series with other performers functioning as host. When *The Loretta Young Show* went into syndication, the introductions were deleted in compliance with Miss Young's wishes. She was concerned that the dresses she had worn for them had become dated with the passage of time.

When this series premiered in September 1953 it was titled *Letter to Loretta*. All of the stories were done as responses to letters that she had received from her fans during the years she had been a motion-picture star. She would read a letter at the beginning of each show and then star in the dramatized answer. Although the title was changed to *The Loretta Young Show* on February 14, 1954, this format was retained through the first two seasons of the series, with Miss Young starring in every episode. At the start of the 1955–1956 season there were a number of changes. The series became a straight dramatic show and the letter concept was dropped. Miss Young, who was recovering from an operation when filming had started in June, was replaced by a succession of guest hosts and stars until her return on Christmas night. After her return, however, she cut back her starring appearances to roughly half of each year's episodes.

Over the years many performers starred, with or without Miss Young, in episodes of this series. Those who had the leads in at least three stories were Eddie Albert, George Nader, Hugh O'Brian, Beverly Washburn, Jock Mahoney, Craig Stevens, Ralph Meeker, James Daly, James Philbrook, Stephen McNally, Pat Crowley, Claude Akins, Barry Atwater, Regis Toomey, Everett Sloane, Ricardo Montalban, and John Newland. The latter two deserve special mention. Ricardo Montalban starred on nine different occasions and John Newland on thirteen. Mr. Newland, in addition to being Loretta's most frequent co-star, from 1957–1959 directed numerous episodes in which he was not acting.

NBC aired reruns of this show on weekday afternoons from February 1960 to December 1964 under the title *The Loretta Young Theatre.*

LORNE GREENE'S LAST OF THE WILD
Wildlife/Nature
BROADCAST HISTORY:
Syndicated only
30 minutes
Produced: *1974–1979* (104 episodes)
Released: *Fall 1974*
HOST/NARRATOR:
Lorne Greene

A wildlife documentary series devoted to endangered species.

LORNE GREENE'S NEW WILDERNESS
Wildlife/Nature
BROADCAST HISTORY:
Syndicated only
30 minutes
Produced: *1982–1986*
Released: *Fall 1982*
HOST/NARRATOR:
Lorne Greene

A wildlife documentary series, similar to *Lorne Greene's Last of the Wild,* hosted by the former star of *Bonanza.* Mr. Greene passed away in the fall of 1987.

LOST IN SPACE
Science Fiction
FIRST TELECAST: *September 15, 1965*
LAST TELECAST: *September 11, 1968*
BROADCAST HISTORY:
Sep 1965–Sep 1968, CBS Wed 7:30–8:30
CAST:
Prof. John Robinson . . . . Guy Williams
Maureen Robinson . . . . June Lockhart
Don West . . . . Mark Goddard
Judy Robinson . . . . Marta Kristen
Will Robinson . . . . Billy Mumy
Penny Robinson . . . . Angela Cartwright
Dr. Zachary Smith . . . . Jonathan Harris
The Robot . . . . Bob May
The Robot's voice . . . . Dick Tufeld

The spaceship *Jupiter II* was supposed to take the Robinson family—Professor John, wife Maureen, and their three children—on a five-year voyage of exploration to a planet in the Alpha Centauri star system. It was, that is, until Dr. Zachary Smith sabotaged the control system so that it could not function properly. The control system was tied into the programming of the robot that went along as part of the exploration team, a friendly, logical, ambulatory machine that was strongly reminiscent of Robby the Robot in the movie *Forbidden Planet.* Smith, apparently in the employ of some foreign government, found himself trapped aboard the ship when it took off, leaving him hopelessly "lost in space" with the Robinsons and the ship's pilot, Major Donald West. An uneasy truce was made between all parties, for none of the scheduled passengers particularly trusted Dr. Smith, knowing what he had done. For three seasons the Robinsons and their unwanted guest wandered from planet to planet, trying to find their way home. The stories were fanciful and rather childish, full of monsters and strange intelligent life forms that were a constant threat, and an endless series of cliff-hanger endings designed to bring viewers back the following week. Dr. Smith was always trying to make a deal with some form of extraterrestrial intelligence to get him back without the others, but his plans never worked out. If he wasn't thwarted by the adults in the party, resourceful little Will Robinson, or the Robot, he managed to botch it up all by himself. He was a rather pompous, cowardly, and inept character.

LOTSA LUCK
Situation Comedy
FIRST TELECAST: *September 10, 1973*
LAST TELECAST: *May 24, 1974*
BROADCAST HISTORY:
Sep 1973–Jan 1974, NBC Mon 8:00–8:30
Jan 1974–May 1974, NBC Fri 8:30–9:00
CAST:
Stanley Belmont . . . . Dom DeLuise
Mrs. Belmont . . . . Kathleen Freeman
Arthur Swann . . . . Wynn Irwin
Olive Swann . . . . Beverly Sanders
Bummy . . . . Jack Knight

Bachelor Stanley Belmont was the custodian of the New York City bus company's lost-and-found department. But it was his home life and not his job that was the source of most of his problems and aggravations. Living with him was his bossy, autocratic mother, his klutzy sister, Olive, and Olive's unemployed husband, Arthur. The fact that Arthur was perfectly content to live off Stanley's earnings, and did not seem particularly interested in finding a job and moving out of Stanley's home, did not endear him to his brother-in-law. One of Stanley's co-workers, his good friend Bummy, was the only other regular in the cast. Based on the British series *On the Busses*.

LOTTERY
Dramatic Anthology
FIRST TELECAST: *September 9, 1983*
LAST TELECAST: *July 12, 1984*
BROADCAST HISTORY:
Sep 1983–Dec 1983, ABC Fri 9:00–10:00
Mar 1984, ABC Thu 9:00–10:00
Jun 1984–Jul 1984, ABC Thu 9:00–10:00
CAST:
Patrick Sean Flaherty . . . . Ben Murphy
Eric Rush . . . . Marshall Colt

Television is a medium of fantasy, and this program offered the favorite fantasy of all: "What if I had a million dollars . . . ?" *Lottery* told two or three stories each week about ordinary people, often struggling to make ends meet, each of whom suddenly won two to four million dollars. The bearer of the good news was Patrick Flaherty, representative of Ireland's Intersweep Lottery, who first had to find the winner, then hand him an envelope containing $5,000 in cash and a check worth millions. With Flaherty was his smiling partner, handsome Eric Rush of the Internal Revenue Service.

No one seemed to mind the presence of the IRS at the joyous moment. Instead, stories centered around the little guy who now could give the big guys their comeuppance, life's losers who were winners at last, various moral dilemmas, and those frantic folks who had lost their all-important Sweepstakes ticket—without which they wouldn't get the money. In all, more than $133 million in make-believe winnings were given away during the short run of this series.

LOU GRANT
Newspaper Drama
FIRST TELECAST: *September 20, 1977*
LAST TELECAST: *September 13, 1982*
BROADCAST HISTORY:
Sep 1977–Jan 1978, CBS Tue 10:00–11:00
Jan 1978–Sep 1982, CBS Mon 10:00–11:00
CAST:
Lou Grant . . . . Edward Asner
Charlie Hume . . . . Mason Adams
Joe Rossi . . . . Robert Walden
Billie Newman McCovey . . . . . . Linda Kelsey
Margaret Pynchon . . . . Nancy Marchand
Art Donovan. . . . . Jack Bannon
Dennis "Animal" Price . . . . . . Daryl Anderson
National Editor (1977–1979) . . . . . Sidney Clute
National Editor (1979–1982) . . Emilio Delgado
Foreign Editor (1977–1980) . Laurence Haddon
Financial Editor (1978–1979) . . . . . Gary Pagett
Adam Wilson (1978–1982) . . . Allen Williams
Photo Editor (1979–1981) . . . . Billy Beck

Carla Mardigian (1977) . . . . . Rebecca Balding
Ted McCovey (1981–1982) . . . . Cliff Potts
Linda (1981–1982) . . . . . Barbara Jane Edelman
Lance (1981–1982) . . . . Lance Guest

In the final episode of *The Mary Tyler Moore Show*, Lou Grant and most of the news staff of WJM-TV in Minneapolis were all fired. Fifty years old, and out of work, Lou moved to Los Angeles where, next season, he got a new job. No longer involved with television news, he became city editor of the *Los Angeles Tribune*, a crusading newspaper under the autocratic rule of its owner-publisher, Margaret Pynchon. Though he officially worked for managing editor Charlie Hume, an old friend, Lou often found himself in a battle of wills with the widowed Mrs. Pynchon, a woman with personality traits—stubbornness, toughness, and determination—very similar to his own. Despite the fireworks that usually erupted when they disagreed, there was an underlying mutual respect between them. Other principals included Joe Rossi, the hotshot, talented young investigative reporter; Carla Mardigian, an ambitious young girl reporter (who lasted only a few weeks, to be replaced by Billie Newman, another young reporter with similar aspirations); Art Donovan, the assistant city editor; and Animal, the staff photographer. Although essentially a dramatic series, *Lou Grant* did have its lighter moments, usually revolving around the interplay between the members of the paper's staff.

The personal life of reporter Billie Newman was the focus of the 1981–1982 season premiere episode of *Lou Grant*, as Billie wed baseball scout Ted McCovey. The series concluded its run the following spring, amid a controversy not radically different from the type that had served as story material for *Lou Grant*. Despite CBS' statement that *Lou Grant* was canceled because of declining ratings, there were many who felt that the political statements of series star Edward Asner were the real reason. Asner himself accused CBS of dropping the show because of his unpopular and highly publicized condemnation of U.S. involvement in Central America.

LOVE, AMERICAN STYLE
Comedy Anthology
FIRST TELECAST: *September 29, 1969*
LAST TELECAST: *January 11, 1974*
BROADCAST HISTORY:
Sep 1969–Jan 1970, ABC Mon 10:00–11:00
Jan 1970–Sep 1970, ABC Fri 10:00–11:00
Sep 1970–Jan 1971, ABC Fri 9:30–10:00
Jan 1971–Jan 1974, ABC Fri 10:00–11:00
REPERTORY COMPANY:
Mary Grover (1969–1970)
Stuart Margolin (1969–1973)
Buzz Cooper (1969–1970)
Barbara Minkus
Bill Callaway (1969–1971)
Lynne Marta (1969–1970)
Tracy Reed (1969–1970, 1972–1974)

Phyllis Davis (1970–1974)
Jaki De Mar (1970–1972)
Richard Williams (1970–1972)
Jim Hampton (1971–1974)
Clifton Davis (1971)
James A. Watson, Jr. (1972–1974)
Jed Allan (1973–1974)

This imaginative anthology was a collection of short comedy playlets, starring all sorts of big names, and dealing with the all-important subject of love. Love was seen from all sides, young and old, rich and poor, unmarried, just married, long married, and multi-married. Generally three or four playlets were presented on each episode, interspersed with short comic "blackouts" by a repertory company of six or seven young performers. In 1972 a tasteful "Lovemate of the Week" centerfold was also added, featuring a different girl each week.

A short list of those appearing in *Love, American Style* reads like a Who's Who of Hollywood: Phyllis Diller, Nanette Fabray, Tammy Grimes, Ann Sothern, Paul Ford, Pat Paulsen, Milton Berle, Sonny & Cher, the Lennon Sisters, George Gobel, Dorothy Lamour, Wally Cox, Tony Randall, Paul Lynde, Burt Reynolds, Harry Morgan, Rich Little, Ozzie & Harriet, Tiny Tim (as a suspected vampire), Sid Caesar, Imogene Coca, Jacqueline Susann, and Martha Raye. Ronny Howard and Anson Williams appeared in a skit entitled "Love and the Happy Days" which served as the pilot for the hit series, *Happy Days*.

The first telecast, on September 29, 1969, was typical of the show's format. Act I, "Love and a Couple of Couples": Michael Callan is a suitor about to propose when his ex-wife turns up, spies the ring, tries it on—and can't get it off. Act II, "Love and the Hustler": Flip Wilson is pool shark "Big Red," who undertakes to instruct a young lady in the fine points of the game. Act III, "Love and the Pill": Bob Cummings and Jane Wyatt are parents worried about their daughter's plans to embark on a "swinger's tour" of Europe with her boyfriend.

Love, American Style reruns were seen in ABC daytime from June 1971 to May 1974.

An updated series of romantic vignettes, titled *New Love, American Style*, was produced for ABC's week-day daytime lineup more than a decade later, running from December 1985 to August 1986.

LOVE & MARRIAGE
Situation Comedy
FIRST TELECAST: *September 21, 1959*
LAST TELECAST: *January 25, 1960*
BROADCAST HISTORY:
Sep 1959–Jan 1960, NBC Mon 8:00–8:30
CAST:
William Harris . . . . William Demarest
Pat Baker . . . . Jeanne Bal
Steve Baker . . . . Murray Hamilton
Sophie . . . . Kay Armen

Stubby Wilson . . . . Stubby Kaye
Susan Baker . . . . Susan Reilly
Jennie Baker . . . . Jennie Lynn

William Harris was an old-time music publisher whose hatred for the currently popular rock 'n' roll music was hurting his business and his health. He loved melodious music and refused to deal with most of the popular songs submitted to him. His progressive son-in-law Steve was a constant source of irritation and his daughter Pat was often left in the role of mediator between her father and her husband. Pat had inveigled herself into partnership with her father so that she could keep an eye on him. Featured in the show were William Harris' secretary, Sophie, and song-plugger Stubby Wilson, who performed many of the songs submitted to the publisher and spent a lot of time reminiscing about the "good old days" in the music-publishing business.

LOVE BOAT, THE
Situation Comedy
FIRST TELECAST: *September 24, 1977*
LAST TELECAST: *September 5, 1986*
BROADCAST HISTORY:
Sep 1977–Jan 1978, ABC Sat 10:00–11:00
Jan 1978–Sep 1985, ABC Sat 9:00–10:00
Sep 1985–May 1986, ABC Sat 10:00–11:00
Jun 1986–Sep 1986, ABC Fri 10:00–11:00
CAST:
Captain Merrill Stubing . . . . . Gavin MacLeod
Ship's Doctor Adam Bricker . . . Bernie Kopell
Yeoman-Purser Burl "Gopher" Smith
. . . . Fred Grandy
Bartender Isaac Washington . . . . . . Ted Lange
Cruise Director Julie McCoy (1977–1984)
. . . . Lauren Tewes
Vicki Stubing (1979–1986) . . . . Jill Whelan
Cruise Director Judy McCoy (1984–1986)
. . . . Pat Klous
Photographer Ashley Covington
Evans (Ace) (1984–1986) . . . Ted McGinley
THE LOVE BOAT MERMAIDS (1985–1986):
Susie . . . . Deborah Bartlett
Maria . . . . Tori Brenno
Jane . . . . Nanci Lynn Hammond
Amy . . . . Terri Hatcher
Patti . . . . Debra Johnson
Sheila . . . . Macarena
Starlight . . . . Andrea Moen
Mary Beth . . . . Beth Myatt
THEME:
"The Love Boat," by Paul Williams and Charles Fox, sung by Jack Jones (1977–1985) and Dionne Warwick (1985–1986).

Love Boat was closely patterned after ABC's hit series *Love, American Style*, which ran from 1969 to 1974. Both programs consisted each week of several short comic sketches dealing with love of all types, young and old, married and unmarried, and both featured famous guest stars in the sketches. The difference was that all of *Love*

Boat's stories were set aboard the *Pacific Princess,* a luxury cruise ship which embarked each week on a romantic, sentimental, and often hilarious voyage across tropic seas. The three or four stories told on each telecast were thus interwoven and often involved the ship's crew, who were seen on the show every week.

Famous movie and TV stars of the past and present were delighted to accept guest roles on *The Love Boat*'s floating sound stage, combining work with travel to exotic locations. Among the many famous names appearing were Raymond Burr, Pearl Bailey, Steve Allen, Janet Gaynor, Greer Garson, Jane Wyman, Don Adams, Helen Hayes, Mildred Natwick, Dick Van Patten and Charo (in the recurring role of singer-guitarist April Lopez). Some stories revolved around the crew, with Capt. Stubing's womanizing brother Marshall (played by MacLeod wearing a toupée) showing up on occasion, and Vicki, Stubing's 12-year-old daughter by a past girlfriend, becoming a regular cast member in 1979.

Most of *Love Boat*'s episodes were filmed on two real cruise ships, the *Pacific Princess* and the *Island Princess,* during their regular voyages from the Virgin Islands to Alaska. Paying passengers were invited to participate as extras, getting a raffle ticket for each day they "worked." Most passengers were delighted to take part, and cruises on which filming was planned were always booked solid long in advance.

Among the highlights of later seasons were voyages to ever more exotic locations—Australia in 1981, the Mediterranean in 1982, and China in 1983. February 1982 saw the first "Love Boat Follies," a shipboard musical extravaganza featuring the regular cast plus Cab Calloway, Carol Channing, Van Johnson, Ethel Merman, Ann Miller, and Della Reese.

A number of changes were made in the fall of 1985, in an attempt to buoy the slowly sinking series. In addition to a new time period and a new theme singer, a group of eight beautiful singer/dancers (The Love Boat Mermaids) were added to the crew, appearing in a weekly musical number and working in the casino that had been added to the *Pacific Princess.* It didn't help. In the spring of 1986, at the end of the original series run, Capt. Stubing romanced and married Emily Heywood, played by Marion Ross. (A number of new two-hour *Love Boat* specials were aired during the following season.)

The series was based on Jeraldine Saunders' novel *The Love Boats* (drawn from her experiences as a cruise hostess), and first aired as a series of specials during the 1976–1977 season. ABC aired reruns of *The Love Boat* on weekday mornings from June 1980 to June 1983.

LOVE ON A ROOFTOP
Situation Comedy
FIRST TELECAST: *September 6, 1966*
LAST TELECAST: *September 8, 1971*

BROADCAST HISTORY:
Sep 1966–Jan 1967, ABC Tue 9:30–10:00
Jan 1967–Apr 1967, ABC Thu 9:00–9:30
Apr 1967–Aug 1967, ABC Thu 9:30–10:00
May 1971–Sep 1971, ABC Wed 9:00–9:30
CAST:
David Willis..................... Peter Deuel
Julie Willis .... Judy Carne
Stan Parker .... Rich Little
Carol Parker .... Barbara Bostock
Phyllis Hammond............ Edith Atwater
Fred Hammond .... Herb Voland
Jim Lucas .... Sandy Kenyon

The joys of young love between a young married couple from different social backgrounds was the theme of this comedy. Art student Julie came from a wealthy family, but when she met $85-a-week apprentice architect David it was love at first sight. They married and moved into a small, windowless, top-floor walkup apartment. Its only asset was an adjacent stairway which led to the roof, and a spectacular view of the San Francisco Bay Area. Also seen were the neighbors, the Parkers (Stan was an "idea" man who composed menus for a living), Julie's unsympathetic parents, the Hammonds, and David's co-worker, Jim.

Reruns of the 1966–1967 series were aired during the summer of 1971.

LOVE, SIDNEY
Situation Comedy
FIRST TELECAST: *October 28, 1981*
LAST TELECAST: *August 29, 1983*

BROADCAST HISTORY:
Oct 1981–Sep 1982, NBC Wed 9:30–10:00
Oct 1982–Dec 1982, NBC Sat 9:30–10:00
Mar 1983–Aug 1983, NBC Mon 8:00–8:30
CAST:
Sidney Shorr .... Tony Randall
Laurie Morgan............... Swoosie Kurtz
Patti Morgan .... Kaleena Kiff
Judge Mort Harris (1981–1982) ... Alan North
Jason Stoller................. Chip Zien
Mrs. Gaffney (1982–1983) ..... Barbara Bryne
Nancy (1982–1983) .... Lynne Thigpen

Series star Tony Randall's role of Sidney Shorr bore a certain resemblance to both Felix Unger from *The Odd Couple* and Judge Walter Franklin from *The Tony Randall Show.* They were all prim, proper, and meticulous to a fault. However, in the made-for-television film on which this series was based Sidney did have one distinctive trait. In that film, *Sidney Shorr,* which aired a few weeks before the series premiered, Sidney was a homosexual. In the series, although homosexuality could have been inferred, it was never mentioned.

Sidney was a middle-aged commercial artist who had been living alone for years. Into his bachelor life had come a perky young actress, Laurie Morgan, who was pregnant and unmarried. Laurie had considered an abortion until Sidney talked her out of it. Now, a few years later, a grateful Laurie and her cute young daughter Patti had moved into Sidney's eight-room Manhattan apartment, and Sidney was in seventh heaven. Into his lonely life, scarred by memories of a domineering mother, had come someone he could love. The relationship between Sidney and Laurie was that of a close brother and sister, and he doted on the precocious Patti like an indulgent uncle. To those who saw Laurie as the nymphomaniac Gloria Trenell on the inane daytime soap opera *As Thus We Are,* her real-life role of loving mother would have come as a surprise.

Jason Stoller was the art director for the Graham and Ludwig Advertising Agency, Sidney's biggest account, Nancy was Jason's secretary, Judge Harris was one of Sidney's neighbors, and Mrs. Gaffney his superintendent's nosy wife, who was romantically attracted to an uninterested and unresponsive Sidney.

LOVE STORY
Anthology
FIRST TELECAST: *April 20, 1954*
LAST TELECAST: *June 29, 1954*
BROADCAST HISTORY:
  Apr 1954–Jun 1954, DUM Tue 8:30–9:00

The teleplays that were aired in this live anthology were all stories that showed the better side of human nature—the affection and concern people could have for one another. Lesser-known actors and actresses were starred.

LOVE STORY
Dramatic Anthology
FIRST TELECAST: *October 3, 1973*
LAST TELECAST: *January 2, 1974*
BROADCAST HISTORY:
  Oct 1973–Jan 1974, NBC Wed 10:00–11:00
THEME:
  "Love Story (Where Do I Begin)," by Francis Lai

In the wake of the best-selling novel and smash-hit 1970 movie starring Ryan O'Neal and Ali MacGraw, NBC felt that *Love Story* was just what was needed for prime time. Unfortunately, the TV series had nothing to do with the book or movie, sharing only the name and that pretty theme song. That may have accounted for its short tenure on the air.

The stories were about people in love, young and old, rich and poor, married and single, and were set in various locations across the U.S. Generally, lesser-known actors and actresses appeared.

LOVE THAT BOB
syndicated title for *Bob Cummings Show, The*

LOVE THAT JILL
Situation Comedy
FIRST TELECAST: *January 20, 1958*
LAST TELECAST: *April 28, 1958*
BROADCAST HISTORY:
  Jan 1958–Apr 1958, ABC Mon 8:00–8:30
CAST:
  Jill Johnson .... Anne Jeffreys
  Jack Gibson .... Robert Sterling
  Richard .... James Lydon
  Pearl........................... Betty Lynn
  Myrtle .... Polly Rose
  Ginger .... Barbara Nichols
  Melody..................... Nancy Hadley
  Peaches .... Kay Elhardt

Real-life husband-and-wife team Robert Sterling and Anne Jeffreys played the heads of rival Manhattan model agencies in this short-lived comedy. Jill was always after one of Jack's clients or models, and vice versa, and Jack would not have minded landing Jill as well. Also seen regularly were Jill's male secretary, Richard, Jack's secretary, Pearl, and a bevy of beautiful models with names such as Melody, Ginger, and Peaches.

LOVE THY NEIGHBOR
Situation Comedy
FIRST TELECAST: *June 15, 1973*
LAST TELECAST: *September 19, 1973*
BROADCAST HISTORY:
  Jun 1973–Jul 1973, ABC Fri 9:30–10:00
  Aug 1973–Sep 1973, ABC Wed 8:00–8:30
CAST:
  Ferguson Bruce .... Harrison Page
  Jackie Bruce.............. Janet MacLachlan
  Charlie Wilson .... Ron Masak
  Peggy Wilson................. Joyce Bulifant
  Murray Bronson .... Milt Kamen
  Harry Mulligan .... Herbie Faye

This integrated comedy revolved around the friendship between a Caucasian family and a young black couple who had just moved into their previously all-white neighborhood. Charlie Wilson was somewhat nonplused when he first discovered that his new neighbor on Friar Tuck Lane in suburban Sherwood Forest Estates (near Los Angeles) was not only black, but was the new efficiency expert at Turner Electronics, the company where he was a union shop steward.

Based on the English TV hit, *Love Thy Neighbor.*

LOVES ME, LOVES ME NOT
Situation Comedy
FIRST TELECAST: *March 20, 1977*
LAST TELECAST: *April 27, 1977*
BROADCAST HISTORY:
  Mar 1977, CBS Sun 10:30–11:00
  Mar 1977–Apr 1977, CBS Wed 8:30–9:00
CAST:
  Jane .... Susan Dey
  Dick .... Kenneth Gilman
  Tom .... Art Metrano
  Sue .... Phyllis Glick

This short romantic-comedy mini-series was about two young single people who were dating each other. Dick and Jane had their ups and their downs and, since their relationship was just getting off the ground, were unsure of their feelings for each other. He was a newspaper reporter and she was a teacher. Tom was Dick's best friend and his editor at the newspaper, and Sue was Tom's wife.

LUCAN

Adventure
FIRST TELECAST: *December 26, 1977*
LAST TELECAST: *December 4, 1978*
BROADCAST HISTORY:
    Dec 1977–Jan 1978, ABC Mon 8:00–9:00
    Jun 1978–Jul 1978, ABC Sun 8:00–9:00
    Nov 1978–Dec 1978, ABC Mon 8:00–9:00
CAST:
    Lucan .... Kevin Brophy
    Dr. Hoagland .... John Randolph
    Prentiss .... Don Gordon

Lucan was the story of a young man of 20 who had been raised in the forest, by wolves. For his first ten years he had never known another human being, and now, though acclimated to the ways of civilization, he still found himself ill at ease in cities. His search for his parents and for his own identity formed the basis for most of the stories.

LUCAS TANNER

School Drama
FIRST TELECAST: *September 11, 1974*
LAST TELECAST: *August 20, 1975*
BROADCAST HISTORY:
    Sep 1974–Aug 1975, NBC Wed 9:00–10:00
CAST:
    Lucas Tanner .... David Hartman
    Margaret Blumenthal ..... Rosemary Murphy
    Glendon Farrell .... Robbie Rist
    Jaytee Drumm .... Alan Abelew
    Cindy Damon .... Trish Soodik
    Terry Klitsner .... Kimberly Beck
    Wally Moore .... Michael Dwight-Smith
    John Hamilton (1975) .... John Randolph

Lucas Tanner had been both a baseball player and a sportswriter but had given up both after the death of his wife and son in an auto accident. Wanting to start a new life, he moved to St. Louis and obtained a job as an English teacher at Harry S Truman Memorial High School in suburban Webster Groves, Mo. There he encountered frustrating resistance to his down-to-earth teaching style, primarily from the more tradition-bound teachers. The support of principal Margaret Blumenthal, who was replaced in January by John Hamilton, and the gratitude of his students were often the only things that kept him from "throwing in the towel." Lucas' warm and understanding nature made him a favorite of the students, who appreciated his ability to treat them as individu-

als. A special friend was little Glendon, a small boy who was one of Lucas' neighbors and who would often come over to visit and talk.

LUCIE ARNAZ SHOW, THE

Situation Comedy
FIRST TELECAST: *April 2, 1985*
LAST TELECAST: *June 11, 1985*
BROADCAST HISTORY:
    Apr 1985, CBS Tue 8:00–8:30
    Jun 1985, CBS Tue 8:00–8:30
CAST:
    Dr. Jane Lucas .... Lucie Arnaz
    Jim Gordon .... Tony Roberts
    Loretta .... Karen Jablons-Alexander
    Jill .... Lee Bryant
    Larry Love .... Todd Waring

Psychologist Jane Lucas had a work schedule that would make most people shudder. Not only did she maintain a private practice in New York City, but Jane also wrote a regular advice column for *Gotham Magazine* and was co-host, with egocentric Larry Love, of radio station WPLE's popular call-in program, the "Love and Lucas Show." It made for a hectic professional life, and didn't leave her with much time for herself, but Jane loved it—at least most of the time. Giving other people advice about their love lives was rewarding, but there were occasions when she would rather have been working on her own love life. The other principal people in Jane's life were Jim Gordon, WPLE's demanding and conniving station manager; Loretta, Jane's secretary at the office; and Jill, her older sister who, in her meddlesome way, was looking out for Jane's best interests.

LUCILLE BALL SHOW, THE

see *Lucy Show, The*

LUCKY PUP

Children's
FIRST TELECAST: *August 23, 1948*
LAST TELECAST: *June 23, 1951*
BROADCAST HISTORY:
    Aug 1948–Sep 1948, CBS Mon/Wed/Fri Various times
    Sep 1948–Sep 1950, CBS Mon–Fri 6:30–6:45
    Jan 1949–Jun 1951, CBS Sat Various half hours between 6:00–7:15
HOSTESS:
    Doris Brown
PUPPETEERS:
    Hope and Morey Bunin

Lucky Pup was one of the more popular puppet shows on early television. It was first previewed between 8:00 P.M. and 9:00 P.M. on two consecutive weeks in 1948 to let parents see what their children would have available to them at an earlier hour, and then began a three-year run in the early evening.

With the exception of hostess and narrator Doris Brown, all of the characters on *Lucky Pup* were puppets. Lucky Pup was a little dog that had inherited $5 million from a recently deceased circus queen. Foodini was the magician who was trying to use his black arts to steal the treasure, Pinhead was Foodini's dumb but friendly stooge, and Jolo was the resident clown. All of the action took place in a circus setting. Gradually Foodini and Pinhead came to dominate the stories, and Lucky Pup himself was seldom seen.

The series ended in June 1951, when Doris Brown married and left television. A charming, modest woman, she later recalled of those early days: "I can't honestly say I miss performing. I never was a real professional at it; just enjoyed myself and often wondered why they ever let me get away with it." The Bunins later returned with a spin-off series called *Foodini the Great*.

LUCY-DESI COMEDY HOUR, THE

Situation Comedy
FIRST TELECAST: *July 2, 1962*
LAST TELECAST: *August 31, 1967*
BROADCAST HISTORY:
  Jul 1962–Sep 1962, CBS Mon 9:00–10:00
  Jun 1963–Sep 1963, CBS Sat 7:30–8:30
  Jun 1964–Sep 1964, CBS Sat 7:30–8:30
  Jun 1965–Sep 1965, CBS Wed 10:00–11:00
  Jun 1967–Aug 1967, CBS Thu 7:30–8:30
CAST:
  Lucy Ricardo .... Lucille Ball
  Ricky Ricardo .... Desi Arnaz
  Ethel Mertz. .... Vivian Vance
  Fred Mertz .... William Frawley
  Little Ricky. .... Richard Keith

At the end of the 1956–1957 season of *I Love Lucy*, the show's stars decided that they wanted to experiment with a longer form of program. Starting on November 14, 1957, and over the course of the next few seasons, all of the *I Love Lucy* regulars starred in a number of full-hour specials. In the specials they traveled to different places and became involved with various guest stars. Collections of these specials were aired as summer series for five years by CBS under the title *The Lucy-Desi Comedy Hour*.

LUCY IN CONNECTICUT

Situation Comedy
FIRST TELECAST: *July 3, 1960*
LAST TELECAST: *September 25, 1960*
BROADCAST HISTORY:
  Jul 1960–Sep 1960, CBS Sun 10:00–10:30
CAST:
  Lucy Ricardo .... Lucille Ball
  Ricky Ricardo .... Desi Arnaz
  Ethel Mertz. .... Vivian Vance
  Fred Mertz .... William Frawley
  Betty Ramsey. .... Mary Jane Croft
  Ralph Ramsey .... Frank Nelson

The episodes that made up this summer series were all reruns of episodes of *I Love Lucy* that covered the period in which Lucy had convinced Ricky that it would be a great idea to move to the country. She got him to make a large down payment on a big home in Westport, Connecticut, and they spent the next several weeks learning about the advantages and disadvantages of suburban living. Mary Jane Croft, who would later replace Vivian Vance as Lucy's friend and companion in mischief on *The Lucy Show*, was showcased here as the Ricardos' next-door neighbor in Westport.

LUCY SHOW, THE

see *I Love Lucy*

LUCY SHOW, THE

Situation Comedy
FIRST TELECAST: *October 1, 1962*
LAST TELECAST: *September 2, 1974*
BROADCAST HISTORY:
  Oct 1962–Jun 1964, CBS Mon 8:30–9:00 (OS)
  Sep 1964–Jul 1965, CBS Mon 9:00–9:30
  Sep 1965–Jun 1967, CBS Mon 8:30–9:00 (OS)
  Sep 1967–Sep 1971, CBS Mon 8:30–9:00
  Sep 1971–Sep 1974, CBS Mon 9:00–9:30
CAST:
  Lucy Carmichael/Carter. .... Lucille Ball
  Vivian Bagley (1962–1965) ..... Vivian Vance
  Mr. Barnsdahl (1962–1963) ..... Charles Lane
  Theodore J. Mooney/Harrison Otis Carter
    (1963–1974) .... Gale Gordon
  Harry Conners (1962–1964). ..... Dick Martin
  Chris Carmichael (1962–1965) .. Candy Moore
  Jerry Carmichael (1962–1966) . Jimmy Garrett
  Sherman Bagley (1962–1965) ..... Ralph Hart
  Harrison Cheever (1965–1968) ... Roy Roberts
  Mary Jane Lewis (1965–1974)
    .... Mary Jane Croft
  Kim Carter (1968–1974) .... Lucie Arnaz
  Craig Carter (1968–1971). ..... Desi Arnaz, Jr.

Tackling a series on her own, without husband Desi Arnaz, Lucille Ball firmly established herself as the first lady of American television with this long-running series. With one exception, the supporting cast underwent numerous changes over the years, and at one time included both of Miss Ball's real-life children. The one exception was Gale Gordon, who provided Lucy with a stubborn, stuffy foil for most of the show's run. The real constant, however, was Lucy and her special brand of slapstick humor, played off of all sorts of guests and regulars. Such was her fame by this time that she could attract Richard Burton and Elizabeth Taylor (and their well-publicized diamond ring) as special guests to open one season (1971), as well as many other stars who normally shunned television.

When it appeared in the fall of 1962, *The Lucy Show* cast its star as a widow with two children, Chris and Jerry, living in suburban Danfield, Connecticut, and sharing her home with a divorced friend, Vivian Bagley, and Vivian's son, Sherman. Both women were desperately looking to snag new husbands and Lucy, in an effort to keep busy and meet eligible men, eventually went to work part-time for Mr. Mooney at the Danfield First National Bank. In September 1965, Lucy moved to San Francisco, as coincidentally did banker Mooney, and again she was working as his secretary, this time at the Westland Bank. Mooney, who had been president of the bank in Connecticut, was a vice-president at the bank in San Francisco, which was run by Harrison Cheever. Lucy's daughter Chris was no longer with the cast and Vivian Bagley, no longer a series regular, appeared only occasionally as a visitor from the East. Lucy's new cohort was friend Mary Jane Lewis. The last episode under this title aired on September 16, 1968.

In September 1968 the show returned with a new title *(Here's Lucy)*, a couple of major cast changes, and a modified story line. Lucy had moved to Los Angeles and her last name was now Carter. She was still a widow with two children, but they were now named Kim and Craig (played by her real-life children, Lucie and Desi). She worked for the Unique Employment Agency, which was owned by her brother-in-law, Harrison "Uncle Harry" Carter. Gale Gordon was thus retained as her blustery, ever-suffering foil. During the summers of 1968–1971 reruns of the earlier *Lucy Shows* were aired (prior to 1968 the series was replaced by various other programs during the summer months).

The program was initially titled *The Lucille Ball Show* when it went on the air in 1962, shortened to *The Lucy Show* after only one month, and then retitled *Here's Lucy* in the fall of 1968.

CBS aired weekday daytime reruns of *The Lucy Show* from September 1968 to September 1972, and of *Here's Lucy* from May to November 1977.

LUX PLAYHOUSE
Dramatic Anthology
FIRST TELECAST: *October 3, 1958*
LAST TELECAST: *September 18, 1959*
BROADCAST HISTORY:
  Oct 1958–Sep 1959, CBS Fri 9:30–10:00

This filmed dramatic-anthology series aired on alternate Fridays with *Schlitz Playhouse*. Content ranged from light comedies, to romance, to melodrama. Generally, better-known performers participated, with Polly Bergen and Rod Taylor in "The Best House in the Valley," Barry Nelson and Audrey Totter in "Drive a Desert Road," Jan Sterling in "Stand-in for Murder," and Gisele MacKenzie and John Forsythe in "The Miss and Missiles" among the presentations.

LUX SHOW STARRING ROSEMARY CLOONEY, THE
Musical Variety
FIRST TELECAST: *September 26, 1957*

LAST TELECAST: *June 19, 1958*
BROADCAST HISTORY:
  Sep 1957–Jun 1958, NBC Thu 10:00–10:30
REGULARS:
  Rosemary Clooney
  Paula Kelly & the Modernaires
  Frank DeVol and His Orchestra
  The Jones Boys (1958)

Rosemary Clooney starred in this variety series that included comedy skits as well as musical numbers. Regulars on the series were the vocal group of Paula Kelly & the Modernaires, who left in March 1958 and were replaced by an all-male group, the Jones Boys.

LUX VIDEO THEATRE
Dramatic Anthology
FIRST TELECAST: *October 2, 1950*
LAST TELECAST: *September 12, 1957*
BROADCAST HISTORY:
  Oct 1950–Jun 1951, CBS Mon 8:00–8:30
  Aug 1951–Mar 1953, CBS Mon 8:00–8:30
  Apr 1953–Jun 1954, CBS Thu 9:00–9:30
  Aug 1954–Sep 1957, NBC Thu 10:00–11:00
HOST:
  James Mason (1954–1955)
  Otto Kruger (1955–1956)
  Gordon MacRae (1956–1957)
  Ken Carpenter (summers 1955–1957)

After 16 years on radio as a weekly dramatic series, *Lux Radio Theatre* became *Lux Video Theatre* on October 2, 1950. The first live play, from New York, was an adaptation of Maxwell Anderson's *Saturday's Children*, starring Joan Caulfield. For three seasons this live dramatic series originated from New York, finally moving to Hollywood with the September 2, 1953, telecast. Major motion-picture stars and Broadway actors performed on the show. Some of the names to appear during this period were Veronica Lake, Zachary Scott, Franchot Tone, Nina Foch, Celeste Holm, Broderick Crawford, Dennis O'Keefe, and young Charlton Heston. The subject matter ranged from contemporary to period, serious to light. On the more literary side, William Faulkner adapted two of his short stories—"The Brooch" and "Shall Not Perish"—for presentation on *Lux Video Theatre* in 1953 and 1954.

When the series moved to NBC in the fall of 1954, there were a number of changes in the format. The length of each telecast was expanded to a full hour, a regular host was added to the program, and adaptations of theatrical films became the principal type of material presented. The host introduced each act and, at the end of the show, conducted short interviews with the stars (female stars always gave plugs for their "Lux Complexion"). When the show had been adapted from a movie, the host also interviewed a principal from the studio whose film had been adapted to plug a current film from that studio.

Film clips from the current film were shown as part of the interview.

A preview of this adaptation of feature films had actually occurred in 1954 while *Lux Video Theatre* was still on CBS. On January 28, 1954, John Derek, Ann Blyth, and Marilyn Erskine had starred in a television version of *A Place in the Sun*, with Ronald Reagan hosting. The first NBC telecast was an abridgement of *To Each His Own*, starring Dorothy Malone and Gene Barry. At the end of the show, Alfred Hitchcock was interviewed about his current film, *Rear Window.* Popular movies that aired in abbreviated versions over the years were *Double Indemnity*, with La-raine Day and Frank Lovejoy; *Sunset Boulevard*, with Miriam Hopkins and James Daly; *Casablanca*, with Paul Douglas, Arlene Dahl, and Hoagy Carmichael; *Mildred Pierce*, with Virginia Bruce and Zachary Scott; *Jezebel*, with Martha Hyer, Charles Drake, and Jack Lord; and *To Have and Have Not*, with Edmond O'Brien and Beverly Garland.

During the summers Ken Carpenter, the regular announcer for the series, doubled as host and the plays presented were short versions of scripts that were under consideration by the studios as possible full-length features. None of them were subsequently produced as feature films.

M

M*A*S*H
Situation Comedy
FIRST TELECAST: *September 17, 1972*
LAST TELECAST: *September 19, 1983*
BROADCAST HISTORY:
Sep 1972–Sep 1973, CBS Sun 8:00–8:30
Sep 1973–Sep 1974, CBS Sat 8:30–9:00
Sep 1974–Sep 1975, CBS Tue 8:30–9:00
Sep 1975–Nov 1975, CBS Fri 8:30–9:00
Dec 1975–Jan 1978, CBS Tue 9:00–9:30
Jan 1978–Sep 1983, CBS Mon 9:00–9:30
CAST:
Capt. Benjamin Franklin Pierce (Hawkeye)
. . . . Alan Alda
Capt. John McIntyre (Trapper John) (1972–1975)
. . . . Wayne Rogers
Maj. Margaret Houlihan (Hot Lips)
. . . . Loretta Swit
Maj. Frank Burns (1972–1977) . . Larry Linville
Cpl. Walter O'Reilly (Radar) (1972–1979)
. . . . Gary Burghoff
Lt. Col. Henry Blake (1972–1975)
. . . . McLean Stevenson
Father John Mulcahy (pilot only)
. . . . '. George Morgan
Father Francis Mulcahy
. . . . William Christopher
Cpl. Maxwell Klinger (1973–1983)
. . . . Jamie Farr
Col. Sherman Potter (1975–1983)
. . . . Harry Morgan
Capt. B. J. Hunnicut (1975–1983)
. . . . Mike Farrell
Maj. Charles Emerson Winchester (1977–1983)
. . . . David Ogden Stiers
Lt. Maggie Dish (1972) . . . . Karen Philipp
Spearchucker Jones (1972) . . . Timothy Brown
Ho-John (1972) . . . . Patrick Adiarte
Ugly John (1972–1973) . . . . John Orchard
Lt. Leslie Scorch (1972–1973)
. . . . Linda Meiklejohn
Gen. Brandon Clayton (1972–1973)
. . . . Herb Voland
Lt. Ginger Ballis (1972–1974)
. . . . Odessa Cleveland
Nurse Margie Cutler (1972–1973)
. . . . Marcia Strassman
Nurse Louise Anderson (1973)
. . . . Kelly Jean Peters
Lt. Nancy Griffin (1973) . . . . . . Lynette Mettey
Various Nurses (1973–1977) . . Bobbie Mitchell
Gen. Mitchell (1973–1974) . . Robert F. Simon
Nurse Kellye (1974–1983) . . . Kellye Nakahara
Various Nurses (1974–1978) . . Patricia Stevens
Various Nurses (1976–1983) . . . . . . Judy Farrell
Igor (1976–1983) . . . . Jeff Maxwell
Nurse Bigelow (1977–1979) . . . . Enid Kent
Sgt. Zale (1977–1979) . . . . Johnny Haymer

Various Nurses (1978–1983) . . . . . . Jan Jordan
Various Nurses (1979–1983) . . . . Gwen Farrell
Various Nurses (1979–1981) . . . . . Connie Izay
Various Nurses (1979–1980) . . . Jennifer Davis
Various Nurses (1980–1983) . . . . . . Shari Sabo
Sgt. Luther Rizzo (1981–1983) . . . G. W. Bailey
Roy (1981–1983) . . . . Roy Goldman
Soon-Lee (1983) . . . . Rosalind Chao
Various Nurses (1981–1983)
. . . . Joann Thompson
Various Nurses (1982–1983)
. . . . Deborah Harmon
THEME:
"Suicide Is Painless," by Johnny Mandel

In 1972 America was still embroiled in a lingering war in Vietnam, a war that had polarized the population. The climate created by an unpopular war was the perfect environment for an antiwar comedy like *M*A*S*H*. The setting was different, Korea in the early 1950s, but the stories and situations could just as easily have been from Vietnam in the 1970s.

The cast of characters in *M*A*S*H* were all members of the 4077th Mobile Army Surgical Hospital, stationed behind the lines during the Korean War. Their job was to treat the wounded being sent to them from the front lines and to try to save as many lives as possible. The environment was depressing; many of the doctors (who had all been drafted) could not really believe they were living under the conditions to which they were being subjected. There was an overwhelming sense of the futility and insanity of war that permeated their daily lives. A certain sense of humor was necessary for survival.

Most of the senior members of the M.A.S.H. unit had wives and families back home, but that never stopped them from propositioning every good-looking nurse they could con into their quarters. After all, they did need something to alleviate the depression that resulted from contact with a constant stream of maimed and dying young GIs. Two of the surgeons were Hawkeye Pierce and Trapper John McIntyre. Like virtually everyone else, they were always breaking regulations. Hawkeye, despite his escapades, was probably the most intellectual of the doctors and was sometimes seen musing on the dehumanizing nature of war and questioning its moral validity.

Among others who were featured was Frank Burns, who was possibly the worst doctor in the unit, and the constant butt of practical jokes perpetrated by Hawkeye and Trapper because of his arrogance and his feigned adherence to military regulations. Hot Lips Houlihan was the head nurse who, despite her admonitions to both her nurses and the doctors about fooling around with each other, had been having an affair with Frank Burns for an extended period. Henry Blake, the commanding officer whose prime concern was the work of the doctors in the operating room, couldn't care less about what they did during their free time. Radar O'Reilly was the extremely shy and bumbling young aide to Col. Blake. There were also numerous nurses who came and went, with the same actress being referred to in different episodes by different names—a large number of actresses were collectively called Nurse Able and Nurse Baker. Dr. Sidney Freedman (Alan Arbus), an army psychiatrist, made sporadic visits to the 4077th M.A.S.H. to check on the mental condition of the staff.

There were changes in the cast over the years. The first significant addition was that of Cpl. Maxwell Klinger, an aide to the doctors in the operating room. There was nothing really wrong with him: it was just that he always dressed in women's clothing in a desperate, though futile, attempt to get himself discharged as mentally unfit. McLean Stevenson left the series in the spring of 1975, to sign a long-term contract with NBC, and his character, Col. Blake, was written out of the show in the last episode of the 1974–1975 season (he was discharged and on his way home, only to have the plane in which he was flying go down in the Sea of Japan). He was replaced by Col. Potter, who was somewhat more sardonic and definitely less silly than his predecessor. In the summer of 1975 Wayne Rogers also left the series, in a contract dispute; his character, Trapper, got a discharge and returned home at the beginning of the 1975–1976 season. B. J. Hunnicut replaced Trapper as Hawkeye's tentmate and co-conspirator.

At the beginning of the 1977–1978 season Larry Linville left, and so Major Burns was written out of the series. Having seen his love affair with Hot Lips end when she married Lt. Col. Donald Penobscott, Frank abruptly went AWOL and was permanently transferred. Replacing him was an aristocratic Bostonian, Maj. Charles Emerson Winchester. Hot Lips' marriage to Col. Penobscott, who was not stationed with the 4077th and who was virtually never seen with his wife after the honeymoon, ended in divorce during the 1978–1979 season. Gary Burghoff, the only member of the cast who had played the same role in the movie version of *M*A*S*H*, departed in the fall of 1979. His character, clairvoyant company clerk Radar O'Reilly, received his discharge and returned to the States. Cpl. Klinger, after a rocky start, settled in as the new company clerk.

On February 28, 1983, the last original episode of *M*A*S*H* aired as a two-and-a-half-hour special. Highly publicized in both print and broadcast media, with TV tributes airing at the local and network level for several days before, this special *M*A*S*H* was a national event, and was seen by the largest audience ever to watch a single television program. The finale brought a dramatic ending to the series regarded by many as one of the finest in television history. In it, the war finally ended, but not before the long years of pressure pushed Hawkeye over the edge and into a chillingly portrayed nervous breakdown. He recovered, but Major Winchester never would recover

from his experience with a group of P.O.W. musicians who had brought a bit of cherished civility to the front—before they were suddenly and senselessly killed. Klinger, on the eve of his long-anticipated departure for home, met and married a beautiful Korean woman named Soon-Lee. As the program came to a close, the men and women of the 4077th departed, one by one, for civilian life. Some of them—Col. Potter, Klinger, Father Mulcahy—would meet again in a sequel the following fall, called *AfterMASH*.

*M*A*S*H* was based on the hit motion picture of the same name, which in turn was taken from the novel. The novel was written by a doctor who had actually served in one of the Korean War M.A.S.H. units, but who used a pseudonym—Richard Hooker—in writing, so as not to compromise his medical standing by his revelations. Reruns of *M*A*S*H* aired on CBS' weekday lineup from September 1978 to September 1979.

MGM PARADE
Documentary
FIRST TELECAST: *September 14, 1955*
LAST TELECAST: *May 2, 1956*
BROADCAST HISTORY:
   Sep 1955–May 1956, ABC Wed 8:30–9:00
HOST:
   George Murphy (1955–1956)
   Walter Pidgeon (1956)

Originally conceived as an opportunity for the viewer to see the workings of a major motion-picture studio, this series was hosted by actor (eventually to become Senator) George Murphy. Segments included interviews with stars, explanations and demonstrations of technical aspects of production, excerpts from current and past MGM productions, and special entertainment featurettes produced specifically for this series by Pete Smith and others. Due to weak ratings, in the spring of 1956 the formant was revised to serialize classic MGM films. Walter Pidgeon took over as host to present *Captains Courageous*, highlights of the work of Greta Garbo, and *The Pirate*.

M SQUAD
Police Drama
FIRST TELECAST: *September 20, 1957*
LAST TELECAST: *September 13, 1960*
BROADCAST HISTORY:
   Sep 1957–Sep 1959, NBC Fri 9:00–9:30
   Sep 1959–Jan 1960, NBC Fri 9:30–10:00
   Jan 1960–Sep 1960, NBC Tue 10:00–10:30
CAST:
   Lt. Frank Ballinger . . . . Lee Marvin
   Capt. Grey . . . . Paul Newlan

The M Squad was an elite group of plainclothes detectives working to fight organized crime in Chicago. Lt. Frank Ballinger was one of these top detectives who worked, as did most of the other members of M Squad, by himself. Ballinger was a hard-nosed cop with no romantic interests. His commanding officer, and the man who assigned him to most of his cases, was Capt. Grey. Lee Marvin starred as Ballinger and also served as narrator of the series.

The original *M Squad* theme had been composed by the show's music director, Stanley Wilson. At the start of *M Squad*'s second season, however, the original theme was replaced by a more jazz-oriented tune composed by Count Basie, which was also known as the "Theme From *M Squad*."

MAC DAVIS SHOW, THE
Musical Variety
FIRST TELECAST: *July 11, 1974*
LAST TELECAST: *June 17, 1976*
BROADCAST HISTORY:
  Jul 1974–Aug 1974, NBC Thu 8:00–9:00
  Dec 1974–Feb 1975, NBC Thu 8:00–9:00
  Mar 1975–May 1975, NBC Thu 9:00–10:00
  Mar 1976–Jun 1976, NBC Thu 8:00–9:00
REGULARS:
  Mac Davis
  Robert Shields and Lorene Yarnell (1976)
  Strutt (1976)
  Ron Silver (1976)
  George Wyle Dancers (1974)
  Tony Mordente Dancers (1974–1975)
  Jim Bates Dancers (1976)
  Mike Post Orchestra (1974–1976)

Country-oriented singer and composer Mac Davis had three tries as host of his own variety series, in the summer of 1974, early 1975, and the spring of 1976. None of the three attempts attracted sufficient audience to stay on the schedule more than a few months. Regular features on all three shows were Mac's singing of his own songs, reminiscing about his growing-up years in Texas, and informal chats with the audience. In fact, he was often seen seated with the audience during part of the show, while he answered questions or sang and played his guitar. He would also improvise songs from title suggestions submitted by the audience. The 1976 edition had, in addition to Mac and his guest stars, three regulars: the mime team of Shields and Yarnell, comedian Ron Silver, and a group of singers and dancers known collectively as Strutt.

MACGRUDER & LOUD
Police Drama
FIRST TELECAST: *January 20, 1985*
LAST TELECAST: *September 3, 1985*
BROADCAST HISTORY:
  Jan 1985, ABC Sun 10:05–11:50
  Jan 1985–Apr 1985, ABC Tue 9:00–10:00
  Apr 1985, ABC Tue 10:00–11:00
  Jun 1985–Sep 1985, ABC Tue 10:00–11:00
CAST:
  Det. Malcolm MacGruder .... John Getz
  Det. Jenny Loud MacGruder
  .... Kathryn Harrold

Sgt. Myhrum .... Frank McCarthy
Det. Sgt. Debbin .... Ted Ross
Naomi .... Gail Grate
Zacharias .... Charles Boswell
Sgt. Hanson .... Lee de Broux
Geller..................... Rick Rossovich

Police Officers in Love could have been the title of this unusual action series. MacGruder and Loud were uniformed officers who shared a patrol car by day, and a passionate love by night. They had secretly married despite department regulations, and now had to hide that fact to stay on the force. There were plenty of high-speed chases, shootouts, and other dangerous assignments in between stolen kisses during the day, but the brass never seemed to catch on to their little secret.

MACGYVER
Foreign Intrigue
FIRST TELECAST: *September 29, 1985*
LAST TELECAST:
BROADCAST HISTORY:
  Sep 1985–Jan 1986, ABC Sun 8:00–9:00
  Jan 1986–Jul 1986, ABC Wed 8:00–9:00
  Aug 1986, ABC Wed 9:00–10:00
  Sep 1986–May 1987, ABC Mon 8:00–9:00
  Jun 1987–Sep 1987, ABC Wed 9:00–10:00
  Sep 1987–May 1988, ABC Mon 8:00–9:00
  Jun 1988–   , ABC Sun 8:00–9:00
CAST:
  MacGyver.......... Richard Dean Anderson
  Peter Thornton .... Dana Elcar
  Jack Dalton (1987–   ) .... Bruce McGill
  Nikki Carpenter (1987–   ) . Elyssa Davalos

Actor Henry Winkler was co-producer of this action-adventure series about a rugged, handsome hero who preferred to use paper clips and candy bars rather than more conventional weapons. MacGyver (no first name) was a former Special Forces agent now working for the Phoenix Foundation, a "think tank" dedicated to righting wrongs and defeating bad guys around the world. A clever fellow, he often slipped past the enemy's defenses and undermined their foul plans with ingenuity rather than brute force, using tidbits of scientific knowledge and ordinary items that happened to be laying around; for example, the paper clip might be used to short-circuit a nuclear missile, the candy bar to stop an acid leak, or a cold capsule to ignite a makeshift bomb, all just in the nick of time. MacGyver could work wonders with the contents of a lady's handbag! His assignments came from Peter Thornton, the Director of Field Operations for the Foundation.

MACKENZIES OF PARADISE COVE, THE
Adventure
FIRST TELECAST: *March 27, 1979*
LAST TELECAST: *May 18, 1979*

  Mar 1979, ABC Tue 8:30–9:30
  Apr 1979, ABC Wed 8:00–9:00
  Apr 1979–May 1979, ABC Fri 8:00–9:00
CAST:
  Cuda Weber.................... Clu Gulager
  Kevin Mackenzie .... Shawn Stevens
  Bridget Mackenzie .... Lory Walsh
  Michael Mackenzie .... Sean Marshall
  Celia Mackenzie................. Randi Kiger
  Timothy Mackenzie .... Keith Mitchell
  Big Ben Kalikini .... Moe Keale
  Mrs. Kalikini .... Leinaala Heine
  Little Ben Kalikini .... Sean Tyler Hall
  Barney .... Harry Chang

Cuda Weber, a crusty old fishing-boat operator in Hawaii, found himself unofficial father to a pack of spirited orphans in this short-lived series. The Mackenzie kids ranged in age from 7-year-old Timothy to 17-year-old twins Kevin and Bridget. Their parents had been lost at sea in a sailing accident, and in an effort to foil the authorities and stay together they persuaded Cuda to pose as their uncle and guardian. From there on in, it was a sort of *Brady Bunch* beneath the palms, with all the little scrapes and adventures of growing kids.

MACKENZIE'S RAIDERS
Western
BROADCAST HISTORY:
  Syndicated only
  30 minutes
  Produced: *1958–1959* (39 episodes)
  Released: *October 1958*
CAST:
  Col. Ranald S. Mackenzie .. Richard Carlson

Richard Carlson, who sneaked around looking for Communists in the long-running *I Led Three Lives*, became a dashing cavalry officer chasing Mexican banditos in this rousing horse opera.

The story was based on historical fact. Col. Ranald Mackenzie was commander of the U.S. Fourth Cavalry stationed at Ft. Clark, Texas, in 1873. Mexican bandits were terrorizing the local settlers, and Mackenzie's secret order from President Grant and General Sheridan was to stop the marauders by pursuing them across the Rio Grande into Mexico if necessary. This had to be done in secret, to avoid an international incident; if Mackenzie was caught inside Mexico, the U.S. would have to disown him. If he succeeded, there would be no glory. Needless to say, the colonel and his troops galloped forth without hesitation, for a season of stealthy attacks and flashing swords.

Mackenzie was one of the most colorful figures in U.S. Army history, and has been written about widely. This series was based primarily on the book *The Mackenzie Raid* by Col. Russell Reeder.

MME LIU TSONG
  see *Gallery Of Madame Liu Tsong, The*

MADAME'S PLACE
Situation Comedy
BROADCAST HISTORY:
  Syndicated only
  30 minutes
  Produced: *1982* (150 episodes)
  Released: *September 1982*
PUPPETEER:
  Wayland Flowers
CAST:
  Sara Joy .... Judy Landers
  Bernadette .... Susan Tolsky
  Pinkerton .... Johnny Haymer
  Buzzy .... Corey Feldman

Puppeteer Wayland Flowers had created the character of Madame, a craggy, cackling, slightly off-color old hussy, and toured with her for many years on the cabaret and TV guest circuit. She was supposed to be an old show-business trouper who had started in vaudeville and then made more than 30 movies, and who still acted very much the glamorous star—despite her appearance. In 1982 the aging queen showed up surrounded by human supporting actors, in this five-night-a-week syndicated comedy, playing the host of a talk show originating from her palatial mansion in Hollywood. There was constant bickering with her neighbors, her network, and her staff, as well as an abundance of lecherous jokes and put-downs of anyone who wandered by.

Despite a large number of bizarre characters passing through (many of them parodies on show-business types), some guest celebrities such as William Shatner and Debbie Reynolds, and very clever puppet work by Flowers (who manipulated his creation with rods rather than strings), *Madame's Place* folded after a short run.

MADE IN AMERICA
Quiz/Audience Participation
FIRST TELECAST: *April 5, 1964*
LAST TELECAST: *May 3, 1964*
BROADCAST HISTORY:
  Apr 1964–May 1964, CBS Sun 9:30–10:00
EMCEE:
  Hans Conried
PANELISTS:
  Jan Sterling
  Walter Slezak
  Don Murray

The goal of the panel on this show was to guess in what manner each of the contestants had made their fortunes. All of the contestants were millionaires and they donated their winnings to charity. The amount they won, up to $600, was dependent on how long it took the panel to identify the source of their incomes. Three contestants appeared on each show.

MADIGAN

Police Drama

FIRST TELECAST: *September 20, 1972*
LAST TELECAST: *August 22, 1973*
BROADCAST HISTORY:
    Sep 1972–Aug 1973, NBC Wed 8:30–10:00
CAST:
    Sgt. Dan Madigan......... Richard Widmark

Dan Madigan was a New York City police detective, and a loner. Superficially abrasive and cool, he had a soft streak that he worked hard to conceal. Although some aspects of his job were unappealing, police work was the only life he knew. His social life was virtually nonexistent and his home was a spartan one-room apartment. At least he got to travel a bit, as cases sometimes took him as far away as London.
    Madigan was one of three elements in the 1972–1973 version of *NBC Wednesday Mystery Movie*, along with *Banacek* and *Cool Million*.

MADISON SQUARE GARDEN

see *Saturday Night at the Garden*

MADISON SQUARE GARDEN HIGHLIGHTS

Sports Commentary

FIRST TELECAST: *June 25, 1953*
LAST TELECAST: *April 15, 1954*
BROADCAST HISTORY:
    Jun 1953–Sep 1953, ABC Thu 9:00–9:30
    Sep 1953–Oct 1953, ABC Sat 8:30–9:00
    Oct 1953–Dec 1953, ABC Sat 10:00–10:30
    Jan 1954, ABC Sat 8:30–9:00
    Feb 1954–Apr 1954, DUM Thu 8:00–8:30
HOSTS:
    Marty Glickman
    Stan Lomax

Sportscasters Marty Glickman and Stan Lomax narrated this weekly collection of filmed highlights of sports events that had taken place the previous week at Madison Square Garden in New York. There was some analysis and commentary mixed in with their narration of the events.

MAGGIE

Situation Comedy

FIRST TELECAST: *October 24, 1981*
LAST TELECAST: *May 21, 1982*
BROADCAST HISTORY:
    Oct 1981–Nov 1981, ABC Sat 8:00–8:30
    Apr 1982–May 1982, ABC Fri 8:30–9:00
CAST:
    Maggie Weston.............. Miriam Flynn
    Len Weston .... James Hampton
    Mark Weston .... Billy Jacoby
    Bruce Weston .... Christian Jacobs
    Loretta....................... Doris Roberts
    Chris .... Margie Impert
    Buffy Croft .... Judith-Marie Bergan
CREATOR/EXECUTIVE PRODUCER:
    Erma Bombeck

Maggie was the television version of the harried suburban housewife made famous in the books of Erma Bombeck. Husband Len was vice principal of schools in Dayton, Ohio, and a perfectly pleasant guy. The children were 8-year-old Bruce, 12-year-old Mark, and 16-year-old L.J., who was never seen because he was always in the bathroom. Their little adventures revolved around clogged drains, notes from the teacher, and Mark's braces, things Maggie liked to chat about during her weekly visits to Loretta's House of Coiffures. It was all very witty and true-to-life in Miss Bombeck's writings, but somehow fell flat on the screen, leading to an early cancellation for this series.

MAGGI'S PRIVATE WIRE

Interview

FIRST TELECAST: *April 12, 1949*
LAST TELECAST: *July 2, 1949*
BROADCAST HISTORY:
    Apr 1949, NBC Tue 7:30–7:45
    May 1949–Jul 1949, NBC Sat 7:30–7:45
HOSTESS:
    Maggi McNellis

Radio and TV personality Maggi McNellis hosted this weekly talk show, interviewing celebrities from show business and other fields.

MAGIC COTTAGE

Children's

FIRST TELECAST: *July 18, 1949*
LAST TELECAST: *February 9, 1951*
BROADCAST HISTORY:
    Jul 1949–Feb 1951, DUM Mon–Fri 6:30–7:00
HOSTESS:
    Pat Meikle

Pat Meikle, who earlier had a daytime program billed as "The TV Babysitter," hosted this storytelling session in 1949–1951. Her cottage had a drawing board, and from the board stepped children's characters from "Jack and the Beanstalk" and "Goldilocks," among other sources, to relate their famous tales, much to the delight of the youthful studio audience. Original stories such as "Oogie the Ogre's Christmas" and the continuing adventures of Wilmer the Pigeon were also presented, and there were games and contests for the kids. *Magic Cottage* was also seen as a daytime program and as a local series in New York.

MAGIC SLATE, THE

Children's

FIRST TELECAST: *June 2, 1950*
LAST TELECAST: *August 25, 1950*
BROADCAST HISTORY:
    Jun 1950–Aug 1950, NBC Fri 8:00–8:30
PRODUCER:
    Norman Gant

These dramatizations of classic and original children's stories were produced under the supervision of Charlotte Chorpenning of the Goodman Children's Theater in Chicago. *The Magic Slate* alternated with *Quiz Kids* on Friday nights in 1950, and then returned in January 1951 as a Sunday afternoon series, which it remained until July. Telecast from Chicago.

MAGICIAN, THE
Adventure
FIRST TELECAST: *October 2, 1973*
LAST TELECAST: *May 20, 1974*
BROADCAST HISTORY:
   Oct 1973–Jan 1974, NBC Tue 9:00–10:00
   Jan 1974–May 1974, NBC Mon 8:00–9:00
CAST:
   Anthony Blake .... Bill Bixby
   Max Pomeroy .... Keene Curtis
   Dennis Pomeroy .... Todd Crespi
   Jerry Wallace .... Jim Watkins
   Dominick .... Joseph Sirola

Earlier in his life, stage magician Tony Blake had spent time in prison for a crime he had not committed. Prison had been a particularly distasteful experience for a man of his background, and had left him with a strong sense of concern for personal freedom and individual rights. Once released, he put his talents as an illusionist and escape artist to use helping people in danger and preventing crimes. Syndicated columnist and novelist Max Pomeroy was a close friend of Tony's and was often responsible for bringing him cases. Max's paraplegic son, Dennis, although confined to a wheelchair, also became involved in the cases, as did Jerry Wallace, the pilot of Tony's private airliner, *The Spirit*.

When this series moved to Monday nights in January 1974, Tony had taken up residence at Hollywood's famous Magic Castle, where many of the most renowned magicians in the world performed, and some of them were seen on this show. The magic acts performed by Blake were also genuine: Bill Bixby was himself an amateur magician.

MAGNAVOX THEATER
Dramatic Anthology
FIRST TELECAST: *September 15, 1950*
LAST TELECAST: *December 8, 1950*
BROADCAST HISTORY:
   Sep 1950–Dec 1950, CBS Fri 9:00–10:00

The first few dramas presented on this series were produced live in New York and aired on alternate Fridays with *Ford Theatre*. Content ranged from serious dramas starring Dane Clark and Geraldine Brooks, to light comedy with Edward Everett Horton. The most notable telecast in *Magnavox Theater*'s short run aired on November 24, 1950. There was nothing spectacular about Magnavox's adaptation of *The Three Musketeers*—which starred "fast-rising" young movie actor Robert Clarke (he had been trying to crash the big time since 1944) and such obscure supporting players as Mel Archer and Marjorie Lord. But this was, according to CBS, the first hour-long film made in Hollywood especially for television. It took just four and a half days to film, and was produced at the Hal Roach Studios, as were the two films which were aired as the last two telecasts of *Magnavox Theater*.

MAGNUM, P.I.
Detective Drama
FIRST TELECAST: *December 11, 1980*
LAST TELECAST:
BROADCAST HISTORY:
   Dec 1980–Aug 1981, CBS Thu 9:00–10:00
   Sep 1981–Apr 1986, CBS Thu 8:00–9:00
   Apr 1986–Jun 1986, CBS Sat 10:00–11:00
   Jun 1986–Aug 1986, CBS Tue 9:00–10:00
   Sep 1986–May 1987, CBS Wed 9:00–10:00
   Jul 1987–Feb 1988, CBS Wed 9:00–10:00
   Jun 1988   , CBS Mon 10:00–11:00
CAST:
   Thomas Sullivan Magnum ...... Tom Selleck
   Jonathan Quayle Higgins III . John Hillerman
   T.C. (Theodore Calvin) ..... Roger E. Mosley
   Rick (Orville Wright) .... Larry Manetti
   *Robin Masters (voice only) (1981–1985)
   .... Orson Welles
   *Mac Reynolds (1981–1982, 1984–1985,
     1987–1988).................. Jeff MacKay
   *Lt. Tanaka (1982–1988) .... Kwan Hi Lim
   *Lt. Maggie Poole (1982–1984, 1986–1988)
   .... Jean Bruce Scott
   Agatha Chumley (1982–1988).... Gillian Dobb
   *Asst. D.A. Carol Baldwin (1983–1988)
   .... Kathleen Lloyd
   *Francis Hofstetler "Ice Pick" (1983–1988)
   .... Elisha Cook, Jr.

*Occasional

For 12 years CBS viewers had been treated to the beautiful Hawaiian scenery on *Hawaii Five-O*. When Steve McGarrett and his special police finally wore out their welcome, *Magnum, P.I.* replaced them on the CBS schedule. It was in the same time period, had the same beautiful backdrop and hard-knuckles action, and it allowed CBS to continue to use the expensive production facilities it had constructed in the mid-1970s for *Hawaii Five-O*. Characters on *Magnum* even referred to McGarrett and his Five-O unit on occasion, as if the older series were still around.

Magnum was a private investigator with an enviable arrangement. In return for helping with the security arrangements for guarding the estate of wealthy writer Robin Masters (never seen on the show), he was provided with free living quarters at the rambling beachfront property on Oahu's north shore. Masters was always away, leaving his stuffy British manservant, Higgins, to run the estate. The laid-back life-style of Magnum was in direct opposition to the strict military discipline that ruled Higgins' life, and there was constant bickering between the two—though there was clearly, underneath, a deep-seated mutual affection.

When Magnum was not romancing the ladies or tooling around the island in Masters' $50,000 Ferrari, he functioned as a traditional detective. A former Vietnam naval intelligence veteran, Tom utilized the services of two of his wartime buddies when he needed help. T.C. was the owner/pilot of Island Hoppers, a helicopter charter service, and Rick (who hated his real name, Orville) ran a Honolulu nightclub patterned after the club run by Humphrey Bogart in *Casablanca*. Early on he sold the club and became the managing partner, with Robin Masters, of the exclusive King Kamehameha Beach Club. Both of them did legwork for Magnum, with Rick's underworld connections, including his relationship with the quasi-legal businessman Ice Pick, coming in handy. Asst. D.A. Carol Baldwin, a friend of Magnum's, who talked him into taking cases that never seemed to generate any fees, showed up once in a while, as did Higgin's English friend, Agatha.

The most unusual semiregular was Magnum's navy buddy Mac Reynolds. Early in the show's run Mac was a lieutenant, stationed at a local navy installation, who provided Magnum with information, until he was killed in a 1982 episode. Two years later a con man who was the spitting image of Mac turned up (initially impersonating the dead officer) to get Magnum into occasional trouble. Colonel Buck Greene (Lance LeGault), an old navy nemesis of Magnum's, turned up about once a season to cause him some kind of trouble. Zeus and Apollo were the two Doberman pinschers who helped Higgins provide security for the Masters estate, often by taking bites out of Magnum's hide.

The producers of *Magnum, P.I.* had anticipated its cancellation in the spring of 1987 and filmed a dramatic and somewhat surrealistic two-part finale, using almost all the occasional players, in which Magnum was shot, died from the wound, and went to heaven. When the series was unexpectedly renewed for a last season, it was explained that he had not died but had instead dreamed of going to heaven in his delirium. The series' real finale aired as a movie in May 1988 and was one of that season's highest rated individual programs, but it still left some loose ends. Magnum was reunited with his long-lost young daughter, quit the private eye business and rejoined the navy, while buddy Rick was married (or was he?) and Higgins was finally revealed to be Robin Masters (or was he?). Fans will have to wait until the *Magnum* reunion to find out.

MAIL STORY, THE
Dramatic Anthology
FIRST TELECAST: *October 7, 1954*

LAST TELECAST: *December 30, 1954*
BROADCAST HISTORY:
    Oct 1954–Dec 1954, ABC Thu 8:00–8:30

There were two completely different types of stories presented on *The Mail Story:* those that dealt with the good and varied services provided by the U.S. Postal Service, which were often in quasi-documentary form; and those that were dramas of people attempting to misuse the postal system and the efforts made by postal authorities to apprehend them. The latter were all based on actual case histories from the Postal Service's files and ranged from stagecoach robbing in the middle 1850s to contemporary mail fraud. This series was subtitled *Handle With Care.*

MAJOR ADAMS, TRAILMASTER
    syndicated title for *Wagon Train*

MAJOR DELL CONWAY OF THE FLYING TIGERS
    Adventure
FIRST TELECAST: *April 7, 1951*
LAST TELECAST: *May 26, 1951*
BROADCAST HISTORY:
    Apr 1951–May 1951, DUM Sat 6:30–7:00
CAST:
    Major Dell Conway .... Eric Fleming
    Major Dell Conway .... Ed Peck
ALSO:
    Luis Van Rooten
    Fran Lee (as *Ma Wong*)
    David Anderson
    Joe Graham
    Harry Kingston
    Bern Hoffman

This live action-adventure series traced the exploits of Major Dell Conway, a heroic pilot who had served with the famous "Flying Tigers" squadron in China during World War II. After the war Conway and some of his buddies, including sidekick Caribou Jones, founded Flying Tiger Airlines on the West Coast. In the series they fought Cold War spies and saboteurs, as well as international criminals.

Flying Tigers was an extremely low-budget production, and it underwent considerable cast and scheduling turmoil during its short run. The original lead, Hollywood B-movie actor Eric Fleming, was replaced almost immediately by Ed Peck, and the supporting cast evidently changed as well (all those who are known to have been regulars are listed above, although their roles have been lost over the years). The program went off for two months after May 26, then returned in late July on Sunday afternoon, where it continued until March 1952. There was a real Flying Tigers, both wartime squadron and postwar airline, which served—loosely—as the basis for this series. The producer was "Gen" Genovese, who himself had been a pilot in China during the war.

MAJORITY RULES

Quiz/Panel

FIRST TELECAST: *September 2, 1949*
LAST TELECAST: *July 30, 1950*
BROADCAST HISTORY:
Sep 1949–Jan 1950, ABC Fri 8:00–8:30
Feb 1950–Mar 1950, ABC Fri 9:30–10:00
Mar 1950–Jul 1950, ABC Sun 8:30–9:00
EMCEE:
Ed Prentiss
Tom Moore
Myron Wallace

A panel of three contestants was posed questions in this Chicago-originated quiz show, with the "right" answer being determined by the majority of two. Several hosts came and went during the run of the series, and a telephone gimmick involving celebrities was also introduced. One of the hosts would himself become a television celebrity in later years. But by then Myron Wallace would have changed his first name to Mike.

MAKE ME LAUGH

Quiz/Audience Participation

FIRST TELECAST: *March 20, 1958*
LAST TELECAST: *June 12, 1958*
BROADCAST HISTORY:
Mar 1958–Jun 1958, ABC Thu 10:00–10:30
EMCEE:
Robert Q. Lewis

The object of this game show was for contestants to refrain from laughing. Each week three different comedians participated in trying to make contestants laugh. One minute was allotted to each comedian. The contestants could win up to $180, one dollar for every second they refrained from laughter.

More than 20 years later, in 1979, a syndicated version of *Make Me Laugh* appeared, hosted by Bobby Van.

MAKE MINE MUSIC

see *Face the Music*

MAKE ROOM FOR DADDY

see *Danny Thomas Show, The*

MAKE ROOM FOR GRANDDADDY

see *Danny Thomas Show, The*

MAKE THAT SPARE

Sports

FIRST TELECAST: *October 8, 1960*
LAST TELECAST: *September 11, 1964*
BROADCAST HISTORY:
Oct 1960–Sep 1963, ABC Sat 10:45–11:00 (OS)
Sep 1963–Sep 1964, ABC Fri 10:45–11:00
COMMENTATOR:
Johnny Johnston (1960–1961, 1962–1964)
Win Elliot (1961–1962)

In this post-fight feature, a top professional bowler, or amateur, had the chance to win up to $5,000 with one roll of the ball by making a hard spare (two or more pins separated in such a way as to require great precision if all were to be knocked down with a single ball). The winner returned the following week—there were usually two bowlers competing each night—to defend his title of "King of the Hill," and individual champions collected as much as $38,000 competing on this show. *Make That Spare* was telecast live from Paramus, New Jersey.

MAKE THE CONNECTION

Quiz/Audience Participation

FIRST TELECAST: *July 7, 1955*
LAST TELECAST: *September 29, 1955*
BROADCAST HISTORY:
Jul 1955–Sep 1955, NBC Thu 8:30–9:00
MODERATOR:
Jim McKay
Gene Rayburn
PANELISTS:
Betty White
Gloria DeHaven
Gene Klavan
Eddie Bracken

The object of this live summer game show was for the panelists to guess the circumstances (when, where, how, and why) that caused the paths of the guests on the program to cross. They tried to *Make the Connection* between the guests. It was a variation on the successful formats of *What's My Line* and *I've Got a Secret*. Jim McKay was the moderator of the show until early in September, when he was replaced by Gene Rayburn.

MAKE YOUR OWN KIND OF MUSIC

Musical Variety

FIRST TELECAST: *July 20, 1971*
LAST TELECAST: *September 7, 1971*
BROADCAST HISTORY:
Jul 1971–Sep 1971, NBC Tue 8:00–9:00
REGULARS:
The Carpenters
Al Hirt
Mark Lindsay
The New Doodletown Pipers
Tom Patchett and Jay Tarses
Allyn Ferguson & the Jack Elliott Orchestra

This summer musical variety series featured popular singers Richard and Karen Carpenter, trumpet player Al Hirt, singer Mark Lindsay (formerly lead singer of the rock group Paul Revere and the Raiders), the New Doodletown Pipers (16-person singing group), and the comedy team of Patchett and Tarses.

The title for this show was taken from a popular song of 1969.

475

MAKIN' IT
Adventure
FIRST TELECAST: *February 1, 1979*
LAST TELECAST: *March 23, 1979*
BROADCAST HISTORY:
Feb 1979, ABC Thu 8:30–9:00
Feb 1979–Mar 1979, ABC Fri 8:00–8:30
CAST:

Billy Manucci	David Naughton
Tony Manucci	Greg Antonacci
Tina Manucci	Denise Miller
Dorothy Manucci	Ellen Travolta
Joseph Manucci	Lou Antonio
Al "Kingfish" Sorrentino	Ralph Seymour
Bernard Fusco	Gary Prendergast
Corky Crandall	Rebecca Balding
Suzanne	Wendy Hoffman
Felice	Diane Robin
Ivy Papastegios	Jennifer Perito

THEME:
"Makin' It," by Dino Fekaris and Freddie Perren, sung by David Naughton

This short-lived series was a thinly disguised TV adaptation of the hit movie *Saturday Night Fever.* The "disco freak" here was young college student Billy Manucci, who was torn between the glittering life of a big man on the dance floor and his more practical desire to complete his education and become a teacher. On the side of the night life were his pals, Bernard and Kingfish, and his laid-back brother, Tony, star dancer at the local disco; urging sober responsibility were his working-class parents, Joseph and Dorothy. Corky was Billy's girlfriend, and Tina his little sister.

To make the connection with the movie as close as possible, the producers used the music of the Bee Gees in the dance sequences, snared Ellen Travolta for one of the roles (since they couldn't get John), and even titled the premiere episode "Stayin' Alive." Robert Stigwood, who produced the movie, was involved with this series as well. None of this helped much, although David Naughton did have a real-life hit record with the show's theme song, in mid-1979.

MAKING A LIVING
see *It's a Living*

MAKING THE GRADE
Situation Comedy
FIRST TELECAST: *April 5, 1982*
LAST TELECAST: *May 10, 1982*
BROADCAST HISTORY:
Apr 1982–May 1982, CBS 9:30–10:00
CAST:

Harry Barnes	James Naughton
Jack Felspar	Graham Jarvis
Sara Conover	Alley Mills
Jeff Kelton	Steve Peterman
Anton Zemeckis	Zane Lasky
Gus Bertoia	George Wendt

David Wasserman	Philip Charles MacKenzie
Janice Reeves	Veronica Redd

Franklin High, a rambling, 4,500-student St. Louis school, was the setting for this short-lived comedy. Harry Barnes was the dedicated Dean of Boys, whose biggest problem was dull, pompous assistant principal Jack Felspar. Felspar's unwillingness to deal with reality was typified by his definition of the "Lord of Death" gang that terrorized students and faculty alike as a "social club." Sara Conover was the beautiful young drama teacher who had to fend off the insistent and unwanted attentions of English teacher David Wasserman, a self-styled ladykiller. Jeff Kelton was an idealistic young English teacher, Anton Zemeckis a Latin teacher who made money on the side as a travel agent, and Gus Bertoia a super-jock physical-education instructor.

MALIBU RUN
see *Aquanauts, The*

MALIBU U
Music
FIRST TELECAST: *July 21, 1967*
LAST TELECAST: *September 1, 1967*
BROADCAST HISTORY:
Jul 1967–Sep 1967, ABC Fri 8:30–9:00
REGULARS:
Rick Nelson
Robie Porter
The Bob Banas Dancers

Popular singer Rick Nelson was the host of this summer music show which originated from the famous Malibu Beach area in Southern California. As "Dean of the Drop-Ins" at this mythical college, Rick invited guest professors—all popular singers—to lecture (sing their hits) to the student body. There was a lot of body to lecture, mostly bikini-clad young girls ("Malibeauties"), and the curriculum for the summer school included such subjects as surfing, sunbathing, girl-watching, and a field trip to a bikini factory (not much going on there). Australian singer Robie Porter was a featured regular.

MAMA
Comedy/Drama
FIRST TELECAST: *July 1, 1949*
LAST TELECAST: *July 27, 1956*
BROADCAST HISTORY:
Jul 1949–Jul 1956, CBS Fri 8:00–8:30 (OS)
CAST:

"Mama" Marta Hansen	Peggy Wood
"Papa" Lars Hansen	Judson Laire
Nels	Dick Van Patten
Katrin	Rosemary Rice
Dagmar (1949)	Iris Mann
Dagmar (1950–1956)	Robin Morgan
Aunt Jenny	Ruth Gates

T. R. Ryan (1952–1956) ...... Kevin Coughlin
Uncle Chris (1949–1951) ...... Malcolm Keen
Uncle Chris (1951–1952) ..... Roland Winters
Uncle Gunnar Gunnerson........ Carl Frank
Aunt Trina Gunnerson .... Alice Frost
Ingeborg (1953–1956) ...... Patty McCormack

THEME MUSIC:
"Holverg Suite" (open), "The Last Spring"
(close), by Edvard Grieg

Mama was one of the best-loved of the early family comedies, and was in many ways the prototype of the "growing family" series which later proliferated on television (Ozzie & Harriet, Danny Thomas, et al.). There were no cheap gags or bumbling parents in *Mama*, but rather a warmhearted, humorous, true-to-life account of a Norwegian-American family of five making their way in turn-of-the-century San Francisco.

The opening each week was in the style of a reminiscence by Katrin, leafing through the pages of the family album, past the pictures she knew so well—"I remember my brother Nels . . . and my little sister Dagmar . . . and of course, Papa. But most of all, I remember Mama."

Mama herself was played to perfection by the noted stage actress, Peggy Wood. Strict yet loving, she epitomized the gentleness which endeared the series to viewers for so many years. Papa was a carpenter who made just enough money to support his family decently, if not richly. Nels, Katrin, and Dagmar were the children. Any member of the family might be the subject of a week's story—Papa's new invention, Dagmar's braces, Mama's attempts to brighten the household—but all shared in the resolution. Each week's episode ended with the family seated around a pot of the sponsor's Maxwell House coffee, sharing the lessons learned.

One of the classic stories, presented each year, was the Christmas episode in which Papa told Dagmar how the animals were given the gift of speech for a few hours each Christmas Eve, as a reward for their protection of the Christ child in Bethlehem. When the rest of the family was asleep, Dagmar slipped out to the stable, to await the special moment.

Other regulars who passed through the Hansens' proper Victorian household on Steiner Street were Aunt Jenny ("Yenny" to all), T. R. Ryan, and Willie, the family dog.

So popular was *Mama* that when CBS announced that it was finally cancelling the show, in 1956, the outcry was sufficient to bring the program back for a short additional run on Sunday afternoons. These episodes, aired from December 1956 through March 1957, were on film and featured the same cast as the prime-time series, except that Toni Campbell took over the role of Dagmar.

Mama was based on a book, *Mama's Bank Account*, which was written by a real-life Kathryn (Forbes). The book had subsequently become a highly successful play (1944) and movie (1948), both of which were titled *I Remember Mama*. Unlike some other early TV comedies such as *The Life of Riley* and *I Love Lucy*, *Mama* was telecast live rather than filmed. So while Lucy will be with us forever, the weekly dramas of life in the big white house on Steiner Street are, for the most part, gone forever. Like Katrin turning the pages of the album, we can only remember.

MAMA MALONE
Situation Comedy
FIRST TELECAST: *March 7, 1984*
LAST TELECAST: *July 21, 1984*
BROADCAST HISTORY:
Mar 1984–Apr 1984, CBS Wed 8:30–9:00
Jun 1984–Jul 1984, CBS Sat 8:00–8:30
CAST:
Mama Renate Malone............. Lila Kaye
Connie Karamakopoulos ..... Randee Heller
Frankie Karamakopoulos ..... Evan Richards
Dino Forresti .... Don Amendolia
Austin .... Raymond Singer
Padre Guardiano .... Ralph Manza
Father Jose Silva .... Richard Yniguez
Ken...................... Pendleton Brown
Harry...................... Mitchell Group
Stanley .... Sam Anderson
Jackie........................ Joey Jupiter

Graham Kerr and Julia Child would never have conducted a cooking show the way Mama Malone did. Not only was it aired live from her fourth-floor walk-up apartment in Brooklyn, but most of her family wandered in regularly while she was on the air and the show would degenerate into a discussion of moral values, social problems, and family happenings—a far cry from the recipes for lasagna, veal scallopini, and fish stew. "Cooking with Mama Malone" was carried by a local TV station in New York and the unplanned visits by family and friends drove her director, Austin, up the wall. Mama, the very Italian widow of an Irish policeman, fussed constantly over her daughter Connie (who was divorced from a Greek), her beloved grandson, Frankie, and her younger brother, Dino, a lounge singer who fancied himself as something of a swinger. Padre Guardiano was the elderly parish priest and Father Silva his handsome young assistant. Stanley was the announcer on the cooking show, and Ken, Harry, and Stanley the production crew.

MAMA ROSA
Situation Comedy
FIRST TELECAST: *May 21, 1950*
LAST TELECAST: *June 11, 1950*
BROADCAST HISTORY:
May 1950–Jun 1950, ABC Sun 9:30–10:00
CAST:
Mama Rosa .... Anna Demetrio
Her daughter .... Beverly Garland

Her son . . . . Richard Anderson
Nikolai . . . . Vito Scotti

This obscure early comedy, which was produced live in Hollywood, was seen briefly on the ABC network in 1950. It was set in a theatrical boardinghouse run by Mama Rosa and located in Hollywood. An assortment of showbiz types passed through, including Nikolai, a violin instructor.

MAMA'S FAMILY
Situation Comedy
FIRST TELECAST: *January 22, 1983*
LAST TELECAST: *August 17, 1985*
BROADCAST HISTORY:
  Jan 1983–Jun 1983, NBC Sat 9:00–9:30
  Aug 1983–Dec 1983, NBC Thu 8:30–9:00
  Jan 1984–May 1984, NBC Sat 9:30–10:00
  Jun 1984–Jul 1984, NBC Sat 9:00–9:30
  Jul 1984–Sep 1984, NBC Sat 9:30–10:00
  Jun 1985–Aug 1985, NBC Sat 9:30–10:00
  (In first-run syndication since September 1986)
CAST:
  Mama (Thelma) Harper . . . . . Vicki Lawrence
  Aunt Fran Crowley (1983–1985)
  . . . . Rue McClanahan
  Vinton Harper . . . . Ken Berry
  Naomi Oates Harper . . . . Dorothy Lyman
  Vinton "Buzz" Harper, Jr. (1983–1985)
  . . . . Eric Brown
  Sonja Harper (1983–1985) . . . . . . Karin Argoud
  Ellen Jackson (1983–1985) . . . . Betty White
  Eunice Higgins (1983–1985) . . . . Carol Burnett
  Ed Higgins (1983–1985) . . . . . . Harvey Korman
  Alistair Quince (1983–1985) . . Harvey Korman
  Bubba Higgins (1986–   ) . . . . . Allan Kayser
  Iola Boylen (1986–   ) . . . . . Beverly Archer

*Occasional

Mama's Family mined comedy from a squabbling family in the Midwestern blue-collar suburb of Raytown. The noisy clan was headed by Mama, a buxom, gray-haired widow with sharp opinions and a sharper tongue who shared her small house with her high-strung sister, Fran, a journalist for a local paper. Mama's lazy, dim-witted son, Vint, a locksmith by trade, moved in at the start of the series with his troublesome teenage children, Buzz and Sonja, after his wife ran off to become a Las Vegas showgirl. Much to Mama's disgust, Vint soon took up with the flirtatious neighbor, Naomi ("that floozy!"). The two were married in early 1983, and Naomi moved in too. Further uproar was caused by the periodic visits of Mama's two married daughters, the foulmouthed Eunice and the snobbish Ellen. Ed was Eunice's dolt of a husband.

The program was based on a series of sketches originally seen on *The Carol Burnett Show* and later made into the high-rated special "Eunice" in 1982. Each episode began with a short, pompous introduction by "your host" Alistair Quince, seen

seated in his armchair. NBC aired reruns of *Mama's Family* during the summer of 1985.

In the fall of 1986 *Mama's Family* returned to TV in first-run syndication. Fran had recently passed away and Ed and Eunice had moved to Florida. They had neglected to mention this to their delinquent son Bubba who, after serving a term in juvenile hall for car theft, ended up living with Mama in Fran's old room, much to the consternation of Naomi and Vinton who thought they were getting it. Iola was the prissy neighbor who barely concealed her romantic designs on Vinton.

MAN AGAINST CRIME
Detective Drama
FIRST TELECAST: *October 7, 1949*
LAST TELECAST: *August 19, 1956*
BROADCAST HISTORY:
  Oct 1949–Mar 1952, CBS Fri 8:30–9:00 (OS)
  Apr 1952–Jun 1952, CBS Thu 9:00–9:30
  Oct 1952–Jun 1953, CBS Wed 9:30–10:00
  Jul 1953–Oct 1953, CBS Fri 8:30–9:00
  Oct 1953–Apr 1954, DUM Sun 10:30–11:00
  Oct 1953–Jul 1954, NBC Sun 10:30–11:00
  Jul 1956–Aug 1956, NBC Sun 10:00–10:30
CAST:
  Mike Barnett (1949–1954) . . . . . Ralph Bellamy
  Mike Barnett (1956) . . . . Frank Lovejoy
  Pat Barnett (1951) . . . . Robert Preston

The "man" was hard-boiled private detective Mike Barnett, who made his first appearance on CBS in the fall of 1949. Mike was a loner who used his brains and especially his fists to solve crimes in this rather violent show. The setting was the New York City area. The show was done live until the fall of 1952, when it went to film. The filmed episodes were all made at the Thomas A. Edison Studios in the Bronx and on location around New York.

When it left CBS in 1953 *Man Against Crime* did something almost unique—it became a regularly scheduled series on two different networks, NBC and DuMont, airing at the same time on both (Sunday, 10:30 P.M.). The program left the air in 1954 but returned in the summer of 1956 as a live program, with Frank Lovejoy in the lead role.

During the summer of 1951, while Ralph Bellamy was on his vacation from the show, Robert Preston filled in for him in the role of his brother, Pat.

MAN AND THE CHALLENGE
Adventure
FIRST TELECAST: *September 12, 1959*
LAST TELECAST: *September 3, 1960*
BROADCAST HISTORY:
  Sep 1959–Sep 1960, NBC Sat 8:30–9:00
CAST:
  Dr. Glenn Barton . . . . George Nader

Dr. Glenn Barton was an athlete, doctor, and research scientist who worked for the government.

Each week he was assigned to help others test the limits of their equipment and themselves under conditions of extreme stress. Barton's curiosity about his varied subjects and the fields with which he became involved occasionally resulted in his subjecting himself to the stresses in question before he would test their effects on others. He helped explorers test advanced jungle-survival techniques, he subjected two volunteers to an extended period in a small capsule to simulate the period in which astronauts await retrieval after returning from space, and he subjected other volunteers to the psychological torture and stress of brainwashing. In many of the episodes an emergency occurred, and Dr. Barton would have to push his own or others' endurance to limits not previously reached to try to save the situation— not always with positive results.

MAN AND THE CITY, THE
Drama
FIRST TELECAST: *September 15, 1971*
LAST TELECAST: *January 5, 1972*
BROADCAST HISTORY:
Sep 1971–Jan 1972, ABC Wed 10:00–11:00
CAST:
Mayor Thomas Jefferson Alcala
.... Anthony Quinn
Andy Hays .... Mike Farrell
Marian Crane .... Mala Powers
Josefina .... Carmen Zapata

Academy Award winner Anthony Quinn starred as the ruggedly independent mayor of a fast-growing contemporary city in the Southwest. Mayor Alcala was no youngster, having been in office for 16 years. His longevity was assured by a constant and personal attention to the needs of individual constituents, whose stories made up this series. The mayor's sensible, button-down aide Andy tried to keep Hizzoner from becoming completely engrossed in individual people's problems, to the detriment of citywide affairs. Marian was the mayor's secretary.

Although the locale of *Man and the City* was not explicitly identified, the program was filmed on location in Albuquerque, New Mexico.

MAN BEHIND THE BADGE, THE
Police Anthology
FIRST TELECAST: *October 11, 1953*
LAST TELECAST: *October 3, 1954*
BROADCAST HISTORY:
Oct 1953–Oct 1954, CBS Sun 9:30–10:00
HOST/NARRATOR:
Norman Rose

Each of the stories told in this live semidocumentary anthology series was a reenactment of an actual case from the files of a law enforcement agency. Although many of the stories were about police officers, they were not the only persons who fell into the category of "man behind the badge." Parole officers, park rangers, public defenders, U.S. Army MPs in Europe, and judges also appeared as leading characters in stories. Crime was not always the theme, either, as rehabilitation, life in a home for boys, and divorce were all touched upon at one time or another. On occasion the "man" behind the badge turned out to be a woman, such as a lady judge or a policewoman in a large city. Lesser-known talent was featured, although some of the actors (Jack Warden, Joey Faye, Bruce Gordon, and young Leslie Nielsen among them) later became well known.

A syndicated film version of *The Man Behind the Badge* was produced after the series had been canceled by CBS. The narrator of the filmed series, which was first seen in January 1955, was Charles Bickford.

MAN CALLED SHENANDOAH, A
Western
FIRST TELECAST: *September 13, 1965*
LAST TELECAST: *September 5, 1966*
BROADCAST HISTORY:
Sep 1965–Sep 1966, ABC Mon 9:00–9:30
CAST:
Shenandoah .... Robert Horton

In the opening episode of this series two buffalo hunters out on the prairie stumbled upon a stranger who had been shot in a gunfight and left to die. Assuming that he might be an outlaw with a price on his head, they hauled the half-dead man into the nearest town. It turned out that he wasn't wanted, but when he recovered from the wound he couldn't remember who he was or why he had been shot. Taking the name Shenandoah, the stranger spent the rest of the season wandering from town to town in search of clues to his real identity. Robert Horton had left *Wagon Train* with the vow never to do another Western, but relented long enough to play the lead in this single-season series.

MAN CALLED SLOANE, A
International Intrigue
FIRST TELECAST: *September 22, 1979*
LAST TELECAST: *September 12, 1980*
BROADCAST HISTORY:
Sep 1979–Dec 1979, NBC Sat 10:00–11:00
Jun 1980–Jul 1980, NBC Fri 10:00–11:00
Sep 1980, NBC Fri 10:00–11:00
CAST:
Thomas Remington Sloane III
.... Robert Conrad
Torque .... Ji-Tu Cumbuka
The Director .... Dan O'Herlihy
Kelly .... Karen Purcill
Effie (voice only) .... Michele Carey

In his successful late 1960s series *The Wild, Wild West,* Robert Conrad played a 19th-century horse-opera version of James Bond. A decade later, he returned with a series in which he played a contemporary James Bond. Thomas Remington Sloane III was the top agent for UNIT, an American counterintelligence team committed to destroying the international criminal organization KARTEL. Suave, romantic, and brilliant, Sloane traveled all over the world to thwart the plans of KARTEL. With him was his trusted aide Torque, a six-foot, five-inch agent with a stainless steel hand that could be adapted to use a myriad of detachable gadgets. Running UNIT headquarters, located behind a toy boutique, was The Director. His only accountability was to the President. At headquarters was a special lab that provided Sloane and Torque with all sorts of devices to help them in emergencies. Lab assistant Kelly, who usually demonstrated the latest devices, occasionally got involved with them on missions. Also at headquarters was the E.F.I. series 3000 multifunction computer ("Effie") that assimilated data and gave its readouts not in print, but over a loudspeaker in a very sexy, very feminine voice.

MAN CALLED X, THE
Intrigue
BROADCAST HISTORY:
Syndicated only
30 minutes
Produced: *1955–1956* (39 episodes)
Released: *January 1956*
CAST:
Agent Ken Thurston .... Barry Sullivan

Barry Sullivan portrayed a U.S. secret agent in this rather standard spy thriller. Thurston (code name "X") trotted off on missions around the world, from Prague to Teheran to Nepal, outwitting enemy agents and rescuing brilliant scientists and beautiful women. There was a certain note of authenticity, however, as the cases were based on real government files and technical supervision was by Ladislas Farago, a former agent of the U.S. Office of Naval Intelligence.

A radio version of *The Man Called X,* starring Herbert Marshall, aired from 1944 to 1952.

MAN FROM ATLANTIS
Adventure
FIRST TELECAST: *September 22, 1977*
LAST TELECAST: *July 25, 1978*
BROADCAST HISTORY:
Sep 1977, NBC Thu 9:00–10:00
Oct 1977–Jan 1978, NBC Tue 8:00–9:00
Apr 1978–Jul 1978, NBC Tue 8:00–9:00
CAST:
Mark Harris.................. Patrick Duffy
Dr. Elizabeth Merrill ... Belinda Montgomery
C. W. Crawford................. Alan Fudge
Mr. Schubert .... Victor Buono
Brent .... Robert Lussier
Jomo..................... Richard Williams
Chuey .... J. Victor Lopez
Jane .... Jean Marie Hon
Allen .... Anson Downes

Mark Harris was the last survivor of the lost continent of Atlantis. Though he appeared to be human, there were distinct differences between Mark and his air-breathing brethren. Having grown up under the sea, Mark possessed gill tissue rather than lungs, which meant that he could survive for only about 12 hours before he had to return to the sea to "breathe." His hands and feet were webbed, he could swim faster than a dolphin, and he had superhuman strength and super-acute senses.

Despite his powers Mark had been washed ashore unconscious, where he was discovered by Dr. Elizabeth Merrill, who nursed him back to health. He then agreed to join her and a team of scientists from the Foundation for Oceanic Research in a project to learn more about life undersea. They traveled about in the "Getacean," a special submersible vehicle, and their adventures included confrontations with extraterrestrial life and numerous evil scientists, notably the diabolical Mr. Schubert and his assistant, Brent. The foundation's director, preoccupied with budget problems, was C. W. Crawford.

Man from Atlantis was first seen in a series of four pilots that aired during the spring and summer of 1977 on varying days of the week. The first of these was telecast on March 4, 1977.

MAN FROM BLACKHAWK, THE
Western
FIRST TELECAST: *October 9, 1959*
LAST TELECAST: *September 23, 1960*
BROADCAST HISTORY:
Oct 1959–Sep 1960, ABC Fri 8:30–9:00
CAST:
Sam Logan .... Robert Rockwell

This was a Western with a twist. Its hero was neither a gunfighter nor a lawman; he was an insurance investigator. Sam Logan, Chicago-based investigator for the Blackhawk Insurance Company, wore a city-slicker outfit complete with string tie and briefcase. He almost never used a gun but often had to resort to his fists as he traveled from place to place investigating attempts to defraud the company and settling claims. In addition to visiting many typical Western frontier towns, Logan also frequently turned up in cities like New Orleans and San Francisco.

MAN FROM INTERPOL
Police Drama
FIRST TELECAST: *January 30, 1960*
LAST TELECAST: *October 22, 1960*
BROADCAST HISTORY:
Jan 1960–Oct 1960, NBC Sat 10:30–11:00
CAST:
Anthony Smith .... Richard Wyler
Superintendent Mercer .... John Longden

Filmed in England, *Man from Interpol* told of the adventures of Anthony Smith, a special agent for the Scotland Yard division of "Interpol," the International Police Force. The crimes he investigated were therefore generally international in scope, sending him trotting around Europe in pursuit of smugglers, counterfeiters, and other border-crossing culprits.

MAN FROM U.N.C.L.E., THE
Spy Spoof
FIRST TELECAST: *September 22, 1964*
LAST TELECAST: *January 15, 1968*
BROADCAST HISTORY:
Sep 1964–Dec 1964, NBC Tue 8:30–9:30
Jan 1965–Sep 1965, NBC Mon 8:00–9:00
Sep 1965–Sep 1966, NBC Fri 10:00–11:00
Sep 1966–Sep 1967, NBC Fri 8:30–9:30
Sep 1967–Jan 1968, NBC Mon 8:00–9:00
CAST:
Napoleon Solo .... Robert Vaughn
Illya Kuryakin .... David McCallum
Mr. Alexander Waverly ...... Leo G. Carroll
Lisa Rogers (1967–1968) ...... Barbara Moore

The Man from U.N.C.L.E. was American television's answer to the very popular James Bond movies. Two superagents, Napoleon Solo and Illya Kuryakin, were teamed to fight the international crime syndicate THRUSH. U.N.C.L.E. (which stood for United Network Command for Law and Enforcement) had its secret American headquarters in New York. Running the office was Mr. Waverly, whose function was to assign agents to cases and coordinate their efforts. The suave, urbane American Solo and the blond, introverted Russian Kuryakin spent most of their time saving the world from THRUSH and, as the series wore on, the plots became more and more farfetched. The pinnacle of silliness was reached in the 1966–1967 season when *The Girl from U.N.C.L.E.* was created, bringing to television two hours of U.N.C.L.E. per week, with plots that were closer to ABC's *Batman* than to any sort of believable spy thriller.

At the end of the 1966–1967 season, *The Girl from U.N.C.L.E.* was dead and *The Man from U.N.C.L.E.* was dying. A transfusion of reality was tried at the start of the 1967–1968 season, with new sets for U.N.C.L.E.'s New York offices and stories that were more traditionally suspenseful, with danger that no longer seemed as if it had just come off the comic-book pages, and with a new regular cast member in Mr. Waverly's secretary Lisa Rogers. Unfortunately it was too late, and the series ended on the evening of January 15, 1968, to be replaced by the biggest hit of the late 1960s, *Rowan & Martin's Laugh-In.*

MAN IN A SUITCASE
Detective Drama
FIRST TELECAST: *May 3, 1968*
LAST TELECAST: *September 20, 1968*
BROADCAST HISTORY:
May 1968–Sep 1968, ABC Fri 8:30–9:30
CAST:
McGill .... Richard Bradford

Filmed in England, as were most of the series about "loners" in the 1960s, *Man in a Suitcase* was the story of a private detective who had once been an American intelligence agent. McGill had been falsely accused of failing to prevent a noted scientist from defecting to Russia, a treasonous offense. The series followed McGill through the European underworld as he searched for the evidence and people that could prove his innocence.

MAN OF THE WEEK
Interview
FIRST TELECAST: *April 20, 1952*
LAST TELECAST: *August 22, 1954*
BROADCAST HISTORY:
Apr 1952–Jan 1953, CBS Sun 6:00–6:30
Jul 1954–Aug 1954, CBS Sun 6:30–7:00
MODERATOR:
Walter Cronkite (1952–1953)
Ron Cochran (1954)

Each week on *Man of the Week*, a prominent public figure was interviewed about subjects of general interest. The program premiered as a Sunday afternoon entry in August 1951, and ran continuously until October 1954, alternating between night-time and afternoon time slots. The night-time telecasts are indicated above. This series was the forerunner of *Face the Nation.*

MAN WHO NEVER WAS, THE
International Intrigue
FIRST TELECAST: *September 7, 1966*
LAST TELECAST: *January 4, 1967*
BROADCAST HISTORY:
Sep 1966–Jan 1967, ABC Wed 9:00–9:30
CAST:
Peter Murphy/Mark Wainwright
.... Robert Lansing
Eva Wainwright .... Dana Wynter
Col. Jack Forbes .... Murray Hamilton
Roger Barry .... Alex Davion
Paul Grant .... Paul Stewart

This spy thriller starred Robert Lansing as an American espionage agent who took another man's identity—and wife, fortune, and life-style. As the series opened Peter Murphy was fleeing from East Berlin with enemy agents in hot pursuit. Taking refuge in a bar, he came upon his exact look-alike, millionaire playboy Mark Wainwright, who was later mistaken for him by the enemy and killed. Sensing an opportunity, Peter assumed Wainwright's identity, his wealth, and his aristocratic wife as a perfect cover for his undercover activities in the glamorous capitals of Europe.

Wainwright's wife Eva knew that Murphy was an impostor, but she went along with him to keep the family fortune, which would have otherwise fallen into the hands of grasping half brother

Roger. Eva even taught Murphy her late husband's habits, so the "cover" would be perfect. Eventually Eva fell in love with her new "husband"—but Peter remained wary. The only other person who knew Murphy's new identity was his boss, Chief of Intelligence Col. Forbes.

Filmed on location in Berlin, Munich, London, Athens, and other cities of Europe.

MAN WITH A CAMERA
Drama
FIRST TELECAST: *October 10, 1958*
LAST TELECAST: *February 29, 1960*
BROADCAST HISTORY:
Oct 1958–Mar 1959, ABC Fri 9:00–9:30
Oct 1959–Feb 1960, ABC Mon 10:30–11:00
CAST:
Mike Kovac .... Charles Bronson
Anton Kovac .... Ludwig Stossel
Lt. Donovan (1959–1960) .... James Flavin

During World War II Mike Kovac had been a combat photographer. Now he was making his living as a free-lance professional lensman. At times it seemed as if he were still in combat. Mike took assignments from newspapers, insurance companies, the police, private individuals, and anyone else who wanted a filmed record of an event. The nature of his assignments often made Mike more private detective than photographer, a situation which was most likely planned by the producers of this series to capitalize on the popularity of detective shows at the time. Occasionally, when he needed advice or help, Mike sought out his father, Anton.

MAN WITHOUT A GUN
Western
BROADCAST HISTORY:
Syndicated only
30 minutes
Produced: *Oct 1957–1959* (52 episodes)
Released: *Fall 1958*
CAST:
Adam MacLean .... Rex Reason
Marshal Frank Tallman .... Mort Mills
Mayor George Dixon ...... Harry Harvey, Sr.
Doc Brannon .... Forrest Taylor

In this syndicated series handsome, brawny Rex Reason starred as a crusading newspaper editor in the Dakota Territory of the 1880s. Bandits, landgrabbers, and miscellaneous troublemakers were all around the town of Yellowstone, but editor MacLean preferred to use persuasion and the columns of *The Yellowstone Sentinel* rather than guns in his campaign for law and order—although a good fistfight now and then helped things along. MacLean also used his office as a schoolroom for the town's youngsters.

MANHATTAN MAHARAJA
Variety
FIRST TELECAST: *October 4, 1950*
LAST TELECAST: *February 26, 1951*
BROADCAST HISTORY:
Oct 1950–Nov 1950, ABC Wed 9:30–10:00
Nov 1950–Feb 1951, ABC Mon 9:15–9:30
REGULARS:
George Ansbro
Joseph Biviano
Ralph Norman

In this odd series, George Ansbro donned the guise of a maharaja in the Arabian Nights vein and in tongue-in-cheek verse touched upon modern topics as they would be seen through the eyes of an Eastern potentate. "Pasha" Joseph Biviano and his Snake Charmers provided upbeat music, while "Sahib" Ralph Norman and his string group played for the maharaja's favorite dancing girls. Seen only on a limited number of ABC network stations during its prime-time run, *Manhattan Maharaja* continued in daytime until 1952.

MANHATTAN SHOWCASE
Musical Variety
FIRST TELECAST: *February 28, 1949*
LAST TELECAST: *June 16, 1949*
BROADCAST HISTORY:
Feb 1949–Apr 1949, CBS Various, 7:15–7:30
Apr 1949–May 1949, CBS Mon/Tue/Thu/Fri 7:45–8:00
May 1949–Jun 1949, CBS Mon/Wed/Thu 7:15–7:30
REGULARS:
Johnny Downs
Helen Gallagher
Virginia Gorski
Evelyn Ward
The Tony Mottola Trio

Manhattan Showcase provided young entertainers with the opportunity to perform before a nationwide audience in the early days of live television. Johnny Downs was the one host who stayed with the show from beginning to end. His female helper was originally Helen Gallagher, who was joined by Virginia Gorski in April; the two of them left in June, to be replaced by Evelyn Ward. The series was initially aired on Mondays, Wednesdays, and Fridays, but later shifted to various combinations of weeknights.

MANHATTAN SPOTLIGHT
Interview
FIRST TELECAST: *January 24, 1949*
LAST TELECAST: *April 20, 1951*
BROADCAST HISTORY:
Jan 1949–Apr 1951, DUM Mon–Fri Various 15-minute spots
Apr 1950–May 1950, DUM Wed 10:00–10:15
May 1950–Jun 1950, DUM Wed 10:30–10:45
HOST:
Chuck Tranum

DuMont Chief Announcer Chuck Tranum was primarily responsible for the station breaks and other announcements made over the fledgling network from its flagship station in New York. He also hosted this nightly 15-minute interview program, which featured ordinary citizens and small-time entertainers with interesting hobbies and talents. Among those appearing were a Mr. Bimstein, who sculpted the Empire State Building in ice, the city's leading umbrella collector, a custom shoe manufacturer, a team of calypso dancers, the head of a lonely hearts club, and a man with a collection of electric eels.

Manhattan Spotlight began in daytime before moving to the nighttime schedule, where it was seen between 7:30 and 8:00 P.M. on various weeknights. There was also a late-night run during April–June 1950. During some periods the show was only seen locally in New York.

MANHATTAN TRANSFER
Variety
FIRST TELECAST: *August 10, 1975*
LAST TELECAST: *August 31, 1975*
BROADCAST HISTORY:
Aug 1975, CBS Sun 7:30–8:30
REGULARS:
Manhattan Transfer
(Laurel Masse, Tim Hauser, Janis Siegel, Alan Paul)
Archie Hahn
Leland Palmer
Fayette Hauser
Laraine Newman
The Ira Newborn Orchestra

The Manhattan Transfer was a popular recording group whose material was impossible to type. Their routines, both musical and comic, spanned the entire 20th century and ran the gamut from semiclassical to rock. This potpourri of songs and humor aired for four weeks in the summer of 1975. Archie Hahn was the most prominent member of their supporting cast, portraying the character Doughie Duck in various comedy sketches.

MANHUNT
Dramatic Anthology
FIRST TELECAST: *July 14, 1951*
LAST TELECAST: *August 23, 1952*
BROADCAST HISTORY:
Jul 1951–Sep 1951, NBC Sat 10:30–11:00
Jul 1952–Aug 1952, NBC Sat 10:30–11:00

Also known as *Assignment Manhunt,* this live dramatic series spent two years as the summer replacement for *Your Hit Parade.* The plays were all adaptations of suspense and adventure stories that had appeared previously in magazines or as books or movies.

MANHUNT
Police Drama

BROADCAST HISTORY:
Syndicated only
30 minutes
Produced: *1959–1961* (78 episodes)
Released: *September 1959*
CAST:
Det. Lt. Howard Finucane .... Victor Jory
Ben Andrews .... Patrick McVey
Det. George Peters (*episodes #1–13*)
.... Charles Bateman
Det. Bruce Hanna (#14–23) ..... Rian Garrick
Det. Dan Kramer (#24–39)
.... Chuck Henderson
Det. Paul Kirk (#40–52) .... Michael Steffany
Det. Phil Burns (#53–65).... Robert Crawford
Det. Carl Spencer (#66–78) . Todd Armstrong

Well-acted, straightforward cops-and-robbers show starring two veteran actors, Victor Jory and Patrick McVey. Jory portrayed a hard-nosed detective with the San Diego Police Dept., and McVey an equally hard-nosed police reporter with the *Chronicle* (similar to his earlier role in *Big Town*). Their easy camaraderie helped lift the series out of the melodramatic rut of murder, mobs, and arson.

Supporting these two old-timers was an up-to-date jazz score and a succession of young police sidekicks for Jory, each of whom appeared in 10 or 15 of the 78 episodes filmed. The producer, Screen Gems, wanted to use this series to expose new talent, but none of the young actors who "tried out" here went on to particularly notable careers.

MANHUNTER, THE
Detective Drama
FIRST TELECAST: *September 11, 1974*
LAST TELECAST: *April 9, 1975*
BROADCAST HISTORY:
Sep 1974–Apr 1975, CBS Wed 10:00–11:00
CAST:
Dave Barrett .... Ken Howard
Sheriff Paul Tate .... Robert Hogan
Lizabeth Barrett .... Hilary Thompson
James Barrett................. Ford Rainey
Mary Barrett .... Claudia Bryar
PRODUCER:
Quinn Martin

The Manhunter was a detective series set in the United States during the depression years of the 1930s. Dave Barrett was an ex-marine whose best friend had been killed by bank robbers during a holdup. Following his friend's death, Dave gave up his Idaho farm and became a private investigator with a mission: to bring to justice as many gangsters of the type that had killed his friend as possible. Tracking down these criminals sent him back and forth across the country, never staying in one place for long, except when he returned home to see his sister Liz and his folks.

MANIMAL

Police Drama/Fantasy
FIRST TELECAST: *September 30, 1983*
LAST TELECAST: *December 31, 1983*
BROADCAST HISTORY:
  Sep 1983–Nov 1983, NBC Fri 9:00–10:00
  Dec 1983, NBC Sat 9:00–10:00
CAST:
  Jonathan Chase .... Simon MacCorkindale
  Brooke McKenzie .... Melody Anderson
  Ty Earle (pilot only) .... Glynn Turman
  Ty Earle .... Michael D. Roberts
  Capt. Nick Rivera .... Reni Santoni

TV superheroes have had many tricks up their sleeves over the years, but Jonathan Chase was really different. He had the ability, inherited from his late father in some faraway jungle, to turn himself into animals—all sorts of animals, from a pussycat to a black panther. To most people he appeared as a wealthy, cultured young professor who taught "animal behavioral sciences" at New York University. To the police, he was a valued consultant on the use of animals in criminology. But to criminals, he was a snarl in the night, the sudden hiss of a cobra, the cry of an observant hawk.

The transformations were at will, and dramatic: his breathing grew heavy, his hands began to show ripples and contractions, his nose grew snouty, and whiskers and fangs began to emerge. All of this was seen in intriguing, unconnected close-ups.

Only two mortals knew of Chase's secret powers, his hip black helper, Ty Earle, with whom he had shared a few scrapes in Vietnam, and a pretty police detective named Brooke. Brooke had stumbled on his secret by accident, and now worked with him on cases. She also found he had a certain—well, animal magnetism, but nothing much came of their budding romance during the short run of this series. Instead, viewers were treated to a steady diet of coy remarks ("I was a real pussycat," "He's probably out catting around"), while the heavy breathing was reserved strictly for business.

MANNIX

Detective Drama
FIRST TELECAST: *September 16, 1967*
LAST TELECAST: *August 27, 1975*
BROADCAST HISTORY:
  Sep 1967–Sep 1971, CBS Sat 10:00–11:00
  Sep 1971–Sep 1972, CBS Wed 10:00–11:00
  Sep 1972–Dec 1972, CBS Sun 9:30–10:30
  Jan 1973–Sep 1974, CBS Sun 8:30–9:30
  Sep 1974–Jun 1975, CBS Sun 9:30–10:30
  Jul 1975–Aug 1975, CBS Wed 10:00–11:00
CAST:
  Joe Mannix .... Mike Connors
  Lou Wickersham (1967–1968)
  .... Joseph Campanella
  Peggy Fair (1968–1975) .... Gail Fisher
  Lt. Adam Tobias (1969–1975).... Robert Reed

Mannix was one of the most violent detective shows of its time, and also one of the longest-running. The original format had Joe Mannix, a Los Angeles–based private detective, employed by a sophisticated detective firm called Intertect. Despite the fact that the company was dedicated to the use of computers and other advanced scientific detection aids, Mannix seemed happiest when working with no implements other than his own intuition and fists. At the start of the second season he had struck out on his own, taking a small office on the first floor of the building in which he lived. Helping him in his new role as an independent investigator was his secretary and girl Friday, Peggy Fair. Her husband, a friend of Mannix's and a former police officer, had been killed in the line of duty. Lou Wickersham, Joe's old boss from Intertect, was also seen occasionally during the second season. Lt. Adam Tobias joined the cast as Joe's friend and contact on the police force at the start of the 1969–1970 season.

The high point of every episode seemed to be a wild brawl, and the body count even in the first few minutes of the show was sometimes appalling. On their radio show, Bob and Ray ran a continuing parody on the series called *Blimmix*, in which the hero always held a polite conversation with some suspect, calmly agreed that mayhem was the only answer, and then was invariably beaten to a pulp.

MANTOVANI

Music
BROADCAST HISTORY:
  Syndicated only
  30 minutes
  Produced: *1958–1959* (39 episodes)
  Released: *January 1959*
HOST:
  John Conte
WITH:
  Mantovani and His Orchestra

English orchestra leader Mantovani was very popular in the U.S. in the 1950s, with a long succession of best-selling albums and even a couple of hit singles ("Charmaine," "Cara Mia") before rock 'n' roll took over the charts. His music was characterized by old favorites, lush arrangements, and a huge string section, all calculated to appeal to the old folks (it put the younger set to sleep). After many concert tours the maestro appeared in this widely seen syndicated TV series, produced in England, with his full 46-piece orchestra. Guest artists trying not to be drowned in all those cascading strings included Connie Francis, Vic Damone, Joni James, Dorothy Collins, the Hi-Lo's, and the Boscoe Holder West Indian Dancers.

Mantovani's real name was Annunzio Paolo Mantovani.

MANY HAPPY RETURNS

Situation Comedy

FIRST TELECAST: *September 21, 1964*
LAST TELECAST: *April 12, 1965*
BROADCAST HISTORY:
Sep 1964–Apr 1965, CBS Mon 9:30–10:00
CAST:

Walter Burnley	John McGiver
Harry Price	Richard Collier
Joan Randall	Elinor Donahue
Wilma Fritter	Jesslyn Fax
Bob Randall	Mark Goddard
Joe Foley	Mickey Manners
Laurie Randall	Andrea Sacino
Lynn Hall	Elena Verdugo

Life was not peaceful for Walter Burnley. He had one of the most thankless jobs in the world, managing the complaint desk at Krockmeyer's department store. Working with him was a staff of four harried souls (Harry, Wilma, Joe, and Lynn), not all of whom managed to maintain their composure under the constant abuse of irate shoppers. Walter was a widower who made his home with his daughter Joan, Joan's husband Bob, and his four-year-old granddaughter Laurie.

MANY LOVES OF DOBIE GILLIS, THE
Situation Comedy
FIRST TELECAST: *September 29, 1959*
LAST TELECAST: *September 18, 1963*
BROADCAST HISTORY:
Sep 1959–Sep 1962, CBS Tue 8:30–9:00
Sep 1962–Sep 1963, CBS Wed 8:30–9:00
CAST:

Dobie Gillis	Dwayne Hickman
Maynard G. Krebs	Bob Denver
Herbert T. Gillis	Frank Faylen
Winifred (Winnie) Gillis	Florida Friebus
Zelda Gilroy	Sheila James
Thalia Menninger (1959–1960)	
	Tuesday Weld
Milton Armitage (1959–1960)	Warren Beatty
Riff Ryan (1959–1960)	Tommy Farrell
Melissa Frome (1959–1960)	Yvonne Lime
Davey Gillis (1959–1960)	Darryl Hickman
Mr. Leander Pomfritt	William Schallert
Clarice Armitage (1959–1960)	Doris Packer
Mrs. Chatsworth Osborne, Sr. (1960–1963)	
	Doris Packer
Chatsworth Osborne, Jr. (1960–1963)	
	Steve Franken
Mrs. Ruth Adams (1959–1960)	Jean Byron
Dr. Burkhart (1961–1963)	Jean Byron
Mrs. Blossom Kenney (1959–1961)	
	Marjorie Bennett
Lt. Merriweather (1961)	Richard Clair
Dean Magruder (1961–1963)	
	Raymond Bailey
Duncan Gillis (1962–1963)	Bobby Diamond

Dobie Gillis was a "typical" American teenager, with three primary interests in life: beautiful women, fancy cars, and money. Unfortunately he was the son of a grocer and not the most attractive of boys, which put a certain crimp in his aspira-

tions. Dobie and his beatnik buddy Maynard—to whom work was a dirty word—did their best to get by with a minimum of effort. Dobie had two real nemeses in his life. The first was intelligent but unattractive Zelda Gilroy, who was constantly trying to get herself married to Dobie. The second, through most of the series, was millionaire Chatsworth Osborne, Jr., a spoiled young man who flaunted his social status, not to mention his money, to snare the attractive girls who eluded Dobie.

When the series premiered in 1959, Dobie had to contend with handsome Milton Armitage for the attention of his favorite girl, the aristocratic (despite her rather modest means) and mercenary Thalia Menninger. She was interested mostly in acquiring "oodles and oodles" of money. To this end she was constantly looking to better Dobie's prospects for supporting her in the style to which she would like to become accustomed. Dobie was also much concerned about his future, and was seen at the beginning and end of each episode in Central City's park next to a statue of *The Thinker*, assuming the same pose while pondering his fate.

In February 1960, Milton Armitage was replaced by Chatsworth Osborne, Jr., with Doris Packer assuming the role of his snobbish, overbearing mother, essentially the same part she had played as Milton's mother when the series began. In March 1961, Dobie and Maynard enlisted in the army, thinking that would help them find themselves. The army hitch lasted only until the first episode of the 1961–1962 season, when they resigned from the service and enrolled in S. Peter Prior Junior College. It was there that they remained, Maynard still fighting the system in his nonconformist way and his "good buddy" Dobie chasing women and trying to find himself, for the last two seasons that *The Many Loves of Dobie Gillis* was on the air.

On May 10, 1977, nearly 15 years after *Dobie Gillis* ended its run, CBS aired the pilot episode for a proposed revival series titled *Whatever Happened to Dobie Gillis?* What had happened was that Dobie had finally been snared by Zelda, become a partner in his family's grocery store, and had a teenaged son, Georgie (played by Stephen Paul). Maynard, now fortyish but still unconventional, came back to visit. The new series never materialized. Another reunion took place in February 1988.

Based on characters created by author Max Shulman.

MARBLEHEAD MANOR
Situation Comedy
BROADCAST HISTORY:
Syndicated only
30 minutes
Produced: *1987–*
Released: *September 1987*
CAST:

Albert Dudley	Paxton Whitehead

485

Hilary Stonehill	Linda Thorson
Randolph Stonehill	Bob Fraser
Jerry Stockton	Phil Morris
Dwayne Stockton	Rodney Scott
Lupe	Dyana Ortelli
Elvis	Humberto Ortiz
Rick	Michael Richards

Randolph Stonehill had made his fortune in the vegetable oil business—a fortune large enough to provide him and his elegant wife, Hilary, with a large, fully staffed estate in this slapstick comedy. The staff was anything but efficient. The butler, Albert Dudley, was a stuffy, uptight Englishman who found it hard to deal with his unbelievably inept subordinates. Handyman Dwayne was always cooking up get-rich-quick schemes that got both him and the others in trouble. He was nothing like his hard-working brother, Jerry, the Stonehill chauffeur, who was going to night school to get his college degree. Others on the staff were Lupe, the well-meaning, if accident prone, household cook; Elvis, her precocious eight-year-old son; and Rick, the klutzy gardner.

Whenever things got out of control—which was often—it was the cool Mrs. Stonehill who kept her short-tempered husband and the staff from coming to blows.

In addition to playing the volatile Randolph Stonehill, Bob Fraser was one of the producers and writers of *Marblehead Manor*.

MARCH OF MEDICINE, THE

Documentary
FIRST TELECAST: *July 8, 1958*
LAST TELECAST: *July 29, 1958*
BROADCAST HISTORY:
Jul 1958, ABC Tue 10:00–10:30
NARRATORS:
Ben Grauer
Eric Sevareid

Public-service films about the mental-health field made up this series.

MARCUS WELBY, M.D.

Medical Drama
FIRST TELECAST: *September 23, 1969*
LAST TELECAST: *May 11, 1976*
BROADCAST HISTORY:
Sep 1969–May 1976, ABC Tue 10:00–11:00
CAST:
Dr. Marcus Welby	Robert Young
Dr. Steven Kiley	James Brolin
Consuelo Lopez	Elena Verdugo
Myra Sherwood (1969–1970)	Anne Baxter
Kathleen Faverty (1974–1976) ..	Sharon Gless
Sandy Porter (1975–1976)	Anne Schedeen
Phil Porter (1975–1976)	Gavin Brendan
Janet Blake (1975–1976)	Pamela Hensley
MEDICAL ADVISOR:
Dr. Robert Forten

CREATOR/PRODUCER:
David Victor

Robert Young was one of the few actors in television history to be closely identified with two highly successful and long-running roles—that of kindly family man Jim Anderson on *Father Knows Best* in the 1950s (8 years) and that of kindly Dr. Marcus Welby in the 1970s (7 years). The 62-year-old Young came out of a seven-year retirement to originate the role of Welby.

Marcus Welby, M.D. portrayed the cases of a veteran general practitioner in Santa Monica, California, whose thoroughness and dedication involved him in the lives of all sorts of patients. Assisting him was young Dr. Steven Kiley, who during the first season contracted to work with Welby for one year before resuming his training as a neurologist (he stayed). Thus the inevitable tension between youth and experience was established, but in this case Welby tended to be the more unorthodox of the two, often confounding the dedicated but textbook-oriented Kiley with his psychiatric approach to medicine. Welby treated the whole patient, his temperament, fears, and family environment, as well as his physical ailments. The ailments were certainly varied for a suburban GP: during the first season alone there were tumors, autistic children, strokes, pernicious anemia, blindness, emphysema, LSD side effects, leukemia, diabetes, Huntington's Chorea, faith healing, dope addiction, an overweight racing jockey, and a diver who kept getting the bends.

A love interest was provided for Dr. Welby during the first season by Myra Sherwood, but this role was soon dropped. The only other suggestion that Welby might have a life of his own came in the last season, when his married daughter (Sandy) and six-year-old grandson (Phil) were occasionally seen. There was no Mrs. Welby. The only other regulars over the years, in fact, were nurses Consuelo Lopez and Kathleen Faverty.

Although romance eluded Dr. Welby it did finally come to young Dr. Kiley, in the person of Janet Blake, public relations director of Hope Memorial Hospital. They were married on the telecast of October 21, 1975.

Marcus Welby premiered in 1969 and soon became the biggest hit in the history of the ABC network up to that time—it was the first ABC series ever to rank number one among all TV programs for a full season (1970–1971). Part of its success, truth to tell, was in scheduling; for its first two years it ran against a CBS news documentary hour and frequently against documentaries on NBC as well *(First Tuesday)*. The limited appeal of these shows practically forfeited the audience to ABC. But once viewers had gotten used to Welby they stayed, against competition soft and strong. The program also won an Emmy and was held in very high esteem by medical groups, with Young serving offscreen as honorary chairman of numerous national fund drives and observances.

MARGE AND GOWER CHAMPION SHOW, THE

Situation Comedy

FIRST TELECAST: *March 31, 1957*
LAST TELECAST: *June 9, 1957*
BROADCAST HISTORY:
  Mar 1957–Jun 1957, CBS Sun 7:30–8:00
CAST:
  Marge Champion .... Herself
  Gower Champion .... Himself
  Marge's Father .... Jack Whiting
  Cozy .... Buddy Rich
  Amanda .... Peg La Centra
  Miss Weatherly .... Barbara Perry
ORCHESTRA:
  Richard Pribor

The format of this comedy series was designed to give the Champions at least one opportunity to dance each week. Gower played a choreographer and Marge his dancing partner, as they were in real life, and the situations used in the series were based on their actual experiences. Drummer Buddy Rich, appropriately, played their drummer and accompanist, and actress-singer Peg La Centra was cast as Marge's close friend and interior decorator. The program aired on alternate Sundays with *The Jack Benny Show*.

MARGE AND JEFF

Situation Comedy

FIRST TELECAST: *September 21, 1953*
LAST TELECAST: *September 24, 1954*
BROADCAST HISTORY:
  Sep 1953–Sep 1954, DUM Mon–Fri 7:15–7:30
CAST:
  Marge .... Marge Greene
  Jeff .... Jess/Jeff Cain

This pleasant 15-minute domestic comedy, presented five nights a week, concerned the day-to-day life of newlyweds Marge and Jeff, starting life together in a big-city apartment. Sharing in their little adventures were occasional neighbors and their cocker spaniel, Paisley. The program was written by Miss Greene, who previously produced a similar local program (called *Marge and Fred*) in Philadelphia.

Because of the confusing similarity of actor Jess Cain's name to that of his character Jeff, the actor had his name legally changed to Jeff shortly after the series began.

MARGIE

Situation Comedy

FIRST TELECAST: *October 12, 1961*
LAST TELECAST: *August 31, 1962*
BROADCAST HISTORY:
  Oct 1961–Apr 1962, ABC Thu 9:30–10:00
  Apr 1962–Aug 1962, ABC Fri 7:30–8:00
CAST:
  Margie Clayton .... Cynthia Pepper
  Maybelle Jackson .... Penney Parker
  Nora Clayton .... Wesley Tackitt

Aunt Phoebe .... Hollis Irving
Harvey Clayton .... Dave Willock
Heywood Botts .... Tommy Ivo
Johnny Green .... Richard Gering
Cornell Clayton .... Johnny Bangert

Growing up in the Roaring Twenties didn't seem to be radically different from growing up in the 1960s, as this series pointed out. The superficial things were different: flappers, bathtub gin, rumble seats, prohibition, raccoon coats, and the Charleston. The real issues were the same: conflicts with parents, troubled love affairs, the hassle of school, and maintaining "true" friends. Margie lived with her parents, her little brother, Cornell, and her aunt Phoebe. Her best friend, Maybelle Jackson, was a flapper, and Heywood and Johnny were the two boys fighting for her affection. To add to the period flavor of the show, *Margie's* producers intermixed silent movie slides that told the audience "Please Pay Attention," "The Plot Thickens," etc., at critical points in the action.

MARIAH

Police Drama

FIRST TELECAST: *April 1, 1987*
LAST TELECAST: *May 13, 1987*
BROADCAST HISTORY:
  Apr 1987–May 1987, ABC Wed 10:00–11:00
CAST:
  Superintendent James Malone
    .... Philip Baker Hall
  Dep. Superintendent Ned Sheffield
    .... John Getz
  Dr. Deena Hertz .... Tovah Feldshuh
  Chaplain Timothy Quinlan ... Chris Wiggins
  Brandis LaSalle .... Kathleen Layman
  Leda Cervantes .... Wanda de Jesus
  Rev. Howard Bouchard
    .... William Allen Young
  Linda Grincato .... Renee Lippin

This earnest but rather grim drama concerned life—and death—at Mariah State Penitentiary. The focus was primarily on the staff, including tough, politically savvy Superintendent Malone and his hard-working young deputy, Sheffield; prison psychiatrist Deena, generally seen running from one suicide attempt to the next, with Father Quinlan close behind; and Brandis, the rich, idealistic activist who worked as a prison volunteer—and also wanted to set up a National Union of Prisoners' Wives and Families headquartered outside the gate. Stories concerned the travails of the staff, political infighting, and sometimes inmates' stories (e.g., a woman prisoner worried about losing her children).

MARIE

Musical Variety

FIRST TELECAST: *December 12, 1980*
LAST TELECAST: *September 26, 1981*

BROADCAST HISTORY:
Dec 1980–Jan 1981, NBC Fri 8:00–9:00
Sep 1981, NBC Sat 9:00–10:00
REGULARS:
Marie Osmond
Howard Itzkowitz
Jeffrey Baron
Jamie Mizada
John Bates
Hennen Chambers
The Lester Wilson Dancers
Doris Hess
Jim Hudson
Greg Norberg
Charlie Gray
Kathe Flinders
Debi Ing
The Bob Rozario Orchestra

At age 21, Marie Osmond was already a veteran performer. She had begun singing with her family, the Osmond Brothers, before entering school and had her first hit record at the age of 14 ("Paper Roses" in 1973). Three years later Marie was starring with her brother Donny in a variety series on ABC *(Donny and Marie)*. This limited-run variety series was Marie's first attempt to go it alone as a single, even if it was produced by Osmond Productions. *Marie* was a mix of music and humor, and was billed as a more sophisticated show than the ABC series had been. Miss Osmond sang songs that ranged from standards to current pop tunes and participated in comedy sketches with a large supporting cast. There were numerous comedy blackouts on each telecast and, reminiscent of *The Carol Burnett Show*, weekly question-and-answer sessions with the studio audience. There were also guests, including Andy Williams, who had given the Osmonds their first TV exposure in the 1960s.

MARILYN MCCOO AND BILLY DAVIS, JR. SHOW, THE
Musical Variety
FIRST TELECAST: *June 15, 1977*
LAST TELECAST: *July 20, 1977*
BROADCAST HISTORY:
Jun 1977–Jul 1977, CBS Wed 8:30–9:00
REGULARS:
Marilyn McCoo
Billy Davis, Jr.
Jay Leno
Lewis Arquette
Tim Reid
The John Myles Orchestra

Summer variety series featuring the husband-and-wife team of McCoo and Davis, who were members of the original Fifth Dimension pop group. This series, with music, comedy, and guest stars, came on the heels of their Grammy Award–winning record "You Don't Have to Be a Star to Be in My Show."

MARK SABER
Detective Drama
FIRST TELECAST: *October 5, 1951*
LAST TELECAST: *May 15, 1960*
BROADCAST HISTORY:
Oct 1951–Apr 1952, ABC Fri 8:00–8:30
Apr 1952–Jun 1952, ABC Wed 9:30–10:00
Oct 1952–Jun 1953, ABC Mon 8:00–8:30
Oct 1953–Jun 1954, ABC Wed 7:30–8:00
Dec 1955–Jun 1957, ABC Fri 9:30–10:00
Sep 1957–Dec 1957, NBC Fri 7:30–8:00
Oct 1958–May 1959, NBC Sun 7:00–7:30
Oct 1959–May 1960, NBC Sun 6:30–7:00
CAST:
Mark Saber (1951–1954) .... Tom Conway
Mark Saber (1955–1960) .... Donald Gray
Sgt. Tim Maloney (1951–1954)... James Burke
Barney O'Keefe (1955–1956) . Michael Balfour
Judy (1956) .... Teresa Thorne
Stephanie Ames (1956–1957) ... Diana Decker
Pete Paulson (1957–1958) ..... Neil McCallum
Pete Paulson (1958) .... Gordon Tanner
Bob Page (1958–1960) .... Robert Arden
Inspector Parker (1957–1960) .... Colin Tapley

Mark Saber was an American cop show with an international flavor. Saber was British, though he worked on the homicide squad of a big-city American police department. Dapper in appearance (with pencil-thin mustache and pinstriped suits) and elegant in speech, he tracked down villains by leaps of brilliant deduction as much as by routine police work. His assistant was a more familiar TV type, the loyal but somewhat thick-headed Sgt. Maloney.

After a three-year run Saber left the air in June 1954, only to return a year and a half later in a series called *The Vise*. This time he was cast as a one-armed private detective in London. The settings were exclusively European, as Saber tracked assorted blackmailers, murderers, and other crooks through London, Paris, along the Riviera, and in other glamorous locales. The cast was all new, with Donald Gray taking the role of Saber and a succession of actors playing his sidekicks, Barney O'Keefe, Judy, Stephanie Ames, Pete Paulson, and Bob Page. Numerous Scotland Yard inspectors came and went as his "official" foil, with Colin Tapley, as Inspector Parker, seen most often.

When first seen in 1951, the program was known as *Mystery Theater*. It was later retitled *Inspector Mark Saber—Homicide Squad* in 1952, *The Vise* in December 1955 (see also under that title for another series by the same name), and *Saber of London* in 1957. It was called *Detective's Diary* in syndication and on NBC from March 1957 to September 1961, when it was rerun on Saturday afternoons.

MARKHAM
Detective Drama
FIRST TELECAST: *May 2, 1959*

LAST TELECAST: *September 22, 1960*
BROADCAST HISTORY:
May 1959–Jan 1960, CBS Sat 10:30–11:00
Jan 1960–Sep 1960, CBS Thu 9:30–10:00
CAST:
Roy Markham .... Ray Milland
John Riggs (1959) .... Simon Scott

Movie star Ray Milland turned private eye for this series. Roy Markham was wealthy, well educated, and a very successful attorney. After spending many years trying cases, he had decided to attempt unraveling them, becoming a private investigator mainly for the excitement of it. Although he was based in New York, his cases took him all over the world on assignments ranging from murder to corporate fraud. Since he had other sources of income, Roy's fees were flexible, sometimes exorbitant and sometimes free, depending on the client. When this series first went on the air, Markham had an assistant named John Riggs who traveled with him and did much of the legwork, but less than two months after the show's premiere, Markham was doing it all by himself.

MARRIAGE, THE
Situation Comedy
FIRST TELECAST: *July 8, 1954*
LAST TELECAST: *August 19, 1954*
BROADCAST HISTORY:
Jul 1954–Aug 1954, NBC Thu 10:00–10:30
CAST:
Ben Marriott .... Hume Cronyn
Liz Marriott .... Jessica Tandy
Pete Marriott .... Malcolm Broderick
Emily Marriott .... Susan Strasberg
Bobby Logan .... William Redfield

To this obscure comedy belongs the distinction of having been the first network series to be regularly telecast in color. *The Marriage* was a live comedy dealing with the home life of New York lawyer Ben Marriott. Ben's practice was moderately successful, allowing his wife Liz, who had been employed previously as a buyer for a department store, to stay home and run the household. Liz's need to keep occupied got her involved in all sorts of community, organizational, and personal projects. The Marriotts had two children, Pete, aged 10, and Emily, aged 15. Cronyn and Tandy had starred in the NBC radio version of this series, which had left the air in the spring of 1954.

MARRIED: THE FIRST YEAR
Drama
FIRST TELECAST: *February 28, 1979*
LAST TELECAST: *March 21, 1979*
BROADCAST HISTORY:
Feb 1979–Mar 1979, CBS Wed 8:00–9:00
CAST:
Billy Baker .... Leigh McCloskey
Joanna Huffman Baker .... Cindy Grover

Barbara Huffman .... Claudette Nevins
Cathy Baker .... K Callan
Bert Baker .... Stanley Grover
Cookie Levin .... Gigi Vorgan
Sharon Kelly .... Stepfanie Kramer
Tom Liberatore .... Gary Epp
Donny Baker .... Stephen Manley
Millie Baker............. Jennifer McAllister
Emily Gorey.............. Christine Belford

Billy and Joanna were young newlyweds trying to make a life for themselves despite families that did not approve of their marrying so young. Joanna had just graduated from high school when she and Billy, only a couple of years older, were wed. They came from different backgrounds, he from a close-knit, blue-collar family, and she from a socially prominent, upper-middle-class one. Joanna's family had a history of divorces and acrimony, which did not help matters.

MARRIED . . . . . . WITH CHILDREN
Situation Comedy
FIRST TELECAST: *April 5, 1987*
LAST TELECAST:
BROADCAST HISTORY:
Apr 1987–Oct 1987, FOX Sun 8:00–8:30
Oct 1987– , FOX Sun 8:30–9:00
CAST:
Al Bundy......................... Ed O'Neill
Peggy Bundy .... Katey Sagal
Kelly Bundy (age 15).... Christina Applegate
Bud Bundy (age 11) .... David Faustino
Steve Rhoades.............. David Garrison
Marcy Rhoades............. Amanda Bearse
THEME:
"Love and Marriage" by Sammy Cahn and Jimmy Van Heusen, sung by Frank Sinatra (1955 recording)

Suburban Chicago was the setting for this domestic comedy that had all the warmth of a boa constrictor. The Bundys were not your typical family. Although they occasionally let it slip that they cared for each other, every member of the household seemed intent on belittling and putting down the others. Al was a lowly but chauvinistic shoe salesman who had been married for 15 years. His wife, Peg, was a lazy housewife who almost never cleaned or cooked, and their semi-delinquent kids Kelly and Bud were forever at each other's throats. Al's bedroom prowess, or lack thereof, was a frequent topic of conversation, and there was constant bickering about money, the kids' activities, and SEX. Their newlywed neighbors, accountants Steve and Marcy Rhoades, were young and gloriously in love until Al started explaining the real world to Steve and Peg did likewise to Marcy. Buck was the Bundy dog.

MARSHAL DILLON
see *Gunsmoke*

MARSHAL OF GUNSIGHT PASS, THE
Western
FIRST TELECAST: *March 12, 1950*
LAST TELECAST: *September 30, 1950*
BROADCAST HISTORY:
　Mar 1950–Sep 1950, ABC Sat 6:30–7:00
CAST:
　Marshal (Mar)...... Russell "Lucky" Hayden
　Marshal Eddie Dean (Mar-Sep) .. Eddie Dean
　Deputy Roscoe .... Roscoe Ates
　Ruth .... Jane Adrian
MUSIC:
Andy Parker and the Plainsmen

Two veterans of Hollywood's Western B-movie factories starred in this obscure oater, which was probably the only network Western action series produced live from a studio. Russell Hayden, best known for his Hopalong Cassidy films, was the original Marshal, replaced after a few weeks by singing cowboy Eddie Dean. Roscoe Ates was the dopey, bug-eyed sidekick, and Ruth was Roscoe's pretty niece. Andy Parker's Western string band provided musical interludes and backup for Eddie's occasional songs.

The series originated from Los Angeles and was seen live on the West Coast, and via kinescope in the rest of the country. The horses and stage-coaches moving (carefully) around an obvious stage setting, the awkwardly staged fight scenes, and the cheap "outdoor" backdrops looked so phony compared to filmed Westerns that the series was considered primitive even for 1950, and soon disappeared from the air.

MARSHALL PLAN IN ACTION, THE
Documentary
FIRST TELECAST: *June 24, 1950*
LAST TELECAST: *February 22, 1953*
BROADCAST HISTORY:
　Jun 1950–Jul 1950, ABC Sat 9:00–9:30
　Jul 1950–Oct 1950, ABC Sun 10:00–10:30
　Oct 1950–Mar 1952, ABC Sun 9:30–10:00
　Jan 1951–Jun 1951, ABC Fri 10:00–10:30 (reruns)
　Jul 1951–Oct 1951, ABC Mon 8:30–9:00 (reruns)
　Apr 1952–Jun 1952, ABC Tue 8:00–8:30
　Jul 1952–Aug 1952, ABC Thu 9:00–9:30
　Sep 1952–Feb 1953, ABC Sun 6:00–6:30

Documentary films prepared by the U.S. government showing the results of Marshall Plan aid to war-ravaged Europe. Each film opened with a statement from Federal Administrator Paul G. Hoffman describing the films as "the story of one successful battle in the series of struggles now going on that have become known as the Cold War."

Impoverished ABC (which could have used some economic aid itself at this time) was sufficiently desperate for inexpensive programming to schedule two showings a week of these films during much of 1951. Effective December 30, 1951, the

series' title was changed to *Strength for a Free World*.

MARTHA RAYE SHOW, THE
Comedy Variety
FIRST TELECAST: *September 20, 1955*
LAST TELECAST: *May 29, 1956*
BROADCAST HISTORY:
　Sep 1955–May 1956, NBC Tue 8:00–9:00
REGULARS:
Martha Raye
Rocky Graziano
Carl Hoff and His Orchestra
The Danny Daniels Dancers

Loud-voiced comedienne and singer Martha Raye first brought her slapstick comedy to TV as one of the stars of NBC's *All Star Revue* in 1951. Between 1953 and 1955 she was seen in a series of specials entitled *The Martha Raye Show*, which served as a periodic replacement for *Your Show of Shows* and *The Milton Berle Show*. Finally, in 1955, she got her own weekly series.

The earlier specials had been relatively unstructured variety shows, with Rocky Graziano regularly appearing as her boyfriend in comedy skits. The 1955–1956 series attempted to tell a complete story each week, in musical variety format. Rocky was once again her boyfriend in each story, and the night's theme was developed in integrated comedy, singing, and musical production numbers. Guest stars also appeared.

MARTHA WRIGHT SHOW, THE
Music
FIRST TELECAST: *April 18, 1954*
LAST TELECAST: *December 5, 1954*
BROADCAST HISTORY:
　Apr 1954–Dec 1954, ABC Sun 9:15–9:30 (OS)
REGULARS:
Martha Wright
Norman Paris
Bobby Hackett and His Band

Songstress Martha Wright was the star of this live music show. Featured with her were pianist Norman Paris and trumpet player Bobby Hackett and his band. Miss Wright, whose show was the replacement for *The Jane Pickens Show* in April, was herself replaced on Miss Pickens' return in July, and replaced Miss Pickens again in September. Also known as *The Packard Showroom*.

MARTIN KANE, PRIVATE EYE
Detective Drama
FIRST TELECAST: *September 1, 1949*
LAST TELECAST: *June 17, 1954*
BROADCAST HISTORY:
　Sep 1949–Jun 1954, NBC Thu 10:00–10:30 (OS)
CAST:
　Martin Kane (1949–1951) .... William Gargan
　Martin Kane (1951–1952) .... Lloyd Nolan
　Martin Kane (1952–1953) .... Lee Tracy

Martin Kane (1953–1954) . . . . . . Mark Stevens
Happy McMann . . . . Walter Kinsella
Don Morrow (1954) . . . . Himself
Lt. Bender (1949–1950). . . . . . . Fred Hillebrand
Capt. Willis (1950–1951) . . . Horace McMahon
Sgt. Ross (1950–1952) . . . . . Nicholas Saunders
Capt. Leonard (1951) . . . . Walter Greaza
Capt. Burke (1951–1952) . . . . . . Frank Thomas
Lt. Grey (1952–1954). . . . . King Calder

This popular, live detective series, which was also heard on radio for several years, underwent several changes of emphasis as well as of cast during its run. William Gargan's original Martin Kane was a smooth, wisecracking operator who worked in close cooperation with the police, an unusual arrangement for TV sleuths. His base of operation was New York, and the crime was usually murder. Later Kanes projected more of a tough-guy image and got less cooperation from the cops, as Lt. Bender gave way to other, more antagonistic officers. In August 1953 the title of the series was shortened to *Martin Kane* and the emphasis shifted to greater mystery and suspense, with less reliance on the somewhat stereotyped situations of earlier seasons.

Throughout most of the run Happy McMann's tobacco shop served as Kane's hangout, and gave him the opportunity to slip in plugs for the sponsor's tobacco products (which included Sano and Encore cigarettes, and Old Briar pipe tobacco). After August 1953 Kane no longer frequented the store, but it remained the setting for the commercials, first by Happy and later (January 1954) by "new owner" Don Morrow.

There was in fact a real Martin Kane. The man who lent his name for use in the show was no sleuth, but an executive with J. Walter Thompson & Co., the advertising agency which produced this series. The real-life Kane later became a senior editor of *Sports Illustrated* magazine and died at the age of 70, in 1977.

Three years after it left the network *Martin Kane* was revived in a syndicated series called *The New Adventures of Martin Kane*, which was sold individually to local stations. In this version Kane was doing his sleuthing in London and sometimes Paris. The title role, ironically enough, was played by William Gargan—the original 1949 Martin Kane.

MARTY FELDMAN COMEDY MACHINE, THE
Comedy Variety
FIRST TELECAST: *April 12, 1972*
LAST TELECAST: *August 16, 1972*
BROADCAST HISTORY:
  Apr 1972–Aug 1972, ABC Wed 9:00–9:30
HOST:
  Marty Feldman
REGULARS:
  Barbara Feldon
  Spike Milligan
  Lenny Schultz

Fred Smoot
Thelma Houston
Orson Welles (frequent guest)

Bug-eyed, shaggy-haired British comedian Marty Feldman starred in this fast-paced half-hour of comedy sketches, blackouts, and music.

MARY
Comedy Variety
FIRST TELECAST: *September 24, 1978*
LAST TELECAST: *October 8, 1978*
BROADCAST HISTORY:
  Sep 1978–Oct 1978, CBS Sun 8:00–9:00
REGULARS:
  Mary Tyler Moore
  Dick Shawn
  James Hampton
  Swoosie Kurtz
  David Letterman
  Judy Kahan
  Michael Keaton
  Tony Stevens Dancers
  Alf Clausen Orchestra

After starring in two highly successful situation comedies, *The Dick Van Dyke Show* in the 1960s and *The Mary Tyler Moore Show* in the 1970s, Miss Moore tried unsuccessfully to launch this comedy variety hour. Relying primarily on a group of repertory players rather than guest stars, much in the manner of the highly successful *Carol Burnett Show*, *Mary* placed strong emphasis on topical sketch comedy. Frequently referred to, but not seen, was Mary's husband, Grant Tinker, who was also the producer of this show.

The program attracted few viewers and was canceled after only three telecasts; Ms. Moore tried again the following spring with *The Mary Tyler Moore Hour*.

MARY
Situation Comedy
FIRST TELECAST: *December 11, 1985*
LAST TELECAST: *April 8, 1986*
BROADCAST HISTORY:
  Dec 1985–Feb 1986, CBS Wed 8:00–8:30
  Mar 1986–Apr 1986, CBS Tue 9:00–9:30
CAST:
  Mary Brenner . . . . Mary Tyler Moore
  Frank DeMarco. . . . . James Farentino
  Jo Tucker . . . . Katey Sagal
  Ed LaSalle . . . . John Astin
  Susan Wilcox . . . . Carlene Watkins
  Lester Mintz . . . . James Tolkan
  Vincent Tully . . . . David Byrd
  Harry Dresden . . . . Harold Sylvester
  Ronnie Dicker . . . . Derek McGrath

More than eight years after the tearful parting of the news staff of WJM-TV in the final episode of *The Mary Tyler Moore Show*, Miss Moore returned to the world of TV sitcoms, again in a news setting. This time she was working for a somewhat sleazy tabloid newspaper, *The Chicago Eagle*. Her character was a divorcée in her 40s who had taken the job at the *Eagle* when the high-fashion magazine for which she worked went out of business. Her "Helpline" column served as a consumer advocate, assisting readers in resolving problems with business and government, often by using the power of the press to cut through red tape. Mary's boss, managing editor Frank DeMarco, emphasized the more exploitive and sensational aspects of the *Eagle*, since that was what sold papers. He was also quite a ladies' man who had an undeniable appeal to Mary, though she was not sure how to deal with that.

Others on the *Eagle* staff included Jo Tucker, the cynical, chain-smoking columnist who sat across from Mary at the office; Ed LaSalle, the rather pompous theater critic; and Tully, the almost-blind copy editor whose job (and he never let you forget it) was protected by the union. On the home front Mary's friend and neighbor was Susan, whose new fiancé, Lester, seemed to have underworld connections.

Mary had its problems. The newspaper was supposed to be called the *Post*, but a lawsuit by the real *Chicago Post*—a small circulation weekly—forced the last-minute name change to the *Eagle*. Despite some positive reviews from columnists, the series did poorly and both its format and timeslot were tinkered with. Mary's home life was minimized, and Susan and Lester were dropped from the cast. The changes didn't help, however, and *Mary* failed to survive its first season.

MARY HARTMAN, MARY HARTMAN
Soap Opera
BROADCAST HISTORY:
Syndicated and Network Late Night
30 minutes
Produced: *1975–1978*
Released: *January 1976*
CAST:

Mary Hartman *(1976–1977)*	Louise Lasser
Tom Hartman	Greg Mullavey
Martha Shumway	Dody Goodman
George Shumway *(1976–1977)*	Philip Bruns
George Shumway *(1977–1978)*	Tab Hunter
Cathy Shumway	Debralee Scott
Heather Hartman	Claudia Lamb
Raymond Larkin	Victor Kilian
Sgt. Dennis Foley *(1976–1977)*	
	Bruce Solomon
Loretta Haggers	Mary Kay Place
Charlie Haggers	Graham Jarvis
Jimmy Joe Jeeter *(1976–1977)*	Sparky Marcus
Merle Jeeter	Dabney Coleman
Wanda Jeeter	Marian Mercer
Garth Gimble *(1976–1977)*	Martin Mull
Pat Gimble *(1976–1977)*	Susan Browning
Eleanor Major *(1977–1978)*	Shelley Fabares
Mac Slattery *(1977–1978)*	Dennis Burkley

Harmon Farinella *(1977–1978)*	
	Richard Hatch
Penny Major *(1977–1978)*	Judy Kahan
Popesco *(1977–1978)*	Severn Darden
Jeffrey DeVito *(1977–1978)*	Randall Carver
Mel Beach *(1977–1978)*	Shelley Berman
Annabelle *(1977–1978)*	Renee Taylor
Reverend Brim *(1977–1978)*	Orson Bean
Dr. Szymon *(1977–1978)*	James Staley

This was the classic soap opera to satirize all soap operas. Mary Hartman was a "typical American housewife" living in the small town of Fernwood, Ohio. She was totally impressionable and rather slow-witted, with the most significant things in her life coming from television commercials, which she believed totally. One of her early concerns was the prospect of "waxy yellow buildup" on her kitchen floor and how to avoid it. Pigtailed and plain, her life was full of one crisis after another—her father (George Shumway) disappeared, her daughter (Heather) was held hostage by a mass murderer, her husband (Tom) was impotent, and her best friend (aspiring country music singer Loretta Haggers) was paralyzed. Eventually Mary's implacable calm collapsed and she had a nervous breakdown, as well as an affair with local cop Dennis Foley. Mary's grandfather, Raymond Larkin, was known to all as the Fernwood Flasher for his penchant for exposing himself in public; her sister, Cathy, was a local swinger; and her mother, Martha, was decidedly flaky. Tom Hartman was an assembly-line worker at the local automobile plant where he worked with Loretta's husband, Charlie. Jimmy Joe Jeeter was an eight-year-old evangelist whose career was cut short when he was electrocuted by a television set that fell into his bathtub. His father, Merle, was Fernwood's mayor.

Mary Hartman, Mary Hartman was the creation of producer Norman Lear and had been offered to the major networks, all of which rejected it as too controversial. Lear then sold the series to local stations as a syndicated entry in 1976 and had a much-publicized success with it. The novelty of a satirical soap opera attracted many viewers (*Mary Hartman, Mary Hartman* ran after the late local news in most cities). When star Louise Lasser left the show in 1977, it continued for another six months under the title *Forever Fernwood* with most of the original cast intact. However, Tab Hunter took over the role of Martha Shumway's husband George (with the explanation that George had fallen into a chemical vat and been restored with plastic surgery); and new characters included Eleanor Major, Tom Hartman's new love interest; Harmon Farinella, who sought an affair with Loretta Haggers; and Mac, the truck driver. CBS, the network that had first rejected it, aired selected reruns of *Mary Hartman, Mary Hartman* as part of its late-night lineup for a few months in 1980. For details of the late-night network run see *The CBS Late Movie*.

MARY KAY AND JOHNNY

Situation Comedy

FIRST TELECAST: *November 18, 1947*

LAST TELECAST: *March 11, 1950*

BROADCAST HISTORY:

Nov 1947–Dec 1947, DUM Tues 9:00–9:15
Jan 1948–Aug 1948, DUM Tue 7:15–7:30
Oct 1948–Feb 1949, NBC Sun 7:00–7:30
Mar 1949–Jun 1949, CBS Wed 9:00–9:30
Jun 1949–Aug 1949, NBC Mon–Fri 7:15–7:30
Aug 1949–Dec 1949, NBC Thu 8:30–9:00
Jan 1950–Feb 1950, NBC Sat 9:00–9:30
Feb 1950–Mar 1950, NBC Sat 7:30–8:00

CAST:

Mary Kay Stearns .... Herself
Johnny Stearns .... Himself
Howie .... Howard Thomas
Mary Kay's mother .... Nydia Westman
Christopher William Stearns (1949–1950)
.... Himself

WRITER:

Johnny Stearns

Live domestic comedy, revolving around young New York newlyweds Mary Kay and Johnny Stearns. She was pretty, pert, and something of a screwball, while he was more serious and always getting her out of various dilemmas. Johnny worked in a bank, but the setting for the action was usually the couple's apartment in Greenwich Village. The Stearns, who were also married in real life, had a baby boy in December 1948, whom they named Christopher. The blessed event was worked into the script and infant Chris was added to the cast less than a month after his birth, appearing in his bassinet. He was surely one of the youngest regular cast members on any show in TV history. Howie was Johnny's best friend, while Nydia Westman played Mary Kay's mother.

In addition to being one of the earliest network situation comedies, the series was notable for its longtime sponsor, Anacin, which even in 1948 was using an outline chart of a human figure with flashing lights to show the product bringing fast, fast relief to every corner of the body.

That sponsors were quite uncertain of the effectiveness of TV at this early stage, however, is illustrated by the following. A few weeks after the program premiered, the sponsor, who had no way of knowing whether anyone was watching (there were no audience ratings), decided to conduct a test by offering a free mirror to the first 200 viewers who wrote in their comments on the program. Just to be safe, the company ordered an extra 200 mirrors so as not to disappoint anyone. 8,960 letters were received!

MARY MARGARET MCBRIDE

Interview

FIRST TELECAST: *September 21, 1948*

LAST TELECAST: *December 14, 1948*

BROADCAST HISTORY:

Sep 1948–Dec 1948, NBC Tue 9:00–9:30

HOSTESS:

Mary Margaret McBride

Interview program featuring the popular radio personality.

MARY TYLER MOORE HOUR, THE

Comedy Variety

FIRST TELECAST: *March 4, 1979*

LAST TELECAST: *June 10, 1979*

BROADCAST HISTORY:

Mar 1979–Jun 1979, CBS Sun 10:00–11:00

CAST:

Mary McKinnon .... Mary Tyler Moore
Iris Chapman .... Joyce Van Patten
Harry Sinclair .... Michael Lombard
Kenneth Christy .... Michael Keaton
Ruby Bell .... Dody Goodman
Mort Zimmick .... Bobby Ramsen

After the disastrous reception given her initial venture into comedy-variety (see *Mary*), Mary Tyler Moore returned in the spring of 1979 with this program, a hybrid that was part variety show and part situation comedy, using a show-within-a-show format.

Mary McKinnon was the star of a fictional network variety series called *The Mary McKinnon Show*. A versatile singer, dancer, and light comedienne, she had a well-established reputation and a large following. Iris was her personal secretary and companion; Harry, the producer of her show; Mort, its head writer; Kenneth, the ambitious young page; and, Ruby, her maid. Stories revolved around the problems encountered in putting a variety show together, including rehearsals and actual numbers from the show itself. Among her "guest stars," all of whom played themselves, were former CBS series stars Lucille Ball, Beatrice Arthur, Nancy Walker, and Dick Van Dyke, and current series stars Linda Lavin, Bonnie Franklin, and Ken Howard. Mike Douglas, Gene Kelly, and Johnny Mathis also showed up to help.

Unfortunately, despite all these friends, *The Mary Tyler Moore Hour* was no more successful than *Mary* had been, and Miss Moore acknowledged that her forte was, indeed, straight situation comedy. She promised to return to CBS in the fall of 1980 with a new situation comedy, to salvage her by now somewhat tarnished reputation. But instead, she tried Broadway, starring in the play *Who's Life Is It, Anyway?*, for which she won a special Tony Award in 1980, and feature films, winning accolades for her performance in *Ordinary People*.

MARY TYLER MOORE SHOW, THE

Situation Comedy

FIRST TELECAST: *September 19, 1970*

LAST TELECAST: *September 3, 1977*

BROADCAST HISTORY:

Sep 1970–Dec 1971, CBS Sat 9:30–10:00
Dec 1971–Sep 1972, CBS Sat 8:30–9:00

Sep 1972–Oct 1976, CBS Sat 9:00–9:30
Nov 1976–Sep 1977, CBS Sat 8:00–8:30

CAST:

Mary Richards .... Mary Tyler Moore
Lou Grant .... Edward Asner
Ted Baxter .... Ted Knight
Murray Slaughter .... Gavin MacLeod
Rhoda Morgenstern (1970–1974)
.... Valerie Harper
Phyllis Lindstrom (1970–1975)
.... Cloris Leachman
Bess Lindstrom (1970–1975) ... Lisa Gerritsen
Gordon (Gordy) Howard (1970–1973)
.... John Amos
Georgette Franklin Baxter (1973–1977)
.... Georgia Engel
Sue Ann Nivens (1973–1977) .... Betty White
Marie Slaughter (1971–1977) ... Joyce Bulifant
Edie Grant (1973–1974) ...... Priscilla Morrill
David Baxter (1976–1977) .... Robbie Rist

The Mary Tyler Moore Show was one of the most literate, realistic, and enduring situation comedies of the 1970s. Unlike the efforts generated by producer Norman Lear, typified by *All in the Family* and *Maude,* there was never a conscious attempt to humiliate or ridicule. Mary Richards was the idealized single career woman. She had come to Minneapolis after breaking up with a man she had been dating for four years. Ambitious, and looking for new friends, she moved into an older apartment building and went to work as an assistant producer of the local news show on television station WJM-TV. In her early 30s, Mary symbolized the independent woman of the 1970s. She would like to find a man and settle down to raise a family, but was not desperately grabbing at any chance for marriage. She would get married, but only if it was to the right man. She was warm, loving, and vulnerable, and although it was never bluntly thrown out at the audience, could spend the night with a man she was not madly in love with.

Mary worked for WJM-TV News producer Lou Grant, an irascible, cantankerous, blustery man whose bark was much worse than his bite. Underneath that harsh exterior beat the heart of a pussycat. Lou had problems with his home life as well as his job. During the 1973–1974 season he separated from his wife Edie and they were later divorced. Though it never developed, there was an underlying feeling that he and Mary might have had a serious relationship, if they could have ever really gotten together.

Murray Slaughter was the head newswriter at the station. He was happily married, had a positive outlook no matter what happened, and was a good friend to all. Anchorman on the WJM-TV News was Ted Baxter, not too bright, prone to put his foot in his mouth both on and off the air, and possessor of such a misplaced sense of his own wonderfulness that he was the butt of everyone's jokes. Ted's long courtship of bland, empty-headed, but well-meaning Georgette Franklin cul-

minated in a marriage he was not quite ready to commit himself to in November 1975. The following spring he and Georgette adopted 8-year-old David, and in the fall of 1976 had a baby of their own.

Mary's closest friend was one of her neighbors, Rhoda Morgenstern, a window dresser for a local department store who, like Mary, was still single though in her 30s. Unlike Mary, however, Rhoda was desperately looking for a husband. Unable to find one in Minneapolis, she moved back home to New York City, and to her own series, *Rhoda,* in the fall of 1974. The other neighbor seen frequently in Mary's apartment was Phyllis Lindstrom. Phyllis was the building's resident busybody, and though it took quite a while to find out, also its landlady (her husband Lars, who was talked about but never seen, actually owned the building). Phyllis was oblivious to everyone else's feelings and had an extremely flaky personality. She, too, got her own series when, following Lars' death, she and her daughter Bess moved to San Francisco in the fall of 1975 (see *Phyllis*), and Mary moved into a more luxurious apartment in a high-rise.

As some of the regulars left the series, including WJM-TV's weatherman Gordy Howard, others took up the slack. Sue Ann Nivens arrived at the station in 1973 with her "Happy Homemaker Show," and Georgette's role was expanded. Sue Ann was in her late 40s and extremely man-hungry. She was constantly trying to get every male in sight into the sack, but primarily Lou Grant. Mary was eventually promoted from associate producer to producer as Lou moved to the job of news director.

Mary Tyler Moore, who, with her husband Grant Tinker, produced *The Mary Tyler Moore Show,* decided that the series would end in 1977, despite its still-large audience. In the last episode new management took over the station and, in an effort to bolster its weak news ratings, fired virtually the entire staff. Ironically, the one survivor was anchorman Ted Baxter, probably the primary cause for the news' low ratings. There were tearful farewells and everyone went their separate ways.

MASK, THE

Crime Drama

FIRST TELECAST: *January 10, 1954*
LAST TELECAST: *May 16, 1954*
BROADCAST HISTORY:

Jan 1954–May 1954, ABC Sun 8:00–9:00
Mar 1954–Apr 1954, ABC Tue/Wed 8:00–9:00

CAST:

Walter Guilfoyle .... Gary Merrill
Peter Guilfoyle .... William Prince

Though short-lived, this program was a pioneer in several ways. It was the first hour-long mystery series to feature a continuing cast of characters—and as such was the father of one of the predominant forms on TV today. It was also, during part of its run, repeated twice a week in prime time, in order that viewers who had missed the original live telecast on Sunday night might see the kinescope repeat on Tuesday or Wednesday (at least on those stations which carried all three).

Unfortunately, the content was not as innovative as the format and scheduling. *The Mask* was a routine crime show centering on two brothers who were attorneys and partners in the firm of Guilfoyle & Guilfoyle. Each week they tackled another case, somewhat in the manner of modern Robin Hoods, unmasking assorted gangsters and rescuing helpless victims. Unable to find a sponsor, and quite expensive to produce, *The Mask* was canceled after four months.

MASLAND AT HOME PARTY
see *Earl Wrightson Show, The*

MASQUERADE
Foreign Intrigue
FIRST TELECAST: *December 15, 1983*
LAST TELECAST: *April 27, 1984*
BROADCAST HISTORY:
   Dec 1983–Jan 1984, ABC Thu 9:00–10:00
   Mar 1984–Apr 1984, ABC Fri 9:00–10:00
CAST:
   Lavender . . . . Rod Taylor
   Casey Collins . . . . Kirstie Alley
   Danny Doyle . . . . Greg Evigan
THEME:
   "Masquerade," by Stu Phillips and Marcia Waldorf, sung by Crystal Gayle

The National Intelligence Agency had a problem. Most of its top agents had suddenly been "neutralized" by the KGB, and NIA chief Lavender needed new recruits quickly, with skills as varied as those of a plumber, a diamond expert, a safecracker, and an electronics wizard. So, naturally enough, he recruited a plumber, a diamond dealer, a safecracker, and an electronics wizard—ordinary citizens whom he persuaded to serve their country as spies-for-a-week. Lavender's superiors thought this a bit irregular, but they had little choice, so each week a new group of Americans with diverse skills was pressed into service chasing foreign agents around the globe; this week they might include a dog trainer or race-car driver, next week a baseball star.

Casey and Danny were Lavender's young assistants who helped keep this unusual package tour together and get everyone home safe and sound after their little adventures with poison darts and stilettos in dark alleyways.

MASQUERADE PARTY
Quiz/Audience Participation
FIRST TELECAST: *July 14, 1952*
LAST TELECAST: *September 16, 1960*
BROADCAST HISTORY:
   Jul 1952–Aug 1952, NBC Mon 8:00–8:30
   Jun 1953–Sep 1953, CBS Mon 9:30–10:00
   Jun 1954–Sep 1954, CBS Mon 9:30–10:00

   Sep 1954–Jun 1956, ABC Wed 9:00–9:30
   Jun 1956–Dec 1956, ABC Sat 10:00–10:30
   Mar 1957–Sep 1957, NBC Wed 8:00–8:30
   Aug 1958–Sep 1958, CBS Mon 8:30–9:00
   Oct 1958–Sep 1959, NBC Thu 10:30–11:00
   Oct 1959–Jan 1960, CBS Mon 7:30–8:00
   Jan 1960–Sep 1960, NBC Fri 9:30–10:00
MODERATOR:
   Bud Collyer (1952)
   Douglas Edwards (1953)
   Peter Donald (1954–1956)
   Eddie Bracken (1957)
   Robert Q. Lewis (1958)
   Bert Parks (1958–1960)
PANELISTS:
   Peter Donald (1952–1953)
   Ilka Chase (1952–1957)
   John S. Young (1952)
   Madge Evans (1952)
   Buff Cobb (1953–1955)
   Ogden Nash (1953–1957)
   Bobby Sherwood (1954–1957)
   Dagmar (1955–1956)
   Mary Healy (1955–1956)
   Betsy Palmer (1956–1957)
   Frank Parker (1957)
   Johnny Johnston (1957–1958)
   Jonathan Winters (1958)
   Jinx Falkenburg (1958)
   Pat Carroll (1958)
   Audrey Meadows (1958–1960)
   Lee Bowman (1958–1960)
   Faye Emerson (1958–1960)
   Sam Levenson (1958–1960)

Well-known celebrities were disguised in elaborate costumes and makeup when they appeared as contestants on *Masquerade Party*. The costume was designed to serve as a clue to the panelists, who questioned the contestants in an attempt to determine their real identities. Any prize money won by contestants was donated to their favorite charities. When contestants answered the panelists' questions, they did so through a special microphone which also disguised their voices. On the air through nine seasons, *Masquerade Party* went through six moderators and a total of 19 regular panelists.

Richard Dawson moderated a syndicated revival of *Masquerade Party* during the 1974–1975 season. Regular panelists were Bill Bixby, Lee Meriwether, and Nipsey Russell.

MASTER, THE
Adventure/Drama
FIRST TELECAST: *January 20, 1984*
LAST TELECAST: *August 31, 1984*
BROADCAST HISTORY:
   Jan 1984–Feb 1984, NBC Fri 9:00–10:00
   Mar 1984–Aug 1984, NBC Fri 8:00–9:00
CAST:
   John Peter McAllister . . . . Lee Van Cleef
   Max Keller . . . . Timothy Van Patten
   Okasa . . . . Sho Kosugi

Stealth and hand-to-hand violence were the hallmarks of this short-lived series. While stationed in Japan as an air force colonel after World War II, John Peter McAllister had become fascinated with the Ninja—a secret and now outlawed society of warriors trained in the martial arts. He entered the sect, and in time became a Ninja Master, the only Westerner ever to do so. When younger members of the sect began to use their deadly skills for evil ends, McAllister left for America, violating his sacred oath never to leave the Ninja. Here he met young Max Keller, a footloose adventurer, and the two of them set out in Max's van, searching for McAllister's long-lost daughter and righting wrongs they encountered along the way. Hard on their heels were deadly Ninja assassins, led by Okasa, after McAllister; but the aging Master, who had trained many of them, dispatched them all with cunning, swift blows, and a variety of exotic weapons such as razor-sharp little wheels that were thrown at the assailant, tiny smoke bombs, and a hand device to ward off blows.

MASTER OF THE GAME
Drama
FIRST TELECAST: *June 6, 1987*
LAST TELECAST: *June 27, 1987*
BROADCAST HISTORY:
　Jun 1987, CBS Sat 8:00–10:00
CAST:
　Kate Blackwell .... Dyan Cannon
　Tony Blackwell .... Harry Hamlin
　Jamie McGregor .... Ian Charleson
　Brad Rogers .... Cliff DeYoung
　George Mellis .... Fernando Allende
　David Blackwell .... David Birney
　Eve/Alexandra Blackwell ... Liane Langland
　Salomon Van der Merwe .. Donald Pleasence
　Margaret Van der Merwe ..... Cherie Lunghi
　Mrs. Talley .... Jean Marsh
　Dr. Harley .... Barry Morse
　Banda .... Johnny Sekka
　Marianne .... Angharad Rees
　Dominique .... Maryam D'Abo
　D'Usseau .... David Suchet
　Solange .... Leslie Caron
　McMillan .... Alan Dobie

Adapted from author Sidney Sheldon's best-selling novel of the same name, *Master of the Game* originally aired as a nine-hour mini-series in February 1984. CBS reran it as a weekly series in the summer of 1987.

The central figure of *Master of the Game* was Kate Blackwell, the matriarch who had been a young girl when her father, Jamie McGregor, moved the family to South Africa in the 1880s to seek his fortune in the diamond mines. His success, overcoming the machinations of greedy Boer merchant Salomon Van der Merwe, provided the foundation for what became Kruger-Brent, Ltd. Over the next 70 years, under Jamie's and then Kate's dynamic leadership, the company grew

prosperous and powerful. Despite her financial success, Kate's failure to establish a family dynasty made her life incomplete. The disagreements, hostilities, and catastrophes that befell her husband, David, her son, Tony, her beautiful twin granddaughters, Eve and Alexandra, her valued assistant, Brad Rogers, and their assorted friends, enemies, lovers, and associates, were all chronicled in this sprawling dramatization that moved from the dirty diamond mines of South Africa to the artsy sections of Paris in the 1940s to the contemporary corporate splendor of Manhattan.

MASTERPIECE PLAYHOUSE
Dramatic Anthology
FIRST TELECAST: *July 23, 1950*
LAST TELECAST: *September 3, 1950*
BROADCAST HISTORY:
　Jul 1950–Sep 1950, NBC Sun 9:00–10:00

Live productions of seven great classics (Ibsen's *Hedda Gabler*, Shakespeare's *Richard III*, etc.), telecast during the summer of 1950. The plays were immaculately produced and used the top talent available to television in those days. Among those appearing were Jessica Tandy, William Windom, and Boris Karloff.

MASTERS OF MAGIC
Magic
FIRST TELECAST: *February 16, 1949*
LAST TELECAST: *May 11, 1949*
BROADCAST HISTORY:
　Feb 1949–May 1949, CBS Wed 7:45–8:00
HOST:
　André Baruch

This live series, which filled the remainder of the half hour in which CBS aired its network news program, gave famous magicians the opportunity to dazzle the viewing audience, and host André Baruch, with their feats of magic.

MATCH GAME P.M.
Quiz/Audience Participation
BROADCAST HISTORY:
　Syndicated and network daytime
　30 minutes
　Produced: *1975–1982*
　Released: *September 1975*
HOST:
　Gene Rayburn
PANELISTS:
　Richard Dawson (1975–1978)
　Brett Somers
　Charles Nelson Reilly
　Betty White
　Fannie Flagg
　Dick Martin
　Richard Paul

This popular game show featured a heavy dose of celebrities and double-entendre questions. A panel of six (count 'em!) celebrities appeared along with two contestants, who won if their answers to the leering questions asked by host Gene Rayburn matched those of the panel. Richard Dawson, Brett Somers, and Charles Nelson Reilly were virtual regulars on the panel, joined frequently by the others listed above.

Match Game aired as a daytime series on NBC from 1962 to 1969, and on CBS from 1973 to 1979. It was revived again as part of *The Match Game—Hollywood Squares Hour* on NBC from October 1983 to July 1984. Gene Rayburn was the host on all versions.

MATLOCK
Law Drama
FIRST TELECAST: *September 20, 1986*
LAST TELECAST:
BROADCAST HISTORY:
  Sep 1986–, NBC Sat 10:00–11:00
  *Sep 1986–   *, NBC Tue 8:00–9:00
CAST:
  Benjamin L. Matlock .... Andy Griffith
  Charlene Matlock (1986–1987) .... Linda Purl
  Tyler Hudson .... Kene Holliday
  Michelle Thomas (1987–)
  .... Nancy Stafford
  Cassie Phillips (1987–   ) .... Kari Lizer
  *Asst. D.A. Julie March (1987) . Julie Sommars
  *D.A. Lloyd Burgess .... Michael Durrell
  *Lt. Bob Brooks .... David Froman
  *Judge Irene Sawyer .... Lucille Meredith
  *Judge Richard Cooksey ..... Richard Newton

*Occasional

Andy Griffith brought his patented "cagey Southerner" portrayal back to TV in this murder-mystery series about an unassuming, but very canny, Harvard-educated lawyer. Ben Matlock was one of the top defense attorneys in Atlanta, and for good reason; like Perry Mason, he always seemed to prove his client innocent, often with some Mason-esque last-minute courtroom revelation. Helping out were his daughter, Charlene, a lawyer; Tyler, a black stock market whiz whom Matlock kept luring away to do his legwork; junior attorney Michelle; and eager law clerk Cassie. When a case bogged down Ben would repair to his handsome, 100-year-old stone house in Willow Springs, Georgia, where he would strum his banjo and ponder clues. Mayberry was not far away, in spirit at least.

MATT DENNIS SHOW, THE
Music
FIRST TELECAST: *June 27, 1955*
LAST TELECAST: *August 29, 1955*
BROADCAST HISTORY:
  Jun 1955–Aug 1955, NBC Mon/Wed/Fri 7:30–7:45
REGULAR:
  Matt Dennis

Versatile singer, composer, and pianist Matt Dennis was the host and star of this summertime musical interlude. Backing Dennis on many of his own hits ("Let's Get Away From It All," "Angel Eyes") was a small, jazz-flavored combo. Guest stars were featured occasionally.

MATT HELM
Detective Drama
FIRST TELECAST: *September 20, 1975*
LAST TELECAST: *January 3, 1976*
BROADCAST HISTORY:
  Sep 1975–Jan 1976, ABC Sat 10:00–11:00
CAST:
  Matt Helm .... Anthony Franciosa
  Claire Kronski .... Laraine Stephens
  Sgt. Hanrahan .... Gene Evans
  Ethel .... Jeff Donnell

Matt Helm was another of the swinging, wisecracking detectives who proliferated during TV's second and third decades. This one was based in Los Angeles (where else?), lived the good life with a fancy foreign sports car and a sexy girlfriend—attorney (Claire), and took on only "high-level" cases around the world. The series certainly had an opulent look, with a posh bachelor pad provided for Matt and much of the outside filming done at private estates around Southern California. Sgt. Hanrahan was the somewhat less highly paid police contact (who nevertheless dined with Matt at the best restaurants), and Ethel the answering-service operator. It was, according to the producer, pure escapist fare.

Based on an extensive collection of detective novels by Donald Hamilton and several movies with Dean Martin in the title role.

MATT HOUSTON
Detective Drama
FIRST TELECAST: *September 26, 1982*
LAST TELECAST: *July 19, 1985*
BROADCAST HISTORY:
  Sep 1982–Aug 1983, ABC Sun 8:00–9:00
  Sep 1983–Jun 1984, ABC Fri 10:00–11:00
  Aug 1984–Mar 1985, ABC Fri 10:00–11:00
  May 1985–Jul 1985, ABC Fri 10:00–11:00
CAST:
  Matlock (Matt) Houston .... Lee Horsley
  C. J. Parsons .... Pamela Hensley
  *Murray Chase .... George Wyner
  Lt. Vince Novelli (1982–1983) .... John Aprea
  Mama Novelli (1982–1983) ..... Penny Santon
  Bo (1982–1983) .... Dennis Frimple
  Lamar Pettybone (1982–1983) .. Paul Brinegar
  Chris (1982–1984) .... Cis Rundle
  Det. Lt. Michael Hoyt (1983–1985)
  .... Lincoln Kilpatrick
  Roy Houston (1984–1985) ...... Buddy Ebsen

*Occasional

ABC described *Matt Houston* as a "stylish, glamorous action/adventure series packed with beautiful women, stunning sets, and freewheeling adventure . . ." In other words, your standard TV adventure show. In this case the handsome private eye was a millionaire's son who had managed his father's oil business in Texas, then moved to California to handle the family's offshore drilling operations. They didn't seem to require much attention, so Matt spent his time on his favorite hobby: detective work. Murray, his business partner, complained that Matt's sleuthing didn't make enough money to cover the $500 license fee, but superrich Matt didn't care. Constantly surrounded by beautiful women, including his gorgeous Harvard-trained lawyer C.J., piloting his own private helicopter to and from his opulent penthouse, or racing around in sexy cars like his cream-colored Excalibur (later a more sedate Mercedes 380SL convertible), Matt evidently found other rewards in the work.

A slightly more down-to-earth flavor was added during the first season by friendly Lt. Novelli and his mom, who never failed to invite Matt in to sample her Italian cooking, as well as Bo and Lamar, two quarreling cowboys who came along from Matt's Texas ranch to help Matt out. Matt's father, Bill, even showed up a couple of times (played by David Wayne). Hominess was out in the second season, however, as Matt turned over his fabulously successful business enterprises to Murray and devoted himself full time to detective work, this time with Lt. Hoyt as his much less cooperative police adversary. Matt's cases usually involved the rich and famous, sometimes with a bizarre twist such as the murdered gourmet found encased in a mold of orange gelatin, or the killer robot, or the beautiful female lifeguards being killed off by a shark.

In the fall of 1984 Matt's uncle Roy, a successful detective in his day, came out of retirement to work with his nephew, C.J., and "Baby" (the nickname for the high-tech computer C.J. accessed to locate information needed in their cases).

MATT LINCOLN
Medical Drama
FIRST TELECAST: *September 24, 1970*
LAST TELECAST: *January 14, 1971*
BROADCAST HISTORY:
  Sep 1970–Jan 1971, ABC Thu 7:30–8:30
CAST:
Dr. Matt Lincoln	Vince Edwards
Tag	Chelsea Brown
Kevin	Michael Larrain
Jimmy	Felton Perry
Ann	June Harding

Matt Lincoln was one of the youthful "relevance" dramas of the early 1970s. Vince Edwards (ex-*Ben Casey*) starred as a hip young psychiatrist who founded and ran a center-city telephone-assistance service for troubled teenagers. His helpers at Hotline were Tag and Jimmy, two equally hip young blacks; Ann; and Kevin, a cynical cop. As

if Hotline didn't get him enough points, Matt also headed a walk-in clinic for those too poor to pay. His own life completed the picture: sports car, bachelor pad at the beach, and a small sailboat. The stories of these beautiful young people, and those they tried to help, formed the plots.

MATTY'S FUNDAY FUNNIES
Cartoon
FIRST TELECAST: *September 30, 1960*
LAST TELECAST: *December 29, 1962*
BROADCAST HISTORY:
  Sep 1960–Sep 1961, ABC Fri 7:30–8:00
  Oct 1961–Dec 1962, ABC Sat 7:00–7:30
CARTOONIST:
  Bob Clampett (for *Beany and Cecil*)

Matty's Funday Funnies was first seen on Sunday afternoons in October 1959, sponsored by the Mattel Toy Co. and "hosted" by cartoon characters Matty and Sisterbelle. The cartoons most frequently seen were those featuring Casper the Friendly Ghost, Little Audrey, Herman the Mouse, Catnip, Tommy the Tortoise, and Buzzy the Crow. Generally two or three cartoons were seen in each half-hour program.

In 1960 the series moved to nighttime television. Then in January 1962 the early characters were dropped and the series became *Matty's Funnies with Beany and Cecil,* starring the familiar characters of Bob Clampett's *Time for Beany* puppet show (which had been in syndication since the early 1950s). This time Beany and his friends were in cartoon form. Beany was the little boy with a big grin and a cap with a propeller on top. He sailed the seven seas with Capt. Huffenpuff on the *Leakin' Lena,* and his best friend was Cecil the Seasick Sea Serpent. Together they had adventures all over the world (and sometimes out of it), encountering such characters as the villainous Dishonest John, Homer the Octopus, Tear-a-Long the Dotted Lion (get it?), Careless the Mexican Hairless, and many others. Cartoonist Clampett always was fond of puns! He also developed his characters with an intelligence and wit that had made *Beany and Cecil* a favorite of many adults, including such diverse fans as Lionel Barrymore and Groucho Marx.

After the first three months the program's title was shortened to simply *Beany and Cecil.* Following its prime-time run during 1962 the show continued on ABC at other times of the day until 1967.

MAUDE
Situation Comedy
FIRST TELECAST: *September 12, 1972*
LAST TELECAST: *April 29, 1978*
BROADCAST HISTORY:
  Sep 1972–Sep 1974, CBS Tue 8:00–8:30
  Sep 1974–Sep 1975, CBS Mon 9:00–9:30
  Sep 1975–Sep 1976, CBS Mon 9:30–10:00
  Sep 1976–Sep 1977, CBS Mon 9:00–9:30

Sep 1977–Nov 1977, CBS Mon 9:30–10:00
Dec 1977–Jan 1978, CBS Mon 9:00–9:30
Jan 1978–Apr 1978, CBS Sat 9:30–10:00
CAST:

Maude Findlay .... Beatrice Arthur
Walter Findlay .... Bill Macy
Carol .... Adrienne Barbeau
Phillip (1972–1977) .... Brian Morrison
Phillip (1977–1978) .... Kraig Metzinger
Dr. Arthur Harmon .... Conrad Bain
Vivian Cavender Harmon .. Rue McClanahan
Florida Evans (1972–1974) ...... Esther Rolle
Henry Evans (1973–1974) .... John Amos
Chris (1973–1974) .... Fred Grandy
Mrs. Nell Naugatuck (1974–1977)
     .... Hermione Baddeley
Bert Beasley (1975–1977) .... J. Pat O'Malley
Victoria Butterfield (1977–1978)
     .... Marlene Warfield
PRODUCER:
Norman Lear

Maude was the first spin-off from producer Norman Lear's enormously successful comedy, All in the Family. Edith Bunker's cousin Maude was upper-middle-class, liberal, and extremely outspoken—a perfect counterpoint to Archie Bunker's blustering, hard-hat bigotry. The character became so popular that in the fall of 1972 Maude was given a series of her own—and it soon became almost as big a hit as All in the Family itself.

Maude lived in suburban Tuckahoe, New York, with her fourth husband, Walter, owner of Findlay's Friendly Appliances. Living with them was Carol, Maude's divorced, 27-year-old daughter, and Carol's 9-year-old son, Phillip.

Even though much of the comedy centered on Maude's determination to represent the independent, even dominant, woman, she herself always had a female servant in the house. In fact, during the course of the series, she ran through three of them. Maude's first maid was Florida, a bright, witty black woman who left early in 1974 to star in her own program, Good Times. (Her husband, Henry, was renamed James in Good Times, even though the same actor continued in the role.) Florida was succeeded by a cynical, hard-drinking Englishwoman, Mrs. Naugatuck. Mrs. Naugatuck was never as popular with viewers as Florida had been, and after marrying Bert Beasley in November 1976 she left the show, ostensibly to return to the British Isles. Her replacement was Victoria Butterfield, who joined the Findlay household in the fall of 1977.

The Findlays' next-door neighbor, and Walter's best friend, was Dr. Arthur Harmon. When the series began Arthur was a widower, but he subsequently began dating Maude's best friend, Vivian (who had just been divorced), and in February 1974 they were married. Everyone on this show seemed to be either married or getting married, except for Maude's daughter Carol. She came close with boyfriend Chris in 1974, but that didn't

work out and he soon disappeared from the cast.

Although this was a comedy show, the subject matter was often on the serious side. During the run, Maude became involved in politics, had a face lift, had an abortion (which drew heavy viewer protest mail), and went through menopause. Walter went through a severe bout with alcoholism, saw his store go bankrupt, and had a nervous breakdown. Maude could be very funny, but in its efforts to be realistic, it could also be controversial and sometimes depressing. Yet for several seasons viewers made it one of the top programs on television.

Finally in 1977–1978 the audience began to decline, and some major cast changes were planned for the next season. The Harmons and Carol were to move out of town, and Walter was to retire from the appliance business. Maude would begin a career in politics, with a new supporting cast. But early in 1978 Bea Arthur announced that she was leaving the series. The producers candidly admitted that no one else could play the role as she had, and so after six years Maude ended its run.

The political career that had been planned for Maude was used as the basis for another proposed series—one that had a very rocky history. See Hanging In for details.

MAVERICK
Western
FIRST TELECAST: September 22, 1957
LAST TELECAST: July 8, 1962
BROADCAST HISTORY:
    Sep 1957–Sep 1961, ABC Sun 7:30–8:30
    Sep 1961–Jul 1962, ABC Sun 6:30–7:30
CAST:
    Bret Maverick (1957–1960) ..... James Garner
    Bart Maverick .... Jack Kelly
    Samantha Crawford (1958–1959)
         .... Diane Brewster
    Cousin Beauregard Maverick (1960–1961)
         .... Roger Moore
    Brent Maverick (1961) .... Robert Colbert

In the days when dozens of staunch TV heroes were chasing lawbreakers in every corner of the Old West, this program was indeed a maverick—a Western with a sense of humor. It didn't start out that way. For the first few episodes Maverick was a fairly straight series about a dapper cardsharp and his adventures on the frontier. Then a bored scriptwriter slipped in some stage directions for star James Garner to look at someone "with his beady little eyes." Garner thought this great fun, and played the scene for laughs. It worked, and soon the whole series was moving toward a satirical orientation. Wisecracking ladies' man Bret was joined by a fairly straight brother, Bart, in November 1957, to keep the series from straying too far from the traditional Western mold (and indeed the series could always be enjoyed as a straight Western). But neither of the

Brothers Maverick was really a hero in the usual sense. They would just as soon slip quietly out of town as face a gunman in an impending showdown; they were usually honest in poker (unless they were dealing); and Bret, in particular, handled a gun rather ineptly.

Bret and Bart alternated as leads, and sometimes appeared together, but Bret clearly had the juicier role and was more visible. Their exploits took them to frontier towns like Hounddog, Apocalypse, and Oblivion, and sometimes out of the country entirely, as when Bret sailed to the South Pacific to inspect an island. Occasionally appearing were Bart's friend Dandy Jim Buckley (played by Efrem Zimbalist, Jr.) and Gentleman Jack Darby (Richard Long). During the second season Bret had a running feud with Samantha Crawford, a pretty slick operator in her own right, to see who could out-con whom. And he would always remind listeners of the advice given him by his "pappy," who said that in the face of overwhelming odds, run. (Pappy, often referred to, actually showed up in one episode, played by Garner!)

Among the high points of *Maverick* were the periodic satires of other TV shows, Western and non-Western alike, such as a takeoff on *Gunsmoke* and another on *Dragnet* (in which Bret intoned a narration in deadpan Joe Friday style). Perhaps the best was a wild parody on *Bonanza,* in which Bart encountered a ranching baron named Joe Wheelwright (played by Jim Backus), owner of the vast Subrosa Ranch, who was trying to marry off his three idiot sons Moose (Hoss), Henry (Adam), and Small Paul (Little Joe). On still another show Bart, in trouble as usual, ran into Clint *(Cheyenne)* Walker, John Russell and his deputy Peter Brown *(Lawman)*, Will *(Sugarfoot)* Hutchins, Ty *(Bronco)* Hardin, and Edd "Kookie" Byrnes, all in one episode. None of them were of any help whatever!

James Garner was a maverick offscreen as well as on. In 1960 he walked out on Warner Brothers Studios, demanding a better contract. In a virtual replay of the confrontation between Warner Brothers and Clint Walker two years before (see *Cheyenne*), the studio refused to give in, and instead hired a new actor to replace him. Enter Cousin Beau Maverick, who was introduced as an expatriate Texan who had fought with valor in the Civil War (unusual behavior for a Maverick), then moved to England, and now returned as a cultured Englishman to further the family fortunes in America.

Unlike the situation in *Cheyenne,* James Garner never did return to *Maverick*. In December 1960 a court ruled that he could not be held to his contract, and he left Warner Brothers (and TV). Cousin Beau and Bart alternated for the rest of the 1960–1961 season, and in the spring of 1961 still another brother, Brent Maverick, was tried out to see if he could fill Garner's shoes. None of this worked out very well, so in 1961–1962, the final season, Bart was seen alone, together with a healthy quantity of reruns of earlier episodes starring Bret and the two brothers together.

MAX HEADROOM
Science Fiction
FIRST TELECAST: *March 31, 1987*
LAST TELECAST: *October 16, 1987*
BROADCAST HISTORY:
  Mar 1987–May 1987, ABC Tue 10:00–11:00
  Aug 1987–Oct 1987, ABC Fri 9:00–10:00
CAST:
  Edison Carter/Max Headroom .. Matt Frewer
  Theora Jones .... Amanda Pays
  Ben Cheviot .... George Coe
  Bryce Lynch .... Chris Young
  Murray .... Jeffrey Tambor
  Blank Reg .... William Morgan Sheppard
  Dominique .... Concetta Tomei
  Ashwell .... Hank Garrett
  Edwards .... Lee Wilkof
  Lauren .... Sharon Barr
  Ms. Formby .... Virginia Kiser

While this unusual series was not a hit, it certainly showed that TV in the '80s had not lost its ability to innovate—or to make fun of itself. The setting was a rather grim futuristic era where television was everywhere, even built into the sides of trash cans in the slums. In fact, it was illegal to turn it off. There were thousands of stations, all vying for viewers; this was the ultimate consumerist society, and advertisers (mostly Japanese, it seemed) ruled the airwaves. "Ratings" were everything, and were reported every second. Any program that started to slip was canceled immediately!

Max Headroom was the ultimate star of this video age, a computer-generated character who popped on to screens at the oddest times, making sarcastic comments about his human creators' foibles. He belonged to top-rated Channel 23, and was created by its brilliant research head Bryce (a young boy!), who had modeled him after ace reporter Edison Carter. Unfortunately Bryce had not yet worked out all the kinks—Max looked a little angular, moved with jerky motions, and spoke with a distinct stutter. But, like Edison, Max had a mind of his own.

Most episodes had Edison chasing around the cold, cruel city to expose the corruption and crime that was evidently rampant. Armed with a powerful minicam (hand-held TV camera) he could uplink into the network from anywhere and go live nationwide, inbetween (or during) shootouts, druggings, and explosions. Back at the control room his beautiful assistant, Theora, monitored his movements from a computer console, while Bryce tried to work out bugs in the all-pervasive computer system, and keep butt-in Max out of the way. Ben Cheviot was the generally supportive head of Channel 23, who sat with the other bosses around a huge oak table in a darkened room staring at a giant screen, on which an advertiser would sometimes appear saying "your ratings have started to slip in the last few minutes . . . get them back up or else, Mr. Cheviot." Then Murray, the newsroom director (do we detect a hint of *The Mary Tyler Moore Show*'s newsroom here?), would fight to get Edison just a little more time to crack the latest scandal wide open.

Edison's chief rivals and sometime allies in the field were Blank Reg and his partner, Dominique, who ran a scruffy underground channel which lacked the power and money of Channel 23, but made up for that with ruthless aggressiveness.

The character of Max Headroom was originally conceived by producer Peter Wagg for a 1984 British TV movie starring actor Frewer, and spread to the U.S. via the Cinemax cable network and heavy use in Coca-Cola commercials.

MAX LIEBMAN PRESENTS
Musical Variety
FIRST TELECAST: *September 12, 1954*
LAST TELECAST: *June 6, 1956*
BROADCAST HISTORY:
Sep 1954–Jun 1956, NBC Sat 9:00–10:30 (OS)
Sep 1954–Jun 1955, NBC Sun 7:30–9:00

In the early 1950s Max Liebman had produced *Your Show of Shows*, one of the most popular variety shows on television. When that series left the air in 1954, Liebman continued to produce lavish variety programming for NBC. His specials aired roughly once every four weeks—for two seasons on Saturday nights in the same time period previously occupied by *Your Show of Shows* and, during 1954–1955, on Sunday nights as well. The Saturday editions of *Max Liebman Presents* were primarily musical comedies. Included among them were *Lady in the Dark* starring Ann Sothern and Paul McGrath; *Best Foot Forward* starring Jeannie Carson, Robert Cummings, and Marilyn Maxwell; *Babes in Toyland* starring Dave Garroway, Dennis Day, Jack E. Leonard, and Wally Cox; *The Merry Widow* starring Anne Jeffreys, Brian Sullivan, Edward Everett Horton, and John Conte; and *Heidi* starring Jeannie Carson, Wally Cox, Elsa Lanchester, and Natalie Wood. The Sunday episodes of *Max Liebman Presents* were musical revues. Among the performers starring in the revues were Judy Holliday, Steve Allen, Dick Shawn, Jimmy Durante, Perry Como, Pat Carroll, Buddy Hackett, Milton Berle, Martha Raye, Ray Bolger, and Frank Sinatra. The dance team of Bambi Linn and Rod Alexander, which had been featured on *Your Show of Shows*, appeared regularly on *Max Liebman Presents*, and Charles Sanford's Orchestra, which had provided the music on Liebman's earlier series, was also used often.

MAXINE BARRAT
see *And Everything Nice*

MAYA
Adventure
FIRST TELECAST: *September 16, 1967*
LAST TELECAST: *February 10, 1968*
BROADCAST HISTORY:
Sep 1967–Feb 1968, NBC Sat 7:30–8:30
CAST:
Terry Bowen . . . . Jay North
Raji . . . . Sajid Khan

Filmed in India, *Maya* was the story of two teenage boys who traveled around that country on the back of an elephant. American Terry Bowen had come to India to be with his father, a professional hunter, only to learn that his father was missing and presumed dead following an attack by a man-eating tiger. Terry refused to accept his father's death and, with the help of Raji, an orphan about his own age, set out to look for the missing man. Raji's faithful elephant Maya was their source of transportation and of much help during their jungle adventures in search of Mr. Bowen, whom the boys never found.

MAYBERRY R.F.D.
Situation Comedy
FIRST TELECAST: *September 23, 1968*
LAST TELECAST: *September 6, 1971*
BROADCAST HISTORY:
Sep 1968–Sep 1971, CBS Mon 9:00–9:30
CAST:
Sam Jones . . . . Ken Berry
Aunt Bee (1968–1970) . . . . Frances Bavier
Goober Pyle . . . . George Lindsey
Howard Sprague . . . . Jack Dodson
Emmett Clark . . . . Paul Hartman
Millie Swanson . . . . Arlene Golonka
Mike Jones . . . . Buddy Foster
Alice (1970–1971) . . . . Alice Ghostley

This was the successor to *The Andy Griffith Show*, in which Andy had starred for eight years as the sheriff of quiet, rural Mayberry, North Carolina. When Griffith decided to call it quits in 1968, CBS kept most of the rest of the cast together, added a new lead in the person of Ken Berry, and continued the show under the title *Mayberry R.F.D.*

Like Griffith's Andy, Berry's Sam Jones was a young widower with a small son, Mike. Sam was a gentleman farmer who had recently taken up residence near Mayberry. Not long after his arrival he found himself elected to the Mayberry Town Council, a position for which he had no prior experience. That hardly mattered in Mayberry, however, as in his friendly, bumbling way he attempted to perform his new duties and tend to the simple needs of the townsfolk. Aunt Bee moved in with him as his housekeeper for two years, then was replaced by Aunt Alice for the 1970–1971 season. Millie Swanson was Sam's romantic interest.

For a couple of years *Mayberry R.F.D.* was virtually as popular as *The Andy Griffith Show* had been. The new program was one of the top four shows on television during its first two years (*Andy Griffith* had reached number one in its final season). It was still in the top 20 when CBS canceled it in 1971, as part of an extensive cutback in "rural"-oriented programming.

MAYOR OF HOLLYWOOD
Variety
FIRST TELECAST: *July 29, 1952*
LAST TELECAST: *September 18, 1952*
BROADCAST HISTORY:
   Jul 1952–Sep 1952, NBC Tue/Thu 7:00–7:30
CAST:
   Walter O'Keefe .... Himself
   Secretary .... Jeanne Dyer
   Campaign Manager .... Lou Crosby
   Campaign Manager .... Bill Baldwin
   Secretary .... Lina Romay

Walter O'Keefe, a well-known radio personality of the 1930s and 1940s, starred as himself in this live series. In his fictional quest to be elected mayor of Hollywood, he took viewers on a tour around the Hollywood area of Los Angeles while trying to drum up support for his campaign. As part of the "tour" he interviewed numerous famous personalities. His original secretary, Jeanne Dyer, was replaced by Lina Romay on August 14, and his campaign manager, Lou Crosby, who was also the show's announcer, was replaced by Bill Baldwin on August 7.

MCCLAIN'S LAW
Police Drama
FIRST TELECAST: *November 20, 1981*
LAST TELECAST: *August 24, 1982*
BROADCAST HISTORY:
   Nov 1981–Feb 1982, NBC Fri 9:00–10:00
   Mar 1982–Apr 1982, NBC Sat 10:00–11:00
   Apr 1982–Jul 1982, NBC Fri 10:00–11:00
   Jul 1982–Aug 1982, NBC Tue 10:00–11:00
CAST:
   Det. Jim McClain .... James Arness
   Det. Harry Gates .... Marshall Colt
   Lt. Edward DeNisco .... George DiCenzo
   Det. Jerry Cross .... Carl Franklin
   Vangie Cruise .... Conchata Ferrell

A leg injury had forced Jim McClain to retire from the San Pedro, California, police force 13 years ago, when he was 39. In the intervening years he had worked as a fisherman and lived in a houseboat on the waterfront. When his fishing partner was robbed and murdered, McClain fought to have himself reinstated, convinced that only he could find the killer. Despite the antagonism of his new boss, Lt. DeNisco, McClain proved himself quite effective in the modern, high-tech world of police work. He quickly gained the respect of most of his fellow officers, including young partner Harry Gates and fellow officer

Jerry Gross. Fortunately for McClain, they tended to look the other way when he reverted to the old-fashioned, physical methods of apprehending criminals. Vangie Cruise ran the dockside cafe where McClain spent much of his spare time.

MCCLOUD
Police Drama
FIRST TELECAST: *September 16, 1970*
LAST TELECAST: *August 28, 1977*
BROADCAST HISTORY:
   Sep 1970–Oct 1970, NBC Wed 9:00–10:00
   Mar 1971–Aug 1971, NBC Wed 9:00–10:00
   Sep 1971–Aug 1972, NBC Wed 8:30–10:00
   Sep 1972–Aug 1975, NBC Sun 8:30–10:00
   Sep 1975–Aug 1976, NBC Sun 9:00–11:00
   Oct 1976–Aug 1977, NBC Sun Various times
CAST:
   Sam McCloud .... Dennis Weaver
   Peter B. Clifford .... J. D. Cannon
   Sgt. Joe Broadhurst .... Terry Carter
   Chris Coughlin .... Diana Muldaur
   Sgt. Grover .... Ken Lynch

McCloud was one of television's more tongue-in-cheek police series. Here was Deputy Marshal Sam McCloud from Taos, New Mexico, driving the New York City police crazy. He had originally arrived in New York to chase a prisoner who had escaped from him, and his direct, rather strong-arm methods were hard for the big-city police to cope with. After capturing his man, McCloud somehow found himself on temporary assignment in Manhattan's 27th Precinct under Chief Peter B. Clifford. Although he was ostensibly there to learn the methods employed by a large metropolitan police department, McCloud usually took things into his own hands and reverted to type, much to the chagrin and frustration of Chief Clifford. Whenever McCloud went on a case he dragged Sgt. Joe Broadhurst with him and, though they usually solved the crime and got along well with each other, Broadhurst's association with McCloud didn't seem to be doing him much good with their mutual superior Clifford. McCloud really looked out of place on the streets of New York, with his cowboy hat, sheepskin jacket, and matching accent. He was full of Western homilies and used the catchphrase "There you go" quite regularly. His romantic interest, not seen in every episode, was writer Chris Coughlin, who was working on a book that related to the fugitive he had chased to New York in the pilot for this series.

McCloud premiered in 1970 as the first of four mini-series aired under the collective title *Four-In-One*—the others being *San Francisco International Airport, Night Gallery,* and *The Psychiatrist.* The following fall it became, along with *Columbo* and *McMillan and Wife,* one of the three original elements in the *NBC Mystery Movie* rotation. It remained with that series throughout the rest of its run.

MCCOY

Detective Drama
FIRST TELECAST: *October 5, 1975*
LAST TELECAST: *March 28, 1976*
BROADCAST HISTORY:
Oct 1975–Mar 1976, NBC Sun 9:00–11:00
CAST:
McCoy .... Tony Curtis
Gideon Gibbs .... Roscoe Lee Browne

The combination of an addiction to gambling, at which he was not particularly successful, and a very expensive life-style prompted McCoy to make a living as a sophisticated con man. He was something of a latter-day Robin Hood, finding ways to relieve wealthy criminals of their ill-gotten gains, then returning most of the loot to those who had been bilked of it, while retaining a healthy fee for his services. He would work elaborate cons on the con men themselves, and would usually take them for so much that after expenses, paying off the many accomplices who worked with him, and reimbursing the original victim, there was still a tidy sum left over for himself. McCoy's principal aide was a nightclub comedian named Gideon Gibbs.

McCoy was seen briefly as one of four rotating elements that made up the 1975–1976 edition of the *NBC Sunday Mystery Movie*. Its resemblance to the hit movie *The Sting* may or may not have been coincidental, but in any event did not help as only four episodes of *McCoy* were actually telecast before the program was canceled.

MCCOYS, THE

syndicated title for *Real McCoys, The*

MCGARRETT

see *Hawaii Five-O*

MCGRAW

see *Meet McGraw*

MCHALE'S NAVY

Situation Comedy
FIRST TELECAST: *October 11, 1962*
LAST TELECAST: *August 30, 1966*
BROADCAST HISTORY:
Oct 1962–Sep 1963, ABC Thu 9:30–10:00
Sep 1963–Aug 1966, ABC Tue 8:30–9:00
CAST:
Lt. Cdr. Quinton McHale .... Ernest Borgnine
Capt. Wallace B. Binghamton ...... Joe Flynn
Ensign Charles Parker .... Tim Conway
Lester Gruber .... Carl Ballantine
George "Christy" Christopher... Gary Vinson
Harrison "Tinker" Bell .... Billy Sands
Virgil Edwards .... Edson Stroll
Nurse Molly Turner (1962–1964).. Jane Dulo
Joseph "Happy" Haines (1962–1964)
.... Gavin MacLeod
Willy Moss (1964–1966) .... John Wright
Fuji Kobiaji .... Yoshio Yoda

Lt. Elroy Carpenter .... Bob Hastings
Col. Douglas Harrigan (1965–1966)
.... Henry Beckman
Gen. Bronson (1965–1966)...... Simon Scott
Dino Baroni (1965–1966) .... Dick Wilson
Mayor Mario Lugatto (1965–1966)
.... Jay Novello
Rosa Giovanni (1965–1966) .... Peggy Mondo

The U.S. Navy was never like this. Lt. Commander Quinton McHale was the commander of a World War II P.T. boat with one of the strangest, most outrageous crews ever assembled. The program was in many respects a copy of Phil Silvers' classic Sgt. Bilko show, its broad humor built on the conflict between the easygoing, regulation-ignoring, con-artist McHale and his long-suffering superior, Capt. Binghamton (known behind his back as "Old Lead Bottom"). The men loved McHale, Binghamton hated him, and the navy put up with him because, in the South Seas where P.T. 73 was based at the island of Taratupa, McHale knew the territory "like the back of his hand."

At the start of *McHale's Navy*'s last season, the entire crew, including Capt. Binghamton, was transferred to Italy, where they helped maintain the occupation of the small town of Voltafiore against the possible incursion of German troops. Not only did Binghamton still have to deal with the incorrigible McHale, but he was now saddled with a conniving Italian mayor, Mario Lugatto, who was almost as adept a con man as McHale himself. Nothing changed but the environment. The gambling that had run rampant in the Pacific now included local residents as well as military personnel.

MCKEEVER & THE COLONEL

Situation Comedy
FIRST TELECAST: *September 23, 1962*
LAST TELECAST: *June 16, 1963*
BROADCAST HISTORY:
Sep 1962–Jun 1963, NBC Sun 6:30–7:00
CAST:
Cadet Gary McKeever .... Scott Lane
Col. Harvey Blackwell .... Allyn Joslyn
Sgt. Barnes .... Jackie Coogan
Mrs. Warner .... Elisabeth Fraser
Tubby .... Keith Taylor
Monk .... Johnny Eimen

Comedy about life in a military school. The cadets—McKeever abetted by his pals Tubby and Monk—were constantly getting into trouble and making it virtually impossible for Col. Blackwell to maintain any semblance of order, decorum, or discipline. Sgt. Barnes was the colonel's aide, Mrs. Warner the head of the school cafeteria.

MCLEAN STEVENSON SHOW, THE

Situation Comedy
FIRST TELECAST: *December 1, 1976*
LAST TELECAST: *March 3, 1977*

BROADCAST HISTORY:
Dec 1976–Jan 1977, NBC Wed 8:30–9:00
Feb 1977–Mar 1977, NBC Wed 9:30–10:00

CAST:

Mac Ferguson	McLean Stevenson
Peggy Ferguson	Barbara Stuart
Grandma	Madge West
Janet	Ayn Ruymen
Chris	Steve Nevil
David	David Hollander
Jason	Jason Whitney

Mac Ferguson was a typical middle-class family man, owner of a hardware store in his hometown of Evanston, Illinois. He and his wife had two grown children who, through circumstances that could not possibly have been anticipated by their parents, were living with them. Janet had separated from her husband and moved in along with her two young children, David and Jason. Chris, after several years of trying to "find" himself, principally spent bumming around in Hawaii, returned home to go back to college part-time, taking up residence in the basement and setting it up as a bachelor pad. If this didn't create enough congestion, Peggy's mother was also a member of the household.

MCMILLAN AND WIFE
Police Drama
FIRST TELECAST: *September 29, 1971*
LAST TELECAST: *August 21, 1977*
BROADCAST HISTORY:
Sep 1971–Aug 1972, NBC Wed 8:30–10:00
Sep 1972–Jul 1974, NBC Sun 8:30–10:00
Sep 1974–Jul 1975, NBC Sun 8:30–10:30
Sep 1975–Aug 1976, NBC Sun 9:00–11:00
Dec 1976–Aug 1977, NBC Sun 8:00–9:30

CAST:

Commissioner Stewart McMillan
.... Rock Hudson
Sally McMillan (1971–1976)
.... Susan Saint James
Sgt. Charles Enright .... John Schuck
Mildred (1971–1976) .... Nancy Walker
Agatha (1976–1977) .... Martha Raye
Sgt. Steve DiMaggio (1976–1977)
.... Richard Gilliland
Maggie (1976–1977) .... Gloria Stroock

San Francisco Police Commissioner Stewart McMillan had a beautiful wife who had a penchant for getting both of them involved in criminal cases which she inadvertently stumbled upon. Mac was very supportive, though occasionally bewildered by the situations Sally got them into, and was often called upon to help solve the cases. This mystery/comedy police series was patterned after the relationship between Nick and Nora Charles in *The Thin Man* movies and TV series of the 1940s and 1950s. There were elements of romance and comedy thrown in with the actual case being solved. Mac's aide was plodding but enthu-

siastic Sgt. Enright, and Mildred was the McMillans' sarcastic, sharp-tongued maid.

McMillan and Wife was one of the three original rotating elements in the *NBC Mystery Movie*—the other two were *McCloud* and *Columbo*—and remained with the series throughout its long run. When Nancy Walker and Susan Saint James left the series at the end of the 1975–1976 season, the former to star in her own series on ABC and the latter in a contract dispute, the title was shortened to *McMillan* and cast changes were made. Sally was written out of the series by having her die in a plane crash, and Mac, now a widower, had a new maid/housekeeper named Agatha, who happened to be Mildred's sister. Mac also acquired a second assistant in Sgt. DiMaggio (the dimwitted Enright had been promoted to lieutenant) and a new secretary named Maggie.

ME AND MAXX
Situation Comedy
FIRST TELECAST: *March 22, 1980*
LAST TELECAST: *September 12, 1980*
BROADCAST HISTORY:
Mar 1980–Apr 1980, NBC Sat 9:30–10:00
May 1980–Jul 1980, NBC Fri 8:30–9:00
Sep 1980, NBC Fri 8:30–9:00

CAST:

Norman Davis	Joe Santos
Maxx Davis	Melissa Michaelsen
Barbara	Jenny Sullivan
Mitch	Jim Weston
Gary	Denny Evans

In this awkward comedy dad was a heel, and his little daughter was a cute but unwanted child who could never get through to him. Norman Davis had walked out on his wife and child years earlier to take up the life of a swinging single. Now his ex-wife had decided that she too was going to "spread her wings," so, unannounced, 11-year-old Maxx showed up at Norman's bachelor pad looking for a home. Maxx was a precocious and sensitive youngster with an extensive vocabulary learned from watching soap operas. Although her initial attitude toward her father was understandably negative, with time, and a little love, she attempted to heal the old wounds. But Norman was irked at having to adjust his bachelor lifestyle to accommodate the presence of a young daughter. The tender "let's make up" scenes at the end of each episode were so cold as to be embarrassing, and the show quickly left the air.

Barbara was Norman's business partner (they brokered tickets to Broadway shows) and occasional girlfriend; Mitch, the swinging next-door neighbor with whom Norman hung out; and Gary, the inept elevator operator.

ME AND MOM
Detective Comedy/Drama
FIRST TELECAST: *April 5, 1985*

LAST TELECAST: *May 17, 1985*
BROADCAST HISTORY:
   Apr 1985–May 1985, ABC Fri 10:00–11:00
CAST:
   Kate Morgan .... Lisa Eilbacher
   Zena Hunnicutt .... Holland Taylor
   Lou Garfield .... James Earl Jones
   Lt. Rojas .... Henry Darrow

Mother and daughter private eyes. Kate was a beautiful, trained criminologist, and Zena her wealthy, socialite mom (you could tell by her ever-present mink coat); Zena was widowed, bored, and looking for a little excitement, so she routinely meddled in Kate's work. Kate's "official" partner, Lou, an ex-cop, helped keep the ladies from getting blown away in this action series. Rojas was their contact on the San Francisco Police Dept.

ME & MRS. C.
Situation Comedy
FIRST TELECAST: *June 21, 1986*
LAST TELECAST: *July 4, 1987*
BROADCAST HISTORY:
   Jun 1986–Jul 1986, NBC Sat 9:30–10:00
   Apr 1987–May 1987, NBC Sat 9:30–10:00
   Jun 1987–Jul 1987, NBC Sat 8:30–9:00
CAST:
   Ethel Conklin (Mrs. C) .... Peg Murray
   Gerri Kilgore .... Misha McK
   Ethan Conklin .... Gary Bayer
   Kathleen Conklin .... Ellen Regan

Mrs. C was a sixty-ish white widow with a problem. She didn't have enough money to meet expenses, so in order to avoid losing her house she took in a boarder—which is when the fun really began. Gerri was a young black girl who was eager to work, but since she was just out of prison found it hard to land a job. In addition, Gerri's streetcorner ways clashed with Mrs C's sedate, old-fashioned life-style, though the two genuinely liked each other. Mrs. C's cold-fish son, Ethan, an efficiency expert, and his snooty wife, Kathleen, were appalled at the arrangement, but did little to help mom out in this somewhat uncomfortable comedy.

ME AND THE CHIMP
Situation Comedy
FIRST TELECAST: *January 13, 1972*
LAST TELECAST: *May 18, 1972*
BROADCAST HISTORY:
   Jan 1972–May 1972, CBS Thu 8:00–8:30
CAST:
   Mike Reynolds .... Ted Bessell
   Liz Reynolds .... Anita Gillette
   Scott Reynolds .... Scott Kolden
   Kitty Reynolds .... Kami Cotler

Mike Reynolds was a happily married dentist living in the suburban Southern California commu-

nity of San Pascal. He and his wife, Liz, had two young children and a small chimpanzee named Buttons. Buttons had been found in a local park by the two Reynolds children, Scott and Kitty, and been brought home as a pet. Despite Mike's objections, Buttons became a regular member of the household, having been given that name because of his infatuation with pushing any and all buttons he found on appliances, radios, cars, dental equipment, or anything else he got his little hands onto. Though very friendly and affectionate, Buttons caused all sorts of problems with his curiosity about almost everything and managed to get the entire household into difficult situations. It always seemed to be Mike's responsibility to get them out.

MEDALLION THEATER
Dramatic Anthology
FIRST TELECAST: *July 11, 1953*
LAST TELECAST: *April 3, 1954*
BROADCAST HISTORY:
   Jul 1953–Apr 1954, CBS Sat 10:00–10:30

This series of adaptations of plays and works from other media was aired live from New York with a different cast each week. The premiere telecast starred Henry Fonda in "The Decision of Arrowsmith," adapted from Sinclair Lewis' novel. Cast in the leads of other presentations were generally well-known performers, including Ronald Reagan, Jack Lemmon, Claude Rains, Robert Preston, Dane Clark, Martha Scott, and Jan Sterling.

MEDIC
Medical Drama
FIRST TELECAST: *September 13, 1954*
LAST TELECAST: *November 19, 1956*
BROADCAST HISTORY:
   Sep 1954–Nov 1956, NBC Mon 9:00–9:30
CAST:
   Dr. Konrad Styner .... Richard Boone
THEME:
   "Blue Star," by Edward Heyman and Victor Young

Case histories from the files of the Los Angeles County Medical Association were dramatized in this filmed series. In its efforts to present the practice of medicine realistically, *Medic* was shot at real hospitals and clinics, and often used real doctors and nurses as part of the cast. Dr. Styner was the host and narrator of the series, as well as a frequent participant in the cases. His introduction to each episode always included this description of the doctor: ". . . guardian of birth, healer of the sick, and comforter of the aged." The dramas generally centered around the struggle to preserve life, and the tragedies and triumphs that resulted.

Medic was a pioneer in TV realism, and was the first starring vehicle for actor Richard Boone. Its pretty theme song, "Blue Star," was quite popular during 1955.

505

MEDICAL CENTER
Medical Drama
FIRST TELECAST: *September 24, 1969*
LAST TELECAST: *September 6, 1976*
BROADCAST HISTORY:
> Sep 1969–May 1973, CBS Wed 9:00–10:00
> May 1973–Sep 1976, CBS Mon 10:00–11:00
CAST:
> Dr. Paul Lochner .... James Daly
> Dr. Joe Gannon .... Chad Everett
> Nurse Chambers (1969–1972)
> .... Jayne Meadows
> Dr. Jeanne Bartlett (1969–1971)
> .... Corinne Camacho
> Nurse Courtland .... Chris Hutson
> Nurse Wilcox (1972–1976) .... Audrey Totter
> Dr. Barnes (1970–1971) .... Fred Holliday
> Nurse Murphy (1971–1972) .... Jane Dulo
> Nurse Holmby (1971–1976)
> .... Barbara Baldavin
> Nurse Canford .... Virginia Hawkins
> Anesthesiologist (1969–1970) ... Daniel Silver
> Dr. Weller (1970–1974) ..... Eugene Peterson
> Dr. Bricker (1970–1974) .... Ed Hall
> Nurse Bascomb (1971–1973)..... Louise Fitch
> Lt. Samuels (1971–1976) .... Martin E. Brooks

Located in the Los Angeles area, Medical Center was an otherwise unnamed hospital complex that was part of a large university campus. Dr. Paul Lochner was the chief of staff, an experienced, professional, compassionate man. Dr. Joe Gannon was a young associate professor of surgery and close friend and colleague of Dr. Lochner. At the start of the show's second season, Dr. Gannon took on the added responsibilities of director of the student health service, an appropriate post for a young physician who could identify closely with the students. A number of other doctors and nurses came and went in the cast; Miss Wilcox, the extremely efficient head nurse, achieved co-star billing in 1972.

The personal and medical stories of the doctors and their patients, as well as others with whom they came into contact, provided the drama in this series. Gannon and Lochner embodied the youth vs. experience tension which seems to be a necessary element of every medical show. The elements certainly worked here, as *Medical Center,* with its seven-year run, was the longest-lasting medical series in the history of prime-time television.

MEDICAL HORIZONS
Public Affairs
FIRST TELECAST: *September 12, 1955*
LAST TELECAST: *March 5, 1956*
BROADCAST HISTORY:
> Sep 1955–Mar 1956, ABC Mon 9:30–10:00
HOST:
> Quincy Howe (1955)
> Don Goddard (1955–1956)

During the 1955–1956 season ABC attempted to bring the television viewer an insight into the advances being made in medicine and an introduction to the people who were responsible for them. Quincy Howe was the original host/narrator, but other commitments forced him to leave this live series after a month. He was replaced by Don Goddard. Each week a different discovery, program of research, or branch of medicine was discussed, with interviews with doctors, technicians, researchers, etc., supplemented by actual scenes of the technique, equipment, or operation.

Medical Horizons returned to the air on Sunday afternoons in September of 1956 and continued until the following June.

MEDICAL STORY
Medical Anthology
FIRST TELECAST: *September 4, 1975*
LAST TELECAST: *January 8, 1976*
BROADCAST HISTORY:
> Sep 1975–Jan 1976, NBC Thu 10:00–11:00

Medical Story attempted to remove the mantle of sainthood from doctors. It dealt with the personal problems and human failings of members of the medical profession, as well as with their skills. Stories confronted many sensitive issues, most notably the mistakes made in hospitals and the selfishness and insensitivity of many doctors. Such a critical view of a profession whose practitioners people want to trust apparently did not sit well with viewers, and the program was dropped after a few months.

MEET CORLISS ARCHER
Situation Comedy
FIRST TELECAST: *July 12, 1951*
LAST TELECAST: *March 29, 1952*
BROADCAST HISTORY:
> Jul 1951–Sep 1951, CBS Thu 9:00–9:30
> Jul 1951–Sep 1951, CBS Fri 10:00–10:30
> Jan 1952–Mar 1952, CBS Sat 6:30–7:00
CAST:
> Corliss Archer.............. Lugene Sanders
> Mr. Harry Archer.............. Fred Shields
> Dexter Franklin .... Bobby Ellis
> Mrs. Janet Archer (1951) .....Frieda Inescort
> Mrs. Janet Archer (1952) ...... Irene Tedrow

Meet Corliss Archer had been on CBS radio since 1943 and was still being aired in the early 1950s when this television version was added in 1951. It was the story of a typical high school girl, her boyfriend, Dexter, and her parents. The stories revolved around the energetic and vivacious Corliss as she made the transition from little girl to young woman. Fred Shields, who had played Mr. Archer through most of the radio run, re-created his role for the new medium, as did Irene Tedrow as Mrs. Archer in part of the television run.

This series was fed to different parts of the country on different days during the summer of

1951. The Thursday shows were seen in the Midwest while the rest of the country was seeing *Your Esso Reporter.* On Friday nights *Meet Corliss Archer* was available to those stations that did not carry it on Thursdays. Since it was done live from Los Angeles, the cast did the same show on consecutive nights.

A syndicated film version of *Meet Corliss Archer* was produced for the 1954–1955 season. The only survivor from the network cast was Bobby Ellis as Dexter. The film Corliss was played by Ann Baker.

MEET MCGRAW
Detective Drama
FIRST TELECAST: *July 2, 1957*
LAST TELECAST: *October 8, 1959*
BROADCAST HISTORY:
  Jul 1957–Jun 1958, NBC Tue 9:00–9:30
  Nov 1958–Dec 1958, ABC Sun 10:00–10:30
  Jan 1959, ABC Sun 9:30–10:00
  Feb 1959–Sep 1959, ABC Sun 10:30–11:00
  Oct 1959, ABC Thu 9:00–9:30
CAST:
  McGraw .... Frank Lovejoy

Although McGraw (that was the only name he used) was not officially a private detective, for all intents and purposes he might as well have been. Tough willing to get into a fight, but never carrying a gun, he accepted all sorts of dangerous jobs for pay. In most of the episodes he regretfully had to leave a pretty woman behind but, as a loner, he just couldn't let himself get tied down. This series premiered on NBC, as *Meet McGraw*, on December 31, 1957, changed its title to *The Adventures of McGraw*, and was rerun on ABC in 1958–1959.

MEET MILLIE
Situation Comedy
FIRST TELECAST: *October 25, 1952*
LAST TELECAST: *March 6, 1956*
BROADCAST HISTORY:
  Oct 1952–Jun 1953, CBS Sat 9:30–10:00
  Jun 1953–Aug 1953, CBS Sat 9:00–9:30
  Aug 1953–Sep 1953, CBS Sat 9:30–10:00
  Oct 1953–Feb 1954, CBS Sat 7:00–7:30
  Mar 1954–Mar 1956, CBS Tue 9:00–9:30
CAST:
  Millie Bronson .... Elena Verdugo
  "Mama" Bronson .... Florence Halop
  Mr. Boone (1952–1953).............. Earl Ross
  Johnny Boone, Jr. (1952–1955) ..... Ross Ford
  Alfred Prinzmetal .... Marvin Kaplan
  Mr. Boone (1953–1956)....... Roland Winters
  Mrs. Boone (1953–1955)..... Isabel Randolph
  Gladys (1956).............. Virginia Vincent

Millie Bronson was a young, attractive, middle-class secretary working in Manhattan. She lived in a brownstone apartment with her mother, who was always promoting Millie to eligible men as a potential spouse. Millie's boyfriend through most of the series' run was Johnny Boone, Jr., the son of her boss. A close friend of the Bronsons, who managed to get involved in most everything, was Alfred Prinzmetal. Alfred was an aspiring author-poet-composer.

Meet Millie had originated on CBS radio in July 1951 with Audrey Totter in the starring role. When her movie studio refused to let her do the TV version, Elena Verdugo took it over and eventually replaced Miss Totter in the radio edition before it expired in 1954. Earl Ross, as her boss, made the transition from radio to TV but was replaced by Roland Winters in June 1953.

MEET MR. MCNUTLEY
  see *Ray Milland Show, The*

MEET THE BOSS
Interview
FIRST TELECAST: *June 10, 1952*
LAST TELECAST: *August 26, 1952*
BROADCAST HISTORY:
  Jun 1952–Aug 1952, DUM Tue 10:30–11:00
HOST:
  Bill Cunningham

Newsman Bill Cunningham interviewed top American executives on their careers and their industries in general, in this paean to big business.

MEET THE CHAMP
  see *Boxing*

MEET THE CHAMPIONS
Sports Interview
FIRST TELECAST: *July 21, 1956*
LAST TELECAST: *January 12, 1957*
BROADCAST HISTORY:
  Jul 1956–Jan 1957, NBC Sat 6:45–7:00
HOST:
  Jack Lescoulie

Each episode of this live program gave viewers the opportunity to see a sports celebrity interviewed by Jack Lescoulie, as well as a second sports-world figure (not necessarily an athlete) making predictions about the outcome of an upcoming athletic event.

MEET THE PRESS
Interview
FIRST TELECAST: *November 20, 1947*
LAST TELECAST: *August 29, 1965*
BROADCAST HISTORY:
  Nov 1947–Dec 1947, NBC Thu 8:00–8:30
  Sep 1948–Feb 1949, NBC Sun 8:30–9:00
  Feb 1949–Jul 1949, NBC Wed 10:00–10:30
  Jul 1949–Sep 1949, NBC Mon 10:00–10:30
  Sep 1949–Feb 1950, NBC Sat Various times
  Oct 1950–May 1952, NBC Sun Various times
  Jun 1951–Sep 1951, NBC Tue 8:00–8:30
  May 1952–Sep 1952, NBC Sun 7:30–8:00
  Oct 1952–Aug 1965, NBC Sun 6:00–6:30

Martha Rountree (1947–1953)
Ned Brooks (1953–1965)
REGULAR PANELISTS:
Lawrence Spivak
Bill Monroe

This NBC public affairs program, which styles itself "America's Press Conference of the Air," is as of this writing the longest-running series on network television. Part of its career (as noted above) has been in prime time, while during other periods it has been telecast on Sunday afternoons.

Meet the Press usually originates from NBC's Washington, D.C., studios. It was created by Martha Rountree and Lawrence Spivak in 1945 as a radio promotion for the *American Mercury Magazine*, of which Spivak was then editor. It started on local television on November 6, 1947, and was first fed over the network (then consisting of two stations) on November 20 of that year. The format has always remained the same: a panel of reporters questions a leading public figure. Over the years virtually every major political figure in the United States has occupied the *Meet the Press* hot seat, and many foreign dignitaries as well. Martha Rountree was the original TV moderator. NBC newsman Ned Brooks took over in 1953, while Spivak remained a regular panelist and occasional moderator. Spivak became the regular moderator in 1965 and served in that capacity for a decade. He was subsequently replaced by Bill Monroe (1975–1984), Marvin Kalb (1984–1987), and current moderator Chris Wallace who has helmed the show since April 1987.

During the summer of 1951, in a move unique to political interview shows of this type, *Meet the Press* aired two times per week, with different guests on each Sunday and Tuesday telecast. Following the end of its nighttime run, in August 1965, *Meet the Press* became a regular fixture on the NBC Sunday afternoon lineup, where it remains to this day.

MEET THE VEEP
Discussion
FIRST TELECAST: *June 30, 1953*
LAST TELECAST: *August 25, 1953*
BROADCAST HISTORY:
Jun 1953–Aug 1953, NBC Tue 10:45–11:00
REGULARS:
Alben W. Barkley
Earl Godwin

Originating live from Washington, D.C., this discussion show featured former Vice President Alben W. Barkley, who had acquired the affectionate nickname "The Veep" during his tenure with Truman, and NBC news commentator Earl Godwin. They would discuss various political issues, reminisce about Mr. Barkley's career, or chat about current nonpolitical issues. On occasion guests appeared on the show to discuss their points of view, be they similar to or different from Mr. Barkley's.

Meet the Veep had premiered as a Sunday afternoon series on NBC in February 1953. After a short spring run it left the air until showing up that June in prime time.

MEET YOUR CONGRESS
Debate
FIRST TELECAST: *July 1, 1949*
LAST TELECAST: *July 4, 1954*
BROADCAST HISTORY:
Jul 1949–Aug 1949, NBC Fri 9:00–9:30
Aug 1949–Oct 1949, NBC Sat 8:00–8:30
Jul 1953–Sep 1953, DUM Wed 9:30–10:00
Oct 1953–Jul 1954, DUM Sun 6:30–7:00
MODERATOR:
Sen. Blair Moody

Public-affairs debate show, in which two Republican and two Democratic Congressmen gave their views on an issue of national importance. The program originated in NBC's Washington, D.C., studios and was first seen as a Sunday afternoon program (March–June 1949). In 1953–1954, it turned up on DuMont. Former Senator Blair Moody of Michigan was the moderator.

MELBA
Situation Comedy
FIRST TELECAST: *January 28, 1986*
LAST TELECAST: *September 13, 1986*
BROADCAST HISTORY:
Jan 1986, CBS Tue 8:00–8:30
Aug 1986–Sep 1986, CBS Sat 8:00–8:30
CAST:
Melba Patterson .... Melba Moore
Tracy Patterson .... Jamilla Perry
Susan Slater................ Gracie Harrison
Mama Rose .... Barbara Meek
Jack .... Lou Jacobi
Gil .... Evan Mirand

Melba was the unqualified disaster of the 1985–1986 TV season. A second-season comedy starring musical-comedy star Melba Moore, it was yanked from the CBS schedule after its premiere telecast and did not show up again until the last few episodes that had been produced were run off during the summer. The storyline dealt with the work and home life of Melba Patterson, the director of New York's Manhattan Visitors' Center. Adapting to life after divorce, Melba was raising her 9-year-old daughter, Tracy, with the help of her mother, Rose, who lived with them. Melba's best friend was her white "sister," Susan—they had both been raised by Rose, who was the housekeeper in the Slater home when they were children. Jack and Gil worked for Melba at the Visitors' Center.

MELBA MOORE-CLIFTON DAVIS SHOW, THE
Musical Variety

FIRST TELECAST: *June 7, 1972*
LAST TELECAST: *July 5, 1972*
BROADCAST HISTORY:
Jun 1972–Jul 1972, CBS Wed 8:00–9:00
REGULARS:
Melba Moore
Clifton Davis
Timmie Rogers
Ron Carey
Dick Libertini
Liz Torres
The Charles H. Coleman Orchestra

Young Broadway stars Melba Moore and Clifton Davis were starred in this summer variety series. With the help of their regular supporting cast and special guest stars they performed skits and did musical numbers. The set for the show was designed to look like the side of an apartment building with the various acts taking place in different apartments.

MELODY, HARMONY & RHYTHM
Music
FIRST TELECAST: *December 13, 1949*
LAST TELECAST: *February 16, 1950*
BROADCAST HISTORY:
Dec 1949–Feb 1950, NBC Tue/Thu 7:30–7:45
REGULARS:
Lynne Barrett
Carol Reed
Charlie Dobson
Tony DeSimone Trio

This musical interlude featured three vocalists and an instrumental trio. It originated from WPTZ, Philadelphia.

MELODY STREET
Music
FIRST TELECAST: *September 23, 1953*
LAST TELECAST: *February 5, 1954*
BROADCAST HISTORY:
Sep 1953–Oct 1953, DUM Wed 8:30–9:00
Nov 1953–Feb 1954, DUM Fri 8:30–9:00
HOST:
Allan Brown (1953)
Elliot Lawrence (1953)
Tony Mottola (1954)
REGULARS:
Lyn Gibbs
Joe Buwen
Roberta McDonald

Another stop in DuMont's never-ending search for low-cost programming was this "musical stroll down Tin Pan Alley," in which a cast of regulars and guests lipsynced (mouthed) the words to a song while a phonograph record was played. The host for most of the run was noted orchestra leader Elliot Lawrence, who was seen sitting at a piano with a cigarette dangling from his mouth, Hoagy Carmichael–style, commenting on the

music. "I was awful," he frankly admits today, "I don't even smoke!" Lawrence soon returned to what he does very well, conducting an orchestra, and guitarist Tony Mottola took over the host's spot for the show's last month.

MELODY TOUR
Musical Variety
FIRST TELECAST: *July 8, 1954*
LAST TELECAST: *September 30, 1954*
BROADCAST HISTORY:
Jul 1954–Sep 1954, ABC Thu 8:00–9:00
REGULARS:
Stan Freeman
Norman Scott
Nellie Fisher
Jorie Remes
Nancy Kenyon
Peter Gladke
Jonathan Lucas
The Harry Sosnik Orchestra

Interesting summer musical series built around the concept of a vacation trip. The premiere took place mostly in a pier setting, as the cast prepared to embark, and subsequent programs highlighted various foreign ports of call. Guests were featured in addition to the regular cast.

MEN, THE
Adventure
FIRST TELECAST: *September 21, 1972*
LAST TELECAST: *September 1, 1973*
BROADCAST HISTORY:
Sep 1972–Jan 1973, ABC Thu 9:00–10:00
Jan 1973–Sep 1973, ABC Sat 10:00–11:00
THEME MUSIC (OVERALL):
Isaac Hayes

This was the umbrella title for three rotating series, *Assignment Vienna*, *Delphi Bureau*, and *Jigsaw*. At first these elements rotated in normal fashion, each one appearing every third week. However, in January 1973, when *The Men* moved to Saturdays, the rotation scheme was changed and each element appeared for several weeks in a row, as follows:

Jan 13–Feb 10: *Assignment Vienna*
Feb 17–Mar 3: *Jigsaw*
Mar 17–Apr 7: *Delphi Bureau*
Apr 14–Jun 9: *Assignment Vienna*
Jun 16–Aug 11: *Jigsaw*
Aug 18–Sep 1: *Delphi Bureau*

See individual element titles for more complete program information.

MEN AT LAW
see *Storefront Lawyers*

MEN FROM SHILOH, THE
see *Virginian, The*

MEN INTO SPACE

Science Fiction

FIRST TELECAST: *September 30, 1959*
LAST TELECAST: *September 7, 1960*
BROADCAST HISTORY:

Sep 1959–Sep 1960, CBS Wed 8:30–9:00
CAST:

Col. Edward McCauley.... William Lundigan

On October 4, 1957, Russia launched the world's first man-made earth satellite. It was too late to get a show about it on television that season, or even the next, but in 1959 CBS was ready to capitalize on the high public interest in and concern about the "space race" with this realistic dramatization of space exploration. *Men into Space* was produced with the cooperation and assistance of the army, navy, air force, and numerous scientific organizations, and every attempt was made to present an accurate picture of man's likely experiences and problems away from Earth. Col. Edward McCauley was the only regular member of the cast. His adventures on the moon base, the space station, other planets within the solar system, and on rocketships in transit provided the stories. Problems with equipment, the environment, and the people involved in the space program all created crisis situations for the indomitable Col. McCauley.

MEN OF TOMORROW

Documentary

FIRST TELECAST: *June 29, 1954*
LAST TELECAST: *September 21, 1954*
BROADCAST HISTORY:

Jun 1954–Sep 1954, ABC Tue 7:30–8:00
REGULARS:

Robert Mitchell Boys Choir

This filmed series was devoted to the Boy Scouts of America. Each episode explored some aspect of the Boy Scout movement, such as the training of young scouts and trips taken by them. Opening and closing music was provided by the Robert Mitchell Boys Choir of Hollywood.

MENASHA THE MAGNIFICENT

Situation Comedy

FIRST TELECAST: *July 3, 1950*
LAST TELECAST: *September 11, 1950*
BROADCAST HISTORY:

Jul 1950–Sep 1950, NBC Mon 8:00–8:30
CAST:

Menasha .... Menasha Skulnik
Mrs. Davis .... Zamah Cunningham

Short-lived situation comedy starring Yiddish comedian Menasha Skulnik, who began each day singing "Oh, What a Beautiful Morning," but usually wound up in trouble. Menasha, a little fellow with a hoplike walk and a tragicomic mien, was cast as the meek manager of a restaurant owned by the domineering, Amazon-like Mrs. Davis. His fate was to be pushed around constantly. Jean Cleveland appeared as Mrs. Davis in the first telecast, but was replaced by Zamah Cunningham the following week.

MEREDITH WILLSON SHOW, THE

Music

FIRST TELECAST: *July 31, 1949*
LAST TELECAST: *August 21, 1949*
BROADCAST HISTORY:

Jul 1949–Aug 1949, NBC Sun 8:30–9:00
REGULARS:

Meredith Willson
Norma Zimmer

Four-week summer musical series, hosted by famed composer and orchestra leader Meredith Willson. Norma Zimmer later became Lawrence Welk's "Champagne Lady."

MERV GRIFFIN SHOW, THE

Talk

FIRST TELECAST: *August 18, 1969*
LAST TELECAST: *February 11, 1972*
BROADCAST HISTORY:

Aug 1969–Feb 1972, CBS Mon–Fri 11:30–1:00 A.M.
REGULARS:

Merv Griffin
Arthur Treacher
Mort Lindsey Orchestra

Merv Griffin had had a highly successful syndicated talk show for several years when CBS chose him to wage war on a network scale with Johnny Carson's *Tonight Show* in 1969. His arrival meant that there were competing late-night talk shows on all three networks, Joey Bishop having started one on ABC in the summer of 1967. A cherubic folksy individual, Merv was a former band singer and veteran of several network daytime talk and game shows, in addition to his syndicated show. His ingratiating manner and aversion to virtually anything that might be considered radical, offensive, or controversial made his show rather bland. It did force Joey Bishop off the air, to be replaced by the dry, intellectual wit of Dick Cavett, but it could never make a dent in Carson's late-night audience. As CBS' first regular late-night entry since *Chronoscope* in the mid-1950s, *The Merv Griffin Show* was never as big an audience-grabber as CBS had hoped and was canceled two and one-half years after its premiere. It was replaced by late-night movies, while Merv returned to the syndicated talk-show world.

Merv's first talk show had been a 55-minute daytime series on NBC from October 1962 to March 1963. Two years later he began the syndicated 90-minute talk show that attracted CBS' attention.

His last daily syndicated *Merv Griffin Show* ran from the summer of 1972 until September of 1986 and, along with a number of successful game shows he had created over the years (including

Jeopardy! and *Wheel of Fortune*), made him a wealthy man.

METROPOLITAN OPERA AUDITIONS OF THE AIR
Talent
FIRST TELECAST: *January 15, 1952*
LAST TELECAST: *April 1, 1952*
BROADCAST HISTORY:
Jan 1952–Apr 1952, ABC Tue 8:30–9:00
COMMENTATOR:
Milton J. Cross

This must have been one of the classiest talent shows in the history of network television, as newcomers competed for a place at the fabled "Met." Similar operatic auditions had been telecast by ABC on a specials basis as early as 1948.

MIAMI VICE
Police Drama
FIRST TELECAST: *September 16, 1984*
LAST TELECAST:
BROADCAST HISTORY:
Sep 1984, NBC Sun 9:00–11:00
Sep 1984–May 1986, NBC Fri 10:00–11:00
Jun 1986–Mar 1988, NBC Fri 9:00–10:00
Apr 1988–   , NBC Fri 10:00–11:00
CAST:
Det. James "Sonny" Crockett ... Don Johnson
Det. Ricardo Tubbs .. Philip Michael Thomas
Lt. Martin Castillo .... Edward James Olmos
Det. Gina Navarro Calabrese
 .... Saundra Santiago
Det. Trudy Joplin .... Olivia Brown
Det. Stan Switek .... Michael Talbott
Det. Larry Zito (1984–1987) .... John Diehl
*Izzy Moreno .... Martin Ferrero
*Caitlin Davies (1987–1988) .... Sheena Easton

*Occasional

The pulse and rhythm of a glamorous resort city was juxtaposed against the seamy haunts of the drug underworld in this gritty action series, which made heavy use of rock music backgrounds and music video effects. Sonny Crockett was a rough-edged Miami vice detective who lived on a sailboat called "St. Vitus' Dance" that was guarded by his dyspeptic pet alligator, Elvis. Ricardo Tubbs was a black ex–New York street cop who had come south to find the drug dealer who murdered his brother. They were an unlikely but effective team, working undercover on the flashy Gold Coast and down the seedy alleyways that made Miami such a city of contrasts. Often they sped around town in Sonny's black Ferrari Spider sports car (later upgraded to a state-of-the-art Ferrari Testarossa). Lt. Castillo was their moody superior, Gina and Trudy a hip, female undercover team, and Stan and Larry more conventional backup.

The stylish, MTV-influenced series (music by rock composer Jan Hammer) was a smash hit, and transformed struggling actor Don Johnson into a major sex symbol in the mid-1980s. His expensive pastel sports jackets worn over a T-shirt, with stubbly beard, no socks, and an angry scowl started a fashion trend for those into the macho/grubby look. Female characters on the show fawned over him—and usually got blown up or shot for their trouble. Sonny's estranged wife, Caroline (played by Belinda Montgomery), and his young son were rarely seen, and a later quickie bride played by rock singer Sheena Easton also appeared infrequently.

The hip series attracted many famous celebrities not normally seen in TV acting roles to do cameos (or more), including singers from the '50s (Little Richard, James Brown) to the '80s (Phil Collins, Ted Nugent, the Fat Boys). Watergate felon G. Gordon Liddy made quite an impression in the role of sneaky Capt. Real Estate; also seen fleetingly were such unlikely folks as boxing promoter Don King, boxing champ Roberto Duran, comic Tommy Chong, Chrysler chairman Lee Iacocca, and the President of NBC-TV (as a bartender!).

MICHAEL NESMITH IN TELEVISION PARTS
Variety
FIRST TELECAST: *June 14, 1985*
LAST TELECAST: *July 5, 1985*
BROADCAST HISTORY:
Jun 1985–Jul 1985, NBC Fri 8:00–8:30
HOST:
Michael Nesmith
REGULARS:
John Hobbs, Musical Director
Donna Ruppert

Did you ever wonder what happened to the Monkees, the pre-fab rock group so popular in the 1960s? One of them, Michael "Wool Hat" Nesmith, was independently wealthy and later began producing avant-garde videos. One of these, *Elephant Parts*, attracted the attention of NBC which decided—unwisely—to try to turn it into a TV series for the masses.

Television Parts was an offbeat mélange of music and comedy. Some of the music was done straight and some as absurdist satire; the comedy consisted largely of surrealistic special effects and incomprehensible bits of comic business. Guest comedians and musicians appeared, with Nesmith providing a degree of continuity both as host (often wandering off the set) and sometimes as participant. Musical Director John Hobbs also appeared on-screen, reworking two familiar songs into a new song each week. Viewers were mystified.

Originally aired as a special on March 7, 1985, *Television Parts* had a short regular run in the summer, with its last three original episodes combined into a 90-minute replacement for *Saturday Night Live* aired on July 27, 1985.

MICHAEL SHAYNE
Detective Drama
FIRST TELECAST: *September 30, 1960*
LAST TELECAST: *September 22, 1961*
BROADCAST HISTORY:
  Sep 1960–Sep 1961, NBC Fri 10:00–11:00
CAST:
  Michael Shayne .... Richard Denning
  Tim Rourke .... Jerry Paris
  Lucy Hamilton (1960–1961)
  .... Patricia Donahue
  Lucy Hamilton (1961) .... Margie Regan
  Will Gentry .... Herbert Rudley
  Dick Hamilton................. Gary Clarke

Michael Shayne was a suave, debonair Miami-based private detective whose cases tended to revolve around bizarre murders. Helping him solve the cases were Tim Rourke, a young newspaper-reporter friend; Will Gentry, the chief of the Miami police department; and Dick Hamilton, the younger brother of Shayne's secretary/girlfriend Lucy. Lucy was not the only love of his life, however, and his fondness for beautiful women often got him into sticky situations. The character of Michael Shayne had been established in a series of detective novels written by Brett Halliday, as well as in a radio series, a dozen movies, and a monthly mystery magazine. Mr. Halliday acted as technical consultant for the series.

MICKEY
Situation Comedy
FIRST TELECAST: *September 16, 1964*
LAST TELECAST: *January 13, 1965*
BROADCAST HISTORY:
  Sep 1964–Jan 1965, ABC Wed 9:00–9:30
CAST:
  Mickey Grady .... Mickey Rooney
  Nora Grady .... Emmaline Henry
  Sammy Ling................. Sammee Tong
  Timmy Grady .... Tim Rooney
  Buddy Grady .... Brian Nash
  Mr. Swidler .... Alan Reed

At the outset of this comedy series Mickey Rooney was cast as a Coast Guard recruiter in landlocked Omaha, who dreamt of a life on the open sea. He got his wish—or at least got close to it—when he inherited a luxurious beachfront hotel in Newport Harbor, California. When the Gradys moved from Omaha to take over the Marina Palms, they thought their money worries and other troubles would be over. Little did they realize that Sammy Ling, the hotel's manager (with a "lifetime contract"), had let it go deeply into debt by letting too many of his relatives in on the operation. The legal work was being done by Ling's shyster cousin and the mortgage was held by the Ling Savings & Loan at an annual rate of 17 percent. Mickey and family set out to straighten things out, in their own comedic way. Mickey Rooney's real-life son, Tim, played his 16-year-old

son Timmy, and Brian Nash played the 8-year-old, Buddy.

MICKEY ROONEY SHOW, THE
Situation Comedy
FIRST TELECAST: *September 4, 1954*
LAST TELECAST: *June 4, 1955*
BROADCAST HISTORY:
  Sep 1954–Jun 1955, NBC Sat 8:00–8:30
CAST:
  Mickey Mulligan .... Mickey Rooney
  Mrs. Mulligan .... Claire Carleton
  Mr. Mulligan .... Regis Toomey
  Pat .... Carla Balenda
  Mr. Brown .... John Hubbard
  Freddie .... Joey Forman
  The Drama Instructor .... Alan Mowbray

Mickey Mulligan was a young man working as a page at the NBC Studios in Hollywood. His aspirations, however, went far beyond his lowly position. He really wanted to be a serious dramatic actor, and was only using the page job as a springboard to bigger things. At night Mickey attended dramatic school, with less-than-spectacular results. By day his thespian ambitions were not encouraged by either his peers or superiors at NBC. But there was no keeping Mickey down. The only people who did encourage him were his father and his girlfriend, Pat, who worked as a secretary at the studios. Mickey lived with his mother, a one-time star in burlesque, and his father, a lifelong cop.

Ironically, in real life the position of page at NBC is widely regarded as an excellent starting job in the broadcasting industry, and many former pages have gone on to become stars or top-level executives.

The official title of this series was *The Mickey Rooney Show;* however, it was also known by its subtitle, *Hey Mulligan.*

MICKEY SPILLANE'S MIKE HAMMER
Detective Drama
BROADCAST HISTORY:
  Syndicated only
  30 minutes
  Produced: *1957–1959* (78 episodes)
  Released: *Late 1957*
CAST:
  Mike Hammer .... Darren McGavin
  Capt. Pat Chambers, N.Y.P.D. ..... Bart Burns

This private-eye series was every bit as violent as the novels that made Mickey Spillane famous. *TV Guide* called it "easily the worst show on TV." *Variety* described it as a "mixture of blood, violence, and sex." A typical plot had a man and a woman thrown down a flight of stairs, a brutal fist fight, a knifing, and a shooting, plus Hammer making what appeared to be a highly successful pass at a married woman. Hammer was usually either kissing them or killing them (Angie Dickinson got bumped off in the premiere episode), while providing a steady stream of smart-alecky wisecracks. The setting was New York City, and episode titles were vintage Spillane such as "Overdose of Lead" and "Music to Die By."

Spillane and McGavin both defended the showing of such violence on TV, but Spillane later admitted that his involvement with this series was minimal. "I just took the money and went home."

MICKEY SPILLANE'S MIKE HAMMER
Detective Drama
FIRST TELECAST: *January 26, 1984*
LAST TELECAST: *September 9, 1987*
BROADCAST HISTORY:
Jan 1984, CBS Thu 9:00–11:00
Jan 1984–Apr 1984, CBS Sat 10:00–11:00
Aug 1984–Sep 1984, CBS Thu 10:00–11:00
Sep 1984–Jan 1985, CBS Sat 9:00–10:00
May 1985–Jul 1985, CBS Sat 10:00–11:00
Apr 1986–May 1986, CBS Tue 9:00–10:00
Sep 1986–Oct 1986, CBS Sat 9:00–10:00
Nov 1986–Sep 1987, CBS Wed 8:00–9:00
CAST:
Mike Hammer . . . . Stacy Keach
Velda . . . . Lindsay Bloom
Capt. Pat Chambers . . . . Don Stroud
Asst. D.A. Lawrence D. Barrington
. . . . Kent Williams
Ozzie the Answer *(1984–1985)*
. . . . Danny Goldman
Jenny the bartender . . . . Lee Benton
Moochie *(1984–1985)* . . . . Ben Powers
Ritchie *(1984–1985)* . . . . Eddie Barth
Hennessey *(1984–1985)* . . . . Eddie Egan
The Face . . . . Donna Denton
THEME:
"Harlem Nocturne," by Earle Hagen

When *Mickey Spillane's Mike Hammer* turned up on network television 25 years after the syndicated version was produced things were little changed. It was still violent, sexist, and full of wisecracks. Mike's secretary, Velda, not seen in the syndicated version, was bustily present, as were a host of other beauties poured into tight, low-cut dresses to emphasize their obvious assets. There was also a regular coterie of street people and contacts, the most prominent of whom was Ozzie the Answer, Mike's most reliable source of information. Jenny was the sexy (what else?) bartender at the Light n' Easy, Mike's favorite hangout. His good buddy Pat, as well as Ritchie and Hennessey were cops on the N.Y.P.D., and Barrington was the assistant D.A. with whom he never saw eye to eye. Mike's best friend, however, was not a person, but the powerful .45 calibre pistol he had nicknamed Betsy and carried with him almost all his waking hours.

Along with the typical cases of murder, extortion, kidnapping, and robbery were cases dealing with drug dealing and problems of the elderly. Regardless of the case, however, Mike always solved it, leaving a trail of bloodied bad guys and swooning women in his wake. There was one thing Mike never did quite solve. At some point in each episode he would catch a glimpse of the same strikingly beautiful brunette (practically the only attractive lady on the show whose assets were only on display from the neck up), but he never got close enough to actually meet her before she disappeared. The show's producers planned to build a 1985 episode around Mike's finally meeting "The Face," but by then star Stacy Keach was serving a six-month jail term in England for cocaine possession, and the 1984–1985 season had to be cut short before the episode was filmed. "Hammer in the Slammer," read the real-life newspaper headlines!

The following season CBS telecast a newly produced TV movie, *The Return of Mickey Spillane's Mike Hammer,* as well as reruns of the original series to test the waters for a possible revival. The series did return in the fall of 1986 as *The New Mike Hammer.* Some changes were made. In an attempt to attract female viewers who had heretofore been offended by the series' blatant sexism, the busty women billowing out of their clothes were gone. However, the violence was, if anything, increased. Claiming they wanted to be true to the original novels (which were *very* violent), the producers made their hero even more brutal than before. In one episode, a fight with a heavyset villain left the criminal clinging precariously to a high ledge; as he struggled to save himself he cried to Hammer, who stood just a few feet away, "for God's sake Hammer, give me a hand!" Our Hero just looked at him coldly—and began to slowly clap. The villain lost his grip and fell screaming to his death. Nice hero.

In the last original episode, which aired the following May, Mike finally met The Face and, after a rather convoluted plot, found out she was an author following him and watching his activities so that she could "fictionalize" his exploits in a series of detective novels. After one memorable romantic evening she disappeared from his life.

MICKIE FINN'S
Musical Variety
FIRST TELECAST: *April 21, 1966*
LAST TELECAST: *September 1, 1966*
BROADCAST HISTORY:
Apr 1966–Sep 1966, NBC Thu 9:30–10:00
REGULARS:
Fred E. Finn
Mickie Finn
The Fred Finn Band
The Mickie Finn Dancers
The Dapper Dans
Harold "Hoot" Connors
Mickey Manners

The set on which this variety series was taped was a replica of the warehouse in San Diego that Fred and Mickie Finn had converted into a "Gay

513

'90s" nightclub. The music played by the band ranged from current hits to ragtime and Dixieland jazz. In addition to the guest stars, the regular cast included Fred, as the proprietor who played piano and led the band, and his wife, Mickie, who played banjo. Harold Connors and Mickey Manners were the bartenders who often provided comic relief.

MIDNIGHT SPECIAL, THE
Music
FIRST TELECAST: *February 2, 1973*
LAST TELECAST: *May 1, 1981*
BROADCAST HISTORY:
   Feb 1973–Sep 1980, NBC Fri 1:00–2:30 A.M.
   Sep 1980–May 1981, NBC Fri 12:30–2:00 A.M.
HOSTESS:
   Helen Reddy (1975–1976)
ANNOUNCER:
   Wolfman Jack

For young people coming home from a Friday night date, or for those who were still up after *The Tonight Show*, *The Midnight Special* provided 90 minutes of taped in-concert popular music. The emphasis was on rock and, when the series first went on the air, everyone was a guest star—there was no regular host. Among the popular stars who hosted the show were Johnny Rivers, Mac Davis, Paul Anka, Lou Rawls, Ray Charles, Jerry Lee Lewis, Chubby Checker, Al Green, Curtis Mayfield, David Bowie, and Charlie Rich. It was Helen Reddy, the hostess of the premiere telecast, however, who finally became permanent host, two years later—in July 1975. Less than a year later she gave up that role and weekly guest hosts returned.

Beginning in the summer of 1975, a regular feature of *The Midnight Special* was "Rock Tribute," a segment that profiled a different rock star each week. Included were scenes of the star in concert, interviews, and various other insights into the star's life.

Another regular feature, added in the fall of 1979, was a weekly comedy segment in which a panel of comics and writers made fun of things that had happened on the previous week's telecast. The following April brought two other new features—"Golden Moments," highlighting clips of great performances from past telecasts of *The Midnight Special*, and "Top 10," a countdown of the week's top hits. The latter feature was dropped six months later.

MIDWESTERN HAYRIDE
Musical Variety
FIRST TELECAST: *June 16, 1951*
LAST TELECAST: *September 6, 1959*
BROADCAST HISTORY:
   Jun 1951–Sep 1951, NBC Sat 9:00–10:00
   Jun 1952–Sep 1952, NBC Tue 8:00–9:00
   Jun 1954–Sep 1954, NBC Tue 8:00–8:30
   May 1955–Sep 1955, NBC Fri 8:00–8:30
   Sep 1955–Jun 1956, NBC Wed 10:00–10:30

   Jul 1957–Oct 1957, ABC Sun 9:30–10:00
   Jun 1958–Sep 1958, ABC Sat 10:00–10:30
   May 1959–Sep 1959, NBC Sun 7:00–7:30
EMCEE:
   Bill Thall (1951–1954)
   Bob Shrede (1951)
   Hugh Cherry (1955–1956)
   Paul Dixon (1957–1958)
   Dean Richards (1959)
REGULARS:
   The County Briar Hoppers (1951–1952)
   Slim King & the Pine Mountain Boys
   Zeke Turner
   Bonnie Lou Ewins (1952–1959)
   The Midwesterners (1954–1959)
   The Hometowners (1957–1959)

This country music hoedown was a night-time summer standby during the 1950s. Originating from the NBC affiliate in Dayton or Cincinnati, Ohio, it featured such talent as a square-dance ensemble (the County Briar Hoppers, later the Midwesterners), yodlers, guitarists, string bands, country comedy acts, etc. Many performers came and went over the years, among them guitarist Jerry Byrd, Ernie Lee, Charlie Gore & the Rangers, Lee Jones, Buddy Ross, the Kentucky Boys, Salty and Mattie (later Billy) Holmes, Freddy Langdon, Tommy Watson, Bobby Bobo, Penny West, Kenny Price, Helen and Billy Scott, and the Lucky Pennies.

Midwestern Hayride was also frequently seen on the network in non-evening hours during the regular season.

MIKE HAMMER
see *Mickey Spillane's Mike Hammer*

MIKE WALLACE INTERVIEWS
Interview
FIRST TELECAST: *April 28, 1957*
LAST TELECAST: *September 14, 1958*
BROADCAST HISTORY:
   Apr 1957–Sep 1957, ABC Sun 10:00–10:30
   Sep 1957–Apr 1958, ABC Sat 10:00–10:30
   Apr 1958–Sep 1958, ABC Sun 10:00–10:30
HOST:
   Mike Wallace

Newsman Mike Wallace conducted this ABC interview program in the aggressive style for which he was to become famous. Among the guests undergoing his grilling were Gloria Swanson, the Imperial Wizard of the Ku Klux Klan, Mickey Cohen, Steve Allen, Arkansas Governor Faubus, stripper Lili St. Cyr, Tennessee Williams, and Major Donald Kehoe, an Air Force expert on Unidentified Flying Objects.

MILLIONAIRE, THE
Dramatic Anthology
FIRST TELECAST: *January 19, 1955*
LAST TELECAST: *September 28, 1960*

BROADCAST HISTORY:
  Jan 1955–Sep 1960, CBS Wed 9:00–9:30
CAST:
  Michael Anthony .... Marvin Miller

Each week eccentric multibillionaire John Beresford Tipton (whose face was never seen on the series) would instruct his personal secretary, Michael Anthony, to present some unsuspecting individual with a cashier's check for one million dollars, tax free. The object was to see how this new-found wealth would change the lives of its recipients. The answers to the question "What would you do if you had a million dollars?" intrigued and entertained audiences for more than five years. Michael Anthony was the only regular member of the cast and functioned more as a host than as a participant in the dramas. The only stipulation that Mr. Anthony made when he presented the checks to their recipients was that they make no attempt to find out who their mysterious benefactor was, or reveal where they got the money to anybody but their spouse. If they did, they would have to forfeit the money.

Viewers never found out who he was, either. Each program opened with Tipton seated in the study of his huge estate, Silverstone, toying with his chessmen. He would call in his faithful secretary, deliver a few philosophical words of wisdom, and hand over the name of the latest recipient. Only the back of Tipton's head or his hand on the arm of a chair was ever seen on camera, and the files do not record who that hand or head belonged to (probably to several people over the years). The deep, authoritative voice of Mr. Tipton was that of a well-known Hollywood announcer, Paul Frees.

Reruns of *The Millionaire* were shown as part of the CBS daytime lineup from October 1959 to August 1963.

MILTON BERLE SHOW, THE
  Comedy Variety
FIRST TELECAST: *June 8, 1948*
LAST TELECAST: *January 6, 1967*
BROADCAST HISTORY:
  Jun 1948–Jun 1956, NBC Tue 8:00–9:00 (OS)
  Oct 1958–May 1959, NBC Wed 9:00–9:30
  Sep 1966–Jan 1967, ABC Fri 9:00–10:00
REGULARS:
  Milton Berle
  Fatso Marco (1948–1952; as *Marko Marcelle* from 1951)
  Ruth Gilbert (1952–1955)
  Bobby Sherwood (1952–1953)
  Arnold Stang (1953–1955)
  Jack Collins (1953–1955)
  Milton Frome (1953–1955)
  Irving Benson (*Sidney Spritzer;* 1966–1967)
COMMERCIAL ANNOUNCER:
  Sid Stone (1948–1951)
  Jimmy Nelson (1952–1953)
  Jack Lescoulie (1954–1955)

ORCHESTRA:
  Alan Roth (1948–1955)
  Victor Young (1955–1956)
  Billy May (1958–1959)
  Mitchell Ayres (1966–1967)
THEME:
  "Near You," by Kermit Goell and Francis Craig

The most popular hour of the week during the early years of TV was Milton Berle's, on Tuesday night. Although Berle was the host on the very first telecast of *Texaco Star Theater,* June 8, 1948, he was not at that time considered the permanent emcee. During the summer of 1948 Harry Richman, Georgie Price, Henny Youngman, Morey Amsterdam, Jack Carter, and Peter Donald rotated in the host's spot. Berle won the "competition" and was made permanent emcee in September 1948.

Milton Berle was not unknown at the time, but he could hardly have been called a big name. He had been on radio since the 1930s, and even in a few films, but hadn't scored a big hit in either medium. On TV, however, he fast developed into something of a national institution—"Mr. Television"—and it is said that he sold more TV sets than any advertising campaign. People bought the newfangled thing just to *see* this crazy comedian everyone was talking about.

The original *Texaco Star Theater* was built along the lines of an old-fashioned vaudeville variety hour, with half a dozen guests each week, including singers, comedians, ventriloquists, acrobats—you name it. But the star was Berle, and he involved himself in many of the acts, adding comedy counterpoint. Soon the basic format was set. Each show opened with the four Texaco Service Men, singing the Texaco jingle ("Oh, we're the men of Texaco, we work from Maine to Mexico . . .") and then working into a musical introduction of Berle, who came on dressed in some outlandish costume. "And now the man with jokes from the Stone Age," and Berle came on dressed as a caveman. "The man who just paid his taxes . . . ," and Berle arrived wearing a barrel. For the sponsor's commercials, old-fashioned pitchman Sid Stone ("Awright, I'll tell ya what I'm gonna do!") would come on stage, set up his sample case, and launch into his spiel—until chased off by a whistle-blowing policeman. And each show would end with Berle singing his theme song, "Near You."

This format changed little during the first four seasons, although the accent was gradually placed more on Berle himself, his sight gags, outlandish costumes, and props. In 1952 young ventriloquist Jimmy Nelson and his dummy Danny O'Day replaced Sid Stone as the commercial announcer. In the fall of 1952 Berle returned with a somewhat different format. There were fewer guest acts, and each show was built around a central theme or comedy plot (often it was the rehearsal for the show itself), involving Berle, his guests, and several regulars. Ruth Gilbert joined the cast as Max, his secretary, and in 1953 Arnold Stang joined as Francis, an NBC stagehand and Max's secret love. In the fall of 1955 the regulars were dropped and an entirely new production staff was hired. The program's format was freer, alternating between straight variety hours, satires, and book musicals (including "State of Confusion" on October 18, 1955, a satirical comedy written for Berle by Gore Vidal). One of the guests during the last few months was Elvis Presley, making two appearances in early 1956.

Title and scheduling underwent several changes in the 1950s. After 1953 Texaco shifted its sponsorship to another night (see the *Jimmy Durante* and *Donald O'Connor* shows) and Berle's hour became the *Buick-Berle Show*. Then from 1954–1956 it was simply *The Milton Berle Show*, which alternated variously with Martha Raye, Bob Hope, and Steve Allen.

By 1956 the steam had run out for "Mr. Television." TV was by then becoming dominated by dramatic-anthology shows, Westerns, and private eyes, and the sight of a grinning comic jumping around in crazy costumes no longer had the appeal it did in 1948, when things were simpler.

Two years after his departure from the Tuesday lineup, Berle returned to prime time with a half-hour variety series on NBC, for Kraft (called *Milton Berle Starring in The Kraft Music Hall*). He was a more restrained performer this time—no slapstick or outrageous costumes—attempting to function more as a host than as the central focus of the show. Each telecast began with an opening monologue, often including informal patter with the evening's guest stars. Later, Berle might perform in skits with his guests. With the exception of the interplay between Milton and bandleader Billy May, the show was a somewhat refined version of *The Red Skelton Show*. Berle's new image did not, however, attract sufficient viewers to warrant renewal for a second season.

After his Kraft show was canceled Berle continued to show up as a guest on other programs, increasingly a nostalgic figure. Then in 1966 he was signed for a new variety series of his own on ABC, and columnists made a great deal of his "comeback." "Can he grab the new generation?" headlined one. To give the show a youthful image singers Bobby Rydell and Donna Loren were signed as regulars (but they soon disappeared), while Irving Benson played the heckler in the audience. The producer was comic Bill Dana, who also appeared periodically as Jose Jiminez. Despite an infusion of top-name guests, Lucille Ball and Bob Hope among them, the program was massacred in the ratings by *The Man from U.N.C.L.E.* and was soon dropped.

MILTON BERLE STARRING IN THE KRAFT MUSIC HALL

see *Milton Berle Show, The*

MISADVENTURES OF SHERIFF LOBO, THE

see *Lobo*

MISFITS OF SCIENCE

Adventure
FIRST TELECAST: *October 4, 1985*
LAST TELECAST: *February 21, 1986*
BROADCAST HISTORY:
Oct 1985–Dec 1985, NBC Fri 9:00–10:00
Dec 1985–Feb 1986, NBC Fri 8:00–9:00
CAST:
Dr. Billy Hayes . . . . Dean Paul Martin
Dr. Elvin "El" Lincoln . . . . . . Kevin Peter Hall
Johnny Bukowski ("Johnny B.")
. . . . Mark Thomas Miller
Gloria Dinallo . . . . Courteney Cox
Jane Miller . . . . Jennifer Holmes
Dick Stetmeyer . . . . Max Wright
Miss Nance . . . . Diane Civita

Misfits of Science was a teen-oriented fantasy adventure that set out to prove that outcasts and freaks could be TV heroes, too. The "freaks" in this case were all young people with bizarre physical abilities, who were being studied by Los Angeles' Humanidyne Institute. Not content to become living laboratory experiments, they formed a team to—what else—fight crime and save the world! Idealistic young scientist Billy Hayes of the Institute was the leader; others included his coworker El Lincoln, a 7-foot, 4-inch black man who had the ability to shrink to just six inches in height by touching the back of his neck; Johnny B., a leather-jacketed rock musician who had once connected with 20,000 volts on stage and now could zap enough electricity from his fingertips to light the city; and reformed delinquent Gloria, whose telekinetic powers could levitate objects.

Dick Stetmeyer was the Institute's director, who wished these nice young people would spend more time on projects he could present to his board of directors. Miss Nance was the office receptionist/secretary who was forever filing her nails, and Jane Miller was Gloria's pregnant probation officer.

MISS WINSLOW AND SON

Situation Comedy
FIRST TELECAST: *March 28, 1979*
LAST TELECAST: *May 2, 1979*
BROADCAST HISTORY:
Mar 1979–May 1979, CBS Wed 8:30–9:00
CAST:
Susan Winslow . . . . Darleen Carr
Harold Devore Neistadter
. . . . Roscoe Lee Browne
Warren Winslow . . . . Elliot Reid
Evelyn Winslow . . . . Sarah Marshall
Mr. Joseph X. Callahan . . . . . . William Bogert
Edmund Hillary Warren Winslow (pilot)
. . . . Benjamin Margolis
Edmund Hillary Warren Winslow
. . . . David Finger & Michael Finger

Rosa Vallone	Ellen Sherman
Angelo Vallone	Joe Rassulo

How times change! In 1952, when Lucille Ball was about to have a baby on *I Love Lucy,* the CBS censors would not even allow the word "pregnant" to be used in the scripts. That, they said, was too sexually suggestive (reluctantly, they used "expecting" instead). By 1979 the same network was ready for Miss Winslow, who was not only pregnant but unwed, having decided not to marry the father of her child.

In the first episode of this comedy she gave birth to a bouncing baby boy, whom she named Eddie. Daddy left for a job in Brazil and Susan, an attractive 23-year-old, set about raising the infant alone, making a living as a free-lance art designer, and dealing with family and friends who did not approve of her decision. Susan sometimes sought the assistance of her neighbor, a rather arrogant and sarcastic author named Harold Neistadter, who grudgingly helped out with the baby when asked. Despite his gruff exterior, he was actually rather fond of Susan and Eddie. Susan's socially prominent parents were aghast at what she'd done and tried to keep the truth from their friends while scrambling to find her a husband. Little Eddie just cooed. Adapted from the British series, *Miss Jones & Son.*

MRS. COLUMBO
see *Kate Loves a Mystery*

MRS. G GOES TO COLLEGE
see *Gertrude Berg Show, The*

MISSION: IMPOSSIBLE
International Intrigue
FIRST TELECAST: *September 17, 1966*
LAST TELECAST: *September 8, 1973*
BROADCAST HISTORY:
    Sep 1966–Jan 1967, CBS Sat 9:00–10:00
    Jan 1967–Sep 1967, CBS Sat 8:30–9:30
    Sep 1967–Sep 1970, CBS Sun 10:00–11:00
    Sep 1970–Sep 1971, CBS Sat 7:30–8:30
    Sep 1971–Dec 1972, CBS Sat 10:00–11:00
    Dec 1972–May 1973, CBS Fri 8:00–9:00
    May 1973–Sep 1973, CBS Sat 10:00–11:00
CAST:

Daniel Briggs (1966–1967)	Steven Hill
Cinnamon Carter (1966–1969)	Barbara Bain
Rollin Hand (1966–1969)	Martin Landau
Barney Collier	Greg Morris
Willie Armitage	Peter Lupus
Voice on Tape	Bob Johnson
James Phelps (1967–1973)	Peter Graves
Paris (1969–1971)	Leonard Nimoy
Doug (1970–1971)	Sam Elliott
Dana Lambert (1970–1971)	Lesley Ann Warren
Casey (1971–1973)	Lynda Day George
Mimi Davis (1972–1973)	Barbara Anderson

THEME:
"Mission: Impossible," by Lalo Schifrin

At the opening of each episode of *Mission: Impossible,* the leader of the Impossible Missions Force, a group of highly specialized government agents, would receive a tape-recorded message outlining instructions for an assignment he was to consider taking. The voice on the tape would give him some background information, usually tied to the pictures of adversaries that were included with the tape, and conclude with "Your mission, Dan, should you decide to accept it, is . . . As always, should you or any member of your I.M. Force be caught or killed, the secretary will disavow any knowledge of your actions. This tape will self-destruct in five seconds." On cue, five seconds later, the tape, and often the small portable recorder that had contained it, went up in a puff of smoke and flame. The leader would then leaf through the dossiers of the various operatives who might be utilized on the mission and pull out the appropriate ones. Except for an occasional guest star, however, he always picked out exactly the same team to work with, which made the entire selection process seem rather superfluous. This opening was so stylized that it was parodied on virtually every comedy show on the air during the period, from *The Carol Burnett Show* to *The Tonight Show.* Over the years it was modified and toward the end of the series' run the process of leafing through dossiers was dropped completely.

The top-secret assignments taken on by this elite group of agents usually involved disrupting the activities of various small foreign powers seeking to create problems for America or the Free World. By the last season the agents had begun to run out of little Communist countries and obscure principalities, so they concentrated their efforts more on dealing with organized crime within the United States. All of the plans executed by the Impossible Missions Force were incredibly complex and depended on split-second timing and an astounding array of sophisticated electronic gadgetry. The leader of the group, Daniel Briggs during the first season and Jim Phelps through the rest of *Mission: Impossible*'s run, devised the complex plans used to accomplish the team's missions. Barney Collier was the electronics expert and Willie Armitage provided muscle throughout the series' run. Rollin Hand was an expert at disguise and Cinnamon Carter was the versatile, beautiful female member of the team. Martin Landau and Barbara Bain, then husband and wife in real life, left the show at the end of the 1968–1969 season in a contract dispute and were replaced by other performers filling their respective functions.

The music for *Mission: Impossible* was written by Lalo Schifrin and had a pulsating, jazz-oriented urgency. The show's theme, which typified the music of the show, was released as a single and was on *Billboard's* "Hot 100" chart for 14 weeks in 1968. There were also two albums of *Mission: Impossible* music released in the late 1960s.

MISSISSIPPI, THE
Law Drama
FIRST TELECAST: *March 25, 1983*
LAST TELECAST: *March 13, 1984*
BROADCAST HISTORY:
   Mar 1983–May 1983, CBS Fri 10:00–11:00
   Sep 1983–Mar 1984, CBS Tue 8:00–9:00
CAST:
   Ben Walker .... Ralph Waite
   Stella McMullen .... Linda G. Miller
   Lafayette "Lafe" Tate .... Stan Shaw

Filmed entirely on location, *The Mississippi* was the story of a highly successful, big-city criminal attorney who sought a more leisurely life. Ben Walker tried to get away from it all by purchasing a sternwheel river tug and making a living with it up and down the Mississippi River. But his former life continued to get in the way as he became involved in criminal proceedings in almost every port. His clients often couldn't pay him for his work, but Ben's sense of justice forced him to get involved. His "crew" consisted of Stella McMullen and Lafe Tate, both of whom were more interested in learning to become lawyers than in running the tug. Stella, one of Ben's former clients, was bright and argumentative, while Lafe, a Vietnam veteran who had had his fill of violence during the war, couldn't keep from getting into fights in civilian life. He did most of the maintenance on the boat, as well as the majority of the legwork on Ben's cases.

MR. ADAMS AND EVE
Situation Comedy
FIRST TELECAST: *January 4, 1957*
LAST TELECAST: *September 23, 1958*
BROADCAST HISTORY:
   Jan 1957–Feb 1958, CBS Fri 9:00–9:30
   Feb 1958–Sep 1958, CBS Tue 8:00–8:30
CAST:
   Eve Drake....................... Ida Lupino
   Howard Adams............... Howard Duff
   Steve .... Hayden Rorke
   Elsie.......................... Olive Carey
   J. B. Hafter...................... Alan Reed

Movie stars Howard Duff and Ida Lupino were married to each other in real life at the time they played husband-and-wife film stars in this series. Happenings at the studio, fights with the studio boss J. B. Hafter, negotiations and dealings with their agent Steve, and the good and troublesome sides of their home life were all shown in *Mr. Adams and Eve*. Though exaggerated for comic effect, many of the stories were based on actual situations that had happened to Duff and Lupino.

MR. & MRS. CARROLL
   see *Most Important People, The*

MR. & MRS. NORTH
Comedy/Mystery
FIRST TELECAST: *October 3, 1952*
LAST TELECAST: *July 20, 1954*
BROADCAST HISTORY:
   Oct 1952–Sep 1953, CBS Fri 10:00–10:30
   Jan 1954–Jul 1954, NBC Tue 10:30–11:00
CAST:
   Pamela North .... Barbara Britton
   Jerry North................ Richard Denning
   Lt. Bill Weigand .... Francis De Sales

Jerry North was a publisher of mystery stories who fancied himself a fairly adept amateur detective. However, his wife, Pamela, an attractive, pleasant, rather naive woman, somehow always seemed to be one step ahead of both him and the police when it came to solving mysterious crimes. The Norths were supposed to be entirely normal Greenwich Village residents, but they seemed to stumble across bodies at every turn. *Mr. & Mrs. North* had long been a favorite on radio, and was also produced as a Broadway play and a movie. The characters were conceived by Richard and Frances Lockridge for a series of stories for *The New Yorker* magazine.

MR. ARSENIC
Talk
FIRST TELECAST: *May 8, 1952*
LAST TELECAST: *June 26, 1952*
BROADCAST HISTORY:
   May 1952–June 1952, ABC Thu 9:00–9:30
HOST:
   Burton Turkus

Burton Turkus, co-author of *Murder, Incorporated* and prosecutor of Murder, Inc., during William O'Dwyer's terms of office as mayor of New York, hosted this program of factual information on current political personalities and gangsters. Mr. Turkus answered questions from an off-camera voice and gave detailed insights into headliners in crime and politics. Definitely not for the squeamish.

MR. BELVEDERE
Situation Comedy
FIRST TELECAST: *March 15, 1985*
LAST TELECAST:
BROADCAST HISTORY:
   Mar 1985–Apr 1985, ABC Fri 8:30–9:00
   Aug 1985–Mar 1987, ABC Fri 8:30–9:00
   May 1987–Sep 1987, ABC Fri 8:30–9:00
   Oct 1987–Jan 1988, ABC Fri 9:00–9:30
   Jan 1988–Feb 1988, ABC Fri 8:30–9:00
   *Mar 1988–   *, ABC Fri 9:00–9:30
CAST:
   Mr. Lynn Belvedere ..... Christopher Hewett
   George Owens.................. Bob Uecker
   Marsha Owens .... Ilene Graff
   Kevin Owens (age 16)........... Rob Stone
   Heather Owens (14)........... Tracy Wells

Wesley Owens (8) .... Brice Beckham
Angela (1986–   ) ...... Michele Matheson
THEME:
  by Judy Hart Angelo and Gary Portnoy, sung by
  Leon Redbone

Clifton Webb's memorably eccentric character
from 1940s films was revived in this routine TV
sitcom in the 1980s. Frumpy sportswriter George
Owens and his wife, Marsha, a lawyer-to-be,
were a two-career couple living in suburban Pittsburgh and having trouble finding time for their
three rambunctious kids—especially "little operator" Wesley. Enter Mr. Belvedere, a witty, debonair, portly English housekeeper who had formerly served such gentry as Winston Churchill; to
everyone's surprise he proved both a genius in the
kitchen and an expert at solving all the little problems of growing up and getting along that fill
"warm family comedies" such as this. Each episode ended with Belvedere writing the lessons of
the day in his diary.
  By the beginning of the 1987–1988 season Marsha had received her degree and begun her first
job as a lawyer, and son Kevin had entered college.
  The character of Mr. Belvedere was originally
created by Gwen Davenport in the novel Belvedere; Clifton Webb played him in three popular
movies, Sitting Pretty (1948), Mr. Belvedere Goes
to College (1949), and Mr. Belvedere Rings the
Bell (1951).
  ABC aired reruns of Mr. Belvedere on weekday
mornings from September 1987 to January 1988.

MR. BLACK
  Mystery Anthology
FIRST TELECAST: *September 19, 1949*
LAST TELECAST: *November 7, 1949*
BROADCAST HISTORY:
  Sep 1949–Oct 1949, ABC Mon 9:30–10:00
  Oct 1949–Nov 1949, ABC Mon 9:00–9:30
CAST:
  Mr. Black .... Andy Christopher

This spooky series always saw that the bad guys
got their due. That was taken care of by Mr.
Black—Lucifer's representative on Earth—who
appeared at the open and close of each show amid
cobwebs and flickering lights. Stories were standard suspense yarns. From Chicago.

MR. BROADWAY
  Drama
FIRST TELECAST: *September 26, 1964*
LAST TELECAST: *December 26, 1964*
BROADCAST HISTORY:
  Sep 1964–Dec 1964, CBS Sat 9:00–9:30
CAST:
  Mike Bell .... Craig Stevens
  Hank McClure .... Horace McMahon
  Toki .... Lani Miyazaki

Michael Bell Associates—Public Relations was a
highly successful venture that numbered among

its clients movie stars, politicians, businessmen,
philanthropists, and even phonies. All of them
had one thing in common, a willingness to pay
well for the creation and maintenance of their
desired public image. That was Mike Bell's job
and it got him into many an exciting, romantic,
dangerous, and frequently amusing situation as
he worked to protect his clients' images. Helping
him were his assistant, ex-newspaperman Hank
McClure, and his attractive and highly efficient
girl Friday, Toki.

MR. CITIZEN
  Dramatic Anthology
FIRST TELECAST: *April 20, 1955*
LAST TELECAST: *July 13, 1955*
BROADCAST HISTORY:
  Apr 1955–Jul 1955, ABC Wed 8:30–9:00
HOST:
  Allyn Edwards

Dramatizations of acts of heroism by real people
were presented each week in this series. Allyn
Edwards introduced the show by providing background on the incident being dramatized. At the
end of each episode, the person whose act of heroism had just been shown appeared in person to
receive the "Mr. Citizen" award for the week.
Each show had a different person in public life
(senators, military personnel, etc.) present the
award.

MR. DEEDS GOES TO TOWN
  Situation Comedy
FIRST TELECAST: *September 26, 1969*
LAST TELECAST: *January 16, 1970*
BROADCAST HISTORY:
  Sep 1969–Jan 1970, ABC Fri 8:30–9:00
CAST:
  Longfellow Deeds .... Monte Markham
  Tony Lawrence .... Pat Harrington, Jr.
  Henry Masterson .... Herb Voland
  George, the butler .... Ivor Barry

Longfellow Deeds, a young newspaper editor in
the small town of Mandrake Falls, suddenly inherited the multimillion-dollar corporation founded
by his uncle, the unscrupulous Alonzo P. Deeds.
Young Mr. Deeds promptly moved to New York to
take over the corporation, and use the money to
right the wrongs his uncle had perpetrated. His
country naivete and extreme honesty almost
brought him down in the cutthroat world of big
business. Tony Lawrence was Uncle Alonzo's former public-relations man who became Longfellow
Deeds' best friend and confidant, and Mr. Masterson was the continually infuriated chairman of the
board of Deeds Enterprises.
  Based rather loosely on the 1936 Gary Cooper
movie of the same name.

MR. DISTRICT ATTORNEY
  Police Drama
FIRST TELECAST: *October 1, 1951*

LAST TELECAST: *June 23, 1952*
BROADCAST HISTORY:
Oct 1951–Jun 1952, ABC Mon 8:00–8:30
CAST:
District Attorney Paul Garrett .... Jay Jostyn
Harrington .... Len Doyle
Miss Miller .... Vicki Vola

Mr. District Attorney was one of the most popular radio crime shows of the 1940s, largely because of its uncanny realism. It was often based on real headlines, and in some cases actually anticipated them. In addition, the lead character was based on a real, and very famous, D.A.—New York's crime-busting Thomas E. Dewey, who later became governor of the state and a two-time candidate for President of the U.S.

The leads in the TV version were the same as those through most of the radio run, Jay Jostyn as the relentless D.A., Len Doyle as an ex-cop who was his investigator, and Vicki Vola as his secretary. Producer Edward C. Byron, who had created the radio show in 1939, also supervised the TV series. The opening lines will be remembered by any fan of either the radio or TV show: "Mister District Attorney! Champion of the people! Guardian of our fundamental rights to life, liberty and the pursuit of happiness!"

Mr. District Attorney was produced live and alternated with *The Amazing Mr. Malone* during the 1951–1952 season. A syndicated version was produced in 1954, with David Brian in the lead role and Jackie Loughery as Miss Miller.

MR. ED
Situation Comedy
FIRST TELECAST: *October 1, 1961*
LAST TELECAST: *September 8, 1965*
BROADCAST HISTORY:
Oct 1961–Sep 1962, CBS Sun 6:30–7:00
Sep 1962–Mar 1963, CBS Thu 7:30–8:00
Mar 1963–Oct 1964, CBS Sun 6:30–7:00
Dec 1964–Sep 1965, CBS Wed 7:30–8:00
CAST:
Wilbur Post .... Alan Young
Carol Post.................... Connie Hines
Roger Addison (1961–1963) .... Larry Keating
Kay Addison (1961–1964) ...... Edna Skinner
Gordon Kirkwood (1963–1965).... Leon Ames
Winnie Kirkwood (1963–1965)
 .... Florence MacMichael
Voice of Mr. Ed .... Allan "Rocky" Lane

One of the more nonsensical TV comedies was this series about a talking horse. Ed belonged to Wilbur Post, a young architect who had decided to move out of the city and get a little closer to nature. The rambling country home Wilbur and his wife bought was everything they had imagined, except for one thing—with it came a palomino that could talk. Mr. Ed didn't talk to everybody; in fact he would only talk to Wilbur, because Wilbur was the first person worth talking

to he had met. The confusion caused by a talking horse, and the situations Ed got Wilbur into, and occasionally out of, formed the stories. Larry Keating was featured as the Posts' next-door neighbor. Unfortunately he passed away shortly after the start of the 1963–1964 season. Edna Skinner, as his wife, remained a while longer but was phased out as the Posts got new neighbors that December. After leaving the nighttime schedule in 1965, *Mr. Ed* continued for one more season, airing on Sundays from 5:30–6:00 P.M. The only regular cast members during the 1965–1966 season were Ed and the Posts. Allan "Rocky" Lane, who provided the resonant, gravelly voice of Mr. Ed, was a retired actor who had starred in scores of low-budget Westerns in the 1930s.

Mr. Ed had actually premiered as a syndicated series, with the same cast as the network version, in January 1961. It was one of the few series to begin in syndication and then be picked by a network for its prime-time lineup.

MR. GARLUND
Adventure
FIRST TELECAST: *October 7, 1960*
LAST TELECAST: *January 13, 1961*
BROADCAST HISTORY:
Oct 1960–Jan 1961, CBS Fri 9:30–10:00
CAST:
Frank Garlund............ Charles Quinlivan
Kam Chang .... Kam Tong

At the age of 30, Frank Garlund had already amassed a considerable fortune. He was a financial wizard whose skill and conspicuous success had brought him into contact with a myriad of people, both honest and dishonest, none of whom were quite the same after their association with him. The young Mr. Garlund had a mysterious background and few close associates. The one person in whom he did confide, and from whom he sought counsel, was his foster brother, Kam Chang. Stories revolved around Garlund's rise in the world of international business and intrigue. The title of this series was changed to *The Garlund Touch* on November 11, 1960.

MR. I MAGINATION
Children's
FIRST TELECAST: *May 29, 1949*
LAST TELECAST: *April 13, 1952*
BROADCAST HISTORY:
May 1949–Jul 1949, CBS Sun 7:00–7:30
Jul 1949, CBS Sun 7:30–8:00
Aug 1949–Sep 1949, CBS Sun 7:30–7:55
Oct 1949–Jun 1951, CBS Sun 6:30–7:00 (OS)
Jan 1952–Feb 1952, CBS Sun 6:30–7:00
Feb 1952–Apr 1952, CBS Sun 6:00–6:30
REGULARS:
Paul Tripp
Ruth Enders
Ted Tiller
Joe Silver

The title role of *Mr. I Magination* was played by the versatile Paul Tripp, author of *Tubby the Tuba* and other stories for children. Not only did he star in the show, but he created it and wrote many of the fantasies which were presented. Children who viewed this live series were asked to send in letters describing something that they wished could happen. Tripp and his fellow regulars would then transform the wishes into television playlets. Each show opened with Tripp in candy-striped overalls, as the engineer of a train carrying children to Imaginationland. The passengers got off at places like Ambitionville, Inventorsville, Seaport City, and "I Wish I Were" Town. That last stop was the point from which plays based on the life of various historical figures were done, with a young (9–12) actor as the historical figure. *Mr. I Magination* began as a local show in New York, and expanded to a four-station network on May 29, 1949, five weeks after its premiere.

MR. LUCKY
Adventure
FIRST TELECAST: *October 24, 1959*
LAST TELECAST: *September 3, 1960*
BROADCAST HISTORY:
  Oct 1959–Sep 1960, CBS Sat 9:00–9:30
CAST:
  Mr. Lucky .... John Vivyan
  Andamo .... Ross Martin
  Lt. Rovacs .... Tom Brown
  Maggie Shank-Rutherford .... Pippa Scott
  Maitre'd .... Joe Scott
THEME:
  "Mr. Lucky," by Henry Mancini

Mr. Lucky was an honest professional gambler who had won a plush floating casino, the ship *Fortuna,* and made it his base of operations. Staying beyond the 12-mile limit, where he could operate a gambling ship legally, Mr. Lucky played host to a wide variety of people, all of whom came to make use of his sumptuous facility. Helping him run the casino was his good friend Andamo. When he got into scrapes that required police assistance, Lt. Rovacs usually provided it. The music from this series, composed by Henry Mancini, produced two successful albums, *The Music from Mr. Lucky* and *Mr. Lucky Goes Latin.* Based on the 1943 movie of the same name starring Cary Grant.

MR. MAGOO
see *Famous Adventures of Mr. Magoo, The*

MR. MERLIN
Situation Comedy
FIRST TELECAST: *October 7, 1981*
LAST TELECAST: *August 18, 1982*
BROADCAST HISTORY:
  Oct 1981–Jan 1982, CBS Wed 8:00–8:30
  Jan 1982–Mar 1982, CBS Mon 8:00–8:30
  Jul 1982–Aug 1982, CBS Wed 8:00–8:30
CAST:
  Max Merlin .... Barnard Hughes
  Zachary Rogers .... Clark Brandon
  Leo Samuels .... Jonathan Prince
  Alexandra .... Elaine Joyce

What better cover for an ageless sorcerer than running a garage in a run-down section of San Francisco? Who would believe that crusty old Max Merlin in his greasy coveralls was the same Merlin renowned in the days of King Arthur's Court? Fifteen-year-old Zac Rogers certainly didn't take Max seriously when the old man offered him the opportunity to become an apprentice sorcerer. But when he found out that this was no joke, Zac figured that learning magic could solve all his problems—with girls, with money, with his grades at school, and with just about anything else. Max believed that Zac could become a responsible sorcerer, and spent an entire TV season trying to train him, despite the troubles that Zac got into—casting the wrong spells, partially casting spells that got out of control, misusing potions, alienating Max's superiors, almost revealing his newfound magical powers to normal people, etc. Leo was Zac's best friend, who often got caught up in the disasters caused by his buddy's imperfect magic, and Alexandra was the beautiful liaison between Max (and Zac) and the all-powerful sorcerers to whom he was responsible.

MR. NOVAK
Drama
FIRST TELECAST: *September 24, 1963*
LAST TELECAST: *August 31, 1965*
BROADCAST HISTORY:
  Sep 1963–Aug 1965, NBC Tue 7:30–8:30
CAST:
  John Novak .... James Franciscus
  Albert Vane .... Dean Jagger
  Jean Pagano (1963–1964) .... Jeanne Bal
  Martin Woodridge (1964–1965)
  .... Burgess Meredith
  Larry Thor .... Jim Hendriks
  Nurse Bromfield (1963–1964) .... Marion Ross
  Mr. Jerry Allen (1963–1964) ... Steve Franken
  Mr. Gallo (1963–1964) .... Donald Barry
  Miss Marilyn Scott .... Marian Collier
  Mr. Pete Butler .... Vince Howard
  Mr. Everett Johns .... André Phillippe
  Mr. Stan Peeples .... Stephen Roberts
  Mrs. Ann Floyd .... Kathleen Ellis
  Miss Rosemary Dorsey (1964–1965)
  .... Marjorie Corley
  Ruth Wilkinson (1964–1965) ... Phyllis Avery
  Mr. Arthur Bradwell (1964–1965)
  .... William Zuckert
  Paul Webb (1964–1965) .... David Sheiner
  Mr. Parkson (1964–1965) .... Peter Hansen
  Mrs. Ring (1965) .... Irene Tedrow

The challenges, accomplishments, and frustrations of a young high school English teacher on his first job provided the stories in this series. John Novak started his career at Jefferson High School in Los Angeles under Principal Albert Vane who, although not in complete agreement with Mr. Novak's approach to teaching, took a strong liking to him as a dedicated teacher. When Vane was elected to the post of state superintendent of schools, he chose Martin Woodridge, another English teacher at Jefferson High, to replace him as principal. A large number of teachers and other school staff members had recurring roles during the two years *Mr. Novak* was on the air.

MR. PEEPERS
Situation Comedy
FIRST TELECAST: *July 3, 1952*
LAST TELECAST: *June 12, 1955*
BROADCAST HISTORY:
Jul 1952–Sep 1952, NBC Thu 9:30–10:00
Oct 1952–Jul 1953, NBC Sun 7:30–8:00
Sep 1953–Jun 1955, NBC Sun 7:30–8:00
CAST:

Robinson Peepers	Wally Cox
Rayola Dean (1952)	Norma Crane
Charlie Burr (1952)	David Tyrell
Mr. Gabriel Gurney (1952–1953)	
	Joseph Foley
Mrs. Gurney	Marion Lorne
Superintendent Bascom	Gage Clark
Nancy Remington	Patricia Benoit
Harvey Weskit	Tony Randall
Mr. Remington	Ernest Truex
Marge Weskit	Georgann Johnson
Mr. Hansen (1953–1954)	Arthur O'Connell
Mrs. Remington (1953–1955)	Sylvia Field
Frank Whip (1953–1955)	Jack Warden
Mom Peepers (1953–1955)	Ruth McDevitt
Agnes Peepers (1953–1955)	Jenny Egan
Aunt Lil (1954)	Reta Shaw

Jefferson High School, located in the small Midwestern town of Jefferson City, was the setting for this live situation comedy. The central character was Robinson Peepers, a shy, quiet, slow-moving science teacher whose efforts to do the right thing always seemed to backfire. He was such a nice guy that everyone on the staff tried to mother him and the students all thought he was great, despite being laughable at times. His best friend was history teacher Harvey Weskit, whose brash self-confidence contrasted with Robinson's low-key personality. Other regulars in the cast were the school nurse, Nancy Remington, English teacher Mrs. Gurney (whose husband was the principal for the first season), and their families.

Mr. Peepers went on the air in the summer of 1952 with a scheduled eight-week run and was slotted for oblivion when the regular fall season began. At the start of the season, however, an NBC filmed series called *Doc Corkle* met with such overwhelming critical and public castigation that it was canceled after only three episodes had been aired. *Mr. Peepers* was rushed back into

production and returned on the last Sunday in October. The one major change was in Robinson's romantic interest. During the summer it had been music appreciation teacher Rayola Dean. Nurse Nancy Remington became his girlfriend that fall. Almost as quiet and unassuming as Robinson, she just seemed "right" for him. Their romance blossomed and at the end of the 1953–1954 season they were married on the air, an event that excited viewers at the time in much the same way that Rhoda's TV marriage would do more than 20 years later.

MR. PRESIDENT
Situation Comedy
FIRST TELECAST: *May 3, 1987*
LAST TELECAST: *April 2, 1988*
BROADCAST HISTORY:
May 1987–Sep 1987, FOX Sun 9:00–9:30
Sep 1987–Oct 1987, FOX Sun 9:30–10:00
Oct 1987–Jan 1988, FOX Sat 8:00–8:30
Jan 1988–Apr 1988, FOX Sat 9:30–10:00
CAST:

President Samuel Arthur Tresch	
	George C. Scott
Meg Tresch (1987)	Carlin Glynn
Cynthia Tresch (age 16)	Maddie Corman
Nick Tresch (age 12)	André Gower
Charlie Ross	Conrad Bain
Lois Gullickson	Madeline Kahn
Daniel Cummings	Allen Williams
Dave	Earl Boen

The return to series television of renowned actor George C. Scott—the man who 23 years earlier, after the failure of his first series, said he would never do another, and the only actor *ever* to refuse an Emmy Award—was a media event in 1987. He was doing it, he said bluntly, for the money.

The series was about the home life of a U.S. President. Former Wisconsin Governor Sam Tresch was newly elected, and living in the White House was quite an adjustment for his entire family. Nobody had any privacy, reporters were always snooping for any sort of story, and the Secret Service was everywhere they looked. Sam was a gruff, somewhat grouchy, very determined man (Scott's patented Patton-esque character), and he could take it. However, his wife, Meg, couldn't, and in the fall of 1987 she left Sam "to find herself," leaving the President and the two rambunctious kids, Cynthia and Nick, to fend for themselves. (An older daughter, Jennifer, was married and rarely seen.) The role of First Lady was assumed by Meg's sister Lois, a flaky woman with delusions of grandeur who had the hots for Sam and thought this was her big chance.

Affable Charlie Ross, who had been with Sam since early in his political career, was the loyal Chief of Staff; Daniel and Dave were others on the squabbling White House staff.

MR. ROBERTS

Comedy/Adventure

FIRST TELECAST: *September 17, 1965*
LAST TELECAST: *September 2, 1966*
BROADCAST HISTORY:

   Sep 1965–Sep 1966, NBC Fri 9:30–10:00

CAST:

   Lt. (j.g.) Douglas Roberts .... Roger Smith
   Ensign Frank Pulver .... Steve Harmon
   Captain John Morton ..... Richard X. Slattery
   Doc .... George Ives
   Seaman D'Angelo .... Richard Sinatra
   Seaman Mannion .... Ronald Starr
   Seaman Reber .... Roy Reese

The adventures of the crew of the *U.S.S. Reluctant,* a cargo ship operating far behind the lines in the South Pacific during World War II, provided the stories for this comedy. Life on board was incredibly dull and monotonous, especially for young Mr. Roberts. He wanted the opportunity to really participate in the war effort, not slosh around in the middle of nowhere on a mangy old tub, and was desperately trying to get transferred to another ship. Ensign Pulver was the crewman who was always scheming to find ways of livening up the otherwise boring existence of the crew—as long as no real work was involved. Stern old Captain Morton was the major concern of most of the crew—they were preoccupied with finding ways to drive him slowly out of his mind.

Based on the book by Thomas Heggen, which was subsequently made into a hit play (1948), and a movie (1955) starring Henry Fonda, Jack Lemmon, and James Cagney.

MR. SMITH

Situation Comedy

FIRST TELECAST: *September 23, 1983*
LAST TELECAST: *December 16, 1983*
BROADCAST HISTORY:

   Sep 1983–Dec 1983, NBC Fri 8:00–8:30

CAST:

   Raymond Holyoke .... Leonard Frey
   Tommy Atwood .... Tim Dunigan
   Ellie Atwood .... Laura Jacoby
   Dr. Judy Tyson .... Terri Garber
   Cha Cha/Mr. Smith
             .... C.J. (voice: Ed Weinberger)
   Dr. Klein .... Stuart Margolin

One of the most talked about but least viewed series of the 1983–1984 season was this light comedy about a talking orangutan. Cha Cha had been an ordinary circus orangutan until his inquisitiveness and thirst (he drank a whole bottle of experimental enzyme) transformed him into a talking primate genius with an I.Q. of 256. The government figured that made him smarter than anybody in Washington, and set him up as a special consultant on such things as nuclear energy and MX missile policy. He was renamed Mr. Smith, given a human wardrobe (except for shoes) and a pair

of spectacles, and moved into a suburban Washington house along with his dimwitted former owner, Tommy, Tommy's smart-alecky kid sister, Ellie, and, eventually, his ordinary brother orangutan Bo Bo.

Attending to Mr. Smith's needs, and keeping a watchful eye on America's newest secret weapon, was prissy Raymond Holyoke, whose previous work had been as personal secretary to presidents and ambassadors. Dr. Judy Tyson was a research scientist from the Institute for Primate Studies who kept track of Mr. Smith's development, and Dr. Klein was her boss. Unfortunately the opportunity for political satire was never really exploited, as stories focused mostly on family contretemps and little misunderstandings, and the series was short-lived.

The orangutan who played Mr. Smith was already a star, having been featured in two Clint Eastwood movies, *Any Which Way You Can* and *Every Which Way But Loose,* and Bo Derek's version of *Tarzan.* Series co-executive producer Ed Weinberger provided his voice.

MR. SMITH GOES TO WASHINGTON

Situation Comedy

FIRST TELECAST: *September 29, 1962*
LAST TELECAST: *March 30, 1963*
BROADCAST HISTORY:

   Sep 1962–Mar 1963, ABC Sat 8:30–9:00

CAST:

   Sen. Eugene Smith .... Fess Parker
   Pat Smith .... Sandra Warner
   Uncle Cooter .... Red Foley
   Arnie .... Stan Irwin
   Miss Kelly .... Rita Lynn

While starring as Davy Crockett in the mid-1950s, Fess Parker was at one point called upon to portray Crockett as a rustic representative to the United States Congress. In this series Parker once again headed for Washington, this time in contemporary garb, but with the same low-keyed, homespun approach to national—and family—politics and problems. Freshman Senator Eugene Smith and his wife Pat were from a small town, and they used the homilies of Middle America to cope with urban, political Washington. Arnie was Senator Smith's chauffeur, Uncle Cooter his philosophical, guitar-strumming uncle, and Miss Kelly his secretary.

Based on the 1939 movie starring James Stewart.

MR. SUNSHINE

Situation Comedy

FIRST TELECAST: *March 28, 1986*
LAST TELECAST: *September 3, 1986*
BROADCAST HISTORY:

   Mar 1986–May 1986, ABC Fri 9:00–9:30
   May 1986, ABC Sat 8:00–8:30
   Jun 1986–Jul 1986, ABC Fri 9:00–9:30
   Aug 1986–Sep 1986, ABC Wed 8:30–9:00

CAST:

Prof. Paul Stark	Jeffrey Tambor
Grace D'Angelo................	Nan Martin
Mrs. June Swinford	Barbara Babcock
Prof. Leon Walters...........	Leonard Frey
Janice Hall...................	Cecilia Hart
Warren Leftwich	David Knell

EXECUTIVE PRODUCERS:

John Rich and Henry Winkler

One of TV's rare attempts to deal with the subject of blindness in a series setting. Paul Stark was a tall, balding, and very acerbic English professor who had suffered two recent blows: he had been blinded in an accident, and divorced by his wife. He coped with his handicap fairly well, physically at least, continuing to teach and even reentering the singles scene (Janice was his chief romantic interest, though by their relationship you might not know it). Mrs. Swinford was his flighty landlady, Grace his caustic personal secretary, and Leon a drama professor. Paul neither asked for nor got pity; sometimes he helped his friends, in his domineering way, and sometimes they helped him.

MR. T. AND TINA
Situation Comedy
FIRST TELECAST: *September 25, 1976*
LAST TELECAST: *October 30, 1976*
BROADCAST HISTORY:
Sep 1976–Oct 1976, ABC Sat 8:30–9:00
CAST:

Taro Takahashi ("Mr. T.")	Pat Morita
Tina Kelly	Susan Blanchard
Michi	Pat Suzuki
Harvard.......................	Ted Lange
Miss Llewellyn	Miriam Byrd-Nethery
Uncle Matsu	"Jerry" Hatsuo Fujikawa
Sachi	June Angela
Aki	Gene Profanato

A comedy of clashing cultures. Mr. T. was a brilliant Japanese inventor who had been transferred by his firm from Tokyo to Chicago. There, he had to cope with the Americanization of his household by a nutty, effervescent, Nebraska-born housekeeper named Tina. Tina was well-intentioned but sometimes her ideas of a happy home were at fearful odds with the traditional, male-dominated society from which the Takahashis had so recently come. Michi was Mr. T.'s sister-in-law, Uncle Matsu the staunch traditionalist, and Sachi and Aki the two children. On the American side were Harvard, the hip handyman, and Miss Llewellyn, the landlady.

MR. TERRIFIC
Situation Comedy
FIRST TELECAST: *January 9, 1967*
LAST TELECAST: *August 28, 1967*
BROADCAST HISTORY:
Jan 1967–Aug 1967, CBS Mon 8:00–8:30

CAST:

Stanley Beamish (Mr. Terrific)	Stephen Strimpell
Barton J. Reed...............	John McGiver
Hal Walters...................	Dick Gautier
Harley Trent	Paul Smith

Stanley Beamish was a young gas station operator whose partner in the service station, as well as his best friend and roommate, was Hal Walters. Stanley did have one secret that he kept from his buddy—with the aid of special top-secret power pills he could become that caped crime fighter, Mr. Terrific. The pills had been developed by the Bureau of Secret Projects, a special government agency. BSP chief Barton J. Reed sent Stanley on his missions and supplied him with the pills. A power pill would give him extraordinary abilities for only one hour. In emergencies he could take two booster pills, each good for an extra 20 minutes, but after that he reverted to normal. He was a nice, soft-spoken, naive guy who, unfortunately for the BSP, was the only person on whom the pills worked. His efforts to serve his government were noble, but not always what Mr. Reed would have liked. Stanley was too gullible, too considerate, and frequently too preoccupied to pay attention to the time limits of his powers. He had a disturbing propensity for returning to normal at the most inopportune times.

MR. WIZARD
see *Watch Mr. Wizard*

MIXED DOUBLES
Drama
FIRST TELECAST: *August 5, 1949*
LAST TELECAST: *October 29, 1949*
BROADCAST HISTORY:
Aug 1949–Sep 1949, NBC Fri 9:00–9:30
Sep 1949–Oct 1949, NBC Sat 8:30–9:00
CAST:

Elaine Coleman (first 2 weeks)	Rhoda Williams
Elaine Coleman	Bonnie Baken
Eddy Coleman...............	Eddy Firestone
Ada Abbott	Ada Friedman
Bill Abbott	Billy Idelson

This early prime-time soap opera was about two newly married couples living side by side in one-room apartments, trying to build their lives on the husbands' meager incomes. Eddy and Bill were both copywriters at large advertising agencies. The program was created by Carleton E. Morse *(One Man's Family)* and first seen locally on the West Coast.

MOBILE ONE
Adventure
FIRST TELECAST: *September 12, 1975*
LAST TELECAST: *December 29, 1975*

   Sep 1975–Oct 1975, ABC Fri 8:00–9:00
   Oct 1975–Dec 1975, ABC Mon 8:00–9:00
CAST:
   Peter Campbell . . . . Jackie Cooper
   Maggie Spencer . . . . Julie Gregg
   Doug McKnight . . . . Mark Wheeler
EXECUTIVE PRODUCER:
   Jack Webb

Jackie Cooper, whose first acting experience was as a member of the *Our Gang* comedies in 1925 (at age 3), played a veteran TV news reporter in this 1975 series. Together with his producer Maggie, cameraman Doug, and the mobile unit from station KONE, he covered hard news and human-interest stories in a large city (not named, but the series was filmed in and around Los Angeles).

MOD SQUAD, THE
Police Drama
FIRST TELECAST: *September 24, 1968*
LAST TELECAST: *August 23, 1973*
BROADCAST HISTORY:
   Sep 1968–Aug 1972, ABC Tue 7:30–8:30
   Sep 1972–Aug 1973, ABC Thu 8:00–9:00
CAST:
   Pete Cochran . . . . Michael Cole
   Linc Hayes . . . . Clarence Williams III
   Julie Barnes . . . . Peggy Lipton
   Capt. Adam Greer . . . . Tige Andrews
CREATOR:
   Bud Ruskin

The Mod Squad was probably the ultimate example of the establishment co-opting the youth movement of the late 1960s. Its three members were "hippie cops," each of them a drop-out from straight society who had had his own brush with the law. Pete was a longhaired youth who had been kicked out by his wealthy Beverly Hills parents and stolen a car; Linc was the Afroed son of a ghetto family of 13, raised in Watts and arrested in the Watts rioting; Julie was the daughter of a San Francisco prostitute who had run away from home and been arrested for vagrancy. All three were on probation and looking for some way to make sense out of their lives when they were approached by Capt. Adam Greer, who recruited them for a special "youth squad." Their purpose was to infiltrate the counterculture and ferret out the adult criminals who preyed upon the young in Southern California (no finking on their own generation, thank you).

A contentious trio, always questioning their own motives and their differing cultural backgrounds, the *Mod Squad* nevertheless proved an effective undercover task force against adult crime. For the first season they rattled around in a battered old 1950 station wagon named "Woody," but this was killed off early in the second season (driven over a cliff).

Strangely enough, *The Mod Squad* was based on the true experiences of creator Bud Ruskin, a former police officer and later private detective. While a member of the Los Angeles Sheriff's Department in the 1950s he was a member of an undercover narcotics squad composed of young officers, which served as the inspiration for *The Mod Squad*. He first wrote a pilot script for the series in 1960, but it took eight more years before it reached the air in this highly successful ABC program.

MODERN SCIENCE THEATER
Documentary
FIRST TELECAST: *January 30, 1958*
LAST TELECAST: *March 13, 1958*
BROADCAST HISTORY:
   Jan 1958–Mar 1958, ABC Thu 10:00–10:30

Documentary films on science and industry.

MOHAWK SHOWROOM
Music
FIRST TELECAST: *May 2, 1949*
LAST TELECAST: *November 23, 1951*
BROADCAST HISTORY:
   May 1949–Dec 1949, NBC Mon–Fri 7:30–7:45
   Dec 1949–Jul 1951, NBC Mon/Wed/Fri 7:30–7:45
   Sep 1951–Nov 1951, NBC Mon/Wed/Fri 7:30–7:45
REGULARS:
   Morton Downey (1949)
   Trio (Carmen Mastren, Jim Ruhl, Trigger Alpert) (1949)
   Roberta Quinlan
   Harry Clark Trio
   Bob Stanton

Live musical program with guest stars. For the first few months Morton Downey was featured on Monday, Wednesday, and Friday, while Roberta Quinlan appeared on Tuesday and Thursday. Beginning in December 1949 Miss Quinlan was the sole host. Sometimes announcer Bob Stanton also took part in the proceedings.

MOMENT OF DECISION
Dramatic Anthology
FIRST TELECAST: *July 3, 1957*
LAST TELECAST: *September 25, 1957*
BROADCAST HISTORY:
   Jul 1957–Sep 1957, ABC Wed 9:30–10:00

The dramas that made up this 1957 summer series consisted of reruns of episodes previously aired on *Ford Theatre*.

MOMENT OF FEAR
Dramatic Anthology
FIRST TELECAST: *July 1, 1960*
LAST TELECAST: *August 10, 1965*
BROADCAST HISTORY:
   Jul 1960–Sep 1960, NBC Fri 10:00–11:00

May 1964–Sep 1964, NBC Tue 8:30–9:00
May 1965–Aug 1965, NBC Tue 8:30–9:00

The 1960 version of *Moment of Fear* consisted of live dramas dealing with individuals who reached emotional crises in their lives. In the summers of 1964 and 1965 *Moment of Fear* was made up of filmed reruns of episodes from other anthology series. In 1964 the reruns were from *G.E. Theater, Schlitz Playhouse, Lux Video Theatre,* and *Studio 57.* In 1965 they came from the above four shows plus *Pepsi Cola Playhouse.*

MOMENTS OF MUSIC
Music
FIRST TELECAST: *July 24, 1951*
LAST TELECAST: *September 11, 1951*
BROADCAST HISTORY:
Jul 1951–Sep 1951, ABC Tue 8:30–8:45

A short, and short-lived, filmed program of music.

MONA MCCLUSKEY
Situation Comedy
FIRST TELECAST: *September 16, 1965*
LAST TELECAST: *April 14, 1966*
BROADCAST HISTORY:
Sep 1965–Apr 1966, NBC Thu 9:30–10:00
CAST:
Mona McCluskey .... Juliet Prowse
Mike McCluskey .... Denny (Scott) Miller
Gen. Crone .... Herb Rudley
Frank Caldwell .... Bartlett Robinson
Sgt. Gruzewsky .... Robert Strauss
Alice Henderson .... Elena Verdugo

Mona Carroll was a beautiful Hollywood star who made the astronomical salary of $5,000 per week. She was married to Mike McCluskey, a sergeant in the air force whose salary was $500 per month. In order to let her husband prove that he could support her, Mona lived with him in a two-room apartment and promised not to use any of her money to supplement his income. Her tastes, coupled with the knowledge that she really had much more money than she could spend, prompted Mona to try all sorts of schemes to improve her husband's financial situation.

MONDAY NIGHT SPECIAL
Varied Format
FIRST TELECAST: *January 10, 1972*
LAST TELECAST: *August 14, 1972*
BROADCAST HISTORY:
Jan 1972–Aug 1972, ABC Mon 8:00–9:00

Throughout most of 1972, ABC set aside the 8:00–9:00 P.M. hour on Monday nights as a place for regular "specials." The programs telecast in this time slot varied greatly in format. Included were Jacques Cousteau nature programs, documentaries on athletics, an occasional circus, and Danny Kaye starring in "The Emperor's New Clothes."

MONDAY SPORTSNITE
Sports News
FIRST TELECAST: *June 1, 1987*
LAST TELECAST: *August 31, 1987*
BROADCAST HISTORY:
Jun 1987–Aug 1987, ABC Mon 12:00–1:00 A.M.
HOST:
Al Trautwig

A 1986 summer series featuring interviews and off-beat moments in the week's sporting events.

MONDAY THEATRE
Anthology
FIRST TELECAST: *July 21, 1969*
LAST TELECAST: *August 10, 1970*
BROADCAST HISTORY:
Jul 1969–Sep 1969, NBC Mon 8:00–8:30
Jul 1970–Aug 1970, NBC Mon 8:00–8:30

Monday Theatre spent two summers as a partial replacement for Rowan & Martin's *Laugh-In.* It was comprised of pilots for projected situation-comedy series in 1969 and projected adventure and drama series in 1970. None of them ever made the jump from pilot to regular series.

MONITOR
News Magazine
FIRST TELECAST: *March 12, 1983*
LAST TELECAST: *April 1, 1984*
BROADCAST HISTORY:
Mar 1983–Aug 1983, NBC Sat 10:00–11:00
Sep 1983–Apr 1984, NBC Sun 7:00–8:00
REGULARS:
Lloyd Dobyns
Steve Delaney
Rebecca Sobel

Lloyd Dobyns was the in-studio anchorman for this weekly news magazine series, with Steve Delaney and Rebecca Sobel filing weekly stories. Some of the stories were serious—"Children Don't Do That," on the problem of child suicide, and "Your Land Is My Land," about the dispute between Arabs and Jews over who had the right to live on the West Bank in Israel. Others were light—"King Pong," a profile of the inventor of Atari, and "The Survival of Peter O'Toole," with the actor reminiscing about his career.

In September 1983 the series changed its name to *First Camera* and moved to Sunday night, in a suicidal attempt to compete head-on with the number-one hit *60 Minutes.* A few months later, *First Camera* was no more.

MONKEES, THE
Situation Comedy
FIRST TELECAST: *September 12, 1966*
LAST TELECAST: *August 19, 1968*
BROADCAST HISTORY:
Sep 1966–Aug 1968, NBC Mon 7:30–8:00

CAST:
Davy (guitar) .... David Jones
Peter (guitar) .... Peter Tork
Micky (drums) .... Micky Dolenz
Mike (guitar) ... Mike Nesmith ("Wool Hat")
MUSIC SUPERVISION:
Don Kirshner

This was a free-form youth-oriented comedy series, inspired by the Beatles' film *A Hard Day's Night* (1964). *The Monkees* was similarly unconventional, utilizing surrealistic film techniques (fast and slow motion, distorted focus, comic film inserts), one-liners, non sequiturs, etc., all delivered at a very fast pace. The Monkees played a rock quartet that got into all sorts of bizarre scrapes as they rescued maidens, ran afoul of dastardly villains, and generally played pranks on the world.

The Monkees simultaneously had a highly successful career on records, a fact which has driven some rock critics into paroxysms of fury since they were so obviously a "manufactured" group. The four members were carefully picked from among nearly 500 applicants in auditions held during the fall of 1965, then drilled and rehearsed until they could pass as reasonably competent musicians (Dolenz and Jones were actors, Tork and Nesmith had some previous musical experience). They were not allowed to play their instruments on their early records, supplying only the vocals, a fact which led to some embarrassment when they went on tour and could not re-create their recorded sound. It also led to dissension among the boys, some of whom had real musical ambitions. Nevertheless their discs, heavily promoted and carefully coordinated with the TV series, sold in the millions. (These included "Last Train to Clarksville," "I'm a Believer," and "Words.") Finally there was a showdown with the program's producers, following a rather remarkable 1967 press conference in which Nesmith bitterly complained that "we're being passed off as something we aren't." The boys were later allowed to "do their own thing" musically. Despite its commercial success, however, the group broke up shortly after the series left the air in 1968.

The Monkees was later seen on CBS in reruns on Saturday mornings, from September 1969 to September 1973. See also *New Monkees*

MONROES, THE
Western
FIRST TELECAST: *September 7, 1966*
LAST TELECAST: *August 30, 1967*
BROADCAST HISTORY:
Sep 1966–Aug 1967, ABC Wed 8:00–9:00
CAST:
Clayt Monroe .... Michael Anderson, Jr.
Kathy Monroe .... Barbara Hershey
Jefferson Monroe .... Keith Schultz
Fennimore Monroe .... Kevin Schultz
Amy Monroe .... Tammy Locke

Major Mapoy .... Liam Sullivan
Dirty Jim .... Ron Soble
Sleeve .... Ben Johnson
Ruel Jaxon .... Jim Westmoreland
Barney Wales .... Robert Middleton
John Bradford ("Brad") .... Buck Taylor

The story of five orphaned youngsters, aged 6 to 18, who fought to establish a homestead in the rugged Wyoming Territory of 1876, after their parents had drowned. Leaders of the crew were Clayt (18) and Kathy (16), who looked after the 13-year-old twins Jeff ("Big Twin") and Fenn ("Little Twin"), 6-year-old Amy, and a dog named Snow. Their ally was the renegade Indian Dirty Jim, and the villain in the piece was wicked British cattle baron Major Mapoy, who wanted their land (heh-heh!). Jaxon was one of Mapoy's cowboys.

Filmed on location in the rugged Grand Teton National Park area of Wyoming.

MONTEFUSCOS, THE
Situation Comedy
FIRST TELECAST: *September 4, 1975*
LAST TELECAST: *October 16, 1975*
BROADCAST HISTORY:
Sep 1975–Oct 1975, NBC Thu 8:00–8:30
CAST:
Tony Montefusco .... Joe Sirola
Rose Montefusco .... Naomi Stevens
Frank Montefusco .... Ron Carey
Joseph Montefusco .... John Aprea
Theresa Montefusco .... Phoebe Dorin
Angela Montefusco Cooney ...... Linda Dano
Jim Cooney .... Bill Cort
Nunzio Montefusco .... Sal Viscuso
Anthony Carmine Montefusco
.... Jeffrey Palladini
Jerome Montefusco .... Robby Paris
Gina Montefusco .... Dominique Pinassi
Anthony Patrick Cooney ..... Damon Raskin

This short-lived series was about Tony Montefusco, a boisterous, middle-class Italian, living in Connecticut, who had his entire family over for dinner every Sunday night. The subjects that came up and situations that developed at, prior to, and following Sunday dinner provided the stories of the series. Tony's wife, Rose, his three sons and one daughter, and their families made up the entire cast. Frankie was a dentist, Joseph a priest, and Nunzio an unemployed actor, while Angela was married to Jim Cooney, the token WASP. Theresa was Frankie's wife.

Carmine, Jerome, and Gina were Frankie's children and Anthony Patrick was Angela's son.

MONTGOMERY'S SUMMER STOCK
see *Robert Montgomery Presents*

MOONLIGHTING
Detective Comedy/Drama
FIRST TELECAST: *March 3, 1985*

LAST TELECAST:
BROADCAST HISTORY:
   Mar 1985, ABC Sun 9:00–11:00
   Mar 1985–Apr 1985, ABC Tue 10:00–11:00
   Aug 1985–   , ABC Tue 9:00–10:00
CAST:
   Maddie Hayes . . . . Cybill Shepherd
   David Addison . . . . Bruce Willis
   Agnes Dipesto . . . . Allyce Beasley
   Herbert Viola (1986–   ) . . Curtis Armstrong
   Virginia Hayes (1987–   ) . Eva Marie Saint
   Alex Hayes (1987–   ) . . . . . Robert Webber
THEME:
   by Lee Holdridge and Al Jarreau, sung by Al
   Jarreau

One of ABC's few major hits in the mid-1980s was
this hip, romantic comedy, which was as much a
TV "in-joke" as a normal detective show. Maddie
was an extremely glamorous, and somewhat icy,
top fashion model who had fallen on hard times
when her manager had cheated her out of her
accumulated fortune. Surveying her few remaining assets she found she owned the Blue Moon
Detective Agency in Los Angeles, a notably unsuccessful venture which she was about to dump,
until its principal employee, cocky David Addison, conned her out of doing so (to save his job).
He then managed to get her involved in the business and the two of them—wisecracking David
and reserved but strong-willed Maddie—became
the city's latest unlikely detective team.

He also lusted for her, in his street-hip way
(with wolf whistles and '60s "girl-watching"
songs), but elegant Maddie resisted. Their uncommon courtship became a main theme of the show;
by the end of the 1985–86 season he finally won a
kiss in a parking garage, but not until the end of
the following season did they finally make love. In
the meantime their rocky relationship survived
breakups, and, in early 1987, her wooing by handsome yuppie Sam Crawford (played by Mark Harmon). Maddie and David each got counseling, she
from Dr. Joyce Brothers and he from Ray Charles.
Eventually, in 1988, she gave birth to David's
baby—although she was married (briefly) to
someone else.

Moonlighting's constant production problems
were widely publicized, and resulted in numerous
repeat episodes. New episodes were eagerly anticipated and were often inventive—for example,
the November 1986 take-off on Shakespeare's
Taming of the Shrew (a dream sequence), with
David as Petruchio and Maddie as Kate. Many
episodes began with the stars doing a little out-of-
character skit, or commenting on the show itself,
before the story began. Sometimes they would
even turn to the camera and talk directly to viewers.

Seen from time to time were Maddie's mother
and father, Virginia and Alex, David's dad, David
Sr. (played by Paul Sorvino), and irresponsible
brother, Richard (Charles Rocket). Agnes was the

slightly daffy, rhyming receptionist, and Herbert
the eager clerk-cum-junior-detective and object of
Agnes' unrequited love.

MOREY AMSTERDAM SHOW, THE
   Comedy Variety
FIRST TELECAST: December 17, 1948
LAST TELECAST: October 12, 1950
BROADCAST HISTORY:
   Dec 1948–Jan 1949, CBS Fri 8:30–9:00
   Jan 1949–Mar 1949, CBS Mon Various
   Apr 1949–Oct 1950, DUM Thu 9:00–9:30
REGULARS:
   Morey Amsterdam
   Art Carney
   Jacqueline Susann
   Johnny Guarnieri Orchestra

In June 1948 Morey Amsterdam premiered a series on the CBS radio network in which he was the
emcee of a small fictional nightclub located in
Times Square in New York City. The club was the
Golden Goose Cafe and the only other regulars in
the series were Art Carney as Charlie the Doorman (later as Newton the Waiter), and Jacqueline
Susann as Lola, the wide-eyed cigarette girl.
Morey told jokes, played his cello, and introduced
guest acts on the show. In December 1948 the
show moved to CBS television, while a separate
radio version continued to be aired. The producer
was Irving Mansfield—Miss Susann's husband.

Then in early 1949 CBS canceled the show, ostensibly not because of low ratings but because
the network already had too many big names to
promote. CBS' loss was DuMont's gain, because
Morey was back a month later with his "yuk-a-
puk" jokes on a Thursday night DuMont variety
show which ran for a year and a half. The setting
changed to the Silver Swan Cafe, but Carney and
Susann remained.

MORK & MINDY
   Situation Comedy
FIRST TELECAST: September 14, 1978
LAST TELECAST: June 10, 1982
BROADCAST HISTORY:
   Sep 1978–Aug 1979, ABC Thu 8:00–8:30
   Aug 1979–Dec 1979, ABC Sun 8:00–8:30
   Jan 1980–Feb 1982, ABC Thu 8:00–8:30
   Apr 1982–May 1982, ABC Thu 8:30–9:00
   May 1982–Jun 1982, ABC Thu 8:00–8:30
CAST:
   Mork . . . . Robin Williams
   Mindy Beth McConnell . . . . Pam Dawber
   Frederick McConnell (1978–1979, 1980–1982)
      . . . . Conrad Janis
   Cora Hudson (1978–1979, 1981–1982)
      . . . . Elizabeth Kerr
   Eugene (1978–1979) . . . . Jeffrey Jacquet
   Orson (voice only) . . . . Ralph James
   Franklin Delano Bickley . . . . Tom Poston
   Remo DaVinci (1979–1981) . . . . Jay Thomas
   Jean DaVinci (1979–1981) . . . . Gina Hecht

528

Nelson Flavor (1979–1981)	Jim Staahl
Exidor	Robert Donner
Glenda Faye "Crissy" Comstock (1980–1981)	
	Crissy Wilzak
Mr. Miles Sternhagen (1981)	Foster Brooks
Mearth (1981–1982)	Jonathan Winters

Mork & Mindy was a spin-off from an episode of *Happy Days* seen in February 1978, in which an alien from the planet Ork landed on Earth and attempted to kidnap Richie. So popular was the nutty character created by Robin Williams that Williams was given his own series in the fall of 1978, and it became an instant hit.

Mork was a misfit on his own planet because of his sense of humor (he was heard to call the Orkan leader, Orson, "cosmic breath"). So the humorless Orkans sent him off to study Earthlings, whose "crazy" customs they had never been able to understand. Mork landed, in a giant eggshell, near Boulder, Colorado. There he was befriended by pretty Mindy McConnell, a clerk at the music store run by her father, Frederick. Mork looked human, but his strange mixture of Orkan and Earthling customs—such as wearing a suit, but putting it on backwards, or sitting in a chair, but upside down—led most people to think of him as just some kind of nut. Mindy knew where he came from, and helped him adjust to Earth's strange ways. She also let him stay in the attic of her apartment house, which scandalized her conservative father, but not her swinging grandmother, Cora.

After a season of simple slapstick and big ratings, both the producers and the network unfortunately got a little cocky and violated one of television's cardinal rules: "Don't tamper with a hit." In the process of doing so, they almost destroyed the program. The producers decided to shift to more "meaningful" stories, opening the second season with a strange, surrealistic episode in which Mork shrunk away to nothing and dropped into a never-never world filled with caricatures of good and evil. At the same time practically the whole supporting cast was changed. Simultaneously ABC decided to move the series from its established Thursday time slot to Sunday, to prop up their sagging schedule on that night. Understandably confused, viewers deserted the show in droves and it lost nearly half its audience.

By December 1979 ABC and the producers were scrambling to undo their mistakes. Mork went back to Thursday, and stories got less complicated. Mindy's father, who had been dumped (along with the grandmother), returned for the third season. He was supposed to have sold the music store and gone on tour as an orchestra conductor, fulfilling a lifelong dream. Now he, but not Cora, was back full-time. Other changes in the second and third seasons included the addition of brother and sister Remo and Jean DaVinci, recently arrived from the Bronx. Remo ran the New York Deli and was helping put Jean through medical school.

Nelson was Mindy's cousin, an uptight young social climber with grandiose political ambitions; Mr. Bickley was the grouchy downstairs neighbor (he had been on before, but his role was enlarged); and Mork's friend Exidor was a crazed prophet and leader of an invisible cult, the Friends of Venus. Mindy, a journalism student, got a job at local TV station KTNS, where her boss was Mr. Sternhagen.

All of this brought back some of the lost viewers, but *Mork & Mindy* never recaptured the enormous following it had during its first season.

The fall of 1981 brought the most surprising developments of all. Mork and Mindy were married, and honeymooned on Ork—which proved to be full of bizarre creatures. Shortly thereafter Mork gave birth, by ejecting a small egg from his navel. The egg grew and grew and finally cracked open to reveal a full-grown Jonathan Winters! Mearth, as they named their first child, weighed 225 pounds and looked middle-aged, but babbled like a baby, calling Mork "Mommy" and Mindy "Shoe." Since things work backwards on Ork, he would gradually grow younger (instead of older) and never want for affection in his waning years.

Despite some hilarious scenes between Robin Williams and his idol Jonathan Winters, the series was by this time losing audience rapidly and left the air at the end of the season. It had succeeded primarily because of the versatile talents of Williams, who mugged, mimicked, and delivered torrents of one-liners and Orkan gibberish. At the end of each episode he reported back to his leader Orson, on Ork, twisting his ears and signing off, "Na nu, na nu"—good-bye in Orkan.

MORNINGSTAR/EVENINGSTAR

Drama

FIRST TELECAST: *March 25, 1986*
LAST TELECAST: *May 6, 1986*
BROADCAST HISTORY:
Mar 1986–May 1986, CBS Tue 8:00–9:00
CAST:

Debbie Flynn	Sherry Hursey
Bob Lane	Darrell Larson
Martha Cameron	Kate Reid
Bill McGregor	Jeff Corey
Binnie Byrd Baylor	Sylvia Sidney
Kathy Kelly	Elizabeth Wilson
Excell Dennis	Scatman Crothers
Gordon Blair	Mason Adams
Nora Blake	Ketty Lester
Alan Bishop	Fred A. Savage
Sarah Bishop	Missy Francis
Kevin Murphy	Chris Peters
Lisa Thurston	Tammy Lauren
Martin Palmer	David Goldsmith
Doug Roberts	Leaf Phoenix
Eugenie Waters	Ebonie Smith

The message of this warm, gentle drama was that there need not be a generation gap between old and young. When a fire destroyed the Morningstar Home, an orphanage administered by social worker Bob Lane, he sought temporary shelter for his waifs in the Eveningstar Home, a well-run senior citizens' facility managed by social worker Debbie Flynn. Bob and Debbie had been friends for a long time, and had mused over the potential advantages of getting the elderly together with the young, to their mutual benefit. The fire had made the experiment a necessity. The senior citizens— Martha, Bill, Binnie, Kathy, Excell, Gordon, and Nora—provided the children with the knowledge and skills acquired over their long lives, while the kids—Alan, Sarah, Kevin, Lisa, Martin, Doug, and Eugenie—provided their elders with a feeling of accomplishment and renewed vitality.

MORTON DOWNEY SHOW, THE
see *Mohawk Showroom, The*

MOSES—THE LAWGIVER
Historical Drama
FIRST TELECAST: *June 21, 1975*
LAST TELECAST: *July 22, 1979*
BROADCAST HISTORY:
 Jun 1975–Aug 1975, CBS Sat 10:00–11:00
 Jun 1979–Jul 1979, CBS Sun 10:00–11:00
CAST:
 Moses .... Burt Lancaster
 Aaron...................... Anthony Quayle
 Miriam .... Ingrid Thulin
 Zipporah .... Irene Papas
 Pharaoh.................... Laurent Terzieff

The story of the book of Exodus had been told twice by Cecil B. DeMille in spectacular feature films, in a silent and a sound version of *The Ten Commandments*. This series of six one-hour programs retold the story of the enslavement of the Jewish people at the hands of the Egyptians, their release by the pharaoh, and the long, arduous journey to the Promised Land. Filmed on location in Italy and Israel, this series was later reedited and released as a theatrical feature. CBS brought it back in the summer of 1979, four years after its original airing.

MOST DEADLY GAME, THE
Detective Drama
FIRST TELECAST: *October 10, 1970*
LAST TELECAST: *January 16, 1971*
BROADCAST HISTORY:
 Oct 1970–Jan 1971, ABC Sat 9:30–10:30
CAST:
 Jonathan Croft.............. George Maharis
 Vanessa Smith .... Yvette Mimieux
 Mr. Arcane................. Ralph Bellamy

A series in the classic whodunit tradition, involving a trio of highly trained criminologists who dealt only in unusual murders ("the most dangerous game"). This elite, and expensive, team was composed of Mr. Arcane, the urbane, cerebral leader; Jonathan, a ruggedly handsome, ex-military intelligence officer; and Vanessa, a beautiful,

college-trained criminologist (formerly Mr. Arcane's ward).

MOST IMPORTANT PEOPLE, THE
Musical Variety
FIRST TELECAST: *October 18, 1950*
LAST TELECAST: *April 13, 1951*
BROADCAST HISTORY:
 Oct 1950–Apr 1951, DUM Wed/Fri 7:30–7:45
REGULARS:
 Jimmy Carroll
 Rita Carroll

This was a 15-minute program of songs and chatter by singer-pianist Jimmy Carroll and his wife Rita, plus guest performers.

The title *The Most Important People* referred to babies, who were indeed important to the sponsor, Gerber's baby food, but had little to do with this show. In December the title was changed to *Mr. and Mrs. Carroll.*

MOST WANTED
Police Drama
FIRST TELECAST: *October 16, 1976*
LAST TELECAST: *April 25, 1977*
BROADCAST HISTORY:
 Oct 1976–Feb 1977, ABC Sat 10:00–11:00
 Mar 1977–Apr 1977, ABC Mon 9:00–10:00
CAST:
 Capt. Linc Evers .... Robert Stack
 Sgt. Charlie Benson .... Shelly Novack
 Officer Kate Manners .... Jo Ann Harris
 Mayor Dan Stoddard.......... Hari Rhodes
PRODUCER:
 Quinn Martin

The "Most Wanted" unit was an elite task force of the Los Angeles Police Department, concentrating exclusively on criminals on the mayor's most-wanted list. By taking on one case at a time, and cutting through normal red tape, Capt. Linc Evers and his two assistants were able to track down the city's most dangerous criminals, often by use of daring undercover work.

MOTHERS-IN-LAW, THE
Situation Comedy
FIRST TELECAST: *September 10, 1967*
LAST TELECAST: *September 7, 1969*
BROADCAST HISTORY:
 Sep 1967–Sep 1969, NBC Sun 8:30–9:00
CAST:
 Eve Hubbard .... Eve Arden
 Kaye Buell .... Kaye Ballard
 Roger Buell (1967–1968) .... Roger Carmel
 Roger Buell (1968–1969) ..... Richard Deacon
 Herb Hubbard.............. Herbert Rudley
 Jerry Buell .... Jerry Fogel
 Susie Hubbard Buell .... Deborah Walley

The Hubbards and the Buells had been neighbors in suburban Los Angeles for 15 years. Herb Hubbard was a successful lawyer and a member of the board of trustees of his alma mater. His wife, Eve, was a great cook, former champion golfer, terrific gardener, and supporter of all the right causes. They were very straight. The Buells, on the other hand, were extremely unconventional. Roger Buell was a television writer who did most of his work at home and would test his scripts on anyone who happened to be available as a sounding board. His wife, Kaye, was not a particularly enthusiastic housekeeper and rather overbearing on occasion. Despite their differences, the Hubbards and the Buells were the best of friends and their children had gotten married to each other. The children, Jerry and Susie, were both in college and had to cope with in-laws who had very different ideas on how they should live. Roger Carmel left the series after the first season, in a contract dispute, and was replaced by Richard Deacon.

MOTOROLA TV THEATRE
Dramatic Anthology
FIRST TELECAST: *December 1, 1953*
LAST TELECAST: *May 18, 1954*
BROADCAST HISTORY:
Dec 1953–May 1954, ABC Tue 9:30–10:30

Live dramas from New York featuring such first-rate talent as Jack Palance, Brian Donlevy, and Sir Cedric Hardwicke in the first three presentations. Later telecasts starred Helen Hayes, Charlie Ruggles, Walter Matthau, and many others. The program alternated with *The U.S. Steel Hour* in the Tuesday 9:30–10:30 P.M. time slot.

MOTOWN REVUE
Musical Variety
FIRST TELECAST: *August 9, 1985*
LAST TELECAST: *September 13, 1985*
BROADCAST HISTORY:
Aug 1985–Sep 1985, NBC Fri 9:00–10:00
HOST:
Smokey Robinson
REGULARS:
Arsenio Hall
Douglas Wood
Cheryl Rhoads
George Solomon
The Hitsville Gang Dancers

The "Motown Sound" was a slickly produced style of black rhythm & blues/rock music pioneered by recording mogul Berry Gordy, Jr., on his Detroit-based Motown and Tamla labels in the 1960s. Many an American teenager in the '60s danced to the music of Motown's artists: the Supremes, the Miracles, Stevie Wonder, the Four Tops, Marvin Gaye, the Jackson Five, and others. Nostalgia for this identifiable "sound of the '60s" erupted in 1983 with NBC's top-rated *Motown 25th Anniversary Special,* and two years later NBC decided to launch a weekly musical variety series based on the unique "sound." Smokey Rob-

inson, onetime lead singer of the Miracles and latter-day solo artist, producer, and songwriter, was the host; guests included many old Motown favorites, newer artists such as Vanity, Chaka Khan, and Natalie Cole, and non-"Motown sound" acts including Weird Al Yankovic, Kim Carnes, Dean Martin, Rick Nelson, Linda Ronstadt, and Boy George. Four young comics were regular cast members.

MOUSE FACTORY
Children's
BROADCAST HISTORY:
Syndicated only
30 minutes
Produced: *1970–1973* (40 episodes)
Released: *January 1971*

The Walt Disney Studios attempted to crack the syndicated-program market with this mixture of animated film clips and live comedy. Mickey Mouse, Donald Duck, Goofy, Pluto, and all the other Disney characters appeared in clips from their films, interspersed with live segments featuring such guest comics as Pat Paulsen, Jonathan Winters, and Phyllis Diller. A different comedian hosted each week. The individual shows generally revolved around a theme, such as alligators or automobiles.

MOVIELAND QUIZ
Quiz/Audience Participation
FIRST TELECAST: *August 15, 1948*
LAST TELECAST: *November 9, 1948*
BROADCAST HISTORY:
Aug 1948–Nov 1948, ABC Tue 7:30–8:00
EMCEE:
Arthur Q. Bryan
Ralph Dumke
Patricia Bright

Studio contestants were asked to identify titles and stars of old-time movies from selected scenes shown on this 1948 quiz show, which was first seen locally in Philadelphia. The set depicted a theater front, with Patricia Bright as ticket seller and Arthur Q. Bryan (later replaced by Ralph Dumke) as emcee.

MOVIES—PRIOR TO 1961

The arrival of commercial television in the mid-1940s was not greeted with much enthusiasm by the major American movie studios. At first they considered television a passing fad that would have no long-range effects on their audience. Then, by the early 1950s, television had become their mortal enemy. Theater owners could not do what some had done in the heyday of radio—stop the film and let the audience listen to *Amos'-n'Andy* over the theater's sound system—all they could do was look at the dwindling attendance figures. On Mondays people stayed home to watch *I Love Lucy*, on Tuesday to watch Milton Berle, on Saturday to watch *The Jackie Gleason Show* and *Your Show of Shows*, and on Sunday to watch *The Toast of the Town*.

In this climate of life-and-death competition, it was no surprise that the motion-picture studios were not willing to provide television with recently released major films. Nor did they look favorably on actors who wanted to try the new medium. Many stars' contracts expressly forbade their appearance on television. Despite the efforts of the studios to restrict the availability of motion pictures for television, there were movies all over the home screen in the early days. They may not have been recent (most were made in the 1930s) or big hits (many were strictly "B" grade), but they filled time. Independent producers and suppliers of B films, such as Monogram, Republic, and RKO, provided television with many of its early movies.

Aged Westerns, including some that had been released as silent films but had sound tracks added, low-budget second features, and imported films (primarily from England) were seen locally, as network fillers, and as network series in the late 1940s and early 1950s. Some were so dreadful that in one city passersby seeing TV for the first time in a shop window were reportedly laughing out loud at the antique two-reelers being aired. One of the earliest network movies series was titled simply *Western Movie*, and aired on the fledgling DuMont network beginning in late 1946. Ironically, the first attempt to get quality films on TV was made not by a network but by an independent station, WPIX-TV in New York. In the spring of 1948 that station signed an agreement with Sir Alexander Korda, the English producer, for the rights to 24 major British films featuring such stars as Vivien Leigh, Laurence Olivier, and Charles Laughton.

Even when major films started becoming available to television, there was a tacit agreement among the producers to limit television films to features released no later than 1948. In this era of old and/or minor films, ABC's package during the summer of 1957, *Hollywood Film Theater*, was the most ambitious effort to date. Among the films aired in that series were *Gunga Din*, *Mr. Blandings Builds His Dream House* and *Bringing Up Baby*, all with Cary Grant, *Top Hat* with Fred Astaire and Ginger Rogers, and the original 1933 version of *King Kong*. Most of television's early efforts at showing theatrical films were not nearly so memorable. It was not until the advent of *Saturday Night at the Movies* on NBC in 1961 that major contemporary films would become part of the television scene (see *Movies—1961 to Date*). Summarized below by title are most of the nighttime network movie series aired between 1948 and 1960. Some were full-length features, some were shorts, and some were serials, but they all had one thing in common—despite their age and/ or quality they had all been released theatrically.

ABC FEATURE FILM
Oct 1948–Apr 1949, ABC Thu 9:00–10:00
May 1949–Jun 1949, ABC Fri 7:30–8:30
May 1949–Sep 1949, ABC Wed 8:00–9:00
ADMISSION FREE
May 1951–Aug 1951, ABC Mon 10:00–11:00
Aug 1951–Dec 1951, ABC Sun 8:00–9:00
ADVENTURE PLAYHOUSE
Apr 1950–May 1950, DUM Wed 8:00–9:00
BUDWEISER SUMMER THEATRE
Jun 1951–Sep 1951, CBS Sat 8:00–9:00
CINEMA-SCOPE
Apr 1952–May 1952, ABC Sun 9:30–10:30
Jun 1952, ABC Sun 10:00–11:00
CINEMA VARIETIES
Sep 1949–Nov 1949, DUM Sun 8:30–9:00
COMEDY PARADE
Apr 1951–May 1951, ABC Mon 8:00–8:30
CURTAIN UP
May 1951–Sep 1951, ABC Tue 10:00–11:00
Oct 1951–Dec 1951, ABC Mon 9:00–10:00
Nov 1951–Dec 1951, ABC Sat 9:00–10:00
ENCORE PLAYHOUSE
May 1952–Oct 1952, ABC Fri 8:30–9:00
FAMOUS FILM FESTIVAL
Sep 1955–Sep 1956, ABC Sun 7:30–9:00
Oct 1956–May 1957, ABC Sat 7:30–9:00
Jun 1957–Jul 1957, ABC Sat 7:30–8:00
Sep 1957, ABC Sat 7:30–8:30
FEATURE FILM
Oct 1950–Jan 1951, ABC Mon 10:00–11:00
Apr 1951, ABC Mon 10:00–11:00
FEATURE PLAYHOUSE
Jun 1952–Aug 1952, ABC Sat 8:30–10:30
Sep 1952–Jan 1953, ABC Sat 8:00–10:00
Feb 1953–Sep 1953, ABC Sat 8:00–9:00
FEATURE THEATRE
Mar 1949–Jun 1949, DUM Tue 8:00–9:00
Aug 1949–Jan 1950, DUM Tue 9:30–10:30
Jan 1950–Aug 1950, DUM Tue 10:00–11:00
Mar 1950–Apr 1950, DUM Thu 8:00–9:00
FILM SHORTS
Dec 1950–Jan 1951, ABC Sun 8:00–8:30
FILM FAIR
Mar 1956–Jul 1956, ABC Mon 9:00–11:00
Jul 1956–Oct 1956, ABC Mon 9:00–10:30
FILM THEATRE OF THE AIR
Mar 1949–Jul 1949, CBS Sat 8:00–9:30
Apr 1951–Oct 1951, CBS Tue 8:00–9:00
Apr 1953–Jun 1953, CBS Tue 8:00–9:00
FIRST NIGHTER
Oct 1950–Jan 1951, ABC Wed 8:00–9:00
FRONTIER THEATRE
May 1950–Sep 1950, DUM Sat 6:30–7:30
HOLLYWOOD ADVENTURE TIME
Jan 1951–Aug 1951, ABC Sun 8:00–9:00
HOLLYWOOD FILM THEATRE
Apr 1957–Sep 1957, ABC Sun 7:30–9:00
HOLLYWOOD MOVIE TIME
Jan 1951–May 1951, ABC Wed 8:00–9:00
Mar 1952–May 1952, ABC Sat 9:00–11:00
HOLLYWOOD MYSTERY TIME
Feb 1951–Jul 1951, ABC Tue 8:00–9:00

HOUR GLASS
  Jun 1956–Sep 1956, ABC Thu 8:00–9:00
INTERNATIONAL PLAYHOUSE
  Apr 1951–May 1951, DUM Mon 7:30–9:00
KING'S CROSSROADS
  Oct 1951–Dec 1951, ABC Wed 10:00–11:00
  Dec 1951–Oct 1952, ABC Sun 8:00–9:00
LIBRARY OF COMEDY FILMS
  see *Comedy Parade*
MYSTERY THEATRE
  Sep 1949–Mar 1950, DUM Thu 8:00–9:00
NBC CINEMA PLAYHOUSE
  Jun 1950–Sep 1950, NBC Tue 8:00–9:00
NBC PRESENTS
  Jun 1948–Aug 1948, NBC Tue 9:00–9:30
  Sep 1948–Oct 1948, NBC Fri 8:00–8:30
  Oct 1948–Dec 1948, NBC Thu 7:30–7:45
NORTHWEST PATROL
  Jun 1951–Aug 1951, ABC Wed 8:00–9:00
PREMIERE PLAYHOUSE
  Mar 1949–Jul 1949, CBS Fri 9:30–10:45
  Jul 1949–Dec 1949, CBS Sat 9:00–10:00
  May 1950–Jul 1950, CBS Sat 10:00–11:00
SADDLE PAL CLUB
  Dec 1951–May 1952, ABC Sat 7:00–7:30
  May 1952–Jun 1952, ABC Sat 6:30–7:30
  Jun 1952–Aug 1952, ABC Sat 7:00–8:00
SCHLITZ FILM FIRSTS
  Jul 1951–Sep 1951, CBS Fri 9:00–10:00
SCREEN MYSTERY
  Apr 1950–Oct 1950, DUM Thu 8:00–9:00
SCREEN SHORTS
  May 1951–Jul 1951, ABC Sun 10:30–11:00
SUMMER CINEMA
  Jun 1952–Oct 1952, CBS Sat 8:00–Conclusion
WASHDAY THEATRE
  Apr 1952–Aug 1952, ABC Mon 8:30–9:30
  Sep 1952–Oct 1952, ABC Mon 9:00–10:00

MOVIES—1961 TO DATE

The evening of September 23, 1961, ushered in a new era in network-television programming. On that night NBC aired the movie *How to Marry a Millionaire* starring Marilyn Monroe, Lauren Bacall, and Betty Grable. It was the premiere telecast of a new series, *Saturday Night at the Movies*, the first movie series composed of films released by major studios after 1948. The war that had existed between the motion-picture community and the television community was finally over. The studios, which had initially feared that television would drive them out of business, were now thriving as the principal suppliers of filmed weekly TV series. It had been only a matter of time before they made the decision to release relatively current theatrical films for network showing.

Unlike previous efforts to program movies on television (ABC's *Hollywood Film Theater* in 1957 had been the most recent), *Saturday Night at the Movies* was very successful. It did, admittedly, have certain advantages over earlier movie

series. For one thing, *Saturday Night at the Movies* was the first movie series that could air color movies in color. But its primary advantage was that it had access to recent movies showcasing currently popular stars, not the poor grade-B films, imports, and dated films previously seen. The popularity of good-quality movies on TV was demonstrated by the rapid growth of such programming. Within a year of the premiere of *Saturday Night at the Movies*, ABC was carrying theatrical films on Sundays and NBC had added a Monday movie to its schedule. By the end of the decade there were as many as nine network movies on each week.

The increased demand for movies on television eventually led to another major development, the made-for-television film. Universal was the first major studio to attempt producing a film expressly for television, during the 1963–1964 season. Their first effort, however, was a brutal film called *The Killers* with Lee Marvin, Angie Dickinson, and Ronald Reagan (in his last film role before entering politics) that was deemed too violent for television and went into theatrical release instead.

The distinction of being the first made-for-television film aired goes to *See How They Run* starring John Forsythe and Senta Berger, originally telecast on October 7, 1964. Many of the early made-for-TV films (and a substantial quantity of those currently being made) were pilots for proposed TV series, one of the most successful being *Fame Is the Name of the Game*, which became the series *Name of the Game*. It was common practice for motion-picture companies to release these tele-features theatrically outside the U.S.

The acceptance of made-for-television films, which had originally been dropped into series that were made up primarily of theatrically released films, resulted in the first series of made-for-television films only, *The ABC Movie of the Week*, in the fall of 1969. The attraction was that every week would be a "world premiere" of a new motion picture. Over the years, a number of series relying on these new films have appeared under titles such as *World Premiere Movie* and *Movie of the Week*, with recent trends tending to minimize the distinction between theatrical and made-for-TV films. In fact, by the 1978–1979 season, with the available supply of theatrical films dwindling while demand for motion pictures on network television remained strong, a milestone was reached. Fifteen years after the first made-for-TV film aired on network television there were more of them aired during an entire season than there were theatrical features. In later seasons, as cable-television airings eroded the ability of theatrical films to generate large audiences when they were eventually run on the networks, all three networks became more dependent on made-for-TV films to fill their movie time slots.

By the 1986–1987 season the shift had reached the point that the networks aired barely more than 100 theatrical features and practically 300 made-for-TV films.

The highest-rated movies since the advent of *Saturday Night at the Movies* in 1961 are ranked below. Following the table is a chronology of network movie series by night of the week. In cases where a series consisted primarily of made-for-television films, and was so advertised to the viewing public, it has been indicated by (TV).

HIGHEST RATED MOVIES ON TELEVISION

1.	*Gone With the Wind* (11/7–8/76)	47.6
2.	*The Day After* (TV) (11/20/83)	46.0
3.	*Airport* (11/11/73)	42.3
	Love Story (10/1/72)	42.3
5.	*Jaws* (11/4/79)	39.1
6.	*The Poseidon Adventure* (10/27/74)	39.0
7.	*True Grit* (11/12/72)	38.9
	The Birds (1/6/68)	38.9
9.	*Patton* (11/19/72)	38.5
10.	*The Bridge on the River Kwai* (9/25/66)	38.3
11.	*The Godfather* (11/16 & 18/74)	38.2
12.	*Jeremiah Johnson* (1/18/76)	37.5
13.	*Ben-Hur* (2/14/71)	37.1
	Rocky (2/4/79)	37.1
15.	*Little Ladies of the Night* (TV) (1/16/77)	36.9
16.	*Helter Skelter* (TV) (4/1–2/76)	36.5
17.	*The Burning Bed* (TV) (10/8/84)	36.2
18.	*The Wizard of Oz* (Rerun) (1/26/64)	35.9
19.	*Planet of the Apes* (9/14/73)	35.2
20.	*The Wizard of Oz* (Rerun) (1/17/65)	34.7
21.	*Born Free* (2/22/70)	34.2
22.	*The Sound of Music* (2/29/76)	33.6
23.	*Bonnie and Clyde* (9/20/73)	33.4
24.	*The Ten Commandments* (2/18/73)	33.2
	The Night Stalker (TV) (1/11/72)	33.2

In addition to the various prime-time movie series, in 1972 CBS premiered *The CBS Late Movie*, a Monday–Friday 11:30 P.M. collection of theatrical and made-for-television reruns; ABC incorporated a large number of made-for-television films in *ABC Late Night* beginning in 1973; and NBC added the *NBC Late Night Movie* on Sunday nights from September 1977–August 1984.

CHRONOLOGY OF NETWORK MOVIES
BY NIGHT OF THE WEEK

Sunday
Apr 1962–Sep 1963 ABC
Sep 1964–Sep 1987 ABC
Jun 1971–Sep 1972 CBS
May 1977–Sep 1977 NBC (TV)
Jul 1977–Sep 1977 CBS
Jan 1979–Feb 1979 CBS
Oct 1981–   NBC
Jan 1986–Jan 1987 CBS
Mar 1987–   CBS
Jan 1988–   ABC

Monday
Feb 1963–Sep 1964 NBC
Sep 1968–Dec 1970 NBC
Jan 1970–Aug 1974 ABC (Jan–Aug Each Year)
Jan 1971–Aug 1971 NBC (TV)
Sep 1971–May 1975 NBC (Sep–May Each Year)
Jan 1975–Feb 1975 ABC
Sep 1975–Jan 1976 NBC
Feb 1976–May 1976 ABC
Sep 1976–May 1981 NBC
Dec 1976–Feb 1977 ABC
Mar 1980–May 1980 ABC
Jul 1980–Aug 1980 ABC
May 1981–Aug 1981 ABC
Aug 1981–   NBC
Jan 1982–May 1982 ABC
Sep 1982–Nov 1982 ABC
Sep 1982–Oct 1982 CBS
Jan 1983–May 1983 ABC
Dec 1983–May 1984 ABC
Dec 1984–May 1985 ABC
Jan 1986–Jun 1986 ABC
Dec 1986–May 1987 ABC
Aug 1987–Sep 1987 ABC
Jan 1988–May 1988 ABC

Tuesday
Sep 1965–Aug 1971 NBC
Sep 1969–Aug 1975 ABC (TV)
Jun 1970–Sep 1970 CBS
Sep 1972–Sep 1974 CBS (TV)
Jan 1973–Aug 1973 NBC
Sep 1974–Sep 1975 NBC (TV)
Jun 1977–Aug 1977 ABC
Jan 1978–Mar 1986 CBS
Sep 1979–Feb 1980 NBC
Jun 1980–Sep 1980 NBC
Sep 1981–Oct 1981 NBC
Aug 1982–Oct 1982 NBC
Aug 1985–Mar 1986 CBS
Aug 1986–Sep 1986 NBC
Sep 1986–Jul 1987 CBS
Jun 1987–Sep 1987 NBC
Apr 1988–   CBS
May 1988–Jun 1988, NBC

Wednesday
Sep 1964–Sep 1965 NBC
Jul 1966–Aug 1966 ABC
Jan 1967–Jan 1970 ABC
Sep 1972–Sep 1975 ABC (TV)
Jan 1974–Aug 1974 NBC
Sep 1976–Nov 1976 NBC (TV)
Nov 1976–Jan 1979 CBS
Mar 1978–May 1978 NBC
Aug 1978–Jan 1979 NBC
Apr 1979–   CBS
Apr 1979–Oct 1979 NBC
Sep 1980–Nov 1980 NBC
Jun 1981–Jul 1981 ABC
May 1984–Jul 1984 ABC
Mar 1986–May 1986 CBS
Aug 1986–Sep 1986 CBS

Thursday

Sep 1965–Nov 1975 CBS
May 1975–Sep 1975 NBC
Jan 1976–Sep 1976 NBC
Apr 1977–Sep 1977 NBC
Jun 1978–Aug 1978 ABC
May 1980–Oct 1981 NBC
Sep 1980–Nov 1980 CBS
Oct 1981 CBS
Jun 1983–Jul 1983 ABC
May 1984–Jun 1984 ABC
Oct 1984–Mar 1985 ABC
May 1985–Sep 1985 ABC
Jul 1987–Sep 1987 CBS
Sep 1987–Mar 1988 ABC
Jan 1988–Mar 1988 ABC
May 1988–Jun 1988 CBS
Jun 1988–   ABC

Friday

Sep 1966–Sep 1971 CBS
Sep 1971–Aug 1972 CBS (TV)
Sep 1971–Dec 1971 NBC (TV)
Jan 1972–Sep 1972 NBC
Sep 1972–Sep 1975 CBS
Jun 1973–Sep 1973 NBC
May 1974–Aug 1974 NBC
Jul 1975–Nov 1981 ABC
Dec 1975–Jan 1977 CBS
Apr 1977–Mar 1978 CBS
Jan 1980–May 1980 NBC
Jun 1981–Nov 1981 NBC
Feb 1982–Apr 1982 NBC
May 1982–Aug 1982 ABC
Dec 1982–Aug 1983 ABC
Nov 1983–Jan 1984 NBC
May 1984–Sep 1984 NBC
May 1985–Sep 1985 CBS
May 1986 ABC
May 1986–Sep 1986 CBS
Mar 1987–Aug 1987 CBS
May 1988–   CBS

Saturday

Sep 1961–Sep 1978 NBC
Sep 1971–May 1972 ABC (TV)
Jun 1972–Aug 1972 ABC
Sep 1973–Aug 1974 ABC (TV)
Jan 1975–Aug 1975 ABC
Apr 1976–Aug 1976 ABC
May 1978–Feb 1980 CBS
May 1980–Nov 1980 CBS
Nov 1980–Jan 1981 NBC
Apr 1981–Jan 1984 CBS
Sep 1981–Oct 1981 NBC
Apr 1984–Sep 1984 CBS
Jul 1985–Apr 1986 CBS
Jun 1986–Aug 1986 ABC
Jun 1986–May 1987 CBS
Jul 1987–Sep 1987 ABC
Nov 1987–Dec 1987 CBS

MOVIN' ON

Adventure

FIRST TELECAST: *September 12, 1974*
LAST TELECAST: *September 14, 1976*
BROADCAST HISTORY:
Sep 1974–May 1975, NBC Thu 10:00–11:00
Sep 1975–Sep 1976, NBC Tue 8:00–9:00
CAST:
Sonny Pruitt.................. Claude Akins
Will Chandler .... Frank Converse
Moose (1975–1976) .... Rosey Grier
Benjy (1975–1976) .... Art Metrano
THEME:
"Movin' On," written and performed by Merle
Haggard

Sonny and Will were two gypsy truck drivers who
came from radically different backgrounds. Sonny
was a burly veteran trucker, owner of the giant rig
that they operated, and prone to settle most of his
arguments with his fists. Will was much younger,
a law school graduate who had turned to trucking
as a means of learning more about himself. His
legal training and quick mind often prevented disagreements from turning into brawls. They were
good for each other; Sonny's outgoing gregarious-
ness counterbalanced Will's quiet, reserved
personality, while Will's rational approach to
problems counteracted Sonny's sucker-prone
willingness to help anyone at any time. Together
they traveled back and forth across the country in
search of adventure and freight to haul. During the
second season another pair of truckers, Moose
and Benjy, were seen frequently. Less than completely ethical, they were two of the most mobile
con men ever seen on television. *Movin' On* was
filmed on location in a different part of the country
each week.

One of the fans of this program was President
Gerald Ford. Once, when *Movin' On* was filming
in Atlanta, Claude Akins happened to be staying
at the same hotel as the President. Approached in
the hotel dining room by a Secret Service agent,
the actor was invited to the President's suite,
where he and Ford chatted about the show for
half an hour. "Now," remarked the President, "I
can tell Betty I know more about *Movin' On* than
she does."

MULLIGAN'S STEW

Comedy/Drama

FIRST TELECAST: *October 25, 1977*
LAST TELECAST: *December 13, 1977*
BROADCAST HISTORY:
Oct 1977–Dec 1977, NBC Tue 9:00–10:00
CAST:
Michael Mulligan .... Lawrence Pressman
Jane Mulligan .... Elinor Donahue
Mark Mulligan .... Johnny Doran
Melinda Mulligan....... Julie Anne Haddock
Jimmy Mulligan .... K. C. Martel
Adam Friedman .... Chris Ciampa
Stevie Friedman .... Suzanne Crough

Kimmy Friedman	Sunshine Lee
Polly Friedman	Lory Kochheim
Polo Polocheck	Jaime Alba

Set in the fictitious Southern California suburban community of Birchfield, *Mulligan's Stew* was the story of Michael and Jane Mulligan and their extended family. The Mulligans had three children of their own, and were managing reasonably well, when Michael's sister and her husband were killed, leaving them with four more children, including a recently adopted five-year-old Vietnamese orphan named Kimmy. The Mulligan home, barely comfortable with its original family of five, was severely overcrowded with nine. The Mulligan children and the Friedman children had been raised with different life-styles and had considerable problems adjusting to each other. Michael's income as a high school teacher/football coach was enough to get by on, but with nine mouths to feed very little was left for luxuries.

MUNSTERS, THE
Situation Comedy
FIRST TELECAST: *September 24, 1964*
LAST TELECAST: *September 1, 1966*
BROADCAST HISTORY:
 Sep 1964–Sep 1966, CBS Thu 7:30–8:00
CAST:
Herman Munster	Fred Gwynne
Lily Munster	Yvonne DeCarlo
Grandpa Munster	Al Lewis
Edward Wolfgang (Eddie) Munster	
....	Butch Patrick
Marilyn Munster (1964)	Beverly Owen
Marilyn Munster (1964–1966)	Pat Priest

At 1313 Mockingbird Lane in Mockingbird Heights stood a musty, cobweb-covered gothic mansion. The residents considered themselves just a normal, everyday American family, but to neighbors—and viewers—they were a bit unusual. Herman, the man of the house, was seven feet tall and bore a striking resemblance to the Frankenstein monster. His wife, Lily, looked very much like a lady vampire; son Eddie looked like he was in the midst of changing from boy to wolf, or vice versa, take your pick; and Grandpa could have passed for an aging, 350-year-old Count Dracula. They all had their idiosyncracies. Grandpa was not above changing into a bat when the situation warranted it. Not only did this family look like monsters, they were monsters—albeit friendly, unassuming ones. They were concerned about their niece Marilyn, who looked somewhat strange to them (to an outsider she was the only normal-looking one of the lot). The effect their physical appearance had on the rest of the world was always predictable, often hilarious, and occasionally poignant. Herman, appropriately, worked in a menial capacity for the funeral home of Gateman, Goodbury & Graves, and was always on the lookout for a better job. Beverly Owen,

who originated the role of Marilyn, left the series in December 1964 to get married, and was replaced by Pat Priest.

MUPPET SHOW, THE
Variety
BROADCAST HISTORY:
 Syndicated only
 30 minutes
 Produced: *1976–1981* (120 episodes)
 Released: *September 1976*
PUPPETEERS:
 Jim Henson
 Frank Oz
 Richard Hunt
 Dave Goelz
 Jerry Nelson
 Erin Ozker (1976–1977)
 Louise Gold (1979–1981)
 Kathryn Muller (1980–1981)
 Steve Whitmire (1980–1981)
THE MUPPETS:
 Kermit the Frog (Henson)
 Miss Piggy (Oz)
 Zoot (Goelz)
 Fozzie Bear (Oz)
 Gonzo (Goelz)
 Sweetums (Hunt)
 Sam the Eagle (Oz)
 The Swedish Chef (Henson & Oz)
 Dr. Teeth (Henson) & the Electric Mayhem
 Floyd (Nelson)
 Animal (Oz)
 Capt. Link Heartthrob (Henson)
 Dr. Strangepork (Nelson)
 Wayne & Wanda (1976–1977)
 Rowlf (Henson)
 Dr. Bunsen Honeydew (Goalz)
 Statler & Waldorf (Hunt & Henson)
 Scooter (Hunt)
 Beauregard (Goelz) (1980–1981)
 Pops (Nelson) (1980–1981)
 Lew Zealand (Nelson) (1980–1981)
 Janice (Hunt)
 Rizzo the Rat (Whitmire) (1980–1981)
MUSICAL DIRECTOR:
 Jack Parnell

This whimsical mixture of puppets and people was probably the most widely viewed television program in the world during the late 1970s. Originated by an American and produced in England, it has been seen in more than 100 countries by upward of 235 million people.

The host was a frog. Kermit presided over a half-hour of chaos each week as the desperate emcee and manager of a theatrical troupe of shaggy animals, monsters, and even humanoid screwballs who seemed to turn every big production number into a shambles. In the troupe was Miss Piggy, corpulent and very determined to be the star (anyone who disagreed got a karate chop); Rowlf, the shaggy, piano-playing dog; Fozzie Bear, with his peaked head and tiny hat; Dr. Teeth and the Electric Mayhem, the resident band, including spaced-out guitarist Floyd and drummer Animal; the maniacal Swedish Chef; Dr. Bunsen Honeydew, the short, balding, and quite mad scientist (modeled after the show's real-life backer, Sir Lew Grade); Gonzo, who always tried to open the show with a trumpet fanfare (but the trumpet would break, explode, emit butterflies, etc.); and a host of others. Observing the tumult with disdain from their box seats, and cracking awful jokes, were the two old geezers, Statler and Waldorf.

A running feature was "Pigs in Space," a soap opera with handsome Capt. Link Heartthrob of the starship *Swinetrek*, doing battle with the evil plots of Dr. Strangepork and the amorous advances of Miss Piggy (who went after almost every male in sight). Miss Piggy bullied her way from a supporting character in the early years of the show to second billing (but don't tell her that!) after Kermit. Guests on *The Muppet Show* ranged from George Burns, Zero Mostel, and Steve Martin to Rudolf Nureyev (dancing a *pas de deux* from "Swine Lake" with Miss Piggy), Elton John (doing "Crocodile Rock" to a chorus of crocodiles), Beverly Sills (in a battle of the sopranos in "Pigaletto"), and Peter Sellers (as a mad German chiropractor who tied a pig into knots, or a pompous actor reciting lines from *Richard III* while squeezing a clucking chicken under each arm).

The gags were often corny, and the skits bizarre to say the least, but what made the show such a hit with adults and children alike was the Muppets themselves, hilarious to look at yet invested with a warmth, wit, and fallibility that made them almost human.

Basically, of course, they *were* human, extensions of the warm and mischievous personality of creator Jim Henson and his associates. Henson was fascinated with puppetry from childhood, and followed *Kukla, Fran & Ollie* and the Baird puppets from the time he first saw a TV set. He had his first short-lived TV puppet show as a senior in high school, on a local station in Maryland. In 1955, as a freshman at the University of Maryland, he and his future wife, Jane Nebel, teamed to present a regular local show on WRC-TV, Washington, called *Sam and Friends*. Henson coined the label "Muppet" at about this time, to indicate the combination of "marionette" and "puppet." Soon he was doing commercials and then making national appearances on such network shows as *Tonight*, *Today*, *Ed Sullivan*, *Jimmy Dean* (where Rowlf was a regular), and *Perry Como*. On his first network appearance (Steve Allen's *Tonight Show* in 1957), a one-year-old Kermit (Henson) sang "I've Grown Accustomed to Your Face" to a purple monster (Nebel), which was so enchanted that it proceeded to eat its own face, and then attempted to devour Kermit, too.

The Muppets gained even greater fame with the debut of *Sesame Street*, on which they were featured, in 1969, but a network show of their own eluded them. Network officials saw the Muppets as strictly for kids, while Henson thought they had broader appeal. Finally English showman Sir Lew Grade offered to back this syndicated series, which has since become a bigger hit than many of the networks' own shows.

By the late 1970s there were more than 400 Muppet characters, of which those listed above were seen most often on *The Muppet Show*. Most were basically hand puppets, made of felt (like Kermit) or foam rubber (like Miss Piggy) and operated by either one or two men each.

In 1979 Henson's horizons expanded even further with the first *Muppet Movie*. There is all manner of Muppet merchandise available, including a famous parody on cheesecake posters featuring the inimitable Miss Piggy.

MURDER, SHE WROTE
Detective Drama
FIRST TELECAST: *September 30, 1984*
LAST TELECAST:
BROADCAST HISTORY:
   Sep 1984–   , CBS Sun 8:00–9:00
CAST:
  Jessica Beatrice Fletcher ... Angela Lansbury
  *Sheriff Amos Tupper .... Tom Bosley
  *Grady Fletcher (1985–   ) .. Michael Horton
  *Dr. Seth Hazlitt (1985–   )
      .... William Windom

*Occasional

Jessica Fletcher was a cherubic, middle-aged widow living in quaint Cabot Cove on the coast of Maine. A former substitute teacher and PTA volunteer, she had attained celebrity late in life through the success of her mystery novels. Not only could Jessica write good stories; she was a talented amateur detective as well. Active and adventuresome, she took advantage of the money and opportunities that her writing had provided and traveled widely. Along the way she frequently got involved in convoluted real-life murder mysteries, which she diligently pursued by piecing together obscure clues to determine the culprit. As in *The Adventures of Ellery Queen*, an earlier television whodunit, viewers had to pay close attention to these clues if they hoped to figure out who the murderer was. The plots were complicated and the pacing brisk, and long-time stage actress Angela Lansbury seemed to be having the time of her life in this, her first television series.

Although Jessica was the series' only regular, there were a few others who turned up periodically—her good friend, and Cabot Cove's sheriff, Amos Tupper; her tax accountant nephew, Grady; and Dr. Seth Hazlitt, with whom she played a spirited game of chess.

MUSEUM OF SCIENCE AND INDUSTRY

Instruction
FIRST TELECAST: *July 30, 1948*
LAST TELECAST: *September 24, 1948*
BROADCAST HISTORY:
Jul 1948–Sep 1948, NBC Fri 8:00–8:30

A live and film program featuring exhibits at a New York City museum.

MUSIC AT THE MEADOWBROOK

Musical Variety
FIRST TELECAST: *May 23, 1953*
LAST TELECAST: *April 19, 1956*
BROADCAST HISTORY:
May 1953–Sep 1953, ABC Sat 7:00–8:00
Oct 1953–Dec 1953, ABC Sat 8:00–9:00
Jan 1956–Apr 1956, ABC Thu 10:00–10:30
HOSTS:
Jimmy Blaine
Bill Williams
Walter Herlihy, and others
REGULAR:
Frank Dailey

This series of band remotes from Frank Dailey's famous Meadowbrook Night Club in Cedar Grove, New Jersey, was reminiscent of radio in the 1930s. In those days the Meadowbrook was one of the chief points of origination for live, nationwide broadcasts by the traveling big bands. In the TV era, however, it—and the big bands—were anachronisms and were televised only briefly, in the 1950s.

In addition to music by a different guest band each week (sometimes one stayed for several weeks) the 1953 series featured a regular college salute, in which students were interviewed and campus talent, such as the glee club, performed. Premiere-night guests in 1953 were Ralph Marterie and His Orchestra, Richard Hayman, and the Douglas Duke Trio. Seen later were such bands as those of Sauter-Finegan, Neal Hefti, Ray McKinley, the Korn Kobblers, Art Mooney, Ralph Flanagan, and King Guion and His Double Rhythm Orchestra, as well as assorted singers, dancers, and other acts.

Jimmy Blaine was the most frequent host in both 1953 and 1956, though others did appear and club owner Frank Dailey also wandered on and off the set.

MUSIC BINGO

Quiz/Audience Participation
FIRST TELECAST: *May 29, 1958*
LAST TELECAST: *September 11, 1958*
BROADCAST HISTORY:
May 1958–Sep 1958, NBC Thu 10:30–11:00
EMCEE:
Johnny Gilbert

Music Bingo was a variation on the highly successful *Name That Tune*. Two contestants would listen to a tune being played and, when the tune was abruptly stopped, would run to an assigned place and push a buzzer. The first one to push the buzzer got the opportunity to identify the song. If correct, the contestant could place his mark—a musical sharp or flat symbol—anyplace on the music bingo board he chose. The first person to successfully complete a bingo, five in a line, was the winner of $500 and would keep facing new contestants until defeated. Three months after the prime-time version left the air, *Music Bingo* returned as an ABC daytime series. The daytime version lasted until January 1960.

MUSIC COUNTRY

see *Dean Martin Presents Music Country*

MUSIC COUNTRY USA

Musical Variety
FIRST TELECAST: *January 17, 1974*
LAST TELECAST: *May 16, 1974*
BROADCAST HISTORY:
Jan 1974–May 1974, NBC Thu 10:00–11:00

The concept of *Music Country USA* was essentially the same as that of *Dean Martin Presents Music Country*, a summer replacement for *The Dean Martin Show*. Country acts performed on the show, which was taped on location in various places around the U.S. There was a different host each week, including Jerry Reed, Lynn Anderson, Marty Robbins, Donna Fargo, Tom T. Hall, Mac Davis, Buck Owens, Wayne Newton, Dionne Warwick, Doug Kershaw, and Charlie Rich. All of them also made frequent appearances as performers on the show.

MUSIC 55

Music
FIRST TELECAST: *July 12, 1955*
LAST TELECAST: *September 13, 1955*
BROADCAST HISTORY:
Jul 1955–Sep 1955, CBS Tue 8:30–9:00
REGULAR:
Stan Kenton

This live weekly summer music series featured the sounds of Stan Kenton and his band. The repertoire included jazz, standards, and contemporary hits. Stan also played host to weekly guest stars.

MUSIC FOR A SUMMER NIGHT

Music
FIRST TELECAST: *June 3, 1959*
LAST TELECAST: *September 21, 1960*
BROADCAST HISTORY:
Jun 1959–Aug 1959, ABC Wed 7:30–8:30
Feb 1960–Mar 1960, ABC Wed 7:30–8:00
Mar 1960–Sep 1960, ABC Wed 7:30–8:30
REGULAR:
Glenn Osser and His Orchestra

ABC salvaged a bit of the prestige it had lost by canceling the *Voice of Firestone* with this replacement program, produced by the same man (Fred Heidler) and containing approximately the same musical ingredients—but on a much lower budget. Like *Voice, Music for a Summer Night* ranged across the "better" musical idioms, principally Broadway show tunes and the classics. Good but not top-name singers were used, such as Betty Ann Grove, Bill Hayes, and Dorothy Collins. Complete productions of *Madame Butterfly, La Traviata,* and *Tosca* (set in Mussolini's Italy) were aired, along with lighter fare such as a visit to summer theaters and musical festivals around the country. A novel touch was the use of John Hoppe's Mobilux creations to introduce numbers.

When the program returned in February 1960, too early to be classified as a summer show, it was titled *Music for a Spring Night*, reverting to its original title in May. ABC documentary news specials preempted this series on an irregular but frequent basis.

MUSIC FROM CHICAGO
Music
FIRST TELECAST: *April 15, 1951*
LAST TELECAST: *June 17, 1951*
BROADCAST HISTORY:
Apr 1951–Jun 1951, DUM Sun 9:30–10:00

A short-lived music series originating in Chicago, which at the time was a fairly important production center for network programs.

MUSIC FROM MANHATTAN
see *Sammy Kaye Show, The*

MUSIC FROM THE MEADOWBROOK
see *Music at the Meadowbrook*

MUSIC HALL
Music
FIRST TELECAST: *July 1, 1952*
LAST TELECAST: *September 25, 1952*
BROADCAST HISTORY:
Jul 1952–Sep 1952, CBS Tue/Thu 7:45–8:00
REGULARS:
Patti Page
Carl Hoff and His Orchestra

Patti Page was the singing star of this twice-weekly 15-minute music show that filled the remainder of the half-hour in which CBS aired its nightly network news program. The show originated from New York and was telecast live.

MUSIC HALL AMERICA
Music
BROADCAST HISTORY:
Syndicated only
60 minutes
Produced: *1976* (26 episodes)
Released: *Fall 1976*

REGULARS:
Dean Rutherford
Sandi Burnett

Country-flavored musical hour, taped at Opryland U.S.A., in Nashville. There was no regular host, but among those guest-starring were Ray Stevens, Jim Stafford, Pat Boone, Charley Pride, Lynn Anderson, and Bobby Goldsboro. The Statler Brothers and the Oak Ridge Boys made repeat appearances.

MUSIC IN VELVET
Music
FIRST TELECAST: *January 16, 1949*
LAST TELECAST: *October 28, 1951*
BROADCAST HISTORY:
Jan 1949–Apr 1949, ABC Sun 9:30–10:00
Jul 1951–Oct 1951, ABC Sun 7:30–8:00
REGULARS:
Johnny Hill* (1949)
The Velveteers (1949)
Don Lindley Orchestra (1949)
Rex Maupin (1951)

*Also given as Johnny Holt

This was another of the easygoing song-and-dance programs that originated from Chicago during TV's early years, when that city was an important network production center. Baritone Johnny Hill was featured during the 1949 run, and Rex Maupin in 1951.

MUSIC ON ICE
Musical Variety
FIRST TELECAST: *May 8, 1960*
LAST TELECAST: *September 11, 1960*
BROADCAST HISTORY:
May 1960–Sep 1960, NBC Sun 8:00–9:00
REGULARS:
Johnny Desmond
Jacqueline du Bief
Ben Dova
The Skip Jacks
The Dancing Blades
The Bob Boucher Orchestra

The melding of a musical variety hour with an ice show in a weekly series was unique. Not all of the numbers in the series were performed on ice, but there were a number of ice-skating features in each program. Johnny Desmond was the host, the Skip Jacks were the regular vocalists, and the Dancing Blades provided regular precision group skating. Guest singers and ice performers were on each show. Perfect for a warm summer's evening.

MUSIC ROOM, THE
see *Jacques Fray Music Room*

MUSIC SCENE, THE
Music

FIRST TELECAST: *September 22, 1969*
LAST TELECAST: *January 12, 1970*
BROADCAST HISTORY:
  Sep 1969–Jan 1970, ABC Mon 7:30–8:15
HOSTS:
  David Steinberg
  Larry Hankin
  Christopher Ross
  Paul Reid Roman
  Chris Bokeno
  Lily Tomlin
  Pat Williams Orchestra

A contemporary popular music program, at first utilizing six rotating hosts, but beginning in November hosted by David Steinberg (and guests) only. Practically every big name in rock music appeared on this short-lived show, with the first telecast alone featuring the Beatles, James Brown, Crosby, Stills, Nash & Young, Buck Owens, Three Dog Night, Oliver, and Tom Jones. Seen in later telecasts were Janis Joplin, Bobby Sherman, Sly & the Family Stone, Isaac Hayes, Stevie Wonder, Mama Cass, and even Groucho Marx, among others. A special feature was performances of the latest hit songs in various fields, such as rock, rhythm & blues, country & western, and comedy, based on *Billboard* magazine's record popularity charts. An improvisational comedy group was also seen.

MUSIC SHOP, THE
Musical Variety
FIRST TELECAST: *January 11, 1959*
LAST TELECAST: *March 8, 1959*
BROADCAST HISTORY:
  Jan 1959–Mar 1959, NBC Sun 7:30–8:00
HOST:
  Buddy Bregman

Most of the singers who appeared on this series had currently popular hit songs, with the emphasis on young performers on the way up. In addition to serving as host, Buddy Bregman accompanied on piano those who performed live. However, the majority lip-synced to their hit records. Among those who appeared were Bobby Darin, Ritchie Valens, the Platters, the Teddy Bears, and Annette Funicello, along with an established, older star each week (Milton Berle, Jerry Lewis, etc.) who would chat and perhaps perform. At the end of each show, Buddy announced the top five records of the week.

MUSIC SHOW, THE
Music
FIRST TELECAST: *May 19, 1953*
LAST TELECAST: *October 17, 1954*
BROADCAST HISTORY:
  May 1953–Jun 1953, DUM Tue 9:00–9:30
  Jul 1953–Oct 1953, DUM Tue 8:30–9:00
  Oct 1953–Jan 1954, DUM Wed 10:30–11:00

Jan 1954–Sep 1954, DUM Wed 10:00–10:30
Sep 1954–Oct 1954, DUM Sun 10:00–10:30
REGULARS:
  Mike Douglas
  Jackie Van
  Henri Noel
  Eleanor Warner (1953–1954)
  Dolores Peterson (1954)
  Robert Trendler Orchestra

This Chicago-originated program was exactly as billed—just music, with no frills, no fancy production, and no gimmicks. Four pleasant-voiced singers shared the vocal honors, with Mike Douglas and Jackie Van handling the more popular tunes and Henri Noel and Eleanor Warner (later replaced by Dolores Peterson) the meatier stuff. Repertoire was primarily standards, including medleys from *Carousel, South Pacific,* and other Broadway shows. Robert Trendler's 34-piece orchestra provided lush accompaniment.

MUSICAL ALMANAC
Music
FIRST TELECAST: *May 10, 1948*
LAST TELECAST: *April 30, 1949*
BROADCAST HISTORY:
  May 1948–Dec 1948, NBC Mon–Thu
    Various nights and times between 7:30–8:00
  May 1948–Aug 1948, NBC Fri 9:00–9:15
  Oct 1948–Dec 1948, NBC Fri 8:00–8:30
  Feb 1949–Apr 1949, NBC Various nights 10:00–
    10:30
EMCEE:
  Harvey Harding

For the first few weeks pianist-singer Harvey Harding "and his musical nostalgia" were featured exclusively on this 15–30-minute musical interlude, but later a variety of cabaret talent appeared from night to night. Among those seen were Ted Steele (from WPTZ, Philadelphia), Barbara Marshall, Verle Mills, and Roberta Quinlan. The program wandered all over the prime-time schedule for about a year in 1948–1949. The title was changed to *Musical Miniatures* in August 1948.

Harding was one of TV's pioneers, having had a similar regular weekly series on New York local television from July 1941 to May 1942.

MUSICAL CHAIRS
Quiz/Audience Participation
FIRST TELECAST: *July 9, 1955*
LAST TELECAST: *September 17, 1955*
BROADCAST HISTORY:
  Jul 1955–Sep 1955, NBC Sat 9:00–9:30
MODERATOR:
  Bill Leyden
PANELISTS:
  Mel Blanc
  Johnny Mercer
  Bobby Troup

SINGERS:
  The Cheerleaders

After two years as a local show in Los Angeles, *Musical Chairs* moved to the NBC network for a summer run in 1955. Viewers of this musical quiz show were encouraged to send in questions to test the knowledge of the panel. Those who submitted questions that stumped the panel won a 21-inch RCA TV. There were four panel members: Mel Blanc, actor and impressionist who was most famous for his work as the voice of Bugs Bunny; composer Johnny Mercer; pianist-orchestra leader Bobby Troup (whose band, the Troup Group, provided the music for this series); and a guest panelist. The questions could have anything to do with music, from arranging, to composing, to performing. Members of the panel were often called on to imitate the singing or playing styles of well-known performers and occasionally collaborated on individual answers.

MUSICAL COMEDY TIME
  Musical Comedy
FIRST TELECAST: *October 2, 1950*
LAST TELECAST: *March 19, 1951*
BROADCAST HISTORY:
  Oct 1950–Mar 1951, NBC Mon 9:30–10:30
REGULARS:
  The Ken Christie Singers
  The Kevin Jonson Dancers
  Harry Sosnik Orchestra

Musical Comedy Time aired on alternate Monday evenings with *Robert Montgomery Presents*. Broadway musical comedies and standard operettas were adapted for presentation as live hour-long TV programs. Among the adaptations were such musical comedies as *Anything Goes* with Martha Raye and John Conte and *No No Nanette* with Jackie Gleason and Anne Crowley, and operettas like *The Merry Widow* with Irra Petina, Wilbur Evans, and Melville Cooper. The principal casts changed from show to show, but the same musical and dance groups were used for all.

MUSICAL MERRY-GO-ROUND
  Music
FIRST TELECAST: *July 25, 1947*
LAST TELECAST: *March 11, 1949*
BROADCAST HISTORY:
  Jul 1947–Sep 1947, NBC Fri 8:00–8:30
  Oct 1947–Jan 1948, NBC Thu 8:00–8:30
  Jan 1948–Feb 1948, NBC Fri 7:45–8:00
  Feb 1948–Mar 1949, NBC Fri 7:30–7:50
REGULARS:
  Jack Kilty
  Frederic (Fritz) DeWilde
  Eve Young (1947)
  Penny Gerard (1948–1949)

One of the earliest regular musical programs on network TV, this extremely simple series was at first called *Disc Magic* and was essentially a disc-jockey show. Viewers watched d.j. Kilty play popular records and occasionally introduce some live entertainment. In 1947, *anything* on the flickering screen seemed interesting to watch. Then in October 1947 the title was changed to *Musical Merry-Go-Round* and the format shifted to live entertainment exclusively, with songs by Kilty, Eve Young (and, later, Penny Gerard), bits by actor Fritz DeWilde, and guest performers. Most of the guests were unknown cabaret talent rather than established stars.

MUSICAL MINIATURES
  see *Musical Almanac*

MY FAVORITE HUSBAND
  Situation Comedy
FIRST TELECAST: *September 12, 1953*
LAST TELECAST: *September 8, 1957*
BROADCAST HISTORY:
  Sep 1953–Jun 1955, CBS Sat 9:30–10:00 (OS)
  Oct 1955–Dec 1955, CBS Tue 10:30–11:00
  Jun 1957–Sep 1957, CBS Sun 7:30–8:00
CAST:
  George Cooper .... Barry Nelson
  Liz Cooper (1953–1955) .... Joan Caulfield
  Liz Cooper (1955) .... Vanessa Brown
  Myra Cobb/Myra Shepard ...... Alix Talton
  Gillmore Cobb (1953–1955) .... Bob Sweeney
  Oliver Shepard (1955) .... Dan Tobin
  Uncle Norman Fildew (1955).... David Burns

George Cooper was a successful bank executive with a fancy suburban home and a beautiful but scatterbrained wife. Living next door were the Cobbs, Gillmore, the peanut magnate, and Myra, the social snob. The Coopers, though wealthy, were rather unpretentious, and the Cobbs were always trying to get them to improve their social image.

Several changes took place at the start of the third season. Vanessa Brown replaced Joan Caulfield in the role of Liz, the next-door neighbors became the Shepards (with Alix Talton still playing the wife), and there was less emphasis on social status. Despite the changes, the program folded three months later. Reruns of this last group of episodes were aired during the summer of 1957.

My Favorite Husband was based on the 1948 radio series of the same name, which starred Lucille Ball as the nutty housewife Liz (the prototype for her long-running Lucy characterization on TV).

MY FAVORITE MARTIAN
  Situation Comedy
FIRST TELECAST: *September 29, 1963*
LAST TELECAST: *September 4, 1966*

Sep 1963–Sep 1966, CBS Sun 7:30–8:00
CAST:

Uncle Martin (The Martian) . . .	Ray Walston
Tim O'Hara	Bill Bixby
Mrs. Lorelei Brown	Pamela Britton
Angela Brown (1963–1964)	Ann Marshall
Mr. Harry Burns (1963–1964) .	J. Pat O'Malley
Det. Bill Brennan (1964–1966) . . .	Alan Hewitt
The Police Chief (1965–1966)	Roy Engle

On the way to cover an assignment for his paper, *The Los Angeles Sun,* reporter Tim O'Hara stumbled upon a Martian whose one-man ship had crashed on Earth. Tim took the dazed Martian back to his rooming house to help him recuperate, while thinking of the fantastic story he would be able to present to his boss, Mr. Burns, about his find. The Martian, however, looked human, spoke English, and refused to admit to anyone but Tim what he was. Tim befriended him, passed him off as his uncle, and had many an interesting adventure with the stranded alien. Uncle Martin had little retractable antennae, could make himself invisible, was telepathic, could move objects just by pointing at them, and had a vast storehouse of advanced technological knowledge. While he was trying to fix his ship he stayed with Tim in Mrs. Brown's rooming house. During the first season, Mrs. Brown's teenage daughter Angela was a cast regular. The following year policeman Bill Brennan joined the cast as Mrs. Brown's boyfriend, a threat to Uncle Martin on two counts—not only was he always a potential discoverer of the Martian's true identity, but Uncle Martin had become romantically interested in Mrs. Brown himself and looked upon Brennan as a rival for her affections.

MY FRIEND FLICKA
Adventure
FIRST TELECAST: *February 10, 1956*
LAST TELECAST: *May 18, 1958*
BROADCAST HISTORY:
Feb 1956–Feb 1957, CBS Fri 7:30–8:00
Mar 1957, CBS Sat 7:00–7:30
Apr 1957–May 1957, CBS Sun 6:00–6:30
Jun 1957–Aug 1957, CBS Wed 7:30–8:00
Sep 1957–Dec 1957, NBC Sun 6:30–7:00
Jan 1958–May 1958, NBC Sun 7:00–7:30
CAST:

Rob McLaughlin	Gene Evans
Nell McLaughlin	Anita Louise
Ken McLaughlin	Johnny Washbrook
Gus Broeberg	Frank Ferguson
Hildy Broeberg (1956)	Pamela Beaird

Set in the ranchlands of Montana around the turn of the century, *My Friend Flicka* was the story of a boy and his horse. Young Ken McLaughlin's best friend was his beloved horse, Flicka. Ken, Flicka, Ken's parents, and ranch hand Gus encountered assorted adventures while struggling to make a

living from the land and dealing with their neighbors and friends. Originally aired as a black-and-white series on CBS, this program, which had been filmed in color, was rerun as a color entry on NBC during the following season. *My Friend Flicka* made the complete circuit, with the reruns showing up on ABC as a late-afternoon entry weekdays during the 1959–1960 season. From the fall of 1961 to the fall of 1966 they were on Saturday afternoons; on CBS during the 1961–1962 season; on ABC from September 1962–December 1963; and back on CBS for two years beginning in September 1964.

Based on the 1943 movie, which had been adapted from the stories of Mary O'Hara.

MY FRIEND IRMA
Situation Comedy
FIRST TELECAST: *January 8, 1952*
LAST TELECAST: *June 25, 1954*
BROADCAST HISTORY:
Jan 1952–Mar 1952, CBS Tue 10:30–11:00
Apr 1952–Jun 1953, CBS Fri 8:30–9:00 (OS)
Oct 1953–Jun 1954, CBS Fri 10:00–10:30
CAST:

Irma Peterson	Marie Wilson
Jane Stacy (1952–1953)	Cathy Lewis
Mrs. O'Reilly	Gloria Gordon
Professor Kropotkin (1952–1953)	Sig Arno
Al (1952–1953)	Sid Tomack
Richard Rhinelander III (1952–1953)	
. . . .	Brooks West
Mrs. Rhinelander (1952–1953)	
. . . .	Margaret Dumont
Mr. Clyde	Don McBride
Joe Vance (1953–1954)	Hal March
Bobby Peterson (1953–1954)	Richard Eyer
Kay Foster (1953–1954)	Mary Shipp
Mr. Corday (1953–1954)	John Carradine

Marie Wilson was TV's—and radio's, and Hollywood's—favorite dumb blonde. She played many similar characters, but her most famous was the title role in *My Friend Irma,* which she created on radio in 1947. Irma Peterson was possibly the kookiest secretary in the entire world. She was friendly, enthusiastic, sexy—and very wacky. She just had no sense of logic. Her roommate was levelheaded Jane Stacy, whose affection for Irma usually overcame the frustrations she met coping with Irma's predicaments. Irma and Jane shared an apartment in Mrs. O'Reilly's run-down Manhattan boardinghouse, where much of the action took place in this live series. Jane's boyfriend was Richard Rhinelander III, her millionaire boss, while Irma's was an impoverished con artist named Al.

When the TV version was added to radio's *My Friend Irma* in 1952, the three female principals—Marie Wilson, Gloria Gordon, and Cathy Lewis—made the transition, with Miss Lewis talking to the audience in the manner of a narrator to set up the scenes as well as participating in them, as she had done on radio. However, the 1953–1954 season brought a number of cast changes. Irma had a new roommate in newspaper reporter Kay Foster' (Jane had moved to Panama), her seven-year-old nephew Bobby had come to live with her, and she had a new boyfriend named Joe Vance. Her original nutty neighbor Professor Kropotkin, the violinist at the Paradise Burlesque, was also gone, replaced by an eccentric actor, Mr. Corday. The only original regulars left in the cast were Irma, her landlady Mrs. O'Reilly, and Mr. Clyde, the blustery, cranky attorney for whom she worked.

MY FRIEND TONY
Detective Drama
FIRST TELECAST: *January 5, 1969*
LAST TELECAST: *September 31, 1969*
BROADCAST HISTORY:
 Jan 1969–Sep 1969, NBC Sun 10:00–11:00
CAST:
 Prof. John Woodruff .... James Whitmore
 Tony Novello .... Enzo Cerusico

When he was in Italy shortly after the end of World War II, John Woodruff almost had his wallet stolen by a street urchin named Tony. Years later, a fully grown Tony arrived in America to join John as half of a private-investigation team. Professor Woodruff, whose academic career in criminology had given him the ability to analyze the most obscure clues to resolve cases, needed Tony to do his legwork and handle the physical side of the business. As they traveled around the country on various assignments, the contrast between Woodruff's stolid, conservative, analytical approach and Tony's carefree romanticism provided a contentious but productive relationship.

MY HERO
Situation Comedy
FIRST TELECAST: *November 8, 1952*
LAST TELECAST: *August 1, 1953*
BROADCAST HISTORY:
 Nov 1952–Apr 1953, NBC Sat 7:30–8:00
 Apr 1953–Aug 1953, NBC Sat 8:00–8:30
CAST:
 Robert S. Beanblossom .... Robert Cummings
 Julie Marshall .... Julie Bishop
 Willis Thackery .... John Litel

Robert S. Beanblossom was a real estate salesman for the Thackery Realty Company. He was not a particularly good salesman, and his carefree attitude tended to create problems, but he was very lucky. In each episode of this filmed series he somehow managed to stumble through a proposed real-estate deal and come out a winner. His luck was helped along by the office secretary, Julie Marshall, who went out of her way to straighten out his mistakes and protect him from the wrath of the boss, Willis Thackery.

MY LITTLE MARGIE
Situation Comedy
FIRST TELECAST: *June 16, 1952*
LAST TELECAST: *August 24, 1955*
BROADCAST HISTORY:
 Jun 1952–Sep 1952, CBS Mon 9:00–9:30
 Oct 1952–Nov 1952, NBC Sat 7:30–8:00
 Jan 1953–July 1953, CBS Thu 10:00–10:30
 Sep 1953–Aug 1955, NBC Wed 8:30–9:00
CAST:
 Margie Albright .... Gale Storm
 Vernon Albright .... Charles Farrell
 Roberta Townsend .... Hillary Brooke
 Freddie Wilson .... Don Hayden
 Mr. George Honeywell .... Clarence Kolb
 Mrs. Odetts .... Gertrude Hoffman
 Charlie .... Willie Best

Vern Albright was a very eligible widower whose 21-year-old daughter was determined to save him from the machinations of various women. An executive with the investment-counseling firm of Honeywell and Todd, Vern was trimly athletic at age 50, and was most often romantically linked with Roberta Townsend. Margie, who shared her father's Fifth Avenue apartment, was always scheming with old Mrs. Odetts, the next-door neighbor, to make Dad more sedate, as well as to circumvent the parental control he vainly tried to maintain over her. Also recruited to help with various subterfuges were Margie's boyfriend, Freddie, and Charlie, the combination handyman and elevator operator in the Albrights' apartment building.

In a somewhat unusual move, *My Little Margie* went from TV to radio in December 1952, airing concurrently on the CBS radio network for the rest of its TV run (not in simulcasts, but in different original episodes). Gale Storm and Charles Farrell also played the leads in the radio version.

MY LIVING DOLL
Situation Comedy
FIRST TELECAST: *September 27, 1964*
LAST TELECAST: *September 8, 1965*
BROADCAST HISTORY:
 Sep 1964–Dec 1964, CBS Sun 9:00–9:30
 Dec 1964–Sep 1965, CBS Wed 8:00–8:30
CAST:
 Dr. Robert McDonald ..... Robert Cummings
 Rhoda Miller .... Julie Newmar
 Peter Robinson .... Jack Mullaney
 Irene Adams .... Doris Dowling

This comedy introduced the ultimate in male fantasy, a sexy, curvaceous, female robot programmed to do anything she was told—absolutely anything. AF 709 was the secret project number that designated this ultimate achievement in space-age technology, a robot that could think on its own and function like a man—well, like a woman. Statuesque Julie Newmar played the robot. She wandered into the office of base psychiatrist Robert McDonald one day and had a pleasant chat with him. Only later did he find out that she was a robot designed by Dr. Carl Miller. When Dr. Miller was called away on assignment to Pakistan he left the robot in Bob's care. Bob named her Rhoda and passed her off as Dr. Miller's niece. She moved into his home, where Bob took on the task of training her to be the "perfect" woman—one that only talked when spoken to, and did what was asked of her. To complicate things, Bob's neighbor Peter fell in love with Rhoda and had to be fended off lest he discover her secret.

MY MOTHER THE CAR
Situation Comedy
FIRST TELECAST: *September 14, 1965*
LAST TELECAST: *September 6, 1966*
BROADCAST HISTORY:
  Sep 1965–Sep 1966, NBC Tue 7:30–8:00
CAST:
  Dave Crabtree . . . . Jerry Van Dyke
  His Mother's Voice . . . . Ann Sothern
  Barbara Crabtree . . . . Maggie Pierce
  Cindy Crabtree . . . . Cindy Eilbacher
  Randy Crabtree . . . . Randy Whipple
  Capt. Mancini . . . . Avery Schreiber

In what was surely one of her more unusual roles, Ann Sothern played a talking car in this 1965 comedy. Dave Crabtree was a small-town lawyer of modest means with a wife (Barbara), two children (Cindy and Randy), and a small dog. On a visit to a used-car lot in search of an inexpensive second-hand car he found himself strangely attracted to an ancient 1928 Porter. When he got behind the wheel, the car talked to him, informing him that it was the reincarnation of his mother. Against the advice of family and friends he bought the car, because he didn't want to lose "Mother." Dave was the only one whom the car would talk to, or who could really hear what it had to say. The "villain" in the series was Capt. Mancini, an antique car collector who was constantly trying to find a way to get the Porter away from Dave.

MY SISTER EILEEN
Situation Comedy
FIRST TELECAST: *October 5, 1960*
LAST TELECAST: *April 12, 1961*
BROADCAST HISTORY:
  Oct 1960–Apr 1961, CBS Wed 9:00–9:30
CAST:
  Ruth Sherwood . . . . Elaine Stritch
  Eileen Sherwood . . . . Shirley Bonne
  Mr. Appopoplous . . . . Leon Belasco
  Chick Adams . . . . Jack Weston
  Bertha . . . . Rose Marie
  Mr. Beaumont . . . . Raymond Bailey
  Marty Scott . . . . Stubby Kaye

Ruth and Eileen Sherwood moved to New York from Ohio in order to further their careers, Ruth as a writer and her younger sister as an aspiring actress. They moved into a Manhattan brownstone, found an agent named Chuck Adams to help them get work, and tried to adjust to life in the big city. Ruth was more serious, more ambitious, and much more sensible than her beautiful younger sister. She got a job working for Mr. Beaumont, a publisher, and made a good friend of her co-worker Bertha. Eileen, on the other hand, was a sucker for every con man and would-be boyfriend who came along. Her life was full of all kinds of propositions, but few real jobs. Ruth spent much of her time trying to watch over her kid sister.

Based on a book by Ruth McKinley and two movies (1942 and 1955) derived from it.

MY SISTER SAM
Situation Comedy
FIRST TELECAST: *October 6, 1986*
LAST TELECAST: *April 12, 1988*
BROADCAST HISTORY:
  Oct 1986–Sep 1987, CBS Mon 8:30–9:00
  Sep 1987–Nov 1987, CBS Sat 8:00–8:30
  Mar 1988–Apr 1988, CBS Tue 9:00–9:30
CAST:
  Samantha "Sam" Russell . . . . Pam Dawber
  Patti Russell . . . . Rebecca Schaeffer
  J.D. Lucas . . . . Joel Brooks
  Dixie Randazzo . . . . Jenny O'Hara
  Jack Kincaid . . . . David Naughton

Perky Samantha Russell was 29 years old and her career as a free-lance commercial photographer in San Francisco was starting to jell. She had a committed, if somewhat fast-talking, agent in J.D. Lucas and a loyal assistant in outspoken Dixie Randazzo. Then her 16-year-old sister, Patti, arrived to take up residence with Sam in the apartment that doubled as her studio. Patti, who reminded Sam of the free spirit she had been as a teenager, was still in high school, and her presence created a number of problems for her older sister. It got in the way of Sam's social life and caused her to wonder about whether she should treat Patti like a sister, a friend, or a daughter—a conflict she never quite resolved. Living across the hall was Sam's good friend Jack Kincaid, a highly successful, globe-trotting photojournalist who provided emotional support when she needed it.

MY SON JEEP
Situation Comedy
FIRST TELECAST: *July 4, 1953*
LAST TELECAST: *September 22, 1953*
BROADCAST HISTORY:
  Jul 1953–Aug 1953, NBC Sat 7:30–8:00
  Sep 1953, NBC Tue 8:00–8:30
CAST:
  Dr. Robert Allison . . . . Jeffrey Lynn
  Jeep Allison . . . . Martin Huston
  Peggy Allison . . . . Betty Lou Keim

Barbara Miller	Anne Sargent
Mrs. Bixby	Leona Powers
Tommy Clifford..............	William Lally
Boots	Richard Wigginton

Grove Falls, U.S.A., was the setting for this live situation comedy that aired during the summer of 1953. "Jeep" Allison was 10 years old and lived with his 13-year-old sister Peggy and their widowed father, Robert. Robert, a physician, tried to be both mother and father to his two children but found them, particularly Jeep, almost too much to handle. The housekeeper, Mrs. Bixby, attempted to maintain some semblance of order at home while Dr. Allison was at the office. Beautiful Barbara Miller, a substitute teacher who also worked part-time as receptionist for Dr. Allison, was the romantic interest, primarily because Jeep liked her and tried to get his father interested in her in more than just a professional manner.

MY THREE SONS

Situation Comedy
FIRST TELECAST: *September 29, 1960*
LAST TELECAST: *August 24, 1972*
BROADCAST HISTORY:

Sep 1960–Sep 1963, ABC Thu 9:00–9:30
Sep 1963–Sep 1965, ABC Thu 8:30–9:00
Sep 1965–Aug 1967, CBS Thu 8:30–9:00
Sep 1967–Sep 1971, CBS Sat 8:30–9:00
Sep 1971–Dec 1971, CBS Mon 10:00–10:30
Jan 1972–Aug 1972, CBS Thu 8:30–9:00

CAST:

Steve Douglas	Fred MacMurray
Mike Douglas (1960–1965)	Tim Considine
Robbie Douglas................	Don Grady
Chip Douglas	Stanley Livingston
Michael Francis "Bub" O'Casey (1960–1964)	
....	William Frawley
Uncle Charley O'Casey (1965–1972)	
....	William Demarest
Jean Pearson (1960–1961)	Cynthia Pepper
Mr. Henry Pearson (1960–1961)	
....	Robert P. Lieb
Mrs. Florence Pearson (1960–1961)	
....	Florence MacMichael
Hank Ferguson (1961–1963)	Peter Brooks
Sudsy Pfeiffer (1961–1963)	Ricky Allen
Mrs. Pfeiffer (1961–1963).......	Olive Dunbar
Mr. Pfeiffer (1961–1963).........	Olan Soule
Sally Ann Morrison Douglas (1963–1965)	
....	Meredith MacRae
Ernie Thompson Douglas (1963–1972)	
....	Barry Livingston
Katie Miller Douglas (1967–1972)..	Tina Cole
Dave Welch (1965–1967).......	John Howard
Dodie Harper Douglas (1969–1972)	
....	Dawn Lyn
Barbara Harper Douglas (1969–1972)	
....	Beverly Garland
Steve Douglas Jr. (1970–1972) ...	Joseph Todd
Charley Douglas (1970–1972)...	Michael Todd
Robbie Douglas II (1970–1972) ..	Daniel Todd
Fergus McBain Douglas (1971–1972)	
....	Fred MacMurray
Terri Dowling (1971–1972)	Anne Francis
Polly Williams Douglas (1970–1972)	
....	Ronne Troup

THEME:
"Theme from *My Three Sons,*" by Frank DeVol

This long-running family comedy had a Disney flavor to it. Fred MacMurray and Tim Considine had starred together in the hit Disney movie *The Shaggy Dog,* and Don Grady was a former *Mickey Mouse Club* mouseketeer. Even little Stanley Livingston was a show-business veteran, having appeared in several episodes of *The Adventures of Ozzie & Harriet.*

The "family" in this case was all-male. Steve Douglas, a consulting aviation engineer, lived in a medium-sized Midwestern city with his children. A widower, he seemed to spend more time raising his three sons than he did at his job, what with the usual growing pains of boys just beginning to date, going on camping trips, and the other "adventures" of middle-class suburbia. Steve also spent a good deal of time fending off attractive women, who wanted to marry him and take over that lovable, ready-made family. Steve's father-in-law was "Bub" O'Casey, a lovable old coot who lived with them and served as a kind of housekeeper to the clan. When he left after five seasons to take a trip to Iceland (William Frawley had passed away during production), he was replaced by his brother, Uncle Charley, a retired sailor whose crusty disposition masked a soft heart. Others joining the cast in the early years were Sally, Mike's girlfriend and later fiancée (the first serious romance he had had since his infatuation with the "girl next door," Jean Pearson); Robbie's friend Hank; and Chip's pals Sudsy Pfeiffer and Ernie Thompson. Tramp was the family dog.

When the series began in 1960, the boys were aged 18 (Mike), 14 (Robbie), and 7 (Chip). By the start of the 1965–1966 season, when the show moved from ABC to CBS, Tim Considine had grown out of the role as oldest son and wanted out of the series. In the first CBS episode, Mike and Sally got married and moved east so that he might accept a job teaching psychology on the college level. To reestablish the "three sons," Steve subsequently adopted the orphaned Ernie. Things went along much as before for the next two seasons.

In the fall of 1967, Steve moved the family from the Midwest to North Hollywood, California, where his job had taken him. Although the adjustment was not completely pleasant—many of the Douglases' new acquaintances were not too friendly at first—there were good sides to the move. Robbie fell in love with Katie Miller, one of his fellow students at college, and their romance blossomed into marriage before the end of the season. (Katie was played by actress Tina Cole, who had been seen, over the previous few seasons, in a number of "high school girl" roles on *My Three Sons*.) In the fall of 1968, the newly-weds discovered that Katie was pregnant and during that season she gave birth to triplets, Steve, Jr., Charley, and Robbie II—three sons, of course. 1969 finally brought new love to father Steve in the person of widow Barbara Harper, one of Ernie's teachers. They were married during the season and Barbara's young daughter, Dodie, joined the family. Even Chip (who was by now 17) got into the act, eloping with his college girlfriend, Polly Williams, in the fall of 1970.

As if the sprawling family had not gotten big enough already, Steve's cousin, Fergus McBain Douglas, arrived in the fall of 1971 in search of a wife to take back home to Scotland. A nobleman in his native land, Lord Fergus fell in love with cocktail waitress Terri Dowling. She felt inadequate to go back to Scotland as royalty, but was eventually persuaded.

In its later years, as the size of the family on *My Three Sons* grew and separated into individual households, episodes could no longer include the entire group. More and more often, they dealt with the specific problems of only a part of the large cast of regulars, with different members taking the spotlight from week to week.

From December 1971 until a few weeks after it ended its prime-time run, CBS ran repeat episodes in its daytime lineup.

MY TRUE STORY
Dramatic Anthology
FIRST TELECAST: *May 5, 1950*
LAST TELECAST: *September 22, 1950*
BROADCAST HISTORY:
  May 1950–Jun 1950, ABC Fri 8:30–9:00
  Jun 1950–Sep 1950, ABC Fri 8:00–8:30

Early television, hungry for inexpensive material, tapped many sources. These romantic dramas were based on first-person stories from the pages of *My True Story* magazine. Examples: the conflict in a woman's mind when she must decide whether to marry for money or love; a forgotten actress makes a comeback and then dies; a man-hungry blonde's predicament.

MY TWO DADS
Situation Comedy
FIRST TELECAST: *September 20, 1987*
LAST TELECAST:
BROADCAST HISTORY:
  Sep 1987–Feb 1988, NBC Sun 8:30–9:00
  *Jun 1988–   *, NBC Sun 8:30–9:00
CAST:
  Michael Taylor .... Paul Reiser
  Joey Harris .... Greg Evigan
  Nicole Bradford .... Staci Keanan
  Judge Wilbur .... Florence Stanley
  Ed Klawicki .... Dick Butkus
  Cory Kupkus .... Vonni Ribisi

546

Another of TV's ad-hoc families. This one had two young single men, uptight yuppie businessman Michael and free-spirited artist Joey, sharing a daughter. The two men had competed for the love of the same woman 13 years before, but had ultimately broken up with her—and parted enemies. Now, after years with no contact, they learned that their ex-flame had died and left them joint custody of her plucky 12-year-old daughter, Nicole. One of them was the father, but nobody knew which one. Putting their obvious life-style differences aside, they moved into Joey's artist's flat (filled with campy pop art) and set about child-rearing by comic compromise. Keeping an eye on things was Judge Wilbur, the sarcastic judge who had awarded them custody and who also happened to own the building. Cory was Nicole's boyfriend, and Klawicki ran the local diner.

MY WORLD AND WELCOME TO IT
Situation Comedy
FIRST TELECAST: *September 15, 1969*
LAST TELECAST: *September 7, 1972*
BROADCAST HISTORY:
  Sep 1969–Sep 1970, NBC Mon 7:30–8:00
  Jun 1972–Sep 1972, CBS Thu 8:00–8:30
CAST:
  John Monroe .... William Windom
  Ellen Monroe .... Joan Hotchkis
  Lydia Monroe .... Lisa Gerritsen
  Hamilton Greeley .... Harold J. Stone
  Philip Jensen .... Henry Morgan

My World and Welcome To It was loosely based on the works of the late James Thurber. John Monroe was a writer and cartoonist whose overly active imagination was often as much of a problem as a blessing. As with most Thurber men, John was vaguely unsatisfied with his work, concerned about the direction his life was taking, and mortified by women. In his imaginary secret world he was king, but in real life he was somewhat dominated by his wife and terrified by his daughter. He would constantly muse about the predatory nature of women and was convinced that their sole function was to make his life miserable. Each episode opened with John making observations on a given situation before walking into an animated Thurberlike home in which his wife was reaching around to devour him. The use of Thurberlike cartoons to picture John's fears, as well as his dream world, gave this series a pleasant aspect of fantasy. Other than John's wife, Ellen, and daughter, Lydia, the only two regulars were his publisher, Hamilton Greeley, and cynical fellow writer Philip Jensen. In the summer of 1972 CBS reran episodes of the original NBC series.

MYSTERIES OF CHINATOWN
Crime Drama
FIRST TELECAST: *December 4, 1949*
LAST TELECAST: *October 23, 1950*

BROADCAST HISTORY:
Dec 1949–May 1950, ABC Sun 9:30–10:00
May 1950–Sep 1950, ABC Sun 9:00–9:30
Sep 1950, ABC Tue 8:30–9:00
Oct 1950, ABC Mon 8:30–9:00
CAST:
Dr. Yat Fu .... Marvin Miller
ALSO:
Robert Bice
Cy Kendall
Ed MacDonald

Marvin Miller portrayed Dr. Yat Fu, proprietor of an herb and curio shop in San Francisco's Chinatown, and an amateur sleuth of some note. The program originated in Hollywood and was seen in the East via kinescope.

MYSTERY IS MY BUSINESS
syndicated title for *Ellery Queen* (1954 edition)

MYSTERY PLAYHOUSE
see *Danger*

MYSTERY PLAYHOUSE STARRING BORIS KARLOFF
see *Starring Boris Karloff*

MYSTERY THEATER
see *Mark Saber*

MYSTERY THEATRE
see *Movies—Prior to 1961*

N

NBC ACTION PLAYHOUSE
Dramatic Anthology
FIRST TELECAST: *June 24, 1971*
LAST TELECAST: *September 5, 1972*
BROADCAST HISTORY:
Jun 1971–Sep 1971, NBC Thu 7:30–8:30
May 1972–Sep 1972, NBC Tue 8:30–9:30
HOST:
Peter Marshall

The filmed dramas presented as *NBC Action Playhouse* were reruns of former episodes of *Bob Hope Presents the Chrysler Theatre*. Peter Marshall taped new introductions for the episodes, to replace the original introductions done by Hope. In 1971 this series was the summer replacement for *The Flip Wilson Show*. In 1972 some of the 1971 episodes were aired again with the same Peter Marshall introductions they had had the previous summer.

NBC ADVENTURE THEATRE
Dramatic Anthology
FIRST TELECAST: *July 24, 1971*
LAST TELECAST: *September 7, 1972*
BROADCAST HISTORY:
Jul 1971–Sep 1971, NBC Sat 7:30–8:30
Jun 1972–Sep 1972, NBC Thu 8:00–9:00
HOST:
Art Fleming (1971)
Ed McMahon (1972)

NBC Adventure Theatre consisted of reruns of episodes of *Bob Hope Presents the Chrysler Theatre*. Art Fleming was the host in 1971 and Ed McMahon in 1972. The introductions that they provided to the filmed dramas replaced the original ones that had been done by Bob Hope. Some of the shows aired in 1972 were repeats of episodes aired in 1971.

NBC CINEMA PLAYHOUSE
see *Movies—Prior to 1961*

NBC COMEDY HOUR
Comedy Variety
FIRST TELECAST: *January 8, 1956*
LAST TELECAST: *June 10, 1956*
BROADCAST HISTORY:
Jan 1956–Jun 1956, NBC Sun 8:00–9:00
REGULARS:
Jonathan Winters
Hy Averback
Gale Storm
Al White Dancers
Tony Charmoli Dancers
Gordon Jenkins Orchestra
Al Goodman Orchestra

When *NBC Comedy Hour* premiered in January of 1956, the network envisioned it as a showcase for new comedy talent. It was a rather unstructured vaudevillian collection of skits, monologues, song-and-dance numbers, one-liners, blackouts, pantomime, etc. There was to be no regular headliner and new young performers were to work with veterans. Initial reaction from both critics and viewers was extremely negative and the concept was altered drastically. The enormous writing staff was reduced substantially, musical production numbers were added, and each show was designed to have more of a sense of continuity than the disorganized, fragmented original. Gale Storm became the regular hostess at the start of February and remained for two months, to be replaced by a succession of weekly hosts. The only two other regular performers were comedian Jonathan Winters and actor-announcer Hy Averback.

NBC COMEDY PLAYHOUSE
Comedy Anthology
FIRST TELECAST: *June 24, 1968*
LAST TELECAST: *September 5, 1970*
BROADCAST HISTORY:
Jun 1968–Aug 1968, NBC Mon 9:00–10:00
Aug 1970–Sep 1970, NBC Sat 7:30–8:30
HOST:
Monty Hall (1968)
Jack Kelly (1970)

The full-hour light comedies presented as *NBC Comedy Playhouse* were reruns of episodes of *Bob Hope Presents the Chrysler Theatre*. Monty Hall was the host of the 1968 edition and Jack Kelly was the host in 1970. They provided introductions to replace the originals that had been done by Bob Hope.

NBC COMEDY THEATER
Comedy Anthology
FIRST TELECAST: *June 7, 1971*
LAST TELECAST: *September 2, 1972*
BROADCAST HISTORY:
Jun 1971–Aug 1971, NBC Mon 8:00–9:00
Jul 1972–Sep 1972, NBC Sat 8:00–9:00
HOST:
Jack Kelly

The light romantic comedies that comprised *NBC Comedy Theater* were filmed reruns of episodes of *Bob Hope Presents the Chrysler Theatre*. Jack Kelly was the host and provided introductions to replace the originals done by Hope. In 1971 this was the summer replacement for *Laugh-In* and in 1972 for *Emergency*.

NBC CONCERT HALL
Music
FIRST TELECAST: *August 29, 1948*
LAST TELECAST: *September 26, 1948*

BROADCAST HISTORY:
Aug 1948–Sep 1948, NBC Sun 9:00–9:30

A brief summer series of excerpts from classical music and ballet, live and on film.

NBC FOLLIES
Comedy Variety
FIRST TELECAST: *September 13, 1973*
LAST TELECAST: *December 27, 1973*
BROADCAST HISTORY:
Sep 1973–Dec 1973, NBC Thu 10:00–11:00
REGULARS:
Sammy Davis, Jr.
Mickey Rooney
Carl Jablonski Dancers
Harper MacKay Orchestra

Although there was no host on *NBC Follies*, Sammy Davis, Jr., and Mickey Rooney were two performers who appeared in virtually every episode. Without a host, the various acts—sketches, comedy monologues, musical numbers, etc.— were arranged to flow in much the same manner that a vaudeville show did, with one turn leading into the next. Guest talent was featured in each show.

NBC MAGAZINE WITH DAVID BRINKLEY
News Magazine
FIRST TELECAST: *September 26, 1980*
LAST TELECAST: *July 31, 1982*
BROADCAST HISTORY:
Sep 1980–Apr 1981, NBC Fri 10:00–11:00
Apr 1981–Sep 1981, NBC Thu 8:00–9:00
Sep 1981–Apr 1982, NBC Fri 8:00–9:00
Apr 1982–Jul 1982, NBC Sat 10:00–11:00
REGULARS:
David Brinkley (1980–1981)
Jack Perkins
Garrick Utley
Douglas Kiker
Betsy Aaron

This series was NBC's third attempt to develop a news magazine that would attract the kind of audience obtained by CBS' highly successful *60 Minutes* (see *Weekend* and *Prime Time Sunday*). It was highly appropriate that NBC chose David Brinkley to anchor this series, for many people felt that he had originated the news-magazine format with the critically acclaimed *David Brinkley's Journal* in 1961. Unlike *60 Minutes*, *NBC Magazine* aired stories that varied widely in length, some running only a few minutes and others as long as half an hour. The stories ranged from hard-news pieces on defective Titan missiles to light stories profiling ballet star Rudolf Nureyev and veteran actor James Cagney. Brinkley provided commentary on topics covered, as well as on other items in the week's news, and engaged in brief round-table discussion with one or more of the regular field reporters—Perkins, Utley, Kiker, and Aaron—following individual stories.

The original scheduling was not ideal, opposite CBS' red-hot soap opera *Dallas*, but as Brinkley wryly remarked on opening night, "This is a new television program for those of us who don't give a damn who shot J.R."

Brinkley's final appearance on the show was on September 18, 1981, prior to his leaving NBC after many years for rival ABC. The following week the series' title was shortened to *NBC Magazine*, with the remaining correspondents thereafter supplying their own commentary.

NBC MYSTERY MOVIE, THE
Police/Detective Drama
FIRST TELECAST: *September 15, 1971*
LAST TELECAST: *September 4, 1977*
BROADCAST HISTORY:
Sep 1971–Jan 1974, NBC Wed 8:30–10:00
Sep 1972–Sep 1974, NBC Sun 8:30–10:00
Jan 1974–Sep 1974, NBC Tue 8:30–10:00
Sep 1974–Sep 1975, NBC Sun 8:30–10:30
Sep 1975–Sep 1976, NBC Sun 9:00–11:00
Oct 1976–Apr 1977, NBC Sun Various times
May 1977–Sep 1977, NBC Sun 8:00–9:30

The NBC Mystery Movie was an umbrella title used to cover a number of rotating series that appeared in the same time slot on different weeks. The first *Mystery Movie* series premiered in 1971 on Wednesday nights, and included *Columbo*, *McCloud*, and *McMillan and Wife*, three series that had considerable success over the years.

Due to the popularity of the *Mystery Movie* concept in the 1971–1972 season, NBC decided to try another one. The three original elements were moved to Sunday night (retitled *The NBC Sunday Mystery Movie*) and three new ones were introduced on Wednesday, under the new blanket title *The NBC Wednesday Mystery Movie*. However, *Madigan, Cool Million*, and *Banacek* were not as successful as their predecessors, nor were any of the elements that were subsequently tried. Following is a listing of all the various *Mystery Movie* elements aired over the years. Details on each will be found under their separate title headings.

1971–1972: *Mystery Movie* (Wed.): *Columbo, McCloud, McMillan and Wife*
1972–1973: *Sunday Mystery Movie: Columbo, McCloud, McMillan, Hec Ramsey* *Wednesday Mystery Movie: Madigan, Cool Million, Banacek*
1973–1974: *Sunday Mystery Movie: Columbo, McCloud, McMillan, Hec Ramsey* *Wednesday Mystery Movie: Madigan, Tenafly, Faraday & Company, The Snoop Sisters.* (Series moved to Tuesday effective January 1972, retitled *NBC Tuesday Mystery Movie.*)
1974–1975: *Sunday Mystery Movie: Columbo, McCloud, McMillan, Amy Prentiss*

1975–1976: *Sunday Mystery Movie: Columbo,*
McCloud, McMillan, McCoy
1976–1977: *Sunday Mystery Movie: Columbo,*
McCloud, McMillan; Quincy, M.E.
(to December 1976); *Lanigan's Rabbi*
(effective January 1977)

NBC NEWS ENCORE
Documentary
FIRST TELECAST: *June 26, 1966*
LAST TELECAST: *August 21, 1966*
BROADCAST HISTORY:
Jun 1966–Aug 1966, NBC Sun 6:30–7:30
HOST:
Robert Abernethy

Host Robert Abernethy introduced and concluded
each of the episodes of *NBC News Encore*, a series of rebroadcasts of selected NBC news documentaries, the bulk of which had originally aired
as *NBC News Actuality Specials*.

NBC NOVELS FOR TELEVISION
Drama
FIRST TELECAST: *February 14, 1979*
LAST TELECAST: *June 28, 1979*
BROADCAST HISTORY:
Feb 1979–Apr 1979, NBC Wed 9:00–11:00
May 1979–Jun 1979, NBC Thu 10:00–11:00

NBC Novels For Television was the umbrella title
used to describe a collection of four mini-series
that were serialized in consecutive weekly installments in 1979. In order of their showing they were:
From Here to Eternity (February 14–February 28);
Studs Lonigan (March 7–March 21); a repeat presentation of *Wheels* (April 4–April 18), which
originally aired in May 1978; and a repeat presentation of *Aspen* under the title *The Innocent and
the Damned* (May 31–June 28). See under individual titles for details.

NBC PLAYHOUSE
see *Variety*

NBC PLAYHOUSE
Dramatic Anthology
FIRST TELECAST: *June 28, 1960*
LAST TELECAST: *September 6, 1960*
BROADCAST HISTORY:
Jun 1960–Sep 1960, NBC Tue 8:30–9:00
HOSTESS:
Jeanne Bal

Actress Jeanne Bal hosted this summer series
composed of reruns of episodes of *The Loretta
Young Show* in which Miss Young had not
starred. *NBC Playhouse* alternated with *The Gas
Company Playhouse*.

NBC PRESENTS
see *Movies—Prior to 1961*

NBC REPERTORY THEATRE
Dramatic Anthology
FIRST TELECAST: *April 17, 1949*
LAST TELECAST: *July 10, 1949*
BROADCAST HISTORY:
Apr 1949–Jul 1949, NBC Sun 9:00–10:00
PRODUCER:
Owen Davis, Jr.

Early live dramatic program, presenting an original TV play or adaptation each week. Many noted
stars appeared during the course of the series,
which did not utilize a repertory company (despite the title) but had a new cast for each telecast. Perhaps the most notable single production
was *Macbeth*, the annual Shakespearean production of The Players, a New York theatrical association. Among those appearing during the course
of the series were Walter Hampden, Joyce Redman, Leo G. Carroll, Ralph Bellamy, John Carradine, David Wayne, and many others.

NBC REPORTS
Documentary
FIRST TELECAST: *September 12, 1972*
LAST TELECAST: *September 4, 1973*
BROADCAST HISTORY:
Sep 1972–Sep 1973, NBC Tue 10:00–11:00

NBC Reports aired on a regular basis during the
1972–1973 season, presenting news documentaries on various subjects of current interest. It had
no permanent host or narrator. Some of the subjects covered were "Pensions: The Broken Promise," "What Price Health," "And When the War Is
Over . . . The American Military in the '70s," "The
Meaning of Watergate" (on May 22, 1973, five
days after the start of the hearings which ran all
that summer), "American Communism Today,"
and, in a special three-hour final telecast, "The
Energy Crisis—An American White Paper." The
title *NBC Reports* has also frequently been used
for irregularly scheduled documentaries.

NBC SPORTS IN ACTION
Sports
FIRST TELECAST: *May 23, 1965*
LAST TELECAST: *September 5, 1965*
BROADCAST HISTORY:
May 1965–Sep 1965, NBC Sun 6:30–7:30
HOST:
Jim Simpson

NBC Sports in Action was an early attempt to
compete with *ABC's Wide World of Sports*. Jim
Simpson was the regular host and narrator of the
series, which covered various types of sporting
events in depth, with action footage of the event
in progress, as well as interviews with and profiles of sports celebrities. Such sports as surfing,
skiing, auto racing, rugby, sailing, and lacrosse—
none of them seen on a regular basis on American
TV—were featured in all or part of various epi-

sodes of this show. Although it aired in the evening only from May to August, *NBC Sports in Action* had actually premiered in January 1965 and ran until June 1966, usually airing on Sunday afternoons.

NBC SPORTS SPOT
Sports Commentary
FIRST TELECAST: *January 10, 1958*
LAST TELECAST: *January 24, 1958*
BROADCAST HISTORY:
Jan 1958, NBC Fri 10:45–11:00

NBC Sports Spot replaced *Fight Beat* as the show filling the time between the end of the bout on *The Gillette Cavalcade of Sports* and the start of the 11:00 P.M. local news. Each week an outstanding nationally known sportswriter was to be host to a famous sports personality whom he would interview. Red Barber served as host for the first two weeks and Bud Palmer was the host on the third. After only three weeks on the air, however, *NBC Sports Spot* was replaced by *Phillies Jackpot Bowling*.

NBC SUNDAY MYSTERY MOVIE, THE
see *NBC Mystery Movie, The*

NBC TUESDAY MYSTERY MOVIE, THE
see *NBC Mystery Movie, The*

NBC WEDNESDAY MYSTERY MOVIE, THE
see *NBC Mystery Movie, The*

NBC'S BEST SELLERS
Drama
FIRST TELECAST: *September 30, 1976*
LAST TELECAST: *April 25, 1977*
BROADCAST HISTORY:
Sep 1976–Jan 1977, NBC Thu 9:00–10:00
Jan 1977–Apr 1977, NBC Thu 9:00–11:00
Apr 1977, NBC Mon 9:00–11:00

NBC's Best Sellers was the umbrella title used to describe a collection of four novels which were serialized in consecutive installments. In order of their showing they were: *Captains and the Kings* (September 30–November 25), *Once an Eagle* (December 2–January 13), *Seventh Avenue* (February 10–24), and *The Rhinemann Exchange* (March 10–24). The first two were aired primarily in one-hour installments, except for the first and last chapters which ran two hours in length, while the latter two ran in two-hour segments. Of the four, only *Captains and the Kings* was repeated, all in two-hour segments, with its concluding chapter running on *NBC's Monday Night at the Movies*. See under individual titles for specific details.

NBC'S SATURDAY NIGHT LIVE
see *Saturday Night Live*

NFL ACTION
Sports
FIRST TELECAST: *May 12, 1971*
LAST TELECAST: *September 8, 1971*
BROADCAST HISTORY:
May 1971–Sep 1971, ABC Wed 10:30–11:00
NARRATOR:
John Facenda (and others)

Football films focusing on various players, teams, and big games.

N.Y.P.D.
Police Drama
FIRST TELECAST: *September 5, 1967*
LAST TELECAST: *September 16, 1969*
BROADCAST HISTORY:
Sep 1967–Sep 1969, ABC Tue 9:30–10:00
CAST:
Det. Lt. Mike Haines . . . . Jack Warden
Det. Jeff Ward . . . . Robert Hooks
Det. Johnny Corso . . . . Frank Converse

New York City was the real star of this police series. Much of the filming was done on location there, and the city's underworld denizens were realistically portrayed. The three N.Y.P.D. plainclothes detectives were experienced Mike Haines, 18 years on the force, the younger Johnny Corso, and black officer Jeff Ward. Together they tracked murderers, extortionists, drug pushers, bombers, rapists, and other thugs around the bustling city. Locales varied from the Bowery to Wall Street, the Empire State Building to Shubert Alley, Greenwich Village to Times Square. The program was commended by real-life Mayor John Lindsay, who permitted filming of some scenes in City Hall. *N.Y.P.D.* was produced with the cooperation of the New York Police Department, with episodes based on actual cases.

NAKED CITY
Police Drama
FIRST TELECAST: *September 30, 1958*
LAST TELECAST: *September 11, 1963*
BROADCAST HISTORY:
Sep 1958–Sep 1959, ABC Tue 9:30–10:00
Oct 1960–Sep 1963, ABC Wed 10:00–11:00
CAST:
Det. Lt. Dan Muldoon (1958–1959)
. . . . John McIntire
Det. Jim Halloran (1958–1959)
. . . . James Franciscus
Janet Halloran (1958–1959) . . . . Suzanne Storrs
Ptlm./Sgt. Frank Arcaro . . . . . . Harry Bellaver
Lt. Mike Parker (1959–1963)
. . . . Horace McMahon
Det. Adam Flint (1960–1963) . . . . . Paul Burke
Libby (1960–1963) . . . . Nancy Malone
THEME (1960–1963):
"Naked City Theme" ("Somewhere in the Night"), by Billy May and Milton Raskin

551

This popular series was shot on location all over the New York City metropolis, from the Staten Island Ferry to Times Square. A feeling of gritty reality pervaded the stories as veteran cop Dan Muldoon and his young sidekick Jim Halloran ran down the murderers and muggers, petty thieves and swindlers who inhabited the city's seamy side.

The program began undergoing cast changes even in its first season. Det. Muldoon was killed in a spectacular chase sequence seen in a March 1959 episode, when his squad car plowed into a gasoline tank truck (stunt men were often used in *Naked City* for such effects). Lt. Mike Parker became the wizened old pro for the remainder of that season, and also returned when the series came back in hour-long form after a year's layoff. With him in the 1960–1963 run was a new young partner, Det. Adam Flint, Flint's girlfriend, Libby, and Sgt. Frank Arcaro (who had been a patrolman from 1958–1959).

Parker, portrayed by steely-eyed Horace McMahon, was the perfect hard-nosed cop for a hard city, and his portrayal helped make the series a success. Added, too, was some dramatic city-at-dawn theme music by Billy May. But the star was New York itself, where, as the narrator intoned, "There are eight million stories in the Naked City . . ."

Based on a story by Mark Hellinger, which was made into a 1948 movie titled *Naked City*.

NAKIA
Police Drama
FIRST TELECAST: *September 21, 1974*
LAST TELECAST: *December 28, 1974*
BROADCAST HISTORY:
Sep 1974–Dec 1974, ABC Sat 10:00–11:00
CAST:
Deputy Nakia Parker .... Robert Forster
Sheriff Sam Jericho .... Arthur Kennedy
Irene James .... Gloria DeHaven
Deputy Hubbel Martin .... Taylor Lacher
Half Cub .... John Tenorio, Jr.

This action series was about a modern-day deputy sheriff in a New Mexico city. Nakia was of Indian heritage, and he frequently found his loyalties divided between ancient tribal customs and modern police methods. Symbolic was his transportation, which alternated between pickup truck and horse rather than a squad car. His cases involved everything from violent demonstrations on the reservation to inflammatory political scheming on the town council. Irene James was the secretary in the sheriff's office.

Filmed in and around Albuquerque, New Mexico.

NAME OF THE GAME, THE
Adventure
FIRST TELECAST: *September 20, 1968*
LAST TELECAST: *September 10, 1971*

BROADCAST HISTORY:
Sep 1968–Sep 1971, NBC Fri 8:30–10:00
CAST:
Glenn Howard .... Gene Barry
Jeff Dillon .... Tony Franciosa
Dan Farrell .... Robert Stack
Peggy Maxwell .... Susan Saint James
Joe Sample .... Ben Murphy
Andy Hill .... Cliff Potter
Ross Craig .... Mark Miller

The Name of the Game was actually three series under one title. Each of the three stars of the show, Robert Stack, Tony Franciosa, and Gene Barry, was featured in his own self-contained episodes. The connection between them was Howard Publications, a Los Angeles–based publishing empire that had been built up from scratch by its dynamic owner, Glenn Howard. Glenn's position of power, his confrontations with business and political enemies, and his own flamboyant lifestyle were portrayed in his portion of *The Name of the Game*. Within the Howard empire were investigative correspondent Jeff Dillon and editor Dan Farrell. Dillon was a superaggressive former newsboy who had clawed his way up to a position of power and respect working for Howard's *People Magazine*. Farrell was a former FBI agent (possibly type-casting for Robert Stack, Eliot Ness in *The Untouchables*) who had gone into the publishing business because it provided a position from which to make the public aware of the threats posed by organized crime. He was the senior editor of *Crime Magazine*. Common to all three elements of *The Name of the Game* was Peggy Maxwell, the bright, ambitious, and occasionally somewhat kooky editorial assistant to all three men. Joe, Andy, and Ross were reporters with recurring, but not weekly, roles. What was "The Name of the Game"? Well, the title of the 1966 TV-movie on which this series was based was more explicit. It was called *Fame Is the Name of the Game*.

NAME THAT TUNE
Quiz/Audience Participation
FIRST TELECAST: *June 29, 1953*
LAST TELECAST: *October 19, 1959*
BROADCAST HISTORY:
Jun 1953–Jun 1954, NBC Mon 8:00–8:30
Sep 1954–Mar 1955, CBS Thu 10:30–11:00
Sep 1955–Sep 1958, CBS Tue 7:30–8:00
Sep 1958–Oct 1959, CBS Mon 7:30–8:00
EMCEE:
Red Benson (1953–1954)
Bill Cullen (1954–1955)
George De Witt (1955–1959)

Contestants on *Name That Tune* competed with each other to identify the title of a song being played by the Harry Salter Orchestra. When a contestant thought he knew the title, he would race his competitor to ring a bell that was 25 feet away to have the opportunity to guess the title. The biggest winner at the end of each show had the opportunity to win a $1,600 jackpot by correctly identifying seven songs in 30 seconds. Viewers submitted the songs used in this "Golden Medley" and won as much money as the contestants if their song list was used. As the era of the big-money quiz show arrived, a variation in this jackpot system was devised. People working in teams could return each week and try to build their winnings up to a possible $25,000 in the renamed "Golden Medley Marathon." They could win $5,000 per week for a maximum of five weeks.

During the 1970–1971 season a syndicated version of *Name That Tune* was produced with Richard Hayes as emcee. NBC revived it as a network daytime series for two short runs, July 1974 to January 1975, emceed by Dennis James, and January 1977 to June 1977, emceed by Tom Kennedy. Kennedy was also host of a separate weekly syndicated version that ran from 1974 to 1981. This syndicated version was retitled *The $100,000 Name That Tune* in 1976 when it instituted a means by which winning contestants could become really big winners. After 1977 the big winner was determined in a season-ending playoff.

This latter syndicated version of *The $100,000 Name That Tune* was revived for the 1984–1985 season, with Jim Lange as emcee.

NAME'S THE SAME, THE
Quiz/Panel
FIRST TELECAST: *December 5, 1951*
LAST TELECAST: *October 7, 1955*
BROADCAST HISTORY:
 Dec 1951–Nov 1952, ABC Wed 7:30–8:00
 Dec 1952–Aug 1954, ABC Tue 10:30–11:00
 Oct 1954–Jun 1955, ABC Mon 7:30–8:00
 Jun 1955–Sep 1955, ABC Tue 10:00–10:30
 Sep 1955–Oct 1955, ABC Fri 10:00–10:30
EMCEE:
 Robert Q. Lewis (1951–1954)
 Dennis James (1954–1955)
 Bob Elliott and Ray Goulding (1955)
 Clifton Fadiman (1955)
PANELISTS:
 Abe Burrows (1951–1952)
 Joan Alexander
 Meredith Willson (1951–1953)
 Bill Stern (1953–1954)
 Gene Rayburn (1953–1955)
 Bess Myerson (1954–1955)
 Roger Price (1954–1955)
 Audrey Meadows (1955)
PRODUCERS:
 Mark Goodson and Bill Todman

This simple variation on *What's My Line* (produced by the same company) could well have been called *What's My Name.* The gimmick was that each of the contestants appearing on the show, whose names the panel had to guess, had the same name as a famous person or an object.

Thus ordinary folks who happened to be named A. Garter, A. Beard, Abraham Lincoln, Mona Lisa, or Napoleon Bonaparte tried to stump the panel.

The regular panel was fairly stable during the program's first two years, but then considerable turnover began to take place. In addition to those listed above (who lasted six months or more), such celebrities as Jerry Lester, Carl Reiner, Basil Rathbone, and Mike Wallace appeared for shorter runs.

NANCY
Situation Comedy
FIRST TELECAST: *September 17, 1970*
LAST TELECAST: *January 7, 1971*
BROADCAST HISTORY:
 Sep 1970–Jan 1971, NBC Thu 9:30–10:00
CAST:
 Nancy Smith .... Renne Jarrett
 Dr. Adam Hudson .... John Fink
 Uncle Everett.............. Robert F. Simon
 Abigail Townsend .... Celeste Holm
 Turner .... William Bassett
 Rodriguez .... Ernesto Macias
 Willie..................... Eddie Applegate
 Tom Daily .... Frank Aletter

Nancy was the attractive young daughter of the President of the United States. She met a young veterinarian from Center City, Iowa, and they fell in love. Unfortunately, being under constant surveillance by secret service agents Turner and Rodriguez did nothing to promote the romance, and Nancy's chaperone, Abigail, and Adam's Uncle Everett also seemed constantly to get in the way, not to mention the press. The President was never shown on camera, but his aides were, and his voice was heard on occasion. The couple got married in the November 5, 1970, episode, but even that could not save the series from cancellation.

NANCY DREW MYSTERIES, THE
Adventure
FIRST TELECAST: *February 6, 1977*
LAST TELECAST: *January 1, 1978*
BROADCAST HISTORY:
 Feb 1977–Jan 1978, ABC Sun 7:00–8:00
CAST:
 Nancy Drew............. Pamela Sue Martin
 Carson Drew .... William Schallert
 Ned Nickerson (1977) .. George O'Hanlon, Jr.
 George Fayne (1977) .... Jean Rasey
 George Fayne (1977–1978) .... Susan Buckner
 Bess .... Ruth Cox

Nancy Drew was the girls' equivalent of *The Hardy Boys Mysteries,* with which it alternated on Sunday nights. Both programs featured teenage sleuths helping adults solve exciting (but not usually violent) mysteries, such as robberies, haunted houses, blackmail attempts on a college football star, etc.

Nancy was 18 and the daughter of famed criminal lawyer Carson Drew, a widower. George (a girl) was her buddy, not particularly brave but willing to stick by Nancy through thick and thin. Ned was her father's law-student assistant, always willing to help (later he became an investigator for the district attorney's office, and more anxious to keep Nancy out of cases than in them). The Drews' home base was River Heights, a suburb of New York, but the mysteries took them far and wide.

In the fall of 1977 Nancy Drew appeared in several joint episodes with the Hardy Boys. Then in February 1978 the two series were combined, at which time Pamela Sue Martin left the program. See *Hardy Boys Mysteries* for further details.

Based on the Nancy Drew books by "Carolyn Keene" (see *Hardy Boys* for true authorship).

NANCY WALKER SHOW, THE
Situation Comedy
FIRST TELECAST: *September 30, 1976*
LAST TELECAST: *December 23, 1976*
BROADCAST HISTORY:
  Sep 1976–Dec 1976, ABC Thu 9:30–10:00
CAST:
  Nancy Kitteridge . . . . Nancy Walker
  Lt. Cdr. Kenneth Kitteridge . William Daniels
  Terry Folson . . . . Ken Olfson
  Lorraine . . . . Beverly Archer
  Glen . . . . James Cromwell
  Michael Futterman. . . . . Sparky Marcus
  Teddy Futterman . . . . William Schallert
EXECUTIVE PRODUCER:
  Norman Lear
THEME:
  "Nancy's Blues," by Marilyn & Alan Bergman and Marvin Hamlisch

Sarcastic, wisecracking Nancy Kitteridge had an ideal life. Ten months of the year she was an active career woman, head of the Nancy Kitteridge Talent Agency which she ran from her Hollywood apartment. Two months of the year, when her navy husband of 29 years returned for his annual shore leave, she was a newlywed, madly in love. Then disaster struck. Hubby came home to stay, and he seemed intent on both bringing navy-style order to her chaotic life and making up for 29 years of lost time romantically. Ken didn't see why that gay, unemployed actor named Terry should be kept around the house (Terry earned his room and board by serving as Nancy's secretary), and in fact he thought she should close down the talent agency entirely. Adding to the confusion was Nancy's handwringing, hypochondriac daughter Lorraine, son-in-law Glen, and Michael, the precocious, six-year-old son of boy-wonder TV network executive Teddy Futterman.

NANETTE FABRAY SHOW, THE
see *Westinghouse Playhouse*

NANNY AND THE PROFESSOR
Situation Comedy

FIRST TELECAST: *January 21, 1970*
LAST TELECAST: *December 27, 1971*
BROADCAST HISTORY:
  Jan 1970–Aug 1970, ABC Wed 7:30–8:00
  Sep 1970–Sep 1971, ABC Fri 8:00–8:30
  Sep 1971–Dec 1971, ABC Mon 8:00–8:30
CAST:
  Phoebe Figalilly . . . . Juliet Mills
  Prof. Howard Everett . . . . Richard Long
  Hal Everett. . . . . David Doremus
  Butch Everett. . . . . Trent Lehman
  Prudence Everett . . . . Kim Richards
  Aunt Henrietta (1971) . . . . Elsa Lanchester
  Francine Fowler . . . . Eileen Baral
  Mrs. Florence Fowler . . . . Patsy Garrett

Phoebe was an uncanny young nanny who breezed in unannounced from England and captivated the Everett household. She arrived just at the right time, as Miss Dunbar, Prof. Everett's fifth housekeeper in a year, had just quit in utter frustration at trying to keep order in the chaotic household. That left the widowed mathematics professor in charge of Hal, a 12-year-old with a fascination for scientific experiments; 8-year-old Butch, who was into everything; and 5-year-old Prudence, a musical prodigy who practiced the same piano piece incessantly; plus Waldo, the family sheepdog, Myrtle, the guinea pig, and other pets. Nanny's sunny disposition and apparently psychic abilities (could she really talk to the animals?) won everybody's heart in this relentlessly cute comedy.

NASH AIRFLYTE THEATER
Dramatic Anthology
FIRST TELECAST: *September 21, 1950*
LAST TELECAST: *March 15, 1951*
BROADCAST HISTORY:
  Sep 1950–Mar 1951, CBS Thu 10:30–11:00
HOST:
  William Gaxton

This live New York–originated anthology series aired during the 1950–1951 season and was hosted by William Gaxton. The range of material was extremely varied. John Payne starred in the premiere telecast, a Western adapted from the O. Henry story "A Double-Dyed Deceiver." Metropolitan Opera soprano Marguerite Piazza starred in an original musical comedy called "The Box Supper," and Patricia Morison was featured in an adaptation of the Gilbert and Sullivan operetta *Trial by Jury*. On the more serious dramatic side, Barbara Bel Geddes starred in the first televised adaptation of a John Steinbeck story, "Molly Morgan." Grace Kelly, Otto Kruger, Fredric March, and Lee Bowman also starred in straight plays on this series.

NASHVILLE 99
Police Drama
FIRST TELECAST: *April 1, 1977*
LAST TELECAST: *April 22, 1977*

Apr 1977, CBS Fri 8:00–9:00
CAST:
Det. Lt. Stonewall Jackson "Stoney" Huff
.... Claude Akins
Det. Trace Mayne .... Jerry Reed
Birdie Huff .... Lucille Benson

Filmed on location in Nashville, and utilizing many country music performers as guest stars playing themselves, *Nashville 99* was the story of a Southern lawman fighting crime in the C&W capital of the world. Stoney Huff was a veteran cop who, with the aid of his partner Trace (played by country music star Jerry Reed), fought organized crime, chased down kidnappers, and performed other law-enforcement duties in this short-lived series.

NASHVILLE ON THE ROAD
Music
BROADCAST HISTORY:
Syndicated only
30 minutes
Produced: *1975–1983* (208 episodes)
Released: *1975*
HOST:
Jim Ed Brown (1975–1981)
Jim Stafford (1981–1983)
REGULARS:
Jerry Clower (1975–1981)
Wendy Holcombe (1975–1981)
The Cates Sisters (1975–1976)
The Fairchilds (1976–1977)
Helen Cornelius (1977–1981)
Rex Allen, Jr. (1981–1983)
Sue Powell (1981–1983)

This popular country music series was filmed at colorful outdoor locations from Florida to Hawaii to Prince Edward Island, Canada—hence the "on the road." Different guest stars were featured each week.

NASHVILLE PALACE, THE
Musical Variety
FIRST TELECAST: *October 24, 1981*
LAST TELECAST: *August 7, 1982*
BROADCAST HISTORY:
Oct 1981–Nov 1981, NBC Sat 9:00–10:00
Jul 1982–Aug 1982, NBC Sat 9:00–10:00
REGULARS:
Slim Pickens
Lynn Hancock
Chuck Bulot
Terri Gardner
Harry Murphy
Kent Perkins
Donna Siegel
Wendy Suits
Hamilton Camp
The Dixie Dozen Dancers
The Charlie McCoy Band

Originating from Opryland U.S.A. in Nashville, and produced by the people responsible for *Hee Haw, The Nashville Palace* was a mix of country music, comedy skits, and big production numbers. Each week a guest host presided over the show, although resident announcer Slim Pickens was on hand to heckle. Lynn Hancock was featured in a weekly visit to the "Boots" honky-tonk, where she was the hostess, Miss Boots. A group of comedians, collectively known as the Nashville Palace Comedy Company, performed in the skits. Guest hosts included Roy Clark, Roy Rogers and Dale Evans, and Joe Namath, with country stars Hank Williams, Jr., Mickey Gilley, Tom T. Hall, and Larry Gatlin among the performers.

NAT "KING" COLE SHOW, THE
Musical Variety
FIRST TELECAST: *November 5, 1956*
LAST TELECAST: *December 17, 1957*
BROADCAST HISTORY:
Nov 1956–Jun 1957, NBC Mon 7:30–7:45
Jul 1957–Sep 1957, NBC Tue 10:00–10:30
Sep 1957–Dec 1957, NBC Tue 7:30–8:00
REGULARS:
Nat "King" Cole
The Boataneers (1956)
The Herman McCoy Singers
The Randy Van Horne Singers (1957)
The Jerry Graff Singers (1957)
The Cheerleaders (1957)
Nelson Riddle and His Orchestra

Nat "King" Cole was a man ahead of his time, and that fact cost him his network series. When his 15-minute show premiered in 1956, he became the first major black performer to headline a network variety series. There had been previous attempts at black series, but they were either short-lived fill-ins with lesser-known talent such as *Sugar Hill Times* in 1949 and *Hazel Scott* in 1950, or rather degrading parodies such as *Beulah* or *Amos 'n' Andy*. Nat's short Monday evening show, which filled the remainder of the half hour in which NBC aired its nightly news program, allowed him little more than the opportunity to sing a couple of songs and occasionally welcome a guest vocalist. The following July, Nat moved to Tuesdays with an expanded half-hour show, allowing time for more variety and guests.

Throughout its run, however, *The Nat "King" Cole Show* was plagued with problems. It failed to attract a significant audience, and therefore sponsors were reluctant to underwrite the show. From 1956–1957 Nat averaged only 19 percent of the viewing audience, compared to the 50 percent who were watching *Robin Hood* on CBS. Nat even trailed a documentary-travelogue on ABC, called *Bold Journey,* which got 21 percent of the audience (the remaining 10 percent were watching non-network programs).

Despite widespread apathy on the part of viewers and sponsors, NBC did not give up on the show, keeping it on the air, at a loss, through the fall of 1957. The performing community was well aware of Nat's sponsor problems, and many stars appeared on the show for minimum fees as personal favors to him, in an effort to save the show. Virtually every black musical star showed up at one time or another, including Count Basie, Mahalia Jackson, Pearl Bailey, Billy Eckstine, Sammy Davis, Jr., the Mills Brothers, Cab Calloway, Ella Fitzgerald, and Harry Belafonte. Nat had his white supporters too, among them Stan Kenton, Frankie Laine, Mel Torme, Peggy Lee, Gogi Grant, Tony Martin, and Tony Bennett. But the effort was in vain. It would be another decade before black entertainers could begin to make a significant dent in the mass medium of television.

NATIONAL BARN DANCE, THE

see *ABC Barn Dance*

NATIONAL BOWLING CHAMPIONS

Sports
FIRST TELECAST: *April 8, 1956*
LAST TELECAST: *December 29, 1957*
BROADCAST HISTORY:
Apr 1956–Dec 1956, NBC Sun 10:30–11:00
Sep 1957–Dec 1957, ABC Sun 8:30–9:00
COMMENTATOR:
"Whispering" Joe Wilson

In 1956 *National Bowling Champions* was telecast live from Chicago. Two professional bowlers competed in a three-game match, the last game and a half telecast on the air. The winner received $1 for every pin knocked down, $10 for every pin in excess of 700 for the series, and $10,000 for a perfect "300" game.

Essentially the same show, with some minor changes, returned on ABC in the fall of 1957, under the title *Bowling Stars*. Also originating from Chicago, the ABC show was filmed in advance, and the winner who, as on NBC, would return the following week to defend his "King of the Hill" title, won a minimum of $1,000. The bonuses for scores in excess of 700 applied to both bowlers, with the loser taking home $1 for every pin knocked down (instead of the flat $500 on NBC), and the $10,000 bonus for a "300" game was still in effect. The series moved to Sunday afternoons in 1958. It remained on Sundays, with the new title *Bowling Stars*, from January 1958 to March 1959 on ABC, and from October 1960 to May 1961 on NBC.

NATIONAL VELVET

Adventure
FIRST TELECAST: *September 18, 1960*
LAST TELECAST: *September 10, 1962*
BROADCAST HISTORY:
Sep 1960–Sep 1961, NBC Sun 8:00–8:30
Sep 1961–Sep 1962, NBC Mon 8:00–8:30
CAST:
Velvet Brown................... Lori Martin
Martha Brown.................. Ann Doran
Mi Taylor................. James McCallion
Herbert Brown .... Arthur Space
Edwina Brown................ Carole Wells
Donald Brown................. Joseph Scott
Teddy .... Carl Crow
John Hadley (1961–1962)...... Rickey Kelman

National Velvet, with its story of a girl and her dreams to run her horse in a championship race, is a classic young people's novel. The movie version (1944) had propelled child actress Elizabeth Taylor to stardom. For TV the setting was changed from England to a Midwestern American dairy farm. Twelve-year-old Velvet had a beautiful chestnut thoroughbred named King, and her greatest dream in the whole world was to train King well enough to run in the Grand National Steeplechase. Velvet's parents, Herbert and Martha, who ran the small dairy farm, shared her love and hopes. Helping her train King was Mi Taylor, an ex-jockey who worked around the farm as a handyman. Also in the cast were Velvet's teenage sister, Winna, her younger brother, Donald, Winna's boyfriend, Teddy, and Donald's friend John. The episodes dealt with the other members of the family on occasion, but centered mostly on Velvet and King.

NATION'S FUTURE, THE

Debate
FIRST TELECAST: *November 12, 1960*
LAST TELECAST: *September 16, 1961*
BROADCAST HISTORY:
Nov 1960–Sep 1961, NBC Sat 9:30–10:30
MODERATOR:
John K. M. McCaffery (1960–1961)
Edwin Newman (1961)

The Nation's Future was a live weekly debate series in which two internationally known public figures, often politicians, expressed their opposing views on a specific issue of national interest. Topics covered ranged from foreign policy and social services to censorship and birth control. On occasion the first half hour of the show was national with local stations filling the second half hour with their own discussion of the issue being covered. John K. M. McCaffery was the moderator through May 27, 1961, and was replaced on June 10, 1961, by Edwin Newman.

NATURE OF THINGS, THE

Instruction
FIRST TELECAST: *February 5, 1948*
LAST TELECAST: *August 29, 1952*
BROADCAST HISTORY:
Feb 1948–Mar 1948, NBC Thu 9:45–10:00
Apr 1948–Dec 1948, NBC Thu 8:15–8:30
Dec 1948–May 1949, NBC Mon Various 15-minute spots
Jul 1949–Aug 1949, NBC Mon 9:30–9:45
Sep 1949–Feb 1950, NBC Sat 7:30–7:45
Mar 1950–Jun 1950, NBC Sat 6:45–7:00

Jun 1950–Sep 1950, NBC Wed 8:15–8:30
Jun 1951–Aug 1951, NBC Fri 10:45–11:00
Jul 1952–Aug 1952, NBC Fri 10:45–11:00

HOST:
Dr. Roy K. Marshall

Dr. Roy K. Marshall of the Fels Planetarium was one of early TV's favorite scientists. His live science program, which was telecast from Philadelphia, featured illustrated talks and interviews on many subjects, including physics, astronomy, and the weather. One early 1948 telecast originated from an observatory, where the camera gave a live telescope's-eye view of the moon and Saturn. Such subjects as the possibility of future space travel were also discussed.

After two and a half years in prime time the program left the air in September 1950. It returned the following January as a Saturday afternoon show, and remained a Saturday/Sunday fixture (aside from some prime-time telecasts in the summers) until 1954.

NAVY LOG
Military Anthology
FIRST TELECAST: *September 20, 1955*
LAST TELECAST: *September 25, 1958*
BROADCAST HISTORY:
Sep 1955–Oct 1955, CBS Tue 8:00–8:30
Nov 1955–Sep 1956, CBS Tue 8:30–9:00
Oct 1956–Oct 1957, ABC Wed 8:30–9:00
Oct 1957–Jan 1958, ABC Thu 10:00–10:30
Jan 1958–Sep 1958, ABC Thu 9:30–10:00

The filmed dramas aired in this series were all reenactments of incidents that had actually happened to U.S. Navy personnel.

The focus was on individual sailors and airmen, often in a battle setting but sometimes in their private lives, as in the story of a mentally disturbed veteran, or a romance disrupted by a sailor's transfer. Most of the subjects were ordinary servicemen, but some famous incidents were dramatized, such as the plan to ambush the plane carrying Admiral Yamamoto, the Japanese commander during World War II, and the sinking of John F. Kennedy's PT-109 in the South Pacific (Kennedy, then a senator, appeared as a special guest on this telecast). Lesser known actors and actresses were featured, although famous personalities sometimes served as host. The stories were all based on official Navy files, and produced with the cooperation of the Navy Department.

NEEDLES AND PINS
Situation Comedy
FIRST TELECAST: *September 21, 1973*
LAST TELECAST: *December 28, 1973*
BROADCAST HISTORY:
Sep 1973–Dec 1973, NBC Fri 9:00–9:30
CAST:
Nathan Davidson .... Norman Fell
Harry Karp .... Louis Nye

Wendy Nelson .... Deirdre Lenihan
Sonia Baker .... Sandra Deel
Charlie Miller .... Bernie Kopell
Max .... Larry Gelman
Myron Russo .... Alex Henteloff
Julius Singer................. Milton Selzer

New York City's famous garment district was the setting for this situation comedy about Nathan Davidson, owner of the Lorelei Fashion House, a manufacturer of women's clothing. Also prominent were Nathan's brother and partner, Harry, and his new designer, Wendy, a Nebraska girl adjusting both to life in the big city and the hectic pace of the fashion industry. Featured in the series were Sonia, the bookkeeper and secretary; Charlie, the firm's salesman; Max, the fabric cutter; Myron, the pattern maker; and Singer, Nathan's principal competitor.

NERO WOLFE
Detective Drama
FIRST TELECAST: *January 16, 1981*
LAST TELECAST: *August 25, 1981*
BROADCAST HISTORY:
Jan 1981–Apr 1981, NBC Fri 9:00–10:00
Apr 1981–Aug 1981, NBC Tue 10:00–11:00
CAST:
Nero Wolfe .... William Conrad
Archie Goodwin .... Lee Horsley
Saul Panzer .... George Wyner
Theodore Horstman........... Robert Coote
Fritz Brenner .... George Voskovec
Inspector Cramer .... Allan Miller

Nero Wolfe was a reclusive, rotund crime-solving genius who rarely ventured out of his lavish New York City brownstone. A wealthy eccentric, Nero seemed most concerned with his prize-winning orchids, spending much of his time tending them in his private greenhouse. But he also had a nose for detective work. Since he rarely left his home, he depended on his trusted assistant, Archie Goodwin, to do most of the legwork and gather the clues. Nero then neatly provided the brilliant analysis and deduction that led to the solution. Others on Nero's staff were Saul Panzer, who helped Archie; Horstman, Nero's valued horticulturist; and Fritz, the gourmet cook.

Although adapted from the extensive series of novels by author Rex Stout, *Nero Wolfe* could actually have been an extension of the character played by star William Conrad in his previous series *Cannon*. Wolfe certainly looked like Cannon in semiretirement. Both men had expensive tastes, were lovers of gourmet food, and had similarly well-developed powers of analytical deduction.

NEW ADVENTURES OF BEANS BAXTER, THE
Adventure/Espionage
FIRST TELECAST: *July 18, 1987*
LAST TELECAST: *April 9, 1988*

BROADCAST HISTORY:
Jul 1987–Oct 1987, FOX Sat 8:30–9:00
Oct 1987–Apr 1988, FOX Sat 9:00–9:30
CAST:
Benjamin "Beans" Baxter, Jr.
.... Jonathan Ward
Number Two .... Jerry Wasserman
Cake Lase .... Karen Mistal
Woodshop .... Stuart Fratkin
Mrs. Susan Baxter .... Elinor Donahue
Scooter Baxter .... Scott Bremner
Mr. Sue .... Kurtwood Smith
Vlodia .... Bruce Wagner
Henry .... David Longworth

Teenager Beans Baxter led a double life in this very tongue-in-cheek espionage series. To the outside world he was a just a student at Upper Georgetown High School in suburban Washington, D.C., living with his mother, Susan, who was oblivious to all that was going on around her, and his little brother, Scooter. Woodshop was Beans' off-beat best friend at school and Cake the beautiful girl who would have gone steady with him if only he wasn't so distracted.

Those distractions stemmed from Beans' other life as a courier-spy for an intelligence agency known as "The Network." His father, Benjamin, (played by Rick Lenz), had been a top courier for The Network—disguised as a mailman—until he was kidnapped by agents for U.G.L.I., the subversive Underground Government Liberation Intergroup. The minions of U.G.L.I., led by the dioboli-cal Mr. Sue, were forever trying to capture Beans, hoping to use the threat of harming him to force his dad to reveal top-secret information. Meanwhile Beans, under the direction of The Network's second-in-command, Number Two, delivered top-secret messages by hiding in vending machines and riding his bicycle into secret hideouts, while trying to find a way to free his dad from the clutches of U.G.L.I.

NEW ADVENTURES OF CHARLIE CHAN, THE
Mystery
BROADCAST HISTORY:
Syndicated only
30 minutes
Produced: *1956–1957* (39 episodes)
Released: *June 1957*
CAST:
Charlie Chan .... J. Carrol Naish
Barry Chan .... James Hong

Earl Derr Biggers' famous philosopher-sleuth came to television only briefly in the 1950s, in this British-made series. In previous productions Chan had been an inspector on the Honolulu Police Force, but here he operated out of London, unraveling complex mysteries with the patience and deduction for which he had become famous. As always, his manners were impeccable. His number-one son and trusted aide was Barry.

New York Irishman J. Carrol Naish was one of a long line of non-Orientals to play Chan. Among the others were Warner Oland, Sydney Toler, and Roland Winters in the movies of the 1930s and 1940s; Walter Connolly, Ed Begley, and Santos Ortega on radio during the same period. There were also Charlie Chan comic strips and comic books. In 1971 there were plans for another TV series, and a pilot movie was made starring Ross Martin, but it was not successful. Even later, there was a somewhat ridiculous Charlie Chan cartoon on CBS' Saturday morning schedule (1972–1974) called *The Amazing Chan and the Chan Clan.*

Charlie Chan was originally modeled on a real person, detective Chang Apana of the Honolulu police.

NEW ADVENTURES OF HUCK FINN, THE
Adventure
FIRST TELECAST: *September 15, 1968*
LAST TELECAST: *September 7, 1969*
BROADCAST HISTORY:
Sep 1968–Sep 1969, NBC Sun 7:00–7:30
CAST:
Huck Finn .... Michael Shea
Becky Thatcher .... Lu Ann Haslam
Tom Sawyer .... Kevin Schultz
Injun Joe .... Ted Cassidy

Much in the style of the highly successful Disney movie *Mary Poppins, The New Adventures of Huck Finn* combined live actors with animated settings. The three young principals, Huck, Becky, and Tom, were confronted with Injun Joe at the start of the first episode. He had sworn to get even with Huck for testifying against him in court and the three youngsters, fearing for their lives, ran away to escape him. As they ran, they began an adventure in which the villain was an animated version of Injun Joe. From episode to episode, the settings varied between contemporary and historical, domestic and foreign. The youngsters were always the only live characters in an otherwise animated adventure series.

NEW ADVENTURES OF MARTIN KANE, THE
see *Martin Kane, Private Eye*

NEW ADVENTURES OF PERRY MASON, THE
see *Perry Mason*

NEW ADVENTURES OF WONDER WOMAN, THE
see *Wonder Woman*

NEW ANDY GRIFFITH SHOW, THE
Situation Comedy
FIRST TELECAST: *January 8, 1971*
LAST TELECAST: *May 21, 1971*
BROADCAST HISTORY:
Jan 1971–May 1971, CBS Fri 8:30–9:00

CAST:

Andy Sawyer	Andy Griffith
Lee Sawyer	Lee Meriwether
Nora	Ann Morgan Guilbert
Lori Sawyer	Lori Rutherford
T. J. Sawyer	Marty McCall
Buff MacKnight	Glen Ash
Verline MacKnight	Susan Davis

Andy Sawyer had been working in a government capacity in the state capital when he was informed that the mayor of his home town of Greenwood was retiring and looking for someone to take over the unexpired portion of his current term. Andy moved home, with his wife, Lee, and his two children, to take the job. Greenwood was a small, rural Southern town and the role of mayor gave star Andy Griffith the opportunity to return to the type of gentle, homespun comedy that had made the original *Andy Griffith Show* so popular. This was on the heels of his failure in the much different title role in *The Headmaster*, but it lasted little longer.

NEW BILL COSBY SHOW, THE
Comedy Variety
FIRST TELECAST: *September 11, 1972*
LAST TELECAST: *May 7, 1973*
BROADCAST HISTORY:
    Sep 1972–May 1973, CBS Mon 10:00–11:00
REGULARS:
    Bill Cosby
    Lola Falana
    Susan Tolsky
    Foster Brooks
    Frank Shaw
    Quincy Jones Orchestra
    Oscar DeGruy
    Pat McCormick
    Mike Elias
    Ronny Graham
    Stan Ross
    Ray Jessel

Comedian Bill Cosby was the star and host of this variety series that showcased guest stars in addition to its regulars. Each episode included a Cosby monologue, several comedy sketches, and one or two musical numbers. Two regular sketches were "The Wife of the Week" and vignettes about "The Dude," a character who was so cool that nothing fazed him. Dancer Lola Falana also functioned as the announcer on this series.

NEW BREED, THE
Police Drama
FIRST TELECAST: *October 3, 1961*
LAST TELECAST: *September 25, 1962*
BROADCAST HISTORY:
    Oct 1961–Nov 1961, ABC Tue 9:00–10:00
    Nov 1961–Sep 1962, ABC Tue 8:30–9:30

CAST:

Lt. Price Adams	Leslie Nielsen
Sgt. Vince Cavelli	John Beradino
Ptlmn. Joe Huddleston	John Clarke
Ptlmn. Pete Garcia	Greg Roman
Capt. Keith Gregory	Byron Morrow

These men were a "new breed" of policeman. They were trained in the use of sophisticated electronic gadgetry to track down criminals who were uncapturable by traditional police methods. As members of the elite Metropolitan Squad of the Los Angeles Police Department, they were under the immediate supervision of Lt. Price Adams. Price was both their superior and leader as they assaulted the underworld in the Southern California area.

NEW CHRISTY MINSTRELS, THE
Musical Variety
FIRST TELECAST: *August 6, 1964*
LAST TELECAST: *September 10, 1964*
BROADCAST HISTORY:
    Aug 1964–Sep 1964, NBC Thu 9:30–10:00
REGULARS:
    The New Christy Minstrels

This five-week summer replacement for *Hazel* was actually titled *Ford Presents the New Christy Minstrels,* in deference to its sponsor. The nine-member folk-singing group was led by Randy Sparks and was quite popular during the mid-1960s. Lead singer was Barry McGuire. Sparks and his group were joined each week by a guest comedian and the shows all had outdoor settings, including two from the New York World's Fair and three from locations in the Los Angeles area. The original Christy Minstrels was a famous minstrel troupe of the mid-1800s which popularized many of Stephen Foster's songs.

NEW COMEDY SHOWCASE
Comedy Anthology
FIRST TELECAST: *August 1, 1960*
LAST TELECAST: *September 19, 1960*
BROADCAST HISTORY:
    Aug 1960–Sep 1960, CBS Mon 10:00–10:30

The situation comedies that were aired in this anthology series were unsold pilots for projected regular series, including one starring Johnny Carson called *Johnny Come Lately* and another with Dick Van Dyke titled *The Trouble with Richard.*

NEW DICK VAN DYKE SHOW, THE
Situation Comedy
FIRST TELECAST: *September 18, 1971*
LAST TELECAST: *September 2, 1974*
BROADCAST HISTORY:
    Sep 1971–Sep 1972, CBS Sat 9:00–9:30
    Sep 1972–Dec 1972, CBS Sun 9:00–9:30
    Jan 1972–Sep 1973, CBS Sun 7:30–8:00
    Sep 1973–Sep 1974, CBS Mon 9:30–10:00

Dick Preston .... Dick Van Dyke
Jenny Preston .... Hope Lange
Bernie Davis (1971–1973) .... Marty Brill
"Mike" Preston (1971–1973) ..... Fannie Flagg
Carol Davis (1971–1973) ..... Nancy Dussault
Ted Atwater (1972–1973) .... David Doyle
Lucas Preston (1971–1973) ..... Michael Shea
Lucas Preston (1973) .... Wendell Burton
Annie Preston .... Angela Powell
Max Mathias (1973–1974)... Dick Van Patten
Dennis Whitehead (1973–1974)
.... Barry Gordon
Alex Montenez (1973–1974) ... Henry Darrow
Richard Richardson (1973–1974)
.... Richard Dawson
Connie Richardson (1973–1974) . Chita Rivera
Margot Brighton (1973–1974) ... Barbara Rush

During its first two seasons on the air, The New Dick Van Dyke Show was filmed on location at Carefree, Arizona. Dick Preston was the host of a local talk show on KXIV-TV, a mythical Phoenix, Arizona, television station. The series revolved around his personal life with his wife, Jenny, and their nine-year-old daughter, and his professional life with the talk show. His manager, Bernie, and Bernie's wife were personal friends and his sister Mike doubled as his secretary. Seen occasionally was Dick's son Lucas, who was away at a private boarding school.

For the third season, the setting of the show moved to Hollywood, and so did its production. Dick moved his family there so that he could take advantage of an opportunity to star in a daytime soap opera, Those Who Care. New series regulars were the soap opera's writer, Dennis Whitehead; its producer, Max Mathias; its stage manager, Alex Montenez; and the soap opera's star, Margot Brighton. In the soap Dick played Dr. Brad Fairmont. At home the Prestons had acquired new neighbors in Richard and Connie Richardson.

NEW DOCTORS, THE
Medical Drama
FIRST TELECAST: September 14, 1969
LAST TELECAST: June 23, 1973
BROADCAST HISTORY:
Sep 1969–Sep 1972, NBC Sun 10:00–11:00
Sep 1972–Jan 1973, NBC Tue 9:00–10:00
May 1973–Jun 1973, NBC Fri 10:00–11:00
CAST:
Dr. David Craig .... E. G. Marshall
Dr. Paul Hunter .... David Hartman
Dr. Ted Stuart (1969–1972) .... John Saxon
Dr. Martin Cohen (1972–1973)
.... Robert Walden

The stories told on The New Doctors took place at the fictional David Craig Institute of New Medicine. The institute was a combination hospital and research center, founded, named after, and run by Dr. David Craig, and dedicated to perfecting new medical techniques. Dr. Craig's expertise in the field had earned him the respect of the profession and had made it possible for him to obtain the funding to pursue new medical breakthroughs. His chief of surgery was brilliant young heart-transplant specialist Dr. Ted Siuart, while Dr. Paul Hunter worked on nonsurgical techniques for treating disease. Dr. Martin Cohen became a regular at the start of the final season, replacing the departed Dr. Stuart. Incidents involving these dedicated men and their patients were dramatized on The New Doctors.

This program was an element of The Bold Ones. It was the only Bold Ones element to be aired throughout that series' entire four-season run, and was, in fact, the only element left in the series during the final season, all of the others having been dropped.

NEW GIDGET, THE
Situation Comedy
BROADCAST HISTORY:
Syndicated only
30 minutes
Produced: 1986–
Released: September 1986
CAST:
Francine* Lawrence Griffin (Gidget)
.... Caryn Richmond
Jeff Griffin (Moondoggie) .... Dean Butler
Danni Collins .... Sydney Penny
Russ Lawrence .... William Schallert
Larue Wilson (1986–1987)....... Jill Jacobson
Gayle Baker.................... Lili Haydn
Murph the Surf (1987–   ) ... David Preston
**Wilton Parmenter (1986–1987)
.... Richard Paul

*Also given as Frances
**Occasional

Twenty years after TV's first Gidget series had left the air this equally sunny syndicated series surfaced. Gidget was now in her late 20s and she and her girlhood idol, Moondoggie, had been married for eight years. They still lived close to the beautiful beach in Santa Monica, but were now a modern working couple. Moondoggie was an architect with the city planning department and Gidget ran her own little travel agency. Working for her at Gidget Travel was her long-time friend Larue.

Most of the stories revolved around the exploits of Gidget's niece, Danni, who was living with the Griffins while her folks were overseas. Danni was the vivacious, impish sort of teenager Gidget herself had been in the earlier series—and like Gidget of yore, she and her best friend, Gayle, were forever getting in trouble. Gidget's dad, Russ, was around to offer sage advice and remind Gidget of how similar she had been to Danni.

The pilot for this series was Gidget's Summer

Reunion, a 1985 made-for-television film starring Richmond and Butler.

NEW KIND OF FAMILY, A
Situation Comedy
FIRST TELECAST: *September 16, 1979*
LAST TELECAST: *January 5, 1980*
BROADCAST HISTORY:
Sep 1979–Oct 1979, ABC Sun 7:30–8:00
Dec 1979–Jan 1980, ABC Sat 8:30–9:00
CAST:
Kit Flanagan .... Eileen Brennan
Andy Flanagan .... David Hollander
Hillary Flanagan .... Lauri Hendler
Tony Flanagan .... Rob Lowe
Abby Stone (Sep–Oct) .... Gwynne Gilford
Jill Stone (Sep–Oct) ...... Connie Ann Hearn
Jess Ashton (Dec–Jan) .... Telma Hopkins
Jojo Ashton (Dec–Jan) .... Janet Jackson
Harold Zimmerman .... Chuck McCann

In this comedy Kit Flanagan, recently widowed, decided to pack up her three children and move from her native New York to Los Angeles. They had rented a house sight unseen, but when they got there they found that someone else had rented it too: divorcée Abby Stone and her daughter Jill. Since neither the Flanagans nor the Stones could afford the place by themselves, they all moved in together—despite the very different life-styles of cynical, free-swinging Kit and conservative, by-the-book (Dr. Spock) Abby. The kids loved the arrangement, especially early adolescents Hillary and Jill, who were the same age. Mr. Zimmerman was the landlord, who also had his own TV show, and Heinz was the family pooch (played by "O.J.").

The series was an instant flop and was pulled from the schedule after only a few weeks. It returned briefly in December–January with new episodes, in which the Stones had been replaced by Jess Ashton and her daughter Jojo.

NEW LAND, THE
Adventure
FIRST TELECAST: *September 14, 1974*
LAST TELECAST: *October 19, 1974*
BROADCAST HISTORY:
Sep 1974–Oct 1974, ABC Sat 8:00–9:00
CAST:
Anna Larsen .... Bonnie Bedelia
Christian Larsen .... Scott Thomas
Tuliff Larsen .... Todd Lookinland
Anneliese Larsen .... Debbie Lytton
Bo .... Kurt Russell
Rev. Lundstrom .... Donald Moffat
Molly Lundstrom .... Gwen Arner
Murdock .... Lou Frizzel

The hardships and triumphs of a courageous family of young Scandinavian immigrants struggling to carve out a life in the hostile wilderness near Solna, Minnesota, in 1858. Anna and Christian were the parents, Tuliff (aged nine) and Anneliese (eight) their children. Rev. Lundstrom and his wife and Murdock, the owner of the general store, also pitched in, but the Larsens' travails lasted for only six weeks before the series was canceled.

Filmed on location in Oregon and California, and based (loosely) on two Swedish movies, *The Emigrants* (1972) and *The New Land* (1973).

NEW LEAVE IT TO BEAVER, THE
Situation Comedy
BROADCAST HISTORY:
The Disney Channel (1985–1986)
WTBS (1986–)
30 minutes
Produced: *1985–*
Released: *September 1985*
CAST:
June Cleaver .... Barbara Billingsley
Theodore "Beaver" Cleaver ... Jerry Mathers
Ward "Kip" Cleaver, Jr. .... Kipp Marcus
Oliver Cleaver................... John Snee
Wally Cleaver .... Tony Dow
Mary Ellen Cleaver .... Janice Kent
Kelly Cleaver .... Kaleena Kiff
*Eddie Haskell .... Ken Osmond
**Freddie Haskell .... Eric Osmond
Bomber Haskell .... Christian Osmond
Gert Haskell .... Ellen Maxted
Clarence "Lumpy" Rutherford ... Frank Bank
Kevin Cleaver (1987–   ) .... Troy Davidson

*Occasional
**Eddie Haskell, Jr. during the 1985–1986 season

Twenty years after *Leave It To Beaver* ended its original run, viewers got a glimpse of what had become of the Cleavers in the March 1983 TV movie *Still the Beaver.* Unlike most TV reunions, this one was bittersweet. Beaver's eternal innocence had not served him well in adult life. At 33, he was out of work, had two young sons he couldn't communicate with, and was being divorced by his wife. Wally was a successful attorney—in fact he handled Beaver's divorce—but he had problems at home as well. Wally's sleazy friend Eddie Haskell had become a crooked contractor. Dad was no longer around to make things right with a few words of sage advice (actor Hugh Beaumont had passed away) and he was sorely missed, by his sons and by his wife, June, who sat by his grave and said "Ward, what would *you* do?"

Despite this dour picture, viewers apparently wanted more of the Cleaver clan, and so the movie led to a series *Still the Beaver* on the pay-cable Disney channel in 1985–1986, and then *The New Leave It to Beaver* on cable superstation WTBS in 1986. Things got somewhat better as time went along. Beaver and his sons (he had custody) moved in with June, who provided some emotional support. He then went to work for Lumpy Rutherford's father and eventually he and

Lumpy formed a highly successful business partnership, although it was never explained exactly what they did. Much of the action shifted to the younger generation—Beaver's boys, teenager Kip and preteen Oliver; Wally's kids, cute Kelly and little Kevin (his mother, Mary Ellen, was pregnant with him for 18 months on the series and three months after his birth he was three years old!); and Eddie's son Freddie, who was Kip's best friend. Although Freddie had picked up some of his father's obnoxious traits, underneath it all he was a pretty good guy. Freddie's brother, Bomber, had been sent off to military school for accidentally spilling grape juice on the white carpeting in the Haskell living room, but showed up periodically. The same gentle, homespun quality that had characterized the original series began to permeate *The New Leave It To Beaver*.

Eddie Haskell's sons were played by actor Ken Osmond's real-life sons.

NEW LORETTA YOUNG SHOW, THE
Drama
FIRST TELECAST: *September 24, 1962*
LAST TELECAST: *March 18, 1963*
BROADCAST HISTORY:
Sep 1962–Mar 1963, CBS Mon 10:00–10:30
CAST:

Christine Massey	Loretta Young
Paul Belzer	James Philbrook
Marnie Massey	Celia Kaye
Vickie Massey	Beverly Washburn
Judy Massey	Sandy Descher
Binkie Massey	Carol Sydes
Dirk Massey	Dirk Rambo
Dack Massey	Dack Rambo
Maria Massey	Tracy Stratford

Christine Massey was a widowed mother of seven children, living in the suburban community of Ellendale, Connecticut. Her children ranged in age from 6 to 18 and were typical of other youngsters of their respective ages in terms of attitudes, wants, and conflicts with each other and with their mother. Christine made her living as a magazine writer, selling stories to various publications. One of those publications, *Belzer's Woman's Journal*, was edited and owned by Paul Belzer, the mature bachelor who was Christine's love interest. They met when she was working on her first assignment for his magazine and their romance continued throughout the six-month run of this series, culminating in marriage on the last telecast, March 18, 1963.

This was Miss Young's sole venture in a continuing role on television. Her previous series, *The Loretta Young Show*, gave her the freedom of playing different people on the occasions in which she starred as well as hosted the show. On this show, she was the center of action in roughly every other episode, with stories centering around individuals in the family on alternate weeks.

NEW MIKE HAMMER, THE
see *Mickey Spillane's Mike Hammer*

NEW MONKEES
Situation Comedy
BROADCAST HISTORY:
Syndicated only
30 minutes
Produced: *1987* (13 episodes)
Released: *September 1987*
CAST:

Larry	Larry Saltis
Dino	Dino Kovas
Jared	Jared Chandler
Marty	Marty Ross
Manford, the butler	Gordon Oas-Heim
Rita, the waitress	Bess Motta
Helen, the lips	Lynne Godfrey

The 1980s was an era of nostalgia, and perhaps the most surprising revival was that of the ultimate "manufactured" rock group of the '60s—the Monkees. Reruns of their '60s TV series on the MTV cable network, a highly publicized concert tour by original members of the group in the summer of 1986, and reissues of their LPs all led trend-conscious producers to think the time was right to bring the public a "new" Monkees. A heavily promoted nationwide talent hunt was staged to find four young men to star in a new version of the '60s series.

The result was this high-tech, special-effects–laden collection of music videos, comic blackouts, and offbeat plots. It was set in a huge gothic mansion in which the four new Monkees (Larry, Dino, Jared, and Marty) lived and frolicked. They had a stuffy butler named Manford and hung out at a diner attached to the mansion, but many of their adventures took place without even leaving home. Commenting on the proceedings was a sarcastic, bodiless pair of lips which appeared on television screens that seemed to be in every room.

The hype didn't work. The New Monkees' album didn't sell and the series didn't attract an audience; apparently the public was more interested in the old Monkees. *New Monkees* was in production for less time than the search for its stars had taken.

NEW ODD COUPLE, THE
see *Odd Couple, The*

NEW PEOPLE, THE
Drama
FIRST TELECAST: *September 22, 1969*
LAST TELECAST: *January 12, 1970*
BROADCAST HISTORY:
Sep 1969–Jan 1970, ABC Mon 8:15–9:00
CAST:

Susan Bradley	Tiffany Bolling
Bob Lee	Zooey Hall
Ginny Loomis	Jill Jaress

Gene Washington .... David Moses
Stanley Gabriel .... Dennis Olivieri
George Potter .... Peter Ratray
CREATOR:
Rod Serling

This fantasy drama centered on a heterogeneous group of 40 young Americans stranded on a South Pacific atoll after a plane crash. The island just happened to be an abandoned U.S. atomic test site, which meant that, though safe, it came complete with buildings, provisions, and all the other physical appurtenances of a modern society—but no people. Inhabiting this eerie world, the young folks, with their differing ethnic and social backgrounds (they were returning from a cultural exchange tour of Southeast Asia), set about organizing their own "new" society, sans adults. A few guest stars did wander on and off their "lost" island, however.

NEW PHIL SILVERS SHOW, THE
Situation Comedy
FIRST TELECAST: *September 28, 1963*
LAST TELECAST: *June 27, 1964*
BROADCAST HISTORY:
Sep 1963–Nov 1963, CBS Sat 8:30–9:00
Nov 1963–Jun 1964, CBS Sat 9:30–10:00
CAST:
Harry Grafton .... Phil Silvers
Brink .... Stafford Repp
Waluska .... Herbie Faye
Roxy .... Pat Renella
Lester .... Jim Shane
Mr. Osborne .... Douglas Dumbrille
Fred Starkey .... Steve Mitchell
Bob .... Bob Williams
Nick .... Buddy Lester
Grabowski .... Norm Grabowski
Audrey (1964) .... Elena Verdugo
Susan (1964) .... Sandy Descher
Andy (1964) .... Ronnie Dapo

The character played by Phil Silvers in his second series was similar to Sgt. Ernie Bilko in the original *Phil Silvers Show*, with one exception—Harry was a civilian. He was the maintenance superintendent of Osborne Industries, a small manufacturing company whose products changed from episode to episode, to suit the plot. Harry was a small-time swindler and office con artist. He would do almost anything to avoid real work, and managed to find angles to provide himself with a little something extra from each job that he and his crew worked on. The boss, Mr. Brink, could only look on helplessly.

NEW SHOW, THE
Comedy Variety
FIRST TELECAST: *January 6, 1984*
LAST TELECAST: *March 23, 1984*
BROADCAST HISTORY:
Jan 1984–Mar 1984, NBC Fri 10:00–11:00

REGULARS:
Buck Henry
Valri Bromfield
Dave Thomas
Maggie Jakobson
Maura Moynihan

The New Show was an hour of offbeat comedy sketches by a cast of regulars and guests. The humor was often topical, as in the regular "Weekend Tonight" mock newscast and in film clips of world leaders with new dialogue dubbed in. Other skits generally emphasized teen-oriented humor; one show opened at the "Restaurant of Revulsion," where a waiter (guest Raul Julia) ceremoniously unveiled for his customers the Catch of the Day, "Tête du Jour"—a severed head on a platter that exclaimed, "(Groan) . . . it's *The New Show!*" Among the guests making multiple appearances were John Candy and Catherine O'-Hara, both alumni of SCTV, and actress Candice Bergen.

A musical spot each week featured rock acts such as the Pretenders and Rick James. *The New Show* was produced by Lorne Michaels, the man who created *Saturday Night Live*, but it failed to capture the novelty or the breakthrough talent of the earlier series, and was soon canceled.

NEW TEMPERATURES RISING SHOW, THE
see *Temperatures Rising*

NEW YORK GIANTS QUARTERBACK HUDDLE
Sports Commentary
FIRST TELECAST: *September 15, 1950*
LAST TELECAST: *November 12, 1953*
BROADCAST HISTORY:
Sep 1950–Dec 1950, ABC Fri 8:30–9:00
Sep 1952–Dec 1952, DUM Wed 7:30–8:00
Oct 1953–Nov 1953, DUM Thu 8:00–8:30
HOST:
Joe Hasel (1950)
Steve Owen (1952–1953)

Highlight films of the New York Giants' game of the previous week, interviews with players, and discussions of more general National Football League news and issues were all included in this weekly show. Sportscaster Joe Hasel hosted the ABC version in 1950, while Steve Owen, coach of the New York Giants team, hosted on DuMont. The 1953 DuMont version continued as a local show until the season ended. Also known as *Pro Football Highlights, Football News,* and *New York Giants Football Huddle.*

NEW YORK TIMES YOUTH FORUM
Discussion
FIRST TELECAST: *October 5, 1952*
LAST TELECAST: *June 21, 1953*
BROADCAST HISTORY:
Oct 1952–Jun 1953, DUM Sun 6:00–7:00

Discussion of topics of importance to young people, by politicians, scientists, and other authorities, including writers from *The New York Times*. Subjects included "Do We Learn Only at School?," "How Does Soviet Policy Affect Us?," "Music: Jazz *vs.* Classics," and "Are Mothers Necessary?"

The series had started one month earlier on Sunday afternoons before shifting to a 6:00 P.M. start. Following the run listed above it returned to Sunday afternoons, where it remained until June 1954.

NEWHART

Situation Comedy
FIRST TELECAST: *October 25, 1982*
LAST TELECAST:
BROADCAST HISTORY:
> Oct 1982–Feb 1983, CBS Mon 9:30–10:00
> Mar 1983–Apr 1983, CBS Sun 9:30–10:00
> Apr 1983–May 1983, CBS Sun 8:30–9:00
> Jun 1983–Aug 1983, CBS Sun 9:30–10:00
> Aug 1983–Sep 1986, CBS Mon 9:30–10:00
> Sep 1986–   , CBS Mon 9:00–9:30

CAST:
Dick Loudon .... Bob Newhart
Joanna Loudon .... Mary Frann
Kirk Devane (1982–1984) . Steven Kampmann
George Utley .... Tom Poston
Leslie Vanderkellen (1982–1983)
.... Jennifer Holmes
Stephanie Vanderkellen (1983–   )
.... Julia Duffy
Larry .... William Sanderson
First Darryl .... Tony Papenfuss
Second Darryl .... John Voldstad
*Jim Dixon .... Thomas Hill
*Chester Wanamaker .... William Lanteau
Cindy Parker Devane (1984) ... Rebecca York
Michael Harris (1984–   ) ..... Peter Scolari
*Harley Estin (1984–   ) .... Jeff Doucette
Elliot Gabler (1984–1985) .... Lee Wilkof
*Bev Dutton (1984–   ) .... Linda Carlson
*Constable Shifflett (1985–   )
.... Todd Susman
*J.J. (1985–1987) .... Fred Applegate
*Bud (1985–   ) .... Ralph Manza

*Occasional

Four years after the highly successful *Bob Newhart Show* had ended its run, Bob Newhart brought his relaxed style, gentle humor, and immaculate comedy timing back to CBS in *Newhart*. Dick Loudon, a New York writer of "How To" books, decided to put his knowledge to practical use by renovating and reopening an authentic colonial inn in scenic Norwich, Vermont. Leaving city life behind, Dick and his somewhat skeptical wife, Joanna, arrived full of anticipation at their new home, the Stratford Inn, built in 1774. It had been shuttered for years and needed a good deal of work, but as a history buff Dick found the building and its past endlessly fascinating.

Dick and Joanna also found that Norwich did not lack eccentric characters. Helping run the inn was crusty and colorful George Utley, whose family had been caretakers there for more than 200 years. Kirk, who ran the Minuteman Cafe and Giftshop next door, was a guilt-ridden compulsive liar who was constantly apologizing for his fibs. After years of searching for the perfect woman, he was finally married in the spring of 1984—to Cindy, a professional clown. Leslie was a pretentious and wealthy student at nearby Dartmouth College, who had taken the part-time job of maid to find out what it was like to be "average." She left to continue her education in England at the end of the first season, and was replaced by her equally attractive cousin, Stephanie. Also seen were three weird brothers who were possibly the world's most inept handymen—Larry, Darryl, and Darryl. Larry was the spokesman for the group, since neither Darryl ever spoke at all.

In the fall of 1984, looking for a little diversity in his life, Dick became the host of "Vermont Today," a talk show on local TV station WPIV. Now, in addition to the folks at the inn, he had to cope with the guests on his TV show and its fast-talking young producer, Michael Harris. When Michael started dating Stephanie—they made the perfect pretentious yuppie couple—Dick had the dubious pleasure of seeing him at the inn almost as much as at the station. Larry, Darryl, and Darryl were around even more than before, since they had taken over the Minuteman Cafe when Kirk left the area.

In this sea of eccentrics, Dick and Joanna were a small island of normalcy, a situation not radically different from that of Newhart and his wife (played by Suzanne Pleshette) in his previous series.

NEWLYWED GAME, THE

Quiz/Audience Participation
FIRST TELECAST: *January 7, 1967*
LAST TELECAST: *August 30, 1971*
BROADCAST HISTORY:
> Jan 1967–Jan 1971, ABC Sat 8:00–8:30
> Jan 1971–Aug 1971, ABC Mon 8:00–8:30

EMCEE:
Bob Eubanks
EXECUTIVE PRODUCER:
Chuck Barris

Each week on *The Newlywed Game* four couples, all married less than one year, competed with each other to win their own special "dream gift," usually appliances or furniture. The emcee asked the wives questions about their husbands, and the husbands questions about their wives, each while the other mate was out of earshot. The couple that correctly guessed the greatest number of each other's answers was the winner. Questions were usually designed to produce embarrassing situations and disagreements between husbands and wives, much to the delight of the audience. For example, "What animal would you compare your mother-in-law to?" or "Would your wife say she sleeps with her toes pointing toward the wall, the ceiling, or the floor?"

There was also a daytime version of the program on ABC from July 1966 to December 1974, and a syndicated version from 1977 until 1980. Bob Eubanks hosted them all. He was still with the show when it surfaced again as *The New Newlywed Game* in the fall of 1985. Despite the name change nothing much had changed, other than the freedom to be somewhat more explicit in the sexual innuendos, a function of the changing mores of American television.

NEWS—ABC

FIRST TELECAST: *August 11, 1948*
LAST TELECAST:
BROADCAST HISTORY:

Aug 1948–Oct 1952, ABC Mon–Sat 7:00–7:15
Oct 1952–Dec 1952, ABC Mon 9:00–10:00
Oct 1952–Dec 1952, ABC Wed 8:00–9:00
Oct 1952–Dec 1952, ABC Thu 8:00–8:30
Oct 1952–Jan 1953, ABC Fri 8:30–9:30
Oct 1952–Aug 1953, ABC Sun 8:00–9:00
Oct 1953–May 1959, ABC Mon–Fri 7:15–7:30
May 1959–Jan 1967, ABC Mon–Fri Various times (15 min.)
Sep 1958–May 1959, ABC Mon–Fri 10:30–10:45
Oct 1961–Jan 1965, ABC Mon–Fri 11:00–11:10
Jan 1965–   , ABC Sat/Sun 11:00–11:15
Jan 1967–   , ABC Mon–Fri Various times (30 min.)
Feb 1973–Jan 1979, ABC Sat 6:30–7:00
Jan 1979–   , ABC Sun 6:30–7:00
Mar 1980–Jan 1981, ABC Mon–Thu 11:30–11:50
Jan 1981–Mar 1981, ABC Mon–Thu 11:30–Midnight
Mar 1981–Apr 1983, ABC Mon–Fri, 11:30–Midnight
Apr 1983–Feb 1984, ABC Mon–Fri, 11:30–12:30 A.M.
Feb 1984–   , ABC Mon–Fri 11:30–Midnight
Jan 1985–   , ABC Sat 6:30–7:00

ABC's first regularly scheduled nightly newscast was *News and Views,* which premiered in August 1948 with H. R. Baukhage and Jim Gibbons sharing the anchor position. Aired six nights each week, it lasted three years, and was succeeded by *After the Deadlines* in April 1951.

The program that succeeded *After the Deadlines* was the most ambitious news show in the early days of television. In an attempt to offer news as an alternative to prime-time entertainment, ABC introduced *All Star News* in October 1952. This offered four and one-half hours of national news coverage per week, a full hour on some nights, all running in the middle of the evening against NBC's and CBS' top entertainment shows. Featured were Bryson Rash, Pauline Frederick, Gordon Fraser, and Leo Cherne. In addition to straight headline reporting, *All Star News* provided analysis and interviews with newsmakers, and had a documentary quality to much of its

coverage. It was a noble effort, but it attracted few viewers against *Ed Sullivan, Arthur Godfrey,* and *I Love Lucy,* and by early 1953 only the Sunday night edition remained on the air.

Smarting from this expensive disaster, ABC reverted to a 15-minute early evening news in October 1953. The anchor was veteran newsman John Daly, who was brought over from CBS. About the only distinctive feature of ABC News at this time was that Daly stood at a podium as he delivered the news, rather than being seated at a desk as were the other networks' anchormen. An interesting sidelight is that even while Daly was anchoring ABC's nightly news, he remained moderator of CBS' top-rated quiz show, *What's My Line.* Daly remained in the ABC anchor position for more than seven years, except for one short stint from 1958–1959 when he anchored a short-lived 10:30 P.M. newscast, and Don Goddard filled in at 7:15 P.M. When Daly left ABC in December 1960, a trio of anchormen took over the early news, Bill Lawrence, Al Mann, and former NBC anchorman John Cameron Swayze.

In the fall of 1961 ABC introduced its first 11:00 P.M. newscast, running from Monday to Friday. The first anchor was Ron Cochran, succeeded by Murphy Martin in 1963 and Bob Young in 1964. In January 1965 ABC dropped this newscast and substituted an 11 P.M. Saturday/Sunday news instead. Called *The ABC Weekend News,* this has remained on the air ever since, although after a short tenure by Bob Young (1965–1966) there was no regular anchor until the mid-1970s; Tom Jarriel has been ABC's principal late weekend anchor since then, although Bill Beutel, Sylvia Chase, Max Robinson, and Britt Hume have also anchored or co-anchored for varying lengths of time.

Weekends also saw the addition of an early evening news on Saturday in 1973. At first called *The Reasoner Report,* this was taken over by Ted Koppel in the summer of 1975, followed by Tom Jarriel and Sylvia Chase in 1977 and Sam Donaldson in 1979 (when the program moved to Sunday). Donaldson has remained with the Sunday early newscast ever since. A new early Saturday edition was begun in January 1985, with Kathleen Sullivan as anchor, later succeeded by Barry Serafin. Capitalizing on the heightened interest in news during the 1979 Iranian crisis, ABC also began regular "Iran reports," Monday through Thursday at 11:30 P.M., in November 1979. These were converted into a regular newscast called *Nightline* with Ted Koppel in March 1980.

There has been, over the years, considerable turnover in anchormen on ABC's early evening news. Ron Cochran took over in January 1963. He was replaced by youthful Peter Jennings in February 1965, and Jennings was still with the newscast when it expanded from 15 minutes to a half hour on January 9, 1967. Bob Young replaced Jennings in January 1968, and Frank Reynolds took over in May 1968. A year later ABC decided to try two anchors, and Howard K. Smith joined Reynolds. In December 1970 it became *The ABC Evening*

News with *Howard K. Smith and Harry Reasoner,* Reasoner having been hired away from CBS (where, it seemed, he was never going to get the chance to succeed the venerable Walter Cronkite). The Smith-Reasoner team lasted almost five years, with Reasoner going it alone in September 1975. In October 1976 he was joined, amid a blaze of publicity, by former NBC newswoman Barbara Walters, who reportedly got an annual salary of $1,000,000 to make the switch. Reasoner and Walters did not work well together, however, and in the summer of 1978 the network decided to try a four-person arrangement called *World News Tonight,* originating from four different cities each night: Max Robinson from Chicago, Frank Reynolds from Washington, Peter Jennings (remember him?) from London, and Barbara Walters doing periodic features from New York. This last change, together with the general momentum provided by ABC's sudden success in prime time, apparently made a difference, as ABC's traditionally third-place news finally began to gain in audience and challenged NBC for second place, behind top-ranked CBS.

The next major change took place in mid-1983, when Frank Reynolds died unexpectedly. The multi-city approach was dropped and Peter Jennings became the sole anchor in August, resuming the position he had held more than 15 years before.

NEWS—CBS

FIRST TELECAST: *May 3, 1948*
LAST TELECAST:
BROADCAST HISTORY:
  May 1948–Sep 1955, CBS Mon–Fri 7:30–7:45
  Aug 1948–Dec 1948, CBS Sun Various times (15 min.) 7:00–8:00
  Jan 1949–Jun 1950, CBS Sun Various times (15 min.) 10:00–11:00
  Jan 1949–Mar 1950, CBS Sat 7:30–7:45
  Jun 1950–Sep 1950, CBS Sat 6:15–6:30
  Aug 1950–Sept 1950, CBS Sun 10:00–10:15
  Sep 1950–Jan 1951, CBS Sat 7:30–7:45
  Jan 1951–   , CBS Sun 11:00–11:15
  Oct 1951–Nov 1951, CBS Sat 6:30–6:45
  Nov 1951–Jan 1952, CBS Sat 6:45–7:00
  Sep 1955–Aug 1963, CBS Mon–Fri 7:15–7:30
  Sep 1963–   , CBS Mon–Fri Various times (30 min.)
  Jan 1966–   , CBS Sat 6:30–7:00
  Jan 1970–Sep 1972, CBS Sun 6:00–6:30 (Jan–Sep each year)
  Jan 1976–   , CBS Sun 6:00–6:30
  Oct 1982–   , CBS Mon–Thu 2:00–6:00 A.M.

Doug Edwards had been doing television news for the CBS station in New York since the mid-1940s and, when it was decided to produce a nightly network newscast, his local show became CBS' first network news show. Edwards remained with the weekday evening news until 1962. One month short of Edwards' 14th anniversary with the series

Walter Cronkite took over, on April 16, 1962. Cronkite lasted even longer than Edwards. When he finally left the show, on March 6, 1981, he had spent almost two decades coming into our living rooms five nights a week. He had become an institution and a celebrity, whose soft-spoken manner and clear, concise delivery had also made him, according to at least one poll, the most trusted man in America. It was with a sad sense of passing that his audience heard him utter "and that's the way it is" at the end of his final newscast. The mantle passed to Dan Rather, who had the unenviable task of trying to replace a living legend in American broadcasting.

Compared to the extreme stability of the weekday news, CBS' weekend shows have gone through many more changes of personnel. The Saturday early news debuted in January 1949 with Quincy Howe reporting. *Quincy Howe with the News* lasted 15 months and was replaced in the summer of 1950 by *The Week in Review,* a filmed newsreel summary of the happenings of the past week. That September *The Saturday News Special,* anchored by Don Hollenbeck, replaced the newsreels for slightly over three months. *Up to the Minute* arrived in October 1951, with Edward P. Morgan anchoring for the first three weeks and Walter Cronkite for the last two months. After no Saturday news program for 14 years, *The CBS Saturday News* arrived on January 12, 1966. Roger Mudd was the original anchor of this show, replaced in July 1973 by Dan Rather, who was in turn replaced by Bob Schieffer in November 1976.

CBS' initial news offering on Sundays, running from August 1948 to June 1950, was the filmed newsreel *The Week in Review.* John Daly had a brief turn with a Sunday weekly news summary show that fall, but the long-lasting 11:00 P.M. Sunday news did not actually start until January 1951. It has been in that time slot ever since. Walter Cronkite was at the helm for more than 11 years, leaving to take over *The CBS Evening News* in April 1962. Cronkite, therefore, was on continuous view as a CBS anchorman from the time he began on *Up to the Minute* in 1951 until 1981. None of the Sunday anchormen who succeeded Cronkite had his endurance. Eric Sevareid was his initial replacement (lasting only nine months), followed by Harry Reasoner (February 1963–November 1970), Dan Rather (November 1970–July 1973), Bob Schieffer (July 1973–August 1974), Rather again (September 1974–December 1975), Morton Dean (December 1975–December 1976), Ed Bradley (December 1976–May 1981), Charles Osgood (June 1981–December 1987), and Susan Spencer (since December 1987). In addition to the late Sunday news, there was an early evening version for parts of 1970 and 1971 with Roger Mudd anchoring, and in 1976 with Bob Schieffer. Schieffer departed in November of that year, with Morton Dean moving over from the late Sunday news to the earlier edition, where he remained until December 1984. Susan Spencer became a semiregular anchor on the *CBS Sunday News* in April 1985, alternating mostly with Bill Redeker and Bruce Morton in 1985, with Bob Schieffer and Forrest Sawyer in 1986, and almost exclusively with Sawyer until she became sole anchor in September of 1987.

In addition to these famous names, CBS News gave short-lived celebrity to another newscaster, albeit unintentionally. During a 13-day performers' union strike in March 1967, CBS and others were forced to put some of their office staff on the air to fill in for striking talent. The honor of sitting in for Walter Cronkite fell to a bespectacled young CBS lawyer named Arnold Zenker, who so caught the fancy of viewers (if not of the union) that he became something of a fad, with Arnold Zenker buttons and jokes abounding. He later tried to parlay this unexpected fame into a show-business career of his own, hosting local news and talk programs in Boston and Baltimore, but lately he has dropped from sight. "Uncle Walters' " reputation as the premiere television anchorman appears to be safe.

Concern about the impact of the 24-hour news service provided to cable television subscribers by Ted Turner's Cable News Network, coupled with expansion in the news programming of NBC and ABC, prompted CBS to add an overnight network news service in late 1982. Premiering in October of that year, and anchored by the team of Harold Dow, Felicia Jeter, Christopher Glenn, Karen Stone, and Mary Jo West, *CBS News Nightwatch* aired weeknights from 2:00 to 6:00 A.M. When the original anchor team departed in January 1984, Charlie Rose and Lark McCarthy took the reins, with McCarthy leaving before the end of the year and Rose staying on as the sole full-time anchor.

NEWS—DUMONT

FIRST TELECAST: *August 25, 1947*
LAST TELECAST: *April 1, 1955*
BROADCAST HISTORY:

Aug 1947–May 1948, DUM Mon–Fri 6:45–7:00
Jan 1948–Jan 1949, DUM Mon–Fri 7:30–7:45
Jan 1948–Jan 1949, DUM Tue 7:45–8:00
Nov 1948–Feb 1949, DUM Sun 6:30–7:00
Feb 1949–May 1950, DUM Mon 8:00–8:30
Sep 1954–Apr 1955, DUM Mon–Fri 7:15–7:30

DuMont never had the financial resources of the other television networks and, though it was second only to NBC with a regularly scheduled evening news program, the DuMont news never developed into the complex and comprehensive effort that its competitors were to become by the early 1950s. The first DuMont network news show, carried on a two-station network, was 1947's *Walter Compton News*. The first network news series to originate from Washington, D.C., where it had been seen since June 1947, *Walter Compton News* became a network program when it was seen simultaneously in New York starting in August. The production was minimal, with

Compton reading from a script and only occasional slides being shown.

In January 1948 *Camera Headlines,* a filmed 15-minute newsreel, was added to the DuMont schedule at 7:30 P.M. Since *Camera Headlines* dealt only with domestic stories, *INS Telenews* followed it on Tuesday nights to provide world news coverage. The *INS Telenews* newsreel was a wrap-up of the major world news stories of the week, provided to DuMont by Hearst's *I*nternational *N*ews *S*ervice, essentially a print service similar to U.P.I. and A.P.

Not precisely a hard-news show, *Newsweek Analysis* premiered in November 1948. Moderated by senior *Newsweek* editor Ernest K. Lindley, it was an interview program in which various editors of the magazine chatted with personalities in the news. When the series moved from Sundays to Mondays the following February, the title was changed to *Newsweek Views the News.*

In the fall of 1954, after an absence of almost five years, regularly scheduled nightly news returned to the DuMont network. Anchored by Morgan Beatty, this show remained on the air until the crumbling DuMont network virtually ceased functioning the following April.

NEWS—NBC

FIRST TELECAST: *April 10, 1944*
LAST TELECAST:
BROADCAST HISTORY:

Apr 1944–Jul 1944, NBC Mon Various times (10 or 15 min. between 8:00–9:00 P.M.)
Aug 1944–Jul 1945, NBC Mon 8:00–8:10
Jul 1945–Jun 1946, NBC Sun 8:00–8:15
Jun 1946–Dec 1946, NBC Mon/Thu 7:50–8:00
Dec 1946–Oct 1947, NBC Mon 9:00–9:10
Dec 1946–Oct 1947, NBC Thu 7:50–8:00
Nov 1947–Dec 1947, NBC Wed 8:45–9:00
Feb 1948–Feb 1949, NBC Mon–Fri 7:50–8:00
Jun 1948–Sep 1948, NBC Sun 7:50–8:00
Sep 1948–Feb 1949, NBC Sun 7:20–7:30
Feb 1949–Sep 1957, NBC Mon–Fri 7:45–8:00
Apr 1949–Feb 1950, NBC Sat 7:45–8:00
Jul 1949–Oct 1949, NBC Sun 7:00–7:30
Sep 1957–Sep 1963, NBC Mon–Fri 6:45–7:00
Oct 1961–Oct 1965, NBC Sat 6:00–6:15
Sep 1963–   , NBC Mon–Fri Various times (30 min.)
Sep 1965–Aug 1967, NBC Sun 6:00–6:30
Oct 1965–   , NBC Sat 6:30–7:00
Sep 1967–   , NBC Sun 6:30–7:00
Jul 1982–Dec 1983, NBC Mon–Thu 1:30–2:30 A.M.
Jul 1982–Dec 1983, NBC Fri 2:00–3:00 A.M.

NBC, which pioneered television networking, was also the first to carry a regular network newscast. This was an outgrowth of the local newscasts that had begun on NBC's New York station almost as soon as the first regular TV service began in 1939 (see Introduction). Lowell Thomas, a nationally known radio commentator, had frequently simulcast his regular weeknight *Sonoco News* on radio and local TV between February and July 1940 (and occasionally thereafter); and there was also a weekly *Esso Television Reporter* from March until May 1940 (the NBC files indicate that "news photos, maps and graphic diagrams" were used, and that "an organ will supply a musical background"). William Spargrove was the reporter. From July 1941 to May 1942 Sam Cuff provided a weekly news commentary on *Face of the War.*

During late 1942 and 1943 television operations were curtailed drastically because of World War II, but February 21, 1944, saw the debut of a new weekly program called *The War As It Happens—* and NBC-TV news has been on the air more or less continuously ever since. At first *The War As It Happens* was a local telecast, like its predecessors, but the NBC files indicate that beginning in April 1944 it was fed to Philadelphia and Schenectady, thus becoming the first TV newscast regularly seen in multiple cities.

What viewers saw on their tiny screens in 1944 was far different from what we see today. Broadcasters did not then have film crews to send out to cover stories, and, in fact, the entire broadcast news apparatus—radio and television—was tiny compared to that maintained by newspapers, newsreels, and the wire services. The first breakthrough came in 1944 when John F. Royal, the first head of television at NBC, acquired rights to U.S. Army Signal Corps footage. Using this footage, *The War As It Happens* followed basically a newsreel format: several minutes of government-supplied film about the war effort, with background music and subtitles, interspersed with Ray Forrest in the studio explaining the latest developments with the help of maps on an easel. Narration for the film was provided by Paul Alley, a former newsreel man. Alley recalls signing off each telecast by saying, "This is the NBC Television Network—WNBT, New York; WPTZ, Philadelphia; and WRGB, Schenectady," after which he read the megacycle band on which each station was operating. Imagine an anchorman doing that today, with more than 200 stations on the network! (While this newscast was definitely seen on a three-city network from April 1944 until January 1945, the files are unclear as to whether it remained a network hookup or reverted to a local broadcast during 1945. NBC news was in any event being telecast over a network from early 1946 on.)

In August 1945, with the war over, the Sunday newscast was retitled *NBC Television Newsreel.* In mid-1946 it was rescheduled to two nights a week, Monday and Thursday, and gained a sponsor, becoming *The Esso Newsreel.*

November 1947 brought *Current Opinion* to the NBC Wednesday night schedule for a one-month run. Hosted by Robert McCormick from Washington, D.C., it was one of the earliest examples of a news commentary program, with opinions rather than fact taking the spotlight. In February 1948, NBC began a Monday–Friday evening news show

called the *Camel Newsreel Theatre.* It was only 10 minutes long, and was not much different from *Esso Newsreel,* which it succeeded, but it was the genesis of the *Camel News Caravan* which took its place a year later. When that happened, John Cameron Swayze, one of the announcers behind the newsreels, moved in front of the camera and became an "anchorman." The sponsor was so nervous about this radical departure from the traditional newsreel concept of TV news that it insisted on including fashion shows and other light features to maintain visual interest and attract female viewers. These were soon phased out, but the background music—another holdover from newsreels—remained until the mid-1950s, as did the film narration by a second, newsreel-style announcer. Nevertheless John Cameron Swayze became America's best-known individual newscaster. His nightly sign-off, "Glad we could get together," was one of early television's most familiar phrases.

Swayze was essentially a newsreader, however. By the mid-1950s television had become a news-gathering force in its own right, and NBC (feeling pressure from CBS) felt it necessary to put someone with more field experience in front of the cameras. So in October 1956 Swayze was replaced by Chet Huntley and David Brinkley, both of whom had years of experience as reporters and who had proven a charismatic team covering the political conventions that summer. They were the first superstars of TV news: the stolid, sober Huntley providing a perfect counterpoint to the wry, sometimes caustic Brinkley. Their habitual closing, "Good Night, Chet . . . Good Night, David," became more famous than Swayze's. By 1965 a poll showed that they were recognized by more adults than Cary Grant, James Stewart, or the Beatles.

The Huntley-Brinkley Report became a national institution, running almost 14 years. It expanded to a half hour on September 9, 1963 (a week after CBS had done the same thing), and added a Saturday telecast in 1969. After Chet Huntley retired in July 1970, NBC experimented for a year with a system in which Brinkley, John Chancellor, and Frank McGee rotated as anchormen seven nights a week, under the blanket title *The NBC Nightly News.* In August 1971 Chancellor emerged as the sole Monday–Friday anchor, remaining in the anchor chair for the next 11 years (joined by Brinkley as co-anchor from 1976 to 1979). He was succeeded in April 1982 by Tom Brokaw, who was at first paired with a recent arrival from CBS, Roger Mudd, but became sole anchor in late 1983.

Saturday newscasts have been more erratic on NBC. The first was *Leon Pearson and the News* in 1949–1950, followed by a hiatus of more than a decade. NBC returned to Saturday newscasting with Sander Vanocur in October 1961. Subsequent Saturday anchormen have included Ray Scherer and Robert MacNeil (1965), Frank McGee

(1967), Garrick Utley (1971), Tom Brokaw (1975), and John Hart (1976). Sunday newscasts resumed in 1965, with anchors including Frank McGee (1965), Garrick Utley (1971), Floyd Kalber (1973), Tom Snyder (1975), and John Hart (1976).

It was at the start of 1977 that women anchors began to be featured on NBC weekend news shows, beginning with Catherine Mackin and followed by Jessica Savitch (November 1977), Jane Pauley (1980), and Connie Chung (1983). Chris Wallace (1982, 1986), John Palmer (1984), and Garrick Utley (1987) have also had stints on the Sunday edition.

A short-lived addition to NBC's roster of regular newscasts was *NBC News Overnight*, which ran from 1:30 to 2:30 A.M. Monday–Thursday, and 2:00–3:00 A.M. on Friday, beginning July 1982—primarily as a response to the growing popularity of 24-hour cable news networks. Lloyd Dobyns and Linda Ellerbee were the original anchors, with Dobyns replaced by Bill Schechner in November 1982. It was a hip, unconventional newscast, but not enough people were viewing at that hour to make the expense worthwhile, and it faded from the air in December 1983.

NEWS IS THE NEWS, THE
Comedy Variety
FIRST TELECAST: *June 15, 1983*
LAST TELECAST: *July 13, 1983*
BROADCAST HISTORY:
Jun 1983–Jul 1983, NBC Wed 10:00–10:30
REGULARS:
Michael Davis
Simon Jones
Charlotte Moore
Lynne Thigpen
Trey Wilson

Mix a little bit of *Saturday Night Live's* "Weekend Update" and a dash of the satiric weekly 1960s series *That Was the Week That Was* and you had *The News Is the News*. Like its predecessors, it was produced live from New York and satirized the current week's headlines with a team of "newspersons" doing most of the sendups, abetted by an occasional guest correspondent. It may have been topical, but it certainly wasn't very funny. The regulars often seemed uncomfortable with the material and the show had a depressingly unfinished look. It was abruptly canceled after only a month on the air.

NEWSSTAND THEATRE
Dramatic Anthology
FIRST TELECAST: *January 16, 1952*
LAST TELECAST: *February 6, 1952*
BROADCAST HISTORY:
Jan 1952–Feb 1952, ABC Wed 9:30–10:00

Four-week series of dramatizations of short stories from national magazines. Included was "Size

12 Tantrum," starring Jack Lemmon and his then wife, Cynthia Stone.

NEXT STEP BEYOND, THE
see *Alcoa Presents*

NICHOLS
Western
FIRST TELECAST: *September 16, 1971*
LAST TELECAST: *August 1, 1972*
BROADCAST HISTORY:
Sep 1971–Nov 1971, NBC Thu 9:00–10:00
Nov 1971–Aug 1972, NBC Tue 9:30–10:30
CAST:
Nichols .... James Garner
Ma Ketcham .... Neva Patterson
Ketcham .... John Beck
Mitch .... Stuart Margolin
Ruth .... Margot Kidder
Bertha .... Alice Ghostley

This was one TV series in which the hero really was shot because of low ratings—as in the movie *Network*. The setting was Nichols, Arizona, in 1914. Nichols (he never did have a first name) returned to the town his family had founded only to discover that it had been taken over by the powerful Ketcham family, dominated by matriarchal Ma Ketcham. He was promptly blackmailed by Ma into serving as sheriff, a powerless but hazardous position where she could keep an eye on him. Although Nichols had spent 18 years in the army, he really hated violence and didn't even carry a gun. His real aim in life was to find a means to get rich, and he concocted all sorts of schemes toward that end. Mitch was the town bully, Ma Ketcham's son, and Nichols' not-too-honest deputy; Ruth, the barmaid, was Nichols' girlfriend; and Bertha was the proprietor of the saloon where Ruth worked. The program had an interesting early-20th-century Western background, with Nichols using an auto and motorcycle rather than the traditional horse.

In the last episode Nichols was shot down, only to be avenged by his identical twin brother Jim Nichols (yes, *he* had a first name) also played by James Garner. At the time that the last episode was filmed it was assumed that, despite marginal ratings, the series would be renewed. By replacing the avaricious Nichols with his stronger, more traditionally heroic twin brother, it was felt that the next season's program would be more successful. By the time the episode actually aired, however, establishing a real hero for the series had become a moot point—*Nichols* had been given the ax.

Effective with the October 25, 1971, telecast, the official title of the series became *James Garner as Nichols*, in the hopes that the drawing power of its star would boost ratings.

NICK KENNY SHOW, THE
Talk/Music
FIRST TELECAST: *July 18, 1951*

LAST TELECAST: *January 1, 1952*
BROADCAST HISTORY:
Jul 1951–Aug 1951, NBC Wed 11:00–11:15
Aug 1951–Jan 1952, NBC Tue 11:00–11:15
REGULARS:
Nick Kenny
Irene Walsh
Don Tippen

Nick Kenny was a columnist for the *New York Daily Mirror* and this series was set in a replica of his newspaper office. Each week he read some of his original poetry, sang, chatted with guests from the worlds of theater and sports, and philosophized about life. Irene Walsh was his secretary and assistant while Don Tippen provided piano background and accompaniment for singers. The show returned for a couple of months in the spring of 1952 on Saturday afternoons.

NIGHT COURT
Situation Comedy
FIRST TELECAST: *January 4, 1984*
LAST TELECAST:
BROADCAST HISTORY:
Jan 1984–Mar 1984, NBC Wed 9:30–10:00
May 1984–May 1986, NBC Thu 9:30–10:00
Jun 1986–Mar 1987, NBC Thu 9:30–10:00
Mar 1987–Jun 1987, NBC Wed 9:00–9:30
Jun 1987–Jul 1987, NBC Wed 9:30–10:00
Jul 1987–Aug 1987, NBC Wed 9:00–9:30
Aug 1987–Mar 1988, NBC Thu 9:30–10:00
Mar 1988–Apr 1988, NBC Fri 9:00–9:30
*May 1988–   *, NBC Thu 9:30–10:00
CAST:
Judge Harry Stone .... Harry Anderson
Court Clerk Lana Wagner (1984)
.... Karen Austin
Selma Hacker (1984–1985) ... Selma Diamond
Bailiff Bull Shannon .... Richard Moll
Asst. D.A. Dan Fielding .... John Larroquette
Liz Williams (1984) .... Paula Kelly
Court Clerk Mac Robinson (1984–   )
.... Charlie Robinson
Billie Young (1984–1985) .... Ellen Foley
*Al Craven (1984) .... Terry Kiser
Christine Sullivan (1985–   ) .. Markie Post
Florence Kleiner (1985–1986)
.... Florence Halop
*Phil the Derelict (1985–1986) ... William Utay
*Leon (1985–1986) .... Bumper Robinson
*Art (1986–   ) .... Mike Finneran
Roz Russell (1986–   ) .... Marsha Warfield

*Occasional

This courtroom comedy revolved around Harry Stone, a boyish, blue-jeaned judge who had been appointed to New York's Manhattan Night Court almost by accident. His unconventional, flippant style dismayed his staff, but often produced unexpectedly positive results with the loonies who paraded through his nocturnal court. Lana was the perky clerk, secretly in love with the cute judge; Selma the caustic, chain-smoking matron; and Bull the bald, towering bailiff. Representing the state was nattily dressed, sex-starved Assistant D.A. Dan Fielding, and the defense, black legal-aid lawyer Liz Williams.

There was a good deal of turnover in the supporting cast, with Lana replaced by sensible Mac, Selma by Florence and then Roz, and Liz by Billie and then Christine (for whose sexy body Dan, and even Harry, lusted). A number of recurring characters were seen occasionally in the carnival-like courtroom, among them obnoxious newspaper reporter Al Craven, who snooped around for stories during the first season; Phil the derelict; runaway orphan Leon; and maintenance man Art. Quon Lee (Denice Kumagai) was seen a few times each season as Mac's Asian wife.

NIGHT EDITOR
Dramatic Anthology
FIRST TELECAST: *March 14, 1954*
LAST TELECAST: *September 8, 1954*
BROADCAST HISTORY:
Mar 1954–Jul 1954, DUM Sun 10:45–11:00
Jul 1954–Sep 1954, DUM Wed 10:30–10:45
HOST:
Hal Burdick

This was one of many attempts by DuMont to devise low-cost TV programming. In this case there was one actor and one set. Hal Burdick, the night editor of an unidentified newspaper, was seen in his office narrating a short crime or human interest story. As he spoke he would sit at his desk or walk around the room, changing his voice to differentiate between characters. The stories ranged across many periods and subjects, including an old policeman on school-crossing duty who had an adventure on his last day on the force; a Korean War veteran who got a medal undeservedly; and a Civil War sentry who fell asleep at his post.

Films of *Night Editor* had been seen locally and in late night for several years before this prime-time network run.

NIGHT GALLERY
Supernatural Anthology
FIRST TELECAST: *December 16, 1970*
LAST TELECAST: *August 12, 1973*
BROADCAST HISTORY:
Dec 1970–Sep 1972, NBC Wed 10:00–11:00
Sep 1972–Jan 1973, NBC Sun 10:00–10:30
May 1973–Aug 1973, NBC Sun 10:00–10:30
HOST:
Rod Serling

Night Gallery was one of the original elements in the 1970–1971 NBC series *Four in One*. It aired for six weeks from December 16, 1970, to January 20, 1971, and was rerun on a rotating basis with the other three elements of the series—*McCloud, San*

Francisco International Airport, and *The Psychiatrist*—from April through the end of the season. It remained in the Wednesday time slot by itself during the 1971–1972 season and was then moved to Sunday nights.

Night Gallery was a weekly collection of short, supernatural vignettes. Rod Serling introduced each one from a bizarre gallery, in which grotesque paintings foreshadowed the stories to follow. Not all of the stories were frightening, and many times humorous blackouts were used between more serious stories. In many respects, *Night Gallery* was the supernatural equivalent of *Love, American Style.*

NIGHT HEAT
Police Drama
FIRST TELECAST: *January 31, 1985*
LAST TELECAST:
BROADCAST HISTORY:
  Jan 1985–Mar 1985, CBS Thu 11:30–12:40 A.M.
  May 1985, CBS Thu 11:30–12:40 A.M.
  Jun 1985–Jul 1985, CBS Wed 11:30–12:40 A.M.
  Sep 1985–Jul 1987, CBS Thu 11:30–12:40 A.M.
  Aug 1987–Sep 1987, CBS Tue 10:00–11:00
  *Sep 1987–   *, CBS Thu 11:30–12:40 A.M.
CAST:
  Det. Kevin O'Brien . . . . Scott Hylands
  Tom Kirkwood . . . . Allan Royal
  Det. Frank Giambone . . . . Jeff Wincott
  Nicole "Nickie" Rimbaud . . . . . Susan Hogan
  Prosecutor Dorothy Fredericks (1985)
  . . . . Wendy Crewson
  Det. Fleece Toland (1985)
  . . . . Lynda Mason Green
  Det. Freddie Carson . . . . Stephen Mendel
  Det. Colby Burns . . . . Eugene Clark
  Lt. Jim Hogan . . . . Sean McCann
  Whitey Low . . . . Tony Rosato
  Prosecutor Elaine Jeffers . . . . Deborah Grover
  Det. Stephanie "Stevie" Brody (1985–1986)
  . . . . Louise Vallance
  Det. Dave Jefferson (1986–   )
  . . . . Clark Johnson
  Det. Christine Meadows (1987–   )
  . . . . Laura Robinson

Filmed entirely on location in Toronto, Canada, *Night Heat* was a straightforward action series about the professional, and occasionally personal, lives of a group of police detectives working in a large metropolitan city—as seen through the eyes of their friend, newspaper columnist Tom Kirkwood. Tom's popular column, "Night Heat," was carried in the major newspaper in town, *The Eagle.* The series focused on two men: Kevin was the veteran, a divorced cop who had seen it all, while Frank was his hot-tempered, skirt-chasing young partner. They worked out of the Mid South precinct and Lt. Hogan, once Kevin's partner, was their boss. Kevin's girlfriend, Nickie, the widow of another cop, was the owner of Nicole's, the lounge where most of the detectives hung out. Whitey

was a street snitch who worked and lived in the sleazy neighborhood in which much of the criminal activity in this series took place.

NIGHTLIFE
Talk
BROADCAST HISTORY:
  Syndicated only
  30 minutes
  Produced: *September 1986–May 1987*
  Released: *September 8, 1986*
HOST:
  David Brenner
MUSICAL DIRECTOR:
  Billy Preston

Offbeat ethnic comedian David Brenner, who had been a frequent guest and occasional guest host on *The Tonight Show Starring Johnny Carson,* got the opportunity to host his own syndicated talk show—briefly—in 1986.

NINE THIRTY CURTAIN
Dramatic Anthology
FIRST TELECAST: *October 13, 1953*
LAST TELECAST: *January 1, 1954*
BROADCAST HISTORY:
  Oct 1953–Jan 1954, DUM Fri 9:30–10:00

A series of 30-minute filmed dramas starring lesser-known actors and actresses. After its network run *Nine Thirty Curtain* was seen for a time as a local show in New York.

9 TO 5
Situation Comedy
FIRST TELECAST: *March 25, 1982*
LAST TELECAST: *October 27, 1983*
BROADCAST HISTORY:
  Mar 1982–Apr 1982, ABC Thu 9:00–9:30
  Sep 1982–Sep 1983, ABC Tue 9:30–10:00
  Sep 1983–Oct 1983, ABC Thu 9:00–9:30
  (In first-run syndication since September 1986)
CAST:
  Violet Newstead (1982–1983) . . . . Rita Moreno
  Doralee Rhodes Brooks . . . . Rachel Dennison
  Judy Bernly . . . . Valerie Curtin
  Franklin Hart (1982) . . . . Jeffrey Tambor
  Franklin Hart (1982–1983) . . . . . . Peter Bonerz
  Roz Keith (1982–1983) . . . . Jean Marsh
  Harry Nussbaum (1982–1983) . Herb Edelman
  Clair (1982–1983) . . . . Ann Weldon
  Michael Henderson (1983) . . . . . George Deloy
  Linda Bowman (1983) . . . . Leah Ayres
  Tommy (1983) . . . . Tony Latorra
  Marsha McMurray Shrimpton (1986–   )
  . . . . Sally Struthers
  William "Bud" Coleman (1986–   )
  . . . . Edward Winter
  Charmin Cunningham (1986–1987)
  . . . . Dorian Lopinto
  Russ Merman (1986–   ) . . . . Peter Evans
  Morgan (1986–   ) . . . . Art Evans

James (1986–   )........... James Martinez
E. Nelson Felb (1987–   )... Fred Applegate
THEME:
"9 To 5," written by Dolly Parton, sung by
Phoebe Snow (1982) and later by Dolly Parton

Three put-upon secretaries matched wits with
their overbearing, sexist boss in this contemporary comedy. Franklin Hart, vice-president of
Midwestern Sales for Consolidated Companies,
was an inept executive who viewed the girls in
the outer office as either sex objects or mere
flunkies to use in his climb upward. Facing him
every day were Violet, a fiery Latin, single (widowed) mother, and 12-year veteran of the company; Doralee, a good-hearted country girl with a
fullsome figure; and Judy, an incredibly smart college graduate with no common sense. Roz, the
office manager, was Mr. Hart's ally and in-house
snoop, though she got little in return for her trouble.

There was a good deal of turnover onscreen
and off during the run of this series. The actor
playing Hart was replaced after the initial spring
1982 tryout run. Harry Nussbaum was added in
the fall as the company's fatherly, good-natured
top salesman, always ready to cheer up the girls
with a joke or bit of help in their schemes. When
the second full season began in September 1983,
Judy had been replaced by Linda, a free-spirited
young woman in her 20s who also moved in to
share an apartment with Violet and Doralee. At
the same time, Violet's 12-year-old son, Tommy,
joined the cast, Roz was gone, and good old Harry
Nussbaum was replaced by a decidedly sexier
young salesman named Michael. Somewhere
along the way, the company changed its name to
American House. Offscreen, actress/activist Jane
Fonda, who was the initial co-producer, was replaced by veteran sitcom producer James Komack. The revised show lasted barely over a
month before being canceled.

Three years later 9 To 5 resurfaced in first-run
syndication. Only Doralee and Judy were back
from the original cast, with the former now married and the latter still desperately trying to find
a boyfriend. New to the secretarial group was
Marsha, a sweet, lovable, but incredibly inept
divorcée with two young children. The company
they were working for was now Barkley Foods
International and among the staff were Judy's
boss, womanizing Russ Merman, Director of Foreign Acquisitions; Marsha's boss, ambitious
young administrative executive Charmin Cunningham (and later obnoxious V.P. of Foreign
Sales, Mr. Felb); and Doralee's boss, Vice-President Bud Coleman.

The series was based on the hit 1980 movie 9 To
5, which starred Jane Fonda, Dolly Parton (Rachel
Dennison's sister), and Lily Tomlin.

1986
News Magazine

FIRST TELECAST: *June 10, 1986*
LAST TELECAST: *December 30, 1986*
BROADCAST HISTORY:
  Jun 1986–Dec 1986, NBC Tue 10:00–11:00
CO-ANCHORS:
  Roger Mudd
  Connie Chung
PRINCIPAL CORRESPONDENTS:
  Ed Rabel
  Lucky Severson
  Maria Shriver
  Peter Kent

NBC's fifteenth attempt to launch a prime-time
news magazine similar to CBS' top-rated *60 Minutes* was no more successful than the previous 14
tries. The format was standard, with NBC correspondents contributing filmed reports on various
issues of the day.

90 BRISTOL COURT
Situation Comedy
FIRST TELECAST: *October 5, 1964*
LAST TELECAST: *January 4, 1965*
BROADCAST HISTORY:
  Oct 1964–Jan 1965, NBC Mon 7:30–9:00

90 Bristol Court was actually three situation
comedies airing in consecutive half-hours. They
were tied together by the fact that the principal
characters in each lived in the same apartment
complex at 90 Bristol Court. For specific information see the titles of the individual situation comedies—*Karen, Harris against the World,* and *Tom,
Dick and Mary.* Although the overall series failed,
one of the three parts—*Karen*—was successful
enough to finish out the season after the other two
elements were canceled in January. A thread of
continuity between the three individual comedies
was provided in the person of the complex's
handyman, Cliff Murdoch, portrayed by Guy Raymond. He was generally seen greeting the residents of the three focal apartments and working
around the complex.

NO HOLDS BARRED
Comedy Variety
FIRST TELECAST: *September 12, 1980*
LAST TELECAST: *October 3, 1980*
BROADCAST HISTORY:
  Sep 1980–Oct 1980, CBS Fri 11:30–12:40 A.M.
HOST:
  Kelly Monteith

This short-lived series attempted to be a little bit
like *60 Minutes,* a little bit like *NBC's Saturday
Night Live,* and a little bit like *Fridays,* its direct
competition on ABC. Hosted by comedian Kelly
Monteith, *No Holds Barred* was a mixture of offbeat short documentary features, animated and
filmed comedy sketches, rock music, and interviews. Segments covered such topics as young
comedians at work, a cable TV show that served

as a video dating service, the plight of a Deadwood, South Dakota, madam whose brothel had been closed, and a preacher who used magic in his services. None of the comics or musical groups who performed on *No Holds Barred* were well known, most of them being struggling performers looking for a break.

NO SOAP, RADIO
Situation Comedy
FIRST TELECAST: *April 15, 1982*
LAST TELECAST: *May 13, 1982*
BROADCAST HISTORY:
  Apr 1982–May 1982, ABC Thu 8:00–8:30
CAST:
  Roger .... Steve Guttenberg
  Karen .... Hillary Bailey
  Mr. Plitzky .... Bill Dana
  Mrs. Belmont .... Fran Ryan
  Morris .... Jerry Maren
  Tuttle .... Stuart Pankin
  Marion .... Edie McClurg
  Rico .... Phil Rubenstein

No Soap, Radio might best be described as the *Twilight Zone* of situation comedies. There was a story of sorts in each episode, but it was frequently interrupted by sight gags, blackouts, and surrealistic skits that might or might not have anything to do with anything else. The setting was the seedy Pelican Hotel in Atlantic City, where you might open the door to your room and find yourself standing in the woods, or pass a glass-enclosed fire station in the corridor and notice a live fireman inside. Riding in the elevator was always interesting, as you could never tell what would be revealed on each floor as the doors opened; Miami Beach, perhaps, or a coronation ball?

Presiding over this house of non sequiturs was the pleasant young manager, Roger, assisted by Karen and Tuttle, the house detective. They hardly batted an eye at such goings-on as the chase after a man-eating chair, the little old lady who was attacked by a submarine, the frustrations of a gunfighter whose opponent overslept, or the pause for a preview of the new science-fiction movie "The Day Everyone's Name Became Al." As for the series' title, *No Soap, Radio*—why should that make any more sense than anything else?

NO TIME FOR SERGEANTS
Situation Comedy
FIRST TELECAST: *September 14, 1964*
LAST TELECAST: *September 6, 1965*
BROADCAST HISTORY:
  Sep 1964–Sep 1965, ABC Mon 8:30–9:00
CAST:
  Airman Will Stockdale ...... Sammy Jackson
  Sgt. King .... Harry Hickox
  Airman Ben Whitledge .... Kevin O'Neal
  Millie Anderson .... Laurie Sibbald
  Capt. Martin .... Paul Smith
  Col. Farnsworth .... Hayden Rorke
  Grandpa Jim Anderson .... Andy Clyde
  Pvt. Jack Langdon .... Michael McDonald
  Capt. Krupnick .... George Murdock
  Pvt. Blanchard .... Greg Benedict
  Pvt. Mike Neddick .... Joey Tata

Comedy about a simpleminded but resourceful hillbilly who found new worlds to conquer in the air force. Airman Will Stockdale didn't have much in the way of rank, but he always seemed to be "improving" things around Oliver Air Force Base, usually to the exasperation of the brass. In the opening episode, for example, he was assigned to permanent K.P., whereupon the food in the mess hall improved so much that the officers began eating there along with the enlisted men. When the colonel inspected the kitchen he discovered that Will had been trading with the local farmers for choice meat and produce—but it was *what* Will had been trading away that upset the colonel when he discovered equipment missing. Sgt. King was Will's incredulous NCO, while Ben was his buddy and Millie his sexy girlfriend.

Based on the novel by Mac Hyman, which was subsequently made into a hit play (1955) and movie (1958), both starring Andy Griffith.

NO WARNING
Dramatic Anthology
FIRST TELECAST: *April 6, 1958*
LAST TELECAST: *September 7, 1958*
BROADCAST HISTORY:
  Apr 1958–Sep 1958, NBC Sun 7:30–8:00
NARRATOR:
  Westbrook Van Voorhis

People involved in sudden, unanticipated crisis situations were the protagonists in *No Warning.* At the start of each story the focal character was established, along with the crisis that was thrust upon him. The remainder of the story presented the resolution of the crisis. All of the episodes dealt with personal and emotional crises, rather than with the threat of violence.

NOAH'S ARK
Medical Drama
FIRST TELECAST: *September 18, 1956*
LAST TELECAST: *October 5, 1958*
BROADCAST HISTORY:
  Sep 1956–Feb 1957, NBC Tue 8:30–9:00
  Jun 1958–Oct 1958, NBC Sun 7:00–7:30
CAST:
  Dr. Noah McCann .... Paul Burke
  Dr. Sam Rinehart .... Vic Rodman
  Liz Clark .... May Wynn
PRODUCER/DIRECTOR:
  Jack Webb

Produced in cooperation with the Southern California Veterinary Medical Association and the American Humane Association, *Noah's Ark* was the story of two veterinarians, the veterinary hospital where they worked, and the animals they treated. Dr. Sam Rinehart was an older man confined to a wheelchair. His young assistant and partner was Dr. Noah McCann. Their secretary and all-purpose assistant was Liz Clark. The relationships that developed between the regulars were as much a part of the story as the collection of animals that they treated. Reruns of the series were aired in the summer of 1958.

NOBODY'S PERFECT
Situation Comedy
FIRST TELECAST: *June 26, 1980*
LAST TELECAST: *August 28, 1980*
BROADCAST HISTORY:
 Jun 1980–Aug 1980, ABC Thu 9:30–10:00
CAST:

Det. Inspector Roger Hart	Ron Moody
Det. Jennifer Dempsey	Cassie Yates
Lt. Vince de Gennaro	Michael Durrell
Det. Jacobi	Victor Brandt
Det. Grauer	Tom Williams
Det. Ramsey	Renny Roker

Roger Hart was an elegant anachronism, an urbane Scotland Yard detective on loan to the San Francisco Police Department, where he worked with decidedly earthier U.S. cops. Hart was a bit confusing to his hosts. On the one hand he seemed klutzy and accident-prone—objects in his vicinity tended to tip over, fall apart, spill, run dry, unravel, or burst into flames. But in a pinch, he could be a man of unexpected talents—bomb expert, pilot, swordsman, or master of disguise. His boss, Lt. Vince de Gennaro, teamed the tall, grinning Englishman with another problem person on the squad, Det. Jennifer Dempsey, and off they went to surprise San Franciscans. On their first assignment Hart so surprised a would-be suicide on the Golden Gate Bridge that the man did indeed jump. Bring up the laugh track.

Jacobi, Grauer, and Ramsey were other detectives on the squad.

NORBY
Situation Comedy
FIRST TELECAST: *January 5, 1955*
LAST TELECAST: *April 6, 1955*
BROADCAST HISTORY:
 Jan 1955–Apr 1955, NBC Wed 7:00–7:30
CAST:

Pearson Norby	David Wayne
Helen Norby	Joan Lorring
Diane Norby	Susan Hallaran
Hank Norby	Evan Elliott
Wahleen Johnson	Janice Mars
Mr. Rudge	Ralph Dunn
Mrs. Maude Endles	Carol Veazie
Bobo	Jack Warden
Maureen	Maxine Stuart

Pearson Norby was vice-president in charge of small loans at the Pearl River First National Bank,

in Pearl River, a small town in upstate New York. He lived there with his wife, Helen, and his two children, Diane and Hank. The problems Pearson had on the job and situations involving his wife and his children were subjects for episodes. Featured were three of the bank's employees, president Maud Endles, vice-president and efficiency expert Mr. Rudge, and switchboard operator Wahleen Johnson. Bobo and Maureen were their next-door neighbors. *Norby* was the first television series to be filmed in color and was, appropriately, sponsored by the Eastman Kodak Company.

NORTHWEST PASSAGE
Adventure
FIRST TELECAST: *September 14, 1958*
LAST TELECAST: *September 8, 1959*
BROADCAST HISTORY:
 Sep 1958–Jan 1959, NBC Sun 7:30–8:00
 Jan 1959–Jul 1959, NBC Fri 7:30–8:00
 Jul 1959–Sep 1959, NBC Tue 7:30–8:00
CAST:

Major Robert Rogers	Keith Larsen
Sgt. Hunk Marriner	Buddy Ebsen
Ensign Langdon Towne	Don Burnett
Gen. Amherst	Philip Tonge

The actual historical search for an inland waterway that would enable boat traffic to cross the breadth of America was the focal point of *Northwest Passage*, which was set during the French and Indian War (1754–1759). Major Robert Rogers, an experienced explorer and Indian fighter, had organized Rogers' Rangers to help him search for that mythical route. The adventures of these men, exploring, fighting Indians, and battling the American wilderness, provided the stories. Chief among the troops were veteran Indian fighter and long-time friend Hunk Marriner, and Langdon Towne, a Harvard graduate from a well-to-do Eastern family who had become the company mapmaker. They never found the Northwest Passage, but did do a lot of fighting with both the French and the Indians in the course of helping settlers in the area now known as New York state and Eastern Canada.

NORTHWEST PATROL
see *Movies—Prior To 1961*

NOT FOR PUBLICATION
Newspaper Drama
FIRST TELECAST: *May 1, 1951*
LAST TELECAST: *May 27, 1952*
BROADCAST HISTORY:
 May 1951–Sep 1951, DUM Mon/Thu 7:45–8:00
 Dec 1951–Mar 1952, DUM Fri 8:30–9:00
 Mar 1952–May 1952, DUM Tue 10:00–10:30
CAST:

Collins (May–Sep 1951)	William Adler
Collins (Dec 1951–May 1952)	Jerome Cowan
Luchek (1952)	Jon Silo

Human-interest stories and adventures in the lives of ordinary people as seen through the eyes of kind-hearted reporter Collins of the big-city newspaper, *The Ledger*. Among the stories were those of an actor who agreed to impersonate an ambassador whose life was in danger; a baseball player who set out to clear his father's name; and a doctor who faced conflict in the operating room. Generally lesser-known actors and actresses appeared in these short dramas, although one February 1952 telecast was billed as the dramatic acting debut of Morey Amsterdam.

NOTHING BUT THE BEST
Musical Variety
FIRST TELECAST: *July 7, 1953*
LAST TELECAST: *September 13, 1953*
BROADCAST HISTORY:
Jul 1953–Aug 1953, NBC Tue 9:00–9:30
Aug 1953–Sep 1953, NBC Sun 10:00–10:30
REGULARS:
Eddie Albert
Skitch Henderson & His Orchestra

Eddie Albert was the star and emcee of this live musical variety show that started out on Tuesday evenings as the summer replacement for *Fireside Theater* and then moved to Sundays.

The acts, each billed as the best in their field, were introduced by Mr. Albert, who chatted with the performers and then left them to perform. As he had said on his opening show: "I have the dream spot on TV this season for the sponsor told me to go out and get my favorite talent and to let them do on the show what they feel is the best of their career—for the show is *Nothing but the Best.*"

NOTHING BUT THE TRUTH
see *To Tell the Truth*

NOTHING IN COMMON
Situation Comedy
FIRST TELECAST: *April 2, 1987*
LAST TELECAST: *June 3, 1987*
BROADCAST HISTORY:
Apr 1987–May 1987, NBC Thu 9:30–10:00
Jun 1987, NBC Wed 9:30–10:00
CAST:
David Basner .... Todd Waring
Max Basner .... Bill Macy
Jacqueline North .... Wendy Kilbourne
Norma Starr .... Mona Lyden
Mark Glick .... Bill Applebaum
Victoria Upton-Smythe .... Elizabeth Bennett
Myron Nipper .... Patrick Richwood
Joey D. .... Billy Wirth
Wally .... Allan Kent
Autumn .... Julie Paris

Based on the 1986 movie of the same name, this frothy comedy followed the travails of nutty young ad-agency head David Basner and his irresponsible, unemployed father, Max, who

mooched off him unmercifully. Stories concerned such burning questions as "should David cancel a long-planned fishing trip with his father to save a sausage account?" A typical cast of TV loonies inhabited David's agency, among them sexy new agency executive Jacqueline, neurotic copywriters Norma and Mark, and leather-jacketed young cameraman Joey D.

NOTHING IS EASY
see *Together We Stand*

NOW
Documentary
FIRST TELECAST: *May 9, 1954*
LAST TELECAST: *September 14, 1970*
BROADCAST HISTORY:
May 1954–Jun 1954, ABC Sun 7:30–8:00
Mar 1970–Sep 1970, ABC Mon 10:30–11:00
EXECUTIVE PRODUCER:
Arthur Holch (1970)

Two unrelated summer documentary series were aired under the title *Now*. The 1954 version consisted of assorted documentary films. The 1970 series was produced by ABC News and hosted by a different ABC newsman each week. It covered such subjects as communes, Women's Liberation, and "A Black Mayor in Dixie."

NUMBER 96
Drama
FIRST TELECAST: *December 10, 1980*
LAST TELECAST: *January 2, 1981*
BROADCAST HISTORY:
Dec 1980, NBC Wed 10:00–11:00
Dec 1980, NBC Thu 10:00–11:00
Dec 1980–Jan 1981, NBC Fri 9:00–10:00
CAST:
Horace Batterson .... Barney Martin
Lisa Brendon .... Christine Jones
Mark Keaton .... Howard McGillin
Jill Keaton .... Sherry Hursey
Sharon St. Clair .... Hilary Thompson
Chick Walden .... John Reilly
Anthea Bryan . Rosina Widdowson-Reynolds
Roger Busky .... James Murtaugh
Ginny Ramirez .... Maria O'Brien
Maureen Galloway .... Betsy Palmer
Sandy Galloway .... Jill Choder
Marion Quintzel .... Randee Heller
Max Quintzel .... Greg Mullavey
Dr. Robert Leon .... Brian Curran
Nathan Sugarman .... Todd Susman
Lou Sugarman .... Eddie Barth
Rita Sugarman .... Ellen Travolta
Lyle Bixler .... Charles Bloom

Life at Number 96 Pacific Way, a Southern California apartment complex, was full of sex, gossip, and all sorts of miscellaneous personal problems. The people who lived there had bizarre lives, though, in all fairness, a soap opera would be dull if its characters were normal. Among the residents were recently divorced Roger Busky, a salesman trying to become a swinging single; retired navy commander Horace Batterson, the resident voyeur; the Quintzels, a couple experimenting with "open marriage"; psychologist Robert Leon, also a transvestite; Nurse Sandy Galloway, living with her widowed, alcoholic mother; and professional con man Chick Walden. Everyone at 96 Pacific Way seemed to be involved with someone else there, either professionally, socially, or sexually, with the strongest emphasis on the latter.

Number 96 was adapted for American television from an Australian series of the same name. Although it tried to retain the flavor of the original, the American version was considerably tamer. The Australian *Number 96* created a sensation when it went on the air in 1972, dealing graphically with homosexuality, drug and alcohol addictions, ambitious and promiscuous people, insanity, rape, and sex—mostly sex. Perhaps its greatest notoriety came from its display of full frontal nudity, something American networks were not ready to attempt. NBC ran a huge promotional campaign for its version of *Number 96*, designed to titillate potential viewers, and premiered the series on three consecutive nights. Despite the hype, it lasted less than a month.

NURSE
Medical Drama
FIRST TELECAST: *April 2, 1981*
LAST TELECAST: *May 21, 1982*
BROADCAST HISTORY:
   Apr 1981–May 1981, CBS Thu 10:00–11:00
   Sep 1981–Oct 1981, CBS Thu 9:00–10:00
   Nov 1981–Dec 1981, CBS Wed 9:00–10:00
   Dec 1981–Mar 1982, CBS Thu 10:00–11:00
   Apr 1982–May 1982, CBS Fri 10:00–11:00
CAST:
   Nurse Mary Benjamin . . . . . . Michael Learned
   Dr. Adam Rose . . . . Robert Reed
   Nurse Toni Gilette . . . . Hattie Winston
   Nurse Penny Brooks . . . . Bonnie Hellman
   Nurse Betty LaSada . . . . . Hortensia Colorado
   Nurse Bailey (1981) . . . . Clarice Taylor
   Chip Benjamin . . . . Christopher Marcantel
   Joe Calvo . . . . Dennis Boutsikaris
   Dr. Greg Manning . . . . Rex Robbins

Fictional Grant Memorial Hospital in New York City was the setting for this medical drama. It was there that former head nurse Mary Benjamin returned to work following the death of her husband, a physician on Grant Memorial's staff. As a supervising floor nurse, Mary was responsible for a considerable staff of nurses and orderlies. But the stories on *Nurse* dealt frequently with Mary's personal life, as she adjusted to life alone, as well as with medical crises at the hospital. A mature and somewhat motherly type, she offered wise counsel to those around her in meeting their problems, while she herself turned to good friend Dr. Adam Rose, a staff physician at the hospital, for help in making her own difficult adjustments. Mary's college student son, Chip, strong-willed and independent, was alternately a comfort and a trial to her. In the fall of 1981 Mary acquired a new neighbor, young lawyer Joe Calvo. He moved into the apartment next door and the two became quite friendly. While Mary dealt with the daily problems at the hospital, Joe got involved in assorted idealistic causes, trying to help the poor and disenfranchised.

NURSES, THE
Medical Drama
FIRST TELECAST: *September 27, 1962*
LAST TELECAST: *September 7, 1965*
BROADCAST HISTORY:
   Sep 1962–Dec 1962, CBS Thu 9:00–10:00
   Jan 1963–Sep 1964, CBS Thu 10:00–11:00
   Sep 1964–Sep 1965, CBS Tue 10:00–11:00
CAST:
   Liz Thorpe . . . . Shirl Conway
   Gail Lucas . . . . Zina Bethune
   Dr. Anson Kiley (1962–1964) . . Edward Binns
   Dr. Ned Lowry (1963–1964) . . Stephen Brooks
   Dr. Alex Tazinski (1964–1965)
   . . . . Michael Tolan
   Dr. Ted Steffen (1964–1965)
   . . . . Joseph Campanella

Filmed on location in New York, *The Nurses* dealt primarily with the personal and professional lives of two nurses working in a large metropolitan hospital. Liz Thorpe was the older, more experienced head nurse and Gail Lucas (played by 17-year-old Zina Bethune) was the somewhat naive student nurse. Two doctors, one older (Steffen) and one a young resident (Tazinski), joined the program when it moved to Tuesday nights in the fall of 1964. They made efforts to help the nurses with their medical and moral problems and the series title was changed to *The Doctors and the Nurses* to include them.

The Nurses was seen as a daytime serial following its nighttime run. The cast changed but the setting (New York City's Alden General Hospital) remained the same. The daytime serial ran from September 1965 to March 1967.

O

O.K. CRACKERBY

Situation Comedy
FIRST TELECAST: *September 16, 1965*
LAST TELECAST: *January 6, 1966*
BROADCAST HISTORY:
Sep 1965–Jan 1966, ABC Thu 8:30–9:00
CAST:

O. K. Crackerby .... Burl Ives
St. John Quincy .... Hal Buckley
O. K., Jr. .... Brian Corcoran
Cynthia Crackerby .... Brooke Adams
Hobart Crackerby .... Joel Davison
Susan Wentworth .... Laraine Stephens
Slim .... Dick Foran
The Chauffeur .... John Indrisano
CREATED BY:
Cleveland Amory and Abe Burrows

Widower O. K. Crackerby was the richest man in
the world, but he lacked the one thing he wanted
above all else—acceptance in the world of high
society. A rough-and-tumble Oklahoman, he
lacked certain qualities that the refined snobs
who controlled the Social Register deemed necessary. To help his kids "get into polite society,"
O. K. hired an unemployed Harvard graduate, St.
John Quincy, as a tutor. Traveling from one society playground to another, the two men split their
time fighting with each other on an intellectual
level and banding together to battle the social
snobs on a personal level. Susan was St. John's
girlfriend, and Slim was O. K.'s business pal.

Although they would probably rather not be
reminded of it, this short-lived comedy was the
creation of Cleveland Amory, who skewered
many a TV series in print during his long tenure
as *TV Guide*'s chief critic and reviewer, and
noted playwright Abe Burrows.

O.S.S.

War Drama
FIRST TELECAST: *September 26, 1957*
LAST TELECAST: *March 17, 1958*
BROADCAST HISTORY:
Sep 1957–Jan 1958, ABC Thu 9:30–10:00
Jan 1958–Mar 1958, ABC Mon 7:30–8:00
CAST:

Capt. Frank Hawthorn .... Ron Randell
The Chief .... Lionel Murton
Sgt. O'Brien .... Robert Gallico

After just about every police file in the country
had been raided for "true stories," ABC came up
with an obvious source of true-life high adventure:
the Office of Strategic Services (OSS), America's
World War II superspy agency. Since the OSS had
been dissolved by executive order after the war,
to be replaced by the CIA, its files were open to

the public. Authenticity was insured by co-producer Colonel William Eliscu, who had been real-
life aide to OSS Chief General "Wild Bill" Donovan during the war.

In this series, agent Frank Hawthorn engaged in
considerable derring-do behind German lines,
often in cahoots with the French Resistance. Sgt.
O'Brien was his assistant. Filmed in England and
France.

OBOLER COMEDY THEATRE

Comedy Anthology
FIRST TELECAST: *October 11, 1949*
LAST TELECAST: *November 20, 1949*
BROADCAST HISTORY:
Oct 1949, ABC Tue 9:00–9:30
Nov 1949, ABC Sun 7:30–8:00

A short series of original stories by Arch Oboler,
the noted radio writer.

OCCASIONAL WIFE

Situation Comedy
FIRST TELECAST: *September 13, 1966*
LAST TELECAST: *August 29, 1967*
BROADCAST HISTORY:
Sep 1966–Aug 1967, NBC Tue 8:30–9:00
CAST:

Peter Christopher .... Michael Callan
Greta Patterson .... Patricia Harty
Max Brahms .... Jack Collins
Mrs. Brahms .... Joan Tompkins
Mrs. Christopher .... Sara Seegar
Man-in-Middle .... Bryan O'Byrne
Bernie .... Stuart Margolin
Wally Frick .... Jack Riley
Vera .... Susan Silo
Marilyn .... Chris Noel

Peter Christopher was a young executive at the
Brahms Baby Food Company whose single status
had prevented him from getting numerous promotions. Due to the nature of its product, the Brahms
Company was a strong believer in marriage and
family. Peter hit upon the idea of having someone
pose as his wife, whenever his boss was around,
so that he could move up in the company and still
retain his bachelor status. To that end, he convinced Greta Patterson, an aspiring young painter
who was temporarily working as a hat-check girl,
to take the "job" of his "occasional wife." In return, he set her up in an apartment two floors
above his and agreed to pay for her art lessons
and a pair of contact lenses. She had to be in his
apartment whenever his boss dropped by and appear at his office from time to time, as well as
attend company functions with him.

The problems caused by this arrangement,
which often saw one or both of them on the fire
escape between their apartments, provided most
of the material for episodes. The poor man who
lived in the apartment between them, and was
often witness to the constant traffic on the fire

escape, remained totally confused by the goings-on. Sportscaster Vin Scully served as narrator for the series, commenting on the increasingly complicated problems created by the arrangement between Peter and Greta.

OCEANQUEST
Documentary
FIRST TELECAST: *August 18, 1985*
LAST TELECAST: *September 15, 1985*
BROADCAST HISTORY:
  Aug 1985–Sep 1985, NBC Sun 8:00–9:00
REGULARS:
  Shawn Weatherly
  Al Giddings

Former Miss Universe Shawn Weatherly and underwater cinematographer Al Giddings were featured in this documentary mini-series which explored the flora and fauna of the six oceans of the world. Miss Weatherly had no experience as a diver before signing on for the around-the-world voyage (which took nearly a year), but she learned the equipment and techniques and dove and endured the elements along with the professionals, from the tropics to the icy Antarctic.

ODD COUPLE, THE
Situation Comedy
FIRST TELECAST: *September 24, 1970*
LAST TELECAST: *June 16, 1983*
BROADCAST HISTORY:
  Sep 1970–Jan 1971, ABC Thu 9:30–10:00
  Jan 1971–Jun 1973, ABC Fri 9:30–10:00
  Jun 1973–Jan 1974, ABC Fri 8:30–9:00
  Jan 1974–Sep 1974, ABC Fri 9:30–10:00
  Sep 1974–Jan 1975, ABC Thu 8:00–8:30
  Jan 1975–Jul 1975, ABC Fri 9:30–10:00
  Oct 1982–Feb 1983, ABC Fri 8:30–9:00
  May 1983, ABC Fri 8:00–8:30
  May 1983–Jun 1983, ABC Thu 8:30–9:00
CAST (1970–1975):
  Felix Unger .... Tony Randall
  Oscar Madison .... Jack Klugman
  Murray Greshner .... Al Molinaro
  Speed (1970–1974) .... Garry Walberg
  Vinnie .... Larry Gelman
  Roger (1973–1974) .... Archie Hahn
  Roy (1970–1971) .... Ryan McDonald
  Cecily Pigeon (1970–1971) .... Monica Evans
  Gwendolyn Pigeon (1970–1971) .. Carol Shelly
  Dr. Nancy Cunningham (1970–1972)
  .... Joan Hotchkis
  Gloria Unger (1971–1975) ...... Janis Hansen
  *Blanche Madison .... Brett Somers
  Myrna Turner (1971–1975) ... Penny Marshall
  Miriam Welby (1972–1974) .. Elinor Donahue
CAST (1982–1983):
  Felix Unger .... Ron Glass
  Oscar Madison .... Demond Wilson
  Murray .... John Schuck
  Speed .... Christopher Joy
  Roy .... Bart Braverman

  Cecily Pigeon .... Sheila Anderson
  Gwendolyn Pigeon .... Ronalda Douglas
  Maria .... Liz Torres
  Mona .... Jo Marie Payton-France

*Occasional

If comedy thrives on contrasts, *The Odd Couple* offered a perfect situation. Felix was a prim, fastidious photographer, a compulsive cleaner; Oscar was a gruff, sloppy sportswriter for the fictional *New York Herald*, to whom a floor was a place to toss things. Both were divorced, and only a mutual need for companionship and a place to stay brought them together to live in the same apartment. Well, coexist in the same apartment. The conflicts were obvious and endless, as each upset the other's way of life and attempted to mix with the other's friends. Frequently seen were Oscar's poker partners, notably Murray the cop, Speed the compulsive gambler, and meek Vinnie. Nancy Cunningham was Oscar's girlfriend during the first season, and Myrna his secretary. The Pigeon Sisters were two nutty English girls who lived upstairs, and Christopher Shea for a time played the obnoxious kid next door. Oscar's ex-wife, Blanche, was played by Jack Klugman's real-life wife, Brett Somers, in occasional appearances. Seen infrequently was Felix's daughter, Edna (played by Pamelyn Ferdin in the first few seasons and Doney Oatman later).

For a couple of seasons Miriam served as Felix's girlfriend, but by the final season he had reconciled with his ex-wife, Gloria. The situation on which the series had been built was neatly resolved in the final episode when Felix moved out to remarry Gloria. Oscar returned to the apartment alone, looked around, and exploded into noisy, messy celebration at the prospect of uninhibited chaos—at last!

Notwithstanding this clear-cut ending to the original *Odd Couple*'s run, the series returned to the ABC schedule seven years later as *The New Odd Couple*, with an all-new cast. This time the principals were black, with Ron Glass as fussy photographer Felix and Demond Wilson as sloppy sportswriter Oscar. The setting was the same, and many of the favorite supporting characters were back, although Felix's ex-wife was now called Frances (played in a couple of episodes by Telma Hopkins). It was no more successful than most other revivals of former hit series.

An animated spin-off of this series, titled *The Oddball Couple* and starring a neat cat and a sloppy dog, ran as a weekend daytime entry on ABC from September 1975 to September 1977.

The Odd Couple was based on Neil Simon's hit Broadway play (1965), which was made into a movie (1968) starring Walter Matthau and Jack Lemmon. *The New Odd Couple* marked ABC's second unsuccessful attempt to stage a Neil Simon comedy with black actors—the first being *Barefoot in the Park*.

OF MANY THINGS
Discussion
FIRST TELECAST: *October 5, 1953*
LAST TELECAST: *January 11, 1954*
BROADCAST HISTORY:
Oct 1953–Jan 1954, ABC Mon 8:30–9:00
HOST:
Dr. Bergen Evans

Discussion program that ranged over many subjects, from the capture of the German submarine *U-505* on the high seas during World War II (with a Navy admiral as guest), to American popular music (with Mitch Miller), to the art of practical joking. From WBKB-TV, Chicago.

OFF THE RACK
Situation Comedy
FIRST TELECAST: *March 15, 1985*
LAST TELECAST: *September 6, 1985*
BROADCAST HISTORY:
Mar 1985–Apr 1985, ABC Fri 9:30–10:00
Aug 1985–Sep 1985, ABC Fri 9:30–10:00
CAST:
Sam Waltman . . . . Edward Asner
Kate Halloran . . . . Eileen Brennan
Shannon Halloran (age 16) . . . Claudia Wells
Timothy Halloran (7) . . . . Corey Yothers
Brenda Patagorski . . . . Pamela Brull
Cletus Maxwell . . . . Dennis Haysbert
Skip Wagner . . . . Sandy Simpson

Comedy set in a struggling, small-time Los Angeles garment factory. Sam, the gruff co-owner, thought he would have to run the place alone when his long-time partner Dan died, but he was soon confronted with an even worse prospect: Dan's strong-willed widow Kate. Her husband had left her no money, so she was determined to work at the place, despite Sam's chauvinistic objections, to help keep it afloat. Lots of yelling ensued. Shannon and Timothy were Kate's children, to whom Sam became a sort of grouchy surrogate father.

OFF TO SEE THE WIZARD
Children's Films
FIRST TELECAST: *September 8, 1967*
LAST TELECAST: *September 20, 1968*
BROADCAST HISTORY:
Sep 1967–Sep 1968, ABC Fri 7:30–8:30

This series was a collection of films, geared specifically to appeal to children. Among the movies aired, often in two parts if they were full-length theatrical features, were *Flipper, Clarence, the Cross-eyed Lion,* and *The Adventures of Huckleberry Finn.* In addition, a number of films were made especially for this series. Most of these were nature documentaries, but one was an engaging hour entitled "Who's Afraid of Mother Goose," featuring such stars as Frankie Avalon and Nancy Sinatra as Jack and Jill, Rowan & Mar-

tin as Simple Simon and the Pieman, the Three Stooges as Three Men in a Tub, and other major names in storybook roles.

The title *Off to See the Wizard* derived from the use of animated characters from *The Wizard of Oz* to host each telecast—Dorothy, the Tin Woodman, the Cowardly Lion, the Scarecrow, Toto, the Wicked Witch of the West, the Wizard, and others.

OH, BOY
Music
FIRST TELECAST: *July 16, 1959*
LAST TELECAST: *September 3, 1959*
BROADCAST HISTORY:
Jul 1959–Sep 1959, ABC Thu 7:30–8:00
HOST:
Tony Hall

Filmed in England, and featuring popular vocal groups from Great Britain plus American guest stars, this series of half-hour musical programs aired on ABC for an eight-week period during the summer of 1959. Among those most frequently featured were Cliff Richard and the Drifters, the Dallas Boys, Marty Wilde, Cherry Wainer, and Dickie Pride. Jimmy Henny was co-host of the program for the last few weeks.

OH MADELINE
Situation Comedy
FIRST TELECAST: *September 27, 1983*
LAST TELECAST: *May 15, 1984*
BROADCAST HISTORY:
Sep 1983–May 1984, ABC Tue 9:30–10:00
CAST:
Madeline Wayne . . . . Madeline Kahn
Charlie Wayne . . . . James Sloyan
Robert Leone . . . . Louis Giambalvo
Doris Leone . . . . Jesse Welles
Annie McIntyre . . . . Francine Tacker

After ten years of marriage, Madeline was bored. Not with husband Charlie, a sweet but square guy who made his living writing steamy romance novels under the name Crystal Love. Not with best friend Doris, a timid divorcée formerly married to Charlie's best friend, a middle-aged swinger named Bob. Just with her sedate, predictable existence in a middle-class suburb. Wanting to put some zip in her life, Madeline decided to try every trendy diversion that came along, whether it was health foods made of seaweed, exercise clubs that seemed intent on bodily destruction, or "ladies only" clubs featuring male strippers. There was plenty of slapstick comedy in this series, along with marital-misunderstanding plots reminiscent of *I Love Lucy.* Annie was Charlie's amorous editor, who seemed to want more than just his manuscripts.

Based on the British television series, *Pig in the Middle.*

579

OH, SUSANNA

syndicated title for *Gale Storm Show, The*

OH, THOSE BELLS

Situation Comedy
FIRST TELECAST: *March 8, 1962*
LAST TELECAST: *May 31, 1962*
BROADCAST HISTORY:
  Mar 1962–May 1962, CBS Thu 7:30–8:00
CAST:
  Herbie Bell.................. Herbert Wiere
  Harry Bell .... Harry Wiere
  Sylvie Bell .... Sylvester Wiere
  Henry Slocum .... Henry Norell
  Kitty Mathews .... Carol Byron
  Mrs. Stanfield .... Reta Shaw

This series was a loosely structured attempt to bring contemporary slapstick humor to television. The Wiere Brothers, an internationally known trio of slapstick comedians, portrayed the last living members of a family with a long history as theatrical prop, costume, and wig makers. They worked in a Hollywood prop shop, run by irascible Henry Slocum with the help of his sweet, understanding secretary, Kitty. Despite their gentle natures, the brothers managed to turn simple everyday situations into frenetic disasters. When things started to go wrong their world looked like it had been taken over by The Three Stooges in their prime.

OHARA

Police/Detective Drama
FIRST TELECAST: *January 17, 1987*
LAST TELECAST:
BROADCAST HISTORY:
  Jan 1987–May 1987, ABC Sat 9:00–10:00
  Oct 1987–Nov 1987, ABC Sat 9:00–10:00
  Dec 1987–Jan 1988, ABC Sat 8:00–9:00
  Jan 1988–   , ABC Sat 9:00–10:00
CAST:
  Lt. Ohara .... Pat Morita
  Capt. Lloyd Hamilton (1987) ... Kevin Conroy
  Capt. Ross (1987) .... Jon Polito
  Gussie Lemmons (1987) ...... Madge Sinclair
  Lt. Jessie Guerrera (1987)... Richard Yniguez
  Lt. Cricket Sideris (1987) .. Catherine Keener
  Sgt. Phil O'Brien (1987)........ Jack Wallace
  Lt. George Shaver (1987-   )
  .... Robert Clohessy
  Asst. U.S. Attorney Teresa Storm
  .... Rachel Ticotin
  Roxy (1987) .... Meagan Fay

ABC really wanted this show to work—so much so that they kept changing its format trying to find *Ohara* an audience. When the series premiered its star was a cop unlike any seen on American television. Lt. Ohara (pronounced "Oh-Har-Ra") was a Japanese-American policeman in Los Angeles who almost never used a gun, preferred patience and persuasion to violence, and didn't even drive a car. A widower, he had a traditional shrine in his home, believed in daily meditation,

and was always ready with a sage saying ("When the going gets tough, the wise get help"). His fellow officers were skeptical, but Ohara's patient methods worked most of the time—and when they didn't he could always resort to the martial arts. Ohara's friend Gussie ran the White Orchid restaurant where the lieutenant could often be found when not on duty.

In the fall of 1987 the format was changed and the entire cast, with the exception of star Pat Morita, was dropped. Ohara was assigned to a federal task force headed by determined lady D.A. Teresa Storm, and his new partner was a brash young officer named Shaver. Though still contemplative, Ohara had suddenly become a more conventional cop—he used his gun and drove his own car, though when on assignment Shaver usually did the driving in his aging convertible. The ratings still were lousy so, in February 1988, the format was changed yet again. After being frustrated by the law enforcement system's bureaucracy—resulting in the murder of a friend—the Lieutenant and his partner both resigned from the force, and short, thoughtful Ohara and tall, hunky Shaver became private eyes.

O'HARA, U.S. TREASURY

Police Drama
FIRST TELECAST: *September 17, 1971*
LAST TELECAST: *September 8, 1972*
BROADCAST HISTORY:
  Sep 1971–Dec 1971, CBS Fri 8:30–9:30
  Jan 1972–Sep 1972, CBS Fri 8:00–9:00
CAST:
  Jim O'Hara.................. David Janssen

Produced with the approval and cooperation of all of the various branches of the Department of the Treasury, this series followed the adventures of special agent Jim O'Hara. Working in pursuit of violators of federal laws, sometimes undercover, Jim served all five of the enforcement agencies of the department: Bureau of Customs, Secret Service, Internal Revenue Service Intelligence Division, Internal Revenue Service Inspection Division, and Internal Revenue Service, Alcohol, Tobacco, and Firearms Division.

OKY DOKY RANCH

see *Adventures of Oky Doky*

OLD AMERICAN BARN DANCE

Music
FIRST TELECAST: *July 5, 1953*
LAST TELECAST: *August 9, 1953*
BROADCAST HISTORY:
  Jul 1953–Aug 1953, DUM Sun 10:30–11:00
EMCEE:
  Bill Bailey

Filmed summertime country music show, featuring Pee Wee King, Tennessee Ernie Ford, and others.

OLD FASHIONED MEETING
Religion
FIRST TELECAST: *October 8, 1950*
LAST TELECAST: *April 1, 1951*
BROADCAST HISTORY:
Oct 1950–Apr 1951, ABC Sun 10:00–10:30

An old-fashioned religious revival hour, sponsored by the Gospel Broadcasting Association.

OLDEST ROOKIE, THE
Police Drama
FIRST TELECAST: *September 16, 1987*
LAST TELECAST: *January 6, 1988*
BROADCAST HISTORY:
Sep 1987–Jan 1988, CBS Wed 8:00–9:00
CAST:

Det. Ike Porter.................. Paul Sorvino
Det. Tony Jonas .... D.W. Moffett
Lt. Marco Zaga .... Raymond J. Barry
Det. Gordon Lane .... Marshall Bell
Chief Black .... Patrick Cronin

After 25 years on the administrative side of police work Ike Porter, Deputy Chief of Police in Charge of Public Affairs, decided to give up the cushy life and get back to the basics of law enforcement. Despite the misgivings of his friends and colleagues, Ike put himself through the rigors of training at the police academy and, much to the surprise of almost everyone, his 50-year-old body survived. Using his connections in the department he got himself and his young rookie partner, Tony Jonas, assigned to the detective division. Their new boss, grizzled veteran Lt. Zaga, wasn't thrilled about having the former P.R. head under his command, and neither was Zaga's second-in-command, Det. Lane, who had been a classmate of Ike's when he had originally joined the force. Despite the problem, Ike and Tony proved to be an effective team.

OLDSMOBILE MUSIC THEATRE
Anthology with Music
FIRST TELECAST: *March 26, 1959*
LAST TELECAST: *May 7, 1959*
BROADCAST HISTORY:
Mar 1959–May 1959, NBC Thu 8:30–9:00
HOSTS:
Bill Hayes
Florence Henderson

This anthology series presented live plays in which a musical element was woven into the storyline, as in musical comedies or dramas with incidental songs. None of the music used was original, however. Hosts Bill Hayes and Florence Henderson appeared in some presentations, along with such stars as Carol Lawrence and Roddy McDowall. The series premiered as *Oldsmobile Music Theatre,* had a single telecast on April 16 as *Oldsmobile Theatre,* and on April 23 became *Oldsmobile Presents.*

OMNIBUS
Culture
FIRST TELECAST: *October 4, 1953*
LAST TELECAST: *March 31, 1957*
BROADCAST HISTORY:
Oct 1953–Apr 1956, CBS Sun 5:00–6:30 (OS)
Oct 1956–Mar 1957, ABC Sun 9:00–10:30
HOST:
Alistair Cooke

Omnibus was the most outstanding and longest-running cultural series in the history of commercial network television. It premiered on November 9, 1952, as a late Sunday afternoon offering on CBS, running from 4:30–6:00 P.M. for its first season. That premiere telecast set the tone for the diversity that would make *Omnibus* a unique program throughout its run. William Saroyan narrated an adaptation of his short story "The Bad Men," there were excerpts from Gilbert and Sullivan's *The Mikado,* and Rex Harrison and his then wife, Lilli Palmer, starred in Maxwell Anderson's "The Trial of Anne Boleyn"—all in one 90-minute program.

As in that first telecast, the range of subject matter presented on *Omnibus* was quite impressive. Opera, symphony, ballet, dramatic plays, and true-life adventure films prepared by the New York Zoological Society and the American Museum of Natural History were but a few of the offerings of this award-winning show. The financing came from the Ford Foundation TV-Radio Workshop, and enabled the producers to devote the full 90 minutes of each show to program content—there were no commercials on *Omnibus,* a rarity in commercial television.

In the fall of 1953, the start time of *Omnibus* was moved up to 5:00 P.M. and, since it ran until 6:30 P.M., it is eligible for inclusion in this book as an evening program. That first evening season presented dramas based on the works of William Inge, James Thurber, Stephen Vincent Benét, Ernest Hemingway, Carson McCullers, John Steinbeck, and T. S. Eliot. Performing were such talents as Hume Cronyn, Jessica Tandy, Carol Channing, Yul Brynner, Walter Slezak, Elsa Lanchester, Anne Bancroft, Mel Ferrer, Helen Hayes, Claude Rains, E. G. Marshall, John Cassavetes, Susan Strasberg, and Thomas Mitchell. But there was much, much more that season. Orson Welles starred in *King Lear,* Jack Benny in a full 90-minute re-creation of his film role in *The Horn Blows at Midnight,* and Victor Borge in a solo segment showing his piano and comedic mastery. Jacques Cousteau, who would have many popular documentaries aired on television in the 1970s, had his first network exposure in January 1954 with "Undersea Archaeology." There were excerpts from the musical *Oklahoma!,* a performance by the Azumi Kabuki Dancers from Japan, a demonstration of the recording techniques used by popular performers Les Paul and Mary Ford, and the ballet *Billy the Kid* with music by Aaron Copland performed by the Ballet Theatre Company. Informational pieces included discussions of the medical uses of X-ray photography and new techniques for determining art forgeries.

Omnibus had a little bit of everything. In subsequent seasons Leonard Bernstein made his television debut with a technical explanation of Beethoven's *Fifth Symphony*, George C. Scott played Robespierre, Peter Ustinov played Samuel Johnson, and Kim Stanley played Joan of Arc. When it left the evening hours in the spring of 1957, it was only to return on Sunday afternoons that fall on NBC, where it remained on an increasingly irregular schedule until its final telecast on April 16, 1961. When it left the air, something wonderful about television went with it, creating a void that was not to be filled until the emergence of network Public Television a decade later.

ABC made a half-hearted attempt at reviving *Omnibus* in 1981, with a few irregularly scheduled special telecasts in prime time.

ON BROADWAY TONIGHT
Talent/Variety
FIRST TELECAST: *July 8, 1964*
LAST TELECAST: *March 12, 1965*
BROADCAST HISTORY:
Jul 1964–Sep 1964, CBS Wed 10:00–11:00
Jan 1965–Mar 1965, CBS Fri 8:30–9:30
EMCEE:
Rudy Vallee

Many talented young performers were given their first national television exposure on this show. Host Rudy Vallee would interview each of the six acts that were performing on a given week's telecast, and then let them do their routines. A special feature of each show was the appearance of a well-known celebrity who would chat with Mr. Vallee about his or her big break in show business. Interestingly, most of the young performers on this series who later became successful were comedians. Among them were Rich Little, Richard Pryor, Marilyn Michaels, Rodney Dangerfield, George Carlin, Jo Anne Worley, and Renee Taylor. Singer Adam Wade, however, made more appearances on the show than anyone else.

ON GUARD
Documentary
FIRST TELECAST: *April 28, 1952*
LAST TELECAST: *May 29, 1954*
BROADCAST HISTORY:
Apr 1952–Aug 1952, ABC Mon 9:30–10:00
Sep 1952–Dec 1952, ABC Thu 9:30–10:00
Dec 1952–Apr 1953, ABC Sun 6:00–6:30
Dec 1953–May 1954, ABC Sat 10:00–10:30

This program consisted of documentary films about the military, produced by the army, navy, and air force.

ON OUR OWN
Situation Comedy

FIRST TELECAST: *October 9, 1977*
LAST TELECAST: *August 20, 1978*
BROADCAST HISTORY:
Oct 1977–Aug 1978, CBS Sun 8:30–9:00
CAST:
Maria Teresa Bonino .... Lynnie Greene
Julia Peters .... Bess Armstrong
Toni McBain .... Gretchen Wyler
April Baxter .... Dixie Carter
Craig Boatwright .... Dan Resin
Eddie Barnes .... John Christopher Jones
J. M. Bedford .... Bob Randall

On Our Own, the story of two young women trying to make it in the New York advertising world, was the only prime-time series actually being produced in New York as of the start of the 1977–1978 season. Maria and Julia had both just been promoted from the secretarial positions they had previously held at the Bedford Advertising Agency, Maria to art director and Julia to copywriter. They were enthusiastic and energetic, if a bit naive and inexperienced, and wanted desperately to take full advantage of their first big step up the corporate ladder. Others in the agency were copywriter April Baxter, beautiful, sexy, and worldly wise with all sorts of advice about men; Eddie Barnes, creative producer of television commercials; and salesman Craig Boatwright. Running the whole operation was sophisticated, slogan-making Toni McBain, the head of the agency. The only person she had to please was board chairman J. M. Bedford.

ON PARADE
Musical Variety
FIRST TELECAST: *July 17, 1964*
LAST TELECAST: *September 18, 1964*
BROADCAST HISTORY:
Jul 1964–Sep 1964, NBC Fri 9:30–10:00

On Parade was originally produced by the Canadian Broadcasting Company. Each telecast spotlighted a particular performer or group of performers from the American musical world such as Rosemary Clooney, Henry Mancini, Diahann Carroll, and the Limeliters. Production numbers, comedy sketches, and interviews were all part of the regular format.

ON STAGE AMERICA
Variety/Magazine
BROADCAST HISTORY:
Syndicated only
120 minutes
Produced: *1984* (13 episodes)
Released: *April 1984*
HOSTS:
Susie Bono
Todd Christianson
Steve Edwards
Randi Oakes

John Barbour
Minnie Pearl

This unusual variety series not only gave its weekly guests the opportunity to perform, but offered viewers in-depth profiles of many of them. Some of the profiles were informative and serious while others looked like fluff pieces from *Lifestyles of the Rich and Famous,* a series that had premiered only a couple of months earlier. Among the more notable personalities appearing were Dean Martin, Barbara Mandrell, Shelley Berman, Jackie Mason, Suzanne Somers, Neil Sedaka, Lisa Hartman, Sid Caesar, Tina Turner, Paul Anka, Diahann Carroll, and David Brenner.

ON THE BOARDWALK WITH PAUL WHITEMAN
Variety
FIRST TELECAST: *May 30, 1954*
LAST TELECAST: *August 1, 1954*
BROADCAST HISTORY:
  May 1954–Aug 1954, ABC Sun 8:00–9:00
EMCEE:
  Paul Whiteman
MUSICAL DIRECTOR:
  Bernie Lowe

Telecast live from the famous Steel Pier in Atlantic City, New Jersey, this program was a variation on *The Original Amateur Hour.* During the first half hour of each show, eight young acts auditioned briefly and were rated by a panel of four people from show business. The four acts with the greatest potential would then return the following week to perform again after they had had a full week of professional coaching.

ON THE CORNER
Variety
FIRST TELECAST: *April 18, 1948*
LAST TELECAST: *May 16, 1948*
BROADCAST HISTORY:
  Apr 1948–May 1948, ABC Sun 6:30–7:00
HOST:
  Henry Morgan

A modest variety program which is said by ABC to have been the first ABC network series. The network at the time consisted of four stations: WFIL in Philadelphia (where *On the Corner* originated); WMAR, Baltimore; WMAL, Washington; and WABC, New York. The latter was a DuMont station, since ABC's own New York outlet was not yet on the air.

Henry Morgan was a major radio star in the 1940s, and was one of the first performers to try the new medium of television on a regular basis. *On the Corner* showed him thumbing the pages of *Variety,* turning up the names of his guests—who generally turned out to be little-known, and sometimes second-rate, nightclub performers. Appear-

ing on the first telecast were George Guest with his marionettes, puppeteer Virginia Austin, impersonator Roy Davis, and the Clark Sisters singing quartet. Laced through it all was Morgan's sardonic wit, which included jibes at the sponsor's commercials. Apparently Admiral Corporation was not amused, as *On the Corner* was canceled after only five weeks of its projected 13-week run.

ON THE LINE WITH CONSIDINE
News Interview
FIRST TELECAST: *January 8, 1952*
LAST TELECAST: *August 29, 1954*
BROADCAST HISTORY:
  Jan 1952–Jun 1953, NBC Tue 10:45–11:00
  Jun 1953–Jan 1954, NBC Tue 10:30–10:45
  Jul 1954–Aug 1954, ABC Sun 9:00–9:15
HOST:
  Bob Considine

After a long career as a journalist, both in print and on radio, Bob Considine came to television. His show, *On the Line with Considine,* actually premiered on Saturday, January 20, 1951, at 5:45 P.M. After a year in that time slot, it moved to Tuesday evening where it remained on NBC for two years. After the show was canceled, it returned for the summer of 1954 on ABC. The format of the show consisted of Bob Considine reading the current news headlines, with occasional comment, and then conducting a short interview with a prominent figure about a pertinent issue of current interest.

ON THE ROAD WITH CHARLES KURALT
Magazine
FIRST TELECAST: *June 26, 1983*
LAST TELECAST: *August 23, 1983*
BROADCAST HISTORY:
  June 1983, CBS Sun 8:00–8:30
  Jun 1983–Aug 1983, CBS Tue 8:00–8:30
HOST/CORRESPONDENT:
  Charles Kuralt

For years CBS correspondent Charles Kuralt had contributed whimsical segments to the *CBS Evening News* and other news series such as 1977's *Who's Who.* These "On the Road" stories were vignettes about the people, places, and bits of history he had encountered while traveling around the country. In the summer of 1983 he got the opportunity to expand the "On the Road" feature with longer pieces in a weekly series of his own.

Much in the style of *Real People,* which may have stolen part of its concept from him, Kuralt had chats with, among others, a man who had traveled around the country for almost 12 years blowing bubbles of all sorts for anyone who cared to watch; the world's record holder in the art of domino-toppling; an Ohio man who had built everything from a Ferris wheel to a grandfather clock—out of toothpicks; a group of real-life cowboys describing what life on the range was truly like; and a man in Denver who collected junk mail by the bagful to use as fuel in his iron stove.

ON THE ROCKS
Situation Comedy
FIRST TELECAST: *September 11, 1975*
LAST TELECAST: *May 17, 1976*
BROADCAST HISTORY:
  Sep 1975–Jan 1976, ABC Thu 8:30–9:00
  Jan 1976–May 1976, ABC Mon 8:00–8:30
CAST:
  Hector Fuentes .... Jose Perez
  DeMott .... Hal Williams
  Cleaver .... Rick Hurst
  Nicky Palik .... Bobby Sandler
  Mr. Gibson .... Mel Stewart
  Mr. Sullivan .... Tom Poston
  Gabby .... Pat Cranshaw
  Baxter .... Jack Grimes
  Warden Wilbur Poindexter ... Logan Ramsey

Comedy centering on the inmates of Alamesa Minimum Security Prison, a "low-risk" institution apparently run as much by the prisoners as by the authorities. The usual setting was the cell containing Hector, the resourceful Latin; his friend DeMott; Cleaver, the eternal optimist; and Nicky, a juvenile offender. Nearby was Gabby, a toothless, elderly inmate. Mr. Gibson was the hard-nosed corrections officer, whose attempts at keeping the boys in line were often unintentionally thwarted by Mr. Sullivan, a mild-mannered guard.

Taped before a live audience and originally telecast immediately following TV's leading cop comedy, *Barney Miller*, which prompted ABC to promote the two shows together with the line "funny cops, and funny robbers." The series was based on the British show *Porridge*.

ON TRIAL
  see *Joseph Cotten Show, The*

ON TRIAL
Debate
FIRST TELECAST: *November 22, 1948*
LAST TELECAST: *August 12, 1952*
BROADCAST HISTORY:
  Nov 1948–Feb 1950, ABC Various nights and times, 30 minutes
  Mar 1950–Sep 1950, ABC Wed 8:00–8:30
  Oct 1950–Sep 1951, ABC Mon 9:30–10:00
  Oct 1951–Jun 1952, ABC Tue 9:30–10:00
  Jun 1952–Aug 1952, ABC Tue 8:00–8:30
MODERATOR:
  David Levitan

Public-affairs debate in the manner of a courtroom trial, with a real-life judge presiding; affirmative and negative counsel and expert witnesses (guest authorities) argued the various points of an issue. Later the format was altered slightly to provide for affirmative arguments one week followed by negative arguments the next. The first issue "on trial" in November 1948 was "Should Wiretapping Be Prohibited?"

For its first 15 months *On Trial* was shifted all over the ABC schedule, seldom spending more than two months in any one time slot. Beginning in early 1950 it settled down to longer runs on various weeknights.

ON YOUR WAY
Quiz/Talent
FIRST TELECAST: *September 9, 1953*
LAST TELECAST: *April 17, 1954*
BROADCAST HISTORY:
  Sep 1953–Jan 1954, DUM Wed 9:30–10:00
  Jan 1954–Apr 1954, ABC Sat 7:00–7:30
EMCEE:
  Bud Collyer (1953–1954)
  Kathy Godfrey (1954)
  John Reed King (1954)

On Your Way began as an audience-participation quiz show in which contestants were given the opportunity to win free transportation to a destination of their choice (thus sending them "on their way"). Bud Collyer was the original host. On January 23, 1954, the program moved to ABC, with new hosts and (two weeks later) a new format. Kathy Godfrey, Arthur Godfrey's younger sister, interviewed four aspiring young performers who then competed in a talent show, under the supervision of emcee John Reed King. In its talent-show format the program was supposed to send winners "on their way" in show business. Unfortunately, not many of them ever gained any sort of fame, although one contestant—a 16-year-old guitarist named Charlie Gracie—later became an important rock star in the late 1950s.

ONCE A HERO
Fantasy/Adventure
FIRST TELECAST: *September 19, 1987*
LAST TELECAST: *October 3, 1987*
BROADCAST HISTORY:
  Sep 1987–Oct 1987, ABC Sat 8:00–9:00
CAST:
  Captain Justice/Brad Steele ...... Jeff Lester
  Abner Bevis .... Milo O'Shea
  Emma Greely .... Caitlin Clarke
  Woody Greely .... Josh Blake
  Gumshoe .... Robert Forster
  Eddie Kybo .... David Wohl
  Rachel Kirk .... Dianne Kay
  Gent .... William Griffis

The first cancellation of the 1987–1988 season was this fantasy-adventure about a cartoon superhero who crossed the "Forbidden Zone" into the real world because he feared his comic strip was about to be canceled. Captain Justice (and his alter ego, mild-mannered professor Brad Steele) hoped to revitalize his creator, legendary cartoonist Abner, with real-world adventures. However, he found that once he was here his super-powers didn't work; no crashing through walls, no deflected bullets, and no one awed by his bright red tights. Cartoon detective Gumshoe (that's right, floppy hat, Sam Spade sneer) also came from fictional Pleasantville into the real world to help Justice battle such adversaries as Max Mayhem and Lobsterman, but it was all uphill. Emma was a suspicious newspaper reporter, and Woody her 12-year-old son.

Once a Hero was canceled after only three weeks, before an already-filmed episode guest starring Adam West ("Batman") could even air. It's tough in the real world.

ONCE AN EAGLE
Military Drama
FIRST TELECAST: *December 2, 1976*
LAST TELECAST: *January 13, 1977*
BROADCAST HISTORY:
 Dec 1976–Jan 1977, NBC Tue 9:00–10:00
CAST:
 Sam Damon .... Sam Elliott
 Courtney Massengale .... Cliff Potts
 Tommy Caldwell Damon ...... Darleen Carr
 George Caldwell .... Glenn Ford
 Lt. Merrick .... Clu Gulager
 Emily Massengale .... Amy Irving
 Jinny Massengale .... Melanie Griffith
 Donny Damon .... Andrew Damon

Adapted from Anton Myrer's novel, *Once an Eagle* was the story of two men's careers in the military over a 30-year period. Sam Damon was a dedicated soldier who cared little for the comforts of home, prestige, power, and the other affectations of rank. Relishing front-line combat, he was a soldier who regarded the military life as a profession to be handled to the best of his ability. Courtney Massengale, on the other hand, was a conniver and maneuverer. More concerned about appearance than substance, he was always on the lookout for a contact to help boost him further up on the ladder to power and prestige. The two men had started out in similar situations as young officers in World War I and individual chapters of *Once an Eagle* showed how their respective lives changed and developed during the intervening period to, and through, World War II.

Once an Eagle was one of four novels dramatized under the collective title *NBC's Best Sellers*. Although individual chapters generally ran only one hour, as indicated in the broadcast history above, the first and last chapters ran from 9:00–11:00 P.M.

ONCE UPON A FENCE
Children's
FIRST TELECAST: *April 13, 1952*
LAST TELECAST: *July 20, 1952*
BROADCAST HISTORY:
 Apr 1952–Jul 1952, NBC Sun 6:30–7:00

REGULARS:
 Dave Kaigler
 Katherine Heger

Music, stories, and magical adventures were all part of this live children's show that originated from Philadelphia during the summer of 1952. The show starred Dave Kaigler, a singer and guitar player who was aided by Eric the Bluebird, an imaginary pet, and Princess Katherine of Storyland, played by Katherine Heger. Miss Heger was a dancer and actress who told stories to the children by acting out all the parts.

ONCE UPON A TUNE
Musical Anthology
FIRST TELECAST: *March 6, 1951*
LAST TELECAST: *May 15, 1951*
BROADCAST HISTORY:
 Mar 1951–May 1951, DUM Tue 10:00–11:00
REGULARS:
 Phil Hanna
 Holly Harris
 Reginald Beane
 Bernice Parks
 Ed Holmes

This bright, though somewhat amateurish, program presented a complete musical every week, usually a takeoff on a current Broadway show or a famous story (for instance, "Little Red Riding Hood"). Various young performers were seen, in addition to the regulars listed above. The program was previously seen locally in New York.

ONE BIG FAMILY
Situation Comedy
BROADCAST HISTORY:
 Syndicated only
 30 minutes
 Produced: *1986–1987*
 Released: *September 1986*
CAST:
 Jake Hatton .... Danny Thomas
 Don Hatton .... Anthony Starke
 Jan Hatton .... Kim Gillingham
 Marianne Hatton (age 19)
 .... Anastasia Fielding
 Brian Hatton (17) .... Michael DeLuise
 Kate Hatton (14) .... Alison McMillan
 Roger Hatton (8) .... Gabriel Damon

This multigeneration family comedy brought Danny Thomas back to series TV—but not for long. Jake was a semiretired nightclub comedian (do they ever really retire?) who moved to Seattle to help out when his son and daughter-in-law were killed in an auto accident. Did we say help out? The five orphaned children ranged in age from eight to adult, and already had surrogate parents in eldest son Don, a policeman, and his new bride Jan. Though grandfather Jake was a peacemaker at times, he also sparked many an uproar, was generally cranky, and was not above running off for an occasional liaison with a mature lady friend.

ONE DAY AT A TIME
Situation Comedy
FIRST TELECAST: *December 16, 1975*
LAST TELECAST: *September 2, 1984*
BROADCAST HISTORY:

Dec 1975–Jul 1976, CBS Tue 9:30–10:00
Sep 1976–Jan 1978, CBS Tue 9:30–10:00
Jan 1978–Jan 1979, CBS Mon 9:30–10:00
Jan 1979–Mar 1979, CBS Wed 9:00–9:30
Mar 1979–Sep 1982, CBS Sun 8:30–9:00
Sep 1982–Mar 1983, CBS Sun 9:30–10:00
Mar 1983–May 1983, CBS Mon 9:30–10:00
Jun 1983–Feb 1984, CBS Sun 8:30–9:00
Mar 1984–May 1984, CBS Wed 8:00–8:30
May 1984–Aug 1984, CBS Mon 9:00–9:30
Aug 1984–Sep 1984, CBS Sun 8:00–8:30

CAST:

Ann Romano Royer . . . . Bonnie Franklin
Julie Cooper Horvath (1975–1980, 1981–1983)
. . . . Mackenzie Phillips
Barbara Cooper Royer . . . . . Valerie Bertinelli
Dwayne Schneider . . . . Pat Harrington, Jr.
David Kane (1975–1976) . . . . . . Richard Masur
Ginny Wrobliki (1976–1977)
. . . . Mary Louise Wilson
Mr. Jerry Davenport (1976–1979)
. . . . Charles Siebert
Max Horvath (1979–1980, 1981–1984)
. . . . Michael Lembeck
Grandma Katherine Romano (1979–1984)
. . . . Nanette Fabray
Nick Handris (1980–1981) . . . . Ron Rifkin
Alex Handris (1980–1983) . . . . Glenn Scarpelli
Francine Webster (1981–1984)
. . . . Shelley Fabares
Mark Royer (1981–1984) . . . . Boyd Gaines
Sam Royer (1982–1984) . . . Howard Hesseman
Annie Horvath (1983–1984)
. . . . Lauren/Paige Maloney

After 17 years of marriage, Ann Romano found herself divorced and living with her two teenage daughters in an apartment building in her hometown of Indianapolis. The problems of trying to keep a job and be an understanding mother to two headstrong girls provided the plots for most episodes of this series. Ann resumed use of her maiden name while both 17-year-old Julie and 15-year-old Barbara kept their father's. The building's super, who regarded himself as the Rudolph Valentino of Indianapolis, was Dwayne Schneider. His first name was virtually never used—all the tenants referred to him only as Schneider. David Kane was Ann's romantic interest during the first season, and at one point they did almost get married, but he departed early in the fall of 1976. Not long after his departure, Ann acquired an outspoken, brassy new neighbor in

Ginny Wrobliki, but she only lasted one season in the cast. It was during that season, however, that Ann found herself a substantial job working as an account executive for the advertising agency of Connors and Davenport. Although not a regular in the series, Joseph Campanella made occasional appearances as Ann's ex-husband, Ed Cooper.

In 1979, while still in college, Julie married Max Horvath, an airline flight steward. No sooner did they get married than he got laid off from his job, forcing the newlyweds to move in temporarily with Ann and Barbara. Max did get back to work and, when he got promoted to a new position in Houston, he and Julie moved away from Indianapolis (series star Mackenzie Phillips had developed a serious drug problem during the 1979–1980 season and was written out of the show to allow her to rehabilitate herself). When Ann left the advertising agency in the fall of 1980 she started a new professional, and eventually personal, involvement with Nick Handris. They became partners doing free-lance advertising—Ann writing copy and Nick doing the art work—and despite initial hostility, romance did bloom. Nick was divorced with a young son, Alex. Ann's mother, Katherine, also became a frequent visitor to the Romano household, especially after her husband died and she moved to Indianapolis to be close to her daughter.

As the 1981–1982 season began, Ann was getting over the shock of Nick's tragic death in an auto accident. Since Nick's ex-wife, Felicia (guest star Elinor Donahue), had moved to Chicago and remarried, Ann was talked into letting Alex move in with her and Barbara until things settled down. Francine Webster, Ann's old nemesis from the days at Connors and Davenport, turned up and convinced her to go into a partnership similar to the one she had had with Nick. Julie and Max also returned to Indianapolis, where he got a job as a travel agent while trying to make extra money as a writer. Barbara and her new boyfriend, dental student Mark Royer, got married in the fall of 1982 and, soon thereafter, Julie gave birth to a daughter, Annie. The following spring, in an effort to economize, Barbara and Julie and their families decided to share a house.

Then, following a courtship that had begun several months earlier, Ann married Mark's divorced father, architect Sam Royer. With Alex moving to Chicago to be with his mother, and her daughters sharing their own house, Ann had no children at home for the first time in years. The only thing to mar her happiness was the sudden disappearance of Julie, who walked out of her home, leaving Max, Barbara, and Mark, now a practicing dentist, to care for little Annie. (Mackenzie Phillips, suffering severe weight loss and other physical problems, was written out of the show for the second time.)

Knowing that stars Bonnie Franklin and Valerie Bertinelli planned to leave the series at the end of the 1983–1984 season, the producers of *One Day at a Time* ended the show's run with a couple of dramatic changes. Ann, having received a fantastic job offer in London, moved overseas with her husband, Sam, and Schneider moved to Florida to raise his orphaned niece and nephew following the unexpected death of his brother.

Reruns of *One Day at a Time* were seen on the CBS daytime lineup from September 1979 to September 1982.

ONE HAPPY FAMILY
Situation Comedy
FIRST TELECAST: *January 13, 1961*
LAST TELECAST: *September 8, 1961*
BROADCAST HISTORY:
  Jan 1961–Mar 1961, NBC Fri 8:00–8:30
  May 1961–Sep 1961, NBC Fri 8:00–8:30
CAST:
  Dick Cooper .... Dick Sargent
  Penny Cooper .... Jody Warner
  Barney Hogan .... Chick Chandler
  Mildred Hogan .... Elisabeth Fraser
  Charlie Hackett .... Jack Kirkwood
  Lovey Hackett .... Cheerio Meredith

Newlyweds Dick and Penny Cooper moved in with Penny's family for a night and somehow ended up as permanent residents. Also part of the household were Penny's grandparents, the Hacketts. Dick was a meterorologist whose good nature was often strained by the efforts of his assembled in-laws to be "helpful," despite their protestations that they would let the young couple lead their own lives. Penny's father, Barney Hogan, was a successful plumbing contractor with an extremely energetic wife, Mildred. Grandfather Charlie Hackett was a strong-willed old coot with a nutty, fun-loving wife named Lovey. The conflicts between the three generations making up *One Happy Family* generated most of the humor in this series.

100 GRAND
Quiz/Audience Participation
FIRST TELECAST: *September 15, 1963*
LAST TELECAST: *September 29, 1963*
BROADCAST HISTORY:
  Sep 1963, ABC Sun 10:00–10:30
EMCEE:
  Jack Clark

Promoted by ABC as the return of the "big-money" quiz show (none had been aired since the 1958 quiz show scandals), this program offered contestants the chance to win up to $100,000. Each contestant challenged a panel of five professional authorities in his particular field of knowledge and, if successful, was to contend with five questions submitted by viewers to the show. The concept didn't work very well and the ratings were so low that the show was canceled after only three weeks on the air.

$128,000 QUESTION, THE
Quiz/Audience Participation
BROADCAST HISTORY:
  Syndicated only
  30 minutes
  Produced: *1976–1978* (81 episodes)
  Released: *September 1976*
HOST:
  Mike Darrow (1976–1977)
  Alex Trebek (1977–1978)

This was a rather limp revival of the quiz-show sensation of the 1950s, *The $64,000 Question*. Besides adjusting the top prize upward for inflation, there was a new host (Hal March having passed away) and questions and answers were fed from a distant point—to lessen the chance of collusion. Otherwise the format was more or less unchanged, with contestants tackling difficult questions in a category of their choosing over a period of weeks, for continuously doubling amounts ($2,000, $4,000, $8,000, etc.). What was lacking was both novelty and suspense. The original had gone on live each week, and anything could happen right there in front of the whole country. The revival was pretaped weeks in advance and shipped around the country for different stations to play at different times.

ONE IN A MILLION
Situation Comedy
FIRST TELECAST: *January 8, 1980*
LAST TELECAST: *June 23, 1980*
BROADCAST HISTORY:
  Jan 1980, ABC Tue 8:30–9:00
  Jan 1980–Mar 1980, ABC Sat 8:00–8:30
  Jun 1980, ABC Mon 8:00–8:30
CAST:
  Shirley Simmons .... Shirley Hemphill
  Barton Stone .... Richard Paul
  Mr. Cushing .... Keene Curtis
  Max Kellerman .... Carl Ballantine
  Nancy Boyer .... Dorothy Fielding
  Duke .... Ralph Wilcox
  Edna .... Ann Weldon
  Raymond .... Mel Stewart
  Dennis .... Billy Wallace

Shirley Hemphill, who played the overpowering black waitress on *What's Happening,* got her own comedy series in 1980. In *One in a Million* down-to-earth cabdriver Shirley Simmons happened to inherit Grayson Enterprises, a multi-million-dollar, white-run conglomerate, when one of her customers died. Bald, scowling Mr. Cushing found this quite inexplicable, as he had planned to take over himself, and he was doubly vexed when scrappy Shirley decided to teach the big "en-dustrialists" how to look out for the ordinary people. Barton Stone was the somewhat naive nephew of the late Mr. Grayson; Nancy, Grayson's secretary and Shirley's ally; Max, the owner of a deli where

Shirley hung out; and Edna and Raymond, her parents.

ONE MAN'S FAMILY
Soap Opera
FIRST TELECAST: *November 4, 1949*
LAST TELECAST: *June 21, 1952*
BROADCAST HISTORY:
  Nov 1949–Jan 1950, NBC Fri 8:00–8:30
  Jan 1950–May 1950, NBC Thu 8:30–9:00
  Jul 1950–Jun 1952, NBC Sat 7:30–8:00 (OS)
CAST:
  Henry Barbour .... Bert Lytell
  Fanny Barbour .... Marjorie Gateson
  Paul Barbour .... Russell Thorson
  Hazel Barbour/Herbert .... Lillian Schaaf
  Claudia Barbour (1949–1950)
  .... Nancy Franklin
  Claudia Barbour/Roberts (1950–1952)
  .... Eva Marie Saint
  Cliff Barbour (1949) .... Frank Thomas, Jr.
  Cliff Barbour (1949) .... Billy Idelson
  Cliff Barbour (1949–1952) .... James Lee
  Jack Barbour (1949–1950) ..... Arthur Cassell
  Jack Barbour (1951–1952) . Richard Wigginton
  Judge Hunter (1949) .... Calvin Thomas
  Dr. Thompson (1949–1950) .. Luis Van Rooten
  Johnny Roberts (1949–1951) .. Michael Higgins
  Beth Holly (1949–1950)
  .... Mercedes McCambridge
  Beth Holly (1950–1952) .... Susan Shaw
  Mrs. Roberts (1950–1951) .... Mona Bruns
  Mr. Roberts (1950–1952) .... Ralph Locke
  Betty Carter (1950) ..... Norma Jean Marlowe
  Judith Richardson (1950) ...... Athena Lorde
  Danny Frank (1950) .... John Newland
  Mac (1950–1952) .... Tony Randall
  Joe Yarbourogh (1950–1952) .... Jim Boles
  Bill Herbert (1950) .... Les Tremayne
  Bill Herbert (1950–1952) ...... Walter Brooke
  Teddy Lawton (1951–1952)
  .... Madeline Belgard
  Ann Waite (1951–1952) ...... Nancy Franklin
  Burton (1951–1952) .... Billy Greene
  Capt. Nicholas Lacey (1952) .. Lloyd Bochner
  Sgt. Tony Adams (1952) .. Michael McAloney
  Sir Guy Vane (1952) .... Maurice Manson
  Jo Collier (1952) .... Gina Holland
CREATOR/WRITER:
  Carleton E. Morse
THEME:
  "Deserted Mansion"

Television version of the favorite radio serial, which began in 1932. None of the radio cast initially carried over into the TV version, but the story remained essentially the same. It was the saga of San Francisco banker Henry Barbour and his clan, set at the Barbours' suburban home in Sea Cliff, overlooking the Golden Gate Bridge. Paul, the eldest son, was the philosophical member of the family, serving as confidant for the other children and the person they turned to when

in trouble (which was often). He was single and a pilot by profession (he had been wounded in World War II). Hazel, the eldest daughter, was 28 when the TV series began and rather anxious to find a husband—which she finally did, in Bill Herbert. Claudia and Cliff were the twins, students at Stanford University, and somewhat rebellious against their father's old-fashioned ways. Jack was the youngest child, aged 10, mischievous and loved by all.

Among the central plot developments during the program's three-year run in prime time were the stormy marriages of Hazel and Claudia, Paul's adopting the orphan Teddy Lawson, Claudia's adventures in Paris where she met the sinister Sir Guy Vane, and assorted illnesses, family feuds, and intrigues. Long-time fans of the radio *One Man's Family* must have had the strange feeling that they were going back in time when watching the TV version—for the action was a full generation behind the continuing radio serial. Ten-year-old Jack was 32 years old on radio, and had six children; the college-age twins were 37 on radio, each having been through two marriages and endless traumas; Paul had been a pilot in World War I on radio—and so on.

The TV version was also seen as a daytime serial from 1954–1955. The program continued on radio until 1959.

ONE MINUTE PLEASE
Quiz/Audience Participation
FIRST TELECAST: *July 6, 1954*
LAST TELECAST: *February 17, 1955*
BROADCAST HISTORY:
  Jul 1954–Oct 1954, DUM Tue 8:30–9:00
  Oct 1954, DUM Tue 9:00–9:30
  Nov 1954–Jan 1955, DUM Fri 9:30–10:00
  Jan 1955–Feb 1955, DUM Thu 9:30–10:00
MODERATOR:
  John K. M. McCaffery (1954)
  Allyn Edwards
REGULAR PANELISTS:
  Hermione Gingold
  Alice Pearce
  Cleveland Amory
  Ernie Kovacs
  Marc Connelly

The object of *One Minute Please* was to see how well the panelists could do at talking nonstop for a full minute on subjects of which they had little knowledge. Such topics as "How to Make Glue," "Breeding Guppies," "Whale Blubber," and "Why I Ride Sidesaddle" were representative of the nonsense talked about. The panelist who managed to say the most in one minute was the winner for the week. Effective November 19, 1954, Allyn Edwards replaced John K. M. McCaffery as permanent moderator.

ONE OF THE BOYS
Situation Comedy

FIRST TELECAST: *January 23, 1982*
LAST TELECAST: *August 20, 1982*
BROADCAST HISTORY:
> *Jan 1982–Apr 1982,* NBC Sat 8:00–8:30
> *Apr 1982–Jun 1982,* NBC Sat 8:30–9:00
> *Aug 1982,* NBC Fri 8:00–8:30

CAST:
> Oliver Nugent .... Mickey Rooney
> Adam Shields .... Dana Carvey
> Jonathan Burns .... Nathan Lane
> Mrs. Green .... Francine Beers
> Bernard Solomon .... Scatman Crothers
> Jane .... Meg Ryan

There was no generation gap here. Sixty-six-year-old Oliver Nugent was retired, energetic, and full of fun. His grandson, Adam, a student at Sheffield College in New Jersey, decided that Gramps was too young at heart to be cooped up at the nearby Bayview Acres retirement home, so he invited Oliver to move in with him and his roommate, Jonathan. He didn't have to ask twice. Coeds thought the old guy was cute, while Mrs. Green, the divorcée who owned their apartment building, found Oliver both attractive and eligible. Oliver's closest friend was Bernard, a retired entertainer with whom he performed occasionally at the local soda shop to entertain the kids. Adam's girlfriend Jane was one of Oliver's biggest fans.

ONE ON ONE
Interview
FIRST TELECAST: *April 25, 1983*
LAST TELECAST: *July 29, 1983*
BROADCAST HISTORY:
> *Apr 1983–Jul 1983,* ABC Mon–Fri 12:30–1:00 A.M.
HOST:
> Greg Jackson

Following the demise of his late-night series *The Last Word,* Greg Jackson briefly hosted this half-hour series in which he interviewed current newsmakers. Only the guest was seen, with Jackson asking the questions from offscreen.

ONE STEP BEYOND
syndicated title for *Alcoa Presents*

1, 2, 3 GO
Educational Children's
FIRST TELECAST: *October 8, 1961*
LAST TELECAST: *May 27, 1962*
BROADCAST HISTORY:
> *Oct 1961–May 1962,* NBC Sun 6:30–7:00
REGULARS:
> Richard Thomas
> Jack Lescoulie

Hosts of this educational program for children were 10-year-old Richard and his adult friend Jack, who traveled around the country learning about our society and the people who comprise it. Trips were taken to such diverse places as NASA

headquarters in Houston, the Treasury Department in Washington, D.C., and an Eskimo village in Alaska. Although informative to viewers of all ages, the emphasis of the show was on professions, skills, and environments that would be of particular interest to young children. Young Richard later went on to fame as John-Boy on *The Waltons.*

O'NEILLS, THE
Drama
FIRST TELECAST: *September 6, 1949*
LAST TELECAST: *January 10, 1950*
BROADCAST HISTORY:
> *Sep 1949–Jan 1950,* DUM Tue 9:00–9:30
CAST:
> Peggy O'Neill.................... Vera Allen
> Janice O'Neill .... Janice Gilbert
> Eddie O'Neill.............. Michael Lawson
> Uncle Bill .... Ian Martin
> Mrs. Bailey .... Jane West
> Morris Levy .... Ben Fishbein
> Mrs. Levy .... Celia Budkin

The O'Neills was an attempt to re-create on television one of the most popular radio serials of the 1930s. Although the radio version had been off the air since 1943, TV brought back many of the characters, including dress designer Peggy O'Neill, who was struggling to raise two fatherless children, cantankerous Uncle Bill, nosy Mrs. Bailey, and the next-door neighbors, the Levys. Actresses Janice Gilbert and Jane West were veterans of the radio show, but their presence was not enough to save the video version of it, which folded after a few months.

OPEN ALL NIGHT
Situation Comedy
FIRST TELECAST: *November 28, 1981*
LAST TELECAST: *March 5, 1982*
BROADCAST HISTORY:
> *Nov 1981–Jan 1982,* ABC Sat 8:00–8:30
> *Feb 1982–Mar 1982,* ABC Fri 8:30–9:00
CAST:
> Gordon Feester .... George Dzundza
> Gretchen Feester .... Susan Tyrrell
> Terry Feester................... Sam Whipple
> Robin .... Bubba Smith
> Officer Steve .... Jay Tarses
> Officer Edie .... Bever-Leigh Banfield

An all-night grocery store might not seem to be a natural setting for comedy, unless it's packed with loonies as this one was. Gordon Feester was the pudgy owner, a semi-failure at everything else he'd done and working on a repeat performance managing the local "364 Store" (closed Christmas). His wife Gretchen helped out, which is more than could be said for their addlebrained teenage son, Terry, who created havoc by just thinking about work. Robin was the towering, black night manager, and Officers Steve and Edie the local cops who were better at helping themselves to coffee and doughnuts than at catching shoplifters. Passing through was a parade of bumbling holdup men, scam artists, hostile midgets, and other assorted weirdos.

Whether in a fit of versatility or just to save money, the co-creator of this show, Jay Tarses, also produced and wrote episodes, co-authored the lyrics to the theme, and appeared on screen as Officer Steve. His creator partner, Tom Patchett, produced, wrote, and directed.

OPEN END
see *David Susskind Show, The*

OPEN HEARING
Public Affairs
FIRST TELECAST: *February 1, 1954*
LAST TELECAST: *September 28, 1958*
BROADCAST HISTORY:
  Feb 1954–Jul 1954, ABC Thu 9:00–9:30
  Feb 1957–Mar 1957, ABC Sun 8:30–9:00
  Nov 1957–Jan 1958, ABC Sun 9:00–9:30
  Jan 1958–Mar 1958, ABC Sun 7:00–7:30
  Jun 1958–Sep 1958, ABC Sun 9:30–10:00
HOST/MODERATOR:
  John Daly (1954)
  John Secondari (1957–1958)

The first ABC program called *Open Hearing* consisted of filmed documentaries and commentary on various topics of general interest, such as the Army-McCarthy controversy, corporate stockholders' meetings, and Alcoholics Anonymous. The 1957–1958 version was a live interview program in which public figures were either interviewed by ABC newsmen, or participated in debates on subjects of current interest. Among the non-politicians appearing were disc jockey Dick Clark, commenting on teenagers and rock 'n' roll, and academician Dr. Henry Kissinger on the state of the nation in 1958. In addition to the prime-time telecasts listed above, this latter version was frequently seen on Sunday afternoons, where it continued until 1960.

For an earlier series on CBS called *Open Hearing* see *The Facts We Face*.

OPENING NIGHT
Dramatic Anthology
FIRST TELECAST: *June 14, 1958*
LAST TELECAST: *September 8, 1958*
BROADCAST HISTORY:
  Jun 1958–Sep 1958, NBC Sat 9:00–9:30
HOSTESS:
  Arlene Dahl

The filmed dramas presented on *Opening Night* were reruns of episodes of the ABC series *Ford Theatre*. Arlene Dahl introduced the plays, which aired on alternate Saturdays with *Club Oasis*.

OPERA CAMEOS
Music

FIRST TELECAST: *January 10, 1954*
LAST TELECAST: *November 21, 1954*
BROADCAST HISTORY:
  Jan 1954–Nov 1954, DUM Sun 7:30–8:00 (OS)
COMMENTATOR:
  Giovanni Martinelli
CONDUCTOR:
  Maestro Guiseppe Bamboschek (and others)

Grand opera has been a rare commodity on American television, but this program of excerpts from famous operas was a fixture on New York TV for many years beginning in 1950. For several months in 1954 (and perhaps for other short periods as well) it was also fed out on the DuMont network. The host, retired Metropolitan Opera star tenor Giovanni Martinelli, introduced the presentations, describing the plot and setting. A mixture of established and younger, lesser-known operatic talent was featured, including some who were billed as future superstars (whatever *did* happen to Gianni Iaia, "the next Caruso"?), some who later did have important careers (such as Beverly Sills), and some whose connection with grand opera was tenuous at best (such as movie vocalist Marni Nixon). Martinelli himself did not appear in the productions, which generally included standard repertoire such as *Tosca, Cavalleria Rusticana, Madame Butterfly, Carmen*, and the like.

OPERA VS. JAZZ
Music
FIRST TELECAST: *May 25, 1953*
LAST TELECAST: *September 21, 1953*
BROADCAST HISTORY:
  May 1953–Sep 1953, ABC Mon 7:30–8:00
REGULARS:
  Nancy Kenyon
  ABC Piano Quartet

This was not really a competition, but simply a mixed presentation of popular tunes (not "jazz") and standard operatic arias, performed by a different pair of guests each week. Nancy Kenyon gave the musical introductions, and accompaniment was by the ABC Piano Quartet, four pianos on a revolving stage. Among those representing the popular field were Alan Dale, Don Cornell, Karen Chandler, and Jerry Vale; the operatic, Jan Peerce, Thomas Hayward, Robert Merrill, and Virginia MacWatters.

OPERATION: ENTERTAINMENT
Variety
FIRST TELECAST: *January 5, 1968*
LAST TELECAST: *January 31, 1969*
BROADCAST HISTORY:
  Jan 1968–Apr 1968, ABC Fri 8:30–9:30
  Sep 1968–Jan 1969, ABC Fri 7:30–8:30
REGULARS:
  The Operation Entertainment Girls
  The Terry Gibbs Band

EXECUTIVE PRODUCER:
  Chuck Barris

With a different guest host and new guest stars each week, this series of filmed variety shows traveled around the world to entertain U.S. military personnel at army, navy, and air force bases, much in the manner of the Bob Hope Christmas shows. Rich Little was host of the first telecast, from Camp Pendleton, California, and such stars as Tim Conway, Jimmy Dean, and Ed Ames appeared on subsequent telecasts.

OPERATION INFORMATION
  Instruction
FIRST TELECAST: *July 17, 1952*
LAST TELECAST: *September 18, 1952*
BROADCAST HISTORY:
  Jul 1952–Sep 1952, DUM Thu 8:00–8:30

Korean War era informational program for veterans, designed to acquaint them with their benefit rights.

OPERATION NEPTUNE
  Science Fiction
FIRST TELECAST: *June 28, 1953*
LAST TELECAST: *August 16, 1953*
BROADCAST HISTORY:
  Jun 1953–Aug 1953, NBC Sun 7:00–7:30
CAST:
  Commander Bill Hollister ...... Todd Griffin
  Dink Saunders .... Richard Holland
  Kebeda .... Harold Conklin
  Mersennus .... Dehl Berti
  Admiral Bigelow .... Rusty Lane
  Thirza .... Margaret Stewart
  Trychus .... Humphrey Davis

Operation Neptune was a live science-fiction series with a strong children's orientation. After the disappearance of a number of ships, the navy concluded that certain evil forces were operating from under the seas to destroy the people living on the surface of Earth. Bill Hollister, who had the nickname "Captain Neptune" for his extensive undersea survey work, was called upon by the navy to track down the source of the trouble, which turned out to be the evil Kebeda and his henchman Mersennus. Helping Captain Neptune was his young assistant and protégé, Dink Saunders.

OPERATION PETTICOAT
  Situation Comedy
FIRST TELECAST: *September 17, 1977*
LAST TELECAST: *August 10, 1979*
BROADCAST HISTORY:
  Sep 1977–May 1978, ABC Sat 8:30–9:00
  May 1978–Jun 1978, ABC Thu 8:30–9:00
  Jun 1978–Aug 1978, ABC Fri 8:30–9:00
  Sep 1978–Oct 1978, ABC Mon 8:30–9:00
  Jun 1979–Aug 1979, ABC Fri 8:00–8:30

CAST:
  Lt. Cdr. Matthew Sherman (1977–1978)
  .... John Astin
  Lt. Nick Holden (1977–1978)
  .... Richard Gilliland
  Major Edna Howard (1977–1978)
  .... Yvonne Wilder
  Lt. Dolores Crandell .... Melinda Naud
  Lt. Barbara Duran (1977–1978)
  .... Jamie Lee Curtis
  Lt. Ruth Colfax (1977–1978) .. Dorrie Thomson
  Lt. Claire Reid (1977–1978) .... Bond Gideon
  Yeoman Hunkle .... Richard Brestoff
  Ensign Stovall (1977–1978)
  .... Christopher J. Brown
  Seaman Dooley (1977–1978).... Kraig Cassity
  Ramon Gallardo (1977–1978) ..... Jesse Dizon
  Chief Herbert Molumphrey (1977–1978)
  .... Wayne Long
  Pharmacist's Mate Williams (1977–1978)
  .... Richard Marion
  Radioman Gossett (1977–1978)
  .... Michael Mazes
  Chief Machinist's Mate Tostin (1977–1978)
  .... Jack Murdock
  Seaman Horwich (1977–1978) ... Peter Schuck
  Lt. Watson (1977–1978) ..... Raymond Singer
  Seaman Broom .... Jim Varney
  Lt. Mike Bender (1978–1979)
  .... Randolph Mantooth
  Lt. Comdr. Haller (1978–1979) .. Robert Hogan
  Lt. Katherine O'Hara (1978–1979)
  .... Jo Ann Pflug
  Lt. Betty Wheeler (1978–1979)
  .... Hilary Thompson
  Chief Engineer Dobritch (1978–1979)
  .... Warren Berlinger
  Seaman Horner (1978–1979)...... Don Sparks
  Doplos (1978–1979) .... Fred Kareman
  Seaman Dixon (1978–1979)... Scott McGinnis

This was a World War II comedy set in the Pacific. Lt. Cdr. Matthew Sherman was a navy career officer anxious to see action before the war was over. When he finally was assigned to command the submarine *Sea Tiger*, however, he arrived to find the craft sunk at dockside. No sooner did he get it patched up and half painted, with pink undercoating, than he had to put to sea quickly to avoid another air raid—hence the navy's first pink submarine. Compounding his problems on board were five army nurses, whom he had rescued, and a wheeler-dealer supply officer, Lt. Holden, who wanted to avoid combat as much as Sherman wanted to find it.

Operation Petticoat was as leaky in the ratings as it was at sea, and when it returned for a second season virtually the entire cast had been changed. Lt. Cdr. Haller was the new skipper, and Lt. Bender his wheeler-dealer executive officer. There were new nurses, led by Lt. O'Hara, new crew members, and also a new mission. The *Sea Tiger* was now assigned to patrol the Pacific for downed airmen and sailors. It didn't help. The

591

series was canceled after only four episodes with the new crew. Repeats aired during the summer of 1979, along with one new episode.

Based on the 1959 movie starring Cary Grant and Tony Curtis, whose daughter, Jamie Lee Curtis, played one of the nurses in this series during the 1977–1978 season.

OPERATION: RUNAWAY
see *Runaways, The*

OPERATION SUCCESS
Information
FIRST TELECAST: *September 21, 1948*
LAST TELECAST: *June 23, 1949*
BROADCAST HISTORY:
Sep 1948–Oct 1948, DUM Tue 8:00–8:30
Jan 1949–Jun 1949, DUM Thu 8:00–8:30
HOST:
Bob Pfeiffer

Public-service program in which host Bob Pfeiffer and others interviewed disabled veterans, and then asked the audience to come forward with job offers. One-hundred-percent placement was claimed.

ORCHID AWARD, THE
Musical Variety
FIRST TELECAST: *May 24, 1953*
LAST TELECAST: *January 24, 1954*
BROADCAST HISTORY:
May 1953–Jul 1953, ABC Sun 6:45–7:00
Jul 1953–Jan 1954, ABC Sun 9:15–9:30
EMCEE:
Bert Lytell (1953)
Ronald Reagan (1953–1954)
Donald Woods (1953–1954)
Paul Weston Orchestra

This musical variety show formed a half-hour block with Walter Winchell's news and gossip program. After Winchell had finished "throwing orchids" at leading entertainers in his commentary, *The Orchid Award* presented one with a real orchid and had him or her perform. Originally *The Orchid Award* presented a performer's biography in music, with Rosemary Clooney being the first guest. Later it became a straight (though short) variety show, with such guests as Rex Harrison, Teresa Brewer, Victor Borge, Lauritz Melchior, Eddie Fisher, and others. Bert Lytell was the original host, replaced in July by alternating hosts Ronald Reagan from Hollywood and Donald Woods from New York. Also known as *The Orchid Room.*

OREGON TRAIL, THE
Western
FIRST TELECAST: *September 21, 1977*
LAST TELECAST: *October 26, 1977*
BROADCAST HISTORY:
Sep 1977–Oct 1977, NBC Wed 9:00–10:00

CAST:
Evan Thorpe .... Rod Taylor
Margaret Devlin .... Darleen Carr
Luther Sprague .... Charles Napier
Andrew Thorpe............ Andrew Stevens
William Thorpe .... Tony Becker
Rachel Thorpe............ Gina Marie Smika

In 1842 widower Evan Thorpe decided to leave his native Illinois with his three children—Andy, age 17; William, age 12; and Rachel, age 10—in search of a new life in the Oregon Territory. He joined a wagon train heading west, was soon elected its captain when the original leader proved to be unreliable, and found a new romantic interest in fellow traveler Margaret Devlin. As the train moved west it was beset with all the traditional enemies—bad weather, unfriendly Indians, rough terrain, and dishonest con men. Luther Sprague was the hardened scout who had little tolerance for the citified travelers' lack of preparedness for the rigors of the trip.

ORIGINAL AMATEUR HOUR, THE
Talent
FIRST TELECAST: *January 18, 1948*
LAST TELECAST: *September 26, 1960*
BROADCAST HISTORY:
Jan 1948–Sep 1949, DUM Sun 7:00–8:00
Oct 1949–Jan 1952, NBC Tue 10:00–11:00
Jan 1952–Sep 1952, NBC Tue 10:00–10:45
Apr 1953–Sep 1954, NBC Sat 8:30–9:00
Oct 1955–Dec 1955, ABC Sun 9:30–10:00
Jan 1956–Feb 1956, ABC Sun 9:30–10:30
Mar 1956–Sep 1956, ABC Sun 9:00–10:00
Oct 1956–Mar 1957, ABC Sun 7:30–8:30
Apr 1957–Jun 1957, ABC Sun 9:00–10:00
Jul 1957–Sep 1957, NBC Mon 10:00–10:30
Sep 1957–Dec 1957, NBC Sun 7:00–7:30
Feb 1958–Oct 1958, NBC Sat 10:00–10:30
May 1959–Jun 1959, CBS Fri 8:30–9:00
Jul 1959–Oct 1959, CBS Fri 10:30–11:00
Mar 1960–Sep 1960, ABC Mon 10:30–11:00
EMCEE:
Ted Mack
ANNOUNCER:
Dennis James

Ted Mack's durable talent show made the rounds of all four networks during its 22 sporadic years on television, including ten (1960–1970) on Sunday afternoons. It was first brought to television on the DuMont network in 1948, a year and a half after the original radio version had ended due to the death of Major Bowes, the founder and original host. It quickly became a Sunday night institution (the radio version was also revived, from 1948 to 1952). The *Amateur Hour* was DuMont's most popular program, and one of the few that was competitive with NBC and CBS—so it was soon stolen away by NBC, in 1949. (This was a pattern which was often repeated during the existence of the DuMont network—whenever a successful program was developed, one of the major networks lured it away with the promise of much more money.)

The format was taken directly from radio's *Major Bowes' Amateur Hour,* on which Mack had been an assistant. Mack, in fact, used the same booking staff and even the same Wheel of Fortune ("Round and round she goes, and where she stops, nobody knows"). He presided over the weekly parade of mimics, kazoo players, and one-man bands with genial good humor. Viewers voted for their favorites by telephone or postcard, and the finalists were awarded scholarships.

Although thousands of hopefuls appeared on the *Original Amateur Hour* over the years and hundreds were winners, surprisingly few ever went on to major or even minor stardom in show business. Probably the most famous "find" of radio days was Frank Sinatra, in 1937. On TV, seven-year-old Gladys Knight and 18-year-old college sophomore Pat Boone were among the grand prize winners. On August 10, 1954, the program celebrated its 1,001st broadcast with a lineup of all-time talent who had graduated from the show.

A familiar feature during the early TV days (1948–1952) was the dancing Old Gold cigarette pack and matchbook (with very shapely legs!) of sponsor P. Lorillard Tobacco Company.

OSMOND FAMILY SHOW, THE
see *Donny and Marie*

OTHER LANDS, OTHER PLACES
Travelogue
FIRST TELECAST: *July 24, 1951*
LAST TELECAST: *May 17, 1953*
BROADCAST HISTORY:
Jul 1951–Sep 1951, ABC Tue 8:45–9:00
Nov 1951–Dec 1951, ABC Sun 9:00–9:30
Apr 1953–May 1953, ABC Sun 7:30–7:45

Documentary travel films. Also known as *Other Lands, Other People,* and also seen locally in New York at various times.

OTHERWORLD
Science Fiction
FIRST TELECAST: *January 26, 1985*
LAST TELECAST: *March 16, 1985*
BROADCAST HISTORY:
Jan 1985–Mar 1985, CBS Sat 8:00–9:00
CAST:
Hal Sterling .... Sam Groom
June Sterling .... Gretchen Corbett
Trace Sterling .... Tony O'Dell
Gina Sterling .... Jonna Lee
Smith Sterling .... Brandon Crane
Kommander Nuveen Kroll ... Jonathan Banks

Hal and June Sterling were on a sightseeing trip with their three children—Trace (18), Gina (17), and Smith (11)—when their lives took a most bi-

zarre twist. While touring the Great Pyramid of Cheops in Egypt they inadvertently passed through a portal to a strange parallel universe. The land in which they found themselves was full of radically different societies, each inhabiting its own area. There were, among others, a mining town run by human-appearing androids, a society in which families were against the law, and a pleasure resort that killed its guests to obtain from their bodies a substance that could give eternal youth to others. Each week the Sterlings found themselves in a new environment where they had to try to fit in, and keep their identities secret, as they searched for the capital city of Imar. There the Supreme Governors of Otherworld had the power to return them to their own world. Hot on their trail was the malevolent Kommander Kroll, whose mysterious "access crystal" they had stolen when they first stumbled into Otherworld.

OUR FAMILY HONOR
Drama
FIRST TELECAST: *September 17, 1985*
LAST TELECAST: *January 3, 1986*
BROADCAST HISTORY:
Sep 1985–Oct 1985, ABC Tue 10:00–11:00
Nov 1985–Jan 1986, ABC Fri 10:00–11:00
CAST:
Commissioner Patrick McKay
.... Kenneth McMillan
Vincent Danzig .... Eli Wallach
Det. Sgt Frank McKay .... Tom Mason
Officer Liz McKay .... Daphne Ashbrook
Katherine McKay .... Georgann Johnson
Augie Danzig .... Michael Madsen
Marianne Danzig .... Barbara Stuart
Jerry Cole (Danzig) .... Michael Woods
Officer Ed Santini .... Ray Liotta
Rita Danzig .... Sheree J. Wilson
Jonas Jones .... Dick Anthony Williams
George Bennett .... Ron Karabatsos

One critic called it "a series you can't refuse," but viewers evidently felt otherwise about this soap opera about two families, one involved in organized crime and the other stalwarts of the New York City Police Department. The McKay clan was headed by Commissioner Patrick, whose hotheaded son, Frank, was a detective and niece, Liz, a recent graduate of the academy. Liz had been assigned to street patrol, where she was partnered with Off. Ed Santini. On the other side of the law were the Danzigs, headed by ruthless crime lord Vincent, whom Commissioner McKay had known since childhood. Augie was Vincent's inept but dangerous son and heir apparent, killing people to please his father. Among the worried wives were Katherine (Patrick's), Marianne (Vincent's), and Rita (Augie's).

Principal stories included Liz's star-crossed love affair with Jerry Cole, who proved to be Vincent's rebel son; the Danzigs' involvement in the death of a contractor whom Jerry tried to help;

and Augie's death (in the last episode) in a struggle with Frank, who was trying to take him in for killing Rita's lover.

OUR HOUSE
Drama
FIRST TELECAST: *September 11, 1986*
LAST TELECAST: *June 26, 1988*
BROADCAST HISTORY:
> *Sep 1986*, NBC Thu 8:30–9:30
> *Sep 1986–May 1987*, NBC Sun 7:00–8:00
> *May 1987–Jun 1987*, NBC Sun 8:00–9:00
> *Jun 1987–   *, NBC Sun 7:00–8:00

CAST:
> *Gus Witherspoon* .... Wilford Brimley
> *Jesse Witherspoon* .... Deidre Hall
> *Kris Witherspoon (15)*..... Shannen Doherty
> *David Witherspoon (12)* .... Chad Allen
> *Molly Witherspoon (8)* .... Keri Houlihan
> *Joe Kaplan* .... Gerald S. O'Loughlin
> *Bertha* .... Nicole DuBuc
> *Crimshaw* .... Owen Bush
> *Cliff*............................. Bob Hoy
> *Mark (1987)* .... Thomas Wilson Brown
> *J.R. Dutton (1987–   )* ... David Mendenhall

*Occasional

The Associated Press called this homey series "a family show suitable for framing." It was certainly warm and old-fashioned, a gentle story about getting along and growing up. Gus was a cantankerous 65-year-old grandpa with a walrus mustache who treasured his privacy living alone in his handsome, tree-shaded Victorian house. However, when his married son died, Gus was faced with the prospect of taking in his distraught widow Jesse—who had no funds—and her three rambunctious children. That was the end of serenity in Gus' house. It was now, as he told Jesse, "our house."

Jesse worked at various jobs, including that of free-lance photographer. Granddaughter Kris had Gus' strong will, and aimed to become an air force test pilot someday; David was headstrong too, but unsure of himself at age 12; and Molly was just a sweet girl who wanted everyone to get along. Joe was Gus' long-time pal. Stories revolved around the compromises made by three generations living under one roof, and the lessons learned by all, including the grumpy, heart-of-gold granddad.

OUR MAN HIGGINS
Situation Comedy
FIRST TELECAST: *October 3, 1962*
LAST TELECAST: *September 11, 1963*
BROADCAST HISTORY:
> *Oct 1962–Sep 1963*, ABC Wed 9:30–10:00

CAST:
> *Higgins* .... Stanley Holloway
> *Alice MacRoberts* .... Audrey Totter
> *Duncan MacRoberts* .... Frank Maxwell
> *Tommy MacRoberts* .... Rickey Kelman
> *Dinghy MacRoberts* .... K. C. Butts
> *Joanie MacRoberts* .... Regina Groves

Stanley Holloway, the veteran British music-hall comic who achieved fame in America in the role of Eliza Doolittle's father in *My Fair Lady*, was the star of this comedy. He played Higgins, a gentleman butler from Scotland who found himself sent to America to serve a suburban couple, the MacRoberts. They had "inherited" him as part of an ancestral bequest. The couple and their three children, Tommy, Dinghy, and Joanie, were constantly being saved from various predicaments by the ever-resourceful Higgins.

OUR MISS BROOKS
Situation Comedy
FIRST TELECAST: *October 3, 1952*
LAST TELECAST: *September 21, 1956*
BROADCAST HISTORY:
> *Oct 1952–Jun 1953*, CBS Fri 9:30–10:00
> *Oct 1953–Jun 1955*, CBS Fri 9:30–10:00
> *Oct 1955–Sep 1956*, CBS Fri 8:30–9:00

CAST:
> *Connie Brooks* .... Eve Arden
> *Osgood Conklin* .... Gale Gordon
> *Philip Boynton* .... Robert Rockwell
> *Walter Denton (1952–1955)* .. Richard Crenna
> *Mrs. Margaret Davis* .... Jane Morgan
> *Harriet Conklin (1952–1955)*
> .... Gloria McMillan
> *Stretch Snodgrass (1952–1955)*
> .... Leonard Smith
> *Miss Daisy Enright (1952–1954)*
> .... Mary Jane Croft
> *Mrs. Martha Conklin (1952–1953)*
> .... Virginia Gordon
> *Mrs. Martha Conklin (1953–1956)*
> .... Paula Winslowe
> *Superintendent Stone (1953–1955)*
> .... Joseph Kearns
> *Angela (1954–1956)* .... Jesslyn Fax
> *Ricky Velasco (1954–1955)*....... Ricky Vera
> *Mr. Oliver Munsey (1955–1956)*
> .... Bob Sweeney
> *Mrs. Nestor (1955)* .... Nana Bryant
> *Mrs. Nestor (1955–1956)* .... Isabel Randolph
> *Gene Talbot (1955–1956)*........ Gene Barry
> *Clint Albright (1955–1956)* .... William Ching
> *Benny Romero (1955–1956)* ...... Ricky Vera
> *Mr. Romero (1956)* .... Hy Averback

Our Miss Brooks had originated on CBS radio in 1948, and was heard on both radio and TV throughout the mid-1950s with essentially the same cast. It was one of the period's most popular and loved comedies, and gave Eve Arden a role with which she will forever be identified. She played Connie Brooks, the wisecracking English teacher at Madison High. Her nemesis was crusty, blustery principal Osgood P. Conklin, who was constantly blowing his stack at her for something. Mr. Boynton, the handsome but incredibly shy biology teacher, was the potential husband she was always trying to snag—without success. Connie rented a room from kindly old Mrs. Davis and rode to school each morning with one of her students, the somewhat dimwitted Walter Denton. Her interaction with these varied regulars, played by an excellent supporting cast, comprised the stories. No one in *Our Miss Brooks* was an out-and-out lunatic, as is so often the case in TV comedies, but everyone had some pronounced but realistic idiosyncrasy that viewers could identify with, thus making the show's principals a perfect TV "family." Eve Arden herself was much in demand to speak to educational groups and at PTA meetings, and even received a dozen offers of positions as an English teacher at real high schools. They could hardly have afforded her, as she was by then making $200,000 per year!

By the start of the 1955–1956 season the ratings were beginning to slip and the setting was changed. Madison High was razed for a highway project and Miss Brooks found a new job at Mrs. Nestor's Private Elementary School nearby. For some reason, Mr. Conklin had acquired the job of principal there, and he and other cast members remained on the show to harass her. Connie's new love interest was the young physical education teacher, Gene Talbot, who was chasing her, quite a turnaround from Mr. Boynton's shy indifference. Somehow the revised format seemed to limp along and Mr. Boynton was brought back in the spring of 1956. His return did not help, however, and the show ended its run shortly thereafter.

Connie's long pursuit of Mr. Boynton did finally pay off, though not in the TV series. In a 1956 Warner Brothers movie based on the series, he finally proposed, and she became Mrs. Philip Boynton.

OUR NEIGHBORS TO THE NORTH
Documentary
FIRST TELECAST: *June 15, 1952*
LAST TELECAST: *August 29, 1952*
BROADCAST HISTORY:
 Jun 1952, ABC Sun 10:00–10:30
 Aug 1952, ABC Fri 8:00–8:30

This was a series of film shorts about Canada, produced by the Canadian government.

OUR PLACE
Musical Variety
FIRST TELECAST: *July 2, 1967*
LAST TELECAST: *September 3, 1967*
BROADCAST HISTORY:
 Jul 1967–Sep 1967, CBS Sun 9:00–10:00
REGULARS:
 The Doodletown Pipers
 Jack Burns
 Avery Schreiber
 The George Wilkins Orchestra

Narrated by a huge puppet dog named Rowlf, one of Jim Henson's Muppets, this musical and comedy variety series was the 1967 summer replacement for *The Smothers Brothers Comedy Hour*. It featured the singing of the Doodletown Pipers and the comic antics of the team of Burns & Schreiber.

OUR PRIVATE WORLD
Soap Opera
FIRST TELECAST: *May 5, 1965*
LAST TELECAST: *September 10, 1965*
BROADCAST HISTORY:
 May 1965–Sep 1965, CBS Wed 9:30–10:00
 May 1965–Sep 1965, CBS Fri 9:00–9:30
CAST:
 Lisa Hughes .... Eileen Fulton
 Helen Eldredge .... Geraldine Fitzgerald
 John Eldredge .... Nicolas Coster
 Eve Eldredge .... Julienne Marie
 Tom Eldredge .... Sam Groom
 Brad Robinson .... Robert Drivas
 Dr. Tony Larson .... David O'Brien
 Sandy Larson .... Sandy Smith
 Franny Martin .... Pamela Murphy
 Dick Robinson .... Ken Tobey
 Pat .... Kathy Dunn

In the wake of ABC's great success with its prime-time soap opera *Peyton Place*, CBS decided to try its own version of the form during the summer of 1965. This series was a spin-off from the highly successful daytime serial *As the World Turns*, and focused on Lisa Hughes, one of *World's* leading characters. Young divorcée Lisa decided to find a new life for herself by leaving her small hometown and moving to Chicago, where she found a job in the admitting room of a hospital. The two major plot lines involved her life and associations at the hospital and the machinations of the Eldredges, a socially prominent and extremely wealthy family living in the exclusive suburb of Lake Forest. The CBS experiment proved not to be very successful and the series was canceled at the end of the summer, leaving actress Eileen Fulton to her daytime role only.

OUR SECRET WEAPON—THE TRUTH
Discussion
FIRST TELECAST: *February 6, 1951*
LAST TELECAST: *April 17, 1951*
BROADCAST HISTORY:
 Feb 1951–Apr 1951, DUM Tue 7:30–8:00
PANELISTS:
 Leo Cherne
 Ralph de Toledano

This propaganda program had been presented on CBS radio during World War II as a forum for debunking Nazi claims against America. It was revived during the Korean War for use against a new enemy, with regulars Leo Cherne and Ralph de Toledano on hand each week to "answer Communist lies about us" with facts and testimony from special guests. Previously a local program in New York.

OUR TIME
Variety
FIRST TELECAST: *July 27, 1985*
LAST TELECAST: *September 7, 1985*
BROADCAST HISTORY:
    Jul 1985–Aug 1985, NBC Sat 8:00–8:30
    Aug 1985, NBC Sat 8:30–9:00
    Sep 1985, NBC Sat 9:30–10:00
HOST:
    Karen Valentine
REGULARS:
    Tim Stack
    Patti Lee
    Zane Buzby
    Phil Hartman
    Denny Evans
    Harry Anderson

Nostalgia for the 1960s was the theme of this light-weight summer series, hosted by actress Karen Valentine with a different co-host each week. Fads of the era were satirized in comedy sketches, and TV and music stars of the '60s paraded through the show, some as featured guests and others in cameos. Old films clips of guests in their TV series of the past were used in a regular "then and now" feature to show how they had aged. Among the "TV kids" of the '60s who received this treatment were Tim Considine, Don Grady, and Barry and Stanley Livingston (from *My Three Sons*), Dwayne Hickman and Sheila James *(The Many Loves of Dobie Gillis)*, Jay North *(Dennis the Menace),* Jon Provost *(Lassie),* Ken Osmond and Frank Bank *(Leave It to Beaver),* Noreen Corcoran *(Bachelor Father),* Marc Copage *(Julia),* and Butch Patrick *(The Munsters).* Musical performers appearing included such moldy oldies as Frankie Avalon, The Coasters, Johnny Rivers, Leslie Gore, Mitch Ryder, and Paul Revere and the Raiders. Co-hosts included Paul Petersen, Sonny Bono, and John Sebastian. No doubt they all appreciated the work.

OUR TIMES WITH BILL MOYERS
Documentary
FIRST TELECAST: *June 26, 1983*
LAST TELECAST: *August 23, 1983*
BROADCAST HISTORY:
    Jun 1983, CBS Sun 8:30–9:00
    Jun 1983–Aug 1983, CBS Tue 8:30–9:00
HOST/CORRESPONDENT:
    Bill Moyers

Each episode of this summer series featured CBS correspondent Bill Moyers talking with people about a social problem in modern-day America. Among them: residents of Gadsden, Alabama, discussed trying to get by in a community dependent on the depressed rubber and steel industries; a profile of Dina Rasor, who revealed information

to the public about Pentagon waste and inefficiency; the search for a cure for A.I.D.S. (Acquired Immune Deficiency Syndrome); the reflections of a number of people who heard Martin Luther King, Jr.'s "I Have A Dream" speech in Washington in 1963, about what the speech had meant to them.

OUR WORLD
Documentary
FIRST TELECAST: *September 25, 1986*
LAST TELECAST: *September 3, 1987*
BROADCAST HISTORY:
    Sep 1986–Jul 1987, ABC Thu 8:00–9:00
    Jul 1987–Sep 1987, ABC Thu 9:00–10:00
HOSTS:
    Linda Ellerbee
    Ray Gandolf

ABC had a problem . . . how to compete against the red-hot *Cosby Show* and not lose a fortune in the process. The answer: raid the news division's vaults, string together old film footage from a specific period, and package it with some glitzy graphics and intelligent commentary. *Our World* was probably the cheapest hour on prime-time TV, yet it was the darling of critics (and a small but vociferous group of fans) who saw it as a worthwhile alternative to the escapist hits on NBC and CBS. In addition to news clips, the show featured first-hand "witness" commentary from people who were there, music, TV and radio entertainment of the era, and even some docudrama "recreations" of famous events. Periods spotlighted ranged from October 1938 (approaching war in Europe, *The War of the Worlds* radio broadcast at home), to the summer of 1969 (Vietnam and the "Woodstock Generation"), and beyond.

OUT OF THE BLUE
Situation Comedy
FIRST TELECAST: *September 9, 1979*
LAST TELECAST: *December 16, 1979*
BROADCAST HISTORY:
    Sep 1979–Oct 1979, ABC Sun 7:00–7:30
    Dec 1979, ABC Sun 7:30–8:00
CAST:
    Random . . . . Jimmy Brogan
    Aunt Marion . . . . Dixie Carter
    Chris Richards (16) . . . . Clark Brandon
    Laura Richards (13) . . . . Olivia Barash
    Stacey Richards (10) . . . . Tammy Lauren
    Jason Richards (8) . . . . Jason Keller
    Shane Richards (8) . . . . Shane Keller
    Gladys . . . . Hannah Dean
    Boss Angel . . . . Eileen Heckart

Kiddie comedy in the style of *Bewitched* and *My Favorite Martian.* In this one, an inept angel was dispatched to help a harried Chicago woman cope with her five adorable nieces and nephews, after their parents had died in a plane crash. Aunt Marion decided to accept a boarder, to help meet expenses, so Random moved in. The fact that he was an angel, with magical powers, was the kids' secret. Random could move people and places around with a twinkle, and he used his powers to teach the kids little lessons about growing up. Gladys was the black housekeeper.

OUT OF THE FOG
Drama
FIRST TELECAST: *April 7, 1952*
LAST TELECAST: *September 22, 1952*
BROADCAST HISTORY:
Apr 1952–Sep 1952, ABC Mon 8:00–8:30

This was a short-lived series of mystery films, which alternated with *Mr. District Attorney* from April through June, then was seen weekly.

OUT OF THIS WORLD
Situation Comedy
BROADCAST HISTORY:
Syndicated only
30 minutes
Produced: *1987–*
Released: *September 1987*
CAST:
Donna Garland . . . . Donna Pescow
Evie Garland (age 13) . . . . Maureen Flannigan
Mayor Kyle Applegate . . . . Doug McClure
Beano Froelich . . . . Joe Alaskey
Buzz . . . . Buzz Belmondo
Troy (voice only) . . . . Burt Reynolds
*Lindsay Selkirk . . . . Christina Nigra
*Phil . . . . John Roarke
*Quigley Handlesman . . . . Carl Steven
*Chris Fuller . . . . Stephen J. Burke

*Occasional

Donna Garland ran a private school for gifted children in the town of Marlowe, near Carmel, California, but none was more gifted than her daughter Evie. Evie was starting to develop powers she had inherited from her father Troy, an extraterrestrial visitor from the planet Antareus who had married her mother and then been called back to his home planet shortly after her birth. Evie's powers included the ability to stop time (freezing people in mid-sentence was a favorite trick) and to materialize things simply by willing them into existence. Whenever she had problems dealing with her powers she could communicate with her dad through a special cube that functioned as an interstellar phone. The only other person who knew about Troy was Donna's brother, Beano, the rotund owner of "Beano's Diet Clinic." Anyone else who happened to see Evie's remarkable powers at work simply thought that she—or they—were crazy.

Buzz was the eccentric character who ran the clinic for Beano, and Mayor Kyle an egocentric former TV star who had turned to politics.

OUT THERE
Science Fiction Anthology
FIRST TELECAST: *October 28, 1951*
LAST TELECAST: *January 13, 1952*
BROADCAST HISTORY:
Oct 1951–Jan 1952, CBS Sun 6:00–6:30

A live anthology series which used filmed special effects, *Out There* sought to bridge the gap between serious drama and the juvenile science fiction of such shows as *Captain Video* and *Tom Corbet—Space Cadet*. All of the episodes were adapted from stories by prominent science-fiction writers and were presented in such a way as to attract an adult audience but still be exciting enough to hold the attention of children.

OUTCASTS, THE
Western
FIRST TELECAST: *September 23, 1968*
LAST TELECAST: *September 15, 1969*
BROADCAST HISTORY:
Sep 1968–Sep 1969, ABC Mon 9:00–10:00
CAST:
Earl Corey . . . . Don Murray
Jemal David . . . . Otis Young

This violent Western teamed a Virginia aristocrat-turned-gunman-and-drifter with a freed slave-turned-bounty hunter, in the years after the Civil War. The two of them had an uneasy relationship at best, often erupting into fights and arguments, as they pursued a common goal of making money by tracking down wanted criminals. Corey was the white man, and David the black.

OUTER LIMITS, THE
Science Fiction Anthology
FIRST TELECAST: *September 16, 1963*
LAST TELECAST: *January 16, 1965*
BROADCAST HISTORY:
Sep 1963–Sep 1964, ABC Mon 7:30–8:30
Sep 1964–Jan 1965, ABC Sat 7:30–8:30
CREATOR/EXECUTIVE PRODUCER:
Leslie Stevens

At the opening of each episode in this anthology series the picture on the TV screen started to do funny things and a deep voice intoned: "There is nothing wrong with your TV set. We are controlling transmission. We can control the vertical. We can control the horizontal. For the next hour we will control all that you see and hear and think. You are watching a drama that reaches from the inner mind to . . . *The Outer Limits.*" The special effects were good, the alien costumes interesting, and the plots tolerable. Unfortunately, at the end of each episode, before the control voice returned your television set to you, it felt compelled to end the story with a moral, often ruining the effect of the whole show.

OUTLAWS
Detective Drama
FIRST TELECAST: *December 28, 1986*
LAST TELECAST: *May 30, 1987*
BROADCAST HISTORY:
Dec 1986, CBS Sun 9:00–11:00
Jan 1987–May 1987, CBS Sat 8:00–9:00
CAST:
John Grail .... Rod Taylor
Harland Pike .... William Lucking
Wolfson "Wolf" Lucas .... Charles Napier
Isaiah "Ice" McAdams ... Richard Roundtree
Billy Pike .... Patrick Houser
Lt. Maggie Randall .... Christine Belford

It was 1899 and Texas Sheriff John Grail was leading a posse after a gang of bank robbers led by Harland Pike—a gang he had been a member of before he had gone straight and become a peace officer. Caught in a freak electrical storm, Grail and the gang were catapulted through time to contemporary Texas, a totally alien world to the one they knew. Realizing what had happened, though having no idea how, they reconciled their differences, used the gold coins from the robbery to buy a ranch they named the Double Eagle, and attempted to adjust to the modern world. Under Grail's urging they opened the Double Eagle Detective Agency, literally bringing old-fashioned justice to Houston and the Southwest. Their biggest problem was keeping Harland's hot-headed kid brother, Billy, under control. These guys were a little hard to take. They wore outfits that, though newly made, were replicas of the clothes they had worn at the turn of the century; they still used their dated weapons; and they never seemed to get shot by the bad guys despite their penchant for striding side-by-side into gunfights. Maggie Randall was the contemporary Houston police officer who befriended them, got them out of trouble, and had a soft spot for John Grail.

OUTLAWS, THE
Western
FIRST TELECAST: *September 29, 1960*
LAST TELECAST: *September 13, 1962*
BROADCAST HISTORY:
Sep 1960–Sep 1962, NBC Thu 7:30–8:30
CAST:
U.S. Marshall Frank Caine (1960–1961)
.... Barton MacLane
Deputy Marshal Will Forman .... Don Collier
Deputy Marshal Heck Martin (1960–1961)
.... Jock Gaynor
Deputy Marshal Chalk Breeson (1961–1962)
.... Bruce Yarnell
Slim (1961–1962) .... Slim Pickens
Connie Masters (1961–1962) ..... Judy Lewis

In its first season, *The Outlaws* approached the struggle between law officers of the Old West and the desperadoes they chased from a novel point of view. Although Marshal Frank Caine and his two deputies, Will Forman and Heck Martin, were the series regulars, each episode was seen through the eyes of the outlaws they were pursuing. The setting for the series was the Oklahoma Territory in the 1890s, when the Dalton Boys, the Jennings Gang, and other outlaws made it one of the most lawless of all the West's frontiers.

When *The Outlaws* returned in the fall of 1961 there were a number of changes. Gone were Caine and Martin, and Will Forman was a full marshal with his own deputy. The perspective of the series was now from the side of the marshals and the honest citizens rather than the criminals. The action was based in the town of Stillwater, Oklahoma, where the marshals were headquartered. Connie Masters worked at the Wells Fargo office, and Slim was the town character.

OUTLOOK
see *Chet Huntley Reporting*

OUTSIDE U.S.A.
Documentary
FIRST TELECAST: *September 1, 1955*
LAST TELECAST: *June 3, 1956*
BROADCAST HISTORY:
Sep 1955–Oct 1955, ABC Thu 10:00–10:30
Nov 1955–Jan 1956, ABC Tue 10:00–10:30
Jan 1956–Mar 1956, ABC Mon 10:00–10:30
Apr 1956–Jun 1956, ABC Sun 10:00–10:30
NARRATOR/COMMENTATOR:
Quincy Howe

Each week Mr. Howe introduced filmed coverage of an event or issue in world politics. Following the film he would analyze or evaluate the situation being covered.

OUTSIDER, THE
Detective Drama
FIRST TELECAST: *September 18, 1968*
LAST TELECAST: *September 3, 1969*
BROADCAST HISTORY:
Sep 1968–Sep 1969, NBC Wed 10:00–11:00
CAST:
David Ross .... Darren McGavin

David Ross was not the stereotyped glamorous private detective. He did not make much money, lived in a run-down Los Angeles apartment building, drove a beat-up 10-year-old car, and often got beat up himself while on cases. Ross was a loner who had never finished high school and had been orphaned when a small child. As an adult, he had served six years in prison on a trumped-up murder charge, before being pardoned. In short Ross had found the world a very unfriendly place—he was an "outsider." Nevertheless he turned private eye to tackle other people's problems, and proved an extremely thorough and productive investigator.

OVERLAND TRAIL, THE

Western

FIRST TELECAST: *February 7, 1960*
LAST TELECAST: *September 11, 1960*
BROADCAST HISTORY:
    Feb 1960–Sep 1960, NBC Sun 7:00–8:00
CAST:
    Frederick Thomas Kelly ..... William Bendix
    Frank "Flip" Flippen .... Doug McClure

The opening of the Overland Trail, one of the major stage routes to the West, and the effort to push that route all the way to the Pacific Ocean, served as the backdrop for this series. The two men charged with moving the stage line from Missouri, over the Rockies, and through to California were Frederick Thomas Kelly and Frank Flippen. Kelly was a crusty former civil engineer and Union Army guerrilla who found getting the Overland Stage Line into operation the most exciting challenge of his life. His young friend and aide, nicknamed Flip, had been brought up by Indians and was full of an adventurous enthusiasm that complemented Kelly's cautious nature. Their adventures and the adventures of their passengers provided the stories for this series.

OVERSEAS ADVENTURE

see *Foreign Intrigue*

OWEN MARSHALL, COUNSELOR AT LAW

Law Drama

FIRST TELECAST: *September 16, 1971*
LAST TELECAST: *August 24, 1974*
BROADCAST HISTORY:
    Sep 1971–Jan 1973, ABC Thu 10:00–11:00
    Jan 1973–Jan 1974, ABC Wed 10:00–11:00
    Jan 1974–Aug 1974, ABC Sat 10:00–11:00
CAST:
    Owen Marshall .... Arthur Hill
    Jess Brandon .... Lee Majors
    Danny Paterno (1973–1974) ..... Reni Santoni
    Ted Warrick (1974) .... David Soul
    Melissa Marshall .... Christine Matchett
    Frieda Krause .... Joan Darling

This popular lawyer drama depicted the life and trials of Owen Marshall, a compassionate defense attorney practicing in a small town in California. Marshall's cases ranged from civil suits to murder, but were always marked by a warmth and consideration for the accused. In a way, *Owen Marshall* was the courtroom equivalent of medicine's kindly *Marcus Welby*, and, in fact, the two series sometimes had joint episodes. In 1972 Marshall found himself defending the father of one of Dr. Welby's patients against a murder charge, and in 1974 he defended Dr. Kiley, Welby's associate, against a paternity suit.

Owen Marshall had several young law partners during his run, the first of whom was Jess Brandon. For a time in 1973–1974 Lee Majors, the actor portraying Brandon, was starring in two ABC series, this one and *The Six Million Dollar Man*. He was finally replaced in February 1974 by another future star, David Soul, in the role of Ted Warrick. In addition, Danny Paterno was seen as a partner during the final season. Melissa was widower Marshall's 12-year-old daughter, and Frieda his loyal law clerk.

Owen Marshall was well regarded by real-life legal associations, and won several public-service awards. Its co-creators were David Victor and University of Wisconsin law professor Jerry McNeely.

OZARK JUBILEE

Country Music

FIRST TELECAST: *January 22, 1955*
LAST TELECAST: *September 24, 1960*
BROADCAST HISTORY:
    Jan 1955–Jun 1955, ABC Sat 9:00–10:00
    Jul 1955–Sep 1956, ABC Sat 7:30–9:00
    Oct 1956–Dec 1956, ABC Thu 10:00–11:00
    Dec 1956–Jun 1957, ABC Sat 10:00–11:00
    Jun 1957–Sep 1957, ABC Sat 10:00–10:30
    Sep 1957–Sep 1959, ABC Sat 8:00–9:00
    Sep 1958–Oct 1958, ABC Mon 7:30–8:30
    Oct 1959–Sep 1960, ABC Sat 10:00–11:00
REGULARS:
    Red Foley
    Webb Pierce (occasional 1955–1956)
    Jean Shepard (1955)
    Hawkshaw Hawkins (1955)
    Tommy Sosebee (1955)
    Porter Wagoner (1955–1956)
    Foggy River Boys/Marksmen (1955–1959)
    Pete Stamper (1956)
    Oklahoma Wranglers (1955)
    Bud Isaac (1955)
    Uncle Cyp & Aunt Sap Brasfield (1956–1960)
    Flash & Whistler (1956–1957)
    Tadpoles (1956)
    Bobby Lord (1957–1960)
    Jim Wilson (1957)
    Marvin Rainwater (1957)
    Bill Wimberly's Country Rhythm Boys (1956–1957)
    Slim Wilson's Jubilee Band (1958–1960)
    Wanda Jackson (1957–1960)
    Billy Walker (1957)
    Tall Timber Trio (1957–1960)
    Bill McMain (1957)
    Norma Jean (1958)
    Leroy Van Dyke (1958)
    Suzi Arden (1958–1959)
    Smiley Burnette (1959)
    The Promenaders (1959–1960)
    Shug Fisher (1960)
    Lew Childre (1960)
THEME:
    "Sugarfoot Rag," by Hank Garland

Country and western music had a major showcase on network television in the late 1950s in this weekly hoedown from Springfield, Missouri. The host was genial country singer Red Foley, a veteran of the *Grand Ole Opry*, who projected a good-natured warmth and sincerity which characterized the whole proceedings. Appearing on *Jubilee* were many of the top names in country music, including regulars Webb Pierce (who was once-a-month host for a time in 1955–1956), the Foggy River Boys vocal quartet (renamed the Marksmen in 1957), comic Pete Stamper, and Porter Wagoner. Among the regular features were square dancing by the Tadpoles, a group of two-to-ten year olds, and the cornpone comedy act of Uncle Cyp and Aunt Sap, who portrayed an elderly married couple who were always throwing ancient jokes at one another. The "Junior Jubilee" portion of the show gave exposure to younger talent. Perhaps its biggest discovery was a sweet-as-peaches little 11-year-old with a booming voice, named Brenda Lee. She made her first appearance in March 1956, quickly became a *Jubilee* favorite,

and later went on to stardom in both the country and popular music fields.

Jubilee ran until 1960, when it was abruptly canceled by ABC. The official reason was that the network had acquired the Gillette fights and wanted to carry them in *Jubilee*'s time slot. The real reason, however, was that host Red Foley had been indicted for tax fraud and was about to stand trial—a situation hardly consonant with the down-home sincerity he projected on the show (Foley's first trial ended in a hung jury, and a second, in 1961, in acquittal).

Ozark Jubilee underwent two name changes during its run, becoming *Country Music Jubilee* in July 1957 and *Jubilee U.S.A.* in August 1958.

OZZIE AND HARRIET
see *Adventures of Ozzie & Harriet, The*

OZZIE'S GIRLS
see *Adventures of Ozzie & Harriet, The*

P

PM MAGAZINE
Magazine
BROADCAST HISTORY:
Syndicated only
30 minutes
Produced: *1978–*
Released: *September 1978*

PM Magazine was an unusual hybrid of local and national programming. Each city had its own version of the show, with local hosts who introduced short, entertaining pieces featuring tips for better living, interesting people, and unusual places. A typical week's stories might include a profile of Alan Alda, a man's reunion with girlfriends from his past, a recipe for gooseberry compote, and ways to reduce stress. Some features were produced locally, but many of them came from other cities and even foreign countries, giving *PM Magazine* a very cosmopolitan look for a locally originated show. The show also stressed mobility—stories were introduced outdoors and taped on location using small, portable "minicam" TV cameras that allowed maximum maneuverability. The viewer never saw the inside of a TV studio.

These rather expensive production techniques were made possible on local TV by a unique experiment in interstation cooperation. The idea for the series originated in August 1976 as a local show called *Evening Magazine* on KPIX in San Francisco, a station owned by the Westinghouse company. Four other stations owned by Westinghouse soon began their own versions, and in the fall of 1978 the company offered the idea to stations across the country, on the following basis: each station was to use two local co-hosts (so that the show, not the host, would be the chief attraction), follow certain guidelines as to the show's format, and—most importantly—contribute at least one locally produced segment each week to a national pool. In return the station would get access to the best tapes other stations had contributed to the pool, the use of the *PM Magazine* name and graphics, and the help of an experienced national staff in producing its local version of the show. A station could thus concentrate on producing only a few good segments each week, and still have enough first-rate material to fill its own five-nights-a-week *PM Magazine*.

PABST BLUE RIBBON BOUTS
see *Boxing*

PACKARD SHOWROOM, THE
see *Martha Wright Show, The*

PALL MALL PLAYHOUSE
Western Anthology

FIRST TELECAST: *July 20, 1955*
LAST TELECAST: *September 7, 1955*
BROADCAST HISTORY:
Jul 1955–Sep 1955, ABC Wed 8:30–9:00

This summer series was comprised of a collection of unsold pilots for dramatic Westerns. Among those starring were John Ireland, Carolyn Jones, and Will Rogers, Jr.

PALMERSTOWN, U.S.A.
Drama
FIRST TELECAST: *March 20, 1980*
LAST TELECAST: *June 9, 1981*
BROADCAST HISTORY:
Mar 1980–May 1980, CBS Thu 8:00–9:00
Mar 1981–June 1981, CBS Tue 8:00–9:00
CAST:
Bessie Freeman .... Jonelle Allen
Luther Freeman .... Bill Duke
Diana Freeman ...... Star-Shemah Bobatoon
Booker T. Freeman .. Jermain Hodge Johnson
W. D. Hall .... Beeson Carroll
Coralee Hall .... Janice St. John
Willy-Joe Hall .... Michael J. Fox
David Hall .... Brian Godfrey Wilson
The Sheriff .... Kenneth White
Widder Brown (1981) .... Iris Korn

Booker T. Freeman and David Hall were nine-year-old boys growing up together in the rural Southern community of Palmerstown during the Depression of the 1930s. They were best friends, despite the fact that Brooker T. was black and David was white. Booker T.'s father, Luther, was the town blacksmith and David's father, W.D., was the local grocer. Diana was Booker T.'s older sister and Willy-Joe was David's older brother. Because of the fast friendship between the two boys their families had become quite close, despite the racial animosities prevalent at the time. In the middle of the South, in the middle of the Depression, they proved that blacks and whites could get along with each other. Most of what happened in Palmerstown was seen through the eyes of the two young friends.

Palmerstown, U.S.A. was co-produced by veteran TV producer Norman Lear and award-winning author Alex Haley, whose book and TV miniseries *Roots* were huge successes during the mid-1970s. For Haley this series was somewhat autobiographical, since he had grown up with a close white friend in an integrated Southern town during the Depression.

In March 1981 the title of the program was shortened to *Palmerstown*.

PANIC
Dramatic Anthology
FIRST TELECAST: *March 5, 1957*
LAST TELECAST: *September 17, 1957*
BROADCAST HISTORY:
Mar 1957–Sep 1957, NBC Tue 8:30–9:00

Westbrook Van Voorhis

At the outset of each episode of *Panic* an individual was put into a sudden crisis situation which posed threats of an emotional or physical nature to him. The remainder of each episode delineated how well he reacted to and coped with the crisis. For example, a young man found himself on the brink of suicide; a vaudeville dancer was stalked by a murderer; and a family was trapped in their home. Appearing were such stars as June Havoc, Darryl Hickman, and James and Pamela Mason.

PANTOMIME QUIZ
Quiz/Audience Participation
FIRST TELECAST: *July 3, 1950*
LAST TELECAST: *September 16, 1963*
BROADCAST HISTORY:
Jul 1950, CBS Mon 9:30–10:00
Jul 1950–Sep 1950, CBS Mon 8:00–8:30
Jul 1951–Aug 1951, CBS Mon 8:00–8:30
Jan 1952, NBC Wed 10:30–11:00
Jan 1952–Mar 1952, NBC Wed 10:00–10:30
Jul 1952–Sep 1952, CBS Fri 8:30–9:00
Jul 1953–Aug 1953, CBS Fri 8:00–8:30
Oct 1953–Apr 1954, DUM Tue 8:30–9:00
Jul 1954–Aug 1954, CBS Fri 8:00–8:30
Jan 1955–Mar 1955, ABC Sun 9:30–10:00
Jul 1955–Sep 1955, CBS Fri 8:00–8:30
Jul 1956–Sep 1956, CBS Fri 10:30–11:00
Jul 1957–Sep 1957, CBS Fri 10:30–11:00
Apr 1958–Sep 1958, ABC Tue 9:30–10:00
Jun 1959–Sep 1959, ABC Mon 9:00–9:30
Sep 1962–Sep 1963, CBS Mon 10:30–11:00
HOST:
Mike Stokey
Pat Harrington, Jr. (1962)
REGULARS:
Hans Conried (1950–1952, 1955–1957, 1962–1963)
Vincent Price (1950–1952)
Adele Jergens (1950–1952)
Jackie Coogan (1950–1955)
John Barrymore, Jr. (1953–1954)
Dave Willock (1953–1954)
Rocky Graziano (1954–1956)
Dorothy Hart (1953–1958)
Robert Clary (1954–1957)
Peter Donald (1953–1955, 1957)
Carol Haney (1955–1956)
Milt Kamen (1957–1959)
Jan Clayton (1953–1954, 1962–1963)
Elaine Stritch (1953–1955, 1958)
Jerry Lester (1953–1955)
Carol Burnett (1958–1959)
Stubby Kaye (1958–1959, 1962–1963)
Dick Van Dyke (1958–1959)

Pantomime Quiz was the perennial summer-replacement series. Created by Mike Stokey, who was its producer and host, it had premiered as a local show in Los Angeles in 1947. The game itself was a variation on the parlor game of charades.

Two teams of four members each, three regulars and one guest, competed with each other in attempting to act out famous phrases, mottos, literary quotes, etc. The team that took the least amount of time solving the total of four or five phrases that each team was given during a telecast was declared the winner. Home viewers were asked to send in suggestions for phrases to be used on the show and won cash if their submissions were used, and a bonus if the team trying to solve it could not do so within the two-minute time limit.

The durability of *Pantomime Quiz* is evident in its survival on network television for more than a decade, generally running during the summers. It was one of only four series to have aired on all four networks. When it was revived for the last time, for a full-season run on CBS in 1962–1963, the title was changed to *Stump the Stars* and Pat Harrington, Jr., became the host. He lasted less than three months in that role, however, being replaced by program producer Mike Stokey on December 10, 1962.

The turnover among regular charaders on *Pantomime Quiz* was extremely high. The list of regulars shown above only includes those who were with the show for at least two different runs. Among the other personalities who were regulars for a single season were Fred Clark, Robert Stack, Angela Lansbury, Orson Bean, Rose Marie, John Carradine, Howard Morris, Tom Poston, Beverly Garland, Sebastian Cabot, Ross Martin, Diana Dors, Mickey Manners, and Ruta Lee.

PAPER CHASE, THE
Drama
FIRST TELECAST: *September 9, 1978*
LAST TELECAST: *July 17, 1979*
BROADCAST HISTORY:
Sep 1978, CBS Sat 8:00–9:00
Sep 1978–Jan 1979, CBS Tue 8:00–9:00
Feb 1979, CBS Tue 10:00–11:00
Mar 1979–Jul 1979, CBS Tue 8:00–9:00
(New episodes produced for cable TV 1983–1985)
CAST:
Professor Charles W. Kingsfield, Jr.
.... John Houseman
James T. Hart .... James Stephens
Franklin Ford III .... Tom Fitzsimmons
Thomas Craig Anderson .... Robert Ginty
Willis Bell .... James Keane
Jonathan Brooks (1978) .... Jonathan Segal
Elizabeth Logan .... Francine Tacker
Asheley Brooks (1978) .... Deka Beaudine
Ernie .... Charles Hallahan
Carol .... Carole Goldman
Mrs. Nottingham .... Betty Harford
Dean Rutherford .... Jack Manning
Mallison .... Jessica Salem
Gagarian .... Stanley De Santis
THEME:
"The First Years," by Charles Fox and Norman Gimbel, sung by Seals and Crofts

James T. Hart was a first-year law student whose upbringing in rural Iowa had not prepared him for the intensity and ruthlessness that he found at a highly competitive law school. His nemesis was Professor Charles Kingsfield, the world's leading authority on contract law, who inspired both awe and terror in his students with his imperious and authoritarian manner. To help cope with the heavy work load, Hart joined a study group consisting of other students who were working together sharing notes and assignments. The group had been organized by Franklin Ford III, a would-be third generation lawyer from a socially prominent family. Others in the group were Anderson, Bell, Logan, and Brooks. Brooks, the only married member of the group, left school after he got caught cheating.

Even with his heavy work load, Hart had to find time for a part-time job at Ernie's pizza joint. There he met Carol, a waitress who admired him but couldn't understand his dedication to his studies. Also seen occasionally was Mrs. Nottingham, Professor Kingsfield's secretary.

Despite being hailed by critics as the most praiseworthy new series of the 1978–1979 season, *The Paper Chase* never attracted a competitive audience and was canceled at the end of the year. PBS aired reruns of *The Paper Chase* for a few years following its departure from CBS and, in the first case of its kind, the pay-cable television service Showtime revived it in the spring of 1983. The new episodes produced for Showtime, under the title *The Paper Chase: The Second Year,* featured Houseman, Stephens, Fitzsimmons, and Keane from the network cast.

The series was based on the movie of the same name, for which John Houseman (as Kingsfield) won a supporting-actor Academy Award. Although the movie took place at Harvard, no mention was made of a specific university in the television series.

PAPER DOLLS
Drama
FIRST TELECAST: *September 23, 1984*
LAST TELECAST: *December 25, 1984*
BROADCAST HISTORY:
  Sep 1984, ABC Sun 9:00–11:00
  Sep 1984–Nov 1984, ABC Tue 9:00–10:00
  Nov 1984–Dec 1984, ABC Tue 10:00–11:00
CAST:
  Grant Harper .... Lloyd Bridges
  Wesley Harper .... Dack Rambo
  Blair Harper-Fenton .... Mimi Rogers
  David Fenton .... Richard Beymer
  Racine .... Morgan Fairchild
  Taryn Blake .... Nicollette Sheridan
  Julia Blake .... Brenda Vaccaro
  Laurie Caswell .... Terry Farrell
  Dinah Caswell............... Jennifer Warren
  Michael Caswell........ John Bennett Perry
  Marjorie Harper .... Nancy Olson
  Sara Frank .... Anne Schedeen
  Colette Ferrier .... Lauren Hutton

  Steve .... Geoffrey Blake
  Mark Bailey.................... Roscoe Born
  Chris York .... Don Bowren
  Sandy Parris .... Jonathan Frakes
  Dr. Van Adams .... Alan Fudge
  Gabrielle...................... Joyce Gittlin
  Grayson Carr................. Larry Linville
  Lewis Crosby.............. Thom Matthews
  Jenna .... Amy Resnick
  Conrad.................... Jeffrey Richman

Paper Dolls was another of television's sagas of power, lust, and family, this time set in the glamorous world of New York's modeling and cosmetics industry. Grant Harper was the mogul who manipulated all; his womanizing son, Wesley, was president of Harper Cosmetics, while his beautiful daughter, Blair, was a top model and the loving wife of hard-working young executive David Fenton, head of Tempus Sportswear. Wesley and David were bitter rivals, both looking for an exclusive fresh new face that would sell their products and free them from Grant's domination. Both were also clients of Racine, the powerful and shrewd head of a top modeling agency, whose hottest property, teenage superstar Taryn Blake, was on the verge of burnout. Although she was only 16, Taryn's frequent temper tantrums and the demands of her aggressive mother and manager, Julia, made the young starlet likely to be pushed aside when the next discovery came along.

That discovery arrived in the person of Laurie Caswell, also 16 and fresh from the suburbs, who projected an innocent beauty and enthusiasm. Laurie's mother and father, Dinah and Michael, worried about what the high pressure life of a model would do to their daughter, but soon they too were drawn into the high-stakes corporate and personal intrigues of Madison Avenue. Colette Ferrier, who ran Ferrier Cosmetics, was one of Harper Cosmetics' chief rivals.

Paper Dolls was based on the 1982 TV movie of the same name.

PAPER MOON
Situation Comedy
FIRST TELECAST: *September 12, 1974*
LAST TELECAST: *January 2, 1975*
BROADCAST HISTORY:
  Sep 1974–Jan 1975, ABC Thu 8:30–9:00
CAST:
  Moses (Moze) Pray .... Christopher Connelly
  Addie Pray .... Jodie Foster
THEME:
  "It's Only a Paper Moon," by Harold Arlen, Yip Harburg, and Billy Rose

This was a gentle comedy about an itinerant Bible salesman/con artist and his precocious 11-year-old daughter, traveling across Kansas during the Depression years. If Moze and Addie never had much money, it wasn't for lack of trying every fast-buck scheme in the book. Though they just "got by," and were often only one step ahead of the law, they at least had each other. Much period flavor was featured in this series, including an authentic 1933 theme song. The series was filmed on location in Kansas.

Based on the 1973 hit movie starring Ryan and Tatum O'Neal, which had in turn been taken from the novel *Addie Pray* by Joe David Brown.

PARENT GAME, THE
Quiz/Audience Participation
BROADCAST HISTORY:
Syndicated only
30 minutes
Produced: *1972–1974*
Released: *Fall 1972*
HOST:
Clark Race
EXECUTIVE PRODUCER:
Chuck Barris

Three pairs of young parents or parents-to-be competed in this game show. The questions all concerned how to handle familiar and funny situations that arise in raising children. Answers were matched with those of an expert on child care (University of Southern California child psychologist Dorothy Thompson), and the couple with the most "matches" won.

PARIS
Police Drama
FIRST TELECAST: *September 29, 1979*
LAST TELECAST: *January 15, 1980*
BROADCAST HISTORY:
Sep 1979–Oct 1979, CBS Sat 10:00–11:00
Dec 1979–Jan 1980, CBS Tue 10:00–11:00
CAST:
Woody Paris .... James Earl Jones
Barbara Paris .... Lee Chamberlain
Deputy Chief Jerome Bench ... Hank Garrett
Stacey Erickson .... Cecilia Hart
Charlie Bogart................ Jake Mitchell
Willie Miller .... Mike Warren
Ernie Villas .... Frank Ramirez

Woody Paris was an erudite and highly principled black police captain whose interests went beyond simple law enforcement. By night he taught a course in criminology at a local university. He even had a home life—unlike most TV cops—shared with his understanding wife, Barbara. On the job, Paris reported to Deputy Chief Jerome Bench, a longtime friend, and ran a special Metro Squad assigned to break touch cases. Assigned to his squad were four young officers, Stacey, Charlie, Willie, and Ernie.

What Paris lacked, unfortunately, was a little bit of believability. James Earl Jones, a highly respected actor, strutted through this role speaking in booming, stentorian tones, as if it were *Richard III*. Despite good reviews from an awed press, *Paris* did not attract much of an audience, and was soon canceled.

PARIS CAVALCADE OF FASHIONS
Fashion Show
FIRST TELECAST: *November 11, 1948*
LAST TELECAST: *January 20, 1949*
BROADCAST HISTORY:
Nov 1948–Jan 1949, NBC Thu 7:15–7:30
NARRATOR:
Faye Emerson (Nov–Dec 1948)
Julie Gibson (Dec 1948–Jan 1949)

Films of the latest Paris creations. The series was formerly seen locally on WNBT, New York.

PARIS 7000
Adventure
FIRST TELECAST: *January 22, 1970*
LAST TELECAST: *June 4, 1970*
BROADCAST HISTORY:
Jan 1970–Jun 1970, ABC Thu 10:00–11:00
CAST:
Jack Brennan .... George Hamilton
Robert Stevens .... Gene Raymond
Jules Maurois .... Jacques Aubuchon

Movie star George Hamilton starred in this series as a State Department employee attached to the U.S. Embassy in Paris, whose job it was to help Americans in trouble. The number to call for help: Paris 7000. Robert Stevens was his aide, and Maurois the contact on the local gendarmerie.

PARK PLACE
Situation Comedy
FIRST TELECAST: *April 9, 1981*
LAST TELECAST: *April 30, 1981*
BROADCAST HISTORY:
Apr 1981, CBS Thu 8:30–9:00
CAST:
David Ross.................... Harold Gould
Jeff O'Neil.................... David Clennon
Howard "Howie" Beech .... Don Calfa
Frances Heine .... Alice Drummond
Ernie Rice .... Cal Gibson
Joel "Jo" Keene .... Mary Elaine Monti
Aaron "Mac" MacRae .... Lionel Smith
Brad Lincoln .... James Widdoes

Patterned after such successful urban "gang comedies" as *Barney Miller* and *Taxi*, *Park Place* was the story of a motley group of lawyers working at a New York City legal aid clinic. Into the Park Place Division of the New York City Legal Assistance Bureau came the poor, the ignorant, and the downright obnoxious—all seeking free legal help. In charge, more or less, was senior attorney David Ross. Five young attorneys made up his staff: Jeff O'Neil, the naive eager beaver; Howie Beech, the status-seeking opportunist; Jo Keene, the aggressive women's libber; Mac MacRae, the wheelchair-ridden black Vietnam veteran; and Brad Lincoln, the inexperienced young Harvard graduate trying to obtain some recognition from his peers. Frances, the efficient but spaced-out secretary, and Ernie, the hip receptionist, rounded out the cast.

PARTNERS, THE
Situation Comedy
FIRST TELECAST: *September 18, 1971*
LAST TELECAST: *September 8, 1972*
BROADCAST HISTORY:
Sep 1971–Jan 1972, NBC Sat 8:00–8:30
Jul 1972–Sep 1972, NBC Fri 8:00–8:30
CAST:
Det. Lennie Crooke .... Don Adams
Det. George Robinson .... Rupert Crosse
Capt. Andrews .... John Doucette
Sgt. Higgenbottom .... Dick Van Patten
Freddie Butler .... Robert Karvelas

Lennie Crooke and George Robinson were a pair of police detectives who were always getting into crazy situations while investigating crimes. In their enthusiasm, they would occasionally get themselves into more trouble than did the criminals they were after. Their boss, Captain Andrews, was constantly frustrated and confounded by their activities which, despite all, somehow resulted in their solving the crimes. Sgt. Higgenbottom, who was trying to ingratiate himself with the captain, spent much of his time belittling Lennie and George. A recurring nuisance was Freddie Butler, a compulsive confessor who claimed responsibility for everything from murder to shoplifting.

PARTNERS IN CRIME
Detective Drama
FIRST TELECAST: *September 22, 1984*
LAST TELECAST: *December 29, 1984*
BROADCAST HISTORY:
Sep 1984–Nov 1984, NBC Sat 9:00–10:00
Nov 1984–Dec 1984, NBC Sat 10:00–11:00
CAST:
Carole Stanwyck .... Lynda Carter
Sydney Kovak .... Loni Anderson
Lt. Ed Vronsky .... Leo Rossi
Harmon Shain .... Walter Olkewicz
Jeanine .... Eileen Heckart

Two beautiful women—both ex-wives of the same man—joined forces to solve his murder in this light mystery series set in San Francisco. Carole was a professional photographer, a former heiress, and a rather proper brunette; Sydney was a jazz bass player, an amateur pickpocket, and a fun-loving blonde. Their ex-hubby, eccentric detective Raymond Caulfield, had left them as a joint bequest his fine old Victorian house and his thriving detective agency. After solving Raymond's last case, the girls decided to continue the business themselves. The series featured glamorous fashions, catty chatter about being married to the same man, and beautiful San Francisco locations. Lt. Vronsky, their contact on the S.F.P.D., was always after a date with Sydney; Shain was

their dense helper; and Jeanine was Raymond's mother, an amateur sleuth and busybody who ran a mystery bookshop called—what else—"Partners In Crime."

PARTRIDGE FAMILY, THE
Situation Comedy
FIRST TELECAST: *September 25, 1970*
LAST TELECAST: *August 31, 1974*
BROADCAST HISTORY:
Sep 1970–Jun 1973, ABC Fri 8:30–9:00
Jun 1973–Aug 1974, ABC Sat 8:00–8:30
CAST:
Shirley Partridge .... Shirley Jones
Keith Partridge .... David Cassidy
Laurie Partridge .... Susan Dey
Danny Partridge .... Danny Bonaduce
Christopher Partridge (1970–1971)
.... Jeremy Gelbwaks
Christopher Partridge (1971–1974)
.... Brian Forster
Tracy Partridge .... Suzanne Crough
Reuben Kinkaid .... David Madden
Ricky Stevens (1973–1974) ...... Ricky Segall
Alan Kinkaid (1973–1974) .... Alan Bursky
THEME:
"When We're Singin'," music by Wes Farrell, lyrics by Diane Hilderbrand (1970); new lyrics and title "Come On, Get Happy," by Danny Janssen (1972)

Oscar-winner Shirley Jones and her stepson, David Cassidy, starred in this comedy about a family that hit the big time in the music business. Shirley Partridge was just another widowed suburban mother with a houseful of rambunctious kids, until one day the kids asked her to take part in an impromptu recording session they were holding in the garage. Seems they needed a vocalist. The song they were recording was "I Think I Love You," and to everyone's surprise they sold it to a record company, the record became a smash hit, and the Partridges were soon setting off in a wildly painted old school bus to perform around the country. They were authentic members of the rock generation. Stories depicted their exploits on the road, and in their California hometown.

Besides Shirley and 16-year-old Keith (Cassidy), the band included Laurie (15), Danny (10, and the freckle-faced con man of the family), Christopher (7), and Tracy (5). Reuben Kinkaid was their fast-talking, child-hating agent—and perpetual foil for Danny. During the 1973–1974 season a neighbor's son, 4-year-old Ricky, joined the cast, and he sang too. Simone was the family pooch.

The Partridges were heavily promoted in the real-life music business, and they caught on with several hit singles, including "I Think I Love You," which sold four million copies, as well as albums. David Cassidy became the hero of the subteen set and had considerable success as a single act. Unlike the Monkees, the Partridges had no artistic pretensions—none of them were professional musicians—and the backgrounds on their records were in fact done by professional studio musicians, with Shirley and David providing the vocals. Their success was as spectacular on the record charts as on TV, but it did not last long in either case.

An animated Saturday morning sequel, *The Partridge Family, 2200 A.D.*, ran on ABC from September 1974 to September 1975.

The Partridge Family was loosely based on the experiences of a real-life popular recording family, the Cowsills.

PARTY LINE
Quiz/Audience Participation
FIRST TELECAST: *June 8, 1947*
LAST TELECAST: *August 31, 1947*
BROADCAST HISTORY:
Jun 1947–Aug 1947, NBC Sun 8:30–9:00
EMCEE:
Bert Parks

Bert Parks, one of the most familiar faces on early TV, hosted this primitive phone-in quiz show which occupied half of the Sunday 8:00–9:00 P.M. Bristol-Myers hour during the summer of 1947. (For the other half, see *Tex and Jinx*.) Bert would ask a question, sometimes illustrated with a short film or performed by actors in the studio, and then would call a number at random from among the cards sent in by viewers. If the person called was watching and could answer the question, he won a prize of $5 and a box of Bristol-Myers products.

The program was sponsored on a two-station network consisting of WNBT, New York, and WPTZ, Philadelphia.

PARTY TIME AT CLUB ROMA
Variety
FIRST TELECAST: *October 14, 1950*
LAST TELECAST: *January 6, 1951*
BROADCAST HISTORY:
Oct 1950–Jan 1951, NBC Sat 11:00–11:30
REGULARS:
Ben Alexander
Pat Emery
Chris Emery
Camille Leong
Doodles and Spicer
The Cheerleaders

Set in the mythical Club Roma in San Francisco, where this series was actually filmed, *Party Time at Club Roma* started out as a variation on *Beat the Clock*, with emcee Alexander inviting guests at the club to join in attempting various stunts or playing games in which they might win small merchandise prizes. His assistants included a pair of identical twins (Pat and Chris), a beautiful girl from San Francisco's Chinatown (Camille), and the pantomime team of Doodles and Spicer. The format was soon changed to a talent contest with

emcee Alexander picking acts out of the audience to perform for the crowd at the club. The winners were chosen by applause meter.

An interesting sidelight to this series is that it was also produced by Ben Alexander. A former child star in films, he was an account executive with Foote, Cone & Belding, the advertising agency for the sponsor, Roma Wines, and this was his first exposure to network television. He subsequently left the agency and played Jack Webb's partner on *Dragnet*.

PASSPORT TO DANGER
Intrigue
BROADCAST HISTORY:
Syndicated only
30 minutes
Produced: *Apr 1954–1956* (39 episodes)
Released: *November 1954*
CAST:
Steve McQuinn . . . . Cesar Romero

The principal attraction of this foreign-adventure series was Cesar Romero, whose debonair good looks and sly sense of humor (he evidently didn't take the role too seriously) lifted it a bit above the ordinary. Otherwise it was the usual international-intrigue series. Glamorous locales, beautiful but mysterious women, and dangerous incidents swirled around diplomatic courier Steve McQuinn as he went about his appointed rounds delivering top-secret messages to U.S. embassies from Rome to Rangoon.

PASSWORD
Quiz/Audience Participation
FIRST TELECAST: *January 2, 1962*
LAST TELECAST: *May 22, 1967*
BROADCAST HISTORY:
Jan 1962–Sep 1962, CBS Tue 8:00–8:30
Sep 1962–Mar 1963, CBS Sun 6:30–7:00
Mar 1963–Sep 1963, CBS Mon 10:00–10:30
Sep 1963–Sep 1964, CBS Thu 7:30–8:00
Sep 1964–Sep 1965, CBS Thu 9:00–9:30
Apr 1967–May 1967, CBS Mon 10:30–11:00
EMCEE:
Allen Ludden

Password was a word-association game. Two teams, each composed of one celebrity and one non-celebrity contestant, competed in trying to identify the "password" with the least number of clues. The "password," usually a common word, was handed to one member of each team and these two people would then take turns giving their partners one-word clues to make them guess the word. After the first clue a correct response was worth ten points, after the second clue, nine points, and so forth. The first team to accumulate 25 points won the round. In the "Lightning Round" one member of each team would have 60 seconds to get his partner to properly associate a total of five "passwords." Winners got cash prizes and the chance to return to face a new challenging team.

The daytime version of *Password* premiered in October 1961 and ran on CBS until 1967. It was syndicated from 1967 to 1969, ran on ABC from 1969 to 1975, and aired on NBC from January 1979 to March 1982. Allen Ludden hosted all versions until suffering a debilitating stroke in 1980 (he died in 1981). He was replaced by Tom Kennedy, who remained with the show until it was canceled. When NBC revived it in the fall of 1984, as a weekday daytime series titled *Super Password,* Bert Convy was the host.

PAT BOONE-CHEVY SHOWROOM, THE
Musical Variety
FIRST TELECAST: *October 3, 1957*
LAST TELECAST: *June 23, 1960*
BROADCAST HISTORY:
Oct 1957–Jun 1960, ABC Thu 9:00–9:30 (OS)
REGULARS:
Pat Boone
Louise O'Brien (1959)
Artie Malvin Chorus (1958–1960)
Mort Lindsey Orchestra

Pat Boone was one of the fastest-rising stars in show business when this series went on the air. He had just completed a long stint with Arthur Godfrey, his records were selling in the millions ("Love Letters in the Sand" was riding high on the charts just as the show premiered), and his movies were box-office hits. The publicity about him was enormous. Kids loved him and so did adults, for his smooth, super-wholesome appearance and that deep, rich voice. A somewhat jaded *TV Guide* reviewer called his new ABC show "about as exciting as a milkshake with two straws," but that didn't matter to viewers. The show continued for three seasons, without the benefit of a large supporting cast or fancy production.

Guests tended to the "nicer" popular singers, such as the Four Lads, Johnny Mathis, Nat "King" Cole, and Gogi Grant (though Danny and the Juniors did slip in), together with such well-scrubbed acts as the Texas Boys' Choir. Most shows ended with an inspirational tune. In 1959 a regular was added in the person of singer Louise O'Brien, a former Miss Oklahoma, but Pat really needed no supporting cast and she soon became an occasional guest.

Believe it or not, one of the staff writers for this show was a young Woody Allen (Pat hardly ever used his material). The head writer was Larry Gelbart, who later created *M*A*S*H.*

PAT PAULSEN'S HALF A COMEDY HOUR
Comedy Variety
FIRST TELECAST: *January 22, 1970*
LAST TELECAST: *April 16, 1970*
BROADCAST HISTORY:
Jan 1970–Apr 1970, ABC Thu 7:30–8:00

REGULARS:
Pat Paulsen
Hal Smith
Bob Einstein
Sherry Miles
Jean Byron
George Spell
The Denny Vaughn Orchestra
Joan Gerber
Pepe Brown
Pedro Regas
Vanetta Rogers

Comedian Pat Paulsen's *Half a Comedy Hour* lasted for less than half a season in early 1970. Pat and his cast of mostly youthful comics were seen in skits such as "Children's Letters to the Devil," and with guest stars. Guesting on the first telecast were Debbie Reynolds, former Vice President Hubert H. Humphrey, and Daffy Duck.

PATRICE MUNSEL SHOW, THE
Musical Variety
FIRST TELECAST: *October 18, 1957*
LAST TELECAST: *June 13, 1958*
BROADCAST HISTORY:
Oct 1957–Dec 1957, ABC Fri 8:30–9:00
Jan 1958–Jun 1958, ABC Fri 9:30–10:00
REGULARS:
Patrice Munsel
The Martins Quartet
The Charles Sanford Orchestra

Metropolitan Opera soprano Patrice Munsel demonstrated her versatility as a singer in this live variety show. Show tunes, popular songs, and operatic excerpts were all part of her repertoire in addition to comedy sketches with her weekly guest stars.

PATRICIA BOWMAN SHOW, THE
Dance/Music
FIRST TELECAST: *August 11, 1951*
LAST TELECAST: *November 3, 1951*
BROADCAST HISTORY:
Aug 1951–Nov 1951, CBS Sat 6:45–7:00
REGULARS:
Patricia Bowman
Paul Shelley
The Norman Paris Trio

This live dance-and-music show was hosted by famous American ballerina Patricia Bowman. Each show featured Miss Bowman and her guest stars performing various types of dances, from ballroom, to jazz, to modern, to ballet.

PATTI PAGE OLDS SHOW, THE
Musical Variety
FIRST TELECAST: *September 24, 1958*
LAST TELECAST: *March 16, 1959*

BROADCAST HISTORY:
Sep 1958–Nov 1958, ABC Wed 9:30–10:00
Dec 1958–Mar 1959, ABC Mon 10:00–10:30
REGULARS:
Patti Page
Rocky Cole
The Jerry Packer Singers
The Matt Mattox Dancers
The Vic Schoen Orchestra

Popular singer Patti Page was the hostess and star of this live musical variety show that featured her singing, regular guest stars, and the dance numbers of the Matt Mattox Dancers. When Patti sang ballads her pianist/accompanist Rocky Cole was featured.

PATTI PAGE SHOW, THE
Musical Variety
FIRST TELECAST: *June 16, 1956*
LAST TELECAST: *July 7, 1956*
BROADCAST HISTORY:
Jun 1956–Jul 1956, NBC Sat 8:00–9:00
REGULARS:
Patti Page
The Frank Lewis Dancers
The Spellbinders
The Carl Hoff Orchestra

Patti Page was one of three stars who filled in for *The Perry Como Show* during the summer of 1956, the other two being Julius LaRosa and Tony Bennett. They shared the services of the Frank Lewis Dancers and the vocal group the Spellbinders. Each star had his/her own guest stars and the show included production numbers, songs by the star, and performances by each week's guests.

PATTY DUKE SHOW, THE
Situation Comedy
FIRST TELECAST: *September 18, 1963*
LAST TELECAST: *August 31, 1966*
BROADCAST HISTORY:
Sep 1963–Aug 1966, ABC Wed 8:00–8:30
CAST:
Patty/Cathy Lane .... Patty Duke
Martin Lane .... William Schallert
Natalie Masters .... Jean Byron
Ross Lane .... Paul O'Keefe
Richard Harrison .... Eddie Applegate
J. R. Castle (1963–1964) .... John McGiver
Nicki Lee (1963–1964) .... Susan Melvin
Sue Ellen (1963–1965) .... Kitty Sullivan
Ted (1963–1965) .... Skip Hinnant
Maggie (1963–1965) .... Alberta Grant
Gloria (1964–1965) .... Kelly Wood
Eileen (1965–1966) .... Ann Alford
Roz (1965–1966) .... Robyn Miller

Teenage actress Patty Duke, fresh from her motion-picture triumph in *The Miracle Worker* (for which she won an Academy Award), starred in a dual role in this light family comedy. As Patty

Lane she was a perky, bubble-gum-chewing teenager who dug Paul Anka records and "slumber parties" with her girlfriends. As Cathy, she was Patty's intellectual Scottish cousin, newly arrived from overseas to live with the Lanes, complete with bagpipes and burr. The girls confused everybody in their middle-class Brooklyn Heights, New York, neighborhood by mischievously switching personalities at critical moments. Since they were exact look-alikes, no one could tell them apart. Martin Lane was Patty's harried father, a newspaper editor; Natalie the mother; and 12-year-old Ross the younger brother, who was constantly at war with the girls. Richard was Patty's boyfriend, a part-time Western Union messenger (she liked men in uniform).

Guest appearances by popular singing stars such as Bobby Vinton, Chad and Jeremy, and Frankie Avalon helped boost this series' popularity among teenagers.

Having one actress play two parts did present certain problems, especially when both girls were in the same scene. The young woman who served as Patty/Cathy's double, and was seen from the back as one girl while Patty Duke faced the camera as the other, was Rita McLaughlin.

PAUL ARNOLD SHOW, THE
Music
FIRST TELECAST: *October 24, 1949*
LAST TELECAST: *June 23, 1950*
BROADCAST HISTORY:
Oct 1949–Dec 1949, CBS Mon/Wed/Fri 7:15–7:30
Jan 1950, CBS Mon/Wed/Thu/Fri 7:15–7:30
Jan 1950–Jun 1950, CBS Mon–Fri 7:15–7:30
STAR:
Paul Arnold

This thrice-weekly 15-minute program gave Mr. Arnold an opportunity to sing a few country and western and rural songs, play his guitar, relate a little homespun philosophy, and chat with an occasional guest. Originating live from New York, it added a fourth day of the week the first week in January and became a five-day-a-week series three weeks later.

PAUL DIXON SHOW, THE
Variety
FIRST TELECAST: *August 8, 1951*
LAST TELECAST: *September 24, 1952*
BROADCAST HISTORY:
Aug 1951–Sep 1951, ABC Wed 8:00–9:00
Sep 1951–Oct 1951, ABC Mon 9:00–10:00
Oct 1951–Jan 1952, ABC Thu 10:00–10:30
Oct 1951–Sep 1952, ABC Wed 8:00–9:00
REGULARS:
Paul Dixon
Dotty Mack
Wanda Lewis
Len Goorian

608

Paul Dixon, one of the most popular radio and TV personalities in the Midwest, was brought to network television by ABC for a prime-time run from 1951–1952. The program was similar in format to his long-running local variety show in Cincinnati, which began in 1949: fun and games with the audience, occasional guests, and his specialty, pantomiming to popular records. Paul contorted his face and mouthed the words as the top singers of the day sang their big hits, on record. Dotty Mack also did musical pantomimes (she later had her own network series doing this), and Wanda Lewis drew pictures as the records were played. Other features in this folksy show included "Visits for Interviews," both light and serious, and "People in Your Life"—the mailman, milkman, policeman, etc. At one time Paul was on two nights a week, for a total of 90 minutes with this potpourri.

In addition to the prime-time show, there was a weekday edition from February to May 1952 on ABC, and from October 1952 until April 1955 on DuMont. Nearly two decades later, in 1973, Dixon returned to the national scene with a similarly formatted syndicated show, which lasted only a year.

PAUL HARVEY NEWS
News and Comment
FIRST TELECAST: *November 16, 1952*
LAST TELECAST: *August 9, 1953*
BROADCAST HISTORY:
  Nov 1952–Aug 1953, ABC Sun 11:00–11:15
NEWSCASTER:
  Paul Harvey

Famed radio commentator Paul Harvey presented news and his own highly individual opinions on current events in this 1952–1953 ABC series, which originated live from Chicago. Harvey always ended his newscasts with an upbeat "Good . . . day!"

PAUL LYNDE SHOW, THE
Situation Comedy
FIRST TELECAST: *September 13, 1972*
LAST TELECAST: *September 8, 1973*
BROADCAST HISTORY:
  Sep 1972–May 1973, ABC Wed 8:00–8:30
  Jun 1973–Sep 1973, ABC Sat 8:30–9:00
CAST:
  Paul Simms .... Paul Lynde
  Martha Simms .... Elizabeth Allen
  Sally Simms .... Pamelyn Ferdin
  Barbara Simms Dickerson ...... Jane Actman
  Howie Dickerson .... John Calvin
  Barney Dickerson .... Jerry Stiller
  Grace Dickerson .... Anne Meara
  T. J. McNish .... Herb Voland
  T. R. Scott .... James Gregory
  Alice .... Allison McKay

Comedian Paul Lynde, a familiar face on TV for many years in guest-star and supporting roles,

starred in this situation comedy. He portrayed Paul Simms, a quiet, respectable attorney living with his wife, Martha, and two daughters in Ocean Grove, California. Quiet—until one day the household was invaded by Howie, a blond, shaggy-haired, blue-jeaned, eccentric university student with an IQ of 185—Paul's new son-in-law. Howie and his bride, Barbara, took up residence in the Simms home, for while the new family genius was a whiz at just about anything he tried—and he tried to offer advice on everything—he couldn't seem to hold a job. All of this drove Paul to distraction, and gave Mr. Lynde plenty of opportunities to do that slow burn for which he was so famous.

Jerry Stiller and Anne Meara were seen occasionally as Howie's parents, the Dickersons.

PAUL SAND IN FRIENDS AND LOVERS
Situation Comedy
FIRST TELECAST: *September 14, 1974*
LAST TELECAST: *January 4, 1975*
BROADCAST HISTORY:
  Sep 1974–Jan 1975, CBS Sat 8:30–9:00
CAST:
  Robert Dreyfuss .... Paul Sand
  Charlie Dreyfuss............. Michael Pataki
  Janice Dreyfuss .... Penny Marshall
  Jack Riordan .... Dick Wesson
  Fred Meyerbach .... Steve Landesberg
  Mason Woodruff .... Craig Richard Nelson
  Ben Dreyfuss .... Jack Gilford

Robert Dreyfuss was a bass violinist with the Boston Symphony Orchestra. A young, unaggressive, incurable romantic whose shyness always made success with women difficult, Robert was nevertheless constantly falling in love with just about every pretty girl he met. His emotional opposite was his older brother Charlie—aggressive, loud, and overprotective of Robert. Charlie's wife Janice was forever making fun of Robert's girl problems.

PAUL WHITEMAN'S GOODYEAR REVUE
Musical Variety
FIRST TELECAST: *November 6, 1949*
LAST TELECAST: *March 30, 1952*
BROADCAST HISTORY:
  Nov 1949–Mar 1952, ABC Sun 7:00–7:30 (OS 1950)
REGULARS:
  Paul Whiteman
  Earl Wrightson (1950–1952)
  Maureen Cannon (1951–1952)
  Glenn Osser conducting the Paul Whiteman Orchestra (summer 1951)
THEME:
  "Rhapsody In Blue," by George Gershwin

At the same time that *Paul Whiteman's TV Teen Club* was a Saturday night fixture during the early 1950s, the bandleader was also seen on Sunday nights with his *Goodyear Revue*. The format was that of a standard musical variety show, with guests such as Victor Borge, Jane Froman, Mel Torme, Charles Laughton, Mindy Carson, and numerous others. Eleven-year-old Junie Keegan of the *TV Teen Club* was a semiregular at the outset of the show, and vocalists Earl Wrightson and Maureen Cannon later became regulars. Dancers and choral groups were also featured.

During the summer of 1951, while Whiteman was on vacation, the program was hosted by regulars Earl Wrightson and Maureen Cannon and renamed *The Goodyear Summertime Revue*.

PAUL WHITEMAN'S TV TEEN CLUB
Talent
FIRST TELECAST: *April 2, 1949*
LAST TELECAST: *March 28, 1954*
BROADCAST HISTORY:
  Apr 1949–Aug 1949, ABC Sat 9:00–10:00
  Sep 1949–Dec 1951, ABC Sat 8:00–9:00
  Dec 1951–Aug 1952, ABC Sat 8:00–8:30
  Sep 1952–Oct 1952, ABC Sat 7:30–8:00
  Oct 1952–Dec 1953, ABC Sat 7:00–7:30 (OS)
  Dec 1953–Mar 1954, ABC Sun 7:30–8:00
REGULARS:
  Paul Whiteman
  Margo Whiteman (1949–1950)
  Nancy Lewis (1950–1953)
  Junie Keegan (1949–1953)
  Stanley Klet (1950–1953)
  Andrea McLaughlin
  Sonny Graham (1950)
  Bobby Rydell (1951–1953)
MUSICAL DIRECTOR:
  Bernie Lowe (1952)
PRODUCER/DIRECTOR:
  Edmund "Skipper" Dawes

Paul Whiteman, one of the great innovators in American popular music, was something of a musical institution by the time television came along in the late 1940s. During the 1920s he had led a fabulously successful dance and concert band, which had been a veritable hotbed of new talent and musical innovation. He was dubbed, with some poetic license, "The King of Jazz." In the 1930s and 1940s he appeared regularly on radio and in films, and when TV came along he plunged enthusiastically into that medium too. From 1949 until the mid-1950s he was frequently seen on the new ABC-TV network, as host of several programs, and he was also ABC's vice president in charge of music.

Paul Whiteman's TV Teen Club provided a second childhood for the rotund, gregarious bandleader. The idea for a teenage talent contest had originated in an antidelinquency program he had begun in his hometown of Lambertville, Pennsylvania. In 1949 he moved the talent show to the ABC network, live from Philadelphia. Each week a series of youthful singers, tap dancers, and instrumentalists would perform, with the winners

being given professional coaching and returning for subsequent appearances. Special contests were also held, such as a *TV Guide*–Paul Whiteman Talent Search in 1952 which brought in 1,500 applications.

Youngsters not only performed on the *TV Teen Club,* but helped run it as well. Whiteman's daughter Margo was the original co-emcee, later replaced by 14-year-old Nancy Lewis. Singer Stan Klet (also 14) became a regular, as did "Pop's" youngest protégée, 4-year-old Andrea McLaughlin. Whiteman's most famous discovery in the 1920s had been young Bing Crosby, and while no one on the TV show equalled that "find" he did have one youngster of whom he was particularly proud: 11-year-old singer Junie Keegan. A notable moment in Junie's career came in June 1950 when she was honored on the show by the National Confectioners' Association as their "Crown Princess of Candyland." She received from Pops "a crown of gumdrops, an all-day sucker, and a giant peppermint-stick scepter" as the fitting symbols of her installation as "The Sweetest Girl in America"—an auspicious, if somewhat gooey, beginning to any girl's career. Junie later made guest appearances on other TV shows, had her own show in New York, and a Decca recording contract.

Better known in later years was a nine-year-old from South Philadelphia who joined the cast in 1951. Robert Ridarelli—who later changed his name to Bobby Rydell—went on to become one of the major pop singers of the late 1950s and early 1960s. The young staff announcer who read the show's Tootsie Roll commercials in 1952 also later became something of a force in rock 'n' roll. His name was Dick Clark.

The dynamo who kept things rolling on the *Teen Club,* however, was Pops himself. Dressed in a flamboyant shirt and an even louder sports jacket, he delighted in using the kids' own catchphrases ("Real gone!") and dispensing the sponsor's Tootsie Rolls and chewing gum from a paper bag. Since he couldn't remember all the kids' names, they variously became "Junior," "Brains," "Pardner," or "Squidgage." One day when he overdid it a bit, little Andrea shot back, "Oh Pops, how corny can we get!"

But Pops didn't mind. "The way to feel young," he confided to a reporter, "is to stay around young people."

During its last few months on the air the show's format was altered to include "at home" and "on camera" guest celebrities who judged the performances (previously this had been done by audience applause). The *TV Teen Club* finally left the air in early 1954, after a five-year run. The concept was revived during the following summer for Whiteman's *On the Boardwalk*.

PAUL WINCHELL—JERRY MAHONEY SHOW, THE
Comedy Variety

FIRST TELECAST: *September 18, 1950*
LAST TELECAST: *May 23, 1954*
BROADCAST HISTORY:
  Sep 1950–Jun 1953, NBC Mon 8:00–8:30 (OS)
  Aug 1953–May 1954, NBC Sun 7:00–7:30
REGULARS:
  Paul Winchell
  Dorothy Claire (1951–1952)
  Diane Sinclair and Ken Spaulding (1951–1953)
  Mary Ellen Terry (1953–1954)
  Margaret Hamilton (1953–1954)
  John Gart Orchestra
ANNOUNCER:
  Jimmy Blaine (1950)
  Ted Brown (1951–1954)

Ventriloquist Paul Winchell and his dummy Jerry Mahoney were the stars of this variety series, which mixed comedy, music, quiz show, and even dramatic elements during its four-year run. At first the program opened with a comedy routine by Winchell and Mahoney, followed by a quiz segment called "What's My Name?", which they emceed. The questions all had to do with famous personalities, and guest stars appeared to act out or sing the clues. Contestants were drawn from the studio audience and viewers could also be called at home if they had sent in their name and phone number.

Gradually the entertainment element took over an increasing portion of the show, and the quiz portion was dropped altogether by 1953. Featured in the variety segments were Winchell and his dummies Jerry, Knucklehead, Oswald, and others, plus vocalist Dorothy Claire, dancers Sinclair and Spaulding, other regulars, and guests.

During the fall of 1953 the program added a filmed dramatic vignette of approximately 10 minutes' duration, starring a well-known actor or actress in a serious short story (Winchell was often seen in a supporting role). This odd insertion lasted until November, when the show returned to a straight comedy-variety format for the rest of its run.

The annual *Look* Magazine TV Awards were presented on special telecasts of this series in December 1952 and December 1953, with many top names appearing.

The *Winchell-Mahoney* show was known as the *Speidel Show* during its first year and a half on the air (until December 1951), and was also sometimes referred to by the quiz element, *What's My Name?*

Following their departure from prime time, Winchell and Mahoney moved to weekend daytime where they could still entertain their primary audience—children. They were seen on CBS' Saturday lineup from November 1954 to June 1956 and then moved to ABC's Sunday lineup from September 1957 to April 1961.

PAULINE FREDERICK'S GUESTBOOK
Interviews

FIRST TELECAST: *January 12, 1949*
LAST TELECAST: *April 13, 1949*
BROADCAST HISTORY:
  Jan 1949–Apr 1949, ABC Wed 9:15–9:30
HOSTESS:
  Pauline Frederick

Interviews with guests from business, political, and cultural life. The program had been seen locally in New York since August 1948.

PEAK OF THE SPORTS NEWS, THE
  see *Red Barber's Corner*

PEARL BAILEY SHOW, THE
Musical Variety
FIRST TELECAST: *January 23, 1971*
LAST TELECAST: *May 8, 1971*
BROADCAST HISTORY:
  Jan 1971–May 1971, ABC Sat 8:30–9:30
REGULARS:
  Pearl Bailey
  The Allan Davies Singers
  The Robert Sidney Dancers
  Louis Bellson & His Orchestra

Pearl Bailey's sole venture into series television was this musical variety series in which she starred during early 1971. Her husband, drummer Louis Bellson, directed the orchestra and Pearlie Mae entertained with an assortment of celebrity guest stars, including Bing Crosby, Louis Armstrong, Andy Williams, Kate Smith, and B.B. King.

PECK'S BAD GIRL
Situation Comedy
FIRST TELECAST: *May 5, 1959*
LAST TELECAST: *September 29, 1960*
BROADCAST HISTORY:
  May 1959–Aug 1959, CBS Tue 9:00–9:30
  Jun 1960–Sep 1960, CBS Tue 8:00–8:30
  Sep 1960, CBS Thu 9:30–10:00
CAST:
  Steve Peck .... Wendell Corey
  Jennifer Peck .... Marsha Hunt
  Torey Peck .... Patty McCormack
  Roger Peck .... Ray Ferrell
  Francesca .... Reba Waters
  Jeannie .... Bernadette Withers

Research physicist Steve Peck was a typical middle-class American with a typical middle-class family. He had a charming wife, two children, and a home in the suburbs. Torey, his 12-year-old, was at that awkward age. She wasn't quite sure whether she was going to become a young lady or stay an aggressive tomboy. Her indecision and inconsistency were very trying on her parents, who tried to understand and give useful advice, and completely mind-boggling to her little brother, who never quite figured out what was going on. The episodes telecast by CBS during the summer of 1960 were all reruns.

The title and format were a variation on the *Peck's Bad Boy* movies of the 1920s and 1930s starring Jackie Cooper.

PEE WEE KING SHOW
Musical Variety
FIRST TELECAST: *May 23, 1955*
LAST TELECAST: *September 5, 1955*
BROADCAST HISTORY:
   May 1955–Sep 1955, ABC Mon 9:00–10:30
REGULARS:
   Pee Wee King and His Golden West Cowboys
   Redd Stewart
   Little Eller Long
   Neal Burris

Ninety-minute country music-variety show from WEWS, Cleveland, Ohio, featuring best-selling country bandleader King ("Tennessee Waltz," "Slow Poke"), his vocalist Redd Stewart, six-foot-five comedienne Little Eller Long, "shuffling cowboy singer" Neal Burris, and a square-dance unit, among others.

PENDULUM, THE
syndicated title for *Vise, The*

PENNY TO A MILLION
Quiz
FIRST TELECAST: *May 4, 1955*
LAST TELECAST: *October 5, 1955*
BROADCAST HISTORY:
   May 1955–Oct 1955, ABC Wed 9:30–10:00
EMCEE:
   Bill Goodwin

The first question in the play-off round of this summer quiz show was worth exactly one cent. However, each subsequent question doubled in value until a contestant could win as much as a million pennies ($10,000). Contestants were chosen in a preliminary round from two teams drawn from the studio audience.

PENTAGON
Interview
FIRST TELECAST: *May 13, 1951*
LAST TELECAST: *November 24, 1952*
BROADCAST HISTORY:
   May 1951–Nov 1951, DUM Sun 8:30–9:00
   Dec 1951–Nov 1952, DUM Mon 8:00–8:30

Korean War era interview program in which top Pentagon brass and other officials discussed the war effort with reporters.

PENTAGON U.S.A.
Dramatic Anthology
FIRST TELECAST: *August 6, 1953*
LAST TELECAST: *September 24, 1953*
BROADCAST HISTORY:
   Aug 1953–Sep 1953, CBS Thu 10:00–10:30

CAST:
   The Colonel .... Addison Richards

The dramas presented in this live summer anthology series were adaptations of cases from the criminal investigation files of the U.S. Army. At the beginning of each episode, the Colonel assigned the investigators who were to handle that week's case and gave them a rundown on what or who they were looking for. His office was located in the Pentagon, in Washington.

PENTHOUSE PARTY
Variety
FIRST TELECAST: *September 15, 1950*
LAST TELECAST: *June 8, 1951*
BROADCAST HISTORY:
   Sep 1950–Dec 1950, ABC Fri 10:00–10:30
   Jan 1951–Jun 1951, ABC Fri 8:30–9:00
REGULARS:
   Betty Furness
   Don Cherry
   Buddy Weed Trio

Betty Furness opened this weekly gathering with the words, "Come on inside and meet all the folks." The "folks," her guests, were generally celebrities from the New York music and theater world who, with little coaxing, would demonstrate unsuspected talents for the viewing audience. Matinee idol Hurd Hatfield did a Hindu dance, British actor Arthur Treacher sang "Ragtime Cowboy Joe," and actress Joan Blondell, famous for her wisecracking blonde chorine characterization in films, whipped up a casserole. It all took place in the style of a swell party in Betty's New York penthouse.

PEOPLE
News Magazine
FIRST TELECAST: *September 18, 1978*
LAST TELECAST: *November 6, 1978*
BROADCAST HISTORY:
   Sep 1978–Nov 1978, CBS Mon 8:30–9:00
REGULARS:
   Phyllis George
   Mark Shaw

People was a televised version of the magazine of the same name and, in fact, was produced by the television production arm of Time Inc., the publishers of the magazine. Hosted by former Miss America Phyllis George, *People* provided short interviews and profiles of people in the news, especially show-business personalities. Despite its half-hour length, *People* offered fleeting glimpses of many celebrities in each episode. One telecast included Jimmy Durante, Carroll O'Connor, Bette Midler, Francesco Scavullo, Cheryl Tiegs, Kristy McNichol, Bill Cosby, Merv Griffin, Rob Reiner, and several lesser-known folk. As with the magazine, the coverage here tended to be fast, flashy, and without much substance. Mark Shaw was a regular contributor, traveling around the country to visit interesting places and interview subjects.

PEOPLE ARE FUNNY
Quiz/Audience Participation
FIRST TELECAST: *September 19, 1954*
LAST TELECAST: *July 21, 1984*
BROADCAST HISTORY:
Sep 1954–Sep 1955, NBC Sun 7:00–7:30
Sep 1955–Sep 1956, NBC Sat 9:00–9:30
Sep 1956–Sep 1959, NBC Sat 7:30–8:00
Sep 1959–Apr 1960, NBC Fri 7:30–8:00
Apr 1960–Sep 1960, NBC Wed 10:30–11:00
Sep 1960–Apr 1961, NBC Sun 6:30–7:00
Mar 1984–May 1984, NBC Sat 9:00–9:30
Jun 1984–Jul 1984, NBC Sat 9:30–10:00
EMCEE:
Art Linkletter (1954–1961)
Flip Wilson (1984)

Contestants on the original *People Are Funny* were picked from the studio audience by host Art Linkletter prior to the filming of each week's episode. On the air they would be interviewed by Art and then asked to get involved in some stunt that would prove that "people are funny." Some stunts, including tests of memory, greed, decision-making or some other trait, took place in the studio—and often ended in pie-throwing, water-dousing, or the like as the penalty. In others, contestants were given an assignment to complete before the next week's telecast, ususally a trick on or test of unsuspecting outsiders—for example, trying to cash a check written on a 40-pound watermelon, or simply trying to give away money to passersby (that can be surprisingly hard). On the next show the contestant would report back with the often hilarious results.

People Are Funny began on radio in 1942. During its first three seasons on TV the radio broadcasts continued, consisting of the sound track from the TV version. Later the TV version was a film of the previously aired radio show. In the 1956–1957 season a computer-dating feature was added, in which a couple, matched by Univac computer, got to know each other while answering questions in a quiz-show segment of the program.

More than 20 years after the original *People Are Funny* ended its run, NBC aired a short-lived revival hosted by Flip Wilson. The stunts were similar, but this time conducted entirely outside the studio, mostly on the streets of Los Angeles. Among the gags were two men trying to get passersby to join them "fishing" in an open manhole, while they caught healthy-looking trout; a little girl in a restaurant who tried to get a patron to eat her "icky" vegetables for her, before her mother came back; and a woman who tried to persuade a delivery boy to disrobe before entering a "nudist condominium" to make a delivery.

PEOPLE DO THE CRAZIEST THINGS
Humor/Audience Participation
FIRST TELECAST: *September 20, 1984*
LAST TELECAST: *August 2, 1985*
BROADCAST HISTORY:
Sep 1984, ABC Thu 8:00–8:30
Dec 1984–May 1985, ABC Various (occasional)
May 1985–Aug 1985, ABC Fri 9:30–10:00
HOST:
Bert Convy
REGULARS:
Bob Perlow
Wendy Cutler

Patterned after Allen Funt's long-running *Candid Camera*, *People Do the Craziest Things* attempted to show how easy it is to get people to make fools of themselves. Women got hysterical when they were weighed on a scale that registered absurdly high weights, motorists overreacted to parking lot gates that refused to open, and assorted other situations were contrived to confuse and embarrass "average folks." If anything, *People Do the Craziest Things* was more heartless than *Candid Camera*, lacking the inoffensive vignettes that appeared on the earlier show.

Bert Convy was the in-studio host of the series, assisted by Bob Perlow and Wendy Cutler, who were often seen on location setting up the situations. The series was pulled from the schedule only two weeks after its premiere, then run infrequently, to fill holes in the ABC schedule, for the rest of the 1984–1985 season.

PEOPLE'S CHOICE, THE
Situation Comedy
FIRST TELECAST: *October 6, 1955*
LAST TELECAST: *September 25, 1958*
BROADCAST HISTORY:
Oct 1955–Dec 1955, NBC Thu 8:30–9:00
Jan 1956–Sep 1958, NBC Thu 9:00–9:30
CAST:
Socrates "Sock" Miller . . . . Jackie Cooper
Amanda "Mandy" Peoples Miller
. . . . Pat Breslin
Aunt Gus . . . . Margaret Irving
Mayor John Peoples . . . . Paul Maxey
Roger Crutcher (1955–1957) . John Stephenson
Pierre (1955–1956) . . . . Leonid Kinskey
Rollo (1956–1958) . . . . Dick Wesson
Cleo . . . . Herself (voice: Mary Jane Croft)

Socrates (Sock) Miller was a government naturalist who had been elected to the city council, a job he took with great seriousness. His interest in helping the community occasionally got him in trouble with Mayor Peoples, a problem that was compounded by the fact that the mayor's daughter, Mandy, was Sock's girlfriend. Making numerous observations to the audience, although no one in the cast could hear her, was Cleo, Sock's pet basset hound. At the end of the 1956–1957 season Sock and Mandy were secretly married. They made it public early in the 1957–1958 season, following his graduation from law school. He got a job selling homes in the neighboring community of Barkerville, for the developer Mr. Barker, and he and Mandy were given one of the homes to live in. Moving in with them was Sock's freeloading friend Rollo. After the move, neither the mayor nor Sock's Aunt Gus were seen on a weekly basis.

PEOPLE'S COURT, THE
Courtroom
BROADCAST HISTORY:
Syndicated only
30 minutes
Produced: *1981–*
Released: *September 1981*
REGULARS:
Judge Joseph A. Wapner (ret.)
Doug Llewelyn
Rusty Burrell, bailiff

One of television's oldest low-budget traditions was real-life courtroom drama, as featured in such 1950s series as *They Stand Accused, Famous Jury Trials,* and *Traffic Court.* It offered a perfect mix of TV's favorite elements: a focus on individuals, realism, high drama, and low production costs. *The People's Court* brought the format back in the 1980s, with an ingenious twist. The plaintiffs were ordinary people who had taken their grievances to Los Angeles area small claims courts, then agreed (along with the defendants) to have their cases heard by an arbitrator—retired Superior Court Judge Joseph Wapner. For their trouble they got speedy disposition of their claims, a moment on national TV, and reimbursement whatever the outcome.

Although strictly speaking this was a private arbitration proceeding, it was staged in a courtroom setting with Judge Wapner on the bench, a bailiff, and spectators in the gallery. As in small claims court, there was no legal counsel or jury. The citizen stated his case to the understanding but firm judge, who rendered a verdict immediately after the next commercial.

Cases revolved around such everyday contretemps as broken contracts, faulty merchandise, and arguments over who owned some shrubbery. Many had odd twists, however: the mother who refused to pay a clown she had hired to appear at her child's party as a Smurf (he had showed up as a towering purple monster and terrified the kiddies); the woman who wanted a stud fee after her poodle mated with a stranger's; the befuddled old gent who wanted his money back when the car he bought proved to have a tiller instead of a steering wheel. All cases were within the small claims court's $1,500 limit.

After each case—one or two per show—reporter Doug Llewelyn interviewed the opposing parties on their way out of the courtroom, and sometimes also reported the "people's verdict" based on a poll of the spectators. Then he closed the show with lines like these: "Remember, when you get mad, don't take the law into your own hands. Take 'em to court."

PEOPLE'S PLATFORM
Discussion
FIRST TELECAST: *August 17, 1948*
LAST TELECAST: *August 11, 1950*
BROADCAST HISTORY:
Aug 1948–Dec 1948, CBS Tue 9:30–10:00
Jan 1949–Sep 1949, CBS Mon Various times
Oct 1949–Aug 1950, CBS Fri 10:00–10:30
MODERATOR:
Quincy Howe

This long-running public-affairs program was begun by the noted educator Dr. Lyman Bryson on CBS radio in 1938, and continued on radio until 1952. It was first seen on TV as a local New York program in May 1948, and moved to the network three months later.

The format was that of a simple debate between major political or other public figures on an important issue of the day. Each side stated its opening arguments, followed by rebuttals. The program was seen on Mondays during most of 1949, but the time varied from week to week (usually between 8:30 and 10:00 P.M.). It continued on TV as a Sunday afternoon feature until July 1951.

PEPSI-COLA PLAYHOUSE
Dramatic Anthology
FIRST TELECAST: *October 2, 1953*
LAST TELECAST: *June 26, 1955*
BROADCAST HISTORY:
Oct 1953–Jun 1954, ABC Fri 8:30–9:00
Jul 1954–Jun 1955, ABC Sun 7:30–8:00
HOSTESS:
Arlene Dahl (1953–1954)
Anita Colby (1954)
Polly Bergen (1954–1955)

Arlene Dahl was the original hostess of this dramatic series which began as a live show and switched to film in the middle of its first season. Miss Colby took over the hostess function in April 1954 and was in turn succeeded by Polly Bergen in October 1954.

The stories ranged from melodrama to comedy, and generally featured lesser-known (and thus inexpensive) actors and actresses. Such stars as Craig Stevens, Lee Marvin, Vera Miles, Hans Conried, and Charles Bronson made early TV appearances here.

PERFECT CRIME, THE
see *Telltale Clue, The*

PERFECT STRANGERS
Situation Comedy
FIRST TELECAST: *March 25, 1986*
LAST TELECAST:
BROADCAST HISTORY:
Mar 1986–Apr 1986, ABC Tue 8:30–9:00

Aug 1986–Feb 1988, ABC Wed 8:00–8:30
Mar 1988–Apr 1988, ABC Fri 8:00–8:30
*May 1988–   *, ABC Tue 8:30–9:00

CAST:
Larry Appleton .... Mark Linn-Baker
Balki Bartokomous......... Bronson Pinchot
Mr. Donald Twinkacetti ("Twinkie")
   (1986–1987) .... Ernie Sabella
Edwina Twinkacetti (1986–1987)
   .... Belita Moreno
Susan Campbell (1986) .... Lise Cutter
Mary Anne .... Rebeca Arthur
Jennifer .... Melanie Wilson
Harriette Winslow (1987–   )
   .... Jo Marie Payton-France
Lydia Markham (1987–   ) .. Belita Moreno
Harry Burns (1987–   ) ...... Eugene Roche

THEME:
"Nothing's Gonna Stop Me Now," by Jesse
Frederick and Bennett Salvay, performed by
David Pomeranz

A "buddy comedy" that explored the wonderment
of a newly arrived immigrant at the ways of
America—"The land of the Whopper." Balki was
a young shepherd from the Mediterranean island
of Mypos, who showed up unexpectedly at the
Chicago apartment of his distant cousin, bachelor
Larry. Balki's wide-eyed, fun-loving manner, and
tendency to take everything Americans told him
quite literally, promised considerable disruption
for Larry's carefully organized life, but Larry took
him in. After all, getting started as a shepherd in
Chicago was not going to be easy.

Larry was just getting started himself, hoping to
become a photojournalist. For the time being he
worked downstairs at the Ritz Discount Shop, run
by a greedy, insensitive man named "Twinkie"
(Twinkie on blind people: "Give somebody a
white cane, they think they own the streets").
Susan was Larry's friend, a nurse who lived upstairs. She was soon replaced by Mary Anne and
Jennifer, two stewardesses who lived in the building.

Stories involved Balki's comic misadventures
as he learned about America, studied citizenship
at night school, and chased girls with Larry. His
answer to every problem: "Don't be ridikalus!" At
first Larry got crazy Balki a job in Twinkie's store,
but in the fall of 1987 they both went to work for
The Chicago Chronicle, Larry as a cub reporter
and Balki in the mail room. Harriette was the elevator operator at the paper, Harry the occasionally seen editor, and Lydia—who looked a lot like
Twinkie's wife of the previous season!—the advice columnist.

PERRY COMO SHOW, THE
Musical Variety
FIRST TELECAST: *December 24, 1948*
LAST TELECAST: *June 12, 1963*
BROADCAST HISTORY:
Dec 1948–Jan 1949, NBC Fri 7:00–7:15

Jan 1949–Jun 1949, NBC Fri 11:00–11:15
Oct 1949–Jun 1950, NBC Sun 8:00–8:30
Oct 1950–Jun 1955, CBS Mon/Wed/Fri 7:45–8:00
   (OS)
Sep 1955–Jun 1959, NBC Sat 8:00–9:00 (OS)
Sep 1959–Jun 1963, NBC Wed 9:00–10:00 (OS)

REGULARS:
Perry Como
Fontane Sisters (1948–1954)
Ray Charles Singers (1950–1963)
Louis Da Pron Dancers (1955–1960)
Peter Gennaro Dancers (1960–1963)
Mitchell Ayres Orchestra

KRAFT MUSIC HALL PLAYERS:
Kaye Ballard (1961–1963)
Don Adams (1961–1963)
Sandy Stewart (1961–1963)
Jack Duffy (1961–1963)
Paul Lynde (1961–1962)
Pierre Olaf (1962–1963)

ANNOUNCER:
Martin Block (1948–1950)
Durward Kirby (1950–1951)
Dick Stark (1951–1955)
Frank Gallop (1955–1963)
Ed Herlihy (1959–1963)

THEME (1955–1963):
"Dream Along with Me (I'm on My Way to a
Star)," by Carl Sigman

Perry Como was one of the hottest properties in
show business, with a four-year string of hit records and an NBC radio series already to his credit,
when his first TV series began in 1948. The *Chesterfield Supper Club* premiered in the Friday 7:00–
7:15 P.M. time slot on December 24, 1948, but
stayed there only three weeks before moving to
11:00 P.M. on January 14, 1949. It was at first a
simulcast of Perry's popular radio show and made
few concessions to the new medium. Cameras
were simply brought into the radio studio and
Como and his guests were seen in front of a radio
microphone, with scripts and music stands in full
view. In succeeding months this was gradually
modified, with simple back-drops and props being
added. The basic format remained Perry's easygoing crooning, often of his latest hit record, with
interludes by regulars the Fontane Sisters (Marge,
Bea, and Geri) and assorted guest stars. The guest
on the very first show, Christmas Eve 1948, was a
boys' choir, which included Perry's eight-year-old
son, Ronnie. Subsequent guest spots tended also
to be filled by singers, some headliners such as
Nat "King" Cole, Burl Ives, Patti Page, etc., and
some less well-known, including an early appearance by the black rhythm and blues group, the
Ravens. Personalities from other areas of show
business, such as comedians and actors, were
also seen.

In 1950 Perry moved to CBS with a thrice
weekly 15-minute program called *The Perry Como
Show.* Then in 1955 he finally graduated to a full
prime-time variety hour on Saturday nights, on

615

NBC. The basic format remained unchanged for the next eight years. Perry opened with his new theme, "Dream along with me, I'm on my way to a star ...," there was a request spot introduced by girls singing "Letters, we get letters, we get stacks and stacks of letters!", and top-name guest stars engaging in easy banter with the relaxed Mr. C. The show would frequently close with Perry singing a religious or serious number, blending into the closing theme, "You are never far away from me ..." In 1961 Kraft took over sponsorship and a group of young players was added, backing Perry and his guests in regular comedy skits. Announcer Frank Gallop also assumed a regular role on the show over the years, as a comic foil to Perry. Gallop was generally heard off camera, his voice booming as if in an echo chamber.

Although Perry's regular weekly series ended in 1963, he remained popular with TV viewers and was seen every five or six weeks in Kraft Music Hall specials from 1963 to 1967. Since then his specials have been somewhat less frequent.

PERRY MASON
Law Drama
FIRST TELECAST: *September 21, 1957*
LAST TELECAST: *January 27, 1974*
BROADCAST HISTORY:

> *Sep 1957–Sep 1962*, CBS Sat 7:30–8:30
> *Sep 1962–Sep 1963*, CBS Thu 8:00–9:00
> *Sep 1963–Sep 1964*, CBS Thu 9:00–10:00
> *Sep 1964–Sep 1965*, CBS Thu 8:00–9:00
> *Sep 1965–Sep 1966*, CBS Sun 9:00–10:00
> *Sep 1973–Jan 1974*, CBS Sun 7:30–8:30

CAST (1957–1966):

Perry Mason . . . . Raymond Burr
Della Street . . . . Barbara Hale
Paul Drake . . . . William Hopper
Hamilton Burger . . . . William Talman
Lt. Arthur Tragg (1957–1965) . . . . . Ray Collins
David Gideon (1960–1962) . . . . Karl Held
Lt. Anderson (1961–1965) . . . . Wesley Lau
Lt. Steve Drumm (1965–1966)
. . . . Richard Anderson
Sgt. Brice (1965–1966) . . . . Lee Miller
Terrence Clay (1965–1966) . . . . Dan Tobin

CAST (1973–1974):

Perry Mason . . . . Monte Markham
Della Street . . . . Sharon Acker
Paul Drake . . . . Albert Stratton
Lt. Arthur Tragg . . . . Dane Clark
Hamilton Burger . . . . Harry Guardino
Gertrude Lade . . . . Brett Somers

CREATED BY:
Erle Stanley Gardner

Perry Mason was television's most successful and longest-running lawyer series. For nine seasons during the 1950s and 1960s Erle Stanley Gardner's famous defense attorney solved murder mysteries in the courtroom. With the aid of his personal investigator Paul Drake and his devoted secretary Della Street, Perry always managed to piece together the puzzle just in time to thwart District Attorney Hamilton Burger, his perpetual adversary. The format was certainly predictable, which may have accounted for much of its appeal. Every case culminated in a courtroom trial, and every trial culminated in the guilty party taking the witness stand, only to break down in a dramatic confession under Mason's battering cross-examination ("But if you were at home on the night of the murder, Mr. Jones, then *how could you have known that ...*" To which the shell-shocked culprit could only sob, "I didn't mean to kill her"). Judges never seemed to object to these histrionics, and in fact looked on with as much fascination as the viewing audience. Often the deciding clue would be rushed into the courtroom at the last moment by Paul Drake. At the end of every episode, Perry, Della, and Paul would gather to recap and explain what had led to the solution, a neat little coda which often sorted things out for confused viewers.

Mason never lost a case and it seemed that the accumulated frustrations made D.A. Burger determined to convict at least one of Perry's clients. Once actor Raymond Burr was confronted by a fan who demanded to know how it was that he won every case. "But madam," he replied smoothly, "you only see the cases I try on Saturday." Actually, Perry did lose one trial, in 1963, when his client refused to reveal the evidence that would save her. Mason found the real culprit anyway, and eventually exonerated his client, despite herself.

Perry Mason was revived in 1973 with an all-new cast (Burr was by that time sleuthing around in a wheelchair on *Ironside*). A new regular was his receptionist, Gertie (a character who had been played, on a very occasional basis, by Connie Cezon during the long run of the original *Perry Mason*). However, *The New Adventures of Perry Mason* could not recapture the magic of the old, and the revival soon folded.

Twelve years later, in December 1985, NBC aired a reunion movie, *Perry Mason Returns*, starring Burr and Hale. Its success led to a series (two or three a year) of new feature-length *Perry Mason* cases.

The Perry Mason character has an interesting background. The fictional alter ego of lawyer-novelist Erle Stanley Gardner, he first became famous in a series of best-selling novels, then in a CBS radio series which ran from 1943 to 1955. The radio series was part soap opera and part detective story (it ran five days a week), and when the time came to move to TV Gardner opted to shift the emphasis to pure sleuthing. The original format also went on TV, in 1956, as *The Edge of Night* (complete with the *Perry Mason* radio production staff and most of the cast, who were given new names). This continued in daytime until December 1984. The name Perry Mason was used for the Raymond Burr series, which had a whole new cast and which dropped the soap-opera elements.

PERRY PRESENTS

Musical Variety

FIRST TELECAST: *June 13, 1959*
LAST TELECAST: *September 5, 1959*
BROADCAST HISTORY:

Jun 1959–Sep 1959, NBC Sat 8:00–9:00

REGULARS:

Teresa Brewer
Tony Bennett
The Four Lads
Jaye P. Morgan
The Modernaires
The Mel Pahl Chorus
The Louis Da Pron Dancers
Mitchell Ayres Orchestra

Following *The Perry Como Show*'s last season on Saturday nights, *Perry Presents* aired as the summer replacement. It was a musical variety show starring Teresa Brewer and Tony Bennett, who also acted as hosts, and the Four Lads. Miss Brewer left the show on July 4 and the Four Lads departed on July 25. On August 1, Jaye P. Morgan and the Modernaires were added to the regular cast. Each show attempted to treat events in history and issues of current interest musically, with songs and production numbers as well as comedy skits.

PERSON TO PERSON

Interview

FIRST TELECAST: *October 2, 1953*
LAST TELECAST: *September 15, 1961*
BROADCAST HISTORY:

Oct 1953–Jun 1959, CBS Fri 10:30–11:00 (OS)
Oct 1959–Sep 1960, CBS Fri 10:30–11:00
Sep 1960–Dec 1960, CBS Thu 10:00–10:30
Jun 1961–Sep 1961, CBS Fri 10:30–11:00

HOST:

Edward R. Murrow (1953–1959)
Charles Collingwood (1959–1961)

Being chosen as one of Ed Murrow's subjects on *Person to Person* was both an honor and an ordeal. Each Friday night Ed would "visit" with two celebrities at their homes. The interviews were all done live, with Ed seated in a comfortable chair in the studio while the subject showed him around his or her home—via the immediacy of live television. At the midpoint of the show Ed would shift to a different personality, who could well be in a different part of the country entirely. TV cameras were bulky and inconvenient to move around those days, meaning that a technical crew virtually had to take over the home of the subject several days in advance, running heavy cables from room to room and carefully mapping out every movement to be used on the night of the broadcast, to avoid tangles and confusion.

Among the people who chatted informally with Murrow were Marilyn Monroe, Zsa Zsa Gabor, A. C. Nielsen of the ratings company, Fidel Castro, Margaret Mead, John Steinbeck, Sam Rayburn,

Tom Dewey, and then-Senator John F. Kennedy. Actors and actresses, politicians, diplomats, heads of state, inventors, scientists, musicians, and high church officials were all "visited" on the series. When Charles Collingwood took over for Murrow at the start of the 1959–1960 season, enabling Ed to ease off on his busy schedule, the show did more world traveling and many of the interviews were filmed or taped on location.

PERSONAL APPEARANCE

Dramatic Anthology

FIRST TELECAST: *July 4, 1958*
LAST TELECAST: *September 19, 1958*
BROADCAST HISTORY:

Jul 1958–Sep 1958, CBS Fri 10:30–11:00

The filmed dramas telecast in this summer replacement for *Person to Person* were all reruns of shows that had originally aired as episodes of *Schlitz Playhouse* and *Screen Director's Playhouse*.

PERSONAL APPEARANCE THEATER

Dramatic Anthology

FIRST TELECAST: *October 27, 1951*
LAST TELECAST: *May 23, 1952*
BROADCAST HISTORY:

Oct 1951–Nov 1951, ABC Sat 7:00–7:30
Dec 1951–Jan 1952, ABC Fri 9:30–10:00
May 1952, ABC Fri 8:30–9:00

A collection of 30-minute comedy and mystery films starring lesser-known actors and actresses, such as Franklin Pangborn, Jane Darwell, Robert Clarke, and Anita Louise.

PERSONAL APPEARANCE THEATRE

see *Joseph Schildkraut Presents*

PERSONALITY PUZZLE

Quiz/Panel

FIRST TELECAST: *March 19, 1953*
LAST TELECAST: *June 25, 1953*
BROADCAST HISTORY:

Mar 1953–Jun 1953, ABC Thu 10:30–11:00

EMCEE:

Robert Alda

REGULAR PANELIST:

Lisa Ferraday

Quiz in which the panelists were given personal possessions of a famous celebrity, who was seated behind them, and then had to guess who the celebrity was. Various guests appeared on the panel from week to week along with regular Lisa Ferraday. The program alternated with the similar *Quick as a Flash*.

PERSPECTIVE

Discussion

FIRST TELECAST: *November 13, 1952*
LAST TELECAST: *April 6, 1953*

BROADCAST HISTORY:

Nov 1952–Jan 1953, ABC Thu 9:00–9:30
Jan 1953–Apr 1953, ABC Mon 9:00–9:30

Live public-affairs program produced in cooperation with the Bar Association of the City of New York, and featuring experts from politics, education, science, and industry discussing how their fields could benefit society.

PERSUADERS, THE

Adventure
FIRST TELECAST: *September 18, 1971*
LAST TELECAST: *June 14, 1972*
BROADCAST HISTORY:
Sep 1971–Jan 1972, ABC Sat 10:00–11:00
Jan 1972–Jun 1972, ABC Wed 9:30–10:30
CAST:
Danny Wilde .... Tony Curtis
Lord Brett Sinclair .... Roger Moore
Judge Fulton .... Laurence Naismith
THEME:
"The Persuaders," by John Barry

Danny and Brett were two wealthy playboys who had attained their wealth in very different ways. Danny Wilde was an American, born and raised in Brooklyn, who was a self-made man. Although he had made a great deal of money in the stock market, he was still a "poor kid" underneath. As a member of the British aristocracy, Brett Sinclair was born to great wealth. They were brought together at a Riviera party by retired Judge Fulton, who persuaded them to tackle criminal cases which the legal authorities couldn't handle. So they set out, half serious and half on a lark, traveling around Europe looking for romance, adventure, and wrongs to right. The contrast in their styles and backgrounds was always apparent, as when they went camping out. There was Danny, under the stars with nothing but a blanket for protection, while Brett had a deluxe tent, complete with bar and freezer.

The show was produced in England.

PET SHOP

Animals
FIRST TELECAST: *December 1, 1951*
LAST TELECAST: *March 14, 1953*
BROADCAST HISTORY:
Dec 1951–Mar 1953, DUM Sat 7:30–8:00
REGULARS:
Gail Compton
Gay Compton
George Menard (1953)

This gentle pet show was presided over by Gail Compton and his young daughter, Gay. They exhibited a variety of domestic animals, welcomed guests with their performing pets, and encouraged adoptions (more than 3,000 homeless dogs were placed during the first nine months alone). Among the regulars were Sissie the poodle, Snooky the

squirrel monkey, Mac the macaw, and Tin Can the goat.

George Menard was host for the show's last four weeks on the network. From Chicago.

PETE AND GLADYS

Situation Comedy
FIRST TELECAST: *September 19, 1960*
LAST TELECAST: *September 10, 1962*
BROADCAST HISTORY:
Sep 1960–Sep 1962, CBS Mon 8:00–8:30
CAST:
Pete Porter .... Harry Morgan
Gladys Porter .... Cara Williams
Hilda Crocker (1960–1961) ..... Verna Felton
Alice (1960–1961) .... Barbara Stuart
George Colton .... Peter Leeds
Janet Colton .... Shirley Mitchell
Pop (1961) .... Ernest Truex
Peggy Briggs (1961–1962) .... Mina Kolb
Ernie Briggs (1961–1962) .... Joe Mantell
Uncle Paul .... Gale Gordon
Nancy (1961–1962) .... Frances Rafferty

During his years as the sardonic next-door neighbor on *December Bride,* Pete Porter was always complaining about his scatterbrained, ineffectual wife, Gladys. She was never seen on that series but became the co-star, in the person of Cara Williams, in this successor to *December Bride.* Along from the original series was Hilda Crocker, the nosy older woman friend who had tried to defend Gladys when Pete made some nasty comment about his wife. Gladys' Uncle Paul was seen occasionally during the first season and became a regular the second, as did the Porters' next-door neighbors and Gladys' friend Nancy (played by *December Bride* regular Frances Rafferty, in a different role). The conflict between the sincere, ingenuous, and often confused Gladys and sarcastic, deprecating Pete formed the crux of the stories in this series.

Reruns of *Pete and Gladys* were on CBS' daytime lineup from October 1962 to October 1964.

PETE KELLY'S BLUES

Drama
FIRST TELECAST: *April 5, 1959*
LAST TELECAST: *September 4, 1959*
BROADCAST HISTORY:
Apr 1959–Jul 1959, NBC Sun 8:30–9:00
Jul 1959–Sep 1959, NBC Fri 7:30–8:00
CAST:
Pete Kelly .... William Reynolds
Savannah Brown .... Connee Boswell
George Lupo .... Than Wyenn
Fred .... Phil Gordon
Johnny Cassiano ...... Fred (Anthony) Eisley
PRODUCER:
Jack Webb

Life in Kansas City during the Roaring Twenties, from the standpoint of a musician working in a speakeasy, was the subject of *Pete Kelly's Blues*. Pete was a trumpet player and the leader of Pete Kelly's Original Big Seven Band. His best friend was the band's pianist, Fred, and his closest female friend was Savannah Brown, a blues singer at another speakeasy. Pete worked for George Lupo, who was essentially a nice guy but had become rather jaded since opening his own place on Cherry Street. The stories revolved around the adventures Pete had as he ran into people who got him involved in murder, tracking down missing people, and other non-musical exploits.

Jack Webb, who produced this series, had been the original Pete Kelly in the radio series of the same name, which ran for six months in 1951, and also starred in the movie version which was released in 1955. The offscreen trumpet player who dubbed in Pete's solos was Dick Cathcart, a well-regarded jazz performer of the period. He had originally been picked by Webb for the radio series and also appeared with him in the movie.

PETER AND MARY SHOW, THE

see *Peter Lind Hayes Show, The*

PETER GUNN

Detective Drama
FIRST TELECAST: *September 22, 1958*
LAST TELECAST: *September 25, 1961*
BROADCAST HISTORY:
 Sep 1958–Sep 1960, NBC Mon 9:00–9:30
 Oct 1960–Sep 1961, ABC Mon 10:30–11:00
CAST:
 Peter Gunn .... Craig Stevens
 Edie Hart .... Lola Albright
 Lt. Jacoby .... Herschel Bernardi
 "Mother" (1958–1959) .... Hope Emerson
 "Mother" (1959–1961) .... Minerva Urecal
THEME:
 "Peter Gunn," by Henry Mancini

Peter Gunn was one of the first suave, aggressive, lady-killer private detectives to be seen on television. Working to get his clients out of trouble, and to solve crimes, he often found himself on the short end of a fight but somehow managed to come out on top, often through the intervention of his friend, police lieutenant Jacoby. Gunn spent much of his free time at a jazz nightclub called "Mother's," where his girlfriend Edie was the featured singer.

Original jazz themes by Henry Mancini punctuated the action and conveyed mood in this detective series, setting a pattern that was followed by many of the other detective shows of the late 1950s and early 1960s. RCA released two very successful albums of music from this series, *The Music from Peter Gunn* and *More Music from Peter Gunn*.

PETER LIND HAYES SHOW, THE

Situation Comedy
FIRST TELECAST: *November 23, 1950*

LAST TELECAST: *March 29, 1951*
BROADCAST HISTORY:
 Nov 1950–Mar 1951, NBC Thu 8:30–9:00
REGULARS:
 Peter Lind Hayes
 Mary Healy
 Mary Wickes (1950)
 Claude Stroud (1950)

The set for this live series was a replica of the New Rochelle, New York, home of its stars, Peter Lind Hayes and Mary Healy. At the start of each episode, a guest star would be seen apologizing over the phone to someone with whom he could not have dinner that evening because of a previous commitment to have dinner with Peter and Mary. The guest star(s) then went to Peter and Mary's "house" for dinner where the talents they possessed—singing, dancing, comedy, etc.—were worked into the script. The series had actually premiered as *The Peter and Mary Show* but was changed to *The Peter Lind Hayes Show* on December 14. Mary Wickes was their housekeeper and Claude Stroud an unemployed comedian who had come for a visit and become a permanent member of the household. Both of them were last seen in the December 28 telecast.

PETER LOVES MARY

Situation Comedy
FIRST TELECAST: *October 12, 1960*
LAST TELECAST: *May 31, 1961*
BROADCAST HISTORY:
 Oct 1960–May 1961, NBC Wed 10:00–10:30
CAST:
 Peter Lindsey .... Peter Lind Hayes
 Mary Lindsey .... Mary Healy
 Wilma .... Bea Benaderet
 Leslie Lindsey .... Merry Martin
 Steve Lindsey .... Gil Smith
 Happy Richman .... Alan Reed
 Horace Gibney .... Howard Smith
 Charlie .... Arch Johnson

Peter Lind Hayes and Mary Healy, husband and wife in real life, here played a show-business couple adjusting to a move to the suburbs. The move from Manhattan to Oakdale affected the members of the household in different ways. Peter longed for the exciting life of the city, where all the show-business people with whom they were friendly congregated in such hangouts as Lindy's. Mary wanted to become involved in all the traditional suburban activities—local government, P.T.A., social causes, etc. The conflicts between their work in the city and their suburban life with housekeeper Wilma and their two children, Leslie and Steve, provided the material for the stories in this series.

PETER MARSHALL VARIETY SHOW, THE

Talk/Variety

BROADCAST HISTORY:
Syndicated only
90 minutes
Produced: *1976* (19 episodes)
Released: *September 1976*
REGULARS:
Peter Marshall
Rod Gist & Denny Evans
Chapter 5
Alan Copeland Orchestra

Peter Marshall was best known as quizmaster on *The Hollywood Squares* when this big budget variety show was made. He still is. *The Peter Marshall Variety Show* debuted with nationwide coverage and made a big initial splash, then promptly sank after only 19 weeks. The format was standard-issue variety show (which may have been the problem): Peter chatting amiably and singing pleasantly; relentlessly middle-of-the-road guests such as Charles Nelson Reilly, John Byner, Patti Page, and Betty White; two bright young sketch comics who were never heard of again (Rod Gist and Denny Evans); and a forgettable singing group with the usual clever name, the Chapter 5. There were even home movies. The program was run in many cities on Saturday or Sunday night at 11:30 P.M., and viewers were evidently asleep by the time Peter said hello.

PETER POTTER SHOW, THE
Music/Discussion
FIRST TELECAST: *September 13, 1953*
LAST TELECAST: *March 28, 1954*
BROADCAST HISTORY:
Sep 1953–Jan 1954, ABC Sun 9:30–10:30
Jan 1954–Mar 1954, ABC Sun 9:30–10:00
HOST:
Peter Potter

Hollywood disc jockey Peter Potter brought his *Juke Box Jury* to national television in 1953. It consisted of the playing of new records, with ensuing discussion by a panel of celebrities from movies, theater, TV, and the recording industry. The studio audience also participated in the voting on each new record—"Will it be a hit (bong!) ... or a miss (clunk!)?" Some live performances were also included.

The program was known during its first month by the familiar title *Juke Box Jury*, then switched to *The Peter Potter Show*.

PETROCELLI
Law Drama
FIRST TELECAST: *September 11, 1974*
LAST TELECAST: *March 3, 1976*
BROADCAST HISTORY:
Sep 1974–Mar 1976, NBC Wed 10:00–11:00
CAST:
Tony Petrocelli .... Barry Newman
Maggie Petrocelli .... Susan Howard
Pete Ritter .... Albert Salmi
Lt. John Ponce .... David Huddleston

Set in the fictional Southwestern town of San Remo, *Petrocelli* was not quite a typical legal series. Harvard-educated Tony Petrocelli had decided to practice law in a part of the country that was not always receptive to big-city, Eastern ways. He and his wife moved to the Southwest, set up housekeeping in a camper-trailer, and opened up his law practice in the middle of wide-open cattle country. Tony hired Pete Ritter, a local cowboy, as his investigator. Tony's propensity for taking on cases whether or not his clients could really afford his services often made it rather hard for him and his wife to make ends meet. Lt. Ponce of the local police, a good friend of Tony's despite the fact that they found themselves in adversary positions in the courtroom, was often involved in investigating the cases Tony was working on. An interesting technique used in this series was showing the actual crime in flashbacks from the perspective of various people involved. The flashbacks, naturally, differed depending on whose recollections were being shown.

Barry Newman created the role of Petrocelli in a 1970 movie called *The Lawyer*, which was loosely based on the Sam Sheppard murder case.

PETTICOAT JUNCTION
Situation Comedy
FIRST TELECAST: *September 24, 1963*
LAST TELECAST: *September 12, 1970*
BROADCAST HISTORY:
Sep 1963–Sep 1964, CBS Tue 9:00–9:30
Sep 1964–Aug 1967, CBS Tue 9:30–10:00
Sep 1967–Sep 1970, CBS Sat 9:30–10:00
CAST:
Kate Bradley (1963–1968) ..... Bea Benaderet
Uncle Joe Carson .... Edgar Buchanan
Billie Jo Bradley (1963–1965).. Jeannine Riley
Billie Jo Bradley (1965–1966).. Gunilla Hutton
Billie Jo Bradley (1966–1970)
.... Meredith MacRae
Bobbie Jo Bradley (1963–1965) .. Pat Woodell
Bobbie Jo Bradley (1965–1970)
.... Lori Saunders
Betty Jo Bradley Elliott
.... Linda Kaye (Henning)
Charlie Pratt (1963–1967) .... Smiley Burnette
Floyd Smoot (1963–1968) .... Rufe Davis
Homer Bedloe (1963–1968) ..... Charles Lane
Sam Drucker .... Frank Cady
Norman Curtis (1963–1964) ..... Roy Roberts
Newt Kiley (1964–1970)......... Kay E. Kuter
Selma Plout (1964–1965) .... Virginia Sale
Selma Plout (1965–1970) .... Elvia Allman
Henrietta Plout (1965–1966) ... Susan Walther
Henrietta Plout (1966–1970) ...Lynette Winter
Steve Elliott (1966–1970)........ Mike Minor
Eb Dawson (1966–1970)......... Tom Lester
Dr. Barton Stuart (1968–1969) . Regis Toomey
Dr. Janet Craig (1968–1970) .... June Lockhart

Wendell Gibbs (1968–1970)	Byron Foulger
Bert Smedley (1968–1969)	Paul Hartman
Kathy Jo Elliott (1968–1970)	Elna Hubbell
Jeff Powers (1968)	Geoff Edwards
Orrin Pike (1969–1970)	Jonathan Daly

The small farming community of Hooterville provided the setting for this highly successful rural situation comedy. Kate Bradley was the widowed owner of the only transient housing in town, the Shady Rest Hotel. Helping her run the hotel were her three beautiful daughters, Billie Jo, Bobbie Jo, and Betty Jo. Also assisting was the girls' Uncle Joe, who had assumed the title of manager. In addition to her involvement with the hotel, the romantic lives of her daughters, and her associations with the townspeople, Kate was constantly at odds with Homer Bedloe, vice-president of the C.F. & W. Railroad. Homer was determined to close down the steam-driven branch of the railroad that ran through Hooterville, scrap its lone engine (the Cannonball), and put its two engineers (Charlie Pratt and Floyd Smoot) out of jobs.

Two years after the premiere of *Petticoat Junction*, CBS added *Green Acres* to its lineup. This situation comedy was the story of a Manhattan businessman who gave up big-city life and bought a farm near Hooterville. For the remainder of their existences there was a certain interplay between the characters of the two shows. The two characters from *Green Acres* who most frequently showed up on *Petticoat Junction* were farmer Newt Kiley and handyman Eb Dawson.

In the fall of 1966 pilot Steve Elliott crashed outside Hooterville and was nursed back to health by the Bradley girls. He later became romantically involved with Betty Jo and eventually married her. They set up housekeeping not far from the hotel, and had a daughter, Kathy Jo. This despite the efforts of Kate's hated adversary, Selma Plout, to get Steve interested in her daughter, Henrietta.

Bea Benaderet passed away soon after production began for the 1968–1969 season and her absence left the show without a unifying center of attention. To fill the void, the role of Dr. Janet Craig, a mature woman doctor who became the town physician when old Dr. Stuart retired, was added late in 1968. The chemistry was not there anymore, however, and the show was canceled in 1970.

One of the distinguishing aspects of *Petticoat Junction* was the turnover in its cast. In addition to those roles that were played by more than one performer as listed in the credits above, a number of actors had appeared, albeit infrequently, as Dr. Stuart and barber Bert Smedley. Not only that, but several people who eventually became regulars on the show—Elvia Allman, Mike Minor, and Byron Foulger—had shown up previously on *Petticoat Junction* in other roles. The one regular who was most likely to stay, however, was Linda Kaye

Henning. Her father, Paul Henning, was the producer of *Petticoat Junction* as well as *Green Acres.*

PEYTON PLACE
Drama
FIRST TELECAST: *September 15, 1964*
LAST TELECAST: *June 2, 1969*
BROADCAST HISTORY:
Sep 1964–Jun 1965, ABC Tue/Thu 9:30–10:00
Jun 1965–Oct 1965, ABC Tue/Thu/Fri 9:30–10:00
Nov 1965–Aug 1966, ABC Mon/Tue/Thu 9:30–10:00
Sep 1966–Jan 1967, ABC Mon/Wed 9:30–10:00
Jan 1967–Aug 1967, ABC Mon/Tue 9:30–10:00
Sep 1967–Sep 1968, ABC Mon/Thu 9:30–10:00
Sep 1968–Jan 1969, ABC Mon 9:00–9:30 Wed 8:30–9:00
Feb 1969–Jun 1969, ABC Mon 9:00–9:30
CAST:
Constance Mackenzie/Carson (1964–1968)
.... Dorothy Malone
Allison Mackenzie (1964–1966) ... Mia Farrow
Dr. Michael Rossi .... Ed Nelson
Matthew Swain, editor of The Clarion *(1964–1965)* .... Warner Anderson
Leslie Harrington (1964–1968) .. Paul Langton
Rodney Harrington, Leslie's oldest son
.... Ryan O'Neal
Norman Harrington, Leslie's younger son
.... Christopher Connelly
Betty Anderson/Harrington/Cord/Harrington
.... Barbara Parkins
Julie Anderson, Betty's mother
.... Kasey Rogers
George Anderson, her father (1964–1965)
.... Henry Beckman
Dr. Robert Morton (1964–1965) ... Kent Smith
Steven Cord .... James Douglas
Hannah Cord, Steven's mother (1965–1967)
.... Ruth Warrick
Paul Hanley (1965) .... Richard Evans
Elliott Carson (1965–1968) .... Tim O'Connor
Eli Carson, Elliott's father ... Frank Ferguson
Nurse Choate (1965–1968)
.... Erin O'Brien-Moore
Dr. Claire Morton (1965) ... Mariette Hartley
Dr. Vincent Markham (1965) ... Leslie Nielsen
Rita Jacks/Harrington (1965–1969)
.... Patricia Morrow
Ada Jacks, Rita's mother (1965–1969)
.... Evelyn Scott
David Schuster (1965–1966)
.... William Smithers
Doris Schuster, his wife (1965) .... Gail Kobe
Kim Schuster, his deaf, 6-year-old child (1965) .... Kimberly Beck
Theodore Dowell, attorney (1965)
.... Patrick Whyte
Stella Chernak (1965–1966) .... Lee Grant
Joe Chernak (1965) .... Don Quine
Gus Chernak (1965–1966) ...... Bruce Gordon
Dr. Russ Gehring (1965–1966) .. David Canary

621

District Attorney John Fowler (1965–1966)
.... John Kerr
Marian Fowler, his wife (1965–1966)
.... Joan Blackman
Martin Peyton (1965–1968)
.... George Macready
Martin Peyton (temporary replacement, 1967)
.... Wilfred Hyde-White
Sandy Webber (1966–1967) ...... Lana Wood
Chris Webber (1966–1967) ..... Gary Haynes
Lee Webber (1966–1968) ..... Stephen Oliver
Ann Howard (1966) .... Susan Oliver
Rachael Welles (1966–1967)
.... Leigh Taylor-Young
Jack Chandler (1966–1967) ...... John Kellogg
Adrienne Van Leyden (1967)
.... Gena Rowlands
Eddie Jacks, Rita's father (1967–1968)
.... Dan Duryea
Carolyn Russell (1968–1969)
.... Elizabeth "Tippy" Walker
Fred Russell (1968–1969)......... Joe Maross
Marsha Russell (1968–1969).... Barbara Rush
Rev. Tom Winter (1968–1969) .... Bob Hogan
Susan Winter, his wife (1968–1969)
.... Diana Hyland
Dr. Harry Miles (1968–1969)
.... Percy Rodriguez
Alma Miles, Harry's wife (1968–1969)
.... Ruby Dee
Lew Miles, Harry's teenage son (1968–1969)
.... Glynn Turman
Jill Smith/Rossi (1968) .... Joyce Jillson
Joe Rossi, Dr. Rossi's brother (1968)
.... Michael Christian

EXECUTIVE PRODUCER:
Paul Monash

Based on the novel *Peyton Place,* by Grace Metalious, this continuing romantic drama was set in the small New England town of Peyton Place, a community that was apparently seething with extramarital affairs, dark secrets, and assorted skulduggery. *Peyton Place* was the first soap opera to become a major hit in prime time. It aired up to three times per week, and every one of the 514 telecasts during its five-year run was an original episode.

Receiving top billing (though not necessarily the most prominent role) was Dorothy Malone as bookshop proprietress Constance Mackenzie, whose own dark secret involved the circumstances surrounding the birth of her daughter Allison 18 years earlier. In May 1965 Constance was finally able to marry Allison's real father, Elliott Carson, upon his release from prison. Meanwhile Allison experienced her own romantic entanglements, leading to a romance with wealthy Rodney Harrington in early 1966. But by August Allison had mysteriously "disappeared" (Mia Farrow had decided to leave the series). Her character was not soon forgotten. First a young girl named Rachael turned up with a clue to Allison's disappear-

ance (a bracelet), setting off a long investigation. Then in 1968 another girl, Jill, arrived in town with what she claimed was Allison's baby.

Other major stories revolved around Rodney Harrington, who was tried for murder in an extended story from 1965–1966. Rodney's lawyer was Steven Cord, another young man with a past, who soon found himself embroiled in the town's active romantic life. So did Dr. Michael Rossi, a young physician who had arrived in Peyton Place on the first telecast in 1964, and who was facing his own murder trial when the series ended in 1969.

And there were many, many more: Betty Anderson, who was married successively to Rodney Harrington (October 1964), Steven Cord (April 1966), and then Rodney Harrington again (June 1968); tavernkeeper's daughter Rita Jacks, who married Norman Harrington (January 1966); David Schuster, who took over the management of the Peyton Mills when Leslie Harrington, Rodney and Norman's father, was sacked by owner Martin Peyton; Rev. Tom Winter, whose affairs were more than clerical; and, toward the end, in a bow to relevance, Dr. Harry Miles, a black neurosurgeon with *his* family and problems.

Aging Martin Peyton, the town's patriarch, was not seen at first. He first appeared in November 1965, as his grandson Rodney Harrington was about to go on trial for murder. Over the next two years Peyton was an important character. An extended story in late 1967 had newcomer Adrienne Van Leyden all set to marry the old codger and collect his loot, until she was killed during a confrontation with Betty (December 1967), resulting in an investigation with multiple consequences. Shortly thereafter Martin Peyton departed for a Boston clinic, where he died in November 1968, and was buried in a funeral attended by most of the town. (Notwithstanding this fact, he was brought back to life when *Peyton Place* was revived as a daytime serial from 1972 to 1974.)

The regular cast of *Peyton Place* would fill a telephone book. One ABC cast credits card lists over 100 "regulars." Those shown above figured most prominently in the various continuing stories. At the outset of the series Dorothy Malone, in the role of Constance Mackenzie, received top billing. A year later, in September 1965, Miss Malone suddenly fell ill and the role was taken over temporarily by Lola Albright. Miss Malone returned in January 1966 and continued for another two and a half years. After she left in June 1968, Ed Nelson, as heartthrob Dr. Michael Rossi, was given top billing.

Probably the two most famous discoveries of *Peyton Place,* however, were Mia Farrow and Ryan O'Neal. Miss Farrow, as the alluring Allison, was seen only during the first two seasons, but O'Neal, as Rodney, continued for virtually the full run of the series.

PHIL HANNA SINGS
see *Starlit Time*

PHIL SILVERS SHOW, THE

Situation Comedy
FIRST TELECAST: *September 20, 1955*
LAST TELECAST: *September 11, 1959*
BROADCAST HISTORY:
  Sep 1955–Oct 1955, CBS Tue 8:30–9:00
  Nov 1955–Feb 1958, CBS Tue 8:00–8:30
  Feb 1958–Sep 1959, CBS Fri 9:00–9:30
CAST:
  M/Sgt. Ernie Bilko . . . . Phil Silvers
  Cpl. Rocco Barbella . . . . Harvey Lembeck
  Pvt. Sam Fender . . . . Herbie Faye
  Col. John Hall . . . . Paul Ford
  Pvt. Duane Doberman . . . . . . Maurice Gosfield
  Sgt. Rupert Ritzik . . . . Joe E. Ross
  Cpl. Henshaw . . . . Allan Melvin
  Pvt. Dino Paparelli . . . . Billy Sands
  Pvt. Zimmerman . . . . Mickey Freeman
  Nell Hall . . . . Hope Sansberry
  Sgt. Grover . . . . Jimmy Little
  Sgt. Joan Hogan (1955–1958)
  . . . . Elisabeth Fraser

Mythical Fort Baxter, Kansas, was the setting for this outrageous satire on military life. Master Sergeant Ernie Bilko was the biggest con man on the post. With little to do in the wilds of Middle America, Bilko spent most of his time gambling, conjuring up assorted money-making schemes, and outmaneuvering his immediate superior, Colonel Hall. Loud, brash, and highly resourceful, Ernie could talk his way out of almost any situation. His attitude and approach filtered down to most of the members of his platoon, and collectively they ran roughshod over the rest of the men stationed at Fort Baxter. WAC Joan Hogan, who worked in the base's office, was Bilko's mild romantic interest during the first three seasons, but was phased out. The original title of the series was *You'll Never Get Rich*, which remained as the subtitle when the series became *The Phil Silvers Show* less than two months after its premiere.

PHILCO TV PLAYHOUSE

Dramatic Anthology
FIRST TELECAST: *October 3, 1948*
LAST TELECAST: *October 2, 1955*
BROADCAST HISTORY:
  Oct 1948–Oct 1955, NBC Sun 9:00–10:00
HOST:
  Bert Lytell (1948–1949)

This live dramatic-anthology series featured top-name actors and actresses in original TV plays and adaptations of novels, short stories, and plays. The first season was produced under the aegis of the Actors' Equity Association, and concentrated on TV adaptations of Broadway dramas and musicals, often with original cast members appearing. Former Equity president Bert Lytell was the host. Perhaps the most elaborate production during the first season was an adaptation of *Cyrano de Bergerac* with Jose Ferrer and a large supporting cast, which used seven sets (including street scenes) to re-create 17th-century Paris. This, remember, was on *live* television. Other first-season productions included adaptations of *Dinner at Eight* with Peggy Wood and Dennis King, and *Counsellor at Law* starring Paul Muni (his TV debut, recreating the role that had brought him fame on Broadway 17 years earlier).

During the second season Equity was no longer involved, but instead an arrangement was made with the Book-of-the-Month Club to present each week a dramatization of a different novel, usually one which was currently popular. After 1950 this theme was dropped and offerings ran the gamut between original and adapted plays, musicals, and occasional true-life documentaries, always meticulously produced. Among the many top stars who appeared on *Philco* were Anthony Quinn, Grace Kelly, young Brandon De Wilde, Lillian Gish (narrating "The Birth of the Movies," a documentary), Walter Matthau, Julie Harris, Rod Steiger, Paul Newman (as Billy the Kid), and Charlton Heston. The last *Philco* telecast was a rough waterfront drama called "A Man Is Ten Feet Tall" with Sidney Poitier, one of the few instances of a black actor appearing in a starring role in a 1950s drama.

From 1951–1955 *Philco TV Playhouse* alternated with *Goodyear TV Playhouse* which presented similar productions.

PHILIP MARLOWE

Detective Drama
FIRST TELECAST: *October 6, 1959*
LAST TELECAST: *March 29, 1960*
BROADCAST HISTORY:
  Oct 1959–Mar 1960, ABC Tue 9:30–10:00
CAST:
  Philip Marlowe . . . . Philip Carey

When author Raymond Chandler wrote his first Philip Marlowe stories in the late 1930s, the detective hero was a hard-bitten loner, rough around the edges, and particularly aggressive. When Philip Marlowe reached television in 1959 he had been laundered considerably. He was still a rather independent loner but had become a much more gentlemanly sort than on the printed page. Working to protect people, solve crimes, and track down missing persons, he moved freely from place to place without getting entangled in any lasting personal relationships.

PHILIP MORRIS PLAYHOUSE

Dramatic Anthology
FIRST TELECAST: *October 8, 1953*
LAST TELECAST: *March 4, 1954*
BROADCAST HISTORY:
  Oct 1953–Mar 1954, CBS Thu 10:00–10:30

This live dramatic series, with individual plays ranging in tone from comedies to melodramas, was aired from New York. Lorne Greene, Eddie

623

Albert, and Constance Ford starred in the premiere telecast, titled "Journey to Nowhere," and Nina Foch, Franchot Tone, Sterling Hayden, Vincent Price, and Otto Kruger appeared in subsequent episodes.

PHILLIES JACKPOT BOWLING
see *Jackpot Bowling Starring Milton Berle*

PHOENIX, THE
Science Fiction
FIRST TELECAST: *March 19, 1982*
LAST TELECAST: *September 15, 1982*
BROADCAST HISTORY:
Mar 1982–Apr 1982, ABC Fri 9:00–10:00
Aug 1982–Sep 1982, ABC Wed 8:00–9:00
CAST:
Bennu of the Golden Light . . . . . . Judson Scott
Preminger . . . . Richard Lynch

Though he looked like a rather concerned young beach bum (frequently bare-chested), Bennu was in fact a messenger from an alien world, far away and long ago. He had come to the earth 1,500 years before as a scout from a dying civilization, and had been entombed in a pre-Incan sarcophagus in the Andes. Centuries later, when modern scientists had stumbled upon him and revived him, his goal became finding Mira, his partner, now in some other ancient burial ground somewhere in North America. Along the way he lent his exceptional powers, vested in the amulet he wore around his neck, to people in distress, and talked frequently of his concern for the environment—which seemed to be in as much danger here as it had been on his home planet.

None of this impressed a hard-nosed government agent named Preminger, whose goal was to capture Bennu and control his special powers.

The Phoenix was first seen as a movie special on April 26, 1981, and returned for a short run as a series in early 1982.

PHOTOCRIME
Crime Drama
FIRST TELECAST: *September 21, 1949*
LAST TELECAST: *December 14, 1949*
BROADCAST HISTORY:
Sep 1949–Dec 1949, ABC Wed 8:30–9:00
CAST:
Inspector Hannibal Cobb . . . . Chuck Webster
ALSO:
Diana Douglas
Joe DeSantis

Easygoing Inspector Hannibal Cobb was the long arm of the law in this mystery series, which was produced in cooperation with *Look* magazine. Also known as *Look Photocrime*.

PHOTOGRAPHIC HORIZONS
Instruction
FIRST TELECAST: *January 12, 1949*

LAST TELECAST: *March 7, 1949*
BROADCAST HISTORY:
Jan 1949–Mar 1949, DUM Mon 8:00–8:30
REGULARS:
Joe Costa
Peggy Corday

Many unusual program formats were tried in the early days of television, including that of the TV camera club. It seemed like a natural for the new medium. Not only could expert photographers describe picture-taking techniques, home-darkroom procedures, etc., they could actually show the results. *Photographic Horizons* began as a local show on DuMont's New York station in December 1947, and was quite popular with early set owners. There were interviews and demonstrations, and a succession of lovely models didn't hurt viewership. The models posed before special backgrounds and viewers at home were encouraged to take pictures of them off the TV screen. Joe Costa, president of the National Press Photographers Association, was host, and 23-year-old Peggy Corday his chief model. Maxine Barrat also frequently modeled for home shutterbugs.

PHOTOPLAY TIME
see *Wendy Barrie Show, The*

PHYL & MIKHY
Situation Comedy
FIRST TELECAST: *May 26, 1980*
LAST TELECAST: *June 30, 1980*
BROADCAST HISTORY:
May 1980–Jun 1980, CBS Mon 8:30–9:00
CAST:
Phyllis Wilson ("Phyl") . . . . . . Murphy Cross
Mikhail Orlov ("Mikhy") . . . . . . Rick Lohman
Max Wilson . . . . Larry Haines
Vladimir Gimenko . . . . Michael Pataki
Edgar "Truck" Morley . . . . Jack Dodson
Connie . . . . Deborah Pratt

Phyllis Wilson and Mikhail Orlov were two young track stars who fell in love and wanted to get married. There were complications. Mikhail was a Russian, so he had to defect to the United States. Since the newlyweds had no money, they moved in with Phyl's widowed father Max, who was somewhat dubious about his new Russian son-in-law. Mikhy, for his part, had to learn to cope with the strange American life-style—not to mention all the unfamiliar appliances in the kitchen. They all had to put up with Gimenko, a representative of the Russian government who kept trying to get Mikhy to return to Mother Russia. Truck Morley was Max's boss and Connie was a friend of Phyl's.

Phyl & Mikhy was originally intended as a topical series to be broadcast prior to coverage of the 1980 Summer Olympics from Moscow, on NBC. But when Russia invaded Afghanistan, the U.S. withdrew its team and Olympic coverage was canceled. CBS considered dropping this series (which it had already paid for), but finally decided to run the six episodes it had. It didn't get much of an audience.

Rick Lohman and Larry Haines had both been on the daytime soap opera *Search for Tomorrow*, where Lohman played Haines' grandson.

PHYLLIS
Situation Comedy
FIRST TELECAST: *September 8, 1975*
LAST TELECAST: *August 30, 1977*
BROADCAST HISTORY:
Sep 1975–Jan 1977, CBS Mon 8:30–9:00
Jan 1977–Jul 1977, CBS Sun 8:30–9:00
Aug 1977, CBS Tue 8:30–9:00
CAST:
Phyllis Lindstrom .... Cloris Leachman
Bess Lindstrom .... Lisa Gerritsen
Julie Erskine (1975–1976) .... Liz Torres
Leo Heatherton (1975–1976).. Richard Schaal
Audrey Dexter................... Jane Rose
Judge Jonathan Dexter .... Henry Jones
Sally "Mother" Dexter .... Judith Lowry
Leonard Marsh (1976–1977) ..... John Lawlor
Harriet Hastings (1976–1977).. Garn Stephens
Dan Valenti (1976–1977) ..... Carmine Caridi
Arthur Lanson (1976)............ Burt Mustin
Mark Valenti (1977)......... Craig Wasson

After five years playing Mary Richards' neighbor, friend, and landlady on *The Mary Tyler Moore Show*, Cloris Leachman began her own spin-off series. Phyllis Lindstrom returned to her hometown of San Francisco following the death of her husband Lars. In her mid-40s, and with a teenage daughter to support, Phyllis moved in with Lars' scatterbrained mother, Audrey, and Audrey's second husband, Judge Jonathan Dexter. Though not a member of the household when the series started, Judge Dexter's mother was also living with them before the first season's end.

Phyllis found a job working as assistant to Julie Erskine at Erskine's Commercial Photography Studio. Also working as a photographer for Julie was Leo Heatherton. (Barbara Colby was the actress originally signed for the role of Julie Erskine but only appeared in the first episode of the series. Miss Colby was brutally murdered soon after production had started and was replaced by Liz Torres.) This job, with Phyllis being her busybody, self-centered, oblivious self, lasted only one season.

At the start of the 1976–1977 season, in an effort to improve upon the mediocre ratings of the first season, Phyllis was given a new job as administrative assistant to Dan Valenti, a member of the San Francisco Board of Supervisors. She worked in an office with another supervisor, Leonard Marsh, and his assistant Harriet. On the home front things were also changing. Witty, sharp-tongued Mother Dexter, far and away the best member of the family when it came to putting down

Phyllis, had become involved with a man. She was 87 and Arthur was 92, but love flowered and they were married in December 1976. Ironically, elderly actress Judith Lowry had died while on vacation in New York during a break in production early in December, before the episode aired, and Bert Mustin, who was too ill to see it, died not long after. Bess also found a man, in the person of Phyllis' boss's nephew Mark. They sneaked off to Las Vegas and were married in the spring. The changes in cast and multiple marriages didn't help the ratings enough to save the series. It was canceled at the end of the 1976–1977 season.

PHYLLIS DILLER SHOW, THE
see *Pruitts of Southampton, The*

PICCADILLY PALACE, THE
Musical Variety
FIRST TELECAST: *May 20, 1967*
LAST TELECAST: *September 9, 1967*
BROADCAST HISTORY:
May 1967–Sep 1967, ABC Sat 9:30–10:30
REGULARS:
Millicent Martin
Eric Morecambe
Ernie Wise
The Paddy Stone Dancers
The Michael Sammes Singers
The Jack Parnell Orchestra

The Piccadilly Palace was produced in London and was the 1967 summer replacement for *The Hollywood Palace*. It followed a similar format, but with regular hosts—who also performed—and with young popular singers (primarily) as guests. The hosts were singer Millicent Martin and the comedy team of Morecambe and Wise, who were seen each week introducing the guests, performing with them, and performing on their own.

PICK THE WINNER
Political
FIRST TELECAST: *August 14, 1952*
LAST TELECAST: *October 31, 1956*
BROADCAST HISTORY:
Aug 1952–Oct 1952, CBS/DUM Thu 9:00–9:30
Nov 1952, CBS/DUM Mon 10:00–10:30
Sep 1956–Oct 1956, CBS Wed 7:30–8:00
HOST:
Walter Cronkite

In both the 1952 and 1956 Presidential election years, CBS newsman Walter Cronkite hosted a series of political telecasts that enabled the candidates and various spokesmen for the parties to discuss the issues and explain their respective positions. The 1952 edition, which was sponsored by Westinghouse Electric as a public service, was carried simultaneously on both the CBS and DuMont networks. After the conclusion of the regular 1956 series, a special telecast was aired from 10:45–11:00 P.M. on the night before the election in which CBS correspondents made analyses of various races and predicted winners.

PICTURE THIS
Cartoons
FIRST TELECAST: *November 17, 1948*
LAST TELECAST: *February 9, 1949*
BROADCAST HISTORY:
Nov 1948–Feb 1949, NBC Wed 8:20–8:30
HOSTESS:
Wendy Barrie

This was a live program, each week featuring a different guest cartoonist who would draw sketches to accompany stories or jokes, some of them submitted by the viewing audience.

PICTURE THIS
Quiz/Audience Participation
FIRST TELECAST: *June 25, 1963*
LAST TELECAST: *September 17, 1963*
BROADCAST HISTORY:
Jun 1963–Sep 1963, CBS Tue 9:30–10:00
EMCEE:
Jerry Van Dyke

This summer game show featured two teams, each composed of a celebrity and non-celebrity contestant. One member of each team was given a secret phrase, then had to direct the drawing of a picture which was supposed to provide his partner with a clue to the phrase. The first partner to guess the phrase won for his team, while the emerging picture and the byplay between contestants provided the laughs.

This was the first regular series for Jerry Van Dyke, who had previously appeared in a few episodes of his brother's popular series, *The Dick Van Dyke Show.*

PINK LADY
Comedy Variety
FIRST TELECAST: *March 1, 1980*
LAST TELECAST: *April 4, 1980*
BROADCAST HISTORY:
Mar 1980, NBC Sat 10:00–11:00
Mar 1980–Apr 1980, NBC Fri 9:00–10:00
REGULARS:
Pink Lady (Mie Nemoto and Kei Masuda)
Jeff Altman
Cheri Eichen
Anna Mathias
Jim Varney
Ed Nakamoto
The Peacock Dancers

Something must have been lost in the translation. Pink Lady was a Japanese rock duo that was a big hit in Japan and even had one moderately popular record in the U.S.A. ("Kiss in the Dark"). The singers were Mie and Kei ("Me" and "Kay"), two sexy young ladies who spoke very little English and who were depicted in comedy sketches as trying

to learn about American customs. Helping them was young comic Jeff Altman, who acted as their guide and interpreter. The show had guest stars, songs, comedy sketches with a regular supporting cast, and a scene at the end of each program with Mie and Kei in bikinis in a hot tub. What it didn't have, unfortunately, was an audience.

PINKY LEE SHOW, THE
Situation Comedy
FIRST TELECAST: *April 5, 1950*
LAST TELECAST: *November 9, 1950*
BROADCAST HISTORY:
Apr 1950–May 1950, NBC Wed 8:30–9:00
Jun 1950–Aug 1950, NBC Wed 10:30–11:00
Sep 1950–Oct 1950, NBC Sat 6:30–7:00
Oct 1950–Nov 1950, NBC Thu 8:30–9:00
CAST:
The Stagehand .... Pinky Lee
The Stage Manager .... William Bakewell

Pinky Lee (real name: Pincus Leff) first came to network TV in 1950. This series was a loosely structured situation comedy, set in a vaudeville theater. Pinky appeared as a stagehand, dressed in baggy clothes, who usually managed to fumble every assignment, but who was nevertheless called upon to fill in for singers and comedians who couldn't make it—thus giving him the opportunity to appear on stage in a variety of roles.

The program originated in Hollywood and was seen in the rest of the country via kinescope. Pinky later starred in the comedy *Those Two* from 1951 to 1953 and in various weekday afternoon and Saturday morning children's shows from 1954 to 1957.

PIONEERS, THE
see *Death Valley Days*

PISTOLS 'N' PETTICOATS
Situation Comedy
FIRST TELECAST: *September 17, 1966*
LAST TELECAST: *August 19, 1967*
BROADCAST HISTORY:
Sep 1966–Jan 1967, CBS Sat 8:30–9:00
Jan 1967–Aug 1967, CBS Sat 9:30–10:00
CAST:
Henrietta Hanks .... Ann Sheridan
Grandpa .... Douglas Fowley
Grandma.................... Ruth McDevitt
Lucy Hanks .... Carole Wells
Sheriff Harold Sikes .... Gary Vinson
Buss Courtney .... Robert Lowery
Chief Eagle Shadow .... Lon Chaney, Jr.
Gray Hawk .... Marc Cavell
Little Bear .... Alex Henteloff

Set in and around the town of Wretched, Colorado, in the 1870s, this Western situation comedy told the story of the Hanks family, three generations strong. Despite their respective ages and sex, all the members of the Hanks family, with the exception of Henrietta's city-bred daughter Lucy, were remarkably adept with guns. They could outdraw and outshoot any desperadoes and hotshot gunslingers within 500 miles of their home. It was extremely embarrassing for a reputedly dangerous outlaw to be subdued by an attractive woman and her grandparents, but that was a common occurrence around Wretched, especially since inept and bumbling young Sheriff Sikes offered little resistance. The Hanks family was so tough, in fact, that normal household pets were too tame for them. So what did they have for a pet? Would you believe, a wolf named Bowser?

PLACE THE FACE
Quiz/Audience Participation
FIRST TELECAST: *July 2, 1953*
LAST TELECAST: *September 13, 1955*
BROADCAST HISTORY:
Jul 1953–Aug 1953, NBC Tue 8:30–9:00
Aug 1953–Aug 1954, CBS Thu 10:30–11:00
Sep 1954–Dec 1954, NBC Sat 8:00–8:30
Jun 1955–Sep 1955, NBC Tue 8:00–8:30
EMCEE:
Jack Smith (1953)
Jack Bailey (1953–1954)
Bill Cullen (1954–1955)

Contestants on *Place the Face* were confronted with an individual from their past, who had encountered them in a specific situation, and asked to identify the face within a short time limit. The associations were such things as the person who had walked next to the contestant at his high school graduation, a policeman who had given him or her a ticket, a former teacher, etc. Clues were given by the emcee and the contestant could ask questions requiring only a yes or no answer of the individual. When Jack Smith was the emcee, the majority of the contestants were not celebrities and won prizes dependent on how quickly they made the identification. Jack Bailey took over as interim host in November 1953 and Bill Cullen became the permanent emcee the following February. By the time Cullen took over most of the contestants were celebrities, the prize aspect was minimized, and the emcee chatted at length with each contestant before the game began.

PLACES PLEASE
Talent Variety
FIRST TELECAST: *August 16, 1948*
LAST TELECAST: *February 25, 1949*
BROADCAST HISTORY:
Aug 1948–Feb 1949, CBS Mon/Wed/Fri 7:15–7:30
HOST:
Barry Wood

This live talent show was produced and emceed by Barry Wood. Each week he would introduce a number of young performers who were then given the opportunity to do their acts on network television. The show had originated as a local show in New York during early July 1948. It had three network telecasts at different times during the week of July 13–16 and then reverted to local status for another month before becoming a regular network feature.

PLAINCLOTHESMAN, THE
Police Drama
FIRST TELECAST: *October 12, 1949*
LAST TELECAST: *September 19, 1954*
BROADCAST HISTORY:
Oct 1949–May 1950, DUM Wed 9:00–9:30
May 1950–May 1951, DUM Wed 9:30–10:00
Jun 1951–Sep 1954, DUM Sun 9:30–10:00
CAST:
The Lieutenant .... Ken Lynch
Sgt. Brady .... Jack Orrison
Annie, the waitress (1952) ..... Helen Gillette

A number of series over the years have featured an unseen character—Bracken in *Bracken's World*, Charlie in *Charlie's Angels*—but this was one of the few series in which the lead role went to someone who was never seen on screen. The technique was camera-as-actor, in which the viewer saw everything exactly as the Lieutenant would. If he lit his cigar, a hand (his) came toward the camera with a lighted match (even the tip of his cigar could be seen jutting out at the bottom of the screen); if he was knocked down, the viewer looked up from floor level; if he got something in his eye, the camera blinked, flickered, and winked clear again. A punch in the nose provided the most spectacular effect for home viewers.

Aside from the novel effects, *The Plainclothesman* was a straightforward big-city crime drama, with the unnamed Lieutenant and his sidekick Sgt. Brady working out of homicide to solve assorted murders. Scientific crime-detection techniques were used.

Oh, yes, the unseen Lieutenant, in reality a handsome actor named Ken Lynch, *was* seen at least once—in a July 1952 episode which featured a series of flashbacks.

PLANET OF THE APES, THE
Science Fiction
FIRST TELECAST: *September 13, 1974*
LAST TELECAST: *December 27, 1974*
BROADCAST HISTORY:
Sep 1974–Dec 1974, CBS Fri 8:00–9:00
CAST:
Galen .... Roddy McDowall
Alan Virdon .... Ron Harper
Pete Burke .... James Naughton
Urko .... Mark Lenard
Zaius .... Booth Colman

Astronauts Alan Virdon and Pete Burke, hurled through the time barrier by some unexplained force, found themselves crash-landed on an Earth of the far future. This future Earth was ruled by apes who regarded humans as representatives of a destructive and dangerous past civilization. In the ape civilization, gorillas like Urko comprised the military class and orangutans like Zaius were the ruling class. Befriended by a curious chimpanzee named Galen, the astronauts sought to find acceptance in their strange new world. The threat they posed to the ape civilization made them hunted quarry and forced them into the life of fugitives. Roddy McDowall re-created the role he had played in a number of the highly successful *Planet of the Apes* theatrical films, upon which this rather less-successful television series was based. The movie, in turn, was adapted from a novel by Pierre Boulle.

An animated version of this series, titled *Beyond the Planet of the Apes,* aired Saturday mornings on NBC from September 1975 to September 1976.

PLAY THE GAME
Charades
FIRST TELECAST: *September 24, 1946*
LAST TELECAST: *December 17, 1946*
BROADCAST HISTORY:
Sep 1946–Dec 1946, DUM Tue 8:00–8:30
HOST:
Dr. Harvey Zorbaugh

Dr. Harvey Zorbaugh, Professor of Educational Sociology at New York University, was something of a minor celebrity among the small band of TV-set owners during the early and mid-1940s. His charade show was seen locally on the NBC station in New York as early as 1941, had a 13-week run on DuMont in 1946, and was seen locally again on ABC in 1948. It was charades, pure and simple, with celebrity guests such as Ireene Wicker, Ray Knight, and Will Mullin performing. Viewers were invited to phone in their guesses to certain charades.

Although seen over DuMont's two-station network, this version was produced by ABC. That network did not yet have any stations of its own on the air, and so bought time on other stations in order to allow its production crews to gain experience against the day when ABC's own facilities would open.

Also known as *Let's Play the Game.*

PLAY YOUR HUNCH
Quiz/Audience Participation
FIRST TELECAST: *April 15, 1960*
LAST TELECAST: *September 26, 1962*
BROADCAST HISTORY:
Apr 1960–Jun 1960, NBC Fri 7:30–8:00
Jun 1960–Sep 1960, NBC Fri 9:00–9:30
Jun 1962–Sep 1962, NBC Wed 10:00–10:30
EMCEE:
Merv Griffin
ANNOUNCER:
Johnny Olsen

Two teams of related contestants—father and son, husband and wife, etc.—competed in this game. Various problems were presented to them and they pooled their knowledge to try to come up with the solutions. Each correct solution was worth a point and the first team to score three points won the game. The winners kept playing until they lost a game. Each point was worth $100 and the losers kept whatever money they had won.

Play Your Hunch also ran in daytime, making a tour of all three networks between June 1958 and September 1963. Merv Griffin, Robert Q. Lewis, Richard Hayes, and Gene Rayburn each had stints as emcee of the daytime version.

PLAYERS, THE
see *Variety*

PLAYHOUSE, THE
syndicated title for *Schlitz Playhouse of Stars*

PLAYHOUSE, THE
Dramatic Anthology
FIRST TELECAST: *September 3, 1957*
LAST TELECAST: *September 24, 1959*
BROADCAST HISTORY:
Sep 1957, CBS Tue 10:30–11:00
Jul 1959–Sep 1959, CBS Wed/Thu 7:30–8:00

The films aired on this summer anthology series were all reruns of episodes previously seen on other anthology programs, primarily *Schlitz Playhouse of Stars.* The 1957 edition lasted only four weeks. When *The Playhouse* returned as a summer series two years later, it was aired on Wednesdays and Thursdays. To distinguish between the days, the Wednesday episodes were titled *Wednesday Playhouse* while the Thursday films went under the generic title *The Playhouse.*

PLAYHOUSE 90
Dramatic Anthology
FIRST TELECAST: *October 4, 1956*
LAST TELECAST: *September 19, 1961*
BROADCAST HISTORY:
Oct 1956–Jan 1960, CBS Thu 9:30–11:00
Jul 1961–Sep 1961, CBS Tue 9:30–11:00

Of all the fine dramatic-anthology series to grace television in the 1950s, *Playhouse 90* was the most ambitious and remains the standard against which all the others are judged. Each week this series aired a complete 90-minute drama. Blessed with a very high budget, *Playhouse 90* could afford to hire the best actors, producers, directors, and writers that money could buy. The logistics of doing such a long show every week—usually live—gave the series' principal director, John Frankenheimer, a task worthy of a military strategist. The sets, the camera movements, the action, the timing were all planned so precisely that even the slightest slip could mean disaster. Yet there were few disasters, and the very first season produced such classics as "Requiem for a Heavyweight" starring Jack Palance (the series' second telecast), "The Miracle Worker" with young Patty McCormack, "The Comedian" with Mickey Rooney, "Charley's Aunt" with Art Carney, and "The Helen Morgan Story" with Polly Bergen. Directors for these and later telecasts included Fred Coe, Franklin Schaffner, George Roy Hill, Alex Segal, and Robert Stevens. Plays included adaptations from Hemingway, Shaw, Faulkner, and Saroyan and originals by Rod Serling (who wrote "Requiem"), Reginald Rose, and others.

In succeeding seasons there were "Point of No Return," "Bitter Heritage," "The Plot to Kill Stalin," "The Days of Wine and Roses," "Judgment at Nuremberg," and a two-part "For Whom the Bell Tolls." Aired weekly for three seasons, *Playhouse 90* was cut back to alternate-week status in the fall of 1959, sharing the time period with *The Big Party*. Its last telecast as a regular series was on January 21, 1960. A total of eight more shows aired on an irregular basis in different time slots through May 18, 1960, and a series of reruns was presented weekly during the summer of 1961.

All of the first season's presentations were done live. During the 1957–1958 season, to give the production team an occasional breather, roughly one drama each month was filmed in advance, by different production teams, and during the third season many of the *Playhouse 90*s were done using the relatively new process of videotape. Even in later seasons some of the productions were done live, however, and *Playhouse 90* is still remembered as the pinnacle of live drama from TV's "Golden Age."

PLAYHOUSE # 7
see *ABC Dramatic Shorts—1952–1953*

PLAYHOUSE OF MYSTERY
see *Johnson's Wax Theater*

PLAYHOUSE OF MYSTERY
Dramatic Anthology
FIRST TELECAST: *February 10, 1959*
LAST TELECAST: *September 15, 1959*
BROADCAST HISTORY:
  Feb 1959–Mar 1959, CBS Tue 8:00–8:30
  May 1959–Sep 1959, CBS Tue 8:00–8:30

The dramas telecast in this filmed anthology series were all reruns of previously aired episodes from other anthology series. They all had one element in common—the plot was designed to keep viewers in suspense until the action resolved itself.

PLAYHOUSE OF STARS
Dramatic Anthology
FIRST TELECAST: *July 21, 1960*
LAST TELECAST: *September 1, 1960*

BROADCAST HISTORY:
  Jul 1960–Sep 1960, CBS Thu 8:00–8:30

The filmed episodes of this summer anthology series were made up of reruns of episodes from other series.

PLAYROOM
Children's
FIRST TELECAST: *January 9, 1948*
LAST TELECAST: *May 28, 1948*
BROADCAST HISTORY:
  Jan 1948–May 1948, DUM Fri 7:00–7:30

This was an early children's program, about which no specific information is available.

PLAY'S THE THING, THE
see *Actors Studio*

PLEASE DON'T EAT THE DAISIES
Situation Comedy
FIRST TELECAST: *September 14, 1965*
LAST TELECAST: *September 2, 1967*
BROADCAST HISTORY:
  Sep 1965–Aug 1966, NBC Tue 8:00–8:30
  Sep 1966–Sep 1967, NBC Sat 8:00–8:30
CAST:
  Joan Nash .... Patricia Crowley
  James (Jim) Nash .... Mark Miller
  Kyle Nash .... Kim Tyler
  Joel Nash .... Brian Nash
  Tracey Nash .... Joe Fithian
  Trevor Nash.................... Jeff Fithian
  Marge Thornton .... Shirley Mitchell
  Herb Thornton (1965–1966) .... Harry Hickox
  Herb Thornton (1966–1967) ... King Donovan
  Ed Hewley (1965–1966) .... Dub Taylor
  Martha O'Reilly .... Ellen Corby
  Dean Gerald Carter (1966–1967)... Bill Quinn
  Ethel Carter (1966–1967)..... Jean VanderPyl

Based on the best-selling book and popular Doris Day movie of the same title, *Please Don't Eat the Daisies* was author Jean Kerr's story of an unusual suburban family. Jim Nash was a professor of English at Ridgemont College in Ridgemont, New York, the community in which he lived with his family. Wife Joan was a newspaper columnist who hated housework, didn't like to cook, and was totally unconcerned about how her traditional suburban housewife neighbors felt about it. She got up at noon and did whatever moved her at the moment. Completing the household were the four Nash children, all boys, including mischievous seven-year-old twins; Martha, the family maid; and a huge 150-pound sheep dog named Ladadog. The Thorntons were next-door neighbors of the Nashes.

PLYMOUTH PLAYHOUSE
Various
FIRST TELECAST: *April 12, 1953*

LAST TELECAST: *June 21, 1953*
BROADCAST HISTORY:
Apr 1953–Jun 1953, ABC Sun 7:30–8:00
HOST:
Donald Cook

This series of auditions for possible series was presented by ABC in hopes of attracting sponsor interest for the fall 1953 season. The productions used top-named talent and expensive budgets (ABC wanted to show that it could produce "big-time programming," just like CBS and NBC) and, indeed, three of the efforts became series. Unfortunately, only one of them aired on ABC—*Jamie*, starring child actor Brandon De Wilde. DuMont picked up *Colonel Humphrey Flack* with Alan Mowbray for its fall lineup, and *Justice*, based on the files of the Legal Aid Society and starring Paul Douglas and Lee Grant, turned up on NBC for a two-year run in the fall of 1954. (See those titles for details.)

Other productions included an elaborate, live, two-part adaptation of *A Tale of Two Cities* starring John Ireland, Wendell Corey, and Joanne Dru, with original music by Dmitri Tiomkin; "Mr. Glencannon Takes All," directed by Sir Cedric Hardwicke and starring Robert Newton; and a series of four classic short stories produced by Hardwicke. Other stars appearing included Robert Preston, Janis Paige, and Walter Matthau. Some productions were live, others on film.

The series was first known as *ABC Album*, but switched to *Plymouth Playhouse* when a sponsor came aboard beginning with the third telecast.

PLYMOUTH SHOW, THE
see *Lawrence Welk's Top Tunes and New Talent*

POLICE SQUAD
Situation Comedy
FIRST TELECAST: *March 4, 1982*
LAST TELECAST: *September 2, 1982*
BROADCAST HISTORY:
Mar 1982, ABC Thu 8:00–8:30
Jul 1982–Aug 1982, ABC Thu 9:30–10:00
Sep 1982, ABC Thu 9:30–10:00
CAST:
Det. Frank Drebin .... Leslie Nielsen
Capt. Ed Hocken .... Alan North
Ted Olson .... Ed Williams
Johnny the Snitch .... William Duell

The creators of the hit movie *Airplane!* brought their bent humor to television in this short-lived series, which, like the movie, starred Leslie Nielsen. The setting this time was a "large American city," where straight-faced Detective Frank Drebin and his loyal Captain Hocken investigated puzzling cases filled with sight-gags and non sequiturs. In the opening episode they arrived at the scene of a murder to find a chalk outline of the body with Egyptian hieroglyphics alongside, the

police photographer taking a picture of a grinning policeman posing with the corpse, and a witness who had a hard time talking through her braces. Parked nearby was a police car, with big letters on the hood reading—of course—POLICE CAR.

Sometimes police scientist Ted Olson might offer dubious help, as when he identified the sounds in the background of a ransom tape as "a foghorn and a bell buoy"—they must be at the harbor! But en route to storm the waterfront with a small army of cops, Drebin stopped for gas and noticed an uncanny similarity between the "bell buoy" and the bell on the gas pump. And that foghorn, was it really a tuba? So they went off to find a tuba next to a gas station, to storm that instead.

Then there was the clue found in a note tied to a window, thrown into a pile of rocks. And so on. Johnny was the shoeshine boy and street snitch, who could give them incredible inside information—for a price.

Where did the creators of this odd program—two brothers named Zucker—get their offbeat approach to comedy? "A lot of our humor was developed as a self-defense for not being good in school," said one of them. "The only difference between then and now is that now we are getting paid for what used to get us kicked out of class."

POLICE STORY
Police Anthology
FIRST TELECAST: *April 4, 1952*
LAST TELECAST: *September 26, 1952*
BROADCAST HISTORY:
Apr 1952–Sep 1952, CBS Fri 10:00–10:30
NARRATOR:
Norman Rose

Case histories were drawn from the files of various law-enforcement agencies and adapted for television presentation in this live dramatic series that originated from New York. Not only were crime-detection stories presented but episodes devoted to crime prevention were included as well. The actors playing lead roles were chosen for their resemblance to the actual officers who had been involved in the cases and used the officers' real names. Settings were various big cities and rural areas around the country with both local and state police operations shown. Generally lesser-known performers participated, with James Gregory, Edward Binns, and E. G. Marshall the most familiar.

POLICE STORY
Police Anthology
FIRST TELECAST: *September 25, 1973*
LAST TELECAST: *August 23, 1977*
BROADCAST HISTORY:
Oct 1973–Sep 1975, NBC Tue 10:00–11:00
Sep 1975–Oct 1975, NBC Tue 9:00–10:00
Nov 1975–Aug 1976, NBC Fri 10:00–11:00
Aug 1976–Aug 1977, NBC Tue 10:00–11:00

CREATOR:
Joseph Wambaugh

One of the more realistic police series to be seen on television was *Police Story,* created by former Los Angeles policeman Joseph Wambaugh. After retiring from the force, Wambaugh had written two highly successful novels about police operations, *The New Centurions* and *The Blue Knight* (the latter also became a TV series in its own right). Wambaugh served as a consultant to this series, insuring that everything was treated with utmost authenticity. Stories covered the more mundane aspects of police work as well as the excitement. They probed the psychology of individual police officers and even dealt with their home lives, how their jobs affected their families, and personal problems such as drinking, injuries, and forced retirement.

Two episodes from *Police Story* went on to become series of their own. "The Gamble" was aired on March 26, 1974, with Angie Dickinson in the role of policewoman Lisa Beaumont. That fall, with her name changed to Pepper Anderson, she became *Police Woman.* "The Return of Joe Forrester," aired as a special 90-minute episode on May 6, 1975, became *Joe Forrester* that fall, with Lloyd Bridges re-creating his role. Although *Police Story* was an anthology, characters occasionally made return appearances. The most notable examples were Tony Lo Bianco (as Tony Calabrese) and Don Meredith (as Bert Jameson). During its first two seasons on the air, these two appeared four times as partners and once each separately as detectives on various cases. Despite the frequency of their visits, they never got a series of their own. NBC aired occasional two-hour *Police Story* specials after the series ceased weekly production.

POLICE SURGEON
see *Dr. Simon Locke.*

POLICE WOMAN
Police Drama
FIRST TELECAST: *September 13, 1974*
LAST TELECAST: *August 30, 1978*
BROADCAST HISTORY:
  Sep 1974–Oct 1975, NBC Fri 10:00–11:00
  Nov 1975–Aug 1977, NBC Tue 9:00–10:00
  Oct 1977–Dec 1977, NBC Tue 10:00–11:00
  Dec 1977–Mar 1978, NBC Wed 10:00–11:00
  Mar 1978–May 1978, NBC Thu 10:00–11:00
  Jun 1978–Aug 1978, NBC Wed 10:00–11:00
CAST:
Sgt. Suzanne "Pepper" Anderson
  .... Angie Dickinson
Lt. Bill Crowley .... Earl Holliman
Det. Joe Styles................. Ed Bernard
Det. Pete Royster .... Charles Dierkop
Lt. Paul Marsh (1974–1976) ..... Val Bisoglio

Sexy Sgt. Pepper Anderson was an undercover agent for the criminal conspiracy department of the Los Angeles Police Department. Working on a vice-squad team that included Joe Styles and Pete Royster, two other undercover cops, she was called on to pose as everything from a prostitute to a gangster's girlfriend. The team reported directly to Lt. Bill Crowley, who was the coordinator of its operations. Although not seen on a regular basis, Pepper's autistic younger sister Cheryl, played by Nichole Kallis, was visited occasionally at the Austin School for the Handicapped during the first season of *Police Woman.* Her role was dropped in the fall of 1975.

The pilot for *Police Woman,* which starred Angie Dickinson and all of the series regulars except Earl Holliman, aired as an episode of *Police Story* titled "The Gamble."

POLITICS ON TRIAL
Debate
FIRST TELECAST: *September 4, 1952*
LAST TELECAST: *October 30, 1952*
BROADCAST HISTORY:
  Sep 1952–Oct 1952, ABC Thu 9:00–9:30

This was a public-affairs debate in the style of a courtroom trial, and was presented in the weeks leading up to the 1952 Presidential election. A prominent Republican or Democrat presented his party's position on a major issue, which was then attacked by "opposing counsel" and defended by his own "counsel." A real-life judge presided.

POLKA-GO-ROUND
Music
FIRST TELECAST: *June 23, 1958*
LAST TELECAST: *September 28, 1959*
BROADCAST HISTORY:
  Jun 1958–Sep 1958, ABC Mon 9:30–10:30
  Oct 1958–Dec 1958, ABC Mon 7:30–8:30
  Dec 1958–May 1959, ABC Mon 8:00–8:30
  Jun 1959–Sep 1959, ABC Mon 7:30–8:30
REGULARS:
  Bob Lewandowski
  Carolyn DeZurik
  Lou Prohut
  The Polka Rounders
  Caine Dancers
  Tom "Stubby" Fouts
  The Singing Waiters
  Georgia Drake

A full hour of polka music in network prime time every week? That's what this program provided throughout most of its run. The colorfully costumed singers and dancers performed in an outdoor cafe setting. Telecast from Chicago.

POLKA TIME
Music
FIRST TELECAST: *July 13, 1956*
LAST TELECAST: *September 24, 1957*

631

BROADCAST HISTORY:
Jul 1956–Oct 1956, ABC Fri 10:00–10:30
Oct 1956–Sep 1957, ABC Tue 10:00–10:30
REGULARS:
Bruno (Junior) Zielinski
Carolyn DeZurik
Richard (Hodyl) and Mildred (Lawnik)
Wally Moore and Chick Hurt
Rusty Gill
Stan Wolowic's Polka Chips

A half hour of authentic Polish music and dancing, telecast from Chicago. Also known as *It's Polka Time.*

POLLY BERGEN SHOW, THE
Musical Variety
FIRST TELECAST: *September 21, 1957*
LAST TELECAST: *May 31, 1958*
BROADCAST HISTORY:
Sep 1957–May 1958, NBC Sat 9:00–9:30
REGULARS:
Polly Bergen
Peter Gennaro Dancers
Bill Bergen
The Luther Henderson, Jr., Orchestra

Singer Polly Bergen starred in this musical variety series which featured Peter Gennaro and his dancers, special guest stars, and, from November through February, her father Bill Bergen. Each show was tailored to the talents of the guest stars, be they singers, dancers, comedians, etc., but always included some songs by Miss Bergen.

PONDEROSA
see *Bonanza*

PONDS THEATER
Dramatic Anthology
FIRST TELECAST: *January 13, 1955*
LAST TELECAST: *July 7, 1955*
BROADCAST HISTORY:
Jan 1955–Jul 1955, ABC Thu 9:30–10:30

For 15 months, the Kraft Corporation had been sponsoring two live plays a week, both titled *Kraft Television Theater.* The NBC version, which aired on Wednesday nights at 9:00 P.M. and had been in that time period since the late 1940s, was by far the more successful. When Kraft decided to drop the Thursday night version on ABC, Ponds took over sponsorship and retitled the series *Ponds Theater.* The dramas continued to be produced live in New York, and included such leading talent as Joanne Woodward, E. G. Marshall, Ed Begley, Roddy McDowall, Eva Gabor, Lee Grant, and Ernest Truex.

PONTIAC PRESENTS PLAYWRIGHTS 56
Dramatic Anthology
FIRST TELECAST: *October 4, 1955*
LAST TELECAST: *June 19, 1956*

BROADCAST HISTORY:
Oct 1955–Jun 1956, NBC Tue 9:30–10:30

During the 1955–1956 season *Pontiac Presents Playwrights 56* aired live plays on alternate Tuesdays with *Armstrong Circle Theatre.* The plays in this series were all adapted from the works of such famous writers as Irwin Shaw, Ernest Hemingway, and F. Scott Fitzgerald, and were somewhat more traditional in form than the documentary-dramas presented on *Armstrong Circle Theatre.*

POP! GOES THE COUNTRY
Music
BROADCAST HISTORY:
Syndicated only
30 minutes
Produced: *1974–1982* (234 episodes)
Released: *1974*
HOST:
Ralph Emery (1974–1980)
Tom T. Hall (1980–1982)
Jim Varney (1982)

One of the more widely circulated country music programs was *Pop! Goes the Country,* taped at the shrine of country music, Opryland U.S.A. in Nashville. It featured all the old Opry favorites—Ray Price, Loretta Lynn, Tammy Wynette and George Jones, Johnny Paycheck, Dolly Parton, Merle Haggard, Hank Williams, Jr., *et al.*

The original host was Ralph Emery, succeeded in 1980 by Tom T. Hall (the "Old Storyteller"). Rubber-faced comedian Jim Varney joined as a regular for the final season. Also in 1982 the setting was changed from a studio to Opryland's Gaslight Theatre, to give the show a more intimate "club" look, and the series' title was changed to *Tom T.'s Pop! Goes the Country Club.*

POPCORN KID, THE
Situation Comedy
FIRST TELECAST: *March 23, 1987*
LAST TELECAST: *April 24, 1987*
BROADCAST HISTORY:
Mar 1987, CBS Mon 8:30–9:00
Mar 1987–Apr 1987, CBS Fri 8:30–9:00
CAST:
Scott Creasman................ Bruce Norris
Leonard Brown .... Raye Birk
Willie Dawson .... Jeffrey Joseph
Gwen Stottlemeyer .... Penelope Ann Miller
Marlin Bond......... John Christopher Jones
Lynn Holly Brickhouse .... Faith Ford

The venerable old Majestic movie house, a revival theater in Kansas City, was the setting for this comedy about teenagers. It was the Majestic's policy to hire local high school kids to man the concession stand, and they were a motley group. Scott loved movies and dreamt of becoming a star himself someday; Willie wanted people to see him as more than just a great athlete; Gwen was the "intellectual," a good student who had a secret crush on Scott; and Lynn Holly was the stereotypical dumb bombshell whose beauty was a turn-on for Scott, despite the fact that he was too shy to ask her out. Marlin was the Majestic's spaced-out projectionist and Leonard its married manager who had no kids of his own—which suited him just fine.

POPI
Situation Comedy
FIRST TELECAST: *January 20, 1976*
LAST TELECAST: *August 24, 1976*
BROADCAST HISTORY:
   Jan 1976–Feb 1976, CBS Tue 8:30–9:00
   Jul 1976–Aug 1976, CBS Tue 8:00–8:30
CAST:
   Abraham Rodriguez......... Hector Elizondo
   Lupe .... Edith Diaz
   Junior Rodriguez .... Anthony Perez
   Luis Rodriguez .... Dennis Vasquez
   Maggio .... Lou Criscuolo

Abraham Rodriguez was a poor Puerto Rican immigrant who held three part-time jobs to make enough money to support his family. A widower with two young sons, he lived in a small apartment. One of his neighbors in the building was Lupe, the woman he was dating. Life in New York City was not easy for him, but he managed somehow to survive and maintain his self-respect and dignity. The first five episodes of this series aired early in 1976 but did so poorly that the show was canceled. During the following summer the remaining original episodes were aired, along with a few reruns.

POPSICLE PARADE OF STARS, THE
Variety
FIRST TELECAST: *May 15, 1950*
LAST TELECAST: *July 17, 1950*
BROADCAST HISTORY:
   May 1950–Jul 1950, CBS Mon 7:45–8:00

A different guest star appeared every week on this short-lived, 15-minute variety show sponsored by the Popsicle company. Each star performed his own specialty, whether it was singing, dancing, playing an instrument, or doing comedy sketches, aiming his material at both adults and children—both, hopefully, being consumers of the sponsor's product.

PORTRAIT
Interview
FIRST TELECAST: *August 9, 1963*
LAST TELECAST: *September 6, 1963*
BROADCAST HISTORY:
   Aug 1963–Sep 1963, CBS Fri 10:30–11:00
HOST:
   Charles Collingwood

Host Charles Collingwood interviewed guests from many walks of life in this series, including comedian Peter Sellers, commentator H. V. Kaltenborn, General Curtis E. LeMay, Oregon Governor Mark Hatfield, and actor Jimmy Stewart. The program was first seen in February 1963, and continued irregularly until the end of September. For five weeks during August and September, however, it was seen as a regular weekly feature.

PORTRAIT OF AMERICA
Interview
FIRST TELECAST: *December 8, 1949*
LAST TELECAST: *December 29, 1949*
BROADCAST HISTORY:
   Dec 1949, NBC Thu 8:00–8:30
HOST:
   Norman Barry

Four-week documentary series in which NBC's cameras visited a different "typical American family" at home each week.

POST FIGHT BEAT
   see *Fight Beat*

POWER OF WOMEN, THE
Discussion
FIRST TELECAST: *July 1, 1952*
LAST TELECAST: *November 11, 1952*
BROADCAST HISTORY:
   Jul 1952–Nov 1952, DUM Tue 8:00–8:30
   Sep 1952–Oct 1952, DUM Mon 8:00–8:30
HOSTESS:
   Vivien Kellems
   Mrs. John G. Lee

Discussion of politics and social problems from the woman's point of view, by Vivien Kellems, president of the Liberty Belles. Sometimes guests appeared, sometimes it was a one-woman show. In October Mrs. John G. Lee, president of the League of Women Voters, took over as moderator. The final telecast, on the week after the 1952 Presidential election, the topic was "Who Cares?"

POWERS OF MATTHEW STAR, THE
Science Fiction
FIRST TELECAST: *September 17, 1982*
LAST TELECAST: *September 11, 1983*
BROADCAST HISTORY:
   Sep 1982–Aug 1983, NBC Fri 8:00–9:00
   Aug 1983–Sep 1983, NBC Sun 7:00–8:00
CAST:
   Matthew Starr................. Peter Barton
   Walt Shephard .... Louis Gossett, Jr.
   Pam Elliott (1982)................ Amy Steel
   Bob Alexander (1982) .... Chip Frye
   Major Wymore (1983) .... James Karen

He may have looked just like any other student at Crestridge High, but he was not what he appeared to be. Matthew Star was actually a crown prince from the planet Quadris who, when his father was overthrown by tyrants, had been sent to Earth to allow his powers of telepathy and telekinesis to develop. Eventually, when he was ready, Matthew would return to fight the oppressors. In the meantime, he and his guardian, Walt Shephard, were forced to hide from their Quadrian foes, who might appear at any time in human, robot, or other form.

Despite the danger, Matthew tried to lead a normal life as a student. He excelled at sports and even had a cute girlfriend named Pam and friend named Bob. Walt was a science teacher and football coach at Crestridge and posed as Matthew's legal guardian. By midseason Matthew's powers were expanding—he had added astral projection (sending part of himself to another place, while his body did not move) and transmutation to his repertoire—and his activities were no longer based at the school. He now utilized his powers to help the government fight espionage and other crimes, on assignments from Maj. Wymore.

The Powers of Matthew Star was originally scheduled to premiere in the fall of 1981. It was delayed for a season when star Peter Barton was seriously burned during the filming of one of the early episodes.

PRACTICE, THE
  Situation Comedy
FIRST TELECAST: *January 30, 1976*
LAST TELECAST: *January 26, 1977*
BROADCAST HISTORY:
  Jan 1976–Jul 1976, NBC Fri 8:30–9:00
  Oct 1976–Nov 1976, NBC Wed 8:00–8:30
  Dec 1976–Jan 1977, NBC Wed 9:30–10:00
CAST:
  Dr. Jules Bedford .... Danny Thomas
  Molly Gibbons .... Dena Dietrich
  Jenny Bedford .... Shelley Fabares
  Dr. David Bedford .... David Spielberg
  Helen .... Didi Conn
  Paul Bedford .... Allen Price
  Tony Bedford................ Damon Raskin
  Dr. Roland Caine .... John Byner
  Nate .... Sam Laws
  Lenny........................ Mike Evans

There were two doctors in the Bedford family, but they had radically different approaches to the practice of medicine. The elder Bedford, Jules, was really from the old school. He was a little absentminded, could be grouchy and preoccupied, but was a warm, concerned individual with a love of people and a willingness to help, whether or not there was money to be made. Jules' office was on Manhattan's middle-class West Side. His nurse, Molly, had been with him for years and had an obvious crush on the widowed doctor; the outer office was "run" by a young, slightly daft receptionist named Helen. Son David Bedford, on the other hand, had set up practice on exclusive Park Avenue, was making money hand

over fist, and was always after his dad to move in and share office space with him. Completing the cast were David's wife, Jenny, and his two young boys.

PRACTICE TEE
  Golf Lesson
FIRST TELECAST: *August 5, 1949*
LAST TELECAST: *September 9, 1949*
BROADCAST HISTORY:
  Aug 1949–Sep 1949, NBC Fri 7:30–7:45
HOST:
  William P. Barbour

Fifteen-minute golf lesson, notable mostly for being the first regular network TV series to originate from Cleveland. Host William P. Barbour served as golf pro.

PREMIERE
  Dramatic Anthology
FIRST TELECAST: *July 1, 1968*
LAST TELECAST: *September 9, 1968*
BROADCAST HISTORY:
  Jul 1968–Sep 1968, CBS Mon 10:00–11:00

The full-hour dramas that were aired in this summer replacement for *The Carol Burnett Show* were all pilots for dramatic series that had not been bought by any of the networks. Among the stars who did not make it, this time around, were Burt Reynolds in "Lassiter," Carl Betz and Susan Strasberg in "Crisis," and Sally Kellerman and John McMartin in "Higher and Higher." "Call to Danger," made some years earlier as the pilot film for *Mission: Impossible*, was also included.

PREMIERE PLAYHOUSE
  see *Movies-Prior to 1961*

PRESENTING SUSAN ANTON
  Musical Variety
FIRST TELECAST: *April 26, 1979*
LAST TELECAST: *May 17, 1979*
BROADCAST HISTORY:
  Apr 1979–May 1979, NBC Thu 10:00–11:00
REGULARS:
  Susan Anton
  Jack Fletcher (as *Robert Tibidas*)
  Jack Knight
  Dick Wilson
  Terry McGovern (as *Bruce Larson*)
  The Walter Painter Dancers
  Jimmy Martinez
  Buddy Powell
  Donovan Scott

This limited-run variety series starred statuesque singer-dancer Susan Anton, who had first achieved notice as the successor to Edie Adams doing commercials for Muriel Cigars. There was an even mix of comedy and musical numbers, with a recurring sketch about the Disco Monks

(Martinez, Powell, and Scott), three religious men attempting to modernize their order to make it more appealing to contemporary men. In the first episode they decided to offer two alternatives to the vow of silence—the vow of backgammon or the vow of jogging. Guest stars appeared with Miss Anton and her regulars on each telecast.

PRESIDENT EISENHOWER'S NEWS CONFERENCE
News
FIRST TELECAST: *February 2, 1955*
LAST TELECAST: *September 11, 1955*
BROADCAST HISTORY:
   Feb 1955–May 1955, ABC Wed 10:00–10:30
   Feb 1955–Sep 1955, ABC Sun 8:30–9:00

Coverage of President Eisenhower's weekly news conferences was provided by ABC during most of 1955. On weeks when there was no news conference a half-hour filmed drama was presented. From the latter part of February through the end of May these filmed news conferences were offered on both Wednesdays and Sundays, after which they were telecast on Sundays only.

PRESIDENTIAL COUNTDOWN
Political
FIRST TELECAST: *September 12, 1960*
LAST TELECAST: *October 31, 1960*
BROADCAST HISTORY:
   Sep 1960–Oct 1960, CBS Mon 10:30–11:00
ANCHORMAN:
   Walter Cronkite

As the 1960 Presidential campaign moved toward its conclusion, CBS aired a weekly summary program that covered candidates Nixon and Kennedy. Results of CBS News polls on the mood of the voters in various parts of the country were also part of the show. Walter Cronkite anchored the series with regular contributions from other CBS News correspondents. On Friday, November 4, a final telecast was aired in which the contributing reporters summed up what they had seen and felt throughout the campaign.

PRESIDENTIAL STRAWS IN THE WIND
Political
FIRST TELECAST: *August 24, 1948*
LAST TELECAST: *October 5, 1948*
BROADCAST HISTORY:
   Aug 1948–Oct 1948, CBS Tue 9:30–10:00
FEATURED:
   Elmo Roper
HOST:
   Lyman Bryson

Pollster Elmo Roper was the star of this pre-election series that broadcast the results of public-opinion polls his organization had taken on various issues, and on the popularity of the candidates themselves. Four members of the stu-

dio audience were brought on stage and asked the same questions that had been asked in the poll, so that viewers could see how the poll had been taken, and the results of the actual poll were then analyzed by Mr. Roper. The first telecast of this series had aired as a local program in New York on August 10, then it expanded to the full network for the four succeeding biweekly telecasts.

PRESIDENTIAL TIMBER
Public Affairs
FIRST TELECAST: *May 27, 1948*
LAST TELECAST: *June 20, 1952*
BROADCAST HISTORY:
   May 1948–Jul 1948, CBS Thu 9:00–9:30
   Apr 1952–Jun 1952, CBS Fri 10:30–11:00
MODERATOR:
   Robert Trout (1952)

Presidential Timber gave candidates for the nation's highest office, or their authorized representatives, the opportunity to present their platforms and programs to a nationwide television audience. This live program did not air each week, only when there was a candidate who wanted to speak. The series was patterned after the CBS radio program of the same name that had been aired during previous Presidential election years.

PRESS CONFERENCE
Interview
FIRST TELECAST: *July 4, 1956* ·
LAST TELECAST: *July 15, 1957*
BROADCAST HISTORY:
   Jul 1956–Sep 1956, NBC Wed 8:00–8:30
   Oct 1956–Dec 1956, ABC Sun 8:30–9:00
   Apr 1957–Jul 1957, ABC Mon 9:00–9:30
MODERATOR:
   Martha Rountree

In a format similar to that of *Meet the Press,* this series brought people in the news, generally the political news, to a weekly news conference. Some of them made opening statements and others simply began by asking for the first question. Martha Rountree was the moderator and called on various members of the press for questions. At the end of each program, she summed up the key points for the viewing audience. The series moved from NBC to ABC in the fall of 1956, moved from prime time to Sunday afternoons for three months at the beginning of 1957, and returned to prime time in April with the title changed to *Martha Rountree's Press Conference.*

PRESS CORRESPONDENTS PANEL
Discussion
FIRST TELECAST: *April 10, 1949*
LAST TELECAST: *May 22, 1949*
BROADCAST HISTORY:
   Apr 1949, CBS Sun 6:30–7:00
   Apr 1949–May 1949, CBS Sun 6:00–6:30

This live weekly program gave news correspondents an opportunity to discuss the events of the week in a round-table discussion fashion.

PREVIEW TONIGHT
Dramatic Anthology
FIRST TELECAST: *August 14, 1966*
LAST TELECAST: *September 11, 1966*
BROADCAST HISTORY:
Aug 1966–Sep 1966, ABC Sun 8:00–9:00

This was a collection of unsold pilots for proposed series which never made the network's schedule. It was, in other words, a "preview" of series which never happened. Perhaps the most unusual was *Great Bible Adventures*, starring Hugh O'Brian as Joseph leading the Jews in Egypt.

PRICE IS RIGHT, THE
Quiz/Audience Participation
FIRST TELECAST: *September 23, 1957*
LAST TELECAST: *September 18, 1986*
BROADCAST HISTORY:
Sep 1957–Jun 1958, NBC Mon 7:30–8:00
Jun 1958–Sep 1958, NBC Thu 10:00–10:30
Sep 1958–Sep 1961, NBC Wed 8:30–9:00
Sep 1961–Sep 1962, NBC Mon 8:30–9:00
Sep 1962–Jan 1963, NBC Mon 9:30–10:00
Feb 1963–Sep 1963, NBC Fri 9:30–10:00
Sep 1963–Nov 1963, ABC Wed 8:30–9:00
Dec 1963–Sep 1964, ABC Fri 9:30–10:00
Aug 1986–Sep 1986, CBS Thu 8:00–9:00
EMCEE:
Bill Cullen (1957–1964)
Bob Barker (1986)
PRODUCERS:
Mark Goodson and Bill Todman

Four contestants competed with each other on *The Price Is Right.* They tried to guess the retail price of merchandise prizes, which were displayed by two beautiful models. The contestant who came closest to the retail price, without going over it, won the merchandise. Most prizes were open to continuously rising price guesses until either the contestants decided to stop, or an undefined time limit forced them to make final bids. If a contestant wanted to hold at a final bid, he could "freeze" at that level and wait until the bidding was over to see if he had won. An added attraction was a home-viewer game in which TV watchers sent in their to-the-nearest-penny price estimates for a group of prizes, which they might then win.

The Price Is Right also ran in daytime on NBC from November 1956 until September 1965. It returned to daytime in the fall of 1972 with a modified format in which different kinds of pricing games were employed. This new version, emceed by Bob Barker, has been a fixture on the CBS daytime lineup ever since. In addition, a syndicated version was produced from 1972 to 1979, with Dennis James serving as emcee until 1976

and Bob Barker taking the reins for the last three seasons. A new syndicated version aired during the 1985–1986 season, emceed by Tom Kennedy. At the end of that season *The Price Is Right* was given a brief prime-time run on CBS, with daytime host Barker doing double duty.

PRIDE OF THE FAMILY, THE
Situation Comedy
FIRST TELECAST: *October 2, 1953*
LAST TELECAST: *July 10, 1955*
BROADCAST HISTORY:
Oct 1953–Sep 1954, ABC Fri 9:00–9:30
Jun 1955–Jul 1955, CBS Sun 7:00–7:30
CAST:
Albie Morrison .... Paul Hartman
Catherine Morrison .... Fay Wray
Ann Morrison .... Natalie Wood
Junior Morrison................ Bobby Hyatt

Albie Morrison worked in the advertising department of the newspaper in the small town in which he lived. He was married and had two teenage children, Ann and Junior. Despite the best of intentions, Albie somehow managed to ruin almost everything he tried to do, whether it was something industrious at the office or an attempt to prove how handy he was around the house. His wife still loved him and, except for the occasions when they resented his attempts to prevent them from being as independent as they would have liked, so did his children. Reruns of this filmed ABC series were aired on CBS for a short time during the summer of 1955.

PRIME TIME SUNDAY
News Magazine
FIRST TELECAST: *June 24, 1979*
LAST TELECAST: *July 5, 1980*
BROADCAST HISTORY:
Jun 1979–Dec 1979, NBC Sun 10:00–11:00
Dec 1979–Jul 1980, NBC Sat 10:00–11:00
REGULARS:
Tom Snyder
Jack Perkins
Jessica Savitch
Bob Dotson
John Dancy (1980)
Chris Wallace
Sandy Gilmour (1980)

Prime Time Sunday was another NBC attempt to produce a successful prime-time magazine series, replacing the departed *Weekend*. Unlike *Weekend*, which had a somewhat irreverent approach to its subject matter (see separate listing), *Prime Time* was a more traditional, hard-hitting news program. Tom Snyder, the sometimes abrasive anchorman, was seen in a control-room atmosphere, with the technical aspects of the show visible to viewers to heighten the sense of immediacy. Each telecast opened with the director counting down to the program start and cueing

tmeirion—a favorite retreat of such writers as
trand Russell, George Bernard Shaw, Noel
ward . . . and Patrick McGoohan. The series
s rerun during the summer of 1969.

RIVATE BENJAMIN
Situation Comedy
RST TELECAST: *April 6, 1981*
AST TELECAST: *September 5, 1983*
ROADCAST HISTORY:
  Apr 1981, CBS Mon 8:00–8:30
  Oct 1981–Jan 1982, CBS Mon 8:00–8:30
  Jan 1982–Mar 1982, CBS Mon 8:30–9:00
  Apr 1982–Sep 1982, CBS Mon 8:00–8:30
  Sep 1982–Jan 1983, CBS Mon 8:30–9:00
  May 1983–Sep 1983, CBS Mon 8:30–9:00
CAST:
  Pvt. Judy Benjamin . . . . Lorna Patterson
  Capt. Doreen Lewis . . . . Eileen Brennan
  Sgt. Major Lucien C. (Ted) Ross
  . . . . Hal Williams
  Pvt. Carol Winter (1981–1982) . . Ann Ryerson
  Pvt. Barbara Ann Glass (1981) . . Joan Roberts
  Pvt. Rayleen White (1981) . . . . Joyce Little
  Pvt. Maria Gianelli . . . . Lisa Raggio
  Pvt. Luanne Hubble (1981–1982) . . Lucy Webb
  Pvt. Harriet Dorsey (1981)
  . . . . Francesca Roberts
  Pvt. Jackie Sims (1981–1983)
  . . . . Damita Jo Freeman
  Col. Lawrence Fielding (1982–1983)
  . . . . Robert Mandan
  Lt. Billy Dean (1982) . . . . Joel Brooks
  Pvt. Stacy Kouchalakas (1982–1983)
  . . . . Wendie Jo Sperber

Practically every major movie hit seems to spawn
TV imitations—either directly or in disguise—and
Goldie Hawn's box office smash *Private Benjamin* was no exception. Goldie wasn't available
for the TV counterpart, so a little-known actress
named Lorna Patterson (previously of *Working
Stiffs* and *Goodtime Girls*) assumed the role of
the spoiled New York socialite who decided to
tackle the U.S. Army. Trading in her designer
clothes for olive drab, and giving up haute cuisine
for such delicacies as chipped beef on toast, Judy
found it difficult to adapt to life in "Today's Modern Army." Yet here she was, at Fort Bradley,
outside Biloxi, Mississippi, determined to make it
through basic training. The unfortunate task of
rying to mold Judy into a soldier fell to her frus-
rated company commander, Capt. Doreen Lewis.
ellow recruits included street-wise Maria Gia-
elli, who chose the army as an alternative to jail;
ayleen White, a bright, ambitious child of the
etroit ghettos; Barbara Ann Glass, a hayseed
no often felt compelled to sing obscure country
gs; and Carol Winter, a brown-nosing, obnox-
s brat. Sgt. Ted Ross was their no-nonsense
l instructor.
ol. Fielding, the base commander, an unctu-

ous, publicity-hungry officer of marginal compe-
tence, became a regular early in 1982. Capt. Lewis
was promoted to Fort Bradley's public affairs officer, and Judy ended up working for her. Amazingly, Pvt. Gianelli became an MP.

Eileen Brennan and Hal Williams re-created
their movie roles for this series. Brennan was seriously hurt in October 1982 when she was struck
by a car, and Polly Holliday was added to the
show's cast as a temporary replacement. She only
appeared in a single episode before *Private Benjamin* was canceled.

PRIVATE EYE
Detective
FIRST TELECAST: *September 13, 1987*
LAST TELECAST: *January 8, 1988*
BROADCAST HISTORY:
  Sep 1987, NBC Sun 9:15–11:15
  Sep 1987–Jan 1988, NBC Fri 10:00–11:00
CAST:
  Jack Cleary . . . . Michael Woods
  Johnny Betts . . . . Josh Brolin
  Lt. Charlie Fontana . . . . Bill Sadler
  Dottie Dworski . . . . Lisa Jane Persky

Having successfully launched one stylish crime
series set in the '80s *(Miami Vice)*, and another in
the '60s *(Crime Story)*, NBC tried the '50s with this
rather violent show. There was lots of period atmosphere: chrome-laden cars, primeval rock 'n'
roll, ducktail haircuts, and everybody dragging on
cigarettes. Jack Cleary was a moody, scruffy ex-
cop, wrongfully busted from the Los Angeles police force, who inherited his brother's detective
agency upon the latter's violent demise. Although
he was later cleared and offered his badge back,
he declined, preferring the fast life of a private
eye. Johnny Betts was a greasy-haired, leather-
jacketed rock 'n' roller who helped out with such
necessities of the trade as hot-wiring cars and
squealing on the younger generation. Fontana
was Cleary's former police partner and contact,
and Dottie his gum-cracking secretary.

PRIVATE SECRETARY
Situation Comedy
FIRST TELECAST: *February 1, 1953*
LAST TELECAST: *September 10, 1957*
BROADCAST HISTORY:
  Feb 1953–Jun 1953, CBS Sun 7:30–8:00
  Jun 1953–Sep 1953, NBC Sat 10:30–11:00
  Sep 1953–Jun 1954, CBS Sun 7:30–8:00
  Jun 1954–Sep 1954, NBC Sat 10:30–11:00
  Sep 1954–Mar 1957, CBS Sun 7:30–8:00
  Apr 1957–Sep 1957, CBS Tue 8:30–9:00
CAST:
  Susie McNamera . . . . Ann Sothern
  Peter Sands . . . . Don Porter
  Vi Praskins . . . . Ann Tyrrell
  Cagey Calhoun . . . . Jesse White
  Sylvia . . . . Joan Banks

Snyder, and closed with a shot of a technician pulling the switch that faded the picture to black.

Each episode of *Prime Time Sunday* contained at least three feature stories, usually narrated by field reporters Jack Perkins and Chris Wallace (son of *60 Minutes'* Mike Wallace). Perkins' stories tended to be human interest and whimsical (profiles of commercial creators Dick Orkin and Bert Berdis, of former cowboy star and current owner of the California Angels baseball team Gene Autry, and of three rodeo cowboys; a piece on a Swedish law making it illegal to spank kids), while Wallace did investigative reporting (on parole-board policies, legal clinics that advertise, and safety problems with commuter airlines). There were also live in-studio panel discussions and updates on breaking news stories. Jessica Savitch became a frequent reporter in the fall of 1979, as did Bob Dotson. Chris Wallace left early in 1980 to be replaced by John Dancy and Sandy Gilmour. The title of the program was changed to *Prime Time Saturday* in December 1979.

PRIMUS
Adventure
BROADCAST HISTORY:
Syndicated only
30 minutes
Produced: *1971* (26 episodes)
Released: *Fall 1971*
CAST:
Carter Primus . . . . Robert Brown
Charlie Kingman . . . . Will Kuluva
Toni Hayden . . . . Eva Renzi
PRODUCER:
Ivan Tors

Producer Ivan Tors *(Sea Hunt, Flipper)* tried to revive the underwater-adventure genre with this 1971 syndicated series. Carter Primus was a global underwater troubleshooter, like *Sea Hunt's* Mike Nelson, but he had a lot more gadgets—an underwater robot called Big Kate, a little exploration and photography sub called *Pegasus,* and a nifty little runabout sea sled. He also had a crusty, bewhiskered sidekick named Charlie, and a pretty assistant, Toni. Unfortunately the plots and acting were strictly kid stuff, and the show, though widely carried at first, lasted for only 26 episodes.

PRINCESS SAGAPHI
Travelogue
FIRST TELECAST: *September 6, 1948*
LAST TELECAST: *January 7, 1949*
BROADCAST HISTORY:
Sep 1948, NBC Mon 8:00–8:15
Sep 1948–Dec 1948, NBC Thu 8:00–8:15
Dec 1948–Jan 1949, NBC Mon 8:45–9:00
HOSTESS:
Princess Annette Sagaphi

Princess Sagaphi, an authority on the Far East, narrated these travelogue films of faraway places.

PRISONER, THE
Mystery/Adventure
FIRST TELECAST: *June 1, 1968*
LAST TELECAST: *September 11, 1969*
BROADCAST HISTORY:
Jun 1968–Sep 1968, CBS Sat 7:30–8:3(
May 1969–Sep 1969, CBS Thu 8:00–9:
CAST:
The Prisoner (Number 6) . Patrick M
The Butler . . . . Angelo

The Prisoner was one of the most original seen on U.S. television. Perhaps it was to nal, for it lasted for only two summers. Film England, it was the story of a government who abruptly resigned his position, only to b ducted and imprisoned in a strange, Kafkae community. His mind held top-secret informa which somebody obviously wanted—but who was he simply being tested? His captors were dom seen, and when they were, their faces we always different. The village itself was a beauti little hamlet, set on a hilly peninsula, ringed mountains, forest, and the sea. But there was leaving. Anyone who got close to the perimete was set upon by strange, glowing spheres ("rov ers") that floated overhead and kept an eye on everyone in the village.

The inhabitants were enigmas too. Some, like the hero (who was known only as "Number 6"), were prisoners, resisting the brainwashing attempts of their captors. Others had already been brainwashed of their secrets and were condemned to spend the rest of their days in the comfortable and peaceful, but eerie, village. Others might be spies. Which was which? Standing alone in a clearing was the Castle, used both as a hospital and interrogation center by the mysterious "Number 1" and his chief agent (played by different actors in different episodes, but invariably designated "Number 2").

Number 6, though he could not escape, outwitted his captors at every turn. Finally, in the las episode, they not only admitted defeat but mad an astonishing offer: they wanted him to be the leader. Skeptical, he was at last led into the Cas to meet Number 1—and into a trap. With his a the silent Butler (the only other regular in the ries), and two other rebels, he managed to es as the Castle and its inhabitants and their m rious world were destroyed.

The Prisoner was created and produced star, Patrick McGoohan, who also wrot episodes. Although it was not explicitly the series was widely believed to be a McGoohan's earlier show *Secret Agent,* he played a character named Drake. (N *oner* fans believe that the hero here w addressed in one episode as "Drake' others argue that what was said is " resume during the morning . . . *brea* turesque "village" used in the filmin a resort on Cardigan Bay in North

Susie McNamera was private secretary to Peter Sands, a very successful New York talent agent. She was attractive, efficient, and conscientious, but she also had one serious failing. Susie couldn't tell when her responsibilities to her boss ended, and, as a result, kept getting mixed up in his personal life. Her efforts to help him with personal problems usually led to confusion and misunderstanding, despite their good intent. Vi Praskins, the agency's receptionist/switchboard operator, was Susie's friend, as was Sylvia, although the latter was often vying with Susie for the affections of a particularly attractive man. Peter's chief competition in the talent business was fast-talking, loudmouthed, cigar-smoking Cagey Calhoun.

The CBS episodes aired during the winter season were rerun by NBC during the summers of 1953 and 1954. During the winter seasons from the fall of 1954 through the spring of 1957, *Private Secretary* aired on alternate Sundays with *The Jack Benny Show.* While Benny was on vacation during the summers, *Private Secretary* played every week.

PRIZE PERFORMANCE
Talent Variety
FIRST TELECAST: *July 3, 1950*
LAST TELECAST: *September 12, 1950*
BROADCAST HISTORY:
    Jul 1950–Aug 1950, CBS Mon 8:30–9:00
    Aug 1950–Sep 1950, CBS Tue 10:00–10:30
HOST:
    Cedric Adams
PANELISTS:
    Arlene Francis
    Peter Donald

Each week four professional child entertainers competed on this live talent show. Arlene Francis and Peter Donald were the judges, evaluating the talent and picking the week's winner. Every five weeks a grand prize of a $500 scholarship was awarded after a special competition among the weekly winners from the four preceding weeks.

PRO FOOTBALL HIGHLIGHTS
    see *New York Giants Quarterback Huddle*

PROBE
Mystery
FIRST TELECAST: *March 7, 1988*
LAST TELECAST: *June 29, 1988*
BROADCAST HISTORY:
    Mar 1988, ABC Mon 9:00–11:00
    Mar 1988–May 1988, ABC Thu 8:00–9:00
    June 1988, ABC Sat 8:00–9:00
CAST:
    Austin James . . . . Parker Stevenson
    Mickey Castle . . . . Ashley Crow

Famed science-fiction writer Isaac Asimov co-created this literate series. Austin James was a brilliant young scientist who operated out of a warehouse laboratory nicknamed the "batcave"; his secretary and helper was the ever-amazed Mickey. With cocky self-confidence, the ability to analyze physical clues in his high-tech lab, and deductive reasoning worthy of Sherlock Holmes, Austin managed to unravel crimes perpetrated by the world's most clever criminals.

The most distinctive aspect of this series was the plots, all based on scientific principles—a computer whose artificial intelligence program had run amok, a murder plot utilizing genetic engineering, a super-intelligent ape accused of murder (in an episode titled "Metamorphic Anthropoidic Prototype Over You"). The police simply shook their heads and arrested whomever Austin fingered.

The series was created by Asimov and former *Hill Street Blues* story editor Michael Wagner.

PRODUCER'S CHOICE
Dramatic Anthology
FIRST TELECAST: *March 31, 1960*
LAST TELECAST: *September 15, 1960*
BROADCAST HISTORY:
    Mar 1960–Sep 1960, NBC Thu 8:30–9:00

The filmed dramas shown on this summer series consisted of reruns of former episodes of *G.E. Theatre, Lux Playhouse, Schlitz Playhouse,* and *Lux Video Theatre.*

PRODUCERS' SHOWCASE
Anthology
FIRST TELECAST: *October 18, 1954*
LAST TELECAST: *May 27, 1957*
BROADCAST HISTORY:
    Oct 1954–May 1957, NBC Mon 8:00–9:30

Live 90-minute productions were aired under this title every fourth Monday on NBC for three seasons. The productions were lavish and included many memorable performances by top stars. *Peter Pan* was presented on this series on March 7, 1955, with Mary Martin and Cyril Ritchard in the lead roles. So popular was this family show that it was repeated live on the same series less than a year later (January 9, 1956), with Miss Martin and Ritchard repeating their roles. Humphrey Bogart and Lauren Bacall made their TV dramatic debuts in an adaptation of *The Petrified Forest,* which also starred Henry Fonda. Bogie's role was the same one that had propelled him to stardom on Broadway more than twenty years previously, and one that he had played on the silver screen as well.

Thornton Wilder's *Our Town* had been adapted for television on *Robert Montgomery Presents* in 1950, but the musical version of the play that aired on *Producer's Showcase* in 1955 is the best-remembered TV version of this classic. It starred Paul Newman and Eva Marie Saint, with Frank

Sinatra (as the stage manager) singing most of the songs, including "Love and Marriage," which became a major hit record for him.

The range of material was vast. Margot Fonteyn and Michael Somes starred in two ballets, *Sleeping Beauty* and *Cinderella. Romeo and Juliet* was presented with Claire Bloom, Paul Rogers, and John Neville heading the cast. Fredric March, Claire Trevor, and Geraldine Fitzgerald starred in an adaptation of *Dodsworth.* The most unusual telecast in the series, because of its contrast to the general tone of the show, was probably the premiere of *Wide Wide World.* The conceptualization of dynamic NBC President Pat Weaver, *Wide Wide World* sought to take full advantage of the technical marvel of live television. Hosted by Dave Garroway, who would remain with it during its run as a late Sunday afternoon series during the latter half of the 1950s, this premiere telecast of *Wide Wide World* enabled the audience to see live entertainment from three countries—the United States, Canada, and Mexico—on the same show, the first inter-American telecast in the history of television.

PRODUCTION FOR FREEDOM
Documentary
FIRST TELECAST: *June 22, 1952*
LAST TELECAST: *September 21, 1952*
BROADCAST HISTORY:
 Jun 1952–Jul 1952, ABC Sun 9:30–10:00
 Jul 1952–Sep 1952, ABC Sun 10:30–11:00

Documentary films about leading power companies and industries of America.

PROFESSIONAL FATHER
Situation Comedy
FIRST TELECAST: *January 8, 1955*
LAST TELECAST: *July 2, 1955*
BROADCAST HISTORY:
 Jan 1955–Jul 1955, CBS Sat 10:00–10:30
CAST:
 Thomas Wilson, M.D. . . . . Steve Dunne
 Helen Wilson . . . . Barbara Billingsley
 Thomas (Twig) Wilson, Jr. . . . . Ted Marc
 Kathryn (Kit) Wilson . . . . Beverly Washburn
 Nurse Madge Allen . . . . Phyllis Coates
 Nana . . . . Ann O'Neal

Tom Wilson was a highly successful child psychologist. At the office he spoke with the wisdom ˅ of Solomon as he resolved family problems that were causing aggravation and suffering to the many parents who sought his services. At home, however, it was a completely different story. All the good judgment and analytical skills that had made him so proficient at his profession deserted him when he tried to cope with his own family.

PROFILES IN COURAGE
Biography
FIRST TELECAST: *November 8, 1964*

LAST TELECAST: *May 9, 1965*
BROADCAST HISTORY:
 Nov 1964–May 1965, NBC Sun 6:30–7:30

This program marked the first time that a President of the United States was directly involved in the production of a television dramatic series. John F. Kennedy's Pulitzer Prize–winning book *Profiles in Courage* was first adapted for TV in 1956, in a special based on the chapter concerning the senator who cast the deciding vote against the impeachment of President Andrew Johnson. Kennedy, then a U.S. Senator, served as a consultant for the broadcast. Eight years later, after Kennedy's death, this anthology series dramatized additional chapters from the book, as well as the stories of other Americans who had also displayed extraordinary personal courage. Prior to his death, President Kennedy himself had stipulated that more biographies be added to those in his book so that the scope of the series would be broader than politics. He had approved of all the additions and read all of the scripts to make sure that they conformed to the Kennedy definition of a "Profile in Courage."

PROGRAM PLAYHOUSE
Various
FIRST TELECAST: *June 22, 1949*
LAST TELECAST: *September 14, 1949*
BROADCAST HISTORY:
 Jun 1949–Sep 1949, DUM Wed 9:00–9:30

This was a series of tryouts for potential series on the DuMont network. At least one of them, *The Hands of Murder,* later became reasonably successful as an independent series. Among the others were "Trouble, Inc." starring Earl Hammond as an amateur private eye, Ernest Truex in a live comedy called "The Timid Soul," and Roscoe Karns in his first TV effort (before *Rocky King*), playing comedy in "Roscoe Karns and Inky Poo." This family comedy had Karns being followed around by his conscience, dressed in a clown suit and called "Inky Poo."

PROJECT: ADVENTURE
syndicated title for *Adventure Theater*

PROJECT U.F.O.
Drama
FIRST TELECAST: *February 19, 1978*
LAST TELECAST: *August 30, 1979*
BROADCAST HISTORY:
 Feb 1978–Sep 1978, NBC Sun 8:00–9:00
 Sep 1978–Jan 1979, NBC Thu 8:00–9:00
 Jul 1979–Aug 1979, NBC Thu 8:00–9:00
CAST:
 Maj. Jake Gatlin (1978) . . . . . . William Jordan
 Capt. Ben Ryan . . . . Edward Winter
 Staff Sgt. Harry Fitz . . . . Caskey Swaim
 Libby Virdon . . . . Aldine King

EXECUTIVE PRODUCER:
 Jack Webb
PRODUCER:
 Col. William T. Coleman

Jack Webb applied his highly successful drama-documentary technique to the unlikely subject of unidentified flying objects (i.e., flying saucers) in this 1978 series. To prepare the series Webb spent eight months poring over the files of the real-life U.S. Air Force investigation into U.F.O.'s, Project Blue Book, which had been disbanded in 1969. Many of the sightings had turned out to be mistaken or simply fraudulent, but about 30 percent remained unexplained—and it was those that Webb dramatized in this series.

Regulars were Maj. Jake Gatlin and S/Sgt. Harry Fitz, Project Blue Book's stolid investigators, who traveled around the country interviewing people who had reported seeing a U.F.O. Some of the stories verged on character studies of these people, but there was always a certain amount of hardware seen, including vivid re-creations of the flying saucers and spacemen that the people had claimed seeing. Offscreen narration reinforced the series' appearance of authenticity.

Maj. Gatlin was replaced in the fall of 1978 by Capt. Ben Ryan as Project Blue-book's chief. Libby was Gatlin's, and later Ryan's, secretary. Colonel William T. Coleman, who had headed the real-life Project Blue-Book, was producer of the series.

PROTECTORS, THE
Police Drama
FIRST TELECAST: *September 28, 1969*
LAST TELECAST: *September 6, 1970*
BROADCAST HISTORY:
 Sep 1969–Sep 1970, NBC Sun 10:00–11:00
CAST:
 Sam Danforth .... Leslie Nielsen
 William Washburn .... Hari Rhodes

Deputy Police Chief Sam Danforth and District Attorney William Washburn were both committed to enforcing the law, but approached that enforcement from very different positions. Chief Danforth followed the rules that had always worked in the past, though they were being sorely tested in the changing moral climate of a modern big city. D.A. Washburn, a black who had used his political savvy to reach his current post, dealt with issues on a more human basis, as objectively and honestly as he could. Each of these men believed that his way of handling situations was right, and they were often in conflict with each other. Each, in his own way, was a dedicated public servant attempting to protect the society he served.

The Protectors was one of three rotating elements that comprised *The Bold Ones* during the 1969–1970 season. The other two were *The New Doctors* and *The Lawyers*.

PROTECTORS, THE
Adventure
BROADCAST HISTORY:
 Syndicated only
 30 minutes
 Produced: *1972–1973* (52 episodes)
 Released: *Fall 1972*
CAST:
 Harry Rule .... Robert Vaughn
 Contessa di Contini ...... Nyree Dawn Porter
 Paul Buchet .... Tony Anholt

This stylish adventure series brought back *The Man From U.N.C.L.E.*'s Robert Vaughn in the not dissimilar role of Harry Rule, one of a three-person team of "protectors" fighting high-level crime in Europe. There was also a dash of *The Avengers* in the Contessa di Contini's high-fashion wardrobe, and of James Bond in the breakneck pace of the stories, which mostly involved murders, espionage, drug rings, and the like. Harry's fellow protectors were the Contessa, a British noblewoman and widow of a wealthy Italian, and Paul Buchet, a Frenchman.

Clipped dialogue, fancy cars, and picturesque European locales added to the *élan*, but star Robert Vaughn complained that it was all rather thin stuff and he would not do another show like it again. But then, he had said after *The Man From U.N.C.L.E.* that he would never do another TV series, period.

Filmed in Europe.

PRUDENTIAL FAMILY PLAYHOUSE, THE
Dramatic Anthology
FIRST TELECAST: *October 10, 1950*
LAST TELECAST: *March 27, 1951*
BROADCAST HISTORY:
 Oct 1950–Mar 1951, CBS Tue 8:00–9:00

This live hour-long dramatic presentation aired on alternate Tuesdays with *Sure as Fate*. The policy was to present top stars in outstanding dramas. Among the stars who appeared were Gertrude Lawrence, Ruth Chatterton, Helen Hayes, Walter Abel, Bert Lahr, and Grace Kelly.

PRUITTS OF SOUTHAMPTON, THE
Situation Comedy
FIRST TELECAST: *September 6, 1966*
LAST TELECAST: *September 1, 1967*
BROADCAST HISTORY:
 Sep 1966–Jan 1967, ABC Tue 9:00–9:30
 Jan 1967–Sep 1967, ABC Fri 9:30–10:00
CAST:
 Phyllis (Mrs. Poindexter) Pruitt
 .... Phyllis Diller
 Uncle Ned Pruitt .... Reginald Gardiner
 Stephanie Pruitt .... Pam Freeman
 Regina Wentworth .... Gypsy Rose Lee
 Maxwell .... Charles Lane
 Sturgis .... Grady Sutton
 Rudy Pruitt (1967) .... John Astin

Norman Krump (1967) .... Marty Ingels
Harvey (1967) .... Paul Lynde
Mr. Baldwin (1967).......... Richard Deacon
Vernon Bradley (1967) .... Billy DeWolfe

Phyllis Diller, whose trademarks were a fright wig and an uproarious cackle, was cast as the widowed matriarch of a down-on-their-luck Long Island society family in this frantic comedy. The Pruitts could live life to the hilt in their 60-room Southampton mansion, despite the fact that they were $10 million in debt to the government, so long as they kept the secret. Seems an unusually understanding I.R.S. would rather let them maintain the fiction that they were fabulously wealthy than risk a stock-market tumble with news of the Pruitts' bankruptcy. Phyllis spent most of her time on harebrained schemes to keep the family afloat, and keep the secret. Ned was her octogenarian uncle, Regina Wentworth her nosy neighbor and archrival, Sturgis the butler, and Stephanie her 22-year-old daughter.

In January 1967 the program title was changed to *The Phyllis Diller Show,* and the mansion became an elegant boardinghouse in an attempt to raise money to pay off the government. Neighborhood Mr. Fixit Norman Krump was a boarder, while Harvey was introduced as Phyllis' ne'er-do-well brother. Occasional roles were star boarder Vernon Bradley, an author; Mr. Baldwin of the I.R.S.; and assorted relatives played by such guest stars as Louis Nye.

Based on the novel *House Party* by Patrick Dennis.

PSYCHIATRIST, THE
Medical Drama
FIRST TELECAST: *February 3, 1971*
LAST TELECAST: *September 1, 1971*
BROADCAST HISTORY:
Feb 1971–Sep 1971, NBC Wed 10:00–11:00
CAST:
Dr. James Whitman .... Roy Thinnes
Dr. Bernard Altman .... Luther Adler

Jim Whitman was a young psychiatrist working in association with a Los Angeles–based institute. His use of modern techniques to help emotionally troubled people, through personal and group therapy, were explored in this series. His older colleague, Dr. Bernard Altman, worked with Jim in evaluating procedures and the progress of various patients. *The Psychiatrist* was one of the four elements that were all aired under the overall title *Four in One.*

PUBLIC DEFENDER, THE
Law Drama
FIRST TELECAST: *March 11, 1954*
LAST TELECAST: *June 23, 1955*
BROADCAST HISTORY:
Mar 1954–Jul 1954, CBS Thu 10:00–10:30

Jul 1954–Sep 1954, CBS Mon 9:00–9:30
Sep 1954–Jun 1955, CBS Thu 10:00–10:30
CAST:
Bart Matthews .... Reed Hadley

Actor Reed Hadley had most recently been seen in the role of a police officer who tracked down confidence men in *Racket Squad.* Here, he portrayed another side of the law—an attorney defending destitute individuals who had been charged with a crime and could not afford their own legal counsel. As a public defender he tried to help these people prove their innocence. The cases adapted for this series were all based on files from public-defender agencies throughout the country and a feature of each episode was a salute to a real public defender who had made some outstanding effort to exonerate a falsely accused person.

PUBLIC LIFE OF CLIFF NORTON, THE
Comedy
FIRST TELECAST: *January 7, 1952*
LAST TELECAST: *February 29, 1952*
BROADCAST HISTORY:
Jan 1952–Feb 1952, NBC Mon–Fri 11:10–11:15
REGULAR:
Cliff Norton

Veteran comic Cliff Norton appeared five times per week, giving short, humorous talks about the problems of everyday life.

PUBLIC PROSECUTOR
see *Crawford Mystery Theatre*

PULITZER PRIZE PLAYHOUSE
Dramatic Anthology
FIRST TELECAST: *October 6, 1950*
LAST TELECAST: *June 4, 1952*
BROADCAST HISTORY:
Oct 1950–Jun 1951, ABC Fri 9:00–10:00
Dec 1951–Jun 1952, ABC Wed 10:00–10:30

This was one of ABC's most prestigious programming efforts in the early 1950s, presenting top-quality dramas written or adapted for television and starring first-rate talent. Among those appearing were Helen Hayes in her TV debut, Melvyn Douglas, Raymond Massey, Edmond O'Brien, Peggy Wood, and Mildred Natwick. The first telecast was an adaptation of the Moss Hart–George S. Kaufman classic *You Can't Take It with You.* Equally famous writers (many of them Pulitzer Prize winners) such as Maxwell Anderson, Thornton Wilder, Marc Connelly, Edna Ferber, and James A. Michener were later represented. There were also original TV plays by Budd Schulberg and Lawrence Hazard, among others.

During its second season *Pulitzer Prize Playhouse* alternated with *Celanese Theatre* on Wednesday nights.

PUNKY BREWSTER

Situation Comedy

FIRST TELECAST: *September 16, 1984*
LAST TELECAST: *September 7, 1986*
BROADCAST HISTORY:

Sep 1984–May 1985, NBC Sun 7:30–8:00
Jun 1985–Apr 1986, NBC Sun 7:00–7:30
May 1986–Sep 1986, NBC Sun 7:30–8:00

CAST:

Penelope "Punky" Brewster
.... Soleil Moon Frye
Henry Warnimont .... George Gaynes
Eddie Malvin (1984).......... Eddie Deezen
Cherie Johnson .... Cherie Johnson
Mrs. Betty Johnson............ Susie Garrett
Margaux Kramer .... Ami Foster
*Mrs. Kramer (1984–1985)....... Loyita Chapel
Allen Anderson............... Casey Ellison
*Mrs. Morton (1984–1985)..... Dody Goodman
Mike Fulton (1985–1986) .... T.K. Carter

*Occasional

Punky was a cute seven-year-old Chicago girl with a lot of problems, but a sunny outlook on life. Abandoned by her parents, spunky Punky and her adorable puppy set up housekeeping in an empty apartment, where they were soon discovered by the building manager, Henry Warnimont, a dour old bachelor. He was about to turn them over to the authorities when—well, those big eyes, that winning smile, that loving heart, who could resist? Somehow he persuaded the skeptical authorities to let Punky stay with him for a while, and the little girl began to bring sunshine into Henry's world. Stories revolved around their adjustments to each other, and Henry's professional work as a photographer. Eddie was the kooky building maintenance man, Cherie was Punky's playmate, Margaux the stuck-up classmate at school, Allen another of Punky's friends, and Mrs. Morton her teacher. Punky got a new teacher, Mike Fulton, for the 1985–1986 season.

According to reports published when this series was announced, there was a real Punky Brewster, though not quite as depicted in the show. NBC programming head Brandon Tartikoff, while a youth, had had a crush on a tomboyish older girl by that name. Years later he nicknamed his own first child Punky. He also thought it would make a great name for a TV series, so when this show went into development, Punky it was—after NBC's lawyers tracked down the real Punky and got permission to use her name (she was married to a lawyer in Connecticut, received a royalty for the use of her name, and even appeared once in a cameo role as one of the teachers at Punky's school). And the puppy who followed Punky around on the show? Its name was "Brandon."

NBC aired an animated version of this series, titled *It's Punky Brewster,* on Saturday mornings from September 1985–September 1987.

PUREX SUMMER SPECIALS

Anthology

FIRST TELECAST: *July 11, 1961*
LAST TELECAST: *September 12, 1963*
BROADCAST HISTORY:

Jul 1961–Sep 1961, NBC Tue 10:00–11:00
Jul 1962–Sep 1962, NBC Fri 9:30–10:30
Jun 1963–Sep 1963, NBC Thu 10:00–11:00

For three summers, NBC aired a series comprised of reruns of special programs that the Purex Corporation had originally sponsored. During 1961 and 1962 approximately half of the shows were reruns of various *Purex Special for Women* telecasts, and the remainder were profiles of famous people, some historical and some current showbusiness personalities. In 1963 the majority of the shows were profiles, and aired under the general title *The World of. . . .*

PURSUIT

Dramatic Anthology

FIRST TELECAST: *October 22, 1958*
LAST TELECAST: *January 14, 1959*
BROADCAST HISTORY:

Oct 1958–Jan 1959, CBS Wed 8:00–9:00

The plays that were aired on this live dramatic series had one element in common—they all told in some way the story of a man, or group, being pursued. The circumstances varied from show to show, but the element of the hunter and the hunted was present in each episode. The casting was strong and several of the authors were well known. A Daphne duMaurier story, "Kiss Me Again, Stranger," featured Jeffrey Hunter, Margaret O'Brien, and Mort Sahl; a Ross Macdonald thriller entitled "Epitaph for a Golden Girl" starred Michael Rennie, Rick Jason, Rip Torn, Sally Forrest, and Joan Bennett; and Rod Serling provided "The Last Night of August" with Franchot Tone, Dennis Hopper, and Cameron Mitchell.

PURSUIT OF HAPPINESS

Situation Comedy

FIRST TELECAST: *October 30, 1987*
LAST TELECAST: *January 8, 1988*
BROADCAST HISTORY:

Oct 1987–Jan 1988, ABC Fri 9:30–10:00

CAST:

Asst. Prof. David Hanley ..... Paul Provenza
Prof. Roland G. Duncan .... Brian Keith
Sara Duncan .... Judie Aronson
Margaret Callahan........ Wendel Meldrum
Vernon Morris........... Wesley Thompson
Prof. Stevens .... John Petlock
Earvin "Magic" Johnson............. himself
Thomas Jefferson .... Kevin Scannell
Mrs. Lopez .... Wanda de Jesus

A short-lived comedy about an idealistic young history teacher who, after years of wandering around the country searching for "meaning," decided to see if he could find it teaching history at a small Philadelphia college. David was especially anxious to meet his idol, noted historian and author Roland G. Duncan. Duncan was not what he expected, gruff and very practical ("They can't fire *me*—I've got tenure!") but he nevertheless became the older man's protégé. Other eccentrics inhabiting David's new world were Margaret, a brilliant Egyptian studies scholar unable to cope with everyday life; Duncan's sexy, not-too-bright teenaged daughter, Sara; and David's college buddy Vernon. David had two other role models—the intellectual in him idolized President Thomas Jefferson and the sports lover idolized Los Angeles Laker basketball star Magic Johnson. Whenever he had a problem, both of his idols would "come to life" to offer David advice. Since their approaches were very different, Thomas and Magic would often disagree about which course of action he should take.

PUTTIN' ON THE HITS
Music/Competition
BROADCAST HISTORY:
Syndicated only
30 minutes
Produced: *1985–*
Released: *Fall 1985*
HOST:
Allen Fawcett
EXECUTIVE PRODUCERS:
Dick Clark
Chris Bearde

Contestants on this series competed by doing elaborate pantomimes to songs by professional singers. There were celebrity judges to score each contestant on three factors—originality, appearance, and lip-sync. Weekly first-round winners won $1,000 and during the season-long competition could advance through several rounds to win the annual grand prize of $25,000.

Q

Q.E.D.
Quiz/Panel
FIRST TELECAST: *April 3, 1951*
LAST TELECAST: *October 9, 1951*
BROADCAST HISTORY:
Apr 1951–Sep 1951, ABC Tue 9:00–9:30
Oct 1951, ABC Tue 10:00–10:30
MODERATOR:
Doug Browning
Fred Uttal
REGULAR PANELISTS:
Hy Brown
Nina Foch
Harold Hoffman

This show presented its panel with a short mystery story, sketch, or playlet, submitted by a viewer, which stopped just before the solution to the mystery was revealed. The panel was then supposed to guess the outcome, based on the clues within the story and a limited number of questions which could be answered with a yes or no. *Q.E.D.* stands for *quod erat demonstrandum* in Latin, or, in English, "which was to be proved." Doug Browning was moderator for the first telecast only, replaced on April 10 by Fred Uttal. The program was also known as *Mystery File.*

Q.E.D.
Adventure
FIRST TELECAST: *March 23, 1982*
LAST TELECAST: *April 27, 1982*
BROADCAST HISTORY:
Mar 1982–Apr 1982, CBS Tue 8:00–9:00
CAST:
Quentin E. Deverill .... Sam Waterston
Phipps .... George Innes
Charlie Andrews .... A. C. Weary
Dr. Stefan Kilkiss .... Julian Glover
Jenny Martin .... Caroline Langrishe

Q.E.D. resembled the hit 1960s series *The Wild, Wild West,* only it was set in England in 1912. Like the earlier program, it was an adventure filled with scientific marvels which seemed far ahead of their time, and an evil genius—Dr. Kilkiss—bent on world domination. Fighting Kilkiss and other international villains was a brilliant American professor named Quentin E. Deverill, whose ability to construct incredible scientific gadgets was exceeded only by his analytical skills as an amateur sleuth. Helping out were: Phipps, his Cockney chauffeur and butler; Jenny, his beautiful and resourceful secretary; and a snooping American reporter named Charlie.

The series was produced in England by John Hawkesworth, who was also responsible for the acclaimed PBS series *Upstairs, Downstairs* and *The Duchess of Duke Street.*

QUADRANGLE, THE
see *Campus Corner*

QUARK
Situation Comedy
FIRST TELECAST: *February 24, 1978*
LAST TELECAST: *April 14, 1978*
BROADCAST HISTORY:
Feb 1978–Apr 1978, NBC Fri 8:00–8:30
CAST:
Adam Quark .... Richard Benjamin
Gene/Jean .... Tim Thomerson
Ficus .... Richard Kelton
Betty I .... Tricia Barnstable
Betty II .... Cyb Barnstable
Andy the Robot............... Bobby Porter
Otto Palindrome .... Conrad Janis
The Head .... Alan Caillou

Quark was a parody on space adventure epics, which were highly popular at this time due to the success of the movie *Star Wars.* The setting was the year 2222 A.D. on the giant space station Perma One, where Adam Quark had been given command of a vital, though not necessarily romantic, mission: to clean up the garbage in outer space. His assignments came from The Head, a disembodied head who governed the universe, and who was seen only on a TV screen; and from Otto Palindrome, the fussy chief architect of Perma One. Quark's crew included first officer Gene/Jean, a transmute with both male and female characteristics; science officer Ficus, a kind of humanoid vegetable; co-pilots Betty I and Betty II, two sexy and identical girls, one of whom was a clone of the other (nobody knew which was which); and Andy the Robot, a walking junkpile.

Though Quark was supposed to stick to his sanitation patrols, he often met adventure with such colorful space denizens as the evil High Gorgon, Zoltar the Magnificent, and Zorgon the Malevolent. A strange mixture of sex, intellectual jokes, and basic slapstick comedy, *Quark* failed to attract a substantial audience and was soon canceled.

QUEEN AND I, THE
Situation Comedy
FIRST TELECAST: *January 16, 1969*
LAST TELECAST: *May 1, 1969*
BROADCAST HISTORY:
Jan 1969–May 1969, CBS Thu 7:30–8:00
CAST:
Charles Duffy .... Larry Storch
Oliver Nelson .... Billy DeWolfe
Becker .... Carl Ballantine
Barney .... Pat Morita
Wilma Winslow .... Barbara Stuart

Max Kowalski	Dave Morick
Capt. Washburn	Liam Dunn
Ozzie	Dave Willock

The *Amsterdam Queen* was an aging ocean liner whose owners had decided to retire and sell her for scrap. Fighting the inevitable was the ship's purser, Charles Duffy, who was not above trying anything to save the boat and his job. The various ways in which he had been able to supplement his income with the ship—making it available for weddings and bar mitzvahs when it was in port, shaming the passengers into giving bigger tips, etc.—made him particularly desperate to save it. Most of the crew members were enthusiastic about his efforts, with the exception of First Mate Nelson, who had never been able to catch Charlie at any of his shenanigans but who would be happy to see him out of a job.

QUEST, THE
Western
FIRST TELECAST: *September 22, 1976*
LAST TELECAST: *December 29, 1976*
BROADCAST HISTORY:
 Sep 1976–Dec 1976, NBC Wed 10:00–11:00
CAST:

Morgan Beaudine	Kurt Russell
Quentin Beaudine	Tim Matheson

Set in the West during the 1890s, *The Quest* was the story of two young brothers in search of their long-lost sister. Several years before, Morgan Beaudine and his sister Patricia had been captured by Cheyenne Indians and become separated. Morgan had been raised by the Cheyenne but was now living in the white man's world, though he actually trusted the Indians more than he did the whites. His brother Quentin, meanwhile, was educated in San Francisco and planned to be a doctor. Together these two young men set out in search of their sister. Morgan affected Indian dress, spoke fluent Cheyenne, and understood Indian customs well enough to get them out of dangerous situations when they encountered unfriendly red men. He even had an Indian name, Two Persons.

The time seemed ripe for a successful Western when this series premiered. The season before had seen not a single Western on prime-time network television, for the first time in more than 20 years. There was plenty of action and violence on *The Quest,* but it could not compete with the pulchritude on ABC's new entry opposite it, *Charlie's Angels.*

QUEST, THE
Adventure
FIRST TELECAST: *October 22, 1982*
LAST TELECAST: *November 19, 1982*
BROADCAST HISTORY:
 Oct 1982–Nov 1982, ABC Fri 10:00–11:00

CAST:

Dan Underwood	Perry King
Art Henley	Noah Beery
Cody Johnson	Ray Vitte
Carrie Welby	Karen Austin
Count Louis Dardinay	Michael Billington
Sir Edward	John Rhys Davies
King Charles	Ralph Michael

The tiny Mediterranean principality of Glendora was due to be absorbed by neighboring France when aging King Charles passed away. If, that is, he had no royal successors. So the king's advisor, Sir Edward, studied the family tree and discovered four Americans, each of whom was distantly related to His Majesty and could rightfully claim the throne—if they could pass a 13th-century test of skill and worthiness. Thus began the quest, in which four ordinary Americans each tried to prove himself and inherit a beautiful little seaside country.

Dan was a handsome international sports photographer, a veritable magnet for beautiful girls; Art a gruff, down-to-earth retired cop from Wilko, Kansas; Cody a slick, black con man and hustler with a heart of gold; and Carrie (can you hear the producers saying, "We need a bimbo!") a good-looking New York department store buyer. Sir Edward gave them their assignment each week, usually in cryptic verse, and off they went, sometimes racing, sometimes helping each other as well as the people they met. The quest, you see, was not only a race but a test of their valor and good deeds. Trying to foil them was the exiled and villainous Count Dardinay, who stood to regain his lands only if none of them won and the country *did* become part of France.

QUEST FOR ADVENTURE
 see *ABC Presents*

QUICK AS A FLASH
Quiz/Panel
FIRST TELECAST: *March 12, 1953*
LAST TELECAST: *February 25, 1954*
BROADCAST HISTORY:
 Mar 1953–Jul 1953, ABC Thu 10:30–11:00
 Sep 1953–Feb 1954, ABC Thu 8:00–8:30
MODERATOR:
 Bobby Sherwood
 Bud Collyer
REGULAR PANELISTS:
 Jimmy Nelson
 Faye Emerson

Quick as a Flash was designed to test the panel's speed in guessing the significance or outcome of a short, specially prepared film. The film might depict a person, event, or a mystery playlet. The program was based on the long-running (1944–1951) radio quiz of the same name, but unlike the radio version it utilized celebrity panelists. Many guest panelists appeared, in addition to the regulars shown above. Bud Collyer replaced Bobby Sherwood as host in May.

The program was telecast live from New York, and alternated with *Personality Puzzle*.

QUICK ON THE DRAW
Quiz/Panel
FIRST TELECAST: *January 15, 1952*
LAST TELECAST: *December 9, 1952*
BROADCAST HISTORY:
Jan 1952–Dec 1952, DUM Tue 9:30–10:00
HOSTESS:
Robin Chandler
CARTOONIST:
Bob Dunn

This panel show used cartoons suggested by viewers and drawn by cartoonist Bob Dunn to provide pictorial clues to familiar words and phrases. The clues were usually in the form of puns or plays on words, for example a comedian on a stage taking off his clothes (representing "a newspaper term"); a baseball player about to swing a rolled-up venetian blind (for "a well-known expression"); or a man putting a tuxedo on a rabbit (for "an occupation"). (See below for the correct answers.) A different panel of celebrities appeared each week.

Quick on the Draw had been seen locally in New York since 1950.

Answers: (1) comic strip; (2) "blind as a bat"; (3) hair (hare) dresser.

QUINCY, M.E.
Police Drama
FIRST TELECAST: *October 3, 1976*
LAST TELECAST: *September 5, 1983*
BROADCAST HISTORY:
Oct 1976–Nov 1976, NBC Sun 9:30–11:00
Feb 1977–May 1977, NBC Fri 10:00–11:00
Jun 1977–Jul 1977, NBC Fri 9:30–11:00
Jul 1977–Aug 1978, NBC Fri 10:00–11:00
Sep 1978–Apr 1980, NBC Thu 9:00–10:00
Apr 1980–Jun 1983, NBC Wed 10:00–11:00
Jun 1983–Sep 1983, NBC Sat 9:00–10:00
Sep 1983, NBC Mon 10:00–11:00
CAST:
Quincy, M.E. .... Jack Klugman
Lt. Frank Monahan .... Garry Walberg
Sam Fujiyama .... Robert Ito
Lee Potter (1976–1977) .... Lynette Mettey
Danny Tovo .... Val Bisoglio
Dr. Robert Astin .... John S. Ragin
Sgt. Brill .... Joseph Roman
Eddie .... Ed Garrett
Diane, the waitress (1980–1983)
.... Diane Markoff
Marc (1978–1983) .... Marc Scott Taylor
Dr. Emily Hanover (1982–1983)
.... Anita Gillette

Quincy was a man with a strong sense of principle. He had given up a lucrative private medical practice to join the Los Angeles County Coroner's Office as a medical examiner ("M.E."). His understanding of forensic medicine led him to conclude that many of the supposed "normal" deaths that he was assigned to investigate were actually murders. Whenever this happened, Quincy tended to resemble a detective more than a pathologist, as he sought evidence to prove his contentions. These wanderings out of his field into the province of the police did not endear Quincy to Dr. Astin, his vacuous, pompous, and insecure superior in the coroner's office. It also alienated many of the police officers who were involved in the investigations and got in the way of his social life, much to the consternation of his girlfriend, Lee. None of this seemed to bother Quincy, however, as he and his young assistant Sam plugged away at solving the cases. Quincy lived on a boat and spent much of his free time at Danny's Place, the bar adjacent to the marina where the boat was docked.

Over the years some things changed. Dr. Astin became less obnoxious and, in fact, actually became almost likable. His problems with Quincy's tendency to play detective never ended, however, and much of his time was spent trying to defend his star pathologist's activities to the police, the local government, the medical board, and the press. He never could get Quincy to conform, and the exasperation showed. Quincy's love life, after Lee's departure, was quite active until he fell for Emily Hanover (played by the same actress who had portrayed his deceased first wife in a 1979 flashback episode), an attractive psychiatrist who provided him with help on some of his cases. They were married in the spring of 1983, after a courtship that suffered because of his preoccupation with his work.

Although Quincy's first name was never mentioned on the show, he did, apparently, have a first initial. His business card was seen briefly in one episode and it read "Dr. R. Quincy."

Quincy was one of the four rotating elements in the 1976–1977 edition of *The NBC Sunday Mystery Movie*—the others being *Columbo, McCloud*, and *McMillan*. It proved so popular during the fall of 1976, however, that after the first of the year it moved to Friday nights as a weekly series.

QUIZ KIDS
Quiz/Panel
FIRST TELECAST: *March 1, 1949*
LAST TELECAST: *September 27, 1956*
BROADCAST HISTORY:
Mar 1949–May 1949, NBC Tue 8:00–8:30 (Midwest net only)
Jun 1949–Sep 1949, NBC Wed 8:00–8:30
Sep 1949–Jan 1950, NBC Mon 10:00–10:30
Jan 1950–Oct 1951, NBC Fri 8:00–8:30
Jul 1952–Sep 1952, NBC Mon 8:00–8:30
Jan 1953–Jul 1953, CBS Sat 10:00–10:30
Jul 1953–Nov 1953, CBS Sun 7:00–7:30
Jan 1956–Sep 1956, CBS Thu 10:30–11:00

Joe Kelly (1949–1953)
Clifton Fadiman (1956)

This popular series had started on radio in 1940 and was brought intact to television, first as a local program on WNBQ, Chicago (January 1949) and later as a network entry (March 1949). The format was simple: a panel of four or five youngsters, chosen through a battery of tests, answered difficult questions requiring both general and specific knowledge. One youngster might be an "arithmetic expert," another a "music expert," etc. Panelists were as young as six, and a child could remain on the show as long as his answering rank remained high or until he or she reached 16. Celebrity guests sometimes appeared, and periodic contests were held for viewers (e.g., describe your "teacher of the year"). Viewers also submitted questions for the panel and received cash prizes if the young intellects failed to come up with the correct answers. *Quiz Kids* was sometimes scheduled in afternoon time slots during its long run; only the prime-time telecasts are reflected above.

One of the great ironies of the show was that Joe Kelly, who was quizmaster from the early 1940s until 1953, had only a third-grade education himself.

Possibly the most famous of the gifted children who appeared as panelists on *Quiz Kids* was young Robert Strom, who became a regular on the show in March 1956 when he was nine years old.

His specialty on *Quiz Kids* was astronomy, but during the next two years his general knowledge of mathematics and physics won him huge sums of money on *The $64,000 Question, The $64,000 Challenge,* and other big-money quiz shows.

A syndicated version of *Quiz Kids* was produced in 1978, with Jim McKrell as emcee.

QUIZZING THE NEWS
Quiz/Panel
FIRST TELECAST: *August 16, 1948*
LAST TELECAST: *March 5, 1949*
BROADCAST HISTORY:
Aug 1948–Sep 1948, ABC Mon 7:30–8:00
Sep 1948–Oct 1948, ABC Mon 8:00–8:30
Nov 1948–Jan 1949, ABC Wed 8:30–9:00
Jan 1949–Mar 1949, ABC Sat 8:30–9:00
EMCEE:
Allen Prescott

A panel of guest celebrities attempted to identify news events from cartoon clues in this early ABC quiz show. Viewers could also participate, and win prizes. *Quizzing the News* was one of the programs produced locally in New York by ABC production crews, using the facilities of an independent station, so that the ABC personnel could gain working experience in TV prior to the opening of ABC's own flagship station. As soon as ABC's own station opened on August 10, 1948, the program moved over intact and was fed to the newly established network.

R

RCA VICTOR SHOW, THE
Various
FIRST TELECAST: *November 23, 1951*
LAST TELECAST: *August 2, 1954*
BROADCAST HISTORY:
Nov 1951–Jun 1953, NBC Fri 8:00–8:30 (OS)
Oct 1953–Aug 1954, NBC Mon 9:00–9:30
CAST:
Ezio Pinza (1951–1952) .... Himself
Dennis Day (1952–1954) .... Himself
Mrs. Day (1952) .... Verna Felton
Kathy (1952).................. Kathy Phillips
Charley Weaver (1952–1954) ... Cliff Arquette
Lois Sterling (1952–1953) .... Lois Butler
Mrs. Pratt (1952–1953) .... Minerva Urecal
Hal March (1952–1953) .... Himself
Susan Sterling (1952–1954) .... Jeri Lou James
Lavinia (1953–1954) .... Ida Moore
Marian (1953–1954) .... Carol Richards
Peggy (1953–1954) .... Barbara Ruick

When *The RCA Victor Show* premiered, its sole star was singer Ezio Pinza. Each episode of the loosely formatted show opened with urbane bachelor Pinza in his luxurious penthouse apartment, from which he would chat with the audience and sing a song or two. He would then leave the apartment, encounter the evening's guest star, and the two would return to his home. Pinza and guest would perform musical numbers separately and together, and the show closed with Mr. Pinza alone at home singing a last song.

On February 8, 1952, Dennis Day made his first appearance as the alternate-week star of *The RCA Victor Show*. His shows were more traditional situation comedies. Dennis played himself as a singer whose mother felt that he had been underpaid working on Jack Benny's radio program and should look for a career of his own. The only person who had real love and faith in him was his girlfriend, Kathy.

On April 11, 1952, the format of the Ezio Pinza part of the show was changed. Each episode starred Mr. Pinza in a dramatic story with guest stars and appropriate songs woven into the general plot line. When *The RCA Victor Show* returned in the fall of 1952, after a summer hiatus, Dennis Day was its sole star, the Ezio Pinza episodes having been dropped.

The format for the Dennis Day situation comedy had also changed. He played himself again, but was a young bachelor living in a luxurious apartment building in Hollywood. He couldn't really afford it, but felt that it was necessary for his image in the quest to get ahead in show business. Charley Weaver was the janitor, Mrs. Pratt his landlady, Hal March a girl-crazy neighbor, and Lois Sterling his girlfriend who lived with her little sister.

In the fall of 1953, the show returned with essentially the same format under the new title *The Dennis Day Show*. Previously live, it was now filmed. Charley Weaver had acquired a girlfriend named Lavinia, and Dennis went through two new girlfriends, Marian and Peggy. Although Lois Sterling was gone, her little sister Susan was still in the cast as Dennis's youngest fan.

R.F.D. AMERICA
Instruction
FIRST TELECAST: *May 26, 1949*
LAST TELECAST: *September 15, 1949*
BROADCAST HISTORY:
May 1949–Sep 1949, NBC Thu 8:00–8:30
EMCEE:
Bob Murphy

A "how to" program dealing with plants and animals, and originating from Chicago (where it began as a local show in January 1949). Host Murphy interviewed various guest experts on raising cattle, watering plants, carving meat, etc., and occasionally displayed live examples of the animal subject at hand. For example, the premiere telecast was said to be the first time in history that an entire herd of cattle was driven into a studio to be seen on live television.

RACKET SQUAD
Police Drama
FIRST TELECAST: *June 7, 1951*
LAST TELECAST: *September 28, 1953*
BROADCAST HISTORY:
Jun 1951–Dec 1952, CBS Thu 10:00–10:30
Jan 1953–Jul 1953, CBS Thu 10:30–11:00
Jul 1953–Sep 1953, CBS Mon 9:00–9:30
CAST:
Capt. John Braddock .... Reed Hadley

Capt. John Braddock worked in the racket squad of a large metropolitan police department. He did not deal with crimes of violence but instead sought to protect the public from the various confidence rackets that were a more direct threat to them than outright robbery. The series was based on actual case records from police departments around the country and described in detail the means by which shady characters fleeced unsuspecting people of their money. Reed Hadley, in addition to his role as star, provided the narration for each episode. Hadley had previously been seen in a syndicated version of *Racket Squad* that was produced in 1950, a year before CBS decided to give the series network exposure.

RAFFERTY
Medical Drama
FIRST TELECAST: *September 5, 1977*
LAST TELECAST: *November 28, 1977*

Sep 1977–Nov 1977, CBS Mon 10:00–11:00
CAST:
Sid Rafferty, M.D. .... Patrick McGoohan
Nurse Vera Wales .... Millie Slavin
Daniel Gentry, M.D. .... John Getz
Dr. Calvin .... David Clemmon
Nurse Keynes .... Joan Pringle
Nurse Koscinski .... Eddie Benton

After 23 years as a doctor in the U.S. Army, Sid Rafferty had retired from the service to open a private practice. Used to military discipline, and possessed of a very short temper, the idealistic and stubborn Rafferty was not the easiest person to get along with. He did things his way, resented the clubbiness of other doctors—particularly their tendency to cover up for each other's shortcomings and mistakes—and was often at odds with the staff of City General Hospital, where he performed surgery. Rafferty's young associate in his private practice was Daniel Gentry, whose freewheeling personal life was in marked contrast to Rafferty's more conservative approach. Their nurse/receptionist was Vera Wales, thoroughly professional in the office but also madly in love with widower Rafferty.

RAGS TO RICHES
Comedy Drama
FIRST TELECAST: *March 9, 1987*
LAST TELECAST:
BROADCAST HISTORY:
Mar 1987, NBC Mon 8:00–10:00
Mar 1987–May 1987, NBC Sun 8:00–9:00
Jul 1987, NBC Sun 8:00–9:00
Aug 1987–Jan 1988, NBC Fri 8:00–9:00
*July 1988–   *, NBC Sun 7:00–8:00
CAST:
Nick Foley .... Joseph Bologna
John Clapper, the butler ...... Douglas Seale
Rose (16) .... Kimiko Gelman
Marva (15) .... Tisha Campbell
Diane (15) .... Bridget Michele
Patty (13) .... Bianca DeGarr
Mickey (7) .... Heidi Zeigler
Nina (pilot only) .... Heather McAdam

The '60s were fun and games for a group of young orphans in this frothy TV version of a B-movie musical, set in 1961. Nick was the millionaire bachelor playboy-businessman who adopted them, in order to look more respectable (seems he could close more deals that way); and Clapper was the elderly Cockney butler who looked after them all in Nick's huge Los Angeles mansion. The five girls were strong-willed Rose, often the ringleader; charming Diane; wisecracking Marva, who wanted to follow in Nick's entrepreneurial footsteps; tomboy Patty; and insufferably cute little Mickey. They all engaged in lots of singing and dancing, often '60s tunes with new lyrics that commented on the story.

RAMAR OF THE JUNGLE
Adventure
BROADCAST HISTORY:
Syndicated only
30 minutes
Produced: *1952–1954* (52 episodes)
Released: *October 1952*
CAST:
Dr. Tom Reynolds (Ramar) .... Jon Hall
Professor Howard Ogden ... Ray Montgomery
ALSO:
James Fairfax
M'liss McClure
Nick Stewart

Adults shook their heads at this one, but kids thought it was *neat* and made *Ramar of the Jungle* one of the leading children's adventure shows of the 1950s. Dr. Tom Reynolds was the son of missionaries who returned to the jungle as head of a medical-research expedition. There he stayed, tending to the natives as if they were little children and fighting off at least one real bad guy every episode (poachers, crooks who wanted to steal the opals right off the natives' idol, etc.). Ramar, as any under-12-year-old could tell you, meant "White Medicine Man" ... or "Great White Doctor," or something like that. Ray Montgomery played his companion.

The plots and dialogue were pretty primitive; for example:

NATIVE CHIEF: Gun make no boom-boom.
RAMAR: You mean it made no sound?
CHIEF: No boom-boom!
RAMAR: Hmmm . . . The gun must have been equipped with a silencer.

It was all good, clean fun, with lots of exciting animal shots. Hall, who knew his juvenile audience, insisted on historical and geographical accuracy (episodes were set in both Africa and India) and no sex. "Kids get smarter every day," he said. "You can't fool them ... even our African dialects are genuine. As for sex, who needs it at their age?" The program was produced on a rock-bottom budget and, together with the merchandising of pith helmets, games, and other Ramar paraphernalia, made a lot of money for former B-movie actor Hall. Some of the *Ramar* TV films were also strung together and released theatrically in the late 1950s and early 1960s.

RANGE RIDER, THE
Western
BROADCAST HISTORY:
Syndicated and network reruns
30 minutes
Produced: *1951–1952* (78 episodes)
Released: *Fall 1952*
CAST:
The Range Rider .... Jock Mahoney
Dick West .... Dick Jones

"Home on the Range"

Six-foot four-inch former stuntman and cowboy star Jock Mahoney headed this early kids' Western. With his youthful sidekick Dick West, he ranged all over the old frontier, righting wrongs and helping out everyone from Arizona Navajos to Canadian Mounties. There was a lot of hard riding and flying tackles, but relatively little gunplay.

The Rider's trusty horse was Rawhide, while Dick's was Lucky. The series was produced by Gene Autry's Flying A Productions, which also sold buckskin shirts and other Range Rider gear in a merchandise tie-in.

Reruns of *Range Rider* appeared on the ABC network on Sunday afternoons from September to December 1965.

RANGO
Situation Comedy
FIRST TELECAST: *January 13, 1967*
LAST TELECAST: *September 1, 1967*
BROADCAST HISTORY:
Jan 1967–Sep 1967, ABC Fri 9:00–9:30
CAST:
Rango .... Tim Conway
Pink Cloud .... Guy Marks
Capt. Horton .... Norman Alden
THEME:
"Rango," by Earle Hagen and Ben Raleigh, sung by Frankie Laine

Rango was a Western comedy about the Texas Ranger that legends don't talk about. He was an inept, bumbling lawman who had been assigned to Deep Wells Ranger Station, the quietest post in the state, in an attempt to keep him out of trouble. But trouble came with him. Criminal activity sprouted in a town which had been quiet for 20 years. Rango's assistant in the post supply room was Pink Cloud, a "chicken" Indian who had discovered that the white man's ways were much to his liking—an interesting book in a comfortable bed was much better than skulking around the plains. "Rango say him return when sun high over teepee," grunted the red man. "By that, I presume he meant he would be back by noon."

Rango's nemesis was Captain Horton, the post commander, who would have dearly loved to have him transferred, but couldn't, because Rango's father happened to be head of the Texas Rangers.

RANSOM SHERMAN SHOW, THE
Comedy Variety
FIRST TELECAST: *July 3, 1950*
LAST TELECAST: *August 25, 1950*
BROADCAST HISTORY:
Jul 1950–Aug 1950, NBC Mon–Fri 7:00–7:30
REGULARS:
Ransom Sherman
Nancy Wright

Johnny Bradford
Art Van Damme Quintet

Radio emcee and comic Ransom Sherman brought his wide-ranging monologues to television in 1950, as a summer replacement for *Kukla, Fran & Ollie*. A variety of vocalists provided musical entertainment, including Nancy Wright, Johnny Bradford, and four different vocal groups who rotated from night to night. One of these groups, the Four Lads, later became famous in their own right.

Sherman was later seen in an afternoon series on NBC from October 1950 to January 1951.

RAT PATROL, THE
War Drama
FIRST TELECAST: *September 12, 1966*
LAST TELECAST: *September 16, 1968*
BROADCAST HISTORY:
Sep 1966–Sep 1968, ABC Mon 8:30–9:00·
CAST:
Sgt. Sam Troy .... Chris George
Sgt. Jack Moffitt .... Gary Raymond
Pvt. Mark Hitchcock .... Lawrence Casey
Pvt. Tully Pettigrew .... Justin Tarr
Capt. Hauptman Hans Dietrich
.... Hans Gudegast

"Leapin' jeeps!" *The Rat Patrol* came roaring onto TV screens in 1966 as a wartime action-adventure series with a touch of humor. The Rat Patrollers were four young commandos, three Americans and one Englishman, fighting General Rommel's elite Afrika Korps in the North African desert early in World War II. Sam Troy was the head rat, Jack Moffitt his very British demolitions expert (and there was a lot of demolition in *Rat Patrol*), Mark Hitchcock the young private trying to live down a "sissy" reputation, and Tully Pettigrew the charming con man of the group. They traveled over the burning sands in two machine-gun-mounted jeeps, working as an independent team because no organized unit could hold them. Capt. Dietrich, C.O. of a German armored unit, was their usual enemy, though sometimes the two sides had to join forces to fight off the Arabs.

The Rat Patrol was filmed in part on the deserts of Spain, where a great deal of war materiel left over from the filming of the movies *Battle of the Bulge* and *The Great Escape* was used for backdrop.

RAWHIDE
Western
FIRST TELECAST: *January 9, 1959*
LAST TELECAST: *January 4, 1966*
BROADCAST HISTORY:
Jan 1959–Apr 1959, CBS Fri 8:00–9:00
May 1959–Sep 1963, CBS Fri 7:30–8:30
Sep 1963–Sep 1964, CBS Thu 8:00–9:00
Sep 1964–Sep 1965, CBS Fri 7:30–8:30
Sep 1965–Jan 1966, CBS Tue 7:30–8:30

CAST:

Rowdy Yates .... Clint Eastwood
Gil Favor (1959–1965) .... Eric Fleming
Pete Nolan (1959–1965) .... Sheb Wooley
Wishbone .... Paul Brinegar
Jim Quince .... Steve Raines
Joe Scarlett (1959–1964) ...... Rocky Shahan
Harkness "Mushy" Mushgrove (1959–1965)
.... James Murdock
Hey Soos Patines (1961–1964) .. Robert Cabal
Clay Forrester (1962–1963) ..... Charles Gray
Ian Cabot (1965–1966) .... David Watson
Jed Colby (1965–1966) .... John Ireland
Solomon King (1965–1966)
.... Raymond St. Jacques

THEME:

"Rawhide," by Ned Washington and Dmitri Tiomkin, sung over credits by Frankie Laine

Rawhide was the cattleman's answer to *Wagon Train.* Whereas *Wagon Train* told of the adventures of people traveling across the Great Plains in wagons, *Rawhide* took its regular performers back and forth across the country as organizers and runners of communal cattle drives. The constant traveling allowed both series to tell stories of people met along the way and those who joined the regulars in transit. Gil Favor was the trail boss, the supervisor of the entire cattle-drive operation. His right-hand man, and second-in-command, was Rowdy Yates. Other regulars were the cooks, drovers, and scouts who helped the cattle drive stay together and avoid possible dangers. In the fall of 1965 Rowdy Yates took over as trail boss and organized his own team to start another drive. This last one, however, only made it part way, or wherever it was when it was canceled in January 1966.

RAY ANTHONY SHOW, THE
Musical Variety
FIRST TELECAST: *October 12, 1956*
LAST TELECAST: *May 3, 1957*
BROADCAST HISTORY:
Oct 1956–Apr 1957, ABC Fri 10:00–11:00
Apr 1957–May 1957, ABC Fri 10:00–10:30
REGULARS:
Ray Anthony and His Orchestra
Frank Leahy
The Four Freshmen
Don Durant
Med Flory
Gene Merlino
Belvederes
Leroy Anthony
The Savoys

ABC, which had struck gold with bandleader Lawrence Welk the previous summer, was reportedly trying to repeat its success by signing up Ray Anthony in 1956. Unfortunately Anthony did not possess quite the same magic, but he did provide a season's worth of pleasing entertainment with a somewhat more sophisticated brand of music than Welk's. A few guests were seen, but mostly it was just Anthony, his trumpet, orchestra, and regulars. Former Notre Dame coach Frank Leahy added an unusual touch with a regular sports feature. Live from Hollywood.

Ray Anthony has also been seen in three syndicated series over the years, in the summer of 1956 (just before this network entry), in 1962, and in 1968. Vocalist Vikki Carr was featured on the last two.

RAY BOLGER SHOW, THE
Situation Comedy
FIRST TELECAST: *October 8, 1953*
LAST TELECAST: *June 10, 1955*
BROADCAST HISTORY:
Oct 1953–Jul 1954, ABC Thu 8:30–9:00
Sep 1954–Jun 1955, ABC Fri 8:30–9:00
CAST:
Raymond Wallace .... Ray Bolger
Jonathan (1953–1954) .... Allyn Joslyn
Pete Morrisey .... Richard Erdman
June (1953–1954) .... Betty Lynn
Susan (1954–1955) .... Marjie Millar
Katie Jones (1954–1955)..... Christine Nelson
Artie Herman (1954–1955) .... Charlie Cantor
Ray's dancing partner .... Sylvia Lewis

Singer-dancer Ray Bolger tried two situation-comedy formats in two successive years in the mid-1950s, and had little luck with either. The 1953–1954 edition, called *Where's Raymond,* cast him as a musical-comedy star with a bright, infectious personality but an unfortunate tendency to arrive at the theater at the last possible moment before the show began—causing constant pandemonium. Jonathan was his meticulous agent (and brother), Pete his pal, and June a friend who ran a restaurant near the theater. This format was little more than an excuse to get Ray into one of his dance routines in each show, often employing one of his famous characterizations such as his role in the Broadway show *Where's Charley* (where he introduced "Once in Love with Amy") or the scarecrow from *The Wizard of Oz.*

In the fall of 1954 the program became *The Ray Bolger Show.* It still had Ray cast as a Broadway star, but this time he was in love with a young lass from Iowa (Susan) who was trying to achieve fame in the big city as a writer. His attempts to help her inevitably backfired. Of the previous year's supporting cast, Pete returned, being joined by Susan, her roommate Katie, and Ray's new friend Artie. Sylvia Lewis, who served as Ray's dancing partner in the big production numbers, was the choreographer for Ray's show throughout its two-year run.

RAY MILLAND SHOW, THE
Situation Comedy
FIRST TELECAST: *September 17, 1953*
LAST TELECAST: *September 30, 1955*

652

BROADCAST HISTORY:
Sep 1953–Jun 1955, CBS Thu 8:00–8:30 (OS)
Jul 1955–Sep 1955, CBS Fri 9:30–10:00
CAST:
Prof. Ray McNutley/McNulty . . . Ray Milland
Peggy McNutley/McNulty . . . . . Phyllis Avery
Dean Josephine Bradley (1953–1954)
. . . . Minerva Urecal
Pete Thompson (1953–1954) . . . . Gordon Jones

During its first season the title of this series was
Meet Mr. McNutley. Ray McNutley was the married, but very attractive, head of the English department of Lynnhaven College, an exclusive
women's school. In fact, the only female on campus who was not distracted by his suave manners
was stern, matronly Dean Bradley. Constantly
getting McNutley into trouble was his hulking
friend, Pete Thompson.

When the show returned in the fall of 1954, a
number of changes had been made. Ray's last
name was now McNulty, he was now teaching at
coeducational Comstock University, and he was
now a drama professor rather than an English
teacher. The show's title had also been changed,
to *The Ray Milland Show.* The basic plot, however, remained the same. He was still an attractive professor whose female acquaintances were
somewhat infatuated with him, he still had the
same loving and supportive wife, and still had his
problems with other members of the faculty.

RAY SCHERER'S SUNDAY REPORT
News/Documentary
FIRST TELECAST: *June 23, 1963*
LAST TELECAST: *August 25, 1963*
BROADCAST HISTORY:
Jun 1963–Aug 1963, NBC Sun 6:30–7:00
HOST:
Ray Scherer

NBC White House correspondent Ray Scherer
opened each show with about five minutes of hard
news and spent the rest of the half hour reviewing
in detail the major event, or events, of the past
week. Subject matter of these expanded stories
ranged from politics to science to international
affairs.

RAY STEVENS SHOW, THE
see *Andy Williams Presents Ray Stevens*

RAYMOND BURR SHOW, THE
syndicated title for *Ironside*

REAL MCCOYS, THE
Situation Comedy
FIRST TELECAST: *October 3, 1957*
LAST TELECAST: *September 22, 1963*
BROADCAST HISTORY:
Oct 1957–Sep 1962, ABC Thu 8:30–9:00
Sep 1962–Sep 1963, CBS Sun 9:00–9:30

CAST:
Grandpa Amos McCoy . . . . . . Walter Brennan
Luke McCoy . . . . Richard Crenna
Kate McCoy (1957–1962) . . . . Kathy Nolan
"Aunt" Hassie . . . . Lydia Reed
Little Luke (1957–1962) . . Michael Winkleman
Pepino Garcia . . . . Tony Martinez
George MacMichael . . . . Andy Clyde
Flora MacMichael . . . . Madge Blake
Aggie Larkin (1959–1960) . . . . Betty Garde
Louise Howard (1963) . . . . Janet De Gore
Greg Howard (1963) . . . . Butch Patrick
Winifred Jordan (1963) . . . . Joan Blondell

When this rural comedy was first proposed to the
networks by writers Irving and Norman Pincus,
the experts said it would never work. Okay for the
sticks, maybe, but no good for city viewers. NBC,
at first interested, finally turned the series down
cold. Walter Brennan, their intended star, wanted
nothing to do with it. But the Pincus brothers persevered. Brennan was finally won over, financing
was obtained from Danny Thomas Productions,
and a spot was found on ABC's impoverished
schedule. The two New York–bred Pincuses had
the last laugh, as *The Real McCoys* became one
of the biggest hits on TV for the next six years,
and started a major trend toward rural comedy
shows which lasted through the 1960s. This was
the inspiration for *The Andy Griffith Show, Beverly Hillbillies, Petticoat Junction, Green Acres,*
and several others.

The premise was simple: a happy-go-lucky
West Virginia mountain family picks up stakes
and moves to a ranch in California's San Fernando Valley. Center of the action, and undisputed star of the show, was Grandpa, a porchrockin', gol-darnin', consarnin' old codger with a
wheezy voice who liked to meddle in practically
everybody's affairs, neighbors and kin alike.
Three-time Academy Award–winner Walter
Brennan (who was 63 when the series began)
played the role to perfection. His kin were grandson Luke and his new bride, Kate; Luke's teenage
sister, "Aunt" Hassie; and Luke's 11-year-old
brother, Little Luke (their parents were deceased).
Completing the regular cast were Pepino, the
musically inclined farm hand, and George MacMichael, their argumentative neighbor. George's
spinster sister Flora had eyes for Grandpa, but
she never did snare him.

In 1962, when the series moved to CBS, Luke
became a widower and many of the plots began
to revolve around Grandpa's attempts to match
him up with a new wife. The series ended its run
in 1963.

CBS aired reruns of this series, with the title
shortened to *The McCoys,* from October 1962 to
September 1966 on weekday mornings.

REAL PEOPLE
Human Interest/Audience Participation
FIRST TELECAST: *April 18, 1979*

LAST TELECAST: *July 4, 1984*
BROADCAST HISTORY:
  Apr 1979–Jul 1984, NBC Wed 8:00–9:00
REGULARS:
  Fred Willard (1979, 1981–1983)
  Sarah Purcell
  John Barbour (1979–1982)
  Mark Russell
  Skip Stephenson
  Bill Rafferty
  Byron Allen
  Kerry Millerick (1982–1983)
  Peter Billingsley (1982–1984)

Producer George Schlatter was truly one of television's comic innovators. In 1968 he introduced *Rowan & Martin's Laugh-In,* a classic series that mixed burlesque with topical satire, and in 1979 he was responsible for this trend-setter. As the title implied, the stars of this series were not celebrities but "real people" with offbeat professions, hobbies, and interests. Each episode opened with the hosts roaming the studio audience soliciting comments and opinions (which led to a short-lived off-shoot series called *Speak Up, America*). Then a succession of "real people" were profiled in filmed reports, among them the world's fastest artist (more than 83,000 paintings), a man who ate soil, a man who went through life walking backward, and a shapely lady truck driver. There were features on a hollering convention, barbershop quartets, and a disco class for senior citizens. Some of the segments were heartwarming, others bizarre. The hosts, who went on location to film the stories, chatted about them in the studio and generally maintained a lighthearted pace. In between segments they read humorous letters from viewers, and showed photos of strange signs, unusual names, and funny typographical errors from newspapers and magazines—all submitted by viewers. Each one used won its sender a *Real People* T-shirt. On occasion, the subject of one of the stories would be present in the studio, presumably to prove that he *was* real.

Real People premiered as a limited series in the spring of 1979. When it returned that fall Fred Willard, one of the original hosts, had been replaced by Byron Allen. Allen, Sarah Purcell, John Barbour, and Skip Stephenson appeared regularly in the studio and on location in the filmed stories. Bill Rafferty was a roving reporter who did all of his commentary on film, never appearing in the studio, and political satirist Mark Russell made pungent comments on the federal bureaucracy, from Washington. Fred Willard returned to the show for two seasons, starting in 1981, and the following fall young Peter Billingsley was added to the roster to cover stories with particular emphasis on children. Kerry Millerick, another roving reporter, was also added in 1982, but appeared infrequently. When Kerry was added, former roving reporter Bill Rafferty began to appear in the

studio, as well as on location. Only moderately successful when it began, *Real People* soon grew into one of the top hits on television, spawning a host of imitators—*That's Incredible, Those Amazing Animals,* and *That's My Line* among them.

REBEL, THE
  Western
FIRST TELECAST: *October 4, 1959*
LAST TELECAST: *September 12, 1962*
BROADCAST HISTORY:
  Oct 1959–Sep 1961, ABC Sun 9:00–9:30
  Jun 1962–Sep 1962, NBC Wed 8:30–9:00
CAST:
  Johnny Yuma .... Nick Adams
THEME:
  "The Ballad of Johnny Yuma," by Andrew J. Fenady and Dick Markowitz

Johnny Yuma was an ex-Confederate soldier whose adventures on the Western frontier, following the end of the Civil War, were the basis of the stories in this series. As the only regular in the series, he traveled from town to town, getting involved with people and functioning, in an unofficial way, as an arbiter of justice. Not only did he get involved in criminal issues, but moral ones as well. The theme song was sung over the opening credits of each episode by popular singer Johnny Cash. In the summer of 1962, NBC aired reruns of episodes that had previously been seen on ABC.

REBOUND
  Dramatic Anthology
FIRST TELECAST: *February 8, 1952*
LAST TELECAST: *January 16, 1953*
BROADCAST HISTORY:
  Feb 1952–Jun 1952, ABC Fri 9:00–9:30
  Nov 1952–Jan 1953, DUM Fri 8:30–9:00

This filmed anthology series presented short stories of mystery and suspense, always with a trick O. Henry–type ending. The films were made in Hollywood by Bing Crosby Enterprises, and featured lesser-known (at the time) talent such as Onslow Stevens, Lee Marvin, John Doucette, and Rita Johnson.

RECKONING
  Dramatic Anthology
FIRST TELECAST: *July 11, 1959*
LAST TELECAST: *September 18, 1963*
BROADCAST HISTORY:
  Jul 1959–Sep 1959, CBS Sat 7:30–8:30
  Jun 1960–Aug 1960, CBS Wed 7:30–8:30
  Jun 1963–Sep 1963, CBS Wed 10:00–11:00

The dramas presented in this summer series were all reruns of episodes previously shown on *Pursuit, Climax!,* and *Studio One in Hollywood.* All of the originals had aired in 1958.

RED BARBER'S CORNER

Sports Commentary

FIRST TELECAST: *July 2, 1949*

LAST TELECAST: *January 3, 1958*

BROADCAST HISTORY:

Jul 1949–Feb 1950, CBS Sat 6:30–6:45
Sep 1950–Oct 1950, CBS Tue 10:30–10:45
Sep 1953–Dec 1953, CBS Sat 6:45–7:00
Dec 1954–May 1955, CBS Wed 10:45–11:00
May 1955–Jun 1955, NBC Fri 10:45–11:00
Sep 1955–Jan 1958, NBC Fri 10:45–11:00

REPORTER:

Red Barber

Sportscaster Red Barber, the "Old Redhead," was reporter, interviewer, and analyst on this weekly sports news program. In 1949 and 1950 it went under the title *Red Barber's Clubhouse*, and in the fall of 1953 it was *The Peak of the Sports News*. During that period Red was director of sports for CBS. From the fall of 1954 on CBS, then on NBC through the winter of 1958, under the title *Red Barber's Corner*, this series was used to fill the time between the conclusion of the boxing match and the start of the local 11:00 P.M. news. The format remained relatively constant. There were feature pieces on sports or individual athletes, interviews with sports figures, and bulletins on and scores of current contests.

RED BUTTONS SHOW, THE

Comedy Variety

FIRST TELECAST: *October 14, 1952*

LAST TELECAST: *May 13, 1955*

BROADCAST HISTORY:

Oct 1952–Dec 1952, CBS Tue 8:30–9:00
Dec 1952–Jan 1953, CBS Sat 9:00–9:30
Jan 1953–Jun 1954, CBS Mon 9:30–10:00 (OS)
Oct 1954–May 1955, NBC Fri 8:00–8:30

REGULARS:

Red Buttons
Dorothy Jolliffe (1952)
Pat Carroll (1952–1953)
Beverly Dennis (1952–1953)
Allan Walker (1952–1953)
Joe Silver
Betty Ann Grove (1953–1954)
Phyllis Kirk (1955)
Paul Lynde (1955)
Bobby Sherwood (1955)
The Elliot Lawrence Orchestra

The most memorable thing about *The Red Buttons Show* was an inane little song that Red sang called the "Ho-Ho" song. He would put his hands together in what appeared to be a gesture of supplication, lean his head against them at a funny angle, and hop around the stage singing "Ho! Ho! . . . He! He! . . . Ha! Ha! . . . Strange things are happening." For a time that song became a national craze that infected millions of children around the country. The show itself featured monologues and dance numbers by Red, and

sketches with his regulars and any guest stars. Some of the recurring characters portrayed by Red were Rocky Buttons, a punchy boxer; the Kupke Kid, a lovable little boy; the Sad Sack; and Keeglefarven, a dumb, blundering German. There were also regular sketches about Red and his wife (in a style that was to be imitated by George Gobel later in the 1950s) with Dorothy Jolliffe as his wife when the show first started. She was replaced in October by Beverly Dennis, and Miss Dennis gave way to Betty Ann Grove at the start of the 1953–1954 season.

A smash hit in its first season, *The Red Buttons Show* began to fade in its second year on CBS and was picked up by NBC after it had been canceled. The NBC series started as a variety show with guests but no regulars other than Red. That didn't seem to work so the format was changed to a situation comedy at the end of January. Red played himself as a TV comic who was always getting into troubles of one sort or another. Phyllis Kirk was his new wife, Bobby Sherwood his pal and director of the TV show, and Paul Lynde played Mr. Standish, a network vice-president with whom Red had constant run-ins. Nothing seemed to help and Red, who had gone through literally dozens of writers in his quest to find a workable format, left the air that spring.

RED SKELTON SHOW, THE

Comedy Variety

FIRST TELECAST: *September 30, 1951*

LAST TELECAST: *August 29, 1971*

BROADCAST HISTORY:

Sep 1951–Jun 1952, NBC Sun 10:00–10:30
Sep 1952–Jun 1953, NBC Sun 7:00–7:30
Sep 1953–Jun 1954, CBS Tue 8:30–9:00
Jul 1954–Sep 1954, CBS Wed 8:00–9:00
Sep 1954–Dec 1954, CBS Tue 8:00–8:30
Jan 1955–Jun 1961, CBS Tue 9:30–10:00 (OS)
Sep 1961–Jun 1962, CBS Tue 9:00–9:30
Sep 1962–Jun 1963, CBS Tue 8:30–9:30
Sep 1963–Jun 1964, CBS Tue 8:00–9:00
Sep 1964–Jun 1970, CBS Tue 8:30–9:30
Sep 1970–Mar 1971, NBC Mon 7:30–8:00
Jun 1971–Aug 1971, NBC Sun 8:30–9:00

REGULARS:

Red Skelton
David Rose and His Orchestra
Carol Worthington (1970–1971)
Chanin Hale (1970–1971)
Jan Arvan (1970–1971)
Bob Duggan (1970–1971)
Peggy Rea (1970–1971)
Brad Logan (1970–1971)
The Burgundy Street Singers (1970–1971)

THEMES:

"Holiday for Strings" (main); "Lovable Clown" (Freeloader skits); "Our Waltz" (intermittent), all by David Rose

Comedian Red Skelton, son of a circus clown, was one of the brightest young stars in radio during the

1940s. While many of radio's big names never fully made the transition to television, Red did. He had been essentially a visual comedian all along. In September 1951, almost ten years to the day after he had first appeared with his own show on network radio, he arrived on TV, and remained a TV superstar for the next 20 years.

Most of Red's repertoire of regular characters had been developed on radio, before a live audience, and they worked just as well on television. Among the best known were The Mean Widdle Kid, who left chaos wherever he went (his favorite expression: "I dood it!"); Clem Kadiddlehopper, the befuddled rustic; Sheriff Deadeye, the scourge of the West; boxer Cauliflower McPugg; Willie Lump-Lump, the drunk; San Fernando Red, the con man; and Bolivar Shagnasty. The one major addition to Red's character list for the TV show was Freddie the Freeloader, a hobo who never spoke. The sketches with Freddie were always pantomimed, and would, therefore, have been completely lost on a radio audience.

The format of the show consisted of an opening monologue by Red, performances by his guest stars, and comedy sketches with them. The only other regular on the show was orchestra leader David Rose, who had been with Red on radio and stayed with him throughout his 20 years on television. This finally changed for Red's last season on NBC, when he worked with a regular repertory cast. In general the humor was broad, but occasionally it could be touching and warm, particularly in the mime sketches with Freddie the Freeloader. These were often included in the completely pantomimed "Silent Spot," which for years was written for Red by Mort Greene.

Skelton was a warm, human performer who loved his audience as much as they loved him. His closing line was always a sincere, "God bless."

REDD FOXX
Comedy Variety
FIRST TELECAST: *September 15, 1977*
LAST TELECAST: *January 26, 1978*
BROADCAST HISTORY:
Sep 1977–Jan 1978, ABC Thu 10:00–11:00
REGULARS:
Redd Foxx
Gerald Wilson Orchestra

Old trouper Redd Foxx had been an obscure stand-up comic for decades before he got his first big break as the star of *Sanford and Son* in 1972. He had to clean up his act considerably for the television medium, as he had previously been known for his off-color humor and "party" albums, but the public loved his crochety old Fred Sanford characterization and the show became a major hit.

In 1977 Foxx left that series and turned up on ABC in the kind of program he had wanted to do all along, his own comedy variety hour with a strong black orientation. Among the regular features were "Redd's Corner," in which he spotlighted old show-business friends who had not had much TV exposure (usually for good reason— they were awful) and "The History of the Black in America," Redd's view of how things *really* happened. Among Redd's semiregular guests were comedian Slappy White, songstress Damita Jo, and Redd's comic partner from *Sanford and Son*, LaWanda Page. Gravel-voiced Redd also frequently offered a song or two.

REDD FOXX SHOW, THE
Situation Comedy
FIRST TELECAST: *January 18, 1986*
LAST TELECAST: *April 19, 1986*
BROADCAST HISTORY:
Jan 1986–Apr 1986, ABC Sat 8:00–8:30
CAST:
Al Hughes	Redd Foxx
Toni Rutledge	Pamela Segall
Diana Olmos	Rosana DeSoto
Sgt. Dwight Stryker	Barry Van Dyke
Jim-Jam	Nathaniel Taylor
Jim-Jam (as of Feb 22)	Theodore Wilson
Felicia Clemmons-Hughes	Beverly Todd
Byron Lightfoot	Sinbad
Duds	Iron Jaw Wilson

Redd Foxx attempted a comeback in this funky little comedy about a small-time businessman in New York City. Al Hughes was a gruff old codger who ran a combination diner/newsstand in a black, inner-city neighborhood. Hanging around the counter were Toni, a white street kid he had adopted as a foster daughter; Diana, the waitress; Jim-Jam, a friend; and Dwight, a local cop. There was a lot of street life in the neighborhood, and early episodes were enlivened by a group of four young harmonizing black kids (played by Ron Jaxon, Phil Perry, Theo Forsett, and Oren Waters) who worked as movers and constituted the "Mulberry St. Du-Wop Moving Company."

Major cast changes were made in March in a vain attempt to improve the program's sagging ratings. Diana and Toni departed (the latter to boarding school), and Al was descended upon by his sharp-tongued ex-wife Felicia, who demanded a half-interest in the business in lieu of the alimony he had never paid her. Byron was a new foster son.

REDIGO
Western
FIRST TELECAST: *September 24, 1963*
LAST TELECAST: *December 31, 1963*
BROADCAST HISTORY:
Sep 1963–Dec 1963, NBC Tue 8:30–9:00
CAST:
Jim Redigo	Richard Egan
Mike	Roger Davis
Frank Martinez	Rudy Solari
Gerry	Elena Verdugo
Linda Martinez	Mina Martinez

Empire had failed during the 1962–1963 season but its focal character, Jim Redigo, survived to try it on his own. In *Empire* he had been the manager of the vast Garret ranch in the contemporary Southwest. Now he was the owner and operator of his own small ranch in the same area at roughly the same time. The problems of making the ranch profitable and the relationships between people on it provided the story material. The two most prominent employees on the Redigo ranch were Mike and Frank, and Jim's casual romantic interest (despite the fact that she was seriously in love with him) was Gerry, manager of the Gran Quivera Hotel in the nearby town of Mesa. Frank's wife Linda was the ranch's cook.

REEL GAME, THE
Quiz/Audience Participation
FIRST TELECAST: *January 18, 1971*
LAST TELECAST: *May 3, 1971*
BROADCAST HISTORY:
  Jan 1971–May 1971, ABC Mon 8:30–9:00
EMCEE:
  Jack Barry

Each of the three contestants in this quiz show was given a sum of money and then asked to bet portions of it on his knowledge of famous people and events. The answers were then compared with newsreels or film clips of the right answers.

The program was created by Jack Barry, who was said to have been involved in the creation and production of 30 different quiz, game, and audience-participation shows up to this time.

REGGIE
Situation Comedy
FIRST TELECAST: *August 2, 1983*
LAST TELECAST: *September 1, 1983*
BROADCAST HISTORY:
  Aug 1983, ABC Tue 9:30–10:00
  Aug 1983–Sep 1983, ABC Thu 9:00–9:30
CAST:
  Reggie Potter .... Richard Mulligan
  Elizabeth Potter .... Barbara Barrie
  Mark Potter .... Timothy Busfield
  Linda Potter Lockett .... Dianne Kay
  Tom Lockett................. Timothy Stack
  C. J. Wilcox .... Chip Zien
  Joan Reynolds .... Jean Smart

Reggie was based on a British television series that had begun with an interesting premise: a frustrated, middle-aged executive, exhausted by the pressures and monotony of his life, faked his own suicide by walking into the ocean. He then came back in all manner of outrageous disguises to snoop on his family and friends (who were mourning him—sort of) and ended up romancing and marrying his own "widowed" wife, before the ruse was discovered. The American series never tried that innovative plot, but it did depict a frustrated Reggie trying to cope with his perpetual midlife crisis through daydream fantasies that viewers saw and that sometimes came true.

Reggie's job at the Funtime Ice Cream Company gave him the most woe, especially his incredibly overbearing young boss, C.J., and his luscious secretary, Joan, about whom he had been having sexual fantasies for years (unknown to Reggie, she had been having the same fantasies about him). He worried about his sexual prowess with his wife, Elizabeth, worried about his daughter, Linda, and her obnoxious husband, Tom, lusted for his son Mark's girlfriend, and confided his darkest secrets to Monty, a large stuffed toy fox attired in English hunting habit.

Based on the British series *The Fall and Rise of Reginald Perrin,* and David Nobbs' book of the same name.

REHEARSAL CALL
Variety
FIRST TELECAST: *March 20, 1949*
LAST TELECAST: *April 24, 1949*
BROADCAST HISTORY:
  Mar 1949–Apr 1949, ABC Sun 9:15–9:30
HOSTESS:
  Dee Parker
REGULARS:
  Leonard Stanley Trio

Short-lived 15-minute variety program originating from Detroit.

REMINGTON STEELE
Detective Drama
FIRST TELECAST: *October 1, 1982*
LAST TELECAST: *March 9, 1987*
BROADCAST HISTORY:
  Oct 1982–Mar 1983, NBC Fri 10:00–11:00
  Mar 1983–Dec 1983, NBC Tue 9:00–10:00
  Jan 1984–Feb 1986, NBC Tue 10:00–11:00
  Feb 1986–Aug 1986, NBC Sat 10:00–11:00
  Feb 1987, NBC Tue 10:00–11:00
  Mar 1987, NBC Mon 10:00–11:00
CAST:
  Laura Holt .... Stephanie Zimbalist
  Remington Steele .... Pierce Brosnan
  Murphy Michaels (1982–1983).... James Read
  Bernice Foxe (1982–1983) ...... Janet DeMay
  Mildred Krebs (1983–1987)..... Doris Roberts

Laura Holt and Remington Steele had come together quite by accident, but they made a great pair of sleuths. She was smart, brassy, and attractive; he was cultured, handsome, and extremely charming. Together they solved complex murder mysteries in high society, while maintaining a relationship that bordered on the romantic. Actually, Remington had begun as a figment of Laura's imagination. Opening her own investigation agency, she found that a woman's name did not bring in assignments, so she invented an imaginary boss—Remington Steele—and business boomed. Trouble was, wealthy clients kept wanting to meet this supersleuth whose name was on the door. Along came an incredibly handsome chap with a suave manner and a mysterious background; just what she needed. Steele (his real name and background remained a mystery) bumbled a lot at first, but learned the private eye's trade quickly and soon was more than a front man for Laura. A fan of old Hollywood movies, he often pursued a case by playing out a scene from a classic film like *The Thin Man*, *Notorious*, or *Key Largo*. With easy banter and close teamwork, and occasional comic interludes, the stylish pair proved that romance and mystery did still mix.

There were changes in the supporting cast for the second season, as Bernice the secretary ran off with a saxophone player and was replaced by Mildred, an ex-I.R.S. agent who had lost her government job after letting Remington beat a tax-evasion charge; and Murphy, Laura's original partner, left to form his own agency.

Remington Steele's last regular season was 1985–1986. However, in early 1987 NBC aired two new two-hour movies in which Laura and Remington solved international mysteries, and finally consummated their relationship.

RENDEZVOUS
International Intrigue
FIRST TELECAST: *February 13, 1952*
LAST TELECAST: *March 5, 1952*
BROADCAST HISTORY:
  Feb 1952–Mar 1952, ABC Wed 9:30–10:00
CAST:
  Nikki Angell .... Ilona Massey
ALSO:
  David McKay

This short-lived series starred gorgeous Hungarian-born film star Ilona Massey as the owner and chief attraction at Chez Nikki, a posh nightclub in Paris. She had been a French underground agent during World War II, and was now engaged in international espionage on the Continent, foiling Communist agents and incidentally romancing newspaperman David McKay. Miss Massey also had an opportunity to sing one or two songs in each episode, in her sultry style.

RENDEZVOUS WITH MUSIC
Music
FIRST TELECAST: *July 11, 1950*
LAST TELECAST: *August 8, 1950*
BROADCAST HISTORY:
  Jul 1950–Aug 1950, NBC Tue 9:00–9:30
REGULARS:
  Carol Reed
  Don Gallagher
  Tony DeSimone Trio

This was a musical interlude, reflecting "the varied tempos of summertime." Emcee Carol Reed was also featured as a singer on the show.

RENEGADES
Police Drama
FIRST TELECAST: *March 4, 1983*
LAST TELECAST: *April 8, 1983*
BROADCAST HISTORY:
  Mar 1983–Apr 1983, ABC Fri 9:00–10:00
CAST:
  Bandit .... Patrick Swayze
  Eagle .... Randy Brooks
  J.T. .... Paul Mones
  Tracy .... Tracy Scoggins
  Dancer..................... Robert Thaler
  Dragon..................... Brian Tochi
  Gaucho .... Fausto Bara
  Lt. Marciano .... James Luisi
  Capt. Scanlon .... Kurtwood Smith

With a premise reminiscent of *The Mod Squad*, this short-run series brought together a group of seven tough young gang leaders and a hip cop named Lt. Marciano to fight crime in the big city. The incentive was to clear their records, and Marciano was a tough taskmaster. Their undercover operations often included finking on their own generation (infiltrating gangs, high schools, etc.), although there usually was a crooked adult behind it all. Capt. Scanlon was dubious about the whole idea, and was constantly on Marciano's back to give it up.

The Renegades was originally seen as a TV-movie on August 11, 1982.

REPORT CARD FOR PARENTS
Discussion
FIRST TELECAST: *December 1, 1952*
LAST TELECAST: *February 2, 1953*
BROADCAST HISTORY:
  Dec 1952–Feb 1953, DUM Mon 8:00–8:30

Panel-discussion program on the problems of bringing up children, with different guests each week.

REPORT FROM . . .
News/Travelogue
FIRST TELECAST: *July 9, 1963*
LAST TELECAST: *September 10, 1963*
BROADCAST HISTORY:
  Jul 1963–Sep 1963, NBC Tue 10:30–11:00

Film portraits of 11 cities around the world, hosted by the NBC News correspondent in each city.

REPORT ON . . .
Documentary
FIRST TELECAST: *March 13, 1949*
LAST TELECAST: *April 3, 1949*
BROADCAST HISTORY:
  Mar 1949–Apr 1949, CBS Sun 6:30–7:00
NARRATOR:
  Charles Hodges

This four-week documentary series, hosted and narrated by CBS News correspondent Charles Hodges, analyzed the current world political situation. The reports were on Moscow, the North Atlantic Pact, Italy, and a United Nations press conference.

REPORT TO MURPHY
Situation Comedy
FIRST TELECAST: *April 5, 1982*
LAST TELECAST: *May 31, 1982*
BROADCAST HISTORY:
  Apr 1982–May 1982, CBS Mon 8:30–9:00
CAST:
  Murphy .... Michael Keaton
  Blanche .... Olivia Cole
  Lucy .... Donna Ponterotto
  Charlie .... Donnelly Rhodes
  Baker .... Margot Rose
  Big Walter .... Ken Foree

Short-lived comedy about the trials of an idealistic young parole officer. Murphy was new to the profession and was not yet as disillusioned as his fellow parole officers. His enthusiasm and willingness to try unorthodox approaches in dealing with parolees were ridiculed by veteran, by-the-book Charlie, the office sourpuss. Even his supervisor, Blanche, and his fellow parole officer, Lucy, sometimes found it hard to understand why Murphy got so personally involved with his "clients." Baker was a pretty young assistant district attorney with whom Murphy had an on-again/off-again relationship, depending on whether or not she was prosecuting one of his parolees, and Big Walter was a car thief who was one of Murphy's favorite "clients."

REPORTER, THE
Newspaper Drama
FIRST TELECAST: *September 25, 1964*
LAST TELECAST: *December 18, 1964*
BROADCAST HISTORY:
  Sep 1964–Dec 1964, CBS Fri 10:00–11:00
CAST:
  Danny Taylor .... Harry Guardino
  Lou Sheldon .... Gary Merrill
  Artie Burns............... George O'Hanlon
  Ike Dawson .... Remo Pisani

Danny Taylor was a reporter for *The New York Globe*, a Manhattan daily. He was young, tough, and determined, all qualities necessary for a newsman in "The Big Apple." City editor Lou Sheldon was Danny's boss. He was also the father figure who understood what made Danny tick and could use his knowledge of the workings of the younger man's mind to drive him to dig deeper and harder into a story. Artie Burns was the friendly cabbie who was always available to take Danny off on a story, and Ike Dawson ran the Press Box, a bar where newspaper people gathered in their off hours.

REPORTER COLLINS
  see *Not for Publication*

RESCUE 8
Adventure
BROADCAST HISTORY:
  Syndicated only
  30 minutes
  Produced: *1958–1959* (73 episodes)
  Released: *September 1958*
CAST:
  Wes Cameron .... Jim Davis
  Skip Johnson .... Lang Jeffries
  Patty Johnson .... Nancy Rennick

This predecessor of *Emergency*, *240-Robert*, and other "rescue" shows was based on the files of the Los Angeles County Fire Department's rescue squads. Wes Cameron headed the two-man team that inched its way into all sorts of precarious situations to save people in awkward straits (scaffolds, Ferris wheels, cliffs, etc.). Skip was the junior member of the team, whose wife, Patty, wished he'd do something less dangerous for a living.

RESTLESS GUN, THE
Western
FIRST TELECAST: *September 23, 1957*
LAST TELECAST: *September 14, 1959*
BROADCAST HISTORY:
  Sep 1957–Sep 1959, NBC Mon 8:00–8:30
CAST:
  Vint Bonner .... John Payne

The adventures of a loner traveling through the post–Civil War Southwest provided the stories told in *The Restless Gun*. Vint Bonner was a cowboy who just couldn't seem to stay in one place too long. Although he was a very proficient gunfighter, Vint was basically a quiet, idealistic individual who preferred not to fight if there was an acceptable alternative. Unfortunately, there often was no alternative.

ABC aired reruns of *The Restless Gun* weekdays from October 1959 to September 1960, and Saturday mornings from November 1959 to March 1960.

RETURN ENGAGEMENT
  see *ABC Dramatic Shorts—1952–1953*

RETURN ENGAGEMENT
  syndicated title for *Fireside Theater*

RETURN OF THE SAINT
  see *Saint, The*

REVLON MIRROR THEATRE
Dramatic Anthology
FIRST TELECAST: *June 23, 1953*
LAST TELECAST: *December 12, 1953*

BROADCAST HISTORY:
Jun 1953–Sep 1953, NBC Tue 8:00–8:30
Sep 1953–Dec 1953, CBS Sat 10:30–11:00
HOSTESS:
Robin Chandler

During the summer of 1953, Revlon sponsored a series of live dramas that aired on NBC on Tuesday nights. When the series moved to CBS in September, the plays shown were on film. During the NBC run, Eddie Albert, Martha Scott, Jackie Cooper, and Peggy Ann Garner appeared. Joan Crawford made her TV dramatic debut in the first CBS episode, and subsequent telecasts featured such stars as Agnes Moorehead, Dane Clark, Angela Lansbury, and Charles Bickford. Hostess Robin Chandler was also the commercial spokeswoman for Revlon Cosmetics, the show's sponsor.

REVLON REVUE, THE
Variety
FIRST TELECAST: *January 28, 1960*
LAST TELECAST: *June 16, 1960*
BROADCAST HISTORY:
Jan 1960–Jun 1960, CBS Thu 10:00–11:00

This series was a collection of variety specials, each of which starred different performers. It presented both comedy and music with the emphasis of a particular show depending on the makeup of its cast. Among the stars of individual telecasts were Mickey Rooney, Maurice Chevalier, Jackie Cooper, Gordon and Sheila MacRae, and Peggy Lee. Miss Lee starred in several shows, while the others were in only one each. On March 24 the show's title was changed to *Revlon Presents* and, effective May 12, when it began a series of musical specials, to *Revlon Spring Music Festival.*

RHINEMANN EXCHANGE, THE
Foreign Intrigue
FIRST TELECAST: *March 10, 1977*
LAST TELECAST: *March 24, 1977*
BROADCAST HISTORY:
Mar 1977, NBC Tue 9:00–11:00
CAST:
David Spaulding .... Stephen Collins
Leslie Hawkewood........... Lauren Hutton
Bobby Ballard .... Roddy McDowall
Walter Kendall .... Claude Akins
Geoffrey Moore .... Jeremy Kemp
Ambassador Granville .... John Huston
Gen. Swanson .... Vince Edwards
Erich Rhinemann .... Jose Ferrer
Heinrik Stoltz .... Bo Brundin

Adapted from Robert Ludlum's best-selling novel of World War II espionage, *The Rhinemann Exchange* was the story of the exploits of David Spaulding, a young intelligence officer who had covered Europe on concert tours with his late father prior to the start of the war. His familiarity

with the Continent and knowledge of many European tongues made him an invaluable wartime agent for the U.S. His biggest assignment developed when he was sent to Argentina to set up a deal between the Americans and certain dissident elements in Hitler's Germany for the exchange of materiel desperately needed to facilitate the successful conduct of the war by the Allies.

The Rhinemann Exchange was one of four novels dramatized under the collective title *NBC's Best Sellers.*

RHODA
Situation Comedy
FIRST TELECAST: *September 9, 1974*
LAST TELECAST: *December 9, 1978*
BROADCAST HISTORY:
Sep 1974–Sep 1975, CBS Mon 9:30–10:00
Sep 1975–Jan 1977, CBS Mon 8:00–8:30
Jan 1977–Sep 1978, CBS Sun 8:00–8:30
Sep 1978–Dec 1978, CBS Sat 8:00–8:30
CAST:
Rhoda Morgenstern Gerard ... Valerie Harper
Brenda Morgenstern .... Julie Kavner
Joe Gerard (1974–1977) .... David Groh
Ida Morgenstern (1974–1976, 1977–1978)
.... Nancy Walker
Martin Morgenstern (1974–1976, 1977–1978)
.... Harold J. Gould
Carlton the Doorman (voice only)
.... Lorenzo Music
Mae (1974–1975) .... Cara Williams
Alice Barth (1974–1975) ...... Candy Azzara
Donny Gerard (1974) .... Todd Turquand
Myrna Morgenstein (1974–1976)
.... Barbara Sharma
Justin Culp (1975–1976) .... Scoey Mitchlll
Gary Levy (1976–1978) .... Ron Silver
Sally Gallagher (1976–1977)..... Anne Meara
Johnny Venture (1977–1978).. Michael Delano
Benny Goodwin (1977–1978) .. Ray Buktenica
Jack Doyle (1977–1978) .... Ken McMillan
Ramón Diaz, Jr. (1977–1978) . Rafael Campos
Tina Molinari (1978) .... Nancy Lane

As Mary Richards' friend and neighbor on *The Mary Tyler Moore Show,* Rhoda had been somewhat overweight, insecure in her relationships with men, and jealous of the trim Mary. Over the years, however, she had slimmed down, and when she returned home to New York for a visit at the start of *Rhoda* in the fall of 1974, she was a more attractive and self-confident person. The visit turned into a permanent change of residence when she met and fell in love with Joe Gerard. Joe was the owner of the New York Wrecking Company, divorced, and the father of a 10-year-old son. Rhoda moved in with her sister Brenda, since living with her parents Ida and Martin was just not working out, and got a job as a window dresser for a department store. The romance blossomed and, in a special full-hour telecast on Octo-

660

ber 28, 1974, Rhoda Morgenstern the husband-hunter became Rhoda Gerard.

The newlyweds moved into the same building in which Brenda and Rhoda had been living. Joe went off every day to the office to deal with his partner Justin while Rhoda was a relatively unoccupied housewife. Boredom precipitated her decision to start her own window-dressing business with a high school friend, shy Myrna, as a partner. With Rhoda happily married, the comedy shifted to her chubby sister, Brenda, a bank teller with constant problems trying to get a boyfriend, sort of a younger version of the Rhoda who started on *The Mary Tyler Moore Show* in 1970.

After two years of stories about wedded bliss the producers of *Rhoda* decided that a happily married couple was just not as funny as two single people trying to cope with the world. In order to create more flexibility in Rhoda's role, she and Joe separated soon after the start of the 1976–1977 season. Now they were able to make new friends, suffer the adjustments of living apart, and again deal with the world of the lonely "single." Joe was gradually phased out of the show, preparatory to the inevitable divorce, and Rhoda joined her sister at mixers and singles bars. She found a new friend in 39-year-old divorced airline stewardess Sally Gallagher, and both she and Brenda were frequently escorted by platonic friend Gary Levy. In the middle of that season Rhoda began an off-again, on-again romance with egocentric Las Vegas-based entertainer Johnny Venture.

The 1977–1978 season brought another raft of changes. Rhoda found a new job working at the Doyle Costume Company, a run-down business struggling to survive. Jack Doyle was the owner of the company and his assistant was Ramón. Brenda had a new boyfriend in Benny Goodwin, (who replaced the infrequently seen Las Vegas musician Nick Lobo, played by Richard Masur, who had romanced her from 1975 to 1977) and mother Ida had just returned from a year's traveling around the country. By the start of the last season Ida too was single, having been deserted by Martin.

RHYTHM RODEO
Music
FIRST TELECAST: *August 6, 1950*
LAST TELECAST: *January 7, 1951*
BROADCAST HISTORY:
Aug 1950–Jan 1951, DUM Sun 8:00–8:30
REGULARS:
Art Jarrett
Paula Wray
The Star Noters

Art Jarrett, a band singer with a career stretching back into the 1920s, hosted this early, low-budget musical program from Chicago. Although the motif was supposed to be "Western," all types of songs were featured. Running opposite Ed Sul-livan's *Toast of the Town*, it didn't really matter what they did.

RICH LITTLE SHOW, THE
Comedy Variety
FIRST TELECAST: *February 2, 1976*
LAST TELECAST: *July 19, 1976*
BROADCAST HISTORY:
Feb 1976–Jul 1976, NBC Mon 8:00–9:00
REGULARS:
Rich Little
Charlotte Rae
Julie McWhirter
R. G. Brown
Mel Bishop
Joe Baker
The Robert E. Hughes Orchestra

Impressionist Rich Little was the host and star of this comedy variety series. Each episode contained a monologue, a number of comedy sketches, and performances by the week's guest stars. The one running character that appeared on each episode was Julie McWhirter's Family Hour Good Fairy (a satire on the TV networks' recently announced policy of reserving 8:00–9:00 P.M. each night for wholesome "family entertainment" rather than violence). For a four-week period in the middle of this show's run, from May 24 to June 14, it was replaced by a mini-series, *The John Davidson Show*.

RICH MAN, POOR MAN—BOOK I
Drama
FIRST TELECAST: *February 1, 1976*
LAST TELECAST: *June 21, 1977*
BROADCAST HISTORY:
Feb 1976–Mar 1976, ABC Mon 10:00–11:00
May 1977–Jun 1977, ABC Tue 9:00–11:00
CAST:
Rudy Jordache .... Peter Strauss
Tom Jordache .... Nick Nolte
Julie Prescott Abbott Jordache
.... Susan Blakely
Axel Jordache .... Edward Asner
Mary Jordache .... Dorothy McGuire
Willie Abbott .... Bill Bixby
Duncan Calderwood .... Ray Milland
Teddy Boylan .... Robert Reed
Virginia Calderwood............ Kim Darby
Sue Prescott................. Gloria Grahame
Asher Berg .... Craig Stevens
Joey Quales .... George Maharis
Linda Quales .... Lynda Day George
Nichols .... Steve Allen
Smitty .... Norman Fell
Teresa Sanjoro .... Talia Shire
Marsh Goodwin .... Van Johnson
Irene Goodwin .... Dorothy Malone
Kate Jordache .... Kay Lenz
Sid Gossett............... Murray Hamilton
Arnold Simms .... Mike Evans
Al Fanducci .... Dick Butkus

661

Clothilde...............	Fionnula Flanagan
Brad Knight	Tim McIntire
Bill Denton.............	Lawrence Pressman
Claude Tinker................	Dennis Dugan
Gloria Bartley...............	Jo Ann Harris
Pete Tierney	Roy Jenson
Lou Martin	Anthony Carbone
Papadakis......................	Ed Barth
Ray Dwyer............	Herbert Jefferson, Jr.
Arthur Falconetti	William Smith
Col. Deiner................	Andrew Duggan
Pinky	Harvey Jason
Martha	Helen Craig
Phil McGee	Gavan O'Herlihy
Billy	Leigh McCloskey
Wesley	Michael Morgan

MUSIC:
Alex North

If it had not been overshadowed so quickly by
Roots, Rich Man, Poor Man would probably be
ranked today as the biggest dramatic spectacular
in the history of television. It was an enormous
hit, not only spawning a separate series the following season (see Rich Man, Poor Man—Book
II) but also stimulating a rash of novels-for-televi-
sion.

The source was Irwin Shaw's sprawling (720-
page) 1970 best-seller about the divergent careers
of two brothers in the years from 1945 to the 1960s.
Rudy Jordache was the "rich man," the ambitious,
educated entrepreneur who triumphed over his
impoverished immigrant background to build a
business and political empire. Tom was the "poor
man," the trouble-prone rebel who turned boxer
for a time, and was eventually murdered in the
last episode by the vicious Falconetti. Axel and
Mary were the parents, and Julie, Rudy's lifelong
love. An enormous, all-star cast paraded through
the 12-hour presentation as lovers, enemies,
scoundrels, and friends. The entire 12 hours was
repeated in May–June 1977.

RICH MAN, POOR MAN—BOOK II
Drama
FIRST TELECAST: September 21, 1976
LAST TELECAST: March 8, 1977
BROADCAST HISTORY:
Sep 1976–Mar 1977, ABC Tue 9:00–10:00
CAST:

Senator Rudy Jordache........	Peter Strauss
Wesley Jordache	Gregg Henry
Billy Abbott	James Carroll Jordan
Maggie Porter	Susan Sullivan
Arthur Falconetti	William Smith
Marie Falconetti..............	Dimitra Arliss
Ramona Scott	Penny Peyser
Scotty	John Anderson
Charles Estep	Peter Haskell
Phil Greenberg	Sorrell Booke
Annie Adams.................	Cassie Yates
Diane Porter	Kimberly Beck
Arthur Raymond...............	Peter Donat

Claire Estep..............	Laraine Stephens
Senator Paxton	Barry Sullivan
Kate Jordache	Kay Lenz
John Franklin................	Philip Abbott
Max Vincent	George Gaynes
Al Barber	Ken Swofford
Senator Dillon...............	G. D. Spradlin

This sequel to the 1976 mini-series began in the
year 1965, after the death of Tom Jordache, and
followed brother Rudy's further career as a U.S.
Senator. Rudy was now surrogate father to a family consisting of Wesley (Tom's boy) and Billy
(Julie's boy, by one of her marriages), two young
men ambitious for futures of their own. Much of
the action in Book II involved their entanglements, and Senator Rudy's protracted battle
against the greedy, power-hungry, and mysterious
billionaire Estep, owner of Tricorp. Falconetti
was back, apparently intent on killing off all the
Jordaches. Backgrounds of Las Vegas, Aspen, and
other haunts of the rich gave this melodrama a
lavish appearance, but it was soap opera nevertheless.

In the last original episode, Rudy and Falconetti
faced each other with guns in hand and shot it out,
apparently leaving the two of them lying bleeding
to death on a sidewalk.

RICHARD BOONE SHOW, THE
Dramatic Anthology
FIRST TELECAST: September 24, 1963
LAST TELECAST: September 15, 1964
BROADCAST HISTORY:
Sep 1963–Sep 1964, NBC Tue 9:00–10:00
REGULARS:
Richard Boone
Robert Blake
Lloyd Bochner
Laura Devon
June Harding
Bethel Leslie
Harry Morgan
Jeanette Nolan
Ford Rainey
Warren Stevens
Guy Stockwell

The Richard Boone Show was television's equivalent of repertory theater. Although there were no
continuing roles in this anthology series, the same
group of actors and actresses played parts in almost all the plays. Richard Boone was the host for
all episodes and starred in roughly half of the
shows. Each of the regulars had an opportunity to
star in at least one of the episodes, in addition to
having supporting roles in many of them.

RICHARD DIAMOND, PRIVATE DETECTIVE
Detective Drama
FIRST TELECAST: July 1, 1957
LAST TELECAST: September 6, 1960

Jul 1957–Sep 1957, CBS Mon 9:30–10:00
Jan 1958–Sep 1958, CBS Thu 8:00–8:30
Feb. 1959–Sep 1959, CBS Sun 10:00–10:30
Oct 1959–Jan 1960, NBC Mon 7:30–8:00
Jun 1960–Sep 1960, NBC Tue 9:00–9:30
CAST:
Richard Diamond .... David Janssen
Lt. McGough (1957–1958) ..... Regis Toomey
Karen Wells (1959) .... Barbara Bain
Lt. Kile (1959–1960) .... Russ Conway
"Sam" (1959) .... Mary Tyler Moore
"Sam" (1959–1960) .... Roxanne Brooks

Richard Diamond was an ex–New York City policeman who had turned in his badge to go into private practice as a detective. His familiarity with the force and his friends on it, most notably Lt. McGough, gave him access to information and help not normally afforded private detectives. In February 1959 he relocated to Hollywood, acquired a semiregular girlfriend in Karen Wells, and began using an answering service to get his messages. His contact at the answering service was a sultry-voiced woman whom he called "Sam." Her voice was heard and her body was seen from the waist down, to show off her legs, but her identity was not revealed in the screen credits at the end of each episode. The first actress to play "Sam" was young Mary Tyler Moore, a fact that was revealed to readers of *TV Guide* when an article appeared in May 1959 in which she modeled the latest in women's hosiery. It was in the middle of that month that she left the series to be replaced by another unbilled leggy actress. "Sam" was important to Richard Diamond since she often reached him in his car, which had a built-in phone, to warn of impending danger.

Dick Powell, whose Four Star Productions produced this series, had starred as Richard Diamond on the radio from 1949–1952.

RICHARD PRYOR SHOW, THE
Comedy Variety
FIRST TELECAST: *September 13, 1977*
LAST TELECAST: *October 20, 1977*
BROADCAST HISTORY:
Sep 1977–Oct 1977, NBC Tue 8:00–9:00
Oct 1977, NBC Thu 9:00–10:00
REGULARS:
Richard Pryor
Allegra Allison
David Banks
Sandra Bernhard
Victor Dunlop
Argus Hamilton
Jimmy Martinez
Paul Mooney
Tim Reid
Marsha Warfield
Robin Williams
"Detroit" John Witherspoon

The career of young black comic Richard Pryor was definitely on the rise when production started on his first regular television series during the summer of 1977. He had become successful as a nightclub performer, was seen regularly on television's talk shows, and had begun a career in motion pictures. His original commitment had been to do a minimum of ten variety shows for the series but, with the demands for his time growing after the success of two 1977 films, *Silver Streak* and *Greased Lightning*, coupled with censorship problems he had with NBC management, it was mutually agreed that he would do only five shows.

Although considered one of the most inventive, offbeat, and satirical performers around, Pryor's background as a nightclub comic led him to try material that might be considered in questionable taste for television. There were constant disagreements on what material was acceptable, and the opening sequence from his first show—in which he was shown nude from the waist up commenting that he had lost nothing in his battles with the network censors, followed by a pan down his body in which he appeared to be both completely nude and emasculated (he was actually wearing a body stocking)—was censored before the show was aired. His feud with NBC was highly publicized in the press but did little to attract viewers from ABC's *Happy Days*, his prime competition, which had twice as large an audience as *The Richard Pryor Show*.

RICHIE BROCKELMAN, PRIVATE EYE
Detective Drama
FIRST TELECAST: *March 17, 1978*
LAST TELECAST: *August 24, 1978*
BROADCAST HISTORY:
Mar 1978–Apr 1978, NBC Fri 9:00–10:00
Aug 1978, NBC Thu 9:00–10:00
CAST:
Richie Brockelman .... Dennis Dugan
Sgt. Ted Coopersmith .... Robert Hogan
Sharon Deterson .... Barbara Bosson

Richie Brockelman didn't look like a detective and that, as he put it, was his "trump card." Since almost no one, criminal or police, took the youthful-looking sleuth seriously, he was able to talk his way into and out of all sorts of dangerous situations in the course of his investigations. But Brockelman was indeed for real, a glib, 23-year-old, college-educated private investigator with his own, admittedly small, agency. Sharon was his trusted secretary and Sgt. Coppersmith his skeptical police contact.

The series was a spin-off of *The Rockford Files*, on which Brockelman had appeared on occasion to help out Jim Rockford.

RIDDLE ME THIS
see *Celebrity Time*

RIFLEMAN, THE
Western
FIRST TELECAST: *September 30, 1958*
LAST TELECAST: *July 1, 1963*
BROADCAST HISTORY:
  Sep 1958–Sep 1960, ABC Tue 9:00–9:30
  Sep 1960–Sep 1961, ABC Tue 8:00–8:30
  Oct 1961–Jul 1963, ABC Mon 8:30–9:00 (OS)
CAST:
  Lucas McCain .... Chuck Connors
  Mark McCain .... Johnny Crawford
  Marshal Micah Torrance .... Paul Fix
  Miss Milly Scott (1960–1962)..... Joan Taylor
  Lou Mallory (1962–1963) .... Patricia Blair
  Sweeney, the bartender .... Bill Quinn
  Hattie Denton .... Hope Summers

The Rifleman was the saga of Lucas McCain, a homesteader in the Old West struggling to make a living off his ranch and make a man out of his motherless son, Mark. Chuck Connors, a former professional baseball player, won critical acclaim for his portrayal of Lucas, and young Johnny Crawford was also started on a successful career by this series. The setting was the town of North Fork, New Mexico, whose marshal seemed incapable of handling any of the numerous desperados who infested the series (as they did all Western series) without the help of Lucas. Helpful, too, was the trick rifle that Lucas always carried, a modified Winchester with a large ring which cocked it as he drew. Supposedly, he could fire off his first round in three-tenths of a second, which certainly helped in a showdown.

Though quite successful at first, the series began to slip in its third season, due to a number of reasons including Lucas' rather righteous tone. To "humanize" him the producers brought Miss Milly to North Fork, to serve as storekeeper and McCain's love interest. In 1962 a somewhat pushier female arrived: Lou Mallory, a kind of con-artist-with-a-heart-of-gold hotel keeper who began buying up the property around town and took out a lease on Lucas as well. In addition, Mark began to experience problems associated with adolescence (he had been 12 when the series started).

RIKER
Police Drama
FIRST TELECAST: *March 14, 1981*
LAST TELECAST: *April 11, 1981*
BROADCAST HISTORY:
  Mar 1981–Apr 1981, CBS Sat 10:00–11:00
CAST:
  Frank Riker .... Josh Taylor
  Brice Landis.............. Michael Shannon

To the general public, and to his former fellow officers on the Los Angeles Police Department, Frank Riker was a busted cop, expelled from the force for blatant disregard of rules and regulations. What they didn't know was that Frank had secretly been offered the chance to work under-cover for California Deputy Attorney General Brice Landis—Frank's former partner. Landis gave him assignments, and was the only person besides the governor who knew of Frank's special status. Everyone else seemed to hate Riker, which didn't stop the two-fisted investigator from infiltrating smuggling operations, prostitution rings, and other unsavory activities.

RIN TIN TIN
  see *Adventures of Rin Tin Tin, The*

RIPCORD
Adventure
BROADCAST HISTORY:
  Syndicated only
  30 minutes
  Produced: *1961–1963* (76 episodes)
  Released: *September 1961*
CAST:
  Ted McKeever................ Larry Pennell
  Jim Buckley .... Ken Curtis
  Chuck Lambert (1961–1962) .... Paul Comi
  Charlie Kern (1962–1963) .... Shug Fisher

The youthful heroes of this series literally jumped into a new adventure every week. Ted and Jim ran Ripcord, Inc., which taught skydiving and also hired out for rescues, recovery work, and other situations where parachutists were needed. Often they landed right in the middle of a crime in progress, and solved that too—who would expect the good guys to come floating down out of the sky? Chuck was their original pilot, replaced midway through the first season by Charlie Kern.

The series featured a lot of spectacular skydiving scenes, including one involving a fistfight in midair (shot by a cameraman in free-fall with the actors). At one point, two planes accidentally crashed while filming scenes for the program. With a little script adjustment, the footage of the crash was later used in the series.

RIPLEY'S BELIEVE IT OR NOT
Variety/Drama
FIRST TELECAST: *March 1, 1949*
LAST TELECAST: *September 4, 1986*
BROADCAST HISTORY:
  Mar 1949–Jun 1949, NBC Tue 9:30–10:00
  Jul 1949–Sep 1949, NBC Wed 10:00–10:30
  Oct 1949–Nov 1949, NBC Various times
  Jan 1950–May 1950, NBC Wed 8:00–8:30
  May 1950–Sep 1950, NBC Thu 8:00–8:30
  Sep 1982–Jan 1986, ABC Sun 7:00–8:00
  May 1985–Jun 1985, ABC Fri 8:30–9:00
  Jan 1986–Sep 1986, ABC Thu 8:00–9:00
HOST:
  Robert L. Ripley (Mar–May 1949)
  Robert St. John (Jul–Nov 1949)
  Jack Palance (1982–1986)
CO-HOST:
  Catherine Shirriff (1982–1983)
  Holly Palance (1983–1985)
  Marie Osmond (1985–1986)

This highly successful radio series moved to television in March 1949. Seen seated in a living room decorated with oriental antiques and mementos of his worldwide travels, Ripley recounted for viewers a number of strange stories each week, sometimes with the aid of exhibits or dramatizations. At times the program had a freak-show atmosphere. Among the early guests were Kuda Bux, the Indian fakir with "X-ray vision"; a man who could thread a needle with one hand while balancing his body parallel to the floor with the other; and a four-eyed Mongolian. However, there were also stories of ordinary people who had triumphed over great adversity to lead normal, and even exceptional, lives.

On May 27, 1949, less than three months after the series began, Bob Ripley died suddenly. He had already prepared the next week's program and it was presented, along with a tribute to his long career. The series continued, hosted by "guest custodians" of Ripley's sketchbook until Robert St. John became permanent host in July 1949. The program left the air briefly at the end of the year and returned in January 1950 as a dramatic series loosely based on Ripley's stories. Each week a guest cast enacted one of his remarkable true tales, usually one involving murder, romance, or both.

Thirty-two years after the original television run of *Believe It Or Not,* the series returned under the title *Ripley's Believe It Or Not,* with Jack Palance as host. The show still used much original Ripley material, and had the full cooperation of the Ripley estate. Now, however, film crews scoured the world for new and up-to-date oddities, and Palance and his co-host, Catherine Shirriff (later replaced by Palance's daughter Holly), were seen on location marveling over the bizarre phenomena they uncovered. Palance loved to skulk about the ruins, and add a sinister tone to his narration of the stories. Among them: the skeleton queen of Portugal, albino gorillas, Mad King Ludwig of Bavaria, drive-in funerals, a museum of torture in Peru, secret weapons of World War II, strange rituals in various parts of the globe, and the Texas millionairess who specified in her will that she be buried in her Ferrari, wearing her sexiest nightgown. Some features were lighter, such as the first showing of a long-lost production number featuring young Judy Garland, Ray Bolger, Bert Lahr, and Jack Haley that had been cut from the 1939 movie classic *The Wizard of Oz.* Others were up-to-date, including wonders of outer space and zero-gravity life aboard the Skylab space station.

The syndicated newspaper column on which all this was based was begun by Robert L. Ripley in 1918. Believe it or not.

RIPTIDE
Detective Drama
FIRST TELECAST: *January 3, 1984*
LAST TELECAST: *April 18, 1986*

BROADCAST HISTORY:
Jan 1984–Feb 1986, NBC Tue 9:00–10:00
Mar 1986–Apr 1986, NBC Fri 8:00–9:00
CAST:
Cody Allen .... Perry King
Nick Ryder .... Joe Penny
Murray "Boz" Bozinsky .... Thom Bray
Mama Jo (occasional, 1984).... Anne Francis
Lt. Ted Quinlan (1984–1985) .... Jack Ging
Kirk "The Dool" Dooley (1984–1985)
.... Ken Orlandt
Lt. Joanna Parisi (1985–1986).. June Chadwick

Nick and Cody were two Southern California beach bums who decided to go into the private-detective business. Working from Cody's cabin cruiser, the *Riptide,* docked at Pier 56 in King's Harbor, or from their hangout, the Straightaways Restaurant, they had at least two advantages over the competition: Cody's speedboat, the *Ebbtide,* and Nick's aging but serviceable helicopter, the *Screaming Mimi* (a bulky Sikorsky, painted pink with a gaping mouth on the front).

The boys knew that this was the high-tech era, so they recruited one more element, an army buddy named Boz, a mousy computer nerd who happened to be a genius with electronics. Well, almost; he never could get his computerized robot, Roboz, to work right. The three of them tackled cases that invariably involved high-speed chases, explosions, and beautiful girls in bikinis. Sometimes they enlisted the help of Mama Jo and the all-girl crew of her charter boat, the *Barefoot Contessa,* which was moored next to theirs. The Dool was a dockboy who occasionally did some of their legwork.

It was a tough job, but someone had to do it. On August 22, 1986, four months after the series had been dropped from the lineup, a final repeat episode of *Riptide* was aired on NBC.

RITUALS
Drama
BROADCAST HISTORY:
Syndicated only
30 minutes
Produced: *1984–1985*
Released: *September 1984*
CAST:
Patrick Chapin .... Dennis Patrick
Taylor Chapin Field Von Platen (1984)
.... Jo Ann Pflug
Taylor Chapin Field Von Platen (1984–1985)
.... Tina Louise
Julia Field .... Andrea Moar
Brady Chapin (1984) .... Marc Poppel
Brady Chapin (1984–1985) ..... Jon Lindstrom
Carter Robertson .... Monte Markham
Christina Robertson......... Christine Jones
Jeff Robertson .... Tim Maier
Eddie Gallagher .... Greg Mullavey
Sara Gallagher (1984) .... Lorinne Vozoff
Sara Gallagher (1984–1985) .... Laurie Burton
Tom Gallagher .... Kevin Blair

Mike Gallagher	Kin Shriner
Noel Gallagher	Karen Kelly
Lacey Jarrett	Philece Sampler
Dakota "Koty" Lane (1984)	Claire Yarlett
Dakota "Koty" Lane (1984–1985)	
	Mary Beth Evans
Cherry Lane	Sharon Farrell
Logan Williams	George Lazenby
Diandra Santiago Gallagher	Gina Gallego
Marissa Mallory (1984)	Patti Davis
Marissa Mallory (1984–1985)	Janice Heiden
Bernhardt	Cameron Smith
Patty Dupont	Winifred Freedman
Clay Travis	Michael Weldon
C.J. Field (1985)	Peter Haskell
Lt. Lucas Gates (1985)	Antony Ponzini
Lisa Thompson (1985)	Wesley Ann Pfenning
Maddie Washington (1985)	Lynn Hamilton
Lucky Washington (1985)	
	Lawrence-Hilton Jacobs

Rituals was an expensive experiment that failed. In the wake of the success of prime-time network soap operas like *Dallas*, *Dynasty*, and *Knots Landing*, the producers of this series felt that the time was ripe for a syndicated nightly prime-time soap opera. *Rituals* represented an investment of tens of millions of dollars that attracted a minimal audience and limped through a single year on the air.

Set in fictional Wingfield, Virginia, outside of Washington, D.C., *Rituals* focused on three families—the wealthy Chapins; the middle-class Gallaghers, who ran a motel on the other side of town; and the Robertsons, whose head, Carter, was the conniving president of Haddon Hall, a local women's college that had been founded by the Chapin family.

The mortality rate was rather high among the early principals on this series. Patrick Chapin, the powerful patriarch who owned Wingfield Mills and and Chapin Industries, had just been widowed as the series began; a few months later he died of heart disease, resulting in another round of bequests and in-fighting. None of Patrick's children had turned out well. His greedy, scheming daughter, Taylor, had gone through five husbands and had a daughter, Julia, who hated her. A principal troublemaker during *Rituals'* early months, Taylor departed for Paris midway through the run. Patrick's young son, Brady, was a spoiled playboy who had affairs with Noel Gallagher and actress Koty Lane. Then there was the inevitable son nobody knew about—none other than manipulative Carter Robertson, who turned out to be Patrick's illegitimate offspring—a Chapin! Even before this was revealed Carter had wormed his way into Chapin Industries.

Eddie Gallagher, a violent man involved with criminal elements, survived only until February, when his daughter, Noel, murdered him to get even for years of abuse. Other members of Eddie's family were Sara, his long-suffering wife, son

Tom, a relatively honest cop, and half-brother Mike, a slightly flaky artist. Others prominently featured included Carter's wife, Christina (Sara's sister), another schemer, and their dishonest son, Jeff; Tom Gallagher's girlfriend and later wife, Diandra, the daughter of a Latin dictator, who was involved with revolutionaries; Lacey, the teacher who married Mike but couldn't have his baby (so Koty did); writer Logan, one of Taylor's former paramours; and another of Taylor's exes, billionaire C.J. Field. Much of the latter part of the series was consumed by the battle between C.J. and Carter for control of everybody and everything; as the series ended Carter got most of the booty, but C.J. had just been elected governor of Virginia.

RIVERBOAT
Adventure

FIRST TELECAST: *September 13, 1959*
LAST TELECAST: *January 16, 1961*
BROADCAST HISTORY:
   Sep 1959–Jan 1960, NBC Sun 7:00–8:00
   Feb 1960–Jan 1961, NBC Mon 7:30–8:30
CAST:

Grey Holden	Darren McGavin
Ben Frazer (1959–1960)	Burt Reynolds
Travis (1959–1960)	William D. Gordon
Carney	Richard Wessell
Joshua	Jack Lambert
Chip (1959–1960)	Mike McGreevey
Pickalong (1959–1960)	Jack Mitchum
Terry Blake (1959–1960)	Bart Patten
Bill Blake (1960–1961)	Noah Beery, Jr.

The *Enterprise* was a 100-foot-long stern-wheeler that churned up and down the Mississippi, Missouri, and Ohio rivers during the 1840s. The captain and owner of the boat was Grey Holden, a former fighter, rumrunner, swordsman, dock foreman, and soldier. A fun-loving romantic, he had won the boat in a poker game and was determined to make it a profitable venture, carrying passengers, hauling freight, and doing anything else it could to generate revenue. Boat pilot Ben Frazer was the co-lead when *Riverboat* first aired, an orphan whose entire life had been spent along the Mississippi. Both he and crew member Travis were written out of the series in the middle of its first season. When it returned in the fall of 1960, *Riverboat* had a new co-lead in Bill Blake, as a pilot who had bought 49 percent of the *Enterprise* and was constantly seeking to take controlling interest. First mate Joshua and crew member Carney were still in the cast, but gone were cabin boy Chip; Pickalong, the ballad singing cook; and Terry Blake, the cub-pilot who had replaced Ben Frazer. Captain Holden spent more time away from the boat and got involved in more romantic entanglements than during the first season.

ROAD WEST, THE
Western

FIRST TELECAST: *September 12, 1966*
LAST TELECAST: *August 28, 1967*
BROADCAST HISTORY:
    Sep 1966–Aug 1967, NBC Mon 9:00–10:00
CAST:
    Benjamin Pride .... Barry Sullivan
    Timothy Pride .... Andrew Prine
    Midge Pride .... Brenda Scott
    Kip Pride .... Kelly Corcoran
    Grandpa Pride................. Charles Seel
    Chance Reynolds .... Glenn Corbett
    Elizabeth Reynolds .... Kathryn Hays

Benjamin Pride was a widower who had taken his family from Springfield, Ohio, where they had lived for generations, and moved them to the Kansas Territory shortly after the end of the Civil War. The problems encountered by this pioneering family in the fertile but lawless West provided the stories in this series. Benjamin's family consisted of his 24-year-old son, Timothy, his daughter, Midge (18), and son, Kip (8), Elizabeth Reynolds, and her younger brother, Chance. Elizabeth, the daughter of a doctor, had become Benjamin's second wife just prior to his move to Kansas. Her brother had gone with the Prides in search of excitement and adventure.

ROAR OF THE RAILS, THE
Adventure
FIRST TELECAST: *October 26, 1948*
LAST TELECAST: *December 12, 1949*
BROADCAST HISTORY:
    Oct 1948–Dec 1948, CBS Tue 7:00–7:15
    Oct 1949–Dec 1949, CBS Mon 7:00–7:15

The object of this live adventure/documentary series was to dramatize the events that had made railroad history. Veteran railroad men appeared to explain what their jobs were like and the dramatizations were carried out with model trains and a miniature set that included mountains and tunnels. Not coincidentally, the program's sponsor was the A. C. Gilbert Company, manufacturer of American Flyer model trains. The sponsor had created the miniature set that was used in the series.
    Rival trainmaker Lionel sponsored a similar program on ABC, called *Tales of the Red Caboose*.

ROARING TWENTIES, THE
Newspaper Drama
FIRST TELECAST: *October 15, 1960*
LAST TELECAST: *September 21, 1962*
BROADCAST HISTORY:
    Oct 1960–Jan 1962, ABC Sat 7:30–8:30
    Sep 1962, ABC Fri 7:30–8:30
CAST:
    Scott Norris .... Rex Reason
    Pat Garrison .... Donald May
    Pinky Pinkham .... Dorothy Provine
    Chris Higbee .... Gary Vinson
    Jim Duke Williams .... John Dehner

Lt. Joe Switolski .... Mike Road
Robert Howard .... James Flavin

This adventure series was set in New York City in the 1920s and, in an attempt at documentary-style authenticity, included newsreel footage of events that had actually happened during that period. Pat and Scott were investigative reporters for the *New York Record* who, with the assistance of their young copy boy and friend, Chris, sought big scoops by infiltrating the underworld and exposing the hoods who were controlling the city during the Prohibition era. They were often seen at the Charleston Club, a posh speakeasy where the leading attraction was beautiful songstress Pinky Pinkham. Working in a club that was frequented by mobsters, Pinky often had tips that would help the reporters break their cases. Whenever they got in over their heads, Lt. Switolski of the N.Y.P.D. would bail them out.
    If this format sounds slightly familiar don't be surprised. Except for the fact that the leads in the series were reporters rather than detectives, *The Roaring Twenties* was interchangeable with any of the other formula series Warner Brothers produced for ABC in the late 1950s and early 1960s, the most successful of which were *77 Sunset Strip*, *Hawaiian Eye*, and *Surfside Six*. Canceled early in 1962, *The Roaring Twenties* returned for a few weeks that September with reruns.

ROBBINS NEST, THE
Comedy Variety
FIRST TELECAST: *September 29, 1950*
LAST TELECAST: *December 22, 1950*
BROADCAST HISTORY:
    Sep 1950–Dec 1950, ABC Fri 11:00–11:15
REGULARS:
    Fred Robbins
    Nate Cantor
    Fran Gregory

New York disc jockey Fred Robbins, known for his hip slang, tried TV comedy in this late-night program. Robbins and his supporting players appeared in various skits, and he also sang (passably), but the humor was rather weak. A typical gag had Robbins telling his secretary Fran to file a letter, whereupon she pulled out a metal file and began honing away. The program lasted three months.

ROBERT MONTGOMERY PRESENTS
Dramatic Anthology
FIRST TELECAST: *January 30, 1950*
LAST TELECAST: *June 24, 1957*
BROADCAST HISTORY:
    Jan 1950–Jun 1957, NBC Mon 9:30–10:30
HOST/EXECUTIVE PRODUCER:
    Robert Montgomery
SUMMER REPERTORY PLAYERS:
    John Newland (1952–1954)
    Vaughn Taylor (1952–1954)

667

Margaret Hayes (1952–1953)
Elizabeth Montgomery (1953–1954, 1956)
Jan Miner (1954–1956)
Anne Seymour (1954)
Cliff Robertson (1954)
Charles Drake (1955–1956)
Augusta Dabney (1955)
House Jameson (1955)
Dorothy Blackburn (1955)
Eric Sinclair (1955)
Mary K. Wells (1956)
John Gibson (1956)
Tom Middleton (1956)

One of the best-remembered big-budget live dramatic series of TV's golden age. Hollywood actor-director-producer Robert Montgomery introduced each telecast, sometimes interviewing one of the stars and sometimes appearing in the play himself. The series had a Hollywood flavor, with many familiar names from the screen appearing in leading roles. At first it presented adaptations of classic motion pictures, such as *Rebecca*, *A Star Is Born*, and *Dark Victory*, all of which were done within the first few months. Later original TV plays and adaptations of stage plays, books, and short stories were used due to copyright rules which prevented the kinescoping of any production based on a motion picture—these could be telecast on a live basis only. (Kinescopes were needed so that the program could be seen on some non-interconnected affiliates.)

The first telecast was an adaptation of W. Somerset Maugham's classic *The Letter*, and the quality of the scripts remained similarly high throughout the run of the series. The program won many awards. Jane Wyatt, Zachary Scott, and Montgomery's daughter, Elizabeth (later of *Bewitched* fame), made their TV debuts on this program. Claudette Colbert made one of her rare appearances in the medium, as did James Cagney. Helen Hayes and other famous stars, as well as newer talent, were also featured.

Some of the productions were truly spectacular for live television, such as a drama built around the destruction of the great dirigible *Hindenburg*, followed by interviews with some of the actual survivors.

Beginning in 1952, during the summers, *Robert Montgomery Presents* adopted a summer-stock format, with a repertory company of regulars appearing in starring or supporting roles in each production. Among these regulars were both newcomers such as Elizabeth Montgomery, Cliff Robertson, and John Newland, and some old-timers as well.

While the series was generally known as *Robert Montgomery Presents* the actual title varied from week to week according to the sponsor: *Robert Montgomery Presents Your Lucky Strike Theater*, . . . *the Johnson's Wax Program*, . . . *the Richard Hudnut Summer Theater*, etc. It alternated with various other programs during its first

two years on the air, then became a weekly series in December 1951.

ROBERT Q. LEWIS SHOW, THE
Comedy/Talk
FIRST TELECAST: *July 16, 1950*
LAST TELECAST: *January 7, 1951*
BROADCAST HISTORY:
    Jul 1950–Sep 1950, CBS Sun 9:00–9:15
    Sep 1950–Jan 1951, CBS Sun 11:00–11:15
HOST:
    Robert Q. Lewis

While still functioning as emcee on *The Show Goes On*, comedian Robert Q. Lewis added this informal show to his list of television credits. The live 15-minute show gave him the opportunity to chat with guest stars and introduce the weekly "Breadwinner of the Week," an individual performing an unusual job somewhere in the New York City area.

ROBERT TAYLOR'S DETECTIVES
    see *Detectives, Starring Robert Taylor, The*

ROBERT YOUNG, FAMILY DOCTOR
    syndicated title for *Marcus Welby, M.D.*

ROBIN HOOD
    see *Adventures of Robin Hood, The*

ROCK AND ROLL YEARS, THE
    see *Dick Clark Presents The Rock and Roll Years*

ROCK 'N' ROLL EVENING NEWS, THE
News/Information
BROADCAST HISTORY:
    Syndicated only
    60 minutes
    Produced: *Fall 1986–January 1987*
    Released: *September 1986*
HOST/ANCHOR:
    Steve Kmetko
CORRESPONDENTS:
    Adrienne Meltzer
    Eleanor Mondale
    Nelson George
    Richard Blade
    Marjorie Wallace
    Robert Hilburn
    Marianne Rogers
    Clarence

The Rock 'n' Roll Evening News was a weekly potpourri of interviews, gossipy news about the happenings in the rock music world, and performances by established and new rock groups. It had a large number of regular correspondents and an expensive high-tech look. To keep current, it was taped only a couple of days before airing (late on Saturday nights in most cities). What it didn't have was a large audience. An ambitious failure, it ceased production less than four months after its premiere.

ROCK 'N' ROLL SUMMER ACTION
Musical Variety
FIRST TELECAST: *July 17, 1985*
LAST TELECAST: *August 28, 1985*
BROADCAST HISTORY:
Jul 1985–Aug 1985, ABC Wed 8:00–9:00
HOST:
Christopher Atkins
REGULARS:
Paul Revere & the Raiders
The Action Kids '85 (dancers)
EXECUTIVE PRODUCER:
Dick Clark

Another of Dick Clark's innumerable lightweight rock 'n' roll series, this one set outdoors on California's Malibu Beach. There were plenty of bikinis, Frisbee-throwing, offbeat contests (e.g., the "bury-your-boyfriend-in-the-sand contest"), hip young stand-up comics, and clips of the kooky fashions and rock stars of yesteryear. Guests included Kim Carnes, Jan and Dean, the New Edition, Weird Al Yankovic, Stephanie Mills, and the Commodores.

For a similar series in 1967, see *Malibu U.*

ROCKFORD FILES, THE
Detective Drama
FIRST TELECAST: *September 13, 1974*
LAST TELECAST: *July 25, 1980*
BROADCAST HISTORY:
Sep 1974–May 1977, NBC Fri 9:00–10:00
Jun 1977, NBC Fri 8:30–9:30
Jul 1977–Jan 1979, NBC Fri 9:00–10:00
Feb 1979–Mar 1979, NBC Sat 10:00–11:00
Apr 1979–Dec 1979, NBC Fri 9:00–10:00
Mar 1980–Apr 1980, NBC Thu 10:00–11:00
Jun 1980–Jul 1980, NBC Fri 9:00–10:00
CAST:
Jim Rockford .... James Garner
Joseph "Rocky" Rockford.... Noah Beery, Jr.
Det. Dennis Becker .... Joe Santos
Beth Davenport (1974–1978)
.... Gretchen Corbett
Evelyn "Angel" Martin ...... Stuart Margolin
John Cooper (1978–1979) .... Bo Hopkins
Lt. Alex Diehl (1974–1976) .... Tom Atkins
Lt. Doug Chapman (1976–1980) ... James Luisi
*Lance White (1979–1980) .... Tom Selleck

*Occasional
THEME:
"The Rockford Files," by Mike Post and C. Carpenter

Jim Rockford was a private detective with a difference. He was an ex-convict. Once imprisoned for a crime he had not committed, but eventually exonerated when new evidence turned up, Jim had a penchant for taking cases that were closed—those the police were sure had been resolved. His knack for turning up information that might reverse the already established verdict did not endear him to the police, particularly to Det. Dennis Becker with whom he had a love-hate relationship. Jim was always getting Dennis involved in situations he would have preferred to avoid, aggravating the cop who, despite it all, had a personal affection for him. Jim lived in, and worked out of, a house trailer at the beach in the Los Angeles area and was not the cheapest detective available, charging $200 per day plus expenses. His father, a retired trucker, helped him on occasions and his girlfriend, attorney Beth Davenport, was always around to bail him out when he ran afoul of the law. Having been in prison, Jim had many ex-con friends. One of them, his former cellmate, Angel Martin, was constantly in need of Jim's help because of his tendency to get involved with his former criminal associates. Another friend was John Cooper, a disbarred lawyer whose ties to the Corporation for Legal Research proved useful.

Jim used all the seamier ploys for which detectives are known—impersonating others to get information, cheap disguises, petty bribery, eavesdropping—but his powers of reasoning and dogged hard work usually solved the case. If, along the way, he got beaten up, had his car damaged, and got shot at—well, he had a sense of humor. He resented fellow private investigator Lance White who, during *The Rockford Files'* last season, always seemed intuitively to know all the answers and have everything fall into his lap without effort. That final season was cut short when Garner, tired of the role and suffering from a variety of ailments, abruptly quit the show.

The theme song from this series was on the hit parade in mid-1975.

ROCKY AND HIS FRIENDS
see *Bullwinkle Show, The*

ROCKY KING, INSIDE DETECTIVE
Police Drama
FIRST TELECAST: *January 14, 1950*
LAST TELECAST: *December 26, 1954*
BROADCAST HISTORY:
Jan 1950–Jul 1950, DUM Sat 8:30–9:00
Jul 1950–Mar 1951, DUM Fri 9:30–10:00
Mar 1951–Dec 1954, DUM Sun 9:00–9:30
CAST:
Det. Rocky King .... Roscoe Karns
Mabel King .... Grace Carney
Sgt. Lane (1950–1953) .... Earl Hammond
Det. Hart (1953–1954) .... Todd Karns

Rocky King was probably the most popular continuing dramatic show to come out of the DuMont network. It never had the opportunity to attain top nationwide ratings, due to DuMont's limited station lineup and severely restricted production budgets (you never saw a big-name guest star acting in a *Rocky King* episode!), but it did attract a loyal and enthusiastic following which kept it on the air for five years, nearly until the end of Du-Mont operations.

The program centered on hard-working Rocky King, a detective on the New York City Homicide Squad, and was in most respects a standard low-budget cops-and-robbers show. What set it apart were its lead, Roscoe Karns; its sense of believability; and its touches of humor. Those who think that *Dragnet* brought realism to TV cop shows obviously never saw *Rocky King*. Rocky had no flashes of brilliant deduction or unbelievably lucky breaks, nor did he tackle impossibly convoluted cases. He simply tracked down the facts, doggedly, and pieced them together until they made sense—and pointed to the culprit. There was plenty of action in *Rocky King* too, but it usually came after some good, hard work.

Rocky also had a family, which generated a good deal of interest, because they were heard but never seen on camera. This began as an economy measure (typical of DuMont), when an actress who was playing a role in a mystery was asked to double as Rocky's wife at home. Since there was no time to change clothes or makeup (the show was live), she spoke from offscreen. Viewers liked the touch and Grace Carney became a permanent feature, her off-camera presence always bringing Rocky back to earth with her problems around the house. For a time there was also an unseen son, named Junior.

Roscoe Karns, who had had a long career in Hollywood as a second banana, was appreciative of the opportunity to extend his career via TV (he frankly said that *Rocky King* had "rescued" him from enforced retirement) and stayed with the show until its demise. During the final year of its run, his son, Todd Karns, played his sidekick, Det. Hart. Roscoe Karns later had a leading role in *Hennessey.* He died in 1970.

ROCKY'S CORNER
see *Henny & Rocky Show, The*

ROD SERLING'S NIGHT GALLERY
see *Night Gallery*

ROGER MILLER SHOW, THE
Musical Variety
FIRST TELECAST: *September 12, 1966*
LAST TELECAST: *December 26, 1966*
BROADCAST HISTORY:
 Sep 1966–Dec 1966, NBC Mon 8:30–9:00
REGULARS:
 Roger Miller
 The Eddie Karam Orchestra

Singer-composer Roger Miller, who had won five 1965 Grammy Awards for his recordings, starred in this short-lived variety show. In addition to singing popular songs and the country and western tunes which had made him so popular, he

introduced and performed with one or two guests stars each week. There were no other regulars, but the Doodletown Pipers made a number of appearances during the less than four months the show was on the air.

ROGUES, THE
Comedy/Drama
FIRST TELECAST: *September 13, 1964*
LAST TELECAST: *September 5, 1965*
BROADCAST HISTORY:
 Sep 1964–Sep 1965, NBC Sun 10:00–11:00
CAST:
 Tony Fleming..................... Gig Young
 Alec Fleming .... David Niven
 Marcel St. Clair .... Charles Boyer
 Timmy St. Clair .... Robert Coote
 Margaret St. Clair .... Gladys Cooper
 Inspector Briscoe .... John Williams

"Honor before Honesty" was the credo of the Flemings and the St. Clairs, the two most successful families of scoundrels the civilized world had ever known. Their lines had been forever crossed when Sir Giles Fleming and la Comtesse Juliette St. Clair had met and fallen in love while both were independently trying to lift a jewel box from Marie Antoinette of France in 1789. The modern descendants of these aristocratic jewel thieves and con men, whose primary activity was relieving the rich of their wealth, were spread all over the world. Tony was the dashing young American member of the family, who worked out of New York and had been hand-picked to take over the family "throne" from his English cousin, Alec, when the latter went into semiretirement. Alec had moved to Montego Bay but was still active for special deals. Marcel was the head of the French branch of the family and Timmy, a master of disguises, was on hand to help each of the principals. His mother, Aunt Margaret, was the planner and coordinator of most of the heists and cons, all of which were finalized at her home across from Buckingham Palace.

ROLL OUT
Situation Comedy
FIRST TELECAST: *October 5, 1973*
LAST TELECAST: *January 4, 1974*
BROADCAST HISTORY:
 Oct 1973–Dec 1973, CBS Fri 8:30–9:00
 Jan 1974, CBS Fri 8:00–8:30
CAST:
 Cpl. "Sweet" Williams .... Stu Gilliam
 Pfc. Jed Brooks .... Hilly Hicks
 Sgt. B. J. Bryant .... Mel Stewart
 Capt. Rocco Calvelli .... Val Bisoglio
 Lt. Robert W. Chapman .... Ed Begley, Jr.
 "Wheels" .... Garrett Morris
 Jersey........................ Darrow Igus
 Phone Booth...................... Rod Gist
 High Strung .... Theodore Wilson
 Madam Delacort.............. Penny Santon

Set in France during World War II, *Roll Out* was the story of the men of the 5050th Trucking Company, the "Red Ball Express," an army trucking unit that managed to get supplies through to troops at the front despite any and all problems. Military discipline meant little to these rowdy men, whose prime purpose was to move war supplies no matter how they did it. Capt. Calvelli was the leader of the unit, which was mostly black. Sweet and Jed were two of his best drivers, and Sgt. Bryant the tough, crusty career military man. When not on assignment, the men of the 5050th sought recreation at the nightclub adjacent to their base camp, run by Madam Delacort.

Based on the story of an actual World War II transportation unit.

ROLLER DERBY
Sports
FIRST TELECAST: *March 24, 1949*
LAST TELECAST: *August 16, 1951*
BROADCAST HISTORY:
  Mar 1949–Jun 1949, ABC Thu 10:00–11:15
  Mar 1949–May 1949, ABC Sat 10:00–11:00
  May 1949–Jun 1949, ABC Mon 9:30–Conclusion
  May 1949–Jul 1949, ABC Fri 10:00–Conclusion
  Sep 1949–Nov 1949, ABC Mon/Fri 10:00–Conclusion
  Sep 1949–Sep 1950, ABC Thu 10:00–Conclusion
  Nov 1949–May 1951, ABC Sat 9:00–Conclusion
  Jun 1950–Sep 1950, ABC Fri 8:30–9:30
  Sep 1950–May 1951, ABC Tue/Thu 10:00–11:15
  Jul 1951–Aug 1951, ABC Thu 10:00–11:15
ANNOUNCER:
  Ken Nydell
  Joe Hasel (1949–1950)
  Howard Myles (1950–1951)
  Ed Begley (1951)

Roller Derby was at one time the most popular program on the ABC schedule, that is if amount of air time occupied is a measure of popularity. The sport, which sometimes seemed more like a head-bashing free-for-all than a test of athletic skill, combined elements of skating, football, rugby, and wrestling, aired as often as three times a week. The show originated from such exotic locations as the 14th Regiment Armory in Brooklyn, and other similar places around New York City and adjacent areas of Long Island and New Jersey. The resident announcer was Ken Nydell, who did the play by play throughout the run, sometimes by himself and sometimes with an assistant. The New York Chiefs were always the home team, playing the San Francisco Bay Bombers, the Midwest Pioneers, and others.

ROLLER GIRLS, THE
Situation Comedy
FIRST TELECAST: *April 24, 1978*
LAST TELECAST: *May 10, 1978*
BROADCAST HISTORY:
  Apr 1978–May 1978, NBC Mon 8:00–8:30
  May 1978, NBC Wed 8:00–8:30
CAST:
  Don Mitchell .... Terry Kiser
  Mongo Sue Lampert .... Rhonda Bates
  J. B. Johnson .... Candy Ann Brown
  Selma "Books" Cassidy ..... Joanna Cassidy
  Honey Bee Novak .... Marcy Hanson
  Shana "Pipeline" Akira ..... Marilyn Tokuda
  Howie Devine .... James Murtaugh

The Pittsburgh Pitts were an all-girl roller derby team, owned and managed by conniving Don Mitchell, who was constantly looking for ways to save the foundering team—and his investment. The Pitts were a sexy, but sometimes inept crew: towering Mongo, feisty J.B. (the token black), sophisticated "Books," dizzy blonde Honey Bee, and innocent "Pipeline," an Eskimo-American. Announcer for the team's raucous games was the snobbish Howie Devine, a down-on-his-luck former opera commentator who would do anything for a buck.

ROLLIN' ON THE RIVER
Music
BROADCAST HISTORY:
Syndicated only
30 minutes
Produced: *1971–1973* (52 episodes)
Released: *Fall 1971*
REGULARS:
  Kenny Rogers and the First Edition (Terry Williams, guitar; Kin Vassey, rhythm guitar; Mickey Jones, drums; Mary Arnold, vocals)

Kenny Rogers and the First Edition, a group formed by ex-members of the New Christy Minstrels, had several soft-rock hits during the late 1960s and early 1970s, including "Ruby, Don't Take Your Love to Town" and "Just Dropped In." After network appearances on *The Smothers Brothers Comedy Hour* and other series, they showed their versatility in this Canadian-produced syndicated program of their own. It included contemporary music, comedy bits, and guests of a generally youthful persuasion—Kris Kristofferson, B. J. Thomas, Mac Davis, Bill Withers, Gladys Knight and the Pips, etc. The program was shot in front of a bright riverboat set.

The title was based on a line from the 1969 Creedence Clearwater Revival hit, "Proud Mary." It was shortened in the second season to *Rollin'*.

The pressures of taping a weekly show led to problems for the group, and after four hitless years they disbanded in 1976. Kenny Rogers then went on to an even bigger solo career acting and singing ballads such as "The Gambler" and "Lady."

ROMANCE
Dramatic Anthology

FIRST TELECAST: *November 3, 1949*
LAST TELECAST: *December 29, 1949*
BROADCAST HISTORY:
    Nov 1949–Dec 1949, CBS Thu 8:30–9:00

Premiering with an updated version of *Camille,* this live anthology series presented television adaptations of famous love stories. *Romance* aired on alternate Thursdays with *Inside U.S.A. with Chevrolet.*

ROOKIES, THE
Police Drama
FIRST TELECAST: *September 11, 1972*
LAST TELECAST: *June 29, 1976*
BROADCAST HISTORY:
    Sep 1972–Sep 1975, ABC Mon 8:00–9:00
    Sep 1975–Apr 1976, ABC Tue 9:00–10:00
    May 1976–Jun 1976, ABC Tue 10:00–11:00
CAST:
Officer Terry Webster
    . . . . Georg Stanford Brown
Officer Willie Gillis (1972–1974)
    . . . . .Michael Ontkean
Officer Mike Danko . . . . Sam Melville
Jill Danko . . . . Kate Jackson
Lt. Eddie Ryker . . . . Gerald S. O'Loughlin
Officer Chris Owens (1974–1976)
    . . . . Bruce Fairbairn

Three wet-behind-the-ears rookie cops in a large Southern California city provided the focus on this series. The trio, variously fresh out of college, a government social program, and the army, were dedicated to the new, more humane methods of law enforcement, which often put them at odds with their hard-nosed mentor, Lt. Ryker. The combination of their youthful enthusiasm and Ryker's experienced guidance helped mold them into effective officers. The only married one of the three was Mike, whose wife, Jill, was a registered nurse. In 1974 a cast change occurred when Willie was replaced by Chris Owens, a new recruit.

ROOM FOR ONE MORE
Situation Comedy
FIRST TELECAST: *January 27, 1962*
LAST TELECAST: *September 22, 1962*
BROADCAST HISTORY:
    Jan 1962–Sep 1962, ABC Sat 8:00–8:30
CAST:
George Rose . . . . Andrew Duggan
Anna Rose . . . . Peggy McCay
Flip Rose . . . . Ronnie Dapo
Laurie Rose . . . . Carol Nicholson
Mary Rose . . . . Anna Carri
Jeff Rose . . . . Timmy Rooney
Walter Burton . . . . Jack Albertson
Ruth Burton . . . . Maxine Stuart

This family comedy was about a middle-class couple, George and Anna Rose, their two natural children, Flip and Laurie, and their adopted children, Mary and Jeff (the latter played by Mickey Rooney's son Timmy). The Roses' easygoing ways and sympathy for children in general kept bringing other homeless waifs in and out of the household as well—they always had "room for one more." Tramp was the family dog, and Ruth a family friend (Jack Albertson appeared briefly as her husband).

Adapted from the autobiography of Anna Perrott Rose, which was also made into a 1952 movie (originally titled *Room for One More,* later retitled *The Easy Way*) starring Cary Grant.

ROOM 222
School Drama
FIRST TELECAST: *September 17, 1969*
LAST TELECAST: *January 11, 1974*
BROADCAST HISTORY:
    Sep 1969–Jan 1971, ABC Wed 8:30–9:00
    Jan 1971–Sep 1971, ABC Wed 8:00–8:30
    Sep 1971–Jan 1974, ABC Fri 9:00–9:30
CAST:
Pete Dixon . . . . Lloyd Haynes
Liz McIntyre . . . . Denise Nicholas
Seymour Kaufman . . . . . Michael Constantine
Alice Johnson . . . . Karen Valentine
Richie Lane (1969–1971) . . . . Howard Rice
Helen Loomis . . . . Judy Strangis
Jason Allen . . . . Heshimu
Al Cowley (1969–1971) . . . . Pendrant Netherly
Bernie (1970–1974) . . . . David Jolliffe
Pam (1970–1972) . . . . Ta-Tanisha
Larry (1971–1973) . . . . Eric Laneuville

Schoolroom drama about Pete Dixon, a black history teacher in an integrated big-city high school. An idealist, Pete instilled his students at Walt Whitman High with gentle lessons in tolerance and understanding. The number of his home room was 222, but wherever he went he was surrounded by a cluster of kids. They loved him for his easygoing manner and willingness to side with them when he knew they were being short-changed by the system. Seymour Kaufman was the cool, slightly sarcastic principal, Liz McIntyre Pete's girlfriend and a school counselor, and Alice Johnson an exuberant student teacher (in the second season she was promoted to full-fledged English teacher). The rest of the regulars were students.

The program was highly regarded for tackling current problems relevant to today's youth (prejudice, drugs, dropping out, etc.) and it received many awards and commendations from educational and civil rights groups. Its sense of reality was heightened by the fact that it was based on, and partially filmed at, 3,000-student Los Angeles High School.

ROOMIES
Situation Comedy
FIRST TELECAST: *March 19, 1987*
LAST TELECAST: *May 15, 1987*

Mar 1987, NBC Thu 9:10–9:40
Mar 1987–May 1987, NBC Fri 8:00–8:30
CAST:
Nick Chase.................... Burt Young
Matthew Wiggins.............. Corey Haim
Ms. Adler .... Jane Daly
Sheldon .... Joshua Nelson
Carl .... Sean Gregory Sullivan
Singing Freshmen
   Michael Lesco, Robert Rheames, Larry Wray

Two unlikely college freshmen shared a dorm room in this "odd couple" comedy. Nick was a burly, balding, 42-year-old former drill sergeant, who had retired after 20 years in the marine corps and entered Saginaw University a little late. Matthew was a 14-year-old genius who got there a little early. His main passion was rare fish. Both had adjustments to make—Nick to the unaccustomed chaos of dorm life, Matthew to the fact that almost everyone was older than he was, and brains alone do not a "cool guy" make. Among the dorm inhabitants were a nutty trio of "Singing Freshmen" who harmonized through the hallways.

Based on the movie of the same name.

ROOTS
Drama
FIRST TELECAST: *January 23, 1977*
LAST TELECAST: *September 10, 1978*
BROADCAST HISTORY:
Jan 1977, ABC 9:00–11:00 or 10:00–11:00 each night for eight days
Sep 1978, ABC 8:00–11:00 or 9:00–11:00 each night for five days
CAST:
Kunta Kinte (as a boy) .... LeVar Burton
Kunta Kinte (Toby; adult) .... John Amos
Binta .... Cicely Tyson
Omoro .... Thalmus Rasulala
Nyo Boto..................... Maya Angelou
Kadi Touray .... O. J. Simpson
The Wrestler .... Ji-Tu Cumbuka
Kintango .... Moses Gunn
Brima Cesay .... Hari Rhodes
Fanta .... Ren Woods
Fanta (later)................. Beverly Todd
Capt. Davies .... Edward Asner
Third Mate Slater .... Ralph Waite
Gardner...................... William Watson
Fiddler.................... Louis Gossett, Jr.
John Reynolds .... Lorne Greene
Mrs. Reynolds .... Lynda Day George
Ames .... Vic Morrow
Carrington .... Paul Shenar
Dr. William Reynolds .... Robert Reed
Bell.......................... Madge Sinclair
Grill .... Gary Collins
The Drummer .... Raymond St. Jacques
Tom Moore .... Chuck Connors
Missy Anne .... Sandy Duncan

Noah .... Lawrence-Hilton Jacobs
Ordell .... John Schuck
Kizzy .... Leslie Uggams
Squire James .... Macdonald Carey
Mathilda .... Olivia Cole
Mingo .... Scatman Crothers
Stephen Bennett .... George Hamilton
Mrs. Moore .... Carolyn Jones
Sir Eric Russell............... Ian McShane
Sister Sara .... Lillian Randolph
Sam Bennett .... Richard Roundtree
Chicken George .... Ben Vereen
Evan Brent .... Lloyd Bridges
Tom .... Georg Stanford Brown
Ol' George Johnson .... Brad Davis
Lewis .... Hilly Hicks
Jemmy Brent .... Doug McClure
Irene........................ Lynne Moody
Martha .... Lane Binkley
Justin .... Burl Ives
PRODUCER:
Stan Margulies
ADAPTED FOR TV BY:
William Blinn

Under the usual definition of a "series," *Roots* would not be included in this book—it was really an extended special. But the fact that it was the most-watched dramatic show in TV history, and its considerable impact on viewers, warrant an exception.

Roots' success was unprecedented. Approximately 100 million viewers saw the concluding installment, and it must be considered an event of considerable magnitude when nearly half the entire population of the U.S. can be assembled in front of its TV sets to watch a single dramatic presentation. No one, not even ABC, was prepared for anything that big. In fact, one of the reasons given for scheduling *Roots* on eight consecutive nights was that if it were a flop it would be over with quickly.

Alex Haley's novel of his own roots was 12 years in the writing. Its story began in 1750 in Gambia, West Africa, with the birth of Kunta Kinte to Binta and Omoro. Kunta grew up free and happy until, at the age of 17, he was taken prisoner by white slave catchers and shipped to America on a vessel commanded by the conscience-stricken Capt. Davies and his cruel third mate, Slater. Kunta remained rebellious for the rest of his life, making several attempts to escape and eventually losing a foot in the process. Then his daughter, Kizzy, was born. She grew to womanhood and bore a son (after she was raped by her owner), later to be named Chicken George. Chicken George was sent into servitude in England in the 1820s, as rumors of slave rebellions swept the American South. Thirty years later he returned, an old but free man, only to find America on the brink of Civil War. George's son, Tom, a blacksmith, was recruited into the army, but after emancipation found that freedom meant little in a land of hooded nightriders and economic exploitation. As the series ended, Tom—the great-grandson of Kunta Kinte—struck out to start a new life in Tennessee, and sow the roots for a better life for his free descendants.

The TV *Roots* was daring in many ways, including its massive historical sweep, its often mature content (including bare breasts in the early African segments), and its scheduling over a full week. However, it was not for rape or nudity that *Roots* received most of its criticism, but for distortion of history, particularly its sensationalized version of black-white relations in the slave era (one critic called it ABC's "shackles, whips and lust" view of slavery). It was pointed out that much of the cruelty attributed to racism was in reality the cruelty of the 18th and 19th centuries, which affected whites fully as much as it did blacks; and that the slave trade rested largely on African blacks selling their own brothers into slavery, not on "white slave parties."

Whether or not the TV *Roots* was pseudo-history, it reached and affected an unprecedented audience, and its effect on future TV programming was profound. That kind of success is not ignored by TV's programmers.

Roots was repeated in September 1978, again as a one-week special.

ROOTS: THE NEXT GENERATIONS
Drama
FIRST TELECAST: *February 18, 1979*
LAST TELECAST: *July 12, 1981*
BROADCAST HISTORY:
Feb 1979, ABC 8:00–10:00 or 9:00–10:00 each night for seven days
May 1981–Jul 1981, ABC Sun 7:00–9:00
CAST:

Tom Harvey	Georg Stanford Brown
Irene Harvey	Lynne Moody
Elizabeth Harvey	Debbi Morgan
Cynthia Harvey Palmer	Bever-Leigh Banfield
Cynthia Harvey Palmer (old)	Beah Richards
Col. Warner	Henry Fonda
Mrs. Warner	Olivia de Havilland
Jim Warner	Richard Thomas
Andy Warner	Marc Singer
Will Palmer	Stan Shaw
Bertha Palmer Haley	Irene Cara
Chicken George Moore	Avon Long
Earl Crowther	Paul Koslo
Lee Garnett	Roger E. Mosley
Bob Campbell	Harry Morgan
Simon Haley	Dorian Harewood
Queen Haley	Ruby Dee
Big Slew Johnson	Rosey Grier
Dr. Horace Huguley	Paul Winfield
Alex Haley (child)	Christoff St. John
Alex Haley (young man)	Damon Evans
Alex Haley (adult)	James Earl Jones
Nan Branch Haley	Debbie Allen
Malcolm X	Al Freeman, Jr.
George Lincoln Rockwell	Marlon Brando
Cousin Georgia	Lynn Hamilton

PRODUCER:
Stan Margulies

Two years after *Roots* made television history, this sequel continued the saga, again attracting large audiences. The story resumed in 1882, by which time Tom Harvey, great-grandson of Kunta Kinte, had established a marginal existence as a blacksmith in Henning, Tennessee. Relations between the races were strained, and old prejudices survived. Tom forbade his daughter's marriage to a light-skinned Negro because he was "too white"; and town patriarch Col. Warner disowned his own son Jim when he dared to marry a black schoolteacher. Before long "literacy tests" were being used to deny blacks their recently won right to vote, and lynch law had reappeared.

Tom's younger daughter, Cynthia, married a hard-working young man named Will Palmer, who, despite the oppression, had risen to ownership of the local lumberyard. In time Will would succeed Tom as leader of the local black community, as Ku Klux Klan terror swept the South. Will and Cynthia's daughter, Bertha, became the first descendant of Kunta Kinte to enter college. There, in 1912, she met ambitious young Simon Haley, son of a sharecropper, whose education was being sponsored by a philanthropic white man. After serving in a segregated combat unit during World War I, Simon returned to wed Bertha and begin teaching agriculture at a black college in Alabama. While Simon was organizing farmers during the New Deal, his son, Alex, soaked up family lore from the older generation.

As World War II approached, Alex enlisted in the Coast Guard, where he spent the next 20 years. When he retired in 1960 he turned to writing, interviewing such national figures as black activist Malcolm X, whose "autobiography" he helped write, and American Nazi leader George Lincoln Rockwell—who held a gun on him throughout their conversation. Then a visit to his boyhood home of Henning reignited his interest in his family's past, all the way back to the "Old African" Kunta Kinte, and started him on a journey to Africa to begin his greatest work.

Roots: The Next Generations was first shown during the eight-day period in February 1979, and was repeated as a weekly series from May to July 1981.

ROPERS, THE
Situation Comedy
FIRST TELECAST: *March 13, 1979*
LAST TELECAST: *May 22, 1980*
BROADCAST HISTORY:
Mar 1979–Apr 1979, ABC Tue 10:00–10:30
Aug 1979–Sep 1979, ABC Sun 8:30–9:00
Sep 1979–Jan 1980, ABC Sat 8:00–8:30
Jan 1980–Mar 1980, ABC Sat 8:30–9:00
May 1980, ABC Thu 9:30–10:00

CAST:

Stanley Roper	Norman Fell
Helen Roper	Audra Lindley
Jeffrey P. Brookes III	Jeffrey Tambor
Anne Brookes	Patricia McCormack
David Brookes	Evan Cohen
Ethel	Dena Dietrich
Hubert	Rod Colbin
Jenny Ballinger (1980)	Louise Vallance

In this spin-off from *Three's Company,* landlord Stanley Roper sold his apartment building in Santa Monica and bought a condominium town house in posh Cheviot Hills. His new foil was balding realtor Jeffrey P. Brooks III, who felt that the earthy Roper was downgrading the neighborhood. Helen Roper, socially aspiring but ever frustrated by Stanley's crass ways, found a supportive friend in Jeffrey's wife, Anne, however. David was the Brookes' young son; Jenny, an attractive art student who rented a room; and Ethel, Helen's snobbish sister. Muffin was Helen's little dog.

Just as *Three's Company* was based on the English TV hit *Man About the House, The Ropers* was based on its spin-off, *George & Mildred.*

ROSCOE KARNS, INSIDE DETECTIVE

see *Rocky King, Inside Detective*

ROSEMARY CLOONEY LUX SHOW, THE

see *Lux Show Starring Rosemary Clooney, The*

ROSETTI AND RYAN

Law Drama
FIRST TELECAST: *September 22, 1977*
LAST TELECAST: *November 10, 1977*
BROADCAST HISTORY:
  Sep 1977–Nov 1977, NBC Thu 10:00–11:00
CAST:

Joseph Rosetti	Tony Roberts
Frank Ryan	Squire Fridell
Jessica Hornesby	Jane Elliot
Judge Hardcastle	Dick O'Neill
Judge Black	William Marshall

They were both single and good-looking, they were both attorneys (in fact, partners), but they had very different personalities. Rosetti had been born to the comfortable life of an upper-middle-class family. He wore the finest clothes, considered himself a gourmet, and was a smooth operator around attractive women. He was also brash, arrogant, and egocentric. Ryan was a former cop who had worked his way through law school at night. He was introspective, modest, and a dogged, persistent researcher—the perfect complement to his glib, impulsive partner. The combination was highly successful, usually to the consternation of Assistant District Attorney Jessica Hornesby, their frequent opponent in the courtroom.

ROUGH RIDERS, THE

Western
FIRST TELECAST: *October 2, 1958*
LAST TELECAST: *September 24, 1959*
BROADCAST HISTORY:
  Oct 1958–Sep 1959, ABC Thu 9:30–10:00
CAST:

Capt. Jim Flagg	Kent Taylor
Lt. Kirby	Jan Merlin
Sgt. Buck Sinclair	Peter Whitney

At the end of the Civil War three soldiers, each of whom planned to move west in search of a new life, joined forces for mutual companionship and protection on the trip. Jim Flagg and Buck Sinclair were veterans of the Union Army, and Lt. Kirby had served the Confederacy. As they crossed the country they encountered numerous bands of outlaws, renegade Indians, and deserters from both armies.

ROUNDERS, THE

Comedy/Western
FIRST TELECAST: *September 6, 1966*
LAST TELECAST: *January 3, 1967*
BROADCAST HISTORY:
  Sep 1966–Jan 1967, ABC Tue 8:30–9:00
CAST:

Ben Jones	Ron Hayes
Howdy Lewis	Patrick Wayne
Jim Ed Love	Chill Wills
Ada	Bobbi Jordan
Sally	Janis Hansen
Shorty Dawes	Jason Wingreen
Regan	Walker Edmiston
Vince	J. Pat O'Malley

Robust comedy, set in the contemporary West. Ben Jones and Howdy Lewis were two rowdy, fun-loving cowpokes who found themselves hog-tied and in debt to unscrupulous Jim Ed Love, owner of a vast ranch and reputedly the second richest man in Texas (Andy Devine made a single guest appearance as Honest John Denton, the first richest man). Jim Ed, a fast-talking wheeler-dealer, dressed in custom-tailored white cowboy suits and rode the range in a souped-up station wagon, while Ben and Howdy had to put up with a mean old roan named Old Fooler. They got some relief at the Longhorn Cafe in the nearby town of Hi Lo, which they tore up every Saturday night, with the assistance of their girlfriends, Ada and Sally.

Based on the novel by Max Evans, which was made into a 1965 movie co-starring Chill Wills in the same role he played on TV.

ROUSTERS, THE

Adventure
FIRST TELECAST: *October 1, 1983*
LAST TELECAST: *July 21, 1984*
BROADCAST HISTORY:
  Oct 1983, NBC Sat 9:00–10:00
  Jun 1984–Jul 1984, NBC Sat 10:00–11:00

CAST:

Wyatt Earp III	Chad Everett
Evan Earp	Jim Varney
Amanda Earp	Maxine Stuart
Michael Earp	Timothy Gibbs
Cactus Jack Slade	Hoyt Axton
Ellen Slade	Mimi Rogers

It was a far cry from the life led by his famous great-grandfather, but Wyatt Earp III made a living working for a traveling carnival show in the modern-day Southwest. He served as a patch (combination bouncer, peacekeeper, and second-in-command) for Cactus Jack's Sladetown Carnival. His lunatic family had other ideas about how to make a living, however, which constantly got the long-suffering Wyatt into trouble. Brother Evan fancied himself a mechanical genius, but always managed to "fix" things so they would never work again. Their feisty and eccentric mother, Amanda, couldn't fry an egg, but was determined to keep alive the "Earp legend" (which was mostly bunk) by chasing modern-day varmints—as a bounty hunter. Wyatt's girlfriend, Ellen Slade, was the boss's daughter as well as a lion tamer and schoolteacher for the children traveling with the carnival. Michael was Wyatt's semi-normal young son.

ROUTE 66
Adventure
FIRST TELECAST: *October 7, 1960*
LAST TELECAST: *September 18, 1964*
BROADCAST HISTORY:
  Oct 1960–Sep 1964, CBS Fri 8:30–9:30
CAST:

Tod Stiles	Martin Milner
Buz Murdock (1960–1963)	George Maharis
Linc Case (1963–1964)	Glenn Corbett

Tod Stiles and Buz Murdock were two young men who traveled around the country together in Tod's Corvette in search of adventure. They came from radically different backgrounds but had become good friends. Tod was born to wealth, but when his father had died unexpectedly, he discovered that most of the money was gone. Buz had grown up in the jungle of New York's Hell's Kitchen and had been employed by Tod's father prior to his death. The series was filmed on location as they crisscrossed the United States in their destinationless travels, meeting all sorts of people and getting into all kinds of situations: romantic, dangerous, amusing, etc. George Maharis left the series in November 1962, while production was still in progress for the 1962–1963 season, because of the lingering effects of a case of hepatitis. He was seen intermittently in episodes aired through March 1963. In the episode aired on March 22, 1963, Linc Case, who was to take over as Tod's traveling companion, was introduced. He was a Vietnam war hero from Houston who returned to the United States unsure of what he was looking

for in life. He joined Tod while trying to find himself and stayed with him throughout the remainder of the series.

Nelson Riddle's recording of his theme music for the show, a driving jazz melody which sounded like the open road, was on the hit parade in 1962.

ROWAN AND MARTIN SHOW, THE
  see *Dean Martin Summer Show, The*

ROWAN & MARTIN'S LAUGH-IN
Comedy Variety
FIRST TELECAST: *January 22, 1968*
LAST TELECAST: *May 14, 1973*
BROADCAST HISTORY:
  Jan 1968–May 1973, NBC Mon 8:00–9:00 (OS)
REGULARS:
  Dan Rowan
  Dick Martin
  Gary Owens
  Ruth Buzzi
  Judy Carne (1968–1970)
  Eileen Brennan (1968)
  Goldie Hawn (1968–1970)
  Arte Johnson (1968–1971)
  Henry Gibson (1968–1971)
  Roddy-Maude Roxby (1968)
  Jo Anne Worley (1968–1970)
  Larry Hovis (1968, 1971–1972)
  Pigmeat Markham (1968–1969)
  Charlie Brill (1968–1969)
  Dick Whittington (1968–1969)
  Mitzi McCall (1968–1969)
  Chelsea Brown (1968–1969)
  Alan Sues (1968–1972)
  Dave Madden (1968–1969)
  Teresa Graves (1969–1970)
  Jeremy Lloyd (1969–1970)
  Pamela Rodgers (1969–1970)
  Byron Gilliam (1969–1970)
  Ann Elder (1970–1972)
  Lily Tomlin (1970–1973)
  Johnny Brown (1970–1972)
  Dennis Allen (1970–1973)
  Nancy Phillips (1970–1971)
  Barbara Sharma (1970–1972)
  Harvey Jason (1970–1971)
  Richard Dawson (1971–1973)
  Moosie Drier (1971–1973)
  Patti Deutsch (1972–1973)
  Jud Strunk (1972–1973)
  Brian Bressler (1972–1973)
  Sarah Kennedy (1972–1973)
  Donna Jean Young (1972–1973)
  Tod Bass (1972–1973)
  Lisa Farringer (1972–1973)
  Willie Tyler & Lester (1972–1973)

Rowan & Martin's Laugh-In was one of TV's classics, one of those rare programs which was not only an overnight sensation, but was highly innovative, created a raft of new stars, and started trends in comedy which other programs would follow. In some ways, it was not original at all, being a cross between Olsen & Johnson's *Helzapoppin'* (which in turn traced its lineage to the frantic, knockabout comedy of the Keystone Cops) and the highly topical satire of *That Was the Week That Was.* But *Laugh-In* crystallized a kind of contemporary, fast-paced, unstructured comedy "happening" that was exactly what an agitated America wanted in 1968.

Laugh-In was first seen as a one-time special on September 9, 1967. It was such an enormous hit that it inevitably led to a series premiering the following January. Its lightning-fast pace took full advantage of the technical capabilities of television and videotape. Blackouts, sketches, one-liners, and cameo appearances by famous show-business celebrities and even national politicians were all edited into a frenetic whole. The regular cast was large and the turnover high, and of the 40 regulars who appeared in the series only four were with it from beginning to end—the two hosts, announcer Gary Owens, and Ruth Buzzi.

The essence of *Laugh-In* was *shtick,* a comic routine or trademark repeated over and over until it was closely associated with a performer. People love it, come to expect it, and talk about it the next morning after the show. All great comedians have at least one, but what was remarkable about *Laugh-In* was that it developed a whole repertoire of sight gags and catchphrases using little-known talent exclusively (though some of them became quite famous later). Among the favorites: Arte Johnson as the German soldier, peering out from behind a potted palm and murmuring, "Verrry interesting!"; Ruth Buzzi as the little old lady with an umbrella, forever whacking the equally decrepit old man who snuggled up beside her on a park bench; Lily Tomlin as the sarcastic, nasal telephone operator (even the phone company wanted to hire her to do commercials using that routine—she wouldn't); Gary Owens as the outrageously overmodulated announcer, facing the microphone, hand cupped to ear; Alan Sues as the grinning moron of a sports announcer; Goldie Hawn as the giggling dumb blonde, and so on.

Some of the devices of the show were the Cocktail Party, Letters to Laugh-In, The Flying Fickle Finger of Fate Award, Laugh-In Looks at the News (of the past, present, and future), Hollywood News with Ruth Buzzi, the gags written on the undulating body of a girl in a bikini, and the joke wall at the close of each show, in which cast members kept popping out of windows to throw each other one-liners—or a bucket of water.

Many catchphrases came out of the sketches and blackouts on *Laugh-In,* and some became national bywords. It is said that a foreign delegate at the United Nations once approached an American member of that organization to ask, in all seriousness, "I have heard a phrase in your country that I do not understand. What is it you mean by 'bippy'?" Besides "You bet your bippy," there

were: "Sock it to me" (splash!), "Look that up in your Funk and Wagnalls," "Beautiful Downtown Burbank," and even "Here come de judge!"

The pace never let up. If it wasn't a short clip of a raincoated adult falling off a tricycle, it was a shot of Richard M. Nixon solemnly declaring "Sock it to me." It didn't even end at the closing credits, as jokes kept flying and, finally, one pair of hands was heard clapping until a station break forcibly took over.

Laugh-In went straight to the top of the TV ratings and was the number one program on the air for its first two full seasons, 1968–1970. It then began to drop off as the best talent left to pursue newfound careers, and finally ended its run in 1973.

ROXIE
Situation Comedy
FIRST TELECAST: *April 1, 1987*
LAST TELECAST: *April 8, 1987*
BROADCAST HISTORY:
   Apr 1987, CBS Wed 8:00–8:30
CAST:
   Roxie Brinkerhoff . . . . Andrea Martin
   Marcie McKinley . . . . Teresa Ganzel
   Michael Brinkerhoff . . . . Mitchell Laurance
   Vito Carteri . . . . Ernie Sabella
   Randy Grant . . . . Jerry Pavlon
   Leon Buchanan . . . . Jack Riley

Roxie was the program director for WNYU, a struggling UHF TV station in New York City. Working with her at the station were Marcie, the secretary and bookkeeper; Vito, the technical genius who operated and fixed all the broadcasting equipment; Randy, the impressionable young gofer; and Leon, the cynical, aging station manager who was also—ironically—the star of WNYU's afternoon children's show. Roxie's husband, Michael, was a schoolteacher.

Roxie and the program that followed it, *Take Five,* were the disasters of the 1986–1987 season. They were both canceled after only two weeks on the air, never to be seen again.

ROY ROGERS & DALE EVANS SHOW, THE
Musical Variety
FIRST TELECAST: *September 29, 1962*
LAST TELECAST: *December 29, 1962*
BROADCAST HISTORY:
   Sep 1962–Dec 1962, ABC Sat 7:30–8:30
REGULARS:
   Roy Rogers & Dale Evans
   Pat Brady
   Sons of the Pioneers
   Kirby Buchanon
   Kathy Taylor
   Cliff Arquette (as *Charley Weaver*)
   Ralph Carmichael Orchestra

This short-lived series featured "The King of the Cowboys" with his wife, Dale Evans, plus regulars and guests in a very wholesome musical variety hour. Regulars included Roy's old sidekick, Pat Brady, rodeo-rider-turned-singer Kirby Buchanon, folk singer Kathy Taylor, and comic Cliff Arquette. Circus and horse-show acts were also included.

ROY ROGERS SHOW, THE
Western
FIRST TELECAST: *December 30, 1951*
LAST TELECAST: *June 23, 1957*
BROADCAST HISTORY:
   Dec 1951–Jun 1952, NBC Sun 6:30–7:00
   Aug 1952–Jun 1957, NBC Sun 6:30–7:00
REGULARS:
   Roy Rogers
   Dale Evans
   Pat Brady
THEME:
   "Happy Trails to You," by Dale Evans

Singing Western movie actor Roy Rogers, who, ironically, was born and raised in Cincinnati, Ohio, struck gold as the most popular television cowboy of the early and mid-1950s. The "King of the Cowboys" was joined by his wife, Dale Evans, and bumbling sidekick, Pat Brady, in his fight for law and order in the contemporary West. In addition to the people, Roy's horse Trigger, Dale's horse Buttermilk, dog Bullet, and Pat's cantankerous jeep Nellybelle were regular members of the cast around the ol' Double R Bar Ranch.

Reruns of *The Roy Rogers Show* turned up on CBS' Saturday morning lineup in January 1961 and remained there until September 1964.

ROYAL PLAYHOUSE
   see *DuMont Royal Theater*

ROYAL PLAYHOUSE
   syndicated title for *Fireside Theater*

RUGGLES, THE
Situation Comedy
FIRST TELECAST: *November 3, 1949*
LAST TELECAST: *June 19, 1952*
BROADCAST HISTORY:
   Nov 1949–Dec 1949, ABC Thu 9:30–10:00
   Dec 1949–Mar 1950, ABC Fri 8:30–9:00
   Apr 1950–Jun 1950, ABC Sun 10:00–10:30
   Jun 1950–Aug 1950, ABC Thu 9:30–10:00
   Sep 1950–Dec 1950, ABC Sun 6:30–7:00
   Jan 1951–Mar 1951, ABC Mon 8:30–9:00
   Mar 1951–Jun 1951, ABC Wed 8:00–8:30
   Jun 1951–Sep 1951, ABC Fri 8:30–9:00
   Oct 1951–Nov 1951, ABC Sat 7:00–7:30
   Dec 1951–Jan 1952, ABC Sun 6:30–7:00
   Jan 1952–Apr 1952, ABC Wed 9:00–9:30
   Apr 1952–Jun 1952, ABC Thu 8:00–8:30
CAST:
   Charlie Ruggles.................... Himself
   Margaret Ruggles (1949)....... Irene Tedrow

   Margaret Ruggles (1950–1952)
   .... Erin O'Brien-Moore
   Sharon Ruggles............. Margaret Kerry
   Chuck Ruggles.............. Tommy Bernard
   Donna Ruggles .... Judy Nugent
   Donald Ruggles............. Jimmy Hawkins

Veteran Hollywood character actor Charlie Ruggles portrayed an insurance salesman and harassed hubby in this early family comedy. The family, which was the source of Charlie's dilemmas around the house, consisted of his wife, Margaret, teenagers Sharon and Chuck, and the cute twins Donna and Donald. Stories revolved around such gentle subjects as who got to use the bathroom first in the morning, how the kids got dad to go square dancing, Sharon's and Chuck's first dates, etc.

The program was produced live at ABC's Hollywood station, KECA-TV, premiering on a seven-station West Coast network on Sunday, October 23, 1949. Shortly thereafter it began airing on ABC's East and Midwest network, using kinescopes of the live West Coast show. The poor quality of these dim kinescopes, and the constant movement of the series all over the ABC schedule, may have contributed to *The Ruggles'* failure to become a hit.

RUN BUDDY RUN
Situation Comedy
FIRST TELECAST: *September 12, 1966*
LAST TELECAST: *January 2, 1967*
BROADCAST HISTORY:
   Sep 1966–Jan 1967, CBS Mon 8:00–8:30
CAST:
   Buddy Overstreet .... Jack Sheldon
   Devere (Mr. D.)............... Bruce Gordon
   Junior........................ Jim Connell
   Wendell .... Nick Georgiade
   Harry....................... Gregg Palmer

Buddy Overstreet was a very average person. He had made one mistake, however, which altered his entire life. While relaxing at a Turkish bath he accidentally overheard syndicate gangsters discussing a proposed rub-out. They realized that he had heard their code phrase—"chicken little"—and spent the rest of the season trying to capture him because he knew too much. They were not particularly adept at this and kept fouling it up. The front for their organization was Devere Enterprises, where Mr. Devere's son, Junior, proved to be inept at running either the legitimate or criminal side of the business.

RUN FOR YOUR LIFE
Adventure
FIRST TELECAST: *September 13, 1965*
LAST TELECAST: *September 11, 1968*
BROADCAST HISTORY:
   Sep 1965–Sep 1967, NBC Mon 10:00–11:00
   Sep 1967–Sep 1968, NBC Wed 10:00–11:00

CAST:

Paul Bryan .... Ben Gazzara

Paul Bryan was a very successful 35-year-old lawyer who had everything a man could want—intelligence, good looks, popularity, and money. He also had something that nobody wants—an incurable disease. Told by doctors that he had, at most, two years to live, Paul closed down his law practice and started traveling around the world in the hope of cramming a lifetime of adventure and excitement into the limited time he had left. With money no problem, he went from one exotic and fascinating place to another and encountered all sorts of people. He had come to terms with his problem and, rather than running away from life, he ran toward it. The show ran three years, even though he supposedly had only two years to live, and he was still running when it faded from the screen in 1968. The series was based on an episode of *Kraft Suspense Theater,* which was telecast in April 1965.

RUNAWAYS, THE

Drama
FIRST TELECAST: *April 27, 1978*
LAST TELECAST: *September 4, 1979*
BROADCAST HISTORY:
  Apr 1978–May 1978, NBC Thu 9:00–10:00
  Aug 1978, NBC Thu 10:00–11:00
  May 1979–Sep 1979, NBC Tue 8:00–9:00
CAST:

David McKay (1978) .... Robert Reed
Steve Arizzio (1979) .... Alan Feinstein
Karen Wingate .... Karen Machon
Mark Johnson .... Michael Biehn
Susan Donovan (1978)............. Ruth Cox
Debbie Shaw (1979) ....: Patti Cohoon
Sgt. Hal Grady (1979) .... James Callahan

Each year in the U.S. between one and two million teenagers run away from home. This socially conscious program dramatized that phenomenon, through fictional stories of youngsters trying to escape from the demands of insensitive parents, broken homes, the shame of unwanted pregnancies, or other problems that were more than they could face.

The central character was David McKay, a psychologist who maintained an office on the campus of Westwood University in Los Angeles. His travels in search of runaway youngsters took him up and down the West Coast. David's girlfriend, Karen Wingate, was Dean of Women at the college. Mark and Susan were his two wards, former runaways who had built lives of their own under David's care. Both were now college students nearing graduation.

The series began with a limited run in the spring of 1978, under the title *Operation: Runaway.* There were plans to bring it back as a regular series in the fall, but it was pulled at the last minute. It finally reappeared in the spring of 1979,

retitled *The Runaways* and starring Alan Feinstein as psychologist Steve Arizzio. Unlike McKay, Arizzio was more concerned with tracking down the runaways than in discerning their psychological motivations. He had two former runaways living with him, Mark (who had been McKay's ward) and Debbie. Helping him trace the missing youngsters was Sgt. Grady of the Los Angeles Police Department.

RUSS HODGES' SCOREBOARD

Sports News
FIRST TELECAST: *April 14, 1948*
LAST TELECAST: *May 22, 1949*
BROADCAST HISTORY:
  Apr 1948–Jan 1949, DUM Mon–Fri 6:30–6:45
  Jan 1949–Mar 1949, DUM Mon–Fri 6:45–7:00
  Mar 1949–May 1949, DUM Mon–Fri 7:45–8:00
REPORTER:
  Russ Hodges

Latest news from the world of sports. Game scores, observation, and commentary by Russ Hodges, and his interviews with sports celebrities were all part of this nightly show.

RUSS MORGAN SHOW, THE

Music
FIRST TELECAST: *July 7, 1956*
LAST TELECAST: *September 1, 1956*
BROADCAST HISTORY:
  Jul 1956–Sep 1956, CBS Sat 9:30–10:00
REGULARS:
  Russ Morgan
  Helen O'Connell

Bandleader Russ Morgan was the host and star of this live summer music show that featured the singing of Helen O'Connell.

RUTHIE ON THE TELEPHONE

Comedy
FIRST TELECAST: *August 7, 1949*
LAST TELECAST: *November 5, 1949*
BROADCAST HISTORY:
  Aug 1949–Sep 1949, CBS Mon/Tue/Thu/Sat/
    Sun 7:55–8:00
  Sep 1949–Nov 1949, CBS Mon/Tue/Thu/Sat
    7:55–8:00
CAST:

Ruthie .... Ruth Gilbert
Richard .... Philip Reed

Ruthie was a young lady much in love with Richard, a man she had never met and who was not interested in meeting her. Regardless, every night for five minutes she tried to inspire Richard over the phone while he tried to avoid her. Split-screen technique was used in this live show, enabling the viewer to see both Ruthie at home and Richard at his desk at the advertising agency where he worked. The idea for this series originated on the Robert Q. Lewis radio program, on which Ruthie's telephone adventures had been featured for about a year.

RYAN'S FOUR
Medical Drama
FIRST TELECAST: *April 6, 1983*
LAST TELECAST: *April 27, 1983*
BROADCAST HISTORY:
　Apr 1983, ABC Wed 9:00–10:00
CAST:
　Dr. Thomas Ryan . . . . Tom Skerritt
　Dr. Ingrid Sorenson . . . . Lisa Eilbacher
　Dr. Edward Gillian . . . . Timothy Daly
　Dr. Terry Wilson . . . . Albert Hall
　Dr. Norman Rostov . . . . Dirk Blocker
　Dr. Morris Whitford . . . . Nicolas Coster

Ryan's four were four young interns working under the supervision of experienced Dr. Thomas Ryan, who had two important goals: to make them the best doctors possible, and to make sure they did not suffer the fate of his son, an intern who had cracked under the incredible pressure of medical training and then committed suicide. The four were: Ingrid, a brilliant young doctor who needed to learn that compassion is as necessary as skill; Gillian, rich and spoiled; Terry, the black whose marriage was in jeopardy because of his long hours; and Norman, whose working-class background had given him a sense of inferiority. Dr. Whitford was the hospital's medical director, to whom Ryan, as director of interns, reported, and who wanted the interns to be shown no favors.

The series was co-produced by David Victor, who was also responsible for *Dr. Kildare* and *Marcus Welby, M.D.*, and actor-producer Henry Winkler.

S

SCTV NETWORK 90
Comedy
FIRST TELECAST: *May 15, 1981*
LAST TELECAST: *June 24, 1983*
BROADCAST HISTORY:
May 1981–Jun 1983, NBC Fri 12:30–2:00 A.M.
(New episodes produced for cable TV 1983–1984)
REGULARS:
Joe Flaherty
Andrea Martin
John Candy
Eugene Levy
Rick Moranis (1981–1982)
Catherine O'Hara (1981–1982)
Dave Thomas (1981–1982)
Martin Short (1982–1983)
Mary Charlotte Wilcox (1982–1983)

In 1981 the syndicated series *Second City TV* moved to the NBC network, expanding from 30 to 90 minutes and changing its name to *SCTV Network 90* in the process. The length of skits, the number of features on each show, and the variety of roles played by each member of the *SCTV* repertory troupe increased significantly as a result. Weekly musical guests were also added, with their performances integrated into the skits.

Station president Guy Caballero (Joe) and station manager Edith Prickley (Andrea) were still around, along with "The Happy Wanderers," a polka variety show hosted by Stan (Eugene) and Yosh (John) Shmenge; Gil Fisher (John), the "Fishin' Musician"; "Great White North," a talk show for beer-drinking Canadian hunters, starring Bob (Rick) and Doug (Dave) MacKenzie; "Mel's Rock Pile," a satire on *Don Kirshner's Rock Concert* hosted by Mel Slurp (Eugene); "The Sammy Maudlin Show," with star Sammy (Joe) and his announcer, William B. (John); a send-up of *The Merv Griffin Show* with Rick as Mr. Griffin; and the continuing soap opera "The Days of the Week" with the entire cast.

The series shortened its title to *SCTV Network* in the fall of 1981. In the fall of 1983, after being canceled by NBC, *SCTV* surfaced for one more season on the pay-cable television service Cinemax, with new episodes and some changes in the cast. The only regulars on the Cinemax version were Flaherty, Martin, Levy, and Short. All version of the series, syndicated, network, and cable TV, were produced in Canada.

S.R.O. PLAYHOUSE
Dramatic Anthology
FIRST TELECAST: *May 11, 1957*
LAST TELECAST: *September 7, 1957*

BROADCAST HISTORY:
May 1957–Sep 1957, CBS Sat 9:30–10:00

The dramas telecast in this summer series were all reruns of episodes that had originally aired on *Schlitz Playhouse*.

S.S. HOLIDAY
see *Starlit Time*

S.W.A.T.
Police Drama
FIRST TELECAST: *February 24, 1975*
LAST TELECAST: *June 29, 1976*
BROADCAST HISTORY:
Feb 1975–Aug 1975, ABC Mon 9:00–10:00
Aug 1975–Apr 1976, ABC Sat 9:00–10:00
Apr 1976–Jun 1976, ABC Tue 9:00–10:00
CAST:
Lt. Dan "Hondo" Harrelson.... Steve Forrest
Sgt. David "Deacon" Kay .... Rod Perry
Officer Jim Street .... Robert Urich
Officer Dominic Luca .... Mark Shera
Officer T. J. McCabe .... James Coleman
Betty Harrelson .... Ellen Weston
Matt Harrelson .... Michael Harland
Kevin Harrelson .... David Adams
THEME:
"Theme from 'S.W.A.T.,' " by Barry DeVorzon

This series brought army-style warfare to big-city police work. S.W.A.T. stood for *S*pecial *W*eapons *A*nd *T*actics, whose job it was to tackle situations—usually violent ones—that line police couldn't handle, with whatever weaponry was necessary. Vietnam veterans all, the S.W.A.T. squad dressed in semimilitary attire, and were organized along the lines of a front-line patrol. Lt. Harrelson was the C.O., Sgt. Kay the observer and communicator, Jim the team scout, Dominic the marksman, and T.J. the backup. Often the young junior officers were a bit too eager to use their firepower, and Harrelson had to hold them back. But as often as not, it was blast away. The team traveled in a specially equipped van, since tanks don't work too well in urban locales.

Filmed in Southern California, and based, loosely at least, on real-life S.W.A.T. teams formed in several large American cities following the disturbances of the late 1960s.

SABER OF LONDON
see *Mark Saber*

SABLE
Adventure
FIRST TELECAST: *November 7, 1987*
LAST TELECAST: *January 2, 1988*
BROADCAST HISTORY:
Nov 1987, ABC Sat 8:00–9:00
Dec 1987–Jan 1988, ABC Sat 9:00–10:00

CAST:

Jon Sable/Nicholas Flemming
.... Lewis Van Bergen
Eden Kendall................... Rene Russo
Joe "Cheesecake" Tyson .... Ken Page
Myke Blackmon .... Holly Fulger
Cynthia .... Marge Kotlisky

What does one make of a slender, rather bookish man who wears stripes of black greasepaint on his face, a black jumpsuit and hood, and a perpetual scowl? Though in his nocturnal getup he looked like a nervous second-story man (or a dropout from army jungle training), this was actually two men—by day Nicholas Flemming, business-suited, successful author of children's books, by night Sable, black-clad crime-fighter and freelance avenger of wrongs. Sable was unusual among TV heroes in that he worried a great deal. A trauma in his past (he had once *killed* a man!) left him with an aversion to violence, and that perpetual scowl. Mostly he was seen being attacked by others, clinging to window ledges, etc.

There were other problems. Whenever he would bed down with his supportive girlfriend and literary agent, Eden, after a hard night's work, that d****d greasepaint would rub off on everything! Cheesecake, a corpulent, blind computer hacker, was his main source of information and the only other person who knew Sable's true identity.

Myke was the illustrator of Flemming's stories, and Cynthia his secretary. The series was filmed on location in Chicago.

SADDLE PAL CLUB
see *Movies—Prior to 1961*

SAFARI TO ADVENTURE
Documentary
BROADCAST HISTORY:
Syndicated only
30 minutes
Produced: *1969–1975* (156 episodes)
Released: *1969*
NARRATOR:
Bill Burrud

This long-running wildlife documentary was produced by Bill Burrud, who has made a career out of such shows. Typical subjects were "Sea Otters and Brown Bears in Alaska," "Life Cycle of a Salmon," "Reindeer Roundup in Lapland," and "Pink Porpoises of the Amazon."

SAINT, THE
Mystery/Adventure
FIRST TELECAST: *May 21, 1967*
LAST TELECAST: *September 12, 1969*
BROADCAST HISTORY:
May 1967–Sep 1967, NBC Sun 10:00–11:00
Feb 1968–Sep 1968, NBC Sat 7:30–8:30
Apr 1969–Sep 1969, NBC Fri 10:00–11:00

CAST:

Simon Templar (1967–1969) ..... Roger Moore
Simon Templar (1978) .... Ian Ogilvy
Inspector Claude Teal (1967–1969)
.... Ivor Dean

Simon Templar was a dashing figure, urbane, sophisticated, and independently wealthy. He was also a crook, but a gentlemanly, modern-day Robin Hood–type crook who took on the causes of those who had been robbed, swindled, or in other ways taken advantage of by their fellow man. He pursued his quest for adventure throughout Europe and the world. His calling card, a stick figure with a halo (representing a "saint"), was equally well known in society circles and among the police of six continents. The police generally regarded him as a mixed blessing, for although he was dedicated to justice, he often used extralegal means to achieve his ends.

The Saint had long been a popular character in fiction, first in the best-selling mystery novels of Leslie Charteris and later in a series of movies and a radio show in the 1930s and 1940s. This television version was produced in England and was first seen in syndication in the U.S. in the early 1960s. It made its network television debut, with all new episodes, in 1967. A decade after the Roger Moore version left the air, CBS added *Return of the Saint* to its *Late Movie* lineup. Ian Ogilvy replaced Moore in the title role (these episodes had been produced in England in 1978). CBS also aired reruns of the original Roger Moore episodes during the summer and fall of 1980 and, for a time, both series were running simultaneously (on different nights of the week) on *The CBS Late Movie*. See that series for specific schedule details.

ST. ELSEWHERE
Medical Drama
FIRST TELECAST: *October 26, 1982*
LAST TELECAST: *May 25, 1988*
BROADCAST HISTORY:
Oct 1982–Aug 1983, NBC Tue 10:00–11:00
Aug 1983–May 1988, NBC Wed 10:00–11:00
CAST:

Dr. Donald Westphall .... Ed Flanders
Dr. Mark Craig .... William Daniels
Dr. Ben Samuels (1982–1983)... David Birney
Dr. Victor Ehrlich .... Ed Begley, Jr.
Dr. Jack Morrison.............. David Morse
Dr. Annie Cavanero (1982–1985)
.... Cynthia Sikes
Dr. Wayne Fiscus............ Howie Mandel
Dr. Cathy Martin (1982–1986)
.... Barbara Whinnery
Dr. Peter White (1982–1985) ... Terence Knox
Dr. Hugh Beale (1982–1983) ..... G.W. Bailey
Nurse Helen Rosenthal..... Christina Pickles
Dr. Phillip Chandler .... Denzel Washington
Dr. V. J. Kochar (1982–1984) .... Kavi Raz
Dr. Wendy Armstrong (1982–1984)
.... Kim Miyori

Dr. Daniel Auschlander	Norman Lloyd
Nurse Shirley Daniels (1982–1985)..	Ellen Bry
Orderly Luther Hawkins	Eric Laneuville
Joan Halloran (1983–1984)	Nancy Stafford
Dr. Robert Caldwell (1983–1986)	
....	Mark Harmon
Dr. Michael Ridley (1983–1984) ...	Paul Sand
Mrs. Ellen Craig	Bonnie Bartlett
Dr. Elliot Axelrod (1983–1988) .	Stephen Furst
Nurse Lucy Papandrao	Jennifer Savidge
Dr. Jaqueline Wade (1983–1988)	
....	Sagan Lewis
Orderly Warren Coolidge (1984–1988)	
....	Byron Stewart
Dr. Emily Humes (1984–1985) .	Judith Hansen
Dr. Alan Poe (1984–1985)	Brian Tochi
Nurse Peggy Shotwell (1984–1986)	
....	Saundra Sharp
Mrs. Hufnagel (1984–1985) ...	Florence Halop
Dr. Roxanne Turner (1985–1987)	
....	Alfre Woodard
Ken Valere (1985–1986)........	George Deloy
Terri Valere (1985–1986).......	Deborah May
Dr. Seth Griffin (1986–1988)	
....	Bruce Greenwood
Dr. Paulette Kiem (1986–1988) .	France Nuyen
Dr. Carol Novino (1986–1988) ..	Cindy Pickett
Dr. John Gideon (1987–1988)	Ronny Cox

St. Elsewhere was a hospital drama with a difference. There was high emotion, there were dedicated, caring physicians, but there were no miracles. Sometimes the patient made it, sometimes not. And they weren't always brave about it. As in real life.

St. Eligius was one of the seedier hospitals on TV, a big-city dumping ground for patients not wanted by the higher-class (and more expensive) medical facilities in Boston. In a typical day the staff might have to deal with a doctor being mugged in the emergency room, a mentally ill patient who wandered away, a drug addict trying to raid the pharmacy, and the wealthy, snobbish parents of an ill child who insisted that she be transferred immediately to a fancier hospital.

Whatever the reputation of St. Eligius, its staff was first-rate. Dr. Westphall was the chief of staff, a seasoned doctor and father figure to the young interns and residents completing their training there; Dr. Craig, an egotistical heart surgeon who was a brilliant doctor, but totally oblivious to his patients' feelings; and Dr. Auschlander, a veteran physician who found he must fight his own battle with cancer. Among the younger doctors, Samuels was a free spirit who had slept with practically every nurse in the hospital; Fiscus was having an affair with pathologist Cathy Martin, who insisted on making love on a slab in the morgue, among the sheet-draped corpses; Morrison was so dedicated to his work that he neglected his young wife, who died tragically in 1983; Cavanero tended to become too involved with her patients; Axelrod was constantly fighting obesity; and Chandler, the

black resident, was always afraid he did not quite measure up to the high standards of medicine. A given episode might combine black comedy and tragedy. For example, in one well-remembered May 1984 episode, sexually active Caldwell decided to dispense with underwear, and promptly caught his most sensitive appendage in the zipper of his fly—whereupon it had to be surgically freed and stitched up by a female colleague while he tried not to become, er, excited; meanwhile, in a more somber story, young resident Armstrong, overwhelmed by the pressure and the rage of a woman whose baby was lost through her misdiagnosis, committed suicide. She left a pathetic note saying, "Why must life always begin tomorrow?"

Continuing stories included Auschlander's coming to terms with his own illness, Nurse Rosenthal and her breast surgery, and Ehrlich's gradual progression from a bright but inexperienced young graduate to a confident doctor and new husband (he was married in early 1984). Peter White was a particularly troubled young doctor who, after experiencing marriage difficulties, turned rapist—and was eventually shot to death by Nurse Daniels.

In the fall of 1987 St. Eligius was taken over by the huge, profit-oriented Ecumena Hospitals Corporation, subjecting the staff more than ever to the pressures of the "business" of medicine. The new Chief of Services, Dr. Gideon, orchestrated a showdown with Westphall, who responded by "mooning" him—and quitting. Craig, meanwhile, pursued an artificial heart project (the "Craig 9000"), but found his marriage to Ellen Craig collapsing. The series' final original episode, in May 1988, was bizarre. Auschlander saved the hospital from closing, then died of a stroke; Westphall returned; Craig moved to Cleveland; and in a final, surrealistic scene, the entire six year saga of *St. Elsewhere* appeared to have been a figment of the imagination of Westphall's uncommunicative, autistic young son.

St. Elsewhere was produced by the same company responsible for *Hill Street Blues*, and it had much of the same gritty reality and cinéma-vérité technique of the police series. Although never a top-ten hit, it had an exceptionally loyal audience and won several Emmy Awards.

SAINTS AND SINNERS
Newspaper Drama
FIRST TELECAST: *September 17, 1962*
LAST TELECAST: *January 28, 1963*
BROADCAST HISTORY:
  Sep 1962–Jan 1963, NBC Mon 8:30–9:30
CAST:

Nick Alexander...............	Nick Adams
Mark Grainger	John Larkin
Lizzie Hogan	Barbara Rush
Klugie	Richard Erdman
Dave Tabak	Robert F. Simon
Polly.......................	Sharon Farrell
Charlie	Nicky Blair

Newspaper action-drama centering on Nick Alexander, crusading reporter for the *New York Bulletin*. Also seen were editor Mark Grainger, staff photographer Klugie, copy editor Dave Tabak, and Washington correspondent Lizzie Hogan.

SALLY

Situation Comedy
FIRST TELECAST: *September 15, 1957*
LAST TELECAST: *March 30, 1958*
BROADCAST HISTORY:
Sep 1957–Mar 1958, NBC Sun 7:30–8:00
CAST:
Sally Truesdale.............. Joan Caulfield
Mrs. Myrtle Banford .... Marion Lorne
Bascomb Bleacher (1958) .... Gale Gordon
Jim Kendall (1958) .... Johnny Desmond
Bascomb Bleacher, Jr. (1958)... Arte Johnson

When this series premiered, Sally Truesdale was a former department store salesgirl who had become the traveling companion of a wealthy widow named Myrtle Banford. The matronly Mrs. Banford was slightly wacky and always getting into scrapes of one sort or another as she and Sally moved from city to city around the world. When they returned home, in the February 16, 1958, episode, the format changed. Sally and Mrs. Banford spent most of their time helping to run the Banford-Bleacher Department Store, of which Mrs. Banford was part owner. Added to the cast were Mr. Bleacher and his incompetent but lovable son, and Jim Kendall, an artist in the store's advertising department who became Sally's love interest.

SALVAGE I

Adventure
FIRST TELECAST: *January 20, 1979*
LAST TELECAST: *November 11, 1979*
BROADCAST HISTORY:
Jan 1979, ABC Sat 9:00–11:00
Jan 1979–May 1979, ABC Mon 8:00–9:00
Jun 1979–Aug 1979, ABC Sun 8:00–9:00
Nov 1979, ABC Sun 7:00–8:00
CAST:
Harry Broderick .... Andy Griffith
Skip Carmichael............... Joel Higgins
Melanie Slozar .... Trish Stewart
Mack .... J. Jay Saunders
Klinger..................... Richard Jaeckel
Hank Beddoes .... Lee De Broux

Harry Broderick was TV's first adventurer in search of junk. His Jettison Scrap and Salvage Company, headquartered in Southern California, specialized in such exotic missions as retrieving old B-52s from a jungle, oil from dried-out oil wells, diamonds from an active volcano, and icebergs from the polar ice cap (which he could steer to a drought-stricken island). His most spectacular forays were into outer space, however, using

a Vulture rocket to lasso abandoned, gold-encased satellites and recover scientific "junk" on the moon. Harry's young partners were Skip, a former member of the NASA space team, and Melanie. Klinger was his FBI friend.

SAM

Police Drama
FIRST TELECAST: *March 14, 1978*
LAST TELECAST: *April 18, 1978*
BROADCAST HISTORY:
Mar 1978–Apr 1978, CBS Tue 8:00–8:30
CAST:
Officer Mike Breen .... Mark Harmon
Captain Tom Clagett.......... Len Wayland

An unusual variation on police series, *Sam* dealt with the exploits of a man-and-dog patrol car team of the Los Angeles Police Department. Mike Breen was the human half of the team and Sam was the yellow Labrador retriever police dog with which he was partnered. They patrolled in a police car designated Two-Henry-Six and made much use of Sam's uncommon skills in detection (his speed, maneuverability, and keen senses of smell and hearing) in their pursuit of criminals. Despite their record of performance, Mike's boss Capt. Clagett had his doubts about Sam's abilities as a crime fighter.

SAM BENEDICT

Law Drama
FIRST TELECAST: *September 15, 1962*
LAST TELECAST: *September 7, 1963*
BROADCAST HISTORY:
Sep 1962–Sep 1963, NBC Sat 7:30–8:30
CAST:
Sam Benedict .... Edmond O'Brien
Hank Tabor .... Richard Rust
Trudy Wagner............... Joan Tompkins

Courtroom drama series loosely based on the career of famed real-life trial lawyer Jacob W. "Jake" Erlich. Set in San Francisco, the program was notable for its intermixing of human-interest and comic elements with the standard lawyer-as-sleuth format. Hank was Sam's assistant, and Trudy his secretary.

The real Erlich served as "technical consultant" for the show.

SAM LEVENSON SHOW, THE

Comedy
FIRST TELECAST: *January 27, 1951*
LAST TELECAST: *June 10, 1952*
BROADCAST HISTORY:
Jan 1951–Jun 1951, CBS Sat 7:00–7:30
Feb 1952–Apr 1952, CBS Sun 6:30–7:00
Apr 1952–Jun 1952, CBS Tue 8:00–8:30
REGULAR:
Sam Levenson

Former schoolteacher Sam Levenson was the star and only regular performer in this informal comedy series aired live from New York. His gentle humor manifested itself in monologues about his growing up in New York, family life in general, and the experiences he had had as a teacher. A regular feature of the program was a visit by a guest celebrity and his or her child.

SAMMY AND COMPANY
Talk/Variety
BROADCAST HISTORY:
Syndicated only
90 minutes
Produced: *1975–1977* (55 episodes)
Released: *Early 1975*
REGULARS:
Sammy Davis, Jr.
William B. Williams
Avery Schreiber
George Rhodes Orchestra

Sammy Davis, Jr., tried to get a foothold in the lucrative syndicated talk-show market with this Las Vegas–styled series, which was run in the late evening on most stations. William B. Williams was his right-hand man and Avery Schreiber the resident comedian, but Sammy's high-energy imprint was on the whole enterprise—as it is in everything he does—and in the long run that may have proved too much for weary viewers (most successful talk/variety show hosts are fairly laidback).

Guests were mostly performers, such as Sandy Duncan, Wayne Newton, Flip Wilson, Freddie Prinze, and Ray Charles. The program was taped in Las Vegas, Lake Tahoe, Acapulco, and other glamour spots.

SAMMY DAVIS JR. SHOW, THE
Musical Variety
FIRST TELECAST: *January 7, 1966*
LAST TELECAST: *April 22, 1966*
BROADCAST HISTORY:
Jan 1966–Apr 1966, NBC Fri 8:30–9:30
REGULARS:
Sammy Davis, Jr.
The Lester Wilson Dancers
The George Rhodes Orchestra

The multitalented Sammy Davis, Jr., starred in this short-lived musical variety series. In addition to regular guest stars, the series was a showcase for Mr. Davis as singer, dancer, comedian, musician, and impressionist. An unusual situation occurred at the start of this series. Mr. Davis had a prior commitment to do a special on ABC with the stipulation that he could not appear on television during the three weeks preceding the special. For that reason, he was seen on the premiere of *The Sammy Davis Jr. Show*, had substitute hosts for

the three succeeding telecasts, and returned to the show on February 11. The substitute hosts were Johnny Carson, Sean Connery, and Jerry Lewis.

SAMMY KAYE SHOW, THE
Musical Variety
FIRST TELECAST: *June 11, 1950*
LAST TELECAST: *June 13, 1959*
BROADCAST HISTORY:
Jun 1950–Jul 1950, NBC Sun 8:00–8:30
Jul 1951–Jul 1952, CBS Sat 7:00–7:30
Aug 1953–Sep 1953, NBC Sat 8:00–8:30
Aug 1954–Jan 1955, ABC Thu 9:00–9:30
Sep 1958–Feb 1959, ABC Sat 10:00–10:30
Feb 1959–Apr 1959, ABC Thu 10:00–10:30
Apr 1959–Jun 1959, ABC Sat 10:00–10:30
REGULARS:
Sammy Kaye
Tony Alamo (1950–1955)
Judy Johnson (1950)
Barbara Benson (1951–1952)
Peggy Powers (1953)
Ray Michaels (1958–1959)
Lynn Roberts (1958–1959)
Susan Silo (1958–1959)
J. Blasingame Bond & the Dixieland Quartet (1958–1959)
Larry Ellis (1958–1959)
Hank Kanui (1958–1959)
Johnny McAfee (1958–1959)
Harry Reser (1958–1959)
The Kaydets
Sammy Kaye Choir

Bandleader Sammy Kaye first brought his swing-and-sway music to television in 1949, with two specials. He later appeared in several series during the 1950s, on various networks. Kaye's most famous trademark was his "So You Want to Lead a Band" audience-participation routine, which he had used for years in personal appearances and on radio, and it was also featured in most of his TV series. In it, Kaye chose half a dozen members of the studio audience to try their hands at bandleading. The band did exactly what the "leader's" baton indicated, sometimes with hilarious effect. The best bandleader was chosen by audience applause and awarded a prize. Kaye also provided straight entertainment with his orchestra, vocalists, and guests, and often led a community sing. He ended each program with an inspirational poem.

The various Sammy Kaye series, though essentially similar in format, went under a number of titles over the years. The 1950 edition was called *So You Want to Lead a Band*. In 1951–1952 it was *The Sammy Kaye Variety Show*, in 1953 *The Sammy Kaye Show*, and in 1954–1955 *So You Want to Lead a Band*. The 1958 series was first called *Sammy Kaye's Music from Manhattan* (the sponsor was Manhattan shirts), then in January 1959 switched to *The Sammy Kaye Show* and in

April 1959 to *Music from Manhattan*. You would never have known the difference by watching them.

SAN FRANCISCO BEAT
syndicated title for *Lineup, The*

SAN FRANCISCO INTERNATIONAL AIRPORT
Suspense Drama
FIRST TELECAST: *October 28, 1970*
LAST TELECAST: *August 25, 1971*
BROADCAST HISTORY:
Oct 1970–Dec 1970, NBC Wed 10:00–11:00
Mar 1971–Aug 1971, NBC Wed 10:00–11:00
CAST:
Jim Conrad .... Lloyd Bridges
Bob Hatten .... Clu Gulager
June .... Barbara Werle
Suzie Conrad .... Barbara Sigel

San Francisco International Airport attempted to portray the problems and challenges involved in running one of the larger airports in the nation, and probably the world. "SFX" employed 35,000 workers, and 15 million passengers used it annually. Jim Conrad was the airport manager, Bob Hatten its chief of security, and June was Mr. Conrad's secretary. Real problems in airport life were depicted—mechanical crises, demonstrations, security issues, etc. *San Francisco International Airport* was one of four elements in the NBC series *Four in One*. Each of the elements aired for a six-week period in the first part of the 1970–1971 TV season and the reruns were aired on a rotating basis.

SAN PEDRO BEACH BUMS, THE
Situation Comedy
FIRST TELECAST: *September 19, 1977*
LAST TELECAST: *December 19, 1977*
BROADCAST HISTORY:
Sep 1977–Dec 1977, ABC Mon 8:00–9:00
CAST:
Buddy .... Christopher Murney
Stuf .... Stuart Pankin
Dancer .... John Mark Robinson
Moose .... Darryl McCullough
Boychick .... Chris De Rose
Louise .... Louise Hoven
Suzi .... Susan Mullen
Margie .... Lisa Reeves
Ralphie .... Christoff St. John
Julie .... Nancy Morgan

Knockabout comedy about five carefree young "beach bums" in sunny California, living on a houseboat called "Our Boat." The five boys, who had been buddies since their high school days, were the ever-confident Buddy, self-proclaimed leader of the group; the shy and nervous Dancer (so named because he couldn't sit still); Stuf, a compulsive eater who believed that heavy is beautiful; the muscular but very gentle Moose; and Boychick, the beach bums' answer to Clark Gable.

SANDY DREAMS
Children's Variety
FIRST TELECAST: *October 7, 1950*
LAST TELECAST: *December 2, 1950*
BROADCAST HISTORY:
Oct 1950–Dec 1950, ABC Sat 7:00–7:30

A musical fantasy in which Sandy, an eight-year-old girl, dreamt of adventure and travel. As she drifted off to sleep viewers were transported along with her to a program of sketches and songs and dances, performed by a changing cast of youngsters. Previously seen as a local program in Los Angeles.

SANDY DUNCAN SHOW, THE
Situation Comedy
FIRST TELECAST: *September 17, 1972*
LAST TELECAST: *December 31, 1972*
BROADCAST HISTORY:
Sep 1972–Dec 1972, CBS Sun 8:30–9:00
CAST:
Sandy Stockton .... Sandy Duncan
Bert Quinn .... Tom Bosley
Kay Fox .... Marian Mercer
Alex Lembeck .... M. Emmet Walsh
Hilary .... Pam Zarit
Ben Hampton .... Eric Christmas

Sandy Stockton was a cute young woman working for Quinn & Cohen, a small advertising agency. She lived in an apartment building where two of her neighbors, Kay and Alex, were also close friends. Alex was a somewhat overprotective motorcycle cop who was worried about what could happen to a young single girl living alone. Sandy was always trying to help people out and frequently got into trouble because of it.

The character of Sandy Stockton had previously appeared in Miss Duncan's 1971 series *Funny Face*, which was no more successful than this attempt.

SANDY STRONG
Children's
FIRST TELECAST: *September 25, 1950*
LAST TELECAST: *March 23, 1951*
BROADCAST HISTORY:
Sep 1950–Mar 1951, ABC Mon–Fri 6:15–6:30
CAST:
Sandy Strong and:
Mr. Mack (1950) .... Ray Suber
Mr. Mack (1950–1951) .... Forrest Lewis

Children's puppet program from Chicago.

SANFORD
Situation Comedy
FIRST TELECAST: *March 15, 1980*
LAST TELECAST: *July 10, 1981*
BROADCAST HISTORY:
Mar 1980–Jul 1980, NBC Sat 9:00–9:30
Aug 1980–Sep 1980, NBC Wed 9:30–10:00

Jan 1981, NBC Fri 8:30–9:00
May 1981–Jul 1981, NBC Fri 8:30–9:00

CAST:

Fred Sanford	Redd Foxx
Cal Pettie	Dennis Burkley
Evelyn "Eve" Lewis	Marguerite Ray
Rollo Larson	Nathaniel Taylor
Cissy Lewis	Suzanne Stone
Clara	Cathy Cooper
Winston	Percy Rodriguez
Cliff Anderson	Clinton Derricks-Carroll

One of the most successful comedy series of the 1970s was *Sanford and Son,* the saga of Fred Sanford, a cantankerous, conniving Los Angeles junk dealer. Its run ended not because of failing ratings, but because star Redd Foxx left the series to star in a variety show on ABC. The variety show lasted less than a season and, three years after leaving the role, Redd attempted to revive *Sanford.* Fred was still running his Watts junkyard but, since son Lamont was away working on the Alaskan pipeline, he had two new partners, both friends of Lamont. Rollo was a holdover from the original *Sanford and Son,* and Cal was an obese white Southerner who invested $2,000 to become part owner of "The Sanford Empire." Fred also had an unlikely new girlfriend in Eve Lewis, a wealthy Beverly Hills widow. What she saw in Fred nobody could understand, especially her daughter, Cissy, her brother, Winston, and her outspoken maid, Clara. Fred's place got a little crowded as first Cal and then Aunt Esther's college-student son, Cliff, moved in to keep him company. Unfortunately for Fred, he had very little company among viewers at home and, after three short runs, *Sanford* quietly passed from view.

SANFORD AND SON

Situation Comedy

FIRST TELECAST: *January 14, 1972*
LAST TELECAST: *September 2, 1977*
BROADCAST HISTORY:

Jan 1972–Sep 1977, NBC Fri 8:00–8:30
Apr 1976–Aug 1976, NBC Wed 9:00–9:30

CAST:

Fred Sanford	Redd Foxx
Lamont Sanford	Demond Wilson
Melvin (1972)	Slappy White
Bubba Hoover	Don Bexley
Officer Swanhauser (1972)	Noam Pitlik
Officer Smith ("Smitty") (1972–1976)	
....	Hal Williams
Aunt Ethel (1972)	Beah Richards
Julio Fuentes (1972–1975)	Gregory Sierra
Rollo Larson	Nathaniel Taylor
Aunt Esther Anderson (1973–1977)	
....	LaWanda Page
Grady Wilson (1973–1977) ...	Whitman Mayo
Donna Harris	Lynn Hamilton
Officer Hopkins ("Happy") (1972–1976)	
....	Howard Platt
Ah Chew (1974–1975)	Pat Morita

Janet Lawson (1976–1977)	Marlene Clark
Woody Anderson (1976–1977)	
....	Raymond Allen
Roger Lawson (1976–1977)	
....	Edward Crawford

PRODUCER:
Norman Lear

Fred Sanford was a 65-year-old Los Angeles junk dealer whose 34-year-old son, Lamont, was his partner, a situation that Lamont was not always happy with. At his advanced age, Fred was very happy with his little business and the marginal income it provided him. Lamont, on the other hand, was looking to better himself by getting out of the junk business and trying something more challenging and, hopefully, more lucrative. Fred, whose wife, Elizabeth, had died some years before, would do anything to keep his son from deserting him and the business. Every time Lamont threatened to leave, Fred would fake a heart attack and start moaning, "I'm coming, Elizabeth, I'm coming." Lamont wasn't really fooled by his father's machinations but he did love him and, despite what he said about his future, really wouldn't have left the old man or the business.

Sanford and Son was producer Norman Lear's second major hit (*All in the Family* was the first) and, like *All in the Family,* was based on a successful British TV comedy. *Sanford and Son's* source was called *Steptoe and Son. Sanford and Son* was an instantaneous hit and ranked among the top ten programs throughout its run. Fred had a steady girlfriend in Nurse Donna Harris, whom he was always promising to marry, and was constantly at odds with Aunt Esther, who ran the Sanford Arms, a run-down rooming house that was located next to the junkyard. Early in 1976 Lamont found a serious romantic interest in Janet, a divorcée with a young son, and they became engaged at the end of the 1976–1977 season. The marriage never took place, however, as the series left the air in the fall of 1977. Redd Foxx had committed himself to do a variety show for ABC and co-star Demond Wilson left the series in a dispute over his remuneration as the sole star of the series after Foxx's departure. With the two stars gone, NBC premiered *The Sanford Arms* (named after Aunt Esther's rooming house) in the fall of 1977, which featured most of the supporting players from *Sanford and Son.*

For a three-month period during the summer of 1976, a second episode of *Sanford and Son* was seen each week on Wednesday nights. The second episodes were reruns from previous seasons and titled *The Best of Sanford and Son.* Reruns were also telecast weekdays on NBC from June 1976 to July 1978.

SANFORD ARMS, THE

Situation Comedy

FIRST TELECAST: *September 16, 1977*
LAST TELECAST: *October 14, 1977*

Sep 1977–Oct 1977, NBC Fri 8:00–8:30

CAST:

Phil Wheeler	Theodore Wilson
Esther Anderson	LaWanda Page
Jeannie	Bebe Drake-Hooks
Grady Wilson	Whitman Mayo
Dolly Wilson	Norma Miller
Bubba Hoover	Don Bexley
Woody Anderson	Raymond Allen
Angie Wheeler	Tina Andrews
Nat Wheeler	John Earl

In 1977 NBC's highly successful comedy *Sanford and Son* lost both of its stars—Redd Foxx to a variety series of his own on ABC, and Demond Wilson because the producers would not meet his salary demands. With most of the supporting players still around, however, *The Sanford Arms* took its place. The new lead character was Phil Wheeler, a widower with two teenage children. He had made a down payment on the entire Sanford property—house, junkyard, and rooming house—and attempted to turn the latter into a successful residential hotel. With Fred and Lamont Sanford having moved to Arizona, Fred's sister-in-law Esther was left to watch over the property and collect the monthly mortgage payments. Also carried over from the *Sanford and Son* cast of characters were Esther's husband, Woody, Fred's friend Grady (who had married Dolly), and Bubba, who worked at the Sanford Arms as both bellboy and maintenance man. Newcomers to the cast in addition to Phil Wheeler were his children Angie and Nat, and his girlfriend Jeannie.

If anything proved more difficult than getting customers for the hotel, it was finding an audience for the series. The attempt to salvage the series without its two departed stars was a total failure and it lasted less than a month.

SARA
Western

FIRST TELECAST: *February 13, 1976*
LAST TELECAST: *July 30, 1976*
BROADCAST HISTORY:
Feb 1976–Jul 1976, CBS Fri 8:00–9:00
CAST:

Sara Yarnell	Brenda Vaccaro
Emmet Ferguson	Bert Kramer
Martin Pope	Albert Stratton
Claude Barstow	William Phipps
George Bailey	William Wintersole
Julia Bailey	Mariclare Costello
Martha Higgins	Louise Latham
Georgie Bailey	Kraig Metzinger
Debbie Higgins	Debbie Lytton
Emma Higgins	Hallie Morgan

Set in the frontier town of Independence, Colorado, in the 1870s, *Sara* was the story of a strong-willed young schoolteacher who had given up a dull, predictable existence in the East for the challenge of the West. A fighter, Sara battled ignorance and prejudice, to the horror of many of the more conservative townspeople who had expected a passive "schoolmarm" for their children. Her actions drew mixed reviews from the school board members, Emmett Ferguson, Claude Barstow, and George Bailey; the approval of newspaper editor Martin Pope and her friend Julia Bailey; and the disapproval of her landlady, Martha Higgins. Most important to Sara, however, was the fact that she had the endorsement and enthusiastic interest of her students in the one-room school where she was the only teacher.

SARA
Situation Comedy

FIRST TELECAST: *January 23, 1985*
LAST TELECAST: *June 15, 1988*
BROADCAST HISTORY:
Jan 1985–May 1985, NBC Wed 9:30–10:00
June 1988, NBC Wed 9:30–10:00
CAST:

Sara McKenna	Geena Davis
Rozalyn Dupree	Alfre Woodard
Marty Lang	Bill Maher
Dennis Kemper	Bronson Pinchot
Stuart Webber	Mark Hudson
Jesse Webber	Matthew Lawrence
Helen Newcomb	Ronnie Claire Edwards

Sara was a comedy about the professional and personal life of a young, attractive single woman in San Francisco. Sara was a lawyer who shared a storefront office with three other attorneys. One of them, Rozalyn, was also her best friend and full of advice on how Sara should run her social life. The other two were men—sleazy Marty, whose ambition often got in the way of his principles and, unfortunately, won; and Dennis, the obligatory gay (it was, after all, San Francisco), whose honesty and integrity often put him at odds with Marty. Helen was the office secretary and surrogate mother to them all. Stuart, who lived in Sara's apartment building, was a recently divorced single parent trying to get back into the single world while raising his four-year-old son, Jesse.

NBC aired reruns of Sara briefly in 1988.

SARGE
Drama

FIRST TELECAST: *September 21, 1971*
LAST TELECAST: *January 11, 1972*
BROADCAST HISTORY:
Sep 1971–Nov 1971, NBC Tue 8:30–9:30
Nov 1971–Jan 1972, NBC Tue 7:30–8:30
CAST:

Father Samuel Cavanaugh (Sarge)

	George Kennedy
Valerie	Sallie Shockley
Kenji Takichi	Harold Sakata
Barney Verick	Ramon Bieri

Set in San Diego, *Sarge* was the story of Father Samuel Cavanaugh, a priest at St. Aloysius Parish. Father Cavanaugh had spent nine years as a member of the San Diego Police Department, part of the time as a homicide detective in the same area in which he was now a priest. He was known as "Sarge" because of his police background, which often helped him provide guidance to his parishioners in their struggle to cope with the problems of a metropolitan environment. The other members of the parish staff seen regularly were Kenji, the rectory cook, and Valerie, the parish secretary. Barney Verick, chief of detectives and long-time friend of Father Cavanaugh, often sought the priest's help when members of the parish were involved in criminal cases.

SATURDAY NIGHT AT THE GARDEN
Sports
FIRST TELECAST: *October 7, 1950*
LAST TELECAST: *March 31, 1951*
BROADCAST HISTORY:
Oct 1950–Mar 1951, DUM Sat 8:30–11:00

Back when Saturday night viewing was dominated by Sid Caesar and Imogene Coca's *Your Show of Shows* on NBC, DuMont offered this weekly program as an alternative to those who preferred sports. Aired live from New York City's Madison Square Garden, *Saturday Night at the Garden* presented whatever event was being staged there, in its entirety. The first three telecasts consisted of a rodeo at which Gene Autry was the guest star, with Don Russell functioning as emcee, and there was one week devoted to a horse show, but most of the remaining telecasts were of more conventional sporting contests. The majority of the broadcasts were basketball games, both professional and college, including the then prestigious NIT College Basketball Tournament, with Curt Gowdy and Don Dunphy doing the commentary. Several track meets were also aired in the spring.

Originally titled *Madison Square Garden*, the series' name was changed to *Saturday Night at the Garden* in November.

SATURDAY NIGHT DANCE PARTY
Variety
FIRST TELECAST: *June 7, 1952*
LAST TELECAST: *August 30, 1952*
BROADCAST HISTORY:
Jun 1952–Jul 1952, NBC Sat 9:30–10:30
Jul 1952–Aug 1952, NBC Sat 9:00–10:30
HOST:
Jerry Lester

This series was the 1952 summer replacement for *Your Show of Shows*. It was a comedy and music variety show that was hosted by comedian Jerry Lester. Each week his guests included a different name band and a number of variety acts.

SATURDAY NIGHT FIGHTS, THE
see *Boxing*

SATURDAY NIGHT HOLLYWOOD PALACE, THE
see *Hollywood Palace, The*

SATURDAY NIGHT JAMBOREE
Country Music
FIRST TELECAST: *December 4, 1948*
LAST TELECAST: *July 2, 1949*
BROADCAST HISTORY:
Dec 1948–Jan 1949, NBC Sat 8:00–9:00
Jan 1949–Apr 1949, NBC Sat 8:00–8:30
Apr 1949–Jul 1949, NBC Sat 9:30–10:00
EMCEE:
Elton Britt (1948)
Boyd Heath (1949)
REGULARS:
Chubby Chuck Roe, comic
Sophrony Garen, vocals
Ted Grant, violin
Eddie Howard, banjo
John Havens, guitar
Edwin Smith, accordion
Gabe Drake, bass

Country music program, with a heavy leavening of cornpone humor. Yodler Elton Britt was the original host, but he skedaddled after three telecasts and no other major stars from the country field associated themselves with this New York–based program during its brief run.

SATURDAY NIGHT LIVE
Comedy Variety
FIRST TELECAST: *October 11, 1975*
LAST TELECAST:
BROADCAST HISTORY:
Oct 1975–   , NBC Sat 11:30–1:00
Oct 1979–Mar 1980, NBC Wed 10:00–11:00
Mar 1980–Apr 1980, NBC Fri 10:00–11:00
REGULARS:
Chevy Chase (1975–1976)
John Belushi (1975–1979)
Dan Aykroyd (1975–1979)
Gilda Radner (1975–1980)
Garrett Morris (1975–1980)
Jane Curtin (1975–1980)
Laraine Newman (1975–1980)
Bill Murray (1977–1980)
Albert Brooks (1975–1976)
Gary Weis (1976–1977)
Jim Henson's Muppets (1975–1976)
Don Novello (1978–1980, 1985–1986)
Paul Shaffer (1978–1980)
Al Franken (1979–1980)
Tom Davis (1979–1980)
Denny Dillon (1980–1981)
Gilbert Gottfried (1980–1981)
Gail Matthius (1980–1981)
Joe Piscopo (1980–1984)
Ann Risley (1980–1981)

Charles Rocket (1980–1981)
Eddie Murphy (1981–1984)
Robin Duke (1981–1984)
Tim Kazurinsky (1981–1984)
Tony Rosato (1981–1982)
Christine Ebersole (1981–1982)
Brian Doyle-Murray (1981–1982)
Mary Gross (1981–1985)
Brad Hall (1982–1984)
Gary Kroeger (1982–1985)
Julia Louis-Dreyfus (1982–1985)
Jim Belushi (1983–1985)
Billy Crystal (1984–1985)
Christopher Guest (1984–1985)
Harry Shearer (1984–1985)
Rich Hall (1984–1985)
Martin Short (1984–1985)
Pamela Stephenson (1984–1985)
Anthony Michael Hall (1985–1986)
Randy Quaid (1985–1986)
Joan Cusack (1985–1986)
Robert Downey (1985–1986)
Nora Dunn (1985–   )
Terry Sweeney (1985–1986)
Jon Lovitz (1985–   )
Damon Wayans (1985–1986)
Danitra Vance (1985–1986)
Dennis Miller (1985–   )
Dana Carvey (1986–   )
Phil Hartman (1986–   )
Jan Hooks (1986–   )
Victoria Jackson (1986–   )
A. Whitney Brown (1986–   )
Kevin Nealon (1986–   )

ANNOUNCER:
Don Pardo (1975–1981, 1982–   )

Saturday Night Live was one of the landmark programs of the 1970s, an attempt to bring fresh, often outrageous comedy and the excitement of live TV to late-night viewers. It featured "The Not Ready for Prime Time Players," a repertory company of wacky comics who presented 90 minutes of topical satire, straight comedy, and music every Saturday night. Each week a different guest star served as the host and the person around whom many of the sketches were written. Some of the more familiar guests were George Carlin (host of the first telecast), Candice Bergen, Buck Henry, Elliott Gould, Lily Tomlin, Dick Cavett, Steve Martin, Eric Idle, Richard Dreyfuss, and Paul Simon. Some hosts weren't from the entertainment world at all, such as New York Mayor Ed Koch, consumer advocate Ralph Nader, football star Fran Tarkenton, Georgia legislator Julian Bond, and even Presidential Press Secretary Ron Nessen (in a controversial but good-humored appearance). Perhaps most unusual was 80-year-old Mrs. Miskel Spillman, who happened to win an "Anyone Can Host" write-in contest during the 1977–1978 season.

Each week also had a musical guest, ranging from some truly offbeat and eccentric musicians

to such major rock stars as Blondie and the Rolling Stones.

The chief "discovery" of *Saturday Night Live* during its initial season was comic Chevy Chase, famous for his opening pratfall and his role as the earnest young newsman reporting preposterous headlines on "Weekend Update." His trademark line was "Good evening. I'm Chevy Chase and you're not." Jane Curtin took over the role as newscaster after Chevy left the show in November 1976, and was later joined by Dan Aykroyd when an anchor team was instituted. Other frequent bits included Chevy as bumbling President Ford; Dan as candidate, and later President, Jimmy Carter; Gilda Radner as a lisping Barbara Walters (Ba Ba Wawa), a confused Emily Litella making editorial replies on Weekend Update, and later as rambling, loudmouthed newscaster Rosanne Rosanna-Dana; John Belushi as a Samurai warrior; Aykroyd and Belushi as the Blues Brothers; Don Novello as Father Guido Sarducci; and practically everyone in ridiculous costumes as the Bees or the alien Coneheads.

Originally Jim Henson's Muppets were a regular feature, as was a short, offbeat film produced each week by Albert Brooks (later the films were by Gary Weis). Still later came the "Mr. Bill" films, about the hapless little puppet made of dough who was always being squashed or dismembered by Sluggo. These evolved from a short film submitted by a young man named Walter Williams. And of course there were the ersatz "commercials," satirizing everything from the telephone company to milk.

Over the years *Saturday Night Live* developed a large and loyal audience, and by the 1977–1978 season it was by far the most popular program in late-night television, surpassing the longtime champ *The Tonight Show*. With the success of the show came success for its stars, and eventually the departure of the entire original cast. Chevy Chase left in the fall of 1976 to pursue a career in films and prime-time specials. Three years later Belushi (a major film star in *Animal House*) and Aykroyd left to make a large-screen production based on the Blues Brothers characters they had developed on *Saturday Night Live*. By the spring of 1980 producer Lorne Michaels decided to leave and the remainder of the original cast went with him. A new producer, Jean Doumanian, a new cast, and new writers took over in the fall of 1980, to generally poor reviews. Declining audiences resulted in considerable behind-the-scenes turmoil, with more cast changes and a new production team taking over in 1981. Michaels returned in 1985.

The major discovery of the recast *Saturday Night Live* was youthful black comic Eddie Murphy, whose career exploded with the success of his first feature film, *48 Hrs.*, in 1982. Later favorite characters included Jon Lovitz's pathological liar Tommy Flanagan ("That's the ticket!") and Billy Crystal's oily interviewer Fernando ("Mahvelous, mahvelous!"). A frequent musical guest in the mid-'80s was David Johansen as gravelly voiced singer Buster Poindexter.

Edited reruns of *Saturday Night Live* were telecast in prime time in 1979–1980, under the title *The Best of Saturday Night Live*.

SATURDAY NIGHT LIVE WITH HOWARD COSELL
Variety
FIRST TELECAST: *September 20, 1975*
LAST TELECAST: *January 17, 1976*
BROADCAST HISTORY:
Sep 1975–Jan 1976, ABC Sat 8:00–9:00
REGULARS:
Howard Cosell
Elliot Lawrence Orchestra
"EXECUTIVE IN CHARGE OF COMEDY":
Alan King

This is the kind of program ABC used to put on before it became a big-league network. Howard Cosell, the acerbic sportscaster who had been a regular for years on *Monday Night Football*, was chosen as host apparently on the dubious premise that familiarity equals popularity. Polls showed him to be one of the best-known personalities in all of television. More people also said that they couldn't stand him than practically anyone else in TV.

He presided over this variety hour with awkward unease and, despite the presence of all sorts of top-name talent, the whole affair had a very amateurish air to it (Ed Sullivan, from whose old theater *Saturday Night Live* originated, was awkward too, but at least he sounded like he knew show business inside out—as indeed he did.) The program was produced by the head of ABC Sports, and was telecast live, which was highly unusual for TV at the time. This was supposed to give it a greater "immediacy," but apparently viewers didn't notice the difference.

The premiere featured the U.S. TV debut of one of the hottest groups in popular music, the Bay City Rollers, live via satellite, who drove a teeny-bopper audience to frenzy. Frank Sinatra, John Denver, and John Wayne showed up, as did such sports stars as Evel Knievel, Alex Karras, Jimmy Connors, and Muhammed Ali and Joe Frazier, live by satellite from Manila on the eve of their championship fight. Cosell even offered Shamu the 5,000-pound killer whale, in a pickup from San Diego's Seaworld Oceanarium.

Howard tried hard—he even sang on one telecast, coached by Andy Williams—but bad is not good, and the show folded after half a season.

SATURDAY NIGHT REVUE
Variety
FIRST TELECAST: *June 6, 1953*
LAST TELECAST: *September 18, 1954*
BROADCAST HISTORY:
Jun 1953–Sep 1953, NBC Sat 9:00–10:30
Jun 1954–Sep 1954, NBC Sat 9:00–10:30
REGULARS:
Hoagy Carmichael (1953)
Eddie Albert (1954)
Ben Blue (1954)
Alan Young (1954)
Pat Carroll (1954)
The Sauter-Finegan Band (1954)

This live series was the summer replacement for *Your Show of Shows* in 1953 and 1954. The 1953 edition starred Hoagy Carmichael, who opened the show from his penthouse apartment (a set) where he informally entertained his friends. In the same building was a nightclub called the Sky Room, to which Hoagy invited his guests to see the dinner show. The locale then switched to the nightclub set where the various acts on the evening's program performed. Emphasis was on introducing and showcasing new talent.

The 1954 version starred Eddie Albert and was more of a straight revue. Albert would introduce the acts, sing, dance, and act in sketches himself. The guest artists, in addition to solo performances, also participated in sketches and production numbers with regular members of the cast. As in 1953, the focus was on showcasing new talent.

SATURDAY NIGHT REVUE, THE
see *Jack Carter Show, The* and *Your Show of Shows*

SATURDAY ROUNDUP
Western Anthology
FIRST TELECAST: *June 10, 1951*
LAST TELECAST: *September 1, 1951*
BROADCAST HISTORY:
Jun 1951–Sep 1951, NBC Sat 8:00–9:00
REGULAR:
Kermit Maynard

The stories of James Oliver Curwood were dramatized in this filmed Western anthology. Although Kermit Maynard starred in all of them, the character that he played varied from show to show.

Maynard was a onetime world's champion rodeo rider, and had appeared in many grade-B Westerns in the 1930s. He was the younger brother of cowboy star Ken Maynard.

SATURDAY SPORTS FINAL, THE
Sports News
FIRST TELECAST: *July 7, 1962*
LAST TELECAST: *October 6, 1962*
BROADCAST HISTORY:
Jul 1962–Oct 1962, ABC Sat 10:45–11:00
SPORTSCASTER:
Merle Harmon

Weekly wrap-up of news from the world of sports, including filmed highlights of major events. Harmon also interviewed guest sports celebrities.

SATURDAY SPORTS MIRROR

Sports News
FIRST TELECAST: *July 14, 1956*
LAST TELECAST: *September 15, 1956*
BROADCAST HISTORY:
  Jul 1956–Sep 1956, CBS Sat 7:00–7:30
REGULARS:
  Jack Drees
  Bill Hickey

This summer sports series featured sportscasters Drees and Hickey with a summary of the week's sports news, interviews with sports celebrities, and occasional coverage of events in progress on the day of the telecast.

SATURDAY SQUARE

Variety
FIRST TELECAST: *January 7, 1950*
LAST TELECAST: *February 18, 1950*
BROADCAST HISTORY:
  Jan 1950–Feb 1950, NBC Sat 8:00–9:00

Short-lived musical variety program which originated from Chicago and incorporated elements from *Chicago Jazz* and *Stud's Place*, which it replaced. In *Saturday Square*, a central figure, at first a policeman but in later telecasts a street-corner loafer, directed the viewer to different spots around the square where entertainment was being offered. The viewer was then transported to one of those spots: a musical rehearsal hall where a jam session was in progress, a stylish penthouse party, to Studs Terkel's pub, etc. Various talent appeared as guests.

SAWYER VIEWS HOLLYWOOD

Musical Variety
FIRST TELECAST: *June 29, 1951*
LAST TELECAST: *August 31, 1951*
BROADCAST HISTORY:
  Jun 1951–Aug 1951, ABC Fri 10:00–10:30
REGULARS:
  Hal Sawyer
  Gaylord Carter Trio

Musical variety program, featuring Hal Sawyer's interviews with Hollywood stars. Previously seen in daytime as *Hal in Hollywood* starting in April 1951.

SAY IT WITH ACTING

Charades
FIRST TELECAST: *January 6, 1951*
LAST TELECAST: *February 22, 1952*
BROADCAST HISTORY:
  Jan 1951–May 1951, NBC Sat 6:30–7:00
  Aug 1951–Feb 1952, ABC Fri 7:30–8:00
TEAM CAPTAINS:
  Maggi McNellis (1951)
  Bud Collyer (1951)

Celebrity charades, featuring two teams of actors and actresses from current Broadway productions. Team captains for the NBC series were Maggi McNellis and Bud Collyer, while team members varied. Formerly a local program in New York, where it began in January 1949 under the title *Look Ma, I'm Acting*, then became *Act It Out*, and finally *Say It with Acting*.

SCARECROW AND MRS. KING

Adventure/Espionage
FIRST TELECAST: *October 3, 1983*
LAST TELECAST: *September 10, 1987*
BROADCAST HISTORY:
  Oct 1983–Sep 1986, CBS Mon 8:00–9:00
  Sep 1986–Feb 1987, CBS Fri 8:00–9:00
  May 1987–Sep 1987, CBS Thu 8:00–9:00
CAST:
  Lee Stetson ("Scarecrow").. Bruce Boxleitner
  Amanda King .... Kate Jackson
  Dotty West .... Beverly Garland
  Billy Melrose .... Mel Stewart
  Francine Desmond .... Martha Smith
  Philip King .... Paul Stout
  Jamie King .... Greg Morton
  T.P. Aquinas (1986–1987) ...... Raleigh Bond
  Dr. Smyth (1986–1987) .... Myron Natwick

Amanda was just another bored, suburban divorcée and mother—until a handsome, mysterious man thrust a package into her hands at a train station and disappeared. It turned out he was "Scarecrow," an agent for a secret government organization called "The Agency," and he needed her help dodging Russian spies. She proved to be so good at it that he convinced her to become his partner, much to the skepticism of his boss, Melrose, and the confusion of Amanda's family, who were never quite sure what was going on (as she was sworn to secrecy).

Chasing foreign spies was certainly more exciting than vacuuming and P.T.A. meetings in the Washington, D.C., suburbs, and Amanda warmed to the challenge of her double life, as well as to the handsome Scarecrow himself. Their relationship was full of quips and the hint of mutual interest, which inspired much curiosity in her mother, Dotty. Were they friends? Lovers? What did this mysterious acquaintance do for a living? Francine was a wisecracking operative of "The Agency," and Philip and Jamie, Amanda's two young children. In order to deflect her friends' questions, Amanda got a part-time job at the International Federal Film Company—which happened to be the "cover" firm for the Agency office out of which Lee worked. Eventually she went through the Agency's training program and officially became Lee's partner.

In 1986 Lee's favorite and most reliable source of information, T.P. Aquinas, became a regular, and the head of the Agency, Dr. Smyth, also made several appearances. The romantic tension between Amanda and Lee finally reached its logical conclusion when, in February 1987, they were married. Unfortunately, in true spy fashion, no one could be told in order to protect Amanda's family from the Agency's many enemies.

SCENE OF THE CRIME
Detective Anthology
FIRST TELECAST: *April 14, 1985*
LAST TELECAST: *May 26, 1985*
BROADCAST HISTORY:
 Apr 1985, NBC Sun 10:00–11:00
 May 1985, NBC Sun 8:00–9:00
HOST:
 Orson Welles

NBC attempted to solve an unusual problem with this series. The network had two unrelated half-hour shows, neither of which was suitable for the schedule. So the programmers stitched the two together, added some continuity in the form of host Orson Welles, and tried to pass the result off as a new, one-hour series. The public didn't bite.

The first half hour was a standard whodunit, with the audience supposed to guess the perpetrator from in the story, before he or she was revealed. The story told in the second half hour (with a different cast) always ended with an O. Henry twist. Generally lesser-known performers were featured, with Barbara Rush, John Davidson, Michelle Phillips, and Dennis Dugan among the more familiar.

SCHLITZ FILM FIRSTS
 see *Movies—Prior to 1961*

SCHLITZ PLAYHOUSE OF STARS
Dramatic Anthology
FIRST TELECAST: *October 5, 1951*
LAST TELECAST: *March 27, 1959*
BROADCAST HISTORY:
 Oct 1951–Mar 1952, CBS Fri 9:00–10:00
 Apr 1952–Sep 1955, CBS Fri 9:00–9:30
 Oct 1955–Mar 1959, CBS Fri 9:30–10:00
HOSTESS:
 Irene Dunne (1952)

For eight seasons, the Schlitz Brewing Company sponsored a regular Friday night dramatic-anthology series on CBS. When it premiered in October 1951, under the title *Schlitz Playhouse of Stars,* it was an hour-long live drama from New York. The premiere telecast starred Helen Hayes and David Niven in "Not a Chance," and CBS heavily promoted the fact that Miss Hayes had signed an exclusive contract to perform only for this series. She did make two other appearances during 1951, but was never seen again on this show. The hour version produced some substantial dramas. Walter Hampden and Chester Morris starred in an adaptation of Herman Melville's *Billy Budd,* Dane Clark in Ernest Hemingway's "Fifty Grand,"

and Margaret Sullavan and Wendell Corey in a version of *Still Life,* the first Noel Coward play adapted for television.

In April 1952 the length of the plays presented was cut from an hour to 30 minutes and the literary merit of the material started to slip. There were still occasional plays like W. Somerset Maugham's "A String of Beads" starring Joan Caulfield and Tom Drake; and experiments like "Autumn in New York," a musical love story with Polly Bergen and Skip Homeier; but potboilers like "The Ordeal of Dr. Sutton" with Raymond Burr and Marilyn Erskine became progressively more common. For roughly six months, in the second half of 1952, Irene Dunne was on hand as a regular hostess, but that function was dropped in favor of letting one of the week's stars introduce the play, and then that too was phased out.

Although this was essentially a live series, filmed episodes started showing up in the summer of 1953, at first on an infrequent basis, then for the entire summer of 1954, and accounting for more than half of the telecasts during the 1954–1955 season. By the fall of 1956 there were no live episodes at all, and that November the title was shortened to *Schlitz Playhouse.* It remained weekly until the start of its last season, when it aired on an alternate-week basis with *Lux Playhouse.*

With a run of almost eight years, countless stars appeared on *Schlitz Playhouse of Stars.* Young James Dean made one of his rare television appearances as the star of "The Unlighted Road" in 1955, and in 1957 Gene Kelly made his television dramatic debut in "The Life You Save" with Agnes Moorehead and Janice Rule. Two episodes were turned into series—"The Restless Gun" starring John Payne and "A Tale of Wells Fargo" starring Dale Robertson—both Westerns aired during the 1956–1957 season. They turned up on NBC's lineup in the fall of 1957.

SCHOOL HOUSE
Comedy Variety
FIRST TELECAST: *January 18, 1949*
LAST TELECAST: *April 19, 1949*
BROADCAST HISTORY:
 Jan 1949–Apr 1949, DUM Tue 9:00–9:30
EMCEE ("TEACHER"):
 Kenny Delmar
APPEARING:
 Arnold Stang
 Wally Cox
 Tommy Dix
 Betty Anne Nyman
 Kenny Bowers
 Maureen Cannon
 Roger Price
 Wendy Drew
 Mary Ann Reeve
 Aileen Stanley, Jr.
 Russell Arms

Beverly Fite
Patty Adair
Buddy Hackett

Early television sometimes looked back into show-business history—*way* back—for material. Gus Edwards' "School Days" routine had been a sensation in vaudeville just after the turn of the century, producing such future stars as Georgie Jessel, Groucho Marx, Eleanor Powell, Ray Bolger, and Mae Murray. Evidently DuMont felt that it might be a hit all over again for video viewers in 1949. The format was a comedy variety show set in a schoolhouse, with a constantly beset "teacher" as emcee and a class full of talented youngsters as "students" (plus some older acts). Arnold Stang and Wally Cox were among the comical students on this TV version, and such notable performers as Buddy Hackett and Russell Arms also appeared. Except for "teacher" Kenny Delmar, the cast was constantly changing and those listed above are a sampling of the talent that performed.

Also seen as a local New York program during 1948, under the title *School Days*, with Happy Felton as "teacher."

SCIENCE CIRCUS
Instruction
FIRST TELECAST: *July 4, 1949*
LAST TELECAST: *September 12, 1949*
BROADCAST HISTORY:
   Jul 1949–Sep 1949, ABC Mon 8:30–9:00
HOST:
   Bob Brown

Children's instructional program featuring Bob Brown in the role of an absentminded science professor presenting scientific stunts and experiments in front of a studio audience. From Chicago.

SCIENCE FICTION THEATER
Science Fiction Anthology
BROADCAST HISTORY:
   Syndicated only
   30 minutes
   Produced: *1955–1957* (78 episodes)
   Released: *April 1955*
NARRATOR:
   Truman Bradley
PRODUCER:
   Ivan Tors

This semidocumentary anthology series explored the "what ifs" of modern science. Each drama was based on scientific fact, dealing with such subjects as UFOs, mental telepathy, psychokinesis, robots, man's first flight into outer space, and the possibility of thawing out frozen prehistoric animals. Actors included such Hollywood standbys as Howard Duff, Gene Barry, Basil Rathbone, and William Lundigan, and the narrator was news commentator Truman Bradley.

The series was one of the first produced by Ivan Tors, a man with a healthy regard for science and nature. He later went on to create such hits as *Sea Hunt, Daktari, Flipper,* and *Gentle Ben.* Real-life scientific experts served as advisors to this series to insure authenticity.

SCOTLAND YARD
Police Anthology
FIRST TELECAST: *November 17, 1957*
LAST TELECAST: *October 3, 1958*
BROADCAST HISTORY:
   Nov 1957–Mar 1958, ABC Sun 10:00–10:30
   May 1958–Jun 1958, ABC Wed 9:30–10:00
   Aug 1958–Oct 1958, ABC Fri 10:00–10:30
HOST:
   Edgar Lustgarten

Filmed in England, this series presented dramas based on actual cases from the files of Scotland Yard, Britain's world-renowned crime investigation unit. Series host Edgar Lustgarten was a noted English criminologist. No regular characters appeared in this series—there seemed to be a different superintendent, inspector, or sergeant on the case every week—but one role, that of Inspector Duggan (played by Russell Napier), did recur in about half a dozen episodes.

SCOTT ISLAND
see *Harbourmaster*

SCOTT MUSIC HALL
Musical Variety
FIRST TELECAST: *October 8, 1952*
LAST TELECAST: *August 26, 1953*
BROADCAST HISTORY:
   Oct 1952–Aug 1953, NBC Wed 8:30–9:00
REGULARS:
   Patti Page
   Frank Fontaine
   Mary Ellen Terry
   The Carl Hoff Orchestra

Patti Page had come to prominence in the late 1940s singing country-flavored tunes and employing an unusual recording technique which allowed her to sing in harmony with herself, or even in whole choruses of her own voice. Her biggest hit, from 1950–1951, was "The Tennessee Waltz." In this network variety program she initially co-starred with Frank Fontaine, Fontaine providing the comedy and Miss Page ("The Singing Rage") the songs. Guests were also seen. In February 1953 Fontaine was phased out of the show and Miss Page became its sole star. The only other regular on the show was featured dancer Mary Ellen Terry.

SCRAPBOOK JUNIOR EDITION
Children's
FIRST TELECAST: *June 27, 1948*
LAST TELECAST: *November 14, 1948*

BROADCAST HISTORY:
Jun 1948–Nov 1948, CBS Sun 6:00–6:30
HOSTS:
Jini Boyd O'Conner
Scotty MacGregor

This children's show invited viewers to send in information or examples of their hobbies and interests so that the TV audience could learn from them. The show started as a local program in October 1947 and remained on the air until May 1949 at an earlier time on Sunday afternoons. A feature which enabled viewers to win prizes was the puzzle tune contest. A child was called on the phone and asked to identify what was wrong with a picture that represented a nursery rhyme. If he or she identified the flaw it was worth anything from a pet dog, to a camping set, to a new bicycle.

SCREEN DIRECTORS PLAYHOUSE
Anthology
FIRST TELECAST: *October 5, 1955*
LAST TELECAST: *September 26, 1956*
BROADCAST HISTORY:
Oct 1955–Jun 1956, NBC Wed 8:00–8:30
Jul 1956–Sep 1956, ABC Wed 9:00–9:30

The one distinguishing characteristic of this filmed anthology series was that each of the dramatizations was directed by an outstanding director of Hollywood motion pictures. Among the participating directors were John Ford, Leo McCarey, Ida Lupino, and George Stevens. The scope of the series ranged from serious dramas to Westerns to comedies, and the players from relative newcomers such as Cloris Leachman, Alan Young, and Pat Hitchcock (Alfred's daughter) to such old-timers as Walter Brennan and Edgar Buchanan.

SCREEN MYSTERY
see *Movies—Prior to 1961*

SCREEN SHORTS
see *Movies—Prior to 1961*

SEA HUNT
Adventure
BROADCAST HISTORY:
Syndicated only
30 minutes
Produced: *Feb 1957–1961* (156 episodes)
Released: *January 1958*
CAST:
Mike Nelson .... Lloyd Bridges
PRODUCER:
Ivan Tors

"*Sea Hunt,*" said the *New York Times,* "may best be described as an adventure series in depth." *TV Guide* called it "an epic so watery that Lloyd Bridges' colleagues tell him they have to drain their TV sets after watching his show." Beyond the inevitable jokes, *Sea Hunt* was one of the best-remembered programs of the 1950s, and one of the most successful syndicated series of all time. The networks, in fact, had turned it down because they felt the possibilities of a weekly series set underwater were too limited. They let a big one get away.

The premise was simple. Mike Nelson was an ex-navy frogman who had become a free-lance undersea investigator. Traveling around the world on jobs, he rescued a trapped flyer in a sunken plane, brought up stolen goods, located hidden clues, and encountered an amazing number of underwater criminals (including one ingenious fellow who was going to blast his way into the vault of a seaside bank). His employers were insurance companies, salvage firms, a Hollywood moviemaker, and sometimes the U.S. government. During later seasons, in fact, when the plausible excuses for dangerous civilian assignments began to run out, he more and more frequently went on missions connected with national security, a job one might expect the navy to do. There was a good deal of action, including underwater fights and occasional chases on a sea scooter. But mostly, the attraction was simply the surreal world of the deep. When the series began perhaps 25 percent of the action took place there. "We weren't sure at first how much underwater stuff we could get by with," commented producer Ivan Tors. "But we soon found out that was what the audience wanted—water, water, and more water." Soon more than half the show took place beneath the waves, with much of the remainder aboard Mike Nelson's boat, the *Argonaut.*

Sea Hunt certainly presented some of Hollywood's more unusual production problems. Filming had to be moved around, from Southern California to Florida to the Caribbean, to follow the warm water. As a result, this was one of the more expensive half-hour series of its day, costing about $40,000 per episode, despite the small cast (Bridges was the only regular). Filming was normally done at depths of 20 to 40 feet—beyond that stuntmen were used—and only three crew members went down with the actors, cameraman, director, and producer. There were remarkably few close scrapes. Barracudas swam within camera range, but none took a bite (they usually attack only near the surface). Seasick actors were a greater problem. "Their faces get so green you can't shoot them," complained Tors. "It would be too ghastly to put on television" (although *Sea Hunt* was filmed in black-and-white).

Advising the program on matters of authenticity were a number of experts, including ex-navy frogman Jon Lindbergh, son of flyer Col. Charles Lindbergh. Underwater photography was by Lamar Boren, one of the country's leading undersea cameramen. Nevertheless, authenticity was not always possible; the wrong kind of fish would swim by for the locale where the story was supposedly taking place—you just couldn't control what happened on the "set"—and, worst of all,

Mike always dived alone, something professionals never do.

Such quibbles hardly mattered. Viewers made *Sea Hunt* a major hit during its four years of original production, and watched countless reruns throughout the 1960s. Actor Bridges thoroughly enjoyed making it, too. An all-around athlete in college, he took to skindiving like a fish. "Surefire way to escape Los Angeles smog . . . I love every minute of it." He even used his young son Beau Bridges in several episodes.

SEA HUNT
Adventure
BROADCAST HISTORY:
Syndicated only
30 minutes
Produced: *1987–*
Released: *September 1987*
CAST:
Mike Nelson .... Ron Ely
Jennifer Nelson .... Kimberly Sissons

More than 25 years after the original *Sea Hunt* had left the air, a new version bubbled to the surface with former TV Tarzan Ron Ely in the starring role. This time around Mike Nelson was a widower who used his boat, the *Sea Hunt* (hence the series title?) for assorted private and commercial uses—charters, research, salvage jobs, etc. His attractive daughter, Jennifer, who was a college student majoring in marine biology, somehow found time to take part in many of the adventures with her dad. The underwater scenes were filmed in the Bahamas, while the rest of the series was shot on location in British Columbia.

SEARCH
Adventure
FIRST TELECAST: *September 13, 1972*
LAST TELECAST: *August 29, 1973*
BROADCAST HISTORY:
Sep 1972–Aug 1973, NBC Wed 10:00–11:00
CAST:
Hugh Lockwood .... Hugh O'Brian
Nick Bianco .... Tony Franciosa
C. R. Grover .... Doug McClure
Cameron .... Burgess Meredith
Gloria Harding .... Angel Tompkins
Dr. Barnett (1972) .... Ford Rainey
Dr. Barnett (1973) .... Keith Andes
Miss Keach (1972) .... Ginny Golden
Ramos .... Tony De Costa
Kuroda .... Byron Chung
Griffin .... Albert Popwell
Carlos .... Ron Castro
Murdock .... Amy Farrell
Harris (1973) .... Tom Hallick
Miss James (1973)............. Pamela Jones

The Probe Division of World Securities had reached the ultimate in sophistication and technological development in equipping its agents as they traveled around the world on missions. Each agent had a transmitter and earphone implanted in one ear, enabling him to keep in constant contact with mission control. He also carried a miniaturized scanning device, in a ring or tie clip, that provided visual contact as well. The staff at mission control could maintain complete surveillance on whatever was happening to any of the agents. Hugh Lockwood, Nick Bianco, and C. R. Grover were the three agents whose exploits were shown, on a rotating basis, from week to week. Their assignments usually involved finding and/or protecting some valuable object or person, often with political implications. The control staff was headed by Cameron and included Gloria Harding, a telemetry specialist. Her function was to monitor the agents' vital signs. Mission control also provided the agents with computer support, status reports, warnings of impending danger, and the advice of the many experts on its permanent staff who were on hand to assist them.

SEARCH, THE
Documentary
FIRST TELECAST: *July 12, 1955*
LAST TELECAST: *October 5, 1958*
BROADCAST HISTORY:
Jul 1955–Sep 1955, CBS Tue 10:30–11:00
Jun 1958–Oct 1958, CBS Sun 6:00–6:30
NARRATOR:
Charles Romine

Produced in cooperation with a number of American universities, this series spotlighted the research projects that were being carried out in such diverse fields as speech therapy, marriage counseling, automobile safety, and robotics. All of the episodes were filmed at the respective schools where the research was in progress. The series had actually premiered in October 1954 on Sunday afternoons before moving into prime time for the summer of 1955. All of the episodes aired in 1958 were reruns of the earlier series.

SEARCH FOR THE NILE, THE
Historical Drama
FIRST TELECAST: *January 25, 1972*
LAST TELECAST: *February 29, 1972*
BROADCAST HISTORY:
Jan 1972–Feb 1972, NBC Tue 7:30–8:30
NARRATOR:
James Mason
CAST:
Sir Richard Burton .... Kenneth Haigh
John Hanning Speke .... John Quentin
Capt. James Grant .... Ian McCulloch
Dr. David Livingstone .... Michael Gough
Samuel Baker .... Norman Rossington
Florence Baker .... Catherine Schell
Henry Stanley .... Keith Buckley
Isabel Arundell Burton .. Barbara Leigh-Hunt
Sir Roderick Murchison
.... Andre van Gyseghem

Bombay......................	Seth Adagala
King Mutesa	Oliver Litonde

Filmed on location in Africa by the BBC, this mini-series chronicled the efforts of six mid-19th-century adventurers to trace the source of the Nile River. The six, all members of England's Royal Geographic Society, were explorer Sir Richard Burton; soldier-adventurer John Hanning Speke and his traveling companion, James Grant; missionary David Livingstone; sportsman Samuel Baker (who traveled with his wife); and American writer Henry Stanley. Most of the scenes were filmed as near as possible to the actual site where the events had taken place and the scripts were adapted from the writings of the principal explorers.

SECOND CHANCE
Situation Comedy
FIRST TELECAST: *September 26, 1987*
LAST TELECAST: *July 2, 1988*
BROADCAST HISTORY:
Sep 1987–Oct 1987, FOX Sat 9:00–9:30
Oct 1987–Jan 1988, FOX Sat 9:30–10:00
Jan 1988–Apr 1988, FOX Sat 8:00–8:30
Apr 1988–Jul 1988, FOX Sat 8:30–9:00
CAST:

Charles Russell/Time (1987)	Kiel Martin
Chazz Russell	Matthew L. Perry
Helen Russell	Randee Heller
Francis "Booch" Lottabucci...	William Gallo
Eugene Blooberman	Demian Slade
St. Peter (1987)	Joseph Maher
Debbie Miller (1988–)	Terri Ivens
Alex (1988–)	Adam Sadowsky

When *Second Chance* premiered it was a fantasy about a man caught between heaven and hell. Charles Russell died in the year 2011 in a hovercraft accident. When St. Peter attempted to determine where Charles' soul should be sent, he found that Mr. Russell was not good enough for heaven or bad enough for hell. To resolve the situation Charles was given a second chance—returning to earth 24 years earlier to provide moral guidance to his own younger self, under the watchful eye of St. Peter. Hopefully he could earn his way into heaven.

Charles assumed the last name Time (from the magazine), and rented the room over the garage at the Venice, California, home in which he had grown up. His divorced mother Helen, who thought he looked familiar, needed the money. The proximity to his younger self, Chazz, gave him plenty of opportunity to help the teenager become a more responsible adult than Charles had turned out to be. Chazz's best friends were Booch, a worldly wise, black-leather-jacketed womanizer reminiscent of *Happy Days'* Fonzie; and Eugene, an incredibly naive nerd.

Unhappy with the original format, the producers dropped the fantasy element and the original

star, Kiel Martin. In January 1988 the series was retitled *Boys Will Be Boys* and the focus shifted to the escapades of the three teens—Chazz, Booch, and Eugene. Though still in high school, Chazz and Booch, whose alcoholic father had recently died, became roommates. They were living in that room over Mrs. Russell's garage (more shades of *Happy Days*) that Charles had lived in. Chazz also had a new girlfriend in perky, next-door neighbor Debbie Miller.

SECOND CITY TV
Comedy
BROADCAST HISTORY:
Syndicated only
30 minutes
Produced: *1977–1981* (78 episodes)
Released: *September 1977*
CAST:

Guy Caballero.................	Joe Flaherty
Edith Prickly	Andrea Martin
Moe Green (1977–1978)........	Harold Ramis
Johnny LaRue (1977–1979)	John Candy
Earl Camembert	Eugene Levy
Lola Heatherton/Lorna Minnelli (1977–1980)	
....	Catherine O'Hara
Angus Crock/various famous stars	
....	Dave Thomas
Rabbi Karlov (1980–1981)......	Rick Moranis
Marcello (1980–1981)	Tony Rosato
Molly Earl (1980–1981)	Robin Duke

Second City TV was a TV parody on TV. Each program consisted of a group of sketches set at the "SCTV Studios," Channel 109, in which cast members did devastating takeoffs on quiz shows, farm reports, and anything else on the tube from *Ben-Hur* to *Leave It to Beaver,* interspersed with commercials for sponsors such as "The Evelyn Wolf School of Speed Eating." Guy Caballero was the unlikely Argentinian station owner; Edith Prickly, the know-it-all manager (succeeding Moe Green, after the latter was kidnapped in 1978); Johnny LaRue, the inept features man; and Earl Camembert, the announcer-newscaster. Dave Thomas and Catherine O'Hara played an assortment of roles. For example, "Lee A. Iacocca's Rock Concert," a twin parody of *Don Kirshner's Rock Concert* and the financially troubled Chrysler Corp., featured Thomas as the host of a rock show which was three billion dollars over budget. Later additions to the cast included Marcello the cowboy star and Molly Earl with her crazy crafts.

The Second City troupe began as an improvisational-comedy theater company performing in a defunct Chinese laundry in Chicago in 1959 (it was so named because Chicago was America's "second city," after New York). A branch sprang up in Toronto, and it was the Toronto group that began the SCTV series in 1977. Second City alumni over the years have included such famous names as Valerie Harper, Alan Arkin, Joan Rivers, Mike Nichols and Elaine May, Robert Klein,

David Steinberg, and *Saturday Night Live's* Gilda Radner, John Belushi, and Dan Aykroyd.

Early in 1981 it was announced that SCTV was finally coming to network television, as part of NBC's late-night lineup—(see *SCTV Network 90*).

SECOND HUNDRED YEARS, THE
Situation Comedy
FIRST TELECAST: *September 6, 1967*
LAST TELECAST: *September 19, 1968*
BROADCAST HISTORY:
Sep 1967–Feb 1968, ABC Wed 8:30–9:00
Mar 1968–Sep 1968, ABC Thu 7:30–8:00
CAST:
Luke Carpenter/Ken Carpenter
.... Monte Markham
Edwin Carpenter .... Arthur O'Connell
Col. Garroway.............. Frank Maxwell
Marcia Garroway.............. Karen Black
Nurse Lucille Anderson ...... Bridget Hanley

In the year 1900 Luke Carpenter, 33, bid farewell to his wife and his infant son Edwin and set out to prospect for gold in Alaska. He was lost in a glacier slide. Sixty-seven years later, by some freak of nature, Luke thawed out, revived, and was brought to the home of his now-aging son in Woodland Oaks, California. Chronologically Luke was 101, but he hadn't aged while in deep freeze and was physiologically still 33—younger than his own son.

In fact, he was younger in spirit, at least, than his 33-year-old grandson Ken, who was his exact look-alike (both parts were played by Monte Markham). Ken was stuffy and conservative, while Luke was ebullient, full of fun, and a rugged individualist.

The comedy centered both on the contrast between them and on Luke's problems in adapting to the modern world, while his origin was kept a military secret (Col. Garroway, an army doctor, was assigned to look after him). The first thing Luke had seen on awakening in Edwin's home was a 1967 TV set with what appeared to be little people aiming guns at him. He applied his simple, individualistic ways to the problems of the 20th century with some success, though he never could get used to a modern job.

SECRET AGENT
International Intrigue
FIRST TELECAST: *April 3, 1965*
LAST TELECAST: *September 10, 1966*
BROADCAST HISTORY:
Apr 1965–Sep 1965, CBS Sat 9:00–10:00
Dec 1965–Sep 1966, CBS Sat 8:30–9:30
CAST:
John Drake.............. Patrick McGoohan
THEME:
"Secret Agent Man," by Phil Sloan and Steve Barri

John Drake was a special security agent working for the British government as a professional spy. He traveled throughout Europe on various cases and had the usual confrontations with enemy agents and beautiful women. His supposed function was to "preserve world peace and promote brotherhood and better understanding between people and nations." He was one of the more violent "peaceful" people seen on television during the 1960s. Somehow, preserving peace always demanded beating people up and shooting them. This series was produced in England and had been popular in Europe before its importation by CBS. Popular singer Johnny Rivers had a highly successful recording of "Secret Agent Man," the theme song which he sang over the opening titles of this series. *Secret Agent* was actually an expanded version of *Danger Man*, another British series. Patrick McGoohan played the same character in both.

SECRET EMPIRE, THE
Serial
FIRST TELECAST: *February 27, 1979*
LAST TELECAST: *May 1, 1979*
BROADCAST HISTORY:
Feb 1979–May 1979, NBC Tue 8:20–8:40
CAST:
Marshal Jim Donner .... Geoffrey Scott
Billy .... Tiger Williams
Millie .... Carlene Watkins
Jess Keller .... Peter Breck
Maya .... Pamela Brull
Princess Tara (Feb–Apr) ..... Diane Markoff
Princess Tara (Apr–May).. Stepfanie Kramer
Emperor Thorval .... Mark Lenard
Roe .... Peter Tomarken
Hator .... David Opatoshu
Yannuck .... Sean Garrison

This "cliff-hanger" serial was part science fiction and part Western. In the 1880s, Cheyenne Marshal Jim Donner was trying to track down a group of gold-shipment-stealing desperadoes known as the Phantom Riders, when he stumbled upon the entrance to the hidden underground city of Chimera. The people of Chimera were visitors from another planet, living in futuristic splendor marred only by the dictatorial rule of the evil Thorval. Thorval maintained control over his subjects with the use of the compliatron, a device that enslaved minds and was powered by the gold stolen by his soldiers. Thorval's daughter Tara was spoiled and self-indulgent, and his aide, Hator, almost as power-hungry as he. Struggling to free their people from the rule of Thorval was a group known as the Partisans, led by Roe and the beautiful Maya. Most of the folks around Cheyenne had no idea that they were neighbors of aliens. Only Donner's friends Millie and Billy knew, as did gold miner Jess Keller, who planned to provide Thorval with gold in exchange for an army of slaves with which to take over the surface world.

The daring marshal tried both to help the Partisans overthrow Thorval and to stop the gold robberies on the surface. In the last episode aired, in true cliff-hanger fashion, Donner was chased into the generator room in Chimera, where there was a power overload explosion. TO BE CONTINUED flashed on the screen but, since the series had been canceled, the audience never found out how or if he had survived.

The Secret Empire was one of three serials aired under the umbrella title *Cliff Hangers*. A nice touch, used only with *The Secret Empire*, was that all of the scenes around Cheyenne, on the surface of the Earth, were filmed in black-and-white, while in the futuristic world of Chimera everything was in color.

SECRET FILES OF CAPTAIN VIDEO, THE
see *Captain Video and His Video Rangers*

SECRETS OF MIDLAND HEIGHTS
Drama
FIRST TELECAST: *December 6, 1980*
LAST TELECAST: *January 25, 1981*
BROADCAST HISTORY:
Dec 1980–Jan 1981, CBS Sat 10:00–11:00
CAST:
Dorothy Wheeler . . . . Bibi Besch
Guy Millington . . . . Jordan Christopher
Nathan Welsh . . . . Robert Hogan
Calvin Richardson . . . . Mark Pinter
Burt Carroll . . . . Lorenzo Lamas
Ann Dulles . . . . Doran Clark
Holly Wheeler . . . . Marilyn Jones
Lisa Rogers . . . . Linda Hamilton
John Grey . . . . Jim Youngs
Teddy Welsh . . . . Daniel Zippi
Danny Welsh . . . . Stephen Manley
Micki Carroll . . . . Melora Hardin
Margaret Millington . . . . Martha Scott
Lucy Dexter . . . . Jenny O'Hara
Mark Hudson . . . . Bill Thornbury
Eric Dexter . . . . Fred Weiss
Etta Bormann . . . . Bea Silvern
Max Bormann . . . .: . . . Gordon Clark
Serena Costin . . . . Erica Yohn
Sue . . . . Irene Arranga

Set in a sleepy Midwestern college town, this was another entry in the *Dallas*-inspired soap-opera boom of the early 1980s. The principal variation was an emphasis on the local teenage population, which led some to characterize this as the first "teenage soap." All the usual elements were there. Sex: rampant, with married people cheating on their spouses and the kids cheating on their boyfriends and girlfriends. Class struggle: the wealthy Millingtons ruthlessly maintained their power over the community. Power struggle: within the Millington family, devious Guy Milling-

ton manipulated people and events to make sure he would inherit the family fortune. Lack of an audience undid them all, as the series was canceled in less than two months.

SEE IT NOW
Documentary
FIRST TELECAST: *April 20, 1952*
LAST TELECAST: *July 5, 1955*
BROADCAST HISTORY:
Apr 1952–Jun 1953, CBS Sun 6:30–7:00 (OS)
Sep 1953–Jul 1955, CBS Tue 10:30–11:00 (OS)
HOST:
Edward R. Murrow

See It Now was the prototype of the in-depth quality television documentary. It had started as a Sunday afternoon program on November 18, 1951. On that first telecast, Edward R. Murrow showed a live camera shot of the Atlantic Ocean, followed by a live shot of the Pacific Ocean, and then commented: "We are impressed by a medium through which a man sitting in his living room has been able for the first time to look at two oceans at once." The subject matter could be as serious as his famous essay on Senator Joe McCarthy or as light as an interview with painter Grandma Moses. Despite the fact that many of the personalities covered in this series could also have been on his other weekly series, *Person to Person*, the tone of *See It Now* was more serious and informative. The thing that distinguished *See It Now* was its penchant for taking controversial positions and dealing directly with major, and often unpopular, issues. In addition to his attacks on McCarthyism and the threat it posed in a free society, Murrow's documentaries detailed the recriminations of atomic scientist J. Robert Oppenheimer over the course of nuclear technology, and the relationship between cigarette smoking and cancer (despite the fact that Murrow himself was a chain smoker). His in-person visit to GIs on the front lines in Korea was a memorable telecast. Each broadcast ended with "Good night . . . and good luck."

Six months after its premiere, *See It Now* moved into the evening lineup, where it remained for more than three years. When it returned in the fall of 1955 it was no longer a weekly half-hour, but had become an irregularly scheduled hour. The longer format enabled more complete coverage of an issue. The last telecast of *See It Now* was on July 7, 1958. Murrow made occasional appearances on its successor, *CBS Reports*.

SEMINAR
see *Columbia University Seminar*

SEMI-TOUGH
Situation Comedy
FIRST TELECAST: *May 29, 1980*
LAST TELECAST: *June 19, 1980*

BROADCAST HISTORY:
May 1980–Jun 1980, ABC Thu 9:30–10:00
CAST:

Billy Clyde Pucket	Bruce McGill
Shake Tiller	David Hasselhoff
Barbara Jane Bookman	Markie Post
Big Ed Bookman	Hugh Gillin
Big Barb	Mary Jo Catlett
Burt Danby	Jim McKrell
Coach Cooper	Ed Peck
Puddin	Bubba Smith
Story Time	Freeman King

Billy Clyde and Shake were two hulking members of football's losingest team, the New York Bulls, who happened to share their apartment—platonically, of course—with a pretty young thing named Barbara Jane. This slapstick comedy was based on the novel by Dan Jenkins, which had previously been made into a hit movie starring Burt Reynolds.

SENATOR, THE
Political Drama
FIRST TELECAST: *September 13, 1970*
LAST TELECAST: *August 22, 1971*
BROADCAST HISTORY:
Sep 1970–Aug 1971, NBC Sun 10:00–11:00
CAST:

Sen. Hayes Stowe	Hal Holbrook
Jordan Boyle	Michael Tolan
Erin Stowe	Sharon Acker
Norma Stowe	Cindy Eilbacher

Junior Senator Hayes Stowe was a very idealistic politician. His goals were the betterment of society and the environment in which we live. His affinity for getting involved with causes and issues of public concern did not endear him to the old-line professional politicians he had to deal with in Washington. In trying to resolve problems he often stepped on the toes of entrenched business interests with impressive political connections. With the help of Jordan Boyle, his administrative aide, and the support of his wife (Erin) and his daughter (Norma), Hayes relentlessly fought for what he believed was right and just.

The Senator was one of the three rotating elements that comprised *The Bold Ones* during the 1970–1971 season. The other two were *The New Doctors* and *The Lawyers.*

SERENADE
see *Sing-Co-Pation*

SERGEANT BILKO
syndicated title for *Phil Silvers Show, The*

SERGEANT PRESTON OF THE YUKON
Police Drama/Adventure
FIRST TELECAST: *September 29, 1955*
LAST TELECAST: *September 25, 1958*

BROADCAST HISTORY:
Sep 1955–Sep 1958, CBS Thu 7:30–8:00
CAST:

Sgt. Preston	Richard Simmons

THEME MUSIC:
"Donna Diana Overture," by Emil Von Reznicek

"On, King! On, you huskies," he cried, and Sergeant Preston was off across the snow to single-handedly enforce law and order on Canada's frozen frontier. The time was the turn of the century, and the place was the Yukon Territory, where thieves and scoundrels preyed upon the gold miners and settlers who had come to open up the wilderness. Aided only by his remarkably intelligent malamute dog, Yukon King, and his black horse, Rex, Preston represented the long arm of the Royal Northwest Mounted Police. He cut a splendid figure in his smart red uniform (even in black-and-white!), his broad-brimmed hat, and his pencil-thin mustache.

The series was filmed in color in mountainous sections of California and Colorado, against a spectacularly scenic backdrop. It was widely seen in reruns, including a season on Saturday afternoons on the NBC network in 1963–1964.

Sergeant Preston had originated on radio in 1947, and was created by George W. Trendle and Fran Striker (who were also responsible for the Lone Ranger and the Green Hornet). It continued on radio until 1955.

SERPICO
Police Drama
FIRST TELECAST: *September 24, 1976*
LAST TELECAST: *January 28, 1977*
BROADCAST HISTORY:
Sep 1976–Jan 1977, NBC Fri 10:00–11:00
CAST:

Frank Serpico	David Birney
Tom Sullivan	Tom Atkins

Frank Serpico was a New York City cop who may have been too idealistic for the system through which he had to work. He often went undercover to track down drug dealers, break up numbers racket operations, and cut down the illegal traffic in weapons. He was also very involved in efforts to prove that various police officers and officials, some in very high places, were on the take from organized crime. Tom Sullivan was a full-time undercover agent who worked with Frank and was his contact with the police when he was on an undercover assignment.

There was a real Frank Serpico, on whose career this series was based. His search for, and exposure of, corruption in the New York City Police Department did not endear him to his fellow officers, many of whom expressed their hatred of him as a "troublemaker." On February 3, 1971, he was shot in the face by a dope pusher, and he subsequently retired from the force on a disability pension. He left with a profound sense of disillusionment and a permit to carry a gun for his own protection, possibly from other police personnel. He later was the subject of a book titled *Serpico* which was the story of his experiences as a police officer. The book was made into a movie of the same name, starring Al Pacino, and that in turn, was the basis for this series.

SERVING THROUGH SCIENCE
Instruction
FIRST TELECAST: *June 18, 1946*
LAST TELECAST: *May 27, 1947*
BROADCAST HISTORY:
  Jun 1946–May 1947, DUM Tue 9:00–9:30 (approx.)
HOST:
  Dr. Guthrie McClintock (also given as Dr. Miller McClintock)

This was an early experiment in educational programming, consisting of short films from the Encyclopedia Britannica with discussion by Dr. McClintock and guests. The setting was Dr. McClintock's study. Shortly after the program began *Television* magazine conducted a poll of its readers that indicated that while everyone thought the presentation worthwhile, some found it to be rather boring. ("It made us very sleepy," wrote one respondent.) So the sponsor added a musical segment with performances by promising young artists, which had nothing whatever to do with the subject at hand but was supposed to "liven things up." This mishmash lasted only a few weeks before the program was finally dropped.

As with some other early programs, it is not known whether *Serving through Science* was fed over the network from the beginning, though it was on the network by the beginning of 1947 at the latest. Sponsor U.S. Rubber had presented similar educational TV shows locally in New York in 1945 and perhaps earlier.

SESSIONS
  see *Chicago Jazz*

SEVEN AT ELEVEN
Comedy Variety
FIRST TELECAST: *May 28, 1951*
LAST TELECAST: *June 27, 1951*
BROADCAST HISTORY:
  May 1951–Jun 1951, NBC Mon/Wed 11:00–Midnight
REGULARS:
  George De Witt
  Sid Gould
  George Freems
  Sammy Petrillo
  Dorothy Keller
  Jane Scott
  Denise Lor
  Betty Luster & Jack Stanton

Jackie Loughery
Herbie Faye
Milton Delugg & His Sextet

Short-lived live comedy variety series originating from New York.

SEVEN BRIDES FOR SEVEN BROTHERS
Adventure
FIRST TELECAST: *September 19, 1982*
LAST TELECAST: *July 2, 1983*
BROADCAST HISTORY:
  Sep 1982, CBS Sun 8:00–9:30
  Sep 1982–Mar 1983, CBS Wed 8:00–9:00
  Jun 1983–Jul 1983, CBS Sat 8:00–9:00
CAST:
  Adam McFadden ... Richard Dean Anderson
  Daniel McFadden (age 18) ..... Roger Wilson
  Crane McFadden (age 21) ...... Peter Horton
  Brian McFadden (age 25) .... Drake Hogestyn
  Ford McFadden (age 15) .... Bryan Utman
  Evan McFadden (age 16) .... Tim Topper
  Guthrie McFadden (age 12) .... River Phoenix
  Hannah McFadden .... Terri Treas
  Marie .... Joan Kjar
ORIGINAL MUSIC:
  by Jimmy Webb

There was singing and dancing, hootin' and hollerin' in this lively, updated revival of the hit 1954 MGM movie classic. While the movie was set on the frontier, this series took place in contemporary times, as a parentless family of boys tried to go it alone on a ranch in northern California. Only the eldest brother, 27-year-old Adam, was married, and his new bride, Hannah, faced the unmanageable task of living with this rowdy, unkempt houseful of brothers. Fortunately, Hannah was high-spirited herself, and got their attention the first day by dumping an entire table full of food in their laps. Besides hijinks around the house, stories revolved around struggles to keep the ranch solvent, personal squabbles, and romances. Despite all the singing, dancing, and romancing, none of the other six McFadden brothers found a bride during the one season *Seven Brides for Seven Brothers* was on the air.

SEVENTH AVENUE
Drama
FIRST TELECAST: *February 10, 1977*
LAST TELECAST: *February 24, 1977*
BROADCAST HISTORY:
  Feb 1977, NBC Thu 9:00–11:00
CAST:
  Jay Blackman .... Steven Keats
  Rhoda Gold .... Dori Brenner
  Myrna Gold .... Anne Archer
  Joe Vitelli .... Herschel Bernardi
  Harry Lee .... Alan King
  Marty Cass .... John Pleshette
  Eva Meyers .... Jane Seymour
  Al Blackman .... Kristoffer Tabori

Celia Blackman .... Anna Berger
Morris Blackman .... Mike Kellin
Frank Topo .... Richard Dimitri

Adapted from Norman Bogner's novel, *Seventh Avenue* was the story of Jay Blackman, a poor young man from New York's Lower East Side who succeeded in becoming a major force in the garment industry in the 1940s and 1950s. His rise to power from humble beginnings and involvements with organized crime as well as his marital problems and affairs were all chronicled.

Seventh Avenue was one of four novels dramatized under the collective title *NBC's Best Sellers*.

77 SUNSET STRIP
Detective Drama
FIRST TELECAST: *October 10, 1958*
LAST TELECAST: *September 9, 1964*
BROADCAST HISTORY:

Oct 1958–Oct 1959, ABC Fri 9:30–10:30
Oct 1959–Sep 1962, ABC Fri 9:00–10:00
Sep 1962–Sep 1963, ABC Fri 9:30–10:30
Sep 1963–Feb 1964, ABC Fri 7:30–8:30
Apr 1964–Sep 1964, ABC Wed 10:00–11:00
CAST:

Stuart Bailey .... Efrem Zimbalist, Jr.
Jeff Spencer (1958–1963) .... Roger Smith
Gerald Lloyd Kookson III ("Kookie") (1958–1963) .... Edd Byrnes
Roscoe (1958–1963) .... Louis Quinn
Suzanne Fabray (1958–1963) . Jacqueline Beer
Lt. Gilmore (1958–1963) .... Byron Keith
Rex Randolph (1960–1961) ..... Richard Long
J. R. Hale (1961–1963) .... Robert Logan
Hannah (1963–1964) .... Joan Staley
THEME:
"77 Sunset Strip," by Mack David and Jerry Livingston

77 Sunset Strip was the prototype for a rash of glamorous private-detective teams in the late 1950s and early 1960s. Half the team was Stu Bailey, a suave, cultured former OSS officer who was an expert in languages. An Ivy League Ph.D., he had intended to become a college professor but turned private investigator instead. The other half was Jeff Spencer, also a former government undercover agent, who had a degree in law. Both of them were judo experts. They worked out of an office at No. 77 Sunset Strip, in Hollywood, though their cases took them to glamour spots all over the world.

Next door to No. 77 was Dino's, a posh restaurant whose maître d', Mario, was seen occasionally in the series. Seen often was Dino's parking lot attendant, a gangling, jive-talking youth named Kookie, who longed to be a private detective himself and who often helped Stu and Jeff on their cases. Kookie provided comic relief for the series, and his "Kookie-isms" became a trademark. For example: "the ginchiest" (the greatest); "piling up the Z's" (sleeping); "keep the eyeballs

rolling" (be on the lookout); "play like a pigeon" (deliver a message); "a dark seven" (a depressing week); and "headache grapplers" (aspirin).

Other regulars included Roscoe the racetrack tout and Suzanne the beautiful French switchboard operator. But it was Kookie who caught the public's fancy and propelled the show into the top ten. In the first telecast of the 1959–1960 season he helped Stu Bailey catch a jewel thief by staging a revue, in which he sang a novelty song called "Kookie, Kookie, Lend Me Your Comb" (after his habit of constantly combing his hair). The song was released on record as a duet between Byrnes and Connie Stevens, and became a smash hit. Byrnes soon began to overshadow the series' principals as a popular celebrity, a kind of "Fonzie" of the 1950s.

Unsatisfied with his secondary role in the show, the young actor demanded a bigger part and eventually walked out. Warner Brothers at first replaced him with Troy Donahue as a long-haired bookworm, about as far from the Kookie character as you could get. But Byrnes came back a few months later and was promoted to a full-fledged partner in the detective firm at the start of the 1961–1962 season. His permanent replacement at the parking lot was J. R. Hale. Previously, for a single season, Rex Randolph had been seen as a third partner in the firm.

Kookie was not the only one who tried parlaying the show's success into a hit record. Following his example, actor Roger Smith put out an album called *Beach Romance* (which bombed), and even Efrem Zimbalist, Jr., who was no singer but who had perhaps the best musical background of the lot (he was the son of a famous concert violinist and a famous opera singer), was lured into a studio to record "Adeste Fideles" in English and Latin. Also, the finger-snapping theme music from the series was made into a best-selling album.

By 1963 the novelty had worn off and the show was in decline. In an attempt to save it, Jack Webb was brought in as producer, and William Conrad as director, and drastic changes were made. The entire cast was dropped with the exception of Efrem Zimbalist, Jr., who became a free-lance investigator traveling around the world on cases. Lavish production values were featured. The season opened with a five-part chase-thriller featuring two dozen big-name guest stars and written by eight top writers. Stu Bailey was seen pursuing operatives of a gigantic smuggling ring across two continents. The rest of the season was spent on the road as well, with Stu acquiring a permanent secretary named Hannah, but it didn't help.

Reruns of *77 Sunset Strip* were seen during the summer of 1964.

77TH BENGAL LANCERS, THE
see *Tales of the 77th Bengal Lancers*

SHA NA NA
Musical Variety

BROADCAST HISTORY:
Syndicated only
30 minutes
Produced: *1977–1981* (97 episodes)
Released: *September 1977*
MEMBERS OF SHA NA NA:
Jon "Bowzer" Bauman
Lennie Baker
Johnny Contardo
Frederick "Dennis" Greene
"Dirty Dan" McBride (1977–1980)
John "Jocko" Marcellino
Dave "Chico" Ryan
"Screamin' Scott" Simon
Tony Santini (Scott Powell)
Donald "Donny" York
OTHER REGULARS:
Avery Schreiber (1977–1978)
Pam Myers
Kenneth Mars (1977–1978)
Phil Roth (1977–1978)
Jane Dulo
June Gable (1978–1981)
Soupy Sales (1978–1981)
Karen Hartman (1980–1981)
Michael Sklar (1978–1979)

This exuberant mixture of 1950s good-time rock 'n' roll and cornball comedy sketches was one of the surprise hits of the late 1970s. The setting was a city street, and the 10 members of Sha Na Na all played variations on the dumb-but-lovable 1950s "greaser"—like Fonzie on *Happy Days*—with ducktail haircuts, leather jackets, or hairy chests under cutaway undershirts. The emcee and unofficial leader was Bowzer, who would strike a pose and flex imaginary muscles in his skinny arm, while grinning with a mouthful of crooked teeth.

The jokes were awful and the comedy skits usually silly, but done with infectious enthusiasm. The boys performed energetically, and obviously didn't take anything or anybody too seriously, which helped make this a very appealing half hour. *TV Guide* said, "They seem like nothing so much as ten little boys—average age late 20s—having fun in Hollywood." Each had his own personality. Bowzer was the smarter-than-he-looks leader; Lennie, the jolly, bearded sax player; Johnny, the sexy, baby-faced Italian; Denny Greene, the only black; Dirty Dan, another youthful goodlooker; Jocko, chunky and a bit on the crazy side; Chico, a handsome, macho type; Screamin' Scott, the balding piano player who looked a bit like Elton John; Santini, also balding and on the heavy side (he used to be called Captain Outrageous, and before that Scott Powell); and Donny, the spaced-out guy in dark glasses.

When they launched into an upbeat oldie like "At the Hop" or "Book of Love," there might be cut-ups, but they were definitely not mocking the music. "They have a lot of fun," said singer Bobby Vee after doing the show, "but they're doing the music of the 50s in the spirit it was intended." And when sexy Johnny did a dreamy ballad like "Our Day Will Come"—well, girls in the audience just wet their pants.

Helping out were all sorts of guests, from Phyllis Diller and Ethel Merman to Dr. Joyce Brothers (who offered to give the boys psychiatric counseling). Many were authentic 1950s rock artists such as Chuck Berry, Bo Diddley, Freddy Cannon, the Shirelles, Chubby Checker, and Brenda Lee. A backup cast of comics, including Pam Myers, the gum-chewing dizzy blonde, was also seen.

Sha Na Na was founded in 1969 by 12 Columbia University students, who did a cappella oldies first on campus, and then in professional engagements. The group was first called the Kingsmen, then changed their name to avoid confusion with another group with the same name (the one that recorded "Louie, Louie"). Sha Na Na—the name came from the background chant in a 1950s hit by the Silhouettes, called "Get a Job"—was a surprise hit with the spaced-out, acid-rock generation, scoring a major triumph at Woodstock in the summer of 1969. However, since they did only other people's hits, the novelty soon began to wear off and they were in decline when their manager pushed them into television—and a whole new comedy/rock career. Only four of the group's original members remained by then—Greene, Marcellino, Santini, and York. Thorough professionals, but still kids at heart, they closed each week with the slogan, "Grease for peace!"

SHADOW CHASERS
Comedy Fantasy
FIRST TELECAST: *November 14, 1985*
LAST TELECAST: *January 16, 1986*
BROADCAST HISTORY:
Nov 1985–Jan 1986, ABC Thu 8:00–9:00
CAST:
Prof. Jonathon MacKensie . . . . Trevor Eve
Edgar (Benny) Benedek . . . . Dennis Dugan
Dr. Juliana Moorhouse . . . . Nina Foch

Ghosts, zombies, graverobbers, and nutty curses filled this obvious but unacknowledged ripoff of the hit comedy movie *Ghostbusters*. The young parapsychology investigators in this case were Prof. MacKensie, an anthropologist with the Georgetown Institute of Science, and Benny, a wisecracking reporter for the tabloid *The National Register* (and you thought they made that stuff up!). Dictatorial Dr. Moorhouse, who worked in a dark, cluttered cave of an office, sent them off on their missions to neutralize the spirits among us.

SHADOW OF THE CLOAK
International Intrigue
FIRST TELECAST: *June 6, 1951*
LAST TELECAST: *April 3, 1952*
BROADCAST HISTORY:
Jun 1951–Nov 1951, DUM Wed 9:30–10:00
Dec 1951–Apr 1952, DUM Thu 9:00–9:30

CAST:

Peter House .... Helmut Dantine

Helmut Dantine, who played the arrogant Nazi in many Hollywood films during the 1940s, starred as the chief agent of International Security Intelligence in this espionage series. He tangled with an assortment of spies, traitors, and other international villains. Despite scripts by a number of notable writers, including Mel London and a young Rod Serling, the series disappeared in less than a year. During its last three months it alternated with *Gruen Playhouse*.

SHAFT

Detective Drama
FIRST TELECAST: *October 9, 1973*
LAST TELECAST: *August 20, 1974*
BROADCAST HISTORY:
    Oct 1973–Aug 1974, CBS Tue 9:30–11:00
CAST:
    John Shaft .... Richard Roundtree
    Lt. Al Rossi .... Ed Barth
THEME:
    "Theme from 'Shaft,'" by Isaac Hayes

John Shaft was a flamboyant, streetwise black private detective working in New York City, although his cases often took him far from the "Big Apple." Smooth, imperturbable, and deadly efficient, he was sought out by all sorts of people when they needed help. His source of information, when he needed it, was police lieutenant Al Rossi, with whom he had a friendly working relationship.

Shaft was one of three elements that rotated in the Tuesday 9:30–11:00 P.M. time period on CBS during the 1973–1974 season. The other two were *Hawkins* and *The New CBS Tuesday Night Movies*. Richard Roundtree brought John Shaft to television after a series of highly successful theatrical features in which he had played the part. The theme for the television series was written for the first *Shaft* movie, and had won composer Hayes an Academy Award.

SHANE

Western
FIRST TELECAST: *September 10, 1966*
LAST TELECAST: *December 31, 1966*
BROADCAST HISTORY:
    Sep 1966–Dec 1966, ABC Sat 7:30–8:30
CAST:
    Shane .... David Carradine
    Marian Starett .... Jill Ireland
    Tom Starett .... Tom Tully
    Joey Starett .... Christopher Shea
    Rufe Ryker .... Bert Freed
    Sam Grafton .... Sam Gilman

The 1953 Western movie *Shane* is considered one of the classics of the cinema. It was the story of a young boy's idolization of a wandering gun-fighter who stops to help the boy's family but who must, in time, move on. In the poignant final scene he did, as the boy (played by Brandon De Wilde) cried out, "Shane . . . come back!"

Shane did come back, for a few months anyway, in this 1966 TV version starring David Carradine as the silent, brooding gunfighter and Christopher Shea as the eight-year-old rancher's son, Joey. Marian Starett was recently widowed and was having a difficult time protecting her homestead against the ravages of nature and of the vicious rancher Ryker. It was the classic confrontation between the cattle ranchers who first claimed the land (Ryker) and the homesteaders who followed (the Staretts). Though Shane was there to help them in their battle, the Staretts knew that he might at any time move on. Tom, Marian's father-in-law, and Sam Grafton, the saloonkeeper, were the only other regulars.

SHANNON

Police Drama
FIRST TELECAST: *November 11, 1981*
LAST TELECAST: *April 7, 1982*
BROADCAST HISTORY:
    Nov 1981–Dec 1981, CBS Wed 10:00–11:00
    Mar 1982–Apr 1982, CBS Wed 10:00–11:00
CAST:
    Det. Jack Shannon .... Kevin Dobson
    Det. Norm White .... William Lucking
    Lt. Moraga .... Michael Durrell
    Inspector Schmidt .... Bruce Kirby
    Johnny Shannon .... Charlie Fields
    Paul Locatelli .... Al Ruscio
    Irene Locatelli .... Karen Kondazian

Following the untimely death of his young wife, N.Y.P.D. plainclothes detective Jack Shannon moved to San Francisco with his ten-year-old son, Johnny. The move served two purposes—it provided a change of scene to help him get over his grief and, since his wife's parents (the Locatellis) lived there, it gave him some assistance in the raising of Johnny. With the help of some of his former superiors in New York (which fostered initial resentment) Jack obtained a position with the S.F.P.D. Special Squad of Investigators. Norm White was his partner and Lt. Moraga was their immediate superior.

SHAPING UP

Situation Comedy
FIRST TELECAST: *March 20, 1984*
LAST TELECAST: *April 17, 1984*
BROADCAST HISTORY:
    Mar 1984–Apr 1984, ABC Tue 9:30–10:00
CAST:
    Buddy Fox .... Leslie Nielsen
    Ben Zachary .... Michael Fontaine
    Shannon Winters .... Jennifer Tilly
    Melissa McDonald .... Shawn Weatherly
    Zoya Antonova .... Cathie Shirriff

Buddy Fox was a graying but physically fit health-club owner who served the sweat-band set with the help of an athletic young manager, Ben, and two curvaceous aerobics instructors, Shannon and Melissa. Despite ample displays of pulchritude in motion, the series quickly died.

SHEENA, QUEEN OF THE JUNGLE
Adventure
BROADCAST HISTORY:
Syndicated only
30 minutes
Produced: *1955–1956* (26 episodes)
Released: *1955*
CAST:
Sheena........................ Irish McCalla
Bob........................ Christian Drake

Sheena had something for everyone. For kids, it was full of jungle excitement, with wild animals and brave heroes battling the bad guys. For adults, it was so trite it was absolutely hilarious, a cliché-ridden parody on *Tarzan*. For boys just entering adolescence—well, Sheena, with her voluptuous figure and skimpy leotard, was something else entirely.

The setting was Kenya, where statuesque Sheena played White Goddess and protector to the beasts and natives. Since she couldn't manage the Tarzan yell, she carried a hunting horn to ward off danger. Her pet chimpanzee was named Chim (played by Neal the Chimp), and Bob was her trader friend. Robbers and interlopers turned up regularly, often capturing Bob. Always, he would get rescued by Sheena. And that's all he got.

The series was shot in Mexico, where some of Sheena's tree-swinging stunts were actually done by men in wigs. The series was based on the popular comic strip created by S. M. Iger and Will Eisner in the late 1930s.

What ever happened to Sheena? Irish McCalla made a few B-movies in the late 1950s and early 1960s, and then became a successful painter.

SHEILAH GRAHAM IN HOLLYWOOD
Talk
FIRST TELECAST: *January 20, 1951*
LAST TELECAST: *July 14, 1951*
BROADCAST HISTORY:
Jan 1951–Jul 1951, NBC Sat 11:00–11:15
HOSTESS:
Sheilah Graham

Syndicated Hollywood gossip columnist Sheilah Graham had been doing a weekly live show in Los Angeles for several months before NBC decided it would be interesting to give it a try on the network. The show combined straight movie news, gossip, fashion information, and chats with visiting stars. Aired live in Los Angeles on Tuesday evenings, with a kinescope made and flown to New York for telecast by NBC on the following Saturday at 11:00 P.M.

SHELL GAME
Comedy Drama
FIRST TELECAST: *January 8, 1987*
LAST TELECAST: *June 17, 1987*
BROADCAST HISTORY:
Jan 1987–Feb 1987, CBS Thu 8:00–9:00
Jun 1987, CBS Wed 9:00–10:00
CAST:
Jennie Jerome .... Margot Kidder
John Reid .... James Read
Bert Luna .... Chip Zien
William Bauer................. Rod McCary
Natalie Thayer .... Marg Heigenberger
Vince Vanneman .... Fred McCarren

Jennie and John had worked together as husband-and-wife con artists but had gone their separate ways when their marriage broke up. He had gone straight and become the producer of *Solutions*, a *60 Minutes*–type series on a local TV station in Santa Ana, California. When Jennie, who was still running scams for personal gain, ran into John and his film crew, she wangled her way onto the team. Together again, they used their well-honed skills to expose corruption and collect information for exposé segments on the TV show. Jennie's presence did not sit well with John's fiancée, Natalie Thayer, the station owner's daughter who feared the two of them would get back together. Others at the office were station manager Bert Luna, *Solution*'s arrogant host William Bauer, and Vince Vanneman.

SHERIFF OF COCHISE, THE
Police Drama
BROADCAST HISTORY:
Syndicated only
30 minutes
Produced: *1956–1960* (156 episodes)
Released: *Fall 1956*
CAST:
Sheriff/Marshal Frank Morgan
.... John Bromfield
Deputy Olson (1956–1958) .... Stan Jones
Deputy Blake (1958)........ Robert Brubaker
Deputy Tom Ferguson (1959–1960)
.... James Griffith

John Bromfield played a jut-jawed, no-nonsense lawman in this contemporary Western set in Cochise County, Arizona. The emphasis was on high-speed chases and fistfights rather than on gunplay, and the scripts were generally interchangeable with those of *Highway Patrol* or *State Trooper*. Actor-songwriter Stan Jones created the series and originally played the deputy, but left when Sheriff Morgan was promoted to U.S. Marshal and given the run of the whole state, in 1958. The series title was also changed to *U.S. Marshal* at this time.

Among the future stars playing supporting roles in episodes of this series were Gavin MacLeod, David Janssen, Michael Landon, Stacy Keach,

Charles Bronson, Jack Lord, Doug McClure, Ross Martin, and Martin Milner.

SHE'S THE SHERIFF
Situation Comedy
BROADCAST HISTORY:
Syndicated only
30 minutes
Produced: *1987–*
Released: *September 1987*
CAST:
Sheriff Hildy Granger ...... Suzanne Somers
Dep. Max Rubin .... George Wyner
Gussie Holt .... Pat Carroll
Allison Granger .... Nicky Rose
Kenny Granger .... Taliesin Jaffe
Dep. Dennis Putnam .... Lou Richards
Dep. Hugh Mulcahy........... Guich Koock
Dep. Alvin Wiggins .... Leonard Lightfoot

Following the death of her husband Jim, Hildy Granger succeeded him as sheriff of Lakes County, Nevada, in the beautiful mountain country near Lake Tahoe. As a widow with two young children (Allison and Kenny) to support, Hildy definitely needed the job. Unfortunately her second in command, obnoxious Max Rubin, was a constant thorn in her side. The other male deputies accepted her, but Max was constantly trying to undermine her authority and embarrass her, in a never-ending quest to get the job that was rightfully his. Helping out on the home front was Hildy's bubbly mother, Gussie, who moved to Lakes County to take care of her grandchildren while her daughter was at work.

SHIELDS AND YARNELL
Variety
FIRST TELECAST: *June 13, 1977*
LAST TELECAST: *March 28, 1978*
BROADCAST HISTORY:
Jun 1977–Jul 1977, CBS Mon 8:30–9:00
Jan 1978–Mar 1978, CBS Tue 8:30–9:00
REGULARS:
Robert Shields
Lorene Yarnell
Ted Zeigler (1977)
Joanna Cassidy (1977)
Gailard Sartain (1978)
Flip Reade (1978)
Norman Maney Orchestra

The talented young mime team of Shields and Yarnell first starred in a brief summer series which featured, in addition to mime, dancing and comedy sketches. A recurring sketch concerned the adventures of the Clinkers, a pair of clumsy robots adjusting to life in their new suburban home. The show was one of the major hits of the summer of 1977, and promised a bright future in TV for the young performers. That future was temporarily dimmed when they returned in January 1978 opposite ABC's top-rated *Laverne & Shirley*

and lasted only two months before being replaced.

SHINDIG
Music
FIRST TELECAST: *September 16, 1964*
LAST TELECAST: *January 8, 1966*
BROADCAST HISTORY:
Sep 1964–Jan 1965, ABC Wed 8:30–9:00
Jan 1965–Sep 1965, ABC Wed 8:30–9:30
Sep 1965–Jan 1966, ABC Thu/Sat 7:30–8:00
REGULARS:
Jimmy O'Neill
The Shindig Dancers
FREQUENTLY SEEN:
Bobby Sherman
Righteous Brothers
The Wellingtons
Everly Brothers
Donna Loren
Glen Campbell
Sonny & Cher

Shindig was one of two rock 'n' roll shows seen in prime time during the mid-1960s (the other: NBC's *Hullabaloo*). It was a fast-paced, youthful program and, like its NBC counterpart, featured many of the top names in popular music performing their latest hits, while platoons of dancers staged elaborate production numbers. There was also a "disc pick of the week" feature.

The premiere telecast starred Sam Cooke and featured such acts as the Everly Brothers, Righteous Brothers, the Wellingtons, Bobby Sherman (a *Shindig* "discovery"), and comic Alan Sues. The second season had an even bigger opening, as the show expanded to two nights a week and opened with the Rolling Stones. Although none of the rock stars seen on *Shindig* were weekly regulars, some (noted above) returned many times. Others appearing included such superstars as the Beatles, the Beach Boys, Chuck Berry, Neil Sedaka, and even old-timer Louis Armstrong. They couldn't get the biggest rock star of all, however—nobody could get Elvis—so in May 1965 *Shindig* devoted an entire telecast to his songs, as a tribute to Elvis' tenth anniversary in show business.

During the 1965–1966 season guest stars from other areas of show business also began to appear, such as Mickey Rooney, Zsa Zsa Gabor, Ed Wynn, and, on Halloween, Boris Karloff.

SHIRLEY
Comedy/Drama
FIRST TELECAST: *October 26, 1979*
LAST TELECAST: *January 25, 1980*
BROADCAST HISTORY:
Oct 1979–Jan 1980, NBC Fri 8:00–9:00
CAST:
Shirley Miller .... Shirley Jones
Lew Armitage .... Patrick Wayne
Bill Miller..................... Peter Barton
Debra Miller .... Rosanna Arquette

Hemm Miller	Bret Shryer
Michelle Miller	Tracey Gold
Dutch McHenry	John McIntire
Charlotte McHenry	Ann Doran
Tracey McCord	Cindy Eilbacher

The Miller family had planned to move out of the congestion of New York City, and had gone so far as to put a down payment on a rambling old house at scenic Lake Tahoe, California, when Jack Miller died unexpectedly. His widow, Shirley, decided to make her late husband's dream come true, even if he could not be there to share it with her. There were adjustments for all of the Millers to make in moving from a large city to a small-town environment. Shirley, who had taught school in New York, could not get a full-time position at the local high school, and had to settle for odd jobs for income. Her stepson, Bill, was a high school senior, and still somewhat resentful of his stepmother. Shirley's own three children were Debra (16), Hemm (10), and Michelle (8). Debra's best new friend at school was Tracey, who had an instant crush on Bill. The Millers also discovered that their new home had a resident housekeeper named Charlotte, whose cranky ex-husband ran the local sandwich shop, owned a boat-rental business, and was an all-purpose repairman. Lew Armitage was Shirley's new romantic interest, and a friend to the entire family. A free spirit, he worked as a ski instructor in the winter and a rodeo rider in the summer. Oregano was the family dog.

SHIRLEY TEMPLE'S STORYBOOK
Children's Anthology
FIRST TELECAST: *January 12, 1959*
LAST TELECAST: *September 10, 1961*
BROADCAST HISTORY:
  Jan 1959–Dec 1959, ABC Mon 7:30–8:30 (OS)
  Sep 1960–Sep 1961, NBC Sun 7:00–8:00
HOSTESS/OCCASIONAL STAR:
  Shirley Temple

Shirley Temple, the popular child star of movies in the 1930s, came to television as narrator, hostess, and sometimes star of this series of dramatized fairy tales. Among the stories adapted (often in musical form) for this family entertainment program were "Winnie the Pooh," "The Prince and the Pauper," "Babes in Toyland," and "The Reluctant Dragon." Many famous stars appeared in the productions, including Claire Bloom, Charlton Heston, Jonathan Winters, and Agnes Moorehead.

The show was first seen as a series of 16 specials which aired on ABC on various nights between January and December 1958. In January 1959 the program began to run regularly every third Monday night, alternating with *Cheyenne*. When it moved to NBC in 1960 it was a weekly series and was renamed *The Shirley Temple Show*.

SHIRLEY'S WORLD
Situation Comedy
FIRST TELECAST: *September 15, 1971*
LAST TELECAST: *January 5, 1972*
BROADCAST HISTORY:
  Sep 1971–Jan 1972, ABC Wed 9:30–10:00
CAST:
  Shirley Logan .... Shirley MacLaine
  Dennis Croft .... John Gregson

Movie actress Shirley MacLaine starred as a mod young reporter-photographer in this, her first TV series. Shirley Logan was based in London, but her assignments for *World Illustrated* magazine took her all over the world. She was saucy, bubbly, and impulsive, and her knack for getting involved with her subjects, be they spies or movie queens, often led to hilarious results, much to the despair of her editor, Dennis Croft.

Filmed in England, Scotland, Tokyo, Hong Kong, and other locales.

SHORT SHORT DRAMAS
Dramatic Anthology
FIRST TELECAST: *September 30, 1952*
LAST TELECAST: *April 9, 1953*
BROADCAST HISTORY:
  Sep 1952–Apr 1953, NBC Tue/Thu 7:15–7:30
HOSTESS:
  Ruth Woods

Model and cover girl Ruth Woods hosted this filmed series of one-act plays that aired twice weekly during the 1952–1953 season. At the start of each episode she would introduce a different storyteller, who would set the scene for the play to follow. By establishing the background in this way the producer hoped to compress into a short time period a story that would otherwise require at least half an hour to do. Once the background had been set the storyteller, who was one of the stars in the short drama, joined the rest of the cast and the play began. Some of the stories were serious and others light, but none of them particularly memorable. Among the stars performing in this series were Leslie Nielsen, Neva Patterson, E. G. Marshall, Cliff Robertson, Tony Randall, and Bethel Leslie.

SHORT STORY PLAYHOUSE
Dramatic Anthology
FIRST TELECAST: *July 5, 1951*
LAST TELECAST: *August 23, 1951*
BROADCAST HISTORY:
  Jul 1951–Aug 1951, NBC Thu 10:30–11:00
NARRATOR:
  Robert Breen

Originating live from Chicago, this was aired only on the NBC Midwest network, as a summer replacement for *The Wayne King Show*. The off-screen voice of Robert Breen was heard throughout the productions, serving to add story elements and to tie together loose ends. The performers were not well known, but many of the stories were adapted from works by major authors—Sinclair Lewis's "The Good Sport," James Thurber's "My Life and Hard Times," and Pearl Buck's "Ransom" being the most noteworthy.

SHOTGUN SLADE
Western
BROADCAST HISTORY:
Syndicated only
30 minutes
Produced: *1959–1961* (78 episodes)
Released: *November 1959*
CAST:
Shotgun Slade .... Scott Brady

Shotgun Slade was an odd mixture of swinging private eye and Western hero. Slade was a detective in the Old West, in fact, working on horseback for clients like Wells Fargo, insurance companies, banks, saloon owners, and others who wanted crimes solved. His weapon was a unique two-in-one shotgun.

A pulsating jazz score, and Slade's way with women, gave the series overtones of *77 Sunset Strip*. Still, there was plenty of Western-style action; one single episode had an ambush, a mine explosion, a knock-down fight in a saloon, a hanging, and lots of gunfire. Another oddity about the series was its casting of unlikely people in supporting roles. Ernie Kovacs played a bewhiskered desert rat in the first episode; others included football star Elroy "Crazylegs" Hirsch as a saloonkeeper, World War II ace Gregory "Pappy" Boyington as a wealthy rancher, recording stars Johnny Cash, Tex Ritter, and Jimmy Wakely as sheriffs, and golfer Paul Hahn, baseball players Chuck Essegian and Wally Moon, and heavyweight boxer Lou Nova in other roles.

SHOW BUSINESS, INC.
Variety
FIRST TELECAST: *March 20, 1947*
LAST TELECAST: *May 4, 1947*
BROADCAST HISTORY:
Mar 1947, NBC Thu 8:00–8:30
Apr 1947–May 1947, NBC Sun 8:00–8:30
REGULARS:
Helen V. Parrish
John Graham

Early music and variety show, telecast only four times in early 1947 over NBC's fledgling East Coast network. There was apparently no regular host, but the performers listed above appeared on all four telecasts.

The title was also used briefly for a series hosted by columnist Danton Walker in 1949 (see *Broadway Spotlight*).

SHOW FOR A SUMMER EVENING
Dramatic Anthology

FIRST TELECAST: *July 16, 1957*
LAST TELECAST: *September 10, 1957*
BROADCAST HISTORY:
Jul 1957–Sep 1957, NBC Tue 9:30–10:00

Show for a Summer Evening alternated with *Armstrong Summer Playhouse* on Tuesday nights during the summer of 1957. All of the dramas shown on it were filmed reruns of episodes from a syndicated series, *Heinz Playhouse*.

SHOW GOES ON, THE
Variety
FIRST TELECAST: *January 19, 1950*
LAST TELECAST: *February 16, 1952*
BROADCAST HISTORY:
Jan 1950–Mar 1950, CBS Thu Various times
Mar 1950–Nov 1950, CBS Thu 8:00–9:00
Nov 1950–Jun 1951, CBS Thu 8:30–9:00
Jun 1951–Feb 1952, CBS Sat 9:30–10:00
HOST:
Robert Q. Lewis

The format of this talent show had young hopefuls performing their acts for a group of interested talented "buyers," who were on hand to appraise the acts and sign up the best ones for actual theater and nightclub bookings. Impresario Max Gordon and bandleader Guy Lombardo were among those who appeared on the show in that capacity. Talent ranged from acrobats, to singers, to comics.

Robert Q. Lewis, who had substituted for Arthur Godfrey on *Arthur Godfrey's Talent Scouts* during the summertime, had his own first starring role with this series. When it first went on the air in January 1950, *The Show Goes On* wandered all over the CBS Thursday night schedule in 30- and 60-minute versions. It finally stabilized in March at a full hour from 8:00 P.M. to 9:00 P.M., and was cut back to a half hour the following fall.

SHOWCASE '68
Variety
FIRST TELECAST: *June 11, 1968*
LAST TELECAST: *September 3, 1968*
BROADCAST HISTORY:
Jun 1968–Sep 1968, NBC Tue 8:00–8:30
HOST:
Lloyd Thaxton

Each week *Showcase '68* originated from a different city in the United States, introducing talented young performers to the viewing audience. All of them were under 22 years of age and made their television debuts on the show. In addition to the young performers, an established star appeared on each telecast. At the end of each show a panel of judges selected the performer with the greatest potential for success. On its last telecast *Showcase '68* expanded to a full hour (8:00–9:00 P.M.) and the ten weekly winners competed for a final $10,000 prize. The winner of the grand prize was rock group Sly and the Family Stone (which already had its first hit on the record charts while this show was on the air). Among the runners-up were Julie Budd, the Chambers Brothers, and the American Breed.

SHOWCASE THEATER
Dramatic Anthology
FIRST TELECAST: *September 12, 1953*
LAST TELECAST: *November 20, 1953*
BROADCAST HISTORY:
  Sep 1953–Oct 1953, ABC Sat 8:00–8:30
  Oct 1953–Nov 1953, ABC Fri 10:00–10:30

This was a filmed anthology series.

SHOWER OF STARS
Musical Variety
FIRST TELECAST: *September 30, 1954*
LAST TELECAST: *April 17, 1958*
BROADCAST HISTORY:
  Sep 1954–Apr 1958, CBS Thu 8:30–9:30 (OS)
HOST:
  William Lundigan

This live musical series aired approximately once per month in the time period normally occupied by the dramatic anthology series *Climax*. Both series were sponsored by Chrysler Corporation and shared the same host, William Lundigan. In contrast to the heavy dramas seen on *Climax*, *Shower of Stars* offered viewers light entertainment featuring some of the biggest names in comedy and music. Although there were occasional plays—*Lend an Ear* with Edgar Bergen, Sheree North, and Mario Lanza; and *A Christmas Carol* with Fredric March and Basil Rathbone (which was broadcast live three straight years)—most of the telecasts were musical-comedy revues. Among the performers who made multiple appearances in these were Betty Grable and her husband Harry James, Ed Wynn, Ethel Merman, Red Skelton, Shirley MacLaine, Frankie Laine, Van Johnson, and Bob Crosby. The most familiar face on *Shower of Stars*, however, belonged to Jack Benny. He first appeared on the show as the star of *Time Out for Ginger*, the play that opened the 1955–1956 season, and after that turned up as one of the principal stars of virtually every telecast of *Shower of Stars* until it left the air in 1958.

SHOWTIME
Variety
FIRST TELECAST: *June 11, 1968*
LAST TELECAST: *September 17, 1968*
BROADCAST HISTORY:
  Jun 1968–Sep 1968, CBS Tue 8:30–9:30
REGULARS:
  The Mike Sammes Singers
  The London Line Dancers
  Jack Parnell and His Orchestra

This 1968 summer replacement for *The Red Skelton Hour* was produced in London and featured a different roster of guest performers each week. Most of the headliners, with the exceptions of Englishmen Terry-Thomas and Dave Allen and South African-born Juliet Prowse, were Americans. Of the Americans, most were comics—Don Knotts, Phyllis Diller, Godfrey Cambridge, Steve Allen, and George Gobel among them.

SHOWTIME AT THE APOLLO
  see *It's Showtime at the Apollo*

SHOWTIME, U.S.A.
Variety
FIRST TELECAST: *October 1, 1950*
LAST TELECAST: *June 24, 1951*
BROADCAST HISTORY:
  Oct 1950–Jun 1951, ABC Sun 7:30–8:00
PRODUCER/EMCEE:
  Vinton Freedley

This weekly variety show was a plug for Broadway. Produced and co-hosted by Vinton Freedley, president of the American National Theatre Academy, it featured scenes from top (and usually current) Broadway productions performed by the original stars. One of the stars would serve as co-host each week. The first telecast had Helen Hayes, Carol Channing, Alec Templeton, Grace and Paul Hartman, Henry Fonda, and the chorus from the currently running *Kiss Me Kate*. Later shows presented Gertrude Lawrence in scenes from *Susan and God*, Fonda in *Mr. Roberts*, and a host of others.

SID CAESAR INVITES YOU
Comedy Variety
FIRST TELECAST: *January 26, 1958*
LAST TELECAST: *May 25, 1958*
BROADCAST HISTORY:
  Jan 1958–May 1958, ABC Sun 9:00–9:30
REGULARS:
  Sid Caesar
  Imogene Coca
  Carl Reiner
  Paul Reed
  Milt Kamen
  Bernie Green Orchestra

Sid Caesar and Imogene Coca had become two of the most famous comedians in America, thanks to *Your Show of Shows* in the early 1950s. When that series ended its run in 1954 Caesar and Coca went their separate ways, hoping to build independent careers with separate series. But alone, neither one could capture the magic they had created together, and so in 1958 they were briefly reunited in this live comedy program. As in the days of old, they appeared in sketches and pantomime, with excellent support from regulars, including Carl Reiner, and writers, including Neil Simon and Mel Brooks. But classic comedy is a fragile commodity which cannot easily be revived, and this attempt ended in failure after only a four-month run.

SID CAESAR SHOW, THE
see *Caesar's Hour*

SID CAESAR SHOW, THE
Comedy Variety
FIRST TELECAST: *October 3, 1963*
LAST TELECAST: *March 12, 1964*
BROADCAST HISTORY:
Oct 1963–Mar 1964, ABC Thu 10:00–10:30
REGULARS:
Sid Caesar
Joey Forman
Gisele MacKenzie
Marilyn Hanold

Sid Caesar's inventive sketch comedy filled this Thursday night half hour on alternate weeks during the 1963–1964 TV season. Singer Edie Adams starred in a musical variety half-hour on the alternate weeks. To start the season they both starred together in a full-hour variety special that ran from 10:00 to 11:00 P.M. on September 19. Sid's regulars included comic Joey Forman and singer Gisele MacKenzie, with frequent visits by a gorgeous lass named Marilyn Hanold—who never spoke, only looked beautiful. Although the production team was first-rate (including head writer Goodman Ace and producer-director Greg Garrison), the program failed to catch on and ended after a single season.

SIDEKICKS
Police Drama
FIRST TELECAST: *September 19, 1986*
LAST TELECAST: *June 27, 1987*
BROADCAST HISTORY:
Sep 1986–Nov 1986, ABC Fri 9:00–9:30
Nov 1986–Mar 1987, ABC Sat 8:00–8:30
Jun 1987, ABC Sat 8:30–9:00
CAST:
Sgt. Jake Rizzo .... Gil Gerard
Ernie Lee .... Ernie Reyes, Jr.
Patricia Blake .... Nancy Stafford
Det. R.T. Mooney .... Frank Bonner
Sabasan .... Keye Luke
Capt. Blanks .... Vinny Argiro

Jake Rizzo was your typical bachelor cop—dedicated and hard-working, personal life empty, apartment a mess. Into his rather routine existence came a most unusual bundle of energy, a polite but determined ten-year-old named Ernie, who was deposited on his doorstep by Ernie's dying grandfather. Granddad had spied Jake through a window and thought he'd make a good foster father for the parentless child. An unusual situation? Just wait. Pint-sized Ernie happened to be a karate expert, able to mow down a whole crowd of burly bad guys with his flying feet; moreover, he was endowed with mystical powers by grandfather "Sabasan," who, before he died, passed on to him the Patasani title of "The Last Electric Knight."
All of this seemed rather dubious to grumpy

Jake, not to mention social worker Patricia, who was all set to place Ernie in an orphanage. But one doesn't argue with Electric Knights, so Jake became a foster dad, coping with Ernie's enthusiasm for a new life as well as with his occasional loneliness for his Sabasan and his Asian cultural heritage. Ernie constantly got involved in Jake's cases, where the kid's martial arts expertise, and those powers, often saved the day. Patricia stayed around to help, providing some much-needed female companionship for Jake.
Young actor Ernie Reyes, Jr., was in real life a juvenile black belt and a veteran of martial arts competitions. The karate sequences in the series were choreographed by his father, Ernie Reyes, Sr.

SIERRA
Dramatic Adventure
FIRST TELECAST: *September 12, 1974*
LAST TELECAST: *December 12, 1974*
BROADCAST HISTORY:
Sep 1974–Dec 1974, NBC Thu 8:00–9:00
CAST:
Ranger Tim Cassidy ... James G. Richardson
Ranger Matt Harper ...... Ernest Thompson
Chief Ranger Jack Moore........ Jack Hogan
Ranger P. J. Lewis .... Mike Warren
Ranger Julie Beck.............. Susan Foster

The work of rangers employed by the National Park Service at fictitious Sierra National Park was dramatized in this series. The problems and satisfactions of supervisor Jack Moore and his staff, consisting of rangers Cassidy, Harper, Lewis, and Beck, were shown. Their problems stemmed from the conflict between trying to preserve the natural beauty of the wilderness and accommodating the flood of tourists wanting to utilize the resources of the park. The campers, skiers, hikers, and climbers came in all shapes and sizes. Some were friendly, some stubborn, and some nasty and cruel. Tracking people who had gotten lost, coping with the visitor who got into a situation he couldn't really handle, and enforcing park regulations were all part of the job. *Sierra* was filmed on location, primarily at Yosemite National Park, in cooperation with the National Park Service. Cruncher was the park's troublemaking bear.

SILENT FORCE, THE
Police Drama
FIRST TELECAST: *September 21, 1970*
LAST TELECAST: *January 11, 1971*
BROADCAST HISTORY:
Sep 1970–Jan 1971, ABC Mon 8:30–9:00
CAST:
Ward Fuller .... Ed Nelson
Jason Hart .... Percy Rodriguez
Amelia Cole .... Lynda Day

The Silent Force was a strike force of government agents assigned to fight organized crime. Ward, Jason, and Amelia were the agents, working mostly undercover to infiltrate "the mob" and expose its operations which preyed on innocent citizens. On several occasions they became involved with companies or individuals who were being pressured by the syndicate, and in the first telecast they exposed a candidate for governor who was actually a member of the syndicate.

Set in Southern California.

SILENT SERVICE, THE
Dramatic Anthology
BROADCAST HISTORY:
Syndicated only
30 minutes
Produced: *1956–1958* (78 episodes)
Released: *March 1957*
HOST/NARRATOR:
Rear Adm. (ret.) Thomas M. Dykers

This series consisted of documentary-style dramas about the exploits of the U.S. Navy's submarine fleet. All were based on fact, and the realism was heightened by the use of actual combat footage from the Navy's files. Most of the stories took place in the South Pacific during World War II, but some were from the Korean War or had a peacetime context. There were no continuing characters, and in fact the acting was pretty much limited to terse commands ("Up periscope" . . . "All secure, sir") and worried looks at dangerous moments.

The series was the brainchild of Rear Adm. Thomas M. Dykers, who retired from the Navy in 1949 after 22 years of service, most of it in the submarine service. After serving as technical advisor for several Hollywood movies, he produced this syndicated show himself, with the full cooperation of the Navy (which loaned him the U.S.S. *Sawfish* for filming).

SILENTS PLEASE
Silent Movies
FIRST TELECAST: *August 4, 1960*
LAST TELECAST: *October 5, 1961*
BROADCAST HISTORY:
Aug 1960–Oct 1960, ABC Thu 10:30–11:00
Mar 1961–Oct 1961, ABC Thu 10:30–11:00
HOST:
Ernie Kovacs (1961)

Classic silent films, some in their entirety, some condensed to fit the confines of a half-hour time slot, were aired in this series. The films included the work of Buster Keaton, Charlie Chaplin, Laurel and Hardy, Lillian Gish, and Douglas Fairbanks, Sr. When it was first telecast in the summer of 1960 there was no host. Ernie Kovacs, whose show *Take a Good Look* had aired in this time slot from October 1960 until *Silents Please* returned the following March, became the host of the show during its second run.

SILVER SPOONS
Situation Comedy

FIRST TELECAST: *September 25, 1982*
LAST TELECAST: *September 7, 1986*
BROADCAST HISTORY:
Sep 1982–Sep 1984, NBC Sat 8:30–9:00
Sep 1984–May 1985, NBC Sun 7:00–7:30
Jun 1985–Mar 1986, NBC Sun 7:30–8:00
May 1986–Sep 1986, NBC Sun 7:00–7:30
(In first-run syndication during the 1986–1987 season)
CAST:
Ricky Stratton . . . . Ricky Schroder
Edward Stratton III . . . . Joel Higgins
Kate Summers Stratton . . . . Erin Gray
Leonard Rollins *(1982–1983)*
. . . . Leonard Lightfoot
Dexter Stuffins . . . . Franklyn Seales
Derek Taylor *(1982–1984)* . . . . . Jason Bateman
Freddy Lippincottleman *(1983–1985)*
. . . . Corky Pigeon
Alfonso Spears *(1984–1987)* . . Alfonso Ribeiro
*J.T. Martin *(1983–1984)* . . . . Bobby Fite
Grandfather Edward Stratton II
. . . . John Houseman
Uncle Harry Summers *(1985)* . . Ray Walston
*Brad *(1985–1986)* . . . . Billy Jacoby

*Occasional

A mature 12-year-old and his childlike father found that they could learn from each other in this comedy. Ricky was an uncommonly bright, attractive youngster who had been brought up by his divorced mother, then dumped in a military school. Finagling an invitation to move in with his wealthy father, whom he had never known, he discovered that his 35-year-old dad was more of a child than he was. Stratton's palatial home was filled with video games, stuffed animals, and a miniature railroad on which he rode through the rooms. They had a lot of love to give each other, and Ricky soon helped Edward learn to be a father, while Edward taught his son a little about enjoying life.

Kate was Edward's amorous secretary (who did, finally, become Mrs. Stratton in February 1985), Leonard his lawyer, and Dexter his fussy business manager and a family friend. Stopping in periodically was the formidable Grandfather Stratton, a stuffy tycoon who had been estranged from his immature son but now found better communication with the help of Ricky. Derek was Ricky's conniving school chum, and Freddie and J.T. were also friends. Dexter's nephew, Alfonso, arrived in 1984, and became Ricky's new best friend.

NBC aired reruns of *Silver Spoons* on weekday mornings during the summer of 1985.

SILVER THEATER, THE
Dramatic Anthology
FIRST TELECAST: *October 3, 1949*
LAST TELECAST: *June 26, 1950*
BROADCAST HISTORY:
Oct 1949–June 1950, CBS Mon 8:00–8:30

HOST:
Conrad Nagel

The teleplays in this series, most of which were aired live, emphasized romance—the humorous, silly, frustrating, futile, and rewarding aspects of it. Famous stars such as Burgess Meredith, Paul Lucas, Glenda Farrell, and Geraldine Brooks appeared in the dramas and Conrad Nagel was the host. The sponsor, the International Silver Company, whence came the title, had also sponsored a radio version of this show during the 1930s and 1940s. A special feature of this program was the monthly "Silver Award" presented to the most deserving supporting performer in the dramas aired in the series during the month. A panel of drama critics determined the monthly winner.

SIMON & SIMON

Detective Drama

FIRST TELECAST: *November 24, 1981*
LAST TELECAST:
BROADCAST HISTORY:
Nov 1981–Mar 1982, CBS Tue 8:00–9:00
Apr 1982, CBS Thu 9:00–10:00
Jul 1982–Apr 1986, CBS Thu 9:00–10:00
Apr 1986–Jun 1986, CBS Thu 8:00–9:00
Jun 1986–Sep 1986, CBS Tue 8:00–9:00
Sep 1986–Nov 1986, CBS Thu 8:00–9:00
Dec 1986–Jan 1987, CBS Thu 8:30–9:30
Jan 1987–May 1987, CBS Thy 9:00–10:00
Jul 1987–Sep 1987, CBS Tue 8:00–9:00
*Dec 1987–   *, CBS Thu 9:00–10:00
CAST:
Andrew Jackson (A.J.) Simon
.... Jameson Parker
Rick Simon................ Gerald McRaney
Cecilia Simon .... Mary Carver
Janet Fowler (1981–1983) .... Jeannie Wilson
Myron Fowler (1981–1983) .... Eddie Barth
Det. Marcel "Downtown" Brown (1983–1987)
.... Tim Reid
Officer Nixon (1986–   ) ...... Scott Murphy
Lt. Abigail Marsh (1987–   )
.... Joan McMurtrey

A.J. and Rick were brothers, but you'd never have known it by looking at them. A.J. was conservative, dedicated, clean-cut, and ambitious. Rick was eccentric, grubby, and laid-back to the point of being lazy. A.J. drove an immaculate convertible and kept his apartment (located behind their office) in spotless condition. Rick bummed around San Diego in a beat-up pickup truck, lived like a slob on a houseboat, and was more interested in pickin' on his guitar than working. Despite their different life-styles, A.J. and Rick were partners in a small, struggling detective agency, with A.J. spending much of his time trying, however hopelessly, to get Rick into a more "corporate" mold. There was much sibling rivalry—Rick tended to exasperate his younger brother—as well as occasional disapproval from their mother, Cecilia,

who wasn't thrilled when they took cases that didn't pay them much.

Across the street from their office was a rival agency run by crabby Myron Fowler. Myron's daughter, Janet, who worked for her dad as a secretary, got an occasional chance to play detective by helping Rick and A.J. on some of their cases, much to Myron's consternation. After graduating from law school Janet became a local assistant district attorney, which strained her relationship with the Simons when she was prosecuting one of their clients. Myron, meanwhile, had closed his detective agency and retired, only to show up as a part-time legman for Rick and A.J. when he got bored with inactivity. Undercover police detective Downtown, whose unorthodox techniques for dealing with criminals and obtaining information appealed to Rick and appalled A.J., was around to help out—as long as he got something out of it. As he told them, "You do for me, and I'll do for you."

When Downtown departed in the fall of 1987 (Tim Reid had moved on to star in his own series, *Frank's Place*), he was replaced on the force by the much less friendly, by-the-book Lt. Abby Marsh.

SING ALONG

Music

FIRST TELECAST: *June 4, 1958*
LAST TELECAST: *July 9, 1958*
BROADCAST HISTORY:
Jun 1958–Jul 1958, CBS Wed 7:30–8:00
REGULARS:
Jim Lowe
Tina Robin
Florence Henderson
Somethin' Smith
The Redheads
Harry Sosnik Orchestra

Jim Lowe, a radio personality whose one hit record was a novelty item called "The Green Door," was the host of this live weekly music show. The regular singers were joined by guest stars and the studio and home audience was invited to "sing along." The lyrics were provided by various forms of cue cards so that everyone would know what to sing. Apparently Lowe was a few years ahead of his time. This show had a mere six-week run and then disappeared forever, but while it was on the air an obscure Columbia record album by Mitch Miller called "Sing Along with Mitch" first began attracting attention. Three years and several million records later, Miller brought the idea back to television, and was a national sensation.

SING ALONG WITH MITCH

Musical Variety

FIRST TELECAST: *January 27, 1961*
LAST TELECAST: *September 2, 1966*
BROADCAST HISTORY:
Jan 1961–Apr 1961, NBC Fri 9:00–10:00
Sep 1961–Sep 1962, NBC Thu 10:00–11:00

Sep 1962–Sep 1963, NBC Fri 8:30–9:30
Sep 1963–Sep 1964, NBC Mon 10:00–11:00
Apr 1966–Sep 1966, NBC Fri 8:30–9:30
REGULARS:
  Mitch Miller
  The Sing Along Gang
  The Sing Along Kids
  Leslie Uggams
  Diana Trask (1961–1962)
  Carolyn Conway (1962–1963)
  Gloria Lambert
  Louise O'Brien
  Sandy Stewart (1963–1964)
  The James Starbuck Dancers
THEME:
  "Sing Along," by Robert Allen

Bearded record producer Mitch Miller was responsible for a large proportion of America's popular music during the 1950s. As head of recording for mighty Columbia Records, he launched literally dozens of stars and trends in music, and even had a choral hit under his own name ("The Yellow Rose of Texas" in 1955). But Mitch didn't like rock 'n' roll, and when the teen beat began swamping the business in the late 1950s *his* kind of music—melodic and stylish—went into a severe decline. In 1958 he conceived the idea of packaging "Singalong" LPs consisting of old favorites with the words printed on the album cover so the listener could sing along with the chorus. This ran contrary to everything that was happening in popular music, but it found a large, obviously frustrated audience, and the albums became enormous sellers. In 1961 Miller tried the idea on television. Overnight, Mitch Miller, who had for decades been a behind-the-scenes man, became a national celebrity. During the first season his show alternated with *The Bell Telephone Hour.* It became such a large ratings success that when it returned in the fall of 1961 it was a weekly show. Old favorites and some currently popular songs were sung by Mitch's Sing Along Gang, the pre-teenaged Sing Along Kids, and by featured vocalists doing solos. Mitch himself said very little, simply standing there waving his baton. For all the group songs, the lyrics would be flashed on the screen so that the home audience could also sing along. In addition to the regulars, occasional guest stars and lavish production numbers were a part of the show. Three of Mitch's "discoveries," Leslie Uggams, Diana Trask, and Sandy Stewart, went on to considerable success in the music business.

The 1966 summer series was made up entirely of reruns.

SING-CO-PATION
Music
FIRST TELECAST: *January 23, 1949*
LAST TELECAST: *October 30, 1949*
BROADCAST HISTORY:
  Jan 1949–Mar 1949, ABC Sun 7:45–8:00

Mar 1949–Aug 1949, ABC Sun 9:00–9:15
Sep 1949–Oct 1949, ABC Sun 6:45–7:00
HOST:
  Jack Brand
REGULARS:
  Dolores Marshall
  George Barnes Trio
  Jack Fascinato Trio

Musical interlude from Chicago, featuring vocalist Dolores Marshall. During the program's final month the title was changed to *Serenade.*

SING IT AGAIN
Quiz/Audience Participation
FIRST TELECAST: *September 2, 1950*
LAST TELECAST: *June 23, 1951*
BROADCAST HISTORY:
  Sep 1950, CBS Sat 10:00–10:30
  Oct 1950–Jun 1951, CBS Sat 10:00–11:00
EMCEE:
  Dan Seymour (1950–1951)
  Jan Murray (1951)
REGULARS:
  Alan Dale
  Judy Lynn
  Bob Howard
  Ray Bloch Orchestra
  The Riddlers
  Betty Luster
  Jack Stanton

This musical quiz show was simulcast on the CBS Radio and Television networks. Dan Seymour was the host when the radio show expanded to both media and was replaced in February by Jan Murray. The regulars, both singers and dancers, stayed with the show throughout most of its TV run. Musical questions were asked of studio audience members and viewers at home. A special feature was the Phantom Voice, in which home viewers attempted to guess the identity of a celebrity, not known as a singer, when they were called. Correct identification could be worth a $15,000 jackpot. Each week a new clue to the identity of the Phantom Voice was given by the emcee.

SINGING LADY, THE
Children's
FIRST TELECAST: *November 7, 1948*
LAST TELECAST: *August 6, 1950*
BROADCAST HISTORY:
  Nov 1948–Sep 1949, ABC Sun 6:30–7:00
  Oct 1949–Aug 1950, ABC Sun 6:00–6:30
HOSTESS:
  Ireene Wicker
ANNOUNCER:
  Bob Dixon (in costume) (1949)
  Dick Collier (1949)
  John Griggs (1950)
REGULARS:
  The Suzari Marionettes

Ireene Wicker was one of the most famous—and least likely—victims of the political blacklisting which disgraced television in the early 1950s. She had been a radio favorite for nearly 20 years with her gentle children's stories and lessons in good behavior when she first appeared on the ABC-TV network in 1948. Her program, as on radio, consisted of songs and fairy tales, acted out with the aid of the Suzari Marionettes. Some were true stories of American history, such as Betsy Ross and the flag.

In February 1950 her program was renewed for another year. Then in June a right-wing publication called *Red Channels* listed her among a large group of actors and actresses who had allegedly been associated with left-wing causes. In August, her program was abruptly canceled.

The principal charge, that she had in 1945 signed a petition for the election of Communist candidate Benjamin J. Davis to the New York City Council, turned out to be totally erroneous. An investigation was made of the 30,000 signatures on his petitions and her name was not there (Miss Wicker herself said that she had never heard of Benjamin Davis). Another citation, that she had sided with leftist causes in the Spanish Civil War, turned out to refer to her support of a fund-raising drive for Spanish refugee children. In Miss Wicker's defense, it was pointed out that she had performed playlets emphasizing good citizenship, had conducted an "I'm glad I'm an American because..." contest for children, and even recorded a series of records based on American history. Her accusers reluctantly admitted that *perhaps* a mistake had been made.

But the damage had been done. Advertisers and their agencies did not want to be associated with anyone "controversial." No network could find a spot for her. Her only work in this period was at a small radio station in western Massachusetts, and a couple of guest appearances. Finally from 1953–1954 ABC found a sponsor for a Sunday morning show for her, which lasted a single year. A bright and worthwhile career, built laboriously over two decades, had been destroyed by innuendo.

SIR FRANCIS DRAKE

see *Adventures of Sir Francis Drake, The*

SIR LANCELOT

see *Adventures of Sir Lancelot, The*

SIROTA'S COURT

Situation Comedy
FIRST TELECAST: *December 1, 1976*
LAST TELECAST: *April 13, 1977*
BROADCAST HISTORY:
  Dec 1976–Jan 1977, NBC Wed 9:00–9:30
  Apr 1977, NBC Wed 9:30–10:00
CAST:
  Matthew J. Sirota ...... Michael Constantine
  Maureen O'Connor .... Cynthia Harris
  Gail Goodman .... Kathleen Miller

Bud Nugent .... Fred Willard
Sawyer Dabney .... Ted Ross
Bailiff John Bellson .... Owen Bush

Matthew J. Sirota was a night-court judge in a large metropolitan city, and far from the traditional serious, austere justices of most TV series. He had a sense of humor, was often more concerned with the practical rather than strictly legal resolution of cases, and was considered a character by many of his associates. For years he had been having an on-again, off-again affair with court clerk Maureen O'Connor, and periodically seemed on the verge of marriage. Others seen regularly in his court were super-liberal public defender Gail Goodman, forever the idealist but lacking the skills to be really successful; District Attorney Bud Nugent, whose incredible ambition and vanity blinded him to his own incompetence; Sawyer Dabney, an attorney who would handle any case if the price were right; and John, Sirota's bailiff, who treated the judge with the adoration of one who believed him to be Solomon.

SIT OR MISS

Quiz/Audience Participation
FIRST TELECAST: *August 6, 1950*
LAST TELECAST: *October 29, 1950*
BROADCAST HISTORY:
  Aug 1950–Oct 1950, ABC Sun 8:30–9:00
EMCEES:
  Kay Westfall
  George Sotos
MUSICAL ACCOMPANIMENT:
  Porter Heaps

This was a TV variation on the old parlor game of musical chairs. Five contestants competed. Each time one of them missed a chair, he was faced with a question, and if he missed the question he had to perform a stunt to win a $10 prize. At the end of the game all five contestants had a chance at a $75 jackpot by guessing, from a verbal clue, the contents of a mystery box. From Chicago.

SIX MILLION DOLLAR MAN, THE

Adventure
FIRST TELECAST: *January 18, 1974*
LAST TELECAST: *March 6, 1978*
BROADCAST HISTORY:
  Jan 1974–Oct 1974, ABC Fri 8:30–9:30
  Nov 1974–Jan 1975, ABC Fri 9:00–10:00
  Jan 1975–Aug 1975, ABC Sun 7:30–8:30
  Sep 1975–Jan 1978, ABC Sun 8:00–9:00
  Jan 1978–Mar 1978, ABC Mon 8:00–9:00
CAST:
  Col. Steve Austin .... Lee Majors
  Oscar Goldman .... Richard Anderson
  Dr. Rudy Wells (1974–1975)
  .... Alan Oppenheimer
  Dr. Rudy Wells (1975–1978)
  .... Martin E. Brooks

The Six Million Dollar Man touched off a wave of superheroes on TV in the mid-1970s. It was first seen as a series of 90-minute movies run on ABC in March, October, and November 1973 (part of the *ABC Suspense Movie* package), then became a regular weekly series in January 1974. At first the ratings were mediocre, but the program grew steadily until by 1975 it was one of TV's biggest hits.

Handsome, athletic Steve Austin was a U.S. astronaut who had been critically injured when the moon-landing craft he was testing over a Southwestern desert crashed to the ground. Fighting to save his life, government doctors decided to try a new type of operation devised by Dr. Rudy Wells—the replacement of certain human parts by atomic-powered electromechanical devices, capable of superhuman performance. Steve lived and became a cyborg—part human, part machine, endowed with powerful legs that permitted him great speed, a right arm of incredible strength, and a left eye of penetrating vision (it even had a built-in grid screen!). Armed with these weapons, Steve set out on dangerous missions for the Office of Scientific Information, battling international villains, mad scientists, and even a few alien monsters such as Bigfoot.

Early in the series Steve learned that he was not the only bionic wonder around. It seemed that Dr. Wells had built a *seven*-million-dollar man as backup for Steve, using an injured race-car driver named Barney Miller (played by Monte Markham). Unfortunately the other superman ran amok, and Steve had to find a way to dispatch him, in a battle of the bionic men. A few months later, in January 1975, Jaime Sommers (Lindsay Wagner) was introduced as Steve's love interest and a former tennis pro who had been grievously injured in a sky-diving accident. She was reconstructed into the Bionic Woman. Unfortunately her body rejected its bionic parts, and she died— at least Steve (and viewers) thought she did, until she was brought back ("out of a coma") for several more episodes in the fall. Then she got her own spin-off series called *The Bionic Woman*.

Steve and Jaime's romance seemed destined never to be fulfilled, but nevertheless in November 1976 the series did produce a bionic boy—not theirs, but 16-year-old athlete Andy Sheffield (played by Vincent Van Patten) whose paralyzed legs were replaced by Dr. Wells. Using his new powers the boy promptly set out on a crusade to clear his dead father's name.

Oscar Goldman appeared as Steve's government boss, and Peggy Callahan (Jennifer Darling) was seen occasionally as his secretary. The role of Dr. Rudy Wells was played by a number of actors, including Martin Balsam in the movie pilot and Alan Oppenheimer and Martin E. Brooks in the series.

Based on the novel *Cyborg*, by Martin Caidin.

SIX WIVES OF HENRY VIII, THE
Historical Drama

FIRST TELECAST: *August 1, 1971*
LAST TELECAST: *September 5, 1971*
BROADCAST HISTORY:
    Aug 1971–Sep 1971, CBS Sun 9:30–11:00
CAST:
    Henry VIII . . . . Keith Michell
    Catherine of Aragon (divorced)
        . . . . Annette Crosbie
    Anne Boleyn (beheaded) . . . . . Dorothy Tutin
    Jane Seymour (natural death)
        . . . . Anne Stallybrass
    Anne of Cleves (divorced) . . . . Elvi Hale
    Catherine Howard (beheaded)
        . . . . Angela Pleasence
    Catherine Parr (outlived him)
        . . . . Rosalie Crutchley
    Duke of Norfolk . . . . Patrick Troughton
    Oliver Cromwell . . . . Wolfe Morris
    Archbishop Cranmer . . . . Bernard Hepton
NARRATOR:
Anthony Quayle

This series of six 90-minute programs had been produced in England by the BBC and won the British equivalent of the Emmy award in five categories. CBS brought it to American television in the summer of 1971. The one addition to the American version was narrator Anthony Quayle. He introduced and concluded each telecast and provided historical background. During his reign as English monarch, Henry VIII had two wives beheaded for adultery, saw one die of natural causes, was divorced from two others, and, when he died in 1547 at the age of 56, was survived by his sixth, Catherine Parr.

SIXTH SENSE, THE
Occult
FIRST TELECAST: *January 15, 1972*
LAST TELECAST: *December 30, 1972*
BROADCAST HISTORY:
    Jan 1972–Dec 1972, ABC Sat 10:00–11:00 (OS)
CAST:
    Dr. Michael Rhodes . . . . Gary Collins
    Nancy Murphy (Jan–May) . . Catherine Ferrar

"You enter a strange room for the first time, yet you know you've been there before. You dream about an event that happens some days later. Someone begins to talk, and you already know what they're going to say. A coincidence? Maybe. But more than likely it's extrasensory perception, a sixth sense that many scientists believe we all possess, but rarely use."

That quotation from a press release pretty well sums up the kind of stories told on *The Sixth Sense*. Dr. Michael Rhodes' studies in parapsychology at a major university took him into the uncharted world of ESP, telepathy, and other psychic phenomena every week, sometimes leading to eerie adventures. Perhaps his most useful exploit was communicating an escape plan to an American prisoner of war in Vietnam, by thought transference. Nancy Murphy was his research assistant during the series' first few months.

$64,000 CHALLENGE, THE
Quiz/Audience Participation
FIRST TELECAST: *April 8, 1956*
LAST TELECAST: *September 7, 1958*
BROADCAST HISTORY:
Apr 1956–Sep 1958, CBS Sun 10:00–10:30
EMCEE:
Sonny Fox (1956)
Ralph Story (1956–1958)

This was a highly successful spin-off of CBS' popular big-money quiz show *The $64,000 Question.* Any of the winners from the original show whose earnings had been at least $8,000 were eligible to be challenged on this series, in the field of knowledge in which they had already demonstrated their skill. The same questions were asked of champion and challenger, each in a separate isolation booth. If one of them missed a question at any level, and the other answered it correctly, the loser was then eliminated. The contestant who had answered correctly continued alone until he also missed a question, quit, or reached the $64,-000 question. In any event, he was guaranteed no less than the amount at which he had defeated his opponent. A successful challenger could be challenged by others. On occasion a defeated champion returned as a challenger and won. Through this format, contestants could multiply their winnings from a prior round several times over.

The biggest winner in the era of big-money quiz shows became a regular on this show. Teddy Nadler was a $70-per-week civil service clerk from St. Louis who happened to have a photographic memory. He had, apparently, memorized a complete encyclopedia and could dredge up the most obscure information. By the time *The $64,000 Challenge* left the air in 1958, he had won $252,000 and was still going strong. He became such a celebrity on the show that he was often competing with two or three different people, on totally unrelated topics, all at the same time.

$64,000 QUESTION, THE
Quiz/Audience Participation
FIRST TELECAST: *June 7, 1955*
LAST TELECAST: *November 2, 1958*
BROADCAST HISTORY:
Jun 1955–Jun 1958, CBS Tue 10:00–10:30
Sep 1958–Nov 1958, CBS Sun 10:00–10:30
EMCEE:
Hal March
ASSISTANT:
Lynn Dollar
QUESTION AUTHORITY:
Dr. Bergen Evans

The era of the big-money quiz show arrived during the summer of 1955 in the form of *The $64,000 Question.* A much-inflated variation on radio's

$64 Question, it offered contestants the opportunity to win vast sums of money by answering extremely complex questions on whatever subject they professed to be experts. A contestant first went through preliminary rounds up to the $4,000 level, with each question, starting at $64, worth twice as much as the preceding question. At that point the contestant would go home and return to answer one question a week until missing or reaching $64,000. The consolation prize for missing after reaching the $8,000 plateau was a new Cadillac. Contestants could quit at any time and leave with their winnings. In order to enable the contestants to concentrate completely, and to avoid any possible answers shouted from the studio audience, all questions from $8,000 on up were asked while contestants were sealed inside a Revlon isolation booth (named for the sponsor).

The appeal of seeing ordinary people sweating through complex questions to reach huge sums of money was enormous, and *The $64,000 Question* became an overnight sensation. It shot to number one among all programs on TV in its first season on the air, displacing *I Love Lucy,* and it spawned many imitators in the big-money sweepstakes. Among them were *Twenty-One* and, from Louis G. Cowan, the man who had started it all here, *The Big Surprise* and *The $64,000 Challenge.*

Many of the contestants were interesting people and generated tremendous empathy from the audience. One of the early winners was New York City policeman Redmond O'Hanlon, an expert on Shakespeare, who took home $16,000. Gino Prato, a shoemaker from the Bronx, took home $32,000 for his knowledge of opera. Catherine Kreitzer was a housewife who won $32,000 on the subject of the Bible, and was then signed to do a series of Bible readings on *The Ed Sullivan Show.* Jockey Billy Pearson was an early winner of $64,000—his subject was art. Many of the winners on *The $64,000 Question* went on to make extra money on its companion show, *The $64,000 Challenge.* One of those was a young psychologist, Dr. Joyce Brothers, who parlayed her knowledge of boxing to the grand prize of $64,000 here, another $70,000 on *Challenge,* and a long and successful career as a radio and television personality. The biggest winner on *The $64,000 Question,* however, was young Robert Strom, an 11-year-old genius who amassed $192,000 during a period when, in order to hold onto its audience amid the competing shows, three new plateaus were added to *The $64,000 Question* making the maximum possible winnings $256,000. Strom's total quiz-show winnings, $224,000 including money won on other shows, made him the second biggest winner of the big-money quiz-show era. Only Teddy Nadler's $252,000 on *The $64,000 Challenge* was higher.

The money angle was a magic attraction, especially during the early days of the giant giveaway shows. *TV Guide* kept a running total of the amount given away on this show—$750,000 and 10 Cadillacs in the first year and $1,000,000 by

November 1956—and published numerous articles about the show and its contestants. There were always rumors that the series was rigged, that the desire to put interesting personalities on the air, rather than brilliant but dull geniuses, resulted in the producers providing answers in advance to some, but not all, of the contestants. As early as September 1956 there was a lengthy article in *TV Guide* in which the producers of *Question, Challenge,* and *The Big Surprise* adamantly denied that there was anything misleading or dishonest about the shows, but in the fall of 1958 the bubble burst. A disgruntled loser on *Dotto,* another giveaway show, announced that the show was rigged, and precipitated the quiz-show scandal that eventually forced all of them off the air. No longer would contestants sweat and ponder in the "isolation booths" that kept them from hearing what was going on in the outside world while searching for answers to incredibly complicated questions.

For a syndicated revival of this program in the 1970s, see *The $128,000 Question.*

60 MINUTES
News Magazine
FIRST TELECAST: *September 24, 1968*
LAST TELECAST:
BROADCAST HISTORY:
> *Sep 1968–Jun 1971,* CBS Tue 10:00–11:00 (OS)
> *Jan 1972–Jun 1972,* CBS Sun 6:00–7:00
> *Jan 1973–Jun 1973,* CBS Sun 6:00–7:00
> *Jun 1973–Sep 1973,* CBS Fri 8:00–9:00
> *Jan 1974–Jun 1974,* CBS Sun 6:00–7:00
> *Jul 1974–Sep 1974,* CBS Sun 9:30–10:30
> *Sep 1974–Jun 1975,* CBS Sun 6:00–7:00
> *Jul 1975–Sep 1975,* CBS Sun 9:30–10:30
> *Dec 1975–   ,* CBS Sun 7:00–8:00

CORRESPONDENTS:
> Mike Wallace
> Harry Reasoner (1968–1970, 1978–   )
> Morley Safer (1970–   )
> Dan Rather (1975–1981)
> Andrew Rooney (1978–   )
> Ed Bradley (1981–   )
> Diane Sawyer (1984–   )

DEBATERS:
> James J. Kilpatrick (1971–1979)
> Nicholas Von Hoffman (1971–1974)
> Shana Alexander (1975–1979)

60 Minutes was the *Time* magazine of the air. Each telecast opened with a "table of contents" (brief excerpts from the three or more stories that would be covered on that episode) superimposed on what appeared to be a magazine cover. Also superimposed at various times, usually between stories, was a moving stopwatch letting viewers know precisely how much of that night's "60 Minutes" was left. Within the magazine trappings lay a documentary series with remarkable scope. There were pieces on politics and politicians; the workings of governments, both domestic and for-

eign; personality profiles on artists, athletes, and citizens whose stories had mass appeal; and light feature pieces on everything from trade shows, to new inventions, to the shopping phenomenon that was Bloomingdale's department store. Indeed, *60 Minutes* was sufficiently diversified that, like each issue of a successful magazine, it had something to appeal to, concern, or interest almost everybody.

Among the more provocative stories featured in segments of *60 Minutes* were numerous items on politics in the Middle East; a 1971 feature on the situation in the Gulf of Tonkin; "The Poppy Fields of Turkey—The Heroin Labs of Marseilles—The N.Y. Connection" (1972); "The Selling of Colonel Herbert" (1973); "The End of a Salesman" (1974); "Local News and the Ratings War" (1974); several items on, and interviews with, participants in the Watergate scandal during 1974–1976; a controversial story on the plight of Jordanian Jews (1976); a feature on the brain damage suffered by workers in a chemical plant manufacturing Kepone (1976); and a dramatic report by Dan Rather from inside the sealed borders of Afghanistan, reporting on resistance to the Soviet invasion (1980).

60 Minutes spent its first three seasons on an alternate-week schedule with *CBS News Hour.* It was during this period that one of the original two correspondents, Harry Reasoner, left the show to join ABC News. His last appearance was on November 24, 1970. Two weeks later, Morley Safer joined Mike Wallace. When it moved into its own weekly time slot on Sunday evenings, a new regular feature called "Point Counterpoint" was added. Each week two columnists at opposite ends of the ideological spectrum—conservative James J. Kilpatrick and liberal Nicholas Von Hoffman (replaced by Shana Alexander in 1975)—would debate a current issue. They never agreed about anything. Dan Rather joined the show in December 1975, when it moved into the prime 7:00–8:00 P.M. hour, expanding the correspondent team from a duet to a trio. It was here that *60 Minutes* became a major hit, violating the traditional rule that documentary programs are marginal audience attractions. The summer of 1978 saw the addition of "Three Minutes or So with Andy Rooney" as a weekly feature filling in for the vacationing debaters from "Point Counterpoint." At the start of the 1978–1979 season Mr. Rooney's musings shared time with "Point Counterpoint," each feature airing on alternate weeks. It was also that fall that Harry Reasoner returned to *60 Minutes,* bringing the number of correspondents to four.

In the spring of 1979 Shana Alexander decided to leave *60 Minutes* and, although there was an attempt to find a new liberal to debate James Kilpatrick, the "Point Counterpoint" feature was dropped from the show (last telecast May 29, 1979) and Andy Rooney's observations became a weekly feature. The 1979–1980 season was a milestone for *60 Minutes* as it became the highest-rated series in all of prime time. It was in the spring of 1980 that CBS announced Dan Rather would leave. Despite leaving *60 Minutes* to anchor the CBS News in the spring of 1981, Rather had already recorded enough features to remain a *60 Minutes* regular through the end of the 1980–1981 season. Ed Bradley replaced Rather in 1982 and Diane Sawyer joined in late 1984.

The conclusion of *60 Minutes* telecasts, in true magazine fashion, consisted of one of the correspondents reading a collection of letters to the editors, followed by that ever-moving stopwatch signaling the end of the hour while the closing credits rolled.

SKAG
Drama
FIRST TELECAST: *January 6, 1980*
LAST TELECAST: *February 21, 1980*
BROADCAST HISTORY:
  Jan 1980–Feb 1980, NBC Thu 10:00–11:00
CAST:
  Pete "Skag" Skagska........... Karl Malden
  Jo Skagska .... Piper Laurie
  David Skagska .... Craig Wasson
  John Skagska............... Peter Gallagher
  Patricia Skagska.......... Kathryn Holcomb
  Barbara Skagska .... Leslie Ackerman
  Petar Skagska .... George Voskovec
  Whalen.................... Powers Boothe
  Paczka.................. Frank Campanella
  Dottie Jessup .... Shirley Stoler

Pete Skagska was a 56-year-old union foreman at a steel mill in Pittsburgh. It was a hard life, but the only one he knew, until he almost lost it when a crippling stroke temporarily forced him to stay home and try to put his life back together. He did have problems. He was concerned about his second wife, Jo, the only Jewish member of an otherwise staunchly Serbian Orthodox Catholic household, and 12 years his junior. His relationships with his children were troubled. The eldest, David, worked with him at the mill but felt uncomfortable about it; 24-year-old John was in medical school and more concerned with making money than with his family; 18-year-old Patricia was extremely shy and insecure; and 15-year-old Barbara was sleeping around to make herself popular despite her obesity. Skag's elderly father, Petar, left speechless and partially incapacitated by a major stroke of his own, also lived in the Skagska household. Whalen was the young steelworker who had taken over Skag's crew while he recovered from the stroke and coveted the job on a permanent basis. All the while, Skag, the stubborn traditionalist, was trying to adjust to a changing world whose values he did not fully understand.

The issues dramatized on *Skag* made for heavy viewing: impotence, senility, prostitution, labor problems, jealousy, family discord, and the conflicts caused by different value structures. The critics loved the show. They called it the season's most thought-provoking, realistic depiction of contemporary life. Boosted by tremendous advance publicity, the special Sunday three-hour premiere of *Skag* attracted a large audience. Unfortunately, the viewers did not stay with it when it moved to its regular Thursday time slot. Maybe it was too depressing to see that much hard reality. The producers of the show took out full-page newspaper ads in major cities beseeching the public to save *Skag*, but it didn't help. After its original limited run, *Skag* expired, rejected by the viewing public.

SKIP FARRELL SHOW, THE
Music
FIRST TELECAST: *January 17, 1949*
LAST TELECAST: *August 28, 1949*
BROADCAST HISTORY:
  Jan 1949–Feb 1949, ABC Mon 9:00–9:30
  Feb 1949–May 1949, ABC Mon 9:15–9:30
  May 1949–Jun 1949, ABC Mon 9:00–9:30
  Jul 1949–Aug 1949, ABC Sun 9:30–10:00
REGULARS:
  Skip Farrell
  The Honeydreamers
  Adele Scott Trio
  Bill Moss Orchestra
  George Barnes Trio
  Joanelle James

Musical program from Chicago, starring singer Skip Farrell.

SKY KING
Western
FIRST TELECAST: *September 21, 1953*
LAST TELECAST: *September 12, 1954*
BROADCAST HISTORY:
  Sep 1953–Sep 1954, ABC Mon 8:00–8:30
  Aug 1954–Sep 1954, ABC Sun 6:00–6:30
CAST:
  Sky King .... Kirby Grant
  Penny........................ Gloria Winters
  Clipper .... Ron Hagerthy

Sky King was a contemporary Western, starring Kirby Grant as an Arizona pilot-rancher who used an airplane instead of a horse to fight wrongdoers. With him on the Flying Crown Ranch were his teenage niece Penny and nephew Clipper. Sky's twin-engine Cessna was called *The Songbird.*

Sky King wandered all over the weekend daytime schedule before touching down in prime time in 1953. It was seen Sunday afternoons on NBC from 1951–1952 and Saturday afternoons on ABC in 1952–1953. Later, from 1959–1966, the same films showed up Saturday afternoons on CBS. The program was also heard on radio from 1946–1954.

SLAP MAXWELL STORY, THE
Situation Comedy
FIRST TELECAST: *September 23, 1987*

BROADCAST HISTORY:
Sep 1987–Mar 1988, ABC Wed 9:30–10:00
Jun 1988–   , ABC Wed 9:30–10:00
CAST:
Slap Maxwell .... Dabney Coleman
Judy Ralston .... Megan Gallagher
Annie Maxwell .... Susan Anspach
Nelson Kruger .... Brian Smiar
The Dutchman .... Bill Cobbs
Charlie Wilson .... Bill Calvert

Dabney Coleman has made a career of playing interesting reprobates (e.g., *Buffalo Bill*), and he essayed another in this 1987 comedy. "Slap" Maxwell was an unbelievably egocentric sportswriter working for a second-rate newspaper, *The Ledger,* located in the Southwest. His column "Slap Shots" was pecked out on an old typewriter (*The Ledger* refused to modernize), and it was certainly lively; however, its rumors and innuendo tended to draw lawsuits, giving editor Nelson Kruger fits. That often got Slap fired, though he'd always come crawling back. Despite his monumental insensitivity to everyone around him, Slap had an on-again, off-again girlfriend in Judy, the newspaper's secretary. Annie, who knew better, was his estranged wife, and Dutchman was the friendly bartender at the local tavern. They all managed to put up with Slap's bluster and bravado, which in the end, of course, got him nowhere.

In case the point of the series was not clear enough, each episode opened with shots of Slap getting slapped around—by (in producer Jay Tarses' words) "An athlete, a nun, or someone hurling a salami in anger."

SLATTERY'S PEOPLE
Political Drama
FIRST TELECAST: *September 21, 1964*
LAST TELECAST: *November 26, 1965*
BROADCAST HISTORY:
Sep 1964–Dec 1964, CBS Mon 10:00–11:00
Dec 1964–Nov 1965, CBS Fri 10:00–11:00
CAST:
James Slattery .... Richard Crenna
Frank Radcliff .... Edward Asner
Johnny Ramos .... Paul Geary
B. J. Clawson .... Maxine Stuart
Speaker Bert Metcalf .... Tol Avery
Liz Andrews (1965) .... Kathie Browne
Mike Valera (1965) .... Alejandro Rey
Wendy Wendkowski (1965) ... Francine York

The professional and personal conflicts and activities of the minority leader in a fictional state legislature were depicted in *Slattery's People.* James Slattery was an idealistic, concerned state representative who was very interested in governmental reforms and constantly found himself involved in causes. With the help of his aide, Johnny Ramos, and his secretary, B.J., he at-

tempted to push legislation that would better the lot of his constituents. House Speaker Bert Metcalf of the stronger opposition party, was his friendly enemy. When this series returned for an abbreviated second season, Slattery had a new aide (Mike Valera), a new secretary (Wendy Wendkowski), and a regular girlfriend in Liz Andrews.

SLEDGE HAMMER!
Situation Comedy
FIRST TELECAST: *September 23, 1986*
LAST TELECAST: *Jun 30, 1988*
BROADCAST HISTORY:
Sep 1986, ABC Tue 8:30–9:00
Sep 1986–Nov 1986, ABC Fri 9:30–10:00
Nov 1986–Mar 1987, ABC Sat 8:30–9:00
Apr 1987, ABC Tue 8:30–9:00
Jun 1987–Jul 1987, ABC Fri 8:00–8:30
Aug 1987–Jan 1988, ABC Thu 8:00–8:30
Jan 1988–Feb 1988, ABC Fri 9:30–10:00
Mar 1988, ABC Thu 8:30–9:00
Jun 1988, ABC Thu 8:00–8:30
CAST:
Det. Insp. Sledge Hammer ..... David Rasche
Off. Dori Doreau .... Anne-Marie Martin
Capt. Trunk .... Harrison Page
Off. Mayjoy .... Leslie Morris
Off. Daley (1987–1988) .... Patti Tippo
Norman Blates (1986–1987) .... Kurt Paul

Satire, they say in theatrical circles, is what closes on Saturday night. Nevertheless, this wild burlesque on tough-cop shows (particularly the *Dirty Harry* type) managed to hang on the ABC schedule for an extended period. Sledge was the ultimate tough cop: square-jawed, totally self-confident, with no mercy for the wimps and scum who infested his fair city. That included jaywalkers and litterers, who deserved to be shot like all the rest. In one episode he forced a miscreant, at gunpoint, to punch *himself* silly. Sledge's appearance was distinctive, with his reflecting sunglasses, striped shirts, and loud, mismatched ties. But his one true love was his giant, pearl-handled .44 Magnum—named "Gun." Each episode opened with the camera caressing this gleaming weapon, while ominous music thundered in the background. Sledge even talked to it. To others he would say, "Trust me ... I know what I'm doing."

Though he was often suspended from the force, Sledge was always reinstated and got his man—although it was usually his savvy partner, Off. Dori Doreau (a woman!), who actually solved the case. Capt. Trunk was their migraine-ridden, bellowing superior.

What did all this mean? Creator/producer Alan Spencer said that much as *Get Smart* poked fun at the spy mania of its day, this show did the same for the current crop of rebel police reactionary movies and TV shows. "Ultimately," he said, "what the show is about ... is a half hour."

SLEEPY JOE

Children's

FIRST TELECAST: *October 3, 1949*
LAST TELECAST: *October 28, 1949*
BROADCAST HISTORY:
Oct 1949, ABC Mon–Fri 6:45–7:00
HOST:
Jimmy Scribner

Jimmy Scribner—a white man—had a long career on radio in the 1930s and 1940s playing comic Southern darkies. On his long-running series *The Johnson Family* (a kind of rural *Amos 'n' Andy*) he portrayed a whole townful, switching voices as necessary. Scribner appeared on television in the late 1940s with a short-lived puppet show on the ABC network, telling Uncle Remus–type stories for the kids. Later he had a syndicated puppet show built around similar Southern stories for which he did all the character voices.

SMALL & FRYE

Situation Comedy

FIRST TELECAST: *March 7, 1983*
LAST TELECAST: *June 15, 1983*
BROADCAST HISTORY:
Mar 1983, CBS Mon 8:30–9:00
Jun 1983, CBS Wed 8:00–8:30
CAST:

Nick Small	Darren McGavin
Chip Frye	Jack Blessing
Phoebe Small	Debbie Zipp
Dr. Hanratty	Bill Daily
Eddie	Warren Berlinger
Vicki, the waitress	Victoria Carroll
The drunken bar fly	Dick Wilson

Nick Small was an old-line private eye who had never adjusted to the modern world. He was right out of the 1930s, hard-nosed, trench-coated, and patterned after the likes of Mike Hammer and Sam Spade. His eager young partner, Chip Frye, was more contemporary, and also brought something else to the partnership. As a result of a freak laboratory accident, Chip could shrink to a height of only six inches by using a special ring device. This gave Small & Frye the ability to get into places their competition couldn't. There was one minor glitch: outside factors like lightning, minerals in certain foods, and his own hiccups could cause Chip to shrink at the most inopportune times.

Phoebe, Nick's young daughter, served as the office receptionist and was Chip's girlfriend. Dr. Hanratty was the eccentric head of the Police Criminal Lab and Eddie was the proprietor of Nick's favorite local hangout, Eddie's Bar and Grill.

SMALL FRY CLUB

Children's

FIRST TELECAST: *March 11, 1947*
LAST TELECAST: *June 15, 1951*
BROADCAST HISTORY:
Mar 1947–Apr 1947, DUM Tue 7:00–8:00
Apr 1947–Jan 1948, DUM Mon–Fri 7:00–7:30
Jan 1948–Apr 1948, DUM Mon–Fri 6:15–6:45
Apr 1948–Jun 1951, DUM Mon–Fri 6:00–6:30
HOST:
Bob Emery

DuMont's *Small Fry Club* was one of the gentlest and most widely lauded children's shows of TV's early days. To an adult viewer it might be pure corn: letters from the little tykes read over the air, with their pictures shown; lessons on good behavior, safety, drinking more milk, etc.; and sketches by a studio cast of actors representing different animals. For the kindergarten set, however, it was *their* show. Its host, a remarkable man who went by the name of "Big Brother" Bob Emery, had spent his whole life entertaining youngsters while imparting lessons of good behavior. From the time he began his "club" on a radio station in Medford, Massachusetts, in 1921, he stressed involvement rather than one-way entertainment, and his young listeners flocked to obtain official membership cards, wrote him letters, sent in pictures and drawings, and joined in contests.

Emery (he then spelled it Emory) later came to New York and got into television on the ground floor, as announcer and producer at DuMont's WABD. He assumed his radio role of "Big Brother" on the station's Christmas show in 1946, and in March 1947 began his first video series, called *Movies for Small Fry*. At first it was just that, cartoons and other children's films, with voiceover narration by Bob—he was not even seen. But soon the program expanded to five days a week (possibly the first ever to do so) and a regular studio setting was developed. Membership cards were offered and letters came pouring in. If anyone doubted the effectiveness of the new medium in reaching an audience, they had only to look at the figures for the *Small Fry Club:* 1,200 cards sent out by May 1947, 15,000 by January 1948, 150,000 "active" members by 1950. Some of these were the children of parents who had themselves been *Small Fry Club* members in the 1920s. Contests drew enormous responses, including 150 returns a week for a jingle contest in 1947, 10,000 drawings by 1948 (these were regularly shown on the air), and 24,000 letters to name a new member of the cast in 1951. (She became Trina the Kitten.)

Other regulars with Bob were Honey the Bunny, Mr. Mischief the Panda, Willy the Wiz, and Peggy the Penguin. Big Brother himself always appeared in a business suit, with heavy, dark-rimmed glasses—the picture of a kindly uncle. In addition to skits such as "Columbus and Isabella" and "Washington at Mt. Vernon," educational films and advice for kids were offered.

As with some other early shows, it is not known whether the *Small Fry Club* was fed over the network from the start; in any event, it was on the network (i.e., two stations) by late 1947. Bob

Emery left DuMont in 1951 to return to Boston, where he later was seen in a series of local programs.

SMALL WONDER
Situation Comedy
BROADCAST HISTORY:
Syndicated only
30 minutes
Produced: *1985–*
Released: *September 1985*
CAST:

Ted Lawson	Dick Christie
Joan Lawson	Marla Pennington
Jamie Lawson	Jerry Supiran
Vicki	Tiffany Brissette
Reggie Williams	Paul C. Scott
Harriet Brindle	Emily Schulman
*Bonnie Brindle (1985–1986)	Edie McClurg
*Warren (1986–1987)	Daryl T. Bartley
*Jessica (1986–)	Lihann Jones
Brandon Brindle (1986–)	William Bogert

*Occasional

Ted Lawson was a research engineer with United Robotronics. He had secretly developed a robot that, superficially, looked exactly like a cute little 10-year-old girl. Ted took the robot, a "Voice Input Child Identicon" which he had nicknamed Vicki, home to his wife and young son Jamie, so that he could get the kinks out of its programming. Vicki generally talked in a monotone, was totally logical, and given to taking anything that was said quite literally—resulting in confusion and embarrassment for Ted and his family when others were around. She was extremely strong, a quality that endeared her to "brother" Jamie when he had to deal with the neighborhood bully. She was also given to repeating things that others had said, much like a parrot. Only Ted's family knew she was not human and they were hard-pressed to keep others from finding out. Reggie was Jamie's friend and Harriet the obnoxious girl next door who was almost as nosy as her mother. Harriet's father, Brandon, was Ted's overbearing boss at United Robotronics.

In the second season Jamie went to junior high school and Vicki went too, creating problems for the other students who didn't have her perfect memory. His life at school was also complicated by having his mom show up frequently as a substitute teacher, falling in puppy-love with gold-digging Jessica (age 11), and coping with another kid in his class, obnoxious Warren.

SMALL WORLD
Discussion
FIRST TELECAST: *October 12, 1958*
LAST TELECAST: *May 29, 1960*
BROADCAST HISTORY:
Oct 1958–May 1960, CBS Sun 6:00–6:30 (OS)

MODERATOR:
Edward R. Murrow

Each week on this filmed series, moderator Edward R. Murrow conducted an informal, unrehearsed discussion with three or four world celebrities. The celebrities were located at widely divergent places around the world and it was only through the use of advanced electronic technology that these people could get together "face to face." Serious discussions on world politics might include Thomas E. Dewey, Jawaharlal Nehru, and writer Aldous Huxley, as on the premiere telecast. Lighter shows might involve actress Ingrid Bergman, *New York Times* film critic Bosley Crowther, and producer Darryl F. Zanuck chatting about the state of the motion-picture industry.

SMILIN' ED MCCONNELL AND HIS BUSTER BROWN GANG
Children's
FIRST TELECAST: *August 26, 1950*
LAST TELECAST: *May 19, 1951*
BROADCAST HISTORY:
Aug 1950–May 1951, NBC Sat 6:30–7:00
HOST:
Ed McConnell

Children's program, based on McConnell's radio show, which featured him playing the piano, singing and telling stories from his storybook—sometimes in the form of films, always with a moral. In the cast were Midnight the tabby cat, Squeaky the mouse, Old Grandie the talking piano, and Uncle Fishface, the world's greatest storyteller. After its prime-time run the series returned to television on Saturday mornings from 1953–1955, with Andy Devine replacing McConnell upon the latter's death in 1954.

The Saturday morning version was retitled *Andy's Gang* when it returned as a local show in the fall of 1955. It continued through the end of 1960, primarily as a local show, with the exception of the 1957–1958 season when it ran on the full NBC network.

SMITH FAMILY, THE
Drama
FIRST TELECAST: *January 20, 1971*
LAST TELECAST: *June 14, 1972*
BROADCAST HISTORY:
Jan 1971–Sep 1971, ABC Wed 8:30–9:00
Sep 1971–Jan 1972, ABC Wed 9:00–9:30
Apr 1972–Jun 1972, ABC Wed 8:30–9:00
CAST:

Det. Sgt. Chad Smith	Henry Fonda
Betty Smith	Janet Blair
Cindy Smith	Darleen Carr
Bob Smith	Ronny Howard
Brian Smith	Michael-James Wixted
Capt. Hughes	Charles McGraw
Sgt. Ray Martin	John Carter

"Primrose Lane," by W. Shanklin and G. Callendar, sung by Mike Minor

Henry Fonda starred in this family drama about the home life of a big-city cop. Det. Sgt. Chad Smith was a Los Angeles plainclothesman, 25 years on the force, who worked on burglaries, drug busts, runaway children, bomb threats, and, occasionally, homicides. His suburban family consisted of wife Betty; 18-year-old daughter Cindy, an L.A. City College student with marriage on her mind; 15-year-old son Bob; and 7-year-old son Brian. Stories touched on the generation gap and the problems of youth as much as on Chad's police work, which did include some dangerous situations but not really much hard action. His captain and partner, Sgt. Martin, were only seen occasionally.

SMITHSONIAN, THE
Documentary
FIRST TELECAST: *June 25, 1967*
LAST TELECAST: *August 27, 1967*
BROADCAST HISTORY:
Jun 1967–Aug 1967, NBC Sun 6:30–7:00
HOST:
Bill Ryan

The vast Smithsonian Museum complex in Washington, D.C., was the starting point for this series. Each week a specific exhibit in one of the Smithsonian buildings opened a filmed exploratory journey into history or some field of scientific endeavor. NBC newsman Bill Ryan narrated the background material with on-location film footage, stills, and animation. The series had originally aired from October 1966 to April 1967 on Saturdays at 12:30 P.M. The episodes seen on Sunday evenings during the summer of 1967 were all reruns.

SMOTHERS BROTHERS COMEDY HOUR, THE
Comedy Variety
FIRST TELECAST: *February 5, 1967*
LAST TELECAST: *May 26, 1975*
BROADCAST HISTORY:
Feb 1967–Jun 1969, CBS Sun 9:00–10:00 (OS)
Jul 1970–Sep 1970, ABC Wed 10:00–11:00
Jan 1975–May 1975, NBC Mon 8:00–9:00
REGULARS:
Tom Smothers
Dick Smothers
Pat Paulsen
Leigh French (1967–1969, 1975)
Bob Einstein (as *Officer Judy;* 1967–1969, 1975)
The Louis Da Pron Dancers (1967–1968)
The Ron Poindexter Dancers (1968–1969)
The Anita Kerr Singers (1967)
The Jimmy Joyce Singers (1967–1969)
Nelson Riddle and His Orchestra (1967–1969)
The Denny Vaughn Orchestra (1970)
Mason Williams (1967–1969)

Jennifer Warnes (Warren) (1967–1969)
John Hartford (1968–1969)
Sally Struthers (1970)
Spencer Quinn (1970)
Betty Aberlin (1975)
Don Novello (1975)
Steve Martin (1975)
Nino Senporty (1975)
The Marty Paich Orchestra (1975)

Tom and Dick Smothers had been a very popular comedy/singing team in the early and mid-1960s with a number of successful, offbeat comedy albums. Tom, who played the guitar, acted the role of the dullard, unable to think logically, making all sorts of inane remarks, and being generally impossible to deal with. Dick, who played bass, was, by contrast, calm, reasonable, and hard pressed to retain his composure when confronted by his brother's stupidity and silliness. Extremely popular with young people, they were an immediate hit with their irreverent variety series on CBS in 1967. Abetted by Pat Paulsen's low-keyed "editorials" and other material, which at times rivaled Tom for the evening's silliest moments, and a large supporting cast, *The Smothers Brothers Comedy Hour* poked fun at virtually all the hallowed institutions of American society—motherhood, church, politics, government, etc. It was topical, it was funny, and occasionally it was in bad taste.

There were always problems getting program material cleared with the CBS censors, and the adamant position taken by the show's stars over what they considered was acceptable did not endear them to CBS management. First there were minor skirmishes. Pat Paulsen had started a campaign for President on their summer series in 1968 *(The Summer Brothers Smothers Show)* with the slogan "If nominated I will not run, and if elected I will not serve." It was a joke but CBS, fearing demands for equal time from real candidates, kept him off the show until after the election. Pete Seeger, a controversial folk singer long blacklisted on television, made several appearances on the show and got them into trouble with his Vietnam protest song "Waist Deep in the Big Muddy." Early in 1969 they did a comedy sketch making fun of religion that outraged the clergy and forced an on-air apology.

CBS had had enough. The ratings were still high, but CBS management finally concluded that *The Smothers Brothers Comedy Hour* was just not worth the trouble. The brothers' choice of guests, predominantly antiwar, left-wing, and outspoken; their fights over material; and their repeated failure to deliver finished programs early enough in the week for the censors to get them edited by air time on Sunday were all advanced as reasons when the series was abruptly canceled. There was a good deal of furor over freedom of speech and the like, but the CBS decision stuck. The Smothers Brothers were replaced by *Hee Haw.*

Thirteen months later, *The Smothers Summer Show* turned up on ABC. Apparently their time had passed, and the show (which included three repeats of episodes from the original CBS series) did not make it to the ABC fall schedule. The following fall Tom turned up by himself as the star of a syndicated half-hour comedy series titled *Tom Smothers' Organic Prime Time Space Ride.* It tried to be irreverent and satirical, but did not attract much of an audience and was not renewed. In 1975 NBC gave Tom and Dick yet another chance, with a new variety series simply titled *The Smothers Brothers Show*. There were no real problems with the NBC censors, probably because the biting edge was gone from their material. The closest they came to anything controversial on the premiere telecast was when Tom announced that they had an "iron-clad" 13-week contract. It got off to a strong start, due more to audience curiosity about what had happened to Tom and Dick in the five years since they had last been on network television than to the merits of the program, but quickly sank into obscurity.

SMOTHERS BROTHERS COMEDY HOUR, THE
Comedy Variety
FIRST TELECAST: *March 30, 1988*
LAST TELECAST: *May 25, 1988*
BROADCAST HISTORY:
Mar 1988–May 1988, CBS Wed 8:00–9:00
REGULARS:
Tom Smothers
Dick Smothers
Pat Paulsen
Jim Stafford
The Larry Cansler Orchestra

Yesterday once more. On February 3, 1988, CBS aired "The Smothers Brothers Comedy Hour 20th Reunion Show," a nostalgic look back at the contentious variety series of the '60s. (So what if it was actually twenty-*one* years since the original series premiered?) The special, which brought together many regulars and writers from the original show, drew a sizeable audience and good reviews, and CBS decided to try it as a series—again. The new effort was sharply written and topical, but there was certainly a sense of *déjà vu*—Tom and Dick's sibling rivalry was as strong as ever, Pat Paulsen was running for president again, and former regulars Jennifer Warnes and Leigh French turned up as guest stars. Even the set looked the same. Regularly featured was a segment in which Tom showed off his considerable skills with the yo-yo, as "The Yo-Yo Man."

SMOTHERS BROTHERS SHOW, THE
Situation Comedy
FIRST TELECAST: *September 17, 1965*
LAST TELECAST: *September 9, 1966*
BROADCAST HISTORY:
Sep 1965–Sep 1966, CBS Fri 9:30–10:00

CAST:
Tom Smothers .... Himself
Dick Smothers .... Himself
Leonard J. Costello .... Roland Winters
Mrs. Costello .... Harriet MacGibbon
Janet .... Ann Elder

As a rising young executive at Pandora Publications, working for publisher Leonard J. Costello, Dick Smothers should have been enjoying the life of a prosperous bachelor. But one little thing kept getting in the way—his brother Tom. Not in ordinary ways, either. Tom had been lost at sea and two years later showed up as an apprentice angel, assigned to do good works on Earth to become a full-fledged regular angel. His efforts to help people did not always seem to work out the way he had planned, and he was forever seeking the aid of his earthly brother to help bail him out of some blunder he had created.

SNEAK PREVIEW
Anthology
FIRST TELECAST: *July 3, 1956*
LAST TELECAST: *August 7, 1956*
BROADCAST HISTORY:
Jul 1956–Aug 1956, NBC Tue 9:00–9:30
HOST:
Nelson Case

The implication of this series was that the viewer would be seeing pilot films for series which might turn up on the fall schedule. None of them made it, however. Included were half-hour comedies starring Zsa Zsa Gabor, Ann Sheridan, and Celeste Holm. *Sneak Preview* was the 1956 summer replacement for *Jane Wyman's Fireside Theater.*

SNOOP SISTERS, THE
Detective Drama
FIRST TELECAST: *December 19, 1973*
LAST TELECAST: *August 20, 1974*
BROADCAST HISTORY:
Dec 1973, NBC Wed 8:30–10:00
Jan 1974–Aug 1974, NBC Tue 8:30–10:00
CAST:
Ernesta Snoop .... Helen Hayes
Gwen Snoop .... Mildred Natwick
Barney .... Lou Antonio
Lt. Steve Ostrowski .... Bert Convy

Ernesta and Gwen Snoop were two elderly sisters who were well named. Despite the fact that they were very successful mystery writers, or possibly because of it, they could not resist getting involved in real mysteries. Their experience working with clues in the fictitious stories they wrote for a living stood them in good stead when they were confronted with the urge to try to solve real crimes. All the physical work was handled for them by Barney, their combination chauffeur and bodyguard, and their nephew, police lieutenant Ostrowski. *The Snoop Sisters* was one of the four rotating elements in the 1973–1974 version of *The NBC Wednesday/Tuesday Mystery Movie*. The others were *Banacek*, *Faraday and Company*, and *Tenafly*.

SO THIS IS HOLLYWOOD
Situation Comedy
FIRST TELECAST: *January 1, 1955*
LAST TELECAST: *August 19, 1955*
BROADCAST HISTORY:
   Jan 1955–Jun 1955, NBC Sat 8:30–9:00
   Jul 1955–Aug 1955, NBC Fri 10:30–11:00
CAST:
   Queenie Dugan .... Mitzi Green
   Kim Tracy .... Virginia Gibson
   Andy Boone .... Jimmy Lydon
   Hubie Dodd .... Gordon Jones
   April Adams .... Peggy Knudsen

So This Is Hollywood was the story of two young women trying to make it in show business. Queenie Dugan was a stunt woman who had been around Hollywood long enough to know how to avoid being hustled and to realize that she wasn't ever going to be a star herself. Her roommate, Kim Tracy, was a young starlet and movie extra who, despite the efforts of her agent, Andy, seemed unable to get the one big break that would make her a star. Queenie was always trying to find ways to promote Kim's career, as were both Andy and Queenie's stunt-man boyfriend Hubie.

SO YOU WANT TO LEAD A BAND
see *Sammy Kaye Show, The*

SOAP
Situation Comedy
FIRST TELECAST: *September 13, 1977*
LAST TELECAST: *April 20, 1981*
BROADCAST HISTORY:
   Sep 1977–Mar 1978, ABC Tue 9:30–10:00
   Sep 1978–Mar 1979, ABC Thu 9:30–10:00
   Sep 1979–Mar 1980, ABC Thu 9:30–10:00
   Oct 1980–Jan 1981, ABC Wed 9:30–10:00
   Mar 1981–Apr 1981, ABC Mon 10:00–11:00
CAST:
   Chester Tate .... Robert Mandan
   Jessica Tate .... Katherine Helmond
   Corrine Tate (1977–1980) ..... Diana Canova
   Eunice Tate .... Jennifer Salt
   Billy Tate .... Jimmy Baio
   Benson (1977–1979) .... Robert Guillaume
   The Major .... Arthur Peterson
   Mary Dallas Campbell ...... Cathryn Damon
   Burt Campbell .... Richard Mulligan
   Jodie Dallas .... Billy Crystal
   Danny Dallas .... Ted Wass
   The Godfather (1977–1978).. Richard Libertini
   Claire (1977–1978) .... Kathryn Reynolds
   Peter Campbell (1977) .... Robert Urich
   Chuck/Bob Campbell .... Jay Johnson
   Dennis Phillips (1978) .... Bob Seagren

Father Timothy Flotsky (1978–1979)
   .... Sal Viscuso
Carol David (1978–1981) .... Rebecca Balding
Elaine Lefkowitz (1978–1979) .. Dinah Manoff
Dutch (1978–1981) .... Donnelly Rhodes
Sally (1978–1979) ...... Caroline McWilliams
Detective Donahue (1978–1980) .. John Byner
Alice (1979) .... Randee Heller
Mrs. David (1979–1981) .... Peggy Pope
Millie (1979) .... Candace Azzara
Leslie Walker (1979–1981) . Marla Pennington
Polly Dawson (1979–1981) ..... Lynne Moody
Saunders (1980–1981).... Roscoe Lee Browne
Dr. Alan Posner (1980–1981) .... Allan Miller
Attorney E. Ronald Mallu (1978–1981)
   .... Eugene Roche
Carlos "El Puerco" Valdez (1980–1981)
   .... Gregory Sierra
Maggie Chandler (1980–1981)
   .... Barbara Rhoades
Gwen (1980–1981) .... Jesse Welles

Soap was undoubtedly the most controversial new series of the 1977–1978 "season of sex." Even before it went on the air ABC had received 32,000 letters about the show—all but nine of them against it—ABC affiliates had been picketed for planning to air it, and sponsors had been urged to boycott the show (which a few did). Some ABC affiliates refused to carry it, and many who did ran it late at night.

The object of all this ire was a half-hour comedy which was billed as a satire on soap operas. It had a continuing story line of sorts, but was populated by a cast such as was seldom seen on any serious dramatic show. Stories centered on the wealthy Tates and the blue-collar Campbells. Chester Tate was a pompous businessman with an affinity for extramarital affairs; no wonder, since his wife, Jessica, was a spaced-out, fluttery idiot. Of their three children, sexy Corrine was always putting her best attributes forward; Eunice was quieter and more conservative; and Billy, 14, was a wise-cracking brat. Living with the Tates were Jessica's father, "the Major," who crawled around the floor in his old army uniform, still fighting World War II; and Benson, the insolent and obnoxious black servant and cook, who commented on the proceedings.

Across town lived Jessica's sister, Mary Campbell. Her husband, Burt, was a "working stiff" whose main problem lay in dealing with stepsons Jodie (who was gay) and Danny (who was involved with organized crime). Surreptitious sex was on practically everyone's mind, and formed the basis of many of the stories.

The major development during the first season was the murder of Peter, the handsome tennis pro (and Burt's son), who had been luring most of his female students into bed with him. First Corrine was accused, but then Jessica was arrested and subsequently convicted of the crime. In the last episode of the 1977–1978 season, an off-screen narrator informed viewers that she didn't really do it, and as the following season opened, Chester confessed to the crime.

Chester was sent to prison but soon escaped with Dutch, a convicted murderer. Soon thereafter Chester lost his memory and wandered out west, where he became a fry cook. Dutch, on the other hand, eloped with Eunice. Jessica fell in love with Detective Donahue, whom she had hired to find Chester, and when Chester finally returned she had to choose between them. She chose Chester, but only for a while; after a fling with South American revolutionary "El Puerco," she and Chester were divorced.

Life was not dull for the rest of the family, either. Benson the butler departed for greener pastures (his own series) in 1979, after rescuing Billy from a religious cult, the Sunnies. The new butler was named Saunders. Daughter Corrine Tate married ex-priest Timothy Flotsky, but their union produced—after six weeks—a baby possessed by the devil, and the Tates had to band together to exorcise the spirit. Across town, Burt found himself kidnapped and cloned by aliens; at least Mary got a few nights of uninhibited sex from the clone. But who, then, was the father of the baby that resulted? Joe, Burt's gay son, decided that women are fun too and sired his own baby by Carol, but wound up in an ugly custody fight. Then Burt got himself elected sheriff, resulting in a run-in with the racketeer Tibbs and his hooker, Gwen. Danny, who had previously been in love with Elaine, Millie, and Polly, sort of liked her.

Soap attracted a large and loyal audience, and the controversy over it was confined largely to the first season. ABC intimated that the program represented a major breakthrough in TV comedy, and claimed that "through the Campbells and the Tates many of today's social concerns will be dealt with in a comedic manner." Others considered *Soap* nothing more than an extended dirty joke being piped into America's living rooms. Much of the opposition to the program was led by religious groups, including the National Council of Churches. Rev. Everett Parker, a longtime critic of TV, called *Soap* "a deliberate effort to break down any resistance to whatever the industry wants to put into prime time. . . . Who else besides the churches is going to stand against the effort of television to tear down our moral values and make all of us into mere consumers?"

See *ABC Late Night* for summer rerun dates for this series.

SOAP BOX THEATRE
Dramatic Anthology
FIRST TELECAST: *June 24, 1950*
LAST TELECAST: *December 3, 1950*
BROADCAST HISTORY:
 Jun 1950–Oct 1950, ABC Sun 9:30–10:00
 Oct 1950–Dec 1950, ABC Sun 9:00–9:30

This was a series of filmed dramas.

SOLDIER PARADE
see *Talent Patrol*

SOLDIERS, THE
Situation Comedy
FIRST TELECAST: *June 25, 1955*
LAST TELECAST: *September 3, 1955*
BROADCAST HISTORY:
 Jun 1955–Sep 1955, NBC Sat 8:00–8:30
CAST:
 Hal .... Hal March
 Tom .... Tom D'Andrea

This live summer comedy series, originating from Hollywood, starred Hal March and Tom D'Andrea in the roles they had played over the years on numerous variety shows. As two typical GIs who found nothing but trouble in the Army, Tom and Hal complained about almost everything—the regimentation, the food, their superior officers, etc. Each episode contained one or more vignettes about a specific aspect of life in the army: getting letters from home, trying to get passes, being sent to an isolated location for a special assignment, and the problems of adjusting to civilian life after getting discharged.

SOLDIERS OF FORTUNE
Adventure
BROADCAST HISTORY:
 Syndicated only
 30 minutes
 Produced: *1955–1956* (52 episodes)
 Released: *Early 1955*
CAST:
 Tim Kelly .... John Russell
 Toubo Smith .... Chick Chandler

Tim Kelly and Toubo Smith were two rugged adventurers-for-hire in this action series. They went anywhere for a price, and a typical episode might find them tramping through the African jungle, fighting their way out of a barroom brawl in Singapore, or pearl diving in the South Seas. Kelly was the serious one, a big, handsome hunk; and Toubo was the older, humorous sidekick.

SOLID GOLD
Music
BROADCAST HISTORY:
 Syndicated only
 60 minutes
 Produced: *1980–*
 Released: *September 1980*
HOSTS:
 Dionne Warwick (1980–1981, 1985–1986)
 Marilyn McCoo (1981–1984, 1986–   )
 Andy Gibb (1981–1982)
 Rex Smith (1982–1983)
 Rick Dees (1984–1985)
REGULARS:
 The Solid Gold Dancers
 Wayland Flowers and Madame (1980–1984)

Marty Cohen (1980–1981)
Mack & Jamie (1982)
Jeff Altman (1982–1983)
Nina Blackwood (1986–   )

Solid Gold was a countdown of the top ten records of the week, most of them accompanied by the high-energy dancing of the athletic and sexy Solid Gold Dancers. Also featured were other new releases, pick hits, and an occasional oldie. Some numbers were seen performed by the artists themselves, either in a video or in the studio, and there was even an occasional "joke" video of ordinary people lip-syncing to some famous hit. Even the star performances were lip-synced, in fact; unlike the situation in the prerock days of *Your Hit Parade,* the record (often an elaborate production), not the song, was now the hit.

There were a number of hosts on the program, most of them singers in their own right. During the first season Dionne Warwick hosted with the help of a different guest star each week. She was replaced by the team of Andy Gibb and Marilyn McCoo. Teenage heartthrob Gibb became increasingly unreliable by the end of the second season, missing several shows, and was replaced by Rex Smith for 1982–1983. Finally Miss McCoo—a beautiful woman who had once been a member of the group the Fifth Dimension—took over as sole host in 1983. Regulars included comedians Marty Cohen, Mack & Jamie, Jeff Altman, and Wayland Flowers and his foulmouthed puppet, Madame.

In the fall of 1984 disc jockey Rick Dees succeeded Miss McCoo as *Solid Gold*'s host, the first non-singer in that role. His tenure lasted one year, followed by the return of Dionne Warwick for the 1985–1986 season, and the return of Miss McCoo in the fall of 1986. That fall there were two new features added to *Solid Gold*—an interview segment in which disc jockey Nina Blackwood chatted with current rock stars and "Flashback," an opportunity for rock stars from the '50s, '60s, and '70s to recreate their big hits. The series was retitled *Solid Gold in Concert* at the start of the 1987–1988 season to reflect an increase in the number of live performances by the artists whose songs were performed on the show.

For a short time, during the summer of 1984, actor Grant Goodeve hosted a weekday half-hour spinoff series titled *Solid Gold Hits.*

SOMERSET MAUGHAM TV THEATRE
Dramatic Anthology
FIRST TELECAST: *October 18, 1950*
LAST TELECAST: *December 10, 1951*
BROADCAST HISTORY:
  Oct 1950–Mar 1951, CBS Wed 9:00–9:30
  Apr 1951–Jun 1951, NBC Mon 9:30–10:30
  Jul 1951–Aug 1951, NBC Mon 9:30–10:00
  Sep 1951–Dec 1951, NBC Mon 9:30–10:30
HOST:
  W. Somerset Maugham

This anthology series had the distinction of having as host the author of the novels and short stories that had been adapted for television presentation. The plays themselves were live, originating from New York, but the opening and closing remarks by the author had all been filmed prior to the start of the season at his home on the French Riviera. He would introduce each play and return at the end to thank the audience for watching and to announce the title of the next week's production. When it premiered on CBS as a half-hour series, its title was *Teller of Tales.* After three telecasts the title was changed to *Somerset Maugham TV Theatre.* On NBC during the spring and fall of 1951, a full-hour version of the show aired on alternate weeks with *Robert Montgomery Presents.* It ran during the summer of 1951 as a half-hour show every week.

SONG AND DANCE
Music
FIRST TELECAST: *December 17, 1948*
LAST TELECAST: *June 21, 1949*
BROADCAST HISTORY:
  Dec 1948–Jan 1949, NBC Fri 8:00–8:30
  Jan 1949–Mar 1949, NBC Mon 8:00–8:30
  Mar 1949–Apr 1949, NBC Mon 8:15–8:30
  May 1949–Jun 1949, NBC Various nights and
    times
EMCEE:
  Roberta Quinlan (1948–1949)
  Barbara Marshall (1949)
DANCERS:
  Ellsworth & Fairchild

Live musical interlude featuring songs and dancing. Quite a number of "regular" singers and dancers came and went during the program's short run. Roberta Quinlan was the original hostess, replaced by Barbara Marshall in April 1949.

SONG SNAPSHOTS ON A SUMMER HOLIDAY
see *Summer Holiday*

SONGS AT TWILIGHT
Music
FIRST TELECAST: *July 3, 1951*
LAST TELECAST: *August 31, 1951*
BROADCAST HISTORY:
  Jul 1951–Aug 1951, NBC Mon–Fri 7:30–7:45
REGULARS:
  Bob Carroll
  Buddy Greco
  Johnny Andrews

Songs at Twilight was a live informal 15 minutes of song and talk by its host and his guest star of the evening. It spent the summer of 1951 filling the remainder of the half hour in which NBC aired its network news program. Holding on to a host was a problem for this series. When it premiered, singer Bob Carroll had the job. On July 16 he was replaced by singer-pianist Buddy Greco, who was replaced on July 30 by singer Johnny Andrews. Andrews somehow managed to last until the program went off the air.

SONGS FOR SALE
Music
FIRST TELECAST: *July 7, 1950*
LAST TELECAST: *June 28, 1952*
BROADCAST HISTORY:
Jul 1950–Sep 1950, CBS Fri 9:00–10:00
Feb 1951, CBS Sat 7:30–8:00
Jun 1951–Feb 1952, CBS Sat 10:00–11:00
Mar 1952–Jun 1952, CBS Sat 9:30–11:00
Jun 1952, CBS Sat 8:00–9:00
EMCEE:
Jan Murray (1950–1951)
Steve Allen (1951–1952)
REGULARS:
Rosemary Clooney (1950–1951)
Tony Bennett (1950)
Richard Hayes (1950–1951)
Ray Bloch and His Orchestra
Mitch Miller (1951)
Peggy Lee (1951–1952)
Barry Gray (1952)

Songs for Sale was a showcase for the efforts of aspiring amateur songwriters. Each week a number of them (usually three) had their songs performed by professional singers and rated by a panel of judges. The winning song was guaranteed to be published, and the runners-up might be if a publisher who was listening liked them. The show, needless to say, was swamped with submissions. Originally there were two permanent singers on the show, and a rotating panel of judges. Rosemary Clooney and Tony Bennett were relatively unknown when the series began, but both immediately attracted considerable attention and went on to become major stars—they were probably more important "discoveries" of this show than any of the songs. (Both had previously been winners on *Arthur Godfrey's Talent Scouts*.) Bennett left the show after a month, but Rosemary Clooney continued, joined by Richard Hayes. Both of them remained until the show was temporarily shelved in the fall of 1950.

When it returned in 1951 singers were generally rotated, though Peggy Lee became a regular in December 1951 and remained for several months. Panelists changed too. For a period in the spring of 1951 Mitch Miller was a regular panelist, and Barry Gray served in a similar capacity in the spring of 1952. From its inception until September 1951, *Songs for Sale* was simulcast on radio and TV.

During its last season there were cash awards, up to $1,000, available to weekly winners whose songs also won a special run-off held once every five or six weeks, before an enlarged panel of judges.

SONGTIME
Religion
FIRST TELECAST: *October 6, 1951*
LAST TELECAST: *May 17, 1952*
BROADCAST HISTORY:
Oct 1951–May 1952, ABC Sat 11:00–11:30
HOST:
Jack Wyrtzen

Hymns, gospel songs, and inspirational talks by youth leader Jack Wyrtzen. The program began locally in New York in November 1950, and was seen live over the network during the 1951–1952 season. Also known as *The Word of Life Songtime*.

SONNY AND CHER COMEDY HOUR, THE
Musical Variety
FIRST TELECAST: *August 1, 1971*
LAST TELECAST: *August 29, 1977*
BROADCAST HISTORY:
Aug 1971–Sep 1971, CBS Sun 8:30–9:30
Dec 1971–Jun 1972, CBS Mon 10:00–11:00
Sep 1972–Dec 1972, CBS Fri 8:00–9:00
Dec 1972–May 1974, CBS Wed 8:00–9:00
Feb 1976–Jan 1977, CBS Sun 8:00–9:00
Jan 1977–Mar 1977, CBS Fri 9:00–10:00
May 1977–Aug 1977, CBS Mon 10:00–11:00
REGULARS:
Sonny Bono
Cher Bono
Ted Zeigler
Chastity Bono (1973–1977)
Tom Solari (1971–1972)
Clark Carr (1971–1972)
Murray Langston (1971–1974)
Freeman King (1971–1974)
Peter Cullen (1971–1974)
The Jimmy Dale Orchestra (1971–1973)
The Marty Paich Orchestra (1973–1974)
Steve Martin (1972–1973)
Teri Garr (1973–1974)
Billy Van (1973–1976)
Bob Einstein (1973–1974)
Gailard Sartain (1976)
Jack Harrell (1976)
Robert Shields and Lorene Yarnell (1976–1977)
The Tony Mordente Dancers (1971–1974)
The Earl Brown Singers (1971–1974)
The Harold Battiste Orchestra (1976–1977)
THEME:
"The Beat Goes On," by Sonny Bono

After almost a decade performing in clubs and auditoriums, Sonny and Cher were given their own summer variety series on CBS. The interplay between the two stars—Sonny's ebullient enthusiasm and Cher's sardonic wit and continual putdowns of her husband—was one of the strong points of the program. The summer show did well and returned that December to become a hit regular series. During its initial run, *The Sonny and Cher Comedy Hour* utilized several recurring comedy sketches. There was a "Vamp" segment in which Cher would portray several of the more notorious women throughout history; a "Sonny's Pizza" segment featuring Sonny as the dumb owner of a pizzeria and Cher as his sexy, beautiful waitress Rosa; the "Dirty Linen" segment with housewife Laverne (Cher) giving her views on men to her friend Olivia (Teri Garr) at the laundromat; and a segment in which news headlines, both current and past, were treated in blackouts. Frequently seen were full-scale operettas based on legitimate operas, television commercials, types of TV programs, and almost anything else that could be spoofed.

All was going well, the ratings were good, the couple seemed to be the picture of happiness (they had even made their daughter a semiregular at the show's close when they would sing their record hit "I've Got You Babe"). Unfortunately, reality and appearances were two different things. The Bonos were having marital problems, and it was announced in the spring of 1974 that they were getting divorced and would give up the series. They went their separate ways. Sonny failed with *The Sonny Comedy Revue,* his own show on ABC that fall, and Cher had only middling success with *Cher,* her solo effort that began on CBS the following January. With her solo venture limping along after less than a year on the air, a professional reconciliation was arranged with Sonny so that they might work together again. Cher had since married rock singer Greg Allman and given birth to a son. The new venture was titled *The Sonny and Cher Show,* but it could never regain the magic of the original. Cher's putdowns of Sonny, which seemed funny when they were married, just didn't work as well after they were divorced. The new series limped along for two seasons and was canceled in the summer of 1977.

SONNY COMEDY REVUE, THE
Comedy Variety
FIRST TELECAST: *September 22, 1974*
LAST TELECAST: *December 29, 1974*
BROADCAST HISTORY:
Sep 1974–Dec 1974, ABC Sun 8:00–9:00
REGULARS:
Sonny Bono
Ted Zeigler
Billy Van
Peter Cullen
Freeman King
Murray Langston
Teri Garr
Lex De Azevedo Orchestra

After Sonny and Cher broke up their successful act, and marriage, in 1974, each of them tried continuing on their own. Sonny's effort was this short-lived comedy variety show in which he was supposed to play the Chaplinesque "little man," always beset by troubles, and always the underdog. A repertory company of young comedians appeared with him in sketches, as did assorted guests.

SONNY KENDIS SHOW, THE
Music
FIRST TELECAST: *April 18, 1949*
LAST TELECAST: *January 6, 1950*
BROADCAST HISTORY:
Apr 1949–May 1949, CBS Mon/Wed 7:15–7:30
May 1949–Sep 1949, CBS Tue/Thu 7:45–7:55
Sep 1949–Jan 1950, CBS Mon/Tue/Thu/Fri 7:45–7:55
REGULARS:
Sonny Kendis
Gigi Durston

Pianist Sonny Kendis starred in this twice-to-four-times-per-week live musical series. His featured vocalist was Gigi Durston. Sonny was reputed to have such fast hands that they appeared to be a blur on the television screen when he played the piano rapidly.

SONNY SPOON
Detective Drama
FIRST TELECAST: *February 12, 1988*
LAST TELECAST:
BROADCAST HISTORY:
Feb 1988–Mar 1988, NBC Fri 10:00–11:00
May 1988– , Fri 9:00–10:00
CAST:
Sonny Spoon .... Mario Van Peebles
Asst. D.A. Carolyn Gilder .... Terry Donahoe
Lucius DeLuce.................... Joe Shea
Monique .... Jordana Capra
Johnny Skates .... Bob Wieland

"He's a scam, he's a sham, he's a flim-flam man," said the ad, which was bad, for this hip black lad. Sonny Spoon was certainly street-hip (though he didn't always rhyme), a smooth operator who had put his talents to work as a private eye. His office was a phone booth, and his friends and information sources mostly street people—Lucius the rotund newsstand operator, Monique the helpful hooker, and Skates, a legless man who zipped through crowds on a skateboard. When he needed a little heavy artillery Sonny turned to Carolyn, a rising star in the D.A.'s office who was skeptical about his scams, but liked the results he got. He was particularly good at disguises, and might turn up, in the course of an episode, as anything from a bewildered Arab tourist, to a clergyman, to an old, fat woman. They all fit in with his bizarre cases, which were peopled with characters like Lame Larry, Insane Wayne, Tonsillitis (a blues singer), and an adorable little waif called Marilyn Monroe. Audiences could hardly keep up.

Hey, Sonny, keep shuckin' and jivin' . . . or else your ratings may start divin'.

SONS AND DAUGHTERS
Drama
FIRST TELECAST: *September 11, 1974*

728

LAST TELECAST: *November 6, 1974*
BROADCAST HISTORY:
Sep 1974–Nov 1974, CBS Wed 8:00–9:00
CAST:
Jeff Reed .... Gary Frank
Anita Cramer .... Glynnis O'Connor
Lucille Reed .... Jay W. Macintosh
Walter Cramer .... John S. Ragin
Ruth Cramer .... Jan Shutan
Danny Reed .... Michael Morgan
Stash Melnyck .... Scott Colomby
Murray "Moose" Kerner ... Barry Livingston
Mary Anne .... Laura Siegel
Charlie Riddel .... Lionel Johnston
Evie Martinson .... Debralee Scott
Cody .... Christopher Nelson

In almost soap-opera fashion, *Sons and Daughters* attempted to portray what it was like to be teenagers in love in the mid-1950s. The two in love were Jeff and Anita, 16-year-old sweethearts and students at southwest High School in Stockton, California. Jeff's dad had recently passed away and Anita's mother had just left her husband and moved in with another man. Their adjustments to the sudden changes in their home lives and the good and bad times they had with each other, with their friends, and with their families were told in the series. The peripheral relationships and involvements of the other cast members, despite the central focus on Jeff and Anita, gave *Sons and Daughters* an almost *Peyton Place* quality.

SOUND OFF TIME
see *Chesterfield Sound Off Time*

SOUPY SALES
Children's
FIRST TELECAST: *July 4, 1955*
LAST TELECAST: *April 13, 1962*
BROADCAST HISTORY:
Jul 1955–Aug 1955, ABC Mon–Fri 7:00–7:15
Jan 1962–Apr 1962, ABC Fri 7:30–8:00
HOST:
Soupy Sales
ASSISTANT:
Clyde Adler

Soupy Sales, the world's leading authority on pie-throwing, seen in a number of local and network series over the years, including two which ran in nighttime hours. His comedy featured outrageous puns, slapstick sketches, and a regular cast of puppet characters including White Fang, the giant dog (only his paw was seen); Black Tooth, the kindest dog in the U.S.; Marilyn Monwolf, a curvaceous friend of White Fang and Black Tooth; Herman the Flea; Willie the Worm; Pookie the Lion; and Hippy the Hippo.

Beginning with a local show, *Soupy's On,* in Detroit in 1953, he then had a 1955 summer series on the ABC network that originated live from that city. From 1959 to 1961 he was seen on the ABC

network on Saturday afternoons in *Lunch with Soupy Sales,* and then in early 1962, Friday at 7:30 P.M., live from Hollywood. Soupy then moved to New York and held forth with a local show that premiered in 1964 and went into syndication the following year. By the late 1970s he was back on the West Coast, where a new syndicated series was produced in 1978–1979.

Remarkably, despite the more than 25-year span of his TV career, the late 1970s versions of *The Soupy Sales Show*—and Soupy himself—looked only slightly different from the original local version in Detroit in 1953.

SOUTHERNAIRES QUARTET
Music
FIRST TELECAST: *September 19, 1948*
LAST TELECAST: *November 21, 1948*
BROADCAST HISTORY:
Sep 1948–Oct 1948, ABC Sun 9:00–9:30
Oct 1948–Nov 1948, ABC Sun 7:30–8:00
REGULARS:
The Southernaires

The Southernaires were a black gospel quartet who had been heard on radio throughout the 1940s. Members of the quartet were Roy Yeates, Lowell Peters, Jay Stone Toney, and William Edmunson, with accompaniment by pianist-arranger Clarence Jones. Their prime-time musical program in the fall of 1948 was one of the earliest network series starring black performers.

SPACE
Drama
FIRST TELECAST: *July 4, 1987*
LAST TELECAST: *July 25, 1987*
BROADCAST HISTORY:
Jul 1987, CBS Sat 8:00–10:00
CAST:
Norman Grant .... James Garner
Elinor Grant .... Susan Anspach
Penny Hardesty Pope .... Blair Brown
Stanley Mott .... Bruce Dern
Rachel Mott .... Melinda Dillon
Leopold Strabismus (née Martin Scorcella)
.... David Dukes
Dieter Kolff .... Michael York
Liesl Kolff .... Barbara Sukowa
Randy Claggett .... Beau Bridges
Debbie Dee Claggett ...... Stephanie Faracy
John Pope .... Harry Hamlin
Senator Glancey .... Martin Balsam
Finnerty .... James Sutorius
Tucker Thomas .... G.D. Spradlin
Cindy Rhee .... Maggie Han
Funkhauser .... Wolf Kahler
Marcia Grant .... Jennifer Runyon
Skip Morgan .... David Spielberg

Originally aired as a five-part, 13-hour mini-series in April 1985, a re-edited 9-hour version of James A. Michener's *Space* was rerun on CBS during the summer of 1987.

This novelization of the evolution of the American space program began at the end of World War II, when the U.S. and Russians both sought to obtain the best German rocket scientists, and continued through the exploration of the moon in the early 1970s.

The central focus of *Space* was World War II naval hero Norman Grant who, after becoming a senator, used the space program as a platform to build a long-term power base. Norman's wife, Elinor, who never liked politics, became an alcoholic and got herself involved with con man Leopold Strabismus, who took advantage of the public's fascination with outer space, U.F.O.s, and extraterrestrials. Penny Pope was an ambitious lawyer working for the Senate Space Committee, chaired by Grant, with whom she had an affair. Her husband, John, and his buddy Randy Claggett, were fighter pilots in Korea, test pilots, and later astronauts. Most important to the success of the space program were the German rocket scientists, led by Dieter Kolff, who had been brought to the U.S. after the war. The man responsible for liberating the Germans, Georgia Tech astrophysicist Stanley Mott, continued to work with them over the years, despite the inherent problems dealing with both the federal bureaucracy and the rivalries among the different military services. It was their perseverance, along with the changing political climate, that eventually led to the creation of NASA under the Eisenhower administration and the highly successful space program of the 1960s. In the climactic episode of *Space,* astronauts Pope and Claggett were teamed on the successful voyage to the dark side of the moon.

SPACE CADET
see *Tom Corbett—Space Cadet*

SPACE: 1999
Science Fiction
BROADCAST HISTORY:
Syndicated only
60 minutes
Produced: *1974–1976* (48 episodes)
Released: *September 1975*
CAST:
Commander John Koenig ..... Martin Landau
Dr. Helena Russell .... Barbara Bain
Prof. Victor Bergman (1975–1976)
.... Barry Morse
Maya (1976–1977) .... Catherine Schell
First Officer Tony Verdeschi (1976–1977)
.... Tony Anholt
Capt. Alan Carter .... Nick Tate
Paul Morrow .... Prentis Hancock
David .... Clifton Jones
Sandra .... Zienia Merton

Moonbase Alpha was a research colony on the surface of the moon. When John Koenig was appointed base commander in September 1999, his orders were to oversee the launch of a deep-space probe. Unfortunately, due to the accidental detonation of nuclear wastes stored on the moon, there was a gigantic explosion and Koenig found himself launched into space, along with his 310 base colleagues. Their spaceship was the moon itself, blasted free from the Earth's gravitational force and hurtling toward distant galaxies.

En route they encountered all the alien life forms and intergalactic dangers familiar to sci-fi fans. Among them: a gigantic, people-swallowing squid; a blob of living foam; a man-turned-machine named Gwent; the sexy robots of the planet Piri; and the fearsome and mysterious Arra (played by Margaret Leighton), queen of the huge planet Astheria. There was plenty of futuristic hardware, including laser beams, giant spaceships, "Queller Drive" engines, "Camelot Locator" beams, and an omnipotent talking computer—which, in moments of crisis, was prone to bark lines like "Not enough data to formulate parameters. Human decision required."

Besides the stolid Koenig, the cast included stylish Dr. Helena Russell, chief medical officer of the base; Prof. Bergman, who had established the base and was Koenig's mentor; and Capt. Carter, the chief astronaut, responsible for reconnaissance missions. Bergman was written out of the show after the first season, as having died. Joining the cast for the second season were First Officer Tony Verdeschi, irreverent and sharp-tongued second in command, and his love interest Maya, a sensual alien from the planet Psychon. She had the unusual ability to transform herself into other forms for short periods, such as a gorilla, a lioness, or even an orange tree, by "rearranging molecules."

All this hokum arrived on TV screens in 1975 amid a huge splash of publicity, brought on by the fact that this was the most expensively produced show of its kind in the history of television (around $300,000 per episode). There were spectacular special effects by England's Brian Johnson. The large cast was headed by husband-and-wife stars Landau and Bain, making a triumphal return to television after their success in *Mission: Impossible.* Even the futuristic, unisex jumpsuits they all wore were by the famous designer Rudi Gernreich. The program was set to run in more than 100 countries around the world. Nevertheless, all three U.S. networks had turned it down. So the English producers took it directly to individual stations, via syndication, and got it scheduled in practically every city in the country. Many stations preempted network programs to put it on, and there was much gloating in the press about how the all-powerful networks were about to get their comeuppance.

It didn't work out that way, however. After heavy curiosity viewing, audiences realized that *Space: 1999* had the same problem as most space epics: all hardware and no character development. The lovely Miss Bain, for one, walked through her role like a zombie. There were efforts made to remedy this in the second season, as Koenig and Russell developed a more explicit love life, as did Carter and his elusive love Maya, but by then it was too late. *Space: 1999* never became the hit its makers anticipated, and production was stopped after 48 expensive episodes.

SPACE PATROL
Children's
FIRST TELECAST: *June 9, 1951*
LAST TELECAST: *June 1, 1952*
BROADCAST HISTORY:
    Jun 1951–Sep 1951, ABC Sat 6:00–6:30
    Dec 1951–Jun 1952, ABC Sun 6:00–6:30
CAST:
    Commander Buzz Corey . . . . Ed Kemmer
    Cadet Happy . . . . Lyn Osborn
    Carol Karlyle . . . . Virginia Hewitt
    Tonga . . . . Nina Bara
    Major Robbie Robertson . . . . Ken Mayer
    Secretary General of the United Planets
        . . . . Norman Jolley
    Mr. Proteus . . . . Marvin Miller
    Prince Baccarratti, alias the Black Falcon
        . . . . Bella Kovacs
CREATED BY:
    Mike Moser

Space Patrol began in early 1950 as a local program on the West Coast, and was seen until 1955. During most of its run it was an ABC network Saturday or Sunday daytime series. However, during the two periods shown above it was run at 6:00 P.M., and thus qualifies as a "nighttime" series.

Set in the 30th century A.D., *Space Patrol* made much use of time travel, depositing its heroes in various historical periods. Commander of the Space Patrol was Buzz Corey (played by real-life World War II flying hero Ed Kemmer), who battled assorted villains in the name of the United Planets of the Universe. His youthful sidekick, Cadet Happy, was always ready with a colorful rejoinder ("Smokin' rockets, Commander!") or a simplistic question to allow Buzz to explain some obvious truth to home viewers. Other leading characters were Carol, pretty daughter of the Secretary General of the United Planets, who had romantic designs on Buzz; Tonga, a beautiful villainess-turned-heroine; and frequent villains Mr. Proteus (played by Marvin Miller, later of *The Millionaire* fame), and Prince Baccarratti.

No one ever got killed on *Space Patrol*. The worst fate was to be rendered inanimate by Buzz's Paralyzer Ray Gun, and then shown the path of truth and justice by the Brainograph. Replicas of these and other devices were available to viewers as premiums. In what was perhaps the most spectacular of all the space-opera promotions, in 1954 a 30-foot model of Buzz's spaceship, the *Terra*, toured the U.S. (on the ground) and then was given away to a lucky viewer.

SPARRING PARTNERS WITH WALTER KIERNAN
Quiz
FIRST TELECAST: *April 8, 1949*
LAST TELECAST: *May 6, 1949*
BROADCAST HISTORY:
    Apr 1949–May 1949, ABC Fri 9:30–10:00
EMCEE:
    Walter Kiernan

This short-lived quiz show pitted a team of men against a team of women in a game using puppets in a miniature boxing ring.

SPEAK UP, AMERICA
Human Interest/Audience Participation
FIRST TELECAST: *August 1, 1980*
LAST TELECAST: *October 10, 1980*
BROADCAST HISTORY:
    Aug 1980–Oct 1980, NBC Fri 10:00–11:00
REGULARS:
    Marjoe Gortner
    Jayne Kennedy
    Rhonda Bates
    Sergio Aragones

This was one series in which the audience really got involved—in fact, the audience was the whole show. Each week audience reaction to a number of subjects and issues was solicited by the show's hosts, Marjoe Gortner (a hyperkinetic former evangelist), Jayne Kennedy, and Rhonda Bates (the tall, skinny one). Some of those asked for opinions were in the live studio audience and others appeared in segments filmed on location. Satirical cartoonist Sergio Aragones sketched appropriate scenes, depending on subject matter, after the segments. Although people with vested interests in specific issues were sometimes asked their opinions, for the most part *Speak Up, America* sought the attitudes of "ordinary, average Americans." Topics discussed included the 1980 Democratic and Republican conventions, the Equal Rights Amendment, whales facing extinction, the J.F.K. assassination, sex among the elderly in nursing homes, the actors' boycott of the Emmy Awards show, an all-nudist apartment house, the problems of the American automobile industry, and TV reruns.

On April 22 and 29, 1980, several months before this series premiered, NBC aired two *Speak Up, America* specials. Only Marjoe Gortner appeared on both the specials and the series. The other hosts on the specials were KNBC newswoman Felicia Jeter and U.S. Olympic hockey coach Herb Brooks.

SPEAKING OF EVERYTHING
Interview/Discussion
BROADCAST HISTORY:
    Syndicated only
    60 minutes

Produced: *1988–*
Released: *January 1988*
HOST:
Howard Cosell

After a television career that had been centered almost completely on sports—as a reporter, football analyst, boxing commentator, and interviewer—Howard Cosell came out of broadcast retirement to host this series in which he chatted with personalities from, as its title would suggest, all walks of life. The literate, controversial, and outspoken Cosell, referred to by his detractors as "the mouth that roared," could be friendly or contentious, depending on his mood and his guests. Among them were columnist Liz Smith, his former boss at ABC Roone Arledge, General William Westmoreland, ABC White House correspondent Sam Donaldson, and comedian Billy Crystal.

SPEIDEL SHOW, THE
see *Paul Winchell—Jerry Mahoney Show*

SPENCER
Situation Comedy
FIRST TELECAST: *December 1, 1984*
LAST TELECAST: *July 5, 1985*
BROADCAST HISTORY:
Dec 1984–Jan 1985, NBC Sat 9:30–10:00
Mar 1985–May 1985, NBC Sat 9:30–10:00
Jun 1985–Jul 1985, NBC Fri 8:30–9:00
CAST:
Spencer Winger .... Chad Lowe
Spencer Winger (1985) .... Ross Harris
Doris Winger................ Mimi Kennedy
George Winger .... Ronny Cox
Andrea Winger .... Amy Locane
Ben Sprague (1985) .... Harold Gould
Millie Sprague (1985) ... Frances Sternhagen
Benjamin Beanley .... Richard Sanders
Miss Spier .... Beverly Archer
Wayne....................... Grant Heslov
Herbie Bailey .... Dean Cameron

Spencer was a teenager coping with the pains of adolescence. At 16, he was a bit eccentric, tended to become involved with causes, and incidentally was having trouble finding the right girl. His chief nemesis was Mr. Beanley, the high school guidance counselor, who just didn't understand that Spencer was making a moral statement when he set free the laboratory mice to prevent them from being dissected. Spencer's parents, George and Doris, were understanding, but bewildered. Andrea was his rather mature younger sister, and Wayne and Herbie were two buddies.

When star Chad Lowe abruptly quit the show in a salary dispute after only a few episodes NBC decided to recast the role, alter the format, and change the title to *Under One Roof.* In this new version George had run off with a 23-year-old girl, leaving Doris to raise the kids alone. Doris' parents, Ben and Millie, moved in to help, taking

Spencer's bedroom and forcing him to sleep in a room in the attic (more problems!). Mr. Beanley had become the school principal, and Miss Spier, who had been an English teacher in *Spencer,* now taught Spanish.

The reworked series was short-lived. To further confuse matters, reruns of the original *Spencer* aired in June and July.

SPENCER'S PILOTS
Adventure
FIRST TELECAST: *September 17, 1976*
LAST TELECAST: *November 19, 1976*
BROADCAST HISTORY:
Sep 1976–Nov 1976, CBS Fri 8:00–9:00
CAST:
Cass Garrett .... Christopher Stone
Stan Lewis .... Todd Susman
Spencer Parish .... Gene Evans
Linda Dann .... Margaret Impert
Mickey Wiggins .... Britt Leach

Spencer Aviation was a small charter airline service located in Southern California that would do everything from crop-dusting to transporting convicted criminals from one location to another for the police. Spencer Parish was the owner, Cass and Stan his two pilots, Linda the office manager, and Mickey the company's mechanic. This series never got off the ground, and was canceled after only two months on the air.

SPENSER: FOR HIRE
Detective
FIRST TELECAST: *September 20, 1985*
LAST TELECAST:
BROADCAST HISTORY:
Sep 1985–Oct 1985, ABC Fri 10:00–11:00
Oct 1985–Sep 1986, ABC Tue 10:00–11:00
Sep 1986–May 1987, ABC Sat 10:00–11:00
Jun 1987–Sep 1987, ABC Tue 10:00–11:00
Sep 1987–Jan 1988, ABC Sun 8:00–9:00
Jan 1988–Jun 1988, ABC Sat 10:00–11:00
Jun 1988–   , ABC Wed 10:00–11:00
CAST:
Spenser .... Robert Urich
Hawk .... Avery Brooks
Susan Silverman (1985–1986, 1987–   )
.... Barbara Stock
Lt. Martin Quirk (1985–1987)
.... Richard Jaeckel
Sgt. Frank Belson .... Ron McLarty
Asst. D.A. Rita Fiori (1986–1987)
.... Carolyn McCormick

Robert B. Parker's literate Boston detective was brought to television in this carefully crated series. Spenser was not only well-read, he was a gourmet cook, an ex-boxer, and a former Boston policeman. Operating out of a converted firehouse (which the City of Boston took back at the start of the second season), he drove around town in a vintage Mustang solving crimes and protecting those who wanted a little class with their private detecting. His chief street contact and sometime backup was even more eccentric—a tall, menacing, yet intelligent black man who operated on both sides of the law. Hawk was a free-lance enforcer who would slowly call from the shadows, "Spen-sah!," in a way that made you wonder whose side he was on, just before he blew somebody away with his oversized Magnum pistol.

Lt. Quirk was Spenser's hard-nosed buddy on the Boston Police Dept., and Belson his slovenly, wisecracking subordinate. When Quirk was forced to retire after suffering a heart attack, Belson became Spenser's chief contact on the force. Spenser's girlfriend, Susan (he had asked her to marry him but she was afraid to marry a man who was always getting shot at), was a school guidance counselor; she left for San Francisco in the second season, to "think things over," but returned in the third. While she was gone Spenser's chief female foil was Asst. D.A. Rita, with whom he was often at odds. To give the series a more "literary" feel, Spenser himself functioned as narrator, as well as dispensing pretentious quotes from the classics in each episode.

Novelist Robert B. Parker served as a consultant and occasional writer for the series, but harbored no illusions about its fidelity to his original. In an interesting June 1987 *TV Guide* article he reflected on the differences between the Spenser of his books and that of the TV show, concluding that comparisons between the two media were pointless. "The business of television is to put on good television, not to replicate my books," he observed. "A thing is, after all, what it is, and not something else."

Filmed on location in Boston.

SPIES

Espionage/Foreign Intrigue
FIRST TELECAST: *March 3, 1987*
LAST TELECAST: *April 14, 1987*
BROADCAST HISTORY:
  Mar 1987–Apr 1987, CBS Tue 8:00–9:00
CAST:
  Ian Stone .... George Hamilton
  Ben Smythe .... Gary Kroeger
  Thomas Brady .... Barry Corbin

Ian Stone had once been the most renowned spy in the world, and he was still irresistably suave, debonair, and handsome. But the years had taken their toll. Ian had degenerated to being little more than a lazy, cynical womanizer. Thomas Brady, Ian's boss at the agency—referred to by his men as "C. of B." (Chairman of the Board)—would have fired him were it not for the intervention of Ben Smythe, an idealistic young agent to whom Ian's past exploits were legendary. Smythe became Ian's partner, more to keep him out of trouble than to help him on their assignments. Ian tried to get the uptight younger man to loosen up a little, and took great pleasure in managing to get

away from Smythe for liaisons with assorted beautiful women. George Hamilton was perfectly cast for his role in this tongue-in-cheek espionage series, deftly caricaturing his real-life public image.

SPIKE JONES SHOW, THE

Comedy Variety
FIRST TELECAST: *January 2, 1954*
LAST TELECAST: *September 25, 1961*
BROADCAST HISTORY:
  Jan 1954–May 1954, NBC Sat 8:00–8:30
  Apr 1957–Aug 1957, CBS Tue 10:30–11:00
  Aug 1960–Sep 1960, CBS Mon 9:30–10:00
  Jul 1961–Sep 1961, CBS Mon 9:00–9:30
REGULARS:
  Spike Jones
  Helen Grayco
  Billy Barty (1954, 1957)
  Bill Dana (1960)
  Joyce Jameson (1960)
  Len Weinrib (1960)

Spike Jones and his singer wife, Helen Grayco, along with Spike's City Slicker Band, starred in this weekly fill-in series that appeared in four different seasons. Cowbells, foghorns, slide whistles, and other paraphernalia were the featured instruments in Spike's band, as virtually every type of music was reduced to mayhem. Spike, in his striped suit, presided over the merry band of musical lunatics. The nature of their work could probably best be described by one of their album titles—*Dinner Music for People Who Aren't Very Hungry*. The series included, along with the outrageous musical numbers, straight singing by Helen Grayco, appearances by guest stars, and comedy sketches. During the summer of 1960 there was a regular group of supporting comedians, the most famous being Bill Dana in his role as Jose Jimenez. Dana also produced the show. The members of the band all participated in the comedy skits and in general contributed to the frenetic nuttiness of the show.

SPIN THE PICTURE

Quiz/Audience Participation
FIRST TELECAST: *June 18, 1949*
LAST TELECAST: *February 4, 1950*
BROADCAST HISTORY:
  Jun 1949–Jan 1950, DUM Sat 8:00–9:00
  Jan 1950–Feb 1950, DUM Sat 8:00–8:30
EMCEE:
  Carl Caruso (1949)
  Eddie Dunn (1949)
  Kathi Norris
REGULARS:
  Gordon Dilworth
  Shaye Cogan
  Bob Dunn
  Jerry Shad's Quartet
  Alan Scott Trio

This was one early quiz show that gave away fairly large prizes. The first jackpot winner, who identified a "spinning picture" of composer Richard Rodgers, took home a cool $7,635. The bulk of the hour-long show consisted of dramatic sketches, songs, and other entertainment, with each act providing a clue to the name of a famous person, event, movie, etc. After each segment the host would call a viewer and ask if they could identify the name (viewers were asked to send in their phone numbers on postcards, and more than 25,000 did during the first weeks alone). The jackpot round presented a quickly flashed picture of a mystery celebrity, along with verbal clues to his identity.

SPORTS CAMERA
Sports Anthology
FIRST TELECAST: *September 12, 1950*
LAST TELECAST: *May 24, 1952*
BROADCAST HISTORY:
  Sep 1950, ABC Tue 9:30–10:00
  Sep 1951, ABC Thu 10:45–11:00
  Dec 1951–May 1952, ABC Sat 8:30–9:00
  May 1952, ABC Sat 10:30–11:00

A collection of filmed short subjects on various sports and sports personalities. Known from December 1951 to March 1952 as *Sports on Parade*.

SPORTS FOCUS
Sports News/Commentary
FIRST TELECAST: *June 3, 1957*
LAST TELECAST: *September 12, 1958*
BROADCAST HISTORY:
  Jun 1957–Jul 1957, ABC Mon–Fri 7:00–7:15
  Sep 1957–Sep 1958, ABC Mon–Fri 7:00–7:15
REPORTER:
  Howard Cosell

Broadcast live from New York, this was Howard Cosell's first foray into the world of network television sports. Each night he summed up the day's news in the sports world, provided personal commentary on any currently controversial issues, and conducted interviews with sports personalities.

SPORTS FOR ALL
see *Fishing and Hunting Club*

SPORTS NEWSREEL
see *Gillette Summer Sports Reel*

SPORTS ON PARADE
see *Sports Camera*

SPORTS SPOT
Sports Commentary
FIRST TELECAST: *June 13, 1951*
LAST TELECAST: *November 24, 1954*
BROADCAST HISTORY:
  Jun 1951–Nov 1954, CBS Wed 10:45–11:00

HOST:
  Jim McKay (1951)
  Mel Allen (1951–1954)

This short live-sports program filled the time between the end of *Pabst Blue Ribbon Bouts* and the start of the local 11:00 P.M. news. It was primarily an interview show in which a sports celebrity chatted with the host about his career or sports in general. Jim McKay was the original host, and was succeeded by Mel Allen in October 1951.

SPORTS WITH JOE HASEL
Sports News
FIRST TELECAST: *August 21, 1948*
LAST TELECAST: *April 26, 1949*
BROADCAST HISTORY:
  Aug 1948–Jan 1949, ABC Sat 7:30–7:45
  Jan 1949–Mar 1949, ABC Fri 9:30–9:45
  Mar 1949–Apr 1949, ABC Tue 7:15–7:30
COMMENTATOR:
  Joe Hasel

Weekly summary of the news from the world of sports—scores, commentary, and interviews with celebrities from various games.

SPORTSMAN'S QUIZ
Sports Information
FIRST TELECAST: *April 26, 1948*
LAST TELECAST: *April 25, 1949*
BROADCAST HISTORY:
  Apr 1948–Aug 1948, CBS Mon 8:00–8:05
  Aug 1948–Dec 1948, CBS Fri 8:00–8:05
  Dec 1948–Jan 1949, CBS Fri 8:30–8:35
  Jan 1949–Apr 1949, CBS Mon 7:10–7:15
REGULARS:
  Don Baker
  Bernard Dudley

With the cooperation and assistance of the staff of *Sports Afield* magazine, the program's sponsor, this short weekly series posed questions about hunting, fishing, conservation, and wildlife, and then answered them with drawings, pictures, diagrams, or other visual aids. Bernard Dudley asked the questions and Don Baker provided the answers. Viewers were invited to send in questions of their own.

SPORTSREEL
see *Gillette Summer Sports Reel*

SPORTSWOMAN OF THE WEEK
Interview
FIRST TELECAST: *September 9, 1948*
LAST TELECAST: *December 2, 1948*
BROADCAST HISTORY:
  Sep 1948–Dec 1948, NBC Thu 7:45–7:50
HOSTESS:
  Sarah Palfrey Cooke

This brief program was originally a documentary about a different notable woman each week, but soon changed to a straight interview show with tennis champion Sarah Cooke playing host to an outstanding woman guest from the world of sports. It was at first called *Girl of the Week*.

SPOTLIGHT
Comedy Variety
FIRST TELECAST: *July 4, 1967*
LAST TELECAST: *August 29, 1967*
BROADCAST HISTORY:
  Jul 1967–Aug 1967, CBS Tue 8:30–9:30
REGULARS:
  The Mike Sammes Singers
  The Lionel Blair Dancers
  Jack Parnell and His Orchestra

Produced in London, this 1967 summer replacement for *The Red Skelton Show* each week featured a different cast of stars in a variety format. At least one of the stars was a singer and at least one of them was a comic. The emphasis shifted depending on the talents of the performers, from music to comedy, with the majority of the shows highlighting the latter. Although the supporting acts were from all over the world, most of the stars were from America, especially the comics. Phil Silvers, Shelley Berman, Jack Carter, Frank Gorshin, and Bill Dana were among them. The singers included Barbara McNair, Paul Anka, Trini Lopez, Vikki Carr, Robert Goulet, Lainie Kazan, and then husband and wife Eddie Fisher and Connie Stevens. Welsh singer Tom Jones appeared as one of the stars, sharing that function with American Fran Jeffries, and eventually got a series of his own, *This Is Tom Jones*, on ABC.

SPOTLIGHT ON SPORTS
Sports
FIRST TELECAST: *July 8, 1950*
LAST TELECAST: *September 3, 1950*
BROADCAST HISTORY:
  Jul 1950, NBC Sat 7:30–8:00
  Aug 1950–Sep 1950, NBC Sun 8:30–9:00
HOST:
  Bill Stern

An interview and discussion program with various celebrities from the sports world. Bill Stern, NBC Sports Director, appeared on many telecasts on the network, including pre- and postgame shows and regular nightly reports, from 1949 through the 1950s. See the performer index for his other series.

SPOTLIGHT PLAYHOUSE
Dramatic Anthology
FIRST TELECAST: *June 21, 1955*
LAST TELECAST: *September 22, 1959*
BROADCAST HISTORY:
  Jun 1955–Sep 1959, CBS Tue 9:30–10:00 (Summer Only)

HOST:
  Anita Louise (1958)
  Julia Meade (1959)
  Zachary Scott (1959)

For five summers *Spotlight Playhouse* filled in for the vacationing Red Skelton. All of the episodes telecast in the series were filmed reruns from other anthology series. During the first two seasons most of the plays came from *Schlitz Playhouse of Stars*. When reruns from *The Loretta Young Show* were used in 1958, Anita Louise was on hand to host the series. The following summer, with episodes coming from *G.E. Theater*, *Schlitz Playhouse*, and *The Jane Wyman Show*, Julia Meade and Zachary Scott served as hosts on alternate weeks.

SQUARE PEGS
Situation Comedy
FIRST TELECAST: *September 27, 1982*
LAST TELECAST: *September 12, 1983*
BROADCAST HISTORY:
  Sep 1982–Mar 1983, CBS Mon 8:00–8:30
  Apr 1983–May 1983, CBS Wed 8:30–9:00
  May 1983–Sep 1983, CBS Mon 8:00–8:30
CAST:
  Patty Greene .... Sarah Jessica Parker
  Lauren Hutchinson .... Amy Linker
  Johnny Slash .... Merritt Butrick
  Marshall Blechtman .... John Femia
  Jennifer DeNuccio .... Tracy Nelson
  Muffy Tepperman .... Jami Gertz
  LaDonna Fredericks .... Claudette Wells
  Vinnie Pasetta .... Jon Caliri
  Principal Dingleman .... Basil Hoffman
  Mr. Donovan .... Steven Peterman
  Ms. Loomis .... Catlin Adams
THEME:
  "Square Pegs," written and performed by the Waitresses

The trials of high school life were the focus of this youthful comedy. Patty and Lauren were best friends who were new freshmen at Weemawee High School. They desperately wanted to be popular and to get into the right social clique, but were not quite cool enough to do it. Patty was skinny and wore glasses, and Lauren, horror of horrors, still had braces on her teeth. Marshall, the resident class clown, was one of their best friends, and even had a bit of a crush on Lauren. Johnny, the New Wave music freak, was Marshall's best friend and also spent much of his spare time with the girls. Then there were the people they could never get close to—wealthy Jennifer, whose life revolved around clothes and guys; Muffy, the preppie head cheerleader; LaDonna, the bigoted black sophisticate; and Vinnie, Weemawee's answer to John Travolta, a self-centered obnoxious hunk who knew he was God's gift to women.

STACCATO

see *Johnny Staccato*

STAGE A NUMBER

Talent
FIRST TELECAST: *September 17, 1952*
LAST TELECAST: *May 20, 1953*
BROADCAST HISTORY:
  Sep 1952–Apr 1953, DUM Wed 9:00–10:00
  Apr 1953–May 1953, DUM Wed 8:30–9:00
EMCEE:
  Bill Wendell

This was one of many low-budget talent shows on TV during the early years. The acts presented were young professionals, or aspiring professionals, who were introduced by a "sponsor" and then "staged their number" before a panel of show-business judges (producers, actors, etc.). Backdrops were simple, and accompaniment was usually just a piano or organ. The acts tended to be theatrical, such as dramatic acting or ballet, with several appearances by the Nina Youshkevitch Ballet Workshop, among others.

STAGE DOOR, THE

Drama
FIRST TELECAST: *February 7, 1950*
LAST TELECAST: *March 28, 1950*
BROADCAST HISTORY:
  Feb 1950–Mar 1950, CBS Tue 9:00–9:30
CAST:
  Celia Knox .... Louise Allbritton
  Hank Merlin .... Scott McKay
  Rocco .... Tom Pedi

Life in and around the Broadway theater, as seen through the eyes of two young and aspiring performers, was the subject of this live dramatic series. It was based on the play *Stage Door* by Edna Ferber and George S. Kaufman. In addition to being struggling young performers, Celia and Hank, the two principals, were also madly in love with each other. The problems they had, both on- and offstage, were portrayed each week.

STAGE ENTRANCE

Interview
FIRST TELECAST: *May 2, 1951*
LAST TELECAST: *March 9, 1952*
BROADCAST HISTORY:
  May 1951–Aug 1951, DUM Wed 7:45–8:00
  Sep 1951–Dec 1951, DUM Mon 8:00–8:30
  Dec 1951–Mar 1952, DUM Sun 7:00–7:30
HOST:
  Earl Wilson

Broadway columnist Earl Wilson ("The Midnight Earl") interviewed established stars and young hopefuls, and gave news of show business in this 1951–1952 TV version of his *New York Post* newspaper column.

STAGE 7

Dramatic Anthology
FIRST TELECAST: *December 12, 1954*
LAST TELECAST: *September 25, 1955*
BROADCAST HISTORY:
  Dec 1954–Sep 1955, CBS Sun 9:30–10:00

This filmed anthology series featured Hollywood stars and a varied format that ranged from comedy, to Westerns, to melodrama. When it premiered in December 1954, its title was *Your Favorite Playhouse* and it was composed of reruns from other anthologies. Effective with the play that aired on January 30, 1955, the title changed to *Stage 7* and the plays were new ones created for this series. The best-known leading players that appeared were Frank Lovejoy, Vanessa Brown, Pat O'Brien, Dennis Morgan, Regis Toomey, George Brent, Alexis Smith, and Angela Lansbury.

STAGE SHOW

Musical Variety
FIRST TELECAST: *July 3, 1954*
LAST TELECAST: *September 22, 1956*
BROADCAST HISTORY:
  Jul 1954–Sep 1954, CBS Sat 8:00–9:00
  Oct 1955–Feb 1956, CBS Sat 8:00–8:30
  Feb 1956–Sep 1956, CBS Sat 8:30–9:00
REGULARS:
  Tommy Dorsey
  Jimmy Dorsey
  The June Taylor Dancers
THEME:
  "I'm Getting Sentimental over You," by Ned Washington and George Bassman

The opening of *Stage Show* was done with the camera used as the eyes of the home viewer. It entered the theater, moved down the aisle to their seats, and then awaited the start of the show. The theme song was "I'm Getting Sentimental over You," long identified with the Dorsey brothers. Tommy and Jimmy alternated as hosts and the show featured various guest stars. At the end of the program, the camera again became the eyes of the viewer, rising from his seat, leaving the theater, and moving out into the bustle of Manhattan on a Saturday night.

Stage Show was produced under the supervision of Jackie Gleason, and was the 1954 summer replacement for Gleason's Saturday night show. It aired intermittently in the Gleason time slot as a special during the 1954–1955 season, and when the half-hour *Honeymooners* became Gleason's regular series in the fall of 1955, *Stage Show* was used to fill the remainder of the hour every week. Gleason himself did the booking for the show.

Probably the most memorable night in the entire run was January 28, 1956, when the guest was a young country-rock singer from Memphis who was just beginning to attract national attention. This was the TV debut of Elvis Presley, the first time he had been seen or heard by most Americans, and he created pandemonium. He sang "Heartbreak Hotel" on that first telecast; released as a single record, it quickly became a multimillion seller. Elvis was booked for a total of six consecutive appearances on *Stage Show*, then went on to a career that dwarfed even that of the fabulous Dorseys. Ironically, the biggest superstar in the history of rock was introduced by two greats of the big-band swing era, in one of their last professional appearances.

Both Tommy and Jimmy Dorsey passed away shortly after this series ended its run, Tommy in November 1956 and brother Jimmy in June 1957.

STAGE 13
Dramatic Anthology
FIRST TELECAST: *April 19, 1950*
LAST TELECAST: *June 28, 1950*
BROADCAST HISTORY:
Apr 1950–Jun 1950, CBS Wed 9:30–10:00

Tales of mystery and suspense were told in this live anthology series that originated from New York. The title was supposed to convey the general feeling of the show, since 13 is an unlucky number and was avoided in numbering building floors, rooms, and the stages on movie lots. It was not particularly lucky for this series, either, which did not last even 13 weeks.

STAGE TWO REVUE
Musical Variety
FIRST TELECAST: *July 30, 1950*
LAST TELECAST: *September 24, 1950*
BROADCAST HISTORY:
Jul 1950–Sep 1950, ABC Sun 8:00–8:30
REGULARS:
Georgia Lee
Buzz Adlam's Orchestra
Arlene Harris
Bob Carroll

Summer variety show, featuring Buzz Adlam's Orchestra, vocals by Georgia Lee, and guest acts.

STAGECOACH WEST
Western
FIRST TELECAST: *October 4, 1960*
LAST TELECAST: *September 26, 1961*
BROADCAST HISTORY:
Oct 1960–Sep 1961, ABC Tue 9:00–10:00
CAST:
Luke Perry .... Wayne Rogers
Simon Kane .... Robert Bray
David Kane .... Richard Eyer

There were very few Western series that paid any attention at all to the people who drove the stagecoaches back and forth from Missouri to California, in the days before the expanding railroad system made their jobs obsolete. This series focused on three. Luke Perry and Simon Kane

were a team of drivers and Simon's son, David, went along to keep them company. The passengers they carried, the people they met, and the things that happened to them en route provided the stories told in this series.

STAINED GLASS WINDOWS
Religion
FIRST TELECAST: *September 26, 1948*
LAST TELECAST: *October 16, 1949*
BROADCAST HISTORY:
Sep 1948–Nov 1948, ABC Sun 6:30–7:00
Jan 1949–Mar 1949, ABC Sun 7:15–7:45
Mar 1949–Oct 1949, ABC Sun 7:00–7:30

This early religious program included dramatizations, discussions dealing with viewers' moral problems, and films illustrating mission work around the world. The supervisor was Rev. Everett Parker of the Joint Radio-TV Commission.

STAND BY FOR CRIME
Police Drama
FIRST TELECAST: *January 11, 1949*
LAST TELECAST: *August 27, 1949*
BROADCAST HISTORY:
Jan 1949–Apr 1949, ABC Sat 9:30–10:00
May 1949–Aug 1949, ABC Sat 8:00–8:30
CAST:
Inspector Webb (Jan–Apr) ...... Boris Aplon
Lt. Anthony Kidd (May–Aug)
 .... Myron Wallace
Sgt. Kramer (May–Aug) .... George Cisar

On January 11, 1949, New York and Chicago were first linked by television and this was the first program transmitted to Eastern audiences from Chicago. Though it was popular enough in the Midwest, Eastern reviewers found it rather crudely produced, and it did not last long.

It was a crime show with a novel twist. The drama was seen up to the point of the murder, with Inspector Webb (later Lt. Kidd of the homicide squad, whose assistant was Sgt. Kramer) sifting through the clues. Before the culprit was revealed, however, the action stopped and viewers were invited to phone in their guesses as to whodunit.

For a time guest "detectives" (celebrities) also appeared to offer their guesses as to who the guilty party might be.

The young actor who played Lt. Anthony Kidd would become one of television's most recognizable figures, but not until he gave up acting to return to his first love, journalism, and changed his first name from Myron to Mike. This was Mike Wallace's first network television exposure.

STAND UP AND CHEER
see *Johnny Mann's Stand Up and Cheer*

STANLEY
Situation Comedy

737

BROADCAST HISTORY:
  Sep 1956–Mar 1957, NBC Mon 8:30–9:00
CAST:
  Stanley Peck .... Buddy Hackett
  Horace Fenton (voice only) ...... Paul Lynde
  Celia .... Carol Burnett
  Marvin .... Reedy Talton
  Mr. Phillips .... Frederic Tozere
  Jane .... Jane Connell

Stanley Peck was the outgoing proprietor of a newsstand in a fancy New York hotel, the Sussex-Fenton. Because of his friendly nature he was also the hotel guests' source of all sorts of inside information on what to do and where to go in New York, and a confidant to his co-workers. Despite being short and fat, his personality made him very popular, and he was constantly involved in trying to help other people. The degree of this involvement often got him in trouble with his girlfriend, Celia, and with Mr. Phillips, the hotel's manager. Horace Fenton, the owner of the hotel chain, although never seen on camera, was heard regularly giving orders to members of the staff. *Stanley* was aired live from New York.

STAR GAMES, THE
Sports
BROADCAST HISTORY:
  Syndicated only
  60 minutes
  Produced: *1985*
  Released: *October 1985*
HOSTS:
  Bruce Jenner
  Pamela Sue Martin
REFEREE:
  Dick Butkus

The Star Games was a variation on the concept that had been pioneered by ABC in its series of *Battle of the Network Stars* specials. Each week three teams of actors, each from a different television series, would compete in assorted sports events with the winners moving up in an elimination tournament. The sports included touch football, tennis, bicycle racing, swimming, and running events. Bruce Jenner and Pamela Sue Martin co-hosted, with former football player Dick Butkus serving as a rather cantankerous referee.

STAR OF THE FAMILY
Comedy Variety
FIRST TELECAST: *September 22, 1950*
LAST TELECAST: *June 26, 1952*
BROADCAST HISTORY:
  Sep 1950–Jun 1951, CBS Fri 10:00–10:30
  Jul 1951–Jan 1952, CBS Sun 6:30–7:00
  Jan 1952–Jun 1952, CBS Thu 8:00–8:30
HOSTS:
  Morton Downey (1950–1951)
  Peter Lind Hayes (1951–1952)

Mary Healy (1951–1952)
Carl Hoff Orchestra

The gimmick in this variety show was unique. The host of the show interviewed people who were related to famous celebrities without disclosing who the celebrities were. After the family members had chatted with the host, the "star of their family" was introduced, joined the conversation, and performed for the audience. Singer Morton Downey was the host during the first season, adding his songs to provide a change of pace from the interviews. He was replaced by Peter Lind Hayes and Mary Healy in the summer of 1951, and the emphasis shifted from music to comedy, depending of course on the talents of the celebrities whose relatives appeared on each week's telecast.

STAR OF THE FAMILY
Situation Comedy
FIRST TELECAST: *September 30, 1982*
LAST TELECAST: *December 23, 1982*
BROADCAST HISTORY:
  Sep 1982–Dec 1982, ABC Thu 8:30–9:00
CAST:
  Buddy Krebs .... Brian Dennehy
  Jennie Lee Krebs .... Kathy Maisnik
  Douggie Krebs .... Michael Dudikoff
  Feldman .... Todd Susman
  Frank Rosetti .... George Deloy
  Max .... Danny Mora
  Moose .... Judy Pioli

The star of this family was 16-year-old Jennie Lee, whose singing talents (in the country/pop vein) were good enough to begin getting her show-business offers. Her dad, grumpy Fire Captain Buddy Krebs, was proud but worried, not wanting his little angel to grow up too soon—not for at least the next 20 or 30 years. That was only one of Buddy's troubles, though. His wife had run off with a bellhop, his 17-year-old son, Douggie, had muscles where he should have had brains, and his young charges down at the firehouse were a bunch of flakes: Feldman wrote to his mother telling her that he was a cardiologist, Rosetti had sex on the brain, and Max was a hotheaded Hispanic whose English was fractured. Then there was Moose, his daughter's amazon of a manager. You think you got troubles?

STAR PERFORMANCE
  syndicated title for *Four Star Playhouse*

STAR SEARCH
Talent
BROADCAST HISTORY:
  Syndicated only
  60 minutes
  Produced: *1983–*
  Released: *September 1983*
HOST:
  Ed McMahon

Ed McMahon hosted this big, glossy talent show, which gave aspiring young performers a chance to compete in various categories: male and female vocalist, musical group, stand-up comedian, dance, dramatic, and "TV spokesmodel." The actors played a scene with a guest star like Joan Collins or Tony Geary, while the spokesmodel posed glamorously for a fashion photographer and read the rules of the competition. Each of the hopefuls was rated by a panel of producers and talent agents, with the winners coming back to face new challengers the following week. Some, like baby-faced vocalist Sam Harris, seemed to triumph week after week, while others (especially the comedians, who generally used up their best material quickly) were on and off in a week. Those who managed to survive to the end-of-season finals could win as much as $100,000.

Unlike some prior TV talent shows, *Star Search* produced many alumni who have gone on to careers in show business—according to some sources, 90% of those who appeared found employment in the field. Among the better-known alumni have been the country/rock group Sawyer Brown, pop singer Tiffany, and actors Brian Bloom *(As the World Turns)*, Sinbad *(A Different World)*, Amy Stock *(Dallas)*, Joseph Gian *(Hooperman)*, and Amy Dolenz *(General Hospital)*.

STAR STAGE
Dramatic Anthology
FIRST TELECAST: *September 9, 1955*
LAST TELECAST: *September 7, 1956*
BROADCAST HISTORY:
Sep 1955–Aug 1956, NBC Fri 9:30–10:00
Sep 1956, NBC Fri 9:00–9:30
HOST:
Jeffrey Lynn

Approximately two-thirds of the two-act plays aired on *Star Stage* were live and the remainder were filmed. The live dramas originated from both Hollywood and New York. Initially, there was no host, until Jeffrey Lynn assumed that post on November 18, 1955. One of the early telecasts was "On Trial" starring Joseph Cotten. He later hosted and starred in a courtroom series of the same name. A February 1956 telecast titled "Killer on Horseback," starring Rod Cameron, was the pilot for Cameron's syndicated series *State Trooper*. Others who were seen on *Star Stage* included Sylvia Sidney, Alan Young, Lorne Greene, Jeanne Crain, Dan Duryea, Ward Bond, Wendell Corey, and Polly Bergen.

STAR TIME
Musical Variety
FIRST TELECAST: *September 5, 1950*
LAST TELECAST: *February 27, 1951*
BROADCAST HISTORY:
Sep 1950–Feb 1951, DUM Tue 10:00–11:00
REGULARS:
Frances Langford
Benny Goodman Sextet
Lew Parker
Kathryn Lee

In the fall of 1950 DuMont made another of its feeble efforts to launch a full-fledged prime-time variety hour with this series. Like most of the other attempts, it lacked the lure of a big-name (or rising) star who could attract viewers, and soon folded.

Star Time did have some good talent, however, including singer Frances Langford and the Benny Goodman Sextet as regulars. Comic Lew Parker and dancer Kathryn Lee also contributed, along with assorted, but not usually top-name, guests.

STAR TIME PLAYHOUSE
Dramatic Anthology
FIRST TELECAST: *July 12, 1955*
LAST TELECAST: *September 13, 1955*
BROADCAST HISTORY:
Jul 1955–Sep 1955, CBS Tue 8:00–8:30

The filmed dramas in this series had never before been aired on television, tended to be on the serious side, and were headlined by well-known performers. Victor Jory starred in "The Man Who Escaped Devil's Island," and Ronald Reagan and Neville Brand in "Edge of Battle." Others appearing were Peter Lorre, Basil Rathbone, Broderick Crawford, and Angela Lansbury—she being the only woman to have star billing throughout *Star Time Playhouse*'s summer run.

STAR TONIGHT
Dramatic Anthology
FIRST TELECAST: *February 3, 1955*
LAST TELECAST: *August 9, 1956*
BROADCAST HISTORY:
Feb 1955–Aug 1956, ABC Thu 9:00–9:30

Star Tonight was designed as a showcase for young actors and actresses working in New York. Each week a live play was telecast with a relative unknown in the lead, hopefully as a springboard to future stardom. The plays were chosen specifically for the individual young "stars" or written to suit their talents. Some of those who went on to greater things were Bruce Gordon, Joanne Woodward, Theodore Bikel, Neva Patterson, Kay Medford, and Robert Culp.

STAR TREK
Science Fiction
FIRST TELECAST: *September 8, 1966*
LAST TELECAST: *September 2, 1969*
BROADCAST HISTORY:
Sep 1966–Aug 1967, NBC Thu 8:30–9:30
Sep 1967–Aug 1968, NBC Fri 8:30–9:30
Sep 1968–Apr 1969, NBC Fri 10:00–11:00
Jun 1969–Sep 1969, NBC Tue 7:30–8:30
CAST:
Capt. James T. Kirk . . . . William Shatner
Mr. Spock . . . . Leonard Nimoy
Dr. Leonard McCoy . . . . DeForest Kelley

Yeoman Janice Rand (1966–1967)
.... Grace Lee Whitney
Sulu .... George Takei
Uhura..................... Nichelle Nichols
Engineer Montgomery Scott .. James Doohan
Nurse Christine Chapel .... Majel Barrett
Ensign Pavel Chekov (1967–1969)
.... Walter Koenig

Set in the 23rd century, *Star Trek* followed the adventures of the starship U.S.S. *Enterprise,* a cruiser-sized spacecraft whose mission included reconnaissance of previously unexplored worlds and transporting supplies to Earth colonies in space. Confrontations with two alien races, Klingons and Romulans, provided recurring conflicts and there were numerous encounters with other "strange" forms of alien life as well. *Star Trek* differed from previous series such as *Captain Video* in that stories were often well written, serious science-fiction short stories, dealing with current social issues thinly disguised in extraterrestrial settings.

Captain James Kirk was cast in the classic hero mold but, if the truth were known, his alien first officer, Mr. Spock, had a following almost as large. Spock, a half-breed Vulcan whose father was an ambassador and mother was an Earth woman, had pointed ears, a decidedly green complexion, and a totally logical mind. His lack of emotion was in perfect contrast to Kirk's impetuousness. Despite his Satanic appearance, Spock quickly became a favorite of viewers. The third principal cast member was Dr. Leonard "Bones" McCoy, a fine surgeon and diagnostician (no doubt helped by the advanced technology at his disposal) with a sarcastic sense of humor. Although Spock and McCoy did not always see eye to eye, they had great underlying respect for each other and were fiercely loyal to Captain Kirk. Supporting regulars were Sulu, the chief navigator; Lt. Uhura, the communications officer; Lt. Commander Montgomery "Scotty" Scott, the chief engineer; Dr. McCoy's assistant, Christine Chapel; and young Ensign Pavel Chekov, assistant navigator and aspiring executive officer. During the first season Yeoman Janice Rand was a regular, but her character never seemed to develop and was dropped.

Although many of today's fans believe that *Star Trek* must have been a big hit, because of all the publicity about it, it was actually not very successful in its original run. It was regularly beaten in its time period by all sorts of competition, and it placed number 52 among all series in 1966–1967, its peak season, behind such programs as *Iron Horse* and *Mr. Terrific. Star Trek* was finally canceled by NBC in 1969 due to gradually declining audiences and the heavy proportion of teenagers and children in its viewership, which made it unattractive to network advertisers.

Since then, however, the program has been very successful in reruns, and developed a fanatical cult following in the 1970s. Its new fans, dubbed "trekkies," organized themselves, lobbied to get the series brought back to network television, and even sponsored annual conventions in the U.S. and England. Probably no prime-time series has had such a well-publicized "life after death" as *Star Trek;* it is practically the embodiment of TV nostalgia for the 1960s.

Star Trek did in fact return to the NBC-TV network, in modified form, as an animated cartoon series on Saturday morning, from 1973 to 1975. Original cast members supplied the voices. Then, in 1979, the years of lobbying, coupled with the box-office success of *Star Wars* and *Close Encounters of the Third Kind,* culminated in a theatrical motion-picture version of *Star Trek.* It reunited most of the original cast, cost some $40,000,000 to produce, and was a major disappointment to all concerned—especially its producer, Paramount Pictures. Despite the marginal success of the first film, a second, *Star Trek II: The Wrath of Khan,* reached theaters in 1982. Essentially a sequel to the "Space Seed" episode from the TV series, with "Space Seed" guest star Ricardo Montalban reprising his role, it was far more successful than the first film and was the basis for a continuing series of *Star Trek* motion pictures.

STAR TREK: THE NEXT GENERATION
Science Fiction
BROADCAST HISTORY:
Syndicated only
60 minutes
Produced: *1987–*
Released: *October 1987*
CAST:
Capt. Jean-Luc Picard .... Patrick Stewart
Cdr. William Riker .... Jonathan Frakes
Lt. Geordi La Forge .... LeVar Burton
Lt. Tasha Yar (1987–1988) .... Denise Crosby
Lt. Worf .... Michael Dorn
Dr. Beverly Crusher........ Gates McFadden
Counselor Deanna Troi .... Marina Sirtis
Lt. Cmdr. Data .... Brent Spiner
Wesley Crusher .... Wil Wheaton

Over the years there had been numerous rumors that Paramount Pictures would bring *Star Trek* back to TV—the *Star Trek* motion pictures had become money-makers for the studio and the ancillary marketing of anything that could be associated with the series and films had become quite lucrative. Finally *Star Trek: The Next Generation* reached the air in 1987, 18 years after the original had ended.

There was a new *Enterprise,* a new crew, and better special effects. Most importantly, the man whose vision had been responsible for *Star Trek* in the first place, creator Gene Roddenberry, was back as executive producer of the new series. He used his influence to see that, as with the original series, the new *Star Trek* had a social conscience and relied heavily on stories which made moral points.

Star Trek: The Next Generation was set in the

24th century, 78 years after the original series. The new *Enterprise* was much larger than its twenty-third century predecessor—more than twice as long and with eight times as much interior space. Accordingly, the ship's crew, which now included children, numbered more than 2,000 people. Commanding the *Enterprise* was Captain Jean-Luc Picard, a more formal, fatherly, and much less emotional leader than Captain Kirk had been on the original series. Unlike Kirk, he generally preferred to remain on board and let his senior officers deal first-hand with crises that required a team to leave the ship. Second in command was Cdr. William Riker, the impetuous Kirk clone on this series. Riker and half-Betazoid Counselor Deanna Troi, who could sense the emotions of any living creature, were former lovers with the potential for rekindling their romance. Other officers on Picard's staff were Lt. Geordi La Forge, the blind helmsman who could "see" with the aid of high-tech electronic sunglasses; Lt. Worf, the ship's Klingon officer (the Federation had made peace with the Klingons in the decades since Kirk's *Enterprise* had fought them); Lt. Tasha Yar, head of security; Lt. Cdr. Data, an android with total recall and the desire to become more "human"; and Dr. Beverly Crusher, the ship's medical officer with a soft spot for the captain. Dr. Crusher's son, Wesley, a brilliant and inventive youth who wanted eventually to become a Starfleet officer himself, helped get the crew out of jams on more than one occasion. When Tasha was killed by an alien in the spring of 1988 Lt. Worf assumed the duties of head of security.

STARLAND VOCAL BAND SHOW, THE
Variety
FIRST TELECAST: *July 31, 1977*
LAST TELECAST: *September 2, 1977*
BROADCAST HISTORY:
Jul 1977–Aug 1977, CBS Sun 8:30–9:00
Aug 1977–Sep 1977, CBS Fri 8:30–9:00
REGULARS:
Bill Danoff
Taffy Danoff
Margot Chapman
Jon Caroll
Mark Russell
Dave Letterman
Jeff Altman
Phil Proctor
Peter Bergman
Milt Okun and His Orchestra

The four members of the popular music group The Starland Vocal Band (Bill, Taffy, Margot, and Jon) starred in this whimsical variety show which featured music and satirical comedy sketches. Political satirist Mark Russell was also a cast regular in this series, which was taped on locations in such diverse places as a concert at Georgetown University in Washington, D.C., and at an outdoor picnic in Great Falls, Virginia. The group's main claim to fame, and the reason they got this summer series, was a 1976 hit record called "Afternoon Delight." Featured regularly in comedy sketches were three of the show's writers—Dave Letterman, Phil Proctor, and Peter Bergman.

STARLIGHT THEATRE
Dramatic Anthology
FIRST TELECAST: *April 2, 1950*
LAST TELECAST: *October 4, 1951*
BROADCAST HISTORY:
Apr 1950–Jun 1950, CBS Sun 7:00–7:30
Jul 1950, CBS Mon 8:00–8:30
Jul 1950–Sep 1950, CBS Thu 9:00–9:30
Sep 1950, CBS Thu 9:30–10:00
Oct 1950, CBS Wed 9:00–9:30
Nov 1950–Oct 1951, CBS Thu 8:00–8:30

Stories of romance were presented on this live anthology series that bounced all over the CBS schedule during the 18 months it was on. The players came from both the legitimate theater and the motion-picture world. During its longest run in a single time slot, from November 1950 through October 1951, *Starlight Theatre* was reduced from a weekly to a biweekly series, alternating with *The George Burns and Gracie Allen Show*. Among the more familiar faces that showed up during the run were Barry Nelson, Mary Sinclair, Ernest Truex, Melvyn Douglas, Eve Arden, Julie Harris, Wally Cox, and John Forsythe.

STARLIT TIME
Musical Variety
FIRST TELECAST: *April 9, 1950*
LAST TELECAST: *November 26, 1950*
BROADCAST HISTORY:
Apr 1950, DUM Sun 6:00–8:00
Apr 1950–Nov 1950, DUM Sun 7:00–8:00
REGULARS:
Bill Williams
Phil Hanna
Minnie Jo Curtis
Gordon Dilworth
Bibi Osterwald
Holly Harris
Allen Prescott
Ralph Stantley
Sondra Lee & Sam Steen
Roberto & Alicia
Eddie Holmes
Reggie Beane Trio
Cy Coleman Trio

Starlit Time was an early attempt by DuMont to compete in the Sunday night variety-show sweepstakes. Unfortunately a severe lack of budget, and therefore of big-name stars, hampered the show considerably. It premiered as an ambitious, two-hour affair consisting of two one-hour segments, "Welcome Mat," emceed by disc jockey Bill Williams, and "Phil Hanna Sings," emceed by vocalist Hanna. The two parts were linked together by Minnie Jo Curtis, who did a running bit as a celestial switchboard operator and who introduced some of the acts. Two hours proved unwieldy for such lightweight talent, and *Starlit Time* was soon reduced to a one-hour variety show co-hosted by Williams and Hanna. Among the regulars were folk singer Gordon Dilworth, dance teams Sondra Lee & Sam Steen and Roberto & Alicia, and assorted comics and vocalists.

During the summer months *Starlit Time* was known as *S.S. Holiday*.

STARMAN
Science Fiction
FIRST TELECAST: *September 19, 1986*
LAST TELECAST: *September 4, 1987*
BROADCAST HISTORY:
  Sep 1986–Mar 1987, ABC Fri 10:00–11:00
  Mar 1987–May 1987, ABC Sat 8:00–9:00
  Jun 1987, ABC Sat 10:00–11:00
  Jul 1987, ABC Sat 8:00–9:00
  Aug 1987–Sep 1987, ABC Fri 10:00–11:00
CAST:
  Paul Forrester ("Starman") ..... Robert Hays
  Scott Hayden................... C.B. Barnes
  George Fox............. Michael Cavanaugh

In this TV sequel to the 1984 theatrical movie of the same name, an alien who had fathered a child by an Earth woman returned—14 years later—to find his love, and help raise his son. Upon his arrival, the Starman (who apparently had no corporeal form of his own) assumed the body of Paul Forrester, a free-lance photographer who had been killed in a wilderness plane crash. He then located his son, Scott, in an orphanage, and together man and boy set out in search of Jenny, who had disappeared many years before.

Scott was naturally a bit skeptical about his alien origins, but was convinced when he saw Paul's unusual powers—and his own emerging paranormal abilities—which were triggered by the small, glowing spheres that Paul carried. It *was* handy at times to be able to levitate objects, or unlock doors without a key. In return, young Scott helped the innocent Paul understand Earth ways, sometimes in comical fashion. As they followed clues to Jenny's whereabouts they met and helped many people along the way, and the series took on an anthology quality. They could not stay anywhere for long; hot on their heels was the inevitable government agent, Fox, who had learned Starman's secret and was determined to capture him and take him to the lab "for testing." Some people have no sense of humor.

Everything turned out for the best in the end, however. In the final episode Starman and Scott finally found Jenny (played by Erin Gray), and they all went happily into cancellation together.

STARRING BORIS KARLOFF
Suspense Anthology
FIRST TELECAST: *September 22, 1949*
LAST TELECAST: *December 15, 1949*
BROADCAST HISTORY:
  Sep 1949–Oct 1949, ABC Thu 9:30–10:00
  Nov 1949–Dec 1949, ABC Thu 9:00–9:30
STAR:
  Boris Karloff
ORGANIST:
  George Henniger

Tales of horror, starring Hollywood's best-known practitioner of that genre. The first telecast, titled "Five Golden Guineas," is illustrative. An English hangman unduly enjoys his work, which brings him payment of five guineas per hanging. He revels in the snap of the victim's neck, and the dangling arms. When his pregnant wife discovers his true occupation she leaves him. Twenty years later the hangman is called upon to execute a young man, which he does with pleasure, despite the fact that he has secret evidence that the youth is in fact innocent. Only then is he confronted by his ex-wife, who tells him that he has just hanged his own son. Enraged, he strangles his wife—and is subsequently sent to the gallows himself. Another hangman collects five golden guineas.

The title of this anthology series was changed to *Mystery Playhouse Starring Boris Karloff* effective with the October 27 telecast.

STARS IN ACTION
Dramatic Anthology
FIRST TELECAST: *September 30, 1958*
LAST TELECAST: *September 29, 1959*
BROADCAST HISTORY:
  Sep 1958–Sep 1959, CBS Tue 7:30–8:00

The filmed plays that were aired in this anthology series were reruns of episodes originally telecast on *Schlitz Playhouse,* an unusual practice for the start of a season. Reruns were frequently repackaged and retitled for use in the summer but rarely to fill a time slot for an entire season.

STARS OF JAZZ
Music
FIRST TELECAST: *April 18, 1958*
LAST TELECAST: *November 30, 1958*
BROADCAST HISTORY:
  Apr 1958–Jun 1958, ABC Fri 8:30–9:00
  Jun 1958–Sep 1958, ABC Mon 9:00–9:30
  Sep 1958–Oct 1958, ABC Thu 10:00–10:30
  Nov 1958, ABC Sun 9:30–10:00
HOST:
  Bobby Troup

Each week a different jazz musician or group was featured on this music series. Host Bobby Troup, himself a jazz musician, would introduce the week's guests, chat with them about their work, and sit back while they played for the audience.

STARS ON PARADE
Musical Variety
FIRST TELECAST: *November 4, 1953*

LAST TELECAST: *June 30, 1954*
BROADCAST HISTORY:
Nov 1953–Jan 1954, DUM Wed 10:00–10:30
Jan 1954–May 1954, DUM Wed 9:30–10:00
May 1954–Jun 1954, DUM Wed 9:00–9:30
EMCEE:
Don Russell (1953)
Bobby Sherwood (1953–1954)
REGULAR:
Elliot Lawrence

Another of the military variety shows on television in the early 1950s. In addition to military bands, which were rehearsed for the occasion by civilian bandleader Elliot Lawrence, the talent included such stars as Perry Como, June Valli, Sarah Vaughan, and Errol Garner. The Glenn Miller Army Air Force Band also made an appearance. Don Russell was host for the first two telecasts only, being replaced on November 18 by Bobby Sherwood.

STARS OVER HOLLYWOOD
Anthology
FIRST TELECAST: *September 6, 1950*
LAST TELECAST: *August 29, 1951*
BROADCAST HISTORY:
Sep 1950–Aug 1951, NBC Wed 10:30–11:00

Early filmed dramatic series, produced in Hollywood and generally featuring lesser-known actors and actresses. The star of the first presentation ("Beauty Is a Joy") was Mary Stuart, later to become the central character in CBS' long-running daytime serial *Search for Tomorrow*. Future star Raymond Burr was seen in two 1951 productions.

STARSKY AND HUTCH
Police Drama
FIRST TELECAST: *September 3, 1975*
LAST TELECAST: *August 21, 1979*
BROADCAST HISTORY:
Sep 1975–Sep 1976, ABC Wed 10:00–11:00
Sep 1976–Jan 1978, ABC Sat 9:00–10:00
Jan 1978–Aug 1978, ABC Wed 10:00–11:00
Sep 1978–May 1979, ABC Tue 10:00–11:00
Aug 1979, ABC Tue 10:00–11:00
CAST:
Det. Dave Starsky ...... Paul Michael Glaser
Det. Ken Hutchinson ("Hutch") .. David Soul
Capt. Harold Dobey........ Bernie Hamilton
Huggy Bear .... Antonio Fargas
MUSIC:
Lalo Schifrin; Tom Scott, Mark Snow

Starsky and Hutch was one of the light, youth-oriented police-action shows that populated TV in the 1970s. The two young plainclothes cops were both swinging bachelors, and their personalities meshed perfectly—they almost seemed to operate as one. Starsky was the streetwise member of the team, and Hutch the better-edu-

cated, soft-spoken one. Together they tackled cases in the roughest neighborhood in town (presumably Los Angeles), full of pimps, muggers, dope pushers, and big-time hoodlums. Sometimes they went undercover, but often they were highly visible, racing around the city, tires squealing, in Starsky's bright red hot-rod (a 1974 Ford Torino). Capt. Dobey was their quick-tempered but understanding boss, and Huggy Bear their flamboyant informant.

START OF SOMETHING BIG, THE
Information/Interview
BROADCAST HISTORY:
Syndicated only
60 minutes
Produced: *1985–1986*
Released: *April 1985*
HOST:
Steve Allen

The primary focus of this series was on the roots of celebrity—how successful performers got started in show business. In addition to chatting with performers about the struggles, or lack thereof, early in their careers, host Steve Allen narrated feature pieces on the development of individual series like *Laugh-In*, *The Tonight Show*, *M*A*S*H*, and *Star Trek*. To provide a little variety, the inquisitive Mr. Allen also offered viewers segments on the origins of such things as the Boy Scouts, the bicycle, ice cream, the Barbie doll, credit cards, the Olympics, chocolate, and the toothbrush.

STARTIME
Variety
FIRST TELECAST: *October 6, 1959*
LAST TELECAST: *May 31, 1960*
BROADCAST HISTORY:
Oct 1959–Jan 1960, NBC Tue 9:30–10:30
Jan 1960–May 1960, NBC Tue 8:30–9:30
PRODUCER:
Hubbell Robinson

The Ford Motor Company was the sponsor of this potpourri of hour-long specials that ran as a series during the 1959–1960 season. When it was sponsored by the Ford Division its full title was *Ford Startime—TV's Finest Hour*. When it was sponsored by the Lincoln-Mercury Division the title became *Lincoln-Mercury Startime*.

Serious dramatic presentations, musical comedies, and musical variety shows were all presented under the generic title *Startime*. One of the specials in this series that eventually became a series on its own was "Sing Along with Mitch," telecast on May 24, 1960, and back as a series the following January. Dean Martin, who would also eventually have a variety series on NBC, starred twice with variety specials. His former partner, Jerry Lewis, was also on *Startime*, but in the dramatic role of "The Jazz Singer," a version of Al

Jolson's classic film. Ingrid Bergman made her American TV dramatic debut in "The Turn of the Screw" and so did Alec Guinness in "The Wicked Scheme of Jebal Deeks." The list of top-rank stars on this series was almost endless. Jimmy Stewart starred in "Cindy's Fella," a Western musical based loosely on "Cinderella," and Ed Wynn and Bert Lahr were featured in a straight comedy, "The Greatest Man Alive." Three of the most popular comedians of the century—Jack Benny, George Burns, and Eddie Cantor—starred together in a musical comedy revue.

STATE TROOPER
Police Drama
BROADCAST HISTORY:
Syndicated only
30 minutes
Produced: *1956–1959* (104 episodes)
Released: *January 1957*
CAST:
Trooper Rod Blake............ Rod Cameron

Lanky Rod Cameron brawled his way through murder cases, kidnappings, and other criminal investigations in this popular action series. Trooper Blake was chief investigator for the Nevada State Police, and as such got to track criminals in Las Vegas, Reno, Lake Tahoe, and across the Mojave Desert. Often he went undercover, assuming a variety of disguises to trap culprits.

State Trooper was supposedly based on actual Nevada police files. The pilot ran as an episode of NBC's *Star Stage* anthology in February 1956, but the series did not make the network schedule and was sold through syndication to local stations.

STEVE ALLEN COMEDY HOUR, THE
Comedy Variety
FIRST TELECAST: *June 14, 1967*
LAST TELECAST: *August 16, 1967*
BROADCAST HISTORY:
Jun 1967–Aug 1967, CBS Wed 10:00–11:00
REGULARS:
Steve Allen
Jayne Meadows
Louis Nye
Ruth Buzzi
David Winters Dancers
John Byner
The Terry Gibbs Band

After an absence of several seasons, Steve Allen returned to prime-time television with this summer comedy variety series. With him were his wife, Jayne Meadows, comedian Louis Nye, comedienne Ruth Buzzi, and the David Winters Dancers. Although there was music in the series, the emphasis, regardless of who the week's guest stars were, was on comedy. Among the featured routines used regularly was the "Man on the Street Interview" in which Louis Nye played the

suave, smug Gordon Hathaway. Although not listed by CBS as a regular, John Byner appeared in most of the episodes.

STEVE ALLEN COMEDY HOUR, THE
Comedy Variety
FIRST TELECAST: *October 18, 1980*
LAST TELECAST: *January 10, 1981*
BROADCAST HISTORY:
Oct 1980, NBC Sat 10:00–11:00
Dec 1980, NBC Tue 10:00–11:00
Jan 1981, NBC Sat 10:00–11:00
CAST:
Steve Allen
Joe Baker
Joey Forman
Tom Leopold
Bill Saluga
Bob Shaw
Helen Brooks
Carol Donelly
Fred Smoot
Nancy Steen
Catherine O'Hara
Kaye Ballard
Doris Hess
Tim Lund
Tim Gibbon
Terry Gibbs and His Band

Funnyman Steve Allen had been a fixture on network television throughout the 1950s, both in prime time and as host of the original *Tonight Show*. Following the cancellation of his prime-time variety hour on ABC in 1961, Steve's projects had been mostly of the syndicated variety. On two occasions (1962–1964 and 1967–1969) he had hosted syndicated 90-minute variety series along the lines of *The Tonight Show* and in 1976 a variation on that type called *Steve Allen's Laugh Back*, in which his guests were all performers who had appeared with him in the 1950s. Steve had also produced and hosted the award-winning *Meeting of Minds* series for PBS starting in 1977, where he interviewed actors made up as historical figures. But, with the exception of a summer run on CBS in 1967 (see above), this was Steve's first commercial network prime-time series in almost two decades.

This *Steve Allen Comedy Hour* featured a large group of resident comics, collectively known as the Krelman Players. There were three recurring sketches on the show—a satirical spoof of local "Eyewitness News" shows, a revival of Steve's classic "Man on the Street" interviews, and "Camera on the Street," in which Steve ad-libbed observations about people and situations captured on tape by a hidden camera outside the studio at Hollywood and Vine in Los Angeles. There were guest stars, including Allen alumni Steve Lawrence and Tom Poston, but the thrust of the show was comedy, not personality. This series had a rather strange broadcast history, premiering in October with a single telecast, returning for the month of December, and closing with a single encore in mid-January.

STEVE ALLEN SHOW, THE
Comedy Variety
FIRST TELECAST: *December 25, 1950*
LAST TELECAST: *September 11, 1952*
BROADCAST HISTORY:
Dec 1950–Mar 1951, CBS Mon–Fri 7:00–7:30
Jul 1952–Sep 1952, CBS Thu 8:30–9:00
REGULAR:
Steve Allen

Steve Allen got his first network exposure on CBS with a live series that aired Monday–Friday at 7:00 P.M. and premiered on Christmas Day 1950. He played the piano, chatted with one or two guest stars, and had funny ad-lib interviews with both the guests and random members of the studio audience. When it left the early evening at the start of March 1951, the series was expanded to a full hour from 11:30 A.M. to 12:30 P.M. weekdays. He returned to CBS' nighttime lineup during the summer of 1952 on Thursday nights, running on alternate weeks with *Amos 'n' Andy*.

STEVE ALLEN SHOW, THE
Comedy Variety
FIRST TELECAST: *June 24, 1956*
LAST TELECAST: *December 27, 1961*
BROADCAST HISTORY:
Jun 1956–Jun 1958, NBC Sun 8:00–9:00
Sep 1958–Mar 1959, NBC Sun 8:00–9:00
Mar 1959, NBC Sun 7:30–9:00
Apr 1959–Jun 1959, NBC Sun 7:30–8:30
Sep 1959–Jun 1960, NBC Mon 10:00–11:00
Sep 1961–Dec 1961, ABC Wed 7:30–8:30
REGULARS:
Steve Allen
Louis Nye
Gene Rayburn (1956–1959)
Skitch Henderson (1956–1959)
Marilyn Jacobs (1956–1957)
Tom Poston (1956–1959, 1961)
Gabe Dell (1956–1957, 1958–1961)
Don Knotts (1956–1960)
Dayton Allen (1958–1961)
Pat Harrington, Jr. (1958–1961)
Cal Howard (1959–1960)
Bill Dana (1959–1960)
Joey Forman (1961)
Buck Henry (1961)
Jayne Meadows (1961)
John Cameron Swayze (1957–1958)
The Smothers Brothers (1961)
Tim Conway (1961)
Don Penny (1961)
Les Brown and His Band (1959–1961)

The multitalented Steve Allen—musician, composer, singer, comedian, author—was the star of this live weekly variety series that bore a strong resemblance to his informal, late-night *Tonight Show*. Although the program had elements of music and serious aspects, comedy was far and away its major component. Steve had with him one of the most versatile and talented collections of improvisational comics ever assembled. Among the features that were used at one time or another on a semi-regular basis were: "Letters to the Editor," "The Allen Report to the Nation," "Mad-Libs," "Crazy Shots," "Where Are They Now," "The Question Man," "The Allen Bureau of Standards," and "The Allen All Stars."

The most frequently used feature, and by far the most memorable, was the "Man on the Street Interview." It was here that the comics on the show developed their best-remembered characters: Louis Nye as suave, smug Gordon Hathaway, Tom Poston as the man who can't remember his own name, Skitch Henderson as Sidney Ferguson, Don Knotts as the extremely nervous and fidgety Mr. Morrison, Pat Harrington as Italian golf pro Guido Panzini, and Bill Dana as shy Jose Jimenez.

The Steve Allen Show spent three years on Sunday evenings in head-to-head competition with *The Ed Sullivan Show*. On its second telecast, as a matter of fact, one of the guest stars was young rock 'n' roll singer Elvis Presley, a performer whose three appearances later that fall on Sullivan's show are better remembered than his stint with Steve Allen. In the fall of 1959, when the show moved to Monday evenings, it was retitled *The Steve Allen Plymouth Show*, a sop to its new full sponsor. When ABC picked up the show for a short run on Wednesdays in the fall of 1961, the title reverted to *The Steve Allen Show*. The series had originated from New York throughout its Sunday evening run but moved to Hollywood when it shifted to Mondays in the fall of 1959.

STEVE CANYON
Adventure
FIRST TELECAST: *September 13, 1958*
LAST TELECAST: *September 8, 1960*
BROADCAST HISTORY:
Sep 1958–Jan 1959, NBC Sat 9:00–9:30
Jan 1959–Mar 1959, NBC Thu 8:00–8:30
Mar 1959–Sep 1959, NBC Tue 8:00–8:30
Apr 1960–Sep 1960, ABC Thu 7:30–8:00
CAST:
Lt. Col. Stevenson B. Canyon
.... Dean Fredericks
Police Chief Hagedorn (1959–1960)
.... Ted DeCorsia
Major "Willie" Williston (1959–1960)
.... Jerry Paris
Airman Abel Featherstone (1959–1960)
.... Abel Fernandez
Sgt. Charley Berger (1959–1960) .. Robert Hoy
Ingrid (1959–1960) .... Ingrid Goude

Milton Caniff's popular comic strip *Steve Canyon* was already 11 years old when this filmed series went on the air in the fall of 1958. Steve Canyon was a command pilot and troubleshooter for the air force and traveled from base to base around the country in the course of his work. Actual on-location footage of air force bases was used in the series, which had government approval and was considered a possible aid in recruiting drives. On January 3, 1959, Steve settled down as commanding officer of Big Thunder Air Force Base and acquired a regular supporting cast. Although based at Big Thunder in California, he still flew all over the world on special assignments. ABC aired reruns of the NBC series during the summer of 1960.

STEVE LAWRENCE-EYDIE GORME SHOW, THE
Musical Variety
FIRST TELECAST: *July 13, 1958*
LAST TELECAST: *August 31, 1958*
BROADCAST HISTORY:
Jul 1958–Aug 1958, NBC Sun 8:00–9:00
REGULARS:
Steve Lawrence
Eydie Gorme
Gene Rayburn
The Artie Malvin Singers
The Jack Kane Orchestra

The husband-and-wife singing team of Steve Lawrence and Eydie Gorme starred in this 1958 summer replacement for *The Steve Allen Show*. They sang separately and together, introduced and participated with their various guest stars in song, and occasionally acted in comedy skits. Gene Rayburn was the show's announcer.

The full title was *Steve Allen Presents the Steve Lawrence-Eydie Gorme Show*.

STEVE LAWRENCE SHOW, THE
Musical Variety
FIRST TELECAST: *September 13, 1965*
LAST TELECAST: *December 13, 1965*
BROADCAST HISTORY:
Sep 1965–Dec 1965, CBS Mon 10:00–11:00
REGULARS:
Steve Lawrence
Charles Nelson Reilly
Betty Walker
The Ernie Flatt Dancers
The Dick Williams Singers
The Joe Guercio Orchestra

Singer Steve Lawrence was the host and star of this musical variety series. It featured appearances by guest stars, songs, comedy sketches, and production numbers. Comics Charles Nelson Reilly and Betty Walker were originally supposed to be featured regulars in the show, but were both gone by the end of September, leaving Steve and his guest stars to fend for themselves.

STEVE RANDALL
Detective Drama

FIRST TELECAST: *November 7, 1952*
LAST TELECAST: *January 30, 1953*
BROADCAST HISTORY:
Nov 1952–Jan 1953, DUM Fri 8:00–8:30
CAST:
Steve Randall . . . . Melvyn Douglas

In this filmed series screen star Melvyn Douglas appeared as a disbarred lawyer who had turned sleuth in an attempt to regain his right to practice law. A suave, mustachioed detective, he greased his way through assorted cases of blackmail and murder before finally reaching his goal—reinstatement as a lawyer—in the final episode. There this short series ended.

Prior to the network run, some episodes of *Steve Randall* were seen locally under the title *Hollywood Off Beat*.

STILL THE BEAVER
see *New Leave it to Beaver, The*

STINGRAY
Drama
FIRST TELECAST: *March 4, 1986*
LAST TELECAST: *July 31, 1987*
BROADCAST HISTORY:
Mar 1986–May 1986, NBC Tue 10:00–11:00
Jun 1986–Aug 1986, NBC Fri 10:00–11:00
Jan 1987–Mar 1987, NBC Fri 8:00–9:00
Mar 1987–May 1987, NBC Fri 10:00–11:00
Jun 1987–Jul 1987, NBC Fri 8:00–9:00
CAST:
Stingray. . . . . Nick Mancuso

"He's a Lone Ranger in a black sportscar!" trumpeted the ads. Stingray was an enigmatic adventurer with no traceable past who traveled from place to place fighting crime and helping people in trouble. He never charged for his services, but informed those he helped that someday he would need a favor from them, no questions asked; the favor would be used to help someone else. His real name was never revealed and he was known only by the vintage 1965 Corvette Stingray he drove; the curious were able to trace the registration only as far as the "White House West Coast motor pool."

STIR CRAZY
Comedy Adventure
FIRST TELECAST: *September 18, 1985*
LAST TELECAST: *January 7, 1986*
BROADCAST HISTORY:
Sep 1985–Oct 1985, CBS Wed 8:00–9:00
Dec 1985–Jan 1986, CBS Tue 8:00–9:00
CAST:
Harry Fletcher . . . . Larry Riley
Skip Harrington . . . . Joseph Guzaldo
Captain Betty (pilot only) . . . . Polly Holliday
Captain Betty (1985) . . . . Jeannie Wilson
Crawford (pilot only) . . . . . . Royce Applegate
Crawford (1985) . . . . Marc Silver

Harry and Skip were best friends who left their home in New York to pursue the American dream by starting a chain of ice cream stores in Glendale, Texas. Unfortunately, while trying to raise money, they got involved in a murder for which they were falsely accused, convicted, and sentenced to 132 years in prison. Undeterred, they escaped from a chain gang and set out, in bumbling fashion, after Crawford, the tattooed cowboy who had actually committed the murder. Hot on their trail, and determined to take them back into custody, was the humorless Captain Betty.

Although this series was loosely based on the 1980 theatrical film of the same name, which had starred Richard Pryor and Gene Wilder, *Stir Crazy* looked more like a silly version of *The Fugitive*.

STOCK CAR RACES
Sports
FIRST TELECAST: *June 24, 1952*
LAST TELECAST: *August 26, 1952*
BROADCAST HISTORY:
  Jun 1952–Aug 1952, ABC Tue 9:00–10:30
ANNOUNCER:
  Chick Hearn

Live coverage of weekly late-model automobile racing from the 87th Street Speedway in Chicago.

STOCKARD CHANNING IN JUST FRIENDS
Situation Comedy
FIRST TELECAST: *March 4, 1979*
LAST TELECAST: *August 11, 1979*
BROADCAST HISTORY:
  Mar 1979–Jun 1979, CBS Sun 9:30–10:00
  Jun 1979–Aug 1979, CBS Sat 8:30–9:00
CAST:
  Susan Hughes . . . . Stockard Channing
  Milt D'Angelo . . . . Lou Criscuolo
  Leonard Scribner . . . . Gerrit Graham
  Victoria . . . . Mimi Kennedy
  Coral . . . . Sydney Goldsmith
  Mrs. Fischer . . . . Joan Tolentino
  Miss Yarnell . . . . Linda Rose
  Mrs. Blanchard . . . . Rhonda Foxx

After separating from her husband, Susan Hughes decided to leave Boston and make a fresh start in sunny Los Angeles. There she found herself an apartment, a kooky neighbor named Leonard, and a job at a Beverly Hills health spa called the Fountain of Youth. Her boss at the spa was Milt D'Angelo, an oddball physical-fitness freak who resembled a mid-forties parody of Jack LaLanne. His fervor when discussing the merits of conditioning and exercise was pretty hard for anyone to take, including Susan, but he nevertheless liked his spunky new employee and quickly promoted her from exercise instructor to assistant manager. Susan's wealthy sister, Victoria, was always on the lookout for a nice, successful professional man for Susan, someone who would get her out of that horrid job and into a classy neighborhood. Coral was one of the instructors at the spa, and Mrs. Fischer, Mrs. Blanchard, and Miss Yarnell some of the patrons.

STOCKARD CHANNING SHOW, THE
Situation Comedy
FIRST TELECAST: *March 24, 1980*
LAST TELECAST: *June 28, 1980*
BROADCAST HISTORY:
  Mar 1980–Apr 1980, CBS Mon 8:30–9:00
  Jun 1980, CBS Sat 8:30–9:00
CAST:
  Susan Goodenow . . . . Stockard Channing
  Brad Gabriel . . . . Ron Silver
  Earline Cunningham . . . . . Sydney Goldsmith
  Gus Clyde . . . . Max Showalter
  Mr. Kramer . . . . Jack Somack

This series was CBS' second attempt in less than a year to make a star out of Stockard Channing. The first venture, *Stockard Channing in Just Friends,* had cast the actress as a recently divorced woman working at a Beverly Hills health spa. This series cast her as a recently divorced woman working for a consumer advocate at a Los Angeles television station. Susan Goodenow had landed her job working for egotistical crusader Brad Gabriel because her friend Earline was a secretary at the station that aired Brad's program, "The Big Rip-Off." Mr. Clyde was the general manager of the station, which was owned by his wife. Mr. Kramer was the owner of the old apartment building in West Hollywood where Susan and Earline lived. His fatherly interest in Susan compensated for a notable lack of skill as a handyman.

There were many similarities between this series and Stockard Channing's previous effort. In both shows she was named Susan, she had recently ended a marriage, she was starting a new job in Los Angeles, and her friend and co-worker was played by Sydney Goldsmith. The most telling similarity, however, was that neither show lasted more than a few months. CBS did not try again.

STONE
Police Drama
FIRST TELECAST: *January 14, 1980*
LAST TELECAST: *March 17, 1980*
BROADCAST HISTORY:
  Jan 1980–Feb 1980, ABC Mon 9:00–10:00
  Mar 1980, ABC Mon 10:00–11:00
CAST:
  Det. Sgt. Daniel Stone . . . . Dennis Weaver
  Chief Paulton . . . . Pat Hingle
  Det. Buck Rogers . . . . Robby Weaver

Stone was a celebrity cop. His best-selling novels about police work, based on his own experiences, had made a lot of money and won him a host of female admirers who turned up wherever he went. Chief Paulton, his one-time mentor, was not too happy about that, but there was not much he could do about it; as long as Stone's writing was done on his own time, it was his private affair. In any event, Stone still managed to solve one tough case after another.

Rookie detective Buck Rogers was played by Dennis Weaver's son Robby.

STONEY BURKE

Western
FIRST TELECAST: *October 1, 1962*
LAST TELECAST: *September 2, 1963*
BROADCAST HISTORY:
Oct 1962–Sep 1963, ABC Mon 9:00–10:00
CAST:
Stoney Burke .... Jack Lord
Cody Bristol .... Robert Dowdell
E. J. Stocker .... Bruce Dern
Ves Painter .... Warren Oates
Red .... Bill Hart

Professional rodeo rider Stoney Burke was after one thing—the Golden Buckle, the award given to the world's champion saddle bronco rider. Unfortunately he didn't make it during the first season, which is as long as this contemporary Western series lasted, although he did survive a considerable array of violence and villainy along the way. Filmed in the Southwest.

STOP, LOOK AND LISTEN

see *Celebrity Time*

STOP ME IF YOU'VE HEARD THIS ONE

Quiz/Panel
FIRST TELECAST: *March 4, 1948*
LAST TELECAST: *April 22, 1949*
BROADCAST HISTORY:
Mar 1948–Dec 1948, NBC Fri 8:30–9:00
Jan 1949–Apr 1949, NBC Fri 9:00–9:30
EMCEE:
Roger Bower (1948)
Leon Janney (1948–1949)
REGULAR PANELISTS:
Cal Tinney
Lew Lehr (1948)
Morey Amsterdam (1948)
Benny Rubin
George Givot (1949)

Live comedy game show in which the emcee read jokes sent in by viewers to a panel of three comedians. If one of the comics recognized the joke he would immediately shout "Stop!" and continue the story himself up to the punch line. For every wrong ending supplied by the comedians the viewer won a prize. Guest comedians were also sometimes seen on the panel of "gag-busters."

Based on the radio program of the same name, which was first heard in 1939 with Milton Berle as its star gagster.

STOP SUSAN WILLIAMS

Serial
FIRST TELECAST: *February 27, 1979*
LAST TELECAST: *May 1, 1979*
BROADCAST HISTORY:
Feb 1979–Mar 1979, NBC Tue 8:00–8:20
Mar 1979–May 1979, NBC Tue 8:40–9:00
CAST:
Susan Williams .... Susan Anton
Bob Richards .... Ray Walston
Jack Schoengarth .... Michael Swan
Jennifer Selden .... Marj Dusay
Anthony Korf .... Albert Paulsen
Gold Tooth .... John Hancock
Ti .... Ti Miratti

Beautiful young newspaper photographer Susan Williams was after the men who killed her brother in this "cliff-hanging" serial. Alan Williams, a reporter for the same Washington, D.C., newspaper that Susan worked for, had been on the verge of exposing a fiendish international conspiracy to set off a nuclear bomb near Camp David while the world's leaders were attending a peace conference there. Masterminding the plot was importer Anthony Korf, whose evil henchmen, Gold Tooth and Ti, tried to kill Susan in virtually every episode. Susan chased them all over the world, from Marrakesh to Nairobi to Switzerland. She barely escaped death by cobra bite, in a lion pit, going over a cliff in a sidecar, and in the final chapter telecast, she was trapped in the mine shaft where the nuclear bomb was about to explode. The episode of May 1, 1980, was supposed "to be continued," but it never was, so whatever became of Susan Williams is lost in the video hereafter.

Bob Richards was Susan's editor (who turned out to be in cahoots with the bad guys) and Jennifer Selden was the owner of the paper. Jack Schoengarth, an old friend of her brother, helped Susan with her search. *Stop Susan Williams* was one of three serials telecast under the umbrella title *Cliff Hangers*.

STOP THE MUSIC

Quiz/Audience Participation
FIRST TELECAST: *May 5, 1949*
LAST TELECAST: *June 14, 1956*
BROADCAST HISTORY:
May 1949–Apr 1952, ABC Thu 8:00–9:00
Sep 1954–May 1955, ABC Tue 10:30–11:00
Sep 1955–Jun 1956, ABC Thu 8:30–9:00
EMCEE:
Bert Parks
VOCALISTS:
Estelle Loring (1949–1950)
Jimmy Blaine (1949–1952)
Betty Ann Grove (1949–1955)
Marion Morgan (1950–1951)
June Valli (1952)
Jaye P. Morgan (1954–1955)

ORCHESTRA:
Harry Salter

Stop the Music was introduced on radio in 1948, where it was an overnight sensation. The following year ABC brought it to TV, complete with Bert Parks and Harry Salter's orchestra, and it was a major hit there. It continued on radio as well.

The format was a mixture of musical entertainment and quiz. Bert, a cast of regular singers, and the orchestra would perform parts of songs, which contestants from the audience would be asked to identify for cash prizes. Viewers at home could get into the act by sending in official entry blanks with their names and phone numbers. Three lovely operators on stage would begin placing calls as Bert crooned a tune, and as soon as a connection was made, someone would yell, "Stop the music!" The home viewer would then be given a chance to identify the tune. It could be worth knowing, too, as a correct answer might be worth a jackpot of $20,000 or more. Mink coats and trips to Paris were also frequent prizes.

Various modifications in the basic format took place from time to time, such as a "mystery medley" and a completion between a contestant in the studio and a viewer at home on the telephone. There was also a good deal of turnover among vocalists on the show, with Betty Ann Grove having the longest run. Guest singers also appeared, and there were segments with straight musical entertainment and comedy sketches and interviews.

STOREFRONT LAWYERS
Law Drama
FIRST TELECAST: *September 16, 1970*
LAST TELECAST: *September 1, 1971*
BROADCAST HISTORY:
 Sep 1970–Sep 1971, CBS Wed 7:30–8:30
CAST:
 David Hansen .... Robert Foxworth
 Deborah Sullivan .... Sheila Larkin
 Gabriel Kaye .... David Arkin
 Roberto Alvarez .... A Martinez
 Gloria Byrd .... Pauline Myers
 Devlin McNeil .... Gerald S. O'Loughlin

1970 was the year of relevance, and no series tried to be more relevant than *Storefront Lawyers*. In its premiere episode, young lawyer David Hansen gave up his position with the prestigious law firm of Horton, Troy, McNeil, Carroll and Clark, in plush Century City, California, to join two other young attorneys in a nonprofit practice. He, Deborah Sullivan, and Gabriel Kaye set up an office in a small store in a poor section of Los Angeles and offered their services to poor people who needed legal help but could not afford an expensive attorney. Following an unsuccessful fall, and a three-week hiatus in January, the series returned on February 3, 1971, with a new title, *Men at Law*, and a new format. The three young attorneys

were now working for the fancy law firm that Hansen had left in the fall, under the guidance of senior partner Devlin McNeil, and the cases were more conventional. They still worked on cases involving the underprivileged, but also took on those of more affluent members of the community. At this point, the amount of each episode that actually took place in the courtroom also increased substantially.

STORK CLUB, THE
Talk
FIRST TELECAST: *July 7, 1950*
LAST TELECAST: *July 24, 1955*
BROADCAST HISTORY:
 Jul 1950, CBS Wed/Fri 7:45–8:00
 Jul 1950–Sep 1950, CBS Mon/Wed/Fri 7:45–8:00
 Sep 1950–Dec 1950, CBS Mon–Fri 7:00–7:30
 Dec 1950–Jan 1951, CBS Tue/Thu/Sat 7:45–8:00
 Jan 1951–Jun 1952, CBS Tue/Thu 7:45–8:00
 Jul 1952–Oct 1953, CBS Sat 7:00–7:30
 Sep 1954–Mar 1955, ABC Sat 10:00–10:30
 Mar 1955–Jun 1955, ABC Sun 9:15–10:00
 Jul 1955, ABC Sun 9:30–10:00
REGULARS:
 Sherman Billingsley
 Peter Lind Hayes (1950)
 Mary Healy (1950)
 Johnny Johnston (1950–1951)
 Virginia Peine (1950–1951)

Stork Club owner Sherman Billingsley became a television celebrity through this series. It was unique in that it was broadcast live from a specially designed permanent set at the club itself. Guest celebrities were informally interviewed at the special "Table 50" and were often given Welsh terriers and boxers as gifts for appearing. Home viewers could also receive one of the pets by sending in particularly interesting questions to be asked of a specific guest. When the series began, Peter Lind Hayes and Mary Healy were regulars. They left in the fall of 1950, around the time Johnny Johnston and Virginia Peine (wife of writer Quentin Reynolds) were added. Johnny lasted only a couple of months and Miss Peine was on until the following June. At that point Sherman Billingsley decided to become the sole host of the show.

STORY OF THE WEEK
Interview
FIRST TELECAST: *January 7, 1948*
LAST TELECAST: *January 5, 1949*
BROADCAST HISTORY:
 Jan 1948–Nov 1948, NBC Wed 8:45–9:00
 Nov 1948–Jan 1949, NBC Wed 7:15–7:30
HOST:
 Richard Harkness

Public-affairs program from Washington, D.C. NBC political analyst Richard Harkness interviewed prominent public figures and commented on the latest events in the capital. Among the many notable guests was freshman Congressman Richard M. Nixon (Rep-Calif.), who commented on his solution to the problem of Communism.

STRAIGHTAWAY
Adventure
FIRST TELECAST: *October 6, 1961*
LAST TELECAST: *July 4, 1962*
BROADCAST HISTORY:
 Oct 1961–Dec 1961, ABC Fri 7:30–8:00
 Jan 1962–Jul 1962, ABC Wed 8:00–8:30
CAST:
 Scott Ross .... Brian Kelly
 Clipper Hamilton .... John Ashley

Scott and Clipper were partners in the Straightaway Garage, where they designed, built, and serviced racing cars. Scott was primarily a designer, and Clipper was the better mechanic. Their involvement with lovers of speed and racing led to the adventures depicted in this series. Originally, the title was to be *The Racers,* but it had to be changed because of sponsor problems. Autolite, the maker of spark plugs, loved racing. But the Ford Motor Company bought up Autolite between the commitment for the series and its actual premiere date. Ford makes cars and loves safety. The title had to be changed and many racing clips in the ten already finished episodes deleted before broadcast, due to Ford's objections.

STRANGE REPORT
Detective Drama
FIRST TELECAST: *January 8, 1971*
LAST TELECAST: *September 10, 1971*
BROADCAST HISTORY:
 Jan 1971–Sep 1971, NBC Fri 10:00–11:00
CAST:
 Adam Strange .... Anthony Quayle
 Hamlyn Gynt................... Kaz Garas
 Evelyn McLean .... Anneke Wills

Strange Report showcased the use of advanced scientific analytic methods as aids in the solution of complex crimes. Adam Strange was renowned as being the foremost authority on the workings of the criminal mind in the entire Western world. Operating out of his flat in the Paddington section of London, he handled special "problem" cases that the British government could not afford to be officially involved in. Adam and Hamlyn "Ham" Gynt, his American companion and assistant, traveled around town in Adam's unlicensed English taxicab working on cases. Gynt was a former Rhodes scholar whose formal job was in the research department of a London museum. Evelyn McLean, one of Adam's neighbors, was a model and aspiring artist whose friendship with him got her involved in many of his bizarre cases.

STRANGER, THE
Crime Drama
FIRST TELECAST: *June 25, 1954*

LAST TELECAST: *February 11, 1955*
BROADCAST HISTORY:
 Jun 1954–Feb 1955, DUM Fri 9:00–9:30
CAST:
 The Stranger .... Robert Carroll

Mystery series dramatizing the adventures of a benevolent stranger who entered into the lives of people threatened by evildoers. The first episode told of a member of a ship's crew pursued by thieves who wanted his collection of beer steins from various ports. The sailor didn't know why they were after him, but "the stranger" did. Later episodes dealt with murder, kidnapping, etc., and at one point "the stranger" even went behind the Iron Curtain. He never accepted payment for his services, and disappeared as mysteriously as he had come after each case was solved.

STRAUSS FAMILY, THE
Romantic Drama
FIRST TELECAST: *May 5, 1973*
LAST TELECAST: *June 16, 1973*
BROADCAST HISTORY:
 May 1973–Jun 1973, ABC Sat 9:00–10:00
CAST:
 Johann Strauss, Sr.............. Eric Woolfe
 Johann Strauss, Jr. .... Stuart Wilson
 Anna Strauss .... Anne Stallybrass
 Emilie Trampusch .... Barbara Ferris
 Lanner .... Derek Jacobi
 Josef .... Nicholas Simmonds
 Hetti..................... Margaret Whiting
 Edi .... Tony Anholt
 Annele .... Hilary Hardiman
 Theresa .... Amanda Walker

True saga of the fabulous "waltz kings" of 19th-century Vienna, produced in England and aired in the U.S. as a seven-part mini-series. The family's history was certainly the stuff of good soap opera. Johann, Sr., was a famous composer and the toast of Vienna, but he was gradually being overshadowed by his ambitious son, who wrote such immortal melodies as "The Blue Danube Waltz" and "Tales from the Vienna Woods." Father and son clashed not only over musical prestige but over politics, women, and just about everything else, and Johann, Sr.'s wife, Anna, was torn between the two. Eventually she left Sr. to his mistress, Emilie, and devoted her full attention to aiding Jr.'s growing career. Romance, death, unfaithful lovers, and great political struggles swept through this epic, along with dozens of cast members, the most prominent of whom are listed above. Music was provided by members of the London Symphony Orchestra.

STRAW HAT THEATRE
 see *ABC Dramatic Shorts—1952–1953*

STRAWHATTERS, THE
Variety
FIRST TELECAST: *May 27, 1953*

LAST TELECAST: *September 8, 1954*
BROADCAST HISTORY:
May 1953–Sep 1953, DUM Wed 8:30–9:30
Jun 1954–Sep 1954, DUM Wed 9:00–10:00
EMCEE:
Johnny Olsen (1953)
Virginia Graham (1954)

This was essentially an hour-long advertisement for Palisades Amusement Park, located in New Jersey, across the Hudson River from New York City. It was (and looked like) a super-cheap production, consisting of a talent show, diving exhibitions in the park's big pool, musical entertainment in the ballroom, and pickups from other locations around the park. Much of the show was done outdoors.

The program was seen locally in New York in 1952 and went out over the full DuMont network (such as it was) from 1953–1954. The 1954 version was called *Summer in the Park*.

STREET, THE
Police Drama
BROADCAST HISTORY:
Syndicated only
30 minutes
Produced: *1988–*
Released: *April 1988*
CAST:
Officer Bud Peluso .... Bruce MacVittie
Officer Arthur Scolari .... Stanley Tucci
Officer Jack Runyon .... Ron J. Ryan
Officer Shepard Scott .... Michael Beach

Shot on location in Newark and other cities of northern New Jersey, *The Street* was a five-nights-a-week cop show that focussed on several patrol car officers, both on and off duty. It was filmed mostly at night with hand-held cameras to give it a documentary/news look, and it exuded a gritty reality that made some viewers wince. Linking the segments together was patrol car 260, used by Peluso and Scolari on the 3:00–11:00 P.M. shift and Runyon and Cooper from 11:00 P.M.–7:00 A.M. The series began with Cooper being shot in the genitals with his own gun, by a female traffic offender with whom he tried to trade the ticket for sex. Runyon, with his somewhat racist attitudes, was none too comfortable to then be paired with black officer Scott, while waiting for Cooper to recover. Peluso and Scolari were squabbling friends, who had been best buddies since parochial school.

In addition to its cinema-verité look, *The Street* used very frank language (there was an on-screen warning to this effect), and showed its officers to have real prejudices and shortcomings. Because of the subject matter and language, most stations aired it after 11:00 P.M.

STREET HAWK
Police Drama
FIRST TELECAST: *January 4, 1985*

LAST TELECAST: *May 16, 1985*
BROADCAST HISTORY:
Jan 1985–Mar 1985, ABC Fri 9:00–10:00
May 1985, ABC Thu 8:00–9:00
CAST:
Off. Jesse Mach .... Rex Smith
Norman Tuttle .... Joe Regalbuto
Capt. Leo Altobelli .... Richard Venture
Rachel Adams .... Jeannie Wilson

There's an old saying that there are two types of motorcyclists—those who have had an accident, and those who will have one. Jesse Mach evidently wanted to be in both groups. Jesse had been a top motorcycle cop until he was seriously injured, and assigned to desk duty. He was then approached by Norman, inventor of the super-secret Street Hawk police bike, with an offer he couldn't refuse: Norman would arrange for "experimental surgery" to repair Jesse's shattered leg if Jesse would agree to become the secret "test pilot" for Norman's incredible new baby. And so by night Jesse donned a futuristic black helmet and fought crime on city streets on the Street Hawk, with its 300 m.p.h. speed, computerized targeting system, high-energy particle beam (to blow things up), and ability to leap through the air. By day he maintained his cover at a desk in the police public information office. Drive carefully, Jesse.

STREETS OF SAN FRANCISCO, THE
Police Drama
FIRST TELECAST: *September 16, 1972*
LAST TELECAST: *June 23, 1977*
BROADCAST HISTORY:
Sep 1972–Jan 1973, ABC Sat 9:00–10:00
Jan 1973–Aug 1974, ABC Thu 10:00–11:00
Sep 1974–Sep 1976, ABC Thu 9:00–10:00
Sep 1976–Jun 1977, ABC Thu 10:00–11:00
CAST:
Det. Lt. Mike Stone .... Karl Malden
Inspector Steve Keller (1972–1976)
.... Michael Douglas
Inspector Dan Robbins (1976–1977)
.... Richard Hatch
Lt. Lessing .... Lee Harris
EXECUTIVE PRODUCER:
Quinn Martin

There always seems to be room on TV for a police show set in San Francisco (remember *The Lineup?*). *The Streets of San Francisco* was such a show for the 1970s, following the cases of Lt. Mike Stone and his young partner as they used modern police methods to track down criminals, against the backdrop of the Bay Area. Mike was a 23-year veteran of the force, a widower, assigned to the Bureau of Inspectors Division of the San Francisco Police Department. His original partner was 28-year-old Steve Keller, a smart, college-educated man who rose from assistant inspector to inspector during his tenure on the show. In 1976 he left ("to enter teaching") and was replaced by the athletic Dan Robbins.

Mike's co-ed daughter was seen occasionally during the early years (played by Darleen Carr), but later the emphasis was shifted to the cases, rather than the home lives, of the principals. Some scenes in the series were filmed in actual San Francisco police buildings, such as the communications center, the morgue, etc.

Based on characters from the novel *Poor, Poor Ophelia*, by Carolyn Weston.

STRENGTH FOR A FREE WORLD
see *Marshall Plan in Action, The*

STRICTLY FOR LAUGHS
Music
FIRST TELECAST: *November 22, 1949*
LAST TELECAST: *June 23, 1950*
BROADCAST HISTORY:
   Nov 1949–Dec 1949, CBS Tue/Wed/Fri 7:00–7:15
   Dec 1949, CBS Mon/Tue/Wed/Fri 7:00–7:15
   Jan 1950, CBS Mon/Wed/Thu/Fri 7:00–7:15
   Jan 1950–Jun 1950, CBS Mon–Fri 7:00–7:15
REGULARS:
   The Kirby Stone Quintet

The light-hearted harmonizing of the Kirby Stone Quintet was featured in this live 15-minute musical program. Their songs were often pleasantly amusing, though not up to the level of silliness attained by the likes of Spike Jones. Rather, the lyrics tended to have subtle twists. Occasionally they were joined by guest performers. Effective with the telecast of April 3, 1950, the title of the series was changed to *The Kirby Stone Quintet*.

STRIKE FORCE
Police
FIRST TELECAST: *November 13, 1981*
LAST TELECAST: *September 24, 1982*
BROADCAST HISTORY:
   Nov 1981–May 1982, ABC Fri 10:00–11:00
   Sep 1982, ABC Fri 10:00–11:00
CAST:
   Capt. Frank Murphy . . . . Robert Stack
   Det. Paul Strobber . . . . Dorian Harewood
   Lt. Charlie Gunzer . . . . Richard Romanus
   Det. Mark Osborn . . . . Michael Goodwin
   Det. Rosie Johnson . . . . Trisha Noble
   Deputy Commissioner Herbert Klein
   . . . . Herb Edelman

Capt. Frank Murphy headed this special unit within the Los Angeles Police Department dedicated to solving the toughest cases. Tackling only one case at a time, these men spent much of their time undercover, tracking mad bombers, rapists, assassins, fanatical cult leaders, and other undesirables who had proven too elusive for ordinary cops.

STRIKE IT RICH
Quiz/Audience Participation
FIRST TELECAST: *July 4, 1951*
LAST TELECAST: *January 12, 1955*
BROADCAST HISTORY:
   Jul 1951–Jan 1955, CBS Wed 9:00–9:30
EMCEE:
   Warren Hull

Strike It Rich was one of the most hotly debated programs on television during the 1950s. To some it was TV's noblest hour, helping those less fortunate than most through the charity and goodwill of viewers. To others it was one of the most sickening spectacles ever seen on a TV screen, exploiting those same unfortunates for the vicarious thrill of viewers and the selfish gain of advertisers, a kind of video "kick the cripple." It was investigated by governmental bodies, limned by charitable organizations, and defended by others. Whichever way you looked at it, though, it was certainly popular, and perhaps the ultimate example of viewer-participation television.

Strike It Rich was created by producer Walt Framer and was first heard on CBS radio in 1947. It consisted of a quiz show whose contestants were exclusively people in need of money—for medical treatment, for a destitute family, for a crippled children's hospital, for a little girl who had lost her dog. About a quarter of the contestants were actually representing someone else who was in need. The questions were easy and most contestants were winners—if you could classify anyone on a show like this a "winner"—but even if they lost, there was always the "Heart Line." After they told their tale of woe, emcee Hull would open up the telephone lines and ask viewers to pitch in what they could. And they did, thousands of dollars every broadcast, expensive therapeutic equipment, clothes, and furniture for those who had none, an endless stream of gifts from all over America to help ease the contestant's suffering.

The problem, besides the obvious ethical one, was that the program seemed to promise more than it could deliver. For every charity case that got on the air, hundreds were turned away (only "appealing" or "interesting" cases were wanted). From 3,000 to 5,000 letters a week poured in from desperate people, and despite the program's repeated advice to the contrary, dozens of them journeyed to New York in hopes of being picked out of the studio audience. Most of these wound up stranded in the city, and were forced to go to welfare agencies or the Salvation Army—which complained bitterly about the effect the show was having. The New York City Commissioner of Welfare called *Strike It Rich* "a disgusting spectacle and a national disgrace," and demanded that it be investigated. The supervisor of the Travelers Aid Society said, "We don't know if the successes on the show balance off against the human misery caused by it. But from what we see, I'd say they didn't. . . . Putting human misery on display can hardly be called right." The General Director of the Family Service Association of America said flatly, "Victims of poverty, illness, and everyday misfortune should not be made a public spectacle or seemingly be put in the position of begging for charity." A New York State legislative committee did look into the controversy, but then washed its hands of the affair, claiming that it did not have jurisdiction. As for CBS and NBC, the networks that carried the show on television and radio respectively, they were unconcerned. "We don't want to do anything that would antagonize the sponsor," said NBC.

And so the program that *TV Guide* called "a despicable travesty on the very nature of charity" continued untouched until it ended its normal run.

Strike It Rich remained on CBS' daytime TV schedule until January 1958. There were two attempts to revive it as a syndicated program in the 1970s, with Bert Parks as host in 1973 and Tom Kelly as host in 1978. Neither revival was successful.

Joe Garagiola hosted a syndicated quiz show that used the title *Strike It Rich* during the 1986–1987 season.

STRUCK BY LIGHTNING
Situation Comedy
FIRST TELECAST: *September 19, 1979*
LAST TELECAST: *October 3, 1979*
BROADCAST HISTORY:
   Sep 1979–Oct 1979, CBS Wed 8:30–9:00
CAST:
   Ted Stein . . . . Jeffrey Kramer
   Frank . . . . Jack Elam
   Nora . . . . Millie Slavin
   Glenn Diamond . . . . Bill Erwin
   Brian . . . . Jeff Cotler
   Walt Calvin . . . . Richard Stahl

Jack Elam played Frankenstein for laughs in this extremely short-lived comedy. "Frank" was the caretaker of the ramshackle Brightwater Inn, on the Old Boston Post Road in modern-day rural Massachusetts. Ted Stein, a young science teacher who had recently inherited the inn, planned to sell it until he found out that Frank was in fact the 231-year-old Frankenstein monster, and that he, Ted, was the great-great-grandson of the original Dr. Frankenstein. Frank convinced Ted to keep the inn open and try to re-create his ancestor's life-sustaining formula. Unlike the monster of legend, Frank was kind and gentle, if a bit clumsy. Hanging out around the inn was Nora, who had been running the place before Ted arrived, her young son, Brian, a long-time boarder named Glenn, and real-estate agent Walt Calvin, who wanted Ted to sell the place through him.

Struck by Lightning wasn't, and the program was canceled after only three telecasts.

STU ERWIN SHOW, THE
Situation Comedy
FIRST TELECAST: *October 21, 1950*
LAST TELECAST: *April 13, 1955*
BROADCAST HISTORY:
   Oct 1950–Sep 1951, ABC Sat 7:30–8:00
   Oct 1951–Apr 1952, ABC Fri 8:30–9:00
   May 1952–Oct 1954, ABC Fri 7:30–8:00
   Oct 1954–Apr 1955, ABC Wed 8:30–9:00
CAST:
   Stu Erwin . . . . Himself
   June Erwin . . . . June Collyer
   Jackie Erwin . . . . Sheila James
   Joyce Erwin (1950–1954) . . . . Ann Todd
   Joyce Erwin (1954–1955) . . . . . . Merry Anders
   Willie . . . . Willie Best
   Harry (1954–1955) . . . . Harry Hayden
   Jimmy Clark (1954–1955) . . . . . . Martin Milner

This was perhaps TV's leading bumbling-father series in the 1950s. Stu Erwin had made a long career of similar roles in movies and on radio before he came to TV in 1950. He was perfect for the role: he looked and acted like a well-meaning, folksy, but completely incompetent middle-aged suburban parent.

Stu was principal of Hamilton High School, which often served to get him involved in various civic activities. But most of the action was around the Erwins' own home, where Stu's every attempt to fix or improve things, surprise someone, or bring up the kids turned to disaster. Wife June (played by Erwin's real-life wife, June Collyer) generally came to the rescue. Teenage Joyce and tomboy Jackie rounded out the family, while Willie was the handyman and various neighbors came and went.

In 1954 Joyce began going steady with Jimmy Clark, and in a December telecast they were married. Also in the 1954–1955 season the producers made an effort to portray Stu as a little less blundering than he had been—something devoutly wished for by actor Erwin—but the series had run its course by early 1955.

The series was first known as *Life with the Erwins,* and later *The Trouble with Father* (which continued as its subtitle). During the final season, to emphasize the changes, it became *The New Stu Erwin Show.*

STUDIO 57
Dramatic Anthology
FIRST TELECAST: *September 21, 1954*
LAST TELECAST: *September 6, 1955*
BROADCAST HISTORY:
   Sep 1954–Oct 1954, DUM Tue 9:00–9:30
   Oct 1954–Sep 1955, DUM Tue 8:30–9:00

This filmed dramatic series had few distinctions—the scripts were weak, the actors generally lesser known (at the time)—except that it was one of the last regularly scheduled series ever carried on the crumbling DuMont network. Only *What's* the *Story*, among non-sports series, lasted a few weeks longer. The title derived from the sponsor, "Heinz 57 Varieties."

Stories on *Studio 57* were generally mysteries or melodramas, set in various historical periods. Among the actors and actresses appearing were Craig Stevens, Natalie Wood, Hugh O'Brian, Pat Carroll, Peter Graves, Charles Coburn, and Brian Keith.

STUDIO ONE

Dramatic Anthology

FIRST TELECAST: *November 7, 1948*
LAST TELECAST: *September 29, 1958*
BROADCAST HISTORY:
  Nov 1948–Mar 1949, CBS Sun 7:30–8:30
  Mar 1949–May 1949, CBS Sun 7:00–8:00
  May 1949–Sep 1949, CBS Wed 10:00–11:00
  Sep 1949–Sep 1958, CBS Mon 10:00–11:00
COMMERCIAL SPOKESPERSON:
  Betty Furness (1949–1958)

When *Studio One* premiered on CBS radio in the spring of 1947, there was little immediate concern at the network over the possible incursion of television as a competing medium. Little priority was given to TV, as CBS did not yet have a TV network. All that changed after the success of NBC's video coverage of the 1947 World Series. There was a crash development program at CBS and one of the principal components in that development was to be a live dramatic-anthology series. The radio version of *Studio One* lasted less than a year, but under the dynamic early leadership of producer Worthington Miner the new TV version became a major success, lasting for almost a full decade.

Miner's approach to television was somewhat different from that of many of the other producers of early dramatic shows. His concern was with the visual impact of the stories, for television was a visual medium, and he placed a greater emphasis on that than on the literary merit of the story. It was not that he produced second-rate plays—to the contrary, many of them were adaptations of classics and from the best young writers available (Miner personally did many of the adaptations during his tenure with *Studio One*)—but Miner's major contribution to television drama was more in his experimentation with camera techniques and other innovations in what the viewer saw, rather than in what was heard.

The premiere telecast of *Studio One,* on November 7, 1948, was an adaptation of the mystery play *The Storm,* starring stage and screen actress Margaret Sullavan, one of the few established stars who was willing to perform on the new medium, especially considering the lowly pay (a maximum of $500 was budgeted for talent on early telecasts). The budgetary problems resulted in other interesting innovations. *Julius Caesar* was done twice in the spring of 1949, with Robert Keith in the lead and young Charlton Heston in a minor role, but lack of money forced the producers to stage it in modern dress. In 1955, with more cash available, *Julius Caesar* was done for a third time, in traditional period costumes, with Theodore Bikel starring.

Studio One had gone on the air without a sponsor, but it gained one in Westinghouse Electric in early 1949. On Westinghouse's third telecast the commercials were done by an actress named Betty Furness. She went on to become the most recognized and famous commercial spokesperson in the history of television. She would remain with the series until its cancellation in 1958 and continued with its successor, *Westinghouse Desilu Playhouse.* The picture of her demonstrating a range or opening a refrigerator and the slogan "You Can Be Sure If It's Westinghouse" were ingrained with a generation of Americans.

In the early years of *Studio One,* three performers were seen far more often than any others— Charlton Heston, Mary Sinclair, and Maria Riva—each with the lead roles in at least a dozen plays. Heston starred in adaptations of *Of Human Bondage, Jane Eyre* with Miss Sinclair, *The Taming of the Shrew* with Phyllis Kirk, and *Wuthering Heights,* again with Miss Sinclair, and many lesser-known plays. Many of the better plays were repeated. The premiere presentation, *The Storm,* was redone in 1949 with Marsha Hunt in the lead role; *Jane Eyre* was done again in 1952; "Flowers from a Stranger" starred Yul Brynner in both 1949 and 1950; and *Julius Caesar,* as mentioned above, was done three times.

Doing live shows often presented problems. In a 1953 story, "Dry Run," whole sections of a submarine were built in the studio and the entire cast was almost electrocuted when the water that was used for special effects got very close to the power cables. Many young directors, such as Frank Schaffner, George Roy Hill, Sidney Lumet, and Paul Nickell, got their baptism under fire with this hectic live series. Authors like Rod Serling, Gore Vidal, Paul Monash, and Reginald Rose contributed teleplays for *Studio One* and it was Rose's "The Twelve Angry Men" in 1954 that won Emmys for writing (Rose), direction (Frank Schaffner), and performance by an actor in a drama (Bob Cummings).

Two months after "The Twelve Angry Men," another episode of *Studio One* aired that is remembered not for its dramatic merit, but for a song. The producers were planning to do a drama about skulduggery in the record industry and they needed a song, so they turned to Mitch Miller, head of recording for CBS' subsidiary, Columbia Records. Miller gave them an obscure ballad called "Let Me Go, Devil," and urged that it be sung on the soundtrack by an unknown songstress rather than by an established star, to heighten the dramatic impact. With remarkable foresight he then saw to it that, prior to the telecast, record stores were well stocked with her Columbia recording of the song.

There was little demand for the record until the night of the telecast (November 15, 1954). Now called "Let Me Go, Lover," and emotionally sung by Joan Weber, it was woven skillfully throughout the drama. The next morning record stores were deluged with customers wanting "that song that was on TV last night"—and "Let Me Go, Lover" became a phenomenal hit, selling more than 500,000 copies in the next five days (it eventually sold over one million). It was one of the few times in the history of television that a single telecast was directly responsible for a major song hit.

People appeared on *Studio One* who may now seem to have been somewhat out of place. Newsman Mike Wallace appeared in two dramas. Jackie Gleason and Art Carney, while still doing their live variety show, took time to star in a serious drama called "The Laugh Maker" in the spring of 1953, and later made other occasional appearances on the show separately. Ironically, Elizabeth Montgomery showed up on *Studio One* a few times in the mid-1950s. Her father was the host of *Robert Montgomery Presents,* the NBC Monday night dramatic showcase that was in direct competition with *Studio One* for most of its run. Even Edward R. Murrow was featured on the series, though not as an actor. He was the narrator of a 1957 documentary-drama, "The Night America Trembled," about Orson Welles' 1938 broadcast of "War of the Worlds."

With the first telecast in January 1958, *Studio One* moved to Hollywood, with the title appropriately changed to *Studio One in Hollywood.* It had moved because that was where the talent was, and the facilities for production were better than in New York. It was still done live, but only remained on the air for another nine months. Live drama was dying, as was New York origination of TV series.

In its decade on the air, *Studio One* presented nearly 500 plays. Literally thousands of actors and actresses appeared, but only a few of them were featured in at least half a dozen plays. Other than those already mentioned above, they were Katherine Bard, Richard Kiley, Priscilla Gillette, Judson Laire, Harry Townes, John Forsythe, Nina Foch, Hildy Parks, Sheppard Strudwick, Leslie Nielsen, James Daly, Everett Sloane, Betsy Palmer, Skip Homeier, James Gregory, Cathleen Nesbitt, Edward Andrews, Barbara O'Neill, Burt Brinckerhoff, Cliff Norton, Stanley Ridges, and Felicia Montealegre.

During the summers, when the regular *Studio One* production team was vacationing, the series was variously titled *Summer Theatre, Westinghouse Summer Theatre,* and *Studio One Summer Theatre.*

STUDS LONIGAN
Drama
FIRST TELECAST: *March 7, 1979*
LAST TELECAST: *March 21, 1979*

BROADCAST HISTORY:
Mar 1979, NBC Wed 9:00–11:00
CAST:
Studs Lonigan .... Harry Hamlin
Mrs. Lonigan .... Colleen Dewhurst
Mr. Lonigan .... Charles Durning
Martin .... John Friedrich
Lucy Scanlon .... Lisa Pelikan
Danny O'Neill .... Brad Dourif
Weary .... David Wilson
Loretta .... Jessica Harper
Fran .... Devon Ericson
Eileen .... Laurie Heineman
Paulie .... Michael Mullins
Catherine Banahan .... Diana Scarwid
Davey Cohen .... Sam Weisman
Phil Rolfe .... Jed Cooper

Set in Chicago, *Studs Lonigan* was the saga of an Irish-American family from the latter stages of World War I until the onset of the Great Depression, in 1930. It was an earthy story centering on young Studs, who was struggling into adulthood in a brawling city full of temptations. He watched as his buddies drifted away into various careers and greater success than he himself found. His social life was split between two extremes—quiet, sensitive Catherine and lusty, sensual Lucy. Underlying it all, as the prologue stated, was "a passionate and realistic echo of urban America as it used to be."

Studs Lonigan was based on the trilogy written by James T. Farrell. It aired as one of the *NBC Novels for Television.*

STUDS' PLACE
Variety
FIRST TELECAST: *November 26, 1949*
LAST TELECAST: *January 28, 1952*
BROADCAST HISTORY:
Nov 1949–Dec 1949, NBC Sat 8:45–9:00
Apr 1950–May 1950, NBC Thu 8:00–8:30
May 1950–Aug 1950, NBC Thu 8:30–9:00
Oct 1950–Aug 1951, ABC Fri 10:30–11:00
Aug 1951–Jan 1952, ABC Mon 10:30–11:00
CAST:
Studs Terkel .... Himself
Grace, the Waitress (1950) . Beverly Younger
Wynn (1950–1952).............. Win Stracke
Mr. Lord (1950) .... Phil Lord
Mr. Denby (1950) .... Jonathan Hole
Pianist (1950–1952).............. Chet Roble

Studs Terkel presided over this affable program of songs and stories, which was at first set in Studs' bar in New York, with Studs as the bartender. This version ran only about a month, and was then incorporated as a regular segment in the Saturday night series *Saturday Square.* When *Saturday Square* was canceled Studs returned again with his own series, this time cast as the proprietor of a Chicago barbecue restaurant frequented by a number of regulars. Among them were Wynn the folk-singing handyman, and Chet the jazz pianist. Both series were loosely plotted, with Studs' garrulous, philosophical ramblings the center of attention.

Telecast from Chicago.

STUMP THE AUTHORS
Stories
FIRST TELECAST: *January 15, 1949*
LAST TELECAST: *April 2, 1949*
BROADCAST HISTORY:
Jan 1949–Apr 1949, ABC Sat 9:00–9:30
EDITOR: Syd Breeze
AUTHORS:
Lou Zara
Dorothy Day
Jack Payne
Angel Casey

Ad-lib storytelling session in which three or four authors tried to spin yarns based on props given to them, which they had never seen before. From Chicago.

STUMP THE STARS
see *Pantomime Quiz*

SUGAR HILL TIMES
Musical Variety
FIRST TELECAST: *September 13, 1949*
LAST TELECAST: *October 20, 1949*
BROADCAST HISTORY:
Sep 1949, CBS Tue 8:00–9:00
Oct 1949, CBS Thu 8:30–9:00
REGULARS:
Willie Bryant
Harry Bellafonte
Timmie Rogers
The Jubileers
Don Redman and His Orchestra

Sugar Hill Times was one of network television's first, short-lived attempts at show-casing black talent. All of the performers in the live weekly musical variety show were black. It aired three times as a full-hour show, and each time had a different title, premiering as *Uptown Jubilee,* changing to *Harlem Jubilee,* and finally settling on *Sugar Hill Times,* the title it also used during its two half-hour telecasts on October 6 and 20. It may have been an unintentional oversight on the part of the CBS press department at the time, but every press release for the show spelled singer Harry Belafonte's name as it's listed above, with two *l*'s.

SUGAR TIME!
Situation Comedy
FIRST TELECAST: *August 13, 1977*
LAST TELECAST: *May 29, 1978*
BROADCAST HISTORY:
Aug 1977–Sep 1977, ABC Sat 8:30–9:00
Apr 1978–May 1978, ABC Mon 8:00–8:30

CAST:
Maxx .... Barbi Benton
Maggie .... Marianne Black
Diane .... Didi Carr
Al Marks .... Wynn Irwin
Paul Landson .... Mark Winkworth

Popular singer/composer Paul Williams wrote original songs and was musical supervisor for this comedy series about three beautiful young girls who were aspiring rock singers. The talented trio called themselves Sugar, and shared an apartment in California where they were attempting to launch their act, without pay, at Al Marks' Tryout Room. Maxx, beautiful and naive, worked as a hat-check girl; Diane, a wise-cracking native of the Bronx, was a dental hygienist; and Maggie, the practical one, taught dancing to children. A constant threat to the group's success was Diane's indecision over whether she should marry her favorite dentist.

SUGARFOOT
Western
FIRST TELECAST: *September 17, 1957*
LAST TELECAST: *July 3, 1961*
BROADCAST HISTORY:
Sep 1957–Sep 1960, ABC Tue 7:30–8:30
Oct 1960–Jul 1961, ABC Mon 7:30–8:30
CAST:
Tom "Sugarfoot" Brewster ..... Will Hutchins

Western about the exploits of a young correspondence-school law student who rode west in search of adventure. Unfortunately, Tom Brewster was somewhat inept as a cowboy, and he promptly earned the nickname "Sugarfoot"—one grade lower than a tenderfoot—in the first episode. Undeterred, and with a redeeming sense of humor, he set out to lasso some outlaws and round up a few pretty girls, if possible.

Although it was a Western in the traditional sense, with plenty of action, *Sugarfoot* always had a light touch which set it apart from most examples of the genre. It ran on an alternate-week basis with *Cheyenne* from 1957–1959, with *Bronco* from 1959–1960, and then became one of three rotating elements of the *Cheyenne* anthology for its final season.

SUMMER BROTHERS SMOTHERS SHOW, THE
Comedy Variety
FIRST TELECAST: *June 23, 1968*
LAST TELECAST: *September 8, 1968*
BROADCAST HISTORY:
Jun 1968–Sep 1968, CBS Sun 9:00–10:00
REGULARS:
Glen Campbell
Pat Paulsen
Leigh French
John Hartford
The Jimmy Joyce Singers
Nelson Riddle & His Orchestra

This 1968 summer replacement for *The Smothers Brothers Comedy Hour* starred country singer Glen Campbell, who was later to get a regular series of his own, and two of the regulars from the Smothers Brothers group, comics Pat Paulsen and Leigh French. Regular features of the show were comedy sketches featuring Leigh French as a hippie, and Pat Paulsen doing improbable editorials and campaigning for President.

SUMMER CINEMA
see Movies—Prior to 1961

SUMMER FAIR
see ABC Dramatic Shorts—*1952–1953*

SUMMER FOCUS
Documentary
FIRST TELECAST: *May 18, 1967*
LAST TELECAST: *August 31, 1967*
BROADCAST HISTORY:
　May 1967–Aug 1967, ABC Thu 10:00–11:00

This series of documentaries included an examination of political protest in America, a debate on the limits of free speech in a democracy, a pictorial study of the paintings of Leonardo Da Vinci, an examination of health-care problems in America, and a look at the pollution problems facing both small and large cities.

SUMMER FUN
Comedy Anthology
FIRST TELECAST: *July 22, 1966*
LAST TELECAST: *September 2, 1966*
BROADCAST HISTORY:
　Jul 1966–Sep 1966, ABC Fri 8:00–8:30

ABC aired a collection of unsold pilots for projected situation comedy series for seven consecutive Fridays during the summer of 1966. Among them were shows starring Cliff Arquette, Bert Lahr, and Shelley Fabares.

SUMMER HOLIDAY
Music
FIRST TELECAST: *June 24, 1954*
LAST TELECAST: *September 9, 1954*
BROADCAST HISTORY:
　Jun 1954–Sep 1954, CBS Thu 7:45–8:00
　Jul 1954–Aug 1954, CBS Tue 7:45–8:00
REGULARS:
　Merv Griffin
　Betty Ann Grove

This twice-weekly summer replacement for both *The Jo Stafford Show* and *The Jane Froman Show* was a live musical interlude that filled the remainder of the half hour in which CBS aired its network news program. The Tuesday edition was titled *Summer Holiday* and the Thursday edition *Song Snapshots on a Summer Holiday*. The format had the two singing stars portray camera

bugs on an around-the-world tour, with sets and costumes of an appropriate nature, all to serve as a backdrop for their solos and duets.

SUMMER IN THE PARK
see *Strawhatters, The*

SUMMER NIGHT THEATER
Anthology
FIRST TELECAST: *July 7, 1953*
LAST TELECAST: *July 28, 1953*
BROADCAST HISTORY:
　Jul 1953, DUM Tue 10:00–10:30

A four-week series of filmed dramas, starring Gale Storm, Lloyd Bridges, and others. The series continued to be seen locally in New York for the remainder of the summer.

SUMMER PLAYHOUSE
Anthology
FIRST TELECAST: *July 6, 1954*
LAST TELECAST: *September 6, 1965*
BROADCAST HISTORY:
　July 1954–Aug 1954, NBC Tue 9:00–9:30
　Jul 1957–Sep 1957, NBC Tue 9:30–10:00
　Jul 1964–Sep 1964, CBS Sat 9:30–10:00
　Jun 1965–Sep 1965, CBS Mon 8:30–9:00
HOST:
　Nelson Case (1954)
　Jane Wyman (1957)

These were all summer anthology series used to fill time until the fall season started. On the two occasions a program with the title *Summer Playhouse* aired on NBC, the episodes were reruns from other anthology series. The two CBS versions in the 1960s were made up of unsold pilots for projected regular series.

SUMMER SPORTS SPECTACULAR, THE
Sports Anthology
FIRST TELECAST: *April 27, 1961*
LAST TELECAST: *September 28, 1961*
BROADCAST HISTORY:
　Apr 1961–Sep 1961, CBS Thu 7:30–8:30
HOST:
　Bud Palmer

CBS had premiered a weekly sports anthology on Sunday afternoons in January 1960 titled *The Sunday Sports Spectacular*. During the summer of 1961 it moved to Thursday evenings as *The Summer Sports Spectacular*. Host Bud Palmer covered a different type of sporting event each week. The premiere telecast was a figure-skating memorial tribute to the members of the 1960 U.S. Olympic figure skating team who had died tragically in an airplane crash. Subsequent episodes covered spring training with one of the two brand-new American League Baseball teams—Gene Autry's Los Angeles Angels—coverage of the European soccer championships, the Army-Navy lacrosse game, a gymnastics meet between the U.S. and Japan, and a motorcycle rally. In addition to actual event coverage, each telecast included background on the sport and interviews with participants.

The Sunday Sports Spectacular changed its name to *The CBS Sports Spectacular* in January 1963 and continued to run on a seasonal basis until the fall of 1967. It returned in January 1973 and has been on ever since, changing its name to *CBS Sports Saturday* and *CBS Sports Sunday* when it started airing episodes on both Saturdays and Sundays in the spring of 1981.

SUMMER SUNDAY U.S.A.
News Magazine
FIRST TELECAST: *July 1, 1984*
LAST TELECAST: *September 7, 1984*
BROADCAST HISTORY:
Jul 1984–Sep 1984, NBC Sun 7:00–8:00
ANCHORS:
Andrea Mitchell
Linda Ellerbee

Summer Sunday was one of a long series of attempts by NBC to establish a prime-time news magazine program, but its scheduling directly opposite CBS' enormously popular *60 Minutes* was fatal. It was certainly different from NBC's previous efforts, however. The program originated live each week from outdoor locations around the country, and included such features as short quiz segments between the stories and "Trading Places," in which politicians were given a chance to question the reporters.

SUMMER THEATRE
see *Studio One*

SUMMER THEATRE
Dramatic Anthology
FIRST TELECAST: *July 10, 1953*
LAST TELECAST: *September 11, 1953*
BROADCAST HISTORY:
Jul 1953–Sep 1953, ABC Fri 8:00–8:30

This filmed anthology series aired on ABC during the summer of 1953 as the replacement for *The Adventures of Ozzie & Harriet*. The title alternated from week to week because of sponsorship. One week it was *Summer Theatre* and on the alternate week it was *Interlude*. Among the presentations were "Myrt and Marge" with Franklin Pangborn and Lyle Talbot and "Foo Young" with Richard Loo.

SUMMERTIME U.S.A.
Music
FIRST TELECAST: *July 7, 1953*
LAST TELECAST: *August 27, 1953*
BROADCAST HISTORY:
Jul 1953–Aug 1953, CBS Tue/Thu 7:45–8:00

REGULARS:
Teresa Brewer
Mel Torme
The Honeydreamers
Ray Bloch & His Orchestra

This series was the 1953 summer replacement for another music series, *Jane Froman's U.S.A. Canteen*. The two stars, Teresa Brewer and Mel Torme, were seen in a different resort setting for each of the live telecasts. The scenic backgrounds ranged from Atlantic City and Niagara Falls on the domestic side, to Rio, Havana, and the Casbah on the international side.

SUNDAY AT HOME
Music
FIRST TELECAST: *July 3, 1949*
LAST TELECAST: *July 31, 1949*
BROADCAST HISTORY:
Jul 1949, NBC Sun 7:15–7:30
FEATURED:
The Pickard Family

Short-lived summer show which presented the Pickard family (Mom, Dad, and four children) singing hymns and old favorite songs. Filmed in Hollywood.

SUNDAY DATE
Music
FIRST TELECAST: *August 21, 1949*
LAST TELECAST: *October 9, 1949*
BROADCAST HISTORY:
Aug 1949–Oct 1949, NBC Sun 7:15–7:30

Live musical interlude featuring an assortment of young, lesser-known singers and instrumentalists, and set in an imaginary sidewalk cafe just off New York's Central Park.

SUNDAY LUCY SHOW, THE
see *I Love Lucy*

SUNDAY MYSTERY HOUR, THE
see *Chevy Mystery Show, The*

SUNDAY SHOWCASE
Variety
FIRST TELECAST: *September 20, 1959*
LAST TELECAST: *May 1, 1960*
BROADCAST HISTORY:
Sep 1959–May 1960, NBC Sun 8:00–9:00

Sunday Showcase was actually a varied series of specials that aired in the 8:00–9:00 P.M. hour on Sunday evenings during the 1959–1960 season. Some of them were dramatic plays, some were comedy variety shows (such as "The Milton Berle Show"), some were musical comedies, and some were historical dramas (such as "Our American Heritage"). Among the other notable telecasts were a two-part version of Budd Schulberg's novel *What Makes Sammy Run* and the premiere offering, a "poetic drama" by S. Lee Pogostin called "People Kill People Sometimes," starring George C. Scott, Geraldine Page, and Jason Robards, Jr.

SUNSHINE
Situation Comedy
FIRST TELECAST: *March 6, 1975*
LAST TELECAST: *June 19, 1975*
BROADCAST HISTORY:
  Mar 1975–Jun 1975, NBC Thu 8:00–8:30
CAST:
  Sam Hayden .... Cliff DeYoung
  Jill .... Elizabeth Cheshire
  Weaver .... Bill Mumy
  Givits .... Corey Fischer
  Nora .... Meg Foster
THEME:
  "Sunshine on My Shoulder," by John Denver, Dick Kniss, and Mike Taylor

Set in Vancouver, British Columbia, *Sunshine* was the story of a young widower and his daughter trying to make ends meet. Sam Hayden's wife had died of cancer, leaving him to care for Jill, her five-year-old daughter by a previous marriage. Sam was a composer and, along with his two friends, Weaver and Givits, a member of a singing trio. With his musical career not generating much money, Sam sought all sorts of odd jobs to help support Jill and himself. He also tried to be both mother and father to Jill, who was always on the lookout for a likely candidate to marry her father. Helping Sam out, in addition to his two long-haired partners, was his neighbor and friend Nora. The easy and contemporary life-style led by Sam and Jill was cheered by some and condemned by others, and caused concern among those who felt it was not good for Jill's welfare. The title of the series referred to Jill's mother's favorite song.

SUPER, THE
Situation Comedy
FIRST TELECAST: *June 21, 1972*
LAST TELECAST: *August 23, 1972*
BROADCAST HISTORY:
  Jun 1972–Aug 1972, ABC Wed 8:00–8:30
CAST:
  Joe Girelli .... Richard Castellano
  Francesca Girelli .... Ardell Sheridan
  Joanne Girelli .... Margaret Castellano
  Anthony Girelli .... Bruce Kirby, Jr.
  Frankie Girelli .... Phil Mishkin
  Officer Clark .... Ed Peck
  Dottie Clark .... Virginia Vincent
  Mrs. Stein .... Janet Brandt
  Louie .... Louis Basile

All Joe wanted was a cold can of beer, a pizza, and a TV set. But big Joe (260 pounds) was superintendent of an old, walk-up apartment building in a lower-middle-class section of New York City, so what he got was tenants banging on the pipes, tenants complaining about him and about each other, a family that wouldn't leave him alone, and a city that wanted to condemn his building. Richard Castellano starred with his real-life daughter Margaret in this ethnic comedy (among the tenants were Italians, Irish, Poles, Jews, blacks, Puerto Ricans, homosexuals, social workers, cops, and revolutionaries). Francesca was his wife, Joanne and Anthony his disrespectful kids, and Frankie his big-shot lawyer brother.

SUPER GHOST
Quiz/Audience Participation
FIRST TELECAST: *July 27, 1952*
LAST TELECAST: *September 6, 1953*
BROADCAST HISTORY:
  Jul 1952–Sep 1952, NBC Sun 7:00–7:30
  Jul 1953–Sep 1953, NBC Sun 7:30–8:00
EMCEE:
  Bergen Evans
PANELISTS:
  Sherl Stern
  Robert Pollack

Super Ghost was a live game show from Chicago, based on the old word game "ghost." Each of the contestants stood before a blackboard and was given three letters of the word being used. They would add letters, one at a time, the object of the game being to avoid completing the designated word. Each time they completed a word they would become one-third a ghost and when they had completed three words they became full ghosts and "disappeared" from the game. Home viewers submitted words for the show and won money if the panel members ended up completing their word. The only two panelists who were regulars throughout the two-summer run of *Super Ghost* were a local Chicago housewife, Sherl Stern, and former drama critic Robert Pollack. A variety of guests filled the other two seats on the panel.

SUPERCARRIER
Military Drama
FIRST TELECAST: *March 6, 1988*
LAST TELECAST:
BROADCAST HISTORY:
  Mar 1988–Apr 1988, ABC Sun 8:00–9:00
  *Jul 1988–   *, ABC Sat 8:00–9:00
CAST:
  Capt. Jim Coleman .... Robert Hooks
  Capt. Henry K. "Hank" Madigan ... Dale Dye
  Lt. Jack "Sierra" DiPalma .... Ken Olandt
  Lt. Doyle "Anzac" Sampson
        .... John David Bland
  Lt. Cdr. Ruth "Beebee" Rutkowski
        .... Cec Verrell
  Master Chief Sam Rivers .... Richard Jaeckel
  Master-at-Arms 1st Class Luis Cruz
        .... Gerardo Mejia

Ocean Specialist 1st Class Donald
    Willoughby .... Michael Stuart Sharrett
Seaman Apprentice Raymond Lafitte
    .... Matthew Walker
Yeoman 1st Class Rosie Henriques
    .... Tasia Valenza
Billie Costello .... Marie Windsor

The above-and-below-deck world of the modern, peacetime navy was glorified in this Sunday action show. The handsome young fighter pilots were straight out of the hit movie *Top Gun*— "Sierra," "Anzac" and "Beebee" (the latter a woman who was better than any of them, but couldn't get sea duty because of her sex). In command of the pilots was Capt. Coleman, a black officer on his first big assignment, and worried about it. The ship's commander was Capt. Madigan; its equivalent of a town cop was Cruz, an earnest young military policeman who wanted to become a boxer; Rosie was a giggly medical assistant; and Willoughby was the expert young radarman.

The real star of the series, however, was the gigantic aircraft carrier itself, the U.S.S. *Georgetown*. How big? As the navy likes to say, "a floating city," 17 stories tall, population 5,630. There were plenty of shots of screaming jets being catapulted from its vast flight deck, or its towering bow looming over smaller craft nearby. It was the pride of San Miguel Naval Base, where off-duty personnel were welcomed by warm beds (and spouses) and by Billie's Bar, run by salty old Billie Costello.

The series was based on the book *Supercarrier* by George C. Wilson. At first the U.S. Navy cooperated fully with the producers, providing technical assistance, loaning aircraft, and allowing filming on the real-life U.S.S. *Kennedy*. However, upset by such non-regulation stories as an on-board love scene (which was deleted), hot-shot pilots crashing $20 million jets into the sea, and the discovery of cocaine on board, the navy later withdrew its support.

SUPERMAN
see *Adventures of Superman, The*

SUPERTRAIN
Dramatic Anthology
FIRST TELECAST: *February 7, 1979*
LAST TELECAST: *July 28, 1979*
BROADCAST HISTORY:
    Feb 1979–Mar 1979, NBC Wed 8:00–9:00
    Apr 1979–Jul 1979, NBC Sat 10:00–11:00
CAST:
    Conductor Harry Flood.... Edward Andrews
    Dave Noonan................ Patrick Collins
    Dr. Dan Lewis .... Robert Alda
    Rose Casey .... Nita Talbot
    Porter George Boone .... Harrison Page
    Bartender Lou Atkins .... Michael Delano
    Robert, the hairdresser......... Charlie Brill

Gilda .... Aarika Wells
Wally..................... William Nuckols
Engineer T.C. .... Anthony Palmer
Social Director Penny Whitaker .. Ilene Graff
Wayne Randall................ Joey Aresco

Supertrain was one of the most expensive failures in the history of network television. It was an anthology series set on a gigantic high-speed train that was appointed like a luxury liner. The massive locomotive pulled nine huge coaches from coast to coast at speeds in excess of 200 miles per hour. The train's passengers could use a 22-by-14-foot swimming pool, a gymnasium equipped with a steam room, a completely staffed and equipped medical center, and a swinging discotheque. The sets utilized in the production of *Supertrain*, both interiors and miniatures, were elaborate and expensive, costing millions of dollars. The train, apparently, was supposed to be the star of the show. Stories were an uneven mix of comedy, mystery, and adventure, and featured assorted guest stars, all interwoven with the activities of the regular train crew (as on ABC's *Love Boat*). Despite extensive advance publicity, which attracted a large audience of curious viewers to its premiere, *Supertrain's* rating dropped like a rock in subsequent weeks and it was pulled from the NBC schedule barely one month after it had begun. Efforts were made to rework the concept, including cutting down on the number of regular crew members. When it returned after a month's hiatus, only conductor Harry Flood, Dr. Lewis, and chief porter Boone were left from the original crew. Two new members—chief operations officer Wayne Randall and social director Penny Whitaker—were added, and the behind-the-scenes production team had been changed, but it didn't help. Less than six months after its premiere, *Supertrain* was derailed for good.

SURE AS FATE
Dramatic Anthology
FIRST TELECAST: *July 4, 1950*
LAST TELECAST: *April 3, 1951*
BROADCAST HISTORY:
    Jul 1950, CBS Tue 8:00–9:00
    Sep 1950–Apr 1951, CBS Tue 8:00–9:00

The themes that predominated in this live anthology series were of a melodramatic nature—stories of people confronted with situations not of their own making. *Sure as Fate* was tried for two weeks in July, received encouraging responses from the critics, and returned in September as a regular series. After a month as a weekly program it was cut back to alternate-week status with *Prudential Family Playhouse*. Among the performers featured were Rod Steiger, Leslie Nielsen, John Carradine, Kim Stanley, and Marsha Hunt.

SURFSIDE SIX
Detective Drama

FIRST TELECAST: *October 3, 1960*
LAST TELECAST: *September 24, 1962*
BROADCAST HISTORY:
  Oct 1960–Sep 1961, ABC Mon 8:30–9:30
  Oct 1961–Sep 1962, ABC Mon 9:00–10:00
CAST:
  Ken Madison .... Van Williams
  Dave Thorne .... Lee Patterson
  Sandy Winfield II .... Troy Donahue
  Daphne Dutton .... Diane McBain
  Cha Cha O'Brien .... Margarita Sierra
  Lt. Snedigar (1960–1961) ...... Donald Barry
  Lt. Gene Plehan (1961–1962) .. Richard Crane
  Mousie .... Mousie Garner

The success of *77 Sunset Strip* had prompted both
its producers, Warner Brothers, and its network,
ABC, to try a series of cookie-cutter copies. *Surfside Six* fit the pattern. Just as in *Sunset Strip*, a
trio of sexy, young private detectives (Ken, Dave,
and Sandy) lived in an exciting city (Miami) and
spent much time with beautiful women (Daphne
and Cha Cha). All that was missing was a jive-
talking parking-lot attendant. Surfside Six was
the Miami telephone exchange that included the
number of the houseboat that served as both
home and office to the detectives. Anchored next
to it was the yacht of kooky socialite Daphne Dutton, and across from it was the fabulous Foun-
tainebleau Hotel, where Cha Cha worked as an
entertainer in the Boom Boom Room.

Detective Ken Madison was a survivor of another private-eye show that had been seen in the
same time slot during the previous season—*Bourbon Street Beat*. His Bourbon Street partner, Rex
Randolph, latched on to another job too, joining
the team on *77 Sunset Strip*. Warner Brothers certainly made the most of its characters.

SURVIVAL—ANGLIA, LTD. SERIES
Wildlife/Nature
FIRST TELECAST: *June 24, 1976*
LAST TELECAST: *September 16, 1976*
BROADCAST HISTORY:
  Jun 1976–Sep 1976, NBC Thu 8:00–9:00

This summer series was composed of a collection
of documentaries on various animals. Some of
them were originals and others were repeats of
specials that had already aired on network television. Included were "Gorilla," narrated by David
Niven, "Magnificent Monsters of the Deep," narrated by Orson Welles, and "Come into My Parlor" (about spiders), narrated by Peter Ustinov.

SURVIVORS, THE
Drama
FIRST TELECAST: *September 29, 1969*
LAST TELECAST: *September 17, 1970*
BROADCAST HISTORY:
  Sep 1969–Jan 1970, ABC Mon 9:00–10:00
  Jun 1970–Sep 1970, ABC Thu 10:00–11:00

CAST:
  Tracy Carlyle Hastings .... Lana Turner
  Philip Hastings .... Kevin McCarthy
  Jeffrey Hastings ...... Jan-Michael Vincent
  Baylor Carlyle .... Ralph Bellamy
  Duncan Carlyle .... George Hamilton
  Belle .... Diana Muldaur
  Jonathan .... Louis Hayward
  Jean Vale .... Louise Sorel
  Antaeus Riakos .... Rossano Brazzi
  Miguel Santerra .... Robert Viharo
  Marguerita .... Donna Baccala
  Shelia .... Kathy Cannon
  Tom .... Robert Lipton
  Sen. Mark Jennings .... Clu Gulager
  Eleanor Carlyle .... Natalie Schafer

Movie queen Lana Turner made her TV series
debut—and swan song—in this adaptation of
Harold Robbins' novel of love and lust among the
jet set. Lana, as Tracy Hastings, was the center of
the action as she struggled to protect her teenage
son Jeffrey from (as the press release put it) "the
forces that could destroy him." Among the other
major protagonists were Tracy's philandering
husband, Philip; her father, banking czar Baylor;
and her playboy half brother, Duncan. Continuing
story lines unfolded in a new "chapter" each
week, and involved the Carlyles' entanglement
with South American revolutionary Miguel Santerra, Tracy's old flame Riakos (eventually revealed to be Jeffrey's real father), Baylor's lingering death, and everybody's attempts to get their
hands on his millions. Pure soap opera.

The Survivors was a big-name bust, lasting
only three and a half months. ABC recouped some
of its cost by running repeats during the summer
of 1970.

The official title of the series was *Harold Robbins' "The Survivors."*

SUSAN RAYE
Music
FIRST TELECAST: *October 2, 1950*
LAST TELECAST: *November 20, 1950*
BROADCAST HISTORY:
  Oct 1950, DUM Mon/Fri 7:45–8:00
  Oct 1950–Nov 1950, DUM Mon 7:30–7:45
HOSTESS:
  Susan Raye

Musical interlude featuring the singing and piano
stylings of Miss Raye.

SUSIE
syndicated title for *Private Secretary*

SUSPENSE
Dramatic Anthology
FIRST TELECAST: *March 1, 1949*
LAST TELECAST: *September 9, 1964*
BROADCAST HISTORY:
  Mar 1949–Jun 1950, CBS Tue 9:30–10:00 (OS)

Aug 1950–Aug 1954, CBS Tue 9:30–10:00
Mar 1964–Sep 1964, CBS Wed 8:30–9:00
HOST:
  Sebastian Cabot (1964)

Suspense had been a fixture on the CBS Radio Network since 1942 (where it remained for 20 years). The radio version had won a Peabody Award and a special citation from the Mystery Writers of America. In the spring of 1949 it came to television. The television plays were broadcast live from New York and featured many well-known Hollywood and Broadway actors. All of the stories dealt with people in dangerous and threatening situations of one kind or another. Some were adaptations of classic horror tales like *Dr. Jekyll and Mr. Hyde,* done in 1950 with Ralph Bell in the lead role and again a year later with Basil Rathbone. A version of *Suspicion* starred Ernest Truex and his wife, Sylvia Field, William Prince had the lead in "The Waxworks," John Forsythe in Robert Louis Stevenson's "The Beach of Falsea," and Peter Lorre in "The Tortured Hand." Frequent performers during the live run of the series were Nina Foch, Mildred Natwick, Tom Drake, Barry Sullivan, and horror veterans Boris Karloff, John Carradine, and Henry Hull.

Not all of the stories were of the horror genre. Though the works of Poe and Lovecraft were adapted frequently, there were straight mysteries by Charlotte Armstrong and Quentin Reynolds, among others. Rudyard Kipling's "The Man Who Would Be King" and numerous stories by Charles Dickens were also presented. On the more contemporary side, Grace Kelly starred in "50 Beautiful Girls," Arlene Francis and Lloyd Bridges in "Her Last Adventure," and Eva Gabor and Sidney Blackmer in a two-parter titled "This Is Your Confession." Jackie Cooper starred on occasion, and Cloris Leachman, Jacqueline Susann, and Mike Wallace showed up on *Suspense* as well.

In the spring of 1964, almost a full decade after the live version of *Suspense* left the air, a new series of filmed *Suspense* dramas arrived on CBS with Sebastian Cabot as host (there had never been a regular host for the live show). Some of the stars of these new stories—E. G. Marshall, James Daly, Basil Rathbone, and Skip Homeier—were returning home, as they had also starred in episodes of the live series in the 1950s. By the end of June, however, there were no new episodes being produced. Although it was still called *Suspense,* and Sebastian Cabot remained as host, all of the telecasts aired from July to September were actually reruns from *Schlitz Playhouse of Stars.*

SUSPENSE PLAYHOUSE
Dramatic Anthology
FIRST TELECAST: *May 24, 1971*
LAST TELECAST: *July 31, 1972*
BROADCAST HISTORY:
  May 1971–Jul 1971, CBS Mon 10:00–11:00
  Jul 1972, CBS Mon 10:00–11:00

The filmed plays presented in this summer anthology series were all reruns of episodes originally telecast on *Premiere* during the summer of 1968. They were all unsold pilots for proposed regular series. The three episodes that aired in the summer of 1972 had also been seen within the 1971 run.

SUSPICION
Suspense Anthology
FIRST TELECAST: *September 30, 1957*
LAST TELECAST: *September 6, 1959*
BROADCAST HISTORY:
  Sep 1957–Sep 1958, NBC Mon 10:00–11:00
  Jun 1959–Sep 1959, NBC Sun 7:30–8:30
HOST:
  Dennis O'Keefe (1957)
  Walter Abel (1959)

Suspicion was comprised of 20 filmed dramas and 20 live dramas that aired on NBC during the 1957–1958 season. The stories were meant to fascinate, mystify, and confound the audience, and generally dealt with people's fears and suspicions, often concerning murder. Alfred Hitchcock, who had his own series on CBS at this time, produced half of the filmed episodes. When it premiered, Dennis O'Keefe was to be the permanent host of the show. After two weeks, however, he left the series and was not replaced. In the summer of 1959 a number of the original episodes were rerun, with Walter Abel hosting them.

SUZANNE PLESHETTE IS MAGGIE BRIGGS
Situation Comedy
FIRST TELECAST: *March 4, 1984*
LAST TELECAST: *April 15, 1984*
BROADCAST HISTORY:
  Mar 1984–Apr 1984, CBS Sun 8:00–8:30
CAST:
  Maggie Briggs .... Suzanne Pleshette
  Walter Holden .... Kenneth McMillan
  Connie Piscipoli .... Shera Danese
  Sherman Milslagle .... Stephen Lee
  Geoff Bennett.................... John Getz
  Melanie Bitterman .... Alison LaPlaca
  Donny Bauer .... Roger Bowen
  Diana Barstow .... Michelle Nicastro

After 15 years as a hard-news reporter, Maggie Briggs was making the difficult adjustment to being a feature writer for the Modern Living Section of the *New York Examiner.* She really hadn't wanted to make the move but, out of loyalty to her friend and mentor, Walter Holden, who had also been transferred, she felt obligated to give it a chance. Working on human-interest stories was quite a change from her former criminal and political bylines. With her in her new area were Sherman, the neurotic food critic; Donny the religion editor; and fellow feature writers Melanie and Diana. Her new boss, editor of the Modern Living Section, was young, straight-arrow company man

Geoff Bennett. Maggie's best friend was sexy but flaky clothing model Connie Piscipoli.

$WEEPSTAKE$
Dramatic Anthology
FIRST TELECAST: *January 26, 1979*
LAST TELECAST: *March 30, 1979*
BROADCAST HISTORY:
  Jan 1979–Mar 1979, NBC Fri 10:00–11:00
CAST:
  The Emcee .... Edd Byrnes

CBS had been quite successful in the 1950s with a series called *The Millionaire,* which each week showed a different recipient of a million dollars adjusting to sudden wealth. *$weepstake$* was an attempt to update the concept. Each week a different group of twelve finalists was in the running for $1 million tax-free, top prize in a state lottery. Every episode of *$weepstake$* concentrated on the lives of three of the finalists as the drawing approached and showed how the amount they won, whether it was the jackpot or the $1,000 given runners-up, affected their lives. Some of the stories were funny and some serious, and the most deserving people did not always win. Edd Byrnes, as the lottery drawing's emcee, was the only series regular. Among the performers appearing were Elaine Joyce, Frankie Avalon, Patrick Macnee, Adrienne Barbeau, Gary Burghoff, Elinor Donahue, Nipsey Russell, and Jack Jones.

SWEET SURRENDER
Situation Comedy
FIRST TELECAST: *April 18, 1987*
LAST TELECAST: *July 8, 1987*
BROADCAST HISTORY:
  Apr 1987–May 1987, NBC Sat 8:30–9:00
  Jul 1987, NBC Wed 9:30–10:00
CAST:
  Georgia Holden .... Dana Delany
  Ken Holden .... Mark Blum
  Bart Holden .... Edan Gross
  Lynnie Holden .... Rebecca and Sarah Simms
  Vaughn Parker .... Christopher Rich
  Frank Macklin .... David Doyle
  Joyce Holden .... Marjorie Lord
  Marty Gafney .... Thom Sharp
  Lyla Gafney .... Louise Williams
  Taylor Gafney .... Victor DiMattia
  Cak .... Viveka Davis

Domesticity was rampant in this routine little comedy about a wife (Georgia) who decided to put her business career on hold and become a full-time mom to her newborn baby Lynnie and young son, Bart. Hubby Ken was understanding, although his swaggering single friend (and co-worker) Vaughn was constantly on hand to remind them that bachelorhood was more fun. Frank was Georgia's dad, Joyce was Ken's mother, the Gafneys were friends, and Cak the flaky teenage babysitter. Everybody offered ad-

vice, but nobody really understood just how *hard* a full-time mom's life could be!

SWIFT SHOW, THE
Musical Variety
FIRST TELECAST: *April 1, 1948*
LAST TELECAST: *August 4, 1949*
BROADCAST HISTORY:
  Apr 1948–Aug 1949, NBC Thu 8:30–9:00
REGULARS:
  Lanny Ross
  Martha Logan
  Sandra Gable (1948)
  Eileen Barton (1948)
  Susan Shaw (1948)
  Martha Wright (1949)
  Dulcy Jordan (1949)
  Max Showalter (1949)
  Ricki Hamilton (1949)
  Frank Fontaine (1949)
  Harry Simeone Orchestra & Chorus

Swift and Company, which had pioneered daytime commercial network television with the *Swift Home Service Club* in 1947, moved to prime time in early 1948 with a Thursday night half hour starring crooner Lanny Ross. Although music and light comedy remained the central theme of the show throughout its run, the specific format changed several times during the next year.

At first the program was a combination of music and a quiz segment called the "Eye-Cue Game," which had been brought over from the *Swift Home Service Club.* Contestants were asked to identify various names, places, or events from a series of visual clues. By September the quiz segment had been dropped and the setting became Lanny's elegant penthouse apartment, with regular friends and special guests dropping by to entertain. Eileen Barton played the small-town girlfriend with a crush on Lanny. Soon Lanny began to get out of his apartment, in fanciful dreams set to music, and on dates with various girlfriends.

In March 1949 the penthouse and the dating story lines were dropped and the program became a straight musical revue, with Lanny singing songs and entertaining guests.

Two carryovers from the *Swift Home Service Club* were Martha Logan, who gave demonstrations and commercials in the Swift Kitchen (during the "apartment" phase she was the girl upstairs), and Sandra Gable, who modeled fashions and gave home-decorating ideas.

SWIFT SHOW WAGON, THE
Variety
FIRST TELECAST: *January 8, 1955*
LAST TELECAST: *October 1, 1955*
BROADCAST HISTORY:
  Jan 1955–Oct 1955, NBC Sat 7:30–8:00
HOST:
  Horace Heidt

Each week this talent and variety show starring veteran bandleader Horace Heidt originated from a different state. It highlighted performers from that state, included interviews with local civic leaders, and presented one or two native sons who had gone on to become nationally known celebrities. Each show also included a salute to the "personality of the week," someone in the state who had performed a heroic deed. The show's title derived from the fact that it moved, not unlike a wagon, from place to place across the country. The full title was *The Swift Show Wagon with Horace Heidt and the American Way*.

SWISS FAMILY ROBINSON
Adventure
FIRST TELECAST: *September 14, 1975*
LAST TELECAST: *April 11, 1976*
BROADCAST HISTORY:
Sep 1975–Apr 1976, ABC Sun 7:00–8:00
CAST:
Karl Robinson .... Martin Milner
Lotte Robinson .... Pat Delany
Fred Robinson .... Willie Aames
Ernie Robinson .... Eric Olson
Jeremiah Worth .... Cameron Mitchell
Helga Wagner .... Helen Hunt
PRODUCER:
Irwin Allen

Johann Wyss' classic children's story of a family shipwrecked in the early 1800s was brought to TV in this 1975 series. It didn't look much like the book, however. The TV *Swiss Family Robinson* was produced by Irwin Allen, famed for his "disaster" movies. Although he claimed that this was not going to be a "disaster of the week" series, there did seem to be a tidal wave, typhoon, earthquake, volcanic eruption, wild animal, or other natural calamity besetting the poor Robinsons in every episode—usually staged in a rather tacky fashion (you just don't have those movie budgets in TV). In their remarkably well-equipped tree house, Karl and Lotte Robinson were stoic through it all, while their children Fred and Ernie hung on for dear life in the teeth of every gale. Jeremiah was a rascally old sailor who had previously been marooned on the island, and Helga was the only other survivor of the Robinsons' shipwreck (she was the daughter of the captain).

Quite a few visitors passed through the Robinsons' "lost" island, including pirate Jean Lafitte, who stopped off to pick up some buried treasure on his way to help General Andrew Jackson at the Battle of New Orleans.

SWITCH
Detective Drama
FIRST TELECAST: *September 9, 1975*
LAST TELECAST: *September 3, 1978*
BROADCAST HISTORY:
Sep 1975–Nov 1975, CBS Tue 9:00–10:00
Dec 1975–Jan 1977, CBS Tue 10:00–11:00

Jan 1977–Sep 1977, CBS Sun 9:00–10:00
Sep 1977, CBS Fri 10:00–11:00
Dec 1977–Jan 1978, CBS Mon 10:00–11:00
Jun 1978–Sep 1978, CBS Sun 10:00–11:00
CAST:
Pete Ryan .... Robert Wagner
Frank McBride .... Eddie Albert
Malcolm Argos .... Charlie Callas
Maggie .... Sharon Gless
Revel .... Mindi Miller
Lt. Griffin (1975–1976) .... Ken Swofford
Lt. Modeer (1976–1977) ... Richard X. Slattery
Lt. Shilton (1976–1978)....... William Bryant
Wang (1977–1978) .... James Hong

It was an unusual partnership. Pete was a former con man and Frank was a retired bunco cop. Together they had formed a private detective agency that specialized in pulling "switches" on the other con men still operating on the wrong side of the law. They would concoct elaborate schemes that would, hopefully, result in the swindlers swindling themselves. Based in Los Angeles, the two of them traveled far and wide on assorted cases. Malcolm, a small-time thief and con man who had gone straight and opened a restaurant was recruited by Pete and Frank to help them on cases, and Maggie was the firm's combination secretary-receptionist and all-around girl Friday.

By the middle of its second season, *Switch* had become a somewhat more traditional detective series, with fewer of the elaborate con games, and in the fall of 1977 Pete moved into a new apartment above Malcolm's bouzouki bar, where Revel was the hostess and Wang the new cook.

SWORD OF JUSTICE
Adventure
FIRST TELECAST: *September 10, 1978*
LAST TELECAST: *August 11, 1979*
BROADCAST HISTORY:
Sep 1978, NBC Sun 8:00–10:00
Oct 1978, NBC Sat 10:00–11:00
Dec 1978, NBC Sun 10:00–11:00
Jul 1979, NBC Sun 9:00–10:00
Aug 1979, NBC Sat 10:00–11:00
CAST:
Jack Cole .... Dack Rambo
Hector Ramirez................ Bert Rosario
Arthur Woods .... Alex Courtney
Buckner..................... Colby Chester

This series was billed as *Zorro* in contemporary garb. Jack Cole was not masked, but he certainly was an avenger, out to fight crime in high places, both public and private. Cole's motivation for this noble crusade was clear enough. A Park Avenue playboy, and heir to a great industrial fortune, he had suddenly been thrust from his pampered, jet-set existence into prison on a trumped-up charge of embezzlement after his father's death. While behind bars he learned the skills of the criminal's trade, lock picking, telephone bugging, and all the rest, and when he emerged he was determined to use these skills against the kind of white-collar criminals who had framed him. He resumed his playboy image, but only as a front for his (mostly) nocturnal crime-busting. His sign: a playing card. Helping was Hector, Jack's wise-cracking Puerto Rican ex-cellmate, and always one step behind was Arthur Woods, formerly the Cole family attorney and now part of a government task force fighting high-level crime. Working with Woods was Federal Agent Buckner.

SYMPHONY, THE
see *Chicago Symphony Chamber Orchestra*

SZYSZNYK
Situation Comedy
FIRST TELECAST: *August 1, 1977*
LAST TELECAST: *January 25, 1978*
BROADCAST HISTORY:
Aug 1977, CBS Mon 8:30–9:00
Dec 1977–Jan 1978, CBS Wed 8:30–9:00

CAST:

Nick Szysznyk	Ned Beatty
Ms. Harrison	Olivia Cole
Sandi Chandler (1977)	Susan Lanier
Leonard Kriegler	Leonard Barr
Ralph	Jarrod Johnson
Fortwengler	Barry Miller
Tony La Placa	Scott Colomby
Ray Gun	Thomas Carter

Nick Szysznyk was a retired marine, used to the discipline and order of military life, who had taken on a new job as playground supervisor at the Northeast Community Center in a poor neighborhood in Washington, D.C. Coping with the bureaucracy in the city government that funded the center, his co-workers, and the street kids who used the center, all proved challenging to him—and to them as well. Highly successful in its initial run against repeat programming during the summer, *Szysznyk* returned in December 1977 against stronger competition and lasted only two months.

T

T. AND T.
Detective Drama
BROADCAST HISTORY:
Syndicated only
30 minutes
Produced: *1987–*
Released: *January 1988*
CAST:

T.S. Turner	Mr. T
Amanda "Amy" Taler	Alex Amini
Dick Decker	David Nerman
Det. Ted Jones	Ken James
Aunt Martha Robinson	Jackie Richardson
Renee	Rachael Crawford
Sophie	Catherine Disher

The A-Team muscleman Mr. T in pinstripes. T.S. Turner was a tough former boxer who worked as a detective/investigator for attorney Amanda Taler. Though he still sported that distinctive Mohawk haircut, this time T was nattily attired in suits that were hard-pressed to contain his bulging muscles. However, when the need arose—and it did at least once in every episode—T.S. would charge off to his locker, change into a studded leather, street-chic outfit, and hunt down the bad guys. Not surprisingly, he found that the criminals were more intimidated by leather than pinstripes. Decker was a good friend who ran the gym where T.S. went to work out, Det. Jones, the cop who had developed a grudging respect for T.S., and Sophie, the secretary who worked for Amy. A bachelor, T.S. lived with his Aunt Martha and her attractive teenaged daughter, Renee.

T.H.E. CAT
Adventure
FIRST TELECAST: *September 16, 1966*
LAST TELECAST: *September 1, 1967*
BROADCAST HISTORY:
Sep 1966–Sep 1967, NBC Fri 9:30–10:00
CAST:

Thomas Hewitt Edward Cat . . .	Robert Loggia
Capt. MacAllister	R. G. Armstrong
Pepe	Robert Carricart

T.H.E. Cat was a former circus aerialist and ex-cat burglar whose name fit him very well. His current profession was that of professional bodyguard. He fought crime by guarding those clients who had been marked for death. Only T.H.E. Cat stood between them and their would-be assassins. Declining to use weapons himself, Cat relied on his quickness and agility to protect his clients and himself. Living in San Francisco, he maintained an "office" at the Casa del Gato, a nightclub owned by his friend Pepe. Pepe was a Spanish gypsy whose life had once been saved by T.H.E. Cat, and he would remain loyal to Cat until the day he died. Capt. MacAllister was the police officer with whom Cat worked most closely.

T.J. HOOKER
Police Drama
FIRST TELECAST: *March 13, 1982*
LAST TELECAST: *September 17, 1987*
BROADCAST HISTORY:
Mar 1982–Apr 1982, ABC Sat 8:00–9:00
Sep 1982–Sep 1985, ABC Sat 8:00–9:00
Sep 1985–Sep 1986, CBS Wed 11:30–12:40 A.M.
Sep 1986–Dec 1986, CBS Fri 11:30–12:40 A.M.
Dec 1986–Sep 1987, CBS Tue 11:30–12:40 A.M.
Sep 1987, CBS Tue-Thu 1:00–2:00 A.M.
CAST:

Sgt. T. J. Hooker	William Shatner
Officer Vince Romano (1982–1985)	
. . . .	Adrian Zmed
Officer Stacy Sheridan	Heather Locklear
*Capt. Dennis Sheridan (1982–1985)	
. . . .	Richard Herd
Fran Hooker (1982–1983)	Lee Bryant
Vicki Taylor (1982)	April Clough
Officer Jim Corrigan (1983–1986)	
. . . .	James Darren

*Occasional

Star Trek's Captain Kirk (William Shatner) was back in uniform in this 1982 police show—but this time as a sergeant. Actually, Sgt. T. J. Hooker had been a detective, but gave up his gold shield and civvies for a uniformed street patrol, because that's where he was needed. He was assigned to the Academy Precinct of the "L.C.P.D.," where he could lend advice to police trainees like Stacy and rookies like his eager new partner, Officer Vince Romano.

Hooker taught them more than street smarts, however. There was a good deal of anguish over the rights and wrongs of police work in this series. Hooker stood for traditional values, despite his own disappointments—a former partner killed in the line of duty, and a marriage that had ended in divorce (though he was still on good terms with his ex-wife, Fran). His two daughters, Cathy (played by Susan McClung) and Chrissie (Nicole Eggert), were seen occasionally. Captain Sheridan was the by-the-book superior, and Stacy's father. In a February 1983 episode Hooker also encountered a familiar face from other times and other places—Leonard Nimoy, as a cop going off the deep end because his daughter had been raped. Celebrities such as Jerry Lee Lewis and the Beach Boys also had cameos from time to time.

In the fall of 1983 Stacy graduated to street patrol, with veteran patrolman Jim Corrigan as her partner. When ABC canceled *T.J. Hooker* in the spring of 1985, CBS picked it up, with new episodes, as an addition to its late-night schedule.

The series went out of production at the end of the 1985–1986 season, but reruns continued to air on *CBS Late Night* for another year.

TV READER'S DIGEST
Dramatic Anthology
FIRST TELECAST: *January 17, 1955*
LAST TELECAST: *July 9, 1956*
BROADCAST HISTORY:
Jan 1955–Jul 1956, ABC Mon 8:00–8:30
HOST:
Hugh Reilly (1955)
Gene Raymond (1956)

Wholesome, frequently patriotic true stories from the pages of the *Reader's Digest* were dramatized in this filmed series. As in the *Digest*, little incidents from history and cameos from contemporary life were favorite subjects, and almost everything had a moral. Included were dramatizations of Stephen Foster's last days, the life of Pocahontas, the Scopes "Monkey" Trial of the 1920s, brainwashing attempts by the Communists in Korea, the story of a retired, old-time six-gun sheriff who was recalled by his town to stop a crime wave, etc. Performers were generally lesser known, but included some future stars such as Peter Graves, Chuck Connors, and Lee Marvin.

TV RECITAL HALL
Music
FIRST TELECAST: *July 1, 1951*
LAST TELECAST: *September 6, 1954*
BROADCAST HISTORY:
Jul 1951–Aug 1951, NBC Sun 8:30–9:00
Aug 1954–Sep 1954, NBC Mon 9:00–9:30

Live performances of classical music, featuring performers in a recital-hall–type setting, were presented on a weekly basis. They originated from New York with a live audience and the selections and performers were introduced by an offstage announcer. Between August 1951 and August 1954 this show was seen on an intermittent basis, occasionally for periods on Sunday afternoons and sometimes as a one-time-only special. It returned in August 1954 with the title shortened to *Recital Hall*. Following its last prime-time telecast, it returned to Sunday afternoons, where it remained until July 1955.

TV SOUNDSTAGE
see *Campbell Soundstage*

TV'S BLOOPERS & PRACTICAL JOKES
Comedy
FIRST TELECAST: *January 9, 1984*
LAST TELECAST:
BROADCAST HISTORY:
Jan 1984–Feb 1986, NBC Mon 8:00–9:00
Feb 1986, NBC Mon 10:00–11:00
May 1988–   , NBC Fri 8:00–9:00
HOSTS:
Ed McMahon
Dick Clark
REGULARS:
Julie Dees (1984)
Robert Klein (1984–1985)
Thom Sharp
Len Cella
Wil Shriner (1985–1986)

Bloopers, unintended pratfalls, and fluffed lines captured on film have been favorite showbiz entertainment for years, both behind the scenes and (at least for the cleaner clips) as features on various shows. In May 1981 NBC began a series of specials called "TV's Censored Bloopers" which proved so popular that the idea was spun off into a weekly series—which was promptly copied by ABC for a nearly identical show (see *Foul-Ups, Bleeps & Blunders*).

In addition to outtakes from movies, TV shows, and newscasts, the series featured classic commercials, humorous comments by children (interviewed by Julie Dees), and people on the street (interviewed by Robert Klein and David Letterman in New York and, beginning in the fall of 1984, by Thom Sharp in Hollywood). There were popular songs set to ironic visual clips, and Len Cella hosted a regular segment of short films that took an offbeat look at everyday life. A popular segment was practical jokes played on famous stars, while hidden cameras looked on; for example, Connie Sellecca of *Hotel* asked to take delivery of a truckload of pigs, Christopher Atkins of *Dallas* stopped by a cop for driving a "stolen" car, or James Coburn entering an apartment which then appeared to have no exit.

Johnny Carson, whose company co-produced this show (with Dick Clark Productions), occasionally narrated clips from *The Tonight Show*.

Whatever else could be said about this mélange, it knew its roots. Each episode ended with a tribute to Kermit Schafer, the producer-writer who first popularized bloopers from radio in the 1940s and 1950s.

NBC aired selected reruns of this series during the summer of 1988.

TV'S TOP TUNES
Music
FIRST TELECAST: *July 2, 1951*
LAST TELECAST: *September 3, 1955*
BROADCAST HISTORY:
Jul 1951–Aug 1951, CBS Mon/Wed/Fri 7:45–8:00
Jun 1953–Aug 1953, CBS Mon/Wed/Fri 7:45–8:00
Jun 1954–Aug 1954, CBS Mon/Wed/Fri 7:45–8:00
Jul 1955–Sep 1955, CBS Sat 10:00–10:30
REGULARS:
Peggy Lee (1951)
Mel Torme (1951)

The Fontane Sisters (1951)
Mitchell Ayres Orchestra (1951, 1955)
The Skyliners (1954)
The Anthony Choir (1954)
Helen O'Connell (1953)
Bob Eberly (1953)
Ray Anthony & His Orchestra (1953, 1954)
Tommy Mercer (1954)
Marcie Mills (1954)
Julius LaRosa (1955)

In 1951, 1953, and 1954 various artists filled in for the vacationing Perry Como on *TV's Top Tunes*, a live thrice-weekly music show that filled the remainder of the half hour in which CBS aired its network news program. During the summer of 1955, when this series was expanded to a full half hour on Saturday nights, its star, Julius LaRosa, had another series, *The Julius LaRosa Show*, airing three times a week in the time period that *TV's Top Tunes* had occupied during previous summers.

TAB HUNTER SHOW, THE
Situation Comedy
FIRST TELECAST: *September 18, 1960*
LAST TELECAST: *September 10, 1961*
BROADCAST HISTORY:
Sep 1960–Sep 1961, NBC Sun 8:30–9:00
CAST:
Paul Morgan .... Tab Hunter
Peter Fairfield III .... Richard Erdman
John Larsen .... Jerome Cowan
Thelma .... Reta Shaw

Paul Morgan was a swinging young bachelor who had made a living out of his life-style. As a cartoonist for Comics, Inc., he was the creator of the strip "Bachelor-at-Large," which detailed the adventures of an amorous young man living the good life in Southern California. The strip read almost like a diary, which it was, of the romantic exploits of its author. Paul's boss, John Larsen, never ceased to be amazed by the situations into which his prize cartoonist got himself. Paul's best friend was the wealthy, eligible, and stingy Peter Fairfield III, a fashion plate and car enthusiast who was regularly mixed up in Paul's romantic adventures. Keeping Paul's Malibu Beach apartment in order was his housekeeper, Thelma, who did not approve of his never-ending stream of beautiful women.

TABITHA
Situation Comedy
FIRST TELECAST: *November 12, 1977*
LAST TELECAST: *August 25, 1978*
BROADCAST HISTORY:
Nov 1977–Jan 1978, ABC Sat 8:00–8:30
Jun 1978–Aug 1978, ABC Fri 8:00–8:30
CAST:
Tabitha Stephens .... Lisa Hartman
Paul Thurston .... Robert Urich

Marvin Decker .... Mel Stewart
Adam Stephens .... David Ankrum
Aunt Minerva .... Karen Morrow

This briefly seen comedy was a spin-off from ABC's long-running hit *Bewitched*. Tabitha was the daughter of Samantha, the leading character on *Bewitched*. She was seen as a child on that series, but by the time this one began she had grown into a bright young woman, just beginning her career as a television production assistant at station KLXA, in California. Tabitha worked for producer Marvin Decker, and her chief assignment was *The Paul Thurston Show*. Thurston was the station's handsome, but not-too-bright, star newscaster. Adam was Tabitha's brother and a fellow employee at KLXA, and Minerva was her meddlesome aunt.

Despite the similarity to *The Mary Tyler Moore Show*, Tabitha had something extra: as a witch, she could perform feats of magic, and get her own way, with a twitch of the nose. It didn't help. The series soon disappeared in a puff of Nielsen ratings.

TAG THE GAG
Quiz/Audience Participation
FIRST TELECAST: *August 13, 1951*
LAST TELECAST: *August 20, 1951*
BROADCAST HISTORY:
Aug 1951, NBC Mon 8:00–8:30
MODERATOR:
Hal Block

In this comedy-quiz show a panel of comedians tried to guess the punch lines to jokes that were acted out by a group of performers. The performers would set up the punch line and it was up to the panelists to "tag the gag." Hal Block, who served as moderator, had created the idea for the show but, apparently, the joke was on him—it only lasted two weeks. The only panelist to appear on both telecasts was funnyman Morey Amsterdam.

TAKE A CHANCE
Quiz/Audience Participation
FIRST TELECAST: *October 1, 1950*
LAST TELECAST: *December 24, 1950*
BROADCAST HISTORY:
Oct 1950–Dec 1950, NBC Sun 10:30–11:00
EMCEE:
Don Ameche

Each contestant on this live quiz program was drawn from the studio audience and given an initial $5. He was then asked a series of four questions. A correct answer to the first one enabled the contestant to keep the $5 and receive a small prize. Answers to the subsequent questions were worth unspecified other winnings, some big and some small. The contestant could quit whenever he or she no longer wanted to "take a chance," but there was an incentive to go on. Correctly answering all four questions gave the contestant a shot at the jackpot question—worth $1,000 in cash and 1,000 cakes of Sweetheart soap. If a question was not answered correctly, however, the contestant had to forfeit his last prize.

TAKE A GOOD LOOK
Quiz/Panel
FIRST TELECAST: *October 22, 1959*
LAST TELECAST: *March 16, 1961*
BROADCAST HISTORY:
Oct 1959–Mar 1961, ABC Thu 10:30–11:00
HOST:
Ernie Kovacs
PANELISTS:
Hans Conried
Cesar Romero
Edie Adams (1960–1961)
Ben Alexander (1960)
Carl Reiner (1960–1961)
ACTORS:
Peggy Connelly
Bobby Lauher
Jolene Brand

Panelists were advised to "take a good look" at the contestants on this quiz show. Although they were relatively unknown, each of the contestants had once been a central figure in a headline-making news event, and the panel had to guess just who they were. To help, clues such as film clips or recordings were played, or Ernie Kovacs and a team of regulars acted out the clues. In addition to the regular panelists guest celebrities frequently appeared.

TAKE A GUESS
Quiz/Audience Participation
FIRST TELECAST: *June 11, 1953*
LAST TELECAST: *September 10, 1953*
BROADCAST HISTORY:
Jun 1953–Sep 1953, CBS Thu 8:00–8:30
MODERATOR:
John K. M. McCaffery
PANELISTS:
Margaret Lindsay
Ernie Kovacs
Dorothy Hart
John Crawford
Robin Chandler
Hans Conried

Contestants on this summer quiz show were aided by members of a celebrity panel in trying to identify something that was known only to the moderator and the audience. Each contestant started with $150. As he looked on, the panel asked questions of the moderator to determine the identity of the mystery object. However, $5 was deducted from the $150 each time one of their questions received a "yes" answer, so the contestant had an incentive to guess as quickly as possible (he could

take a maximum of four guesses). The contestant won whatever was left of the original $150 after the money for the "yes" answers was subtracted. If the entire $150 was used up (due to 30 "yes" answers), or the contestant had made four incorrect answers, there were no winnings at all.

TAKE FIVE
Situation Comedy
FIRST TELECAST: *April 1, 1987*
LAST TELECAST: *April 8, 1987*
BROADCAST HISTORY:
Apr 1987, CBS Wed 8:30–9:00
CAST:
Andy Kooper .... George Segal
Dr. Noah Wolf .... Severn Darden
Al .... Derek McGrath
Monty .... Bruce Jarchow
Lenny Goodman .... Jim Haynie
Laraine McDermott .... Melanie Chartoff
Kevin Davis .... Todd Field
Max Davis .... Eugene Roche

Life was not going well for lanky Andy Kooper. His wife had divorced him and her father had fired him from his public relations job. Andy tried to get a handle on things by picking and singing with his buddies in the Lenny Goodman Quartet, a semi-pro Dixieland jazz band in which he sang and played banjo. The others in the quartet were Lenny, piano; Al, saxophone; and Monty, drums. The fact that Monty was dating Andy's ex-wife was a sour note but, hey, Andy could handle it. Andy did find a new job with Davis & Son public relations—where old Max Davis was retired and the new boss, his son Kevin, was incompetent. Unfortunately, the brightest person there, Laraine, hated Andy because she had pitched for the job he had gotten. Dr. Wolf was the psychiatrist to whom Andy told all.

Star George Segal, who played regularly with a Dixieland band much like the one in this series when he was not acting, managed to combine both his vocation and his avocation here—but not for long. *Take Five* never even got to five. It was canceled after only two episodes had aired.

TAKE IT FROM ME
Situation Comedy
FIRST TELECAST: *November 4, 1953*
LAST TELECAST: *January 20, 1954*
BROADCAST HISTORY:
Nov 1953–Jan 1954, ABC Wed 9:00–9:30
CAST:
Wife .... Jean Carroll
Husband (Herbie).............. Alan Carney
Daughter .... Lynn Loring

Stand-up comedienne Jean Carroll starred as an "average" New York City housewife, complete with bumbling husband and moppet daughter, in this comedy. She opened each show with a monologue, then spiced the night's sketch with comic asides to the audience. Many of the stories involved her sly schemes to trick husband Herbie into doing whatever she wanted. The action took place in the couple's apartment and the surrounding neighborhood, which, though never identified, was presumably in Brooklyn or The Bronx. This New York orientation may have limited the show's appeal west of the Hudson River, and it lasted less than three months.

Also known as *The Jean Carroll Show.*

TALENT JACKPOT
Talent
FIRST TELECAST: *July 19, 1949*
LAST TELECAST: *August 23, 1949*
BROADCAST HISTORY:
 Jul 1949–Aug 1949, DUM Tue 9:00–9:30
EMCEE:
 Vinton Freedley
ASSISTANT:
 Bud Collyer

Summer talent show for aspiring professionals, emceed by Broadway producer Vinton Freedley and offering a maximum prize of $250 for each of the night's five acts. The amount each act won depended on the level reached by an audience applause meter. The top winner of the night got his own winnings as well as whatever was left over from the other acts' $250 maximums.

TALENT PATROL
Talent/Variety
FIRST TELECAST: *January 19, 1953*
LAST TELECAST: *September 8, 1955*
BROADCAST HISTORY:
 Jan 1953–Jul 1953, ABC Mon 9:30–10:00
 Jul 1953–Aug 1953, ABC Mon 8:00–8:30
 Sep 1953–Oct 1953, ABC Wed 8:00–8:30
 Oct 1953–Jan 1954, ABC Sat 8:00–8:30
 Jan 1954–Mar 1954, ABC Thu 9:00–9:30
 Apr 1954–Jul 1954, ABC Thu 8:00–8:30
 Jul 1954–Oct 1954, ABC Wed 7:30–8:00
 Oct 1954–Nov 1954, ABC Sun 9:30–10:00
 Dec 1954–Jan 1955, ABC Mon 8:00–8:30
 Jan 1955–Jun 1955, ABC Thu 8:00–8:30
 Jun 1955–Sep 1955, ABC Thu 8:00–9:00
EMCEE:
 Steve Allen (1953)
 Bud Collyer (1953)
 Arlene Francis (1953–1955)
 Richard Hayes (1955)

Talent Patrol began as a military talent show, sponsored by the army over the 88 stations of the ABC network as an aid to recruiting. All the contestants were GIs, performing a wide variety of nonmilitary skills—impersonations, folk singing, playing musical instruments, trampoline acts, and even hula dancing! Winners got a night on the town with a pretty actress. Even the runners-up came out ahead, however, with national TV exposure, not to mention a five-day pass to go to New

York and rehearse for the show. Army bands provided the musical accompaniment.

In mid-1954 the program became more of a straight variety show, featuring army professional talent as well as celebrity guests, and the title was changed to *Soldier Parade.*

Steve Allen was the original host of the series, replaced "temporarily" by Bud Collyer after only three months and permanently by Arlene Francis in June 1953. When the program expanded to a full hour in June 1955 singer Richard Hayes, in the Army himself at the time, joined Miss Francis in the capacity of co-host.

TALENT SCOUTS
Talent/Variety
FIRST TELECAST: *July 3, 1962*
LAST TELECAST: *September 17, 1963*
BROADCAST HISTORY:
 Jul 1962–Sep 1962, CBS Tue 10:00–11:00
 Jul 1963–Sep 1963, CBS Tue 8:30–9:30
HOST:
 Jim Backus (1962)
 Merv Griffin (1963)

Each week a number of guest celebrities appeared on this show to introduce young professional performers who were being given their first network exposure on the series. In 1962 this was the summer replacement for *The Garry Moore Show* and in 1963 for *The Red Skelton Hour.* The most immediate success story from this series was impressionist Vaughn Meader. He did his imitation of President Kennedy on the first telecast of the 1962 series and had a subsequent smash recording—*The First Family.* Among the other young performers who appeared as newcomers were George Carlin, Charles Nelson Reilly, Louise Lasser, and Vic Dana.

This summer series was a revival of *Arthur Godfrey's Talent Scouts,* which had had a ten-year run on CBS ending in 1958.

TALENT VARIETIES
Variety
FIRST TELECAST: *June 28, 1955*
LAST TELECAST: *November 1, 1955*
BROADCAST HISTORY:
 Jun 1955–Sep 1955, ABC Tue 7:30–8:30
 Sep 1955–Nov 1955, ABC Tue 10:00–10:30
REGULARS:
 Slim Wilson
 The Tall Timber Trio

Originating from Springfield, Missouri, this variety show had a country-and-western flavor. Each week emcee and singer Slim Wilson introduced assorted amateur talent and occasionally performed himself.

TALES FROM THE DARKSIDE
Horror/Supernatural

BROADCAST HISTORY:
Syndicated only
30 minutes
Produced: *1984–*
Released: *September 1984*
NARRATOR:
Paul Sparer

Stylish if rather low-budget anthology of horror stories, many with O. Henry-ish surprise endings. *Tales From the Darkside* resembled the more macabre episodes of *The Twilight Zone* but, unlike the latter series, it never aired stories of a whimsical/fantasy nature. Watching it regularly could become a depressing experience. Performers were generally lesser-knowns or veteran character actors, among them Arnold Stang, Connie Stevens, Keenan Wynn, Fritz Weaver, Justine Bateman, Eddie Bracken, Peggy Cass, Harry Anderson, Jean Marsh, Bill Macy, Darren McGavin, and Phyllis Diller.

TALES OF E.S.P.
see *E.S.P.*

TALES OF THE CITY
see *Willys Theater Presenting Ben Hecht's Tales of the City*

TALES OF THE GOLD MONKEY
Adventure
FIRST TELECAST: *September 22, 1982*
LAST TELECAST: *July 6, 1983*
BROADCAST HISTORY:
Sep 1982–Feb 1983, ABC Wed 8:00–9:00
Mar 1983–Apr 1983, ABC Fri 10:00–11:00
Jun 1983–Jul 1983, ABC Wed 9:00–10:00
CAST:
Jake Cutter .... Stephen Collins
Corky .... Jeff MacKay
Sarah Stickney White ..... Caitlin O'Heaney
Bon Chance Louis .... Roddy McDowall
Rev. Willie Tenboom .... John Calvin
Princess Koji .... Marta DuBois
Todo .... John Fujioka

The year was 1938, and the setting the tropical Marivella Islands in the South Pacific. Spies and schemers of many nationalities were found throughout the islands, especially in the languid port of Boragora. Their chief gathering spot was the elegant Monkey Bar, filled with wood carvings, tinkling piano music, and whispered information. Everyone in the place seemed to have a mysterious past, including Jake Cutter, whose worn leather flight jacket bore a Flying Tigers patch—legacy of past adventures. Jake was an American soldier of fortune and pilot with a wry sense of humor, whose battered seaplane, a Grumman Goose, provided the only inter-island air transportation. From this romantic setting Jake set out on a new adventure each week, rescuing kidnaped travelers, recovering stolen booty, and foiling the German and Japanese spies who infested the area.

Jake had two sidekicks, his loyal but frequently inebriated mechanic, Corky, and a one-eyed terrier named Jack (who never would forgive Jake for gambling away his jeweled glass eye). A shifty ally was the dapper but roguish Bon Chance Louis, the French magistrate in Boragora and proprietor of the Monkey Bar. Sarah was the willowy, contrary American singer at the bar, whose attraction to Jake kept getting in the way of her real purpose—she was an American agent keeping an eye on things in the islands. Others in the colorful cast were Rev. Willie Tenboom, a pompous Dutch minister who was really a German spy; Princess Koji, a beautiful Dragon Lady who maintained a large fleet of trading ships at Matuka in the Japanese sector of the island chain; and Todo, the fierce Samurai commander of the princess' private army.

TALES OF THE RED CABOOSE
Adventure
FIRST TELECAST: *October 29, 1948*
LAST TELECAST: *January 14, 1949*
BROADCAST HISTORY:
Oct 1948–Jan 1949, ABC Fri 7:30–7:45

Early TV advertisers did not know what kind of use could be made of the new medium, and so can be forgiven shows like this one. *Tales of the Red Caboose* was sponsored by Lionel Trains, and consisted simply of model trains racing around on their tracks. Various races and miniaturized "adventures" were depicted, and a narrator, "Don Magee," spun yarns based on the lore of railroads.

For a similar program sponsored by rival A. C. Gilbert Co. (American Flyer) see *Roar of the Rails.*

TALES OF THE 77TH BENGAL LANCERS
Adventure
FIRST TELECAST: *October 21, 1956*
LAST TELECAST: *June 2, 1957*
BROADCAST HISTORY:
Oct 1956–Jun 1957, NBC Sun 7:00–7:30
CAST:
Lt. Michael Rhodes .... Phil Carey
Lt. William Storm .... Warren Stevens
Col. Standish .... Patrick Whyte

Set in India in the late 19th century, the stories of this fictional outfit were based on the exploits of the real Bengal Lancers, the famed British Cavalry unit. Col. Standish was the commander of the "77th" and working under him were two lieutenants who were also close friends, Michael Rhodes and William Storm. Rhodes was portrayed as a Canadian because New Jersey–born Phil Carey had trouble mastering an English accent.

TALES OF THE TEXAS RANGERS
Western

LAST TELECAST: *May 25, 1959*
BROADCAST HISTORY:
  Dec 1958–May 1959, ABC Mon 7:30–8:00
CAST:
  Ranger Jace Pearson .... Willard Parker
  Ranger Clay Morgan .... Harry Lauter

As the title suggests, these were straightforward adventure stories concerning the exploits of one of America's most famous law-enforcement agencies. Although Rangers Pearson and Morgan were regulars, they appeared in a different setting each week, ranging from the Old West of the 1830s to modern-day Texas, using crime-detection methods appropriate to each era. The program was, in effect, a survey of the Rangers' activities over its 120-year history.

Tales of the Texas Rangers was seen on Saturday afternoons on CBS from September 1955 to May 1957. It then moved to ABC, where it ran at 5:00 P.M. on Sundays (September 1957 to June 1958) and later Thursdays (October 1958 to December 1958), just prior to its prime-time run. *Tales of the Texas Rangers* was also heard as a radio series in the early 1950s, with Joel McCrea in the lead role of Ranger Pearson.

TALES OF THE UNEXPECTED

Suspense Anthology
FIRST TELECAST: *February 2, 1977*
LAST TELECAST: *August 24, 1977*
BROADCAST HISTORY:
  Feb 1977–Mar 1977, NBC Wed 10:00–11:00
  Mar 1977, NBC Sun 9:00–11:00
  Aug 1977, NBC Wed 10:00–11:00
NARRATOR:
  William Conrad
EXECUTIVE PRODUCER:
  Quinn Martin

This anthology show dealt in both psychological and occult suspense stories, all of which had unusual O. Henry–like twists to prolong the suspense until the very end of the episode. After five weeks on Wednesdays, the final two-hour episode of this series aired on a Sunday. Five months later, *Tales of the Unexpected* returned to its original time slot for two weeks with new episodes.

TALES OF THE UNKNOWN

see *Journey to the Unknown*

TALES OF TOMORROW

Science Fiction Anthology
FIRST TELECAST: *August 3, 1951*
LAST TELECAST: *June 12, 1953*
BROADCAST HISTORY:
  Aug 1951–Jun 1953, ABC Fri 9:30–10:00

Tales of Tomorrow was one of TV's earliest adult science-fiction series, using both classic and modern stories of strange and supernatural happen-

ings. Among the stories were "The Monsters" (from Mars), "The Dark Angel" (about a woman who never aged), H. G. Wells' "The Crystal Egg," "The Flying Saucer," "Frankenstein," and a two-part version of Jules Verne's *20,000 Leagues Under the Sea.* The program was produced by George F. Foley, Jr., and used such talent as Franchot Tone, Lon Chaney, Jr., Veronica Lake, Boris Karloff, Eva Gabor, Leslie Nielsen, and Lee J. Cobb.

During 1951 and 1953 it alternated with other series. For a time during early 1953 the program was also heard on radio.

TALES OF WELLS FARGO

Western
FIRST TELECAST: *March 18, 1957*
LAST TELECAST: *September 8, 1962*
BROADCAST HISTORY:
  Mar 1957–Jul 1957, NBC Mon 8:30–9:00
  Sep 1957–Sep 1961, NBC Mon 8:30–9:00
  Sep 1961–Sep 1962, NBC Sat 7:30–8:30
CAST:
  Jim Hardie .... Dale Robertson
  Beau McCloud (1961–1962) .... Jack Ging
  Jeb Gaine (1961–1962) ..... William Demarest
  Ovie (1961–1962) .... Virginia Christine
  Mary Gee (1961–1962) ... Mary Jane Saunders
  Tina (1961–1962) .... Lory Patrick

During the five seasons in which *Tales of Wells Fargo* ran on Monday nights it had a single regular cast member, Wells Fargo agent Jim Hardie. Jim was a troubleshooter for the company, whose assignments ranged from helping employees out of personal jams to functioning as an unofficial lawman by fighting criminals who preyed on Wells Fargo shipments and passengers.

In the fall of 1961, *Tales of Wells Fargo* moved to Saturday nights and was expanded to a full hour. Also expanded was the regular cast. Although still a Wells Fargo agent, Jim Hardie was now also the owner of a ranch just outside of San Francisco. He had acquired a young assistant in Beau McCloud and a ranch foreman named Jeb Gaine. The ranch next door to his was owned by Widow Ovie, who lived with her two attractive daughters, Mary Gee and Tina. Ovie had her eye on Jeb as a possible second husband, despite his lack of interest. Most of the shows during this last season took place on the Hardie ranch and in San Francisco, although Jim still went on an occasional assignment in other parts of the West.

TALL MAN, THE

Western
FIRST TELECAST: *September 10, 1960*
LAST TELECAST: *September 1, 1962*
BROADCAST HISTORY:
  Sep 1960–Sep 1962, NBC Sat 8:30–9:00
CAST:
  Billy the Kid .... Clu Gulager
  Dep. Sheriff Pat Garrett ...... Barry Sullivan

Set in New Mexico during the 1870s, *The Tall Man* told fictionalized stories of the adventures of two real-life characters, Sheriff Pat Garrett and William H. Bonney. The latter was more popularly known as Billy the Kid, a youthful gunfighter with a penchant for getting himself into trouble. Billy and Pat, whose honesty and forthrightness had earned him the nickname "The Tall Man," were close friends despite the fact that they were often on opposite sides of the law. Pat looked upon Billy as a younger brother or son, but knew in the back of his mind that they would eventually be forced into a showdown. Although he too was pretty handy with a gun, Pat regarded it as a tool only to be used in an emergency where there was no alternative. Billy, on the other hand, looked at his gun as the great equalizer, compensating for his inferiority in size, strength, or intelligence. His criminal activities kept bringing him and Pat closer to the day of reckoning which, although never shown on the series, culminated in Pat's killing Billy.

TAMMY

Situation Comedy
FIRST TELECAST: *September 17, 1965*
LAST TELECAST: *July 15, 1966*
BROADCAST HISTORY:
  Sep 1965–Jul 1966, ABC Fri 8:00–8:30
CAST:
  Tammy Tarleton .... Debbie Watson
  Grandpa Tarleton .... Denver Pyle
  Uncle Lucius .... Frank McGrath
  John Brent .... Donald Woods
  Steven Brent .... Jay Sheffield
  Lavinia Tate .... Dorothy Green
  Gloria Tate .... Linda Marshall
  Peter Tate .... David Macklin
  Dwayne Whitt .... George Furth
  Cousin Cletus Tarleton .... Dennis Robertson
  Mrs. Brent .... Doris Packer

Tammy was the story of a winsome, 18-year-old backwoods girl who moved back and forth between two worlds. One was the bayou houseboat where she and her kin lived. The other was "The Bowers," the plantation owned by wealthy John Brent, where she worked as Brent's secretary. Tammy's wistful, beguiling ways endeared her to almost everyone—except Lavinia Tate, the blue-blooded neighbor of the Brents who was always scheming to snatch some juicy plum away from Tammy for her own daughter, Gloria. Steven was John Brent's son, and Peter was Lavinia's son. Tammy's own kin included old codger Grandpa and scalawag Uncle Lucius, who had raised her after the death of her parents.

Based on the 1957 movie *Tammy and the Bachelor,* which starred Debbie Reynolds, and the movie sequels starring Sandra Dee. In 1967 there was a feature-length theatrical motion picture called *Tammy and the Millionaire,* in which Miss Watson and most of the principals from the series appeared in their TV roles.

TAMMY GRIMES SHOW, THE

Situation Comedy
FIRST TELECAST: *September 8, 1966*
LAST TELECAST: *September 29, 1966*
BROADCAST HISTORY:
  Sep 1966, ABC Thu 8:30–9:00
CAST:
  Tammy Ward .... Tammy Grimes
  Uncle Simon .... Hiram Sherman
  Terrence Ward .... Dick Sargent
  Mrs. Ratchett .... Maudie Prickett

Tammy Ward was what the ABC press releases referred to as "a madcap heiress." Given her own way, she would have spent oodles of money on just anything that hit her fancy, regardless of how useful it might be. Trying to keep the purse strings from being opened too far was her banker, Uncle Simon, a much more pecunious soul than Tammy. In addition to not being able to get her hands on her money, she had to cope with an incredibly square twin brother named Terrence and a nosy housekeeper named Mrs. Ratchett. Both Tammy and Terrence worked for Uncle Simon at the Perpetual Bank of America. This series lasted just four weeks.

TARGET

Dramatic Anthology
BROADCAST HISTORY:
  Syndicated only
  30 minutes
  Produced: *1957–1958*
  Released: *March 1958*
HOST/OCCASIONAL STAR:
  Adolphe Menjou

This anthology series featured stories of terror and suspense in which some ruthless force pursued its target—a man, a family, a place. In one, a helpless invalid became the target of a "mercy killer"; in another, a respected man was the target of a mining swindle. Adolphe Menjou, who had earlier presided over the somewhat gentler *Favorite Story* anthology series, was host and frequent star. Others appearing included Howard Duff, Kent Taylor, Hans Conried, Marie Windsor, and Lon Chaney, Jr.

TARGET: THE CORRUPTORS

Newspaper Drama
FIRST TELECAST: *September 29, 1961*
LAST TELECAST: *September 21, 1962*
BROADCAST HISTORY:
  Sep 1961–Sep 1962, ABC Fri 10:00–11:00
CAST:
  Paul Marino .... Stephen McNally
  Jack Flood .... Robert Harland

Paul Marino was an investigative rackets reporter and Jack Flood was his undercover agent, sent to infiltrate suspected criminal-controlled or -threatened businesses to provide Marino with material for his newspaper exposes and for the police. A different form of underworld corruption was detailed each week in this dramatic series—everything from bookmaking and prostitution to phony charities and protection rackets.

TARZAN
Adventure
FIRST TELECAST: *September 8, 1966*
LAST TELECAST: *September 10, 1969*
BROADCAST HISTORY:
   Sep 1966, NBC Thu 7:30–8:30
   Sep 1966–Sep 1968, NBC Fri 7:30–8:30
   Jun 1969–Sep 1969, CBS Wed 7:30–8:30
CAST:
   Tarzan .... Ron Ely
   Jai .... Manuel Padilla, Jr.

Edgar Rice Burroughs' famous "Tarzan" character came to television in the person of Ron Ely, the 14th actor to play the role since *Tarzan of the Apes* had first been made as a silent movie almost half a century before. In the TV series Tarzan, who was actually the Earl of Greystoke, returned to his native jungle forest after years of formal schooling. Living among the wild creatures, with whom he could communicate, and possessed of incredibly acute senses, Tarzan waged war on renegades, poachers, and other interlopers in the jungle. Familiar with the civilized world, Tarzan preferred the honesty and openness of life in the jungle. His closest friend was the chimp Cheetah, but he was fond of all the creatures of the wilds. He was also very close to a small orphan boy named Jai. Ron Ely did many of his own stunts for this series. The famous Tarzan yell was actually a recording by another Tarzan, Johnny Weissmuller. CBS aired reruns of the NBC series during the summer of 1969, and some episodes were strung together and actually shown in theaters as feature-length films.

The character of Jane and the crude English Tarzan had used in the movie versions ("Me Tarzan—you Jane") were dropped for the purposes of this TV series.

TATE
Western
FIRST TELECAST: *June 8, 1960*
LAST TELECAST: *September 28, 1960*
BROADCAST HISTORY:
   Jun 1960–Sep 1960, NBC Wed 9:30–10:00
CAST:
   Tate .... David McLean

Tate was the 1960 summer replacement for the second half hour of *The Perry Como Show*, the first half hour being occupied by a situation comedy called *Happy*. Tate was a casualty of the Civil War. His left arm had been blasted into uselessness by an explosion during his wartime service. With only one good arm, he had found it almost impossible to get a job after the war ended.

With little choice, he had become a wandering gunfighter, traveling from town to town looking for work as a fast gun. He was an imposing figure, with his shattered left arm wrapped in a rawhide-stitched black leather casing that ran from his fingertips to above the elbow.

TAXI
Situation Comedy
FIRST TELECAST: *September 12, 1978*
LAST TELECAST: *July 27, 1983*
BROADCAST HISTORY:
   Sep 1978–Oct 1980, ABC Tue 9:30–10:00
   Nov 1980–Jan 1981, ABC Wed 9:00–9:30
   Feb 1981–Jun 1982, ABC Thu 9:30–10:00
   Sep 1982–Dec 1982, NBC Thu 9:30–10:00
   Jan 1983–Feb 1983, NBC Sat 9:30–10:00
   Mar 1983–May 1983, NBC Wed 9:30–10:00
   Jun 1983–Jul 1983, NBC Wed 10:30–11:00
CAST:
   Alex Rieger .... Judd Hirsch
   Bobby Wheeler (1978–1981) .... Jeff Conaway
   Louie De Palma .... Danny DeVito
   Elaine Nardo .... Marilu Henner
   Tony Banta .... Tony Danza
   John Burns (1978–1979) ...... Randall Carver
   Latka Gravas .... Andy Kaufman
   "Reverend Jim" Ignatowski (1979–1983)
      .... Christopher Lloyd
   Simka Gravas (1981–1983) .... Carol Kane

The happy cabbies of New York's Sunshine Cab Company were the focal point of this comedy. Cab driving may be fun, but it was just a job for this crew, most of whom were working part-time as they tried to make it in other fields. Alex, the most experienced and most conservative of the group, was the only full-time driver. Bobby was a frustrated actor, waiting for his big break; Elaine was an art gallery receptionist, trying to pick up a few extra bucks; Tony, the boxer who never won a fight; and John, the student and all-around lost soul. Latka was the company's mechanic, of indeterminate nationality and fractured English, and Louie was the dispatcher, a pint-sized petty tyrant who ran things from a wire cage in the center of the garage. Joining the cast as a regular driver in the second season was Reverend Jim, a spaced-out ex-hippie.

During the 1980–1981 season Latka started to date a rather scatterbrained lady from his homeland named Simka, and at the end of that season they were married. Falling ratings led ABC to cancel *Taxi* in the spring of 1982 and, for a time, it seemed that the pay-cable network Home Box Office would pick up the series. That was not to be, however, as NBC decided to give *Taxi* a new life. Promotional announcements on NBC during the summer of 1982 showed series star Danny DeVito looking up at the camera and gloating, "Same time, better network!" Despite critical acclaim for the ensemble acting, the wit and charm of the writing, and the faith of a new network,

Taxi obtained the same low ratings on NBC as it had in its last season on ABC, and faded from sight the following summer.

TEACHERS ONLY
Situation Comedy
FIRST TELECAST: *April 14, 1982*
LAST TELECAST: *May 21, 1983*
BROADCAST HISTORY:
Apr 1982–Jun 1982, NBC Wed 9:30–10:00
Sep 1982, NBC Thu 9:30–10:00
Feb 1983–May 1983, NBC Sat 9:30–10:00
CAST:
Diana Swanson . . . . Lynn Redgrave
Ben Cooper . . . . Norman Fell
Michael Dreyfuss (1982) . . . . Adam Arkin
Mr. Pafko (1982) . . . . Richard Karron
Mr. Brody (1982) . . . . Norman Bartold
Gwen Edwards (1982) . . . . . Van Nessa Clarke
Lois McCardle (1982) . . . . Kit McDonough
Samantha "Sam" Keating (1983)
. . . . Teresa Ganzel
Michael Horne (1983) . . . . Tim Reid
Spud Le Boone (1983) . . . . Joel Brooks
Shari (1983) . . . . Jean Smart

Most of the action in this short-lived school comedy took place in the faculty lunchroom and lounge, which was off limits to the students—hence the series title, *Teachers Only.* It was there that the faculty and staff of Millard Filmore High School talked about their successes and failures, both professional and personal. Diana Swanson was a high-principled, dedicated English teacher, popular with her students despite the rigors of her curriculum. Ben Cooper was the gruff, stubborn, but warm-hearted school principal who had developed an ulcer after many years of trying to balance the needs and wants of students, parents, faculty, and staff. Michael and Gwen were fellow teachers, Mr. Brody the assistant principal, and Mr. Pafko the janitor.

When *Teachers Only* returned in the spring of 1983 there were a number of changes. It was still set in Los Angeles, but the school (with no on-air explanation) was now Woodrow Wilson High. Only Diana, now a guidance counselor, and Ben, still the principal, returned. The remainder of the cast, teachers Sam Keating, Michael Horne, and Barney Betelman; gym teacher and coach Spud Le Boone; and Ben's secretary, Shari, were all new. Apparently, the problem with the series was its premise, not its cast. Despite the infusion of new cast members, ratings as low as those it had obtained a year earlier prompted *Teachers Only* to be canceled again.

TED KNIGHT SHOW, THE
Situation Comedy
FIRST TELECAST: *April 8, 1978*
LAST TELECAST: *May 13, 1978*
BROADCAST HISTORY:
Apr 1978–May 1978, CBS Sat 8:30–9:00

CAST:
Roger Dennis . . . . Ted Knight
Burt Dennis . . . . Normann Burton
Winston Dennis . . . . Thomas Leopold
Dottie . . . . Iris Adrian
Graziella . . . . Cissy Colpitts
Honey . . . . Fawne Harriman
Irma . . . . Ellen Regan
Philadelphia Phil Brown . . . . Tanya Boyd
Cheryl . . . . Janice Kent
Joy . . . . Deborah Harmon
Hobart Nalven . . . . Claude Stroud

Ted Knight, the handsome, empty-headed newscaster on *The Mary Tyler Moore Show,* landed his own series with this frothy comedy about an escort service in New York City. Dennis Escorts was a strictly high-class outfit, located in a posh Manhattan apartment building. It was staffed by some lovely young ladies, and headed by the suave, middle-aged Roger Dennis, who clucked over his brood like a mother hen. Complicating matters was Roger's no-nonsense businessman/brother, Burt, who had financed the enterprise and had incidentally saddled it with his wisecracking sister-in-law Dottie (who served as receptionist). Other cast members were Roger's college-age son, Winston, who was trying to break into the business and make time with the girls, and the mailman, Hobart, who had his eyes on Dottie.

TED KNIGHT SHOW, THE
see *Too Close For Comfort*

TED MACK FAMILY HOUR, THE
Musical Variety
FIRST TELECAST: *January 7, 1951*
LAST TELECAST: *November 25, 1951*
BROADCAST HISTORY:
Jan 1951–Nov 1951, ABC Sun 6:00–7:00
REGULARS:
Ted Mack
The Mack Triplets
Jean Steel
Dick Byrd
Andy Roberts

Ted Mack, who was most famous for his *Original Amateur Hour,* also hosted this live Sunday night variety show during 1951. The emphasis was on family entertainment, and guest stars were generally cabaret and stage talent such as pianist Vincent Lopez, songstress Betty Ann Grove, and actor Bert Lytell. An occasional *Amateur Hour* champion also made his professional debut here.

TED STEELE SHOW, THE
Music
FIRST TELECAST: *September 29, 1948*
LAST TELECAST: *August 3, 1949*
BROADCAST HISTORY:
Sep 1948–Oct 1948, NBC Wed/Fri Various 15 minute

Feb 1949–Apr 1949, DUM Sun 6:30–7:00
Apr 1949–Jul 1949, DUM Tue 9:00–9:30
Jul 1949–Aug 1949, CBS Tue/Wed/Thu 7:15–7:30
REGULARS:
Ted Steele
Mardi Bryant
Helen Wood
Michael Rich

Ted Steele was a versatile young (31) musician who had a blossoming career on radio in the 1940s. He was orchestra leader for several years on Perry Como's *Chesterfield Supper Club,* was a composer of some note ("Smoke Rings"), and also a singer, pianist, organist, and novachordist. His first break on TV came with a series of musical interludes on NBC, which originated in the WPTZ studios in Philadelphia. Ted later switched to DuMont, then to CBS, then became a local personality in New York.

TEEN TIME TUNES
Music
FIRST TELECAST: *March 14, 1949*
LAST TELECAST: *July 15, 1949*
BROADCAST HISTORY:
Mar 1949–Jul 1949, DUM Mon–Fri 6:30–6:45
REGULARS:
Sue Benjamin (Bennett)
Alan Logan Trio

A pretty young vocalist named Sue Benjamin, just out of college, was the featured singer on this early program. It was typical of the extremely low-budget musical interludes favored by the networks—especially cash-poor ABC and Dumont—in the early days of TV. Miss Benjamin recalls that it was produced in a corner of the same studio used for Vincent Lopez, *The Small Fry Club,* Wendy Barrie, and others, and the set really consisted of no more than a drape with the musical trio (pianist Alan Logan, guitar, and bass) and herself in front. The program was just a superclub combo on TV. Despite the "Teen" in the title, they played mostly standards and opened with an inane little ditty that went something like, "It's time, time, time/Time for "Teen Time Tunes'!" Hardly a precursor of *American Bandstand!*

Miss Benjamin later changed her professional name to Sue Bennett and had a successful career on *Kay Kyser's Kollege of Musical Knowledge* and *Your Hit Parade.*

TEENAGE BOOK CLUB
Discussion
FIRST TELECAST: *August 27, 1948*
LAST TELECAST: *October 29, 1948*
BROADCAST HISTORY:
Aug 1948–Oct 1948, ABC Fri 7:30–8:00
Oct 1948, ABC Fri 8:00–8:30

One of ABC's earlier series was this discussion program on books of interest to teenagers. Among the titles considered were Betty Betz's *Your Manners Are Showing,* Harry Haenigsen's comic strips, and a few classics such as *David Copperfield* and *Hamlet.*

TELEPHONE TIME
Dramatic Anthology
FIRST TELECAST: *April 8, 1956*
LAST TELECAST: *April 1, 1958*
BROADCAST HISTORY:
Apr 1956–Mar 1957, CBS Sun 6:00–6:30
Apr 1957–Jun 1957, ABC Thu 10:00–10:30
Jun 1957–Apr 1958, ABC Tue 9:30–10:00
HOST:
John Nesbitt (1956–1957)
Dr. Frank Baxter (1957–1958)

The plays presented in this film series had all been adapted from short stories by author John Nesbitt, who also served as the host of the show, introducing each episode. The subject matter ranged from contemporary to historical, with emphasis on the varied natures and qualities of people, both good and bad. He remained as the host of the series when it moved from CBS to ABC in the spring of 1957, although by this time the works of other authors had been included among the presentations. He was replaced as host in September 1957 by Dr. Frank Baxter. There were occasional appearances by such name talents as Judith Anderson, Thomas Mitchell, and Claudette Colbert, but most of the players in this series were not, at the time, major stars. A number of them—including Cloris Leachman, Michael Landon, Martin Milner, and Robert Vaughn—did become stars of their own television series in the 1960s and 1970s. On an unusual note, famed clown Emmett Kelly made his dramatic debut here in a story titled "Captain from Kopenick."

TELE-VARIETIES
see *Bristol-Myers Tele-Varieties*

TELEVISION: INSIDE AND OUT
Magazine
FIRST TELECAST: *December 5, 1981*
LAST TELECAST: *January 2, 1982*
BROADCAST HISTORY:
Dec 1981–Jan 1982, NBC Sat 10:00–11:00
REGULARS:
Rona Barrett
Wil Shriner
Sylvester L. "Pat" Weaver
Gary Deeb

Hollywood gossip columnist Rona Barrett hosted this mix of information, opinion, reportage, and gossip about television. Pat Weaver, former chairman of the board of NBC, was on hand to do features about the past and present of TV, sometimes making editorial commentary and other times doing straight information pieces—as when he narrated a report on A. C. Nielsen, Jr., and his rating system. Humorist Wil Shriner looked at the funny side of the medium, and syndicated TV columnist Gary Deeb did a weekly report about current programs and personalities on TV. Rona did interviews à la Barbara Walters, with celebrities ranging from singers Mick Jagger and Lena Horne to actors Rock Hudson and Edward Asner.

TELEVISION PLAYHOUSE
see *Philco TV Playhouse*

TELEVISION PLAYHOUSE
Dramatic Anthology
FIRST TELECAST: *December 4, 1947*
LAST TELECAST: *April 11, 1948*
BROADCAST HISTORY:
Dec 1947–Apr 1948, NBC Sun 8:40–9:10

This was an early series of live television dramas presented by NBC in cooperation with the American National Theater and Academy (ANTA), a federally sponsored theater group. Both light and serious fare were presented, many by famous authors but few starring actors of any note (they would not go near television in 1947). The first presentation was "The Last of My Solid Gold Watches" by Tennessee Williams. *Television Playhouse* was a semiregular program, generally appearing every third Sunday night during the period indicated.

TELEVISION SCREEN MAGAZINE
Various
FIRST TELECAST: *November 17, 1946*
LAST TELECAST: *July 23, 1949*
BROADCAST HISTORY:
Nov 1946–Dec 1946, NBC Sun 8:00–8:30
Dec 1947–Mar 1948, NBC Thu Various 30 minutes
Mar 1948–Sep 1948, NBC Tue Various 30 minutes
Oct 1948–Jul 1949, NBC Sat Various 30 minutes
EMCEE/"EDITOR":
George Putnam (1948)
Alan Scott (1948, 1949)
John K. M. McCaffery (1948)
Millicent Fenwick (1948)
Bob Stanton (1948)
Ray Forrest (1948–1949)
REGULAR:
Bill Berns

This grab bag of features, presented magazine-style once a week, was one of NBC's earliest network series and was seen initially in three cities (New York, Philadelphia, Schenectady). At first the format was highly informal and the guests were often ordinary people—seemingly anyone who could be lured into the studio. NBC employee Walter Law and his stamp collection was an early favorite, and the very first telecast (November 17, 1946) featured the Police Athletic League Chorus. Later the program became more tightly structured, with a regular host or "editor," occasional film

features, and regular segments such as Bill Berns' "While Berns Roams."

The magazine format was emphasized by a shot of pages being flipped before each feature, and regular departments such as the fashion page, personality interviews, etc.

TELL IT TO GROUCHO
Comedy/Interview
FIRST TELECAST: *January 11, 1962*
LAST TELECAST: *May 31, 1962*
BROADCAST HISTORY:
Jan 1962–May 1962, CBS Thu 9:00–9:30
REGULARS:
Groucho Marx
Jack Wheeler
Patty Harmon

This filmed series was the short-lived successor to Groucho's long-running *You Bet Your Life*. It was a vehicle designed to let Groucho demonstrate his wit by zinging the guests who appeared on the show to "tell it to Groucho." Guests were interviewed by Groucho about their hobbies, problems, and/or jobs. Assisting Groucho, and participating in the discussions with the guests, were two teenagers who had been "discovered" by Groucho when they had appeared as contestants on *You Bet Your Life*.

TELL IT TO THE CAMERA
Interview
FIRST TELECAST: *December 25, 1963*
LAST TELECAST: *March 18, 1964*
BROADCAST HISTORY:
Dec 1963–Mar 1964, CBS Wed 8:30–9:00
HOST:
Red Rowe

Tell It to the Camera enabled everyday people from around the country to voice their opinions on network television. The filmed series sent a mobile unit to random locations at plants, shopping centers, schools, etc., and invited passersby to let their opinions be known, register complaints about almost anything that was bothering them, or tell what they felt were amusing or interesting stories. There was more than a coincidental resemblance between *Tell It to the Camera* and another series on the CBS schedule, *Candid Camera*. They were both produced by Allen Funt, whose entire career was wrapped up in showing normal people reacting to normal and abnormal situations.

TELLER OF TALES
see *Somerset Maugham TV Theater*

TELLTALE CLUE, THE
Police Drama
FIRST TELECAST: *July 8, 1954*
LAST TELECAST: *September 23, 1954*
BROADCAST HISTORY:
Jul 1954–Sep 1954, CBS Thu 10:00–10:30

CAST:
    Det. Lt. Richard Hale .... Anthony Ross

Detective Lieutenant Richard Hale was the head
of the criminology department of the police department of a large, unnamed city. He used all of
the scientific equipment and analytical skills at
his disposal to find the flaws in what would have
otherwise been "perfect" crimes. The step-by-
step process by which he isolated the evidence
that eventually led to an arrest enabled the home
viewers to become familiar with modern police
technology and, in certain respects, made this series a variation on the Ellery Queen–style whodunit.

TEMPERATURES RISING
Situation Comedy
FIRST TELECAST: *September 12, 1972*
LAST TELECAST: *August 29, 1974*
BROADCAST HISTORY:
    Sep 1972–Jan 1974, ABC Tue 8:00–8:30
    Jul 1974–Aug 1974, ABC Thu 8:00–8:30
CAST (1972–1973):
    Dr. Vincent Campanelli .... James Whitmore
    Dr. Jerry Noland .... Cleavon Little
    Nurse Annie Carlisle .... Joan Van Ark
    Nurse Mildred MacInerny .... Reva Rose
    Student Nurse Ellen Turner ...... Nancy Fox
    Dr. David Amherst .... David Bailey
CAST (1973–1974)
    Dr. Paul Mercy .... Paul Lynde
    Dr. Jerry Noland .... Cleavon Little
    Martha Mercy .... Sudie Bond
    Miss Tillis .... Barbara Cason
    Nurse "Windy" Winchester . Jennifer Darling
    Dr. Lloyd Axton .... Jeff Morrow
    Dr. Charles Cleveland Claver... John Dehner
CAST (SUMMER 1974):
    Dr. Paul Mercy .... Paul Lynde
    Dr. Jerry Noland .... Cleavon Little
    Edwina Moffitt .... Alice Ghostley
    Nurse Ellen Turner .... Nancy Fox
    Nurse Amanda Kelly .... Barbara Rucker

ABC evidently had a good deal of faith in this
medical comedy, trying three different casts and
formats in two years before finally giving up. For
the first season the show was set at Capital General Hospital in Washington, D.C., presided over
by no-nonsense chief of surgery Dr. Vincent Cam-
panelli and his all-nonsense staff. The latter consisted of prankster Jerry Noland, a free-swinging
product of the ghetto and the hospital's chief
bookie; sexy young nurse Annie Carlisle; her mischievous companion Mildred MacInerny; and Dr.
David Amherst, the handsome love interest of
practically every female in the place. There were
also the patients: the old codger who liked to drag-
race in his wheelchair, the paranoid young man
who wanted his medication pretasted and then
slipped under the door, etc.
    The program returned for its second season

retitled *The New Temperatures Rising Show,*
with new producers, and almost completely recast. Capital General was now a private hospital,
run by penny-pinching Dr. Paul Mercy (played by
Paul Lynde) and owned by his meddlesome
mother, Martha, who was permanently in residence and who kept calling her son via a beeper
on his belt. Miss Tillis was the efficient accountant, "Windy" Winchester, the romantically inclined nurse, and Dr. Axton, the cheerfully fraudulent surgeon who had recently published two
books, *Profit in Healing* and *Malpractice and Its
Defense.* Only intern Jerry Noland remained from
the first season.
    The second version of *Temperatures Rising*
was no more successful than the first, however,
and lasted only through mid-season. Apparently
viewers did not appreciate seeing doctors as the
butt of comedy. The show did come back for another short run in the summer of 1974, with more
new episodes, and still more changes in cast and
plot. This time the meddling mother was gone, and
Dr. Mercy ran the place with the help of his sister,
Edwina. Intern Jerry Noland was back, along with
a couple of nurses.

TEMPLE HOUSTON
Western
FIRST TELECAST: *September 19, 1963*
LAST TELECAST: *September 10, 1964*
BROADCAST HISTORY:
    Sep 1963–Sep 1964, NBC Thu 7:30–8:30
CAST:
    Temple Houston .... Jeffrey Hunter
    George Taggart .... Jack Elam

Traveling the circuit courts in the Southwest during the 1880s was Temple Houston, the handsome
attorney son of Texas immortal Sam Houston.
Temple found his clients, both civil and criminal,
wherever the circuit court happened to be in session. In spite of his vocation as a lawyer, Temple
was also quite adept as a fast-shooting gunman.
His appearance was one of elegance and his ora-
torical skills were renowned throughout the
Southwest. Also traveling with the circuit court
was George Taggart, an itinerant U.S. marshal
and over-the-hill gunfighter. Taggart hired himself
to the local towns and was either friend or foe of
Houston, depending on the interests of Temple's
clients. The real-life Temple Houston was a contemporary of both Bat Masterson and Billy the
Kid, and was known to have engaged in shooting
matches with them.

TENAFLY
Detective Drama
FIRST TELECAST: *October 10, 1973*
LAST TELECAST: *August 6, 1974*
BROADCAST HISTORY:
    Oct 1973–Jan 1974, NBC Wed 8:30–10:00
    Apr 1974–Aug 1974, NBC Tue 8:30–10:00

CAST:
Harry Tenafly .... James McEachin
Ruth Tenafly .... Lillian Lehman
Herb Tenafly .... Paul Jackson
Lorrie .... Rosanna Huffman
Lt. Sam Church .... David Huddleston

Harry Tenafly was a rarity among television's private detectives: he was black, and a dedicated and happy family man. He lived in Los Angeles with his wife, Ruth, and their son, Herb. The action in the series was divided between his home and his office life. His friend and confidant at the police department was Lt. Sam Church, who often got Harry out of jams. Unlike most private detectives, Harry was neither chasing nor being chased by beautiful women. He was happy with his family and saw his job as only a job. *Tenafly* was one of the four rotating elements in the 1973–1974 edition of *NBC Wednesday/Tuesday Mystery Movie*.

TENNESSEE ERNIE FORD SHOW, THE
see *Ford Show Starring Tennessee Ernie Ford, The*

TENSPEED AND BROWN SHOE
Detective Drama
FIRST TELECAST: *January 27, 1980*
LAST TELECAST: *June 27, 1980*
BROADCAST HISTORY:
Jan 1980–Mar 1980, ABC Sun 8:00–9:00
May 1980–Jun 1980, ABC Fri 10:00–11:00
CAST:
E. L. Turner ("Tenspeed") .... Ben Vereen
Lionel Whitney ("Brown Shoe")
.... Jeff Goldblum

This was the odd couple of detective work. "Tenspeed" was a charming hustler and master of disguises, for whom legitimate employment (as a detective) was necessary to meet his parole requirements. "Brown Shoe"—an old term for bankers, stockbrokers, and other "straight" types—was his well-to-do and somewhat naive foil, a romantic whose idea of sleuthing was rooted in 1940s novels and old Bogart movies. This unlikely pair joined forces in their own agency, located two blocks off Sunset Boulevard in Los Angeles, and with lots of undercover work and high-speed chases they managed to crack all sorts of cases.

Tenspeed and Brown Shoe was launched with a tremendous promotional blitz in early 1980, and attracted a large audience for its first couple of episodes. It then declined rapidly and was soon canceled. The producer of this series was Stephen J. Cannell, whose name was used as "the author" of all the blood-and-guts detective novels Lionel was forever reading to help him hone his detective's skills.

TEX AND JINX
Talk

FIRST TELECAST: *April 20, 1947*
LAST TELECAST: *September 5, 1949*
BROADCAST HISTORY:
Apr 1947–Jun 1947, NBC Sun 8:00–8:15
Jun 1947–Aug 1947, NBC Sun 8:00–8:30
Mar 1949–Jul 1949, CBS Mon 8:00–8:30
Jul 1949–Sep 1949, CBS Mon 9:00–9:30
REGULARS:
Tex McCrary
Jinx Falkenburg

Newspaper columnist Tex McCrary and his actress-wife Jinx Falkenburg were frequently seen during the early days of television, both in guest appearances and as hosts of their own celebrity-interview series. First seen on NBC, they later moved to CBS, where their program was billed as *Preview*, "the living television magazine." In addition to these prime-time appearances they hosted *The Swift Home Service Club* (1947–1948), which NBC says was the first sponsored network daytime program, an NBC radio series and various local programs in New York. Later, in the 1950s, they returned to daytime television.

Their prime-time programs were variously known as *At Home with Tex and Jinx*, *The Tex and Jinx Film*, and *Preview with Tex and Jinx* in addition to *Tex and Jinx*.

TEXACO STAR THEATER
see *Milton Berle Show, The*

TEXACO STAR THEATER STARRING DONALD O'CONNOR, THE
see *Donald O'Connor Texaco Show, The*

TEXACO STAR THEATER STARRING JIMMY DURANTE, THE
see *Jimmy Durante Show, The*

TEXAN, THE
Western
FIRST TELECAST: *September 29, 1958*
LAST TELECAST: *September 12, 1960*
BROADCAST HISTORY:
Sep 1958–Sep 1960, CBS Mon 8:00–8:30
CAST:
Bill Longley .... Rory Calhoun

He was not a law officer, but Big Bill Longley was often confronted with situations in which he might as well have been. In the years following the Civil War he made a name for himself throughout the state of Texas. He was a fast gun, a loyal and devoted friend, and a mortal enemy to those who broke the law or harassed those people whom he felt close to. As he traveled from town to town he helped those in need and found adventure, danger, and even an occasional romance.

ABC aired reruns of *The Texan* in its weekday daytime lineup from October 1960 to March 1962 and its Saturday morning lineup from February to May 1962.

TEXAS RODEO

Sports Event
FIRST TELECAST: *April 30, 1959*
LAST TELECAST: *July 2, 1959*
BROADCAST HISTORY:
   Apr 1959–Jul 1959, NBC Thu 7:30–8:00
COMMENTATOR:
   Paul Crutchfield

All of the standard rodeo events were shown in this weekly series filmed on location before arena audiences at rodeos in Texas and elsewhere in the Southwest. Calf roping, bronc riding, bull riding, and steer wrestling were all standard features. Such special events as wild-cow milking and barrel racing were also included in some telecasts. Veteran rodeo announcer Paul Crutchfield did the commentary for this series.

TEXAS WHEELERS, THE

Situation Comedy
FIRST TELECAST: *September 13, 1974*
LAST TELECAST: *July 24, 1975*
BROADCAST HISTORY:
   Sep 1974–Oct 1974, ABC Fri 9:30–10:00
   Jun 1975–Jul 1975, ABC Thu 8:30–9:00
CAST:
   Zack Wheeler .... Jack Elam
   Truckie Wheeler .... Gary Busey
   Doobie Wheeler .... Mark Hamill
   Boo Wheeler .... Karen Oberdiear
   T. J. Wheeler .... Tony Becker
   Sally .... Lisa Eilbacher
   Bud .... Dennis Burkley
   Lyle .... Bruce Kimball
THEME:
   "Illegal Smile," composed and sung by John Prine (1974)

Earthy comedy about the four motherless Wheeler children and their no-account, cantankerous, "but lovable" father Zack. With Zack spending most of his time thinking of ways to avoid work, eldest son Truckie, 24, led the clan, which consisted of Doobie (16), Boo (12), and T.J. (10). Their adventures living in rural Texas, without much money but with a lot of spirit, provided the stories for this short-lived series.

THAT GIRL

Situation Comedy
FIRST TELECAST: *September 8, 1966*
LAST TELECAST: *September 10, 1971*
BROADCAST HISTORY:
   Sep 1966–Apr 1967, ABC Thu 9:30–10:00
   Apr 1967–Jan 1969, ABC Thu 9:00–9:30
   Feb 1969–Sep 1970, ABC Thu 8:00–8:30
   Sep 1970–Sep 1971, ABC Fri 9:00–9:30
CAST:
   Ann Marie .... Marlo Thomas
   Don Hollinger .... Ted Bessell
   Lou Marie .... Lew Parker
   Helen Marie (1966–1970) . Rosemary DeCamp
   Judy Bessemer (1966–1967) ..... Bonnie Scott
   Dr. Leon Bessemer (1966–1967)
   .... Dabney Coleman
   Jerry Bauman .... Bernie Kopell
   Ruth Bauman (1967–1969).... Carolyn Daniels
   Ruth Bauman (1969–1971)...... Alice Borden
   Harvey Peck (1966–1967) ...... Ronnie Schell
   George Lester (1966–1967) ..... George Carlin
   Seymour Schwimmer (1967–1968)
   .... Don Penny
   Margie "Pete" Peterson (1967–1968)
   .... Ruth Buzzi

Danny Thomas' daughter Marlo started a trend in TV comedies with this series. *That Girl* was the prototype for a wave of "independent woman" series, including *The Doris Day Show*, *Mary Tyler Moore*, and *Rhoda*. Marlo played Ann Marie, a high-spirited young actress who had left the comfort of her parents' home in rural Brewster, New York, to build a career in the big city. Her "big breaks" usually consisted of roles in TV commercials and bit parts in plays, so she supported herself with odd jobs in offices and department stores. New York City did bring one big break for Ann, however, as on the first telecast she met Don Hollinger, a junior executive for *Newsview* magazine, who became her first romance. They finally became engaged on a September 1970 telecast, but Don never did get to marry "that girl"—although he got as far as a stag party before the 1970–1971 season ended.

Others in Ann's world at various times were her parents, Lou (a restaurant owner) and Helen; her neighbors, the Bessemers; her friends the Baumans; and her agents, Harvey and George. Marcy (played by Reva Rose) was seen briefly as Ann Marie's married friend, during the 1970–1971 season. Danny Thomas made a few cameo appearances in the series in various roles.

Reruns of *That Girl* were shown as part of ABC's daytime lineup from June 1969 to March 1972.

THAT GOOD OLE NASHVILLE MUSIC

Music
BROADCAST HISTORY:
   Syndicated only
   30 minutes
   Produced: *1970–1985*
   Released: *1970*

Widely carried country music series, featuring a different guest star each week. Produced in association with WSM-TV and Opryland U.S.A., in Nashville. Also known as *That Nashville Music*.

THAT REMINDS ME

Stories
FIRST TELECAST: *August 13, 1948*
LAST TELECAST: *October 1, 1948*
BROADCAST HISTORY:
   Aug 1948–Oct 1948, ABC Fri 8:30–9:00

Walter Kiernan
Governor Harold Hoffman
"Uncle Jim" Harkins

This was simply a storytelling session with newsman Walter Kiernan joined by ex–New Jersey Governor Harold Hoffman and "Uncle Jim" Harkins. The stories were generally about humorous incidents in the lives of famous people, and members of the celebrity's family were often on hand to embellish the tales. It seemed like a good idea for TV in 1948.

THAT WAS THE WEEK THAT WAS
News Satire
FIRST TELECAST: *January 10, 1964*
LAST TELECAST: *May 4, 1965*
BROADCAST HISTORY:
Jan 1964–Jul 1964, NBC Fri 9:30–10:00
Sep 1964–May 1965, NBC Tue 9:30–10:00
REGULARS:
Elliot Reid (1964)
Nancy Ames
David Frost
Henry Morgan (1964)
Phyllis Newman
Pat Englund
Buck Henry
Bob Dishy
Doro Merande (1964)
Alan Alda (1964)
Sandy Baron (1964)
Tom Bosley (1964)
Jerry Damon
Stanley Grover (1964)
Burr Tillstrom's Puppets
The Norman Paris Orchestra

Political satire came to American TV for the first time in this pioneering NBC series, known affectionately as "TW3." Based on a 1963 British TV series of the same name, it was first seen here as a special in November 1963, and premiered as a weekly series the following January. The setting and atmosphere resembled that of a cabaret, and the live origination (from New York) allowed the program to be highly topical.

Singer Nancy Ames was the "TW3" girl and sang the opening and closing numbers in addition to participating in the body of the show. The emphasis of the show was on poking fun at people in high places. Included in the format were comedy sketches, blackouts, musical production numbers, and news reports. Elliot Reid was the host during its first season. David Frost, who had hosted the British version of TW3 and been a contributor to the American series from the start, took over as host in the fall of 1964.

The satire could be very brutal. In one scene two good friends, a Catholic and a Jew, were discussing the fact that the Vatican had just ex-onerated the Jews from responsibility for Jesus' death. Well, they were off the hook for that one, after 2,000 years, but no, the Jew still couldn't join the Catholic's country club—that one hadn't been worked out yet. Then there was the news report from Jackson, Mississippi, where UN paratroopers had just been dropped by Guatemalan Air Force planes, to rescue Negro ministers, missionaries, and civil rights workers. The musical numbers were no less offensive. One telecast had "The Dance of the Liberal Republicans," and other such songs by writer-composer Tom Lehrer (who later recorded them on an album) as "National Brotherhood Week," "The Folk Song Army," "Smut," "Pollution," "Whatever Became of Hubert?" (Vice President Humphrey), and "The Vatican Rag."

TW3 attracted considerable attention and large audiences during its first few months on the air, and was easily renewed for the 1964–1965 season. But 1964 was an election year, and politicians—including Republican Presidential candidate Barry Goldwater—were among the show's favorite targets. Perhaps by chance, perhaps by design, TW3 was repeatedly preempted during the fall and replaced with low-rated political speeches and documentaries paid for by the Republicans. By the time the show reappeared after the election, its momentum was gone, and audiences had switched to the competition (*Peyton Place* on ABC and *Petticoat Junction* on CBS). TW3—and with it topical TV—was gone by the end of the season, but the example had been set. Political satire would appear in later years in *The Smothers Brothers Comedy Hour*, NBC's *Saturday Night Live*, and many other programs.

THAT WONDERFUL GUY
Situation Comedy
FIRST TELECAST: *December 28, 1949*
LAST TELECAST: *April 28, 1950*
BROADCAST HISTORY:
Dec 1949–Mar 1950, ABC Wed 9:00–9:30
Mar 1950–Apr 1950, ABC Fri 8:30–9:00
CAST:
Harold .... Jack Lemmon
Franklin Westbrook .... Neil Hamilton
Harold's girlfriend .... Cynthia Stone

A young Jack Lemmon starred in this early situation comedy about a pompous theatrical critic and his eager but bumbling valet. Lemmon, as the valet, was a lad fresh out of a Midwestern dramatic school and fresh into New York, looking for a chance to break into the Broadway big time as an actor. While waiting for opportunity to knock, he worked for suave, cynical drama critic Franklin Westbrook. Despite slick production and smooth performances by newcomer Lemmon and old pro Neil Hamilton, this series did not attract a sponsor and lasted only four months.

Lemmon himself did somewhat better than the valet he played here. After several more television roles (see Index) he landed a part in a Broadway play in 1953, then went to Hollywood in 1954 to begin a stellar motion-picture career.

Cynthia Stone, who played Harold's girlfriend, was Jack Lemmon's girlfriend in real life. Later in 1950 they were married.

THAT'S HOLLYWOOD
Documentary
BROADCAST HISTORY:
Syndicated only
30 minutes
Produced: *1976–1982* (74 episodes)
Released: *Fall 1977*
NARRATOR:
Tom Bosley

This was a spin-off from the hit movie *That's Entertainment,* and was produced by Jack Haley, Jr., the same man responsible for the movie. Essentially, it was the same thing in small-screen format: scenes from great 20th Century–Fox movies of the past, strung together at a fast clip. Each show was built around a single theme, such as disaster scenes, popular detectives, musicals, amusing outtakes, etc. Two pilot episodes were aired on some stations during the 1976–1977 season (with Tony Franciosa as host of one), with the series proper debuting in the fall of 1977, with Tom Bosley as host.

THAT'S INCREDIBLE!
Documentary
FIRST TELECAST: *March 3, 1980*
LAST TELECAST: *April 30, 1984*
BROADCAST HISTORY:
Mar 1980–Feb 1984, ABC Mon 8:00–9:00 (OS)
Apr 1984, ABC Thu 8:00–9:00
Apr 1984, ABC Mon 8:00–9:00
HOSTS:
John Davidson
Cathy Lee Crosby
Fran Tarkenton

A dentist who cures pain with clothespins! A man who catches arrows with his bare hands! An acrobat who leaps over cars speeding at him at 60 m.p.h.! A dog that catches sharks! A skydiver who jumps out of an airplane handcuffed and straitjacketed! A daredevil who catches a bullet in his teeth! (Six others lost their lives trying that last one.) ABC's *That's Incredible!,* conceived as an imitation of NBC's hit program *Real People,* seemed to be the freak-show annex of the earlier series. From a yogi sandwiched between two slabs of nails (sealed with a sledgehammer) to the band of karate experts leveling a barn, this show had less to do with "real people" than with those craving attention at any cost. When *Time* magazine announced its 1980 dubious achievement awards, "Most Sadistic Show" went to "ABC's *That's Incredible!,* which, in the search for thrills and ratings, had caused one man nearly to lose a

foot, another to burn his fingers to stumps, and a third to suffer several fractures and a ruptured aorta." Even an exposé in a May 1982 issue of *TV Guide,* which revealed several of the program's stunts to be rigged or outright frauds, did not faze the series' producers.

To be fair, there were informative segments on breakthroughs in medicine and people overcoming their handicaps. But the show was perhaps best represented by the picture of a man juggling whirring chain saws, while a caption on the screen read, "Do not try this yourself!"

THAT'S LIFE
Music/Comedy
FIRST TELECAST: *September 24, 1968*
LAST TELECAST: *May 20, 1969*
BROADCAST HISTORY:
Sep 1968–May 1969, ABC Tue 10:00–11:00
CAST:
Robert Dickson . . . . Robert Morse
Gloria Quigley Dickson . . . . E. J. Peaker
MUSICAL DIRECTOR:
Elliot Lawrence
CHOREOGRAPHER:
Tony Mordente

This unusual comedy followed the romance and married life of a young couple through sketches, monologues, music, and dance. Though set in the mythical town of Ridgeville, it was otherwise relatively unstructured—in a sense, a predecessor of *Love, American Style,* which premiered the following fall. Both shows made heavy use of guest celebrities in cameo roles. For example, the first episode of *That's Life* opened with a monologue by George Burns, punctuated by short songs, dances, and skits. There followed a dream sequence in which Gloria imagined herself married to Rodney Wonderful (Tony Randall). Later, back in reality, Rodney arranged a blind date for Gloria and she met Bobby at a discotheque, where the music was provided by the rock group the Turtles. Their romance began, and was followed through subsequent shows as they married, set up housekeeping, had their first child, etc.

Other stars making appearances on *That's Life* included Sid Caesar, Paul Lynde, Ethel Merman, Alan King, Mahalia Jackson, Robert Goulet, Phil Silvers, the Muppets, Flip Wilson, Goldie Hawn, Louis Armstrong, Wally Cox, and many others. Creator and executive producer of the show was Marvin Marx, who was for many years Jackie Gleason's head writer.

THAT'S MY BOY
Situation Comedy
FIRST TELECAST: *April 10, 1954*
LAST TELECAST: *September 13, 1959*
BROADCAST HISTORY:
Apr 1954–Jan 1955, CBS Sat 10:00–10:30
Jun 1959–Sep 1959, CBS Sun 7:30–8:00

"Jarring" Jack Jackson ...... Eddie Mayehoff
Alice Jackson.............. Rochelle Hudson
Junior Jackson .... Gil Stratton, Jr.
Henrietta Patterson .... Mabel Albertson
Bill Baker .... John Smith

"Jarring" Jack Jackson was a junior partner in the firm of Patterson and Jackson, made a comfortable living, and had a pleasant home in the suburbs. An ex-football star, and married to a former tennis star, Jack had delusions of grandeur about the future potential of his son, Junior, as an athlete. Unfortunately, Junior had neither the interest nor the ability to excel at sports. A quiet, intellectual sort, he was constantly hounded and prodded by his father into doing things he was not capable of succeeding at. Jack not only made life miserable for his son, but treating the world and everyone in it as though he was still calling signals in a football game, he also managed to make himself pretty hard for everyone else to take. During the summer of 1959, reruns of the original series were aired on Sunday evenings.

Based on the 1951 movie of the same name, which also starred Mayehoff (with Jerry Lewis as his son).

THAT'S MY LINE
Comedy Variety
FIRST TELECAST: *August 9, 1980*
LAST TELECAST: *April 11, 1981*
BROADCAST HISTORY:
Aug 1980, CBS Sat 8:00–9:00
Feb 1981–Mar 1981, CBS Tue 8:00–9:00
Apr 1981, CBS Sat 9:00–10:00
REGULARS:
Bob Barker
Tiiu Leek
Suzanne Childs
Kerry Millerick (1981)

In the wake of NBC's hit series about *Real People* with unusual occupations, the producers of the 1950s and 1960s panel show *What's My Line* decided to bring back their old program—with a twist. Instead of making it a guessing game, they did filmed reports—à la *Real People*—on actual people with unusual ways of making a living. Among those seen were the world's fastest typist, a rodeo clown, professional flag raisers in Washington, D.C., a blind cabinetmaker, a man who designed skirts for men, the world's greatest hoaxer, and a 76-year-old man who delivered newspapers from an airplane.

Bob Barker was the host of *That's My Line*, and Tiiu Leek and Suzanne Childs were field reporters. When the series returned in 1981, following an initial three-week run the previous summer, a third reporter, Kerry Millerick, had been added. The thrust of the show also seemed to have changed: its initial effort to cover unusual occupations of all types had given way to an emphasis on the funny, bizarre, or ridiculous.

THAT'S MY MAMA
Situation Comedy
FIRST TELECAST: *September 4, 1974*
LAST TELECAST: *December 24, 1975*
BROADCAST HISTORY:
Sep 1974–Sep 1975, ABC Wed 8:00–8:30
Sep 1975–Dec 1975, ABC Wed 8:30–9:00
CAST:
Clifton Curtis .... Clifton Davis
"Mama" Eloise Curtis .... Theresa Merritt
Earl Chambers .... Theodore Wilson
Tracy Curtis Taylor (1974–1975)
.... Lynne Moody
Tracy Curtis Taylor (1975) ..... Joan Pringle
Leonard Taylor .... Lisle Wilson
Wildcat .... Jester Hairston
Josh .... DeForest Covan
Junior .... Ted Lange

This ethnic comedy centered on the world of Clifton Curtis, a young, hip barber in a black middle-class neighborhood of Washington, D.C. Clifton had inherited the family barbershop, "Oscar's," after the death of his father. He liked his trade and his life as a bachelor, but Mama had different ideas for him, wanting him to find a nice, conservative mate, as his sister Tracy had done. Tracy's husband Leonard was successful, all right (he was an engineer), but far too square for Clifton. Others around the shop were Clifton's buddy Earl, the postman; old-timers Wildcat and Josh, who stopped in for jokes, checkers, and faulty advice; and Junior, the irrepressible street philosopher.

There were several cast changes in the fall of 1975, and Earl, the big talker with unworkable schemes, became Clifton's partner in the barbershop. (Note: Ed Bernard played Earl in the first two telecasts in 1974, while Theodore Wilson had another role in those episodes only.)

THEATER OF THE MIND
Discussion
FIRST TELECAST: *July 14, 1949*
LAST TELECAST: *September 15, 1949*
BROADCAST HISTORY:
Jul 1949–Aug 1949, NBC Thu 9:30–10:00
Aug 1949–Sep 1949, NBC Thu 9:00–9:30
MODERATOR:
Dr. Houston Peterson

An early attempt to use television to help viewers meet emotional problems of home life. The first half of each telecast consisted of a playlet revolving around a problem such as a child's adjustment to a new baby in the home, inferiority complexes, domineering parents, old age, alcoholism, etc. After the dramatization a panel of psychiatrists and other experts discussed how the problem could be faced.

THEATER TIME
Dramatic Anthology
FIRST TELECAST: *July 25, 1957*
LAST TELECAST: *September 26, 1957*
BROADCAST HISTORY:
Jul 1957–Sep 1957, ABC Thu 9:00–9:30
HOSTESS:
Anita Louise

The plays shown in this filmed series were all reruns of episodes originally aired as part of other anthology programs.

THEN CAME BRONSON
Adventure
FIRST TELECAST: *September 17, 1969*
LAST TELECAST: *September 9, 1970*
BROADCAST HISTORY:
Sep 1969–Sep 1970, NBC Wed 10:00–11:00
CAST:
Jim Bronson .... Michael Parks

Following the suicide of his best friend, big-city reporter Jim Bronson pondered the meaning of his life and wondered about the satisfaction he was getting out of it. The conclusion he reached was that he really yearned to be free of the traditional commitments of urban living. So, he gave up his job, divested himself of most of his material possessions, and left town on his deceased friend's motorcycle in search of a more meaningful existence. The places he traveled to, the people he met, and the odd jobs he took to support himself in his wanderings across the country, provided the stories in this adventure series.

THEY STAND ACCUSED
Courtroom Drama
FIRST TELECAST: *January 18, 1949*
LAST TELECAST: *December 30, 1954*
BROADCAST HISTORY:
Jan 1949–May 1949, CBS Tue 8:00–9:00
Sep 1949–Mar 1950, DUM Sun 9:00–10:00
Jun 1950–Oct 1950, DUM Sun 9:00–10:00
Oct 1950–Apr 1951, DUM Sun 10:00–11:00
Apr 1951–May 1951, DUM Sat 9:00–10:00
May 1951–Sep 1951, DUM Tue 10:00–11:00
Sep 1951–Oct 1952, DUM Sun 10:00–11:00
Sep 1954–Dec 1954, DUM Thu 8:00–9:00

They Stand Accused was one of the earliest and more popular network series to originate from Chicago. It was an unscripted, spontaneous courtroom trial with real lawyers and judges, and actors playing the parts of defendants and witnesses. Everyone ad-libbed his lines as he went along, according to the developing action. The studio audience served as the "jury," and determined the outcome of each case. Even the cases, though fictitious, had a ring of authenticity. They were plotted out by William Wines, Assistant Attorney General of the State of Illinois, who briefed the participants before each show as if they were principals in a real case about to go to trial, and then let the trial run its course.

Wines' cases sometimes involved murder, but just as often were property claims, divorces, or other civil matters. One week the jury might be deciding custody of a child; on another, whether a wealthy eccentric was capable of managing his own affairs. When it was murder there never was a question of who did it, but rather if self-defense, accident, or temporary insanity was a valid defense. So realistic was the presentation that many viewers were convinced that they were watching a real trial in progress.

They Stand Accused was first seen locally over WGN-TV in Chicago, in April 1948. One week after Chicago and New York were linked by coaxial cable in January 1949 the program was fed out to the CBS network, under the title *Cross Question.* It later moved to DuMont and changed its name to *They Stand Accused* in January 1950.

THEY'RE OFF
Quiz
FIRST TELECAST: *June 30, 1949*
LAST TELECAST: *August 18, 1949*
BROADCAST HISTORY:
Jun 1949–Aug 1949, DUM Thu 8:30–9:00
EMCEE:
Tom Shirley
RACE CALLER:
Byron Field

Contestants were tested on films of historic horse races on this obscure early quiz show.

THICKE OF THE NIGHT
Talk/Variety
BROADCAST HISTORY:
Syndicated only
90 minutes
Produced: *1983–1984*
Released: *September 5, 1983*
HOST:
Alan Thicke
REGULARS:
Richard Belzer
Isabel Grandin
Mike McManus
Charles Fleischer
Chloe Webb (1983)
Gilbert Gottfried (1983)
Arsenio Hall (1984)
The Tom Canning Band
The John Toben Band (1984)
RECURRING PLAYERS:
Kent Skov
Bill Hudnut
Fred Willard
Rick Ducommun
Carl Wolfson
Cecille Frenette

Thicke of the Night arrived in the fall of 1983 amid a barrage of publicity: move over, Johnny Carson, a new, youth-oriented King of Late Night was here, produced by television's most famous programmer, Fred Silverman! More than one hundred stations agreed to carry the new Monday–Friday show, a few of them preempting Carson in the process and most of the rest running it in direct competition with *The Tonight Show.*

Johnny needn't have worried. Thicke, an amiable, good-looking Canadian who had been hovering around the U.S. television business for years (as an actor, producer, and songwriter), proved to be no competition. His show aimed for a more contemporary, improvisational feel than the *Tonight Show,* with rock songs, skits, and chatter among the regulars, as well as segments with guest stars like John Ritter, Rick Nelson, James Brown, Teri Copley, and Mr. T. Some guests turned up repeatedly, among them TV columnists Richard Hack and R. Couri Hay, talk-show host Wally George, rock-show emcee Kasey Kasem, and Thicke's wife at the time, actress-singer Gloria Loring. A large, open set, reminiscent of scaffolding (as if it were still under construction), added to the wide-open atmosphere. Despite energetic rock songs by Thicke and off-the-wall skits by a host of young comics, the show drew poor reviews and a small audience.

THICKER THAN WATER
Situation Comedy
FIRST TELECAST: *June 13, 1973*
LAST TELECAST: *August 8, 1973*
BROADCAST HISTORY:
  Jun 1973–Aug 1973, ABC Wed 8:00–8:30
CAST:
  Nellie Paine .... Julie Harris
  Ernie Paine .... Richard Long
  Jonas Paine .... Malcolm Atterbury
  Lily .... Jessica Myerson
  Walter .... Lou Fant

This family comedy pitted a swinging brother (Ernie) and a staid, spinster sister (Nellie) in a battle of wits. The two were brought together by their ailing, octogenarian father, Jonas, who promised them each a $75,000 inheritance if they could both live at his home and together run the family pickle factory ("Paine's Pure Pickles") for five years. As it turned out, old Jonas not only hung on to watch them bicker, but was probably going to outlive them both.

Lily was a cousin and Walter her husband. Based on the English TV series *Nearest and Dearest.*

THIN MAN, THE
Detective/Comedy
FIRST TELECAST: *September 20, 1957*
LAST TELECAST: *June 26, 1959*

BROADCAST HISTORY:
  Sep 1957–Jun 1959, NBC Fri 9:30–10:00
CAST:
  Nick Charles .... Peter Lawford
  Nora Charles .... Phyllis Kirk
  Lt. Ralph Raines (1957–1958)... Stafford Repp
  Lt. Steve King (1957–1958) .... Tol Avery
  Lt. Harry Evans (1958–1959) .. Jack Albertson
  Beatrice Dane (1958–1959) .... Nita Talbot
  Hazel (1958–1959) .... Pat Donahue

Nick and Nora Charles were wealthy New York socialites living with their wire-haired fox terrier, Asta, in a luxurious Park Avenue apartment. When he married Nora, Nick retired from his occupation as a private detective, but his underworld friends were still around to haunt him. Out of her love for Nick, Nora tried to be hospitable to his friends from the seamier side of life. The friend she had the most trouble being courteous to was Beatrice Dane, a beautiful con-artist friend of Nick's who used the alias "Blondie Collins." Asta, with the mistaken notion that he was a bloodhound, spent much of his time sniffing out clues and suspects. Nick, Nora, and Asta were a team of super-sleuths, solving crimes together for the pure enjoyment of it.

Based on the characters created by novelist Dashiell Hammett, and portrayed in films for many years by William Powell and Myrna Loy. The name "thin man" did not refer to Nick Charles, incidentally, but to another character in the first (1934) *Thin Man* movie.

NBC aired reruns of *The Thin Man* as part of its daytime lineup from September 1959 to February 1960.

THINK FAST
Quiz/Panel
FIRST TELECAST: *March 26, 1949*
LAST TELECAST: *October 8, 1950*
BROADCAST HISTORY:
  Mar 1949–Apr 1949, ABC Sat 8:30–9:00
  May 1949–Sep 1949, ABC Fri 8:00–8:30
  Sep 1949–Jul 1950, ABC Sun 8:00–8:30
  Jul 1950–Oct 1950, ABC Sun 7:00–7:30
MODERATOR:
  Dr. Mason Gross (1949–1950)
  Gypsy Rose Lee (1950)
PANELISTS:
  Leon Janney
  David Broekman
  Eloise McElhone

The five panelists (three regulars and two guests) on this wordy quiz circled a large table, each getting a chance at the "King's" throne by outtalking the others on subjects thrown out by the host.

THIRD MAN, THE
Intrigue

BROADCAST HISTORY:
Syndicated only
30 minutes
Produced: *1959–1962* (77 episodes)
Released (U.S.): *Fall 1960*
CAST:
Harry Lime .... Michael Rennie
Bradford Webster .... Jonathan Harris

Harry Lime was one of those sinister characters of literature who was cleaned up considerably for television (for two other notable examples, see *Boston Blackie* and *Hopalong Cassidy*). As introduced in Graham Greene's novel *The Third Man,* and portrayed by Orson Welles in the famous 1950 movie of the same name, Lime was a dark and treacherous man, a double-dealer whose only saving grace was that he usually swindled con men who were even more distasteful than himself. Harry could be very charming, but he always had an angle somewhere.

Television turned this blackheart into a suave and debonair ladies' man, the head of an import-export company in Vienna who traveled around the world acquiring works of art and solving mysteries. His criminal past was acknowledged, and he could still be a bit on the shady side. But, as actor Michael Rennie put it, "Justice is Harry Lime's major concern, his primary motive." Graham Greene must have howled at that! Bradford Webster, played by Jonathan Harris (later of *Lost in Space*), was Harry's sometime assistant.

The Third Man was an unusual joint British-American production, with approximately half the episodes filmed in England under the auspices of the BBC, and the other half in Hollywood by National Telefilm Associates. A radio version of *The Third Man,* starring Orson Welles, was syndicated in the early 1950s.

13 QUEENS BOULEVARD
Situation Comedy
FIRST TELECAST: *March 20, 1979*
LAST TELECAST: *July 24, 1979*
BROADCAST HISTORY:
Mar 1979–Apr 1979, ABC Tue 10:30–11:00
Jul 1979, ABC Tue 10:00–10:30
CAST:
Felicia Winters .... Eileen Brennan
Steven Winters .... Jerry Van Dyke
Elaine Dowling .... Marcia Rodd
Mildred Capestro .... Helen Page Camp
Annie Capestro .... Susan Elliot
Jill .... Louise Williams
Camille .... Karen Rushmore
Lois .... Frances Lee McCain

Adult comedy set in a garden apartment complex in Queens, a middle-class, residential borough of New York City. Felicia and Steven had been happily married for 15 years. Their neighbors included Felicia's best friend Elaine, a divorcée; Mildred Capestro; and Mildred's daughter, Jill.

After a four-week run in March–April, the series returned in July with three additional episodes.

THIRTYSOMETHING
Comedy/Drama
FIRST TELECAST: *September 29, 1987*
LAST TELECAST:
BROADCAST HISTORY:
Sep 1987–   , ABC Tue 10:00–11:00
CAST:
Michael Steadman .... Ken Olin
Hope Murdoch Steadman .... Mel Harris
Elliot Weston .... Timothy Busfield
Nancy Weston .... Patricia Wettig
Melissa Steadman .... Melanie Mayron
Ellyn .... Polly Draper
Prof. Gary Shepherd .... Peter Horton

Ever since the term "Yuppie" became popular the networks have been trying to fashion a series about this elusive—and presumably heavy-consuming—audience segment. *thirtysomething* (sic) was the very picture of the viewers ABC wanted in its audience: 30-ish, upwardly mobile, preferably with children, and spending lots of money on consumer goods. Stories traced the relationships between two couples and three singles in Philadelphia, all friends. Michael and Elliot had worked together at a large advertising agency, then left to open their own. Michael's wife, Hope, a glamorous, driven, overachiever from Princeton, wanted to be a superstar in publishing but—for now—was raising their newborn baby, Janey. Elliot's wife, Nancy, a flower child of the '60s, had dreams of being an artist, but wound up raising their now school-age children, Ethan and Brittany; by early 1988 Elliot and Nancy were going through a painful separation. Melissa was Michael's sex-starved, want-it-all single cousin (an aging "JAP"), a photographer; Ellyn was Hope's girlhood friend, a worried career woman; and Gary, a long-haired, fun-loving Assistant Professor of Classics at a nearby college, who was Michael's best buddy.

All these pampered people worried constantly about the true meaning of their lives and marriages, pined for the youth they had left behind, and ran to see why the babies were crying. It was enough to make the Yuppies tune over to *Crime Story* on NBC.

THIS COULD BE YOU
see *Bill Gwinn Show, The*

THIS IS BROADWAY
see *This Is Show Business*

THIS IS GALEN DRAKE
see *Galen Drake Show, The*

THIS IS MUSIC
Music
FIRST TELECAST: *November 29, 1951*

786

LAST TELECAST: *October 9, 1952*
BROADCAST HISTORY:
  Nov 1951–Jun 1952, DUM Thu 8:00–8:30
  Jun 1952–Oct 1952, DUM Thu 10:00–10:30
HOST:
  Alexander Gray
REGULARS:
  Nancy Carr
  Bruce Foote
  Lucille Reed
  Jackie Van (1952)
  Jacqueline James (1952)
  Bill Snary
  Robert Trendler Orchestra

DuMont favored pleasant, unassuming musical programs such as this one because they cost very little to telecast and could be relied upon to attract a respectable, if not really large, audience. The format consisted primarily of popular songs sung by a young cast of regulars.

THIS IS MUSIC
  Music
FIRST TELECAST: *June 13, 1958*
LAST TELECAST: *May 21, 1959*
BROADCAST HISTORY:
  Jun 1958–Sep 1958, ABC Fri 8:30–9:00
  Sep 1958, ABC Mon 7:30–8:00
  Oct 1958, ABC Mon 10:00–10:30
  Nov 1958–Feb 1959, ABC Thu 10:00–10:30
  Mar 1959, ABC Mon 9:30–10:00
  Apr 1959–May 1959, ABC Thu 10:00–10:30
EMCEE:
  Colin Male
REGULARS:
  Ramona Burnett
  Lee Fogel
  Paula Jane
  Wanda Lewis
  The O'Neill Dancers
  Bud Chase
  Bob Smith
  Gail Johnson
  Bob Shreeve

When the original artists mouthed the words to their hit records, as they did on *American Bandstand,* to make sure that it sounded right, it was called lip-syncing. On this live series, which originated from Cincinnati, Ohio, a group of regular performers did the same thing, but to records made famous by other artists. They mouthed the words while the records were played. *This Is Music* hopped all over the ABC schedule during the 1958–1959 season, filling otherwise empty time slots. Many of the larger stations, which scheduled syndicated programs to fill time slots that the network did not program on a regular basis, did not air this series.

THIS IS MY SONG
  see *Bill Gwinn Show, The*

THIS IS NBC NEWS
  News
FIRST TELECAST: *June 3, 1962*
LAST TELECAST: *September 16, 1962*
BROADCAST HISTORY:
  Jun 1962–Sep 1962, NBC Sun 6:30–7:00
HOST:
  Ray Scherer

Anchorman Ray Scherer opened each edition of the 1962 summer season of *This Is NBC News* with a five-minute wrap-up of the day's news. The body of the show was then devoted to a series of reports by various NBC News correspondents, on tape or filmed, covering offbeat or entertaining news events from all over the world. At the end of each show, a short summary of the major news events that had occurred during the previous week was given by Mr. Scherer. A slightly different version of this show had aired earlier on Sunday evenings during the previous summer and this version continued on Sunday afternoons until March 24, 1963.

THIS IS SHOW BUSINESS
  Variety
FIRST TELECAST: *July 15, 1949*
LAST TELECAST: *September 11, 1956*
BROADCAST HISTORY:
  Jul 1949–Sep 1949, CBS Fri Fri 9:00–10:00
  Oct 1949–Jan 1953, CBS Sun 7:30–8:00 (OS)
  Jan 1953–Jun 1953, CBS Sat 9:00–9:30
  Sep 1953–Mar 1954, CBS Tue 9:00–9:30
  Jun 1956–Sep 1956, NBC Tue 8:30–9:00
EMCEE:
  Clifton Fadiman
PANELISTS:
  George S. Kaufman
  Abe Burrows (1949–1951, 1956)
  Sam Levenson (1951–1954)
  Walter Slezak (1956)

The various entertainers who performed on this series were introduced by host/emcee Clifton Fadiman, who chatted with them briefly before they did their acts. Following each act—there were usually three on each show—the entertainers received the opportunity to ask the panel, composed of three show-business veterans, a few questions about the contestants' own acts or on general subjects related to the entertainment world. The title of this series was *This Is Broadway* during its Friday night run in the summer of 1949. When it moved to Sunday evenings that October the title was changed to *This Is Show Business.* During the period in which it was called *This Is Broadway,* the show was simulcast on radio and television. The NBC revival, for the summer of 1956, aired on alternate Tuesdays with *The Chevy Show.*

Probably the most famous moment in the entire run of the series came on the 1952 Christmas show, when acerbic author and panelist George S.

Kaufman remarked on the commercialization of Christmas and then said, "Let's make this one program on which no one sings 'Silent Night.' " CBS received several hundred letters expressing viewer outrage at the comment, and Kaufman was briefly dropped from the show amid considerable publicity. Cooler heads prevailed, however, and he was soon reinstated.

THIS IS THE LIFE
Religious Drama
FIRST TELECAST: *September 9, 1952*
LAST TELECAST: *October 26, 1953*
BROADCAST HISTORY:
  Sep 1952–Oct 1952, DUM Fri 8:00–8:30
  Oct 1952–Sep 1953, ABC Sun 9:30–10:00
  Apr 1953–Aug 1953, DUM Mon 8:30–9:00
  Sep 1953–Oct 1953, ABC Mon 10:00–10:30
CAST:
  Mr. Fisher .... Onslow Stevens
  Mrs. Fisher .... Nan Boardman
  Emily Fisher (18) .... Randy Stuart
  Pete Fisher (16) .... Michael Hall
  Freddie Fisher (10) .... David Kasday
  Grandpa Fisher .... Forrest Taylor
  Pastor Martin .... Nelson Leigh

This religious series was produced by the Lutheran Church's Missouri Synod and depicted a Christian family's attempts to deal with the moral problems of everyday life. The "typical family" was the Fishers, who lived in the town of Middleburg, somewhere in the Midwest. Into their lives came a basketball player who had betrayed the trust of his team, a person victimized by rumors, a couple contemplating divorce, and others. The problem was unfolded in a dramatic presentation, then one member of the family, usually Grandpa or eldest child Emily, would deliver the "pitch"—the Christian solution.

The shows were provided free to any station that would air them, and were seen locally in many cities as well as in the ABC and DuMont runs indicated above. The series was described by *TV Guide* in 1954 as "the most widely circulated TV show in the world."

This Is the Life has continued in production to the present day, making it one of the longest-running series in television history. It has won more than 70 awards, including four Emmies. The Fisher family was phased out in January 1956, and the title shortened from the original *This Is the Life Presents "The Fisher Family"* to simply *This Is the Life*. Since that time the program has followed an anthology format, with a different cast and setting each week. However, the objective remains the same: to illustrate through an interesting weekly drama the Christian solution to the problems of life.

THIS IS TOM JONES
Musical Variety
FIRST TELECAST: *February 7, 1969*

LAST TELECAST: *January 15, 1971*
BROADCAST HISTORY:
  Feb 1969–May 1969, ABC Fri 7:30–8:30
  May 1969–Sep 1970, ABC Thu 9:00–10:00
  Sep 1970–Jan 1971, ABC Fri 10:00–11:00
REGULARS:
  Tom Jones
  The Ace Trucking Company (1970–1971)
  Big Jim Sullivan (1970–1971)
  The Norman Maen Dancers
  The Jack Parnell Orchestra (1969–1970)
  The Johnnie Spence Orchestra (1970–1971)

Pop singer Tom Jones, he of the booming baritone, raw, driving energy, and ability to turn grown women into putty (read "sex appeal"), starred in his own musical variety series from 1969–1971. Jones is a Welshman and the first few telecasts originated in London and featured many English stars. Later the origination alternated between London and Hollywood, and top American stars, especially popular musicians, appeared as well. The show had a very contemporary quality, especially during the second season when the Ace Trucking Company, an improvisational comedy troupe consisting of four boys and one girl, joined as regulars.

After the last big, brassy musical number, dynamic Tom would wish his viewers good night in traditional Welsh, saying, "Gwyn eich byd a dymunaf i chwi lawenydd bob amser." Although there was some speculation about what he was really saying (how many Americans understand Welsh?), it meant, simply, "May you always be well and be happy."

THIS IS YOUR LIFE
Testimonial
FIRST TELECAST: *October 1, 1952*
LAST TELECAST: *September 3, 1961*
BROADCAST HISTORY:
  Oct 1952–Jun 1953, NBC Wed 10:00–10:30
  Jun 1953–Aug 1953, NBC Tue 9:30–10:00
  Jul 1953–Jun 1958, NBC Wed 9:30–10:00
  Sep 1958–Sep 1960, NBC Wed 10:00–10:30
  Sep 1960–Sep 1961, NBC Sun 10:30–11:00
HOST:
  Ralph Edwards
ANNOUNCER:
  Bob Warren

This Is Your Life was created by Ralph Edwards in the late 1940s and aired for one year each on NBC and CBS radio. It came to television in 1952 and remained on the air for nine seasons. Ralph Edwards was the host throughout the long network run and returned a decade later with a syndicated version.

The format of *This Is Your Life* was quite simple. Each show opened with Edwards surprising an unsuspecting individual, either in the studio or at some location not too far from it, and informing him or her that "this is your life." The guest of honor was then transported to the program's studio, where his life story was presented. Edwards would read from the honored guest's *This Is Your Life* book, chronologically covering the high points in his life, and would pause periodically in the narrative for the voice of an offstage guest. The guest of honor would try to guess whose voice it was—a relative, friend, teacher, minister, business associate, etc.—and then the offstage guest would come out to reminisce about their shared experiences. This would go on until the entire life story was unfolded.

At the end of the show, Ralph Edwards gathered all the guests together on the stage and personally presented the guest of honor with mementoes—a film of the show, a camera and projector to show it on, a charm bracelet with each charm depicting a significant event in the guest of honor's life, and various other prizes. After the show, the friends and family were taken to a party at the hotel where all out-of-town guests had been staying prior to the telecast. The subjects varied from ordinary people, to show-business celebrities, to well-known businessmen. *This Is Your Life* was presented live until the start of the 1959–1960 season, at which point many of the episodes were prerecorded.

Edwards' narration of the biographies of the subjects on *This Is Your Life* tended to wring the maximum amount of emotion from both subject and audience and there was plenty of nostalgic crying done by subjects and guests. To most of the guests of honor, the confrontation with Edwards came as a complete surprise, but there were a few exceptions. Eddie Cantor was told in advance because he had a heart condition and Edwards did not want to shock him into an attack. The most celebrated subject in the long history of *This Is Your Life*, singer Lillian Roth, was also told ahead of time, but for a very different reason. She had waged a long, successful battle with alcoholism and her story was just too personal to spring on her as a surprise. That telecast was extremely inspirational, had the full sanction of Alcoholics Anonymous, and was the only episode to be aired three times, twice on kinescopes after its original live presentation in 1953.

There was always a backup kinescope ready to roll in case something went wrong when Edwards sprang his little surprise on an unsuspecting guest, but it was never needed. There were occasions, though, when the plans had to be scrapped because the subject found out in advance what was being planned. According to the *This Is Your Life* staff, Ann Sheridan was one whose biography was canceled for this reason. There was one person who was definitely off limits—Ralph Edwards himself. He had told his staff, and he meant it, that he would fire every one of them if they ever tried to pull the switch and surprise him with his "life."

The first syndicated edition of *This Is Your Life* lasted only the 1971–1972 season. In the fall of 1983 a new syndicated version of *This Is Your Life*

appeared, produced by Ralph Edwards but hosted by actor Joseph Campanella.

THIS WEEK IN COUNTRY MUSIC
Magazine
BROADCAST HISTORY:
Syndicated only
30 minutes
Produced: *1983–1987*
Released: *September 1983*
HOSTS:
Lorianne Crook
Charlie Chase

This series aimed to do for country music what *Entertainment Tonight* did for the larger world of show business: provide news, gossip, and features on the stars and happenings in the field, on an up-to-the-minute basis. It was fed once a week via satellite to stations around the country.

THIS WEEK IN SPORTS
Sports News
FIRST TELECAST: *September 20, 1949*
LAST TELECAST: *December 13, 1949*
BROADCAST HISTORY:
Sep 1949–Dec 1949, CBS Tue 10:00–10:15

Newsreel highlights of the week's activities in the world of sports were telecast in this series. Included were highlights from various events, films of outstanding individual plays, and short profiles of well-known sports personalities.

THIS WORLD—1954
Documentary
FIRST TELECAST: *August 4, 1954*
LAST TELECAST: *September 22, 1954*
BROADCAST HISTORY:
Aug 1954–Sep 1954, ABC Wed 9:00–9:30

Documentary films produced by the federal government on such subjects as Communism, good government, democracy, etc.

THORNS, THE
Situation Comedy
FIRST TELECAST: *January 15, 1988*
LAST TELECAST: *March 11, 1988*
BROADCAST HISTORY:
Jan 1988–Feb 1988, ABC Fri 9:00–9:30
Mar 1988, ABC Fri 9:30–10:00
CAST:
Sloan Thorn . . . . Tony Roberts
Ginger Thorn . . . . Kelly Bishop
Rose Thorn . . . . Marilyn Cooper
Cricket . . . . Lori Petty
Toinette . . . . Mary Louise Wilson
Chad Thorn (age 16) . . . . Adam Biesk
Joey Thorn (14) . . . . Lisa Rieffel
Edmund Thorn (7) . . . . Jesse Tendler
Peggy/Mrs. Hamilton . . . . Maureen Stapleton
Katina Pappas . . . . Kathryn Marcopulos

"We're All Right" by John Kander and Fred Ebb, sung by Dorothy Loudon in an opening nightclub scene.

Mike Nichols produced this caviar comedy about a family of rich, social-climbing snobs. Sharing an elegant New York City townhouse were Sloan, an insensitive, self-absorbed public relations executive; Ginger, his status-seeking wife; and their three insufferable children, Chad (a junior snob at 16), Joey, and Edmund. The most frequent form of parental discipline was to buy the kids off; the most frequent social activity, buying and lying one's way into all the right affairs. Cricket was the shapely mother's helper, and Toinette the contemptuous French maid.

Introducing a modicum of common sense were Sloan's no-nonsense mother, Rose, who moved in (horrors!) when her Brooklyn apartment burned down; and Peggy, the sensible maid to a fabulously rich, reclusive widow who lived nearby. (It turned out that Peggy was the widow herself, in disguise.)

Mike Nichols' previous contribution to television was the acclaimed dramatic series *Family*. With luck, this one will mercifully be forgotten.

THOSE AMAZING ANIMALS
Animals
FIRST TELECAST: *August 24, 1980*
LAST TELECAST: *August 23, 1981*
BROADCAST HISTORY:
Aug 1980, ABC Sun 8:00–9:00
Sep 1980–May 1981, ABC Sun 7:00–8:00
July 1981–Aug 1981, ABC Sun 7:00–8:00
HOSTS:
Burgess Meredith
Priscilla Presley
Jim Stafford
REGULAR CONTRIBUTORS:
Jacques-Yves Cousteau
Joan Embrey
Ron and Valerie Taylor

Those Amazing Animals was a spinoff from the animal segments of *That's Incredible!* Like the parent program, and unlike most previous nature series (*Wild Kingdom*, etc.), it followed a news-magazine format, with separate live or taped reports linked by studio discussion. There was also a studio audience.

Those Amazing Animals tried to play up the sensational aspects of wildlife wherever possible (A horse that can count! An elephant walks on Jim Stafford! "Reptile Man" hypnotizes hungry crocodiles! A 121-pound dog that chomps rearview mirrors off of passing cars!). Still, most of the reports were instructive, especially those contributed by world-famous explorer Jacques-Yves Cousteau, leading undersea photographers Ron and Valerie Taylor, and Joan Embrey of the San Diego Zoo. The program's hosts seemed to have been chosen

mostly for their diversity: Burgess Meredith, the venerable actor, Priscilla Presley, ex-wife of Elvis, and Jim Stafford, a popular singer whose biggest hit was something called "Spiders and Snakes."

THOSE ENDEARING YOUNG CHARMS
Situation Comedy
FIRST TELECAST: *March 30, 1952*
LAST TELECAST: *June 17, 1952*
BROADCAST HISTORY:
Mar 1952–Apr 1952, NBC Sun 6:30–7:00
May 1952–Jun 1952, NBC Tue/Thu 7:15–7:30
CAST:
Ralph Charm .... Maurice Copeland
Abbe Charm .... Fern Persons
Connie Charm .... Charon Follett
Clem Charm .... Gerald Garvey
Uncle Duff .... Clarence Hartzell

This live series, originating from Chicago, told of the adventures of the Charm family, who ran a mail-order business catering to collectors of household gadgets. The family business was run by Ralph Charm and his wife, Abbe, but all of the members of the household participated in it, including daughter Connie and son Clem. The strangest member of the household was Uncle Duff, whose hobby was memorizing mail-order catalogues. *Those Endearing Young Charms* had premiered on Sunday afternoons at the end of December 1951. It spent only two weeks in the 6:30–7:00 P.M. Sunday time slot and then returned early in May.

THOSE TWO
Situation Comedy
FIRST TELECAST: *November 26, 1951*
LAST TELECAST: *April 24, 1953*
BROADCAST HISTORY:
Nov 1951–Apr 1953, NBC Mon/Wed/Fri 7:30–7:45
REGULARS:
Pinky Lee
Vivian Blaine (1951–1952)
Martha Stewart (1952–1953)

This live, loosely structured musical situation-comedy series was used to fill the remainder of the half hour in which NBC aired its network news program. Vivian was a nightclub singer whose accompanist, Pinky, was madly in love with her. Unfortunately for Pinky, she was in love with another man. The vestigial plot was primarily a backdrop allowing the stars to sing solos and duets. Miss Blaine left the series in May 1952 and was replaced by Martha Stewart.

THOSE WHITING GIRLS
Situation Comedy
FIRST TELECAST: *July 4, 1955*
LAST TELECAST: *September 30, 1957*

BROADCAST HISTORY:
Jul 1955–Sep 1955, CBS Mon 9:00–9:30
Jul 1957–Sep 1957, CBS Mon 9:00–9:30
CAST:
Margaret Whiting .... Herself
Barbara Whiting .... Herself
Mrs. Whiting .... Mabel Albertson
Artie (1957) .... Jerry Paris

There were many similarities between the real lives of the Whiting sisters, Margaret and Barbara, and the roles they portrayed in this summer replacement for *I Love Lucy*. Margaret was, and played, a popular singer and Barbara was, and played, her younger sister. They lived in Los Angeles with their mother, and Barbara was a coed at UCLA. The adventures of the two girls and their relationship with their "mother" formed the bases for the stories told in the series. When it returned in 1957, Margaret had acquired an accompanist named Artie who was the one new regular in the cast.

THREE ABOUT TOWN
Music
FIRST TELECAST: *August 11, 1948*
LAST TELECAST: *October 27, 1948*
BROADCAST HISTORY:
Aug 1948–Sep 1948, ABC Wed 7:15–7:30
Sep 1948–Oct 1948, ABC Wed 8:45–9:00
HOSTESS:
Betsi Allison

Musical interlude featuring vocalist Betsi Allison and twin pianos, with songs and chatter about the theatrical world. Also seen as a local program in New York at various times during 1948.

THREE FLAMES SHOW, THE
Music
FIRST TELECAST: *June 13, 1949*
LAST TELECAST: *August 20, 1949*
BROADCAST HISTORY:
Jun 1949, NBC Mon 10:00–10:30
Jul 1949–Aug 1949, NBC Mon 9:45–10:00
Jul 1949–Aug 1949, NBC Sat 10:00–10:30
REGULARS:
The Three Flames (Tiger Haynes, guitar; Roy Testamark, piano; Bill Pollard, bass)

Live program of music and patter by the Three Flames, a popular black vocal and instrumental trio whose biggest hit was the 1947 novelty "Open the Door, Richard." They performed, appropriately enough, before a backdrop of flames. Many, though not all, of their guests were black, including trumpet players Hot Lips Page and Dizzy Gillespie, singer Dinah Washington, and pianist Errol Garner.

The Three Flames were previously seen locally in New York as well as in a daytime program. They were among the first, if not *the* first, black performers to have a regular network series.

THREE FOR THE ROAD
Adventure
FIRST TELECAST: *September 14, 1975*
LAST TELECAST: *November 30, 1975*
BROADCAST HISTORY:
Sep 1975–Nov 1975, CBS Sun 7:00–8:00
CAST:
Pete Karras .... Alex Rocco
John Karras .... Vincent Van Patten
Endy Karras .... Leif Garrett

Free-lance photographer Pete Karras, a widower with two teenage sons, traveled around the country on various assignments. His mode of travel, and the means by which he kept his family together, was a mobile home. The nature of Pete's job and the people that he and his sons encountered in their travels provided the material for the stories in this series, which often tended to the moralistic (after beating a bad guy to a pulp, Pete told the boys that violence is not the answer, etc.) The series had a short run.

3 GIRLS 3
Variety
FIRST TELECAST: *March 30, 1977*
LAST TELECAST: *June 29, 1977*
BROADCAST HISTORY:
Mar 1977, NBC Wed 9:00–10:00
Jun 1977, NBC Wed 9:00–10:00
REGULARS:
Debbie Allen
Ellen Foley
Mimi Kennedy
Oliver Clark
Richard Byrd
Alan Johnson Dancers
Marvin Laird Orchestra

A novel programming idea, *3 Girls 3* was part musical variety show and part situation comedy. The three young stars, none of whom had any previous television experience, played three unknowns who auditioned for, and won, the starring roles in a network variety series. Part of each telecast consisted of their "show," where they were seen singing, dancing, and doing comedy sketches, and part depicted scenes at rehearsals and in their personal lives. Originally scheduled as a four-week mini-series in the spring of 1977, only the first telecast aired, with the three remaining episodes shown in June. A critical success, praised as a programming innovation, *3 Girls 3* never found much of an audience against *Baretta* and CBS movies.

THREE'S A CROWD
Situation Comedy
FIRST TELECAST: *September 25, 1984*
LAST TELECAST: *September 10, 1985*
BROADCAST HISTORY:
Sep 1984–Oct 1984, ABC Tue 8:30–9:00

Oct 1984–Jul 1985, ABC Tue 8:00–8:30
Aug 1985–Sep 1985, ABC Tue 8:30–9:00

CAST:

Jack Tripper .... John Ritter
Vicky Bradford .... Mary Cadorette
James Bradford .... Robert Mandan
E. Z. Taylor .... Alan Campbell

After years of living platonically with two female roommates and chasing after a succession of beautiful girls, Jack Tripper finally found true love. He was smitten with pert flight attendant Vicky Bradford, much to the chagrin of her wealthy and straitlaced father, James. When Jack's roommates moved out, Jack decided it was finally time to get married. Unfortunately Vicky didn't agree—her parents' marriage had been turbulent and ended in divorce—and she preferred that she and Jack live together. Jack had misgivings, but they moved into an apartment over Jack's Bistro, the restaurant he now owned. Vicky's dad was apoplectic. In an effort to break them up, he bought the building, thus becoming their landlord, 10 percent owner of the restaurant, and constant surprise visitor. Beach bum E.Z. was Jack's eccentric assistant chef. Jessica Walter was seen occasionally as Vicky's mother, Claudia.

Three's a Crowd, a spin-off from the long-running hit series Three's Company, was adapted from the British series Robin's Nest.

ABC aired reruns of Three's a Crowd on weekday mornings from September 1985–January 1986.

THREE'S COMPANY
Music

FIRST TELECAST: May 18, 1950
LAST TELECAST: September 29, 1950
BROADCAST HISTORY:
    May 1950–Jun 1950, CBS Thu 7:45–8:00
    Jun 1950, CBS Wed/Thu 7:45–8:00
    Jul 1950–Sep 1950, CBS Tue/Thu 7:45–8:00
    Sep 1950, CBS Mon/Wed/Fri 7:45–8:00
    Sep 1950, CBS Sun 9:15–9:30
REGULARS:
    Martha Wright
    Cy Walter
    Stan Freeman
    Judy Lynn

This live 15-minute music show, which filled the remainder of the half hour in which CBS aired its network news program during the summer of 1950, featured pianists Cy Walter and Stan Freeman and the vocals of Martha Wright. When Miss Wright left the show she was replaced, effective June 28, by Judy Lynn.

THREE'S COMPANY
Situation Comedy

FIRST TELECAST: March 15, 1977
LAST TELECAST: September 18, 1984
BROADCAST HISTORY:
    Mar 1977–Apr 1977, ABC Thu 9:30–10:00

Aug 1977–Sep 1977, ABC Thu 9:30–10:00
Sep 1977–May 1984, ABC Tue 9:00–9:30
May 1984–Sep 1984, ABC Tue 8:30–9:00

CAST:

Jack Tripper .... John Ritter
Janet Wood .... Joyce DeWitt
Chrissy Snow (1977–1981) .. Suzanne Somers
Helen Roper (1977–1979) ..... Audra Lindley
Stanley Roper (1977–1979) ...... Norman Fell
Larry Dallas (1978–1984) ...... Richard Kline
Ralph Furley (1979–1984) .... Don Knotts
Lana Shields (1979–1980) .. Ann Wedgeworth
Cindy Snow (1980–1982) ..... Jenilee Harrison
Terri Alden (1981–1984) ..... Priscilla Barnes
Mike the bartender (occasional, 1981–1984)
    .... Brad Blaisdell

THEME:

"Three's Company," by Don Nicholl and Joe Raposo, sung by Ray Charles and Julia Rinker

In this comedy, two contemporary young single girls found themselves in need of a roommate for their Santa Monica apartment so they decided to settle for the man they found sleeping in their bathtub—after a going-away party for their last roommate. Jack was harmless enough, but the problem was in convincing everyone else of that.

Parents objected and humorous misunderstandings abounded, but Jack stayed. In addition to his other virtues, he was the only one of the three roommates who could cook. His favorite ploy was to intimate that he was a homosexual, and therefore uninterested in the two sexy girls (in fact, nothing did go on between them). The landlady, Mrs. Roper, who lived downstairs, worried less about what was going on upstairs than about the fact that nothing was going on in her love life with her husband, Stanley. Away from their confused home life, Jack was studying for (and eventually got) his chef's diploma; Janet, the brunette, worked in a florist shop; and Chrissy, the frivolous blonde, was a typist.

After a short run in the spring of 1977 Three's Company was picked up as a regular series on ABC's fall 1977 schedule. The comedy was based almost entirely on sexual double-entendres, and religious leaders and critics found the program almost as objectionable as Soap, which followed it on the Tuesday night schedule. Nevertheless viewers made it one of the major hits of the 1977–1978 season, especially after it was featured on the cover of Newsweek magazine in February 1978. The cover photo was a staged shot of Chrissy with her undergarment seemingly falling off, and Jack leering over her shoulder—something that never happened on the show.

Norman Fell and Audra Lindley left the series in 1979 for their own show (see The Ropers), and were replaced by Don Knotts as the new landlord. Then, in 1980, Suzanne Somers, who had become a media celebrity as a result of this series, demanded a huge increase in salary plus a piece of the profits in recognition of her new importance.

The producers adamantly refused, and her role was reduced to an occasional brief scene in which she was seen phoning her roommates long distance (she was supposed to be in Fresno caring for her sick mother). Eventually Somers was written out of the show altogether, and her career went into decline.

Jack and Janet promptly found a new roommate in Cindy, who was introduced as Chrissy's cute but clumsy cousin. She moved out in 1981 in order to study veterinary medicine at UCLA, though she continued to visit for another season. Her replacement was a smart, vivacious nurse named Terri.

Meanwhile Jack pursued his career as a chef, first at Angelino's Restaurant (whose owner, Frank Angelino, played by Jordan Charney, was seen occasionally). In 1982 Mr. Angelino and landlord Ralph Furley put up the money to open Jack's own place, called Jack's Bistro, specializing in French cuisine. When not at the restaurant or the apartment, the gang hung out at the Regal Beagle, a neighborhood pub.

When he lost his roommates (Janet got married and Terri moved to Hawaii) Jack moved in with his new girlfriend and a new series began in the fall of 1984. See *Three's A Crowd* for details.

Three's Company was based on the British series *Man About the House*.

ABC aired reruns on weekday mornings from June to September 1981.

THRILL SEEKERS
Documentary
BROADCAST HISTORY:
Syndicated only
30 minutes
Produced: *1972–1974* (52 episodes)
Released: *January 1973*
HOST/NARRATOR:
Chuck Connors

This documentary focused on stunts, with films of motorcycle daredevils, cliff divers in Acapulco, practitioners of the Oriental martial arts, and others who sought danger for their kicks. Chuck Connors' excited narration tried to make everything seem equally death-defying, even a little girl with her pet lion.

THRILLER
Suspense Anthology
FIRST TELECAST: *September 13, 1960*
LAST TELECAST: *July 9, 1962*
BROADCAST HISTORY:
Sep 1960–Sep 1961, NBC Tue 9:00–10:00
Sep 1961–Jul 1962, NBC Mon 10:00–11:00
HOST:
Boris Karloff

Stories of normal, everyday people caught in unexpected, often terrifying, situations were broadcast weekly on *Thriller*. Famous horror-movie star Boris Karloff was the host of the series,

introducing all of the stories and occasionally starring in them. Generally lesser-known actors and actresses appeared in most of the productions, which bore such evocative titles as "Parasite Mansions," "The Terror in Teakwood," "Pigeons from Hell," and "The Premature Burial."

THROB
Situation Comedy
BROADCAST HISTORY:
Syndicated only
30 minutes
Produced: *1986–*
Released: *September 1986*
CAST:
Sandy Beatty .... Diana Canova
Jeremy Beatty (1986–1987) ... Paul W. Walker
Jeremy Beatty (1987–   ) ... Sean de Veritch
Zachary Armstrong .... Jonathan Prince
Meredith .... Maryedith Burrell
Blue (Prudence Anne Bartlett) .. Jane Leeves
Phil Gaines .... Richard Cummings, Jr.
THEME:
"Throb," written by Paul Cooper and performed by The Nylons and Diana Canova

A comedy that satirized the youth-oriented record business. Sandy was only 33, a divorcée with a teenage son, Jeremy, but she felt old when she went to work at New York's Throb Records. Throb was a small outfit with offices in a Manhattan loft, and it specialized in the more bizarre punk rock acts (you could tell them by their pink hair). The label was run by a very short and very energetic young man named Zachary. An eternal optimist, Zach had more than a platonic affection for Sandy, despite the fact that she was both older and taller than he. The other principal staffers at Throb were Phil, a hip but businesslike black, and Blue, a flighty young English girl who was more punk than most of the groups that paraded through the office. Meredeth was Sandy's best friend, a single teacher who lived in Sandy's building.

In the fall of 1987 Sandy fell in love with the newly vacated penthouse apartment in her building and took Blue in as a roommate to help with the rent. The conflicts between conservative Sandy and free-spirited Blue became even more pronounced when they were both living and working together.

THROUGH THE CRYSTAL BALL
Dance
FIRST TELECAST: *April 18, 1949*
LAST TELECAST: *July 4, 1949*
BROADCAST HISTORY:
Apr 1949–Jul 1949, CBS Mon 9:00–9:30
REGULAR:
Jimmy Savo

Dramatizations in dance form of popular fables were presented live on *Through the Crystal Ball*.

Pantomimist Jimmy Savo was the original star, host, and narrator of the series. After he left in May there were no regular cast members. Various choreographers worked on the dance interpretation of such fables as *Alice in Wonderland*, "Cinderella," "Ali Baba," and "Casey at the Bat."

THROUGH THE CURTAIN
Discussion
FIRST TELECAST: *October 21, 1953*
LAST TELECAST: *February 24, 1954*
BROADCAST HISTORY:
  Oct 1953–Feb 1954, ABC Wed 8:15–8:30
HOST:
  George Hamilton Combs
REGULAR:
  Leo Gruliow

The curtain referred to here was the Iron Curtain. The program's object was to bring to the American viewer a concise summary of what the Soviet citizen got in his newspapers and magazines each week, with an analysis of what these publications revealed about Soviet society. Gruliow was editor of the *Current Digest of the Soviet Press*.

THROUGH WENDY'S WINDOW
  see *Wendy Barrie Show, The*

TIC TAC DOUGH
Quiz/Audience Participation
FIRST TELECAST: *September 12, 1957*
LAST TELECAST: *December 29, 1958*
BROADCAST HISTORY:
  Sep 1957–Oct 1958, NBC Thu 7:30–8:00
  Oct 1958–Dec 1958, NBC Mon 7:30–8:00
EMCEE:
  Jay Jackson (1957)
  Win Elliot

The format of this nighttime quiz show was essentially the same as that of its daytime counterpart. Jay Jackson hosted the nighttime show, but only for its premiere episode. He was replaced the following week by Win Elliot, who remained with it until it was canceled. The game itself was a variation of tic-tac-toe in which each contestant put his *X* or *O* in a given box by answering a question in the category covering that box. After each round (one question for each contestant) the categories were rotated to different boxes. The value of the outside-box questions was $300 and the tougher center-box question was worth $500. The winner kept the cash value of the correct questions he had answered. In a tie game, the winnings were added to the value of the next game.

NBC aired a weekday daytime edition of *Tic Tac Dough* from July 1956 to October 1959. Emcees of the daytime version were Jack Barry, Gene Rayburn, and Bill Wendell. Nearly 20 years later, in 1978, *Tic Tac Dough* was revived as a daytime series on CBS and, simultaneously, a five-episodes-per-week syndicated series. Wink Martindale emceed both, with his work load cut in half when the CBS version was canceled in September after less than two months on the air. The syndicated version, however, remained in production through the 1985–1986 season. Jim Caldwell replaced Wink Martindale as emcee in the fall of 1985.

TIGHTROPE
Police Drama
FIRST TELECAST: *September 8, 1959*
LAST TELECAST: *September 13, 1960*
BROADCAST HISTORY:
  Sep 1959–Sep 1960, CBS Tue 9:00–9:30
CAST:
  Undercover Agent .... Mike Connors

The task of infiltrating organized crime to expose its leaders and prevent the spread of corruption was the job of the unnamed police undercover agent who was the focus of this series. The "tightrope" he walked was treacherous, for many of the police he aided had no idea who he was and would have shot him in various situations without realizing he was working on their side.

The name used by the agent was part of his cover, and changed with each episode. Originally he was supposed to be named Nick Stone, but this idea was dropped before the first telecast and thereafter only occasionally was his real name mentioned—as "Nick."

TIM CONWAY COMEDY HOUR, THE
Comedy Variety
FIRST TELECAST: *September 20, 1970*
LAST TELECAST: *December 13, 1970*
BROADCAST HISTORY:
  Sep 1970–Dec 1970, CBS Sun 10:00–11:00
REGULARS:
  Tim Conway
  McLean Stevenson
  Art Metrano
  The Tom Hansen Dancers
  Sally Struthers
  Bonnie Boland
  Bruce Belland and Dave Somerville
  The Jimmy Joyce Singers
  The Nelson Riddle Orchestra

Comedian Tim Conway was the host and star of this variety show, which stressed sketch comedy. Tim's offbeat comedy did not attract much of an audience—many people were probably bewildered by musical production numbers in which Sally Struthers was the entire dancing chorus—and the show was canceled after only thirteen weeks.

TIM CONWAY SHOW, THE
Situation Comedy
FIRST TELECAST: *January 30, 1970*
LAST TELECAST: *June 19, 1970*

Jan 1970–Jun 1970, CBS Fri 8:00–8:30

CAST:

Spud Barrett	Tim Conway
Herbert T. Kenworth	Joe Flynn
Mrs. K. J. Crawford	Anne Seymour
Ronnie Crawford	Johnnie Collins III
Becky Parks	Emily Banks
Harry Wetzel	Fabian Dean
Sherman Bell	Dennis Robertson

Spud Barrett was the clumsy, oafish, but well-meaning chief pilot for Triple-A, that is, Anywhere, Anytime Airline. He was the chief pilot primarily because he was also the only pilot. Owner of the airline, and Spud's boss, was cranky Herb Kenworth, who, despite being in the air-charter business, was terrified of flying. The airport out of which they flew was owned by Mrs. Crawford, who also ran her own more prosperous charter service.

TIM CONWAY SHOW, THE

Comedy Variety

FIRST TELECAST: *March 22, 1980*
LAST TELECAST: *August 31, 1981*
BROADCAST HISTORY:
Mar 1980–May 1980, CBS Sat 8:00–9:00
Aug 1980–Sep 1980, CBS Sat 8:30–9:00
Sep 1980–Oct 1980, CBS Sat 8:00–8:30
Nov 1980–Mar 1981, CBS Mon 8:30–9:00
Jun 1981–Aug 1981, CBS Mon 8:30–9:00
REGULARS:
Tim Conway
Eric Boardman (1980)
Jack Riley (1980)
Maggie Roswell
Miriam Flynn
Dick Orkin
Bert Berdis
Harvey Korman
The Peter Matz Orchestra
The Don Crichton Dancers
The Artie Malvin Singers

Tim Conway's second attempt at his own prime-time variety hour was essentially an offshoot of *The Carol Burnett Show,* on which he had been a supporting regular for several years. As with Carol's show, this *Tim Conway Show* relied on a small group of regulars in comedy sketches, supplemented by musical numbers and occasional guest stars. Since the series was produced by Miss Burnett's husband, Joe Hamilton, the similarity of formats was not surprising. An unusual feature was the dance group, the Don Crichton Dancers, all youngsters between the ages of 8 and 13.

The Tim Conway Show premiered as a full hour in the spring of 1980, but was trimmed to half an hour that summer. Carol Burnett, Vicki Lawrence, and Harvey Korman made guest appearances, with Harvey becoming a regular co-star late in 1980. These alumni of the *Burnett* show even resurrected old running sketches from the former program when they guested here.

TIME EXPRESS

Drama/Supernatural

FIRST TELECAST: *April 26, 1979*
LAST TELECAST: *May 17, 1979*
BROADCAST HISTORY:
Apr 1979–May 1979, CBS Thu 8:00–9:00
CAST:

Jason	Vincent Price
Margaret	Coral Browne
Conductor R. J. Walker	James Reynolds
Engineer Callahan	William Phipps
Ticket Clerk	Woodrow Parfey

This peculiar program was a sort of supernatural variation on *Fantasy Island.* Passengers who boarded the gleaming Time Express found themselves on an eerie train ride through a mist-filled sky, going back through time to destinations that were turning points in their lives. There they could disembark and attempt to alter decisions they had made long ago, in hopes of changing all that had subsequently happened to them as a result. The charming but mysterious couple who escorted the passengers to their destinations were Jason and Margaret, played by real-life married couple Vincent Price and Coral Browne. Among the voyagers who traveled back through time in this limited-run series were an advertising copywriter who wanted to recapture a romance he had forsaken, a rodeo cowboy seeking to find the daughter he had lost after a serious accident, and a former boxer who had thrown a championship fight and wanted to go back and win it after all.

TIME FOR REFLECTION

Poetry

FIRST TELECAST: *May 7, 1950*
LAST TELECAST: *October 22, 1950*
BROADCAST HISTORY:
May 1950–Oct 1950, DUM Sun 6:45–7:00
HOST:
David Ross

Poetry readings by David Ross.

TIME TO SMILE

see *Alan Young Show, The* and *Ken Murray Show, The*

TIME TUNNEL, THE

Science Fiction

FIRST TELECAST: *September 9, 1966*
LAST TELECAST: *September 1, 1967*
BROADCAST HISTORY:
Sep 1966–Jul 1967, ABC Fri 8:00–9:00
Jul 1967–Sep 1967, ABC Fri 7:30–8:30
CAST:

Dr. Tony Newman	James Darren
Dr. Doug Phillips	Robert Colbert

Dr. Ann MacGregor	Lee Meriwether
Gen. Heywood Kirk	Whit Bissel
Dr. Raymond Swain	John Zaremba

CREATOR/PRODUCER:
Irwin Allen

Tony Newman and Doug Phillips were two young scientists working on a top-secret government project, deep below the Arizona desert. Their goal: to build a laser-actuated "time tunnel," leading to ages past and future. Unfortunately they were forced to plunge into the tunnel before it was fully tested, and found themselves lost in history, able to move from one point in time to another, but unable to get back to their starting point in the present.

While their associates, Drs. MacGregor and Swain, worked feverishly to free them from their bondage, Tony and Doug found themselves plunged into one famous historical event after another, always knowing the outcome in advance, but unable to change it. First they were deposited on the deck of the *Titanic*, just before you-know-what. Then it was in and out of the shadows of great events from the siege of Troy (500 B.C.) to a futuristic space flight to Mars. They tried to save Marie Antoinette and President Lincoln, opposed Cortez, and watched the Battle of Jericho as the walls came a-tumbling down. They chased one villain clear from one million B.C. to one million A.D. Who wanted to go back to Arizona?

TIME WILL TELL

Quiz/Audience Participation
FIRST TELECAST: *August 20, 1954*
LAST TELECAST: *October 15, 1954*
BROADCAST HISTORY:
 Aug 1954–Oct 1954, DUM Fri 10:30–11:00
EMCEE:
 Ernie Kovacs
ANNOUNCER:
 Bob Russell

This short-lived quiz show was intended to give comic Ernie Kovacs a chance to clown around with the contestants. And, indeed, Kovacs' interviews and asides were the principal attraction. The quiz portion consisted simply of a series of questions, most requiring one-word answers, delivered rapid-fire to a panel of three contestants for 90 seconds. The contestant with the most correct answers won.

TIMMY AND LASSIE

syndicated title for *Lassie*

TIN PAN ALLEY TV

Musical Variety
FIRST TELECAST: *April 28, 1950*
LAST TELECAST: *September 29, 1950*
BROADCAST HISTORY:
 Apr 1950–Sep 1950, ABC Fri 9:30–10:00

REGULARS:
 Johnny Desmond
 Gloria Van
 Chet Roble, piano
 Rex Maupin's Orchestra

This live musical program from Chicago showcased the songs of a different composer or lyricist each week. The one so honored was usually on hand; for example, lyricist Mitchell Parish watched the cast perform his "Deep Purple," "Star Dust," "Organ Grinder's Swing," and other standards on the premiere telecast. By early TV standards the production was quite elaborate, which at first gave the inexperienced studio crew some problems. *Variety* reported that on the premiere the singers were continually interrupted by loud thuds and clunks from offstage, that a dance team performing behind a vocalist worked nicely "when the camera could find them," and that a group of kids dancing around the man playing the organ grinder in "Organ Grinder's Swing" kept dancing right off the screen. Such were the problems of live TV in 1950. Presumably the problems were overcome as the series continued through the summer.

TO ROME WITH LOVE

Situation Comedy
FIRST TELECAST: *September 28, 1969*
LAST TELECAST: *September 21, 1971*
BROADCAST HISTORY:
 Sep 1969–Sep 1970, CBS Sun 7:30–8:00
 Sep 1970–Jan 1971, CBS Tue 9:30–10:00
 Jan 1971–Sep 1971, CBS Wed 8:30–9:00
CAST:

Michael Endicott	John Forsythe
Aunt Harriet Endicott (1969–1970)	
. . . .	Kay Medford
Alison Endicott	Joyce Menges
Penny Endicott	Susan Neher
Mary Jane (Pokey) Endicott	
. . . .	Melanie Fullerton
Mama Vitale	Peggy Mondo
Gino Mancini	Vito Scotti
Nico	Gerald Michenaud
Grandpa Andy Pruitt (1970–1971)	
. . . .	Walter Brennan

Following the death of his wife, college professor Michael Endicott decided to leave his native Iowa to accept a teaching position at the American Overseas School in Rome. The adjustments made by Michael and his three daughters to a wholly alien but fascinating environment provided much of the gentle humor of this series. Michael's sister Harriet, who tried constantly to get the family to return to Iowa, was living with them in their Rome apartment through the first half of the 1969–1970 season but gave up and returned home alone. At the start of the second season Andy Pruitt, the father of Michael's late wife, joined the cast. A crotchety Iowa farmer who had sold his farm in anticipation of moving to a retirement community, he arrived for a visit in Rome and somehow never left.

TO TELL THE TRUTH
Quiz/Audience Participation
FIRST TELECAST: *December 18, 1956*
LAST TELECAST: *May 22, 1967*
BROADCAST HISTORY:
Dec 1956–Sep 1958, CBS Tue 9:00–9:30
Sep 1958–Sep 1959, CBS Tue 8:30–9:00
Oct 1959–Jun 1960, CBS Thu 7:30–8:00
Jul 1960–Sep 1960, CBS Thu 10:30–11:00
Sep 1960–Sep 1966, CBS Mon 7:30–8:00
Dec 1966–May 1967, CBS Mon 10:00–10:30
EMCEE:
Bud Collyer
PANELISTS:
Polly Bergen (1956–1961)
Hy Gardner (1956–1959)
Hildy Parks (1956–1957)
Kitty Carlisle
Ralph Bellamy (1957–1959)
Tom Poston (1958–1967)
Orson Bean (1964–1967)
Peggy Cass (1964–1967)
PRODUCERS:
Mark Goodson and Bill Todman

Contestants on *To Tell the Truth* were introduced in threes. All of them purported to be the same individual. Following the introduction, emcee Bud Collyer would read an affidavit describing the life, activities, and/or unique experiences of the person who all the contestants claimed to be. The panel then spent an amount of time asking questions of the three contestants, trying to determine which one was telling the truth and which two were lying. Following the question session, each panelist had to vote for whom he thought was really the person described in the affidavit. Wrong guesses were worth money to all three contestants, who split the winnings equally. The original title, which lasted only one episode, was *Nothing but the Truth*. The person whose description was read in the affidavit had to tell the truth, but the impostors, who had been given a briefing by the person they were pretending to be, could say anything. The famous closing line for each round: "Will the real ―――― please stand up!"

To Tell the Truth was also seen in daytime on CBS from June 1962 to September 1968. The emcee of the daytime version was also Bud Collyer and the regular panelists were the same ones as on the prime-time edition.

Two of the regular panelists who were with the show when it left CBS in 1968—Kitty Carlisle and Peggy Cass—practically made careers out of *To Tell the Truth*. In the fall of 1969 it turned up in syndication with the two of them and Bill Cullen as regular panelists. They remained with the syndicated version until it left the air in 1977. Garry Moore was the emcee until the last year, with Joe

Garagiola taking over at the end. Yet another syndicated version was produced during the 1980–1981 season with young Robin Ward as emcee, but without Carlisle and Cass.

TO THE QUEEN'S TASTE
Cooking
FIRST TELECAST: *May 3, 1948*
LAST TELECAST: *December 29, 1949*
BROADCAST HISTORY:
May 1948–Aug 1948, CBS Mon 8:05–8:30
Aug 1948–Apr 1949, CBS Thu 8:00–8:30
May 1949–Jul 1949, CBS Thu 9:30–10:00
Jul 1949–Sep 1949, CBS Mon 8:00–8:30
Oct 1949–Dec 1949, CBS Thu 7:00–7:30
CHEF:
Dione Lucas

This early cooking show began as a local program in New York on October 9, 1947, originating from the Cordon Bleu (a Manhattan restaurant owned by Dione Lucas). Seven months later the show became a CBS network series. Cooking expert Lucas, the Julia Child of her day, showed viewers how to prepare exotic and tasty culinary treats from varied cuisines. This series was also known as *The Dione Lucas Show*, a title that was used for later local versions after it left the CBS network.

TOAST OF THE TOWN, THE
see *Ed Sullivan Show, The*

TODAY'S F.B.I.
Police Drama
FIRST TELECAST: *October 25, 1981*
LAST TELECAST: *August 14, 1982*
BROADCAST HISTORY:
Oct 1981–Apr 1982, ABC Sun 8:00–9:00
Apr 1982, ABC Mon 8:00–9:00
Jun 1982–Aug 1982, ABC Sat 8:00–9:00
CAST:
Ben Slater.................... Mike Connors
Nick Frazier.................... Joseph Cali
Al Gordean .... Richard Hill
Dwayne Thompson (pilot only)
.... Charles Brown
Dwayne Thompson .... Harold Sylvester
Maggie Clinton .... Carol Potter

Today's F.B.I. was ABC's attempt to update its popular 1960s series, *The F.B.I.* Ben Slater, a 20-year veteran of the bureau, was the father figure and leader of a team of four bright young agents: Nick, a sometimes overeager young stud with a talent for undercover work; Al, an athletic type; Dwayne, a former marine intelligence officer; and Maggie, a trained psychologist who—in case that didn't work—was also a crack shot. They were all terribly efficient and, as *TV Guide* commented, "such a clean-cut bunch they could sell milk in the commercials." Their cases were often pursued with a moralistic zeal as well, accompanied by little lectures about how nuisances like First Amendment guarantees and restrictions on wiretaps got in the way of capturing slimy criminals. Organized crime, pornographers, kidnapers, and religious fanatics were typical villains, often caught through elaborate undercover operations.

This highly favorable portrait of the bureau was monitored and "approved" by the real-life FBI, which allowed use of its files for ideas for episodes.

TOGETHER WE STAND
Situation Comedy
FIRST TELECAST: *September 22, 1986*
LAST TELECAST: *April 24, 1987*
BROADCAST HISTORY:
 Sep 1986–   , CBS Mon 8:30–9:00
 Oct 1986–   , CBS Wed 8:00–8:30
 Oct 1986–   , CBS Wed 8:30–9:00
 Feb 1987–   , CBS Sun 9:30–10:00
 Mar 1987–Apr 1987, CBS Fri 8:00–8:30
CAST:
 David Randall (1986) . . . . Elliott Gould
 Lori Randall . . . . Dee Wallace Stone
 Jack Randall (age 14) . . . . Scott Grimes
 Amy Randall (16) . . . . Katie O'Neill
 Sam (14) . . . . Ke Huy Quan
 Sally (6) . . . . Natasha Bobo
 Marion (1987) . . . . Julia Migenes

One of TV's many amalgam-family comedies, *Together We Stand* had a short, disrupted run during the 1986–1987 season. Originally it starred Elliott Gould as a former pro basketball coach for the Portland Trailblazers, who stayed in the area after retiring to open a sporting goods store. Most of the action took place at home, where he and his wife, Lori, had a houseful of kids acquired from various sources. Amy, the oldest, had been adopted before Jack, the natural son they thought they could not have ("it was a miracle") was born. Seeing how well they did mixing a natural and adopted child, a pushy social worker then foisted on them two more adoptees, Asian-American Sam and a cute little black girl, Sally. Stories revolved around the cultural differences among the members of this suddenly multi-ethnic family and the adjustments that had to be made by all—Sam and Sally having parents for the first time, and Jack and Amy having to compete with the new arrivals for their folks' time and affection.

After a low-rated and often preempted fall season, *Together We Stand* was pulled from the schedule. It returned in February with a new title, *Nothing Is Easy,* and without star Elliott Gould. Lori was now a widow (David had been killed in an auto accident), coping with this United Nations of kids alone. She had gone back to work, was taking courses at night school to become a legal stenographer, and had to fend off the adoption agency, which had begun to think this was all a bit much for one woman. At least she gained a next-door neighbor, cynical Marion, who was a divorcée and also a single parent.

TOM CORBETT, SPACE CADET
Children's Science Fiction
FIRST TELECAST: *October 2, 1950*
LAST TELECAST: *September 26, 1952*
BROADCAST HISTORY:
 Oct 1950–Dec 1950, CBS Mon/Wed/Fri 6:45–7:00
 Jan 1951–Sep 1952, ABC Mon/Wed/Fri 6:30–6:45
 Jul 1951–Sep 1951, NBC Sat 7:00–7:30
CAST:
 Tom Corbett . . . . Frankie Thomas
 Capt. Steve Strong (1950) . . . . Michael Harvey
 Capt. Steve Strong (1951–1952)
 . . . . Edward Bryce
 Astro the Venusian . . . . Al Markim
 Roger Manning . . . . Jan Merlin
 Dr. Joan Dale . . . . Margaret Garland
TECHNICAL ADVISOR:
Willie Ley
WRITERS:
Frankie Thomas, Stu Brynes, Ray Morse

Tom Corbett was conceived by CBS in late 1950 to cash in on the enormous popularity of DuMont's *Captain Video.* The two programs were not directly competitive—in fact *Tom Corbett* (6:45–7:00 P.M.) led into *Captain Video* (7:00–7:30 P.M.) three nights a week—and they differed in substantial ways. *Tom Corbett* had a much larger budget and thus more realistic special effects, such as blastoffs, weightlessness, etc., all done live through various techniques of video hocuspocus. And the emphasis was less on futuristic hardware (though there was plenty) and more on the adventures of the young cast.

Tom Corbett, curly-headed teenage cadet at the Space Academy, four centuries hence, was a figure with whom youngsters could identify. With him in training to become Solar Guards were wisecracking Cadet Roger Manning ("So what happens now, space heroes?" "Aw, go blow your jets!") and the quieter Astro, a Venusian (planetary boundaries were rather less important in the 24th century). Every week they blasted off in the spaceship *Polaris* to new adventures somewhere in space, usually against natural forces rather than the space villains who populated *Captain Video.* Their exploits were instructive as well as exciting. Program advisor Willie Ley, a noted scientist and author, worked in legitimate concepts such as variable gravity forces, asteroid belts, and anti-matter.

After three months on CBS *Tom Corbett* moved to ABC for a run of nearly two years. In addition kinescopes of the weekday serial were run on Saturdays on NBC during the summer of 1951—as summer replacement for Victor Borge! The series was also heard on ABC radio during 1952, with the same cast as the TV version. The *Tom Corbett* cast also made personal appearances to promote merchandise connected with the show (wonder if they offered the most popular of the Cadets' 24th-century aids—the Study Machine?). Late in 1952 the series moved to Saturday daytime, where it continued, off and on, until the summer of 1955.

Based on the novel *Space Cadet* by Robert A. Heinlein.

TOM, DICK AND MARY
Situation Comedy
FIRST TELECAST: *October 5, 1964*
LAST TELECAST: *January 4, 1965*
BROADCAST HISTORY:
Oct 1964–Jan 1965, NBC Mon 8:30–9:00
CAST:
Dr. Tom Gentry.............. Don Galloway
Mary Gentry .... Joyce Bulifant
Dr. Dick Moran.............. Steve Franken
Dr. Krevoy .... John Hoyt
Horace Moran.......... J. Edward McKinley

There is one thing you can always say for group living: it helps spread the costs of housing. It was for that reason that young Dr. Tom Gentry and his recent bride, Mary, were sharing an apartment with Tom's best friend, Dick. With Tom working as an intern and Mary as a medical secretary, the family income did not quite stretch far enough to afford their apartment at 90 Bristol Court. Dick was also an intern who had moved in with the Gentrys to share the costs of the apartment. The newlyweds were not thrilled having an extra person around, except when the rent was due. *Tom, Dick and Mary* was one of the three situation comedies that collectively made up the series *90 Bristol Court*. The other two were *Karen* and *Harris Against the World*.

TOM EWELL SHOW, THE
Situation Comedy
FIRST TELECAST: *September 27, 1960*
LAST TELECAST: *July 18, 1961*
BROADCAST HISTORY:
Sep 1960–Jul 1961, CBS Tue 9:00–9:30
CAST:
Tom Potter .... Tom Ewell
Fran Potter .... Marilyn Erskine
Irene Brady .... Mabel Albertson
Carol Potter .... Cindy Robbins
Debbie Potter .... Sherry Alberoni
Sissie Potter.................. Eileen Chesis

Tom Potter was a real estate agent whose entire life, away from the office, was dominated by women. His household resembled a multi-generational girl's dormitory. In addition to his wife Fran, and his three daughters (Carol, 15; Debbie, 11; and Sissie, 7), he had to cope with a live-in mother-in-law, Grandma Brady. The problems he had living in a woman's world provided the focus of this series.

TOM SMOTHERS' ORGANIC PRIME TIME SPACE RIDE
see *Smothers Brothers Comedy Hour, The*

TOMA
Police Drama
FIRST TELECAST: *October 4, 1973*
LAST TELECAST: *September 6, 1974*
BROADCAST HISTORY:
Oct 1973–Jan 1974, ABC Thu 8:00–9:00
Jan 1974–Sep 1974, ABC Fri 10:00–11:00
CAST:
Det. David Toma .... Tony Musante
Inspector Spooner .... Simon Oakland
Patty Toma .... Susan Strasberg
Jimmy Toma .... Sean Manning
Donna Toma .... Michelle Livingston

Like *Serpico* a few years later, *Toma* was based on the exploits of a real-life big-city cop, Det. David Toma of the Newark, New Jersey, police department. Toma was a loner, continually bucking the system, and in many ways a headache to his boss, Inspector Spooner. But he was also a master of disguise, and his quick-wittedness and unorthodox methods won him national fame as a highly effective undercover agent. His targets were usually crime syndicates, racketeers, and the like. Patty Toma was his worried wife, and Jimmy and Donna his young children.

The real-life Dave Toma played bit parts in this series.

In a rather unusual move, actor Tony Musante left the program after only one season because he just didn't like the weekly grind of production. ABC was not unhappy with the show's performance and planned to bring *Toma* back with a new actor in the lead role. It was originally to be called *Toma Starring Robert Blake*, but despite the strong similarities in the lead role, a number of minor changes in the format resulted in a new series titled *Baretta*.

TOMBSTONE TERRITORY
Western
FIRST TELECAST: *October 16, 1957*
LAST TELECAST: *October 9, 1959*
BROADCAST HISTORY:
Oct 1957–Sep 1958, ABC Wed 8:30–9:00
Mar 1959–Oct 1959, ABC Fri 9:00–9:30
CAST:
Sheriff Clay Hollister .... Pat Conway
Harris Claibourne .... Richard Eastham
Deputy Riggs (1957) .... Gil Rankin

Western adventure set in Tombstone, Arizona, "the town too tough to die." Sheriff Hollister was the strong arm of the law, and Harris Claibourne, editor of *The Epitaph,* was the voice of the press. In addition to playing Claibourne, Eastham was also host/narrator of the series.

In an unusual move, new episodes of this series

continued to be produced for a year after the program left the network, for sale in syndication.

TOMORROW SHOW, THE
Talk
FIRST TELECAST: *October 15, 1973*
LAST TELECAST: *January 28, 1982*
BROADCAST HISTORY:
Oct 1973–Sep 1980, NBC Mon–Thu 1:00–2:00 A.M.
Sep 1980–Jan 1982, NBC Mon–Thu 12:30–2:00 A.M.
HOST:
Tom Snyder
Rona Barrett (1980–1981)
REGULAR:
Nancy Friday (1980–1981)

For those insomniacs who were still looking for something other than old movies to watch in the wee hours, NBC offered *The Tomorrow Show* four nights each week. Hosted by brash newsman Tom Snyder, the topics covered ranged from nudism (including a remote pickup at a California nudist colony), to discussions with draft dodgers living in Canada, to all aspects of changing American life-styles with a panel of psychologists. Tom Snyder's choreography often seemed to borrow a little from Edward R. Murrow's incisiveness and vintage Alan Burke guest-baiting. Tom could be sweet and ingenuous one moment, relentlessly probing the next.

Tomorrow was originally produced in Los Angeles, where host Snyder worked as an anchorman on the local KNBC-TV news. When it first went on the air there was no studio audience present at the taping, a situation that changed in less than four months. After an audience had been added, Snyder would often invite its members to ask questions of his guests. When his local news anchor duties shifted to New York, in December 1974, *The Tomorrow Show* went with him. In June 1977, Tom and the show returned to California, only to come back again to New York when Snyder became host of the news magazine *Prime Time Sunday* in 1979.

In the fall of 1980 *The Tomorrow Show* expanded from an hour to 90 minutes, as part of a general restructuring of NBC's late-night lineup. With an extra half-hour to fill, the *Tomorrow* staff was expanded and two new on-air personalities were added, Nancy Friday and Rona Barrett, and contemporary musical guests performed on most telecasts. Miss Friday, a psychologist who had been an occasional guest of Tom's in the past, became a semiregular as the resident "human relations commentator." Miss Barrett, the noted Hollywood gossip columnist, joined *Tomorrow* at the end of October (she had just left ABC's *Good Morning, America* to sign a long-term contract with NBC) as the West Coast–based co-host with Tom. She and Tom didn't get along well, with their strong egos conflicting almost immediately. Their feud boiled over on November 10, 1980, only two weeks after her first appearance on *Tomorrow*, when she refused to appear on the air. It took two months to resolve the dispute, and when Rona returned to the show on January 12, 1981, it had been retitled *Tomorrow Coast to Coast*. She left again later that year.

To those skeptical of the practicality of televising anything this late at night, *Tomorrow*'s success was surprising. During its first two seasons it attracted an average of approximately three million viewers per night.

TOMORROW'S BOXING CHAMPIONS
see *Boxing*

TOMORROW'S CAREERS
Informational
FIRST TELECAST: *March 26, 1955*
LAST TELECAST: *May 29, 1956*
BROADCAST HISTORY:
Mar 1955–Jun 1955, ABC Sat 7:00–7:30
Sep 1955–Jan 1956, ABC Sat 10:00–10:30
Jan 1956–May 1956, ABC Tue 10:00–10:30
HOST:
Lynn Poole

Each week Mr. Poole discussed opportunities in a particular career area with experts in that field. One week, it might be jobs in the antique field; another week, jobs with airlines; a third week, opportunities in movie direction. Emphasis was placed on openings for students graduating from school and for those in their middle years seeking to change career paths. During its March through June 1955 run, the title of this program was simply *Tomorrow*.

TONI TWIN TIME
Variety
FIRST TELECAST: *April 5, 1950*
LAST TELECAST: *September 20, 1950*
BROADCAST HISTORY:
Apr 1950–Sep 1950, CBS Wed 9:00–9:30
HOST:
Jack Lemmon
REGULARS:
Arlene Terry
Ardelle Terry
Ray Bloch Orchestra

This live variety show, hosted by young actor Jack Lemmon, alternated with *What's My Line* on Wednesday evenings during the summer of 1950. It was designed as a showcase for young talent, with Mr. Lemmon providing continuity and introductions. The "Toni Twins," Arlene and Ardelle Terry, acted as hostesses and did the commercials for the sponsor, whose slogan "Which Twin Has the Toni?" made home-permanent history in the late 1940s.

TONIGHT ON BROADWAY
Interview/Play Excerpts
FIRST TELECAST: *April 20, 1948*

LAST TELECAST: *December 25, 1949*
BROADCAST HISTORY:
   Apr 1948–May 1948, CBS Tue 7:00–7:30
   Oct 1949–Dec 1949, CBS Sun 7:00–7:30
HOST:
   John Mason Brown

Excerpts from current Broadway shows and interviews with the stars of those shows, broadcast directly from the stages of the theaters where the shows were being performed, were presented weekly on this series. It had originally begun as an experimental concept which premiered locally in New York on April 6, 1948, from the theater where *Mr. Roberts* was playing, moved to the CBS network two weeks later with *High Button Shoes,* and returned in the fall of 1949 for a three-month run. John Mason Brown, the host/interviewer/commentator of the series, was the president of the New York Drama Critics Circle.

TONIGHT SHOW, THE
Talk/Variety
FIRST TELECAST: *September 27, 1954*
LAST TELECAST:
BROADCAST HISTORY:
   Sep 1954–Oct 1956, NBC Mon–Fri 11:30–1:00
   Oct 1956–Jan 1957, NBC Mon–Fri 11:30–12:30
   Jan 1957–Dec 1966, NBC Mon–Fri 11:15–1:00
   Jan 1965–Sep 1966, NBC Sat or Sun 11:15–1:00
   Sep 1966–Sep 1975, NBC Sat or Sun 11:30–1:00
   Jan 1967–Sep 1980, NBC Mon–Fri 11:30–1:00
   Sep 1980–   , NBC Mon–Fri 11:30–12:30

Because of the unusual nature of *The Tonight Show*—the several complete overhauls of its cast and format—each of the individual versions is treated separately below:

TONIGHT
(September 27, 1954–January 25, 1957)
HOST:
   Steve Allen
   Ernie Kovacs (1956–1957)
REGULARS:
   Gene Rayburn
   Steve Lawrence
   Eydie Gorme
   Andy Williams
   Pat Marshall (1954–1955)
   Pat Kirby (1955–1957)
   Hy Averback (1955)
   Skitch Henderson and His Orchestra
   Peter Hanley (1956–1957)
   Maureen Arthur (1956–1957)
   Bill Wendell (1956–1957)
   Barbara Loden (1956–1957)
   LeRoy Holmes & Orchestra (1956–1957)

Tonight began in June 1953 as a local show on WNBT-TV, the NBC flagship station in New York. Steve Allen was the original host, and he remained with the show when it moved to the network 15 months later. Under Allen, *Tonight* was very informal. He would open each evening seated at the piano, chatting and playing some of his own compositions (his most famous song, "This Could Be the Start of Something," was often heard). He then went to his desk, where he talked about anything that seemed to interest him. There were guest stars, in addition to his semiregulars—only announcer Gene Rayburn and orchestra leader Skitch Henderson were on every night—but the emphasis was on Steve and his comedic ad-libbing. He would go into the audience, work up impromptu sketches with other members of the cast, and do remotes outside the studio. Many of the remotes were comic man-in-the-street routines, but perhaps the most famous incident occurred when *Tonight* was doing some telecasts from Miami. Allen somehow talked the U.S. Marines into staging a nighttime landing on Miami Beach, for the benefit of his cameras—panicking tourists in nearby hotels, who thought an invasion was underway. In addition to the special features, there was a regular news summary given at about 12:30 A.M. by Gene Rayburn. The entire show was done live.

When Allen's prime-time series premiered in the summer of 1956, he cut back his *Tonight* appearances to Wednesday through Friday. A series of guest hosts filled in on Mondays and Tuesdays until October 1st, when Ernie Kovacs took over as permanent Monday–Tuesday host. Kovacs had his own complete cast: Bill Wendell as announcer, and Peter Hanley, Maureen Arthur, and Barbara Loden as regulars. Ernie's format was very similar to that of his various prime-time shows, with most of the same characters, as well as blackouts, satires, and slapstick humor.

TONIGHT! AMERICA AFTER DARK
(January 28, 1957–July 26, 1957)
HOST:
   Jack Lescoulie (Jan–Jun)
   Al "Jazzbo" Collins (Jun–Jul)
REGULARS:
   Judy Johnson (Mar–Jul)
   Lou Stein Trio (Jan–Mar)
   Mort Lindsey Quartet (Mar–Jun)
   Johnny Guarnieri Quartet (Jun–Jul)
   Hy Gardner
   Bob Considine
   Earl Wilson (Jan–Jun)
   Irv Kupcinet
   Vernon Scott (Jan–Feb)
   Paul Coates
   Lee Giroux (Mar–Jun)

When Steve Allen left in January 1957, *Tonight* was replaced by a totally different type of program. It became much more like the early-morning *Today Show,* with an emphasis on news items. Its original host was *Today* veteran Jack Lescoulie. There were reports by contributing columnists in New York, Chicago, and Los Angeles, with live coverage from all three cities and elsewhere via remotes. Interviews with personalities in the news, in politics, or in show business were interspersed with live visits to nightclubs, Broadway openings, or such places as research hospitals and planetariums. Regular features were Bob Considine's summary of the news of the day, "The World Tonight"; a Hy Gardner interview segment, "Face to Face"; news of the entertainment world on "Hy Gardner Time"; and news commentary, human interest stories, and interviews on "Considine's Corner."

JACK PAAR SHOW, THE
(July 29, 1957–March 30, 1962)
HOST:
  Jack Paar
REGULARS:
  Hugh Downs
  Jose Melis & Orchestra
  Tedi Thurman (1957)
  Dody Goodman (1957–1958)
SEMI-REGULARS:
  Elsa Maxwell (1957–1958)
  Bil Baird Puppets (1957–1958)
  Betty Johnson (1957–1958)
  Genevieve (1958–1962)
  Cliff Arquette as *Charley Weaver* (1958–1962)
  Pat Harrington, Jr., as *Guido Panzini*
    (1959–1962)
  Hans Conried (1959–1962)
  Peggy Cass (1958–1962)
  Alexander King (1958–1962)
  Joey Bishop (1958–1962)
  Hermione Gingold (1958–1962)
  Florence Henderson (1958–1962)
  Buddy Hackett (1958–1962)
  Renee Taylor (1959–1962)
  Betty White (1959–1962)

Tonight! America After Dark was not successful with viewers or critics, so it was decided to return to a format closer to the original. The new host, a young comic named Jack Paar, was raided from CBS, where he had hosted several game and talk shows. Paar took over *The Tonight Show* six months after Steve Allen had left. Whereas Allen had depended on a frenetic pace and sketch comedy, Paar was at his best interviewing. He was incisive, witty, and highly emotional. He could easily get emotionally involved with his guests and their stories, and was not above crying on the air when he was moved. There were still sketches, and Paar would sometimes go into the audience for interviews. "It's All Relative" was a periodic spot in which a relative of a famous person would appear and the other guests would try to figure out who he was related to; "What Is It?" was a feature in which Paar would produce some strange-looking object and then explain what it was used for; there was a routine where baby pictures were shown to the audience and Paar would come up with funny captions for them; and Jose Melis had

a "telephone game" in which he improvised melodies based on the last four digits of an audience member's telephone number.

Besides the fun and games, the show had a serious side. At one point Paar went on an extended crusade against the Batista dictatorship in Cuba, lauding Castro's revolution; later he tried to arrange a swap of tractors for prisoners from the Bay of Pigs invasion; several telecasts originated from the Berlin Wall; and presidential candidates Kennedy and Nixon were both guests, on separate occasions.

Paar's emotional outbursts were a major attraction of the show, and the cause of many of the controversies surrounding him. When he had first taken over as host, *The Tonight Show* was still being done live. Not too long after, it began taping early in the evening that it would be aired. It was NBC's ability to edit the tapes before air time that precipitated Paar's famous tearful walkout on the February 11, 1960, program. A "water closet" joke he had told the night before was considered in bad taste by the NBC censors and had been removed. Paar didn't think the joke was offensive and he left the show for a month. He later had a feud with Ed Sullivan over the fees paid guest stars—Paar's $320 versus Sullivan's several thousand—and eventually feuded with several newspaper columnists, notably Dorothy Kilgallen. Videotape did have its advantages, however, as it enabled Paar to cut down to a four-day week. Starting July 10, 1959, the Friday show was retitled *The Best of Paar* and was composed of reruns of previous shows.

TONIGHT SHOW, THE
(April 2, 1962–September 28, 1962)
ANNOUNCERS:
  Hugh Downs
  Jack Haskell
  Ed Herlihy
ORCHESTRA:
  Skitch Henderson

After Jack Paar's departure from the series in March 1962, *The Tonight Show* aired with a succession of substitute hosts, while awaiting the arrival of Johnny Carson (who had to wait out an ABC contract). Hosts during this period were Art Linkletter, Joey Bishop, Bob Cummings, Merv Griffin, Jack Carter, Jan Murray, Peter Lind Hayes and Mary Healy, Soupy Sales, Mort Sahl, Steve Lawrence, Jerry Lewis, Jimmy Dean, Arlene Francis, Jack E. Leonard, Hugh Downs, Groucho Marx, Hal March, and Donald O'Connor. The format was unchanged.

TONIGHT SHOW STARRING JOHNNY
  CARSON, THE
(October 2, 1962–   )
HOST:
  Johnny Carson

Ed McMahon
Skitch Henderson (1962–1966)
Milton Delugg (1966–1967)
Doc Severinsen (1967–)
Tommy Newsom (1968–)
REGULAR GUEST HOST:
Joan Rivers (1983–1986)
THEME:
"Johnny's Theme," by Paul Anka and Johnny
Carson

The contrast between Jack Paar and Johnny Carson was marked. As emotional and likely to blow up as Paar was, that is how calm and unflappable Carson was. Like Paar, Carson had been spirited away from another network; in fact he had previously had shows on both CBS and ABC. His biggest asset, other than his durability, was probably his knack for salvaging disasters with a perfect reaction take (a comic expression of resignation whenever something would not work). Carson opened each show with a monologue and then spent most of the remainder of the evening chatting with guests. Unlike Paar, Carson tended to avoid anything controversial and was usually content to keep his audience amused. Features that were used on his show with varying frequency included "Stump the Band," in which members of the studio audience would ask the band to try to play obscure songs by giving them only the titles; "Carnac the Magnificent" (first seen in 1964), with Carson as an inept magician; "Aunt Blabby" (1964); "The Mighty Carson Art Players" (1966), spoofing movies, TV shows, or events in the news; "Carswell" (1967), with Carson as a psychic predicting the future; "The Great Carsoni" (1967); "Faharishi" (1968), with Carson as a yogi; "The Art Fern Tea Time Movie" (1971), with Carol Wayne as the "Matinee Lady"; superpatriot "Floyd R. Turbo" (1977); "Father Time" (1977); and the one holdover from Paar, periodic displays of strange-looking contraptions with even stranger functions.

Perhaps the most celebrated telecast, and certainly the one with the most enormous audience, was that of December 17, 1969, on which Tiny Tim married Miss Vicki. Other highlights were seen on annual anniversary shows, in which Carson reprised often embarrassing moments from past years.

When Carson started, the show was originating from New York and was taped on the same evening that it aired. Johnny was on all five nights and began his monologue when the show began, at 11:15 P.M. In February 1965 he refused to do the 11:15–11:30 P.M. segment any longer, leaving that to Ed McMahon and Skitch Henderson. Many local stations carried local news until 11:30 P.M., preempting the first fifteen minutes of The Tonight Show, and Carson wanted to save his monologue until the full network was in place. Two years later, on January 2, 1967, this first 15 minutes was

dropped altogether. A few months later, in March 1967, Carson fought another skirmish with NBC, this time over money. This led to his walkout, which lasted for several weeks until he was finally lured back with a contract reported to provide more than $1 million per year.

In May 1972 The Tonight Show moved permanently from New York to Burbank (previously periodic telecasts were done from the West Coast), and for a time after that taping was done a day before the show aired. Because so much immediacy was lost, Tonight returned to same-night taping in May 1974. Carson also started cutting back on his appearances at about this time. After July 1971 he was no longer seen on Mondays. Then in March 1978 he obtained a highly publicized new $3-million-per-year contract that required him to work only three nights per week. In 1980, after threats of a walkout, the program was cut back to an hour per night, with Carson on Tuesday through Friday. (Steve Allen had worked only three hours per week for a time in 1956, although he also had a prime-time show to do.) Carson's irregular appearances opened the way for a large number of substitute hosts, some of whom have become almost as familiar to viewers as Johnny himself. Seen most often during the first 21 years were Joey Bishop (177 appearances as guest host), followed by Joan Rivers (93), Bob Newhart (87), John Davidson (87), David Brenner (70), McLean Stevenson (58), Jerry Lewis (52), and David Letterman (51). Joan Rivers was the "permanent" (and only) guest host from September 1983 until 1986, when she quit to launch her own ill-fated late-night show opposite Carson. The Tonight Show reverted to various guest hosts after Joan left, with Jay Leno the most frequent.

For more than a decade, from January 1965 until September 1975, taped repeats of The Tonight Show were offered to NBC stations for airing after the 11:00 P.M. news on Saturday or Sunday.

In the fall of 1985 a collection of edited comedy sketches from The Tonight Show was syndicated to local stations under the title Carson Comedy Classics.

TONY BENNETT SHOW, THE
Musical Variety
FIRST TELECAST: August 11, 1956
LAST TELECAST: September 8, 1956
BROADCAST HISTORY:
Aug 1956–Sep 1956, NBC Sat 8:00–9:00
REGULARS:
Tony Bennett
The Frank Lewis Dancers
The Spellbinders
The Carl Hoff Orchestra

The Tony Bennett Show was one of three musical variety shows that served as 1956 summer replacement for The Perry Como Show. All three of them featured the Frank Lewis Dancers and the singing of the Spellbinders. The only difference between them was their star and host. Patti Page starred for the first month of the summer, and was followed by Julius LaRosa, who in turn was followed by Tony Bennett.

TONY MARTIN SHOW, THE
Music
FIRST TELECAST: *April 26, 1954*
LAST TELECAST: *February 27, 1956*
BROADCAST HISTORY:
   Apr 1954–Jun 1955, NBC Mon 7:30–7:45
   Sep 1955–Feb 1956, NBC Mon 7:30–7:45
REGULARS:
   Tony Martin
   The Interludes
   The Hal Bourne Orchestra (1954–1955)
   David Rose and His Orchestra (1955–1956)

Singer Tony Martin starred in this live music series that filled the remainder of the half hour in which NBC aired its network news program. Backing up Mr. Martin was a mixed vocal group, the Interludes. The show originated from Hollywood and Mr. Martin had occasional guest stars who either performed or chatted with him or both.

TONY ORLANDO AND DAWN
Musical Variety
FIRST TELECAST: *July 3, 1974*
LAST TELECAST: *December 28, 1976*
BROADCAST HISTORY:
   Jul 1974, CBS Wed 8:00–9:00
   Dec 1974–Jun 1976, CBS Wed 8:00–9:00
   Sep 1976–Dec 1976, CBS Tue 8:00–9:00
REGULARS:
   Tony Orlando
   Telma Hopkins
   Joyce Vincent Wilson
   Alice Nunn
   Lonnie Schorr
   Adam Wade (1976)
   George Carlin (1976)
   Nancy Steen (1976)
   Bob Holt (1976)
   Susan Lanier (1976)
   Jimmy Martinez (1976)
   Edie McClurg (1976)
   Jerry Jackson Singers
   Bob Rozario Orchestra

After a number of hit records, most notably "Tie a Yellow Ribbon 'Round the Old Oak Tree," the singing group Tony Orlando and Dawn (Telma Hopkins and Joyce Vincent Wilson) was given a summer variety hour on CBS in the time slot that had been vacated by Sonny and Cher. The emphasis was on music, with guest stars joining the trio in song and comedy skits. A summer hit, it returned in December and had a very successful first year, but started to slip in the second. When it moved to Tuesday nights in the fall of 1976, there were a number of changes, including the title, which became *The Tony Orlando and Dawn*

Rainbow Hour. Comedian George Carlin was added as a regular with a weekly comedy monologue, and a group of comics was also added to participate in sketches. Emphasis was shifted from music to comedy, but the series failed to last past the end of the year.

TONY RANDALL SHOW, THE
Situation Comedy
FIRST TELECAST: *September 23, 1976*
LAST TELECAST: *March 25, 1978*
BROADCAST HISTORY:
   Sep 1976–Dec 1976, ABC Thu 9:00–9:30
   Dec 1976–Mar 1977, ABC Thu 9:30–10:00
   Sep 1977–Jan 1978, CBS Sat 9:30–10:00
   Jan 1978–Mar 1978, CBS Sat 8:30–9:00
CAST:
   Judge Walter Franklin .... Tony Randall
   Jack Terwilliger .... Barney Martin
   Miss Janet Reubner ...... Allyn Ann McLerie
   Roberta "Bobby" Franklin (1976–1977)
   .... Devon Scott
   Roberta "Bobby" Franklin (1977–1978)
   .... Penny Peyser
   Oliver Wendell Franklin .... Brad Savage
   Mrs. Bonnie McClellan ...... Rachel Roberts
   Mario Lanza .... Zane Lasky
   Judge Eleanor Hooper .... Diana Muldaur
   Wyatt Franklin (1977–1978) .... Hans Conried

This comedy concerned the courtroom and home life of a middle-aged Philadelphia judge. Court of Common Pleas Judge Walter Franklin was serious about his work, sometimes a bit stuffy, but kind at heart and always had a twinkle in his eye. After two years as a widower Walter was ready for a little romance, and his attempts to both keep his dignity and charm his dates provided much of the humor. Walter played the field, although Judge Eleanor Hooper was a recurring love interest.

Jack Terwilliger was Walter's longtime, ultra-accurate court reporter; Miss Reubner, the sharp-tongued, motherly secretary; Mario Lanza, the obnoxiously ingratiating assistant to the assistant District Attorney; and Mrs. McClellan, the nutty housekeeper. Walter's family consisted of 18-year-old daughter Bobby, who was very much involved with current issues, and precocious 11-year-old son Oliver. Wyatt Franklin was Walter's liberal-minded father, who considered his son something of a stuffed shirt.

TOO CLOSE FOR COMFORT
Situation Comedy
FIRST TELECAST: *November 11, 1980*
LAST TELECAST: *September 15, 1983*
BROADCAST HISTORY:
   Nov 1980–Sep 1982, ABC Tue 9:30–10:00
   Sep 1982–Jun 1983, ABC Thu 9:00–9:30
   Aug 1983–Sep 1983, ABC Thu 8:30–9:00
   Sep 1983, ABC Thu 8:00–8:30
   (In first-run syndication as *Too Close for Comfort* from January 1984–September 1985; and

as *The Ted Knight Show* from April 1986–September 1986)

CAST:

Henry Rush	Ted Knight
Muriel Rush	Nancy Dussault
Jackie Rush (1980–1985)	
	Deborah Van Valkenburgh
Sara Rush (1980–1985)	Lydia Cornell
Arthur Wainwright (1981)	Hamilton Camp
Monroe Ficus	JM J. Bullock
April Rush (1981–1982)	Deena Freeman
Iris Martin (1982–1983)	Audrey Meadows
Andrew Rush (1983–1984)	
	William Thomas Cannon
Andrew Rush (1983–1984)	
	Michael Philip Cannon
Andrew Rush (1984–1986)	Joshua Goodwin
Lisa Flores (1986)	Lisa Antille
Hope Stinson (1986)	Pat Carroll

Henry Rush was a middle-aged, conservative, and very orderly professional illustrator. His greatest regret was that years ago he had gotten caught up in doing a kiddie cartoon called "Cosmic Cow," and now it seemed to rule his life. His second greatest regret was that his two college-aged daughters, wanting a little independence, had talked him into letting them live in the downstairs apartment of his two-apartment San Francisco town house. As boyfriends came and went, Henry agonized over his two little lambs.

Jackie, the brunette, worked at a bank; Sara, the blonde sex kitten, was a freshman at San Francisco State College. Among the others who drifted around this sex farce were Muriel, the understanding mom (an independent type who had once been a band singer and now was a successful free-lance photographer; Mr. Wainwright, Henry's diminutive boss at the newspaper; Monroe, Sara's flaky student friend; and Henry's hand puppet, from which he derived inspiration for his comic strip and commiseration for his worries about his pretty daughters. Appearing occasionally was Mildred Rafkin (Selma Diamond), sister of the former downstairs tenant.

Among the developments in the second and third seasons were the arrival of April, Henry's hippie niece from Delaware, who stayed with the family for a year; and Muriel's pregnancy at age 42, culminating in the birth of a son, Andrew. Also arriving in 1982 were Muriel's nagging mother, Iris, who added further grief to Henry's life, and Jackie's fiancé, policeman Brad Turner (Jordan Suffin), who was seen occasionally.

Too Close For Comfort continued in production after being canceled by ABC in 1983, with the new episodes offered to local stations on a syndicated basis. With the title change to *The Ted Knight Show* came a change in format. Henry had purchased 49% of a weekly newspaper, *The Marin Bugler*, and he, Muriel, and Andrew had moved to a house in Mill Valley, north of San Francisco, to be close to his new place of business. Monroe,

who had worked as a security guard after college, was still around, attempting to help out at the *Bugler*, where Muriel was also working as staff photographer, but Sara and Jackie (who had been dropped from the cast) were off on their own. New to the cast were the Rushes' hispanic housekeeper, Lisa, and the publisher of the *Bugler*, Mrs. Stinson. She still owned 51% and loved her regular editorial disputes with Henry, her new partner and editor. *The Ted Knight Show* was scheduled to go into its second season of production when its star, who had been ill for several months, passed away during the summer of 1986.

ABC aired reruns of *Too Close for Comfort* on weekday mornings from June to September 1983.

Based on the British series *Keep It in the Family*.

TOO YOUNG TO GO STEADY

Situation Comedy

FIRST TELECAST: *May 14, 1959*
LAST TELECAST: *June 25, 1959*
BROADCAST HISTORY:

May 1959–Jun 1959, NBC Thu 8:30–9:00
CAST:

Mary Blake	Joan Bennett
Tom Blake	Donald Cook
Pam Blake	Brigid Bazlen
Johnny Blake	Martin Huston
Timmy	Lorna Gillam

The problems of teenagers Pam and Johnny Blake were the focal points of this live series that aired in the spring of 1959. Pam was a 14-year-old trying to make the transition from tomboy to young lady. Her older brother, Johnny, got into almost as much trouble trying to help her as he did with his own life. Pam and her girlfriend Timmy were at that stage when love—or was it infatuation?—was the most important thing in their lives. Pam and Johnny's father, attorney Tom Blake, and their mother, Mary, kept a watchful eye on the activities of the kids and were generally understanding and interested in their happiness.

TOP CAT

Cartoon

FIRST TELECAST: *September 27, 1961*
LAST TELECAST: *September 26, 1962*
BROADCAST HISTORY:

Sep 1961–Sep 1962, ABC Wed 8:30–9:00
VOICES:

Top Cat	Arnold Stang
Benny the Ball	Maurice Gosfield
Choo Choo	Marvin Kaplan
Spook/The Brain	Leo DeLyon
Fancy-Fancy	John Stephenson
Officer Dibble	Allen Jenkins

Top Cat was the sophisticated, opportunistic leader of a pack of Broadway alley cats. Their homes were well-equipped ash cans, they made all their phone calls from the police phone on a nearby pole, got their milk and newspapers from nearby doorsteps, and ate scraps from the neighborhood delicatessen. Their only problem was Officer Dibble, the cop on the local beat. He did his best to control them but seldom succeeded.

Reruns of *Top Cat* aired for several years on Saturday mornings—on ABC from October 1962 to March 1963 and on NBC from April 1965 to May 1969.

TOP DOLLAR
Quiz/Audience Participation
FIRST TELECAST: *March 29, 1958*
LAST TELECAST: *August 30, 1958*
BROADCAST HISTORY:
   Mar 1958–Aug 1958, CBS Sat 8:30–9:00
EMCEE:
   Toby Reed
WORD AUTHORITY:
   Dr. Bergen Evans

Three contestants participated in each round of this word-spelling game that was a variation on the old party game "ghost." The object of the game was to keep adding letters to a potential word without completing it. Each letter, after the first three, was worth $100 to the winner, and after the first person was eliminated by making a word the two remaining contestants competed to determine the winner. As long as a contestant remained undefeated, he could continue to play. Dr. Bergen Evans was the final authority on whether or not a word had been made. An added attraction for home viewers was the announcement at the end of each telecast of the serial number of a dollar bill that, if presented to the show's producers, was worth $5,000 to the bearer. The serial number was determined by the regular game. The first eight letters of the "top dollar" word of the night (the longest one created by the contestants on the show) were matched to a telephone dial and converted to the digits of the jackpot serial number for the week.

CBS started a daytime version of *Top Dollar* two weeks before the prime-time version left the air. The daytime version lasted until October 1959. Toby Reed also emceed the daytime version, but was succeeded by Jack Narz during its run.

TOP OF THE POPS
Music
FIRST TELECAST: *September 25, 1987*
LAST TELECAST: *March 25, 1988*
BROADCAST HISTORY:
   Sep 1987–Mar 1988, CBS Fri 11:30–12:30 A.M.
HOSTS:
   Gary Davies
   Nia Peeples

Top of the Pops was the third pop-music series CBS had aired in this Friday late-night time period in less than a year. Unlike the first two—*Keep on Cruisin'* and *In Person from the Palace*— which

had been produced by American Dick Clark, this one was from the people responsible for the British series *Top of the Pops*. That venerable pop-music showcase had been running for 23 years at the time its American counterpart premiered. The American version was twice as long as the British version and actually consisted of two half-hour shows, one from London hosted by Gary Davies, and one from Los Angeles hosted by Nia Peeples. Among the performers appearing were Mick Jagger, Bananarama, David Bowie, Los Lobos, REO Speedwagon, Steve Winwood, Cliff Richard, Def Leppard, Bon Jovi, Kiss, Sting, Santana, Squeeze, Pet Shop Boys, and the Bee Gees.

TOP PLAYS OF 1954
Dramatic Anthology
FIRST TELECAST: *June 1, 1954*
LAST TELECAST: *August 24, 1954*
BROADCAST HISTORY:
   Jun 1954–Aug 1954, NBC Tue 9:30–10:00

This filmed anthology series was the 1954 summer replacement for *Armstrong Circle Theatre*. The plays which aired under this title were all reruns of episodes of *Ford Theatre* that had been telecast during the first half of 1954.

TOP PRO GOLF
Sports
FIRST TELECAST: *April 6, 1959*
LAST TELECAST: *September 28, 1959*
BROADCAST HISTORY:
   Apr 1959–Sep 1959, ABC Mon 9:30–10:30
COMMENTATOR:
   Dick Danehe

Each week two professional golfers competed in an 18-hole match. The winner won $1,500 and the right to return the following week to defend his championship, while the loser took home $500. Filmed on location at various golf courses in Florida and Georgia, *Top Pro Golf* showed only the highlights of the round, avoiding coverage of holes that did not bear significantly on the outcome of the match. The big winner on this series was veteran Sam Snead. He had appeared early in the show's run and lost, but when he got another shot early in August he really took advantage of it. He won the last eight matches on this series.

The episodes that aired on Monday evenings as *Top Pro Golf* were actually reruns of a Saturday afternoon series on ABC titled *All Star Golf*. These episodes had first been seen during the 1958–1959 winter season on that series.

TOP TEN LUCY SHOWS, THE
   see *I Love Lucy*

TOPPER
Situation Comedy
FIRST TELECAST: *October 9, 1953*

BROADCAST HISTORY:
   Oct 1953–Sep 1955, CBS Fri 8:30–9:00
   Oct 1955–Mar 1956, ABC Mon 7:30–8:00
   Jun 1956–Oct 1956, NBC Sun 7:00–7:30
CAST:
   Marion Kerby .... Anne Jeffreys
   George Kerby .... Robert Sterling
   Cosmo Topper .... Leo G. Carroll
   Henrietta Topper .... Lee Patrick
   Katie, the maid (1953–1954)
   .... Kathleen Freeman
   Mr. Schuyler .... Thurston Hall
   Maggie, the cook (1954–1955) .. Edna Skinner

On a skiing vacation in Europe, George and Marion Kerby were trapped in an avalance along with their would-be rescuer, a St. Bernard named Neil. All three of them died—only to return to the United States to haunt their former home, now occupied by banker Cosmo Topper. George and Marion developed quite an affection for the very proper Mr. Topper, but felt that he needed to be a little less stuffy. They did everything in their powers, and those powers were considerable, to help Cosmo loosen up. Between their antics and the wanderings of the ghostly Neil, who had a penchant for oversized, brim-full brandy snifters, life in the Topper household was kept very chaotic.

After two seasons on CBS, this series was canceled, only to show up in reruns for a full season on ABC and a summer on NBC. *Topper* was based on characters created by novelist Thorne Smith. These characters were also seen later in a series of movies. The one member of the TV cast that had not appeared in Mr. Smith's novels or the movies was Neil. In the original Smith story the Kerbys died in an automobile accident, not while skiing. Since no dog died with them, there was no dog to haunt with them.

TORTELLIS, THE
Situation Comedy
FIRST TELECAST: *January 22, 1987*
LAST TELECAST: *May 12, 1987*
BROADCAST HISTORY:
   Jan 1987, NBC Thu 9:30–10:00
   Jan 1987–Apr 1987, NBC Wed 9:30–10:00
   Apr 1987–May 1987, NBC Tue 9:30–10:00
CAST:
   Nick Tortelli .... Dan Hedaya
   Loretta Tortelli .... Jean Kasem
   Anthony Tortelli .... Timothy Williams
   Annie Tortelli .... Mandy Ingber
   Charlotte Cooper .... Carlene Watkins
   Mark Cooper .... Aaron Moffatt

In this spin-off from *Cheers,* slimy Nick Tortelli (onetime husband of Carla) moved to Las Vegas to try to reconcile with his new wife, a spaced-out blonde named Loretta who was trying to launch a show-biz career there. He swore he'd turned over a new leaf, but Loretta's level-headed sister Charlotte, who lived with them, was skeptical. Anthony was Nick's dumb teenaged son, who helped him in his TV repair business, and Annie was Anthony's young bride.

TOUCH OF GRACE, A
Situation Comedy
FIRST TELECAST: *January 20, 1973*
LAST TELECAST: *June 16, 1973*
BROADCAST HISTORY:
   Jan 1973–Jun 1973, ABC Sat 8:30–9:00
CAST:
   Grace Simpson .... Shirley Booth
   Herbert Morrison .... J. Patrick O'Malley
   Walter Bradley .... Warren Berlinger
   Myra Bradley .... Marian Mercer

Oscar, Emmy, and Tony winner Shirley Booth starred in this comedy as a recently widowed, sixtyish woman who moved in with her daughter and son-in-law. There the battle of the generations began—between Grace, a perky youngster at heart, and the young couple, a pair of conservative "squares," older than their years. Grace did a lot of dating, but her steady boyfriend was Herbert, a gravedigger. In the final telecast, he proposed and Grace accepted.

Based on the British TV series *For the Love of Ada.*

TOUGH COOKIES
Situation Comedy
FIRST TELECAST: *March 5, 1986*
LAST TELECAST: *April 23, 1986*
BROADCAST HISTORY:
   Mar 1986–Apr 1986, CBS Wed 8:30–9:00
CAST:
   Det. Cliff Brady.............. Robby Benson
   Rita .... Lainie Kazan
   Danny Polchek .... Adam Arkin
   Richie Messina .... Matt Craven
   Lt. Iverson .... Art Metrano
   Off. Connie Rivera .... Elizabeth Pena
   Father McCaskey .... Alan North

Juvenile film star Robby Benson, just turned 30 but still saddled with a kid's image (one unkind critic called him "Cute as Bambi and twice as smarmy"), tried to establish an "adult" image by playing a tough cop in this 1986 series. It didn't work. Plainclothes detective Cliff Brady was on home turf, assigned to the precinct in a tough Southside Chicago neighborhood where he had grown up. He lived nearby, kept in touch with old friends, and tried to keep the area from deteriorating still further. His favored hangout (all tough cops have hangouts) was The Windbreaker, a local saloon run by outspoken Rita, a sort of surrogate mother. Boyhood friend Richie worked there as a bartender and another buddy, smooth-talking bookmaker Danny, hung out. Lt. Iverson was Cliff's even-tougher superior, Father McCaskey the understanding police chaplain, and Connie a fellow officer who couldn't have been more concerned about the welfare of the cute—er, tough—detective if she had been his sister.

TRACEY ULLMAN SHOW, THE
Comedy Variety
FIRST TELECAST: *April 5, 1987*
LAST TELECAST:
BROADCAST HISTORY:
Apr 1987–May 1987, FOX Sun 8:30–9:00
May 1987–Sep 1987, FOX Sun 9:30–10:00
Sep 1987–Feb 1988, FOX Sun 9:00–9:30
Mar 1988–Jul 1988, FOX Sun 10:00–10:30
Jul 1988–   , FOX Sun 9:30–10:00
REGULARS:
Tracey Ullman
Julie Kavner
Dan Castellaneta
Joe Malone
Sam McMurray
ANIMATION:
Gabor Csupo
Matt Groening

The multitalented British import Tracey Ullman—singer, dancer, actress, comedienne—starred in this critically acclaimed variety series. Each episode contained two or three comedy "playlets" featuring Miss Ullman and her small repertory group. Her recurring characterizations included South African golf pro Kiki Howard-Smith; materialistic Yuppie Sara Downey; anthropologist Ceci Beckwith, who was living with monkeys in the wilds of Africa; divorcée Ginny Tillman; Francesca, a teenager living with her gay father and his lover; Kay, an insecure spinster living with her mother; and Tina the postal worker. Short, bizarre animated segments aired between the live-action sketches; after a few months these began to focus on a rather strange family. At the close of each show Miss Ullman came on stage without makeup, in her housecoat, to talk briefly to the studio audience. There was never any doubt when she was through, since her parting words were always the same—"Go home!!"

The Tracey Ullman Show was the only Fox Broadcasting series to be nominated for Emmy Awards during the fledgling fourth network's first season.

TRACKDOWN
Western
FIRST TELECAST: *October 4, 1957*
LAST TELECAST: *September 23, 1959*
BROADCAST HISTORY:
Oct 1957–Jan 1959, CBS Fri 8:00–8:30
Feb 1959–Sep 1959, CBS Wed 8:30–9:00
CAST:
Hoby Gilman .... Robert Culp

Set in the Southwest during the 1870s, *Trackdown* detailed the adventures of a mythical Texas

Ranger, Hoby Gilman. Many of the stories told in the series were adapted from cases in the files of the Texas Rangers and it was for that reason that the show had the official approval of the State of Texas and the Rangers. That was a distinction that could be claimed by no other Western on the air.

TRAFFIC COURT
Courtroom Drama
FIRST TELECAST: *June 18, 1958*
LAST TELECAST: *March 30, 1959*
BROADCAST HISTORY:
Jun 1958–Jul 1958, ABC Wed 9:30–10:00
Jul 1958–Oct 1958, ABC Sun 9:00–9:30
Oct 1958–Nov 1958, ABC Thu 10:00–10:30
Nov 1958, ABC Mon 10:00–10:30
Mar 1959, ABC Mon 10:00–10:30
CAST:
The Judge .... Edgar Allan Jones, Jr.
Bailiff .... Frank Chandler McClure
Court Clerk .... Samuel Whitson

This filmed series had a regular run during the summer of 1958, and was then used to fill numerous holes in the ABC schedule during the 1958–1959 season. It presented reenactments of actual traffic-court trials and arraignments. The judge was Edgar Allan Jones, Jr., who in real life was assistant dean of the U.C.L.A. law school.

TRAILMASTER
see *Wagon Train*

TRAILS WEST
see *Death Valley Days*

TRAP, THE
Dramatic Anthology
FIRST TELECAST: *April 29, 1950*
LAST TELECAST: *June 24, 1950*
BROADCAST HISTORY:
Apr 1950–Jun 1950, CBS Sat 9:00–10:00
NARRATOR:
Joseph DeSantis

The melodramas that were presented in this live anthology series were all concerned with people who had gotten themselves into situations over which they no longer had control. Fate would be the determinant of their future, of whether or not they survived the perilous predicament into which they had gotten themselves "trapped."

TRAPPER JOHN, M.D.
Medical Drama
FIRST TELECAST: *September 23, 1979*
LAST TELECAST: *September 4, 1986*
BROADCAST HISTORY:
Sep 1979–Jan 1986, CBS Sun 10:00–11:00
Feb 1986–Mar 1986, CBS Tue 8:00–9:00
Jun 1986, CBS Thu 9:00–10:00
Aug 1986–Sep 1986, CBS Thu 10:00–11:00

CAST:

Dr. John McIntyre ("Trapper John")
.... Pernell Roberts
Dr. George Alonzo Gates ("Gonzo")
.... Gregory Harrison
Nurse Clara Willoughly ("Starch")
(1979–1980) .... Mary McCarty
Nurse Gloria Brancusi ("Ripples")
(1979–1985) .... Christopher Norris
Dr. Stanley Riverside II ..... Charles Siebert
Dr. Justin Jackson ("Jackpot")
.... Brian Mitchell
Nurse Shapiro (1979–1980) ...... Marion Yue
Arnold Slocum (1979–1985) .... Simon Scott
Nurse Ernestine Shoop (1980–1986)
.... Madge Sinclair
Dr. Sandler (1980–1984) .... Richard Schaal
Dr. Charlie Nichols (1980–1984)
.... Michael Tucci
Nurse (1981–1985) .... Chris Hutson
Nurse Clover (1981–1984) .... Bebe Kelly
Nurse Andrews (1981–1986)
.... Sarah Cunningham
Andrea Brancusi (1983–1985) ... Robin Ignico
E. J. Riverside (1983–1986) ..... Marcia Rodd
Dr. John ("J.T.") McIntyre (1984–1986)
.... Tim Busfield
Catherine Hackett (1985–1986) ... Janis Paige
Nurse Libby Kegler (1985–1986) ... Lorna Luft
Dr. Andy Pagano (1985–1986) .. Beau Gravitte
Fran Brennan (1985–1986)
.... Andrea Marcovicci

This medical drama was a spin-off, of sorts, from
the popular comedy M*A*S*H. In the 28 years
since he had been discharged from the 4077th
M.A.S.H. unit in Korea, balding Dr. John McIntyre
had mellowed considerably. He not only learned
to stop fighting the system, but became part of it,
as chief of surgery at sprawling San Francisco
Memorial Hospital. His concern for his patients
still sometimes tempted him to violate "established hospital procedures," but Trapper had
learned to mollify the hospital administration,
represented by bookish Arnold Slocum. Working
with Trapper was an admiring young doctor
named Gonzo Gates, whose brash, irreverent attitude and love of life reminded Trapper of his own
youth. Gonzo, the hospital Lothario, had even
served in an army M.A.S.H. unit himself, during
the Vietnam war, and was a talented surgeon.
Also featured was Trapper's scrub nurse, Starch,
who went all the way back to his M.A.S.H. days
(she was replaced by Nurse Shoop when actress
Mary McCarty died during the hiatus between
Trapper John's first and second seasons); sexy
young nurse Gloria Brancusi; and Doctors Jackson
and Riverside, the latter a likable but officious
chief of emergency services who, it was rumored,
owed his job more to his father's position on the
hospital's board of directors than to his own skill.
Major changes occurred in the personal lives of
two of San Francisco Memorial's staff members

early in 1983. Stanley Riverside got married to a
woman dentist who also worked at the hospital,
and Gloria adopted a sickly, homeless waif
named Andrea. Trapper also had to deal with the
occasional intrusions into his life by his ex-wife,
Melanie (played by Jessica Walter).

Their son, J.T., recently graduated from medical
school, arrived in the fall of 1984 to do his intern-
ship at San Francisco Memorial. The following
fall saw the arrival of Libby Kegler to replace
Gloria, attractive, mature Catherine Hackett as
the new administrator, and young surgeon and
emergency service helicopter pilot Andy Pagano.
Early in 1986 Gonzo suffered a stroke (Gregory
Harrison was leaving the series) and, although he
regained most of his faculties, was unable to return to surgery. Trying to put his life back together, and unsure that he wanted to stay in medicine if he could not be a surgeon, Gonzo left the
hospital on an extended vacation with his new
bride, Fran.

TRASH OR TREASURE
see What's It Worth?

TRAUMA CENTER
Medical Drama
FIRST TELECAST: September 22, 1983
LAST TELECAST: December 8, 1983
BROADCAST HISTORY:
Sep 1983–Oct 1983, ABC Thu 8:00–9:00
Nov 1983–Dec 1983, ABC Thu 9:00–10:00
CAST:

Dr. Michael "Cutter" Royce
.... James Naughton
Dr. Nate "Skate" Baylor... Dorian Harewood
Dr. Brigitte Blaine .... Wendie Malick
Dr. "Beaver" Bouvier .... Bill Randolph
Amy Decker.................. Eileen Heckart
Dr. Charles Sternhauser.. Arlen Dean Snyder
John Six .... Lou Ferrigno
Sidney "Hatter" Pacelli .... Alfie Wise
Buck Williams .... Jack Bannon
Nurse Hooter................. Jayne Modean

Life was just one disaster after another for the
medics of Trauma Center. There were generally
three or four "traumas" per show, ranging from an
injured construction worker stuck in a high rise to
golfers struck by lightning, victims of an explosion
at a singles bar, a skyscraper climber whose foot
slipped, and students mangled when the roof
caved in on their high school prom. Youthful doctor "Cutter" Royce dealt with all this at the McKee
Hospital Trauma Center, which had been set up to
make maximum use of the "golden hour"—the
first 60 minutes following an accident, in which
many victims can be saved by fast action. Helping
at the center and on the scene were young doctors
Baylor, Blaine, and Bouvier, nursing supervisor
Amy Decker and her ingenuous assistant Hooter,
helicopter pilot Buck (well, they did have to move
fast), and ambulance drivers Hatter and John Six.

Six was played by brawny Lou Ferrigno, whose real-life partial deafness (and halting speech) was used to advantage in a story about a young boy coming to terms with his own accident-induced deafness. Dr. Sternhauser was the hospital administrator with whom Cutter was constantly fighting for new equipment and additional funds.

TRAVEL CORNER
Documentary
FIRST TELECAST: *December 28, 1953*
LAST TELECAST: *September 4, 1954*
BROADCAST HISTORY:
  Dec 1953–May 1954, ABC Mon 9:30–10:00
  Jun 1954–Sep 1954, ABC Sat 10:00–10:30

Travel films.

TRAVELS OF JAIMIE MCPHEETERS, THE
Western
FIRST TELECAST: *September 15, 1963*
LAST TELECAST: *March 15, 1964*
BROADCAST HISTORY:
  Sep 1963–Mar 1964, ABC Sun 7:30–8:30
CAST:
  "Doc" Sardius McPheeters ... Dan O'Herlihy
  Jaimie McPheeters .... Kurt Russell
  John Murrel .... James Westerfield
  Shep Baggott .... Sandy Kenyon
  Jenny .... Donna Anderson
  Matt Kissel .... Mark Allen
  Mrs. Kissel .... Meg Wyllie
  Kissel Brothers .... Osmond Brothers
  Henry T. Coe .... Hedley Mattingly
  Othello .... Vernett Allen III
  Buck Coulter (1963) .... Michael Witney
  Linc Murdock .... Charles Bronson

This adventure series followed a young boy on a westward-bound wagon train in 1849. Twelve-year-old Jaimie was surrounded by a colorful cast of characters, not the least of whom was his stovepipe-hatted father, an irresponsible scalawag M.D. (they had sneaked out of Paducah, Kentucky, just ahead of their creditors to join the wagon train). Traveling with the McPheeterses in the train was 17-year-old Jenny, a rather sexy orphan; the God-fearin' Kissel family (whose children, Micah, Leviticus, Deuteronomy, and Lamentations, were portrayed by the Osmond Brothers); and blue-blooded Henry T. Coe and his valet, Othello. Continual danger was posed by the Bible-quoting but cunning thief Murrel, and his shady partner, Baggott.

Adventure followed as the wagons made their way north to St. Louis, west across the North Platte River to Ft. Bridger, down to Salt Lake City, across the Humboldt Sink and the Sierra Nevada to the Feather River and finally the gold fields of California! Wagonmaster Buck Coulter lasted only a few weeks, until he was trampled to death in the process of saving Jaimie's life. Linc Mur-

dock, a powerful but troubled man, then became the wagonmaster for the remainder of the show's single-season journey.

Based on Robert Lewis Taylor's 1958 Pulitzer Prize–winning novel of the same name.

TREASURE HUNT
see *What's It Worth?*

TREASURE HUNT
Quiz/Audience Participation
FIRST TELECAST: *September 7, 1956*
LAST TELECAST: *June 17, 1958*
BROADCAST HISTORY:
  Sep 1956–May 1957, ABC Fri 9:00–9:30
  Dec 1957–Jun 1958, NBC Tue 7:30–8:00
EMCEE:
  Jan Murray
ASSISTANT:
  Marian Stafford (1956–1957, 1958)
  Greta Thyssen (1957–1958)

Contestants on *Treasure Hunt,* usually one man and one woman, were asked a series of questions on a designated topic and got $50 for each correct answer. When one of the contestants had defeated the other in the quiz portion of the program, he won the opportunity to go on a "treasure hunt." There were a number of treasure chests on the stage and the winning contestant got to pick one. Whatever was in the chest went to the contestant. The prizes in the chests were not all winners. Everything from a head of cabbage to a check for a large sum of money was contained in various chests. The jackpot check in the ABC version was a flat $25,000. When NBC picked up *Treasure Hunt* for a nighttime version (NBC had begun airing it as a daytime show in August 1957) the jackpot check was a basic $10,000 plus $1,000 for each week that it was not discovered.

Jan Murray's sexy assistant, clad in a scanty pirate costume, was referred to on the show as the Pirate Girl. Marian Stafford was the Pirate Girl when the series was on ABC. Greta Thyssen was the first NBC nighttime pirate girl. When she left the show in January 1958, Marian, who had replaced Pat White in the daytime version in December, returned to the nighttime version as well.

Fourteen years after *Treasure Hunt* departed NBC's daytime lineup in December 1959, Chuck Barris purchased the rights to the title and brought out a syndicated series titled *The New Treasure Hunt,* emceed by Geoff Edwards. There was no quiz, only the opportunity for two contestants to pick the treasure chest with the $25,000 check. It was played to take advantage of the emotions of the contestants, and Barris was proud of the fact that one winner actually passed out on the stage. *The New Treasure Hunt* ran from 1973 to 1976.

TREASURE QUEST
Quiz/Audience Participation

FIRST TELECAST: *April 24, 1949*
LAST TELECAST: *September 2, 1949*
BROADCAST HISTORY:
    Apr 1949–Jun 1949, ABC Sun 9:30–10:00
    Jun 1949–Sep 1949, ABC Fri 8:30–9:00
HOST:
    John Weigel

Quiz show in which contestants were required to identify various locations, from visual and verbal clues, with an expense-paid trip as prize. From Chicago.

Known during its first two weeks as *Bon Voyage*.

TREASURY MEN IN ACTION
Crime Drama
FIRST TELECAST: *September 11, 1950*
LAST TELECAST: *September 30, 1955*
BROADCAST HISTORY:
    Sep 1950–Dec 1950, ABC Mon 8:00–8:30
    Apr 1951–Apr 1954, NBC Thu 8:30–9:00 (OS)
    Oct 1954–Jun 1955, ABC Thu 8:30–9:00
    Jun 1955–Sep 1955, ABC Fri 8:30–9:00
CAST:
    The Chief .... Walter Greaza

Action dramas based on actual cases from the files of the U.S. Treasury Department and telecast live. Walter Greaza portrayed the chief of whatever division was involved in each week's case, running to earth such assorted scoundrels as smugglers, counterfeiters, gunrunners, tax evaders (a favorite!), and moonshiners. The program invariably ended with the moral that the government always wins, and thereby received several awards and commendations from official agencies for its public service. Actual government officials sometimes appeared on the show.

The supporting cast varied from week to week, but over the years included such names as Lee Marvin, Grace Kelly, Jason Robards, Jr., James Dean, Cliff Robertson, Jack Klugman, and Charles Bronson.

TRIAL AND ERROR
Situation Comedy
FIRST TELECAST: *March 15, 1988*
LAST TELECAST: *March 29, 1988*
BROADCAST HISTORY:
    Mar 1988, CBS Tue 8:00–8:30
CAST:
    John Hernandez .... Eddie Velez
    Tony Rivera .... Paul Rodriguez
    Bob Adams .... John de Lancie
    Rhonda .... Debbie Shapiro
    Edmund Kittle .... Stephen Elliott
    Lisa .... Susan Saldivar

These two hispanics had grown up together in the barrio in East L.A., and now they were roommates, but John and Tony had totally different approaches to life. Tony was a free spirit with limited financial aspirations, making a living selling T-shirts from a stand on Olvera Street near downtown Los Angeles. John, on the other hand, was recently graduated from law school and had joined the prestigious law firm of Kittle, Barnes, Fletcher & Gray. Although he disliked being the token hispanic in the firm, and had to deal with condescending fellow attorney Bob Adams, John had the sincere support of senior partner Edmund Kittle. John's secretary, Rhonda, who had been with the firm for several years, knew much more about the internal politics and pecking order than he did. John and Tony were friends and they were roommates, but many were the times when Tony's blue-collar presence conflicted with, and potentially embarrassed, John's pinstripe-suited legal world.

TRIALS OF O'BRIEN, THE
Law Drama
FIRST TELECAST: *September 18, 1965*
LAST TELECAST: *May 6, 1966*
BROADCAST HISTORY:
    Sep 1965–Nov 1965, CBS Sat 8:30–9:30
    Dec 1965–May 1966, CBS Fri 10:00–11:00
CAST:
    Daniel J. O'Brien .... Peter Falk
    Katie .... Joanna Barnes
    The Great McGonigle .... David Burns
    Miss G .... Elaine Stritch
    Margaret .... Ilka Chase
    Lt. Garrison .... Dolph Sweet

The Trials of O'Brien were not confined to those that took place in the court of law. Daniel J. O'Brien was a very talented—and expensive—New York attorney whose personal life was almost more trying than his professional life. He was behind in the rent on his luxurious penthouse apartment, behind in alimony payments to his beautiful ex-wife, Katie, and was one of the most unsuccessful gamblers in the city. Somehow, no matter how fast the money came in, it went out just a little bit faster. His secretary, Miss G., tried to help him maintain a better financial equilibrium, but it never quite worked out. The cases in this series were treated seriously, but O'Brien's personal problems were not. In certain ways, Peter Falk's characterization of O'Brien had parallels with his much more successful portrayal of Columbo in the 1970s. Both were extremely good at their jobs but rather sloppy and disorganized when it came to their personal lives.

TROUBLE WITH FATHER
    syndicated title for *Stu Erwin Show, The*

TROUBLESHOOTERS
Adventure
FIRST TELECAST: *September 11, 1959*
LAST TELECAST: *June 17, 1960*

Sep 1959–Jun 1960, NBC Fri 8:00–8:30
CAST:
Kodiak	Keenan Wynn
Frank Dugan	Bob Mathias
Scotty	Bob Fortier
Skinner	Carey Loftin
Jim	Bob Harris
Slats	Chet Allen

The number one troubleshooter of the Stenrud Corporation, a large heavy-construction firm specializing in both domestic and foreign building projects, was a grizzled old veteran named Kodiak. He had held that post for five years, during which time he had coped with the problems involved in building highways, dams, airfields, skyscrapers, and atomic installations all over the world. The pace had started to become too much for him to take, and he was in the slow process of training his assistant, Frank Dugan, to take over. Frank was all the things that Kodiak was not—well educated, socially polished, soft-spoken, and innocent of the evil ways of the world. As the two of them traveled from assignment to assignment they learned from each other and acquired qualities that would stand them in good stead in the future. Kodiak became somewhat less gruff and uncivilized and Frank became stronger and more assertive. Scotty, Skinner, Jim, and Slats were crew members who made frequent appearances.

TRUE

Syndicated title for *General Electric True Theater*

TRUTH OR CONSEQUENCES

Quiz/Audience Participation
FIRST TELECAST: *September 7, 1950*
LAST TELECAST: *June 6, 1958*
BROADCAST HISTORY:
Sep 1950–May 1951, CBS Thu 10:00–10:30
May 1954–Sep 1955, NBC Tue 10:00–10:30
Sep 1955–Sep 1956, NBC Fri 8:00–8:30
Dec 1957–Jun 1958, NBC Fri 7:30–8:00
EMCEE:
Ralph Edwards (1950–1951)
Jack Bailey (1954–1956)
Steve Dunne (1957–1958)

Truth or Consequences had originally aired in 1940 as an NBC radio program with its creator, Ralph Edwards, as the emcee. A decade later it moved to television, on CBS, with its format and emcee unchanged. Contestants on the show were asked silly trick questions which they almost invariably failed to answer correctly. If they answered incorrectly, or failed to come up with any answer in a short time, Beulah the Buzzer went off. The emcee then told them that since they had failed to tell the truth, they would have to pay the consequences. Consequences consisted of elabo-

rate stunts, some done in the studio and others done outside, some completed on that week's episode and others taking a week or more and requiring the contestant to return when the stunt was completed. Some of the stunts were funny, but more often they were also embarrassing, and occasionally they were sentimental (as when long-separated relatives were reunited within the context of the stunt).

The original TV version of this series, with Edwards as host, lasted only a single season. When it returned three years later on NBC, Jack Bailey was the emcee, later replaced by Steve Dunne. NBC aired a daytime version of the show from 1956 until 1965, first with Jack Bailey as host, succeeded by Bob Barker at the end of 1956. Barker made a career of the show after that, remaining with it through the rest of the daytime run and on into the original syndicated run from 1966 to 1974. A short-lived syndicated revival in 1977–1978 was emceed by Bob Hilton.

A decade later, in the fall of 1987, comic Larry Anderson turned up as the emcee of yet another syndicated *Truth or Consequences.* This version, in which the emcee was assisted by Murray (the Unknown Comic) Langston, quickly faded from the airwaves.

TRY AND DO IT

Variety/Audience Participation
FIRST TELECAST: *July 4, 1948*
LAST TELECAST: *September 5, 1948*
BROADCAST HISTORY:
Jul 1948–Sep 1948, NBC Sun 8:30–9:00
HOST:
Jack Bright
REGULARS:
Thomas Leander Jones' Brass Band

Audience-participation show in which people from the studio audience performed various stunts—whistling through a mouthful of crackers, lacing up a right shoe on the left foot, etc. The program was set in a picnic ground, with Thomas Leander Jones' band providing schmaltzy music from an old-fashioned bandstand.

TUCKER'S WITCH

Detective Drama
FIRST TELECAST: *October 6, 1982*
LAST TELECAST: *August 8, 1983*
BROADCAST HISTORY:
Oct 1982–Nov 1982, CBS Wed 10:00–11:00
Mar 1983–Jun 1983, CBS Thu 10:00–11:00
Jul 1983–Aug 1983, CBS Mon 9:00–10:00
CAST:
Rick Tucker	Tim Matheson
Amanda Tucker	Catherine Hicks
Ellen Hobbes	Barbara Barrie
Lt. Sean Fisk	Bill Morey
Marcia Fulbright	Alfre Woodard
Stucky, the mortician	Duncan Ross

Mix a little bit of *Mr. & Mrs. North* with a dash of *Bewitched* and you know what *Tucker's Witch* was like. Rick and Amanda Tucker were husband-and-wife partners in a private-detective agency. He was the conventional detective, working with evidence and utilizing his analytical skills, while she relied on her "intuition." In Amanda's case, however, there was a pretty substantial basis for her hunches, since she resorted to witchcraft for clues. Unfortunately, her ability to use witchcraft properly to solve cases was not always successful, since some of her spells didn't work exactly as planned, even with the help of her Siamese cat, Dickens, and the occasional assistance of her mother, Ellen, who was also a witch. Marcia was the Tuckers' secretary and Lt. Fisk the homicide detective with whom they were often at odds.

TUGBOAT ANNIE
see *Adventures of Tugboat Annie, The*

TURN OF FATE, A
see *Alcoa Theatre* and *Goodyear TV Playhouse*

TURNABOUT
Situation Comedy
FIRST TELECAST: *January 26, 1979*
LAST TELECAST: *March 23, 1979*
BROADCAST HISTORY:
Jan 1979–Feb 1979, NBC Fri 9:00–9:30
Feb 1979–Mar 1979, NBC Fri 9:30–10:00
CAST:

Sam Alston	John Schuck
Penny Alston	Sharon Gless
Jack Overmeyer	Richard Stahl
Judy Overmeyer	Bobbi Jordan
Geoffrey St. James	James Sikking
Al Brennan	Bruce Kirby

Everyone has, at one time or another, wished that they could change places with somebody else, and lead that other person's life. That was the wish that got Sam and Penny Alston into so much trouble. Over Sam's objections, Penny had purchased a small Buddha-like statue from a gypsy who claimed it had magic powers. Later, in a moment of boredom, the couple chanced to wish they could change places with each other and—*voilá!* the statue granted them their wish. While they slept, Sam's spirit moved into Penny's body and vice versa. Finding out the next morning that they had exchanged bodies was quite a shock—and that was only the beginning. Trying to maintain the illusion of normalcy, until they could get the statue to switch them back to their own bodies, was not easy. Sam (in Penny's body) had to learn all about the cosmetics industry, since she was an executive working for Geoffrey St. James; and Penny (in Sam's body) had to act the part of a gruff sportswriter to deal with boss Al Brennan. They

also had personal habits and gestures that seemed inappropriate in their new bodies. Sam liked to smoke cigars and Penny was very dainty, among other things. The people most likely to notice the sudden "turnabout" were their nosy neighbors, the Overmeyers.

Based on the novel by Thorne Smith, who was also the author of the books on which another whimsical series, *Topper*, was based. The novel was also made into a movie, in 1940.

TURNING POINT
Dramatic Anthology
FIRST TELECAST: *April 12, 1958*
LAST TELECAST: *October 4, 1958*
BROADCAST HISTORY:
Apr 1958–Oct 1958, NBC Sat 9:30–10:00

This was a collection of filmed reruns from other anthology series, with the addition of two unsold pilots for projected (but never scheduled) dramatic series.

TURNING POINT, THE
see *ABC Dramatic Shorts—1952–1953*

TURN-ON
Comedy Variety
FIRST TELECAST: *February 5, 1969*
LAST TELECAST: *February 5, 1969*
BROADCAST HISTORY:
Feb 1969, ABC Wed 8:30–9:00
REPERTORY COMPANY:
Bonnie Boland
Teresa Graves
Maura McGiveney
Cecile Ozorio
Mel Stuart
Alma Murphy
Hamilton Camp
Maxine Greene
Carlos Manteca
Chuck McCann
Bob Staats
Ken Greenwald

Turn-On is remembered as one of the most famous one-telecast fiascos in the history of television. It was publicized as the second coming of *Laugh-In*, and even had the same executive producer, George Schlatter. According to the producer, Digby Wolfe, it was to be a "visual, comedic, sensory assault involving . . . animation, videotape, stop-action film, electronic distortion, computer graphics—even people." The "star" of the show was a mock-up computer. Despite the ballyhoo, what it turned out to be was an exercise in extremely bad taste. When the show's rampant sexual double-entendres and complete depersonalization led many ABC affiliates to refuse to carry it after the first telecast, and Bristol-Myers dropped sponsorship, it was canceled.

Guest star on the first, and only, telecast was Tim Conway.

TWELVE O'CLOCK HIGH
War Drama
FIRST TELECAST: *September 18, 1964*
LAST TELECAST: *January 13, 1967*
BROADCAST HISTORY:
Sep 1964–Jan 1965, ABC Fri 9:30–10:30
Jan 1965–Sep 1965, ABC Fri 10:00–11:00
Sep 1965–Sep 1966, ABC Mon 7:30–8:30
Sep 1966–Jan 1967, ABC Fri 10:00–11:00
CAST:
Brigadier General Frank Savage (1964–1965)
.... Robert Lansing
Major General Wiley Crowe (1964–1965)
.... John Larkin
Major Harvey Stovall .... Frank Overton
Major Joe Cobb (1964–1965)....... Lew Gallo
Major ("Doc") Kaiser .... Barney Phillips
Captain/Major/Colonel Joe Gallagher
.... Paul Burke
Tech. Sgt. Sandy Komansky (1965–1967)
.... Chris Robinson
Brigadier General Ed Britt (1965–1967)
.... Andrew Duggan
EXECUTIVE PRODUCER:
Quinn Martin

This was one wartime action-adventure series in which the top brass did not stay behind the lines. It was the story of the 918th Bombardment Group of the U.S. Eighth Air Force, stationed near London during World War II. During the first season the stories centered on Brigadier General Frank Savage, as he personally led his pilots through bombing raids and narrow escapes over enemy territory. Major General Crowe was his boss, and Major Harvey Stovall his adjutant on the ground.

The action was hot and heavy, and at the start of the second season it got a little too hot for General Savage, who was killed during a mission. Colonel Joe Gallagher then assumed command, and the lead in the series for the rest of its run. (Gallagher zoomed in rank from captain to colonel during the series' run, despite getting off to a bad start in the premiere telecast. He guest-starred then as a brash young man who felt that he deserved special treatment from Savage because his father was a three-star general.) Brigadier General Britt became the new superior officer in the second season, while Tech. Sgt. Komansky was Gallagher's gunner and flight engineer.

Based on the novel by Beirne Lay, Jr., and Sy Bartlett, which was also made into a movie starring Gregory Peck (1949).

20TH CENTURY, THE
Documentary
FIRST TELECAST: *October 20, 1957*
LAST TELECAST: *January 4, 1970*
BROADCAST HISTORY:
Oct 1957–May 1958, CBS Sun 6:30–7:00
Sep 1958–Aug 1961, CBS Sun 6:30–7:00
Sep 1961–Aug 1966, CBS Sun 6:00–6:30
Jan 1967–Oct 1967, CBS Sun 6:00–6:30
Jan 1968–Oct 1968, CBS Sun 6:00–6:30
Jan 1969–Sep 1969, CBS Sun 6:00–6:30
Jan 1970, CBS Sun 6:00–6:30
NARRATOR:
Walter Cronkite

CBS News correspondent Walter Cronkite was the narrator and host of this series throughout its run. The objective of *The 20th Century* was to present filmed reports of the major events, movements, and personalities that had shaped modern world history. The subject matter ranged from politics and war to medicine and the arts. When the series returned to the air to start its tenth season in January 1967, the title and format were altered. Under the new title, *The 21st Century*, the subjects covered looked to the future, rather than the past. Advances that were taking place or were anticipated in medicine, transportation, space exploration, communications, the arts, and living conditions in general were all explored in depth.

20TH CENTURY–FOX HOUR, THE
Dramatic Anthology
FIRST TELECAST: *October 5, 1955*
LAST TELECAST: *September 18, 1957*
BROADCAST HISTORY:
Oct 1955–Sep 1957, CBS Wed 10:00–11:00
HOST:
Joseph Cotten (1955–1956)
Robert Sterling (1956–1957)

The filmed dramas that were presented in this series were produced by 20th Century–Fox in Hollywood. Many of them were short adaptations of films that had been released by Fox over its long history, but generally featured newer, lesser-known actors and actresses (few big-name movie stars appeared in this series). Among the adaptations presented were "The Ox-Bow Incident," "Junior Miss," "The Late George Apley," and "Miracle on 34th Street." *The 20th Century–Fox Hour* aired on alternate weeks with *The U.S. Steel Hour*.

TWENTIETH CENTURY TALES
see *ABC Dramatic Shorts—1952–1953*

21ST CENTURY, THE
see *20th Century, The*

TWENTY-ONE
Quiz/Audience Participation
FIRST TELECAST: *September 12, 1956*
LAST TELECAST: *October 16, 1958*
BROADCAST HISTORY:
Sep 1956–Jan 1957, NBC Wed 10:30–11:00
Jan 1957–Sep 1958, NBC Mon 9:00–9:30
Sep 1958–Oct 1958, NBC Thu 8:30–9:00

Jack Barry

Fifteen months after the premier of *The $64,000 Question,* which was the first and most popular of the big-money quiz shows, *Twenty-One* made its debut. The format was loosely based on the card game of the same name, also known as blackjack. Two contestants competed with each other to reach a point total of 21 and win the game. They were asked the questions while in individual isolation booths. At the start of each round they were informed of the category from which the questions would come and could choose to attempt a question worth from 1 to 11 points, with the difficulty increasing with rising point value. The value of each point was $500, with the winner progressing to face a new opponent. In case of a tie, a new game was started with the value of each point raised by $500, a process which would continue through succeeding ties until there was a winner. The only threat to a champion was that if he lost a future game, the amount of his opponent's winnings would be deducted from his final total.

When the quiz-show scandals surfaced in 1958, initiated by a former contestant on the game show *Dotto, Twenty-One* was one of the biggest losers. Its producers admitted that the game had been rigged; that contestants were often given answers in advance if the producers felt that they were desirable as winners in the sense that they were people the public could identify with; and that a fraud had indeed been perpetrated on the trusting American public. Herb Stempel, a former winner on *Twenty-One,* told the detailed story of how the game had been rigged. The most popular *Twenty-One* winner, college professor Charles Van Doren, who had acquired a regular position on NBC's *Today Show* after being dethroned with winnings of $129,000, was also forced eventually to admit that he had participated in the rigging. He lost his job on *Today,* was relieved of his teaching post, and suffered inestimable embarrassment. When the dust cleared the game shows were gone, but their records of generosity to contestants remained. The biggest winner on *Twenty-One* was Elfrida Von Nardroff, who apparently had not been a participant in the fixing of the show. She came away with a final total of $220,500. In the annals of the big-money quiz shows this total was only exceeded by the $224,000 won by 11-year-old genius Robert Strom and the $252,000 won by Teddy Nadler, both on CBS game shows, *The $64,000 Question* and *The $64,000 Challenge* respectively.

21 BEACON STREET
Detective Drama
FIRST TELECAST: *July 2, 1959*
LAST TELECAST: *March 20, 1960*
BROADCAST HISTORY:
Jul 1959–Sep 1959, NBC Thu 9:30–10:00
Dec 1959–Mar 1960, ABC Sun 10:30–11:00

CAST:
Dennis Chase .... Dennis Morgan
Lola .... Joanna Barnes
Brian .... Brian Kelly
Jim .... James Maloney

Private investigator Dennis Chase operated out of an office at 21 Beacon Street, where he and his staff worked out methods of trapping criminals. The locale was not specified; it could have been any large American metropolis. Chase's staff consisted of sexy Lola, whose beauty could be used to charm information out of people; young law school graduate Brian; and Jim, a handyman with a knack for dialects. Unlike most private-detective shows, *21 Beacon Street* developed its crime situation before the hero entered the story, and then never had him take part in the actual apprehension. Chase preferred to send the police on that errand, after determining who the culprit was. *21 Beacon Street* was the 1959 summer replacement for *The Ford Show,* and was rerun on ABC in the middle of the 1959–1960 season.

21 JUMP STREET
Police Drama
FIRST TELECAST: *April 12, 1987*
LAST TELECAST:
BROADCAST HISTORY:
Apr 1987– , FOX Sun 7:00–8:00
CAST:
Off. Tom Hanson (pilot only) .... Jeff Yagher
Off. Tom Hanson ....Johnny Depp
Off. Doug Penhall ....Peter DeLuise
Off. Judy Hoffs ....Holly Robinson
Off. Harry Truman Ioki ...... Dustin Nguyen
Capt. Richard Jenko (1987) .. Frederic Forest
Capt. Adam Fuller .... Steven Williams

The most popular of fledgling Fox Broadcasting's first-season shows was this teen-oriented police series. The four youthful officers featured were members of a special unit of the Los Angeles Police Department that fought crime in the schools. Hanson, Penhall, Hoffs, and Ioki could all pass as students, and went undercover every week in local high schools to deal with drug trafficking, extortion, school gangs, teenage prostitution, murders, and other "typical" teenage problems. The building in which the special unit was based was an abandoned chapel at 21 Jump Street, hence the show's title. Captain Jenko, an eccentric nonconformist, was the original supervisor of the group. He was killed by a drunk hit-and-run driver and was replaced by Adam Fuller, who preferred to do things by the book.

Most episodes ended with one of the cast members doing a public service announcement suggesting agencies or counseling services that were available to teens facing the problems dramatized in that week's story.

TWENTY QUESTIONS
Quiz/Panel
FIRST TELECAST: *November 26, 1949*
LAST TELECAST: *May 3, 1955*
BROADCAST HISTORY:
  Nov 1949–Dec 1949, NBC Sat 8:00–8:30
  Mar 1950–Jun 1951, ABC Fri 8:00–8:30 (OS)
  Jul 1951–Jun 1952, DUM Fri 8:00–8:30
  Jul 1952–Sep 1952, DUM Fri 8:30–9:00
  Oct 1952–Sep 1953, DUM Fri 10:00–10:30
  Sep 1953–Apr 1954, DUM Mon 8:00–8:30
  Apr 1954–May 1954, DUM Sun 10:00–10:30
  Jul 1954–May 1955, ABC Tue 8:30–9:00
HOST:
  Bill Slater (1949–1952)
  Jay Jackson (1953–1955)
PANELISTS:
  Fred Van De Venter
  Florence Rinard
  Herb Polesie
  Johnnie McPhee (1949–1953)
  Dickie Harrison (1953–1954)
  Bobby McGuire (1954–1955)

This popular quiz show was something of a family affair, having been created by the Van De Venters on radio in 1946 and featuring father (Fred), mother (Florence Rinard), and son (Bobby McGuire) together on the panel at various times. The format was based on the old parlor game of "animal, vegetable, or mineral." The panel, which consisted of four regulars and one celebrity guest, could ask up to 20 questions to identify the subject at hand. Each question would be answered only by a "yes" or "no." Questions were sent in by viewers, who won a prize if they stumped the panel.

Twenty Questions originated on the Mutual Radio Network in 1946 and when first seen on TV in 1949 was simulcast on radio. There was little turnover among regular panelists during its run, except in the "teenage" chair, where Johnny McPhee was replaced by Dickie Harrison, who in turn gave way to the Van De Venters' own son, Bobby McGuire, who had been with the show on radio during the 1940s.

$25,000 PYRAMID, THE
Quiz/Audience Participation
BROADCAST HISTORY:
  Syndicated and Network Daytime
  30 minutes
  Produced: *1974–1979, 1981, 1985–*
  Released: *Fall 1974*
HOST:
  Bill Cullen (1974–1979)
  Dick Clark (1981, 1985–   )

Television's most inflationary game show has worked its way up from *The $10,000 Pyramid*, to *The $20,000 Pyramid*, to *The $25,000 Pyramid*, to *The $50,000 Pyramid*, to *The $100,000 Pyramid* since its premiere in daytime in 1973. The contest was a simple word-association game, played by two teams, each composed of one celebrity and one noncelebrity. One member of each team was given a list of words; the other member then had 30 seconds to identify the words from one-word clues shouted by his or her partner. The winning team (most words identified) then went into a playoff round in which they could follow a similar procedure to work their way up a pyramid of questions to the grand prize.

The daytime version ran on CBS from 1973 to 1974, on ABC from 1974 to 1980, and returned to CBS from the fall of 1982 to the summer of 1988. The top prize on the daytime version was raised from $10,000 to $20,000 in January of 1976, and to $25,000 when it was resurrected by CBS in 1982. The top prize on the original syndicated version was $25,000, rising to $50,000 in 1981, and $100,000 when it was revived in 1985. With the exception of the 1974–1979 syndicated *$25,000 Pyramid*, Dick Clark hosted the series in all its incarnations.

26 MEN
Western
BROADCAST HISTORY:
  Syndicated only
  30 minutes
  Produced: *1957–1959* (78 episodes)
  Released: *October 1957*
CAST:
  Capt. Tom Rynning .... Tris Coffin
  Ranger Clint Travis .... Kelo Henderson

26 Men was the Arizona equivalent of *Tales of the Texas Rangers*. It was based on historical fact; in 1901, the Arizona Territorial Legislature had authorized an armed force consisting of "one captain, one lieutenant, four sergeants, and 20 privates" to maintain law and order. "The reason there was only 26 of us was because the Territory couldn't afford no more," reminisced one of the original members, many years later.

In this straightforward action Western Tris Coffin played the captain, and Kelo Henderson a new recruit. Others of the 26 were seen from time to time, but none were regulars. The series was shot on location in Arizona, and many residents of Phoenix and Tucson were used in supporting roles.

20/20
News Magazine
FIRST TELECAST: *June 6, 1978*
LAST TELECAST:
BROADCAST HISTORY:
  Jun 1978–Aug 1978, ABC Tue 10:00–11:00
  Sep 1978–Apr 1979, ABC Various times
  May 1979–Sep 1987, ABC Thu 10:00–11:00
  *Sep 1987–   *, ABC Fri 10:00–11:00
HOSTS:
  Harold Hayes and Robert Hughes (first telecast only)
  Hugh Downs
  Barbara Walters (1984–   )

REGULAR CORRESPONDENTS:
Dave Marash (1978–1981)
Sylvia Chase (1978–1986)
Dr. Carl Sagan (1978–1980)
Thomas Hoving (1978–1984)
Geraldo Rivera (1978–1985)
Tom Jarriel (1979–   )
Bob Brown (1980–   )
Steve Fox (1980–1983)
Barbara Walters (1981–1984)
John Stossel (1981–   )
Lynn Sherr (1986–   )
Stone Phillips (1986–   )

This ABC news magazine set out to emulate the success of CBS' *60 Minutes*, but got off to a disastrous start. The elements were similar to those in *60 Minutes*—personality profiles, mini-documentaries, hard-hitting investigative reports—but the coverage was so shallow, and the production so full of gimmicks, that the premiere telecast received devastating reviews. *Variety* likened it to *The National Enquirer*. In one of the fastest cast changes in history, producer Bob Shanks fired his two co-hosts—former magazine editor Harold Hayes and Australian art critic Robert Hughes—after just one telecast, brought in old pro Hugh Downs, and began tinkering with the contents. Subsequent shows were better received, though *20/20* never rivaled *60 Minutes* as an audience attraction. Correspondents included Geraldo Rivera with investigative reports and Thomas Hoving on popular culture. ABC correspondents Tom Jarriel and Bob Brown also filed frequent reports. Dr. Carl Sagan, originally announced as a regular contributor on science, was seen relatively infrequently. At the start of the 1984–85 season Barbara Walters was formally promoted from correspondent to co-host.

Nearly every telecast of *20/20* seemed to headline something sensational or celebrity-oriented, such as a profile of the latest rock star or an investigation into the circumstances surrounding the death of Elvis Presley, or something—anything—concerning sex. There were also more substantive features over the years, among them a widely acclaimed special telecast on the secret Iranian hostage negotiations (aired just after the hostages were released), an exposé on the hazards of aluminum wiring, and Geraldo Rivera's report from inside war-torn Laos.

TWILIGHT THEATER
Dramatic Anthology
FIRST TELECAST: *April 2, 1956*
LAST TELECAST: *July 15, 1959*
BROADCAST HISTORY:
Apr 1956–Jul 1956, ABC Mon 7:30–8:00
Jul 1958–Jul 1959, CBS Wed 7:30–8:00

The title *Twilight Theater* has been used several times for filmed prime-time anthology series. In 1953 it was one of the titles under which ABC aired its inventory of miscellaneous dramatic films (see *ABC Dramatic Shorts—1952–1953* for details). ABC revived the name in 1956 for a summer series consisting of 30-minute dramas and comedies featuring such Hollywood standbys as Ethel Waters, Vera Miles, Hans Conried, Charles Coburn, and Hugh O'Brian. From 1958–1959 CBS used the title *Twilight Theater* for a series of reruns of films previously seen on *Schlitz Playhouse of Stars*.

TWILIGHT ZONE, THE
Science Fiction Anthology
FIRST TELECAST: *October 2, 1959*
LAST TELECAST: *July 31, 1987*
BROADCAST HISTORY:
Oct 1959–Sep 1962, CBS Fri 10:00–10:30
Jan 1963–Sep 1963, CBS Thu 9:00–10:00
Sep 1963–Sep 1964, CBS Fri 9:30–10:00
May 1965–Sep 1965, CBS Sun 9:00–10:00
Sep 1985–Apr 1986, CBS Fri 8:00–9:00
Jun 1986–Sep 1986, CBS Fri 8:00–9:00
Sep 1986–Oct 1986, CBS Sat 10:00–11:00
Dec 1986, CBS Thu 8:00–8:30
Jul 1987, CBS Fri 10:00–11:00
HOST:
Rod Serling (1959–1965)
NARRATOR:
Charles Aidman (1985–1987)

Playwright Rod Serling, who in the mid-1950s had been a prolific contributor of fine dramas for almost all of the prestigious live anthology series (his most famous being "Requiem for a Heavyweight" for *Playhouse 90*), turned to the world of science fiction with this series. In addition to serving as series host, he wrote many of the teleplays that were presented on *The Twilight Zone*. The stories were unusual and offbeat, often with ironic twists. For example, there was "Escape Clause," starring David Wayne as a hypochondriac who, in an effort to escape his dependence on pills and fear of his environment, made a pact with the Devil. In exchange for his soul he won immortality. Filled with self-assurance, he killed a man (expecting to be sentenced to die and knowing that was now impossible). Instead of the death penalty he got life imprisonment—an awfully long time for someone who was immortal. Another episode, "Time Enough at Last," starred Burgess Meredith as a bank teller who could never find enough time to read. One day at lunchtime, while he was squirreled away in the bank's vault reading a good book, there was a nuclear attack that killed everybody outside. Now he had all the time in the world to read. A happy ending—until he tripped and broke his glasses! In "The Eye of the Beholder," a young woman who had been born with a horrible facial deformity had just undergone the last possible operation to try and make her less hideous. Her head was swathed in bandages, and all the doctors and nurses were dimly seen standing in the shadows around her bed. Then the bandages were finally removed and there she was, beautiful—at least to us. Only then were the faces of the doctors and nurses revealed to be those of reptiles, for she lived in a world where our "beauty" was considered a horrible deformity. At the end of the telecast she was led away to her society's equivalent of a leper colony.

Some well-known actors appeared on *Twilight Zone,* but it was the stories rather than the performers that made the show work. Serling's original opening narration to the show set the scene appropriately. The opening: "There is a fifth dimension beyond that which is known to man. It is a dimension as vast as space and as timeless as infinity. It is the middle ground between light and shadow, between science and superstition, and it lies between the pit of man's fears and the summit of his knowledge. This is the dimension of imagination. It is an area we call *The Twilight Zone.*"

After three successful seasons in a half-hour format, *The Twilight Zone* expanded to a full hour in January 1963. The longer format was abandoned the following fall, but some of the longer episodes were rerun during the summer of 1965.

In the fall of 1985, following the release of a 1983 theatrical feature of the same title, *The Twilight Zone* returned to TV. It had been two decades since the original had left the air, and a decade since the passing of its driving creative force, Rod Serling. The new version ran in an hour-long format, with two or three stories of varying length in each episode. It still had the same mix of straight science fiction, whimsy, fantasy, and the occult, but it was definitely a different show. It was now in color, the special effects were more elaborate and, although some of the original episodes were redone, most of the stories were new. There was a minor furor when, late in 1985, science fiction writer Harlan Ellison, who had been serving as creative consultant, left the series in a dispute with the network over the content of the Christmas episode.

TWO FOR THE MONEY
Quiz/Audience Participation
FIRST TELECAST: *September 30, 1952*
LAST TELECAST: *September 7, 1957*
BROADCAST HISTORY:
  Sep 1952–Aug 1953, NBC Tue 10:00–10:30
  Aug 1953–Sep 1956, CBS Sat 9:00–9:30
  Mar 1957–Jun 1957, CBS Sat 10:30–11:00
  Jun 1957–Sep 1957, CBS Sat 8:30–9:00
EMCEE:
  Herb Shriner (1952–1956)
  Walter O'Keefe (1954)
  Sam Levenson (1955, 1956, 1957)
QUIZ MODERATOR:
  Dr. Mason Gross

Much in the manner of *You Bet Your Life,* this quiz show was designed more as a vehicle for the comic talents of its emcee than as a straight contest. Herb Shriner, with his country humor and tales of life in Indiana, was the original emcee and remained with the show until the spring of 1956. He was spelled during the summers by Walter O'Keefe in 1954 and Sam Levenson in 1955 and 1956. Levenson returned as the full-time emcee when the show returned in the spring of 1957. Three pairs of contestants vied for cash prizes during the actual quiz portion of the show and Dr. Mason Gross, Provost and Professor of Philosophy at Rutgers University, was the authority on correctness of answers.

240-ROBERT
Adventure
FIRST TELECAST: *August 28, 1979*
LAST TELECAST: *September 19, 1981*
BROADCAST HISTORY:
  Aug 1979, ABC Tue 8:30–10:00
  Sep 1979–Dec 1979, ABC Mon 8:00–9:00
  May 1980–Aug 1980, ABC Sat 8:00–9:00
  Mar 1981, ABC Sat 8:00–9:00
  Sep 1981, ABC Sat 8:00–9:00
CAST:
  Deputy Theodore Roosevelt Applegate III
    ("Trap") .... John Bennett Perry
  Deputy Dwayne Thibideaux (1979–1980)
    .... Mark Harmon
  Deputy Morgan Wainwright (1979–1980)
    .... Joanna Cassidy
  Kestenbaum .... Steve Tannen
  Deputy C.B. (1979–1980) ...... Lew Saunders
  Deputy Roverino (1979–1980) . JoeAl Nicassio
  Terry (1979–1980) .... Thomas Babson
  Deputy Bottendott (1981)
    .... Brant Von Hoffman
  Deputy Brett Cueva (1981) .... Stephan Burns
  Deputy Sandy Harper (1981)
    .... Pamela Hensley

One of TV's periodic "rescue" shows, *240-Robert* followed the exploits of the Los Angeles County Sheriff's Department Emergency Service Detail (E.S.D.). The principal characters were three bright-faced young deputies: Trap, the leader; Morgan, the pretty helicopter pilot; and Thib, the husky helper (played by former UCLA star quarterback Mark Harmon). Using choppers, motorcycles, boats, and a customized four-wheel-drive wagon, they managed to extract hapless citizens from various uncomfortable situations.

After its original run in the fall of 1979, and repeats the following summer, *240-Robert* returned briefly in early 1981 with a new female pilot (Sandy) and helper (Brett).

TWO IN LOVE
Quiz/Audience Participation
FIRST TELECAST: *June 19, 1954*
LAST TELECAST: *September 11, 1954*
BROADCAST HISTORY:
  Jun 1954–Sep 1954, CBS Sat 10:30–11:00
EMCEE:
  Bert Parks

Each week a couple—engaged, newly married, or celebrating a wedding anniversary—were the guests of emcee Bert Parks. Many of their relatives and friends were also invited to be on the show. The relatives and friends participated in an on-the-air discussion of the couple's romance and were asked other questions which, if answered correctly, added to the "nest egg" of cash that would be presented to the couple at the end of the show. After the first couple of weeks it was decided by the producers to have only engaged couples as guests.

TWO MARRIAGES
Drama
FIRST TELECAST: *August 23, 1983*
LAST TELECAST: *April 26, 1984*
BROADCAST HISTORY:
  Aug 1983, ABC Tue 9:30–11:00
  Aug 1983–Sep 1983, ABC Wed 9:00–10:00
  Mar 1984, ABC Thu 8:00–9:00
  Apr 1984, ABC Thu 9:00–10:00
CAST:
  Jim Daley .... Tom Mason
  Ann Daley .... Karen Carlson
  Willie Daley .... Ian Fried
  Kim Daley .... Tiffany Toyoshima
  Scott Morgan .... C. Thomas Howell
  Dr. Art Armstrong .... Michael Murphy
  Nancy Armstrong .... Janet Eilber
  Eric Armstrong .... Kirk Cameron
  Shelby Armstrong .... Louanne
  Woody Daley .... John McLiam

The relationships within and between two middle-class, suburban American families were the subjects of this gentle drama, set in a pleasant Iowa community. The Daleys were the more contemporary couple: Ann was pursuing a successful career as a construction engineer, even while pregnant with another child, and Jim worked at his father Woody's dairy farm. Besides their rambunctious six-year-old, Willie, the bustling Daley household included two children from previous marriages, Jim's 11-year-old Vietnamese-American daughter, Kim, and Ann's rebellious teenage son, Scott. Across the well-mown lawn were their best friends the Armstrongs—Art the busy surgeon and Nancy the vaguely dissatisfied homemaker, who kept herself occupied with volunteer work and was always a bit envious of Ann's independent life-style. Shelby was the Armstrongs' 15-year-old, sensitive and wise beyond her years, and Eric their happy-go-lucky young son.

The contrast between traditional and "modern" marriages, and the joys and pains of families and friendships provided the stories.

TWO OF US, THE
Situation Comedy
FIRST TELECAST: *April 6, 1981*
LAST TELECAST: *August 10, 1982*
BROADCAST HISTORY:
  Apr 1981, CBS Mon 8:30–9:00
  Sep 1981–Jan 1982, CBS Mon 8:30–9:00
  Jan 1982–Feb 1982, CBS Wed 8:30–9:00
  Jun 1982–Aug 1982, CBS Tue 8:30–9:00

CAST:
  Robert Brentwood .... Peter Cook
  Nan Gallagher................ Mimi Kennedy
  Cubby Royce .... Oliver Clark
  Gabrielle "Gabby" Gallagher ...... Dana Hill
  Reggie Cavanaugh (1981–1982)
    .... Tim Thomerson

Robert Brentwood was a very proper English manservant thrust into a free-wheeling American household in this comedy of life-styles. Nan Gallagher was a highly successful, divorced career woman, co-host of the New York City TV talk show "Mid-morning Manhattan." (The other host was the unseen Reggie Philbis—a takeoff on real Los Angeles talk show host Regis Philbin.) Nan's blind spot was housekeeping. Basically, she was a slob around the house, and she desperately needed someone to put her daily life in order. Enter Brentwood, quite by accident. Though initially repelled by the thought of working for a woman (with a child, yet!), he took the challenge. On the one hand sarcastic, sometimes overbearing, and always proper, he also happened to be a gourmet cook, a meticulous organizer, and conversant in several languages—skills which proved invaluable when Nan had to entertain a diverse parade of guests. If only he were a little less pompous! Cubby Royce was Nan's agent.

When *The Two of Us* returned in the fall of 1981 after a limited run in the spring, the name of Nan's co-host had been changed from Philbis to Cavanaugh and he was seen regularly in the person of actor Tim Thomerson. Reggie's ego was as big as all outdoors and he was so obnoxious that he had practically no real friends. Needless to say, Reggie and Nan were not the best of friends off camera.

227
Situation Comedy
FIRST TELECAST: *September 14, 1985*
LAST TELECAST:
BROADCAST HISTORY:
  Sep 1985–Mar 1986, NBC Sat 9:30–10:00
  Apr 1986–Jun 1986, NBC Sat 9:30–10:00
  Jun 1986–May 1987, NBC Sat 8:30–9:00
  Jun 1987–Jul 1987, NBC Sat 8:00–8:30
  *Jul 1987–   *, NBC Sat 8:30–9:00
CAST:
  Mary Jenkins .... Marla Gibbs
  Lester Jenkins .... Hal Williams
  Rose Lee Holloway .... Alaina Reed
  Sandra Clark .... Jackee (Harry)
  Brenda Jenkins (14) .... Regina King
  Tiffany Holloway (12) (1984–1985)
    .... Kia Goodwin
  Pearl Shay .... Helen Martin
  Calvin Dobbs .... Curtis Baldwin

Marla Gibbs, who played the insolent, wisecracking housekeeper on *The Jeffersons* for ten years, brought a somewhat toned-down variation of the character to this popular comedy about family life in a black neighborhood of Washington, D.C. Mary and her best friend, Rose, the landlady, liked to sit on the stoop of their apartment building (No. 227) and gossip about many things—especially the building's resident vamp, Sandra, who had the figure and mannerisms of a modern Mae West. While Sandra wiggled around in her tight dresses, Mary's daughter, Brenda, was just beginning to struggle with the pains of adolescence, her number-one pain being gangly boyfriend Calvin. Lester was Mary's level-headed husband, a small-time contractor, and Pearl a crochety old busybody (and Calvin's grandmother) who often leaned out her window to join in the front-stoop conversations. Tiffany, Rose's daughter and Brenda's friend, was rarely seen after the first season.

The series was based on a play, *227*, in which several of the principals (including Gibbs) had appeared.

TYCOON, THE

Situation Comedy
FIRST TELECAST: *September 15, 1964*

LAST TELECAST: *September 7, 1965*
BROADCAST HISTORY:
Sep 1964–Sep 1965, ABC Tue 9:00–9:30
CAST:

Walter Andrews	Walter Brennan
Pat Burns	Van Williams
Herbert Wilson	Jerome Cowan
Betty Franklin	Janet Lake
Martha Keane	Pat McNulty
Una Fields	Monty Margetts

The chairman of the board of the giant Thunder Corporation was Walter Andrews, a cantankerous and eccentric millionaire. Walter did things his way, and despite the complaints and misgivings of his co-workers and business associates, his approach to problems usually worked. Not one to let protocol affect his operation, Walter was a constant problem for everyone from his young assistant and private pilot Pat Burns, to company president Herbert Wilson. Walter made his home with his cute little granddaughter Martha and housekeeper Una Fields.

U

UFO
Science Fiction
BROADCAST HISTORY:
Syndicated only
60 minutes
Produced: *1970* (26 episodes)
Released (U.S.): *Fall 1972*
CAST:
Cdr. Edward Straker .... Ed Bishop
Col. Alec Freeman .... George Sewell
Capt. Peter Karlin .... Peter Gordeno
Lt. Gay Ellis .... Gabrielle Drake
Col. Paul Foster .... Michael Billington
Gen. Henderson .... Grant Taylor

This science-fiction adventure was set 10 years in
the future—in the year 1980—when it was discovered that unidentified flying objects posed an imminent threat to Earth. The general public was not
yet aware of this unfortunate development, so a
secret multinational defense command was set up
under a movie studio (!) and called SHADO—Supreme Headquarters, Alien Defense Organization. Its commander was Edward Straker, whose
"cover" was that of a movie producer. Others included Col. Freeman, his second-in-command;
Capt. Karlin, pilot of the "remarkable" Seagull
X-ray craft; and Lt. Ellis, in charge of SHADO's
Moon Base Control.

The stories were filled with violence, green-
faced aliens, a number of very sexy females, and
the usual array of scientific hardware. Among the
gimmicks were an underwater airplane launcher,
the ultra-futuristic Moon Base, and a Space Intruder Detector called SID.

The series was produced in England.

U.N.C.L.E.
syndicated title for *Man from U.N.C.L.E., The*
and *Girl from U.N.C.L.E., The*

U.N. CASEBOOK
Documentary
FIRST TELECAST: *September 26, 1948*
LAST TELECAST: *March 6, 1949*
BROADCAST HISTORY:
Sep 1948–Oct 1948, CBS Sun 6:45–7:15
Oct 1948–Mar 1949, CBS Sun 6:30–7:00
MODERATOR:
Dr. Lyman Bryson
Quincy Howe

The many and varied functions of the United Nations were looked at individually in this documentary series. Dr. Lyman Bryson, CBS Counsellor on
Public Affairs, and Quincy Howe interviewed international political and intellectual figures about
the roles that the U.N. played and should play in
its multiple areas of activity.

U.S. HIGHWAY 1954
Travelogue
FIRST TELECAST: *August 2, 1954*
LAST TELECAST: *September 27, 1954*
BROADCAST HISTORY:
Aug 1954–Sep 1954, ABC Mon 7:30–8:00

Travel films on American vacation spots and
scenic areas such as the Grand Canyon, Yosemite
National Park, Cape Cod, etc.

U.S. MARINE BAND
Music
FIRST TELECAST: *July 9, 1949*
LAST TELECAST: *August 20, 1949*
BROADCAST HISTORY:
Jul 1949–Aug 1949, NBC Sat 8:00–8:30

A series of summer concerts originating in Washington, D.C., and featuring the 70-piece Marine
Band, under the direction of Major William San-
telmann.

U.S. MARSHAL
see *Sheriff of Cochise, The*

U.S. ROYAL SHOWCASE, THE
Comedy Variety
FIRST TELECAST: *January 13, 1952*
LAST TELECAST: *June 29, 1952*
BROADCAST HISTORY:
Jan 1952–Jun 1952, NBC Sun 7:00–7:30
HOST:
George Abbott
Jack Carson

This live comedy variety series originated from
New York City. Each show was composed of
three separate acts: a performance by a well-
known star comedian, a singing interlude by a
popular recording artist, and a performance by a
promising young comedian. Broadway producer
George Abbott directed the show and acted as the
host, introducing the evening's performers, but he
relinquished the on-camera hosting chores to comedian Jack Carson on April 13. The new-talent
segment had been dropped from the show by the
time Carson had taken over as host.

U.S. STEEL HOUR, THE
Dramatic Anthology
FIRST TELECAST: *October 27, 1953*
LAST TELECAST: *June 12, 1963*
BROADCAST HISTORY:
Oct 1953–Jun 1955, ABC Tue 9:30–10:30
Jul 1955–Jun 1963, CBS Wed 10:00–11:00

United States Steel's initial venture into broadcast drama had been on ABC radio in 1945. Under
the title *The Theatre Guild on the Air*, it was a
showcase for authors and directors as well as
performers, and presented plays from New York
with distinguished casts. In 1953 The Theatre

Guild moved the series to television, in effect bringing the Broadway stage to the nation's television viewers. Throughout its 10-year run as a live show originating from New York, *The U.S. Steel Hour* aired on alternate weeks with other dramatic anthologies. Ironically, *Armstrong Circle Theater*, the show with which it shared the Wednesday time slot during its eight years on CBS, had been its competition during part of the time it was on ABC.

The two years on ABC produced primarily dramatic presentations. The premiere telecast, "P.O.W." starring Gary Merrill, Richard Kiley, and Sally Forrest, set the tone. Rex Harrison and his then wife, Lilli Palmer, were featured in "The Man in Possession," Tallulah Bankhead in an adaptation of Ibsen's *Hedda Gabler*, Thomas Mitchell and Dorothy Gish in a version of *The Rise and Fall of Silas Lapham*, and Wendell Corey and Keenan Wynn in "The Rack," by frequent contributor Rod Serling. Not all was serious, however, as Andy Griffith starred in "No Time for Sergeants" in 1955, before re-creating the role on both Broadway and film.

With the move to CBS, there was more diversity in the subject matter. To be sure, there were still moving dramas—Paul Newman, Albert Salmi, and George Peppard in "Bang the Drum Slowly" in 1956, almost 20 years before the movie of the same title; Teresa Wright, Dick Van Dyke, and George C. Scott in "Trap for a Stranger"; and Mona Freeman and Cliff Robertson in "The Two Worlds of Charlie Gordon" (which became the 1968 movie *Charly* for which Mr. Robertson received a Best Actor Academy Award for his portrayal of the title role)—but there was much more. Dorothy Collins and Edward Mulhare starred in an adaptation of Oscar Wilde's *The Importance of Being Earnest*, and Jack Carson, Basil Rathbone, Jimmy Boyd, and Florence Henderson were featured in a musical titled "Huck Finn," based on the Mark Twain novel. There was even a musical revue, with Fred MacMurray, Wally Cox, Edie Adams, Carol Burnett, and Hans Conried in a bit of fluff titled "The American Cowboy." Johnny Carson, not known primarily as an actor, appeared twice in light dramas in 1960, the first time with Anne Francis in "Queen of the Orange Bowl."

In ten years on the air, *The U.S. Steel Hour* presented more than 200 live plays, and the list of noted personalities who appeared in them is substantial. Numerous people made multiple appearances and, though some of them have already been mentioned, the names that follow were featured in at least four shows: Eddie Albert, Edward Andrews, Marty Astor, Ed Begley, Ralph Bellamy, Larry Blyden, Geraldine Brooks, Jack Carson, Hans Conried, James Daly, Jeff Donnell, Patty Duke, Faye Emerson, Nina Foch, Mona Freeman, Farley Granger, Arthur Hill, Richard Kiley, June Lockhart, Diana Lynn, Biff McGuire, Barry Morse, Meg Mundy, Betsy Palmer, Gene Raymond, Cliff Robertson, Franchot Tone, and Teresa Wright.

UGLIEST GIRL IN TOWN, THE
Situation Comedy
FIRST TELECAST: *September 26, 1968*
LAST TELECAST: *January 30, 1969*
BROADCAST HISTORY:
Sep 1968–Jan 1969, ABC Thu 7:30–8:00
CAST:
Timothy Blair ("Timmie") ..... Peter Kastner
Julie Renfield .... Patricia Blake
Gene Blair .... Garry Marshall
Sondra Wolston .... Jenny Till
David Courtney............ Nicholas Parsons

This frothy bit of comedy had a male star dressed in women's clothes as its running gag. The situation was all very logical, though somewhat farfetched. It seemed that young Hollywood talent agent Timothy Blair had fallen madly in love with an English starlet named Julie, while Julie was in town making a film. Then she flew back to London, and Timothy did not have the money to follow. Enter Timothy's brother Gene, a professional photographer assigned to shoot pictures of San Francisco hippies for a London magazine. At the last moment Gene's pictures were accidentally destroyed, and in desperation he dressed Timothy in a wig and hippie outfit and took pictures of *him* to send to London. London liked the pictures so much that they wanted that "girl"—for a major "Twiggy"-style modeling assignment.

Timothy (now dubbed "Timmie") went along with the ruse because it meant free airplane fare to England and his Julie, but once there he was faced with the necessity of maintaining the put-on in all sorts of awkward situations. What to do in a nude scene?

In almost less time than it took to explain all this, *The Ugliest Girl in Town* was on and off the ABC schedule.

UNCOVERED
syndicated title for *Vise, The*

UNDER ONE ROOF
see *Spencer*

UNDERCURRENT
Dramatic Anthology
FIRST TELECAST: *July 1, 1955*
LAST TELECAST: *September 19, 1958*
BROADCAST HISTORY:
Jun 1955–Sep 1958, CBS Fri 10:00–10:30 (Summers only)

For four summers *Undercurrent* was the replacement for *The Lineup*. During the first two years, the plays presented were all new to television. Starring in these dramas, which tended to be on the heavy side, were many future stars of television series. Among them were Brian Keith, Craig Stevens, Lloyd Bridges, Dale Robertson, Raymond Burr, and Vince Edwards. None of them, however, were major stars when these films aired. In 1957 and 1958 *Undercurrent* telecast reruns of episodes originally aired on other anthology series, the 1958 edition coming from NBC's *The Web*, which had aired the previous summer.

UNDERSEA WORLD OF JACQUES COUSTEAU, THE

Documentary
FIRST TELECAST: *May 23, 1976*
LAST TELECAST: *June 13, 1976*
BROADCAST HISTORY:
May 1976–Jun 1976, ABC Sun 7:00–8:00
PRODUCER:
Capt. Jacques-Yves Cousteau
NARRATOR:
Joseph Campanella

French scientist and explorer Capt. Jacques Cousteau has been producing TV documentaries longer than most people realize. His first network telecast was a feature on undersea archeology, presented on *Omnibus* on January 17, 1954. Widespread fame came in the late 1960s, however, when he began a long series of prime-time specials for ABC depicting outdoor nature adventures from pole to pole. It was ABC's answer to the *National Geographic Specials*.

At first the program dealt with sea life, as seen from Cousteau's exploration ship *Calypso* (the first special, on January 8, 1968, was "Sharks"). Later, as he began to run out of sea-born subjects, programs were done on land life as well. Rod Serling was the narrator until 1974, when he was replaced by Joseph Campanella.

The dates shown above reflect the single instance in which Cousteau specials ran consecutively for four weeks in the same time slot, qualifying as a "series" for the purposes of this book.

UNITED OR NOT

Interview
FIRST TELECAST: *July 2, 1951*
LAST TELECAST: *October 27, 1952*
BROADCAST HISTORY:
Jul 1951–Sep 1951, ABC Mon 9:00–9:30
Oct 1951–Jun 1952, ABC Tue 9:00–9:30
Jun 1952–Aug 1952, ABC Tue 8:30–9:00
Sep 1952–Oct 1952, ABC Mon 8:30–9:00
MODERATOR:
John MacVane

Interviews and discussions with guests from the United Nations, including ambassadors, specialists from various technical branches, foreign government officials, and the Secretary General, Trygve Lie.

UNITED STATES

Situation Comedy
FIRST TELECAST: *March 11, 1980*
LAST TELECAST: *April 29, 1980*
BROADCAST HISTORY:
Mar 1980–Apr 1980, NBC Tue 10:30–11:00

CAST:
Richard Chapin .... Beau Bridges
Libby Chapin .... Helen Shaver
Dylan Chapin .... Rossie Harris
Nicky Chapin .... Justin Dana

Produced by Larry Gelbart, who had developed *M*A*S*H* for TV nearly a decade earlier, *United States* was supposed to be a breakthrough in its blending of drama and comedy to explore the joys and the problems of contemporary marriage. Richard and Libby Chapin were a young, middle-class couple with two young children, and most of the action took place in their home. The series was certainly not a typical situation comedy. The frank discussions of problems, the open hostilities, and the inability often to reach long-term solutions all made difficult the Chapins' search for "united states," those moments when they felt at one with each other, a single entity. The subjects they discussed included death and dying, Libby's reunion with an old family friend who had molested her when she was eight, the mixed feelings they had had about becoming parents, their differing attitudes about their sexual relationship, and the admission that each of them had been unfaithful. Far from being funny, *United States* was often tedious, boring, and didactic. Viewers tuned out in droves. It lasted less than two months.

UNIVERSAL STAR TIME

syndicated title for *Bob Hope Presents the Chrysler Theatre*

UNIVERSE

Science Magazine
FIRST TELECAST: *July 12, 1980*
LAST TELECAST: *September 14, 1982*
BROADCAST HISTORY:
Jul 1980–Aug 1980, CBS Sat 8:00–9:00
Jun 1981–Sep 1981, CBS Tue 8:30–9:00
Jun 1982–Sep 1982, CBS Tue 8:00–8:30
ANCHORMAN:
Walter Cronkite

This summer series attempted to do for the world of science what *60 Minutes* did for general news subjects. *Universe* offered viewers insights on such topics as how EPA mileage ratings for new cars are computed and tested, the use of wind power in a world of shrinking energy reserves, the special-effects technology of movies like *Star Wars*, and a study of what causes motion sickness. Walter Cronkite was anchorman and chief correspondent, with contributions by other CBS News correspondents including Charles Osgood, Diane Sawyer, and Charles Crawford. In 1981 it was retitled *Walter Cronkite's Universe*.

UNTAMED WORLD

Documentary

Syndicated and network daytime
30 minutes
Produced: *1968–1975* (156 episodes)
Released: *1971*
NARRATOR:
Phil Carey

Nature documentary films about such subjects as
snakes, predators and scavengers, primitive
South American tribes, etc. The series first ran on
NBC on Saturday afternoons from January to August 1969, then went into syndication with both
repeats and new episodes.

UNTOUCHABLES, THE
Police Drama
FIRST TELECAST: *October 15, 1959*
LAST TELECAST: *September 10, 1963*
BROADCAST HISTORY:
Oct 1959–Oct 1961, ABC Thu 9:30–10:30
Oct 1961–Sep 1962, ABC Thu 10:00–11:00
Sep 1962–Sep 1963, ABC Tue 9:30–10:30
CAST:
Eliot Ness .... Robert Stack
Agent Martin Flaherty (1959–1960)
.... Jerry Paris
Agent William Youngfellow . Abel Fernandez
Agent Enrico Rossi .... Nick Georgiade
Agent Cam Allison (1960) .. Anthony George
Agent Lee Hobson (1960–1963) .. Paul Picerni
Agent Rossman (1960–1963).... Steve London
Frank Nitti .... Bruce Gordon
NARRATOR:
Walter Winchell
PRODUCER:
Quinn Martin

With the chatter of machine-gun fire and the
squeal of tires on Chicago streets, *The Untouchables* brought furious controversy—and big ratings—to ABC in the early 1960s. It was perhaps
the most mindlessly violent program ever seen on
TV up to that time. Critics railed and public officials were incensed, but apparently many viewers
enjoyed the weekly bloodbath, which sometimes
included two or three violent shootouts per episode. As *TV Guide* observed, the show was
highly consistent. "In practically every episode a
gang leader winds up stitched to a brick wall and
full of bullets, or face down in a parking lot (and
full of bullets), or face up in a gutter (and still full
of bullets), or hung up in an ice box, or run down
in the street by a mug at the wheel of a big black
Hudson touring car."

How did they get away with it? The first defense was that the program was historically accurate, being based on the life of a real treasury
department gangbuster in the bullet-riddled Prohibition days of the early 1930s. The agent was
Eliot Ness, and he had in fact played an important
role in breaking the power of the notorious Al
Capone in Chicago in 1931. Ness later wrote an

autobiography, which served as the basis for a
two-part semidocumentary dramatization of the
Capone affair, presented on *Desilu Playhouse* in
April 1959.

The special was an enormous hit, and led immediately to an ABC series the next fall. It followed Ness and his small band of incorruptible
agents (dubbed by a Chicago newspaper "the Untouchables") as they battled one major crime lord
after another. Capone had been packed off to
prison at the conclusion of the April special, so
the series began with the battle between his two
top lieutenants, Jake "Greasy Thumb" Guzik and
Frank "The Enforcer" Nitti, for control of his empire. As the series continued, and writers were
pressed to find criminals famous enough for Ness
to tackle, stories wandered farther and farther
from the historical record. (Ness had in real life
disbanded his Untouchables after cracking the
Capone case, and had nothing to do with most of
the cases dramatized on TV.) *The Untouchables*
went after Bugs Moran (in whose garage the St.
Valentine's Day Massacre took place), Ma Barker,
and such East Coast hoods as Mad Dog Coll,
Dutch Schultz, and Philadelphia crime boss Walter Legenza. There was even a two-part dramatization of the events leading up to the attempted
assassination of President-elect Franklin D.
Roosevelt at Miami Beach in 1933.

Some of this dramatic license caused problems,
as when the FBI protested the depiction of Ness
cornering Ma Barker (it was actually FBI agents).
The estate of Al Capone sued the show for $1
million—not for inaccuracy, but for using Capone's name and likeness for profit. Italian-
American groups protested the fact that so many
of the hoods were given Italian names. Prison officials protested an episode which seemed to
show Capone getting soft treatment in the Atlanta
Penitentiary. Eventually the producers appended
a disclaimer to the end of each episode stating
that certain portions of *The Untouchables* had
been "fictionalized."

Historical accuracy (or inaccuracy) aside, *The
Untouchables* had another kind of appeal—and
an excuse for violence. It was almost a fantasy,
played by such colorful characters (the hoods), in
such a one-dimensional style, and with such period trappings, that even the killings did not seem
to be real. Eliot Ness was the upright, virtuous,
and humorless enforcer of the law, and his opponents were greedy, sniveling animals. Robert
Stack frankly admitted that he didn't really act in
his role as Ness, but simply "re-acted" to the over-
played villains around him, and the contrast made
the show work. Many fine character actors guest-
starred as the thugs, such as Bruce Gordon (seen
numerous times as Frank Nitti), Neville Brand (a
look-alike for Capone), Nehemiah Persoff (Guzik),
William Bendix (Legenza), Lloyd Nolan (Bugs
Moran), Clu Gulager (baby-faced Mad Dog Coll),
and Peter Falk (Nate Selko).

The Untouchables' success was spectacular

but relatively short-lived. The program zoomed from the number 43 program on TV during its first season to number 8 in its second, but then, faced with the decidedly less violent competition of *Sing Along with Mitch* from 1961–1962, dropped back to number 41. There was frantic tinkering with the format during the final season—Ness became "more human," and the killings "more motivated." Investigators from other government bureaus began to appear, such as Barbara Stanwyck as a lieutenant from the Bureau of Missing Persons, and Dane Clark as an official of the U.S. Public Health Service. But *The Untouchables* was gone by 1963.

The Untouchables' original Desilu pilot and the initial episodes of the series were supervised by a young staff producer named Quinn Martin, starting a long string of TV crime-show hits for that gentleman.

UP TO PAAR

Quiz/Audience Participation
FIRST TELECAST: *July 28, 1952*
LAST TELECAST: *September 26, 1952*
BROADCAST HISTORY:
  Jul 1952–Sep 1952, NBC Mon/Wed/Fri 7:00–7:30
EMCEE:
  Jack Paar

Contestants on this live quiz show were drawn from the studio audience. They were interviewed by Mr. Paar and then asked a series of five questions based on current news stories. The value of each question increased, from $5 to $50. Winnings were given in the form of silver dollars and the money for each wrong answer went into the jackpot. At the end of the show all the contestants were asked the same jackpot question taken from that day's newspaper. They wrote their answers on a ballot and if anyone had the correct answer, he won $100 plus all the money lost by all the contestants on that night's show. This was Jack Paar's first network television series.

UPBEAT

Music
FIRST TELECAST: *July 5, 1955*
LAST TELECAST: *September 22, 1955*
BROADCAST HISTORY:
  Jul 1955–Sep 1955, CBS Tue/Thu 7:45–8:00
REGULARS:
  The Honeydreamers
  Russ Case Orchestra
  The Tommy Morton Dancers

This twice-weekly summer series, which originated live from New York, filled the remainder of the half hour in which CBS aired its network news program. Each week there was a different singer as host, performing songs he or she had made popular. Among the singers who hosted the show were Tony Bennett, Teresa Brewer, Georgia Gibbs, Polly Bergen, and the Four Lads.

V

Science Fiction

FIRST TELECAST: *October 26, 1984*
LAST TELECAST: *July 5, 1985*
BROADCAST HISTORY:

> *Oct 1984–Jan 1985*, NBC Fri 8:00–9:00
> *Feb 1985–Mar 1985*, NBC Fri 9:00–10:00
> *May 1985*, NBC Fri 8:00–9:00
> *May 1985–Jul 1985*, NBC Fri 9:00–10:00

CAST:

Mike Donovan	Marc Singer
Dr. Julie Parrish	Faye Grant
Diana	Jane Badler
Nathan Bates	Lane Smith
Robin Maxwell	Blair Tefkin
Elizabeth (as teenager)	Jennifer Cooke
Ham Tyler	Michael Ironside
Elias	Michael Wright
Willie	Robert Englund
Kyle Bates	Jeff Yagher
Lydia	June Chadwick
Howard K. Smith	Himself
Sean Donovan	Nicky Katt
Mr. Chiang	Aki Aleong
Charles	Duncan Regehr
Lt. James (1985)	Judson Scott
Martin/Philip (1985)	Frank Ashmore

"V" stood for the "Visitors" in this science-fiction allegory of the takeover of Germany by the Nazis in the 1930s. The Visitors were aliens from a distant planet who came as friends, offering to help the world solve its problems through their high technology. All they asked for in exchange were some needed minerals. With the willing cooperation of a gullible world population and clever manipulation of the media they slowly and insidiously gained total control of Earth and then began methodically eliminating their enemies. As the story unfolded in two widely viewed mini-series broadcast in May 1983 and May 1984, the Visitors were finally unmasked by a small band of resistance fighters who discovered their true plan: to conquer the Earth and eat its population. Underneath the aliens' humanlike faces, they were actually lizards! A climactic battle ensued, and the Visitors were finally driven away with the help of a red dust bacteria.

As the weekly series began, the Visitors' captured leader, Diana, faced a Nuremburg-style trial. But she soon escaped and regained control of the Earth with the help of greedy human collaborators—notably the corrupt industrialist Nathan Bates, whose Scientific Frontiers Corp. (i.e., Krupp?) manufactured the dreaded Red Dust.

Leading the resistance were TV newsman Mike Donovan, who had originally discovered the Visitors' deceit; Julie, a brilliant scientist; and Ham

and Elias. Their hideout was the Club Creole, and their allies included Willie, an alien who had turned against his leaders' diabolical plans. Another ally was a young woman named Robin, who had given birth to a half-human, half-alien baby following an affair with a Visitor. The child, named Elizabeth, had gone through a rapid metamorphosis, emerging as a beautiful teenager with extraordinary powers—and the key to the Visitors' destruction. Kyle was Nathan Bates' rebellious son, who aided the resistance; and Lydia was a Visitor military leader who plotted against Diana. Charles, Lt. James, and Martin were Visitor officers, with the latter sympathetic to and working with the resistance until his death. His twin brother Philip, a Visitor leader, also sided with those fighting for the Earth's freedom. In the last original episode (aired March 22, 1985), despite Diana's best efforts to ruin things, peace was reached between the Visitors and Earth. Elizabeth and Kyle (who stowed away because he loved her) returned to the Visitors' home planet, and Willie, who had grown fond of Earth, remained here with his new friends.

Former newsman Howard K. Smith portrayed himself as the anchorman of the Freedom Network newscast that opened each episode from November to January, with an update on the activities of both Visitors and resistance fighters around the world.

VACATION PLAYHOUSE

Anthology

FIRST TELECAST: *July 22, 1963*
LAST TELECAST: *August 28, 1967*
BROADCAST HISTORY:

> *Jul 1963–Sep 1963*, CBS Mon 8:30–9:00
> *Jun 1964–Sep 1964*, CBS Mon 8:30–9:00
> *Jun 1965–Sep 1965*, CBS Fri 9:30–10:00
> *Jul 1966–Sep 1966*, CBS Mon 8:30–9:00
> *Jul 1967–Aug 1967*, CBS Mon 8:30–9:00

Vacation Playhouse collected pilots for proposed series that had not been sold and aired them as a summer replacement series. In the four years that this show ran on Monday nights it was the replacement for *The Lucy Show* and all of the episodes were situation comedies. In 1965, when it aired as the replacement for *Gomer Pyle U.S.M.C.* on Friday nights, the episodes were adventure and mystery pilots.

VAL DOONICAN SHOW, THE

Musical Variety

FIRST TELECAST: *June 5, 1971*
LAST TELECAST: *August 14, 1971*
BROADCAST HISTORY:

> *Jun 1971–Aug 1971*, ABC Sat 8:30–9:30

REGULARS:

> Val Doonican
> Bernard Cribbins
> Bob Todd
> The Norman Maen Dancers

The Mike Sammes Singers
Kenny Woodman's Orchestra
THEME:
"I Believe My Love Loves Me," by Tom Paxton

Irish singer Val Doonican was the star and host of this summer variety series that was taped in England. Comedians Bernard Cribbins and Bob Todd were featured regulars on the series, which also showcased both American and British guest stars.

VALENTINE'S DAY
Situation Comedy
FIRST TELECAST: *September 18, 1964*
LAST TELECAST: *September 10, 1965*
BROADCAST HISTORY:
 Sep 1964–Sep 1965, ABC Fri 9:00–9:30
CAST:
 Valentine Farrow . . . . Tony Franciosa
 Rockwell "Rocky" Sin . . . . Jack Soo
 Libby Freeman . . . . Janet Waldo
 Molly . . . . Mimi Dillard
 O. D. Dunstall . . . . Jerry Hausner
 Grover Cleveland Fipple . . . . . . Eddie Quillan

The life of Valentine Farrow, a debonair young New York publishing executive, was depicted in this comedy. Valentine was continually being chased by beautiful girls, both in and out of his Park Avenue office at the publishing firm of Brackett and Dunstall, where he was senior nonfiction editor. Libby was his pretty secretary, Molly his receptionist, and O. D. Dunstall his nervous boss. At home, Valentine was no hero to his valet, the scrounging, poker-playing, con man "Rocky" Sin. Rocky had been Valentine's buddy in the army, and had saved his neck. Now he was his chief confidant and bottle-washer. Living in the basement of Valentine's elegant East Side town house was Mr. Fipple, the handyman.

After a series of amorous adventures Valentine finally fell in love in the last episode, with a pretty research assistant at Brackett and Dunstall. The series didn't return for a second season, however, so it never got any further than that.

Seen in a guest role was opera singer Helen Traubel as Valentine's mother, Muriel Farrow.

VALENTINO
Romantic Monologue
FIRST TELECAST: *December 18, 1952*
LAST TELECAST: *March 5, 1953*
BROADCAST HISTORY:
 Dec 1952–Mar 1953, ABC Thu 9:30–10:00
HOST:
 Barry Valentino

Poetry readings, songs, and romantic monologues by Barry Valentino, who even looked a bit like his namesake, Rudolph Valentino. An obvious copy of CBS's soft-lights-and-sweet-music show, *The Continental.*

Also seen for a time as a local program in New York.

VALERIE
Situation Comedy
FIRST TELECAST: *March 1, 1986*
LAST TELECAST:
BROADCAST HISTORY:
 Mar 1986, NBC Sat 8:30–9:00
 Mar 1986–Jun 1986, NBC Mon 8:30–9:00
 Jun 1986–Sep 1986, NBC Mon 8:00–8:30
 Sep 1986–Nov 1986, NBC Sun 8:30–9:00
 Nov 1986–Jan 1987, NBC Sun 8:00–8:30
 Jan 1987–Mar 1987, NBC Sun 8:30–9:00
 Mar 1987– , NBC Mon 8:30–9:00
CAST:
 Valerie Hogan (1986–1987) . . . . Valerie Harper
 David Hogan (age 16) . . . . Jason Bateman
 Willie Hogan (12) . . . . Danny Ponce
 Mark Hogan (12) . . . . Jeremy Licht
 Michael Hogan . . . . Josh Taylor
 Barbara Goodwin (1986) . . Christine Ebersole
 Annie Steck (1986–1987) . . . . Judith Kahan
 Mrs. Patty Poole . . . . Edie McClurg
 *Peter Poole (1987–   ) . . . . Willard Scott
 Sandy Hogan (1987–   ) . . . . . Sandy Duncan
 Rich (1986–   ) . . . . Tom Hodges
 Burt (1987–   ) . . . . Steve Witting

*Occasional
THEME:
"Together Through the Years," by Charles Fox and Stephen Geyer, performed by Roberta Flack

Uproar on and off the screen marked this family sitcom. The premise was straightforward enough—take one harried mom (Valerie), juggling part-time career and full-time responsibility for running a household due to the frequent absence of her husband (Michael), an international airline pilot; add one rambunctious teenager (David) and two super-cute fraternal twins (Willie and Mark). All that was missing was a dog, or a feisty maid.

Valerie did have a career of sorts, first as the manager of an auction house and later as a graphic artist. However, most of the action took place in her suburban Chicago home, where girl-hungry David (the "man of the house"), fun-loving Willie, and brainy Mark could always be counted on to stir things up. Barbara was Valerie's understanding friend, and Mrs. Poole the busybody neighbor.

In the fall of 1987 Valerie Harper abruptly walked off the show in a well-publicized dispute with the producers. NBC decided to continue without her, retitling the series *Valerie's Family* (some suggested "Where's Valerie?" or "Who's Valerie?" might be more appropriate). Valerie was written out of the series as having died, and Michael's divorced sister Sandy moved in to serve as a sort of surrogate mom. Stories began to focus more on the kids, especially teenager David, who the producers hoped would become the next TV heartthrob. Others joining the cast included David's pal Burt, and Mrs. Poole's jovial husband Peter, played on an infrequent basis by *Today* show weatherman Willard Scott.

In June 1988 the title was changed, again, to *The Hogan Family.*

VALIANT YEARS, THE
see *Winston Churchill—The Valiant Years*

VAN CAMP'S LITTLE SHOW
Music
FIRST TELECAST: *June 27, 1950*
LAST TELECAST: *November 22, 1951*
BROADCAST HISTORY:
Jun 1950–Nov 1951, NBC Tue/Thu 7:30–7:45
HOST:
John Conte
REGULARS:
Jesse Bradley Trio

Intimate musical variety program featuring musical-comedy star Conte with a different female vocalist, and sometimes with other guests, on each show. Also known as *John Conte's Little Show* and *The Little Show.*

VAN DYKE AND COMPANY
Comedy Variety
FIRST TELECAST: *September 20, 1976*
LAST TELECAST: *December 30, 1976*
BROADCAST HISTORY:
Sep 1976, NBC Mon 10:00–11:00
Oct 1976, NBC Thu 10:00–11:00
Nov 1976–Dec 1976, NBC Thu 8:00–9:00
REGULARS:
Dick Van Dyke
The L.A. Mime Company
Andy Kaufman
Marilyn Sokol
Pat Proft
Bob Einstein
Richard Kiel
Chuck McCann

This short-lived series starred comedian Dick Van Dyke, whose previous success had been in situation comedies rather than variety programs. A true devotee of the art of pantomime, and renowned for his impression of Stan Laurel, Van Dyke made nonverbal comedy a prime ingredient in this show. In addition to the mime segments, and the recurring "bright family" sketch about the dumbest family in the world, there were appearances by guest stars from the music and comedy worlds.

VARIETY
Various
FIRST TELECAST: *April 11, 1948*
LAST TELECAST: *September 26, 1948*

BROADCAST HISTORY:
Apr 1948–Jun 1948, NBC Sun 8:30–9:00
Jul 1948–Sep 1948, NBC Sun 9:00–9:30

NBC presented what amounted to a series of specials under this umbrella title in 1948. The shows ranged from music and comedy acts to full-scale plays. Some plays were light entertainment, such as Gilbert & Sullivan; others were serious dramas. There was no host or continuing cast.

Variety was also known at times as *NBC Playhouse* or *The Players.*

VAUDEO VARIETIES
Variety
FIRST TELECAST: *January 14, 1949*
LAST TELECAST: *April 15, 1949*
BROADCAST HISTORY:
Jan 1949–Apr 1949, ABC Fri 8:00–9:00
EMCEE:
Eddie Hubbard

Hour-long variety show from Chicago, featuring emcee Eddie Hubbard and five different acts each week.

VAUDEVILLE SHOW
Musical Variety
FIRST TELECAST: *December 9, 1953*
LAST TELECAST: *December 30, 1953*
BROADCAST HISTORY:
Dec 1953, ABC Wed 9:30–10:00
ORCHESTRA:
Glenn Osser

A four-week series of re-creations of an old-time vaudeville show. Each telecast had five acts, including singers, dancers, tumblers, magicians, etc.

VAUGHN MONROE SHOW, THE
Musical Variety
FIRST TELECAST: *October 10, 1950*
LAST TELECAST: *September 8, 1955*
BROADCAST HISTORY:
Oct 1950–Jul 1951, CBS Tue 9:00–9:30
Aug 1954–Sep 1954, NBC Tue/Thu 7:30–7:45
Jul 1955–Sep 1955, NBC Tue/Thu 7:30–7:45
REGULARS:
Vaughn Monroe
Shaye Cogan (1950–1951)
Ziggy Talent (1950–1951)
Olga Suarez (1950–1951)
Kenny Davis (1950–1951)
The Satisfiers (1954)
The Richard Hayman Orchestra (1954)
The Richard Maltby Orchestra (1955)
THEME:
"Racing with the Moon," by Vaughn Monroe, Johnny Watson, and Pauline Pope

Singer and orchestra leader Vaughn Monroe was one of the leading musical stars on radio during the late 1940s and early 1950s with his *Camel*

Caravan, a Saturday night CBS variety show which ran from 1946 to 1954. He took his first plunge into the new medium of television on CBS in 1950, with a half-hour series that featured singer Shaye Cogan and comedian Ziggy Talent, plus guest stars. Most of the crooning was done by Vaughn himself, however, with his deep baritone voice and raft of melodious hits ("Racing with the Moon," "There I've Said It Again," "Ghost Riders in the Sky," etc.). After a single season as a TV series star, he returned to radio and occasional TV guest shots, but in 1954 and 1955 was back with an NBC program that served as summer replacement for *The Dinah Shore Show*. Like the CBS series it was telecast live, but the 15-minute length allowed time for little more than a few songs. By 1955 Vaughn's kind of music was becoming more nostalgic than contemporary, and thereafter he was seen with decreasing frequency in guest appearances on other shows. Perhaps his best-remembered role in TV was as commercial spokesman for RCA products. He died in 1973.

VEGA$

Detective Drama
FIRST TELECAST: *September 20, 1978*
LAST TELECAST: *September 16, 1981*
BROADCAST HISTORY:
Sep 1978–Jun 1981, ABC Wed 10:00–11:00
Aug 1981–Sep 1981, ABC Wed 9:00–10:00
CAST:
Dan Tanna .... Robert Urich
Beatrice Travis .... Phyllis Davis
Binzer (Bobby Borso) .... Bart Braverman
Angie Turner (1978–1979) ...... Judy Landers
Sgt. Bella Archer (1978–1979)
.... Naomi Stevens
Lt. David Nelson (1979–1981) ... Greg Morris
Philip Roth .... Tony Curtis

TV audiences never seem to tire of handsome, wisecracking private eyes, and Dan Tanna was the very latest 1978 model. Blue jeans, a sports car (a vintage red Thunderbird), sexy assistants, glamorous Las Vegas settings, and a new homicide every Wednesday night helped make this one of the hits of the 1978–1979 season. Dan was on retainer to Philip Roth, the fast-talking, millionaire owner of several of Vegas' bigger casino-hotels—including the Desert Inn, on whose grounds Tanna's office/apartment was located. Binzer, a reformed hood, was his inept but enthusiastic legman; Angie, his sexy but not very bright receptionist; and Beatrice, his equally sexy and very efficient secretary/assistant. Both women were also showgirls, though the older Beatrice was more often seen teaching the chorus line routines than participating in them. Dan's original contact on the Vegas police department was Sgt. Archer, who gradually faded from the scene after Lt. Nelson was added to the cast midway through the first season. Seen occasionally were Dan's boss, Philip Roth, who Tanna affectionately nicknamed

"Slick"; Chief Harlon Two Leaf (played by Will Sampson), a friend of Dan's; and a stylish but hefty gambler named Diamond Jim (Victor Buono).

VERDICT IS YOURS, THE

Courtroom Drama
FIRST TELECAST: *July 3, 1958*
LAST TELECAST: *September 25, 1958*
BROADCAST HISTORY:
Jul 1958–Sep 1958, CBS Thu 8:30–9:30
COURT REPORTER:
Jim McKay

Reenactments of actual trials were presented on this nighttime version of *The Verdict Is Yours*. Real lawyers tried the cases and real judges were on the bench. The jury was made up of members of the studio audience. Jim McKay, in the role of court reporter, established the background for each case and filled in missing details during the "trial." He also performed the same task on the daytime version which had premiered in 1957 and ran until 1962.

VERSATILE VARIETIES

Variety/Children's
FIRST TELECAST: *August 26, 1949*
LAST TELECAST: *December 14, 1951*
BROADCAST HISTORY:
Aug 1949–Jan 1951, NBC Fri 9:00–9:30 (OS)
Sep 1951–Dec 1951, ABC Fri 9:30–10:00
EMCEE:
George Givot (1949)
Harold Barry (1949–1950)
Bob Russell (1950–1951)
Lady Iris Mountbatten (1951)
"BONNY MAID":
Anne Francis (1949–1950)
ORCHESTRA:
Jerry Jerome (1949–1950)
Bernie Sands (1950–1951)

This began as a live variety show set in a nightclub, with guest singers, comedians, performing dogs, etc. Nonperforming guest celebrities were sometimes seen seated at ringside tables. George Givot, "the Greek Ambassador of Good Will," was the original host, succeeded after two months by comedian Harold Barry. Singer Bob Russell took over in the fall of 1950, as the program tended more to a presentation of new talent. Anne Francis appeared in the commercials (for floor covering) as "Bonny Maid," assisted by two other Bonny Maids and the team of "Wear and Tear."

Versatile Varieties returned in the fall of 1951 with a somewhat different format, featuring Lady Iris Mountbatten and a cast of kids who presented various children's stories and skits.

During its NBC run the program was also known as *Bonny Maid Versatile Varieties*.

VIC DAMONE SHOW, THE

see *Dean Martin Presents Vic Damone* and *Dean Martin Summer Show, The*

VIC DAMONE SHOW, THE

Musical Variety
FIRST TELECAST: *July 2, 1956*
LAST TELECAST: *September 11, 1957*
BROADCAST HISTORY:
  Jul 1956–Sep 1956, CBS Mon 9:30–10:00
  Jul 1957–Sep 1957, CBS Wed 8:00–9:00
REGULARS:
  Vic Damone
  The Spellbinders (1957)
  The Tutti Camarata Orchestra (1956)
  The Bert Farber Orchestra (1957)

Singer Vic Damone spent the summer of 1956 filling in for *December Bride* with a musical variety show. In addition to songs by himself and his guests, it featured aspects of Vic's personal life and interaction with the guests, many of whom were off-screen friends. The following summer Vic returned on a different night with an expanded, full-hour variety show. The format of the 1957 series was more traditional than his first one had been, with musical and comedy numbers filling the entire hour and no side trips into Vic's personal life. A singing group, the Spellbinders, was featured regularly on the 1957 show.

VICEROY STAR THEATRE

Dramatic Anthology
FIRST TELECAST: *July 2, 1954*
LAST TELECAST: *September 24, 1954*
BROADCAST HISTORY:
  Jul 1954–Sep 1954, CBS Fri 10:00–10:30

The plays presented in this filmed summer anthology series were all on the melodramatic and suspenseful side and starred personalities from the motion-picture world. Appearing were Zachary Scott, Katy Jurado, Lynn Bari, and Dennis Morgan, among others.

VICTOR BORGE SHOW, THE

Comedy Variety
FIRST TELECAST: *February 3, 1951*
LAST TELECAST: *June 30, 1951*
BROADCAST HISTORY:
  Feb 1951–Jun 1951, NBC Sat 7:00–7:30
REGULARS:
  Victor Borge
  The Phil Ingalls Orchestra

Internationally known pianist and comic interpreter of music Victor Borge starred in this live variety series. His satirical interpretations of classical music were only one part of the show, however, and he did play at least one piece in a straight concert rendition each week. Perhaps his most famous routine, and one that he featured periodically, was "Phonetic Punctuation," in which each punctuation mark was represented by a different noise—"Ffftt!," "Sscht!," etc. When he read quickly through an entire paragraph, substituting "Ffftt's" and "Sscht's" for every dash, comma, and period, the effect could be hilarious.

Guest stars were also a regular feature of the show, and would chat with Borge in addition to performing.

VIDEO VILLAGE

Quiz/Audience Participation
FIRST TELECAST: *July 1, 1960*
LAST TELECAST: *September 16, 1960*
BROADCAST HISTORY:
  Jul 1960–Sep 1960, CBS Fri 9:00–9:30
EMCEE:
  Jack Narz
ASSISTANT:
  Joanne Copeland
ANNOUNCER:
  Ken Williams

In a novel approach to television game shows, *Video Village* was a living board game. The contestants were the pieces, moving from square to square as determined by the roll of a giant die in a chuck-a-luck cage. The roll was accomplished with the aid of a friend or relative of the contestant. Various cash and merchandise prizes were awarded for landing on specified squares, while landing on others might cause loss of a turn, having to answer questions, or moving to another part of the board. The first person to reach the end of the board was the winner and started over again with a new contestant. Emcee Jack Narz was the mayor, assistant Joanne Copeland the assistant mayor, and announcer Ken Williams the town crier. The daytime version of this series started one week after the nighttime version and remained on the air through June 1962.

Monty Hall took over for Jack Narz when he left the daytime version, and Eileen Barton similarly replaced Joanne Copeland. There was also a Saturday morning children's version, *Video Village Jr. Edition*, during the 1961–1962 season, with Hall and Barton and a collection of young contestants vying for prizes appropriate for children.

VILLAGE BARN

Musical Variety
FIRST TELECAST: *May 17, 1948*
LAST TELECAST: *May 29, 1950*
BROADCAST HISTORY:
  May 1948–Oct 1948, NBC Mon 9:10–10:00
  Oct 1948–Jan 1949, NBC Wed 10:10–11:00
  Jan 1949–May 1949, NBC Wed 8:30–9:00
  May 1949–Jul 1949, NBC Mon 10:00–10:30
  Jul 1949–Sep 1949, NBC Thu 10:00–10:30
  Jan 1950–May 1950, NBC Mon 9:30–10:00
EMCEE:
  Zebe Carver (1948)
  Dick Thomas & Dick Dudley (1948–1949)
  Dick Dudley (1949)

Bob Stanton (1949)
Ray Forrest (1949)
REGULARS:
  Romolo De Spirito (as The Road Agent, also
    known as The Masked Singer) (1949)
  Piute Pete (1948–1949)
  Pappy Howard and His Tumbleweed Gang
  Bill Long and His Ranch Girls

Country music and down-home humor originating
from New York's Village Barn, a popular night
spot located at 52 West 8th Street. This was perhaps the first regular series to originate live from
an actual nightclub. In addition to the music of
such groups as Pappy Howard and His Tumbleweed Gang, Harry Ranch and His Kernels of
Korn, and Bill Long's Ranch Girls, there was
square dancing (with calls by Piute Pete), audience participation in potato sack, hobby horse,
and kiddie-car races, and other unsophisticated
entertainment.

VINCENT LOPEZ
Musical Variety
FIRST TELECAST: *March 7, 1949*
LAST TELECAST: *July 22, 1950*
BROADCAST HISTORY:
  Mar 1949–May 1949, DUM Mon/Wed/Fri 6:45–
    7:00
  May 1949–Jul 1949, DUM Mon–Fri 6:45–7:00
  Jul 1949–Jun 1950, DUM Mon–Fri 7:30–7:45
  Jan 1950–Jul 1950, DUM Sat 8:00–8:30
REGULARS:
  Vincent Lopez
  Ann Warren (1950)
  Lee Russell (1950)
  Ray Barr
ANNOUNCER:
  Fred Scott

Veteran bandleader and pianist Vincent Lopez
("Lopez speaking!") was seen on two different
programs on the DuMont network from 1949–1950.
The first was an early-evening musical interlude,
running three to five nights a week with Lopez and
Barr on twin pianos. The other, seen during 1950,
was a full-fledged Saturday night variety show
called *Dinner Date with Vincent Lopez* and originating live from the Grill Room of the Hotel Taft
in New York, where Lopez had been holding forth
for many years. Featured was his full orchestra,
guest performers such as Cab Calloway, Arthur
Tracy, and Woody Herman, and his own regular
vocalists, Ann Warren and Lee Russell. In addition to serving as emcee, Lopez did numerous interviews, made song predictions, and improvised
original themes based on the letters or names of
viewers writing in.

VINCENT LOPEZ SHOW, THE
Music
FIRST TELECAST: *February 9, 1957*
LAST TELECAST: *March 9, 1957*

BROADCAST HISTORY:
  Feb 1957–Mar 1957, CBS Sat 7:00–7:30
REGULARS:
  Vincent Lopez
  Danny Davis
  Judy Lynn
  Johnny Messner
  Teddy Norman
  Eddie O'Connor
  Johnny Amorosa
  Joe Ortalano

In October 1956, six years after his departure from
DuMont, Vincent Lopez turned up with an early
Saturday evening music series on CBS' local sta-
tion in New York. After four highly successful
months, *The Vincent Lopez Show* expanded in
February from 45 minutes to an hour, with the
second half hour carried on the full CBS network.
Among the featured vocalists were several mem-
bers of the Lopez band—saxophonist Teddy Nor-
man, guitarist Eddie O'Connor, trumpet player
Johnny Amorosa, and trombonist Joe Ortalano.
Although it only lasted five weeks on the network,
The Vincent Lopez Show remained on the air locally until the end of April.

VIRGINIAN, THE
Western
FIRST TELECAST: *September 19, 1962*
LAST TELECAST: *September 8, 1971*
BROADCAST HISTORY:
  Sep 1962–Sep 1971, NBC Wed 7:30–9:00
CAST:
  Judge Henry Garth (1962–1966)... Lee J. Cobb
  The Virginian .... James Drury
  Trampas .... Doug McClure
  Steve (1962–1964) .... Gary Clarke
  Molly Wood (1962–1963) .... Pippa Scott
  Betsy (1962–1965) .... Roberta Shore
  Randy (1963–1966) .... Randy Boone
  Emmett Ryker (1964–1966, 1967–1968)
  .... Clu Gulager
  Belden (1964–1967) .... L. Q. Jones
  Jennifer (1965–1966) .... Diane Roter
  John Grainger (1966–1967) .. Charles Bickford
  Stacy Grainger (1966–1968) ...... Don Quine
  Elizabeth Grainger (1966–1967).... Sara Lane
  Sheriff Abbott (1967–1970) .... Ross Elliott
  Clay Grainger (1967–1968) ..... John McIntire
  Holly Grainger (1967–1968) ... Jeanette Nolan
  David Sutton (1968–1969) .... David Hartman
  Jim Horn (1969–1970) .... Tim Matheson
  Col. Alan MacKenzie (1970–1971)
  .... Stewart Granger
  Roy Tate (1970–1971)........... Lee Majors
  Parker (1970–1971) .... John McLiam

This long-running drama was the first 90-minute
Western series. It starred James Drury as the laconic, mysterious "Virginian," who never revealed his real name and who "forced his idea of
law and order on a Wyoming Territory commu-

nity in the 1890s"; and Doug McClure as the wild young cowhand Trampas. Setting for the saga was the Shiloh Ranch, owned successively by Judge Garth, the two Grainger brothers (John and Clay), and finally Col. Alan MacKenzie. Col. MacKenzie took over during the last season, at which time the program was retitled *The Men from Shiloh* and the historical period was moved up a few years.

The Virginian was one of the leading "adult Westerns," relying on strong characterizations by both regular cast and guest stars rather than on gimmicks. In many respects it resembled a weekly movie feature. Many actors and actresses appeared in regular supporting roles for varying lengths of time, among them David Hartman in 1968 and Lee Majors in 1970.

The Virginian was based on the classic 1902 novel of the same name by Owen Wister, which had been produced three times as a motion picture (the most famous being the 1929 version starring Gary Cooper and Walter Huston).

An interesting sidelight was that the original pilot for this series, produced in the late 1950s, cast Drury as a Western dandy replete with shiny hunting boots, skintight pants, lace cuffs, and a tiny pistol. It didn't sell, and so was remade several years later without the foppish accoutrements—to become one of TV's biggest hits.

VISE, THE
Suspense Anthology
FIRST TELECAST: *October 1, 1954*
LAST TELECAST: *December 16, 1955*
BROADCAST HISTORY:
  Oct 1954–Dec 1955, ABC Fri 9:30–10:00
HOST:
  Ron Randell

Filmed drama series produced in London, depicting people caught in "the vise" of fate due to their own misdeeds. Schemers, blackmailers, and other unseemly types always got their due in this program, and viewers invariably got a look at some very pretty girls, who always seemed to play roles in each of these internationally flavored stories. The actors were generally lesser-known British performers, but some talented newcomers who would later become internationally famous were seen here, including Honor Blackman, Patrick McGoohan, and Petula Clark. Australian actor Ron Randell was the host.

The series ended in December 1955, after which the time slot and the title *The Vise* were taken over by a new series of *Mark Saber* episodes.

VISIT WITH THE ARMED FORCES
Documentary
FIRST TELECAST: *July 3, 1950*
LAST TELECAST: *January 1, 1951*
BROADCAST HISTORY:
  Jul 1950–Jan 1951, DUM Mon 8:00–8:30

Documentary films about the armed forces.

VISITOR, THE
syndicated title for *Doctor, The*

VIVA VALDEZ
Situation Comedy
FIRST TELECAST: *May 31, 1976*
LAST TELECAST: *September 6, 1976*
BROADCAST HISTORY:
  May 1976–Sep 1976, ABC Mon 8:00–8:30
CAST:
  Luis Valdez .... Rodolfo Hoyos
  Sophia Valdez .... Carmen Zapata
  Victor Valdez .... James Victor
  Ernesto Valdez .... Nelson D. Cuevas
  Connie Valdez.............. Lisa Mordente
  Pepe Valdez.............. Claudio Martinez
  Jerry Ramirez .... Jorge Cervera, Jr.

Noisy "gang" comedy about a close-knit Mexican-American family living in East Los Angeles. Louis ran a plumbing business with his eldest son, Victor. Sophia was the mama; Ernesto, an artistic lad in training with the telephone company; Connie, the irrepressible teenager; and Pepe, the 12-year-old baseball fanatic. Jerry was a cousin newly arrived from Mexico.

VIVIEN KELLEMS
see *Power of Women, The*

VOICE OF FIRESTONE, THE
Music
FIRST TELECAST: *September 5, 1949*
LAST TELECAST: *June 16, 1963*
BROADCAST HISTORY:
  Sep 1949–Jun 1954, NBC Mon 8:30–9:00
  Jun 1954–Jun 1957, ABC Mon 8:30–9:00
  Sep 1957–Jun 1959, ABC Mon 9:00–9:30 (OS)
  Sep 1962–Jun 1963, ABC Sun 10:00–10:30
NARRATOR:
  John Daly (1958–1959)
REGULARS:
  Howard Barlow conducting the Firestone Concert Orchestra
THEME MUSIC:
  "If I Could Tell You" and "In My Garden," both composed by Mrs. Harvey Firestone

Radio's venerable Monday night program of classical and semiclassical music, which had been on the air since 1928, became a TV series in 1949, when regular simulcasts began with the radio program. It survived on TV for a total of twelve seasons, but not without sparking a bitter controversy over the role that ratings and mass-audience appeal should play in TV programming. It was canceled three times, eventually leaving the air permanently in 1963, a victim of the basic rule that on American television "best" is not enough—only "biggest" counts.

The format of *Voice* changed little over the years. Stars of grand opera were the usual guests, although occasionally more "popular" talent would also appear singing Broadway show tunes and pop standards. The 25th anniversary telecast, in 1953, was an especially gala affair, with speeches and performances by many of the great stars who had appeared on *Voice* over the years, including Eleanor Steber, Rise Stevens, Thomas L. Thomas, Brian Sullivan, Robert Rounseville, and Jerome Hines. Worthy causes were frequently promoted on the show, such as highway safety, 4-H, and the UN, and in 1954 there was an essay contest on the theme "I Speak for Democracy." The winner, a 16-year-old Akron, Ohio, schoolgirl, appeared on the program to read her essay.

Though the program was certainly prestigious, to be truthful it was a bit stiff—pleasing to hear, but sometimes boring to watch. Tuxedos and starched shirts were the order of the evening, with staging to match. There were few concessions to popular taste. During the early 1950s only occasional popular talent appeared (notably Jane Froman), but from 1958–1959 a new format was announced which struck a much more equal balance between the classics and the "better" pops on each show. Jo Stafford, Fred Waring, Xavier Cugat, and Gordon MacRae were among those who appeared, along with Carlos Montoya, the Philadelphia Symphony, the Ballet Russe of Monte Carlo, and the Vienna Boys' Choir from the "serious" side. John Daly, urbane and witty as always, was added as narrator.

A further change took place from 1962–1963 when Howard Barlow was phased out as permanent conductor (he still appeared occasionally) and a rotating roster of maestros was introduced. Most frequently seen were Arthur Fiedler, Wilfred Pelletier, and Harry John Brown. James McCracken made his network TV debut during this season, and Rudolf Nureyev also appeared.

Although the audience for *Voice* was relatively small by TV standards (about two to three million viewers per week), the appreciation of those who did watch, and the considerable prestige, made Firestone quite content to continue funding the show. But in 1954, after carrying *Voice* on Monday nights at 8:30 P.M. for 26 years (first on radio and then TV), NBC insisted that a change had to be made. The program's low ratings were affecting the entire Monday night NBC lineup, and the network was finding it impossible to sell the succeeding half hour. Firestone refused to budge, arguing that many of the program's faithful viewers would not be able to watch in a less desirable time period. So the show, both radio and TV versions, moved to ABC the following fall. ABC was at the time happy to have the business, but by 1959 that network too was beginning to taste big ratings in other parts of its schedule. A new, sales-oriented ABC management determined that *Voice* must move to 10:00 P.M. so as not to hurt the shows that followed it. Again, Firestone objected, and this time the show went off the air.

Though the audiences had been small, the hue and cry when *Voice* was dropped was deafening. Sen. Mike Monroney bitterly attacked ABC for following in the footsteps of NBC in dropping the

"best" of TV. There were threats of action through the FCC, and critics were unrelenting. ABC tried to appease them by putting on a similar program called *Music for a Summer Night* using the same producers, but with a smaller budget. It was not the same. All three networks offered various fringe time slots to *Voice*, which Firestone rejected. For an investment of more than $1 million per year, Firestone felt that it deserved the best. Finally in 1962, after a change of management, ABC took it back, this time at 10:00 P.M. Commendations were immediately forthcoming (Sen. Thomas E. Dodd: "You're bringing back *Voice of Firestone*, and I find that commendable"). But again "only" two and a half million viewers chose to watch, and by mid-1963 *Voice* was once again gone—this time for good.

VOICE OF FIRESTONE TELEVUES
Documentary
FIRST TELECAST: *April 10, 1944*
LAST TELECAST: *January 20, 1947*
BROADCAST HISTORY:
> Apr 1944–Jan 1947, NBC Mon Various 10–15 minutes

The Firestone Tire and Rubber Co. was one of television's earliest advertisers, beginning this Monday night series of "Televues" on NBC's New York station on November 29, 1943, and sponsoring it continuously for more than three years. The presentations were a varied selection of short documentary films on different subjects, such as dairy farming, football, vocational guidance, etc. There was a live opening and closing for each show.

The program became one of the first network series when NBC began feeding its Monday night schedule to stations in Philadelphia and Schenectady in April 1944.

VOLUME ONE
Dramatic Anthology
FIRST TELECAST: *June 16, 1949*
LAST TELECAST: *July 21, 1949*
BROADCAST HISTORY:
> Jun 1949–Jul 1949, ABC Thu 9:30–10:00
PRODUCER/DIRECTOR/NARRATOR:
> Wyllis Cooper

Famed radio writer Wyllis Cooper tried his hand at television in this six-telecast series of original dramas. Cooper was the Rod Serling of radio, producing eerie, surrealistic stories of horror and suspense, often based more on psychological terror than on actual violence. He had created, among other shows, *Lights Out* and *Quiet, Please*. His first telecast starred Jack Lescoulie, Nancy Sheridan, and Frank Thomas, Jr., in an intelligent psychological thriller which drew rave reviews. Nevertheless the series lasted for only the scheduled six weeks.

Each telecast was numbered: "Volume One, Number One," "Volume One, Number Two," etc.

The radio title *Quiet, Please* was originally to be used for the series, but had to be dropped at the last minute.

VOYAGE TO THE BOTTOM OF THE SEA
Science Fiction
FIRST TELECAST: *September 14, 1964*
LAST TELECAST: *September 15, 1968*
BROADCAST HISTORY:
   Sep 1964–Sep 1965, ABC Mon 7:30–8:30
   Sep 1965–Sep 1968, ABC Sun 7:00–8:00
CAST:
   Adm. Harriman Nelson ..... Richard Basehart
   Cdr./Capt. Lee Crane .... David Hedison
   Lt. Cdr. Chip Morton .... Robert Dowdell
   Chief Petty Officer Curley Jones (1964–1965)
   .... Henry Kulky
   Chief Sharkey (1965–1968) ...... Terry Becker
   Stu Riley (1965–1967) .... Allan Hunt
   Kowalsky .... Del Monroe
   Crewman Patterson .... Paul Trinka
   Crewman Sparks .... Arch Whiting
   Doctor .... Richard Bull
CREATOR/PRODUCER:
   Irwin Allen

One of TV's all-time favorite science-fiction adventure series, this followed the exploits of the officers and men of the *Seaview,* a glass-nosed atomic submarine that roamed the seven seas fighting villains both human and alien. The *Seaview* was the brainchild of retired Adm. Harriman Nelson, director of the super-secret Nelson Institute of Marine Research at Santa Barbara, California. The time was ten years into the future. Originally there were two subs, but the *Seaview's* sister ship, the *Polidor,* was sunk in the third episode. Nelson's chief assistant and the commander of the *Seaview* then became Cdr. Lee Crane (he was promoted to captain in the second season). Their opponents included such dastardly villains as Dr. Gamma (Theodore Marcuse) and the sneaky Prof. Multiple (Vincent Price)—he came aboard under the pretext of presenting a puppet show, only to have the puppets come to life and run amok—plus assorted unreconstructed Nazis, lost worlds, giant orchids quivering with alien energy, globular masses of "pure intelligence" that threatened to devour the entire sub, and other fantastic creatures (remarkable, what's down there!). Some episodes were less obvious. On one, the *Seaview* picked up Old John (Carroll O'Connor), an enigmatic stranger found floating placidly in a rowboat in the middle of the Pacific.

During the second season the emphasis on gadgetry was increased, with the *Seaview* gaining the *Sea Crab,* a self-propelled two-man explorer, and the *Flying Fish,* a mini-sub which could fly through the air at fantastic speeds. Some cast changes were made, including the addition of fast-talking, handsome young surfer Stu Riley, as a kind of on-shore ally.

The series was based on Irwin Allen's 1961 movie of the same name, and used many of the sets from that film.

VOYAGERS
Science Fiction
FIRST TELECAST: *October 3, 1982*
LAST TELECAST: *July 31, 1983*
BROADCAST HISTORY:
   Oct 1982–Mar 1983, NBC Sun 7:00–8:00
   Jun 1983–Jul 1983, NBC Sun 7:00–8:00
CAST:
   Phineas Bogg .... Jon-Erik Hexum
   Jeffrey Jones .... Meeno Peluce

Designed primarily to appeal to children, this educational science-fiction series chronicled the adventures of two time travelers taking part in great events of human history. The show began with the curious premise that a group of trained travelers, or "Voyagers," journeyed back and forth through the ages making sure that great events turned out as intended. Phineas Bogg was one such Voyager, but a somewhat klutzy one. When his Omni—his time-travel device—malfunctioned, Phineas crashed into the Manhattan bedroom of young Jeffrey Jones. Phineas' guidebook to history was then eaten by Jeffrey's dog, Ralph, leaving the traveler without his source of information on how great events were supposed to turn out. Fortunately young Jeffrey was a history buff, and knew more about the subject than his embarrassed guest, so he agreed to travel with him and help him on assignments.

Most episodes featured two or three notable moments in history, with the Voyagers on hand to keep things on the right track. They gave directions to Lewis and Clark, helped General MacArthur get away from Pearl Harbor just before the Japanese attack in 1941, made sure the baby Moses was discovered by the Pharaoh's daughter, got the Wright Brothers back to working on their airplane, prevented President Teddy Roosevelt from being killed by Billy the Kid, and helped Spartacus escape from jail to lead a revolt against Roman oppression. Because Phineas' Omni was damaged, they could not go any later than the year 1982, except when the Voyagers brought them back to Phineas' home time (never specified) to try him for violating the Voyager code by using Jeffrey as a guide (he was acquitted). At the conclusion of each show, series star Meeno Peluce would suggest to young viewers that they go to the library to get more information about the historical periods featured on that episode.

W

W.E.B.
Drama
FIRST TELECAST: *September 13, 1978*
LAST TELECAST: *October 5, 1978*
BROADCAST HISTORY:
Sep 1978, NBC Wed 10:00–11:00
Sep 1978–Oct 1978, NBC Thu 10:00–11:00
CAST:
Ellen Cunningham .... Pamela Bellwood
Jack Kiley .... Alex Cord
Gus Dunlap .... Richard Basehart
Dan Costello .... Andrew Prine
Walter Matthews .... Howard Witt
Harvey Pearlstein .... Lee Wilkof
Christine .... Tisch Raye
Kevin .... Peter Coffield

Television showed the ability to caricature even itself, in this prime-time soap opera set behind the scenes at a "major television network"—Trans Atlantic Broadcasting. Ellen Cunningham, an ambitious, talented female executive who had clawed her way up in a man's world, was head of Special Events Programming. Surrounding her was an executive suite full of unsavory characters: Jack Kiley, the ruthless head of programming; Gus Dunlap, news chief and a drunken has-been; Dan Costello, fast-talking, inebriated sales chief; Walter Matthews, hard-driving head of operations; and Harvey Pearlstein, the research head obsessed with ratings. There was plenty of backbiting, maneuvering, and high-level treachery behind the smiling screen at T.A.B. This series was no doubt inspired by the movie *Network,* and was produced by Lin Bolen, who in real life had been one of the industry's first female programming chiefs (at NBC).

WKRP IN CINCINNATI
Situation Comedy
FIRST TELECAST: *September 18, 1978*
LAST TELECAST: *September 20, 1982*
BROADCAST HISTORY:
Sep 1978–Nov 1978, CBS Mon 8:00–8:30
Jan 1979–Dec 1979, CBS Mon 9:30–10:00
Dec 1979–Jul 1980, CBS Mon 8:00–8:30
Jul 1980–Aug 1980, CBS Mon 8:30–9:00
Aug 1980–Sep 1980, CBS Sat 8:00–8:30
Sep 1980–Oct 1980, CBS Mon 9:30–10:00
Nov 1980–May 1981, CBS Sat 8:00–8:30
Jun 1981–Sep 1981, CBS Mon 8:00–8:30
Oct 1981–Jan 1982, CBS Wed 8:30–9:00
Jan 1982–Feb 1982, CBS Wed 8:00–8:30
Mar 1982–Apr 1982, CBS Wed 9:00–9:30
Jun 1982–Sep 1982, CBS Mon 8:30–9:00
CAST:
Andy Travis .... Gary Sandy
Arthur Carlson ("Big Guy") .... Gordon Jump
Jennifer Marlowe .... Loni Anderson
Les Nessman .... Richard Sanders
Gordon Sims (Venus Flytrap) ..... Tim Reid
Herb Tarlek .... Frank Bonner
Bailey Quarters .... Jan Smithers
Johnny Caravella (Dr. Johnny Fever)
.... Howard Hesseman
Lillian "Mama" Carlson (pilot only)
.... Sylvia Sidney
Lillian "Mama" Carlson (1979–1982)
.... Carol Bruce

The arrival of a new program director, Andy Travis, brought sudden and dramatic changes to WKRP, a Cincinnati radio station that had been losing money for years by playing sedate music. Andy's decision to turn WKRP into a "top 40" rock 'n' roll station alienated its elderly audience, and also its few sponsors, such as the Shady Hill Rest Home and Barry's Fashions for the Short and Portly. It also created a trying situation for Arthur Carlson, the inept and bumbling general manager who held his job only because his mother owned the station. But Mother Carlson, who had dollar signs in her eyes, decided to give Andy's plan a try—as long as the station turned a profit.

The staff of WKRP was full of offbeat characters. Les Nessman was the naive, gullible, and pompous news director, more concerned with his farm reports than with national and international stories. Bailey Quarters was Andy's enthusiastic young assistant, who handled billing and traffic and was eventually given the added responsibilities of backup news reporter working with Les. The two WKRP disc jockeys seen regularly were morning man Dr. Johnny Fever, a jive-talking counterculture type who seemed constantly spaced out, and night man Venus Flytrap, a hip black who had worked with Andy at other stations.

Jennifer Marlowe, the sexy but efficient receptionist, actually had a lot to do with holding the station together—she knew far more about what was going on than did her boss, Mr. Carlson. Loni Anderson, who played Jennifer, quickly became the star of the show, and one of the major sex symbols of the late 1970s. The Farrah Fawcett-Majors posters of a few years earlier gave way to posters of the buxom Loni. She guested constantly on other programs, and soon landed the juicy role of Jayne Mansfield in a made-for-television movie about the life of that sex symbol of an earlier era. All the adulation went to her—or her agent's—head, and, like Farrah, she quickly demanded a huge increase in salary or she would leave the show. Unlike Farrah, she got it, and stayed.

The final regular was Herb Tarlek, WKRP's high-pressure advertising salesman who, though married, spent much of his time making passes at Jennifer. He proved to be more talk than action, however, as he was totally intimidated when she indicated she was willing to take him up on his offer in one touching episode. Station owner Mrs.

Carlson was a constant threat to them all but, fortunately, only showed up occasionally, usually to complain about something they either were or weren't doing with the station.

WACKIEST SHIP IN THE ARMY, THE
War Adventure
FIRST TELECAST: *September 19, 1965*
LAST TELECAST: *September 4, 1966*
BROADCAST HISTORY:
Sep 1965–Sep 1966, NBC Sun 10:00–11:00
CAST:
Major Simon Butcher .... Jack Warden
Lt. (j.g.) Richard "Rip" Riddle .. Gary Collins
Chief Petty Officer Willie Miller
.... Mike Kellin
Gunner's Mate Sherman Nagurski
.... Rudy Solari
Ship's Cook Charles Tyler....... Don Penny
Radioman Patrick Hollis .... Mark Slade
Machinist's Mate Seymour Trivers
.... Fred Smoot
Gen. Cross .... William Zuckert
Admiral Vincent Beckett ..... Charles Irving

In the spring of 1942, only months after the Japanese bombing of Pearl Harbor, the government of New Zealand presented to the United States the *Kiwi*, a 70-year-old twin-masted schooner. Obsolete and badly in need of repairs, the ship was staffed with a token crew while the U.S. Navy tried to figure out what to do with it. The navy soon discovered that it possessed certain unique qualities that made it a useful espionage weapon. Its wooden hull did not show up on radar, its sailing power did not register on sonar, and its shallow draft allowed it to travel in waters not deep enough for larger ships. And so the *Kiwi* went to war. It was commanded by young Lt. Rip Riddle when at sea and by Maj. Simon Butcher of the Army when in port, a situation which caused numerous problems because Rip and Simon had very different views on war strategy, women, protocol, and their respective roles on the ship. Complicating things even more was the fact that Maj. Butcher, although higher in rank than Lt. Riddle, had to report to the younger man whenever the *Kiwi* was at sea, while their roles were reversed whenever it made port. The adventures of the crew in the South Pacific during the early days of the war constituted the stories, which were based on the real-life exploits of the *Echo*, a leaky two-masted schooner which New Zealand's government gave to the U.S. in 1942. The story of the *Echo* had been made into a comedy-adventure movie in 1960.

WACKY WORLD OF JONATHAN WINTERS, THE
Comedy Variety
BROADCAST HISTORY:
Syndicated only
30 minutes
Produced: *1972–1974* (52 episodes)
Released: *Fall 1972*
REGULARS:
Jonathan Winters
Marian Mercer
Mary Gregory
Soul Sisters (1972–1973)
The Golddiggers (1973–1974)
Van Alexander Orchestra

Comedian Jonathan Winters, who has had a number of network series (see Index), returned to TV in 1972 with this syndicated comedy variety show. The emphasis was on improvisational sketches, with Maudie Frickert and the other fanciful Winters characters appearing frequently. There was a regular supporting cast in the first season, and multiple guest appearances by John Davidson, Tony Orlando and Dawn, Charo, the Staple Singers, John Stewart, the Ding-a-Lings, and Lynn Anderson.

WAGON TRAIN
Western
FIRST TELECAST: *September 18, 1957*
LAST TELECAST: *September 5, 1965*
BROADCAST HISTORY:
Sep 1957–Sep 1962, NBC Wed 7:30–8:30
Sep 1962–Sep 1963, ABC Wed 7:30–8:30
Sep 1963–Sep 1964, ABC Mon 8:30–10:00
Sep 1964–Sep 1965, ABC Sun 7:30–8:30
CAST:
Major Seth Adams (1957–1961)... Ward Bond
Flint McCullough (1957–1962) . Robert Horton
Bill Hawks .... Terry Wilson
Charlie Wooster .... Frank McGrath
Duke Shannon (1961–1964)....... Scott Miller
Christopher Hale (1961–1965) .. John McIntire
Barnaby West (1963–1965).... Michael Burns
Cooper Smith (1963–1965) ..... Robert Fuller

Wagon Train was one of the most popular "big" Western series during the heyday of TV Westerns, in the late 1950s and early 1960s. It was big in scope (the whole American West, it seemed), big in cast (many top-name guests), and big in format (60 minutes most seasons, 90 minutes in one). The setting was a California-bound wagon train in the post–Civil War days, starting out each season from "St. Joe" (St. Joseph, Missouri) and making its way west until reaching California in the spring. In between there were endless adventures on the vast, Indian-controlled Great Plains, the endless deserts, and the towering passes of the Rocky Mountains. But what made *Wagon Train* work were the characters who passed in and out of its episodes. The program was actually a series of character studies, each week revolving around a different member of the party or a different person encountered by the train along the way. Some were God-fearin' settlers, others young adventurers, others scoundrels. The regulars in the cast, who composed the "staff" of the wagon train, were seen in co-starring or some-times even secondary roles.

Wagon Train had only two wagonmasters in its eight years of crisscrossing the country. The first was fatherly Major Adams, replaced in the spring of 1961 by Chris Hale (actor Ward Bond had died the previous November in the middle of shooting the 1960–1961 season's episodes). Flint McCullough was the original frontier scout who rode out ahead to clear the way and make peace, if possible, with often unfriendly Indians. When Robert Horton left the series (supposedly he was "fed up" with Westerns), McCullough was replaced by Duke Shannon and young Cooper Smith. Bill Hawks went all the way as the assistant wagon-master and lead wagon driver, as did grizzled old Charlie Wooster as the cook. Barnaby West joined the regular cast during the last couple of seasons as a 13-year-old orphan boy found trudging along the trail heading west on his own.

Those were the continuing cast members, but the regular infusion of guest stars and the focus on different personalities in each episode made *Wagon Train* seem more like a new Western film every week than an ordinary TV series. The series took a season to catch on, but in its second year it was in the top ten. After three years of placing a close second to *Gunsmoke*, it became the number-one program on television in the 1961–1962 season.

Reruns of the episodes featuring Ward Bond aired as part of the ABC weekday daytime lineup under the title *Major Adams—Trailmaster* from September 1963 to September 1965 and on Sunday afternoons from January 1963 to May 1964.

WAIT TILL YOUR FATHER GETS HOME
Cartoon
BROADCAST HISTORY:
Syndicated only
30 minutes
Produced: *1972–1974* (48 episodes)
Released: *Fall 1972*
VOICES:
Harry Boyle .... Tom Bosley
Irma Boyle .... Joan Gerber
Alice Boyle .... Kristina Holland
Chet Boyle .... David Hayward
Jamie Boyle .... Jackie Haley
Ralph .... Jack Burns

This rather unsubtle animated comedy was an attempt to cash in on the enormous success of *All in the Family*. Harry Boyle was a conservative businessman-father who was continually exasperated by the excesses of his hippie son, Chet, and sexually liberated daughter, Alice. His allies were obedient youngest son, Jamie, and Neanderthal neighbor, Ralph, who gave his family close-order drill against the day of the Communist invasion. Wife Irma was neutral.

A good many celebrities appeared on the show, sometimes voicing cartoon representations of themselves. Among them were Don Knotts, Phyllis Diller, Don Adams, Rich Little, Jonathan Winters, and Monty Hall.

WAITING FOR THE BREAK
Variety
FIRST TELECAST: *March 18, 1950*
LAST TELECAST: *April 8, 1950*
BROADCAST HISTORY:
Mar 1950–Apr 1950, NBC Sat 7:30–8:00
HOST:
Hank Ladd

Four-week variety series featuring the understudies and chorus people from current Broadway hits, performing scenes and songs from their shows.

WALKING TALL
Police Drama
FIRST TELECAST: *January 17, 1981*
LAST TELECAST: *June 6, 1981*
BROADCAST HISTORY:
Jan 1981–Feb 1981, NBC Sat 9:00–10:00
Mar 1981–Apr 1981, NBC Tue 10:00–11:00
Apr 1981–Jun 1981, NBC Sat 10:00–11:00
CAST:
Sheriff Buford Pusser .... Bo Svenson
Michael Pusser .... Rad Daly
Dwana Pusser .... Heather McAdams
Carl Pusser .... Walter Barnes
Deputy Aaron Fairfax ...... Harold Sylvester
Deputy Grady Spooner .... Jeff Lester
Deputy Joan Litton .... Courtney Pledger

Buford Pusser was a man with a deeply moral sense of right and wrong, which he enforced none too subtly with a large club. The sheriff of rural McNeal County, Tennessee, he was a big, two-fisted brawler who often used force to convince wrongdoers of the error of their ways. The local purveyors of gambling and prostitution hated Buford, who, carrying a four-foot-long club to mete out justice (his "pacifier"), was certainly an imposing sight. He had been beaten, threatened, and shot at—one assassination attempt had killed his wife, Pauline, by mistake, leaving Buford to raise his two young children with the help of his father, Carl.

There had been a real Buford Pusser, and his actual exploits were brought to theaters in 1973 in the film version of *Walking Tall*. Joe Don Baker played the role in the original film, and Bo Svenson took it over in the two sequels. Pusser was to have played himself in the second movie sequel, but died in an automobile crash before the film went into production. Although it could not be proven, the nature of the crash led some to suspect that the criminals had finally gotten rid of him.

WALT DISNEY
Anthology

FIRST TELECAST: *October 27, 1954*
LAST TELECAST:
BROADCAST HISTORY:
  Oct 1954–Sep 1958, ABC Wed 7:30–8:30
  Sep 1958–Sep 1959, ABC Fri 8:00–9:00
  Sep 1959–Sep 1960, ABC Fri 7:30–8:00
  Sep 1960–Sep 1961, ABC Sun 6:30–7:30
  Sep 1961–Aug 1975, NBC Sun 7:30–8:30
  Sep 1975–Sep 1981, NBC Sun 7:00–8:00
  Sep 1981–Jan 1983, CBS Sat 8:00–9:00
  Jan 1983–Feb 1983, CBS Tue 8:00–9:00
  Jul 1983–Sep 1983, CBS Sat 8:00–9:00
  Feb 1986–Sep 1987, ABC Sun 7:00–9:00
  *Sep 1987–   *, ABC Sun 7:00–8:00
EXECUTIVE PRODUCER/HOST:
  Walt Disney (1954–1966)
  Michael Eisner (1986–   )

Walt Disney is the longest-running prime-time series in network history. It is also historic for another reason. When it premiered in 1954 it marked the first big plunge by a major Hollywood movie studio into television production. Disney changed the face of television in many ways. Previously the big studios, afraid of competition from the new medium, were television's sworn enemies, not only refusing to produce programming but denying TV the use of any of the latest or best theatrical films. Until Disney led the way, the lavish movie-style series so familiar today were an impossibility.

Luring Disney into television was a major coup for struggling ABC. Both CBS and NBC had negotiated with the moviemaker, but neither could agree to his seemingly exorbitant terms. Among other things, Mr. Disney wanted the network to help finance his proposed amusement park in Anaheim, California. Only ABC was willing to take a chance, paying a then-fabulous $500,000 plus $50,000 per program. ABC won big. Both the TV series and the park, Disneyland, were fabulous successes. The program *Disneyland* was, in fact, ABC's first major hit series.

Disneyland consisted of a mixture of cartoons, live-action adventures, documentaries, and nature stories, some made especially for TV and some former theatrical releases. A liberal number of repeat telecasts was included with each season's originals. At first *Disneyland* was divided into four rotating segments, listed at the beginning of each week's show by the cartoon character Tinkerbell (from *Peter Pan*). They were Frontierland, Fantasyland, Tomorrowland, and Adventureland. The first telecast was a variety show, but what really got *Disneyland* off the ground was a three-part series of Frontierland adventures which began less than two months later—*Davy Crockett*. The exploits of the famed real-life frontiersman of the early 1800s took America by storm. The title role was played by Fess Parker (whom Disney had seen playing a bit part in the horror movie *Them*). Buddy Ebsen played his sidekick, George Russel. *Davy Crockett* lifted

Fess Parker from obscurity to stardom overnight. Davy's trademark coonskin cap and other Crockett merchandise sold like wildfire to the nation's youth, and a recording of the theme song, "The Ballad of Davy Crockett," was one of the biggest hits of the mid-1950s. (Fess Parker recorded the song, but ironically a minor-league singer named Bill Hayes beat him to it and had the big hit recording.)

The three original Crockett episodes were "Davy Crockett, Indian Fighter" (first aired December 15, 1954), "Davy Crockett Goes to Congress" (January 26, 1955), and "Davy Crockett at the Alamo" (February 23, 1955). Crockett was killed in the last episode, which created an embarrassing situation when the public began clamoring for more. Eventually a few more episodes were made, depicting incidents earlier in his life, but Crockett, for some reason, never did become a series in its own right.

Flushed with the spectacular success of Davy Crockett, Disney tried several more times to base multi-part stories on actual Western heroes. In 1958 there was "The Saga of Andy Burnett" (Jerome Courtland as the young frontiersman), followed by "The Nine Lives of Elfego Baca" (starring Robert Loggia as a peace-loving but determined lawman in Tombstone, Arizona), "Texas John Slaughter" (Tom Tryon in the lead role), and "Swamp Fox" (Leslie Nielsen as Francis Marion, the Revolutionary War hero). Even Fess Parker got another shot at superstardom playing John Grayson in the film *Westward Ho! The Wagons*, which later turned up on the TV series. That time Parker made sure he got his recording of the theme song out before Bill Hayes did, but it didn't matter because neither the show nor the song was a hit.

There were many other presentations on *Disneyland* beyond the boundaries of Frontierland. Some were adaptations of classics such as *Alice in Wonderland*, *The Legend of Sleepy Hollow* (narrated by Bing Crosby), *Robin Hood*, *Treasure Island*, and *Babes in Toyland* (with Annette Funicello, Tommy Sands, and Ray Bolger). The animated shows tended to feature well-known Disney characters such as Mickey Mouse (voice provided by Walt himself), Donald Duck, Pluto, and Goofy, sometimes in full-length stories, sometimes "narrating" documentaries on various subjects. When the series moved to NBC in 1961 a new character was added, Professor Ludwig Von Drake (voice by Paul Frees), who was supposed to be Donald's eccentric uncle and who co-hosted many of the shows with Walt.

Documentaries within the series covered subjects ranging from space travel to how cartoons are made, and were always entertainingly presented. And of course there were plenty of plugs for the Disneyland park and, later, its Florida counterpart, Disney World, including reports on construction in progress, big opening galas, and, later, on-location variety shows. One of the latter,

"Disneyland After Dark" in April 1962, marked the network TV debut of the Osmond Brothers, who were then performing at the park.

Every season of *Disney* brought all types of presentations, but the mix changed with the times. In the late 1950s and early 1960s there were many Westerns and other early-American adventures. Then the emphasis shifted more to nature stories, often about animals and their young human companions. *Disney,* in fact, produced quite a menagerie of nonhuman "stars," to wit: "Sammy, the Way Out Seal," "Greta, the Misfit Greyhound," "Ida, the Offbeat Eagle," "Joker, the Amiable Ocelot," "Boomerang, Dog of Many Talents," "Inky the Crow," "The Horse in the Grey Flannel Suit," "Salty, the Hijacked Harbor Seal," "Ringo, the Refugee Raccoon," "Stub, Best Cow Dog in the West," "Deacon, the High Noon Dog," "Twister, Bull from the Sky," and "Lefty, the Ding-a-Ling Linx." Not to mention "The Horse with the Flying Tail" and "The Hound That Thought He Was a Raccoon." The most frequent narrator of these animal stories was cowboy star Rex Allen, although producer-writer Winston Hibler and others were also used.

For many years Walt Disney himself introduced the telecasts, and it was through television that the master showman became a national celebrity. He was such an institution that it was a distinct shock when Walt Disney passed away suddenly on December 15, 1966. On the next Sunday's telecast the prefilmed introductions by Disney were deleted, and tributes by Chet Huntley and Dick Van Dyke were substituted. But the program itself went on as planned—appropriately, it was a tour led by Walt himself through his pride and joy, Disneyland.

In subsequent seasons there was no opening and closing host, simply voice-over narration by announcer Dick Wesson.

In later years *Disney* suffered the same fate as many long-running series, gradually declining in audience because viewers apparently took it for granted, or considered it "old hat." The fact that such programs might continue to provide first-rate entertainment meant little in the quest for "novelty." Each year *Disney*'s renewal became more doubtful until NBC finally announced its cancellation in 1981. The Disney magic refused to die, however. The series was picked up by CBS for two seasons (1981–1983), and then after a two-year hiatus returned to its original network, ABC. This latter version consisted of films (theatrical and made-for-TV), and revived the custom of specially filmed introductions by the head of the Disney studio—now a young executive named Michael D. Eisner.

The Disney series was originally titled *Disneyland,* changed to *Walt Disney Presents* in 1958, to *Walt Disney's Wonderful World of Color* in 1961 (when many of the films previously seen in black-and-white on ABC were repeated in color on NBC), to *The Wonderful World of Disney* in 1969,

and to *Disney's Wonderful World* in 1979. The 1981 CBS version was titled simply *Walt Disney,* and the 1986 ABC revival, *The Disney Sunday Movie.*

WALTER CRONKITE'S UNIVERSE
see *Universe*

WALTER WINCHELL FILE, THE
Crime Anthology
FIRST TELECAST: *October 2, 1957*
LAST TELECAST: *March 28, 1958*
BROADCAST HISTORY:
  Oct 1957–Dec 1957, ABC Wed 9:30–10:00
  Jan 1958–Mar 1958, ABC Fri 10:00–10:30
HOST/NARRATOR:
  Walter Winchell

The crime dramas presented in this anthology were adapted from stories that Walter Winchell had uncovered while working the police beat in New York City. In addition to hosting the show, he functioned as the narrator, tying together the various elements that led to the drama that was actually shown on the air.

WALTER WINCHELL SHOW, THE
News/Commentary
FIRST TELECAST: *October 5, 1952*
LAST TELECAST: *November 6, 1960*
BROADCAST HISTORY:
  Oct 1952–Apr 1953, ABC Sun 6:45–7:00
  Apr 1953–Jul 1953, ABC Sun 6:30–6:45
  Sep 1953–Jan 1954, ABC Mon 7:00–7:15
  Sep 1953–Jun 1955, ABC Sun 9:00–9:15
  Oct 1960–Nov 1960, ABC Sun 10:30–11:00
REPORTER:
  Walter Winchell

Syndicated newspaper columnist Walter Winchell had a highly successful radio series in the 1930s and 1940s which gave him the opportunity to report the headlines he deemed important in his uniquely fast-paced and highly opinionated style. His crusades and grudges were legendary, but everything was delivered with a theatricality (Winchell had once been in vaudeville) that kept listeners entranced. After the war he went on an extended crusade against Communism, and eventually became a staunch supporter of Senator Joseph McCarthy.

In the fall of 1952 Winchell began simulcasting his famous Sunday night news show. The sight of the grizzled reporter was a surprise to many viewers. He always wore his hat while on the air, he was noticeably older (in his 50s) than many had imagined, and he personally ran the telegraph key that was used to punctuate the news and gossip of the world that he related (though the "code" he punched out was actually meaningless garble). Even his opening line, "Good evening, Mr. and Mrs. North and South America and all the ships at sea . . . let's go to press," seemed somewhat dated on TV. The television version of his news show, although not the success that his radio program had been, remained on the air until Winchell resigned in a huff in 1955 after a disagreement with ABC executives. Five years later, it was brought back in a longer version. The revival was an immediate failure and lasted for only six weeks.

Winchell died in 1972.

WALTER WINCHELL SHOW, THE
Variety
FIRST TELECAST: *October 5, 1956*
LAST TELECAST: *December 28, 1956*
BROADCAST HISTORY:
  Oct 1956–Dec 1956, NBC Fri 8:30–9:00
HOST:
  Walter Winchell

In the fall of 1956, NBC gave Walter Winchell the opportunity to show that he could be as successful as his fellow columnist Ed Sullivan as the host of a weekly live variety show. The program originated from New York for its first nine weeks and then moved to Hollywood. Despite the ability of Winchell to attract as guests show-business celebrities who owed him favors, and a reasonably well-paced production, the series never caught on and was canceled after 13 weeks.

WALTONS, THE
Drama
FIRST TELECAST: *September 14, 1972*
LAST TELECAST: *August 20, 1981*
BROADCAST HISTORY:
  Sep 1972–Aug 1981, CBS Thu 8:00–9:00
CAST:
  John Walton................... Ralph Waite
  Olivia Walton (1972–1980).. Michael Learned
  Zeb (Grandpa) Walton (1972–1978)
  .... Will Geer
  Esther (Grandma) Walton (1972–1979)
  ....Ellen Corby
  John Boy Walton (1972–1977)
  .... Richard Thomas
  John Boy Walton (1979–1981)
  .... Robert Wightman
  Mary Ellen Walton Willard
  ....Judy Norton-Taylor
  Jim-Bob Walton .... David W. Harper
  Elizabeth Walton .... Kami Cotler
  Jason Walton................. Jon Walmsley
  Erin Walton ..... Mary Elizabeth McDonough
  Ben Walton .... Eric Scott
  Ike Godsey .... Joe Conley
  Corabeth Godsey (1974–1981)
  .... Ronnie Claire Edwards
  Sheriff Ep Bridges .... John Crawford
  Mamie Baldwin .... Helen Kleeb
  Emily Baldwin .... Mary Jackson
  Verdie Foster............... Lynn Hamilton
  Rev. Matthew Fordwick (1972–1977)
  .... John Ritter

Rosemary Hunter Fordwick (1973–1977)
  .... Mariclare Costello
Yancy Tucker (1972–1979) .... Robert Donner
Flossie Brimmer (1972–1977) .. Nora Marlowe
Maude Gormsley (1973–1979) .... Merie Earle
Dr. Curtis Willard (1976–1978) ... Tom Bower
Rev. Hank Buchanan (1977–1978) .. Peter Fox
J. D. Pickett (1978–1981) ..... Lewis Arquette
John Curtis Willard (alternating; 1978–1981)
  .... Marshall Reed
John Curtis Willard (alternating; 1978–1981)
  .... Michael Reed
Cindy Brunson Walton (1979–1981)
  .... Leslie Winston
Rose Burton (1979–1981).......... Peggy Rea
Serena Burton (1979–1980) .... Martha Nix
Jeffrey Burton (1979–1980) .... Keith Mitchell
Toni Hazleton (1981) .... Lisa Harrison
Arlington Wescott Jones (Jonesy) (1981)
  .... Richard Gilliland
NARRATOR:
  Earl Hamner, Jr.

Life in the South during the Depression was the subject of *The Waltons*. John and Olivia Walton and their seven children all lived together on Walton's Mountain, in the Blue Ridge Mountains of rural Jefferson County, Virginia. The family's modest income came from the lumber mill run by John and Grandpa Zeb. It was a close-knit family, with everyone helping out most of the time, and moralistic homilies abounded. There was no sex, no violence—just a warm family drama. Everything was seen through the eyes of John Boy, the oldest son, who had wanted to be a novelist for as long as he could remember. After high school he had enrolled as an English major at the local college, and at the start of the 1976–1977 season he began publishing his own local paper, *The Blue Ridge Chronicle*. By the end of the season, when his novel had been accepted by a publisher, he decided to move to New York. That season had been full of changes, including the marriage of Mary Ellen, who was in nursing school, to young Dr. Curtis Willard in November, and leading to the birth of their baby in 1978.

At the start of the 1977–1978 season *The Waltons* moved out of the Depression and into World War II. Young Rev. Fordwick enlisted in the army (John Ritter, who played the role, had a starring role in ABC's *Three's Company* that season) and was replaced by young Rev. Buchanan. Grandma Walton was ill (actress Ellen Corby had suffered a stroke) and was not seen until the last episode of the season, when she finally came home to Walton's Mountain, even though she was still partially incapacitated. The reunion was tearful, but brief. In April 1978, shortly after the close of the regular season, actor Will Geer, who played Grandpa Walton, died at the age of 76.

The 1978–1979 season saw much suffering on Walton's Mountain. Mary Ellen's husband, Curt, was killed in the Japanese attack on Pearl Harbor, and Olivia found out she had tuberculosis and went to a sanitarium for treatment (Michael Learned's contract had expired and she asked to be written out of the show to pursue other roles). In the spring Ben eloped with a young girl named Cindy. Olivia returned from the sanitarium and went off to a domestic army hospital to serve as a nurse. With Olivia gone and Grandpa having passed away, Olivia's cousin Rose arrived to run the Walton household—adding her two grandchildren to the group. Jason, John Boy, and Ben were all in the military, and a shortage of both materials and help forced John Walton to close his lumber mill temporarily. As the war drew to a close Jason got engaged to WAC Toni Hazleton (played by Jon Walmsley's real-life wife, Lisa Harrison), and Mary Ellen, taking courses in premed, found a new love with fellow student Jonesy. Her romance was almost aborted when she found that Curt had not died at Pearl Harbor after all, but their marriage was over and she stayed with Jonesy. As the series ended, John sold Walton's Mill to son Ben and moved to Arizona to be with his wife while she recuperated from a relapse of her TB.

Although *The Waltons* stopped production as a series in the spring of 1981, three more episodes aired as made-for-TV movies on NBC in February, May, and November of 1982. Erin Walton married her brother Jason's partner in the lumber business in February, Mary Ellen married Jonesy in May, and the family got together for Thanksgiving in the November episode, which aired almost 11 years after the made-for-TV film "The Homecoming," the original pilot for *The Waltons*.

Author Earl Hamner, Jr., was the creator and narrator of *The Waltons*, which was based on reminiscences of his own childhood. It was the most wholesome of TV programs and, surprisingly, did extremely well in the ratings. When it premiered in 1972 its competition was *The Flip Wilson Show* on NBC, then one of the most popular shows on television. To the surprise of both critics and TV executives *The Waltons* not only survived, but it forced Flip Wilson off the air and itself became one of the most viewed programs on TV. It was never a big hit in large cities, but it struck a chord in middle and rural America that guaranteed it a long and prosperous run.

WANTED
Documentary
FIRST TELECAST: *October 20, 1955*
LAST TELECAST: *January 5, 1956*
BROADCAST HISTORY:
  Oct 1955–Jan 1956, CBS Thu 10:30–11:00
NARRATOR:
  Walter McGraw

There were no actors in *Wanted*. All of the participants played themselves, be they policemen, informers, or witnesses, as this filmed documentary series reenacted the process by which wanted criminals were pursued by law-enforcement officers. Each week an actual case was followed from the criminal act and then through the process of detection. All of the cases, which were drawn from FBI files, were still active, and the criminals whose stories were shown were asked over the air to give themselves up. There were interviews with victims and members of the wanted party's family as well as the crime-and-detection aspects of the show. The narrator, Walter McGraw, also produced *Wanted*.

WANTED: DEAD OR ALIVE
Western
FIRST TELECAST: *September 6, 1958*
LAST TELECAST: *March 29, 1961*
BROADCAST HISTORY:
  Sep 1958–Sep 1960, CBS Sat 8:30–9:00
  Sep 1960–Mar 1961, CBS Wed 8:30–9:00
CAST:
  Josh Randall .... Steve McQueen
  Jason Nichols (1960) .... Wright King

Bounty hunters were very common in the Old West during the last half of the 19th century. They made a living from the rewards offered for capturing wanted criminals. Since it didn't matter whether or not the criminals were brought back alive, bounty hunters were not bound by the constraints that hampered lawmen, and did pretty much as they pleased. Such a man was Josh Randall. He felt little apparent emotion and was a man of few words. He was also adept at using his gun, not a normal pistol but an unusual cross between a hand gun and a rifle. His "Mare's Leg" was a .30–40 sawed-off carbine that could be handled almost like a pistol but had much more explosive impact when its cartridges hit a target. In the spring of 1960 Josh acquired a sidekick in young Jason Nichols. Apparently things didn't work out, for by the fall of that year Josh was once again riding alone.

The pilot for this program was aired in March 1958 as an episode of the series *Trackdown*.

WARNER BROTHERS PRESENTS
Various
FIRST TELECAST: *September 13, 1955*
LAST TELECAST: *September 11, 1956*
BROADCAST HISTORY:
  Sep 1955–Sep 1956, ABC Tue 7:30–8:30
HOST/NARRATOR:
  Gig Young

When ABC first approached the giant Warner Brothers film company it was for the purpose of obtaining the rights to theatrical films for telecasting on the network. But Warner was interested in getting into TV production, and the result was *Warner Brothers Presents*, an umbrella title for three rotating series, each based on a successful movie: *Kings Row, Cheyenne,* and *Casablanca*. From this start Warner Brothers went on to produce dozens of hit programs, and it is today an important producer of TV series.

Warner's first effort was a mixed success, however. Viewers and critics alike objected to the 10–15 minute segment at the end of each week's presentation devoted to plugging current Warner Brothers movies, and this was eventually dropped. (Gig Young was host of this segment, as well as narrator for the entire series.) *Kings Row* proved unsuccessful and was canceled at mid-season, followed soon after by *Casablanca*. Only *Cheyenne* caught on, lasting for a total of eight years on the ABC schedule. The *Warner Brothers Presents* title was discontinued after the 1955–1956 season.

See separate element titles for details.

WARREN HULL SHOW, THE
see *Ben Grauer Show, The*

WASHDAY THEATRE
see *Movies—Prior to 1961*

WASHINGTON EXCLUSIVE
Discussion
FIRST TELECAST: *June 21, 1953*
LAST TELECAST: *November 1, 1953*
BROADCAST HISTORY:
Jun 1953–Nov 1953, DUM Sun 7:30–8:00
MODERATOR:
Frank McNaughton

Public-affairs discussion program in which six former senators discussed the civil and military affairs of the nation. Produced by Martha Rountree and Lawrence Spivak.

WASHINGTON REPORT
Discussion
FIRST TELECAST: *May 22, 1951*
LAST TELECAST: *August 31, 1951*
BROADCAST HISTORY:
May 1951–Aug 1951, DUM Tue/Fri 7:45–8:00
MODERATOR:
Tris Coffin

Newsman Tris Coffin and distinguished guests from government, business, and labor discussed current events in this series originating from Washington, D.C.

WATCH MR. WIZARD
Educational
FIRST TELECAST: *May 26, 1951*
LAST TELECAST: *February 19, 1955*
BROADCAST HISTORY:
May 1951–Feb 1952, NBC Sat 6:30–7:00
Mar 1952–Feb 1955, NBC Sat 7:00–7:30
CAST:
Mr. Wizard .... Don Herbert

Watch Mr. Wizard was one of the longest-running educational children's programs in the his-

tory of television. It originated from Chicago from its inception on March 3, 1951 (late on Saturday afternoons), through the conclusion of the 1954–1955 season. When it moved to New York at the start of the 1955–1956 season, it was part of the NBC Saturday morning lineup. It remained as part of that lineup until June 27, 1965, and was revived for another season from 1971–1972. New episodes, under the title *Mr. Wizard's World,* have been airing on the Nickleodeon cable channel since 1983.

Don Herbert was the star of the show for its entire run. As Mr. Wizard, he would show his young helper how to do interesting scientific experiments with simple things found around the house. In addition to the demonstrations, Mr. Wizard would explain the principles behind them. The original helper was Mr. Wizard's 11-year-old neighbor, a boy named Willy. By the start of the 1953–1954 season, a boy and a girl alternated as Mr. Wizard's assistant. There was considerable turnover in the children who acted as his assistants, but they were all ready with an excited "Gee, Mr. Wizard!" whenever he popped one of his scientific tricks.

WATCH THE WORLD
Documentary
FIRST TELECAST: *July 2, 1950*
LAST TELECAST: *August 20, 1950*
BROADCAST HISTORY:
Jul 1950–Aug 1950, NBC Sun 7:30–8:00
COMMENTATOR:
Don Goddard

Current events and features especially designed for youngsters, produced by NBC News in cooperation with the National Education Association. *Watch the World* was seen on Sunday afternoons during most of its 14-month run (April 1950–June 1951), with John Cameron Swayze and his family hosting. During the program's summer prime-time run, newscaster Don Goddard took over, with the vacationing Swayzes (John, his wife, son, and daughter) continuing to appear in periodic filmed reports.

WATERFRONT
Adventure
BROADCAST HISTORY:
Syndicated only
30 minutes
Produced: *1953–1956* (78 episodes)
Released: *February 1954*
CAST:
Capt. John Herrick .... Preston Foster
May (Mom) Herrick .... Lois Moran
Jim Herrick .... Harry Lauter
Carl Herrick .... Douglas Dick
Tip Hubbard .... Pinky Tomlin
Terry Van Buren .... Kathleen Crowley
Sid .... Allen Jenkins
Willie Slocum .... Willie Best

Tom Bailey	Raymond Haddon
Wally	Sid Saylor
Capt. Winant	Miles Halpin
Joe Johnson	Louis Jean Heydt

One of TV's earlier seagoing adventures was this syndicated series, focusing on tugboat captain Carl Herrick, his crew, and his family. Cap'n John ran the *Cheryl Ann* around San Pedro–Los Angeles harbor, encountering all sorts of smugglers, saboteurs, escaped convicts, and other seaborne criminals. Some episodes revolved around the doings of his family. The large cast included his wife, May, son Jim (a police detective), and the crew of the *Cheryl Ann*—son Carl, Tip, and Willie. Terry was Carl's fiancée, the daughter of a wealthy stockbroker.

Filmed on location in Los Angeles Harbor.

WAVERLY WONDERS, THE
Situation Comedy
FIRST TELECAST: *September 7, 1978*
LAST TELECAST: *October 6, 1978*
BROADCAST HISTORY:
   Sep 1978–Oct 1978, NBC Fri 8:00–8:30
CAST:

Joe Casey	Joe Namath
John Tate	Charles Bloom
Tony Faguzzi	Joshua Grenrock
Connie Rafkin	Kim Lankford
Alan Kerner	James Staley
Hasty Parks	Tierre Turner
Linda Harris	Gwynne Gilford
George Benton	Ben Piazza

Former pro football quarterback Joe Namath took a flyer in TV comedy in this 1978 series. He starred as Joe Casey, a washed-up pro basketball player turned history teacher and coach at Waverly High, in Eastfield, Wisconsin. It was questionable who was more inept, Joe in the classroom (he knew nothing about history) or his team, the Waverly Wonders, on the court (they hadn't won a game in three years). Nice kids, though: Tate, so shy he wouldn't take a shot; Faguzzi, the fumbling "Italian Stallion"; Parks, the fast-talking con artist; and Connie, the cute tomboy who was the best player of the lot. Linda Harris was the attractive principal and George Benton the stodgy former coach, known affectionately as "old prune face."

WAY OUT
Dramatic Anthology
FIRST TELECAST: *March 31, 1961*
LAST TELECAST: *July 14, 1961*
BROADCAST HISTORY:
   Mar 1961–Jul 1961, CBS Fri 9:30–10:00
HOST:
   Roald Dahl

The host for this dramatic anthology was well chosen. Roald Dahl was a writer of short, macabre stories about people in strange and unsettling situations. The dramas in this series all fell into that category. In many respects it was like another CBS anthology series that was being aired in the following half hour, *The Twilight Zone*. *Way Out* was noticeably less successful, however, and lasted for only three and a half months.

WAYNE AND SHUSTER TAKE AN AFFECTIONATE LOOK AT . . .
Documentary
FIRST TELECAST: *June 17, 1966*
LAST TELECAST: *July 29, 1966*
BROADCAST HISTORY:
   Jun 1966–Jul 1966, CBS Fri 10:00–11:00
HOSTS:
   Johnny Wayne
   Frank Shuster

Each week Canadian comedians Wayne and Shuster hosted a documentary that profiled top comedians of the 20th century. Film clips were used to provide background and examples of the work of the comedians being profiled, with Wayne and Shuster providing running commentary. The people whose careers were chronicled were Bob Hope and Bing Crosby, Jack Benny, W.C. Fields, the Marx Brothers, and George Burns. In addition to the profiles of comedians, one episode presented an affectionate look at one movie form native to America, the Western.

WAYNE KING
Music
FIRST TELECAST: *September 29, 1949*
LAST TELECAST: *June 26, 1952*
BROADCAST HISTORY:
   Sep 1949–Jun 1952, NBC Thu 10:30–11:00 (OS)
REGULARS:
   Wayne King
   Nancy Evans (1949–1951)
   Harry Hall
   Gloria Van (1951–1952)
   Barbara Becker (1951–1952)
   Bob Morton (1951–1952)
   The Don Large Chorus

Live program from Chicago featuring the smooth, somewhat sedate music of Wayne King and His Orchestra. Typical, and best known, of his numbers was "The Waltz You Saved for Me." Seen only on NBC's Midwest network.

WE GOT IT MADE
Situation Comedy
FIRST TELECAST: *September 8, 1983*
LAST TELECAST: *March 30, 1984*
BROADCAST HISTORY:
   Sep 1983–Dec 1983, NBC Thu 9:00–9:30
   Jan 1984–Mar 1984, NBC Sat 9:00–9:30
   (In first-run syndication for the 1987–1988 season)

843

CAST:
Mickey McKenzie .... Teri Copley
Jay Bostwick .... Tom Villard
David Tucker (1983–1984) ...... Matt McCoy
David Tucker (1987–1988) ...... John Hillner
Claudia (1983–1984) .... Stepfanie Kramer
Beth Sorenson (1983–1984) .... Bonnie Urseth
Max Papavasilios, Sr. (1987–1988)
.... Ron Karabatsos
Max Papavasilios, Jr. (1987–1988)
.... Lance Wilson-White

Frothy comedy in which two young New York City bachelors hired a sexy live-in maid to clean up their sloppy apartment. David was a button-down lawyer, disgusted by the mess created by goofy roommate Jay, a free-thinking importer and "idea man." Along came Mickey, a bubbly and apparently air-headed blonde who just happened to be a crackerjack housekeeper. David and Jay's girlfriends (neurotic Claudia and ingenuous Beth, respectively) were naturally suspicious, but it was all quite innocent—of course.

Three years after leaving NBC, *We Got It Made* surfaced again with new episodes in first-run syndication. The relationship between Mickey and her bosses had not changed but David and Jay's regular girlfriends were gone. New to the cast were Max, a cop living in the apartment across the hall, and his awkward teenaged son. Max, Jr., who had the hots for Mickey, often sought her advice about dealing with women.

WE TAKE YOUR WORD
Quiz/Audience Participation
FIRST TELECAST: *April 1, 1950*
LAST TELECAST: *June 1, 1951*
BROADCAST HISTORY:
Apr 1950, CBS Sat 9:00–9:30
Jun 1950–Jul 1950, CBS Fri 8:00–8:30
Aug 1950, CBS Sun 9:30–10:00
Aug 1950–Sep 1950, CBS Mon 9:30–10:00
Oct 1950–Jan 1951, CBS Tue 10:30–11:00
Mar 1951–Jun 1951, CBS Fri 10:30–11:00
WORDMASTER:
John K. M. McCaffery
John Daly
PANELISTS:
Abe Burrows
Lyman Bryson (1950)

The panelists on *We Take Your Word* sought to provide the definitions, derivations, and histories of words that were sent in by viewers. Any word used on the program won for its submitter a book prize and, if the panel bungled their attempt to define it, $50. The series began on radio in January 1950 and was tried on television that April. John K. M. McCaffery was the wordmaster (moderator) of the radio version and also of the experimental TV version in April. He was replaced by John Daly when the show returned to television in June. John Daly stayed with the show through Jan-

uary 1951, to be replaced by its original host for its last three months. Initially there were two regular panelists and one guest. When Lyman Bryson left the show at the end of August 1950, Abe Burrows became the sole regular, with two guest panelists each week.

WE, THE PEOPLE
Interview
FIRST TELECAST: *June 1, 1948*
LAST TELECAST: *September 26, 1952*
BROADCAST HISTORY:
Jun 1948–Oct 1949, CBS Tue 9:00–9:30
Nov 1949–Jun 1951, NBC Fri 8:30–9:00
Sep 1951–Sep 1952, NBC Fri 8:30–9:00
HOST:
Dwight Weist (1948–1950)
Dan Seymour (1950–1952)

We, the People had been a feature on radio for 12 years when it moved to television in the summer of 1948. It was the first regularly scheduled series to be simulcast on both network radio and network television. Host Dwight Weist (replaced by Dan Seymour in April 1950) interviewed various guests about important events in their lives. Entertainers, politicians, and ordinary Americans appeared on the series to chat informally, often about experiences of deep personal suffering or triumph over adversaries. Members of public-service organizations and individuals who had done some form of humanitarian work appeared frequently. The guests were introduced with the line, "We, the people . . . speak." The radio-TV simulcasts continued until July 1950, after which date the radio and television versions were aired at different times.

WEB, THE
Dramatic Anthology
FIRST TELECAST: *July 11, 1950*
LAST TELECAST: *October 6, 1957*
BROADCAST HISTORY:
Jul 1950–Aug 1950, CBS Tue 9:30–10:00
Aug 1950–Jul 1952, CBS Wed 9:30–10:00
Sep 1952–Sep 1954, CBS Sun 10:00–10:30
Jul 1957–Oct 1957, NBC Sun 10:00–10:30
HOST/NARRATOR:
Jonathan Blake (1950–1954)
William Bryant (1957)
PRODUCERS:
Mark Goodson and Bill Todman (1950–1954)

Normal, everyday people who found themselves in situations beyond their control populated the dramas telecast in this live CBS anthology series. Its producers, ironically, were Mark Goodson and Bill Todman of game-show fame.

All of the plays were adaptations of stories written by members of the Mystery Writers of America. Walter C. Brown and Hugh Pentecost were frequent contributors and even an occasional Charlotte Armstrong story, like "All the

Way Home," turned up on *The Web.* Most of the actors and actresses appearing on the show were performers based in New York, where the show was produced. Included were Richard Kiley, James Daly, Eli Wallach, James Gregory, Patricia Wheel, Mary Sinclair, John Newland, and Phyllis Kirk.

Some future stars who were seen on *The Web* early in their careers were Grace Kelly in "Mirror of Delusion" in 1950, Jack Palance and Eva Marie Saint in "Last Chance" in 1953, and Paul Newman twice that summer, the second time in "One for the Road" on September 20, at the same time he was appearing on Broadway in the play *Picnic.* Newman's future wife, Joanne Woodward (they would marry in 1958), starred in "Welcome Home," the final telecast of CBS's version of *The Web,* on September 26, 1954.

Hollywood veterans taking lead roles in episodes of *The Web* on CBS included John Carradine, Mildred Dunnock, Sidney Blackmer, Mildred Natwick, Henry Hull, and Chester Morris. On occasion the leads went to performers not noted for their dramatic acting ability, such as singer Jane Morgan in "Rehearsal for Death" and musical-comedy star John Raitt in "The Dark Shore." The real stars on *The Web* were the stories, however, not the performers. The overall quality of the productions was attested to when *The Web* became the first television series to win the Edgar Allan Poe Award for excellence in the presentation of suspense stories during the 1951–1952 season.

In the summer of 1957, NBC revived the title *The Web* for a series of filmed dramas with essentially the same format as the live CBS series of the early 1950s. Again, the emphasis was on story rather than star, with Alexander Scourby, Beverly Garland, James Darren, and Rex Reason the most familiar performers appearing. The NBC edition was the summer replacement for *The Loretta Young Show.*

WEBSTER

Situation Comedy
FIRST TELECAST: *September 16, 1983*
LAST TELECAST: *September 11, 1987*
BROADCAST HISTORY:

Sep 1983–Mar 1985, ABC Fri 8:30–9:00
Mar 1985–Mar 1987, ABC Fri 8:00–8:30
Mar 1987–Apr 1987, ABC Fri 8:30–9:00
May 1987, ABC Fri 8:00–8:30
Jun 1987–Aug 1987, ABC Sat 8:00–8:30
Aug 1987–Sep 1987, ABC Fri 8:00–8:30
(In first-run syndication during the 1987–1988 season)

CAST:

Webster Long .... Emmanuel Lewis
George Papadapolis .... Alex Karras
Katherine Calder-Young Papadapolis
.... Susan Clark
Jerry Silver .... Henry Polic II
Bill Parker (1984–1986) .... Eugene Roche

Cassie Parker (1984–1986) ... Cathryn Damon
Uncle Phillip Long (1984–1985) ... Ben Vereen
*"Papa" Papadapolis (1985–1987)
.... Jack Kruschen
Rob Whitaker/Joiner (1985–1986)
.... Chad Allen
*Tommy (1987) .... Gabe Witcher
*Roger (1986–1987) .... Carl Steven
*Andy (1986–1987) .... Danny McMurphy
*Benny (1987) .... Nick DeMauro
Nicky Papadopolis (1987–1988)
.... Corin "Corky" Nemec

*Occasional
THEME:
"Then Came You" by Steve Nelson and Madeline Sunshine

Emmanuel Lewis was 40 inches tall, cute as a button, and the comic find of the 1983–84 season. He was 12 years old, but looked half that. A network executive spotted him in a Burger King commercial and signed him on the spot—then ordered his writers to think up a series for him fast, before the little fellow grew another inch.

The series they came up with may have been a bit farfetched, but it did showcase young Lewis' talents. George was a burly former pro football player turned sportscaster on WBJX-TV, Katherine a fluttery socialite with a career as a consumer advocate (later she became a psychologist). They had met on a Greek cruise and—though total opposites—married on impulse. George was generally an impulsive guy. No sooner did they arrive back in Chicago than they discovered at their door the result of one of George's past impulses: a cute black seven-year-old named Webster. It seemed that George was Webster's godfather. He had promised the boy's parents, teammate and best friend Travis and his wife Gert, that if anything ever happened to them he would look after their child. Well, something did (they were killed in a car crash), there were no next of kin, and here was Webster.

Adjustments were made by all, particularly Katherine, who was totally inept as a housewife or mother. Webster was cute enough to melt even her Tiffany heart, however, when he told her why he always called her Ma'am—"cause it kinda sounds like 'mom.'" (*Awwwww,* sighs the audience.) As for George, beneath that hulk beat the heart of a pussycat. Most of the stories in this syrupy series were of the "Webster can't sleep without his teddy bear" variety, but a few dealt with more serious subjects such as retarded children, and the day they had to explain to Webster that his parents were not just "away."

Jerry was Katherine's sarcastic male secretary, Cassie and Bill owned the large Victorian house into which the Papadapolises moved in the fall of 1984 (they later bought it), and Phillip was Webster's uncle—who arrived planning to fight for custody of the little guy, much to everyone's discomfort. He later moved to Hollywood to start a movie career. A major change occured in the fall of 1987 when George's brother and sister-in-law decided to relocate to Nigeria to work on a UN agricultural project, and their 14-year-old son Nicky moved in with George and his family. Nicky and Webster got along famously, and the older boy provided Webster with the "brother" he had never had.

ABC aired reruns of *Webster* on weekday mornings from December 1986 to July 1987.

WEDNESDAY NIGHT FIGHTS, THE
see *Boxing*

WEEK IN RELIGION, THE
Religion
FIRST TELECAST: *March 16, 1952*
LAST TELECAST: *October 18, 1954*
BROADCAST HISTORY:
> *Mar 1952–Sep 1952*, DUM Sun 6:00–7:00
> *Jul 1953–Sep 1953*, DUM Sun 6:00–7:00
> *Sep 1953–Oct 1954*, DUM Sun 6:00–6:30

This ecumenical religious program was originally one hour long and divided into three 20-minute segments: 20 minutes for the Protestants, 20 minutes for the Catholics, and 20 minutes for the Jews. A representative of each faith reported on the latest news and happenings in his denomination. There is no record of who, if anyone, got cut when the program was reduced to a half hour.

WEEKEND
News Magazine
FIRST TELECAST: *October 20, 1974*
LAST TELECAST: *April 22, 1979*
BROADCAST HISTORY:
> *Oct 1974–Jun 1978*, NBC Sat 11:30–1:00 A.M.
> *Dec 1978*, NBC Sat 10:00–11:00
> *Jan 1979–Apr 1979*, NBC Sun 10:00–11:00
REGULARS:
> Lloyd Dobyns
> Linda Ellerbee (1978–1979)

Weekend was one of the more unusual news programs attempted in the 1970s. Hosted by sardonic Lloyd Dobyns, it was an odd mixture of serious and frivolous features, packaged in a most irreverent fashion. There were serious investigative stories on killer bees invading Central America, American women in Colombian prisons, and the competition to enter medical school, juxtaposed with topics like "Frisbees Are a Way of Life," "Slots on the Rhine," "The Pigeon Wars," and "My Son-in-Law, the President" (in which people talked about their relatives running for president). Adding to the light flavor of the program was the extensive use of animation, in running cartoon features like "Feeble Fables" and "Mr. Hipp Goes to Town," and in short sequences that commented, often sarcastically, on the main stories.

It was all very hip, and certainly compatible with *NBC's Saturday Night Live*, with which it alternated during most of its late-night run. (*Weekend* aired approximately once every four weeks.) But in 1978, entranced with visions of an irreverent hit show for prime time, NBC moved it to 10 P.M. To the larger (and older) prime-time audience such flippancy seemed out of place on a news program, and *Weekend* did poorly, finally being replaced by the more traditional *Prime Time Sunday* in 1979. Linda Ellerbee appeared as co-host during *Weekend*'s prime-time run.

WELCOME ABOARD
Musical Variety
FIRST TELECAST: *October 3, 1948*
LAST TELECAST: *February 20, 1949*
BROADCAST HISTORY:
> *Oct 1948–Feb 1949*, NBC Sun 7:30–8:00
REGULARS:
> Russ Morgan and His Orchestra (Oct–Nov 1948)
> Vincent Lopez and His Orchestra (Nov 1948–Feb 1949)
THEME:
> "Sailor's Hornpipe"

Live musical variety program with a nautical theme, including the members of the orchestra dressed in sailor suits. Top-name singers and comedians appeared as guests, with Phil Silvers and Martin and Lewis featured on the first telecast. Toward the end of the run one of the guests would serve as the emcee, with bandleader Lopez assuming a background role. The series was originally known as *Admiral Presents the Five Star Revue—Welcome Aboard*, but became *Welcome Aboard* when Admiral dropped sponsorship in December.

WELCOME BACK, KOTTER
Situation Comedy
FIRST TELECAST: *September 9, 1975*
LAST TELECAST: *August 10, 1979*
BROADCAST HISTORY:
> *Sep 1975–Jan 1976*, ABC Tue 8:30–9:00
> *Jan 1976–Aug 1978*, ABC Thu 8:00–8:30
> *Sep 1978–Oct 1978*, ABC Mon 8:00–8:30
> *Oct 1978–Jan 1979*, ABC Sat 8:00–8:30
> *Feb 1979–Mar 1979*, ABC Sat 8:30–9:00
> *May 1979–Aug 1979*, ABC Fri 8:30–9:00
CAST:
> *Gabe Kotter* .... Gabriel Kaplan
> *Julie Kotter* .... Marcia Strassman
> *Vinnie Barbarino* .... John Travolta
> *Juan Luis Pedro Phillipo de Huevos Epstein*
> .... Robert Hegyes
> *Freddie "Boom Boom" Washington*
> .... Lawrence-Hilton Jacobs
> *Arnold Horshack* .... Ron Palillo
> *Mr. Michael Woodman*
> .... John Sylvester White
> *Rosalie Totzie (1975–1976)* .... Debralee Scott
> *Verna Jean (1975–1977)* ...... Vernee Watson
> *Judy Borden (1975–1977)* ... Helaine Lembeck

Todd Ludlow (1975–1977) ..... Dennis Bowen
Maria (1975–1976).......... Catarina Cellino
Angie Globagoski (1978)...... Melonie Haller
Beau De Labarre (1978–1979)
.... Stephen Shortridge
Carvelli (1978–1979)....... Charles Fleischer
Murray (1978–1979) .... Bob Harcum
Mary Johnson (1978–1979) ..... Irene Arranga
CREATED BY:
Gabriel Kaplan and Alan Sacks
THEME:
"Welcome Back," composed and performed by
John Sebastian

Welcome Back, Kotter was one of the more realistic comedies of the 1970s. Gabriel Kaplan portrayed Kotter, a Brooklyn-born teacher who returned to the inner-city high school from which he
had graduated 10 years earlier to teach the toughest cases—a remedial academics group. Gabe's
"sweathogs" were the outcasts of the academic
system, streetwise but unable or unwilling to
make it in normal classes. They were the toughest,
and also the funniest, kids in school. Gabe was
just as hip as they were, and with fine disregard
for rules and a sense of humor he set out to help
them pick up a little bit of practical, if not academic, knowledge, during their years at James Buchanan High. The four original "sweathogs" were
Epstein, the Jewish Puerto Rican; "Boom Boom,"
the hip black; Horshack, the class yo-yo; and Barbarino, the cool, tough leader. John Travolta, playing Barbarino, became a major star through this
series. He branched into popular music, where he
had several hit records beginning in the summer
of 1976 (although the big song hit to come out of
this show was the theme, as recorded by its composer John Sebastian). Travolta also began a successful movie career, with such films as *Carrie*
and *Saturday Night Fever,* while he was still starring on *Kotter.* By 1978 he was seen only occasionally on the series.

Dozens of other students passed through the
series, most seen only briefly. Those with the most
appearances are listed above. Other regulars
were Gabe's wife, Julie, and Mr. Woodman, the
assistant principal. Julie became pregnant at the
end of the 1976–1977 season, and gave birth to
twins Rachel and Robin in the fall of 1977, adding
to the confusion and crowding in the Kotters'
small apartment, and putting new strains on
Gabe's limited income. In other developments,
Angie turned up in early 1978 with the announcement that she was becoming the first female
"sweathog" (she didn't last long), and a slick
southerner, Beau De Labarre, joined the class the
following fall. Also in the fall of 1978 Kotter was
promoted to vice principal and Mr. Woodman to
principal. The sweathogs got part-time jobs, with
Vinnie becoming an orderly at a nearby hospital.

Welcome Back, Kotter was based on a real
high school and the real experiences of Gabriel
Kaplan. Kaplan had once attended the equivalent
of James Buchanan High School, in Bensonhurst,
Brooklyn, New York, and had been a student in a
remedial class there. He credits a Miss Shepard as
the teacher who inspired him, and who led, in-
directly, to *Welcome Back, Kotter.* Like Kotter,
she cared about her "unteachable" students.

WELCOME MAT
see *Starlit Time*

WE'LL GET BY
Situation Comedy
FIRST TELECAST: *March 14, 1975*
LAST TELECAST: *May 30, 1975*
BROADCAST HISTORY:
Mar 1975–May 1975, CBS Fri 8:30–9:00
CAST:
George Platt.................... Paul Sorvino
Liz Platt .... Mitzi Hoag
Muff Platt .... Jerry Houser
Kenny Platt .... Willie Aames
Andrea Platt .... Devon Scott

The Platt family was a normal middle-class group
living in a modest home in the New Jersey suburbs
just outside of New York City, where George Platt
worked as a lawyer. He and his wife, Liz, had
three teenage children. Life in the Platt household,
with all its conflicts, was one of love and understanding. The program was created by Alan Alda.

WELLS FARGO
see *Tales of Wells Fargo*

WENDY AND ME
Situation Comedy
FIRST TELECAST: *September 14, 1964*
LAST TELECAST: *September 6, 1965*
BROADCAST HISTORY:
Sep 1964–Sep 1965, ABC Mon 9:00–9:30
CAST:
George Burns...................... Himself
Wendy Conway .... Connie Stevens
Jeff Conway .... Ron Harper
Danny Adams .... James Callahan
Mr. Bundy .... J. Pat O'Malley
Willard Norton .... Bartlett Robinson

This comedy was roughly patterned after the old
Burns and Allen Show of the 1950s, and was another attempt to find a suitable format for George
Burns after the retirement of his wife, Gracie
Allen. The setting was an apartment house in
Southern California whose principal tenants were
Wendy Conway, a slightly daft young bride, and
her airline-pilot husband Jeff. Jeff's co-pilot and
best friend was Danny, a girl-chasing bachelor
who was inordinately proud of his "little black
book" and "little red book." Mr. Bundy was the
building superintendent.

Into the picture came George Burns, as himself.
He had bought the building so he would have a
place to practice his vaudeville routine—just in

case anyone should ask him to perform it again. George's singing was not exactly widely admired, so he had written into every lease a provision that no tenant could evict the landlord. George, with his familiar cigar in hand, spent most of his time serving as onscreen narrator of the series. He followed Wendy through her day, commenting on the action in asides to the audience. Then he would step into the action himself.

WENDY BARRIE SHOW, THE
Interview
FIRST TELECAST: *March 14, 1949*
LAST TELECAST: *September 27, 1950*
BROADCAST HISTORY:
Mar 1949–Jun 1949, DUM Mon/Wed/Fri 7:00–7:30
Jun 1949–Jul 1949, DUM Wed 7:00–7:30
Sep 1949–Oct 1949, ABC Mon 8:30–9:00
Nov 1949–Dec 1949, ABC Wed 8:00–8:30
Dec 1949–Feb 1950, ABC Thu 9:00–9:30
Feb 1950–Jun 1950, NBC Tue/Thu 7:30–7:45
Jul 1950–Aug 1950, NBC Mon/Wed/Fri 7:30–7:45
Aug 1950–Sep 1950, NBC Wed 8:15–8:30
REGULARS:
Wendy Barrie
Dave Davis (1949)

Celebrity-interview and gossip show, hosted by one-time Hollywood starlet and early TV personality Wendy Barrie. Wendy's movie heyday was past by the time she went into the infant medium of television, but her vivacious charm was quite intact. Each night she welcomed viewers into a plush setting that was supposed to be her own Manhattan apartment, with outstretched arms, and such endearments as "sweet bunny," "sweetie," and "dearie" (her sign-off was always "be a good bunny"). All sorts of celebrities dropped in to chat with Wendy, and sometimes to perform, and there was show-business gossip as well as banter (Wendy had a marvelous sense of humor, even about herself). There was a definite air of glamour about it all.

Her first nighttime network series was produced in cooperation with *Photoplay* magazine and was called *Inside Photoplay*, then *Photoplay Time* (September 1949). Later it became *The Wendy Barrie Show* (December 1949) and finally *Through Wendy's Window* (August 1950). Miss Barrie was later seen on afternoon shows and on local television in New York.

WEREWOLF
Supernatural
FIRST TELECAST: *July 11, 1987*
LAST TELECAST:
BROADCAST HISTORY:
Jul 1987–Aug 1987, FOX Sat 9:00–9:30
Aug 1987–Oct 1987, FOX Sat 8:00–8:30
Oct 1987–Mar 1988, FOX Sun 8:00–8:30
Apr 1988, FOX Sat 9:00–10:00
May 1988– , FOX Sun 10:30–11:00

CAST:
Eric Cord .... John J. York
Alamo Joe Rogan .... Lance LeGault
*Janos Skorzeny (1987–1988) .. Chuck Connors
Nicholas Remy (1988–) . Brian Thompson

*Occasional

Eric Cord was a graduate student in college whose life took a bizarre twist when his best friend Ted asked Eric to kill him with a pistol loaded with a silver bullet—because Ted was a werewolf! Eric thought his friend was off his rocker, but was forced to oblige when Ted turned into a werewolf and attacked him. Unfortunately Eric was bitten in the attack, and found that *he* was now afflicted with the deadly curse. The only way to rid himself of it as to find and kill "the source of the bloodline," the mysterious Captain Janos Skorzeny. Eric embarked on a cross-country hunt for the swaggering Skorzeny while he, in turn, was being tracked by bounty hunter Alamo Joe. Although Eric was now prone to turn into a werewolf under the full moon, fortunately for the honest citizenry he only seemed to attack criminals, evil folk, and other werewolves.

Eric finally found and killed Skorzeny, but another complication arose; it turned out the source of the bloodline was actually Nicholas Remy, a remarkably well-preserved, powerful, and diabolical 2,000-year-old werewolf. Eric's quest to rid himself of his curse continued.

Werewolf was a very atmospheric series with vivid, even terrifying, special effects. The Fox network promoted the show heavily during the fall of 1987, and straight-faced announcements were aired giving viewers a toll-free number to call if they had sighted a werewolf. More than 400,000 calls were received. Later announcements featured Dr. Stephen Kaplan, an instructor of parapsychology, providing information about werewolves.

WESLEY
Situation Comedy
FIRST TELECAST: *May 8, 1949*
LAST TELECAST: *August 30, 1949*
BROADCAST HISTORY:
May 1949–Jul 1949, CBS Sun 7:30–8:00
Jul 1949–Aug 1949, CBS Tue 9:30–10:00
Aug 1949, CBS Tue 8:00–8:30
CAST:
Wesley Eggleston (May–Jul) .. Donald Devlin
Wesley Eggleston (Jul–Aug).. Johnny Stewart
Mr. Eggleston .... Frank Thomas
Mrs. Eggleston.............. Mona Thomas
Grandpa .... Joe Sweeney
Elizabeth Eggleston .... Joy Reese
Alvin .... Billie Nevard

Wesley was a 12-year-old boy who was making, but ever so slowly, the transition from childhood to adulthood. He liked to play with his good buddy, Alvin, with whom he had an almost brotherly relationship, fight with his teenage sister, Elizabeth, and find ways of getting around his parents. This live situation comedy told of his adventures in a small rural community. The relationship between Wesley and his parents was, despite the problems inherent in all parent-child relationships, a warm and loving one. Donald Devlin, the young actor who originated the lead role in this series, left in July and was replaced by Johnny Stewart.

WEST 57TH
News Magazine
FIRST TELECAST: *August 13, 1985*
LAST TELECAST:
BROADCAST HISTORY:
  Aug 1985–Sep 1985, CBS Tue 10:00–11:00
  Apr 1986–Jun 1986, CBS Wed 8:00–9:00
  Jun 1986–Jul 1986, CBS Wed 10:00–11:00
  Apr 1987, CBS Mon 10:00–11:00
  May 1987–Jun 1987, CBS Tue 8:00–9:00
  *Jun 1987–   *, CBS Sat 10:00–11:00
CORRESPONDENTS:
  John Ferrugia
  Bob Sirott
  Meredith Vieira
  Jane Wallace (1985–1988)
  Steve Kroft (1987–   )
  Selina Scott (1987–   )
  Karen Burnes (1988–   )

West 57th premiered as a summer magazine series that was a fast-paced "yuppie" version of *60 Minutes*. The four original correspondents were all under 40, and the stories they covered were oriented to a younger audience. There were multiple pieces on the drug problem—steroids for athletes, the use and abuse of legal "designer" drugs, and the problems with "Angel Dust"; a story on the growing popularity of cosmetic surgery; a feature about the increasing incidence of arson among teens, and coverage of the competition between American and Japanese companies searching for a cure for cancer. On the lighter side were profiles of actors Chuck Norris and John and Angelica Huston, singers Billy Joel and John Cougar Mellencamp, and comic Martin Short, as well as a story on the never-ending labors of an exterminator trying to control the pest population in the Pentagon.

After two years as a summer show, *West 57th* returned to the CBS schedule, in April 1987, on a full-time basis. That fall Steve Kroft joined the correspondents, as did Britisher Selina Scott, whose forte was European-based pieces on the music industry. When Jane Wallace left the show at the end of the year she was replaced by Karen Burnes.

WEST POINT STORY, THE
Military Anthology
FIRST TELECAST: *October 5, 1956*
LAST TELECAST: *July 1, 1958*
BROADCAST HISTORY:
  Oct 1956–Sep 1957, CBS Fri 8:00–8:30
  Oct 1957–Jul 1958, ABC Tue 10:00–10:30
HOST:
  Donald May (as *Cadet Charles C. Thompson*) (1956)

Produced with the cooperation of the Department of Defense, the Department of the Army, and the United States Military Academy, this series dramatized actual events and persons from the files of West Point. The names and dates of the people and situations involved were changed, but the events were real. The dramas showed cadets as real people, with the problems, joys, and tragedies that are part of every person's life. Not all of the episodes were based on contemporary life at the military academy; some looked at the academy at different periods in its history and the men who were a part of that history. Donald May was the host, in character, when *The West Point Story* premiered, but was phased out before the end of 1956.

WESTERN HOUR, THE
  syndicated title for *Rifleman, The* and *Dick Powell's Zane Grey Theater* (packaged as an hour show)

WESTERN STAR THEATRE
  see *Death Valley Days*

WESTERNER, THE
Western
FIRST TELECAST: *September 30, 1960*
LAST TELECAST: *December 30, 1960*
BROADCAST HISTORY:
  Sep 1960–Dec 1960, NBC Fri 8:30–9:00
CAST:
  Dave Blassingame .... Brian Keith
  Burgundy Smith .... John Dehner

Dave Blassingame was one of many adventurers wandering the TV version of the Old West. He was accompanied by a large mongrel named Brown (played by the same dog that had been featured in the Walt Disney movie *Old Yeller*). Though not a particularly friendly or outgoing type, Dave found settlers to defend, villains to fight, and causes to champion throughout the portion of the Southwest along the Mexican border. His avowed aim was to settle down on a ranch of his own and breed quarter horses, but his concern for the exploited pioneers he met constantly kept him postponing that move. One person Dave kept running into as he traveled was Burgundy Smith, an enterprising con man, who was constantly trying to fleece the citizenry.

WESTERNERS, THE
  syndicated title for *Black Saddle, Johnny Ringo, Law of the Plainsman, The,* and *Westerner, The* (packaged as a single series)

WESTINGHOUSE DESILU PLAYHOUSE

Dramatic Anthology

FIRST TELECAST: *October 13, 1958*
LAST TELECAST: *June 10, 1960*
BROADCAST HISTORY:
   Oct 1958–Sep 1959, CBS Mon 10:00–11:00
   Oct 1959–Jun 1960, CBS Fri 9:00–10:00
HOST:
   Desi Arnaz
COMMERCIAL SPOKESPERSON:
   Betty Furness

When *Studio One*'s live weekly anthology series went off the air after almost a full decade, sponsor Westinghouse Electric kept the time period with this series of filmed dramas. Betty Furness, who had been the spokesperson for *Studio One*, continued to show off refrigerators and ranges throughout the two years that *Desilu Playhouse* was on. The premiere telecast featured young Pier Angeli in "Bernadette," but the material ranged from light to serious. During the first season, host Desi Arnaz, whose production company was making the series, made no appearances as a performer, but two of his *I Love Lucy* gang did. Lucille Ball starred with William Lundigan and Aldo Ray in "K.O. Kitty," and William Frawley worked with Dan Duryea in "Comeback." William Bendix and Martin Balsam were featured in "The Time Element," a science-fiction story written by Rod Serling (and possibly the genesis of his later series *The Twilight Zone*). The most memorable program was a two-part story aired on April 20 and 27, 1959. Walter Winchell was the narrator, Robert Stack the star, and Keenan Wynn, Neville Brand, and Barbara Nichols featured players in "The Untouchables," which was destined to become a very successful and highly controversial series on ABC that fall.

Desi himself starred in two plays aired during the second season, "So Tender So Profane" and "Thunder in the Night," and another "Untouchables"-type story, "Meeting at Apalachian" starring Luther Adler, Cameron Mitchell, and Jack Warden and narrated by Bob Considine, was tried. Airing roughly once every five weeks within the series were a number of *Westinghouse Lucille Ball-Desi Arnaz Shows* in which the two stars re-created their roles from *I Love Lucy* along with Vivian Vance, William Frawley, and Richard Keith.

WESTINGHOUSE PLAYHOUSE

Situation Comedy

FIRST TELECAST: *January 6, 1961*
LAST TELECAST: *July 7, 1961*
BROADCAST HISTORY:
   Jan 1961–Apr 1961, NBC Fri 8:30–9:00
   May 1961–Jul 1961, NBC Fri 10:00–10:30
CAST:
   Nan McGovern .... Nanette Fabray
   Dan McGovern .... Wendell Corey
   Buddy .... Bobby Diamond
   Nancy .... Jacklyn O'Donnell
   Mrs. Harper .... Doris Kemper

The full title of this comedy was *Westinghouse Playhouse Starring Nanette Fabray and Wendell Corey*. It was created by Miss Fabray's husband, writer-director Ranald MacDougall, and was based somewhat on her own life. Nan McGovern was a successful Broadway star who fell madly in love with Dan McGovern (whose wife had died six years previously) and married him after a very short courtship. On their way back to his hometown of Hollywood, Dan admitted to Nan that he had not told his children about her. When they arrived at his home in Beverly Hills Nan found herself confronted with two rude and indifferent stepchildren and a less-than-enthusiastic housekeeper. Her efforts to cope with the situation and become close to her new family provided the material for the episodes in this series.

WESTINGHOUSE PREVIEW THEATRE

Comedy Anthology

FIRST TELECAST: *July 14, 1961*
LAST TELECAST: *September 22, 1961*
BROADCAST HISTORY:
   Jul 1961–Sep 1961, NBC Fri 10:00–10:30

This summer series consisted of ten unsold pilots for potential situation comedy series, starring assorted TV and film personalities, and one musical program, "The Benny Goodman Show," which aired on September 15.

WESTINGHOUSE SUMMER THEATRE

see *Studio One*

WESTSIDE MEDICAL

Medical Drama

FIRST TELECAST: *March 15, 1977*
LAST TELECAST: *August 25, 1977*
BROADCAST HISTORY:
   Mar 1977–Apr 1977, ABC Thu 10:00–11:00
   Jun 1977–Aug 1977, ABC Thu 10:00–11:00
CAST:
   Dr. Sam Lanagan .... James Sloyan
   Dr. Janet Cottrell .... Linda Carlson
   Dr. Philip Parker .... Ernest Thompson
   Carrie .... Alice Nunn
TECHNICAL CONSULTANT:
   Walter D. Dishell, M.D.

Set in Southern California, this short-lived medical drama centered around three dedicated young doctors who opened their own clinic to provide total, personalized care to their patients. Carrie was the receptionist. *Westside Medical* returned at the end of June to run for another two months with both original and repeat episodes.

WE'VE GOT EACH OTHER

Situation Comedy

FIRST TELECAST: *October 1, 1977*

BROADCAST HISTORY:
  Oct 1977–Jan 1978, CBS Sat 8:30–9:00
CAST:
  Stuart Hibbard .... Oliver Clark
  Judy Hibbard .... Beverly Archer
  Damon Jerome .... Tom Poston
  Dee Dee Baldwin .... Joan Van Ark
  Donna .... Ren Woods
  Ken Redford................... Martin Kove

The trials of a married couple whose marital roles were somewhat reversed formed the crux of this comedy. Stuart worked at home, as a copywriter for the "Herman Gutman Mail Order Catalogue" (full of improbable and useless gadgets), and did most of the cleaning and cooking. Judy commuted every day to downtown Los Angeles, where she was the assistant to professional photographer Damon Jerome, a hypertense, absentminded man who was great with a camera but terrible at the practical aspects of his business. Both Stuart and Judy had primary sources of aggravation, his being next-door neighbor Ken Redford and hers being model Dee Dee Baldwin, who was sarcastic, demanding, and incredibly self-centered. Donna, the office secretary, tried to maintain an uneasy truce between Judy and Dee Dee, but it was almost impossible.

WHAT A COUNTRY

Situation Comedy
BROADCAST HISTORY:
  Syndicated only
  30 minutes
  Produced: *1986–1987*
  Released: *September 1986*
CAST:
  Nikolai Rostapovich .... Yakov Smirnoff
  Taylor Brown .... Garrett M. Brown
  Principal Joan Courtney ..... Gail Strickland
  Ali Nadeem .... Vijay Amritraj
  Laslo Gabov............... George Murdock
  Robert Muboto .... Harry Waters, Jr.
  Maria Conchita Lopez .... Ada Maris
  Victor Ortega .... Julian Reyes
  Yung Hi..................... Leila Hee Olsen
  Principal F. Jerry "Bud" McPherson (1987)
  .... Don Knotts

Real-life Russian immigrant Yakov Smirnoff starred in this series about resident aliens hoping to become American citizens. The series was set in Los Angeles where young Taylor Brown taught a night school course to help immigrants pass the American citizenship test. The members of his class were Nikolai, an effervescent Russian cab driver; Laslo, a grumpy, retired Hungarian physician; Ali, a Pakistani who took everything quite literally; Robert, the pretentious son of a deposed African king; Maria, the sexy housekeeper for a wealthy Beverly Hills family; Victor, a young hispanic lady-killer in love with Maria; and Yung Hi,

an incredibly shy and sensitive Chinese girl. Joan Courtney was the rather pushy principal of the school (replaced by Bud McPherson early in 1987). Stories revolved around their problems with American language and customs, as well as the ways in which they related to each other.

What a Country was adapted from the British series *Mind Your Language.*

WHAT DO YOU HAVE IN COMMON

Quiz/Audience Participation
FIRST TELECAST: *July 1, 1954*
LAST TELECAST: *September 23, 1954*
BROADCAST HISTORY:
  Jul 1954–Sep 1954, CBS Thu 9:00–9:30
EMCEE:
  Ralph Story

Contestants on *What Do You Have in Common?* were brought to the stage in groups of three and informed by emcee Ralph Story that they had something in common that they must try to figure out by cross-examining each other. The first to figure out their common bond (which had been flashed on the TV screen to the viewers at home) won $500. Three groups of three participated on each show and the group that had taken the least time to figure out what they had in common won the opportunity to try for an extra $1,000 by guessing the similarity in the lives of three pictured celebrities.

WHAT DO YOU THINK?

Discussion
FIRST TELECAST: *January 17, 1949*
LAST TELECAST: *February 14, 1949*
BROADCAST HISTORY:
  Jan 1949–Feb 1949, ABC Mon 8:30–9:00

Book-discussion program produced by the Great Books Foundation Forum. From Chicago.

WHAT HAPPENED

Quiz/Audience Participation
FIRST TELECAST: *August 7, 1952*
LAST TELECAST: *August 21, 1952*
BROADCAST HISTORY:
  Aug 1952, NBC Thu 8:30–9:00
MODERATOR:
  Ben Grauer
PANELISTS:
  Lisa Ferraday
  Roger Price
  Maureen Stapleton
  Frank Gallop

Six weeks after *I've Got a Secret* premiered on CBS this very similar show turned up on the NBC schedule. Contestants on *What Happened* were all people who had had something happen to them that had been reported in a newspaper. The panelists, by asking questions to which the contestant answered yes or no, attempted to guess "what happened" to the contestant that was newsworthy. *I've Got a Secret* lasted 15 years in its original prime-time run. This shabby imitation lasted only three weeks.

WHAT IN THE WORLD
Quiz
FIRST TELECAST: *February 7, 1953*
LAST TELECAST: *September 5, 1953*
BROADCAST HISTORY:
Feb 1953–Sep 1953, CBS Sat 6:30–7:00
MODERATOR:
Dr. Froelich Rainey
PANELISTS:
Dr. Carleton Coon
Dr. Schuyler Cammann

The moderator of this live museum quiz was Dr. Froelich Rainey, director of the University of Pennsylvania Museum. Each week the two regular panelists, both professors in the anthropology department of the University of Pennsylvania, along with a third, guest panelist, were shown works of art from the museum and asked to identify them. The identifications included background on the origins and original uses of the pieces, as well as possible explanations of the circumstances surrounding their discovery. This Peabody Award–winning series, broadcast live from Philadelphia, had actually premiered in April 1951 and continued until March 1955. For most of its run, however, it aired as a Saturday or Sunday afternoon program.

WHAT REALLY HAPPENED TO THE CLASS OF '65?
Dramatic Anthology
FIRST TELECAST: *December 8, 1977*
LAST TELECAST: *July 27, 1978*
BROADCAST HISTORY:
Dec 1977–Mar 1978, NBC Thu 10:00–11:00
May 1978–Jul 1978, NBC Thu 10:00–11:00
CAST:
Sam Ashley .... Tony Bill

A different graduate of Bret Harte High School, class of '65, was the subject of this dramatic anthology each week. Their post–high school stories were told from the perspective of a decade later: the class hustler, who had become a Vietnam War amputee; the class dreamers, who had become involved in a get-rich-quick scheme; "everybody's girl," who could never escape from her reputation for promiscuity.

A different cast appeared each week, with the only continuing role being that of Sam Ashley, who was a graduate of the class himself and who had returned to teach at the school. He served solely as narrator. Others appearing in individual telecasts included Leslie Nielsen, Jane Curtin, Larry Hagman, Linda Purl, and Meredith Baxter-Birney.

The series was based on the book of the same name.

WHAT'S GOING ON?
Quiz/Panel
FIRST TELECAST: *November 28, 1954*
LAST TELECAST: *December 26, 1954*
BROADCAST HISTORY:
Nov 1954–Dec 1954, ABC Sun 9:30–10:00
MODERATOR:
Lee Bowman
PANELISTS:
Kitty Carlisle
Hy Gardner
Audrey Meadows
Cliff Norton
Gene Raymond
Susan Oakland

This show featured a panel of six celebrities, divided into two groups, the "ins" and the "outs." The "ins" remained inside the studio and had to guess what the "outs," gathered outside at some remote location, were doing. The program lasted exactly five weeks.

WHAT'S HAPPENING!!
Situation Comedy
FIRST TELECAST: *August 5, 1976*
LAST TELECAST: *April 28, 1979*
BROADCAST HISTORY:
Aug 1976, ABC Thu 8:30–9:00
Nov 1976–Dec 1976, ABC Sat 8:30–9:00
Dec 1976–Jan 1978, ABC Thu 8:30–9:00
Jan 1978–Apr 1978, ABC Sat 8:00–8:30
Apr 1978–Jan 1979, ABC Thu 8:30–9:00
Feb 1979–Mar 1979, ABC Fri 8:30–9:00
Mar 1979–Apr 1979, ABC Sat 8:00–8:30
(In first-run syndication from September 1985)
CAST:
Roger Thomas ("Raj") .... Ernest Thomas
Freddie Stubbs ("Rerun") (1976–1986)
.... Fred Berry
Dwayne Clemens .... Haywood Nelson
Mrs. Thomas (Mama) (1976–1979)
.... Mabel King
Dee Thomas .... Danielle Spencer
Shirley Wilson .... Shirley Hemphill
Bill Thomas (1976–1977) ... Thalmus Rasulala
Marvin (1976–1977) .... Bryan O'Dell
Big Earl Babcock* (1978–1979) ... John Welsh
Little Earl (1978–1979) ...... David Hollander
"The Snake" (1978–1979) ...... Leland Smith
Nadine Hudson Thomas (1985–   )
.... Anne-Marie Johnson
Carolyn (1985–1986) .... Reina King
Maurice Warfield (1987–   )
.... Martin Lawrence
Darryl (1987–   ) .... Ken Sagoes

*Later called Barnett, then Barrett
MUSIC:
Henry Mancini

852

Urban comedy about three spirited black kids in a big city. Raj was the studious dreamer, who wanted to be a writer; Rerun, the jolly, overweight clown who often wound up with his foot in his mouth; and Dwayne, the shy tag-along, always striving to be "cool." When not involved in some sort of scrape, the three could be found hanging out at Rob's, a diner near their school, where Shirley was the waitress. Family problems arose when Raj clashed with his no-nonsense mother, who worked as a maid, and with his pesky little sister, Dee. Mama's no-good ex-husband Bill, the kids' father, was seen occasionally, as was Marvin, the gossipy reporter for the high school newspaper.

In 1978 Raj and Rerun graduated from high school and moved into a shared apartment nearby, while Raj entered college and Rerun went to work. Their new neighbors were Big Earl, a police detective, and his smart-mouthed son, Little Earl. "The Snake" was the college basketball star.

First seen as a summer replacement show, *What's Happening!!* was given a spot on the regular ABC schedule in the fall of 1976. Six years after leaving ABC in 1979 it returned to television with a new title, *What's Happening Now!!,* and most of the original cast. In the syndicated version Raj was newly married and trying to make it as a writer, and Rerun and Dwayne, now a used car salesman and computer programmer, respectively, were sharing an apartment. Shirley and Raj were also partners running Rob's, and Dee (who only showed up occasionally) was in college. Raj and Nadine, who were living in the house he had grown up in, took in a foster child named Caroline for a time. Added to the cast in the fall of 1987 were a local high school student named Maurice, who worked part-time as a busboy at Rob's, and his buddy, Darryl. It was also during that season that Dwayne gave up corporate life to open a small magic supplies shop.

The series was loosely based on the movie *Cooley High.*

WHAT'S HAPPENING TO AMERICA
Discussion
FIRST TELECAST: *July 12, 1968*
LAST TELECAST: *August 16, 1968*
BROADCAST HISTORY:
   Jul 1968–Aug 1968, NBC Fri 10:00–11:00
HOST:
   Edwin Newman

NBC News correspondent Edwin Newman was the host and moderator of this series of four discussions with prominent figures about the contradictions in American life: the gap between the rich and the poverty-stricken, the disparity between the good times experienced by some and the bad times by others, and the recently apparent tension and violence on the political scene. This series did not air on either August 2 or August 9.

WHAT'S IN A WORD
Quiz/Audience Participation
FIRST TELECAST: *July 22, 1954*
LAST TELECAST: *September 9, 1954*
BROADCAST HISTORY:
   Jul 1954–Sep 1954, CBS Thu 8:00–8:30
MODERATOR:
   Clifton Fadiman
PANELISTS:
   Faye Emerson
   Audrey Meadows
   Jim Moran
   Mike Wallace

Contestants on this word-association panel show made up simple two-word rhymes, like Fickle Pickle or Nice Rice, and won money depending on how successful the panel was at guessing what the rhyme was. The moderator provided clues to the noun portion of the rhyme and, to narrow down the possibilities, the panelists tried to make an association that was correct. The contestant won $5 for each clue used before the panel narrowed down and correctly identified the noun. At that point the moderator would give a definition of the adjective. The contestant then won an additional $5 for each wrong guess until the panel identified the adjective to complete the rhyme.

WHAT'S IT ALL ABOUT, WORLD?
Comedy Variety
FIRST TELECAST: *February 6, 1969*
LAST TELECAST: *May 1, 1969*
BROADCAST HISTORY:
   Feb 1969–May 1969, ABC Thu 9:00–10:00
HOST:
   Dean Jones
REGULARS:
   Dick Clair
   Jenna McMahon
   Gerri Granger
   Alex Dreier
   Dennis Allen
   Scoey Mitchlll
   Ron Prince
   Maureen Arthur
   Bayn Johnson
   Kevin Carlisle Dancers
   Denny Vaughn Orchestra

Not exactly a *Laugh-In,* not as bitingly satirical as *That Was the Week That Was,* not as controversial as *The Smothers Brothers Show, What's It All About, World?* nevertheless had some elements of each of those programs. It was a satirical revue that made fun of contemporary mores and hallowed institutions in a light, relatively inoffensive way. Comedy routines, fake documentaries, and musical production numbers were included, such as "The Rumor Factory" and "Hollywood Behind the Nixons." Among the regulars were the comedy team of Clair and McMahon, singer Gerri

Granger, commentator Alex Dreier, and nine-year-old Bayn Johnson.

The show was produced by Saul Ilson and Ernest Chambers, who were also responsible for *The Smothers Brothers Show* (the Smothers Brothers made a guest appearance here).

WHAT'S IT FOR
Quiz/Panel
FIRST TELECAST: *October 12, 1957*
LAST TELECAST: *January 4, 1958*
BROADCAST HISTORY:
Oct 1957–Jan 1958, NBC Sat 10:00–10:30
EMCEE:
Hal March
PANELISTS:
Betsy Palmer
Hans Conried
Abe Burrows
Toni Gilman (1957)
Lisa Ferraday

Strange inventions with presumably practical uses (an automatic hammock swinger, an umbrella skirt, etc.) were demonstrated each week for the panelists and audience of this program. After the demonstration an offstage announcer would inform the audience what the purpose of the invention was. The panel then had four minutes, one for each panel member, to guess the use of the invention by asking questions of the inventor or the inventor's representative, who had performed the demonstration. If the panel was stumped the inventor received $100, and if they guessed the function of the invention he received $50. The three original regular panel members were Betsy Palmer, Hans Conried, and Abe Burrows, with a rotating fourth member. Toni Gilman became a fourth regular member in November and Lisa Ferraday replaced Miss Gilman in December.

WHAT'S IT WORTH
Art Appraisal
FIRST TELECAST: *May 21, 1948*
LAST TELECAST: *October 11, 1953*
BROADCAST HISTORY:
May 1948–Jun 1948, CBS Fri 9:00–9:30
Jul 1948–Dec 1948, CBS Fri 8:00–8:30
Dec 1948–Jan 1949, CBS Fri 8:30–9:00
Jan 1949–Mar 1949, CBS Tue 9:30–10:00
Oct 1952, DUM Wed 8:30–9:00
Nov 1952–Sep 1953, DUM Thu 9:00–9:30
Sep 1953–Oct 1953, DUM Sun 6:00–6:30
APPRAISER:
Sigmund Rothschild
EMCEE:
Gil Fates (1948–1949)
Nelson Case (1952–1953)
Bill Wendell (1953)

As the resident authority on *What's It Worth?*, art restorer and copyist Sigmund Rothschild invited viewers to submit objects for appraisal. The ob-

jects could be family heirlooms, things discovered buried in attics, pets, or anything else of questionable value. Aided by visiting appraisers, Mr. Rothschild would establish the value of the object and discuss its discovery or history with its owners. The series left network TV in March 1949 but remained on as a local program in New York for another three months.

A little over a year later, on November 9, 1950, Mr. Rothschild made his first appearance as an occasional visitor to the late afternoon weekday daytime series *The Kate Smith Hour*. He did essentially the same thing he had done on CBS—pointing out the distinguishing characteristics that made objects either valuable or worthless. He left Miss Smith in January 1952 but turned up that fall on DuMont with his own show, *Trash or Treasure*, the same title his feature had used within *The Kate Smith Hour*. The DuMont show utilized Nelson Case as emcee until March 1953, and Bill Wendell thereafter. The title was changed to *Treasure Hunt* (not to be confused with the later quiz show of that name) in April 1953.

WHAT'S MY LINE
Quiz/Panel
FIRST TELECAST: *February 16, 1950*
LAST TELECAST: *September 3, 1967*
BROADCAST HISTORY:
Feb 1950–Mar 1950, CBS Thu 8:00–8:30
Apr 1950–Sep 1950, CBS Wed 9:00–9:30
Oct 1950–Sep 1967, CBS Sun 10:30–11:00
MODERATOR:
John Daly
PANELISTS:
Arlene Francis
Dorothy Kilgallen (1950–1965)
Louis Untermeyer (1950–1951)
Hal Block (1950–1953)
Bennett Cerf (1951–1967)
Steve Allen (1953–1954)
Fred Allen (1954–1956)
PRODUCERS:
Mark Goodson and Bill Todman

What's My Line was the longest-running game show in the history of prime-time network television. It ran for 18 seasons, on alternate weeks from February to September 1950, then every Sunday at 10:30 P.M. for the next 17 years. The format was exceedingly simple. Contestants were asked simple yes-or-no questions by the panel members, who tried to determine what interesting or unusual occupation the contestant had. Each time the contestant could answer no to a question, he got $5, and a total of 10 no's ended the game. The panel was forced to don blindfolds for the "mystery guest," a celebrity who tried to avoid identification by disguising his voice.

That little game, by itself, hardly warranted an 18-year run, when other panel shows of the early 1950s came and went every month. But *What's My Line* was something special, both for the witty and engaging panel, and for a certain élan which few other shows have ever captured. There were no flashy celebrities-of-the-moment or empty-headed pretty faces on this panel; they were obviously very intelligent people all, out to have some genteel fun with an amusing parlor game. Like John Daly with his bow tie and perfect manners, it reeked of urbanity ("That's three down and seven to go. Mr. Cerf?").

The panelists who created this special atmosphere were an elite group. The panel on the initial telecast consisted of Park Avenue psychiatrist Dr. Richard Hoffman, poet and critic Louis Untermeyer, former New Jersey Governor Harold Hoffman, and columnist Dorothy Kilgallen. (Their first contestant: a lissome blond hat-check girl from the Stork Club.) Arlene Francis joined the panel on the second telecast, and Bennett Cerf in March 1951. Kilgallen, Cerf, and Francis were continuing regulars for the next 15 years.

Of the other early panelists, Untermeyer was perhaps the most tragic loss—forced off the show, and off television, by McCarthy Era political blacklisting. Gag writer Hal Block was a panelist for a time, as was acerbic Fred Allen and multi-talented Steve Allen (who, in trying to determine size as quickly as possible within the show's yes-or-no format, conjured up the program's classic question: "Is it bigger than a breadbox?"). After the death of Fred Allen in 1956, the fourth seat on the panel was left permanently open for a different guest panelist each week. Little changed until the mid 1960s. In 1965 Dorothy Kilgallen died suddenly, of an overdose of medication, following her appearance on the November 7 program. A much-publicized talent hunt ensued for a permanent replacement, but in the end her chair was also left open, filled by another guest panelist each week.

Finally in 1967, hoary with age, *What's My Line* left the network, only to surface less than a year later in a considerably less sophisticated and more slapstick syndicated version. Arlene Francis was the only holdover, joined by Soupy Sales as a regular panelist and Wally Bruner as moderator (replaced by Larry Blyden in 1972). The syndicated version lasted until 1975.

WHAT'S MY NAME
see *Paul Winchell—Jerry Mahoney Show, The*

WHAT'S NEW
see *Gulf Road Show Starring Bob Smith, The*

WHAT'S ON YOUR MIND
see *How Did They Get That Way*

WHAT'S THE STORY?
Quiz/Panel
FIRST TELECAST: *July 25, 1951*
LAST TELECAST: *September 23, 1955*
BROADCAST HISTORY:
Jul 1951–Oct 1951, DUM Wed 9:00–9:30
Oct 1951–Feb 1952, DUM Tue 8:00–8:30
Feb 1952–May 1952, DUM Tue 10:30–11:00
Jun 1952–May 1953, DUM Thu 9:30–10:00

May 1953–Jun 1953, DUM Wed 7:30–8:00
Jun 1953–Sep 1953, DUM Sun 10:00–10:30
Sep 1953–Apr 1954, DUM Thu 9:00–9:30
Apr 1954–Sep 1954, DUM Thu 8:00–8:30
Sep 1954–Feb 1955, DUM Thu 9:00–9:30
Mar 1955–Jun 1955, DUM Wed 8:00–8:30
Jul 1955–Sep 1955, DUM Fri 7:30–8:00
MODERATOR:
Walt Raney (1951)
Walter Kiernan (1951–1953)
Al Capp (1953)
John K. M. McCaffery (1953–1955)
PANELISTS:
Harriet Van Horne (1952–1955)
Robert Sullivan (1952–1953)
Jimmy Cannon (1952–1955)

To this innocuous panel show belongs the unique distinction of being the last surviving entertainment show on the dying DuMont TV network—only a few scattered sports events were continued into 1956. After *What's the Story?* left the air in September 1955, and the remaining boxing matches petered out in 1956, the DuMont network was but a memory.

For four years, however, *What's the Story?* had a reasonably successful career. It consisted of a celebrity panel which attempted to identify important news events from clues provided by the moderator and his helpers. Panelists were generally well-known newspaper columnists, with Harriet Van Horne of the *New York World Telegram*, Robert Sullivan of the New York *Daily News* and Jimmy Cannon of the *Post* the longest-running regulars. Bosley Crowther of the *New York Times* made frequent guest appearances, and John McCaffery's English bulldog, Porthos, was the show's mascot for a time.

WHAT'S YOUR BID
Auction
FIRST TELECAST: *February 14, 1953*
LAST TELECAST: *July 5, 1953*
BROADCAST HISTORY:
Feb 1953–Apr 1953, ABC Sat 7:30–8:00
May 1953–Jul 1953, DUM Sun 10:00–10:30
HOST:
Leonard Rosen (ABC)
Robert Alda (DUM)
ANNOUNCER:
John Reed King (ABC)
Dick Shepard (DUM)
MODEL:
Roslyn Woods (ABC)

What's Your Bid was a switch on the usual TV giveaway in that the studio audience was supposed to bring its own money to the show—and use it to bid on merchandise such as radios, cars, mink coats, home freezers, etc. Bidders at least got their money's worth (if they bid more than an item was worth, something extra was thrown in) and the proceeds all went to charity. A feature of each show was the auctioning of an item brought in by a famous celebrity, and having some special connection with that celebrity. Some straight giveaway segments were also worked in, but this early form of "pay TV" did not catch on and was soon canceled. Leonard Rosen, the first host and auctioneer, was known on the show as "Liberal Bill."

WHEEL OF FORTUNE
Quiz/Audience Participation
FIRST TELECAST: *July 7, 1953*
LAST TELECAST: *September 15, 1953*
BROADCAST HISTORY:
Jul 1953–Sep 1953, CBS Tue 8:30–9:00
HOST:
Todd Russell

All of the contestants on this early series were people who had distinguished themselves as good samaritans or heroes. They were brought on the show and received rewards for their good deeds. After host Todd Russell related their individual stories for the audience, a giant carnival-type wheel was spun to determine the nature of the "reward" that they would receive. A special "lucky" section on the wheel could bring the contestant a $1,000 bonus if he could answer a special jackpot question correctly. This summer series was identical to the daytime version that had premiered the previous October, and ran until Christmas Day 1953.

WHEEL OF FORTUNE
Quiz
BROADCAST HISTORY:
Syndicated and network daytime
30 minutes
Produced: *1983–*
Released: *September 1983*
HOST:
Pat Sajak
ASSISTANT:
Vanna White

This series was a rather straightforward game show in which contestants spun a large wheel to determine whether they could attempt to fill in one letter of a mystery phrase. Depending on where the wheel stopped, they might win a corresponding amount of money (if the letter they guessed was in the phrase); lose control to another contestant; or go "bankrupt," losing all their winnings to date. The first contestant to guess the phrase got to use his or her accumulated money to buy prizes.

Wheel of Fortune premiered in NBC daytime in January 1975, with Chuck Woolery as host, later replaced by Pat Sajak. A syndicated evening version began production in 1983 and it became the most popular syndicated series of the 1980s. The program was created and produced by Merv Griffin.

WHEELS
Drama
FIRST TELECAST: *April 4, 1979*
LAST TELECAST: *April 18, 1979*
BROADCAST HISTORY:
Apr 1979, NBC Wed 9:00–11:00
CAST:
Adam Trenton .... Rock Hudson
Erica Trenton .... Lee Remick
Greg Trenton .... Howard McGillin
Kirk Trenton .... James Carroll Jordan
Hub Hewitson .... Tim O'Connor
Rusty Horton .... Gerald S. O'Loughlin
Rollie Knight .... Harold Sylvester
Teresa Chapman .... Adele Mara
Lowell Baxter .... Ralph Bellamy
Jody Horton .... Lisa Eilbacher
Smokey Stephenson .... Tony Franciosa
Barbara Lipton .... Blair Brown
Leonard Wingate .... Fred Williamson
Ursula .... Jessica Walter
Newkirk .... Al White

Set in Detroit in the late 1960s, *Wheels* was the story of boardroom intrigue at National Motors, a giant automobile company struggling for its life in a highly competitive industry. The central character was Adam Trenton, Vice President of Product Development, who had put his career on the line by developing and pushing the Hawk, a radically new, sporty model designed to win back the youth market. Opposing him were scheming President Hub Hewitson and conservative Board Chairman Lowell Baxter, Adam's father-in-law. Adam's total commitment to his work put his marriage on the line, as well. His wife, Erica, began an affair with a race driver, his younger son, Greg, ran away from home, and his older son, Kirk, began an affair with Adam's own mistress, Barbara Lipton.

Wheels was based on the best-selling novel by Arthur Hailey. It first aired as a five-part miniseries from May 7–15, 1978, and was highly successful. When it was repeated a year later, however, as part of *NBC Novels for Television,* hardly anyone watched—leading to one of the fastest re-editing jobs ever seen on network television. The repeat was supposed to run for five consecutive weeks, but when the network saw the disastrously low ratings for parts one and two it quickly compressed parts three, four, and five into a single concluding episode. Next week, surprised viewers saw the entire remainder of the novel flash by—and disappear.

WHEN THE WHISTLE BLOWS
Situation Comedy
FIRST TELECAST: *March 14, 1980*
LAST TELECAST: *July 27, 1980*
BROADCAST HISTORY:
Mar 1980–Apr 1980, ABC Fri 8:00–9:00
Jun 1980, ABC Sat 10:00–11:00
Jul 1980, ABC Sun 8:00–9:00

Buzz Dillard .... Doug Barr
Randy Hartford .... Philip Brown
Lucy Davis .... Susan Buckner
Martin "Hunk" Kincaid ...... Tim Rossovich
Norm Jenkins .... Dolph Sweet
Dottie Jenkins .... Alice Hirson
Ted Hanrahan .... Gary Allen
Bulldog .... Noble Willingham
Darlene Ridgeway .... Sue Ane Langdon

Comedy about a gang of young construction workers out to have a good time, on the job and off. Lucy was the only woman on the crew, and just "one of the guys" at that. Randy was the college graduate; Buzz, the complete extrovert; and Hunk, the resident hulk. Others around the ol' construction site were Norm Jenkins, the older guy whose wife, Dottie, wished he would slow down; Bulldog, another worker; Hanrahan, the foreman; and Darlene, the operator of the gang's favorite hangout.

WHEN THINGS WERE ROTTEN
Situation Comedy
FIRST TELECAST: September 10, 1975
LAST TELECAST: December 24, 1975
BROADCAST HISTORY:
Sep 1975–Dec 1975, ABC Wed 8:00–8:30
CAST:
Robin Hood .... Dick Gautier
Friar Tuck .... Dick Van Patten
Alan-a-Dale .... Bernie Kopell
Bertram/Renaldo .... Richard Dimitri
The Sheriff of Nottingham ..... Henry Polic II
Maid Marian .... Misty Rowe
Little John .... David Sabin
Prince John .... Ron Rifkin
Princess Isabelle .... Jane A. Johnston
CREATOR PRODUCER:
Mel Brooks

Mel Brooks created this wild satire on Robin Hood and His Merry Men of Sherwood Forest in 12th-century England. Instead of the boldly heroic Robin of legend, he was portrayed as a complete nitwit, and his men a band of incompetents who only succeeded because of the even greater incompetence of the evil Prince John and his henchman, the sheriff of Nottingham. Much of the humor in this fast-paced, movie-style comedy was based on non sequiturs and historical anachronisms, such as the episode in which Prince John hired the four fastest woodcutters in the kingdom to chop down the entire Sherwood Forest—to make way for a new housing development for wealthy burghers. In the premiere telecast, the prince lured Robin into a trap by staging an archery contest to determine who was the greatest bowman in the land. Robin, vain as ever, came in disguise to win the title but was seized and thrown into the dungeon. Whereupon his men disguised themselves

as a traveling conga band and bongoed their way into the castle to rescue him.

Maid Marian was Robin's sexy but empty-headed love interest.

Critics applauded this series as one of the most inventive of the season, but viewers paid no attention to it and it was soon canceled.

WHERE WAS I?
Quiz/Panel
FIRST TELECAST: September 2, 1952
LAST TELECAST: October 6, 1953
BROADCAST HISTORY:
Sep 1952–May 1953, DUM Tue 9:00–9:30
May 1953–Jun 1953, DUM Tue 10:00–10:30
Jul 1953–Oct 1953, DUM Tue 9:30–10:00
EMCEE:
Dan Seymour (1952)
Ken Roberts (1952)
John Reed King (1952–1953)
PANELISTS:
Nancy Guild
Peter Donald
Samuel Grafton (1953)
Virginia Graham (1952)
Bill Cullen (1953)
Barbara Barondess MacLean (1953)
Skitch Henderson (1953)
Mort Greene (1953)

In this picture quiz the panel had to identify a given location from a set of photographs, and some verbal clues. The original host, Dan Seymour, lasted less than a month, followed by Ken Roberts for about two months and then John Reed King for the remainder of the run of the show. There was quite a bit of turnover in panelists as well.

WHERE'S HUDDLES
Cartoon
FIRST TELECAST: July 1, 1970
LAST TELECAST: September 9, 1970
BROADCAST HISTORY:
Jul 1970–Sep 1970, CBS Wed 7:30–8:00
VOICES:
Bubba McCoy .... Mel Blanc
Sports Announcer .... Dick Enberg
Freight Train .... Herb Jeffries
Claude Pertwee .... Paul Lynde
Fumbles .... Don Messick
Ed Huddles .... Cliff Norton
Mad Dog Maloney .... Alan Reed
Marge Huddles .... Jean VanderPyl
Penny McCoy .... Marie Wilson

This animated summer series was the story of two professional football players for the Rhinos, quarterback Ed Huddles and center Bubba McCoy. They were next-door neighbors and best friends, as well as teammates, and their adventures on and off the field were the subjects of the episodes of the show.

WHERE'S RAYMOND?
see *Ray Bolger Show, The*

WHIPLASH
Western
BROADCAST HISTORY:
Syndicated only
30 minutes
Produced: *1960–1961* (34 episodes)
Released (U.S.): *1961*
CAST:
Christopher Cobb . . . . Peter Graves
Dan . . . . Anthony Wickert

This was an Australian Western. Set in the 1850s, it traced the exploits of American Chris Cobb as he fought gunslingers, robbers, and swindlers to establish Cobb & Co., the first stagecoach line on the continent. Although filmed in Australia, the series did all it could to look American—even the bad guys were émigrés. The locals were mostly reduced to lines like, "You're an American—you're the only one who can stop them." Cobb, at least, showed some sensitivity to local feelings by using bullwhips and boomerangs to corral the villains.

WHIRLYBIRDS, THE
Adventure
BROADCAST HISTORY:
Syndicated only
30 minutes
Produced: *1956–1959* (111 episodes)
Released: *January 1957*
CAST:
Chuck Martin . . . . Ken Tobey
Pete ("P.T.") Moore . . . . Craig Hill
Janet Culver (1956–1957) . . . . . . Sandra Spence
Helen Carter (1957–1959) . . . . Nancy Hale

Helicopters were substituted for horses in this contemporary Western. Chuck and P.T. were pilot partners in an outfit called Whirlybirds, Inc., located in Southern California. They hired out for all sorts of jobs, such as locating lost prospectors, delivering vital supplies, and even chasing a bad guy or two. There were plenty of stunt scenes, where one of the heroes would dangle from the end of a rope to pluck a client out of danger, or even leap from the chopper onto the back of a villain galloping away on horseback. Janet Culver was their original pretty secretary, replaced after the first season by Helen Carter.

The series was originally made to run on the CBS network, but instead was put into syndication by CBS Films. It became a substantial hit with the younger set.

WHISPERING SMITH
Western/Detective
FIRST TELECAST: *May 15, 1961*
LAST TELECAST: *September 18, 1961*
BROADCAST HISTORY:
May 1961–Sep 1961, NBC Mon 9:00–9:30
CAST:
Det. Tom "Whispering" Smith
. . . . Audie Murphy
Det. George Romack . . . . Guy Mitchell
Chief John Richards . . . . Sam Buffington

Set in Denver, Colorado, in the 1870s, *Whispering Smith* was based on the adventures of the first police detective to bring modern methods of analysis, tracing technique, and apprehension to the practice of law enforcement in the West. Denver police detective Tom Smith, better known by his nickname "Whispering," was this pioneer Western criminologist. His partner and sidekick, George Romack, was played by singer-turned-actor Guy Mitchell. Sam Buffington, who played the chief of the Denver Police Department, died during the filming of the series and was seen in only a portion of the episodes. Actual cases from the file of the Denver Police Department provided the cases depicted in *Whispering Smith*.

This series was originally scheduled for the 1959–1960 fall season but, after co-star Guy Mitchell suffered a broken shoulder with only seven episodes completed, it was temporarily postponed.

WHITE CAMELLIA, THE
see *ABC Dramatic Shorts—1952–1953*

WHITE SHADOW, THE
Drama
FIRST TELECAST: *November 27, 1978*
LAST TELECAST: *August 12, 1981*
BROADCAST HISTORY:
Nov 1978–Jan 1979, CBS Mon 8:00–9:00
Jan 1979–Feb 1979, CBS Sat 8:00–9:00
Mar 1979–Dec 1979, CBS Mon 8:00–9:00
Dec 1979–Sep 1980, CBS Tue 8:00–9:00
Dec 1980–Jan 1981, CBS Tue 8:00–9:00
Feb 1981–Mar 1981, CBS Mon 8:00–9:00
Jun 1981–Aug 1981, CBS Wed 8:00–9:00
CAST:
Ken Reeves . . . . Ken Howard
Jim Willis (first episode) . . . . . Jason Bernard
Jim Willis (1978–1980) . . . . Ed Bernard
Sybil Buchanan . . . . Joan Pringle
James Hayward (1978–1980) . . Thomas Carter
Morris Thorpe . . . . Kevin Hooks
Curtis Jackson (1978–1980) . . . . Eric Kilpatrick
Milton Reese (1978–1980) . . . . . . Nathan Cook
Mario Pettrino (Salami)
. . . . Timothy Van Patten
Abner Goldstein (1978–1980)
. . . . Ken Michelman
Ricky Gomez (1978–1980) . . . . . . Ira Angustain
Warren Coolidge . . . . Byron Stewart
Katie Donahue (1978–1979) . . . . . . Robin Rose
Bill Donahue (1978–1979) . . . . Jerry Fogel
Nick Vitaglia (1979–1981) . . . . John Mengatti
Manager Phil Jefferson (1979–1981)
. . . . Russell Phillip Robinson

Wardell Stone (1980–1981)

.... Larry Flash Jenkins
Jesse B. Mitchell (1980–1981)

.... Stoney Jackson
Teddy Rutherford (1980–1981)... Wolfe Perry
Eddie Franklin (1980–1981) ..... Art Holliday
Paddy Falahey (1980–1981) .... John Laughlin

After a succession of knee problems forced Ken Reeves to retire from his job as a forward on the Chicago Bulls professional basketball team, his college friend Jim Willis convinced him to take a shot at being the basketball coach of Carver High in Los Angeles. Carver was in a tough inner-city, lower-middle-class neighborhood, with a racially mixed student body and team. It was a hard job, especially for someone unfamiliar with street-wise kids and coaching them in a game he knew best as a player. Ken could have earned more doing something else, as his sister Katie kept reminding him, but he found greater satisfaction working with these teenagers. Ken's old friend Jim was Carver's principal, and Sybil Buchanan was the vice principal (who became principal in the fall of 1980).

The White Shadow was more than just a basketball show, it was also the story of young people and their adjustments to life in an often hostile world. Within the framework of a high school basketball team were stories of personal conflict, drug problems, teenage crime, and the dangers in a tough area. In fact, in the spring of 1980 one of Ken's players, Curtis Jackson, was shot to death while witnessing a liquor-store holdup. Students moved on, as in real life. In the spring of 1980, after the team had won the Los Angeles City Basketball Championship, several players graduated from Carver and were replaced by new players in the fall. The series treated its subjects realistically and sympathetically, and was lauded by numerous educational organizations, although its audience size remained marginal throughout its run.

WHIZ KIDS

Detective/Adventure
FIRST TELECAST: *October 5, 1983*
LAST TELECAST: *June 2, 1984*
BROADCAST HISTORY:
    Oct 1983–Dec 1983, CBS Wed 8:00–9:00
    Jan 1984–Jun 1984, CBS Sat 8:00–9:00
CAST:
    Richie Adler .... Matthew Laborteaux
    Hamilton Parker............... Todd Porter
    Jeremy Saldino .... Jeffrey Jacquet
    Llewellen Farley, Jr. .... Max Gail
    Alice Tyler................... Andrea Elson
    Cheryl Adler .... Melanie Gaffin
    Lt. Neal Quinn .... A Martinez
    Irene Adler................. Madelyn Cain
    Ms. Vance .... Linda Scruggs
    Carson Marsh (1984) .... Dan O'Herlihy

If you were going to do a show about kids and computers, what better place than California, home of Silicon Valley, high-tech, and trend setters? It was there, in the suburban Los Angeles community of Calabasas, that the *Whiz Kids* lived. Richie was the bright computer "hacker" who, with the aid of Ham, Jeremy, and Alice, his buddies and schoolmates at Canyon High School, worked as an amateur detective in his spare time. Farley was their friend and information source, a reporter with the *Los Angeles Gazette* who sometimes asked them for help on stories he was working on and at other times got involved with cases on which they were already working. Farley's brother-in-law Neal Quinn, who ran the police department's MDT's (Mobile Data Terminals), also provided Farley and the kids with some help, albeit grudgingly, when they needed access to police computer information.

The real star of the show, however, may have been Richie's talking computer, Ralf. With Richie's expert programming, Ralf provided clues, graphic images, answers to problems, and access to other computer information banks that were supposedly protected against unauthorized use. Everyone in Richie's home got involved with technological toys and services. His little sister, Cheryl, had a small robot (instead of a doll) named Herman, and his divorced mother, Irene, had been enrolled (by Richie) in a computer dating service. At midseason the mysterious Carson Marsh was added to the cast, an elderly gentleman who, as head of the Athena Society, had contacts and access to data that not even Richie or the police could get to. Occasionally, when the kids got in over their heads, Carson helped bail them out.

WHO IN THE WORLD

Interview
FIRST TELECAST: *June 24, 1962*
LAST TELECAST: *September 16, 1962*
BROADCAST HISTORY:
    Jun 1962–Sep 1962, CBS Sun 9:30–10:00
HOST:
    Warren Hull

Each week host Warren Hull interviewed three to five people who had made headlines in the nation's newspapers during the previous seven days. At least that was the original idea behind the show. A shortage of available headline-makers forced the area from which guests were drawn to be broadened to include people who had human-interest stories to tell. The program's producer found the world's first airline stewardess and the 1,000th member of the Peace Corps, among others, for Warren Hull to chat with.

WHO PAYS

Quiz/Panel
FIRST TELECAST: *July 2, 1959*
LAST TELECAST: *September 24, 1959*

859

Jul 1959–Sep 1959, NBC Thu 8:00–8:30
EMCEE:
Mike Wallace
PANELISTS:
Gene Klavan
Cedric Hardwicke
Celeste Holm

The object of *Who Pays* was for the three regular panelists to determine which celebrity or public figure was the employer of each pair of contestants. The employees were questioned by the panelists in two rounds. The first round gave each panelist one minute to ask specific questions of the two employees (who were chauffeurs, doctors, gardeners, hair stylists, etc.). At the end of the round the panelists pooled their information and decided whether or not to guess the identity of the employer. If they guessed correctly, the employees split $100 and if they guessed incorrectly the employees split $200. If the panelists felt they had too little information to hazard a guess, a second round was played with the dollar value to the employees doubling.

WHO SAID THAT?
Quiz/Panel
FIRST TELECAST: *December 9, 1948*
LAST TELECAST: *July 26, 1955*
BROADCAST HISTORY:
Dec 1948–Jan 1949, NBC Mon 10:00–10:30
Jan 1949–Mar 1949, NBC Sun 10:30–11:00
Apr 1949–Dec 1949, NBC Sat 9:00–9:30
Jan 1950–Jul 1954, NBC Mon 10:30–11:00
Feb 1955–Apr 1955, ABC Wed 9:00–9:30
May 1955–Jul 1955, ABC Tue 8:30–9:00
EMCEE:
Robert Trout (1948–1951)
Walter Kiernan (1951–1954)
John Daly (1955)
PANELISTS:
John Cameron Swayze (1948–1951)
Bill Henry (1952–1953)
June Lockhart (1952–1955)
Morey Amsterdam (1954)
H. V. Kaltenborn (1954)
Bob Considine (1955)
John Mason Brown (1955)

Live quiz show based on quotations from the news. A panel of newsmen and celebrities was read a quotation from the current headlines, and then asked to identify "who said that," and something about the circumstances. Failure to come up with the correct answer resulted in forfeiture of cash to the prize jackpot, which at one time was represented by a goldfish bowl into which panel members stuffed bills. The jackpot was awarded to a home viewer if the quote had been sent in by one, or to a charity. Variations such as a famous guest who, seen only in silhouette, personally delivered his own quote, famous quotes from the

past, and partial quotes which had to be completed were also introduced from time to time. During most of the show's run there was only a single permanent panelist (or "anchorman"), plus guests, but toward the end several permanent panelists were used. Among the panelists appearing irregularly, but frequently, were Frank Coniff, Earl Wilson, Al Capp, Quentin Reynolds, Bennett Cerf, Oscar Levant, and Kitty Carlisle.

The program was originally edited by Fred Friendly, and was also heard on radio for a time.

WHO'S THE BOSS?
Quiz/Panel
FIRST TELECAST: *February 19, 1954*
LAST TELECAST: *August 20, 1954*
BROADCAST HISTORY:
Feb 1954–Jun 1954, ABC Fri 9:30–10:00
Jul 1954–Aug 1954, ABC Fri 8:30–9:00
EMCEE:
Walter Kiernan (Feb–Jul)
Mike Wallace (Jul–Aug)
PANELISTS:
Peggy McKay
Dick Kollmar
Sylvia Lyons
Horace Sutton

Secretaries to famous personalities from the worlds of show business, politics, and sports were the guests on this show. The panel attempted to identify the names of their bosses through indirect questioning, with prizes being awarded after each round that the secretary continued to stump the panel.

WHO'S THE BOSS?
Situation Comedy
FIRST TELECAST: *September 20, 1984*
LAST TELECAST:
BROADCAST HISTORY:
Sep 1984, ABC Thu 8:30–9:00
Oct 1984–Apr 1985, ABC Tue 8:30–9:00
Apr 1985–Jul 1985, ABC Tue 9:00–9:30
Aug 1985–   , ABC Tue 8:00–8:30
CAST:
Angela Bower .... Judith Light
Tony Micelli .... Tony Danza
Samantha Micelli .... Alyssa Milano
Jonathan Bower .... Danny Pintauro
Mona Robinson......... Katherine Helmond
*Geoffrey Wells (1986–1987) ... Robin Thomas
*Bonnie (1986–   ) .... Shana Lane-Block
*Jesse Nash (1987–   ) .... Scott Bloom

*Occasional role
THEME:
"Brand New Life" by Larry Carlton, Robert Kraft, Martin Cohan, and Blake Hunter

1984 was the year of male role reversal on television. That fall, both *Who's the Boss?* and *Charles in Charge* featured macho guys working as domestics for women who didn't have time to raise the kids. Tony was a former boxer and a widower with a kid of his own, young Samantha. Fed up with the congestion and bustle of New York City, he sought refuge working as a domestic for Angela Bower, the high-powered but somewhat disorganized President of the Wallace and McQuade Advertising Agency, who lived in suburban Connecticut. Angela, a widow with a rambunctious young son named Jonathan, had doubts about the arrangement, but her mother, Mona, quickly observed that "a man can do meaningless, unproductive work as well as a woman." Tony proved to be very good at his new job, bringing order to Angela's chaotic household and providing a needed father figure to Jonathan.

Angela, who worried constantly about her career, was abruptly fired in 1986, whereupon she opened her own ad agency. At about the same time romance entered her life in the person of handsome Geoffrey Wells—which served to bring into focus her growing fondness for Tony. However, for the time being, at least, they would not become an "item." Also in 1986, Samantha entered high school where, a year later, she found a boyfriend in Jesse. Not to be left out Mona was courted, off and on, by mature, dashing Max Muldoon (Leslie Nielsen).

ABC aired reruns of *Who's the Boss?* on weekday mornings from June 1987 to July 1988.

WHO'S THERE
Quiz/Audience Participation
FIRST TELECAST: *July 14, 1952*
LAST TELECAST: *September 15, 1952*
BROADCAST HISTORY:
Jul 1952–Sep 1952, CBS Mon 9:30–10:00
EMCEE:
Arlene Francis
PANELISTS:
Bill Cullen
Robert Coote
Roger Price

The panelists on *Who's There* tried to identify famous celebrities from various articles of clothing or props that had been characteristic of, or identified with, the celebrities. There were two regular panelists—originally Bill Cullen and Robert Coote—and one guest panelist. Cullen was replaced in midsummer by Roger Price.

WHO'S WATCHING THE KIDS
Situation Comedy
FIRST TELECAST: *September 22, 1978*
LAST TELECAST: *December 15, 1978*
BROADCAST HISTORY:
Sep 1978–Dec 1978, NBC Fri 8:30–9:00
CAST:
Stacy Turner .... Caren Kaye
Angie Vitola .... Lynda Goodfriend
Frankie "the Fox" Vitola .... Scott Baio
Melissa Turner .... Tammy Lauren

Mitzi Logan .... Marcia Lewis
Larry Parnell .... Larry Breeding
Memphis O'Hara .... Lorrie Mahaffey
Bert Gunkel .... Jim Belushi
Venus .... Shirley Kirkes
Bridget .... Elaine Bolton

The kids in this comedy were 15-year-old Frankie and 9-year-old Melissa, two hyperactive and worldly-wise youngsters who lived with their showgirl older sisters in a Las Vegas apartment. Angie and Stacy spent much of their time performing at a third-rate local nightspot, the Club Sand Pile, so help was enlisted from neighbor Larry Parnell to "watch the kids." Macho, street-wise Frankie and bookish, know-it-all Melissa were more than a match for all three adults. Larry was a reporter whose ambition was to become a hard-hitting investigative journalist, but so far he had made it only to reading the weather and garden news on a local TV station. Mitzi was the rotund emcee at the Club Sand Pile, and also the girls' landlady; Memphis was a singer at the club.

The pilot for this comedy, which had a slightly different story line, aired on May 19, 1978, under the title *Legs*.

WHO'S WHO
News Magazine
FIRST TELECAST: *January 4, 1977*
LAST TELECAST: *June 26, 1977*
BROADCAST HISTORY:
Jan 1977–May 1977, CBS Tue 8:00–9:00
Jun 1977, CBS Sun 10:00–11:00
REPORTERS:
Dan Rather
Barbara Howar
Charles Kuralt

If *60 Minutes* was the television equivalent of *Time* magazine, this series, produced by the same team, was patterned after *People* magazine. Although *60 Minutes* often did profiles on individuals, it also included in-depth studies of broader issues. *Who's Who* concentrated only on people. Dan Rather and Barbara Howar did pieces on the famous—Richard Burton, Leopold Stokowski, Lily Tomlin, Jodie Foster, Jack Nicklaus, UN Ambassador Andrew Young, and First Lady Rosalynn Carter. Charles Kuralt focused on more obscure subjects. His "On the Road" segment included chats with an 89-year-old kite flyer in Farmland, Indiana; a champion boomerang thrower living on an island in the Gulf of Mexico; a nightclub owner in Vicksburg, Mississippi, who had booked top black jazz performers into his place in the 1930s and 1940s; and the inventor of the supermarket shopping cart, in Oklahoma City.

WHO'S WHOSE
Quiz/Audience Participation
FIRST TELECAST: *June 25, 1951*
LAST TELECAST: *June 25, 1951*

BROADCAST HISTORY:
Jun 1951, CBS Mon 9:30–10:00
EMCEE:
Phil Baker
PANELISTS:
Robin Chandler
Art Ford
Basil Davenport
Emily Kimbrough

The object of this summer show was for the celebrity panel (three regulars and one guest) to guess which of three people was the spouse of a fourth contestant. The panelists had an opportunity to question all four people, three of one sex and the fourth of the other, in the attempt to determine who was whose. Since the show only lasted one week, it obviously did not work too well.

WHODUNNIT?

Quiz/Audience Participation
FIRST TELECAST: *April 12, 1979*
LAST TELECAST: *May 17, 1979*
BROADCAST HISTORY:
Apr 1979, NBC Thu 8:00–8:30
May 1979, NBC Thu 8:30–9:00
EMCEE:
Ed McMahon
REGULAR PANELISTS:
F. Lee Bailey
Melvin Belli

This odd program was a hybrid of drama and quiz show. Each week three contestants and a panel of three experts watched a dramatization of a murder mystery. The action stopped just before the villain was revealed, and the object was for the contestants to match wits with the experts in determining "whodunnit." Clues were provided, some relevant and some not, and the "suspects" were interrogated by a law-enforcement officer. The panel also cross-examined the suspects, but if any contestant could guess the actual murderer before they did he won $10,000. The panel then offered their opinion of who the actual murderer was. With all this information, the contestants made their choices; if they were right, and the panel was wrong, they won $5,000. If they and the panel both nailed the right suspect, they got $2,500.

Ed McMahon hosted the show, and celebrity attorneys F. Lee Bailey and Melvin Belli were the most frequent panelists. An added feature was the appearance of famous guest stars such as Jack Klugman, Erik Estrada, and Loni Anderson as the murder victims.

Although NBC billed this as television's first mystery game show, the format, and variations on it, were in fact rather popular in the very early days of TV: see *Stand By for Crime* (1949), *Chicagoland Mystery Players* (1949), and *Crawford Mystery Theatre* (1951), among others.

WHY?

Quiz/Panel
FIRST TELECAST: *January 12, 1953*
LAST TELECAST: *April 20, 1953*
BROADCAST HISTORY:
Jan 1953–Apr 1953, ABC Mon 10:00–10:30
EMCEE:
John Reed King
ASSISTANT:
Bill Cullen

In this quiz show based on the old "five W's," Bill Cullen read the panel the who, what, where, and when of a situation. The panel then had to guess the "why?" The three members of each night's panel were drawn from all walks of life.

WICHITA TOWN

Western
FIRST TELECAST: *September 30, 1959*
LAST TELECAST: *September 23, 1960*
BROADCAST HISTORY:
Sep 1959–Apr 1960, NBC Wed 10:30–11:00
Jun 1960–Sep 1960, NBC Fri 8:30–9:00
CAST:
Marshal Mike Dunbar .... Joel McCrea
Ben Matheson .... Jody McCrea
Rico Rodriguez .... Carlos Romero
Dr. Nat Wyndham .... George Neise
Aeneas MacLinahan .... Bob Anderson
Joe Kingston.................. Robert Foulk

In the decade following the Civil War the town of Wichita, on the fringes of the lawless Western frontier in the Kansas Territory, was a young city trying to grow and prosper. The town's leading citizen was Mike Dunbar, a man who had led a cattle drive to Wichita and decided to stay on as marshal to help establish law and order in the community. Dunbar was aided by his two deputies, Ben Matheson and Rico Rodriguez, the former a foreman at the nearby Circle J Ranch, and the latter a reformed Mexican gunfighter. Also seen regularly in the series were Dr. Nat Wyndham, Wichita's first doctor, Aeneas MacLinahan, the town blacksmith, and Joe Kingston, the bartender in the local saloon.

Joel and Jody McCrea, who played marshal and deputy in this Western, were in real life father and son.

Wichita Town was based on the 1955 film in which McCrea had played Wyatt Earp.

WIDE COUNTRY, THE

Western
FIRST TELECAST: *September 20, 1962*
LAST TELECAST: *September 12, 1963*
BROADCAST HISTORY:
Sep 1962–Sep 1963, NBC Thu 7:30–8:30
CAST:
Mitch Guthrie .... Earl Holliman
Andy Guthrie................. Andrew Prine

Western drama revolving around champion bronco rider Mitch Guthrie, as he encountered the adventures of contemporary rodeo life, while trying to persuade his kid brother Andy not to become a "rodeo bum" like himself.

WIFE SAVER, THE
Household Hints
FIRST TELECAST: *May 22, 1947*
LAST TELECAST: *June 26, 1947*
BROADCAST HISTORY:
May 1947–Jun 1947, NBC Thu 8:30–9:00
HOST:
Allen Prescott

Longtime radio favorite Allen Prescott tried his popular *Wife Saver* routine (first heard in 1932) on television in 1947. The format consisted of Prescott in the kitchen demonstrating household gadgets and explaining ways of solving problems around the house, such as keeping twine untangled or bureau drawers unstuck, all interspersed with a steady patter of gags. The humor plus the useful hints should have made this a popular show, but it lasted only six weeks.

WILD BILL HICKOK
see *Adventures of Wild Bill Hickok, The*

WILD KINGDOM
Wildlife/Nature
FIRST TELECAST: *January 7, 1968*
LAST TELECAST: *April 11, 1971*
BROADCAST HISTORY:
Jan 1968–Jun 1968, NBC Sun 7:00–7:30
Jan 1969–Jun 1969, NBC Sun 7:00–7:30
Sep 1969–Jun 1970, NBC Sun 7:00–7:30
Sep 1970–Apr 1971, NBC Sun 7:00–7:30
REGULARS:
Marlin Perkins
Jim Fowler
Stan Brock

The full title of this long-running nature series was *Mutual of Omaha's Wild Kingdom*. It starred famed naturalist and zoo director Marlin Perkins, with the aid of fellow naturalist Jim Fowler and, later, Stan Brock. The series covered such diverse topics as animal survival in the wilds, treatment of animals in captivity, the environments of primitive peoples, and the interrelationships between both primitive peoples and their animal neighbors and different species of animals with each other. An outgrowth of an earlier NBC series, *Zoo Parade*, which had originated almost exclusively from Chicago's Lincoln Park Zoo and which also starred Mr. Perkins, *Wild Kingdom* spent much more time away from the zoo setting. When it premiered on January 6, 1963, *Wild Kingdom* was telecast on Sunday afternoons, as its predecessor had been. It moved into the evening hours in January 1968. Following its cancellation by NBC at the end of the 1970–1971 season, *Wild Kingdom* went

into syndication. Although many of the episodes shown in the syndicated version were reruns of those seen previously on NBC, new episodes continue to be produced. Perkins and Fowler were featured in these new episodes until failing health forced Perkins to leave the series in 1985 (he died the following year). Fowler's new assistant was Peter Eros.

WILD WILD WEST, THE
Western
FIRST TELECAST: *September 17, 1965*
LAST TELECAST: *September 7, 1970*
BROADCAST HISTORY:
Sep 1965–Sep 1969, CBS Fri 7:30–8:30
Jul 1970–Sep 1970, CBS Mon 10:00–11:00
CAST:
James T. West .... Robert Conrad
Artemus Gordon .... Ross Martin

James T. West was the James Bond of Westerns. West was an undercover agent for President Grant whose assignments usually involved exposing or undermining the attempts of various radical, revolutionary, or criminal groups to take over all or part of the U.S. Helping him was his fellow Secret Service agent, Artemus Gordon, a master of disguises and dialects. The two of them traveled in a special railroad car that supplied them with the materials to concoct all sorts of bizarre weapons and devices to foil their adversaries. Beautiful women, contrived situations, and fantastic devices populated this series throughout its four-year run. One villain who had a remarkable facility for evading capture, or escaping from prison if caught, was the evil genius Dr. Miguelito Loveless (played by dwarf Michael Dunn). Dr. Loveless was to James West what Prof. Moriarty was to Sherlock Holmes—a brilliant antagonist bent on taking over the world.

CBS aired reruns during the summer of 1970.

WILD, WILD WORLD OF ANIMALS, THE
Wildlife/Nature
BROADCAST HISTORY:
Syndicated only
30 minutes
Produced: *1973–1978* (129 episodes)
Released: *Fall 1973*
NARRATOR:
William Conrad

This popular wildlife documentary series was produced by Time-Life Films.

WILDSIDE
Western
FIRST TELECAST: *March 21, 1985*
LAST TELECAST: *April 25, 1985*
BROADCAST HISTORY:
Mar 1985–Apr 1985, ABC Thu 8:00–9:00

CAST:

Brodie Hollister .... William Smith
Sutton Hollister.............. J. Eddie Peck
Bannister Sparks ..... Howard E. Rollins, Jr.
Varges De La Cosa .... John DiAquinto
Prometheus Jones .... Terry Funk
Cally Oaks .... Meg Ryan
Governor J. Wendell Summerhayes
.... Sandy McPeak
Keye Ahn .... Jon Fong
Elliot Thogmorton .... Kurt Fuller
Alice Freeze.................... Robin Hoff
Skillet .... Timothy Scott
Zeke .... Jason Hervey

Five upstanding citizens of Wildside County, California, constituted the "Wildside Chamber of Commerce"—a secret law-enforcement group—in this action series set in the old West. Brodie was a rancher and the "fastest gun in the west"; Sutton, his son; Bannister, the debonair black explosives expert; Varges, the knife-wielding gunsmith; and Prometheus a gentle giant who was also a veternarian and expert with the lariat. Their assignments generally came from the Governor, and adversaries ranged from local gangs to wandering ex-Confederate platoons and renegade British cavalry units left over from the Crimean War.

WILLY

Law Drama
FIRST TELECAST: September 18, 1954
LAST TELECAST: July 7, 1955
BROADCAST HISTORY:
Sep 1954–Mar 1955, CBS Sat 10:30–11:00
Apr 1955–Jul 1955, CBS Thu 10:30–11:00
CAST:

Willa Dodger................... June Havoc
Franklin Dodger .... Denny Richards, Jr.
Emily Dodger.................. Mary Treen
Papa Dodger .... Lloyd Corrigan
Charlie Bush .... Whitfield Connor
Perry Bannister (1955)............ Hal Peary
Harvey Evelyn (1955) ..... Sterling Holloway

Following her graduation from law school, Willa Dodger opened a legal practice in her hometown of Renfrew, New Hampshire. There were not many exciting cases in that little hamlet so, in mid-season, Willy got an offer to work as legal counsel to a vaudeville organization run by Perry Bannister. She left her family and her boyfriend, Charlie Bush, and relocated to the big city. Her adventures, whether in rural New England or cosmopolitan New York, were on the lighter side and rarely involved her in serious legal cases.

WILLYS THEATRE PRESENTING BEN HECHT'S TALES OF THE CITY

Dramatic Anthology
FIRST TELECAST: June 25, 1953
LAST TELECAST: September 17, 1953
BROADCAST HISTORY:
Jun 1953–Sep 1953, CBS Thu 8:30–9:00

NARRATOR:
Ben Hecht

Author Ben Hecht, whose most famous and award-winning work was the play The Front Page, was the narrator of this anthology series composed of adaptations of his stories. He was never seen onscreen, only heard with his introductions and closing remarks. The live dramas aired on alternate weeks with Four Star Playhouse.

WILTON NORTH REPORT, THE

Comedy/News Magazine
FIRST TELECAST: December 11, 1987
LAST TELECAST: January 8, 1988
BROADCAST HISTORY:
Dec 1987–Jan 1988, FOX Mon-Fri
11:00–12:00 MID
HOSTS:
Phil Cowan
Paul Robins
REGULARS:
Nancy Collins
Greg Jackson
Wayne Satz
Paul Krassner
Jack LaLanne

This example of guerilla television was an odd mixture of serious news features and thoroughly ridiculous stories and comic bits, all in the guise of a nightly news magazine. It was produced by the former producer of Late Night With David Letterman, and was apparently an attempt to see what would happen if someone like Letterman took over 60 Minutes. Hosted by the young comedy team of Phil Cowan and Paul Robins, Wilton North covered in documentary fashion such burning subjects as a woman claiming to be an extraterrestrial who had lived on 37 planets, the funniest inmate in Chino prison, a man who collected things that glowed in the dark, a visit to an alligator farm, lady wrestlers, and a woman who was convinced the devil was living in her toaster. On the more serious side were interviews with a professional matchmaker in New York, the woman president of Motown productions, the daughter of presidential candidate Gary Hart, and FBI informant Jimmie "The Weazel" Fratiano. Although there were many contributors to Wilton North, the most frequently seen were tongue-in-cheek investigative reporter Wayne Satz, satirical commentator Paul Krassner, health and science editor Jack LaLanne, and serious interviewers Nancy Collins and Greg Jackson. The title of the series referred to the location of the Hollywood building from which it was aired.

The Wilton North Report was fraught with problems. Its premiere was delayed for several weeks while producer Barry Sand tried to get the kinks out of the format. When it reached the air television critics crucified it as stupid, disjointed, and amateurish. What Fox executives had hoped would be an appealingly distinctive late-night viewing alternative drew small audiences and was yanked from the schedule less than a month after its first telecast.

WIN, LOSE OR DRAW
Quiz/Panel
BROADCAST HISTORY:
Syndicated and network daytime
30 minutes
Produced: *1987–*
Released: *September 1987*
HOST:
Bert Convy

Movie star Burt Reynolds invented this celebrity game for his friends' amusement in his own living room. The set, with its plush couches and plants, was even supposed to *look* like Burt's living room ("The john's down that way," he volunteered on one show). The game was, essentially, charades with pictures. Two teams competed, three men vs. three women. One person from a team was given a name or phrase (like "Neil Diamond" or "A Heart-to-Heart Talk"), and then had to communicate it to his or her teammates by quickly drawing a series of pictures on a large board. If the team failed to guess the phrase, the other team got to guess it. A speed round consisted of guessing as many words as possible in 90 seconds.

Prizes were not large, but two out of the three members on each team were celebrities, so the appeal was largely in watching the stars in a fast-paced, party-like setting. (The prize money went to the one non-celebrity on the winning team.) Burt himself often appeared, as did his Hollywood friends, including Loni Anderson, Dom DeLuise, Betty White, and other famous faces. A daytime version of *Win, Lose or Draw,* hosted by Vicki Lawrence, aired on NBC beginning in September 1987.

WIN WITH A WINNER
Quiz/Audience Participation
FIRST TELECAST: *June 24, 1958*
LAST TELECAST: *September 9, 1958*
BROADCAST HISTORY:
Jun 1958–Sep 1958, NBC Tue 7:30–8:00
EMCEE:
Sandy Becker
Win Elliot
POSTCARD GIRL:
Marilyn Toomey
Rita Hayes

This rather complicated summer quiz show encouraged home viewers to root for their favorite contestant and possibly share in the prizes. At the end of each show the next week's contestants were introduced, and viewers were invited to write in with their prediction of who would be the top money winner, as well as (during the first month at least) the order of finish. Those with the right choice were candidates for cash prizes, and anyone predicting the entire order of finish got a bonus prize.

The game itself generally resembled a horse race. The five (later four) contestants were each given the same question. A correct answer added the value of that question, usually $100 or $200, to their total, while a wrong answer subtracted the same amount from their previous winnings. In addition one contestant in each round had the opportunity to double his winnings—or losses. A running tally was kept of each contestant's total in the race, but only the top winner got to keep his money. The others got consolation prizes.

A "postcard girl" picked home-viewer predictions out of a large drum during the course of the show, and all those predicting the top contestant would "win with the winner," splitting the same amount of money that he had won.

Sandy Becker and Marilyn Toomey, the original host and postcard girl, were replaced by Win Elliot and Rita Hayes on July 22.

WINDOW ON MAIN STREET
Situation Comedy
FIRST TELECAST: *October 2, 1961*
LAST TELECAST: *September 12, 1962*
BROADCAST HISTORY:
Oct 1961–Feb 1962, CBS Mon 8:30–9:00
Feb 1962–Sep 1962, CBS Wed 8:00–8:30
CAST:
Cameron Garrett Brooks ...... Robert Young
Chris Logan .... Constance Moore
Lloyd Ramsey .... Ford Rainey
Arny Logan .... Brad Berwick
Wally Evans .... James Davidson
Peggy Evans.................... Carol Byron
Miss Wycliffe .... Coleen Gray
Harry McGill................. Warner Jones
Roddy Miller .... Tim Matheson

Writer Cameron Brooks returned to his hometown of Millsburg in search of materials for stories. He moved into the Majestic Hotel and resumed an old friendship with Lloyd Ramsey, editor of the local newspaper. The people he knew, as well as those he met at the hotel, served as subjects for his stories. In the spring, when the Majestic was temporarily closed for renovations, Cameron took a room in the home of Wally and Peggy Evans.

Robert Young, the star of this series, had just completed a six-year run in the highly popular *Father Knows Best* (reruns of which were still being telecast in prime time). He was looking for a different type of series to display his talents, but *Window on Main Street* was not successful and so Young subsequently went into retirement—until 1969, when *Marcus Welby* came along.

WINDOW ON THE WORLD
Variety
FIRST TELECAST: *January 27, 1949*
LAST TELECAST: *April 14, 1949*
BROADCAST HISTORY:
Jan 1949–Apr 1949, DUM Thu 9:00–9:30

REGULAR:
  Merle Kendrick Orchestra

Variety acts from different parts of the world were featured on this program, with film clips of their native lands setting the scene. Among the American performers appearing were Hollywood comedian Gil Lamb and actress-singer Irene Manning. There was no regular emcee.

WINDOWS
Dramatic Anthology
FIRST TELECAST: *July 8, 1955*
LAST TELECAST: *August 26, 1955*
BROADCAST HISTORY:
  Jul 1955–Aug 1955, CBS Fri 10:30–11:00

This live dramatic series, originating from New York, was the 1955 summer replacement for *Person to Person*. Each episode of the series opened on an ordinary window through which the camera moved to begin the unfolding of the story. All of the stories were designed to show real people confronting real problems, such as a woman alcoholic and her effect on her family, a boy's adulation for an ex-circus clown, and an illiterate woman's determined struggle to learn how to read.

WINDY CITY JAMBOREE
Country Music
FIRST TELECAST: *March 19, 1950*
LAST TELECAST: *June 18, 1950*
BROADCAST HISTORY:
  Mar 1950–Jun 1950, DUM Sun 9:00–10:00
REGULARS:
  Danny O'Neil
  Gloria Van
  Julian Stockdale Orchestra

Barn dance with variety acts, originating from Chicago.

WINGO
Quiz/Audience Participation
FIRST TELECAST: *April 1, 1958*
LAST TELECAST: *May 6, 1958*
BROADCAST HISTORY:
  Apr 1958–May 1958, CBS Tue 8:30–9:00
EMCEE:
  Bob Kennedy

This short-lived entry in the big-money quiz-show sweepstakes pitted two contestants against each other in answering questions of general and varied knowledge. The winner of each round won $1,000, the opportunity to continue against a new challenger, and a shot at the "Wingo" portion of the show. This part of the game, which depended on pure luck, offered the ultimate jackpot of $250,-000 to any contestant who succeeded in matching the letters spelling the show's title in an elaborate word game. Contestants who continued to compete risked a part of their winnings in the event

that they were defeated by a subsequent challenger.

WINNER TAKE ALL
Quiz/Audience Participation
FIRST TELECAST: *July 8, 1948*
LAST TELECAST: *October 3, 1950*
BROADCAST HISTORY:
  Jul 1948–Aug 1948, CBS Thu 9:30–10:00
  Aug 1948–Jan 1949, CBS Wed 8:30–9:00
  Apr 1950–Jul 1950, CBS Thu 9:45–10:30
  Jul 1950–Oct 1950, CBS Tue 9:00–9:30
EMCEE:
  Bud Collyer

The format of *Winner Take All* was very simple. Two contestants competed with each other answering questions given them by the emcee. One of them had a bell and the other had a buzzer. The first one to announce his/her readiness to answer (by ringing or buzzing) was given an opportunity to answer the question. Each correct answer was worth a point and three points won the game. The winner won merchandise prizes and the right to meet new challengers until defeated. *Winner Take All* had been on CBS radio since the mid-1940s and the radio version, with a different emcee, was still being aired when the show moved to television in 1948. During the 15 months that it was not on the network, from January 1949 to April 1950, it continued as a local program in New York, returning to the network for its final six months as a nighttime series. It then became a daytime show, running first on CBS (with Barry Gray as emcee) and then on NBC (with Bill Cullen), until its final telecast in April 1952. The daytime version was much different from the evening *Winner Take All*. Regular members of the daytime cast performed sketches to challenge contestants' knowledge, and did song and dance numbers as well.

WINSTON CHURCHILL—THE VALIANT YEARS
Documentary
FIRST TELECAST: *November 27, 1960*
LAST TELECAST: *April 5, 1963*
BROADCAST HISTORY:
  Nov 1960–Jun 1961, ABC Sun 10:30–11:00
  Sep 1962–Dec 1962, ABC Sun 6:30–7:00
  Dec 1962–Apr 1963, ABC Fri 7:30–8:00
NARRATORS:
  Gary Merrill
  Richard Burton

Churchill's role in the years leading into and during World War II was chronicled in this award-winning documentary series. The basis for each episode was the memoirs that Churchill the historian had kept to describe the activities of Churchill the statesman. Old film clips, letters, and contemporary backgrounds were woven together to paint a picture of Churchill's role at that critical period of world history. Gary Merrill was the narrator with Richard Burton reading from Churchill's memoirs. The series was rerun in its entirety during the 1962–1963 season.

WIRE SERVICE

Newspaper Drama
FIRST TELECAST: *October 4, 1956*
LAST TELECAST: *September 13, 1959*
BROADCAST HISTORY:
  Oct 1956–Feb 1957, ABC Thu 9:00–10:00
  Feb 1957–Sep 1957, ABC Mon 7:30–8:30
  Feb 1959–Sep 1959, ABC Sun 9:30–10:30
CAST:
  Dan Miller .... Dane Clark
  Dean Evans .... George Brent
  Katherine Wells .... Mercedes McCambridge

The three stars of this series each played a roving reporter for the Trans-Globe wire service. Each of them traveled all over the country and the world, tracking down stories involving crime and high adventure. The three reporters worked independently and appeared in separate stories, on a rotating basis.

In 1959 the *Wire Service* episodes starring Dane Clark were rerun under the title *Deadline for Action*.

WISDOM OF THE AGES

Discussion
FIRST TELECAST: *December 16, 1952*
LAST TELECAST: *June 30, 1953*
BROADCAST HISTORY:
  Dec 1952–Jun 1953, DUM Tue 9:30–10:00
MODERATOR:
  Jack Barry
PANELISTS:
  Ronnie Mulluzzo (8)
  Marcia Van Dyke (28)
  Leo Cherne (40)
  Mrs. H. V. Kaltenborn (64)
  Thomas Clark (82)

Quizmaster Jack Barry had been highly successful with a panel show featuring youngsters *(Juvenile Jury)* and another with oldsters *(Life Begins at Eighty)*, so it was natural to try a show that spanned all age groups. As on the prototype programs, the format was simply for the panel to discuss, from the perspective of their various generations, the often humorous problems and questions submitted by viewers. The panel consisted of one member under 20, one 20–40, one 40–60, one 60–80, and one over 80. The panelists most frequently seen during the show's six-month run are listed above. Interestingly enough, though each age group had its own unique point of view, it was the two extremes—the 8- and the 82-year-old—who were most often in agreement.

WISEGUY

Police Drama
FIRST TELECAST: *September 16, 1987*
LAST TELECAST:

BROADCAST HISTORY:
  Sep 1987, CBS Wed 9:00–11:00
  Sep 1987–Nov 1987, CBS Thu 9:00–10:00
  Jan 1988–Mar 1988, CBS Mon 10:00–11:00
  Jun 1988–   , CBS Wed 10:00–11:00
CAST:
  Vinnie Terranova .... Ken Wahl
  Frank McPike .... Jonathan Banks
  "Lifeguard"...................... Jim Byrnes
  Fr. Peter Terranova (1987) ... Gerald Anthony
  Sonny Steelgrave (1987) .... Ray Sharkey
  Paul Patrice (1987) .... Joe Dallesandro
  Sid Royce (1987) .... Dennis Lipscomb
  Harry "The Hunchback" Schanstra (1987)
    .... Eric Christmas
  Roger LoCocco (1988) .... William Russ
  Susan Profitt (1988) .... Joan Severance
  Mel Profitt (1988) .... Kevin Spacey
  Herb Ketcher (1988) .... David Spielberg

Vinnie Terranova was an undercover agent for the Organized Crime Bureau who went from assignment to assignment infiltrating the most dangerous criminal organizations in America. Because of his brash attitude and street smarts, Vinnie made a perfect mob lieutenant. His boss at O.C.B. was cynical Frank McPike; "Lifeguard," Vinnie's only link to McPike while he was on assignment, served as a sympathetic conduit, as well as providing Vinnie with the information necessary to maintain his cover. Maintaining that cover was literally a matter of life or death—Vinnie was always "on the edge"—and it meant that everybody Vinnie knew, with the single exception of his brother, Peter (a priest), really thought he had become a crook.

Once he had contributed to the downfall of a mobster Vinnie moved on and, as a result, there was periodic turnover in the supporting cast. His first assignment was to bring down Atlantic City mob boss Sonny Steelgrave (played by Ray Sharkey in a bravura performance). From there he went on to disrupt the international smuggling operation (contraband, munitions, drugs, etc.) of crazed Mel Profitt and his beautiful sister Susan. Mel was involved with a deposed Caribbean dictator who was planning a coup but, when the plan fell apart, he committed suicide. His emotionally unstable sister, Susan, wound up in a mental hospital and Vinnie found out that the coup had in fact been orchestrated as an unauthorized CIA operation by Herb Ketcher through undercover agent Roger LoCocco, who was also a "wiseguy"—posing as a hit man for the Profitts. When the whole tangled affair came out in Senate hearings LoCocco was assassinated (or was he?), Ketcher committed suicide, and Vinnie—disillusioned with the entire U.S. government—contemplated resigning from the O.C.B.

WITH THIS RING

Quiz/Audience Participation
FIRST TELECAST: *January 28, 1951*
LAST TELECAST: *March 18, 1951*

BROADCAST HISTORY:
Jan 1951–Mar 1951, DUM Sun 9:30–10:00
HOST:
Bill Slater
Martin Gabel

This gentle quiz show drew its contestants from lists of young couples who had recently applied for a marriage license. Two couples were chosen and presented with questions about marriage sent in by viewers. After they gave their ideas about how they would handle the situations posed, a pair of celebrity judges—both married and therefore experienced—evaluated the answers. The winning couple got a free honeymoon trip.

Martin Gabel succeeded Bill Slater as host on the last two telecasts. The program was originally known as *Happily Ever After.*

WITNESS, THE

Courtroom Anthology
FIRST TELECAST: *September 29, 1960*
LAST TELECAST: *January 26, 1961*
BROADCAST HISTORY:
Sep 1960–Dec 1960, CBS Thu 7:30–8:30
Dec 1960–Jan 1961, CBS Thu 9:00–10:00
CAST:
Court Reporter .... Verne Collett
Court Clerk .... William Griffis
COMMITTEE MEMBERS:
Charles Haydon
Paul McGrath
William Smithers
Frank Milan

In a format that was similar to a Congressional investigation, this series attempted to dramatize the exploits and life-styles of gangsters and rogues from the past and present. Detailed research was done on all of the "witnesses" who were brought before the committee to explain and/or defend their activities. The first of these hearings starred Telly Savalas as Charles "Lucky" Luciano. Among the other figures whose lives were exposed on this show were Bugsy Siegel, Dutch Schultz, Al Capone, John Dillinger, James Walker (former New York City mayor), and Ma Barker. The committee members asking the questions were all real attorneys and members of the New York Bar Association.

WIZARD, THE

Adventure/Foreign Intrigue
FIRST TELECAST: *September 9, 1986*
LAST TELECAST: *July 7, 1987*
BROADCAST HISTORY:
Sep 1986–Oct 1986, CBS Tue 8:00–9:00
Nov 1986, CBS Sat 8:00–9:00
Dec 1986–Feb 1987, CBS Tue 8:00–9:00
Feb 1987–Apr 1987, CBS Thu 8:00–9:00
Jun 1987–Jul 1987, CBS Tue 8:00–9:00

CAST:
Simon McKay .... David Rappaport
Alex Jagger .... Douglas Barr
Tillie Russell .... Fran Ryan

Although he made his living as an inventor of exotic and ingenious toys, diminutive Simon McKay (just four feet tall) spent much of his time helping people. He was a good samaritan who would track down people in need, design special devices to help the handicapped, and had, in the past, made contraptions for government agencies. It was this latter skill that had prompted the government to assign agent Alex Jagger to work with Simon. They were afraid that criminals or foreign powers who were aware of Simon's talents would kidnap him and force him to work for them. The two of them made quite a pair—impish, fun-loving Simon and serious, almost-humorless Alex. Together they traveled all over the world, at times on Simon's charitable missions and at others fighting the forces of evil. Tillie was the housekeeper who kept Simon's home in perfect order.

WIZARDS AND WARRIORS

Adventure
FIRST TELECAST: *February 26, 1983*
LAST TELECAST: *May 14, 1983*
BROADCAST HISTORY:
Feb 1983–May 1983, CBS Sat 8:00–9:00
CAST:
Prince Erik Greystone .... Jeff Conaway
Marko .... Walter Olkewicz
Prince Dirk Blackpool .... Duncan Regehr
Princess Ariel .... Julia Duffy
Wizard Vector .... Clive Revill
King Baaldorf .... Tom Hill
Wizard Tranquil .... Ian Wolfe
Geoffrey Blackpool .... Tim Dunigan
Justin Greystone .... Jay Kerr
Queen Lattinia .... Julie Payne
Bethel .... Randi Brooks
Cassandra .... Phyllis Katz
Oriental Guard .... Lonnie Wun

This period adventure with a sense of humor was set in the time of King Arthur's Court, when brave knights battled the forces of evil, with magic, sorcery, and sheer courage. The prize was the legendary Kingdom of Camarand, ruled by good King Baaldorf and Queen Lattinia. Their daughter, Princess Ariel, was betrothed to handsome Prince Erik Greystone, who, aided by his burly vassal Marko, was the principal defender of the realm. Evil Prince Dirk Blackpool was the archvillain, seeking to conquer Camarand through the black arts of Wizard Vector and sexy, decadent Witch Bethel. Prince Erik sometimes had the help of aged Wizard Tranquil, but often had to cope with no magical assistance at all. Justin was Erik's ne'er-do-well playboy brother, while Geoffrey was Blackpool's incompetent brother. Elaborate special effects such as ghosts, demons, powerful amulets, and fiery swords added visual impact to this short-lived fantasy.

WOMAN TO REMEMBER, A
Romantic Drama
FIRST TELECAST: *May 2, 1949*
LAST TELECAST: *July 15, 1949*
BROADCAST HISTORY:
  May 1949–Jul 1949, DUM Mon–Fri 7:30–7:45
CAST:
  Christine Baker............... Patricia Wheel
  Steve Hammond .... John Raby
  Charley Anderson .... Frankie Thomas
  Bessie Thatcher .... Ruth McDevitt
  Carol Winstead................. Joan Catlin

A Woman to Remember was an early attempt to bring soap opera—radio soap opera, at that—to early-evening television. The leading character, Christine Baker, was even depicted as a radio soap-opera queen, engaged to handsome Steve Hammond, but beset by scheming rivals, notably shrewish Carol Winstead. Charley Anderson, the young sound man on Christine's show, and Bessie, another actress, were allies.

A Woman to Remember was first seen as a daytime serial, beginning February 21, 1949.

WOMEN IN PRISON
Situation Comedy
FIRST TELECAST: *October 11, 1987*
LAST TELECAST: *April 2, 1988*
BROADCAST HISTORY:
  Oct 1987, FOX Sun 8:30–9:00
  Oct 1987–Apr 1988, FOX Sat 8:30–9:00
CAST:
  Vicki Springer............... Julia Campbell
  Asst. Warden Clint Rafferty ..... Blake Clark
  Dawn Murphy .... C.C.H. Pounder
  Eve Shipley .... Peggy Cass
  Bonnie Harper............. Antoinette Byron
  Pam .... Wendie Jo Sperber
  Meg Bando................... Denny Dillon

Twelve years after ABC failed with a comedy set in a men's prison *(On the Rocks)*, Fox Broadcasting gave women equal time. The setting for this bizarre comedy was Bass Women's Prison in Wisconsin, where the inmates in cellblock J never seemed to be locked in their cells. Among the incarcerated skirts were naive Vicki, a pampered suburban housewife who had been framed for shoplifting by her philandering husband; Dawn, a tough black who had murdered her husband; Bonnie, a sexy, gay English hooker; and Eve, an aging, forgetful bank robber who had lived here for decades. In the adjoining cell, with a computer terminal but no roommates, was Pam, a brilliant but sarcastic woman who was serving time for computer embezzlement. Meg was cellblock J's short, frumpy, sadistic guard, and Warden Rafferty the grumpy boss, for whom Vicki worked as a secretary.

None of this was meant to be taken the least bit seriously, it seems. The garish theme song thundered lines like "So misunderstood, now you're missing a life that was so good. . . . While other girls make dates, you make license plates. . . . you're in JAIL!!"

WONDER WOMAN
Adventure
FIRST TELECAST: *December 18, 1976*
LAST TELECAST: *September 11, 1979*
BROADCAST HISTORY:
  Dec 1976–Jan 1977, ABC Sat 8:00–9:00
  May 1977–Jul 1977, ABC Sat 8:00–9:00
  Sep 1977–Feb 1979, CBS Fri 8:00–9:00
  Aug 1979–Sep 1979, CBS Tue 8:00–9:00
CAST:
  Yeoman Diana Prince/"Wonder Woman"
  .... Lynda Carter
  Maj. Steve Trevor/Steve Trevor, Jr.
  ....Lyle Waggoner
  Gen. Blankenship (1976–1977)
  .... Richard Eastham
  Corp. Etta Candy (1976–1977)
  .... Beatrice Colen
  Joe Atkinson (1977) .... Normann Burton
  Eve (1977–1979).............. Saundra Sharp
  Voice of I.R.A. (1977–1979) .. Tom Kratochzil

Wonder Woman, based on Charles Moulon's comic-book superheroine of the 1940s, developed gradually into a regular TV series. It was first seen as a TV movie in March 1974 (with Cathy Lee Crosby in the title role), then in another try in November 1975 (with Lynda Carter), then in a series of specials called *The New Original Wonder Woman* beginning in March 1976. After popping up in various spots all over the ABC schedule, it had a short consecutive-weeks run in December 1976–January 1977. Finally, in the fall of 1977, it moved to CBS and became a regular weekly series.

The show was comic-strip, pure and simple, set in the 1940s. Wonder Woman came from a "lost" island where a band of Amazon women had fled *ca.* 200 B.C. to escape male domination by the ancient Greeks and Romans. On Paradise Island they found the magic substance Feminum, which when molded into a golden belt gave them superhuman strength and in golden bracelets could deflect bullets. It didn't help their love life much, though, so when Major Steve Trevor of the U.S. army crash-landed on the island during World War II, Wonder Woman fell in love and returned with him to the U.S. in the guise of his secretary. Major Trevor did not know of her powers, but when trouble threatened, Yeoman Prince could disappear for a while, and whirl herself into Wonder Woman! She then reappeared, clad in sexy tights and draped in a cape that looked something like the American flag.

Her opponents were mostly Nazi agents, plus a few aliens from outer space, all of whom were dispatched in slam-bang-biff-pow style. Once the

Nazis even found and occupied Paradise Island in their quest for Feminum, and they had their own Wonder Woman in Fausta. Seen occasionally on Diana's side was her younger sister, Drusilla, the "Wonder Girl" (played by Debra Winger).

When the series moved to CBS in the fall 1977 there were a number of changes made. The title was now *The New Adventures of Wonder Woman* and the period was contemporary, rather than World War II. The heroine returned to America to fight terrorists and subversive elements for the Inter-Agency Defense Command (IADC), where her boss was Joe Atkinson. Working closely with her was Steve Trevor, Jr., the son of the Major Trevor with whom she had been associated during World War II. Since she had not aged at all—residents of Paradise Island had life spans measured in centuries, not decades—and Steve, Jr., was a dead ringer for his father, the couple seemed virtually unchanged. Eve was Steve's secretary. By the end of 1977 Mr. Atkinson had been phased out of the show and Steve had been promoted to Diana Prince's boss, leaving her to go alone on missions. A primary source of information for all IADC agents was the Internal Retrieval Associative computer. This wonderful device, called IRA by the staff, could actually communicate by voice with the agents. Despite the fact that Diana was no longer wearing glasses to conceal her real identity, as she had done in the ABC version of *Wonder Woman*, only IRA knew who she really was.

Lynda Carter, who portrayed Wonder Woman, did fit the part. A former "Miss World—U.S.A.," she was very athletic, tall (5' 10", not 6' as some publicity releases claimed), and extremely well-endowed.

WONDER YEARS, THE
Situation Comedy
FIRST TELECAST: *March 15, 1988*
LAST TELECAST:
BROADCAST HISTORY:
   Mar 1988–Apr 1988, ABC Tues 8:30–9:00
CAST:
   Kevin Arnold (age 12) . . . . Fred Savage
   Kevin (as adult; voice only) . . . . Daniel Stern
   Wayne Arnold. . . . . Jason Hervey
   Karen Arnold. . . . . Olivia d'Abo
   Norma Arnold . . . . Alley Mills
   Jack Arnold . . . . Dan Lauria
   Paul Pfeiffer. . . . . Josh Saviano
   Winnie (Gwendolyn) Cooper
      . . . . Danica McKellar
   Coach Cutlip . . . . Robert Picardo
   Mrs. Ritvo . . . . Linda Hoy

A whimsical view of growing up in suburban America of the '60s, as seen through the eyes of a 12-year-old. In 1968 Kevin was just entering Robert F. Kennedy Junior High School. Vietnam protests, Beatles music and America's space program were in the air, but Kevin's concerns were closer to home. His teenaged brother, Wayne, existed only to torture and humiliate him, or so it seemed; his older sister Karen was in her own world of love beads and social protest. Mom (Norma) and Dad (Jack) were a little distant—especially Dad, an intimidating presense who came home tired from work each day, and always seemed to get in an argument with someone. Fitting in at school was an awesome challenge, shared with best friend Paul and hoped-for girlfriend Winnie. But Kevin, a rambunctious kid with an angelic face, would try.

The series was narrated by an unseen, adult Kevin; news clips and music from the period also contributed to the nostalgic flavor. One critic called it "A *Leave It to Beaver* with bite." A special preview of the series was telecast on January 31, 1988, following the Super Bowl.

WONDERFUL JOHN ACTON, THE
Drama
FIRST TELECAST: *July 5, 1953*
LAST TELECAST: *September 22, 1953*
BROADCAST HISTORY:
   July 1953–Aug 1953, NBC Sun 10:00–10:30
   Sep 1953, NBC Tue 8:30–9:00
CAST:
   John Acton . . . . Harry Holcombe
   Uncle Terrence . . . . Ian Martin
   Julia Acton . . . . Virginia Dwyer
   Kevin Acton. . . . . Ronnie Walken
   Aunt Bessie . . . . Jane Rose
   Peter Bodkin, Sr.. . . . . Pat Harrington
   Birdie Bodkin . . . . Mary Michael
   Narrator . . . . Luis Van Rooten

Set in the Ohio River Valley town of Ludlow, Kentucky, *The Wonderful John Acton* was the story of an Irish family in 1919. John Acton was the county clerk and owned a combination candy and notions store, with his living quarters in the back. The stories were narrated by John's grandson, Kevin Acton, who reminisced about his childhood growing up in small-town America. Kevin revered his grandfather and had always considered him someone "wonderful." As narrator, the adult Kevin was never seen in this live dramatic series.

WONDERFUL WORLD OF DISNEY, THE
see *Walt Disney*

WORD OF LIFE SONGTIME, THE
see *Songtime*

WORDS AND MUSIC
Music
FIRST TELECAST: *August 2, 1949*
LAST TELECAST: *September 8, 1949*
BROADCAST HISTORY:
   Aug 1949–Sep 1949, NBC Tue/Thu 7:30–7:45
REGULARS:
   Barbara Marshall
   Jerry Jerome Trio

Live musical interlude featuring singer-pianist Barbara Marshall.

WORKING STIFFS
Situation Comedy
FIRST TELECAST: *September 15, 1979*
LAST TELECAST: *October 6, 1979*
BROADCAST HISTORY:
    Sep 1979–Oct 1979, CBS Sat 8:00–8:30
CAST:
    Ernie O'Rourke .... Jim Belushi
    Mike O'Rourke .... Michael Keaton
    Al Steckler .... Val Bisoglio
    Frank Falzone .... Phil Rubinstein
    Mitch Hannigan .... Alan Arbus
    Nikki Evashevsky .... Lorna Patterson

One of the first casualties of the 1979–1980 season, *Working Stiffs* was the story of two young brothers trying to get started in the business world. Ernie and Mike O'Rourke were ambitious, but incredibly clumsy janitors planning to work their way up from the bottom in the building-management field. The Chicago office building where they worked was owned by their uncle, Al Steckler, and Frank Falzone was their immediate superior, the building manager. Ernie and Mike lived in a small apartment over the Playland Cafe, where they spent much of their spare time with owner Mitch Hannigan and waitress Nikki Evashevsky. Dismal ratings cut the life of this slapstick comedy to less than a month.

WORLD IN YOUR HOME, THE
Documentary
FIRST TELECAST: *December 22, 1944*
LAST TELECAST: *January 9, 1948*
BROADCAST HISTORY:
    Dec 1944–Jan 1948, NBC Fri 8:45–9:00 (approx.)

One of the very earliest regular network features on TV seems to have been this weekly educational film sponsored by RCA Victor. It ran for more than three years in the same time slot, from 1944 to 1948. Network records are sketchy that far back and it is not known exactly when *The World in Your Home* became a network show (it originated from New York), but New York, Philadelphia, and Schenectady were linked by NBC-TV in 1944 and it is quite possible that it was fed to all three stations from the beginning.

WORLD OF MR. SWEENEY, THE
Situation Comedy
FIRST TELECAST: *June 30, 1954*
LAST TELECAST: *August 20, 1954*
BROADCAST HISTORY:
    Jun 1954–Aug 1954, NBC Tue–Fri 7:30–7:45
CAST:
    Cicero P. Sweeney .... Charlie Ruggles
    Kippy Franklin .... Glenn Walken
    Marge Franklin .... Helen Wagner

Following a season as one of the segments of *The Kate Smith Evening Hour*, *The World of Mr. Sweeney* struck out on its own during the summer of 1954. Cicero P. Sweeney was the owner of a small-town general store who, in addition to providing groceries to the townspeople, was a sounding board for their problems and provider of good advice. Each episode revolved around different members of the local community and Sweeney's solutions to their problems. The only regulars other than Sweeney himself were his grandson, Kippy, and Kippy's mother, Marge. *The World of Mr. Sweeney* was produced live from New York throughout its nighttime run. In October 1954 it moved to the NBC Monday–Friday daytime lineup, where it stayed until December 1955.

Despite its relatively short run, *The World of Mr. Sweeney* was recently cited as holding the all-time record for the largest number of episodes of a comedy series ever presented on the NBC network—mostly because of its 14 months in daytime, where it ran five times a week. In all, 345 installments were presented.

WORLD OF TALENT
see *Dick Clark's World of Talent*

WORLD WAR I
Documentary
FIRST TELECAST: *September 22, 1964*
LAST TELECAST: *September 5, 1965*
BROADCAST HISTORY:
    Sep 1964–Dec 1964, CBS Tue 8:00–8:30
    Dec 1964–Sep 1965, CBS Sun 6:30–7:00
NARRATOR:
    Robert Ryan

This was a documentary series recalling the background causes, conduct, and aftermath of World War I. The emotional reactions of the leaders and peoples most directly involved, as well as the social, political, and economic fabric of the times, were analyzed in depth.

WORLD WIDE '60
Documentary
FIRST TELECAST: *January 23, 1960*
LAST TELECAST: *August 27, 1960*
BROADCAST HISTORY:
    Jan 1960–Aug 1960, NBC Sat 9:30–10:30
HOST:
    Frank McGee

NBC News correspondent Frank McGee served as host and narrator of this series of public-affairs documentaries. The subject matter ranged from alcoholism, to old age, to architecture, to missiles, to jazz, to the problems of refugees. The premiere telecast of this series covered the first year of Fidel Castro's regime in Cuba.

WRANGLER
Western

871

FIRST TELECAST: *August 4, 1960*
LAST TELECAST: *September 15, 1960*
BROADCAST HISTORY:
    Aug 1960–Sep 1960, NBC Thu 9:30–10:00
CAST:
    Pitcairn, the Wrangler .... Jason Evers

Wrangler was the 1960 summer replacement for *The Ford Show Starring Tennessee Ernie Ford.* Pitcairn, the Wrangler, was an adventurer who traveled about the Old West working sometimes as a ranch hand, sometimes as a gunfighter, and sometimes as a good samaritan. This short-lived summer series was filled with rustlers, horse thieves, hostile Indians, and all the other low-brow characters so prevalent in superficial Western shoot-'em-ups.

WREN'S NEST
Situation Comedy
FIRST TELECAST: *January 13, 1949*
LAST TELECAST: *April 30, 1949*
BROADCAST HISTORY:
    Jan 1949–Apr 1949, ABC Thu/Fri/Sat 7:15–7:30
CAST:
    Sam Wren
    Virginia Sale

One of the many "Mr. and Mrs." comedies of early television was this thrice-weekly series about the home life of a suburban New York couple and their 12-year-old twins. The Wrens were also married in real life, and both had appeared in numerous Hollywood films. (Virginia's screen career lasted from the 1920s to the 1960s, and recently, at the age of 80, she completed a one-woman national tour doing her comedy-drama act in theaters, schools, and clubs.)

WRESTLING
Sports
FIRST TELECAST: *July 30, 1948*
LAST TELECAST: *March 5, 1955*
BROADCAST HISTORY:

Monday
    Sep 1949–Jan 1950, DUM 9:30–11:00
    Jan 1950–Feb 1952, DUM 9:00–11:00
    Feb 1952–Mar 1952, DUM 9:30–11:00

Tuesday
    Oct 1948–Jul 1949, NBC 110:00–Conclusion
    Jan 1950–Aug 1950, CBS 10:00–Conclusion

Wednesday
    Aug 1948–Sep 1950, ABC 9:30–Conclusion

    Sep 1950–Apr 1951, ABC 10:00–Conclusion
    Apr 1951–Sep 1951, ABC 9:30–11:00
    Jun 1952–Sep 1952, ABC 10:00–11:15
    Sep 1952–Oct 1953, ABC 9:30–11:15
    Oct 1953–Sep 1954, ABC 10:00–Midnight

Thursday
    Oct 1948–Jan 1949, DUM 9:00–Conclusion

Friday
    Jul 1948–Dec 1948, DUM 9:00–Conclusion

Saturday
    Sep 1949–May 1951, DUM 10:00–Conclusion
    May 1951–Mar 1955, DUM 9:30–Conclusion

Professional wrestling, the world of the "grunt and groaners," was a regular and popular form of entertainment on early, live network television, particularly on ABC and DuMont. Names like Gorgeous George, Antonino "Argentina" Rocca, and The Mighty Atlas were household words among the owners of TV sets in the late 1940s and early 1950s, as well as among those who watched the matches at their local bars. The two longest-running wrestling shows originated from Chicago—Jack Brickhouse doing the play-by-play from Marigold Garden every Saturday night on DuMont for almost six years and Wayne Griffin announcing from Rainbow Arena for ABC for roughly the same length of time. DuMont's other long-running wrestling show originated from various arenas around the New York City area (Jerome Arena, Jamaica Arena, Sunnyside Gardens, and Columbia Park Arena) with Dennis James at the mike. Bill Johnston, Jr., did commentary for CBS's New York–based show (from the Bronx Winter Garden Arena and St. Nicholas Arena), and NBC's show was covered by Bob Stanton (from St. Nicholas Arena).

The most famous of these early wrestling announcers was probably DuMont's Dennis James, whose simplified explanations and infectious enthusiasm made the sport palatable even to little old ladies. His oft-repeated phrase "Okay, Mother" became so identified with him that it was later used for the title of one of his numerous daytime game shows. That a game show emcee like James could become wrestling's most famous commentator was perhaps symbolic of the fact that on TV wrestling was more show business than sport.

WYATT EARP
    see *Life and Legend of Wyatt Earp, The*

X

XAVIER CUGAT SHOW, THE
Music
FIRST TELECAST: *February 27, 1957*
LAST TELECAST: *May 24, 1957*
BROADCAST HISTORY:
  Feb 1957–May 1957, NBC Wed/Fri 7:30–7:45

REGULARS:
  Xavier Cugat
  Abbe Lane

Latin bandleader Xavier Cugat and his then wife, Abbe Lane, starred in this live 15-minute musical variety show that filled the remainder of the half hour in which NBC aired its nightly network news program. Cugie led the band and played his violin, Abbe sang Latin numbers and danced, and occasional guest stars joined them for variety.

Y

YANCY DERRINGER

Action/Adventure
FIRST TELECAST: *October 2, 1958*
LAST TELECAST: *September 24, 1959*
BROADCAST HISTORY:
  Oct 1958–Sep 1959, CBS Thu 8:30–9:00
CAST:
  Yancy Derringer .... Jock Mahoney
  Pahoo-Ka-Ta-Wah .... X. Brands
  John Colton .... Kevin Hagen
  Amanda Eaton .... Julie Adams
  Madame Francine .... Frances Bergen

Set in New Orleans in the years after the Civil War, *Yancy Derringer* followed the exploits of an ex–Confederate soldier turned cardsharp and adventurer in a wide-open city. Yancy did have a steady occupation, that of special agent working for John Colton, civil administrator of the city of New Orleans. His job was to prevent crimes when possible, and to capture the criminals when it was not. Yancy was a smooth operator, dapper and suave with the ladies, and he carried a tiny pistol in his fancy hat. His constant companion and aide was an Indian named Pahoo. Together they formed a team that was not police, not detective, and not secret agent, but a little bit of all three.

YEAR AT THE TOP, A

Situation Comedy
FIRST TELECAST: *August 5, 1977*
LAST TELECAST: *September 4, 1977*
BROADCAST HISTORY:
  Aug 1977, CBS Fri 8:00–8:30
  Aug 1977–Sep 1977, CBS Sun 8:30–9:00
CAST:
  Greg .... Greg Evigan
  Paul .... Paul Shaffer
  Frederick J. Hanover .... Gabriel Dell
  Miss Worley .... Priscilla Morrill
  Trish .... Julie Cobb
  Grandma Belle Durbin .... Nedra Volz
EXECUTIVE PRODUCER:
  Norman Lear
MUSIC SUPERVISOR:
  Don Kirshner

This summer series, long delayed in getting on the air because of production and conceptual problems (it was originally supposed to premiere in January, with a completely different cast), was about two young rock musicians in search of fame and fortune. Greg and Paul moved to Hollywood from their home in Boise, Idaho, and were looking for an agent to help them get their big break. The promoter they found was Frederick J. Hanover, renowned for discovering and creating pop music

stars. He offered them the chance at stardom, but there was one little catch. Hanover was the son of the Devil and, in exchange for their year as pop music superstars, Greg and Paul would have to sign away their souls. Hanover gave them tastes of what their "year at the top" could be like, and tried various ways of tempting them to sign the contract, but circumstances and misgivings on Greg and Paul's part prevented it from happening, at least in the five weeks that *A Year at the Top* ran.

YEAR IN THE LIFE, A

Drama
FIRST TELECAST: *August 24, 1987*
LAST TELECAST: *April 20, 1988*
BROADCAST HISTORY:
  Aug 1987–Sep 1987, NBC Mon 9:00–11:00
  Sep 1987–Feb 1988, NBC Wed 9:00–10:00
  Mar 1988, NBC Wed 10:00–11:00
  Apr 1988, NBC Wed 9:00–10:00
CAST:
  Joe Gardner .... Richard Kiley
  Anne Gardner Maxwell ..... Wendy Phillips
  David Sisk .... Trey Ames
  Sunny Sisk .... Amanda Peterson
  Lindley Gardner Eisenberg .. Jayne Atkinson
  Jim Eisenberg .... Adam Arkin
  Jack Gardner .... Morgan Stevens
  Sam Gardner .... David Oliver
  Kay Ericson Gardner .. Sarah Jessica Parker
  Dr. Alice Foley .... Diana Muldaur

This warm family drama, a spin-off from the acclaimed December 1986, mini-series of the same name, sensitively explored the lives of three generations of a large, prosperous Seattle family. Sam Gardner was the patriarch, a strong-willed but basically decent man who had grown up during the Depression (the kids were never allowed to forget it!) and built the family's successful plastics business. In the mini-series, the death of his wife had brought his four grown children back together, despite their various problems. Anne, 35, was an ex-hippie, who had been shattered by the failure of her second marriage and had moved back into the house with her two teenaged children (David and Sunny) from her first marriage. Daughter Lindley, 31, was struggling to balance her career as a sales representative for Gardner Plastics with being a mother to her new baby, Ruthie, and wife to amiable patent attorney Jim. Jack, 30, was the black sheep of the family, a rebellious drifter still trying to "find himself"—to the disgust of his father. And Sam, 24, was a handsome, conservative preppie-type who had inexplicably married the flighty, free-spirited Kay; he also worked for the family firm and lived in the guest house while saving for a home of his own.

  Stories revolved around the tears and joys of these marriages and family relationships. Alice was Joe's on-again, off-again romantic interest.

YELLOW ROSE, THE

Drama

FIRST TELECAST: *October 2, 1983*
LAST TELECAST: *May 12, 1984*
BROADCAST HISTORY:
   Oct 1983, NBC Sun 10:00–11:00
   Oct 1983–Jan 1984, NBC Sat 10:00–11:00
   Mar 1984–May 1984, NBC Sat 10:00–11:00
CAST:
   Chance McKenzie .... Sam Elliott
   Colleen Champion .... Cybill Shepherd
   Roy Champion .... David Soul
   Quisto Champion .... Edward Albert
   Jeb Hollister................ Chuck Connors
   Juliette Hollister .... Deborah Shelton
   Grace McKenzie (1983)...... Susan Anspach
   Luther Dillard .... Noah Beery, Jr.
   Hoyt Coryell .... Ken Curtis
   Whit Champion .... Tom Schanley
   L. C. Champion .... Michelle Bennett
   Caryn Cabrera .... Kerrie Keane
   John Stronghart.............. Will Sampson

Soap opera set on a huge, modern-day west Texas ranch. All the usual ingredients were there—money, lust, power, mysterious pasts, and family entanglements—along with a few not usually found in modern soaps (cattle drives, campfires out in the wide open spaces). The Yellow Rose, a 200,000 acre spread, had been built by the late Wade Champion, and now his offspring were fighting among themselves and against the world to keep it going. Wade's sons Roy and Quisto (a lawyer), and his 29-year-old widow, Colleen, ran the place. Roy found himself fighting both family arch-enemy Jeb Hollister, who thought the ranch should belong to him, and his own passion for his beautiful young stepmother. Colleen, on the other hand, was drawn to Chance, a lanky, taciturn stranger who arrived in the first episode and was the man with a past; it turned out he (1) had served time for murder, and (2) was Wade's illegitimate son. Other stories involved the smuggling of drugs and illegal aliens across the nearby border.

L.C. ("Love Child") was Colleen's 12-year-old daughter, and Whit was Roy's sexually curious teenage son. Also near the center of things were Grace, the sensual housekeeper, ranch hands Dillard and Coryell, and Jeb's daughter Juliette. Midway through the season it was announced that Jane Russell would join the cast as Chance's long-lost mother, Rose Hollister, but she showed up for only a couple of episodes.

YES YES NANETTE

syndicated title for *Westinghouse Playhouse*

YOU AGAIN?

Situation Comedy

FIRST TELECAST: *February 27, 1986*
LAST TELECAST: *March 30, 1987*
BROADCAST HISTORY:
   Feb 1986, NBC Thu 8:30–9:00
   Mar 1986–Jun 1986, NBC Mon 8:00–8:30
   Jun 1986–Jan 1987, NBC Wed 9:30–10:00
   Mar 1987, NBC Mon 10:30–11:00
CAST:
   Henry Willows .... Jack Klugman
   Matt Willows .... John Stamos
   Enid Tompkins .... Elizabeth Bennett
   Pam .... Valerie Landsburg
   Maggie Davis .... Barbara Rhoades
   Louis Robles .... Luis Avalos
   Harry......................... Guy Marks

Ever since his bitter divorce ten years before, supermarket manager Henry Willows had been leading a quiet, peaceful life—and getting very set in his ways. Until, that is, his 17-year-old son Matt, whom he had not seen since the divorce, turned up on his doorstep. Henry's life was thrown into turmoil. Matt was a girl-chasing, borderline juvenile delinquent, and more than his conservative father could deal with. There was much yelling, and a lot of difficult adjustments to make on both sides, but underneath it all—as in all sitcoms—genuine affection. Henry's sarcastic British housekeeper, Enid, tossed in a few wisecracks from the woman's point of view.

Adapted from the British series *Home to Roost*, which was still running in that country. *You Again?* boasted at least one TV first. Actress Elizabeth Bennett played the same role (Enid) in both series simultaneously, requiring her to regularly commute between Los Angeles and London.

YOU ARE AN ARTIST

see *Ben Grauer Show, The*

YOU ARE AN ARTIST

Art Instruction

FIRST TELECAST: *November 1, 1946*
LAST TELECAST: *January 17, 1950*
BROADCAST HISTORY:
   Nov 1946–Dec 1946, NBC Fri 8:15–8:30
   Dec 1946–Aug 1948, NBC Thu 9:00–9:15
   Sep 1948–Oct 1948, NBC Wed 7:30–7:50
   Nov 1948–Mar 1949, NBC Tue 7:30–7:45
   Mar 1949–Apr 1949, NBC Thu 7:30–7:45
   Jul 1949–Sep 1949, NBC Sat 7:30–7:45
   Jan 1950, NBC Tue 11:00–11:15
HOST:
   Jon Gnagy

Jon Gnagy might seem an unlikely choice to be one of the very first personalities to have his own network television series. An obscure but articulate young artist, he first appeared on NBC's *Radio City Matinee*, a grab bag of features telecast locally over WNBT, New York, in the early and mid-1940s. In November 1946, he was given a 15-minute time slot of his own and his program, *You Are an Artist*, was fed to a small network of stations on the East Coast. A month later the Gulf Oil Company was persuaded to assume sponsorship of the show, thus insuring its survival (and making Gulf one of the first sponsors of a network series).

Sporting a goatee, a plaid shirt, and sometimes a beret, Gnagy would execute drawings before the camera while describing his technique in simple, understandable terms as he went along. Later he added a segment in which he analyzed a famous painting lent by the Museum of Modern Art (and brought into the studio by two armed guards). He varied little from this simple format from 1946 to 1949, but around him the medium of television changed dramatically. In 1949 the program, by then a gentle reminder of an earlier day (only three years back!), quietly moved into daytime, then became a local New York show. It had a final three-week run on the network in January 1950.

Though soon forgotten amid the rush of superproductions and big names flooding into the new medium, Jon Gnagy and *You Are an Artist* were true video pioneers. Gnagy died in 1981.

YOU ARE THERE
Documentary Drama
FIRST TELECAST: *February 1, 1953*
LAST TELECAST: *October 13, 1957*
BROADCAST HISTORY:
    Feb 1953–Jun 1953, CBS Sun 6:00–6:30
    Sep 1953–Oct 1957, CBS Sun 6:30–7:00 (OS)
REPORTER:
    Walter Cronkite

Reenactments of major events in the history of the world, with the emphasis on those of the last century, were presented on this weekly series. CBS News correspondent Walter Cronkite served as the anchorman as the events "occurred" and reports and interviews came in from various reporters. The initial telecast was "The Landing of the Hindenburg" and the last one was "The Scuttling of the Graf Spee." In between there were programs on "The Salem Witchcraft Trials," "The Gettysburg Address," and "The Fall of Troy."

Perhaps best remembered are the program's closing lines: "What sort of a day was it? A day like all days, filled with those events that alter and illuminate our times . . . and you were there."

You Are There was first heard as a CBS radio show in 1947, with John Daly as host.

YOU ASKED FOR IT
Audience Participation
FIRST TELECAST: *December 29, 1950*
LAST TELECAST: *September 27, 1959*
BROADCAST HISTORY:
    Dec 1950–Dec 1951, DUM Fri 8:30–9:00
    Dec 1951–Mar 1952, ABC Mon 9:00–9:30
    Apr 1952–Jan 1958, ABC Sun 7:00–7:30
    Jan 1958–Apr 1958, ABC Sun 9:30–10:00
    Apr 1958–Sep 1959, ABC Sun 7:00–7:30
HOST:
    Art Baker (1950–1958)
    Jack Smith (1958–1959)

When this series premiered on the DuMont television network in December 1950, it was named *The Art Baker Show,* after its creator and host. That title was changed on April 13, 1951, to the more descriptive *You Asked for It.*

The format of the show was very simple. Viewers were asked to send in a postcard describing something they wanted to see and the program's staff made every attempt to provide it. For almost a decade *You Asked for It* thrived, taking viewers into the vault at Fort Knox, bringing to them strange people with unusual talents, showing them $1,000,000 in one-dollar bills, and almost anything else that the viewers wanted to see.

Jack Smith replaced Art Baker as host when the program moved to 9:30 P.M. Sunday night on January 26, 1958.

Although *You Asked for It* is most associated with this particular format, it was actually anticipated by a nearly identical program on NBC from 1948–1949 called *I'd Like to See.*

Jack Smith also hosted the syndicated version of *You Asked for It* that appeared during the 1971–1972 season and which continued in production on an erratic basis until 1977. A new syndicated version surfaced from 1981 to 1983, with impressionist Rich Little as host. Jack Smith was on hand to narrate clips from the older versions, many of them in black-and-white, while Little and his assistant, Jayne Kennedy, narrated the new stories.

YOU BET YOUR LIFE
Quiz/Audience Participation
FIRST TELECAST: *October 5, 1950*
LAST TELECAST: *September 21, 1961*
BROADCAST HISTORY:
    Oct 1950–Jun 1951, NBC Thu 8:00–8:30
    Oct 1951–Sep 1958, NBC Thu 8:00–8:30
    Sep 1958–Sep 1961, NBC Thu 10:00–10:30
EMCEE:
    Groucho Marx
ANNOUNCER:
    George Fenneman
THEME:
    "Hooray for Captain Spaulding," by Bert Kalmar and Harry Ruby

Comedian Groucho Marx, of the rapierlike wit and sarcastic asides, was the emcee and star of this filmed quiz show, which had begun on radio in 1947. Although it was ostensibly a quiz, the series' most important asset was the humor injected by Groucho into the interviews he did with contestants before they had a chance to play the game. Contestants were picked primarily on the potential they had to be foils for Groucho's barbs, which they seemed to love.

At the start of each show the audience was informed of the night's secret word—"It's a common word, something you see every day." If any of the contestants happened to say it while they were on the air, they won an extra $100. When they said the word a dilapidated stuffed duck would drop from the ceiling with the $100 attached. The quiz consisted of question-and-answer rounds in which contestants bet all or part of an initial purse on their ability to answer the questions in a chosen category. The questions were not really difficult, and the two members of a team could collaborate ("Remember, only one answer between you"), but sometimes they lost the whole thing. Then there was always the consolation prize, which could be won by answering a nonsense question like "Who is buried in Grant's Tomb?" As Groucho liked to say, "Nobody leaves here broke."

During the period in which *You Bet Your Life* was aired on both TV and radio, an hour-long session was filmed and then edited down to provide both 30-minute versions of the show—as well as to edit out any risqué remarks by Groucho. The same contestants appeared on both radio and TV versions, though the two were not exactly alike. The reruns that aired on TV during the summer were titled *The Best of Groucho* and the entire program was retitled *The Groucho Show* during its last season.

Along with the title change came a slight change in format. The mangy duck announcing the secret word was still around, but sometimes it was replaced by other ways of revealing the "word"—a pretty girl on a swing, a ballerina dancing across the stage, tumblers dropping from the ceiling with it on a sign, etc.

A syndicated version of *You Bet Your Life*, hosted by comic Buddy Hackett, turned up briefly in the fall of 1980.

YOU CAN'T TAKE IT WITH YOU
Situation Comedy
BROADCAST HISTORY:
Syndicated only
30 minutes
Produced: *1987–*
Released: *September 1987*
CAST:
Martin Vanderhof .... Harry Morgan
Penny Vanderhof Sycamore .. Lois Nettleton
Paul Sycamore .... Richard Sanders
Alice Sycamore.................. Lisa Aliff
Essie Sycamore............ Heather Blodgett
Durwood M. Pinner .... Theodore Wilson

A turn-of-the-century Victorian home in New York City's suburban borough of Staten Island was the setting for this multigenerational comedy about a family of eccentrics. Martin Vanderhof was the patriarch of the clan, an independent curmudgeon who also served as the series' narrator. Martin, a widower, lived with his bubbly, somewhat scatterbrained daughter, Penny, and her family. That family consisted of Penny's husband,

Paul, an inventor of toys with no apparent regular source of income; their idealistic teenaged daughter, Essie; and their older daughter, Alice, who worked for a Manhattan brokerage firm. Mr. Pinner was a neighbor and friend who constructed prototypes for the toys Paul invented.

Adapted from the Pulitzer Prize–winning 1936 play of the same name written by Moss Hart and George S. Kaufman, which will be remembered long after this routine comedy is not.

YOU DON'T SAY
Quiz/Audience Participation
FIRST TELECAST: *January 7, 1964*
LAST TELECAST: *May 5, 1964*
BROADCAST HISTORY:
Jan 1964–May 1964, NBC Tue 8:30–9:00
EMCEE:
Tom Kennedy

You Don't Say was a game in which two teams of two members each (one member being the contestant and the other member a celebrity) competed in trying to guess the name of a famous person. One member of each team would be told the identity of the person and would then give clues to his partner in the form of incomplete sentences, with the missing word at the end of the sentence being the clue. The winner of each game got $100 and the chance to go to the bonus board to win more money. The board contained word clues to a different famous person's name. The clues were revealed, one at a time, and the members of the winning team tried to guess who the famous person was. Correct identification after one clue was worth $300, after two clues worth $200, and after all three clues worth $100. The daytime version of *You Don't Say*, on which the nighttime version was based, ran from April 1963 to September 1969 and was revived for a six-month period in 1975. Tom Kennedy was the emcee of all network versions of the show.

When *You Don't Say* returned to the air on a first-run syndicated basis during the 1978–1979 season, Jim Peck was the new emcee.

YOU WRITE THE SONGS
Music/Competition
BROADCAST HISTORY:
Syndicated only
30 minutes
Produced: *1986–1987*
Released: *September 1986*
HOST:
Ben Vereen
REGULARS:
The New Song Dancers (choreographed by Jaime Rogers)
Sam Harris
Monica Page
Kenny James
Catte Adams

Aspiring songsmiths were given exposure on this weekly series which presented offerings from three different amateur songwriters each week. The songs were performed by the show's regular singers, all alumni from *Star Search,* and were judged by a rotating celebrity panel with the weekly winners advancing toward a $100,000 grand prize. Host Ben Vereen introduced the songs and chatted with the weekly celebrity guests. Among those appearing on the show were Stevie Wonder, Donna Summer, Carol Bayer Sager, Melissa Manchester, Smokey Robinson, and Neil Sedaka.

For a similar series 36 years earlier, see *Songs for Sale.*

YOU'LL NEVER GET RICH
see *Phil Silvers Show, The*

YOUNG AND GAY
see *Girls, The*

YOUNG BROADWAY
Music
FIRST TELECAST: *December 22, 1948*
LAST TELECAST: *June 23, 1949*
BROADCAST HISTORY:
Dec 1948–Mar 1949, NBC Wed 7:30–7:50
Apr 1949–Jun 1949, NBC Thu 10:00–10:30

Live musical program featuring young performers who were just getting their start in show business. For a time each program was built around a current Broadway play, but with the understudies rather than the stars performing the lead roles. Performers as varied as Roberta Quinlan and Marguerite Piazza appeared.

YOUNG DAN'L BOONE
Adventure
FIRST TELECAST: *September 12, 1977*
LAST TELECAST: *October 4, 1977*
BROADCAST HISTORY:
Sep 1977, CBS Mon 8:00–9:00
Oct 1977, CBS Tue 8:00–9:00
CAST:
Daniel Boone .... Rick Moses
Rebecca Bryan .... Devon Ericson
Hawk .... Ji-Tu Cumbuka
Peter Dawes .... John Joseph Thomas
Tsiskwa .... Eloy Phil Casádos

Fess Parker had spent six successful seasons in the latter half of the 1960s playing an older version of the legendary Daniel Boone and CBS brought a younger version of the Kentucky woodsman to television in the fall of 1977. In his mid-20s, and not yet married, Daniel did his exploring with Peter Dawes, a 12-year-old English boy; Hawk, a runaway slave; and a Cherokee Indian friend named Tsiskwa. Waiting for him to settle down was his sweetheart, Rebecca. One of the failures of the 1977–1978 season, *Young Dan'l Boone*

lasted only four weeks, three in its original Monday time slot and a fourth on Tuesday, October 4.

YOUNG LAWYERS, THE
Law Drama
FIRST TELECAST: *September 21, 1970*
LAST TELECAST: *May 5, 1971*
BROADCAST HISTORY:
Sep 1970–Jan 1971, ABC Mon 7:30–8:30
Jan 1971–May 1971, ABC Wed 10:00–11:00
CAST:
Attorney David Barrett .... Lee J. Cobb
Aaron Silverman .... Zalman King
Pat Walters .... Judy Pace
Chris Blake (1971) .... Philip Clark

Drama about law students operating a Boston "Neighborhood Law Office" that provided free legal assistance to indigent clients. Slumlords, drug busts, police brutality, and rip-offs of the poor constituted most of their cases. In TV fashion the crew was suitably mixed: Aaron was the scrappy, tousle-haired young idealist, Pat was the well-educated but street-wise black chick, and Chris the earnest young middle-class WASP who was added to the cast in January, for contrast. Their experienced supervisor was David Barrett.

YOUNG MAVERICK
Western
FIRST TELECAST: *November 28, 1979*
LAST TELECAST: *January 16, 1980*
BROADCAST HISTORY:
Nov 1979–Jan 1980, CBS Wed 8:00–9:00
CAST:
Ben Maverick .... Charles Frank
Nell McGarrahan .... Susan Blanchard
Marshal Edge Troy .... John Dehner

Revivals have had a generally dismal record on network television, and this one was no exception. The original *Maverick* was one of the biggest hits of the late 1950s, and widely remembered for its laid-back, easygoing sense of humor. The secret of its success was James Garner, a magnetic personality with just the right sardonic touch, and when CBS tried to bring it all back without him 20 years later the effect was like sarsaparilla gone flat.

Garner did appear briefly in the opening scene of the first episode, meeting his successor on the trail, but it was Charles Frank who had the unenviable task of trying to fill his boots as the permanent lead. Ben Maverick was Bret's cousin (which brought the number of Maverick kin appearing on the two series up to five: Ben, Beau, Bart, Bret, and Brent). He was Harvard-educated and inheritor of the Maverick family traditions of gambling artistry, disarming good looks, a willingness to bend the law wherever profitable, and an abiding belief in cowardice as the best way to avoid getting killed on the rough frontier. He was a little more of a dandy than Bret, having learned much from his father Beau. Ben's nemesis, partner, and romantic interest was Nell McGarrahan, a pretty slick operator in her own right, who hoped to marry him someday. Marshal Edge Troy always seemed to arrive on the scene just in time to save Ben from bodily harm. He never quite understood Ben's sense of humor, or anybody else's for that matter. He was all business. Marshal Troy's territory was the area of Idaho where Ben and Nell did their gambling and ran an occasional con game.

Series stars Charles Frank and Susan Blanchard were already well acquainted before this series premiered. They had spent several years playing husband and wife on the ABC daytime soap opera *All My Children,* and were married in real life as well.

YOUNG MR. BOBBIN
Situation Comedy
FIRST TELECAST: *August 26, 1951*
LAST TELECAST: *May 18, 1952*
BROADCAST HISTORY:
   Aug 1951–May 1952, NBC Sun 7:30–8:00
CAST:
   Alexander Hawthorne Bobbin ... Jackie Kelk
   Aunt Clara .... Jane Seymour
   Aunt Bertha .... Nydia Westman
   Nancy .... Pat Hosley
   Susie .... Laura Weber
   Mr. Deacon .... Cameron Prud'homme
   Mr. Willis.................... Cort Benson

At age 18, Alexander Bobbin had just graduated from high school and begun seeking his fortune. At his age, however, his aspirations tended to exceed his abilities. This live situation comedy focused on the struggles of the young man to establish himself and attain maturity. Alexander lived in an old house with the two maiden aunts who had raised him: organized, resourceful Aunt Clara, and confused, flighty Aunt Bertha. He was in love with Nancy, the girl next door, who liked him but was determined not to let him think he was the only man in her life. His strongest ally in his effort to win Nancy was Susie, her tomboy sister who tried to help him despite her apparent teasing.

YOUNG PEOPLE'S CHURCH OF THE AIR
see *Youth on the March*

YOUNG REBELS, THE
Adventure
FIRST TELECAST: *September 20, 1970*
LAST TELECAST: *January 3, 1971*
BROADCAST HISTORY:
   Sep 1970–Jan 1971, ABC Sun 7:00–8:00
CAST:
   Jeremy Larkin .... Rick Ely
   Isak Poole................. Louis Gossett, Jr.
   Henry Abington .... Alex Henteloff
   Elizabeth Coates.......... Hilary Thompson
   General the Marquis de Lafayette
      .... Philippe Forquet

This series was supposed to allow the youthful social rebels of the late 1960s and early 1970s (or those who fantasized along with them) to relate to the American Revolution. The four young leads were members of the fictional Yankee Doodle Society, based in Chester, Pennsylvania, in the year 1777. Their goal was to harass the British behind their lines and to serve as spies for the American forces. Everyone was under 30, and British rule was the "system" they sought to overturn. Jeremy, the son of the town's mayor, was the long-haired leader; Elizabeth, his teenage girlfriend and helper; Isak, an ex-slave; and Henry, the brains of the outfit. Henry greatly admired Benjamin Franklin, and even looked a lot like him, with a calm, intellectual detachment and tiny spectacles on his nose. General Lafayette, the 20-year-old French nobleman who had come to aid the rebels, was a frequent ally, and various other youthful patriots also passed through the stories (including that eternal teenager Brandon De Wilde as young Nathan Hale).

YOUR BIG MOMENT
see *Blind Date*

YOUR CHEVROLET SHOWROOM
Variety
FIRST TELECAST: *November 20, 1953*
LAST TELECAST: *February 12, 1954*
BROADCAST HISTORY:
   Nov 1953–Feb 1954, ABC Fri 10:00–11:00
EMCEE:
   Cesar Romero

This hour of music and comedy premiered locally in New York on October 25, 1953, and went on the full ABC network a month later. Unfortunately the biggest name guests appeared on the first few telecasts, which were seen only in New York, and by the time network telecasting had begun, Cesar Romero found himself playing host to good but non-superstar acts such as Earl Wrightson, Connee Boswell, and the Russ Morgan Orchestra, plus legions of unknown singers, dancers, and comedians. The program was known for its first few weeks simply as *Chevrolet Showroom.*

YOUR ESSO REPORTER
News
FIRST TELECAST: *July 12, 1951*
LAST TELECAST: *September 13, 1951*
BROADCAST HISTORY:
   Jul 1951–Sep 1951, CBS Thu 9:00–9:30

Your Esso Reporter had been a regular feature of CBS radio since the late 1930s, and the company had also sponsored one of the very earliest regular network TV newscasts, which began almost as soon as NBC was able to organize its first three-station East Coast network in 1946. During the summer of 1951 Esso sponsored this weekly roundup of the major news events from around the world, with the CBS News correspondents based in various world capitals all participating. In a rather unusual situation, the 1951 series was seen only in the East and the Far West, where Esso was marketed. The Midwest portion of the CBS-TV network got *Meet Corliss Archer* instead.

YOUR FUNNY, FUNNY FILMS
Comedy
FIRST TELECAST: *July 8, 1963*
LAST TELECAST: *September 9, 1963*
BROADCAST HISTORY:
 Jul 1963–Sep 1963, ABC Mon 8:30–9:00
HOST:
 George Fenneman

Home movies taken by amateurs, with the emphasis on intentionally (and sometimes unintentionally) humorous sequences. A few celebrities also appeared with their home movies. The first telecast consisted of (1) a five-year-old's birthday party, as he demolished a cake, then learned to ride a bicycle and roller skate; (2) a World War II "epic" made by a 12-year-old and his friends; (3) some amateur films made in the 1920s. The "Short Shorts" feature consisted of a string of brief clips, such as a youngster experimenting with shoe polish, a woman ostensibly climbing a mountain, a little girl dancing, a wood-chopping scene, and a tiny Romeo trying to steal a kiss from his little girlfriend. A lot of kids were seen in this series, which in some ways resembled *Candid Camera.*

YOUR HIT PARADE
Music
FIRST TELECAST: *July 10, 1950*
LAST TELECAST: *August 30, 1974*
BROADCAST HISTORY:
 Jul 1950–Aug 1950, NBC Mon 9:00–9:30
 Oct 1950–Jun 1958, NBC Sat 10:30–11:00 (OS)
 Oct 1958–Apr 1959, CBS Fri 7:30–8:00
 Aug 1974, CBS Fri 8:00–8:30
VOCALISTS:
 Eileen Wilson (1950–1952)
 Snooky Lanson (1950–1957)
 Dorothy Collins (1950–1957, 1958–1959)
 Sue Bennett (1951–1952)
 June Valli (1952–1953)
 Russell Arms (1952–1957)
 Gisele MacKenzie (1953–1957)
 Tommy Leonetti (1957–1958)
 Jill Corey (1957–1958)
 Alan Copeland (1957–1958)
 Virginia Gibson (1957–1958)
 Johnny Desmond (1958–1959)
 Kelly Garrett (1974)
 Chuck Woolery (1974)
 Sheralee (1974)
DANCERS:
 The Hit Paraders (chorus & dancers) (1950–1958)

Peter Gennaro Dancers (1958–1959)
Tom Hansen Dancers (1974)
ANNOUNCERS:
 Andre Baruch (1950–1957)
 Del Sharbutt (1957–1958)
ORCHESTRA:
 Raymond Scott (1950–1957)
 Harry Sosnik (1958–1959)
 Milton Delugg (1974)
THEME:
 "Lucky Day"; "So Long for Awhile" (closing)

The legendary *Lucky Strike Hit Parade,* which had been a radio standby since 1935, was first seen on television during the summer of 1950, as a four-time-only replacement for *Robert Montgomery Presents.* It became a regular series the following October, simulcast with the radio version.

The format was essentially unchanged from radio, presenting the seven most popular songs in America as performed by a regular cast of singers and the Hit Parade Orchestra. Songs were not necessarily presented in rank order, although the rank of each was prominently featured and number one was always presented last, with great fanfare. Two or three "extras"—usually standards—were also included. Elaborate production numbers marked *Your Hit Parade,* and since many songs stayed on the charts for months, considerable ingenuity was required to vary the treatment of a song from week to week. Among the songs that remained in the number-one spot for long periods in the early 1950s were "Too Young" (12 weeks), "Because of You" (11 weeks), and "Hey There" (10 weeks).

The survey strove to sound official. Each week listeners were told that *"Your Hit Parade* survey checks the best sellers on sheet music and phonograph records, the songs most heard on the air and most played on the automatic coin machines ... an accurate, authentic tabulation of America's taste in popular music." No explanation of exactly how the surveying was done was ever revealed, however, and the actual compiling took place in great secrecy at Batten, Barton, Durstine & Osborne, which was sponsor American Tobacco Company's advertising agency.

The ballads of the early 1950s were fine for TV presentation by a regular cast of singers, but trouble began to brew for *Your Hit Parade* in 1955 when a new kind of music invaded the charts—rock 'n' roll. Not only were the Hit Parade regulars ill-suited to perform this new, raucous music, but the youngsters who bought the records wanted to see only the original performers. There was something ludicrous about Snooky Lanson attempting "Hound Dog" in a different setting each week (usually as a childish novelty).

Although most of the Hit Parade singers were recording artists in their own right, only one of them ever had a hit big enough to appear on the program's top seven while a regular on the show.

That was Gisele MacKenzie's "Hard to Get," which made the list briefly in 1955. Ironically, one-time Hit Parade regular June Valli had the biggest hit of her career, "Crying in the Chapel," only two months after leaving the show in June 1953.

In September 1957 the entire cast was replaced by a younger, more "contemporary" crew, none of whom were popular rock artists, however. The age-old format itself was extensively revamped the following February, with the hit parade reduced to five songs, plus five more melodious "extras" and a big $200,000 "Mystery Tune" contest. None of this tinkering solved the problems created by drastically changing musical styles, and after a final season on CBS (during which the top-tunes list was drawn from *Billboard* magazine) the program expired on April 24, 1959. An abortive attempt was made at reviving the show in the summer of 1974, with the emphasis on *Your Hit Parade* songs from selected broadcasts of specific weeks in the 1940s and 1950s, mixed with currently popular hits performed by the original artists.

YOUR KAISER DEALER PRESENTS KAISER-FRAZER "ADVENTURES IN MYSTERY" STARRING BETTY FURNESS IN "BYLINE"
see *Byline*

YOUR LUCKY CLUE
Quiz/Audience Participation
FIRST TELECAST: *July 13, 1952*
LAST TELECAST: *August 31, 1952*
BROADCAST HISTORY:
Jul 1952–Aug 1952, CBS Sun 7:30–8:00
EMCEE:
Basil Rathbone

Each week two teams competed with each other to solve dramatized mysteries. One team was composed of two professional detectives and the other of two amateur criminologists. The audience was made aware of where the clues were in each dramatization, but the contestants were not. Each team tried to solve the case before the other team did, and before the emcee disclosed the solution. Basil Rathbone, long known as the Sherlock Holmes of motion pictures (he played the role in most of the adaptations of A. Conan Doyle's stories), was a logical choice as emcee.

YOUR LUCKY STRIKE HIT PARADE
see *Your Hit Parade*

YOUR NEIGHBOR THE WORLD
Documentary
FIRST TELECAST: *April 6, 1958*
LAST TELECAST: *October 8, 1959*
BROADCAST HISTORY:
Apr 1958–Jan 1959, ABC Sun Various 30 minute
May 1959–Oct 1959, ABC Thu 10:00–10:30

Documentary films about different peoples and cultures around the world, from high fashion in Paris to natives in the Belgian Congo.

YOUR PLAY TIME
Dramatic Anthology
FIRST TELECAST: *June 14, 1953*
LAST TELECAST: *September 3, 1955*
BROADCAST HISTORY:
Jun 1953–Sep 1953, CBS Sun 7:30–8:00
Jun 1954–Sep 1954, CBS Sun 7:30–8:00
Jun 1955–Sep 1955, NBC Sat 10:30–11:00

For three consecutive summers series bearing the title *Your Play Time* aired as replacements for other shows. In 1953 and 1954, on CBS, the show was the summer replacement for two alternating CBS programs, *The Jack Benny Show* and *Private Secretary*. In 1953 some of the plays were done live and others on film. They tended to be on the melodramatic side with settings in foreign locales. 1954's offerings, both comedy and drama, were entirely on film and generally took place in domestic settings. Featured were such lesser-known stars as George Nader, Hillary Brooke, Jack Haley, Peter Graves, Ruth Warrick, and Tommy Rettig.

The *Your Play Time* that was telecast by NBC in the summer of 1955 was made up of reruns from other anthology series, primarily *Pepsi-Cola Playhouse* and *Studio 57*. It was the summer replacement for *Your Hit Parade*.

YOUR PRIZE STORY
Dramatic Anthology
FIRST TELECAST: *April 2, 1952*
LAST TELECAST: *May 28, 1952*
BROADCAST HISTORY:
Apr 1952–May 1952, NBC Wed 10:00–10:30

This live weekly dramatic show was unique in that its sponsor, Hazel Bishop, requested viewers to submit story ideas. The person sending in a story that was accepted and adapted for television received a cash prize of $1,000. It had to be a true story and literary skill was not required. The viewer was to tell it in his own words and let the program's staff rewrite it for airing. The presentations were done with very little in the way of scenery or props, much in the manner of little-theater performances.

Evidently the public was not bubbling over with good ideas for TV shows, as the series lasted less than two months.

YOUR SHOW OF SHOWS
Comedy Variety
FIRST TELECAST: *February 25, 1950*
LAST TELECAST: *June 5, 1954*
BROADCAST HISTORY:
Feb 1950–Jun 1954, NBC Sat 9:00–10:30
REGULARS:
Sid Caesar
Imogene Coca

Carl Reiner
Howard Morris (1951–1954)
Robert Merrill (1950–1951)
Marguerite Piazza (1950–1953)
Bill Hayes (1950–1953)
Jerry Ross & Nellie Fisher (1950–1952)
Mata & Hari (1950–1953)
Tom Avera (1950)
Hamilton Dancers
Jack Russell
Billy Williams Quartet
Judy Johnson (1950–1953)
Earl Redding (1950–1951)
Aariana Knowles (1951–1952)
Dick DeFreitas (1950–1953)
Bambi Linn & Rod Alexander (1952–1954)
James Starbuck
Show of Shows Ballet Company
Charles Sanford Orchestra
PRODUCER:
Max Liebman
WRITERS:
Mel Brooks, Neil Simon, Woody Allen, Lucille
Kallen, Larry Gelbart, Mel Tolkin, others

One of the classics of television's "Golden Age,"
Your Show of Shows was the successor to Caesar
and Coca's 1949 *Admiral Broadway Revue*. At the
outset, *Your Show of Shows* was actually half of
a larger show, being the New York element of
NBC's *Saturday Night Revue*. The other portion,
from Chicago, was *The Jack Carter Show,* on between 8:00 and 9:00 P.M. At the end of the 1950–
1951 season Carter and the *Saturday Night Revue*
umbrella title were dropped.

Your Show of Shows was surely one of the most
ambitious undertakings on television, *ever*. It was
90 minutes of live, original comedy, every week.
And it was good. In addition to Caesar and Coca's
sketches there was a large corps of regular singers
and dancers, plus top-name guest stars. As a matter of fact, the nominal host of each program was
a different big-name guest star (Burgess Meredith
hosted the first two shows). Ballet sequences and
scenes from grand opera were also featured, to
give the show an undeniably "classy" air.

But it was the comic genius of Caesar and Coca
for which the program is remembered. They appeared in such regular routines as "History As
She Ain't," Caesar's roving reporter, monologues
and mime, as well as in large-scale satires on
current films and other hit TV shows. Caesar and
his writers were movie buffs, and many of Hollywood's most pretentious epics got the full treatment, ranging from antique silent films (the
drunken father) to contemporary hits such as
Shane (in which Caesar played the unbelievably
fearless gunfighter Strange) and *From Here to
Eternity* ("From Here to Obscurity").

Carl Reiner and Howard Morris, who joined the
supporting cast in 1950 and 1951 respectively,
were gradually given more prominent roles and
by the final season Caesar, Coca, Reiner, and

Morris constituted a four-person repertory group
employed in many of the skits. Caesar could take
on many roles. He was the double-talking fo-
reigner (he was a master of dialects), the henpecked husband, or the greasy-haired cad. Coca
was nearly as versatile, while Reiner would most
often be the slick, presumptuous salesman type,
and Howard Morris the little guy determined to
prove that he was as good as *anybody*—even if he
wasn't. Among the notable routines developed
during the show's long run were Caesar and
Coca's husband-and-wife skit, "The Hickenloop-
ers"; the fable of the great clock in the little town
of Baverhoff, Bavaria, whose mechanical figures
always seemed to go haywire when the hour
struck; Coca as the happy-go-lucky tramp; Caesar
as an Italian opera star babbling gibberish in
Galapacci, or as the supercool jazz musician
Progress Hornsby, or as the visiting authority on
almost anything, usually being interviewed at the
airport, with such dialogue as this:

ARCHEOLOGIST: "After many years, I haff found
ze secret of Titten-Totten's Tomb!"

INTERVIEWER (excitedly): "What is it, Professor?"

ARCHEOLOGIST: "I should tell *you?*"

Your Show of Shows finally left the air in June
1954, as Caesar and Coca parted to pursue separate careers. Most series end their runs forgotten
or in reruns, but in what must have been one of the
more unusual farewells in TV history, the last
telecast of *Your Show of Shows* was a big, tearful,
nostalgic recap of the best sketches of the past
years, ending with the by-then famous finale number "Stars over Broadway." Even the president of
NBC, Pat Weaver, showed up to thank everyone
for four excellent years and to wish them well in
their future separate series.

Caesar and Coca never again quite recaptured
the magic of those four years, either separately or
together. The combination of fresh talent, excellent supporting cast, gifted writers (including such
future stars as Mel Brooks, Neil Simon, and a
young Woody Allen), and perhaps the times themselves had been "right"—but only once. Excerpts
from the shows were packaged by producer Max
Liebman as a theatrical movie titled *Ten From
Your Show of Shows,* in 1973, and as a series of
90-minute TV specials syndicated in 1976.

YOUR SHOW TIME
Dramatic Anthology
FIRST TELECAST: *January 21, 1949*
LAST TELECAST: *July 15, 1949*
BROADCAST HISTORY:
Jan 1949–Jul 1949, NBC Fri 9:30–10:00
HOST:
Arthur Shields

Filmed dramatizations of classic short stories by
many of the world's most famous authors, including Guy de Maupassant, Robert Louis Stevenson,
Henry James, and Sir Arthur Conan Doyle. Each

telecast opened in an old bookshop where host Arthur Shields was seen seated behind an old-fashioned desk, from which he introduced to-night's story.

This program was notable as the recipient of the very first Emmy award presented to a network show. The award was for the premiere telecast, "The Necklace," starring John Beal.

YOUR SPORTS SPECIAL
Sports News
FIRST TELECAST: *October 8, 1948*
LAST TELECAST: *November 4, 1949*
BROADCAST HISTORY:
Oct 1948–Jan 1949, CBS Fri 7:00–7:15
Jan 1949–Nov 1949, CBS Various 7:00–7:15
REPORTERS:
Carswell Adams
Dolly Stark

Sports reporter Carswell Adams and former major-league umpire Dolly Stark were the hosts of this sports news and interview show. Originally seen on Friday nights, it expanded in January 1949 to an irregular schedule that varied from two to five times per week for the next ten months.

YOUR STORY THEATRE
Dramatic Anthology
FIRST TELECAST: *December 1, 1950*
LAST TELECAST: *February 2, 1951*
BROADCAST HISTORY:
Dec 1950–Feb 1951, DUM Fri 8:00–8:30

Series of half-hour filmed dramas, starring such Hollywood standbys as Robert Alda, Hurd Hatfield, Marjorie Lord, William Frawley, Sterling Holloway, etc. Stories included both original scripts and adaptations from Henry James, Robert Louis Stevenson, Frank R. Stockton ("The Lady or the Tiger"), and other noted authors.

YOUR —— TV THEATER
syndicated title for *Fireside Theater*

YOUR WITNESS
Courtroom Drama
FIRST TELECAST: *September 19, 1949*
LAST TELECAST: *September 26, 1950*
BROADCAST HISTORY:
Sep 1949–Oct 1949, ABC Mon 8:00–8:30
Dec 1949–May 1950, ABC Sun 9:00–9:30
Aug 1950–Sep 1950, ABC Wed 9:00–9:30
WITH:
Edmund Lowe

Wednesday was courtroom night in 1950, with *Your Witness* following *On Trial* on the ABC schedule, and running opposite *Famous Jury Trials* on DuMont. This was a low-budget courtroom drama/mystery, and originated from Chicago.

YOU'RE IN THE PICTURE
Quiz/Audience Participation
FIRST TELECAST: *January 20, 1961*
LAST TELECAST: *January 20, 1961*
BROADCAST HISTORY:
Jan 1961, CBS Fri 9:30–10:00
HOST:
Jackie Gleason
PANELISTS:
Keenan Wynn
Pat Carroll
Jan Sterling
Arthur Treacher

This was one of those rare series that was so bad it was canceled after exactly one telecast. It was certainly one of the major fiascos in Jackie Gleason's career. The four celebrity panelists on the show were seen situated behind an oversized comic cutout of the kind found in amusement-park photography booths. They had no idea what the picture through which they had stuck their heads, and sometimes their hands, represented. The object was for the panel to guess what the picture was by asking questions of host/emcee Gleason. When they had successfully identified the picture, a new one would be substituted and they would start over. Jackie's wit was supposed to add to the humor of the show, which was played primarily for laughs.

The first telecast was so bad, however, that the program never aired again. On the following Friday night Jackie spent the entire half hour apologizing for the disastrous first episode. For the remainder of the season he filled the time slot with an interview show, hosting different celebrities each week, under the title *The Jackie Gleason Show* (not to be confused with his comedy variety series of the same name). *You're in the Picture* was never heard of again.

YOU'RE INVITED
Comedy Variety
FIRST TELECAST: *July 1, 1948*
LAST TELECAST: *September 20, 1948*
BROADCAST HISTORY:
Jul 1948–Aug 1948, ABC Wed 8:00–8:30
Aug 1948–Sep 1948, ABC Mon 9:00–9:30
EMCEE:
Romo Vincent

Jovial, rotund comic Romo Vincent hosted this early variety show, which took place in a house-party setting. At the start of each show he greeted his audience at the front door and invited them in to see the singers, dancers, and ventriloquists who were that week's guests. There was also an audience-participation segment.

YOU'RE ON YOUR OWN
Quiz/Audience Participation
FIRST TELECAST: *December 22, 1956*
LAST TELECAST: *March 16, 1957*

BROADCAST HISTORY:
Dec 1956–Mar 1957, CBS Sat 10:30–11:00
EMCEE:
Steve Dunne

Contestants on *You're on Your Own* had free access to anything on the stage that would help them find the answers to the questions posed by emcee Steve Dunne. They need not know everything, only be able to use the correct source: directories, record albums, telephone books, etc. The faster they were at ferreting out the correct answers, the more money they could win—as much as $25,000 on a single night.

YOURS FOR A SONG
Quiz/Audience Participation
FIRST TELECAST: *November 14, 1961*
LAST TELECAST: *September 18, 1962*
BROADCAST HISTORY:
Nov 1961–Sep 1962, ABC Tue 9:30–10:00
EMCEE:
Bert Parks

Contestants on this live half-hour game show won money by filling in the missing words to song lyrics that were flashed on a screen. Whenever a contestant won a round, in addition to the prize money he won the right to face a new challenger. In addition to serving as quizmaster, Bert Parks got a chance to sing in this one. A few weeks after this prime-time version premiered, ABC added a daytime version that ran until March 1963.

YOUTH ON THE MARCH
Religion
FIRST TELECAST: *October 9, 1949*
LAST TELECAST: *June 7, 1953*
BROADCAST HISTORY:
Oct 1949–May 1952, ABC Sun 10:30–11:00 (OS)
Oct 1952–Jun 1953, DUM Sun 10:30–11:00
HOST:
Rev. Percy Crawford

This program of inspirational songs, hymns, and sermons was a fixture on Sunday nights for nearly four years, first on ABC and then on DuMont. It was presented by the Young People's Church of the Air and was presided over by Rev. Percy Crawford, with mixed choir and men's glee club.

YOUTH TAKES A STAND
Discussion
FIRST TELECAST: *August 18, 1953*
LAST TELECAST: *September 15, 1953*

BROADCAST HISTORY:
Aug 1953–Sep 1953, CBS Tue 10:30–11:00
MODERATOR:
Marc Cramer
Alan Jackson

In an effort to get intelligent audience feedback to its television news effort, CBS invited four young scholars from high schools and junior colleges to participate in a discussion of current events and world affairs with a different CBS-TV reporter each week. The first moderator for the sessions during the show's prime-time run was the series' co-producer, Marc Cramer. A different panel of students, selected by CBS stations around the country in cooperation with various public, parochial, and private school organizations, appeared on each telecast to chat with such reporters as Charles Collingwood and Douglas Edwards. Mr. Cramer was replaced by CBS News reporter Alan Jackson before the series moved into a late-afternoon time slot on Sundays. It remained on the air until March 1955 with Jim McKay replacing Jackson as moderator in March 1954.

YOUTH WANTS TO KNOW
Forum
FIRST TELECAST: *September 8, 1951*
LAST TELECAST: *August 24, 1954*
BROADCAST HISTORY:
Sep 1951–Oct 1951, NBC Sat 7:00–7:30
Jun 1952–Sep 1952, NBC Wed 8:30–9:00
Jul 1954–Aug 1954, NBC Sat 7:30–8:00
MODERATOR:
Theodore Granik

This series gave high school and college students the opportunity to ask questions of major figures in the world of politics, business, and international affairs. The subjects covered were generally related to major issues that affected large parts of the world and large numbers of its people. *Youth Wants to Know* originated live from Washington, D.C., and students from the Washington area participated. Mr. Granik and the guest were seated on a platform in front of the students and the entire operation was run like a press conference, with Mr. Granik picking the questioners. The students prepared their own questions. When this series premiered in 1951, its title was *The American Youth Forum.* It was changed to *Youth Wants to Know* in January 1952. At times, though not always, it was simulcast on radio, and it continued to run irregularly on Sunday afternoons until October 1958.

Z

ZANE GREY THEATER
see *Dick Powell's Zane Grey Theater*

ZORRO
Western
FIRST TELECAST: *October 10, 1957*
LAST TELECAST: *September 24, 1959*
BROADCAST HISTORY:
Oct 1957–Sep 1959, ABC Thu 8:00–8:30
CAST:
Don Diego de la Vega ("Zorro") . Guy Williams
Don Alejandro .... George J. Lewis
Bernardo .... Gene Sheldon
Capt. Monastario .... Britt Lomond
Sgt. Garcia .... Henry Calvin
Nacho Torres.................. Jan Arvan
Elena Torres .... Eugenia Paul
Magistrate Galindo .... Vinton Hayworth
Anna Maria Verdugo (1958–1959)
.... Jolene Brand
Sénor Gregorio Verdugo (1958–1959)
.... Eduard Franz
Cpl. Reyes (1958–1959) .... Don Diamond
PRODUCER:
Walt Disney
THEME:
"Theme from Zorro," by Norman Foster and
George Burns

Guy Williams starred as a swashbuckling masked
hero in Spanish California in this popular series.
The year was 1820, and young Don Diego, the only
son of wealthy Don Alejandro, was returning
home from Spain in response to his father's ap-
peals. Monastario, a ruthless army officer, had
become commandant of the Fortress de los Angeles, and was tyrannizing the local dons and
their peons. Arriving in California, Don Diego presented himself as a lazy, foppish aristocrat, much
to his father's dismay. Secretly, however, he
donned mask and sword and set out to aid the
oppressed and foil the schemes of the evil Monastario. His name on these forays was Zorro—for
the sign of the "Z" he cut with his sword—and his
loyal manservant was the mute Bernardo, who
pretended to be deaf as well as mute to make it
easier for him to eavesdrop for his master. Only
Zorro knew that Bernardo could really hear.

The plots were pretty simple, and there was a
lot of derring-do (especially in the sword fights),
making *Zorro* a great favorite with children. Helping Zorro's crusade was the fact that his chief
adversaries, Monastario and his henchman, the
fat, dimwitted Sgt. Garcia, were both quite incompetent. Another element of interest was that the
stories continued from episode to episode, in
semi-serial fashion, even though they were so
basic that they could be joined at any point.

Among the other regulars were Anna Maria
Verdugo, Zorro's love interest (introduced in the

second season); Nacho Torres, an escaped political prisoner, and his daughter Elena; and Zorro's
black and white stallions, Tornado and Phantom.
Many characters came and went in three- or four-
installment subplots within the main series, including a young señorita named Anita Cabrillo,
played by Annette Funicello, who even got a
chance to sing a few songs on the show. Her role
was a birthday present from series producer Walt
Disney, who had originally brought Annette to
stardom as a *Mickey Mouse Club* mouseketeer
only a few years before.

The theme song from the show ("Zorro—the fox
so cunning and free/Zorro—make the sign of the
Z!") was a hit-parade favorite in 1958. It was first
recorded by Henry Calvin, of all people (fat Sgt.
Garcia!), but the hit version was by a pop group,
the Chordettes.

ZORRO AND SON
Situation Comedy
FIRST TELECAST: *April 6, 1983*
LAST TELECAST: *June 1, 1983*
BROADCAST HISTORY:
Apr 1983–Jun 1983, CBS Wed 8:00–8:30
CAST:
Don Diego de la Vega (Zorro Sr.)
.... Henry Darrow
Don Carlos de la Vega (Zorro Jr.)
.... Paul Regina
Commandante Paco Pico ..... Gregory Sierra
Sgt. Sepulveda.......... Richard Beauchamp
Bernardo .... Bill Dana
Brothers Napa and Sonoma .. Barney Martin
Corporal Cassette............ John Moschitta
Señorita Anita .... Catherine Parks
Peasant .... Pete Leal

Played pretty much for laughs, this series updated
the legend of Zorro, 20–25 years after the masked
defender of the people had first made his name in
old California. Age had taken its toll on Don Diego
and, when he was injured while trying to live up
to his reputation, his faithful manservant Bernardo decided something had to be done. Bernardo sent to Spain for young Don Carlos, Diego's
son. Unlike his father, Don Carlos was a modern
swinger who, though willing to help out his father,
would not give up his gambling or his girl-chasing.
Not only that, the elder Zorro, a traditionalist, had
great difficulty adjusting to his son's use of guns,
gas bombs, and other modern weapons, instead of
a simple sword. The current oppressor of the people was Commandante Pico, assisted by Sgt.
Sepulveda, and his human recording machine,
Corp. Cassette. *Zorro and Son* was liberally laced
with bad jokes—the Franciscan monk arrested for
"selling wine before its time," young Don Carlos
futilely trying to rally the people in a makeshift
Zorro costume when his regular one was lost,
etc.—and it rarely took itself seriously, despite
being produced by Walt Disney Productions, the
same company responsible for the original *Zorro*
TV series more than 25 years earlier.

PRIME-TIME SCHEDULES: 1946–1987

On the following pages are complete prime-time network schedules for each season from 1946–1947 through 1987–1988. Television programming changes constantly, and schedules such as these can only offer an approximation of what was on during any given week. However, the industry has long had a custom of introducing new series in September or October of each year, and it is these introductory "fall schedules" that are shown here.

During the 1950s and 1960s most of the series introduced in the fall of each year lasted for at least three months, and often for a full year, even when they were unsuccessful. Industry practice was to contract in advance for at least 13 original episodes of a series. In recent years, however, intense network competition has led to the dropping of unsuccessful series as soon as three or four weeks after their premieres, and occasionally a TV dud, like a Broadway flop, will even close on its opening night. The principal fall programs are shown here, no matter how short their actual runs.

Times given are those at which the programs were seen in most cities. Newscasts will be found in the main body of the book under *News,* feature film series under *Movies,* sports events under the name of the sport, etc. (Miscellaneous collections of film shorts, used to fill time, are included on the schedules but are not in the book.) A blank indicates that there was no network programming in the time slot. This does not necessarily mean there was nothing on TV—individual stations usually filled in with their own local or syndicated shows—although in the earliest days there sometimes was only a test pattern to watch.

Abbreviations
A = ABC
C = CBS
D = DuMont
F = Fox
N = NBC

PRIME TIME SCHEDULE: 1946

		7:00 PM	7:30	8:00	8:30	9:00	9:30	10:00	10:30	11:00
SUNDAY	A									
	C									
	D			Western Movie						
	N			Face to Face	Geographically Speaking	Television Screen Magazine				
MONDAY	A									
	C									
	D									
	N			Esso Newsreel	†		Gillette Cavalcade of Sports			
TUESDAY	A									
	C									
	D			Play the Game		Serving Through Science				
	N									
WEDNESDAY	A									
	C									
	D					Faraway Hill				
	N									
THURSDAY	A									
	C									
	D					Cash and Carry				
	N			Esso Newsreel	Hour Glass		Fight Film Filler			
FRIDAY	A									
	C									
	D									
	N				*	I Love to Eat	‡		Gillette Cavalcade of Sports	
SATURDAY	A									
	C									
	D									
	N									

*You Are an Artist / Let's Rhumba   †Voice of Firestone Televues   ‡The World in Your Home

PRIME TIME SCHEDULE: 1947

		7:00 PM	7:30	8:00	8:30	9:00	9:30	10:00	10:30	11:00
SUNDAY	A									
	C									
	D									
	N			Various Special Presentations						
MONDAY	A									
	C									
	D	Small Fry Club	Doorway to Fame							
	N				Americana		Esso Reporter	Gillette Cavalcade of Sports		
TUESDAY	A									
	C									
	D	Small Fry Club		Western Movie			Mary Kay and Johnny			
	N									
WEDNESDAY	A									
	C									
	D	Small Fry Club								
	N		Kraft Television Theatre		*					
THURSDAY	A									
	C									
	D	Small Fry Club	Birthday Party		Charade Quiz					
	N			†	Musical Merry-Go-Round	Eye Witness	You Are an Artist			
FRIDAY	A									
	C									
	D	Small Fry Club								
	N			Campus Hoopla		‡		Gillette Cavalcade of Sports		
SATURDAY	A									
	C									
	D									
	N									

*In the Kelvinator Kitchen   †NBC TV Newsreel   ‡The World in Your Home

PRIME TIME SCHEDULE: 1948

Day	Net	7:00 PM	7:30	8:00	8:30	9:00	9:30	10:00	10:30	11:00
SUNDAY	A	Pauline Frederick	Southernaires Quartet	Hollywood Screen Test	Actors Studio	Movie				
	C	Newsweek in Review	Studio One / Various		Riddle Me This	Toast of the Town		America Speaks	News	
	D	Original Amateur Hour								
	N	Mary Kay and Johnny / News	Welcome Aboard	Author Meets the Critics	Meet the Press	Philco TV Playhouse				
MONDAY	A	News	Kiernan's Corner	Quizzing the News	Film Shorts					
	C	Places Please / News	Face the Music		Arthur Godfrey's Talent Scouts	Basketball				
	D	Doorway to Fame	†† / Champagne and Orchids	Court of Current Issues						
	N	America Song / News	Chevrolet Tele-Theater	Americana	Newsreel	Boxing from St. Nicholas Arena				
TUESDAY	A	News	Movieland Quiz	Film Shorts	America's Town Meeting of the Air					
	C	Roar of the Rails	News / Face the Music			We, the People	People's Platform			
	D	††	INS Telenews	Boxing						
	N	Musical Miniatures / News	Texaco Star Theater		Mary Margaret McBride	News / Films	Wrestling from St. Nicholas Arena			
WEDNESDAY	A	News	Critic at Large	Gay Nineties Revue	Film Shorts / Three About Town	Wrestling from Washington, D.C.				
	C	Places Please / News	Face the Music	Kobbs Korner	Winner Take All	Boxing from Westchester			News	
	D	Birthday Party	†† / Film Shorts	Photographic Horizons	The Growing Paynes	Boxing from Jamaica Arena				
	N	You Are an Artist / News	Girl About Town / Picture This	Ted Steele / Story of the Week	Kraft Television Theatre		News Reel	Village Barn		
THURSDAY	A	News	Film Shorts	Fashion Story	Club Seven	Movie				
	C	News	Face the Music	To the Queen's Taste	Movies / Sports					
	D	Adventures of Okey Doky	††	Film Shorts	Charade Quiz	Wrestling / Football				
	N	‡	Musical Miniatures	* / News	NBC Presents / ♯	Swift Show	Gulf Road Show with Bob Smith	Bigelow Show		
FRIDAY	A	News	Tales of Red Caboose	Film Shorts	Teenage Book Club	Various	Break the Bank			
	C	Your Sports Special	Places Please / News	Face the Music	† / What's It Worth	Cap'n Billy's Mississippi Music Hall				
	D	Key to the Missing	†† / Film Shorts	Fashions on Parade	Film Shorts	Wrestling from Jamaica Arena				
	N	Musical Merry-Go-Round / News	Musical Miniatures	Stop Me If You've Heard This One	I'd Like to See / News	Gillette Cavalcade of Sports				
SATURDAY	A	News	Film Shorts	Sports with Joe Hasel	Play the Game	Film Shorts	Basketball			
	C			Basketball						
	D									
	N		Televison Screen Magazine	Saturday Night Jamboree	Basketball					

890

*Sportswoman of the Week
†Sportsman's Quiz
††Camera Headlines (News)
‡Paris Cavalcade of Fashion
♯The Nature of Things

PRIME TIME SCHEDULE: 1949

Day	Net	7:00 PM	7:30	8:00	8:30	9:00	9:30	10:00	10:30	11:00
SUNDAY	A	Paul Whiteman's Goodyear Revue	ABC Penthouse Players	Think Fast	The Little Revue	Let There Be Stars		Celebrity Time	Youth on the March	
SUNDAY	C	Tonight on Broadway	This is Show Business	Toast of the Town		Fred Waring Show		News		
SUNDAY	D	Front Row Center		Chicagoland Mystery Players	Cinema Varieties	Cross Question				
SUNDAY	N	Leave It to the Girls	Aldrich Family	Chesterfield Supper Club	Colgate Theatre	Philco TV Playhouse		Garroway at Large		
MONDAY	A	News								
MONDAY	C	Roar of the Rails	News / Sonny Kendis *	Silver Theater	Arthur Godfrey's Talent Scouts	Candid Camera	The Goldbergs	Studio One		
MONDAY	D	Captain Video	‡ / Vincent Lopez	Newsweek Views the News	Al Morgan	And Everything Nice	Wrestling			
MONDAY	N	Kukla, Fran & Ollie	† / News	Chevrolet Tele-Theater	Voice of Firestone	Lights Out	Cities Service Band of America	Quiz Kids		
TUESDAY	A	News						Tomorrow's Boxing Champions		
TUESDAY	C	Strictly for Laughs	News / Sonny Kendis *	Movies / Specials		Actors Studio	Suspense	This Week in Sports		
TUESDAY	D	Captain Video	‡ / Vincent Lopez	Court of Current Issues		The O'Neills	Feature Theatre			
TUESDAY	N	Kukla, Fran & Ollie	† / News	Texaco Star Theater		Fireside Theater	Life of Riley	Original Amateur Hour		
WEDNESDAY	A	News		Photoplay Time	Look Photocrime	Author Meets the Critics	Wrestling from Chicago			
WEDNESDAY	C	Strictly for Laughs	News / At Home	Arthur Godfrey & His Friends		Bigelow Show	Boxing from St. Nicholas Arena			
WEDNESDAY	D	Captain Video	‡ / Vincent Lopez	Movies		††	Famous Jury Trials			
WEDNESDAY	N	Kukla, Fran & Ollie	† / News	Crisis	The Clock	Kraft Television Show		Break the Bank		
THURSDAY	A	News	Lone Ranger	Stop the Music		Crusade in Europe	Starring Boris Karloff	Roller Derby		
THURSDAY	C	Dione Lucas	News / Sonny Kendis *	Front Page	Inside U.S.A. / Romance		Boxing from Sunnyside Gardens			
THURSDAY	D	Captain Video	‡ / Vincent Lopez	Mystery Theater		Morey Amsterdam Show				
THURSDAY	N	Kukla, Fran & Ollie	† / News	Hollywood Premiere	Mary Kay and Johnny	Fireball Fun-For-All		Martin Kane Private Eye		
FRIDAY	A	News		Majority Rules	Blind Date	Auction-Aire	Fun for the Money	Roller Derby		
FRIDAY	C	Strictly for Laughs	News / Sonny Kendis *	Mama	Man Against Crime	Ford Theatre / 54th Street Revue		People's Platform	Capitol Cloakroom	
FRIDAY	D	Captain Video	‡ / Vincent Lopez	Hands of Mystery	Headline Clues	Fishing and Hunting Club	Film	Amateur Boxing from Chicago		
FRIDAY	N	Kukla, Fran & Ollie	† / News	One Man's Family	We, the People	Bonny Maid Versatile Varieties	Big Story / Various	Gillette Cavalcade of Sports		
SATURDAY	A		Hollywood Screen Test	Paul Whiteman's TV Teen Club		Roller Derby				
SATURDAY	C		Quincy Home-News / Blues by Bargy *			Premiere Playhouse				
SATURDAY	D			Spin the Picture		Cavalcade of Stars		Wrestling from Chicago		
SATURDAY	N		‡‡ / News	Twenty Questions	Sessions / Stud's Place	Who Said That?	Meet the Press	Black Robé		

*Herb Shriner Show
†Mohawk Showroom
‡Manhattan Spotlight
††The Plainclothesman
‡‡The Nature of Things

PRIME TIME SCHEDULE: 1950

Day		7:00 PM	7:30	8:00	8:30	9:00	9:30	10:00	10:30	11:00
SUNDAY	A	Paul Whiteman's Revue	Showtime, U.S.A.	Hollywood Premiere Theatre	Sit or Miss	Soap Box Theatre	Marshall Plan in Action	Old Fashioned Meeting	Youth on the March	
	C	Gene Autry Show	This is Show Business	Toast of the Town		Fred Waring Show		Celebrity Time	What's My Line	
	D	Starlit Time		Rhythm Rodeo		Arthur Murray Party		They Stand Accused		
	N	Leave it to the Girls	Aldrich Family	Colgate Comedy Hour		Philco TV Playhouse		Garroway at Large	Take a Chance	
MONDAY	A	Club Seven	Hollywood Screen Test	Treasury Men in Action	Dick Tracy	College Bowl	On Trial	Feature Film		
	C	Stork Club	News	Perry Como	Lux Video Theatre	Arthur Godfrey's Talent Scouts	Horace Heidt Show	The Goldbergs	Studio One	
	D	Captain Video	Susan Raye	*	Visit with the Armed Forces	Al Morgan	Wrestling from Columbia Park			
	N	Kukla, Fran & Ollie	†	News	Special Show	Voice of Firestone	Lights Out	Robert Montgomery Presents Lucky Strike Time/ Musical Comedy Time	Who Said That?	
TUESDAY	A	Club Seven	Beulah	Game of the Week	Buck Rogers	Billy Rose Show	Can You Top This?	Life Begins at Eighty	Roller Derby	
	C	Stork Club	News	Faye Emerson	Prudential Family Playhouse / Sure as Fate		Vaughn Monroe Musical Variety	Suspense	Danger	We Take Your Word
	D	Captain Video		Joan Edwards	Court of Current Issues	Johns Hopkins Science Review	Cavalcade of Bands		Star Time	
	N	Kukla, Fran & Ollie	Little Show	News	Texaco Star Theater		Fireside Theatre	Circle Theatre	Original Amateur Hour	
WEDNESDAY	A	Club Seven	Chance of a Lifetime	First Nighter		Don McNeill TV Club		Chicago Wrestling		
	C	Stork Club	News	Perry Como	Arthur Godfrey & His Friends		Teller of Tales		Blue Ribbon Bouts	
	D	Captain Video	Most Important People	*			Famous Jury Trials	The Plain-clothesman	Broadway to Hollywood	
	N	Kukla, Fran & Ollie	†	News	Four Star Revue		Kraft Television Theatre		Break the Bank	Stars Over Hollywood
THURSDAY	A	Club Seven	Lone Ranger	Stop the Music		Holiday Hotel	Blind Date	I Cover Times Square	Roller Derby	
	C	Stork Club	News	Faye Emerson	Show Goes On		Alan Young Show	Big Town	Truth or Consequences	Nash Airflyte Theater
	D	Captain Video	*	Joan Edwards			Adventures of Ellery Queen	Boxing from Dexter Arena		
	N	Kukla, Fran & Ollie	Little Show	News	You Bet Your Life	Hawkins Falls	Kay Kyser's Kollege of Musical Knowledge		Martin Kane, Private Eye	Wayne King
FRIDAY	A	Club Seven	Life with Linkletter	Twenty Questions	Pro Football Highlights	Pulitzer Prize Playhouse		Penthouse Party	Stud's Place	
	C	Stork Club	News	Perry Como	Mama	Man Against Crime	Ford Theatre / Magnavox Theater		Morton Downey Show	Beat the Clock
	D	Captain Video	Most Important People	*	Film Filler	Hold That Camera	Hands of Mystery	Inside Detective	Cavalcade of Stars	
	N	Kukla, Fran & Ollie	†	News	Quiz Kids	We, the People	Bonny Maid Versatile Varieties	Big Story / The Clock	Gillette Cavalcade of Sports	Greatest Fights
SATURDAY	A	Sandy Dreams	Stu Erwin Show	Paul Whiteman's TV Teen Club		Roller Derby				
	C	Big Top	Week in Review	Faye Emerson	Ken Murray Show		Frank Sinatra Show		Sing It Again	
	D	Captain Video		Country Style		Madison Square Garden				
	N	Hank McCune	One Man's Family	Jack Carter Show		Your Show of Shows			Your Hit Parade	

*Manhattan Spotlight †Mohawk Showroom

PRIME TIME SCHEDULE: 1951

Day	Net	7:00 PM	7:30	8:00	8:30	9:00	9:30	10:00	10:30	11:00
SUNDAY	A	Paul Whiteman's Goodyear Revue	Music in Velvet	Admission Free		Film Filler	Marshall Plan in Action	Hour of Decision	Youth on the March	
SUNDAY	C	Gene Autry Show	This is Show Business	Toast of the Town		Fred Waring Show		Goodrich Celebrity Time	What's My Line	
SUNDAY	D					Rocky King, Detective	The Plain-clothesman	They Stand Accused		
SUNDAY	N	Chesterfield Sound Off Time	Young Mr. Bobbin	Colgate Comedy Hour		Philco TV Playhouse / Goodyear TV Playhouse		Red Skelton Show	Leave It to the Girls	
MONDAY	A	News	Hollywood Screen Test	*	Life Begins at Eighty	Curtain Up		Bill Gwinn Show	Stud's Place	
MONDAY	C		News / Perry Como	Lux Video Theatre	Arthur Godfrey's Talent Scouts	I Love Lucy	It's News to Me	Studio One		
MONDAY	D	Captain Video		Stage Entrance	Johns Hopkins Science Review	Wrestling from Columbia Park				
MONDAY	N	Kukla, Fran & Ollie	† / News	Speidel Show	Voice of Firestone	Lights Out	Robert Montgomery Presents/ Somerset Maugham TV Theatre			
TUESDAY	A		Beulah	Charlie Wild, Private Detective	How Did They Get That Way	United or Not	On Trial	Film Filler	Chicago Symphony Chamber Orchestra	
TUESDAY	C		News / Stork Club	Frank Sinatra Show		Crime Syndicated	Suspense	Danger		
TUESDAY	D	Captain Video		What's the Story?	Keep Posted	Cosmopolitan Theatre		Hands of Destiny		
TUESDAY	N	Kukla, Fran & Ollie	Little Show / News	Texaco Star Theater		Fireside Theatre	Armstrong Circle Theatre	Original Amateur Hour		
WEDNESDAY	A	News	Chance of a Lifetime	Paul Dixon Show		Don McNeil's TV Club/Arthur Murray Party	The Clock	Celanese Theatre / King's Crossroads		
WEDNESDAY	C		News / Perry Como	Arthur Godfrey & His Friends		Strike It Rich	The Web	Pabst Blue Ribbon Bouts		Sports Spot
WEDNESDAY	D	Captain Video				Gallery of Mme. Liu-Tsong	Shadow of the Cloak			
WEDNESDAY	N	Kukla, Fran & Ollie	† / News	Kate Smith Evening Hour		Kraft Television Theatre		Break the Bank	Freddy Martin Show	
THURSDAY	A	News	Lone Ranger	Stop the Music		Herb Shriner Show	Gruen Guild Theater	Paul Dixon Show	Masland at Home Show	Carmel Myers Show
THURSDAY	C		News / Stork Club	George Burns & Gracie Allen Show / Garry Moore Show	Amos 'n' Andy	Alan Young Show	Big Town	Racket Squad	Crime Photographer	
THURSDAY	D	Captain Video		Georgetown University Forum	Broadway to Hollywood	Adventures of Ellery Queen		Bigelow Theatre	Football This Week	
THURSDAY	N	Kukla, Fran & Ollie	Little Show / News	You Bet Your Life	Treasury Men in Action	Ford Festival		Martin Kane, Private Eye	Wayne King	
FRIDAY	A	News	Say it with Acting/Life with Linkletter	Mystery Theatre	Stu Erwin Show	Crime with Father	Tales of Tomorrow/ Versatile Varieties	Dell O'Dell Show	America in View	
FRIDAY	C		News / Perry Como	Mama	Man Against Crime	Schlitz Playhouse of Stars		Live Like a Millionaire	Hollywood Opening Night	
FRIDAY	D	Captain Video		Twenty Questions	You Asked for It	Down You Go	Front Page Detective	Cavalcade of Stars		
FRIDAY	N	Kukla, Fran & Ollie	† / News	Quiz Kids	We, the People	Big Story	Aldrich Family	Gillette Cavalcade of Sports		Greatest Fights
SATURDAY	A	Hollywood Theatre Time	Jerry Colonna Show	Paul Whiteman's TV Teen Club		Lesson in Safety	America's Health			
SATURDAY	C	Sammy Kaye Variety Show	Beat the Clock	Ken Murray Show		Faye Emerson's Wonderful Town	Show Goes On	Songs for Sale		
SATURDAY	D						Pro Wrestling from Chicago			
SATURDAY	N	American Youth Forum	One Man's Family	All Star Revue		Your Show of Shows			Your Hit Parade	

*Mr. District Attorney/Amazing Mr. Malone

†Mohawk Showroom

PRIME TIME SCHEDULE: 1952

Day	Net	7:00 PM	7:30	8:00	8:30	9:00	9:30	10:00	10:30 / 11:00
SUNDAY	A	You Asked for It	Hot Seat	All-Star News		Playhouse #7	This is the Life	Hour of Decision / Film Filler	Anywhere, U.S.A.
	C	Gene Autry Show	This is Show Business	Toast of the Town		Fred Waring Show	Break the Bank	The Web	What's My Line
	D	Georgetown University Forum				Rocky King, Detective	The Plain-clothesman	Arthur Murray Show	Youth on the March
	N	Red Skelton Show	Doc Corkle	Colgate Comedy Hour		Philco TV Playhouse / Goodyear TV Playhouse		The Doctor	
MONDAY	A		Hollywood Screen Test	Inspector Mark Saber	United or Not	All-Star News			
	C		News / Perry Como	Lux Video Theatre	Arthur Godfrey's Talent Scouts	I Love Lucy	Life with Luigi	Studio One	
	D	Captain Video		Pentagon	Johns Hopkins Science Review	Guide Right	Football Sidelines / Famous Fights	Boxing from Eastern Parkway	
	N		Those Two / News	What's My Name	Voice of Firestone	Hollywood Opening Night	Robert Montgomery Presents		Who Said That?
TUESDAY	A		Beulah						
	C		News / Heaven for Betsy	Leave it to Larry	Red Buttons Show	Crime Syndicated / City Hospital	Suspense	Danger	
	D	Captain Video		Power of Women	Keep Posted	Where Was I?	Quick on the Draw		
	N	Short Short Dramas	Dinah Shore / News	Texaco Star Theater		Fireside Theatre	Armstrong Circle Theatre	Two for the Money	Club Embassy / On the Line with Considine
WEDNESDAY	A		Name's the Same	All-Star News		Adventures of Ellery Queen	Chicago Wrestling		
	C		News / Perry Como	Arthur Godfrey & His Friends		Strike It Rich	Man Against Crime	Pabst Blue Ribbon Bouts	Sports Spot
	D	Captain Vidoe	New York Giants Quarterback Huddle		Trash or Treasure	Stage a Number			
	N		Those Two / News	I Married Joan	Scott Music Hall/Cavalcade of America	Kraft Television Theatre		This Is Your Life	
THURSDAY	A		Lone Ranger	All-Star News	Chance of a Lifetime	Politics on Trial	On Guard		
	C		News / Heaven for Betsy	George Burns and Gracie Allen Show	Amos 'n' Andy / Four Star Playhouse	Pick the Winner	Big Town	Racket Squad	I've Got a Secret
	D	Captain Video			Broadway to Hollywood	Pick the Winner	What's the Story?	Author Meets the Critics	
	N	Short Short Dramas	Dinah Shore / News	You Bet Your Life	Treasury Men in Action	Dragnet / Gangbusters	Ford Theatre	Martin Kane, Private Eye	
FRIDAY	A		Stu Erwin Show	Adventures of Ozzie & Harriet	All-Star News		Tales of Tomorrow		
	C		News / Perry Como	Mama	My Friend Irma	Schlitz Playhouse of Stars	Our Miss Brooks	Mr. & Mrs. North	
	D	Captain Video		Steve Randall	Dark of Night	Life Begins at Eighty		Twenty Questions	Down You Go
	N	Herman Hickman Show	Those Two / News	RCA Victor Show	Gulf Playhouse	Big Story	Aldrich Story	Gillette Cavalcade of Sports	Greatest Fights
SATURDAY	A	Paul Whiteman's TV Teen Club	Live Like a Millionaire	Feature Playhouse					
	C	Stork Club	Beat the Clock	Jackie Gleason Show		Jane Froman's U.S.A. Canteen	Meet Millie	Balance Your Budget/Quiz Kids	Battle of the Ages
	D		Pet Shop				Pro Wrestling from Chicago		
	N	Mr. Wizard	My Little Margie	All Star Revue		Your Show of Shows			Your Hit Parade

PRIME TIME SCHEDULE: 1953

Day	Net	7:00 PM	7:30	8:00	8:30	9:00	9:30	10:00	10:30	11:00
SUNDAY	A	You Asked for It	Frank Leahy Show	Notre Dame Football		Walter Winchell Show	Orchid Award	Peter Potter Show		Hour of Decision
	C	Quiz Kids	Jack Benny Show / Private Secretary	Toast of the Town		G.E. Theater / Fred Waring Show	Man Behind the Badge	The Web	What's My Line	
	D	Georgetown University Forum	Washington Exclusive			Rocky King, Detective	The Plain-clothesman	Dollar a Second	Man Against Crime	
	N	Paul Winchell Show	Mr. Peepers	Colgate Comedy Hour		Philco TV Playhouse / Goodyear TV Playhouse		Letter to Loretta	Man Against Crime	
MONDAY	A	Walter Winchell / News	Jamie	Sky King	Of Many Things	Junior Press Conference	Big Picture	This is the Life		
	C		News / Perry Como	George Burns and Gracie Allen Show	Arthur Godfrey's Talent Scouts	I Love Lucy	Red Buttons Show	Studio One		
	D	Captain Video		Twenty Questions	Big Issue	Boxing from Eastern Parkway				
	N		Arthur Murray Party / News	Name That Tune	Voice of Firestone	RCA Victor Show Starring Dennis Day	Robert Montgomery Presents		Who Said That?	
TUESDAY	A		News	Cavalcade of America		Make Room for Daddy	U.S. Steel Hour / Motorola TV Theatre		Name's the Same	
	C		News / Jane Froman	Gene Autry Show	Red Skelton Show	This is Show Business	Suspense	Danger	See It Now	
	D	Captain Video		Life is Worth Living	Pantomime Quiz					
	N		Dinah Shore / News	Buick Berle Show		Fireside Theatre	Armstrong Circle Theatre	Judge for Yourself	On the Line with Considine	*
WEDNESDAY	A		News	Inspector Mark Saber	At Issue / Through the Curtain	America in View	Wrestling from Rainbo			
	C		News / Perry Como	Arthur Godfrey & His Friends		Strike It Rich	I've Got a Secret	Pabst Blue Ribbon Bouts	Sports Spot	
	D	Captain Video		Johns Hopkins Science Review	Joseph Schildkraut Presents	Colonel Humphrey Flack	On Your Way	Stars on Parade	Music Show	
	N		Coke Time / News	I Married Joan	My Little Margie	Kraft Television Theatre		This Is Your Life		
THURSDAY	A	News	Lone Ranger	Quick as a Flash	Where's Raymond	Back That Fact	Kraft Television Theatre			
	C		News / Jane Froman	Meet Mr. McNutley	Four Star Playhouse	Lux Video Theatre	Big Town	Philip Morris Playhouse	Place the Face	
	D	Captain Video		New York Giants Quarterback Huddle	Broadway to Hollywood	What's the Story?				
	N		Dinah Shore / News	You Bet Your Life	Treasury Men in Action	Dragnet	Ford Theatre	Martin Kane, Private Eye		
FRIDAY	A	News	Stu Erwin Show	Adventures of Ozzie & Harriet	Pepsi-Cola Playhouse	Pride of the Family	Comeback Story	Showcase Theater		
	C		News / Perry Como	Mama	Topper	Schlitz Playhouse of Stars	Our Miss Brooks	My Friend Irma	Person to Person	
	D	Captain Video		Front Page Detective	Melody Street	Life Begins at Eighty	Nine Thirty Curtain	Chance of a Lifetime	Down You Go	
	N		Coke Time / News	Dave Garroway Show	Life of Riley	Big Story	Campbell Soundstage	Gillette Cavalcade of Sports		Greatest Fights
SATURDAY	A	Paul Whiteman's TV Teen Club	Leave it to the Girls	Talent Patrol	Music at the Meadowbrook	Saturday Night Fights	Fight Talk	Madison Square Garden Highlights		
	C	Meet Millie	Beat the Clock	Jackie Gleason Show		Two for the Money	My Favorite Husband	Medallion Theater	Revlon Mirror Theatre	
	D			Pro Football						
	N	Mr. Wizard	Ethel & Albert	Bonino	Original Amateur Hour	Your Show of Shows			Your Hit Parade	

*It Happened in Sports

PRIME TIME SCHEDULE: 1954

Day	Net	7:00 PM	7:30	8:00	8:30	9:00	9:30	10:00	10:30	11:00
SUNDAY	A	You Asked for It	Pepsi-Cola Playhouse	Flight #7	Big Picture	Walter Winchell Show / Martha Wright Show	Dr. I.Q.	Break the Bank		
	C	Lassie	Jack Benny Show/Private Secretary	Toast of the Town		G.E. Theater	Honestly Celeste	Father Knows Best	What's My Line	
	D	Author Meets the Critic	Opera Cameos			Rocky King Detective	Life Begins at Eighty	Music Show		
	N	People Are Funny	Mr. Peepers	Colgate Comedy Hour		Philco TV Playhouse/Goodyear TV Playhouse		Loretta Young Show	The Hunter	
MONDAY	A	Kukla, Fran & Ollie / News	Name's the Same	Come Closer	Voice of Firestone	Junior Press Conference	Boxing from Eastern Parkway			
	C		News / Perry Como	George Burns and Gracie Allen Show	Arthur Godfrey's Talent Scouts	I Love Lucy	December Bride	Studio One		
	D	Captain Video / News		Ilona Massey Show		Boxing from St. Nicholas Arena				
	N		Tony Martin / News	Caesar's Hour		Medic	Robert Montgomery Presents			
TUESDAY	A	Kukla, Fran & Ollie / News	Cavalcade of America		Twenty Questions	Make Room for Daddy	U.S. Steel Hour / Elgin TV Hour		Stop the Music	
	C		News / Jo Stafford	Red Skelton Show	Halls of Ivy	Meet Millie	Danger	Life with Father	See it Now	
	D	Captain Video / News		Life is Worth Living	Studio 57	One Minute Please				
	N		Dinah Shore / News	Buick Berle Show		Fireside Theatre	Armstrong Circle Theatre	Truth or Consequences	It's a Great Life	
WEDNESDAY	A	Kukla, Fran & Ollie / News	Disneyland		Stu Erwin Show	Masquerade Party	Enterprise			
	C		News / Perry Como	Arthur Godfrey & His Friends		Strike It Rich	I've Got a Secret	Pabst Blue Ribbon Bouts		Sports Spot
	D	Captain Video / News				Chicago Symphony		Down You Go		
	N		Coke Time / News	I Married Joan	My Little Margie	Kraft Television Theatre		This Is Your Life	Big Town	
THURSDAY	A	Kukla, Fran & Ollie / News	Lone Ranger	Mail Story	Treasury Men In Action	So You Want to Lead a Band	Kraft Television Theatre			
	C		News / Jane Froman	Ray Milland Show	Climax		Four Star Playhouse	Public Defender	Name That Tune	
	D	Captain Video / News		They Stand Accused		What's the Story				
	N		Dinah Shore / News	You Bet Your Life	Justice	Dragnet	Ford Theatre	Lux Video Theatre		
FRIDAY	A	Kukla, Fran & Ollie / News	Adventures of Rin Tin Tin	Adventures of Ozzie & Harriet	Ray Bolger Show	Dollar a Second	The Vise			
	C		News / Perry Como	Mama	Topper	Schlitz Playhouse of Stars	Our Miss Brooks	The Lineup	Person to Person	
	D	Captain Video / News				The Stranger		Chance of a Lifetime	Time Will Tell	
	N		Coke Time / News	Red Buttons Show	Life of Riley	Big Story	Dear Phoebe	Gillette Cavalcade of Sports		Great Moments In Sports
SATURDAY	A		Compass	Dotty Mack Show		Saturday Night Fights	Fight Talk	Stork Club		
	C	Gene Autry Show	Beat the Clock	Jackie Gleason Show		Two for the Money	My Favorite Husband	That's My Boy	Willy	
	D		Pro Football							
	N	Mr. Wizard	Ethel & Albert	Mickey Rooney Show	Place the Face	Imogene Coca Show	Texaco Star Theater	George Gobel Show	Your Hit Parade	

PRIME TIME SCHEDULE: 1955

Day		7:00 PM	7:30	8:00	8:30	9:00	9:30	10:00	10:30	11:00
SUNDAY	A	You Asked for It	Famous Film Festival			Chance of a Lifetime	Original Amateur Hour	Life Begins at Eighty		
	C	Lassie	Jack Benny Show / Private Secretary	Ed Sullivan Show		G.E. Theater	Alfred Hitchcock Presents	Appointment with Adventure	What's My Line	
	N	It's a Great Life	Frontier	Colgate Variety Hour		Goodyear TV Playhouse / Alcoa Hour		Loretta Young Show	Justice	
MONDAY	A	Kukla, Fran & Ollie	News	Topper	TV Reader's Digest	Voice of Firestone	Dotty Mack Show	Medical Horizons	Big Picture	
	C		News	Adventures of Robin Hood	George Burns and Gracie Allen Show	Arthur Godfrey's Talent Scouts	I Love Lucy	December Bride	Studio One	
	N		Tony Martin Show / News	Caesar's Hour		Medic	Robert Montgomery Presents			
TUESDAY	A	Kukla, Fran & Ollie	News	Warner Brothers Presents	Life and Legend of Wyatt Earp	Make Room for Daddy	DuPont Cavalcade Theater	Talent Varieties		
	C		News	Name That Tune	Navy Log	You'll Never Get Rich	Meet Millie	Red Skelton Show	$64,000 Question	My Favorite Husband
	N		Dinah Shore Show / News	Martha Raye Show / Milton Berle Show / Chevy Show		Fireside Theatre	Armstrong Circle Theatre / Pontiac Presents Playwrights '56		Big Town	
WEDNESDAY	A	Kukla, Fran & Ollie	News	Disneyland	MGM Parade	Masquerade Party	Break the Bank	Wednesday Night Fights		
	C		News	Brave Eagle	Arthur Godfrey & His Friends	The Millionaire	I've Got a Secret	20th Century-Fox Hour / U.S. Steel Hour		
	N		Coke Time / News	Screen Director's Playhouse	Father Knows Best	Kraft Television Theatre		This Is Your Life	Midwestern Hayride	
THURSDAY	A	Kukla, Fran & Ollie	News	Lone Ranger	Life Is Worth Living	Stop the Music	Star Tonight	Down You Go	Outside U.S.A.	
	C		News	Sgt. Preston of the Yukon	Bob Cummings Show	Climax		Four Star Playhouse	Johnny Carson Show	Wanted
	N		Dinah Shore Show / News	You Bet Your Life	People's Choice	Dragnet	Ford Theatre	Lux Video Theatre		
FRIDAY	A	Kukla, Fran & Ollie	News	Adventures of Rin Tin Tin	Adventures of Ozzie & Harriet	Crossroads	Dollar a Second	The Vise	Ethel & Albert	
	C		News	Adventures of Champion	Mama	Our Miss Brooks	The Crusader	Schlitz Playhouse of Stars	The Lineup	Person to Person
	N		Coke Time / News	Truth or Consequences	Life of Riley	Big Story	Star Stage	Gillette Cavalcade of Sports		Red Barber's Corner
SATURDAY	A		Ozark Jubilee			Lawrence Welk Show		Tomorrow's Careers		
	C	Gene Autry Show	Beat the Clock	Stage Show	The Honeymooners	Two for the Money	It's Always Jan	Gunsmoke	Damon Runyon Theatre	
	N		Big Surprise	Perry Como Show		People Are Funny	Texaco Star Theater Starring Jimmy Durante	George Gobel Show	Your Hit Parade	

897

PRIME TIME SCHEDULE: 1956

Day	Net	7:00 PM	7:30	8:00	8:30	9:00	9:30	10:00	10:30
SUNDAY	A	You Asked for It	Original Amateur Hour		Press Conference	Omnibus			
SUNDAY	C	Lassie	Jack Benny Show / Private Secretary	Ed Sullivan Show		G.E. Theater	Alfred Hitchcock Presents	$64,000 Challenge	What's My Line
SUNDAY	N	Tales of the 77th Bengal Lancers	Circus Boy	Steven Allen Show		Goodyear TV Playhouse / Alcoa Hour		Loretta Young Show	National Bowling Champions
MONDAY	A	Kukla, Fran & Ollie / News	Bold Journey	Danny Thomas Show	Voice of Firestone	Life Is Worth Living	Lawrence Welk Talent Show		
MONDAY	C	News	Adventures of Robin Hood	George Burns and Gracie Allen Show	Arthur Godfrey's Talent Scouts	I Love Lucy	December Bride	Studio One	
MONDAY	N		Nat "King" Cole Show / News	Adventures of Sir Lancelot	Stanley	Medic	Robert Montgomery Presents		
TUESDAY	A	Kukla, Fran & Ollie / News	Conflict / Cheyenne		Life and Legend of Wyatt Earp	Broken Arrow	DuPont Theater	It's Polka Time	
TUESDAY	C	News	Name That Tune	Phil Silvers Show	The Brothers	Herb Shriner Show	Red Skelton Show	$64,000 Question	Do You Trust Your Wife?
TUESDAY	N		Jonathan Winters Show / News	Big Surprise	Noah's Ark	Jane Wyman Show	Armstrong Circle Theatre / Kaiser Aluminum Hour		Break the $250,000 Bank
WEDNESDAY	A	Kukla, Fran & Ollie / News	Disneyland		Navy Log	Adventures of Ozzie & Harriet	Ford Theatre	Wednesday Night Fights	
WEDNESDAY	C	News	Giant Step	Arthur Godfrey Show		The Millionaire	I've Got a Secret	20th Century-Fox Hour / U.S. Steel Hour	
WEDNESDAY	N		Eddie Fisher Show / News	Adventures of Hiram Holliday	Father Knows Best	Kraft Television Theatre		This Is Your Life	Twenty-One
THURSDAY	A	Kukla, Fran & Ollie / News	Lone Ranger	Circus Time		Wire Service		Ozark Jubilee	
THURSDAY	C	News	Sgt. Preston of the Yukon	Bob Cummings Show	Climax		Playhouse 90		
THURSDAY	N		Dinah Shore Show / News	You Bet Your Life	Dragnet	People's Choice	Ford Show Starring Tennessee Ernie Ford	Lux Video Theatre	
FRIDAY	A	Kukla, Fran & Ollie / News	Adventures of Rin Tin Tin	Adventures of Jim Bowie	Crossroads	Treasure Hunt	The Vise	Ray Anthony Show	
FRIDAY	C	News	My Friend Flicka	West Point Story	Dick Powell's Zane Grey Theater	The Crusader	Schlitz Playhouse	The Lineup	Person to Person
FRIDAY	N		Eddie Fisher Show / News	Life of Riley	Walter Winchell Show	On Trial	Big Story	Gillette Cavalcade of Sports	Red Barber's Corner
SATURDAY	A		Famous Film Festival			Lawrence Welk Show		Masquerade Party	
SATURDAY	C	Beat the Clock	The Buccaneers	Jackie Gleason Show		Gale Storm Show	Hey Jeannie	Gunsmoke	High Finance
SATURDAY	N		People Are Funny	Perry Como Show		Caesar's Hour		George Gobel Show	Your Hit Parade

PRIME TIME SCHEDULE: 1957

Day		7:00 PM	7:30	8:00	8:30	9:00	9:30	10:00	10:30	11:00
SUNDAY	A	You Asked for It	Maverick		Bowling Stars	Open Hearing	All-American Football Game of the Week			
	C	Lassie	Jack Benny Show / Bachelor Father	Ed Sullivan Show		G.E. Theater	Alfred Hitchcock Presents	$64,000 Challenge	What's My Line	
	N	Original Amateur Hour	Sally	Steve Allen Show		Dinah Shore Chevy Show		Loretta Young Show		
MONDAY	A	News	American Bandstand	Guy Mitchell Show	Bold Journey	Voice of Firestone	Lawrence Welk's Top Tunes and New Talent Show			
	C	News	Adventures of Robin Hood	George Burns and Gracie Allen Show	Arthur Godfrey's Talent Scouts	Danny Thomas Show	December Bride	Studio One in Hollywood		
	N		Price is Right	Restless Gun	Tales of Wells Fargo	Twenty-One	Turn of Fate	Suspicion		
TUESDAY	A	News	Cheyenne / Sugarfoot		Life and Legend of Wyatt Earp	Broken Arrow	Telephone Time	West Point Story		
	C	News	Name That Tune	Phil Silvers Show	Eve Arden Show	To Tell the Truth	Red Skelton Show	$64,000 Question	Assignment Foreign Legion	
	N		Nat "King" Cole Show	Eddie Fisher Show / George Gobel Show		Meet McGraw	Bob Cummings Show	The Californians		
WEDNESDAY	A	News	Disneyland		Tombstone Territory	Adventures of Ozzie & Harriet	Walter Winchell File	Wednesday Night Fights		Famous Fights
	C	News	I Love Lucy	Big Record		The Millionaire	I've Got a Secret	Armstrong Circle Theatre/ U.S. Steel Hour		
	N		Wagon Train		Father Knows Best	Kraft Television Theatre		This Is Your Life		
THURSDAY	A	News	Circus Boy	Zorro	Real McCoys	Pat Boone—Chevy Showroom	O.S.S.	Navy Log		
	C	News	Sgt. Preston of the Yukon	Harbourmaster	Climax		Playhouse 90			
	N		Tic Tac Dough	You Bet Your Life	Dragnet	People's Choice	Ford Show Starring Tennessee Ernie Ford	Lux Show Starring Rosemary Clooney	Jane Wyman Show	
FRIDAY	A	News	Adventures of Rin Tin Tin	Adventures of Jim Bowie	Patrice Munsel Show	Frank Sinatra Show	Date with the Angels	Colt .45		
	C	News	Leave It to Beaver	Trackdown	Dick Powell's Zane Grey Theatre	Mr. Adams & Eve	Schlitz Playhouse	The Lineup	Person to Person	
	N		Saber of London	Court of Last Resort	Life of Riley	M Squad	Thin Man	Gillette Cavalcade of Sports		Red Barber's Corner
SATURDAY	A		Keep It in the Family	Country Music Jubilee		Lawrence Welk's Dancing Party		Mike Wallace Interviews		
	C		Perry Mason		Dick & the Duchess	Gale Storm Show	Have Gun, Will Travel	Gunsmoke		
	N		People Are Funny	Perry Como Show		Polly Bergen Show / Club Oasis	Gisele MacKenzie Show	What's It For	Your Hit Parade	

PRIME TIME SCHEDULE: 1958

Day	Net	7:00 PM	7:30	8:00	8:30	9:00	9:30	10:00	10:30	11:00
SUNDAY	A	You Asked for It	Maverick		The Lawman	Colt .45	Encounter			
	C	Lassie	Jack Benny Show / Bachelor Father	Ed Sullivan Show		G.E. Theater	Alfred Hitchcock Presents	$64,000 Question	What's My Line	
	N	Saber of London	Northwest Passage	Steve Allen Show		Dinah Shore Chevy Show		Loretta Young Show		
MONDAY	A		News	Jubilee U.S.A.	Bold Journey	Voice of Firestone	Anybody Can Play	This Is Music		
	C		News	Name That Tune	The Texan	Father Knows Best	Danny Thomas Show	Ann Sothern Show	Desilu Playhouse	
	N		Tic Tac Dough	Restless Gun	Tales of Wells Fargo	Peter Gunn	Alcoa / Goodyear TV Playhouse	Arthur Murray Party		
TUESDAY	A		News	Cheyenne / Sugarfoot	Life and Legend of Wyatt Earp	The Rifleman	Naked City	Confession		
	C		News	Stars in Action	Keep Talking	To Tell the Truth	Arthur Godfrey Show	Red Skelton Show	Garry Moore Show	
	N		Dragnet	George Gobel Show / Eddie Fisher Show		George Burns Show	Bob Cummings Show	The Californians		
WEDNESDAY	A		News	Lawrence Welk's Plymouth Show	Adventures of Ozzie & Harriet	Donna Reed Show	Patti Page Olds Show	Wednesday Night Fights		
	C		News	Twilight Theater	Pursuit	The Millionaire	I've Got a Secret	Armstrong Circle Theatre / U.S. Steel Hour		
	N		Wagon Train		Price Is Right	Milton Berle in the Kraft Music Hall	Bat Masterson	This Is Your Life		
THURSDAY	A		News	Leave It to Beaver	Zorro	Real McCoys	Pat Boone—Chevy Showroom	Rough Riders	Traffic Court	
	C		News	I Love Lucy	December Bride	Yancy Derringer	Dick Powell's Zane Grey Theatre	Playhouse 90		
	N		Jefferson Drum	Ed Wynn Show	Twenty-One	Behind Closed Doors	Ford Show Starring Tennessee Ernie Ford	You Bet Your Life	Masquerade Party	
FRIDAY	A		News	Adventures of Rin Tin Tin	Walt Disney Presents	Man with a Camera	77 Sunset Strip			
	C		News	Your Hit Parade	Trackdown	Jackie Gleason Show	Phil Silvers Show	Lux Playhouse/ Schlitz Playhouse	The Lineup	Person to Person
	N		Buckskin	Adventures of Ellery Queen		M Squad	Thin Man	Gillette Cavalcade of Sports		Fight Beat
SATURDAY	A		Dick Clark Show	Jubilee U.S.A.		Lawrence Welk's Dodge Dancing Party		Sammy Kaye's Music from Manhattan		
	C		Perry Mason		Wanted: Dead or Alive	Gale Storm Show	Have Gun, Will Travel	Gunsmoke		
	N		People Are Funny	Perry Como Show		Steve Canyon	Cimarron City		Brains & Brawn	

PRIME TIME SCHEDULE: 1959

		7:00 PM	7:30	8:00	8:30	9:00	9:30	10:00	10:30	11:00
SUNDAY	A	Colt .45	Maverick		The Lawman	The Rebel	The Alaskans		Dick Clark's World of Talent	
SUNDAY	C	Lassie	Dennis the Menace	Ed Sullivan Show		G.E. Theater	Alfred Hitchcock Presents	Jack Benny Show / George Gobel Show	What's My Line	
SUNDAY	N	Riverboat		Sunday Showcase		Dinah Shore Chevy Show		Loretta Young Show		
MONDAY	A		Cheyenne		Bourbon Street Beat		Adventures in Paradise		Man with a Camera	
MONDAY	C	News	Masquerade Party	The Texan	Father Knows Best	Danny Thomas Show	Ann Sothern Show	Hennessey	DuPont Show with June Allyson	
MONDAY	N		Richard Diamond, Private Detective	Love & Marriage	Tales of Wells Fargo	Peter Gunn	Alcoa / Goodyear TV Playhouse	Steve Allen Plymouth Show		
TUESDAY	A		Sugarfoot / Bronco		Life and Legend of Wyatt Earp	The Rifleman	Philip Marlowe	Alcoa Presents	Keep Talking	
TUESDAY	C	News		Dennis O'Keefe Show	Many Loves of Dobie Gillis	Tightrope	Red Skelton Show	Garry Moore Show		
TUESDAY	N		Laramie		Fibber McGee & Molly	Arthur Murray Party	Startime			
WEDNESDAY	A		Court of Last Resort	Hobby Lobby Show	Adventures of Ozzie & Harriet	Hawaiian Eye		Wednesday Night Fights		
WEDNESDAY	C	News	The Lineup		Men into Space	The Millionaire	I've Got a Secret	Armstrong Circle Theatre / U.S. Steel Hour		
WEDNESDAY	N		Wagon Train		Price is Right	Perry Como's Kraft Music Hall		This Is Your Life	Wichita Town	
THURSDAY	A		Gale Storm Show	Donna Reed Show	Real McCoys	Pat Boone—Chevy Showroom	The Untouchables		Take a Good Look	
THURSDAY	C	News	To Tell the Truth	Betty Hutton Show	Johnny Ringo	Dick Powell's Zane Grey Theatre	Playhouse 90 / Big Party			
THURSDAY	N		Law of the Plainsman	Bat Masterson	Staccato	Bachelor Father	Ford Show Starring Tennessee Ernie Ford	You Bet Your Life	The Lawless Years	
FRIDAY	A		Walt Disney Presents		Man from Blackhawk	77 Sunset Strip		Robert Taylor: The Detectives	Black Saddle	
FRIDAY	C	News	Rawhide		Hotel de Paree	Desilu Playhouse		Twilight Zone	Person to Person	
FRIDAY	N		People Are Funny	The Trouble-shooters	Bell Telephone Hour		M Squad	Gillette Cavalcade of Sports		Phillies Jackpot Bowling
SATURDAY	A		Dick Clark Show	High Road	Leave It to Beaver	Lawrence Welk Show		Jubilee U.S.A.		
SATURDAY	C		Perry Mason		Wanted: Dead or Alive	Mr. Lucky	Have Gun, Will Travel	Gunsmoke	Markham	
SATURDAY	N		Bonanza		Man & the Challenge	The Deputy	Five Fingers		It Could Be You	

PRIME TIME SCHEDULE: 1960

Day	Net	7:00 PM	7:30	8:00	8:30	9:00	9:30	10:00	10:30	11:00
SUNDAY	A	Walt Disney Presents		Maverick		The Lawman	The Rebel	The Islanders		Walter Winchell Show
SUNDAY	C	Lassie	Dennis the Menace	Ed Sullivan Show		G.E. Theater	Jack Benny Show	Candid Camera	What's My Line	
SUNDAY	N	Shirley Temple's Storybook		National Velvet	Tab Hunter Show	Dinah Shore Chevy Show		Loretta Young Show		This Is Your Life
MONDAY	A		Cheyenne		Surfside Six		Adventures in Paradise		Peter Gunn	
MONDAY	C	News	To Tell the Truth	Pete & Gladys	Bringing Up Buddy	Danny Thomas Show	Andy Griffith Show	Hennessey	Presidential Countdown	
MONDAY	N		Riverboat		Tales of Wells Fargo	Klondike	Dante	Barbara Stanwyck Show	Jackpot Bowling	
TUESDAY	A	Expedition	Bugs Bunny Show	The Rifleman	Life and Legend of Wyatt Earp	Stagecoach West		Alcoa Presents		
TUESDAY	C	News		Father Knows Best	Many Loves of Dobie Gillis	Tom Ewell Show	Red Skelton Show	Garry Moore Show		
TUESDAY	N		Laramie		Alfred Hitchcock Presents	Thriller				
WEDNESDAY	A		Hong Kong		Adventures of Ozzie & Harriet	Hawaiian Eye		Naked City		
WEDNESDAY	C	News	Aquanauts		Wanted: Dead or Alive	My Sister Eileen	I've Got a Secret	Armstrong Circle Theatre/U.S. Steel Hour		
WEDNESDAY	N		Wagon Train		Price is Right	Perry Como's Kraft Music Hall		Peter Loves Mary		
THURSDAY	A		Guestward Ho!	Donna Reed Show	Real McCoys	My Three Sons	The Untouchables		Take a Good Look	
THURSDAY	C	News	The Witness		Dick Powell's Zane Grey Theatre	Angel	Peck's Bad Girl	Person to Person	DuPont Show with June Allyson	
THURSDAY	N		The Outlaws		Bat Masterson	Bachelor Father	Ford Show Starring Tennessee Ernie Ford	Groucho Show		
FRIDAY	A		Matty's Funday Funnies	Harrigan & Son	The Flintstones	77 Sunset Strip		Robert Taylor: The Detectives	Law & Mr. Jones	
FRIDAY	C	News	Rawhide		Route 66		Mr. Garlund	Twilight Zone	Eyewitness to History	
FRIDAY	N		Dan Raven		The Westerner	Bell Telephone Hour		Michael Shayne		
SATURDAY	A		Roaring Twenties		Leave It to Beaver	Lawrence Welk Show		Fight of the Week		Make That Spare
SATURDAY	C		Perry Mason		Checkmate		Have Gun, Will Travel	Gunsmoke		
SATURDAY	N		Bonanza		Tall Man	The Deputy	Nation's Future			

PRIME TIME SCHEDULE: 1961

Day	Net	7:00 PM	7:30	8:00	8:30	9:00	9:30	10:00	10:30
SUNDAY	A	Maverick	Follow the Sun		The Lawman	Bus Stop		Adventures in Paradise	
SUNDAY	C	Lassie	Dennis the Menace	Ed Sullivan Show		G.E. Theater	Jack Benny Show	Candid Camera	What's My Line
SUNDAY	N	Bullwinkle Show	Walt Disney's Wonderful World of Color		Car 54, Where Are You?	Bonanza		DuPont Show of the Week	
MONDAY	A	Expedition	Cheyenne		The Rifleman	Surfside Six		Ben Casey	
MONDAY	C	News	To Tell the Truth	Pete & Gladys	Window on Main Street	Danny Thomas Show	Andy Griffith Show	Hennessey	I've Got a Secret
MONDAY	N			National Velvet	Price Is Right	87th Precinct		Thriller	
TUESDAY	A		Bugs Bunny Show	Bachelor Father	Calvin & the Colonel	New Breed		Alcoa Premiere	
TUESDAY	C	News	Marshal Dillon	Dick Van Dyke Show	Many Loves of Dobie Gillis	Red Skelton Show	Ichabod & Me	Garry Moore Show	
TUESDAY	N		Laramie		Alfred Hitchcock Presents	Dick Powell Show		Cain's Hundred	
WEDNESDAY	A		Steve Allen Show		Top Cat	Hawaiian Eye		Naked City	
WEDNESDAY	C	News	Alvin Show	Father Knows Best	Checkmate		Mrs. G. Goes to College	U.S. Steel Hour/Armstrong Circle Theatre	
WEDNESDAY	N		Wagon Train		Joey Bishop Show	Perry Como's Kraft Music Hall		Bob Newhart Show	David Brinkley's Journal
THURSDAY	A		Adventures of Ozzie & Harriet	Donna Reed Show	Real McCoys	My Three Sons	Margie	The Untouchables	
THURSDAY	C	News	Frontier Circus		Bob Cummings Show	The Investigators		CBS Reports	
THURSDAY	N		The Outlaws		Dr. Kildare		Hazel	Sing Along with Mitch	
FRIDAY	A		Straightaway	The Hathaways	The Flintstones	77 Sunset Strip		Target: The Corruptors	
FRIDAY	C	News	Rawhide		Route 66		Father of the Bride	Twilight Zone	Eyewitness
FRIDAY	N		International Showtime		Robert Taylor's Detectives		Bell Telephone Hour / Dinah Shore Show		Here & Now
SATURDAY	A	Matty's Funday Funnies	Roaring Twenties		Leave It to Beaver	Lawrence Welk Show		Fight of the Week	Make That Spare
SATURDAY	C		Perry Mason		The Defenders		Have Gun, Will Travel	Gunsmoke	
SATURDAY	N		Tales of Wells Fargo		Tall Man	NBC Saturday Night Movie			

PRIME TIME SCHEDULE: 1962

		7:00 PM	7:30	8:00	8:30	9:00	9:30	10:00	10:30	11:00
SUNDAY	A	Father Knows Best	Jetsons	ABC Sunday Night Movie				Voice of Firestone	Howard K. Smith	
	C	Lassie	Dennis the Menace	Ed Sullivan		Real McCoys	G.E. True Theater	Candid Camera	What's My Line	
	N	Ensign O'Toole	Walt Disney's Wonderful World of Color		Car 54 Where Are You?	Bonanza		DuPont Show of the Week		
MONDAY	A			Cheyenne		Rifleman	Stoney Burke		Ben Casey	
	C		News	To Tell the Truth	I've Got a Secret	Lucy Show	Danny Thomas Show	Andy Griffith Show	New Loretta Young Show	Stump the Stars
	N			It's a Man's World		Saints & Sinners		Price Is Right	David Brinkley's Journal	
TUESDAY	A			Combat		Hawaiian Eye		The Untouchables		Bell & Howell Closeup
	C		News	Marshal Dillon	Lloyd Bridges Show	Red Skelton Hour		Jack Benny Show	Garry Moore Show	
	N			Laramie		Empire		Dick Powell Show		Chet Huntley Reporting
WEDNESDAY	A			Wagon Train		Going My Way		Our Man Higgins	Naked City	
	C		News	CBS Reports		Many Loves of Dobie Gillis	Beverly Hillbillies	Dick Van Dyke Show	Armstrong Circle Theatre/ U.S. Steel Hour	
	N			The Virginian		Perry Como's Kraft Music Hall		Eleventh Hour		
THURSDAY	A			Adventures of Ozzie & Harriet	Donna Reed Show	Leave It to Beaver	My Three Sons	McHale's Navy	Alcoa Premiere	
	C		News	Mr. Ed	Perry Mason		The Nurses		Alfred Hitchcock Hour	
	N			Wide Country		Dr. Kildare		Hazel	Andy Williams Show	
FRIDAY	A			Gallant Men		The Flintstones	I'm Dickens— He's Fenster	77 Sunset Strip		
	C		News	Rawhide		Route 66		Fair Exchange		Eyewitness
	N			International Showtime		Sing Along with Mitch		Don't Call Me Charlie	Jack Paar Show	
SATURDAY	A	Beany & Cecil	Roy Rogers & Dale Evans Show		Mr. Smith Goes to Washington	Lawrence Welk Show		Fight of the Week		Make That Spare
	C		Jackie Gleason Show		Defenders		Have Gun, Will Travel	Gunsmoke		
	N		Sam Benedict		Joey Bishop Show	NBC Saturday Night Movie				

904

PRIME TIME SCHEDULE: 1963

		7:00 PM	7:30	8:00	8:30	9:00	9:30	10:00	10:30	11:00
SUNDAY	A		Travels of Jaimie McPheeters			Arrest and Trial			100 Grand	ABC News Reports
	C	Lassie	My Favorite Martian	Ed Sullivan Show		Judy Garland Show			Candid Camera	What's My Line
	N	Bill Dana Show	Walt Disney's Wonderful World of Color		Grindl	Bonanza		DuPont Show of the Week		
MONDAY	A		Outer Limits			Wagon Train		Breaking Point		
	C		To Tell the Truth	I've Got a Secret	Lucy Show	Danny Thomas Show	Andy Griffith Show	East Side / West Side		
	N		NBC Monday Night Movie				Hollywood & the Stars	Sing Along with Mitch		
TUESDAY	A		Combat		McHale's Navy	Greatest Show on Earth		The Fugitive		
	C		Marshal Dillon	Red Skelton Hour		Petticoat Junction	Jack Benny Show	Garry Moore Show		
	N		Mr. Novak		Redigo	Richard Boone Show		Bell Telephone Hour		
WEDNESDAY	A		Adventures of Ozzie & Harriet	Patty Duke Show	Price Is Right	Ben Casey		Channing		
	C		Chronicle / CBS Reports		Glynis	Beverly Hillbillies	Dick Van Dyke Show	Danny Kaye Show		
	N		The Virginian			Espionage		Eleventh Hour		
THURSDAY	A		The Flintstones	Donna Reed Show	My Three Sons	Jimmy Dean Show		Edie Adams Show / Sid Caesar Show		
	C		Password		Rawhide		Perry Mason		The Nurses	
	N		Temple Houston		Dr. Kildare		Hazel	Kraft Suspense Theater		
FRIDAY	A		77 Sunset Strip		Burke's Law		Farmer's Daughter	Fight of the Week		Make That Spare
	C		Great Adventure		Route 66		Twilight Zone	Alfred Hitchcock Hour		
	N		International Showtime		Bob Hope Presents the Chrysler Theatre		Harry's Girls	Jack Paar Show		
SATURDAY	A		Hootenanny		Lawrence Welk Show		Jerry Lewis Show			
	C		Jackie Gleason Show		Phil Silvers Show	The Defenders		Gunsmoke		
	N		The Lieutenant		Joey Bishop Show	NBC Saturday Night Movie				

905

PRIME TIME SCHEDULE: 1964

Day	Net	7:00 PM	7:30	8:00	8:30	9:00	9:30	10:00	10:30	11:00
SUNDAY	A		Wagon Train		Broadside	ABC Sunday Night Movie				
SUNDAY	C	Lassie	My Favorite Martian	Ed Sullivan Show		My Living Doll	Joey Bishop Show	Candid Camera	What's My Life	
SUNDAY	N	Profiles in Courage	Walt Disney's Wonderful World of Color		Bill Dana Show	Bonanza		The Rogues		
MONDAY	A		Voyage to the Bottom of the Sea		No Time for Sergeants	Wendy and Me	Bing Crosby Show	Ben Casey		
MONDAY	C		To Tell the Truth	I've Got a Secret	Andy Griffith Show	Lucy Show	Many Happy Returns	Slattery's People		
MONDAY	N		90 Bristol Court: Karen/Harris Against the World/ Tom, Dick, and Mary			Andy Williams Show		Alfred Hitchcock Hour		
TUESDAY	A		Combat		McHale's Navy	The Tycoon	Peyton Place	The Fugitive		
TUESDAY	C		Marshal Dillon	World War I	Red Skelton Hour		Petticoat Junction	Doctors and the Nurses		
TUESDAY	N		Mr. Novak		Man from U.N.C.L.E.		That Was the Week That Was	Bell Telephone Hour		
WEDNESDAY	A		Adventures of Ozzie & Harriet	Patty Duke Show	Shindig	Mickey	Burke's Law		ABC Scope	
WEDNESDAY	C		CBS Reports		Beverly Hillbillies	Dick Van Dyke Show	Cara Williams Show	Danny Kaye Show		
WEDNESDAY	N		The Virginian			NBC Wednesday Night Movie				
THURSDAY	A		The Flintstones	Donna Reed Show	My Three Sons	Bewitched	Peyton Place	Jimmy Dean Show		
THURSDAY	C		The Munsters	Perry Mason		Password	Baileys of Balboa	The Defenders		
THURSDAY	N		Daniel Boone		Dr. Kildare		Hazel	Kraft Suspense Theater		
FRIDAY	A		Jonny Quest	Farmer's Daughter	Addams Family	Valentine's Day	Twelve O'Clock High			
FRIDAY	C		Rawhide		The Entertainers		Gomer Pyle, U.S.M.C.	The Reporter		
FRIDAY	N		International Showtime		Bob Hope Presents the Chrysler Theatre		Jack Benny Program	Jack Paar Show		
SATURDAY	A		Outer Limits		Lawrence Welk Show		Hollywood Palace			
SATURDAY	C		Jackie Gleason Show		Gilligan's Island	Mr. Broadway		Gunsmoke		
SATURDAY	N		Flipper	Famous Adventures of Mr. Magoo	Kentucky Jones	NBC Saturday Night Movie				

Day	Net	7:00 PM	7:30	8:00	8:30	9:00	9:30	10:00	10:30	11:00
SUNDAY	A	Voyage to the Bottom of the Sea		The F.B.I.		ABC Sunday Night Movie				
SUNDAY	C	Lassie	My Favorite Martian	Ed Sullivan Show		Perry Mason		Candid Camera	What's My Line	
SUNDAY	N	Bell Telephone Hour/Actuality Specials	Walt Disney's Wonderful World of Color		Branded	Bonanza		Wackiest Ship in the Army		
MONDAY	A		Twelve O'Clock High		Legend of Jesse James	Man Called Shenandoah	Farmer's Daughter	Ben Casey		
MONDAY	C		To Tell the Truth	I've Got a Secret	Lucy Show	Andy Griffith Show	Hazel	Steve Lawrence Show		
MONDAY	N		Hullabaloo	John Forsythe Show	Dr. Kildare	Andy Williams Show		Run for Your Life		
TUESDAY	A		Combat		McHale's Navy	F Troop	Peyton Place	The Fugitive		
TUESDAY	C		Rawhide		Red Skelton Hour		Petticoat Junction	CBS Reports/News Hour		
TUESDAY	N		My Mother the Car	Please Don't Eat the Daisies	Dr. Kildare	NBC Tuesday Night Movie				
WEDNESDAY	A		Adventures of Ozzie & Harriet	Patty Duke Show	Gidget	Big Valley		Amos Burke—Secret Agent		
WEDNESDAY	C		Lost in Space		Beverly Hillbillies	Green Acres	Dick Van Dyke Show	Danny Kaye Show		
WEDNESDAY	N		The Virginian			Bob Hope Presents the Chrysler Theatre		I Spy		
THURSDAY	A		Shindig	Donna Reed Show	O.K. Crackerby	Bewitched	Peyton Place	Long, Hot Summer		
THURSDAY	C		The Munsters	Gilligan's Island	My Three Sons	CBS Thursday Night Movie				
THURSDAY	N		Daniel Boone		Laredo		Mona McCluskey	Dean Martin Show		
FRIDAY	A		The Flintstones	Tammy	Addams Family	Honey West	Peyton Place	Jimmy Dean Show		
FRIDAY	C		Wild Wild West		Hogan's Heroes	Gomer Pyle U.S.M.C.	Smothers Brothers Show	Slattery's People		
FRIDAY	N		Camp Runamuck	Hank	Convoy		Mr. Roberts	Man from U.N.C.L.E.		
SATURDAY	A		Shindig	King Family Show	Lawrence Welk Show		Hollywood Palace		ABC Scope	
SATURDAY	C		Jackie Gleason Show		Trials of O'Brien		The Loner	Gunsmoke		
SATURDAY	N		Flipper	I Dream of Jeannie	Get Smart	NBC Saturday Night Movie				

PRIME TIME SCHEDULE: 1966

Day	Net	7:00 PM	7:30	8:00	8:30	9:00	9:30	10:00	10:30	11:00
SUNDAY	A	Voyage to the Bottom of the Sea		The F.B.I.		ABC Sunday Night Movie				
SUNDAY	C	Lassie	It's About Time	Ed Sullivan Show		Garry Moore Show		Candid Camera	What's My Line	
SUNDAY	N	Actuality Specials/Bell Telephone Hour	Walt Disney's Wonderful World of Color		Hey Landlord	Bonanza		Andy Williams Show		
MONDAY	A		Iron Horse		Rat Patrol	Felony Squad	Peyton Place	Big Valley		
MONDAY	C		Gilligan's Island	Run Buddy Run	Lucy Show	Andy Griffith Show	Family Affair	Jean Arthur Show	I've Got a Secret	
MONDAY	N		The Monkees	I Dream of Jeannie	Roger Miller Show	Road West		Run for Your Life		
TUESDAY	A		Combat		The Rounders	Pruits of Southampton	Love on a Rooftop	The Fugitive		
TUESDAY	C		Daktari		Red Skelton Hour		Petticoat Junction	CBS News Hour		
TUESDAY	N		Girl from U.N.C.L.E.		Occasional Wife	NBC Tuesday Night Movie				
WEDNESDAY	A		Batman	The Monroes		Man Who Never Was	Peyton Place	ABC Stage '67		
WEDNESDAY	C		Lost in Space		Beverly Hillbillies	Green Acres	Gomer Pyle, U.S.M.C.	Danny Kaye Show		
WEDNESDAY	N		The Virginian			Bob Hope Presents the Chrysler Theatre		I Spy		
THURSDAY	A		Batman	F Troop	Tammy Grimes Show	Bewitched	That Girl	Hawk		
THURSDAY	C		Jericho		My Three Sons	CBS Thursday Night Movie				
THURSDAY	N		Daniel Boone		Star Trek		The Hero	Dean Martin Show		
FRIDAY	A		Green Hornet	Time Tunnel		Milton Berle Show		Twelve O'Clock High		
FRIDAY	C		Wild Wild West		Hogan's Heroes	CBS Friday Night Movie				
FRIDAY	N		Tarzan		Man from U.N.C.L.E.		T.H.E. Cat	Laredo		
SATURDAY	A		Shane		Lawrence Welk Show		Hollywood Palace		ABC Scope	
SATURDAY	C		Jackie Gleason Show		Pistols 'n' Petticoats	Mission: Impossible		Gunsmoke		
SATURDAY	N		Flipper	Please Don't Eat the Daisies	Get Smart	NBC Saturday Night Movie				

908

PRIME TIME SCHEDULE: 1967

		7:00 PM	7:30	8:00	8:30	9:00	9:30	10:00	10:30	11:00
SUNDAY	A	Voyage to the Bottom of the Sea		The F.B.I.		ABC Sunday Night Movie				
	C	Lassie	Gentle Ben	Ed Sullivan Show		Smothers Brothers Comedy Hour		Mission: Impossible		
	N	Walt Disney's Wonderful World of Color		Mothers-in-Law		Bonanza		High Chaparral		
MONDAY	A		Cowboy in Africa		Rat Patrol	Felony Squad	Peyton Place	Big Valley		
	C		Gunsmoke		Lucy Show	Andy Griffith Show	Family Affair	Carol Burnett Show		
	N	The Monkees		Man from U.N.C.L.E.		Danny Thomas Hour		I Spy		
TUESDAY	A		Garrison's Gorillas		The Invaders		N.Y.P.D.	Hollywood Palace		
	C		Daktari		Red Skelton Hour		Good Morning, World	CBS News Hour		
	N	I Dream of Jeannie	Jerry Lewis Show		NBC Tuesday Night Movie					
WEDNESDAY	A		Legend of Custer		Second 100 Years	ABC Wednesday Night Movie				
	C		Lost in Space		Beverly Hillbillies	Green Acres	He & She	Dundee and the Culhane		
	N		The Virginian			Kraft Music Hall		Run for Your Life		
THURSDAY	A		Batman	Flying Nun	Bewitched	That Girl	Peyton Place	Good Company		
	C		Cimarron Strip			CBS Thursday Night Movie				
	N		Daniel Boone		Ironside		Dragnet	Dean Martin Show		
FRIDAY	A		Off To See the Wizard		Hondo		Guns of Will Sonnett	Judd, for the Defense		
	C		Wild Wild West		Gomer Pyle, U.S.M.C.	CBS Friday Night Movie				
	N		Tarzan		Star Trek		Accidental Family	Actuality Specials/ Bell Telephone Hour		
SATURDAY	A		Dating Game	Newlywed Game	Lawrence Welk Show		Iron Horse		ABC Scope	
	C		Jackie Gleason Show		My Three Sons	Hogan's Heroes	Petticoat Junction	Mannix		
	N		Maya		Get Smart		NBC Saturday Night Movie			

PRIME TIME SCHEDULE: 1968

		7:00 PM	7:30	8:00	8:30	9:00	9:30	10:00	10:30	11:00
SUNDAY	A	Land of the Giants		The F.B.I.		ABC Sunday Night Movie				
	C	Lassie	Gentle Ben	Ed Sullivan Show		Smothers Brothers Comedy Hour		Mission: Impossible		
	N	New Adventures of Huck Finn	Walt Disney's Wonderful World of Color		Mothers-in-Law	Bonanza		Beautiful Phyllis Diller Show		
MONDAY	A		The Avengers		Peyton Place	The Outcasts		Big Valley		
	C		Gunsmoke		Here's Lucy	Mayberry R.F.D.	Family Affair	Carol Burnett Show		
	N		I Dream of Jeannie	Rowan & Martin's Laugh-In		NBC Monday Night Movie				
TUESDAY	A		Mod Squad		It Takes a Thief		N.Y.P.D.	That's Life		
	C		Lancer		Red Skelton Hour		Doris Day Show	CBS News Hour / 60 Minutes		
	N		Jerry Lewis Show		Julia	NBC Tuesday Night Movie				
WEDNESDAY	A		Here Comes the Brides		Peyton Place	ABC Wednesday Night Movie				
	C		Daktari		Good Guys	Beverly Hillbillies	Green Acres	Jonathan Winters Show		
	N		The Virginian			Kraft Music Hall		The Outsider		
THURSDAY	A		Ugliest Girl in Town	Flying Nun	Bewitched	That Girl	Journey to the Unknown			
	C		Blondie	Hawaii Five-O		CBS Thursday Night Movie				
	N		Daniel Boone		Ironside		Dragnet	Dean Martin Show		
FRIDAY	A		Operation: Entertainment		Felony Squad	Don Rickles Show	Guns of Will Sonnett	Judd, for the Defense		
	C		Wild Wild West		Gomer Pyle, U.S.M.C.	CBS Friday Night Movie				
	N		High Chaparral		Name of the Game			Star Trek		
SATURDAY	A		Dating Game	Newlywed Game	Lawrence Welk Show		Hollywood Palace			
	C		Jackie Gleason Show		My Three Sons	Hogan's Heroes	Petticoat Junction	Mannix		
	N		Adam 12	Get Smart	Ghost & Mrs. Muir	NBC Saturday Night Movie				

PRIME TIME SCHEDULE: 1969

		7:00 PM	7:30	8:00	8:30	9:00	9:30	10:00	10:30	11:00
SUNDAY	A	Land of the Giants		The F.B.I.		ABC Sunday Night Movie				
	C	Lassie	To Rome with Love	Ed Sullivan Show		Leslie Uggams Show		Mission: Impossible		
	N	Wild Kingdom	Walt Disney's Wonderful World of Color		Bill Cosby Show	Bonanza		Bold Ones: The New Doctors/The Lawyers/The Protectors		
MONDAY	A		Music Scene		New People	Harold Robbins' "The Survivors"		Love, American Style		
	C		Gunsmoke		Here's Lucy	Mayberry R.F.D.	Doris Day Show	Carol Burnett Show		
	N		My World and Welcome to It	Rowan & Martin's Laugh-In		NBC Monday Night Movie				
TUESDAY	A		Mod Squad		Movie of the Week			Marcus Welby, M.D.		
	C		Lancer		Red Skelton Hour		Governor & J.J.	CBS News Hour / 60 Minutes		
	N		I Dream of Jeannie	Debbie Reynolds Show	Julia	NBC Tuesday Night Movie				
WEDNESDAY	A		Flying Nun	Courtship of Eddie's Father	Room 222	ABC Wednesday Night Movie				
	C		Glen Campbell Goodtime Hour		Beverly Hillbillies	Medical Center		Hawaii Five-O		
	N		The Virginian			Kraft Music Hall		Then Came Bronson		
THURSDAY	A		Ghost & Mrs. Muir	That Girl	Bewitched	This Is Tom Jones		It Takes a Thief		
	C		Family Affair	Jim Nabors Hour		CBS Thursday Night Movie				
	N		Daniel Boone		Ironside		Dragnet	Dean Martin Show		
FRIDAY	A		Let's Make a Deal	Brady Bunch	Mr. Deeds Goes to Town	Here Comes the Brides		Jimmy Durante Presents Lennon Sisters		
	C		Get Smart	Good Guys	Hogan's Heroes	CBS Friday Night Movie				
	N		High Chaparral		Name of the Game			Bracken's World		
SATURDAY	A		Dating Game	Newlywed Game	Lawrence Welk Show		Hollywood Palace			
	C		Jackie Gleason Show		My Three Sons	Green Acres	Petticoat Junction	Mannix		
	N		Andy Williams Show		Adam 12	NBC Saturday Night Movie				

PRIME TIME SCHEDULE: 1970

		7:00 PM	7:30	8:00	8:30	9:00	9:30	10:00	10:30
SUNDAY	A	Young Rebels		The F.B.I.		ABC Sunday Night Movie			
SUNDAY	C	Lassie	Hogan's Heroes	Ed Sullivan Show		Glen Campbell Goodtime Hour		Tim Conway Comedy Hour	
SUNDAY	N	Wild Kingdom	Wonderful World of Disney		Bill Cosby Show	Bonanza		Bold Ones: The New Doctors/The Lawyers/The Senator	
MONDAY	A		Young Lawyers		Silent Force	ABC Monday Night Football			
MONDAY	C		Gunsmoke		Here's Lucy	Mayberry R.F.D.	Doris Day Show	Carol Burnett Show	
MONDAY	N		Red Skelton Show	Rowan & Martin's Laugh-In		NBC Monday Night Movie			
TUESDAY	A		Mod Squad		Movie of the Week			Marcus Welby, M.D.	
TUESDAY	C		Beverly Hillbillies	Green Acres	Hee Haw		To Rome with Love	CBS News Hour / 60 Minutes	
TUESDAY	N		Don Knotts Show		Julia	NBC Tuesday Night Movie			
WEDNESDAY	A		Courtship of Eddie's Father	Make Room for Granddaddy	Room 222	Johnny Cash Show		Dan August	
WEDNESDAY	C		Storefront Lawyers		Governor & J.J.	Medical Center		Hawaii Five-O	
WEDNESDAY	N		Men from Shiloh			Kraft Music Hall		Four in One: McCloud/San Francisco International Airport/Night Gallery/The Psychiatrist	
THURSDAY	A		Matt Lincoln		Bewitched	Barefoot in the Park	Odd Couple	The Immortal	
THURSDAY	C		Family Affair	Jim Nabors Hour		CBS Thursday Night Movie			
THURSDAY	N		Flip Wilson Show		Ironside		Nancy	Dean Martin Show	
FRIDAY	A		Brady Bunch	Nanny and the Professor	Partridge Family	That Girl	Love, American Style	This Is Tom Jones	
FRIDAY	C		The Interns		The Headmaster	CBS Friday Night Movie			
FRIDAY	N		High Chaparral		Name of the Game			Bracken's World	
SATURDAY	A		Let's Make a Deal	Newlywed Game	Lawrence Welk Show		Most Deadly Game		
SATURDAY	C		Mission: Impossible		My Three Sons	Arnie	Mary Tyler Moore Show	Mannix	
SATURDAY	N		Andy Williams Show		Adam 12	NBC Saturday Night Movie			

PRIME TIME SCHEDULE: 1971

Day	Net	7:00 PM	7:30	8:00	8:30	9:00	9:30	10:00	10:30 – 11:00
SUNDAY	A			The F.B.I.		ABC Sunday Night Movie			
	C		CBS Sunday Night Movie			Cade's County			
	N		Wonderful World of Disney		Jimmy Stewart Show	Bonanza		Bold Ones: The New Doctors/The Lawyers	
MONDAY	A			Nanny & Professor		ABC Monday Night Football			
	C		Gunsmoke			Here's Lucy	Doris Day Show	My Three Sons	Arnie
	N			Rowan & Martin's Laugh-In		NBC Monday Night Movie			
TUESDAY	A		Mod Squad		Movie of the Week			Marcus Welby, M.D.	
	C		Glen Campbell Goodtime Hour		Hawaii Five-O		Cannon		
	N		Ironside		Sarge		The Funny Side		
WEDNESDAY	A			Bewitched	Courtship of Eddie's Father	Smith Family	Shirley's World	Man and the City	
	C			Carol Burnett Show		Medical Center		Mannix	
	N			Adam 12	NBC Mystery Movie: Columbo/McCloud/McMillan and Wife			Night Gallery	
THURSDAY	A			Alias Smith & Jones		Longstreet		Owen Marshall	
	C			Bearcats		CBS Thursday Night Movie			
	N			Flip Wilson Show		Nichols		Dean Martin Show	
FRIDAY	A			Brady Bunch	Partridge Family	Room 222	Odd Couple	Love, American Style	
	C			Chicago Teddy Bears	O'Hara, U.S. Treasury		New CBS Friday Night Movie		
	N			The D.A.	NBC World Premiere Movie				
SATURDAY	A			Getting Together	ABC Movie of the Weekend			The Persuaders	
	C			All in the Family	Funny Face	New Dick Van Dyke Show	Mary Tyler Moore Show	Mission: Impossible	
	N			The Partners	The Good Life	NBC Saturday Night Movie			

PRIME TIME SCHEDULE: 1972

		7:00 PM	7:30	8:00	8:30	9:00	9:30	10:00	10:30	11:00
SUNDAY	A			The F.B.I.		ABC Sunday Night Movie				
	C		Anna and the King	M*A*S*H	Sandy Duncan Show	New Dick Van Dyke Show		Mannix		
	N		Wonderful World of Disney		NBC Sunday Mystery Movie Columbo/McCloud/McMillan and Wife/ Hec Ramsey			Night Gallery		
MONDAY	A			The Rookies		ABC Monday Night Football				
	C			Gunsmoke		Here's Lucy	Doris Day Show	New Bill Cosby Show		
	N			Rowan & Martin's Laugh-In		NBC Monday Night Movie				
TUESDAY	A			Temperatures Rising	Tuesday Movie of the Week			Marcus Welby, M.D.		
	C			Maude	Hawaii Five-O		New CBS Tuesday Night Movie			
	N			Bonanza		Bold Ones: The New Doctors		NBC Reports		
WEDNESDAY	A			Paul Lynde Show	Wednesday Movie of the Week			Julie Andrews Hour		
	C			Carol Burnett Show		Medical Center		Cannon		
	N			Adam 12	NBC Wednesday Mystery Movie: Madigan/Cool Million/Banacek			Search		
THURSDAY	A			Mod Squad		The Men: Assignment Vienna/ Delphi Bureau/Jigsaw		Owen Marshall		
	C			The Waltons		CBS Thursday Night Movie				
	N			Flip Wilson Show		Ironside		Dean Martin Show		
FRIDAY	A			Brady Bunch	Partridge Family	Room 222	Odd Couple	Love, American Style		
	C			Sonny & Cher Comedy Hour		CBS Friday Night Movie				
	N			Sanford & Son	Little People	Ghost Story		Banyon		
SATURDAY	A			Alias Smith & Jones		Streets of San Francisco		The Sixth Sense		
	C			All in the Family	Bridget Loves Bernie	Mary Tyler Moore Show	Bob Newhart Show	Mission: Impossible		
	N			Emergency		NBC Saturday Night Movie				

PRIME TIME SCHEDULE: 1973

		7:00 PM	7:30	8:00	8:30	9:00	9:30	10:00	10:30	11:00
SUNDAY	A			The F.B.I.		ABC Sunday Night Movie				
	C			New Adv. of Perry Mason		Mannix		Barnaby Jones		
	N			Wonderful World of Disney		NBC Sunday Mystery Movie: Columbo/McCloud/McMillan and Wife/Hec Ramsey				
MONDAY	A				The Rookies		ABC Monday Night Football			
	C				Gunsmoke	Here's Lucy	New Dick Van Dyke Show	Medical Center		
	N				Lotsa Luck	Diana	NBC Monday Night Movie			
TUESDAY	A			Temperatures Rising		Tuesday Movie of the Week		Marcus Welby, M.D.		
	C			Maude		Hawaii Five-O		Tuesday Night CBS Movie: Hawkins/Shaft/The New CBS Tuesday Night Movie		
	N			Chase		The Magician		Police Story		
WEDNESDAY	A			Bob & Carol & Ted & Alice		Wednesday Movie of the Week		Owen Marshall		
	C			Sonny & Cher Comedy Hour		Cannon		Kojak		
	N			Adam 12		NBC Wednesday Mystery Movie: Madigan/Tenafly/Faraday & Company/The Snoop Sisters		Love Story		
THURSDAY	A			Toma		Kung Fu		Streets of San Francisco		
	C			The Waltons		CBS Thursday Night Movie				
	N			Flip Wilson Show		Ironside		NBC Follies		
FRIDAY	A			Brady Bunch	Odd Couple	Room 222	Adam's Rib	Love, American Style		
	C			Calucci's Dept.	Roll Out	CBS Friday Night Movie				
	N			Sanford & Son	The Girl with Something Extra	Needles & Pins	Brian Keith Show	Dean Martin Show		
SATURDAY	A			Partridge Family		ABC Suspense Movie		Griff		
	C			All in the Family	M*A*S*H	Mary Tyler Moore Show	Bob Newhart Show	Carol Burnett Show		
	N			Emergency		NBC Saturday Night Movie				

915

PRIME TIME SCHEDULE: 1974

		7:00 PM	7:30	8:00	8:30	9:00	9:30	10:00	10:30	11:00
SUNDAY	A			Sonny Comedy Revue		ABC Sunday Night Movie				
	C		Apple's Way		Kojak		Mannix			
	N		Wonderful World of Disney		NBC Sunday Mystery Movie: Columbo/McCloud/McMillian and Wife/Amy Prentiss					
MONDAY	A			Rookies		ABC Monday Night Football				
	C			Gunsmoke		Maude	Rhoda	Medical Center		
	N			Born Free		NBC Monday Night Movie				
TUESDAY	A			Happy Days	Tuesday Movie of the Week			Marcus Welby, M.D.		
	C			Good Times	M*A*S*H	Hawaii Five-O		Barnaby Jones		
	N			Adam 12	NBC World Premiere Movie			Police Story		
WEDNESDAY	A			That's My Mama	Wednesday Movie of the Week			Get Christie Love		
	C			Sons & Daughters		Cannon		Manhunter		
	N			Little House on the Prairie		Lucas Tanner		Petrocelli		
THURSDAY	A			Odd Couple	Paper Moon	Streets of San Francisco		Harry-O		
	C			The Waltons		CBS Thursday Night Movie				
	N			Sierra		Ironside		Movin' On		
FRIDAY	A			Kodiak	Six Million Dollar Man		Texas Wheelers	Kolchak: The Night Stalker		
	C			Planet of the Apes		CBS Friday Night Movie				
	N			Sanford & Son	Chico and the Man	Rockford Files		Police Woman		
SATURDAY	A			The New Land		Kung Fu		Nakia		
	C			All in the Family	Paul Sand in Friends and Lovers	Mary Tyler Moore Show	Bob Newhart Show	Carol Burnett Show		
	N			Emergency		NBC Saturday Night Movie				

916

PRIME TIME SCHEDULE: 1975

		7:00 PM	7:30	8:00	8:30	9:00	9:30	10:00	10:30	11:00
SUNDAY	A	Swiss Family Robinson		Six Million Dollar Man		ABC Sunday Night Movie				
	C	Three for the Road		Cher		Kojak		Bronk		
	N	Wonderful World of Disney		Family Holvak		NBC Sunday Mystery Movie: Columbo/McCloud/McMillan and Wife/McCoy				
MONDAY	A			Barbary Coast		ABC Monday Night Football				
	C			Rhoda	Phyllis	All in the Family	Maude	Medical Center		
	N			Invisible Man		NBC Monday Night Movie				
TUESDAY	A			Happy Days	Welcome Back, Kotter	The Rookies		Marcus Welby, M.D.		
	C			Good Times	Joe and Sons	Switch		Beacon Hill		
	N			Movin' On		Police Story		Joe Forrester		
WEDNESDAY	A			When Things Were Rotten	That's My Mama	Baretta		Starsky & Hutch		
	C			Tony Orlando & Dawn		Cannon		Kate McShane		
	N			Little House on the Prairie		Doctors' Hospital		Petrocelli		
THURSDAY	A			Barney Miller	On the Rocks	Streets of San Francisco		Harry-O		
	C			The Waltons		CBS Thursday Night Movie				
	N			The Montefuscos	Fay	Ellery Queen		Medical Story		
FRIDAY	A			Mobile One		ABC Friday Night Movie				
	C			Big Eddie	M*A*S*H	Hawaii Five-O		Barnaby Jones		
	N			Sanford & Son	Chico and the Man	Rockford Files		Police Woman		
SATURDAY	A			Saturday Night Live with Howard Cosell		S.W.A.T.		Matt Helm		
	C			The Jeffersons	Doc	Mary Tyler Moore Show	Bob Newhart Show	Carol Burnett Show		
	N			Emergency		NBC Saturday Night Movie				

PRIME TIME SCHEDULE: 1976

		7:00 PM	7:30	8:00	8:30	9:00	9:30	10:00	10:30	11:00
SUNDAY	A	Cos		Six Million Dollar Man		ABC Sunday Night Movie				
	C	60 Minutes		Sonny & Cher Show		Kojak		Delvecchio		
	N	Wonderful World of Disney		NBC Sunday Mystery Movie: Columbo/McCloud/McMillan/Quincy, M.E.				Big Event		
MONDAY	A			Captain and Tennille		ABC Monday Night Football				
	C			Rhoda	Phyllis	Maude	All's Fair	Executive Suite		
	N			Little House on the Prairie		NBC Monday Night Movie				
TUESDAY	A			Happy Days	Laverne & Shirley	Rich Man, Poor Man—Book II		Family		
	C			Tony Orlando & Dawn Rainbow Hour		M*A*S*H	One Day at a Time	Switch		
	N			Baa Baa Black Sheep		Police Woman		Police Story		
WEDNESDAY	A			Bionic Woman		Baretta		Charlie's Angels		
	C			Good Times	Ball Four	All in the Family	Alice	Blue Knight		
	N			The Practice		NBC Movie of the Week		The Quest		
THURSDAY	A			Welcome Back, Kotter	Barney Miller	Tony Randall Show	Nancy Walker Show	Streets of San Francisco		
	C			The Waltons		Hawaii Five-O		Barnaby Jones		
	N			Gemini Man		NBC's Best Sellers		Van Dyke & Company		
FRIDAY	A			Donny & Marie		ABC Friday Night Movie				
	C		Campaign '76	Spencer's Pilots		CBS Friday Night Movie				
	N			Sanford & Son	Chico and the Man	Rockford Files		Serpico		
SATURDAY	A			Holmes & Yo-Yo	Mr. T and Tina	Starsky & Hutch		Most Wanted		
	C			The Jeffersons	Doc	Mary Tyler Moore Show	Bob Newhart Show	Carol Burnett Show		
	N			Emergency		NBC Saturday Night Movie				

PRIME TIME SCHEDULE: 1977

		7:00 PM	7:30	8:00	8:30	9:00	9:30	10:00	10:30	11:00
SUNDAY	A	Hardy Boys Mysteries/ Nancy Drew Mysteries		Six Million Dollar Man		ABC Sunday Movie				
	C	60 Minutes		Rhoda	On Our Own	All in the Family	Alice		Kojak	
	N	Wonderful World of Disney				Big Event				
MONDAY	A			San Pedro Beach Bums		Monday Night Football				
	C			Young Dan'l Boone		Betty White Show	Maude		Rafferty	
	N			Little House on the Prairie		NBC Monday Movie				
TUESDAY	A			Happy Days	Laverne & Shirley	Three's Company	Soap		Family	
	C			The Fitzpatricks		M*A*S*H	One Day at a Time		Lou Grant	
	N			Richard Pryor Show		Mulligan's Stew			Police Woman	
WEDNESDAY	A			Eight is Enough		Charlie's Angels			Baretta	
	C			Good Times	Busting Loose	CBS Wednesday Movie				
	N			Life and Times of Grizzly Adams		Oregon Trail			Big Hawaii	
THURSDAY	A			Welcome Back, Kotter	What's Happening	Barney Miller	Carter Country		Redd Foxx Show	
	C			The Waltons		Hawaii Five-O			Barnaby Jones	
	N			CHiPS		Man from Atlantis			Rosetti and Ryan	
FRIDAY	A			Donny and Marie		ABC Friday Movie				
	C			New Adventures of Wonder Woman		Logan's Run			Switch	
	N			Sanford Arms	Chico and the Man	Rockford Files			Quincy, M.E.	
SATURDAY	A			Fish	Operation Petticoat	Starsky and Hutch			Love Boat	
	C			Bob Newhart Show	We've Got Each Other	The Jeffersons	Tony Randall Show		Carol Burnett Show	
	N			Bionic Woman		NBC Saturday Movie				

PRIME TIME SCHEDULE: 1978

		7:00 PM	7:30	8:00	8:30	9:00	9:30	10:00	10:30	11:00
SUNDAY	A	Hardy Boys Mysteries		Battlestar Galactica		ABC Sunday Movie				
	C	60 Minutes		Mary		All in the Family	Alice	Kaz		
	N	Wonderful World of Disney		Big Event				Lifeline		
MONDAY	A			Welcome Back, Kotter	Operation Petticoat	Monday Night Football				
	C			WKRP in Cincinnati	People	M*A*S*H	One Day at a Time	Lou Grant		
	N			Little House on the Prairie		NBC Monday Movie				
TUESDAY	A			Happy Days	Laverne & Shirley	Three's Company	Taxi	Starsky and Hutch		
	C			Paper Chase		CBS Tuesday Movie				
	N			Grandpa Goes to Washington		Big Event				
WEDNESDAY	A			Eight is Enough		Charlie's Angels		Vega$		
	C			The Jeffersons	In the Beginning	CBS Wednesday Movie				
	N			Dick Clark's Live Wednesday		NBC Wednesday Movie				
THURSDAY	A			Mork & Mindy	What's Happening	Barney Miller	Soap	Family		
	C			The Waltons		Hawaii Five-O		Barnaby Jones		
	N			Project U.F.O.		Quincy, M.E.		W.E.B.		
FRIDAY	A			Donny and Marie		ABC Friday Movie				
	C			New Adventures of Wonder Woman		Incredible Hulk		Flying High		
	N			Waverly Wonders	Who's Watching the Kids	Rockford Files		Eddie Capra Mysteries		
SATURDAY	A			Carter Country	Apple Pie	Love Boat		Fantasy Island		
	C			Rhoda	Good Times	American Girls		Dallas		
	N			CHiPS		Specials		Sword of Justice		

PRIME TIME SCHEDULE: 1979

		7:00 PM	7:30	8:00	8:30	9:00	9:30	10:00	10:30	11:00
SUNDAY	A	Out of the Blue	A New Kind of Family	Mork & Mindy	The Associates	ABC Sunday Movie				
	C	60 Minutes		Archie Bunker's Place	One Day at a Time	Alice	The Jeffersons	Trapper John, M.D.		
	N	Disney's Wonderful World		The Big Event				Prime Time Sunday		
MONDAY	A			240-Robert		Monday Night Football				
	C			White Shadow		M*A*S*H	WKRP in Cincinnati	Lou Grant		
	N			Little House on the Prairie		NBC Monday Movie				
TUESDAY	A			Happy Days	Angie	Three's Company	Taxi	Lazarus Syndrome		
	C			California Fever		CBS Tuesday Movie				
	N			Misadventures of Sheriff Lobo		NBC Tuesday Movie				
WEDNESDAY	A			Eight is Enough		Charlie's Angels		Vega$		
	C			Last Resort	Struck By Lightning	CBS Wednesday Movie				
	N			Real People		Diff'rent Strokes	Hello Larry	Best of Saturday Night Live		
THURSDAY	A			Laverne & Shirley	Benson	Barney Miller	Soap	20/20		
	C			The Waltons		Hawaii Five-O		Barnaby Jones		
	N			Buck Rogers in the 25th Century		Quincy, M.E.		Kate Loves a Mystery		
FRIDAY	A			Fantasy Island		ABC Friday Movie				
	C			Incredible Hulk		Dukes of Hazzard		Dallas		
	N			Shirley		Rockford Files		Eischied		
SATURDAY	A			The Ropers	Detective School	Love Boat		Hart to Hart		
	C			Working Stiffs	Bad News Bears	Big Shamus, Little Shamus		Paris		
	N			CHiPS		B.J. and the Bear		A Man Called Sloane		

PRIME TIME SCHEDULE: 1980*

		7:00 PM	7:30	8:00	8:30	9:00	9:30	10:00	10:30	11:00
SUNDAY	A	Those Amazing Animals		Charlie's Angels		ABC Sunday Movie				
	C	60 Minutes		Archie Bunker's Place	One Day at a Time	Alice	The Jeffersons	Trapper John, M.D.		
	N	Disney's Wonderful World		CHiPS		The Big Event				
MONDAY	A			That's Incredible		Monday Night Football				
	C			Flo	Ladies' Man	M*A*S*H	House Calls	Lou Grant		
	N			Little House on the Prairie		NBC Monday Movie				
TUESDAY	A			Happy Days	Laverne & Shirley	Three's Company	Too Close For Comfort	Hart to Hart		
	C			White Shadow		CBS Tuesday Movie				
	N			Lobo		B.J. and the Bear		Steve Allen Comedy Hour		
WEDNESDAY	A			Eight is Enough		Taxi	Soap	Vega$		
	C			Enos		CBS Wednesday Movie				
	N			Real People		Diff'rent Strokes	Facts of Life	Quincy, M.E.		
THURSDAY	A			Mork & Mindy	Bosom Buddies	Barney Miller	It's a Living	20/20		
	C			The Waltons		Magnum, P.I.		Knots Landing		
	N			Games People Play		NBC Thursday Movie				
FRIDAY	A			Benson	I'm a Big Girl Now	ABC Friday Movie				
	C			Incredible Hulk		Dukes of Hazard		Dallas		
	N			Marie		Speak Up America		NBC Magazine with David Brinkley		
SATURDAY	A			Breaking Away		Love Boat		Fantasy Island		
	C			WKRP in Cincinnati	Tim Conway Show	Freebie and the Bean		Secrets of Midland Heights		
	N			Barbara Mandrell & the Mandrell Sisters		Walking Tall		Hill Street Blues		

922

*An actors' strike delayed the start of the 1980-1981 season for many programs. The shows indicated in this schedule represent the first series with new episodes to appear in each time period. Some of them premiered in September but others may not have started until January 1981.

PRIME TIME SCHEDULE: 1981*

		7:00 PM	7:30	8:00	8:30	9:00	9:30	10:00	10:30	11:00
SUNDAY	A	Code Red		Today's F.B.I.		ABC Sunday Movie				
	C	60 Minutes		Archie Bunker's Place	One Day at a Time	Alice	The Jeffersons	Trapper John, M.D.		
	N	Specials	Here's Boomer	CHiPS		NBC Sunday Movie				
MONDAY	A			That's Incredible		Monday Night Football				
	C			Pvt. Benjamin	Two of Us	M*A*S*H	House Calls	Lou Grant		
	N			Little House on the Prairie		NBC Monday Movie				
TUESDAY	A			Happy Days	Laverne & Shirley	Three's Company	Too Close for Comfort	Hart to Hart		
	C			Simon & Simon		CBS Tuesday Movie				
	N			Father Murphy		Bret Maverick		Flamingo Road		
WEDNESDAY	A			Greatest American Hero		Fall Guy		Dynasty		
	C			Mr. Merlin	WKRP in Cincinnati	Nurse		Shannon		
	N			Real People		Facts of Life	Love, Sidney	Quincy, M.E.		
THURSDAY	A			Mork & Mindy	Best of the West	Barney Miller	Taxi	20/20		
	C			Magnum, P.I.		Knots Landing		Jessica Novak		
	N			Harper Valley	Lewis & Clark	Diff'rent Strokes	Gimme A Break	Hill Street Blues		
FRIDAY	A			Benson	Bosom Buddies	Darkroom		Strike Force		
	C			Incredible Hulk		Dukes of Hazard		Dallas		
	N			NBC Magazine		McClain's Law		Specials		
SATURDAY	A			Maggie	Making a Living	Love Boat		Fantasy Island		
	C			Walt Disney		CBS Saturday Movie				
	N			Barbara Mandrell and The Mandrell Sisters		Nashville Palace		Fitz and Bones		

*A writers' strike delayed the start of the 1981-1982 season for many programs. The shows indicated in this schedule represent the first series with new episodes to appear in each time period. Some of them premiered in September but others may not have started until several months later.

PRIME TIME SCHEDULE: 1982

		7:00 PM	7:30	8:00	8:30	9:00	9:30	10:00	10:30	11:00
SUNDAY	A	Ripley's Believe It or Not		Matt Houston		ABC Sunday Movie				
	C	60 Minutes		Archie Bunker's Place	Gloria	The Jeffersons	One Day at a Time	Trapper John, M.D.		
	N	Voyagers		CHiPS		NBC Sunday Movie				
MONDAY	A			That's Incredible		Monday Night Football				
	C			Square Pegs	Pvt. Benjamin	M*A*S*H	Newhart	Cagney & Lacey		
	N			Little House: A New Beginning		NBC Monday Movie				
TUESDAY	A			Happy Days	Laverne & Shirley	Three's Company	9 to 5	Hart to Hart		
	C			Bring 'Em Back Alive		CBS Tuesday Movie				
	N			Father Murphy		Gavilan		St. Elsewhere		
WEDNESDAY	A			Tales of the Gold Monkey		Fall Guy		Dynasty		
	C			Seven Brides for Seven Brothers		Alice	Filthy Rich	Tucker's Witch		
	N			Real People		Facts of Life	Family Ties	Quincy, M.E.		
THURSDAY	A			Joanie Loves Chachi	Star of the Family	Too Close for Comfort	It Takes Two	20/20		
	C			Magnum, P.I.		Simon & Simon		Knots Landing		
	N			Fame		Cheers	Taxi	Hill Street Blues		
FRIDAY	A			Benson	New Odd Couple	Great American Hero		The Quest		
	C			Dukes of Hazard		Dallas		Falcon Crest		
	N			Powers of Matthew Star		Knight Rider		Remington Steele		
SATURDAY	A			T. J. Hooker		Love Boat		Fantasy Island		
	C			Walt Disney		CBS Saturday Movie				
	N			Diff'rent Strokes	Silver Spoons	Gimme a Break	Love, Sidney	Devlin Connection		

PRIME TIME SCHEDULE: 1983

		7:00 PM	7:30	8:00	8:30	9:00	9:30	10:00	10:30	11:00
SUNDAY	A	Ripley's Believe It or Not		Hardcastle & McCormick		ABC Sunday Movie				
	C	60 Minutes		Alice	One Day at a Time	The Jeffersons	Goodnight, Beantown	Trapper John, M.D.		
	N	First Camera		Knight Rider		NBC Sunday Movie				
MONDAY	A			That's Incredible		Monday Night Football				
	C			Scarecrow & Mrs. King		AfterMASH	Newhart	Emerald Point N.A.S.		
	N			Boone		NBC Monday Movie				
TUESDAY	A			Just Our Luck	Happy Days	Three's Company	Oh, Madeline	Hart to Hart		
	C			The Mississippi		CBS Tuesday Movie				
	N			The A-Team		Remington Steele		Bay City Blues		
WEDNESDAY	A			Fall Guy		Dynasty		Hotel		
	C			Whiz Kids		CBS Wednesday Movie				
	N			Real People		Facts of Life	Family Ties	St. Elsewhere		
THURSDAY	A			Trauma Center		9 to 5	It's Not Easy	20/20		
	C			Magnum, P.I.		Simon & Simon		Knots Landing		
	N			Gimme a Break	Mama's Family	We Got it Made	Cheers	Hill Street Blues		
FRIDAY	A			Benson	Webster	Lottery		Matt Houston		
	C			Dukes of Hazzard		Dallas		Falcon Crest		
	N			Mr. Smith	Jennifer Slept Here	Manimal		For Love and Honor		
SATURDAY	A			T.J. Hooker		Love Boat		Fantasy Island		
	C			Cutter to Houston		CBS Saturday Movie				
	N			Diff'rent Strokes	Silver Spoons	The Rousters		Yellow Rose		

925

PRIME TIME SCHEDULE: 1984

		7:00 PM	7:30	8:00	8:30	9:00	9:30	10:00	10:30	11:00
SUNDAY	A	Ripley's Believe It or Not		Hardcastle & McCormick		ABC Sunday Night Movie				
	C	60 Minutes		Murder, She Wrote		The Jeffersons	Alice	Trapper John, M.D.		
	N	Silver Spoons	Punky Brewster	Knight Rider		NBC Sunday Movie				
MONDAY	A			Call to Glory		Monday Night Football				
	C			Scarecrow & Mrs. King		Kate & Allie	Newhart	Cagney & Lacey		
	N			TV's Bloopers & Practical Jokes		NBC Monday Movie				
TUESDAY	A			Foul-Ups, Bleeps& Blunders	Three's a Crowd	Paper Dolls		Jessie		
	C			AfterMASH	E/R	CBS Tuesday Movie				
	N			The A-Team		Riptide		Remington Steele		
WEDNESDAY	A			Fall Guy		Dynasty		Hotel		
	C			Charles in Charge	Dreams	CBS Wednesday Movie				
	N			Highway to Heaven		Facts of Life	It's Your Move	St. Elsewhere		
THURSDAY	A			People Do the Craziest Things	Who's the Boss	Glitter		20/20		
	C			Magnum P.I.		Simon & Simon		Knots Landing		
	N			Cosby Show	Family Ties	Cheers	Night Court	Hill Street Blues		
FRIDAY	A			Benson	Webster	Hawaiian Heat		Matt Houston		
	C			Dukes of Hazzard		Dallas		Falcon Crest		
	N			V		Hunter		Miami Vice		
SATURDAY	A			T.J. Hooker		Love Boat		Finder of Lost Loves		
	C			Airwolf		Mickey Spillane's Mike Hammer		Cover Up		
	N			Diff'rent Strokes	Gimme a Break	Partners in Crime		Hot Pursuit		

PRIME TIME SCHEDULE: FALL 1985

		7:00 PM	7:30	8:00	8:30	9:00	9:30	10:00	10:30	11:00
SUNDAY	A	Ripley's Believe It or Not		MacGyver		ABC Sunday Movie				
	C	60 Minutes		Murder, She Wrote		Crazy Like a Fox		Trapper John, M.D.		
	N	Punky Brewster	Silver Spoons	Amazing Stories	Alfred Hitchcock Presents	NBC Sunday Movie				
MONDAY	A			Hardcastle & McCormick		Monday Night Football				
	C			Scarecrow & Mrs. King		Kate & Allie	Newhart	Cagney & Lacey		
	N			TV's Bloopers & Practical Jokes		NBC Monday Movie				
TUESDAY	A			Who's the Boss	Growing Pains	Moonlighting		Our Family Honor		
	C			Hometown		CBS Tuesday Movie				
	N			The A-Team		Riptide		Remington Steele		
WEDNESDAY	A			Insiders		Dynasty		Hotel		
	C			Stir Crazy		Charlie & Company	George Burns Comedy Week	The Equalizer		
	N			Highway to Heaven		Helltown		St. Elsewhere		
THURSDAY	A			Fall Guy		Lady Blue		20/20		
	C			Magnum, P.I.		Simon & Simon		Knots Landing		
	N			Cosby Show	Family Ties	Cheers	Night Court	Hill Street Blues		
FRIDAY	A			Webster	Mr. Belvedere	Diff'rent Strokes	Benson	Spenser: For Hire		
	C			Twilight Zone		Dallas		Falcon Crest		
	N			Knight Rider		Misfits of Science		Miami Vice		
SATURDAY	A			Hollywood Beat		Lime Street		Love Boat		
	C			Airwolf		CBS Saturday Movie				
	N			Gimme A Break	Facts of Life	Golden Girls	227	Hunter		

PRIME TIME SCHEDULE: 1986

		7:00 PM	7:30	8:00	8:30	9:00	9:30	10:00	10:30	11:00
SUNDAY	A	Disney Sunday Movie				ABC Sunday Movie				
	C	60 Minutes		Murder, She Wrote		CBS Sunday Movie				
	N	Our House		Easy Street	Valerie	NBC Sunday Movie				
MONDAY	A	MacGyver				Monday Night Football				
	C			Kate & Allie	My Sister Sam	Newhart	Designing Women	Cagney & Lacey		
	N			Alf	Amazing Stories	NBC Monday Movie				
TUESDAY	A			Who's the Boss	Growing Pains	Moonlighting		Jack and Mike		
	C			The Wizard		CBS Tuesday Movie				
	N			Matlock		Crime Story		1986		
WEDNESDAY	A			Perfect Strangers	Head of the Class	Dynasty		Hotel		
	C			Together We Stand	Better Days	Magnum, P.I.		The Equalizer		
	N			Highway to Heaven		Gimme a Break	You Again	St. Elsewhere		
THURSDAY	A			Our World		The Colbys		20/20		
	C			Simon & Simon		Knots Landing		Kay O'Brien		
	N			Cosby Show	Family Ties	Cheers	Night Court	Hill Street Blues		
FRIDAY	A			Webster	Mr. Belvedere	Sidekicks	Sledge Hammer	Starman		
	C			Scarecrow & Mrs. King		Dallas		Falcon Crest		
	N			The A-Team		Miami Vice		L. A. Law		
SATURDAY	A			Life with Lucy	Ellen Burstyn Show	Heart of the City		Spenser: For Hire		
	C			Downtown		New Mike Hammer		Twilight Zone		
	N			Facts of Life	227	Golden Girls	Amen	Hunter		

PRIME TIME SCHEDULE: FALL 1987

Day	Net	7:00 PM	7:30	8:00	8:30	9:00	9:30	10:00	10:30
SUNDAY	A	Disney Sunday Movie		Spenser: For Hire		Dolly		Buck James	
	C	60 Minutes		Murder, She Wrote		CBS Sunday Movie			
	F	21 Jump Street		Werewolf	Married With Children	Tracey Ullman	Duet		
	N	Our House		Family Ties	My Two Dads	NBC Sunday Movie			
MONDAY	A			MacGyver		Monday Night Football			
	C			Frank's Place	Kate & Allie	Newhart	Designing Women	Cagney & Lacey	
	N			Alf	Valerie's Family	NBC Monday Movie			
TUESDAY	A			Who's the Boss	Growing Pains	Moonlighting		Thirtysomething	
	C			Houston Knights		Jake and the Fatman		Law and Harry McGraw	
	N			Matlock		J. J. Starbuck		Crime Story	
WEDNESDAY	A			Perfect Strangers	Head of the Class	Hooperman	Slap Maxwell Story	Dynasty	
	C			Oldest Rookie		Magnum, P.I.		The Equalizer	
	N			Highway to Heaven		A Year in the Life		St. Elsewhere	
THURSDAY	A			Sledge Hammer	The Charmings	ABC Thursday Movie			
	C			Tour of Duty		Wiseguy		Knots Landing	
	N			Cosby Show	A Different World	Cheers	Night Court	L. A. Law	
FRIDAY	A			Full House	I Married Dora	Max Headroom		20/20	
	C			Beauty and the Beast		Dallas		Falcon Crest	
	N			Rags to Riches		Miami Vice		Private Eye	
SATURDAY	A			Once a Hero		Ohara		Hotel	
	C			My Sister Sam	Everything's Relative	Leg Work		West 57th	
	F			Mr. President	Women in Prison	New Adventures of Beans Baxter	Second Chance		
	N			Facts of Life	227	Golden Girls	Amen	Hunter	

EMMY AWARD WINNERS

The "Emmy" awards are given each year in recognition of excellence in television performance and production. The following are the principal awards presented over the years to nighttime network series and the people connected with them, including actors, writers, and directors. Also included, for the sake of completeness, are awards for nighttime "one-time-only" specials and Public Broadcasting Service programs, even though these are not otherwise within the scope of this book.

The National Academy of Television Arts and Sciences also presents many other "Emmy" awards not listed here, in such areas as local programming, daytime and sports programming, and in numerous technical areas such as film editing, sound mixing, and technical direction.

1948 (presented January 25, 1949)
BEST FILM MADE FOR TELEVISION: "The Necklace," *Your Show Time* (NBC)

1949 (presented January 27, 1950)
BEST LIVE SHOW: *The Ed Wynn Show* (CBS)
BEST KINESCOPE SHOW: *Texaco Star Theater* (NBC)
MOST OUTSTANDING LIVE PERSONALITY: Ed Wynn (CBS)
MOST OUTSTANDING KINESCOPE PERSONALITY: Milton Berle (NBC)
BEST FILM MADE FOR AND VIEWED ON TELEVISION: *The Life of Riley* (NBC)

1950 (presented January 23, 1951)
BEST ACTOR: Alan Young (CBS)
BEST ACTRESS: Gertrude Berg (CBS)
MOST OUTSTANDING PERSONALITY: Groucho Marx (NBC)
BEST VARIETY SHOW: *The Alan Young Show* (CBS)
BEST DRAMATIC SHOW: *Pulitzer Prize Playhouse* (ABC)
BEST GAME AND AUDIENCE PARTICIPATION SHOW: *Truth or Consequences* (CBS)

1951 (presented February 18, 1952)
BEST DRAMATIC SHOW: *Studio One* (CBS)
BEST COMEDY SHOW: *The Red Skelton Show* (CBS)
BEST VARIETY SHOW: *Your Show of Shows* (NBC)
BEST ACTOR: Sid Caesar (NBC)
BEST ACTRESS: Imogene Coca (NBC)
BEST COMEDIAN OR COMEDIENNE: Red Skelton (NBC)

1952 (presented February 5, 1953)
BEST DRAMATIC PROGRAM: *Robert Montgomery Presents* (NBC)
BEST VARIETY PROGRAM: *Your Show of Shows* (NBC)
BEST PUBLIC AFFAIRS PROGRAM: *See It Now* (CBS)
BEST MYSTERY, ACTION, OR ADVENTURE PROGRAM: *Dragnet* (NBC)
BEST SITUATION COMEDY: *I Love Lucy* (CBS)
BEST AUDIENCE PARTICIPATION, QUIZ, OR PANEL PROGRAM: *What's My Line* (CBS)
BEST ACTOR: Thomas Mitchell
BEST ACTRESS: Helen Hayes
BEST COMEDIAN: Jimmy Durante (NBC)
BEST COMEDIENNE: Lucille Ball (CBS)
MOST OUTSTANDING PERSONALITY: Bishop Fulton J. Sheen (DUM)

1953 (presented February 11, 1954)
BEST DRAMATIC PROGRAM: *The U.S. Steel Hour* (ABC)
BEST SITUATION COMEDY: *I Love Lucy* (CBS)
BEST VARIETY PROGRAM: *Omnibus* (CBS)
BEST PROGRAM OF NEWS OR SPORTS: *See It Now* (CBS)
BEST PUBLIC AFFAIRS PROGRAM: *Victory at Sea* (NBC)
BEST CHILDREN'S PROGRAM: *Kukla, Fran & Ollie* (NBC)
BEST NEW PROGRAMS: *Make Room for Daddy* (ABC) and *The U.S. Steel Hour* (ABC)
BEST MALE STAR OF REGULAR SERIES: Donald O'Connor, *Colgate Comedy Hour* (NBC)

BEST FEMALE STAR OF REGULAR SERIES: Eve Arden, *Our Miss Brooks* (CBS)
BEST SERIES SUPPORTING ACTOR: Art Carney, *The Jackie Gleason Show* (CBS)
BEST SERIES SUPPORTING ACTRESS: Vivian Vance, *I Love Lucy* (CBS)
BEST MYSTERY, ACTION, OR ADVENTURE PROGRAM: *Dragnet* (NBC)
BEST AUDIENCE PARTICIPATION, QUIZ, OR PANEL PROGRAM: *This Is Your Life* (NBC) and *What's My Line* (CBS)
MOST OUTSTANDING PERSONALITY: Edward R. Murrow (CBS)

1954 (presented March 7, 1955)
MOST OUTSTANDING NEW PERSONALITY: George Gobel (NBC)
BEST CULTURAL, RELIGIOUS, OR EDUCATIONAL PROGRAM: *Omnibus* (CBS)
BEST SPORTS PROGRAM: *The Gillette Cavalcade of Sports* (NBC)
BEST CHILDREN'S PROGRAM: *Lassie* (CBS)
BEST WESTERN OR ADVENTURE SERIES: *Stories of the Century* (syndicated)
BEST NEWS REPORTER OR COMMENTATOR: John Daly (ABC)
BEST AUDIENCE, GUEST PARTICIPATION, OR PANEL PROGRAM: *This Is Your Life* (NBC)
BEST ACTOR IN A SINGLE PERFORMANCE: Robert Cummings, "Twelve Angry Men," *Studio One* (CBS)
BEST ACTRESS IN A SINGLE PERFORMANCE: Judith Anderson, "Macbeth," *Hallmark Hall of Fame* (NBC)
BEST MALE SINGER: Perry Como (CBS)
BEST FEMALE SINGER: Dinah Shore (NBC)
BEST SUPPORTING ACTOR IN A REGULAR SERIES: Art Carney, *The Jackie Gleason Show* (CBS)
BEST SUPPORTING ACTRESS IN A REGULAR SERIES: Audrey Meadows, *The Jackie Gleason Show* (CBS)
BEST ACTOR STARRING IN A REGULAR SERIES: Danny Thomas, *Make Room for Daddy* (ABC)
BEST ACTRESS STARRING IN A REGULAR SERIES: Loretta Young, *The Loretta Young Show* (NBC)
BEST MYSTERY OR INTRIGUE SERIES: *Dragnet* (NBC)
BEST VARIETY SERIES INCLUDING MUSICAL VARIETIES: *Disneyland* (ABC)
BEST SITUATION COMEDY SERIES: *Make Room for Daddy* (ABC)
BEST DRAMATIC SERIES: *The U.S. Steel Hour* (ABC)
BEST INDIVIDUAL PROGRAM OF THE YEAR: "Operation Undersea," *Disneyland* (ABC)
BEST WRITTEN DRAMATIC MATERIAL: Reginald Rose, "Twelve Angry Men," *Studio One* (CBS)
BEST WRITTEN COMEDY MATERIAL: James Allardice, Jack Douglas, Hal Kanter, and Harry Winkler, *The George Gobel Show* (NBC)
BEST DIRECTION: Franklin Schaffner, "Twelve Angry Men," *Studio One* (CBS)

1955 (presented March 17, 1956)
BEST CHILDREN'S SERIES: *Lassie* (CBS)
BEST DOCUMENTARY PROGRAM (RELIGIOUS, INFORMATIONAL, EDUCATIONAL, OR INTERVIEW): *Omnibus* (CBS)
BEST AUDIENCE PARTICIPATION SERIES (QUIZ, PANEL, ETC.): *The $64,000 Question* (CBS)
BEST ACTION OR ADVENTURE SERIES: *Disneyland* (ABC)
BEST COMEDY SERIES: *The Phil Silvers Show* (CBS)
BEST VARIETY SERIES: *The Ed Sullivan Show* (CBS)
BEST MUSIC SERIES: *Your Hit Parade* (NBC)
BEST DRAMATIC SERIES: *Producers' Showcase* (NBC)
BEST SINGLE PROGRAM OF THE YEAR: "Peter Pan," *Producers' Showcase* (NBC)
BEST ACTOR (SINGLE PERFORMANCE): Lloyd Nolan, "The Caine Mutiny Court-Martial," *Ford Star Jubilee* (CBS)
BEST ACTRESS (SINGLE PERFORMANCE): Mary Martin, "Peter Pan," *Producers' Showcase* (NBC)
BEST ACTOR (CONTINUING PERFORMANCE): Phil Silvers, *The Phil Silvers Show* (CBS)
BEST ACTRESS (CONTINUING PERFORMANCE): Lucille Ball, *I Love Lucy* (CBS)
BEST ACTOR IN A SUPPORTING ROLE: Art Carney, *The Jackie Gleason Show* (CBS)
BEST ACTRESS IN A SUPPORTING ROLE: Nanette Fabray, *Caesar's Hour* (NBC)
BEST COMEDIAN: Phil Silvers (CBS)
BEST COMEDIENNE: Nanette Fabray (NBC)
BEST MALE SINGER: Perry Como (NBC)
BEST FEMALE SINGER: Dinah Shore (NBC)
BEST MC OR PROGRAM HOST (MALE OR FEMALE): Perry Como (NBC)
BEST NEWS COMMENTATOR OR REPORTER: Edward R. Murrow (CBS)
BEST ORIGINAL TELEPLAY WRITING: Rod Serling, "Patterns," *Kraft Television Theatre* (NBC)
BEST COMEDY WRITING: Nat Hiken, Barry Blitser, Arnold Auerbach, Harvey Orkin, Vincent Bogert, Arnold Rosen, Coleman Jacoby, Tony Webster, and Terry Ryan, *The Phil Silvers Show* (CBS)
BEST TELEVISION ADAPTATION: Paul Gregory and Franklin Schaffner, "The Caine Mutiny Court-Martial," *Ford Star Jubilee* (CBS)

BEST PRODUCER (LIVE SERIES): Fred Coe, *Producers' Showcase* (NBC)
BEST PRODUCER (FILM SERIES): Walt Disney, *Disneyland* (ABC)
BEST DIRECTOR (LIVE SERIES): Franklin Schaffner, "The Caine Mutiny Court-Martial," *Ford Star Jubilee* (CBS)
BEST DIRECTOR (FILM SERIES): Nat Hiken, *The Phil Silvers Show* (CBS)

1956 (presented March 16, 1957)

BEST SINGLE PROGRAM OF THE YEAR: "Requiem for a Heavyweight," *Playhouse 90* (CBS)
BEST NEW PROGRAM SERIES: *Playhouse 90* (CBS)
BEST SERIES (HALF HOUR OR LESS): *The Phil Silvers Show* (CBS)
BEST SERIES (ONE HOUR OR MORE): *Caesar's Hour* (NBC)
BEST PUBLIC SERVICE SERIES: *See It Now* (CBS)
BEST CONTINUING PERFORMANCE BY AN ACTOR IN A DRAMATIC SERIES: Robert Young, *Father Knows Best* (NBC)
BEST CONTINUING PERFORMANCE BY AN ACTRESS IN A DRAMATIC SERIES: Loretta Young, *The Loretta Young Show* (NBC)
BEST CONTINUING PERFORMANCE BY A COMEDIAN IN A SERIES: Sid Caesar, *Caesar's Hour* (NBC)
BEST CONTINUING PERFORMANCE BY A COMEDIENNE IN A SERIES: Nanette Fabray, *Caesar's Hour* (NBC)
BEST SINGLE PERFORMANCE BY AN ACTOR: Jack Palance, "Requiem for a Heavyweight," *Playhouse 90* (CBS)
BEST SINGLE PERFORMANCE BY AN ACTRESS: Claire Trevor, "Dodsworth," *Producers' Showcase* (NBC)
BEST SUPPORTING PERFORMANCE BY AN ACTOR: Carl Reiner, *Caesar's Hour* (NBC)
BEST SUPPORTING PERFORMANCE BY AN ACTRESS: Pat Carroll, *Caesar's Hour* (NBC)
BEST MALE PERSONALITY (CONTINUING PERFORMANCE): Perry Como (NBC)
BEST FEMALE PERSONALITY (CONTINUING PERFORMANCE): Dinah Shore (NBC)
BEST NEWS COMMENTATOR: Edward R. Murrow (CBS)
BEST TELEPLAY WRITING (HALF HOUR OR LESS): James P. Cavanagh, "Fog Closes In," *Alfred Hitchcock Presents* (CBS)
BEST TELEPLAY WRITING (ONE HOUR OR MORE): Rod Serling, "Requiem for a Heavyweight," *Playhouse 90* (CBS)
BEST COMEDY WRITING (VARIETY OR SITUATION COMEDY): Nat Hiken, Billy Friedberg, Tony Webster, Leonard Stern, Arnold Rosen, and Coleman Jacoby, *The Phil Silvers Show* (CBS)
BEST DIRECTION (HALF HOUR OR LESS): Sheldon Leonard, "Danny's Comeback," *The Danny Thomas Show* (ABC)
BEST DIRECTION (ONE HOUR OR MORE): Ralph Nelson, "Requiem for a Heavyweight," *Playhouse 90* (CBS)

1957 (presented April 15, 1958)

BEST SINGLE PROGRAM OF THE YEAR: "The Comedian," *Playhouse 90* (CBS)
BEST NEW PROGRAM SERIES OF THE YEAR: *The Seven Lively Arts* (CBS)
BEST DRAMATIC ANTHOLOGY SERIES: *Playhouse 90* (CBS)
BEST DRAMATIC SERIES WITH CONTINUING CHARACTERS: *Gunsmoke* (CBS)
BEST COMEDY SERIES: *The Phil Silvers Show* (CBS)
BEST MUSICAL, VARIETY, AUDIENCE PARTICIPATION, OR QUIZ SERIES: *The Dinah Shore Chevy Show* (NBC)
BEST PUBLIC SERVICE PROGRAM OR SERIES: *Omnibus* (ABC and NBC)
BEST CONTINUING PERFORMANCE BY AN ACTOR IN A LEADING ROLE IN A DRAMATIC OR COMEDY SERIES: Robert Young, *Father Knows Best* (NBC)
BEST CONTINUING PERFORMANCE BY AN ACTRESS IN A LEADING ROLE IN A DRAMATIC OR COMEDY SERIES: Jane Wyatt, *Father Knows Best* (NBC)
BEST CONTINUING PERFORMANCE (MALE) IN A SERIES BY A COMEDIAN, SINGER, HOST, DANCER, MC, ANNOUNCER, NARRATOR, PANELIST, OR ANY PERSON WHO ESSENTIALLY PLAYS HIMSELF: Jack Benny, *The Jack Benny Show* (CBS)
BEST CONTINUING PERFORMANCE (FEMALE) IN A SERIES BY A COMEDIENNE, SINGER, HOSTESS, DANCER, MC, ANNOUNCER, NARRATOR, PANELIST, OR ANY PERSON WHO ESSENTIALLY PLAYS HERSELF: Dinah Shore, *The Dinah Shore Chevy Show* (NBC)
ACTOR—BEST SINGLE PERFORMANCE (LEAD OR SUPPORT): Peter Ustinov, "The Life of Samuel Johnson," *Omnibus* (NBC)
ACTRESS—BEST SINGLE PERFORMANCE (LEAD OR SUPPORT): Polly Bergen, "The Helen Morgan Story," *Playhouse 90* (CBS)
BEST CONTINUING SUPPORTING PERFORMANCE BY AN ACTOR IN A DRAMATIC OR COMEDY SERIES: Carl Reiner, *Caesar's Hour* (NBC)
BEST CONTINUING SUPPORTING PERFORMANCE BY AN ACTRESS IN A DRAMATIC OR COMEDY SERIES: Ann B. Davis, *The Bob Cummings Show* (CBS and NBC)
BEST NEWS COMMENTARY: Edward R. Murrow, *See It Now* (CBS)

BEST TELEPLAY WRITING (HALF HOUR OR LESS): Paul Monash, "The Lonely Wizard," *Schlitz Playhouse of Stars* (CBS)

BEST TELEPLAY WRITING (ONE HOUR OR MORE): Rod Serling, "The Comedian," *Playhouse 90* (CBS)

BEST COMEDY WRITING: Nat Hiken, Billy Friedberg, Phil Sharp, Terry Ryan, Coleman Jacoby, Arnold Rosen, Sydney Zelinka, A. J. Russell, and Tony Webster, *The Phil Silvers Show* (CBS)

BEST DIRECTION (HALF HOUR OR LESS): Robert Stevens, "The Glass Eye," *Alfred Hitchcock Presents* (CBS)

BEST DIRECTION (ONE HOUR OR MORE): Bob Banner, *The Dinah Shore Chevy Show* (NBC)

1958–1959 (presented May 6, 1959)

MOST OUTSTANDING SINGLE PROGRAM OF THE YEAR: "An Evening with Fred Astaire" (NBC)

BEST DRAMATIC SERIES (ONE HOUR OR LONGER): *Playhouse 90* (CBS)

BEST DRAMATIC SERIES (LESS THAN ONE HOUR): *Alcoa-Goodyear Theatre* (NBC)

BEST COMEDY SERIES: *The Jack Benny Show* (CBS)

BEST MUSICAL OR VARIETY SERIES: *The Dinah Shore Chevy Show* (NBC)

BEST WESTERN SERIES: *Maverick* (ABC)

BEST PUBLIC SERVICE PROGRAM OR SERIES: *Omnibus* (NBC)

BEST NEWS REPORTING SERIES: *The Huntley-Brinkley Report* (NBC)

BEST PANEL, QUIZ, OR AUDIENCE PARTICIPATION SERIES: *What's My Line* (CBS)

BEST SPECIAL DRAMATIC PROGRAM (ONE HOUR OR LONGER): "Little Moon of Alban," *Hallmark Hall of Fame* (NBC)

BEST SPECIAL MUSICAL OR VARIETY PROGRAM (ONE HOUR OR LONGER): "An Evening with Fred Astaire" (NBC)

BEST ACTOR IN A LEADING ROLE (CONTINUING CHARACTER) IN A DRAMATIC SERIES: Raymond Burr, *Perry Mason* (CBS)

BEST ACTRESS IN A LEADING ROLE (CONTINUING CHARACTER) IN A DRAMATIC SERIES: Loretta Young, *The Loretta Young Show* (NBC)

BEST ACTOR IN A LEADING ROLE (CONTINUING CHARACTER) IN A COMEDY SERIES: Jack Benny, *The Jack Benny Show* (CBS)

BEST ACTRESS IN A LEADING ROLE (CONTINUING CHARACTER) IN A COMEDY SERIES: Jane Wyatt, *Father Knows Best* (CBS and NBC)

BEST SUPPORTING ACTOR (CONTINUING CHARACTER) IN A DRAMATIC SERIES: Dennis Weaver, *Gunsmoke* (CBS)

BEST SUPPORTING ACTRESS (CONTINUING CHARACTER) IN A DRAMATIC SERIES: Barbara Hale, *Perry Mason* (CBS)

BEST SUPPORTING ACTOR (CONTINUING CHARACTER) IN A COMEDY SERIES: Tom Poston, *The Steve Allen Show* (NBC)

BEST SUPPORTING ACTRESS (CONTINUING CHARACTER) IN A COMEDY SERIES: Ann B. Davis, *The Bob Cummings Show* (NBC)

BEST PERFORMANCE BY AN ACTOR (CONTINUING CHARACTER) IN A MUSICAL OR VARIETY SERIES: Perry Como, *The Perry Como Show* (NBC)

BEST PERFORMANCE BY AN ACTRESS (CONTINUING CHARACTER) IN A MUSICAL OR VARIETY SERIES: Dinah Shore, *The Dinah Shore Chevy Show* (NBC)

BEST SINGLE PERFORMANCE BY AN ACTOR: Fred Astaire, "An Evening with Fred Astaire" (NBC)

BEST SINGLE PERFORMANCE BY AN ACTRESS: Julie Harris, "Little Moon of Alban," *Hallmark Hall of Fame* (NBC)

BEST NEWS COMMENTATOR OR ANALYST: Edward R. Murrow (CBS)

BEST DIRECTION OF A SINGLE PROGRAM OF A DRAMATIC SERIES (LESS THAN ONE HOUR): Jack Smight, "Eddie," *Alcoa-Goodyear Theatre* (NBC)

BEST DIRECTION OF A SINGLE DRAMATIC PROGRAM (ONE HOUR OR LONGER): George Schaefer, "Little Moon of Alban," *Hallmark Hall of Fame* (NBC)

BEST DIRECTION OF A SINGLE PROGRAM OF A COMEDY SERIES: Peter Tewksbury, "Medal for Margaret," *Father Knows Best* (CBS)

BEST DIRECTION OF A SINGLE MUSICAL OR VARIETY PROGRAM: Bud Yorkin, "An Evening with Fred Astaire" (NBC)

BEST WRITING OF A SINGLE PROGRAM OF A DRAMATIC SERIES (LESS THAN ONE HOUR): Alfred Brenner and Ken Hughes, "Eddie," *Alcoa-Goodyear Theatre* (NBC)

BEST WRITING OF A SINGLE DRAMATIC PROGRAM (ONE HOUR OR LONGER): James Costigan, "Little Moon of Alban," *Hallmark Hall of Fame* (NBC)

BEST WRITING OF A SINGLE PROGRAM OF A COMEDY SERIES: Sam Perrin, George Balzer, Hal Goldman, and Al Gordon, "Jack Benny Show with Ernie Kovacs," *The Jack Benny Show* (CBS)

BEST WRITING OF A SINGLE MUSICAL OR VARIETY PROGRAM: Bud Yorkin and Herbert Baker, "An Evening with Fred Astaire" (NBC)

933

1959–1960 (presented June 20, 1960)
OUTSTANDING PROGRAM ACHIEVEMENT IN THE FIELD OF HUMOR: "The Art Carney Special" (NBC)
OUTSTANDING PROGRAM ACHIEVEMENT IN THE FIELD OF DRAMA: *Playhouse 90* (CBS)
OUTSTANDING PROGRAM ACHIEVEMENT IN THE FIELD OF VARIETY: " 'The "Fabulous Fifties' " (CBS)
OUTSTANDING PROGRAM ACHIEVEMENT IN THE FIELD OF NEWS: *The Huntley-Brinkley Report* (NBC)
OUTSTANDING PROGRAM ACHIEVEMENT IN THE FIELD OF PUBLIC AFFAIRS AND EDUCATION: *The Twentieth Century* (CBS)
OUTSTANDING SINGLE PERFORMANCE BY AN ACTOR (LEAD OR SUPPORT): Laurence Olivier, "The Moon and Sixpence" (NBC)
OUTSTANDING SINGLE PERFORMANCE BY AN ACTRESS (LEAD OR SUPPORT): Ingrid Bergman, "The Turn of the Screw," *Ford Startime* (NBC)
OUTSTANDING PERFORMANCE BY AN ACTOR IN A SERIES (LEAD OR SUPPORT): Robert Stack, *The Untouchables* (ABC)
OUTSTANDING PERFORMANCE BY AN ACTRESS IN A SERIES (LEAD OR SUPPORT): Jane Wyatt, *Father Knows Best* (CBS)
OUTSTANDING PERFORMANCE IN A VARIETY OR MUSICAL PROGRAM OR SERIES: Harry Belafonte, "Tonight with Belafonte," *The Revlon Revue* (CBS)
OUTSTANDING WRITING ACHIEVEMENT IN DRAMA: Rod Serling, *The Twilight Zone* (CBS)
OUTSTANDING WRITING ACHIEVEMENT IN COMEDY: Sam Perrin, George Balzer, Al Gordon, and Hal Goldman, *The Jack Benny Show* (CBS)
OUTSTANDING WRITING ACHIEVEMENT IN THE DOCUMENTARY FIELD: Howard K. Smith and Av Westin, "The Population Explosion" (CBS)
OUTSTANDING DIRECTORIAL ACHIEVEMENT IN DRAMA: Robert Mulligan, "The Moon and Sixpence" (NBC)
OUTSTANDING DIRECTORIAL ACHIEVEMENT IN COMEDY: Ralph Levy and Bud Yorkin, *The Jack Benny Hour Specials* (CBS)

1960–1961 (presented May 16, 1961)
THE PROGRAM OF THE YEAR: "Macbeth," *Hallmark Hall of Fame* (NBC)
OUTSTANDING PROGRAM ACHIEVEMENT IN THE FIELD OF HUMOR: *The Jack Benny Show* (CBS)
OUTSTANDING PROGRAM ACHIEVEMENT IN THE FIELD OF DRAMA: "Macbeth," *Hallmark Hall of Fame* (NBC)
OUTSTANDING PROGRAM ACHIEVEMENT IN THE FIELD OF VARIETY: "Astaire Time" (NBC)
OUTSTANDING PROGRAM ACHIEVEMENT IN THE FIELD OF NEWS: *The Huntley-Brinkley Report* (NBC)
OUTSTANDING PROGRAM ACHIEVEMENT IN THE FIELD OF PUBLIC AFFAIRS AND EDUCATION: *The Twentieth Century* (CBS)
OUTSTANDING SINGLE PERFORMANCE BY AN ACTOR IN A LEADING ROLE: Maurice Evans, "Macbeth," *Hallmark Hall of Fame* (NBC)
OUTSTANDING SINGLE PERFORMANCE BY AN ACTRESS IN A LEADING ROLE: Judith Anderson, "Macbeth," *Hallmark Hall of Fame* (NBC)
OUTSTANDING PERFORMANCE BY AN ACTOR IN A SERIES (LEAD): Raymond Burr, *Perry Mason* (CBS)
OUTSTANDING PERFORMANCE BY AN ACTRESS IN A SERIES (LEAD): Barbara Stanwyck, *The Barbara Stanwyck Show* (NBC)
OUTSTANDING PERFORMANCE IN A SUPPORTING ROLE BY AN ACTOR OR ACTRESS IN A SINGLE PROGRAM: Roddy McDowall, "Not Without Honor," *Equitable's American Heritage* (NBC)
OUTSTANDING PERFORMANCE IN A SUPPORTING ROLE BY AN ACTOR OR ACTRESS IN A SERIES: Don Knotts, *The Andy Griffith Show* (CBS)
OUTSTANDING PERFORMANCE IN A VARIETY OR MUSICAL PROGRAM OR SERIES: Fred Astaire, "Astaire Time" (NBC)
OUTSTANDING WRITING ACHIEVEMENT IN DRAMA: Rod Serling, *The Twilight Zone* (CBS)
OUTSTANDING WRITING ACHIEVEMENT IN COMEDY: Sherwood Schwartz, Dave O'Brien, Al Schwartz, Martin Ragaway, and Red Skelton, *The Red Skelton Show* (CBS)
OUTSTANDING WRITING ACHIEVEMENT IN THE DOCUMENTARY FIELD: Victor Wolfson, *Winston Churchill—The Valiant Years* (ABC)
OUTSTANDING DIRECTORIAL ACHIEVEMENT IN DRAMA: George Schaefer, "Macbeth," *Hallmark Hall of Fame* (NBC)
OUTSTANDING DIRECTORIAL ACHIEVEMENT IN COMEDY: Sheldon Leonard, *The Danny Thomas Show* (CBS)

1961–1962 (presented May 22, 1962)
THE PROGRAM OF THE YEAR: "Victoria Regina," *Hallmark Hall of Fame* (NBC)
OUTSTANDING PROGRAM ACHIEVEMENT IN THE FIELD OF HUMOR: *The Bob Newhart Show* (NBC)
OUTSTANDING PROGRAM ACHIEVEMENT IN THE FIELD OF DRAMA: *The Defenders* (CBS)
OUTSTANDING PROGRAM ACHIEVEMENT IN THE FIELD OF VARIETY: *The Garry Moore Show* (CBS)

OUTSTANDING PROGRAM ACHIEVEMENT IN THE FIELD OF NEWS: *The Huntley-Brinkley Report* (NBC)

OUTSTANDING PROGRAM ACHIEVEMENT IN THE FIELD OF EDUCATIONAL AND PUBLIC AFFAIRS PROGRAMMING: *David Brinkley's Journal* (NBC)

OUTSTANDING SINGLE PERFORMANCE BY AN ACTOR IN A LEADING ROLE: Peter Falk, "The Price of Tomatoes," *The Dick Powell Show* (NBC)

OUTSTANDING SINGLE PERFORMANCE BY AN ACTRESS IN A LEADING ROLE: Julie Harris, "Victoria Regina," *Hallmark Hall of Fame* (NBC)

OUTSTANDING CONTINUED PERFORMANCE BY AN ACTOR IN A SERIES (LEAD): E. G. Marshall, *The Defenders* (CBS)

OUTSTANDING CONTINUED PERFORMANCE BY AN ACTRESS IN A SERIES (LEAD): Shirley Booth, *Hazel* (NBC)

OUTSTANDING PERFORMANCE IN A SUPPORTING ROLE BY AN ACTOR: Don Knotts, *The Andy Griffith Show* (CBS)

OUTSTANDING PERFORMANCE IN A SUPPORTING ROLE BY AN ACTRESS: Pamela Brown, "Victoria Regina," *Hallmark Hall of Fame* (NBC)

OUTSTANDING PERFORMANCE IN A VARIETY OR MUSICAL PROGRAM OR SERIES: Carol Burnett, *The Garry Moore Show* (CBS)

OUTSTANDING WRITING ACHIEVEMENT IN DRAMA: Reginald Rose, *The Defenders* (CBS)

OUTSTANDING WRITING ACHIEVEMENT IN COMEDY: Carl Reiner, *The Dick Van Dyke Show* (CBS)

OUTSTANDING WRITING ACHIEVEMENT IN THE DOCUMENTARY FIELD: Lou Hazam, "Vincent Van Gogh: A Self-Portrait" (NBC)

OUTSTANDING DIRECTORIAL ACHIEVEMENT IN DRAMA: Franklin Schaffner, *The Defenders* (CBS)

OUTSTANDING DIRECTORIAL ACHIEVEMENT IN COMEDY: Nat Hiken, *Car 54, Where Are You?* (NBC)

1962–1963 (presented May 26, 1963)

THE PROGRAM OF THE YEAR: "The Tunnel" (NBC)

OUTSTANDING PROGRAM ACHIEVEMENT IN THE FIELD OF HUMOR: *The Dick Van Dyke Show* (CBS)

OUTSTANDING PROGRAM ACHIEVEMENT IN THE FIELD OF DRAMA: *The Defenders* (CBS)

OUTSTANDING PROGRAM ACHIEVEMENT IN THE FIELD OF MUSIC: "Julie and Carol at Carnegie Hall" (CBS)

OUTSTANDING ACHIEVEMENT IN THE FIELD OF VARIETY: *The Andy Williams Show* (NBC)

OUTSTANDING PROGRAM ACHIEVEMENT IN THE FIELD OF PANEL, QUIZ, OR AUDIENCE PARTICIPATION: *The G. E. College Bowl* (CBS)

OUTSTANDING PROGRAM ACHIEVEMENT IN THE FIELD OF CHILDREN'S PROGRAMMING: *Walt Disney's Wonderful World of Color* (NBC)

OUTSTANDING ACHIEVEMENT IN THE FIELD OF DOCUMENTARY PROGRAMS: "The Tunnel," Reuven Frank (NBC)

OUTSTANDING ACHIEVEMENT IN THE FIELD OF NEWS: *The Huntley-Brinkley Report* (NBC)

OUTSTANDING PROGRAM ACHIEVEMENT IN THE FIELD OF NEWS COMMENTARY OR PUBLIC AFFAIRS: *David Brinkley's Journal* (NBC)

OUTSTANDING ACHIEVEMENT IN INTERNATIONAL REPORTING OR COMMENTARY: Piers Anderson, Berlin correspondent, "The Tunnel" (NBC)

OUTSTANDING SINGLE PERFORMANCE BY AN ACTOR IN A LEADING ROLE: Trevor Howard, "The Invincible Mr. Disraeli," *Hallmark Hall of Fame* (NBC)

OUTSTANDING SINGLE PERFORMANCE BY AN ACTRESS IN A LEADING ROLE: Kim Stanley, "A Cardinal Act of Mercy," *Ben Casey* (ABC)

OUTSTANDING CONTINUED PERFORMANCE BY AN ACTOR IN A SERIES (LEAD): E. G. Marshall, *The Defenders* (CBS)

OUTSTANDING CONTINUED PERFORMANCE BY AN ACTRESS IN A SERIES (LEAD): Shirley Booth, *Hazel* (NBC)

OUTSTANDING PERFORMANCE IN A SUPPORTING ROLE BY AN ACTOR: Don Knotts, *The Andy Griffith Show* (CBS)

OUTSTANDING PERFORMANCE IN A SUPPORTING ROLE BY AN ACTRESS: Glenda Farrell, "A Cardinal Act of Mercy," *Ben Casey* (ABC)

OUTSTANDING PERFORMANCE IN A VARIETY OR MUSICAL PROGRAM OR SERIES: Carol Burnett, "Julie and Carol at Carnegie Hall" (CBS) and "Carol and Company" (CBS)

OUTSTANDING WRITING ACHIEVEMENT IN DRAMA: Robert Thom and Reginald Rose, "The Madman," *The Defenders* (CBS)

OUTSTANDING WRITING ACHIEVEMENT IN COMEDY: Carl Reiner, *The Dick Van Dyke Show* (CBS)

OUTSTANDING DIRECTORIAL ACHIEVEMENT IN DRAMA: Stuart Rosenberg, "The Madman," *The Defenders* (CBS)

OUTSTANDING DIRECTORIAL ACHIEVEMENT IN COMEDY: John Rich, *The Dick Van Dyke Show* (CBS)

1963–1964 (presented May 25, 1964)

THE PROGRAM OF THE YEAR: "The Making of the President 1960" (ABC)

OUTSTANDING PROGRAM ACHIEVEMENT IN THE FIELD OF COMEDY: *The Dick Van Dyke Show* (CBS)

OUTSTANDING PROGRAM ACHIEVEMENT IN THE FIELD OF DRAMA: *The Defenders* (CBS)

OUTSTANDING PROGRAM ACHIEVEMENT IN THE FIELD OF MUSIC: *The Bell Telephone Hour* (NBC)

OUTSTANDING PROGRAM ACHIEVEMENT IN THE FIELD OF VARIETY: *The Danny Kaye Show* (CBS)

OUTSTANDING ACHIEVEMENT IN THE FIELD OF DOCUMENTARY PROGRAMS: "The Making of the President 1960" (ABC)

OUTSTANDING PROGRAM ACHIEVEMENT IN THE FIELD OF NEWS REPORTS: *The Huntley-Brinkley Report* (NBC)

OUTSTANDING PROGRAM ACHIEVEMENT IN THE FIELD OF NEWS COMMENTARY OR PUBLIC AFFAIRS: "Cuba: Parts I and II—The Bay of Pigs and the Missile Crisis," *NBC White Paper* (NBC)

OUTSTANDING SINGLE PERFORMANCE BY AN ACTOR IN A LEADING ROLE: Jack Klugman, "Blacklist," *The Defenders* (CBS)

OUTSTANDING SINGLE PERFORMANCE BY AN ACTRESS IN A LEADING ROLE: Shelley Winters, "Two Is the Number," *Bob Hope Presents the Chrysler Theatre* (NBC)

OUTSTANDING CONTINUED PERFORMANCE BY AN ACTOR IN A SERIES (LEAD): Dick Van Dyke, *The Dick Van Dyke Show* (CBS)

OUTSTANDING CONTINUED PERFORMANCE BY AN ACTRESS IN A SERIES (LEAD): Mary Tyler Moore, *The Dick Van Dyke Show* (CBS)

OUTSTANDING PERFORMANCE IN A SUPPORTING ROLE BY AN ACTOR: Albert Paulsen, "One Day in the Life of Ivan Denisovich," *Bob Hope Presents the Chrysler Theatre* (NBC)

OUTSTANDING PERFORMANCE IN A SUPPORTING ROLE BY AN ACTRESS: Ruth White, "Little Moon of Alban," *Hallmark Hall of Fame* (NBC)

OUTSTANDING PERFORMANCE IN A VARIETY OR MUSICAL PROGRAM OR SERIES: Danny Kaye, *The Danny Kaye Show* (CBS)

OUTSTANDING WRITING ACHIEVEMENT IN DRAMA (ORIGINAL): Ernest Kinoy, "Blacklist," *The Defenders* (CBS)

OUTSTANDING WRITING ACHIEVEMENT IN DRAMA (ADAPTATION): Rod Serling, "It's Mental Work" (from the story by John O'Hara), *Bob Hope Presents the Chrysler Theatre* (NBC)

OUTSTANDING WRITING ACHIEVEMENT IN COMEDY OR VARIETY: Carl Reiner, Sam Denoff, and Bill Persky, *The Dick Van Dyke Show* (CBS)

OUTSTANDING DIRECTORIAL ACHIEVEMENT IN DRAMA: Tom Gries, "Who Do You Kill," *East Side/West Side* (CBS)

OUTSTANDING DIRECTORIAL ACHIEVEMENT IN COMEDY: Jerry Paris, *The Dick Van Dyke Show* (CBS)

OUTSTANDING DIRECTORIAL ACHIEVEMENT IN VARIETY OR MUSIC: Robert Scheerer, *The Danny Kaye Show* (CBS)

1964–1965 (presented September 12, 1965)

OUTSTANDING PROGRAM ACHIEVEMENTS IN ENTERTAINMENT: *The Dick Van Dyke Show,* Carl Reiner, producer (CBS); "The Magnificent Yankee," *Hallmark Hall of Fame,* George Schaefer, producer (NBC); "My Name Is Barbra," Richard Lewine, producer (CBS)

OUTSTANDING INDIVIDUAL ACHIEVEMENTS IN ENTERTAINMENT (ACTORS AND PERFORMERS): Lynn Fontanne, "The Magnificent Yankee," *Hallmark Hall of Fame* (NBC); Alfred Lunt, "The Magnificent Yankee," *Hallmark Hall of Fame* (NBC); Barbra Streisand, "My Name Is Barbra" (CBS); Dick Van Dyke, *The Dick Van Dyke Show* (CBS)

OUTSTANDING INDIVIDUAL ACHIEVEMENT IN ENTERTAINMENT (WRITER): David Karp, "The 700-Year-Old Gang," *The Defenders* (CBS)

OUTSTANDING INDIVIDUAL ACHIEVEMENT IN ENTERTAINMENT (DIRECTOR): Paul Bogart, "The 700-Year-Old Gang," *The Defenders* (CBS)

OUTSTANDING PROGRAM ACHIEVEMENTS IN NEWS, DOCUMENTARIES, INFORMATION, AND SPORTS: "I, Leonardo da Vinci," *The Saga of Western Man,* John H. Secondari and Helen Jean Rogers, producers (ABC); "The Louvre," Lucy Jarvis, producer, and John J. Sughrue, co-producer (NBC)

OUTSTANDING INDIVIDUAL ACHIEVEMENT IN NEWS, DOCUMENTARIES, INFORMATION, AND SPORTS (DIRECTOR): John J. Sughrue, "The Louvre" (NBC)

OUTSTANDING INDIVIDUAL ACHIEVEMENT IN NEWS, DOCUMENTARIES, INFORMATION, AND SPORTS (WRITER): Sidney Carroll, "The Louvre" (NBC)

1965–1966 (presented May 22, 1966)

OUTSTANDING COMEDY SERIES: *The Dick Van Dyke Show,* Carl Reiner, producer (CBS)

OUTSTANDING VARIETY SERIES: *The Andy Williams Show,* Bob Finkel, producer (NBC)

OUTSTANDING VARIETY SPECIAL: "Chrysler Presents the Bob Hope Christmas Special," Bob Hope, executive producer (NBC)

OUTSTANDING DRAMATIC SERIES: *The Fugitive,* Alan Armer, producer (ABC)

OUTSTANDING DRAMATIC PROGRAM: "The Ages of Man," David Susskind and Daniel Melnick, producers (CBS)

936

OUTSTANDING MUSICAL PROGRAM: "Frank Sinatra: A Man and His Music," Dwight Hemion, producer (NBC)

OUTSTANDING CHILDREN'S PROGRAM: "A Charlie Brown Christmas," Lee Mendelson and Bill Melendez, producers (CBS)

OUTSTANDING PERFORMANCE BY AN ACTOR IN A LEADING ROLE IN A DRAMA: Cliff Robertson, "The Game," *Bob Hope Presents the Chrysler Theatre* (NBC)

OUTSTANDING PERFORMANCE BY AN ACTRESS IN A LEADING ROLE IN A DRAMA: Simone Signoret, "A Small Rebellion," *Bob Hope Presents the Chrysler Theatre* (NBC)

OUTSTANDING CONTINUED PERFORMANCE BY AN ACTOR IN A LEADING ROLE IN A DRAMATIC SERIES: Bill Cosby, *I Spy* (NBC)

OUTSTANDING CONTINUED PERFORMANCE BY AN ACTRESS IN A LEADING ROLE IN A DRAMATIC SERIES: Barbara Stanwyck, *The Big Valley* (ABC)

OUTSTANDING CONTINUED PERFORMANCE BY AN ACTOR IN A LEADING ROLE IN A COMEDY SERIES: Dick Van Dyke, *The Dick Van Dyke Show* (CBS)

OUTSTANDING CONTINUED PERFORMANCE BY AN ACTRESS IN A LEADING ROLE IN A COMEDY SERIES: Mary Tyler Moore, *The Dick Van Dyke Show* (CBS)

OUTSTANDING PERFORMANCE BY AN ACTOR IN A SUPPORTING ROLE IN A DRAMA: James Daly, "Eagle in a Cage," *Hallmark Hall of Fame* (NBC)

OUTSTANDING PERFORMANCE BY AN ACTRESS IN A SUPPORTING ROLE IN A DRAMA: Lee Grant, *Peyton Place* (ABC)

OUTSTANDING PERFORMANCE BY AN ACTOR IN A SUPPORTING ROLE IN A COMEDY: Don Knotts, "The Return of Barney Fife," *The Andy Griffith Show* (CBS)

OUTSTANDING PERFORMANCE BY AN ACTRESS IN A SUPPORTING ROLE IN A COMEDY: Alice Pearce, *Bewitched* (ABC)

OUTSTANDING WRITING ACHIEVEMENT IN DRAMA: Millard Lampell, "Eagle in a Cage," *Hallmark Hall of Fame* (NBC)

OUTSTANDING WRITING ACHIEVEMENT IN COMEDY: Bill Persky and Sam Denoff, "Coast to Coast Big Mouth," *The Dick Van Dyke Show* (CBS)

OUTSTANDING WRITING ACHIEVEMENT IN VARIETY: Al Gordon, Hal Goldman, and Sheldon Keller, "An Evening with Carol Channing" (CBS)

OUTSTANDING DIRECTORIAL ACHIEVEMENT IN DRAMA: Sidney Pollack, "The Game," *Bob Hope Presents the Chrysler Theatre* (NBC)

OUTSTANDING DIRECTORIAL ACHIEVEMENT IN COMEDY: William Asher, *Bewitched* (ABC)

OUTSTANDING DIRECTORIAL ACHIEVEMENT IN VARIETY OR MUSIC: Alan Handley, "The Julie Andrews Show" (NBC)

ACHIEVEMENTS IN NEWS AND DOCUMENTARIES (PROGRAMS): "American White Paper: United States Foreign Policy," Fred Freed, producer (NBC); "KKK—The Invisible Empire," *CBS Reports,* David Lowe, producer (CBS); "Senate Hearings on Vietnam," Chet Hagen, producer (NBC)

SPECIAL CLASSIFICATIONS OF INDIVIDUAL ACHIEVEMENTS: Burr Tillstrom, "Berlin Wall" hand ballet, *That Was The Week That Was* (NBC)

1966–1967 (presented June 4, 1967)

OUTSTANDING COMEDY SERIES: *The Monkees,* Bert Schneider and Bob Rafelson, producers (NBC)

OUTSTANDING VARIETY SERIES: *The Andy Williams Show,* Edward Stephenson and Bob Finkel, producers (NBC)

OUTSTANDING VARIETY SPECIAL: "The Sid Caesar, Imogene Coca, Carl Reiner, Howard Morris Special," Jack Arnold, producer (CBS)

OUTSTANDING DRAMATIC SERIES: *Mission: Impossible,* Joseph Gantman and Bruce Geller, producers (CBS)

OUTSTANDING DRAMATIC PROGRAM: "Death of a Salesman," David Susskind and Daniel Melnick, producers (CBS)

OUTSTANDING MUSICAL PROGRAM: "Brigadoon," Fielder Cook, producer (ABC)

OUTSTANDING CHILDREN'S PROGRAM: "Jack and the Beanstalk," Gene Kelly, producer (NBC)

OUTSTANDING SINGLE PERFORMANCE BY AN ACTOR IN A LEADING ROLE IN A DRAMA: Peter Ustinov, "Barefoot in Athens," *Hallmark Hall of Fame* (NBC)

OUTSTANDING SINGLE PERFORMANCE BY AN ACTRESS IN A LEADING ROLE IN A DRAMA: Geraldine Page, "A Christmas Memory," *ABC Stage 67* (ABC)

OUTSTANDING CONTINUED PERFORMANCE BY AN ACTOR IN A LEADING ROLE IN A DRAMATIC SERIES: Bill Cosby, *I Spy* (NBC)

OUTSTANDING CONTINUED PERFORMANCE BY AN ACTRESS IN A LEADING ROLE IN A DRAMATIC SERIES: Barbara Bain, *Mission: Impossible* (CBS)

OUTSTANDING CONTINUED PERFORMANCE BY AN ACTOR IN A LEADING ROLE IN A COMEDY SERIES: Don Adams, *Get Smart* (NBC)

OUTSTANDING CONTINUED PERFORMANCE BY AN ACTRESS IN A LEADING ROLE IN A COMEDY SERIES: Lucille Ball, *The Lucy Show* (CBS)

OUTSTANDING PERFORMANCE BY AN ACTOR IN A SUPPORTING ROLE IN A DRAMA: Eli Wallach, "The Poppy Is Also a Flower," *Xerox Special* (ABC)

OUTSTANDING PERFORMANCE BY AN ACTRESS IN A SUPPORTING ROLE IN A DRAMA: Agnes Moorehead, "Night of the Vicious Valentine," *The Wild Wild West* (CBS)

OUTSTANDING PERFORMANCE BY AN ACTOR IN A SUPPORTING ROLE IN A COMEDY: Don Knotts, "Barney Comes to Mayberry," *The Andy Griffith Show* (CBS)

OUTSTANDING PERFORMANCE BY AN ACTRESS IN A SUPPORTING ROLE IN A COMEDY: Frances Bavier, *The Andy Griffith Show* (CBS)

OUTSTANDING WRITING ACHIEVEMENT IN DRAMA: Bruce Geller, *Mission: Impossible* (CBS)

OUTSTANDING WRITING ACHIEVEMENT IN COMEDY: Buck Henry and Leonard Stern, "Ship of Spies," *Get Smart* (NBC)

OUTSTANDING WRITING ACHIEVEMENT IN VARIETY: Mel Brooks, Sam Denoff, Bill Persky, Carl Reiner, and Mel Tolkin, "The Sid Caesar, Imogene Coca, Carl Reiner, Howard Morris Special" (CBS)

OUTSTANDING DIRECTORIAL ACHIEVEMENT IN DRAMA: Alex Segal, "Death of a Salesman" (CBS)

OUTSTANDING DIRECTORIAL ACHIEVEMENT IN COMEDY: James Frawley, "Royal Flush," *The Monkees* (NBC)

OUTSTANDING DIRECTORIAL ACHIEVEMENT IN VARIETY OR MUSIC: Fielder Cook, "Brigadoon" (ABC)

ACHIEVEMENTS IN NEWS AND DOCUMENTARIES (PROGRAMS): "China: The Roots of Madness," Mel Stuart, producer (syndicated); "Hall of Kings," Harry Rasky, producer (ABC); "The Italians," Bernard Birnbaum, producer (CBS)

ACHIEVEMENTS IN NEWS AND DOCUMENTARIES (INDIVIDUAL): Theodore H. White, writer, "China: The Roots of Madness" (syndicated)

SPECIAL CLASSIFICATIONS OF INDIVIDUAL ACHIEVEMENTS: Art Carney, *The Jackie Gleason Show* (CBS); Truman Capote and Eleanor Perry, adaptation of "A Christmas Memory," *ABC Stage 67* (ABC); Arthur Miller, adaptation of "Death of a Salesman" (CBS)

1967–1968 (presented May 19, 1968)

OUTSTANDING ACHIEVEMENT WITHIN REGULARLY SCHEDULED NEWS PROGRAMS: "1st Cavalry, Con Thien," and other segments, *The CBS Evening News with Walter Cronkite,* CBS news correspondent John Laurence and CBS news cameraman Keith Kay (CBS); "Crisis in the Cities," *Public Broadcast Laboratory,* Av Westin, executive producer (NET)

OUTSTANDING ACHIEVEMENT IN NEWS DOCUMENTARIES: "Africa," James Fleming, executive producer (ABC); "Summer '67: What We Learned," Fred Freed, producer (NBC); "CBS Reports: What about Ronald Reagan?" *CBS News Hour,* Harry Reasoner, writer (CBS); "Same Mud, Same Blood," Vo Huynh, cameraman (NBC)

OUTSTANDING ACHIEVEMENT IN CULTURAL DOCUMENTARIES: "Eric Hoffer, the Passionate State of Mind," *CBS News Hour,* Jack Beck, producer (CBS); "Gauguin in Tahiti: The Search for Paradise," *CBS News Hour,* Martin Carr, producer (CBS); "John Steinbeck's America and the Americans," Lee Mendelson, producer (NBC); "Dylan Thomas: The World I Breathe," *NET Festival,* Perry Miller Adato, producer (NET); Nathaniel Dorsky, art photographer, "Gauguin in Tahiti: The Search for Paradise," *CBS News Hour* (CBS); Harry Morgan, writer, "The Wyeth Phenomenon," *Who, What, When, Where, Why* (CBS); Thomas A. Priestley, director of photography, and Robert Loweree, film editor, "John Steinbeck's America and the Americans" (NBC)

OTHER OUTSTANDING NEWS AND DOCUMENTARY ACHIEVEMENTS: *The Twenty-first Century,* Isaac Kleinerman, producer (CBS); "Science and Religion: Who Will Play God?" *CBS News Special,* Ben Flynn, producer (CBS); *Our World,* George Delerue, composer (NET)

OUTSTANDING COMEDY SERIES: *Get Smart,* Burt Nodella, producer (NBC)

OUTSTANDING DRAMATIC SERIES: *Mission: Impossible,* Joseph E. Gantman, producer (CBS)

OUTSTANDING DRAMATIC PROGRAM: "Elizabeth the Queen," *Hallmark Hall of Fame,* George Schaefer, producer (NBC)

OUTSTANDING MUSICAL OR VARIETY SERIES: *Rowan and Martin's Laugh-In,* George Schlatter, producer (NBC)

OUTSTANDING MUSICAL OR VARIETY PROGRAM: "Rowan and Martin's Laugh-In Special," George Schlatter, producer (NBC)

OUTSTANDING SINGLE PERFORMANCE BY AN ACTOR IN A LEADING ROLE IN A DRAMA: Melvin Douglas, "Do Not Go Gentle into That Good Night," *CBS Playhouse* (CBS)

OUTSTANDING SINGLE PERFORMANCE BY AN ACTRESS IN A LEADING ROLE IN A DRAMA: Maureen Stapleton, "Among the Paths to Eden," *Xerox Special Event* (ABC)

OUTSTANDING CONTINUED PERFORMANCE BY AN ACTOR IN A LEADING ROLE IN A DRAMATIC SERIES: Bill Cosby, *I Spy* (NBC)

938

OUTSTANDING CONTINUED PERFORMANCE BY AN ACTRESS IN A LEADING ROLE IN A DRAMATIC SE-RIES: Barbara Bain, *Mission: Impossible* (CBS)

OUTSTANDING CONTINUED PERFORMANCE BY AN ACTOR IN A LEADING ROLE IN A COMEDY SERIES: Don Adams, *Get Smart* (NBC)

OUTSTANDING CONTINUED PERFORMANCE BY AN ACTRESS IN A LEADING ROLE IN A COMEDY SERIES: Lucille Ball, *The Lucy Show* (CBS)

OUTSTANDING PERFORMANCE BY AN ACTOR IN A SUPPORTING ROLE IN A DRAMA: Milburn Stone, *Gunsmoke* (CBS)

OUTSTANDING PERFORMANCE BY AN ACTRESS IN A SUPPORTING ROLE IN A DRAMA: Barbara Anderson, *Ironside* (NBC)

OUTSTANDING PERFORMANCE BY AN ACTOR IN A SUPPORTING ROLE IN A COMEDY: Werner Klemperer, *Hogan's Heroes* (CBS)

OUTSTANDING PERFORMANCE BY AN ACTRESS IN A SUPPORTING ROLE IN A COMEDY: Marion Lorne, *Bewitched* (ABC)

OUTSTANDING WRITING ACHIEVEMENT IN DRAMA: Loring Mandel, "Do Not Go Gentle into That Good Night," *CBS Playhouse* (CBS)

OUTSTANDING WRITING ACHIEVEMENT IN COMEDY: Alan Burns and Chris Hayward, "The Coming-Out Party," *He & She* (CBS)

OUTSTANDING WRITING ACHIEVEMENT IN MUSIC OR VARIETY: Paul Keyes, Hugh Wedlock, Allan Manings, Chris Beard, David Panich, Phil Hahn, Jack Hanrahan, Coslough Johnson, Marc London, and Digby Wolfe, *Rowan and Martin's Laugh-In* (NBC)

OUTSTANDING DIRECTORIAL ACHIEVEMENT IN DRAMA: Paul Bogart, "Dear Friends," *CBS Playhouse* (CBS)

OUTSTANDING DIRECTORIAL ACHIEVEMENT IN COMEDY: Bruce Bilson, "Maxwell Smart, Private Eye," *Get Smart* (NBC)

OUTSTANDING DIRECTORIAL ACHIEVEMENT IN MUSIC OR VARIETY: Jack Haley, Jr., "Movin' with Nancy" (NBC)

SPECIAL CLASSIFICATION OF OUTSTANDING INDIVIDUAL ACHIEVEMENT: Art Carney, *The Jackie Gleason Show* (CBS); Pat Paulsen, *The Smothers Brothers Comedy Hour* (CBS)

1968–1969 (presented June 8, 1969)

OUTSTANDING COMEDY SERIES: *Get Smart,* Arne Sultan, executive producer; Burt Nodella, producer (NBC)

OUTSTANDING DRAMATIC SERIES: *NET Playhouse,* Curtis Davis, executive producer (NET)

OUTSTANDING DRAMATIC PROGRAM: "Teacher, Teacher," Henry Jaffe, executive producer; George Lefferts, producer, *Hallmark Hall of Fame* (NBC)

OUTSTANDING MUSICAL OR VARIETY SERIES: *Rowan and Martin's Laugh-In,* George Schlatter, executive producer; Paul Keyes and Carolyn Raskin, producers (NBC)

OUTSTANDING VARIETY OR MUSICAL PROGRAM: "The Bill Cosby Special," Roy Silver, executive producer; Bill Hobin, Bill Persky, and Sam Denoff, producers (NBC)

OUTSTANDING SINGLE PERFORMANCE BY AN ACTOR IN A LEADING ROLE: Paul Scofield, "The Male of the Species," *Prudential's On Stage* (NBC)

OUTSTANDING SINGLE PERFORMANCE BY AN ACTRESS IN A LEADING ROLE: Geraldine Page, "The Thanksgiving Visitor" (ABC)

OUTSTANDING CONTINUED PERFORMANCE BY AN ACTOR IN A LEADING ROLE IN A DRAMATIC SERIES: Carl Betz, *Judd, for the Defense* (ABC)

OUTSTANDING CONTINUED PERFORMANCE BY AN ACTRESS IN A LEADING ROLE IN A DRAMATIC SE-RIES: Barbara Bain, *Mission: Impossible* (CBS)

OUTSTANDING CONTINUED PERFORMANCE BY AN ACTOR IN A LEADING ROLE IN A COMEDY SERIES: Don Adams, *Get Smart* (NBC)

OUTSTANDING CONTINUED PERFORMANCE BY AN ACTRESS IN A LEADING ROLE IN A COMEDY SERIES: Hope Lange, *The Ghost and Mrs. Muir* (NBC)

OUTSTANDING SINGLE PERFORMANCE BY AN ACTOR IN A SUPPORTING ROLE: no award given

OUTSTANDING SINGLE PERFORMANCE BY AN ACTRESS IN A SUPPORTING ROLE: Anna Calder-Marshall, "The Male of the Species," *Prudential's On Stage* (NBC)

OUTSTANDING CONTINUED PERFORMANCE BY AN ACTOR IN A SUPPORTING ROLE IN A SERIES: Werner Klemperer, *Hogan's Heroes* (CBS)

OUTSTANDING CONTINUED PERFORMANCE BY AN ACTRESS IN A SUPPORTING ROLE IN A SERIES: Susan Saint James, *The Name of the Game* (NBC)

OUTSTANDING WRITING ACHIEVEMENT IN DRAMA: J. P. Miller, "The People Next Door," *CBS Playhouse* (CBS)

OUTSTANDING WRITING ACHIEVEMENT IN COMEDY, VARIETY, OR MUSIC: Alan Blye, Bob Einstein, Murray Roman, Carl Gottlieb, Jerry Music, Steve Martin, Cecil Tuck, Paul Wayne, Cy Howard, and Mason Williams, *The Smothers Brothers Comedy Hour* (CBS)

OUTSTANDING DIRECTORIAL ACHIEVEMENT IN DRAMA: David Greene, "The People Next Door," *CBS Playhouse* (CBS)

OUTSTANDING PROGRAM ACHIEVEMENT (SPECIAL CLASSIFICATION): *Firing Line with William F. Buckley, Jr.,* Warren Steibel, producer (syndicated); *Wild Kingdom,* Don Meier, producer (NBC)

OUTSTANDING INDIVIDUAL ACHIEVEMENT (SPECIAL CLASSIFICATION): Arte Johnson, *Rowan and Martin's Laugh-In* (NBC); Harvey Korman, *The Carol Burnett Show* (CBS)

OUTSTANDING ACHIEVEMENT WITHIN REGULARLY SCHEDULED NEWS PROGRAMS: "Coverage of Hunger in the United States," *The Huntley-Brinkley Report,* Wallace Westfeldt, executive producer (NBC). "On the Road," *The CBS Evening News with Walter Cronkite,* Charles Kuralt, correspondent; James Wilson, cameraman; Robert Funk, soundman (CBS). "Police After Chicago," *The CBS Evening News with Walter Cronkite,* John Laurence, correspondent (CBS)

OUTSTANDING ACHIEVEMENT IN COVERAGE OF SPECIAL EVENTS: "Coverage of Martin Luther King Assassination and Aftermath," *CBS News Special Reports* and Broadcasts, Robert Wussler, Ernest Leiser, Don Hewitt, and Burton Benjamin, executive producers (CBS)

OUTSTANDING NEWS DOCUMENTARY PROGRAM ACHIEVEMENTS: "CBS Reports: Hunger in America," *CBS News Hour,* Martin Carr, producer (CBS); "Law and Order," *Public Broadcast Laboratory,* Frederick Wiseman, producer (NET)

OUTSTANDING NEWS DOCUMENTARY INDIVIDUAL ACHIEVEMENT: Perry Wolff and Andrew A. Rooney, writers, "Black History: Lost, Stolen or Strayed" [*Of Black America Series*], *CBS News Hour* (CBS)

OUTSTANDING CULTURAL DOCUMENTARY AND "MAGAZINE TYPE" PROGRAM OR SERIES ACHIEVEMENT (PROGRAMS): "Don't Count the Candles," *CBS News Hour,* William K. McClure, producer (CBS); "Justice Black and the Bill of Rights," *CBS News Special,* Burton Benjamin, producer (CBS); "Man Who Dances: Edward Villela," *The Bell Telephone Hour,* Robert Drew and Mike Jackson, producers (NBC); "The Great American Novel," *CBS News Hour,* Arthur Barron, producer (CBS)

OUTSTANDING CULTURAL DOCUMENTARY AND "MAGAZINE TYPE" PROGRAM OR SERIES ACHIEVEMENT (INDIVIDUAL): Walter Dombrow and Jerry Sims, cinematographers, "The Great American Novel," *CBS News Hour* (CBS); Tom Pettit, producer, "CBW: The Secrets of Secrecy," *First Tuesday* (NBC); Lord Snowden, cinematographer, "Don't Count the Candles," *CBS News Hour* (CBS)

1969–1970 (presented June 7, 1970)

OUTSTANDING COMEDY SERIES: *My World and Welcome to It,* Sheldon Leonard, executive producer; Danny Arnold, producer (NBC)

OUTSTANDING DRAMATIC SERIES: *Marcus Welby, M.D.,* David Victor, executive producer; David J. O'Connell, producer (ABC)

OUTSTANDING DRAMATIC PROGRAM: "A Storm in Summer," *Hallmark Hall of Fame,* M. J. Rifkin, executive producer; Alan Landsburg, producer (NBC)

OUTSTANDING VARIETY OR MUSICAL SERIES: *The David Frost Show,* Peter Baker, producer (syndicated)

OUTSTANDING VARIETY OR MUSICAL PROGRAM (VARIETY AND POPULAR MUSIC): "Annie, the Women in the Life of a Man," Joseph Cates, executive producer; Martin Charnin, producer (CBS)

OUTSTANDING VARIETY OR MUSICAL PROGRAM (CLASSICAL MUSIC): "Cinderella," John Barnes and Curtis Davis, executive producers; Norman Campbell, producer (NET)

OUTSTANDING NEW SERIES: *Room 222,* Gene Reynolds, producer (ABC)

OUTSTANDING SINGLE PERFORMANCE BY AN ACTOR IN A LEADING ROLE: Peter Ustinov, "A Storm in Summer," *Hallmark Hall of Fame* (NBC)

OUTSTANDING SINGLE PERFORMANCE BY AN ACTRESS IN A LEADING ROLE: Patty Duke, "My Sweet Charlie," *NBC World Premiere Movie* (NBC)

OUTSTANDING CONTINUED PERFORMANCE BY AN ACTOR IN A LEADING ROLE IN A DRAMATIC SERIES: Robert Young, *Marcus Welby, M.D.* (ABC)

OUTSTANDING CONTINUED PERFORMANCE BY AN ACTRESS IN A LEADING ROLE IN A DRAMATIC SERIES: Susan Hampshire, *The Forsythe Saga* (NET)

OUTSTANDING CONTINUED PERFORMANCE BY AN ACTOR IN A LEADING ROLE IN A COMEDY SERIES: William Windom, *My World and Welcome to It* (NBC)

OUTSTANDING CONTINUED PERFORMANCE BY AN ACTRESS IN A LEADING ROLE IN A COMEDY SERIES: Hope Lange, *The Ghost and Mrs. Muir* (ABC)

OUTSTANDING PERFORMANCE BY AN ACTOR IN A SUPPORTING ROLE IN DRAMA: James Brolin, *Marcus Welby, M.D.* (ABC)

OUTSTANDING PERFORMANCE BY AN ACTRESS IN A SUPPORTING ROLE IN DRAMA: Gail Fisher, *Mannix* (CBS)

OUTSTANDING PERFORMANCE BY AN ACTOR IN A SUPPORTING ROLE IN COMEDY: Michael Constantine, *Room 222* (ABC)

OUTSTANDING PERFORMANCE BY AN ACTRESS IN A SUPPORTING ROLE IN COMEDY: Karen Valentine, *Room 222* (ABC)

OUTSTANDING WRITING ACHIEVEMENT IN DRAMA: Richard Levinson and William Link, "My Sweet Charlie," *NBC World Premiere Movie* (NBC)

OUTSTANDING WRITING ACHIEVEMENT IN COMEDY, VARIETY, OR MUSIC: Gary Belkin, Peter Bellwood, Herb Sargent, Thomas Meehan, and Judith Viorst, "Annie, the Women in the Life of a Man" (CBS)

OUTSTANDING DIRECTORIAL ACHIEVEMENT IN DRAMA: Paul Bogart, "Shadow Game," *CBS Playhouse* (CBS)

OUTSTANDING DIRECTORIAL ACHIEVEMENT IN COMEDY, VARIETY, OR MUSIC: Dwight Hemion, "The Sound of Burt Bacharach," *Kraft Music Hall* (NBC)

SPECIAL CLASSIFICATION OF OUTSTANDING PROGRAM AND INDIVIDUAL ACHIEVEMENT: *Wild Kingdom*, Don Meier, producer (NBC)

OUTSTANDING ACHIEVEMENT WITHIN REGULARLY SCHEDULED NEWS PROGRAMS: "An Investigation of Teenage Drug Addiction—Odyssey House," *The Huntley-Brinkley Report*, Wallace Westfeldt, executive producer; Les Crystal, producer (NBC). "Can the World Be Saved?," *The CBS Evening News with Walter Cronkite*, Ronald Bonn, producer (CBS)

OUTSTANDING ACHIEVEMENT IN MAGAZINE-TYPE PROGRAMMING: *Black Journal*, William Greaves, executive producer (NET); Tom Pettit, reporter-writer, "Some Footnotes to 25 Nuclear Years," *First Tuesday* (NBC)

OUTSTANDING ACHIEVEMENT IN NEWS DOCUMENTARY PROGRAMMING: "Hospital," *NET Journal*, Frederick Wiseman, producer (NET). "The Making of the President 1968," M. J. Rifkin, executive producer; Mel Stuart, producer (CBS)

OUTSTANDING ACHIEVEMENT IN CULTURAL DOCUMENTARY PROGRAMMING: "Artur Rubinstein," George A. Vicas, producer (NBC). Artur Rubinstein, commentator, "Artur Rubinstein" (NBC). "Fathers and Sons," *CBS News Hour*, Ernest Leiser, executive producer; Harry Morgan, producer (CBS). "The Japanese," *CBS News Hour*, Perry Wolff, executive producer; Igor Oganesoff, producer (CBS). Edwin O. Reischauer, commentator, "The Japanese," *CBS News Hour* (CBS)

1970–1971 (presented May 9, 1971)

OUTSTANDING SERIES—COMEDY: *All in the Family*, Norman Lear, producer (CBS)

OUTSTANDING SERIES—DRAMA: *The Senator* [*The Bold Ones*], David Levinson, producer (NBC)

OUTSTANDING SINGLE PROGRAM—DRAMA OR COMEDY: "The Andersonville Trial," *Hollywood Television Theatre*, Lewis Freedman, producer (PBS)

OUTSTANDING VARIETY SERIES—MUSICAL: *The Flip Wilson Show*, Monte Kay, executive producer; Bob Henry, producer (NBC)

OUTSTANDING VARIETY SERIES—TALK: *The David Frost Show*, Peter Baker, producer (syndicated)

OUTSTANDING SINGLE PROGRAM—VARIETY OR MUSICAL (VARIETY AND POPULAR MUSIC): "Singer Presents Burt Bacharach," Gary Smith and Dwight Hemion, producers (CBS)

OUTSTANDING SINGLE PROGRAM—VARIETY OR MUSICAL (CLASSICAL MUSIC): "Leopold Stokowski," *NET Festival*, Curtis W. Davis, executive producer; Thomas Stevin, producer (PBS)

OUTSTANDING NEW SERIES: *All in the Family*, Norman Lear, producer (CBS)

OUTSTANDING SINGLE PERFORMANCE BY AN ACTOR IN A LEADING ROLE: George C. Scott, "The Price," *Hallmark Hall of Fame* (NBC)

OUTSTANDING SINGLE PERFORMANCE BY AN ACTRESS IN A LEADING ROLE: Lee Grant, "The Neon Ceiling," *World Premiere NBC Monday Night at the Movies* (NBC)

OUTSTANDING CONTINUED PERFORMANCE BY AN ACTOR IN A LEADING ROLE IN A DRAMATIC SERIES: Hal Holbrook, *The Senator* [*The Bold Ones*] (NBC)

OUTSTANDING CONTINUED PERFORMANCE BY AN ACTRESS IN A LEADING ROLE IN A DRAMATIC SERIES: Susan Hampshire, *The First Churchills* [*Masterpiece Theatre*] (PBS)

OUTSTANDING CONTINUED PERFORMANCE BY AN ACTOR IN A LEADING ROLE IN A COMEDY SERIES: Jack Klugman, *The Odd Couple* (ABC)

OUTSTANDING CONTINUED PERFORMANCE BY AN ACTRESS IN A LEADING ROLE IN A COMEDY SERIES: Jean Stapleton, *All in the Family* (CBS)

OUTSTANDING PERFORMANCE BY AN ACTOR IN A SUPPORTING ROLE IN DRAMA: David Burns, "The Price," *Hallmark Hall of Fame* (NBC)

OUTSTANDING PERFORMANCE BY AN ACTRESS IN A SUPPORTING ROLE IN DRAMA: Margaret Leighton, "Hamlet," *Hallmark Hall of Fame* (NBC)

OUTSTANDING PERFORMANCE BY AN ACTOR IN A SUPPORTING ROLE IN COMEDY: Edward Asner, *The Mary Tyler Moore Show* (CBS)

OUTSTANDING PERFORMANCE BY AN ACTRESS IN A SUPPORTING ROLE IN COMEDY: Valerie Harper, *The Mary Tyler Moore Show* (CBS)

OUTSTANDING DIRECTORIAL ACHIEVEMENT IN DRAMA (SERIES): Daryl Duke, "The Day the Lion Died," *The Senator* [*The Bold Ones*] (NBC)

OUTSTANDING DIRECTORIAL ACHIEVEMENT IN DRAMA (SINGLE PROGRAM): Fielder Cook, "The Price," *Hallmark Hall of Fame* (NBC)

OUTSTANDING DIRECTORIAL ACHIEVEMENT IN COMEDY (SERIES): Jay Sandrich, "Toulouse-Lautrec Is One of My Favorite Artists," *The Mary Tyler Moore Show* (CBS)

OUTSTANDING DIRECTORIAL ACHIEVEMENT IN VARIETY OR MUSIC (SERIES): Mark Warren, *Rowan and Martin's Laugh-In,* 10/26/70 (NBC)

OUTSTANDING DIRECTORIAL ACHIEVEMENT IN VARIETY OR MUSIC (SPECIAL): Sterling Johnson, "Timex Presents Peggy Fleming at Sun Valley" (NBC)

OUTSTANDING WRITING ACHIEVEMENT IN DRAMA (SERIES): Joel Oliansky, "To Taste of Death but Once," *The Senator [The Bold Ones]* (NBC)

OUTSTANDING WRITING ACHIEVEMENT IN DRAMA, ORIGINAL TELEPLAY (SPECIAL): Tracy Keenan Wynn and Marvin Schwartz, "Tribes," *Movie of the Week* (ABC)

OUTSTANDING WRITING ACHIEVEMENT IN DRAMA, ADAPTATION (SPECIAL): Saul Levitt, "The Andersonville Trial" (PBS)

OUTSTANDING WRITING ACHIEVEMENT IN COMEDY (SERIES): James L. Brooks and Allan Burns, "Support Your Local Mother," *The Mary Tyler Moore Show* (CBS)

OUTSTANDING WRITING ACHIEVEMENT IN VARIETY OR MUSIC (SERIES): Herbert Baker, Hal Goodman, Larry Klein, Bob Weiskopf, Bob Schiller, Norman Steinberg, and Flip Wilson, *The Flip Wilson Show,* with Lena Horne and Tony Randall, 12/10/70 (NBC)

OUTSTANDING WRITING ACHIEVEMENT IN COMEDY, VARIETY, OR MUSIC (SPECIAL): Bob Ellison and Marty Farrell, "Singer Presents Burt Bacharach" (CBS)

OUTSTANDING ACHIEVEMENT WITHIN REGULARLY SCHEDULED NEWS PROGRAMS (PROGRAMS): "Five Part Investigation of Welfare," *The NBC Nightly News,* Wallace Westfeldt, executive producer; David Teitelbaum, producer (NBC)

OUTSTANDING ACHIEVEMENT WITHIN REGULARLY SCHEDULED NEWS PROGRAMS (INDIVIDUALS): Bruce Morton, correspondent, "Reports from the Lt. Calley Trial," *The CBS Evening News with Walter Cronkite* (CBS)

OUTSTANDING ACHIEVEMENT IN NEWS DOCUMENTARY PROGRAMMING (PROGRAMS): "The Selling of the Pentagon," Perry Wolff, executive producer; Peter Davis, producer (CBS). "The World of Charlie Company," Ernest Leiser, executive producer; Russ Bensley, producer (CBS). "NBC White Paper: Pollution Is a Matter of Choice," Fred Freed, producer (NBC)

OUTSTANDING ACHIEVEMENT IN NEWS DOCUMENTARY PROGRAMMING (INDIVIDUALS): John Laurence, correspondent, "The World of Charlie Company" (CBS); Fred Freed, writer, "NBC News White Paper: Pollution Is a Matter of Choice" (NBC)

OUTSTANDING ACHIEVEMENT IN MAGAZINE-TYPE PROGRAMMING (PROGRAMS): "Gulf of Tonkin Segment," *60 Minutes,* Joseph Wershba, producer; *The Great American Dream Machine,* A. H. Perlmutter and Jack Willis, executive producers (PBS)

OUTSTANDING ACHIEVEMENT IN MAGAZINE-TYPE PROGRAMMING (INDIVIDUALS): Mike Wallace, correspondent, *60 Minutes* (CBS)

OUTSTANDING ACHIEVEMENT IN CULTURAL DOCUMENTARY PROGRAMMING (PROGRAMS): "The Everglades," Craig Fisher, producer (NBC); "The Making of Butch Cassidy & the Sundance Kid," Ronald Preissman, producer (NBC); "Arthur Penn, 1922– : Themes and Variants," Robert Hughes, producer (PBS)

OUTSTANDING ACHIEVEMENT IN CULTURAL DOCUMENTARY PROGRAMMING (INDIVIDUALS): Nana Mahomo, narrator, "A Black View of South Africa" (CBS); Robert Guenette and Theodore H. Strauss, writers, "They've Killed President Lincoln" (NBC); Robert Young, director, "The Eskimo: Fight for Life" (CBS)

SPECIAL CLASSIFICATION OF OUTSTANDING INDIVIDUAL ACHIEVEMENT: Harvey Korman, *The Carol Burnett Show* (CBS)

1971–1972 (presented May 6, 1972)

OUTSTANDING SERIES—COMEDY: *All in the Family,* Norman Lear, producer (CBS)

OUTSTANDING SERIES—DRAMA: *Elizabeth R [Masterpiece Theatre],* Christopher Sarson, executive producer; Roderick Graham, producer (PBS)

OUTSTANDING SINGLE PROGRAM—DRAMA OR COMEDY: "Brian's Song," *Movie of the Week,* Paul Junger Witt, producer (ABC)

OUTSTANDING VARIETY SERIES—MUSICAL: *The Carol Burnett Show,* Joe Hamilton, executive producer; Arnie Rosen, producer (CBS)

OUTSTANDING VARIETY SERIES—TALK: *The Dick Cavett Show,* John Gilroy, producer (ABC)

OUTSTANDING SINGLE PROGRAM (VARIETY AND POPULAR MUSIC): "Jack Lemmon in 'S Wonderful, 'S Marvelous, 'S Gershwin," *Bell System Family Theatre,* Joseph Cates, executive producer; Martin Charnin, producer (NBC)

OUTSTANDING SINGLE PROGRAM (CLASSICAL MUSIC): "Beethoven's Birthday: A Celebration in Vienna with Leonard Bernstein," James Krayer, executive producer; Humphrey Burton, producer (CBS)

OUTSTANDING NEW SERIES: *Elizabeth R* [*Masterpiece Theatre*], Christopher Sarson, executive producer; Roderick Graham, producer (PBS)

OUTSTANDING SINGLE PERFORMANCE BY AN ACTOR IN A LEADING ROLE: Keith Michell, "Catherine Howard," *The Six Wives of Henry VIII* (CBS)

OUTSTANDING SINGLE PERFORMANCE BY AN ACTRESS IN A LEADING ROLE: Glenda Jackson, "Shadow in the Sun," *Elizabeth R* [*Masterpiece Theatre*] (PBS)

OUTSTANDING CONTINUED PERFORMANCE BY AN ACTOR IN A LEADING ROLE IN A DRAMATIC SERIES: Peter Falk, *Columbo* [*NBC Mystery Movie*] (NBC)

OUTSTANDING CONTINUED PERFORMANCE BY AN ACTRESS IN A LEADING ROLE IN A DRAMATIC SERIES: Glenda Jackson, *Elizabeth R* [*Masterpiece Theatre*] (PBS)

OUTSTANDING CONTINUED PERFORMANCE BY AN ACTOR IN A LEADING ROLE IN A COMEDY SERIES: Carroll O'Connor, *All in the Family* (CBS)

OUTSTANDING CONTINUED PERFORMANCE BY AN ACTRESS IN A LEADING ROLE IN A COMEDY SERIES: Jean Stapleton, *All in the Family* (CBS)

OUTSTANDING PERFORMANCE BY AN ACTOR IN A SUPPORTING ROLE IN DRAMA: Jack Warden, "Brian's Song," *Movie of the Week* (ABC)

OUTSTANDING PERFORMANCE BY AN ACTRESS IN A SUPPORTING ROLE IN DRAMA: Jenny Agutter, "The Snow Goose," *Hallmark Hall of Fame* (NBC)

OUTSTANDING PERFORMANCE BY AN ACTOR IN A SUPPORTING ROLE IN COMEDY: Edward Asner, *The Mary Tyler Moore Show* (CBS)

OUTSTANDING PERFORMANCE BY AN ACTRESS IN A SUPPORTING ROLE IN COMEDY: (TIE) Valerie Harper, *The Mary Tyler Moore Show* (CBS); Sally Struthers, *All in the Family* (CBS)

OUTSTANDING ACHIEVEMENT BY A PERFORMER IN MUSIC OR VARIETY: Harvey Korman, *The Carol Burnett Show* (CBS)

OUTSTANDING ACHIEVEMENT WITHIN REGULARLY SCHEDULED NEWS PROGRAMS (PROGRAMS): "Defeat of Dacca," *The NBC Nightly News,* Wallace Westfeldt, executive producer; Robert Mulholland and David Teitelbaum, producers (NBC)

OUTSTANDING ACHIEVEMENT WITHIN REGULARLY SCHEDULED NEWS PROGRAMS (INDIVIDUALS): Phil Brady, reporter, "Defeat of Dacca," *The NBC Nightly News* (NBC); Bob Schieffer, Phil Jones, Don Webster, and Bill Plante, correspondents, "The Air War," *The CBS Evening News with Walter Cronkite* (CBS)

OUTSTANDING ACHIEVEMENT FOR REGULARLY SCHEDULED MAGAZINE-TYPE PROGRAMS (PROGRAMS): *The Great American Dream Machine,* A. H. Perlmutter, executive producer (PBS); *Chronolog,* Eliot Frankel, executive producer (NBC)

OUTSTANDING ACHIEVEMENT FOR REGULARLY SCHEDULED MAGAZINE-TYPE PROGRAMS (INDIVIDUALS): Mike Wallace, correspondent, *60 Minutes* (CBS)

OUTSTANDING DOCUMENTARY PROGRAM ACHIEVEMENT (PROGRAMS OF CURRENT SIGNIFICANCE): "A Night in Jail, A Night in Court," *CBS Reports,* Burton Benjamin, executive producer; John Sharnik, producer (CBS). "This Child Is Rated X: An NBC News White Paper on Juvenile Justice," Martin Carr, producer (NBC)

OUTSTANDING DOCUMENTARY PROGRAM ACHIEVEMENT (CULTURAL PROGRAMS): "Hollywood: The Dream Factory," *The Monday Night Special,* Nicolas Noxon, executive producer; Irwin Rosten and Bud Friedman, producers (ABC). "A Sound of Dolphins," *The Undersea World of Jacques Cousteau,* Jacques Cousteau and Marshall Flaum, executive producers; Andy White, producer (ABC). "The Unsinkable Sea Otter," *The Undersea World of Jacques Cousteau,* Jacques Cousteau and Marshall Flaum, executive producers; Andy White, producer (ABC)

OUTSTANDING DOCUMENTARY PROGRAM ACHIEVEMENT (INDIVIDUALS): Louis J. Hazam, writer, "Venice Be Damned" (NBC); Robert Northshield, writer, "Suffer the Little Children—An NBC News White Paper on Northern Ireland" (NBC)

OUTSTANDING DIRECTORIAL ACHIEVEMENT IN DRAMA (SERIES): Alexander Singer, "The Invasion of Kevin Ireland," *The Lawyers* [*The Bold Ones*] (NBC)

OUTSTANDING DIRECTORIAL ACHIEVEMENT IN DRAMA (SINGLE PROGRAM): Tom Gries, "The Glass House," *The New CBS Friday Night Movies* (CBS)

OUTSTANDING DIRECTORIAL ACHIEVEMENT IN COMEDY (SERIES): John Rich, "Sammy's Visit," *All in the Family* (CBS)

OUTSTANDING DIRECTORIAL ACHIEVEMENT IN VARIETY OR MUSIC (SERIES): Art Fisher, *The Sonny and Cher Comedy Hour,* with Tony Randall, 1/31/72 (CBS)

OUTSTANDING DIRECTORIAL ACHIEVEMENT IN COMEDY, VARIETY, OR MUSIC (SPECIAL): Walter C. Miller and Martin Charnin, "Jack Lemmon in 'S Wonderful, 'S Marvelous, 'S Gershwin," *Bell System Family Theatre* (NBC)

OUTSTANDING WRITING ACHIEVEMENT IN DRAMA (SERIES): Richard L. Levinson and William Link, "Death Lends a Hand," *Columbo* [*NBC Mystery Movie*] (NBC)

OUTSTANDING WRITING ACHIEVEMENT IN DRAMA, ORIGINAL TELEPLAY: Allan Sloane, "To All My Friends on Shore" (CBS)

OUTSTANDING WRITING ACHIEVEMENT IN DRAMA, ADAPTATION: William Blinn, "Brian's Song," *Movie of the Week* (ABC)

OUTSTANDING WRITING ACHIEVEMENT IN COMEDY (SERIES): Burt Styler, "Edith's Problem," *All in the Family* (CBS)

OUTSTANDING WRITING ACHIEVEMENT IN VARIETY OR MUSIC (SERIES): Don Hinkley, Stan Hart, Larry Siegel, Woody Kling, Roger Beatty, Art Baer, Ben Joelson, Stan Burns, Mike Marmer, and Arnie Rosen, *The Carol Burnett Show,* with Tim Conway and Ray Charles, 1/26/72 (CBS)

OUTSTANDING WRITING ACHIEVEMENT IN COMEDY, VARIETY, OR MUSIC (SPECIAL): Anne Howard Bailey, "The Trial of Mary Lincoln," *NET Opera Theatre* (PBS)

SPECIAL CLASSIFICATION OF OUTSTANDING PROGRAM AND INDIVIDUAL ACHIEVEMENT (GENERAL PRO-GRAMMING): "The Pentagon Papers," *PBS Special,* David Prowitt, executive producer; Martin Clancy, producer (PBS)

SPECIAL CLASSIFICATION OF OUTSTANDING PROGRAM AND INDIVIDUAL ACHIEVEMENT (DOCU-DRAMA): "-The Search for the Nile—Parts I–VI," Christopher Railing, producer (NBC)

SPECIAL CLASSIFICATION OF OUTSTANDING PROGRAM AND INDIVIDUAL ACHIEVEMENT (INDIVIDUALS): Michael Hastings and Derek Marlowe, writers, "The Search for the Nile—Parts I–VI" (NBC)

1972–1973 (presented May 22, 1973)

OUTSTANDING COMEDY SERIES: *All in the Family,* Norman Lear, executive producer; John Rich, producer (CBS)

OUTSTANDING DRAMA SERIES—CONTINUING: *The Waltons,* Lee Rich, executive producer; Robert L. Jacks, producer (CBS)

OUTSTANDING DRAMA/COMEDY—LIMITED EPISODES: *Tom Brown's Schooldays* [*Masterpiece Theatre*], John D. McRae, producer (PBS)

OUTSTANDING VARIETY MUSICAL SERIES: *The Julie Andrews Hour,* Nick Vanoff and William O. Harbach, producers (ABC)

OUTSTANDING SINGLE PROGRAM—DRAMA OR COMEDY: "A War of Children," *The New CBS Tuesday Night Movies,* Roger Gimbel, executive producer; George Schaefer, producer (CBS)

OUTSTANDING SINGLE PROGRAM—VARIETY AND POPULAR MUSIC: "Singer Presents Liza with a 'Z'," Bob Fosse and Fred Ebb, producers (NBC)

OUTSTANDING SINGLE PROGRAM—CLASSICAL MUSIC: "The Sleeping Beauty," J. W. Barnes and Robert Kotlowitz, executive producers; Norman Campbell, producer (PBS)

OUTSTANDING NEW SERIES: *America,* Michael Gill, producer (NBC)

OUTSTANDING SINGLE PERFORMANCE BY AN ACTOR IN A LEADING ROLE: Laurence Olivier, "A Long Day's Journey into Night" (ABC)

OUTSTANDING SINGLE PERFORMANCE BY AN ACTRESS IN A LEADING ROLE: Cloris Leachman, "A Brand New Life," *Tuesday Movie of the Week* (ABC)

OUTSTANDING CONTINUED PERFORMANCE BY AN ACTOR IN A LEADING ROLE (DRAMA SERIES—CONTINUING): Richard Thomas, *The Waltons* (CBS)

OUTSTANDING CONTINUED PERFORMANCE BY AN ACTOR IN A LEADING ROLE (DRAMA/COMEDY—LIMITED EPISODES): Anthony Murphy, *Tom Brown's Schooldays* [*Masterpiece Theatre*] (PBS)

OUTSTANDING CONTINUED PERFORMANCE BY AN ACTRESS IN A LEADING ROLE (DRAMA SERIES—CONTINUING): Michael Learned, *The Waltons* (CBS)

OUTSTANDING CONTINUED PERFORMANCE BY AN ACTRESS IN A LEADING ROLE (DRAMA/COMEDY—LIMITED EPISODES): Susan Hampshire, *Vanity Fair* [*Masterpiece Theatre*] (PBS)

OUTSTANDING CONTINUED PERFORMANCE BY AN ACTOR IN A LEADING ROLE IN A COMEDY SERIES: Jack Klugman, *The Odd Couple* (ABC)

OUTSTANDING CONTINUED PERFORMANCE BY AN ACTRESS IN A LEADING ROLE IN A COMEDY SERIES: Mary Tyler Moore, *The Mary Tyler Moore Show* (CBS)

OUTSTANDING PERFORMANCE BY AN ACTOR IN A SUPPORTING ROLE IN DRAMA: Scott Jacoby, "That Certain Summer," *Wednesday Movie of the Week* (ABC)

OUTSTANDING PERFORMANCE BY AN ACTRESS IN A SUPPORTING ROLE IN DRAMA: Ellen Corby, *The Waltons* (CBS)

OUTSTANDING PERFORMANCE BY AN ACTOR IN A SUPPORTING ROLE IN COMEDY: Ted Knight, *The Mary Tyler Moore Show* (CBS)

OUTSTANDING PERFORMANCE BY AN ACTRESS IN A SUPPORTING ROLE IN COMEDY: Valerie Harper, *The Mary Tyler Moore Show* (CBS)

OUTSTANDING ACHIEVEMENT BY A SUPPORTING PERFORMER IN MUSIC OR VARIETY: Tim Conway, *The Carol Burnett Show,* 2/17/73 (CBS)

OUTSTANDING DIRECTORIAL ACHIEVEMENT IN DRAMA (SERIES): Jerry Thorpe, "An Eye for an Eye," *Kung Fu* (ABC)

OUTSTANDING DIRECTORIAL ACHIEVEMENT IN DRAMA (SINGLE PROGRAM): Joseph Sargent, "The Marcus-Nelson Murders," *The CBS Thursday Night Movies* (CBS)

OUTSTANDING DIRECTORIAL ACHIEVEMENT IN COMEDY (SERIES): Jay Sandrich, "It's Whether You Win or Lose," *The Mary Tyler Moore Show* (CBS)

OUTSTANDING DIRECTORIAL ACHIEVEMENT IN VARIETY OR MUSIC (SERIES): Bill Davis, *The Julie Andrews Hour*, with "Liza Doolittle" and "Mary Poppins," 9/13/72 (ABC)

OUTSTANDING DIRECTORIAL ACHIEVEMENT IN VARIETY OR MUSIC (SPECIAL): Bob Fosse, "Singer Presents Liza with a 'Z' " (NBC)

OUTSTANDING WRITING ACHIEVEMENT IN DRAMA (SERIES): John McGreevey, "The Scholar," *The Waltons* (CBS)

OUTSTANDING WRITING ACHIEVEMENT IN DRAMA, ORIGINAL TELEPLAY (SINGLE PROGRAM): Abby Mann, "The Marcus-Nelson Murders," *The CBS Thursday Night Movies* (CBS)

OUTSTANDING WRITING ACHIEVEMENT IN DRAMA, ADAPTATION (SINGLE PROGRAM): Eleanor Perry, "The House without a Christmas Tree" (CBS)

OUTSTANDING WRITING ACHIEVEMENT IN COMEDY (SERIES): Michael Ross, Bernie West, and Lee Kalcheim, "The Bunkers and the Swingers," *All in the Family* (CBS)

OUTSTANDING WRITING ACHIEVEMENT IN VARIETY OR MUSIC (SERIES): Stan Hart, Larry Siegel, Gail Parent, Woody Kling, Roger Beatty, Tom Patchett, Jay Tarses, Robert Hilliard, Arnie Kogen, Bill Angelos, and Buz Kohan, *The Carol Burnett Show*, with Steve Lawrence and Lily Tomlin, 11/8/72 (CBS)

OUTSTANDING WRITING ACHIEVEMENT IN COMEDY, VARIETY, OR MUSIC (SPECIAL): Renee Taylor and Joseph Bologna, "Acts of Love—And Other Comedies" (ABC)

OUTSTANDING ACHIEVEMENT WITHIN REGULARLY SCHEDULED NEWS PROGRAMS (PROGRAM SEGMENTS): "The U.S./Soviet Wheat Deal: Is There a Scandal?" *The CBS Evening News with Walter Cronkite*, Paul Greenberg and Russ Bensley, executive producers; Stanhope Gould and Linda Mason, producers (CBS)

OUTSTANDING ACHIEVEMENT WITHIN REGULARLY SCHEDULED NEWS PROGRAMS (INDIVIDUALS): Walter Cronkite, Dan Rather, Daniel Schorr, and Joel Blocker, correspondents, "The Watergate Affair," *CBS Evening News with Walter Cronkite* (CBS); David Dick, Dan Rather, Roger Mudd, and Walter Cronkite, correspondents, "Coverage of the Shooting of Governor Wallace," *CBS Evening News with Walter Cronkite* (CBS); Eric Sevareid, correspondent, "LBJ—The Man and the President," *CBS Evening News with Walter Cronkite* (CBS)

OUTSTANDING ACHIEVEMENT FOR REGULARLY SCHEDULED MAGAZINE-TYPE PROGRAMS (PROGRAMS): "Poppy Fields of Turkey—The Heroin Labs of Marseilles—The New York Connection," *60 Minutes*, Don Hewitt, executive producer; William McClure, John Tiffin, and Philip Scheffler, producers (CBS). "The Selling of Colonel Herbert," *60 Minutes*, Don Hewitt, executive producer; Barry Lando, producer (CBS). *60 Minutes*, Don Hewitt, executive producer (CBS)

OUTSTANDING ACHIEVEMENT FOR REGULARLY SCHEDULED MAGAZINE-TYPE PROGRAMS (INDIVIDUALS): Mike Wallace, correspondent, "The Selling of Colonel Herbert," *60 Minutes* (CBS); Mike Wallace, correspondent, *60 Minutes* (CBS)

OUTSTANDING ACHIEVEMENT IN COVERAGE OF SPECIAL EVENTS (INDIVIDUALS): Jim McKay, commentator, "Coverage of the Munich Olympic Tragedy," *ABC Special* (ABC)

OUTSTANDING DOCUMENTARY PROGRAM ACHIEVEMENT (CURRENT EVENTS): "The Blue Collar Trap," *NBC News White Paper*, Fred Freed, producer (NBC). "The Mexican Connection," *CBS Reports*, Burton Benjamin, executive producer; Jay McMullen, producer (CBS). "One Billion Dollar Weapon and Now the War Is Over—The American Military in the 1970's," *NBC Reports*, Fred Freed, executive producer; Al Davis, producer (NBC)

OUTSTANDING DOCUMENTARY PROGRAM ACHIEVEMENT (CULTURAL): *America*, Michael Gill, executive producer (NBC). "Jane Goodall and the World of Animal Behavior—The Wild Dogs of Africa," Marshall Flaum, executive producer; Hugo Van Lawick, Bill Travers, and James Hill, producers (ABC)

OUTSTANDING DOCUMENTARY PROGRAM ACHIEVEMENT (INDIVIDUALS): Alistair Cooke, narrator, *America* (NBC); Alistair Cooke, writer, "A Fireball in the Night," *America* (NBC); Hugo Van Lawick, director, "Jane Goodall and the World of Animal Behavior—The Wild Dogs of Africa" (ABC)

SPECIAL CLASSIFICATION OF OUTSTANDING PROGRAM AND INDIVIDUAL ACHIEVEMENT: *The Advocates*, Greg Harney, executive producer; Tom Burrows, Russ Morash, and Peter McGhee, producers (PBS). "VD Blues," *The Special of the Week*, Don Fouser, producer (PBS)

1973–1974 (presented May 28, 1974)

OUTSTANDING COMEDY SERIES: *M*A*S*H*, Gene Reynolds and Larry Gelbart, producers (CBS)

OUTSTANDING DRAMA SERIES: *Upstairs, Downstairs* [*Masterpiece Theatre*], Rex Firkin, executive producer; John Hawkesworth, producer (PBS)

OUTSTANDING MUSIC-VARIETY SERIES: *The Carol Burnett Show*, Joe Hamilton, executive producer; Ed Simmons, producer (CBS)

OUTSTANDING LIMITED SERIES: *Columbo* [*NBC Sunday Mystery Movie*], Dean Hargrove and Roland Kibbee, executive producers; Douglas Benton, Robert F. O'Neill, and Edward K. Dodds, producers (NBC)

945

OUTSTANDING SPECIAL—COMEDY OR DRAMA (SINGLE SPECIAL PROGRAM): "The Autobiography of Miss Jane Pittman," Robert Christiansen and Rick Rosenberg, producers (CBS)
OUTSTANDING COMEDY-VARIETY, VARIETY, OR MUSIC SPECIAL (SINGLE SPECIAL PROGRAM): "Lily," Irene Pinn, executive producer; Herb Sargent and Jerry McPhie, producers (CBS)
OUTSTANDING CHILDREN'S SPECIAL (EVENING): "Marlo Thomas and Friends in Free to Be . . . You and Me," Marlo Thomas and Carole Hart, producers (ABC)
BEST LEAD ACTOR IN A COMEDY SERIES: Alan Alda, *M*A*S*H* (CBS)
BEST LEAD ACTOR IN A DRAMA SERIES: Telly Savalas, *Kojak* (CBS)
BEST LEAD ACTOR IN A LIMITED SERIES: William Holden, *The Blue Knight* (NBC)
BEST LEAD ACTOR IN A DRAMA (FOR A SPECIAL PROGRAM—COMEDY OR DRAMA; OR A SINGLE APPEARANCE IN A COMEDY OR DRAMA SERIES): Hal Holbrook, "Pueblo," *ABC Theatre* (ABC)
ACTOR OF THE YEAR—SERIES: Alan Alda, *M*A*S*H* (CBS)
ACTOR OF THE YEAR—SPECIAL: Hal Holbrook, "Pueblo," *ABC Theatre* (ABC)
BEST LEAD ACTRESS IN A COMEDY SERIES: Mary Tyler Moore, *The Mary Tyler Moore Show* (CBS)
BEST LEAD ACTRESS IN A DRAMA SERIES: Michael Learned, *The Waltons* (CBS)
BEST LEAD ACTRESS IN A LIMITED SERIES: Mildred Natwick, *The Snoop Sisters* [*NBC Tuesday Mystery Movie*] (NBC)
BEST LEAD ACTRESS IN A DRAMA (FOR A SPECIAL PROGRAM—COMEDY OR DRAMA; OR A SINGLE APPEARANCE IN A COMEDY OR DRAMA SERIES): Cicely Tyson, "The Autobiography of Miss Jane Pittman" (CBS)
ACTRESS OF THE YEAR—SERIES: Mary Tyler Moore, *The Mary Tyler Moore Show* (CBS)
ACTRESS OF THE YEAR—SPECIAL: Cicely Tyson, "The Autobiography of Miss Jane Pittman" (CBS)
BEST SUPPORTING ACTOR IN COMEDY (FOR A SPECIAL PROGRAM; A ONE-TIME APPEARANCE IN A SERIES; OR A CONTINUING ROLE): Rob Reiner, *All in the Family* (CBS)
BEST SUPPORTING ACTOR IN DRAMA (FOR A SPECIAL PROGRAM; A ONE-TIME APPEARANCE IN A SERIES; OR A CONTINUING ROLE): Michael Moriarty, "The Glass Menagerie" (ABC)
BEST SUPPORTING ACTOR IN COMEDY-VARIETY, VARIETY, OR MUSIC (FOR A SPECIAL PROGRAM; A ONE-TIME APPEARANCE IN A SERIES; OR A CONTINUING ROLE): Harvey Korman, *The Carol Burnett Show* (CBS)
SUPPORTING ACTOR OF THE YEAR: Michael Moriarty, "The Glass Menagerie" (ABC)
BEST SUPPORTING ACTRESS IN COMEDY (FOR A SPECIAL PROGRAM; A ONE-TIME APPEARANCE IN A SERIES; OR A CONTINUING ROLE): Cloris Leachman, "The Lars Affair," *The Mary Tyler Moore Show*, 9/15/73 (CBS)
BEST SUPPORTING ACTRESS IN DRAMA (FOR A SPECIAL PROGRAM; A ONE-TIME APPEARANCE IN A SERIES; OR A CONTINUING ROLE): Joanna Miles, "The Glass Menagerie" (ABC)
BEST SUPPORTING ACTRESS IN COMEDY-VARIETY, VARIETY OR MUSIC (FOR A SPECIAL PROGRAM; A ONE-TIME APPEARANCE IN A SERIES; OR A CONTINUING ROLE): Brenda Vaccaro, "The Shape of Things" (CBS)
SUPPORTING ACTRESS OF THE YEAR: Joanna Miles, "The Glass Menagerie" (ABC)
BEST DIRECTING IN DRAMA (A SINGLE PROGRAM OF A SERIES WITH CONTINUING CHARACTERS AND/OR THEME): Robert Butler, *The Blue Knight*, PART III, 11/15/73 (NBC)
BEST DIRECTING IN DRAMA (A SINGLE PROGRAM—COMEDY OR DRAMA): John Korty, "The Autobiography of Miss Jane Pittman" (CBS)
BEST DIRECTING IN COMEDY (A SINGLE PROGRAM OF A SERIES WITH CONTINUING CHARACTERS AND/OR THEME): Jackie Cooper, "Carry On Hawkeye," *M*A*S*H*, 11/24/73 (CBS)
BEST DIRECTING IN VARIETY OR MUSIC (A SINGLE PROGRAM OF A SERIES): Dave Powers, "The Australia Show," *The Carol Burnett Show*, 12/8/73 (CBS)
BEST DIRECTING IN COMEDY-VARIETY, VARIETY, OR MUSIC (A SPECIAL PROGRAM): Dwight Hemion, "Barbra Streisand . . . And Other Musical Instruments" (CBS)
DIRECTOR OF THE YEAR—SERIES: Robert Butler, *The Blue Knight*, Part III, 11/15/73 (NBC)
DIRECTOR OF THE YEAR—SPECIAL: Dwight Hemion, "Barbra Streisand . . . And Other Musical Instruments" (CBS)
BEST WRITING IN DRAMA (A SINGLE PROGRAM OF A SERIES WITH CONTINUING CHARACTERS AND/OR THEME): Joanna Lee, "The Thanksgiving Story," *The Waltons*, 11/15/73 (CBS)
BEST WRITING IN DRAMA, ORIGINAL TELEPLAY (A SINGLE PROGRAM—COMEDY OR DRAMA): Fay Kanin, "Tell Me Where It Hurts," *G.E. Theater* (CBS)
BEST WRITING IN DRAMA, ADAPTATION (A SINGLE PROGRAM—COMEDY OR DRAMA): Tracy Keenan Wynn, "The Autobiography of Miss Jane Pittman" (CBS)
BEST WRITING IN COMEDY (A SINGLE PROGRAM OF A SERIES WITH CONTINUING CHARACTERS AND/OR THEME): Treva Silverman, "The Lou and Edie Story," *The Mary Tyler Moore Show*, 10/6/73 (CBS)
BEST WRITING IN VARIETY OR MUSIC (A SINGLE PROGRAM OF A SERIES): Ed Simmons, Gary Belkin, Roger Beatty, Arnie Kogen, Bill Richmond, Gene Perret, Rudy De Luca, Barry Levinson, Dick Clair, Jenna McMahon, and Barry Harman, *The Carol Burnett Show*, with Tim Conway and Bernadette Peters, 2/16/74 (CBS)

946

BEST WRITING IN COMEDY-VARIETY, VARIETY, OR MUSIC (A SPECIAL PROGRAM): Herb Sargent, Rosalyn Drexler, Lorne Michaels, Richard Pryor, Jim Rusk, James R. Stein, Robert Illes, Lily Tomlin, George Yanok, Jane Wagner, Rod Warren, Ann Elder, and Karyl Geld, "Lily" (CBS)

WRITER OF THE YEAR—SERIES: Treva Silverman, "The Lou and Edie Story," *The Mary Tyler Moore Show*, 10/6/73 (CBS)

WRITER OF THE YEAR—SPECIAL: Fay Kanin, "Tell Me Where It Hurts," *G.E. Theater* (CBS)

SPECIAL CLASSIFICATION OF OUTSTANDING PROGRAM AND INDIVIDUAL ACHIEVEMENT: *The Dick Cavett Show*, John Gilroy, producer (ABC); Tom Snyder, host, *Tomorrow* (NBC)

OUTSTANDING INDIVIDUAL ACHIEVEMENT IN CHILDREN'S PROGRAMMING: Charles M. Schultz, writer, "A Charlie Brown Thanksgiving" (CBS)

OUTSTANDING ACHIEVEMENT WITHIN REGULARLY SCHEDULED NEWS PROGRAMS: "Coverage of the October War from Israel's Northern Front," *CBS Evening News with Walter Cronkite*, John Laurence, correspondent, October 1973 (CBS). "The Agnew Resignation," *CBS Evening News with Walter Cronkite*, Paul Greenberg, executive producer; Ron Bonn, Ed Fouhy, John Lane, Don Bowers, John Armstrong, and Robert Mean, producers; Walter Cronkite, Robert Schakne, Fred Graham, Robert Pierpoint, Roger Mudd, Dan Rather, John Hart, and Eric Sevareid, correspondents, 10/10/73 (CBS). "The Key Biscayne Bank Charter Struggle," *CBS Evening News with Walter Cronkite*, Ed Fouhy, producer; Robert Pierpoint, correspondent, 10/15–10/17/73 (CBS). "Reports on World Hunger," *NBC Nightly News*, Lester M. Crystal, executive producer; Richard Fischer and Joseph Angotti, producers; Tom Streithorst, Phil Brady, John Palmer, and Liz Trotta, correspondents, March–June 1974 (NBC)

OUTSTANDING ACHIEVEMENT FOR REGULARLY SCHEDULED MAGAZINE-TYPE PROGRAMS: "America's Nerve Gas Arsenal," *First Tuesday*, Eliot Frankel, executive producer; William B. Hill and Anthony Potter, producers; Tom Pettit, correspondent, 6/5/73 (NBC). "The Adversaries," *Behind the Lines*, Carey Winfrey, executive producer; Peter Forbath, producer/reporter; Brendan Gill, host/moderator, 3/28/74 (PBS); "A Question of Impeachment," *Bill Moyers' Journal*, Jerome Toobin, executive producer; Martin Clancy, producer; Bill Moyers, broadcaster, 1/22/74 (PBS)

OUTSTANDING DOCUMENTARY PROGRAM ACHIEVEMENTS (CURRENT EVENTS): "Fire!," *ABC News Close Up*, Pamela Hill, producer; Jules Bergman, correspondent/narrator (ABC). "CBS News Special Report: The Senate and the Watergate Affair," Lesley Midgley, executive producer; Hal Haley, Bernard Birnbaum, and David Browning, producers; Dan Rather, Roger Mudd, Daniel Schorr, and Fred Graham, correspondents (CBS)

OUTSTANDING DOCUMENTARY PROGRAM ACHIEVEMENTS (CULTURAL): "Journey to the Outer Limits," *National Geographic Specials*, Nicholas Clapp and Dennis Kane, executive producers; Alex Grasshoff, producer (ABC). *The World at War*, Jeremy Isaacs, producer (syndicated). CBS "Reports: The Rockefellers," Burton Benjamin, executive producer; Howard Stringer, producer; Walter Cronkite, correspondent (CBS)

OUTSTANDING INTERVIEW PROGRAM (FOR A SINGLE PROGRAM OF A SERIES): "Solzhenitsyn," *CBS News Special*, Burton Benjamin, producer; Walter Cronkite, correspondent, 6/24/74 (CBS). "Henry Steele Commager," *Bill Moyers' Journal*, Jerome Toobin, executive producer; Martin Clancy, producer; Bill Moyers, broadcaster, 3/26/74 (PBS)

OUTSTANDING TELEVISION NEWS BROADCASTER: Harry Reasoner, *ABC News* (ABC); Bill Moyers, "Essay on Watergate," *Bill Moyers' Journal*, 10/31/73 (PBS)

1974–1975 (presented May 19, 1975)

OUTSTANDING COMEDY SERIES: *The Mary Tyler Moore Show*, James L. Brooks and Allan Burns, executive producers; Ed Weinberger and Stan Daniels, producers (CBS)

OUTSTANDING DRAMA SERIES: *Upstairs, Downstairs* [*Masterpiece Theatre*], Rex Firkin, executive producer; John Hawkesworth, producer (PBS)

OUTSTANDING COMEDY-VARIETY OR MUSIC SERIES: *The Carol Burnett Show*, Joe Hamilton, executive producer; Ed Simmons, producer (CBS)

OUTSTANDING LIMITED SERIES: *Benjamin Franklin*, Lewis Freedman, executive producer; George Lefferts and Glenn Jordan, producers (CBS)

OUTSTANDING SPECIAL—DRAMA OR COMEDY: "The Law," *NBC World Premiere Movie*, William Sackheim, producer, 10/22/74 (NBC)

OUTSTANDING SPECIAL—COMEDY-VARIETY OR MUSIC: "An Evening with John Denver," Jerry Weintraub, executive producer; Al Rogers and Rich Eustis, producers (ABC)

OUTSTANDING CLASSICAL MUSIC PROGRAM (FOR A SPECIAL PROGRAM OR FOR A SERIES): "Profile in Music: Beverly Sills," *Festival '75*, Patricia Foy, producer, 3/10/75 (PBS)

OUTSTANDING LEAD ACTOR IN A COMEDY SERIES: Tony Randall, *The Odd Couple* (ABC)

OUTSTANDING LEAD ACTOR IN A DRAMA SERIES: Robert Blake, *Baretta* (ABC)

OUTSTANDING LEAD ACTOR IN A LIMITED SERIES: Peter Falk, *Columbo* [*NBC Sunday Mystery Movie*] (NBC)

OUTSTANDING LEAD ACTOR IN A SPECIAL PROGRAM—DRAMA OR COMEDY (FOR A SPECIAL PROGRAM; OR

A SINGLE APPEARANCE IN A DRAMA OR COMEDY SERIES): Laurence Olivier, "Love Among the Ruins," *ABC Theatre* (ABC)

OUTSTANDING LEAD ACTRESS IN A COMEDY SERIES: Valerie Harper, *Rhoda* (CBS)

OUTSTANDING LEAD ACTRESS IN A DRAMA SERIES: Jean Marsh, *Upstairs, Downstairs* [*Masterpiece Theatre*] (PBS)

OUTSTANDING LEAD ACTRESS IN A LIMITED SERIES: Jessica Walter, *Amy Prentiss* [*NBC Sunday Mystery Movie*] (NBC)

OUTSTANDING LEAD ACTRESS IN A SPECIAL PROGRAM—DRAMA OR COMEDY (FOR A SPECIAL PROGRAM; OR A SINGLE APPEARANCE IN A DRAMA OR COMEDY SERIES): Katharine Hepburn, "Love Among the Ruins," *ABC Theatre* (ABC)

OUTSTANDING CONTINUING PERFORMANCE BY A SUPPORTING ACTOR IN A COMEDY SERIES: Ed Asner, *The Mary Tyler Moore Show* (CBS)

OUTSTANDING CONTINUING PERFORMANCE BY A SUPPORTING ACTOR IN A DRAMA SERIES: Will Geer, *The Waltons* (CBS)

OUTSTANDING CONTINUING OR SINGLE PERFORMANCE BY A SUPPORTING ACTOR IN VARIETY OR MUSIC (FOR A CONTINUING ROLE IN A REGULAR OR LIMITED SERIES; OR A ONE-TIME APPEARANCE IN A SERIES; OR A SPECIAL): Jack Albertson, *Cher*, 3/2/75 (CBS)

OUTSTANDING SINGLE PERFORMANCE BY A SUPPORTING ACTOR IN A COMEDY OR DRAMA SPECIAL: Anthony Quayle, "QB VII," Parts 1 & 2, *ABC Movie Special* (ABC)

OUTSTANDING SINGLE PERFORMANCE BY A SUPPORTING ACTOR IN A COMEDY OR DRAMA SERIES (FOR A ONE-TIME APPEARANCE IN A REGULAR OR LIMITED SERIES): Patrick McGoohan, "By Dawn's Early Light," *Columbo* [*NBC Sunday Mystery Movie*], 10/27/74 (NBC)

OUTSTANDING CONTINUING PERFORMANCE BY A SUPPORTING ACTRESS IN A COMEDY SERIES: Betty White, *The Mary Tyler Moore Show* (CBS)

OUTSTANDING CONTINUING PERFORMANCE BY A SUPPORTING ACTRESS IN A DRAMA SERIES: Ellen Corby, *The Waltons* (CBS)

OUTSTANDING CONTINUING OR SINGLE PERFORMANCE BY A SUPPORTING ACTRESS IN VARIETY OR MUSIC (FOR A CONTINUING ROLE IN A REGULAR OR LIMITED SERIES; OR A ONE-TIME APPEARANCE IN A SERIES; OR A SPECIAL): Cloris Leachman, *Cher*, 3/2/75 (CBS)

OUTSTANDING SINGLE PERFORMANCE BY A SUPPORTING ACTRESS IN A COMEDY OR DRAMA SPECIAL: Juliet Mills, "QB VII," Parts 1 & 2, *ABC Movie Special* (ABC)

OUTSTANDING SINGLE PERFORMANCE BY A SUPPORTING ACTRESS IN A COMEDY OR DRAMA SERIES (FOR A ONE-TIME APPEARANCE IN A REGULAR OR LIMITED SERIES): (TIE) Cloris Leachman, "Phyllis Whips Inflation," *The Mary Tyler Moore Show*, 1/18/75 (CBS); Zohra Lampert, "Queen of the Gypsies," *Kojak*, 1/19/75 (CBS)

OUTSTANDING DIRECTING IN A DRAMA SERIES (A SINGLE EPISODE OF A REGULAR OR LIMITED SERIES WITH CONTINUING CHARACTERS AND/OR THEME): Bill Bain, "A Sudden Storm," *Upstairs, Downstairs* [*Masterpiece Theatre*], 12/22/74 (PBS)

OUTSTANDING DIRECTING IN A COMEDY SERIES (A SINGLE EPISODE OF A REGULAR OR LIMITED SERIES WITH CONTINUING CHARACTERS AND/OR THEME): Gene Reynolds, "O.R." *M*A*S*H*, 10/8/74 (CBS)

OUTSTANDING DIRECTING IN A COMEDY-VARIETY OR MUSIC SERIES (A SINGLE EPISODE OF A REGULAR OR LIMITED SERIES): Dave Powers, *The Carol Burnett Show*, with Alan Alda, 12/21/74 (CBS)

OUTSTANDING DIRECTING IN A COMEDY-VARIETY OR MUSICAL SPECIAL: Bill Davis, "An Evening with John Denver" (ABC)

OUTSTANDING DIRECTING IN A SPECIAL PROGRAM—DRAMA OR COMEDY: George Cukor, "Love Among the Ruins," *ABC Theatre* (ABC)

OUTSTANDING WRITING IN A DRAMA SERIES (A SINGLE EPISODE OF A REGULAR OR LIMITED SERIES WITH CONTINUING CHARACTERS AND/OR THEME): Howard Fast, "The Ambassador," *Benjamin Franklin*, 11/21/74 (CBS)

OUTSTANDING WRITING IN A COMEDY SERIES (A SINGLE EPISODE OF A REGULAR OR LIMITED SERIES WITH CONTINUING CHARACTERS AND/OR THEME): Ed Weinberger and Stan Daniels, "Mary Richards Goes to Jail," *The Mary Tyler Moore Show*, 9/14/74 (CBS)

OUTSTANDING WRITING IN A COMEDY-VARIETY OR MUSIC SERIES (A SINGLE EPISODE OF A REGULAR OR LIMITED SERIES): Ed Simmons, Gary Belkin, Roger Beatty, Arnie Kogen, Bill Richmond, Gene Perret, Rudy De Luca, Barry Levinson, Dick Clair, and Jenna McMahon, *The Carol Burnett Show*, with Alan Alda, 12/21/74 (CBS)

OUTSTANDING WRITING IN A COMEDY-VARIETY OR MUSIC SPECIAL: Bob Wells, John Bradford, and Cy Coleman, "Shirley MacLaine: If They Could See Me Now" (CBS)

OUTSTANDING WRITING IN A SPECIAL PROGRAM—DRAMA OR COMEDY—ORIGINAL TELEPLAY: James Costigan, "Love Among the Ruins," *ABC Theatre* (ABC)

OUTSTANDING WRITING IN A SPECIAL PROGRAM—DRAMA OR COMEDY—ADAPTATION: David W. Rintels, "IBM Presents Clarence Darrow" (NBC)

OUTSTANDING CHILDREN'S SPECIAL (EVENING): "Yes Virginia, There Is a Santa Claus," Burt Rosen, executive producer; Bill Melendez and Mort Green, producers (ABC)

SPECIAL CLASSIFICATION OF OUTSTANDING PROGRAM ACHIEVEMENT: "The American Film Institute Salute to James Cagney," George Stevens, Jr., executive producer; Paul W. Keyes, producer (CBS)

SPECIAL CLASSIFICATION OF OUTSTANDING INDIVIDUAL ACHIEVEMENT: Alistair Cooke, host, *Masterpiece Theatre* (PBS)

1975–1976 (presented May 17, 1976)

OUTSTANDING COMEDY SERIES: *The Mary Tyler Moore Show,* James L. Brooks and Allan Burns, executive producers; Ed Weinberger and Stan Daniels, producers (CBS)

OUTSTANDING DRAMA SERIES: *Police Story,* David Gerber and Stanley Kallis, executive producers; Liam O'Brien and Carl Pingitore, producers (NBC)

OUTSTANDING COMEDY-VARIETY OR MUSIC SERIES: *NBC's Saturday Night Live,* Lorne Michaels, producer (NBC)

OUTSTANDING LIMITED SERIES: *Upstairs, Downstairs* [*Masterpiece Theatre*], Rex Firkin, executive producer; John Hawkesworth, producer (PBS)

OUTSTANDING SPECIAL—DRAMA OR COMEDY: "Eleanor and Franklin," *ABC Theatre,* David Susskind, executive producer; Harry Sherman and Audrey Mass, producers (ABC)

OUTSTANDING SPECIAL—COMEDY-VARIETY OR MUSIC: "Gypsy in My Soul," William O. Harbach, executive producer; Cy Coleman and Fred Ebb, producers (CBS)

OUTSTANDING CLASSICAL MUSIC PROGRAM: "Bernstein and the New York Philharmonic," *Great Performances,* Klaus Hallig and Harry Kraut, executive producers; David Griffiths, producer, 11/26/75 (PBS)

OUTSTANDING LEAD ACTOR IN A COMEDY SERIES: Jack Albertson, *Chico and the Man* (NBC)

OUTSTANDING LEAD ACTOR IN A DRAMA SERIES: Peter Falk, *Columbo* [*NBC Sunday Mystery Movie*] (NBC)

OUTSTANDING LEAD ACTOR IN A LIMITED SERIES: Hal Holbrook, "Sandburg's Lincoln" (NBC)

OUTSTANDING LEAD ACTOR IN A DRAMA OR COMEDY SPECIAL: Anthony Hopkins, "The Lindbergh Kidnapping Case," *NBC World Premiere Movie* (NBC)

OUTSTANDING LEAD ACTOR FOR A SINGLE APPEARANCE IN A DRAMA OR COMEDY SERIES: Edward Asner, *Rich Man, Poor Man,* 2/1/76 (ABC)

OUTSTANDING LEAD ACTRESS IN A COMEDY SERIES: Mary Tyler Moore, *The Mary Tyler Moore Show* (CBS)

OUTSTANDING LEAD ACTRESS IN A DRAMA SERIES: Michael Learned, *The Waltons* (CBS)

OUTSTANDING LEAD ACTRESS IN A LIMITED SERIES: Rosemary Harris, *Notorious Woman* [*Masterpiece Theatre*] (PBS)

OUTSTANDING LEAD ACTRESS IN A DRAMA OR COMEDY SPECIAL: Susan Clark, "Babe" (CBS)

OUTSTANDING LEAD ACTRESS FOR A SINGLE APPEARANCE IN A DRAMA OR COMEDY SERIES: Kathryn Walker, "John Adams, Lawyer," *The Adams Chronicles,* 1/20/76 (PBS)

OUTSTANDING CONTINUING PERFORMANCE BY A SUPPORTING ACTOR IN A COMEDY SERIES: Ted Knight, *The Mary Tyler Moore Show* (CBS)

OUTSTANDING CONTINUING PERFORMANCE BY A SUPPORTING ACTOR IN A DRAMA SERIES: Anthony Zerbe, *Harry-O* (ABC)

OUTSTANDING CONTINUING OR SINGLE PERFORMANCE BY A SUPPORTING ACTOR IN VARIETY OR MUSIC: Chevy Chase, *NBC's Saturday Night Live,* 1/17/76 (NBC)

OUTSTANDING SINGLE PERFORMANCE BY A SUPPORTING ACTOR IN A COMEDY OR DRAMA SPECIAL: Ed Flanders, "A Moon for the Misbegotten," *ABC Theatre* (ABC)

OUTSTANDING SINGLE PERFORMANCE BY A SUPPORTING ACTOR IN A COMEDY OR DRAMA SERIES: Gordon Jackson, "The Beastly Hun," *Upstairs, Downstairs* [*Masterpiece Theatre*], 1/18/76 (PBS)

OUTSTANDING CONTINUING PERFORMANCE BY A SUPPORTING ACTRESS IN A COMEDY SERIES: Betty White, *The Mary Tyler Moore Show* (CBS)

OUTSTANDING CONTINUING PERFORMANCE BY A SUPPORTING ACTRESS IN A DRAMA SERIES: Ellen Corby, *The Waltons* (CBS)

OUTSTANDING CONTINUING OR SINGLE PERFORMANCE BY A SUPPORTING ACTRESS IN VARIETY OR MUSIC: Vicki Lawrence, *The Carol Burnett Show,* 2/7/76 (CBS)

OUTSTANDING SINGLE PERFORMANCE BY A SUPPORTING ACTRESS IN A COMEDY OR DRAMA SPECIAL: Rosemary Murphy, "Eleanor and Franklin," *ABC Theatre* (ABC)

OUTSTANDING SINGLE PERFORMANCE BY A SUPPORTING ACTRESS IN A COMEDY OR DRAMA SERIES: Fionnula Flanagan, *Rich Man, Poor Man,* 2/2/76 (ABC)

OUTSTANDING DIRECTING IN A DRAMA SERIES (A SINGLE EPISODE OF A REGULAR OR LIMITED SERIES WITH CONTINUING CHARACTERS AND/OR THEME): David Greene, "Episode 8," *Rich Man, Poor Man,* 3/15/76 (ABC)

OUTSTANDING DIRECTING IN A COMEDY SERIES (A SINGLE EPISODE OF A REGULAR OR LIMITED SERIES WITH

CONTINUING CHARACTERS AND/OR THEME): Gene Reynolds, "Welcome to Korea," *M*A*S*H,* 9/12/75 (CBS)

OUTSTANDING DIRECTING IN A COMEDY-VARIETY OR MUSIC SERIES (A SINGLE EPISODE OF A REGULAR OR LIMITED SERIES): Dave Wilson, *NBC's Saturday Night Live,* with host Paul Simon, 10/18/75 (NBC)

OUTSTANDING DIRECTING IN A COMEDY-VARIETY OR MUSIC SPECIAL: Dwight Hemion, "Steve and Eydie: 'Our Love Is Here to Stay' " (CBS)

OUTSTANDING DIRECTING IN A SPECIAL PROGRAM—DRAMA OR COMEDY: Daniel Petrie, "Eleanor and Franklin," *ABC Theatre* (ABC)

OUTSTANDING WRITING IN A DRAMA SERIES (A SINGLE EPISODE OF A REGULAR OR LIMITED SERIES WITH CONTINUING CHARACTERS AND/OR THEME): Sherman Yellen, "John Adams, Lawyer," *The Adams Chronicles,* 1/20/76 (PBS)

OUTSTANDING WRITING IN A COMEDY SERIES (A SINGLE EPISODE OF A REGULAR OR LIMITED SERIES WITH CONTINUING CHARACTERS AND/OR THEME): David Lloyd, "Chuckles Bites the Dust," *The Mary Tyler Moore Show,* 10/25/75 (CBS)

OUTSTANDING WRITING IN A COMEDY-VARIETY OR MUSIC SERIES (A SINGLE EPISODE OF A REGULAR OR LIMITED SERIES): Anne Beatts, Chevy Chase, Al Franken, Tom Davis, Lorne Michaels, Marilyn Suzanne Miller, Michael O'Donoghue, Herb Sargent, Tom Schiller, Rosie Schuster, and Alan Zweibel, *NBC's Saturday Night Live,* with host Elliott Gould, 1/10/76 (NBC)

OUTSTANDING WRITING IN A COMEDY-VARIETY OR MUSIC SPECIAL: Jane Wagner, Lorne Michaels, Ann Elder, Christopher Guest, Earl Pomerantz, Jim Rusk, Lily Tomlin, Rod Warren, and George Yanok, "Lily Tomlin" (ABC)

OUTSTANDING WRITING IN A SPECIAL PROGRAM—DRAMA OR COMEDY—ORIGINAL TELEPLAY: James Costigan, "Eleanor and Franklin," *ABC Theatre* (ABC)

OUTSTANDING WRITING IN A SPECIAL PROGRAM—DRAMA OR COMEDY—ADAPTATION: David W. Rintels, "Fear on Trial" (CBS)

OUTSTANDING EVENING CHILDREN'S SPECIAL: "You're a Good Sport, Charlie Brown," Lee Mendelson, executive producer; Bill Melendez, producer (CBS). "Huckleberry Finn," Steven North, producer (ABC)

SPECIAL CLASSIFICATION OF OUTSTANDING PROGRAM AND INDIVIDUAL ACHIEVEMENT: *Bicentennial Minutes,* Bob Markell, executive producer; Gareth Davies and Paul Walgner, producers (CBS). *The Tonight Show Starring Johnny Carson,* Fred De Cordova, producer (NBC). Ann Marcus, Jerry Adelman, and Daniel Gregory Browne, writers, *Mary Hartman, Mary Hartman* (syndicated)

1976–1977 (presented September 12, 1977)

OUTSTANDING COMEDY SERIES: *The Mary Tyler Moore Show,* Allan Burns and James L. Brooks, executive producers; Ed Weinberger and Stan Daniels, producers (CBS)

OUTSTANDING DRAMA SERIES: *Upstairs, Downstairs* [*Masterpiece Theatre*], John Hawkesworth and Joan Sullivan, producers (PBS)

OUTSTANDING COMEDY-VARIETY OR MUSIC SERIES: *Van Dyke and Company,* Byron Paul, executive producer; Alan Blye and Bob Einstein, producers (NBC)

OUTSTANDING LIMITED SERIES: *Roots* [*ABC Novel for Television*], David L. Wolper, executive producer; Stan Margulies, producer (ABC)

OUTSTANDING SPECIAL—DRAMA OR COMEDY: "Eleanor and Franklin: The White House Years," *ABC Theatre,* David Susskind, executive producer; Harry R. Sherman, producer (ABC). "Sybil," *The Big Event/NBC World Premiere Movie,* Peter Dunne and Philip Capice, executive producers; Jacqueline Babbin, producer (NBC)

OUTSTANDING SPECIAL—COMEDY-VARIETY OR MUSIC: "The Barry Manilow Special," Miles Lourie, executive producer; Steve Binder, producer (ABC)

OUTSTANDING CLASSICAL PROGRAM IN THE PERFORMING ARTS: "American Ballet Theatre: Swan Lake Live from Lincoln Center," *Great Performances,* John Goberman, producer, 6/30/76 (PBS)

OUTSTANDING LEAD ACTOR IN A COMEDY SERIES: Carroll O'Connor, *All in the Family* (CBS)

OUTSTANDING LEAD ACTOR IN A DRAMA SERIES: James Garner, *The Rockford Files* (NBC)

OUTSTANDING LEAD ACTOR IN A LIMITED SERIES: Christopher Plummer, "The Moneychangers," *The Big Event/NBC World Premiere Movie* (NBC)

OUTSTANDING LEAD ACTOR IN A DRAMA OR COMEDY SPECIAL: Ed Flanders, "Harry S Truman: Plain Speaking" (PBS)

OUTSTANDING LEAD ACTOR FOR A SINGLE APPEARANCE IN A DRAMA OR COMEDY SERIES: Louis Gossett, Jr., *Roots*—Part Two, 1/24/77 (ABC)

OUTSTANDING LEAD ACTRESS IN A COMEDY SERIES: Beatrice Arthur, *Maude* (CBS)

OUTSTANDING LEAD ACTRESS IN A DRAMA SERIES: Lindsay Wagner, *The Bionic Woman* (ABC)

OUTSTANDING LEAD ACTRESS IN A LIMITED SERIES: Patty Duke Astin, *Captains and the Kings, NBC's Best Sellers* (NBC)

OUTSTANDING LEAD ACTRESS IN A DRAMA OR COMEDY SPECIAL: Sally Field, "Sybil," *The Big Event/NBC World Premiere Movie* (NBC)

950

OUTSTANDING LEAD ACTRESS FOR A SINGLE APPEARANCE IN A DRAMA OR COMEDY SERIES: Beulah Bondi, "The Pony Cart," *The Waltons*, 12/2/76 (CBS)

OUTSTANDING CONTINUING PERFORMANCE BY A SUPPORTING ACTOR IN A COMEDY SERIES: Gary Burghoff, *M*A*S*H* (CBS)

OUTSTANDING CONTINUING PERFORMANCE BY A SUPPORTING ACTOR IN A DRAMA SERIES: Gary Frank, *Family* (ABC)

OUTSTANDING CONTINUING OR SINGLE PERFORMANCE BY A SUPPORTING ACTOR IN VARIETY OR MUSIC: Tim Conway, *The Carol Burnett Show* (CBS)

OUTSTANDING PERFORMANCE BY A SUPPORTING ACTOR IN A COMEDY OR DRAMA SPECIAL: Burgess Meredith, "Tailgunner Joe," *The Big Event*, 2/6/77 (NBC)

OUTSTANDING SINGLE PERFORMANCE BY A SUPPORTING ACTOR IN A COMEDY OR DRAMA SERIES: Edward Asner, *Roots*—Part One, 1/23/77 (ABC)

OUTSTANDING CONTINUING PERFORMANCE BY A SUPPORTING ACTRESS IN A COMEDY SERIES: Mary Kay Place, *Mary Hartman, Mary Hartman* (syndicated)

OUTSTANDING CONTINUING PERFORMANCE BY A SUPPORTING ACTRESS IN A DRAMA SERIES: Kristy McNichol, *Family* (ABC)

OUTSTANDING CONTINUING OR SINGLE PERFORMANCE BY A SUPPORTING ACTRESS IN VARIETY OR MUSIC: Rita Moreno, *The Muppet Show* (syndicated)

OUTSTANDING PERFORMANCE BY A SUPPORTING ACTRESS IN A COMEDY OR DRAMA SPECIAL: Diana Hyland, "The Boy in the Plastic Bubble," *The ABC Friday Night Movie*, 11/12/76 (ABC)

OUTSTANDING SINGLE PERFORMANCE BY A SUPPORTING ACTRESS IN A COMEDY OR DRAMA SERIES: Olivia Cole, *Roots*—Part Eight, 1/30/77 (ABC)

OUTSTANDING DIRECTING IN A DRAMA SERIES (A SINGLE EPISODE OF A REGULAR OR LIMITED SERIES WITH CONTINUING CHARACTERS AND/OR THEME): David Greene, *Roots*—Part One, 1/23/77 (ABC)

OUTSTANDING DIRECTING IN A COMEDY SERIES (A SINGLE EPISODE OF A REGULAR OR LIMITED SERIES WITH CONTINUING CHARACTERS AND/OR THEME): Alan Alda, "Dear Sigmund," *M*A*S*H*, 11/9/76 (CBS)

OUTSTANDING DIRECTING IN A COMEDY-VARIETY OR MUSIC SERIES (A SINGLE EPISODE OF A REGULAR OR LIMITED SERIES): Dave Powers, *The Carol Burnett Show*, with Eydie Gorme, 2/12/77 (CBS)

OUTSTANDING DIRECTING IN A COMEDY-VARIETY OR MUSIC SPECIAL: Dwight Hemion, "America Salutes Richard Rodgers: The Sound of His Music" (CBS)

OUTSTANDING DIRECTING IN A SPECIAL PROGRAM—DRAMA OR COMEDY: Daniel Petrie, "Eleanor and Franklin: The White House Years," *ABC Theatre* (ABC)

OUTSTANDING WRITING IN A DRAMA SERIES (A SINGLE EPISODE OF A REGULAR OR LIMITED SERIES WITH CONTINUING CHARACTERS ANDOR THEME): William Blinn, *Roots*—Part Two, 1/24/77 (ABC)

OUTSTANDING WRITING IN A COMEDY SERIES (A SINGLE EPISODE OF A REGULAR OR LIMITED SERIES WITH CONTINUING CHARACTERS AND/OR THEME): Allan Burns, James L. Brooks, Ed Weinberger, Stan Daniels, David Lloyd, and Bob Ellison, "The Final Show," *The Mary Tyler Moore Show*, 3/19/77 (CBS)

OUTSTANDING WRITING IN A COMEDY-VARIETY OR MUSIC SERIES (A SINGLE EPISODE OF A REGULAR OR LIMITED SERIES): Anne Beatts, Dan Aykroyd, Al Franken, Tom Davis, James Downey, Lorne Michaels, Marilyn Suzanne Miller, Michael O'Donoghue, Herb Sargent, Tom Schiller, Rosie Schuster, Alan Zweibel, John Belushi, and Bill Murray, *NBC's Saturday Night Live*, with host Sissy Spacek, 3/12/77 (NBC)

OUTSTANDING WRITING IN A COMEDY-VARIETY OR MUSIC SPECIAL: Alan Buz Kohan and Ted Strauss, "America Salutes Richard Rodgers: The Sound of His Music" (CBS)

OUTSTANDING WRITING IN A SPECIAL PROGRAM—DRAMA OR COMEDY—ORIGINAL TELEPLAY: Lane Slate, "Tailgunner Joe," *The Big Event*, 2/6/77 (NBC)

OUTSTANDING WRITING IN A SPECIAL PROGRAM—DRAMA OR COMEDY—ADAPTATION: Stewart Stern, "Sybil," *The Big Event/NBC World Premiere Movie* (NBC)

OUTSTANDING EVENING CHILDREN'S SPECIAL: "Ballet Shoes, Parts 1 & 2," *Piccadilly Circus*, 12/27 & 12/28/76 (PBS)

SPECIAL CLASSIFICATION OF OUTSTANDING PROGRAM ACHIEVEMENT: *The Tonight Show Starring Johnny Carson*, Fred De Cordova, producer (NBC)

1977–1978 (presented September 17, 1978)

OUTSTANDING COMEDY SERIES: *All in the Family*, Mort Lachman, executive producer; Milt Josefsberg, producer (CBS)

OUTSTANDING DRAMA SERIES: *The Rockford Files*, Meta Rosenberg, executive producer; Stephen J. Cannell, supervising producer; David Chase and Charles F. Johnson, producers (NBC)

OUTSTANDING COMEDY-VARIETY OR MUSIC SERIES: *The Muppet Show*, David Lazer, executive producer; Jim Henson, producer; The Muppets—Frank Oz, Jerry Nelson, Richard Hunt, Dave Goelz, and Jim Henson, stars (syndicated)

OUTSTANDING LIMITED SERIES: *Holocaust*, Herbert Brodkin, executive producer; Robert Berger, producer (NBC)

OUTSTANDING INFORMATION SERIES: *The Body Human,* Thomas W. Moore, executive producer; Alfred R. Kelman, producer (CBS)

OUTSTANDING SPECIAL—DRAMA OR COMEDY: "The Gathering," Joseph Barbera, executive producer; Harry R. Sherman, producer (ABC)

OUTSTANDING SPECIAL—COMEDY-VARIETY OR MUSIC: "Bette Midler—Old Red Hair Is Back," Aaron Russo, executive producer; Gary Smith and Dwight Hemion, producers; Bette Midler, star (NBC)

OUTSTANDING INFORMATION SPECIAL: "The Great Whales: National Geographic," Thomas Skinner and Dennis B. Kane, executive producers; Nicolas Noxon, producer (PBS)

OUTSTANDING CLASSICAL PROGRAM IN THE PERFORMING ARTS: "American Ballet Theatre; 'Giselle' Live from Lincoln Center," John Goberman, producer, 6/2/77 (PBS)

OUTSTANDING LEAD ACTOR IN A COMEDY SERIES: Carroll O'Connor, *All in the Family* (CBS)

OUTSTANDING LEAD ACTOR IN A DRAMA SERIES: Ed Asner, *Lou Grant* (CBS)

OUTSTANDING LEAD ACTOR IN A LIMITED SERIES: Michael Moriarty, *Holocaust* (NBC)

OUTSTANDING LEAD ACTOR IN A DRAMA OR COMEDY SPECIAL: Fred Astaire, "A Family Upside Down" (NBC)

OUTSTANDING LEAD ACTOR FOR A SINGLE APPEARANCE IN A DRAMA OR COMEDY SERIES: Barnard Hughes, "Judge," *Lou Grant,* 11/15/77 (CBS)

OUTSTANDING LEAD ACTRESS IN A COMEDY SERIES: Jean Stapleton, *All in the Family* (CBS)

OUTSTANDING LEAD ACTRESS IN A DRAMA SERIES: Sada Thompson, *Family* (ABC)

OUTSTANDING LEAD ACTRESS IN A LIMITED SERIES: Meryl Streep, *Holocaust* (NBC)

OUTSTANDING LEAD ACTRESS IN A DRAMA OR COMEDY SPECIAL: Joanne Woodward, "See How She Runs," *General Electric Theater* (CBS)

OUTSTANDING LEAD ACTRESS FOR A SINGLE APPEARANCE IN A DRAMA OR COMEDY SERIES: Rita Moreno, "The Paper Palace," *The Rockford Files,* 1/20/78 (NBC)

OUTSTANDING CONTINUING PERFORMANCE BY A SUPPORTING ACTOR IN A COMEDY SERIES: Rob Reiner, *All in the Family* (CBS)

OUTSTANDING CONTINUING PERFORMANCE BY A SUPPORTING ACTOR IN A DRAMA SERIES: Robert Vaughn, *Washington: Behind Closed Doors* (ABC)

OUTSTANDING CONTINUING OR SINGLE PERFORMANCE BY A SUPPORTING ACTOR IN VARIETY OR MUSIC: Tim Conway, *The Carol Burnett Show* (CBS)

OUTSTANDING PERFORMANCE BY A SUPPORTING ACTOR IN A COMEDY OR DRAMA SPECIAL: Howard Da Silva, "Verna: USO Girl," *Great Performances,* 1/25/78 (PBS)

OUTSTANDING SINGLE PERFORMANCE BY A SUPPORTING ACTOR IN A COMEDY OR DRAMA SERIES: Ricardo Montalban, *How the West Was Won*—Part II, 2/19/78 (ABC)

OUTSTANDING CONTINUING PERFORMANCE BY A SUPPORTING ACTRESS IN A COMEDY SERIES: Julie Kavner, *Rhoda* (CBS)

OUTSTANDING CONTINUING PERFORMANCE BY A SUPPORTING ACTRESS IN A DRAMA SERIES: Nancy Marchand, *Lou Grant* (CBS)

OUTSTANDING CONTINUING OR SINGLE PERFORMANCE BY A SUPPORTING ACTRESS IN VARIETY OR MUSIC: Gilda Radner, *NBC's Saturday Night Live* (NBC)

OUTSTANDING PERFORMANCE BY A SUPPORTING ACTRESS IN A COMEDY OR DRAMA SPECIAL: Eva La Gallienne, "The Royal Family," 11/9/77 (PBS)

OUTSTANDING SINGLE PERFORMANCE BY A SUPPORTING ACTRESS IN A COMEDY OR DRAMA SERIES: Blanche Baker, *Holocaust*—Part I, 4/16/78 (NBC)

OUTSTANDING DIRECTING IN A DRAMA SERIES (A SINGLE EPISODE OF A REGULAR OR LIMITED SERIES WITH CONTINUING CHARACTERS AND/OR THEME): Marvin J. Chomsky, *Holocaust,* entire series (NBC)

OUTSTANDING DIRECTING IN A COMEDY SERIES (A SINGLE EPISODE OF A REGULAR OR LIMITED SERIES WITH CONTINUING CHARACTERS AND/OR THEME): Paul Bogart, "Edith's 50th Birthday," *All in the Family,* 10/16/77 (CBS)

OUTSTANDING DIRECTING IN A COMEDY-VARIETY OR MUSIC SERIES (A SINGLE EPISODE OF A REGULAR OR LIMITED SERIES): Dave Powers, *The Carol Burnett Show,* with Steve Martin and Betty White, 3/5/78 (CBS)

OUTSTANDING DIRECTING IN A COMEDY-VARIETY OR MUSIC SPECIAL: Dwight Hemion, "The Sentry Collection Presents Ben Vereen—His Roots," 3/2/78 (ABC)

OUTSTANDING DIRECTING IN A SPECIAL PROGRAM—DRAMA OR COMEDY: David Lowell Rich, "The Defection of Simas Kudirka," 1/23/78 (CBS)

OUTSTANDING WRITING IN A DRAMA SERIES (A SINGLE EPISODE OF A REGULAR OR LIMITED SERIES WITH CONTINUING CHARACTERS AND/OR THEME): Gerald Green, *Holocaust,* entire series (NBC)

OUTSTANDING WRITING IN A COMEDY SERIES (A SINGLE EPISODE OF A REGULAR OR LIMITED SERIES WITH CONTINUING CHARACTERS AND/OR THEME): Bob Weiskopf, Bob Schiller, Barry Harmon, and Harve Broston, "Cousin Liz," *All in the Family,* 10/9/77 (CBS)

OUTSTANDING WRITING IN A COMEDY-VARIETY OR MUSIC SERIES (A SINGLE EPISODE OF A REGULAR OR LIMITED SERIES): Ed Simmons, Roger Beatty, Rick Hawkins, Liz Sage, Robert Illes, James Stein, Franelle

Silver, Larry Siegel, Tim Conway, Bill Richmond, Gene Perret, Dick Clair, and Jenna McMahon, *The Carol Burnett Show,* with Steve Martin and Betty White, 3/5/78 (CBS)

OUTSTANDING WRITING IN A COMEDY-VARIETY OR MUSIC SPECIAL: Chevy Chase, Tom Davis, Al Franken, Charles Grodin, Lorne Michaels, Paul Simon, Lily Tomlin, and Alan Zweibel, "The Paul Simon Special," 12/8/77 (NBC)

OUTSTANDING WRITING IN A SPECIAL PROGRAM—DRAMA OR COMEDY—ORIGINAL TELEPLAY: George Rubino, "The Last Tenant," 6/25/78 (ABC)

OUTSTANDING WRITING IN A SPECIAL PROGRAM—DRAMA OR COMEDY—ADAPTATION: Caryl Ledner, "Mary White," 11/18/77 (ABC)

OUTSTANDING EVENING CHILDREN'S SPECIAL: "Halloween Is Grinch Night," David H. DePatie and Fritz Freleng, executive producers; Ted Geisel, producer, 10/29/77 (CBS)

SPECIAL CLASSIFICATION OF OUTSTANDING PROGRAM ACHIEVEMENT: *The Tonight Show Starring Johnny Carson,* Fred De Cordova, producer; Johnny Carson, star (NBC)

FIRST ANNUAL ATAS GOVERNOR'S AWARD: William S. Paley, Chairman of the Board, CBS

1978–1979 (presented September 9, 1979)

OUTSTANDING COMEDY SERIES: *Taxi,* James L. Brooks, Stan Daniels, David Davis, and Ed Weinberger, executive producers; Glen Charles and Les Charles, producers (ABC)

OUTSTANDING DRAMA SERIES: *Lou Grant,* Gene Reynolds, executive producer; Seth Freeman and Gary David Goldberg, producers (CBS)

OUTSTANDING LIMITED SERIES: *Roots: The Next Generations,* David L. Wolper, executive producer; Stan Margulies, producer (ABC)

OUTSTANDING SPECIAL—DRAMA OR COMEDY: "Friendly Fire," Martin Starger, executive producer; Philip Barry and Fay Kanin, producers (ABC)

OUTSTANDING COMEDY-VARIETY OR MUSIC PROGRAM (SPECIAL OR SERIES): "Steve & Eydie Celebrate Irving Berlin," Steve Lawrence and Gary Smith, executive producers; Gary Smith and Dwight Hemion, producers; Steve Lawrence and Eydie Gorme, stars, 8/22/78 (NBC)

OUTSTANDING INFORMATION PROGRAM (SPECIAL OR SERIES): "Scared Straight," Arnold Shapiro, producer (syndicated)

OUTSTANDING CLASSICAL PROGRAM IN THE PERFORMING ARTS: "Balanchine IV Dance in America," *Great Performances,* Jac Venza, executive producer; Merrill Brockway, series producer; Emile Ardolino, series coordinating producer; Judy Kunberg, producer, 3/7/79 (PBS)

OUTSTANDING ANIMATED PROGRAM (SPECIAL OR SERIES): "The Lion, the Witch, and the Wardrobe," David Connell, executive producer; Steve Melendez, producer (CBS)

OUTSTANDING CHILDREN'S PROGRAM (SPECIAL OR SERIES): "Christmas Eve on Sesame Street," Jon Stone, executive producer; Dulcy Singer, producer, 12/3/78 (PBS)

OUTSTANDING PROGRAM ACHIEVEMENT—SPECIAL EVENTS: "51st Annual Awards Presentation of the Academy of Motion Picture Arts and Sciences," Jack Haley, Jr., producer, 4/9/79 (ABC)

OUTSTANDING LEAD ACTOR IN A COMEDY SERIES (FOR A CONTINUING OR SINGLE PERFORMANCE IN A REGULAR SERIES): Carroll O'Connor, *All in the Family* (CBS)

OUTSTANDING LEAD ACTOR IN A DRAMA SERIES (FOR A CONTINUING OR SINGLE PERFORMANCE IN A REGULAR SERIES): Ron Leibman, *Kaz* (CBS)

OUTSTANDING LEAD ACTOR IN A LIMITED SERIES OR A SPECIAL: Peter Strauss, "The Jericho Mile," 3/18/79 (ABC)

OUTSTANDING LEAD ACTRESS IN A COMEDY SERIES (FOR A CONTINUING OR SINGLE PERFORMANCE IN A REGULAR SERIES): Ruth Gordon, "Sugar Mama," *Taxi,* 1/16/79 (ABC)

OUTSTANDING LEAD ACTRESS IN A DRAMA SERIES (FOR A CONTINUING OR SINGLE PERFORMANCE IN A REGULAR SERIES): Mariette Hartley, "Married," *The Incredible Hulk,* 9/23/78 (CBS)

OUTSTANDING LEAD ACTRESS IN A LIMITED SERIES OR A SPECIAL: Bette Davis, "Strangers: The Story of a Mother and Daughter," 5/13/79 (CBS)

OUTSTANDING SUPPORTING ACTOR IN A COMEDY OR COMEDY-VARIETY OR MUSIC SERIES (FOR A CONTINUING OR SINGLE PERFORMANCE IN A REGULAR SERIES): Robert Guillaume, *Soap* (ABC)

OUTSTANDING SUPPORTING ACTOR IN A DRAMA SERIES (FOR A CONTINUING OR SINGLE PERFORMANCE IN A REGULAR SERIES): Stuart Margolin, *The Rockford Files* (NBC)

OUTSTANDING SUPPORTING ACTOR IN A LIMITED SERIES OR A SPECIAL: Marlon Brando, *Roots: The Next Generations*—Episode Seven, 2/25/79 (ABC)

OUTSTANDING SUPPORTING ACTRESS IN A COMEDY OR COMEDY-VARIETY OR MUSIC SERIES (FOR A CONTINUING OR SINGLE PERFORMANCE IN A REGULAR SERIES): Sally Struthers, "California Here We Are," *All in the Family,* 12/17/78 (CBS)

OUTSTANDING SUPPORTING ACTRESS IN A DRAMA SERIES (FOR A CONTINUING OR SINGLE PERFORMANCE IN A REGULAR SERIES): Kristy McNichol, *Family* (ABC)

OUTSTANDING SUPPORTING ACTRESS IN A LIMITED SERIES OR A SPECIAL: Esther Rolle, "Summer of My German Soldier," 10/30/78 (NBC)

OUTSTANDING INDIVIDUAL ACHIEVEMENT—INFORMATIONAL PROGRAM: John Korty, director; "Who Are the Debolts—And Where Did They Get 19 Kids?," 12/17/78 (ABC)

OUTSTANDING INDIVIDUAL ACHIEVEMENT—SPECIAL EVENTS: Mikhail Baryshnikov, star; "Baryshnikov at the White House," 4/15/79 (PBS)

OUTSTANDING DIRECTING IN A COMEDY OR COMEDY-VARIETY OR MUSIC SERIES (A SINGLE EPISODE OF A REGULAR SERIES): Noam Pitlik, "The Harris Incident," *Barney Miller,* 11/30/78 (ABC)

OUTSTANDING DIRECTING IN A DRAMA SERIES (A SINGLE EPISODE OF A REGULAR SERIES): Jackie Cooper, "Pilot," *The White Shadow,* 11/27/78 (CBS)

OUTSTANDING DIRECTING IN A LIMITED SERIES OR A SPECIAL: David Greene, "Friendly Fire," 4/22/79 (ABC)

OUTSTANDING WRITING IN A COMEDY OR COMEDY-VARIETY OR MUSIC SERIES (A SINGLE EPISODE OF A REGULAR SERIES): Alan Alda, "Inga," *M*A*S*H,* 1/8/79 (CBS)

OUTSTANDING WRITING IN A DRAMA SERIES (A SINGLE EPISODE OF A REGULAR SERIES): Michele Gallery, "Dying," *Lou Grant,* 11/6/78 (CBS)

OUTSTANDING WRITING IN A LIMITED SERIES OR A SPECIAL: Patrick Nolan and Michael Mann, "The Jericho Mile," 3/18/79 (ABC)

SPECIAL CLASSIFICATION OF OUTSTANDING PROGRAM ACHIEVEMENT: *The Tonight Show Starring Johnny Carson,* Fred De Cordova, producer; Johnny Carson, star. *Lifeline,* Thomas W. Moore and Robert E. Fuisz, M.D., executive producers; Alfred Kelman and Geof Bartz, producers (NBC)

SECOND ANNUAL ATAS GOVERNOR'S AWARD: Walter Cronkite

1979–1980 (presented September 7, 1980)

OUTSTANDING COMEDY SERIES: *Taxi,* James L. Brooks, Stan Daniels, and Ed Weinberger, executive producers; Glen Charles and Les Charles, producers (ABC)

OUTSTANDING DRAMA SERIES: *Lou Grant,* Gene Reynolds, executive producer; Seth Freeman, producer (CBS)

OUTSTANDING LIMITED SERIES: *Edward & Mrs. Simpson,* Andrew Brown, producer (syndicated)

OUTSTANDING SPECIAL—DRAMA OR COMEDY: "The Miracle Worker," Raymond Katz and Sandy Gallin, executive producers; Fred Coe, producer, 10/14/79 (NBC)

OUTSTANDING VARIETY OR MUSIC PROGRAM (SPECIAL OR SERIES): "IBM Presents Baryshnikov on Broadway," Herman Krawitz, executive producer; Gary Smith and Dwight Hemion, producers; Mikhail Baryshnikov, star, 4/24/80 (ABC)

OUTSTANDING INFORMATION PROGRAM (SPECIAL OR SERIES): "The Body Human: The Magic Sense," Thomas W. Moore, executive producer; Alfred R. Kelman, Robert E. Fuisz, M.D., Charles A. Bangert, and Vivian R. Moss, producers, 9/6/79 (CBS)

OUTSTANDING CLASSICAL PROGRAM IN THE PERFORMING ARTS: "Live from Studio 8H: A Tribute to Toscanini," Alvin Cooperman and Judith De Paul, producers, 1/9/80 (NBC)

OUTSTANDING ANIMATED PROGRAM (SPECIAL OR SERIES): "Carlton, Your Doorman," Lorenzo Music and Barton Dean, producers, 5/21/80 (CBS)

OUTSTANDING PROGRAM ACHIEVEMENT—SPECIAL EVENTS: "The 34th Annual Tony Awards," Alexander H. Cohen, executive producer; Hildy Parks and Roy A. Somlyo, producers, 6/8/80 (CBS)

OUTSTANDING LEAD ACTOR IN A COMEDY SERIES (FOR A CONTINUING OR SINGLE PERFORMANCE IN A REGULAR SERIES): Richard Mulligan, *Soap* (ABC)

OUTSTANDING LEAD ACTOR IN A DRAMA SERIES (FOR A CONTINUING OR SINGLE PERFORMANCE IN A REGULAR SERIES): Ed Asner, *Lou Grant* (CBS)

OUTSTANDING LEAD ACTOR IN A LIMITED SERIES OR A SPECIAL: Powers Boothe, "Guyana Tragedy," 4/15–16/80 (CBS)

OUTSTANDING LEAD ACTRESS IN A COMEDY SERIES (FOR A CONTINUING OR SINGLE PERFORMANCE IN A REGULAR SERIES): Cathryn Damon, *Soap* (ABC)

OUTSTANDING LEAD ACTRESS IN A DRAMA SERIES (FOR A CONTINUING OR SINGLE PERFORMANCE IN A REGULAR SERIES): Barbara Bel Geddes, *Dallas* (CBS)

OUTSTANDING LEAD ACTRESS IN A LIMITED SERIES OR A SPECIAL: Patty Duke Astin, "The Miracle Worker," 10/14/79 (NBC)

OUTSTANDING SUPPORTING ACTOR IN A COMEDY OR COMEDY-VARIETY OR MUSIC SERIES (FOR A CONTINUING OR SINGLE PERFORMANCE IN A REGULAR SERIES): Harry Morgan, *M*A*S*H* (CBS)

OUTSTANDING SUPPORTING ACTOR IN A DRAMA SERIES (FOR A CONTINUING OR SINGLE PERFORMANCE IN A REGULAR SERIES): Stuart Margolin, *The Rockford Files* (NBC)

OUTSTANDING SUPPORTING ACTOR IN A LIMITED SERIES OR A SPECIAL: George Grizzard, "The Oldest Living Graduate," 4/7/80 (NBC)

OUTSTANDING SUPPORTING ACTRESS IN A COMEDY OR COMEDY-VARIETY OR MUSIC SERIES (FOR A CONTINUING OR SINGLE PERFORMANCE IN A REGULAR SERIES): Loretta Swit, *M*A*S*H* (CBS)

OUTSTANDING SUPPORTING ACTRESS IN A DRAMA SERIES (FOR A CONTINUING OR SINGLE PERFORMANCE IN A REGULAR SERIES): Nancy Marchand, *Lou Grant* (CBS)

OUTSTANDING SUPPORTING ACTRESS IN A LIMITED SERIES OR A SPECIAL: Mare Winningham, "Amber Waves," 3/9/80 (ABC)
OUTSTANDING INDIVIDUAL ACHIEVEMENT—SPECIAL CLASS: "Operation: Lifeline," Dr. James "Red" Duke, 8/13/79 (NBC)
OUTSTANDING DIRECTING IN A COMEDY SERIES (A SINGLE EPISODE OF A REGULAR SERIES): James Burrows, *Taxi*, 9/11/79 (ABC)
OUTSTANDING DIRECTING IN A DRAMA SERIES (A SINGLE EPISODE OF A REGULAR SERIES): Roger Young, "Cop," *Lou Grant*, 9/17/79 (CBS)
OUTSTANDING DIRECTING IN A LIMITED SERIES OR A SPECIAL: Marvin J. Chomsky, "Attica," 3/2/80 (ABC)
OUTSTANDING DIRECTING IN A VARIETY OR MUSIC PROGRAM (A SINGLE EPISODE OF A REGULAR OR LIMITED SERIES, OR FOR A SPECIAL): Dwight Hemion, "Baryshnikov on Broadway," 4/24/80 (ABC)
OUTSTANDING WRITING IN A COMEDY SERIES (A SINGLE EPISODE OF A REGULAR SERIES): Bob Colleary, "Photographer," *Barney Miller*, 9/20/79 (ABC)
OUTSTANDING WRITING IN A DRAMA SERIES (A SINGLE EPISODE OF A REGULAR SERIES): Seth Freeman, "Cop," *Lou Grant*, 9/17/79 (CBS)
OUTSTANDING WRITING IN A LIMITED SERIES OR A SPECIAL: David Chase, "Off the Minnesota Strip," 5/5/80 (ABC)
OUTSTANDING WRITING IN A VARIETY OR MUSIC PROGRAM (A SINGLE EPISODE OF A REGULAR OR LIMITED SERIES, OR FOR A SPECIAL): Buz Kohan and Shirley MacLaine, "Every Little Movement," 5/22/80 (CBS)
SPECIAL CLASSIFICATION OF OUTSTANDING PROGRAM ACHIEVEMENT: "Fred Astaire, Change Partners and Dance," David Heeley, producer, 3/14/80 (PBS)
THIRD ANNUAL ATAS GOVERNOR'S AWARD: Johnny Carson

1980–1981 (presented September 13, 1981)

OUTSTANDING COMEDY SERIES: *Taxi*, James L. Brooks, Stan Daniels, and Ed Weinberger, executive producers; Glen Charles and Les Charles, producers (ABC)
OUTSTANDING DRAMA SERIES: *Hill Street Blues*, Steven Bochco and Michael Kozoll, executive producers; Gregory Hoblit, producer (NBC)
OUTSTANDING LIMITED SERIES: *Shogun*, James Clavell, executive producer; Eric Bercovici, producer (NBC)
OUTSTANDING VARIETY, MUSIC OR COMEDY PROGRAM: "Lily: Sold Out," Lily Tomlin and Jane Wagner, executive producers; Rocco Urbisci, producer (CBS)
OUTSTANDING DRAMA SPECIAL: "Playing for Time," Linda Yellen, executive producer; John E. Quill, co-producer (CBS)
OUTSTANDING INFORMATIONAL SERIES: *Steve Allen's Meeting of Minds*, Loring d'Usseau, producer (PBS)
OUTSTANDING INFORMATIONAL SPECIAL: "The Body Human: The Bionic Breakthrough," Thomas W. Moore, executive producer; Alfred R. Kelman and Robert E. Fuisz, M.D., producers; Charles A. Bangert and Nancy Smith, co-producers (CBS)
OUTSTANDING CLASSICAL PROGRAM IN THE PERFORMING ARTS: "Live from Studio 8H: An Evening of Jerome Robbins' Ballets with Members of the New York City Ballet," Alvin Cooperman and Judith De Paul, producers (NBC)
OUTSTANDING CHILDREN'S PROGRAM: "Donahue and Kids. Project Peacock," Walter Bartlett, executive producer; Don Mischer, producer; Jan Cornell, co-producer (NBC)
OUTSTANDING ANIMATED PROGRAM: "Life Is a Circus, Charlie Brown," Lee Mendelson, executive producer; Bill Melendez, producer (CBS)
OUTSTANDING LEAD ACTOR IN A DRAMA SERIES: Daniel J. Travanti, *Hill Street Blues* (NBC)
OUTSTANDING LEAD ACTOR IN A COMEDY SERIES: Judd Hirsch, *Taxi* (ABC)
OUTSTANDING LEAD ACTOR IN A LIMITED SERIES OR A SPECIAL: Anthony Hopkins, "The Bunker" (CBS)
OUTSTANDING LEAD ACTRESS IN A DRAMA SERIES: Barbara Babcock, *Hill Street Blues* (NBC)
OUTSTANDING LEAD ACTRESS IN A COMEDY SERIES: Isabel Sanford, *The Jeffersons* (CBS)
OUTSTANDING LEAD ACTRESS IN A LIMITED SERIES OR A SPECIAL: Vanessa Redgrave, "Playing for Time" (CBS)
OUTSTANDING SUPPORTING ACTOR IN A DRAMA SERIES: Michael Conrad, *Hill Street Blues* (NBC)
OUTSTANDING SUPPORTING ACTOR IN A COMEDY OR VARIETY OR MUSIC SERIES: Danny DeVito, *Taxi* (ABC)
OUTSTANDING SUPPORTING ACTOR IN A LIMITED SERIES OR A SPECIAL: David Warner, *Masada* (ABC)
OUTSTANDING SUPPORTING ACTRESS IN A DRAMA SERIES: Nancy Marchand, *Lou Grant* (CBS)
OUTSTANDING SUPPORTING ACTRESS IN A COMEDY OR VARIETY OR MUSIC SERIES: Eileen Brennan, *Private Benjamin* (CBS)
OUTSTANDING SUPPORTING ACTRESS IN A LIMITED SERIES OR A SPECIAL: Jane Alexander, "Playing for Time" (CBS)
OUTSTANDING INDIVIDUAL ACHIEVEMENT—SPECIAL CLASS: Sarah Vaughan, performer, "Rhapsody and Song—A Tribute to George Gershwin" (PBS)

OUTSTANDING DIRECTING IN A DRAMA SERIES (SINGLE EPISODE): Robert Butler, "Hill Street Station," *Hill Street Blues* (NBC)

OUTSTANDING DIRECTING IN A COMEDY SERIES (SINGLE EPISODE): James Burrows, "Elaine's Strange Triangle," *Taxi* (ABC)

OUTSTANDING DIRECTING IN A LIMITED SERIES OR A SPECIAL: James Goldstone, "Kent State" (NBC)

OUTSTANDING DIRECTING IN A VARIETY, MUSIC OR COMEDY PROGRAM: Don Mischer, "The Kennedy Center Honors: A National Celebration of the Performing Arts" (CBS)

OUTSTANDING WRITING IN A DRAMA SERIES (SINGLE EPISODE): Michael Kozoll and Steven Bochco, "Hill Street Station," *Hill Street Blues* (NBC)

OUTSTANDING WRITING IN A COMEDY SERIES (SINGLE EPISODE): Michael Leeson, "Tony's Sister and Jim," *Taxi* (ABC)

OUTSTANDING WRITING IN A LIMITED SERIES OR A SPECIAL: Arthur Miller, "Playing for Time" (CBS)

OUTSTANDING WRITING IN A VARIETY, MUSIC OR COMEDY PROGRAM: Jerry Juhl, David O'Dell, Chris Langham, Jim Henson, and Don Hinkley; "The Muppet Show with Carol Burnett" (syndicated)

FOURTH ANNUAL ATAS GOVERNOR'S AWARD: Elton H. Rule, President, American Broadcasting Company

1981–1982 (presented September 19, 1982)

OUTSTANDING COMEDY SERIES: *Barney Miller,* Danny Arnold and Roland Kibbee, executive producers; Frank Dungan and Jeff Stein, producers; Gary Shaw, co-producer (ABC)

OUTSTANDING DRAMA SERIES: *Hill Street Blues,* Steven Bochco, executive producer; Gregory Hoblit, supervising producer; David Anspaugh and Anthony Yerkovich, producers (NBC)

OUTSTANDING LIMITED SERIES: *Marco Polo,* Vincenzo Labella, producer (NBC)

OUTSTANDING VARIETY, MUSIC OR COMEDY PROGRAM: "Night of 100 Stars," Alexander H. Cohen, executive producer; Hildy Parks, producer; Roy A. Somlyo, co-producer (ABC)

OUTSTANDING DRAMA SPECIAL: "A Woman Called Golda," Harve Bennett, executive producer; Gene Corman, producer (syndicated)

OUTSTANDING INFORMATIONAL SERIES: *Creativity with Bill Moyers,* Merton Koplin and Charles Grinker, executive producers; Betsy McCarthy, coordinating producer (PBS)

OUTSTANDING INFORMATIONAL SPECIAL: "Making of *Raiders of the Lost Ark,*" Sidney Ganis, executive producer; Howard Kazanjian, producer (PBS)

OUTSTANDING CLASSICAL PROGRAM IN THE PERFORMING ARTS: "*La Bohème,* Live from the Met," Michael Bronson, executive producer; Clement d'Alessio, producer (PBS)

OUTSTANDING CHILDREN'S PROGRAM: "The Wave," Virginia L. Carter, executive producer; Fern Field, producer (ABC)

OUTSTANDING ANIMATED PROGRAM: "Grinch Grinches the Cat in the Hat," David H. DePatie, executive producer; Ted Geisel and Fritz Freleng, producers (ABC)

OUTSTANDING LEAD ACTOR IN A DRAMA SERIES: Daniel J. Travanti, *Hill Street Blues* (NBC)

OUTSTANDING LEAD ACTOR IN A COMEDY SERIES: Alan Alda, *M*A*S*H* (CBS)

OUTSTANDING LEAD ACTOR IN A LIMITED SERIES OR A SPECIAL: Mickey Rooney, "Bill" (CBS)

OUTSTANDING LEAD ACTRESS IN A DRAMA SERIES: Michael Learned, *Nurse* (CBS)

OUTSTANDING LEAD ACTRESS IN A COMEDY SERIES: Carol Kane, "Simka Returns," *Taxi* (ABC)

OUTSTANDING LEAD ACTRESS IN A LIMITED SERIES OR A SPECIAL: Ingrid Bergman, "A Woman Called Golda" (syndicated)

OUTSTANDING SUPPORTING ACTOR IN A DRAMA SERIES: Michael Conrad, *Hill Street Blues* (NBC)

OUTSTANDING SUPPORTING ACTOR IN A COMEDY OR VARIETY OR MUSIC SERIES: Christopher Lloyd, *Taxi* (ABC)

OUTSTANDING SUPPORTING ACTOR IN A LIMITED SERIES OR A SPECIAL: Laurence Olivier, *Brideshead Revisited* (PBS)

OUTSTANDING SUPPORTING ACTRESS IN A DRAMA SERIES: Nancy Marchand, *Lou Grant* (CBS)

OUTSTANDING SUPPORTING ACTRESS IN A COMEDY OR VARIETY OR MUSIC SERIES: Loretta Swit, *M*A*S*H* (CBS)

OUTSTANDING SUPPORTING ACTRESS IN A LIMITED SERIES OR A SPECIAL: Penny Fuller, "The Elephant Man" (ABC)

OUTSTANDING INDIVIDUAL ACHIEVEMENT—SPECIAL CLASS: Nell Carter, performer, "Ain't Misbehavin' " (NBC); Andre De Shields, performer, "Ain't Misbehavin' " (NBC)

OUTSTANDING DIRECTING IN A DRAMA SERIES (SINGLE EPISODE): Harry Harris, "To Soar and Never Falter," *Fame* (NBC)

OUTSTANDING DIRECTING IN A COMEDY SERIES (SINGLE EPISODE): Alan Rafkin, "Barbara's Crisis," *One Day at a Time* (CBS)

OUTSTANDING DIRECTING IN A LIMITED SERIES OR A SPECIAL: Marvin J. Chomsky, "Inside the Third Reich" (ABC)

OUTSTANDING WRITING IN A DRAMA SERIES (SINGLE EPISODE): Steven Bochco, Anthony Yerkovich, Jeffrey Lewis, and Michael Wagner, teleplay; Michael Kozoll and Steven Bochco, story; "Freedom's Last Stand," *Hill Street Blues* (NBC)

OUTSTANDING WRITING IN A COMEDY SERIES (SINGLE EPISODE): Ken Estin, "Elegant Iggy," *Taxi* (ABC)

OUTSTANDING WRITING IN A LIMITED SERIES OR A SPECIAL: Corey Blechman, teleplay; Barry Morrow, story; "Bill" (CBS)

FIFTH ANNUAL ATAS GOVERNOR'S AWARD: *The Hallmark Hall of Fame*

1982–1983 (presented September 25, 1983)

OUTSTANDING COMEDY SERIES: *Cheers,* James Burrows, Glen Charles, and Les Charles, producers; Ken Levine and David Isaacs, co-producers (NBC)

OUTSTANDING DRAMA SERIES: *Hill Street Blues,* Steven Bochco, executive producer; Gregory Hoblit, co-executive producer; Anthony Yerkovich, supervising producer; David Anspaugh and Scott Brazil, producers (NBC)

OUTSTANDING LIMITED SERIES: *Nicholas Nickleby,* Colin Callender, producer (syndicated)

OUTSTANDING VARIETY, MUSIC OR COMEDY PROGRAM: "Motown 25: Yesterday, Today, Forever," Suzanne de Passe, executive producer; Don Mischer and Buz Kohan, producers; Suzanne Coston, producer for Motown (NBC)

OUTSTANDING DRAMA SPECIAL: "Special Bulletin," Don Ohlmeyer, executive producer; Marshall Herskovitz and Edward Zwick, producers (NBC)

OUTSTANDING INFORMATIONAL SERIES: *The Barbara Walters Specials,* Beth Polson, producer; Barbara Walters, host (ABC)

OUTSTANDING INFORMATIONAL SPECIAL: "The Body Human: The Living Code," Thomas W. Moore, executive producer; Robert E. Fuisz, M.D., and Alfred R. Kelman, M.D., producers; Charles A. Bangert, Franklin Getchell, and Nancy Smith, co-producers (CBS)

OUTSTANDING CLASSICAL PROGRAM IN THE PERFORMING ARTS: "Pavarotti in Philadelphia: *La Bohème,*" Margaret Anne Everitt, executive producer; Clement D'Alessio, producer; Luciano Pavarotti, star (PBS)

OUTSTANDING CHILDREN'S PROGRAM: "Big Bird in China," Jon Stone, executive producer; David Liu, Kuo Bao-Xiang, and Xu Ja-Cha, producers (NBC)

OUTSTANDING ANIMATED PROGRAM: "Ziggy's Gift," Lena Tabori, executive producer; Richard Williams, Tom Wilson, and Lena Tabori, producers (ABC)

OUTSTANDING LEAD ACTOR IN A DRAMA SERIES: Ed Flanders, *St. Elsewhere* (NBC)

OUTSTANDING LEAD ACTOR IN A COMEDY SERIES: Judd Hirsch, *Taxi* (NBC)

OUTSTANDING LEAD ACTOR IN A LIMITED SERIES OR A SPECIAL: Tommy Lee Jones, "The Executioner's Song," (NBC)

OUTSTANDING LEAD ACTRESS IN A DRAMA SERIES: Tyne Daly, *Cagney & Lacey* (CBS)

OUTSTANDING LEAD ACTRESS IN A COMEDY SERIES: Shelley Long, *Cheers* (NBC)

OUTSTANDING LEAD ACTRESS IN A LIMITED SERIES OR A SPECIAL: Barbara Stanwyck, *The Thorn Birds*— Part 1 (ABC)

OUTSTANDING SUPPORTING ACTOR IN A DRAMA SERIES: James Coco, "Cora and Arnie," *St. Elsewhere* (NBC)

OUTSTANDING SUPPORTING ACTOR IN A COMEDY, VARIETY OR MUSIC SERIES: Christopher Lloyd, *Taxi* (NBC)

OUTSTANDING SUPPORTING ACTOR IN A LIMITED SERIES OR A SPECIAL: Richard Kiley, *The Thorn Birds*— Part 1 (ABC)

OUTSTANDING SUPPORTING ACTRESS IN A DRAMA SERIES: Doris Roberts, "Cora and Arnie," *St. Elsewhere* (NBC)

OUTSTANDING SUPPORTING ACTRESS IN A COMEDY, VARIETY OR MUSIC SERIES: Carol Kane, *Taxi* (NBC)

OUTSTANDING SUPPORTING ACTRESS IN A LIMITED SERIES OR A SPECIAL: Jean Simmons, *The Thorn Birds* (ABC)

OUTSTANDING INDIVIDUAL PERFORMANCE IN A VARIETY OR MUSIC PROGRAM: Leontyne Price, "Live from Lincoln Center: Leontyne Price, Zubin Mehta, and the New York Philharmonic" (PBS)

OUTSTANDING INDIVIDUAL ACHIEVEMENT—INFORMATIONAL PROGRAMMING: Alfred R. Kelman, M.D., and Charles Bangert, directors, "The Body Human: The Living Code"; Louis H. Gorfain and Robert E. Fuisz, M.D., writers, "The Body Human: The Living Code" (CBS)

OUTSTANDING DIRECTING IN A DRAMA SERIES (SINGLE EPISODE): Jeff Bleckner, "Life in the Minors," *Hill Street Blues* (NBC)

OUTSTANDING DIRECTING IN A COMEDY SERIES (SINGLE EPISODE): James Burrows, "Showdown, Part 2," *Cheers* (NBC)

OUTSTANDING DIRECTING IN A LIMITED SERIES OR A SPECIAL: John Erman, "Who Will Love My Children" (ABC)

OUTSTANDING DIRECTING IN A VARIETY OR MUSICAL PROGRAM: Dwight Hemion, "Sheena Easton, Act I" (NBC)

OUTSTANDING WRITING IN A DRAMA SERIES (SINGLE EPISODE): David Milch, "Trial By Fury," *Hill Street Blues* (NBC)

OUTSTANDING WRITING IN A COMEDY SERIES (SINGLE EPISODE): Glen Charles and Les Charles, "Give Me a Ring Sometime," *Cheers* (NBC)

OUTSTANDING WRITING IN A LIMITED SERIES OR A SPECIAL: Marshall Herskovitz, teleplay; Edward Zwick and Marshall Herskovitz, story; "Special Bulletin" (NBC)

OUTSTANDING WRITING IN A VARIETY OR MUSICAL PROGRAM: John Candy, Joe Flaherty, Eugene Levy, Andrea Martin, Martin Short, Dick Blasucci, Paul Flaherty, John McAndrew, Doug Steckler, Bob Dolman, Michael Short, and Mary Charlotte Wilcox; "The Energy Ball/Sweeps Week," *SCTV Network* (NBC)

SIXTH ANNUAL ATLAS GOVERNOR'S AWARD: Sylvester L. "Pat" Weaver, Jr., former President of the National Broadcasting Company

1983–1984 (presented September 23, 1984)

OUTSTANDING COMEDY SERIES: *Cheers,* James Burrows, Glen Charles, and Les Charles, producers (NBC)

OUTSTANDING DRAMA SERIES: *Hill Street Blues,* Steven Bochco, executive producer; Gregory Hoblit, co-executive producer; Scott Brazil, supervising producer; Jeff Lewis and Sascha Schneider, producers; David Latt, co-producer (NBC)

OUTSTANDING LIMITED SERIES: "Concealed Enemies," *American Playhouse,* Lindsay Law and David Elstein, executive producers; Peter Cook, producer (PBS)

OUTSTANDING VARIETY, MUSIC OR COMEDY PROGRAM: Nick Vanoff and George Stevens, Jr., producers; "The 6th Annual Kennedy Center Honors: A Celebration of the Performing Arts (CBS)

OUTSTANDING DRAMA SPECIAL: "Something About Amelia," Leonard Goldberg, executive producer; Michele Rappaport, producer (ABC)

OUTSTANDING INFORMATIONAL SERIES: *A Walk Through the 20th Century,* Merton Y. Koplin, senior executive producer; Charles Grinker and Sanford H. Fisher, producers; Betsy McCarthy, coordinating producer; David Grubin and Ronald Blumer, producers; Bill Moyers, host (PBS)

OUTSTANDING INFORMATIONAL SPECIAL: "America Remembers John F. Kennedy," Thomas F. Horton, producer (syndicated)

OUTSTANDING CLASSICAL PROGRAM IN THE PERFORMING ARTS: "Placido Domingo Celebrates Saville." *Great Performances,* Horant H. Holfeld, executive producer; David Griffiths, producer; Placido Domingo, host (PBS)

OUTSTANDING CHILDREN'S PROGRAM: "He Makes Me Feel Like Dancin'," Edgar J. Scherick and Scott Rudin, executive producers; Emile Ardolino and Judy Kinberg, producers (NBC)

OUTSTANDING ANIMATED PROGRAM: "Garfield on the Town," Jay Poynor, executive producer; Lee Mendelson and Bill Melendez, producers (CBS)

OUTSTANDING LEAD ACTOR IN A DRAMA SERIES: Tom Selleck, *Magnum, P.I.* (CBS)

OUTSTANDING LEAD ACTOR IN A COMEDY SERIES: John Ritter, *Three's Company* (ABC)

OUTSTANDING LEAD ACTOR IN A LIMITED SERIES OR A SPECIAL: Sir Laurence Olivier, *King Lear* (syndicated)

OUTSTANDING LEAD ACTRESS IN A DRAMA SERIES: Tyne Daly, *Cagney & Lacey* (CBS)

OUTSTANDING LEAD ACTRESS IN A COMEDY SERIES: Jane Curtin, *Kate & Allie* (CBS)

OUTSTANDING LEAD ACTRESS IN A LIMITED SERIES OR A SPECIAL: Jane Fonda, *The Dollmaker* (ABC)

OUTSTANDING SUPPORTING ACTOR IN A DRAMA SERIES: Bruce Weitz, *Hill Street Blues* (CBS)

OUTSTANDING SUPPORTING ACTOR IN A COMEDY, VARIETY OR MUSIC SERIES: Pat Harrington, Jr., *One Day at a Time* (CBS)

OUTSTANDING SUPPORTING ACTOR IN A LIMITED SERIES OR A SPECIAL: Art Carney, "Terrible Joe Moran" (CBS)

OUTSTANDING SUPPORTING ACTRESS IN A DRAMA SERIES: Alfre Woodard, "Doris in Wonderland," *Hill Street Blues* (NBC)

OUTSTANDING SUPPORTING ACTRESS IN A COMEDY, VARIETY OR MUSIC SERIES: Rhea Perlman, *Cheers* (NBC)

OUTSTANDING SUPPORTING ACTRESS IN A LIMITED SERIES OR A SPECIAL: Roxana Zal, "Something About Amelia" (ABC)

OUTSTANDING INDIVIDUAL PERFORMANCE IN A VARIETY OR MUSIC PROGRAM: Cloris Leachman, "Screen Actors Guild 50th Anniversary Celebration" (CBS)

OUTSTANDING INDIVIDUAL ACHIEVEMENT—INFORMATIONAL PROGRAMMING: Emile Ardolino, director; "He Makes Me Feel Like Dancin' " (NBC) and Bill Moyers, writer; "Marshall, Texas—Marshall Texas" (PBS)

OUTSTANDING DIRECTING IN A DRAMA SERIES (SINGLE EPISODE): Corey Allen, "Goodbye Mr. Scripps," *Hill Street Blues* (NBC)

OUTSTANDING DIRECTING IN A COMEDY SERIES (SINGLE EPISODE): Bill Persky, "Very Loud Family," *Kate & Allie* (CBS)

OUTSTANDING DIRECTING IN A LIMITED SERIES OR A SPECIAL: Jeff Bleckner, "Concealed Enemies," *American Playhouse* (PBS)

OUTSTANDING DIRECTING IN A VARIETY, MUSIC OR COMEDY PROGRAM: Dwight Hemion, "Here's Television Entertainment" (PBS)

958

OUTSTANDING WRITING IN A DRAMA SERIES (SINGLE EPISODE): John Ford Noonan, teleplay; John Masius and Tom Fontana, story; "The Women," *St. Elsewhere* (NBC)

OUTSTANDING WRITING IN A COMEDY SERIES (SINGLE EPISODE): David Angell, "Old Flames," *Cheers* (NBC)

OUTSTANDING WRITING IN A LIMITED SERIES OR A SPECIAL: William Hanley, "Something About Amelia" (ABC)

OUTSTANDING WRITING IN A VARIETY, MUSIC OR COMEDY PROGRAM: Steve O'Donnell, Gerard Mulligan, Sandy Frank, Joe Toplyn, Chris Elliott, Matt Wickline, Jeff Martin, Todd Greenberg, David Yazbek, Merrill Markoe, and David Letterman; *Late Night with David Letterman,* with Dr. Ruth Westheimer and Teri Garr, 11/15/83 (NBC)

SEVENTH ANNUAL ATLAS GOVERNOR'S AWARD: Bob Hope

1984–1985 (presented September 22, 1985)

OUTSTANDING COMEDY SERIES: *The Cosby Show,* Marcy Carsey and Tom Werner, executive producers; Earl Pomerantz and Elliot Schoenman, co-executive producers; John Markus, supervising producer; Caryn Sneider, producer; Earl Hyman, Jerry Ross, and Michael Loman, co-producers (NBC)

OUTSTANDING DRAMA SERIES: *Cagney & Lacey,* Barney Rosenzweig, executive producer; Steve Brown, Terry Louise Fisher, and Peter Lefcourt, producers (CBS)

OUTSTANDING LIMITED SERIES: "The Jewel in the Crown," *Masterpiece Theatre,* Denis Forman, executive producer; Christopher Morahan, producer (PBS)

OUTSTANDING VARIETY, MUSIC OR COMEDY PROGRAM: "Motown Returns to the Apollo," Suzanne de Passe, executive producer; Don Mischer, producer; Suzanne Coston and Michael Weisbarth, co-producers (NBC)

OUTSTANDING DRAMA/COMEDY SPECIAL: "Do You remember Love?," Dave Bell, executive producer; Marilyn Hall, co-executive producer; Wayne Threm and James E. Thompson, producers; Walter Halsey Davis, co-producer (CBS)

OUTSTANDING INFORMATIONAL SERIES: *The Living Planet: A Portrait of Earth,* Richard Brock, executive producer; Adrian Warren, Ned Kelly, Andrew Neal, and Richard Brock, producers (PBS)

OUTSTANDING INFORMATIONAL SPECIAL: "Cousteau: Mississippi," Jacques-Yves Cousteau and Jean-Michel Cousteau, executive producers; Andrew Solt, producer; Jacques-Yves Cousteau, host (SYN)

OUTSTANDING CLASSICAL PROGRAM IN THE PERFORMING ARTS: *"Tosca,* Live From the Met," Michael Bronson, executive producer; Samuel J. Paul, producer (PBS)

OUTSTANDING CHILDREN'S PROGRAM: "Displaced Person," *American Playhouse,* Allison Maher, Barry Solomon, Rick Traum, and Patrick Lynch, executive producers; Patrick Dromgoole, supervising executive producer; Barry Levinson, producer (PBS)

OUTSTANDING ANIMATED PROGRAM: "Garfield in the Rough," Jay Poynor, executive producer; Phil Roman, producer; Jim Davis, writer; Phil Roman, director (CBS)

OUTSTANDING LEAD ACTOR IN A DRAMA SERIES: William Daniels, *St. Elsewhere* (NBC)

OUTSTANDING LEAD ACTOR IN A COMEDY SERIES: Robert Guillaume, *Benson* (ABC)

OUTSTANDING LEAD ACTOR IN A LIMITED SERIES OR A SPECIAL: Richard Crenna, "The Rape of Richard Beck," *ABC Theatre* (ABC)

OUTSTANDING LEAD ACTRESS IN A DRAMA SERIES: Tyne Daly, *Cagney & Lacey* (CBS)

OUTSTANDING LEAD ACTRESS IN A COMEDY SERIES: Jane Curtin, *Kate & Allie* (CBS)

OUTSTANDING LEAD ACTRESS IN A LIMITED SERIES OR A SPECIAL: Joanne Woodward, "Do You Remember Love?" (CBS)

OUTSTANDING SUPPORTING ACTOR IN A DRAMA SERIES: Edward James Olmos, *Miami Vice* (NBC)

OUTSTANDING SUPPORTING ACTOR IN A COMEDY SERIES: John Larroquette, *Night Court* (NBC)

OUTSTANDING SUPPORTING ACTOR IN A LIMITED SERIES OR A SPECIAL: Karl Malden, "Fatal Vision" (NBC)

OUTSTANDING SUPPORTING ACTRESS IN A DRAMA SERIES: Betty Thomas, *Hill Street Blues* (NBC)

OUTSTANDING SUPPORTING ACTRESS IN A COMEDY SERIES: Rhea Perlman, *Cheers* (NBC)

OUTSTANDING SUPPORTING ACTRESS IN A LIMITED SERIES OR A SPECIAL: Kim Stanley, "Cat on a Hot Tin Roof," *American Playhouse* (PBS)

OUTSTANDING INDIVIDUAL PERFORMANCE IN A VARIETY OR MUSIC PROGRAM: George Hearns, "Sweeney Todd," *Great Performances* (PBS)

OUTSTANDING INDIVIDUAL ACHIEVEMENT—INFORMATIONAL PROGRAMMING—WRITING: Howard Enders, John G. Fox, Michael Joseloff, and Marc Siegel; "The Crucible of Europe," *Heritage: Civilization and the Jews* (PBS) and Brian Wilson, "Out of the Ashes," *Heritage: Civilization and the Jews* (PBS)

OUTSTANDING DIRECTING IN A DRAMA SERIES (SINGLE EPISODE): Arthur Karen, "Heat," *Cagney & Lacey* (CBS)

OUTSTANDING DIRECTING IN A COMEDY SERIES (SINGLE EPISODE): Jay Sandrich, "The Younger Woman," *The Cosby Show* (NBC)

OUTSTANDING DIRECTING IN A LIMITED SERIES OR A SPECIAL: Lamont Johnson, "Wallenberg: A Hero's Story" (NBC)

OUTSTANDING DIRECTING IN A VARIETY, OR MUSIC PROGRAM: Terry Hughes, "Sweeney Todd," *Great Performances* (PBS)

OUTSTANDING WRITING IN A DRAMA SERIES (SINGLE EPISODE): Patricia M. Green, "Who Said It's Fair—Part II," *Cagney & Lacey* (CBS)

OUTSTANDING WRITING IN A COMEDY SERIES (SINGLE EPISODE): Ed Weinberg and Michael Leeson, premiere episode, *The Cosby Show* (NBC)

OUTSTANDING WRITING IN A LIMITED SERIES OR A SPECIAL: Vickie Patik, "Do You Remember Love?" (CBS)

OUTSTANDING WRITING IN A VARIETY, MUSIC PROGRAM: Gerard Mulligan, Sandy Frank, Joe Toplyn, Chris Elliott, Matt Wickline, Jeff Martin, Eddie Gorodetsky, Randy Cohen, Larry Jacobson, Kevin Curran, Fred Graver, Merrill Markoe, and David Letterman; "Christmas with the Lettermans," show #491 *Late Night with David Letterman* (NBC)

EIGHTH ANNUAL ATAS GOVERNOR'S AWARD: Alistaire Cooke

1985–1986 (presented September 20, 1986)

OUTSTANDING COMEDY SERIES: *The Golden Girls,* Paul Junger Witt and Tony Thomas executive producers; Paul Bogart, supervising producer; Paul Junger Witt, Tony Thomas, Kathy Speer, and Terry Grossman producers; Marsha Posner Williams co-producer (NBC)

OUTSTANDING DRAMA SERIES: *Cagney & Lacey,* Barney Rosenzweig, executive producer; Liz Coe, supervising producer; Ralph Singleton, Patricia Green, and Steve Brown, producers; P. K. Knelman, co-producer (CBS)

OUTSTANDING MINISERIES: "Peter the Great," Marvin J. Chomsky, producer; Konstantin Theoren, line producer (NBC)

OUTSTANDING VARIETY, MUSIC OR COMEDY PROGRAM: "The Kennedy Center Honors: A Celebration of the Performing Arts," Nick Vanoff and George Stevens, Jr., producers (CBS)

OUTSTANDING DRAMA/COMEDY SPECIAL: "Love Is Never Silent," Marian Rees, executive producer; Juliana Field, co-executive producer (NBC)

OUTSTANDING INFORMATIONAL SERIES: *Laurence Olivier—A Life,* Nick Evans and Nick Elliott, executive producers; Bob Bee, producer (PBS) *Planet Earth,* Thomas Skinner, executive producer; Gregory Andorfer, series producer; Georgann Kane, coordinating producer (PBS)

OUTSTANDING INFORMATIONAL SPECIAL: "W. C. Fields Straight Up," Robert B. Weide, executive producer; Ronald J. Fields, co-producer (PBS)

OUTSTANDING CLASSICAL PROGRAM IN THE PERFORMING ARTS: "Wolftrap Presents the Kirov: Swan Lake," Michael B. Styer, executive producer; Phillip Byrd, senior producer; John T. Potthast, producer (PBS)

OUTSTANDING CHILDREN'S PROGRAM: *Anne of Green Gables—Wonderworks,* Kevin Sullivan and Lee Polk executive producers; Kevin Sullivan and Ian McDougall producers (PBS)

OUTSTANDING ANIMATED PROGRAM: "Garfield's Halloween Adventure," Jay Poynor, executive producer (CBS)

OUTSTANDING LEAD ACTOR IN A DRAMA SERIES: William Daniels, *St. Elsewhere* (NBC)

OUTSTANDING LEAD ACTOR IN A COMEDY SERIES: Michael J. Fox, *Family Ties* (NBC)

OUTSTANDING LEAD ACTOR IN A MINI SERIES OR A SPECIAL: Dustin Hoffman, "Death of a Salesman" (CBS)

OUTSTANDING LEAD ACTRESS IN A DRAMA SERIES: Sharon Gless, *Cagney & Lacey* (CBS)

OUTSTANDING LEAD ACTRESS IN A COMEDY SERIES: Betty White, *The Golden Girls* (NBC)

OUTSTANDING LEAD ACTRESS IN A MINISERIES OR A SPECIAL: Marlo Thomas, "Nobody's Child" (NBC)

OUTSTANDING SUPPORTING ACTOR IN A DRAMA SERIES: John Karlen, *Cagney & Lacey* (CBS)

OUTSTANDING SUPPORTING ACTOR IN A COMEDY SERIES: John Larroquette, *Night Court* (NBC)

OUTSTANDING SUPPORTING ACTOR IN A MINISERIES OR A SPECIAL: John Malkovich, "Death of a Salesman" (CBS)

OUTSTANDING SUPPORTING ACTRESS IN A DRAMA SERIES: Bonnie Bartlett, *St. Elsewhere* (NBC)

OUTSTANDING SUPPORTING ACTRESS IN A COMEDY SERIES: Rhea Perlman, *Cheers* (NBC)

OUTSTANDING SUPPORTING ACTRESS IN A MINISERIES OR A SPECIAL: Colleen Dewhurst, "Between Two Women" (ABC)

OUTSTANDING INDIVIDUAL PERFORMANCE IN A VARIETY OR MUSIC PROGRAM: Whitney Houston, "The 28th Annual Grammy Awards" (CBS)

OUTSTANDING GUEST PERFORMER IN A DRAMA SERIES: John Lithgow, *Amazing Stories* (NBC)

OUTSTANDING GUEST PERFORMER IN A COMEDY SERIES: Roscoe Lee Browne, *The Cosby Show* (NBC)

OUTSTANDING INDIVIDUAL ACHIEVEMENT IN CLASSICAL MUSIC/DANCE PROGRAMMING-PERFORMING: Placido Domingo, "Cavalleria Rustiana," *Great Performances* (PBS)

OUTSTANDING INDIVIDUAL ACHIEVEMENT—INFORMATIONAL PROGRAMMING—WRITING: John L. Miller, "The Spencer Tracy Legacy: A Tribute by Katharine Hepburn" (PBS)

OUTSTANDING DIRECTING IN A DRAMA SERIES (SINGLE EPISODE): Georg Stanford Brown, "Parting Shots," *Cagney & Lacey* (CBS)

OUTSTANDING DIRECTING IN A COMEDY SERIES (SINGLE EPISODE): Jay Sandrich, "Denise's Friend," *The Cosby Show* (NBC)

OUTSTANDING DIRECTING IN A MINISERIES OR A SPECIAL: Joseph Sargent, "Love Is Never Silent," *Hallmark Hall of Fame* (NBC)

OUTSTANDING DIRECTING IN A VARIETY, OR MUSIC PROGRAM: Waris Hussein, "Copacabana," (CBS)

OUTSTANDING WRITING IN A DRAMA SERIES (SINGLE EPISODE): Tom Fontana, John Tinker, and John Masius, "Time Heals," *St. Elsewhere* (NBC)

OUTSTANDING WRITING IN A COMEDY SERIES (SINGLE EPISODE): Barry Fanaro and Mort Nathan, "A Little Romance," *The Golden Girls* (NBC)

OUTSTANDING WRITING IN A MINISERIES OR A SPECIAL: Ron Cowen and Daniel Lipman, teleplay; Sherman Yellen, story; "An Early Frost," (NBC)

OUTSTANDING WRITING IN A VARIETY, MUSIC PROGRAM: David Letterman, Joe O'Donnell, Sandy Frank, Joe Toplyn, Chris Elliott, Matt Wickline, Jeff Martin, Gerard Mulligan, Randy Cohen, Larry Jacobson, Kevin Curran, Fred Graver, and Merrill Markoe; Fourth Anniversary Show, *Late Night with David Letterman* (NBC)

OUTSTANDING INDIVIDUAL ACHIEVEMENT IN CLASSICAL MUSIC/DANCE PROGRAMMING-WRITING: John Ardlon, "Gala of Stars 1986" (PBS)

NINTH ANNUAL ATAS GOVERNOR'S AWARD: Red Skelton

1986–1987 (presented September 20, 1987)

OUTSTANDING COMEDY SERIES: *The Golden Girls,* Paul Junger Witt, Tony Thomas, and Susan Harris, executive producers; Kathy Speer and Terry Grossman, producers; Mort Nathan, Barry Fanaro, Winifred Hervey, and Marsha Posner Williams, co-producers (NBC)

OUTSTANDING DRAMA SERIES: *L.A. Law,* Steven Bochco, executive producer; Gregory Hoblit, co-executive producer; Terry Louise Fisher, supervising producer; Ellen S. Pressman and Scott Goldstein, producers; Phillip M. Goldfarb, coordinating producer (NBC)

OUTSTANDING MINISERIES: "A Year in the Life," Joshua Brand and John Falsey, executive producers; Stephen Cragg, producer (NBC)

OUTSTANDING VARIETY, MUSIC OR COMEDY PROGRAM: "The 1987 Tony Awards," Don Mischer, executive producer; David J. Goldberg, producer (CBS)

OUTSTANDING DRAMA/COMEDY SPECIAL: "Promise," *Hallmark Hall of Fame,* Peter K. Duchow and James Garner, executive producers; Glenn Jordan, producer; Richard Friedenberg, co-producer (CBS)

OUTSTANDING INFORMATIONAL SERIES: *Smithsonian World,* Adrian Malone, executive producer; David Grubin, producer (PBS). "Unknown Chaplin," *American Masters,* Kevin Brownlow and David Gill, producers (PBS)

OUTSTANDING INFORMATIONAL SPECIAL: "Dance in America: Agnes, The Indomitable De Mille," *Great Performances,* Jac Venza, executive producer; Judy Kinberg, producer (PBS)

OUTSTANDING CLASSICAL PROGRAM IN THE PERFORMING ARTS: "Vladimir Horowitz: The Last Romantic," Peter Gelb, executive producer; Susan Froemke, producer; Vladimir Horowitz, star (PBS)

OUTSTANDING CHILDREN'S PROGRAM: *Jim Henson's the Storyteller,* "Hans My Hedgehog," Jim Henson, executive producer; Mark Shivas, producer (NBC)

OUTSTANDING ANIMATED PROGRAM: "Cathy," Lee Mendelson, executive producer; Bill Melendez, producer; Cathy Guisewite, writer (CBS)

OUTSTANDING LEAD ACTOR IN A DRAMA SERIES: Bruce Willis, *Moonlighting* (ABC)

OUTSTANDING LEAD ACTOR IN A COMEDY SERIES: Michael J. Fox, *Family Ties* (NBC)

OUTSTANDING LEAD ACTOR IN A MINI SERIES OR A SPECIAL: James Woods, "Promise," *Hallmark Hall of Fame* (CBS)

OUTSTANDING LEAD ACTRESS IN A DRAMA SERIES: Sharon Gless, *Cagney & Lacey* (CBS)

OUTSTANDING LEAD ACTRESS IN A COMEDY SERIES: Rue McClanahan, *The Golden Girls* (NBC)

OUTSTANDING LEAD ACTRESS IN A MINISERIES OR A SPECIAL: Gena Rowlands, "The Betty Ford Story" (ABC)

OUTSTANDING SUPPORTING ACTOR IN A DRAMA SERIES: John Hillerman, *Magnum, P.I.* (CBS)

OUTSTANDING SUPPORTING ACTOR IN A COMEDY SERIES: John Larroquette, *Night Court* (NBC)

OUTSTANDING SUPPORTING ACTOR IN A MINISERIES OR A SPECIAL: Dabney Coleman, "Sworn to Silence" (ABC)

OUTSTANDING SUPPORTING ACTRESS IN A DRAMA SERIES: Bonnie Bartlett, *St. Elsewhere* (NBC)

OUTSTANDING SUPPORTING ACTRESS IN A COMEDY SERIES: Jackee Harry, *227* (NBC)

OUTSTANDING SUPPORTING ACTRESS IN A MINISERIES OR A SPECIAL: Piper Laurie, "Promise," *Hallmark Hall of Fame* (CBS)

OUTSTANDING INDIVIDUAL PERFORMANCE IN A VARIETY OR MUSIC PROGRAM: Robin Williams, "A Carol Burnett Special: Carol, Carl, Whoopi & Robin" (ABC)

OUTSTANDING GUEST PERFORMER IN A DRAMA SERIES: Alfre Woodard, *L.A. Law* (NBC)

OUTSTANDING GUEST PERFORMER IN A COMEDY SERIES: John Cleese, *Cheers* (NBC)

OUTSTANDING INDIVIDUAL ACHIEVEMENT IN CLASSICAL MUSIC/DANCE PROGRAMMING: Albert Maysles and David Maysles, directors; "Vladimir Horowitz: The Last Romantic" (PBS)

OUTSTANDING INDIVIDUAL ACHIEVEMENT IN INFORMATIONAL PROGRAMMING: Robert McCrum and Robert MacNeil, writers; *The Story of English,* "A Muse of Fire" (PBS)

OUTSTANDING DIRECTING IN A DRAMA SERIES (SINGLE EPISODE): Gregory Hoblit, "Pilot," *L.A. Law* (NBC)

OUTSTANDING DIRECTING IN A COMEDY SERIES (SINGLE EPISODE): Terry Hughes, "Isn't It Romantic," *The Golden Girls* (NBC)

OUTSTANDING DIRECTING IN A MINISERIES OR A SPECIAL: Glenn Jordan, "Promise," *Hallmark Hall of Fame* (CBS)

OUTSTANDING DIRECTING IN A VARIETY, OR MUSIC PROGRAM: Don Mischer, "The Kennedy Center Honors: A Celebration of the Performing Arts" (CBS)

OUTSTANDING WRITING IN A DRAMA SERIES (SINGLE EPISODE): Terry Louise Fisher, "Venus Butterfly," *L.A. Law* (NBC)

OUTSTANDING WRITING IN A COMEDY SERIES (SINGLE EPISODE): Gary David Goldberg and Alan Uger, "My Name is Alex," *Family Ties* (NBC)

OUTSTANDING WRITING IN A MINISERIES OR A SPECIAL: Richard Friedenberg, teleplay; Kenneth Blackwell, Tennyson Flowers, and Richard Friedenberg, story; "Promise," *Hallmark Hall of Fame* (CBS)

OUTSTANDING WRITING IN A VARIETY, MUSIC PROGRAM: Steve O'Donnell, Sandy Frank, Joe Toplyn, Chris Elliott, Matt Wickline, Jeff Martin, Gerard Mulligan, Randy Cohen, Larry Jacobson, Kevin Curran, Fred Graver, Adam Resnick, and David Letterman; Fifth Anniversary Special, *Late Night with David Letterman* (NBC)

TENTH ANNUAL ATAS GOVERNOR'S AWARD: Grant Tinker

TOP-RATED PROGRAMS BY SEASON

The following are listings of the top-rated evening series during each season, ranked by audience size. The Nielsen rating is the percent of all TV-equipped homes tuned to the program on an average night, as measured by the A. C. Nielsen Company. Thus a rating of 61.6 for the *Texaco Star Theater* from 1950–1951 means that on the average, 61.6 percent of all homes that had a TV were tuned to this show.

A. C. Nielsen changed its system of computing ratings in 1960, so ratings prior to and after that date are not precisely comparable. It should also be noted that since the Nielsen system is basically a service for advertisers, only sponsored programs are measured. However, it is unlikely that any unsponsored series (usually public affairs or news) has ever regularly achieved audience levels comparable to those of the commercial programs shown here.

October 1950–April 1951

	Program	Network	Rating
1.	Texaco Star Theater	NBC	61.6
2.	Fireside Theatre	NBC	52.6
3.	Philco TV Playhouse	NBC	45.3
4.	Your Show of Shows	NBC	42.6
5.	The Colgate Comedy Hour	NBC	42.0
6.	Gillette Cavalcade of Sports	NBC	41.3
7.	The Lone Ranger	ABC	41.2
8.	Arthur Godfrey's Talent Scouts	CBS	40.6
9.	Hopalong Cassidy	NBC	39.9
10.	Mama	CBS	39.7
11.	Robert Montgomery Presents	NBC	38.8
12.	Martin Kane, Private Eye	NBC	37.8
13.	Man Against Crime	CBS	37.4
14.	Kraft Television Theatre	NBC	37.0
15.	The Toast of the Town	CBS	36.5
16.	The Aldrich Family	NBC	36.1
17.	You Bet Your Life	NBC	36.0
18.	Arthur Godfrey and His Friends	CBS	35.9
19.	Armstrong Circle Theatre	NBC	35.6
	Lights Out	NBC	35.6
	Big Town	CBS	35.6
22.	The Alan Young Show	CBS	34.4
23.	Stop the Music	ABC	34.0
24.	Studio One	CBS	33.8
25.	The Big Story	NBC	33.7

October 1951–April 1952

	Program	Network	Rating
1.	Arthur Godfrey's Talent Scouts	CBS	53.8
2.	Texaco Star Theater	NBC	52.0
3.	I Love Lucy	CBS	50.9
4.	The Red Skelton Show	NBC	50.2
5.	The Colgate Comedy Hour	NBC	45.3
6.	Arthur Godfrey and His Friends	CBS	43.3
7.	Fireside Theatre	NBC	43.1
8.	Your Show of Shows	NBC	43.0
9.	The Jack Benny Show	CBS	42.8
10.	You Bet Your Life	NBC	42.1
11.	Mama	CBS	41.3
12.	Philco TV Playhouse	NBC	40.4
13.	Amos 'n' Andy	CBS	38.9
14.	Gangbusters	NBC	38.7
15.	Big Town	CBS	38.5
16.	Goodyear TV Playhouse	NBC	37.8
17.	Pabst Blue Ribbon Bouts	CBS	37.5
18.	The Lone Ranger	ABC	36.8
19.	Gillette Cavalcade of Sports	NBC	36.5
20.	All Star Revue	NBC	36.3
	Dragnet	NBC	36.3
22.	The Alan Young Show	CBS	35.8
23.	Kraft Television Theatre	NBC	34.8
24.	Armstrong Circle Theatre	NBC	34.7
25.	Strike It Rich	CBS	34.5

October 1952–April 1953

	Program	Network	Rating
1.	I Love Lucy	CBS	67.3
2.	Arthur Godfrey's Talent Scouts	CBS	54.7
3.	Arthur Godfrey and His Friends	CBS	47.1
4.	Dragnet	NBC	46.8
5.	Texaco Star Theater	NBC	46.7
6.	The Buick Circus Hour	NBC	46.0
7.	The Colgate Comedy Hour	NBC	44.3
8.	Gangbusters	NBC	42.4
9.	You Bet Your Life	NBC	41.6
10.	Fireside Theatre	NBC	40.6
11.	The Red Buttons Show	CBS	40.2
12.	The Jack Benny Show	CBS	39.0
13.	Life with Luigi	CBS	38.5
14.	Pabst Blue Ribbon Bouts	CBS	37.9
15.	Goodyear TV Playhouse	NBC	37.8
16.	The Life of Riley	NBC	37.4
17.	Philco TV Playhouse	NBC	37.3
18.	Mama	CBS	37.0
19.	Your Show of Shows	NBC	36.0
20.	What's My Line	CBS	35.3
	Strike It Rich	CBS	35.3
22.	Our Miss Brooks	CBS	35.0
	The Big Story	NBC	35.0
24.	Gillette Cavalcade of Sports	NBC	34.7
25.	Amos 'n' Andy	CBS	34.4

October 1953–April 1954

	Program	Network	Rating
1.	I Love Lucy	CBS	58.8
2.	Dragnet	NBC	53.2
3.	Arthur Godfrey's Talent Scouts	CBS	43.6
	You Bet Your Life	NBC	43.6
5.	The Milton Berle Show	NBC	40.2
6.	Arthur Godfrey and His Friends	CBS	38.9
7.	Ford Theatre	NBC	38.8
8.	The Jackie Gleason Show	CBS	38.1
9.	Fireside Theatre	NBC	36.4
10.	The Colgate Comedy Hour	NBC	36.2
	This Is Your Life	NBC	36.2
12.	The Red Buttons Show	CBS	35.3
13.	The Life of Riley	NBC	35.0
14.	Our Miss Brooks	CBS	34.2
15.	Treasury Men in Action	NBC	33.9
16.	The Jack Benny Show	CBS	33.3
17.	The Toast of the Town	CBS	33.0
18.	Gillette Cavalcade of Sports	NBC	32.7
19.	Philco TV Playhouse	NBC	32.5
20.	The George Burns and Gracie Allen Show	CBS	32.4
21.	Kraft Television Theatre	NBC	31.3
22.	Goodyear TV Playhouse	NBC	31.0
23.	Pabst Blue Ribbon Bouts	CBS	30.9
24.	Private Secretary	CBS	30.3
25.	I Married Joan	NBC	30.2
	Mama	CBS	30.2

October 1954–April 1955

	Program	Network	Rating
1.	I Love Lucy	CBS	49.3
2.	The Jackie Gleason Show	CBS	42.4
3.	Dragnet	NBC	42.1
4.	You Bet Your Life	NBC	41.0
5.	The Toast of the Town	CBS	39.6
6.	Disneyland	ABC	39.1
7.	The Jack Benny Show	CBS	38.3
8.	The George Gobel Show	NBC	35.2
9.	Ford Theatre	NBC	34.9
10.	December Bride	CBS	34.7
11.	Buick-Berle Show	NBC	34.6
12.	This Is Your Life	NBC	34.5
13.	I've Got a Secret	CBS	34.0
14.	Two for the Money	CBS	33.9
15.	Your Hit Parade	NBC	33.6
16.	The Millionaire	CBS	33.0
17.	General Electric Theater	CBS	32.6
18.	Arthur Godfrey's Talent Scouts	CBS	32.5
19.	Private Secretary	CBS	32.2
20.	Fireside Theatre	NBC	31.1
21.	The Life of Riley	NBC	30.9
22.	Arthur Godfrey and His Friends	CBS	29.8
23.	The Adventures of Rin Tin Tin	ABC	29.5
24.	Topper	CBS	29.4
25.	Pabst Blue Ribbon Bouts	CBS	29.1

October 1955–April 1956

Program	Network	Rating
1. The $64,000 Question	CBS	47.5
2. I Love Lucy	CBS	46.1
3. The Ed Sullivan Show	CBS	39.5
4. Disneyland	ABC	37.4
5. The Jack Benny Show	CBS	37.2
6. December Bride	CBS	37.0
7. You Bet Your Life	NBC	35.4
8. Dragnet	NBC	35.0
9. The Millionaire	CBS	33.8
10. I've Got a Secret	CBS	33.5
11. General Electric Theater	CBS	32.9
12. Private Secretary	CBS	32.4
Ford Theatre	NBC	32.4
14. The Red Skelton Show	CBS	32.3

Program	Network	Rating
15. The George Gobel Show	NBC	31.9
16. Arthur Godfrey's Talent Scouts	CBS	31.1
17. The Lineup	CBS	30.8
18. The Perry Como Show	NBC	30.3
19. The Honeymooners	CBS	30.2
20. The Adventures of Robin Hood	CBS	30.1
21. The Life of Riley	NBC	29.9
22. Climax	CBS	29.6
23. Your Hit Parade	NBC	29.1
24. Fireside Theatre	NBC	29.0
25. Lux Video Theatre	NBC	28.9

October 1956–April 1957

Program	Network	Rating
1. I Love Lucy	CBS	43.7
2. The Ed Sullivan Show	CBS	38.4
3. General Electric Theater	CBS	36.9
4. The $64,000 Question	CBS	36.4
5. December Bride	CBS	35.2
6. Alfred Hitchcock Presents	CBS	33.9
7. I've Got a Secret	CBS	32.7
Gunsmoke	CBS	32.7
9. The Perry Como Show	NBC	32.6
10. The Jack Benny Show	CBS	32.3
11. Dragnet	NBC	32.1
12. Arthur Godfrey's Talent Scouts	CBS	31.9
13. The Millionaire	CBS	31.8

Program	Network	Rating
Disneyland	ABC	31.8
15. The Red Skelton Show	CBS	31.4
The Lineup	CBS	31.4
17. You Bet Your Life	NBC	31.1
18. The Life & Legend of Wyatt Earp	ABC	31.0
19. The Ford Show	NBC	30.7
20. The Adventures of Robin Hood	CBS	30.3
21. People Are Funny	NBC	30.2
22. The $64,000 Challenge	CBS	29.7
The Phil Silvers Show	CBS	29.7
24. Lassie	CBS	29.5
25. Private Secretary	CBS	29.0

October 1957–April 1958

Program	Network	Rating
1. Gunsmoke	CBS	43.1
2. The Danny Thomas Show	CBS	35.3
3. Tales of Wells Fargo	NBC	35.2
4. Have Gun Will Travel	CBS	33.7
5. I've Got a Secret	CBS	33.4
6. The Life and Legend of Wyatt Earp	ABC	32.6
7. General Electric Theater	CBS	31.5
8. The Restless Gun	NBC	31.4
9. December Bride	CBS	30.7
10. You Bet Your Life	NBC	30.6
11. The Perry Como Show	NBC	30.5
12. Alfred Hitchcock Presents	CBS	30.3

Program	Network	Rating
Cheyenne	ABC	30.3
14. The Ford Show	NBC	29.7
15. The Red Skelton Show	CBS	28.9
16. The Gale Storm Show	CBS	28.8
17. The Millionaire	CBS	28.5
18. The Lineup	CBS	28.4
19. This Is Your Life	NBC	28.1
The $64,000 Question	CBS	28.1
21. Zane Grey Theater	CBS	27.9
22. Lassie	CBS	27.8
23. Wagon Train	NBC	27.7
Sugarfoot	ABC	27.7
Father Knows Best	NBC	27.7

October 1958–April 1959

Program	Network	Rating	Program	Network	Rating
1. Gunsmoke	CBS	39.6	Father Knows Best	CBS	28.3
2. Wagon Train	NBC	36.1	15. The Texan	CBS	28.2
3. Have Gun Will Travel	CBS	34.3	16. Wanted: Dead or Alive	CBS	28.0
4. The Rifleman	ABC	33.1	Peter Gunn	NBC	28.0
5. The Danny Thomas Show	CBS	32.8	18. Cheyenne	ABC	27.9
6. Maverick	ABC	30.4	19. Perry Mason	CBS	27.5
7. Tales of Wells Fargo	NBC	30.2	20. The Ford Show	NBC	27.2
8. The Real McCoys	ABC	30.1	21. Sugarfoot	ABC	27.0
9. I've Got a Secret	CBS	29.8	The Ann Sothern Show	CBS	27.0
10. The Life and Legend of Wyatt			The Perry Como Show	NBC	27.0
Earp	ABC	29.1	24. Alfred Hitchcock Presents	CBS	26.8
11. The Price Is Right	NBC	28.6	25. Name That Tune	CBS	26.7
12. The Red Skelton Show	CBS	28.5	General Electric Theatre	CBS	26.7
13. Zane Grey Theater	CBS	28.3			

October 1959–April 1960

Program	Network	Rating	Program	Network	Rating
1. Gunsmoke	CBS	40.3	14. The Ford Show	NBC	27.4
2. Wagon Train	NBC	38.4	15. The Lawman	ABC	26.2
3. Have Gun Will Travel	CBS	34.7	16. Dennis the Menace	CBS	26.0
4. The Danny Thomas Show	CBS	31.1	17. Cheyenne	ABC	25.9
5. The Red Skelton Show	CBS	30.8	18. Rawhide	CBS	25.8
6. Father Knows Best	CBS	29.7	19. Maverick	ABC	25.2
77 Sunset Strip	ABC	29.7	20. The Life and Legend of Wyatt		
8. The Price Is Right	NBC	29.2	Earp	ABC	25.0
9. Wanted: Dead or Alive	CBS	28.7	21. Mr. Lucky	CBS	24.4
10. Perry Mason	CBS	28.3	Zane Grey Theater	CBS	24.4
11. The Real McCoys	ABC	28.2	General Electric Theater	CBS	24.4
12. The Ed Sullivan Show	CBS	28.0	24. The Ann Sothern Show	CBS	24.2
13. The Rifleman	ABC	27.5	25. Alfred Hitchcock Presents	CBS	24.1

October 1960–April 1961

Program	Network	Rating	Program	Network	Rating
1. Gunsmoke	CBS	37.3	77 Sunset Strip	ABC	25.8
2. Wagon Train	NBC	34.2	15. The Ed Sullivan Show	CBS	25.0
3. Have Gun Will Travel	CBS	30.9	16. Perry Mason	CBS	24.9
4. The Andy Griffith Show	CBS	27.8	17. Bonanza	NBC	24.8
5. The Real McCoys	ABC	27.7	18. The Flintstones	ABC	24.3
6. Rawhide	CBS	27.5	19. The Red Skelton Show	CBS	24.0
7. Candid Camera	CBS	27.3	20. General Electric Theater	CBS	23.4
8. The Untouchables	ABC	27.0	21. Checkmate	CBS	23.2
The Price Is Right	NBC	27.0	22. What's My Line	CBS	23.1
10. The Jack Benny Show	CBS	26.2	23. The Many Loves of Dobie		
11. Dennis the Menace	CBS	26.1	Gillis	CBS	23.0
12. The Danny Thomas Show	CBS	25.9	24. The Ford Show	NBC	22.9
13. My Three Sons	ABC	25.8	25. The Garry Moore Show	CBS	22.7

October 1961–April 1962

	Program	Network	Rating		Program	Network	Rating
1.	Wagon Train	NBC	32.1	15.	Lassie	CBS	24.0
2.	Bonanza	NBC	30.0		Sing Along with Mitch	NBC	24.0
3.	Gunsmoke	CBS	28.3	17.	Dennis the Menace	CBS	23.8
4.	Hazel	NBC	27.7	18.	Ben Casey	ABC	23.7
5.	Perry Mason	CBS	27.3	19.	The Ed Sullivan Show	CBS	23.5
6.	The Red Skelton Show	CBS	27.1	20.	Car 54, Where Are You?	NBC	23.2
7.	The Andy Griffith Show	CBS	27.0	21.	The Flintstones	ABC	22.9
8.	The Danny Thomas Show	CBS	26.1		The Many Loves of Dobie		
9.	Dr. Kildare	NBC	25.6		Gillis	CBS	22.9
10.	Candid Camera	CBS	25.5	23.	Walt Disney's Wonderful		
11.	My Three Sons	ABC	24.7		World of Color	NBC	22.7
12.	The Garry Moore Show	CBS	24.6	24.	The Joey Bishop Show	NBC	22.6
13.	Rawhide	CBS	24.5	25.	The Perry Como Show	NBC	22.5
14.	The Real McCoys	ABC	24.2				

October 1962–April 1963

	Program	Network	Rating		Program	Network	Rating
1.	The Beverly Hillbillies	CBS	36.0	14.	The Ed Sullivan Show	CBS	25.3
2.	Candid Camera	CBS	31.1	15.	Hazel	NBC	25.1
	The Red Skelton Show	CBS	31.1	16.	I've Got a Secret	CBS	24.9
4.	Bonanza	NBC	29.8	17.	The Jackie Gleason Show	CBS	24.1
	The Lucy Show	CBS	29.8	18.	The Defenders	CBS	23.9
6.	The Andy Griffith Show	CBS	29.7	19.	The Garry Moore Show	CBS	23.3
7.	Ben Casey	ABC	28.7		To Tell the Truth	CBS	23.3
	The Danny Thomas Show	CBS	28.7		Lassie	CBS	23.3
9.	The Dick Van Dyke Show	CBS	27.1	22.	Rawhide	CBS	22.8
10.	Gunsmoke	CBS	27.0	23.	Perry Mason	CBS	22.4
11.	Dr. Kildare	NBC	26.2	24.	Walt Disney's Wonderful		
	The Jack Benny Show	CBS	26.2		World of Color	NBC	22.3
13.	What's My Line	CBS	25.5	25.	Wagon Train	ABC	22.0

October 1963–April 1964

	Program	Network	Rating		Program	Network	Rating
1.	The Beverly Hillbillies	CBS	39.1		The Jack Benny Show	CBS	25.0
2.	Bonanza	NBC	36.9	15.	The Jackie Gleason Show	CBS	24.6
3.	The Dick Van Dyke Show	CBS	33.3	16.	The Donna Reed Show	ABC	24.5
4.	Petticoat Junction	CBS	30.3	17.	The Virginian	NBC	24.0
5.	The Andy Griffith Show	CBS	29.4	18.	The Patty Duke Show	ABC	23.9
6.	The Lucy Show	CBS	28.1	19.	Dr. Kildare	NBC	23.6
7.	Candid Camera	CBS	27.7	20.	Gunsmoke	CBS	23.5
8.	The Ed Sullivan Show	CBS	27.5	21.	Walt Disney's Wonderful		
9.	The Danny Thomas Show	CBS	26.7		World of Color	NBC	23.0
10.	My Favorite Martian	CBS	26.3	22.	Hazel	NBC	22.8
11.	The Red Skelton Show	CBS	25.7		McHale's Navy	ABC	22.8
12.	I've Got a Secret	CBS	25.0	24.	To Tell the Truth	CBS	22.6
	Lassie	CBS	25.0		What's My Line	CBS	22.6

October 1964–April 1965

Program	Network	Rating
1. Bonanza	NBC	36.3
2. Bewitched	ABC	31.0
3. Gomer Pyle, U.S.M.C.	CBS	30.7
4. The Andy Griffith Show	CBS	28.3
5. The Fugitive	ABC	27.9
6. The Red Skelton Hour	CBS	27.4
7. The Dick Van Dyke Show	CBS	27.1
8. The Lucy Show	CBS	26.6
9. Peyton Place II	ABC	26.4
10. Combat	ABC	26.1
11. Walt Disney's Wonderful World of Color	NBC	25.7
12. The Beverly Hillbillies	CBS	25.6

Program	Network	Rating
13. My Three Sons	ABC	25.5
14. Branded	NBC	25.3
15. Petticoat Junction	CBS	25.2
The Ed Sullivan Show	CBS	25.2
17. Lassie	CBS	25.1
18. The Munsters	CBS	24.7
Gilligan's Island	CBS	24.7
20. Peyton Place I	ABC	24.6
21. The Jackie Gleason Show	CBS	24.4
22. The Virginian	NBC	24.0
23. The Addams Family	ABC	23.9
24. My Favorite Martian	CBS	23.7
25. Flipper	NBC	23.4

October 1965–April 1966

Program	Network	Rating
1. Bonanza	NBC	31.8
2. Gomer Pyle, U.S.M.C.	CBS	27.8
3. The Lucy Show	CBS	27.7
4. The Red Skelton Hour	CBS	27.6
5. Batman (Thurs.)	ABC	27.0
6. The Andy Griffith Show	CBS	26.9
7. Bewitched	ABC	25.9
The Beverly Hillbillies	CBS	25.9
9. Hogan's Heroes	CBS	24.9
10. Batman (Wed.)	ABC	24.7
11. Green Acres	CBS	24.6
12. Get Smart	NBC	24.5
13. The Man from U.N.C.L.E.	NBC	24.0

Program	Network	Rating
14. Daktari	CBS	23.9
15. My Three Sons	CBS	23.8
16. The Dick Van Dyke Show	CBS	23.6
17. Walt Disney's Wonderful World of Color	NBC	23.2
The Ed Sullivan Show	CBS	23.2
19. The Lawrence Welk Show	ABC	22.4
I've Got a Secret	CBS	22.4
21. Petticoat Junction	CBS	22.3
22. Gilligan's Island	CBS	22.1
23. Wild, Wild West	CBS	22.0
The Jackie Gleason Show	CBS	22.0
The Virginian	NBC	22.0

October 1966–April 1967

Program	Network	Rating
1. Bonanza	NBC	29.1
2. The Red Skelton Hour	CBS	28.2
3. The Andy Griffith Show	CBS	27.4
4. The Lucy Show	CBS	26.2
5. The Jackie Gleason Show	CBS	25.3
6. Green Acres	CBS	24.6
7. Daktari	CBS	23.4
Bewitched	ABC	23.4
9. The Beverly Hillbillies	CBS	23.4
10. Gomer Pyle, U.S.M.C.	CBS	22.8
The Virginian	NBC	22.8
The Lawrence Welk Show	ABC	22.8
The Ed Sullivan Show	CBS	22.8
14. The Dean Martin Show	NBC	22.6

Program	Network	Rating
Family Affair	CBS	22.6
16. The Smothers Brothers Comedy Hour	CBS	22.2
17. Friday Night Movies	CBS	21.8
Hogan's Heroes	CBS	21.8
19. Walt Disney's Wonderful World of Color	NBC	21.5
20. Saturday Night at the Movies	NBC	21.4
21. Dragnet	NBC	21.2
22. Get Smart	NBC	21.0
23. Petticoat Junction	CBS	20.9
Rat Patrol	ABC	20.9
25. Daniel Boone	NBC	20.8

October 1967–April 1968

	Program	Network	Rating		Program	Network	Rating
1.	The Andy Griffith Show	CBS	27.6	15.	Friday Night Movie	CBS	22.8
2.	The Lucy Show	CBS	27.0		Green Acres	CBS	22.8
3.	Gomer Pyle, U.S.M.C.	CBS	25.6	17.	The Lawrence Welk Show	ABC	21.9
4.	Gunsmoke	CBS	25.5	18.	The Smothers Brothers		
	Family Affair	CBS	25.5		Comedy Hour	CBS	21.7
	Bonanza	NBC	25.5	19.	Gentle Ben	CBS	21.5
7.	The Red Skelton Show	CBS	25.3	20.	Tuesday Night at the Movies	NBC	21.4
8.	The Dean Martin Show	NBC	24.8	21.	Rowan & Martin's Laugh-In	NBC	21.3
9.	The Jackie Gleason Show	CBS	23.9	22.	The F.B.I.	ABC	21.2
10.	Saturday Night at the Movies	NBC	23.6	23.	Thursday Night Movie	CBS	21.1
11.	Bewitched	ABC	23.5	24.	My Three Sons	CBS	20.8
12.	The Beverly Hillbillies	CBS	23.3	25.	Walt Disney's Wonderful		
13.	The Ed Sullivan Show	CBS	23.2		World of Color	NBC	20.7
14.	The Virginian	NBC	22.9				

October 1968–April 1969

	Program	Network	Rating		Program	Network	Rating
1.	Rowan & Martin's Laugh-In	NBC	31.8	15.	The Glen Campbell Goodtime		
2.	Gomer Pyle, U.S.M.C.	CBS	27.2		Hour	CBS	22.5
3.	Bonanza	NBC	26.6	16.	Ironside	NBC	22.3
4.	Mayberry R.F.D.	CBS	25.4	17.	The Virginian	NBC	21.8
5.	Family Affair	CBS	25.2	18.	The F.B.I.	ABC	21.7
6.	Gunsmoke	CBS	24.9	19.	Green Acres	CBS	21.6
7.	Julia	NBC	24.6	20.	Dragnet	NBC	21.4
8.	The Dean Martin Show	NBC	24.1	21.	Daniel Boone	NBC	21.3
9.	Here's Lucy	CBS	23.8		Walt Disney's Wonderful		
10.	The Beverly Hillbillies	CBS	23.5		World of Color	NBC	21.3
11.	Mission: Impossible	CBS	23.3	23.	The Ed Sullivan Show	CBS	21.2
	Bewitched	ABC	23.3	24.	The Carol Burnett Show	CBS	20.8
	The Red Skelton Hour	CBS	23.3		The Jackie Gleason Show	CBS	20.8
14.	My Three Sons	CBS	22.8				

October 1969–April 1970

	Program	Network	Rating		Program	Network	Rating
1.	Rowan & Martin's Laugh-In	NBC	26.3	14.	The Dean Martin Show	NBC	21.9
2.	Gunsmoke	CBS	25.9	15.	My Three Sons	CBS	21.8
3.	Bonanza	NBC	24.8		Ironside	NBC	21.8
4.	Mayberry R.F.D.	CBS	24.4		The Johnny Cash Show	ABC	21.8
5.	Family Affair	CBS	24.2	18.	The Beverly Hillbillies	CBS	21.7
6.	Here's Lucy	CBS	23.9	19.	Hawaii Five-O	CBS	21.1
7.	The Red Skelton Hour	CBS	23.8	20.	The Glen Campbell Goodtime		
8.	Marcus Welby, M.D.	ABC	23.7		Hour	CBS	21.0
9.	Walt Disney's Wonderful				Hee Haw	CBS	21.0
	World of Color	NBC	23.6	22.	Movie of the Week	ABC	20.9
10.	The Doris Day Show	CBS	22.8	23.	Mod Squad	ABC	20.8
11.	The Bill Cosby Show	NBC	22.7	24.	Saturday Night Movie	NBC	20.6
12.	The Jim Nabors Hour	CBS	22.4		Bewitched	ABC	20.6
13.	The Carol Burnett Show	CBS	22.1		The F.B.I.	ABC	20.6

October 1970–April 1971

Program	Network	Rating		Program	Network	Rating
1. Marcus Welby, M.D.	ABC	29.6		Disney	NBC	22.4
2. The Flip Wilson Show	NBC	27.9	15.	Mayberry R.F.D.	CBS	22.3
3. Here's Lucy	CBS	26.1	16.	Hee Haw	CBS	21.4
4. Ironside	NBC	25.7	17.	Mannix	CBS	21.3
5. Gunsmoke	CBS	25.5	18.	The Men from Shiloh	NBC	21.2
6. ABC Movie of the Week	ABC	25.1	19.	My Three Sons	CBS	20.8
7. Hawaii Five-O	CBS	25.0	20.	The Doris Day Show	CBS	20.7
8. Medical Center	CBS	24.5	21.	The Smith Family	ABC	20.6
9. Bonanza	NBC	23.9	22.	The Mary Tyler Moore Show	CBS	20.3
10. The F.B.I.	ABC	23.0	23.	NBC Saturday Movie	NBC	20.1
11. Mod Squad	ABC	22.7	24.	The Dean Martin Show	NBC	20.0
12. Adam-12	NBC	22.6	25.	The Carol Burnett Show	CBS	19.8
13. Rowan & Martin's Laugh-In	NBC	22.4		The Partridge Family	ABC	19.8
The Wonderful World of				NBC Monday Movie	NBC	19.8

October 1971–April 1972

Program	Network	Rating		Program	Network	Rating
1. All in the Family	CBS	34.0	15.	Ironside	NBC	23.0
2. The Flip Wilson Show	NBC	28.2	16.	The Partridge Family	ABC	22.6
3. Marcus Welby, M.D.	ABC	27.8	17.	The F.B.I.	ABC	22.4
4. Gunsmoke	CBS	26.0	18.	The New Dick Van Dyke		
5. ABC Movie of the Week	ABC	25.6		Show	CBS	22.2
6. Sanford and Son	NBC	25.2	19.	The Wonderful World of		
7. Mannix	CBS	24.8		Disney	NBC	22.0
8. Funny Face	CBS	23.9	20.	Bonanza	NBC	21.9
Adam 12	NBC	23.9	21.	Mod Squad	ABC	21.5
10. The Mary Tyler Moore Show	CBS	23.7	22.	Rowan & Martin's Laugh-In	NBC	21.4
Here's Lucy	CBS	23.7	23.	The Carol Burnett Show	CBS	21.2
12. Hawaii Five-O	CBS	23.6		The Doris Day Show	CBS	21.2
13. Medical Center	CBS	23.5	25.	Monday Night Football	ABC	20.9
14. The NBC Mystery Movie	NBC	23.2				

October 1972–April 1973

Program	Network	Rating		Program	Network	Rating
1. All in the Family	CBS	33.3	15.	Here's Lucy	CBS	21.9
2. Sanford and Son	NBC	27.6	16.	The Bob Newhart Show	CBS	21.8
3. Hawaii Five-O	CBS	25.2	17.	Tuesday Movie of the Week	ABC	21.5
4. Maude	CBS	24.7	18.	Monday Night Football	ABC	21.0
5. Bridget Loves Bernie	CBS	24.2	19.	The Partridge Family	ABC	20.6
The NBC Sunday Mystery				The Waltons	CBS	20.6
Movie	NBC	24.2	21.	Medical Center	CBS	20.6
7. The Mary Tyler Moore Show	CBS	23.6	22.	The Carol Burnett Show	CBS	20.3
Gunsmoke	CBS	23.6	23.	ABC Sunday Movie	ABC	20.0
9. The Wonderful World of				The Rookies	ABC	20.0
Disney	NBC	23.5	25.	Escape	NBC	19.9
10. Ironside	NBC	23.4		Barnaby Jones	CBS	19.9
11. Adam 12	NBC	23.3		The Little People	NBC	19.9
12. The Flip Wilson Show	NBC	23.1		ABC Wednesday Movie of the		
13. Marcus Welby, M.D.	ABC	22.9		Week	ABC	19.9
14. Cannon	CBS	22.4				

September 1973–April 1974

Program	Network	Rating
1. All in the Family	CBS	31.2
2. The Waltons	CBS	28.1
3. Sanford and Son	NBC	27.5
4. M*A*S*H	CBS	25.7
5. Hawaii Five-O	CBS	24.0
6. Maude	CBS	23.5
7. Kojak	CBS	23.3
The Sonny and Cher Comedy Hour	CBS	23.3
9. The Mary Tyler Moore Show	CBS	23.1
Cannon	CBS	23.1
11. The Six Million Dollar Man	ABC	22.7
12. The Bob Newhart Show	CBS	22.3
The Wonderful World of Disney	NBC	22.3
14. The NBC Sunday Mystery Movie	NBC	22.2
15. Gunsmoke	CBS	22.1
16. Happy Days	ABC	21.5
17. Good Times	CBS	21.4
Barnaby Jones	CBS	21.4
19. Monday Night Football	ABC	21.2
CBS Friday Night Movie	CBS	21.2
21. Tuesday Movie of the Week	ABC	21.0
22. The Streets of San Francisco	ABC	20.8
23. Adam 12	NBC	20.7
ABC Sunday Night Movie	ABC	20.7
25. The Rookies	ABC	20.3

September 1974–April 1975

Program	Network	Rating
1. All in the Family	CBS	30.2
2. Sanford and Son	NBC	29.6
3. Chico and The Man	NBC	28.5
4. The Jeffersons	CBS	27.6
5. M*A*S*H	CBS	27.4
6. Rhoda	CBS	26.3
7. Good Times	CBS	25.8
8. The Waltons	CBS	25.5
9. Maude	CBS	24.9
10. Hawaii Five-O	CBS	24.8
11. The Mary Tyler Moore Show	CBS	24.0
12. The Rockford Files	NBC	23.7
13. Little House on the Prairie	NBC	23.5
14. Kojak	CBS	23.3
15. Police Woman	NBC	22.8
16. S.W.A.T.	ABC	22.6
17. The Bob Newhart Show	CBS	22.4
18. The Wonderful World of Disney	NBC	22.0
The Rookies	ABC	22.0
20. Mannix	CBS	21.6
Cannon	CBS	21.6
22. Cher	CBS	21.3
The Streets of San Francisco	ABC	21.3
The NBC Sunday Mystery Movie	NBC	21.3
25. Paul Sand in Friends and Lovers	CBS	20.7
Tony Orlando & Dawn	CBS	20.7

September 1975–April 1976

Program	Network	Rating
1. All in the Family	CBS	30.1
2. Rich Man, Poor Man	ABC	28.0
3. Laverne & Shirley	ABC	27.5
4. Maude	CBS	25.0
5. The Bionic Woman	ABC	24.9
6. Phyllis	CBS	24.5
7. Sanford and Son	NBC	24.4
Rhoda	CBS	24.4
9. The Six Million Dollar Man	ABC	24.3
10. ABC Monday Night Movie	ABC	24.2
11. Happy Days	ABC	23.9
12. One Day at a Time	CBS	23.1
13. ABC Sunday Night Movie	ABC	23.0
14. The Waltons	CBS	22.9
M*A*S*H	CBS	22.9
16. Starsky and Hutch	ABC	22.5
Good Heavens	ABC	22.5
18. Welcome Back, Kotter	ABC	22.1
19. The Mary Tyler Moore Show	CBS	21.9
20. Kojak	CBS	21.8
21. The Jeffersons	CBS	21.5
22. Baretta	ABC	21.3
23. The Sonny & Cher Show	CBS	21.2
24. Good Times	CBS	21.0
25. Chico and the Man	NBC	20.8

September 1976–April 1977

	Program	Network	Rating
1.	Happy Days	ABC	31.5
2.	Laverne & Shirley	ABC	30.9
3.	ABC Monday Night Movie	ABC	26.0
4.	M*A*S*H	CBS	25.9
5.	Charlie's Angels	ABC	25.8
6.	The Big Event	NBC	24.4
7.	The Six Million Dollar Man	ABC	24.2
8.	ABC Sunday Night Movie	ABC	23.4
	Baretta	ABC	23.4
	One Day at a Time	CBS	23.4
11.	Three's Company	ABC	23.1
12.	All in the Family	CBS	22.9
13.	Welcome Back, Kotter	ABC	22.7
14.	The Bionic Woman	ABC	22.4
15.	The Waltons	CBS	22.3
	Little House on the Prairie	NBC	22.3
17.	Barney Miller	ABC	22.2
18.	60 Minutes	CBS	21.9
	Hawaii Five-O	CBS	21.9
20.	NBC Monday Night Movie	NBC	21.8
21.	Rich Man, Poor Man, Book II	ABC	21.6
22.	Monday Night Football	ABC	21.2
23.	Eight Is Enough	ABC	21.1
24.	The Jeffersons	CBS	21.0
25.	What's Happening	ABC	20.9

September 1977–April 1978

	Program	Network	Rating
1.	Laverne & Shirley	ABC	31.6
2.	Happy Days	ABC	31.4
3.	Three's Company	ABC	28.3
4.	60 Minutes	CBS	24.4
	Charlie's Angels	ABC	24.4
	All in the Family	CBS	24.4
7.	Little House on the Prairie	NBC	24.1
8.	Alice	CBS	23.2
	M*A*S*H	CBS	23.2
10.	One Day at a Time	CBS	23.0
11.	How the West Was Won	ABC	22.5
12.	Eight Is Enough	ABC	22.2
13.	Soap	ABC	22.0
14.	The Love Boat	ABC	21.9
15.	NBC Monday Night Movie	NBC	21.7
16.	Monday Night Football	ABC	21.5
17.	Fantasy Island	ABC	21.4
	Barney Miller	ABC	21.4
19.	Project U.F.O.	NBC	21.2
20.	ABC Sunday Night Movie	ABC	20.8
	The Waltons	CBS	20.8
22.	Barnaby Jones	CBS	20.6
23.	Hawaii Five-O	CBS	20.4
24.	ABC Monday Night Movie	ABC	20.3
25.	Rhoda	CBS	20.1

September 1978–April 1979

	Program	Network	Rating
1.	Laverne & Shirley	ABC	30.5
2.	Three's Company	ABC	30.3
3.	Mork & Mindy	ABC	28.6
	Happy Days	ABC	28.6
5.	Angie	ABC	26.7
6.	60 Minutes	CBS	25.5
7.	M*A*S*H	CBS	25.4
8.	The Ropers	ABC	25.2
9.	All in the Family	CBS	24.9
	Taxi	ABC	24.9
11.	Eight Is Enough	ABC	24.8
12.	Charlie's Angels	ABC	24.4
13.	Alice	CBS	23.2
14.	Little House on the Prairie	NBC	23.1
15.	ABC Sunday Night Movie	ABC	22.6
	Barney Miller	ABC	22.6
17.	The Love Boat	ABC	22.1
18.	One Day at a Time	CBS	21.6
19.	Soap	ABC	21.3
20.	The Dukes of Hazzard	CBS	21.0
21.	NBC Monday Night Movie	NBC	20.9
22.	Fantasy Island	ABC	20.8
23.	Vega$	ABC	20.6
24.	Barnaby Jones	CBS	20.5
25.	CHiPS	NBC	20.3

September 1979–April 1980

Program	Network	Rating		Program	Network	Rating
1. 60 Minutes	CBS	28.4	14.	House Calls	CBS	22.1
2. Three's Company	ABC	26.3		Real People	NBC	22.1
3. That's Incredible	ABC	25.8	16.	Little House on the Prairie	NBC	21.8
4. Alice	CBS	25.3	17.	Happy Days	ABC	21.7
M*A*S*H	CBS	25.3	18.	CHiPS	NBC	21.5
6. Dallas	CBS	25.0	19.	Trapper John, M.D.	CBS	21.2
7. Flo	CBS	24.4	20.	Charlie's Angels	ABC	20.9
8. The Jeffersons	CBS	24.3		Barney Miller	ABC	20.9
9. The Dukes of Hazzard	CBS	24.1	22.	WKRP in Cincinnati	CBS	20.7
10. One Day at a Time	CBS	23.0	23.	Benson	ABC	20.6
11. Archie Bunker's Place	CBS	22.9		The Love Boat	ABC	20.6
12. Eight Is Enough	ABC	22.8	25.	Soap	ABC	20.5
13. Taxi	ABC	22.4				

September 1980–April 1981

Program	Network	Rating		Program	Network	Rating
1. Dallas	CBS	34.5	14.	Magnum, P.I.	CBS	21.0
2. The Dukes of Hazzard	CBS	27.3	15.	Happy Days	ABC	20.8
3. 60 Minutes	CBS	27.0		Too Close for Comfort	ABC	20.8
4. M*A*S*H	CBS	25.7	17.	Fantasy Island	ABC	20.7
5. The Love Boat	ABC	24.3		Trapper John, M.D.	CBS	20.7
6. The Jeffersons	CBS	23.5		Diff'rent Strokes	NBC	20.7
7. Alice	CBS	22.9	20.	Monday Night Football	ABC	20.6
8. House Calls	CBS	22.4		Laverne & Shirley	ABC	20.6
Three's Company	ABC	22.4	22.	That's Incredible	ABC	20.5
10. Little House On the Prairie	NBC	22.1	23.	Hart to Hart	ABC	19.9
11. One Day at a Time	CBS	22.0	24.	ABC Sunday Night Movie	ABC	19.4
12. Real People	NBC	21.5		CHiPS	NBC	19.4
13. Archie Bunker's Place	CBS	21.4				

September 1981–April 1982

Program	Network	Rating		Program	Network	Rating
1. Dallas	CBS	28.4	14.	The Love Boat	ABC	21.2
2. 60 Minutes	CBS	27.7	15.	Hart to Hart	ABC	21.1
3. The Jeffersons	CBS	23.4		Trapper John, M.D.	CBS	21.1
4. Three's Company	ABC	23.3	17.	Magnum, P.I.	CBS	20.9
5. Alice	CBS	22.7	18.	Happy Days	ABC	20.6
6. The Dukes of Hazzard	CBS	22.6	19.	Dynasty	ABC	20.2
Too Close for Comfort	ABC	22.6	20.	Laverne & Shirley	ABC	19.9
8. ABC Monday Night Movie	ABC	22.5	21.	Real People	NBC	19.7
9. M*A*S*H	CBS	22.3	22.	ABC Sunday Night Movie	ABC	19.5
10. One Day at a Time	CBS	22.0	23.	House Calls	CBS	19.2
11. Monday Night Football	ABC	21.8	24.	The Facts of Life	NBC	19.1
12. Archie Bunker's Place	CBS	21.6		Little House on the Prairie	NBC	19.1
13. Falcon Crest	CBS	21.4				

September 1982–April 1983

Program	Network	Rating	Program	Network	Rating
1. 60 Minutes	CBS	25.5	14. The Fall Guy	ABC	19.4
2. Dallas	CBS	24.6	15. 9 To 5	ABC	19.3
3. M*A*S*H	CBS	22.6	16. One Day at a Time	CBS	19.1
Magnum, P.I.	CBS	22.6	17. Hart to Hart	ABC	18.9
5. Dynasty	ABC	22.4	18. Gloria	CBS	18.7
6. Three's Company	ABC	21.2	Trapper John, M.D.	CBS	18.7
7. Simon & Simon	CBS	21.0	20. Knots Landing	CBS	18.6
8. Falcon Crest	CBS	20.7	21. Hill Street Blues	NBC	18.4
9. The Love Boat	ABC	20.3	22. That's Incredible	ABC	18.3
10. The A-Team	NBC	20.1	Archie Bunker's Place	CBS	18.3
Monday Night Football	ABC	20.1	24. ABC Monday Night Movie	ABC	18.0
12. The Jeffersons	CBS	20.0	25. Laverne & Shirley	ABC	17.8
Newhart	CBS	20.0			

September 1983–April 1984

Program	Network	Rating	Program	Network	Rating
1. Dallas	CBS	25.7	15. AfterMASH	CBS	20.1
2. 60 Minutes	CBS	24.2	16. The Fall Guy	ABC	19.9
3. Dynasty	ABC	24.1	17. The Love Boat	ABC	19.0
4. The A-Team	NBC	24.0	18. Riptide	NBC	18.8
5. Simon & Simon	CBS	23.8	19. The Jeffersons	CBS	18.6
6. Magnum, P.I.	CBS	22.4	20. Scarecrow & Mrs. King	CBS	18.3
7. Falcon Crest	CBS	22.0	21. Monday Night Football	ABC	18.1
8. Kate & Allie	CBS	21.9	NBC Monday Night Movie	NBC	18.1
9. Hotel	ABC	21.1	23. Newhart	CBS	18.0
10. Cagney & Lacey	CBS	20.9	24. The Facts of Life	NBC	17.3
11. Knots Landing	CBS	20.8	25. CBS Tuesday Night Movie	CBS	17.2
12. ABC Sunday Night Movie	ABC	20.4	Webster	ABC	17.2
ABC Monday Night Movie	ABC	20.4	Alice	CBS	17.2
14. TV's Bloopers & Practical			Knight Rider	NBC	17.2
Jokes	NBC	20.3	Hardcastle & McCormick	ABC	17.2

September 1984–April 1985

Program	Network	Rating	Program	Network	Rating
1. Dynasty	ABC	25.0	15. Magnum, P.I.	CBS	19.1
2. Dallas	CBS	24.7	16. Newhart	CBS	18.4
3. The Cosby Show	NBC	24.2	17. Kate & Allie	CBS	18.3
4. 60 Minutes	CBS	22.2	18. NBC Monday Night Movie	NBC	18.2
5. Family Ties	NBC	22.1	19. Highway to Heaven	NBC	17.7
6. The A-Team	NBC	21.9	20. Night Court	NBC	17.6
7. Simon & Simon	CBS	21.8	21. ABC Sunday Night Movie	ABC	17.5
8. Murder, She Wrote	CBS	20.1	22. Scarecrow & Mrs. King	CBS	17.1
9. Knots Landing	CBS	20.0	TV's Bloopers & Practical		
10. Falcon Crest	CBS	19.9	Jokes	NBC	17.1
Crazy Like a Fox	CBS	19.9	The Fall Guy	ABC	17.1
12. Hotel	ABC	19.7	25. Monday Night Football	ABC	17.0
Cheers	NBC	19.7	Remington Steele	NBC	17.0
14. Riptide	NBC	19.2	Webster	ABC	17.0

September 1985–April 1986

	Program	Network	Rating		Program	Network	Rating
1.	The Cosby Show	NBC	33.7	14.	Kate & Allie	CBS	20.0
2.	Family Ties	NBC	30.0	15.	Monday Night Football	ABC	19.8
3.	Murder, She Wrote	CBS	25.3	16.	Newhart	CBS	19.6
4.	60 Minutes	CBS	23.9	17.	Knots Landing	CBS	19.5
5.	Cheers	NBC	23.7		Growing Pains	ABC	19.5
6.	Dallas	CBS	21.9	19.	You Again	NBC	19.2
7.	Dynasty	ABC	21.8	20.	227	NBC	18.8
	The Golden Girls	NBC	21.8	21.	NBC Sunday Night Movie	NBC	18.5
9.	Miami Vice	NBC	21.3	22.	Hotel	ABC	18.3
10.	Who's the Boss?	ABC	21.1		NBC Monday Night Movie	NBC	18.3
11.	Night Court	NBC	20.9	24.	Moonlighting	ABC	18.1
12.	CBS Sunday Night Movie	CBS	20.5		Falcon Crest	CBS	18.1
13.	Highway to Heaven	NBC	20.1		Valerie	NBC	18.1

September 1986–April 1987

	Program	Network	Rating		Program	Network	Rating
1.	The Cosby Show	NBC	34.9	14.	227	NBC	18.9
2.	Family Ties	NBC	32.7	15.	Matlock	NBC	18.6
3.	Cheers	NBC	27.2		CBS Sunday Night Movie	CBS	18.6
4.	Murder, She Wrote	CBS	25.4		NBC Monday Night Movie	NBC	18.6
5.	The Golden Girls	NBC	24.5	18.	Monday Night Football	ABC	18.4
6.	60 Minutes	CBS	23.3	19.	Kate & Allie	CBS	18.3
7.	Night Court	NBC	23.2	20.	NBC Sunday Night Movie	NBC	18.2
8.	Growing Pains	ABC	22.7	21.	L.A. Law	NBC	17.4
9.	Moonlighting	ABC	22.4		My Sister Sam	CBS	17.4
10.	Who's the Boss?	ABC	22.0	23.	Falcon Crest	CBS	17.3
11.	Dallas	CBS	21.3	24.	Highway to Heaven	NBC	17.2
12.	Newhart	CBS	19.5		Dynasty	ABC	17.2
13.	Amen	NBC	19.4				

September 1987–April 1988

	Program	Network	Rating		Program	Network	Rating
1.	The Cosby Show	NBC	27.8	14.	Matlock	NBC	17.8
2.	A Different World	NBC	25.0	15.	Amen	NBC	17.5
3.	Cheers	NBC	23.4	16.	Monday Night Football	ABC	17.4
4.	The Golden Girls	NBC	21.8	17.	Family Ties	NBC	17.3
5.	Growing Pains	ABC	21.3	18.	CBS Sunday Night Movie	CBS	17.2
6.	Who's the Boss	ABC	21.2	19.	In the Heat of the Night	NBC	17.0
7.	Night Court	NBC	20.8	20.	My Two Dads	NBC	16.9
8.	60 Minutes	CBS	20.6		Valerie's Family	NBC	16.9
9.	Murder, She Wrote	CBS	20.2	22.	Dallas	CBS	16.8
10.	Alf	NBC	18.8	23.	NBC Sunday Night Movie	NBC	16.7
	The Wonder Years	ABC	18.8		Head of the Class	ABC	16.7
12.	Moonlighting	ABC	18.3	25.	Newhart	CBS	16.5
	L.A. Law	NBC	18.3				

LONGEST-RUNNING SERIES

The following is a listing of the longest-running series on nighttime network television, excluding movies and newscasts. A series is counted as having aired in a season if it was on for at least two months during that season. Seasons in which a series aired at other times of the day (for example, in the daytime), or on local stations, are not counted. Also not counted are late-night reruns (on *ABC Late Night* and *The CBS Late Night Movies*) of series that originally aired in prime time (for example, *Baretta, Police Woman,* and *M*A*S*H*).

Meet the Press is the longest-running series in all of television, having been on the air continuously since 1947. Only the eighteen seasons which it spent on the nighttime schedule (post 6:00 P.M.) are counted here, however.

Alternate titles are given in parentheses. The 1987–1988 season is the last one counted.

34 Seasons

The Tonight Show

32 Seasons

Walt Disney

24 Seasons

The Ed Sullivan Show (The Toast of the Town)

20 Seasons

Gunsmoke
The Red Skelton Show (The Red Skelton Hour)
60 Minutes

18 Seasons

Meet the Press
Monday Night Football
What's My Line

17 Seasons

Lassie
The Lawrence Welk Show (Lawrence Welk's Dodge Dancing Party)
Monday Night Baseball

16 Seasons

Kraft Television Theatre (Kraft Suspense Theater, Kraft Mystery Theater)

15 Seasons

I've Got a Secret
The Jack Benny Show
The Jackie Gleason Show (The Honeymooners)
The Perry Como Show (Chesterfield Supper Club)

14 Seasons

The Adventures of Ozzie & Harriet
Armstrong Circle Theatre (Circle Theatre)
Bonanza
The Gillette Cavalcade of Sports (The Cavalcade of Sports)

13 Seasons

All in the Family (Archie Bunker's Place)
The Danny Thomas Show (Make Room for Daddy, Make Room for Granddaddy)
The Dinah Shore Show (The Dinah Shore Chevy Show)
Saturday Night Live

12 Seasons

Dragnet
Hawaii Five-O
The Lucy Show (Here's Lucy)
My Three Sons
The Original Amateur Hour
Pabst Blue Ribbon Bouts (International Boxing Club Bouts, The Wednesday Night Fights)
The 20th Century (The 21st Century)

11 Seasons

Alfred Hitchcock Presents (The Alfred Hitchcock Hour)
Arthur Godfrey's Talent Scouts
The Arthur Murray Party
CBS Reports/News Hour/News Special
Candid Camera (Candid Microphone)
The Carol Burnett Show
Fireside Theatre (Jane Wyman's Fireside Theater, The Jane Wyman Show)
General Electric Theater (General Electric True)
Happy Days
The Jeffersons
M*A*S*H
The Milton Berle Show (The Texaco Star

Theater, The Buick-Berle Show, Milton Berle
Starring in the Kraft Music Hall)
Pantomime Quiz (Stump the Stars)
To Tell the Truth
20/20
The Voice of Firestone
You Bet Your Life (The Groucho Show)

10 Seasons

Arthur Godfrey and His Friends (The Arthur
Godfrey Show)
Dallas
Perry Mason (The New Adventures of Perry
Mason)
The Steve Allen Show (The Steve Allen
Comedy Hour)
Studio One
The U.S. Steel Hour
Your Hit Parade

9 Seasons

Alice
The Andy Williams Show
Beat the Clock
The Beverly Hillbillies
Break the Bank
The Dean Martin Show
The F.B.I.
The Facts of Life
Father Knows Best
Goodyear TV Playhouse (Goodyear Theater)
Knots Landing
Little House on the Prairie (Little House: A
New Beginning)
The Love Boat
Masquerade Party
The Midnight Special
One Day at a Time
This Is Your Life
Three's Company (Three's A Crowd)
The Tomorrow Show
The Virginian (The Men from Shiloh)
The Waltons
You Asked for It (The Art Baker Show)

8 Seasons

The Alcoa Hour (Alcoa Theatre, Alcoa
Presents, Alcoa Premiere)
The Andy Griffith Show
Barnaby Jones
Barney Miller
The Bell Telephone Hour
Bewitched
The Big Story
Cheyenne
Diff'rent Strokes
The Donna Reed Show
Dynasty

The Garry Moore Show
The George Burns and Gracie Allen Show
I Love Lucy (The Sunday Lucy Show, The Top
10 Lucy Shows)
Ironside
Laverne & Shirley
The Lone Ranger
The Loretta Young Show (A Letter to Loretta)
Lux Video Theatre (Lux Playhouse)
Magnum, P.I.
Mama
Mannix
Mark Saber (Mystery Theater, Inspector Mark
Saber—Homicide Squad, The Vise, Saber of
London)
Midwestern Hayride
People Are Funny
Person to Person
Rawhide
Robert Montgomery Presents
Schlitz Playhouse of Stars (Schlitz Playhouse)
The Twilight Zone
Wagon Train

7 Seasons

Adam 12
Benson
Cagney & Lacey
Captain Video and His Video Rangers
The Dukes of Hazzard
The Eddie Fisher Show (Coke Time with Eddie
Fisher)
Falcon Crest
Fantasy Island
Ford Theatre
The Gene Autry Show
Hill Street Blues
The Hollywood Palace
Kukla, Fran & Ollie
Late Night with David Letterman
Life Begins at Eighty
The Life of Riley
Marcus Welby, M.D.
The Mary Tyler Moore Show
McCloud
Medical Center
Mission: Impossible
Name That Tune
Petticoat Junction
Philco TV Playhouse
The Price Is Right
Quincy, M.E.
The Quiz Kids
Red Barber's Corner (Red Barber's Clubhouse,
The Peak of the Sports News)
Simon & Simon
Suspense
This Is Show Business
Trapper John, M.D.
Who Said That?

6 Seasons

The Author Meets the Critics
Big Town
The Bob Newhart Show
Broadway to Hollywood—Headline Clues
Cheers
CHiPs
The Colgate Comedy Hour
Columbo
Daniel Boone
December Bride
Dick Powell's Zane Grey Theater
Down You Go
Emergency
Family Ties
The Flintstones
Focus
The Fred Waring Show
The George Gobel Show
The Gillette Summer Sports Reel
Gimme a Break
The Goldbergs
Gomer Pyle, U.S.M.C.
Good Times
Green Acres
Have Gun Will Travel
Hogan's Heroes
Hollywood Screen Test
Leave It to Beaver

The Life and Legend of Wyatt Earp
Life Is Worth Living
The Lineup
Man Against Crime
Maude
McMillan and Wife (McMillan)
The Millionaire
NBC Mystery Movie (NBC Sunday/
    Tuesday/Wednesday Mystery Movie)
Newhart
Ozark Jubilee (Country Music Jubilee, Jubilee
    U.S.A.)
Paul Whiteman's TV Teen Club
The Real McCoys
Real People
The Rockford Files
Rocky King, Inside Detective (Inside Detective)
Rowan & Martin's Laugh-In
The Roy Rogers Show
The Sammy Kaye Show (So You Want to Lead
    a Band, Music from Manhattan)
Sanford and Son
77 Sunset Strip
The Sonny and Cher Comedy Hour (The Sonny
    and Cher Show)
Stop the Music
Tales of Wells Fargo
Twenty Questions
The Web

THE TOP 100 SERIES OF ALL TIME

In 1985 we published a small paperback book called *TV's Greatest Hits*, which contained our first-ever ranking of the most popular TV series of all time. The following is an updated version of that ranking, including data through the 1987–1988 season. It reflects not our choices, but those of you, the viewer. It was compiled by assigning each prime-time series points based on the number of seasons it was telecast, and its audience size ranking each year. (Detailed information on these two measures will be found in the "Top-Rated Programs By Season" and "Longest-Running Series" appendixes.) Thus, series were given credit for both popularity and longevity.

Some series currently on the air are still moving up the list; *60 Minutes,* which ranked number nine on the 1985 all-time list, is by virtue of its continued popularity now up to number three. It has quite a way to go before it will reach number one, however; *Gunsmoke* is the number one series of all time by a wide margin.

Program	Network(s)	From	To
1. Gunsmoke	CBS	1955	1975
2. The Red Skelton Show	CBS, NBC	1951	1971
3. 60 Minutes	CBS	1968	—
4. Bonanza	NBC	1959	1973
5. All in the Family/Archie Bunker's Place	CBS	1971	1983
6. The Ed Sullivan Show/Toast of the Town	CBS	1948	1971
7. Walt Disney	ABC, NBC, CBS	1954	—
8. The Lucy Show/Here's Lucy	CBS	1962	1974
9. M*A*S*H	CBS	1972	1983
10. Dallas	CBS	1978	—
11. The Andy Griffith Show	CBS	1960	1968
12. The Jack Benny Show	CBS, NBC	1950	1965
13. Three's Company/Three's a Crowd	ABC	1977	1985
14. I Love Lucy	CBS	1951	1961
15. The Danny Thomas Show	ABC, CBS	1953	1971
16. The Beverly Hillbillies	CBS	1962	1971
17. You Bet Your Life	NBC	1950	1961
18. Happy Days	ABC	1974	1984
19. I've Got a Secret	CBS	1952	1967
20. Dragnet/Dragnet '67	NBC	1952	1970
21. Arthur Godfrey's Talent Scouts	CBS	1948	1958
22. The Jeffersons	CBS	1975	1985
23. Hawaii Five-O	CBS	1968	1980
24. The Jackie Gleason Show	CBS	1952	1970
25. One Day at a Time	CBS	1975	1984
26. Laverne & Shirley	ABC	1976	1983
27. The Milton Berle Show	NBC, ABC	1948	1967
28. Sanford and Son	NBC	1972	1977
29. Gomer Pyle, U.S.M.C.	CBS	1964	1970
30. Alice	CBS	1976	1985
31. Dynasty	ABC	1981	—
32. Wagon Train	NBC, ABC	1957	1965
33. My Three Sons	ABC, CBS	1960	1972
34. Bewitched	ABC	1964	1972
35. The Love Boat	ABC	1977	1986
36. Fireside Theatre	NBC, ABC	1949	1963
37. Little House on the Prairie	NBC	1974	1983
38. The Cosby Show	NBC	1984	—
39. The Waltons	CBS	1972	1981
40. Have Gun, Will Travel	CBS	1957	1963
41. Candid Camera	CBS, NBC, ABC	1948	1967
42. General Electric Theater	CBS	1953	1962
43. Arthur Godfrey and His Friends	CBS	1949	1959
44. The Mary Tyler Moore Show	CBS	1970	1977

45.	Falcon Crest	CBS	1981	—
46.	Maude	CBS	1972	1978
47.	Marcus Welby, M.D.	ABC	1969	1976
48.	Magnum, P.I.	CBS	1980	1988
49.	Cheers	NBC	1982	—
50.	Family Ties	NBC	1982	—
51.	Ironside	NBC	1967	1975
52.	Rowan & Martin's Laugh-In	NBC	1968	1973
53.	The Colgate Comedy Hour	NBC	1950	1955
54.	Murder, She Wrote	CBS	1984	—
55.	December Bride	CBS	1954	1960
56.	Family Affair	CBS	1966	1971
57.	The Dean Martin Show	NBC	1965	1974
58.	The Dukes of Hazzard	CBS	1979	1985
59.	The Virginian	NBC	1962	1971
60.	The Dick Van Dyke Show	CBS	1961	1966
61.	Lassie	CBS	1954	1971
62.	The Real McCoys	ABC, CBS	1957	1963
63.	Perry Mason	CBS	1957	1974
64.	Newhart	CBS	1982	—
65.	The Perry Como Show	NBC, CBS	1948	1963
66.	Knots Landing	CBS	1979	—
67.	Simon & Simon	CBS	1981	—
68.	Charlie's Angels	ABC	1976	1981
69.	The Flip Wilson Show	NBC	1970	1974
70.	Philco TV Playhouse	NBC	1948	1955
71.	Adam 12	NBC	1968	1975
72.	The A-Team	NBC	1983	1987
73.	Night Court	NBC	1984	—
74.	The Lawrence Welk Show	ABC	1955	1971
75.	Green Acres	CBS	1965	1971
76.	The Golden Girls	NBC	1985	—
77.	The Price Is Right	NBC, ABC	1957	1964
78.	The F.B.I.	ABC	1965	1974
79.	Ford Theatre	CBS, NBC, ABC	1949	1957
80.	The $64,000 Question	CBS	1955	1958
81.	The Life and Legend of Wyatt Earp	ABC	1955	1961
82.	Mayberry, R.F.D.	CBS	1968	1971
83.	What's My Line	CBS	1950	1967
84.	Rawhide	CBS	1959	1966
85.	McCloud	NBC	1970	1977
86.	The Millionaire	CBS	1955	1960
87.	The Six Million Dollar Man	ABC	1974	1978
88.	Eight is Enough	ABC	1977	1981
89.	Who's the Boss?	ABC	1984	—
90.	Mama	CBS	1949	1956
91.	McMillan and Wife	NBC	1971	1977
92.	Columbo	NBC	1971	1977
93.	Alfred Hitchcock Presents/Hour	CBS, NBC	1955	1986
94.	Petticoat Junction	CBS	1963	1970
95.	Your Show of Shows	NBC	1950	1954
96.	The Carol Burnett Show	CBS	1967	1978
97.	Barnaby Jones	CBS	1973	1980
98.	Growing Pains	ABC	1985	—
99.	This Is Your Life	NBC	1952	1961
100.	Barney Miller	ABC	1975	1982

PRIME TIME SERIES REUNION TELECASTS

A successful TV series is something to be treasured, remembered, and, often, revived. Although reunions took place as early as the 1960s, gathering together the casts of past series has become increasingly popular in the 1980s, as producers seek to capitalize on today's wave of TV nostalgia. Sometimes these reunions test the waters for series revivals (*Make Room For Granddaddy* and *The New Leave It to Beaver* were launched this way), but more often they are one-time affairs. A unique case is *Perry Mason;* its 1985 reunion movie led to a continuing series of made-for-TV movies, with two or three new ones produced each year thereafter.

Following is a list of network TV series whose casts were reunited in a TV movie or special long after the series had left the air. Following the name of the original series is the title of the reunion episode, and the date on which it aired. To qualify for this list the reunion must have occured at least two years after the original series ended (eliminating quick follow-ups such as those for *Emergency, Little House on the Prairie, The Love Boat,* and *The Waltons*); it must have been produced for TV (not for the theater, as was the *Peter Gunn* film *Gunn* and the *Get Smart* film *The Nude Bomb*); and it must have featured a majority of the original series' cast (no *The New Gidget* or *Bonanza: The Next Generation* allowed). Additionally, only series with a continuing storyline and cast are included; revivals of variety or anthology programs such as *Alfred Hitchcock Presents, Candid Camera, The Smothers Brothers Comedy Hour, That's Incredible,* and *This Is Your Life* have been excluded.

The Addams Family—"Halloween with the Addams Family" (10/30/77)
The Adventures of Ozzie and Harriet—"Ozzie's Girls" (9/10/72)
The Andy Griffith Show—"Return to Mayberry" (4/13/86)
The Beverly Hillbillies—"The Return of the Beverly Hillbillies" (10/6/81)
The Bionic Woman—"The Return of the Six Million Dollar Man and the Bionic Woman" (5/17/87)
Cannon—"The Return of Frank Cannon" (11/1/80)
The Danny Thomas Show—"Make More Room For Daddy" (11/6/67)
The Danny Thomas Show—"Make Room For Granddaddy" (9/14/69)
Eight Is Enough—"Eight Is Enough: A Family Reunion" (10/18/87)
Father Knows Best—"The Father Knows Best Reunion" (5/15/77)
Father Knows Best—"Father Knows Best: Home For Christmas" (12/18/77)
Gilligan's Island—"Rescue From Gilligan's Island" (10/14 & 21/78)
Gilligan's Island—"The Castaways on Gilligan's Island" (5/3/79)
Gilligan's Island—"The Harlem Globetrotters on Gilligan's Island" (5/15/81)
Gunsmoke—"Gunsmoke: Return to Dodge" (9/26/87)
The Honeymooners—"The Honeymooners Second Honeymoon" (2/2/76)
The Honeymooners—"The Honeymooners Christmas" (11/28/77)
The Honeymooners—"The Honeymooners Valentine Special" (2/13/78)
The Honeymooners—"The Honeymooners Christmas Special" (12/10/78)
I Dream of Jeannie—"I Dream of Jeannie: 15 Years Later" (10/20/85)
The Incredible Hulk—"The Incredible Hulk Returns" (5/24/88)
Kojak—"Kojak: The Belarus File" (2/16/85)
Kojak—"Kojak: The Price of Justice" (2/21/87)
Kung Fu—"Kung Fu The Movie" (2/1/86)
Leave it to Beaver—"Still the Beaver" (3/19/83)
The Man From U.N.C.L.E.—"The Return of the Man From U.N.C.L.E.: The 15 Years Later Affair" (4/5/83)
The Many Loves of Dobie Gillis—"Whatever Happened to Dobie Gillis" (5/10/77)
The Many Loves of Dobie Gillis—"Bring Me the Head of Dobie Gillis" (2/21/88)
Marcus Welby, M.D.—"The Return of Marcus Welby" (5/16/84)
Maverick—"The New Maverick" (9/3/78)
The Mod Squad—"The Return of the Mod Squad" (5/18/79)
The Munsters—"The Munsters' Revenge" (2/27/81)
My Three Sons—"The Partridge Family—My Three Sons Reunion" (11/25/77)
The Partridge Family—"The Partridge Family—My Three Sons Reunion" (11/25/77)
Perry Mason—"Perry Mason Returns" (12/1/85)
Peyton Place—"Peyton Place: The Next Generation" (5/13/85)

The Six Million Dollar Man—"The Return of the Six Million Dollar Man and the Bionic Woman (5/17/87)
The Wild, Wild West—"The Wild, Wild West Revisited" (5/9/79)
The Wild, Wild West—"More Wild, Wild West" (10/7 & 8/80)

SERIES AIRING IN PRIME TIME ON MORE THAN ONE NETWORK

On 4 Networks

The Arthur Murray Party
Down You Go
The Original Amateur Hour
Pantomime Quiz

On 3 Networks

The Adventures of Ellery Queen (DUM, ABC, NBC)
The Andy Williams Show (ABC, CBS, NBC)
Animal World (NBC, CBS, ABC)
Author Meets the Critics (NBC, ABC, DUM)
Bachelor Father (CBS, NBC, ABC)
Big Town (CBS, DUM, NBC)
Blind Date (Your Big Moment) (ABC, NBC, DUM)
Break the Bank (ABC, NBC, CBS)
Candid Camera (ABC, NBC, CBS)
Charlie Wild, Private Detective (CBS, ABC, DUM)
Dollar a Second (DUM, NBC, ABC)
The Eddy Arnold Show (CBS, NBC, ABC)
Ethel and Albert (NBC, CBS, ABC)
Father Knows Best (CBS, NBC, ABC)
Ford Theatre (CBS,NBC, ABC)
The Goldbergs (CBS, NBC, DUM)
Life Begins at Eighty (NBC, ABC, DUM)
Man Against Crime (CBS, DUM, NBC)
Mary Kay and Johnny (DUM, NBC, CBS)
Masquerade Party (NBC, CBS, ABC)
The Sammy Kaye Show (So You Want to Lead a Band, Music from Manhattan) (NBC, CBS, ABC)
The Smothers Brothers Comedy Hour (The Smothers Brothers Summer Show, The Smothers Brothers Show) (CBS, ABC, NBC)
The Steve Allen Show (CBS, NBC, ABC)
The Ted Steele Show (NBC, DUM, CBS)
Tom Corbett: Space Cadet (CBS, ABC, NBC)
Topper (CBS, ABC, NBC)
Twenty Questions (NBC, ABC, DUM)
Walt Disney (ABC, NBC, CBS)
The Wendy Barrie Show (Inside Photoplay, Photoplay Time, Through Wendy's Window) (DUM, ABC, NBC)

On 2 Networks

Actor's Studio (The Play's the Thing) (ABC, CBS)
Adventure Theater (NBC, CBS)
The Alan Dale Show (DUM, CBS)
Alfred Hitchcock Presents (The Alfred Hitchcock Hour) (CBS, NBC)
The Amazing Dunninger (The Dunninger Show (ABC, NBC)
Armstrong Circle Theatre (NBC, CBS)
Bank on the Stars (CBS, NBC)

The Battle of the Ages (DUM, CBS)
The Bigelow Show (NBC, CBS)
Bigelow Theatre (CBS, DUM)
The Bionic Woman (ABC, NBC)
The Black Saddle (NBC, ABC)
Blondie (CBS, NBC)
The Bob Cummings Show (NBC, CBS)
Bosom Buddies (ABC, NBC)
Cavalcade of America (DuPont Cavalcade Theater, DuPont Theater) (NBC, ABC)
Celebrity Time (Goodrich Celebrity Time) (CBS, ABC)
Chance of a Lifetime (ABC, DUM)
The Charlie Farrell Show (CBS, NBC)
Circus Boy (NBC, ABC)
Claudia, The Story of a Marriage (NBC, CBS)
The Clock (NBC, ABC)
The Continental (CBS, ABC)
The Court of Last Resort (NBC, ABC)
Dan August (ABC, CBS)
The Danny Thomas Show (Make Room for Daddy) (ABC, CBS)
The Detectives Starring Robert Taylor (Robert Taylor's Detectives) (ABC, NBC)
Diff'rent Strokes (NBC, ABC)
Doorway to Danger (NBC, ABC)
The Dotty Mack Show (Girl Alone) (DUM, ABC)
Drew Pearson (ABC, DUM)
The Earl Wrightson Show (Earl Wrightson at Home, The at Home Show, The Masland at Home Party) (ABC, CBS)
Eddie Condon's Floor Show (NBC, CBS)
Empire (NBC, ABC)
Ensign O'Toole (NBC, ABC)
The Ernie Kovacs Show (CBS, NBC)
The Family Holvak (NBC, CBS)
Famous Fights (DUM, ABC)
The Faye Emerson Show (Fifteen with Faye) (CBS, NBC)
Fireside Theatre (NBC, ABC)
The Gale Storm Show (CBS, ABC)
The George Gobel Show (NBC, CBS)
Get Smart (NBC, CBS)
The Ghost and Mrs. Muir (NBC, ABC)
Harbourmaster (CBS, ABC)
Hawk (ABC, NBC)
Hazel (NBC, CBS)
The Herb Shriner Show (CBS, ABC)
Hey Jeannie (CBS, ABC)
Hollywood Opening Night (CBS, NBC)
The Hunter (CBS, NBC)
It Pays to Be Ignorant (CBS, NBC)
The Jack Benny Show (CBS, NBC)
The Jimmy Dean Show (CBS, ABC)
The Jimmy Durante Show (NBC, CBS)
The Joey Bishop Show (NBC, CBS)

The John Davidson Show (ABC, NBC)
The Johnny Cash Show (ABC, CBS)
Johnny Staccato (NBC, ABC)
The Johns Hopkins Science Review (CBS, DUM)
The Joseph Cotten Show (On Trial) (NBC, CBS)
Juvenile Jury (NBC, CBS)
Keep Talking (CBS, ABC)
Kraft Television Theatre (NBC, ABC)
Kukla, Fran & Ollie (NBC, ABC)
Law of the Plainsman (NBC, ABC)
Leave It to Beaver (CBS, ABC)
Leave It to the Girls (NBC, ABC)
Let's Make a Deal (NBC, ABC)
The Liberace Show (NBC, CBS)
Life Is Worth Living (DUM, ABC)
Live Like a Millionaire (CBS, ABC)
Lux Video Theatre (Lux Playhouse) (CBS, NBC)
Madison Square Garden Highlights (ABC, DUM)
Mark Saber (ABC, NBC)
Meet McGraw (NBC, ABC)
Meet Your Congress (NBC, DUM)
Midwestern Hayride (NBC, ABC)
The Milton Berle Show (NBC, ABC)
Mr. & Mrs. North (CBS, NBC)
The Morey Amsterdam Show (CBS, DUM)
My Friend Flicka (CBS, NBC)
My Little Margie (CBS, NBC)
My Three Sons (ABC, CBS)
My World and Welcome to It (NBC, CBS)
Name That Tune (NBC, CBS)
Navy Log (CBS, ABC)
Omnibus (CBS, ABC)
On the Line with Considine (NBC, ABC)
On Your Way (DUM, ABC)
The Perry Como Show (The Chesterfield Supper Club) (NBC, CBS)
Peter Gunn (NBC, ABC)
Pick the Winner (CBS, DUM)
Place the Face (NBC, CBS)
Press Conference (Martha Rountree's Press Conference) (NBC, ABC)
The Price Is Right (NBC, ABC)
The Pride of the Family (ABC, CBS)
Private Secretary (CBS, NBC)
Quiz Kids (NBC, CBS)
The Real McCoys (ABC, CBS)

The Rebel (ABC, NBC)
Rebound (ABC, DUM)
Red Barber's Corner (Red Barber's Clubhouse, The Peak of the Sports News) (CBS, NBC)
The Red Buttons Show (CBS, NBC)
The Red Skelton Show (NBC, CBS)
Revlon Mirror Theatre (NBC, CBS)
Richard Diamond, Private Detective (CBS, NBC)
Say It with Acting (NBC, ABC)
Screen Director's Playhouse (NBC, ABC)
Shirley Temple's Storybook (ABC, NBC)
Somerset Maugham TV Theatre (Teller of Tales) (CBS, NBC)
The Spike Jones Show (NBC, CBS)
Steve Canyon (NBC, ABC)
The Stork Club (CBS, ABC)
Stud's Place (NBC, ABC)
Tarzan (NBC, CBS)
Taxi (ABC, NBC)
Telephone Time (CBS, ABC)
Tex and Jinx (NBC, CBS)
They Stand Accused (CBS, DUM)
This Is Show Business (CBS, NBC)
This Is the Life (DUM, ABC)
The Tony Randall Show (ABC, CBS)
Treasure Hunt (ABC, NBC)
Treasury Men in Action (ABC, NBC)
Truth or Consequences (CBS, NBC)
21 Beacon Street (NBC, ABC)
Two for the Money (NBC, CBS)
The U.S. Steel Hour (ABC, CBS)
The Vaughn Monroe Show (CBS, NBC)
Versatile Varieties (NBC, ABC)
The Voice of Firestone (NBC, ABC)
Wagon Train (NBC, ABC)
We, the People (CBS, NBC)
The Web (CBS, NBC)
The West Point Story (CBS, ABC)
What's It Worth (Trash or Treasure, Treasure Hunt) (CBS, DUM)
What's Your Bid (ABC, DUM)
Who Said That? (NBC, ABC)
Wonder Woman (ABC, CBS)
You Asked for It (DUM, ABC)
Your Hit Parade (NBC, CBS)
Your Play Time (CBS, NBC)
Youth on the March (ABC, DUM)

PRIME-TIME SPIN-OFFS

Listed below are the prime-time network series that are spin-offs from other prime-time network series. A spin-off occurred when one or more characters from a series, usually supporting characters, subsequently appeared on another series. In most, but not all, cases the supporting characters from the original series became the stars of the spin-off series, and ceased to appear in the original series (assuming that the original series was still in production). In some cases, particularly when the spin-off was set in a period several years apart from the original series or was actually produced many years after the original series had ceased production, the common characters were portrayed by different actors in the spin-off than had portrayed them in the original.

A variation on the idea of a spinoff is sometimes used by the producers of a successful show when they want to launch another, essentially unrelated series. Characters who appeared only infrequently on the established show—not regulars—become the stars of the new show, which otherwise has nothing to do with the earlier series. Often, in fact, their appearance is nothing more than a promotion for the upcoming series; for example, Robin Williams appeared just once on *Happy Days* as the alien Mork before beginning his own series, *Mork & Mindy*. These "semi-spin-offs" based on occasional characters and one-time guests are indicated by an asterisk (*).

In the listing below, the spin-off series appears first, with the series from which it was spun off listed second.

The Adventures of Champion from The Gene Autry Show
AfterMASH from M*A*S*H
*The Andy Griffith Show from The Danny Thomas Show
Benson from Soap
Beverly Hills Buntz from Hill Street Blues
The Bionic Woman from The Six Million Dollar Man
The Brady Brides from The Brady Bunch
Bret Maverick from Maverick
Checking In from The Jeffersons
The Colbys from Dynasty
A Different World from The Cosby Show
*Dirty Sally from Gunsmoke
Enos from The Dukes of Hazzard
The Facts of Life from Diff'rent Strokes
Fish from Barney Miller
Flo from Alice
*Getting Together from The Partridge Family
The Girl from U.N.C.L.E. from The Man from U.N.C.L.E.
Gloria from All in the Family
Gomer Pyle, U.S.M.C. from The Andy Griffith Show
Good Times from Maude
Grady from Sanford and Son
Green Acres from Petticoat Junction
*Honey West from Burke's Law
The Jeffersons from All in the Family
Joanie Loves Chachi from Happy Days
Knots Landing from Dallas
*Laverne & Shirley from Happy Days
*The Law and Harry McGraw from Murder, She Wrote
*Law of the Plainsman from The Rifleman
Lou Grant from The Mary Tyler Moore Show
*Maude from All in the Family
Mayberry R.F.D. from The Andy Griffith Show
The Misadventures of Sheriff Lobo from B.J. & the Bear
*Mork & Mindy from Happy Days
*Out of the Blue from Happy Days
Pete and Gladys from December Bride

Phyllis from **The Mary Tyler Moore Show**
The Prisoner from **Secret Agent**
Redigo from **Empire**
Rhoda from **The Mary Tyler Moore Show**
*Richie Brockelman, Private Eye from **The Rockford Files**
The Ropers from **Three's Company**
The Sandy Duncan Show from **Funny Face**
Sanford from **Sanford and Son**
The Sanford Arms from **Sanford and Son**
*Sarge from **Ironside**
The $64,000 Challenge from **The $64,000 Question**
Surfside Six from **Bourbon Street Beat**
Tabitha from **Bewitched**
Three's a Crowd from **Three's Company**
*The Tortellis from **Cheers**
Trapper John, M.D. from **M*A*S*H**
*Wanted: Dead or Alive from **Trackdown**
Young Maverick from **Maverick**
Zorro and Son from **Zorro**

PRIME-TIME NETWORK TV SERIES THAT ALSO AIRED ON NETWORK RADIO

The ideas for network TV series come from many sources. Some are original creations and others are adapted from other media—novels, short stories, magazine articles, motion pictures, comic strips, etc. One of the most popular sources for series ideas, particularly in the early days of television, was network radio. Many of radio's most popular, and in some cases least popular, series found their way to television in the 1940s and 1950s. On rare occasions television returned the favor. *Have Gun, Will Travel* was first seen on CBS television in 1957—the following year an audio version turned up on CBS radio.

Following is a list of network TV series that also aired on network radio. In cases where the radio title differed from the title of the TV series, the radio title is in parentheses. Each listing includes the radio networks on which the series was aired (in alphabetical order, not sequential order) and the years in which the radio version was in production. In addition to the three networks familiar to TV viewers—ABC, CBS, and NBC—there is a fourth radio network, the Mutual Broadcasting System (MBS). It should be noted that ABC was formed in 1943 when NBC, which previously owned two separate radio networks, the "red" network and the "blue" network, sold the "blue" network to Edward J. Noble. The network indications in the listing below, for all programs aired prior to 1943, refer to the NBC red network as "NBC" and to the NBC blue network as "BLUE."

In addition to the network series that aired on network radio, this listing also includes radio entries for any syndicated TV series which have been included in the body of *The Complete Directory.* To distinguish the listings for syndicated TV series from their network TV counterparts, they are all preceded by an asterisk.

The sources for this radio information were three books—*Tune in Yesterday,* by John Dunning, Prentice-Hall, Inc., 1976: *The Big Broadcast,* by Frank Buxton and Bill Owen, the Viking Press, 1972; and *A Thirty Year History of Programs Carried on National Radio Networks in the United States 1926–1956* by Harrison B. Summers, Arno Press and The New York Times, 1972.

*The Abbott and Costello Show; ABC, NBC; 1940, 1942–1949
The Adventures of Ellery Queen (Ellery Queen); ABC, CBS, NBC; 1939–1948
*The Adventures of Fu Manchu (Fu Manchu); CBS, Syndicated; 1932–1933, 1939–1940
The Adventures of Ozzie and Harriet; ABC, CBS, NBC; 1944–1954
The Adventures of Rin Tin Tin (Rin-Tin-Tin); BLUE, CBS, MBS; 1930–1934, 1955–1956
*The Adventures of Superman; ABC, MBS; 1940–1951
*The Adventures of Wild Bill Hickock (Wild Bill Hickock); MBS; 1951–1956
The Alan Young Show; ABC, NBC; 1944–1949
The Aldrich Family; BLUE, NBC; 1939–1953
The Amazing Dunninger (Dunninger the Mentalist); ABC; 1943–1944
The Amazing Mr. Malone (Murder and Mr. Malone); ABC; 1947–1950
American Forum of the Air; MBS, NBC; 1937–1956
America's Town Meeting (America's Town Meeting of the Air); ABC, NBC; 1935–1956
Amos 'n' Andy; BLUE, CBS, NBC; 1929–1960
Arthur Godfrey's Talent Scouts; CBS; 1946–1958
Author Meets the Critics; ABC, MBS, NBC; 1946–1950
Beat the Clock; CBS; 1948–1950
Believe It Or Not; ABC, BLUE, CBS, MBS, NBC; 1930–1938, 1942–1947
The Bell Telephone Hour; NBC; 1940–1958
Beulah; ABC, CBS, NBC; 1945–1954
The Big Story; NBC; 1947–1955
Big Town; CBS, NBC; 1937–1952
Blind Date; ABC, NBC; 1943–1946
Blondie; ABC, CBS, NBC; 1939–1950
Bob and Ray; ABC, CBS, MBS, NBC; 1951–1960
The Bob Hope Show; NBC; 1938–1958
*Bold Venture; Syndicated; 1950–1951
*Boston Blackie; NBC, Syndicated; 1944–1945
Break the Bank; ABC, MBS, NBC; 1945–1955

Buck Rogers (Buck Rogers in the Twenty-Fifth Century); CBS, MBS; 1932–1936, 1939–1947
Can You Top This; ABC, MBS, NBC; 1942–1954
Candid Camera (Candid Microphone); ABC; 1947–1948, 1950
Capitol Cloak Room (Capitol Cloakroom); CBS, MBS; 1948–1956
Cavalcade of America; CBS, NBC; 1935–1953
Chance of a Lifetime; ABC; 1949–1952
Charlie Wild, Private Detective; CBS; 1950–1951
*The Cisco Kid; MBS; 1942–1943, 1946–1947
Cities Service Band of America (Cities Service Concerts); NBC; 1926–1956
City Hospital; CBS; 1951–1956
The Clock; ABC; 1946–1948
Coke Time with Eddie Fisher (The Eddie Fisher Show); ABC, MBS; 1952–1957
Crime Photographer (Casey, Crime Photographer); CBS; 1943–1950, 1953–1955
*Dangerous Assignment; NBC; 1950–1953
The Danny Kaye Show; CBS; 1945–1946
A Date with Judy; ABC, NBC; 1941–1950
The Dave Garroway Show; NBC; 1949–1953
*Death Valley Days; BLUE, CBS; 1930–1945
Dick Powell's Zane Grey Theater (The Zane Grey Show); MBS; 1947–1948
Dick Tracy; ABC, MBS, NBC; 1935–1939, 1943–1948
The Dinah Shore Show; CBS, NBC; 1939–1947, 1953–1955
Dr. I.Q. (Dr. I.Q., The Mental Banker); ABC, NBC; 1939–1950
Dr. Kildare; MBS, Syndicated; 1949, 1951–1952
Don McNeill TV Club (The Breakfast Club); ABC, BLUE; 1933–1968
Double or Nothing; CBS, MBS, NBC; 1940–1952
Down You Go; MBS; 1952–1953
Dragnet; NBC; 1949–1956
Earn Your Vacation; CBS; 1949–1950
Easy Aces; BLUE, CBS; 1931–1945, 1948–1949
Escape; CBS; 1948–1954
Ethel and Albert; ABC; 1944–1950
Face the Nation; CBS; 1954–
Famous Jury Trials; ABC, BLUE, MBS, NBC; 1936–1949
Father Knows Best; NBC; 1949–1954
*Favorite Story; Syndicated; 1946–1949
Fibber McGee and Molly; BLUE, NBC; 1935–1957
*Flash Gordon; MBS; 1935–1936
Ford Show (The Tennessee Ernie Ford Show); ABC, CBS; 1952–1955
Ford Theatre; CBS, NBC; 1947–1949
The Frank Sinatra Show; ABC, CBS, NBC; 1944–1947, 1949, 1951, 1956–1958
The Fred Waring Show; CBS, NBC; 1932–1952
The Galen Drake Show; ABC, CBS; 1945–1955
Gangbusters (Gang Busters); ABC, BLUE, CBS, MBS, NBC; 1936–1957
The Garry Moore Show; CBS; 1949–1950
The Gay Nineties Review; CBS; 1940–1944
The George Burns and Gracie Allen Show (Burns and Allen); CBS, NBC; 1932–1950
The Goldbergs; CBS, MBS, NBC; 1929–1934, 1937–1945, 1949–1950
Grand Ole Opry; NBC; 1939–1957
The Green Hornet; ABC, BLUE, MBS, NBC; 1936–1952
Gunsmoke; CBS; 1952–1961
The Halls of Ivy; NBC; 1950–1952
Have Gun, Will Travel; CBS; 1958–1960
Hayloft Hoedown; ABC; 1945–1949
Herb Shriner Time; CBS; 1948–1949
Hobby Lobby; BLUE, CBS, MBS; 1937–1949
Hopalong Cassidy; CBS, MBS; 1950–1952
The Horace Heidt Show; ABC, CBS, NBC; 1932–1953
The Hour of Decision; ABC, MBS; 1950–1956
Information Please; BLUE, CBS, MBS, NBC; 1938–1948
It Pays to Be Ignorant; CBS, MBS; 1942–1949
It's Alec Templeton Time (Alec Templeton Time); BLUE, CBS, NBC; 1939–1943, 1947
The Jack Benny Show; BLUE, CBS, NBC; 1932–1958
The Jane Pickens Show; NBC; 1952–1956

The Jimmy Durante Show; CBS, NBC; 1943–1950
Juvenile Jury; MBS, NBC; 1946–1953
The Kate Smith Show; ABC, CBS, MBS, NBC; 1930–1951, 1957–1958
Kay Kyser's Kollege of Musical Knowledge; ABC, MBS, NBC; 1938–1949
The Kraft Music Hall; NBC; 1933–1949
Ladies Be Seated; ABC; 1943–1950
Lassie; ABC, NBC; 1947–1950
The Lawrence Welk Show; ABC; 1949–1956
Leave It to the Girls; MBS; 1945–1949
Life Begins at 80; ABC, MBS; 1948–1949
The Life of Riley; NBC; 1943–1951
Life with Linkletter (Art Linkletter's House Party); CBS; 1945–1967
Life with Luigi; CBS; 1948–1953
Lights Out; CBS, MBS, NBC; 1935–1947
The Lineup; CBS; 1950–1953
The Little Show; CBS; 1947
Life Like a Millionaire; ABC; 1950–1953
The Lone Ranger; ABC, BLUE, NBC, Syndicated; 1933–1955
Lux Video Theatre (The Lux Radio Theatre); CBS, NBC; 1934–1955
*The Man Called X; CBS, NBC; 1944–1948, 1950–1952
The Marriage; NBC; 1953–1954
Martin Kane, Private Eye (Martin Kane, Private Detective); MBS; 1949–1952
Mary Margaret McBride; ABC, CBS, NBC; 1937–1954
Meet Corliss Archer; ABC, CBS; 1943–1955
Meet Millie; CBS; 1951–1954
Meet the Press; NBC; 1945–
Michael Shayne; ABC, MBS; 1946–1952
The Milton Berle Show; NBC; 1941–1942, 1947–1948
Mr. and Mrs. North; CBS, NBC; 1941–1956
Mr. District Attorney; ABC, BLUE, NBC; 1939–1953
The Morey Amsterdam Show; CBS; 1948–1949
My Favorite Husband; CBS; 1948–1951
My Friend Irma; CBS; 1947–1954
My Little Margie; CBS, MBS; 1952–1955
My True Story; ABC, NBC; 1943–1961
Name That Tune; NBC; 1952–1953
The Nat "King" Cole Show ("King" Cole Trio Time); NBC; 1947–1948
The National Barn Dance; ABC, BLUE, NBC; 1933–1950
Nero Wolfe (The Adventures of Nero Wolfe); ABC, BLUE NBC; 1943–1946, 1950–1951
*The New Adventures of Charlie Chan (Charlie Chan); ABC, BLUE, MBS; 1932–1933, 1937–1938,
   1944–1948
Oboler Comedy Theatre (Arch Oboler Plays) MBS, NBC; 1939–1940, 1945
One Man's Family; NBC; 1932–1959
The O'Neills; CBS, MBS, NBC; 1934–1943
The Original Amateur Hour (Major Bowes' Original Amateur Hour); ABC, CBS, NBC; 1935–1946,
   1948–1952
Our Miss Brooks; CBS; 1948–1957
Our Secret Weapon—The Truth; CBS; 1942–1943
The Paul Winchell and Jerry Mahoney Show; MBS; 1943–1944
The Pee Wee King Show; NBC; 1952–1955
People Are Funny; CBS, NBC; 1942–1959
The People's Platform; CBS; 1938–1952
The Perry Como Show (Chesterfield Supper Club); NBC; 1944–1950
Perry Mason; CBS; 1943–1955
Pete Kelly's Blues; NBC; 1951
The Peter Potter Show (Jukebox Jury); CBS; 1954–1956
Philip Marlowe (The Adventures of Philip Marlowe); CBS, NBC; 1947–1950
Presidential Timber; CBS; 1948
Public Prosecutor; MBS; 1954–1956
Pursuit; CBS; 1949–1952
Q.E.D. (Mystery File); ABC; 1950–1951
Quick as a Flash; ABC, MBS; 1944–1951
The Quiz Kids; ABC, BLUE, CBS, NBC; 1940–1953

The RCA Victor Show (A Day in the Life of Dennis Day); NBC; 1946–1951
RFD America; MBS, NBC; 1947–1949
The Ray Bolger Show; CBS; 1945
The Ray Milland Show (Meet Mr. McNutley); CBS; 1953–1954
The Red Skelton Show; CBS, NBC; 1941–1953
Richard Diamond, Private Detective; ABC, NBC; 1949–1952
The Robert Q. Lewis Show; CBS; 1951–1955
Romance; CBS; 1947–1960
The Roy Rogers Show; MBS, NBC; 1944–1955
The Saint; CBS, MBS, NBC; 1945–1952
The Screen Directors' Playhouse; NBC; 1949–1951
See It Now (Hear It Now); CBS; 1950–1951
Sergeant Preston of the Yukon; ABC, MBS; 1947–1955
Sheilah Graham in Hollywood (The Sheilah Graham Show); MBS; 1949–1950
The Show Goes On; CBS; 1949–1950
The Silver Theatre; CBS; 1937–1946
Sing It Again; CBS; 1948–1951
The Singing Lady (The Singing Story Lady); ABC, BLUE, MBS, NBC; 1932–1950
Sky King; ABC, MBS; 1946–1954
Smilin' Ed McConnell and His Buster Brown Gang; NBC; 1944–1952
Songs For Sale; CBS; 1950–1951
Space Patrol; ABC; 1950–1955
The Spike Jones Show; CBS; 1947–1949
Stars Over Hollywood; CBS; 1941–1954
The Steve Allen Show; CBS; 1952–1953
Stop Me If You've Heard This One; MBS, NBC; 1939–1940, 1947–1948
Stop the Music; ABC, CBS; 1948–1955
Strike It Rich; CBS, NBC; 1947–1958
Studio One; CBS; 1947–1948
Suspense; CBS; 1942–1962
The TV Reader's Digest (The Radio Reader's Digest); CBS; 1942–1948
Tales of the Texas Rangers; NBC; 1950–1952
Tales of Tomorrow; ABC, CBS; 1953
Tarzan; CBS; 1952–1953
The Ted Steele Show; MBS; 1954–1955
Tex and Jinx (Meet Tex and Jinx); NBC; 1947–1948
The Thin Man (The Adventures of the Thin Man); ABC, CBS, NBC; 1941–1950
Think Fast; ABC; 1949–1950
*The Third Man; Syndicated; 1950–1951
This Is Show Business; CBS; 1949–1954
This Is Your Life; NBC; 1948–1950
Tom Corbett, Space Cadet; ABC; 1952
Topper (The Adventures of Topper); NBC; 1945
Truth or Consequences; CBS, NBC; 1940–1957
Twenty Questions; MBS; 1946–1954
Two For the Money; CBS; 1952–1957
The U.S. Steel Hour; ABC, NBC; 1945–1953
Valentino; ABC; 1952–1956
The Victor Borge Show; NBC; 1945–1947
Vincent Lopez; ABC, MBS; 1949–1956
The Voice of Firestone; ABC, NBC; 1928–1956
The Walter Winchell Show (Walter Winchell's Journal); ABC, BLUE, MBS; 1932–1956
We Take Your Word; CBS; 1950–1951
We, The People; CBS, NBC; 1936–1951
What's My Line; CBS; 1952–1953
What's My Name; ABC, MBS, NBC; 1938–1942, 1949–1950
Who Said That; NBC; 1948–1950
The Wife Saver; NBC; 1932–1942
Winner Take All; CBS; 1946–1952
You Are There; (CBS Is There); CBS; 1947–1950
You Bet Your Life; ABC, CBS, NBC; 1947–1959
Your Hit Parade; NBC; 1935–1959
Youth Wants to Know; NBC; 1951–1955

HIT THEME SONGS FROM SERIES

Listed here are TV theme songs which reached *Billboard's* top 60. For detailed information on TV themes over the years, the reader is referred to the article "Trends in Recorded Television Themes" by Steve Gelfand in *Goldmine* magazine, September 1979.

All in the Family
("Those Were the Days"), Carroll O'Connor & Jean Stapleton (1971, #43)

Angie
("Different Worlds"), Maureen McGovern (1979, #18)

Baretta
("Keep Your Eye on the Sparrow") Rhythm Heritage (1976, #20)

Batman, The Marketts (1966, #17) Neal Hefti & Orchestra (1966, #35)

Ben Casey, Valjean (1962, #28)

Beverly Hillbillies
("The Ballad of Jed Clampett") Lester Flatt & Earl Scruggs (1962, #44)

Bonanza, Al Caiola (1961, #19)

Charlie's Angels, Henry Mancini (1977, #45)

Dr. Kildare
("Three Stars Will Shine Tonight") Richard Chamberlain (1962, #10)

Dragnet, Ray Anthony Orchestra (1953, #3)

The Dukes of Hazzard, Waylon Jennings (1980, #21)

Dynasty, Bill Conti (1982, #52)

The Greatest American Hero
("Believe It or Not") Joey Scarbury (1981, #2)

Happy Days, Pratt & McClain (1976, #5)

Have Gun Will Travel
("Ballad of Paladin") Duane Eddy (1962, #33)

Hawaii Five-O, The Ventures (1969, #4)

Here Come the Brides
("Seattle") Perry Como (1969, #38)

Hill Street Blues, Mike Post, featuring Larry Carlton, guitar (1981, #10)

I Love Lucy
("Disco Lucy"), Wilton Place Street Band (1977, #24)

Laverne and Shirley
("Making Our Dreams Come True") Cyndi Grecco (1976, #25)

Magnum, P.I., Mike Post (1982, #25)

Makin' It, David Naughton (1979, #5)

Medic
  ("Blue Star"), Felicia Sanders (1955, #29)

The Men, Isaac Hayes (1972, #38)

Miami Vice, Jan Hammer (1985, #1)

Mission: Impossible, Lalo Schifrin (1968, #41)

Mr. Lucky, Henry Mancini Orchestra (1960, #21)

Moonlighting, Al Jarreau (1987, #23)

My Three Sons, Lawrence Welk Orchestra (1961, #55)

Peter Gunn, Ray Anthony Orchestra (1959, #8), Duane Eddy (1960, #27), The Art of Noise (1986, #50)

The Rockford Files, Mike Post (1975, #10)

Route 66, Nelson Riddle Orchestra (1962, #30)

S.W.A.T., Rhythm Heritage (1975, #1)

Secret Agent
  ("Secret Agent Man") Johnny Rivers (1966, #3), The Ventures (1966, #54)

Welcome Back, Kotter
  ("Welcome Back") John Sebastian (1976, #1)

Zorro, The Chordettes (1958, #17)

INDEX

Note: Bold face numerals designate Emmy-Award winners.

Baker, Art, 237, 876
Baker, Blanche, **952**
Baker, Carroll, 183
Baker, Cathy, 335
Baker, David Lain, 124
Baker, Diane, 339
Baker, Don, 734
Baker, Don "Red," 453
Baker, Herbert, **933, 942**
Baker, Jay, 75
Baker, Jim B., 269
Baker, Joby, 305
Baker, Joe, 1, 83, 424, 661, 744
Baker, Joe Don, 233, 837
Baker, Josephine, 412
Baker, Kirsten, 388
Baker, Lennie, 703
Baker, Peter, **940, 941**
Baker, Phil, 862
Baker, Ray, 334
Bakewell, William, 626
Bakula, Scott, 234, 315
Bal, Jeanne, 56, 461, 521, 550
Balanchine, George, **953**
Baldavin, Barbara, 506
Balding, Rebecca, 460, 476, 724
Baldwin, Alec, 176, 420
Baldwin, Bill, 502
Baldwin, Curtis, 819
Baldwin, Judith, 297
Balenda, Carla, 14, 512
Balfour, Michael, 488
Ball, Dee Dee, 371
Ball, Lucille, xv, 185, 187, 192,
    230, 365, 366, 373, 450, 465, 466,
    493, 516, 541, 850, **930, 931, 938,
    939**
Ball, Sue, 443
Ballantine, Carl, 503, 587, 645
Ballantine, Eddie, 212
Ballard, Kaye, 215, 338, 530, 615,
    744
Ballard, Michael, 25
Ballet Russe of Monte Carlo, The,
    833
Ballet Theatre Company, 581
Balsam, Martin, xv, 9, 22, 26, 28,
    307, 350, 715, 729, 850
Balson, Allison, 453
Baltzell, Deborah, 368
Balzer, George, **933, 934**
Bamber, Judy, 42
Bamboschek, Maestro Guiseppe,
    590
Bananarama, 806
Banas, Bob, 404, 476
Bancroft, Anne, 581
Bancroft, Griffing, 129
Band of America, 153
Banfield, Bever-Leigh, 175, 589,
    674
Bangert, Charles A., **954, 955, 957**

Bangert, Johnny, 487
Banghart, Ken, 296
Banham, Russ, 399
Bank, Frank, 441, 561, 596
Bankhead, Tallulah, 28, 82, 822
Banks, C. Tillery, 327
Banks, David, 663
Banks, Emily, 795
Banks, Heidi, 315
Banks, Joan, 638
Banks, Jonathan, 246, 287, 593,
    867
Banks, Tyler, 178
Banner, Bob, **933**
Banner, John, 147, 346
Bannister, Jeff, 50
Bannon, Jack, 460, 809
Bannon, Jim, 13
Bao-Xiang, Kuo, **957**
Bar-Yotam, Reuven, 133
Bara, Fausto, 658
Bara, Nina, 731
Baragrey, John, 426
Baral, Eileen, 554
Barash, Olivia, 249, 370, 596
Barbeau, Adrienne, 499, 763
Barber, Ava, 439
Barber, Bobby, 7
Barber, Glynis, 194
Barber, Red, 551, 655
Barbera, Joseph, 268, 322, 393,
    405, **952**
Barbour, John, 583, 654
Barbour, William P., 634
Barbutti, Pete, 289, 400
Bard, Katherine, 442, 755
Bardette, Trevor, 446
Bardolph, Dana, 122
Bardolph, Paige, 122
Bargy, Jean, 92
Bargy, Roy, 92, 396
Bari, Lenny, 265
Bari, Lynn, 85, 100, 197, 272, 830
Barker, Bob, 237, 636, 783, 812
Barker, Ma, 824, 868
Barkley, Alben W., 508
Barlow, Howard, 832, 833
Barnard, Pat, 15
Barnes, Ann, 90
Barnes, C. B., 188, 742
Barnes, Emily, 169
Barnes, George, 713, 718
Barnes, Georgene, 404
Barnes, Joanna, 811, 815
Barnes, John W., **940, 944**
Barnes, Priscilla, 33, 792
Barnes, Walter, 837
Barnouw, Erik, 354
Barnstable, Cyb, 645
Barnstable, Tricia, 645
Barnum, P. T., 69, 448
Baron, Jeffrey, 488

Baron, Sandy, 341, 781
Barr, Douglas, 249, 856, 868
Barr, Leonard, 765
Barr, Ray, 831
Barr, Sharon, 500
Barrat, Maxine, 37, 624
Barrett, Lynne, 509
Barrett, Majel, 739
Barrett, Monte, 15
Barrett, Ray, 296, 326
Barrett, Rona, 239, 776, 800
Barri, Steve, 698
Barrie, Barbara, 57, 62, 105, 198,
    217, 657, 812
Barrie, Wendy, 15, 626, 776, 848
Barrier, Edgar, 224
Barris, Chuck, 150, 186, 209, 210,
    303, 304, 564, 591, 604, 810
Barris, Marty, 163, 436
Barron, Arthur, **940**
Barry, Donald, 521, 761
Barry, Gene, 43, 64, 115, 201, 264,
    350, 372, 467, 552, 594, 694
Barry, Harold, 829
Barry, Ivor, 106, 519
Barry, J. J., 167
Barry, Jack, 84, 104, 164, 291, 343,
    404, 409, 448, 657, 794, 815, 867
Barry, Jeff, 252, 390
Barry, John, 618
Barry, Matthew, 381
Barry, Norman, 633
Barry, Patricia, 327
Barry, Peter, 264
Barry, Philip, **953**
Barry, Raymond J., 581
Barry, Robert, 23
Barrymore, Drew, 31
Barrymore, John, Jr., 602
Barrymore, Lionel, 498
Barstow, Edith, 278
Bartel, Paul, 31
Barth, Eddie, 362, 513, 575, 661,
    704, 712
Bartlett, Bonnie, 453, 682, **960, 961**
Bartlett, Deborah, 461
Bartlett, Diana, 77
Bartlett, Sy, 814
Bartlett, Walter, **955**
Bartley, Daryl T., 721
Bartold, Norman, 10, 11, 775
Barton, Dan, 182
Barton, Earl, 108
Barton, Eileen, 108, 763, 830
Barton, Joan, 169
Barton, Peter, 633, 634, 706
Barton, Tod, 453
Barty, Billy, 9, 152, 155, 273, 733
Bartz, Geof, **954**
Baruch, André, 496, 880
Baryshnikov, Mikhail, **954, 955**
Basch, Harry, 246

Basehart, Richard, 9, 834, 835
Basie, Count, 35, 349, 392, 470, 556
Basile, Louis, 759
Basinger, Kim, 209, 281
Bass, Emory, 40
Bass, Tod, 676
Bassett, Skye, 177
Bassett, William, 553
Bassman, George, 736
Bastedo, Alexandra, 138
Bateman, Charles, 483
Bateman, Jason, 381, 453, 711, 827
Bateman, Justine, 252, 771
Bates, Barbara, 377
Bates, Jeanne, 71
Bates, Jim, 470
Bates, Jimmy, 257
Bates, John, 488
Bates, Lulu, 289
Bates, Rhonda, 89, 414, 671, 731
Batinkoff, Randall, 75
Batista, Fulgencio, 802
Battiste, Harold, 727
Bauer, Charita, 23
Bauer, Jaime Lyn, 60
Bauer, Louis H., 354
Baukhage, H. R., 565
Bauman, Jon "Bowzer," 350, 703
Baumann, Kathrine, 414
Baur, Elizabeth, 375, 430
Bavaar, Tony, 155
Bavier, Frances, 38, 240, 377, 501, **938**
Baxter, Anne, 291, 356, 486
Baxter, Billy, 376
Baxter, Carol, 175
Baxter, Frank, 776
Baxter, Warner, 152
Baxter-Birney, Meredith, 106, 107, 250, 252, 852
Bay City Rollers, 691
Bayer, Gary, 505
Baylor, Hal, 446
Bazlen, Brigid, 805
Beach, Michael, 751
Beach Boys, The, 706, 766
Beacham, Stephanie, 157
Beaird, Barbara, 261
Beaird, Betty, 407
Beaird, Pamela, 542
Beal, John, 883
Bean, Orson, 74, 91, 381, 415, 492, 602, 797
Beane, Reginald, 585, 741
Beard, James, 366
Bearde, Chris, 304, 644, **939**
Bearse, Amanda, 489
Beasley, Allyce, 528
Beastie Boys, The, 370, 381
Beaters, The, 414
Beatles, The, 230, 238, 280, 360, 527, 540, 568, 706, 870

Beatts, Anne, **950, 951**
Beatty, Morgan, 567
Beatty, Ned, 765
Beatty, Roger, **944, 945, 946, 948, 952**
Beatty, Warren, 485
Beauchamp, Richard, 121, 361, 885
Beaudine, Deka, 602
Beaumont, Chris, 339
Beaumont, Hugh, 441, 561
Beavers, Louise, 76, 77
Bechet, Sidney, 231
Beck, Billy, 460
Beck, Jack, **938**
Beck, Jackson, 139, 451
Beck, John, 178, 266, 569
Beck, Kimberly, 464, 621, 662
Beck, Michael, 358
Becker, Barbara, 843
Becker, George, 289
Becker, Sandy, 44, 865
Becker, Terry, 834
Becker, Tony, 272, 592, 780
Beckham, Brice, 518
Beckley, William, 225
Beckman, Henry, 110, 142, 284, 339, 369, 446, 503, 621
Bedelia, Bonnie, 561
Bedford, Brian, 167
Bedford-Lloyd, John, 351
Bee, Bob, **960**
Bee, Molly, 396
Bee Gees, The, 334, 476, 806
Beecham, Sir Thomas, 137
Beer, Jacqueline, 702
Beers, Francine, 589
Beery, Noah, Jr., 152, 206, 351, 646, 666, 669, 875
Beery, Wallace, 19
Beethoven, Ludwig van, 219, 582, **942**
Bega, Leslie, 333
Begley, Ed, 442, 558, 632, 671, 822
Begley, Ed, Jr., 670, 682
Bel Geddes, Barbara, 178, 554, **954**
Belack, Doris, 58
Belafonte, Harry, 556, 756, **934**
Belafonte-Harper, Shari, 356
Belasco, Leon, 544
Belford, Christine, 59, 236, 489, 598
Belgard, Madeline, 588
Belkin, Gary, **941, 946, 948**
Bell, Darryl, 203
Bell, Dave, **959**
Bell, Edward, 420
Bell, Marshall, 581
Bell, Michael, 178
Bell, Ralph, 762
Bell, Rex, 171

Bell, Tita, 322
Bell Telephone Orchestra, The, 71
Bellamann, Henry, 418
Bellamy, Ralph, 193, 234, 283, 307, 356, 361, 410, 478, 530, 550, 761, 797, 822, 856
Belland, Bruce, 794
Bellaver, Harry, 551
Beller, Kathleen, 110, 225
Beller, Mary Linn, 186
Bellflower, Nellie, 415
Belli, Melvin, 862
Bellini, Cal, 198
Bellson, Louis, 611
Bellwood, Pamela, 225, 835
Bellwood, Peter, **941**
Belmondo, Buzz, 597
Beltran, Alma, 73
Belushi, Jim, 689, 861, 871
Belushi, John, 194, 689, 690, 697, **951**
Belvederes, 652
Belzer, Richard, 784
Benaderet, Bea, 77, 268, 291, 292, 619–621
Benben, Brian, 287, 413
Bench, Johnny, 286
Bender, Gary, 63
Bendix, William, 264, 449, 599, 824, 850
Benedict, Dirk, 6, 66, 150
Benedict, Greg, 573
Benedict, Paul, 390
Benét, Stephen Vincent, 581
Beniades, Ted, 37
Benjamin, Burton, **940, 943, 945, 947**
Benjamin, Julia, 332
Benjamin, Richard, 333, 645
Benjamin, Sue, 776
Benjamin, Susan, 8
Bennett, Donn, 81
Bennett, Elizabeth, 575, 875
Bennett, Harve, **956**
Bennett, Joan, 74, 148, 643, 805
Bennett, Marjorie, 485
Bennett, Michelle, 875
Bennett, Peter, 17
Bennett, Sue, 412, 776, 880
Bennett, Tony, 48, 314, 407, 556, 608, 617, 727, 803, 825
Benny, Jack, xiii, xv, 162, 291, 293, 383, 384, 396, 407, 423, 487, 581, 639, 649, 709, 743, 843, 881, **932, 933, 934**
Benoit, Patricia, 522
Bensley, Russ, **942, 945**
Benson, Barbara, 685
Benson, Cort, 879
Benson, Irving, 515, 516
Benson, Lucille, 99, 555

Benson, Pat, 398
Benson, Red, 552
Benson, Robby, 807
Bentley, Beverly, 68, 69
Benton, Barbi, 136, 335, 756
Benton, Douglas, **945**
Benton, Eddie, 209, 650
Benton, Lee, 513
Beradino, John, 364, 559
Bercovici, Eric, **955**
Berdis, Bert, 637, 795
Berg, Gertrude, 145, 234, 294, 302, **930**
Bergan, Judith-Marie, 28, 211, 472
Bergen, Bill, 632
Bergen, Candice, 563, 690
Bergen, Edgar, 205, 357, 368, 709
Bergen, Frances, 874
Bergen, Jerry, 116
Bergen, Polly, 43, 155, 234, 466, 614, 628, 632, 693, 739, 797, 825, **932**
Berger, Anna, 701
Berger, Helmut, 225
Berger, Robert, **951**
Berger, Senta, 533
Bergere, Lee, 225, 355
Bergman, Alan, 25, 554
Bergman, Ingrid, 721, 743, **934, 956**
Bergman, Jules, **947**
Bergman, Marilyn, 25, 554
Bergman, Peter, 741
Bergman, Richard, 258
Bergmeier, Jane, 415
Beria, Lavrenti Pavlovich, 449
Berle, Milton, xiii, xiv, 11, 31, 60, 81, 85, 114, 135, 145, 170, 185, 211, 244, 277, 349, 357, 358, 365, 384, 386, 387, 403, 423, 461, 490, 501, 515, 516, 531, 540, 748, 758, **930**
Berlin, Irving, 71, 230, **953**
Berlinger, Warren, 284, 399, 591, 720, 807
Berman, Shelley, 5, 224, 492, 583, 735
Bernard, Crystal, 322, 378
Bernard, Dorothy, 450
Bernard, Ed, 167, 631, 783, 858
Bernard, Jason, 122, 342, 858
Bernard, Tommy, 678
Bernardi, Herschel, 45, 318, 393, 619, 701
Berner, Sara, 321
Bernhard, Sandra, 435, 663
Bernie, Al, 261, 262
Bernier, Daisy, 278
Berns, Bill, 777
Bernsen, Corbin, 429
Bernstein, Leonard, 582, **942, 949**
Berry, Chuck, 80, 150, 200, 211, 703, 706
Berry, Fred, 852

Berry, Ken, 38, 41, 94, 132, 243, 415, 478, 501
Berthrong, Deirdre, 388
Berti, Dehl, 99, 112, 591
Bertinelli, Valerie, 586
Berwick, Brad, 865
Berwick, Ray, 339
Besch, Bibi, 320, 699
Bessell, Ted, 1, 303, 305, 318, 378, 505, 780
Besser, Joe, 7, 357, 399, 415
Best, James, 223
Best, Willie, 543, 753, 842
Beswick, Martine, 372
Bethune, Ivy, 258
Bethune, Zina, 576
Bettger, Lyle, 170
Betts, Jack, 143
Betz, Betty, 301, 776
Betz, Carl, 213, 405, 634, **939**
Beutel, Bill, 565
Bexley, Don, 687, 688
Beyer, Troy, 225
Beyers, Bill, 398
Beymer, Richard, 603
Biberman, Abner, 422
Bice, Robert, 547
Bickford, Charles, 479, 660, 831
Biehn, Michael, 679
Biener, Tom, 387, 394
Bieri, Ramon, 105, 399, 688
Biesk, Adam, 789
Big Show Ice Skaters, The, 83
Big Show Water Ballet, The, 83
Bigelow, Donald N., 160
Bigelow, Joe, 135
Biggers, Earl Derr, 558
Bikel, Theodore, 739, 754
Bill, Tony, 852
Billingsley, Barbara, 441, 561, 640
Billingsley, Kelly, 335
Billingsley, Peter, 654
Billingsley, Sherman, 749
Billington, Michael, 646, 821
Bilson, Bruce, **939**
Binder, Steve, **950**
Binkley, Lane, 673
Binns, Edward, 105, 376, 576, 630
Birch, Paul, 170
Birch, Peter, 389
Bird, Billie, 73, 377
Birk, Raye, 632
Birkett, Bernadette, 379
Birman, Len, 208
Birnbaum, Bernard, **938, 947**
Birney, David, 106, 107, 300, 496, 682, 700
Bishop, Ed, 821
Bishop, Jennifer, 335
Bishop, Joey, 2, 399, 400, 415, 445, 510, 802, 803
Bishop, John, 447

Bishop, Julie, 543
Bishop, Kelly, 789
Bishop, Mel, 661
Bishop, Stephen, 381, 414
Bishop, William, 377
Bisoglio, Val, 631, 647, 670, 871
Bissel, Whit, 795
Biviano, Joseph, 138, 482
Bixby, Bill, xvii, 98, 170, 306, 315, 371, 399, 473, 495, 542, 661
Black, Fischer, 75
Black, Gerry, 344
Black, Hugo L., 120, **940**
Black, Karen, 136, 698
Black, Marianne, 756
Black Sabbath, 211
Blackburn, Dorothy, 667
Blackburn, Harriet, 371
Blackman, Honor, 52, 832
Blackman, Joan, 621
Blackmer, Sidney, 762, 845
Blackmore, Stephanie, 178
Blackton, Jay, 373
Blackwell, Kenneth, **962**
Blackwood, Nina, 725, 726
Blacque, Taurean, 344
Blade, Jimmy, 199
Blade, Richard, 668
Blaine, Jimmy, 87, 346, 347, 395, 538, 611, 748
Blaine, Vivian, 138, 181, 290, 790
Blair, Frank, 294, 340
Blair, Janet, 23, 122, 145, 442, 721
Blair, June, 15
Blair, Kevin, 665
Blair, Lionel, 735
Blair, Nicky, 683
Blair, Patricia, 183, 664
Blaire and Deane, 273
Blaisdell, Brad, 792
Blake, Amanda, 316
Blake, Geoffrey, 603
Blake, Jonathan, 844
Blake, Josh, 584
Blake, Madge, 65, 399, 653
Blake, Oliver, 111
Blake, Patricia, 822
Blake, Robert, 61, 336, 662, 799, **947**
Blake, Sondra, 61
Blake, Whitney, 187, 332
Blakely, Susan, 661
Blakeney, Olive, 206
Blanc, Mel, 112, 114, 268, 383, 393, 394, 540, 541, 857
Blanchard, Mari, 419
Blanchard, Susan, 524, 878, 879
Bland, John David, 759
Blankfield, Mark, 280
Blasucci, Dick, **958**
Blattner, Buddy, 64
Blechman, Corey, **957**

Bradley, Truman, 694
Brady, Pat, 677, 678
Brady, Phil, **943**, **947**
Brady, Scott, xvi, 708
Brake, Patricia, 822
Bramley, Raymond, 215
Brand, Jack, 9, 713
Brand, Jolene, 314, 769, 885
Brand, Joshua, **961**
Brand, Max, 196
Brand, Neville, 290, 431, 739, 824, 850
Brand, Oscar, 220
Brando, Marlon, 9, 18, 674, **953**
Brandon, Clark, 265, 521, 596
Brandon, Michael, 194, 235
Brands, X., 874
Brandt, Hank, 407
Brandt, Janet, 759
Brandt, Mel, 255
Brandt, Victor, 574
Brandt, Willy, 166
Brannum, Hugh, 278
Brasfield, Aunt Sap, 599
Brasfield, Rod, 308
Brasfield, Uncle Cyp, 599
Brasselle, Keefe, 67, 68, 414
Braun, Bob, 216
Brauner, Asher, 54
Braverman, Bart, 578, 829
Bravo, Danny, 404
Bray, Robert, 432, 737
Bray, Thom, 105, 328, 665
Brazil, Scott, **957**, **958**
Brazzi, Rossano, 225, 761
Brecht, Susan, 216
Breck, Peter, 85, 89, 698
Breeding, Larry, 434, 861
Breen, Patrick, 408
Breen, Robert, 218, 707
Breese, Lou, 384
Breeze, Syd, 756
Bregman, Buddy, 232, 540
Bregman, Martin, 276
Bremner, Scott, 558
Brendan, Gavin, 486
Brenna, Bettina, 77
Brennan, Eileen, 561, 579, 638, 676, 786, **955**
Brennan, Frederick Hazlitt, 446
Brennan, Walter, 316, 653, 695, 796, 820
Brenner, Alfred, **933**
Brenner, David, 571, 583, 803
Brenner, Dori, 134, 141, 701
Brenno, Tori, 461
Brent, George, 264, 736, 867
Bresler, Jerry, 46, 48
Breslin, Jimmy, 200, 395
Breslin, Pat, 613
Bressler, Brian, 676
Brestoff, Richard, 591
Brewer, Betty, 129, 347

Brewer, Teresa, 314, 592, 617, 758, 825
Brewster, Diane, 371, 375, 441, 499
Brewster, Punky, 643
Brewton, Maia, 452
Brian, David, 369, 520
Brickell, Beth, 291
Brickhouse, Jack, 872
Bricusse, Leslie, 369
Bridge, Lois, 450
Bridges, Beau, 237, 696, 729, 823
Bridges, Lloyd, 85, 272, 309, 398, 425, 455, 457, 603, 631, 673, 686, 695, 696, 757, 762, 822
Bridges, Todd, 202, 265
Bright, Jack, 812
Bright, Patricia, 98, 220, 262, 315, 379, 531
Briles, Charles, 85
Brill, Charlie, 676, 760
Brill, Marty, 559
Brill, Patti, 444
Brimley, Wilford, 594
Brinckerhoff, Burt, 755
Brinegar, Paul, 430, 446, 497, 651
Brinkley, David, 187, 264, 265, 549, 568, **933**, **934**, **935**, **936**, **940**, **941**
Brisebois, Danielle, 26, 420
Brissette, Tiffany, 721
Britt, Elton, 689
Brittany, Morgan, 178, 300
Britton, Barbara, 518
Britton, Pamela, 90, 542
Brock, Jimmy, 159
Brock, Lou, 63
Brock, Maurice C., 130
Brock, Richard, **959**
Brock, Stan, 863
Brock, Stanley, 340
Brockway, Merrill, **953**
Broderick, James, 105, 250
Broderick, Malcolm, 489
Brodie, Steve, 446
Brodkin, Herbert, **951**
Broekman, David, 785
Brogan, Jimmy, 596
Brokaw, Tom, 568
Brokenshire, Norman, 75, 161, 221, 276
Brolin, James, 356, 486, **940**
Brolin, Josh, 638
Bromfield, John, 705
Bromfield, Lois, 414
Bromfield, Valri, 40, 74, 95, 563
Bromley, Sheila, 321, 367
Bronson, Charles, 236, 482, 614, 705, 810, 811
Bronson, Lillian, 186, 418
Bronson, Michael, **956**, **959**
Bronson, Milt, 7
Brook, Faith, 153

Brooke, Hillary, 7, 543, 881
Brooke, Walter, 311, 588
Brookes, Jacqueline, 383
Brooks, Albert, 50, 190, 689, 690
Brooks, Avery, 732
Brooks, Elizabeth, 209
Brooks, Foster, 95, 98, 190, 529, 559
Brooks, Geraldine, 224, 255, 299, 410, 473, 712, 822
Brooks, Helen, 744
Brooks, Herb, 731
Brooks, James L., **942**, **947**, **949**, **950**, **951**, **953**, **954**, **955**
Brooks, Joe, 243
Brooks, Joel, 318, 544, 638, 775
Brooks, Martin E., 88, 178, 506, 714, 715
Brooks, Mel, 211, 295, 709, 857, 882, **938**
Brooks, Ned, 508
Brooks, Peter, 545
Brooks, Rand, 16
Brooks, Randi, 433, 868
Brooks, Randy, 111, 658
Brooks, Roxanne, 663
Brooks, Stephen, 243, 373, 576
Brookshier, Tom, 136
Brophy, Kevin, 464
Brophy, Sallie, 113
Brosnan, Pierce, 657
Broston, Harve, **952**
Brothers, Dr. Joyce, 303, 408, 528, 703, 716
Brough, Candi, 54
Brough, Randi, 54
Brown, A. Whitney, 689
Brown, Allan, 509
Brown, Andrew, **954**
Brown, Blair, 1, 130, 189, 729, 856
Brown, Bob, 817
Brown, Bob (1940s), 694
Brown, Bob (1980s), 817
Brown, Candy Ann, 671
Brown, Charles, 797
Brown, Chelsea, 498, 676
Brown, Christopher J., 591
Brown, Doris, 464, 465
Brown, Earl, 184, 198, 404, 727
Brown, Eric, 478
Brown, Garrett M., 851
Brown, Georg Stanford, 672–674, **960**
Brown, Harry John, 833
Brown, Hy, 645
Brown, James, 16
Brown, James (actor), 16
Brown, James (singer), 187, 381, 511, 540, 785
Brown, Jim Ed, 555
Brown, Joe David, 604
Brown, Joe E., 114, 230, 290
Brown, John, 291, 292, 449

Busfield, Timothy, 657, 786, 808
Bush, Owen, 594, 714
Bush, Tommy, 105
Bushkin, Joe, 169
Butkus, Dick, 92, 319, 546, 661, 738
Butler, Daws, 393
Butler, Dean, 453, 560, 561
Butler, Johnny, 412
Butler, Lois, 649
Butler, Paul, 173
Butler, Robert, **946, 956**
Butrick, Merritt, 735
Butterfield, Herb, 319
Butterfield, Wally, 102
Butterworth, Shane, 57
Buttons, Red, 162, 217, 420, 655
Buttram, Pat, 290, 311
Butts, K. C., 594
Buwen, Joe, 509
Bux, Kuda, 31, 368, 426, 665
Buxton, Frank, 987
Buzby, Zane, 596
Buzzi, Ruth, 98, 161, 238, 676, 677, 744, 780
Byington, Spring, 85, 192, 431
Byner, John, 3, 95, 289, 400, 423, 620, 634, 724, 744
Byrd, David, 342, 491
Byrd, Dick, 775
Byrd, Jerry, 514
Byrd, Phillip, **960**
Byrd, Ralph, 202
Byrd, Richard, 791
Byrd, Tom, 98
Byrd-Nethery, Miriam, 524
Byrne, Bobby, 155
Byrnes, Burke, 178
Byrnes, Edd, 500, 702, 763
Byrnes, Jim, 867
Byron, Antoinette, 869
Byron, Carol, 580, 865
Byron, Edward C., 520
Byron, Jean, 485, 607, 608

C

Caan, James, 279
Cabal, Robert, 651
Cabot, Sebastian, 143, 251, 295, 296, 602, 762
Cabot, Susan, 350
Caddigan, James, 130
Cadorette, Mary, 792
Cady, Frank, 15, 311, 620
Caesar, Dave, 122
Caesar, Jimmy, 414
Caesar, Julius, 79
Caesar, Sid, xiv, 11, 31, 83, 122, 135, 232, 239, 277, 349, 384, 461, 583, 689, 709, 710, 782, 881, 882, **930, 931, 932, 937, 938**
Cafritz, Gwen, 368

Cagney, James, 523, 549, 668, **949**
Cahill, Cathy, 190
Cahill, Wash, 192
Cahn, Sammy, 188, 489
Caidin, Martin, 88, 715
Caillou, Alan, 645
Cain, Jess/Jeff, 487
Cain, Madelyn, 859
Caine, Howard, 124
Caine Dancers, 631
Caiola, Al, 991
Calame, Bob, 439
Calder, King, 490
Calder-Marshall, Anna, **939**
Caldwell, Jim, 794
Caldwell, Taylor, 130
Calfa, Don, 443, 604
Calhoun, Rory, 127, 192, 779
Cali, Joseph, 267, 797
Californians, The, 120
Caliri, Jon, 217, 735
Call, Brandon, 141
Callahan, Bill, 384
Callahan, James, 139, 166, 308, 679, 847
Callahan, John, 246
Callan, K, 176, 399, 489
Callan, Michael, 461, 577
Callas, Charlie, 1, 39, 210, 764
Callaway, Bill, 460
Callaway, Cheryl, 206
Callaway, Thomas, 246
Callendar, G., 722
Callender, Colin, **957**
Calloway, Cab, 150, 426, 462, 556, 831
Calmer, Ned, 370
Calvert, Bill, 256, 719
Calvert, Henry, 355
Calvin, Henry, 885
Calvin, John, 281, 609, 771
Camacho, Corinne, 506
Camarata, Tutti, 830
Cambridge, Godfrey, 709
Cameron, Candace, 284
Cameron, Dean, 256, 732
Cameron, Kirk, 312, 819
Cameron, Rod, 153, 350, 739, 744
Cammann, Schuyler, 852
Camp, Colleen, 180
Camp, Hamilton, 156, 333, 408, 555, 805, 813
Camp, Helen Page, 437, 786
Campanella, Frank, 718
Campanella, Joseph, 157, 440, 484, 576, 586, 789, 823
Campbell, Alan, 387, 792
Campbell, Archie, 335
Campbell, Dean, 127
Campbell, Duane R., 25
Campbell, Flora, 186, 255
Campbell, Glen, 300, 396, 402, 706, 756

Campbell, Julia, 869
Campbell, Mark, 435
Campbell, Nicholas, 198, 373
Campbell, Norman, **940, 944**
Campbell, Tisha, 650
Campbell, Toni, 477
Campbell, William, 173, 225
Campo, Pupi, 385
Campos, Rafael, 137, 660
Campos, Victor, 121, 209
Canary, David, 97, 621
Candoli, Pete, 403
Candy, John, 563, 681, 697, **958**
Canfield, Curtis, 8
Canfield, Mary Grace, 250, 311, 329
Caniff, Milton, 745
Cannell, Stephen J., 779, **951**
Canning, Tom, 784
Cannon, Dyan, 496
Cannon, Freddy, 703
Cannon, Glenn, 330
Cannon, J. D., 124, 502
Cannon, Jimmy, 5, 44, 855
Cannon, Katherine, 55, 166, 258, 334, 761
Cannon, Maureen, 108, 609, 610, 693
Cannon, Michael Philip, 805
Cannon, William Thomas, 805
Canova, Diana, 204, 271, 368, 369, 724, 793
Canova, Judy, 371
Cansler, Larry, 723
Cantor, Charlie, 652
Cantor, Eddie, xiv, 158, 231, 743, 789
Cantor, Nate, 667
Cantu, Carlos, 420
Capers, Virginia, 219, 278
Capice, Philip, **950**
Capone, Al, 824, 868
Caposella, Fred, 296
Capote, Truman, 2, **938**
Capp, Al, 42, 51, 259, 855, 860
Capps, Lisa, 312
Cappy, Ted, 317
Capra, Jordana, 728
Captain and Tennille, 211
Cara, Irene, 674
Carafotes, Paul, 420
Carbone, Anthony, 661
Card, Kathryn, 140
Cardi, Pat, 379
Carere, Christine, 91
Carey, Harry, 456
Carey, MacDonald, 405, 410, 456, 673
Carey, Michele, 479
Carey, Olive, 456, 518
Carey, Philip, 431, 623, 771, 824
Carey, Ron, 62, 167, 509, 527
Carhart, Georgiana, 448

1003

Cauldwell, Alan, 381
Caulfield, Joan, 466, 541, 684, 693
Caulfield, Maxwell, 157
Cavanagh, James P., **932**
Cavanaugh, Michael, 361, 742
Cavell, Marc, 626
Cavett, Dick, 2, 199, 200, 392, 395, 510, 690, **942, 947**
Cawdron, Robert, 281
Cazenove, Christopher, 225
Cella, Len, 767
Cellini, Karen, 225
Cellino, Catarina, 846
Cerf, Bennett, 51, 174, 854, 855, 860
Cerf, Phyllis, 218
Cerusico, Enzo, 543
Cervantes, Don, 309
Cervera, Jorge, Jr., 832
Cerveris, Michael, 249
Cesana, Renzo, 166
Cezon, Connie, 616
Chad and Jeremy, 608
Chadwick, June, 665, 826
Chagrin, Julian, 190
Chakiris, George, 178
Chamberlain, Lee, 29, 604
Chamberlain, Richard, 137, 207, 991
Chambers, Ernest, 854
Chambers, Everett, 54
Chambers, Hennen, 488
Chambers, Michael, 210
Chambers, Phil, 309
Chambers Brothers, The, 708
Chamblis, Woody, 316
Champion, Gower, 11, 71, 487
Champion, Marge, 11, 71, 487
Champlin, Irene, 267
Chancellor, John, 568
Chandler, Chick, 587, 725
Chandler, George, 368, 432
Chandler, Jared, 562
Chandler, Karen, 590
Chandler, Loretta, 249
Chandler, Raymond, 623
Chandler, Robin, 647, 660, 769, 862
Chandu the Magician, 314
Chaney, Lon, Jr., 169, 626, 772, 773
Chang, Harry, 471
Channing, Carol, 462, 581, 709, **937**
Channing, Stockard, 747
Chao, Rosalind, 19, 202, 468
Chapel, Bette, 288
Chapel, Loyita, 70, 643
Chapin, Lauren, 257
Chaplin, Charlie, 21, 711
Chapman, Graham, 83
Chapman, Jean Anne, 394
Chapman, Joseph, 420
Chapman, Lonny, 273, 374

Chapman, Margot, 741
Chapman, Mark Lindsay, 178
Chapman, Robert, 257
Chappell, John, 19
Chapter 5, 620
Charbonneau, Patricia, 173
Charles, Glen, **953, 954, 955, 957, 958**
Charles, Les, **953, 954, 955, 957, 958**
Charles, Lewis, 260
Charles, Ray (conductor), 400, 615
Charles, Ray (singer), 114, 514, 528, 685, 792, **944**
Charleson, Ian, 496
Charmoli, Tony, 83, 144, 184, 204, 404, 407, 548
Charney, Jordan, 37, 246, 793
Charnin, Martin, **940, 942, 943**
Charo, 148, 462, 836
Charteris, Leslie, 682
Chartoff, Melanie, 280, 769
Chase, Barrie, 94
Chase, Bud, 787
Chase, Charlie, 789
Chase, Chevy, 275, 280, 689, 690, **949, 950, 953**
Chase, David, **951, 955**
Chase, Eric, 339
Chase, Erin, 6
Chase, Ilka, 137, 299, 415, 495, 811
Chase, Mary, 259
Chase, Sylvia, 565, 817
Chastain, Don, 192, 232
Chatterton, Ruth, 641
Chavez, Robert, 188
Chayefsky, Paddy, 307
Checker, Chubby, 514, 703
Cheek, Molly, 146, 379
Cheerleaders, The, 288, 307, 412, 541, 555, 606
Cheong, George Lee, 107
Cher, 214, 360, 461, 706, 727, 728, 804, **943, 948**
Cherne, Leo, 565, 595, 867
Cherry, Byron, 223
Cherry, Don, 191, 612
Cherry, Hugh, 514
Cheshire, Elizabeth, 252, 759
Chesis, Eileen, 799
Chesney, Diana, 246
Chester, Colby, 764
Chester, George Randolph, 100
Chevalier, Maurice, 660
Chi, Chau-Li, 246
Chicago, 200
Child, Julia, 477, 797
Childre, Lew, 599
Childress, Alvin, 36, 37
Childs, Suzanne, 783
Chiles, Linden, 166, 388
Chiles, Lois, 178

Ching, William, 594
Choder, Jill, 575
Chomsky, Marvin J., **952, 955, 956, 960**
Chong, Tommy, 511
Chordettes, The, xv, 46–48, 885, 992
Chorpenning, Charlotte, 473
Christian, Claudia, 73
Christian, Michael, 621
Christian, P.A., 342
Christiansen, Robert, **946**
Christianson, Todd, 582
Christie, Agatha, 425
Christie, Audrey, 131, 246, 313, 400
Christie, Dick, 9, 721
Christie, Dinah, 142
Christie, Ken, 541
Christie, Marcia, 333
Christine, Virginia, 772
Christmas, Eric, 686, 867
Christopher, Andy, 519
Christopher, Jordan, 699
Christopher, Thom, 112
Christopher, William, 19, 303, 468
Christy, Julie, 255
Chung, Byron, 55, 696
Chung, Connie, 569, 572
Church, Elaine, 209
Churchill, Winston, 88, 243, 866, **934**
Ciampa, Chris, 535
Ciannelli, Eduardo, 403
Ciardi, John, 8
Cioffi, Charles, 50, 294
Cirillo, Al, 101
Cirillo, Joe, 233
Cisar, George, 195, 737
City Slicker Band, 155, 733
Civita, Diane, 516
C.J., 523
Claghorn, Senator, 291
Clair, Dick, 284, 853, **946, 948, 953**
Clair, Richard, 485
Claire, Dorothy, 338, 611
Clampett, Bob, 498
Clancy, Martin, **944, 947**
Clapp, Gordon, 142
Clapp, Nicholas, **947**
Clare, Diane, 169
Clarence, 668
Claridge, Shaaron, 10
Clark, Alex, 153
Clark, Blake, 869
Clark, Candy, 292
Clark, Cliff, 161
Clark, Dane, 43, 96, 405, 473, 505, 616, 660, 693, 825, 867
Clark, Dick, 32, 33, 200, 201, 370, 372, 414, 426, 590, 610, 644, 669, 767, 806, 816
Clark, Doran, 235, 418, 699

Clark, Ernest, 207
Clark, Eugene, 571
Clark, Fred, 217, 291, 292, 602
Clark, Gage, 186, 329, 522
Clark, Gordon, 699
Clark, Harry, 525
Clark, Jack, 174, 189, 422, 587
Clark, Marlene, 687
Clark, Matt, 209
Clark, Oliver, 94, 410, 791, 819, 851
Clark, Patty, 300
Clark, Petula, 832
Clark, Philip, 878
Clark, Roy, 48, 335, 336, 410, 555
Clark, Susan, 845, **949**
Clark, Thomas, 448, 867
Clark Sisters, The, 583
Clarke, Brian Patrick, 193, 232
Clarke, Caitlin, 584
Clarke, Gary, 351, 512, 831
Clarke, John, 559
Clarke, Patrick James, 442
Clarke, Robert, 473, 617
Clarke, Van Nessa, 775
Clary, Robert, 346, 602
Clausen, Alf, 491
Clavell, James, **955**
Clawson, Connie, 455
Clawson, Cynthia, 120
Clay, Andrew, 173
Clay, Cassius. *See* Mohammed Ali
Clayton, Bob, 164
Clayton, Jan, 432, 602
Clayton, Merry, 122
Cleese, John, **961**
Clemmon, David, 650
Clennon, David, 604
Clerk, Clive, 322
Cleveland, George, 432
Cleveland, Jean, 510
Cleveland, Odessa, 468
Cliburn, Van, 71
Cliff Quartet, 128
Cline, Patsy, 48
Clinger, Debra, 33
Clohessy, Robert, 344, 580
Clooney, Betty, 385
Clooney, George, 228, 245
Clooney, Rosemary, 48, 231, 466, 582, 592, 727
Clough, April, 766
Clower, Jerry, 555
Clute, Sidney, 122, 460
Clyde, Andy, 354, 432, 573, 653
Clyde, Jeremy, 608
Coasters, The, 150, 596
Coates, Phyllis, 222
Coates, Paul, 801
Coates, Phyllis, 17, 18, 640
Cobb, Buff, 26, 495
Cobb, Julie, 139, 177, 874

Cobb, Lee J., 772, 831, 878
Cobbs, Bill, 719
Coburn, Charles, 74, 76, 138, 231, 274, 754, 817
Coburn, James, 8, 110, 186, 201, 286, 419, 767
Coca, Imogene, 11, 116, 135, 264, 312, 349, 369, 379, 384, 461, 689, 709, 881, 882, **930, 937, 938**
Cochran, Ron, 3, 44, 481, 565
Cochrane, Robert, 403
Coco, James, 124, 224, **957**
Coe, Barry, 271
Coe, Fred, 98, 307, 452, 628, **932**
Coe, George, 306, 500
Coe, Liz, **960**
Coffield, Peter, 835
Coffin, Tris, 18, 816, 842
Cogan, Shaye, 244, 733, 828
Cohan, George M., 224
Cohan, Martin, 860
Cohen, Alexander H., **954, 956**
Cohen, Evan, 380, 674
Cohen, Jill, 420
Cohen, Marty, 387, 725, 726
Cohen, Mickey, 514
Cohen, Randy, **960, 961, 962**
Cohn, Mindy, 245
Cohoon, Patti, 43, 339, 679
Colasanto, Nicholas, 143
Colbert, Claudette, 74, 274, 668, 776
Colbert, Robert, 499, 795
Colbin, Rod, 674
Colby, Anita, 614
Colby, Barbara, 625
Colby, Carroll "Kib," 86
Colby, Marion, 108, 214, 337, 338
Cole, Alexander, 220
Cole, Carol, 308
Cole, Dennis, 68, 102, 260
Cole, Harry, 335
Cole, Michael, 525
Cole, Nat "King," 274, 555, 607, 615
Cole, Natalie, 381, 531
Cole, Olivia, 57, 659, 673, 765, **951**
Cole, Rocky, 608
Cole, Tina, 545
Coleman, Carole, 244
Coleman, Charles H., 509
Coleman, Cy, 5, 741, **948, 949**
Coleman, Dabney, 43, 113, 492, 719, 780, **961**
Coleman, Emil, 48
Coleman, Gary, 202, 203
Coleman, Jack, 225
Coleman, James, 681
Coleman, William T., 641
Colen, Beatrice, 322, 869
Colicos, John, 66
Colin, Margaret, 270, 442
Coll, Vincent "Mad Dog," 824

Colleary, Bob, **955**
Collett, Verne, 868
Colley, Don Pedro, 183, 223
Collier, Dick, 138, 713
Collier, Don, 341, 598
Collier, Lois, 100
Collier, Marian, 521
Collier, Richard, 485
Collingwood, Charles, 12, 83, 150, 242, 617, 633, 884
Collins, Al "Jazzbo," 801
Collins, Dorothy, 128, 484, 539, 822, 880
Collins, Gary, 99, 375, 673, 715, 836
Collins, Jack, 515, 577
Collins, Joan, 225, 739
Collins, Johnnie, III, 795
Collins, Nancy, 864
Collins, Pat, 381
Collins, Patrick, 142, 760
Collins, Phil, 511
Collins, Ray, 319, 616
Collins, Stephen, 660, 771
Collins, Ted, 412
Collyer, Bud, 18, 68, 69, 104, 495, 584, 646, 692, 770, 797, 866
Collyer, June, 753
Colman, Booth, 627
Colman, Ronald, 259, 277, 319
Colomby, Bobby, 370
Colomby, Scott, 729, 765
Colonna, Jerry, 357, 392
Colorado, Hortensia, 576
Colpitts, Cissy, 775
Colt, Mackenzie, 335
Colt, Marshall, 460, 502
Colvin, Jack, 371
Combs, George Hamilton, 794
Comegys, Kathleen, 388
Comets, Bill Haley & His, 323
Comi, Paul, 664
Commager, Henry Steele, **947**
Commodores, The, 669
Como, Perry, xv, 29, 93, 144, 216, 229, 232, 277, 300, 353, 407, 423–425, 501, 537, 608, 615–617, 743, 767, 774, 776, 803, **931, 932, 933,** 991
Compton, Forrest, 303
Compton, Gail, 618
Compton, Gay, 618
Compton, John, 177
Compton, Walter, 567
Comstock, Frank, 395
Conaway, Jeff, 73, 774, 868
Condon, Eddie, 231
Coniff, Frank, 44, 860
Conklin, Harold "Hal," 130, 591
Conley, Joe, 840
Conn, Didi, 73, 414, 634
Connell, David, **953**
Connell, Jane, 224, 738

Connell, Jim, 214, 678
Connelly, Christopher, 603, 621
Connelly, Marc, 9, 221, 588, 642
Connelly, Peggy, 769
Conner, Betty, 296
Connery, Sean, 685
Connolly, Walter, 558
Connor, Whitfield, 864
Connors, Chuck, xvi, 45, 104, 171, 664, 673, 767, 793, 848, 875
Connors, Harold "Hoot," 513
Connors, Jimmy, 691
Connors, Mike, 484, 794, 797
Conover Cover Girls, The, 256
Conrad, Christian, 342
Conrad, Joan, 342
Conrad, Michael, 194, 344, 345, 955, 956
Conrad, Nancy, 55
Conrad, Robert, 50, 55, 137, 177, 223, 331, 342, 479, 863
Conrad, Shane, 342
Conrad, William, 113, 114, 128, 284, 316, 387, 557, 702, 772, 863
Conried, Hans, 1, 33, 114, 184, 185, 471, 602, 614, 769, 773, 802, 804, 817, 822, 854
Conroy, Kevin, 580
Considine, Bob, 583, 801, 850, 860
Considine, Tim, 545, 596
Constantine, Michael, 341, 672, 714, 940
Contardo, Johnny, 703
Conte, John, 484, 501, 541, 828
Conte, Richard, 224, 389
Conti, Bill, 226, 991
Conti, Vince, 422
Continental Showcase Dancers, The, 166
Contreras, Roberto, 341
Converse, Frank, 167, 253, 535, 551
Converse-Roberts, William, 189
Convy, Bert, 380, 436, 607, 613, 723, 865
Conway, Carolyn, 713
Conway, Gary, 115, 430
Conway, Pat (female), 310, 415
Conway, Pat (male), 799
Conway, Russ, 663
Conway, Shirl, 122, 397, 576
Conway, Tim, 9, 132, 315, 401, 503, 591, 651, 745, 794, 795, 814, 944, 946, 951, 952, 953
Conway, Tom, 76, 488
Conwell, Patricia, 223
Coogan, Jackie, 11, 503, 602
Coogan, Richard, 124, 130
Cook, Bob, 262
Cook, Donald, 630, 805
Cook, Elisha, Jr., 473
Cook, Fielder, 425, 937, 938, 941
Cook, Nathan, 356, 858

Cook, Perry, 361
Cook, Peter, 819, 958
Cooke, Alistair, 32, 581, 945, 949, 960
Cooke, Jennifer, 826
Cooke, Sam, 381, 706
Cooke, Sarah Palfrey, 734
Cooksey, Danny, 136, 202
Cooksey, Darryl, 235
Cookson, Gary, 193
Coolidge, Philip, 256
Coon, Carleton, 852
Cooper, Ann, 92
Cooper, Buzz, 460
Cooper, Cathy, 687
Cooper, Charles, 258, 325
Cooper, Gary, 519, 832
Cooper, Gladys, 670
Cooper, Jackie, 189, 307, 309, 337, 340, 525, 612, 613, 660, 762, 946, 954
Cooper, Jeanne, 102
Cooper, Jed, 755
Cooper, Jeff, 178
Cooper, Maggie, 246, 363
Cooper, Marilyn, 789
Cooper, Melville, 381, 541
Cooper, Paul, 793
Cooper, Roy, 68
Cooper, Wyllis, 833
Cooperman, Alvin, 954, 955
Coote, Robert, 557, 670, 861
Copage, Marc, 407, 596
Copeland, Alan, 322, 414, 620, 880
Copeland, Joanne, 830
Copeland, Maurice, 790
Copeland, Raye, 15
Copland, Aaron, 581
Copley, Teri, 363, 785, 843
Coppola, Frank, 399
Corbett, Glenn, 178, 378, 667, 676
Corbett, Gretchen, 593, 669
Corbin, Barry, 98, 733
Corby, Ellen, 629, 840, 944, 948, 949
Corcoran, Brian, 577
Corcoran, Kelly, 667
Corcoran, Noreen, 56, 596
Cord, Alex, 20, 134, 835
Corday, Barbara, 123
Corday, Jo, 122
Corday, Peggy, 624
Corden, Henry, 415
Core, Natalie, 336, 338
Corey, Joe, 191
Corey, Irwin, 39, 205
Corey, Jeff, 336, 529
Corey, Jill, 288, 401, 880
Corey, Wendell, 22, 234, 324, 611, 630, 693, 739, 822, 850
Cori, Lisa, 123
Corley, Al, 225
Corley, Marjorie, 521

Corley, Pat, 67, 340
Corman, Gene, 956
Corman, Maddie, 522
Cornelius, Helen, 555
Cornell, Don, 201, 590
Cornell, Jan, 955
Cornell, Lydia, 805
Cornthwaite, Robert, 14
Correll, Charles, 36, 37, 125
Correll, Richard, 441
Corrigan, Lloyd, 74, 321, 322, 446, 864
Corrigan, Ray Crash, 172
Corsaut, Aneta, 38, 294, 358
Cort, Bill, 5, 225, 527
Cosby, Bill, 85, 168, 203, 367, 381, 559, 612, 937, 938, 939
Cosell, Howard, 63, 64, 271, 272, 691, 732, 734
Coss, Stewart, 122
Cossart, Valerie, 329
Costa, Cosie, 123
Costa, Joe, 624
Costa, Mary, 154
Costa, Peter, 168
Costanzo, Robert, 142, 398, 434
Costello, Lou, xiv, 7, 158, 351
Costello, Mariclare, 265, 688, 840
Costello, Pat, 7
Coster, Nicolas, 246, 456, 595, 680
Costigan, James, 933, 948, 950
Costner, Kevin, 31
Coston, Suzanne, 957, 959
Cotler, Jeff, 753
Cotler, Kami, 505, 840
Cotten, Joseph, 225, 264, 309, 348, 405, 739, 814
Cotten, Susan, 111
Coughlan, Dick, 114
Coughlin, Francis, 218, 219
Coughlin, Kevin, 476
Coulier, David, 284
Coulton, Jim, 424
Country Lads, The, 395
Country Rhythm Boys, The, 599
County Briar Hoppers, The, 514
Court, Hazel, 199
Courtland, Jerome, 838
Courtney, Alex, 764
Cousins, Christian, 420
Cousins, Joseph, 420
Cousteau, Jacques-Yves, 526, 581, 790, 823, 943, 959
Cousteau, Jean-Michel, 959
Covan, DeForest, 783
Cover, Franklin, 390
Cowan, Jerome, 574, 768, 820
Cowan, Louis G., 716
Cowan, Phil, 864
Coward, Noel, 274, 637, 693
Cowen, Ron, 961
Cowling, Sam, 212
Cowsills, The, 606

Cox, Courteney, 252, 516
Cox, Richard, 241
Cox, Ronny, 43, 682, 732
Cox, Ruth, 325, 553, 679
Cox, Wally, 14, 350, 461, 501, 522, 693, 741, 782, 822
Coxe, George Harmon, 172
Coy, Walter, 282
Crabbe, Buster, 112, 267
Cragg, Stephen, **961**
Craig, Don, 347
Craig, Francis, 515
Craig, Helen, 661
Craig, Col. John D., 241
Craig, Yvonne, 65
Crain, Jeanne, 739
Cramer, Marc, 884
Crampton, Cydney, 456
Crane, Bob, 93, 213, 346, 350, 401
Crane, Brandon, 593
Crane, Harry, 135
Crane, Les, 2, 4, 5
Crane, Norma, 522
Crane, Richard, 761
Cranshaw, Pat, 19, 25, 584
Craven, Matt, 328, 807
Crawford, Bobby, Jr., 431
Crawford, Broderick, 94, 290, 343, 373, 418, 466, 739
Crawford, Charles, 823
Crawford, Edward, 687
Crawford, Joan, 267, 660
Crawford, John, 769, 840
Crawford, Johnny, 664
Crawford, Katherine, 130, 290
Crawford, Michael, 17
Crawford, Percy, 884
Crawford, Rachael, 766
Crawford, Robert, 483
Creasey, John, 63
Creators, The, 72
Creedence Clearwater Revival, 671
Crenna, Richard, 29, 137, 377, 594, 653, 719, **959**
Crespi, Todd, 473
Crewson, Wendy, 325, 571
Cribbins, Bernard, 826, 827
Crichton, Don, 238, 395, 795
Crile, George, 126
Criscuolo, Lou, 633, 747
Cristal, Linda, 341
Crittenden, James, 156, 358
Croce, Jim, 200
Crockett, Davy, 15
Crockett, Jan, 395
Croft, Mary Jane, 15, 365, 465, 594, 613
Cromwell, James, 26, 229, 355, 433, 554
Cronin, Lois, 371
Cronin, Patrick J., 25, 581
Cronkite, Kathy, 345

Cronkite, Walter, 20, 126, 242, 246, 345, 380, 481, 565–567, 625, 635, 814, 823, 876, **938, 940, 941, 942, 943, 944, 945, 947, 954**
Cronyn, Hume, 274, 410, 489, 581
Crook, Lorianne, 789
Crosbie, Annette, 715
Crosby, Bing, 71, 87, 160, 301, 349, 351, 423, 610, 611, 654, 838, 843
Crosby, Bob, 35, 93, 709
Crosby, Cathy Lee, 782, 869
Crosby, David, 540
Crosby, Denise, 740
Crosby, Gary, 10, 86, 142, 349
Crosby, John, 47
Crosby, Lou, 502
Crosby, Mary (actress), 111, 178
Crosby, Mary (singer), 395
Crosby, Norm, 69, 162, 445
Crosby, Stills, Nash & Young, 540
Cross, Dennis, 91
Cross, Milton J., 511
Cross, Murphy, 624
Crosse, Rupert, 605
Crothers, Scatman, 133, 148, 529, 589, 673
Crough, Suzanne, 535, 605
Crow, Ashley, 639
Crow, Carl, 556
Crowe, Cameron, 257
Crowe, Tonya, 420
Crowley, Anne, 541
Crowley, Kathleen, 842
Crowley, Patricia, 186, 225, 398, 459, 629
Crowther, Bosley, 174, 721, 855
Cruikshank, Rufus, 17
Crutchfield, Paul, 780
Crutchley, Rosalie, 715
Cruz, Brandon, 170
Crystal, Billy, 87, 689, 690, 724, 732
Crystal, Lester M., **941, 947**
Csupo, Gabor, 808
Cuervo, Alma, 5
Cuevas, Nelson D., 832
Cuff, Sam, 567
Cuff, Simon, 207
Cugat, Xavier, 35, 833, 873
Cukor, George, **948**
Culea, Melinda, 6, 162, 300
Cullen, Bill, 59, 218, 219, 381, 382, 404, 552, 627, 636, 797, 816, 857, 861, 862, 866
Cullen, Brett, 149, 246
Cullen, Peter, 727, 728
Cullen, William Kirby, 359
Cullum, John, 112
Cully, Zara, 390
Culp, Robert, 8, 35, 145, 309, 367, 410, 739, 808
Culture Club, 280
Culver, Howard, 316

Cumbuka, Ji-Tu, 479, 673, 878
Cummings, Bob, 93, 290, 309, 461, 501, 543, 754, 802, **931, 932, 933**
Cummings, Quinn, 80, 250, 318
Cummings, Richard, Jr., 793
Cunningham, Bill, 507
Cunningham, Bob, 173
Cunningham, Ronnie, 11
Cunningham, Sarah, 808
Cunningham, Zamah, 510
Curb, Mike, 300
Curfew Boys, The, 299
Curran, Brian, 575
Curran, Kevin, **960, 961, 962**
Curreri, Lee, 249, 250
Curtain Calls, The, 69
Curtin, Jane, 411, 689, 690, 852, **958, 959**
Curtin, Valerie, 394, 571
Curtis, Barry, 13
Curtis, Bob (actor), 246
Curtis, Bob (pianist), 384
Curtis, Dick, 39, 404
Curtis, Donald, 197
Curtis, Helen, 385
Curtis, Jamie Lee, 591, 592
Curtis, Janet Lynn, 456
Curtis, Keene, 30, 473, 587
Curtis, Ken, 316, 664, 875
Curtis, Liane, 75
Curtis, Minnie Jo, 741
Curtis, Scott, 6
Curtis, Tony, 290, 304, 503, 592, 618, 829
Curtis, Virginia, 122
Curwood, James Oliver, 691
Curzon, Clifford, 71
Cusack, Joan, 689
Custer, George A., 175
Cutler, Jon, 111
Cutler, Wendy, 613
Cutter, Lise, 615
Cutts, Patricia, 218
Cypher, Jon, 344, 420
Cyphers, Charles, 76
Czonka, Larry, 86

D

Da Pron, Louis, 407, 615, 617, 722
Da Silva, Howard, 273, 349, **952**
Da Vinci, Leonardo, 757
Dabney, Augusta, 667
D'Abo, Maryam, 496
d'Abo, Olivia, 870
Dagmar, 108, 177, 495
Dahl, Arlene, 467, 590, 614
Dahl, Roald, 843
Dailey, Dan, 255, 308
Dailey, Frank, 538
Daily, Bill, 29, 94, 162, 363, 720
Dale, Alan, 21, 201, 590, 713

1007

Dale, Dick, 439
Dale, Jimmy, 95, 144, 415, 727
d'Alessio, Clement, **956**, **957**
Dali, Salvador, 434
Dalio, Marcel, 133
Dallas Boys, The, 579
Dallesandro, Joe, 275, 867
Dallimore, Maurice, 246
Dalton, Abby, 62, 145, 246, 337, 399, 404
Dalton, Darren, 75
Dalton, Susanna, 193
Dalton, Timothy, 137
Daly, James, 224, 274, 275, 459, 467, 506, 755, 762, 822, 844, **937**
Daly, Jane, 673
Daly, John, 36, 137, 282, 380, 565, 566, 590, 832, 833, 844, 854, 855, 860, 876, **931**
Daly, Jonathan, 121, 397, 620
Daly, Rad, 57, 837
Daly, Timothy, 680
Daly, Tyne, 122, **957**, **958**, **959**
Damon, Andrew, 585
Damon, Cathryn, 724, 845, **954**
Damon, Gabriel, 124, 585
Damon, Jerry, 781
Damon, Stuart, 138
Damone, Vic, 22, 191, 401, 455, 484, 830
d'Amore, Rose, 340
Dana, Barbara, 328
Dana, Bill, 86, 161, 185, 516, 573, 733, 735, 745, 885
Dana, Dick, 214
Dana, Justin, 420, 823
Dana, Vic, 770
Dancing Blades, The, 539
Dancy, John, 636, 637
D'Andrea, Tom, 185, 449, 725
Dandridge, Dorothy, 274
Dandridge, Ruby, 258
Dane, Frank, 332
Danehe, Dick, 806
Danese, Shera, 9, 762
Dangcil, Linda, 270
D'Angelo, Beverly, 130
Dangerfield, Rodney, 190, 582
Daniel, Eliot, 365
Daniels, Billy, 87
Daniels, Carolyn, 780
Daniels, Charlie, 370
Daniels, Danny, 490
Daniels, Stan, **947**, **948**, **949**, **950**, **951**, **953**, **954**, **955**
Daniels, William, 129, 162, 279, 419, 554, 682, **959**, **960**
Daniely, Lisa, 374
Dannay, Frederic, 13
Danner, Blythe, 10
Danny and the Juniors, 200, 607
Dano, Linda, 527
Danoff, Bill, 741
Danoff, Taffy, 741

Danova, Cesare, 287
Danson, Ted, 143, 162
Dante, Michael, 175
Dantine, Helmut, 703
Danton, Ray, 22
Danza, Tony, 280, 774, 860
Danziger, Cory, 69
Dapo, Ronnie, 563, 672
Dapper Dans, The, 513
Darby, Kim, 433, 661
Darcel, Denise, 286
Darcy, Georgine, 327
Darden, Severn, 79, 492, 769
Darin, Bobby, 80, 95, 182, 190, 212, 386, 423, 540
Dark, Danny, 220
Dark, Johnny, 214, 387
Darling, Jean, 356
Darling, Jennifer, 88, 232, 715, 778
Darling, Joan, 599
Darren, James, 766, 795, 845
Darrieux, Danielle, 266
Darrow, Barbara, 209
Darrow, Clarence, **948**
Darrow, Henry, 328, 341, 505, 559, 885
Darrow, Mike, 221, 587
Darwell, Jane, 617
D'Avalos, 445
Davalos, Dick, 35
Davalos, Elyssa, 470
Davenport, Basil, 218, 862
Davenport, Gwen, 519
Davi, Robert, 287
David, Brad, 263
David, Jeff, 112
David, Larry, 280
David, Mack, 702
Davidson, Ben, 58, 156
Davidson, James, 865
Davidson, John, 238, 298, 350, 400, 423, 425, 661, 693, 782, 803, 836
Davidson, Troy, 561
Davies, Allan, 611
Davies, Gareth, **950**
Davies, Gary, 806
Davies, Geoffrey, 207
Davies, Geraint Wyn, 20
Davies, Irving, 237
Davies, Jane, 371
Davies, John Rhys, 646
Davion, Alex, 481
Davis, Al, **945**
Davis, Ann B., 93, 103, 401, 414, **932**, **933**
Davis, Benjamin J., 714
Davis, Bette, 225, 291, 307, 348, 356, **953**
Davis, Bill, **945**, **948**
Davis, Billy, Jr., 488
Davis, Brad, 673
Davis, Buster, 289
Davis, Buzz, 127
Davis, Clifton, 31, 32, 460, 509, 783

Davis, Curtis, **939**, **940**, **941**
Davis, Danny, 831
Davis, Dave, 848
Davis, David, **953**
Davis, Donald, 9
Davis, Fred, 103
Davis, Gail, 41
Davis, Geena, 113, 688
Davis, Humphrey, 591
Davis, Janette, 46
Davis, Jennifer, 468
Davis, Jim (writer), **959**
Davis, Jim (actor), 171, 178, 180, 659
Davis, Jo, 395
Davis, Joan, 367
Davis, Josie, 139
Davis, Kenny, 828
Davis, Lisa, 292
Davis, Mac, 470, 514, 538, 671
Davis, Marty, 437
Davis, Michael, 569
Davis, Nancy, 274, 290
Davis, Owen, Jr., 550
Davis, Patsy, 256
Davis, Patti, 665
Davis, Peter, **942**
Davis, Phyllis, 460, 829
Davis, Roger, 24, 25, 286, 372, 656
Davis, Roy, 583
Davis, Rufe, 620
Davis, Sammy, Jr., 61, 82, 349, 392, 549, 556, 685
Davis, Susan, 559
Davis, Tom, 689, **950**, **951**, **953**
Davis, Viveka, 763
Davis, Walter Halsey, **959**
Davison, Bruce, 361
Davison, Joel, 577
Dawber, Pam, 528, 544
Dawes, Edmund "Skipper," 610
Dawn, 804, 836
Dawson, Greg, 15
Dawson, Richard, 127, 251, 252, 346, 381, 495, 496, 559, 676
Day, Clarence, Jr., 450
Day, Dennis, 29, 357, 383, 384, 501, 649
Day, Dianne, 182
Day, Doris, 215, 629, 780
Day, Dorothy, 756
Day, Jack, 332
Day, Laraine, 189, 350, 381, 467
Day, Lynda, 517, 661, 673, 710
Day, Marilyn, 256, 262
Daydreamers, The, 288
Dayton, Danny, 26, 400, 415
Dayton, June, 23
de Azevedo, Lex, 399, 728
de Broux, Lee, 470, 684
De Cordova, Fred, **950**, **951**, **953**, **954**
De Costa, Tony, 696
De Craft, Joseph, 99

De Gore, Janet, 438, 653
De Grosa, John, 417
de Havilland, Olivia, 674
de Jesus, Wanda, 487, 643
de Lancie, John, 811
de León, Ponce, 69
De Luca, Rudy, **946, 948**
De Mar, Jaki, 460
de Marney, Terence, 403
de Maupassant, Guy, 882
de Mauro, Gino, 188
De Mave, Jack, 432
De Mille, Agnes, **961**
de Passe, Suzanne, **957, 959**
De Paul, Judith, **954, 955**
de Rochemont, Richard, 174
De Rose, Chris, 686
De Sales, Francis, 518
De Santis, Stanley, 602
De Shields, Andre, **956**
De Spirito, Romolo, 831
de Toledano, Ralph, 595
de Veritch, Sean, 793
De Wilde, Brandon, 388, 623, 630,
    704, 879
de Winter, Jo, 301
de Witt, George, 26, 67, 68, 552,
    701
De Zurick Sisters, 1
Deacon, Richard, 54, 140, 186,
    202, 441, 530, 531, 641
Dean, Abner, 220
Dean, Barton, **954**
Dean, Eddie, 490
Dean, Fabian, 795
Dean, Hannah, 596
Dean, Ivor, 682
Dean, James, 68, 126, 183, 200,
    425, 693, 811
Dean, Jimmy, 183, 383, 395, 402,
    537, 591, 802
Dean, Larry, 439
Dean, Morton, 34, 566
Dean, Ron, 173, 430
Dean, Suzi, 326
Debutones, The, 407
DeCamp, Rosemary, 93, 192, 449,
    780
DeCarlo, Yvonne, 452, 536
Decker, Diana, 488
DeCorsia, Ted, 745
Dee, Joey, 372
Dee, Ruby, 621, 674
Dee, Sandra, 296, 773
Deeb, Gary, 776
Deel, Sandra, 122, 557
Deems, Mickey, 212, 345
Deep River Boys, 108
Dees, Julie, 767
Dees, Rick, 725, 726
Deezen, Eddie, 643
Def Leppard, 806
DeFore, Don, 15, 332, 351
DeForest, Calvert, 434

DeFreitas, Dick, 881
DeGarr, Bianca, 650
DeGruy, Oscar, 559
DeHaven, Gloria, 475, 552
Dehner, John, 58, 60, 81, 212, 215,
    237, 667, 778, 849, 878
Deignan, Martina, 156
deKova, Frank, 243
Del Regno, John, 58
Delaney, Steve, 526
Delano, Michael, 263, 660, 760
Delany, Dana, 763
Delany, Pat, 764
Delerue, George, **938**
Delevanti, Cyril, 390
Delfino, Frank, 260
Delgado, Emilio, 99, 460
Delgado, Luis, 105
Delgado, Roger, 17
Delgarde, Dominick, 161
Dell, Charlie, 223
Dell, Gabriel, 167, 745, 874
Dell, Myrna, 148, 149
Dell and Abbott, 108
Dell Vikings, The, 152
Delmar, Kenny, 693
Deloy, George, 571, 682, 738
Delugg, Milton, 8, 108, 150, 177,
    214, 303, 406, 701, 803, 880
DeLuise, Dom, 190, 191, 210, 211,
    238, 300, 459, 865
DeLuise, Michael, 585
DeLuise, Peter, 815
DeLyon, Leo, 377, 805
Demarest, William, 461, 545, 772
DeMauro, Nick, 845
DeMay, Janet, 657
Demetrio, Anna, 477
DeMille, Cecil B., 530
Demosthenes, 423
Dempsey, Patrick, 256
Denison, Anthony, 173
Dennehy, Brian, 83, 738
Denning, Richard, 330, 410, 512,
    518
Dennis, Beverly, 655
Dennis, Matt, 497
Dennis, Nick, 71
Dennis, Patrick, 642
Dennison, Rachel, 571, 572
Dennison, Richard, 210
Denny, George V., Jr., 36
Denoff, Sam, **936, 937, 938, 939**
Denton, Donna, 513
Denver, Bob, 225, 297, 304, 485
Denver, John, 691, 759, **947, 948**
DePatie, David H., **953, 956**
Depp, Johnny, 815
Der, Ricky, 416
Derek, Bo, 523
Derek, John, 283, 467
Dern, Bruce, 729, 748
Derr, Richard, 254
Derricks-Carroll, Clinton, 687

DeSantis, Joe, 624, 808
Descher, Sandy, 562, 563
Desiderio, Robert, 334
DeSimone, Tony, 239, 509, 658
Desmond, Johnny, 22, 89, 212, 244,
    300, 356, 385, 539, 684, 796, 880
DeSoto, Rosana, 656
Despo, 381
Despotovich, Nada, 408
Deuel, Peter, 24, 25, 296, 462
Deutsch, Patti, 400, 676
Devane, William, 281, 420
DeVarona, Donna, 286
Devine, Andy, 19, 60, 269, 675, 721
Devine, Loretta, 203
DeVito, Danny, 774, **955**
Devlin, Dean, 325
Devlin, Donald, 848
Devlin, Joe, 202
DeVol, Frank, 76, 125, 204, 260,
    293, 369, 412, 466, 545
Devon, Laura, 662
Devore, Cain, 221
DeVorzon, Barry, 681
Dewey, Thomas E., 520, 617, 721
Dewhurst, Colleen, 755, **960**
DeWilde, Frederic Fritz, 541
DeWindt, Sheila, 54
DeWitt, Alan, 379
DeWitt, Fay, 327
DeWitt, Joyce, 792
DeWolfe, Billy, 76, 305, 641, 645
Dexter, Jerry, 322
Dey, Susan, 235, 429, 463, 605
DeYoung, Cliff, 137, 496, 759
Dezina, Kate, 320
DeZurik, Carolyn, 631, 632
Dhiegh, Khigh, 416
Diamond, Barry, 319
Diamond, Bobby, 485, 850
Diamond, Don, 15, 243, 885
Diamond, Neil, 865
Diamond, Peter, 17
Diamond, Selma, 570, 805
Diamonds, The, 48
DiAquinto, John, 864
Diaz, Edith, 633
Dibbs, Kem, 112
DiCenzo, George, 225, 372, 502
Dick, David, **945**
Dick, Douglas, 842
Dickens, Charles, 22, 253, 762
Dickens, Jimmy, 308
Dickens Sisters, The, 232
Dickerson, Nat, 46
Dickinson, Angie, 94, 134, 512,
    533, 631
Diddley, Bo, 200, 703
Diehl, John, 511
Diener, Joan, 262
Dierdorf, Dan, 271
Dierkop, Charles, 631
Dietrich, Dena, 10, 11, 410, 634,
    674

Dietrich, Marlene, 196
Diffring, Anton, 50
Dillard, Mimi, 827
Diller, Phyllis, 69, 303, 304, 396, 461, 531, 641, 703, 709, 771, 837
Dillinger, John, 868
Dillman, Bradford, 169, 246, 418
Dillon, Brendon, 26
Dillon, Denny, 689, 869
Dillon, Melinda, 729
Dilworth, Gordon, 169, 733, 741
DiMattia, Victor, 763
Dimitri, Richard, 701, 857
Dinehart, Mason Alan, III, 446
Ding-a-Ling Sisters, The, 190
Ding-a-Lings, The, 836
Dinsdale, Shirley, 406
Dirksen, Everett, 304
Disco Dozen, The, 214
Dishell, Walter D., 850
Disher, Catherine, 766
Dishy, Bob, 781
Disney, Walt, xiv, 88, 154, 183, 230, 315, 338, 531, 545, 558, 838, 839, 849, 885, 932, 935
Dix, Tommy, 693
Dixie Dozen Dancers, The, 555
Dixieland Quartet, The, 685
Dixon, Bob, 713
Dixon, Donna, 73, 99
Dixon, Franklin W., 326
Dixon, Ivan, 346
Dixon, Macintyre, 163
Dixon, Paul, 216, 514, 608
Dizon, Jesse, 591
Dizon, J.P., 188
Dobb, Gillian, 473
Dobie, Alan, 496
Dobson, Charlie, 509
Dobson, Kevin, 420, 422, 704
Dobyns, Lloyd, 526, 569, 846
Dodd, Thomas E., 833
Dodds, Edward K., 945
Dodson, Jack, 29, 38, 370, 501, 624
Dodson, Rhonda, 336
Doerr-Hutchinson Dancers, 395
Doherty, Shannen, 453, 594
Doig, Barry, 255
Dolce, John, 1
Dolenz, Amy, 739
Dolenz, Mickey, 152, 527
Dollar, Lynn, 716
Dolman, Bob, 958
Dombrow, Walter, 940
Domingo, Placido, 958, 960
Dominicans, The, 98
Domino, Fats, 16, 80, 323
Donahoe, Terry, 728
Donahue, Elinor, 38, 162, 257, 485, 535, 558, 578, 586, 763
Donahue, Patricia, 512, 785
Donahue, Phil, 380, 434, 955
Donahue, Troy, 331, 702, 761

Donald, Juli, 437
Donald, Peter, 4, 10, 127, 495, 515, 602, 639, 857
Donaldson, Sam, 565, 732
Donaldson, Walter, 412
Donat, Peter, 266, 662
Donelly, Carol, 744
DonHowe, Gwyda, 241
Donlevy, Brian, 183, 531
Donnell, Jeff, 293, 497, 822
Donnelly, Tim, 235
Donner, Robert, 528, 840
Donovan, Bill, 577
Donovan, King, 93, 629
Doodles and Spicer, 606
Doodletown Pipers, The, 595, 670
Doohan, James, 739
Dooley, Paul, 163, 210
Doonican, Val, 826, 827
Doors, The, 280
DoQui, Robert, 260
Doran, Ann, 443, 458, 556, 706
Doran, Johnny, 535
Doran, Nancy, 454
Doremus, David, 554
Dorin, Phoebe, 527
Dorn, Michael, 149, 740
Dors, Diana, 602
Dorsey, Arnold George, 237
Dorsey, Jimmy, 230, 736, 737
Dorsey, Tommy, 230, 412, 736, 737
Dorsky, Nathaniel, 938
D'Orso, Wisa, 191, 322, 404
Dotrice, Roy, 69
Dotson, Bob, 636, 637
Double Daters, The, 37
Doucette, Jeff, 228, 564
Doucette, John, 74, 84, 456, 605, 654
Douglas, Diana, 171, 624
Douglas, Donna, 77
Douglas, Jack (writer), 931
Douglas, Jack (host), 96
Douglas, Jack D., 424
Douglas, James, 621
Douglas, Lloyd C., 206
Douglas, Melvyn, 90, 283, 642, 741, 746, 938
Douglas, Michael, 751
Douglas, Mike, 260, 412, 413, 493, 540
Douglas, Paul, 12, 307, 357, 467, 630
Douglas, Ronalda, 578
Douglas, Sarah, 246
Douglass, Robyn, 66, 358
Doumanian, Jean, 690
Dourif, Brad, 755
Dova, Ben, 539
Dow, Harold, 567
Dow, Tony, 441, 561
Dowdell, Robert, 748, 834
Dowling, Doris, 543

Dowling, Eddie, 43
Downes, Anson, 480
Downey, James, 951
Downey, Morton, 448, 525, 738
Downey, Robert, 689
Downing, David, 57
Downing, Wilfrid, 111
Downs, Hugh, 122, 164, 802, 816, 817
Downs, Johnny, 129, 298, 482
Doxee, Diane, 199
Doyle, Arthur Conan, 881, 882
Doyle, David, 106, 141, 559, 763
Doyle, Len, 520
Doyle, Robert, 431
Doyle-Murray, Brian, 689
Draeger, Jason, 27
Draeger, Justin, 27
Dragon, Carmen, 129
Dragon, Daryl, 129, 210
Drake, Alfred, 87, 136
Drake, Charles, 467, 667
Drake, Christian, 705
Drake, Ellen, 429
Drake, Gabe, 689
Drake, Gabrielle, 821
Drake, Galen, 285
Drake, Georgia, 631
Drake, Larry, 429
Drake, Sir Francis, 17
Drake, Tom, 74, 693, 762
Drake-Hooks, Bebe, 688
Dramarama, 182
Draney, John, 448
Draper, Polly, 786
Drees, Jack, 101, 102, 384, 692
Dreier, Alex, 853
Dressler, Marie, 19
Drew, Paula, 282
Drew, Robert, 940
Drew, Wendy, 396, 693
Drexler, Rosalyn, 947
Dreyfuss, Randy, 377
Dreyfuss, Richard, 218, 410, 690
Drier, Moosie, 676
Drifters, The, 579
Driggs, William King, 417
Driscoll, Patricia, 17
Drivas, Robert, 595
Dromgoole, Patrick, 959
Dru, Joanne, 314, 350, 630
Drummond, Alice, 604
Drury, James, 192, 263, 831, 832
Dryden, Mack, 161
Dryer, Fred, 361
Drysdale, Don, 22, 63, 64
du Bief, Jacqueline, 539
DuArt, Louise, 177
Duback, Bob, 163
DuBarry, Denise, 55
Dubin, Gary, 102
DuBois, Ja'net, 305, 390
DuBois, Marta, 771

DuBuc, Nicole, 594
Duchow, Peter K., **961**
Ducommun, Rick, 414, 433, 784
Duddy, Lynn, 278
Dudikoff, Michael, 738
Dudley, Bernard, 734
Dudley, Dick, 830
Duell, William, 630
Duff, Howard, 178, 185, 260, 266, 277, 420, 518, 694, 773
Duffy, Jack, 95, 615
Duffy, Julia, 564, 868
Duffy, Patrick, 178, 181, 480
Dugan, Dennis, 236, 661, 663, 693, 703
Duggan, Andrew, 57, 100, 224, 430, 661, 672, 814
Duggan, Bob, 655
Duggan, Tom, 49
Duke, Bill, 601
Duke, Daryl, **941**
Duke, Douglas, 538
Duke, Dr. James "Red," **955**
Duke, Patty, 318, 411, 608, 822, **940, 950, 954.** *See also* Patty Duke Astin
Duke, Robin, 689, 697
Dukes, David, 68, 729
Dulo, Jane, 294, 297, 340, 503, 506, 703
duMaurier, Daphne, 643
Dumbrille, Douglas, 148, 149, 449, 563
Dumke, Ralph, 129, 531
DuMont, Allen B., xiii
Dumont, Margaret, 542
Dunbar, Olive, 545
Duncan, Angus, 372
Duncan, Archie, 17
Duncan, Arlene, 413
Duncan, Art, 439, 440
Duncan, Lee, 16
Duncan, Sandy, 284, 673, 685, 686, 827
Dungan, Frank, **956**
Dunigan, Tim, 6, 523, 868
Dunlap, Richard, 425
Dunlop, Victor, 319, 326, 663
Dunn, Bill, 245
Dunn, Bob, 647, 733
Dunn, Eddie, 245, 733
Dunn, Elaine, 108
Dunn, George, 125, 151
Dunn, James, 377
Dunn. Kathy, 595
Dunn, Kevin, 383
Dunn, Liam, 129, 198, 645
Dunn, Michael, 863
Dunn, Nora, 689
Dunn, Pete, 151
Dunn, Ralph, 574
Dunnam, Stephanie, 235
Dunne, Irene, 693

Dunne, James P., 397
Dunne, Peter, **950**
Dunne, Steve, 640, 812, 884
Dunnham, Stephanie, 225
Dunning, John, 987
Dunninger, Joseph, 30, 31, 85
Dunnock, Mildred, 845
Dunphy, Don, 63, 64, 102, 262, 296, 297, 689
Duran, Duran, 280
Duran, Roberto, 511
Durant, Don, 403, 652
Durante, Jimmy, xiv, 28, 29, 155, 158, 213, 349, 396, 501, 516, 612, **930**
Durante Girls, The, 396
Durning, Charles, 130, 167, 242, 755
Durocher, Leo, 386
Durrell, Michael, 25, 368, 497, 574, 704
Durston, Gigi, 728
Duryea, Dan, 148, 264, 621, 739, 850
Dusay, Marj, 105, 246, 748
Dusenberry, Ann, 253, 450, 455
Duskin, Ruthie, 378
Dussault, Nancy, 559, 805
d'Usseau, Loring, **955**
Duvall, Robert, 309
Duvall, Susan, 40
Dwight-Smith, Michael, 464
Dwyer, Virginia, 870
Dye, Dale, 759
Dyer, Jeanne, 502
Dykers, Thomas M., 711
Dykstra, John, 66
Dylan, Bob, 253
Dysart, Richard, 429
Dziubinska, Anulka, 60
Dzundza, George, 589

E

Eadie and Rack, 155
Earhart, Amelia, 370
Earl, John, 688
Earle, Merie, 393, 840
Earle, Robert, 285
Earp, Wyatt, 64, 446, 862
Easterbrook, Leslie, 437
Eastham, Richard, 246, 799, 869
Easton, Sheena, 511, **957**
Eastwood, Clint, 31, 361, 523, 651
Eaton, Evelyn, 357
Ebb, Fred, 789, **944, 949**
Eben, Al, 330
Eberly, Bob, 767
Ebersole, Christine, 136, 689, 827
Ebert, Roger, 51
Ebsen, Bonnie, 410

Ebsen, Buddy, 1, 61, 77, 121, 410, 497, 574, 838
Echevarria, Rocky, 281
Echoes, The, 157
Eckstine, Billy, 556
Eddy, Duane, 200, 991, 992
Edelman, Barbara Jane, 460
Edelman, Herb, 303, 304, 429, 571, 752
Eden, Barbara, xvii, 326, 327, 360, 363
Edison, Thomas A., 290, 478
Edmiston, Walker, 675
Edmonds, Don, 107
Edmund, Lada, Jr., 360
Edmunds, Noel, 275
Edmunson, William, 729
Edwards, Allyn, 169, 519, 588
Edwards, Anthony, 377
Edwards, Cliff, 154, 262
Edwards, Douglas, 44, 137, 244, 495, 566, 884
Edwards, Gail, 378
Edwards, Geoff, 95, 620, 810
Edwards, Gerald, 171
Edwards, Gus, 693
Edwards, Joan, 397
Edwards, Ralph, 174, 237, 788, 789, 812
Edwards, Rick, 342
Edwards, Ronnie Claire, 98, 408, 688, 840
Edwards, Stephanie, 298, 360
Edwards, Steve, 238, 582
Edwards, Vince, 71, 498, 660, 822
Efron, Marshall, 200
Egan, Eddie, 233, 398, 513
Egan, Jenny, 522
Egan, Richard, 236, 656
Eggar, Samantha, 41, 292
Eggert, Nicole, 139, 766
Egnor, Virginia Ruth, 109
Ego, Sandra, 121
Ehlers, Beth, 75
Eichen, Cheri, 626
Eiding, Paul, 141
Eikenberry, Jill, 429
Eilbacher, Cindy, 544, 700, 706
Eilbacher, Lisa, 325, 505, 680, 780, 856
Eilber, Janet, 75, 819
Eimen, Johnny, 503
Einstein, Bob, 399, 607, 722, 727, 828, **939, 950**
Eiseley, Loren, 40
Eisenhower, Dwight D., 42, 57, 174, 635, 730
Eisenmann, Al, 42
Eisenmann, Ike, 254
Eisley, Anthony, 97, 331, 618
Eisley, Fred, 97
Eisner, Michael D., 838, 839
Eisner, Will, 705

Flannigan, Maureen, 597
Flash & Whistler, 599
Flatt, Ernest, 132, 238, 289, 406, 746
Flatt, Lester, 78, 991
Flaum, Marshall, **943**, **945**
Flavin, James, 482, 667
Fleer, Alicia, 281
Fleetwood Mac, 211
Fleicher, Walter, 256
Fleischer, Charles, 414, 784, 846
Fleming, Art, 124, 391, 548
Fleming, Eric, 474, 651
Fleming, Ian, 240
Fleming, James, **938**
Fleming, Peggy, 83, **942**
Fletcher, Aaron, 445
Fletcher, Jack, 93, 124, 308, 634
Fletcher, Tom, 108
Flinders, Kathe, 488
Flippen, Jay C., 237
Flippin, Lucy Lee, 269, 433, 453
Flock of Seagulls, 4
Floradora Girls, The, 289
Floren, Myron, 439, 440
Flory, Med, 342, 652
Flowers, Tennyson, **962**
Flowers, Wayland, 39, 414, 436, 471, 725, 726
Fluegel, Darlanne, 173
Flynn, Ben, **938**
Flynn, Errol, 307
Flynn, Joe, 15, 94, 293, 376, 399, 503, 795
Flynn, Miriam, 472, 795
Flynn, Salli, 439
Foch, Nina, 183, 380, 466, 623, 645, 703, 755, 762, 822
Fogel, Jerry, 530, 858
Fogel, Lee, 787
Foggy River Boys, The, 600
Foley, Ellen, 570, 791
Foley, George F., Jr., 772
Foley, Joseph, 23, 522
Foley, Red, 523, 599, 600
Folk Dancers, The, 169
Follett, Charon, 790
Follows, Megan, 67, 211
Fonda, Henry, 195, 505, 523, 639, 674, 709, 721, 722
Fonda, Jane, 572, **958**
Fong, Brian, 142
Fong, Harold, 353
Fong, Jon, 864
Fong, Kam, 330
Fontaine, Eddie, 286
Fontaine, Frank, 282, 385, 386, 694, 763
Fontaine, Joan, 277, 405
Fontaine, Michael, 704
Fontana, Tom, **959**, **961**
Fontane, Bea, 615
Fontane, Char, 398
Fontane, Geri, 615

Fontane, Marge, 615
Fontane Sisters, The, 80, 615, 767
Fontanne, Lynn, **936**
Fonteyn, Margot, 640
Foody, Ralph, 430
Foote, Bruce, 787
Foraker, Lois, 19, 210
Foran, Dick, 577
Foray, June, 114
Forbath, Peter, **947**
Forbes, Kathryn, 477
Forbes, Kenneth, 299
Forbes, Scott, xvi, 14
Ford, Art, 46, 862
Ford, Betty, 226, 535, **961**
Ford, Charlie, 72
Ford, Constance, 623
Ford, Ed, 127
Ford, Faith, 632
Ford, Gerald, 126, 177, 226, 535, 690
Ford, Glenn, 121, 122, 252, 281, 585
Ford, Janie, 21
Ford, John, 22, 359, 695
Ford, Mary, 581
Ford, Olga, 294
Ford, Paul, 58, 461, 623
Ford, Peter, 121
Ford, Ross, 507
Ford, Tennessee Ernie, 60, 210, 273, 309, 412, 413, 580, 872
Ford, Wallace, 195
Foree, Ken, 659
Foreman, Percy, 405
Forest, Frederic, 815
Forester, C. S., 22
Forman, Denis, **959**
Forman, Joey, 399, 512, 710, 744, 745
Forquet, Philippe, 879
Forrest, Gregg, 57
Forrest, Ray, 101, 568, 777, 830
Forrest, Sally, 643, 822
Forrest, Steve, 63, 178, 681
Forsett, Theo, 656
Forster, Brian, 605
Forster, Robert, 59, 552, 584
Forsythe, Brooke, 401
Forsythe, Henderson, 234
Forsythe, John, 56, 141, 225, 234, 401, 466, 533, 741, 755, 762, 796
Forsythe, Page, 401
Forte, Fabian, 116
Forte, Joe, 451
Forten, Dr. Robert, 486
Fortier, Bob, 812
Fosse, Bob, 262, **944**, **945**
Fosse and Niles, 262
Foster, Ami, 643
Foster, Bill, 414, 424
Foster, Buddy, 351, 501
Foster, Connie, 146
Foster, Donald, 332

Foster, Jodie, 92, 170, 603, 861
Foster, Linda, 321
Foster, Meg, 122, 123, 759
Foster, Norman, 885
Foster, Phil, 122, 436, 437
Foster, Preston, 316, 350, 842
Foster, Stephen, 559
Foster, Stuart, 285
Foster, Susan, 710
Fouhy, Ed, **947**
Foulger, Byron, 129, 620, 621
Foulk, Robert, 257, 862
Fountain, Pete, 439, 440
Four Aces, The, 201
Four Freshmen, The, 652
Four Lads, The, 607, 617, 651, 825
Four Tops, The, 531
Fouser, Don, **945**
Fouts, Tom "Stubby," 631
Fowler, Jim, 863
Fowley, Douglas, 197, 446, 626
Fox, Bernard, 78
Fox, Charles, 40, 323, 437, 461, 602, 827
Fox, John G., **959**
Fox, Michael, 133
Fox, Michael J., 252, 601, **960**, **961**
Fox, Nancy, 778
Fox, Peter, 193, 420, 840
Fox, Sonny, 716
Fox, Steve, 817
Foxworth, Robert, 246, 749
Foxx, Redd, 656, 687, 688
Foxx, Rhonda, 747
Foy, Eddie, Jr., 94, 246
Foy, Fred, 199
Foy, Patricia, **947**
Frakes, Jonathan, 60, 603, 740
Framer, Walt, 752
France, Dick, 454
Francine, Anne, 326
Franciosa, Tony, 263, 372, 497, 552, 696, 782, 827, 856
Francis, Anne, 178, 352, 545, 665, 822, 829
Francis, Arlene, 42, 90, 116, 117, 161, 639, 762, 770, 802, 854, 855, 861
Francis, Connie, 48, 80, 323, 395, 484
Francis, Genie, 60, 61
Francis, Ivor, 225
Francis, Missy, 399, 453, 529
Franciscus, James, 206, 361, 374, 458, 521, 551
Francks, Don, 392
Frank, Allan, 139
Frank, Carl, 476
Frank, Charles, 149, 235, 262, 878, 879
Frank, Gary, 250, 729, **951**
Frank, Joanna, 429
Frank, Reuven, **935**
Frank, Sandy, **959**, **960**, **961**, **962**

Frankel, Eliot, **943, 947**
Franken, Al, 689, **950, 951, 953**
Franken, Rose, 154
Franken, Steve, 446, 485, 521, 799
Frankenheimer, John, 183, 628
Franklin, Benjamin, 134
Franklin, Bonnie, 493, 586
Franklin, Carl, 132, 254, 502
Franklin, Cass, 282
Franklin, Nancy, 588
Franklin, Susan, 209
Frann, Mary, 418, 564
Franz, Dennis, 67, 78, 146, 344
Franz, Eduard, 105, 885
Fraser, Bob, 485, 486
Fraser, Elisabeth, 261, 313, 503, 587, 623
Fraser, Gordon, 565
Fratiano, Jimmie "The Weazel," 864
Fratkin, Stuart, 558
Frawley, James, **938**
Frawley, William, 365, 465, 545, 850, 883
Fray, Jacques, 387
Frazee, Jane, 76
Frazer, Dan, 422
Frazier, Joe, 691
Frazier, Sheila, 441
Freberg, Stan, 31, 145, 219, 231
Frederick, Hal, 99, 373
Frederick, Jesse, 615
Frederick, Pauline, 565, 611
Fredericks, Dean, 745
Freed, Alan, 80
Freed, Bert, 704
Freed, Fred, **937, 938, 942, 945**
Freed, Sam, 411
Freedley, Vinton, 709, 770
Freedman, Lewis, **941, 947**
Freedman, Winifred, 397, 665
Freeman, Al, Jr., 355, 674
Freeman, Damita Jo, 638
Freeman, Deena, 805
Freeman, J. Paul, 246
Freeman, Joan, 115
Freeman, Kathleen, 77, 284, 379, 459, 807
Freeman, Lucy, 393
Freeman, Mickey, 623
Freeman, Mona, 822
Freeman, Pam, 641
Freeman, Sandy, 221
Freeman, Seth, **953, 954, 955**
Freeman, Stan, 509, 792
Freeman, Ticker, 204
Freems, George, 701
Frees, Paul, 114, 125, 253, 515, 838
Freleng, Fritz, **953, 956**
Fremin, Jourdan, 50
French, Leigh, 200, 722, 723, 756
French, Susan, 60
French, Victor, 133, 294, 340, 343, 453, 454

Frenette, Cecille, 784
Frewer, Matt, 500, 501
Frey, Leonard, 74, 523
Friday, Nancy, 800
Fridell, Squire, 675
Friebus, Florida, 94, 485
Fried, Ian, 258, 819
Fried, Myra, 413
Friedberg, Billy, **932, 933**
Friedenberg, Richard, **961, 962**
Friedman, Ada, 524
Friedman, Bud, **943**
Friedman, David, 453
Friedrich, John, 755
Friendly, Fred, 120, 860
Frimple, Dennis, 497
Frischman, Dan, 333
Fritts, Stan, 422
Frivolous Five, The, 350
Frizzel, Lou, 97, 150, 561
Froemke, Susan, **961**
Froman, David, 497
Froman, Jane, 389, 610, 757, 833
Frome, Milton, 77, 515
Frost, Alice, 476
Frost, David, 4, 187, 188, 333, 781, **940, 941**
Frye, Chip, 633
Frye, Soleil Moon, 643
Fuccello, Tom, 178
Fudge, Alan, 233, 480, 603
Fujikawa, "Jerry" Hatsuo, 524
Fujioka, John, 434, 771
Fuisz, Robert E., **954, 955, 957**
Fulger, Holly, 383, 682
Fuller, Kurt, 864
Fuller, Penny, 60, 275, **956**
Fuller, Robert, 235, 431, 836
Fullerton, Melanie, 796
Fulmer, Ray, 332
Fulton, Eileen, 595
Fulton, Julie, 452
Fulton, Wendy, 60, 420
Funicello, Annette, 115, 184, 229, 360, 540, 838, 885
Funk, Robert, **940**
Funk, Terry, 864
Funt, Allen, 127, 128, 289, 452, 613, 777
Furlong, Kirby, 397
Furness, Betty, 4, 74, 117, 612, 754, 850
Furst, Stephen, 193, 682
Furth, George, 107, 224, 304, 773
Fusco, Paul, 24

G

Gabb, Peter, 370
Gabel, Martin, 868
Gable, Clark, 686
Gable, June, 62, 436, 703
Gable, Sandra, 763

Gabler, Munroe, 255
Gabor, Eva, 106, 311, 632, 762, 772
Gabor, Zsa Zsa, 211, 346, 617, 706, 723
Gabrielle, 285
Gaffin, Melanie, 859
Gail, Max, 62, 859
Gaillard, Slim, 150
Gainer, Richard, 100
Gaines, Boyd, 586
Gaines, Jimmy, 39
Gale, Bill, 255
Gale, Bobby, 424
Galik, Denise, 266, 420
Gallagher, 83, 87
Gallagher, Don, 4, 658
Gallagher, Helen, 482
Gallagher, Keeley Mari, 252
Gallagher, Meg, 178
Gallagher, Megan, 344, 719
Gallagher, Peter, 718
Gallego, Gina, 266, 665
Gallery, James, 86
Gallery, Michele, **954**
Galliart, Melville, 255
Gallichio, Joseph, 288
Gallico, Paolo, 448
Gallico, Paul, 137
Gallico, Robert, 577
Gallin, Sandy, **954**
Gallo, Lew, 814
Gallo, Mario, 194
Gallo, William, 697
Gallop, Frank, 108, 114, 424, 452, 615, 616, 851
Galloway, Don, 45, 314, 345, 375, 799
Galloway, Michael, 91
Gallu, Sam, 91
Gallup, George, 32
Ganas, Monica, 87
Gandolf, Ray, 596
Ganis, Sidney, **956**
Gant, Norman, 472
Gantman, Joseph E., **937, 938**
Ganzel, Teresa, 222, 677, 775
Garagiola, Joe, 63, 64, 286, 753, 797
Garas, Kaz, 750
Garber, Terri, 225, 523
Garber, Victor, 189, 363
Garbo, Greta, 469
Garde, Betty, 229, 422, 653
Gardenia, Vincent, 26, 105
Gardiner, Reginald, 641
Gardner, Ava, 420
Gardner, Craig, 142
Gardner, Erle Stanley, 170, 616
Gardner, Hy, 797, 801, 852
Gardner, Terri, 555
Garen, Sophrony, 689
Garfield, Gil, 10
Gargan, William, 490, 491

Ginsburg, Robin, 420
Ginty, Robert, 55, 331, 602
Giovanni, Jim, 436
Girard, Henry, 23
Girard, Wendy, 19
Girardin, Ray, 140
Giroux, Lee, 801
Gish, Dorothy, 307, 822
Gish, Lillian, 126, 136, 274, 307, 623, 711
Gist, Robert, 337
Gist, Rod, 620, 670
Gittlin, Joyce, 603
Givens, Robin, 333
Givot, George, 748, 829
Gladke, Peter, 509
Glaser, Paul Michael, 743
Glass, Ned, 106, 407
Glass, Ron, 62, 578
Glazer, Vic, 229
Glea-Girls, The, 385, 386
Gleason, Jackie, xiii, xv, 35, 53, 116, 122, 135, 166, 268, 286, 351–353, 385, 386, 432, 449, 531, 541, 736, 755, 782, 883, **931, 938, 939**
Gleason, Joanna, 337
Glenn, Christopher, 567
Glenn, Louise, 214
Gless, Sharon, 122, 123, 137, 255, 358, 433, 486, 764, 813, **960, 961**
Glick, Phyllis, 463
Glickman, Marty, 172, 311, 472
Glover, Bruce, 331
Glover, Julian, 645
Gluskin, Lud, 230, 401
Glut, Donald F., 130
Glynn, Carlin, 522
Gnagy, Jon, 72, 875, 876
Gobel, George, 37, 232, 236, 261, 292, 293, 317, 326, 461, 655, 709, **931**
Goberman, John, **950, 952**
Goddard, Don, 270, 506, 565, 842
Goddard, Mark, 197, 403, 459, 485
Godfrey, Arthur, xiii, xv, 26, 46–48, 81, 127, 212, 278, 288, 384, 403, 455, 565, 584, 607, 708, 727, 770
Godfrey, Kathy, 584
Godfrey, Lynne, 562
Godkin, Paul, 232, 289
Godwin, Earl, 508
Goell, Kermit, 515
Goelz, Dave, 536, **951**
Goetz, Peter Michael, 19, 136
Goins, Jesse D., 309
Gold, Brandy, 55
Gold, Louise, 536
Gold, Missy, 73
Gold, Tracey, 306, 312, 706
Goldberg, Bernard, 275
Goldberg, David J., **961**
Goldberg, Gary David, **953, 962**

Goldberg, Jason, 246
Goldberg, Leonard, **958**
Goldberg, Whoopi, 210
Goldblum, Jeff, 779
Golddiggers, The, 190, 836
Golden, Ginny, 696
Golden West Cowboys, The, 612
Goldfarb, Phillip M., **961**
Goldin, Ricky Paul, 318
Goldman, Carole, 602
Goldman, Danny, 116, 305, 513
Goldman, Hal, **933, 934, 937**
Goldman, Roy, 468
Goldman, Wendy, 193
Goldsboro, Bobby, 95, 210, 403, 539
Goldsmith, Clifford, 23
Goldsmith, David, 529
Goldsmith, Jonathan, 178, 420
Goldsmith, Merwin, 307
Goldsmith, Sydney, 747
Goldstein, Scott, **961**
Goldstone, James, **956**
Goldwater, Barry, 385, 781
Golonka, Arlene, 398, 501
Gonzales, Claudia, 5
Gonzales, Martha, 5
Good Humor Company, The, 120
Good Time Singers, The, 39
Goodall, Jane, **945**
Goode, Richard, 221
Goodeve, Grant, 225, 232, 726
Goodfriend, Lynda, 89, 322, 861
Goodman, Al, 263, 548
Goodman, Benny, 71, 426, 739, 850
Goodman, Diana, 335
Goodman, Dody, 202, 445, 492, 493, 643, 802
Goodman, Frank, 417
Goodman, Hal, **942**
Goodrow, Michael, 232
Goodson, Mark, 68, 382, 553, 636, 797, 844, 854
Goodwin, Bill, 96, 291, 292, 612
Goodwin, Joshua, 805
Goodwin, Kia, 819
Goodwin, Michael, 320, 752
Goorian, Len, 608
Gorall, Leslie, 354
Gorden, Hayes, 256
Gordeno, Peter, 821
Gordon, Al, **933, 934, 937**
Gordon, Anita, 415
Gordon, Barry, 26, 213, 265, 305, 559
Gordon, Bruce, 70, 479, 621, 678, 739, 824
Gordon, Colin, 63
Gordon, Don, 91, 166, 464
Gordon, Gale, 111, 195, 267, 450, 451, 465, 466, 594, 618, 684
Gordon, Gerald, 342

Gordon, Glen, 14
Gordon, Gloria, 542
Gordon, Joann, 281
Gordon, Leo V., 152, 237
Gordon, Mark, 188
Gordon, Max, 708
Gordon, Phil, 77, 618
Gordon, Richard, 207
Gordon, Ruth, **953**
Gordon, Virginia, 594
Gordon, William D., 666
Gordon and Williams, 334
Gordy, Berry, Jr., 531
Gore, Charlie, 514
Gore, Leslie, 596
Gore, Michael, 250
Gorfain, Louis H., **957**
Gorman, Mari, 326, 340
Gorme, Eydie, 314, 423, 450, 746, 801, **950, 951, 953**
Gormley, Jim, 131
Gorodetsky, Eddie, **960**
Gorshin, Frank, 1, 65, 735
Gorski, Virginia, 262, 482
Gortner, Marjoe, 246, 731
Gosch, Martin, 159
Gosden, Freeman, 36, 37, 125
Gosfield, Maurice, 623, 805
Gossett, Louis, Jr., 57, 441, 633, 673, 879, **950**
Gothie, Robert, 286
Gottfried, Gilbert, 689, 784
Gottlieb, Alex, 7
Gottlieb, Carl, 415, **939**
Gottlieb, Stan, 355
Gottlieb, Brother Theodore, 87
Gottschalk, Vim, 378
Goude, Ingrid, 93, 745
Gough, Lloyd, 311
Gough, Michael, 696
Gould, Chester, 202
Gould, Elliott, 228, 690, 798, **950**
Gould, Harold, 260, 271, 333, 604, 660, 732
Gould, Sandra, 78
Gould, Sid, 122, 701
Gould, Stanhope, **945**
Goulding, Ray, 92, 155, 322, 484, 553
Goulet, Robert, 91, 735, 782
Gounod, Charles-Francois, 24
Gowdy, Curt, 63, 64, 689
Gower, André, 55, 258, 522
Gozier, Bernie, 96
Grable, Betty, 274, 360, 533, 709
Grabowski, Norm, 563
Grace, Mary, 379
Gracie, Charlie, 584
Grade, Sir Lew, 537
Grady, Don, 545, 596
Graff, David, 340
Graff, Ilene, 445, 518, 760
Graff, Jerry, 555

Graff, Robert D., 243
Grafton, Samuel, 857
Graham, Billy, 87, 187, 358
Graham, Fred, **947**
Graham, Gerrit, 747
Graham, Joe, 474
Graham, John, 708
Graham, June, 347
Graham, Roderick, **942, 943**
Graham, Ronny, 93, 148, 360, 559
Graham, Sheilah, 705
Graham, Sonny, 610
Graham, Virginia, 751, 857
Graham, William, 425
Grahame, Gloria, 661
Grammer, Kelsey, 143
Grandin, Isabel, 336, 784
Grandy, Fred, 461, 499
Granger, Farley, 822
Granger, Gerri, 853
Granger, Stewart, 356, 831
Granik, Theodore, 33, 884
Grant, Alberta, 608
Grant, Cary, 521, 532, 568, 592, 672
Grant, Faye, 309, 826
Grant, Gogi, 80, 182, 371, 556, 607
Grant, Harvey, 450
Grant, Kirby, 718
Grant, Lee, 57, 183, 259, 309, 621, 630, 632, **937, 941**
Grant, Marshall, 402
Grant, Ted, 689
Grasshoff, Alex, **947**
Grassle, Karen, 453
Grate, Gail, 470
Graubart, Judy, 163
Grauer, Ben, 35, 72, 83, 84, 242, 412, 486, 851
Graver, Fred, **960, 961, 962**
Graves, Leslie, 339
Graves, Peter, 169, 517, 754, 767, 858, 881
Graves, Teresa, 284, 294, 676, 813
Gravitte, Beau, 808
Gray, Alexander, 787
Gray, Barry, 727, 866
Gray, Billy, 257
Gray, Charles, 316, 651
Gray, Charlie, 488
Gray, Coleen, 865
Gray, Dolores, 114
Gray, Donald, 488
Gray, Erin, 112, 711, 742
Gray, Linda, 178
Gray, Michael, 106
Gray, Robert, 326
Grayco, Helen, 155, 733
Graziano, Rocky, 101, 337, 338, 414, 490, 602
Greaves, William, **941**
Greaza, Walter, 490, 811

Grecco, Cyndi, 437, 991
Greco, Buddy, 53, 108, 400, 726
Green, Al, 514
Green, Bernie, 46, 289, 347, 709
Green, Bud, 288
Green, Dorothy, 773
Green, Gerald, **952**
Green, John, 89
Green, Lynda Mason, 571
Green, Milt, 21
Green, Mitzi, 724
Green, Patricia M., **960**
Green and White Vocal Quartette, 153
Greenberg, Paul, **945, 947**
Greenberg, Todd, **959**
Greenbush, Lindsay, 453
Greenbush, Sidney, 453
Greene, Billy, 588
Greene, Brian, 420
Greene, Daniel, 246
Greene, David, **940, 949, 951, 954**
Greene, Frederick "Dennis," 703
Greene, Graham, 786
Greene, James, 189
Greene, Karen, 240
Greene, Kim Morgan, 157
Greene, Laura, 163
Greene, Lorne, 10, 66, 97, 156, 312, 423, 459, 623, 673, 739
Greene, Lynnie, 582
Greene, Marge, 487
Greene, Maxine, 813
Greene, Michele, 67, 216, 429
Greene, Mike, 178
Greene, Miss, 487
Greene, Mort, 656, 857, **949**
Greene, Richard, 17
Greene, Shecky, 98, 161, 436
Greene, Sid, 424
Greener, Dorothy, 347
Greenlee, David, 69, 249
Greenwald, Ken, 813
Greenwood, Bruce, 443, 682
Greer, Brodie, 149
Greer, Dabbs, 316, 321, 453
Greer, Michael, 95
Greer, Robin, 246
Gregg, Julie, 59, 525
Gregg, Virginia, 125, 455
Gregory, Benji, 24
Gregory, Fran, 667
Gregory, James, 62, 197, 438, 609, 630, 755, 844
Gregory, Mary, 836
Gregory, Paul, **931**
Gregson, Jack, 51, 102
Gregson, John, 707
Grenrock, Joshua, 843
Grey, Zane, 196, 201, 283
Grice, Wayne, 331
Grieg, Edvard, 476
Grier, David Alan, 28

Grier, Roosevelt "Rosey," 183, 184, 185, 535, 674
Gries, Tom, **936, 943**
Griffeth, Simone, 30, 105, 429
Griffin, Merv, 86, 118, 187, 188, 260, 279, 339, 345, 391, 415, 510, 612, 628, 681, 757, 770, 802
Griffin, Todd, 591
Griffin, Wayne, 872
Griffis, William, 584, 868
Griffith, Andy, 38, 137, 196, 303, 334, 394, 403, 415, 497, 501, 559, 573, 653, 684, 822, **934, 935, 937, 938**
Griffith, James, 705
Griffith, Melanie, 133, 585
Griffiths, David, **949, 958**
Griggs, John, 399, 713
Grimes, Jack, 584
Grimes, Jackie, 23
Grimes, Scott, 798
Grimes, Tammy, 186, 461, 773
Grimm, Paul, 83
Grinker, Charles, **956, 958**
Grinnage, Jack, 94, 423
Grizzard, George, **954**
Grodin, Charles, **953**
Groening, Matt, 808
Groh, David, 42, 660
Groom, Sam, 208, 593, 595
Gross, Ben, 47
Gross, Edan, 763
Gross, Mary, 689
Gross, Mason, 51, 785, 818
Gross, Michael, 252
Grossman, Gary, 18
Grossman, Scott, 220
Grossman, Terry, **960, 961**
Grove, Betty Ann, 82, 152, 539, 655, 748, 749, 757, 775
Grover, Cindy, 489
Grover, Deborah, 571
Grover, Edward, 61
Grover, Mary, 460
Grover, Stanley, 489, 781
Groves, Regina, 594
Grubbs, Gary, 272, 319
Grubin, David, **958, 961**
Gruliow, Leo, 794
Grusin, Dave, 39
Guardino, Harry, 616, 659
Guardino, Jerome, 131
Guarnieri, Johnny, 315, 528, 801
Gudegast, Hans, 651
Guenette, Robert, **942**
Guercio, Joe, 746
Guerrero, Evelyn, 366
Guest, Christopher, 689, **950**
Guest, George, 583
Guest, Lance, 460
Guest, Nicholas, 258
Guest, William, 299
Guilbert, Ann Morgan, 202, 559

Guild, Nancy, 857
Guillaume, Robert, 73, 724, **953, 959**
Guinness, Sir Alec, 435, 743
Guion, King, 538
Guisewite, Cathy, **961**
Gulager, Clu, 471, 585, 686, 761, 772, 824, 831
Gumbel, Bryant, 286
Gunn, Moses, 166, 171, 258, 305, 673
Gunther, John, 401
Gunton, Bob, 163
Guthrie, Arlo, 402
Guttenberg, Steve, 86, 573
Guy, Jasmine, 203
Guzaldo, Joseph, 746
Guzik, Jake, 824
Gwinn, Bill, 86
Gwinn, William, 8
Gwynne, Fred, 131, 536

H

Hack, Richard, 785
Hack, Shelley, 141, 176, 383
Hacker, Joseph, 420
Hackett, Bobby, 20, 337, 338, 490
Hackett, Buddy, 182, 385, 386, 501, 693, 738, 802, 877
Hackett, Joan, 42, 193
Haddock, Julie Anne, 98, 245, 535
Haddon, Laurence, 460
Haddon, Raymond, 842
Hadley, Nancy, 111, 399, 463
Hadley, Reed, 642, 649
Haenigsen, Harry, 776
Hagedorn, Carol, 46
Hagen, Chet, **937**
Hagen, Earle, 513, 651
Hagen, Jean, 184
Hagen, Kevin, 430, 453, 874
Hagen, Ross, 178
Hager, Jim, 335
Hager, Jon, 335
Hagerthy, Ron, 718
Haggard, Merle, 191, 402, 535, 632
Haggerty, Dan, 322, 447, 448
Haggerty, Don, 446
Hagman, Heidi, 26
Hagman, Larry, xvii, 178, 181, 305, 339, 363, 852
Hague, Albert, 249, 250
Hague, Steven, 106
Hagy, Ruth Geri, 408
Hahn, Archie, 483, 578
Hahn, Paul, 708
Hahn, Phil, **939**
Haid, Charles, 194, 344, 412
Haigh, Kenneth, 696
Hailey, Arthur, 356, 856

Haim, Corey, 673
Haines, Larry, 624, 625
Hairston, Jester, 31, 783
Haje, Khrystyne, 333
Hakeem, 258
Hale, Alan, Jr., 80, 297, 304
Hale, Barbara, 272, 616, **933**
Hale, Chanin, 655
Hale, Elvi, 715
Hale, Lee, 238
Hale, Nancy, 858
Haleloke, 46, 47
Haley, Alex, 601, 673
Haley, Bill, 216, 323, 324
Haley, Hal, **947**
Haley, Jack, Jr., 88, 782, **939, 953**
Haley, Jack, Sr., 274, 665, 881
Haley, Jackie, 837
Haley, Jackie Earle, 105
Hall, Albert, 680
Hall, Anthony Michael, 689
Hall, Arsenio, 319, 435, 531, 784
Hall, Brad, 689
Hall, Cliff, 172
Hall, Deidre, 594
Hall, Ed, 55, 506
Hall, Harry, 843
Hall, Huntz, 147
Hall, Jon, 650
Hall, Juanita, 129
Hall, Kevin Peter, 516
Hall, LaSaundra, 75
Hall, Marilyn, **959**
Hall, Michael, 788
Hall, Monty, 69, 171, 415, 444, 548, 830, 837
Hall, Philip Baker, 487
Hall, Radcliff, 296
Hall, Rich, 689
Hall, Sean Tyler, 106, 471
Hall, Thurston, 807
Hall, Tom T., 327, 538, 555, 632
Hall, Tony, 579
Hall, Zooey, 562
Hallahan, Charles, 361, 602
Hallaran, Susan, 574
Haller, Melonie, 846
Halley, Rudolph, 173
Hallick, Tom, 238, 696
Halliday, Brett, 512
Hallig, Klaus, **949**
Hallman, Victoria, 335
Halloran, Jack, 255
Halop, Billy, 26
Halop, Florence, 347, 507, 570, 682
Halpin, Helen, 139
Halpin, Luke, 269
Halpin, Miles, 842
Halsey, Brett, 271
Hamel, Veronica, 200, 344
Hamer, Rusty, 184
Hamill, Dorothy, 83, 286

Hamill, Mark, 31, 780
Hamilton, Alexa, 318
Hamilton, Antony, 170, 171
Hamilton, Argus, 663
Hamilton, Barbara, 142
Hamilton, Bernie, 743
Hamilton, Bob, 39, 289
Hamilton, Carrie, 249
Hamilton, Donald, 497
Hamilton, George, 225, 604, 673, 733, 761
Hamilton, Henry, 44
Hamilton, Joe, 795, **942, 945, 947**
Hamilton, John, 17
Hamilton, Linda, 69, 418, 699
Hamilton, Lynn, 665, 674, 687, 840
Hamilton, Margaret, 611
Hamilton, Murray, 54, 318, 461, 481, 661
Hamilton, Neil, 65, 349, 781
Hamilton, Ray, 418
Hamilton, Richard, 105
Hamilton, Ricki, 763
Hamilton Dancers, 881
Hamlin, Harry, 429, 496, 729, 755
Hamlisch, Marvin, 206, 554
Hammer, Jan, 511
Hammer, Jay, 390
Hammerstein, Oscar, II, 41, 230, 444
Hammett, Dashiell, 785
Hammond, Earl, 10, 640, 669
Hammond, Helen, 371
Hammond, Nanci Lynn, 461
Hammond, Nicholas, 31
Hammond, Peter, 111
Hamner, Earl, Jr., 840, 841
Hampden, Burford, xi
Hampden, Walter, 550, 693
Hampshire, Susan, **940, 941, 944**
Hampton, James, 215, 243, 460, 472, 491
Hampton, Lionel, 135
Han, Maggie, 729
Hancock, John, 325, 358, 748
Hancock, Lynn, 555
Hancock, Prentis, 730
Handleman, Stanley Myron, 184, 190
Handley, Alan, **937**
Haney, Anne, 452
Haney, Carol, 602
Hankboner, Sara, 190
Hankin, Larry, 540
Hanks, Steve, 54
Hanks, Tom, 99
Hanley, Bridget, 326, 339, 698
Hanley, Peter, 232, 239, 801
Hanley, Robert, 172
Hanley, William, **959**
Hanna, Elizabeth, 142
Hanna, Mark, 313
Hanna, Phil, 585, 741

Hanna, William, 268, 322, 393, 405
Hannah, Page, 249
Hanold, Marilyn, 710
Hanrahan, Jack, **939**
Hansard, Paul, 111
Hansen, Janis, 578, 675
Hansen, Judith, 344, 682
Hansen, Peter, 521
Hansen, Tom, 794, 880
Hanson, Marcy, 671
Hanson, Peter, 14
Happy Days Band, The, 322
Happy Days Singers, The, 322
Happy-Am-I Choir, 234
Harbach, Otto, 292
Harbach, William O., **944, 949**
Harburg, Yip, 603
Harcum, Bob, 846
Harding, Harvey, 540
Harden, Ernest, Jr., 390
Hardiman, Hilary, 750
Hardin, Jerry, 262
Hardin, Melora, 75, 253, 699
Hardin, Ty, 110, 146, 500
Harding, Harvey, 540
Harding, June, 498, 662
Hardison, Kadeem, 203
Hardt, Eloise, 194
Hardwicke, Sir Cedric, 14, 115, 291, 294, 531, 630, 860
Hardy, Oliver, 711
Harewood, Dorian, 300, 674, 752, 809
Harford, Betty, 602
Hargitay, Mariska, 219, 246
Hargrove, Dean, **945**
Harkins, Jim, 781
Harkins, John, 205
Harkness, Richard, 749
Harland, Michael, 681
Harland, Robert, 773
Harlem Globetrotters, The, 297
Harman, Barry, **946**
Harmer, Shirley, 288
Harmon, Barry, **946, 952**
Harmon, Deborah, 443, 468, 775
Harmon, Jim, 130
Harmon, Kelly, 67
Harmon, Kristin, 15
Harmon, Mark, 137, 266, 528, 682, 684, 818
Harmon, Merle, 691
Harmon, Patty, 777
Harmon, Steve, 523
Harms, Carl, 402
Harney, Greg, **945**
Harper, Constance, 15
Harper, David W., 840
Harper, Jessica, 372, 455, 755
Harper, John, 316
Harper, Robert, 278
Harper, Ron, 233, 287, 389, 627, 847

Harper, Valerie, 494, 660, 697, 827, **941, 943, 944, 948**
Harrell, Jack, 727
Harrelson, Woody, 143
Harriman, Averill, 187
Harriman, Fawne, 775
Harrington, Al, 330
Harrington, Bill, 347
Harrington, Pat, Jr., 1, 136, 162, 184, 519, 586, 602, 745, 802, **958**
Harrington, Pat, Sr., 169, 870
Harris, Arlene, 737
Harris, Bill, 51, 239
Harris, Bob, 812
Harris, Cynthia, 362, 429, 714
Harris, Debby, 182
Harris, Donald, 97
Harris, Harry, **956**
Harris, Holly, 585, 741
Harris, Howard "Stony," 172
Harris, Jed, 87
Harris, Jo Ann, 197, 530, 661
Harris, Jonathan, 86, 459, 786
Harris, Joshua, 178
Harris, Julie, 9, 57, 252, 307, 420, 623, 741, 785, **933, 935**
Harris, Lee, 751
Harris, Mel, 786
Harris, Percy (Bud), 76
Harris, Phil, 244
Harris, Robert H., 170, 302
Harris, Rosemary, 149, **949**
Harris, Ross, 732
Harris, Rossie, 823
Harris, Sam, 739, 877
Harris, Stacy, 215, 446
Harris, Susan, 318, **961**
Harrison, Dickie, 816
Harrison, Gracie, 508
Harrison, Gregory, 137, 456, 808, 809
Harrison, Jenilee, 178, 792
Harrison, Joan, 405
Harrison, Linda, 102
Harrison, Lisa, 840, 841
Harrison, Noel, 298
Harrison, Ray, 32
Harrison, Rex, 145, 295, 581, 592, 822
Harrold, Kathryn, 110, 470
Harron, Don, 335
Harry, Jackee, 819, **961**
Harsch, Joseph C., 56
Hart, Bill, 748
Hart, Carole, **946**
Hart, Cecilia, 523, 604
Hart, Clay, 439
Hart, David, 370
Hart, Dorothy, 602, 769
Hart, Gary, 864
Hart, John (actor), 323, 457
Hart, John (newsman), 120, 568, **947**
Hart, Mary, 238

Hart, Moss, 42, 642, 877
Hart, Ralph, 465
Hart, Richard, 13
Hart, Stan, **944, 945**
Hart, Trisha, 93
Hartford, John, 300, 722, 756
Hartley, Mariette, 306, 340, 621, **953**
Hartley, Ted, 150
Hartman, David, 464, 560, 831, 832
Hartman, Grace, 329, 709
Hartman, Karen, 703
Hartman, Lisa, 342, 420, 583, 768
Hartman, Paul, 38, 329, 501, 620, 636, 709
Hartman, Phil, 596, 689
Hartmann, Ena, 181
Harty, Patricia, 90, 338, 577
Hartzell, Clarence, 121, 790
Harvey, Harry, Sr., 378, 482
Harvey, Jane, 108, 444
Harvey, John, 313
Harvey, Laurence, 22
Harvey, Michael, 798
Harvey, Ned, 215
Harvey, Paul, 609
Hasel, Joe, 101, 563, 671, 734
Haskell, Jack, 288, 802
Haskell, Jimmie, 425
Haskell, Peter, 102, 437, 662, 665
Haslam, Lu Ann, 558
Hasselhoff, David, 419, 420, 700
Hastings, Bob, 26, 189, 503
Hastings, Don, 130
Hastings, Hal, 145
Hastings, Michael, **944**
Hatch, Richard, 66, 492, 751
Hatcher, Terri, 411, 461
Hatfield, Hurd, 612, 883
Hatfield, Mark, 633
Hathaway, Noah, 66
Hatrak, Ernie, 239
Haufrect, Alan, 25
Hauser, Fayette, 483
Hauser, Tim, 483
Hauser, Wings, 433
Hausner, Jerry, 827
Havel Brothers, 274
Havens, John, 689
Havoc, June, 291, 602, 864
Hawkesworth, John, 645, **945, 947, 949, 950**
Hawkins, Dale, 80
Hawkins, Dolores, 317
Hawkins, Hawkshaw, 599
Hawkins, Jimmy, 41, 368, 678
Hawkins, Rick, **952**
Hawkins, Virginia, 506
Hawley, Adelaide, 256
Hawn, Goldie, 275, 305, 638, 676, 677, 782
Hay, R. Couri, 785
Hayden, Don, 543

Hickman, Herman, 137, 340
Hickok, Wild Bill, 19, 309
Hickox, Harry, 573, 629
Hicks, Catherine, 57, 812
Hicks, Hilly, 670, 673
Higgins, Joe, 45, 402
Higgins, Joel, 74, 684, 711
Higgins, Michael, 588
Hiken, Nat, 131, **931, 932, 933, 935**
Hilber, Burt, 15
Hilburn, Robert, 668
Hilderbrand, Diane, 605
Hilgemeier, Edward, Jr., 216
Hill, Arthur, 300, 309, 318, 599, 822
Hill, Benny, 72
Hill, Charlie, 83
Hill, Craig, 858
Hill, Dana, 819
Hill, George Roy, 425, 628, 754
Hill, Goldie, 308
Hill, James, **945**
Hill, Johnny, 539
Hill, Pamela, **947**
Hill, Richard, 797
Hill, Steven, 517
Hill, Thomas, 564
Hill, Tom, 868
Hill, William B., **947**
Hillaire, Marcel, 13
Hillebrand, Fred, 490
Hillerman, John, 13, 76, 161, 473, **961**
Hilliard, Robert, **945**
Hillis, Margaret, 147
Hillner, John, 843
Hills, Dick, 424
Hilton, Bob, 812
Hinckley, John, 310
Hindle, Art, 73, 178, 418
Hines, Connie, 520
Hines, Janear, 407
Hines, Jerome, 833
Hines, John B., 427
Hines, Theodore, 108
Hingle, Pat, 747
Hinkley, Don, **944, 956**
Hinnant, Skip, 608
Hinton, Darby, 183
Hinton, Ed, 364
Hinton, James David, 393
Hirsch, Elroy "Crazylegs," 708
Hirsch, Judd, 194, 196, 774, **955, 957**
Hirsch, Louis A., 292
Hirsch, Steven, 420
Hirschfield, Bert, 372
Hirschfield, Robert, 344
Hirson, Alice, 178, 856
Hirt, Al, 254, 312, 475
Hit Paraders, The, 880
Hitchcock, Alfred, 24, 154, 405, 467, 695, 762, **932, 933**
Hitchcock, Pat, 695

Hitler, Adolph, 88
Hitsville Gang Dancers, The, 531
Ho, Don, 424
Hoag, Mitzi, 339, 847
Hobbs, John, 511
Hobin, Bill, **939**
Hoblit, Gregory, **955, 956, 957, 958, 961, 962**
Hobson, Laura, 381
Hoctor, Danny, 155
Hodge, Al, 130
Hodges, Charles, 42, 658, 659
Hodges, Russ, 101, 102, 679
Hodges, Tom, 827
Hodgins, Earle, 314
Hodiak, John, 349
Hodson, Jim, 8
Hodyl, Richard, 632
Hoff, Carl, 93, 274, 369, 407, 412, 490, 539, 608, 694, 738, 803
Hoff, Robin, 864
Hoffer, Eric, 120, **938**
Hoffman, Basil, 735
Hoffman, Bern, 474
Hoffman, Dustin, **960**
Hoffman, Gertrude, 543
Hoffman, Harold, 645, 781, 855
Hoffman, Paul G., 490
Hoffman, Richard, 855
Hoffman, Wendy, 476
Hogan, Bob, 621
Hogan, Jack, 10, 161, 710
Hogan, Robert, 213, 483, 591, 663, 699
Hogan, Susan, 571
Hogestyn, Drake, 701
Holbrook, Hal, 195, 700, **941, 946, 949**
Holch, Arthur, 575
Holcomb, Kathryn, 359, 718
Holcombe, Harry, 61, 870
Holcombe, Wendy, 445, 555
Holden, James, 13
Holden, Rebecca, 419
Holden, William, 91, **946**
Holder, Boscoe, 484
Holdridge, Lee, 528
Hole, Jonathan, 755
Holfeld, Horant H., **958**
Holiday, Billie, 381
Holland, Gina, 588
Holland, Kristina, 170, 837
Holland, Maury, 425
Holland, Richard, 591
Holland, Steve, 267
Holland, W. S., 402
Hollander, David, 124, 445, 504, 561, 852
Hollander, Lorin, 201
Hollenbeck, Don, 566
Holliday, Art, 858
Holliday, Fred, 506
Holliday, Judy, 501

Holliday, Kene, 133, 497
Holliday, Polly, 25, 269, 638, 746
Hollies, The, 280
Holliman, Earl, xvi, 356, 631, 862
Hollis, Jeff, 121
Holloway, Joan, 159
Holloway, Stanley, 594
Holloway, Sterling, 58, 349, 449, 864, 883
Hollowell, Todd, 245
Holly, Buddy, 48
Holm, Celeste, 57, 193, 246, 352, 393, 466, 553, 723, 860
Holman, Bill, 220
Holmes, Billy, 514
Holmes, Clint, 435
Holmes, Dennis, 431
Holmes, Ed, 313, 585
Holmes, Eddie, 741
Holmes, Jennifer, 516, 564
Holmes, LeRoy, 801
Holmes, Mattie, 514
Holmes, Oliver Wendell, 438
Holmes, Salty, 514
Holmes, Tony, 55
Holt, Bob, 804
Holt, Johnny, 539
Homeier, Skip, 182, 373, 693, 755, 762
Homer, Ben, 288
Homer and Jethro, 396
Hometowners, The, 514
Homolka, Oscar, 224
Hon, Jean Marie, 480
Honeydreamers, The, 108, 412, 718, 758, 825
Hong, James, 394, 558, 764
Hood, Darla, 415
Hood, Noel, 281
Hook, Dr., 211
Hooker, Richard, 469
Hooks, Jan, 319, 689
Hooks, Kevin, 340, 858
Hooks, Robert, 57, 551, 759
Hooper, Larry, 439, 440
Hoover, J. Edgar, 243, 364
Hope, Bob, xiv, 28, 59, 94, 144, 145, 158, 185, 200, 230, 278, 351, 396, 407, 516, 548, 591, 843, **936, 937, 959**
Hope, Leslie, 73, 420
Hopkins, Anthony, **949, 955**
Hopkins, Bo, 206, 225, 372, 669
Hopkins, Miriam, 467
Hopkins, Telma, 99, 297, 561, 578, 804
Hoppe, John, 539
Hopper, Dennis, 240, 643
Hopper, William, 616
Horan, Barbra, 54
Horan, Bobby, 340
Horgan, Patrick, 133
Horne, Lena, 230, 776, **942**

Ichino, Laurie, 184
Idelson, Billy, 524, 588
Idle, Eric, 690
Idol, Billy, 4
Iger, S. M., 705
Ignico, Robin, 808
Igus, Darrow, 280, 670
Illes, Robert, **947, 952**
Ilson, Saul, 854
Imel, Jack, 439, 440
Imperato, Carlo, 249
Impert, Margaret, 472, 732
Indrisano, John, 577
Inescort, Frieda, 506
Ing, Debi, 488
Ingalls, Phil, 830
Ingber, Mandy, 196, 807
Inge, William, 116, 581
Ingels, Marty, 369, 641
Innes, George, 645
Insana, Tino, 87
Interludes, The, 804
Ireland, Jill, 704
Ireland, John, 134, 264, 601, 630, 651
Ironside, Michael, 826
Irving, Amy, 585
Irving, Charles, 836
Irving, George S., 187, 224
Irving, Hollis, 487
Irving, Jay, 220
Irving, Margaret, 613
Irwin, Stan, 523
Irwin, Wynn, 459, 756
Isaac, Bud, 599
Isaacs, David, **957**
Isaacs, Jeremy, **947**
Isacksen, Peter, 121, 162, 319, 393
Ito, Robert, 647
Itzkowitz, Howard, 488
Ivar, Stan, 453
Ivens, Terri, 697
Ives, Burl, 9, 343, 440, 577, 615, 673
Ives, George, 523
Ivey, Dana, 229
Ivo, Tommy, 487
Izay, Connie, 468

J

Ja-Cha, Xu, **957**
Jablons-Alexander, Karen, 464
Jablonski, Carl, 198, 549
Jack, Wolfman, 514
Jack and Jill, 273
Jackee, 819
Jackie and Gayle, 425
Jacko, 344
Jacks, Robert L., **944**
Jackson, Alan, 884
Jackson, Andrew, 15
Jackson, Anne, 206, 241

Jackson, Clydine, 188
Jackson, Eddie, 396
Jackson, Freddie, 381
Jackson, Glenda, 358, **943**
Jackson, Gordon, **949**
Jackson, Greg, 434, 589, 864
Jackson, Jackie, 387
Jackson, Janet, 202, 249, 305, 387, 561
Jackson, Jay, 794, 816
Jackson, Jerry, 804
Jackson, Kate, 141, 672, 692
Jackson, Keith, 63, 64, 271, 272
Jackson, LaToya, 387
Jackson, Lia, 327
Jackson, Mahalia, 71, 556, 782
Jackson, Marlon, 387
Jackson, Mary, 325, 840
Jackson, Michael, 280, 387
Jackson, Mike, **940**
Jackson, Paul, 778
Jackson, Randy, 387
Jackson, Rebie Maureen, 387
Jackson, Reggie, 136, 286
Jackson, Sammy, 573
Jackson, Selmer, 446
Jackson, Sherry, 184
Jackson, Slim, 26
Jackson, Stoney, 373, 858
Jackson, Tito, 387
Jackson, Victoria, 319, 689
Jackson, Wanda, 599
Jackson Five, The, 387, 531
Jacobi, Derek, 750
Jacobi, Lou, 190, 381, 508
Jacobs, Beth, 358
Jacobs, Christian, 301, 472
Jacobs, Johnny, 76
Jacobs, Lawrence-Hilton, 186, 665, 673, 846
Jacobs, Marilyn, 745
Jacobs, Parker, 136
Jacobs, Rachael, 312, 380
Jacobson, Jill, 246, 560
Jacobson, Larry, 435, **960, 961, 962**
Jacoby, Billy, 57, 380, 472, 711
Jacoby, Bobby, 420
Jacoby, Coleman, **931, 932, 933**
Jacoby, Laura, 523
Jacoby, Scott, **944**
Jacqueline, 51
Jacquet, Jeffrey, 528, 859
Jaeckel, Richard, 50, 59, 263, 283, 684, 732, 759
Jaffe, Henry, 71, **939**
Jaffe, Sam, 71
Jaffe, Taliesin, 318, 706
Jagger, Dean, 521
Jagger, Mick, 211, 776, 806
Jakobson, Maggie, 563
Jalbert, Pierre, 161
James, Art, 164
James, Clifton, 153, 445

James, Dennis, 102, 127, 134, 139, 254, 342, 406, 553, 592, 636, 872
James, Harry, 392, 709
James, Henry, 882, 883
James, Jacqueline, 787
James, Jeri Lou, 379, 649
James, Joanelle, 718
James, John, 157, 225
James, Joni, 484
James, Ken, 766
James, Kenny, 877
James, Olga, 85
James, Ralph, 528
James, Rick, 563
James, Sheila, 107, 485, 596, 753
James, Stephanie, 407
Jameson, House, 23, 667
Jameson, Joyce, 155, 733
Jamison, Mikki, 10
Jan and Dean, 669
Jane, Paula, 787
Janes, Sallie, 436
Janis, Conrad, 97, 396, 528, 645
Jann, Gerald, 353
Janney, Leon, 331, 748, 785
Jannis, Vivi, 257
Janssen, Danny, 605
Janssen, David, 88, 137, 283, 328, 580, 663, 705
Jarchow, Bruce, 769
Jaress, Jill, 562
Jarnac, Dorothy, 338
Jarreau, Al, 381, 528, 992
Jarrett, Art, 661
Jarrett, Renne, 553
Jarriel, Tom, 565, 817
Jarrin, Mauricio, 168
Jarvis, Graham, 249, 476, 492
Jarvis, Lucy, **936**
Jason, George, 129
Jason, Harvey, 107, 130, 661, 676
Jason, Rick, 161, 643
Jaxon, Ron, 656
Jean, Norma, 599
Jefferson, Herbert, Jr., 66, 197, 661
Jefferson, Thomas, 8, 644
Jeffreys, Anne, 193, 263, 463, 501, 807
Jeffries, Dean, 312
Jeffries, Fran, 735
Jeffries, Herb, 857
Jeffries, Lang, 659
Jellison, Bob, 69
Jenkins, Allen, 222, 340, 805, 842
Jenkins, Carol Mayo, 249
Jenkins, Dan, 700
Jenkins, Gordon, 347, 548
Jenkins, Larry Flash, 67, 263, 858
Jenkins, Mark, 207
Jenks, Frank, 159, 160
Jenner, Barry, 178
Jenner, Bruce, 149, 286, 738
Jennings, Peter, 565

Kageyama, Rodney, 315
Kahan, Judy, 29, 205, 279, 491, 492, 827
Kahan, Steve, 73, 420
Kahler, Wolf, 729
Kahn, Madeline, 1, 163, 522, 579
Kai, Lani, 13
Kaigler, Dave, 585
Kajuna, Nelson, 99
Kalb, Marvin, 508
Kalber, Floyd, 568
Kalcheim, Lee, 945
Kalember, Patricia, 408, 413
Kallen, Kitty, 135, 406
Kallen, Lucille, 882
Kallis, Nichole, 631
Kallis, Stanley, 949
Kallman, Dick, 321
Kalmar, Bert, 876
Kaltenborn, H. V., 633, 860
Kaltenborn, Mrs. H. V., 867
Kamen, Milt, 122, 463, 602, 709
Kampmann, Steven, 564
Kanaly, Steve, 178
Kander, John, 789
Kane, Bob, 65
Kane, Carol, 28, 774, 956, 957
Kane, Dennis B., 947, 952
Kane, Georgann, 960
Kane, Jack, 39, 746
Kane, Martin, 491
Kanin, Fay, 946, 947, 953
Kanter, Hal, 931
Kantor, Richard, 263
Kanui, Hank, 685
Kaper, Bronislaw, 243
Kaplan, Gabriel, 445, 846, 847
Kaplan, Marvin, 25, 147, 507, 805
Kaplan, Stephen, 848
Karabatsos, Ron, 221, 593, 843
Karam, Eddie, 190, 394, 670
Kareman, Fred, 591
Karen, Arthur, 959
Karen, James, 633
Karl, Martin, 46
Karlen, Betty, 110
Karlen, John, 122, 960
Karloff, Boris, 74, 218, 234, 373, 452, 496, 706, 742, 762, 772, 793
Karnes, Robert, 438
Karnilova, Maria, 381
Karns, Roscoe, 337, 640, 669, 670
Karns, Todd, 669, 670
Karp, David, 936
Karras, Alex, 137, 271, 691, 845
Karron, Richard, 140, 305, 775
Karvelas, Robert, 294, 605
Kasday, David, 788
Kasem, Jean, 807
Kasem, Kasey, 785
Kastner, Peter, 193, 822
Kasznar, Kurt, 430
Katan, Roseanne, 308

Katt, Nicky, 338, 826
Katt, William, 309
Katz, Omri, 178
Katz, Phyllis, 87, 868
Katz, Raymond, 954
Kaufman, Andy, 280, 774, 828
Kaufman, George S., 642, 736, 787, 877
Kava, Caroline, 381
Kavner, Julie, 660, 808, 952
Kay, Beatrice, 125
Kay, Dianne, 232, 300, 584, 657
Kay, Keith, 938
Kay, Linda, 620
Kay, Monte, 941
Kaydets, The, 685
Kaye, Caren, 76, 89, 236, 381, 861
Kaye, Celia, 562
Kaye, Danny, 184, 200, 401, 526, 936
Kaye, Lila, 477
Kaye, Mandy, 313, 400
Kaye, Sammy, 35, 412, 414, 426, 685
Kaye, Stubby, 461, 544, 602
Kayser, Allan, 478
Kazan, Lainie, 191, 411, 735, 807
Kazanjian, Howard, 956
Kazann, Zitto, 336
Kazurinsky, Tim, 689
Keach, Stacy, 132, 294, 513, 705
Keale, Moe, 81, 330, 471
Kean, Betty, 442
Kean, Jane, 22, 352, 353, 385, 386
Keanan, Staci, 546
Keane, James, 602, 603
Keane, John, 414
Keane, Kerrie, 355, 875
Keane, Tom, 414
Kearns, Joseph, 195, 594
Kearns, Sandra, 266
Keating, Larry, 291, 292, 321, 520
Keaton, Buster, 7, 161, 230, 231, 711
Keaton, Michael, 29, 491, 493, 659, 871
Keats, Steven, 701
Keefer, Don, 39
Keegan, Chris, 84
Keegan, Junie, 610
Keel, Howard, 178
Keeler, Donald, 432
Keen, Malcolm, 476
Keen, Noah, 45
Keene, Carolyn, 326, 554
Keener, Catherine, 580
Keens, Michael, 324
Keep, Stephen, 269
Kehoe, Donald, 514
Keim, Betty Lou, 195, 544
Keith, Brian, xvi, 22, 44, 74, 106, 126, 137, 174, 251, 325, 643, 754, 822, 849

Keith, Byron, 702
Keith, David, 156
Keith, Larry, 66
Keith, Richard, 365, 465, 850
Keith, Robert, 754
Keith, Ronald, 450
Kelk, Jackie, 23, 879
Kellems, Vivien, 633
Keller, Dorothy, 701
Keller, Jack, 339
Keller, Jason, 596
Keller, Mary Page, 222
Keller, Shane, 596
Keller, Sheldon, 937
Kellerman, Sally, 137, 634
Kelley, Barry, 84
Kelley, DeForest, 739
Kellin, Mike, 97, 265, 352, 701, 836
Kellogg, John, 621
Kellogg, Ray, 77
Kelly, Al, 56, 239
Kelly, Bebe, 808
Kelly, Brian, 269, 750, 815
Kelly, Emmett, 224, 776
Kelly, Gene (actor), 83, 284, 301, 493, 693, 937
Kelly, Gene (sportscaster), 296
Kelly, Grace, 80, 183, 307, 350, 425, 554, 623, 641, 762, 811, 845
Kelly, Jack, 206, 294, 325, 418, 499, 548
Kelly, Joe, 647, 648
Kelly, Karen, 665
Kelly, Ned, 959
Kelly, Patsy, 167
Kelly, Paula (actress), 570
Kelly, Paula (singer), 466
Kelly, Roz, 323
Kelly, Sean, 171
Kelly, Tom, 753
Kelman, Alfred R., 451, 951, 954, 955, 957
Kelman, Rickey, 194, 556, 594
Kelsey, Linda, 188, 460
Kelton, Pert, 135, 338, 352
Kelton, Richard, 645
Kemelman, Harry, 431
Kemmer, Ed, 731
Kemp, Brandis, 19, 280
Kemp, Jeremy, 660
Kemper, Doris, 850
Kendall, Cy, 547
Kendis, Sonny, 728
Kendrick, Merle, 866
Kenin, Alexa, 156
Kennedy, Adam, 124
Kennedy, Arthur, 22, 224, 240, 243, 552
Kennedy, Betty, 429
Kennedy, Bob, 866
Kennedy, George, 57, 91, 169, 688
Kennedy, Jayne, 731, 876

Kobe, Gail, 621
Kober, Jeff, 246
Kobin, Bill, 3
Koch, Ed, 690
Kochheim, Lory, 535
Koehler, Frederick, 411
Koenig, Josh A. Andrew, 312
Koenig, Walter, 739
Kogen, Arnie, **945, 946, 948**
Kohan, Alan Buz, **945, 951, 955, 957**
Kolb, Clarence, 543
Kolb, Mina, 618
Kolden, Scott, 505
Kollmar, Dick, 100, 109, 313, 860
Komack, James, 170, 337, 572
Kondazian, Karen, 704
Konrad, Dorothy, 434
Koock, Guich, 133, 149, 445, 706
Koop, Ted, 244
Kopell, Bernie, 215, 294, 461, 557, 780, 857
Kopins, Karen, 178
Koplin, Merton Y., **956, 958**
Koppel, Ted, 177, 565
Korda, Sir Alexander, 532
Korman, Harvey, 4, 132, 184, 292, 443, 478, 795, **940, 942, 943, 946**
Korn, Iris, 601
Korn Kobblers, The, 422, 538
Korty, John, **946, 954**
Koslo, Paul, 674
Kostal, Irwin, 289
Kosugi, Sho, 495
Kotero, Patricia "Apollonia," 246
Kotlisky, Marge, 682
Kotlowitz, Robert, **944**
Kotto, Yaphet, 272
Koufax, Sandy, 63
Koury, Rex, 316
Kovacs, Bella, 731
Kovacs, Ernie, xv, 239, 286, 435, 588, 708, 711, 769, 796, 801, **933**
Kovacs, Jonathan Hall, 253
Kovas, Dino, 562
Kove, Martin, 122, 156, 851
Kowanko, Pete, 272
Kozoll, Michael, **955, 956**
Kraft, Robert, 860
Kramer, Bert, 265, 688
Kramer, Jeffrey, 325, 753
Kramer, Stepfanie, 361, 489, 698, 843
Krassner, Paul, 864
Kratochzil, Tom, 869
Kraut, Harry, **949**
Krawitz, Herman, **954**
Krayer, James, **942**
Kreitzer, Catherine, 716
Krenn, Sherrie, 245
Kreppel, Paul, 378
Kreskin, 31
Kristen, Marta, 459

Kristofferson, Kris, 671
Kroeger, Gary, 689, 733
Krofft, Marty, 60, 177, 214
Krofft, Sid, 60, 177, 214
Krofft Puppets, The, 60, 177, 214
Kroft, Steve, 849
Kruger, Otto, 466, 554, 623
Krupa, Gene, 231
Kruschen, Jack, 116, 353, 845
Kubek, Tony, 63, 64
Kubelik, Rafael, 147
Kudirka, Simas, **952**
Kuhlman, Ron, 103
Kulik, Buzz, 425
Kulky, Henry, 337, 449, 834
Kulp, Nancy, 77, 93, 106
Kuluva, Will, 637
Kumagai, Denice, 570
Kunberg, Judy, **953**
Kupcinet, Irv, 801
Kupcinet, Karyn, 294
Kuralt, Charles, 34, 120, 242, 583, 861, **940**
Kuroda, Emily K., 315
Kurtis, Bill, 34
Kurty, Lee, 207
Kurtz, Swoosie, 462, 491
Kurtzman, Katy, 225
Kusatsu, Clyde, 107
Kutash, Jeff, 200
Kuter, Kay E., 311, 620
Kuyper, George, 147
Kuzyk, Mimi, 344
Kyser, Kay, 274, 412, 776

L

La Centra, Peg, 487
La Gallienne, Eva, **952**
La Guardia, Fiorello, 88
L.A. Mime Company, The, 828
La Rue, Lash, 432, 446
La Torre, Tony, 122
Labella, Vincenzo, **956**
Laborteaux, Matthew, 453, 859
Laborteaux, Patrick, 453
LaBrie, Donna, 73
Labriola, Tony, 415
Lacey, Laara, 322, 415
Lacher, Taylor, 121, 398, 552
Lachman, Mort, **951**
Lack, Andrew, 34
Ladd, Alan, 291
Ladd, Cheryl, 141, 415
Ladd, Diane, 25
Ladd, Hank, 45, 837
Ladd, Margaret, 246
Lafitte, Jean, 15
Lahr, Bert, 74, 274, 357, 641, 665, 743, 757
Lai, Francis, 463
Laine, Frankie, 278, 556, 651, 709

Laird, Marvin, 791
Laire, Judson, 11, 12, 476, 755
Lake, Arthur, 90
Lake, Janet, 820
Lake, Veronica, 307, 466, 772
LaLanne, Jack, 747, 864
Lally, Michael David, 73
Lally, William, 544
LaMarche, Maurice, 177
Lamas, Lorenzo, 123, 182, 246, 699
Lamb, Claudia, 492
Lamb, Gil, 351, 866
Lambert, Gloria, 713
Lambert, Jack, 666
Lambert, Paul, 241
Lambie, Joe, 246
LaMotta, John, 24
Lamour, Dorothy, 461
L'Amour, Louis, 352
Lampell, Millard, **937**
Lampert, Zohra, 209, 298, **948**
Lampkin, Charles, 278
Lampley, Jim, 63
Lancaster, Burt, 281, 530
Lanchester, Elsa, 401, 501, 554, 581
Landau, Martin, 517, 730
Lander, David L., 437
Lander, Diane, 358
Landers, Audrey, 178, 342
Landers, Harry, 71
Landers, Judy, 54, 162, 471, 829
Landesberg, Steve, 62, 190, 609
Landis, Monte, 260
Lando, Barry, **945**
Lando, Brian, 195
Landon, Leslie, 453, 454
Landon, Margaret, 41
Landon, Michael, 15, 97, 258, 290, 343, 344, 453, 454, 705, 776
Landsberg, David, 121
Landsburg, Alan, **940**
Landsburg, Valerie, 28, 249, 356, 875
Lane, Abbe, 873
Lane, Allan "Rocky," 520
Lane, Charles, 191, 410, 465, 620, 641
Lane, Don, 415
Lane, Doris, 256
Lane, John, **947**
Lane, Ken, 190
Lane, Nancy, 40, 222, 660
Lane, Nathan, 589
Lane, Rusty, 173, 396, 591
Lane, Sara, 831
Lane, Scott, 503
Lane-Block, Shana, 860
Laneuville, Eric, 167, 672, 682
Lang, Howard, 17
Lang, Perry, 67
Lang, Shirley, 19
Lang, Stephen, 173

Langan, Glenn, 100
Langard, Janet, 213
Langdon, Freddy, 514
Langdon, Harry, 161
Langdon, Sue Ane, 45, 56, 309, 385, 856
Lange, Ann, 163
Lange, Hope, 56, 295, 559, **939, 940**
Lange, Jim, 138, 186, 553
Lange, Ted, 461, 524, 783
Langford, Frances, 44, 739
Langham, Chris, **956**
Langland, Liane, 496
Langrishe, Caroline, 645
Langston, Murray, 210, 304, 727, 728, 812
Langton, Paul, 621
Lanier, Susan, 765, 804
Lanin, Jay, 271
Lankford, Kim, 420, 843
Lannom, Les, 137, 149, 328
Lansbury, Angela, 537, 602, 660, 736, 739
Lansing, Joi, 78, 93, 419
Lansing, Robert, 52, 233, 239, 481, 814
Lanson, Snooky, 145, 266, 880
Lanteau, William, 564
Lanza, Mario, 709
LaPlaca, Alison, 222, 762
Larch, John, 45, 166
Lardner, Ring, 9
Large, Don, 843
Larkin, Dick, 454
Larkin, John, 683, 814
Larkin, Sheila, 749
LaRoche, Mary, 410
LaRosa, Julius, xv, 46, 47, 407, 425, 444, 608, 767, 768, 803
Larrain, Michael, 498
Larroquette, John, 55, 161, 209, 570, **959, 960, 961**
Larsen, Keith, 43, 104, 361, 362, 574
Larsen, Larry, 214
Larson, Darrell, 334, 529
Larson, Dennis, 397
Larson, Glen A., 24, 54, 249, 344
Larson, Jack, 17
LaRue, Jack, 452
LaRussa, Adrienne, 137
Lascoe, Henry, 239
Laskey, Kathleen, 142
Lasky, Zane, 434, 476, 804
Lasser, Louise, 378, 492, 770
LaStarza, Roland, 286
Late, Jason, 258
Latham, Louise, 166, 688
Latorra, Tony, 571
Latt, David, **958**
Lau, Wesley, 616
Laughlin, John, 858

Laughton, Charles, 230, 274, 322, 532, 610
Lauher, Bobby, 769
Launer, John, 170
Lauper, Cyndi, 4
Laurance, Matthew, 222
Laurance, Mitchell, 677
Laurel, Stan, 711, 828
Laurel & Hardy, 351
Lauren, Tammy, 40, 75, 529, 596, 861
Laurence, John, **938, 940, 942, 947**
Lauria, Dan, 870
Laurie, Joe, Jr., 127
Laurie, Piper, 718, **961**
Lauter, Ed, 54
Lauter, Harry, 772, 842
·Lavalle, Paul, 153
Lavin, Linda, 25, 62, 493
Law, Lindsay, **958**
Law, Walter, 777
Lawford, Peter, 191, 264, 274, 307, 785
Lawlor, John, 245, 625
Lawnik, Mildred, 632
Lawrence, Bill (newsman), 565
Lawrence, Bill (singer), 46
Lawrence, Carol, 71, 191, 581
Lawrence, David, 78
Lawrence, Elliot, 5, 20, 314, 509, 655, 691, 743, 782
Lawrence, Gertrude, x, 641, 709
Lawrence, Greg, 78
Lawrence, Joey, 297, 298
Lawrence, Mark, 26
Lawrence, Martin, 852
Lawrence, Mary, 93
Lawrence, Matthew, 297, 688
Lawrence, Mort, 82
Lawrence, Steve, 48, 132, 275, 314, 423, 744, 746, 801, 802, **945, 950, 953**
Lawrence, Vicki, 132, 174, 395, 478, 795, 865, **949**
Laws, Barry, 122
Laws, Sam, 634
Lawson, Linda, 13, 214
Lawson, Michael, 589
Lawson, Richard, 146, 225
Lay, Beirne, Jr., 814
Lay, Rodney, 335
Layman, Kathleen, 487
Layton, George, 207
Lazarus, Bill, 57, 124
Lazenby, George, 665
Lazer, David, **951**
Le Beauf, Sabrina, 168
Le Blanc, Christian, 370
Le May, John D., 280
Le Roy, Gloria, 355, 413
Le Sueur, Larry, 150
Leach, Britt, 732
Leach, Robin, 177, 452

Leachman, Cloris, 9, 57, 92, 140, 183, 245, 346, 425, 432, 494, 625, 695, 762, 776, **944, 946, 948, 958**
Leahy, Frank, 277, 652
Leal, Pete, 885
Leaming, Jim, 296
Lear, Norman, 5, 27, 67, 260, 261, 274, 305, 320, 355, 390, 492, 494, 499, 554, 601, 687, 874, **941, 942, 944**
Learned, Michael, 576, 840, 841, **944, 946, 949, 956**
Leary, Brianne, 55, 149
Leary, Dr. Timothy, 187
Lebieg, Earl, 278
Led Zeppelin, 211
Lederer, Bill, 238
Lederer, Suzanne, 233
Ledford, Judy, 6
Ledner, Caryl, **953**
Lee, Anna, 380
Lee, Brenda, 600, 703
Lee, Bruce, 311, 428, 458
Lee, Cherylene, 416
Lee, Christopher, 14
Lee, Ernie, 514
Lee, Fran, 474
Lee, Gene, 442
Lee, Georgia, 737
Lee, Gypsy Rose, 346, 641, 785
Lee, James, 588
Lee, Joanna, **946**
Lee, Johnny, 36
Lee, Jonna, 593
Lee, Kathryn, 739
Lee, Manfred Bennington, 13
Lee, Michele, 400, 420
Lee, Mrs. John G., 633
Lee, Patsy, 212
Lee, Patti, 596
Lee, Peggy, 135, 278, 357, 556, 660, 727, 767
Lee, Pinky, 349, 626, 790
Lee, Roberta, 277
Lee, Ruta, 163, 602
Lee, Sondra, 741
Lee, Stan, 31, 372
Lee, Stephen, 315, 762
Lee, Sunshine, 535
Leeds, Elissa, 216
Leeds, Peter, 618
Leeds, Phil, 282, 381
Leek, Tiiu, 783
Leeson, Michael, **956, 960**
Leeves, Jane, 793
Lefcourt, Peter, **959**
Leff, Pincus, 626
Lefferts, George, **939, 947**
LeGault, Lance, 6, 474, 848
Lehman, Lillian, 259, 778
Lehman, Trent, 554
Lehne, Fredric, 178
Lehr, Lew, 748

Lehrer, Tom, 781
Lei, Lydia, 172
Leibman, Ron, 413, **953**
Leifer, Carol, 435
Leigh, Nelson, 788
Leigh, Vivien, 532
Leigh-Hunt, Barbara, 696
Leigh-Hunt, Ronald, 17
Leighton, Bernie, 139
Leighton, Frances Spatz, 57
Leighton, Isabelle, 359
Leighton, Margaret, 730, **941**
Leiser, Ernest, **940, 941, 942**
Leiston, Freddie, 450
LeMay, General Curtis E., 633
Lembeck, Harvey, 237, 329, 623
Lembeck, Helaine, 846
Lembeck, Michael, 270, 284, 586
Lemmon, Chris, 111, 222
Lemmon, Jack, 10, 23, 126, 183,
    199, 274, 307, 335, 425, 505, 523,
    569, 578, 781, 782, 800, **942, 943**
Lemon, Meadowlark, 31, 337
LeMond, Bob, 37
Lenard, Mark, 339, 627, 698
Lenihan, Deirdre, 557
Lennon, Dianne, 396, 439, 440
Lennon, Janet, 396, 439
Lennon, Kathy, 396, 439
Lennon, Peggy, 396, 439
Lennon Sisters, The, 39, 95, 396,
    439, 440, 461
Leno, Jay, 435, 488, 803
LeNoire, Rosetta, 31, 124, 297
Lenz, Kay, 661, 662
Lenz, Richard, 335
Lenz, Rick, 558
Leonard, Jack, 108, 109, 384
Leonard, Jack E., 201, 501, 802
Leonard, Lu, 387
Leonard, Sheldon, 80, 184, 185,
    202, 222, **932, 934, 940**
Leonetti, Tommy, 303, 880
Leong, Camille, 606
Leopold, Thomas, 744, 775
Lerman, April, 139
Lerner, Max, 5
Leroy, Philippe, 449
Lesco, Michael, 673
Lescoulie, Jack, 103, 385, 507, 515,
    589, 801, 833
Leslie, Aleen, 186
Leslie, Bethel, 299, 662, 707
Leslie, Nan, 124, 418
Leslie, William, 453
Lessy, Ben, 184
Lester, Buddy, 563
Lester, Jeff, 584, 837
Lester, Jerry, 108, 109, 135, 144,
    158, 177, 553, 602, 689
Lester, Ketty, 453, 529
Lester, Tom, 311, 620

Letner, Ken, 246
Letterman, David, 434, 491, 741,
    767, 803, 864, **959, 960, 961, 962**
Levant, Oscar, 285, 373, 860
Level 42, 370
Levenson, Sam, 136, 495, 684, 787,
    818
Leversee, Loretta, 23
Levien, Phil, 209
Levin, Charles, 25, 306, 411
Levine, Anna, 157
Levine, Jerry, 110
Levine, Ken, **957**
Levine, Ted, 173
Levinson, Barry, **946, 948, 959**
Levinson, David, **941**
Levinson, Richard L., **941, 943**
Levitan, David, 584
Levitt, Saul, **942**
Levy, Eugene, 681, 697, **958**
Levy, Ralph, **934**
Levy, Weaver, 13
Lewandowski, Bob, 631
Lewine, Richard, 354, **936**
Lewis, Al, 131, 536
Lewis, Cathy, 261, 332, 542
Lewis, David P., 255
Lewis, Dawnn, 203
Lewis, Emmanuel, 845
Lewis, Forrest, 368, 686
Lewis, Frank, 407, 608, 803
Lewis, Gary, 360
Lewis, Geoffrey, 269, 315
Lewis, George J., 885
Lewis, Huey, 4
Lewis, Jeanne, 177, 178
Lewis, Jeffrey, **956, 958**
Lewis, Jennie. *See* Dagmar
Lewis, Jenny, 450
Lewis, Jerry, xiv, 158, 230, 351,
    360, 392, 423, 540, 685, 743, 783,
    802, 803, 846
Lewis, Jerry Lee, 80, 514, 766
Lewis, Jim, 46
Lewis, Judy, 598
Lewis, Juliette, 366
Lewis, Marcia, 307, 861
Lewis, Minnabess, 139
Lewis, Nancy, 610
Lewis, Richard, 328, 435
Lewis, Robert Q., 475, 495, 553,
    628, 668, 679, 708
Lewis, Sagan, 682
Lewis, Sinclair, 505, 707
Lewis, Sylvia, 652
Lewis, Wanda, 608, 609, 787
Lewis, William, 122
Ley, Willie, 798
Leyden, Bill, 376, 540
Leyton, John, 392
Liberace, 356, 446
Liberace, George, 446

Libertini, Richard, 252, 509, **724**
Licht, Jeremy, 827
Liddy, G. Gordon, 511
Lido, Bob, 439
Lie, Trygve, 823
Lieb, Robert P., 332, 545
Liebman, Max, 11, 501, 882
Lifford, Tina, 420
Light, Enoch, 315
Light, Judith, 860
Lightfoot, Leonard, 706, 711
Lim, Kwan Hi, 473
Lime, Yvonne, 257, 322, 485
Limeliters, The, 354, 582
Lindbergh, Charles, 695
Lindbergh, Jon, 695
Linden, Hal, 62, 89
Lindgren, Lisa, 42
Lindine, Jack, 156
Lindley, Audra, 106, 205, 259, 674,
    792
Lindley, Don, 539
Lindley, Ernest K., 567
Lindsay, John V., 5, 551
Lindsay, Margaret, 769
Lindsay, Mark, 475
Lindsey, George, 38, 335, 501
Lindsey, Lee, 159
Lindsey, Mort, 39, 254, 406, 510,
    607, 801
Lindstrom, Jon, 665
Linero, Jeannie, 73, 355
Ling, Mung, 355
Linhart, Buzzy, 168
Link, Frank, 115
Link, Michael, 407
Link, William, **941, 943**
Linke, Paul, 149
Linker, Amy, 445, 735
Linkletter, Art, 46, 350, 409, 450,
    613, 802
Linkletter, Jack, 318, 354
Linn, Bambi, 501, 881
Linn-Baker, Mark, 163, 615
Linville, Joanne, 70
Linville, Larry, 142, 309, 338, 468,
    469, 603
Liotta, Ray, 133, 593
Lipman, Daniel, **961**
Lipman, Paul, 452
Lippin, Renee, 94, 279, 487
Lippman, David, 138
Lippman, Mort, 38
Lipscomb, Dennis, 370, 867
Lipton, Lynn, 163, 187
Lipton, Michael, 113
Lipton, Peggy, 401, 525
Lipton, Robert, 761
Lisa, Anna, 89
List, Eugene, 230
Lister, Chez, 258
Liston, Sonny, 392

Litel, John, 543
Lithgow, John, **960**
Litonde, Oliver, 696
Little, Cleavon, 162, 187, 321, 778
Little, Jimmy, 623
Little, Joyce, 638
Little, Rich, 1, 59, 163, 187, 400, 407, 461, 462, 582, 591, 661, 837, 876
Little, Tiny, Jr., 439
Little Anthony, 414
Little Richard, 200, 511
Littlefield, Lucien, 90
Liu, David, **957**
Lively, Robyn, 98
Lively Set, The, 425
Livingston, Barry, 545, 596, 729
Livingston, Jay, 97
Livingston, Jerry, 702
Livingston, Michelle, 799
Livingston, Stanley, 545, 596
Livingstone, Mary, 383, 384
Livoti, Joe, 439
Lizer, Kari, 497
Llewelyn, Doug, 614
Lloyd, Christopher, 774, **956, 957**
Lloyd, David, **950, 951**
Lloyd, Jeremy, 676
Lloyd, Kathleen, 287, 473
Lloyd, Norman, 682
Lloyd, Sue, 63
Lo Bianco, Tony, 162, 397, 631
Lobbin, Peggy, 173
Locane, Amy, 732
Lockard, Tom, 46
Locke, Ralph, 588
Locke, Tammy, 527
Lockhart, Anne, 66
Lockhart, Gene, 264
Lockhart, June, 186, 274, 405, 432, 459, 620, 822, 860
Lockin, Danny, 190
Locklear, Heather, 225, 766
Lockridge, Frances, 518
Lockridge, Richard, 518
Lockwood, Gary, 271, 446
Loden, Barbara, 239, 801
Loeb, Philip, 23, 302
Loesser, Frank, 439
Loftin, Carey, 812
Logan, Alan, 776
Logan, Brad, 655
Logan, Martha, 763
Logan, Robert, 183, 702
Loggia, Robert, 235, 766, 838
Logran, Tommy, 102
Lohman, Rick, 624, 625
Lohr, Aaron, 116
Lollobrigida, Gina, 246
Loman, Hal, 282
Loman, Michael, **959**
Lomax, Stan, 311, 472

Lombard, Michael, 262, 493
Lombardo, Guy, 135, 317, 708
Lomond, Britt, 446, 885
Lon, Alice, 439, 440
London, Dirk, 446
London, Julie, 235, 236
London, Marc, 340, **939**
London, Mel, 704
London, Steve, 824
London Line Dancers, The, 709
Lonergan, Leonore, 347
Lonergan, Lester, Jr., 313
Long, Avon, 674
Long, Bill, 831
Long, Huey, 88
Long, Little Eller, 612
Long, Mary, 162
Long, Richard, 85, 100, 500, 554, 702, 785
Long, Shelley, 143, **957**
Long, Wayne, 591
Longden, John, 480
Longo, Tony, 25, 336
Longworth, David, 558
Lonow, Claudia, 420
Lonow, Mark, 362
Lontoc, Leon, 115
Loo, Richard, 758
Lookinland, Mike, 103
Lookinland, Todd, 561
Loose, William, 213
Lopez, J. Victor, 480
Lopez, Marco, 235
Lopez, Mario, 5
Lopez, Priscilla, 370, 413
Lopez, Trini, 735
Lopez, Vincent, 256, 775, 776, 831, 846
Lopinto, Dorian, 571
Lor, Denise, 82, 221, 288, 314, 701
Lord, Bobby, 599
Lord, Jack, 94, 165, 330, 467, 705, 748
Lord, Marjorie, 184, 473, 763, 883
Lord, Phil, 332, 755
Lord, Phillips H., 287
Lorde, Athena, 588
Loren, Donna, 516, 706
Loring, Estelle, 11, 748
Loring, Gloria, 245, 785
Loring, Lisa, 11
Loring, Lynn, 243, 246, 769
Lorne, Marion, 78, 289, 522, 684, **939**
Lorre, Peter, 74, 231, 739, 762
Lorring, Joan, 574
Los Angeles Philharmonic Orchestra, The, 66
Los Lobos, 806
Louanne, 819
Loudon, Dorothy, 216, 289, 377, 436, 789

Loughery, Jackie, 520, 701
Louis-Dreyfus, Julia, 188, 689
Louise, Anita, 1, 542, 617, 735, 784
Louise, Tina, 178, 297, 388, 389, 665
Lourie, Miles, **950**
Louvin Brothers, The, 308
Lovato, Beto, 5
Love, Keland, 103
Lovecraft, H. P., 762
Lovejoy, Frank, 274, 277, 467, 478, 507, 736
Lovitz, Jon, 270, 689, 690
Low, Ben, 255
Low, Theodore, 416
Lowe, Bernie, 583, 610
Lowe, Chad, 732
Lowe, David, **937**
Lowe, Edmund, 282, 883
Lowe, Jim, 712
Lowe, Rob, 561
Lowell, Tom, 161
Loweree, Robert, **938**
Lowery, Robert, 152, 626
Lowry, Judith, 625
Loy, Myrna, 291, 785
Lu, Lisa, 41, 329
Lubran, Kathryn, 420
Lubran, Tiffany, 420
Lucas, Clarence, 36
Lucas, Dione, 797
Lucas, Jim, 164
Lucas, Jonathan, 509
Lucas, Paul, 712
Lucchesi, Vincent, 344
Luchsinger, Chuck, 133
Luchsinger, Jack, 133
Luciano, Charles "Lucky," 287, 868
Luck, Susan, 19
Luckinbill, Laurence, 193
Lucking, William, 6, 81, 393, 598, 704
Lucky Pennies, The, 514
Lud and Lester, 396
Ludden, Allen, 285, 445, 606, 607
Ludlum, Robert, 660
Luez, Laurette, 14
Luft, Lorna, 808
Lui-Tsong, Wong, 286
Luisi, James, 327, 658, 669
Lujack, Johnny, 49
Luke, Keye, 41, 328, 416, 427, 710
Lukoye, Peter, 99
Lulu, 39
Lulu Belle Scotty, 1
Lum and Abner, 396
Lumb, Geoffrey, 352
Lumbly, Carl, 122
Lumet, Sidney, 183, 754
Lumley, Joanna, 52
Lummis, Dayton, 438

1031

Lund, Art, 415
Lund, Deanna, 430
Lund, Lee, 72
Lund, Tim, 744
Lund, Trigger, 239
Lundigan, William, 154, 510, 694, 709, 850
Lunghi, Cherie, 496
Lunt, Alfred, **936**
Lupino, Ida, 274, 276, 518, 695
Lupton, John, 109
Lupus, Peter, 517
Lurie, Dan, 84
Lussier, Robert, 480
Luster, Betty, 701, 713
Lustgarten, Edgar, 694
Luxton, Bill, 31
Luz, Franc, 351, 413
Lyden, Mona, 575
Lydon, Jimmy, 463, 724
Lyman, Dorothy, 478
Lymon, Frankie, 80
Lyn, Dawn, 545
Lynch, Ken, 502, 627
Lynch, Patrick, **959**
Lynch, Peg, 240, 412
Lynch, Richard, 66, 624
Lynde, Paul, 78, 190, 214, 244, 350, 404, 461, 609, 615, 641, 655, 738, 778, 782, 857
Lynley, Carol, 369
Lynn, Betty, 38, 463, 652
Lynn, Cynthia, 346
Lynn, Diana, 154, 822
Lynn, Dick, 210
Lynn, Jeffrey, 544, 739
Lynn, Jennie, 461
Lynn, Jonathan, 207
Lynn, Judy, 713, 792, 831
Lynn, Loretta, 190, 336, 632
Lynn, Rita, 523
Lyons, Gene, 375
Lyons, Sylvia, 860
Lytell, Bert, 349, 588, 592, 623, 775
Lytton, Debbie, 561, 688

M

Mabley, Moms, 381
MacKenzie, Gisele, 466
Macarena, 461
MacArthur, Charles, 282
MacArthur, Douglas, 834
MacArthur, James, 330
MacAteer, Alan, 424
Macchio, Ralph, 232
MacCorkindale, Simon, 246, 484
MacDonald, Aimi, 400
MacDonald, Ed, 547
MacDonald, Ross, 44, 643
MacDonnell, Kyle, 137, 273, 298, 346, 347

MacDougall, Ranald, 850
MacGibbon, Harriet, 77, 723
MacGraw, Ali, 225, 463
MacGregor, Jeff, 186
MacGregor, Katherine, 453
MacGregor, Scotty, 695
MacGregor Brothers, The, 424
Machon, Karen, 679
Macht, Stephen, 33, 122, 420
Macias, Ernesto, 553
Macintosh, Jay W., 729
Mack, Dotty, 216, 608, 609
Mack, Gilbert, 402
Mack, Jack, 435
Mack, Ted, xiii, 299, 592, 775
Mack & Jamie, 725
Mack Triplets, The, 775
MacKay, Harper, 549
MacKay, Jeff, 55, 473, 771
Mackenzie, Gisele, 145, 299, 408, 425, 710, 880
MacKenzie, Phil, 394
MacKenzie, Philip Charles, 476
Mackenzie, Col. Ranald, 471
Mackenzie, Will, 94
Mackie, Bob, 214
Mackin, Catherine, 569
Macklin, Albert, 221
Macklin, David, 327, 773
MacLachlan, Janet, 26, 281, 463
MacLaine, Shirley, 187, 707, 709, **948, 955**
MacLane, Barton, 363, 598
MacLane, Kerry, 171
MacLean, Barbara Barondess, 857
MacLeod, Gavin, 461, 462, 494, 503, 705
MacLeod, Murray, 410
MacMichael, Florence, 520, 545
MacMurray, Fred, 545, 822
Macnee, Patrick, 52, 236, 237, 289, 763
MacNeil, Robert, 10, 568, **962**
MacRae, Gordon, 158, 307, 466, 660, 833
MacRae, Meredith, 545, 620
MacRae, Sheila, 352, 353, 385, 386, 660
Macready, George, 621
Macredy, Renee, xi
MacVane, John, 823
MacVittie, Bruce, 751
MacWatters, Virginia, 590
Macy, Bill, 320, 321, 499, 575, 771
Madden, Dave, 25, 125, 605, 676
Maddern, Victor, 246
Maddox, Lester, 199
Madison, Guy, 19, 154
Madsen, Michael, 593
Maen, Norman, 788, 826
Magee, Don, 771
Maggart, Brandon, 391

Maguire, Mady, 77
Mahaffey, Lorrie, 861
Maharis, George, 530, 661, 676
Maher, Allison, **959**
Maher, Bill, 688
Maher, Joseph, 217, 697
Mahler, Bruce, 280
Mahomo, Nana, **942**
Mahoney, Jock, 459, 650, 874
Mahoney, John, 146
Maier, Tim, 665
Maisnik, Kathy, 738
Majors, Lee, 85, 249, 599, 714, 831, 832
Mako, 331
Malden, Karl, 718, 751, **959**
Male, Colin, 216, 787
Malenkov, Georgi, 449
Malet, Arthur, 133, 229
Malick, Wendie, 809
Malis, Claire, 246, 281
Malkovich, John, **960**
Malone, Adrian, **961**
Malone, Dorothy, 264, 467, 621, 622, 661
Malone, Joe, 808
Malone, Mary, 23, 299
Malone, Nancy, 458, 551
Malone, Pick, 34
Malone, Ray, 108, 177
Maloney, James, 815
Maloney, Paige, 586
Malooly, Maggie, 455
Maltby, Richard, 828
Maltin, Leonard, 238
Malvin, Artie, 407, 607, 746, 795
Manard, Biff, 387
Manchester, Melissa, 878
Mancini, Henry, 39, 356, 521, 582, 619, 852, 991, 992
Mancuso, Nick, 746
Mandan, Robert, 132, 638, 724, 792
Mandel, Howie, 682
Mandel, Johnny, 468
Mandel, Loring, **939**
Mandrell, Barbara, 60, 583
Mandrell, Irlene, 60, 335
Mandrell, Louise, 60
Manetti, Larry, 55, 223, 473
Maney, Norman, 706
Mangione, Chuck, 300
Mango, Alex, 111
Manhattan Transfer, The, 87, 483
Manilow, Barry, **950**
Manings, Allan, **939**
Mankiewiez, Joseph L., 266
Manley, Stephen, 489, 699
Mann, Abby, **945**
Mann, Al, 565
Mann, Anita, 144, 414
Mann, Howard, 402
Mann, Iris, 476

Mann, Johnny, 184, 232, 293, 360, 400, 403
Mann, Larry D., 8, 208
Mann, Michael, 397, **954**
Mann, Peanuts, 214
Manne, Shelly, 403
Manners, Mickey, 94, 485, 513, 602
Manning, Irene, 866
Manning, Jack, 602
Manning, Ruth, 305
Manning, Sean, 799
Manoff, Dinah, 724
Mansfield, Irving, 528
Mansfield, Jayne, 218, 219, 386, 835
Mansfield, Sally, 56
Manson, Maurice, 588
Manteca, Carlos, 813
Mantee, Paul, 122
Mantegna, Joe, 163
Mantell, Joe, 618
Mantley, John, 359
Mantooth, Randolph, 197, 235, 591
Mantovani, Annunzio Paolo, 484
Manz, Linda, 216
Manza, Ralph, 5, 59, 177, 477, 564
Mara, Adele, 167, 856
Marash, Dave, 817
Marc, Ted, 640
Marcantel, Christopher, 576
Marcelino, Mario, 246
Marcelle, Marco, 515
Marcellino, John "Jocko," 703
Marcellino, Muzzy, 450
March, Alex, 425
March, Fredric, 74, 274, 554, 640, 709
March, Hal, 291, 292, 369, 436, 542, 587, 649, 716, 725, 802, 854
Marchand, Nancy, 68, 460, **952, 954, 955, 956**
Marciano, Rocky, 101
Marco, Fatso, 515
Marcopulos, Kathryn, 789
Marcovicci, Andrea, 73, 808
Marcus, Ann, **950**
Marcus, Kipp, 561
Marcus, Sparky, 57, 307, 309, 492, 554
Marcuse, Theodore, 834
Mardi, Danielle, 77
Maren, Jerry, 573
Margetts, Monty, 820
Margolin, Janet, 431
Margolin, Stuart, 105, 106, 460, 523, 569, 577, 669, **953, 954**
Margolis, Benjamin, 516
Margulies, Stan, 673, 674, **950, 953**
Marie, Julienne, 595
Marie, Rose, 161, 202, 215, 371, 544, 602

Marihugh, Tammy Lea, 93
Marinaro, Ed, 344, 437
Marine, Joe, 278
Mariners, The, 46, 47
Marion, Richard, 591
Maris, Ada, 851
Maris, Herbert L., 456
Mark, Flip, 246, 314
Markell, Bob, **950**
Marketts, The, 991
Markey, Enid, 107
Markham, Monte, 178, 519, 616, 665, 698, 715
Markham, Pigmeat, 676
Markim, Al, 798
Markland, Ted, 341
Markoe, Merrill, **959, 960, 961**
Markoff, Diane, 647, 698
Markowitz, Dick, 654
Marks, Guy, 399, 401, 651, 875
Marksmen, 600
Markus, John, **959**
Marlowe, Christian, 342
Marlowe, Derek, **944**
Marlowe, Hugh, 13
Marlowe, Marion, xv, 46, 47
Marlowe, Nora, 308, 438, 840
Marlowe, Norma Jean, 588
Marmer, Mike, **944**
Maross, Joe, 156, 621
Marr, Eddie, 152
Mars, Janice, 574
Mars, Kenneth, 132, 212, 245, 333, 703
Marsh, Jean, 496, 571, 771, **948**
Marshall, Ann, 542
Marshall, Barbara, 540, 726, 870
Marshall, Connie, 205
Marshall, Dolores, 713
Marshall, Don, 430
Marshall, E. G., 126, 145, 193, 287, 425, 560, 581, 630, 632, 707, 762, **935**
Marshall, Garry, 350, 822
Marshall, Gloria, 93
Marshall, Gregory, 449
Marshall, Herbert, 480
Marshall, Joan, 96
Marshall, Linda, 773
Marshall, Mort, 224, 262, 346, 396
Marshall, Pat, 801
Marshall, Penny, 94, 437, 578, 609
Marshall, Peter, 350, 356, 444, 548, 620
Marshall, Red, 214
Marshall, Rex, 151, 340, 426
Marshall, Roy K., 274, 412, 557
Marshall, Sarah, 516
Marshall, Sean, 265, 471
Marshall, William, 675
Marta, Lynne, 460
Martel, K. C., 75, 312, 535
Martell, Anita, 359

Marterie, Ralph, 538
Martin, Andrea, 677, 681, 697, **958**
Martin, Anne-Marie, 719
Martin, Barney, 424, 575, 804, 885
Martin, Bobby, 313
Martin, Dean, xiv, 83, 155, 158, 189–191, 211, 230, 319, 351, 423, 497, 531, 538, 583, 743, 846
Martin, Dean Paul, 516
Martin, Dick, 145, 191, 293, 335, 406, 436, 465, 481, 496, 526, 579, 654, 676, **938, 939, 940, 942**
Martin, Eugene, 390
Martin, Freddy, 136, 279
Martin, Gail, 190, 191
Martin, Helen, 55, 819
Martin, Ian, 589, 870
Martin, Jared, 178, 254
Martin, Jeff, **959, 960, 961, 962**
Martin, John, 432
Martin, Kiel, 344, 697
Martin, Lori, 556
Martin, Mary, 274, 639, **931**
Martin, Merry, 619
Martin, Millicent, 219, 281, 625
Martin, Murphy, 565
Martin, Nan, 523
Martin, Pamela, 602
Martin, Pamela Sue, 225, 325, 326, 553, 554, 738
Martin, Quinn, 62, 74, 243, 283, 374, 483, 530, 751, 772, 814, 824, 825
Martin, Ron, 396
Martin, Ross, 521, 558, 602, 705, 863
Martin, Russ, 209
Martin, Steve, 39, 144, 211, 402, 415, 443, 537, 690, 722, 727, **939, 952, 953**
Martin, Strother, 331, 356
Martin, Tony, 158, 556, 804
Martin and Lewis, 158, 351, 846
Martin Men, The, 279
Martindale, Wink, 127, 408, 794
Martinelli, Giovanni, 590
Martinez, A, 99, 134, 137, 171, 749, 859
Martinez, Claudio, 832
Martinez, James, 571
Martinez, Jimmy, 634, 663, 804
Martinez, Manuel, 381
Martinez, Mina, 656
Martinez, Tony, 653
Martino, Al, 48
Martins Quartet, The, 607
Marvin, Lee, 22, 138, 206, 425, 469, 533, 614, 654, 767, 811
Marvin, Tony, xv, 46–48
Marx, Chico, 85, 159
Marx, Groucho, xv, 5, 199, 349, 423, 498, 540, 693, 777, 802, 876, 877, **930**

Miratti, Ti, 748
Mischer, Don, **955, 956, 957, 959, 961, 962**
Mishkin, Phil, 759
Mistal, Karen, 558
Mitchell, Andrea, 758
Mitchell, Bobbie, 468
Mitchell, Brian, 358, 808
Mitchell, Cameron, 126, 341, 643, 764, 850
Mitchell, Chad, 354
Mitchell, Don, 375
Mitchell, Ewing, 13
Mitchell, Guy, 317, 858
Mitchell, Gwenn, 37
Mitchell, Jake, 604
Mitchell, Keith, 315, 471, 840
Mitchell, Paul, 232
Mitchell, Red, 403
Mitchell, Robert, 510
Mitchell, Shirley, 56, 618, 629
Mitchell, Steve, 563
Mitchell, Thomas, 274, 307, 581, 776, 822, **930**
Mitchlll, Scoey, 61, 660, 853
Mitchum, Jack, 666
Mix, Tom, 196
Mixon, Alan, 37
Miya, Jo Anne, 45
Miyazaki, Lani, 519
Miyori, Kim, 682
Mizada, Jamie, 488
Mizzy, Vic, 212
Moar, Andrea, 665
Mobley, Mary Ann, 67, 68, 202
Modean, Jayne, 809
Modernaires, The, 293, 466, 617
Moen, Andrea, 461
Moffat, Donald, 456, 561
Moffat, Kitty, 98
Moffatt, Aaron, 807
Moffett, D.W., 581
Mohr, Gerald, 274, 275
Mokihana, 29
Molière, 437
Molinaro, Al, 322, 397, 578
Moll, Richard, 570
Monash, Paul, 621, 754, **933**
Mond, Steven, 202
Mondale, Eleanor, 668
Mondale, Walter, 126
Mondo, Peggy, 503, 796
Mones, Paul, 658
Money, Eddie, 370, 414
Monica, Corbett, 399
Monkees, The, 212, 511, 527, 562, 605, **937, 938**
Monkhouse, Bob, 97
Monroe, Bill, 165, 508
Monroe, Del, 834
Monroe, Marilyn, 360, 533, 617
Monroe, Vaughn, 20, 828
Monroney, Mike, 833

Montagne, Edward J., 108
Montalban, Ricardo, 157, 254, 309, 350, 459, 740, **952**
Monte, Vinnie, 72
Montealegre, Felicia, 755
Monteith, Kelly, 415, 572
Montenaro, Tony, Jr., 314
Montenegro, Hugo, 339
Montgomery, Barbara, 31
Montgomery, Belinda, 6, 480, 511
Montgomery, Elizabeth, 22, 78, 79, 667, 668, 755
Montgomery, George, 151
Montgomery, Mark, 175
Montgomery, Ray, 650
Montgomery, Robert, 242, 264, 541, 639, 667, 726, 755, 880, **930**
Monti, Mary Elaine, 604
Montoya, Carlos, 833
Montrose, Belle, 329
Monty, Gloria, 320
Moody, Blair, 508
Moody, King, 294
Moody, Lynne, 228, 420, 673, 674, 724, 783
Moody, Ron, 574
Moody Blues, 360
Moon, Georgina, 446
Moon, Wally, 708
Mooney, Art, 426, 444, 538
Mooney, Paul, 663
Moore, Alvy, 311
Moore, Archie, 101
Moore, Barbara, 481
Moore, Candy, 465
Moore, Charlotte, 569
Moore, Clayton, 457
Moore, Constance, 865
Moore, Del, 56, 76, 392, 450
Moore, Garry, 128, 288, 289, 294, 381, 382, 406, 414, 770, 797, **934, 935**
Moore, Ida, 649
Moore, Mary Tyler, xviii, 76, 202, 215, 306, 460, 491, 493, 494, 501, 625, 660, 663, 768, 775, 780, **936, 937, 941, 942, 943, 944, 945, 946, 947, 948, 949, 950, 951**
Moore, Melba, 381, 508, 509
Moore, Monica, 282
Moore, Robert, 198
Moore, Roger, 22, 499, 618, 682
Moore, Terry, 236
Moore, Thomas W., **952, 954, 955, 957**
Moore, Tim, 36
Moore, Tom, 429, 475
Moore, Wally, 632
Moorehead, Agnes, 23, 74, 78, 145, 660, 693, 707, **938**
Mora, Danny, 738
Morahan, Christopher, **959**
Moran, Erin, 178, 213, 322, 397

Moran, Jim, 853
Moran, Lois, 842
Moranis, Rick, 681, 697
Morash, Russ, **945**
Mordente, Lisa, 205, 832
Mordente, Tony, 115, 394, 395, 470, 727, 782
Morecambe, Eric, 625
Moreno, Belita, 615
Moreno, Rita, 571, **951, 952**
Morey, Bill, 812
Morgan, Al, 21
Morgan, Cindy, 107, 246
Morgan, Debbi, 70, 674
Morgan, Dennis, 146, 736, 815, 830
Morgan, Edward P., 150, 566
Morgan, George, 468
Morgan, Hallie, 688
Morgan, Harry, 19, 57, 89, 177, 192, 219, 220, 335, 416, 461, 468, 618, 662, 674, 877, **954**
Morgan, Harry (writer/producer), **938, 941**
Morgan, Helen, 628, **932**
Morgan, Henry, xii, 51, 220, 338, 381, 382, 442, 546, 583, 781
Morgan, Jane, 594, 845
Morgan, Jaye P., 150, 210, 303, 304, 389, 617, 748
Morgan, Marion, 44, 748
Morgan, Melissa, 182
Morgan, Michael, 661, 729
Morgan, Nancy, 686
Morgan, Norman, 425
Morgan, Ray, 34, 368
Morgan, Read, 195
Morgan, Robin, 476
Morgan, Russ, 371, 679, 846, 879
Morgan, Sean, 15
Morgan, Terence, 17
Morgan, Wesley, 449
Morgan Brothers, The, 389
Moriarty, Michael, **946, 952**
Morick, Dave, 645
Morin, Alberto, 178
Morison, Patricia, 554
Morita, Pat, 89, 90, 322, 323, 524, 580, 645, 687
Morley, Virginia, 278
Mormon Tabernacle Choir, 214
Morrill, Priscilla, 55, 105, 216, 370, 494, 874
Morris, Anita, 73, 218
Morris, Chester, 100, 198, 693, 845
Morris, Garrett, 361, 381, 670, 689
Morris, Gary, 157
Morris, Greg, 211, 517, 829
Morris, Howard, 122, 167, 253, 393, 602, 881, 882, **937, 938**
Morris, Leslie, 719
Morris, Phil, 485
Morris, Wolfe, 715
Morrison, Brian, 499

Morrison, Shelley, 270
Morriss, Ann, 111
Morrow, Barry, **957**
Morrow, Buddy, 395
Morrow, Byron, 241, 559
Morrow, Don, 490, 491
Morrow, Jeff, 350, 778
Morrow, Karen, 281, 394, 429, 768
Morrow, Patricia, 364, 621
Morrow, Vic, 54, 130, 161, 673
Morse, Barry, 237, 283, 496, 730, 822
Morse, Carleton E., 524, 588
Morse, David, 682
Morse, Ray, 798
Morse, Robert, 782
Morton, Bob, 843
Morton, Bruce, 566, **942**
Morton, Greg, 692
Morton, Howard, 297
Morton, Joe, 308
Morton, Tommy, 159, 825
Mosby, John Singleton, 309
Moschitta, John, 319, 885
Moser, James, 72
Moser, Mike, 731
Moses, David, 562
Moses, Grandma, 699
Moses, Rick, 878
Moses, William R., 246
Mosley, Philip E., 354
Mosley, Roger E., 473, 674
Moss, Bill, 718
Moss, Stewart, 259
Moss, Vivian R., **954**
Mossen, Brad, 130
Mossman, Doug, 331
Most, Donny, 322, 324
Mostel, Josh, 50, 193, 194
Mostel, Zero, 194, 537
Motion, 182
Motta, Bess, 562
Mottola, Tony, 154, 172, 244, 482, 509
Moulton, Charles, 869
Moultrie, Emily, 55
Mountain, Johnny, 242
Mountbatten, Lady Iris, 829
Mowbray, Alan, 159, 185, 512, 630
Moyer, Paul, 242
Moyers, Bill, 34, 596, **947, 956, 958**
Moynihan, Maura, 563
Mozart, Wolfgang Amadeus, 260
Mudd, Roger, 566, 568, 572, **945, 947**
Muir, Gavin, 76
Muir, Jean, 23
Muldaur, Diana, 99, 265, 345, 502, 761, 804, 874
Mule Deer, Gary, 204
Mulford, Clarence E., 354
Mulgrew, Kate, 143, 334, 411
Mulhall, Jack, 415

Mulhare, Edward, 295, 419, 822
Mulhern, Scott, 70
Mulholland, Jim, 7
Mulholland, Robert, **943**
Mull, Martin, 177, 211, 260, 292, 492
Mullally, Megan, 235
Mullaney, Jack, 41, 237, 379, 543
Mullavey, Greg, 492, 575, 665
Mullen, Susan, 686
Muller, George, 435
Muller, Kathryn, 536
Mulligan, Gerard, 435, **959, 960, 961, 962**
Mulligan, Richard, 198, 340, 657, 724, **954**
Mulligan, Robert, **934**
Mullin, Will, 628
Mullins, Michael, 755
Mulluzzo, Ronnie, 867
Mulqueen, Kathleen, 195
Mulrooney, John, 163, 435
Mumy, Billy, 459, 759
Mundy, Meg, 822
Muni, Paul, 145, 623
Muni, Scott, 279
Munro, C. Pete, 237
Munsel, Patrice, 607
Munson, Warren, 258
Muppets, The, 98, 537, 689, 690, 782, **951, 956**
Murdock, George, 62, 573, 851
Murdock, Jack, 267, 591
Murdock, James, 651
Murney, Christopher, 686
Murphy, Alma, 813
Murphy, Anthony, **944**
Murphy, Audie, 196, 858
Murphy, Ben, 24, 73, 149, 290, 312, 460, 552
Murphy, Bob, 649
Murphy, Diane, 78, 79
Murphy, Eddie, 689, 690
Murphy, Erin, 78, 79
Murphy, George, 469
Murphy, Harry, 555
Murphy, Mary, 374
Murphy, Maureen, 210
Murphy, Michael, 325, 819
Murphy, Pamela, 595
Murphy, Rosemary, 464, **949**
Murphy, Scott, 712
Murphy, Timothy Patrick, 178, 300
Murray, Arthur, 48, 49, 64
Murray, Bill, 689, **951**
Murray, Don, 420, 471, 597
Murray, Jan, 90, 209, 301, 388, 389, 713, 727, 802, 810
Murray, Kathryn, 48
Murray, Ken, 22, 224, 406, 415
Murray, Mae, 693
Murray, Peg, 505

Murray, Wynn, 262
Murray Sisters, The, 332
Murrow, Edward R., 120, 304, 404, 617, 699, 721, 755, 800, **931, 932, 933**
Murtaugh, James, 575, 671
Murtaugh, Kate, 378
Murton, Lionel, 577
Musante, Tony, 61, 799
Muscat, Angelo, 637
Muse, Clarence, 133
Music, Jerry, **939**
Music, Lorenzo, 660, **954**
Mussolini, Benito, 539
Mustin, Burt, 26, 38, 186, 284, 368, 625
Mutrux, Ashley, 157
Myatt, Beth, 461
Myers, Carmel, 132
Myers, Pamela, 83, 703
Myers, Pauline, 749
Myers, Susan, 388
Myerson, Bess, 82, 127, 381, 382, 387, 553
Myerson, Jessica, 785
Myles, Howard, 671
Myles, John, 488
Myrer, Anton, 433, 585

N

Nabors, Jim, 38, 132, 303, 394
Nabors Kids, The, 394
Nader, George, 13, 14, 74, 459, 478, 881
Nader, Michael, 225, 296
Nader, Ralph, 690
Nadler, Teddy, 716, 815
Nagel, Conrad, 109, 137, 712
Naish, J. Carrol, 314, 451, 558
Naismith, Laurence, 618
Nakahara, Kellye, 468
Nakamoto, Ed, 626
Nalle, Bill, 299
Namath, Joe, 271, 555, 843
Napier, Alan, 65, 214
Napier, Charles, 592, 598
Napier, Russell, 694
Nardini, James, 256
Nardini, Tom, 171
Narz, Jack, 69, 216, 299, 412, 450, 806, 830
Nash, Brian, 512, 629
Nash, Graham, 540
Nash, Joe, 267
Nash, Johnny, 211
Nash, Noreen, 140
Nash, Ogden, 495
Nashville Edition, The, 335
Nathan, Mort, **961**
Nathan, Steve, 116
National Gallery Orchestra, 340

Natoli, Sarah, 265
Natural Gas, 211
Natwick, Mildred, 206, 455, 462, 642, 723, 762, 845, **946**
Natwick, Myron, 692
Naud, Melinda, 197, 591
Naughton, David, 50, 476, 544, 991
Naughton, James, 255, 476, 627, 809
Navin, John P., Jr., 391
Naylor, Jason, 177
Neal, Andrew, **959**
Neal, Patricia, 240
Nealon, Kevin, 689
Nebel, Jane, 537
Nedwell, Robin, 207
Needham, Connie, 232
Neenan, Audrie J., 163
Negron, Taylor, 197
Neher, Susan, 295, 796
Nehru, Jawaharlal, 721
Neil, Gloria, 455
Neill, Noel, 17, 18
Neise, George, 862
Nelkin, Stacey, 149, 433
Nelson, Ann, 249
Nelson, Barry, 154, 361, 362, 466, 541, 741
Nelson, Bek, 438
Nelson, Billy, 18
Nelson, Christine, 652
Nelson, Christopher, 156, 729
Nelson, Craig Richard, 132, 609
Nelson, Craig T., 124, 146
Nelson, David, 15, 16
Nelson, Ed, 209, 621, 622, 710
Nelson, Frank, 76, 321, 365, 383, 384, 393, 465
Nelson, Harriet, xv, 15, 200, 288, 323, 461, 476, 545, 758
Nelson, Haywood, 308, 852
Nelson, Jerry, 536, **951**
Nelson, Jessica, 26
Nelson, Jimmy, 59, 161, 218, 219, 515, 646
Nelson, John, 455
Nelson, Joshua, 673
Nelson, Kenneth, 23
Nelson, Lindsay, 296
Nelson, Lori, 360
Nelson, Miriam, 53
Nelson, Ozzie, xv, 15, 16, 200, 264, 288, 323, 461, 476, 545, 758
Nelson, Ralph, **932**
Nelson, Rick, 15, 16, 200, 476, 531, 785
Nelson, Steve, 845
Nelson, Tracy, 300, 735
Nelson, Willie, 210, 300
Nelson's Cats, 34
Nemec, Corin "Corky," 845
Nemes, Grant, 379

Nemoto, Mie, 626
Nerman, David, 766
Nesbitt, Cathleen, 256, 755
Nesbitt, John, 776
Nesbitt, Susan, 229
Nesmith, Michael, 511, 527
Ness, Eliot, 824
Nessen, Ron, 690
Netherly, Pendrant, 672
Netherton, Tom, 439
Nettleton, Lois, 8, 137, 309, 877
Neuhaus, Lacey, 281
Neumann, Dorothy, 321
Neun, Mike, 204
Neuwirth, Bebe, 143
Nevard, Billie, 848
Nevil, Steve, 504
Neville, John, 640
Nevins, Claudette, 70, 334, 362, 489
Nevins, Natalie, 439
Newhart, Bob, 94
New Christy Minstrels, The, 39, 559, 671
New Doodletown Pipers, The, 475
New Edition, The, 414, 669
New Faces, The, 424
New Monkees, The, 562
New Seekers, The, 415
New Song Dancers, The, 877
New York Philharmonic, The, **957**
New York Symphony Orchestra, The, 71
Newborn, Ira, 483
Newell, Patrick, 52, 424
Newhart, Bob, 94, 211, 238, 349, 564, 803, **934**
Newlan, Paul, 469
Newland, John, 22, 459, 588, 667, 668, 844
Newman, Barry, 620
Newman, Edwin, 10, 164, 232, 556, 853
Newman, Elmer, 332
Newman, Laraine, 292, 483, 689
Newman, Paul, 43, 122, 183, 187, 307, 348, 410, 425, 623, 639, 822, 845
Newman, Phyllis, 163, 198, 781
Newmar, Julie, 65, 543
Newmark, Matthew, 420
Newsom, Tommy, 803
Newton, Richard, 497
Newton, Robert, 630
Newton, Wayne, 423, 538, 685
Nguyen, Dustin, 815
Nicassio, JoeAl, 818
Nicastro, Michelle, 762
Nicholas, Denise, 55, 672
Nicholas Brothers, The, 381
Nicholl, Don, 792
Nicholls, Anthony, 138

Nichols, Barbara, 108, 109, 122, 463, 850
Nichols, Mike, 436, 697, 789
Nichols, Nichelle, 739
Nicholson, Carol, 672
Nicholson, Jack, 177
Nickell, Paul, 754
Nickerson, Dawn, 328
Nicklaus, Jack, 861
Nielsen, A. C., 617
Nielsen, A. C., Jr., 776
Nielsen, Leslie, 57, 102, 208, 241, 452, 479, 559, 621, 630, 641, 704, 707, 755, 760, 772, 838, 852, 861
Nigh, Jane, 84
Nigra, Christina, 597
Niles, Mary Ann, 262
Niles, Wendell, 376
Nilsson, Harry, 170
Nimmo, Bill, 414
Nimoy, Leonard, 370, 517, 739, 766
Nirvana, Yana, 433
Nitti, Frank, 824
Nittoli, Tony Deacon, 241
Niven, David, 23, 136, 188, 225, 276, 289, 307, 349, 373, 670, 693, 761
Niven, Paul, 244
Niverson, Elaine, 439
Nix, Martha, 840
Nixon, Marni, 590
Nixon, Richard M., ix, 34, 125, 177, 385, 415, 635, 677, 749, 802, 853
Nobbs, David, 657
Noble, Edward J., 987
Noble, James, 73
Noble, Trisha, 241, 752
Noble, William, 425
Nodella, Burt, **938**, **939**
Noel, Chris, 446, 577
Noel, Dick, 378
Noel, Frank, 149
Noel, Henri, 540
Nolan, James, 185
Nolan, Jeanette, 204, 356, 662, 831
Nolan, Kathy, 107, 388, 653
Nolan, Lloyd, 60, 224, 274, 407, 490, 824, **931**
Nolan, Patrick, **954**
Nolan, Tom, 393
Nolan, Tommy, 113
Nolan, William F., 457
Nolte, Nick, 218, 661
Nomkeena, Keena, 104
Noonan, John Ford, **959**
Noonan, Tom, 444
Norberg, Greg, 488
Norden, Tommy, 269
Nordine, Ken, 147
Norell, Henry, 580
Norell, Michael, 235

Norman, B. G., 450
Norman, Ralph, 482
Norman, Teddy, 831
Norris, Bruce, 632
Norris, Christopher, 808
Norris, Chuck, 849
Norris, Jan, 378
Norris, Kathi, 733
North, Alan, 462, 630, 807
North, Alex, 662
North, Jay, 195, 501, 596
North, Sheree, 67, 80, 368, 709
North, Steven, 950
North, Zeme, 217
Northrop, Wayne, 225
Northshield, Robert, 943
Northup, Harry, 420
Norton, Cliff, 122, 288, 379, 642, 755, 852, 857
Norton, John K., 42
Norton, Ken, 303
Norton-Taylor, Judy, 840
Norvo, Red, 403
Notables, The, 204
Nouri, Michael, 67, 68, 175, 219, 287, 433
Nova, Lou, 708
Novack, Shelly, 243, 530
Novak, Kim, 246
Novelites, The, 388, 389
Novello, Don, 689, 690, 722
Novello, Jay, 74, 503
Novins, Stuart, 244
Noxon, Nicolas, 943, 952
Nuckols, William, 760
Nugent, Judy, 678
Nugent, Ted, 511
Nunez, Charles, 57
Nunez, Danny, 57
Nunn, Alice, 125, 804, 850
Nureyev, Rudolf, 71, 537, 549, 833
Nusser, James, 316
Nutt, Rev. Grady, 162, 335
Nuyen, France, 682
Nydell, Ken, 671
Nye, Louis, 41, 77, 210, 322, 557, 642, 744, 745
Nylons, The, 370, 793
Nyman, Betty Anne, 693
Nype, Russell, 216

O

Oak Ridge Boys, The, 210, 336, 539
Oakes, Randi, 149, 582
Oakland, Simon, 55, 187, 423, 799
Oakland, Sue, 442, 852
Oakley, Annie, 41, 42
Oas-Heim, Gordon, 562
Oates, Warren, 748
Oatman, Doney, 578

Ober, Philip, 363
Oberdiear, Karen, 780
O'Berlin, Bill, 322
Oberon, Merle, 49, 74, 277, 350
Oboler, Arch, 577
O'Bourne, Bryan, 90
O'Brian, Hugh, xvi, 94, 224, 446, 459, 636, 696, 754, 817
O'Brien, Clay, 171
O'Brien, Cubby, 440
O'Brien, Dave, 934
O'Brien, David, 595
O'Brien, Edmond, 458, 467, 642, 684
O'Brien, Liam, 949
O'Brien, Louise, 607, 713
O'Brien, Margaret, 293, 643
O'Brien, Maria, 575
O'Brien, Pat, 327, 736
O'Brien, Rory, 256
O'Brien, Thomas, 124
O'Brien-Moore, Erin, 621, 678
O'Byrne, Bryan, 577
O'Connell, Arthur, 307, 522, 698
O'Connell, David J., 940
O'Connell, Helen, 231, 336, 679, 767
O'Connell, Taaffe, 89
O'Conner, Jini Boyd, 695
O'Connor, Carroll, 26, 370, 371, 612, 834, 943, 950, 952, 953, 991
O'Connor, Des, 424
O'Connor, Donald, 158, 213, 356, 396, 516, 802, 930
O'Connor, Eddie, 831
O'Connor, Glynnis, 729
O'Connor, Hugh, 370
O'Connor, Tim, 112, 621, 856
O'Conor, Sen. Herbert R., 173
O'Dell, Bryan, 852
O'Dell, David, 956
O'Dell, Dell, 193
O'Dell, Tony, 333, 593
O'Demus, Nick, 36
O'Donnell, Gene, 62
O'Donnell, Jacklyn, 231, 850
O'Donnell, Joe, 961
O'Donnell, Rosie, 297
O'Donnell, Steve, 435, 959, 962
O'Donoghue, Michael, 950, 951
O'Dwyer, William, 518
Ofarim, Abi, 166
Ofarim, Esther, 166
O'Farrell, Bernadette, 17
O'Flynn, Damian, 446
Oganesoff, Igor, 941
Ogilvy, Ian, 682
O'Grady, Lani, 232, 334
O'Halloran, Hal, 1
O'Halloran, Michael, 455
O'Hanlon, George, 4, 393, 449, 659
O'Hanlon, George, Jr., 553
O'Hanlon, Redmond, 716

O'Hara, Catherine, 563, 681, 697, 744
O'Hara, Jenny, 245, 342, 544, 699
O'Hara, John, 296, 936
O'Hara, Mary, 542
O'Hara, Quinn, 455
O'Heaney, Caitlin, 43, 141, 771
O'Herlihy, Dan, 458, 479, 810, 859
O'Herlihy, Gavan, 322, 661
Ohlmeyer, Don, 957
Oingo Boingo, 256, 414
Okazaki, Bob, 26
O'Keefe, Dennis, 194, 466, 762
O'Keefe, Paul, 608
O'Keefe, Walter, 29, 502, 818
Oklahoma Wranglers, 599
Okun, Milt, 741
Olaf, Pierre, 615
Oland, Warner, 558
Olandt, Ken, 759
Olfson, Ken, 269, 554
Oliansky, Joel, 942
Olin, Ken, 67, 246, 344, 786
Oliver, 540
Oliver, David, 874
Oliver, Stephen, 102, 621
Oliver, Susan, 621
Olivier, Sir Laurence, 4, 532, 934, 944, 948, 956, 958, 960
Olivieri, Dennis, 562
Olkewicz, Walter, 434, 605, 868
Olmos, Edward James, 511, 959
O'Loughlin, Gerald S., 52, 594, 672, 749, 856
Olsen, Ashley Fuller, 284
Olsen, J. C., 263
Olsen, Johnny, 215, 284, 347, 385, 414, 628, 751
Olsen, Leila Hee, 851
Olsen, Mary Kate, 284
Olsen, Merlin, 6, 258, 453, 454
Olsen, Ole, xiv, 28, 263, 676
Olsen, Susan, 103
Olsen & Johnson, xiv, 28, 263, 676
Olson, Eric, 43, 764
Olson, Nancy, 418, 603
O'Malley, J. Pat, 307, 499, 542, 675, 847
O'Malley, Pat J., 807
O'Mara, Kate, 225
O'Morrison, Kevin, 140
O'Neal, Ann, 640
O'Neal, Frederick, 131
O'Neal, Kevin, 573
O'Neal, Patrick, 198, 199, 235, 313, 413
O'Neal, Ron, 107, 239
O'Neal, Ryan, 236, 463, 604, 621, 622
O'Neal, Tatum, 58, 604
O'Neil, Cathryn, 156
O'Neil, Danny, 866
O'Neill, Barbara, 755

Pratt & McClain, 991
Preissman, Ronald, **942**
Preminger, Michael, 204
Prendergast, Gary, 476
Prentis, Lou, 112
Prentiss, Ann, 129
Prentiss, Ed, 9, 206, 475
Prentiss, Paula, 333
Prescott, Allen, 648, 741, 863
Presley, Elvis, xv, 48, 200, 216, 230, 285, 425, 516, 706, 736, 745, 790, 817
Presley, Priscilla, 178, 790
Pressman, Ellen S., **961**
Pressman, Lawrence, 429, 535, 661
Prestidge, Mel, 331
Preston, Billy, 571
Preston, David, 560
Preston, J. A., 29, 344
Preston, Kelly, 272
Preston, Mike, 355
Preston, Robert, 43, 149, 478, 505, 630
Preston, Wayde, 160
Pretenders, The, 563
Preville, Anne, 274, 275
Pribor, Richard, 487
Price, Allen, 634
Price, Georgie, 515
Price, Kenny, 335, 336, 514
Price, Leontyne, **957**
Price, Marc, 165, 252
Price, Paul B., 116
Price, Ray, 632
Price, Roger, 221, 359, 396, 553, 693, 851, 861
Price, Vincent, 1, 65, 145, 174, 228, 264, 602, 623, 795, 834
Prickett, Maudie, 186, 332, 773
Pride, Charley, 60, 539
Pride, Dickie, 579
Priest, Pat, 536
Priestley, Thomas A., **938**
Primus, Barry, 122
Prince, 4, 373
Prince, Bob, 63, 64
Prince, Jack, 401
Prince, Jonathan, 25, 521, 793
Prince, Ron, 853
Prince, William, 33, 372, 408, 494, 762
Principal, Victoria, 178
Prine, Andrew, 667, 835, 862
Prine, John, 780
Pringle, Joan, 375, 650, 783, 858
Prinze, Freddie, 148, 261, 685
Pritchett, Florence, 442
Proctor, Phil, 741
Profanato, Gene, 524
Proft, Pat, 197, 399, 828
Prohaska, Janos, 39
Prohut, Lou, 631

Promenaders, The, 266, 599
Prosky, Robert, 344
Provenza, Paul, 163, 245, 643
Provine, Dorothy, 22, 667
Provost, Jon, 432, 596
Prowitt, David, **944**
Prowse, Juliet, 526, 709
Prud'homme, Cameron, 879
Pryor, Ainslie, 14
Pryor, Joe, 299
Pryor, Nicholas, 110, 233
Pryor, Richard, 116, 582, 663, 747, **947**
Puck, Larry, 47
Pudgy, 163
Pugh, Madelyn, 365
Pulliam, Keshia Knight, 168
Pupa, Piccola, 185
Purcell, Sarah, 654
Purcill, Karen, 479
Purl, Linda, 68, 121, 322, 497, 852
Pusser, Buford, 837
Pustil, Jeff, 142
Putnam, George, 109, 777
Pyl, Jean Vander, 268
Pyle, Denver, 215, 223, 410, 446–448, 773

Q

Quade, John, 267
Quaid, Randy, 689
Quan, Ke Huy, 798
Quarry, Robert, 349, 350
Quarterflash, 280
Quatro, Suzi, 323
Quayle, Anthony, 240, 530, 715, 750, **948**
Quentin, John, 696
Quill, John E., **955**
Quillan, Eddie, 336, 407, 827
Quine, Don, 621, 831
Quinlan, Roberta, 525, 540, 726, 878
Quinlan, Siobhan, 207
Quinlivan, Charles, 520
Quinn, Anthony, 183, 199, 479, 623
Quinn, Bill, 26, 629, 664
Quinn, Carmel, 46–48
Quinn, Louis, 702
Quinn, Spencer, 393, 722
Quinn, Stanley, 425
Quinn, Teddy, 8, 410
Quinn, Thomas, 58
Quinones, Adolfo, 83

R

R E O Speedwagon, 806
Rabel, Ed, 572

Raby, John, 869
Race, Clark, 604
Rachins, Alan, 429
Racimo, Victoria, 149, 246
Radner, Gilda, 689, 690, 697, **952**
Rae, Charlotte, 131, 202, 245, 355, 661
Rafelson, Bob, **937**
Rafferty, Bill, 436, 654
Rafferty, Frances, 1, 126, 192, 618
Raffin, Deborah, 275, 433
Rafkin, Alan, **956**
Raft, George, 322, 369
Ragaway, Martin, **934**
Raggio, Lisa, 638
Ragin, John S., 647, 729
Ragland, Larry, 414
Railing, Christopher, **944**
Railsback, Steve, 281
Raine, Norman Reilly, 19
Raines, Cristina, 137, 266
Raines, Ella, 389
Raines, Steve, 651
Rainey, Ford, 88, 483, 662, 696, 865
Rainey, Froelich, 852
Rainger, Ralph, 383
Rainmakers, The, 182
Rains, Claude, 224, 410, 505, 581
Rainwater, Marvin, 599
Raisch, Bill, 283
Raitt, John, 114, 145, 845
Raleigh, Ben, 651
Raleigh, Sir Walter, 17
Ralph, Sheryl Lee, 156, 378
Ralston, Bob, 439
Rambo, Dack, 178, 204, 316, 562, 603, 764
Rambo, Dirk, 562
Ramirez, Connie, 73
Ramirez, Frank, 604
Ramis, Harold, 697
Ramones, The, 211
Ramos, Rudy, 341, 361
Ramsen, Bobby, 493
Ramsey, Logan, 584
Ramsey, Marion, 168, 414
Ramus, Nick, 149, 246
Rance, Howard, 291
Ranch, Harry, 356, 831
Ranch Girls, The, 831
Ranch Square Dancers, 332
Randall, Ann, 335
Randall, Bob, 582
Randall, Charlotte "Rebel," 51
Randall, Frankie, 191
Randall, Stuart, 151, 431
Randall, Sue, 441
Randall, Tony, 43, 83, 307, 322, 461, 462, 522, 578, 588, 707, 782, 804, **942, 943, 947**
Randell, Ron, 577, 832
Randolph, Amanda, 36, 184, 441

Robinson, Fran, 140
Robinson, Holly, 815
Robinson, Hubbell, 743
Robinson, John Mark, 686
Robinson, Larry, 302
Robinson, Laura, 571
Robinson, Max, 565
Robinson, Roger, 281
Robinson, Russell Phillip, 858
Robinson, Smokey, 87, 370, 531, 878
Robinson, Sugar Ray, 101
Roble, Chet, 755, 796
Rocca, Antonino "Argentina," 187, 872
Rocco, Alex, 246, 791
Roche, Eugene, 167, 305, 615, 724, 769, 845
Rock, Blossom, 11
Rocket, Charles, 528, 689
Rockne, Knute, 88
Rockwell, George Lincoln, 674
Rockwell, Robert, 18, 126, 480, 594
Rockwell, Rocky, 439
Rodd, Marcia, 187, 224, 266, 276, 786, 808
Roddenberry, Gene, 740
Rodgers, Jimmie (contemporary), 395
Rodgers, Jimmie (1920s), 402
Rodgers, Pamela, 341, 404, 676
Rodgers, Richard, 41, 132, 230, 310, 444, 733, **951**
Rodman, Vic, 573
Rodriguez, Marco, 67
Rodriguez, Paul, 5, 811
Rodriguez, Percy, 241, 621, 687, 710
Roe, Chubby Chuck, 689
Rogers, Al, **947**
Rogers, Buddy, 135
Rogers, Ginger, 225, 400, 532
Rogers, Helen Jean, **936**
Rogers, Jaime, 39, 336, 360, 415, 877
Rogers, Jesse, 332
Rogers, Kasey, 78, 621
Rogers, Kenny, 60, 671
Rogers, Marianne Gordon, 335, 668
Rogers, Michael, 413
Rogers, Mimi, 603, 675
Rogers, Paul, 640
Rogers, Roy, 423, 555, 677, 678
Rogers, Steven, 161
Rogers, Timmie, 509, 756
Rogers, Vanetta, 607
Rogers, Wayne, xvi, 153, 358, 468, 469, 737
Rogers, Will, 338
Rogers, Will, Jr., 192, 601
Rohmer, Sax, 14
Roker, Renny, 574

Roker, Roxie, 390
Roland, Gilbert, 152
Roland, Will, 46, 48
Rolfe, Sam, 329
Rolike, Hank, 433
Rolin, Judi, 191
Rolle, Esther, 186, 305, 306, 499, 953
Rolling Stones, The, 187, 211, 349, 690, 706
Rollins, Howard E., Jr., 370, 864
Roman, Greg, 559
Roman, Joseph, 647
Roman, Lulu, 335, 336
Roman, Murray, **939**
Roman, Paul Reid, 540
Roman, Phil, **959**
Roman, Ruth, 420, 458
Romano, Andy, 281, 294
Romanus, Richard, 275, 752
Romanus, Robert, 245, 249
Romay, Lina, 502
Romero, Carlos, 246, 862
Romero, Cesar, 1, 65, 85, 126, 148, 152, 246, 384, 606, 769, 879
Romero, Ned, 177, 181
Romine, Charles, 696
Romoff, Colin, 39
Rondo, Don, 80
Ronettes, The, 360
Ronstadt, Linda, 402, 531
Rooney, Andrew, 177, 717, **940**
Rooney, Mickey, 94, 136, 349, 386, 406, 436, 512, 549, 589, 628, 660, 672, 706, **956**
Rooney, Tim,, 512, 672
Roosevelt, Eleanor, 243, **949, 950, 951**
Roosevelt, Franklin D., xi, 243, 824, **949, 950, 951**
Roosevelt, Teddy, 63, 834
Roper, Elmo, 635
Rorke, Hayden, 363, 518, 573
Rosario, Bert, 5, 764
Rosario, Joe, 26
Rosato, Tony, 30, 198, 571, 689, 697
Rose, Anna Perrott, 672
Rose, Billy, 11, 87, 174, 603
Rose, Charlie, 567
Rose, David, 655, 656, 804
Rose, George, 68
Rose, Jamie, 246, 430
Rose, Jane, 156, 625, 870
Rose, Linda, 747
Rose, Margot, 340, 659
Rose, Nicky, 706
Rose, Norman, 83, 479, 630
Rose, Polly, 463
Rose, Reginald, 193, 628, 754, **931, 935**
Rose, Reva, 778, 780
Rose, Robin, 858
Rosedale, Dolores, 69

Rosen, Arnie, **931, 932, 933, 942, 944**
Rosen, Burt, **949**
Rosen, Daniel, 435
Rosen, Leonard, 855, 856
Rosenberg, Arthur, 361
Rosenberg, Meta, **951**
Rosenberg, Rick, **946**
Rosenberg, Stuart, **935**
Rosenbloom, Slapsie Maxie, 137
Rosenfield, Joe, 169
Rosengarden, Bobby, 199
Rosenthal, Joseph, 448
Rosenzweig, Barney, 122, **959, 960**
Ross, Anthony, 778
Ross, Betsy, 714
Ross, Buddy, 514
Ross, Christopher, 540
Ross, David, 795
Ross, Diana, 80
Ross, Duncan, 812
Ross, Earl, 507
Ross, Jerry, 881, **959**
Ross, Joe E., 131, 379, 623
Ross, Katherine, 157
Ross, Lanny, 448, 763
Ross, Marion, 294, 322, 450, 462, 521
Ross, Marty, 562
Ross, Michael, **945**
Ross, Shavar, 202
Ross, Stan, 559
Ross, Stanley Ralph, 410
Ross, Ted, 470, 714
Ross-Leming, Eugenie, 342
Rossi, Leo, 605
Rossington, Norman, 696
Rossini, G., 457
Rossovich, Rick, 470
Rossovich, Tim, 856
Rosten, Irwin, **943**
Rosten, Leo, 166
Roswell, Maggie, 795
Roter, Diane, 831
Roth, Alan, 515
Roth, Jack, 396
Roth, Lillian, 789
Roth, Phil, 703
Rothschild, Sigmund, 854
Rounds, David, 68
Roundtree, Richard, 598, 673, 704
Rounseville, Robert, 833
Rountree, Martha, 81, 415, 442, 508, 635, 842
Rowan, Dan, xviii, 145, 191, 293, 335, 406, 436, 481, 526, 579, 654, 676, **938, 939, 940, 942**
Rowe, Misty, 322, 335, 336, 399, 857
Rowe, Red, 777
Rowe, Verne, 260
Rowland, Dave, 210
Rowland, Jada, 320
Rowlands, Gena, 43, 233, 621, **961**

Rowles, Polly, 193, 388
Roxanne, 69
Roxby, Roddy-Maude, 676
Royal, Allan, 571
Royal, John F., 568
Royal Canadians, The, 317
Roylance, Pamela, 453
Rozario, Bob, 488, 804
Ruben, Tom, 121
Rubenstein, Phil, 573
Rubes, Jan, 413
Rubin, Andrew, 351, 393, 398
Rubin, Benny, 72, 748
Rubino, George, **953**
Rubinstein, Artur, **941**
Rubinstein, John, 172, 250
Rubinstein, Phil, 871
Rubio, Edie Marie, 5
Ruby, Harry, 185, 876
Rucker, Barbara, 778
Rucker, Dennis, 294, 335
Rudd, Paul, 68, 420
Rudin, Scott, **958**
Ruditsky, Barney, 438
Rudley, Herbert, 124, 512, 526, 530
Rudner, Rita, 163, 435
Ruggles, Charles, 114, 531, 678, 871
Rugulo, Pete, 260
Ruhl, Jim, 525
Ruick, Barbara, 159, 392, 401, 649
Ruick, Melville, 153, 215
Ruiz, Isaac, 148
Rule, Elton H., **956**
Rule, Janice, 693
Ruman, Sig, 451
Rundle, Cis, 497
Rundle, Robbie, 156
Runyon, Damon, 181
Runyon, Jennifer, 139, 729
Ruppert, Donna, 511
Ruscio, Al, 704
Rush, Barbara, 266, 559, 621, 683, 693
Rushmore, Karen, 786
Rusk, Jim, **947**, **950**
Ruskin, Bud, 525
Ruskin, Shimen, 167
Russ, Tim, 344
Russ, William, 867
Russel, Del, 45
Russell, A. J., **933**
Russell, Andy, 38
Russell, Bertrand, 637
Russell, Bob, 796, 829
Russell, Connie, 155, 288
Russell, Della, 38
Russell, Don, 314, 689, 743
Russell, Henry, 319
Russell, Jack, 881
Russell, Jane, 875
Russell, Jeannie, 195

Russell, John, 438, 500, 725
Russell, Kimberly, 333
Russell, Kurt, 561, 646, 810
Russell, Lee, 831
Russell, Mark (actor), 422
Russell, Mark (humorist), 654, 741
Russell, Nipsey, 5, 61, 131, 189, 190, 495, 763
Russell, Rosalind, 276
Russell, Todd, 856
Russell, William, 17
Russell and Aura, 288, 387
Russo, Aaron, **952**
Russo, Rene, 682
Rust, Richard, 684
Ruth, Babe, 88
Rutherford, Angelo, 291
Rutherford, Ann, 1, 126, 442
Rutherford, Dean, 539
Rutherford, Lori, 559
Ruttan, Susan, 429
Ruymen, Ayn, 504
Ryan, Bill, 722
Ryan, Dave "Chico," 703
Ryan, Fran, 215, 311, 316, 573, 868
Ryan, Irene, 77
Ryan, John P., 44
Ryan, Meg, 589, 864
Ryan, Mitchell, 142, 149, 241, 330, 342
Ryan, Natasha, 429
Ryan, Peggy, 330
Ryan, Robert, 23, 307, 871
Ryan, Ron J., 751
Ryan, Roz, 31
Ryan, Steve, 173, 775
Ryan, Terry, **931**, **933**
Rydell, Bobby, 516, 610
Ryder, Eddie, 194, 207
Ryder, Mitch, 596
Ryerson, Ann, 638

S

S.O.S. Band, The, 181
Saam, Byrum, 296
Sabatino, Michael, 70, 420
Sabella, Ernie, 381, 615, 677
Sabin, David, 857
Sabo, Shari, 468
Sacino, Andrea, 485
Sackheim, William, **947**
Sacks, Alan, 847
Saddler, Don, 347
Sadler, Bill, 638
Sadowsky, Adam, 381, 697
Safer, Morley, 717
Safranski, Eddie, 294, 404
Sagal, Jean, 217
Sagal, Katey, 489, 491
Sagal, Liz, 217
Sagan, Carl, 817

Sagaphi, Princess Annette, 637
Sage, Liz, **952**
Sage Riders, 1
Seger, Carol Bayer, 878
Saget, Bob, 163, 284
Sagoes, Ken, 852
Sahl, Mort, 82, 392, 643, 802
Saint, Eva Marie, 127, 307, 528, 588, 639, 845
St. Cyr, Lili, 514
St. Jacques, Raymond, 246, 651, 673
Saint James, Susan, 280, 411, 504, 552, **939**
St. John, Al "Fuzzy," 432
St. John, Howard, 321, 374
St. John, Janice, 601
St. John, Jill, 235
St. John, Kristoff, 57, 140, 674, 686
St. John, Marco, 58
St. John, Robert, 664, 665
Sajak, Pat, 856
Sakata, Harold, 342, 688
Salata, Gregory, 411
Salcido, Michael A., 187
Saldivar, Susan, 811
Sale, Virginia, 620, 872
Salem, Jessica, 602
Salem, Kario, 137, 334
Salerno, Charlene, 15
Sales, Clifford, 76
Sales, Soupy, 59, 703, 729, 802, 855
Salmi, Albert, 183, 620, 822
Salt, Jennifer, 724
Salter, Harry, 552, 749
Saltis, Larry, 562
Saluga, Bill, 744
Salvay, Bennett, 615
Sammes, Mike, 424, 625, 709, 735, 826
Samms, Emma, 157, 225
Sampler, Philece, 665
Samples, Alvin "Junior," 335
Sampley, Jameson, 225
Sampson, Robert, 106, 246
Sampson, Will, 99, 281, 829, 875
Samuels, Jim, 387
San Juan, Guillermo, 99
Sand, Barry, 864
Sand, Paul, 297, 609, 682
Sandburg, Carl, **949**
Sande, Walter, 19
Sanders, Beverly, 121, 459
Sanders, Felicia, 992
Sanders, George, 293
Sanders, Jay O., 19, 173
Sanders, Kelly, 258, 323
Sanders, Lugene, 449, 506
Sanders, Ray, 335
Sanders, Richard, 73, 732, 835, 877
Sanderson, William, 564
Sandler, Bobby, 584

Scott, Pippa, 394, 521, 831
Scott, Raymond, 880
Scott, Rodney, 485
Scott, Selina, 849
Scott, Simon, 489, 503, 808
Scott, Synda, 274
Scott, Timothy, 864
Scott, Tom, 252, 743
Scott, Vernon, 801
Scott, Willard, 827, 828
Scott, Zachary, 145, 224, 290, 466, 467, 668, 735, 830
Scotti, Vito, 61, 270, 477, 796
Scotty, 1
Scourby, Alexander, 845
Scribner, Jimmy, 720
Scroggins, Bobby, 17
Scruggs, Earl, 78, 991
Scruggs, Langhorn, 167
Scruggs, Linda, 859
Scudder, Billy, 210
Scully, Vin, 578
Sedaka, Neil, 706
Seagram, Lisa, 77
Seagren, Bob, 724
Seale, Douglas, 650
Seales, Franklyn, 31, 711
Seals and Crofts, 602
Sears, "Big Al," 80
Sears, Bill, 417
Sears, Peggy, 120
Seatle, Dixie, 11
Sebastian, John, 596, 847, 992
Sebesky, Don, 395
Secondari, John H., 590, **936**
Sedaka, Neil, 583, 878
Sedan, Rolfe, 291, 292
Seegar, Sara, 195, 577
Seeger, Pete, 187, 354, 402, 722
Seel, Charles, 316, 667
Seeley, Eileen, 218
Seely, John, 213
Seer, Richard, 193
Seff, Richard, 139
Segal, Alex, 22, 628, **938**
Segal, George, 769
Segal, Jonathan, 602
Segall, Pamela, 245, 656
Segall, Ricky, 605
Segers, Harry, 166
Seigel, Irma, 260
Sekka, Johnny, 496
Selburg, David, 344
Selby, David, 246, 266
Selby, Sarah, 257, 316
Seligman, Selig J., 9
Selko, Nate, 824
Sellecca, Connie, 79, 269, 309, 356, 767
Selleck, Tom, 372, 473, 669, **958**
Sellers, Peter, 4, 14, 537, 633
Seltzer, Will, 345, 410
Selzer, Milton, 557

Semon, Larry, 155
Sen Yung, Victor, 56, 97
Sennett, Mack, 39, 131
Sennett, Susan, 16
Senporty, Nino, 722
Sepe, Michelle, 122
Serafian, Richard C., 270
Serafin, Barry, 565
Serling, Rod, 31, 414, 425, 445, 562, 570, 571, 628, 643, 704, 754, 817, 818, 822, 823, 850, **931, 932, 933, 934, 936**
Serpico, Frank, 700
Server, Eric, 54, 112
Sevarance, Joan, 867
Sevareid, Eric, 35, 129, 166, 486, 566, **945, 947**
Seven, Johnny, 37, 375
Severinsen, Doc, 803
Severson, Lucky, 572
Seville, David, 30
Sewell, George, 821
Seymour, Anne, 236, 667, 795
Seymour, Dan, 133, 713, 844, 857
Seymour, Jane (1950s), 879
Seymour, Jane (1970s), 130, 701
Seymour, Ralph, 476
Sha Na Na, 350, 703
Shabba-Doo, 83
Shackelford, Ted, 178, 420
Shackleford, Lynn, 29
Shad, Jerry, 733
Shadel, Bill, 129, 246, 270
Shafer, Ross, 435
Shaffer, Paul, 434, 435, 689, 874
Shahan, Rocky, 651
Shakespeare, William, 8, 425, 496, 528, 550, 716
Shandling, Gary, 379, 380
Shane, Jim, 563
Shanklin, W., 722
Shanks, Bob, 817
Shanks, Don, 447
Shannon, Del, 173
Shannon, Michael, 664
Shapiro, Arnold, **953**
Shapiro, Debbie, 811
Sharbutt, Del, 880
Sharkey, Ray, 867
Sharma, Barbara, 300, 660, 676
Sharnik, John, **943**
Sharp, Phil, **933**
Sharp, Saundra, 682, 869
Sharp, Thom, 319, 763, 767
Sharpe, Karen, 363, 403
Sharrett, Michael, 399
Sharrett, Michael Stuart, 759
Shatner, William, 31, 60, 94, 193, 208, 273, 471, 739, 766
Shaughnessy, Mickey, 147
Shaver, Helen, 393, 823
Shaw, Bob, 744
Shaw, Frank, 559

Shaw, Gary, **956**
Shaw, George Bernard, 628, 637
Shaw, Irwin, 9, 632, 662
Shaw, Mark, 612
Shaw, Martin, 207
Shaw, Reta, 41, 76, 131, 295, 368, 522, 580, 768
Shaw, Robert, 111
Shaw, Stan, 518, 674
Shaw, Steve, 420
Shaw, Susan, 588, 763
Shawlee, Joan, 7, 76, 260
Shawley, Bob, 329
Shawn, Dick, 318, 396, 491, 501
Shayne, Robert, 17
Shea, Christopher, 578, 704
Shea, Eric, 41
Shea, Joe, 728
Shea, John, 433
Shea, Michael, 558, 559
Shear, Pearl, 163
Shearer, Harry, 441, 689
Shearin, John, 105, 266, 361
Shearing, George, 161
Sheehan, Douglas, 188, 420
Sheen, Charlie, 31
Sheen, Bishop Fulton J., 448, 449, **930**
Sheffer, Craig, 320
Sheffield, Jay, 773
Sheffield, Jeanne, 394
Sheiner, David, 198, 521
Sheldon, Ernie, 339
Sheldon, Gene, 885
Sheldon, Jack, 131, 298, 678
Sheldon, Sidney, 329, 496
Shellabarger, Jill, 146
Shelley, Joshua, 54, 347
Shelley, Paul, 607
Shelly, Carol, 578
Shelton, Deborah, 178, 875
Shelton, Earl, 273
Shelton, George, 376
Shenar, Paul, 673
Shepard, Bob, 139
Shepard, Dick, 855
Shepard, Jean, 599
Shepherd, Cybill, 528, 875
Shepley, Michael, 199
Shepodd, Jon, 432
Sheppard, Sam, 620
Sheppard, William Morgan, 500
Shera, Mark, 61, 681
Sheralee, 880
Sheridan, Ann, 274, 626, 723, 789
Sheridan, Ardell, 759
Sheridan, Dan, 438
Sheridan, Liz, 24
Sheridan, Nancy, 833
Sheridan, Nicollette, 420, 603
Sherman, Allan, 345, 382
Sherman, Bobby, 295, 339, 540, 706

Sparks, Dana, 170, 246
Sparks, David, 174
Sparks, Don, 591
Sparks, Randy, 39, 559
Spaulding, Ken, 288, 412, 611
Spear, Charlie, 135
Spear, Sammy, 135, 210, 282, 385
Spector, Ronnie, 414
Speer, Kathy, **960, 961**
Spell, George, 607
Spellbinders, The, 407, 608, 803, 830
Spelling, Aaron, 263
Spelman, Sharon, 40, 167
Spence, Johnnie, 788
Spence, Sandra, 858
Spencer, Alan, 719
Spencer, Danielle, 852
Spencer, Glenn, 316
Spencer, Susan, 566
Sperber, Wendie Jo, 99, 638, 869
Spicer, Bart, 372
Spielberg, David, 33, 92, 281, 393, 634, 729, 867
Spielberg, Steven, 31
Spies, Adrian, 173
Spillane, Mickey, 512, 513
Spillman, Mrs. Miskel, 690
Spiner, Brent, 740
Spiridakis, Tony, 67
Spivak, Lawrence, 81, 415, 508, 842
Spock, Dr. Benjamin, 561
Spound, Michael, 356
Spradlin, G. D., 662, 729
Squeeze, 806
Staahl, Jim, 306, 528
Staats, Bob, 813
Stabilizers, The, 182
Stack, Robert, 94, 246, 530, 552, 602, 752, 824, 850, **934**
Stack, Timothy, 596, 657
Stacy, James, 15, 430
Stadlen, Lewis J., 73
Stafford, Jim, 394, 539, 555, 723, 790
Stafford, Jo, 155, 397, 757, 833
Stafford, Marian, 810
Stafford, Nancy, 497, 682, 710
Stahl, Leslie, 244
Stahl, Richard, 378, 394, 753, 813
Staley, James, 492, 843
Staley, Joan, 107, 455, 702
Stalin, Josef, 449, 629
Stallybrass, Anne, 715, 750
Stalmaster, Lyn, 84
Stamos, John, 221, 284, 875
Stamper, Pete, 599, 600
Stander, Lionel, 328
Standing, John, 452
Standish, Lorna, 448
Stang, Arnold, 107, 205, 338, 515, 693, 771, 805

Stanis, BernNadette, 305
Stanley, Aileen, Jr., 693
Stanley, Florence, 62, 265, 398, 546
Stanley, Kim, 183, 307, 582, 760, **935, 959**
Stanley, Leonard, 657
Stantley, Ralph, 741
Stanton, Bob, 45, 64, 101, 127, 525, 777, 830, 872
Stanton, Jack, 701, 713
Stanwyck, Barbara, 60, 85, 157, 291, 825, **934, 937, 957**
Staple Singers, The, 836
Stapleton, Jean, 26, 27, **941, 943,** 952, 991
Stapleton, Maureen, 22, 789, 851, **938**
Star Noters, The, 661
Starbuck, James, 39, 278, 713, 881
Starger, Martin, **953**
Stark, Charles, 387, 425
Stark, Dolly, 883
Stark, Lenny, 400
Stark, Richard, 182, 615
Starke, Anthony, 585
Starke, Todd, 215
Starland Vocal Band, The, 741
Starlighters, The, 397
Starliters, The, 372
Starr, Don, 178
Starr, Kay, 155, 323
Starr, Ronald, 523
Statler Brothers, The, 336, 402, 539
Stearns, Christopher William, 493
Stearns, Johnny, 493
Stearns, Mary Kay, 493
Stearns, Roger, 256
Steber, Eleanor, 833
Steckler, Doug, **958**
Steel, Amy, 272, 633
Steel, Jean, 775
Steele, Bob, 243
Steele, Richard, 407
Steele, Stephanie, 45
Steele, Ted, 135, 540, 776
Steelman, Dr. John, 66
Steen, Nancy, 744, 804
Steen, Sam, 741
Stefan, Virginia, 364, 365
Steffany, Michael, 483
Steffen, Sirry, 77
Steibel, Warren, **940**
Steiger, Rod, 183, 307, 371, 425, 623, 760
Stein, Fred, 448
Stein, James R., **947, 952**
Stein, Jeff, **956**
Stein, Lou, 801
Steinbeck, John, 554, 581, 617, **938**
Steinberg, David, 188, 540, 697

Steinberg, Norman, **942**
Steinfeld, Jerry, 73
Stell, Ann, 255
Stella, Antoinette, 175
Stempel, Herb, 815
Stephens, Garn, 625
Stephens, James, 602, 603
Stephens, Laraine, 102, 497, 577, 662
Stephenson, Edward, **937**
Stephenson, John, 96, 404, 613, 805
Stephenson, Pamela, 689
Stephenson, Skip, 654
Sterling, Jack, 84, 261, 262
Sterling, Jan, 57, 466, 471, 505, 883
Sterling, Philip, 153
Sterling, Robert, 368, 463, 807, 814
Stern, Bill, 44, 102, 326, 553, 735
Stern, Daniel, 351, 870
Stern, Leonard, 351, 359, **932, 938**
Stern, Sandor, 206
Stern, Sherl, 218, 378, 759
Stern, Stewart, **951**
Stern, Wes, 295
Sternhagen, Frances, 732
Steven, Carl, 597, 845
Stevens, Andrew, 156, 178, 235, 592
Stevens, Connie, 331, 356, 424, 702, 735, 771, 847
Stevens, Craig, 178, 375, 459, 519, 614, 619, 661, 754, 822
Stevens, Frank, 127
Stevens, George, 695
Stevens, George, Jr., **949, 958, 960**
Stevens, Inger, 256
Stevens, Julie, 84
Stevens, Kay, 392
Stevens, Leslie, 597
Stevens, Mark, 84, 85, 490
Stevens, Morgan, 60, 249, 874
Stevens, Naomi, 215, 527, 829
Stevens, Onslow, 1, 654, 788
Stevens, Patricia, 468
Stevens, Ray, 39, 190, 539
Stevens, Rise, 833
Stevens, Robert, 628, **933**
Stevens, Ronnie, 199
Stevens, Rusty, 441
Stevens, Shadoe, 350
Stevens, Shawn, 433, 471
Stevens, Stella, 71, 266
Stevens, Tony, 491
Stevens, Warren, 70, 102, 145, 662, 771
Stevens, William, 10
Stevenson, Jim, 310
Stevenson, McLean, 136, 165, 215, 337, 356, 370, 468, 469, 504, 794, 803
Stevenson, Parker, 246, 325, 639

Stevenson, Robert, 390
Stevenson, Robert Louis, 762, 882, 883
Stevenson, Valerie, 221
Stevin, Thomas, **941**
Stewart, Byron, 682, 858
Stewart, Chad, 608
Stewart, Charlotte, 453
Stewart, Horace, 36
Stewart, James, 22, 196, 290, 331, 397, 523, 568, 633, 743
Stewart, Jay, 444
Stewart, John, 836
Stewart, Johnny, 848
Stewart, Lynne Marie, 362
Stewart, Margaret, 591
Stewart, Martha, 790
Stewart, Mel, 26, 279, 584, 587, 670, 692, 768
Stewart, Nick, 650
Stewart, Patrick, 740
Stewart, Paul, 481
Stewart, Ray, 5
Stewart, Redd, 612
Stewart, Sandy, 615, 713
Stewart, Trish, 684
Stich, Patricia, 312
Stiers, David Ogden, 205, 468
Stigwood, Robert, 476
Stiller, Jerry, 398, 412, 609
Stills, Stephen, 540
Stillwell, Jack, 1
Stilwell, Diane, 319
Sting, 373, 806
Stiteler, Elena, 112
Stock, Alan, 166
Stock, Amy, 178, 739
Stock, Barbara, 732
Stockdale, Julian, 866
Stockton, Frank R., 883
Stockwell, Guy, 13, 662
Stoker, Mike, 235
Stokey, Mike, xv, 602
Stokowski, Leopold, 861, **941**
Stoler, Shirley, 718
Stone, Carol, 446
Stone, Christopher, 178, 326, 373, 732
Stone, Cynthia, 10, 335, 569, 781, 782
Stone, Dee Wallace, 798
Stone, Ezra, 51, 263
Stone, Gail, 240
Stone, Harold J., 94, 106, 302, 329, 546
Stone, I. F., 199
Stone, Irving, 290
Stone, Jon, **953, 957**
Stone, Karen, 567
Stone, Kirby, 108, 109, 395, 752
Stone, Leonard, 125, 389
Stone, Milburn, 316, **939**
Stone, Paddy, 625
Stone, Rob, 518

Stone, Sharon, 67
Stone, Sid, 515
Stone, Steve, 63
Stone, Suzanne, 687
Stone, Sylvester "Sly," 540, 708
Stoneman, Roni, 335
Stoppelmoor, Cheryl, 415
Storch, Larry, 135, 162, 243, 432, 645
Stordahl, Axel, 157, 188, 277, 299
Storm, Gale, 85, 272, 285, 351, 543, 548, 757
Storrs, Suzanne, 551
Story, Ralph, 24, 716, 851
Stossel, John, 817
Stossel, Ludwig, 133, 482
Stout, Paul, 692
Stout, Rex, 557
Stowe, Madeline, 287
Stracke, Win, 332, 755
Straight, Beatrice, 68, 418
Stralser, Lucia, 81
Strand, Robin, 73
Strange, Glenn, 316
Strangis, Judy, 672
Strasberg, Susan, 208, 489, 581, 634, 799
Strassman, Marcia, 228, 254, 305, 468, 846
Stratemeyer, Edward, 326
Stratford, Tracy, 401, 562
Strathairn, David, 189
Stratton, Albert, 616, 688
Stratton, Gil, Jr., 783
Stratton, W. K., 55
Strauss, Johann, 48
Strauss, Peter, 661, 662, **953**
Strauss, Robert, 526
Strauss, Ted, 951
Strauss, Theodore H., **942**
Streep, Meryl, **952**
Street, Dave, 108
Streisand, Barbra, 260, 414, **936, 946**
Streithorst, Tom, **947**
Strickland, Amzie, 133
Strickland, Gail, 334, 373, 851
Striders, The, 356
Striker, Fran, 457, 700
Strimpell, Stephen, 524
Stringbean, 335
Stringer, Howard, **947**
Stritch, Elaine, 235, 313, 544, 602, 811
Stroll, Edson, 503
Strom, Robert, 648, 716, 815
Stromsoe, Fred, 10
Stromstedt, Ulla, 269
Stroock, Gloria, 299, 504
Stroud, Claude, 222, 619, 775
Stroud, Don, 411, 513
Strouse (composer), 27
Strudwick, Sheppard, 755
Strunk, Jud, 676

Struthers, Sally, 26, 27, 301, 571, 722, 794, **943, 953**
Strutt, 470
Stuart, Barbara, 303, 504, 593, 618, 645
Stuart, Mary, 743
Stuart, Maxine, 209, 241, 318, 574, 672, 675, 719
Stuart, Mel, 813, **938, 941**
Stuart, Patrick, 66
Stuart, Randy, 80, 446, 788
Stuart, Roy, 303
Studer, Hal, 255
Stumpf, Randy, 267
Stuthman, Fred, 337
Styer, Michael B., **960**
Styler, Burt, **944**
Styles, Susan, 176
Styne, Jule, 132
Styx, 280
Suarez, Olga, 828
Suber, Ray, 686
Sublette, Linda, 400
Sucari Marionettes, The, 713
Suchet, David, 496
Sues, Alan, 676, 677, 706
Suffin, Jordan, 805
Sugar, 245
Sughrue, John J., **936**
Suits, Wendy, 555
Sukowa, Barbara, 729
Sulds, Irvin Paul, 170
Sullavan, Margaret, 693, 754
Sullivan, Ann, 313
Sullivan, Barry, 274, 324, 480, 662, 667, 762, 772
Sullivan, Big Jim, 788
Sullivan, Brian, 501, 833
Sullivan, Ed, xiii, 11, 47, 135, 158, 229, 230, 278, 349, 357, 416, 439, 537, 565, 661, 691, 716, 745, 802, 840, **931**
Sullivan, Francis L., 196
Sullivan, Jenny, 504
Sullivan, Joan, **950**
Sullivan, Kathleen, 565
Sullivan, Kathy, 439
Sullivan, Kevin, **960**
Sullivan, Kitty, 608
Sullivan, Liam, 527
Sullivan, Mady, 72
Sullivan, Maxine, 108
Sullivan, Owen, 83
Sullivan, Paul, 441
Sullivan, Robert, 855
Sullivan, Sean Gregory, 673
Sullivan, Susan, 246, 330, 378, 662
Sultan, Arne, **939**
Sumac, Yma, 371
Summer, Donna, 878
Summers, Harrison B., 987
Summers, Hope, 38, 42, 332, 664
Summers, Marc, 251
Summers, Yale, 178